מסורה

ArtScroll® Mesorah Series

Rabbi Nosson Scherman / Rabbi Meir Zlotowitz

General Editors

באור על התורה לרבי עובדיה ספורנו

COMMENTARY ON THE TORAH

Published by

Mesorah Publications, ltd

A PROJECT OF THE

Mesorah Heritage Foundation

SFORNO

Translation and explanatory notes
by Rabbi Raphael Pelcovitz

VOLUME I FIRST EDITION
First Impression . . . December 1987
Second Impression . . . January 1989

VOLUME II FIRST EDITION
First Impression . . . May 1989

ONE VOLUME EDITION
First Impression . . . January 1993

ONE VOLUME EDITION — WITH TRANSLATION OF THE TORAH
Four Impressions . . . February 1997 — February 2009
Fifth Impression . . . January 2014

Published and Distributed by
MESORAH PUBLICATIONS, Ltd.
4401 Second Avenue
Brooklyn, New York 11232

Distributed in Europe by
LEHMANNS
Unit E, Viking Business Park
Rolling Mill Road
Jarrow, Tyne & Wear NE32 3DP
England

Distributed in Australia & New Zealand by
GOLDS WORLD OF JUDAICA
3-13 William Street
Balaclava, Melbourne 3183
Victoria Australia

Distributed in Israel by
SIFRIATI / A. GITLER — BOOKS
6 Hayarkon Street
Bnei Brak 51127, Israel

Distributed in South Africa by
KOLLEL BOOKSHOP
Northfield Centre, 17 Northfield Avenue
Glenhazel 2192, Johannesburg, South Africa

THE ARTSCROLL® MESORAH SERIES
SFORNO — COMMENTARY ON THE TORAH
COMPLETE IN ONE VOLUME — WITH TRANSLATION OF THE TORAH

ISBN 10: 0-89906-268-7 / ISBN 13: 978-0-89906-268-6

Typography by CompuScribe at ArtScroll Studios, Ltd.
4401 Second Avenue / Brooklyn, N.Y. 11232 / (718) 921-9000

Printed in the United States of America by Noble Book Press
Bound by Sefercraft, Inc., Brooklyn, NY

מוקדש לזכר נשמת אשת נעורי

״מנשים באהל תבורך״

פרומא בת יצחק ליב ע״ה

י״ג תשרי תשמ״ז

Dedicated to the everlasting memory of

My Beloved Wife

FRUMI PELCOVITZ

Who encouraged me to undertake this project

and whose blessed memory inspired me

to complete it.

תנצב״ה

⚜ Preface

This project was begun in תשכ"ו (1966), although my interest in the *Sforno* dates back to my earlier years when I was studying and teaching *Chumash* and commentaries. Since my background is also one which was steeped in the *Mussar* movement, whose teachers quoted the *Sforno* constantly, it is understandable that this 16th-century Torah commentator attracted and intrigued me. The idea of translating the *Sforno* and writing explanatory notes, although started in 1966 in Jerusalem, was set aside due to the many demands on my time and the varied pressures associated with my rabbinical position.

When my congregation granted me a sabbatical in תשמ"ו (1985-86), I decided to resume this project and dedicate my time and energy to it, spurred on by the willingness of Mesorah Publications to publish this work.

The Mosad HaRav Kook edition of the *Sforno's Chumash* commentary, published in תש"מ (1980), edited and annotated by Avrohom Darom ז"ל and Zev Gottlieb ז"ל, served as an invaluable source and guide to this work. It should be noted that their version is a most definitive one, based as it is on nine different manuscripts. The perceptive reader will note that there are certain commentaries of the *Sforno* found in their work, and in this translation, which do not appear in the מקראות גדולות (the standard *Chumash* with commentaries) edition.

This translation of the *Sforno* is basically a literal one, retaining the original flavor and also permitting the reader to refer to it while studying the *Sforno* in the original Hebrew. Parenthesized words and phrases are inserted by the translator to enhance the grammatical flow, and for the purpose of clarification, recognizing that an English translation of Medieval Hebrew, were it totally a literal one, would at times be obscure, awkward and even incomprehensible. The explanatory notes will, hopefully, elucidate, explain and clarify the meaning, sense and intent of the author.

This work is dedicated to the memory of my beloved wife Frumi ע"ה. The translation of the first three books — *Bereishis, Shemos* and *Vayikra* — were completed during our Sabbatical in the States and Jerusalem, a period of tranquility, contentment and fulfillment with her at my side. Her sudden passing caused me to put aside this work for a period of time, but I was determined to resume and finish it לזכר נשמתה — in her beloved memory, as a tribute to a most outstanding and special woman.

Our Sages, who were extremely sensitive to the unique worth and value of a true *Aishes Chayil,* and profoundly understood the vital role she plays in her husband's life, state: "A man who has no wife lives without joy, without blessing, without good, without Torah and without peace" (Tractate *Yevamos* 62). My wife's passing indeed left me deprived of these many blessings, save one. I learned that the study of Torah can, and must, be salvaged, and only through it can one's equilibrium and clarity of mind be retained. King David, in his great wisdom,

summed it up beautifully when he said: *Had Your Torah not been my pursuit, I would have perished in my affliction* (*Psalms* 119:92).

Let it be recorded that the total support of my children, grandchildren, friends and congregants gave me much needed encouragement and strength, enabling me to fulfill my manifold duties, and above all, to proceed with the completion of this work on the *Sforno.*

It is my sincere hope and prayer that the students and scholars who will read and study this *sefer* will come to appreciate the פשטות ועמקות (the reasoned logic and profound depth) of the *Sforno's* commentary on the Torah. If this English translation and explanatory notes will help them better understand and appreciate the *Sforno*, that will be my greatest source of satisfaction and fulfillment.

Acknowledgments to the First Edition — Volume One

The author wishes to express his heartfelt thanks and appreciation to the editors of the ArtScroll series, Rabbi Nosson Scherman and Rabbi Meir Zlotowitz, for their invaluable assistance; to Rabbi Sheah Brander, who was in charge of the beautiful design and layout of this work; and to Rabbi Avie Gold for his painstaking proofreading and most helpful suggestions.

During my stay in Israel, Rabbi Samuel Stern and Rabbi Heshie Leiman were most helpful in supplying me with the necessary *seforim* not available to me in my temporary residence in Jerusalem. I am also most thankful to my assistant, Rabbi David Weinberger, to Rabbi Aaron Brafman, and to my daughter, Ethel Gottlieb, for their careful reading of the galley proofs, and their valuable suggestions and corrections. I am especially appreciative to Eleanor Klein for the many hours spent in preparing the manuscript of the Introductory Essay.

A special *yasher koach* is extended to my congregation, Knesseth Israel of Far Rockaway, N.Y., for giving me the opportunity to spend so much time on this work. May we all merit to attain חלקנו בתורתך, *our portion in Your Torah.*

Raphael Pelcovitz

Tammuz, 5747

Acknowledgments to the First Edition — Volume Two

The first volume of the Sforno's commentary on the Torah, covering the Books of Bereishis and Shemos, was well received by a large number of readers, among whom are respected Rabbonim, educators and learned laymen. I have found this acceptance and approval on their part to be most gratifying, and I wish to thank all those who were kind enough to share their feelings with me, and express their appreciation to me.

In the preparation of this second volume, which completes the Sforno's commentary on the Chumash, I was assisted by a number of individuals whom I wish to thank. I am indebted to my dear daughter Ethel Gottlieb for her careful reading of the manuscript and to Belle Koenigsberg for her secretarial assistance during the editing and rewriting process. Above all, I am beholden to my dear wife Shirley שתחי׳ for her tremendous help in editing and refining the final version of this second volume. She gave me the strength, support and inspiration I needed, during a difficult period in my life, helping me to bring this work to its completion. Her Torah erudition, coupled with a gifted, graceful command of the English language, proved to be a considerable help to me. I am profoundly grateful to her.

Rabbi Avie Gold of Mesorah Publications was extremely helpful to me during the final phases of this publication, as were the editors of the ArtScroll Series, Rabbi Nosson Scherman and Rabbi Meir Zlotowitz, and Rabbi Sheah Brander who designed the beautiful layout of this work.

At the completion of a Sefer of Torah on Shabbos, we stand up and recite חזק חזק ונתחזק — *Be strong, be strong and let us strengthen ourselves.* My prayer to Hashem is that He grant me the strength to continue to disseminate Torah, through the spoken and written word, in tranquility, good health and with peace of mind.

Raphael Pelcovitz

Adar II, 5749

Note to the Reader

The translation of the Chumash text is taken from the Stone Edition of the Chumash. In certain instances, it may not conform with Sforno's interpretation.

INTRODUCTION

Ovadiah ben Yaacov Sforno

◆§ Biographical Data and Historical Period

Ovadiah Sforno (referred to respectfully as "the *Sforno*") was born in Cesena, Italy, in the year 5230 (1470) or 5235 (1475) [the records regarding the date are unclear]. He received his Jewish education in the city of his birth and, from his prestigious works on the Torah as well as the Talmudic knowledge for which he was famous, one can assume that his Torah education was most thorough. From Cesena he moved to Rome where he attended the university, and studied philosophy, mathematics and medicine, receiving his medical degree in 1501. For thirty years the *Sforno* lived in Rome, where he was a great *marbitz Torah* (a teacher and disseminator of Torah), as well as the author of many works on Jewish philosophy and commentaries on *Tanach*. A number of rabbis consulted with him regarding halachic problems and we find him quoted in their responsa, including a responsum of the Torah luminary, Maharam of Padua (Rabbi Meir Katzenellenbogen).

While living in Rome, the *Sforno* came into contact with the Christian community and, apparently, moved with ease and comfort in high society. For example, he was retained by Johann Reuchlin, the well-known German scholar and humanist, to teach him the Hebrew language. Indeed, the *Sforno* had a marked influence on Reuchlin who, during the critical period when Jews were under attack by the Church, became a spirited defender of the Talmud and the Jews.

The *Sforno* dedicated his commentaries on *Shir HaShirim* (Song of Songs) and *Koheles* (Ecclesiastes) to Henry II of France, and after writing his famous philosophical work *Ohr Amim* (Light of Nations), he translated it into Latin and sent it to King Henry, indicating that there was a close relationship between them.

This was a relatively peaceful period, thanks to the liberal climate fostered by the popes who headed the Church at that time. The fact that the *Sforno* was able to attend the university and associate with prominent men and even kings, indicates that it was a period of intellectual openness and tolerance. As usually happens, such freedom also proved detrimental to the loyalties and commitments of the Jewish community, which we can deduce from the *Sforno's* introduction to his commentary on Torah. In this introduction, he explains that he was motivated to undertake this commentary

> ... because our people dwell in an alien land and concentrate their efforts on the accumulation of wealth, feeling that this will protect them from the exigencies of their time. This in turn results in a condition where they have no proper time to consider the wonders and wisdom of our Torah, and even brings them to question the importance of our holy Torah, becoming critical of its teachings for they do not understand it properly.

From these words of the *Sforno*, we detect the Jewish intellectual and spiritual poverty of his fellow Jews, which prompted him to write his commentary on the Torah in the hope that he would be able to arouse their interest and develop in them an appreciation for the word of *Hashem*.

In addition to his major work on the Five Books of Moses, and his philosophical treatise, *Ohr Amim*, the *Sforno* also wrote commentaries on the books of *Psalms*, *Job*, *Jonah*, *Zechariah* and *Habakuk*, as well as a commentary on *Avos* (Ethics of the Fathers). He later moved from Rome and lived for a time in Reggio, prior to settling in Bologna where his banker brother, Chananel, supported him financially and urged him to complete his commentary on the Torah. In Bologna the *Sforno* apparently practiced medicine, for we find him described as the *Abir Harofim* (the mightiest physician) in various records of that time. He established a Beth Medrash in Bologna, where he taught Torah until the end of his life, in 1550.

Although the early period of his life was, as we have noted, a relatively peaceful one, wherein Jews in Italy were able to enter the professions and participate in the business and banking world, nonetheless, the clouds gathering in other countries would also affect Italian Jewry. The Expulsion from Spain 1492 affected the Jews in Sicily and Sardinia as well, for these islands were under the rule of the Aragonese. In addition to Spanish Jews who were expelled from their native land, a large number of Sicilian Jews emigrated to Italy. This had an impact upon the *Sforno*, who was a witness to these persecutions and, no doubt, he sensed the beginnings of a deteriorating Christian-Jewish relationship even in Italy. As early as 1510, the kingdom of Naples, under Spanish rule, expelled the Jews, and the Venice ghetto was established in 1516.

Indeed, the *Sforno* lived at a critical juncture in Jewish history, a period of volatile change. Although the serious persecution of Jews in Italy did not begin until after his death, his later years were clouded by the many difficulties that confronted the Jewish population. The popes who headed the Church from 1549 to 1559 were particularly antagonistic to the Jews. Among the anti-Jewish measures instigated during this period was the burning of the Talmud in 1553. The Counter Reformation also had a deleterious effect upon Jews who were suspected of sympathizing with the Protestants against the Catholics. Many of these events were brewing in the *Sforno's* later years and are reflected in his writings, where he alludes to the difficult conditions of his fellow Jews and strives to encourage and strengthen them with words of hope and faith in the ultimate triumph of Israel over Esau (Edom), which is synonymous with Rome, as every Jewish reader of that time understood. See his commentary on *Genesis* 25:26 and 32:29 regarding the names of Jacob and Israel.

◆§ Method and Style of the Sforno's Exegesis

The *Sforno's derech* (method) of commentary is that which is known as *pshat* — the interpretation of a verse in accordance with the grammatical and linguistic connotation of the words. However, he often goes beyond the simple, straightforward meaning of a verse, offering expositions that are scientific or philosophical and often ethical. He usually avoids philological analyses of individual words and is more interested in elucidating the sense of a complete passage. Rather than spelling out the difficulties inherent in a verse, he resolves them through a comment that anticipates the questions and problems that may trouble the student. He also emphasizes the inner connection between different but similar parts of a verse, and thus removes the problem of *kaphel lashon* (duplication in phraseology). He is not averse at times to interpret sections of the Torah allegorically or mystically, based upon the *Zohar*. See, for example, *Exodus* 13:15, *Numbers* 12:2, and *Exodus* 12:22.

His approach is in keeping with his motivation and intent as spelled out in his Introduction, namely to demonstrate that the Torah is reasoned, logical, ordered and not redundant, and also to refute the argument that our Torah speaks only of material rewards while remaining silent regarding the World to Come, immortality of the soul

and eternal reward, as opposed to the Christian faith which stresses these latter elements so strongly.

In addition to the general introduction to his commentary on the Torah, the *Sforno* wrote a lengthy introduction to Torah, which he entitled *Kavanos HaTorah* (the intent and meaning of Torah). In that essay, he explains that the reason the Torah was given to Israel was to sanctify them as an eternal people, a goal that would be realized

> ... by their being like unto Him in thought and deed ... and to attain this exalted level, the Almighty gave us in His Torah, a theoretical section called "Torah" and a second section dealing with practical, pragmatic actions called "Mitzvah." The portion of the Torah which is theoretical has as its primary purpose to understand, comprehend and find proof of the existence of God, Who is non-corporeal, Creator of all, Omniscient and Omnipotent. This knowledge of God's greatness will bring man to revere and fear Him while also accepting the concept of reward and punishment.

This section of the Torah is also meant

> ... to bring man to an appreciation of God's mercy and kindness, His concern for all creation and especially for the human race, which He created in His image and after His likeness. Through the knowledge of these two fundamentals — recognition of God's existence and of His goodness and kindness — the Torah grants us life in this world and eternal life in the world to come. By studying Torah, one learns to strive to emulate *Hashem* in all His ways, to imitate His goodness and kindness to others and to be holy as He is holy. By so doing, we attain the goal meant for all mankind and especially for Israel, His people, whom He created in His image and after His likeness.

This *hashkafah* (point of view) of the *Sforno* is found time and again in his commentary. He is committed to the concept of universal man, which in no way however diminishes his fierce faith in the status of Israel as God's chosen people. Many, therefore, have referred to the *Sforno* as a humanist, but this lends itself to misinterpretation. Humanism, the attitude of mind which attaches primary importance to man and which was a characteristic attitude of the Renaissance, was in many ways a reaction to the Church's belittling of man's natural condition. The *Sforno's* commitment, however, to the dignity of man is drawn totally from our Torah and our Sages. The verse, *Let us make man in our image and our form* (*Genesis* 1:26), is of sufficient import to cause him to accept universal man — his role in the world, his importance and his place in the Divine pattern of this world. The expression, "Precious is man who was created in the Divine image" (*Avos* 3:18), buttresses this belief and is a theme which is repeated time and again in the *Sforno's* commentaries. Nonetheless, he fully recognizes Israel's special role: that although the Almighty had hoped originally to realize His purpose through mankind in general, this hope was ultimately shattered and *Hashem* therefore chose Abraham and his seed to realize the original intent of *Hashem* in the creation of man.

Toward that end the Torah also contains the second section of which the *Sforno* speaks in his *Kavanos HaTorah*, the one dealing with deeds and actions that are meant "to prepare man, especially the people of Israel, toward the goal of God's original intent." To explain this section the *Sforno* submits that the *mitzvos* are built upon seven pillars, among them *mitzvos* that are meant to create a pure heart in man, others which are meant as deterrents, and some that have as their purpose the regulation of man's reproductive behavior. Another section of *mitzvos* concerns dietary disciplines, while other observances serve as signs and symbols teaching us that we are *Hashem's* people — such as circumcision and Sabbath, which are signs of the Covenant. The last two

pillars consist of "reminders" that we are servants of God, which include *tzitzis, tefillin* and *mezuzah;* and *mitzvos* that are meant to correct and control domestic, social and political behavior, such as the ordinances and laws. It is interesting to note that Rabbi Samson Raphael Hirsch's *Horeb* in many ways follows this order.

We see that the *Sforno*, in order to refute the argument of those who felt that the Torah was unclear and disorganized, applied himself to explain and clarify the intent and purpose of the Torah. As for the second argument that the Torah speaks only of material and not eternal reward, he stresses, in his *Kavanos HaTorah*, the concepts that "the reward of a *mitzvah* is not given in this world" (*Kiddushin* 39b) and that "the reward of a *mitzvah* is another *mitzvah*" (*Avos* 4:2). He emphasizes that the treasures awaiting the righteous in the next world have never been revealed to man and, therefore, remain a mystery to which the Torah does not address itself, but he reassures us that the soul of man is immortal. He also vigorously defends the eternal character and obligation of *mitzvos* and the everlasting viability, vitality and legitimacy of the covenant between God and Israel, which was never supplanted by a "new covenant" or a "new Israel" as claimed by the Church. Of course, it was extremely important to convey this message to sixteenth-century Italian Jewry.

The literary style of the *Sforno*, who was famed for his proficiency in the Hebrew language, is succinct, precise and clear. It is simple yet elegant, and at times poetic. He paraphrases many expressions from the *Tanach* and the Talmud, often quoting directly from these sources, while drawing parallels from verses in *Tanach* to the verse at hand. It is for this reason that the phrase *k'inyan* (similar to) appears very frequently.

Although the *Sforno's* knowledge of *Tanach* and Talmud is all-encompassing, nonetheless there are times when he deviates from the interpretation of our Sages or other commentators who preceded him, and offers an original, fresh approach. However, this is always done in the spirit of tradition and never negates the accepted principles of Torah, nor questions the discipline and authority of Torah. The *Sforno* is known for his brevity, but there are times when he deviates from this style and presents a lengthy discourse on a subject that he feels is important for his readers to understand, especially if it represents a fundamental and critical aspect of Torah *hashkafah*. Some examples are: *Genesis* 1:27 regarding man's creation in the image of God; *Exodus* 19:9 regarding the prophetic spirit granted to the people of Israel at Sinai; *Leviticus* 13:27 regarding נִגְעֵי בְגָדִים *(plague of garments); Leviticus* 18:6 regarding forbidden sexual unions; *Numbers* 19:2 regarding the red cow and *Numbers* chapter 20 regarding the episode of the waters of Meribah.

He often draws a moral lesson from an episode and underscores the ethical teachings underlying an event, a law, a commandment or an ordinance of the Torah. A few examples are in *Genesis* 2:9, 33:11 and 35:1. There are many more, which will be apparent to the reader of his Torah commentary. It is for this reason that the masters of *Mussar* in the nineteenth and twentieth centuries looked to the *Sforno* as a classical source for their moral and ethical discourses. The method of the *Mussar* masters is to delve deeply into every episode related in the Torah and Prophets in an attempt to detect the motivation of the personae who are meant to serve as our models, and also to analyze the nuances and subtleties of expression used in the Torah, which reveal a much more profound meaning than one can gain through a superficial reading. This is precisely what the *Sforno* does time and time again. He is sensitive to every moral and ethical lesson which one can derive from events recorded in the Torah, as well as the underlying purpose and goal of various *mitzvos*, which the masters of *Mussar* incorporated into their teachings as well.

Through his commentary on the Torah the *Sforno* stresses themes that are at the heart of the *Mussar* approach: the paramount importance of man; the purpose of man; the

complexity of his emotions and motivations; and the major role of *teshuvah* (repentance) in man's experience. These themes represent the core of *Mussar* teachings; hence, it is no wonder that the Lithuanian School of *Mussar*, in particular, drew from the *Sforno* so extensively.

The *Sforno* was familiar with, and often reflects, the commentaries of the *Ramban, Rashi, Ibn Ezra, Rashbam, Chizkuni* and, especially, *Abarbanel*, whose commentary he very often parallels. He was also well versed in the writings of *Rambam*, especially his *Guide for the Perplexed*. Strangely, the *Sforno* does not quote any of these great commentators or attribute any interpretation to his predecessors by name. This failure to quote or attribute was apparently an accepted practice of his time. He also was knowledgeable in the teachings of *Kabbalah* and the *Zohar*, which he incorporates in his commentary. See, for example, his commentary on *Exodus* 12:22. His genius lies in his ability to digest and distill the essence of these great classic commentators while adding his own distinct, unique flavor to them.

◆§ Major Recurrent Themes

These are the major recurring themes that the careful reader and serious student will find in the *Sforno's* commentary:

1. *Universal Man and Israel.*

Man plays an extremely important role in the *hashkafah* of the *Sforno*. In addition to the concept of universal man — without denying the special role played by Israel — the *Sforno* stresses the concept of יִשְׂמַח ה׳ בְּמַעֲשָׂיו *(God rejoices in His creations)*. God's greatest delight is to rejoice with His creation and especially with man, the crown of His creation, and, of course, with Israel who represents the most precious jewel in this crown. Hence, it is our duty to conduct ourselves in a manner that will afford God this *simchah*. As he states in *Kavanos HaTorah*, "When we fulfill His will and are worthy to be rewarded, God rejoices for He desires to do kindness. Conversely, when we sin, God is brought to עַצְבוּת *(sorrow)*, as it is written, וַיִּתְעַצֵּב אֶל לִבּוֹ *(and it grieved Him at his heart)*, for He does not desire the death of the sinner."

This latter expression, that God does not desire the sinner's death, is based on *Ezekiel* 18:23, and is repeated time and again in the *Sforno's* commentary, to emphasize God's love, compassion and kindness, and His readiness to accept man's repentance. Man is frail and is prone to transgress and sin. God's desire is for man to repent, for His desire is not to punish the wicked, but rather that they return to Him. This is found in the *Sforno's* commentary on the Ten Plagues in Egypt as well as in the story of the Golden Calf.

The greatness of the human being, according to him, lies in the fact that "he alone among all creatures is predisposed to be like the Creator in intellect and deed" *(Leviticus* 13:47). Nonetheless, not all people are privileged to be subject to God's Divine Providence [הַשְׁגָּחָה פְּרָטִית] in a particular, individualistic fashion. As the *Sforno* explains in his commentary on the aforementioned verse in *Leviticus*, "Mankind as a whole is controlled by the natural order and heavenly forces . . . similar to the destiny of other living creatures who are not subject to God's providence individually but only as a species." Israel, the chosen people, on the other hand, is distinctive and as such is under the Almighty's direct, personal supervision. However, not all Jews are worthy of this special Divine Providence in a particular sense. Indeed, "the majority of Israel, except for chosen individuals, are doubtless controlled by the natural order similar to all gentiles" (ibid.).

In the view of the *Sforno*, בְּחִירָה חָפְשִׁית (freedom of choice) and Divine Providence are interwoven. The man who strives to imitate God and attempts to adopt His will as

his own has utilized the gift of free will as intended by God and therefore deserves to be under His protection and providence. In *Ohr Amim* the *Sforno* presents this theory succinctly and clearly:

> Being that Israel is more readily prepared for this (i.e., to fulfill God's intent and purpose here on earth) because they are children of the covenant, therefore God is referred to as "the God of Israel," meaning that He watches over them in a particular, personal fashion . . . (but) when the nations will ultimately call in the Name of Hashem and serve Him in unison, He will be called "the God of the entire world."

In other words, universal man has the potential to realize God's purpose in His creation of mankind. Until that time, however, Israel is the people chosen to reach this goal more readily and, as such, is worthy of special Divine consideration and concern. The *Sforno* expresses this thought in *Deuteronomy* 26:18: "You (Israel) have been granted the advantage of being chosen to observe His commandments, through which you will find favor in His eyes, whereas the other nations are not worthy or prepared to do so." He perceives that the purpose of man is to imitate God, i.e., to imitate His *ways*. As the Talmud *(Shabbos* 133b) states: "Abba Shaul says: *V'anvayhu* (וְאַנְוֵהוּ), be like Him. As He is merciful and gracious, so shall you be merciful and gracious."

In *Ohr Amim* the *Sforno* writes, "The intended purpose of the human race is that man shall be like his Creator in his behavior and intelligence, to the extent possible, as the Torah attests, *Let us make man in Our image, after Our likeness (Genesis* 1:26). [Therefore man] must choose to walk in His path and follow the well-ordered ways of His conduct in this world, to the extent possible." In his commentary on *Genesis* 1:26 the *Sforno* develops this theme. He points out that, unlike the angels, man has freedom of choice, which is a power equal to that of the Creator Himself, Who is the ultimate Master of Free Will. On the other hand, unlike God, man does not always choose well. Nonetheless, man is entitled to be called one who is "in His likeness and image." Hence, the mission and purpose of man is to strive to emulate God's *ways*, for it is impossible to imitate God Himself.

The charge given to Israel to be holy (קְדוֹשִׁים תִּהְיוּ) is explained by the *Sforno* in a similar vein: "The purpose of all these laws (i.e., regarding sexual morality, purity and impurity, dietary disciplines, etc.) is that [the Jewish people] be holy, in order to become like their Creator, to the extent possible. This was indeed the Divine intent in creating man as it says, *Let us make man in Our image, after Our likeness* (*Genesis* 1:26); *For I, your God, am holy (Leviticus* 19:2), therefore it is fitting that you be like Me in thought and deed."

2. *Israel Among the Nations*

To some extent the *Sforno's* own life reflected the general state of Israel in exile, a most difficult and perilous condition in his time, including as it did the expulsion of Jews from Spain and the establishment of ghettos in Italy. Consequently, he injects in his commentary words of comfort and encouragement to his fellow Jews. He stresses this topical theme in his commentary on various verses, especially when he explains the reason for the names Yaakov and Yisrael. The former name refers to the end of time, indicating that Jacob will survive and exist even after all others have disappeared from the stage of history, while the latter indicates the status of our people in the Messianic period. He attempts to combat the sense of despair which doubtless enveloped many of his co-religionists at that time and reassures them that God's providence has never been removed and that He cares and is concerned for them. See, for example, *Exodus* 12:42. However, in spite of his great faith in the ultimate victory of Israel, he is doubtful whether statehood is for Israel's optimum benefit. In his commentary on *Genesis* 27:29,

he makes the interesting suggestion that it may be more beneficial for Jacob to live under the protection of Esau, lest by becoming involved in the demands of statehood, Jacob will have to forsake his pursuit of the spiritual!

This theme of the interrelationship between brothers is expressed in a different manner regarding the interaction and relationship between Issachar and Zevulun, wherein the former pursues the study of Torah and is supported by the latter. This, no doubt, is a reflection of his own warm relationship with his brother, Hananel, and mirrors the economic problems which confronted him, preventing his exclusive pursuit of Torah scholarship, before Hananel stepped in. This is also mirrored in his commentary on *Genesis* 28:20 and 49:13.

3. *Medicine and the Natural Sciences*

The *Sforno's* medical knowledge is reflected in a number of his commentaries and, at times, is extremely original and advanced for his period. For example, regarding Sarah's and Rachel's difficulty in conceiving, which caused each of them to offer her handmaiden to her husband as a co-wife, the *Sforno* comments that, by involving themselves in the rearing of the children of Hagar and Bilhah respectively, they hoped that their own fertility and reproductive capabilities would be enhanced. This concept is accepted even today and has been proven to be beneficial. Many women who adopt a baby, eventually are able to conceive their own. The *Sforno's* grasp of this psychosomatic factor is most impressive.

At times he includes the opinion of medical experts in his interpretation of Biblical verses such as *Leviticus* 13:19, regarding skin ailments, and *Numbers* 13:18, regarding the effect of climate on population growth. He cites the importance of climate in other verses as well, for example regarding Jethro's reluctance to join Moses and Israel in their journey to the Promised Land, as well as in *Numbers* 10:30 where the spies speak of the climate of *Eretz Yisrael* in a disparaging manner. His knowledge of the natural sciences is apparent in his discussion regarding the rainbow (*Genesis* 9:13), as well as in his commentary on *Exodus* 35:20 regarding the spinning of the goat's hair for use in the construction of the Sanctuary. His pharmaceutical skills are demonstrated in his commentary on *Exodus* 30:34.

4. *Aesthetics*

In a number of places, the *Sforno* points out the aesthetic dimension of Torah. A prime example is in *Genesis* 2:9 regarding the Tree of Knowledge, which the Torah describes as being "pleasant to look at." The *Sforno* comments that this would expand man's heart and sensitize his mind to receive the "intellectual flow" emanating from on High. Similarly, in the episode when Jacob enters the room of his blind father Isaac, wearing Esau's clothes, the Torah tells us that Isaac *smelled the aroma of his clothes, which was the aroma of the fields* (*Genesis* 27:27). The *Sforno* comments that this pleasant experience enhanced Isaac's spiritual capacity, and he quotes the statement of our Sages that man's soul gains pleasure and enjoyment from the sense of smell. Scripture's description of Isaac's enjoyment of the aroma is followed immediately by the words, *and he blessed him,* implying that Isaac was Divinely inspired by this aesthetic experience. The *Sforno* adds that Isaac urges his son to consider carefully the ability of man to smell the aroma of a field, and thereby enjoy God's gifts of nature. The sense of smell provides an added dimension to the practical benefit derived by man from the produce of the field. The latter satisfies his material needs while the former nurtures his spirit of life and his soul (רוּחַ חִיּוּנִי וָנֶפֶשׁ).

It is important to remember that the *Sforno* lived at the time of the Renaissance, a period when people were exposed to great art, classical music and literature, all of which

appeal to man's aesthetic sense. It is understandable therefore that in addressing his contemporaries he considered it important to demonstrate that the Torah was sensitive to man's emotions, sensitivities and feelings. The *Sforno* was writing for the readers of his time, just as *Rambam* in his *Guide For The Perplexed* spoke to his contemporaries in their language, attempting to resolve their problems and answer their questions in a manner to which they could relate, thereby more effectively conveying to them the truth of Torah. R' Samson Raphael Hirsch did the same in the nineteenth century in his *Horeb* and so the *Sforno* in the sixteenth century. All great commentators and teachers must gear their style and approach to the audience at hand, for they must be relevant and reasonable in order to appeal to the minds and hearts of their students. It is amazing that even though *Sforno* spoke to his contemporaries four centuries ago, his comments are as fresh, engaging and modern as if they had been written today.

We detect in the introduction to his commentary that there were many commentators who preceded him, who, in his opinion, did not address themselves to the needs of the time. He expresses this criticism in a frank and open fashion. "Their attempts were, at times, not sufficiently clear and at times insufficient to resolve doubts, thereby resulting in the embarrassment of these authors." He was determined to avoid these pitfalls and engage the minds and hearts of his readers, by using the tools of his time, while always remaining steadfast in his loyalty to Torah and reverence for the Almighty.

5. *Biblical Narratives*

Ramban explains that Biblical narratives serve a most important purpose. As he puts it, מַעֲשֵׂה אָבוֹת סִימָן לַבָּנִים *(The events of our fathers are a portent and guide for their children).* The *Sforno* similarly stresses this idea in his *Kavanos HaTorah* and in the body of his Bible commentary. In *Kavanos HaTorah* he states,

> The purpose of the [narrative] section of the Torah, which relates various events and episodes, is to instruct us in the ways of the righteous ones among the ancients — their tests, trials, and actions that found favor in God's eyes — so that we, in turn, shall strive to emulate them. The Torah also relates how tests were accepted and passed by individuals and by Israel as a people, thereby establishing their superiority even over the angels, as the angel himself admits to Abraham after the binding of Isaac (the *Akeidah),* and the exalted position of Israel attested to by God, when He stated that Israel was put to the test of wandering in the wilderness so that His angels might know that Israel is superior to them. (See *Deuteronomy* 13:4 and the *Sforno's* interpretation of the phrase *to know.)*
>
> We are also told the reverse: The evil deeds of wicked ones serve as a warning to us to avoid and reject such actions, which resulted in terrible and destructive consequences, such as the sin of Adam which brought the decree of death in its wake; the sins of the generation of the Flood which caused major disruptions in nature and decreased man's longevity; the sin of the generation of dispersion which resulted in the Babel of tongues and further shortened man's longevity; the sins of Sodom, which was the choicest of all areas at that time and became desolate and a wasteland; and the sin of the Golden Calf which thwarted the intent of God, Who, through the giving of Torah, meant to return us to the level of Adam before the sin.

This theme of *maaseh avos* (the events of our forefathers) and their symbolism for the future repeats itself quite frequently in the *Sforno's* commentary on the Torah. For example, see *Genesis* 16:6, 21:12; 32:25, 32; 33:4, 41:14 and 46:5; and *Exodus* 12:42.

6. Leadership and Authority

As mentioned above, the *Sforno* moved in circles of leadership and power. He had frequent contact with royalty and Church personalities. This exposure no doubt impacted on his attitude toward authority and made him sensitive to the important role leadership plays in the security and stability of society. It is understandable that among Jews there was always a fear of general unrest and resultant anarchy in the host society, which would have a deleterious effect upon the Jewish community. The *Sforno*, therefore, emphasizes in his commentary the impact a leader has on his people (see *Genesis* 26:10); the influence of his behavior and conduct upon society (see *Genesis* 45:14 and 47:17); and above all, the great responsibility which the leader bears and cannot evade (see *Genesis* 21:26). In general, he emphasizes that just as God "establishes the earth with justice," so everyone who is in a position of authority and power must emulate the Almighty and strengthen the foundation of justice in his society.

Given this attitude, one can understand why the *Sforno* stresses the obligation of those who live under the authority of a leader to show him respect as indicated in his commentary on *Exodus* 22:27, where he states, "The evil which befalls the king will, in most cases, cause great evil and harm to the community as well." This echoes his comment in *Genesis* 26:10 regarding Abimelech, where he states, "When the leader of the generation is punished, great harm befalls those who find protection under his wings."

It is interesting to note that the *Sforno's* high regard for leadership qualities is also incorporated in his definition of what he calls the completeness and perfection of the truly wise man *(chacham hashalem)*. In *Genesis* 49:14, he speaks of Issachar as one who symbolizes the wise man embodying completeness and perfection in his intellectual and personal qualities. "Issachar shall carry the yoke of Torah, the yoke of earthly pursuits *(derech eretz)* and that of community leadership." This may well be his definition, informed by Torah teaching, of the ideal state of what his gentile contemporaries called Renaissance Man.

◆§ Fundamentals of Faith in the Sforno's Hashkafah

There are a number of fundamental principles of Judaism that are reflected in the *Sforno's* commentary on the Torah and that serve as an index to his basic *hashkafos*. Among them are:

1. *Freedom of Choice and Ability to Repent*

Belief in man's freedom of choice is inexorably linked to the concept of repentance in Judaism. In *Sefer Bamidbar* (the Book of Numbers) the Torah records various sins and transgressions committed by the people of Israel, which the *Sforno* uses as a springboard for his philosophy regarding sin and repentance. For example, in *Numbers* 11:23 he stresses that God will never deny man his freedom of choice, for if this were to happen, he would also automatically be denied the ability to repent. The *Sforno* also cites these episodes as revealing the frailty of man. In *Numbers* 5:28 he comments regarding the *sotah*, a wife who is suspected of being unfaithful, that God desires to clear her of such unfounded accusations, for "He knows man's evil inclinations and man's weakness."

Very often the *Sforno* quotes from the Prophet Ezekiel that God does not desire the death of the wicked, but rather that he turn away from evil and return to Him. Even regarding Israel's bondage and suffering in Egypt, he is careful to point out that the plagues visited upon the Egyptians were not meant as punishment for their cruel deeds, but as an inducement for them to repent. This, he submits, is the symbolism of the burning bush *(Exodus* 3:7) which is not consumed. According to his interpretation, the

bush is meant to represent Egypt (not the Jews!) who will be subjected to the fire of Divine punishment but will not be consumed thereby.

The theme of repentance is also found in his commentary regarding the episode of the Golden Calf (*Exodus* 32:15), where the *Sforno* explains the reason why Moses brought down the Tablets of Testimony, even though he had already been told by God that Israel had sinned. Moses thought that if he returned to them, they would repent, and if not, he would shatter the tablets of stone in their presence so as to shock them into repenting.

2. *The Power of Prophecy*

Regarding the gift of prophecy that God has granted man, the *Sforno* stresses that the epitome of the prophetic spirit in man is found in Moses our Teacher. Although others were granted this power of prophecy, none attained the special level reached by Moses, who communicated with God "face to face" and who was in a state of total awareness when the Almighty spoke to him. Other prophets received God's message in a dream or in a trance but not while in command of their senses. Only one other person came close to Moses' powers of prophecy and that, strangely, was Balaam. However, there was a time in history when, according to the *Sforno*, an entire people reached the level of Moses in their ability to prophesy and receive the spirit of *Hashem*. That people was the people of Israel, and the time and place was when God descended on Mt. Sinai to give the Ten Commandments to Israel and, through them, to mankind at large.

The *Sforno* is of the opinion, as stated in *Exodus* 19:9, that the people of Israel were granted this unique gift of prophecy, if only for a brief period of time, so that their own experience would convince them that God spoke to Moses, not through a vision or a dream, but indeed "face to face." The sin of the Golden Calf, however, caused this power of Israel's prophecy to become dissipated, and from that moment forward only select individuals were granted this power of prophecy, and even then on a much lower level than the one which Israel experienced at Sinai.

3. *The Shechinah* (Divine Presence)

Just as God's communication with Israel was adversely affected when they sinned with the Golden Calf, the nature of His Presence (the *Shechinah*) in their midst was also altered. The *Sforno* submits that God's original intent was to dwell in our midst without the need for a Sanctuary, priestly services or sacrifices. This original intent was thwarted as a result of Israel's sin. According to the *Sforno*, the Sanctuary is not a sign of God's forgiveness for the sin of the Golden Calf, as explained by other commentators, but it is an imperfect substitute for what was originally meant to be a far greater gift — namely His Presence in Israel's midst without need for a special structure.

In *Kavanos HaTorah* he expresses this idea as follows:

> It is important to note that prior to the sin of the Golden Calf, it was unnecessary to have a Sanctuary, priestly services or sacrifices in order to merit *Hashem's* Presence in their midst. No intermediary was needed, nor any special structure, nor any mandatory offerings. When they would wish to bring a peace offering, it could be brought on an altar of earth and wherever God's Name would be mentioned, including houses of study, He would come. However, after the sin of the Golden Calf, although Moses intervened with his prayers and was successful to the extent that the Divine Presence did not depart from the camp of Israel, nonetheless it was now necessary to build a Sanctuary and appoint priests to offer sacrifices, since Israel had descended from their exalted, unique status and God no longer was willing to have a direct relationship with them as had been His initial intent.

4. *The Centrality of Kedushah*

Although Israel had fallen from their "exalted, unique status," as the *Sforno* puts it, nonetheless the *Shechinah* still came to rest in their midst through the medium of the *Mishkan* (Sanctuary), for God still desired to keep Israel as His people and was willing to dwell with them even *in the midst of their uncleanliness* (*Leviticus* 16:16). This was, no doubt, due to the fact that they were still a holy people, as God had stated when He gave the Torah. The concept of *kedushah* (holiness) is a very important one. The Torah commands us to be holy for God is holy. This is indeed our primary mission and from it flow all of our other responsibilities toward mankind.

The *Sforno* adds a most interesting and unique dimension to the concept of *kedushah* as it applies to God and to Israel. The added dimension is that of eternity. In *Exodus* 15:11 he states, "The ultimate in holiness is everlasting and eternal," a concept which is taught to us by our Sages in *Sanhedrin* 92a, and which they base upon a verse in the Prophets (*Isaiah* 4:3). Since the Almighty states that the people of Israel shall be unto Him *a kingdom of priests and a holy people* (*Exodus* 19:6), the nation will never perish for it possesses the force of eternity, which is an integral aspect of *kedushah*. See the *Sforno's* commentary on *Exodus* 19:6, where he posits this idea and also his commentary on *Leviticus* 11:42 and *Deuteronomy* 26:19. By linking the eternity of Israel to its sanctity, the *Sforno* once again gave encouragement to his people at a time when they needed it desperately, thereby strengthening their faith in God and confidence in their future as a people.

◈ The Sforno as an Eclectic Exegete

As one studies the commentary of the *Sforno* on the Torah, one finds a treasure house of original and unusual interpretations of verses. It is worthwhile for the student to examine carefully a number of these commentaries which reflect his knowledge of the natural sciences, of the Kabbalah, and also his willingness to interpret verses and events in a most original and unique manner.

For example, his commentary regarding the rainbow in *Genesis* 9:13 is in keeping with the scientific teachings of the twentieth century as well as that of the sixteenth century. In *Exodus* 12:22, the *Sforno* explains the sprinkling of the blood of the *pesach* lamb on the lintel and doorpost in accordance with the teachings of the *Zohar*. In the following chapter (13:14-15), the *Sforno* offers a most unique explanation of the commandment of the Torah regarding the redemption of a firstborn donkey. Many find this *mitzvah* inexplicable since the ass is an unclean animal and, therefore, should not have the sanctity that would necessitate redemption. He explains this in a most original and brilliant allegorical manner.

Other examples of his originality of approach can be found in *Exodus* 32:29, regarding the call of Moses to the Levites to rally around him on behalf of God in the aftermath of the sin of the Golden Calf. There the *Sforno* explains the words *each one against his son and his brother* as referring to the willingness of the Levites to circumcise their children even while they were in the Wilderness! In *Exodus* 6:14-25, the *Sforno* explains that the development of the character of Moses and Aaron was due to a great extent to the longevity of their great-great-grandfather, Levi. He thereby instructs us in the influence that older generations can wield on grandchildren and even great-grandchildren.

◈ Olam Haba and Eternal Reward

Toward the end of *Kavanos HaTorah*, the *Sforno* addresses himself to a definition of what our Sages mean when they speak in terms of "the life of the World to Come" (*chayei olam haba*). He bases his explanation upon numerous statements of our Sages

regarding *the world which is all Sabbath* (*Rosh Hashanah* 31a). It is a purely spiritual world, in which there is "neither food nor drink, but where the righteous sit with crowns on their heads and enjoy the radiance of the *Shechinah*" (*Berachos* 17a). The *Sforno* tells us that regarding *Olam Haba,* we really have no way to grasp or comprehend it, for no eye has seen it, not even that of a prophet, nor has anyone been granted the power to envision it. This, however, we do know, he continues: that all the promised rewards and punishments found in the Torah are not experienced in this life as a direct result of our actions, for indeed our Sages have taught us "today to perform them, but it is not today that you receive their reward" (*Avodah Zarah* 3a). Rather, the immediate result of our good deeds is that the condition and quality of our life is of such a nature that one is afforded the opportunity to live the good life of Torah without hindrance or obstacles, while the consequence of deviation is one's vulnerability to the nations and הֶסְתֵּר פָּנִים (the concealment of God's face). This concealment may well spur us to repent, which will ultimately redound to our own benefit. In respect of performance of *mitzvos* and study of Torah, the *Sforno* stresses that each of us acts on a different level, for each person is granted different powers of intellect and spirit, and each of us develops his potential differently, so that even among the righteous in the world to come, there are levels and gradations. As our Sages tell us in *Bava Basra* 75a: "The Holy One, Blessed is He, will make for everyone a canopy corresponding to his rank (of honor and glory), and everyone one will be burnt by reason of the (superior) canopy of his friend." From this saying of our Sages, the *Sforno* proves that honor in the World to Come is contingent upon one's superior rank, which in turn depends upon what he has accomplished in this world — the only world where a man can prepare for the World to Come, as our Sages say, "Happy is he who comes here with his Torah knowledge in his hands" (*Pesachim* 50a).

The *Sforno* also discusses, in addition to man's quest for ultimate honor, his desire to attain joy (*simchah*). As the *Sforno* sees it, *simchah* is realized when one attains that which he truly desires and wants, whereas *atzvus* (melancholy) results when his desires are frustrated. Hence, when mankind fulfills God's will, they bring joy to Him, as it were: *Let HASHEM rejoice in His works* (*Psalms* 104:31), because God wants man to serve Him. The opposite occurred when mankind rebelled against God causing Him to *grieve at His heart* (*Genesis* 6:6), for then God brought retribution upon mankind, which He did not desire to do, since He *does not desire the death of the wicked.*

Since, according to this definition, joy is the attainment of one's desire and is comparable to the attainment of superior rank, the ultimate honor in *Olam Haba,* it therefore follows that in *Olam Haba* where there is no eating or drinking, enjoyment will be derived from "the brightness of the Divine Presence"; and this represents man's ultimate joy in the World to Come. The *Sforno* views *Olam Haba* as a world where man will enjoy the rewards of honor and joy to the degree that he has prepared himself for this eternal reward by his actions in this world.

He concludes by stating, "Lest we find ourselves cast into despair when we consider that even the righteous will be ashamed of one another in *Olam Haba* due to their deeds and shortcomings," nonetheless he urges us not to lose hope, but to consider that as long as we have done our best and striven to realize our potential, even though we may have fallen short, "*HASHEM* in His kindness will grant us favor and honor. As our Sages relate, when Rabbi Yochanan visited Rabbi Eleazar, who had fallen ill, Rabbi Yochanan noticed him weeping and said to him, 'Why do you weep? Is it because you did not study enough Torah? Surely we learn: the one who sacrifices much and the one who sacrifices little have the same merit provided that the heart is directed to heaven' (*Berachos* 5b)." On this note, the *Sforno* completes *Kavanos HaTorah.*

The appeal of the *Sforno* has not diminished with the passage of time. Each generation has come to appreciate his unique contribution to Torah commentary. As mentioned above, his concise style, penetrating analysis of Torah phraseology, the major themes that he develops, and his original, unique interpretations have captured the imagination of Bible scholars, students, and learned laymen for the past four centuries. The excellence of his commentary motivated editors and publishers to include his commentary in most editions of *Mikraos Gedolos,* together with the classical commentaries of *Rashi, Ramban* and other early and later masters of Bible commentary.

In spite of this popularity and although the *Sforno* is basically an adherent of *p'shat*, nonetheless serious students have often found his commentary difficult to comprehend. As they read it, they sense that there are nuggets of wisdom buried in his words, but, confronted by the imponderable, they often skip his commentary, thereby depriving themselves of his great elucidation and clarification of Biblical verses. Also, with the passage of time, a new group of Bible students has appeared on the American scene whose proficiency in Hebrew is inadequate to grasp the meaning, and certainly the nuances and allusions, of the *Sforno* in the original.

This present work attempts to overcome both of these obstacles. The English translation will, it is hoped, open the door to the masterful work of one of the great Bible exegetes of the Middle Ages, while the explanatory notes will prove to be of considerable assistance, even to those who are conversant with the original Hebrew text.

Many exegetes of the early sixteenth century do not appeal to the twentieth-century reader and student. Not so the *Sforno*. His intellectual clarity, philosophical insights, and the religious fervor and profound faith that forms his commentary are as fresh, meaningful and stimulating today as they were 420 years ago, when his commentary was first published in Venice. His purpose in writing the commentary, as he explains in his introduction, is also relevant to our time. Considering that it was meant to demonstrate the truth of Torah and its timeless message for all ages, and to encourage Israel to adhere to its eternal teachings, it is of paramount importance to introduce this remarkable commentary to a wider audience, especially to those who have in recent years manifested a thirst for Torah knowledge.

The Five Books of Moses represent the foundation of our Torah. A classic commentary such as the *Sforno's* grants us profound understanding and brilliant insights, while affording us a valuable aid to our comprehension of *Chumash*. This work will hopefully provide many serious students of Bible with an opportunity to expand their knowledge and appreciation of the eternal wisdom and inspiring message of God's Torah.

Raphael Pelcovitz

סיון תשמ״ז
Sivan, 5747

באור על התורה לרבי עובדיה ספורנו

SFORNO

COMMENTARY ON THE TORAH

Sforno's Introduction

I Ovadiah, the young one,[1] may my Rock and Redeemer watch over me,[2] son of my honored master and teacher Jacob Sforno, may his memory be unto the life of the World to Come[3] (hearkening) to the voice (and) words of my honored teacher, my brother Rav Chananel, may his Rock and Redeemer watch over him, who in his zeal to defend the Torah from insult (inflicted by) irresponsible heretics, "children in whom there is no faithfulness"[4] who discredit and give blemished explanations to the reasoned words, stories and order of Torah, (which in reality is) a wholly precious treasure, straightforward to all who discern (and understand) and there are none to say, Restore![5] (did) awaken and convince me to find desirable words which would relate (Torah) in a straightforward manner, removing all obstacles so that its righteousness might shine forth brightly. Then I said, I will present a particle[6] of what I have attained toward that end. Behold, the little I will present may arouse many more honorable than I to present pleasing words as "a memorial in the book"[7] to enlarge Torah and ennoble it.

For indeed (as a result) of impatience of the spirit, bondage and the preoccupation of our people in a land which is not theirs, confronted by oppressors who pressure them daily to incapacitate and destroy them, they all as one have concentrated their attention, eyes and hearts to (amass) wealth, (which will) shelter and protect them from the daily alien stream which envelops them as bees, so that there is no proper place or time to consider the wonders of our Torah. Therefore they have become like "dreamers" (deluded) in the midst of the nations, drawing nigh as disputers, saying: "What profit and gain is there in the promise of our holy Torah, considering that it (deals) only with the material (i.e., this world) devoid of hope for eternal life? And to what avail its many stories, which at times are without chronological order?"

---

1. The Hebrew term הַצָּעִיר, *the young one,* is used by many authors as an expression of "diminishment," which is another meaning of צָעִיר. It is meant to indicate one's sense of humility.

2. The abbreviation used is יצ"ו which represents יִשְׁמְרֵנִי צוּרִי וְגוֹאֲלִי, *may my Rock, etc.* The term "Rock" as a name for God is based on *Deut.* 32:18.

3. The Hebrew expression זִכְרוֹנוֹ לְחַיֵּי הָעוֹלָם הַבָּא is written in its abbreviated form זלה"ה.

4. Based on *Deut.* 32:20.

5. An expression based on *Isaiah* 42:22.

6. Based on *Job* 4:12.

7. Based on *Exodus* 17:14.

The "myriad holy ones then came forth,"[1] a remnant of Torah scholars (to defend and explain the Torah). (However) at times the commentary of these early scholars is not sufficiently clear and at times (their) answers are inadequate to resolve the doubts, resulting in their humiliation.

As for us, how shall we justify ourselves to God when He will hold us accountable for the honor of His Name? (Only) by relating the wonders of His Torah, which illuminate the eyes of every intelligent (person) through its tales and order, its division of books and their conclusions, demonstrating the great righteousness and goodness of *Hashem*, the Blessed One, through telling of His supreme kindness when He granted salvation after total despair. For indeed He commanded His covenant forever, to understand and teach through pure words which are established on a foundation (lit., "sockets") of analysis and deed, as He, Blessed is He, testified, saying "The Torah and the commandments which I have written to teach them" *(Exodus* 24:12). For through it He told us the purpose and intent of existence in general, and the choice of His people, and the time to give His Torah, (all of which are matters) over which many have marveled; "they have seen and wondered."

Now, being that the goal of contemplation is to understand and know the greatness of the Holy God, whereby His reverence will be experienced by all discerning people, and by knowing His ways of goodness and kindness, especially toward the human race, for which there is (the greatest) love — as it becomes clear that God, Blessed is He, indeed attempts through the generations to elevate man and correct what he has distorted — every intelligent person will then love to make God's will his will[2] and with these two (attributes), reverence and love (of God), he will perfect the area of observance[3] intended (for him) by God.

Therefore, He, the Blessed One, undertook (consented) to explain through reasoned evidence, in His first book which is *Genesis*, (the story of Creation etc.).

---

1. Based on *Deut.* 33:2.

2. *Avos*, Chapter 2, Mishnah 4.

3. Love of God will bring man to perform the positive commandments. Reverence will insure the observance of the negative commandments.

ספר בראשית

Bereishis / Genesis

Sforno's Introduction

(This book relates) the story of Creation and the general and individual providence (of God). (It also relates) the existence of (angels) who are "separated from matter" (i.e., totally spiritual) and among them are those who move the spheres; man's power of intellect; (and) that all emanates from Him with intent and will for a specific purpose.

(The Torah) then explains how precious is His loving-kindness toward the human race, for indeed He remedies their needs in each generation to the extent possible, but (man's sins) increased, thereby bringing destruction upon himself. (The Torah) first relates how the Blessed One created man in His image after His likeness,[1] that he might choose to imitate his Maker to the extent possible, for in this manner he will perfect himself, and his deeds will be more perfect and more honored than all other creatures, as is the intent of the Blessed One, that man be superior to all other (living) creatures. God in His mercy and compassion granted man his needs without any pain, placing him in the Garden of Eden, until "he perverted his ways and destroyed his livelihood,"[2] whereupon God, the Blessed One, drove him forth from there to work the earth and to occupy himself with many labors in order to earn bread for himself.[3]

The second story relates that in spite of all this, God did not choose to destroy him. The produce of the earth was beneficial and sufficient for his food needs to the extent that man lived close to a thousand years, until the wickedness of the generation increased and they were sentenced to be destroyed with the earth (6:13). (In turn) the nature of earth's elements was corrupted, its vegetation and that of all living creatures, resulting in an insufficiency of food to sustain man, as it did originally.[4]

The third story (tells us) that in spite of all the above He took pity on the remnant (of the human race) and permitted them to eat the flesh of all living creatures, save that of humans. He ordained that (control of) the earth be given to man, to the extent that the dread of man should be upon every beast of the earth.[5] In spite of all these radical changes, man's life span was four hundred years or more, until they gathered together to call upon the name of a certain strange god, chosen by them, and to place his image in a tower so that all the people would seek him out (for worship). This would have caused the Name of God, the Blessed One,

1. "In His image, after His likeness" — 1:26. The image of God means the intelligence of man who can understand and discern, thereby meriting the designation of "His likeness," to be like God though not equal to Him.

2. This expression is based upon Tractate *Kiddushin* 82b.

3. See Tractate *Berachos* 58a.

4. The effect of the deluge upon the longevity of man was most radical. The reduction first was from one thousand to four hundred and then two hundred, after which it diminished further with the passage of time.

5. *Genesis* 9:2,3.

to no longer be remembered among them.[1] Consequently, (God) dispersed them, and their life span was halved to about two hundred years — diminishing even further with the passing of time. The Torah then tells us that when it was apparent that there was no longer any hope that the human race as a whole would repent, having thwarted the Divine plan on their behalf on two and three different occasions, God then chose a pious man from among the entire species (of man), Abraham[2] and his seed, to attain through them the goal intended by Him from the moment man had been placed on earth, as explained above.

Now this three-ply cord, Abraham, his son (Isaac) and grandson (Jacob) who filled the earth with God's glory, by proclaiming His Name, found favor in His eyes, (so that) He entered into a covenant with them to be a God to them and their descendants after them eternally, and to give a place[3] (i.e., *Eretz Yisrael*) to their seed, when they would become a people of sufficient size to warrant a state in which they would unite to serve Him with common accord.

Because of the perfection of these three (patriarchs), the episodes regarding them related in the Torah serve to instruct (later) generations through these principal happenings (for they are symbolic lessons) augmented by some other (events) such as the use of the rod[4] (of Moses and Aaron) with which the signs and wonders in Egypt were performed and the episode of (Elisha and Yoash): יְרֵה וַיּוֹר, *"Shoot!" And he shot* (*II Kings* 13:17).[5]

Thus, the history of Israel is (divided into three periods). (The first) from the time they left Egypt until the building of the First Temple, during which time four altars were constructed — namely, the Sanctuary in the Wilderness, Shiloh, Nov, and Givon — which mirror the events of Abraham from the time he left Ur Casdim to go to Canaan where he (also) built four altars.[6] (The second being) the events of the period of the First Temple which mirror the events of Isaac who built only one altar.[7] The events of the First Temple period, and the subsequent exile followed by the future redemption, during which time the Second Temple was built and the future (one) may it be built "speedily in our days," are similar to the events of Jacob, our Father, who built two altars[8] and is the third period. After despair, he merited at the end to witness "good."[9] Thus, the first Book concludes.

1. *Genesis* 11:1-6.

2. *Genesis* 12.

3. *Genesis* 15:18.

4. *Exodus* 4:17.

5. The prophet Elisha tells Yoash, the king of Israel, to take a bow and arrow and shoot the arrow through the window. He tells him that this is the arrow of salvation, symbolizing victory over Aram. The *Sforno* uses this episode in various sections of his commentary (e.g. *Genesis* 16:9, 32:25) to demonstrate that episodes and events of our ancestors are symbolic of future events. Indeed these symbolic acts often prepare the way for the future.

6. *Genesis* 12:7, 12:8, 13:18, 22:9.

7. *Genesis* 26:25.

8. *Genesis* 33:20, 35:7.

9. Jacob lived through many troubles and was confronted by a myriad of problems both external and internal. However after many years of pain, sorrow and frustrations, his life ends in honor and a sense of fulfillment. This also is symbolic of the history of the people of Israel.

פרשת בראשית

א א־ב בְּרֵאשִׁית בָּרָא אֱלֹהִים אֵת הַשָּׁמַיִם וְאֵת הָאָרֶץ: וְהָאָרֶץ הָיְתָה תֹהוּ וָבֹהוּ

I

1. בְּרֵאשִׁית — *In the beginning.* (This means) at the beginning of time, the very first moment which could not be a part of time, since time did not exist prior to it (i.e., that moment).

בָּרָא — *Of God's creating.* He made "something" from "nothing," hence the concept of time cannot apply (to this) at all.

אֱלֹהִים — *Elohim.* The term אֱלוֹהַּ, *Eloha,* denotes the eternal and everlasting. That is why the שֵׁדִים *(demons)* who are mortal like human beings, as our Sages testify (*Chagigah* 16a), are called לַשֵּׁדִים לֹא אֱלֹהַּ, *to demons, no-gods (Deut.* 32:17), whereas God, the Blessed One, is called אֱלוֹהַּ for He is surely (definitively) eternal as it says, וַיִּטֹּשׁ אֱלוֹהַּ עָשָׂהוּ, *and he forsook God Who made him* (ibid. verse 15). He is called אֱלֹהִים, *Elohim,* in the plural form to teach us that He is "the form of all forms," be they everlasting or otherwise, as it says, מְלֹא כָל הָאָרֶץ כְּבוֹדוֹ, *the whole earth is full of His glory (Isaiah* 6:3), for nothing can exist except that which is reserved from His existence; and there can be no being without His Being, as it says, וְאַתָּה מְחַיֶּה אֶת כֻּלָּם, *and You preserve them all (Nehemiah* 9:6). In a similar sense, all who are separated from matter (i.e., the angels) are called *Elohim.* Expert judges are also called *Elohim,* when they judge (guided by) the "image of God." To indicate God's superior Being as the Eternal, from Whom emanates the everlasting power of others who are separated from matter (i.e., the angels), we read in *Deuteronomy* 10:17, הוּא אֱלֹהֵי הָאֱלֹהִים, *He is the God of gods.*

אֵת הַשָּׁמַיִם — *The heavens.* The word שָׁם, *there,* denotes a far, distant place. Whenever a word is changed from the singular to the plural (i.e., by adding the letters י and ם) preceded by a *pasach,* it indicates two that are equal. Therefore, the word שָׁמַיִם indicates an object

NOTES

In the first chapter of the Torah, the *Sforno* reflects, to a great extent, the teachings of the *Rambam* (Maimonides) in his *Guide of the Perplexed* (מורה נבוכים). These notes will often refer to the *Guide,* in explaining the commentary of the *Sforno.*

I

1. בְּרֵאשִׁית – *In the beginning.* The *Rambam (Guide* II:30) states that the world was not created in "a temporal beginning" for "time belongs to the created things." There are, of course, many philosophers — Aristotle among them, and even some of our Sages (*Bereishis Rabbah* III) — who believe that time existed before the creation of the world. This doctrine of the "eternity of the world," however, is vigorously rejected by the *Rambam.* Judaism asserts that just as the Almighty created the world *ex nihilo,* something out of nothingness, so must one accept that there was no concept of time until Creation. As mentioned above, time itself was *created,* and did not exist before. It is to this that the *Sforno* alludes when he states that בְּרֵאשִׁית means *at the beginning of time,* the first instant, not a point in time separate from what previously existed. It is this idea which the *Sforno* is referring to in his interpretation of the phrase בָּרָא *(created),* where he uses the Hebrew phrase אֵינוֹ יֶשְׁנוֹ which is the equivalent of the more common term יֵשׁ מֵאַיִן, both meaning *something (that which is) from nothing.* By rejecting the doctrine of the existence of prior matter one also rejects the doctrine of the eternity of the world. This in turn compels us to accept the idea of time itself being one of the created things, as has already been explained (see the *Guide* II:13).

אֱלֹהִים – *Elohim.* The phrase צוּרַת כָּל הַצּוּרוֹת, *the form of all forms,* is used by the *Rambam (Guide* I:69) and the concept presented here by the *Sforno* in explaining the plural form אֱלֹהִים, *Elohim,* is developed by the *Rambam* there. "(God) is that One upon Whom the existence and stability of every form in the world ultimately reposes and by which they are constituted." What the *Sforno* calls הַנֶּאֱצָל, *that which is separated and shared by God,* the *Rambam* calls שֶׁפַע, *the overflowing.* The existence of all things, both the everlasting and the perishable (mortal), flows from God and is dependent

PARASHAS BEREISHIS

1 [1] *In the beginning of God's creating the heavens and the earth —*
[2] *and the earth was desolate and void, with darkness upon the*

---

far removed from our point of perspective, on two sides, both equidistant from all sides. This can only be true of a sphere which revolves in a perfect circle. Therefore, (the Torah states) that (God) created this object which is now equidistant (to our naked eye) from all sides. This is the גַּלְגַּל, *the celestial sphere* (the sphere of the Zodiac), and that is why it does not say בָּרָא שָׁמַיִם, *He created heaven* (rather אֵת הַשָּׁמַיִם), for (the term שָׁמַיִם) is not one that can be expressed independently by itself but only in relationship to our place (i.e., the earth). The Torah then says וְאֵת הָאָרֶץ, *and the earth,* i.e., the central point which is fitting for the celestial sphere.

2. וְהָאָרֶץ הָיְתָה תֹהוּ וָבֹהוּ — *And the earth was desolate and void.* That earth, which was created, was an amalgam of primeval matter called תֹּהוּ and primeval form called בֹּהוּ, for it would not be suitable (possible) for primeval matter to exist without being clothed in some form. This, then, was the first amalgam perforce, of matter and substance (form). The Torah is explaining that primeval matter was a totally new creation (there being no "matter" preceding the world's creation). The matter in this initial amalgam is called תֹּהוּ for it only possesses potential but no actuality, as it says כִּי תֹהוּ הֵמָּה, *for they are vain (I Samuel* 12:21), that is, something not existing in reality, only in the imagination. The form of that initial amalgam is called בֹּהוּ for *in it* the תֹּהוּ is found, in actuality. The prophet calls אַבְנֵי בֹהוּ, *stones sunken in the primeval mire (Isaiah* 34:11), any object which does not remain in a given form for an appreciable period of time, just as we call the initial form בֹּהוּ which immediately clothed itself in a variety of forms (namely, the four elements).

NOTES

upon Him not only as the "Maker" but as the "Cause," in an ongoing sense. Without His continuous will they would cease, unlike the carpenter and his handiwork, which exists even after he departs. This is what the *Sforno* is referring to when he quotes the verses from *Isaiah* and *Nehemiah.* The former verse establishes the idea that (as the *Rambam* puts it in the *Guide* I:19): "The whole earth bears witness to His perfection" for without Him the earth, and all which is in it, could not exist. The latter verse supports this thesis by emphasizing that God is the חַי עוֹלָמִים, *Living of the World,* meaning that He is the life of the world, for all life and existence emanates from Him, not only as the original cause but as the ongoing one.

The *Sforno,* however, also adds an important explanation of the term *Elohim.* As he explains, the source of this word is אֱלוֹהַּ, *Eloha,* signifying the eternal and everlasting, as well as that which is separated from matter, and is perfect (see the *Sforno* on verse 27). This term can then be applied to the angels and even judges when they reflect Divine intelligence. In this manner the *Sforno* explains the difficult term אֱלֹהֵי הָאֱלֹהִים, *God of gods,* for it is not praiseworthy or proper to speak of Hashem in relationship to other gods! Rather it is to be understood as God being the source of the eternal and everlasting, as well as of Divine intelligence, from which emanate similar qualities to others (compare this to the *Rambam's Guide* II:6).

אֵת הַשָּׁמַיִם — *The heavens.* The *Sforno* derives the word שָׁמַיִם from שָׁם, *there.* The heaven above, from our perspective on earth, is *there.* To us everything in heaven *appears* to be the same distance away, even though in reality it is not so. Now since this thing called שָׁמַיִם, *heaven,* is so named, only in relationship to man on earth, the Torah cannot state *He created heaven,* but must precede it with the indefinite article אֵת, thereby indicating that it is so called relative to our perception. In keeping with this interpretation the *Sforno* explains הָאָרֶץ, written with the definite article ה, as indicating that *this* earth is to be considered as the center of the sphere of the Zodiac, so destined to be, by God's will. The *Sforno* is proposing the theory that the world is geocentric.

2. וְהָאָרֶץ הָיְתָה תֹהוּ וָבֹהוּ — *And the earth was desolate and void.* The *Sforno* explains the two words תֹּהוּ *(tohu)* and בֹּהוּ *(bohu)* in the following manner. All matter had to be created by God since we reject the theory of the eternity of matter. Matter, as such, only had potential (כֹּחַ) and was not actual. This is called תֹּהוּ in the Hebrew language. An idol

ג וְחֹשֶׁךְ עַל־פְּנֵי תְהוֹם וְרוּחַ אֱלֹהִים מְרַחֶפֶת עַל־פְּנֵי הַמָּיִם: וַיֹּאמֶר אֱלֹהִים
ד יְהִי־אוֹר וַיְהִי־אוֹר: וַיַּרְא אֱלֹהִים אֶת־הָאוֹר כִּי־טוֹב וַיַּבְדֵּל אֱלֹהִים בֵּין
ה הָאוֹר וּבֵין הַחֹשֶׁךְ: וַיִּקְרָא אֱלֹהִים ׀ לָאוֹר יוֹם וְלַחֹשֶׁךְ קָרָא לָיְלָה
וַיְהִי־עֶרֶב וַיְהִי־בֹקֶר יוֹם אֶחָד:
ו וַיֹּאמֶר אֱלֹהִים יְהִי רָקִיעַ בְּתוֹךְ הַמָּיִם וִיהִי מַבְדִּיל בֵּין מַיִם לָמָיִם:
ז וַיַּעַשׂ אֱלֹהִים אֶת־הָרָקִיעַ וַיַּבְדֵּל בֵּין הַמַּיִם אֲשֶׁר מִתַּחַת לָרָקִיעַ וּבֵין

וְחֹשֶׁךְ עַל פְּנֵי תְהוֹם — *With darkness upon the surface of the deep.* The dark air which emanated from the first amalgam was on the surface of the two lower elements (water and earth) which also emanated from the first amalgam; these encircled one another.

וְרוּחַ אֱלֹהִים מְרַחֶפֶת עַל פְּנֵי הַמָּיִם — *And the Divine Presence hovered upon the surface of the waters.* The (angels) that moved the spheres who are called רוּחַ, *wind,* as it says, עֹשֶׂה מַלְאָכָיו רוחות, *Who makes wind His angels (messengers)* (*Psalms* 104:4) moved the dark air over the surface of the water, which then encompassed the foundation of the earth. As a result, the inner part (of the dark air) close to the orb overheated through the friction of its movement and that became the element of fire, while that part (of the dark air) close to the water was cooled by the water, except for a small portion thereof which became heated, thereby forming sparks which gave forth light.

3. יְהִי אוֹר — *Let there be light.* This is the light of the seven days (of Creation) for the purpose of generating growth without the benefit of seed. This (phenomenon) will also come to pass at the end of days (lit., "the future") for our Sages tell us that this hidden light will be used for the purpose of bringing forth cakes and woolen robes without the medium of planted seed (*Shabbos* 30b).

4. וַיַּרְא אֱלֹהִים אֶת הָאוֹר כִּי טוֹב — *God saw that the light was good.* And so it was, for God *saw* (comprehended) (that light was good) and He chose its existence toward the end of

NOTES

is called תֹּהוּ because it has no substance. The phrase בֹּהוּ is a combination of two words, בו and הוּא, *it is in it.* Hence the word בֹּהוּ means the form which contains within it בֹּהוּ, *primeval matter.* This in turn is comprised of the four primeval elements of fire, air, water, and dust. The potential of תֹּהוּ became actual through the בֹּהוּ — the initial form. Said form did not remain inflexible but kept changing until it eventually reached its final state, on the subsequent days of Creation. At the beginning of Creation, heaven, earth and all which is in them were created at one time, בְּכֹחַ, *in potentia;* afterward, this potential was formed into the substantive, each on its day, as chosen by God.

וְחֹשֶׁךְ עַל פְּנֵי תְהוֹם – *With darkness upon the surface of the deep.* The sequence of events recorded in this verse, as interpreted by the *Sforno,* is to be understood as follows: *Darkness* is not to be understood as the absence of light but as a specific object of God's creation. It was composed of fire and air, two of the fundamental elements. The תְּהוֹם, *the deep,* contained the other two elements, water and dust. These four elements emanated from the first amalgam. Now there were two intersecting circles, the outer being fire and the inner air, which hovered over the surface of the deep, which was composed of water and dust. The light mentioned in the next verse resulted from the sparks created by the movement of the sphere, said movement being caused by the angels, i.e., the wind sent by God. As the *Rambam* says (*Guide* II:6), "All forces (of God) are (called) angels."

3. יְהִי אוֹר – *Let there be light.* The statement of our Sages in Tractate *Shabbos* that *Eretz Yisrael,* the Land of Israel, in future time will bring forth "cakes and woolen robes," is explained by the *Sforno* as resulting from the unique powerful light of the seven days of Creation, which was capable of generating growth without the benefit of seed, and which will shine again in future time. According to tradition, this special light was deemed fit only for the righteous and was therefore "stored" away by God, to be used at the end of days. It is this unique generative light that our Sages refer to in the above-cited passage of the Talmud.

4. וַיַּרְא אֱלֹהִים אֶת הָאוֹר כִּי טוֹב – *God saw that the light was good.* One cannot say of God, as one would say of a human being, that after an object is

surface of the deep, and the Divine Presence hovered upon the surface of
the waters — 3 *God said, "Let there be light," and there was light.* 4 *God*
saw that the light was good, and God separated between the light and the
darkness. 5 *God called to the light: "Day," and to the darkness He called:*
"Night." And there was evening and there was morning, one day.
6 *God said, "Let there be a firmament in the midst of the waters, and let*
it separate between water and water." 7 *So God made the firmament, and*
separated between the waters which were beneath the firmament and the

---

the achievement of *good*, and He brought it (light) into being through His knowledge which is the "efficient cause" (that alone brought it into actuality).

וַיַּבְדֵּל אֱלֹהִים בֵּין הָאוֹר וּבֵין הַחֹשֶׁךְ — *And God separated between the light and the darkness.* During those days that the primeval light served the world, there were periods of light and periods of darkness without the revolution of the spheres. It was so only through Divine Will which separated between the "time" of light and the "time" of darkness.

5. וַיִּקְרָא אֱלֹהִים לָאוֹר יוֹם — *God called to the light: "Day."* Although the periods of light and darkness did not function at that time in the same manner as they do today, when we call (these periods) by their names of day and night, nonetheless ...

וַיְהִי עֶרֶב וַיְהִי בֹקֶר — *And there was evening and there was morning.* Although God separated light and darkness so that they might serve at different times, without benefit of the revolution of the spheres, nonetheless He separated (these periods of light and darkness) in a gradual manner so that there was a time called "evening" as night arrived and a time called "morning" as day came.

6. יְהִי רָקִיעַ בְּתוֹךְ הַמָּיִם — *Let there be a firmament in the midst of the waters.* Let the nature of the elemental waters become as though the form of a wheel is girdling it, separating one part from the other, in such a manner that a portion of the upper waters adjacent to the air mass change once again to the nature of vapor. In this manner, they will be elevated to a (higher) area of the elemental air. This air will now perforce somehow be made into a place for that portion (of water) which changed to vapor. It will expand considerably into a larger area than it was originally (and become the firmament).

7. וַיַּעַשׂ אֱלֹהִים אֶת הָרָקִיעַ — *So God made the firmament.* Now, since the rest of the foundation waters — which remained below those waters that vaporized — gathered together, as it says, יִקָּווּ הַמַּיִם מִתַּחַת הַשָּׁמַיִם, *let the waters beneath the heaven be gathered,* it should

NOTES

formed or a certain matter fashioned, it is examined and found to be good. Hence the expression וַיַּרְא אֱלֹהִים, *and God saw,* does not mean He saw His handiwork, i.e., light, and found it to His liking, for it was good. Rather וַיַּרְא means: because God knew that light was good for the world and its inhabitants, therefore He created it. As the *Rambam* says (*Guide* II:30), "The meaning of the words 'that it was good' is that the thing in question is externally visible and of manifest utility for the existence and permanence of that which exists." The expression יְדִיעָתוֹ הַפּוֹעֶלֶת, *His knowledge which is the efficient cause,* means that God does not have to order something to happen through a command, but as soon as He "knows," in the sense of the "potential," it becomes "actual."

5. וַיִּקְרָא אֱלֹהִים לָאוֹר יוֹם – *God called to the light: "Day."* Although the periods of light and darkness functioned arbitrarily, by the will of God, and were separated by His decree — not as a result of the revolution of the spheres — nonetheless the changeover from light to darkness and darkness to light did not occur abruptly but happened gradually, as it does now; evening leading into darkness and dawn into the light of day. This, also, was due to the kindness of Hashem for the benefit of the world — even before there was man or living creatures.

7. וַיַּעַשׂ אֱלֹהִים אֶת הָרָקִיעַ – *So God made the firmament.* Since the lower waters gathered into one area leaving a vacuum, by right the upper

ח הַמַּיִם אֲשֶׁר מֵעַל לָרָקִיעַ וַיְהִי־כֵן: וַיִּקְרָא אֱלֹהִים לָרָקִיעַ שָׁמָיִם וַיְהִי־
עֶרֶב וַיְהִי־בֹקֶר יוֹם שֵׁנִי:
ט וַיֹּאמֶר אֱלֹהִים יִקָּווּ הַמַּיִם מִתַּחַת הַשָּׁמַיִם אֶל־מָקוֹם אֶחָד וְתֵרָאֶה
י הַיַּבָּשָׁה וַיְהִי־כֵן: וַיִּקְרָא אֱלֹהִים | לַיַּבָּשָׁה אֶרֶץ וּלְמִקְוֵה הַמַּיִם קָרָא
יא יַמִּים וַיַּרְא אֱלֹהִים כִּי־טוֹב: וַיֹּאמֶר אֱלֹהִים תַּדְשֵׁא הָאָרֶץ דֶּשֶׁא
עֵשֶׂב מַזְרִיעַ זֶרַע עֵץ פְּרִי עֹשֶׂה פְּרִי לְמִינוֹ אֲשֶׁר זַרְעוֹ־בוֹ עַל־הָאָרֶץ
יב וַיְהִי־כֵן: וַתּוֹצֵא הָאָרֶץ דֶּשֶׁא עֵשֶׂב מַזְרִיעַ זֶרַע לְמִינֵהוּ וְעֵץ עֹשֶׂה־
יג פְּרִי אֲשֶׁר זַרְעוֹ־בוֹ לְמִינֵהוּ וַיַּרְא אֱלֹהִים כִּי־טוֹב: וַיְהִי־עֶרֶב וַיְהִי־
יד בֹקֶר יוֹם שְׁלִישִׁי: וַיֹּאמֶר אֱלֹהִים יְהִי מְאֹרֹת בִּרְקִיעַ הַשָּׁמַיִם לְהַבְדִּיל
טו בֵּין הַיּוֹם וּבֵין הַלָּיְלָה וְהָיוּ לְאֹתֹת וּלְמוֹעֲדִים וּלְיָמִים וְשָׁנִים: וְהָיוּ

---

follow that the upper waters which became vapor would have filled the vacuum left by the departure of the waters. However, He made the רָקִיעַ which separated (the higher and lower waters), in such a manner that it (the רָקִיעַ) was given the power of restraint, preventing the vapor portion — that is, the water which was above the firmament — from descending; in a manner that the (newly) fashioned atmosphere did fill the void while the vapor remained in its initial position. Now, when the moist vaporized water becomes dense, it brings forth rain, snow and hail as it becomes laden heavily (with water) and descends (to the earth), as it says, לְקוֹל תִּתּוֹ הֲמוֹן מַיִם בַּשָּׁמַיִם, *At the sound of His giving a multitude of waters in the heavens (Jeremiah* 10:13). What is meant by the term הַשָּׁמַיִם *(the heavens)* is the firmament which holds back the vapor portion, as it says, *And God called the firmament heaven* (verse 8). And when the smoke-laden mist comes there, it results in thunder and lightning as it says, וַיַּעֲלֶה נְשִׂאִים מִקְצֵה הָאָרֶץ בְּרָקִים לַמָּטָר עָשָׂה, *He causes the clouds to ascend from the ends of the earth, He makes lightning for the rain (Jeremiah* 10:13). Since the elemental waters, which are denser, are above the light air, this condition is contrary to nature, indicating that it is an act performed by God's Will, directed without a doubt toward a (good) purpose and end, as it says, וּמַעֲשֵׂה יָדָיו מַגִּיד הָרָקִיעַ, *the firmament shows His handiwork (Psalms* 19:2).

וַיְהִי כֵן — *And it was so.* It remained so contrary to its (own) nature.

8. וַיִּקְרָא אֱלֹהִים לָרָקִיעַ שָׁמָיִם — *God called to the firmament: "Heaven"* ... because the heavenly functionings reach the earth through the medium (of the רָקִיעַ), as it says: *And God set them in the firmament of the heaven to give light upon the earth, to dominate by day and by night, and to separate, etc.* (verses 17, 18).

9. יִקָּווּ הַמַּיִם אֶל מָקוֹם אֶחָד — *Let the waters be gathered into one area.* This drying

NOTES

waters should have come down to fill that void. The firmament, however, held them back, and instead, the air, replaced by the upper waters which had become vapor, came down and filled the void with atmosphere. The vapor is heavier than air, still it remains above (restrained by the firmament) except when it rains or snows. This is one of the great wonders of the Creator, done for the benefit of the world and its inhabitants.

8. וַיִּקְרָא אֱלֹהִים לָרָקִיעַ שָׁמָיִם — *God called to the firmament: "Heaven."* The *Sforno* is explaining why the רָקִיעַ, *firmament,* is called שָׁמַיִם, *heaven.* Since the light of the luminaries, which are *heavenly* bodies, reach the earth *through* the firmament, it is called שָׁמַיִם, *heaven.*

9. יִקָּווּ הַמַּיִם ... — *Let the waters be gathered.* The ocean waters do not go beyond the boundary of sand on the shore. God established this border to protect the integrity of the dry land.

10. וַיִּקְרָא אֱלֹהִים לַיַּבָּשָׁה אֶרֶץ — *God called to the dry land: "Earth."* The name אֶרֶץ was already given to the earth, in the first verse of this chapter. This verse, which states that *dry land* was called אֶרֶץ, *earth,* signifies that although earth is a general

waters which were above the firmament. And it was so. 8 *God called to the*
firmament: "Heaven." And there was evening and there was morning, a
second day.
9 *God said, "Let the waters beneath the heaven be gathered into one*
area, and let the dry land appear." And it was so. 10 *God called to the dry*
land: "Earth," and to the gathering of waters He called: "Seas." And God
saw that it was good. 11 *God said, "Let the earth sprout vegetation:*
herbage yielding seed, fruit trees yielding fruit each after its kind,
containing its own seed on the earth." And it was so. 12 *And the earth*
brought forth vegetation: herbage yielding seed after its kind, and trees
yielding fruit, each containing its seed after its kind. And God saw that it
was good. 13 *And there was evening and there was morning, a third day.*
14 *God said, "Let there be luminaries in the firmament of the heaven to*
separate between the day and between the night; and they shall serve as
signs, and for festivals, and for days and years; 15 *and they shall serve as*

(process) by which the exposed (dry) land occurred, was not due to the effect of the constellations (מַעֲרָכוֹת הַשָּׁמַיִם), as many may think, rather (God) commanded that (the waters) be gathered in order that they not transgress (their bounds). Therefore, though they are higher than the earth they do not descend upon it, as our senses testify, as it says, גְּבוּל שַׂמְתָּ בַּל יַעֲבֹרוּן בַּל יְשׁוּבוּן לְכַסּוֹת הָאָרֶץ, *You set a bound which they do not pass over, that they may not return to cover the earth (Psalms* 104:9).

10. וַיִּקְרָא אֱלֹהִים לַיַּבָּשָׁה אֶרֶץ — *God called to the dry land: "Earth."*
He called that specific area (i.e., dry land) by its (original) general name (i.e., אֶרֶץ, *earth*), since that area was the principal-intended part of the entire earth, as it states: לָשֶׁבֶת יְצָרָהּ, *He formed it to be inhabited (Isaiah* 45:18).

וַיַּרְא אֱלֹהִים כִּי טוֹב — *And God saw that it was good.* He so wanted it, toward the intended end (which was) *good.*

11. דֶּשֶׁא — *Vegetation.* This refers to a variety of herbage fit for animals, as it says: כִּי דָשְׁאוּ נְאוֹת מִדְבָּר, *For the pastures of the wilderness spring forth abundant growth (Joel* 2:22).

עֵשֶׂב מַזְרִיעַ זֶרַע — *Herbage yielding seed.* For man to eat.

עֵץ פְּרִי עֹשֶׂה פְּרִי לְמִינוֹ — *Fruit trees yielding fruit each after its kind.* A hybrid of two kinds will not reproduce.

וַיְהִי כֵן — *And it was so.* So it was established (and remained) that it not (be able) to accept less (than its inherent nature) or more (of a different species) so that if perchance there be a hybrid from two kinds, it will not reproduce.

14. יְהִי מְאֹרֹת בִּרְקִיעַ הַשָּׁמַיִם — *Let there be luminaries in the firmament of the heaven.* Let there be the spark of light from the luminaries in that firmament created on the second day, and let it increase and refract so as to work upon the lower (terrestrial) land, as related in this chapter. We see through our (own) senses that there is an increase of light when it passes through clear (pure) water.

NOTES

term incorporating the totality of the planet Earth, it is the dry land which represents the primary purpose for which the earth was created, as we see from the verse of *Isaiah* quoted by the *Sforno.*

וַיַּרְא אֱלֹהִים כִּי טוֹב — *And God saw that it was good.* As explained in verse 4, the word וַיַּרְא, *He saw,* does not mean He saw *after* the creation of dry land but signifies the *reason* for God's decision to gather the waters and expose dry land, namely, to realize His original intent of bringing "good" to the world and its inhabitants.

טז לִמְאוֹרֹת בִּרְקִיעַ הַשָּׁמַיִם לְהָאִיר עַל־הָאָרֶץ וַיְהִי־כֵן׃ וַיַּעַשׂ אֱלֹהִים
אֶת־שְׁנֵי הַמְּאֹרֹת הַגְּדֹלִים אֶת־הַמָּאוֹר הַגָּדֹל לְמֶמְשֶׁלֶת הַיּוֹם וְאֶת־
יז הַמָּאוֹר הַקָּטֹן לְמֶמְשֶׁלֶת הַלַּיְלָה וְאֵת הַכּוֹכָבִים׃ וַיִּתֵּן אֹתָם אֱלֹהִים
יח בִּרְקִיעַ הַשָּׁמָיִם לְהָאִיר עַל־הָאָרֶץ׃ וְלִמְשֹׁל בַּיּוֹם וּבַלַּיְלָה וּלְהַבְדִּיל בֵּין
יט הָאוֹר וּבֵין הַחֹשֶׁךְ וַיַּרְא אֱלֹהִים כִּי־טוֹב׃ וַיְהִי־עֶרֶב וַיְהִי־בֹקֶר יוֹם רְבִיעִי׃
כ וַיֹּאמֶר אֱלֹהִים יִשְׁרְצוּ הַמַּיִם שֶׁרֶץ נֶפֶשׁ חַיָּה וְעוֹף יְעוֹפֵף עַל־הָאָרֶץ עַל־
כא פְּנֵי רְקִיעַ הַשָּׁמָיִם׃ וַיִּבְרָא אֱלֹהִים אֶת־הַתַּנִּינִם הַגְּדֹלִים וְאֵת כָּל־נֶפֶשׁ
הַחַיָּה ׀ הָרֹמֶשֶׂת אֲשֶׁר שָׁרְצוּ הַמַּיִם לְמִינֵהֶם וְאֵת כָּל־עוֹף כָּנָף לְמִינֵהוּ
כב וַיַּרְא אֱלֹהִים כִּי־טוֹב׃ וַיְבָרֶךְ אֹתָם אֱלֹהִים לֵאמֹר פְּרוּ וּרְבוּ וּמִלְאוּ
כג אֶת־הַמַּיִם בַּיַּמִּים וְהָעוֹף יִרֶב בָּאָרֶץ׃ וַיְהִי־עֶרֶב וַיְהִי־בֹקֶר יוֹם חֲמִישִׁי׃
כד וַיֹּאמֶר אֱלֹהִים תּוֹצֵא הָאָרֶץ נֶפֶשׁ חַיָּה לְמִינָהּ בְּהֵמָה וָרֶמֶשׂ וְחַיְתוֹ־
כה אֶרֶץ לְמִינָהּ וַיְהִי־כֵן׃ וַיַּעַשׂ אֱלֹהִים אֶת־חַיַּת הָאָרֶץ לְמִינָהּ וְאֶת־

---

15. לְהָאִיר עַל הָאָרֶץ — *To shine upon the earth.* That blended (filtered) light shall shine (upon the earth in a manner) suitable for its inhabitants.

וַיְהִי כֵן — *And it was so.* That blend (of light filtered through the firmament), which came about perforce by God's command, was established and remained (for all time).

16-18. וַיַּעַשׂ . . . וַיִּתֵּן . . . לְהָאִיר . . . וְלִמְשֹׁל . . . וּלְהַבְדִּיל . . . כִּי טוֹב — *And [God] made . . . And [God] set . . . to give light . . . to dominate . . . and to separate . . . that it was good.* Regarding the luminaries and other stars (the phrase used) is וַיַּעַשׂ, *And [God] made,* for they were already (created) as part of the spheres, or of the heavens, the creation of which the Torah already related (in verse 1), therefore the verb *create* is not used, but *make.*

Now, the reason why they were made (different than the other spheres and orbs) in round forms and as shining ones, is because, כִּי טוֹב, *that it was good,* i.e., God's intent was for the good (of mankind) which was the proper ultimate purpose of His act.

וְלִמְשֹׁל בַּיּוֹם וּבַלַּיְלָה — *To dominate by day and by night.* (They dominate by) generating existences (creatures) in the (terrestrial) lower world. This (light) was necessary to function with the primeval light to bring living creatures into being, for they are more important (and complex) than the plant (world).

וּלְהַבְדִּיל בֵּין הָאוֹר וּבֵין הַחֹשֶׁךְ — *And to separate between the light and between the darkness.* (This means) to separate, in the lower (terrestrial) world, through its rising and setting,

NOTES

14-15. יְהִי מְאֹרֹת בִּרְקִיעַ הַשָּׁמַיִם . . . לְהָאִיר עַל הָאָרֶץ — *Let there be luminaries in the firmament . . . to shine upon the earth.* The source of the light emanating from the luminaries is in the higher heavens. However, it comes to earth through the firmament, thereby radiating and refracting and increasing its efficacy. That is why both terms are used — רָקִיעַ and שָׁמַיִם.

16-18. This commentary of the *Sforno* does not appear in the *Mikraos Gedolos* edition, but does appear in the *Mosad Harav Kook* edition which is based on a number of different manuscripts.

20. יְעוֹפֵף עַל הָאָרֶץ עַל פְּנֵי רְקִיעַ הַשָּׁמָיִם — *(And fowl) that fly about over the earth across the expanse of the heavens.* The *Sforno* is of the opinion that there was a residue of mist and vapor generated by the heat working on the moisture of the firmament. The birds' wings act as fans circulating these vapors and clear the air for the benefit of mankind.

21-22. וַיִּבְרָא אֱלֹהִים אֶת הַתַּנִּינִם — *And God created the great sea-giants.* The phrase וַיִּבְרָא, *(And God) created,* is used here for the first time since the first day. It denotes that a new כֹּחַ, *potential force,* had to be introduced into the waters to produce such huge sea-creatures. A special blessing was also necessary, so as to realize the end purpose for which they were created.

24. תּוֹצֵא הָאָרֶץ נֶפֶשׁ חַיָּה — *Let the earth bring forth living creatures.* Beyond the דּוֹמֵם, *inanimate, min-*

luminaries in the firmament of the heaven to shine upon the earth." And it was so. [16] *And God made the two great luminaries, the greater luminary to dominate the day and the lesser luminary to dominate the night; and the stars.* [17] *And God set them in the firmament of the heaven to give light upon the earth,* [18] *to dominate by day and by night, and to separate between the light and between the darkness. And God saw that it was good.* [19] *And there was evening and there was morning, a fourth day.*

[20] *God said, "Let the waters teem with teeming living creatures, and fowl that fly about over the earth across the expanse of the heavens."* [21] *And God created the great sea-giants and every living being that creeps, with which the waters teemed after their kinds; and all winged fowl after its kind. And God saw that it was good.* [22] *God blessed them, saying, "Be fruitful and multiply, and fill the waters in the seas; but the fowl shall increase on the earth."* [23] *And there was evening and there was morning, a fifth day.*

[24] *God said, "Let the earth bring forth living creatures after its kind: animal, and creeping thing, and beast of the land each according to its kind." And it was so.* [25] *God made the beast of the earth after its kind,*

---

between the period of light which was called day and the period of darkness which was called night, as it says above *to separate between the day and between the night* (verse 14).

20. וְעוֹף יְעוֹפֵף עַל הָאָרֶץ עַל פְּנֵי רְקִיעַ הַשָּׁמָיִם — *(And fowl) that fly about over the earth across the expanse of the heavens.* (They) cleanse the air (atmosphere) of the earth, on behalf of its inhabitants, of extraneous moisture coming from the firmament, which was created on the second day, through the medium of the sparks which worked upon it.

21. וַיִּבְרָא אֱלֹהִים אֶת הַתַּנִּינִם — *And God created the great sea-giants.* The generative potential which was present in the water (as endowed by God), was not sufficient (in power) to bring forth the first sea-giants without seed, until (God) created at that time sufficient potential (power) to do so.

22. וַיְבָרֶךְ אֹתָם אֱלֹהִים — *God blessed them.* Their end purpose would not be realized unless they were numerous.

24. תּוֹצֵא הָאָרֶץ נֶפֶשׁ חַיָּה — *Let the earth bring forth living creatures.* A living soul in addition to the (living) plants which grow.

וַיְהִי כֵן — *And it was so.* Nothing was added or diminished; and if a new hybrid be crossbred from two species it will not be capable of reproducing.

25. וַיַּעַשׂ אֱלֹהִים אֶת חַיַּת הָאָרֶץ לְמִינָהּ — *God made the beast of the earth after its kind.* He endowed each species with whatever senses and faculties were required by that species.

NOTES

eral, and the צוֹמֵחַ, *growing plants,* are חַי, *living,* i.e., creatures which possess the spark of life; free, living, breathing beings. This characteristic, which makes them superior to the two lower categories, is called נֶפֶשׁ, a *soul,* by the Torah. It is to this that the *Sforno* alludes when he states, "a living soul in addition to the (living) plants which grow."

וַיְהִי כֵן – *And it was so.* The expression וַיְהִי כֵן, *and it was so,* is used here and above in verse 11, as it is used in verses 7, 9, 15 and 30; however, the *Sforno* apparently feels the need to comment only here and in verse 11, where the Torah speaks of *after its kind.* It is his opinion that כֵן implies something that is immutably set, firmly established in the nature of the plant and animal kingdoms, regarding their reproductive capacity. What is common to both is the exactness and absolute preciseness of each species and kind created by the Almighty — neither too little or too much. Hence, if an attempt is made to graft or crossbreed, though a hybrid may result, it will not be able to reproduce!

הַבְּהֵמָה֙ לְמִינָ֔הּ וְאֵ֛ת כָּל־רֶ֥מֶשׂ הָֽאֲדָמָ֖ה לְמִינֵ֑הוּ וַיַּ֥רְא אֱלֹהִ֖ים כִּי־טֽוֹב:

כו וַיֹּ֣אמֶר אֱלֹהִ֗ים נַֽעֲשֶׂ֥ה אָדָ֛ם בְּצַלְמֵ֖נוּ כִּדְמוּתֵ֑נוּ וְיִרְדּוּ֩ בִדְגַ֨ת הַיָּ֜ם וּבְע֣וֹף

כז הַשָּׁמַ֗יִם וּבַבְּהֵמָה֙ וּבְכָל־הָאָ֔רֶץ וּבְכָל־הָרֶ֖מֶשׂ הָֽרֹמֵ֣שׂ עַל־הָאָֽרֶץ: וַיִּבְרָ֨א

אֱלֹהִ֤ים ׀ אֶת־הָֽאָדָם֙ בְּצַלְמ֔וֹ בְּצֶ֥לֶם אֱלֹהִ֖ים בָּרָ֣א אֹת֑וֹ זָכָ֥ר וּנְקֵבָ֖ה בָּרָ֥א

26. וַיֹּאמֶר אֱלֹהִים נַעֲשֶׂה — *And God said, "Let us make (man)."* He then endowed His פַּמַלְיָא, *His heavenly host*, with the power to impart the (heavenly) image to the subject which was prepared for it (i.e., man).

אָדָם — *Man.* (Man is) a species of the "living being" species, which I (already) formed (verse 24), whose name is "Adam," as it says, *And man became a living creature.* Let us make him ...

בְּצַלְמֵנוּ — *In our image.* (Who shall be) one (lit., "an object") that is everlasting (נִצְחִי) and (endowed with) reason (שִׂכְלִי); and thus God, the Blessed One, gave man an opening in His Torah to acquire knowledge regarding those separated from matter (i.e., the angels) through the (intuitive) knowledge of our souls.

כִּדְמוּתֵנוּ — *As our likeness ...* indeed — that he be in a small way like the "Heavenly host," insofar as they function with knowledge and recognition (understanding). However, their actions (i.e., the angels) are (performed) without (freedom) of choice, and in this sense man is not like them. In a limited manner, man is (also) like God, the Blessed One, Who acts with choice. However, God's choice is always (to do) good, but man's choice is not (always) so. In this (area) the Divine (freedom of choice) is far superior to man's (freedom of) choice. Therefore it says, כִּדְמוּתֵנוּ, *"as"* our likeness, not בִּדְמוּתֵנוּ, *"in"* our likeness (which would mean it is so) in truth.

NOTES

26. וַיֹּאמֶר אֱלֹהִים נַעֲשֶׂה — *And God said, "Let us make (man)."* The phrase נַעֲשֶׂה, *let us make,* is in the plural, which obviously presents a great difficulty, considering the "oneness" and "unity" of the Almighty. Rashi's explanation, based upon the interpretation of our Sages, is well known, namely, to teach us a great lesson in humility, that a superior consult with his inferiors. The *Sforno,* however, follows the interpretation of the *Rambam* in his *Guide* (II:6) based on the Talmud (*Sanhedrin* 38b) which states that "The Holy One, Blessed is He, does nothing without consulting the 'famalya' (*host* or *families*) above." This does not mean that God consults or asks the opinion of His "Heavenly household." The meaning is rather that God acts and governs through the intermediary vehicle of angels, "for all forces are angels" (the words used by the *Rambam*). Angels are "intellects separate from matter" (*Guide* I:49) and these separate intellects are God's intermediaries. This then explains the plural form of נַעֲשֶׂה אָדָם, *Let "us" make man,* i.e., God creates through His intermediaries (angels) as explained. By *image* (צֶלֶם) the *Sforno* means the power of "intellectual apprehension" (intuitive understanding) imparted to man through the angels, as the *Rambam* explains in his *Guide* I:1.

אָדָם — *Man.* Included in the general species of *living beings* was a species called "Adam." This is

clearly stated in 2:7. What this species was is not yet clarified or described. The vessel (his body) was in existence waiting for further development. When God says, "Let us make this species called Adam, *in our image, after our likeness,"* the identity of "Adam," his special unique character and position in the scheme of Creation, becomes clear. This interpretation of the *Sforno* reconciles this verse with that of 2:7, in a manner which demonstrates the two are not redundant.

בְּצַלְמֵנוּ — *In our image.* To understand what the *Sforno* is saying regarding the term צֶלֶם in relation to man, one must examine the Rambam's *Guide* I:1. There Maimonides explains that the term צֶלֶם (image) in Hebrew does not denote the shape and configuration of a thing. The proper term designating that form is תּוֹאַר. Image, on the other hand, "is applied to the natural form." In man this refers to his "intellectual apprehension." This is what the *Sforno* means by שִׂכְלִי, *reason* or *intellect.* Through this power of the intellect, man now possesses an "image" similar to that of the angels — hence בְּצַלְמֵנוּ, *in our image.*

The term נִצְחִי means that which has eternal existence, enduring and immutable. In connection with Adam it refers to his immortal soul.

כִּדְמוּתֵנוּ — *As our likeness.* Whereas צַלְמֵנוּ, *our image,* refers to man's intellectual apprehension,

and the animal after its kind, and every creeping being of the ground after its kind. And God saw that it was good.

26 *And God said, "Let us make man in our image, as our likeness. They shall rule over the fish of the sea, the birds of the sky, and over the animal, the whole earth, and every creeping thing that creeps upon the earth."*
27 *So God created man in His image, in the image of God He created him; male and female He created them.*

---

27. בְּצֶלֶם אֱלֹהִים — *In the image of God.* The term *Elohim* used in a comparable sense (or as a counterpart) can be applied to every intelligent force (object) separated from matter which is perfect (complete) and (can function) in actuality and as such, is perforce everlasting. Therefore (this term) is used regarding God, the Blessed One, and His angels. It is also applied to judges (reflecting) their power of reason which is suitable for them. However, even though human reasoning functions without any material medium, expanding to the extrasensory and to a limited extent, even into the future, nor does (this power) weaken through much use or with age but increases in strength, which demonstrates that man's reason is also without a doubt separated from matter — seeing that the opposite is true of all physical material powers — nonetheless, before man contemplates and thinks deeply, lacking the perfection and completeness prepared for him, he cannot be called *Elohim*, but can only be called the *image* of *Elohim* — until he attains perfection. (This is) especially (so until he attains) the wisdom which brings to the love and awe of God. Only then will he become one who is intellectually apprehensive in deed (action); perfect and separated from matter, resulting in immortality, existing even after the death of his body. Now since man can choose to attain this perfection, by striving to delve into the aforementioned wisdom (it follows) that if he restrains himself from (this perfection) his intellectual powers will remain (only) potential, deprived of all perfection in the actual (as it was in the beginning), resulting in his desolation and destruction, as it says: אָדָם בִּיקָר וְלֹא יָבִין נִמְשַׁל כַּבְּהֵמוֹת נִדְמוּ, *Man is in his splendor (honor) but does not understand, he is like the beasts that perish (Psalms 49:21).* All this, God, the Blessed One, taught us in these two words, saying בְּצֶלֶם אֱלֹהִים, *in the image of Elohim.*

NOTES

כִּדְמוּתֵנוּ, *as our likeness*, refers to the actions of men and the angels. The reason why the expression used is כִּדְמוּתֵנוּ, *as our likeness*, and not בִּדְמוּתֵנוּ, *in our likeness*, is because man is only "similar to" the angels in his actions, but not "the same," for man is tempted by his evil inclination and has freedom of choice in fulfilling God's commandments, whereas the angels do not, being compelled by their nature and essence to obey the Almighty. In this respect man is "higher than the angels." This freedom of choice granted to man is a reflection of God Himself, Who is the ultimate in רָצוֹן, *will* — for all that He does is by His choice. In this respect also man is only "similar" but certainly not "the same," for God's choices are always טוֹב, *good*, whereas man chooses both good and evil. Hence man is *as our likeness*, i.e., כִּדְמוּתֵנוּ but not בִּדְמוּתֵנוּ, considering that he is similar to God — but not in every respect; and he is similar to the angels — but not the same.

27. בְּצֶלֶם אֱלֹהִים — *In the image of God.* The *Sforno* is explaining why the term *Elohim* is not applied to man, only that of the image of *Elohim*, considering that this term *(Elohim)* is not reserved for God alone, but is applied to angels and judges as well. After all, if man is similar to God and the angels, having been created in their "image and likeness," why then is he only an "image" of *Elohim*? The argument can even be strengthened, as the *Sforno* does here, by pointing out the reasoning power and intellectual capacity of man which is comparable to the angels, to the extent that these qualities function, akin to theirs, without benefit of any physical limb or organ, as the *Rambam* states in his *Guide* and in the *Mishnah Torah (Yesodei HaTorah* 4:8). However, all this is true only in man's potential but does not become actual, unless he chooses to attain perfection, separate himself from matter (as such) and translate his intellectual apprehension into action — all of these being the

כח אֹתָם: וַיְבָרֶךְ אֹתָם אֱלֹהִים וַיֹּאמֶר לָהֶם אֱלֹהִים פְּרוּ וּרְבוּ וּמִלְאוּ
אֶת־הָאָרֶץ וְכִבְשֻׁהָ וּרְדוּ בִּדְגַת הַיָּם וּבְעוֹף הַשָּׁמַיִם וּבְכָל־חַיָּה הָרֹמֶשֶׂת
כט עַל־הָאָרֶץ: וַיֹּאמֶר אֱלֹהִים הִנֵּה נָתַתִּי לָכֶם אֶת־כָּל־עֵשֶׂב ׀ זֹרֵעַ זֶרַע
אֲשֶׁר עַל־פְּנֵי כָל־הָאָרֶץ וְאֶת־כָּל־הָעֵץ אֲשֶׁר־בּוֹ פְרִי־עֵץ זֹרֵעַ זָרַע לָכֶם
ל יִהְיֶה לְאָכְלָה: וּלְכָל־חַיַּת הָאָרֶץ וּלְכָל־עוֹף הַשָּׁמַיִם וּלְכֹל ׀ רוֹמֵשׂ
לא עַל־הָאָרֶץ אֲשֶׁר־בּוֹ נֶפֶשׁ חַיָּה אֶת־כָּל־יֶרֶק עֵשֶׂב לְאָכְלָה וַיְהִי־כֵן: וַיַּרְא
אֱלֹהִים אֶת־כָּל־אֲשֶׁר עָשָׂה וְהִנֵּה־טוֹב מְאֹד וַיְהִי־עֶרֶב וַיְהִי־בֹקֶר יוֹם
הַשִּׁשִּׁי:

ב א־ב וַיְכֻלּוּ הַשָּׁמַיִם וְהָאָרֶץ וְכָל־צְבָאָם: וַיְכַל אֱלֹהִים בַּיּוֹם הַשְּׁבִיעִי
מְלַאכְתּוֹ אֲשֶׁר עָשָׂה וַיִּשְׁבֹּת בַּיּוֹם הַשְּׁבִיעִי מִכָּל־מְלַאכְתּוֹ אֲשֶׁר עָשָׂה:

28. וְכִבְשֻׁהָ וּרְדוּ — *And subdue it; and rule* . . . to protect it with your intelligence, and prevent the beasts from entering your limits (boundaries), for you will rule over them with nets and snares, to subject them to your service.

29. הִנֵּה נָתַתִּי לָכֶם — *Behold, I have given to you* . . . for human consumption.

30. וּלְכָל חַיַּת הָאָרֶץ — *And to every beast of the earth.* But for all the beasts of the earth, and the animals and birds I have given . . .

אֶת כָּל יֶרֶק עֵשֶׂב לְאָכְלָה — *Every green herb for food.* Species of herbs which are not planted by seeds.

31. אֶת כָּל אֲשֶׁר עָשָׂה וְהִנֵּה טוֹב מְאֹד — *All that He had made, and behold it was very good.* The end (result) of existence *in toto* was far greater than the end result of each particular part which was intended for the general purpose.

יוֹם הַשִּׁשִּׁי — *The sixth day.* The first (sixth day) which was the beginning of all *sixth days (Erev Shabbos)* when all deeds are completed so as to rest on Shabbos, as it says, וְעָשִׂיתָ

NOTES

three characteristics of angels, i.e., separation from matter, perfection, and actuality (force). Until this comes to pass, man can only be called צֶלֶם אֱלֹהִים, an *image* of *Elohim,* having not as yet merited the name *Elohim* itself! The *Sforno* also underlines the tragic consequences resulting from the squandering of these great potential forces and abilities, with which man was endowed, the ultimate goal being the attainment of the greatest wisdom of all — the love and fear (reverence) of the Almighty, which insures man's immortality. To ignore and reject his spiritual and intellectual potential is to reject the noble, unique status of אָדָם, *man* — as opposed to בְּהֵמָה, *animal* — and makes of him a mere physical being, no different than an animal.

28. וְכִבְשֻׁהָ וּרְדוּ — *And subdue it; and rule.* The two expressions *to subdue* and *to rule* refer to two separate areas of man's dominion over the animal kingdom. One is the power to prevent the beasts from overrunning man's domain, thanks to the special fear of man implanted by God in the beasts. The second is man's ability to subject animals, and channel their strength into his service.

29-30. הִנֵּה נָתַתִּי לָכֶם . . . וּלְכָל חַיַּת הָאָרֶץ — *Behold, I have given to you . . . And to every beast of the earth.* For human food consumption, God gave herbage yielding seed and seed-yielding fruit, whereas the beasts of the earth and the fowl of the heaven were confined to green herbage, which grows wild, independent of the need to be planted by man.

31. אֶת כָּל אֲשֶׁר עָשָׂה וְהִנֵּה טוֹב מְאֹד — *All that He had made, and behold it was very good.* The *Rambam (Guide* III:13) explains the expression *"And God saw that it was good,"* which is repeated a number of times in the Creation chapter (verses 10, 12, 18, 21, 25), as meaning that the existence of every *part* in the world "conformed to its purpose." He stresses that the expression טוֹב, *good,* is applied to whatever conforms to its purpose, said expression being used about man as well. The expression טוֹב מְאֹד, *very good,* used in this verse, regarding the whole of Creation, comes to teach us that whereas "sometimes a thing is good by itself and conforms for a time to our purpose," nonetheless "afterwards the goal is missed." Not so with the process of Creation where all things made

[28] *God blessed them and God said to them, "Be fruitful and multiply, fill the earth and subdue it; and rule over the fish of the sea, the bird of the sky, and every living thing that moves on the earth."*

[29] *God said, "Behold, I have given to you all herbage yielding seed that is on the surface of the entire earth, and every tree that has seed-yielding fruit; it shall be yours for food.* [30] *And to every beast of the earth, to every bird of the sky, and to everything that moves on the earth, within which there is a living soul, every green herb for food." And it was so.* [31] *And God saw all that He had made, and behold it was very good. And there was evening and there was morning, the sixth day.*

2
[1] *Thus the heaven and the earth were finished, and all their array.* [2] *By the seventh day God completed His work which He had done, and He rested on the seventh day from all His work which He had done.*

כָּל מְלַאכְתֶּךָ, *And do all your work (Exodus* 20:9) (followed by), וְיוֹם הַשְּׁבִיעִי שַׁבָּת, *but the seventh day is a Sabbath* (ibid. verse 10).

II

1. וַיְכֻלּוּ — *Were finished* ... having reached the end purpose of existence (Creation) in general.

2. וַיְכַל אֱלֹהִים בַּיּוֹם הַשְּׁבִיעִי — *By the seventh day God completed.* God completed all creative activity at the (exact) beginning of the seventh day, at the indivisible moment which marked the inception of the future time, but yet was not part of it, as our Sages said, "He entered into it by a hair's-breadth" *(Bereishis Rabbah).*

וַיִּשְׁבֹּת בַּיּוֹם הַשְּׁבִיעִי — *And He rested on the seventh day.* That entire day was distinguished from the first six days by abstention (from creative activity).

NOTES

"conformed to His intention and purpose," and continue so "without ceasing to correspond to what was intended." The *Sforno* in his commentary on this verse is expressing the same thought, adding a succinct summary, namely, that the whole represents more than the sum of its parts, and that is characterized as being *very good.*

יוֹם הַשִּׁשִּׁי — *The sixth day.* The prefix ה at the beginning of the word הַשִּׁשִּׁי, *the sixth,* is explained by our Sages (*Shabbos* 88a) as alluding to *the* sixth day of Sivan when the Torah was given, indicating that the existence of the world depends upon Israel's acceptance of the Torah. The *Sforno,* however, explains the use of the definite article as an allusion to all subsequent "sixth days," i.e., the sixth day of the week, *Erev Shabbos,* for this day will for all times carry a special character. On this day each week a Jew must feel that all his work is done so that he may rest, with ease and tranquility, on Shabbos. This echoes the statement of the *Mechilta,* quoted by *Rashi* in *Exodus* 20:9: "When Shabbos arrives, let it be in your eyes as though *all* your work is done, and put any thoughts of labor out of your mind." The end of verse 9 and the beginning of verse 10 in *Exodus* 20 are thus linked.

II

1. וַיְכֻלּוּ – *Were finished.* The expression *were finished* does not mean to imply the material completion of the creation of heaven and earth. Rather it indicates that just as every aspect and part of Creation has its purpose, so too the totality of Creation met the goal set for it by the Almighty. At the end of six days, the process of creation was "finished" in the sense that it had achieved the general purpose of Creation, as the *Sforno* puts it.

2. וַיְכַל אֱלֹהִים בַּיּוֹם הַשְּׁבִיעִי –*By the seventh day God completed.* The expression רֶגַע בִּלְתִּי מִתְחַלֵּק, *an indivisible moment,* was used by the *Sforno* in the first verse of *Bereishis* and is repeated here. The implication is a precise, exact moment in time which is compared by our Sages to a "hair's-breadth." In the case of the seventh day — Shabbos — it teaches us that the six days of Creation were total and complete, while the seventh day was total and complete in its character of rest and cessation of labor. Both are perfect and whole with

ג וַיְבָרֶךְ אֱלֹהִים אֶת־יוֹם הַשְּׁבִיעִי וַיְקַדֵּשׁ אֹתוֹ כִּי בוֹ שָׁבַת מִכָּל־מְלַאכְתּוֹ
אֲשֶׁר־בָּרָא אֱלֹהִים לַעֲשׂוֹת:
שני ד אֵלֶּה תוֹלְדוֹת הַשָּׁמַיִם וְהָאָרֶץ בְּהִבָּרְאָם בְּיוֹם עֲשׂוֹת יהוה אֱלֹהִים אֶרֶץ
ה וְשָׁמָיִם: וְכֹל ׀ שִׂיחַ הַשָּׂדֶה טֶרֶם יִהְיֶה בָאָרֶץ וְכָל־עֵשֶׂב הַשָּׂדֶה טֶרֶם
יִצְמָח כִּי לֹא הִמְטִיר יהוה אֱלֹהִים עַל־הָאָרֶץ וְאָדָם אַיִן לַעֲבֹד
ו־ז אֶת־הָאֲדָמָה: וְאֵד יַעֲלֶה מִן־הָאָרֶץ וְהִשְׁקָה אֶת־כָּל־פְּנֵי הָאֲדָמָה: וַיִּיצֶר
יהוה אֱלֹהִים אֶת־הָאָדָם עָפָר מִן־הָאֲדָמָה וַיִּפַּח בְּאַפָּיו נִשְׁמַת חַיִּים וַיְהִי
ח הָאָדָם לְנֶפֶשׁ חַיָּה: וַיִּטַּע יהוה אֱלֹהִים גַּן בְּעֵדֶן מִקֶּדֶם וַיָּשֶׂם שָׁם

3. וַיְבָרֶךְ אֱלֹהִים אֶת יוֹם הַשְּׁבִיעִי — *God blessed the seventh day.* Every future seventh day was blessed with an "added soul" so that it be more prepared than any other day to be *illuminated by the light of life* (based on *Job* 33:30) as our Sages state, כיון ששבת ווי אבדה נפש, *"When Shabbos ends, woe! The (additional) soul is lost"* (*Beitzah* 16a).

4. אֵלֶּה תוֹלְדוֹת הַשָּׁמַיִם וְהָאָרֶץ בְּהִבָּרְאָם — *These are the products of the heaven and the earth when they were created.* These plants and living creatures, which we have already mentioned, were the products of heaven and earth *in potentia*, and (were) contained within them from the time of their creation, from which time (all) active and passive, eternal and perishable powers were present, as it says (verse 1) אֵת הַשָּׁמַיִם, *the heavens* (preceded by the indefinite article אֵת). This is to be understood as an amplification, i.e., including its "offspring" (heavenly bodies and constellations). וְאֵת הָאָרֶץ, *and the earth,* which similarly is an amplification including its "offspring" (the trees, herbage and living creatures). However, all these only became actual ...

בְּיוֹם עֲשׂוֹת ה׳ אֱלֹהִים אֶרֶץ וְשָׁמָיִם — *On the day that* HASHEM *God made earth and heaven.* On that day He set in order, from heaven, the permanent natural laws of the earth and its "offspring." This was after the six days of Creation. He is then called ה׳ אֱלֹהִים, *HASHEM, Elohim,* for by setting this order, He made its existence permanent.

NOTES

total integrity. This is the meaning of the verse in *Exodus* 20:11: *In six days God made it ... and He rested on the seventh day.* Six *complete* days God made the heavens and the earth and the *entire* seventh day He rested. This also explains the expression *And He rested on the seventh day* in our verse; it implies the entire seventh day, since no part of the six days impinged upon the seventh day, nor did the seventh day impinge upon the six days.

3. וַיְבָרֶךְ אֱלֹהִים אֶת יוֹם הַשְּׁבִיעִי — *God blessed the seventh day.* The definite article ה is used before the word שְׁבִיעִי, *seventh,* to indicate that every seventh day, for all time, is blessed with an "added soul" (נְשָׁמָה יְתֵרָה). The Talmud explains this as being the reason for lamenting the end of the Shabbos, for then one loses this great gift — until the following Shabbos.

4. אֵלֶּה תוֹלְדוֹת הַשָּׁמַיִם וְהָאָרֶץ בְּהִבָּרְאָם בְּיוֹם עֲשׂוֹת ה׳ אֱלֹהִים אֶרֶץ וְשָׁמָיִם — *These are the products of the heaven and the earth when they were created on the day that* HASHEM *God made earth and heaven.* As *Rashi* points out in 1:14, everything in heaven and on earth was created *in potentia* on the first day, following which, on their appropriate days, they were brought from the potential to the actual. To this theory the *Sforno* adds that the permanent order of all these things in heaven and earth were established as laws of nature, after the six days of Creation. The reason this twofold name of God is used, i.e., ה׳ אֱלֹהִים, is explained by the *Sforno* as reflecting God's overflowing powers of eternal existence with which He endows all living matter and creatures. As the *Sforno* explained in 1:1, the name *Elohim* implies precisely that, while the name ה׳ (which in Hebrew is called הֲוָיָ׳, *to be)* indicates the ongoing permanent order of living nature — its existence flowing from the Eternal "Being."

6. וְאֵד יַעֲלֶה מִן הָאָרֶץ — *A mist ascended from the earth.* The *Sforno* is of the opinion that the mist ascended after the six days of Creation. The *Rambam (Guide* II:6), however, interprets this verse as being a description of "the first state of matters obtaining before the command of 'Let the earth bring forth grass' " (I:11). *Onkelos* also is of the

[3] *God blessed the seventh day and sanctified it because on it He rested from all His work which God created to make.*

[4] *These are the products of the heaven and the earth when they were created on the day that* HASHEM *God made earth and heaven —* [5] *now all the trees of the field were not yet on the earth and all the herb of the field had not yet sprouted, for* HASHEM *God had not sent rain upon the earth and there was no man to work the soil.* [6] *A mist ascended from the earth and watered the whole surface of the soil.* [7] *And* HASHEM *God formed the man of dust from the ground, and He blew into his nostrils the soul of life; and man became a living being.*

[8] HASHEM *God planted a garden in Eden, to the east, and placed there*

---

5. טֶרֶם יִהְיֶה בָאָרֶץ — *Were not yet on the earth.* The reason that the trees were only in their potential and not actual state when they were created, in such a manner that there were as yet no tree of the field, and so also . . .

וְכָל עֵשֶׂב הַשָּׂדֶה — *And all the herb of the field . . .* had as yet not sprouted.

כִּי לֹא הִמְטִיר — *For (Hashem) had not sent rain.* Hence the "material" was not prepared to realize its complete potential, for it lacked rain and work of the soil (by man).

6. וְאֵד יַעֲלֶה מִן הָאָרֶץ — *A mist ascended from the earth.* When (God) established (lit., "set in order") as a continual order (plant life), a mist (vapor) came up from the earth which (caused) dew, as a blessing, to water the earth, bring forth and bud, without benefit of rain or (man's) working of the soil.

7. וַיִּיצֶר ה' אֱלֹהִים — *And* HASHEM *God formed.* However, to bring forth living creatures, it was not sufficient (to use the earlier method and powers). The Creator utilized different ways and methods (to create all living creatures). To form man He chose (to use) . . .

עָפָר מִן הָאֲדָמָה — *Dust from the ground.* A distinguished part (of the ground).

וַיִּפַּח בְּאַפָּיו נִשְׁמַת חַיִּים — *And He blew into his nostrils the soul of life . . .* a vivifying soul ready to receive the "image of God," as it says: וְנִשְׁמַת שַׁדַּי תְּבִינֵם, *And the breath of the Almighty that gives them understanding (Job* 32:8), nonetheless . . .

וַיְהִי הָאָדָם לְנֶפֶשׁ חַיָּה — *And man became a living being.* In spite of all this (his special forming by God), he was still only a living creature, unable to speak, until he was created in (God's) image and likeness.

8. אֲשֶׁר יָצָר — *Whom He had formed.* After He formed him in the distinguished manner already mentioned, He placed him there (in the garden), being a place suitable for man to

NOTES

same opinion, translating our verse, *And there had gone up a mist etc.* The preceding verse, however, seems to bear out the *Sforno's* interpretation for it states *all the trees of the field were not yet on the earth,* nor any herb of the field until rain fell, and rain in turn was caused by the vapor ascending. Hence all this occurred at the end of the six days of Creation, not at the beginning as the *Rambam* states.

7-8. וַיִּיצֶר ה' אֱלֹהִים . . . אֲשֶׁר יָצָר — *And* HASHEM *God formed . . . Whom He had formed.* All living creatures, as compared to the mineral and plant kingdom, needed a special "forming" by God to be brought into being. This was especially true of man. Each, according to the *Sforno*, was fashioned in a different manner by God, with man's raw material (dust) chosen carefully from a special part of the earth, namely the eventual place of the Altar on Mt. Moriah. Now, the process of man's creation was in two phases. First man was formed as a higher, more advanced living creature, granted a "soul of life." However, he was not as yet endowed with the "image of God" until God placed him in the Garden of Eden, a place conducive for Adam to receive this image thanks to its unique character. The *Sforno* interprets this "image" as meaning the flow of reason and intelligence emanating from God.

ט אֶת־הָאָדָם אֲשֶׁר יָצָר: וַיַּצְמַח יְהוָה אֱלֹהִים מִן־הָאֲדָמָה כָּל־עֵץ נֶחְמָד
י לְמַרְאֶה וְטוֹב לְמַאֲכָל וְעֵץ הַחַיִּים בְּתוֹךְ הַגָּן וְעֵץ הַדַּעַת טוֹב וָרָע: וְנָהָר
יא יֹצֵא מֵעֵדֶן לְהַשְׁקוֹת אֶת־הַגָּן וּמִשָּׁם יִפָּרֵד וְהָיָה לְאַרְבָּעָה רָאשִׁים: שֵׁם
יב הָאֶחָד פִּישׁוֹן הוּא הַסֹּבֵב אֵת כָּל־אֶרֶץ הַחֲוִילָה אֲשֶׁר־שָׁם הַזָּהָב: וּזֲהַב
יג הָאָרֶץ הַהִוא טוֹב שָׁם הַבְּדֹלַח וְאֶבֶן הַשֹּׁהַם: וְשֵׁם־הַנָּהָר הַשֵּׁנִי גִּיחוֹן הוּא
יד הַסּוֹבֵב אֵת כָּל־אֶרֶץ כּוּשׁ: וְשֵׁם הַנָּהָר הַשְּׁלִישִׁי חִדֶּקֶל הוּא הַהֹלֵךְ קִדְמַת
טו אַשּׁוּר וְהַנָּהָר הָרְבִיעִי הוּא פְרָת: וַיִּקַּח יְהוָה אֱלֹהִים אֶת־הָאָדָם וַיַּנִּחֵהוּ
טז בְגַן־עֵדֶן לְעָבְדָהּ וּלְשָׁמְרָהּ: וַיְצַו יְהוָה אֱלֹהִים עַל־הָאָדָם לֵאמֹר מִכֹּל
יז עֵץ־הַגָּן אָכֹל תֹּאכֵל: וּמֵעֵץ הַדַּעַת טוֹב וָרָע לֹא תֹאכַל מִמֶּנּוּ כִּי בְּיוֹם

receive God's image and acquire intellectual reasoning (functioning) powers, (through) its atmosphere and food.

9. וַיַּצְמַח ה׳ — *And* H*ASHEM caused to sprout . . .* his food, without toil (lit., "suffering").

נֶחְמָד לְמַרְאֶה — *Pleasing to the sight . . .* gladdening and broadening the heart, preparing it (and) making it receptive to the flow of intelligence, as it says, וְהָיָה כְּנַגֵּן הַמְנַגֵּן וַתְּהִי עָלָיו יַד ה׳, *And it came to pass when the minstrel played that the hand of* H*ASHEM came upon him (II Kings* 3:15).

וְעֵץ הַדַּעַת — *And the Tree of Knowledge. Knowledge* to give one's attention to and focus one's heart on (what is) good and evil. From this (source of the word דַּעַת) we also find, *And Adam knew* (4:1), i.e., he became aware and concentrated his heart on her. (This is also) why we call a relative מוֹדַע, as it says מוֹדַע לְאִישָׁהּ, *a relative of her husband (Ruth* 2:1), for it is natural that one concerns himself for the needs of his relative, as it says וְאָח לְצָרָה יִוָּלֵד, *And a brother is born for adversity* (*Proverbs* 17:17).

טוֹב וָרָע — *Good and Bad.* To choose the sweet even when it is harmful and reject the bitter even when it is beneficial.

NOTES

9. נֶחְמָד לְמַרְאֶה — *Pleasing to the sight.* The spirit of prophecy, according to our Sages, can only come to rest upon one who is in a state of *simchah,* happiness and contentment. God's intention was for man to dwell in the garden, where his material needs would be taken care of and he would be able to occupy himself with the pursuit of דַּעַת ה׳, *the knowledge of God.* The *Sforno* therefore explains the reason for God's planting trees in the garden pleasant to the sight, as being for the purpose of preparing Adam to receive the spirit of *Hashem,* since by appealing to his aesthetic sense Adam would be more receptive to the overflow of the intellect emanating from God. The quote from *Kings* refers to Elisha who was unable to receive prophecy until his mood was changed, and his spirit elevated by the music of the minstrel which dispelled his gloom and gladdened his heart.

טוֹב וָרָע — *Good and Bad.* The *Rambam* in his *Guide* (I:2) explains that man was originally granted an "overflow of the intellect" allowing him "to distinguish between truth and falsehood." Only after the sin of eating from the Tree of Knowledge did man develop a taste for good and evil, or "fine and bad" as the *Rambam* puts it. The term "good and evil," however, does not mean good and evil in the moral sense. Rather, that which is sweet and pleasant to man's physical senses he now considers "good," even though, as the *Sforno* says, it is harmful; and what is bitter, or difficult, is rejected by man, and considered "evil," even though it is really beneficial for him. It is in this sense that the forbidden fruit of this prohibited tree caused man to give his heart, not to truth and falsehood, but to good and bad. As Onkelos translates, it was a tree "of the knowledge of good and bad," *not* a "tree of knowledge."

15. לְעָבְדָהּ וּלְשָׁמְרָהּ — *To work it and to guard it. To work it* does not refer to the garden, for it was not necessary for man to *work it* as explained by the *Sforno* in verses 9-10. Rather *it* refers to man's *soul of life* mentioned in verse 7. In the Garden of Eden man was meant to develop himself, expanding his spirit and broadening his knowledge of Hashem, thereby receiving the "image of God" for which he was destined. The expression *to guard it* is also

the man whom He had formed. [9] *And* HASHEM *God caused to sprout from the ground every tree that was pleasing to the sight and good for food; also the Tree of Life in the midst of the garden, and the Tree of Knowledge of Good and Bad.*

[10] *A river issues forth from Eden to water the garden, and from there it is divided and becomes four headwaters.* [11] *The name of the first is Pishon, the one that encircles the whole land of Havilah, where the gold is.* [12] *The gold of that land is good; bedolach is there, and the shoham stone.* [13] *The name of the second river is Gihon, the one that encircles the whole land of Cush.* [14] *The name of the third river is Hiddekel, the one that flows toward the east of Assyria; and the fourth river is the Euphrates.*

[15] HASHEM *God took the man and placed him in the Garden of Eden, to work it and to guard it.* [16] *And* HASHEM *God commanded the man, saying, "Of every tree of the garden you may freely eat;* [17] *but of the Tree of Knowledge of Good and Bad, you must not eat thereof; for on the day*

---

10. וְנָהָר יֹצֵא מֵעֵדֶן — *A river issues forth from Eden* ... without need (lit., pain) of rain or the toil (labor) of man.

11. שֵׁם הָאֶחָד פִּישׁוֹן — *The name of the first is Pishon.* The (Torah) tells us how praiseworthy was the river that watered the garden, (the name of) which is unknown to us, by informing us of (the names of) the rivers branching out from it, which are well known to us as commendable for their size and the quality of their waters and fruits.

15. לְעָבְדָהּ — *To work it.* To work (to perfect) his *soul of life,* as it says: *And He blew into his nostrils the soul of life* (verse 7).

וּלְשָׁמְרָהּ — *And to guard it* ... that it (i.e., his *soul of life)* not be diminished through the impact of nature's heat upon his fundamental vitality; this (therapeutic aid) coming from the esteemed fruits which constantly replaced what man's constitution lost, for (these fruits) never rotted.

16. מִכֹּל עֵץ הַגָּן — *Of every tree of the garden* ... according to the changing seasons, as affected by the stars, as it says, לָחֳדָשָׁיו יְבַכֵּר, *It shall bring forth new fruit every month (Ezekiel* 47:12).

17. וּמֵעֵץ הַדַּעַת — *But of the Tree of Knowledge* ... which was situated in the midst of the garden near the Tree of Life mentioned above, as it says, *the Tree of Life in the midst of the garden* (verse 9). (This is) in keeping with, הַחַיִּים וְהַמָּוֶת נָתַתִּי לְפָנֶיךָ, *I have set before you life and death (Deut.* 30:19).

NOTES

interpreted by the *Sforno* as referring to man's "soul of life." Through the precious, unusual fruits of the garden, man's well-being would be guarded and preserved.

16. מִכֹּל עֵץ הַגָּן *–Of every tree of the garden.* The expression *Of "every" tree of the garden* is interpreted by the *Sforno* as implying a variety of fruits in different seasons, thereby satisfying man's inherent desire for variety.

17. וּמֵעֵץ הַדַּעַת *– But of the Tree of Knowledge.* In verse 9 the Torah implies that not only was the Tree of Life *in the midst of the garden* but also the *Tree of the Knowledge of Good and Bad,* for these two are placed in juxtaposition, following one another in the same verse. 3:3 also states that the tree was *in the center of the garden.* The *Sforno* sees in this a great moral lesson; man was given the choice between life and death, for he alone has been granted freedom of choice. Had man chosen to eat from the Tree of Life, rather than the Tree of the Knowledge of Good and Bad, he apparently would have been granted eternal life. Because he chose the sweet and pleasant, which was forbidden to him, he also chose death over life, as the verse in *Deuteronomy* states.

יח אֲכָלְךָ מִמֶּנּוּ מוֹת תָּמוּת: וַיֹּאמֶר יְהוָה אֱלֹהִים לֹא־טוֹב הֱיוֹת הָאָדָם
יט לְבַדּוֹ אֶעֱשֶׂה־לּוֹ עֵזֶר כְּנֶגְדּוֹ: וַיִּצֶר יְהוָה אֱלֹהִים מִן־הָאֲדָמָה כָּל־חַיַּת
הַשָּׂדֶה וְאֵת כָּל־עוֹף הַשָּׁמַיִם וַיָּבֵא אֶל־הָאָדָם לִרְאוֹת מַה־יִּקְרָא־לוֹ
כ וְכֹל אֲשֶׁר יִקְרָא־לוֹ הָאָדָם נֶפֶשׁ חַיָּה הוּא שְׁמוֹ: וַיִּקְרָא הָאָדָם שֵׁמוֹת שלישי
לְכָל־הַבְּהֵמָה וּלְעוֹף הַשָּׁמַיִם וּלְכֹל חַיַּת הַשָּׂדֶה וּלְאָדָם לֹא־מָצָא עֵזֶר
כא כְּנֶגְדּוֹ: וַיַּפֵּל יְהוָה אֱלֹהִים ׀ תַּרְדֵּמָה עַל־הָאָדָם וַיִּישָׁן וַיִּקַּח אַחַת
כב מִצַּלְעֹתָיו וַיִּסְגֹּר בָּשָׂר תַּחְתֶּנָּה: וַיִּבֶן יְהוָה אֱלֹהִים ׀ אֶת־הַצֵּלָע אֲשֶׁר־
כג לָקַח מִן־הָאָדָם לְאִשָּׁה וַיְבִאֶהָ אֶל־הָאָדָם: וַיֹּאמֶר הָאָדָם זֹאת הַפַּעַם
עֶצֶם מֵעֲצָמַי וּבָשָׂר מִבְּשָׂרִי לְזֹאת יִקָּרֵא אִשָּׁה כִּי מֵאִישׁ לֻקְחָה־זֹּאת:
כד עַל־כֵּן יַעֲזָב־אִישׁ אֶת־אָבִיו וְאֶת־אִמּוֹ וְדָבַק בְּאִשְׁתּוֹ וְהָיוּ לְבָשָׂר אֶחָד:

18. לֹא טוֹב הֱיוֹת הָאָדָם לְבַדּוֹ — *It is not good that man be alone.* The (goal and) purpose intended in his being in the likeness and image (of God) will not be realized if (man) will have to occupy himself alone, to supply the needs of life.

עֵזֶר כְּנֶגְדּוֹ — *A helper corresponding to him.* (This means) a helper that will be, as it were, equal to him in image and likeness. This was mandatory so that (the helper) would appreciate his needs and meet them at the proper time. The word כְּנֶגְדּוֹ, *opposite him,* implies that when an object is placed on one side of a scale it will be even with the object on the other side providing they are both equal in weight. Only then is it נֶגְדּוֹ, *opposite,* on a straight line. However, if they are unequal in weight, they will not be opposite one another on a straight line; rather, one will go up and the other down (higher and lower). This is what is meant by our Sages when they state, "Moshe was equal to all of Israel" (*Mechilta*). It would, however, not have been proper for the helper to be completely equal to him for then one would not be properly able to work for and serve the other.

19. וַיִּצֶר ה׳ אֱלֹהִים מִן הָאֲדָמָה כָּל חַיַּת הַשָּׂדֶה — *HASHEM God had formed out of the ground every beast of the field.* He gave them a complete form as feeling (creatures); the heavenly force not being sufficient to do so without the help of the natural reproductive (lit., "seed") force.

וַיָּבֵא אֶל הָאָדָם — *And brought (them) to the man* . . . so that he (man) might recognize (appreciate) that he needed a new creation (as a mate) seeing that there was none among the living creatures to serve him suitably.

לִרְאוֹת מַה יִּקְרָא לוֹ — *To see what he would call each one* . . . so that he might see and discern what name was proper for each one of them, according to the function most suitable to its form (essential being).

נֶפֶשׁ חַיָּה הוּא שְׁמוֹ — *Living creature, that remained its name.* The particular name by which

NOTES

18. עֵזֶר כְּנֶגְדּוֹ — *A helper corresponding to him.* Were the Torah to have said נֶגְדּוֹ, without the prefix כ, it would have meant that woman was to be fully equal to man. This was not God's intent, for then she could not be his עֵזֶר, *helper.* Rather she was meant to be like him, similar but not completely equal. Still, since both of them fulfill the roles destined for them, they are "equal in weight," on a straight line, striking a proper balance for their mutual benefit.

19. וַיִּצֶר ה׳ אֱלֹהִים — *HASHEM God had formed.* The *first* beasts had to be formed by Hashem's direct intervention, after which they could reproduce themselves, from the seed within them.

לִרְאוֹת מַה יִּקְרָא לוֹ — *To see what he would call each one.* God did not need Adam to decide which name to give to each of these living creatures. This was meant as an object lesson for Adam to understand the essential form of each animal and beast to better discern its purpose. By so doing, man also came to recognize that none of these creatures could be his mate and helper and would thereby

you eat of it, you shall surely die."
18 *HASHEM God said, "It is not good that man be alone; I will make him*
a helper corresponding to him." 19 *Now, HASHEM God had formed out of*
the ground every beast of the field and every bird of the sky, and brought
[them] to the man to see what he would call each one; and whatever the
man called each living creature, that remained its name. 20 *And the man*
assigned names to all the cattle and to the birds of the sky and to every beast
of the field; but as for man, he did not find a helper corresponding to him.
21 *So HASHEM God cast a deep sleep upon the man and he slept; and He*
took one of his sides and He filled in flesh in its place. 22 *Then HASHEM God*
fashioned the side that He had taken from the man into a woman, and He
brought her to the man. 23 *And the man said, "This time it is bone of my*
bones and flesh of my flesh. This shall be called woman, for from man was
she taken." 24 *Therefore a man shall leave his father and his mother and*
cling to his wife and they shall become one flesh.

---

it was called indicated the form of that living creature, i.e., the essence of its living soul which represents its actuality in existence.

21. וַיַּפֵּל ה׳ אֱלֹהִים תַּרְדֵּמָה עַל הָאָדָם — *So HASHEM God cast a deep sleep upon the man . . .* so he should not be afraid or experience pain.

וַיִּקַּח אַחַת מִצַּלְעֹתָיו — *And He took one of his sides.* Since the choicest dust had been gathered and all proper material (matter) went into man's living form, therefore, when God wanted to fashion the female form, which was almost similar to him (Adam), it was fitting to take some of his material being (body), namely one of his sides.

22. וַיִּבֶן ה׳ אֱלֹהִים אֶת הַצֵּלָע . . . לְאִשָּׁה — *Then HASHEM God fashioned the side . . . into a woman . . .* that she may have the form of man and his faculties (qualities), differing from him only in "the physical vessels" (i.e., sex) — this being the difference between them, (otherwise) both have the possibility for (the attainment of) perfection, (be the measure) abundant or meager.

23. זֹאת — *This.* This female.

הַפַּעַם — *Time.* This time it is . . .

עֶצֶם מֵעֲצָמַי וּבָשָׂר מִבְּשָׂרִי — *Bone of my bone and flesh of my flesh.* Henceforth, however, the female of the human species will not be so (she will be formed separately from man).

לְזֹאת — *This.* Every female woman, in the future . . .

יִקָּרֵא אִשָּׁה — *Shall be called woman . . .* even though she will not be a part of man.

כִּי מֵאִישׁ לֻקֳחָה זֹּאת — *For from man was she taken . . .* the first one of all (women).

24. עַל כֵּן — *Therefore . . .* since the first woman was intended by God to be similar to man as much as possible (to such an extent) that He formed her from (man's) body.

NOTES

appreciate the loving-kindness of God in creating a new person, and yet taken from him, as his helper who (as the *Sforno* states in verse 18) would appreciate his needs and fulfill them.

23. זֹאת הַפַּעַם עֶצֶם מֵעֲצָמַי — *This time it is bone of my bone.* The *Sforno* interprets and explains the repetition of the word זאת — in this verse. Before she was called אִשָּׁה — woman — she is referred to as זאת — the feminine form of *this.* Therefore the words זאת and הַפַּעַם are not linked, rather we connect הַפַּעַם to עֶצֶם מֵעֲצָמַי, *bone of my bone.* The sense of the verse is as follows: Only this time is "this" female literally "flesh of my flesh" and therefore rightfully called אִשָּׁה, having been taken from אִישׁ. In the future, however, she will still be called אִשָּׁה since the first one was taken from him.

ג כה־א וַיִּהְיוּ שְׁנֵיהֶם עֲרוּמִּים הָאָדָם וְאִשְׁתּוֹ וְלֹא יִתְבֹּשָׁשׁוּ׃ וְהַנָּחָשׁ הָיָה עָרוּם
מִכֹּל חַיַּת הַשָּׂדֶה אֲשֶׁר עָשָׂה יהוה אֱלֹהִים וַיֹּאמֶר אֶל־הָאִשָּׁה אַף כִּי־
ב אָמַר אֱלֹהִים לֹא תֹאכְלוּ מִכֹּל עֵץ הַגָּן׃ וַתֹּאמֶר הָאִשָּׁה אֶל־הַנָּחָשׁ מִפְּרִי
ג עֵץ־הַגָּן נֹאכֵל׃ וּמִפְּרִי הָעֵץ אֲשֶׁר בְּתוֹךְ־הַגָּן אָמַר אֱלֹהִים לֹא תֹאכְלוּ
ד מִמֶּנּוּ וְלֹא תִגְּעוּ בּוֹ פֶּן תְּמֻתוּן׃ וַיֹּאמֶר הַנָּחָשׁ אֶל־הָאִשָּׁה לֹא־מוֹת
ה תְּמֻתוּן׃ כִּי יֹדֵעַ אֱלֹהִים כִּי בְּיוֹם אֲכָלְכֶם מִמֶּנּוּ וְנִפְקְחוּ עֵינֵיכֶם וִהְיִיתֶם

יַעֲזָב אִישׁ אֶת אָבִיו וְאֶת אִמּוֹ וְדָבַק בְּאִשְׁתּוֹ — *A man shall leave his father and his mother and cling to his wife.* It is proper that a man should attempt to marry a woman suitable for him and suitable to cleave to him. (This he shall do) even though it may be necessary to leave his father and mother; there can be no authentic cleaving among those who are not alike; it can only be among those who are similar, for only then can they be of one mind.

וְהָיוּ לְבָשָׂר אֶחָד — *And they shall become one flesh.* In all their actions they will aim to attain the perfection intended by man's creation, as though the two were as only one (flesh).

25. עֲרוּמִּים ... וְלֹא יִתְבֹּשָׁשׁוּ — *Naked ... and they were not ashamed.* At that time, all their organs, limbs and actions were (used for the purpose) of fulfilling God's will exclusively, not to attain physical pleasure at all. (Consequently) the act of sexual congress was to them as normal as that of eating and drinking; therefore their reproductive organs were regarded by them as we regard our mouth, face and hands.

III

1. וְהַנָּחָשׁ — *And the serpent.* "He is Satan, he is the evil prompter" (*Bava Basra* 16a). Although he is small in appearance he does much damage. (The Torah) describes things figuratively by (various names) which are similar to them, just as a king is called "lion," as it says, עָלָה אַרְיֵה מִסֻּבְּכוֹ, *A lion is gone up from his thicket (Jeremiah* 4:7), or enemies who do harm, "serpents, adders," as it says, כִּי הִנְנִי מְשַׁלֵּחַ בָּכֶם נְחָשִׁים צִפְעֹנִים אֲשֶׁר אֵין לָהֶם לָחַשׁ, *For behold I will send serpents, adders, among you which will not be charmed* (ibid. 8:17). In this manner the evil inclination which tempts man is called "serpent," for he is similar to a serpent, which is (an animal) with limited utility but great potential to do harm, though small in appearance. Our Sages have told us that Samael (the accuser; Angel of Death) rode on him (the serpent), meaning that the power of lust, bringing to sin, accomplishes its end through the medium of the power of imagination which brings to man visions of physical, material pleasures, which lead him astray (turning him away) from the way of perfection intended by God, the Blessed One. This power of desire (and base appetites) with the images of pleasure accompanying it are present in the functional physical powers (of man), causing him to frustrate God's will and intent unless the power of reason rises up to combat it, as our Sages state, "the heart and the eye are the two agents

NOTES

24. עַל כֵּן יַעֲזָב ... — *Therefore ... shall leave ...* The *Sforno* submits that only those who are alike can cleave to one another. Since woman was once actually part of man, she is certainly like him, and when man and woman marry they come together once again. The motivation to do so is stronger than the natural desire of man to remain close to his parents. This commentary echoes the words of our Sages who liken man's search for a wife to one who seeks something he has lost. Man lost one of his sides, which God fashioned into woman, so he looks for it until he finds a wife, thereby becoming "whole" once again.

III

1. וְהַנָּחָשׁ — *And the serpent.* The *Sforno* is of the opinion that the serpent is not to be interpreted literally, but figuratively. Just as a lion is used by the prophet to represent King Nebuchadnezzar and adders to represent the enemies of Israel, so the serpent represents Satan and the יֵצֶר הָרַע (the evil inclination) which is within man, leading him

25 *They were both naked, the man and his wife, and they were not ashamed.*

3

1 *And the serpent was cunning beyond any beast of the field that* HASHEM *God had made. He said to the woman, "Although God had said: 'You shall not eat of any tree of the garden'?"*
2 *The woman said to the serpent, "Of the fruit of any tree of the garden*
we may eat. 3 *Of the fruit of the tree which is in the center of the garden*
God has said: 'You shall neither eat of it nor touch it, lest you die.'
4 *The serpent said to the woman, "You will not surely die;* 5 *for God*
knows that on the day you eat of it your eyes will be opened and you will be

---

of sin" (Jerusalem Talmud, *Berachos* 1:8). This is what the Torah cautions against, saying, וְלֹא תָתוּרוּ אַחֲרֵי לְבַבְכֶם וְאַחֲרֵי עֵינֵיכֶם, *Go not after your own heart and your own eyes* (*Numbers* 15:39).

הָיָה עָרוּם מִכֹּל חַיַּת הַשָּׂדֶה — *Was cunning beyond any beast of the field.* For the imaginative powers (in man) which project the image of pleasures to the powers of his base desire is stronger (in man) than in other living creatures as our Sages say, "He who is greater than his fellow, his evil inclination is greater than his" (*Succah* 52a).

וַיֹּאמֶר אֶל הָאִשָּׁה — *He said to the woman.* For her weaker intellect was too indolent to delve deeply to discern (the truth) and could not withstand the false image (of temptation). Rather she pictured in her imagination that even though ...

אַף כִּי אָמַר אֱלֹהִים — *Although God had said.* Although God had said not to eat from the Tree of Knowledge *lest you die,* nonetheless it will not come to pass, and therefore when the serpent, which means her imaginative powers, began to plant a doubt (in her mind), the woman with her weak intellect (first) said — from all ...

2. מִפְּרִי עֵץ הַגָּן נֹאכֵל — *Of the fruit of any tree of the garden we may eat.* And there is no need to expose ourselves to danger by eating from the tree which God, the Blessed One, cautioned us not to eat from, lest we die. However, her imagination overpowered her (reason) thereby attributing jealousy and falsehood (God forbid) to God, the Blessed One, (falsely) picturing (God) as prohibiting the fruit so that they would not attain the purpose of being as *Elohim* (Divine beings), but not because it would result in (their) death. Therefore he said to the woman ...

4-5. לֹא מוֹת תְּמֻתוּן כִּי יֹדֵעַ אֱלֹהִים כִּי בְּיוֹם אֲכָלְכֶם מִמֶּנּוּ וְנִפְקְחוּ עֵינֵיכֶם — *You will not surely die; for God knows that on the day you eat of it your eyes will be opened.* He did not prohibit this fruit at all because it would cause your death. Rather it was because He knows that by eating from it, you will gain added knowledge, and (as a result) be as *Elohim* (Divine beings) perfect in knowledge.

NOTES

astray. This "evil prompter" works through the heart of man (his desires) and his eyes, which see and arouse man's base appetites. Since the evil inclination, Satan and the Angel of Death are one and the same, the imagery used by our Sages when they depict the Angel of Death (Samael) riding on the serpent (*Pirkei Eliezer* 13; *Zohar Chadash)* is an apt one. The original sin of man was caused by his inherent weakness and inability to withstand temptation which ultimately resulted in his death.

1-5. וַיֹּאמֶר ... אַף כִּי אָמַר ... כִּי יֹדֵעַ אֱלֹהִים ... — *He said ..." Although God had said ... For God knows ..."* The *Sforno* depicts the internal struggle within Eve between her reason and desire. At first she reasoned correctly that since there is such a plentiful variety of permitted fruits, why should they expose themselves to the danger of death? But she then was overcome by her appetite and desire, succumbing to the wiles of the "evil prompter," rationalizing that death would not occur, and

ו כֵּאלֹהִ֔ים יֹדְעֵ֖י ט֣וֹב וָרָֽע: וַתֵּ֣רֶא הָֽאִשָּׁ֡ה כִּ֣י טוֹב֩ הָעֵ֨ץ לְמַֽאֲכָ֜ל וְכִ֧י תַֽאֲוָה־ה֣וּא לָעֵינַ֗יִם וְנֶחְמָ֤ד הָעֵץ֙ לְהַשְׂכִּ֔יל וַתִּקַּ֥ח מִפִּרְי֖וֹ וַתֹּאכַ֑ל וַתִּתֵּ֧ן ז גַּם־לְאִישָׁ֛הּ עִמָּ֖הּ וַיֹּאכַֽל: וַתִּפָּקַ֨חְנָה֙ עֵינֵ֣י שְׁנֵיהֶ֔ם וַיֵּ֣דְע֔וּ כִּ֥י עֵֽירֻמִּ֖ם הֵ֑ם ח וַֽיִּתְפְּרוּ֙ עֲלֵ֣ה תְאֵנָ֔ה וַיַּֽעֲשׂ֥וּ לָהֶ֖ם חֲגֹרֹֽת: וַֽיִּשְׁמְע֞וּ אֶת־ק֨וֹל יְהֹוָ֧ה אֱלֹהִ֛ים מִתְהַלֵּ֥ךְ בַּגָּ֖ן לְר֣וּחַ הַיּ֑וֹם וַיִּתְחַבֵּ֨א הָֽאָדָ֜ם וְאִשְׁתּ֗וֹ מִפְּנֵי֙ יְהֹוָ֣ה אֱלֹהִ֔ים ט-י בְּת֖וֹךְ עֵ֥ץ הַגָּֽן: וַיִּקְרָ֛א יְהֹוָ֥ה אֱלֹהִ֖ים אֶל־הָֽאָדָ֑ם וַיֹּ֥אמֶר ל֖וֹ אַיֶּֽכָּה: וַיֹּ֕אמֶר יא אֶת־קֹלְךָ֥ שָׁמַ֖עְתִּי בַּגָּ֑ן וָֽאִירָ֛א כִּֽי־עֵירֹ֥ם אָנֹ֖כִי וָֽאֵֽחָבֵֽא: וַיֹּ֕אמֶר מִ֚י הִגִּ֣יד לְךָ֔ כִּ֥י עֵירֹ֖ם אָ֑תָּה הֲמִן־הָעֵ֗ץ אֲשֶׁ֧ר צִוִּיתִ֛יךָ לְבִלְתִּ֥י אֲכׇל־מִמֶּ֖נּוּ אָכָֽלְתָּ: יב וַיֹּ֖אמֶר הָֽאָדָ֑ם הָֽאִשָּׁה֙ אֲשֶׁ֣ר נָתַ֣תָּה עִמָּדִ֔י הִ֛וא נָֽתְנָה־לִּ֥י מִן־הָעֵ֖ץ וָֽאֹכֵֽל:

---

6. וַתֵּרֶא הָאִשָּׁה כִּי טוֹב הָעֵץ לְמַאֲכָל — *And the woman perceived that the tree was good for eating.* She perceived that it was pleasant (sweet) to eat, because of the nature of its place, atmosphere and the aroma of its fruit.

וְנֶחְמָד הָעֵץ לְהַשְׂכִּיל — *And the tree was desirable as a means of wisdom.* As God Himself said, that it was *a Tree of Knowledge of Good and Bad* (2:9).

גַּם לְאִישָׁהּ עִמָּהּ — *Also to her husband with her.* He was receptive to her request, because he was אִישָׁהּ, *her husband,* and because he was עִמָּהּ, *with her* (in an intimate sense).

7. וַתִּפָּקַחְנָה עֵינֵי שְׁנֵיהֶם — *Then the eyes of both of them were opened.* They turned their attention to what was sweet (pleasant) and pleasurable, even though it was harmful. Attending to and inspecting any matter is called פְּקִיחַת עֵינַיִם, *opening of the eyes,* as it says, אַף עַל זֶה פָּקַחְתָּ עֵינֶךָ, *And you open your eyes upon such a one* (Job 14:3).

וַיֵּדְעוּ כִּי עֵירֻמִּם הֵם — *And they realized that they were naked.* They perceived that it was proper to conceal their private organs inasmuch as their major function had now become for pleasure that was degrading and harmful.

8. מִתְהַלֵּךְ בַּגָּן — *Moving about (manifesting itself) in the garden.* To and fro, according

---

NOTES

justifying her action by convincing herself that God's motivation in prohibiting this tree was to protect His exclusive monopoly of knowledge, Divine wisdom and perfection.

6. גַּם לְאִישָׁהּ עִמָּהּ — *Also to her husband with her.* The two words אִישָׁהּ, *her husband,* and עִמָּהּ, *with her,* are interpreted by the *Sforno* as representing two reasons for Adam's willingness to listen to Eve. First because he was her husband and felt a certain sense of responsibility to accommodate her, and second because he was *with her,* a euphemism for marital intimacy.

7. וַתִּפָּקַחְנָה עֵינֵי שְׁנֵיהֶם וַיֵּדְעוּ — *Then the eyes of both of them were opened and they realized.* Obviously the expression פְּקִיחַת עֵינַיִם, *opening of the eyes,* cannot be understood in a literal sense. Also the expression וַיֵּדְעוּ, *they knew* — or *realized* — rather than וַיִּרְאוּ, *they saw,* is significant. The *Rambam* in his *Guide* (I:2) observes that the choice of words ("knew" rather than "saw") as well as the expression "*opening of the eyes*" indicates that man "entered upon another state in which he

considered as bad things that he had not seen in that light before." The *Sforno* explains this verse in a manner similar to his interpretation of 2:9, where he explains the word דַּעַת, *knowledge,* as pertaining to the concentration of one's attention and concern toward a person, object or issue. He explains the "opening of one's eyes" in similar fashion, i.e., the concentration of their thoughts away from truth and spirituality to the pleasurable and physical. This change in their priorities, in turn, causes them to perceive their bodies in a different light, and they *recognize* (וַיֵּדְעוּ) the need to conceal their private parts. The *Sforno,* therefore, to a certain extent, reflects the *Rambam's* comments in the *Guide.*

8. מִתְהַלֵּךְ בַּגָּן לְרוּחַ הַיּוֹם — *Moving about (manifesting itself) in the garden in the wind of the day.* God's will is supreme; naught can control it. There can also be no aimless movement on His part. Hence the *Sforno* interprets this difficult verse as follows: God's movements in the garden were with purpose, motivated by His

like God, knowing good and bad."

6 *And the woman perceived that the tree was good for eating and that it was a delight to the eyes, and that the tree was desirable as a means to wisdom, and she took of its fruit and ate; and she gave also to her husband with her and he ate.* 7 *Then the eyes of both of them were opened and they realized that they were naked; and they sewed together a fig leaf and made themselves aprons.*

8 *They heard the sound of HASHEM God moving about in the garden in the wind of the day; and the man and his wife hid from HASHEM God among the trees of the garden.* 9 *HASHEM God called out to the man and said to him, "Where are you?"*

10 *He said, "I heard the sound of You in the garden, and I was afraid because I am naked, so I hid."*

11 *And He said, "Who told you that you are naked? Have you eaten of the tree from which I commanded you not to eat?"*

12 *The man said, "The woman whom You gave to be with me — she gave me of the tree, and I ate."*

---

to the intended end (purpose), similar to, הִתְהַלֵּךְ בָּאָרֶץ, *walk through the land* (13:17) and, וַיִּתְהַלְּכוּ מִגּוֹי אֶל גּוֹי, *they went about from nation to nation* (*Psalms* 105:13).

לְרוּחַ הַיּוֹם — *In the wind of the day.* According (to His) will that day, to do the desirable things for that day, just as He did during the other days of Creation, and as He did that day (as well) before they sinned.

וַיִּתְחַבֵּא — *And he hid.* As it says, וְלֹא יִרְאֶה בְךָ עֶרְוַת דָּבָר, *that He see no unseemly thing in you* (*Deut.* 23:15).

9. אַיֶּכָּה — *Where are you?* That you are no longer visible in the garden as heretofore, having now hidden yourself — something you did not do before.

10. וָאִירָא — *And I was afraid.* This also happened to Israel after the sin (of the golden calf) as it says, וַיִּירְאוּ מִגֶּשֶׁת אֵלָיו, *and they were afraid to come near to Him* (*Exodus* 34:30).

11. מִי הִגִּיד לְךָ — *Who told you.* The knowledge of good and bad.

כִּי עֵירֹם אָתָּה — *That you are naked.* That because you are naked it is proper to cover yourself (i.e., that nakedness is shameful).

12. הִיא — *She ...* whom You gave (to me) as a helper, to be useful ...

נָתְנָה לִּי מִן הָעֵץ — *She gave me of the tree.* (She) was an obstacle (stumbling block). And thus he attributed his guilty act to his "Owner" (Hashem) instead of repenting, which would have been proper for him, as David did, when he said to Nathan (the prophet), "חָטָאתִי, *I sinned*" (*II Samuel* 12:13).

NOTES

will, just as they were during the six days of Creation. However, when Adam and Eve sinned, He paused in His activities and addressed Himself to them.

וַיִּתְחַבֵּא — *And he hid.* Although man had sinned, still this noble creation of God is sensitive to the requirements of modesty in the presence of God. This sensitivity is also underscored in verse 10 (see the *Sforno's* comment there).

9. אַיֶּכָּה — *Where are you?* God is not asking Adam where he is. All is known to Him. Rather He is asking Adam to explain the reason for his strange, new behavior. By so doing he will hopefully be led to repent. Unfortunately, Adam blames both Eve and God instead of confessing his guilt and repenting.

יג וַיֹּאמֶר יְהוָה אֱלֹהִים לָאִשָּׁה מַה־זֹּאת עָשִׂית וַתֹּאמֶר הָאִשָּׁה הַנָּחָשׁ
יד הִשִּׁיאַנִי וָאֹכֵל: וַיֹּאמֶר יְהוָה אֱלֹהִים | אֶל־הַנָּחָשׁ כִּי עָשִׂיתָ זֹּאת אָרוּר
אַתָּה מִכָּל־הַבְּהֵמָה וּמִכֹּל חַיַּת הַשָּׂדֶה עַל־גְּחֹנְךָ תֵלֵךְ וְעָפָר תֹּאכַל
טו כָּל־יְמֵי חַיֶּיךָ: וְאֵיבָה | אָשִׁית בֵּינְךָ וּבֵין הָאִשָּׁה וּבֵין זַרְעֲךָ וּבֵין
טז זַרְעָהּ הוּא יְשׁוּפְךָ רֹאשׁ וְאַתָּה תְּשׁוּפֶנּוּ עָקֵב: אֶל־
הָאִשָּׁה אָמַר הַרְבָּה אַרְבֶּה עִצְּבוֹנֵךְ וְהֵרֹנֵךְ בְּעֶצֶב תֵּלְדִי בָנִים וְאֶל־
יז אִישֵׁךְ תְּשׁוּקָתֵךְ וְהוּא יִמְשָׁל־בָּךְ: וּלְאָדָם אָמַר כִּי־
שָׁמַעְתָּ לְקוֹל אִשְׁתֶּךָ וַתֹּאכַל מִן־הָעֵץ אֲשֶׁר צִוִּיתִיךָ לֵאמֹר לֹא תֹאכַל

13. מַה זֹּאת עָשִׂית — *What is this that you have done!* He said this to urge her also toward repentance, *For He does not desire that (the wicked) die but rather that he should return* (based on expressions in *Ezekiel* 18:23 and 32).

14. אָרוּר אַתָּה מִכָּל — *Accursed are you beyond all.* (The serpent) would attain his desires and needs with pain and less pleasure than all other living creatures, as our Sages say, "Have you ever seen a beast or bird with a craft, yet they are sustained without anxiety" (*Kiddushin* 82a), and this He explains, saying . . .

עַל גְּחֹנְךָ תֵלֵךְ — *Upon your belly shall you go.* You will attain your food through suffering, as our Sages say, "Because I have acted evilly and destroyed my livelihood" (ibid.), and (they have also stated), "What labors Adam had to carry out before he obtained bread to eat" (*Berachos* 58a).

וְעָפָר תֹּאכַל — *And dust shall you eat.* You will no longer attain the enjoyment of food, drink and sexual congress, that you experienced before the sin. This also happened to the people of Israel when they sinned, as our Sages say, "(The cessation of) purity has removed taste and fragrance (from the fruits) and (the cessation of) tithes has removed the fatness of corn" (*Sotah* 49a).

15. וְאֵיבָה אָשִׁית — *I will put enmity.* Woman will be abhorrent in the (mind's) eye of one's imagination, even her own, as our Sages say: "A woman (is like) a pitcher full of filth and her mouth is full of blood" (*Shabbos* 152a). This will be so among males and females (alike).

NOTES

14. אָרוּר אַתָּה מִכָּל — *Accursed are you beyond all.* Our Sages were of the opinion that unlike man, all creatures sustain themselves without undue hardship. The curse of the serpent is that he, unlike other creatures, will attain his needs with pain, as a punishment for his sin. Since the *Sforno* interprets the serpent figuratively, as the evil inclination within man, he quotes the saying of our Sages regarding the difficulties of man in obtaining his bread. Apparently, he is linking the cause of man's suffering in finding his sustenance, as do the Sages, with his spiritual shortcomings which in turn are caused by his succumbing to the blandishments of the serpent — i.e., the evil inclination.

15. וְאֵיבָה אָשִׁית — *And I will put enmity.* The *Sforno*, apparently, interprets this enmity as referring to the relationship of Adam and Eve *after* the sin. Adam's attitude toward his wife had changed, and hers toward him as well. The sin created tension, not only between the first man and woman, but left a legacy for future generations as well.

הוּא יְשׁוּפְךָ רֹאשׁ וְאַתָּה תְּשׁוּפֶנּוּ עָקֵב — *He will pound your head, and you will bruise his heel.* The *Sforno*, consistent with his interpretation of the serpent as the evil inclination, interprets the word ראשׁ as *beginning* and עָקֵב as *end*. God is depicting man's ongoing confrontation with his יֵצֶר (inclination-prompter). Even at the *beginning*, before he gives in to his desires and passions, he anticipates the problems that may beset him, thereby diminishing his intensity of pleasure. And afterward, at the *end*, his indulgence may well bring him harm.

16. הַרְבָּה אַרְבֶּה עִצְּבוֹנֵךְ . . . בְּעֶצֶב תֵּלְדִי בָנִים — *I will greatly increase your suffering . . . In pain shall you bear children.* The *Sforno* follows the interpretation of our Sages (*Erubin* 100b) regarding the discomfort of woman's menstrual periods, but whereas the Talmud applies the difficulties associated with rearing children to the word עִצְּבוֹנֵךְ,

13 *And HASHEM God said to the woman, "What is this that you have done!"*

The woman said, "The serpent deceived me, and I ate."

14 *And HASHEM God said to the serpent, "Because you have done this, accursed are you beyond all the cattle and beyond all beasts of the field; upon your belly shall you go, and dust shall you eat all the days of your life.*
15 *I will put enmity between you and the woman, and between your offspring and her offspring. He will pound your head, and you will bruise his heel."*

16 *To the woman He said, "I will greatly increase your suffering and your childbearing; in pain shall you bear children. Yet your craving shall be for your husband, and he shall rule over you."*

17 *To Adam He said, "Because you listened to the voice of your wife and ate of the tree about which I commanded you saying, 'You shall not eat*

וּבֵין זַרְעֲךָ וּבֵין זַרְעָהּ — *And between your offspring and her offspring.* This (enmity) will not be between Adam and Eve alone.

הוּא יְשׁוּפְךָ רֹאשׁ — *He will pound your head.* The power of imagination will diminish pleasure at the very outset of its attainment, due to (man's) mental image and apprehension of harm (resulting from) the quality, quantity and (arrangement) procedure of his pleasure.

וְאַתָּה תְּשׁוּפֶנּוּ עָקֵב — *And you will bruise his heel ...* for the lustful (person), whose (lust) will overpower him, will bring harm (to himself) at the culmination of his pleasure.

16. הַרְבָּה אַרְבֶּה עִצְּבוֹנֵךְ — *I will greatly increase your suffering ...* (This refers to) menstrual blood, which is called נִדַּת דְּוֺתָהּ, *the impurity of her sickness* (*Leviticus* 12:2), for (during this period) she is, כָּל הַיּוֹם דָּוָה, *faint all the day* (*Lamentations* 1:13).

וְהֵרֹנֵךְ — *And your childbearing.* This was the reverse of their condition prior to the sin, as our Sages tell us, "On the very same day they were created, they cohabited and (she) gave birth" (*Bereishis Rabbah* 22:3), and so it shall be in the future, as our Sages say, "In the future a woman will give birth daily" (*Shabbos* 30b), for at that time Israel will find favor with God, the Blessed One, as Adam originally did before he sinned.

בְּעֶצֶב תֵּלְדִי בָנִים — *In pain shall you bear children.* You will rear them with greater pain (trouble) than other living creatures. The word לֵידָה, *to bear,* is (also) used to denote "raising" (children), as it says, חֲמֵשֶׁת בְּנֵי מִיכַל בַּת שָׁאוּל אֲשֶׁר יָלְדָה לְעַדְרִיאֵל בֶּן בַּרְזִלַּי הַמְּחֹלָתִי, *the five sons of Michal, the daughter of Saul, whom she bore to Adriel the son of Barzillai the Meholti* (*II Samuel* 21:8).

17. כִּי שָׁמַעְתָּ לְקוֹל אִשְׁתֶּךָ — *Because you listened to the voice of your wife ...* when she imputed to God falsehood and jealousy.

וַתֹּאכַל מִן הָעֵץ — *And ate of the tree.* You disobeyed and therefore deserve the death penalty, since you were warned. (Yet) you listened to her voice and accepted her opinion that God misled you.

NOTES

your suffering, the *Sforno* applies the area of childraising to the phrase בְּעֶצֶב תֵּלְדִי, consistent with his interpretation in various places (see 25:2) that the word לֵידָה denotes rearing of children, as well as its common meaning of bearing and giving birth to a child.

17. כִּי שָׁמַעְתָּ לְקוֹל אִשְׁתֶּךָ וַתֹּאכַל מִן הָעֵץ — *Because you listened to the voice of your wife and ate of the tree.* God chastises Adam for two transgressions: first, for accepting Eve's false claim that God's intention in prohibiting the fruit of the Tree of Knowledge was to prevent mankind from attaining added knowledge, thereby becoming as *Elohim;* second, for the overt act of eating the fruit of the prohibited tree. This eliminates any question of redundancy in this verse.

יח מִמֶּנּוּ אֲרוּרָה הָאֲדָמָה בַּעֲבוּרֶךָ בְּעִצָּבוֹן תֹּאכְלֶנָּה כֹּל יְמֵי חַיֶּיךָ: וְקוֹץ
יט וְדַרְדַּר תַּצְמִיחַ לָךְ וְאָכַלְתָּ אֶת־עֵשֶׂב הַשָּׂדֶה: בְּזֵעַת אַפֶּיךָ תֹּאכַל לֶחֶם
עַד שׁוּבְךָ אֶל־הָאֲדָמָה כִּי מִמֶּנָּה לֻקָּחְתָּ כִּי־עָפָר אַתָּה וְאֶל־עָפָר תָּשׁוּב:
כ־כא וַיִּקְרָא הָאָדָם שֵׁם אִשְׁתּוֹ חַוָּה כִּי הִוא הָיְתָה אֵם כָּל־חָי: וַיַּעַשׂ יהוה
אֱלֹהִים לְאָדָם וּלְאִשְׁתּוֹ כָּתְנוֹת עוֹר וַיַּלְבִּשֵׁם:
רביעי כב וַיֹּאמֶר ׀ יהוה אֱלֹהִים הֵן הָאָדָם הָיָה כְּאַחַד מִמֶּנּוּ לָדַעַת טוֹב וָרָע וְעַתָּה
כג ׀ פֶּן־יִשְׁלַח יָדוֹ וְלָקַח גַּם מֵעֵץ הַחַיִּים וְאָכַל וָחַי לְעֹלָם: וַיְשַׁלְּחֵהוּ יהוה
כד אֱלֹהִים מִגַּן־עֵדֶן לַעֲבֹד אֶת־הָאֲדָמָה אֲשֶׁר לֻקַּח מִשָּׁם: וַיְגָרֶשׁ
אֶת־הָאָדָם וַיַּשְׁכֵּן מִקֶּדֶם לְגַן־עֵדֶן אֶת־הַכְּרֻבִים וְאֵת לַהַט הַחֶרֶב
ד א הַמִּתְהַפֶּכֶת לִשְׁמֹר אֶת־דֶּרֶךְ עֵץ הַחַיִּים: וְהָאָדָם
יָדַע אֶת־חַוָּה אִשְׁתּוֹ וַתַּהַר וַתֵּלֶד אֶת־קַיִן וַתֹּאמֶר קָנִיתִי אִישׁ
ב אֶת־יהוה: וַתֹּסֶף לָלֶדֶת אֶת־אָחִיו אֶת־הָבֶל וַיְהִי־הֶבֶל רֹעֵה צֹאן

אֲרוּרָה הָאֲדָמָה — *Accursed is the ground.* It will no longer yield up its strength (crop) to you without toil; and because you were disobedient and transgressed His command ...

19. וְאֶל עָפָר תָּשׁוּב — *And to dust shall you return* ... as I forewarned you when I commanded and said, *For on the day you eat of it, you shall surely die* (2:17), i.e., you will become mortal (and *ultimately* die).

20. חַוָּה — *Eve.* Because of her sin, she must sustain (nurture) and raise her children.

כִּי הִיא הָיְתָה אֵם כָּל חָי — *Because she had become the mother of all the living.* Although other women will also be mothers, nonetheless she alone is called by this name, because she was the first of them all.

21. וַיַּעַשׂ ... כָּתְנוֹת עוֹר — *Made ... garments of skin* ... without the efforts of man, as it will come to pass in the future, as our Sages say, "*Eretz Yisrael* will bring forth cakes and woolen garments, in the future" (*Shabbos* 30b).

וַיַּלְבִּשֵׁם — *And He clothed them.* He did not drive them out naked, lest they dress themselves later through their own efforts and thereby think they had an added attainment (of knowledge).

NOTES

19. וְאֶל עָפָר תָּשׁוּב — *And to dust shall you return.* The punishment of death, if man were to eat of the tree, was never meant to be immediate. Rather, the consequence of this act was that man would now become a mortal being, destined eventually and inevitably to die.

20. חַוָּה — *Eve.* The word חַיָּה, in connection with a person's relationship to a child, means to sustain, nurture — *give life* — to the dependent infant. Regarding Yocheved and Miriam, the Torah says וַתְּחַיֶּיןָ, *they "gave life to,"* (i.e., *they sustained*) *the infants (Exodus* 1:17). *Rashi* comments on that verse, "they provided them with water and food." The *Sforno* interprets Eve's name accordingly — חַוָּה derived from חַיָּה — her task now being to sustain, nurture and raise her children.

21. וַיַּלְבִּישֵׁם — *And He clothed them.* Although God's clothing of Adam and Eve is considered by our Sages as an act of *chesed* (kindness) on His part, the *Sforno* gives an additional reason. Since they had eaten of the Tree of Knowledge they might well delude themselves into thinking, were they to clothe themselves on their own, that they had indeed gained a new, higher status of wisdom as the serpent had suggested. Therefore God clothed them before they left the garden, to dispel such an assumption.

22-23. כְּאַחַד מִמֶּנּוּ ... וַיְשַׁלְּחֵהוּ — *As one of us ... and He banished him.* Man was granted freedom of choice. In that sense he is "as one of us" (i.e., Divine beings), still he has physical appetites and desires. Were he to live forever he would pursue his bodily pleasures and reject the spiritual blessings which God intended for him. However, his mortality encourages him to attain knowledge and spiritual perfection in the brief time allotted to him. That is why God banishes them from the garden and

of it,' accursed is the ground because of you; through suffering shall you eat of it all the days of your life.
18 *Thorns and thistles shall it sprout for you, and you shall eat the herb of the field.*
19 *By the sweat of your brow shall you eat bread until you return to the ground, from which you were taken: For you are dust, and to dust shall you return."*

20 *The man called his wife's name Eve, because she had become the mother of all the living.*

21 *And HASHEM God made for Adam and his wife garments of skin, and He clothed them.*

22 *And HASHEM God said, "Behold man has become as one of us, knowing good and bad; and now, lest he put forth his hand and take also of the Tree of Life, and eat and live forever!"*

23 *And HASHEM God banished him from the Garden of Eden, to work the soil from which he was taken.*
24 *And He drove out the man, and He stationed at the east of the Garden of Eden the Cherubim and the flame of the ever-turning sword, to guard the way to the Tree of Life.*

4
1 *Now the man had known his wife Eve, and she conceived and bore Cain, saying, "I have acquired a man with HASHEM."*
2 *And additionally she bore his brother Abel. And Abel became a shepherd,*

---

22. כְּאַחַד מִמֶּנּוּ לָדַעַת טוֹב וָרָע — *As one of us to know good and bad.* He knows good and bad since he is formed in our (the Divine) image. Should he also be immortal, he will pursue (earthly) pleasures all his days and cast aside all intelligent (spiritual) concepts and good deeds, and never attain that spiritual bliss which God intended for him in making him in His image and likeness.

23. וַיְשַׁלְּחֵהוּ — *And He banished.* He commanded them to leave from there (the garden), similar to, לְמַהֵר לְשַׁלְּחָם מִן הָאָרֶץ, *to send them out of the land in haste* (*Exodus* 12:33).

הָאֲדָמָה אֲשֶׁר לֻקַּח מִשָּׁם — *The soil from which he was taken ...* for that place and its atmosphere was suitable to (man's) temperament, food (source) and his needs, more so than other parts of the earth.

24. וַיְגָרֶשׁ אֶת הָאָדָם — *And He drove out the man ...* that neither he nor his descendants should ever return there.

וַיַּשְׁכֵּן — *And He stationed ...* before they had departed.

לִשְׁמֹר אֶת דֶּרֶךְ עֵץ הַחַיִּים — *To guard the way to the Tree of Life ...* so they should not detour to the Tree of Life and partake of it on their way out.

IV

2. וַיְהִי הֶבֶל רֹעֵה צֹאן — *And Abel became a shepherd.* This was a more skilled occupation than that of agriculture.

NOTES

guards the key to the Tree of Life, lest they partake of it *prior* to their departure (see verse 24).

23. הָאֲדָמָה אֲשֶׁר לֻקַּח מִשָּׁם – *The soil from which he was taken.* The *Sforno* (2:7,8) explains that man was formed from the earth outside the garden and then placed therein. Now, he is sent back to the place of his origin for his own benefit. Even as God punishes him He is compassionate, and places him in an environment to which he can readily adjust.

IV

2. וַיְהִי הֶבֶל רֹעֵה צֹאן וְקַיִן הָיָה עֹבֵד אֲדָמָה – *And Abel became a shepherd, and Cain became a tiller of the ground.* Since Cain was older than Abel, his occu-

ג וְקַ֗יִן הָיָ֖ה עֹבֵ֣ד אֲדָמָֽה: וַיְהִ֖י מִקֵּ֣ץ יָמִ֑ים וַיָּבֵ֨א קַ֜יִן מִפְּרִ֧י הָֽאֲדָמָ֛ה מִנְחָ֖ה
ד לַֽיהוָֽה: וְהֶ֨בֶל הֵבִ֥יא גַם־ה֛וּא מִבְּכֹר֥וֹת צֹאנ֖וֹ וּמֵֽחֶלְבֵהֶ֑ן וַיִּ֣שַׁע יְהוָ֔ה
ה אֶל־הֶ֖בֶל וְאֶל־מִנְחָתֽוֹ: וְאֶל־קַ֥יִן וְאֶל־מִנְחָת֖וֹ לֹ֣א שָׁעָ֑ה וַיִּ֤חַר לְקַ֨יִן֙ מְאֹ֔ד
ו-ז וַֽיִּפְּל֖וּ פָּנָֽיו: וַיֹּ֥אמֶר יְהוָ֖ה אֶל־קָ֑יִן לָ֚מָּה חָ֣רָה לָ֔ךְ וְלָ֖מָּה נָֽפְל֥וּ פָנֶֽיךָ: הֲל֤וֹא
אִם־תֵּיטִיב֙ שְׂאֵ֔ת וְאִם֙ לֹ֣א תֵיטִ֔יב לַפֶּ֖תַח חַטָּ֣את רֹבֵ֑ץ וְאֵלֶ֨יךָ֙ תְּשׁ֣וּקָת֔וֹ
ח וְאַתָּ֖ה תִּמְשָׁל־בּֽוֹ: וַיֹּ֥אמֶר קַ֖יִן אֶל־הֶ֣בֶל אָחִ֑יו וַֽיְהִי֙ בִּֽהְיוֹתָ֣ם בַּשָּׂדֶ֔ה
ט וַיָּ֥קָם קַ֛יִן אֶל־הֶ֥בֶל אָחִ֖יו וַיַּֽהַרְגֵֽהוּ: וַיֹּ֤אמֶר יְהוָה֙ אֶל־קַ֔יִן אֵ֖י הֶ֣בֶל אָחִ֑יךָ

וְקַיִן הָיָה עֹבֵד אֲדָמָה — *And Cain became a tiller of the ground* . . . therefore, each brought (an offering to God) from that which came to his hand.

4. אֶל־הֶבֶל וְאֶל־מִנְחָתוֹ — *To Abel and to his offering.* Abel, himself, was pleasing and acceptable, and his offering was also pleasing, for it came from a species worthy to be accepted.

5. וְאֶל־קַיִן וְאֶל־מִנְחָתוֹ לֹא שָׁעָה — *But to Cain and to his offering He did not turn.* He did not turn to Cain, himself, who was not pleasing, nor to the offering, which also was not worthy to be accepted (by God).

וַיִּחַר לְקַיִן מְאֹד — *And Cain was very annoyed (wroth)* . . . jealous of his brother (whose offering) was accepted (by God).

וַיִּפְּלוּ פָּנָיו — *And his countenance fell* . . . in shame, for God had shamed him by not accepting it (his offering).

6. לָמָּה חָרָה לָךְ — *Why are you annoyed (angry).* Why are you jealous of your brother, and concerned that I accepted his offering with good will? This was not an arbitrary decision nor an unjust one.

וְלָמָּה נָפְלוּ פָנֶיךָ — *And why has your countenance fallen?* When a fault can be remedied it is not proper to grieve over what has passed, but rather to try to amend and improve (matters) for the future.

7. הֲלוֹא אִם תֵּיטִיב — *Surely, if you improve (yourself).* (Improve) yourself, and strive that you should also be acceptable (to God).

NOTES

pation should have been mentioned first. The reason Abel's occupation as a shepherd is given precedence is explained by the *Sforno* as reflecting its relative importance, compared to agriculture. The tending of sheep, cattle and animals in general is established at this early stage as a preferred occupation for those who are concerned with spiritual excellence and reaching out to God. The patriarchs, Moshe, David and many other great men of our people were shepherds. Apparently it is a way of life that frees man to come closer to God and meditate on His ways, attaining eventually heightened knowledge of Him. The expression used by the *Sforno*, מְלָאכָת חָכְמָה, *skilled occupation*, literally, *occupation of wisdom*, may well imply not only the skill required, but the higher wisdom eventually attained.

    The expression מִן הַבָּא בְיָדוֹ, *from that which had come in his hand*, is taken by the *Sforno* from 32:14. It implies that which one possesses and can legitimately give as a gift or offering.

4. אֶל־הֶבֶל וְאֶל־מִנְחָתוֹ – *To Abel and to his offering.* Since the Torah mentions both the name of the one who brings the sacrifice, as well as his offering, the implication is that God examined the character and motivation of the person bringing the sacrifice, not only the animal or produce brought. Abel measured up well on both counts, while Cain failed to do so on both.

5-6. וַיִּחַר לְקַיִן מְאֹד וַיִּפְּלוּ פָנָיו . . . לָמָּה חָרָה לָךְ וְלָמָּה נָפְלוּ פָנֶיךָ – *And Cain was very annoyed (wroth), and his countenance fell . . . Why are you annoyed (angry), and why has your countenance fallen?* The *Sforno* interprets the phrase וַיִּחַר, *he was wroth,* as referring to Cain's jealousy of his brother, while וַיִּפְּלוּ פָנָיו (*his countenance fell*) implies shame. It therefore follows that God's questions to Cain are twofold. You have no reason to be jealous since My decision was a just one, and if you are ashamed, let that be channeled into the positive act of self-improvement rather than dwelling on the failure of the past.

and Cain became a tiller of the ground.

3 *After a period of time, Cain brought an offering to* HASHEM *of the fruit of the ground;* 4 *and as for Abel, he also brought of the firstlings of his flock and from their choicest.* HASHEM *turned to Abel and to his offering,* 5 *but to Cain and to his offering He did not turn. And Cain was very annoyed, and his countenance fell.*

6 *And* HASHEM *said to Cain, "Why are you annoyed, and why has your countenance fallen?* 7 *Surely, if you improve [yourself], you will be lifted. But if you do not improve [yourself], sin rests at the door. Its desire is toward you, yet you can conquer it."*

8 *Cain spoke with his brother Abel. And it happened when they were in the field, that Cain rose up against his brother Abel and killed him.*

9 HASHEM *said to Cain, "Where is Abel your brother?"*

שְׂאֵת — *You will be lifted.* Exalted heights and elevated position await you, and will be yours.

וְאִם לֹא תֵיטִיב לַפֶּתַח חַטָּאת רֹבֵץ — *But if you do not improve [yourself], sin rests at the door.* Then sin also awaits you, and you will add iniquity to your sins, for such is the way of the evil inclination.

וְאֵלֶיךָ תְּשׁוּקָתוֹ — *Its desire is toward you.* If you turn to him (the evil inclination) and succumb to your evil desires, as our Sages say, יִצְרוֹ שֶׁל אָדָם מִתְגַּבֵּר עָלָיו בְּכׇל יוֹם, *The evil inclination within man grows stronger from day to day (Succah* 52a).

וְאַתָּה תִּמְשָׁל בּוֹ — *Yet you can conquer it.* You can overpower it (the evil inclination) through the Divine Image (within you) as our Sages say (ibid.), וְאִלְמָלֵא הקב״ה עוֹזְרוֹ אֵינוֹ יָכוֹל לוֹ, שֶׁנֶּאֱמַר: ה׳ לֹא יַעַזְבֶנּוּ בְיָדוֹ, *Were it not that the Holy One, Blessed is He, helps him, he would not be able to withstand it, as it says: "*HASHEM *will not leave him in his hand" (Psalms* 37:33).

8. וַיֹּאמֶר קַיִן אֶל הֶבֶל אָחִיו — *Cain spoke with his brother Abel.* (He told him) how annoyed he was, and how his countenance fell, because of his brother.

וַיְהִי בִּהְיוֹתָם בַּשָּׂדֶה — *And it happened when they were in the field* ... away from the presence of their father and mother.

וַיָּקָם קַיִן — *That Cain rose up* ... without any prior argument, as (we find), וְאָרַב לוֹ וְקָם עָלָיו, *And lie in wait for him, and rise up against him (Deut.* 19:11).

9. אֵי הֶבֶל אָחִיךָ — *Where is Abel your brother?* Where did you bury him? (God) asked this,

NOTES

7. ... וְאִם לֹא תֵיטִיב — *But if you will not improve [yourself]*... The expression used by the *Sforno* — "for such is the way of the evil inclination" — refers to the saying of our Sages (*Shabbos* 105b) regarding the יֵצֶר (the evil tempter): "Today he tells you to do thus and tomorrow thus ... until he eventually tells you to become an idolater!" The Almighty cautions Cain, and through him all mankind, that the evil tempter lies in wait, "crouching at the door," ready to capitalize on man's weakness and vulnerability. Yet man is in reality stronger, and can conquer the יֵצֶר because he possesses the strength of the Divine image within him. The *Sforno* seems to interpret the saying of our Sages (*Succah* 52a), "and were it not for the Holy One, Blessed is He," as referring not only to God Himself, but to the Divine image within man as well.

8. וַיֹּאמֶר קַיִן אֶל הֶבֶל אָחִיו — *Cain spoke with his brother Abel.* The Torah does not tell us what Cain said. The *Sforno* surmises it was the baring of his heart, sharing his deep hurt with Abel.

וַיְהִי בִּהְיוֹתָם בַּשָּׂדֶה — *And it happened when they were in the field.* Although Cain is prepared to harm his brother, he is not so callous and cruel as to do so in the presence of his parents!

וַיָּקָם קַיִן — *That Cain rose up.* The *Sforno* is drawing a parallel from the word וַיָּקָם, *rose up*, to קָם, *rise up*, where the Torah explicitly states that one ambushed his victim without any warning.

י וַיֹּאמֶר לֹא יָדַעְתִּי הֲשֹׁמֵר אָחִי אָנֹכִי: וַיֹּאמֶר מֶה עָשִׂיתָ קוֹל דְּמֵי אָחִיךָ
יא צֹעֲקִים אֵלַי מִן־הָאֲדָמָה: וְעַתָּה אָרוּר אָתָּה מִן־הָאֲדָמָה אֲשֶׁר פָּצְתָה
יב אֶת־פִּיהָ לָקַחַת אֶת־דְּמֵי אָחִיךָ מִיָּדֶךָ: כִּי תַעֲבֹד אֶת־הָאֲדָמָה לֹא־תֹסֵף
יג תֵּת־כֹּחָהּ לָךְ נָע וָנָד תִּהְיֶה בָאָרֶץ: וַיֹּאמֶר קַיִן אֶל־יהוה גָּדוֹל עֲוֺנִי
יד מִנְּשֹׂא: הֵן גֵּרַשְׁתָּ אֹתִי הַיּוֹם מֵעַל פְּנֵי הָאֲדָמָה וּמִפָּנֶיךָ אֶסָּתֵר וְהָיִיתִי
טו נָע וָנָד בָּאָרֶץ וְהָיָה כָל־מֹצְאִי יַהַרְגֵנִי: וַיֹּאמֶר לוֹ יהוה לָכֵן כָּל־הֹרֵג קַיִן
טז שִׁבְעָתַיִם יֻקָּם וַיָּשֶׂם יהוה לְקַיִן אוֹת לְבִלְתִּי הַכּוֹת־אֹתוֹ כָּל־מֹצְאוֹ: וַיֵּצֵא
יז קַיִן מִלִּפְנֵי יהוה וַיֵּשֶׁב בְּאֶרֶץ־נוֹד קִדְמַת־עֵדֶן: וַיֵּדַע קַיִן אֶת־אִשְׁתּוֹ
וַתַּהַר וַתֵּלֶד אֶת־חֲנוֹךְ וַיְהִי בֹּנֶה עִיר וַיִּקְרָא שֵׁם הָעִיר כְּשֵׁם בְּנוֹ חֲנוֹךְ:

so that he (Cain) might repent, for He does not desire the death (of the wicked).

לֹא יָדַעְתִּי — *I do not know.* He thought that the question meant "what happened to him (Abel)?" Since Cain had not sought out God to attain prophecy or acceptance, as he had originally done, he thought (was convinced) that God, the Blessed One, was not aware of (all) human details, except of those who cleaved to Him.

11. אָרוּר אָתָּה מִן הָאֲדָמָה — *You are cursed more than the ground* . . . cursed and deprived of the earth's goodness.

אֲשֶׁר פָּצְתָה אֶת פִּיהָ — *Which opened wide its mouth.* You used the earth to cover (the traces) of the murder of your brother; as punishment you will be unable to use (its strength) as you did heretofore, for your life's needs. (The Torah) does not find it necessary to describe the punishment of the murderer, for the law is clearly defined in nature itself, regarding anyone who inflicts injury, that, כַּאֲשֶׁר עָשָׂה כֵּן יֵעָשֶׂה לוֹ, *as he has done, so shall it be done to him (Leviticus* 24:19).

13. גָּדוֹל עֲוֺנִי מִנְּשֹׂא — *My iniquity is too great to be borne.* After (Cain) realized that God, the Blessed One, observes absolutely every (human) detail, he thought that (God) would surely know that he is (really) not repenting his sin, since his regret was due only to (the fear) of punishment, and even then, only after God entreated him to repent, which he (at

NOTES

9. אֵי הֶבֶל אָחִיךָ – *Where is Abel your brother?* Since God knows all and all is revealed to Him, the question posed to Cain, "Where is your brother?" cannot be interpreted literally. It is only a subtle opening given to Cain, to confess and repent.

לֹא יָדַעְתִּי – *I do not know.* Cain is convinced that God is close to those who are close to Him. As such His providence is extended to them alone, not to those who have distanced themselves from Him. It therefore follows that God is not concerned or aware of the detailed actions of those who transgress. The truth however is that the Almighty oversees, supervises and knows the actions of every human being. This is one of the major lessons taught to us through this episode.

11. אָרוּר אָתָּה מִן הָאֲדָמָה – *You are cursed more than the ground.* The concept of "curse" is one of diminishment and lack, just as that of "blessing" (בְּרָכָה) implies increase and plenty. Because Cain used and abused the earth to conceal his victim, it will no longer be a blessing to him but will withhold its strength from him, thereby depriving Cain of his sustenance. This is what is meant by אָרוּר אָתָּה, *you will be cursed* — not *you* as a person, but your productive relationship to the earth will now be diminished.

אֲשֶׁר פָּצְתָה אֶת פִּיהָ – *Which opened wide its mouth.* Cain murdered his brother and then used the earth to conceal his crime. For the initial crime the Torah finds no need to spell out his punishment. Since the dawn of human history, the enormity of a crime such as murder would perforce bring with it consequences commensurate with the crime — *as he has done so shall it be done to him.* As for the misuse of the earth by Cain, who had heretofore drawn his sustenance from it, God utters the phrase אָרוּר, *cursed.*

13. גָּדוֹל עֲוֺנִי מִנְּשֹׂא – *My iniquity is too great to be borne.* According to *Rashi*, this is a question, "Is my iniquity too great to bear?" However, the *Sforno* interprets Cain's words as a statement, not a question. Since God had admonished and cau-

And he said, "I do not know. Am I my brother's keeper?"
[10] Then He said, "What have you done? The voice of your brother's blood
cries out to Me from the ground! [11] Therefore, you are cursed more than the
ground, which opened wide its mouth to receive your brother's blood from
your hand. [12] When you work the ground, it shall no longer yield its
strength to you. You shall become a vagrant and a wanderer on earth."
[13] Cain said to HASHEM, "My iniquity is too great to be borne! [14] Behold,
You have banished me this day from the face of the earth — can I be hidden
from Your presence? I must become a vagrant and a wanderer on earth;
whoever meets me will kill me!" [15] HASHEM said to him, "Therefore,
whoever slays Cain, twice sevenfold shall he be avenged." And HASHEM
placed a mark upon Cain, so that none that meet him might kill him.
[16] Cain left the presence of HASHEM and settled in the land of Nod, east
of Eden.
[17] And Cain knew his wife, and she conceived and bore Enoch. He
became a city-builder, and he named the city after his son Enoch.

---

first) refused (to do). Therefore, he felt that there was no hope for (true) repentance of his sin which would atone and protect him from the present punishment, as we find by Saul in the episode of Amalek, when he said to Samuel, חָטָאתִי, *I sinned* (*I Samuel* 15:24), (only) after Samuel pleaded and entreated him to repent of his sin, (and so) was punished, as it says, וַיִּמְאָסְךָ מִמֶּלֶךְ, *He has rejected you as king* (ibid. 23).

14. וְהָיָה כָל מֹצְאִי יַהַרְגֵנִי — *Whoever meets me will kill me . . .* hence, my punishment will be greater than what You decreed.

15. כָּל הֹרֵג קַיִן שִׁבְעָתַיִם יֻקָּם — *Whoever slays Cain, twice sevenfold shall he be avenged.* I (i.e., Hashem) say to whoever is to kill Cain, "I decree that the revenge for his sin is 'twice sevenfold.'" Whoever is (only) "prepared to kill" is (also) referred to as a "killer," as it says, וְאֶפְרַיִם לְהוֹצִיא אֶל הֹרֵג בָּנָיו, *Ephraim must bring out his children to slayers* (*Hosea* 9:13), and the word שִׁבְעָתַיִם implies seven times doubled, as we find וְנִמְצָא יְשַׁלֵּם שִׁבְעָתָיִם, *If caught he must pay twice sevenfold* (*Proverbs* 6:31). The decree therefore was that for this murder, where the blood of his brother represented one half or one third of mankind, the revenge (punishment) for the murderer shall be "twice sevenfold," in such a manner that for six generations (Cain) will be a "vagrant and wanderer," (which is) a bad life equal to death, or even more severe, as it says, אַל תַּהַרְגֵם פֶּן יִשְׁכְּחוּ עַמִּי הֲנִיעֵמוֹ בְחֵילְךָ, *Do not kill them lest my people be unmindful; with Your power make wanderers of them* (*Psalms* 59:12). In the end, he (Cain) will be killed, in the seventh generation, as (indeed) happened through Lemech, as is brought in traditional sources (*Tanchuma* 10).

NOTES

tioned him before his murderous act (verse 7) to no avail, then his repentance will surely not atone for his sin nor protect him from punishment. Were he to have repented on his own there would have been hope, but now that he does so only because of God's importuning, as Saul did after Samuel pleaded and pressured him to repent, it is meaningless. In both cases it is too late to avert the punishment.

15. כָּל הֹרֵג קַיִן שִׁבְעָתַיִם יֻקָּם — *Whoever slays Cain, twice sevenfold shall be avenged.* The punishment of wandering and exile is greater than the eventual one of death. Therefore God cautions anyone who may plan to execute Cain to refrain from doing so, since God's decree of banishment and wandering is a far more severe punishment, justified by the enormity of this murder of Abel who represented one half of humankind, if you consider their generation, or one third if you also include Adam. After seven generations the final stage of Cain's punishment will occur, namely, his death at the hands of Lemech.

יח וַיִּוָּלֵד לַחֲנוֹךְ אֶת־עִירָד וְעִירָד יָלַד אֶת־מְחוּיָאֵל וּמְחִיָּיאֵל יָלַד אֶת־
חמישי יט מְתוּשָׁאֵל וּמְתוּשָׁאֵל יָלַד אֶת־לָמֶךְ: וַיִּקַּח־לוֹ לֶמֶךְ שְׁתֵּי נָשִׁים שֵׁם
כ הָאַחַת עָדָה וְשֵׁם הַשֵּׁנִית צִלָּה: וַתֵּלֶד עָדָה אֶת־יָבָל הוּא הָיָה אֲבִי יֹשֵׁב
כא-כב אֹהֶל וּמִקְנֶה: וְשֵׁם אָחִיו יוּבָל הוּא הָיָה אֲבִי כָּל־תֹּפֵשׂ כִּנּוֹר וְעוּגָב: וְצִלָּה
גַם־הִוא יָלְדָה אֶת־תּוּבַל קַיִן לֹטֵשׁ כָּל־חֹרֵשׁ נְחֹשֶׁת וּבַרְזֶל וַאֲחוֹת
כג תּוּבַל־קַיִן נַעֲמָה: וַיֹּאמֶר לֶמֶךְ לְנָשָׁיו עָדָה וְצִלָּה שְׁמַעַן קוֹלִי נְשֵׁי לֶמֶךְ
כד הַאְזֵנָּה אִמְרָתִי כִּי אִישׁ הָרַגְתִּי לְפִצְעִי וְיֶלֶד לְחַבֻּרָתִי: כִּי שִׁבְעָתַיִם
כה יֻקַּם־קָיִן וְלֶמֶךְ שִׁבְעִים וְשִׁבְעָה: וַיֵּדַע אָדָם עוֹד אֶת־אִשְׁתּוֹ וַתֵּלֶד בֵּן
וַתִּקְרָא אֶת־שְׁמוֹ שֵׁת כִּי שָׁת־לִי אֱלֹהִים זֶרַע אַחֵר תַּחַת הֶבֶל כִּי הֲרָגוֹ
כו קָיִן: וּלְשֵׁת גַּם־הוּא יֻלַּד־בֵּן וַיִּקְרָא אֶת־שְׁמוֹ אֱנוֹשׁ אָז הוּחַל לִקְרֹא בְּשֵׁם
ה ששי א יְהוָה: זֶה סֵפֶר תּוֹלְדֹת אָדָם בְּיוֹם בְּרֹא אֱלֹהִים אָדָם
ב בִּדְמוּת אֱלֹהִים עָשָׂה אֹתוֹ: זָכָר וּנְקֵבָה בְּרָאָם וַיְבָרֶךְ אֹתָם וַיִּקְרָא
ג אֶת־שְׁמָם אָדָם בְּיוֹם הִבָּרְאָם: וַיְחִי אָדָם שְׁלֹשִׁים וּמְאַת שָׁנָה וַיּוֹלֶד
ד בִּדְמוּתוֹ כְּצַלְמוֹ וַיִּקְרָא אֶת־שְׁמוֹ שֵׁת: וַיִּהְיוּ יְמֵי־אָדָם אַחֲרֵי הוֹלִידוֹ אֶת־
ה שֵׁת שְׁמֹנֶה מֵאֹת שָׁנָה וַיּוֹלֶד בָּנִים וּבָנוֹת: וַיִּהְיוּ כָּל־יְמֵי אָדָם אֲשֶׁר־חַי

---

23. שְׁמַעַן קוֹלִי נְשֵׁי לֶמֶךְ — *Hear my voice; wives of Lemech* . . . as I cry out in sorrow.

אִמְרָתִי — *My speech.* As I relate my pain.

הָרַגְתִּי לְפִצְעִי — *A man have I slain by my wound.* I actually wounded myself, since the victim was my father.

וְיֶלֶד לְחַבֻּרָתִי — *And a child by my bruise.* I actually bruised myself, since the victim was my son.

24. וְלֶמֶךְ שִׁבְעִים וְשִׁבְעָה — *Then Lemech at seventy-seven.* The pain that I will suffer for these (deaths) all my days will be greater than the pain experienced by Cain when he was a vagrant and a wanderer. The reason is that Lemech suffered all his days for having killed his grandfather Cain and his son Tubal-Cain, as we learn from our traditional sources (ibid.).

26. אָז הוּחַל לִקְרֹא בְּשֵׁם ה׳ — *Then they began to publicly expound the Name of* HASHEM. The righteous of the generation began to expound the Name of HASHEM to the public, similar to, וַיִּקְרָא שָׁם בְּשֵׁם ה׳ אֵל עוֹלָם, *And called there in the Name of* HASHEM *the everlasting God* (21:33). This was necessary to refute the beliefs of the idolaters, who then began (to spread their heresy) as our Sages tell us (*Shabbos* 188b).

NOTES

23. שְׁמַעַן קוֹלִי נְשֵׁי לֶמֶךְ ... אִמְרָתִי – *Hear my voice; wives of Lemech ... My speech.* Two expressions are used by Lemech: *my voice* and *my speech.* The first refers to his cry of sorrow while the second refers to his tale of woe. According to tradition, Lemech killed Cain (accidentally) as well as his own son, Tubal-Cain (see *Rashi*).

24. וְלֶמֶךְ שִׁבְעִים וְשִׁבְעָה – *Then Lemech at seventy-seven.* Lemech bemoans the fact that he killed two relatives, one his forefather (an ancestor) and the second his own son (a descendant). His pain and regret will therefore be greater than that experienced by Cain who killed one person — his brother.

26. אָז הוּחַל לִקְרֹא בְּשֵׁם ה׳ – *Then they began to publicly expound the Name of* HASHEM. The word הוּחַל can be translated *began* or *profane* (from the word חוּלִין, *secular, non-sacred). Rashi,* based on the Midrash, translates *that the Name of* HASHEM *became profaned,* for idolatry had begun. The *Sforno* translates *began to publicly expound the Name of* HASHEM. The righteous ones, observing

18 *To Enoch was born Irad, and Irad begot Mehujael, and Mehujael begot Methushael, and Methushael begot Lamech.*
19 *Lamech took to himself two wives: The name of one was Adah, and the name of the second was Zillah.* 20 *And Adah bore Jabal; he was the first of those who dwell in tents and breed cattle.* 21 *The name of his brother was Jubal; he was the first of all who handle the harp and flute.*
22 *And Zillah, too — she bore Tubal-cain, who sharpened all cutting implements of copper and iron. And the sister of Tubal-cain was Naamah.*
23 *And Lamech said to his wives, "Adah and Zillah, hear my voice; wives of Lemech, give ear to my speech: A man have I slain by my wound and a child by my bruise!* 24 *If Cain shall be avenged twice sevenfold, then Lamech at seventy-seven!"*
25 *Adam knew his wife again, and she bore a son and named him Seth, because: "God has provided me another child in place of Abel, for Cain had killed him."* 26 *And as for Seth, to him also a son was born, and he named him Enosh. Then they began to publicly expound the Name of* HASHEM.

5 1 *This is the book of the descendants of man — on the day that God created man, He made him in the likeness of God.* 2 *He created them male and female. He blessed them and called their name man on the day they were created —* 3 *when Adam had lived one hundred and thirty years, he begot in his likeness and his image, and he named him Seth.* 4 *And the days of Adam after begetting Seth were eight hundred years, and he begot sons and daughters.* 5 *All the days that Adam lived*

V

1. זֶה סֵפֶר תּוֹלְדֹת אָדָם — *This is the book of the descendants of man.* This is the history of the events which befell the human race.

בִּדְמוּת אֱלֹהִים עָשָׂה אֹתוֹ — *He made him in the likeness of God* . . . as one who has freedom of choice. Therefore when (future) generations angered God, the Blessed One, (by their sins,) He punished them.

3. וַיּוֹלֶד בִּדְמוּתוֹ כְּצַלְמוֹ — *He begot in his likeness and his image.* He (Seth) was more righteous than those who preceded him (i.e., Cain and Abel), for even Abel did not bring a sacrifice until Cain did so first.

NOTES

how idolatry was developing, realized the need to counteract this rejection of God's truth by publicly expounding the Name of HASHEM. This is precisely what Abraham did later, in his generation, for the same reason.

V

1. זֶה סֵפֶר תּוֹלְדֹת אָדָם – *This is the book of the descendants of man.* The word תּוֹלְדוֹת lends itself to various translations. The *Sforno* consistently interprets it as the events or "offspring" of one's life activities. See 6:9, 25:19 and 37:2.

The Torah uses the expression סֵפֶר... אָדָם, *book of man,* at this point in the narrative, because with the death of Abel and the eventual decimation of Cain's offspring, the human race is descended from Seth (verse 3).

3. וַיּוֹלֶד בִּדְמוּתוֹ כְּצַלְמוֹ – *He begot in his likeness and his image. Sforno* bases his contention that Seth was more righteous than his brothers on the fact that the Torah does not use the expression *in his likeness and his image* regarding Cain and Abel, as it does regarding Seth.

ו תְּשַׁע מֵאוֹת שָׁנָה וּשְׁלֹשִׁים שָׁנָה וַיָּמֹת׃ וַיְחִי־שֵׁת
ז חָמֵשׁ שָׁנִים וּמְאַת שָׁנָה וַיּוֹלֶד אֶת־אֱנוֹשׁ׃ וַיְחִי־שֵׁת אַחֲרֵי הוֹלִידוֹ אֶת־
ח אֱנוֹשׁ שֶׁבַע שָׁנִים וּשְׁמֹנֶה מֵאוֹת שָׁנָה וַיּוֹלֶד בָּנִים וּבָנוֹת׃ וַיִּהְיוּ כָּל־יְמֵי־
ט שֵׁת שְׁתֵּים עֶשְׂרֵה שָׁנָה וּתְשַׁע מֵאוֹת שָׁנָה וַיָּמֹת׃ וַיְחִי
י אֱנוֹשׁ תִּשְׁעִים שָׁנָה וַיּוֹלֶד אֶת־קֵינָן׃ וַיְחִי אֱנוֹשׁ אַחֲרֵי הוֹלִידוֹ אֶת־קֵינָן
יא חֲמֵשׁ עֶשְׂרֵה שָׁנָה וּשְׁמֹנֶה מֵאוֹת שָׁנָה וַיּוֹלֶד בָּנִים וּבָנוֹת׃ וַיִּהְיוּ כָּל־יְמֵי
יב אֱנוֹשׁ חָמֵשׁ שָׁנִים וּתְשַׁע מֵאוֹת שָׁנָה וַיָּמֹת׃ וַיְחִי קֵינָן
יג שִׁבְעִים שָׁנָה וַיּוֹלֶד אֶת־מַהֲלַלְאֵל׃ וַיְחִי קֵינָן אַחֲרֵי הוֹלִידוֹ אֶת־
יד מַהֲלַלְאֵל אַרְבָּעִים שָׁנָה וּשְׁמֹנֶה מֵאוֹת שָׁנָה וַיּוֹלֶד בָּנִים וּבָנוֹת׃ וַיִּהְיוּ
טו כָּל־יְמֵי קֵינָן עֶשֶׂר שָׁנִים וּתְשַׁע מֵאוֹת שָׁנָה וַיָּמֹת׃ וַיְחִי
טז מַהֲלַלְאֵל חָמֵשׁ שָׁנִים וְשִׁשִּׁים שָׁנָה וַיּוֹלֶד אֶת־יָרֶד׃ וַיְחִי מַהֲלַלְאֵל
אַחֲרֵי הוֹלִידוֹ אֶת־יֶרֶד שְׁלֹשִׁים שָׁנָה וּשְׁמֹנֶה מֵאוֹת שָׁנָה וַיּוֹלֶד בָּנִים
יז וּבָנוֹת׃ וַיִּהְיוּ כָּל־יְמֵי מַהֲלַלְאֵל חָמֵשׁ וְתִשְׁעִים שָׁנָה וּשְׁמֹנֶה מֵאוֹת שָׁנָה
יח וַיָּמֹת׃ וַיְחִי־יֶרֶד שְׁתַּיִם וְשִׁשִּׁים שָׁנָה וּמְאַת שָׁנָה
יט וַיּוֹלֶד אֶת־חֲנוֹךְ׃ וַיְחִי־יֶרֶד אַחֲרֵי הוֹלִידוֹ אֶת־חֲנוֹךְ שְׁמֹנֶה מֵאוֹת שָׁנָה
כ וַיּוֹלֶד בָּנִים וּבָנוֹת׃ וַיִּהְיוּ כָּל־יְמֵי־יֶרֶד שְׁתַּיִם וְשִׁשִּׁים שָׁנָה וּתְשַׁע
כא מֵאוֹת שָׁנָה וַיָּמֹת׃ וַיְחִי חֲנוֹךְ חָמֵשׁ וְשִׁשִּׁים שָׁנָה
כב וַיּוֹלֶד אֶת־מְתוּשָׁלַח׃ וַיִּתְהַלֵּךְ חֲנוֹךְ אֶת־הָאֱלֹהִים אַחֲרֵי הוֹלִידוֹ
כג אֶת־מְתוּשֶׁלַח שְׁלֹשׁ מֵאוֹת שָׁנָה וַיּוֹלֶד בָּנִים וּבָנוֹת׃ וַיְהִי כָּל־יְמֵי חֲנוֹךְ
כד חָמֵשׁ וְשִׁשִּׁים שָׁנָה וּשְׁלֹשׁ מֵאוֹת שָׁנָה׃ וַיִּתְהַלֵּךְ חֲנוֹךְ אֶת־הָאֱלֹהִים
כה וְאֵינֶנּוּ כִּי־לָקַח אֹתוֹ אֱלֹהִים׃ וַיְחִי מְתוּשֶׁלַח שביעי
כו שֶׁבַע וּשְׁמֹנִים שָׁנָה וּמְאַת שָׁנָה וַיּוֹלֶד אֶת־לָמֶךְ׃ וַיְחִי מְתוּשֶׁלַח
אַחֲרֵי הוֹלִידוֹ אֶת־לֶמֶךְ שְׁתַּיִם וּשְׁמוֹנִים שָׁנָה וּשְׁבַע מֵאוֹת שָׁנָה וַיּוֹלֶד
כז בָּנִים וּבָנוֹת׃ וַיִּהְיוּ כָּל־יְמֵי מְתוּשֶׁלַח תֵּשַׁע וְשִׁשִּׁים שָׁנָה וּתְשַׁע
כח מֵאוֹת שָׁנָה וַיָּמֹת׃ וַיְחִי־לֶמֶךְ שְׁתַּיִם וּשְׁמֹנִים
כט שָׁנָה וּמְאַת שָׁנָה וַיּוֹלֶד בֵּן׃ וַיִּקְרָא אֶת־שְׁמוֹ נֹחַ לֵאמֹר *זֶה יְנַחֲמֵנוּ
ל מִמַּעֲשֵׂנוּ וּמֵעִצְּבוֹן יָדֵינוּ מִן־הָאֲדָמָה אֲשֶׁר אֵרְרָהּ יהוה׃ וַיְחִי־לֶמֶךְ
אַחֲרֵי הוֹלִידוֹ אֶת־נֹחַ חָמֵשׁ וְתִשְׁעִים שָׁנָה וַחֲמֵשׁ מֵאֹת שָׁנָה וַיּוֹלֶד בָּנִים
לא וּבָנוֹת׃ וַיְהִי כָּל־יְמֵי־לֶמֶךְ שֶׁבַע וְשִׁבְעִים שָׁנָה וּשְׁבַע מֵאוֹת שָׁנָה
לב וַיָּמֹת׃ וַיְהִי־נֹחַ בֶּן־חֲמֵשׁ מֵאוֹת שָׁנָה וַיּוֹלֶד נֹחַ אֶת־שֵׁם

---

22. וַיִּתְהַלֵּךְ חֲנוֹךְ אֶת הָאֱלֹהִים — *Enoch walked with God.* He walked in His ways, doing good on behalf of others, (through) charitable acts and admonition.

NOTES

22. וַיִּתְהַלֵּךְ חֲנוֹךְ אֶת הָאֱלֹהִים – *Enoch walked with God.* The *Sforno* is of the opinion that to emulate God, one must be kind to others and still admonish them.

29. זֶה יְנַחֲמֵנוּ – *This one will bring us comfort (rest).* The name נֹחַ does not seem to be correctly derived from the word נֶחָמָה, as the Torah implies. Indeed the Midrash comments, "The name does not correspond to its interpretation nor does the interpretation correspond to the name." The

were nine hundred and thirty years; and he died.
6 *Seth lived one hundred and five years and begot Enosh.* 7 *And Seth*
lived eight hundred and seven years after begetting Enosh, and he begot
sons and daughters. 8 *All the days of Seth were nine hundred and twelve*
years; and he died.
9 *Enosh lived ninety years, and begot Kenan.* 10 *And Enosh lived eight*
hundred and fifteen years after begetting Kenan, and he begot sons and
daughters. 11 *All the days of Enosh were nine hundred and five years; and*
he died.
12 *Kenan lived seventy years, and begot Mahalalel.* 13 *And Kenan lived*
eight hundred and forty years after begetting Mahalalel, and he begot
sons and daughters. 14 *All the days of Kenan were nine hundred and ten*
years; and he died.
15 *Mahalalel lived sixty-five years, and begot Jared.* 16 *And Mahalalel*
lived eight hundred and thirty years after begetting Jared, and he begot
sons and daughters. 17 *All the days of Mahalalel were eight hundred and*
ninety-five years; and he died.
18 *Jared lived one hundred and sixty-two years, and begot Enoch.*
19 *And Jared lived eight hundred years after begetting Enoch and he begot*
sons and daughters. 20 *All the days of Jared came to nine hundred and*
sixty-two years; and he died.
21 *Enoch lived sixty-five years, and begot Methuselah.* 22 *Enoch walked*
with God for three hundred years after begetting Methuselah; and he
begot sons and daughters. 23 *All the days of Enoch were three hundred*
and sixty-five years. 24 *And Enoch walked with God; then he was no*
more, for God had taken him.
25 *Methuselah lived one hundred and eighty-seven years, and begot*
Lamech. 26 *And Methuselah lived seven hundred and eighty-two years*
after begetting Lamech, and he begot sons and daughters. 27 *All the days*
of Methuselah were nine hundred and sixty-nine years; and he died.
28 *Lamech lived one hundred and eighty-two years, and begot a son.*
29 *And he called his name Noah, saying, "This one will bring us comfort*
from our work and from the toil of our hands, from the ground which
HASHEM had cursed." 30 *Lamech lived five hundred and ninety-five years*
after begetting Noah, and he begot sons and daughters. 31 *All the days of*
Lamech were seven hundred and seventy-seven years; and he died.
32 *When Noah was five hundred years old, Noah begot Shem, Ham, and*
Japheth.

---

29. זֶה יְנַחֲמֵנוּ — *This one will bring us comfort (rest).* He (Lemech) prayed that this one (Noah) will comfort us by bringing us rest (relief) from our labors. The word נוֹחַ indicates rest, similar to וְנוֹחַ מֵאֹיְבֵיהֶם, *and they rested from their enemies (Esther 9:16).*

NOTES

Sforno, however, reconciles this difficulty, linking the words מְנוּחָה, *rest*, and נֶחָמָה, *comfort*, by interpreting Lemech's "saying" as a prayer: "May this child *comfort* us by bringing us *rest* (relief)." Hence the name נֹחַ is appropriate. Indeed this hope was fulfilled when Noah fashioned agricultural tools, relieving mankind from the toil of farming by hand.

ו א אֶת־חָם וְאֶת־יָפֶת: וַיְהִי כִּי־הֵחֵל הָאָדָם לָרֹב עַל־פְּנֵי הָאֲדָמָה וּבָנוֹת
ב יֻלְּדוּ לָהֶם: וַיִּרְאוּ בְנֵי־הָאֱלֹהִים אֶת־בְּנוֹת הָאָדָם כִּי טֹבֹת הֵנָּה וַיִּקְחוּ
ג לָהֶם נָשִׁים מִכֹּל אֲשֶׁר בָּחָרוּ: וַיֹּאמֶר יהוה לֹא־יָדוֹן רוּחִי בָאָדָם לְעֹלָם
ד בְּשַׁגַּם הוּא בָשָׂר וְהָיוּ יָמָיו מֵאָה וְעֶשְׂרִים שָׁנָה: הַנְּפִלִים הָיוּ בָאָרֶץ
בַּיָּמִים הָהֵם וְגַם אַחֲרֵי־כֵן אֲשֶׁר יָבֹאוּ בְּנֵי הָאֱלֹהִים אֶל־בְּנוֹת הָאָדָם
וְיָלְדוּ לָהֶם הֵמָּה הַגִּבֹּרִים אֲשֶׁר מֵעוֹלָם אַנְשֵׁי הַשֵּׁם:
מפטיר ה וַיַּרְא יהוה כִּי רַבָּה רָעַת הָאָדָם בָּאָרֶץ וְכָל־יֵצֶר מַחְשְׁבֹת לִבּוֹ רַק רַע
ו כָּל־הַיּוֹם: וַיִּנָּחֶם יהוה כִּי־עָשָׂה אֶת־הָאָדָם בָּאָרֶץ וַיִּתְעַצֵּב אֶל־לִבּוֹ:
ז וַיֹּאמֶר יהוה אֶמְחֶה אֶת־הָאָדָם אֲשֶׁר־בָּרָאתִי מֵעַל פְּנֵי הָאֲדָמָה מֵאָדָם
ח עַד־בְּהֵמָה עַד־רֶמֶשׂ וְעַד־עוֹף הַשָּׁמָיִם כִּי נִחַמְתִּי כִּי עֲשִׂיתִם: וְנֹחַ מָצָא
חֵן בְּעֵינֵי יהוה:

VI

3. לֹא יָדוֹן רוּחִי בָאָדָם לְעֹלָם בְּשַׁגַּם הוּא בָשָׂר — *My spirit shall not contend evermore concerning man since he is but flesh.* It is not appropriate that there should forever be contention within Me (concerning man) or that an opportunity be given to those who would dispute Me, saying, "Although man is worthy to be greatly punished for his rebellion (against God) since he is (created) in His image and likeness, nonetheless it is proper to show him mercy since he is, after all, *flesh,* not only (Divine) image and likeness, therefore he is brought to sin ..."

וְהָיוּ יָמָיו — *His days shall be.* He will be granted time to repent.

מֵאָה וְעֶשְׂרִים שָׁנָה — *A hundred and twenty years* ... during which time Noah constructed the ark, admonished them and warned them, as our Sages tell us (*Sanhedrin* 108a).

4. הַנְּפִלִים הָיוּ בָאָרֶץ בַּיָּמִים הָהֵם — *The Nephilim were on the earth in those days.* God gave them this period of time for the purpose of repentance.

וְגַם אַחֲרֵי כֵן — *And also afterward.* They did not repent at all.

5. כִּי רַבָּה רָעַת הָאָדָם — *The wickedness of man was great* ... in the past.

וְכָל יֵצֶר מַחְשְׁבֹת — *And every product of the thoughts of his heart* ... for the future — they did not hearken to the (words) of the admonisher, since there was no hope that they would repent.

6. וַיִּתְעַצֵּב אֶל לִבּוֹ — *And He had heartfelt sadness* (or: *He grieved to His heart*) ... for

NOTES

VI

3. לֹא יָדוֹן רוּחִי בָאָדָם לְעֹלָם בְּשַׁגַּם הוּא בָשָׂר – *My spirit shall not contend evermore concerning man since he is but flesh.* The meaning of this verse, according to the *Sforno,* is that since man is comprised of both physical and spiritual elements, the former causing him to pursue the demands and pleasures of the flesh, while the latter makes him vulnerable to God's anger when he fails to attain his spiritual potential, hence, conflict and tension is now present within God (as it were) and within man. This state of affairs is unacceptable to God. The solution is to hold man accountable for his sins, but also to give him the opportunity to repent. The time allotted would be 120 years, during which time Noah would admonish and caution them of the impending destruction unless they mended their ways. Unfortunately, they did not heed his words.

6. וַיִּתְעַצֵּב אֶל לִבּוֹ – *And He had heartfelt sadness.* The *Sforno,* in this verse as well as 12:2 and 28:3, stresses that God's desire is to rejoice in His works. This will only be if man perfects his deeds and

6 1 *And it came to pass when man began to increase upon the ground and*
daughters were born to them, 2 *the sons of the rulers saw that the*
daughters of man were good and they took themselves wives from
whomever they chose. 3 *And HASHEM said, "My spirit shall not contend*
evermore concerning man since he is but flesh; his days shall be a
hundred and twenty years."
4 *The Nephilim were on the earth in those days — and also afterward*
when the sons of the rulers would consort with the daughters of man, who
would bear to them. They were the mighty who, from old, were men of
devastation.
5 *HASHEM saw that the wickedness of man was great upon the earth,*
and every product of the thoughts of his heart was but evil always. 6 *And*
HASHEM reconsidered having made man on earth, and He had heartfelt
sadness. 7 *And HASHEM said, "I will blot out man whom I created from*
the face of the ground — from man to animal, to creeping things, and to
birds of the sky; for I have reconsidered My having made them." 8 *But*
Noah found grace in the eyes of HASHEM.

He does not desire the death of the wicked, on the contrary, יִשְׂמַח ה׳ בְּמַעֲשָׂיו, *HASHEM rejoices in His works (Psalms* 104:31).

8. וְנֹחַ מָצָא חֵן — *But Noah found grace.* (Sufficient) to save his sons and daughters; not that they were worthy (to be saved in his merit). It was (only) because of God's grace that he merited it, as it says, וְהָיוּ שְׁלֹשֶׁת הָאֲנָשִׁים הָאֵלֶּה בְּתוֹכָהּ נֹחַ דָּנִאֵל וְאִיּוֹב ... חַי אָנִי, נְאֻם ה׳ אֱלֹהִים, אִם בָּנִים וְאִם בָּנוֹת יַצִּילוּ, הֵמָּה לְבַדָּם יִנָּצֵלוּ, *Even if these three men, Noah, Daniel and Job, be in it . . . as I live, declares HASHEM God, they would save neither sons or daughters, they alone would be saved* (*Ezekiel* 14:14,15). The reason is that they did not teach their generations to know God, as Abraham, Moshe and Samuel did (and others as well). As our Sages say, "Elam (i.e., Daniel and his colleagues) merited to study but not to teach" (*Pesachim* 87a). Noah, also, even though he admonished them regarding their corrupt deeds (which were) harmful to the welfare of society, did not teach them to know God, the Blessed One, (and) to walk in His ways, although he (himself) was a righteous and perfect man in thought and practice. A righteous man who perfects himself alone is worthy to rescue himself alone, but one who perfects others as well, merits to save others, because there is then hope that they will repent, as our Sages say, "If you see a Torah scholar who has committed an offense by night, do not cavil at him by day, for he certainly has repented" (*Berachos* 19a).

NOTES

pursues the knowledge of God. When this goal is thwarted by man's evil ways it causes God "heartfelt sadness."

8. וְנֹחַ מָצָא חֵן – *But Noah found grace.* God's grace is necessary when man is unworthy of His providence and protection. Noah, although worthy to be saved in his own merit, did not merit to have his family saved, for he failed to teach his generation the knowledge of God. Had he done so, many of them would have repented and been saved. Therefore the salvation of Noah's family is only due to God's grace and compassion. The selection from *Berachos* quoted by the *Sforno* indicates that a scholar, though he may sin, will certainly repent quickly and not postpone his *teshuvah*. Had Noah, and the others mentioned by Ezekiel, taught and trained their generation, many of their disciples would have become scholars and therefore repented. By failing to do so, these three great men saved only themselves but not their contemporaries. Hence, even Noah needed Divine grace to save his immediate family.

פרשת נח

ט אֵלֶּה תּוֹלְדֹת נֹחַ נֹחַ אִישׁ צַדִּיק תָּמִים הָיָה בְּדֹרֹתָיו אֶת־הָאֱלֹהִים
י הִתְהַלֶּךְ־נֹחַ: וַיּוֹלֶד נֹחַ שְׁלֹשָׁה בָנִים אֶת־שֵׁם אֶת־חָם וְאֶת־יָפֶת:
יא־יב וַתִּשָּׁחֵת הָאָרֶץ לִפְנֵי הָאֱלֹהִים וַתִּמָּלֵא הָאָרֶץ חָמָס: וַיַּרְא אֱלֹהִים
אֶת־הָאָרֶץ וְהִנֵּה נִשְׁחָתָה כִּי־הִשְׁחִית כָּל־בָּשָׂר אֶת־דַּרְכּוֹ עַל־
יג הָאָרֶץ: וַיֹּאמֶר אֱלֹהִים לְנֹחַ קֵץ כָּל־בָּשָׂר בָּא לְפָנַי כִּי־
יד מָלְאָה הָאָרֶץ חָמָס מִפְּנֵיהֶם וְהִנְנִי מַשְׁחִיתָם אֶת־הָאָרֶץ: עֲשֵׂה לְךָ תֵּבַת
טו עֲצֵי־גֹפֶר קִנִּים תַּעֲשֶׂה אֶת־הַתֵּבָה וְכָפַרְתָּ אֹתָהּ מִבַּיִת וּמִחוּץ בַּכֹּפֶר: וְזֶה
אֲשֶׁר תַּעֲשֶׂה אֹתָהּ שְׁלֹשׁ מֵאוֹת אַמָּה אֹרֶךְ הַתֵּבָה חֲמִשִּׁים אַמָּה רָחְבָּהּ
טז וּשְׁלֹשִׁים אַמָּה קוֹמָתָהּ: צֹהַר | תַּעֲשֶׂה לַתֵּבָה וְאֶל־אַמָּה תְּכַלֶּנָּה
מִלְמַעְלָה וּפֶתַח הַתֵּבָה בְּצִדָּהּ תָּשִׂים תַּחְתִּיִּם שְׁנִיִּם וּשְׁלִשִׁים תַּעֲשֶׂהָ:

9. תּוֹלְדֹת נֹחַ — *The toldos* (lit., *offspring*) *of Noah* . . . the events and history of his life.

צַדִּיק — *A righteous man* . . . in deeds.

תָּמִים — *Perfect* . . . in intellectual understanding.

בְּדֹרֹתָיו — *In his generations* . . . according (relative) to his generations. These were the generations of Methuselah, Lemech, his own (Noah's) and the descendants of his contemporaries during the six hundred years (prior to the Deluge).

אֶת הָאֱלֹהִים הִתְהַלֶּךְ נֹחַ — *Noah walked with God.* He walked in His ways, doing good to others and reproving his contemporaries, as our Sages tell us. Barusi the Chaldean also writes so, regarding him (Noah).

10. וַיּוֹלֶד נֹחַ — *Noah had begotten.* When he began admonishing his contemporaries, he was rewarded with children.

12. וְהִנֵּה נִשְׁחָתָה — *And behold it was destroyed (corrupted)* . . . on its own; even without (Divine) punishment it was on the way to destruction, through the corruption of their ways (immorality) which damages (corrupts) one's progeny, and violent robbery which corrupts the social order, similar to וְטַחֲנִי קָמַח, *and grind meal (Isaiah* 47:2).

NOTES

9. תּוֹלְדֹת נֹחַ – *The toldos* (lit., *offspring) of Noah.* Regarding the word תּוֹלְדֹת, see note to 5:1. Various explanations are given by the commentators to explain the seeming digression in this opening section of Noah, where the Torah begins with the genealogy of Noah (continued in verse 10) only to interject a description of Noah's character. However, the *Sforno's* translation of תּוֹלְדֹת as *events* and *history* obviates the difficulty. The Torah's description of Noah as being a *righteous* and *perfect* man, *walking with God*, is an integral part of his life story, hence not a digression at all.

בְּדֹרֹתָיו – *In his generations.* Generations in the plural is explained most logically by the *Sforno* as referring to the various generations that Noah's first 600 years spanned.

. . . אֶת הָאֱלֹהִים – . . . *With God.* Barusi the Chaldean (Berosus the Babylonian) was a historian who lived in the third century B.C.E. He is mentioned a number of times in the works of Josephus, and is purported to have deciphered events recorded by the ancient Mesopotamians on stone tablets. Since every culture has a "Flood story," the *Sforno* feels it is important to cite the writings of a Chaldean historian, who supports the words of our Sages. The *Sforno* cites him again in 9:22.

10. וַיּוֹלֶד נֹחַ – *Noah had begotten.* Noah had no children until a late age. Whatever the reason may have been, he is now blessed with three sons, as a reward for reproving his contemporaries. The concept of מִדָּה כְּנֶגֶד מִדָּה, *measure for measure,* may well be that if one demonstrates his willingness and ability to admonish and instruct, he can also be an effective parent to his children; as Solomon says, *"My son, listen to the* מוּסַר*, admonishment, of your father"* (*Proverbs* 1:8).

12. וְהִנֵּה נִשְׁחָתָה – *And behold it was destroyed (corrupted).* The *Sforno* interprets the phrase וְהִנֵּה נִשְׁחָתָה as meaning *behold it was on the path to (self-) destruction,* translating נִשְׁחָתָה as *destruc-*

PARASHAS NOACH

[9] *These are the offspring of Noah — Noah was a righteous man, perfect in his generations; Noah walked with God. —* [10] *Noah had begotten three sons: Shem, Ham, and Japheth.*

[11] *Now the earth had become corrupt before God; and the earth had become filled with robbery.* [12] *And God saw the earth and behold it was corrupted, for all flesh had corrupted its way upon the earth.*

[13] *God said to Noah, "The end of all flesh has come before Me, for the earth is filled with robbery through them; and behold, I am about to destroy them from the earth.* [14] *Make for yourself an Ark of gopher wood; make the Ark with compartments, and cover it inside and out with pitch.* [15] *This is how you should make it — three hundred cubits the length of the Ark; fifty cubits its width; and thirty cubits its height.* [16] *A window shall you make for the Ark, and to a cubit finish it from above. Put the entrance of the Ark in its side; make it with bottom, second, and third decks.*

---

13. קֵץ כָּל בָּשָׂר — *The end of all flesh* . . . the period of 120 years which I stipulated for them.

בָּא לְפָנַי — *Has come before Me* . . . which I set for their repentance.

כִּי מָלְאָה הָאָרֶץ חָמָס מִפְּנֵיהֶם — *For the earth is filled with robbery through them.* Each robs the other; the landowners rob the sharecroppers forcibly, while the sharecropper robs the landowner through deceit. Thus the earth is producing all its fruit for robbers!

וְהִנְנִי מַשְׁחִיתָם אֶת הָאָרֶץ — *And behold, I am about to destroy them with the earth.* I will destroy them *with* the earth. I will destroy (alter) the climate of the earth and air, i.e., after the deluge the angle of the earth to the sun was altered, (whereas before) the equinox was constant (day and night being of equal length) — as God explained to Job in His rejoinder. As a result, immediately after the Flood, the span of human life was shortened, since weather conditions and fruits were no longer perfect (complete) as before. It is for this reason that man was permitted to eat the meat of living creatures after the Flood.

14. עֲשֵׂה לְךָ תֵּבַת — *Make for yourself an Ark.* During the time stipulated for them, so that they may observe and repent.

16. בְּצִדָּהּ תָּשִׂים — *Put (the entrance) in its side.* Along the breadth (of the Ark) for that is referred to as צַד; the long side is called צֶלַע.

תַּחְתִּיִּם — *Lower (deck).* Customary in (all) ships (boats).

שְׁנִיִּם וּשְׁלִשִׁים — *Second and third (decks).* Similar to the usual lower one (of the average boat).

NOTES

tion rather than *corruption.* His proof from the verse in *Isaiah* is based on the use of the word קֶמַח instead of דָּגָן — *flour* rather than grain. Flour is the *end* product of grinding; still the prophet speaks of grinding *flour*! The answer is that he "calls" it flour עַל שֵׁם סוֹפוֹ, by its eventual, ultimate name. And so in our instance: The earth may seem secure and stable, but it is already on the path to destruction.

13. וְהִנְנִי מַשְׁחִיתָם אֶת הָאָרֶץ – *And behold, I am about to destroy them with the earth.* See verse 3, the *Sforno's* commentary and explanatory notes.

וְהִנְנִי מַשְׁחִיתָם – *And behold, I am about to destroy.* See the *Sforno's* commentary to 8:22. At the time of Creation it was always springtime. The ideal climate, and the equal length of day and night, created a perfect balance which affected man's well-being and the quality of the earth's productivity. The Flood disrupted this balance and as a result adversely affected man and the produce of the land. The *Sforno* interprets the word אֶת in this verse as meaning *with,* i.e., man together with the earth is "destroyed." His reference to Job alludes to God's retort in Chapter 38, where He begins, *"Where were you when I laid the earth's foundations?"* and then proceeds to describe the wonders of nature.

14. עֲשֵׂה לְךָ תֵּבַת – *Make for Yourself an Ark.* As our Sages say in *Sanhedrin* 108b, the Almighty could have saved Noah without imposing upon him the lengthy difficult process of constructing an ark. However the real purpose was to arouse the

יז וַאֲנִי הִנְנִי מֵבִיא אֶת־הַמַּבּוּל מַיִם עַל־הָאָרֶץ לְשַׁחֵת כָּל־בָּשָׂר אֲשֶׁר־בּוֹ
יח רוּחַ חַיִּים מִתַּחַת הַשָּׁמָיִם כֹּל אֲשֶׁר־בָּאָרֶץ יִגְוָע: וַהֲקִמֹתִי אֶת־בְּרִיתִי
יט אִתָּךְ וּבָאתָ אֶל־הַתֵּבָה אַתָּה וּבָנֶיךָ וְאִשְׁתְּךָ וּנְשֵׁי־בָנֶיךָ אִתָּךְ: וּמִכָּל־הָחַי
מִכָּל־בָּשָׂר שְׁנַיִם מִכֹּל תָּבִיא אֶל־הַתֵּבָה לְהַחֲיֹת אִתָּךְ זָכָר וּנְקֵבָה יִהְיוּ:
כ מֵהָעוֹף לְמִינֵהוּ וּמִן־הַבְּהֵמָה לְמִינָהּ מִכֹּל רֶמֶשׂ הָאֲדָמָה לְמִינֵהוּ שְׁנַיִם
כא מִכֹּל יָבֹאוּ אֵלֶיךָ לְהַחֲיוֹת: וְאַתָּה קַח־לְךָ מִכָּל־מַאֲכָל אֲשֶׁר יֵאָכֵל
כב וְאָסַפְתָּ אֵלֶיךָ וְהָיָה לְךָ וְלָהֶם לְאָכְלָה: וַיַּעַשׂ נֹחַ כְּכֹל אֲשֶׁר צִוָּה אֹתוֹ
ז שני א אֱלֹהִים כֵּן עָשָׂה: וַיֹּאמֶר יהוה לְנֹחַ בֹּא־אַתָּה וְכָל־בֵּיתְךָ אֶל־הַתֵּבָה
ב כִּי־אֹתְךָ רָאִיתִי צַדִּיק לְפָנַי בַּדּוֹר הַזֶּה: מִכֹּל | הַבְּהֵמָה הַטְּהוֹרָה תִּקַּח־
לְךָ שִׁבְעָה שִׁבְעָה אִישׁ וְאִשְׁתּוֹ וּמִן־הַבְּהֵמָה אֲשֶׁר לֹא טְהֹרָה הִוא שְׁנַיִם
ג אִישׁ וְאִשְׁתּוֹ: גַּם מֵעוֹף הַשָּׁמַיִם שִׁבְעָה שִׁבְעָה זָכָר וּנְקֵבָה לְחַיּוֹת זֶרַע עַל־
ד פְּנֵי כָל־הָאָרֶץ: כִּי לְיָמִים עוֹד שִׁבְעָה אָנֹכִי מַמְטִיר עַל־הָאָרֶץ אַרְבָּעִים
יוֹם וְאַרְבָּעִים לָיְלָה וּמָחִיתִי אֶת־כָּל־הַיְקוּם אֲשֶׁר עָשִׂיתִי מֵעַל פְּנֵי
ה־ו הָאֲדָמָה: וַיַּעַשׂ נֹחַ כְּכֹל אֲשֶׁר־צִוָּהוּ יהוה: וְנֹחַ בֶּן־שֵׁשׁ מֵאוֹת שָׁנָה
ז וְהַמַּבּוּל הָיָה מַיִם עַל־הָאָרֶץ: וַיָּבֹא נֹחַ וּבָנָיו וְאִשְׁתּוֹ וּנְשֵׁי־בָנָיו אִתּוֹ
ח אֶל־הַתֵּבָה מִפְּנֵי מֵי הַמַּבּוּל: מִן־הַבְּהֵמָה הַטְּהוֹרָה וּמִן־הַבְּהֵמָה אֲשֶׁר
ט אֵינֶנָּה טְהֹרָה וּמִן־הָעוֹף וְכֹל אֲשֶׁר־רֹמֵשׂ עַל־הָאֲדָמָה: שְׁנַיִם שְׁנַיִם
י בָּאוּ אֶל־נֹחַ אֶל־הַתֵּבָה זָכָר וּנְקֵבָה כַּאֲשֶׁר צִוָּה אֱלֹהִים אֶת־נֹחַ: וַיְהִי

---

17. וַאֲנִי הִנְנִי מֵבִיא אֶת הַמַּבּוּל — *And as for Me — Behold, I am about to bring the Flood-waters.* You complete the Ark, and I will immediately bring on the Flood (מַבּוּל). This word (i.e., *mabul)* is a term meaning downfall and loss (catastrophe), similar to the term נְבָלָה, *wither, decay.* (The verse is) saying: I will bring about (by means of water) the downfall and loss (i.e., catastrophe) which I (already) said, *And behold, I am about to destroy them from the earth* (verse 13).

18. וַהֲקִמֹתִי אֶת בְּרִיתִי — *But I will establish My covenant . . .* (which I will make) *after* the Flood.

21. וְאַתָּה — *And as for you . . .* now!

קַח . . . מִכָּל מַאֲכָל — *Take . . . of every food . . .* various foods for the various species.

VII

1. כִּי אֹתְךָ רָאִיתִי צַדִּיק — *For it is* you *that I have seen to be righteous.* You, not your

NOTES

people to question, contemplate and repent.

17. וַאֲנִי הִנְנִי מֵבִיא אֶת הַמַּבּוּל – *And as for Me — Behold, I am about to bring the Flood-waters.* In the *Sforno's* opinion, the word מַבּוּל does not mean "flood" but any catastrophic event which causes a sudden and widespread disaster. In this particular instance the medium used by God was water. Therefore when He promises that there will never again be a מַבּוּל to destroy the earth (9:11) it is all inclusive, not only a flood but through any medium.

18. וַהֲקִמֹתִי אֶת בְּרִיתִי – *But I will establish My covenant.* Many commentators interpret this covenant as one now being made. The *Sforno* is of the opinion, however, that it refers to the covenant which God will establish later, after the Flood (9:9-11).

21. קַח . . . מִכָּל מַאֲכָל – *Take . . . of every food.* The *Sforno* interprets these words as emphasizing that it is Noah's responsibility to make provision for each and every species in his Ark.

VII

1. כִּי אֹתְךָ רָאִיתִי צַדִּיק – *For it is you that I have seen*

17 *"And as for Me — Behold, I am about to bring the Flood-waters upon*
the earth to destroy all flesh in which there is a breath of life from under
the heavens; everything that is in the earth shall expire. 18 *But I will*
establish My covenant with you, and you shall enter the Ark — you, your
sons, your wife, and your sons' wives with you. 19 *And from all that lives,*
of all flesh, two of each shall you bring into the Ark to keep alive with you;
they shall be male and female. 20 *From each bird according to its kind, and*
from each animal according to its kind, and from each thing that creeps
on the ground according to its kind, two of each shall come to you to keep
alive.

21 *"And as for you, take for yourself of every food that is eaten and*
gather it in to yourself, that it shall be as food for you and for them."
22 *Noah did according to everything God commanded him, so he did.*

7 1 *Then HASHEM said to Noah, "Come to the Ark, you and all your*
household, for it is you that I have seen to be righteous before Me in
this generation. 2 *Of every clean animal take unto you seven pairs, a male*
with its mate, and of the animal that is not clean, two, a male with its
mate; 3 *of the birds of the heavens also, seven pairs, male and female, to*
keep seed alive upon the face of all the earth. 4 *For in seven more days'*
time I will send rain upon the earth, forty days and forty nights, and I
will blot out all existence that I have made from upon the face of the
ground." 5 *And Noah did according to everything that HASHEM had*
commanded him.

6 *Noah was six hundred years old when the Flood was water upon the*
earth. 7 *Noah, with his sons, his wife, and his sons' wives with him, went*
into the Ark because of the waters of the Flood. 8 *Of the clean animal, of*
the animal that is not clean, of the birds, and of each thing that creeps
upon the ground, 9 *two by two they came to Noah into the Ark, male and*
female, as God had commanded Noah. 10 *And it came to pass after*

---

household. Nonetheless, "You and all your household" I will save only for your sake.

2. הַטְּהוֹרָה — *Clean (animal).* All (clean animals) were then fit for sacrifice, as our Sages mention to us (*Zevachim* 115b). (These) were also suited for food, as opposed to, וְנִטְמֵתֶם בָּם, *And you will be defiled by them* (*Vayikra* 11:43).

NOTES

to be righteous. The *Sforno* interprets the verse in reverse order. The end of the verse, Noah's personal righteousness, is the reason for the beginning of the verse, where Hashem tells Noah to enter the Ark *with* his household. They were not worthy on their own to be saved, and even Noah's merit was insufficient were it not for God's grace, as the *Sforno* explained above, in 6:8.

2. הַטְּהוֹרָה – *Clean (animal).* (a) The phrase טְהוֹרָה, *clean,* when applied to an animal or fowl, refers to its acceptability as a sacrifice as well as being fit halachically for consumption by man. In this particular instance it would only be applicable to the former, since man was not permitted to eat the flesh of living creatures until after the Flood. Nonetheless, the *Sforno* is of the opinion that since Noah was familiar with the animals and birds of prey, he also discerned which would eventually be טְהוֹרָה, *clean,* for food, when the flesh of animals and birds would be permitted, since the reason certain flesh is prohibited is because it defiles man and makes him dull and insensitive, as our Sages tell us (*Yoma* 39a).

(b) Before the giving of the Torah, all the animals were qualified as sacrifices. It is only later that the Torah limits and restricts it to specific species and kinds. Hence, at the time of the Flood, the quota of seven applied to *all* clean creatures.

יא לְשִׁבְעַת הַיָּמִים וּמֵי הַמַּבּוּל הָיוּ עַל־הָאָרֶץ: בִּשְׁנַת שֵׁשׁ־מֵאוֹת שָׁנָה
לְחַיֵּי־נֹחַ בַּחֹדֶשׁ הַשֵּׁנִי בְּשִׁבְעָה־עָשָׂר יוֹם לַחֹדֶשׁ בַּיּוֹם הַזֶּה נִבְקְעוּ כָּל־
יב מַעְיְנוֹת תְּהוֹם רַבָּה וַאֲרֻבֹּת הַשָּׁמַיִם נִפְתָּחוּ: וַיְהִי הַגֶּשֶׁם עַל־הָאָרֶץ
יג אַרְבָּעִים יוֹם וְאַרְבָּעִים לָיְלָה: בְּעֶצֶם הַיּוֹם הַזֶּה בָּא נֹחַ וְשֵׁם־וְחָם וָיֶפֶת
יד בְּנֵי־נֹחַ וְאֵשֶׁת נֹחַ וּשְׁלֹשֶׁת נְשֵׁי־בָנָיו אִתָּם אֶל־הַתֵּבָה: הֵמָּה וְכָל־הַחַיָּה
לְמִינָהּ וְכָל־הַבְּהֵמָה לְמִינָהּ וְכָל־הָרֶמֶשׂ הָרֹמֵשׂ עַל־הָאָרֶץ לְמִינֵהוּ וְכָל־
טו הָעוֹף לְמִינֵהוּ כֹּל צִפּוֹר כָּל־כָּנָף: וַיָּבֹאוּ אֶל־נֹחַ אֶל־הַתֵּבָה שְׁנַיִם שְׁנַיִם
טז מִכָּל־הַבָּשָׂר אֲשֶׁר־בּוֹ רוּחַ חַיִּים: וְהַבָּאִים זָכָר וּנְקֵבָה מִכָּל־בָּשָׂר בָּאוּ
שלישי יז כַּאֲשֶׁר צִוָּה אֹתוֹ אֱלֹהִים וַיִּסְגֹּר יהוה בַּעֲדוֹ: וַיְהִי הַמַּבּוּל אַרְבָּעִים יוֹם עַל־
יח הָאָרֶץ וַיִּרְבּוּ הַמַּיִם וַיִּשְׂאוּ אֶת־הַתֵּבָה וַתָּרָם מֵעַל הָאָרֶץ: וַיִּגְבְּרוּ הַמַּיִם
יט וַיִּרְבּוּ מְאֹד עַל־הָאָרֶץ וַתֵּלֶךְ הַתֵּבָה עַל־פְּנֵי הַמָּיִם: וְהַמַּיִם גָּבְרוּ מְאֹד
מְאֹד עַל־הָאָרֶץ וַיְכֻסּוּ כָּל־הֶהָרִים הַגְּבֹהִים אֲשֶׁר־תַּחַת כָּל־הַשָּׁמָיִם:
כ-כא חֲמֵשׁ עֶשְׂרֵה אַמָּה מִלְמַעְלָה גָּבְרוּ הַמָּיִם וַיְכֻסּוּ הֶהָרִים: וַיִּגְוַע כָּל־בָּשָׂר ׀
הָרֹמֵשׂ עַל־הָאָרֶץ בָּעוֹף וּבַבְּהֵמָה וּבַחַיָּה וּבְכָל־הַשֶּׁרֶץ הַשֹּׁרֵץ עַל־הָאָרֶץ
כב וְכֹל הָאָדָם: כֹּל אֲשֶׁר נִשְׁמַת־רוּחַ חַיִּים בְּאַפָּיו מִכֹּל אֲשֶׁר בֶּחָרָבָה
כג מֵתוּ: וַיִּמַח אֶת־כָּל־הַיְקוּם ׀ אֲשֶׁר ׀ עַל־פְּנֵי הָאֲדָמָה מֵאָדָם עַד־בְּהֵמָה
עַד־רֶמֶשׂ וְעַד־עוֹף הַשָּׁמַיִם וַיִּמָּחוּ מִן־הָאָרֶץ וַיִּשָּׁאֶר אַךְ־נֹחַ וַאֲשֶׁר
ח כד-א אִתּוֹ בַּתֵּבָה: וַיִּגְבְּרוּ הַמַּיִם עַל־הָאָרֶץ חֲמִשִּׁים וּמְאַת יוֹם: וַיִּזְכֹּר אֱלֹהִים
אֶת־נֹחַ וְאֵת כָּל־הַחַיָּה וְאֶת־כָּל־הַבְּהֵמָה אֲשֶׁר אִתּוֹ בַּתֵּבָה וַיַּעֲבֵר
ב אֱלֹהִים רוּחַ עַל־הָאָרֶץ וַיָּשֹׁכּוּ הַמָּיִם: וַיִּסָּכְרוּ מַעְיְנֹת תְּהוֹם וַאֲרֻבֹּת
ג הַשָּׁמָיִם וַיִּכָּלֵא הַגֶּשֶׁם מִן־הַשָּׁמָיִם: וַיָּשֻׁבוּ הַמַּיִם מֵעַל הָאָרֶץ הָלוֹךְ וָשׁוֹב
ד וַיַּחְסְרוּ הַמַּיִם מִקְצֵה חֲמִשִּׁים וּמְאַת יוֹם: וַתָּנַח הַתֵּבָה בַּחֹדֶשׁ הַשְּׁבִיעִי
ה בְּשִׁבְעָה־עָשָׂר יוֹם לַחֹדֶשׁ עַל הָרֵי אֲרָרָט: וְהַמַּיִם הָיוּ הָלוֹךְ וְחָסוֹר עַד

---

18. וַתֵּלֶךְ הַתֵּבָה — *And the Ark drifted (went).* Pushed by the strong gush (of water) which came from below.

23. וַיִּמַח אֶת כָּל הַיְקוּם — *And He blotted out all existence.* Living creatures; but not herbage, plants or vegetation, as the verse clearly explicates, saying: מֵאָדָם עַד בְּהֵמָה עַד רֶמֶשׂ וְעַד עוֹף הַשָּׁמַיִם, *from man to animal to creeping things and to the bird of the heavens.*

וַיִּמָּחוּ מִן הָאָרֶץ — *And they were blotted out from the earth* ... children, relatives, grandchildren and great-grandchildren.

24. וַיִּגְבְּרוּ ... חֲמִשִּׁים וּמְאַת יוֹם — *And (the waters) prevailed ... a hundred and fifty days.* The water increased in intensity from the start of the rain until it ceased, 150 days from its beginning on the seventeenth day of the second month (Cheshvan), ending on the seventeenth of the seventh month (Nissan) — the 150 days (comprising) a full (complete) five months. The Ark then came to rest since there was (no longer) a strong upsurge to propel it, for from the day the rains commenced the waters began to surge

NOTES

23. וַיִּמַח אֶת כָּל הַיְקוּם – *And He blotted out all existence.* The phrase *blotted out* appears twice in this verse (וַיִּמַח־וַיִּמָּחוּ). According to many commentators this is to indicate total obliteration; everything was wiped away. The *Sforno* interprets the verse differently. He feels that the balance of

the seven-day period that the waters of the Flood were upon the earth.
[11] In the six hundredth year of Noah's life, in the second month, on the
seventeenth day of the month, on that day all the fountains of the great deep
burst forth; and the windows of the heavens were opened. [12] And the rain
was upon the earth forty days and forty nights.
[13] On that very day Noah came, with Shem, Ham, and Japheth, Noah's
sons, with Noah's wife, and the three wives of his sons with them, into the
Ark — [14] they and every beast after its kind, every animal after its kind,
every creeping thing that creeps on the earth after its kind, and every bird
after its kind, and every bird of any kind of wing. [15] They came to Noah into
the Ark; two by two of all flesh in which there was a breath of life. [16] Thus
they that came, came male and female of all flesh, as God had commanded
him. And HASHEM shut it on his behalf.
[17] When the Flood was on the earth forty days, the waters increased and
raised the Ark so that it was lifted above the earth. [18] The waters
strengthened and increased greatly upon the earth, and the Ark drifted
upon the surface of the waters. [19] The waters strengthened very much upon
the earth, all the high mountains which are under the entire heavens were
covered. [20] Fifteen cubits upward did the waters strengthen, and the
mountains were covered. [21] And all flesh that moves upon the earth expired
— among the birds, the animals, the beasts, and all the creeping things that
creep upon the earth, and all mankind. [22] All in whose nostrils was the breath
of the spirit of life, of everything that was on dry land, died. [23] And He
blotted out all existence that was on the face of the ground — from man to
animals to creeping things and to the bird of the heavens; and they
were blotted out from the earth. Only Noah survived, and those with him
in the Ark. [24] And the waters strengthened on the earth a hundred and fifty
days.

8 *[1] God remembered Noah and all the beasts and all the animals that were*
with him in the Ark, and God caused a spirit to pass over the earth, and
the waters subsided. [2] The fountains of the deep and the windows of the
heavens were closed, and the rain from heaven was restrained. [3] The waters
then receded from upon the earth, receding continuously, and the waters
diminished at the end of a hundred and fifty days. [4] And the Ark came to
rest in the seventh month, on the seventeenth day of the month, upon the
mountains of Ararat. [5] The waters were continuously diminishing until the

---

strongly from below, as it says: *All the fountains of the great deep burst forth* (v. 11). In truth, the Ark did not move on the surface of the water until the waters were so high that the Ark was lifted up over the earth. Even when the days of rain were finished and there was only the upsurge of water from below, which continued until the completion of the 150 days (the Ark continued to move). When this upsurge which had propelled the Ark ceased, the Ark (also) came to rest.

NOTES

the verse qualifies the word וַיִּמַח, when it specifies men, animals, creeping things and birds — thereby excluding plants and vegetation. He therefore explains the repetition of the word *blotted out* as meaning the total annihilation of the human race — except for Noah and his family.

ו הַחֹדֶשׁ הָעֲשִׂירִי בָּעֲשִׂירִי בְּאֶחָד לַחֹדֶשׁ נִרְאוּ רָאשֵׁי הֶהָרִים: וַיְהִי מִקֵּץ
ז אַרְבָּעִים יוֹם וַיִּפְתַּח נֹחַ אֶת־חַלּוֹן הַתֵּבָה אֲשֶׁר עָשָׂה: וַיְשַׁלַּח אֶת־הָעֹרֵב
ח וַיֵּצֵא יָצוֹא וָשׁוֹב עַד־יְבֹשֶׁת הַמַּיִם מֵעַל הָאָרֶץ: וַיְשַׁלַּח אֶת־הַיּוֹנָה מֵאִתּוֹ
ט לִרְאוֹת הֲקַלּוּ הַמַּיִם מֵעַל פְּנֵי הָאֲדָמָה: וְלֹא־מָצְאָה הַיּוֹנָה מָנוֹחַ לְכַף־
רַגְלָהּ וַתָּשָׁב אֵלָיו אֶל־הַתֵּבָה כִּי־מַיִם עַל־פְּנֵי כָל־הָאָרֶץ וַיִּשְׁלַח יָדוֹ
י וַיִּקָּחֶהָ וַיָּבֵא אֹתָהּ אֵלָיו אֶל־הַתֵּבָה: וַיָּחֶל עוֹד שִׁבְעַת יָמִים אֲחֵרִים וַיֹּסֶף
יא שַׁלַּח אֶת־הַיּוֹנָה מִן־הַתֵּבָה: וַתָּבֹא אֵלָיו הַיּוֹנָה לְעֵת עֶרֶב וְהִנֵּה עֲלֵה־זַיִת
יב טָרָף בְּפִיהָ וַיֵּדַע נֹחַ כִּי־קַלּוּ הַמַּיִם מֵעַל הָאָרֶץ: וַיִּיָּחֶל עוֹד שִׁבְעַת יָמִים
יג אֲחֵרִים וַיְשַׁלַּח אֶת־הַיּוֹנָה וְלֹא־יָסְפָה שׁוּב־אֵלָיו עוֹד: וַיְהִי בְּאַחַת וְשֵׁשׁ־
מֵאוֹת שָׁנָה בָּרִאשׁוֹן בְּאֶחָד לַחֹדֶשׁ חָרְבוּ הַמַּיִם מֵעַל הָאָרֶץ וַיָּסַר נֹחַ
יד אֶת־מִכְסֵה הַתֵּבָה וַיַּרְא וְהִנֵּה חָרְבוּ פְּנֵי הָאֲדָמָה: וּבַחֹדֶשׁ הַשֵּׁנִי בְּשִׁבְעָה
טו וְעֶשְׂרִים יוֹם לַחֹדֶשׁ יָבְשָׁה הָאָרֶץ: וַיְדַבֵּר אֱלֹהִים אֶל־נֹחַ רביעי
טז־יז לֵאמֹר: צֵא מִן־הַתֵּבָה אַתָּה וְאִשְׁתְּךָ וּבָנֶיךָ וּנְשֵׁי־בָנֶיךָ אִתָּךְ: כָּל־הַחַיָּה
אֲשֶׁר־אִתְּךָ מִכָּל־בָּשָׂר בָּעוֹף וּבַבְּהֵמָה וּבְכָל־הָרֶמֶשׂ הָרֹמֵשׂ עַל־הָאָרֶץ
יח °הוצא אִתָּךְ וְשָׁרְצוּ בָאָרֶץ וּפָרוּ וְרָבוּ עַל־הָאָרֶץ: וַיֵּצֵא־נֹחַ וּבָנָיו וְאִשְׁתּוֹ °הַיְצֵא ק׳
יט וּנְשֵׁי־בָנָיו אִתּוֹ: כָּל־הַחַיָּה כָּל־הָרֶמֶשׂ וְכָל־הָעוֹף כֹּל רוֹמֵשׂ עַל־הָאָרֶץ
כ לְמִשְׁפְּחֹתֵיהֶם יָצְאוּ מִן־הַתֵּבָה: וַיִּבֶן נֹחַ מִזְבֵּחַ לַיהוה וַיִּקַּח מִכֹּל ׀ הַבְּהֵמָה
כא הַטְּהֹרָה וּמִכֹּל הָעוֹף הַטָּהֹר וַיַּעַל עֹלֹת בַּמִּזְבֵּחַ: וַיָּרַח יהוה אֶת־
רֵיחַ הַנִּיחֹחַ וַיֹּאמֶר יהוה אֶל־לִבּוֹ לֹא אֹסִף לְקַלֵּל עוֹד אֶת־הָאֲדָמָה
בַּעֲבוּר הָאָדָם כִּי יֵצֶר לֵב הָאָדָם רַע מִנְּעֻרָיו וְלֹא־אֹסִף עוֹד לְהַכּוֹת

VIII

7. וַיְשַׁלַּח אֶת הָעֹרֵב — *He sent out the raven* ... to see whether, after the tops of the mountains were seen, the atmosphere was dry enough for the raven to accept (endure) it.

וַיֵּצֵא יָצוֹא וָשׁוֹב — *And it kept going and returning* ... for he could not endure it.

8. וַיְשַׁלַּח אֶת הַיּוֹנָה — *Then he sent out the dove* ... the complete species of doves, which were seven pairs.

לִרְאוֹת הֲקַלּוּ — *To see whether the waters had subsided.* If (the waters) had subsided, they would nest on the mountains and towers instinctively (lit., "according to its way").

9. כִּי מַיִם עַל פְּנֵי כָל הָאָרֶץ — *For water was upon the surface of all the earth.* The tops of the mountains which had appeared were still saturated so that even there ... *the dove could not find a resting place for the sole of its foot.*

13. וַיָּסַר נֹחַ אֶת מִכְסֵה הַתֵּבָה — *Noah removed the covering of the Ark.* He thought that the excessive moisture of the air had dried.

NOTES

VIII

8. וַיְשַׁלַּח אֶת הַיּוֹנָה — *Then he sent out the dove.* The sending forth by Noah of all seven pairs is brought in certain manuscripts. It does not appear in our *Mikraos Gedolos* editions. It is difficult to understand why it was necessary for Noah to do so, hence it would seem that our version of the *Sforno* is correct. Nonetheless, since the *Sforno's* commentary regarding the nesting of doves appears in every version, we can speculate that this test would be negated if the doves refused to nest without their mates or even without their fellow doves, since their species is known for loyalty one to another. For this reason Noah had to send *all* of them, to determine whether the waters had subsided.

21. אֶת רֵיחַ הַנִּיחֹחַ — *The pleasing aroma.* The

*tenth month. In the tenth [month], on the first of the month, the tops of the
mountains became visible.*
*6 And it came to pass at the end of forty days, that Noah opened the win-
dow of the Ark which he had made. 7 He sent out the raven, and it kept going and returning until the waters dried from upon the earth. 8 Then he sent
out the dove from him to see whether the waters had subsided from the face
of the ground. 9 But the dove could not find a resting place for the sole of its
foot, and it returned to him to the Ark, for water was upon the surface of all
the earth. So he put forth his hand, and took it, and brought it to him to the
Ark. 10 He waited again another seven days, and again sent out the dove
from the Ark. 11 The dove came back to him in the evening — and behold!
an olive leaf it had plucked with its bill! And Noah knew that the waters had
subsided from upon the earth. 12 Then he waited again another seven days
and sent the dove forth; and it did not return to him any more.*
*13 And it came to pass in the six hundred and first year, in the first
[month], on the first of the month, the waters dried from upon the earth;
Noah removed the covering of the Ark, and looked — and behold! the surface
of the ground had dried. 14 And in the second month, on the twenty-seventh
day of the month, the earth was fully dried.*
*15 God spoke to Noah, saying, 16 "Go forth from the Ark: you and your
wife, your sons, and your sons' wives with you. 17 Every living being that is
with you of all flesh, of birds, of animals, and all moving things that move
on the earth — order them out with you, and let them teem on the earth and
be fruitful and multiply on the earth." 18 So Noah went forth, and his sons,
his wife, and his sons' wives with him. 19 Every living being, every creeping
thing, and every bird, everything that moves on earth came out of the Ark
by their families.*
*20 Then Noah built an altar to HASHEM and took of every clean animal and
of every clean bird, and offered burnt-offerings on the altar. 21 HASHEM
smelled the pleasing aroma, and HASHEM said in His heart: "I will not
continue to curse again the ground because of man, since the imagery of
man's heart is evil from his youth; nor will I again continue to smite*

וְהִנֵּה חָרְבוּ פְּנֵי הָאֲדָמָה — *And behold! the surface of the ground had dried.* But not dry enough to enable him to leave.

21. אֶת רֵיחַ הַנִּיחֹחַ — *The pleasing aroma . . .* for at that time, they (i.e., *all* clean animals and birds) were acceptable for sacrifice.

וַיֹּאמֶר ה׳ אֶל לִבּוֹ — *And HASHEM said in His heart.* He did not reveal it to Noah and his sons until they accepted His commandments and established a covenant.

כִּי יֵצֶר לֵב הָאָדָם רַע מִנְּעֻרָיו — *Since the imagery* (lit., *formation) of man's heart is evil from*

NOTES

Sforno stresses that all clean animals were acceptable as sacrifices (see 7:2). However, in *Leviticus* 1:2 he seemingly retreats from his original position (that at that time *all* clean animals were suitable to be brought as sacrifices) and he interprets our verse to mean "the pleasing aroma of those animals that would eventually be deemed worthy as sacrifices."

וַיֹּאמֶר ה׳ אֶל לִבּוֹ — *And HASHEM said in His heart.* The expression "said in His heart" is not anthropomorphic. As the *Sforno* explains, it is to be understood as a decision of the Almighty which He does not reveal to others.

כִּי יֵצֶר לֵב הָאָדָם רַע מִנְּעֻרָיו — *Since the imagery of man's heart is evil from his youth.* A basic trans-

כב אֶת־כָּל־חַי כַּאֲשֶׁר עָשִׂיתִי: עֹד כָּל־יְמֵי הָאָרֶץ זֶרַע וְקָצִיר וְקֹר וָחֹם
ט א וְקַיִץ וָחֹרֶף וְיוֹם וָלַיְלָה לֹא יִשְׁבֹּתוּ: וַיְבָרֶךְ אֱלֹהִים אֶת־נֹחַ וְאֶת־בָּנָיו
ב וַיֹּאמֶר לָהֶם פְּרוּ וּרְבוּ וּמִלְאוּ אֶת־הָאָרֶץ: וּמוֹרַאֲכֶם וְחִתְּכֶם יִהְיֶה
עַל כָּל־חַיַּת הָאָרֶץ וְעַל כָּל־עוֹף הַשָּׁמָיִם בְּכֹל אֲשֶׁר תִּרְמֹשׂ הָאֲדָמָה
ג וּבְכָל־דְּגֵי הַיָּם בְּיֶדְכֶם נִתָּנוּ: כָּל־רֶמֶשׂ אֲשֶׁר הוּא־חַי לָכֶם יִהְיֶה
ד לְאָכְלָה כְּיֶרֶק עֵשֶׂב נָתַתִּי לָכֶם אֶת־כֹּל: אַךְ־בָּשָׂר בְּנַפְשׁוֹ דָמוֹ לֹא
ה תֹאכֵלוּ: וְאַךְ אֶת־דִּמְכֶם לְנַפְשֹׁתֵיכֶם אֶדְרֹשׁ מִיַּד כָּל־חַיָּה אֶדְרְשֶׁנּוּ
ו וּמִיַּד הָאָדָם מִיַּד אִישׁ אָחִיו אֶדְרֹשׁ אֶת־נֶפֶשׁ הָאָדָם: שֹׁפֵךְ דַּם
ז הָאָדָם בָּאָדָם דָּמוֹ יִשָּׁפֵךְ כִּי בְּצֶלֶם אֱלֹהִים עָשָׂה אֶת־הָאָדָם: וְאַתֶּם

his youth. Since the climate (of the earth) and the temperament (of mankind) will from now on be inferior to conditions prior to the Flood, their intellectual powers will not illuminate them from their youth, as it did before, in a manner (that they might) overcome the base desires which overpower one from his youth.

22. עֹד כָּל יְמֵי הָאָרֶץ זֶרַע וְקָצִיר וְקֹר וָחֹם וְקַיִץ וָחֹרֶף וְיוֹם וָלַיְלָה לֹא יִשְׁבֹּתוּ — *While the earth remains, seedtime and harvest, cold and heat, summer and winter, day and night, shall not cease.* (They will not cease) from continuing in this unnatural fashion, which I set for them after the Flood: that the sun shall revolve spherically, tilted from the equator (hence the equinox will not be constant) and this turning will cause the change of all these seasons. Before the Flood the (angle of the earth) to the sun was such that the equinox was constant, and therefore it was always springtime, which was a general betterment for the elements, vegetation and the span of life of living creatures. (Now, the Torah) says that this will be "while the earth remains," (meaning) until (such time) that God, the Blessed One, will ameliorate the damage caused by the Flood, as He says, הָאָרֶץ הַחֲדָשָׁה אֲשֶׁר אֲנִי עֹשֶׂה, *The new earth which I will make (Isaiah* 66:22), for then the sun will return, once again, to the (permanent) equinox, and there will be a general improvement of the elements, vegetation and living creatures, (including) their length of days. This is the way it was before the Flood, as it says, כִּי הַנַּעַר בֶּן מֵאָה שָׁנָה יָמוּת וְהַחוֹטֶא בֶּן מֵאָה שָׁנָה יְקֻלָּל, *He who dies at a hundred years shall be reckoned a youth, and he who fails to reach a hundred shall be reckoned accursed* (ibid. 65:20); and this is what is meant by, מוֹצָאֵי בֹקֶר וָעֶרֶב תַּרְנִין, *The lands of sunrise and sunset (will) shout for joy* (*Psalms* 65:9).

IX

4. אַךְ בָּשָׂר בְּנַפְשׁוֹ — *But flesh with its soul.* However, the flesh of a living (animal) while it is still with its soul, i.e., alive.

דָּמוֹ — *Its blood* . . . similarly, the blood drawn from a living (animal) . . .

NOTES

formation occurred within man spiritually following the Flood, as it did physically. The evil inclination was now present from birth, whereas the good inclination only develops later in life as one reaches adulthood.

22. עֹד כָּל יְמֵי הָאָרֶץ. . . לֹא יִשְׁבֹּתוּ — *While the earth remains . . . shall not cease.* See the *Sforno's* commentary on 6:13 and the notes. The *Sforno* submits that the various seasons and the ever-changing climate is the result of the Flood, which disrupted the perfect balance of nature that earth and man enjoyed from the time of Creation until the Flood. These ideal conditions will, however, be renewed at the "end of days."

IX

4. אַךְ בָּשָׂר בְּנַפְשׁוֹ — *But flesh with its soul.* The *Sforno* is of the opinion (as is *Rashi)* that the sense of the verse is: There are two prohibitions; both the flesh and the blood taken from a living animal (דַּם מִן הַחַי and אֵבֶר מִן הַחַי) are prohibited to a Noachide. This follows the view of Rav Chaninah ben Gamliel in *Sanhedrin* 59. However, the blood drawn from a dead animal was permitted to him.

every living being, as I have done. 22 *Continuously, all the days of the earth,*
seedtime and harvest, cold and heat, summer and winter, day and night, shall
not cease."

9 1 *God blessed Noah and his sons, and He said to them, "Be fruitful and*
multiply and fill the land. 2 *The fear of you and the dread of you shall*
be upon every beast of the earth and upon every bird of the heavens, in
everything that moves on earth and in all the fish of the sea; in your hand they
are given. 3 *Every moving thing that lives shall be food for you; like the green*
herbage I have given you everything. 4 *But flesh; with its soul its blood you*
shall not eat. 5 *However, your blood which belongs to your souls I will demand,*
of every beast will I demand it; but of man, of every man for that of his brother
I will demand the soul of man. 6 *Whoever sheds the blood of man, by man*
shall his blood be shed; for in the image of God He made man. 7 *And you,*

לֹא תֹאכֵלוּ — *You shall not eat*. However, (blood) drawn from a dead animal is permitted to Noachides.

5. וְאַךְ אֶת דִּמְכֶם לְנַפְשֹׁתֵיכֶם אֶדְרֹשׁ — *However, your blood which belongs to your souls I will demand*. Although I will not demand the blood of other living creatures from your hands, nonetheless I will demand your blood because of your souls which are more precious to Me than the lives of other living creatures. Now, this "demanding" will be in various ways; if the person (the intended victim) is worthy then ...

מִיַּד כָּל חַיָּה אֶדְרְשֶׁנּוּ וּמִיַּד הָאָדָם — *Of every beast will I demand it; and of the hand of man ...* to save him. (This is) comparable to, וְדָרַשְׁתִּי אֶת צֹאנִי מִיָּדָם ... וְהִצַּלְתִּי צֹאנִי מִפִּיהֶם, *I will demand a reckoning for My flock ... for I will rescue My flock from their mouths* (*Ezekiel* 34:10).

מִיַּד אִישׁ אָחִיו אֶדְרֹשׁ אֶת נֶפֶשׁ הָאָדָם — *Of the hand of every man for that of his brother I will demand the soul of man*. If he is not worthy to be saved and is slain by another, I will avenge the victim by punishing the slayer — but not the beast (who kills him).

6. בָּאָדָם דָּמוֹ יִשָּׁפֵךְ — *By man shall his blood be shed* — by the court (here on earth).

כִּי בְּצֶלֶם אֱלֹהִים — *For in the image of God*. The reason I demand (punishment) for the shedding of man's blood but not for the blood of other living creatures is because *in the image of God He made*, i.e., in the image of those who are separated (from material; i.e., angels) who are called *Elohim*, some of the (humans) were made. From the moment that God, the Blessed One, said *Let us make man* (1:26), he gave the power to the "forms separated (from material)," or one of them, to endow with intellectual power, every subject prepared (to receive this power), which includes every human. Now since man (is created) in the image of *Elohim*, which is the human soul by which he becomes a "rational living being" (based on the *Rambam's Guide* I:51), it is proper that his blood and living soul, which serve that image, be considered precious, and (if shed) be demanded of his murderers, more so than the (taking of the) life of all other living creatures.

NOTES

5-6. מִיַּד כָּל חַיָּה אֶדְרְשֶׁנּוּ... כִּי בְּצֶלֶם אֱלֹהִים... — *Of every beast will I demand it ... For in the image of God*. The sense of these two verses, according to the *Sforno*, is thus: Man, who is created in the image of *Elohim*, is far more important and precious than any other living creature. As such, if he is worthy, God will save him from his attacker, be he beast or man. If he is not worthy, God will punish the murderer (if he is a man) but preferably, the court should execute justice. The reason given by the *Sforno* for the importance and value of the physical body of man is that it houses and gives life to the soul and intellect of man, which is called צֶלֶם אֱלֹהִים, the *Divine image*.

חמישי
ח פְּרוּ וּרְבוּ שִׁרְצוּ בָאָרֶץ וּרְבוּ־בָהּ: וַיֹּאמֶר אֱלֹהִים אֶל־נֹחַ
ט וְאֶל־בָּנָיו אִתּוֹ לֵאמֹר: וַאֲנִי הִנְנִי מֵקִים אֶת־בְּרִיתִי אִתְּכֶם וְאֶת־זַרְעֲכֶם
י אַחֲרֵיכֶם: וְאֵת כָּל־נֶפֶשׁ הַחַיָּה אֲשֶׁר אִתְּכֶם בָּעוֹף בַּבְּהֵמָה וּבְכָל־
יא חַיַּת הָאָרֶץ אִתְּכֶם מִכֹּל יֹצְאֵי הַתֵּבָה לְכֹל חַיַּת הָאָרֶץ: וַהֲקִמֹתִי אֶת־
בְּרִיתִי אִתְּכֶם וְלֹא־יִכָּרֵת כָּל־בָּשָׂר עוֹד מִמֵּי הַמַּבּוּל וְלֹא־יִהְיֶה עוֹד
יב מַבּוּל לְשַׁחֵת הָאָרֶץ: וַיֹּאמֶר אֱלֹהִים זֹאת אוֹת־הַבְּרִית אֲשֶׁר־אֲנִי נֹתֵן
יג בֵּינִי וּבֵינֵיכֶם וּבֵין כָּל־נֶפֶשׁ חַיָּה אֲשֶׁר אִתְּכֶם לְדֹרֹת עוֹלָם: אֶת־קַשְׁתִּי
יד נָתַתִּי בֶּעָנָן וְהָיְתָה לְאוֹת בְּרִית בֵּינִי וּבֵין הָאָרֶץ: וְהָיָה בְּעַנְנִי עָנָן עַל־
טו הָאָרֶץ וְנִרְאֲתָה הַקֶּשֶׁת בֶּעָנָן: וְזָכַרְתִּי אֶת־בְּרִיתִי אֲשֶׁר בֵּינִי וּבֵינֵיכֶם וּבֵין
כָּל־נֶפֶשׁ חַיָּה בְּכָל־בָּשָׂר וְלֹא־יִהְיֶה עוֹד הַמַּיִם לְמַבּוּל לְשַׁחֵת כָּל־בָּשָׂר:
טז וְהָיְתָה הַקֶּשֶׁת בֶּעָנָן וּרְאִיתִיהָ לִזְכֹּר בְּרִית עוֹלָם בֵּין אֱלֹהִים וּבֵין כָּל־
יז נֶפֶשׁ חַיָּה בְּכָל־בָּשָׂר אֲשֶׁר עַל־הָאָרֶץ: וַיֹּאמֶר אֱלֹהִים אֶל־נֹחַ זֹאת אוֹת־
הַבְּרִית אֲשֶׁר הֲקִמֹתִי בֵּינִי וּבֵין כָּל־בָּשָׂר אֲשֶׁר עַל־הָאָרֶץ:

---

7. וְאַתֶּם פְּרוּ וּרְבוּ — *And you, be fruitful and multiply . . .* and do not shed the blood of men.

9. וַאֲנִי הִנְנִי מֵקִים אֶת בְּרִיתִי — *And as for Me, behold, I establish My covenant.* On the condition that you not shed innocent blood do I *establish My covenant* not to destroy the earth again, but if there will be innocent blood shed, the earth will be destroyed, as it says, כִּי הַדָּם הוּא יַחֲנִיף אֶת הָאָרֶץ וְלָאָרֶץ לֹא יְכֻפַּר . . ., *For blood pollutes the land, and no expiation can be made for the land, etc.* (*Numbers* 35:33). However, for all other sins, only the sinner will be punished, but the earth shall not be destroyed.

11. וְלֹא יִהְיֶה עוֹד מַבּוּל לְשַׁחֵת הָאָרֶץ — *And never again shall there be a flood to destroy the earth.* There will not be any sort of catastrophe (lit. downfall and loss) to destroy the substance of the earth.

13. אֶת קַשְׁתִּי נָתַתִּי בֶּעָנָן — *I have set My bow in the cloud.* I set it (originally) that it be part of nature.

וְהָיְתָה לְאוֹת בְּרִית — *And it shall be a sign of the covenant . . .* since the bow is double; for indeed scholars and researchers have tried in vain to give a reason for the order of colors of the second bow, which is opposite of the color order of the normal first bow. (The bow)

NOTES

7. וְאַתֶּם פְּרוּ וּרְבוּ — *And you, be fruitful and multiply.* The phrase פְּרוּ וּרְבוּ, *Be fruitful and multiply,* appears in verse 1 and is repeated here. *Rashi* explains that the former is a blessing, while this is a command to procreate. The *Sforno* resolves this difficulty (i.e. why the Torah repeats this phrase) by explaining that the command in this verse is not to procreate but to *preserve* human life. By refraining from shedding blood the human race will be *fruitful and multiply.*

9-11. וַאֲנִי הִנְנִי מֵקִים אֶת בְּרִיתִי . . . וְלֹא יִהְיֶה עוֹד מַבּוּל לְשַׁחֵת הָאָרֶץ — *And as for Me, behold, I establish My covenant . . . And never again shall there be a flood to destroy the earth.* A covenant involves two parties; in this instance God and mankind. A condition is now being made by the Almighty: If man refrains from shedding innocent blood, God in turn will not destroy the inhabitants of the earth again. This pledge, however, is a conditional one, and the covenant demands mutual, reciprocal responsibility. In addition to this promise of God (verse 9) there is another *unconditional* statement made by Him (verse 11) that regardless of man's conduct, the *substance* of the earth will never again be destroyed by a total catastrophe.

13. אֶת קַשְׁתִּי נָתַתִּי בֶּעָנָן וְהָיְתָה לְאוֹת בְּרִית — *I have set My bow in the cloud and it shall be a sign of the covenant.* There is a difference of opinion among the early Torah commentators as to whether the rainbow was brought forth by God after the Flood, or it was part of original Creation. *Saadiah Gaon* and the *Ramban* are of the latter opinion, to which the *Sforno* also subscribes. However, the *Sforno* submits that since a rainbow shows two bands of

be fruitful and multiply; teem on the earth and multiply on it."
8 *And God said to Noah and to his sons with him saying:* 9 *"And as for Me,*
behold, I establish My covenant with you and with your offspring after you,
10 *and with every living being that is with you — with the birds, with the*
animals, and with every beast of the land with you — of all that departed the
Ark, to every beast of the land. 11 *And I will confirm My covenant with you:*
Never again shall all flesh be cut off by the waters of the flood, and never
again shall there be a flood to destroy the earth."
12 *And God said, "This is the sign of the covenant that I give between*
Me and you, and every living being that is with you, to generations forever:
13 *I have set My rainbow in the cloud, and it shall be a sign of the covenant*
between Me and the earth. 14 *And it shall happen, when I place a cloud*
over the earth, and the bow will be seen in the cloud, 15 *I will remember*
My covenant between Me and you and every living being among all
flesh, and the water shall never again become a flood to destroy all flesh.
16 *And the bow shall be in the cloud, and I will look upon it to remember the*
everlasting covenant between God and every living being, among all flesh
that is on earth." 17 *And God said to Noah, "This is the sign of the covenant*
that I have confirmed between Me and all flesh that is upon the earth."

---

will be a sign to the righteous in (each generation), that their generation is guilty, as our Sages say, *"Did the rainbow appear in your days?" (Kesubos* 77b), so that they (the righteous) might pray, admonish and teach the people knowledge (of God).

14. בְּעַנְנִי עָנָן — *When I place a cloud . . .* for the rainbow will not be visible without a thick, heavy cloud, following the moisture and the clearing.

16. וּרְאִיתִיהָ לִזְכֹּר בְּרִית עוֹלָם — *And I will look upon it to remember the everlasting covenant.* I will regard the result of the bow, which is the prayers of the righteous as they stand in the breach to turn away My wrath from destroying (the earth) — similar to, *He remembers the everlasting covenant.*

17. וַיֹּאמֶר אֱלֹהִים אֶל נֹחַ זֹאת אוֹת הַבְּרִית — *And God said to Noah, "This is the sign of the covenant."* This second rainbow is the sign of the covenant, and it is incumbent upon you, and those like you, to bestir yourselves when you see it, to rouse the people to repent and understand to better (themselves).

NOTES

colors, the inner brighter one (called the *primary* bow) and the outer, less distinct one (known as the *secondary* bow), both theories as to the time of the rainbow's origin may be correct. At the time of Creation there was only the primary bow, but after the Flood the secondary one appeared, made visible by God as a "sign of the covenant," for the purpose of alerting the righteous to pray on behalf of their generation and arouse the people to repent. He feels that this interpretation regarding the double bow explains the phenomena of the reverse order of the rainbow's colors. The primary bow has the red coloring on the outside and the violet on the inside of the arch, while in the secondary bow the colors appear just the opposite. The passage from the Tractate *Kesubos* (77b) which he cites alludes to the exchange between Rabbi Shimon Bar Yochai and Rabbi Yehoshua ben Levi. The former asks Rabbi Yehoshua whether the rainbow appeared in his generation. When he answers affirmatively, Rabbi Shimon questions his righteousness, for a truly great *tzaddik* protects his generation so that it is unnecessary for God to give the rainbow as a sign to the righteous to pray and intercede.

14. בְּעַנְנִי עָנָן – *When I place a cloud.* The *Sforno's* observation is scientifically sound. Rainbows vary, some are brighter and others lighter. If the rain has been heavy, the bow will spread all the way across the sky and be more pronounced. This is the meaning of the phrase, *When I place a cloud,* interpreted by the *Sforno* as a thick, heavy cloud which produces heavy rain that is a prerequisite for a full rainbow.

ששי יח־יט וַיִּהְיוּ בְנֵי־נֹחַ הַיֹּצְאִים מִן־הַתֵּבָה שֵׁם וְחָם וָיָפֶת וְחָם הוּא אֲבִי כְנָעַן: שְׁלֹשָׁה
כ אֵלֶּה בְּנֵי־נֹחַ וּמֵאֵלֶּה נָפְצָה כָל־הָאָרֶץ: וַיָּחֶל נֹחַ אִישׁ הָאֲדָמָה וַיִּטַּע כָּרֶם:
כא־כב וַיֵּשְׁתְּ מִן־הַיַּיִן וַיִּשְׁכָּר וַיִּתְגַּל בְּתוֹךְ אָהֳלֹה: וַיַּרְא חָם אֲבִי כְנַעַן אֵת עֶרְוַת
כג אָבִיו וַיַּגֵּד לִשְׁנֵי־אֶחָיו בַּחוּץ: וַיִּקַּח שֵׁם וָיֶפֶת אֶת־הַשִּׂמְלָה וַיָּשִׂימוּ עַל־שְׁכֶם
שְׁנֵיהֶם וַיֵּלְכוּ אֲחֹרַנִּית וַיְכַסּוּ אֵת עֶרְוַת אֲבִיהֶם וּפְנֵיהֶם אֲחֹרַנִּית וְעֶרְוַת
כד אֲבִיהֶם לֹא רָאוּ: וַיִּיקֶץ נֹחַ מִיֵּינוֹ וַיֵּדַע אֵת אֲשֶׁר־עָשָׂה לוֹ בְּנוֹ הַקָּטָן: וַיֹּאמֶר
כה־כו אָרוּר כְּנָעַן עֶבֶד עֲבָדִים יִהְיֶה לְאֶחָיו: וַיֹּאמֶר בָּרוּךְ יהוה אֱלֹהֵי שֵׁם וִיהִי
כז כְנַעַן עֶבֶד לָמוֹ: יַפְתְּ אֱלֹהִים לְיֶפֶת וְיִשְׁכֹּן בְּאָהֳלֵי־שֵׁם וִיהִי כְנַעַן עֶבֶד לָמוֹ:

---

18. וְחָם הוּא אֲבִי כְנָעַן — *And Ham was the father of Canaan.* Akin in his ways to Canaan who is well known for degradation, in such a manner that he (Ham) was truly the *father of Canaan,* and similar to him as well; (this is) comparable to אָבִיךְ הָאֱמֹרִי, *Your father was an Emorite (Ezekiel* 16:3).

19. שְׁלֹשָׁה אֵלֶּה בְּנֵי נֹחַ — *These three were the sons of Noah.* Although a wicked one was among them, since they were the *sons of Noah,* God blessed all of them, saying, *"Be fruitful and multiply and fill the land"* (9:1), the result being that מֵאֵלֶּה נָפְצָה כָל הָאָרֶץ, *from these the whole world was spread out.*

20. וַיָּחֶל נֹחַ — *And Noah (the man of the earth) began.* He began with an unsuitable project, therefore unsavory deeds resulted from it, for indeed, a small fault at the beginning will cause many more at the end, as (often) happens in (the pursuit of) wisdom (sciences) which (are based) on an incorrect premise. This is taught to us (when the Torah) says, וַיָּחֶל הָעָם לִזְנוֹת, *And the people began to commit harlotry (Numbers* 25:1).

22. וַיַּרְא חָם אֲבִי כְנַעַן אֵת עֶרְוַת אָבִיו — *Ham, the father of Canaan, saw his father's nakedness.* He saw the degradation inflicted on him (Noah) by his son Canaan, i.e., emasculation, as some of our Sages say (*Sanhedrin* 70a). Barusi the Chaldean wrote that he emasculated him through sorcery. Ham, in his wickedness, saw (this happening) and did not protest. Truly, shame is termed עֶרְוָה, *nakedness,* as it says, וְעַרְוַת מַלְכָּא לָא אֲרִיךְ לָנָא לְמֶחֱזֵא, *It is improper for us to see the shame (nakedness) of the king (Ezra* 4:14). Also, (the term) עֶרְוַת דָּבָר, *unseemly thing,* is applied to an ugly thing (or act).

וַיַּגֵּד לִשְׁנֵי אֶחָיו — *And told his two brothers outside.* He rejoiced at the act of his son.

NOTES

18. וְחָם הוּא אֲבִי כְנָעַן – *And Ham was the father of Canaan.* Ham had other sons in addition to Canaan. The Torah singles him out to indicate that father and son were strikingly similar in their wickedness. The quote cited by the *Sforno* from *Ezekiel* is to prove that ethnic names are not always used literally but at times figuratively. In that verse the prophet is alluding to their deeds, not their origin; their *actions* were those of Emorites. In our case, the name Canaanite represents degradation and immorality.

19. שְׁלֹשָׁה אֵלֶּה בְּנֵי נֹחַ – *These three were the sons of Noah.* The previous verse enumerates the sons of Noah; why is it necessary to repeat again, *These three were the sons of Noah* from whom the new world spread out? The *Sforno's* answer is that although a wicked one was among them (Ham) since they were the *sons of Noah,* God blessed them, with the result that from all three of them *the whole world was spread out.*

20. וַיָּחֶל נֹחַ – *And Noah began.* The *Sforno* stresses the moral lesson to be learned from Noah's first agricultural project after the Flood. The planting of a vineyard and drinking of its wine may seem innocent, yet this inappropriate act led to far more serious consequences. The proof brought by the *Sforno* from *Numbers* is most telling. The tragic episode of Shitim begins with harlotry, but leads to idolatry, the most serious transgression of all.

22. וַיַּרְא חָם אֲבִי כְנַעַן אֵת עֶרְוַת אָבִיו – *Ham, the father of Canaan, saw his father's nakedness.* Contrary to the interpretation of some of our Sages, and the literal meaning of the verse, the *Sforno* (as *Rashi*) is of the opinion that it was Canaan, not Ham, who inflicted this indignity upon his grandfather. Ham's sin was that he did not prevent or protest; on the contrary — he rejoiced and joyfully told his brothers.

24. בְּנוֹ הַקָּטָן – *His small son.* The *Sforno* suggests three reasons for calling him, *his small son.* Consis-

[18] *The sons of Noah who came out of the Ark were Shem, Ham, and Japheth — Ham being the father of Canaan.* [19] *These three were the sons of Noah, and from these the whole world was spread out.*

[20] *Noah, the man of the earth, debased himself and planted a vineyard.* [21] *He drank of the wine and became drunk, and he uncovered himself within his tent.* [22] *Ham, the father of Canaan, saw his father's nakedness and told his two brothers outside.* [23] *And Shem and Japheth took a garment, laid it upon both their shoulders, and they walked backwards, and covered their father's nakedness; their faces were turned away, and they saw not their father's nakedness.*

[24] *Noah awoke from his wine and realized what his small son had done to him.*

[25] *And he said, "Cursed is Canaan; a slave of slaves shall he be to his brothers."*

[26] *And he said, "Blessed is HASHEM, the God of Shem; and let Canaan be a slave to them.*

[27] *"May God extend Japheth, but he will dwell in the tents of Shem; may Canaan be a slave to them."*

---

23. וּפְנֵיהֶם אֲחֹרַנִּית — *Their faces were turned away.* Even when they were covering (him) at which time there was a need to turn toward him, (nonetheless) they did not turn to look, for that would have increased their pain (sadness).

24. בְּנוֹ הַקָּטָן — *His small son.* Grandchildren are considered as children, and Canaan was the youngest of Ham's sons. Perhaps he (also) was the youngest grandson of Noah; also in his conduct (behavior), קָטֹן... בַּגּוֹיִם בָּזוּי... מְאֹד, *(He was) least among the nations, most despised (Obadiah* 1:2).

25. עֶבֶד עֲבָדִים יִהְיֶה לְאֶחָיו — *A slave of slaves shall he be to his brothers.* Under normal circumstances he should be a slave to his brothers, since he was the least in (moral) stature and the (most) degraded of them all, as it says, וְעֶבֶד אֱוִיל לַחֲכַם לֵב, *A fool shall be slave to the wise hearted (Proverbs* 11:29); therefore when he sinned, the *added* (punishment) was *slave of slaves.*

26. וִיהִי כְנַעַן — *And let Canaan* ... his offspring, be ...

עֶבֶד לָמוֹ — *A slave to them* ... to the God of Shem and the descendants of Shem, as it says, חֹטְבֵי עֵצִים וְשֹׁאֲבֵי מַיִם לָעֵדָה וּלְמִזְבַּח ה׳, *(And they became) choppers of wood and hewers of water for the congregation and the altar of HASHEM (Joshua* 9:27).

27. בְּאָהֳלֵי שֵׁם — *In the tents of Shem.* (This refers to the) houses of study, besides the Temple (lit. "Chosen House").

עֶבֶד לָמוֹ — *A slave to them.* This is repeated (a second time) to indicate both Shem and Japheth, even not at the time of the Temple.

NOTES

tent with his interpretation that Canaan was the perpetrator of this gross act, the *Sforno* submits that he was (a) the youngest of Ham's sons; (b) Noah's youngest grandson; (c) the Torah does not call him small in a chronological sense but refers to his inferior, deficient status.

26-27. וִיהִי כְנַעַן עֶבֶד לָמוֹ... בְּאָהֳלֵי שֵׁם... עֶבֶד לָמוֹ — *And let Canaan be a slave to them ... In the tents of Shem ... a slave to them.* The word לָמוֹ, *to them,* is in the plural. In verse 26 it refers to Canaan's relationship to Shem, therefore the plural term is interpreted by the *Sforno* as alluding to the double duty imposed by Joshua on the Givonim (who were descendants of Canaan), i.e., to do the menial labor for the Sanctuary and to serve Israel as well. The repetition of the phrase לָמוֹ in verse 27 is meant to teach us that Canaan will be a slave to both Shem and Japheth. The *Sforno* is constrained to explain the second לָמוֹ in this manner, since this verse speaks of a time when the Temple no longer exists; hence the initial interpretation of the plural form לָמוֹ is not applicable.

27. בְּאָהֳלֵי שֵׁם — *In the tents of Shem.* The *Sforno* agrees with Rashi that the subject of *and dwell in the tents of Shem* is God. Therefore he explains the plural form (tents) as referring to the Temple and all Houses of Study, where God's presence is found.

כח-כט וַיְחִי־נֹחַ אַחַר הַמַּבּוּל שְׁלֹשׁ מֵאוֹת שָׁנָה וַחֲמִשִּׁים שָׁנָה׃ וַיְהִי כָּל־יְמֵי־נֹחַ
תְּשַׁע מֵאוֹת שָׁנָה וַחֲמִשִּׁים שָׁנָה וַיָּמֹת׃
י א-ב וְאֵלֶּה תּוֹלְדֹת בְּנֵי־נֹחַ שֵׁם חָם וָיָפֶת וַיִּוָּלְדוּ לָהֶם בָּנִים אַחַר הַמַּבּוּל׃ בְּנֵי
ג יֶפֶת גֹּמֶר וּמָגוֹג וּמָדַי וְיָוָן וְתֻבָל וּמֶשֶׁךְ וְתִירָס׃ וּבְנֵי גֹּמֶר אַשְׁכְּנַז וְרִיפַת
ד-ה וְתֹגַרְמָה׃ וּבְנֵי יָוָן אֱלִישָׁה וְתַרְשִׁישׁ כִּתִּים וְדֹדָנִים׃ מֵאֵלֶּה נִפְרְדוּ אִיֵּי
ו הַגּוֹיִם בְּאַרְצֹתָם אִישׁ לִלְשֹׁנוֹ לְמִשְׁפְּחֹתָם בְּגוֹיֵהֶם׃ וּבְנֵי חָם כּוּשׁ וּמִצְרַיִם
ז וּפוּט וּכְנָעַן׃ וּבְנֵי כוּשׁ סְבָא וַחֲוִילָה וְסַבְתָּה וְרַעְמָה וְסַבְתְּכָא וּבְנֵי רַעְמָה
ח-ט שְׁבָא וּדְדָן׃ וְכוּשׁ יָלַד אֶת־נִמְרֹד הוּא הֵחֵל לִהְיוֹת גִּבֹּר בָּאָרֶץ׃ הוּא־הָיָה
י גִבֹּר־צַיִד לִפְנֵי יהוה עַל־כֵּן יֵאָמַר כְּנִמְרֹד גִּבּוֹר צַיִד לִפְנֵי יהוה׃ וַתְּהִי
יא רֵאשִׁית מַמְלַכְתּוֹ בָּבֶל וְאֶרֶךְ וְאַכַּד וְכַלְנֵה בְּאֶרֶץ שִׁנְעָר׃ מִן־הָאָרֶץ
יב הַהִוא יָצָא אַשּׁוּר וַיִּבֶן אֶת־נִינְוֵה וְאֶת־רְחֹבֹת עִיר וְאֶת־כָּלַח׃ וְאֶת־רֶסֶן
יג בֵּין נִינְוֵה וּבֵין כָּלַח הִוא הָעִיר הַגְּדֹלָה׃ וּמִצְרַיִם יָלַד אֶת־לוּדִים וְאֶת־
יד עֲנָמִים וְאֶת־לְהָבִים וְאֶת־נַפְתֻּחִים׃ וְאֶת־פַּתְרֻסִים וְאֶת־כַּסְלֻחִים אֲשֶׁר
טו יָצְאוּ מִשָּׁם פְּלִשְׁתִּים וְאֶת־כַּפְתֹּרִים׃ וּכְנַעַן
טז יָלַד אֶת־צִידֹן בְּכֹרוֹ וְאֶת־חֵת׃ וְאֶת־הַיְבוּסִי וְאֶת־הָאֱמֹרִי וְאֵת
יז-יח הַגִּרְגָּשִׁי׃ וְאֶת־הַחִוִּי וְאֶת־הַעַרְקִי וְאֶת־הַסִּינִי׃ וְאֶת־הָאַרְוָדִי

---

29. וַיָּמֹת — *And he died.* Prior to the major historical event of that era, namely, the awakening of Abraham to call in the name of Hashem.

X

6. וּפוּט וּכְנָעַן — *And Put and Canaan.* His children are not mentioned (i.e., Put's) because all his children formed one people called by his name, as it says, פָּרַס כּוּשׁ וּפוּט אִתָּם, *Among them shall be Persia, Cush and Put (Ezekiel* 38:5).

7. וּבְנֵי כוּשׁ סְבָא וַחֲוִילָה — *The children of Cush; Seba and Havilah.* Each became the afounder of a people, besides those who are called by his name, as it says: כּוּשׁ וּסְבָא תַּחְתֶּיךָ, *Cush and Seba in exchange for you (Isaiah* 43:3).

8. וְכוּשׁ יָלַד אֶת נִמְרֹד — *And Cush begot Nimrod.* Among those who are called by his name he begot an individual known as a mighty man.

9. לִפְנֵי ה׳ — *Before Hashem.* Exceedingly mighty, similar to, עִיר גְּדוֹלָה לֵאלֹהִים, *(Nineveh) an enormously large city (Jonah* 3:3).

NOTES

29. וַיָּמֹת – *And he died.* The phrase וַיָּמֹת, *and he died,* is used to indicate finality and culmination. In 11:11 the *Sforno* points out that the Torah does not use the term *he died* for the generations mentioned in that chapter, i.e., from Noah to Abraham. He states that the reason is that they were all alive when Abraham sought to lead man to the worship of God, as opposed to the ten generations from Adam to Noah who died by the time of the Flood (hence the Torah does use the term *and he died* in *Parashas Bereishis*). Whenever there is a *culmination* of a unit of the Torah's narrative, i.e., "the major historical event of that era," as the *Sforno* phrases it, the word וַיָּמֹת is used. If, however, the central feature of a unit is still in process, the word וַיָּמֹת is not used. This explains the *Sforno's* interpretation here. Although Abraham was 58 years old when Noah died, he had as yet not become known or begun his mission of leading man to God. Therefore, the death of Noah represented the culmination of an era, the central feature of which was the Flood. That is why וַיָּמֹת, *and he died,* is used here.

X

8. וְכוּשׁ יָלַד אֶת נִמְרֹד – *And Cush begot Nimrod.* In the previous verse (7) the children of Cush are listed. The singling out of Nimrod in this verse is explained by the *Sforno* as indicating his unique position among the offspring of Cush.

9. לִפְנֵי ה׳ – *Before* HASHEM. The expression לִפְנֵי ה׳

28 Noah lived after the Flood three hundred fifty years. 29 And all the days
of Noah were nine hundred fifty years; and he died.

10 *1 These are the descendants of the sons of Noah: Shem, Ham, and*
Japheth; sons were born to them after the Flood.
2 The sons of Japheth: Gomer, Magog, Madai, Javan, Tubal, Meshech, and
Tiras. 3 The sons of Gomer: Ashkenaz, Riphath, and Togarmah. 4 The sons of
Javan: Elishah and Tarshish, the Kittim and the Dodanim. 5 From these the
islands of the nations were separated in their lands — each according to its
language, by their families, in their nations.
6 The sons of Ham: Cush, Mizraim, Put, and Canaan. 7 The sons of Cush: Seba,
Havilah, Sabtah, Raamah, and Sabteca. The sons of Raamah: Sheba and Dedan.
8 And Cush begot Nimrod. He was the first to be a mighty man on earth. 9 He
was a mighty hunter before HASHEM; *therefore it is said: "Like Nimrod a*
mighty hunter before HASHEM.*" 10 The beginning of his kingdom was Babel,*
Erech, Accad, and Calneh in the land of Shinar. 11 From that land Ashur went
forth and built Nineveh, Rehovoth-ir, Calah, 12 and Resen between Nineveh
and Calah, that is the great city.
13 And Mizraim begot Ludim, Anamim, Lehabim, Naphtuhim, 14 Path-
rusim, and Casluhim, whence the Philistines came forth, and Caphtorim.
15 Canaan begot Zidon his firstborn, and Heth; 16 and the Jebusite, the
Amorite, the Girgashite, 17 the Hivite, the Arkite, the Sinite, 18 the Arvadite,

עַל כֵּן יֵאָמַר כְּנִמְרֹד גִּבּוֹר צַיִד — *Therefore it is said: "Like Nimrod a mighty hunter."* And because of his reputation as a mighty man he ruled over nations, as it says . . .

10. וַתְּהִי רֵאשִׁית מַמְלַכְתּוֹ בָּבֶל — *The beginning of his kingdom was Babel.* This is to tell (us) that because of his kingdom, it came to pass that various nations came to dwell in Shinar and (consequently) the city and tower were built (11:4) for the purpose of expanding his (Nimrod's) kingdom over the human race through the medium of a universal strange god whom all would worship, similar to the strategy of Jeroboam when he feared the (magnetic) call of the Temple (*I Kings* 12:26).

11. מִן הָאָרֶץ הַהִוא יָצָא אַשּׁוּר — *From that land Ashur went forth.* He rejected (both) the rulership of Nimrod and his wicked vulgar plan, as our Sages tell us (*Midrash*).

וַיִּבֶן אֶת נִינְוֵה — *And built Nineveh* . . . and therefore he merited to build all these cities, as it says, אֶל פָּנָיו יְשַׁלֶּם לוֹ, *He will repay him to his face (Deut.* 7:10).

NOTES

(before HASHEM*)* cannot be translated literally here as meaning "before God" or "in His presence." It is an idiom for anyone or anything which is exceedingly *mighty*, as in the case of Nimrod, or *large*, as in the case of the city Nineveh.

10. וַתְּהִי רֵאשִׁית מַמְלַכְתּוֹ בָּבֶל — *The beginning of his kingdom was Babel.* The plan of Nimrod and his advisors was to consolidate the rulership of Nimrod not only through political allegiance but also through a common religious commitment. The *Sforno* cites the case of Jeroboam, the first king of the northern kingdom — Israel — who feared the effect of the festival pilgrimage to Jerusalem on his people, who might transfer their allegiance to the kingdom of Judah, so he proceeded to erect golden calves in Bethel and Dan to rally his people around these idols, using their commitment to a new faith to buttress their allegiance to him.

11. מִן הָאָרֶץ הַהִוא יָצָא אַשּׁוּר — *From that land Ashur went forth.* Since Ashur refused to support Nimrod in his nefarious plan, although he was not that worthy himself, God rewards him for this one proper act of defiance. The verse cited from *Deuteronomy*, where the expression *to his face* is used, is to be understood as referring to the reward given by God to the wicked in this world, during their lifetime, for any good deed performed by them. Punishment for their sins, on the other hand, will be meted out in the next world.

יט וְאֶת־הַצְּמָרִי וְאֶת־הַחֲמָתִי וְאַחַר נָפֹצוּ מִשְׁפְּחוֹת הַכְּנַעֲנִי׃ וַיְהִי גְּבוּל
הַכְּנַעֲנִי מִצִּידֹן בֹּאֲכָה גְרָרָה עַד־עַזָּה בֹּאֲכָה סְדֹמָה וַעֲמֹרָה וְאַדְמָה
כ וּצְבֹיִם עַד־לָשַׁע׃ אֵלֶּה בְנֵי־חָם לְמִשְׁפְּחֹתָם לִלְשֹׁנֹתָם בְּאַרְצֹתָם
כא בְּגוֹיֵהֶם׃ וּלְשֵׁם יֻלַּד גַּם־הוּא אֲבִי כָּל־בְּנֵי־עֵבֶר אֲחִי יֶפֶת
כב־כג הַגָּדוֹל׃ בְּנֵי שֵׁם עֵילָם וְאַשּׁוּר וְאַרְפַּכְשַׁד וְלוּד וַאֲרָם׃ וּבְנֵי אֲרָם עוּץ וְחוּל
כד־כה וְגֶתֶר וָמַשׁ׃ וְאַרְפַּכְשַׁד יָלַד אֶת־שָׁלַח וְשֶׁלַח יָלַד אֶת־עֵבֶר׃ וּלְעֵבֶר יֻלַּד
כו שְׁנֵי בָנִים שֵׁם הָאֶחָד פֶּלֶג כִּי בְיָמָיו נִפְלְגָה הָאָרֶץ וְשֵׁם אָחִיו יָקְטָן׃ וְיָקְטָן
כז יָלַד אֶת־אַלְמוֹדָד וְאֶת־שָׁלֶף וְאֶת־חֲצַרְמָוֶת וְאֶת־יָרַח׃ וְאֶת־הֲדוֹרָם
כח־כט וְאֶת־אוּזָל וְאֶת־דִּקְלָה׃ וְאֶת־עוֹבָל וְאֶת־אֲבִימָאֵל וְאֶת־שְׁבָא׃ וְאֶת־
ל אוֹפִר וְאֶת־חֲוִילָה וְאֶת־יוֹבָב כָּל־אֵלֶּה בְּנֵי יָקְטָן׃ וַיְהִי מוֹשָׁבָם מִמֵּשָׁא
לא בֹּאֲכָה סְפָרָה הַר הַקֶּדֶם׃ אֵלֶּה בְנֵי־שֵׁם לְמִשְׁפְּחֹתָם לִלְשֹׁנֹתָם בְּאַרְצֹתָם
לב לְגוֹיֵהֶם׃ אֵלֶּה מִשְׁפְּחֹת בְּנֵי־נֹחַ לְתוֹלְדֹתָם בְּגוֹיֵהֶם וּמֵאֵלֶּה נִפְרְדוּ הַגּוֹיִם
בָּאָרֶץ אַחַר הַמַּבּוּל׃

יא שביעי א־ב וַיְהִי כָל־הָאָרֶץ שָׂפָה אֶחָת וּדְבָרִים אֲחָדִים׃ וַיְהִי בְּנָסְעָם מִקֶּדֶם וַיִּמְצְאוּ
ג בִקְעָה בְּאֶרֶץ שִׁנְעָר וַיֵּשְׁבוּ שָׁם׃ וַיֹּאמְרוּ אִישׁ אֶל־רֵעֵהוּ הָבָה נִלְבְּנָה
לְבֵנִים וְנִשְׂרְפָה לִשְׂרֵפָה וַתְּהִי לָהֶם הַלְּבֵנָה לְאָבֶן וְהַחֵמָר הָיָה לָהֶם
ד לַחֹמֶר׃ וַיֹּאמְרוּ הָבָה ׀ נִבְנֶה־לָּנוּ עִיר וּמִגְדָּל וְרֹאשׁוֹ בַשָּׁמַיִם וְנַעֲשֶׂה־לָּנוּ

---

21. וּלְשֵׁם יֻלַּד — *And to Shem was born . . .* a man, virtuous like him, namely Eber.

גַּם הוּא אֲבִי כָּל בְּנֵי עֵבֶר — *He also was the ancestor (father) of all the descendants (children) of Eber.* Although those who hold fast to the belief in God's existence, His power and providence, are called עִבְרִים, *Ivrim,* after עֵבֶר, *Eber,* (their teacher) who endeavored to understand and teach this (belief) as it says, *And he told Abram the Ivri* (14:13), nonetheless *he also,* namely Shem, was the father and teacher of *all the children of Eber.* (This is so) because one who teaches and guides is called *father,* as we find, *He was the "father" of all who handle the harp and flute* (4:21); also, וּמִי אֲבִיהֶם, *And who are their fathers? (I Samuel* 10:12); and the students are called *sons,* as it says, בְּנֵי הַנְּבִיאִים, *The disciples (sons) of the Prophets (I Kings* 20:35).

25. פֶּלֶג כִּי בְיָמָיו נִפְלְגָה הָאָרֶץ — *Peleg, for in his days the earth was divided.* (The Torah) tells us Eber's virtue, that he correctly divined through the holy spirit what was to come to pass in the days of his son. He called his son by the name Peleg to tell (everyone) the cause for the reduced human longevity beginning from Peleg and beyond; the cause being

NOTES

21. וּלְשֵׁם יֻלַּד גַּם הוּא אֲבִי כָּל בְּנֵי עֵבֶר — *And to Shem was born, he also was the ancestor (father) of all the descendants (children) of Eber.* Since it does not say *And Shem begot* but, *and to Shem was born,* which implies a child whose character reflected his father Shem, the *Sforno* interprets this as referring to Eber who possessed the qualifications to transmit the teachings of his great father Shem. The *Sforno* also links the phrase גַּם הוּא *(he also)* to the latter part of the verse, to emphasize the pedagogic role played by Shem in teaching and influencing the followers of Eber. Indeed, in our tradition reference is always made to the "school of Shem and Eber." The *Sforno* stresses that the relationship between a teacher and pupil is akin to that of a father and son, which accounts for the term "the *father* (אֲבִי) of the descendants of Eber," a term used in other instances as well, as cited by the *Sforno.*

25. פֶּלֶג כִּי בְיָמָיו נִפְלְגָה הָאָרֶץ — *Peleg, for in his days the earth was divided.* The word פֶּלֶג means *half.* The name given by Eber to his son פֶּלֶג was meant

the Zemarite, and the Hamathite. Afterward, the families of the Canaan-
ites branched out. 19 *And the Canaanite boundary extended from Zidon*
going toward Gerar, as far as Gaza; going toward Sodom, Gomorrah,
Admah, and Zeboiim, as far as Lasha. 20 *These are the descendants of Ham,*
by their families, by their languages, in their lands, in their nations.

21 *And to Shem, also to him were born; he was the ancestor of all those who*
lived on the other side; the brother of Japheth the elder. 22 *The sons of Shem:*
Elam, Asshur, Arpachshad, Lud, and Aram. 23 *The sons of Aram: Uz, Hul,*
Gether, and Mash. 24 *Arpachshad begot Shelah, and Shelah begot Eber.*
25 *And to Eber were born two sons: The name of the first was Peleg, for in his*
days the earth was divided; and the name of his brother was Joktan.
26 *Joktan begot Almodad, Sheleph, Hazarmaveth, Jerah,* 27 *Hadoram, Uzal,*
Diklah, 28 *Obal, Abimael, Sheba,* 29 *Ophir, Havilah, and Jobab; all these were*
the sons of Joktan. 30 *Their dwelling place extended from Mesha going*
toward Sephar, the mountain to the east. 31 *These are the descendants of*
Shem according to their families, by their languages, in their lands, by their
nations.

32 *These are the families of Noah's descendants, according to their*
generations, by their nations; and from these the nations were separated on
the earth after the Flood.

11 1 *The whole earth was of one language and of common purpose.* 2 *And*
it came to pass, when they migrated from the east they found a valley
in the land of Shinar and settled there. 3 *They said to one another, "Come,*
let us make bricks and burn them in fire." And the brick served them as
stone, and the bitumen served them as mortar. 4 *And they said, "Come, let*
us build us a city, and a tower with its top in the heavens, and let us make

---

the sin of the generation of Dispersion and their (consequent) punishment, for their vitality (was affected) by the sudden change of climates.

XI

2. בְּנָסְעָם מִקֶּדֶם — *When they traveled from the east*... as is the custom of shepherds who travel from place to place in search of suitable pasture.

3. הָבָה נִלְבְּנָה לְבֵנִים — *Come, let us make bricks*... to construct houses and sheepfolds; this was the counsel of individuals among the populace, as it says, *They said to one another.*

4. וַיֹּאמְרוּ הָבָה נִבְנֶה לָּנוּ עִיר — *And they said, "Come, let us build us a city."* This was the counsel of the princes of the generation, (their goal being) to make Nimrod king over the whole human race.

NOTES

to indicate, as *Rashi* states in *Chronicles*, that in his days the lifespan of man was cut in half. The *Sforno* adds that the reason for this reduced longevity was because through man's dispersal, the dislocation and resultant climate changes had a deleterious effect upon his lifespan.

XI

3-4. וַיֹּאמְרוּ הָבָה – *And they said, "Come..."* The introductory phrase, *And they said, "Come,"* (וַיֹּאמְרוּ הָבָה) appears in both verses. The *Sforno* explains that it is not redundant: The first refers to the masses, who are interested in building homes and sheepfolds — the necessities of life; and the second to the princes and leaders who are interested in a base of power for Nimrod, who according to our Sages (*Chullin* 89a) was the initiator of this plan. They also realized that by combining physical grandeur with religious fervor they would insure the success of this grand plan.

ה שָׁם פֶּן־נָפוּץ עַל־פְּנֵי כָל־הָאָרֶץ׃ וַיֵּרֶד יהוה לִרְאֹת אֶת־הָעִיר וְאֶת־
ו הַמִּגְדָּל אֲשֶׁר בָּנוּ בְּנֵי הָאָדָם׃ וַיֹּאמֶר יהוה הֵן עַם אֶחָד וְשָׂפָה אַחַת לְכֻלָּם
ז וְזֶה הַחִלָּם לַעֲשׂוֹת וְעַתָּה לֹא־יִבָּצֵר מֵהֶם כֹּל אֲשֶׁר יָזְמוּ לַעֲשׂוֹת׃ הָבָה
ח נֵרְדָה וְנָבְלָה שָׁם שְׂפָתָם אֲשֶׁר לֹא יִשְׁמְעוּ אִישׁ שְׂפַת רֵעֵהוּ׃ וַיָּפֶץ יהוה
ט אֹתָם מִשָּׁם עַל־פְּנֵי כָל־הָאָרֶץ וַיַּחְדְּלוּ לִבְנֹת הָעִיר׃ עַל־כֵּן קָרָא שְׁמָהּ
בָּבֶל כִּי־שָׁם בָּלַל יהוה שְׂפַת כָּל־הָאָרֶץ וּמִשָּׁם הֱפִיצָם יהוה עַל־פְּנֵי כָּל־
הָאָרֶץ׃
י אֵלֶּה תּוֹלְדֹת שֵׁם שֵׁם בֶּן־מְאַת שָׁנָה וַיּוֹלֶד אֶת־אַרְפַּכְשָׁד שְׁנָתַיִם אַחַר
יא הַמַּבּוּל׃ וַיְחִי־שֵׁם אַחֲרֵי הוֹלִידוֹ אֶת־אַרְפַּכְשָׁד חֲמֵשׁ מֵאוֹת שָׁנָה וַיּוֹלֶד
יב בָּנִים וּבָנוֹת׃ וְאַרְפַּכְשַׁד חַי חָמֵשׁ וּשְׁלֹשִׁים שָׁנָה וַיּוֹלֶד אֶת־שָׁלַח׃

וּמִגְדָּל וְרֹאשׁוֹ בַשָּׁמַיִם וְנַעֲשֶׂה לָּנוּ שֵׁם — *And a tower with its top in the heavens, and let us make a name for ourselves.* "Let us make a name," an idol which will be situated in the tower. The fame of its height, and the huge size of the city, will spread among the whole human race in such a manner that this deity will be considered as the "deity of deities" among mankind, and all will seek it out. The one who would rule over that city would rule over the entire human race, since everyone would seek it out — and this was (indeed) their intent.

5. וַיֵּרֶד ה׳ לִרְאֹת — *And HASHEM came down to see.* The idiom "descending to see" said of God, the blessed One, is used when the action (of the sinner) does not in itself merit punishment, but will inevitably lead to a (more serious) deterioration, (as we find by) בֵּן סוֹרֵר וּמוֹרֶה, *a rebellious, gluttonous son* (*Deut.* 21:18-21), where our Sages explain, "The Torah descended to the depths of his intention" (*Sanhedrin* 72a). The same (is true) of Sodom, where it is written, *I will go down now and see* (18:21), for indeed their wickedness was no greater than that of other people to merit punishing them (so severely) in this world — except in the area of cruelty against poor people, from which total deterioration would eventually result, as it says, הִנֵּה זֶה הָיָה עֲוֹן סְדֹם אֲחוֹתֵךְ . . . וְיַד עָנִי וְאֶבְיוֹן לֹא הֶחֱזִיקָה, *Behold, this was the iniquity of Sodom, your sister (city) . . . she did not support the poor and the needy* (*Ezekiel* 16:49). This was also (true) of the punishment of Israel in their exile, as it says, אֶרְאֶה מָה אַחֲרִיתָם, *I will see what their end shall be* (*Deut.* 32:20).

6. הֵן עַם אֶחָד — *Behold, they are one people.* (Normally) the counsel of nations and their

NOTES

4. וְנַעֲשֶׂה לָּנוּ שֵׁם – *And let us make a name for ourselves.* The *Sforno* interprets the word שֵׁם, *name,* as meaning idolatry, in keeping with the interpretation of our Sages (*Sanhedrin* 109a) and the *Zohar* which explains it as meaning, "let us make an *object of worship.*"

5. וַיֵּרֶד ה׳ לִרְאֹת – *And HASHEM came down to see.* The Almighty has no need to "descend and see"; all is known to Him. The word וַיֵּרֶד, *He descended,* is meant to imply that He sees the *ultimate* consequences of a present act or condition. In the case of the rebellious son cited by the *Sforno*, although the present actions of this son are not serious enough to warrant such severe punishment, God however knows that ultimately he will murder and steal to satisfy his appetites. Even Sodom, wicked and evil as they were, would not have deserved destruction were it not for the ultimate evil which would inevitably result from their present behavior. In the case of the tower, He examines the inevitable results of this project, and determines that it must be prevented through dispersion (see verse 6). The verse cited from *Deuteronomy* is perhaps the key to his interpretation. He does not interpret the phrase *what their end shall be* as meaning the vulnerability of the Jewish people when God will *hide His face from them,* which is the beginning of that particular verse (*Deut.* 32:20). Rather it is the *reason* for God's decision to "hide His face" (to remove His providence). Because He sees what their actions will eventually lead to, He turns away from them — now!

6. הֵן עַם אֶחָד – *Behold, they are one people.* The

a name for ourselves, lest we be dispersed across the whole earth."
5 *HASHEM descended to look at the city and tower which the sons of man*
built, 6 *and HASHEM said, "Behold, they are one people with one language for all, and this they begin to do! And now, should it not be withheld from them all they propose to do?* 7 *Come, let us descend and there confuse their language, that they should not understand one another's language."*
8 *And HASHEM dispersed them from there over the face of the whole earth;*
and they stopped building the city. 9 *That is why it was called Babel, because it was there that HASHEM confused the language of the whole earth, and from there HASHEM scattered them over the face of the whole earth.*
10 *These are the descendants of Shem: Shem was one hundred years old*
when he begot Arpachshad, two years after the Flood. 11 *And Shem lived five*
hundred years after begetting Arpachshad, and he begot sons and daughters.
12 *Arpachshad had lived thirty-five years when he begot Shelah.*

---

plans are thwarted and nullified as a result of divisions which occur between them, caused by (differences) regarding faith, or (lack of a common) language. They, however, were "one people" in the area of religion, for they all agreed (to accept) the philosophy of the Sabians, and they also accepted (one) language.

וְזֶה הַחִלָּם לַעֲשׂוֹת — *And this they begin to do.* They also now have this beginning, which they have all agreed to . . .

וְעַתָּה לֹא יִבָּצֵר מֵהֶם — *And now nothing will be withheld from them.* Therefore there is no deterrent to prevent them from completing their intentions, and the religion (deity) they choose will become universal for the whole human race so that no man will turn to (seek) the knowledge of the Creator, the blessed One, or to understand that He formed all. The opposite of this will happen when there will be division between the nations, regarding their strange gods, for each one of them does believe that there is a "god of gods" with whom all other gods agree, and through him their governance and the governance of all existence reaches perfection, as it says, כִּי מִמִּזְרַח שֶׁמֶשׁ וְעַד מְבוֹאוֹ גָּדוֹל שְׁמִי בַּגּוֹיִם, *From where the sun rises to where it sets, My Name is honored among the nations (Malachi* 1:11).

11. וַיּוֹלֶד בָּנִים וּבָנוֹת — *And he begot sons and daughters.* The phrase וַיָּמֹת, *and he died,* is not mentioned by any one of these ten generations, as it is mentioned of the ten

NOTES

Sforno, in his reference to the Sabians, follows the *Rambam's* approach in his *Guide* (III:29). He explains that their doctrine was "that there is no deity but the stars," and that the "sun is the greatest deity." The *Rambam* always refers, in his *Guide*, to the pagan philosophers of early times as "Sabians" (צאב׳ה). The *Sforno* interprets the phrase עַם אֶחָד as meaning one, both in language and religion, their faith being that of the Sabians.

וְעַתָּה לֹא יִבָּצֵר מֵהֶם – *And now nothing will be withheld from them.* The *Sforno* understands the reason for the Dispersion thus: When people worship deities other than God, such as stars, luminaries, spirits, or even inanimate objects that symbolize, or reflect, these deities, as the *Rambam* explains "in respect of its being an *image* of a thing that is an intermediary between ourselves and God" (*Guide* I:36), they still accept the concept of a אֱלֹהֵי הָאֱלֹהִים, a *god of gods*, i.e., a supreme being. Hence, the possibility exists that some day they will come to the knowledge of God, the Blessed One. The Sages in *Menachos* 110a express this thought in their interpretation of the verse in *Malachi* cited here by the *Sforno*. However, if universal man would have accepted the religion fostered by Nimrod, this monolithic idolatry would have closed the door to further inquiry and speculation, thereby barring mankind's way to return to the true God. The dispersion was meant to disrupt the acceptance of an exclusive false deity, for through dispersion would come diverse religions which would result in a more favorable religious climate, leading ultimately to the day of ה׳ אֶחָד וּשְׁמוֹ אֶחָד, when *God would be One and His Name one (Zechariah* 14:9).

11. וַיּוֹלֶד בָּנִים וּבָנוֹת – *And he begot sons and*

יג וַיְחִ֣י אַרְפַּכְשַׁ֗ד אַֽחֲרֵי֙ הוֹלִידֽ֣וֹ אֶת־שֶׁ֔לַח שָׁלֹ֣שׁ שָׁנִ֔ים וְאַרְבַּ֥ע מֵא֖וֹת שָׁנָ֑ה
יד וַיּ֖וֹלֶד בָּנִ֥ים וּבָנֽוֹת: וְשֶׁ֥לַח חַ֖י שְׁלֹשִׁ֣ים שָׁנָ֑ה וַיּ֖וֹלֶד אֶת־עֵֽבֶר:
טו וַֽיְחִי־שֶׁ֗לַח אַֽחֲרֵי֙ הוֹלִיד֣וֹ אֶת־עֵ֔בֶר שָׁלֹ֣שׁ שָׁנִ֔ים וְאַרְבַּ֥ע מֵא֖וֹת שָׁנָ֑ה וַיּ֥וֹלֶד
טז בָּנִ֥ים וּבָנֽוֹת: וַֽיְחִי־עֵ֕בֶר אַרְבַּ֥ע וּשְׁלֹשִׁ֖ים שָׁנָ֑ה וַיּ֖וֹלֶד אֶת־פָּֽלֶג:
יז וַֽיְחִי־עֵ֗בֶר אַֽחֲרֵי֙ הוֹלִיד֣וֹ אֶת־פֶּ֔לֶג שְׁלֹשִׁ֣ים שָׁנָ֔ה וְאַרְבַּ֥ע מֵא֖וֹת שָׁנָ֑ה וַיּ֥וֹלֶד
יח־יט בָּנִ֥ים וּבָנֽוֹת: וַֽיְחִי־פֶ֖לֶג שְׁלֹשִׁ֣ים שָׁנָ֑ה וַיּ֖וֹלֶד אֶת־רְעֽוּ: וַֽיְחִי־
פֶ֗לֶג אַֽחֲרֵי֙ הוֹלִיד֣וֹ אֶת־רְע֔וּ תֵּ֥שַׁע שָׁנִ֖ים וּמָאתַ֣יִם שָׁנָ֑ה וַיּ֥וֹלֶד בָּנִ֖ים
כ וּבָנֽוֹת: וַיְחִ֣י רְע֔וּ שְׁתַּ֥יִם וּשְׁלֹשִׁ֖ים שָׁנָ֑ה וַיּ֖וֹלֶד אֶת־שְׂרֽוּג:
כא וַיְחִ֣י רְע֗וּ אַֽחֲרֵי֙ הוֹלִיד֣וֹ אֶת־שְׂר֔וּג שֶׁ֥בַע שָׁנִ֖ים וּמָאתַ֣יִם שָׁנָ֑ה וַיּ֥וֹלֶד בָּנִ֖ים
כב־כג וּבָנֽוֹת: וַיְחִ֣י שְׂר֔וּג שְׁלֹשִׁ֖ים שָׁנָ֑ה וַיּ֖וֹלֶד אֶת־נָחֽוֹר: וַיְחִ֣י שְׂר֗וּג
כד אַֽחֲרֵי֙ הוֹלִיד֣וֹ אֶת־נָח֔וֹר מָאתַ֖יִם שָׁנָ֑ה וַיּ֥וֹלֶד בָּנִ֖ים וּבָנֽוֹת: וַיְחִ֣י
כה נָח֔וֹר תֵּ֥שַׁע וְעֶשְׂרִ֖ים שָׁנָ֑ה וַיּ֖וֹלֶד אֶת־תָּֽרַח: וַיְחִ֣י נָח֗וֹר אַֽחֲרֵי֙ הוֹלִיד֣וֹ אֶת־
כו תֶּ֔רַח תְּשַֽׁע־עֶשְׂרֵ֥ה שָׁנָ֖ה וּמְאַ֣ת שָׁנָ֑ה וַיּ֥וֹלֶד בָּנִ֖ים וּבָנֽוֹת: וַֽיְחִי־
כז תֶ֖רַח שִׁבְעִ֣ים שָׁנָ֑ה וַיּ֙וֹלֶד֙ אֶת־אַבְרָ֔ם אֶת־נָח֖וֹר וְאֶת־הָרָֽן: וְאֵ֙לֶּה֙ תּֽוֹלְדֹ֣ת
תֶּ֔רַח תֶּ֚רַח הוֹלִ֣יד אֶת־אַבְרָ֔ם אֶת־נָח֖וֹר וְאֶת־הָרָ֑ן וְהָרָ֖ן הוֹלִ֥יד אֶת־
כח ל֑וֹט: וַיָּ֣מָת הָרָ֗ן עַל־פְּנֵי֙ תֶּ֣רַח אָבִ֔יו בְּאֶ֖רֶץ מֽוֹלַדְתּ֑וֹ בְּא֖וּר כַּשְׂדִּֽים:
כט וַיִּקַּ֨ח אַבְרָ֧ם וְנָח֛וֹר לָהֶ֖ם נָשִׁ֑ים שֵׁ֤ם אֵֽשֶׁת־אַבְרָם֙ שָׂרָ֔י וְשֵׁ֤ם אֵֽשֶׁת־נָחוֹר֙
ל מִלְכָּ֔ה בַּת־הָרָ֥ן אֲבִֽי־מִלְכָּ֖ה וַֽאֲבִ֣י יִסְכָּֽה: וַתְּהִ֥י שָׂרַ֖י עֲקָרָ֑ה אֵ֥ין לָ֖הּ וָלָֽד:
לא וַיִּקַּ֨ח תֶּ֜רַח אֶת־אַבְרָ֣ם בְּנ֗וֹ וְאֶת־ל֤וֹט בֶּן־הָרָן֙ בֶּן־בְּנ֔וֹ וְאֵת֙ שָׂרַ֣י כַּלָּת֔וֹ
אֵ֖שֶׁת אַבְרָ֣ם בְּנ֑וֹ וַיֵּֽצְא֨וּ אִתָּ֜ם מֵא֣וּר כַּשְׂדִּ֗ים לָלֶ֨כֶת֙ אַ֣רְצָה כְּנַ֔עַן וַיָּבֹ֥אוּ
לב עַד־חָרָ֖ן וַיֵּ֣שְׁבוּ שָֽׁם: וַיִּֽהְי֣וּ יְמֵי־תֶ֗רַח חָמֵ֧שׁ שָׁנִ֛ים וּמָאתַ֥יִם שָׁנָ֑ה וַיָּ֥מָת תֶּ֖רַח
בְּחָרָֽן:

מפטיר

---

generations from Adam to Noah. (The reason is) that they all died prior to the major historical event of that era, namely, the Flood. These generations, however, were all still alive when the major historical event began, i.e., when Abraham our father, more so than all the righteous ones of the previous generations, endeavored to call in the Name of Hashem, לְהוֹדִיעַ לִבְנֵי הָאָדָם גְּבוּרֹתָיו וּכְבוֹד הֲדַר מַלְכוּתוֹ, *to make His mighty acts known among men, and the majestic glory of His kingship* (Psalms 145:12), and to draw them with cords of loving-kindness, to serve Him with one accord.

31. לָלֶכֶת אַרְצָה כְּנַעַן — *To go to the land of Canaan.* (This land) was predisposed to bring about intellectual elevation, and was more desirable (spiritually) than all other lands, as it says, אֶרֶץ אֲשֶׁר ה' אֱלֹהֶיךָ דֹּרֵשׁ אֹתָהּ, *A land which* HASHEM *your God cares for* (Deut. 11:12). Its climate had not been adversely affected by the Flood's rains as was that of other lands, as it says, לֹא גֻשְׁמָה בְּיוֹם זָעַם, *not to be washed with rain on the day of indignation* (Ezekiel 22:24), and our Sages (also) have said, "The air of *Eretz Yisrael* makes one wise" (*Bava Basra* 158b).

NOTES

daughters. See the explanatory note to 9:29. The expression *cords of loving-kindness* is derived from *Hosea* 11:4 and that of *one accord* from *Zephaniah* 3:9.

31-32. לָלֶכֶת אַרְצָה כְּנַעַן — *To go to the land of Canaan.* Terach senses that the land of Canaan represented the potential for spiritual excellence and a place which could cause revolutionary change in the

13 *And Arpachshad lived four hundred three years after begetting Shelah; and he begot sons and daughters.*
14 *Shelah had lived thirty years when he begot Eber.* 15 *And Shelah lived four hundred and three years after begetting Eber, and begot sons and daughters.*
16 *When Eber had lived thirty-four years, he begot Peleg.* 17 *And Eber lived four hundred and thirty years after begetting Peleg, and he begot sons and daughters.*
18 *When Peleg had lived thirty years, he begot Reu.* 19 *And Peleg lived two hundred and nine years after begetting Reu, and he begot sons and daughters.*
20 *When Reu had lived thirty-two years, he begot Serug.* 21 *And Reu lived two hundred and seven years after begetting Serug, and he begot sons and daughters.*
22 *When Serug had lived thirty years, he begot Nahor.* 23 *And Serug lived two hundred years after begetting Nahor, and he begot sons and daughters.*
24 *When Nahor had lived twenty-nine years, he begot Terah.* 25 *And Nahor lived one hundred nineteen years after begetting Terah, and he begot sons and daughters.*
26 *When Terah had lived seventy years, he begot Abram, Nahor, and Haran.*
27 *Now these are the chronicles of Terah: Terah begot Abram, Nahor, and Haran; and Haran begot Lot.* 28 *Haran died in the lifetime of Terah his father, in his native land, in Ur Kasdim.* 29 *And Abram and Nahor took themselves wives; the name of Abram's wife was Sarai, and the name of Nahor's wife was Milcah, the daughter of Haran, the father of Milcah and the father of Iscah.* 30 *And Sarai was barren, she had no child.*
31 *Terah took his son Abram, and Lot the son of Haran, his grandson, and his daughter-in-law Sarai, the wife of Abram his son, and they departed with them from Ur Kasdim to go to the land of Canaan; they arrived at Haran and they settled there.*
32 *The days of Terah were two hundred and five years, and Terah died in Haran.*

---

32. וַיָּמָת תֶּרַח בְּחָרָן — *And Terach died in Charan.* And he did not endeavor to achieve what he intended to achieve by journeying from Ur Casdim, (nor) did he come, at all, to (visit) Abraham when he lived in the land of Canaan, calling there *in the name of* HASHEM and (even when) his reputation became widespread. The reverse of this was done by Lot, who for a time (did accompany Abraham) and therefore he and his descendants merited to (share) a portion of Abraham's gifts, whereas the other offspring of Terach, who were as closely related to Abraham, if not more so, did not merit (to share in these gifts).

NOTES

history of mankind. He sets out to go there but never reaches his destination. His son Abraham, however, is destined to realize Terach's dream. Strangely, once Terach's initial plan is frustrated, he loses all desire to go to that special land, even after his son has become "a prince" in the land and his fame as teacher and man of righteousness has spread far and wide. The fact that Lot, of all Abraham's family, does accompany Abraham, is most commendable, and as a result he is rewarded with wealth, while his offspring, Ammon and Moab, are granted an inheritance of the land that was once Canaan.

פרשת לך לך

יב א וַיֹּאמֶר יהוה אֶל־אַבְרָם לֶךְ־לְךָ מֵאַרְצְךָ וּמִמּוֹלַדְתְּךָ וּמִבֵּית אָבִיךָ
ב אֶל־הָאָרֶץ אֲשֶׁר אַרְאֶךָּ: וְאֶעֶשְׂךָ לְגוֹי גָּדוֹל וַאֲבָרֶכְךָ וַאֲגַדְּלָה שְׁמֶךָ
ג וֶהְיֵה בְּרָכָה: וַאֲבָרְכָה מְבָרְכֶיךָ וּמְקַלֶּלְךָ אָאֹר וְנִבְרְכוּ בְךָ כֹּל מִשְׁפְּחֹת
ד הָאֲדָמָה: וַיֵּלֶךְ אַבְרָם כַּאֲשֶׁר דִּבֶּר אֵלָיו יהוה וַיֵּלֶךְ אִתּוֹ לוֹט וְאַבְרָם
ה בֶּן־חָמֵשׁ שָׁנִים וְשִׁבְעִים שָׁנָה בְּצֵאתוֹ מֵחָרָן: וַיִּקַּח אַבְרָם אֶת־שָׂרַי
אִשְׁתּוֹ וְאֶת־לוֹט בֶּן־אָחִיו וְאֶת־כָּל־רְכוּשָׁם אֲשֶׁר רָכָשׁוּ וְאֶת־הַנֶּפֶשׁ
ו אֲשֶׁר־עָשׂוּ בְחָרָן וַיֵּצְאוּ לָלֶכֶת אַרְצָה כְּנַעַן וַיָּבֹאוּ אַרְצָה כְּנָעַן: וַיַּעֲבֹר
ז אַבְרָם בָּאָרֶץ עַד מְקוֹם שְׁכֶם עַד אֵלוֹן מוֹרֶה וְהַכְּנַעֲנִי אָז בָּאָרֶץ: וַיֵּרָא
יהוה אֶל־אַבְרָם וַיֹּאמֶר לְזַרְעֲךָ אֶתֵּן אֶת־הָאָרֶץ הַזֹּאת וַיִּבֶן שָׁם מִזְבֵּחַ
ח לַיהוה הַנִּרְאֶה אֵלָיו: וַיַּעְתֵּק מִשָּׁם הָהָרָה מִקֶּדֶם לְבֵית־אֵל וַיֵּט אָהֳלֹה
בֵּית־אֵל מִיָּם וְהָעַי מִקֶּדֶם וַיִּבֶן־שָׁם מִזְבֵּחַ לַיהוה וַיִּקְרָא בְּשֵׁם יהוה:
ט וַיִּסַּע אַבְרָם הָלוֹךְ וְנָסוֹעַ הַנֶּגְבָּה:
י וַיְהִי רָעָב בָּאָרֶץ וַיֵּרֶד אַבְרָם מִצְרַיְמָה לָגוּר שָׁם כִּי־כָבֵד הָרָעָב בָּאָרֶץ:
יא וַיְהִי כַּאֲשֶׁר הִקְרִיב לָבוֹא מִצְרָיְמָה וַיֹּאמֶר אֶל־שָׂרַי אִשְׁתּוֹ הִנֵּה־נָא

XII

1. אֶל הָאָרֶץ אֲשֶׁר אַרְאֶךָּ — *To the land that I will show you* . . . to a particular place in the land which I will show to you through a Godly vision. He therefore passed through the land but did not pitch his tent until (he came to the) place where God appeared to him, as it says, *Abram passed onto the land as far as the site of Shechem . . . HASHEM appeared to Abram and said, "To your offspring I will give this land"* (verses 6-7).

2. וֶהְיֵה בְּרָכָה — *And you shall be a blessing.* The blessing of God is that He should rejoice in His creation, as our Sages have said, יִשְׁמָעֵאל בְּנִי בָּרְכֵנִי, אָמַרְתִּי לוֹ: יְהִי רָצוֹן מִלְּפָנֶיךָ . . . וְיָגֹלּוּ רַחֲמֶיךָ עַל מִדּוֹתֶיךָ, "(God said to me,) *'Ishmael, My son, bless Me.' I replied, 'May it be Your will . . . and Your mercy may prevail over Your other attributes'* " (*Berachos* 7a). Therefore He (God) says, "Become a blessing to Me by (your) deep understanding (whereby) you will acquire perfection, and teach knowledge (of God) to the people."

5. וַיֵּצְאוּ לָלֶכֶת אַרְצָה כְּנַעַן — *And they embarked for the land of Canaan* . . . which was widely known to them as a land conducive to deep understanding and service of God, the Blessed One.

וַיָּבֹאוּ אַרְצָה כְּנָעַן — *And they came to the land of Canaan* . . . unlike Terach's departure *to go to the land of Canaan* (11:31) when he only came as far as Charan.

NOTES

XII

1. אֶל הָאָרֶץ אֲשֶׁר אַרְאֶךָּ – *To the land that I will show you.* Terach, Abram's father, had set out from Ur Kasdim to go to the land of Canaan because people already knew that this land was conducive to spiritual and intellectual elevation and excellence (see the *Sforno* 11:31). Hence, the Almighty's command to Abram, *to the land that I will show you,* cannot mean that the land was unknown to Abram at the time he set out on his journey. Therefore, the *Sforno* interprets this phrase to mean a particular place in Canaan, which God would *show to him.* Only when this place was revealed to Abram by God would he pitch his tent there.

2. וֶהְיֵה בְּרָכָה – *And you shall be a blessing.* Many find it difficult to comprehend a "blessing" as applied to God. Still we see from the Talmudic statement (*Berachos* 7a), cited by the *Sforno* in this verse, that the Almighty asks to be blessed! The

PARASHAS LECH LECHA

12 *[1]HASHEM said to Abram, "Go for yourself from your land, from your
relatives, and from your father's house to the land that I will show
you. [2]And I will make of you a great nation; I will bless you, and make
your name great, and you shall be a blessing. [3]I will bless those who bless
you, and him who curses you I will curse; and all the families of the earth
shall bless themselves by you."*

*[4] So Abram went as HASHEM had spoken to him, and Lot went with
him; Abram was seventy-five years old when he left Haran. [5] Abram
took his wife Sarai and Lot, his brother's son, and all their wealth that
they had amassed, and the souls they made in Haran; and they left to go
to the land of Canaan, and they came to the land of Canaan. [6] Abram
passed into the land as far as the site of Shechem, until the Plain of Moreh.
The Canaanite was then in the land.*

*[7] HASHEM appeared to Abram and said, "To your offspring I will give
this land." So he built an altar there to HASHEM Who appeared to him.
[8] From there he relocated to the mountain east of Beth-el and pitched his
tent, with Beth-el on the west and Ai on the east; and he built there an
altar to HASHEM and invoked HASHEM by Name. [9] Then Abram journeyed
on, journeying steadily toward the south.*

*[10] There was a famine in the land, and Abram descended to Egypt
to sojourn there, for the famine was severe in the land. [11] And it occurred, as he was about to enter Egypt, he said to his wife Sarai, "See now,*

---

6. וַיַּעֲבֹר אַבְרָם בָּאָרֶץ — *Abram passed into the land.* He did not stop (for any period) in any one place until God, the Blessed One, appeared to him as He had instructed him when He said, *"To the land that I will show you."*

8. בֵּית אֵל מִיָּם וְהָעַי מִקֶּדֶם — *Beth-el on the west and Ai on the east* ... between two large cities, so that many people would come to listen when he called in the name of *HASHEM*.

9. הָלוֹךְ וְנָסוֹעַ הַנֶּגְבָּה — *Journeying steadily toward the south.* As he journeyed from place to place, as is the custom of shepherds, he did not turn eastward or westward so as not to turn away from these two cities (Beth-el and Ai) because a number of its inhabitants had begun to follow him.

10. לָגוּר שָׁם — *To sojourn there* ... but not to settle there permanently.

11. כַּאֲשֶׁר הִקְרִיב — *As he came near* ... close to the necessary time (of arrival) lest she forget (his instructions).

לָבוֹא מִצְרָיְמָה — *To enter Egypt.* Egypt was a place known for its immorality, as it is said of them, אֲשֶׁר בְּשַׂר חֲמוֹרִים בְּשָׂרָם וְזִרְמַת סוּסִים זִרְמָתָם, *Whose flesh is as the flesh of asses, and whose issue is like the issue of horses* (*Ezekiel* 23:20).

NOTES

Sforno, therefore, interprets this to mean that God's greatest "desire" is to rejoice in His creation and above all with mankind. When this happens He is "blessed." This concept is established here in the phrase וֶהְיֵה בְּרָכָה, and is repeated again in 14:20, 28:4, and a number of other places.

5. וַיָּבֹאוּ אַרְצָה כְּנָעַן – *And they came to the land of Canaan.* These three Hebrew words are missing from 11:31. They are the key words which differentiate Abram's journey from his father's.

6. וַיַּעֲבֹר אַבְרָם בָּאָרֶץ – *Abram passed into the land.* See note on verse 1.

יב יָדַעְתִּי כִּי אִשָּׁה יְפַת־מַרְאֶה אָתְּ: וְהָיָה כִּי־יִרְאוּ אֹתָךְ הַמִּצְרִים וְאָמְרוּ
יג אִשְׁתּוֹ זֹאת וְהָרְגוּ אֹתִי וְאֹתָךְ יְחַיּוּ: אִמְרִי־נָא אֲחֹתִי אָתְּ לְמַעַן יִיטַב־לִי
שני יד בַעֲבוּרֵךְ וְחָיְתָה נַפְשִׁי בִּגְלָלֵךְ: וַיְהִי כְּבוֹא אַבְרָם מִצְרָיְמָה וַיִּרְאוּ
טו הַמִּצְרִים אֶת־הָאִשָּׁה כִּי־יָפָה הִוא מְאֹד: וַיִּרְאוּ אֹתָהּ שָׂרֵי פַרְעֹה וַיְהַלְלוּ
טז אֹתָהּ אֶל־פַּרְעֹה וַתֻּקַּח הָאִשָּׁה בֵּית פַּרְעֹה: וּלְאַבְרָם הֵיטִיב בַּעֲבוּרָהּ
יז וַיְהִי־לוֹ צֹאן־וּבָקָר וַחֲמֹרִים וַעֲבָדִים וּשְׁפָחֹת וַאֲתֹנֹת וּגְמַלִּים: וַיְנַגַּע יהוה ׀
יח אֶת־פַּרְעֹה נְגָעִים גְּדֹלִים וְאֶת־בֵּיתוֹ עַל־דְּבַר שָׂרַי אֵשֶׁת אַבְרָם: וַיִּקְרָא
פַרְעֹה לְאַבְרָם וַיֹּאמֶר מַה־זֹּאת עָשִׂיתָ לִּי לָמָּה לֹא־הִגַּדְתָּ לִּי כִּי אִשְׁתְּךָ
יט הִוא: לָמָה אָמַרְתָּ אֲחֹתִי הִוא וָאֶקַּח אֹתָהּ לִי לְאִשָּׁה וְעַתָּה הִנֵּה אִשְׁתְּךָ
כ קַח וָלֵךְ: וַיְצַו עָלָיו פַּרְעֹה אֲנָשִׁים וַיְשַׁלְּחוּ אֹתוֹ וְאֶת־אִשְׁתּוֹ וְאֶת־כָּל־
יג א אֲשֶׁר־לוֹ: וַיַּעַל אַבְרָם מִמִּצְרַיִם הוּא וְאִשְׁתּוֹ וְכָל־אֲשֶׁר־לוֹ וְלוֹט עִמּוֹ
ב־ג הַנֶּגְבָּה: וְאַבְרָם כָּבֵד מְאֹד בַּמִּקְנֶה בַּכֶּסֶף וּבַזָּהָב: וַיֵּלֶךְ לְמַסָּעָיו מִנֶּגֶב

12. וְהָרְגוּ אֹתִי — *Then they will kill me* ... for they cannot hope that I would consent to give you to them.

13. לְמַעַן יִיטַב לִי — *That it may go well with me.* When you will tell them that you are my sister, each one will have hopes of marrying you (with my consent), thereby preventing them from killing me. (On the contrary) it will go well for me as a result of the dowry and gifts (they will give to me), as was the custom at that time, to induce the father of the bride through a dowry and the (bride's) relatives through gifts, to gain their consent to give her in marriage to her suitor. As the Torah tells us, מָהֹר יִמְהָרֶנָּה, *he shall surely pay a dowry* ... אִם מָאֵן יְמָאֵן אָבִיהָ ... כֶּסֶף יִשְׁקֹל, *if her father utterly refuses (to give her) he shall pay money (according to the dowry of virgins)* (Exodus 22:15,16). In the interim, Abram thought, he (and Sarai) would depart from there.

14. וַיִּרְאוּ הַמִּצְרִים — *The Egyptians saw.* As Abram had foreseen, they all gazed at her (beauty, and were attracted to her).

15. וַיִּרְאוּ אֹתָהּ שָׂרֵי פַרְעֹה — *The officials of Pharaoh saw her.* And thwarted the plans of the masses (to take Sarai).

וַתֻּקַּח הָאִשָּׁה — *And the woman was taken* ...

16. וּלְאַבְרָם הֵיטִיב — *And Abram was treated well.* Contrary to the accepted custom, they did not consult with (Abram) first or attempt to induce him (to agree to the match) for they thought it was unnecessary, since it was the king who was marrying her. Now since she claimed to be Abram's sister and marriageable, there could certainly be no better match for her than the king, as he himself attested when he said, "*So that I would take her as my wife*" (verse 19). Therefore, they brought her to the king first, and afterwards the king treated (Abram) well, on her behalf, by giving a dowry and gift, as was the custom.

צֹאן וּבָקָר ... וַעֲבָדִים — *Sheep, oxen ... slaves.* Many ... as befits a king.

NOTES

13. לְמַעַן יִיטַב לִי – *That it may go well with me.* This concluding comment of the *Sforno* explains how Abram, who rejects riches offered to him by man (see his response to the king of Sodom 14:23), can allow himself to say לְמַעַן יִיטַב לִי, *that it may go well with me.* As the *Sforno* sees it, this was only a strategy to forestall an overt act of force to take Sarai, by having her "brother" negotiate for an acceptable dowry, thereby buying time, in the hope that they would be able to leave before anything happened to them. This plan was only effective, however, when dealing with the people, but not with Pharaoh, who took her first and negotiated later (see verses 15-16).

I have known that you are a woman of beautiful appearance. [12] *And it shall occur, when the Egyptians will see you, they will say, 'This is his wife!'; then they will kill me, but you they will let live.* [13] *Please say that you are my sister, that it may go well with me for your sake, and that I may live on account of you."*

[14] *But it occurred, with Abram's coming to Egypt, the Egyptians saw that the woman was very beautiful.* [15] *When the officials of Pharaoh saw her, they lauded her for Pharaoh, and the woman was taken to Pharaoh's house.* [16] *And he treated Abram well for her sake, and he acquired sheep, cattle, donkeys, slaves and maidservants, female donkeys, and camels.*

[17] *But* HASHEM *afflicted Pharaoh along with his household with severe plagues because of the matter of Sarai, the wife of Abram.* [18] *Pharaoh summoned Abram and said, "What is this you have done to me? Why did you not tell me that she is your wife?* [19] *Why did you say, 'She is my sister,' so that I would take her as my wife? Now, here is your wife; take her and go!"* [20] *So Pharaoh gave men orders concerning him, and they escorted him and his wife and all that was his.*

13 [1] *So Abram went up from Egypt, he with his wife and all that was his — and Lot with him — to the south.* [2] *Now Abram was very laden with livestock, silver, and gold.* [3] *He proceeded on his journeys from the south*

17. וַיְנַגַּע ה׳ אֶת פַּרְעֹה נְגָעִים גְּדֹלִים — *HASHEM afflicted Pharaoh with severe plagues.* Only Pharaoh (was afflicted) with "severe plagues."

וְאֶת בֵּיתוֹ — *Along with his household.* His household was also afflicted with plagues, but not as severe as those of Pharaoh's. This demonstrated that only this pious woman (Sarai) was saved (from the plagues) so that all would recognize that this plague was brought on her account, and (hopefully) they would repent of their evil.

18. לָמָּה לֹא הִגַּדְתָּ לִּי — *Why didn't you tell me?* For even if you suspected the masses, you should not have suspected the king who establishes justice in the land (of harming you).

19. לָמָה אָמַרְתָּ אֲחֹתִי הִוא — *Why did you say, 'She is my sister'?* (You said this) even after she was brought to my palace.

וָאֶקַּח אֹתָהּ לִי לְאִשָּׁה — *So that I would take her as my wife . . .* not as a concubine! (True) I did it without your permission, (but that was) because I thought you would be pleased to have your sister marry the king.

XIII

2. וְאַבְרָם כָּבֵד מְאֹד בַּמִּקְנֶה — *Now, Abram was very laden with cattle.* He was forced to lead (his flocks) slowly even though he was anxious to return quickly to the place of (his) altar, in that place to understand (God) and teach (others) as before. Therefore . . .

3. וַיֵּלֶךְ לְמַסָּעָיו — *He proceeded on his journeys.* A shepherd's journey, traveling from place to place; leaving the first place (for a second) when the pasture was exhausted.

NOTES

17. וַיְנַגַּע ה׳ אֶת פַּרְעֹה נְגָעִים גְּדֹלִים — *HASHEM afflicted Pharaoh with severe plagues.* The reason the *Sforno* interprets the word גְּדֹלִים, *severe,* as referring only to Pharaoh is because if it is an adjective describing נְגָעִים, *plagues,* the words נְגָעִים גְּדֹלִים, *severe plagues,* should be placed after וְאֶת בֵּיתוֹ, *and his household,* not following פַּרְעֹה. This then indicates that *severe* plagues refers *only* to Pharaoh.

וְעַד־בֵּית־אֵל עַד־הַמָּקוֹם אֲשֶׁר־הָיָה שָׁם אָהֳלֹה בַּתְּחִלָּה בֵּין בֵּית־אֵל
ד וּבֵין הָעָי׃ אֶל־מְקוֹם הַמִּזְבֵּחַ אֲשֶׁר־עָשָׂה שָׁם בָּרִאשֹׁנָה וַיִּקְרָא שָׁם
שלישי ה אַבְרָם בְּשֵׁם יהוה׃ וְגַם־לְלוֹט הַהֹלֵךְ אֶת־אַבְרָם הָיָה צֹאן־וּבָקָר
ו וְאֹהָלִים׃ וְלֹא־נָשָׂא אֹתָם הָאָרֶץ לָשֶׁבֶת יַחְדָּו כִּי־הָיָה רְכוּשָׁם רָב וְלֹא
ז יָכְלוּ לָשֶׁבֶת יַחְדָּו׃ וַיְהִי־רִיב בֵּין רֹעֵי מִקְנֵה־אַבְרָם וּבֵין רֹעֵי מִקְנֵה־לוֹט
ח וְהַכְּנַעֲנִי וְהַפְּרִזִּי אָז יֹשֵׁב בָּאָרֶץ׃ וַיֹּאמֶר אַבְרָם אֶל־לוֹט אַל־נָא תְהִי
ט מְרִיבָה בֵּינִי וּבֵינֶךָ וּבֵין רֹעַי וּבֵין רֹעֶיךָ כִּי־אֲנָשִׁים אַחִים אֲנָחְנוּ׃ הֲלֹא
כָל־הָאָרֶץ לְפָנֶיךָ הִפָּרֶד נָא מֵעָלָי אִם־הַשְּׂמֹאל וְאֵימִנָה וְאִם־הַיָּמִין
י וְאַשְׂמְאִילָה׃ וַיִּשָּׂא־לוֹט אֶת־עֵינָיו וַיַּרְא אֶת־כָּל־כִּכַּר הַיַּרְדֵּן כִּי כֻלָּהּ
מַשְׁקֶה לִפְנֵי ׀ שַׁחֵת יהוה אֶת־סְדֹם וְאֶת־עֲמֹרָה כְּגַן־יהוה כְּאֶרֶץ מִצְרַיִם
יא בֹּאֲכָה צֹעַר׃ וַיִּבְחַר־לוֹ לוֹט אֵת כָּל־כִּכַּר הַיַּרְדֵּן וַיִּסַּע לוֹט מִקֶּדֶם
יב וַיִּפָּרְדוּ אִישׁ מֵעַל אָחִיו׃ אַבְרָם יָשַׁב בְּאֶרֶץ־כְּנָעַן וְלוֹט יָשַׁב בְּעָרֵי
יג הַכִּכָּר וַיֶּאֱהַל עַד־סְדֹם׃ וְאַנְשֵׁי סְדֹם רָעִים וְחַטָּאִים לַיהוה מְאֹד׃

6. וְלֹא נָשָׂא אֹתָם הָאָרֶץ — *And the land could not support them.* There was insufficient pasture for both, therefore . . .

7. וַיְהִי רִיב בֵּין רֹעֵי מִקְנֵה אַבְרָם וּבֵין רֹעֵי מִקְנֵה לוֹט — *And there was quarreling between the herdsmen of Abram's flocks and the herdsmen of Lot's flocks.* The quarrel was to see who would be forced out by whom from the pasture available.

וְהַכְּנַעֲנִי וְהַפְּרִזִּי אָז יֹשֵׁב בָּאָרֶץ — *And the Canaanite and the Perizzite were then dwelling in the land.* The quarrel between two relatives who were strangers in the land was odious in the eyes of the native dwellers who would consider them as argumentative men, and would assume that if they quarrel among themselves how much more so will they quarrel with the native dwellers.

8. אַל נָא תְהִי מְרִיבָה בֵּינִי וּבֵינֶךָ — *Please let there be no quarrel between me and you . . .* in the future, when one chooses a piece of ground for pasture which the other also wants.

וּבֵין רֹעַי וּבֵין רֹעֶיךָ — *And between my herdsmen and your herdsmen . . .* also now, while we are still here together.

9. הֲלֹא כָל הָאָרֶץ לְפָנֶיךָ — *Is not all the land before you?* You can choose the place you want, therefore . . .

הִפָּרֶד נָא מֵעָלָי — *Please separate from me.* You separate yourself to the side you choose, and I will journey in the opposite direction.

NOTES

XIII

7. וְהַכְּנַעֲנִי וְהַפְּרִזִּי אָז יֹשֵׁב בָּאָרֶץ — *And the Canaanite and the Perizzite were then dwelling in the land.* This phrase is seemingly added to this verse unnecessarily. The commentators suggest various explanations. The *Sforno* offers his interpretation, that since Abram and Lot were dwelling in the midst of other people, who were in the majority, the quarrel between them would expose them to the contempt and eventual enmity of the inhabitants of the land.

8. אַל נָא תְהִי מְרִיבָה בֵּינִי וּבֵינֶךָ — *Let there be no quarrel between me and you . . .* The argument was between the herdsmen, not Lot and Abram. Why then does Abram say *between me and you*? The answer is that he is anticipating a future argument, which he would like to avoid.

9. הֲלֹא כָל הָאָרֶץ לְפָנֶיךָ — *Is not all the land before you?* Neither Abram or Lot had a legal claim to the land at that time — hence the suggestion, made by Abram, that each choose a place for their flocks and herds to graze, could only apply to the accepted right of nomadic shepherds to seek out pastureland. That is why the *Sforno* stresses here "to seek out pasture," and in verse 11 explains that the agreement between Lot and Abram was regarding the exclusive right to seek out pasture

to Beth-el to the place where his tent had been at first, between Beth-el and Ai, [4] to the site of the altar which he had erected there at first; and there Abram invoked HASHEM *by Name.*

[5] *Also Lot who went with Abram had flocks, cattle, and tents.* [6] *And the land could not support them dwelling together for their possessions were abundant and they were unable to dwell together.* [7] *And there was quarreling between the herdsmen of Abram's livestock and the herdsmen of Lot's livestock — and the Canaanite and the Perizzite were then dwelling in the land.*

[8] *So Abram said to Lot: "Please let there be no strife between me and you, and between my herdsmen and your herdsmen, for we are kinsmen.* [9] *Is not all the land before you? Please separate from me: If you go left then I will go right, and if you go right then I will go left."* [10] *So Lot raised his eyes and saw the entire plain of the Jordan that it was well watered everywhere — before* HASHEM *destroyed Sodom and Gomorrah —like the garden of* HASHEM, *like the land of Egypt, going toward Zoar.* [11] *So Lot chose for himself the whole plain of the Jordan, and Lot journeyed from the east; thus they parted, one from his brother.*

[12] *Abram dwelled in the land of Canaan while Lot dwelled in the cities of the plain and pitched tents as far as Sodom.* [13] *Now the people of Sodom were wicked and sinful toward* HASHEM, *exceedingly.*

אִם הַשְּׂמֹאל — *If you go left.* If you choose to seek out pasture on the left.

וְאֵימְנָה – *Then I will go right.* I will seek on the right.

11. וַיִּבְחַר לוֹ לוֹט אֵת כָּל כִּכַּר הַיַּרְדֵּן — *So Lot chose for himself the whole plain of the Jordan.* He chose a place where only he and his herdsmen would have the right to seek out pasture, while Abram and his herdsmen would not be permitted to do so.

וַיִּסַּע לוֹט מִקֶּדֶם — *And Lot journeyed from the east.* He did not turn to the right or the left, which would have been the north or south, but he journeyed from east to west, so as to distance himself from Abram whose dwelling place was in eastern *Eretz Yisrael* close to Ai. (This is) where the tribes came up into the land initially, upon crossing over from the east of the Jordan.

וַיִּפָּרְדוּ אִישׁ מֵעַל אָחִיו — *And they parted, one from another* not only insofar as pasture, but also (insofar as) their dwelling places.

12. אַבְרָם יָשַׁב בְּאֶרֶץ כְּנָעַן — *Abram remained in the land of Canaan.* Although Sodom and its neighboring towns were also part of Canaan, nevertheless its inhabitants at that time were not Canaanites. (The Torah tells us) Abram chose to dwell in that part of the land where the Canaanites lived, since they were not as wicked as the Sodomites; and (Abram) did not come close to the environs of Sodom.

NOTES

in a given area.

11. וַיִּסַּע לוֹט מִקֶּדֶם – *And Lot journeyed from the east.* When Abram and Lot discussed their decision to separate, they were in the east facing westward. Right would then be north, and left would be south. Lot, however, chose neither direction and opted instead to journey west, which the Torah interprets as being motivated by Lot's desire to distance himself from Abram *totally,* not only regarding the issue of pasture, but a separation in spirit as well.

12. אַבְרָם יָשַׁב בְּאֶרֶץ כְּנָעַן – *Abram remained in the land of Canaan.* The expression *Abram remained in . . . Canaan* implies that Lot did not. However, this is not so since Sodom is also part of Canaan. The answer must perforce be that the Torah is

יד וַיהֹוָ֞ה אָמַ֣ר אֶל־אַבְרָ֗ם אַחֲרֵי֙ הִפָּֽרֶד־ל֣וֹט מֵֽעִמּ֔וֹ שָׂא־נָ֤א עֵינֶ֙יךָ֙ וּרְאֵ֔ה
טו מִן־הַמָּק֖וֹם אֲשֶׁר־אַתָּ֣ה שָׁ֑ם צָפֹ֥נָה וָנֶ֖גְבָּה וָקֵ֥דְמָה וָיָֽמָּה׃ כִּ֧י אֶת־כָּל־
טז הָאָ֛רֶץ אֲשֶׁר־אַתָּ֥ה רֹאֶ֖ה לְךָ֣ אֶתְּנֶ֑נָּה וּֽלְזַרְעֲךָ֖ עַד־עוֹלָֽם׃ וְשַׂמְתִּ֥י
אֶֽת־זַרְעֲךָ֖ כַּעֲפַ֣ר הָאָ֑רֶץ אֲשֶׁ֣ר ׀ אִם־יוּכַ֣ל אִ֗ישׁ לִמְנוֹת֙ אֶת־עֲפַ֣ר הָאָ֔רֶץ
יז גַּ֥ם זַרְעֲךָ֖ יִמָּנֶֽה׃ ק֚וּם הִתְהַלֵּ֣ךְ בָּאָ֔רֶץ לְאָרְכָּ֖הּ וּלְרָחְבָּ֑הּ כִּ֥י לְךָ֖ אֶתְּנֶֽנָּה׃
יח וַיֶּאֱהַ֣ל אַבְרָ֗ם וַיָּבֹ֛א וַיֵּ֛שֶׁב בְּאֵלֹנֵ֥י מַמְרֵ֖א אֲשֶׁ֣ר בְּחֶבְר֑וֹן וַיִּֽבֶן־שָׁ֥ם מִזְבֵּ֖חַ
לַֽיהֹוָֽה׃

יד רביעי א וַיְהִ֗י בִּימֵ֤י אַמְרָפֶל֙ מֶֽלֶךְ־שִׁנְעָ֔ר אַרְי֖וֹךְ מֶ֣לֶךְ אֶלָּסָ֑ר כְּדָרְלָעֹ֙מֶר֙ מֶ֣לֶךְ
ב עֵילָ֔ם וְתִדְעָ֖ל מֶ֥לֶךְ גּוֹיִֽם׃ עָשׂ֣וּ מִלְחָמָ֗ה אֶת־בֶּ֙רַע֙ מֶ֣לֶךְ סְדֹ֔ם וְאֶת־בִּרְשַׁ֖ע
°צְבוֹיִם ק׳ מֶ֣לֶךְ עֲמֹרָ֑ה שִׁנְאָ֣ב ׀ מֶ֣לֶךְ אַדְמָ֗ה וְשֶׁמְאֵ֙בֶר֙ מֶ֣לֶךְ °צביים וּמֶ֥לֶךְ בֶּ֖לַע
ג-ד הִיא־צֹֽעַר׃ כָּל־אֵ֙לֶּה֙ חָֽבְר֔וּ אֶל־עֵ֖מֶק הַשִּׂדִּ֑ים ה֖וּא יָ֥ם הַמֶּֽלַח׃ שְׁתֵּ֤ים
ה עֶשְׂרֵה֙ שָׁנָ֔ה עָֽבְד֖וּ אֶת־כְּדָרְלָעֹ֑מֶר וּשְׁלֹשׁ־עֶשְׂרֵ֥ה שָׁנָ֖ה מָרָֽדוּ׃ וּבְאַרְבַּ֩ע
עֶשְׂרֵ֨ה שָׁנָ֜ה בָּ֣א כְדָרְלָעֹ֗מֶר וְהַמְּלָכִים֙ אֲשֶׁ֣ר אִתּ֔וֹ וַיַּכּ֤וּ אֶת־רְפָאִים֙
ו בְּעַשְׁתְּרֹ֣ת קַרְנַ֔יִם וְאֶת־הַזּוּזִ֖ים בְּהָ֑ם וְאֵת֙ הָֽאֵימִ֔ים בְּשָׁוֵ֖ה קִרְיָתָֽיִם׃ וְאֶת־
ז הַֽחֹרִ֖י בְּהַרְרָ֣ם שֵׂעִ֑יר עַ֚ד אֵ֣יל פָּארָ֔ן אֲשֶׁ֖ר עַל־הַמִּדְבָּֽר׃ וַיָּשֻׁ֜בוּ וַיָּבֹ֨אוּ
אֶל־עֵ֤ין מִשְׁפָּט֙ הִ֣וא קָדֵ֔שׁ וַיַּכּ֕וּ אֶֽת־כָּל־שְׂדֵ֖ה הָעֲמָלֵקִ֑י וְגַם֙ אֶת־הָ֣אֱמֹרִ֔י
ח הַיֹּשֵׁ֖ב בְּחַֽצְצֹ֥ן תָּמָֽר׃ וַיֵּצֵ֨א מֶֽלֶךְ־סְדֹ֜ם וּמֶ֣לֶךְ עֲמֹרָ֗ה וּמֶ֤לֶךְ אַדְמָה֙ וּמֶ֣לֶךְ
°צְבוֹיִם ק׳ ט °צביים וּמֶ֖לֶךְ בֶּ֣לַע הִוא־צֹ֑עַר וַיַּעַרְכ֤וּ אִתָּם֙ מִלְחָמָ֔ה בְּעֵ֖מֶק הַשִּׂדִּֽים׃ אֵ֣ת

---

14. אַחֲרֵי הִפָּרֶד לוֹט — *After Lot had parted.* This (renewed promise of the land) was not given while Lot was still with them, lest Lot and his herdsmen expropriate Abram's honored role and with arrogant pride be encouraged to rob (land for pasture).

17. לְךָ אֶתְּנֶנָּה — *To you will I give it.* Even in your days the inhabitants of the land will consider you as an honored prince of God.

18. וַיֶּאֱהַל אַבְרָם — *And Abram moved his tent.* He arranged the tents (for his) cattle here and there (on different sites).

וַיָּבֹא וַיֵּשֶׁב בְּאֵלֹנֵי מַמְרֵא — *And he came to dwell in the plains of Mamre . . .* and later he came and established his own dwelling place in the plains of Mamre.

XIV

1. וַיְהִי בִּימֵי אַמְרָפֶל מֶלֶךְ שִׁנְעָר — *And it happened in the days of Amraphel, king of Shinar.* He was a great, prominent king in that generation, as well as later. In his days, Arioch, Chedorlaomer and Tidal arose and waged war with Bera and his allies. Afterward . . .

NOTES

referring to the *residents* of the land, not the land per se.

14. אַחֲרֵי הִפָּרֶד לוֹט — *After Lot had parted. Rashi,* quoting the *Midrash,* tells us that Lot's herdsmen justified their grazing on other people's pastures, basing their right to do so on the fact that some day the land would belong to Lot as the only heir of Abram. Therefore, God does not renew His promise of the land to Abram while Lot is still with him, for then Lot's herdsmen would be encouraged all the more so to engage in the robbery of private pastures.

17. לְךָ אֶתְּנֶנָּה — *To you will I give it.* The expression, *to you will I give it,* implies that this will be fulfilled in Abram's lifetime. The *Sforno* therefore explains it to mean that Abram will gain recognition and honor from the inhabitants of Canaan.

XIV

1. וַיְהִי בִּימֵי אַמְרָפֶל מֶלֶךְ שִׁנְעָר — *And it happened*

[14] *HASHEM said to Abram after Lot had parted from him, "Raise now your eyes and look out from where you are: northward, southward, eastward and westward.* [15] *For all the land that you see, to you will I give it, and to your descendants forever.* [16] *I will make your offspring as the dust of the earth so that if one can count the dust of the earth, then your offspring, too, can be counted.* [17] *Arise, walk about the land through its length and breadth! For to you will I give it."* [18] *And Abram moved his tent and came and dwelled in the plains of Mamre which are in Hebron; and he built there an altar to HASHEM.*

14

[1] *And it happened in the days of Amraphel, king of Shinar; Arioch, king of Ellasar; Chedorlaomer, king of Elam, and Tidal, king of Goiim,* [2] *that these made war on Bera, king of Sodom; Birsha, king of Gomorrah; Shinab, king of Admah; Shemeber, king of Zeboiim; and the king of Bela, which is Zoar.* [3] *All these had joined at the Valley of Siddim, now the Salt Sea.* [4] *Twelve years they served Chedorlaomer, and they rebelled thirteen years.* [5] *In the fourteenth year, Chedorlaomer and the kings who were with him came and struck the Rephaim at Ashteroth-karnaim, the Zuzim in Ham, the Emim at Shaveh-kiriathaim;* [6] *and the Horites in their mountains of Seir, as far as the Plain of Paran which is by the desert.* [7] *Then they turned back and came to En-mishpat, which is Kadesh; they struck all the territory of the Amalekites; and also the Amorites who dwell in Hazazon-tamar.*

[8] *And the king of Sodom went forth with the king of Gomorrah, the king of Admah, the king of Zeboiim and the king of Bela, which is Zoar, and engaged them in battle in the Valley of Siddim:* [9] *With Chedorlaomer,*

3. כָּל אֵלֶּה — *All these* ... Amraphel and the two contending forces.

חָבְרוּ אֶל עֵמֶק הַשִּׂדִּים — *Joined in the Valley of Sidim* ... entering into an alliance (made a compromise) as a result of which the five kings who were losing the war ...

4. עָבְדוּ אֶת כְּדָרְלָעֹמֶר — *They served Chedorlaomer.* As a result of the compromise (treaty) they (served) for twelve years, and then rebelled.

5. וְהַמְּלָכִים אֲשֶׁר אִתּוֹ — *And the kings who were with him* ... those who had joined the alliance in the Valley of Sidim, among them being Amraphel.

וַיַּכּוּ אֶת רְפָאִים ... וְאֶת הַזּוּזִים ... וְאֵת הָאֵימִים — *And smote the Rephaim ... and the Zuzim ... and the Emim.* These all served the five kings and fought on their side. (The Torah) is telling us how great these five kings were, and how powerful were the four kings who defeated them. Now we can know (judge) the great might of Abram and his military skill, as well as the great kindness shown to his relative (Lot), by his willingness to sacrifice himself to overcome them (the four kings) so as to save his nephew and his possessions from them, wresting the prey from their jaws and achieving even more than he had hoped for, thanks to the mercy of God.

NOTES

in the days of Amraphel, king of Shinar. The episode related here involves many kings; still, the opening statement, setting the historical time frame, calls it בִּימֵי אַמְרָפֶל, *the days of Amraphel.* The reason given by the *Sforno* is that being the most prominent of all these leaders, this age is called by his name. Following this reasoning, the *Sforno* singles out Amraphel when he explains the compromise (alliance) in verse 3 and again in verse 5.

כְּדָרְלָעֹמֶר מֶלֶךְ עֵילָם וְתִדְעָל מֶלֶךְ גּוֹיִם וְאַמְרָפֶל מֶלֶךְ שִׁנְעָר וְאַרְיוֹךְ
י מֶלֶךְ אֶלָּסָר אַרְבָּעָה מְלָכִים אֶת־הַחֲמִשָּׁה: וְעֵמֶק הַשִּׂדִּים בֶּאֱרֹת בֶּאֱרֹת
יא חֵמָר וַיָּנֻסוּ מֶלֶךְ־סְדֹם וַעֲמֹרָה וַיִּפְּלוּ־שָׁמָּה וְהַנִּשְׁאָרִים הֶרָה נָּסוּ: וַיִּקְחוּ
יב אֶת־כָּל־רְכֻשׁ סְדֹם וַעֲמֹרָה וְאֶת־כָּל־אָכְלָם וַיֵּלֵכוּ: וַיִּקְחוּ אֶת־לוֹט
יג וְאֶת־רְכֻשׁוֹ בֶּן־אֲחִי אַבְרָם וַיֵּלֵכוּ וְהוּא יֹשֵׁב בִּסְדֹם: וַיָּבֹא הַפָּלִיט
וַיַּגֵּד לְאַבְרָם הָעִבְרִי וְהוּא שֹׁכֵן בְּאֵלֹנֵי מַמְרֵא הָאֱמֹרִי אֲחִי אֶשְׁכֹּל וַאֲחִי
יד עָנֵר וְהֵם בַּעֲלֵי בְרִית־אַבְרָם: וַיִּשְׁמַע אַבְרָם כִּי נִשְׁבָּה אָחִיו
וַיָּרֶק אֶת־חֲנִיכָיו יְלִידֵי בֵיתוֹ שְׁמֹנָה עָשָׂר וּשְׁלֹשׁ מֵאוֹת וַיִּרְדֹּף עַד־דָּן:
טו וַיֵּחָלֵק עֲלֵיהֶם ׀ לַיְלָה הוּא וַעֲבָדָיו וַיַּכֵּם וַיִּרְדְּפֵם עַד־חוֹבָה אֲשֶׁר
טז מִשְּׂמֹאל לְדַמָּשֶׂק: וַיָּשֶׁב אֵת כָּל־הָרְכֻשׁ וְגַם אֶת־לוֹט אָחִיו וּרְכֻשׁוֹ
יז הֵשִׁיב וְגַם אֶת־הַנָּשִׁים וְאֶת־הָעָם: וַיֵּצֵא מֶלֶךְ־סְדֹם לִקְרָאתוֹ אַחֲרֵי
שׁוּבוֹ מֵהַכּוֹת אֶת־כְּדָרְלָעֹמֶר וְאֶת־הַמְּלָכִים אֲשֶׁר אִתּוֹ אֶל־עֵמֶק שָׁוֵה
יח הוּא עֵמֶק הַמֶּלֶךְ: וּמַלְכִּי־צֶדֶק מֶלֶךְ שָׁלֵם הוֹצִיא לֶחֶם וָיָיִן וְהוּא כֹהֵן
יט לְאֵל עֶלְיוֹן: וַיְבָרְכֵהוּ וַיֹּאמַר בָּרוּךְ אַבְרָם לְאֵל עֶלְיוֹן קֹנֵה שָׁמַיִם
כ וָאָרֶץ: וּבָרוּךְ אֵל עֶלְיוֹן אֲשֶׁר־מִגֵּן צָרֶיךָ בְּיָדֶךָ וַיִּתֶּן־לוֹ מַעֲשֵׂר מִכֹּל:

---

10. וַיָּנֻסוּ מֶלֶךְ סְדֹם וַעֲמֹרָה — *The kings of Sodom and Gomorrah fled.* This would explain why Abram had no faith in them (in his effort to) rescue Lot.

וְהַנִּשְׁאָרִים הֶרָה נָּסוּ — *And those who remained fled to the mountain* ... i.e., the three remaining kings.

12. וַיִּקְחוּ אֶת לוֹט וְאֶת רְכֻשׁוֹ בֶּן אֲחִי אַבְרָם — *And they captured Lot, Abram's nephew, and his possessions.* They tried especially to capture Lot, because he was Abram's nephew, and being aware of Abram's wealth they hoped to receive a huge ransom.

13. וַיַּגֵּד לְאַבְרָם הָעִבְרִי — *And told Abram, the Ivri.* The fugitive did not know that Abram was Lot's relative. He knew only that he was a believer in the religion of Eber, as was Abram.

וְהוּא שֹׁכֵן בְּאֵלֹנֵי מַמְרֵא — *And he dwelt in the plains of Mamre.* Therefore, Aner, Eshcol, and Mamre joined him (Abram) in battle, as it says: *Aner, Eshcol, and Mamre — they will take their portion* (verse 24).

14. וַיִּרְדֹּף עַד דָּן — *And he pursued them as far as Dan* ... in great haste, so as to attack them suddenly.

15. וַיֵּחָלֵק עֲלֵיהֶם — *And deployed against them.* As part of his strategy, so that they would think they were being attacked from all sides, as Aram thought when they said, הִנֵּה שָׂכַר עָלֵינוּ מֶלֶךְ יִשְׂרָאֵל, *The king of Israel has hired against us* ... *(II Kings 7:6).*

לַיְלָה — *At night.* This was also part of his strategy, that they should not see how few they were in number, just as Achitofel advised, when he said, וְאֶרְדְּפָה אַחֲרֵי דָוִד הַלָּיְלָה, *And I will rise and pursue David at night (II Samuel 17:1).*

NOTES

13. וַיַּגֵּד לְאַבְרָם הָעִבְרִי — *And told Abram, the Ivri.* The *Sforno* interprets this verse thus because it does not say, *Abram, the relative of Lot,* which would account for the fugitive seeking him out to relate the capture of Lot. Apparently, Og (who was the fugitive) did not know of their relationship, but did know they shared the same religious beliefs. This the verse indicates by saying *Abram, the Ivri.*

15. וַיַּכֵּם — *And struck them.* The word וַיַּכֵּם normally means to smite one and kill him. In our case

king of Elam; Tidal, king of Goiim; Amraphel, king of Shinar; and Arioch, king of Ellasar — four kings against five.

10 *The Valley of Siddim was full of bitumen wells. The kings of Sodom and Gomorrah fled and fell into them while the rest fled to a mountain.*
11 *They seized all the wealth of Sodom and Gomorrah and all their food and they departed.* 12 *And they captured Lot and his possessions — Abram's nephew — and they left; for he was residing in Sodom.*

13 *Then there came the fugitive and told Abram, the Ivri, who dwelt in the plains of Mamre, the Amorite, the brother of Eshcol and the brother of Aner, these being Abram's allies.* 14 *And when Abram heard that his kinsman was taken captive, he armed his disciples who had been born in his house — three hundred and eighteen — and he pursued them as far as Dan.* 15 *And he with his servants deployed against them at night and struck them; he pursued them as far as Hobah which is to the north of Damascus.* 16 *He brought back all the possessions; he also brought back his kinsman, Lot, with his possessions, as well as the women and the people.*

17 *The king of Sodom went out to meet him after his return from defeating Chedorlaomer and the kings that were with him, to the Valley of Shaveh which is the king's valley.* 18 *But Malchi-zedek, king of Salem, brought out bread and wine; he was a priest of God, the Most High.* 19 *He blessed him saying: "Blessed is Abram of God, the Most High, Maker of heaven and earth;* 20 *and blessed be God, the Most High, Who has delivered your foes into your hand"; and he gave him a tenth of everything.*

וַיַּכֵּם — *And struck them* . . . a blow which caused them to flee.

וַיִּרְדְּפֵם — *He pursued them.* "Flight is the beginning of defeat" (*Sotah* 44a).

16. וְגַם אֶת הַנָּשִׁים — *As well as the women.* Lot's (wives) whom he had to ransom.

וְאֶת הָעָם — *And the people* . . . the Sodomites who were taken captive. These are the ones to whom the king of Sodom was referring when he said to Abram, "*Give me the people*" (verse 21).

18. הוֹצִיא לֶחֶם וָיָיִן — *Brought out bread and wine* . . . to the returning battle-weary.

וְהוּא כֹהֵן — *He was a priest* . . . and thus, it was proper (fitting) for him to give a blessing.

19. וַיְבָרְכֵהוּ וַיֹּאמַר בָּרוּךְ אַבְרָם לְאֵל עֶלְיוֹן — *He blessed him saying: Blessed is Abram of God, the Most High.* First he blessed him. Afterward he said: Even without my blessing, Abram is *blessed of God the Most High,* as it is said, וַאֲבָרֶכְךָ, *I will bless you* (12:2).

קֹנֵה שָׁמַיִם וָאָרֶץ — *Possessor of heaven and earth.* Heaven and earth are God's possessions (acquisitions) to do with them as He wills, for they did not come into existence through any natural cause (as some philosophers and scientists believe) but (it is only) He Who dictates their existence through His will, and works them as He wills.

20. וּבָרוּךְ אֵל עֶלְיוֹן — *And Blessed is God the Most High.* This act which He wrought, i.e., the mighty victory of Abram over his enemies, is a blessing for Him, the Blessed One, for He rejoices with His creations when the wicked are destroyed; and the righteous rejoice

NOTES

it cannot be translated thus, for then how could a dead person flee and be pursued (וַיִּרְדְּפֵם)? For this reason the *Sforno* interprets וַיַּכֵּם as a blow, instilling fear followed by flight.

חמישי כא-כב *וַיֹּאמֶר מֶלֶךְ־סְדֹם אֶל־אַבְרָם תֶּן־לִי הַנֶּפֶשׁ וְהָרְכֻשׁ קַח־לָךְ: וַיֹּאמֶר
אַבְרָם אֶל־מֶלֶךְ סְדֹם הֲרִמֹתִי יָדִי אֶל־יהוה אֵל עֶלְיוֹן קֹנֵה שָׁמַיִם וָאָרֶץ:
כג אִם־מִחוּט וְעַד שְׂרוֹךְ־נַעַל וְאִם־אֶקַּח מִכָּל־אֲשֶׁר־לָךְ וְלֹא תֹאמַר אֲנִי
כד הֶעֱשַׁרְתִּי אֶת־אַבְרָם: בִּלְעָדַי רַק אֲשֶׁר אָכְלוּ הַנְּעָרִים וְחֵלֶק הָאֲנָשִׁים
טו א אֲשֶׁר הָלְכוּ אִתִּי עָנֵר אֶשְׁכֹּל וּמַמְרֵא הֵם יִקְחוּ חֶלְקָם: אַחַר ׀
הַדְּבָרִים הָאֵלֶּה הָיָה דְבַר־יהוה אֶל־אַבְרָם בַּמַּחֲזֶה לֵאמֹר אַל־תִּירָא
ב אַבְרָם אָנֹכִי מָגֵן לָךְ שְׂכָרְךָ הַרְבֵּה מְאֹד: וַיֹּאמֶר אַבְרָם אֲדֹנָי יֱהֹוִה
מַה־תִּתֶּן־לִי וְאָנֹכִי הוֹלֵךְ עֲרִירִי וּבֶן־מֶשֶׁק בֵּיתִי הוּא דַּמֶּשֶׂק אֱלִיעֶזֶר:
ג-ד וַיֹּאמֶר אַבְרָם הֵן לִי לֹא נָתַתָּה זָרַע וְהִנֵּה בֶן־בֵּיתִי יוֹרֵשׁ אֹתִי: וְהִנֵּה
דְבַר־יהוה אֵלָיו לֵאמֹר לֹא יִירָשְׁךָ זֶה כִּי־אִם אֲשֶׁר יֵצֵא מִמֵּעֶיךָ הוּא

(exult) as we find, שַׁבְּחוּהוּ כָּל הָאֻמִּים כִּי גָבַר עָלֵינוּ חַסְדּוֹ, *Laud Him all you people, for His mercy is great toward us* (*Psalms* 117:1-2).

23. אִם מִחוּט וְעַד שְׂרוֹךְ נַעַל — *If so much as a thread or a shoestrap.* Throughout the Torah, the word אִם, *if*, where it is not followed by a condition, replaces the phrase, *I will not*. Therefore, the meaning is: "I lift up my hand to Hashem, that I cannot give you so much as a thread or shoestrap" for I have nothing (of the booty). And, also, "I will not take anything of yours." Similarly, אִם יִרְאוּ אֶת הָאָרֶץ, *If they will see the land* (*Numbers* 14:23), meaning *they will* not *see*; אִם אַתֶּם תָּבֹאוּ, *If you will come* (*Numbers* 14:30), meaning *they will* not *come*; חַי ה׳ אִם יוּמָת, *As HASHEM lives if he will die* (*I Samuel* 19:6), meaning *he will* not *die*; חַי ה׳ אֲשֶׁר עָמַדְתִּי לְפָנָיו אִם אֶקָּח, *As HASHEM lives, before whom I stand, if I will take* (*II Kings* 5:16), meaning *I will* not *take*, and many more (such examples).

24. בִּלְעָדַי — *Far from me (without me).* You said, "*Give me the people.*" Even without my permission you can take them, for I am keeping nothing for myself.

רַק אֲשֶׁר אָכְלוּ הַנְּעָרִים וְחֵלֶק הָאֲנָשִׁים — *Only what the young men have eaten, and the share of the men.* Only this will I accept from you: the expenses incurred in feeding the young men. I will also take the share of the men who accompanied me, but . . .

עָנֵר אֶשְׁכֹּל וּמַמְרֵא הֵם יִקְחוּ חֶלְקָם — *Aner, Eshcol, and Mamre — they will take their portion.* I will not (be the one) to give them a share, nor will I take a portion for them, rather they themselves shall take (their portion) as (befits) leaders.

XV

1. אַל תִּירָא אַבְרָם — *Fear not, Abram.* Fear not that the four kings will seek revenge from you (for their defeat at your hand).

שְׂכָרְךָ— *Your reward.* Not only have your merits not been diminished by the victory

NOTES

23. אִם מִחוּט וְעַד שְׂרוֹךְ נַעַל — *If so much as a thread or a shoestrap.* Based upon the *Sforno's* general principle that the word אִם, if not followed by a condition, has the implication of an oath, the meaning being *I will not*, it follows that (unlike the simple interpretation) the phrase *so much as a thread or a shoestrap* is not connected to אִם אֶקַּח, *if I should take*, but means *I cannot* give *to* you (the king of Sodom) anything — not even a small item such as a thread or a shoestrap. The phrase אִם אֶקַּח begins a new thought, i.e., I will also take nothing *from* you.

24. רַק אֲשֶׁר אָכְלוּ הַנְּעָרִים וְחֵלֶק הָאֲנָשִׁים. . . עָנֵר אֶשְׁכֹּל וּמַמְרֵא הֵם יִקְחוּ חֶלְקָם — *Only what the young men have eaten, and the share of the men . . . Aner, Eshcol, and Mamre — they will take their portion.* Abram is willing to act as intermediary on behalf of his young men and those men who accompanied him, to collect their share and apportion it among them. He will not do so, however, on behalf of his friends, Aner, Eshcol, and Mamre, for this would be insulting to them. They are respected and honored men who should be dealt with directly, as befits their status and position.

[21] *The king of Sodom said to Abram: "Give me the people and take the possessions for yourself."*

[22] *Abram said to the king of Sodom: "I lift up my hand to* HASHEM, *God, the Most High, Maker of heaven and earth,* [23] *if so much as a thread to a shoestrap; or if I shall take from anything of yours! So you shall not say, 'It is I who made Abram rich.'* [24] *Far from me! Only what the young men have eaten, and the share of the men who accompanied me: Aner, Eshcol, and Mamre — they will take their portion."*

15 [1] *After these events, the word of* HASHEM *came to Abram in a vision, saying, "Fear not, Abram, I am a shield for you; your reward is very great."*

[2] *And Abram said, "My Lord,* HASHEM/ELOHIM: *What can You give me seeing that I go childless, and the steward of my house is the Damascene Eliezer?"*

[3] *Then Abram said, "See, to me You have given no offspring; and see, my steward inherits me . . ."*

[4] *Suddenly, the word of* HASHEM *came to him, saying: "That one will not inherit you. Only him that shall come forth from within you shall*

granted to you (by God), but you have earned a reward for the act of kindness shown to your relative and others, by saving these victims from their oppressors.

הַרְבֵּה מְאֹד — *Very great.* In this world, and the world to come (lit., "eternal life"), as our Sages say, אֵלּוּ דְבָרִים שֶׁאָדָם אוֹכֵל פֵּרוֹתֵיהֶם בָּעוֹלָם הַזֶּה וְהַקֶּרֶן קַיֶּמֶת לָעוֹלָם הַבָּא, *These are the things, the fruits of which a man enjoys in this world and the stock remains for him in the world to come (Peah* 1:1), and among these we find acts of loving-kindness (as Abram demonstrated to Lot and the others).

2. מַה תִּתֶּן לִי — *What can you give me?* In this world.

עֲרִירִי — *Childless.* I have no son to succeed me and be in charge of my affairs, as it says, כִּתְבוּ אֶת הָאִישׁ הַזֶּה עֲרִירִי גֶּבֶר לֹא יִצְלַח בְּיָמָיו כִּי לֹא יִצְלַח מִזַּרְעוֹ אִישׁ יֹשֵׁב עַל כִּסֵּא דָוִד, *Write this man childless, a man that shall not prosper in his days, for no man of his seed shall prosper sitting upon the throne of David (Jeremiah* 22:30).

וּבֶן מֶשֶׁק בֵּיתִי הוּא דַּמֶּשֶׂק אֱלִיעֶזֶר — *And the steward of my house is Damascus Eliezer . . .* who is a slave known only by the name of his city, without a (true) name of his own, and without a doubt there is a vast difference between a servant conducting the affairs of a household motivated by fear, as compared to a son's conducting (these affairs) motivated by love.

3. בֶּן בֵּיתִי יוֹרֵשׁ אֹתִי — *My steward is my heir.* Even were You to grant me offspring eventually, as You said, *"To your offspring I will give this land"* (12:7), he will be young after my demise and unprepared to conduct (financial) affairs. (Therefore) my steward will be in charge and (in effect) be the heir — as often happens.

4. לֹא יִירָשְׁךָ זֶה כִּי אִם אֲשֶׁר יֵצֵא מִמֵּעֶיךָ — *That one will not inherit you, but he who comes forth from within you.* Your son will successfully conduct your affairs even in your

NOTES

XV

1. שְׂכָרְךָ הַרְבֵּה מְאֹד — *Your reward is very great.* The *Sforno* interprets הַרְבֵּה, *great*, as referring to reward in this world, while the adverb "very" is added, to indicate reward in the world to come. He bases this upon the Mishnah in *Peah*, which he quotes, where we find that the reward for גְּמִילַת חֲסָדִים, acts of loving-kindness, such as that of Abram in the rescue operation, is both in this world and the next.

ה יִרָשֶׁךָ: וַיּוֹצֵא אֹתוֹ הַחוּצָה וַיֹּאמֶר הַבֶּט־נָא הַשָּׁמַיְמָה וּסְפֹר הַכּוֹכָבִים
ו אִם־תּוּכַל לִסְפֹּר אֹתָם וַיֹּאמֶר לוֹ כֹּה יִהְיֶה זַרְעֶךָ: וְהֶאֱמִן בַּיהוָה
ששי ז וַיַּחְשְׁבֶהָ לּוֹ צְדָקָה: וַיֹּאמֶר אֵלָיו אֲנִי יהוה אֲשֶׁר הוֹצֵאתִיךָ מֵאוּר
ח כַּשְׂדִּים לָתֶת לְךָ אֶת־הָאָרֶץ הַזֹּאת לְרִשְׁתָּהּ: וַיֹּאמַר אֲדֹנָי יֱהוִה
ט בַּמָּה אֵדַע כִּי אִירָשֶׁנָּה: וַיֹּאמֶר אֵלָיו קְחָה לִי עֶגְלָה מְשֻׁלֶּשֶׁת וְעֵז
י מְשֻׁלֶּשֶׁת וְאַיִל מְשֻׁלָּשׁ וְתֹר וְגוֹזָל: וַיִּקַּח־לוֹ אֶת־כָּל־אֵלֶּה וַיְבַתֵּר
אֹתָם בַּתָּוֶךְ וַיִּתֵּן אִישׁ־בִּתְרוֹ לִקְרַאת רֵעֵהוּ וְאֶת־הַצִּפֹּר לֹא בָתָר: וַיֵּרֶד
יא־יב הָעַיִט עַל־הַפְּגָרִים וַיַּשֵּׁב אֹתָם אַבְרָם: וַיְהִי הַשֶּׁמֶשׁ לָבוֹא
וְתַרְדֵּמָה נָפְלָה עַל־אַבְרָם וְהִנֵּה אֵימָה חֲשֵׁכָה גְדֹלָה נֹפֶלֶת עָלָיו:
יג וַיֹּאמֶר לְאַבְרָם יָדֹעַ תֵּדַע כִּי־גֵר ׀ יִהְיֶה זַרְעֲךָ בְּאֶרֶץ לֹא לָהֶם וַעֲבָדוּם

---

lifetime, as it says, *And Abraham gave all that he had to Isaac* (25:5); *and he sent them* (i.e., the sons borne to him by Keturah) *away from his son Isaac, while he yet lived* (25:6).

6. וְהֶאֱמִן בַּה׳ — *And he trusted in* HASHEM. He believed without a doubt that (God) would do as He said, even though it was highly improbable according to the laws of nature.

וַיַּחְשְׁבֶהָ לּוֹ צְדָקָה — *He reckoned it to him as righteousness.* God, the Blessed One, reckoned this trust in Him as righteousness and to the merit of Abram. We are, then, being told that when Abram later asked, "בַּמָּה אֵדַע כִּי אִירָשֶׁנָּה, *Whereby shall I know that I am to inherit it?*" (verse 8), he did not lose his faith (in this promise) at all, for if he had, his (original) faith would not have been considered as righteousness, as it says, וּבְשׁוּב צַדִּיק מִצִּדְקָתוֹ וְעָשָׂה עָוֶל כְּכֹל הַתּוֹעֵבוֹת אֲשֶׁר עָשָׂה הָרָשָׁע יַעֲשֶׂה וָחָי כָּל צִדְקֹתָו אֲשֶׁר עָשָׂה לֹא תִזָּכַרְנָה, *But when the righteous turns away from his righteousness and commits iniquity ... none of his righteous deeds that he has done shall be remembered (Ezekiel* 18:24).

7. אֲשֶׁר הוֹצֵאתִיךָ מֵאוּר כַּשְׂדִּים לָתֶת לְךָ אֶת הָאָרֶץ הַזֹּאת — *Who brought you out of Ur Kasdim to give you this land* ... that you, yourself, should take possession of it (the land) through חֲזָקָה (an act of acquisition).

לְרִשְׁתָּהּ — *To inherit it* ... so that your children will inherit it from you as an inheritance which is never ending.

8. בַּמָּה אֵדַע — *Whereby shall I know.* Perhaps my children will sin and not merit to inherit it.

9. קְחָה לִי עֶגְלָה מְשֻׁלֶּשֶׁת — *Bring me three heifers* ... to enter a covenant, so that my word become a decree with the status of an irrevocable oath, as our Sages teach us (*Rosh*

NOTES

6. וְהֶאֱמִן בַּה׳ – *And he trusted in* HASHEM. Faith and trust in God, to be considered as righteousness, must be abiding. Therefore the *Sforno* stresses that Abram's question, "*How shall I know, etc.,*" is to be understood, as he later explains in his commentary on verse 8, that perhaps his children will sin and not be worthy to inherit the land. At no time, however, does Abram doubt God's promise.

7. אֲשֶׁר הוֹצֵאתִיךָ מֵאוּר כַּשְׂדִּים לָתֶת לְךָ אֶת הָאָרֶץ הַזֹּאת – *Who brought you out of Ur Kasdim to give you this land.* One of the methods of חֲזָקָה, *acquisition*, is to walk through the length and breadth of a newly purchased field (*Bava Basra* 100). God had already commanded Abram (13:17) to *walk about the land* for this purpose. This is what the *Sforno* is referring to. God had taken Abram out of Ur Kasdim, brought him to *Eretz Yisrael*, and commanded him to perform an act of possession in the land thereby acquiring it, after which he can transmit it to his children as an eternal inheritance.

9. קְחָה לִי עֶגְלָה מְשֻׁלֶּשֶׁת – *Bring me three heifers.* The Talmud (*Rosh Hashanah* 18) establishes the principle that when a final sentence is pronounced it can still be rescinded, unless it is accompanied by an oath. The *Sforno* paraphrases this Talmudic statement, applying it to the covenant God entered

inherit you." 5 *And He took him outside, and said, "Gaze, now, toward*
the Heavens, and count the stars if you are able to count them!" And He
said to him, "So shall your offspring be!" 6 *And he trusted in HASHEM,*
and He reckoned it to him as righteousness.
7 *He said to him, "I am HASHEM Who brought you out of Ur Kasdim to give you this land to inherit it."*
8 *He said, "My Lord, HASHEM/ELOHIM: Whereby shall I know that I am to inherit it?"*
9 *And He said to him, "Take to Me three heifers, three goats, three*
rams, a turtledove, and a young dove." 10 *He took all these to Him: he cut*
them in the center, and placed each piece opposite its counterpart. The
birds, however, he did not cut up.
11 *Birds of prey descended upon the carcasses, and Abram drove them away.*
12 *And it happened, as the sun was about to set, a deep sleep fell upon Abram; and behold — a dread! great darkness fell upon him.*
13 *And He said to Abram, "Know with certainty that your offspring shall be aliens in a land not their own — and they will serve them,*

Hashanah 18), (it was to this that) Moses our Teacher referred when he said, *"It is not for your righteousness . . . but because of the wickedness of these nations HASHEM is driving them out, and in order to fulfill the oath that He swore"* (based on *Deut.* 9:5).

13. יָדֹעַ תֵּדַע — *Know with certainty.* He told him the reason for the delay in the inheriting (of the land) by his children, which is: כִּי לֹא שָׁלֵם עֲוֹן הָאֱמֹרִי, *Because the iniquity of the Emorite is not yet full* (v. 16), and it is not right to expel a nation from its land until its "measure (of wickedness) is full." Therefore (God) says, "Know with certainty" that even though I have sworn to give this land to your children, it will not be immediately.

כִּי גֵר יִהְיֶה זַרְעֲךָ בְּאֶרֶץ לֹא לָהֶם — *For your offspring shall be aliens in a land not their own . . .* until the time that the iniquity of the Emorites will be full. (Abram) is being told the future events of servitude and affliction which will befall some of his offspring in their burdensome state. This will (however) not occur during the generation of the righteous, for as long as one of the tribes (Jacob's sons) was alive the servitude did not begin, until they (the Israelites) corrupted their ways, as the Prophet testifies, וַיַּמְרוּ בִי וְלֹא אָבוּ לִשְׁמֹעַ אֵלַי, אִישׁ אֶת שִׁקּוּצֵי עֵינֵיהֶם לֹא הִשְׁלִיכוּ, וְאֶת גִּלּוּלֵי מִצְרַיִם לֹא עָזָבוּ, וָאֹמַר לִשְׁפֹּךְ חֲמָתִי עֲלֵיהֶם, לְכַלּוֹת אַפִּי בָּהֶם בְּתוֹךְ אֶרֶץ מִצְרָיִם, וָאַעַשׂ לְמַעַן שְׁמִי, *But they rebelled against Me, and would not hearken to Me; they did not, every man, cast away the detestable things of their eyes, neither did they forsake the idols of Egypt; then I said I would pour out My fury upon them in the midst of the land of Egypt* (*Ezekiel* 20:8-9). All this He revealed (to Abram) so that the last generation should know, through tradition, that this is (because of) God's word, and not attribute it to other causes, as the Prophet says, וָאַגִּיד לְךָ מֵאָז בְּטֶרֶם תָּבוֹא הִשְׁמַעְתִּיךָ פֶּן תֹּאמַר

NOTES

into with Abram. The ritual followed here, as described in this chapter, is the equivalent of an oath; therefore the promise made to give Abram's children *Eretz Yisrael* is irrevocable. Even if they will be unworthy, the covenant is unbroken, and the promise remains. It is this oath that Moses alludes to in the verse quoted by the *Sforno*.

13. כִּי גֵר יִהְיֶה זַרְעֲךָ בְּאֶרֶץ לֹא לָהֶם — *For your offspring shall be aliens in a land not their own.* The *Sforno* points out that the status of aliens in a strange land is not always a precarious and difficult one. The Israelites lived in Egypt quite securely and prospered, even though they were aliens. God's statement, therefore, must be under-

יד וְעַנּוּ אֹתָם אַרְבַּע מֵאוֹת שָׁנָה: וְגַם אֶת־הַגּוֹי אֲשֶׁר יַעֲבֹדוּ דָּן אָנֹכִי
טו וְאַחֲרֵי־כֵן יֵצְאוּ בִּרְכֻשׁ גָּדוֹל: וְאַתָּה תָּבוֹא אֶל־אֲבֹתֶיךָ בְּשָׁלוֹם תִּקָּבֵר
טז בְּשֵׂיבָה טוֹבָה: וְדוֹר רְבִיעִי יָשׁוּבוּ הֵנָּה כִּי לֹא־שָׁלֵם עֲוֺן הָאֱמֹרִי
יז עַד־הֵנָּה: וַיְהִי הַשֶּׁמֶשׁ בָּאָה וַעֲלָטָה הָיָה וְהִנֵּה תַנּוּר עָשָׁן וְלַפִּיד אֵשׁ
יח אֲשֶׁר עָבַר בֵּין הַגְּזָרִים הָאֵלֶּה: בַּיּוֹם הַהוּא כָּרַת יהוה אֶת־אַבְרָם בְּרִית
לֵאמֹר לְזַרְעֲךָ נָתַתִּי אֶת־הָאָרֶץ הַזֹּאת מִנְּהַר מִצְרַיִם עַד־הַנָּהָר הַגָּדֹל
יט-כ נְהַר־פְּרָת: אֶת־הַקֵּינִי וְאֶת־הַקְּנִזִּי וְאֵת הַקַּדְמֹנִי: וְאֶת־הַחִתִּי וְאֶת־
כא הַפְּרִזִּי וְאֶת־הָרְפָאִים: וְאֶת־הָאֱמֹרִי וְאֶת־הַכְּנַעֲנִי וְאֶת־הַגִּרְגָּשִׁי וְאֶת־
טז א הַיְבוּסִי: וְשָׂרַי אֵשֶׁת אַבְרָם לֹא יָלְדָה לוֹ וְלָהּ שִׁפְחָה
ב מִצְרִית וּשְׁמָהּ הָגָר: וַתֹּאמֶר שָׂרַי אֶל־אַבְרָם הִנֵּה־נָא עֲצָרַנִי יהוה
מִלֶּדֶת בֹּא־נָא אֶל־שִׁפְחָתִי אוּלַי אִבָּנֶה מִמֶּנָּה וַיִּשְׁמַע אַבְרָם לְקוֹל
ג שָׂרָי: וַתִּקַּח שָׂרַי אֵשֶׁת־אַבְרָם אֶת־הָגָר הַמִּצְרִית שִׁפְחָתָהּ מִקֵּץ עֶשֶׂר
שָׁנִים לְשֶׁבֶת אַבְרָם בְּאֶרֶץ כְּנָעַן וַתִּתֵּן אֹתָהּ לְאַבְרָם אִישָׁהּ לוֹ לְאִשָּׁה:
ד-ה וַיָּבֹא אֶל־הָגָר וַתַּהַר וַתֵּרֶא כִּי הָרָתָה וַתֵּקַל גְּבִרְתָּהּ בְּעֵינֶיהָ: וַתֹּאמֶר
שָׂרַי אֶל־אַבְרָם חֲמָסִי עָלֶיךָ אָנֹכִי נָתַתִּי שִׁפְחָתִי בְּחֵיקֶךָ וַתֵּרֶא כִּי
ו הָרָתָה וָאֵקַל בְּעֵינֶיהָ יִשְׁפֹּט יהוה בֵּינִי וּבֵינֶיךָ: וַיֹּאמֶר אַבְרָם אֶל־שָׂרַי
הִנֵּה שִׁפְחָתֵךְ בְּיָדֵךְ עֲשִׂי־לָהּ הַטּוֹב בְּעֵינָיִךְ וַתְּעַנֶּהָ שָׂרַי וַתִּבְרַח מִפָּנֶיהָ:

עָצְבִּי עָשָׂם, *I have already from the beginning told it to you; announced things to you before they happened; lest you say, "My idol has caused them"* (*Isaiah* 48:5).

14. וְגַם אֶת הַגּוֹי אֲשֶׁר יַעֲבֹדוּ דָּן אָנֹכִי — *But also upon the nation which they shall serve will I execute judgment.* Just as I shall judge your children for their wickedness, (visiting upon them) affliction and servitude, so shall I execute judgment upon the nation, Egypt, that will enslave them.

XVI

2. הִנֵּא נָא עֲצָרַנִי ה׳ מִלֶּדֶת — *See, now, HASHEM has restrained me from bearing.* Although He promised you offspring, as it says, *"To your offspring I will give this land"* (12:7), He has not said that this offspring will issue from me.

אוּלַי אִבָּנֶה מִמֶּנָּה — *Perhaps I will be built up through her.* Perhaps my jealousy of her will stimulate (my) potential powers of reproduction into functioning, and I will be able to have offspring.

לְקוֹל שָׂרָי — *To the voice of Sarai.* He considered that her suggestion was correct; therefore he complied with her wish, not because he wanted to consort with (enjoy) another woman.

NOTES

stood as being applicable only to a number of generations, and even after the death of the שְׁבָטִים (*the tribes,* i.e., the sons of Jacob) the offspring of Abram could have been spared the pain of exile, had they not sinned! It was important for God to reveal all this to Abram, so that future generations would know that the bondage in Egypt was ordained by God and that it was so severe because of their transgressions. Indeed, our Sages tell us that the Israelites were not redeemed from Egypt until they had repented of their sins.

XVI

2. הִנֵּה נָא עֲצָרַנִי ה׳ מִלֶּדֶת – *See, now, HASHEM has restrained me from bearing.* Sarai, whose faith was perfect, never questioned God's promise to Abram that he would have children. She merely points out that these children were not promised specifically through her. This thought is echoed by Rivkah in 25:22. See the *Sforno's* commentary on that verse.

אוּלַי אִבָּנֶה מִמֶּנָּה – *Perhaps I will be built up through her.* When Sarai says, "Perhaps I will be

and they will oppress them — four hundred years. [14]*But also the nation that they will serve, I shall judge, and afterwards they will leave with great wealth.* [15] *As for you: You shall come to your ancestors in peace; you shall be buried in a good old age.* [16] *And the fourth generation shall return here, for the iniquity of the Amorite shall not yet be full until then."*

[17] *So it happened: The sun set, and it was very dark. Behold — there was a smoky furnace and a torch of fire which passed between these pieces.* [18]*On that day HASHEM made a covenant with Abram, saying, "To your descendants have I given this land, from the river of Egypt to the great river, the Euphrates River:* [19] *the Kennite, the Kenizzite, and the Kadmonite;* [20] *the Hittite, the Perizzite, and the Rephaim;* [21] *the Emorite, the Canaanite, the Girgashite, and the Jebusite."*

16

[1] *Now Sarai, Abram's wife, had borne him no children. She had an Egyptian maidservant whose name was Hagar.* [2] *And Sarai said to Abram, "See, now, HASHEM has restrained me from bearing; consort, now, with my maidservant, perhaps I will be built up through her." And Abram heeded the voice of Sarai.*

[3] *So Sarai, Abram's wife, took Hagar the Egyptian, her maidservant — after ten years of Abram's dwelling in the Land of Canaan — and gave her to Abram her husband, to him as a wife.* [4]*He consorted with Hagar and she conceived; and when she saw that she had conceived, her mistress was lowered in her esteem.* [5] *So Sarai said to Abram, "The outrage against me is due to you! It was I who gave my maidservant into your bosom, and now that she sees that she has conceived, I became lowered in her esteem. Let HASHEM judge between me and you!"*

[6] *Abram said to Sarai, "Behold! — your maidservant is in your hand; do to her as you see fit." And Sarai dealt harshly with her, so she fled from her.*

---

5. חֲמָסִי עָלֶיךָ — *My violence is upon you.* You should have admonished her, since she is (now) your wife, when she treated me so lightly once she became pregnant.

6. שִׁפְחָתֵךְ בְּיָדֵךְ — *Your maidservant is in your hand.* She has not been set free by you.

וַתְּעַנֶּהָ שָׂרַי — *And Sarai dealt harshly with her* ... so she should recognize her subordinate position and cease insulting her mistress. This (incident) is symbolic of all who demean

NOTES

built up through her," she does not mean to say that she will rear the child born to Hagar. She is expressing the hope that the jealousy she will experience may serve as a powerful catharsis awakening her potential to conceive. Rachel expresses a similar hope in 30:3. In both cases the word מִמֶּנָּה, *from her*, is to be understood literally, i.e., *from* Hagar's conception, Sarai may ultimately conceive, and "from" Bilhah's, Rachel may also conceive.

לְקוֹל שָׂרַי — *To the voice of Sarai.* In Hebrew the difference between בְּקוֹל and לְקוֹל is that the former means "to obey," whereas the latter means "to understand and agree." Since the phrase used here is וַיִּשְׁמַע אַבְרָם לְקוֹל, the *Sforno* interprets it to mean the latter.

5. חֲמָסִי עָלֶיךָ — *My violence is upon you.* Had Sarai freed Hagar, she would no longer have control over her. Since she had not, Abram correctly said to her, "Even though she is now my wife, she is still your maidservant, hence under your authority." Leah and Rachel, however, did free their maidservants Zilpah and Bilhah when they urged Jacob to take them as wives (see the *Sforno* 30:6).

6. וַתְּעַנֶּהָ שָׂרַי — *And Sarai dealt harshly with her.* Both in this verse and in verse 9, the *Sforno* sees the

ז־ח וַיִּמְצָאָהּ מַלְאַ֣ךְ יהוה עַל־עֵ֥ין הַמַּ֖יִם בַּמִּדְבָּ֑ר עַל־הָעַ֖יִן בְּדֶ֥רֶךְ שֽׁוּר: וַיֹּאמַ֗ר
הָגָ֞ר שִׁפְחַ֤ת שָׂרַי֙ אֵֽי־מִזֶּ֣ה בָ֔את וְאָ֖נָה תֵלֵ֑כִי וַתֹּ֕אמֶר מִפְּנֵי֙ שָׂרַ֣י גְּבִרְתִּ֔י
ט אָנֹכִ֖י בֹּרַֽחַת: וַיֹּ֤אמֶר לָהּ֙ מַלְאַ֣ךְ יהוה שׁ֖וּבִי אֶל־גְּבִרְתֵּ֑ךְ וְהִתְעַנִּ֖י תַּ֥חַת
י יָדֶֽיהָ: וַיֹּ֤אמֶר לָהּ֙ מַלְאַ֣ךְ יהוה הַרְבָּ֥ה אַרְבֶּ֖ה אֶת־זַרְעֵ֑ךְ וְלֹ֥א יִסָּפֵ֖ר מֵרֹֽב:
יא וַיֹּ֨אמֶר לָ֜הּ מַלְאַ֣ךְ יהוה הִנָּ֥ךְ הָרָ֖ה וְיֹלַ֣דְתְּ בֵּ֑ן וְקָרָ֤את שְׁמוֹ֙ יִשְׁמָעֵ֔אל כִּֽי־
יב שָׁמַ֥ע יהוה אֶל־עָנְיֵֽךְ: וְה֤וּא יִֽהְיֶה֙ פֶּ֣רֶא אָדָ֔ם יָד֣וֹ בַכֹּ֔ל וְיַ֥ד כֹּ֖ל בּ֑וֹ וְעַל־פְּנֵ֥י
יג כָל־אֶחָ֖יו יִשְׁכֹּֽן: וַתִּקְרָ֤א שֵׁם־יהוה֙ הַדֹּבֵ֣ר אֵלֶ֔יהָ אַתָּ֖ה אֵ֣ל רֳאִ֑י כִּ֣י אָֽמְרָ֔ה
יד הֲגַ֥ם הֲלֹ֛ם רָאִ֖יתִי אַֽחֲרֵ֥י רֹאִֽי: עַל־כֵּן֙ קָרָ֣א לַבְּאֵ֔ר בְּאֵ֥ר לַחַ֖י רֹאִ֑י הִנֵּ֥ה
טו בֵֽין־קָדֵ֖שׁ וּבֵ֥ין בָּֽרֶד: וַתֵּ֧לֶד הָגָ֛ר לְאַבְרָ֖ם בֵּ֑ן וַיִּקְרָ֨א אַבְרָ֧ם שֶׁם־בְּנ֛וֹ

Israel, as it says, וְהִשְׁתַּֽחֲו֤וּ עַל־כַּפּ֣וֹת רַגְלַ֔יִךְ כָּל־מְנַֽאֲצָ֖יִךְ, *And all who despised you will bow down at the soles of your feet* (Isaiah 60:14).

7. וַיִּמְצָאָהּ מַלְאַךְ ה' — *An angel of* HASHEM *found her.* He found her ready for the Divine vision and therefore appeared to her.

עַל עֵין הַמַּיִם — *At the spring of water.* (She was) praying, as implied in verse 11, *for* HASHEM *has heard your prayer.*

עַל הָעַיִן — *At the spring.* At the crossroad. When there are two roads, it is called עֵינַיִם (in Hebrew). Where the two roads start, it is called פֶּתַח עֵינַיִם; while our Sages refer to it as פָּרָשַׁת דְּרָכִים, *the dividing (forking) of the roads.*

בְּדֶרֶךְ שׁוּר — *On the road to Shur.* (Shur) is identical to חַגְרָא, as Onkelos translates. It is a town on the border of *Eretz Yisrael*, or across the border, as our Sages tell us (*Gittin* 2a). We are being told (by the Torah) that her intention was to leave *Eretz Yisrael*.

8. אֵי מִזֶּה בָאת וְאָנָה תֵלֵכִי — *Where have you come from, and where are you going?* The meaning is: Consider well "from where you are traveling," a holy place and a house of the righteous; and you are going outside the Land, to an unclean place of wicked people!

אָנֹכִי בֹּרַחַת — *I am running away.* I have no particular destination. I am merely fleeing.

9. וְהִתְעַנִּי — *And submit yourself (be afflicted).* This indicates future events, similar to יְרֵה וַיּוֹר, *"Shoot!" and he shot* (II Kings 13:17), for so the king has decreed.

NOTES

incident of Sarai and Hagar as mirroring the eventual roles and relationship of Israel with the Ishmaelites. Ultimately, the latter will have to subjugate themselves to the former, as Hagar did to Sarai.

7. וַיִּמְצָאָהּ מַלְאַךְ ה' — *An angel of* HASHEM *found her.* One cannot translate the word וַיִּמְצָאָהּ, *and he found her*, literally, for that would be an inappropriate statement to make regarding an angel of God, who need not *search* for someone. Therefore the word must be understood as finding Hagar in a certain condition and frame of mind. He *found* her ready for Divine vision. And the reason she was ready was because she had prepared herself through prayer.

עַל הָעַיִן — *At the spring.* The phrase עֵין in this verse connotes purity of mind and heart, while the

word עַיִן means a road. Normally a different word for road may have been used but here it is a play on words — עֵין and עַיִן.

8. אָנֹכִי בֹּרַחַת — *I am running away.* Hagar answers the angel succinctly and sharply. He admonishes her for leaving a holy place for an impure one. She retorts, "I am not making a free choice. I am simply fleeing my mistress and have no destination in mind."

9. וְהִתְעַנִּי — *And submit yourself.* The quote from the Book of *Kings* is from an episode wherein the prophet Elisha commands King Yoash to shoot an arrow through the window ("*Shoot!" and he shot*) which he calls "the arrow of salvation," symbolizing Israel's victory over Aram. The *Sforno* is bringing proof from this episode that a seemingly simple act can have great historical significance. And

7 *An angel of HASHEM found her by the spring of water in the desert, at the spring on the road to Shur.* 8 *And he said, "Hagar, maidservant of Sarai, where have you come from and where are you going?" And she said, "I am running away from Sarai my mistress."*

9 *And an angel of HASHEM said to her, "Return to your mistress, and submit yourself to her domination."*

10 *And an angel of HASHEM said to her, "I will greatly increase your offspring, and they will not be counted for abundance."*

11 *And an angel of HASHEM said to her, "Behold, you will conceive, and give birth to a son; you shall name him Ishmael, for HASHEM has heard your prayer.* 12 *And he shall be a wild-ass of a man: his hand against everyone, and everyone's hand against him; and over all his brothers shall he dwell."*

13 *And she called the Name of HASHEM Who spoke to her "You are the God of Vision," for she said, "Could I have seen even here after having seen?"* 14 *Therefore the well was called "The Well of the Living One Appearing to Me." It is between Kadesh and Bered.*

15 *Hagar bore Abram a son and Abram called the name of his son*

12. פֶּרֶא אָדָם — *A wild ass of a man.* פֶּרֶא is a wild ass. He will be as an ass, in temperament, (acquired) from his mother the Egyptian, as it is said of the Egyptians, אֲשֶׁר בְּשַׂר חֲמוֹרִים בְּשָׂרָם, *Whose flesh is as the flesh of asses* (*Ezekiel* 23:20). (He will be) a wild ass, dwelling in the desert, as it says, *And he grew up and he dwelt in the desert* (21:20). (However) he will also be an אָדָם, *a man,* (acquiring this) from his father (Abram), as our Sages tell us, 'Ishmael repented' (*Baba Basra* 16).

13. וַתִּקְרָא שֵׁם ה׳ — *And she called the name of HASHEM.* Calling the name of HASHEM signifies prayer, (for one should first) praise the Holy One, Blessed is He, in thought or words (before praying) as our Sages teach us: 'A man should always first recount the praise of the Holy One, Blessed is He, and then pray' (*Berachos* 32). In this manner the worshiper will concentrate on God, as we find, שִׁוִּיתִי ה׳ לְנֶגְדִּי תָמִיד, *I have set HASHEM before me always* (*Psalms* 16:8). (We find this phrase, *calling the name of HASHEM*) also in, קָרָאתִי שִׁמְךָ ה׳, *I have called upon Your Name, HASHEM* (*Lamentations* 3:55); also in, וּשְׁמוּאֵל בְּקֹרְאֵי שְׁמוֹ, *And Samuel among them that call upon His Name* (*Psalms* 99:6); also in, כִּי שֵׁם ה׳ אֶקְרָא, *for I will proclaim the name of HASHEM* (*Deut.* 32:3). (The Torah) is then telling us that when she prayed, she (first) recounted the praises of God, Who had spoken to her; this she did by stating . . .

אַתָּה אֵל רֳאִי — *You are the God of vision.* You are the God Who sees everywhere, not only in the house of Abram, as our Sages tell us, 'All gates are locked, except the gates (through which pass the cries) of wrongdoing' (*Baba Metzia* 59a).

15. שֵׁם בְּנוֹ אֲשֶׁר יָלְדָה הָגָר יִשְׁמָעֵאל — *(Abram) named his son that Hagar bore him, Ishmael.* This name was appropriate for both (i.e., Abram and Hagar) — on account of Abram, who later prayed on his behalf, and (God answered), וּלְיִשְׁמָעֵאל שְׁמַעְתִּיךָ, *As for Ishmael, I have heard you* (17:20); and also on account of Hagar, as the angel had told her (verse 11).

NOTES

so the one (Heb.) word spoken to Hagar — וְהִתְעַנִּי, *submit yourself* — will one day be fulfilled on a vast scale when the descendants of Ishmael will submit to the children of Israel, just as Hagar is told to submit to Sarai.

15. שֵׁם בְּנוֹ אֲשֶׁר יָלְדָה הָגָר יִשְׁמָעֵאל – *(Abram) named his son that Hagar bore him, Ishmael.* The name יִשְׁמָעֵאל is comprised of two words — יִשְׁמַע, *to hear,* and אֵל, *God.* The angel of God tells Hagar specifically to name her son יִשְׁמָעֵאל, for God had

טז אֲשֶׁר־יָלְדָה הָגָר יִשְׁמָעֵאל׃ וְאַבְרָם בֶּן־שְׁמֹנִים שָׁנָה וְשֵׁשׁ שָׁנִים
יז א בְּלֶדֶת־הָגָר אֶת־יִשְׁמָעֵאל לְאַבְרָם׃ וַיְהִי אַבְרָם
בֶּן־תִּשְׁעִים שָׁנָה וְתֵשַׁע שָׁנִים וַיֵּרָא יהוה אֶל־אַבְרָם וַיֹּאמֶר אֵלָיו
ב אֲנִי־אֵל שַׁדַּי הִתְהַלֵּךְ לְפָנַי וֶהְיֵה תָמִים׃ וְאֶתְּנָה בְרִיתִי בֵּינִי וּבֵינֶךָ
ג וְאַרְבֶּה אוֹתְךָ בִּמְאֹד מְאֹד׃ וַיִּפֹּל אַבְרָם עַל־פָּנָיו וַיְדַבֵּר אִתּוֹ אֱלֹהִים
ד־ה לֵאמֹר׃ אֲנִי הִנֵּה בְרִיתִי אִתָּךְ וְהָיִיתָ לְאַב הֲמוֹן גּוֹיִם׃ וְלֹא־יִקָּרֵא
עוֹד אֶת־שִׁמְךָ אַבְרָם וְהָיָה שִׁמְךָ אַבְרָהָם כִּי אַב־הֲמוֹן גּוֹיִם נְתַתִּיךָ׃
ו וְהִפְרֵתִי אֹתְךָ בִּמְאֹד מְאֹד וּנְתַתִּיךָ לְגוֹיִם וּמְלָכִים מִמְּךָ יֵצֵאוּ׃

XVII

1. וַיֵּרָא ה׳ — *Hashem appeared.* The phrase מַרְאָה — *vision* or *appearance* — always denotes a lower degree of prophecy. This is what (God) said (to Moses), וּשְׁמִי ה׳ לֹא נוֹדַעְתִּי לָהֶם, *But My Name, Hashem, I made not known to them (Exodus* 6:3).

אֲנִי אֵל שַׁדַּי — *I am El-Shaddai.* I am He, that has sufficiency in My existence, to uniquely create (all Creation) even though there was no other prior matter or substance — implying that the Creator needs naught (in existence) to act (and create). The reverse is true of all others, except the Creator, who can perform no act without a recipient, nor can they be the objects of an action unless there is some being (or force) to act upon them. From all this, perforce, there is clear proof to all thorough thinkers of the existence of the Creator, His uniqueness and the perfection of His work, as compared to all other creative acts. All this, God taught to the Patriarchs. However, He did not make known the (mysterious) reason behind Creation, which emanated from His singular Name, until Moses our Teacher, as it says, וָאֵרָא . . . וּשְׁמִי ה׳ לֹא נוֹדַעְתִּי לָהֶם, *I appeared . . . but My Name, Hashem, I made not known to them (Exodus* 6:3).

הִתְהַלֵּךְ לְפָנַי — *Walk before Me.* Wherever you go (and turn) as it were, gaze at Me, to know My ways, to the full extent of your capacity, as we find, שִׁוִּיתִי ה׳ לְנֶגְדִּי תָמִיד, *I have set Hashem before me always (Psalms* 16:8).

NOTES

listened to her prayer. Later Abram prays for his son, and God assures him that He has heard his prayer. Hence the name Ishmael is an appropriate one to be chosen by Abram, indicated by the word בְּנוֹ, *his son,* and also for Hagar, indicated by the phrase אֲשֶׁר יָלְדָה הָגָר, *that Hagar bore him.*

XVII

1. וַיֵּרָא ה׳ — *Hashem appeared.* Before Abram enters *Eretz Yisrael,* God speaks to him but only His voice is "heard." In the land of Canaan, God "appears" as well. There is, to a certain extent, "visibility," hence the word וַיֵּרָא is used. Not until Moses, the man chosen to receive and transmit the Torah, is there "prophecy" and also "open miracles" transcending nature. This is expressed through the four-letter Name, which transmits the idea of God as the essence of all existence and that nothing can exist without His will. This Name is revealed not to the Patriarchs, but to Moses when God says to him אֶהְיֶה אֲשֶׁר אֶהְיֶה, *I am that I am (Exodus* 3:14).

אֲנִי אֵל שַׁדַּי — *I am El-Shaddai.* The name שַׁדַּי, *Shaddai,* is used here for the first time in the Torah. Subsequently, it can be found in a number of other verses (28:3; 35:11; 43:14) as well. *Rashi* explains this Name of God as indicating *sufficiency* (from the word דַּי, *enough).* Its meaning varies according to the context of its usage. At times it is the sufficiency of His Divinity, at others of His Blessings and at others of His Mercy. The *Sforno* interprets it to mean the sufficiency of His Existence. Similar to the *Rambam's* approach in his writings, the *Sforno* interprets the name *Shaddai* to mean, "He Who is self-sufficient, independent of all other beings." As such, only God could create a world *ex nihilo,* יֵשׁ מֵאַיִן, *something from nothing.* This concept of שַׁדַּי, *Shaddai,* was made known to the Patriarchs, as we see here and in the other verses cited. It is the Divine Name with its special connotations mentioned above which was not revealed to them, but to Moses.

וֶהְיֵה תָמִים — *And be perfect.* The Almighty's being

that Hagar bore him Ishmael. [16] *And Abram was eighty-six years old when Hagar bore Ishmael to Abram.*

17 [1] *When Abram was ninety-nine years old, HASHEM appeared to Abram and said to him, "I am El-Shaddai; walk before Me and be perfect.* [2] *I will set My covenant between Me and you, and I will increase you most exceedingly."*

[3] *Abram threw himself upon his face, and God spoke with him saying,* [4] *"As for Me, this is My covenant with you: You shall be a father of a multitude of nations;* [5] *your name shall no longer be called Abram, but your name shall be Abraham, for I have made you the father of a multitude of nations;* [6] *I will make you most exceedingly fruitful, and make nations of you; and kings shall descend from you.*

וֶהְיֵה תָמִים — *And be perfect.* Seek to attain the perfection attainable to man, i.e., knowing Me through My ways and emulating Me, to the degree possible for you, for the actions of every being reflects his essence, as it says, הוֹדִעֵנִי נָא אֶת דְּרָכֶךָ וְאֵדָעֲךָ, *Show me Your ways, that I may know You (Exodus* 33:13). This, then, is man's ultimate perfection and God's purpose in Creation, as it says, נַעֲשֶׂה אָדָם בְּצַלְמֵנוּ כִּדְמוּתֵנוּ, *Let us make man in our image, after our likeness* (1:26).

2. וְאֶתְּנָה בְרִיתִי בֵּינִי וּבֵינֶךָ — *I will set My covenant between Me and you.* In this manner, I will establish a covenant with you, to be a God to you and your offspring after you, for you will teach them (the fundamentals of faith).

3. וַיִּפֹּל אַבְרָם עַל פָּנָיו — *Abram fell upon his face . . .* in acceptance of, and gratitude to God, for this covenant.

4. אֲנִי הִנֵּה בְרִיתִי אִתָּךְ — *As for Me, this is My covenant with you.* I will now do what I (already) said, to establish the covenant.

5. וְהָיָה שִׁמְךָ אַבְרָהָם — *Your name shall be Abraham . . .* starting now.

כִּי אַב הֲמוֹן גּוֹיִם נְתַתִּיךָ — *For I have made you the father of a multitude of nations.* The significance of this (new) name starts today, for I have already made you the father of a multitude of nations, therefore, *you shall no longer be called by your name Abram* at all; forever. This will not be so regarding the name of Israel, since the main purpose of the name Israel is (meant) for the distant future, as will be explained in its proper place (32:39 and 35:10).

NOTES

and essence cannot possibly be grasped by man's finite mind. We *know* Him only as manifested through His ways. The verse quoted by the *Sforno* regarding Moses' request of God to show him His ways is to be understood thus: Moses is not asking God to literally show him His essence and being, rather to show him His ways so that he in turn can emulate God. In this manner he will know Him, to the extent that man can ever know God! To inquire, search and seek this knowledge of God is proper and commendable. To attain it is "perfection," and indeed, this is the ultimate purpose of man's creation.

5. כִּי אַב הֲמוֹן גּוֹיִם נְתַתִּיךָ — *For I have made you the father of a multitude of nations.* The order used in the commentary is in accordance with the *Sforno's* interpretation of the sequence. When God changes Abram's name to Abraham it takes effect immediately, for the significance of this new name, i.e., *father of a multitude of nations,* begins at once, since God has already set this process in motion. Therefore there is no hiatus, and it is prohibited to call him by his original name, Abram (see *Berachos* 13). That is also why the past tense is used — נְתַתִּיךָ, and וְהָיָה. This however is not the case with Jacob, whose name is changed to Israel by the angel and concurred with by God. In that instance, both names will continue to be used. Only at the "end of days" will "Jacob" be discontinued and "Israel" will supplant it (see *Sforno* 32:39 and 35:10).

ז וַהֲקִמֹתִי אֶת־בְּרִיתִי בֵּינִי וּבֵינֶךָ וּבֵין זַרְעֲךָ אַחֲרֶיךָ לְדֹרֹתָם לִבְרִית עוֹלָם שביעי
ח לִהְיוֹת לְךָ לֵאלֹהִים וּלְזַרְעֲךָ אַחֲרֶיךָ: וְנָתַתִּי לְךָ וּלְזַרְעֲךָ אַחֲרֶיךָ אֵת ׀
אֶרֶץ מְגֻרֶיךָ אֵת כָּל־אֶרֶץ כְּנַעַן לַאֲחֻזַּת עוֹלָם וְהָיִיתִי לָהֶם לֵאלֹהִים:
ט וַיֹּאמֶר אֱלֹהִים אֶל־אַבְרָהָם וְאַתָּה אֶת־בְּרִיתִי תִשְׁמֹר אַתָּה וְזַרְעֲךָ
י אַחֲרֶיךָ לְדֹרֹתָם: זֹאת בְּרִיתִי אֲשֶׁר תִּשְׁמְרוּ בֵּינִי וּבֵינֵיכֶם וּבֵין זַרְעֲךָ
יא אַחֲרֶיךָ הִמּוֹל לָכֶם כָּל־זָכָר: וּנְמַלְתֶּם אֵת בְּשַׂר עָרְלַתְכֶם וְהָיָה לְאוֹת
יב בְּרִית בֵּינִי וּבֵינֵיכֶם: וּבֶן־שְׁמֹנַת יָמִים יִמּוֹל לָכֶם כָּל־זָכָר לְדֹרֹתֵיכֶם יְלִיד
יג בָּיִת וּמִקְנַת־כֶּסֶף מִכֹּל בֶּן־נֵכָר אֲשֶׁר לֹא מִזַּרְעֲךָ הוּא: הִמּוֹל ׀ יִמּוֹל יְלִיד
יד בֵּיתְךָ וּמִקְנַת כַּסְפֶּךָ וְהָיְתָה בְרִיתִי בִּבְשַׂרְכֶם לִבְרִית עוֹלָם: וְעָרֵל ׀ זָכָר
אֲשֶׁר לֹא־יִמּוֹל אֶת־בְּשַׂר עָרְלָתוֹ וְנִכְרְתָה הַנֶּפֶשׁ הַהִוא מֵעַמֶּיהָ אֶת־
טו בְּרִיתִי הֵפַר: וַיֹּאמֶר אֱלֹהִים אֶל־אַבְרָהָם שָׂרַי
טז אִשְׁתְּךָ לֹא־תִקְרָא אֶת־שְׁמָהּ שָׂרָי כִּי שָׂרָה שְׁמָהּ: וּבֵרַכְתִּי אֹתָהּ וְגַם
נָתַתִּי מִמֶּנָּה לְךָ בֵּן וּבֵרַכְתִּיהָ וְהָיְתָה לְגוֹיִם מַלְכֵי עַמִּים מִמֶּנָּה יִהְיוּ:
יז וַיִּפֹּל אַבְרָהָם עַל־פָּנָיו וַיִּצְחָק וַיֹּאמֶר בְּלִבּוֹ הַלְּבֶן מֵאָה־שָׁנָה יִוָּלֵד וְאִם־

7. לִהְיוֹת לְךָ לֵאלֹהִים וּלְזַרְעֲךָ אַחֲרֶיךָ — *To be a God to you and to your offspring after you.* I will associate My Name with yours without an intermediary, as I associate it with all that is eternal, as it says, כִּי כָּל אֲשֶׁר יַעֲשֶׂה הָאֱלֹהִים הוּא יִהְיֶה לְעוֹלָם, *For whatever God does, it shall be forever (Ecclesiastes* 3:14). Whatever is perishable (subject to decay or destruction) is not God's direct work or action, but (functions) through an intermediary. Therefore, (God is saying) that with the establishment and keeping of the covenant, he (Abraham) and his offspring will forever be before Him as individuals (lit., "as a man").

8. לַאֲחֻזַּת עוֹלָם — *As an everlasting possession* . . . and I will be their God, so that you will be able to fulfill My will in it (the land) as we find, וַיִּתֵּן לָהֶם אַרְצוֹת גּוֹיִם . . . בַּעֲבוּר יִשְׁמְרוּ חֻקָּיו, *And He gave them the lands of nations . . . that they might keep His statutes (Psalms* 105:44,45). In this manner I will be your God, that you be everlasting as individuals (lit., "as a man").

9. וְאַתָּה אֶת בְּרִיתִי תִשְׁמֹר — *And as for you, you shall keep My covenant.* Just as (v. 4), אֲנִי הִנֵּה בְרִיתִי אִתָּךְ, *As for Me, this is My covenant with you,* you (in turn) shall keep My covenant, otherwise the covenant will not be valid.

NOTES

7-8. לִהְיוֹת לְךָ לֵאלֹהִים . . . וְהָיִיתִי לָהֶם לֵאלֹהִים — *To be a God to you . . . And I shall be a God to them.* In these two verses the phrase *to be a God to you* (or *to them)* is repeated. The first refers to the covenant between the Almighty and Abraham's descendants; the second to the promise of the Land. In the first case God pledges Himself to הַשְׁגָּחָה פְּרָטִית, *individualized, direct involvement and supervision* of the people of Israel. As such, the Jewish people will be an everlasting one, for only that which is under the control and supervision of Divine intermediaries, as opposed to that under God's direct supervision, is subject to destruction. Abraham is also being assured that this special providence is not only a general one, but also (at times) a particular one — such as the association of God's Name with the Patriarchs, i.e., *God of Abraham, God of Isaac and God of Jacob.* In the second verse, the phrase *and I will be a God to them* is to be understood as the purpose for which the Land is being given to the offspring of Abraham, namely to fulfill God's will and, by conducting themselves as a holy nation, become a light to the nations of the world. In this manner the people and the Land of Israel will be everlasting as well.

9. וְאַתָּה אֶת בְּרִיתִי תִשְׁמֹר — *And as for you, you shall keep My covenant.* Every covenant, to be

[7] *I will ratify My covenant between Me and you and between your offspring after you, throughout their generations, as an everlasting covenant, to be a God to you and to your offspring after you;*
[8] *and I will give to you and to your offspring after you the land of your sojourns — the whole of the land of Canaan — as an everlasting possession; and I shall be a God to them."*

[9] *God said to Abraham, "And as for you, you shall keep My covenant — you and your offspring after you throughout their generations.*
[10] *This is My covenant which you shall keep between Me and you and your descendants after you: Every male among you shall be circumcised.*
[11] *You shall circumcise the flesh of your foreskin, and that shall be the sign of the covenant between Me and you.*
[12] *At the age of eight days every male among you shall be circumcised, throughout your generations — he that is born in the household or purchased with money from any stranger who is not of your offspring.*
[13] *He that is born in your household or purchased with your money shall surely be circumcised. Thus, My covenant shall be in your flesh for an everlasting covenant.*
[14] *An uncircumcised male the flesh of whose foreskin shall not be circumcised — that soul shall be cut off from its people; he has invalidated My covenant."*

[15] *And God said to Abraham, "As for Sarai your wife — do not call her name Sarai, for Sarah is her name.*
[16] *I will bless her; indeed, I will give you a son through her; I will bless her and she shall give rise to nations; kings of peoples will rise from her."*

[17] *And Abraham threw himself upon his face and laughed; and he thought, "Shall a child be born to a hundred-year-old man? And shall*

---

11. לְאוֹת בְּרִית — *The sign of the covenant* . . . a perpetual reminder to walk in His ways, it being as it were the master's seal on his servant.

13. בִּבְשַׂרְכֶם — *In your flesh.* The word בָּשָׂר, *flesh,* is a euphemism in the holy tongue for the organ of procreation; similar to גִּדְלֵי בָשָׂר, *great of flesh* (*Ezekiel* 16:26); זָב מִבְּשָׂרוֹ, *an issue out of his flesh,* and אוֹ הֶחְתִּים בְּשָׂרוֹ מִזּוֹבוֹ, *or his flesh be stopped from his issue* (*Lev.* 15:2,3) and other examples. Since the sign of the covenant is (in the physical sense) in the organ whereby the species is perpetuated, it symbolizes the eternity associated with this covenant. (And) since this organ is the reproductive one, the sign impressed upon it symbolizes the continuity of the covenant among later generations.

16. וּבֵרַכְתִּיהָ — *I will bless her.* She will carry, give birth and rear her son without suffering, contrary to the curse pronounced over Eve, בְּעֶצֶב תֵּלְדִי בָנִים, *In pain you shall bring forth children* (3:16). Sarah will carry, give birth and bring up her son without suffering, as our Sages tell us, אֲשֶׁר פָּדָה אֶת אַבְרָהָם, *Who redeemed Abraham* (*Isaiah* 29:22), 'He was redeemed from the suffering of child rearing' (*Sanhedrin* 19b).

17. הַלְּבֶן מֵאָה שָׁנָה יִוָּלֵד — *Shall a child be born to a hundred-year-old man?* Although it

NOTES

valid, must be a mutual agreement with both parties accepting responsibilities upon themselves. Verse 4 represents God's acceptance, while this verse represents Abraham's.

17. הַלְּבֶן מֵאָה שָׁנָה יִוָּלֵד — *Shall a child be born to a hundred-year-old man?* Abraham wonders how it is possible for him, an old man, and Sarah, an old woman, to have a child born to them. Each

יח שָׂרָה הֲבַת־תִּשְׁעִים שָׁנָה תֵּלֵד׃ וַיֹּאמֶר אַבְרָהָם אֶל־הָאֱלֹהִים לוּ
יט יִשְׁמָעֵאל יִחְיֶה לְפָנֶיךָ׃ וַיֹּאמֶר אֱלֹהִים אֲבָל שָׂרָה אִשְׁתְּךָ יֹלֶדֶת לְךָ בֵּן
וְקָרָאתָ אֶת־שְׁמוֹ יִצְחָק וַהֲקִמֹתִי אֶת־בְּרִיתִי אִתּוֹ לִבְרִית עוֹלָם לְזַרְעוֹ
כ אַחֲרָיו׃ וּלְיִשְׁמָעֵאל שְׁמַעְתִּיךָ הִנֵּה ׀ בֵּרַכְתִּי אֹתוֹ וְהִפְרֵיתִי אֹתוֹ וְהִרְבֵּיתִי
אֹתוֹ בִּמְאֹד מְאֹד שְׁנֵים־עָשָׂר נְשִׂיאִם יוֹלִיד וּנְתַתִּיו לְגוֹי גָּדוֹל׃
כא וְאֶת־בְּרִיתִי אָקִים אֶת־יִצְחָק אֲשֶׁר תֵּלֵד לְךָ שָׂרָה לַמּוֹעֵד הַזֶּה בַּשָּׁנָה
כב־כג הָאַחֶרֶת׃ וַיְכַל לְדַבֵּר אִתּוֹ וַיַּעַל אֱלֹהִים מֵעַל אַבְרָהָם׃ וַיִּקַּח אַבְרָהָם
אֶת־יִשְׁמָעֵאל בְּנוֹ וְאֵת כָּל־יְלִידֵי בֵיתוֹ וְאֵת כָּל־מִקְנַת כַּסְפּוֹ כָּל־זָכָר
בְּאַנְשֵׁי בֵּית אַבְרָהָם וַיָּמָל אֶת־בְּשַׂר עָרְלָתָם בְּעֶצֶם הַיּוֹם הַזֶּה כַּאֲשֶׁר
מפטיר כד דִּבֶּר אִתּוֹ אֱלֹהִים׃ וְאַבְרָהָם בֶּן־תִּשְׁעִים וָתֵשַׁע שָׁנָה בְּהִמֹּלוֹ בְּשַׂר
כה עָרְלָתוֹ׃ וְיִשְׁמָעֵאל בְּנוֹ בֶּן־שְׁלֹשׁ עֶשְׂרֵה שָׁנָה בְּהִמֹּלוֹ אֵת בְּשַׂר עָרְלָתוֹ׃
כו־כז בְּעֶצֶם הַיּוֹם הַזֶּה נִמּוֹל אַבְרָהָם וְיִשְׁמָעֵאל בְּנוֹ׃ וְכָל־אַנְשֵׁי בֵיתוֹ יְלִיד
בָּיִת וּמִקְנַת־כֶּסֶף מֵאֵת בֶּן־נֵכָר נִמֹּלוּ אִתּוֹ׃

---

is possible for a woman past her youth to conceive, it is usually from a young man, not an old one.

הֲבַת תִּשְׁעִים שָׁנָה תֵּלֵד — *Shall a ninety-year-old woman give birth?* ... from any man, even a young one.

NOTES

separately, with a younger mate, perhaps — but not the two of them together.

22. וַיַּעַל אֱלֹהִים מֵעַל אַבְרָהָם – *God ascended from upon Abraham.* Unlike Cain, who did

Sarah — a ninety-year-old woman — give birth?" 18 *And Abraham said to God, "O that Ishmael might live before You!"* 19 *God said, "Nonetheless, your wife Sarah will bear you a son and you shall call his name Isaac; and I will fulfill My covenant with him as an everlasting covenant for his offspring after him.* 20 *But regarding Ishmael I have heard you: I have blessed him, will make him fruitful, and will increase him most exceedingly; he will beget twelve princes and I will make him into a great nation.* 21 *But I will maintain My covenant through Isaac whom Sarah will bear to you by this time next year."* 22 *And when He had finished speaking with him, God ascended from upon Abraham.*

23 *Then Abraham took his son Ishmael and all those servants born in his household and all those he had purchased for money — all the male members of Abraham's house — and he circumcised the flesh of their surplusage on that very day as God had spoken with him.* 24 *Abraham was ninety-nine when he was circumcised on the flesh of his surplusage;* 25 *And his son Ishmael was thirteen years old when he was circumcised on the flesh of his surplusage.* 26 *On that very day was Abraham circumcised with Ishmael his son,* 27 *and all the people of his household, born in his household and purchased for money from a stranger, were circumcised with him.*

---

22. וַיַּעַל אֱלֹהִים מֵעַל אַבְרָהָם — *God ascended from upon Abraham.* (This was) the reverse (of Cain, as it says), וַיֵּצֵא קַיִן מִלִּפְנֵי ה׳, *And Cain went out from the presence of* HASHEM (4:16).

23. בְּעֶצֶם הַיּוֹם הַזֶּה — *On that very day.* He did not postpone (it).

NOTES

not wait for God to ascend but left His presence, Abraham, showing honor to God, waits until He has ascended and only then does Abraham leave.

פרשת וירא

יח א־ב וַיֵּרָא אֵלָיו יהוה בְּאֵלֹנֵי מַמְרֵא וְהוּא יֹשֵׁב פֶּתַח־הָאֹהֶל כְּחֹם הַיּוֹם: וַיִּשָּׂא
עֵינָיו וַיַּרְא וְהִנֵּה שְׁלֹשָׁה אֲנָשִׁים נִצָּבִים עָלָיו וַיַּרְא וַיָּרָץ לִקְרָאתָם
ג מִפֶּתַח הָאֹהֶל וַיִּשְׁתַּחוּ אָרְצָה: וַיֹּאמַר אֲדֹנָי אִם־נָא מָצָאתִי חֵן בְּעֵינֶיךָ
ד אַל־נָא תַעֲבֹר מֵעַל עַבְדֶּךָ: יֻקַּח־נָא מְעַט־מַיִם וְרַחֲצוּ רַגְלֵיכֶם וְהִשָּׁעֲנוּ
ה תַּחַת הָעֵץ: וְאֶקְחָה פַת־לֶחֶם וְסַעֲדוּ לִבְּכֶם אַחַר תַּעֲבֹרוּ כִּי־עַל־כֵּן
ו עֲבַרְתֶּם עַל־עַבְדְּכֶם וַיֹּאמְרוּ כֵּן תַּעֲשֶׂה כַּאֲשֶׁר דִּבַּרְתָּ: וַיְמַהֵר אַבְרָהָם
הָאֹהֱלָה אֶל־שָׂרָה וַיֹּאמֶר מַהֲרִי שְׁלֹשׁ סְאִים קֶמַח סֹלֶת לוּשִׁי וַעֲשִׂי
ז עֻגוֹת: וְאֶל־הַבָּקָר רָץ אַבְרָהָם וַיִּקַּח בֶּן־בָּקָר רַךְ וָטוֹב וַיִּתֵּן אֶל־הַנַּעַר
ח וַיְמַהֵר לַעֲשׂוֹת אֹתוֹ: וַיִּקַּח חֶמְאָה וְחָלָב וּבֶן־הַבָּקָר אֲשֶׁר עָשָׂה וַיִּתֵּן
ט לִפְנֵיהֶם וְהוּא עֹמֵד עֲלֵיהֶם תַּחַת הָעֵץ וַיֹּאכֵלוּ: וַיֹּאמְרוּ *אֵלָיו אַיֵּה
י שָׂרָה אִשְׁתֶּךָ וַיֹּאמֶר הִנֵּה בָאֹהֶל: וַיֹּאמֶר שׁוֹב אָשׁוּב אֵלֶיךָ כָּעֵת חַיָּה
וְהִנֵּה־בֵן לְשָׂרָה אִשְׁתֶּךָ וְשָׂרָה שֹׁמַעַת פֶּתַח הָאֹהֶל וְהוּא אַחֲרָיו:

XVIII

1. וַיֵּרָא אֵלָיו ה׳ בְּאֵלֹנֵי מַמְרֵא — *HASHEM appeared to him in the plains of Mamre* . . . because there Abraham and his household were circumcised, and there God's Divine Presence revealed itself, to *stand* there (confirming) the covenant, as was the practice of all who entered a covenant. (This is) similar to אַתֶּם נִצָּבִים . . . לְעָבְרְךָ בִּבְרִית, *You are* standing . . . *to enter into the covenant* (*Deut.* 29:9,11), and וַיִּכְרֹת . . . לִפְנֵי ה׳ . . . וַיַּעֲמֹד כָּל הָעָם בַּבְּרִית, *And made a covenant before HASHEM . . . and all the people* stood *to the covenant* (*II Kings* 23:3). He *appeared* (however only to) Abraham, for he (Abraham) was more prepared than the others to see the visions. This was also the case (with Moses), וַיִּפְגְּשֵׁהוּ ה׳, *HASHEM met him* (*Exodus* 4:24), at which time God did not appear to speak with Moses but to be present, and accept the covenant (of circumcision) of his son, as it says: . . . בֵּינִי וּבֵינֵיכֶם לְדֹרֹתֵיכֶם, *Between Me and you . . . throughout your generations* (17:11,12). Possibly that is the reason for the custom of preparing a (special) chair at a circumcision.

2. וַיִּשָּׂא עֵינָיו — *He lifted his eyes* . . . with intent to observe.

נִצָּבִים עָלָיו — *Standing over him* . . . turning toward him, as though waiting to speak with him when he would be available, following the glorious vision. Whoever waits in the presence of another to speak to him is referred to as נִצָּבִים עָלָיו, *standing over him*, similar to לְהִתְאַפֵּק לְכֹל הַנִּצָּבִים עָלָיו, *Joseph could not refrain himself, before all them that stood over him* (45:1), and וְכָל הָעָם נִצָּב עָלֶיךָ, *and all the people stand over you* (*Exodus* 18:14).

וַיָּרָץ לִקְרָאתָם — *He ran toward them* . . . even before they approached to speak with him.

NOTES

XVIII

1. וַיֵּרָא אֵלָיו – *HASHEM appeared to him.* We do not find God appearing without a direct communication immediately following. In this verse (וַיֵּרָא), God "appears" for some reason other than communication. *Rashi*, quoting the Talmud, tells us the purpose was to visit Abraham who was sick, recuperating from his circumcision. The *Sforno*, however, interprets this "appearance" as being linked to the *covenant* of circumcision, where God as a party to the covenant comes to participate and confirm it, as it were. The custom of setting up a "chair of Elijah" at every *bris* is to symbolize God's presence, through His representative, Elijah.

2. וַיָּרָץ . . . וַיִּשְׁתַּחוּ – *He ran . . . and bowed.* Unlike *Rashi*, who says that the three men appeared as Arabs (based on *Bava Metzia* 86), the *Sforno* feels that even when angels appear as men their countenance is awe inspiring, and that is why Abraham ran to greet them and bowed down to them.

PARASHAS VAYEIRA

18
[1] *Hashem appeared to him in the plains of Mamre while he was sitting
at the entrance of the tent in the heat of the day.* [2] *He lifted his eyes
and saw: And behold! three men were standing over him. He perceived,
so he ran toward them from the entrance of the tent, and bowed toward
the ground.* [3] *And he said, "My Lord, if I find favor in Your eyes, please
pass not away from Your servant."*
[4] *"Let some water be brought and wash your feet, and recline beneath
the tree.* [5] *I will fetch a morsel of bread that you may sustain yourselves,
then go on — inasmuch as you have passed your servant's way." They
said, "Do so, just as you have said."*
[6] *So Abraham hastened to the tent to Sarah and said, "Hurry! Three
se'ahs of meal, fine flour! Knead and make cakes!"* [7] *Then Abraham ran
to the cattle, took a calf, tender and good, and gave it to the youth who
hurried to prepare it.* [8] *He took cream and milk and the calf which he had
prepared, and placed these before them; he stood over them beneath the
tree and they ate.*
[9] *They said to him, "Where is Sarah your wife?" And he said, "Behold!
— in the tent!"*
[10] *And he said, "I will surely return to you at this time next year, and
behold Sarah your wife will have a son." Now Sarah was listening at the
entrance of the tent which was behind him.*

מִפֶּתַח הָאֹהֶל — *From the entrance of the tent.* He began to run from the entrance in their honor, for one's alacrity and eagerness to do something indicates the importance of that deed in his eyes, as we find, וַיְמַהֵר מֹשֶׁה וַיִּקֹּד אַרְצָה וַיִּשְׁתָּחוּ, *And Moses made haste and bowed toward the earth* (*Exodus* 34:8).

וַיִּשְׁתַּחוּ אָרְצָה — *And bowed toward the ground* . . . for their appearance was awesome, as it says, וּמַרְאֵהוּ כְּמַרְאֵה מַלְאַךְ הָאֱלֹהִים נוֹרָא מְאֹד, *And his appearance was like the countenance of an angel of God, very awesome* (*Judges* 13:6). (Abraham) thought they were the messengers of some king.

3. אַל נָא תַעֲבֹר — *Please pass not away.* You, the head of the messengers, do not hasten to pass away, as is the custom of every messenger who is in a hurry to bring a report back to the one who sent him.

5. כֵּן תַּעֲשֶׂה — *Do so.* But do not keep us beyond this; therefore (Abraham) runs and says (to Sarah), מַהֲרִי, *Hurry* (verse 6).

9. אַיֵּה שָׂרָה — *Where is Sarah?* The purpose of their mission was to inform Sarah (personally) so she might rejoice and thank God, for (in this manner) her pregnancy will be more perfect. Abraham had already been told this tiding by God (17:16). They inquired regarding Sarah *through* Abraham, as our Sages have said (advised us to do) (*Bava Metzia* 87a).

10. שׁוֹב אָשׁוּב אֵלֶיךָ — *I will surely return to you* . . . at the time of each and every circumcision.

NOTES

9. אַיֵּה שָׂרָה — *Where is Sarah?* The Talmud (*Bava Metzia* 87) tells us that one should not inquire after the health of a man's wife directly, except through her husband.

10. וְהוּא אַחֲרָיו — *Which was behind him.* Although one does not address himself directly to a married woman, as mentioned in the previous note, it is proper to do so if one is transmitting a

יא וְאַבְרָהָם וְשָׂרָה זְקֵנִים בָּאִים בַּיָּמִים חָדַל לִהְיוֹת לְשָׂרָה אֹרַח כַּנָּשִׁים:
יב וַתִּצְחַק שָׂרָה בְּקִרְבָּהּ לֵאמֹר אַחֲרֵי בְלֹתִי הָיְתָה־לִּי עֶדְנָה וַאדֹנִי זָקֵן:
יג וַיֹּאמֶר יהוה אֶל־אַבְרָהָם לָמָּה זֶּה צָחֲקָה שָׂרָה לֵאמֹר הַאַף אֻמְנָם
יד אֵלֵד וַאֲנִי זָקַנְתִּי: הֲיִפָּלֵא מֵיהוה דָּבָר לַמּוֹעֵד אָשׁוּב אֵלֶיךָ כָּעֵת חַיָּה
שני טו וּלְשָׂרָה בֵן: וַתְּכַחֵשׁ שָׂרָה ׀ לֵאמֹר לֹא צָחַקְתִּי כִּי ׀ יָרֵאָה וַיֹּאמֶר ׀ לֹא
טז כִּי צָחָקְתְּ: וַיָּקֻמוּ מִשָּׁם הָאֲנָשִׁים וַיַּשְׁקִפוּ עַל־פְּנֵי סְדֹם וְאַבְרָהָם הֹלֵךְ
יז עִמָּם לְשַׁלְּחָם: וַיהוה אָמָר הַמְכַסֶּה אֲנִי מֵאַבְרָהָם אֲשֶׁר אֲנִי עֹשֶׂה:
יח־יט וְאַבְרָהָם הָיוֹ יִהְיֶה לְגוֹי גָּדוֹל וְעָצוּם וְנִבְרְכוּ־בוֹ כֹּל גּוֹיֵי הָאָרֶץ: כִּי יְדַעְתִּיו
לְמַעַן אֲשֶׁר יְצַוֶּה אֶת־בָּנָיו וְאֶת־בֵּיתוֹ אַחֲרָיו וְשָׁמְרוּ דֶּרֶךְ יהוה לַעֲשׂוֹת
צְדָקָה וּמִשְׁפָּט לְמַעַן הָבִיא יהוה עַל־אַבְרָהָם אֵת אֲשֶׁר־דִּבֶּר עָלָיו:

וְהוּא אַחֲרָיו — *Which was behind him.* The entrance (to the tent) where Sarah was listening was behind the angel who was speaking, therefore he did not speak directly (to her) as did Elisha (*II Kings* 4:15).

12. וַתִּצְחַק שָׂרָה — *And Sarah laughed.* She thought that the angel's words were only akin to the blessing of a prophet, similar to the episode of Elisha (*II Kings* 4:16), not a prophecy sent by God, the Blessed One. She thought that since they were (both) old, even if a prophet should bless them, it was unattainable. Such a rejuvenation, given their old age, would be like the revival of the dead, which could only be accomplished through the command of God Himself, or through prayer which would find special favor with Him.

14. הֲיִפָּלֵא מֵה׳ דָּבָר — *Is anything beyond* H*ASHEM*? The angel did not make this statement as a blessing, but (he) brought tidings in the name (of God).

15. כִּי יָרֵאָה — *For she was frightened* ... to say, "I have sinned." However, in her heart (inwardly) she repented.

וַיֹּאמֶר לֹא — *But he said, "No."* For he (Abraham) knew that, לֹא אִישׁ אֵל וִיכַזֵּב, *God is not a man, that He should lie* (*Numbers* 23:19), and he did not believe her, at all.

16-17. וַיַּשְׁקִפוּ — *And they gazed* ... gazing for the purpose of bringing evil.

עַל פְּנֵי סְדֹם — *Down, toward Sodom.* In contrast to the house of Abraham, as the Prophet testifies, saying, הִנֵּה זֶה הָיָה עֲוֹן סְדֹם אֲחוֹתֵךְ, גָּאוֹן שִׂבְעַת לֶחֶם וְשַׁלְוַת הַשְׁקֵט הָיָה לָהּ וְלִבְנוֹתֶיהָ, וְיַד עָנִי וְאֶבְיוֹן לֹא הֶחֱזִיקָה, *Behold this was the iniquity of your sister Sodom, pride, fullness of bread and quiet ease was in her and her daughter; neither did she strengthen the hand of the poor and needy* (*Ezekiel* 16:49).

וְאַבְרָהָם הֹלֵךְ . . . וַה׳ אָמָר — *While Abraham walked . . . And* H*ASHEM said.* (While) he was occupied with the precept (*mitzvah*) of acts of loving-kindness, i.e., accompanying his guests, God said (that) He would reveal Himself to him "so that he will command his

NOTES

promise from God, or giving a blessing. When Elisha spoke to the Shunamis promising her a child, he did so directly. The only reason the angel did not do so was because Sarah was standing in the entrance of the tent behind him.

12. וַתִּצְחַק שָׂרָה – *And Sarah laughed.* The unique power of prayer resulting in the birth of a child, mentioned by the *Sforno*, refers to the prayers of Rebecca and Hannah.

15. וַיֹּאמֶר לֹא – *But he said, "No."* The commentators have different opinions regarding the word וַיֹּאמֶר, *He said.* Some feel it is God, Who is speaking to Sarah. The *Sforno*, however, interprets it as Abraham chiding his wife.

16-17. וְאַבְרָהָם הֹלֵךְ . . . וַה׳ אָמָר – *While Abraham walked . . . And* H*ASHEM said.* These two verses are linked with the letter *vav* (וַה׳), being a וָי״ו הַחִבּוּר — because Abraham performed the *mitzvah* of hos-

11 *Now Abraham and Sarah were old, well on in years; the manner of women had ceased to be with Sarah —*

12 *And Sarah laughed at herself, saying, "After I have withered shall I again have delicate skin? And my husband is old!"*

13 *Then HASHEM said to Abraham, "Why is it that Sarah laughed, saying: 'Shall I in truth bear a child, though I have aged?'* 14 *— Is anything beyond HASHEM?! At the appointed time I will return to you at this time next year, and Sarah will have a son."*

15 *Sarah denied it, saying, "I did not laugh," for she was frightened. But he said, "No, you laughed indeed."*

16 *So the men got up from there, and gazed down toward Sodom, while Abraham walked with them to escort them.*

17 *And HASHEM said, "Shall I conceal from Abraham what I do,* 18 *now that Abraham is surely to become a great and mighty nation, and all the nations of the earth shall bless themselves by him?* 19 *For I have loved him, because he commands his children and his household after him that they keep the way of HASHEM, doing charity and justice, in order that HASHEM might then bring upon Abraham that which He had spoken of him."*

---

children," as our Sages say, שְׂכַר מִצְוָה מִצְוָה, *The reward of one mitzvah is another mitzvah* (*Avos* 4:2).

הַמְכַסֶּה אֲנִי — *Shall I conceal?* It is proper that I should not conceal My attribute of goodness from Abraham, and inform him that if indeed there are a number of righteous men in the midst of the wicked ones, through whom there is hope the wicked may repent, I would tilt (the scale) toward loving-kindness and be forbearing, even toward the wicked, in the hope that they might repent. (God) *does not desire the death of the wicked* (based on *Ezekiel* 18:32); only if there is no hope for repentance will He exact justice.

18. וְאַבְרָהָם הָיוֹ יִהְיֶה — *Now that Abraham will surely be.* As one who shall be a standard for many nations, his teachings (admonition) will be most effective.

19. כִּי יְדַעְתִּיו — *For I have known him.* I admonish him with directness.

לְמַעַן אֲשֶׁר יְצַוֶּה אֶת בָּנָיו — *Because he commands his children.* All this (the blessings in the previous verse), God says He shall do — so that Abraham, observing the great loving-kindness (of God) even toward the wicked, and His justice against those who do not repent (will teach his children) . . .

וְשָׁמְרוּ . . . לַעֲשׂוֹת צְדָקָה וּמִשְׁפָּט לְמַעַן הָבִיא ה׳ עַל אַבְרָהָם אֵת אֲשֶׁר דִּבֶּר עָלָיו — *That they keep . . . doing charity and justice, in order that HASHEM might then bring upon Abraham that which He had spoken of him.* The ultimate purpose intended by the Almighty was to bring upon Abraham that which He had spoken, when He said, "*To be a God to you and to your offspring after you*" (17:7).

NOTES

pitality including the accompanying of his guests as they were leaving, God reveals His plan, and reason, for punishing Sodom so that Abraham will be able to teach his children the ways of God, that they might act in accordance with His will.

17. הַמְכַסֶּה אֲנִי – *Shall I conceal?* The phrase used here by the *Sforno* — "I would tilt (the scales) toward (*chesed*) loving-kindness" — is based upon Tractate *Rosh Hashanah*, 17. Our Sages tell us that there are times when the scales of justice may be balanced, evil and good being equal. The Almighty, in His infinite compassion, tilts the scales in our favor.

19. וְשָׁמְרוּ . . . לַעֲשׂוֹת צְדָקָה וּמִשְׁפָּט – *That they keep . . . doing charity and justice.* The fate of Sodom is a dramatic forceful lesson for Abraham

כ וַיֹּאמֶר יהוה זַעֲקַת סְדֹם וַעֲמֹרָה כִּי־רָבָּה וְחַטָּאתָם כִּי כָבְדָה מְאֹד:
כא אֵרְדָה־נָּא וְאֶרְאֶה הַכְּצַעֲקָתָהּ הַבָּאָה אֵלַי עָשׂוּ | כָּלָה וְאִם־לֹא אֵדָעָה:
כב־כג וַיִּפְנוּ מִשָּׁם הָאֲנָשִׁים וַיֵּלְכוּ סְדֹמָה וְאַבְרָהָם עוֹדֶנּוּ עֹמֵד לִפְנֵי יהוה: וַיִּגַּשׁ
כד אַבְרָהָם וַיֹּאמַר הַאַף תִּסְפֶּה צַדִּיק עִם־רָשָׁע: אוּלַי יֵשׁ חֲמִשִּׁים צַדִּיקִם
בְּתוֹךְ הָעִיר הַאַף תִּסְפֶּה וְלֹא־תִשָּׂא לַמָּקוֹם לְמַעַן חֲמִשִּׁים הַצַּדִּיקִם
כה אֲשֶׁר בְּקִרְבָּהּ: חָלִלָה לְּךָ מֵעֲשֹׂת | כַּדָּבָר הַזֶּה לְהָמִית צַדִּיק עִם־רָשָׁע
וְהָיָה כַצַּדִּיק כָּרָשָׁע חָלִלָה לָּךְ הֲשֹׁפֵט כָּל־הָאָרֶץ לֹא יַעֲשֶׂה מִשְׁפָּט:

---

20. וַיֹּאמֶר ה׳ — *So* HASHEM *said.* (With this expression וַיֹּאמֶר) a higher degree of prophecy than the vision mentioned in verse 1, i.e., וַיֵּרָא אֵלָיו, *appeared to him,* begins.

21. אֵרְדָה נָּא — *I will descend.* I will delve into the ultimate consequences of their wickedness, which progresses from evil to evil, similar to, הָבָה נֵרְדָה וְנָבְלָה שָׁם שְׂפָתָם, *Come, let us go down and there confound their language* (11:7), as explained earlier.

וְאֶרְאֶה הַכְּצַעֲקָתָהּ — *And see, (whether) in accordance with its outcry.* I will demonstrate this (evil) concretely, when they openly reveal (their wickedness) by rising up against Lot's hospitality; then all will know (recognize) that this great punishment was not for naught.

עָשׂוּ כָּלָה — *They have all done.* They have all done (evil) and there is none among them to protest, similar to כָּלָה גָּרֵשׁ יְגָרֵשׁ, *He shall thrust all of you out (Exodus* 11:1), (the word כָּלָה) meaning, *all of you.* This was also demonstrated through the visit of the angels, where it is written, כָּל הָעָם מִקָּצֶה, *all the people from every quarter* (19:4), none being ashamed.

22. וַיִּפְנוּ מִשָּׁם הָאֲנָשִׁים — *And the men turned from there.* They turned from the house of kindness.

וְאַבְרָהָם עוֹדֶנּוּ עֹמֵד — *While Abraham was still standing.* Although the angels who were sent to destroy (Sodom) had already reached Sodom, Abraham still stood (in prayer) to beseech (God) for mercy on their behalf and seek merits (for them), as our Sages tell us, "One must not desist from asking (God's) mercy, even when a sharp sword is on his

NOTES

and his descendants. God decides to reveal to Abraham the reasoning behind this Divine decision so that he in turn can use it as an example when instructing his children the fundamentals of דַּרְכֵּי ה׳, *the Ways of Hashem.* The *Sforno,* consistent with his commentary in the previous verses, explains that the expressions צְדָקָה, *righteousness,* and מִשְׁפָּט, *justice,* which are the two key teachings to be transmitted by Abraham, are reflected in the ways of God with Sodom. He was prepared to be benevolent, even with the wicked, but not to the extent of ignoring the demands of justice toward those who refuse to repent. The חֶסֶד the *Sforno* mentions is the equivalent of צְדָקָה, while the מִשְׁפָּט He metes out to Sodom is the same מִשְׁפָּט Abraham is to teach to his children. The Sodom episode demonstrates the vital need for both צְדָקָה and מִשְׁפָּט.

20. וַיֹּאמֶר ה׳ – *So* HASHEM *said.* Heretofore God only "appears" to Abraham in a vision. For the first time the phrase וַיֹּאמֶר, *he said* — a more direct and higher level of prophecy — is used.

21. אֵרְדָה נָּא – *I will descend.* There is no need, obviously, for the Almighty to descend in order to see what is happening on earth. All is known to Him. The expression אֵרְדָה must therefore be understood as projection into the future: What will eventually come forth from their present evil behavior? To determine this, God tests the people of Sodom with the visit of the angels, giving them one last chance to repent. Unfortunately, they all fail the test.

עָשׂוּ כָּלָה – *They have all done.* The word כָּלָה is translated by most commentators as *destruction.* They interpret the verse to mean, *if they are indeed guilty, then I will decree destruction.* The Sforno, however, translates כָּלָה as synonymous with כֻּלָּה, *all of it.* The verse accordingly means "Have they *all* done this evil — or are there still

20 *So* Hashem *said, "Because the outcry of Sodom and Gomorrah has become great, and because their sin has been very grave,* 21 *I will descend and see: If they act in accordance with its outcry which has come to Me — then destruction! And if not, I will know."*

22 *The men had turned from there and went to Sodom, while Abraham was still standing before* Hashem.

23 *Abraham came forward and said, "Will You also stamp out the righteous along with the wicked?* 24 *What if there should be fifty righteous people in the midst of the city? Would You still stamp it out rather than spare the place for the sake of the fifty righteous people within it?* 25 *It would be sacrilege to You to do such a thing, to bring death upon the righteous along with the wicked; so the righteous will be like the wicked. It would be sacrilege to You! Shall the Judge of all the earth not do justice?"*

---

neck" (*Berachos* 10a). We also find regarding those condemned to death, "We bring him back (from the execution place) even four or five times, providing he presents a substantive defense" (*Sanhedrin* 42b).

23. הַאַף תִּסְפֶּה צַדִּיק עִם רָשָׁע — *Will You also stamp out the righteous with the wicked?* Since You said, *"The outcry of Sodom and Gomorrah has become great"* (verse 20), (the implication is) that You are judging the entire place according to the (actions) of the majority, not of the sinners alone.

24. הַאַף תִּסְפֶּה וְלֹא תִשָּׂא לַמָּקוֹם — *Would You still stamp it out rather than spare the place?* Even though You will stamp out and not spare the wicked (in the merit of) the righteous, it would be sacrilegious for You to bring death upon the righteous.

25. וְהָיָה כַצַּדִּיק כָּרָשָׁע — *And it would be like the righteous as the wicked ...* subject to the (destructive) event, even though there be some righteous in the midst of the wicked.

הֲשֹׁפֵט כָּל הָאָרֶץ — *Shall the Judge of all the earth.* Considering that You are the Judge of all the earth, if You decide the fate of all by following the majority, You will, without a doubt, destroy all, since the majority of people are wicked!

NOTES

some righteous among them?"

22. וַיִּפְנוּ מִשָּׁם הָאֲנָשִׁים — *And the men turned from there.* The word וַיִּפְנוּ, *they turned,* is not to be understood in the physical sense, for they were angels. Rather it means they considered and compared Abraham's home of kindness with the wickedness of Sodom, where the people could not abide Lot's willingness to extend hospitality to strangers.

וְאַבְרָהָם עוֹדֶנּוּ עֹמֵד — *While Abraham was still standing.* The verse explicitly states that the men had already gone to Sodom — וַיֵּלְכוּ סְדֹמָה — following which we are told that Abraham was still standing and praying. Though Heavenly sentence had been passed, there was still a remote chance it could be changed. Abraham therefore refuses to accept the finality of Sodom's destruction and pleads with God to rescind His decision, which He would have done if only there were a sufficient number of righteous men to make a difference. (See *Sforno's* commentary on 19:1.)

23. הַאַף תִּסְפֶּה צַדִּיק עִם רָשָׁע — *Will You also stamp out the righteous with the wicked?* Abraham's concern is that God seems to be judging them *collectively*, not individually. He argues (in verses 24-25) that even if God is not willing to save the wicked in the merit of the righteous, at least let not the righteous be swept along in the wake of destruction visited upon the wicked. God answers (verse 26) that He is prepared to spare the entire place, including the wicked who are the majority, providing there is a sufficient number of righteous men in their midst.

כו וַיֹּאמֶר יְהוָה אִם־אֶמְצָא בִסְדֹם חֲמִשִּׁים צַדִּיקִם בְּתוֹךְ הָעִיר וְנָשָׂאתִי
כז לְכָל־הַמָּקוֹם בַּעֲבוּרָם: וַיַּעַן אַבְרָהָם וַיֹּאמַר הִנֵּה־נָא הוֹאַלְתִּי לְדַבֵּר
כח אֶל־אֲדֹנָי וְאָנֹכִי עָפָר וָאֵפֶר: אוּלַי יַחְסְרוּן חֲמִשִּׁים הַצַּדִּיקִם חֲמִשָּׁה
הֲתַשְׁחִית בַּחֲמִשָּׁה אֶת־כָּל־הָעִיר וַיֹּאמֶר לֹא אַשְׁחִית אִם־אֶמְצָא
כט שָׁם אַרְבָּעִים וַחֲמִשָּׁה: וַיֹּסֶף עוֹד לְדַבֵּר אֵלָיו וַיֹּאמַר אוּלַי יִמָּצְאוּן שָׁם
ל אַרְבָּעִים וַיֹּאמֶר לֹא אֶעֱשֶׂה בַּעֲבוּר הָאַרְבָּעִים: וַיֹּאמֶר אַל־נָא יִחַר
לַאדֹנָי וַאֲדַבֵּרָה אוּלַי יִמָּצְאוּן שָׁם שְׁלֹשִׁים וַיֹּאמֶר לֹא אֶעֱשֶׂה
לא אִם־אֶמְצָא שָׁם שְׁלֹשִׁים: וַיֹּאמֶר הִנֵּה־נָא הוֹאַלְתִּי לְדַבֵּר אֶל־אֲדֹנָי
אוּלַי יִמָּצְאוּן שָׁם עֶשְׂרִים וַיֹּאמֶר לֹא אַשְׁחִית בַּעֲבוּר הָעֶשְׂרִים:
לב וַיֹּאמֶר אַל־נָא יִחַר לַאדֹנָי וַאֲדַבְּרָה אַךְ־הַפַּעַם אוּלַי יִמָּצְאוּן שָׁם
לג עֲשָׂרָה וַיֹּאמֶר לֹא אַשְׁחִית בַּעֲבוּר הָעֲשָׂרָה: וַיֵּלֶךְ יְהוָה כַּאֲשֶׁר כִּלָּה
יט שלישי א לְדַבֵּר אֶל־אַבְרָהָם וְאַבְרָהָם שָׁב לִמְקֹמוֹ: וַיָּבֹאוּ שְׁנֵי הַמַּלְאָכִים סְדֹמָה
בָּעֶרֶב וְלוֹט יֹשֵׁב בְּשַׁעַר־סְדֹם וַיַּרְא־לוֹט וַיָּקָם לִקְרָאתָם וַיִּשְׁתַּחוּ

---

26. אִם אֶמְצָא בִסְדֹם — *If I find in Sodom.* Now, when I test them through (the visit) of the angels whom I sent, if I find fifty righteous men who will protest against the wicked ones of Sodom, which is the major city of the area, as it says סְדֹם וּבְנוֹתֶיהָ, *Sodom and her suburbs (Ezekiel* 16:46) where the leaders of the people from all the cities of the area gather together (then . . .)

וְנָשָׂאתִי לְכָל הַמָּקוֹם — *Then I would spare the entire place.* Not only the righteous.

27. הִנֵּה נָא הוֹאַלְתִּי לְדַבֵּר — *Behold, now, I have taken upon me to speak . . .* to ask (You) regarding the doubts I have in my mind about the manner of God's justice.

וְאָנֹכִי עָפָר וָאֵפֶר — *Although I am but dust and ashes . . .* (and as such) I have still not been able to fathom the implications (meaning) of Your answer.

28. הֲתַשְׁחִית בַּחֲמִשָּׁה אֶת כָּל הָעִיר — *Would You destroy the entire city because of the five?* Tell me whether this number (ten) is an exact one, for if a city has less than ten (righteous men) it lacks "a saving congregation," and accordingly You will destroy the fifth city, which is the most guilty, lacking a saving congregation (and God) says . . .

לֹא אַשְׁחִית — *I will not destroy.* The fifth one.

30. לֹא אֶעֱשֶׂה — *I will not act.* I will do no evil at all to the three *least* guilty cities.

31-32. לֹא אַשְׁחִית בַּעֲבוּר הָעֶשְׂרִים . . . הָעֲשָׂרָה . . . — *I will not destroy on account of the twenty . . . of the ten.* For if three (of the five) are destroyed, the remaining two cannot

NOTES

28. הֲתַשְׁחִית בַּחֲמִשָּׁה אֶת כָּל הָעִיר – *Would You destroy the entire city because of the five?* The expression עֵדָה מַצֶּלֶת, *a saving congregation,* is based upon the Sages' interpretation of the verses in *Numbers* 35:24,25 where the phrases וְשָׁפְטוּ הָעֵדָה, *and the congregation shall judge,* and וְהִצִּילוּ הָעֵדָה, *and the congregation shall deliver (save),* are used. This juxtaposition teaches us that wherever possible to do so within the law, we attempt to exonerate the accused. The *Sforno* applies this concept to the episode at hand. Ten righteous men represent a congregation, which is of sufficient weight to tilt the scales and save the community.

28-30. לֹא אַשְׁחִית . . . לֹא אֶעֱשֶׂה – *I will not destroy . . . I will not act.* According to the *Sforno,* the responses of God are to be understood in the following manner: In response to Abraham's question as to what the fate of the fifth city would be, God answers, "*I will not destroy it,* but I will still punish it" (v. 28). As for the three cities that are relatively less sinful, He answers, "*I will not act* (at all)." Here (v. 30) the word used is אֶעֱשֶׂה, *to do* or *act,* not אַשְׁחִית, *to destroy,* which accounts for the *Sforno's* subtle change of interpretation. When, however, the number of righteous men is reduced to a mere twenty or ten, God's mercy increases

[26] *And HASHEM said, "If I find in Sodom fifty righteous people in the midst of the city, then I would spare the entire place on their account."*
[27] *Abraham responded and said, "Behold, now, I desired to speak to my Lord although I am but dust and ash.* [28] *What if the fifty righteous people should lack five? Would You destroy the entire city because of the five?" And He said, "I will not destroy if I find there forty-five."*
[29] *He further continued to speak to Him and he said, "What if forty would be found there?" And He said, "I will not act on account of the forty."*
[30] *And he said, "Let not my Lord be annoyed and I will speak: What if thirty would be found there?" And He said, "I will not act if I find there thirty."*
[31] *So he said, "Behold, now, I desired to speak to my Lord: What if twenty would be found there?" And He said, "I will not destroy on account of the twenty."*
[32] *So he said, "Let not my Lord be annoyed and I will speak but this once: What if ten would be found there?" And He said, "I will not destroy on account of the ten."*
[33] *HASHEM departed when He had finished speaking to Abraham, and Abraham returned to his place.*

19 [1] *The two angels came to Sodom in the evening and Lot was sitting at the gate of Sodom; now Lot saw and stood up to meet them and he bowed,*

---

escape harm and damage as a result of the destruction of the neighboring towns, as it says, "Babylon is cursed, her neighbors are (also) cursed" (*Berachos* 58a).

33. וַיֵּלֶךְ ה׳ — *And HASHEM departed.* Abraham waited there and did not interrupt his prophetic concentration until the Divine presence left; (this being) the reverse of, וַיֵּצֵא קַיִן מִלִּפְנֵי ה׳, *And Cain went out from the presence of HASHEM* (4:16).

וְאַבְרָהָם שָׁב — *And Abraham returned.* He returned from the place to which he had accompanied the angels, for it was there that God had spoken to him.

לִמְקֹמוֹ — *To his place.* To his house.

XIX

1. וַיָּבֹאוּ שְׁנֵי הַמַּלְאָכִים סְדֹמָה בָּעֶרֶב — *The two angels came to Sodom in the evening.* Although they arrived there without delay, as our Sages tell us, גַּבְרִיאֵל בִּשְׁתַּיִם מִיכָאֵל בְּאַחַת, *Gabriel (reaches his goal) in two flights, Michael in one* (*Berachos* 4b), and we are (also) told this above, *and they went to Sodom* (18:22), nonetheless, they did not *enter* Sodom until the evening, (delaying) until Abraham's intercession had been denied and the final (Divine) sentence passed.

NOTES

perforce, for as the *Sforno* explains, the one or two cities worthy of salvation will still be doomed if all the others are destroyed, since they cannot survive in an area of total destruction (verses 31-32).

33. לִמְקֹמוֹ – *To his place.* See note to 17:22. The word שָׁב, *returned*, denotes *from* a certain place, whereas לִמְקֹמוֹ, *to his place*, is to go *toward* a certain destination. The former word is therefore to be understood as departing from the place to which he had accompanied the angels and communicated with God, while the latter refers to his return home.

XIX

1. וַיָּבֹאוּ שְׁנֵי הַמַּלְאָכִים סְדֹמָה בָּעֶרֶב – *The two angels came to Sodom in the evening.* The *Sforno* quotes the Talmudic saying regarding the angels

ב אַפַּיִם אָרְצָה: וַיֹּאמֶר הִנֶּה נָּא־אֲדֹנַי סוּרוּ נָא אֶל־בֵּית עַבְדְּכֶם וְלִינוּ
וְרַחֲצוּ רַגְלֵיכֶם וְהִשְׁכַּמְתֶּם וַהֲלַכְתֶּם לְדַרְכְּכֶם וַיֹּאמְרוּ *לֹּא כִּי בָרְחוֹב
ג נָלִין: וַיִּפְצַר־בָּם מְאֹד וַיָּסֻרוּ אֵלָיו וַיָּבֹאוּ אֶל־בֵּיתוֹ וַיַּעַשׂ לָהֶם מִשְׁתֶּה
ד וּמַצּוֹת אָפָה וַיֹּאכֵלוּ: טֶרֶם יִשְׁכָּבוּ וְאַנְשֵׁי הָעִיר אַנְשֵׁי סְדֹם נָסַבּוּ עַל־
ה הַבַּיִת מִנַּעַר וְעַד־זָקֵן כָּל־הָעָם מִקָּצֶה: וַיִּקְרְאוּ אֶל־לוֹט וַיֹּאמְרוּ לוֹ אַיֵּה
ו הָאֲנָשִׁים אֲשֶׁר־בָּאוּ אֵלֶיךָ הַלָּיְלָה הוֹצִיאֵם אֵלֵינוּ וְנֵדְעָה אֹתָם: וַיֵּצֵא
ז־ח אֲלֵהֶם לוֹט הַפֶּתְחָה וְהַדֶּלֶת סָגַר אַחֲרָיו: וַיֹּאמַר אַל־נָא אַחַי תָּרֵעוּ: הִנֵּה־
נָא לִי שְׁתֵּי בָנוֹת אֲשֶׁר לֹא־יָדְעוּ אִישׁ אוֹצִיאָה־נָּא אֶתְהֶן אֲלֵיכֶם וַעֲשׂוּ
לָהֶן כַּטּוֹב בְּעֵינֵיכֶם רַק לָאֲנָשִׁים הָאֵל אַל־תַּעֲשׂוּ דָבָר כִּי־עַל־כֵּן בָּאוּ
ט בְּצֵל קֹרָתִי: וַיֹּאמְרוּ | גֶּשׁ־הָלְאָה וַיֹּאמְרוּ הָאֶחָד בָּא־לָגוּר וַיִּשְׁפֹּט שָׁפוֹט
עַתָּה נָרַע לְךָ מֵהֶם וַיִּפְצְרוּ בָאִישׁ בְּלוֹט מְאֹד וַיִּגְּשׁוּ לִשְׁבֹּר הַדָּלֶת:
י וַיִּשְׁלְחוּ הָאֲנָשִׁים אֶת־יָדָם וַיָּבִיאוּ אֶת־לוֹט אֲלֵיהֶם הַבָּיְתָה וְאֶת־הַדֶּלֶת
יא סָגָרוּ: וְאֶת־הָאֲנָשִׁים אֲשֶׁר־פֶּתַח הַבַּיִת הִכּוּ בַּסַּנְוֵרִים מִקָּטֹן וְעַד־גָּדוֹל
יב וַיִּלְאוּ לִמְצֹא הַפָּתַח: וַיֹּאמְרוּ הָאֲנָשִׁים אֶל־לוֹט עֹד מִי־לְךָ פֹה חָתָן וּבָנֶיךָ
יג וּבְנֹתֶיךָ וְכֹל אֲשֶׁר־לְךָ בָּעִיר הוֹצֵא מִן־הַמָּקוֹם: כִּי־מַשְׁחִתִים אֲנַחְנוּ
אֶת־הַמָּקוֹם הַזֶּה כִּי־גָדְלָה צַעֲקָתָם אֶת־פְּנֵי יהוה וַיְשַׁלְּחֵנוּ יהוה לְשַׁחֲתָהּ:

וַיָּקָם לִקְרָאתָם — *And stood up to meet them* . . . lest they spend the night in the streets, as was the custom in those cities where there was no hospitality extended, and (by so doing expose themselves) to harm by the wicked townspeople.

וַיִּשְׁתַּחוּ אַפַּיִם אָרְצָה — *And he bowed, face to the ground* . . . for their countenance was, without a doubt, awe inspiring.

3. מִשְׁתֶּה — *A feast.* A feast centered on wine, of which he was fond, as later events prove. Abraham, however, did not prepare a feast (of wine) for them, doing so only on the day Isaac was weaned (21:8) with the participation of the leaders of that generation who were accustomed to drink (quantities of) wine on their joyous occasions, as our Sages tell us, קָמֵי דְשָׁתָא חַמְרָא — חַמְרָא, *For one accustomed to drink wine — bring (him) wine* (*Sotah* 10a).

8. אוֹצִיאָה נָּא אֶתְהֶן אֲלֵיכֶם — *I shall bring them out to you.* He was certain that the men betrothed to his daughters would rise up (to defend their honor) and there would be tumult among them (thereby deterring the crowd).

9. גֶּשׁ הָלְאָה — *Stand back!* . . . from the opening and we will break down the door.

הָאֶחָד בָּא לָגוּר — *This one came to sojourn.* Is there anyone who would (dare) do such a thing?

NOTES

Gabriel and Michael, for they were two of the three who came to Abraham and subsequently went on to Sodom (*Yoma* 37). In the previous chapter (18:22) the *Sforno* established that the angels had already arrived at the gates of Sodom well before evening. He therefore explains the reason for their delaying their actual entrance to the city.

וַיָּקָם לִקְרָאתָם – *And stood up to meet them.* The *Sforno* in 28:11 describes the custom of wayfarers to spend the night in the village square. The reason Lot insists that they not do so in Sodom is because of the danger to which they will be exposed, given the wickedness of the inhabitants.

3. מִשְׁתֶּה – *A feast.* The phrase מִשְׁתֶּה (from the root שתה, *drink)* is used only regarding Lot, but not when Abraham entertained them. The word connotes a "feast" focused on wine. The *Sforno* is of the opinion that the Torah is hinting to the important role that wine will later play, in the episode of Lot and his daughters (verse 32).

face to the ground. 2 And he said, "Behold now, my lords; turn about, please, to your servant's house; spend the night and wash your feet, then wake up early and go your way!" And they said, "No, rather we will spend the night in the square."

3 And he urged them very much, so they turned toward him and came to his house; he made a feast for them and baked matzos, and they ate. 4 They had not yet lain down when the townspeople, Sodomites, converged upon the house, from young to old, all the people from every quarter. 5 And they called to Lot and said to him, "Where are the men who came to you tonight? Bring them out to us that we may know them." 6 Lot went out to them to the entrance, and shut the door behind him. 7 And he said, "I beg you, my brothers, do not act wickedly. 8 See, now, I have two daughters who have never known a man. I shall bring them out to you and do to them as you please; but to these men do nothing inasmuch as they have come under the shelter of my roof."

9 And they said, "Stand back!" Then they said, "This fellow came to sojourn and would act as a judge? Now we will treat you worse than them!" They pressed exceedingly upon the man, upon Lot, and they approached to break the door.

10 The men stretched out their hand and brought Lot into the house with them, and closed the door. 11 And the men who were at the entrance of the house they struck with blindness, from small to great; and they tried vainly to find the entrance. 12 Then the men said to Lot, "Whom else do you have here — a son-in-law, your sons, or your daughters? All that you have in the city remove from the place, 13 for we are about to destroy this place; for their outcry has become great before HASHEM, so HASHEM has sent us to destroy it."

---

10. וְאֶת הַדֶּלֶת סָגָרוּ — *And closed the door* ... so that they will (be forced) to weary themselves in vain to locate the entrance, and thus their utter wickedness would be demonstrated.

11. וַיִּלְאוּ לִמְצֹא הַפָּתַח — *They wearied themselves in vain to find the entrance.* Although they were stricken with blindness, they exerted themselves to find the entrance so as to break down the door, as our Sages tell us: "The wicked do not repent even at the entrance of *Gehinnom* (Hell)" (*Eruvin* 19a).

NOTES

8. אוֹצִיאָה נָּא אֶתְהֶן אֲלֵיכֶם — *I shall bring them out to you.* It is incomprehensible that a father would sacrifice his daughters to a mob, instead of defending their honor. Various answers are given by the commentators to resolve this difficulty. The *Sforno* gives his unique interpretation, that this was a strategic ploy to create a confrontation between his daughters' fiances and the mob, and in the ensuing confusion he would spirit away his guests.

10-11. וְאֶת הַדֶּלֶת סָגָרוּ . . . וַיִּלְאוּ לִמְצֹא הַפָּתַח — *And closed the door . . . they wearied themselves in vain to find the entrance.* The *Sforno* established in the previous chapter (verse 21) that the angels came to Lot's house to test the reaction of the populace and to give them one last chance to repent. The closing of the door by the angels is meant to underscore the townspeople's wickedness and demonstrate how corrupted they were, that even when blinded, their passion does not subside. The saying of the Sages quoted by the *Sforno* is a play on words — the Sodomites stand at "the entrance," as do the wicked at "the entrance" of Hell — and fail to repent.

יד וַיֵּצֵא לוֹט וַיְדַבֵּר ׀ אֶל־חֲתָנָיו ׀ לֹקְחֵי בְנֹתָיו וַיֹּאמֶר קוּמוּ *צְּאוּ מִן־הַמָּקוֹם
טו הַזֶּה כִּי־מַשְׁחִית יהוה אֶת־הָעִיר וַיְהִי כִמְצַחֵק בְּעֵינֵי חֲתָנָיו: וּכְמוֹ הַשַּׁחַר
עָלָה וַיָּאִיצוּ הַמַּלְאָכִים בְּלוֹט לֵאמֹר קוּם קַח אֶת־אִשְׁתְּךָ וְאֶת־שְׁתֵּי
טז בְנֹתֶיךָ הַנִּמְצָאֹת פֶּן־תִּסָּפֶה בַּעֲוֹן הָעִיר: וַיִּתְמַהְמָהּ ׀ וַיַּחֲזִיקוּ הָאֲנָשִׁים
בְּיָדוֹ וּבְיַד־אִשְׁתּוֹ וּבְיַד שְׁתֵּי בְנֹתָיו בְּחֶמְלַת יהוה עָלָיו וַיֹּצִאֻהוּ וַיַּנִּחֻהוּ
יז מִחוּץ לָעִיר: וַיְהִי כְהוֹצִיאָם אֹתָם הַחוּצָה וַיֹּאמֶר הִמָּלֵט עַל־נַפְשֶׁךָ
אַל־תַּבִּיט אַחֲרֶיךָ וְאַל־תַּעֲמֹד בְּכָל־הַכִּכָּר הָהָרָה הִמָּלֵט פֶּן־תִּסָּפֶה:
יח־יט וַיֹּאמֶר לוֹט אֲלֵהֶם אַל־נָא אֲדֹנָי: הִנֵּה־נָא מָצָא עַבְדְּךָ חֵן בְּעֵינֶיךָ וַתַּגְדֵּל
חַסְדְּךָ אֲשֶׁר עָשִׂיתָ עִמָּדִי לְהַחֲיוֹת אֶת־נַפְשִׁי וְאָנֹכִי לֹא אוּכַל לְהִמָּלֵט
כ הָהָרָה פֶּן־תִּדְבָּקַנִי הָרָעָה וָמַתִּי: הִנֵּה־נָא הָעִיר הַזֹּאת קְרֹבָה לָנוּס שָׁמָּה
כא וְהִוא מִצְעָר אִמָּלְטָה נָּא שָׁמָּה הֲלֹא מִצְעָר הִוא וּתְחִי נַפְשִׁי: וַיֹּאמֶר אֵלָיו רביעי
הִנֵּה נָשָׂאתִי פָנֶיךָ גַּם לַדָּבָר הַזֶּה לְבִלְתִּי הָפְכִּי אֶת־הָעִיר אֲשֶׁר דִּבַּרְתָּ:
כב מַהֵר הִמָּלֵט שָׁמָּה כִּי לֹא אוּכַל לַעֲשׂוֹת דָּבָר עַד־בֹּאֲךָ שָׁמָּה עַל־כֵּן
כג־כד קָרָא שֵׁם־הָעִיר צוֹעַר: הַשֶּׁמֶשׁ יָצָא עַל־הָאָרֶץ וְלוֹט בָּא צֹעֲרָה: וַיהוה
כה הִמְטִיר עַל־סְדֹם וְעַל־עֲמֹרָה גָּפְרִית וָאֵשׁ מֵאֵת יהוה מִן־הַשָּׁמָיִם: וַיַּהֲפֹךְ
אֶת־הֶעָרִים הָאֵל וְאֵת כָּל־הַכִּכָּר וְאֵת כָּל־יֹשְׁבֵי הֶעָרִים וְצֶמַח הָאֲדָמָה:
כו־כז וַתַּבֵּט אִשְׁתּוֹ מֵאַחֲרָיו וַתְּהִי נְצִיב מֶלַח: וַיַּשְׁכֵּם אַבְרָהָם בַּבֹּקֶר
כח אֶל־הַמָּקוֹם אֲשֶׁר־עָמַד שָׁם אֶת־פְּנֵי יהוה: וַיַּשְׁקֵף עַל־פְּנֵי סְדֹם וַעֲמֹרָה
וְעַל כָּל־פְּנֵי אֶרֶץ הַכִּכָּר וַיַּרְא וְהִנֵּה עָלָה קִיטֹר הָאָרֶץ כְּקִיטֹר הַכִּבְשָׁן:

---

14. וַיֵּצֵא לוֹט — *So Lot went out* . . . after they failed (to find the entrance) and left.

15. וַיָּאִיצוּ — *(The angels) urged.* So that their misfortune (calamity) befall them (precisely) at sunrise, when their great deity (the sun) appears, as our Sages tell us, "At the time when the sun rises and all the kings . . . bow down to the sun, the Holy One, Blessed is He, becomes angry immediately" (*Berachos* 7a).

16. בְּחֶמְלַת ה׳ עָלָיו — *In HASHEM's mercy on him.* Although he was saved in the merit of Abraham, as it states, *God remembered Abraham, so he sent Lot from amidst the upheaval* (verse 29), nonetheless, since he tarried and lingered after the angels warned him, he deserved to be swept away. However, (God) had mercy on him, because he was not motivated by a rebellious spirit or defiance, rather (this was) a result of lethargy and bewilderment.

17. אַל תַּבִּיט אַחֲרֶיךָ — *Do not look behind you.* The evil will spread to you as if it were following you, but will not harm you. However, if you stop to peer (behind you), it will (overtake you) and cleave to you, as indeed happened to his wife, as it says, *and she became a pillar of salt* (verse 26).

24. מֵאֵת ה׳ מִן הַשָּׁמָיִם — *From HASHEM, out of heaven.* He did not cause clouds to form from the ends of the earth that would traverse the atmosphere, as is the natural phenomenon with lightning and hail.

25. וַיַּהֲפֹךְ — *He overturned* (lit., *changed*). The nature of the land and its inhabitants *changed* to brimstone and fire, similar to הָפַךְ אֶת מֵימֵיהֶם לְדָם, *He changed their waters to*

NOTES

16. בְּחֶמְלַת ה׳ עָלָיו — *In HASHEM's mercy on him.* The expression בְּחֶמְלַת ה׳, *in HASHEM's mercy,* is not to be understood as the *reason* for Lot's deliverance. That was due to the merit of Abraham, his uncle. God's mercy is necessary only to prevent punishment for Lot's procrastination.

[14] *So Lot went out and spoke to his sons-in-law, [and] the betrothed of his daughters, and he said, "Get up and leave this place, for HASHEM is about to destroy the city!" But he seemed like a jester in the eyes of his sons-in-law.*

[15] *And just as dawn was breaking, the angels urged Lot on saying: "Get up — take your wife and your two daughters who are present, lest you be swept away because of the sin of the city!"*

[16] *Still he lingered — so the men grasped him by his hand, his wife's hand, and the hand of his two daughters in HASHEM's mercy on him; and*
they took him out and left him outside the city. [17] *And it was as they took*
them out that one said: "Flee for your life! Do not look behind you nor stop anywhere in all the plain; flee to the mountain lest you be swept away."

[18] *Lot said to them: "Please, no! My Lord —* [19] *See, now, Your servant has*
found grace in Your eyes and Your kindness was great which You did with me to save my life; but I cannot escape to the mountain lest the evil attach
itself to me and I die. [20] *Behold, please, this city is near enough to escape*
there and it is small; I shall flee there. Is it not small? — and I will live."

[21] *And He replied to him: "Behold, I have granted you consideration even regarding this, that I not overturn the city about which you have*
spoken. [22] *Hurry, flee there, for I cannot do a thing until you arrive there."*
He therefore called the name of the city Zoar.

[23] *The sun rose upon the earth and Lot arrived at Zoar.* [24] *Now HASHEM*
had caused sulfur and fire to rain upon Sodom and Gomorrah, from
HASHEM, out of heaven. [25] *He overturned these cities and the entire plain,*
with all the inhabitants of the cities and the vegetation of the soil. [26] *His*
wife peered behind him and she became a pillar of salt.

[27] *Abraham arose early in the morning to the place where he had*
stood before HASHEM. [28] *And he gazed down upon Sodom and*
Gomorrah and the entire surface of the land of the plain; and saw — and behold! the smoke of the earth rose like the smoke of a kiln.

---

blood (*Psalms* 105:29). In their case, the dew which forms before sunrise changed from its natural state to one of salt, as it is written, גָּפְרִית וָמֶלַח שְׂרֵפָה כָל אַרְצָהּ, *The whole land thereof is brimstone and salt, with a burning* (*Deut.* 29:22), as is the case with all neutral moisture when mixed with burnt particles.

27. אֶל הַמָּקוֹם אֲשֶׁר עָמַד שָׁם אֶת פְּנֵי ה׳ — *To the place where he had stood before HASHEM* ... to the place to which he had accompanied the angels (18:16), for it was there that the "hand of *HASHEM*" had come to rest upon him. Since he had failed to find justification for them (Sodom) in law, he thought to plead for mercy on their behalf.

28. וַיַּשְׁקֵף — *He gazed* ... a gaze of animosity because of their great wickedness.

וַיַּרְא וְהִנֵּה עָלָה קִיטֹר הָאָרֶץ — *And he saw, and behold, the smoke of the earth rose.* Therefore he realized there was no longer any reason to pray on their behalf.

NOTES

24. מֵאֵת ה׳ מִן הַשָּׁמָיִם — *From HASHEM, out of heaven.* This phrase seems superfluous since we are told at the beginning of the verse that God caused sulphur and fire to rain upon Sodom and Gomorrah. The *Sforno* explains that the Torah is emphasizing that this was not a natural phenomenon but a Divine punishment, *from HASHEM, out of heaven.*

כט וַיְהִי בְּשַׁחֵת אֱלֹהִים אֶת־עָרֵי הַכִּכָּר וַיִּזְכֹּר אֱלֹהִים אֶת־אַבְרָהָם וַיְשַׁלַּח
ל אֶת־לוֹט מִתּוֹךְ הַהֲפֵכָה בַּהֲפֹךְ אֶת־הֶעָרִים אֲשֶׁר־יָשַׁב בָּהֵן לוֹט: וַיַּעַל
לוֹט מִצּוֹעַר וַיֵּשֶׁב בָּהָר וּשְׁתֵּי בְנֹתָיו עִמּוֹ כִּי יָרֵא לָשֶׁבֶת בְּצוֹעַר וַיֵּשֶׁב
לא בַּמְּעָרָה הוּא וּשְׁתֵּי בְנֹתָיו: וַתֹּאמֶר הַבְּכִירָה אֶל־הַצְּעִירָה אָבִינוּ זָקֵן
לב וְאִישׁ אֵין בָּאָרֶץ לָבוֹא עָלֵינוּ כְּדֶרֶךְ כָּל־הָאָרֶץ: לְכָה נַשְׁקֶה אֶת־אָבִינוּ
לג יַיִן וְנִשְׁכְּבָה עִמּוֹ וּנְחַיֶּה מֵאָבִינוּ זָרַע: וַתַּשְׁקֶיןָ אֶת־אֲבִיהֶן יַיִן בַּלַּיְלָה הוּא
לד וַתָּבֹא הַבְּכִירָה וַתִּשְׁכַּב אֶת־אָבִיהָ וְלֹא־יָדַע בְּשִׁכְבָהּ וּבְקוּמָהּ: וַיְהִי
מִמָּחֳרָת וַתֹּאמֶר הַבְּכִירָה אֶל־הַצְּעִירָה הֵן־שָׁכַבְתִּי אֶמֶשׁ אֶת־אָבִי
לה נַשְׁקֶנּוּ יַיִן גַּם־הַלַּיְלָה וּבֹאִי שִׁכְבִי עִמּוֹ וּנְחַיֶּה מֵאָבִינוּ זָרַע: וַתַּשְׁקֶיןָ גַּם
בַּלַּיְלָה הַהוּא אֶת־אֲבִיהֶן יָיִן וַתָּקָם הַצְּעִירָה וַתִּשְׁכַּב עִמּוֹ וְלֹא־יָדַע
לו-לז בְּשִׁכְבָהּ וּבְקֻמָהּ: וַתַּהֲרֶיןָ שְׁתֵּי בְנוֹת־לוֹט מֵאֲבִיהֶן: וַתֵּלֶד הַבְּכִירָה בֵּן
לח וַתִּקְרָא שְׁמוֹ מוֹאָב הוּא אֲבִי־מוֹאָב עַד־הַיּוֹם: וְהַצְּעִירָה גַם־הִוא יָלְדָה
כ א בֵּן וַתִּקְרָא שְׁמוֹ בֶּן־עַמִּי הוּא אֲבִי בְנֵי־עַמּוֹן עַד־הַיּוֹם: וַיִּסַּע
מִשָּׁם אַבְרָהָם אַרְצָה הַנֶּגֶב וַיֵּשֶׁב בֵּין־קָדֵשׁ וּבֵין שׁוּר וַיָּגָר בִּגְרָר:
ב וַיֹּאמֶר אַבְרָהָם אֶל־שָׂרָה אִשְׁתּוֹ אֲחֹתִי הִוא וַיִּשְׁלַח אֲבִימֶלֶךְ מֶלֶךְ גְּרָר

29. מִתּוֹךְ הַהֲפֵכָה בַּהֲפֹךְ אֶת הֶעָרִים — *From amidst the upheaval when He overturned the cities.* Since (Lot) was saved in the merit of Abraham from the midst of the upheaval, even while God was overturning these cities before Lot had left the area; and he (on his own) would never have merited (such salvation) being that he did not flee *before* the catastrophe struck, due to his lethargy, as it says, וַיִּתְמַהְמָה, *Still he lingered* (verse 16), therefore he was afraid to dwell in Zoar, for he thought that its upheaval would only be delayed until he (Lot) departed from it, (also) in the merit of Abraham, but once he left, the upheaval would spread to Zoar (as well).

30. וַיֵּשֶׁב בָּהָר — *And settled on the mountain* . . . for he thought that the upheaval would spread throughout the area up to (but not including) the mountain, as the angel had indicated when he said, *flee to the mountain* (verse 17).

31. אָבִינוּ זָקֵן — *Our father is old* . . . and he will not exert himself to travel on to a different land.

וְאִישׁ אֵין בָּאָרֶץ לָבוֹא עָלֵינוּ — *And there is no man in the land to marry us.* There is no man in this region worthy to marry us.

כְּדֶרֶךְ כָּל הָאָרֶץ — *In the manner of all the land* . . . for it was customary that a woman would only marry a (man) who was proper for her.

37-38. וַתִּקְרָא שְׁמוֹ מוֹאָב — *And she named him Moab* (lit., *from father*) . . .

NOTES

29. מִתּוֹךְ הַהֲפֵכָה בַּהֲפֹךְ אֶת הֶעָרִים — *From amidst the upheaval when He overturned the cities.* Lot was convinced that Zoar was also marked for destruction. The only reason it was spared was due to his dwelling there and not because of his merit but the merit of Abraham, which is mentioned here in this verse, followed by the cryptic statement in the next verse *and Lot went up from Zoar.* The *Sforno* interprets the *order* of the two verses as explained above. Lot does not choose to dwell too long in such a precarious place, so he moves to the mountain, which he believes is safer, since the angel had indeed suggested it to him as a haven, when they first fled Sodom.

31-38. אָבִינוּ זָקֵן וְאִישׁ אֵין בָּאָרֶץ . . . הוּא אֲבִי מוֹאָב . . . הוּא אֲבִי בְנֵי עַמּוֹן — *Our father is old and there is no man in the land to marry us . . . he is the ancestor of the Moabites . . . he is the ancestor of*

29 *And so it was when God destroyed the cities of the plain that God remembered Abraham; so He sent Lot from amidst the upheaval when He overturned the cities in which Lot had lived.*

30 *Now Lot went up from Zoar and settled on the mountain, his two daughters with him, for he was afraid to remain in Zoar; he dwelt in a cave,*
he with his two daughters. 31 *The older one said to the younger, "Our father is old and there is no man in the land to marry us in the usual manner.*
32 *Come, let us ply our father with wine and lay with him that we may give life to offspring through our father."*

33 *So they plied their father with wine on that night; and the older one came and lay with her father, and he was not aware of her lying down and of her getting up.*

34 *And it was on the next day that the older one said to the younger, "Behold, I lay with my father last night; let us ply him with wine tonight as well, and you come lay with him that we may give life to offspring through our father."*

35 *So they plied their father with wine that night also; and the younger one got up and lay with him, and he was not aware of her lying down and of her getting up.*

36 *Thus, Lot's two daughters conceived from their father.*

37 *The older bore a son and she called his name Moab; he is the ancestor*
of Moab until this day. 38 *And the younger one also bore a son and she called his name Ben-Ammi; he is the ancestor of the children of Ammon until this day.*

20

1 *Abraham journeyed from there to the region of the south and settled between Kadesh and Shur, and he sojourned in Gerar.* 2 *Abraham*
said of Sarah his wife, "She is my sister"; so Abimelech, king of Gerar, sent,

---

וַתִּקְרָא שְׁמוֹ בֶּן עַמִּי — *And she named him Ben-Ami* (lit., *son of my people*) ... to indicate that they had not conceived from one who was unworthy (improper).

הוּא אֲבִי מוֹאָב... הוּא אֲבִי בְנֵי עַמּוֹן — *He is the ancestor of the Moabites ... he is the ancestor of the people of Ammon* ... who inherited the land. Because the motivation of these women was acceptable, their offspring became two nations who were partially Abraham's heirs, as our Sages tell us, בְּכָל דְּרָכֶיךָ דָעֵהוּ, *In all your ways acknowledge Him (Proverbs* 3:6) — even for a matter of transgression (*Berachos* 63a).

XX

1. וַיֵּשֶׁב בֵּין קָדֵשׁ וּבֵין שׁוּר — *And settled between Kadesh and Shur.* (He settled) between two large cities to invoke HASHEM, the Eternal One, by Name, as he later did, *to strengthen the covenant with many* (based on *Daniel* 9:27).

NOTES

the people of Ammon. Departing from *Rashi's* interpretation of this episode, the *Sforno* explains that: (a) the advanced age of their father precluded his journeying on to another community where suitable husbands might be found for them; (b) even under these extremely difficult circumstances they were concerned to conceive only from a man (or men) worthy to marry them; (c) their motivation was "for the sake of heaven," and though the act itself was immodest and unchaste, their reward is not denied them, and their children become the founders of two nations. Compare the term "Abraham's heirs" to the *Sforno's* commentary on 11:32.

ג וַיִּקַּח אֶת־שָׂרָה: וַיָּבֹא אֱלֹהִים אֶל־אֲבִימֶלֶךְ בַּחֲלוֹם הַלָּיְלָה וַיֹּאמֶר לוֹ
ד הִנְּךָ מֵת עַל־הָאִשָּׁה אֲשֶׁר־לָקַחְתָּ וְהִוא בְּעֻלַת בָּעַל: וַאֲבִימֶלֶךְ לֹא
ה קָרַב אֵלֶיהָ וַיֹּאמַר אֲדֹנָי הֲגוֹי גַּם־צַדִּיק תַּהֲרֹג: הֲלֹא הוּא אָמַר־לִי
אֲחֹתִי הִוא וְהִיא־גַם־הִוא אָמְרָה אָחִי הוּא בְּתָם־לְבָבִי וּבְנִקְיֹן כַּפַּי
ו עָשִׂיתִי זֹאת: וַיֹּאמֶר אֵלָיו הָאֱלֹהִים בַּחֲלֹם גַּם אָנֹכִי יָדַעְתִּי כִּי
בְתָם־לְבָבְךָ עָשִׂיתָ זֹּאת וָאֶחְשֹׂךְ גַּם־אָנֹכִי אוֹתְךָ מֵחֲטוֹ־לִי עַל־כֵּן
ז לֹא־נְתַתִּיךָ לִנְגֹּעַ אֵלֶיהָ: וְעַתָּה הָשֵׁב אֵשֶׁת־הָאִישׁ כִּי־נָבִיא הוּא
וְיִתְפַּלֵּל בַּעַדְךָ וֶחְיֵה וְאִם־אֵינְךָ מֵשִׁיב דַּע כִּי־מוֹת תָּמוּת אַתָּה
ח וְכָל־אֲשֶׁר־לָךְ: וַיַּשְׁכֵּם אֲבִימֶלֶךְ בַּבֹּקֶר וַיִּקְרָא לְכָל־עֲבָדָיו וַיְדַבֵּר
ט אֶת־כָּל־הַדְּבָרִים הָאֵלֶּה בְּאָזְנֵיהֶם וַיִּירְאוּ הָאֲנָשִׁים מְאֹד: וַיִּקְרָא
אֲבִימֶלֶךְ לְאַבְרָהָם וַיֹּאמֶר לוֹ מֶה־עָשִׂיתָ לָּנוּ וּמֶה־חָטָאתִי לָךְ
כִּי־הֵבֵאתָ עָלַי וְעַל־מַמְלַכְתִּי חֲטָאָה גְדֹלָה מַעֲשִׂים אֲשֶׁר לֹא־יֵעָשׂוּ
י עָשִׂיתָ עִמָּדִי: וַיֹּאמֶר אֲבִימֶלֶךְ אֶל־אַבְרָהָם מָה רָאִיתָ כִּי עָשִׂיתָ
יא אֶת־הַדָּבָר הַזֶּה: וַיֹּאמֶר אַבְרָהָם כִּי אָמַרְתִּי רַק אֵין־יִרְאַת אֱלֹהִים
יב בַּמָּקוֹם הַזֶּה וַהֲרָגוּנִי עַל־דְּבַר אִשְׁתִּי: וְגַם־אָמְנָה אֲחֹתִי בַת־אָבִי הִוא
יג אַךְ לֹא בַת־אִמִּי וַתְּהִי־לִי לְאִשָּׁה: וַיְהִי כַּאֲשֶׁר הִתְעוּ אֹתִי אֱלֹהִים

---

3. וַיָּבֹא אֱלֹהִים אֶל אֲבִימֶלֶךְ — *And God came to Abimelech.* (This expression, *came,*) is also used by Laban and Bilaam. The expressions וַיֵּרָא, *He appeared to him,* and מַרְאוֹת אֱלֹהִים, *visions of God,* are not mentioned, nor is דִּבּוּר, *speaking,* as we do find with the Patriarchs and other prophets, as it says, בַּמַּרְאָה אֵלָיו אֶתְוַדָּע בַּחֲלוֹם אֲדַבֶּר בּוֹ, *I make Myself known to him in a vision; I speak to him in a dream* (*Numbers* 12:6). God did not *appear* to them (Abimelech, Laban and Bilaam) at all; only a voice came to them.

הִנְּךָ מֵת — *Behold you are to die.* You will fade away and die from this illness which has already commenced, for God had *completely restrained (every womb of Abimelech's household* — verse 18).

4. הֲגוֹי גַּם צַדִּיק תַּהֲרֹג — *Will You slay a people though it is righteous?* — Is it proper for You to destroy a people by slaying their king; (and) to slay the king who is righteous in this regard, having not sinned?

7. וְעַתָּה הָשֵׁב אֵשֶׁת הָאִישׁ — *But now, return the man's wife.* Before you are wiped out by this illness.

וֶחְיֵה — *And you will live.* You will be healed, similar to, עַד חֲיוֹתָם, *till they were whole* (*Joshua* 5:8).

אַתָּה וְכָל אֲשֶׁר לָךְ — *You and all that is yours* . . . the embryos in the wombs of your wife and your maidservants.

NOTES

XX

3. וַיָּבֹא אֱלֹהִים אֶל אֲבִימֶלֶךְ – *And God came to Abimelech.* There are various levels of prophecy which the *Sforno* touched upon at the beginning of this *sidrah* (17:1). He feels it is important to emphasize that God's communication with those who were not righteous men, such as Abimelech, Laban and Bilaam, was only through the medium of "a voice," never on *any* level of prophecy, which was reserved exclusively for the Patriarchs and other prophets.

4. הֲגוֹי גַּם צַדִּיק תַּהֲרֹג – *Will You slay a people though it is righteous?*

(a) Although only Abimelech and his immediate household were afflicted (verse 17), still if the king is punished it affects all the people.

(b) Abimelech does not claim to be a perfect man, without blemish. When he refers to himself

and took Sarah. [3] *And God came to Abimelech in a dream by night and said to him, "Behold you are to die because of the woman you have taken; moreover she is a married woman."*

[4] *Now Abimelech had not approached her; so he said, "O my Lord, will You slay a nation even though it is righteous?* [5] *Did not he himself tell me: 'She is my sister'? And she, too, herself said: 'He is my brother!' In the innocence of my heart and integrity of my hands have I done this."*

[6] *And God said to him in the dream, "I, too, knew that it was in the innocence of your heart that you did this, and I, too, prevented you from sinning against Me; that is why I did not permit you to touch her.* [7] *But now, return the man's wife for he is a prophet, and he will pray for you and you will live, but if you do not return her, be aware that you shall surely die: you and all that is yours."*

[8] *Abimelech arose early next morning; he summoned all his servants and told them all of these things in their ears, and the people were very frightened.* [9] *Then Abimelech summoned Abraham and said to him, "What have you done to us? How have I sinned against you that you brought upon me and my kingdom such great sin? Deeds that ought not to be done have you done to me!"* [10] *And Abimelech said to Abraham, "What did you see that you did such a thing?"*

[11] *And Abraham said, "Because I said, 'There is but no fear of God in this place and they will slay me because of my wife.'* [12] *Moreover, she is indeed my sister, my father's daughter, though not my mother's daughter; and she became my wife.* [13] *And so it was, when God caused me to wander*

---

9. מַעֲשִׂים אֲשֶׁר לֹא יֵעָשׂוּ — *Deeds that ought not to be done* . . . to cause harm to a man you have not known before, and with whom you have no quarrel. All this will in no way benefit you, (therefore) it is most unusual to act thus.

11. רַק אֵין יִרְאַת אֱלֹהִים בַּמָּקוֹם הַזֶּה — *There is no fear of Elohim in this place.* There is no fear of the ruling authority, for the Philistine chieftains were not really kings (accepted or) feared by the people, as we see from Goliath who said, הֲלוֹא אָנֹכִי הַפְּלִשְׁתִּי, וְאַתֶּם עֲבָדִים לְשָׁאוּל, *Behold I am the Philistine, while you are slaves to Saul* (*I Samuel* 17:8).

12. וְגַם אָמְנָה — *And moreover.* And even you the king, who is the righteous one among them, sinned by taking this woman because I told you she was my sister. (By right) you should have inquired whether she was also my wife, for in truth she is (both) my "sister" and my wife.

13. הִתְעוּ אֹתִי אֱלֹהִים — *When Elohim caused me to wander.* Because of the strange gods whom I abhorred, I was caused to leave my father's home for an unknown destination, not a specific chosen one. Therefore it is called תוֹעָה, *to wander.*

NOTES

as a צַדִּיק, *righteous one,* he only pleads innocence in this particular case, since he was misled and is blameless.

11. רַק אֵין יִרְאַת אֱלֹהִים בַּמָּקוֹם הַזֶּה – *There is no fear of Elohim in this place.* The *Sforno,* unlike other commentators, interprets the word אֱלֹהִים as meaning, *ruler, judge* or *monarch,* not the Deity. He feels that Abraham's justification for his actions was not predicated on a religious base but a social-political one.

13. הִתְעוּ אֹתִי אֱלֹהִים – *When Elohim caused me to wander.* In this verse, the *Sforno* interprets the name אֱלֹהִים as a deity in the non-sacred sense, referring to the false gods revered by Abraham's father. *Rashi,* and others, however, interpret it as meaning *God.*

מִבֵּית אָבִי וָאֹמַר לָהּ זֶה חַסְדֵּךְ אֲשֶׁר תַּעֲשִׂי עִמָּדִי אֶל כָּל־הַמָּקוֹם אֲשֶׁר
יד נָבוֹא שָׁמָּה אִמְרִי־לִי אָחִי הוּא׃ וַיִּקַּח אֲבִימֶלֶךְ צֹאן וּבָקָר וַעֲבָדִים
טו וּשְׁפָחֹת וַיִּתֵּן לְאַבְרָהָם וַיָּשֶׁב לוֹ אֵת שָׂרָה אִשְׁתּוֹ׃ וַיֹּאמֶר אֲבִימֶלֶךְ הִנֵּה
טז אַרְצִי לְפָנֶיךָ בַּטּוֹב בְּעֵינֶיךָ שֵׁב׃ וּלְשָׂרָה אָמַר הִנֵּה נָתַתִּי אֶלֶף כֶּסֶף
לְאָחִיךְ הִנֵּה הוּא־לָךְ כְּסוּת עֵינַיִם לְכֹל אֲשֶׁר אִתָּךְ וְאֵת כֹּל וְנֹכָחַת׃
יז וַיִּתְפַּלֵּל אַבְרָהָם אֶל־הָאֱלֹהִים וַיִּרְפָּא אֱלֹהִים אֶת־אֲבִימֶלֶךְ וְאֶת־אִשְׁתּוֹ
יח וְאַמְהֹתָיו וַיֵּלֵדוּ׃ כִּי־עָצֹר עָצַר יהוה בְּעַד כָּל־רֶחֶם לְבֵית אֲבִימֶלֶךְ
כא א עַל־דְּבַר שָׂרָה אֵשֶׁת אַבְרָהָם׃ וַיהוָה פָּקַד אֶת־
ב שָׂרָה כַּאֲשֶׁר אָמָר וַיַּעַשׂ יהוה לְשָׂרָה כַּאֲשֶׁר דִּבֵּר׃ וַתַּהַר וַתֵּלֶד שָׂרָה
ג לְאַבְרָהָם בֵּן לִזְקֻנָיו לַמּוֹעֵד אֲשֶׁר־דִּבֶּר אֹתוֹ אֱלֹהִים׃ וַיִּקְרָא אַבְרָהָם
ד אֶת־שֶׁם־בְּנוֹ הַנּוֹלַד־לוֹ אֲשֶׁר־יָלְדָה־לּוֹ שָׂרָה יִצְחָק׃ וַיָּמָל אַבְרָהָם אֶת־
חמישי ה יִצְחָק בְּנוֹ בֶּן־שְׁמֹנַת יָמִים כַּאֲשֶׁר צִוָּה אֹתוֹ אֱלֹהִים׃ וְאַבְרָהָם בֶּן־
ו מְאַת שָׁנָה בְּהִוָּלֶד לוֹ אֵת יִצְחָק בְּנוֹ׃ וַתֹּאמֶר שָׂרָה צְחֹק עָשָׂה לִי אֱלֹהִים

---

16. הִנֵּה נָתַתִּי אֶלֶף כֶּסֶף לְאָחִיךְ — *Behold, I have given your brother a thousand pieces of silver* ... as a dowry, as was the custom when one married a man's daughter or sister.

הִנֵּה הוּא לָךְ כְּסוּת עֵינַיִם — *Let it be for you an eye-covering* ... a multicolored garment which women wore as an honored apparel. The dowry I give you demonstrates the honor (in which you are held) and that I did not take you as a courtesan or a concubine, but as a wife, and I would never have released you so quickly were it not that God was with you, and I had to return you!

לְכֹל אֲשֶׁר אִתָּךְ — *For all who are with you* ... in the eyes (presence) of all who are with you and the members of your household.

וְאֵת כֹּל וְנֹכָחַת — *And to all, you will be vindicated* ... in the eyes of all who heard (of this episode), (as well) as in the eyes of all those present who might seek to disgrace you, as is the custom of women who chasten and disparage one another regarding sexual immorality.

18. כִּי עָצֹר עָצַר ה׳ בְּעַד כָּל רֶחֶם — *For HASHEM had completely restrained every womb* ... to destroy the embryos had Abimelech not repented. This is in accord with the warning given to him: *Be aware that you will surely die, you and all that is yours* (verse 7).

XXI

1. וַה׳ פָּקַד — *HASHEM had remembered (Sarah)* ... when Abraham prayed on Abimelech's behalf, then *HASHEM remembered Sarah*, as it says, וַה׳ שָׁב אֶת שְׁבוּת אִיּוֹב בְּהִתְפַּלְלוֹ בְּעַד רֵעֵהוּ, *And HASHEM changed the fortune of Job, when he prayed for his friends (Job 42:10).*

NOTES

16. הִנֵּה נָתַתִּי . . . וְאֵת כֹּל וְנֹכָחַת — *Behold, I have given ... and to all, you will be vindicated.* The flow of this verse, according to the *Sforno*, is: Since Abraham's greatest fear would be that people would say the king used Sarah and then discarded her, something must be done to defend her honor and dignity. To prove that she was taken by the king with the intent to wed her, a dowry is now offered, and to demonstrate her status, and the king's great respect for her, she is clothed in a garment reserved for women of high position. All this will hopefully prevent the spreading of malicious gossip which would damage Sarah's reputation.

XXI

1. וַה׳ פָּקַד — *HASHEM had remembered.* Similar to (18:16,17) the letter *vav* (וַה׳ פָּקַד) is a וי״ו הַדְּרִית, linking the previous verses which tell us of Abraham's intercession on behalf of Abimelech, to Sarah's conception. The Talmudic dictum which

from my father's house, I said to her, 'Let this be your kindness which you shall do for me — to whatever place we come, say of me: He is my brother.' "

14 *So Abimelech took flocks and cattle and servants and maidservants and gave them to Abraham; and he returned his wife Sarah to him.*

15 *And Abimelech said, "Behold, my land is before you: Settle wherever you see fit."* 16 *And to Sarah he said, "Behold, I have given your brother a thousand pieces of silver. Behold! Let it be for you an eye-covering for all who are with you; and to all, you will be vindicated."*

17 *Abraham prayed to God, and God healed Abimelech, his wife, and his maids, and they were relieved;* 18 *for* HASHEM *had completely restrained every orifice of the household of Abimelech, because of Sarah, the wife of Abraham.*

21 1 HASHEM *had remembered Sarah as He had said; and* HASHEM *did for Sarah as He had spoken.* 2 *Sarah conceived and bore a son unto Abraham in his old age, at the appointed time which God had spoken.* 3 *Abraham called the name of his son who was born to him — whom Sarah had borne him — Isaac.*

4 *Abraham circumcised his son Isaac at the age of eight days as God had commanded him.* 5 *And Abraham was a hundred years old when his son Isaac was born to him.* 6 *Sarah said, "God has made laughter for me;*

כַּאֲשֶׁר אָמָר — *As He had said* ... when He said *I will bless her* (17:16), meaning that the curse of Eve, i.e., (the difficulties associated with) pregnancy, childbirth and child raising, were all removed from her (Sarah) as it says, *I will greatly multiply your pain and travail* (3:16).

וַיַּעַשׂ ה׳ לְשָׂרָה כַּאֲשֶׁר דִּבֵּר — *And* HASHEM *did for Sarah as He had spoken* ... as He said, *"Indeed, I will give you a son through her"* (17:16). (This is) contrary to the usual occurrence when an older woman gives birth, for the majority (of such births) are females.

4. וַיָּמָל אַבְרָהָם אֶת יִצְחָק בְּנוֹ — *And Abraham circumcised his son Isaac ...*

5. וְאַבְרָהָם בֶּן מְאַת שָׁנָה — *And Abraham was a hundred years old* ... and yet he circumcised his son, and did not have tender concern for the infant of his old age.

6. צְחֹק עָשָׂה לִי אֱלֹהִים — *God has made laughter for me.* Although there is pain associated with the circumcision of the infant, God, the Blessed One, has given joy to my heart, therefore ...

NOTES

Rashi quotes is echoed in the *Sforno's* commentary as well, i.e., "He who prays on behalf of his fellow, and is himself in need of the same help, is answered first" (*Bava Kama* 92). The Talmud proves this concept from our verses, whereas the *Sforno* strengthens it from the verse in *Job*; when Job prays for others, he himself is blessed.

כַּאֲשֶׁר אָמָר – *As He had said.* The two phrases used, כַּאֲשֶׁר אָמָר, *as He had said*, and כַּאֲשֶׁר דִּבֵּר, *as He had spoken*, are not redundant. The former refers to Sarah's special blessing from God relieving her from Eve's curse, which is true of all righteous women, as our Sages tell us in *Sotah* 14. The latter refers to her bearing a son rather than a daughter, which was contrary to the norm, as the *Sforno* explains. In both cases, Sarah is granted special favor and grace.

5. וְאַבְרָהָם בֶּן מְאַת שָׁנָה – *And Abraham was a hundred years old.* We already know how old Abraham was when Isaac was born, since we have already been told that he was ninety-nine when he himself was circumcised and Isaac was born a year later. The reason we are told that Abraham was one hundred years old when he circumcised his son is to emphasize his righteousness and great trust in Hashem, as the *Sforno* explains.

ז כָּל־הַשֹּׁמֵעַ יִצְחַק־לִי: וַתֹּאמֶר מִי מִלֵּל לְאַבְרָהָם הֵינִיקָה בָנִים שָׂרָה
ח כִּי־יָלַדְתִּי בֵן לִזְקֻנָיו: וַיִּגְדַּל הַיֶּלֶד וַיִּגָּמַל וַיַּעַשׂ אַבְרָהָם מִשְׁתֶּה
ט גָדוֹל בְּיוֹם הִגָּמֵל אֶת־יִצְחָק: וַתֵּרֶא שָׂרָה אֶת־בֶּן־הָגָר הַמִּצְרִית
י אֲשֶׁר־יָלְדָה לְאַבְרָהָם מְצַחֵק: וַתֹּאמֶר לְאַבְרָהָם גָּרֵשׁ הָאָמָה הַזֹּאת
יא וְאֶת־בְּנָהּ כִּי לֹא יִירַשׁ בֶּן־הָאָמָה הַזֹּאת עִם־בְּנִי עִם־יִצְחָק: וַיֵּרַע
יב הַדָּבָר מְאֹד בְּעֵינֵי אַבְרָהָם עַל אוֹדֹת בְּנוֹ: וַיֹּאמֶר אֱלֹהִים אֶל־אַבְרָהָם
אַל־יֵרַע בְּעֵינֶיךָ עַל־הַנַּעַר וְעַל־אֲמָתֶךָ כֹּל אֲשֶׁר תֹּאמַר אֵלֶיךָ שָׂרָה
יג שְׁמַע בְּקֹלָהּ כִּי בְיִצְחָק יִקָּרֵא לְךָ זָרַע: וְגַם אֶת־בֶּן־הָאָמָה לְגוֹי
יד אֲשִׂימֶנּוּ כִּי זַרְעֲךָ הוּא: וַיַּשְׁכֵּם אַבְרָהָם ׀ בַּבֹּקֶר וַיִּקַּח־לֶחֶם וְחֵמַת
מַיִם וַיִּתֵּן אֶל־הָגָר שָׂם עַל־שִׁכְמָהּ וְאֶת־הַיֶּלֶד וַיְשַׁלְּחֶהָ וַתֵּלֶךְ
טו וַתֵּתַע בְּמִדְבַּר בְּאֵר שָׁבַע: וַיִּכְלוּ הַמַּיִם מִן־הַחֵמֶת וַתַּשְׁלֵךְ אֶת־הַיֶּלֶד

כָּל הַשֹּׁמֵעַ יִצְחַק לִי — *Whoever hears will laugh for me* . . . rejoicing for me, and will not be concerned for the pain of the circumcision.

9. אֶת בֶּן הָגָר הַמִּצְרִית — *The son of Hagar the Egyptian.* Sarah assumed that this scoffing was instigated by (Hagar) his mother, from whom he first heard it, as our Sages say, שׁוּתָא דְּרִינוֹקָא בְּשׁוּקָא אוֹ דַּאֲבוּהִי אוֹ דְאִמֵּיהּ, *The talk of a child in the marketplace is either that of his father or that of his mother (Succah* 56b).

מְצַחֵק — *Mocking* . . . scoffing at the feast made in Abraham's house (upon the weaning of Isaac), for he said, (Sarah) conceived from Abimelech. The reason he did not claim this at the time of Isaac's birth was because Ishmael heard it later from the "scoffers of the time," or perhaps even if he did mock at the time of (Isaac's) birth, Sarah was not aware of it since she was preoccupied at that time.

10. גָּרֵשׁ הָאָמָה הַזֹּאת וְאֶת בְּנָהּ — *Drive out this slavewoman with her son.* It was her advice which caused him to slander (me) so that her son should inherit all (from you), therefore drive (her out) because it is not right for him to even inherit a portion (of your estate).

כִּי לֹא יִירַשׁ בֶּן הָאָמָה — *For the son of this slavewoman shall not inherit* . . . inasmuch that he is not considered genealogically yours, for "the child follows the status of the tainted (פָּגוּם) parent" (*Kiddushin* 66b).

12. אַל יֵרַע בְּעֵינֶיךָ עַל הַנַּעַר וְעַל אֲמָתֶךָ כֹּל אֲשֶׁר תֹּאמַר אֵלֶיךָ שָׂרָה — *Be not distressed over the youth or your slavewoman: Whatever Sarah tells you.* Do not be distressed by her demands regarding the youth and the slavewoman, i.e., to drive them out with a sign of (their status) as slaves, as it says, *he placed them on her shoulder* (verse 14 — see explanation ahead).

שְׁמַע בְּקֹלָהּ — *Heed her voice* . . . for she is justified in telling you to do so.

כִּי בְיִצְחָק יִקָּרֵא לְךָ זָרַע — *Since through Isaac will offspring be considered yours* . . . and not through him (Ishmael).

NOTES

9. אֶת בֶּן הָגָר הַמִּצְרִית – *The son of Hagar the Egyptian.* Since we are not told that Ishmael mocked, but *the son of Hagar*, the implication must be that his behavior was influenced by his mother. She, of course, had an ulterior motive in questioning Abraham's paternity of Isaac, for then her son would be the sole heir of Abraham's considerable wealth.

10. גָּרֵשׁ הָאָמָה הַזֹּאת וְאֶת בְּנָהּ – *Drive out this slavewoman with her son.* The *Sforno's* interpretation explains why Sarah said בְּנָהּ, *her son*, implying, not yours, insofar as inheritance is concerned. Hagar questioned Abraham's paternity of Isaac; Sarah denied Hagar's son (Ishmael) the patrimony of Abraham. Halachically her argument was sound. Since Hagar had not been set free by Sarah,

whoever hears will laugh for me." [7] *And she said, "Who is the One Who said to Abraham, 'Sarah would nurse children'? For I have borne a son in his old age!"*

[8] *The child grew and was weaned. Abraham made a great feast on the day Isaac was weaned.*

[9] *Sarah saw the son of Hagar, the Egyptian, whom she had born to Abraham, mocking.* [10] *So she said to Abraham, "Drive out this slavewoman with her son, for the son of that slavewoman shall not inherit with my son, with Isaac!"*

[11] *The matter greatly distressed Abraham regarding his son.* [12] *So God said to Abraham, "Be not distressed over the youth or your slavewoman: Whatever Sarah tells you, heed her voice, since through Isaac will offspring be considered yours.* [13] *But the son of the slavewoman as well will I make into a nation for he is your offspring."*

[14] *So Abraham awoke early in the morning, took bread and a skin of water, and gave them to Hagar. He placed them on her shoulder along with the boy, and sent her off. She departed, and strayed in the desert of Beer-sheba.*

[15] *When the water of the skin was consumed, she cast off the boy*

---

13. וְגַם אֶת בֶּן הָאָמָה — *But the son of the slavewoman as well.* Do not worry over driving out the son, for you are driving out *the son of the slavewoman,* not *your* son, nonetheless . . .

לְגוֹי אֲשִׂימֶנּוּ כִּי זַרְעֲךָ הוּא — *I will make him into a nation for he is your offspring . . .* but he himself is not worthy to be a nation.

14. שָׂם עַל שִׁכְמָהּ — *He placed them on her shoulder . . .* the "skin of water"; as a sign that she is a bondwoman, similar to, וְהִתְעַנִּי תַּחַת יָדֶיהָ — *submit yourself to her domination* (16:9). However, this righteous man (Abraham) did not refrain from providing them with all their needs, as our Sages tell us, *God was with the youth* (verse 20) — this teaches us to amplify the verse to include his asses, camels and laborers (*Bereishis Rabbah* 53:15). Therefore, they lacked naught except for water when they strayed in the wilderness, and once they found water he dwelled in the wilderness according to his nature which was that of a פֶּרֶא אָדָם, *wild ass of a man.*

וְאֶת הַיֶּלֶד — *And the boy.* He also gave her the boy.

וַיְשַׁלְּחֶהָ — *And he saw her off.* In his great kindness he accompanied her, similar to, *while Abraham walked with them to see them off* (18:16).

NOTES

her status of slavewoman establishes the status of her son as well, based upon the Talmudic decision in *Kiddushin* cited by the *Sforno.*

14. שָׂם עַל שִׁכְמָהּ – *He placed them on her shoulder.* Abraham placed the skin of water on Hagar's shoulder, not to burden her, for there were beasts of burden at her disposal as the *Midrash* cited by the *Sforno* indicates. This was done only as a symbolic act, to establish her continuing status as a slavewoman.

וְאֶת הַיֶּלֶד – *And the boy.* The expression וְאֶת הַיֶּלֶד, *and the boy,* is not to be understood as placing him on her shoulder as well. It simply means that he gave along the boy with her, to be in her care.

וַיְשַׁלְּחֶהָ – *And he saw her off* (lit., *sent her away*). The Hebrew word לְשַׁלֵּחַ, *to send away,* at times has a different connotation. We see the word used when Abraham accompanied the angels וְאַבְרָהָם הֹלֵךְ עִמָּם לְשַׁלְּחָם, which certainly does not mean that he sent them away. Here also Abraham did not callously send Hagar and Ishmael away. The phrase וַיְשַׁלְּחֶהָ is interpreted by the *Sforno* as *he accompanied her,* similar to the expression used in 18:16.

טז תַּחַת אַחַד הַשִּׂיחִם׃ וַתֵּלֶךְ וַתֵּשֶׁב לָהּ מִנֶּגֶד הַרְחֵק כִּמְטַחֲוֵי קֶשֶׁת כִּי
אָמְרָה אַל־אֶרְאֶה בְּמוֹת הַיָּלֶד וַתֵּשֶׁב מִנֶּגֶד וַתִּשָּׂא אֶת־קֹלָהּ וַתֵּבְךְּ׃
יז וַיִּשְׁמַע אֱלֹהִים אֶת־קוֹל הַנַּעַר וַיִּקְרָא מַלְאַךְ אֱלֹהִים ׀ אֶל־הָגָר מִן־
הַשָּׁמַיִם וַיֹּאמֶר לָהּ מַה־לָּךְ הָגָר אַל־תִּירְאִי כִּי־שָׁמַע אֱלֹהִים אֶל־קוֹל
יח הַנַּעַר בַּאֲשֶׁר הוּא־שָׁם׃ קוּמִי שְׂאִי אֶת־הַנַּעַר וְהַחֲזִיקִי אֶת־יָדֵךְ בּוֹ כִּי־
יט לְגוֹי גָּדוֹל אֲשִׂימֶנּוּ׃ וַיִּפְקַח אֱלֹהִים אֶת־עֵינֶיהָ וַתֵּרֶא בְּאֵר מָיִם וַתֵּלֶךְ
כ וַתְּמַלֵּא אֶת־הַחֵמֶת מַיִם וַתַּשְׁקְ אֶת־הַנָּעַר׃ וַיְהִי אֱלֹהִים אֶת־הַנַּעַר
כא וַיִּגְדָּל וַיֵּשֶׁב בַּמִּדְבָּר וַיְהִי רֹבֶה קַשָּׁת׃ וַיֵּשֶׁב בְּמִדְבַּר פָּארָן וַתִּקַּח־לוֹ
אִמּוֹ אִשָּׁה מֵאֶרֶץ מִצְרָיִם׃
כב וַיְהִי בָּעֵת הַהִוא וַיֹּאמֶר אֲבִימֶלֶךְ וּפִיכֹל שַׂר־צְבָאוֹ אֶל־אַבְרָהָם לֵאמֹר ששי
כג אֱלֹהִים עִמְּךָ בְּכֹל אֲשֶׁר־אַתָּה עֹשֶׂה׃ וְעַתָּה הִשָּׁבְעָה לִּי בֵאלֹהִים
הֵנָּה אִם־תִּשְׁקֹר לִי וּלְנִינִי וּלְנֶכְדִּי כַּחֶסֶד אֲשֶׁר־עָשִׂיתִי עִמְּךָ תַּעֲשֶׂה
כד־כה עִמָּדִי וְעִם־הָאָרֶץ אֲשֶׁר־גַּרְתָּה בָּהּ׃ וַיֹּאמֶר אַבְרָהָם אָנֹכִי אִשָּׁבֵעַ׃ וְהוֹכִחַ
אַבְרָהָם אֶת־אֲבִימֶלֶךְ עַל־אֹדוֹת בְּאֵר הַמַּיִם אֲשֶׁר גָּזְלוּ עַבְדֵי אֲבִימֶלֶךְ׃
כו וַיֹּאמֶר אֲבִימֶלֶךְ לֹא יָדַעְתִּי מִי עָשָׂה אֶת־הַדָּבָר הַזֶּה וְגַם־אַתָּה
כז לֹא־הִגַּדְתָּ לִּי וְגַם אָנֹכִי לֹא שָׁמַעְתִּי בִּלְתִּי הַיּוֹם׃ וַיִּקַּח אַבְרָהָם
כח צֹאן וּבָקָר וַיִּתֵּן לַאֲבִימֶלֶךְ וַיִּכְרְתוּ שְׁנֵיהֶם בְּרִית׃ וַיַּצֵּב אַבְרָהָם אֶת־
כט שֶׁבַע כִּבְשֹׂת הַצֹּאן לְבַדְּהֶן׃ וַיֹּאמֶר אֲבִימֶלֶךְ אֶל־אַבְרָהָם מָה הֵנָּה
ל שֶׁבַע כְּבָשֹׂת הָאֵלֶּה אֲשֶׁר הִצַּבְתָּ לְבַדָּנָה׃ וַיֹּאמֶר כִּי אֶת־שֶׁבַע
כְּבָשֹׂת תִּקַּח מִיָּדִי בַּעֲבוּר תִּהְיֶה־לִּי לְעֵדָה כִּי חָפַרְתִּי אֶת־הַבְּאֵר
לא הַזֹּאת׃ עַל־כֵּן קָרָא לַמָּקוֹם הַהוּא בְּאֵר שָׁבַע כִּי שָׁם נִשְׁבְּעוּ שְׁנֵיהֶם׃

---

19. וַיִּפְקַח אֱלֹהִים אֶת עֵינֶיהָ — *Then God opened her eyes.* He gave her understanding to perceive that water was in that place; for she was not blind before that.

22. אֱלֹהִים עִמְּךָ — *God is with you.* Therefore I fear you and desire a treaty with you, not because of your might or wealth.

23. כַּחֶסֶד אֲשֶׁר עָשִׂיתִי עִמְּךָ תַּעֲשֶׂה עִמָּדִי — *According to the kindness that I have done with you, do with me.* Do this kindness with me, and take an oath on behalf of your children.

24. אָנֹכִי אִשָּׁבֵעַ — *I will swear.* I will do this kindness and swear, but you did not do any kindness to me as you claim, for your servants stole (my well).

25. אֲשֶׁר גָּזְלוּ עַבְדֵי אֲבִימֶלֶךְ — *That Abimelech's servants stole.* He rebuked him, as king, for the violent robbery committed without shame in his land, and also for keeping wicked men in his household, which is not the way of the righteous, as it says, לֹא יֵשֵׁב בְּקֶרֶב בֵּיתִי עֹשֵׂה רְמִיָּה, *He that is deceitful shall not dwell within my house (Psalms* 101:7).

26. לֹא יָדַעְתִּי מִי עָשָׂה — *I do not know who did (this thing).* Even now that you tell me my servants committed this violence, I have no idea who (among them) could have done

NOTES

30. כִּי אֶת שֶׁבַע כְּבָשֹׂת תִּקַּח מִיָּדִי — *Because you are to take these seven ewes from me.* The animals given by Abraham to Abimelech are not meant as a gift. That would not fit into the context of this event. Rather it is meant to be a means of exchange (חֲלִיפִין) whereby one party gives an item of value to the second party which consummates the transaction. This is done when property or goods are

beneath one of the trees. 16 *She went and sat herself down at a distance,*
some bowshots away, for she said, "Let me not see the death of the child."
And she sat at a distance, lifted her voice, and wept.
17 *God heard the cry of the youth, and an angel of God called to Hagar*
from heaven and said to her, "What troubles you, Hagar? Fear not, for God
has heeded the cry of the youth in his present state. 18 *Arise, lift up the*
youth and grasp your hand upon him, for I will make a great nation of him."
19 *Then God opened her eyes and she perceived a well of water; she went*
and filled the skin with water and gave the youth to drink.
20 *God was with the youth and he grew up; he dwelt in the desert and*
became an accomplished archer. 21 *He lived in the desert of Paran, and his*
mother took a wife for him from the land of Egypt.
22 *At that time, Abimelech and Phicol his general said to Abraham, "God*
is with you in all that you do. 23 *Now swear to me here by God that you will*
not deal falsely with me nor with my son nor with my grandson; according
to the kindness that I have done with you, do with me, and with the land
in which you have sojourned." 24 *And Abraham said, "I will swear."*
25 *Then Abraham disputed with Abimelech regarding the well of water*
that Abimelech's servants had seized. 26 *But Abimelech said, "I do not*
know who did this thing; furthermore, you have never told me, and
moreover, I myself have heard nothing of it except for today."
27 *So Abraham took flocks and cattle and gave them to Abimelech; and*
the two of them entered into a covenant. 28 *Abraham set seven ewes of the*
flock by themselves. 29 *And Abimelech said to Abraham, "What are these*
seven ewes which you have set by themselves?"
30 *And he replied, "Because you are to take these seven ewes from me,*
that it may serve me as testimony that I dug this well." 31 *Therefore that*
place was called Beer-sheba because there the two of them took an oath.

---

it, for there is no one among them I suspect (of such an act). Were there (one) who was suspect, he would not be a member of my household.

וְגַם אַתָּה לֹא הִגַּדְתָּ לִּי וְגַם אָנֹכִי לֹא שָׁמַעְתִּי — *Furthermore, you have never told me, and moreover, I myself have heard nothing of it.* Regarding your reproof that as king I should have relieved the oppressed, certainly the king can only react to one of two circumstances: either to the cry of the victim of violence, or to the outcry of the populace protesting such violence, and (in this case) you (the victim) never told me, and moreover I have heard no public outcry regarding this matter.

30. כִּי אֶת שֶׁבַע כְּבָשֹׂת תִּקַּח מִיָּדִי — *Because you are to take these seven ewes from me.* Similar to, שָׁלַף אִישׁ נַעֲלוֹ וְנָתַן לְרֵעֵהוּ וְזֹאת הַתְּעוּדָה, *one would draw off his shoe and give it to his friend (Ruth* 4:7), (as a symbolic act) testifying to the agreement of the parties and their acknowledgment of the matter (at hand).

בַּעֲבוּר תִּהְיֶה לִּי — *That it may serve me* ... this covenant ...

לְעֵדָה כִּי חָפַרְתִּי אֶת הַבְּאֵר הַזֹּאת — *as testimony* ... of your acknowledgement *that I dug this well.*

NOTES

sold or given as a gift. It also was done to finalize an agreement or treaty, as in this case. The source of this *halachah* is found in the Book of *Ruth,* cited by the *Sforno,* where Boaz and his relative reach an understanding regarding Ruth and the land of Elimelech.

לב וַיִּכְרְתוּ בְרִית בִּבְאֵר שָׁבַע וַיָּקָם אֲבִימֶלֶךְ וּפִיכֹל שַׂר־צְבָאוֹ וַיָּשֻׁבוּ אֶל־
לג אֶרֶץ פְּלִשְׁתִּים: וַיִּטַּע אֶשֶׁל בִּבְאֵר שָׁבַע וַיִּקְרָא־שָׁם בְּשֵׁם יהוה אֵל
לד עוֹלָם: וַיָּגָר אַבְרָהָם בְּאֶרֶץ פְּלִשְׁתִּים יָמִים רַבִּים:
כב שביעי א וַיְהִי אַחַר הַדְּבָרִים הָאֵלֶּה וְהָאֱלֹהִים נִסָּה אֶת־אַבְרָהָם וַיֹּאמֶר אֵלָיו
ב אַבְרָהָם וַיֹּאמֶר הִנֵּנִי: וַיֹּאמֶר קַח־נָא אֶת־בִּנְךָ אֶת־יְחִידְךָ אֲשֶׁר־אָהַבְתָּ
אֶת־יִצְחָק וְלֶךְ־לְךָ אֶל־אֶרֶץ הַמֹּרִיָּה וְהַעֲלֵהוּ שָׁם לְעֹלָה עַל אַחַד
ג הֶהָרִים אֲשֶׁר אֹמַר אֵלֶיךָ: וַיַּשְׁכֵּם אַבְרָהָם בַּבֹּקֶר וַיַּחֲבֹשׁ אֶת־חֲמֹרוֹ
וַיִּקַּח אֶת־שְׁנֵי נְעָרָיו אִתּוֹ וְאֵת יִצְחָק בְּנוֹ וַיְבַקַּע עֲצֵי עֹלָה וַיָּקָם וַיֵּלֶךְ
ד אֶל־הַמָּקוֹם אֲשֶׁר־אָמַר־לוֹ הָאֱלֹהִים: בַּיּוֹם הַשְּׁלִישִׁי וַיִּשָּׂא אַבְרָהָם
ה אֶת־עֵינָיו וַיַּרְא אֶת־הַמָּקוֹם מֵרָחֹק: וַיֹּאמֶר אַבְרָהָם אֶל־נְעָרָיו שְׁבוּ־
לָכֶם פֹּה עִם־הַחֲמוֹר וַאֲנִי וְהַנַּעַר נֵלְכָה עַד־כֹּה וְנִשְׁתַּחֲוֶה וְנָשׁוּבָה
ו אֲלֵיכֶם: וַיִּקַּח אַבְרָהָם אֶת־עֲצֵי הָעֹלָה וַיָּשֶׂם עַל־יִצְחָק בְּנוֹ וַיִּקַּח בְּיָדוֹ
ז אֶת־הָאֵשׁ וְאֶת־הַמַּאֲכֶלֶת וַיֵּלְכוּ שְׁנֵיהֶם יַחְדָּו: וַיֹּאמֶר יִצְחָק אֶל־
אַבְרָהָם אָבִיו וַיֹּאמֶר אָבִי וַיֹּאמֶר הִנֶּנִּי בְנִי וַיֹּאמֶר הִנֵּה הָאֵשׁ וְהָעֵצִים
ח וְאַיֵּה הַשֶּׂה לְעֹלָה: וַיֹּאמֶר אַבְרָהָם אֱלֹהִים יִרְאֶה־לּוֹ הַשֶּׂה לְעֹלָה בְּנִי
ט וַיֵּלְכוּ שְׁנֵיהֶם יַחְדָּו: וַיָּבֹאוּ אֶל־הַמָּקוֹם אֲשֶׁר אָמַר־לוֹ הָאֱלֹהִים וַיִּבֶן

---

32. וַיָּשֻׁבוּ אֶל אֶרֶץ פְּלִשְׁתִּים — *And they returned to the land of the Philistines.* They returned from Beer-sheba, which was not part of the land of the Philistines. They came there to speak to Abraham, who (in turn) had come there to oversee his herds. It was there that he gave them sheep, cattle and ewes to establish the covenant.

33. וַיִּקְרָא שָׁם בְּשֵׁם ה׳ אֵל עוֹלָם — *And there he proclaimed the name of* H*ASHEM*, *God of eternity.* He proclaimed and made known to the populace that the Almighty is the God Who not only directs time, but preceded and created it, a concept contrary to that of early and later scholars of the nations.

XXII

1. נִסָּה אֶת אַבְרָהָם — *Tested Abraham.* (God's) intention was that he (Abraham) should translate his love and reverence (of God) from the potential to the actual. In this manner he would be similar to his Creator, Who is good to this world in actuality, for the purpose of man's existence is to imitate his Creator as far as possible, as the (Torah) testifies, in saying: נַעֲשֶׂה אָדָם בְּצַלְמֵנוּ כִּדְמוּתֵנוּ, *Let us make man in our image, after our likeness* (1:26).

3. וַיֵּלֶךְ אֶל הַמָּקוֹם — *And he went to the place* . . . to the Land of Moriah.

NOTES

32. וַיָּשֻׁבוּ אֶל אֶרֶץ פְּלִשְׁתִּים – *And they returned to the land of the Philistines.* The word *returned* presents a difficulty to some commentators, who consider Beer-sheba to be a part of the land of the Philistines. The *Sforno* however considers this clear proof that Beer-sheba never was part of that land, but only bordered on it.

33. וַיִּקְרָא שָׁם בְּשֵׁם ה׳ אֵל עוֹלָם – *And there he proclaimed the Name of* H*ASHEM*, *God of eternity.* Most commentators understand the term אֵל עוֹלָם as *God of the Universe.* However, the *Sforno* translates it as *Eternal God.* Hence Abraham is teaching the populace the concept of God as the First Cause, Who is Eternal and existed before the creation of time. The *Sforno* is alluding to this idea in his commentary on this verse.

XXII

1. נִסָּה אֶת אַבְרָהָם – *Tested Abraham.* Since God foresees everything, and nothing is unknown to Him, there is no need for Him to test man to see whether he will meet the test. The concept of נִסָּיוֹן,

32 Thus, they entered into a covenant at Beer-sheba; Abimelech then arose,
with Phicol, his general, and they returned to the land of the Philistines.
33 He planted an "eshel" in Beer-sheba, and there he proclaimed the
Name of HASHEM, God of the Universe. 34 And Abraham sojourned in the
land of the Philistines many years.

22 *1 And it happened after these things that God tested Abraham and said*
to him, "Abraham," and he replied, "Here I am."
2 And He said, "Please take your son, your only one, whom you love —
Isaac — and go to the land of Moriah; bring him up there as an offering upon
one of the mountains which I shall tell you."
3 So Abraham woke up early in the morning and he saddled his donkey;
he took his two young men with him and Isaac, his son; he split the wood
for the offering, and stood up and went to the place of which God had
spoken to him.
4 On the third day, Abraham raised his eyes and perceived the place
from afar. 5 And Abraham said to his young men, "Stay here by yourselves
with the donkey, while I and the lad will go yonder; we will worship and
we will return to you."
6 And Abraham took the wood for the offering, and placed it on Isaac,
his son. He took in his hand the fire and the knife, and the two of them went
together. 7 Then Isaac spoke to Abraham his father and said, "Father —"
And he said, "Here I am, my son."
And he said, "Here are the fire and the wood, but where is the lamb for
the offering?"
8 And Abraham said, "God will seek out for Himself the lamb for the
offering, my son." And the two of them went together.
9 They arrived at the place of which God had spoken to him; Abraham

---

4. וַיִּשָּׂא אַבְרָהָם אֶת עֵינָיו וַיַּרְא אֶת הַמָּקוֹם — *Abraham looked up and perceived the place . . .* the place for the sacrifice on Mount Moriah.

מֵרָחֹק — *From afar.* By the will of God he was granted the ability to see clearly from afar, as we find (by Moses), וַיַּרְאֵהוּ ה׳ אֶת כָּל הָאָרֶץ, *HASHEM showed him all the land* (*Deut.* 34:1). He therefore understood that that particular place was to be the place of sacrifice.

5. שְׁבוּ לָכֶם פֹּה — *Stay here by yourselves . . .* so that they should not prevent him or interfere with him in bringing this sacrifice.

NOTES

test, has therefore given Torah commentators pause, and presented numerous difficulties, which they have answered with a variety of explanations. The *Sforno*, in this verse, offers a quite simple, but profound, explanation. God is not testing Abraham to determine whether he will sacrifice his son or not. Rather he is drawing forth the potential inner powers of faith and trust which are latent in Abraham, bringing them to the fore and translating them into actuality through the *Akeidah* (the binding of Isaac). In this manner, man also fulfills his purpose, which is to imitate his Creator, who manifests Himself in this world בְּפוֹעַל, *through the actual* (i.e., His works) and not only בְּכֹחַ, *in potential.*

3-4. וַיֵּלֶךְ אֶל הַמָּקוֹם . . . וַיַּרְא אֶת הַמָּקוֹם מֵרָחֹק — *And he went to the place . . . and perceived the place from afar.* The word מָקוֹם, *place,* is used in both verses. The first refers to the Land of Moriah; the second to the particular place on the mountain where the sacrifice is to be held. The very fact that God granted Abraham (an old man) such unusual vision to be able to see the place from so far was a clear indication that this was indeed the place chosen by Him for the *Akeidah.*

שָׁם אַבְרָהָם אֶת־הַמִּזְבֵּחַ וַיַּעֲרֹךְ אֶת־הָעֵצִים וַיַּעֲקֹד אֶת־יִצְחָק בְּנוֹ
י וַיָּשֶׂם אֹתוֹ עַל־הַמִּזְבֵּחַ מִמַּעַל לָעֵצִים: וַיִּשְׁלַח אַבְרָהָם אֶת־יָדוֹ וַיִּקַּח
יא אֶת־הַמַּאֲכֶלֶת לִשְׁחֹט אֶת־בְּנוֹ: וַיִּקְרָא אֵלָיו מַלְאַךְ יהוה מִן־הַשָּׁמַיִם
יב וַיֹּאמֶר אַבְרָהָם | אַבְרָהָם וַיֹּאמֶר הִנֵּנִי: וַיֹּאמֶר אַל־תִּשְׁלַח יָדְךָ
אֶל־הַנַּעַר וְאַל־תַּעַשׂ לוֹ מְאוּמָה כִּי | עַתָּה יָדַעְתִּי כִּי־יְרֵא אֱלֹהִים
יג אַתָּה וְלֹא חָשַׂכְתָּ אֶת־בִּנְךָ אֶת־יְחִידְךָ מִמֶּנִּי: וַיִּשָּׂא אַבְרָהָם אֶת־עֵינָיו
וַיַּרְא וְהִנֵּה־אַיִל אַחַר נֶאֱחַז בַּסְּבַךְ בְּקַרְנָיו וַיֵּלֶךְ אַבְרָהָם וַיִּקַּח
יד אֶת־הָאַיִל וַיַּעֲלֵהוּ לְעֹלָה תַּחַת בְּנוֹ: וַיִּקְרָא אַבְרָהָם שֵׁם־הַמָּקוֹם הַהוּא
טו יהוה | יִרְאֶה אֲשֶׁר יֵאָמֵר הַיּוֹם בְּהַר יהוה יֵרָאֶה: וַיִּקְרָא מַלְאַךְ יהוה
טז אֶל־אַבְרָהָם שֵׁנִית מִן־הַשָּׁמָיִם: וַיֹּאמֶר בִּי נִשְׁבַּעְתִּי נְאֻם־יהוה כִּי יַעַן
יז אֲשֶׁר עָשִׂיתָ אֶת־הַדָּבָר הַזֶּה וְלֹא חָשַׂכְתָּ אֶת־בִּנְךָ אֶת־יְחִידֶךָ: כִּי־בָרֵךְ
אֲבָרֶכְךָ וְהַרְבָּה אַרְבֶּה אֶת־זַרְעֲךָ כְּכוֹכְבֵי הַשָּׁמַיִם וְכַחוֹל אֲשֶׁר
יח עַל־שְׂפַת הַיָּם וְיִרַשׁ זַרְעֲךָ אֵת שַׁעַר אֹיְבָיו: וְהִתְבָּרְכוּ בְזַרְעֲךָ כֹּל גּוֹיֵי
יט הָאָרֶץ עֵקֶב אֲשֶׁר שָׁמַעְתָּ בְּקֹלִי: וַיָּשָׁב אַבְרָהָם אֶל־נְעָרָיו וַיָּקֻמוּ וַיֵּלְכוּ
יַחְדָּו אֶל־בְּאֵר שָׁבַע וַיֵּשֶׁב אַבְרָהָם בִּבְאֵר שָׁבַע:

---

12. עַתָּה יָדַעְתִּי — *Now I know.* I, the angel, now know God is justified in considering you greater than His angels, as our Sages say, "The righteous are greater than the ministering angels" (*Sanhedrin* 93a).

מִמֶּנִּי — *Than I.* (I now know that) you fear God "more than I," an angel, and hence you are more worthy of elevated status than I, as our Sages state, "the righteous are greater, etc." You (have proven) in actuality that you are God fearing. The Almighty had prior knowledge of your potential as a God-fearing (man), but an angel's actual knowledge can only be drawn from what is actual (not potential).

13. וְהִנֵּה אַיִל אַחַר נֶאֱחַז בַּסְּבַךְ — *Behold a ram, afterward, caught in the thicket.* Since he did not see a ram there before (the angel intervened) — only immediately afterward — caught in the thicket, he realized that the ram had been sent through the will of God and there was no fear of theft (attached to his taking it).

תַּחַת בְּנוֹ — *Instead of his son.* As exchange (for him) since he had committed himself to offer his son (as a sacrifice) in keeping with, וְדֹבֵר אֱמֶת בִּלְבָבוֹ, *And speaks truth in his heart* (*Psalms* 15:2).

14. אֲשֶׁר יֵאָמֵר הַיּוֹם — *As it is said this day.* That place which Israel referred to on the day the Torah was written, as being the mountain (on which) *HASHEM* is seen, (meaning) when He will reveal its location, as it says, וְהָיָה הַמָּקוֹם אֲשֶׁר יִבְחַר, *Then it shall come to pass that the place which (God) shall choose* (*Deut.* 12:11), (and this was in the time of David); that place, Abraham called ה׳ יִרְאֶה, *HASHEM yireh.*

NOTES

12. עַתָּה יָדַעְתִּי ... מִמֶּנִּי – *Now I know ... than I.* The *Sforno* interprets this verse as recording the words of the angel, speaking on his own, and not as the messenger of God, speaking in His Name. עַתָּה יָדַעְתִּי means *now I know* that man can be "higher than the angels," and superior מִמֶּנִּי, *than I*, in יִרְאַת ה׳, *the fear of HASHEM*. The word מִמֶּנִּי, according to the *Sforno*, is not linked to, *you have not withheld your son from Me* (the word *Me* referring to God); rather this word reverts back to *you are a God-fearing man*. The sense of the sentence is: The angel states that he now realizes that Abraham is superior to him in the fear of *Hashem*, which he proved by not withholding his son from Him.

*built the altar there, and arranged the wood; he bound Isaac, his son, and
he placed him on the altar atop the wood.* 10 *Abraham stretched out his
hand, and took the knife to slaughter his son.*
11 *And an angel of HASHEM called to him from heaven, and said,
"Abraham! Abraham!"*
And he said, "Here I am."
12 *And he said, "Do not stretch out your hand against the lad nor do
anything to him for now I know that you are a God-fearing man, since
you have not withheld your son, your only one, from Me."*
13 *And Abraham raised his eyes and saw — behold, a ram! —
afterwards, caught in the thicket by its horns; so Abraham went and took
the ram and offered it up as an offering instead of his son.* 14 *And
Abraham called the name of that site "HASHEM Yireh," as it is said this
day, on the mountain HASHEM will be seen.*
15 *The angel of HASHEM called to Abraham a second time from heaven.*
16 *And he said, "By Myself I swear — the word of HASHEM — that because
you have done this thing, and have not withheld your son, your only one,*
17 *that I shall surely bless you and greatly increase your offspring like the
stars of the heavens and like the sand on the seashore; and your offspring
shall inherit the gate of its enemy.* 18 *And all the nations of the earth shall
bless themselves by your offspring, because you have listened to My
voice."*
19 *Abraham returned to his young men, and they stood up and went
together to Beer-sheba, and Abraham stayed at Beer-sheba.*

---

16. בִּי נִשְׁבַּעְתִּי — *By Myself, I swear* . . . that I will bless you.

נְאֻם ה׳ כִּי יַעַן אֲשֶׁר עָשִׂיתָ — *Declared HASHEM, That since you have done (this thing).* I, God, say that since you have done this thing . . .

17. כִּי בָרֵךְ אֲבָרֶכְךָ — *That I shall surely bless you.*

18. וְהִתְבָּרְכוּ בְזַרְעֲךָ כֹּל גּוֹיֵי הָאָרֶץ — *And all the nations of the earth shall bless themselves by your offspring.* When the nations will all call upon God's Name to serve Him with one accord (based on *Zephaniah* 3:9), they will all seek blessings through your seed and endeavor to emulate them.

עֵקֶב אֲשֶׁר שָׁמַעְתָּ בְּקֹלִי — *Because you have listened to My voice.* Because שְׂכַר מִצְוָה מִצְוָה, *the reward of one mitzvah is another mitzvah* (*Avos* 4:2), therefore you will merit (through this willingness to sacrifice Isaac) that your children will be a "banner for the nations," teaching them to serve the Almighty, and this will be considered as a righteousness for you.

NOTES

13. וְהִנֵּה אַיִל אַחַר נֶאֱחַז בַּסְּבַךְ – *Behold a ram, afterward, caught in the thicket.* The word אַחַר, *afterward,* refers to the sequence of events. Abraham did not see any ram there, until the angel commanded him to desist from sacrificing Isaac. Only *afterward* did he see the ram, and realized that it had been sent by God to be used as a sacrifice in place of Isaac. By sacrificing the ram, Abraham will fulfill his commitment to bring an offering.

14. אֲשֶׁר יֵאָמֵר הַיּוֹם – *As it is said this day.* The flow of the verse is to be understood thus, according to the *Sforno:* Abraham called the name of the place *HASHEM Yireh,* God will see and seek out this place for the dwelling of His *Shechinah* (see *Onkelos).* This place is the one which the Torah alludes to as *the place which God shall choose.* This in turn did not happen until the time of David. And it is in this place that ה׳ יֵרָאֶה, *HASHEM is seen (always).*

מפטיר

כ וַיְהִ֗י אַחֲרֵי֙ הַדְּבָרִ֣ים הָאֵ֔לֶּה וַיֻּגַּ֥ד לְאַבְרָהָ֖ם לֵאמֹ֑ר הִ֠נֵּה יָלְדָ֨ה מִלְכָּ֥ה
כא גַם־הִ֛וא בָּנִ֖ים לְנָח֥וֹר אָחִֽיךָ׃ אֶת־ע֥וּץ בְּכֹר֖וֹ וְאֶת־בּ֣וּז אָחִ֑יו וְאֶת־קְמוּאֵ֖ל
כב אֲבִ֥י אֲרָֽם׃ וְאֶת־כֶּ֣שֶׂד וְאֶת־חֲז֔וֹ וְאֶת־פִּלְדָּ֖שׁ וְאֶת־יִדְלָ֑ף וְאֵ֖ת בְּתוּאֵֽל׃
כג וּבְתוּאֵ֖ל יָלַ֣ד אֶת־רִבְקָ֑ה שְׁמֹנָ֥ה אֵ֙לֶּה֙ יָלְדָ֣ה מִלְכָּ֔ה לְנָח֖וֹר אֲחִ֥י אַבְרָהָֽם׃
כד וּפִֽילַגְשׁ֖וֹ וּשְׁמָ֣הּ רְאוּמָ֑ה וַתֵּ֣לֶד גַּם־הִ֗וא אֶת־טֶ֙בַח֙ וְאֶת־גַּ֔חַם וְאֶת־תַּ֖חַשׁ
וְאֶת־מַעֲכָֽה׃

---

20. הִנֵּה יָלְדָה מִלְכָּה — *Behold, Milcah too has borne children.* Behold, you already know that Milcah gave birth to children.

גַּם הִוא — *She also* . . . in addition to his (Nachor's) concubine.

23. וּבְתוּאֵל יָלַד אֶת רִבְקָה — *And Bethuel begot Rebecca.* The reporter told (Abraham) that Bethuel, who was a son of the wife (of Nachor, not of his concubine), begot Rebecca. This tiding came to (tell Abraham) that he would be able to find a wife for his son in

[20] *It came to pass after these things, that Abraham was told, saying:
Behold, Milcah too has borne children to Nahor, your brother:* [21] *Uz, his
firstborn; Buz, his brother; Kemuel, the father of Aram;* [22] *and Chesed,
Hazo, Pildash, Jidlaph, and Bethuel;* [23] *And Bethuel begot Rebecca. These
eight Milcah bore to Nahor, Abraham's brother.* [24] *And his concubine,
whose name was Reumah, also bore children: Tebah, Gaham, Tahash,
and Maacah.*

---

his father's house, and would not have to become associated (through marriage) with Canaan.

24. וּפִילַגְשׁוֹ . . . וַתֵּלֶד גַּם הִוא — *And his concubine . . . also bore children.* The reporter told (Abraham) that his (Nachor's) concubine gave birth to Maacah, who was also worthy to wed his son if he chose not to marry Rebecca, and it would not be necessary to (take a wife) from the seed of Canaan.

פרשת חיי שרה

כג
א־ב וַיִּהְיוּ חַיֵּי שָׂרָה מֵאָה שָׁנָה וְעֶשְׂרִים שָׁנָה וְשֶׁבַע שָׁנִים שְׁנֵי חַיֵּי שָׂרָה: וַתָּמָת
שָׂרָה בְּקִרְיַת אַרְבַּע הִוא חֶבְרוֹן בְּאֶרֶץ כְּנָעַן וַיָּבֹא אַבְרָהָם לִסְפֹּד לְשָׂרָה
ג־ד וְלִבְכֹּתָהּ: וַיָּקָם אַבְרָהָם מֵעַל פְּנֵי מֵתוֹ וַיְדַבֵּר אֶל־בְּנֵי־חֵת לֵאמֹר: גֵּר־
וְתוֹשָׁב אָנֹכִי עִמָּכֶם תְּנוּ לִי אֲחֻזַּת־קֶבֶר עִמָּכֶם וְאֶקְבְּרָה מֵתִי מִלְּפָנָי:
ה־ו וַיַּעֲנוּ בְנֵי־חֵת אֶת־אַבְרָהָם לֵאמֹר לוֹ: שְׁמָעֵנוּ | אֲדֹנִי נְשִׂיא אֱלֹהִים
אַתָּה בְּתוֹכֵנוּ בְּמִבְחַר קְבָרֵינוּ קְבֹר אֶת־מֵתֶךָ אִישׁ מִמֶּנּוּ אֶת־קִבְרוֹ לֹא־
ז יִכְלֶה מִמְּךָ מִקְּבֹר מֵתֶךָ: וַיָּקָם אַבְרָהָם וַיִּשְׁתַּחוּ לְעַם־הָאָרֶץ לִבְנֵי־חֵת:
ח וַיְדַבֵּר אִתָּם לֵאמֹר אִם־יֵשׁ אֶת־נַפְשְׁכֶם לִקְבֹּר אֶת־מֵתִי מִלְּפָנַי שְׁמָעוּנִי
ט וּפִגְעוּ־לִי בְּעֶפְרוֹן בֶּן־צֹחַר: וְיִתֶּן־לִי אֶת־מְעָרַת הַמַּכְפֵּלָה אֲשֶׁר־לוֹ

XXIII

2. וַתָּמָת שָׂרָה — *And Sarah died.* After Rebecca — who is fit to replace Sarah — is born, and Abraham is notified, Sarah dies. As (our Sages tell us), "One righteous person does not die before another is born, as it is written, וְזָרַח הַשֶּׁמֶשׁ וּבָא הַשָּׁמֶשׁ, *and the sun rises, and the sun sets (Ecclesiastes* 1:5)" *(Yoma* 38b).

לִסְפֹּד לְשָׂרָה — *To eulogize Sarah* ... on her behalf and in her honor, as (our Sages) tell us, "The eulogy is for the honor of the deceased" *(Sanhedrin* 46b).

3. מֵעַל פְּנֵי מֵתוֹ וַיְדַבֵּר אֶל בְּנֵי חֵת — *From the presence of his dead, and spoke to the children of Heth.* The laws of mourning had not yet gone into effect; therefore he was permitted to leave his residence and speak to the children of Heth.

4. גֵּר וְתוֹשָׁב — *An alien and a resident.* Since I am a stranger I have no gravesite here, as it is written, וּמִי לְךָ פֹּה כִּי חָצַבְתָּ לְּךָ פֹּה קָבֶר, *Whom do you have here that you have hewed out a sepulcher here for yourself? (Isaiah* 22:16). The reason I wish to purchase one is because I reside among you and my intention is to establish myself here in your midst.

תְּנוּ לִי אֲחֻזַּת קֶבֶר — *Grant me an estate for a burial site.* Please agree to give me the right to have a possession of a grave as is written, *Unto Abraham for a possession of a burying place by the children of Heth* (v. 20).

6. בְּמִבְחַר קְבָרֵינוּ קְבֹר — *In the choicest of our burial places bury* ... and do not wait until you have made your purchase, as (our Sages) have taught us, כָּל הַמֵּתִים כֻּלָּם הַמִּדְחָה מִטָּתָם

NOTES

XXIII

2. וַתָּמָת שָׂרָה — *And Sarah died.* The *Sforno* links the conclusion of the previous *sidrah* (וַיֵּרָא) to the beginning of this *sidrah.* After Abraham is informed of the birth of Rebecca, the Torah relates that Sarah died. From heaven it is ordained that a righteous person leaves this earth only after another righteous one is born to take his or her place. Only after the new sun of Rebecca has risen does the sun of Sarah set.

לִסְפֹּד לְשָׂרָה — *To eulogize (for) Sarah.* The phraseology in this verse is a bit awkward and difficult to reconcile with the rules of Hebrew grammar. It should have been written לִסְפֹּד אֶת שָׂרָה, *to eulogize Sarah,* not לְשָׂרָה, *for Sarah.* The Torah, however, is teaching us that the opinion of those who contend that every eulogy is meant for the honor of the dead, and not for the living, is correct; hence לִסְפֹּד לְשָׂרָה, *for Sarah,* on her behalf, not in accordance with those who contend that the eulogy is for the honor of the living.

3. מֵעַל פְּנֵי מֵתוֹ וַיְדַבֵּר אֶל בְּנֵי חֵת — *From the presence of his dead, and spoke to the children of Heth.* Upon the death of a relative for whom one is obligated to mourn, one's status is that of an *onen.* Only after burial does one become an *avel.* Unlike an *avel,* a mourner, who is prohibited to leave his house or engage in any business transaction, an *onen* is permitted to do so providing it is in conjunction with the needs and honor of the deceased. There-

PARASHAS CHAYEI SARAH

23 *1 Sarah's lifetime was one hundred years, twenty years, and seven years; the years of Sarah's life. 2 Sarah died in Kiriath-arba which is Hebron in the land of Canaan; and Abraham came to eulogize Sarah and to bewail her. 3 Abraham rose up from the presence of his dead, and spoke to the children of Heth, saying: 4 "I am an alien and a resident among you; grant me an estate for a burial site with you, that I may bury my dead from before me."*

5 And the children of Heth answered Abraham, saying to him: 6 "Hear us, my lord: You are a prince of God in our midst; in the choicest of our burial places bury your dead, any of us will not withhold his burial place from you, from burying your dead."

7 Then Abraham rose up and bowed down to the members of the council, to the children of Heth. 8 He spoke to them saying: "If it is truly your will to bury my dead from before me, heed me, and intercede for me with Ephron son of Zohar. 9 Let him grant me the Cave of Machpelah which is his,

---

הֲרֵי זֶה מְשֻׁבָּח, *Regarding all deceased, he who hastens to inter them is praiseworthy* (*Moed Katan* 22a).

7. וַיִּשְׁתַּחוּ לְעַם הָאָרֶץ — *And he bowed to the people of the land* . . . to the assembled chiefs who represented the populace.

8. אִם יֵשׁ אֶת נַפְשְׁכֶם לִקְבֹּר — *If it is your will to bury.* If indeed you wish me to bury my dead quickly and not tarry as you indicated by saying, *In the choice of our sepulcher bury* (v. 6), then . . .

שְׁמָעוּנִי — *Hear me.* Assist me in the acquisition of a burying place.

וּפִגְעוּ לִי בְּעֶפְרוֹן — *And intercede for me with Ephron* . . . that he shall sell me (a parcel of his land) though it is unseemly for a distinguished person to sell any part of his patrimony, as Naboth states, חָלִילָה לִּי מֵה׳ מִתִּתִּי אֶת נַחֲלַת אֲבֹתַי לָךְ, *a profanation to me from* HASHEM *from giving the inheritance of my fathers to you* (*I Kings* 21:3).

9. מְעָרַת הַמַּכְפֵּלָה — *The cave of Machpelah.* (It is located in) a place named Machpelah, as it is written, וַיָּקָם שְׂדֵה עֶפְרוֹן אֲשֶׁר בַּמַּכְפֵּלָה, *The field of Ephron which was in Machpelah* (v. 17).

NOTES

fore Abraham is permitted to approach the children of Heth and negotiate the purchase of a gravesite for his wife Sarah.

4. גֵּר וְתוֹשָׁב — *An alien and a resident.* The custom of the land and the culture of the Hittites was that strangers were not permitted to bury their dead in their midst, since this would be considered staking out a claim to that particular parcel of land, a right reserved only for residents. Abraham appreciated this obstacle confronting him and assured the children of Heth that he intended to change his status and take up permanent residence in this land. Indeed, he was not misleading them, for this land would some day become the permanent residence of his descendants. The children of Heth might not have grasped the subtle truth of Abraham's statement, and interpreted it their way. Abraham was telling the truth; they were the victims of self-deception.

6. בְּמִבְחַר קְבָרֵינוּ קְבֹר — *In the choicest of our burial places bury* . . . The Talmud teaches us that a deceased relative should be buried as quickly as possible. This was apparently the ancient custom of the Hittites as well; therefore they urged Abraham to bury his wife at once, even before he had concluded the purchase of the gravesite.

7. וַיִּשְׁתַּחוּ לְעַם הָאָרֶץ — *And he bowed to the people of the land* . . . Abraham did not bow down to *all* the people of the land. However, since he did so to the leaders, it is as though he bowed to the populace.

9. מְעָרַת הַמַּכְפֵּלָה . . . בְּכֶסֶף מָלֵא — *The cave of Machpelah . . . for its full price.* A careful examination of the verses will show that Machpelah was

י אֲשֶׁר בִּקְצֵה שָׂדֵהוּ בְּכֶסֶף מָלֵא יִתְּנֶנָּה לִּי בְּתוֹכְכֶם לַאֲחֻזַּת־קָבֶר: וְעֶפְרוֹן
יֹשֵׁב בְּתוֹךְ בְּנֵי־חֵת וַיַּעַן עֶפְרוֹן הַחִתִּי אֶת־אַבְרָהָם בְּאָזְנֵי בְנֵי־חֵת לְכֹל
יא בָּאֵי שַׁעַר־עִירוֹ לֵאמֹר: לֹא־אֲדֹנִי שְׁמָעֵנִי הַשָּׂדֶה נָתַתִּי לָךְ וְהַמְּעָרָה אֲשֶׁר־
יב בּוֹ לְךָ נְתַתִּיהָ לְעֵינֵי בְנֵי־עַמִּי נְתַתִּיהָ לָּךְ קְבֹר מֵתֶךָ: וַיִּשְׁתַּחוּ אַבְרָהָם לִפְנֵי
יג עַם־הָאָרֶץ: וַיְדַבֵּר אֶל־עֶפְרוֹן בְּאָזְנֵי עַם־הָאָרֶץ לֵאמֹר אַךְ אִם־אַתָּה לוּ
יד שְׁמָעֵנִי נָתַתִּי כֶּסֶף הַשָּׂדֶה קַח מִמֶּנִּי וְאֶקְבְּרָה אֶת־מֵתִי שָׁמָּה: וַיַּעַן עֶפְרוֹן
טו אֶת־אַבְרָהָם לֵאמֹר לוֹ: אֲדֹנִי שְׁמָעֵנִי אֶרֶץ אַרְבַּע מֵאֹת שֶׁקֶל־כֶּסֶף בֵּינִי
טז וּבֵינְךָ מַה־הִוא וְאֶת־מֵתְךָ קְבֹר: וַיִּשְׁמַע אַבְרָהָם אֶל־עֶפְרוֹן וַיִּשְׁקֹל
אַבְרָהָם לְעֶפְרֹן אֶת־הַכֶּסֶף אֲשֶׁר דִּבֶּר בְּאָזְנֵי בְנֵי־חֵת אַרְבַּע מֵאוֹת שֶׁקֶל
שני יז כֶּסֶף עֹבֵר לַסֹּחֵר: וַיָּקָם ׀ שְׂדֵה עֶפְרוֹן אֲשֶׁר בַּמַּכְפֵּלָה אֲשֶׁר לִפְנֵי מַמְרֵא
הַשָּׂדֶה וְהַמְּעָרָה אֲשֶׁר־בּוֹ וְכָל־הָעֵץ אֲשֶׁר בַּשָּׂדֶה אֲשֶׁר בְּכָל־גְּבֻלוֹ סָבִיב:

אֲשֶׁר בִּקְצֵה שָׂדֵהוּ — *Which is on the edge of his field* . . . therefore the sale of it will not impair his estate.

בְּכֶסֶף מָלֵא — *For its full price.* I do not want him to reduce the price in your honor.

בְּתוֹכְכֶם — *In your midst.* (This means) in your presence. I do not ask for time but will pay immediately; and so he did, as it says, *and Abraham weighed to Ephron the silver, in the presence of the children of Heth* (vs. 16 and 18).

לַאֲחֻזַּת קָבֶר — *For a possession of a burying place.* Even though he (Ephron) may agree to sell me a portion of his estate, he may object to my using it for a burying site; therefore I want it understood that it is to be used for that purpose.

11. לֹא אֲדֹנִי — *No, my lord.* It is not necessary for the leaders of the populace to intercede and entreat me.

שְׁמָעֵנִי — *Hear me.* Listen to me directly; there is no need for any intermediary.

הַשָּׂדֶה נָתַתִּי לָךְ — *I have given you the field.* As soon as you spoke I mentally gave it to you.

וְהַמְּעָרָה אֲשֶׁר בּוֹ — *And the cave that is in it* . . . so you need not go through the field of another to bury your dead.

לְעֵינֵי בְנֵי עַמִּי נְתַתִּיהָ לָּךְ קְבֹר מֵתֶךָ — *In the presence of the children of my people I give it to you; bury your dead.* In their presence do I give it to you for the explicit purpose of burying your dead, as you requested when you said, *"For a possession of a burying place."*

12. וַיִּשְׁתַּחוּ אַבְרָהָם לִפְנֵי עַם הָאָרֶץ — *And Abraham bowed down before the people of the land.* He bowed down in gratitude to them to indicate that it was in their honor that

NOTES

the name of an area. In that area there was a field and in that field a cave was located. The phrase מְעָרַת הַמַּכְפֵּלָה does not mean, *the cave of Machpelah,* rather the cave situated in the field which was located in Machpelah.

בְּכֶסֶף מָלֵא — *For its full price.* Abraham had already demonstrated, following the Battle of the Kings, that he adamantly refused to accept anything from others, even when it was richly deserved. So here also he rejected the offer of Ephron to give him a grave and insisted upon paying immediately in full. He did so, wisely, in the presence of the populace who would serve as witness, with the clear understanding that this cave will be used for a burying place, so that Ephron will not be able to renege. (See verse 13.)

11. הַשָּׂדֶה נָתַתִּי לָךְ — *I have given you the field.* Even though Abraham has only requested the cave, Ephron includes the field as well, so that Abraham will have access to the cave without the need to acquire a right of way from another landowner.

12. וַיִּשְׁתַּחוּ אַבְרָהָם לִפְנֵי עַם הָאָרֶץ — *And Abraham bowed down before the people of the land.* Ephron

*on the edge of his field; let him grant it to me for its full price, in your midst,
as an estate for a burial site."*
10 *Now, Ephron was sitting in the midst of the children of Heth; and
Ephron the Hittite responded to Abraham in the hearing of the children of
Heth, for all who come to the gate of his city, saying:* 11 *"No, my lord; heed
me! I have given you the field, and as for the cave that is in it, I have given
it to you; In the view of the children of my people have I given it to you;
bury your dead."* 12 *So Abraham bowed down before the members of the
council.* 13 *He spoke to Ephron in the hearing of the members of the council,
saying: "Rather, if only you would heed me! I give you the price of the field,
accept it from me, that I may bury my dead there."*
14 *And Ephron replied to Abraham, saying to him:* 15 *"My lord, heed me!
Land worth four hundred silver shekels; between me and you — what is it?
Bury your dead."*
16 *Abraham heeded Ephron, and Abraham weighed out to Ephron the
price which he had mentioned in the hearing of the children of Heth, four
hundred silver shekels in negotiable currency.* 17 *And Ephron's field, which
was in Machpelah, facing Mamre, the field and the cave within it and all
the trees in the field, within all its surrounding boundaries, was confirmed*

Ephron agreed to accede to his request, as (our Sages) tell us, "If one knows that his father is highly regarded in a certain place he should not say, 'Hasten to serve me or release me for my sake,' but 'for my father's sake' " (*Kiddushin* 31b).

13. אַךְ אִם... נָתַתִּי כֶּסֶף הַשָּׂדֶה — *But if only you . . . I give you the price of the field.* I will do as you say and bury my dead in your field but only if I will (be permitted) to pay the price, otherwise I will not bury her there.

אַתָּה לוּ שְׁמָעֵנִי — *If only you would heed me.* Please listen to me.

קַח מִמֶּנִּי וְאֶקְבְּרָה — *Accept it from me that I may bury my dead there.* Only after you accept the silver will I bury her.

15. מַה הִוא — *What is it.* It is such a paltry sum that our word will suffice, and (even) prior to payment you can proceed to bury your dead.

16. וַיִּשְׁמַע אַבְרָהָם אֶל עֶפְרוֹן — *And Abraham heeded Ephron.* He accepted Ephron's valuation of the field.

וַיִּשְׁקֹל — *And weighed out . . .* (i.e.,) he paid, as we find, כִּכַּר כֶּסֶף תִּשְׁקוֹל, *You shall pay* (lit., *weigh out*) *a talent of silver (I Kings* 20:39).

17-18. וַיָּקָם שְׂדֵה... לְאַבְרָהָם לְמִקְנָה — *And the field was secured . . . to Abraham as a purchase.* The deed of purchase was validated by its signatories.

NOTES

was most generous and Abraham should have thanked *him*, not the children of Heth, but he bowed to them in gratitude, not to Ephron! The *Sforno* explains that Abraham was convinced that Ephron's magnanimity was motivated by his desire to impress his countrymen, hence he expressed his gratitude to them, rather than directly to Ephron.

13. See note on verse 9.

16. וַיִּשְׁמַע אַבְרָהָם אֶל עֶפְרוֹן — *And Abraham heeded Ephron.* Since Abraham refused to accept Ephron's offer to bury Sarah prior to payment, why does the Torah tell us that *he listened to Ephron*? The *Sforno* explains that this refers only to his acceptance of the price, not the *conditions* of the sale set forth by Ephron.

16-20. וַיִּשְׁקֹל... וַיָּקָם הַשָּׂדֶה... מֵאֵת בְּנֵי חֵת — *And weighed out . . . and the field was secured . . . from*

יח-יט לְאַבְרָהָם לְמִקְנָה לְעֵינֵי בְנֵי־חֵת בְּכֹל בָּאֵי שַׁעַר־עִירוֹ: וְאַחֲרֵי־כֵן קָבַר
אַבְרָהָם אֶת־שָׂרָה אִשְׁתּוֹ אֶל־מְעָרַת שְׂדֵה הַמַּכְפֵּלָה עַל־פְּנֵי מַמְרֵא
כ הִוא חֶבְרוֹן בְּאֶרֶץ כְּנָעַן: וַיָּקָם הַשָּׂדֶה וְהַמְּעָרָה אֲשֶׁר־בּוֹ לְאַבְרָהָם
כד א לַאֲחֻזַּת־קָבֶר מֵאֵת בְּנֵי־חֵת: וְאַבְרָהָם זָקֵן בָּא בַּיָּמִים
ב וַיהוָה בֵּרַךְ אֶת־אַבְרָהָם בַּכֹּל: וַיֹּאמֶר אַבְרָהָם אֶל־עַבְדּוֹ זְקַן בֵּיתוֹ
ג הַמֹּשֵׁל בְּכָל־אֲשֶׁר־לוֹ שִׂים־נָא יָדְךָ תַּחַת יְרֵכִי: וְאַשְׁבִּיעֲךָ בַּיהוָה אֱלֹהֵי
הַשָּׁמַיִם וֵאלֹהֵי הָאָרֶץ אֲשֶׁר לֹא־תִקַּח אִשָּׁה לִבְנִי מִבְּנוֹת הַכְּנַעֲנִי
ד אֲשֶׁר אָנֹכִי יוֹשֵׁב בְּקִרְבּוֹ: כִּי אֶל־אַרְצִי וְאֶל־מוֹלַדְתִּי תֵּלֵךְ וְלָקַחְתָּ
ה אִשָּׁה לִבְנִי לְיִצְחָק: וַיֹּאמֶר אֵלָיו הָעֶבֶד אוּלַי לֹא־תֹאבֶה הָאִשָּׁה לָלֶכֶת
אַחֲרַי אֶל־הָאָרֶץ הַזֹּאת הֶהָשֵׁב אָשִׁיב אֶת־בִּנְךָ אֶל־הָאָרֶץ אֲשֶׁר־
ו יָצָאתָ מִשָּׁם: וַיֹּאמֶר אֵלָיו אַבְרָהָם הִשָּׁמֶר לְךָ פֶּן־תָּשִׁיב אֶת־בְּנִי שָׁמָּה:
ז יְהוָה | אֱלֹהֵי הַשָּׁמַיִם אֲשֶׁר לְקָחַנִי מִבֵּית אָבִי וּמֵאֶרֶץ מוֹלַדְתִּי וַאֲשֶׁר
דִּבֶּר־לִי וַאֲשֶׁר נִשְׁבַּע־לִי לֵאמֹר לְזַרְעֲךָ אֶתֵּן אֶת־הָאָרֶץ הַזֹּאת הוּא
ח יִשְׁלַח מַלְאָכוֹ לְפָנֶיךָ וְלָקַחְתָּ אִשָּׁה לִבְנִי מִשָּׁם: וְאִם־לֹא תֹאבֶה הָאִשָּׁה
לָלֶכֶת אַחֲרֶיךָ וְנִקִּיתָ מִשְּׁבֻעָתִי זֹאת רַק אֶת־בְּנִי לֹא תָשֵׁב שָׁמָּה:
ט וַיָּשֶׂם הָעֶבֶד אֶת־יָדוֹ תַּחַת יֶרֶךְ אַבְרָהָם אֲדֹנָיו וַיִּשָּׁבַע לוֹ עַל־הַדָּבָר
שלישי י הַזֶּה: וַיִּקַּח הָעֶבֶד עֲשָׂרָה גְמַלִּים מִגְּמַלֵּי אֲדֹנָיו וַיֵּלֶךְ וְכָל־טוּב אֲדֹנָיו

20. וַיָּקָם הַשָּׂדֶה . . . מֵאֵת בְּנֵי חֵת — *And the field was secured . . . from the children of Heth.* The whole community agreed that it should be his for a burial place.

XXIV

1. וְאַבְרָהָם זָקֵן . . . וַה׳ בֵּרַךְ אֶת אַבְרָהָם — *And Abraham was old . . . and HASHEM had blessed Abraham.* The Torah explains the reasons which motivated Abraham to send his servant to another land to find a wife for his son, and why he had to adjure him with an oath. Firstly, since he was old he was concerned lest he die before a match was arranged for his son, and since he was convinced that there was no worthy wife for his son (in Canaan) he sent (Eliezer) to another land. Also, since Abraham was wealthy he feared that someone might bribe his servant to select an unfit wife for Isaac; hence he made him swear.

3. אֱלֹהֵי הַשָּׁמַיִם וֵאלֹהֵי הָאָרֶץ — *God of heaven and God of earth.* Should you prove false to the oath, He will punish you in this world (*earth*) and in the next *(heaven).*

5. אֲשֶׁר יָצָאתָ מִשָּׁם — *To the land from which you departed . . .* which you have rejected by your departure from there! Now if I swear to find a proper wife (and betroth her on behalf of Isaac) and she refuses to come back with me to Canaan, then Isaac will be

NOTES

the children of Heth. So that there be no question of the legality and validity of this sale, a number of steps were taken by Abraham. The silver was weighed and paid, the deed was validated and the entire community concurred that this cave might be used as a burial place.

XXIV

1-3. וְאַבְרָהָם זָקֵן . . . וַה׳ בֵּרַךְ אֶת אַבְרָהָם — *And Abraham was old . . . and HASHEM had blessed Abraham.* The *Sforno* reads into these verses three reasons for Abraham's decision to send Eliezer to Haran to find a bride for his son and for the need to administer an oath to him: (a) He was old and time was running out (זָקֵן); (b) he was determined not to have Isaac marry one of the Canaanite women (מִבְּנוֹת הַכְּנַעֲנִי); and (c) because he was rich he was afraid that there will be unscrupulous people who will try to become part of his family through marriage, hence וְאַשְׁבִּיעֲךָ, *I adjure you.*

5. אֲשֶׁר יָצָאתָ מִשָּׁם — *To the land from which you*

[18] *as Abraham's as a purchase in the view of the children of Heth, among
all who came to the gate of his city.* [19] *And afterwards Abraham buried
Sarah his wife in the cave of the field of Machpelah facing Mamre, which
is Hebron, in the land of Canaan.* [20] *Thus, the field with its cave confirmed
as Abraham's as an estate for a burial site, from the children of Heth.*

24 [1] *Now Abraham was old, well on in years, and HASHEM had blessed
Abraham with everything.* [2] *And Abraham said to his servant, the
elder of his household who controlled all that was his: "Place now your
hand under my thigh.* [3] *And I will have you swear by HASHEM, God of
heaven and God of earth, that you not take a wife for my son from the
daughters of the Canaanites, among whom I dwell.* [4] *Rather, to my land
and to my kindred shall you go and take a wife for my son for Isaac."*
[5] *The servant said to him: "Perhaps the woman shall not wish to follow
me to this land; shall I take your son back to the land from which you
departed?"* [6] *Abraham answered him, "Beware not to return my son to
there.* [7] *HASHEM, God of heaven, Who took me from the house of my father
and from the land of my birth; Who spoke concerning me, and Who swore
to me saying, 'To your offspring will I give this land,' He will send His angel
before you, and you will take a wife for my son from there.* [8] *But if the
woman will not wish to follow you, you shall then be absolved of this oath
of mine. However, do not return my son to there."*
[9] *So the servant placed his hand under the thigh of Abraham his master
and swore to him regarding this matter.* [10] *Then the servant took ten camels
of his master's camels and set out with all the bounty of his master*

---

obligated to fulfill all the duties of a husband, i.e., food, clothing, and marital duties, and be obligated to travel there. If not, he would betray the wife of his youth.

7. אֱלֹהֵי הַשָּׁמַיִם ... יִשְׁלַח מַלְאָכוֹ — *The God of heaven ... will send His angel.* May it be His will to send His angel from on High; since He took me forth from that land, and to Him all deeds are known, He will arrange matters so that my son need not return there.

וַאֲשֶׁר דִּבֶּר לִי — *And Who spoke to me ...* in addition to which He spoke to me, saying, כִּי בְיִצְחָק יִקָּרֵא לְךָ זָרַע, *Through Isaac will offspring be considered yours* (21:12).

וַאֲשֶׁר נִשְׁבַּע לִי — *And Who swore to me.* Since He swore to me He will not renege, and without a doubt He will assure (the success of this mission), that my son wed a woman fitting for him so as to bring into the world worthy children who are prepared to fulfill the oath given by God.

9. וַיִּשָּׁבַע לוֹ עַל הַדָּבָר הַזֶּה — *And swore to him regarding this matter.* He swore, including in his oath all the conditions made by Abraham.

10. וַיִּקַּח הָעֶבֶד עֲשָׂרָה גְמַלִּים מִגְּמַלֵּי אֲדֹנָיו וַיֵּלֶךְ — *And the servant took ten camels of his master, and departed.* He requested permission of his master to depart, after preparing the

NOTES

departed. Eliezer was sent not only to *find* a bride but also to betroth her on behalf of Isaac, acting as a שָׁלִיחַ, *agent;* hence, if she would refuse to accompany him back to Canaan after he betroths her, serious problems would arise.

7. אֱלֹהֵי הַשָּׁמַיִם — *The God of heaven.* In verse 3 the God of heaven and earth is invoked, whereas here only the God of heaven. The reason, as given by the *Sforno*, is because Abraham is referring to the intervention of the Almighty from on High.

10. וַיִּקַּח הָעֶבֶד ... וַיֵּלֶךְ ... וַיָּקָם וַיֵּלֶךְ – *And the servant took ... and departed ... and he arose and*

יא בְּיָדוֹ וַיָּקָם וַיֵּלֶךְ אֶל־אֲרַם נַהֲרַיִם אֶל־עִיר נָחוֹר: וַיַּבְרֵךְ הַגְּמַלִּים מִחוּץ
יב לָעִיר אֶל־בְּאֵר הַמָּיִם לְעֵת עֶרֶב לְעֵת צֵאת הַשֹּׁאֲבֹת: וַיֹּאמַר ׀ יהוה
אֱלֹהֵי אֲדֹנִי אַבְרָהָם הַקְרֵה־נָא לְפָנַי הַיּוֹם וַעֲשֵׂה־חֶסֶד עִם אֲדֹנִי אַבְרָהָם:
יג הִנֵּה אָנֹכִי נִצָּב עַל־עֵין הַמָּיִם וּבְנוֹת אַנְשֵׁי הָעִיר יֹצְאֹת לִשְׁאֹב מָיִם:
יד וְהָיָה הַנַּעֲרָ אֲשֶׁר אֹמַר אֵלֶיהָ הַטִּי־נָא כַדֵּךְ וְאֶשְׁתֶּה וְאָמְרָה שְׁתֵה
וְגַם־גְּמַלֶּיךָ אַשְׁקֶה אֹתָהּ הֹכַחְתָּ לְעַבְדְּךָ לְיִצְחָק וּבָהּ אֵדַע כִּי־עָשִׂיתָ
טו חֶסֶד עִם־אֲדֹנִי: וַיְהִי־הוּא טֶרֶם כִּלָּה לְדַבֵּר וְהִנֵּה רִבְקָה יֹצֵאת אֲשֶׁר
יֻלְּדָה לִבְתוּאֵל בֶּן־מִלְכָּה אֵשֶׁת נָחוֹר אֲחִי אַבְרָהָם וְכַדָּהּ עַל־שִׁכְמָהּ:
טז וְהַנַּעֲרָ טֹבַת מַרְאֶה מְאֹד בְּתוּלָה וְאִישׁ לֹא יְדָעָהּ וַתֵּרֶד הָעַיְנָה וַתְּמַלֵּא
יז כַדָּהּ וַתָּעַל: וַיָּרָץ הָעֶבֶד לִקְרָאתָהּ וַיֹּאמֶר הַגְמִיאִינִי נָא מְעַט־מַיִם
יח־יט מִכַּדֵּךְ: וַתֹּאמֶר שְׁתֵה אֲדֹנִי וַתְּמַהֵר וַתֹּרֶד כַּדָּהּ עַל־יָדָהּ וַתַּשְׁקֵהוּ: וַתְּכַל
כ לְהַשְׁקֹתוֹ וַתֹּאמֶר גַּם לִגְמַלֶּיךָ אֶשְׁאָב עַד אִם־כִּלּוּ לִשְׁתֹּת: וַתְּמַהֵר
וַתְּעַר כַּדָּהּ אֶל־הַשֹּׁקֶת וַתָּרָץ עוֹד אֶל־הַבְּאֵר לִשְׁאֹב וַתִּשְׁאַב לְכָל־
כא גְּמַלָּיו: וְהָאִישׁ מִשְׁתָּאֵה לָהּ מַחֲרִישׁ לָדַעַת הַהִצְלִיחַ יהוה דַּרְכּוֹ אִם־לֹא:

(ten) camels, and left.

וְכָל טוּב אֲדֹנָיו בְּיָדוֹ — *With all the bounty of his master in his hand.* He took with him gold, silver and garments. There was no need to get permission to do so, since the affairs of Abraham's household were in his hands and his authority was unquestioned.

וַיָּקָם וַיֵּלֶךְ — *And he arose and departed* ... on his journey.

14. וְהָיָה הַנַּעֲרָה אֲשֶׁר אֹמַר אֵלֶיהָ — *So let it be that the maiden to whom I shall say.* He did not make this a sign whereby he might recognize Isaac's destined wife, because that would be divination (נַחַשׁ), rather he prayed that it might fall out so; and so it was with Jonathan the son of Saul (see *I Samuel* 14:8-12). As for the saying of our Sages, כָּל נַחַשׁ שֶׁאֵינוֹ כֶּאֱלִיעֶזֶר עֶבֶד אַבְרָהָם וִיהוֹנָתָן בֶּן שָׁאוּל אֵינוֹ נַחַשׁ, *An omen which is not as that pronounced by Abraham's servant Eliezer, or by Jonathan the son of Saul, is not considered a divination (Chullin* 95b), their intent and meaning is: If the individual says it not as a prayer, but as divination, i.e., "If thus and thus happens then I shall do this," then he is guilty of divination (נַחַשׁ).

וְגַם גְּמַלֶּיךָ אַשְׁקֶה — *And I will even water your camels.* One who asks should request less than he actually needs so as not to overly bother others, while the person responding should go beyond it and offer all, or more, than is needed.

אֹתָהּ הֹכַחְתָּ — *She has been instructed* (lit., *designated) by You.* You have taught her proper ethical understanding so that she is indeed worthy to be Isaac's wife.

15. טֶרֶם כִּלָּה — *Before he had finished speaking* ... even before he finished, similar to, וְהָיָה טֶרֶם יִקְרָאוּ וַאֲנִי אֶעֱנֶה, *Before they call I will answer (Isaiah* 65:24).

NOTES

departed. The phrase וַיֵּלֶךְ, *he departed,* is used twice in this verse. The first means he asked permission to go; the second means he went.

14. וְהָיָה הַנַּעֲרָה אֲשֶׁר אֹמַר אֵלֶיהָ — *So let it be that the maiden to whom I shall say.* The Talmud *(Chullin* 95b) discusses the episodes of Eliezer and Jonathan son of Saul. In both cases it would seem that they are "divining," i.e., relying upon a sign to determine their ultimate action. Since this is prohibited, *Tosafos* asks how they allowed themselves to do so. He explains the reasoning used by Eliezer and Jonathan, but the *Sforno* answers this question quite simply. In both cases they are but praying that it might fall out so. It is interesting to note that the *Rambam* and *Raavad* also disagree as to how to interpret this passage in the Talmud. Again, the *Sforno's* interpretation would reconcile the difficulties they both encounter.

in his hand and made his way to Aram Naharaim to the city of Nahor.
11 *He made the camels kneel down outside the city towards a well of water at evening time, the time when women come out to draw.*
12 *And he said, "HASHEM, God of my master Abraham, may You so arrange it for me this day that You do kindness with my master Abraham.*
13 *See, I stand here by the spring of water and the daughters of the townsmen come out to draw.*
14 *Let it be that the maiden to whom I shall say, 'Please tip over your jug so I may drink,' and who replies, 'Drink, and I will even water your camels,' her will You have designated for Your servant, for Isaac; and may I know through her that You have done kindness with my master."*

15 *And it was when he had not yet finished speaking that suddenly Rebecca was coming out — she who had been born to Bethuel the son of Milcah the wife of Nahor, brother of Abraham — with her jug upon her shoulder.*
16 *Now the maiden was very fair to look upon; a virgin whom no man had known. She descended to the spring, filled her jug and ascended.*
17 *The servant ran towards her and said, "Let me sip, if you please, a little water from your jug."*
18 *She said, "Drink, my lord," and quickly she lowered her jug to her hand and gave him drink.*

19 *When she finished giving him drink, she said, "I will draw water even for your camels until they have finished drinking."*
20 *So she hurried and emptied her jug into the trough and kept running to the well to draw water; and she drew for all his camels.*
21 *The man was astonished at her, reflecting silently to know whether HASHEM had made his journey successful or not.*

אֲשֶׁר יָלְדָה לִבְתוּאֵל בֶּן מִלְכָּה — *Who was born to Bethuel the son of Milcah* . . . the son of the wife, not of Reumah the concubine (22:23,24).

16. טֹבַת מַרְאֶה — *Fair to look upon.* (She had a) beautiful complexion.

19. וַתְּכַל לְהַשְׁקֹתוֹ וַתֹּאמֶר — *When she finished giving him drink, she said.* She waited until he had finished drinking before speaking to him, as our Sages say, אֵין מְשִׂיחִין בִּסְעוּדָה שֶׁמָּא יַקְדִּים קָנֶה לְוֶשֶׁט, *One should not converse at meals, lest the windpipe acts before the gullet* (*Taanis* 5b).

20. וַתְּמַהֵר — *So she hurried.* Haste in serving another is a sign of regard and respect.

וַתָּרָץ עוֹד אֶל הַבְּאֵר — *And ran again to the well* . . . the well in front of the fountain from whence the animals drink.

21. מִשְׁתָּאֵה — *Looked wonderingly.* He wondered at the alacrity with which she hastened to do this kindness.

מַחֲרִישׁ — *Maintaining silence.* He did not urge her to desist from exerting herself, as would have been proper.

לָדַעַת — *To learn* . . . to determine and judge from her act of kindness and haste to perform it.

NOTES

אֹתָהּ הֹכַחְתָּ — *She has been instructed by You.* The word הוֹכָחָה can mean *to prove, to appoint, to admonish,* or *to instruct.* The *Sforno* chooses the latter interpretation. If Rebecca should demonstrate unusual kindness, then Eliezer attributes this virtue to a unique aspect of her character granted her by the Almighty, Who was also (כביכול) her instructor, since she had no other teacher from her family.

15. אֲשֶׁר יָלְדָה לִבְתוּאֵל — *Who was born to Bethuel.* Born to *Bethuel the son of Nahor* would have been more appropriate than *son of Milcah.* The answer must be that the Torah is stressing that Rebecca's father is the son of Nahor's wife, not his concubine.

כב וַיְהִי כַּאֲשֶׁר כִּלּוּ הַגְּמַלִּים לִשְׁתּוֹת וַיִּקַּח הָאִישׁ נֶזֶם זָהָב בֶּקַע מִשְׁקָלוֹ
כג וּשְׁנֵי צְמִידִים עַל־יָדֶיהָ עֲשָׂרָה זָהָב מִשְׁקָלָם: וַיֹּאמֶר בַּת־מִי אַתְּ הַגִּידִי
כד נָא לִי הֲיֵשׁ בֵּית־אָבִיךְ מָקוֹם לָנוּ לָלִין: וַתֹּאמֶר אֵלָיו בַּת־בְּתוּאֵל אָנֹכִי
כה בֶּן־מִלְכָּה אֲשֶׁר יָלְדָה לְנָחוֹר: וַתֹּאמֶר אֵלָיו גַּם־תֶּבֶן גַּם־מִסְפּוֹא רַב
*רביעי כו־כז עִמָּנוּ גַּם־מָקוֹם לָלוּן: וַיִּקֹּד הָאִישׁ וַיִּשְׁתַּחוּ לַיהוה: * וַיֹּאמֶר בָּרוּךְ יהוה
אֱלֹהֵי אֲדֹנִי אַבְרָהָם אֲשֶׁר לֹא־עָזַב חַסְדּוֹ וַאֲמִתּוֹ מֵעִם אֲדֹנִי אָנֹכִי
כח בַּדֶּרֶךְ נָחַנִי יהוה בֵּית אֲחֵי אֲדֹנִי: וַתָּרָץ הַנַּעֲרָ וַתַּגֵּד לְבֵית אִמָּהּ
כט כַּדְּבָרִים הָאֵלֶּה: וּלְרִבְקָה אָח וּשְׁמוֹ לָבָן וַיָּרָץ לָבָן אֶל־הָאִישׁ הַחוּצָה
ל אֶל־הָעָיִן: וַיְהִי ׀ כִּרְאֹת אֶת־הַנֶּזֶם וְאֶת־הַצְּמִדִים עַל־יְדֵי אֲחֹתוֹ וּכְשָׁמְעוֹ
אֶת־דִּבְרֵי רִבְקָה אֲחֹתוֹ לֵאמֹר כֹּה־דִבֶּר אֵלַי הָאִישׁ וַיָּבֹא אֶל־הָאִישׁ
לא וְהִנֵּה עֹמֵד עַל־הַגְּמַלִּים עַל־הָעָיִן: וַיֹּאמֶר בּוֹא בְּרוּךְ יהוה לָמָּה תַעֲמֹד
לב בַּחוּץ וְאָנֹכִי פִּנִּיתִי הַבַּיִת וּמָקוֹם לַגְּמַלִּים: וַיָּבֹא הָאִישׁ הַבַּיְתָה וַיְפַתַּח
הַגְּמַלִּים וַיִּתֵּן תֶּבֶן וּמִסְפּוֹא לַגְּמַלִּים וּמַיִם לִרְחֹץ רַגְלָיו וְרַגְלֵי הָאֲנָשִׁים
°וַיּוּשַׂם ק׳ לג אֲשֶׁר אִתּוֹ: °ויישם לְפָנָיו לֶאֱכֹל וַיֹּאמֶר לֹא אֹכַל עַד אִם־דִּבַּרְתִּי דְּבָרָי
לד־לה וַיֹּאמֶר דַּבֵּר: וַיֹּאמַר עֶבֶד אַבְרָהָם אָנֹכִי: וַיהוה בֵּרַךְ אֶת־אֲדֹנִי מְאֹד
וַיִּגְדָּל וַיִּתֶּן־לוֹ צֹאן וּבָקָר וְכֶסֶף וְזָהָב וַעֲבָדִם וּשְׁפָחֹת וּגְמַלִּים וַחֲמֹרִים:

הַהִצְלִיחַ ה׳ דַּרְכּוֹ אִם לֹא — *Whether God had made his journey successful* ... whether she was motivated by natural kindness or by the hope of reward.

22. כַּאֲשֶׁר כִּלּוּ הַגְּמַלִּים לִשְׁתּוֹת — *And it was when the camels had finished drinking.* (Although this) took considerable time, still she did not ask for aught, doing it purely from a motivation of kindness.

וּשְׁנֵי צְמִידִים עַל יָדֶיהָ — *And two bracelets on her arms.* They proved to be a perfect fit (for her hands) similar to, וְעָשִׂיתָ עַל הַחֹשֶׁן שַׁרְשֹׁת גַּבְלֻת, *And you shall make upon the breastplate plaited chains (Exodus* 28:22), and וְעָשִׂיתָ עָלָיו זֵר זָהָב, *And make upon it a crown of gold* (ibid. 25:11), (meaning) a proper fit (for the חֹשֶׁן and אָרוֹן).

23. הֲיֵשׁ בֵּית אָבִיךְ מָקוֹם — *Is there room in your father's house* ... available for guest lodging, as was then the custom.

לָלִין — *To lodge in* ... where we may stable (our camels).

25. גַּם תֶּבֶן גַּם מִסְפּוֹא — *Even straw and feed.* Not only place to stable them but provender to feed them as well.

גַּם מָקוֹם לָלוּן — *And room to lodge in* ... for you and your people.

29. וַיָּרָץ לָבָן אֶל הָאִישׁ — *And Laban ran out to the man.* He ran to see the wealthy visitor, not to offer him hospitality.

30. וַיְהִי כִּרְאֹת אֶת הַנֶּזֶם וְאֶת הַצְּמִדִים עַל יְדֵי אֲחֹתוֹ — *When he saw the nose ring and the bracelets on his sister's arm.* He did not wish to be ungrateful.

NOTES

22. וּשְׁנֵי צְמִידִים עַל יָדֶיהָ — *And two bracelets on her arms.* As the *Ramban* points out, this verse lacks a verb, i.e., וַיִּתֵּן, *and he gave,* or וַיָּשֶׂם, *and he placed.* All it states is *two bracelets on her hands.* The answer perforce is that these bracelets were destined for her hands, fitting her wrists perfectly, indicating that this match of Rebecca and Isaac is also destined.

23-25. מָקוֹם לָלִין ... מָקוֹם לָלוּן — *Room to lodge in ... room to lodge in.* לָלִין, *to lodge in,* is written in the הִפְעִיל, as a transitive verb, whereas לָלוּן is a

22 *And it was, when the camels had finished drinking, the man took a
golden nose ring, its weight was a beka, and two bracelets on her arms, ten
gold shekels was their weight.* 23 *And he said, "Whose daughter are you?
Pray tell me. Is there room in your father's house for us to spend the night?"*
24 *She said to him, "I am the daughter of Bethuel the son of Milcah whom
she bore to Nahor."* 25 *And she said to him, "Even straw and feed is
plentiful with us as well as place to lodge."*
26 *So the man bowed low and prostrated himself to* HASHEM. 27 *He said,
"Blessed is* HASHEM, *God of my master Abraham, Who has not withheld
His kindness and truth from my master. As for me,* HASHEM *has guided me
on the way to the house of my master's brothers."*
28 *The maiden ran and told her mother's household according to these
events.* 29 *Rebecca had a brother whose name was Laban: Laban ran to the
man, outside to the spring.* 30 *For upon seeing the nose ring, and the
bracelets on his sister's hands, and upon his hearing his sister Rebecca's
words, saying, "Thus has the man spoken to me," he approached the man,
who was still standing by the camels by the spring.* 31 *He said, "Come, O
blessed of* HASHEM! *Why should you stand outside when I have cleared the
house, and place for the camels?"*
32 *So the man entered the house, and unmuzzled the camels. He gave
straw and feed for the camels, and water to bathe his feet and the feet of the
men who were with him.* 33 *Food was set before him, but he said, "I will not
eat until I have spoken my piece."*
And he said, "Speak."
34 *Then he said, "A servant of Abraham am I.* 35 HASHEM *has greatly
blessed my master, and he prospered; He has given him flocks, cattle, silver and gold, servants and maidservants, camels and donkeys.*

וּכְשָׁמְעוֹ אֶת דִּבְרֵי רִבְקָה אֲחֹתוֹ לֵאמֹר כֹּה דִבֶּר אֵלַי הָאִישׁ — *And when he heard the word of Rebecca his sister saying, thus spoke the man to me* ... asking her, *"Is there room in your father's house for us to lodge in?"* (v. 23).

וַיָּבֹא אֶל הָאִישׁ — *And he approached the man* ... to invite him into his house.

וְהִנֵּה עֹמֵד עַל הַגְּמַלִּים — *Who was still standing by the camels* ... to attend to their needs. He did not intend to lodge in Rebecca's father's house, unless invited by him.

31. לָמָּה תַעֲמֹד בַּחוּץ — *Why should you stand outside?* You only asked lodging for your camels, but why should you and your men remain outside?

וְאָנֹכִי פִּנִּיתִי הַבַּיִת — *I have cleared the house* ... for you and your men.

וּמָקוֹם לַגְּמַלִּים — *And made room for the camels* ... as well as for your camels.

35. בֵּרַךְ אֶת אֲדֹנִי מְאֹד — *Has blessed my master greatly* ... and without a doubt many in our country would be glad to marry into his family.

NOTES

simple verb in the light קַל form. The former is applicable to the camels, while the latter is fitting for Eliezer and his men.

31. לָמָּה תַעֲמֹד בַּחוּץ — *Why should you stand outside?* The question poses a difficulty, for it is obvious that a person will not enter unless invited to do so. Therefore the interpretation must be, as the *Sforno* says, that Laban remonstrated with Eliezer, saying to him, "Why did you only concern yourself with a place for your camels and not for yourself and your men?"

לו וַתֵּלֶד שָׂרָה אֵשֶׁת אֲדֹנִי בֵן לַאדֹנִי אַחֲרֵי זִקְנָתָהּ וַיִּתֶּן־לוֹ אֶת־כָּל־אֲשֶׁר־
לז לוֹ: וַיַּשְׁבִּעֵנִי אֲדֹנִי לֵאמֹר לֹא־תִקַּח אִשָּׁה לִבְנִי מִבְּנוֹת הַכְּנַעֲנִי אֲשֶׁר
לח אָנֹכִי יֹשֵׁב בְּאַרְצוֹ: אִם־לֹא אֶל־בֵּית־אָבִי תֵּלֵךְ וְאֶל־מִשְׁפַּחְתִּי וְלָקַחְתָּ
לט-מ אִשָּׁה לִבְנִי: וָאֹמַר אֶל־אֲדֹנִי אֻלַי לֹא־תֵלֵךְ הָאִשָּׁה אַחֲרָי: וַיֹּאמֶר
אֵלָי יהוה אֲשֶׁר־הִתְהַלַּכְתִּי לְפָנָיו יִשְׁלַח מַלְאָכוֹ אִתָּךְ וְהִצְלִיחַ דַּרְכֶּךָ
מא וְלָקַחְתָּ אִשָּׁה לִבְנִי מִמִּשְׁפַּחְתִּי וּמִבֵּית אָבִי: אָז תִּנָּקֶה מֵאָלָתִי כִּי תָבוֹא
מב אֶל־מִשְׁפַּחְתִּי וְאִם־לֹא יִתְּנוּ לָךְ וְהָיִיתָ נָקִי מֵאָלָתִי: וָאָבֹא הַיּוֹם אֶל־
הָעָיִן וָאֹמַר יהוה אֱלֹהֵי אֲדֹנִי אַבְרָהָם אִם־יֶשְׁךָ־נָּא מַצְלִיחַ דַּרְכִּי אֲשֶׁר
מג אָנֹכִי הֹלֵךְ עָלֶיהָ: הִנֵּה אָנֹכִי נִצָּב עַל־עֵין הַמָּיִם וְהָיָה הָעַלְמָה הַיֹּצֵאת
מד לִשְׁאֹב וְאָמַרְתִּי אֵלֶיהָ הַשְׁקִינִי־נָא מְעַט־מַיִם מִכַּדֵּךְ: וְאָמְרָה אֵלַי גַּם־
אַתָּה שְׁתֵה וְגַם לִגְמַלֶּיךָ אֶשְׁאָב הִוא הָאִשָּׁה אֲשֶׁר־הֹכִיחַ יהוה לְבֶן־
מה אֲדֹנִי: אֲנִי טֶרֶם אֲכַלֶּה לְדַבֵּר אֶל־לִבִּי וְהִנֵּה רִבְקָה יֹצֵאת וְכַדָּהּ עַל־
מו שִׁכְמָהּ וַתֵּרֶד הָעַיְנָה וַתִּשְׁאָב וָאֹמַר אֵלֶיהָ הַשְׁקִינִי נָא: וַתְּמַהֵר וַתּוֹרֶד
כַּדָּהּ מֵעָלֶיהָ וַתֹּאמֶר שְׁתֵה וְגַם־גְּמַלֶּיךָ אַשְׁקֶה וָאֵשְׁתְּ וְגַם הַגְּמַלִּים
מז הִשְׁקָתָה: וָאֶשְׁאַל אֹתָהּ וָאֹמַר בַּת־מִי אַתְּ וַתֹּאמֶר בַּת־בְּתוּאֵל בֶּן־
נָחוֹר אֲשֶׁר יָלְדָה־לּוֹ מִלְכָּה וָאָשִׂם הַנֶּזֶם עַל־אַפָּהּ וְהַצְּמִידִים עַל־יָדֶיהָ:
מח וָאֶקֹּד וָאֶשְׁתַּחֲוֶה לַיהוה וָאֲבָרֵךְ אֶת־יהוה אֱלֹהֵי אֲדֹנִי אַבְרָהָם אֲשֶׁר
מט הִנְחַנִי בְּדֶרֶךְ אֱמֶת לָקַחַת אֶת־בַּת־אֲחִי אֲדֹנִי לִבְנוֹ: וְעַתָּה אִם־יֶשְׁכֶם
עֹשִׂים חֶסֶד וֶאֱמֶת אֶת־אֲדֹנִי הַגִּידוּ לִי וְאִם־לֹא הַגִּידוּ לִי וְאֶפְנֶה
נ עַל־יָמִין אוֹ עַל־שְׂמֹאל: וַיַּעַן לָבָן וּבְתוּאֵל וַיֹּאמְרוּ מֵיהוה יָצָא הַדָּבָר
נא לֹא נוּכַל דַּבֵּר אֵלֶיךָ רַע אוֹ־טוֹב: הִנֵּה־רִבְקָה לְפָנֶיךָ קַח וָלֵךְ וּתְהִי
נב אִשָּׁה לְבֶן־אֲדֹנֶיךָ כַּאֲשֶׁר דִּבֶּר יהוה: וַיְהִי כַּאֲשֶׁר שָׁמַע עֶבֶד אַבְרָהָם

---

36. אַחֲרֵי זִקְנָתָהּ — *When she was old.* This made him (Isaac) all the more beloved.

37. וַיַּשְׁבִּעֵנִי אֲדֹנִי — *And my master made me take an oath.* I come to you because my master has rejected the families in Canaan in favor of those here, but not because there is a lack of potential wives in Canaan.

44. הִוא הָאִשָּׁה אֲשֶׁר הֹכִיחַ — *She is the woman designated (by God).* As our Sages state, בַּת קוֹל מַכְרֶזֶת וְאוֹמֶרֶת בַּת פְּלוֹנִי לִפְלוֹנִי, *A heavenly voice proclaims, "The daughter of this man (is destined) for this man"* (Sotah 2a).

45. אֲנִי טֶרֶם אֲכַלֶּה לְדַבֵּר — *And before I had finished meditating.* This proved that she was destined by the Almighty (to be Isaac's wife).

49. אִם יֶשְׁכֶם עֹשִׂים חֶסֶד — *If you intend to do kindness.* If you are prepared to allow your daughter to go so far away, and forgo your preference that she wed a man closer to home, so as to fulfill the wish of my master . . .

וֶאֱמֶת — *And truthfulness* . . . while at the same time considering her *true* interests by bringing honor and position to your daughter, i.e., by bringing her into Abraham's house.

NOTES

44. הִוא הָאִשָּׁה אֲשֶׁר הֹכִיחַ — *She is the woman designated (by God).* Here the *Sforno* interprets the word הוֹכִיחַ in a different manner than he does in verse 14. The reason may be because when Eliezer related the episode to Bethuel and Laban he wished to impress upon them that Rebecca is destined from heaven to become the wife of Isaac, as we see in the very next verse.

36 Sarah, my master's wife, bore my master a son after she had grown old, and he gave him all that he possesses. 37 And my master had me take an oath saying, 'Do not take a wife for my son from the daughters of the Canaanites in whose land I dwell. 38 Unless you go to my father's house and to my family and take a wife for my son.' 39 And I said to my master, 'Perhaps the woman will not follow me?' 40 He replied to me, 'HASHEM, before Whom I have walked, will send His angel with you and make your journey successful, and you will take a wife for my son from my family and my father's house. 41 Then will you be absolved from my oath when you have come to my family; and if they will not give her to you, then, you shall be absolved from my oath.'

42 "I came today to the spring and said, 'HASHEM, God of my master Abraham, if You would graciously make successful the way on which I go. 43 Behold, I am standing by the spring of water; let it be that the young woman who comes out to draw and to whom I shall say, "Please give me some water to drink from your jug," 44 and who will answer, "You may also drink and I will draw water for your camels, too," she shall be the woman whom HASHEM has designated for my master's son.' 45 I had not yet finished meditating when suddenly Rebecca came out with a jug on her shoulder, and descended to the spring and drew water. Then I said to her, 'Please give me a drink.' 46 She hurried and lowered her jug from upon herself and said, 'Drink, and I will even water your camels.' So I drank and she watered the camels also.

47 "Then I questioned her and said, 'Whose daughter are you?' And she said, 'The daughter of Bethuel, son of Nahor, whom Milcah bore to him.' And I placed the ring on her nose and the bracelets on her hands. 48 Then I bowed and prostrated myself to HASHEM and blessed HASHEM, God of my master Abraham, Who led me on a true path to take the daughter of my master's brother for his son. 49 And now, if you intend to do kindness and truth with my master, tell me; and if not, tell me, and I will turn to the right or to the left."

50 Then Laban and Bethuel answered and said, "The matter stemmed from HASHEM! We can say to you neither bad nor good. 51 Here, Rebecca is before you; take her and go, and let her be a wife to your master's son as HASHEM has spoken." 52 And it was, when Abraham's servant heard

---

50. לֹא נוּכַל דַּבֵּר אֵלֶיךָ רַע אוֹ טוֹב — *We can say to you neither bad nor good.* It is God's decree which we can neither annul nor confirm, because it does not depend on us.

51. קַח וָלֵךְ — *Take her and go* ... even without our permission.

כַּאֲשֶׁר דִּבֶּר ה׳ — *As the Lord has spoken* ... Who decreed בַּת פְּלוֹנִי לִפְלוֹנִי, *the daughter of this man (is destined) for this man,* for has He not given a sign that this is His will?

NOTES

49. אִם יֶשְׁכֶם עֹשִׂים חֶסֶד וֶאֱמֶת — *If you intend to do kindness and truthfulness.* חֶסֶד is a kindness; אֱמֶת is an act dictated by the reality of a situation. Eliezer pointed out to Bethuel and Laban that by agreeing to let Rebecca go to Abraham's house they would do both; a *kindness* to Abraham who was so anxious to see his son wed to the proper woman before he dies, while at the same time it was *truly* a benefit to her, and for their prestige, to have her become a part of this princely household.

חמישי נג אֶת־דִּבְרֵיהֶם וַיִּשְׁתַּחוּ אַרְצָה לַיהוָה: וַיּוֹצֵא הָעֶבֶד כְּלֵי־כֶסֶף וּכְלֵי זָהָב
נד וּבְגָדִים וַיִּתֵּן לְרִבְקָה וּמִגְדָּנֹת נָתַן לְאָחִיהָ וּלְאִמָּהּ: וַיֹּאכְלוּ וַיִּשְׁתּוּ הוּא
נה וְהָאֲנָשִׁים אֲשֶׁר־עִמּוֹ וַיָּלִינוּ וַיָּקוּמוּ בַבֹּקֶר וַיֹּאמֶר שַׁלְּחֻנִי לַאדֹנִי: וַיֹּאמֶר
נו אָחִיהָ וְאִמָּהּ תֵּשֵׁב הַנַּעֲרָ אִתָּנוּ יָמִים אוֹ עָשׂוֹר אַחַר תֵּלֵךְ: וַיֹּאמֶר אֲלֵהֶם
נז אַל־תְּאַחֲרוּ אֹתִי וַיהוָה הִצְלִיחַ דַּרְכִּי שַׁלְּחוּנִי וְאֵלְכָה לַאדֹנִי: וַיֹּאמְרוּ
נח נִקְרָא לַנַּעֲרָ וְנִשְׁאֲלָה אֶת־פִּיהָ: וַיִּקְרְאוּ לְרִבְקָה וַיֹּאמְרוּ אֵלֶיהָ הֲתֵלְכִי עִם־
נט הָאִישׁ הַזֶּה וַתֹּאמֶר אֵלֵךְ: וַיְשַׁלְּחוּ אֶת־רִבְקָה אֲחֹתָם וְאֶת־מֵנִקְתָּהּ וְאֶת־
ס עֶבֶד אַבְרָהָם וְאֶת־אֲנָשָׁיו: וַיְבָרְכוּ אֶת־רִבְקָה וַיֹּאמְרוּ לָהּ אֲחֹתֵנוּ אַתְּ הֲיִי
סא לְאַלְפֵי רְבָבָה וְיִירַשׁ זַרְעֵךְ אֵת שַׁעַר שֹׂנְאָיו: וַתָּקָם רִבְקָה וְנַעֲרֹתֶיהָ
וַתִּרְכַּבְנָה עַל־הַגְּמַלִּים וַתֵּלַכְנָה אַחֲרֵי הָאִישׁ וַיִּקַּח הָעֶבֶד אֶת־רִבְקָה וַיֵּלַךְ:
סב־סג וְיִצְחָק בָּא מִבּוֹא בְּאֵר לַחַי רֹאִי וְהוּא יוֹשֵׁב בְּאֶרֶץ הַנֶּגֶב: וַיֵּצֵא יִצְחָק לָשׂוּחַ
סד בַּשָּׂדֶה לִפְנוֹת עָרֶב וַיִּשָּׂא עֵינָיו וַיַּרְא וְהִנֵּה גְמַלִּים בָּאִים: וַתִּשָּׂא רִבְקָה
סה אֶת־עֵינֶיהָ וַתֵּרֶא אֶת־יִצְחָק וַתִּפֹּל מֵעַל הַגָּמָל: וַתֹּאמֶר אֶל־הָעֶבֶד מִי־
הָאִישׁ הַלָּזֶה הַהֹלֵךְ בַּשָּׂדֶה לִקְרָאתֵנוּ וַיֹּאמֶר הָעֶבֶד הוּא אֲדֹנִי וַתִּקַּח
סו־סז הַצָּעִיף וַתִּתְכָּס: וַיְסַפֵּר הָעֶבֶד לְיִצְחָק אֵת כָּל־הַדְּבָרִים אֲשֶׁר עָשָׂה: וַיְבִאֶהָ

---

55. יָמִים אוֹ עָשׂוֹר — *A year or ten [months].* They asked for the delay in order to help Rebecca gradually accustom herself to the idea of leaving home for such a long journey, since such a radical change is difficult to accept.

57. וְנִשְׁאֲלָה אֶת פִּיהָ — *And inquire of her mouth ...* whether she is capable of going immediately (in spite of the trauma of going so far away).

60. אַתְּ הֲיִי לְאַלְפֵי רְבָבָה וְיִירַשׁ זַרְעֵךְ — *May you be the mother of thousands, of ten thousands, and may your offspring inherit (the gates).* Be you acceptable and cherished by your husband as a result of your good conduct, so that only through you will the blessing given by God to Abraham (*Your seed shall possess the gates of his enemies;* 22:17) be fulfilled, and not through another wife.

61. וַיִּקַּח הָעֶבֶד אֶת רִבְקָה — *The servant took Rebecca.* Eliezer, as the agent of Isaac (the husband), took her into his custody, from the agent of her father. In this manner she now becomes wedded to Isaac; hence she is now Eliezer's mistress and he is her servant.

62. בָּא מִבּוֹא בְּאֵר לַחַי רֹאִי — *Came from having gone to Be'er-lahai-ro'i . . .* to pray in the place where Hagar's prayer had been heard (16:14). But before he even prayed, his prayer had already been answered and his wife was approaching, as we read, טֶרֶם יִקְרָאוּ וַאֲנִי אֶעֱנֶה, *Before they call I will answer (Isaiah* 65:24).

וְהוּא יוֹשֵׁב בְּאֶרֶץ הַנֶּגֶב — *For he dwelt in the land of the south.* Isaac was still living to the south of Be'er-lahai-ro'i (with his father) and did not establish his residence there at that time (until later, see 25:11).

63. וַיֵּצֵא יִצְחָק לָשׂוּחַ בַּשָּׂדֶה — *And Isaac went out to supplicate in the field.* He turned away from the public path so as not to be interrupted by wayfarers, and went into the field

NOTES

60. אַתְּ הֲיִי לְאַלְפֵי רְבָבָה — *May you be the mother of thousands, of ten thousands.* They were not giving her a blessing. They were rather urging her to conduct herself in such a manner that she be worthy of God's blessings!

61. וַיִּקַּח הָעֶבֶד אֶת רִבְקָה — *The servant took Rebecca.* The Torah refers to Eliezer as אִישׁ, *man,* the majority of the time, in relating the story of his efforts to arrange the match between Isaac and Rebecca. Still, in this verse the term אִישׁ suddenly changes to that of

their words, he prostrated himself to the ground unto HASHEM. 53 The servant brought out objects of silver and gold, and garments, and gave them to Rebecca; and delicious fruits he gave to her brother and her mother. 54 They ate and drank, he and the men who were with him, and they spent the night; when they arose next morning, he said, "Send me to my master."

55 Her brother and mother said, "Let the maiden remain with us a year or ten [months]; then she will go." 56 He said to them, "Do not delay me now that HASHEM had made my journey successful. Send me, and I will go to my master." 57 And they said, "Let us call the maiden and ask her decision."

58 They called Rebecca and said to her, "Will you go with this man?"

And she said, "I will go."

59 So they escorted Rebecca their sister, and her nurse, as well as Abraham's servant and his men. 60 They blessed Rebecca and said to her, "Our sister, may you come to be thousands of myriads, and may your offspring inherit the gate of its foes."

61 Then Rebecca arose with her maidens; they rode upon the camels and proceeded after the man; the servant took Rebecca and went.

62 Now Isaac came from having gone to Be'er-lahai-ro'i, for he dwelt in the south country. 63 Isaac went out to supplicate in the field towards evening and he raised his eyes and saw, and behold! camels were coming. 64 And Rebecca raised her eyes and saw Isaac; she inclined while upon the camel. 65 And she said to the servant, "Who is that man walking in the field toward us?"

And the servant said, "He is my master." She then took the veil and covered herself. 66 The servant told Isaac all the things he had done. 67 And Isaac

---

to pray, even though he had already prayed in Be'er-lahai-ro'i. But before he prayed he was answered, similar to, מִן הַיּוֹם הָרִאשׁוֹן אֲשֶׁר נָתַתָּ אֶת לִבְּךָ לְהָבִין וּלְהִתְעַנּוֹת... נִשְׁמְעוּ דְבָרֶיךָ, *From the first day that you set your heart to understand and humble yourself... your words were heard (Daniel* 10:12).

וְהִנֵּה גְמַלִּים בָּאִים — *And behold there were camels coming.* When he went forth to meditate (pray), his direction took him toward them (Eliezer and Rebecca), as it states הַהֹלֵךְ בַּשָּׂדֶה לִקְרָאתֵנוּ, *that walks in the field to meet us* (v. 65). When Isaac returned home from Be'er-lahai-ro'i he traveled from north to south; those who were coming from Haran to Abraham's house traveled from east to west. When Isaac turned away from the road, going north-south, he went eastward which brought him toward the caravan conveying Rebecca, who thought that he was coming to welcome her.

64. וַתִּפֹּל מֵעַל הַגָּמָל — *She inclined while upon the camel.* She bowed her head to Isaac from her seat on the camel, as a sign of respect. This is similar to the episode of Naaman, וַיִּפֹּל מֵעַל הַמֶּרְכָּבָה לִקְרָאתוֹ, *He alighted from the chariot to meet him (II Kings* 5:21).

65. וַתִּתְכָּס — *And covered herself...* because she was afraid to look (upon Isaac), as we find, וַיַּסְתֵּר מֹשֶׁה פָּנָיו, *And Moses hid his face (Exodus* 3:6).

NOTES

עֶבֶד — i.e., *and she followed the "man," and the "servant" took Rebecca.* The answer given by the *Sforno* is that until Rebecca is taken by Eliezer as Isaac's wife, his relationship to her is simply that of אִישׁ, *a man;* however, once he, as Isaac's agent, takes her into the domain of the husband she now becomes Eliezer's mistress (as the wife of his master) and his status vis-a-vis Rebecca is that of an עֶבֶד, *a servant.*

65. וַתִּתְכָּס — *And covered herself.* Isaac was an עוֹלָה תְמִימָה, *an offering to God without blemish.* His piety and sanctity of being was such that his appearance

יִצְחָק הָאֹהֱלָה שָׂרָה אִמּוֹ וַיִּקַּח אֶת־רִבְקָה וַתְּהִי־לוֹ לְאִשָּׁה וַיֶּאֱהָבֶהָ וַיִּנָּחֵם
יִצְחָק אַחֲרֵי אִמּוֹ׃

כה ששי א־ב וַיֹּסֶף אַבְרָהָם וַיִּקַּח אִשָּׁה וּשְׁמָהּ קְטוּרָה׃ וַתֵּלֶד לוֹ אֶת־זִמְרָן וְאֶת־יָקְשָׁן
ג וְאֶת־מְדָן וְאֶת־מִדְיָן וְאֶת־יִשְׁבָּק וְאֶת־שׁוּחַ׃ וְיָקְשָׁן יָלַד אֶת־שְׁבָא וְאֶת־
ד דְּדָן וּבְנֵי דְדָן הָיוּ אַשּׁוּרִם וּלְטוּשִׁם וּלְאֻמִּים׃ וּבְנֵי מִדְיָן עֵיפָה וָעֵפֶר וַחֲנֹךְ
ה וַאֲבִידָע וְאֶלְדָּעָה כָּל־אֵלֶּה בְּנֵי קְטוּרָה׃ וַיִּתֵּן אַבְרָהָם אֶת־כָּל־אֲשֶׁר־לוֹ
ו לְיִצְחָק׃ וְלִבְנֵי הַפִּילַגְשִׁים אֲשֶׁר לְאַבְרָהָם נָתַן אַבְרָהָם מַתָּנֹת וַיְשַׁלְּחֵם
ז מֵעַל יִצְחָק בְּנוֹ בְּעוֹדֶנּוּ חַי קֵדְמָה אֶל־אֶרֶץ קֶדֶם׃ וְאֵלֶּה יְמֵי שְׁנֵי־חַיֵּי
ח אַבְרָהָם אֲשֶׁר־חָי מְאַת שָׁנָה וְשִׁבְעִים שָׁנָה וְחָמֵשׁ שָׁנִים׃ וַיִּגְוַע וַיָּמָת
ט אַבְרָהָם בְּשֵׂיבָה טוֹבָה זָקֵן וְשָׂבֵעַ וַיֵּאָסֶף אֶל־עַמָּיו׃ וַיִּקְבְּרוּ אֹתוֹ יִצְחָק
וְיִשְׁמָעֵאל בָּנָיו אֶל־מְעָרַת הַמַּכְפֵּלָה אֶל־שְׂדֵה עֶפְרֹן בֶּן־צֹחַר הַחִתִּי אֲשֶׁר
י עַל־פְּנֵי מַמְרֵא׃ הַשָּׂדֶה אֲשֶׁר־קָנָה אַבְרָהָם מֵאֵת בְּנֵי־חֵת שָׁמָּה קֻבַּר
יא אַבְרָהָם וְשָׂרָה אִשְׁתּוֹ׃ וַיְהִי אַחֲרֵי מוֹת אַבְרָהָם וַיְבָרֶךְ אֱלֹהִים אֶת־יִצְחָק
בְּנוֹ וַיֵּשֶׁב יִצְחָק עִם־בְּאֵר לַחַי רֹאִי׃

שביעי יב וְאֵלֶּה תֹּלְדֹת יִשְׁמָעֵאל בֶּן־אַבְרָהָם אֲשֶׁר יָלְדָה הָגָר הַמִּצְרִית שִׁפְחַת שָׂרָה
יג לְאַבְרָהָם׃ וְאֵלֶּה שְׁמוֹת בְּנֵי יִשְׁמָעֵאל בִּשְׁמֹתָם לְתוֹלְדֹתָם בְּכֹר יִשְׁמָעֵאל
יד־טו נְבָיֹת וְקֵדָר וְאַדְבְּאֵל וּמִבְשָׂם׃ וּמִשְׁמָע וְדוּמָה וּמַשָּׂא׃ חֲדַד וְתֵימָא יְטוּר
מפטיר טז נָפִישׁ וָקֵדְמָה׃ אֵלֶּה הֵם בְּנֵי יִשְׁמָעֵאל וְאֵלֶּה שְׁמֹתָם בְּחַצְרֵיהֶם וּבְטִירֹתָם
יז שְׁנֵים־עָשָׂר נְשִׂיאִם לְאֻמֹּתָם׃ וְאֵלֶּה שְׁנֵי חַיֵּי יִשְׁמָעֵאל מְאַת שָׁנָה וּשְׁלֹשִׁים
יח שָׁנָה וְשֶׁבַע שָׁנִים וַיִּגְוַע וַיָּמָת וַיֵּאָסֶף אֶל־עַמָּיו׃ וַיִּשְׁכְּנוּ מֵחֲוִילָה עַד־שׁוּר
אֲשֶׁר עַל־פְּנֵי מִצְרַיִם בֹּאֲכָה אַשּׁוּרָה עַל־פְּנֵי כָל־אֶחָיו נָפָל׃

---

67. וַיִּנָּחֵם יִצְחָק אַחֲרֵי אִמּוֹ — *And Isaac was comforted after his mother.* Until now he could not be comforted, for he had loved and respected his mother so much.

XXV

2. וַתֵּלֶד לוֹ אֶת זִמְרָן — *And she bore him Zimran.* She brought them up in his house, but they were not his children, similar to חֲמֵשֶׁת בְּנֵי מִיכַל . . . אֲשֶׁר יָלְדָה לְעַדְרִיאֵל, *The five sons of Michal, whom she bore to Adriel* (*II Samuel* 21:8), which also means she brought them up, but they were not her children. Abraham only begot two, Isaac and Ishmael, as it is recorded, בְּנֵי אַבְרָהָם יִצְחָק וְיִשְׁמָעֵאל, *The sons of Abraham — Isaac and Ishmael* (whereas Zimran et al. are recorded as בְּנֵי קְטוּרָה, *The children of Keturah — I Chronicles* 1:28, 32).

6. נָתַן אַבְרָהָם מַתָּנֹת — *Abraham gave gifts.* These were given not as an inheritance (but a gift) so that it be legal and binding (at once).

NOTES

inspired awe and reverence in others. The impact made by him upon Rebecca was similar to that of God's appearance in the burning bush upon Moses.

XXV

2. וַתֵּלֶד לוֹ אֶת זִמְרָן — *And she bore him Zimran.* To prove that the word וַתֵּלֶד need not mean *she gave birth* but *she raised*, the *Sforno* cites the verse in *II Samuel* where five sons of Michal the daughter of Saul are mentioned, which perforce must be translated *to raise* since Michal had no children of her own.

6. נָתַן אַבְרָהָם מַתָּנֹת — *Abraham gave gifts.* The Mishnah in *Bava Basra* (12b) teaches us that if a man gives property to any of his children as a gift, in his lifetime, it is valid — providing he does not call it "an inheritance." This Abraham did with the children of the concubines.

brought her into the tent of Sarah his mother; he married Rebecca, she be-
came his wife, and he loved her; and thus was Isaac consoled after his mother.
25 [1] *Abraham proceeded and took a wife whose name was Keturah.* [2] *She*
bore him Zimran, Jokshan, Medan, Midian, Ishbak and Shuah.
[3] *Jokshan begot Sheba and Dedan, and the children of Dedan were Asshurim,*
Letushim, and Leummim. [4] *And the children of Midian: Ephah [and] Epher,*
Hanoch, Abida, and Eldaah; all these were the descendants of Keturah.
[5] *Abraham gave all that he had to Isaac.* [6] *But to the concubine-children who*
were Abraham's, Abraham gave gifts; then he sent them away from Isaac
his son, while he was still alive, eastward to the land of the east.
[7] *Now these are the days of the years of Abraham's life which he lived: a*
hundred years, seventy years, and five years. [8] *And Abraham expired and*
died at a good old age, mature and content, and he was gathered to his people.
[9] *His sons Isaac and Ishmael buried him in the cave of Machpelah, in the field*
of Ephron the son of Zohar the Hittite, facing Mamre. [10] *The field that*
Abraham had bought from the children of Heth, there Abraham was buried,
and Sarah his wife. [11] *And it was after the death of Abraham that God blessed*
Isaac his son, and Isaac settled near Be'er-lahai-ro'i.
[12] *These are the descendants of Ishmael, Abraham's son, whom Hagar the*
Egyptian, Sarah's maidservant, bore to Abraham. [13] *These are the names of*
the sons of Ishmael by their names, in order of their birth: Ishmael's firstborn
Nebaioth, Kedar, Adbeel, and Mibsam, [14] *Mishma, Dumah, and Massa,*
[15] *Hadad and Tema, Jetur, Naphish, and Kedem.* [16] *These are the sons of*
Ishmael, and these are their names by their open cities and by their
strongholds, twelve chieftains for their nations.
[17] *These were the years of Ishmael's life: a hundred and thirty-seven years,*
when he expired and died, and was gathered to his people. [18] *They dwelt from*
Havilah to Shur — which is near Egypt — toward Assyria; over all his
brothers he dwelt.

בְּעוֹדֶנּוּ חַי — *While he was still alive.* He did not rely upon a will or a disposition of property by testament.

8. וְשָׂבֵעַ — *And content.* He saw all the desires of his heart fulfilled, and was satisfied with all he wished to see and do.

וַיֵּאָסֶף אֶל עַמָּיו — *And was gathered to his people.* He was gathered into the bond of eternal life together with the righteous of all generations who, being like him in that respect, were his people. The word עַמָּיו is in the plural, however, to indicate that even the righteous are on different levels, even though they all merit the eternal life, as our Sages teach us, שֶׁכָּל אֶחָד וְאֶחָד נִכְוָה מֵחֻפָּתוֹ שֶׁל חֲבֵירוֹ, *Each one will be burned by reason of his envy of the superior canopy of his fellow* (*Bava Basra* 75a).

NOTES

8. וַיֵּאָסֶף אֶל עַמָּיו — *And was gathered to his people.* The expression *to his people* is a bit difficult to understand. Who are *his people,* since it cannot mean his ancestors who were far from being righteous? The *Sforno* answers that in the generations preceding Abraham there *were* righteous men and in that respect they are called *his people,* even though they may not have reached Abraham's level of wisdom, piety and spirituality. Our Sages tell us that in the world to come, each righteous person will be given a canopy, where he shall "dwell," according to his rank. These canopies will not be equal; hence there will be envy among them. This lesson of the Talmud is brought by the *Sforno* to prove that there are different levels of the righteous, even in the bond of eternal life.

פרשת תולדות

יט־כ וְאֵלֶּה תּוֹלְדֹת יִצְחָק בֶּן־אַבְרָהָם אַבְרָהָם הוֹלִיד אֶת־יִצְחָק: וַיְהִי יִצְחָק
בֶּן־אַרְבָּעִים שָׁנָה בְּקַחְתּוֹ אֶת־רִבְקָה בַּת־בְּתוּאֵל הָאֲרַמִּי מִפַּדַּן אֲרָם
כא אֲחוֹת לָבָן הָאֲרַמִּי לוֹ לְאִשָּׁה: וַיֶּעְתַּר יִצְחָק לַיהוה לְנֹכַח אִשְׁתּוֹ כִּי
כב עֲקָרָה הִוא וַיֵּעָתֶר לוֹ יהוה וַתַּהַר רִבְקָה אִשְׁתּוֹ: וַיִּתְרֹצְצוּ הַבָּנִים בְּקִרְבָּהּ
כג וַתֹּאמֶר אִם־כֵּן לָמָּה זֶּה אָנֹכִי וַתֵּלֶךְ לִדְרֹשׁ אֶת־יהוה: וַיֹּאמֶר יהוה לָהּ
°גוֹיִם ק׳ שְׁנֵי °גיים בְּבִטְנֵךְ וּשְׁנֵי לְאֻמִּים מִמֵּעַיִךְ יִפָּרֵדוּ וּלְאֹם מִלְאֹם יֶאֱמָץ וְרַב
כד־כה יַעֲבֹד צָעִיר: וַיִּמְלְאוּ יָמֶיהָ לָלֶדֶת וְהִנֵּה תוֹמִם בְּבִטְנָהּ: וַיֵּצֵא הָרִאשׁוֹן
כו אַדְמוֹנִי כֻּלּוֹ כְּאַדֶּרֶת שֵׂעָר וַיִּקְרְאוּ שְׁמוֹ עֵשָׂו: וְאַחֲרֵי־כֵן יָצָא אָחִיו וְיָדוֹ
אֹחֶזֶת בַּעֲקֵב עֵשָׂו וַיִּקְרָא שְׁמוֹ יַעֲקֹב וְיִצְחָק בֶּן־שִׁשִּׁים שָׁנָה בְּלֶדֶת אֹתָם:

XXV

19. וְאֵלֶּה תּוֹלְדֹת יִצְחָק — *And these are the offspring of Isaac . . .* the events to which his days gave birth (i.e., the historical events of his life).

אַבְרָהָם הוֹלִיד אֶת יִצְחָק — *Abraham begot Isaac.* He (Isaac) alone is considered the seed of Abraham.

20. אֲחוֹת לָבָן הָאֲרַמִּי — *The sister of Laban the Aramean.* From her Esau was born. (He) resembled his mother's brother.

21. לְנֹכַח אִשְׁתּוֹ — *Opposite his wife (for his wife).* Even though he had been assured children, he prayed to God that it be from this worthy woman who stood opposite him.

22. וַתֹּאמֶר אִם כֵּן — *And she said, "If so."* Since they are struggling (within her) and there is the possibility that one will die, I will be in danger at the time of birth, as often happens when a dead infant is delivered.

לָמָּה זֶּה אָנֹכִי — *"Why am I thus?"* Why did my family so desire that the children of Isaac be born through me, as it is written, *Be thou the mother of thousands and tens of thousands* (24:60) and why did my husband pray that I bear his children?

NOTES

XXV

19. וְאֵלֶּה תּוֹלְדֹת יִצְחָק — *And these are the offspring of Isaac.* The *Sforno* departs from *Rashi's* interpretation of this verse. Whereas the word תּוֹלְדוֹת is explained by *Rashi* as referring to Jacob and Esau the offspring of Isaac, the *Sforno* translates it as meaning the "life story" of Isaac, the events which represent the offspring of his activities, just as children are one's offspring.

אַבְרָהָם הוֹלִיד אֶת יִצְחָק — *Abraham begot Isaac.* This second part of the verse is explained by *Rashi* as refuting the canard that Isaac was not the child of Abraham but of Abimelech (based on the Talmud, *Bava Metzia* 87). The *Sforno* gives a simple answer to the question: why does the Torah have to state *Abraham begot Isaac,* since we are told that Isaac was the son of Abraham? This is meant to tell us that only Isaac is considered to be the true and worthy seed of Abraham, akin to, כִּי בְיִצְחָק יִקָּרֵא לְךָ זָרַע, *for in Isaac shall seed be called to you* (21:12), i.e., Isaac and not Ishmael, even though he is also the son of Abraham.

20. אֲחוֹת לָבָן הָאֲרַמִּי — *The sister of Laban the Aramean.* Here again *Sforno* differs from *Rashi.* Whereas *Rashi* explains that the reason the Torah tells us, once again, that Rebecca is the sister of Laban is to praise her piety even though she was raised in such an evil household, the *Sforno* interprets the phrase as explaining how two such *tzaddikim* as Isaac and Rebecca could have given birth to a son such as Esau. The answer is that her brother was Laban and our Rabbis teach us, "Most sons are like their mother's brother" (*Bava Basra* 110b). This interpretation may well answer the question *Rashi* poses in 28:5 where the Torah tells us, . . . *and he went . . . to Laban the brother of Rebecca, the mother of Jacob and Esau. Rashi* comments, "I do not know what this comes to teach us." However, using the *Sforno's* interpretation here the answer might well be that the Torah is telling us how it is

PARASHAS TOLDOS

19 *And these are the offspring of Isaac son of Abraham — Abraham begot*
Isaac. 20 *Isaac was forty years old when he took Rebecca, daughter of*
Bethuel the Aramean from Paddan Aram, sister of Laban the Aramean, as
a wife for himself. 21 *Isaac entreated HASHEM opposite his wife, because she*
was barren. HASHEM allowed Himself to be entreated by him, and his wife
Rebecca conceived.
22 *The children agitated within her, and she said, "If so, why am I thus?" And she went to inquire of HASHEM.*
23 *And HASHEM said to her: "Two nations are in your womb; two regimes from your insides shall be separated; the might shall pass from one regime to the other, and the elder shall serve the younger."*
24 *When her term to bear grew full, then behold! there were twins in her*
womb. 25 *The first one emerged red, entirely like a hairy mantle; so they*
named him Esau. 26 *After that his brother emerged with his hand grasping*
on to the heel of Esau; so he called his name Jacob; Isaac was sixty years old
when she bore them.

---

23. שְׁנֵי גוֹיִם בְּבִטְנֵךְ — *Two nations are in your womb.* The cause of the struggling within you is because they are destined to be two nations with opposing ideas of religion.

וּשְׁנֵי לְאֻמִּים — *And two peoples.* They will also be two peoples who have opposing ideas of nationalism.

מִמֵּעַיִךְ יִפָּרֵדוּ — *Shall be separated from your insides.* Neither will die due to their struggling.

24. וְהִנֵּה תוֹמִם בְּבִטְנָהּ — *Behold, there were twins in her womb.* Those who were assisting with the birth recognized, even before the actual birth, that twins were being delivered, and when the first to be born proved to be covered as with a hairy mantle, they realized that his birth should have been more difficult and later than that of the smooth one, therefore they called his name עֵשָׂו (Esau) (as though to say) his brother did it by forcing him out first (עֵשָׂו related to עָשׂוּי, i.e., the efforts exerted by the other infant forced him out).

26. וַיִּקְרָא שְׁמוֹ יַעֲקֹב — *So he named him* (lit., *called his name) Jacob.* (From the root עקב, *the end,* i.e., he will remain at the end.) This was indicated by the fact that his hand held on to his brother's heel. Our Sages tell us that God gave him this name (Jacob) to show that he will survive after the destruction of all the nations, as it is written, כִּי אֶעֱשֶׂה כָלָה בְּכָל הַגּוֹיִם . . . וְאֹתְךָ לֹא אֶעֱשֶׂה כָלָה, *For I will make a full end of all the nations . . . but I will not make a full end of you (Jeremiah* 46:28).

NOTES

possible for a woman like Rebecca to be the mother of both a Jacob and an Esau — because she had a brother Laban!

21. לְנֹכַח אִשְׁתּוֹ – *Opposite his wife (for his wife).* Isaac was assured of children after the *Akeidah,* his binding — (see *Perek* 22:17), hence his prayer cannot be to *have* children; the question is only through whom? He prays that it be from pious Rebecca.

22. וַתֹּאמֶר אִם כֵּן – *And she said, "If so."* She, in turn, although desirous to have Isaac's children, did not want to do so at the price of her own life. She had no objection to his taking another wife, as did his father, and to build his family with her. This explains the phrase לָמָּה זֶּה אָנֹכִי, *why me* — let it be with another that God's promise be fulfilled.

23. שְׁנֵי גוֹיִם בְּבִטְנֵךְ – *Two nations are in your womb.* The Torah uses two terms — גוֹיִם, *nations,* and לְאֻמִּים, *peoples.* The first refers to a community of faith, the second to a political, national entity.

26. וַיִּקְרָא שְׁמוֹ יַעֲקֹב – *So he named him* (lit., *called his name) Jacob.* The name "Jacob" is given by the Almighty. That is why the word וַיִּקְרָא, *and he called,* is in the singular, as opposed to וַיִּקְרְאוּ, *and*

כז וַיִּגְדְּלוּ הַנְּעָרִים וַיְהִי עֵשָׂו אִישׁ יֹדֵעַ צַיִד אִישׁ שָׂדֶה וְיַעֲקֹב אִישׁ תָּם יֹשֵׁב
כח אֹהָלִים: וַיֶּאֱהַב יִצְחָק אֶת־עֵשָׂו כִּי־צַיִד בְּפִיו וְרִבְקָה אֹהֶבֶת אֶת־יַעֲקֹב:
כט־ל וַיָּזֶד יַעֲקֹב נָזִיד וַיָּבֹא עֵשָׂו מִן־הַשָּׂדֶה וְהוּא עָיֵף: וַיֹּאמֶר עֵשָׂו אֶל־יַעֲקֹב
הַלְעִיטֵנִי נָא מִן־הָאָדֹם הָאָדֹם הַזֶּה כִּי עָיֵף אָנֹכִי עַל־כֵּן קָרָא־שְׁמוֹ
לא־לב אֱדוֹם: וַיֹּאמֶר יַעֲקֹב מִכְרָה כַיּוֹם אֶת־בְּכֹרָתְךָ לִי: וַיֹּאמֶר עֵשָׂו הִנֵּה אָנֹכִי
לג הוֹלֵךְ לָמוּת וְלָמָּה־זֶּה לִי בְּכֹרָה: וַיֹּאמֶר יַעֲקֹב הִשָּׁבְעָה לִּי כַּיּוֹם וַיִּשָּׁבַע
לד לוֹ וַיִּמְכֹּר אֶת־בְּכֹרָתוֹ לְיַעֲקֹב: וְיַעֲקֹב נָתַן לְעֵשָׂו לֶחֶם וּנְזִיד עֲדָשִׁים
וַיֹּאכַל וַיֵּשְׁתְּ וַיָּקָם וַיֵּלַךְ וַיִּבֶז עֵשָׂו אֶת־הַבְּכֹרָה:

כו

א וַיְהִי רָעָב בָּאָרֶץ מִלְּבַד הָרָעָב הָרִאשׁוֹן אֲשֶׁר הָיָה בִּימֵי אַבְרָהָם וַיֵּלֶךְ
ב יִצְחָק אֶל־אֲבִימֶלֶךְ מֶלֶךְ־פְּלִשְׁתִּים גְּרָרָה: וַיֵּרָא אֵלָיו יהוה וַיֹּאמֶר אַל־

---

27. אִישׁ שָׂדֶה — *A man of the field* . . . a man skilled in working the earth.

יֹשֵׁב אֹהָלִים — *Abiding in tents* . . . two kinds of tents, one the tent of a shepherd and the second a nonfolding tent of meditation where he learned to know his Maker and to become sanctified in His glory.

28. וַיֶּאֱהַב יִצְחָק אֶת עֵשָׂו — *Now Isaac loved Esau . . . also* Esau; even though he certainly knew that he was not as perfect as Jacob.

וְרִבְקָה אֹהֶבֶת אֶת יַעֲקֹב — *But Rebecca loved Jacob* . . . for she recognized the wickedness of Esau.

30. עַל כֵּן קָרָא שְׁמוֹ אֱדוֹם — *Therefore was his name called Edom* (lit., *Red*). When they saw that Esau was totally committed to coarse meaningless labors not befitting civilized man, to the extent that he was incapable of even recognizing the lentils as such, (knowing only) their color (not their name), they called him אֱדוֹם. This word is to be understood as an imperative: "Be red by the pottage you swallow."

31. מִכְרָה כַיּוֹם — *Sell as this day.* As your time is wholly occupied with your labors (hunting) in such a manner that you are so tired you cannot even identify a pottage of lentils, then doubtless you will not be able to occupy yourself with the responsibilities of the birthright, to serve God as befits a firstborn.

32. הוֹלֵךְ לָמוּת — *I am going to die* . . . through weariness and fatigue.

NOTES

they called, in the plural, regarding Esau. The root of the name is עָקֵב, which means *heel* but also means *the end*, referring to the end of time when Jacob will prevail. God Himself assures us that Jacob and his children will survive all other nations.

27. יֹשֵׁב אֹהָלִים — *Abiding in tents.* The word used is אֹהָלִים, *tents*, in the plural. A man normally resides in one tent, not two. *Rashi* explains that it refers to the tents of Shem and Eber, tents of study. The *Sforno* feels that this would be redundant, therefore he interprets it to mean that one was for Jacob's work as a shepherd while the second was for study and meditation.

30. עַל כֵּן קָרָא שְׁמוֹ אֱדוֹם — *Therefore was his name called Edom* (lit., *Red*). When Esau was born he was אַדְמוֹנִי, *red complexioned.* The name אֱדוֹם was not a new appellation given to him now when he demanded to be fed *"this red food."* Hence the *Sforno* interprets the phrase *therefore was his name called red* (אֱדוֹם) as meaning, "be red by the pottage you swallow," and as a result everyone now called him אֱדוֹם, *Red.*

31. מִכְרָה כַיּוֹם — *Sell as this day.* The key word is כַּיּוֹם, *as the day*, which the *Sforno* understands as *this* day. The experience of "this day" demonstrates that Esau's interests in life are such as to preclude any serious desire for the spiritual service which the birthright demanded. Our Rabbis tell us that the lentils were prepared as a meal of condolence, for Abraham had died that day. The fact that Esau is so insensitive to this tragic event and is concerned only for his hunting and the satisfaction of his appetites underlines his unworthiness to be the *bechor* (firstborn).

33-34. הִשָּׁבְעָה לִּי. . . וְיַעֲקֹב נָתַן לְעֵשָׂו — *Swear to me . . . And Jacob gave Esau (bread and lentils).* Ac-

[27] *The lads grew up and Esau became one who knows hunting, a man of the field; but Jacob was a wholesome man, abiding in tents.* [28] *Isaac loved Esau for game was in his mouth; but Rebecca loved Jacob.*

[29] *Jacob simmered a stew, and Esau came in from the field, and he was exhausted.* [30] *Esau said to Jacob, "Pour into me, now, some of that very red stuff for I am exhausted." (He therefore called his name Edom.)*

[31] *Jacob said, "Sell, as this day, your birthright to me."*

[32] *And Esau said, "Look, I am going to die, so of what use to me is a birthright?"*

[33] *Jacob said, "Swear to me as this day"; he swore to him and sold his birthright to Jacob.* [34] *Jacob gave Esau bread and lentil stew, and he ate and drank, got up and left; thus, Esau spurned the birthright.*

26 [1] *There was a famine in the land, aside from the first famine that was in the days of Abraham; and Isaac went to Abimelech king of the Philistines, to Gerar.* [2] *HASHEM appeared to him and said, "Do not*

33. הִשָּׁבְעָה לִּי — *Swear to me.* Since the transaction involved nothing concrete it was necessary to swear, for there could be no *act* of purchase.

וַיִּמְכֹּר אֶת בְּכֹרָתוֹ — *And he sold his birthright* . . . for the price agreed to, even though the Torah does not reveal it explicitly.

34. וְיַעֲקֹב נָתַן לְעֵשָׂו — *And Jacob gave Esau (bread and lentils).* The lentils, or the vessel in which they were cooked, was used as the means of exchange (חֲלִיפִין) as we find, שָׁלַף אִישׁ נַעֲלוֹ וְנָתַן לְרֵעֵהוּ, *One would draw off his shoe and give it to his friend (Ruth 4:7).*

וַיִּבֶז עֵשָׂו אֶת הַבְּכֹרָה — *Thus, Esau spurned the birthright.* In Esau's eyes the birthright was not worth the price Jacob set, even after the sale; hence the seller was not deceived for to him it had little value.

XXVI

1. אֲשֶׁר הָיָה בִּימֵי אַבְרָהָם — *That was in the days of Abraham.* From the time (of Abraham) until now, there had been no famine so severe as to compel the inhabitants of the land to leave, as Abraham did (in his time).

וַיֵּלֶךְ יִצְחָק אֶל אֲבִימֶלֶךְ — *And Isaac went to Abimelech* . . . as a courtesy, to ask permission of him to leave his land due to the famine.

NOTES

cording to *halachah*, every transaction that entails transfer of ownership requires a *kinyan* (an act of purchase) which varies, depending upon the property being sold or given. To sell the birthright is to transfer rights and responsibilities which have value but no substance until one actually inherits. An oath, however, can be taken and is valid even for דָּבָר שֶׁלֹּא בָא לְעוֹלָם, *that which is not yet in this world.* For this reason Jacob asks Esau to swear. In addition, they also make a *sale of exchange* which is done with a סוּדָר, *a handkerchief*, vessel or any article. The *Sforno*, therefore, suggests that this could have been the role played by the lentils themselves, or the container in which they were cooked, as the means of exchange. This would consummate the deal for which a specific price had been agreed to, willingly, by both parties, and not under duress of hunger and fatigue.

XXVI

1. אֲשֶׁר הָיָה בִּימֵי אַבְרָהָם וַיֵּלֶךְ יִצְחָק אֶל אֲבִימֶלֶךְ — *That was in the days of Abraham, and Isaac went to Abimelech.* There is no need to mention the famine in the days of Abraham, unless it is to underscore the severity of this famine, which was sufficiently serious and exceptional that it caused people to leave, as it had forced Abraham to go down to Egypt in his time. Isaac, who always looked upon his father as a role model, therefore planned to do the same. Since that was his intent, then the reason to go first to Abimelech was as a courtesy, to take leave of him.

ג תֵּרֵד מִצְרָיְמָה שְׁכֹן בָּאָרֶץ אֲשֶׁר אֹמַר אֵלֶיךָ: גּוּר בָּאָרֶץ הַזֹּאת וְאֶהְיֶה
עִמְּךָ וַאֲבָרְכֶךָּ כִּי־לְךָ וּלְזַרְעֲךָ אֶתֵּן אֶת־כָּל־הָאֲרָצֹת הָאֵל וַהֲקִמֹתִי
ד אֶת־הַשְּׁבֻעָה אֲשֶׁר נִשְׁבַּעְתִּי לְאַבְרָהָם אָבִיךָ: וְהִרְבֵּיתִי אֶת־זַרְעֲךָ
כְּכוֹכְבֵי הַשָּׁמַיִם וְנָתַתִּי לְזַרְעֲךָ אֵת כָּל־הָאֲרָצֹת הָאֵל וְהִתְבָּרְכוּ בְזַרְעֲךָ
ה כֹּל גּוֹיֵי הָאָרֶץ: עֵקֶב אֲשֶׁר־שָׁמַע אַבְרָהָם בְּקֹלִי וַיִּשְׁמֹר מִשְׁמַרְתִּי
שני ו־ז מִצְוֹתַי חֻקּוֹתַי וְתוֹרֹתָי: * וַיֵּשֶׁב יִצְחָק בִּגְרָר: וַיִּשְׁאֲלוּ אַנְשֵׁי הַמָּקוֹם
לְאִשְׁתּוֹ וַיֹּאמֶר אֲחֹתִי הִוא כִּי יָרֵא לֵאמֹר אִשְׁתִּי פֶּן־יַהַרְגֻנִי אַנְשֵׁי
ח הַמָּקוֹם עַל־רִבְקָה כִּי־טוֹבַת מַרְאֶה הִוא: וַיְהִי כִּי אָרְכוּ־לוֹ שָׁם הַיָּמִים
וַיַּשְׁקֵף אֲבִימֶלֶךְ מֶלֶךְ פְּלִשְׁתִּים בְּעַד הַחַלּוֹן וַיַּרְא וְהִנֵּה יִצְחָק מְצַחֵק
ט אֵת רִבְקָה אִשְׁתּוֹ: וַיִּקְרָא אֲבִימֶלֶךְ לְיִצְחָק וַיֹּאמֶר אַךְ הִנֵּה אִשְׁתְּךָ הִוא
וְאֵיךְ אָמַרְתָּ אֲחֹתִי הִוא וַיֹּאמֶר אֵלָיו יִצְחָק כִּי אָמַרְתִּי פֶּן־אָמוּת עָלֶיהָ:

---

2. אַל תֵּרֵד מִצְרָיְמָה — *Do not descend to Egypt.* Do not let the lack of pasture persuade you to go there (i.e., Egypt), as we find (regarding the sons of Jacob), *for there is no pasture for your servants' flocks* (47:4).

שְׁכֹן בָּאָרֶץ אֲשֶׁר אֹמַר אֵלֶיךָ — *Dwell in the land that I shall indicate to you.* Set up shepherd's tents for your flocks and cattle in the place where I tell you to dwell (i.e., here in Gerar), for your flocks will also be successful here. (This assurance is given) since the reason he planned to leave was because of the lack of pasture.

3. גּוּר בָּאָרֶץ הַזֹּאת — *Reside in this land.* Reside in this land (of Canaan).

וְאֶהְיֶה עִמְּךָ וַאֲבָרְכֶךָּ — *And I will be with you and bless you.* Even though there is a lack of pasture now in Canaan, I shall be with you and you will have no lack of pasture.

וַאֲבָרְכֶךָּ — *And bless you* ... with money and cattle (here), but not outside the land (of Canaan).

כִּי לְךָ וּלְזַרְעֲךָ אֶתֵּן אֶת כָּל הָאֲרָצֹת הָאֵל וַהֲקִמֹתִי אֶת הַשְּׁבֻעָה — *For to you and your offspring will I give all these lands and establish the oath.* The reason I tell you to reside in this land whereby I will do good for you is because I gave an oath to Abraham to grant him and his descendants this land; therefore by living here you will be a prince in their midst and take possession of it, so as to transmit it (through inheritance) to your children.

NOTES

2-3. שְׁכֹן בָּאָרֶץ אֲשֶׁר אֹמַר אֵלֶיךָ גּוּר בָּאָרֶץ הַזֹּאת — *Dwell in the land that I shall indicate to you. Reside in this land.* The two words used in these verses — שְׁכֹן and גּוּר — are interpreted by the *Sforno* as applicable to different categories. The first refers to *dwelling* in shepherd's tents (which is a temporary abode) while the second is the more permanent term, referring to one's residence.

3. וְאֶהְיֶה עִמְּךָ וַאֲבָרְכֶךָּ — *And I will be with you and bless you.* God's assurances to Isaac are manifold. He promises pastureland for his cattle (וְאֶהְיֶה עִמְּךָ), wealth (וַאֲבָרְכֶךָּ), and the eventual possession of the land. So as not to forfeit his claim to the land, it is vital for Isaac to remain and establish his rights and strengthen his status as a prince in the midst of the populace.

5. עֵקֶב אֲשֶׁר שָׁמַע אַבְרָהָם בְּקֹלִי וַיִּשְׁמֹר מִשְׁמַרְתִּי מִצְוֹתַי חֻקּוֹתַי וְתוֹרֹתָי — *Because Abraham hearkened to My voice and safeguarded My charge, My commandments, My statutes, and My laws.* Multiple phrases are used in the verse, i.e., "hearken," "safeguarding My charge," My "commandments," "statutes" and "laws." The commentators offer a number of interpretations to explain the variety of words depicting Abraham's observance and loyalty to the Almighty. The *Sforno* divides this verse into three parts: the specific commands given to Abraham by God (בְּקֹלִי); the seven Noahide commandments in general (מִצְוֹתַי חֻקּוֹתַי וְתוֹרֹתָי); and מִשְׁמַרְתִּי, *My charge.* The latter is interpreted by the *Sforno* as referring to God's special charge and unique responsibility, i.e., to exercise kindness and

descend to Egypt; dwell in the land that I shall indicate to you. [3] *Sojourn in this land and I will be with you and bless you; for to you and your offspring will I give all these lands, and establish the oath that I swore to Abraham your father:* [4] *'I will increase your offspring like the stars of the heavens; and will give to your offspring all these lands'; and all the nations of the earth shall bless themselves by your offspring.* [5] *Because Abraham obeyed My voice, and observed My safeguards, My commandments, My decrees, and My Torahs."*

[6] *So Isaac settled in Gerar.* [7] *When the men of the place asked about his wife, he said, "She is my sister" — for he was afraid to say "my wife" — "lest the men of the place kill me because of Rebecca for she is fair to look upon!"*

[8] *And it came to pass, as his days there lengthened, that Abimelech king of the Philistines gazed down through the window and saw — behold! Isaac was jesting with his wife Rebecca.* [9] *Abimelech summoned Isaac and said, "But look! She is your wife! How could you say, 'She is my sister?' "*

Isaac said to him, "Because I said that I would be killed because of her."

---

5. עֵקֶב אֲשֶׁר שָׁמַע אַבְרָהָם בְּקֹלִי — *Because Abraham hearkened to My voice . . .* to all that I commanded him.

וַיִּשְׁמֹר מִשְׁמַרְתִּי — *And safeguarded My charge.* He constantly kept My special charge which is to do kindness, as it says, כׇּל אׇרְחוֹת ה׳ חֶסֶד וֶאֱמֶת, *All the paths of God are mercy and truth* (*Psalms* 25:10), and to teach sinners the correct way. This he did when he *called upon the Name of God.* He also kept . . .

מִצְוֹתַי חֻקּוֹתַי וְתוֹרֹתָי — *My commandments, My statutes, and My laws . . .* which were commanded to the "sons of Noah," thereby practicing what he taught and acting as a model to others. We see here that the merit of others is invoked when (God) speaks to Isaac; also when He says, וְהִרְבֵּיתִי אֶת זַרְעֲךָ בַּעֲבוּר אַבְרָהָם עַבְדִּי, *I will multiply your seed for My servant Abraham* (v. 24). Not so with Jacob, and certainly not with Abraham. This, however, was *before* Isaac was inspired to call upon the Name of God, but after he did so it is written, וַאֲבִימֶלֶךְ הָלַךְ אֵלָיו מִגְּרָר, *Abimelech went to him from Gerar* (v. 26), and said, רָאוֹ רָאִינוּ כִּי הָיָה ה׳ עִמָּךְ . . . אַתָּה עַתָּה בְּרוּךְ ה׳, *We saw that God is with you . . . you are now the blessed of God* (vs. 28-29), and he no longer experienced the hardships of envy and quarrels as he had previously. Jacob, however, never had to depend upon the merits of others, for from his youth he dwelled in the tents of Shem and Eber, studying and teaching knowledge (of God) to the people, who doubtless came (to these tents) to seek God.

NOTES

to instruct sinners how to return to the ways of truth. This was precisely what Abraham dedicated himself to, and as such he was *doing God's work* (as it were). This is the meaning of וַיִּשְׁמֹר מִשְׁמַרְתִּי, *Abraham kept and safeguarded My (God's) charge.*

מִצְוֹתַי חֻקּוֹתַי וְתוֹרֹתָי — *My commandments, My statutes, and My laws.* The *Sforno* makes a most important point in his commentary on this verse. Although זְכוּת אָבוֹת, *the merit of ancestors,* is a fundamental concept in our faith, it is only invoked regarding Isaac, among the three Patriarchs. Abraham, as the son of Terach, certainly had to develop his own merits, while Jacob had no need for the merit of fathers since he, like his grandfather, proclaimed the name of God and taught it to others. Isaac, however, practiced his faith in private and as such needed the merit of Abraham (as we see in this verse and verse 24) for his own preservation, and to insure his future. However, once he *calls upon the Name of God,* he is worthy on his own to be blessed by God (verses 28-29).

י וַיֹּאמֶר אֲבִימֶלֶךְ מַה־זֹּאת עָשִׂיתָ לָּנוּ כִּמְעַט שָׁכַב אַחַד הָעָם אֶת־
יא אִשְׁתֶּךָ וְהֵבֵאתָ עָלֵינוּ אָשָׁם׃ וַיְצַו אֲבִימֶלֶךְ אֶת־כָּל־הָעָם לֵאמֹר הַנֹּגֵעַ
יב בָּאִישׁ הַזֶּה וּבְאִשְׁתּוֹ מוֹת יוּמָת׃ וַיִּזְרַע יִצְחָק בָּאָרֶץ הַהִוא וַיִּמְצָא בַּשָּׁנָה
יג הַהִוא מֵאָה שְׁעָרִים וַיְבָרְכֵהוּ יהוה׃ וַיִּגְדַּל הָאִישׁ וַיֵּלֶךְ הָלוֹךְ וְגָדֵל עַד שלישי
יד כִּי־גָדַל מְאֹד׃ וַיְהִי־לוֹ מִקְנֵה־צֹאן וּמִקְנֵה בָקָר וַעֲבֻדָּה רַבָּה וַיְקַנְאוּ אֹתוֹ
טו פְּלִשְׁתִּים׃ וְכָל־הַבְּאֵרֹת אֲשֶׁר חָפְרוּ עַבְדֵי אָבִיו בִּימֵי אַבְרָהָם אָבִיו
טז סִתְּמוּם פְּלִשְׁתִּים וַיְמַלְאוּם עָפָר׃ וַיֹּאמֶר אֲבִימֶלֶךְ אֶל־יִצְחָק לֵךְ מֵעִמָּנוּ
יז כִּי־עָצַמְתָּ מִמֶּנּוּ מְאֹד׃ וַיֵּלֶךְ מִשָּׁם יִצְחָק וַיִּחַן בְּנַחַל־גְּרָר וַיֵּשֶׁב שָׁם׃
יח וַיָּשָׁב יִצְחָק וַיַּחְפֹּר ׀ אֶת־בְּאֵרֹת הַמַּיִם אֲשֶׁר חָפְרוּ בִּימֵי אַבְרָהָם אָבִיו
וַיְסַתְּמוּם פְּלִשְׁתִּים אַחֲרֵי מוֹת אַבְרָהָם וַיִּקְרָא לָהֶן שֵׁמוֹת כַּשֵּׁמֹת אֲשֶׁר־
יט קָרָא לָהֶן אָבִיו׃ וַיַּחְפְּרוּ עַבְדֵי־יִצְחָק בַּנָּחַל וַיִּמְצְאוּ־שָׁם בְּאֵר מַיִם חַיִּים׃
כ וַיָּרִיבוּ רֹעֵי גְרָר עִם־רֹעֵי יִצְחָק לֵאמֹר לָנוּ הַמָּיִם וַיִּקְרָא שֵׁם־הַבְּאֵר עֵשֶׂק
כא כִּי הִתְעַשְּׂקוּ עִמּוֹ׃ וַיַּחְפְּרוּ בְּאֵר אַחֶרֶת וַיָּרִיבוּ גַּם־עָלֶיהָ וַיִּקְרָא שְׁמָהּ
כב שִׂטְנָה׃ וַיַּעְתֵּק מִשָּׁם וַיַּחְפֹּר בְּאֵר אַחֶרֶת וְלֹא רָבוּ עָלֶיהָ וַיִּקְרָא שְׁמָהּ
כג רְחֹבוֹת וַיֹּאמֶר כִּי־עַתָּה הִרְחִיב יהוה לָנוּ וּפָרִינוּ בָאָרֶץ׃ וַיַּעַל מִשָּׁם בְּאֵר רביעי
כד שָׁבַע׃ וַיֵּרָא אֵלָיו יהוה בַּלַּיְלָה הַהוּא וַיֹּאמֶר אָנֹכִי אֱלֹהֵי אַבְרָהָם אָבִיךָ
אַל־תִּירָא כִּי־אִתְּךָ אָנֹכִי וּבֵרַכְתִּיךָ וְהִרְבֵּיתִי אֶת־זַרְעֲךָ בַּעֲבוּר אַבְרָהָם
כה עַבְדִּי׃ וַיִּבֶן שָׁם מִזְבֵּחַ וַיִּקְרָא בְּשֵׁם יהוה וַיֶּט־שָׁם אָהֳלוֹ וַיִּכְרוּ־
כו שָׁם עַבְדֵי־יִצְחָק בְּאֵר׃ וַאֲבִימֶלֶךְ הָלַךְ אֵלָיו מִגְּרָר וַאֲחֻזַּת מֵרֵעֵהוּ

---

10. כִּמְעַט שָׁכַב אַחַד הָעָם — *One of the people has nearly lain.* (אַחַד) refers to the king who is singular among his people; he never thought it was necessary to ask your opinion or desire regarding (Rebecca) for doubtless, considering his exalted position, you would be satisfied to have him marry your sister.

וְהֵבֵאתָ עָלֵינוּ אָשָׁם — *And you would have brought guilt upon us ...* and (by your concealment of her status) you almost brought guilt and punishment upon (all of) us. He said עָלֵינוּ, *all of us,* for when the leader of the generation (the king) is punished, great harm also befalls those who dwell under his protective (rule).

12. וַיִּזְרַע יִצְחָק בָּאָרֶץ הַהִוא — *Isaac sowed in that land.* As God had said to him, *"Reside in this land"* (verse 3).

מֵאָה שְׁעָרִים — *A hundredfold ...* as He had promised, *"And I will be with you and bless you"* (ibid.).

וַיְבָרְכֵהוּ ה׳ — *And God blessed him ...* with wealth, for he sold his produce at a high price. (And) according to what our Sages tell us that "this computation was made for the sake of tithing" (*Bereishis Rabbah* 64), this in turn granted him a blessing, as it is written: הָבִיאוּ אֶת כָּל הַמַּעֲשֵׂר אֶל בֵּית הָאוֹצָר . . . וַהֲרִיקֹתִי לָכֶם בְּרָכָה עַד בְּלִי דָי, *Bring the whole tithe into the storehouse ... and I will pour out a blessing to you that will be more than sufficient* (*Malachi* 3:10).

NOTES

12. וַיְבָרְכֵהוּ ה׳ – *And God blessed him.* The word וַיְבָרְכֵהוּ is in addition to the previous phrase, *and found, that year, a hundredfold;* hence it must mean an added blessing of money, not only the produce of the land. The amount recorded (a hundred) is used to denote that ten percent of this produce was given by Isaac to *tzedakah* (charity). The Torah, by telling us this, indicates that God's blessing was due to this praiseworthy behavior on his part.

10 *Abimelech said, "What is this that you have done to us? One of the
people has nearly lain with your wife, and you would have brought guilt
upon us!"* 11 *Abimelech then warned all the people saying, "Whoever
molests this man or his wife shall surely be put to death."*
12 *Isaac sowed in that land, and in that year he reaped a hundredfold;
thus had HASHEM blessed him.* 13 *The man became great and kept becoming
greater until he was very great.* 14 *He had acquired flocks and herds and
many enterprises; and the Philistines envied him.*
15 *All the wells that his father's servants had dug in the days of Abraham
his father, the Philistines stopped up, and filled them with earth.* 16 *And
Abimelech said to Isaac, "Go away from us for you have become much
mightier than we!"* 17 *So Isaac departed from there and encamped in the
valley of Gerar, and dwelled there.* 18 *And Isaac dug anew the wells of
water which they had dug in the days of Abraham his father and the
Philistines had stopped up after Abraham's death; and he called them by
the same names that his father had called them.*
19 *Isaac's servants dug in the valley and found there a well of fresh
water.* 20 *The herdsmen of Gerar quarreled with Isaac's herdsmen saying,
"The water is ours," so he called the name of that well Esek because they
involved themselves with him.* 21 *Then they dug another well, and they
quarreled over that also; so he called its name Sitnah.* 22 *He relocated from
there and dug another well; they did not quarrel over it, so he called its
name Rehoboth, and said, "For now HASHEM has granted us ample space,
and we can be fruitful in the land."*
23 *He went up from there to Beer-sheba.* 24 *HASHEM appeared to him that
night and said, "I am the God of your father Abraham: Fear not, for I am
with you; I will bless you and increase your offspring because of Abraham
my servant."* 25 *He built an altar there, invoked HASHEM by Name, and
there he pitched his tent; there Isaac's servants dug a well.*
26 *Abimelech went to him from Gerar with a group of his friends and*

---

14. וַעֲבֻדָּה רַבָּה — *And many enterprises* . . . lands ready to be tilled.
וַיְקַנְאוּ אֹתוֹ פְּלִשְׁתִּים — *And the Philistines envied him* . . . because in their fields the opposite was true; they planted much and produced little.

15. סִתְּמוּם פְּלִשְׁתִּים — *The Philistines stopped up.* Fearing to harm Isaac (in person) because of Abimelech's orders, they stopped up the wells, because of envy and animosity.

16. כִּי עָצַמְתָּ מִמֶּנּוּ — *You have become mightier than us.* Your (great) wealth will enable you to rise up against us.

20. הִתְעַשְּׂקוּ עִמּוֹ — *They involved themselves with him.* They endeavored to make Isaac abandon the well.

24. אַל תִּירָא — *Fear not* . . . that your property will be diminished through this strife.
וּבֵרַכְתִּיךָ — *And I will bless you* . . . with additional wealth.

25-26. וַיִּקְרָא בְּשֵׁם ה׳ . . . וַיִּכְרוּ שָׁם עַבְדֵי יִצְחָק בְּאֵר . . . וַאֲבִימֶלֶךְ הָלַךְ אֵלָיו — *And called upon the name of God . . . and there Isaac's servants dug a well . . . Then Abimelech went to*

NOTES

24. וּבֵרַכְתִּיךָ – *And I will bless you.* Consistent with his interpretation of בְּרָכָה, *blessing,* in verse 12, the *Sforno* interprets the word וּבֵרַכְתִּיךָ, *And I will bless you,* similarly — with additional wealth.

כז וּפִיכֹל שַׂר־צְבָאוֹ: וַיֹּאמֶר אֲלֵהֶם יִצְחָק מַדּוּעַ בָּאתֶם אֵלָי וְאַתֶּם שְׂנֵאתֶם
כח אֹתִי וַתְּשַׁלְּחוּנִי מֵאִתְּכֶם: וַיֹּאמְרוּ רָאוֹ רָאִינוּ כִּי־הָיָה יהוה | עִמָּךְ וַנֹּאמֶר
כט תְּהִי נָא אָלָה בֵּינוֹתֵינוּ בֵּינֵינוּ וּבֵינֶךָ וְנִכְרְתָה בְרִית עִמָּךְ: אִם־תַּעֲשֵׂה
עִמָּנוּ רָעָה כַּאֲשֶׁר לֹא נְגַעֲנוּךָ וְכַאֲשֶׁר עָשִׂינוּ עִמְּךָ רַק־טוֹב וַנְּשַׁלֵּחֲךָ
חמישי ל בְּשָׁלוֹם אַתָּה עַתָּה בְּרוּךְ יהוה: וַיַּעַשׂ לָהֶם מִשְׁתֶּה וַיֹּאכְלוּ וַיִּשְׁתּוּ:
לא וַיַּשְׁכִּימוּ בַבֹּקֶר וַיִּשָּׁבְעוּ אִישׁ לְאָחִיו וַיְשַׁלְּחֵם יִצְחָק וַיֵּלְכוּ מֵאִתּוֹ
לב בְּשָׁלוֹם: וַיְהִי | בַּיּוֹם הַהוּא וַיָּבֹאוּ עַבְדֵי יִצְחָק וַיַּגִּדוּ לוֹ עַל־אֹדוֹת הַבְּאֵר
לג אֲשֶׁר חָפָרוּ וַיֹּאמְרוּ לוֹ מָצָאנוּ מָיִם: וַיִּקְרָא אֹתָהּ שִׁבְעָה עַל־כֵּן שֵׁם־
לד הָעִיר בְּאֵר שֶׁבַע עַד הַיּוֹם הַזֶּה: וַיְהִי עֵשָׂו בֶּן־אַרְבָּעִים
שָׁנָה וַיִּקַּח אִשָּׁה אֶת־יְהוּדִית בַּת־בְּאֵרִי הַחִתִּי וְאֶת־בָּשְׂמַת בַּת־
כז לה־א אֵילֹן הַחִתִּי: וַתִּהְיֶיןָ מֹרַת רוּחַ לְיִצְחָק וּלְרִבְקָה: וַיְהִי
כִּי־זָקֵן יִצְחָק וַתִּכְהֶיןָ עֵינָיו מֵרְאֹת וַיִּקְרָא אֶת־עֵשָׂו | בְּנוֹ הַגָּדֹל
ב וַיֹּאמֶר אֵלָיו בְּנִי וַיֹּאמֶר אֵלָיו הִנֵּנִי: וַיֹּאמֶר הִנֵּה־נָא זָקַנְתִּי לֹא יָדַעְתִּי

---

him. After he was inspired to "call upon the name of God," the servants of Isaac successfully dug a well without conflict and Abimelech came to him to make a covenant and no longer harmed him.

28. כִּי הָיָה ה׳ עִמָּךְ — *That God has been with you.* It is not out of fear of you that we make this covenant with you.

29. אִם תַּעֲשֵׂה עִמָּנוּ רָעָה . . . אַתָּה עַתָּה — *If you dare do evil to us . . . Now, you . . .* that you will do us no harm, as we have not molested you.

33. וַיִּקְרָא אֹתָהּ שִׁבְעָה — *And he named it Shivah.* He called the well *shivah* because it was the "seventh" place where he had dug a well; the three of Abraham which the Philistines stopped, as it says, וְכָל הַבְּאֵרֹת . . . סִתְּמוּם פְּלִשְׁתִּים, *All the wells . . . the Philistines had stopped* (verse 15), and the word כָּל, *all,* is never used for less than three; the three wells of Isaac: Esek, Sitnah and Rehoboth; and this was the seventh, which was called *Shivah.*

עַל כֵּן שֵׁם הָעִיר בְּאֵר שֶׁבַע — *Therefore the name of the city is Beer-sheba.* (The word שֶׁבַע), with a סֶגּוֹל (ֶ), indicates both שְׁבוּעָה, *the oath,* and the number שִׁבְעָה, *seven.* In the days of Abraham, however, the name of the city was בְּאֵר שָׁבַע, with a קָמָץ (ָ), indicating only the "oath" (21:31).

34. וַיְהִי עֵשָׂו בֶּן אַרְבָּעִים שָׁנָה — *And Esau was forty years old.* Isaac did not concern himself with wedding him and his brother to appropriate wives.

וַיִּקַּח אִשָּׁה אֶת יְהוּדִית בַּת בְּאֵרִי הַחִתִּי — *And he took to wife Judith the daughter of Be'eri the Hittite.* Isaac did not protest against his marrying these Hittite women, as had his father (24:3).

35. וַתִּהְיֶיןָ מֹרַת רוּחַ — *And they cut short the spirit.* They were as a razor and knife which cut short the spirit in the lives of Isaac and Rebecca. The word מֹרַת is cognate to מוֹרָה, as we

NOTES

34. וַיְהִי עֵשָׂו בֶּן אַרְבָּעִים שָׁנָה וַיִּקַּח אִשָּׁה אֶת יְהוּדִית — *And Esau was forty years old and he took to wife Judith.* Abraham took the initiative and involved himself in finding a proper wife for his son. Unfortunately, Isaac, the private retiring person, did not, and consequently Esau, without parental restraint, married unsuitable wives, causing much distress to his parents.

35. וַתִּהְיֶיןָ מֹרַת רוּחַ — *And they cut short the spirit.* Two expressions are used by the *Sforno:* בְּרָכָה, *blessing,* and עֵצָה, *counsel.* The former refers

Phicol, general of his legion. [27] *Isaac said to him, "Why have you come to me? You hate me and drove me away from you!"*

[28] *And they said, "We have indeed seen that HASHEM has been with you, so we said, 'Let the oath between ourselves now be between us and you, and let us make a covenant with you:* [29] *If you do evil with us. . .! Just as we have not molested you, and just as we have done with you only good, and sent you away in peace — Now, you, O blessed of HASHEM!' "*

[30] *He made them a feast and they ate and drank.* [31] *They awoke early in the morning and swore to one another; then Isaac saw them off and they departed from him in peace.* [32] *And it was on that very day that Isaac's servants came and told him about the well they had dug, and they said to him, "We have found water!"* [33] *And he named it Shibah; therefore, the name of the city is Beer-sheba until this very day.*

[34] *When Esau was forty years old, he took as a wife Judith daughter of Beeri the Hittite, and Basemath daughter of Elon the Hittite;* [35] *and they were a source of spiritual rebellion to Isaac and to Rebecca.*

27 [1] *And it came to pass, when Isaac had become old, and his eyes dimmed from seeing, that he summoned Esau, his older son, and said to him, "My son." And he said to him, "Here I am."* [2] *And he said, "See, now, I have aged; I know*

---

find, וּמוֹרָה לֹא יַעֲלֶה עַל רֹאשׁוֹ, *And no razor shall come upon his head* (*Judges* 13:5). Now, in spite of all this, Isaac did not recognize the great wickedness of Esau, nor did he protest against (these wives). As a result, (Isaac) failed by trying to bless Esau. From this (error) a mishap resulted whereby he (Isaac) gave a blessing and counsel (to Esau) and subsequently hatred increased among his sons, and Jacob was compelled to flee to another country.

XXVII

1. וַתִּכְהֶיןָ עֵינָיו — *And his eyesight dimmed* . . . as happened to Eli who (also) did not restrain (the wickedness) of his sons, as it is written, וְלֹא כִהָה בָּם, *And he did not rebuke them (I Samuel* 3:13), and (as a result), וְעֵינָיו קָמָה וְלֹא יָכוֹל לִרְאוֹת, *His eyes were set and he could not see (* ibid. 4:15). Now this (dimness of sight) did not occur with Abraham or Jacob even when they were older than Isaac or Eli. Of Abraham it is written, וַיֹּסֶף אַבְרָהָם וַיִּקַּח אִשָּׁה, *And Abraham took another wife* (25:1), and as for Jacob, in spite of all his distress and (constant) weeping, it is written, וַיַּרְא יִשְׂרָאֵל אֶת בְּנֵי יוֹסֵף, *And Israel saw Joseph's sons* (48:8). Even though his sight was dim, as it says, וְעֵינֵי יִשְׂרָאֵל כָּבְדוּ מִזֹּקֶן, *The eyes of Israel were dim from old age* (48:10), this was (only) to the extent that he could not *identify* an individual image (but he could distinguish people).

2. לֹא יָדַעְתִּי יוֹם מוֹתִי — *I know not the day of my death.* A blessing is more effective when the one who gives the blessing is close to death, as we find by Jacob and Moses (as well), because the soul is separated from the physical (bonds) more so, at that time.

NOTES

to the blessings recorded in 27:39, i.e., *the fat of the earth* and *the dew of heaven,* while the latter refers to *by thy sword shall you live* (27:40).

XXVII

1. וַתִּכְהֶיןָ עֵינָיו – *And his eyesight dimmed.* The *Sforno* links the physical dimming of one's eyes to the failure to perceive the behavior of one's children and their effect upon the family's future. The *Sforno* is also critical of Isaac's passivity when Esau marries Hittite women (26:34) and his lack of involvement in choosing wives for his sons, as his father had done for him. All this can be termed *the dimming of one's eyes.*

2. לֹא יָדַעְתִּי יוֹם מוֹתִי – *I know not the day of my death.* When a righteous person gives a blessing it

ג יוֹם מוֹתִי: וְעַתָּה שָׂא־נָא כֵלֶיךָ תֶּלְיְךָ וְקַשְׁתֶּךָ וְצֵא הַשָּׂדֶה וְצוּדָה לִּי
ד °צידה: וַעֲשֵׂה־לִי מַטְעַמִּים כַּאֲשֶׁר אָהַבְתִּי וְהָבִיאָה לִּי וְאֹכֵלָה בַּעֲבוּר °צַיִד ק'
ה תְּבָרֶכְךָ נַפְשִׁי בְּטֶרֶם אָמוּת: וְרִבְקָה שֹׁמַעַת בְּדַבֵּר יִצְחָק אֶל־עֵשָׂו בְּנוֹ
ו וַיֵּלֶךְ עֵשָׂו הַשָּׂדֶה לָצוּד צַיִד לְהָבִיא: וְרִבְקָה אָמְרָה אֶל־יַעֲקֹב בְּנָהּ
ז לֵאמֹר הִנֵּה שָׁמַעְתִּי אֶת־אָבִיךָ מְדַבֵּר אֶל־עֵשָׂו אָחִיךָ לֵאמֹר: הָבִיאָה
לִּי צַיִד וַעֲשֵׂה־לִי מַטְעַמִּים וְאֹכֵלָה וַאֲבָרֶכְכָה לִפְנֵי יְהוָה לִפְנֵי מוֹתִי:
ח־ט וְעַתָּה בְנִי שְׁמַע בְּקֹלִי לַאֲשֶׁר אֲנִי מְצַוָּה אֹתָךְ: לֶךְ־נָא אֶל־הַצֹּאן וְקַח־
לִי מִשָּׁם שְׁנֵי גְּדָיֵי עִזִּים טֹבִים וְאֶעֱשֶׂה אֹתָם מַטְעַמִּים לְאָבִיךָ כַּאֲשֶׁר
י־יא אָהֵב: וְהֵבֵאתָ לְאָבִיךָ וְאָכָל בַּעֲבֻר אֲשֶׁר יְבָרֶכְךָ לִפְנֵי מוֹתוֹ: וַיֹּאמֶר
יב יַעֲקֹב אֶל־רִבְקָה אִמּוֹ הֵן עֵשָׂו אָחִי אִישׁ שָׂעִר וְאָנֹכִי אִישׁ חָלָק: אוּלַי
יְמֻשֵּׁנִי אָבִי וְהָיִיתִי בְעֵינָיו כִּמְתַעְתֵּעַ וְהֵבֵאתִי עָלַי קְלָלָה וְלֹא בְרָכָה:
יג־יד וַתֹּאמֶר לוֹ אִמּוֹ עָלַי קִלְלָתְךָ בְּנִי אַךְ שְׁמַע בְּקֹלִי וְלֵךְ קַח־לִי: וַיֵּלֶךְ
טו וַיִּקַּח וַיָּבֵא לְאִמּוֹ וַתַּעַשׂ אִמּוֹ מַטְעַמִּים כַּאֲשֶׁר אָהֵב אָבִיו: וַתִּקַּח רִבְקָה
אֶת־בִּגְדֵי עֵשָׂו בְּנָהּ הַגָּדֹל הַחֲמֻדֹת אֲשֶׁר אִתָּהּ בַּבָּיִת וַתַּלְבֵּשׁ אֶת־
טז יַעֲקֹב בְּנָהּ הַקָּטָן: וְאֵת עֹרֹת גְּדָיֵי הָעִזִּים הִלְבִּישָׁה עַל־יָדָיו וְעַל חֶלְקַת
יז צַוָּארָיו: וַתִּתֵּן אֶת־הַמַּטְעַמִּים וְאֶת־הַלֶּחֶם אֲשֶׁר עָשָׂתָה בְּיַד יַעֲקֹב בְּנָהּ:
יח־יט וַיָּבֹא אֶל־אָבִיו וַיֹּאמֶר אָבִי וַיֹּאמֶר הִנֶּנִּי מִי אַתָּה בְּנִי: וַיֹּאמֶר יַעֲקֹב אֶל־
אָבִיו אָנֹכִי עֵשָׂו בְּכֹרֶךָ עָשִׂיתִי כַּאֲשֶׁר דִּבַּרְתָּ אֵלָי קוּם־נָא שְׁבָה וְאָכְלָה
כ מִצֵּידִי בַּעֲבוּר תְּבָרְכַנִּי נַפְשֶׁךָ: וַיֹּאמֶר יִצְחָק אֶל־בְּנוֹ מַה־זֶּה מִהַרְתָּ
כא לִמְצֹא בְּנִי וַיֹּאמֶר כִּי הִקְרָה יְהוָה אֱלֹהֶיךָ לְפָנָי: וַיֹּאמֶר יִצְחָק אֶל־יַעֲקֹב
כב גְּשָׁה־נָּא וַאֲמֻשְׁךָ בְּנִי הַאַתָּה זֶה בְּנִי עֵשָׂו אִם־לֹא: וַיִּגַּשׁ יַעֲקֹב אֶל־יִצְחָק
כג אָבִיו וַיְמֻשֵּׁהוּ וַיֹּאמֶר הַקֹּל קוֹל יַעֲקֹב וְהַיָּדַיִם יְדֵי עֵשָׂו: וְלֹא הִכִּירוֹ

3. שָׂא נָא כֵלֶיךָ — *Now sharpen, please, your gear . . .* so that you not return empty-handed nor tarry.

4. וַעֲשֵׂה לִי מַטְעַמִּים — *And make me delicacies.* He asked for savory food that (Esau) should occupy himself with כִּבּוּד אָב, *filial honor,* (and be worthy) that the blessing be effective, for even though he did not recognize Esau's great wickedness, nonetheless he did not feel him worthy to receive the blessing that he had in mind to give him. Because of this, when he blessed Jacob later (before he left for Haran) he did not request him to bring savory food, but blessed him at once, saying וְאֵל שַׁדַּי יְבָרֵךְ אֹתְךָ, *And God Almighty bless you* (28:3), for he knew that he was worthy to be blessed.

12. וְלֹא בְרָכָה — *Rather than a blessing.* Even if he has reserved a blessing for me he will not bless me, if I deceive him.

NOTES

is inspired from above. That is why the expression נַפְשִׁי, *my soul,* is used by Isaac (verse 4). The person's spiritual self is purer when unencumbered by his physical being. Thus, before one's death, when the body is weak, the soul is stronger, hence the blessing is more effective. This is why Isaac stresses the imminence of his death in this verse and Rebecca does so, in verse 7, where she also adds the words, לִפְנֵי מוֹתוֹ, *before he dies,* to stress the inspiration from on High when Isaac will give his blessing.

13. עָלַי קִלְלָתְךָ — *Your curse be on me.* The Sages' interpretation of the episode cited by the *Sforno* clarifies the meaning of עָלַי קִלְלָתְךָ, *Your curse be on me,* which implies that one *can* transfer a curse.

not the day of my death. [3] *Now sharpen, if you please, your gear — your sword and your bow — and go out to the field and hunt game for me.* [4] *Then make me delicacies such as I love and bring it to me and I will eat, so that my soul may bless you before I die."*

[5] *Now Rebecca was listening as Isaac spoke to Esau his son; and Esau went to the field to hunt game to bring.* [6] *But Rebecca had said to Jacob her son, saying, "Behold I heard your father speaking to your brother Esau saying,* [7] *'Bring me some game and make me delicacies to eat, and I will bless you in the presence of* H*ASHEM* *before my death.'* [8] *So now, my son, heed my voice to that which I command you.* [9] *Go now to the flock and fetch me from there two choice young kids of the goats, and I will make of them delicacies for your father, as he loves.* [10] *Then bring it to your father and he shall eat, so that he may bless you before his death."*

[11] *Jacob replied to Rebecca, his mother, "But my brother Esau is a hairy man and I am a smooth-skinned man.* [12] *Perhaps my father will feel me and I shall be as a mocker in his eyes; I will thus bring upon myself a curse rather than a blessing."* [13] *But his mother said to him, "Your curse be on me, my son; only heed my voice and go fetch them for me."* [14] *So he went, fetched, and brought to his mother, and his mother made delicacies as his father loved.* [15] *Rebecca then took her older son Esau's clean garments which were with her in the house, and clothed Jacob her young son.* [16] *With the skins of the goat-kids she covered his arms and his smooth-skinned neck.* [17] *She placed the delicacies and the bread which she had made into the hand of her son Jacob.*

[18] *And he came to his father and said, "Father," and he said, "Here I am; who are you, my son?"* [19] *Jacob said to his father, "It is I, Esau your firstborn; I have done as you told me; rise up, please, sit and eat of my game that your soul may bless me."*

[20] *Isaac said to his son, "How is it that you were so quick to find, my son?" And he said, "Because* H*ASHEM* *your God arranged it for me."* [21] *And Isaac said to Jacob, "Come close, if you please, so I can feel you, my son; are you, indeed, my son Esau or not?"*

[22] *So Jacob drew close to Isaac his father who felt him and said, "The voice is Jacob's voice, but the hands are Esau's hands."* [23] *But he did not recognize*

13. עָלַי קִלְלָתְךָ — *Your curse be on me.* I will accept the curse in your place, as our Sages tell us regarding Solomon who accepted upon himself the curses of Joab, and so it came to pass (*Sanhedrin* 48b).

22. וְהַיָּדַיִם יְדֵי עֵשָׂו — *The hands are the hands of Esau.* Doubtless, the skins were prepared in such a fashion that their hair was similar to that of a human, (still) there is a vast

NOTES

When Joab killed Abner, David was appalled and cursed him. Before David died he commanded his son Solomon to avenge the blood of Abner and Amasa. When Solomon prepared to execute Joab, our Sages tell us that Joab argued that since he was cursed he should not be killed, and if Solomon insisted upon slaying him then the curse of David should be transferred to Solomon and the Davidic house. Solomon accepted the curse, Joab was executed, and indeed the curses of David were visited upon various generations of his descendants. Thus we see that Rebecca's willingness to accept any curse pronounced over her son is a valid transfer.

22. וְהַיָּדַיִם יְדֵי עֵשָׂו — *The hands are the hands of Esau.* To prove that in old age one's senses are

כד כִּי־הָיוּ יָדָיו כִּידֵי עֵשָׂו אָחִיו שְׂעִרֹת וַיְבָרְכֵהוּ: וַיֹּאמֶר אַתָּה זֶה בְּנִי עֵשָׂו
כה וַיֹּאמֶר אָנִי: וַיֹּאמֶר הַגִּשָׁה לִּי וְאֹכְלָה מִצֵּיד בְּנִי לְמַעַן תְּבָרֶכְךָ נַפְשִׁי
כו וַיַּגֶּשׁ־לוֹ וַיֹּאכַל וַיָּבֵא לוֹ יַיִן וַיֵּשְׁתְּ: וַיֹּאמֶר אֵלָיו יִצְחָק אָבִיו גְּשָׁה־נָּא
כז וּשְׁקָה־לִּי בְּנִי: וַיִּגַּשׁ וַיִּשַּׁק־לוֹ וַיָּרַח אֶת־רֵיחַ בְּגָדָיו וַיְבָרְכֵהוּ וַיֹּאמֶר רְאֵה
כח רֵיחַ בְּנִי כְּרֵיחַ שָׂדֶה אֲשֶׁר בֵּרְכוֹ יהוה: וְיִתֶּן־לְךָ הָאֱלֹהִים מִטַּל הַשָּׁמַיִם
שׁשׁי
כט וּמִשְׁמַנֵּי הָאָרֶץ וְרֹב דָּגָן וְתִירֹשׁ: יַעַבְדוּךָ עַמִּים °וְיִשְׁתַּחוּ לְךָ לְאֻמִּים הֱוֵה
°וְיִשְׁתַּחֲווּ ק
ל גְּבִיר לְאַחֶיךָ וְיִשְׁתַּחֲווּ לְךָ בְּנֵי אִמֶּךָ אֹרְרֶיךָ אָרוּר וּמְבָרֲכֶיךָ בָּרוּךְ: וַיְהִי
כַּאֲשֶׁר כִּלָּה יִצְחָק לְבָרֵךְ אֶת־יַעֲקֹב וַיְהִי אַךְ יָצֹא יָצָא יַעֲקֹב מֵאֵת פְּנֵי
לא יִצְחָק אָבִיו וְעֵשָׂו אָחִיו בָּא מִצֵּידוֹ: וַיַּעַשׂ גַּם־הוּא מַטְעַמִּים וַיָּבֵא לְאָבִיו

difference between the hair of a man and that of a kid, unless it is thoroughly prepared. Now, we are told that (Jacob's) hands were as the hands of his brother Esau, "hairy." Perhaps (this was so) because (Isaac's) sense of touch was weakened (as was his sight) similar to: אִם יִטְעַם עַבְדְּךָ אֶת אֲשֶׁר אֹכַל, Can I, your servant, taste what I eat? (II Samuel 19:36).

23. שְׂעִרֹת וַיְבָרְכֵהוּ — *Hairy, and he blessed him.* Because he (first) suspected him that he deserved to be cursed, as (Jacob himself) said, *and I shall bring a curse upon me* (verse 12) (therefore he blessed him). As our Sages teach us, הַחוֹשֵׁד אֶת חֲבֵרוֹ בְּדָבָר שֶׁאֵין בּוֹ צָרִיךְ לְפַיְּיסוֹ, וְלֹא עוֹד אֶלָּא שֶׁצָּרִיךְ לְבָרְכוֹ, *One who suspects another of a fault which he has not committed must appease him; even more, he must bless him* (Berachos 31b). (This is) similar to Eli who suspected Hannah of being drunk.

27. וַיָּרַח אֶת רֵיחַ בְּגָדָיו — *And he smelled the fragrance of his garments . . .* so as to expand his soul through the pleasure of the fragrance, as our Sages tell us, אֵיזֶהוּ דָּבָר שֶׁהַנְּשָׁמָה נֶהֱנִית מִמֶּנּוּ וְאֵין הַגּוּף נֶהֱנֶה מִמֶּנּוּ הֱוֵי אוֹמֵר זֶה הָרֵיחַ, *What is it which gives enjoyment to the soul and not to the body? You must say that this refers to a fragrant aroma* (Berachos 43b).

וַיְבָרְכֵהוּ — *And blessed him.* This is similar to, וְהָיָה כְּנַגֵּן הַמְנַגֵּן וַתְּהִי עָלָיו יַד ה', *And it came to pass when the musician played, that the hand of HASHEM was upon him* (II Kings 3:15).

רְאֵה רֵיחַ בְּנִי — *See, the fragrance of my son.* You, my son, see and understand that this aroma is . . .

כְּרֵיחַ שָׂדֶה אֲשֶׁר בֵּרְכוֹ ה' — *Like the fragrance of a field which God has blessed.* Besides the existence in fact (of a field) which provides food for all living creatures, God in His goodness added the pleasant aroma which gives pleasure and satisfies the spiritual and aesthetic needs (of man).

NOTES

dulled, the *Sforno* cites the incident recorded in *II Samuel* where Barzilai respectfully refused David's invitation to become a member of his household in Jerusalem, pleading that he was an old man and could no longer enjoy the physical pleasure of life, for he could not even enjoy food and drink, so he preferred to go home and live simply.

23. שְׂעִרֹת וַיְבָרְכֵהוּ — *Hairy, and he blessed him.* The blessing mentioned in this verse is not the one that follows in verses 28-29, but a separate one given as compensation for suspecting him of a misdeed which he had not committed. Since Isaac was in error (for indeed Jacob had deceived him) the text of this blessing is not revealed to us.

27. וַיָּרַח אֶת רֵיחַ בְּגָדָיו וַיְבָרְכֵהוּ — *And he smelled the fragrance of his garments and blessed him.* In order to bless from the depth of one's inner being it is necessary to be joyful and elevated in spirit. This sense of joy can be aroused through fragrance, which appeals to the soul of man, or through music, which elevated Elisha's spirit, enabling him to prophesy (II Kings chap. 3).

רְאֵה רֵיחַ בְּנִי — *See, the fragrance of my son.* The *Sforno* interprets the word רְאֵה, see, (the imperative form) as being directed by Isaac to Jacob. He urged him to be sensitive to the fragrance of the field, which should be appreciated as a blessing from God, i.e., satisfying man's inherent aesthetic

him because his hands were hairy like those of Esau his brother; so he blessed
him. 24 He said, "You are, indeed, my son Esau!" And he said, "I am." 25 He
said, "Serve me and let me eat of my son's game that my soul may bless you."
So he served him and he ate, and he brought him wine and he drank.
26 Then his father Isaac said to him, "Come close, if you please, and kiss me,
my son." 27 So he drew close and kissed him; he smelled the fragrance of his
garments and blessed him; he said, "See, the fragrance of my son is like the
fragrance of a field which H*ASHEM had blessed — 28 And may God give you of*
the dew of the heavens and of the fatness of the earth, and abundant grain and
wine. 29 Peoples will serve you, and regimes will prostrate themselves to you;
be a lord to your kinsmen, and your mother's sons will prostrate themselves
to you; cursed be they who curse you, and blessed be they who bless you."
30 And it was, when Isaac had finished blessing Jacob, and Jacob had
scarcely left from the presence of Isaac his father, that Esau his brother came
back from his hunt. 31 He, too, made delicacies, and brought them to his father;

28. וְיִתֶּן לְךָ הָאֱלֹהִים — *And may God give you.* When you will consider (and appreciate) this attribute of His goodness, He will give you, as the Creator (הָאֱלֹהִים), a field blessed . . .

מִטַּל הַשָּׁמַיִם — *Of the dew of the heavens.* The dew of heaven will be sufficient (for your needs) gladdening all, for it will not interfere with the comings and goings (of people).

וְרֹב דָּגָן וְתִירֹשׁ — *And abundant grain and wine.* To be able to sustain others, as we find, וְהִלְוִיתָ גּוֹיִם רַבִּים וְאַתָּה לֹא תִלְוֶה, *And you will lend to many nations, but you will not borrow (Deut.* 28:12).

29. וְיִשְׁתַּחֲווּ לְךָ לְאֻמִּים — *And nations will bow down to you.* Even those who will not *serve* you will bow down to you, for you will be superior to the kings of the land.

הֱוֵה גְבִיר לְאַחֶיךָ — *Be a lord to your kinsmen.* (Isaac) felt it would be good and sufficient for Jacob to have *Eretz Yisrael* as his possession, and to live there with a measure of submissiveness, so as not to trouble himself with the demands of leadership (or occupy himself) with passing vanities, as indeed happened to his descendants later on, as it says, מְתָאֵב אָנֹכִי אֶת גְּאוֹן יַעֲקֹב, *I abhor the pride of Jacob (Amos* 6:8). It would (also) be better for him to be subjugated to his brother rather than to another people, as our Sages teach us, אוֹ בְּטוּלָּךְ אוֹ בְּטוּלָא דְבַר עֵשָׂו, *Either in your shadow or in the shadow of the son of Esau (Gittin* 17a). Now since (Isaac) knew that *Eretz Yisrael* was fitting only for Jacob, he therefore omitted the blessings of Abraham and *Eretz Yisrael* in this blessing, which he thought was being given to Esau, and gave it (later) to Jacob, doing so knowingly (28:4).

אֹרְרֶיךָ אָרוּר — *Cursed be they who curse you* . . . for there are many who do curse kings and lords when their requests are not granted. It is for this reason that (the Torah) cautions us, אֱלֹהִים לֹא תְקַלֵּל, *You shall not curse the judges (Exodus* 22:27).

NOTES

needs. This aspect of God's goodness — often overlooked — if considered and appreciated, would cause God to give you the fat of the land and the dew of the heavens. According to the *Sforno*, then, this verse is the prerequisite for the blessings which follow in verses 28-29.

29. הֱוֵה גְבִיר לְאַחֶיךָ — *Be a lord to your kinsmen.* Isaac was under the impression that he was blessing Esau, therefore he did not include בִּרְכַּת אַבְרָהָם, the blessings given by God to Abraham (see *Rashi* 28:4), nor did he mention the inheritance of *Eretz Yisrael.* These were reserved for Jacob, for Isaac knew full well that Esau was not worthy to receive these special, unique spiritual gifts. By the same token he also knew that for Jacob's own good he should be submissive rather than assertive or aggressive, if his mission and purpose in life would be accomplished and fulfilled. That is why he designated Esau as the "lord" over his brother, which would be beneficial for both.

לב וַיֹּאמֶר לְאָבִיו יָקֻם אָבִי וְיֹאכַל מִצֵּיד בְּנוֹ בַּעֲבֻר תְּבָרְכַנִּי נַפְשֶׁךָ: וַיֹּאמֶר
לג לוֹ יִצְחָק אָבִיו מִי־אָתָּה וַיֹּאמֶר אֲנִי בִּנְךָ בְכֹרְךָ עֵשָׂו: וַיֶּחֱרַד יִצְחָק חֲרָדָה
גְּדֹלָה עַד־מְאֹד וַיֹּאמֶר מִי־אֵפוֹא הוּא הַצָּד־צַיִד וַיָּבֵא לִי וָאֹכַל מִכֹּל
לד בְּטֶרֶם תָּבוֹא וָאֲבָרֲכֵהוּ גַּם־בָּרוּךְ יִהְיֶה: כִּשְׁמֹעַ עֵשָׂו אֶת־דִּבְרֵי אָבִיו וַיִּצְעַק
לה צְעָקָה גְּדֹלָה וּמָרָה עַד־מְאֹד וַיֹּאמֶר לְאָבִיו בָּרְכֵנִי גַם־אָנִי אָבִי: וַיֹּאמֶר
לו בָּא אָחִיךָ בְּמִרְמָה וַיִּקַּח בִּרְכָתֶךָ: וַיֹּאמֶר הֲכִי קָרָא שְׁמוֹ יַעֲקֹב וַיַּעְקְבֵנִי
זֶה פַעֲמַיִם אֶת־בְּכֹרָתִי לָקָח וְהִנֵּה עַתָּה לָקַח בִּרְכָתִי וַיֹּאמַר הֲלֹא־
לז אָצַלְתָּ לִּי בְּרָכָה: וַיַּעַן יִצְחָק וַיֹּאמֶר לְעֵשָׂו הֵן גְּבִיר שַׂמְתִּיו לָךְ וְאֶת־כָּל־
אֶחָיו נָתַתִּי לוֹ לַעֲבָדִים וְדָגָן וְתִירֹשׁ סְמַכְתִּיו וּלְכָה אֵפוֹא מָה אֶעֱשֶׂה בְּנִי:
לח וַיֹּאמֶר עֵשָׂו אֶל־אָבִיו הַבְרָכָה אַחַת הִוא־לְךָ אָבִי בָּרְכֵנִי גַם־אָנִי אָבִי
לט וַיִּשָּׂא עֵשָׂו קֹלוֹ וַיֵּבְךְּ: וַיַּעַן יִצְחָק אָבִיו וַיֹּאמֶר אֵלָיו הִנֵּה מִשְׁמַנֵּי הָאָרֶץ
מ יִהְיֶה מוֹשָׁבֶךָ וּמִטַּל הַשָּׁמַיִם מֵעָל: וְעַל־חַרְבְּךָ תִחְיֶה וְאֶת־אָחִיךָ תַּעֲבֹד
מא וְהָיָה כַּאֲשֶׁר תָּרִיד וּפָרַקְתָּ עֻלּוֹ מֵעַל צַוָּארֶךָ: וַיִּשְׂטֹם עֵשָׂו אֶת־יַעֲקֹב
עַל־הַבְּרָכָה אֲשֶׁר בֵּרְכוֹ אָבִיו וַיֹּאמֶר עֵשָׂו בְּלִבּוֹ יִקְרְבוּ יְמֵי אֵבֶל אָבִי
מב וְאַהַרְגָה אֶת־יַעֲקֹב אָחִי: וַיֻּגַּד לְרִבְקָה אֶת־דִּבְרֵי עֵשָׂו בְּנָהּ הַגָּדֹל וַתִּשְׁלַח

---

33. מִי אֵפוֹא הוּא — *If so, who is the one (who hunted game)?* If it is true that you are Esau, who then is he who brought me game? The word אֵפוֹא, spelled with an א at the end, means *if so*, but when אֵיפֹה has a ה at the end, then it means *where*, as we find, אֵיפֹה הֵם רֹעִים, *Where are they feeding the flock* (37:16)?

גַּם בָּרוּךְ יִהְיֶה — *Indeed, he shall remain blessed.* If so, then he who brought me the game did so deceitfully; still he merited to be blessed, for I felt at the time I blessed him that it took effect, similar to what (our Sages tell us) regarding Rabbi Chanina when he prayed for the sick *(Berachos* 34b).

35. וַיִּקַּח בִּרְכָתֶךָ — *And took away your blessing* . . . that blessing which was fitting and proper for you, dealing as it did with things of this world and חוּץ לָאָרֶץ, *outside Eretz Yisrael*, for the blessing of Abraham is not worthy (or fitting) for you.

36. הֲכִי קָרָא שְׁמוֹ יַעֲקֹב וַיַּעְקְבֵנִי — *Is it because he was named Jacob that he outwitted me?* Did the fact that he was named Jacob influence him to deceive me, since שְׁמָא גָּרֵים, *a name can influence one's character (Berachos* 7b)?

הֲלֹא אָצַלְתָּ לִּי בְּרָכָה — *Have you not reserved a blessing for me?* Even though you intended to bless me with the superior blessing, you did not intend for me to have everything while my brother be denied and deprived of all blessing.

37. וְאֶת כָּל אֶחָיו נָתַתִּי לוֹ לַעֲבָדִים — *And all his kin have I given him as servants* . . . the children of Ishmael, Keturah and the kings of the nations, as he said, יַעַבְדוּךָ עַמִּים, *Peoples will serve you* (verse 29).

NOTES

33. גַּם בָּרוּךְ יִהְיֶה — *Indeed, he shall remain blessed.* The Mishnah (*Berachos* 34b) relates that Rabbi Chanina ben Dosa would pray for ill people and then state, "This one will die, this one will live." When asked how he knew this, he answered, "If my prayer comes out fluently, I know it is accepted." And so here Isaac felt that his prayer was effective, for Heaven inspired his words, henc how can he negate it?

39-40. וּמִטַּל הַשָּׁמַיִם מֵעָל. וְעַל חַרְבְּךָ תִחְיֶה — *And of the dew of heaven from above. And by your sword shall you live.* The *Sforno* interprets the phrase *shall you live* as applying both to the

he said to his father, "Let my father rise and eat of his son's game, so that your
soul will bless me."
32 *Isaac his father said to him, "Who are you?" And he said, "I am your*
firstborn son Esau." 33 *Then Isaac trembled in very great perplexity, and said,*
"Who — where — is the one who hunted game, brought it to me, and I partook
of all when you had not yet come, and I blessed him? Indeed, he shall remain
blessed!"
34 *When Esau heard his father's words, he cried out an exceedingly great*
and bitter cry, and said to his father, "Bless me too, Father!"
35 *But he said, "Your brother came with cleverness and took your blessing."*
36 *He said, "Is it because his name was called Jacob that he outwitted me*
these two times? — He took away my birthright and see, now he took away my
blessing!" Then he said, "Have you not reserved a blessing for me?"
37 *Isaac answered, and said to Esau, "Behold, a lord have I made him over*
you, and all his kin have I given him as servants; with grain and wine have I
supported him, and for you, where — what can I do, my son?"
38 *And Esau said to his father, "Have you but one blessing, Father? Bless me*
too, Father!" And Esau raised his voice and wept.
39 *So Isaac his father answered, and said to him: "Behold, of the fatness of*
the earth shall be your dwelling and of the dew of the heavens from above. 40 *By*
your sword you shall live, but your brother you shall serve; yet it shall be that
when you are aggrieved, you may cast off his yoke from upon your neck."
41 *Now Esau harbored hatred toward Jacob because of the blessing with*
which his father had blessed him; and Esau thought, "May the days of
mourning for my father draw near, then I will kill my brother Jacob."
42 *When Rebecca was told of the words of her older son Esau, she sent*

וּלְכָה אֵפוֹא מָה אֶעֱשֶׂה — *What then shall I do for you?*... therefore what can I do for you; what blessing (can I give you) which will be of benefit to you?

39-40. הִנֵּה מִשְׁמַנֵּי הָאָרֶץ יִהְיֶה מוֹשָׁבֶךָ — *Behold, of the fat of the earth shall be your dwelling.* This blessing I can give to you that your dwelling be in a land of fat (plenty) combined with some subservience to your brother.

וּמִטַּל הַשָּׁמַיִם מֵעָל. וְעַל חַרְבְּךָ תִחְיֶה — *And of the dew of heaven from above. And by your sword shall you live.* You shall live from *the dew of heaven,* i.e., you will not have to work the land which requires rain; and you shall also live *by your sword,* as a warrior waging war at the behest of your brother, or others. From this it shall follow ...

וְהָיָה כַּאֲשֶׁר תָּרִיד — *It shall come to pass that when you are aggrieved.* When you will cry out from the violence of your brother who will overly subjugate you ...

וּפָרַקְתָּ עֻלּוֹ מֵעַל צַוָּארֶךָ — *You shall remove his yoke from your neck* ... for you are learned in battle and thus qualified for kingship. However, if during your subjugation you will turn to tilling the soil and other such labors, you will never be free of subjugation to your brother or others.

NOTES

conclusion of verse 39 and the beginning of verse 40. Esau will live from the land, to some extent, but also from his role as warrior. Hence *shall you live* refers to *dew of the heaven* as well as to *by your sword.* Since he is subservient to his brother, however, he cannot initiate a war, but must do battle at his brother's behest. If Jacob's overlordship is, however, unduly harsh, Esau's cry of protest will be heard and Jacob's yoke will be cast off.

וַתִּקְרָא לְיַעֲקֹב בְּנָהּ הַקָּטָן וַתֹּאמֶר אֵלָיו הִנֵּה עֵשָׂו אָחִיךָ מִתְנַחֵם לְךָ
מג־מד לְהָרְגֶךָ: וְעַתָּה בְנִי שְׁמַע בְּקֹלִי וְקוּם בְּרַח־לְךָ אֶל־לָבָן אָחִי חָרָנָה: וְיָשַׁבְתָּ
מה עִמּוֹ יָמִים אֲחָדִים עַד אֲשֶׁר־תָּשׁוּב חֲמַת אָחִיךָ: עַד־שׁוּב אַף־אָחִיךָ מִמְּךָ
וְשָׁכַח אֵת אֲשֶׁר־עָשִׂיתָ לּוֹ וְשָׁלַחְתִּי וּלְקַחְתִּיךָ מִשָּׁם לָמָה אֶשְׁכַּל
מו גַּם־שְׁנֵיכֶם יוֹם אֶחָד: וַתֹּאמֶר רִבְקָה אֶל־יִצְחָק קַצְתִּי בְחַיַּי מִפְּנֵי בְּנוֹת
חֵת אִם־לֹקֵחַ יַעֲקֹב אִשָּׁה מִבְּנוֹת־חֵת כָּאֵלֶּה מִבְּנוֹת הָאָרֶץ לָמָּה לִּי חַיִּים:

כח

א וַיִּקְרָא יִצְחָק אֶל־יַעֲקֹב וַיְבָרֶךְ אֹתוֹ וַיְצַוֵּהוּ וַיֹּאמֶר לוֹ לֹא־תִקַּח אִשָּׁה
ב מִבְּנוֹת כְּנָעַן: קוּם לֵךְ פַּדֶּנָה אֲרָם בֵּיתָה בְתוּאֵל אֲבִי אִמֶּךָ וְקַח־לְךָ מִשָּׁם
ג אִשָּׁה מִבְּנוֹת לָבָן אֲחִי אִמֶּךָ: וְאֵל שַׁדַּי יְבָרֵךְ אֹתְךָ וְיַפְרְךָ וְיַרְבֶּךָ וְהָיִיתָ
ד לִקְהַל עַמִּים: וְיִתֶּן־לְךָ אֶת־בִּרְכַּת אַבְרָהָם לְךָ וּלְזַרְעֲךָ אִתָּךְ לְרִשְׁתְּךָ
שביעי ה אֶת־אֶרֶץ מְגֻרֶיךָ אֲשֶׁר־נָתַן אֱלֹהִים לְאַבְרָהָם: וַיִּשְׁלַח יִצְחָק אֶת־יַעֲקֹב
וַיֵּלֶךְ פַּדֶּנָה אֲרָם אֶל־לָבָן בֶּן־בְּתוּאֵל הָאֲרַמִּי אֲחִי רִבְקָה אֵם יַעֲקֹב וְעֵשָׂו:
ו וַיַּרְא עֵשָׂו כִּי־בֵרַךְ יִצְחָק אֶת־יַעֲקֹב וְשִׁלַּח אֹתוֹ פַּדֶּנָה אֲרָם לָקַחַת־לוֹ
מִשָּׁם אִשָּׁה בְּבָרְכוֹ אֹתוֹ וַיְצַו עָלָיו לֵאמֹר לֹא־תִקַּח אִשָּׁה מִבְּנוֹת כְּנָעַן:
מפטיר ז־ח *וַיִּשְׁמַע יַעֲקֹב אֶל־אָבִיו וְאֶל־אִמּוֹ וַיֵּלֶךְ פַּדֶּנָה אֲרָם: וַיַּרְא עֵשָׂו כִּי רָעוֹת
ט בְּנוֹת כְּנָעַן בְּעֵינֵי יִצְחָק אָבִיו: וַיֵּלֶךְ עֵשָׂו אֶל־יִשְׁמָעֵאל וַיִּקַּח אֶת־מָחֲלַת ׀
בַּת־יִשְׁמָעֵאל בֶּן־אַבְרָהָם אֲחוֹת נְבָיוֹת עַל־נָשָׁיו לוֹ לְאִשָּׁה:

XXVIII

3. וְאֵל שַׁדַּי יְבָרֵךְ אֹתְךָ — *And may God Almighty bless you* . . . with material wealth.

וְיַפְרְךָ — *And make you fruitful* . . . with children.

וְיַרְבֶּךָ — *And multiply you* . . . (with) position and power.

4. וְיִתֶּן לְךָ אֶת בִּרְכַּת אַבְרָהָם — *And give you the blessings of Abraham* . . . as (God) said, "וֶהְיֵה בְּרָכָה, *And you shall be a blessing*" (12:2), which can (only) be by teaching the knowledge (of God) to the people, for in this manner God, the Blessed One, will be blessed.

לְךָ וּלְזַרְעֲךָ אִתָּךְ לְרִשְׁתְּךָ — *To you and to your seed with you that you may inherit the land* . . . for when your children teach the ways of righteousness they will be worthy to inherit (the land), and this is considered sanctification of God's name, rather than the opposite, as we find, יִשְׂרָאֵל אֲשֶׁר בְּךָ אֶתְפָּאָר, *Israel in whom I will be glorified* (*Isaiah* 49:3), for this will bring about יִשְׂמַח ה׳ בְּמַעֲשָׂיו, *Let God rejoice in His works* (*Psalms* 104:31).

אֶרֶץ מְגֻרֶיךָ — *The land of your sojournings* . . . the land of Canaan where you presently reside.

NOTES

XXVIII

3. וְאֵל שַׁדַּי יְבָרֵךְ אֹתְךָ וְיַפְרְךָ וְיַרְבֶּךָ — *And may God Almighty bless you and make you fruitful and multiply you.* Three expressions (יְבָרֵךְ, יַפְרְךָ, יַרְבֶּךָ) are used by Isaac in this blessing. It is a threefold blessing, of material wealth, children and position amongst his fellow men.

4. וְיִתֶּן לְךָ אֶת בִּרְכַּת אַבְרָהָם — *And give you the blessing of Abraham.* In his commentary on the phrase וֶהְיֵה בְּרָכָה, *and you be a blessing* (12:2), the *Sforno* explains that the greatest blessing one can give to God is to teach mankind the knowledge of the Almighty, so that through their moral and ethical behavior they will cause Him to rejoice in His creation. This is the charge given by God to Abraham when he states, "*Be a blessing,*" i.e., give a בְּרָכָה. It is this same admonition which Isaac now gives to Jacob.

6-8. וַיַּרְא עֵשָׂו כִּי בֵרַךְ יִצְחָק . . . כִּי רָעוֹת בְּנוֹת כְּנָעַן בְּעֵינֵי יִצְחָק אָבִיו — *Now Esau saw that Isaac had blessed* . . .

and summoned Jacob her younger son and said to him, "Behold, your brother Esau is consoling himself regarding you to kill you. 43 So now, my son, heed my voice and arise; flee to my brother Laban, to Charan. 44 And remain with him a short while until your brother's wrath subsides. 45 Until your brother's anger against you subsides and he forgets what you have done to him; then I will send and bring you from there; why should I be bereaved of both of you on the same day?"

46 Rebecca said to Isaac, "I am disgusted with my life on account of the daughters of Heth; if Jacob takes a wife of the daughters of Heth like these, of the daughters of the land, what is life to me?"

28 *1 So Isaac summoned Jacob and blessed him; he instructed him, and said to him, "Do not take a wife from the Canaanite women. 2 Arise, go to Paddan-aram, to the house of Bethuel your mother's father, and take a wife from there from the daughters of Laban your mother's brother. 3 And may Almighty God bless you, make you fruitful and make you numerous, and may you be a congregation of peoples. 4 May He grant you the blessing of Abraham to you and to your offspring with you, that you may possess the land of your sojourns which God gave to Abraham." 5 So Isaac sent away Jacob and he went toward Paddan-aram, to Laban the son of Bethuel the Aramean, brother of Rebecca, mother of Jacob and Esau. —*

6 When Esau saw that Isaac had blessed Jacob and sent him off to Paddan-aram to take himself a wife from there, as he blessed him he commanded him, saying, "You shall not take a wife from among the daughters of Canaan"; 7 and that Jacob obeyed his father and mother and went to Paddan-aram; 8 then Esau perceived that the daughters of Canaan were evil in the eyes of Isaac, his father. 9 So Esau went to Ishmael and took Mahalath, the daughter of Ishmael son of Abraham, sister of Nebaioth, in addition to his wives, as a wife for himself.

---

6. וַיַּרְא עֵשָׂו כִּי בֵרַךְ יִצְחָק — *Now Esau saw that Isaac had blessed.* Even though Esau sees that when Isaac blesses Jacob, he commands him not to marry a Canaanite woman which would negate his blessing, still he does not pay serious attention to this (stricture) except he does see . . .

8. כִּי רָעוֹת בְּנוֹת כְּנָעַן בְּעֵינֵי יִצְחָק אָבִיו — *That the daughters of Canaan were evil in the eyes of Isaac his father . . .* But he thought that this was because they opposed the will of his father, as it says, *and they cut short the spirit (of Isaac and Rebecca)* (26:35), so he (then) went to Ishmael (to marry his daughter). With this (the Torah) informs us that Isaac could have opposed Esau when he married the Canaanite women, had he but attended to it, as he does now when Rebecca alerts (and urges) him to (i.e., to warn) Jacob.

NOTES

that the daughters of Canaan were evil in the eyes of Isaac his father. The word וַיַּרְא, *and he saw*, is used at the beginning of each of these two verses. The first refers to the blessing given to Jacob coupled with the admonition not to marry a Canaanite woman, thus indicating Isaac's *preference* for a non-Canaanite wife. The second is Esau's realization that the Hittite women he married (26:31) caused his father's spirit to be cut short. Now the first does not deter him but the second does, and to appease his father he marries "in the family" by taking Ishmael's daughter. We see then that Esau was sensitive to his father's approval or lack of same; hence the *Sforno* feels that the Torah is telling us that Isaac could have influenced and controlled Esau, had he but expressed his strong disapproval of Canaanite wives.

פרשת ויצא

י־יא וַיֵּצֵא יַעֲקֹב מִבְּאֵר שָׁבַע וַיֵּלֶךְ חָרָנָה: וַיִּפְגַּע בַּמָּקוֹם וַיָּלֶן שָׁם כִּי־בָא הַשֶּׁמֶשׁ
יב וַיִּקַּח מֵאַבְנֵי הַמָּקוֹם וַיָּשֶׂם מְרַאֲשֹׁתָיו וַיִּשְׁכַּב בַּמָּקוֹם הַהוּא: וַיַּחֲלֹם וְהִנֵּה
סֻלָּם מֻצָּב אַרְצָה וְרֹאשׁוֹ מַגִּיעַ הַשָּׁמָיְמָה וְהִנֵּה מַלְאֲכֵי אֱלֹהִים עֹלִים וְיֹרְדִים
יג בּוֹ: וְהִנֵּה יהוה נִצָּב עָלָיו וַיֹּאמַר אֲנִי יהוה אֱלֹהֵי אַבְרָהָם אָבִיךָ וֵאלֹהֵי יִצְחָק
יד הָאָרֶץ אֲשֶׁר אַתָּה שֹׁכֵב עָלֶיהָ לְךָ אֶתְּנֶנָּה וּלְזַרְעֶךָ: וְהָיָה זַרְעֲךָ כַּעֲפַר הָאָרֶץ
וּפָרַצְתָּ יָמָּה וָקֵדְמָה וְצָפֹנָה וָנֶגְבָּה וְנִבְרְכוּ בְךָ כָּל־מִשְׁפְּחֹת הָאֲדָמָה
טו וּבְזַרְעֶךָ: וְהִנֵּה אָנֹכִי עִמָּךְ וּשְׁמַרְתִּיךָ בְּכֹל אֲשֶׁר־תֵּלֵךְ וַהֲשִׁבֹתִיךָ אֶל־
הָאֲדָמָה הַזֹּאת כִּי לֹא אֶעֱזָבְךָ עַד אֲשֶׁר אִם־עָשִׂיתִי אֵת אֲשֶׁר־דִּבַּרְתִּי לָךְ:

---

10. וַיֵּצֵא יַעֲקֹב . . . וַיֵּלֶךְ חָרָנָה — *And Jacob departed . . . and went toward Haran.* He went to reach Haran, but before he arrived there the events recorded here occurred.

11. וַיִּפְגַּע בַּמָּקוֹם — *And he encountered the place.* He came to a place which he had not planned on as a destination. The definite article *the place* denotes a place where travelers could spend the night. Such places were to be found in every town, usually on the road. Similarly, the angels say to Lot, "We will spend the night בָּרְחוֹב, *on the road* (19:2)," and so in the episode of the concubine in Givah, רַק בָּרְחוֹב אַל תָּלַן, *but do not spend the night on the road* [where wayfarers customarily stay] (*Judges* 19:20).

מֵאַבְנֵי הַמָּקוֹם — *From the stones of the place . . .* which were prepared there for guests to eat or sit on.

12-13. וְהִנֵּה מַלְאֲכֵי אֱלֹהִים עֹלִים וְיֹרְדִים . . . וְהִנֵּה ה׳ נִצָּב עָלָיו — *And behold angels of God ascending and descending . . . And behold God stood over him.* For indeed as it shall come to pass at the end (of time), the heavenly representatives of the nations after having ascended will fall, but God, the Blessed One, Who stands (guard) eternally (over Israel), will not forsake His people, as it says, כִּי אֶעֱשֶׂה כָלָה בְּכָל הַגּוֹיִם . . . וְאֹתְךָ לֹא אֶעֱשֶׂה כָלָה, *For I will make a full end of all the nations . . . but I will not make a full end of you* (*Jeremiah* 46:28).

הָאָרֶץ אֲשֶׁר אַתָּה שֹׁכֵב עָלֶיהָ — *The ground upon which you are lying . . .* which is the center of the Land of Canaan.

לְךָ אֶתְּנֶנָּה — *To you will I give it.* You will be a "mighty prince" in the midst of its inhabitants as were Abraham and Isaac.

14. וְהָיָה זַרְעֲךָ כַּעֲפַר הָאָרֶץ וּפָרַצְתָּ — *And your offspring shall be as the dust of the earth, and you shall spread abroad.* When your seed will be treated as the dust of the earth, as we read, וַתָּשִׂימִי כָאָרֶץ גֵּוֵךְ וְכַחוּץ לַעֹבְרִים, *And you laid your back as the ground, and as the street to them that go over* (*Isaiah* 51:23), i.e., after they have reached the lowest depths,

NOTES

11. וַיִּפְגַּע בַּמָּקוֹם . . . מֵאַבְנֵי הַמָּקוֹם — *And he encountered the place . . . from the stones of the place.* The word פְּגִיעָה means to chance upon a place which one had not originally planned as his destination. Since according to the *Sforno* this place was one used frequently by travelers, the stones were not lying around aimlessly, but were part of the furnishings put there for the convenience of travelers. Jacob now took some of these stones to place under his head.

12-13. וְהִנֵּה מַלְאֲכֵי אֱלֹהִים עֹלִים וְיֹרְדִים . . . וְהִנֵּה ה׳ נִצָּב עָלָיו — *And behold angels of God ascending and descending . . . And behold God stood over him.* The *Sforno* follows the interpretation of the Midrash *Tanchuma* that the imagery of this dream is symbolic of the rise and fall of empires and of the Eternal One guarding His People who will, unlike all other nations, survive forever.

לְךָ אֶתְּנֶנָּה — *To you will I give it.* The expression *to you will I give it* cannot be meant as a promise, for this has already been given (28:4). Rather it is to be understood as an assurance of Jacob's standing and stature among the inhabitants of this land.

PARASHAS VAYEITZEI

10 *Jacob departed from Beer-sheba and went toward Haran.* 11 *He encountered the place and spent the night there because the sun had set; he took from the stones of the place which he arranged around his head, and lay down in that place.* 12 *And he dreamt, and behold! A ladder was set earthward and its top reached heavenward; and behold! angels of God were ascending and descending on it.*

13 *And behold!* HASHEM *was standing over him, and He said, "I am* HASHEM, *God of Abraham your father and God of Isaac; the ground upon which you are lying, to you will I give it and to your descendants.* 14 *Your offspring shall be as the dust of the earth, and you shall spread out powerfully westward, eastward, northward and southward; and all the families of the earth shall bless themselves by you and by your offspring.* 15 *Behold, I am with you; I will guard you wherever you go, and I will return you to this soil; for I will not forsake you until I will have done what I have spoken about you."*

---

then shall they spread abroad, crossing over the boundaries of this land on which you lie, to every side.

יָמָּה וָקֵדְמָה וְצָפֹנָה וָנֶגְבָּה — *To the west, east, north and south* . . . as it is attested, וְקַרְקַר כָּל בְּנֵי שֵׁת, *and break down all the sons of Seth* (*Numbers* 24:17), for the salvation from God will come only after the present unprecedented degradation of Israel in exile, as our Sages state, "If you see a generation subjected to suffering, engulfing it as a river, wait and observe (the salvation which is nigh), as it is written, כִּי יָבֹא כַנָּהָר צָר, *For distress will come as a river* (*Isaiah* 59:19), followed by, וּבָא לְצִיּוֹן גּוֹאֵל, *And a redeemer will come to Zion*" (ibid. v. 20).

וְנִבְרְכוּ בְךָ כָּל מִשְׁפְּחֹת הָאֲדָמָה וּבְזַרְעֶךָ — *And in you shall all the families of the earth be blessed* . . . in the sense of, וְאַתֶּם כֹּהֲנֵי ה׳ תִּקָּרֵאוּ מְשָׁרְתֵי אֱלֹהֵינוּ יֵאָמֵר לָכֶם, *You shall be named priests of* HASHEM, *they shall call you the ministers of our God* (*Isaiah* 61:6).

15. כִּי לֹא אֶעֱזָבְךָ — *For I will not forsake you.* The assurance I have given to you, that after a lengthy exile you will spread abroad, crossing every boundary, and not be destroyed by the suffering and distress of your exile, is because during that exile I will not leave you, as it is written, לֹא מְאַסְתִּים וְלֹא גְעַלְתִּים, *I will not reject them, neither will I abhor them* (*Lev.* 26:44).

עַד אֲשֶׁר אִם עָשִׂיתִי — *Until I have done.* (I will not leave you) even before I will have done that which I have spoken to you, i.e., וּפָרַצְתָּ, *and you will spread abroad.* The word עַד, *until*, at times means בְּעוֹד, *while* [i.e., while I have not yet done], as we find,

NOTES

14. וְהָיָה זַרְעֲךָ כַּעֲפַר הָאָרֶץ וּפָרַצְתָּ . . . וְנִבְרְכוּ בְךָ כָּל מִשְׁפְּחֹת הָאֲדָמָה — *And your offspring shall be as the dust of the earth, and you shall spread abroad . . . and in you shall all the families of the earth be blessed.* Here again the expression *as the dust of the earth* cannot be meant as a promise of Israel's great numbers since it was already pledged. Therefore, it is to be understood as a *condition* for Jacob's seed to be "spread abroad." Only after they have come to a state of degradation, trampled upon as the dust of the earth, will their salvation come. The *Sforno's* interpretation of וְנִבְרְכוּ, *And in you shall be blessed,* is consistent with his commentary on verse 4. See note there.

15. כִּי לֹא אֶעֱזָבְךָ — *For I will not forsake you.* This expression is not to be understood as part of God's assurance, i.e., a continuation of the promise made in the previous verses (13-14) or the first part of this verse. Rather it is the key to their survival. They will continue to exist in exile because of God's special providence. This unique protection of the Almighty granted to Israel is undeserved — it is a *chesed*, but ultimately it will be earned, at which time God will dwell in their midst.

טז וַיִּיקַץ יַעֲקֹב מִשְּׁנָתוֹ וַיֹּאמֶר אָכֵן יֵשׁ יהוה בַּמָּקוֹם הַזֶּה וְאָנֹכִי לֹא
יז יָדָעְתִּי: וַיִּירָא וַיֹּאמַר מַה־נּוֹרָא הַמָּקוֹם הַזֶּה אֵין זֶה כִּי אִם־בֵּית אֱלֹהִים
יח וְזֶה שַׁעַר הַשָּׁמָיִם: וַיַּשְׁכֵּם יַעֲקֹב בַּבֹּקֶר וַיִּקַּח אֶת־הָאֶבֶן אֲשֶׁר־שָׂם
יט מְרַאֲשֹׁתָיו וַיָּשֶׂם אֹתָהּ מַצֵּבָה וַיִּצֹק שֶׁמֶן עַל־רֹאשָׁהּ: וַיִּקְרָא אֶת־
כ שֵׁם־הַמָּקוֹם הַהוּא בֵּית־אֵל וְאוּלָם לוּז שֵׁם־הָעִיר לָרִאשֹׁנָה: וַיִּדַּר יַעֲקֹב
נֶדֶר לֵאמֹר אִם־יִהְיֶה אֱלֹהִים עִמָּדִי וּשְׁמָרַנִי בַּדֶּרֶךְ הַזֶּה אֲשֶׁר אָנֹכִי
כא הוֹלֵךְ וְנָתַן־לִי לֶחֶם לֶאֱכֹל וּבֶגֶד לִלְבֹּשׁ: וְשַׁבְתִּי בְשָׁלוֹם אֶל־בֵּית אָבִי
כב וְהָיָה יהוה לִי לֵאלֹהִים: וְהָאֶבֶן הַזֹּאת אֲשֶׁר־שַׂמְתִּי מַצֵּבָה יִהְיֶה בֵּית
כט שני א אֱלֹהִים וְכֹל אֲשֶׁר תִּתֶּן־לִי עַשֵּׂר אֲעַשְּׂרֶנּוּ לָךְ: וַיִּשָּׂא

עַד שֶׁהַמֶּלֶךְ בִּמְסִבּוֹ, *While the king was (still) at his table (Song of Songs* 1:12), and עַד לֹא עָשָׂה אֶרֶץ וְחוּצוֹת, *Before He had made the earth and the outside places (Proverbs* 8:26). However, once this great salvation will come, its nature will not only be the (negative) kindness of not leaving (them) but this kindness will abundantly grow to the point where (God) will walk in our midst, as it says, וְהִתְהַלַּכְתִּי בְּתוֹכְכֶם, *And I will walk among you (Lev.* 26:12).

16. אָכֵן יֵשׁ ה׳ בַּמָּקוֹם הַזֶּה — *Surely* H*ASHEM is in this place.* Without a doubt this place is conducive to prophecy, for I have seen such a vision without even preparing myself for prophecy. A change of place and climate can affect man's intellectual capacities, faculties, and spirit, as (our Sages) tell us, אֲוִירָא שֶׁל אֶרֶץ יִשְׂרָאֵל מַחְכִּים, *The atmosphere of Eretz Yisrael makes one wise (Bava Basra* 158b).

וְאָנֹכִי לֹא יָדָעְתִּי — *And I did not know.* Had I known it I would have prepared myself to reach the degree of prophecy (to which such a place is conducive), but I did not.

17. וַיִּירָא — *And he was afraid.* Because of his error.

אֵין זֶה — *This is none other.* The place I saw in the vision where the ladder was standing is none other ...

כִּי אִם בֵּית אֱלֹהִים — *Than the house of God* ... the place of the Holy Temple, as our Sages tell us, "Jacob called it a house" (*Pesachim* 88a).

וְזֶה שַׁעַר הַשָּׁמָיִם — *And this is the gate of heaven.* And this ladder that I saw teaches that

NOTES

16-17. אָכֵן יֵשׁ ה׳ בַּמָּקוֹם הַזֶּה ... וַיִּירָא — *Surely* H*ASHEM is in this place ... and he was afraid.* Prophecy is usually experienced by those who have prepared themselves for it. However, not only must it be the right person but the right place as well. According to our Sages, once the Jewish people established themselves in *Eretz Yisrael,* prophecy can only occur in the Holy Land. The power and efficacy of this place where Jacob lay down to sleep (the place where Isaac was brought as a sacrifice and where the Holy Temple is destined to be built) was already so great, that he beheld a vision even though he had not prepared himself spiritually. This indicated the sacred nature of this place. Had he known and prepared himself, this prophecy would have been even greater and more intense. Jacob considered this lack of knowledge a blemish on his character and he faulted himself for it. Hence he was afraid.

17. כִּי אִם בֵּית אֱלֹהִים – *Than the house of God.* Our Sages tell us that each of the three אָבוֹת, *Patriarchs,* called this place of prayer by different names. Abraham called it הַר, *a mountain,* as we find by the *Akeidah.* Isaac called it שָׂדֶה, *a field,* as we find, *And Isaac went out to meditate in the field* (24:63). Jacob called it בַּיִת, *a house,* as we find here. To Abraham, prayer demanded an extraordinary elevation of the spirit akin to climbing to the mountain top. It also required removing oneself from the mundane so as to reach the heights. Isaac, however, was inspired to commune with the Almighty in the broad, open field, which expanded his heart and mind. Still he also sought out a special place, away from the ordinary and the confined enclosure of his dwelling place. It was Jacob who taught that to concentrate the mind and heart of the worshiper it is better to pray in the confines of a house. He also taught that man can pray to the Almighty in any

[16] *Jacob awoke from his sleep and said, "Surely HASHEM is present in this place and I did not know!"* [17] *And he became frightened and said, "How awesome is this place! This is none other than the abode of God and this is the gate of the heavens!"* [18] *Jacob arose early in the morning and took the stone that he placed around his head and set it up as a pillar; and he poured oil on its top.* [19] *And he named that place Beth-el; however, Luz was the city's name originally.*

[20] *Then Jacob took a vow, saying, "If God will be with me, will guard me on this way that I am going; will give me bread to eat and clothes to wear;* [21] *and I return in peace to my father's house, and HASHEM will be a God to me —* [22] *then this stone which I have set up as a pillar shall become a house of God, and whatever You will give me, I shall repeatedly tithe to You."*

---

from this place where the ladder was, God, Who stood upon it, will hear the prayers of the petitioners, and their prayers will ascend to His holy abode in heaven.

18. וַיָּשֶׂם אֹתָהּ מַצֵּבָה — *And he set it up as a pillar.* He sanctified it by setting it aside to *eventually* be a מַצֵּבָה, when he would dedicate it as such upon his return, as the verse states, *And Jacob set up a pillar in the place where He spoke with him, a pillar of stone, and he poured a libation upon it* (35:14).

20. אִם יִהְיֶה אֱלֹהִים עִמָּדִי — *If God will be with me.* If He will remove from me all oppression and obstacles which bring men to transgress the will of his Maker, as our Sages say, שְׁלֹשָׁה דְבָרִים מַעֲבִירִים אֶת הָאָדָם עַל דַּעְתּוֹ וְעַל דַּעַת קוֹנוֹ . . . גּוֹיִם וְרוּחַ רָעָה וְדִקְדּוּקֵי עֲנִיּוּת, *Three things deprive a man of his senses and a knowledge of his Creator . . . viz. idolaters, an evil spirit and oppressive poverty* (*Eruvin* 41b).

וּשְׁמָרַנִי — *And will keep me . . .* guard me from the evil of the pagans who rise up against me and force me (to transgress).

וְנָתַן לִי לֶחֶם לֶאֱכֹל — *And will give me bread to eat . . .* so that a state of poverty will not bring me to rebel against my own will, the will of my Maker.

21. וְשַׁבְתִּי בְשָׁלוֹם — *And come back in peace.* (Unharmed by) the illnesses which cause a man to transgress. This is the meaning of רוּחַ רָעָה, *an evil spirit,* which our Sages mentioned.

וְהָיָה ה׳ לִי לֵאלֹהִים — *Then shall HASHEM be my God.* Then shall *HASHEM* be my judge if I will not serve Him with all my strength. The letter ו here (וְהָיָה) means *behold* (וְהִנֵּה), i.e., I hereby accept upon myself that *HASHEM,* the compassionate God, will then be to me as אֱלֹהִים, conducting Himself with the attribute of justice.

NOTES

house, thereby creating a House of God through the medium of his prayer.

18. וַיָּשֶׂם אֹתָהּ מַצֵּבָה — *And he set it up as a pillar.* If Jacob had completed the consecration of this stone as a pillar (מַצֵּבָה), the word used should not have been וַיָּשֶׂם, *and he placed,* but וַיַּצֵּב, *and he established.* The *Sforno* therefore explains that Jacob now performed a preliminary act of sanctification (הֶקְדֵּשׁ) by anointing the stone with oil, a method used to sanctify the vessels of the Sanctuary. The actual erection of this stone and its use as a מַצֵּבָה would be later, upon his return. Then, Jacob would consecrate it through the libation (נֶסֶךְ).

20-21. אִם יִהְיֶה אֱלֹהִים עִמָּדִי . . . וְהָיָה ה׳ לִי לֵאלֹהִים — *If God will be with me . . . then shall HASHEM be my God.* Jacob makes a vow. His words in these verses are to be understood as part of the vow, not as conditions. Jacob, however, was aware that difficult conditions of life — such as oppression, poverty and illness — could impair his ability to keep the vow. He prayed that these should not befall him and lead him away from God. If this prayer would be answered then Jacob would be prepared to be judged by God as אֱלֹהִים, denoting justice, if he failed to serve Him with all his might. Until his return, however, he could only hope that God would treat him as ה׳, denoting mercy and compassion.

ב יַעֲקֹב רַגְלָיו וַיֵּלֶךְ אַרְצָה בְנֵי־קֶדֶם: וַיַּרְא וְהִנֵּה בְאֵר בַּשָּׂדֶה וְהִנֵּה־שָׁם
שְׁלֹשָׁה עֶדְרֵי־צֹאן רֹבְצִים עָלֶיהָ כִּי מִן־הַבְּאֵר הַהִוא יַשְׁקוּ הָעֲדָרִים
ג וְהָאֶבֶן גְּדֹלָה עַל־פִּי הַבְּאֵר: וְנֶאֶסְפוּ־שָׁמָּה כָל־הָעֲדָרִים וְגָלֲלוּ
אֶת־הָאֶבֶן מֵעַל פִּי הַבְּאֵר וְהִשְׁקוּ אֶת־הַצֹּאן וְהֵשִׁיבוּ אֶת־הָאֶבֶן עַל־פִּי
ד הַבְּאֵר לִמְקֹמָהּ: וַיֹּאמֶר לָהֶם יַעֲקֹב אַחַי מֵאַיִן אַתֶּם וַיֹּאמְרוּ מֵחָרָן
ה־ו אֲנָחְנוּ: וַיֹּאמֶר לָהֶם הַיְדַעְתֶּם אֶת־לָבָן בֶּן־נָחוֹר וַיֹּאמְרוּ יָדָעְנוּ: וַיֹּאמֶר
ז לָהֶם הֲשָׁלוֹם לוֹ וַיֹּאמְרוּ שָׁלוֹם וְהִנֵּה רָחֵל בִּתּוֹ בָּאָה עִם־הַצֹּאן: וַיֹּאמֶר
הֵן עוֹד הַיּוֹם גָּדוֹל לֹא־עֵת הֵאָסֵף הַמִּקְנֶה הַשְׁקוּ הַצֹּאן וּלְכוּ רְעוּ:
ח וַיֹּאמְרוּ לֹא נוּכַל עַד אֲשֶׁר יֵאָסְפוּ כָּל־הָעֲדָרִים וְגָלְלוּ אֶת־הָאֶבֶן
ט מֵעַל פִּי הַבְּאֵר וְהִשְׁקִינוּ הַצֹּאן: עוֹדֶנּוּ מְדַבֵּר עִמָּם וְרָחֵל ׀ בָּאָה
י עִם־הַצֹּאן אֲשֶׁר לְאָבִיהָ כִּי רֹעָה הִוא: וַיְהִי כַּאֲשֶׁר רָאָה יַעֲקֹב אֶת־
רָחֵל בַּת־לָבָן אֲחִי אִמּוֹ וְאֶת־צֹאן לָבָן אֲחִי אִמּוֹ וַיִּגַּשׁ יַעֲקֹב וַיָּגֶל
יא אֶת־הָאֶבֶן מֵעַל פִּי הַבְּאֵר וַיַּשְׁקְ אֶת־צֹאן לָבָן אֲחִי אִמּוֹ: וַיִּשַּׁק יַעֲקֹב
יב לְרָחֵל וַיִּשָּׂא אֶת־קֹלוֹ וַיֵּבְךְּ: וַיַּגֵּד יַעֲקֹב לְרָחֵל כִּי אֲחִי אָבִיהָ הוּא
יג וְכִי בֶן־רִבְקָה הוּא וַתָּרָץ וַתַּגֵּד לְאָבִיהָ: וַיְהִי כִשְׁמֹעַ לָבָן אֶת־שֵׁמַע ׀
יַעֲקֹב בֶּן־אֲחֹתוֹ וַיָּרָץ לִקְרָאתוֹ וַיְחַבֶּק־לוֹ וַיְנַשֶּׁק־לוֹ וַיְבִיאֵהוּ אֶל־בֵּיתוֹ

XXIX

1. וַיִּשָּׂא יַעֲקֹב רַגְלָיו — *So Jacob lifted his feet.* When a person sets out to go willingly to a chosen destination, we may rightly say of him that he "carries his feet." But if he is forced to leave because of difficulties we may properly say of him that "his feet carry him," similar to, יֹבִלוּהָ רַגְלֶיהָ, *Whose feet carried her* (from afar to sojourn) (*Isaiah* 23:7).

6. הֲשָׁלוֹם לוֹ — *Is it well with him?* He attempted to find out (Laban's) circumstances before visiting him, since a guest's behavior with his host is determined by his (host's) circumstances.

7. הֵן עוֹד הַיּוֹם גָּדוֹל — *Look, the day is yet great.* A righteous man objects to a wrong being done even to strangers, as it is said, תּוֹעֲבַת צַדִּיקִים אִישׁ עָוֶל, *An unjust man is an abomination to the righteous* (*Proverbs* 29:27).

9. כִּי רֹעָה הִוא — *For she was a shepherdess.* She was skilled in the art of tending (sheep).

10. כַּאֲשֶׁר רָאָה יַעֲקֹב אֶת רָחֵל — *And it was when Jacob saw Rachel* . . . but not before, so

NOTES

XXIX

1. וַיִּשָּׂא יַעֲקֹב רַגְלָיו – *So Jacob lifted his feet.* Jacob had just seen a vision of angels, experienced the nearness of the Almighty and received the assurance of God's protection — small wonder that his spirit was elevated. Thus he set out on his journey with confidence and hope. To indicate this the Torah states that Jacob *lifted his feet.* Far from being an awkward, archaic phrase it reveals Jacob's attitude, as the *Sforno* explains. Cheerfully and confidently Jacob *carried his feet,* for he was master of his destiny, capable of making his own decisions, with the assistance of God.

7. הֵן עוֹד הַיּוֹם גָּדוֹל – *Look, the day is yet great.* There is an imperative for every person to protest wrongdoing and attempt to correct it, unafraid of being accused of meddling. This episode of Jacob establishes a precedent for Moses many years later, when he is similarly confronted with the unfair actions of the shepherds against the daughters of Jethro. A righteous man cannot abide to witness injustice in silence.

9. כִּי רֹעָה הִוא – *For she was a shepherdess.* Under normal circumstances it would be immodest for a young girl to tend the flocks. She did so only because she was unusually skilled in the art of shepherding.

29 [1]*So Jacob lifted his feet, and went toward the land of the easterners.* [2] *He*
looked, and behold — a well in the field! And behold! three flocks of sheep lay there beside it, for from that well they would water the flocks, and the stone over the mouth of the well was large. [3] *When all the flocks would be assembled there they would roll the stone from the mouth of the well and water the sheep; then they would put back the stone over the mouth of the well, in its place.*

[4] *Jacob said to them, "My brothers, where are you from?" And they said, "We are from Charan."* [5] *He said to them, "Do you know Laban the son of Nahor?" And they said, "We know."* [6] *Then he said to them, "Is it well with him?" They answered, "It is well; and see — his daughter Rachel is coming with the flock!"*

[7] *He said, "Look, the day is still long; it is not yet time to bring the livestock in; water the flock and go on grazing."* [8] *But they said, "We will be unable to, until all the flocks will have been gathered and they will roll the stone off the mouth of the well; we will then water the flock."*

[9] *While he was still speaking with them, Rachel had arrived with her father's flock, for she was a shepherdess.* [10] *And it was, when Jacob saw Rachel, daughter of Laban his mother's brother, and the flock of Laban his mother's brother, Jacob came forward and rolled the stone off the mouth of the well and watered the sheep of Laban his mother's brother.* [11] *Then Jacob kissed Rachel; and he raised his voice and wept.* [12] *Jacob told Rachel that he was her father's relative, and that he was Rebecca's son; then she ran and told her father.*

[13] *And it was, when Laban heard the news of Jacob his sister's son, he ran toward him, embraced him, kissed him, and took him to his house;*

---

as not to deprive others, for he feared that if he did so sooner (i.e., roll off the stone) the shepherds would water the three flocks and not wait to help others.

11. וַיִּשָּׂא אֶת קֹלוֹ וַיֵּבְךְּ — *And he raised his voice and cried* ... at the thought of his not having merited to marry her in his youth, for he would then have had children born to him as a young man.

12. כִּי אֲחִי אָבִיהָ הוּא — *That he was her father's relative* ... to assure her that he had not acted improperly (immodestly) by kissing her.

וְכִי בֶן רִבְקָה הוּא — *And that he was Rebecca's son.* He mentioned Rebecca, although Rachel did not know her, so that she might inform her father.

13. אֶת שֵׁמַע יַעֲקֹב — *The news of Jacob* ... that he alone had rolled away the stone.

NOTES

11. וַיִּשָּׂא אֶת קֹלוֹ וַיֵּבְךְּ — *And he raised his voice and cried.* Jacob was seventy-seven years old when he first met Rachel. He left home at the age of sixty-three and then spent fourteen years studying at the Academy of Shem and Eber. He realized that it is far better for children to have a young, energetic father. Had he met her earlier, by now he would have had grown children. He wept for those lost years. And that is also the reason for his impatience recorded in verse 21, as interpreted by the *Sforno*.

12. The *halachah* forbids such intimacy even with members of one's family unless they are very young children, except between parent and child (*Even HaEzer* 21:6). *Ramban* points out that Rachel was still too young to arouse one's passion. Moreover, as the Sforno states in verse 18, Jacob had to wait seven years until she would reach marriageable age. This fact, coupled with the fact that he was "her father's relative," prompted his action.

יד וַיְסַפֵּר לְלָבָן אֵת כָּל־הַדְּבָרִים הָאֵלֶּה: וַיֹּאמֶר לוֹ לָבָן אַךְ עַצְמִי וּבְשָׂרִי
טו אָתָּה וַיֵּשֶׁב עִמּוֹ חֹדֶשׁ יָמִים: וַיֹּאמֶר לָבָן לְיַעֲקֹב הֲכִי־אָחִי אַתָּה
טז וַעֲבַדְתַּנִי חִנָּם הַגִּידָה לִּי מַה־מַּשְׂכֻּרְתֶּךָ: וּלְלָבָן שְׁתֵּי בָנוֹת שֵׁם הַגְּדֹלָה
יז לֵאָה וְשֵׁם הַקְּטַנָּה רָחֵל: וְעֵינֵי לֵאָה רַכּוֹת וְרָחֵל הָיְתָה יְפַת־תֹּאַר וִיפַת
שלישי יח מַרְאֶה: וַיֶּאֱהַב יַעֲקֹב אֶת־רָחֵל וַיֹּאמֶר אֶעֱבָדְךָ שֶׁבַע שָׁנִים בְּרָחֵל בִּתְּךָ
יט הַקְּטַנָּה: וַיֹּאמֶר לָבָן טוֹב תִּתִּי אֹתָהּ לָךְ מִתִּתִּי אֹתָהּ לְאִישׁ אַחֵר שְׁבָה
כ עִמָּדִי: וַיַּעֲבֹד יַעֲקֹב בְּרָחֵל שֶׁבַע שָׁנִים וַיִּהְיוּ בְעֵינָיו כְּיָמִים אֲחָדִים
כא בְּאַהֲבָתוֹ אֹתָהּ: וַיֹּאמֶר יַעֲקֹב אֶל־לָבָן הָבָה אֶת־אִשְׁתִּי כִּי מָלְאוּ יָמָי
כב־כג וְאָבוֹאָה אֵלֶיהָ: וַיֶּאֱסֹף לָבָן אֶת־כָּל־אַנְשֵׁי הַמָּקוֹם וַיַּעַשׂ מִשְׁתֶּה: וַיְהִי
כד בָעֶרֶב וַיִּקַּח אֶת־לֵאָה בִתּוֹ וַיָּבֵא אֹתָהּ אֵלָיו וַיָּבֹא אֵלֶיהָ: וַיִּתֵּן לָבָן לָהּ
כה אֶת־זִלְפָּה שִׁפְחָתוֹ לְלֵאָה בִתּוֹ שִׁפְחָה: וַיְהִי בַבֹּקֶר וְהִנֵּה־הִוא לֵאָה
וַיֹּאמֶר אֶל־לָבָן מַה־זֹּאת עָשִׂיתָ לִּי הֲלֹא בְרָחֵל עָבַדְתִּי עִמָּךְ וְלָמָּה
כו רִמִּיתָנִי: וַיֹּאמֶר לָבָן לֹא־יֵעָשֶׂה כֵן בִּמְקוֹמֵנוּ לָתֵת הַצְּעִירָה לִפְנֵי

וַיְסַפֵּר לְלָבָן — *He recounted to Laban* . . . that he had not come to him for a livelihood, but to escape from his brother and live with him (Laban), at the behest of his mother.

14. אַךְ עַצְמִי וּבְשָׂרִי אָתָּה — *Nevertheless, you are my flesh and blood.* Although you can earn your living as a shepherd elsewhere or in some other occupation, since you are *my flesh and blood* you should stay in my house.

וַיֵּשֶׁב עִמּוֹ — *And he stayed with him* . . . working for him as a shepherd, as we find in, שְׁבָה עִמָּדִי, *Remain with me* (v. 19); and in, וַיּוֹאֶל מֹשֶׁה לָשֶׁבֶת אֶת הָאִישׁ, *And Moses was willing to stay with the man (Exodus* 2:21). That is why (Laban) later says to him, "וַעֲבַדְתַּנִי חִנָּם, *Should you serve me for nothing?*" (v. 15).

17. יְפַת תֹּאַר — *Beautiful of form* . . . beautiful features (image) similar to, וּבַמְּחוּגָה יְתָאֳרֵהוּ, *and marks it out with a compass (Isaiah* 44:13).

וִיפַת מַרְאֶה — *And beautiful of appearance* . . . beautiful complexion and radiant appearance; one's natural coloring which appeals to the (beholder's) sense of sight.

18. אֶעֱבָדְךָ שֶׁבַע שָׁנִים בְּרָחֵל — *I will work for you seven years for Rachel.* Without a doubt, this righteous man (Jacob) would not have wed and had children unless he had the wherewithal to support (his wife), specifically her food and clothing, as our Sages state, נוֹשֵׂא אָדָם כַּמָּה נָשִׁים וְהוּא דְאִית לֵיהּ לְמֵיזוֹנִינְהוּ, *A man may marry many wives (in addition to his first) provided he possesses the means to support them (Yevamos* 68a). Laban, in turn, who was a man of means, would not have allowed his daughters to marry a man who could not provide for them. We must therefore say that when (Jacob) said, "*For with my staff I crossed this Jordan*" (32:11), he meant that he had neither flocks nor a way to

NOTES

14. וַיֵּשֶׁב עִמּוֹ – *And he stayed with him.* The expression וַיֵּשֶׁב is not to be understood as "dwelling with his uncle as a guest." Jacob worked for Laban from the outset. He was never a guest enjoying Laban's hospitality.

18. אֶעֱבָדְךָ שֶׁבַע שָׁנִים בְּרָחֵל – *I will work for you seven years for Rachel.* The *Sforno* is convinced that Jacob would never have asked for Rachel's hand in marriage, nor would Laban have consented, if he was impoverished. That is why he interprets the verse as meaning a lack of substantial assets, but still with sufficient means to wed and support a wife. The years of labor are not for this purpose, rather for the purpose of giving a dowry to his prospective father-in-law.

20. וַיִּהְיוּ בְעֵינָיו . . . בְּאַהֲבָתוֹ אֹתָהּ – *And they seemed to him . . . because of his love for her.* Jacob's love for Rachel, and his estimation of her

he recounted to Laban all these events. 14 *Then Laban said to him,*
"Nevertheless, you are my flesh and blood!" And he stayed with him a
month's time.
15 *Then Laban said to Jacob, "Just because you are my relative, should*
you serve me for nothing? Tell me: What are your wages?"
16 *(Laban had two daughters. The name of the older one was Leah and the*
name of the younger one was Rachel. 17 *Leah's eyes were tender, while*
Rachel was beautiful of form and beautiful of appearance.)
18 *Jacob loved Rachel, so he said, "I will work for you seven years, for*
Rachel your younger daughter."
19 *Laban said, "It is better that I give her to you than that I give her to*
another man; remain with me." 20 *So Jacob worked seven years for Rachel*
and they seemed to him a few days because of his love for her.
21 *Jacob said to Laban, "Deliver my wife for my term is fulfilled, and I will*
consort with her."
22 *So Laban gathered all the people of the place and made a feast.* 23 *And*
it was in the evening, that he took Leah his daughter and brought her to him;
and he consorted with her.
24 *— And Laban gave her Zilpah his maidservant — a maidservant to*
Leah his daughter.
25 *And it was, in the morning, that behold it was Leah! So he said to Laban,*
"What is this you have done to me? Was it not for Rachel that I worked for
you? Why have you deceived me?"
26 *Laban said, "Such is not done in our place, to give the younger before*

---

earn a living. The work he did for Rachel was in the form of a dowry to the father of the daughter as it says, אִם מָאֵן יְמָאֵן אָבִיהָ לְתִתָּהּ לוֹ כֶּסֶף יִשְׁקוֹל כְּמֹהַר הַבְּתוּלֹת, *If her father refuses to give her to him, he shall pay money according to the dowry of virgins* (*Exodus* 22:16). And what they meant later by saying, "כִּי מְכָרָנוּ, *For he has sold us*" (31:15), was because in their humility they believed that the dowry was more than they were worth.

בִּתְּךָ הַקְּטַנָּה — *Your younger daughter.* During these seven years (Rachel) would reach marriageable age and in the interim (Laban) would be able to find a husband for the older daughter (Leah).

20. וַיִּהְיוּ בְעֵינָיו כְּיָמִים אֲחָדִים — *And they seemed to him a few days . . .* because he thought that he should have given an even bigger dowry for her.

בְּאַהֲבָתוֹ אֹתָהּ — *Because of his love for her . . .* for "love upsets the rule of normal conduct" (*Sanhedrin* 105b).

21. וְאָבוֹאָה אֵלֶיהָ — *And I will consort with her.* Let us proceed immediately with the marriage, not only the betrothal, for he desired to acquire "the Godly heritage of children."

26. לֹא יֵעָשֶׂה כֵן בִּמְקוֹמֵנוּ — *Such is not done in our place.* The people here would not allow me to keep my word.

NOTES

value, was such that he felt the dowry he was giving (through the seven years of labor) was far too little. The *Sforno*, however, comments that since love affects man's objectivity, perhaps Jacob's willingness to pay this price was in reality a bit extravagant.

21. וְאָבוֹאָה אֵלֶיהָ – *And I will consort with her.* Based on, *Children are a heritage of* HASHEM (*Psalms* 127:3).

כז הַבְּכִירָה: מַלֵּא שְׁבֻעַ זֹאת וְנִתְּנָה לְךָ גַּם־אֶת־זֹאת בַּעֲבֹדָה אֲשֶׁר תַּעֲבֹד
כח עִמָּדִי עוֹד שֶׁבַע־שָׁנִים אֲחֵרוֹת: וַיַּעַשׂ יַעֲקֹב כֵּן וַיְמַלֵּא שְׁבֻעַ זֹאת
כט וַיִּתֶּן־לוֹ אֶת־רָחֵל בִּתּוֹ לוֹ לְאִשָּׁה: וַיִּתֵּן לָבָן לְרָחֵל בִּתּוֹ אֶת־בִּלְהָה
ל שִׁפְחָתוֹ לָהּ לְשִׁפְחָה: וַיָּבֹא גַּם אֶל־רָחֵל וַיֶּאֱהַב גַּם־אֶת־רָחֵל מִלֵּאָה
לא וַיַּעֲבֹד עִמּוֹ עוֹד שֶׁבַע־שָׁנִים אֲחֵרוֹת: וַיַּרְא יהוה כִּי־שְׂנוּאָה לֵאָה וַיִּפְתַּח
לב אֶת־רַחְמָהּ וְרָחֵל עֲקָרָה: וַתַּהַר לֵאָה וַתֵּלֶד בֵּן וַתִּקְרָא שְׁמוֹ רְאוּבֵן
לג כִּי אָמְרָה כִּי־רָאָה יהוה בְּעָנְיִי כִּי עַתָּה יֶאֱהָבַנִי אִישִׁי: וַתַּהַר עוֹד
וַתֵּלֶד בֵּן וַתֹּאמֶר כִּי־שָׁמַע יהוה כִּי־שְׂנוּאָה אָנֹכִי וַיִּתֶּן־לִי גַּם־אֶת־זֶה
לד וַתִּקְרָא שְׁמוֹ שִׁמְעוֹן: וַתַּהַר עוֹד וַתֵּלֶד בֵּן וַתֹּאמֶר עַתָּה הַפַּעַם יִלָּוֶה
לה אִישִׁי אֵלַי כִּי־יָלַדְתִּי לוֹ שְׁלֹשָׁה בָנִים עַל־כֵּן קָרָא־שְׁמוֹ לֵוִי: וַתַּהַר
עוֹד וַתֵּלֶד בֵּן וַתֹּאמֶר הַפַּעַם אוֹדֶה אֶת־יהוה עַל־כֵּן קָרְאָה שְׁמוֹ יְהוּדָה
ל א וַתַּעֲמֹד מִלֶּדֶת: וַתֵּרֶא רָחֵל כִּי לֹא יָלְדָה לְיַעֲקֹב וַתְּקַנֵּא רָחֵל בַּאֲחֹתָהּ
ב וַתֹּאמֶר אֶל־יַעֲקֹב הָבָה־לִּי בָנִים וְאִם־אַיִן מֵתָה אָנֹכִי: וַיִּחַר־אַף
יַעֲקֹב בְּרָחֵל וַיֹּאמֶר הֲתַחַת אֱלֹהִים אָנֹכִי אֲשֶׁר־מָנַע מִמֵּךְ פְּרִי־בָטֶן:

---

27. וְנִתְּנָה לְךָ — *And we will give her to you.* Then the people (of the place) will also agree.

30. וַיֶּאֱהַב גַּם אֶת רָחֵל מִלֵּאָה — *And he also loved Rachel more than Leah* ... not only because of the intimacy of marriage but because she was Rachel; (i.e.,) her deeds which stemmed from her personality. Even though Leah was his first wife, and it is common for a man to find greater contentment with her, as our Sages tell us, "A man finds contentment only with his first wife" (*Yevamos* 63b).

31. כִּי שְׂנוּאָה לֵאָה — *That Leah was unloved.* (Jacob did not love Leah because) after a while he recognized (certain) signs of barrenness in her, as it says, *So He (God) opened her womb,* and he (Jacob) thought that because of this (condition) she had agreed to deceive him.

וְרָחֵל עֲקָרָה — *But Rachel remained barren.* She was by nature barren, and remained so until God opened her womb.

32. בְּעָנְיִי — *In my affliction.* Because my husband suspected me of willfully deceiving him, therefore God, may He be blessed, granted me children as vindication, similar to a *sotah* (a woman suspected of infidelity unjustly, who when cleared conceives — see *Numbers* 5:28).

33. כִּי שְׂנוּאָה אָנֹכִי — *That I am unloved* ... and as compensation for this unfounded suspicion He has granted me this (son) also.

34. הַפַּעַם יִלָּוֶה — *This time (my husband) will become attached (to me).* For I have established that I am capable of having many children, as our Sages teach us, בִּתְלָתָא זִימְנֵי הֲוֵיא חֲזָקָה, *A chazakah (presumption) is established when it occurs three times* (*Yevamos* 64b).

NOTES

30. וַיֶּאֱהַב גַּם אֶת רָחֵל — *And he also loved Rachel more than Leah.* The word גַּם, *also,* is to be understood thus: "He loved" Rachel as his wife, but he "also" loved her for her personal traits and qualities — i.e., for being Rachel.

32. בְּעָנְיִי — *In my affliction.* The name רְאוּבֵן is a bit difficult to understand. Leah said, *God has seen my affliction,* which accounts for the first part of the name, i.e., רְאוּ (from רָאָה), but the concluding part בֵּן can only be explained by accepting the *Sforno's* interpretation. Since Leah was unjustly suspected by Jacob of collusion with her father, she was similar to a *sotah,* hence worthy to be granted a child (בֵּן) as compensation. The name רְאוּבֵן is now quite understandable. By "seeing" my suffering, a "son" was born to me.

the elder. [27] *Complete the week of this one and we will give you the other one too, for the work which you will perform for me yet another seven years."*
[28] *So Jacob did so and he completed the week for her; and he gave him Rachel his daughter to him as a wife.* [29] *And Laban gave Rachel his daughter Bilhah his maidservant — to her as a maidservant.* [30] *He consorted also with Rachel and loved Rachel even more than Leah; and he worked for him yet another seven years.*

[31] *HASHEM saw that Leah was unloved, so He opened her womb; but Rachel remained barren.*

[32] *Leah conceived and bore a son, and she called his name Reuben, as she had declared, "Because HASHEM has discerned my humiliation, for now my husband will love me."*

[33] *And she conceived again and bore a son and declared, "Because HASHEM has heard that I am unloved, He has given me this one also," and she called his name Simeon.*

[34] *Again she conceived, and bore a son and declared, "This time my husband will become attached to me for I have borne him three sons"; therefore He called his name Levi.*

[35] *She conceived again, and bore a son and declared, "This time let me gratefully praise HASHEM"; therefore she called his name Judah; then she stopped giving birth.*

30 [1] *Rachel saw that she had not borne children to Jacob, so Rachel became envious of her sister; she said to Jacob, "Give me children — otherwise I am dead."*

[2] *Jacob's anger flared up at Rachel, and he said, "Am I instead of God Who has withheld from you fruit of the womb?"*

---

35. עַל כֵּן קָרְאָה שְׁמוֹ יְהוּדָה — *Therefore she named him Judah.* This name contains the letters of the honored name of God as well as those of "thankfulness" (praise). It appears that these were names of the ancients, as we find before this, יְהוּדִית בַּת בְּאֵרִי, *Judith the daughter of Be'eri* (26:34), and we also find, שְׁמוּאֵל בֶּן עַמִּיהוּד, *Samuel the son of Amihud* (*Numbers* 34:20), antedating Samuel the prophet. (Apparently) they chose these earlier names which fit events (at the time of their children's birth).

XXX

1. מֵתָה אָנֹכִי — *(Otherwise) I am dead* . . . similar to, הֵן אֲנִי עֵץ יָבֵשׁ, *Behold, I am a dry tree* (*Isaiah* 56:3).

2. וַיִּחַר אַף יַעֲקֹב — *Jacob's anger flared up* . . . for saying, "הָבָה לִּי בָנִים, *Give me children,*" implying that he had the power to do so. In his zeal for the honor of God he disregarded his love for her.

NOTES

XXX

1. מֵתָה אָנֹכִי – *(Otherwise) I am dead.* When Rachel said מֵתָה אָנֹכִי, *I am dead,* her remark is to be understood in the same sense as that of the eunuch who said, "Behold, I am a dry tree," for just as he is unable to have children and is compared to a dry tree which has no life, so one who is childless may be regarded as dead. This is the intent of Rachel's remark. If she is childless, it is as though she was dead. (See *Nedarim* 64b, "Four may be regarded as dead: the leper, the blind, he who is childless and he who is impoverished.")

2. וַיִּחַר אַף יַעֲקֹב – *Jacob's anger flared up.* Jacob was angry with Rachel for saying, "*Give me,*" not

ג וַתֹּאמֶר הִנֵּה אֲמָתִי בִלְהָה בֹּא אֵלֶיהָ וְתֵלֵד עַל־בִּרְכַּי וְאִבָּנֶה גַם־אָנֹכִי
ד־ה מִמֶּנָּה׃ וַתִּתֶּן־לוֹ אֶת־בִּלְהָה שִׁפְחָתָהּ לְאִשָּׁה וַיָּבֹא אֵלֶיהָ יַעֲקֹב׃ וַתַּהַר
ו בִּלְהָה וַתֵּלֶד לְיַעֲקֹב בֵּן׃ וַתֹּאמֶר רָחֵל דָּנַנִּי אֱלֹהִים וְגַם שָׁמַע בְּקֹלִי
ז וַיִּתֶּן־לִי בֵּן עַל־כֵּן קָרְאָה שְׁמוֹ דָּן׃ וַתַּהַר עוֹד וַתֵּלֶד בִּלְהָה שִׁפְחַת
ח רָחֵל בֵּן שֵׁנִי לְיַעֲקֹב׃ וַתֹּאמֶר רָחֵל נַפְתּוּלֵי אֱלֹהִים ׀ נִפְתַּלְתִּי עִם־
ט אֲחֹתִי גַּם־יָכֹלְתִּי וַתִּקְרָא שְׁמוֹ נַפְתָּלִי׃ וַתֵּרֶא לֵאָה כִּי עָמְדָה מִלֶּדֶת
י וַתִּקַּח אֶת־זִלְפָּה שִׁפְחָתָהּ וַתִּתֵּן אֹתָהּ לְיַעֲקֹב לְאִשָּׁה׃ וַתֵּלֶד זִלְפָּה
יא שִׁפְחַת לֵאָה לְיַעֲקֹב בֵּן׃ וַתֹּאמֶר לֵאָה °בגד וַתִּקְרָא אֶת־שְׁמוֹ גָּד׃ °בָּא גָד ק׳

אֲשֶׁר מָנַע מִמֵּךְ — *Who has withheld from you.* (God) has created you barren. He (Jacob) recognized in her the signs of a woman incapable of conception (אַילוֹנִית).

3. בֹּא אֵלֶיהָ — *Consort with her.* This is what I meant when I said, *"Give me children."* I never thought that you possess the key to (open) a barren woman.

וְאִבָּנֶה גַם אָנֹכִי מִמֶּנָּה — *And I too may be built from her . . .* similar to my sister.

מִמֶּנָּה — *From her.* My jealousy of my co-wife may stimulate the nature of my reproductive system [so that it will function normally].

6. דָּנַנִּי אֱלֹהִים — *God has judged me.* God was righteous in His judgment by not granting me a pregnancy . . .

וְגַם שָׁמַע בְּקֹלִי — *He also heard my voice.* But nevertheless He accepted my prayer.

וַיִּתֶּן לִי בֵּן — *And has given me a son.* (He will be) חוּטְרָא לִידָא וּמָרָא לִקְבוּרָה, *A staff in my hand and a spade for my burial* (*Kesubos* 64a), since he was born on my knees (see 50:23). The wives (Rachel and Leah) by these statements (adopting the children of the maidservants as their own) agreed to set them (Bilhah and Zilpah) free. Since these children were accepted as sons, they would not have a status of slaves, since their mothers were no longer maidservants, otherwise it would have been a case of, הָאִשָּׁה וִילָדֶיהָ תִּהְיֶה לַאדֹנֶיהָ, *The wife and her children shall be her master's* (*Exodus* 21:4). For this reason they no longer subjugated (their maidservants) as Sarah did with Hagar, with Abraham's consent, when he said, הִנֵּה שִׁפְחָתֵךְ בְּיָדֵךְ, *Behold your maid is in your hand* (16:6). Therefore, all (the sons) are considered to be "the children of Jacob" to inherit him, and all are worthy to be remembered before God, (inscribed) on the *Ephod* and *Choshen* (breastplate), for each of them is considered to be the legitimate descendant of Jacob. This is not so regarding Ishmael, as it says, כִּי בְיִצְחָק יִקָּרֵא לְךָ זָרַע, *Since through Isaac will offspring be considered yours* (21:12).

NOTES

"Pray for me." The latter request would have been proper; the former was not, since it implied that Jacob had the power to grant that which only God can give. Normally, the great love Jacob had for Rachel would have made him more patient, and he would have controlled his anger. His great zeal for God's honor, however, caused him to set aside his feelings of love for Rachel, for his love of God was greater.

3. מִמֶּנָּה – *From her.* The word מִמֶּנָּה, *from her,* is translated literally by the *Sforno.* From Bilhah's ability to conceive and give birth to a child whom I will raise, the functioning of my reproductive system will hopefully be aroused.

6. וַיִּתֶּן לִי בֵּן – *And has given me a son.* Our Sages use this expression "a staff, etc." in the following sense. By having a son, one is assured of support in old age (if necessary) and someone to attend to his burial when the time comes. The *Sforno* applies this saying to Rachel's gratification at the birth of Dan, whom she intended to raise *on her knees.*

The *Sforno* draws a fine, and vital, distinction between the children born to Jacob through Bilhah and Zilpah and the son that Hagar bore to Abraham. In the former case, the mothers were set free; hence the status of their sons is the same as the sons of their former mistresses. Hagar was not set free by Sarah. As a result, her son Ishmael was the son

[3] *She said, "Here is my maid Bilhah, consort with her, that she may bear upon my knees and I too may be built up through her."*

[4] *So she gave him Bilhah her maidservant as a wife, and Jacob consorted with her.* [5] *Bilhah conceived and bore Jacob a son.* [6] *Then Rachel said, "God has judged me, He has also heard my voice and has given me a son." She therefore called his name Dan.*

[7] *Bilhah, Rachel's maidservant, conceived again and bore Jacob a second son.* [8] *And Rachel said, "Sacred schemes have I maneuvered to equal my sister, and I have also prevailed!" And she called his name Naphtali.*

[9] *When Leah saw that she had stopped giving birth, she took Zilpah her maidservant and gave her to Jacob as a wife.* [10] *Zilpah, Leah's maidservant, bore Jacob a son.* [11] *And Leah declared, "Good luck has come!" So she called his name Gad.*

---

8. נַפְתּוּלֵי אֱלֹהִים נִפְתַּלְתִּי — *With Godly bonds have I been bound.* (נַפְתּוּלֵי) From the expression, צָמִיד פָּתִיל, *tightly bound (Numbers* 19:15). With Godly and sacred cleaving did I cleave to my husband.

עִם אֲחֹתִי — *With my sister* . . . this I did together with my sister, since we both gave our handmaids (to Jacob) to facilitate the birth of the (twelve) tribes. Leah, perforce, had already given Zilpah to Jacob *before* the birth of Naphtali, for in seven years eight tribes were born — six sons to Leah and two to Zilpah. Now if we figure nine months for each pregnancy, it totals seventy-two months, which equals six years, besides the nine months for Dan who preceded (Zilpah's children), totaling eight tribes. From all this we must conclude that Leah gave Zilpah to Jacob (as a wife) prior to Naphtali's birth, otherwise seven years would not suffice for all, unless we assume that every pregnancy was only seven months, and that immediately after each birth they conceived again, (implying) that they did not observe any restrictions regulating post-natal impurity.

גַּם יָכֹלְתִּי — *I have also prevailed.* I have attained my intentions by giving my maidservant to my husband.

11. (בָּגָד) בָּא גָד — *Good luck has come.* He has come by chance, for had I not ceased to bear (children) I had no intention to bring him into the world (through my maidservant). בָּגָד is written as one word, implying "failure," because she *failed* to bear, after she had done so heretofore. (בָּגָד is derived from) אַחַי בָּגְדוּ כְמוֹ נָחַל, *My brethren have dealt deceitfully as a brook (Job* 6:15).

NOTES

of a maidservant and was not considered genealogically equal to his half-brother Isaac.

8. עִם אֲחֹתִי – *With my sister.* The phrase עִם אֲחֹתִי, *with my sister,* is interpreted by the *Sforno* in consonance with his translation of נַפְתּוּלֵי as meaning *bound,* i.e., bound together with her sister Leah in their common endeavor to assist Jacob in bringing twelve tribes into the world. Toward that end, Leah had already given Zilpah to her husband as a wife, prior to Naphtali's birth. The *Sforno* proves this sequence of events by showing that only in this manner could eight tribes be born in seven years. He rejects the unlikely theory (held by some commentators) that a number of these pregnancies were of seven-month duration, as well as the equally unlikely theory of conception following immediately after each birth, which would have negated the observance of the laws of purity governing marital relations after childbirth.

11. בָּא גָד – *Good luck has come.* The explanation of the verse from *Job,* quoted by the *Sforno,* is that there are brooks (wadis) which flow abundantly in the rainy season but dry up completely during the summer. Job complains that similarly there are friends whose sympathy at first flows, then ceases (fails) completely. The Hebrew word for *failure* in that verse is בָּגְדוּ although it can also be associated with *treachery.* Hence the name given by Leah to Zilpah's child, גָד, from בָּא גָד, has a twofold meaning. Written as two words it can mean *Good luck has come.* Written as one (בָּגָד) it is linked to the

יב־יג וַתֵּלֶד זִלְפָּה שִׁפְחַת לֵאָה בֵּן שֵׁנִי לְיַעֲקֹב: וַתֹּאמֶר לֵאָה בְּאָשְׁרִי כִּי
רביעי יד אִשְּׁרוּנִי בָּנוֹת וַתִּקְרָא אֶת־שְׁמוֹ אָשֵׁר: וַיֵּלֶךְ רְאוּבֵן בִּימֵי קְצִיר־חִטִּים
וַיִּמְצָא דוּדָאִים בַּשָּׂדֶה וַיָּבֵא אֹתָם אֶל־לֵאָה אִמּוֹ וַתֹּאמֶר רָחֵל אֶל־
טו לֵאָה תְּנִי־נָא לִי מִדּוּדָאֵי בְּנֵךְ: וַתֹּאמֶר לָהּ הַמְעַט קַחְתֵּךְ אֶת־אִישִׁי
וְלָקַחַת גַּם אֶת־דּוּדָאֵי בְּנִי וַתֹּאמֶר רָחֵל לָכֵן יִשְׁכַּב עִמָּךְ הַלַּיְלָה תַּחַת
טז דּוּדָאֵי בְנֵךְ: וַיָּבֹא יַעֲקֹב מִן־הַשָּׂדֶה בָּעֶרֶב וַתֵּצֵא לֵאָה לִקְרָאתוֹ וַתֹּאמֶר
אֵלַי תָּבוֹא כִּי שָׂכֹר שְׂכַרְתִּיךָ בְּדוּדָאֵי בְּנִי וַיִּשְׁכַּב עִמָּהּ בַּלַּיְלָה הוּא:
יז־יח וַיִּשְׁמַע אֱלֹהִים אֶל־לֵאָה וַתַּהַר וַתֵּלֶד לְיַעֲקֹב בֵּן חֲמִישִׁי: וַתֹּאמֶר לֵאָה
נָתַן אֱלֹהִים שְׂכָרִי אֲשֶׁר־נָתַתִּי שִׁפְחָתִי לְאִישִׁי וַתִּקְרָא שְׁמוֹ יִשָּׂשכָר:
יט־כ וַתַּהַר עוֹד לֵאָה וַתֵּלֶד בֵּן־שִׁשִּׁי לְיַעֲקֹב: וַתֹּאמֶר לֵאָה זְבָדַנִי אֱלֹהִים ׀
אֹתִי זֵבֶד טוֹב הַפַּעַם יִזְבְּלֵנִי אִישִׁי כִּי־יָלַדְתִּי לוֹ שִׁשָּׁה בָנִים וַתִּקְרָא

13. בְּאָשְׁרִי — *In my good fortune.* This son represents another instance of my good fortune, for he also is considered as my son.

14. וַיֵּלֶךְ רְאוּבֵן — *Reuben went out* . . . when he perceived that his mother (Leah) was painfully distressed by the cessation of her childbearing.

וַיִּמְצָא דוּדָאִים — *He found duda'im (mandrakes)* . . . a most fragrant plant which (supposedly) promotes fertility, similar to garlic which our Sages suggested be eaten Friday nights by men (since they increase fertility). The *duda'im* were similar, and even superior, since it also increased the love of (husband and wife) as it is written, שָׁם אֶתֵּן אֶת דֹּדַי לָךְ, הַדּוּדָאִים נָתְנוּ רֵיחַ, *There I will give my love to you; the mandrakes yield fragrance* (*Song of Songs* 7:13,14). We are being told (in this story) that even though Reuben at this time was at most four or five years old, he possessed mature judgment (and sensitivity).

15. הַמְעַט קַחְתֵּךְ אֶת אִישִׁי — *Is it a small matter that you have taken away my husband?* You should never have consented to become my rival-wife, as it says, וְאִשָּׁה אֶל אֲחֹתָהּ לֹא תִקָּח לִצְרֹר, *You shall not take a woman to her sister to be a rival-wife* (*Leviticus* 18:18).

וְלָקַחַת גַּם אֶת דּוּדָאֵי בְּנִי — *And now to take even my son's duda'im* . . . to increase his love for you and hatred for me!

לָכֵן יִשְׁכַּב עִמָּךְ הַלַּיְלָה — *Therefore, he shall lie with you tonight.* Hence, the effectiveness and magical power of these *duda'im* (for me) will be preceded by your (spending the night with Jacob) and so no harm will come to you, by giving me the *duda'im* now; and, as for the future, what is to prevent anyone from finding some for me, since, as our Sages tell us (*Sanhedrin* 99b), these were brought from (הֶפְקֵר) ownerless property (see *Rashi* on verse 14).

16. אֵלַי תָּבוֹא כִּי שָׂכֹר שְׂכַרְתִּיךָ — *It is to me that you must come for I have surely hired you.* You will not be guilty of any wrongdoing by depriving my sister her conjugal rights since she has willingly consented (to relinquish her right). This incident may appear immodest

NOTES

same word in *Job* (6:15) meaning *failed* and *betrayed*, as the *Sforno* explains.

16. וַיִּשְׁכַּב עִמָּהּ בַּלַּיְלָה הוּא — *So he lay with her that night.* The word הוּא at the end of this verse is seemingly superfluous. Our Sages interpreted it as referring to the Almighty's involvement in the conception of Issachar. The *Sforno* interprets it as referring to Jacob, revealing to us that he did not cohabit with Leah because of her arrangement with Rachel, but of his own free will. A positive attitude of both husband and wife is vital to happy and fulfilling marital relations, in the view of the Torah.

17-20. נָתַן אֱלֹהִים שְׂכָרִי אֲשֶׁר נָתַתִּי שִׁפְחָתִי לְאִישִׁי . . . וְזָבַדְנִי אֱלֹהִים — *God has granted my reward because I gave my maidservant to my husband* . . .

[12] *Zilpah, Leah's maidservant, bore a second son to Jacob.* [13] *Leah
declared, "In my good fortune! For women have deemed me fortunate!" So
she called his name Asher.*
[14] *Reuben went out in the days of the wheat harvest; he found dudaim in
the field and brought them to Leah his mother; Rachel said to Leah, "Please
give me some of your son's dudaim."* [15] *But she said to her, "Was your
taking my husband insignificant? — And now to take even my son's
dudaim!" Rachel said, "Therefore, he shall lie with you tonight in return for
your son's dudaim."*
[16] *When Jacob came from the field in the evening, Leah went out to meet
him and said, "It is to me that you must come for I have clearly hired you
with my son's dudaim." So he lay with her that night.*
[17] *God hearkened to Leah; and she conceived and bore Jacob a fifth son.*
[18] *And Leah declared, "God has granted me my reward because I gave my
maidservant to my husband." So she called his name Issachar.*
[19] *Then Leah conceived again and bore Jacob a sixth son.* [20] *Leah said,
"God has endowed me with a good endowment; now my husband will make
his permanent home with me for I have borne him six sons." So she called*

---

to those who brazenly misinterpret (Torah) but it reveals to us that the Patriarchs viewed marital intimacy as innocently as did Adam and Eve before they sinned, for there was no thought or intent of physical gratification at all; they were solely motivated to produce offspring, to serve and honor God. This incident also tells us that the motive of the Matriarchs was acceptable to God, the Blessed One, when they tried (to build the house of Israel) by bringing in co-wives (Bilhah and Zilpah) and the incident of the *duda'im* (as well). Because of their (pure deeds) their prayers were accepted, for it is proper for the *tzaddik* to utilize every possible natural means to attain his goal, combined with prayer, as our Sages tell us, הַקָּדוֹשׁ בָּרוּךְ הוּא מִתְאַוֶּה לִתְפִלָּתָם שֶׁל צַדִּיקִים, *the Holy One, Blessed is He, desires the prayers of the righteous (Yevamos* 64a).

וַיִּשְׁכַּב עִמָּהּ בַּלַּיְלָה הוּא — *So he lay with her that night* ... with his full knowledge and consent, cognizant of Leah's zest and pure motives.

17. וַיִּשְׁמַע אֱלֹהִים אֶל לֵאָה — *And God hearkened to Leah* ... for she had preceded her prayer with (her own) efforts, as she said ...

18. נָתַן אֱלֹהִים שְׂכָרִי אֲשֶׁר נָתַתִּי שִׁפְחָתִי לְאִישִׁי — *God has granted my reward because I gave my maidservant to my husband.* This was my first effort, when I brought this rival-wife into my house.

20. זְבָדַנִי אֱלֹהִים אֹתִי — *God has endowed me.* He has granted me a (generous) portion and rewarded me for my second effort, i.e., with the *duda'im*, for, שְׂכַר מִצְוָה מִצְוָה, *The reward of a mitzvah is a mitzvah (Avos* 4:2).

זֶבֶד טוֹב — *A good endowment* . . . for I (now) have a goodly portion, because I did not have any intention for physical pleasure. (I acted) only for His honor.

NOTES

God has endowed me. The *Sforno* explains that two additional sons were born to Leah as reward for the two efforts she expended — giving Zilpah to her husband as a co-wife and the incident of the *duda'im.* The first child (Issachar) is a reward for the first good deed, while Zebulun is in recognition of the *duda'im.* It is possible that this is so not only because of the sequence of these two events, but also to remove the immediacy of Leah's hiring Jacob with her *duda'im* from the conception of Issachar. Even though the motivation was pure, as mentioned in verse 16, for the sake of modesty it is preferable to let time elapse before Leah is rewarded with a child for the *duda'im* episode.

כא־כב אֶת־שְׁמוֹ זְבֻלוּן: וְאַחַר יָלְדָה בַּת וַתִּקְרָא אֶת־שְׁמָהּ דִּינָה: וַיִּזְכֹּר אֱלֹהִים
כג אֶת־רָחֵל וַיִּשְׁמַע אֵלֶיהָ אֱלֹהִים וַיִּפְתַּח אֶת־רַחְמָהּ: וַתַּהַר וַתֵּלֶד בֵּן
כד וַתֹּאמֶר אָסַף אֱלֹהִים אֶת־חֶרְפָּתִי: וַתִּקְרָא אֶת־שְׁמוֹ יוֹסֵף לֵאמֹר יֹסֵף
כה יְהוָה לִי בֵּן אַחֵר: וַיְהִי כַּאֲשֶׁר יָלְדָה רָחֵל אֶת־יוֹסֵף וַיֹּאמֶר יַעֲקֹב
כו אֶל־לָבָן שַׁלְּחֵנִי וְאֵלְכָה אֶל־מְקוֹמִי וּלְאַרְצִי: תְּנָה אֶת־נָשַׁי וְאֶת־
יְלָדַי אֲשֶׁר עָבַדְתִּי אֹתְךָ בָּהֵן וְאֵלֵכָה כִּי אַתָּה יָדַעְתָּ אֶת־עֲבֹדָתִי
כז אֲשֶׁר עֲבַדְתִּיךָ: וַיֹּאמֶר אֵלָיו לָבָן אִם־נָא מָצָאתִי חֵן בְּעֵינֶיךָ נִחַשְׁתִּי
חמישי כח־כט וַיְבָרְכֵנִי יְהוָה בִּגְלָלֶךָ: *וַיֹּאמַר נָקְבָה שְׂכָרְךָ עָלַי וְאֶתֵּנָה: וַיֹּאמֶר אֵלָיו
ל אַתָּה יָדַעְתָּ אֵת אֲשֶׁר עֲבַדְתִּיךָ וְאֵת אֲשֶׁר־הָיָה מִקְנְךָ אִתִּי: כִּי
מְעַט אֲשֶׁר־הָיָה לְךָ לְפָנַי וַיִּפְרֹץ לָרֹב וַיְבָרֶךְ יְהוָה אֹתְךָ לְרַגְלִי
לא וְעַתָּה מָתַי אֶעֱשֶׂה גַם־אָנֹכִי לְבֵיתִי: וַיֹּאמֶר מָה אֶתֶּן־לָךְ וַיֹּאמֶר
יַעֲקֹב לֹא־תִתֶּן־לִי מְאוּמָה אִם־תַּעֲשֶׂה־לִּי הַדָּבָר הַזֶּה אָשׁוּבָה
לב אֶרְעֶה צֹאנְךָ אֶשְׁמֹר: אֶעֱבֹר בְּכָל־צֹאנְךָ הַיּוֹם הָסֵר מִשָּׁם כָּל־שֶׂה ׀
נָקֹד וְטָלוּא וְכָל־שֶׂה־חוּם בַּכְּשָׂבִים וְטָלוּא וְנָקֹד בָּעִזִּים וְהָיָה שְׂכָרִי:

---

22. וַיִּזְכֹּר אֱלֹהִים אֶת רָחֵל — *God remembered Rachel* ... her efforts to conceive by bringing her handmaiden into the house as a rival-wife and the incident of the *duda'im.*

וַיִּשְׁמַע אֵלֶיהָ אֱלֹהִים — *And God hearkened to her* ... to her prayers, after she had made both efforts.

23. אֶת חֶרְפָּתִי — *My disgrace* ... that God had accepted her sister's prayer and not hers.

24. יֹסֵף ה׳ לִי בֵּן אַחֵר — *May HASHEM add on for me another son* ... (as a reward) for my second effort (i.e., the *duda'im),* as He did for my sister.

25. שַׁלְּחֵנִי וְאֵלְכָה — *Grant me leave that I may go.* Even though (Jacob) had no flocks or cattle at that time, having come only with his staff, still he had sufficient to provide his wives and children with bread, clothing and provision for the road. Otherwise, a wise righteous man (such as Jacob) would never have set out (on this journey) to die from hunger, nor would Laban, who was a rich man, respected in his city, have allowed him to leave with his daughters and family to die in hunger, thirst and deprivation, far from home. Now, Laban implores him (Jacob) to remain for his *own* benefit, as it is said וַיְבָרְכֵנִי ה׳ בִּגְלָלֶךָ, *HASHEM has blessed me on account of you* (verse 27).

27. אִם נָא מָצָאתִי חֵן בְּעֵינֶיךָ — *If I have found favor in your eyes.* If you love me to the degree that our kinship would warrant, you would not leave me, for I have learned by divination that my house has been blessed on account of you, with cattle and other possessions, as our Sages say, תֵּיכֶף לְתַלְמִיד חָכָם בְּרָכָה, *A blessing follows immediately on the (entertaining) of a scholar (Berachos* 42a).

וַיְבָרְכֵנִי ה׳ בִּגְלָלֶךָ — *HASHEM has blessed me on account of you.* And I am also cognizant of the fact that I have realized from my cattle much money and wealth to an abnormal extent, and I know that this is on account of you.

NOTES

23. אֶת חֶרְפָּתִי — *My disgrace.* The righteous Rachel's greatest disgrace is not her barrenness, but that her prayers are not deemed worthy of acceptance by God, while her sister's are!

29-30. אַתָּה יָדַעְתָּ אֵת אֲשֶׁר עֲבַדְתִּיךָ . . . וַיְבָרֶךְ ה׳ אֹתְךָ לְרַגְלִי — *You know how I have served you* ... *HASHEM has blessed you with my coming.* Jacob does not deny that Laban's household has been

his name Zebulun. [21] *Afterwards, she bore a daughter and she called her name Dinah.*

[22] *God remembered Rachel; God hearkened to her and He opened her womb.* [23] *She conceived and bore a son, and said, "God has taken away my disgrace."* [24] *So she called his name Joseph, saying, "May* HASHEM *add on for me another son."*

[25] *And it was, when Rachel had given birth to Joseph, Jacob said to Laban, "Grant me leave that I may go to my place and to my land.* [26] *Give me my wives and my children for whom I have served you, and I will go; for you are aware of my service that I labored for you."*

[27] *But Laban said to him, "If I have found favor in your eyes! — I have learned by divination that* HASHEM *has blessed me on account of you."* [28] *And he said, "Specify your wage to me and I will give it."* [29] *But he said to him, "You know how I served you and what your livestock were with me.* [30] *For the little that you had before I came has expanded substantially as* HASHEM *has blessed you with my coming; and now, when will I also do something for my own house?"*

[31] *He said, "What shall I give you?" And Jacob said, "Do not give me anything; if you will do this thing for me, I will resume pasturing and guarding your flocks:* [32] *Let me pass through your whole flock today. Remove from there every speckled or spotted lamb, every brownish lamb among the sheep and the spotted or speckled among the goats — that will be my wage.*

---

29. אַתָּה יָדַעְתָּ אֵת אֲשֶׁר עֲבַדְתִּיךָ — *You know how I have served you.* Do not attribute the increase in your flocks to divination and good luck, rather attribute it to my (hard) committed labors, performed by skill and much effort in tending the sheep.

וְאֵת אֲשֶׁר הָיָה מִקְנְךָ אִתִּי — *And what your cattle were with me.* There were among them broken and sick ones. I bound the broken ones and healed the sick, as befits an expert shepherd.

30. וַיְבָרֶךְ ה׳ אֹתְךָ לְרַגְלִי — HASHEM *has blessed you with my coming.* However, when you said that God blessed you with my coming, that is without a doubt true.

וְעַתָּה — *And now* . . . since God, the Blessed One, blessed you on my account.

מָתַי אֶעֱשֶׂה גַם אָנֹכִי — *When will I also do something (for my own house)?* When will I (be able) to do something which will bring blessing to my house, just as you have benefited through me; and for that the normal compensation of shepherds will not suffice.

31. מָה אֶתֶּן לָךְ — *What shall I give you?* . . . to compensate for what you expect to get.

לֹא תִתֶּן לִי מְאוּמָה — *You shall give me nothing* . . . because if God will favor me (with His blessing) what you have will not be diminished, as our Sages say, אֵין אָדָם נוֹגֵעַ בַּמּוּכָן לַחֲבֵרוֹ, *No man can touch what is prepared for his fellow (Yoma* 38b).

32. הָסֵר מִשָּׁם כָּל שֶׂה — *Remove from there every (speckled and spotted) sheep* . . . the young ones (lambs and kids), not the mature ones, so that they will reproduce (some) offspring that are similarly (speckled and spotted) which will then belong to me.

NOTES

blessed by God on his account, but he also wants Laban to know that he has labored excessively and skillfully over the years. The *Sforno* constantly stresses the importance of combining one's own efforts with God's blessing and assistance.

לג וְעָנְתָה־בִּי צִדְקָתִי בְּיוֹם מָחָר כִּי־תָבוֹא עַל־שְׂכָרִי לְפָנֶיךָ כֹּל אֲשֶׁר־
לד אֵינֶנּוּ נָקֹד וְטָלוּא בָּעִזִּים וְחוּם בַּכְּשָׂבִים גָּנוּב הוּא אִתִּי׃ וַיֹּאמֶר לָבָן הֵן
לה לוּ יְהִי כִדְבָרֶךָ׃ וַיָּסַר בַּיּוֹם הַהוּא אֶת־הַתְּיָשִׁים הָעֲקֻדִּים וְהַטְּלֻאִים וְאֵת
כָּל־הָעִזִּים הַנְּקֻדּוֹת וְהַטְּלֻאֹת כֹּל אֲשֶׁר־לָבָן בּוֹ וְכָל־חוּם בַּכְּשָׂבִים וַיִּתֵּן
לו בְּיַד־בָּנָיו׃ וַיָּשֶׂם דֶּרֶךְ שְׁלֹשֶׁת יָמִים בֵּינוֹ וּבֵין יַעֲקֹב וְיַעֲקֹב רֹעֶה אֶת־צֹאן
לז לָבָן הַנּוֹתָרֹת׃ וַיִּקַּח־לוֹ יַעֲקֹב מַקַּל לִבְנֶה לַח וְלוּז וְעַרְמוֹן וַיְפַצֵּל בָּהֵן
לח פְּצָלוֹת לְבָנוֹת מַחְשֹׂף הַלָּבָן אֲשֶׁר עַל־הַמַּקְלוֹת׃ וַיַּצֵּג אֶת־הַמַּקְלוֹת
אֲשֶׁר פִּצֵּל בָּרְהָטִים בְּשִׁקֲתוֹת הַמָּיִם אֲשֶׁר תָּבֹאןָ הַצֹּאן לִשְׁתּוֹת לְנֹכַח
לט הַצֹּאן וַיֵּחַמְנָה בְּבֹאָן לִשְׁתּוֹת׃ וַיֶּחֱמוּ הַצֹּאן אֶל־הַמַּקְלוֹת וַתֵּלַדְןָ הַצֹּאן
מ עֲקֻדִּים נְקֻדִּים וּטְלֻאִים׃ וְהַכְּשָׂבִים הִפְרִיד יַעֲקֹב וַיִּתֵּן פְּנֵי הַצֹּאן אֶל־
עָקֹד וְכָל־חוּם בְּצֹאן לָבָן וַיָּשֶׁת לוֹ עֲדָרִים לְבַדּוֹ וְלֹא שָׁתָם עַל־צֹאן
מא לָבָן׃ וְהָיָה בְּכָל־יַחֵם הַצֹּאן הַמְקֻשָּׁרוֹת וְשָׂם יַעֲקֹב אֶת־הַמַּקְלוֹת לְעֵינֵי
מב הַצֹּאן בָּרֳהָטִים לְיַחְמֵנָּה בַּמַּקְלוֹת׃ וּבְהַעֲטִיף הַצֹּאן לֹא יָשִׂים וְהָיָה
מג הָעֲטֻפִים לְלָבָן וְהַקְּשֻׁרִים לְיַעֲקֹב׃ וַיִּפְרֹץ הָאִישׁ מְאֹד מְאֹד וַיְהִי־לוֹ צֹאן
לא א רַבּוֹת וּשְׁפָחוֹת וַעֲבָדִים וּגְמַלִּים וַחֲמֹרִים׃ וַיִּשְׁמַע אֶת־דִּבְרֵי בְנֵי־לָבָן
לֵאמֹר לָקַח יַעֲקֹב אֵת כָּל־אֲשֶׁר לְאָבִינוּ וּמֵאֲשֶׁר לְאָבִינוּ עָשָׂה אֵת כָּל־
ב הַכָּבֹד הַזֶּה׃ וַיַּרְא יַעֲקֹב אֶת־פְּנֵי לָבָן וְהִנֵּה אֵינֶנּוּ עִמּוֹ כִּתְמוֹל שִׁלְשׁוֹם׃
ג וַיֹּאמֶר יהוה אֶל־יַעֲקֹב שׁוּב אֶל־אֶרֶץ אֲבוֹתֶיךָ וּלְמוֹלַדְתֶּךָ וְאֶהְיֶה עִמָּךְ׃

---

33. וְעָנְתָה בִּי צִדְקָתִי . . . כִּי תָבוֹא עַל שְׂכָרִי לְפָנֶיךָ — *Let my integrity testify for me . . . When you will come regarding my wage from you.* When you will come to inspect the additions to my flock, their number will testify to the integrity of my labor, for the Almighty will abnormally increase my share as compensation for my labors.

34. לוּ יְהִי כִדְבָרֶךָ — *If only it would remain as you say.* If only you would be appeased (satisfied) with your statement.

35. וַיָּסַר בַּיּוֹם הַהוּא אֶת הַתְּיָשִׁים — *So he removed on that very day the he-goats.* After (agreeing) and saying, "יְהִי כִדְבָרֶךָ, *let it be as you say,*" he reneged and removed on that very day both the young and mature ones.

38. לְנֹכַח הַצֹּאן — *Facing the sheep.* He set up the rods in front of the sheep so that they should look at this phenomena and picture it in their mind when they conceive, for the picture impressed upon the imagination at that time is a determining factor in the appearance (nature) of the offspring.

40. אֶל עָקֹד וְכָל חוּם בְּצֹאן לָבָן — *The ringed ones and all the brownish ones.* After (Laban) changed his wages, and kept the spotted and brown ones in his own flock.

42. וּבְהַעֲטִיף הַצֹּאן לֹא יָשִׂים — *When the sheep were late bearing he would not place . . .* so that Laban should not think that (Jacob) had deceived him in some manner.

43. וַיִּפְרֹץ הָאִישׁ — *The man became exceedingly prosperous.* He exceeded the limitations of prosperity which would be normal for those occupied with shepherding.

NOTES

33. וְעָנְתָה בִּי צִדְקָתִי . . . כִּי תָבוֹא עַל שְׂכָרִי לְפָנֶיךָ — *Let my integrity testify for me . . . when you will come regarding my wage from you.* There are commentators, including *Rashi,* who interpret the phrase כִּי תָבוֹא as *when it comes,* referring to *my integrity* (צִדְקָתִי). Not so the *Sforno,* who interprets it as referring to Laban — *when you will come* to investigate my flocks, you will see how God has blessed me due to my integrity.

[33] *Let my integrity testify for me in the future when it comes before you regarding my wage; any among the goats that is not speckled or spotted, or among the sheep that is not brownish, is stolen, if in my possession."*

[34] *And Laban said, "Agreed! If only it will be as you say."*

[35] *So he removed on that very day the ringed and spotted he-goats and all the speckled and spotted goats — every one that contained white, as well as all the brownish ones among the sheep — and he left them in charge of his sons.* [36] *And he put a distance of three days between himself and Jacob; and Jacob tended Laban's remaining flock.*

[37] *Jacob then took himself fresh rods of poplar and hazel and chestnut. He peeled white streaks in them, laying bare the white of the rods.* [38] *And he set up the rods which he had peeled, in the runnels — in the watering receptacles to which the flocks came to drink — facing the flocks, so they would become stimulated when they came to drink.* [39] *Then the flocks became stimulated by the rods and the flocks gave birth to ringed ones, speckled ones, and spotted ones.* [40] *Jacob segregated the lambs and he made the flocks face the ringed ones and all the brownish ones among Laban's flocks. He formed separate droves of his own and did not mingle them with Laban's flocks.*

[41] *Whenever it was mating time for the early-bearing flocks, Jacob would place the rods in the runnels, in full view of the flock to stimulate them among the rods.* [42] *But when the sheep were late bearing, he would not emplace; thus, the late-bearing ones went to Laban and the early-bearing ones to Jacob.*

[43] *The man became exceedingly prosperous and he attained fecund flocks, maidservants and servants, camels and donkeys.*

31 [1] *Then he heard the words of Laban's sons, saying, "Jacob has taken all that belonged to our father, and from that which belonged to our father he amassed all this wealth."* [2] *Jacob also noticed Laban's disposition that, behold, it was not toward him as in earlier days.* [3] *And HASHEM said to Jacob, "Return to the land of your fathers and to your native land, and I will be with you."*

XXXI

1. וַיִּשְׁמַע אֶת דִּבְרֵי בְנֵי לָבָן — *Then he heard the words of Laban's sons* ... slanderous remarks against him, caused by their jealousy of him.

2. וַיַּרְא יַעֲקֹב אֶת פְּנֵי — *And Jacob saw the countenance (of Laban).* He perceived that (Laban) had accepted the slander (of his sons).

3. וַיֹּאמֶר ה׳ אֶל יַעֲקֹב שׁוּב — *And HASHEM said to Jacob, Return.* The Torah tells us the three reasons why Jacob fled and did not ask permission of Laban, such behavior being unseemly for a man such as (Jacob). He felt that since Laban had accepted (his sons') slander, then if he would know of his departure he would steal (all from him), as it says, פֶּן תִּגְזֹל אֶת בְּנוֹתֶיךָ, *Perhaps you might steal your daughters (from me)* (v. 31).

וְאֶהְיֶה עִמָּךְ — *And I will be with you* ... that no harm befall you during the journey.

NOTES

XXXI

1-3. וַיִּשְׁמַע ... וַיַּרְא ... וַיֹּאמֶר ה׳ אֶל יַעֲקֹב — *Then he heard ... and saw ... and HASHEM said to Jacob.* Jacob *hears* the slanderous remarks of Laban's sons (Jacob's brothers-in-law); he *sees* the changed countenance of Laban (his father-in-law) and also hears the word of God to return to *Eretz Yisrael.* These are the three reasons for Jacob's precipitous departure.

ד־ה וַיִּשְׁלַח יַעֲקֹב וַיִּקְרָא לְרָחֵל וּלְלֵאָה הַשָּׂדֶה אֶל־צֹאנוֹ: וַיֹּאמֶר לָהֶן רֹאֶה
אָנֹכִי אֶת־פְּנֵי אֲבִיכֶן כִּי־אֵינֶנּוּ אֵלַי כִּתְמֹל שִׁלְשֹׁם וֵאלֹהֵי אָבִי הָיָה עִמָּדִי:
ו־ז וְאַתֵּנָה יְדַעְתֶּן כִּי בְּכָל־כֹּחִי עָבַדְתִּי אֶת־אֲבִיכֶן: וַאֲבִיכֶן הֵתֶל בִּי וְהֶחֱלִף
ח אֶת־מַשְׂכֻּרְתִּי עֲשֶׂרֶת מֹנִים וְלֹא־נְתָנוֹ אֱלֹהִים לְהָרַע עִמָּדִי: אִם־כֹּה
יֹאמַר נְקֻדִּים יִהְיֶה שְׂכָרֶךָ וְיָלְדוּ כָל־הַצֹּאן נְקֻדִּים וְאִם־כֹּה יֹאמַר עֲקֻדִּים
ט יִהְיֶה שְׂכָרֶךָ וְיָלְדוּ כָל־הַצֹּאן עֲקֻדִּים: וַיַּצֵּל אֱלֹהִים אֶת־מִקְנֵה אֲבִיכֶם
י וַיִּתֶּן־לִי: וַיְהִי בְּעֵת יַחֵם הַצֹּאן וָאֶשָּׂא עֵינַי וָאֵרֶא בַּחֲלוֹם וְהִנֵּה הָעַתֻּדִים
יא הָעֹלִים עַל־הַצֹּאן עֲקֻדִּים נְקֻדִּים וּבְרֻדִּים: וַיֹּאמֶר אֵלַי מַלְאַךְ הָאֱלֹהִים
יב בַּחֲלוֹם יַעֲקֹב וָאֹמַר הִנֵּנִי: וַיֹּאמֶר שָׂא־נָא עֵינֶיךָ וּרְאֵה כָּל־הָעַתֻּדִים
הָעֹלִים עַל־הַצֹּאן עֲקֻדִּים נְקֻדִּים וּבְרֻדִּים כִּי רָאִיתִי אֵת כָּל־אֲשֶׁר לָבָן
יג עֹשֶׂה לָּךְ: אָנֹכִי הָאֵל בֵּית־אֵל אֲשֶׁר מָשַׁחְתָּ שָּׁם מַצֵּבָה אֲשֶׁר נָדַרְתָּ לִּי
יד שָׁם נֶדֶר עַתָּה קוּם צֵא מִן־הָאָרֶץ הַזֹּאת וְשׁוּב אֶל־אֶרֶץ מוֹלַדְתֶּךָ: וַתַּעַן
טו רָחֵל וְלֵאָה וַתֹּאמַרְנָה לוֹ הַעוֹד לָנוּ חֵלֶק וְנַחֲלָה בְּבֵית אָבִינוּ: הֲלוֹא
טז נָכְרִיּוֹת נֶחְשַׁבְנוּ לוֹ כִּי מְכָרָנוּ וַיֹּאכַל גַּם־אָכוֹל אֶת־כַּסְפֵּנוּ: כִּי כָל־הָעֹשֶׁר
אֲשֶׁר הִצִּיל אֱלֹהִים מֵאָבִינוּ לָנוּ הוּא וּלְבָנֵינוּ וְעַתָּה כֹּל אֲשֶׁר אָמַר אֱלֹהִים
ששי יז אֵלֶיךָ עֲשֵׂה: וַיָּקָם יַעֲקֹב וַיִּשָּׂא אֶת־בָּנָיו וְאֶת־נָשָׁיו עַל־הַגְּמַלִּים: וַיִּנְהַג
יח אֶת־כָּל־מִקְנֵהוּ וְאֶת־כָּל־רְכֻשׁוֹ אֲשֶׁר רָכָשׁ מִקְנֵה קִנְיָנוֹ אֲשֶׁר רָכַשׁ
יט בְּפַדַּן אֲרָם לָבוֹא אֶל־יִצְחָק אָבִיו אַרְצָה כְּנָעַן: וְלָבָן הָלַךְ לִגְזֹז אֶת־
כ צֹאנוֹ וַתִּגְנֹב רָחֵל אֶת־הַתְּרָפִים אֲשֶׁר לְאָבִיהָ: וַיִּגְנֹב יַעֲקֹב אֶת־לֵב לָבָן
כא הָאֲרַמִּי עַל־בְּלִי הִגִּיד לוֹ כִּי בֹרֵחַ הוּא: וַיִּבְרַח הוּא וְכָל־אֲשֶׁר־לוֹ וַיָּקָם

---

5. כִּי אֵינֶנּוּ אֵלַי כִּתְמֹל שִׁלְשֹׁם — *Is not toward me as yesterday and the day before* ... for he thinks that I have (appropriated) what is his.

וֵאלֹהֵי אָבִי הָיָה עִמָּדִי — *But the God of my father was with me.* God alone has given me what I possess and I have stolen nothing from Laban.

14. הַעוֹד לָנוּ — *Have we then still (a share ...).* How can you even think that it would be difficult for us to leave our father?

16. כִּי כָל הָעֹשֶׁר — *But all the wealth.* Similar to, כִּי צָחָקְתְּ, *But you laughed* (18:15). We have no hope of inheriting from our father. However, all the wealth which God has taken away from him, that alone is ours and our children's.

וְעַתָּה — *So now* ... after you have seen that he has accepted the slander against you, and there is (valid) suspicion that he will steal (all) from you.

כֹּל אֲשֶׁר אָמַר אֱלֹהִים — *Whatever God has said to you* ... that alone must you do. Proceed and go, you do not need (his) permission.

20. וַיִּגְנֹב יַעֲקֹב אֶת לֵב לָבָן — *Jacob deceived Laban.* He did not reveal how he felt regarding Laban's acceptance of the slanderous remarks made against him, nor that he realized that Laban was no longer well disposed toward him as before.

NOTES

16. וְעַתָּה כֹּל אֲשֶׁר אָמַר אֱלֹהִים – *So now, whatever God has said to you.* First Jacob's wives — Laban's daughters — argue that logically there is every reason to leave. But even if these reasons were not valid, God's command must be obeyed. Hence, do not delay; proceed and go!

[4] *Jacob sent and summoned Rachel and Leah to the field, to his flock,*
[5] *and said to them, "I have noticed that your father's disposition is not toward me as in earlier days; but the God of my father was with me.*
[6] *Now you have known that it was with all my might that I served your father,*
[7] *yet your father mocked me and changed my wage a hundred times; but God did not permit him to harm me.*
[8] *If he would stipulate: 'Speckled ones shall be your wages,' then the entire flock bore spotted ones; and if he would stipulate: 'Ringed ones shall be your wages,' then the entire flock bore ringed ones.*
[9] *Thus, God took away your father's livestock, and gave them to me.*
[10] *It once happened at the mating time of the flock that I raised my eyes and saw in a dream — Behold! The he-goats that mounted the flock were ringed, speckled, and checkered.*
[11] *And an angel of God said to me in the dream, 'Jacob!' And I said, 'Here I am.'*
[12] *And he said, 'Raise your eyes, if you please, and see that all the he-goats mounting the flocks are ringed, speckled, and checkered, for I have seen all that Laban is doing to you.*
[13] *I am the God of Bethel where you anointed a pillar and where you made Me a vow. Now — arise, leave this land and return to your native land.' "*

[14] *Then Rachel and Leah replied and said to him, "Have we then still a share and an inheritance in our father's house?*
[15] *Are we not considered by him as strangers? For he has sold us and even totally consumed our money!*
[16] *But, all the wealth that God has taken away from our father belongs to us and to our children; so now, whatever God has said to you, do."*

[17] *Jacob arose and lifted his children and his wives onto the camels.*
[18] *He led away all his livestock and all the wealth which he had amassed — his purchased property which he had amassed in Paddan-aram — to go to his father Isaac, to the land of Canaan.*

[19] *Laban had gone to shear his sheep, and Rachel stole the teraphim that belonged to her father.*
[20] *Jacob deceived Laban the Aramean by not telling him that he was fleeing.*
[21] *Thus, he fled with all he had. He arose*

הָאֲרַמִּי — *The Aramean.* He (Jacob) did thus because he was Laban the Aramean, a cheat (*ramai,* רַמַּאי, a play on the word אֲרַמִּי). If Laban had suspected that Jacob knew anything about (the slander and Laban's change of heart) he would have "counted the steps" of Jacob who would have found no way to flee.

עַל בְּלִי הִגִּיד לוֹ — *Besides not telling him.* Similar to, עַל עֹלַת הַתָּמִיד, *Besides the continual burnt offering (Numbers* 28:10). Jacob acted as though he did not sense the enmity of Laban, *besides* concealing his desire to leave. All this was not unethical but done under duress, because . . .

כִּי בֹרֵחַ הוּא — *That he was fleeing.* He was worried that Laban would steal all from him with the help of his townspeople, as he said later when he defended himself to Laban.

21. וַיִּבְרַח — *He fled.* The word בְּרִיחָה, *fleeing,* is used to indicate flight from a place in anticipation of future danger, and in cases where there is no pursuer. The term נְסָה, *to run away*, is used when one flees from a place due to a clear and present danger, or from a pursuer.

NOTES

20. עַל בְּלִי הִגִּיד לוֹ — *Besides not telling him.* The word עַל in this context does not mean *on,* but *in addition to,* as it does regarding the daily offering and the additional *Shabbos* sacrifice. Jacob, in addition to concealing his determination to leave, also acts as though his relationship with Laban is unchanged.

כב וַיַּעֲבֹר אֶת־הַנָּהָר וַיָּשֶׂם אֶת־פָּנָיו הַר הַגִּלְעָד: וַיֻּגַּד לְלָבָן בַּיּוֹם הַשְּׁלִישִׁי
כג כִּי בָרַח יַעֲקֹב: וַיִּקַּח אֶת־אֶחָיו עִמּוֹ וַיִּרְדֹּף אַחֲרָיו דֶּרֶךְ שִׁבְעַת יָמִים
כד וַיַּדְבֵּק אֹתוֹ בְּהַר הַגִּלְעָד: וַיָּבֹא אֱלֹהִים אֶל־לָבָן הָאֲרַמִּי בַּחֲלֹם הַלָּיְלָה
כה וַיֹּאמֶר לוֹ הִשָּׁמֶר לְךָ פֶּן־תְּדַבֵּר עִם־יַעֲקֹב מִטּוֹב עַד־רָע: וַיַּשֵּׂג לָבָן
אֶת־יַעֲקֹב וְיַעֲקֹב תָּקַע אֶת־אָהֳלוֹ בָּהָר וְלָבָן תָּקַע אֶת־אֶחָיו בְּהַר
כו הַגִּלְעָד: וַיֹּאמֶר לָבָן לְיַעֲקֹב מֶה עָשִׂיתָ וַתִּגְנֹב אֶת־לְבָבִי וַתְּנַהֵג אֶת־
כז בְּנֹתַי כִּשְׁבֻיוֹת חָרֶב: לָמָּה נַחְבֵּאתָ לִבְרֹחַ וַתִּגְנֹב אֹתִי וְלֹא־הִגַּדְתָּ לִּי
כח וָאֲשַׁלֵּחֲךָ בְּשִׂמְחָה וּבְשִׁרִים בְּתֹף וּבְכִנּוֹר: וְלֹא נְטַשְׁתַּנִי לְנַשֵּׁק לְבָנַי
כט וְלִבְנֹתָי עַתָּה הִסְכַּלְתָּ עֲשׂוֹ: יֶשׁ־לְאֵל יָדִי לַעֲשׂוֹת עִמָּכֶם רָע וֵאלֹהֵי
אֲבִיכֶם אֶמֶשׁ | אָמַר אֵלַי לֵאמֹר הִשָּׁמֶר לְךָ מִדַּבֵּר עִם־יַעֲקֹב מִטּוֹב עַד־
ל רָע: וְעַתָּה הָלֹךְ הָלַכְתָּ כִּי־נִכְסֹף נִכְסַפְתָּה לְבֵית אָבִיךָ לָמָּה גָנַבְתָּ אֶת־
לא אֱלֹהָי: וַיַּעַן יַעֲקֹב וַיֹּאמֶר לְלָבָן כִּי יָרֵאתִי כִּי אָמַרְתִּי פֶּן־תִּגְזֹל אֶת־
לב בְּנוֹתֶיךָ מֵעִמִּי: °עִם אֲשֶׁר תִּמְצָא אֶת־אֱלֹהֶיךָ לֹא יִחְיֶה נֶגֶד אַחֵינוּ
לג הַכֶּר־לְךָ מָה עִמָּדִי וְקַח־לָךְ וְלֹא־יָדַע יַעֲקֹב כִּי רָחֵל גְּנָבָתַם: וַיָּבֹא לָבָן
בְּאֹהֶל־יַעֲקֹב | וּבְאֹהֶל לֵאָה וּבְאֹהֶל שְׁתֵּי הָאֲמָהֹת וְלֹא מָצָא וַיֵּצֵא
לד מֵאֹהֶל לֵאָה וַיָּבֹא בְּאֹהֶל רָחֵל: וְרָחֵל לָקְחָה אֶת־הַתְּרָפִים וַתְּשִׂמֵם
בְּכַר הַגָּמָל וַתֵּשֶׁב עֲלֵיהֶם וַיְמַשֵּׁשׁ לָבָן אֶת־כָּל־הָאֹהֶל וְלֹא מָצָא:
לה וַתֹּאמֶר אֶל־אָבִיהָ אַל־יִחַר בְּעֵינֵי אֲדֹנִי כִּי לוֹא אוּכַל לָקוּם מִפָּנֶיךָ כִּי־
לו דֶרֶךְ נָשִׁים לִי וַיְחַפֵּשׂ וְלֹא מָצָא אֶת־הַתְּרָפִים: וַיִּחַר לְיַעֲקֹב וַיָּרֶב בְּלָבָן

---

24. פֶּן תְּדַבֵּר עִם יַעֲקֹב — *Lest you speak with Jacob.* Even speech is forbidden to you.

מִטּוֹב עַד רָע — *Either good or bad.* Do not persuade him to return by giving him hope that you will be good to him, and do not exaggerate the evil that you will do to him (if he refuses to return).

29. וֵאלֹהֵי אֲבִיכֶם — *But the God of your father.* Not in your merit (but in that of the God of your *father),* for you departed without my permission and deceived me in doing so.

30. הָלֹךְ הָלַכְתָּ כִּי נִכְסֹף נִכְסַפְתָּה — *You have left because you longed greatly for your father's house.* Granted that you went in this fashion because of your great desire to return to your father's house, come what may . . .

לָמָּה גָנַבְתָּ אֶת אֱלֹהָי — *But why did you steal my gods?* For this there is no excuse. Your great desire for your father's house cannot justify your stealing my gods.

31. פֶּן תִּגְזֹל אֶת בְּנוֹתֶיךָ — *Perhaps you might steal your daughters . . .* for when you claim that you did not give your daughters to me to have me take them away from you (you will use that as an excuse) to steal them, the children and my possessions from me, as (indeed) he later said, "הַבָּנוֹת בְּנֹתַי וְהַבָּנִים בָּנַי וְהַצֹּאן צֹאנִי, *The daughters are my daughters, the children are my children and the flock is my flock*" (verse 43). Now, all this you could have done with the help of your townspeople if I remained (in Charan) but you will not

NOTES

24. מִטּוֹב עַד רָע – *Either good or bad.* The expression מִטּוֹב עַד רָע, *good or bad,* cannot refer to the content of Laban's remarks to Jacob, since we see that he *did* incorporate both elements in his speech to his son-in-law. The *Sforno* therefore interprets this to mean that Laban is prohibited from making promises or threats to Jacob. This admonition Laban does obey.

and crossed the river, and he set his direction toward Mount Gilead.
22 It was told to Laban on the third day that Jacob had fled. 23 So he took
his kinsmen with him and pursued him a distance of seven days, catching
up with him on Mount Gilead. 24 But God had come to Laban the Aramean
in a dream by night and said to him, "Beware lest you speak with Jacob
either good or bad."
25 Laban overtook Jacob. Jacob had pitched his tent on the mountain,
while Laban had stationed his kinsmen on Mount Gilead. 26 Laban said to
Jacob, "What have you done that you have deceived me and led my
daughters away like captives of the sword? 27 Why have you fled so
stealthily, and cheated me? Nor did you tell me — for I would have sent you
off with gladness, with songs, with timbrel, and with lyre! 28 And you did
not even allow me to kiss my sons and daughters; now you have acted
foolishly. 29 It is in my power to do you all harm; but the God of your father
addressed me last night, saying, 'Beware of speaking with Jacob either good
or bad.' 30 Now — you have left because you longed greatly for your father's
house; but why did you steal my gods?"
31 Jacob answered and said to Laban, "Because I was afraid, for I thought,
perhaps you might steal your daughters from me. 32 With whomever you
find your gods, he shall not live; in the presence of our kinsmen ascertain for
yourself what is with me and take it back." (Now Jacob did not know that
Rachel had stolen them.)
33 Laban came into Jacob's tent, and into Leah's tent, and into the tent of
the two maidservants, but he found nothing. When he had left Leah's tent,
he came into Rachel's tent. 34 Now Rachel had taken the teraphim, put them
into the camel's packsaddle and sat on them. Laban rummaged through the
whole tent, but found nothing. 35 She said to her father, "Let not my lord find
it annoying that I cannot rise up before you, for the way of women is upon
me." Thus he searched but did not find the teraphim.
36 Then Jacob became angered and he took up his grievance with Laban;

---

be able to do so (as readily), once I have left your country.

32. לֹא יִחְיֶה — *He shall not live.* (Jacob) was convinced that one of his servants had stolen it to worship it (in secret) thereby lapsing back into idolatry. This in turn would condemn him to death.

הַכֶּר לְךָ מָה עִמָּדִי — *Ascertain for yourself what is with me* . . . that belongs to you and take it, once you recognize (it is yours).

וְלֹא יָדַע יַעֲקֹב — *And Jacob did not know* . . . for if he had known he would never have had the audacity to deny it, nor would he have said, "לֹא יִחְיֶה, *He shall not live.*"

36. וַיִּחַר לְיַעֲקֹב וַיָּרֶב בְּלָבָן — *Then Jacob became angered and strove with Laban.* Once nothing was found, Jacob thought that the תְּרָפִים, *terafim,* had never been stolen, and that

NOTES

32. לֹא יִחְיֶה – *He shall not live.* The servants in Jacob's household would not have been permitted to accompany him to *Eretz Yisrael* unless they had rejected idolatry, thereby qualifying as גֵּרֵי תוֹשָׁב, *non-Jews who* (agree to observe the seven Noahide laws and) *are permitted to dwell in our midst.* However, if such a person lapsed back into idolatry, the laws regarding idolaters apply, and he is now punishable by death for the transgression of stealing.

לז וַיַּעַן יַעֲקֹב וַיֹּאמֶר לְלָבָן מַה־פִּשְׁעִי מַה חַטָּאתִי כִּי דָלַקְתָּ אַחֲרָי: כִּי־
מִשַּׁשְׁתָּ אֶת־כָּל־כֵּלַי מַה־מָּצָאתָ מִכֹּל כְּלֵי־בֵיתֶךָ שִׂים כֹּה נֶגֶד אַחַי
לח וְאַחֶיךָ וְיוֹכִיחוּ בֵּין שְׁנֵינוּ: זֶה עֶשְׂרִים שָׁנָה אָנֹכִי עִמָּךְ רְחֵלֶיךָ וְעִזֶּיךָ לֹא
לט שִׁכֵּלוּ וְאֵילֵי צֹאנְךָ לֹא אָכָלְתִּי: טְרֵפָה לֹא־הֵבֵאתִי אֵלֶיךָ אָנֹכִי אֲחַטֶּנָּה
מ מִיָּדִי תְּבַקְשֶׁנָּה גְּנֻבְתִי יוֹם וּגְנֻבְתִי לָיְלָה: הָיִיתִי בַיּוֹם אֲכָלַנִי חֹרֶב וְקֶרַח
מא בַּלָּיְלָה וַתִּדַּד שְׁנָתִי מֵעֵינָי: זֶה־לִּי עֶשְׂרִים שָׁנָה בְּבֵיתֶךָ עֲבַדְתִּיךָ אַרְבַּע־
עֶשְׂרֵה שָׁנָה בִּשְׁתֵּי בְנֹתֶיךָ וְשֵׁשׁ שָׁנִים בְּצֹאנֶךָ וַתַּחֲלֵף אֶת־מַשְׂכֻּרְתִּי
מב עֲשֶׂרֶת מֹנִים: לוּלֵי אֱלֹהֵי אָבִי אֱלֹהֵי אַבְרָהָם וּפַחַד יִצְחָק הָיָה לִי כִּי
עַתָּה רֵיקָם שִׁלַּחְתָּנִי אֶת־עָנְיִי וְאֶת־יְגִיעַ כַּפַּי רָאָה אֱלֹהִים וַיּוֹכַח אָמֶשׁ:
שביעי מג וַיַּעַן לָבָן וַיֹּאמֶר אֶל־יַעֲקֹב הַבָּנוֹת בְּנֹתַי וְהַבָּנִים בָּנַי וְהַצֹּאן צֹאנִי וְכֹל
אֲשֶׁר־אַתָּה רֹאֶה לִי־הִוא וְלִבְנֹתַי מָה־אֶעֱשֶׂה לָאֵלֶּה הַיּוֹם אוֹ לִבְנֵיהֶן
מד אֲשֶׁר יָלָדוּ: וְעַתָּה לְכָה נִכְרְתָה בְרִית אֲנִי וָאָתָּה וְהָיָה לְעֵד בֵּינִי וּבֵינֶךָ:
מה־מו וַיִּקַּח יַעֲקֹב אָבֶן וַיְרִימֶהָ מַצֵּבָה: וַיֹּאמֶר יַעֲקֹב לְאֶחָיו לִקְטוּ אֲבָנִים וַיִּקְחוּ
מז אֲבָנִים וַיַּעֲשׂוּ־גָל וַיֹּאכְלוּ שָׁם עַל־הַגָּל: וַיִּקְרָא־לוֹ לָבָן יְגַר שָׂהֲדוּתָא
מח וְיַעֲקֹב קָרָא לוֹ גַּלְעֵד: וַיֹּאמֶר לָבָן הַגַּל הַזֶּה עֵד בֵּינִי וּבֵינְךָ הַיּוֹם
מט עַל־כֵּן קָרָא־שְׁמוֹ גַּלְעֵד: וְהַמִּצְפָּה אֲשֶׁר אָמַר יִצֶף יהוה בֵּינִי וּבֵינֶךָ כִּי

Laban had used this accusation as a pretext to enable him to make a general search, because he suspected (Jacob) of stealing something from him.

מַה פִּשְׁעִי מַה חַטָּאתִי — *What is my transgression? What is my sin?* What wrongdoing have you found me guilty of in the past, that you suspect me now of being a robber?

38. רְחֵלֶיךָ וְעִזֶּיךָ לֹא שִׁכֵּלוּ — *Your ewes and she-goats never miscarried.* The opposite (of theft) is what you have found in my behavior; not only did I serve you faithfully as befits the righteous, but I also benefited you by my efforts to prevent any miscarriages (among your animals).

וְאֵילֵי צֹאנְךָ לֹא אָכָלְתִּי — *Nor did I eat rams of your flock* ... as other shepherds allow themselves to do.

39. לֹא הֵבֵאתִי אֵלֶיךָ אָנֹכִי אֲחַטֶּנָּה — *I did not bring to you, I myself would bear the loss.* (I never brought to you) any animal mangled due to my sinful negligence; but I only brought to you those mangled through (non-preventable accidents) and even so ...

מִיָּדִי תְּבַקְשֶׁנָּה — *From me you would exact it* ... (unjustly) contrary to the law.

41. וַתַּחֲלֵף אֶת מַשְׂכֻּרְתִּי — *And you changed my wage* ... which is contrary to what you say; it is you (not I) who changed my wage.

43. וְהַצֹּאן צֹאנִי — *And the flock is my flock.* Even if I changed your wage, or sent you away empty handed, I would not have been taking away anything from you since everything belongs to me; and whatever you possess is through fraud, not by right.

וְלִבְנֹתַי — *Yet to my daughters* ... and it should go to my daughters as their dowry.

NOTES

36-39. וַיִּחַר לְיַעֲקֹב וַיָּרֶב בְּלָבָן ... לֹא הֵבֵאתִי אֵלֶיךָ — *Then Jacob become angered and strove with Laban ... I did not bring to you.* Jacob is incensed that Laban accuses him of theft, given his record and past performance. He never rationalized, as did other shepherds, that he was justified in taking some animals for his personal use, nor did he ever attempt to evade compensating Laban for any negligence. Indeed, he even paid for losses caused by accidents which were non-preventable (אונס).

Jacob spoke up and said to Laban, "What is my transgression? What is my sin that you have hotly pursued me? [37] *When you rummaged through all my things, what did you find of all your household objects? Set it here before my kinsmen and your kinsmen, and let them decide between the two of us.*

[38] *"These twenty years I have been with you, your ewes and she-goats never miscarried, nor did I eat rams of your flock.* [39] *That which was mangled I never brought you — I myself would bear the loss, from me you would exact it, whether it was stolen by day or stolen by night.* [40] *This is how I was: By day scorching heat consumed me, and frost by night; my sleep drifted from my eyes.* [41] *This is my twenty years in your household: I served you fourteen years for your two daughters, and six years for your flocks; and you changed my wage a hundred times.* [42] *Had not the God of my father — the God of Abraham and the Dread of Isaac — been with me, you would surely have now sent me away empty handed; God saw my wretchedness and the toil of my hands, so He admonished you last night."*

[43] *Then Laban spoke up and said to Jacob, "The daughters are my daughters, the children are my children and the flock is my flock, and all that you see is mine. Yet to my daughters — what could I do to them this day? Or to their children whom they have borne!* [44] *So now, come, let us make a covenant, I and you, and He shall be a witness between me and you."*

[45] *Then Jacob took a stone and raised it up as a monument.* [46] *And Jacob said to his brethren, "Gather stones!" So they took stones and made a mound, and they ate there on the mound.* [47] *Laban called it Jegar-sahadutha, but Jacob called it Galeed.*

[48] *And Laban declared, "This mound is a witness between me and you today"; therefore he called its name Galeed.* [49] *And as for the Mitzpah — because he said, "May HASHEM keep watch between me and you when*

מָה אֶעֱשֶׂה לָאֵלֶּה — *What could I do to them?* Even though I could (rightfully) take away everything from you, what could I (then) do to provide for them in the future?

44. וְעַתָּה — *And now.* Considering that I do not want to harm you.

לְכָה נִכְרְתָה בְרִית — *Come, let us make a covenant* ... that you, in turn, will not harm me.

45. וַיְרִימֶהָ מַצֵּבָה — *And raised it up as a monument* ... to symbolize that the matter would stand permanently.

47. וְיַעֲקֹב קָרָא לוֹ גַּלְעֵד — *But Jacob called it Galeed.* He had not abandoned his (Hebrew) language.

48. וַיֹּאמֶר לָבָן הַגַּל הַזֶּה עֵד — *And Laban declared, "This mound is a witness."* He subordinated himself to Jacob by agreeing to call it by the Hebrew name. He declared that it be a witness of what he was about to say.

49. וְהַמִּצְפָּה — *And as for the Mitzpah* ... and let the adjoining place, Mitzpah (lit., "watchtower"), also be a witness, reminding us what will (now) be said.

אֲשֶׁר אָמַר — *Because he said.* The reason he said that the Mitzpah should also testify to his statement, was because Laban said to Jacob ...

NOTES

49. וְהַמִּצְפָּה — *And as for the Mitzpah.* The name Mitzpah is not being given now. It was an ancient name, but Laban is calling upon this *watch-place* (or tower) to keep watch over their agreement, since fortuitously the name Mitzpah connotes *watching over*, from צפה, *to observe.*

נ נִסָּתֵר אִישׁ מֵרֵעֵהוּ: אִם־תְּעַנֶּה אֶת־בְּנֹתַי וְאִם־תִּקַּח נָשִׁים עַל־בְּנֹתַי אֵין
נא אִישׁ עִמָּנוּ רְאֵה אֱלֹהִים עֵד בֵּינִי וּבֵינֶךָ: וַיֹּאמֶר לָבָן לְיַעֲקֹב הִנֵּה | הַגַּל
נב הַזֶּה וְהִנֵּה הַמַּצֵּבָה אֲשֶׁר יָרִיתִי בֵּינִי וּבֵינֶךָ: עֵד הַגַּל הַזֶּה וְעֵדָה הַמַּצֵּבָה
אִם־אָנִי לֹא־אֶעֱבֹר אֵלֶיךָ אֶת־הַגַּל הַזֶּה וְאִם־אַתָּה לֹא־תַעֲבֹר אֵלַי
נג אֶת־הַגַּל הַזֶּה וְאֶת־הַמַּצֵּבָה הַזֹּאת לְרָעָה: אֱלֹהֵי אַבְרָהָם *וֵאלֹהֵי נָחוֹר
יִשְׁפְּטוּ בֵינֵינוּ *אֱלֹהֵי אֲבִיהֶם וַיִּשָּׁבַע יַעֲקֹב בְּפַחַד אָבִיו יִצְחָק: וַיִּזְבַּח
נד יַעֲקֹב זֶבַח בָּהָר וַיִּקְרָא לְאֶחָיו לֶאֱכָל־לָחֶם וַיֹּאכְלוּ לֶחֶם וַיָּלִינוּ בָּהָר:
לב מפטיר א וַיַּשְׁכֵּם לָבָן בַּבֹּקֶר וַיְנַשֵּׁק לְבָנָיו וְלִבְנוֹתָיו וַיְבָרֶךְ אֶתְהֶם וַיֵּלֶךְ וַיָּשָׁב לָבָן
ב לִמְקֹמוֹ: וְיַעֲקֹב הָלַךְ לְדַרְכּוֹ וַיִּפְגְּעוּ־בוֹ מַלְאֲכֵי אֱלֹהִים: וַיֹּאמֶר יַעֲקֹב
ג כַּאֲשֶׁר רָאָם מַחֲנֵה אֱלֹהִים זֶה וַיִּקְרָא שֵׁם־הַמָּקוֹם הַהוּא מַחֲנָיִם:

יִצֶף ה׳ בֵּינִי וּבֵינֶךָ — *May HASHEM keep watch between me and you* ... and be our Judge and Referee.

50. רְאֵה אֱלֹהִים עֵד — *But see, God is a witness.* Behold, if you will betray me, you trespass against Him, and He will punish you, similar to, וּמָעֲלָה מַעַל בַּה׳ וְכִחֵשׁ בַּעֲמִיתוֹ, *And commit a trespass against God and deal falsely with his neighbor* (*Lev.* 5:21). As our Sages say, (if one deals falsely) *he offends God, (Who is the invisible) Witness among them.* (See *Rashi*, quoting *Sifra*, in *Lev.* 5:21.)

53. אֱלֹהֵי אֲבִיהֶם — *The god of their father.* Laban argued that (Jacob) should not refuse to accept as judge the god of Nahor together with the God of Abraham, since the god of Nahor was also the deity of Terach, who was the father of both Nahor and Abraham.

וַיִּשָּׁבַע יַעֲקֹב בְּפַחַד אָבִיו יִצְחָק — *And Jacob swore by the Dread of his father Isaac* ... for Isaac was not the son of Terach. (Jacob) swears that only the God of Isaac shall judge them if there is any betrayal.

54. וַיִּקְרָא לְאֶחָיו — *And summoned his kinsmen* ... (the kinsmen) of Laban, but there was no need to summon Laban, since he was, at that time, as a father to the House of Jacob.

NOTES

54. וַיִּקְרָא לְאֶחָיו — *And summoned his kinsmen.* It was only necessary to summon to this farewell feast those who were not part of Jacob's family. Therefore the *Sforno* interprets אֶחָיו, *his kinsmen,* to mean the kinsmen of Laban who had accompanied him. However, just as Jacob does not summon his own sons, so he does not find it necessary to summon Laban, who is still considered the head of the household.

XXXII

1. וַיְבָרֶךְ אֶתְהֶם — *And blessed them.* The phrase צֶלֶם אֱלֹהִים, *in the image of God* (1:27), is explained by the *Sforno* as meaning that man has the potential to understand God and perfect himself to the extent of reaching a level of Godliness and immortality. This power is hidden in his נֶפֶשׁ *(soul),* and when this force is released its impact is powerful. When a father blesses his children, the blessing

we are out of each other's sight. 50 *If you will ill-treat my daughters or if you*
will marry wives in addition to my daughters — though no man may be
among us — but see! God is a witness between me and you." 51 *And Laban*
said to Jacob, "Here is this mound, and here is the monument which I have
cast between me and you. 52 *This mound shall be witness and the monument*
shall be witness that I may not cross over to you past this mound, nor may
you cross over to me past this mound and this monument for evil. 53 *May the*
God of Abraham and the god of Nachor judge between us — the god of their
father." And Jacob swore by the Dread of his father Isaac. 54 *Then Jacob*
slaughtered for a feast on the mountain and summoned his kinsmen to
break bread; and they broke bread and spent the night on the mountain.

32 1 *And Laban awoke early in the morning; he kissed his sons and his*
daughters and blessed them; then Laban went and returned to his
place. 2 *Jacob went on his way, and angels of God encountered him.* 3 *Jacob*
said when he saw them, "This is a Godly camp!" So he called the name of
that place Mahanaim.

XXXII

1. וַיְבָרֵךְ אֶתְהֶם — *And blessed them.* (Our Sages) have said, "Even the blessing of a common man should not be treated lightly" (*Megillah* 15a); the Torah tells us of Laban's blessing to his daughters to teach us that a father's blessing is, without a doubt, given with all his soul, and is worthy to be accepted (effective) reflecting as it does the "image of God" within the (father) who blesses, similar to, בַּעֲבוּר תְּבָרֶכְךָ נַפְשִׁי, *That my soul may bless you* (27:4).

3. מַחֲנֵה אֱלֹהִים זֶה — *This is a Godly camp.* Without a doubt my camp, met by the camp of angels, is a camp of God, as we find, *and he called the place* אֵל בֵּית אֵל, (lit., *the God of Beth El) because there, God was revealed to him* (35:7).

מַחֲנָיִם — *Machanaim (two camps)* ... two Godly camps — one of angels, the other his (Jacob's), in keeping with the (grammatical) rule that when the plural suffix יִם is preceded by a *patach* (ַ), and the word is accented on the second to last syllable, it means *two*, e.g., פַּעֲמַיִם, *two times* (from פַּעַם); שְׁבוּעַיִם, *two weeks* (from שָׁבוּעַ); שְׁנָתַיִם, *two years* (from שָׁנָה); etc. (Similarly מַחֲנַיִם, *two camps*, from מַחֲנֶה.)

NOTES

emanates from the depth of his soul and therefore it is extremely effective. This is true whether it be an Isaac or a Laban.

3. מַחֲנֵה אֱלֹהִים זֶה ... מַחֲנָיִם – *This is a Godly camp ... Machanaim (two camps).* The statement *this is a Godly camp* does not refer to the angels' camp but to the camp of Jacob, which is deemed worthy to be met by angels. Wherever God reveals Himself, either directly or through angels, it is a *holy place,* as we see from the name Beth El (House of God) which the Torah explains by stating *because there God was revealed.* We have now established that both camps — Jacob's and the angels — are Godly, hence it is proper to call the place Machanaim — *two camps* — for both are similar in nature and character.

פרשת וישלח

ד וַיִּשְׁלַח יַעֲקֹב מַלְאָכִים לְפָנָיו אֶל־עֵשָׂו אָחִיו אַרְצָה שֵׂעִיר שְׂדֵה אֱדוֹם:
ה וַיְצַו אֹתָם לֵאמֹר כֹּה תֹאמְרוּן לַאדֹנִי לְעֵשָׂו כֹּה אָמַר עַבְדְּךָ יַעֲקֹב
ו עִם־לָבָן גַּרְתִּי וָאֵחַר עַד־עָתָּה: וַיְהִי־לִי שׁוֹר וַחֲמוֹר צֹאן וְעֶבֶד וְשִׁפְחָה
ז וָאֶשְׁלְחָה לְהַגִּיד לַאדֹנִי לִמְצֹא־חֵן בְּעֵינֶיךָ: וַיָּשֻׁבוּ הַמַּלְאָכִים אֶל־יַעֲקֹב
לֵאמֹר בָּאנוּ אֶל־אָחִיךָ אֶל־עֵשָׂו וְגַם הֹלֵךְ לִקְרָאתְךָ וְאַרְבַּע־מֵאוֹת
ח אִישׁ עִמּוֹ: וַיִּירָא יַעֲקֹב מְאֹד וַיֵּצֶר לוֹ וַיַּחַץ אֶת־הָעָם אֲשֶׁר־אִתּוֹ
ט וְאֶת־הַצֹּאן וְאֶת־הַבָּקָר וְהַגְּמַלִּים לִשְׁנֵי מַחֲנוֹת: וַיֹּאמֶר אִם־יָבוֹא עֵשָׂו
י אֶל־הַמַּחֲנֶה הָאַחַת וְהִכָּהוּ וְהָיָה הַמַּחֲנֶה הַנִּשְׁאָר לִפְלֵיטָה: וַיֹּאמֶר יַעֲקֹב
אֱלֹהֵי אָבִי אַבְרָהָם וֵאלֹהֵי אָבִי יִצְחָק יהוה הָאֹמֵר אֵלַי שׁוּב לְאַרְצְךָ
יא וּלְמוֹלַדְתְּךָ וְאֵיטִיבָה עִמָּךְ: קָטֹנְתִּי מִכֹּל הַחֲסָדִים וּמִכָּל־הָאֱמֶת אֲשֶׁר
עָשִׂיתָ אֶת־עַבְדֶּךָ כִּי בְמַקְלִי עָבַרְתִּי אֶת־הַיַּרְדֵּן הַזֶּה וְעַתָּה הָיִיתִי לִשְׁנֵי
יב מַחֲנוֹת: הַצִּילֵנִי נָא מִיַּד אָחִי מִיַּד עֵשָׂו כִּי־יָרֵא אָנֹכִי אֹתוֹ פֶּן־יָבוֹא
יג וְהִכַּנִי אֵם עַל־בָּנִים: וְאַתָּה אָמַרְתָּ הֵיטֵב אֵיטִיב עִמָּךְ וְשַׂמְתִּי אֶת־זַרְעֲךָ

4. וַיִּשְׁלַח יַעֲקֹב מַלְאָכִים — *And Jacob sent angels* ... to learn his brother's plans and his intentions.

אַרְצָה שֵׂעִיר שְׂדֵה אֱדוֹם — *To the land of Seir, the field of Edom* ... to the region called Seir and to the locale called Edom where Esau dwelled, for at that time Esau had as yet not conquered the entire area from the Hori who were the inhabitants of the land.

5. וָאֵחַר עַד עָתָּה — *And have lingered until now.* That is why I did not come to pay my respects (lit., "bow down") sooner.

6. לִמְצֹא חֵן בְּעֵינֶיךָ — *To gain favor in your eyes.* I am confident that you will be pleased to hear of my wealth and honored position, and that I will find favor by telling you this.

7. וְגַם הֹלֵךְ לִקְרָאתְךָ — *And moreover he is heading toward you.* Not only was he not impressed or pleased when we told him of your good fortune, but he is also coming toward you.

וְאַרְבַּע מֵאוֹת אִישׁ עִמּוֹ — *And four hundred men are with him* ... and his intent must be to attack you as we find, וַיֵּצֵא אֱדוֹם לִקְרָאתוֹ בְּעַם כָּבֵד, *and Edom came out against him with many people (Numbers* 20:20).

9. וְהָיָה הַמַּחֲנֶה הַנִּשְׁאָר לִפְלֵיטָה — *Then the camp which is left will survive.* While (the enemy) is descending upon the first camp to pillage, the second will escape with their weapons — or at least will be able to flee.

10. אֱלֹהֵי אָבִי אַבְרָהָם — *O God of my father Abraham.* He began (his prayer) by reciting praises of God's kindness, and he also mentions the merit of his fathers (Abraham and

NOTES

4. אַרְצָה שֵׂעִיר שְׂדֵה אֱדוֹם — *To the land of Seir, the field of Edom.* The expression *the land of Seir, the field of Edom,* is not redundant. Although later on the two are the same, at this particular time the Hori were still in control of Seir, while Esau only ruled over a small section of that land, which was called Edom.

7. וְאַרְבַּע מֵאוֹת אִישׁ עִמּוֹ — *And four hundred men are with him.* It is interesting that the *Sforno* should bring as proof to his interpretation an incident that happened so many years later when Moses was leading Israel close by the land of Edom. He feels that Edom did not change his practice of confronting and attacking his brother — i.e., Esau did not change his spots.

10. אֱלֹהֵי אָבִי אַבְרָהָם — *O God of my father Abraham.* Jacob petitioned God to help him in this difficult hour. The order of prayer ordained by the

PARASHAS VAYISHLACH

4 Then Jacob sent angels ahead of him to Esau his brother to the land of
Seir, the field of Edom. 5 He charged them, saying: "Thus shall you say,
'To my lord, to Esau, so said your servant Jacob: I have sojourned with
Laban and have lingered until now. 6 I have acquired oxen and donkeys,
flocks, servants, and maidservants and I am sending to tell my lord to find
favor in your eyes.' "
7 The angels returned to Jacob, saying, "We came to your brother, to Esau;
moreover, he is heading toward you, and four hundred men are with him."
8 Jacob became very frightened, and it distressed him. So he divided the
people with him, and the cattle, herds, and camels, into two camps. 9 For he
said, "If Esau comes to the one camp and strikes it down, then the remaining
camp shall survive." 10 Then Jacob said, "God of my father Abraham and
God of my father Isaac; HASHEM Who said to me, 'Return to your land and
to your relatives and I will do good with you' — 11 I have been diminished
by all the kindnesses and by all the truth that You have done Your servant;
for with my staff I crossed this Jordan and now I have become two camps.
12 Rescue me, please, from the hand of my brother, from the hand of Esau,
for I fear him lest he come and strike me down, mother and children. 13 And
You had said, 'I will surely do good with you and I will make your offspring

---

Isaac) similar to the order of prayer instituted by the Men of the Great Assembly at the beginning of *Shemoneh Esrei* (the *Amidah*).

11. קָטֹנְתִּי מִכֹּל הַחֲסָדִים וּמִכָּל הָאֱמֶת — *I have been diminished by all the kindnesses and by all the truth.* I was not worthy to be the recipient of all the kindness (shown to me), nor of the good fortune which is mine. In truth, it is because of the merit of my fathers, and because of them You conducted Yourself toward me beyond the requirement of the law (i.e., with *chesed* — undeserved blessing). Now, therefore, do I ask that You save me in the same manner, as it is said, כְּגֹדֶל חַסְדֶּךָ וְכַאֲשֶׁר נָשָׂאתָה לָעָם הַזֶּה, *(Pardon the iniquity of this people) according to the greatness of Your loving-kindness, and as You have forgiven this people, etc. (Numbers* 14:19).

12. וְהִכַּנִי אֵם עַל בָּנִים — *And strike me down, mother and children.* By killing the mother and the children he will smite *me*, even if I personally escape.

13. וְאַתָּה אָמַרְתָּ הֵיטֵב אֵיטִיב עִמָּךְ — *And You have said, 'I will surely do good with you'* . . . and if this comes to pass it will negate the promise to do good with me, as well as the promise of . . .

וְשַׂמְתִּי אֶת זַרְעֲךָ — *And I will make your offspring.* For if my family is exterminated, this will negate the promise made to multiply my offspring; and even if I am unworthy, save

NOTES

Men of the Great Assembly is to invoke the merits of our ancestors, mention the *chesed* of the Almighty, and only then to submit our requests. This order is followed by our father Jacob and could well be the source for the order of our *tefillos*.

11. קָטֹנְתִּי מִכֹּל הַחֲסָדִים וּמִכָּל הָאֱמֶת — *I have been diminished by all the kindnesses and by all the truth.* What God has done for Jacob may be undeserved, hence it is called *chesed*, but what is done in the merit of his fathers is *truth*, and is justified. What he asked for now was to be saved from the clutches of Esau even if it would be but an act of mercy on the part of the Almighty, for since this attribute of mercy was already demonstrated in the past, Jacob felt justified in asking for it once again. To prove that this is proper, the *Sforno* quotes the verse in *Numbers*.

שני יד כְּחוֹל הַיָּם אֲשֶׁר לֹא־יִסָּפֵר מֵרֹב: וַיָּלֶן שָׁם בַּלַּיְלָה הַהוּא וַיִּקַּח מִן־הַבָּא
טו בְיָדוֹ מִנְחָה לְעֵשָׂו אָחִיו: עִזִּים מָאתַיִם וּתְיָשִׁים עֶשְׂרִים רְחֵלִים מָאתַיִם
טז וְאֵילִים עֶשְׂרִים: גְּמַלִּים מֵינִיקוֹת וּבְנֵיהֶם שְׁלֹשִׁים פָּרוֹת אַרְבָּעִים וּפָרִים
יז עֲשָׂרָה אֲתֹנֹת עֶשְׂרִים וַעְיָרִם עֲשָׂרָה: וַיִּתֵּן בְּיַד־עֲבָדָיו עֵדֶר עֵדֶר לְבַדּוֹ
יח וַיֹּאמֶר אֶל־עֲבָדָיו עִבְרוּ לְפָנַי וְרֶוַח תָּשִׂימוּ בֵּין עֵדֶר וּבֵין עֵדֶר: וַיְצַו אֶת־
הָרִאשׁוֹן לֵאמֹר כִּי יִפְגָשְׁךָ עֵשָׂו אָחִי וּשְׁאֵלְךָ לֵאמֹר לְמִי־אַתָּה וְאָנָה
יט תֵלֵךְ וּלְמִי אֵלֶּה לְפָנֶיךָ: וְאָמַרְתָּ לְעַבְדְּךָ לְיַעֲקֹב מִנְחָה הִוא שְׁלוּחָה
כ לַאדֹנִי לְעֵשָׂו וְהִנֵּה גַם־הוּא אַחֲרֵינוּ: וַיְצַו גַּם אֶת־הַשֵּׁנִי גַּם אֶת־הַשְּׁלִישִׁי
גַּם אֶת־כָּל־הַהֹלְכִים אַחֲרֵי הָעֲדָרִים לֵאמֹר כַּדָּבָר הַזֶּה תְּדַבְּרוּן אֶל־
כא עֵשָׂו בְּמֹצַאֲכֶם אֹתוֹ: וַאֲמַרְתֶּם גַּם הִנֵּה עַבְדְּךָ יַעֲקֹב אַחֲרֵינוּ כִּי־
אָמַר אֲכַפְּרָה פָנָיו בַּמִּנְחָה הַהֹלֶכֶת לְפָנָי וְאַחֲרֵי־כֵן אֶרְאֶה פָנָיו אוּלַי
כב יִשָּׂא פָנָי: וַתַּעֲבֹר הַמִּנְחָה עַל־פָּנָיו וְהוּא לָן בַּלַּיְלָה־הַהוּא בַּמַּחֲנֶה:
כג וַיָּקָם | בַּלַּיְלָה הוּא וַיִּקַּח אֶת־שְׁתֵּי נָשָׁיו וְאֶת־שְׁתֵּי שִׁפְחֹתָיו וְאֶת־
כד אַחַד עָשָׂר יְלָדָיו וַיַּעֲבֹר אֵת מַעֲבַר יַבֹּק: וַיִּקָּחֵם וַיַּעֲבִרֵם אֶת־הַנָּחַל
כה וַיַּעֲבֵר אֶת־אֲשֶׁר־לוֹ: וַיִּוָּתֵר יַעֲקֹב לְבַדּוֹ וַיֵּאָבֵק אִישׁ עִמּוֹ עַד עֲלוֹת

---

me for the sake of Your Name, as we find, אִם עֲוֹנֵינוּ עָנוּ בָנוּ ה׳ עֲשֵׂה לְמַעַן שְׁמֶךָ, *Though our iniquities testify against us, HASHEM, do for Your Name's sake (Jeremiah* 14:7).

17. עֵדֶר עֵדֶר לְבַדּוֹ — *Each drove separately* . . . so that (Esau) might see that there was the proper proportion of males and females in each species so that they may yield maximum productivity, as he says, *"Take my blessing"* (33:11), for the gift was so constituted that there would surely be a blessing (of natural increase).

וְרֶוַח תָּשִׂימוּ בֵּין עֵדֶר וּבֵין עֵדֶר — *And leave a space between drove and drove* . . . so that the animals should not wander from drove to drove, preventing the observer from appreciating how wisely the offering was selected and the blessing it would bring.

19. וְאָמַרְתָּ לְעַבְדְּךָ לְיַעֲקֹב — *You shall say, 'They are your servant Jacob's.'* He instructed the messenger not to acknowledge that he recognizes Esau nor that he is being sent to him (en route), lest Esau think that Jacob is aware of his approach and is sending him this gift due to fear. Rather the messenger should act as though he is being sent to the land of Seir, unaware [that the man marching on Jacob's camp] is Esau.

20. כַּדָּבָר הַזֶּה תְּדַבְּרוּן אֶל עֵשָׂו — *In this manner shall you speak to Esau.* He instructed each messenger what to say to Esau. They were to tell him that all these droves were Jacob's, sent as a gift to his older brother.

NOTES

17. עֵדֶר עֵדֶר לְבַדּוֹ — *Each drove separately.* When Jacob urged Esau to accept his offering he did not say, *"Take my gift,"* rather, *"my blessing,"* which indicates the nature and ultimate purpose of the gift. In the case of animals — goats, sheep and camels — blessing is measured by the growth of the flocks and herds through reproduction.

19. וְאָמַרְתָּ לְעַבְדְּךָ לְיַעֲקֹב — *You shall say, 'They are your servant Jacob's.'* Although Jacob was prepared to appease Esau by means of this generous gift he wisely did not want him to believe that he was afraid of him, for a perception of weakness would have increased Jacob's vulnerability. That is why Jacob preferred that Esau believe the gift was being sent to him in his homeland as a gesture of friendship, motivated by a spirit of brotherhood, and not due to fear of an approaching army — which would transform the gift into a bribe.

20. כַּדָּבָר הַזֶּה תְּדַבְּרוּן אֶל עֵשָׂו — *In this manner shall you speak to Esau.* Jacob acknowledges that Esau was the *bechor*, the firstborn son, even though the birthright was sold to him. That is

like the sand of the sea which is too numerous to count.' "
14 *He spent the night there, then he took, from that which had come in his*
hand, a tribute to Esau his brother: 15 *Two hundred she-goats and twenty*
he-goats; two hundred ewes and twenty rams; 16 *thirty nursing camels with*
their colts; forty cows and ten bulls; twenty she-donkeys and ten he-
donkeys. 17 *He put in his servants' charge each drove separately and said*
to his servants, "Pass on ahead of me and leave a space between drove and
drove." 18 *He instructed the first one, saying, "When my brother Esau meets*
you and asks you, saying, 'Whose are you, where are you going, and whose
are these that are before you?' — 19 *You shall say, 'Your servant Jacob's. It*
is a tribute sent to my lord, to Esau, and behold he himself is behind us.' "
20 *He similarly instructed the second, also the third, as well as all who*
followed the droves, saying, "In this manner shall you speak to Esau when
you find him. 21 *And you shall say, 'Moreover — behold your servant Jacob*
is behind us.' " (For he said, "I will appease him with the tribute that
precedes me, and afterwards I will face him; perhaps he will forgive me.")
22 *So the tribute passed on before him while he spent that night in the camp.*
23 *But he got up that night and took his two wives, his two handmaids, and*
his eleven sons and crossed the ford of the Jabbok. 24 *And when he took them*
and had them cross over the stream, he sent over all his possessions.
25 *Jacob was left alone and a man wrestled with him until the break of*

---

21. וַאֲמַרְתֶּם גַּם הִנֵּה עַבְדְּךָ יַעֲקֹב אַחֲרֵינוּ — *And you shall say, 'Moreover, behold, your servant Jacob is behind us.'* Each messenger was told to give a specific answer, but all were told to tell Esau that Jacob was following them. In this manner Esau would find their answers consistent, namely, that Jacob was coming after them to Seir to greet his brother.

כִּי אָמַר אֲכַפְּרָה פָנָיו בַּמִּנְחָה — *For he said, "I will appease him with the tribute."* He instructed his servants to say these words in order to lessen Esau's anger through these words of submission coupled with the tribute.

אֶרְאֶה פָנָיו — *I will face him.* (This is) the accepted manner of appearing before lords, as we find, יֵרָאֶה כָּל זְכוּרְךָ אֶת פְּנֵי הָאָדֹן, *All your males shall appear before the Lord* (*Exodus* 34:23); (also) וְלֹא יֵרָאוּ פָנַי רֵיקָם, *And none shall appear before Me empty-handed* (ibid. 23:15). So (Jacob) says to Esau, *I have seen your face as one sees the face of the Divine* (33:10). It is the custom to greet one's superiors by appearing before them personally bearing gifts.

22. וַתַּעֲבֹר הַמִּנְחָה עַל פָּנָיו — *So the tribute passed before him . . .* to check and make sure that all was in the proper order, so as to insure the desired end.

24. וַיַּעֲבֵר אֶת אֲשֶׁר לוֹ — *And he sent over all his possessions.* He instructed everyone to precede him in crossing over the ford, as we find, וַיַּעֲבוֹר אֶת הַכּוּשִׁי, *And went ahead of the Cushite* (*II Samuel* 18:23).

25. וַיִּוָּתֵר יַעֲקֹב לְבַדּוֹ — *And Jacob was left alone.* He was the last to leave the camp in order to direct everyone to take along all his possessions so that nothing be left behind.

NOTES

why Jacob referred to Esau as אֲדֹנִי, *my lord* (33:8), and to himself as עַבְדְּךָ, *your servant* (33:6). At this moment, Jacob was willing to forgo his own claim to the birthright, so as to save his family.

21. כִּי אָמַר אֲכַפְּרָה פָנָיו בַּמִּנְחָה — *For he said, "I will appease him with the tribute."* Whereas others interpret the phrase, *For he said . . .*, as an *unspoken* explanation of Jacob's motives, the *Sforno* is of the opinion that these words were part of the message; they were to tell Esau that Jacob said, "I will appease him," for this would have a desired effect upon Esau and impress upon him Jacob's sincerity.

כו הַשָּׁחַר: וַיַּרְא כִּי לֹא יָכֹל לוֹ וַיִּגַּע בְּכַף־יְרֵכוֹ וַתֵּקַע כַּף־יֶרֶךְ יַעֲקֹב בְּהֵאָבְקוֹ
כז עִמּוֹ: וַיֹּאמֶר שַׁלְּחֵנִי כִּי עָלָה הַשָּׁחַר וַיֹּאמֶר לֹא אֲשַׁלֵּחֲךָ כִּי אִם־בֵּרַכְתָּנִי:
כח-כט וַיֹּאמֶר אֵלָיו מַה־שְּׁמֶךָ וַיֹּאמֶר יַעֲקֹב: וַיֹּאמֶר לֹא יַעֲקֹב יֵאָמֵר עוֹד שִׁמְךָ
ל כִּי אִם־יִשְׂרָאֵל כִּי־שָׂרִיתָ עִם־אֱלֹהִים וְעִם־אֲנָשִׁים וַתּוּכָל: וַיִּשְׁאַל יַעֲקֹב
וַיֹּאמֶר הַגִּידָה־נָּא שְׁמֶךָ וַיֹּאמֶר לָמָּה זֶּה תִּשְׁאַל לִשְׁמִי וַיְבָרֶךְ אֹתוֹ
שלישי לא שָׁם: וַיִּקְרָא יַעֲקֹב שֵׁם הַמָּקוֹם פְּנִיאֵל כִּי־רָאִיתִי אֱלֹהִים פָּנִים אֶל־פָּנִים
לב וַתִּנָּצֵל נַפְשִׁי: וַיִּזְרַח־לוֹ הַשֶּׁמֶשׁ כַּאֲשֶׁר עָבַר אֶת־פְּנוּאֵל וְהוּא צֹלֵעַ
לג עַל־יְרֵכוֹ: עַל־כֵּן לֹא־יֹאכְלוּ בְנֵי־יִשְׂרָאֵל אֶת־גִּיד הַנָּשֶׁה אֲשֶׁר עַל־כַּף
לג א הַיָּרֵךְ עַד הַיּוֹם הַזֶּה כִּי נָגַע בְּכַף־יֶרֶךְ יַעֲקֹב בְּגִיד הַנָּשֶׁה: וַיִּשָּׂא יַעֲקֹב עֵינָיו
וַיַּרְא וְהִנֵּה עֵשָׂו בָּא וְעִמּוֹ אַרְבַּע מֵאוֹת אִישׁ וַיַּחַץ אֶת־הַיְלָדִים עַל־לֵאָה

וַיֵּאָבֵק אִישׁ עִמּוֹ — *And there wrestled a man with him.* Without a doubt this was the work of an angel sent by God, as we find, יְרֵה וַיּוֹר, *"Shoot!" And he shot* (*II Kings* 13:17). (The purpose of this encounter) was to demonstrate that God will save Jacob and his children (in all their confrontations) with Esau and even though there will be material loss at times, ultimately there will be salvation and blessing, with mastery both in heaven above and here on earth.

26. לֹא יָכֹל לוֹ — *He perceived he could not overcome him . . .* because Jacob cleaved fully and constantly to God in thought and speech.

וַיִּגַּע — *He touched.* (The angel) told him the sins which the future leaders of Israel would commit. His (resultant) concern stopped his concentration on God, enabling the angel to touch the hollow of his thigh as they wrestled.

27. לֹא אֲשַׁלֵּחֲךָ — *I will not let you go . . .* for "the righteous are greater than the angels" (*Sanhedrin* 92a).

29. לֹא יַעֲקֹב יֵאָמֵר עוֹד שִׁמְךָ — *No longer will it be said that your name is Jacob . . .* at the "end of days." You will survive all the nations and therefore the significance of the name "Jacob" will be fulfilled since it implies existence "at the end." Hence the name Jacob is no longer necessary to indicate that you will be there at the "end" of all the nations.

כִּי אִם יִשְׂרָאֵל כִּי שָׂרִיתָ — *But Israel, for you have striven.* You will then be called Israel to show that "you have striven with the Divine and man," as we find, יִפְקֹד ה׳ עַל צְבָא הַמָּרוֹם בַּמָּרוֹם וְעַל מַלְכֵי הָאֲדָמָה עַל הָאֲדָמָה, *HASHEM will punish the host of the high heaven, on high, and the kings of the earth upon the earth* (*Isaiah* 24:21).

NOTES

25. וַיֵּאָבֵק אִישׁ עִמּוֹ — *And there wrestled a man with him.* (a) Even though the word אִישׁ, *man,* is used, it refers to an angel sent by God. However, if so, what is God's purpose? The *Sforno* explains that this encounter is symbolic of the constant conflict between the forces of Israel and Esau, which will harm and damage Israel over the centuries, but in the end Israel will prevail, not only here on earth but in heaven above. In a mystical manner, the representatives of every nation contend with each other in heaven and the outcome above affects the destiny of these nations on earth. This explains the expression used later — *you have striven with the Divine and man,* the phrase *God* referring to שָׂרוֹ שֶׁל עֵשָׂו, *the heavenly lord of Esau.* This concept is alluded to by the *Sforno* in his commentary on verse 29 when he quotes *Isaiah* 24:21.

(b) The verse from *II Kings* 13:17 cited by the *Sforno* speaks of Elisha commanding King Yoash to shoot an arrow through the window, while the prophet rests his hand on the hand of the king. The arrow is called "the arrow of salvation." From this episode proof is being brought that a simple, prosaic act can have profound historic meaning. And so here, the man (angel) who wrestled with Jacob is symbolic of significant truths regarding Israel and Esau.

dawn. [26] *When he perceived that he could not overcome him, he struck the socket of his hip; so Jacob's hip-socket was dislocated as he wrestled with him.* [27] *Then he said, "Let me go, for dawn has broken."*

And he said, "I will not let you go unless you bless me."

[28] *He said to him, "What is your name?"*

He replied, "Jacob."

[29] *He said, "No longer will it be said that your name is Jacob, but Israel, for you have striven with the Divine and with man and have overcome."*

[30] *Then Jacob inquired, and he said, "Divulge, if you please, your name."*

And he said, "Why then do you inquire of my name?" And he blessed him there.

[31] *So Jacob called the name of the place Peniel — "For I have seen the Divine face to face, yet my life was spared."* [32] *The sun rose for him as he passed Penuel and he was limping on his hip.* [33] *Therefore the Children of Israel are not to eat the displaced sinew on the hip-socket to this day, because he struck Jacob's hip-socket on the displaced sinew.*

33 [1] *Jacob raised his eyes and saw — behold, Esau was coming, and with him were four hundred men — so he divided the children among*

30. הַגִּידָה נָּא שְׁמֶךָ — *Tell me, if you please, your name* . . . which indicates your essence and your mission, that I might know why you were sent to confront me, so I will be able to repent and pray (to rectify the sin which caused you to come and confront me).

לָמָּה זֶּה תִּשְׁאַל לִשְׁמִי — *Why then do you inquire of My name?* Our spiritual essence, clothed in human form, cannot be defined in human terminology, as it says, וְהוּא פֶלִאי, *It is hidden* (*Judges* 13:18), and as for the mission, that is according to the will of God.

32. וַיִּזְרַח לוֹ הַשֶּׁמֶשׁ כַּאֲשֶׁר עָבַר אֶת פְּנוּאֵל וְהוּא צֹלֵעַ — *And the sun rose upon him after he passed over Penuel and he limped.* After he passed Penuel limping, the sun rose and its rays healed him, as it will come to pass in the future, as it says, וְזָרְחָה לָכֶם יִרְאֵי שְׁמִי שֶׁמֶשׁ צְדָקָה וּמַרְפֵּא בִּכְנָפֶיהָ, *But to you who fear My name, the sun of righteousness will rise with healing in its wings* (*Malachi* 3:20).

33. עַל כֵּן לֹא יֹאכְלוּ בְנֵי יִשְׂרָאֵל — *Therefore the Children of Israel eat not* . . . to demonstrate that the injury inflicted on the hollow of his thigh is unessential to us.

XXXIII

1. וְעִמּוֹ אַרְבַּע מֵאוֹת אִישׁ — *Accompanied by four hundred men.* The gift had not appeased him.

NOTES

26. לֹא יָכֹל לוֹ — *He perceived he could not overcome him.* The *Sforno* uses the expression פָּסַק הַדִּבּוּק, *his cleaving to God was severed.* Since Jacob's strength was derived from his connection to the Almighty "in thought and speech," when this link was cut, Jacob was vulnerable. We find a similar situation with David and the Angel of Death (*Shabbos* 30b). As long as David was immersed in Torah study the Angel of Death had no power over him; once David paused in his study the Angel of Death was able to conquer him.

30. הַגִּידָה נָּא שְׁמֶךָ — *Tell me, if you please, your name.* Jacob asked the angel to reveal *his name,* which means his mission, for then he would be able to understand why God had sent this adversary. He was not simply curious. Only by knowing what his transgression was would he be able to do *teshuvah,* to repent.

33. עַל כֵּן לֹא יֹאכְלוּ בְנֵי יִשְׂרָאֵל — *Therefore the Children of Israel eat not.* The prohibition to eat the גִּיד הַנָּשֶׁה, *the sinew of the thigh-vein,* is not in memory of this event, but to demonstrate for all time that the damage inflicted upon Jacob by the angel is of no account to us and we eschew it completely to indicate that it is of no importance to us.

ב וְעַל־רָחֵל וְעַל שְׁתֵּי הַשְּׁפָחוֹת: וַיָּשֶׂם אֶת־הַשְּׁפָחוֹת וְאֶת־יַלְדֵיהֶן רִאשֹׁנָה
ג וְאֶת־לֵאָה וִילָדֶיהָ אַחֲרֹנִים וְאֶת־רָחֵל וְאֶת־יוֹסֵף אַחֲרֹנִים: וְהוּא עָבַר
ד לִפְנֵיהֶם וַיִּשְׁתַּחוּ אַרְצָה שֶׁבַע פְּעָמִים עַד־גִּשְׁתּוֹ עַד־אָחִיו: וַיָּרָץ עֵשָׂו
ה לִקְרָאתוֹ וַיְחַבְּקֵהוּ וַיִּפֹּל עַל־צַוָּארָו *וַיִּשָּׁקֵהוּ וַיִּבְכּוּ: וַיִּשָּׂא אֶת־עֵינָיו וַיַּרְא
אֶת־הַנָּשִׁים וְאֶת־הַיְלָדִים וַיֹּאמֶר מִי־אֵלֶּה לָּךְ וַיֹּאמַר הַיְלָדִים אֲשֶׁר־חָנַן
ו־ז אֱלֹהִים אֶת־עַבְדֶּךָ: *וַתִּגַּשְׁןָ הַשְּׁפָחוֹת הֵנָּה וְיַלְדֵיהֶן וַתִּשְׁתַּחֲוֶיןָ: וַתִּגַּשׁ
ח גַּם־לֵאָה וִילָדֶיהָ וַיִּשְׁתַּחֲווּ וְאַחַר נִגַּשׁ יוֹסֵף וְרָחֵל וַיִּשְׁתַּחֲווּ: וַיֹּאמֶר מִי לְךָ
ט כָּל־הַמַּחֲנֶה הַזֶּה אֲשֶׁר פָּגָשְׁתִּי וַיֹּאמֶר לִמְצֹא־חֵן בְּעֵינֵי אֲדֹנִי: וַיֹּאמֶר עֵשָׂו
י יֶשׁ־לִי רָב אָחִי יְהִי לְךָ אֲשֶׁר־לָךְ: וַיֹּאמֶר יַעֲקֹב אַל־נָא אִם־נָא מָצָאתִי
חֵן בְּעֵינֶיךָ וְלָקַחְתָּ מִנְחָתִי מִיָּדִי כִּי עַל־כֵּן רָאִיתִי פָנֶיךָ כִּרְאֹת פְּנֵי אֱלֹהִים
יא וַתִּרְצֵנִי: קַח־נָא אֶת־בִּרְכָתִי אֲשֶׁר הֻבָאת לָךְ כִּי־חַנַּנִי אֱלֹהִים וְכִי יֶשׁ־
יב־יג לִי־כֹל וַיִּפְצַר־בּוֹ וַיִּקָּח: וַיֹּאמֶר נִסְעָה וְנֵלֵכָה וְאֵלְכָה לְנֶגְדֶּךָ: וַיֹּאמֶר אֵלָיו
אֲדֹנִי יֹדֵעַ כִּי־הַיְלָדִים רַכִּים וְהַצֹּאן וְהַבָּקָר עָלוֹת עָלָי וּדְפָקוּם יוֹם אֶחָד

* נקוד על וישקהו

רביעי

4. וַיָּרָץ עֵשָׂו לִקְרָאתוֹ — *Esau ran toward him.* He quickly changed his mind due to Jacob's obeisances. This (episode) reflects our relationship with Esau in exile, who feels, "*Who shall bring me down to the ground?*" (see *Obadiah* 1:3). It teaches us that we will be saved from the sword of (Esau's) pride through submission and gifts, as our Sages tell us regarding Achiyah Hashiloni who "cursed" Israel, comparing them to a reed (*Taanis* 20a) which bends in the wind. Had the zealots (*biryoni*) guarding the city followed this policy in the time of the Second Temple, our Holy Temple would not have been destroyed, as Rabban Yochanan ben Zakkai testifies, when he says, בִּרְיוֹנֵי דְאִית בָּן לָא שַׁבְקִינָן, *The biryoni among us did not let me (Gittin* 56b).

5. מִי אֵלֶּה לָּךְ — *Who are these to you?* He asked: "Are they your children, your servants, or members of your household?"

8. מִי לְךָ כָּל הַמַּחֲנֶה — *What did you intend by that whole camp?* The camp that said to me, "*It is a gift sent to my lord*" (32:19), was it meant as a mark of honor, or as an act of kindness thinking that I might be in need of it?

9. יֶשׁ לִי רָב — *I have plenty . . .* and need naught.

אָחִי יְהִי לְךָ אֲשֶׁר לָךְ — *My brother, let what you have remain yours.* Since you are my brother, you need not honor me with this gift.

10. כִּרְאֹת פְּנֵי אֱלֹהִים — *Like seeing the face of a Divine being.* (Accept it) because it is customary to bring a tribute to a lord (an honored man), as it is written, וְלֹא יֵרָאוּ פָנַי רֵיקָם, *And do not appear before Me empty-handed (Exodus* 23:15).

NOTES

XXXIII

4. וַיָּרָץ עֵשָׂו לִקְרָאתוֹ — *Esau ran toward him.* Although Esau's original intention was to attack his brother, Jacob's submission and gift altered Esau's plans and appeased him. The *Sforno*, citing various selections from the Talmud, interprets this episode as a model lesson for the Jewish people in exile. Although courage and a willingness to do battle is praiseworthy, it is only so in the proper time and circumstances. In general, Israel in exile among the nations will find far greater security if like a reed she will bend with the wind and resist false heroics, which will in most cases accomplish nothing. The "curse" of Achiyah was in reality a blessing, and Rabban Yochanan ben Zakkai accomplished far more with his strategy than the *biryoni* did with theirs. He was able to salvage Yavneh and its Academy, and would perhaps have saved the Temple as well if the *biryoni* had not thwarted his policy of moderation and conciliation.

9. אָחִי יְהִי לְךָ אֲשֶׁר לָךְ — *My brother, let what you have remain yours.* The *Sforno* connects the word

Leah, Rachel, and the two handmaids. 2 *He put the handmaids and their*
children first, Leah and her children next, and Rachel and Joseph last.
3 *Then he himself went on ahead of them and bowed earthward seven times*
until he reached his brother.

4 *Esau ran toward him, embraced him, fell upon his neck, and kissed him;*
then they wept. 5 *He raised his eyes and saw the women and children, and*
he asked, "Who are these to you?"

He answered, "The children whom God has graciously given your servant."

6 *Then the handmaids came forward — they and their children — and*
they bowed down. 7 *Leah, too, came forward with her children and they*
bowed down; and afterwards, Joseph and Rachel came forward and bowed down.

8 *And he asked, "What did you intend by that whole camp that I met?"*
He answered, "To gain favor in my lord's eyes."

9 *Esau said, "I have plenty. My brother, let what you have remain yours."*

10 *But Jacob said, "No, I beg of you! If I have now found favor in your eyes,*
then accept my tribute from me, inasmuch as I have seen your face, which
is like seeing the face of a Divine being, and you were appeased by me.
11 *Please accept my gift which was brought to you, inasmuch as God has*
been gracious to me and inasmuch as I have everything." He urged him, and
he accepted.

12 *And he said, "Travel on and let us go — I will proceed alongside you."*

13 *But he said to him, "My lord knows that the children are tender, and the*
nursing flocks and cattle are upon me; if they will be driven hard for a single

---

וַתִּרְצֵנִי — *And you were appeased by me.* For you received me graciously, similar to, הֲיִרְצְךָ אוֹ הֲיִשָּׂא פָנֶיךָ, *Will he be pleased with you, or will he forgive you? (Malachi* 1:8). And for this reason, also, it is proper that I greet you with a gift.

11. וַיִּפְצַר בּוֹ — *He urged him* . . . to accept it, (knowing that) bribery blinds (the recipient).

וַיִּקָּח — *And he accepted.* The reverse of Elisha, as it says, וַיִּפְצַר בּוֹ לָקַחַת, וַיְמָאֵן, *He urged him to take it, but he refused (II Kings* 5:16).

12. נִסְעָה וְנֵלֵכָה — *Travel on, and let us go.* (Let us go) to Seir, as those who brought the gift said, *'Moreover, behold your servant Jacob is behind us'* (32:21).

13. כִּי הַיְלָדִים רַכִּים וְהַצֹּאן וְהַבָּקָר עָלוֹת עָלָי — *The children are tender and the nursing flocks and herds are upon me.* They are my responsibility.

וּדְפָקוּם — *If they will be driven hard* . . . in your honor, not to delay you on the road.

NOTES

אָחִי, *my brother*, with the latter part of the verse rather than the first. It is not meant to be a title or salutation, it is rather an explanation: "Since we are brothers there is no need for you to honor me with such an extravagant gift."

11. וַיִּפְצַר בּוֹ — *He urged him.* Jacob was not deterred by Esau's protestations. He knew full well that Esau really wanted to keep the gift, and he also appreciated that it would, like any bribe, reduce his enmity and appease him.

12. נִסְעָה וְנֵלֵכָה — *Travel on, and let us go.* In 32:21 the *Sforno* explained that Jacob told the messengers to imply to Esau that the gift was being sent to Esau *in Seir*, and Jacob would follow them there. Hence, Esau now wanted to hold him to his word.

13. עָלָי — *Are upon me.* The word עָלָי, *are upon me*, is linked by the *Sforno* to both the children and the animals. They are *my* responsibility and weigh heavily upon me, hence I must be prudent and ask you to be understanding.

יד וָמֵתוּ כָּל־הַצֹּאן׃ יַעֲבָר־נָא אֲדֹנִי לִפְנֵי עַבְדּוֹ וַאֲנִי אֶתְנָהֲלָה לְאִטִּי לְרֶגֶל
הַמְּלָאכָה אֲשֶׁר־לְפָנַי וּלְרֶגֶל הַיְלָדִים עַד אֲשֶׁר־אָבֹא אֶל־אֲדֹנִי שֵׂעִירָה׃
טו וַיֹּאמֶר עֵשָׂו אַצִּיגָה־נָּא עִמְּךָ מִן־הָעָם אֲשֶׁר אִתִּי וַיֹּאמֶר לָמָּה זֶּה
טז-יז אֶמְצָא־חֵן בְּעֵינֵי אֲדֹנִי׃ וַיָּשָׁב בַּיּוֹם הַהוּא עֵשָׂו לְדַרְכּוֹ שֵׂעִירָה׃ וְיַעֲקֹב
נָסַע סֻכֹּתָה וַיִּבֶן לוֹ בָּיִת וּלְמִקְנֵהוּ עָשָׂה סֻכֹּת עַל־כֵּן קָרָא שֵׁם־הַמָּקוֹם
יח סֻכּוֹת׃ וַיָּבֹא יַעֲקֹב שָׁלֵם עִיר שְׁכֶם אֲשֶׁר בְּאֶרֶץ כְּנַעַן
יט בְּבֹאוֹ מִפַּדַּן אֲרָם וַיִּחַן אֶת־פְּנֵי הָעִיר׃ וַיִּקֶן אֶת־חֶלְקַת הַשָּׂדֶה אֲשֶׁר
כ נָטָה־שָׁם אָהֳלוֹ מִיַּד בְּנֵי־חֲמוֹר אֲבִי שְׁכֶם בְּמֵאָה קְשִׂיטָה׃ וַיַּצֶּב־שָׁם
לד חמישי א מִזְבֵּחַ וַיִּקְרָא־לוֹ אֵל אֱלֹהֵי יִשְׂרָאֵל׃ וַתֵּצֵא דִינָה בַּת־
ב לֵאָה אֲשֶׁר יָלְדָה לְיַעֲקֹב לִרְאוֹת בִּבְנוֹת הָאָרֶץ׃ וַיַּרְא אֹתָהּ שְׁכֶם
ג בֶּן־חֲמוֹר הַחִוִּי נְשִׂיא הָאָרֶץ וַיִּקַּח אֹתָהּ וַיִּשְׁכַּב אֹתָהּ וַיְעַנֶּהָ׃ וַתִּדְבַּק
ד נַפְשׁוֹ בְּדִינָה בַּת־יַעֲקֹב וַיֶּאֱהַב אֶת־הַנַּעֲרָ וַיְדַבֵּר עַל־לֵב הַנַּעֲרָ׃ וַיֹּאמֶר
ה שְׁכֶם אֶל־חֲמוֹר אָבִיו לֵאמֹר קַח־לִי אֶת־הַיַּלְדָּה הַזֹּאת לְאִשָּׁה׃ וְיַעֲקֹב
שָׁמַע כִּי טִמֵּא אֶת־דִּינָה בִתּוֹ וּבָנָיו הָיוּ אֶת־מִקְנֵהוּ בַּשָּׂדֶה וְהֶחֱרִשׁ יַעֲקֹב
ו-ז עַד־בֹּאָם׃ וַיֵּצֵא חֲמוֹר אֲבִי־שְׁכֶם אֶל־יַעֲקֹב לְדַבֵּר אִתּוֹ׃ וּבְנֵי יַעֲקֹב בָּאוּ
מִן־הַשָּׂדֶה כְּשָׁמְעָם וַיִּתְעַצְּבוּ הָאֲנָשִׁים וַיִּחַר לָהֶם מְאֹד כִּי נְבָלָה עָשָׂה

---

18. וַיָּבֹא יַעֲקֹב שָׁלֵם עִיר שְׁכֶם — *Jacob arrived intact at the city of Shechem ...* as soon as he arrived in peace in the Land of Canaan, as he had said, *"And (if) I return in peace"* (28:21). He did not wait (to build an altar) until he reached his father's home.

בְּבֹאוֹ מִפַּדַּן אֲרָם — *Upon arriving from Padan Aram.* While he was still on the way to his father's house, even though he had not yet arrived there, he began to fulfill his vow and built an altar, as he had said, *"And HASHEM will be a God to me"* (28:21).

19-20. וַיִּקֶן אֶת חֶלְקַת הַשָּׂדֶה ... וַיַּצֶּב שָׁם מִזְבֵּחַ — *He bought the parcel of land ... He set up an altar ...* as it is said, אֵיךְ נָשִׁיר אֶת שִׁיר ה׳ עַל אַדְמַת נֵכָר, *How shall we sing the song of HASHEM in a foreign land (Psalms 137:4)?*

וַיִּקְרָא לוֹ אֵל אֱלֹהֵי יִשְׂרָאֵל — *And proclaimed it, "God is the God of Israel."* In his prayers he invoked God as God (of Israel), in keeping with his statement, וְהָיָה ה׳ לִי לֵאלֹהִים, *And HASHEM will be a God to me* (28:21), i.e., when (Jacob) will become "Israel," and the nations will be unable to "deprive him of his senses and of a knowledge of his Creator" as mentioned in his vow (28:20).

NOTES

18. וַיָּבֹא יַעֲקֹב שָׁלֵם עִיר שְׁכֶם ... בְּבֹאוֹ מִפַּדַּן אֲרָם — *Jacob arrived intact at the city of Shechem ... upon arriving from Padan Aram.* The *Sforno* interprets the word שָׁלֵם as שָׁלוֹם *(in peace* rather than *intact),* linking it to the condition of his vow, "וְשַׁבְתִּי בְשָׁלוֹם, *and if I return in peace"* (28:21). Once this had been fulfilled, he immediately kept his promise upon his arrival in Shechem and built an altar. This is also indicated by the words בְּבֹאוֹ מִפַּדַּן אֲרָם, *"upon" arriving from Padan Aram,* i.e., as soon as he arrived in Canaan, even before he had completed the next part of his vow; i.e., אֶל בֵּית אָבִי, *to my father's house.*

19-20. וַיִּקֶן אֶת חֶלְקַת הַשָּׂדֶה... וַיַּצֶּב שָׁם מִזְבֵּחַ וַיִּקְרָא לוֹ אֵל אֱלֹהֵי יִשְׂרָאֵל — *He bought the parcel of land ... He set up an altar and proclaimed it, "God is the God of Israel."* The *Sforno* connects these two verses. Jacob bought a portion of land in *Eretz Yisrael* and only then, שָׁם, *there,* not outside of the land, did he build an altar to God, for "how can he sing the song of HASHEM outside of *Eretz Yisrael?"* Jacob had stated that if God would help him to remain loyal to Him, and not allow the exigencies of exile to undermine his faith, he would then accept God as his Judge *(Elohim),* and forgo God's mercy as HASHEM. This he now did by calling God,

day, then all the flocks will die. [14] *Let my lord go ahead of his servant; I will
make my way at my slow pace according to the gait of the drove before me
and the gait of the children, until I come to my lord at Seir."*
[15] *Then Esau said, "Let me assign to you some of the people who are with
me."*
And he said, "To what purpose? Let me just have favor in my lord's eyes!"
[16] *So Esau started back that day on his way toward Seir.* [17] *But Jacob
journeyed to Succoth and built himself a house, and for his livestock he made
shelters; he therefore called the name of the place Succoth.*
[18] *Jacob arrived intact at the city of Shechem which is in the land of
Canaan, upon arriving from Paddan-aram, and he encamped before the city.*
[19] *He bought the parcel of land upon which he pitched his tent from the
children of Hamor, Shechem's father, for one hundred kesitahs.* [20] *He set up
an altar there and proclaimed, "God, the God of Israel."*

34 [1] *Now Dinah — the daughter of Leah, whom she had borne to Jacob —
went out to look over the daughters of the land.* [2] *Shechem, son of
Hamor the Hivvite, the prince of the region, saw her; he took her, lay with
her, and violated her.* [3] *He became deeply attached to Dinah, daughter of
Jacob; he loved the maiden and appealed to the maiden's emotions.* [4] *So
Shechem spoke to Hamor, his father, saying, "Take me this girl for a wife."*
[5] *Now Jacob heard that he had defiled his daughter Dinah, while his sons
were with his cattle in the field; so Jacob kept silent until their arrival.*
[6] *Hamor, Shechem's father, went out to Jacob to speak to him.* [7] *Jacob's
sons arrived from the field, when they heard; the men were distressed,
and were fired deeply with indignation, for he had committed an outrage*

XXXIV

3. וַתִּדְבַּק נַפְשׁוֹ בְּדִינָה — *And his soul cleaved to Dinah.* The effect in the case of Amnon and Tamar was the reverse, once he violated her.

בַּת יַעֲקֹב — *Daughter of Jacob* . . . because she was the daughter of Jacob, who was a man honored by all, as it later says, *for he wanted Jacob's daughter* (verse 19).

5. וְהֶחֱרִשׁ יַעֲקֹב עַד בֹּאָם — *So Jacob kept silent until their arrival.* He avoided any confrontation until his sons' arrival. Thus, they would be alerted (before the confrontation began, and would be able) to guard themselves against their antagonists.

6. וַיֵּצֵא חֲמוֹר — *Chamor went out.* Observing (Jacob's) silence, he grew worried that he was plotting against him.

7. וַיִּתְעַצְּבוּ הָאֲנָשִׁים וַיִּחַר לָהֶם מְאֹד — *The men were distressed and very angry.* Their distress was due to the outrage which had been perpetrated in Israel. Even though this was not considered a shame among the heathen nations, it was a shameful act in Israel. (Furthermore . . .)

NOTES

Elohim, but also connecting this name to *his* new name — Israel (אֱלֹהֵי יִשְׂרָאֵל) — since this name implied that he was now capable of confronting any and all challenges, and prevailing.

XXXIV

3. וַתִּדְבַּק נַפְשׁוֹ בְּדִינָה — *And his soul cleaved to Dinah.* Once passion was spent, Amnon's love for Tamar changed to שִׂנְאָה, *hatred* (*II Samuel* 13:14, 15). Not so Shechem, who became deeply attached to Dinah *after* he had taken and violated her.

7. וַיִּתְעַצְּבוּ הָאֲנָשִׁים וַיִּחַר לָהֶם מְאֹד — *The men were distressed and very angry.* Two expressions are

ח בְּיִשְׂרָאֵל לִשְׁכַּב אֶת־בַּת־יַעֲקֹב וְכֵן לֹא יֵעָשֶׂה: וַיְדַבֵּר חֲמוֹר אִתָּם
לֵאמֹר שְׁכֶם בְּנִי חָשְׁקָה נַפְשׁוֹ בְּבִתְּכֶם תְּנוּ נָא אֹתָהּ לוֹ לְאִשָּׁה:
ט־י וְהִתְחַתְּנוּ אֹתָנוּ בְּנֹתֵיכֶם תִּתְּנוּ־לָנוּ וְאֶת־בְּנֹתֵינוּ תִּקְחוּ לָכֶם: וְאִתָּנוּ
יא תֵּשֵׁבוּ וְהָאָרֶץ תִּהְיֶה לִפְנֵיכֶם שְׁבוּ וּסְחָרוּהָ וְהֵאָחֲזוּ בָּהּ: וַיֹּאמֶר שְׁכֶם
אֶל־אָבִיהָ וְאֶל־אַחֶיהָ אֶמְצָא־חֵן בְּעֵינֵיכֶם וַאֲשֶׁר תֹּאמְרוּ אֵלַי אֶתֵּן:
יב הַרְבּוּ עָלַי מְאֹד מֹהַר וּמַתָּן וְאֶתְּנָה כַּאֲשֶׁר תֹּאמְרוּ אֵלָי וּתְנוּ־לִי
יג אֶת־הַנַּעֲרָ לְאִשָּׁה: וַיַּעֲנוּ בְנֵי־יַעֲקֹב אֶת־שְׁכֶם וְאֶת־חֲמוֹר אָבִיו בְּמִרְמָה
יד וַיְדַבֵּרוּ אֲשֶׁר טִמֵּא אֵת דִּינָה אֲחֹתָם: וַיֹּאמְרוּ אֲלֵיהֶם לֹא נוּכַל לַעֲשׂוֹת
הַדָּבָר הַזֶּה לָתֵת אֶת־אֲחֹתֵנוּ לְאִישׁ אֲשֶׁר־לוֹ עָרְלָה כִּי־חֶרְפָּה הִוא
טו לָנוּ: אַךְ־בְּזֹאת נֵאוֹת לָכֶם אִם תִּהְיוּ כָמֹנוּ לְהִמֹּל לָכֶם כָּל־זָכָר:
טז וְנָתַנּוּ אֶת־בְּנֹתֵינוּ לָכֶם וְאֶת־בְּנֹתֵיכֶם נִקַּח־לָנוּ וְיָשַׁבְנוּ אִתְּכֶם וְהָיִינוּ
יז לְעַם אֶחָד: וְאִם־לֹא תִשְׁמְעוּ אֵלֵינוּ לְהִמּוֹל וְלָקַחְנוּ אֶת־בִּתֵּנוּ
יח־יט וְהָלָכְנוּ: וַיִּיטְבוּ דִבְרֵיהֶם בְּעֵינֵי חֲמוֹר וּבְעֵינֵי שְׁכֶם בֶּן־חֲמוֹר: וְלֹא־אֵחַר
הַנַּעַר לַעֲשׂוֹת הַדָּבָר כִּי חָפֵץ בְּבַת־יַעֲקֹב וְהוּא נִכְבָּד מִכֹּל בֵּית אָבִיו:
כ וַיָּבֹא חֲמוֹר וּשְׁכֶם בְּנוֹ אֶל־שַׁעַר עִירָם וַיְדַבְּרוּ אֶל־אַנְשֵׁי עִירָם לֵאמֹר:
כא הָאֲנָשִׁים הָאֵלֶּה שְׁלֵמִים הֵם אִתָּנוּ וְיֵשְׁבוּ בָאָרֶץ וְיִסְחֲרוּ אֹתָהּ
וְהָאָרֶץ הִנֵּה רַחֲבַת־יָדַיִם לִפְנֵיהֶם אֶת־בְּנֹתָם נִקַּח־לָנוּ לְנָשִׁים
כב וְאֶת־בְּנֹתֵינוּ נִתֵּן לָהֶם: אַךְ־בְּזֹאת יֵאֹתוּ לָנוּ הָאֲנָשִׁים לָשֶׁבֶת אִתָּנוּ
כג לִהְיוֹת לְעַם אֶחָד בְּהִמּוֹל לָנוּ כָּל־זָכָר כַּאֲשֶׁר הֵם נִמֹּלִים: מִקְנֵהֶם
וְקִנְיָנָם וְכָל־בְּהֶמְתָּם הֲלוֹא לָנוּ הֵם אַךְ נֵאוֹתָה לָהֶם וְיֵשְׁבוּ אִתָּנוּ:

וְכֵן לֹא יֵעָשֶׂה — *Such a thing was not done.* It was most uncommon to violate the daughter of a person of renown, therefore they were extremely angered that it had happened to them.

10. וּסְחָרוּהָ — *And trade in it.* Normally strangers were not allowed to trade, as we find, בַּר מָתָא אַבַּר מָתָא אַחֲרִיתָא מָצֵי מְעַכֵּב, *A local person can prevent an outsider (from trading or doing business)* (*Bava Basra* 21a).

12. הַרְבּוּ עָלַי מְאֹד מֹהַר — *Inflate exceedingly upon me the dowry* ... as compensation for my guilt and transgression against you.

13. בְּמִרְמָה — *Cleverly.* The request that they should circumcise themselves was made either in the belief that they would refuse, or that they would be unable to convince their townspeople to do so.

וַיְדַבֵּרוּ אֲשֶׁר טִמֵּא אֵת דִּינָה — *And they spoke, after he had defiled Dinah.* They answered that the offer of extravagant gifts made by Shechem and his father was inappropriate inasmuch as he had already defiled her, for it would appear as a harlot's hire.

NOTES

used to describe the emotions of the brothers — *distress* and *anger*. The former is a reaction to the moral outrage which was peculiar to them as Israelites. The latter is because even among the heathens respect was shown to a girl who was the daughter of an important personage. This lack of elemental respect for the status and position of their father and family incensed them.

13. וַיְדַבֵּרוּ אֲשֶׁר טִמֵּא אֵת דִּינָה — *And they spoke, after he had defiled Dinah.* According to the Midrash these words, *because he had defiled*

in Israel by lying with a daughter of Jacob — such a thing may not be done!
8 Hamor spoke with them, saying, "Shechem, my son, longs deeply for
your daughter — please give her to him as a wife. 9 And intermarry with us;
give your daughters to us, and take our daughters for yourselves. 10 And
among us you shall dwell; the land will be before you — settle and trade in it, and acquire property in it."
11 Then Shechem said to her father and brothers, "Let me gain favor in
your eyes; and whatever you tell me — I will give. 12 Inflate exceedingly
upon me the marriage settlement and gifts and I will give whatever you tell me; only give me the maiden for a wife."
13 Jacob's sons answered Shechem and his father Hamor cleverly and
they spoke (because he had defiled their sister Dinah). 14 They said to them,
"We cannot do this thing, to give our sister to a man who is uncircumcised,
for that is a disgrace for us. 15 Only on this condition will we acquiesce to
you: If you become like us by letting every male among you become circum-
cised. 16 Then we will give our daughters to you, and take your daughters to
ourselves; we will dwell with you, and become a single people. 17 But if you
will not listen to us to be circumcised, we will take our daughter and go."
18 Their proposal seemed good in the view of Hamor, and in the view of
Shechem, Hamor's son. 19 The youth did not delay doing the thing, for he
wanted Jacob's daughter. Now he was the most respected of all his father's household.
20 Hamor — with his son Shechem — came to the gate of their city and
spoke to the people of their city, saying, 21 "These people are peaceable with
us; let them settle in the land and trade in it, for see, there is ample room in the land for them! Let us take their daughters for ourselves as wives and
give our daughters to them. 22 Only on this condition will the people
acquiesce with us to dwell with us to become a single people: that all our
males become circumcised as they themselves are circumcised. 23 Their
livestock, their possessions, and all their animals — will they not be ours? Let us acquiesce to them and they will settle with us."

---

14. כִּי חֶרְפָּה הִוא לָנוּ — *For that would be a disgrace among us . . .* for it would imply that there is no fitting man among the circumcised who would marry her.

17. וְלָקַחְנוּ אֶת בִּתֵּנוּ — *We will take our daughter.* Though she is still in your house, we will take her from you.

וְהָלָכְנוּ — *And go.* With all our wealth, from which you will derive no benefit.

19. וְהוּא נִכְבָּד — *He was the most respected.* Even so, he did not delay doing the thing (circumcision), for he wanted Jacob's daughter.

21. שְׁלֵמִים הֵם אִתָּנוּ — *These people are peaceable with us.* They are peaceable toward us and do not wish to avenge their humiliation.

NOTES

their sister Dinah, were interjected by the Divine Spirit parenthetically, to justify their "clever" proposal. The *Sforno,* however, interprets these words as having been said by Jacob's sons to Chamor and Shechem. What good is your offer of gifts and dowry since the deed is already done? The word אֲשֶׁר is to be understood here as אַחֲרֵי (*after* he had defiled) similar to, כַּאֲשֶׁר עָבַר אֶת פְּנוּאֵל, *"after" he had passed over Penuel* (32:32).

כד וַיִּשְׁמְעוּ אֶל־חֲמוֹר וְאֶל־שְׁכֶם בְּנוֹ כָּל־יֹצְאֵי שַׁעַר עִירוֹ וַיִּמֹּלוּ כָּל־זָכָר
כה כָּל־יֹצְאֵי שַׁעַר עִירוֹ׃ וַיְהִי בַיּוֹם הַשְּׁלִישִׁי בִּהְיוֹתָם כֹּאֲבִים וַיִּקְחוּ שְׁנֵי־
בְנֵי־יַעֲקֹב שִׁמְעוֹן וְלֵוִי אֲחֵי דִינָה אִישׁ חַרְבּוֹ וַיָּבֹאוּ עַל־הָעִיר בֶּטַח וַיַּהַרְגוּ
כו כָּל־זָכָר׃ וְאֶת־חֲמוֹר וְאֶת־שְׁכֶם בְּנוֹ הָרְגוּ לְפִי־חָרֶב וַיִּקְחוּ אֶת־דִּינָה
כז מִבֵּית שְׁכֶם וַיֵּצֵאוּ׃ בְּנֵי יַעֲקֹב בָּאוּ עַל־הַחֲלָלִים וַיָּבֹזּוּ הָעִיר אֲשֶׁר טִמְּאוּ
כח אֲחוֹתָם׃ אֶת־צֹאנָם וְאֶת־בְּקָרָם וְאֶת־חֲמֹרֵיהֶם וְאֵת אֲשֶׁר־בָּעִיר וְאֶת־
כט אֲשֶׁר בַּשָּׂדֶה לָקָחוּ׃ וְאֶת־כָּל־חֵילָם וְאֶת־כָּל־טַפָּם וְאֶת־נְשֵׁיהֶם שָׁבוּ
ל וַיָּבֹזּוּ וְאֵת כָּל־אֲשֶׁר בַּבָּיִת׃ וַיֹּאמֶר יַעֲקֹב אֶל־שִׁמְעוֹן וְאֶל־לֵוִי עֲכַרְתֶּם
אֹתִי לְהַבְאִישֵׁנִי בְּיֹשֵׁב הָאָרֶץ בַּכְּנַעֲנִי וּבַפְּרִזִּי וַאֲנִי מְתֵי מִסְפָּר וְנֶאֶסְפוּ
לא עָלַי וְהִכּוּנִי וְנִשְׁמַדְתִּי אֲנִי וּבֵיתִי׃ וַיֹּאמְרוּ הַכְזוֹנָה יַעֲשֶׂה אֶת־אֲחוֹתֵנוּ׃

לה

א וַיֹּאמֶר אֱלֹהִים אֶל־יַעֲקֹב קוּם עֲלֵה בֵית־אֵל וְשֶׁב־שָׁם וַעֲשֵׂה־שָׁם מִזְבֵּחַ
ב לָאֵל הַנִּרְאֶה אֵלֶיךָ בְּבָרְחֲךָ מִפְּנֵי עֵשָׂו אָחִיךָ׃ וַיֹּאמֶר יַעֲקֹב אֶל־בֵּיתוֹ
וְאֶל כָּל־אֲשֶׁר עִמּוֹ הָסִרוּ אֶת־אֱלֹהֵי הַנֵּכָר אֲשֶׁר בְּתֹכְכֶם וְהִטַּהֲרוּ
ג וְהַחֲלִיפוּ שִׂמְלֹתֵיכֶם׃ וְנָקוּמָה וְנַעֲלֶה בֵּית־אֵל וְאֶעֱשֶׂה־שָּׁם מִזְבֵּחַ לָאֵל
ד הָעֹנֶה אֹתִי בְּיוֹם צָרָתִי וַיְהִי עִמָּדִי בַּדֶּרֶךְ אֲשֶׁר הָלָכְתִּי׃ וַיִּתְּנוּ אֶל־יַעֲקֹב

25. וַיַּהַרְגוּ כָּל זָכָר — *They killed every male.* For they had circumcised themselves only in the hope of gaining their livestock and possessions, as Chamor and Shechem had said to them (verse 23).

26. וְאֶת חֲמוֹר וְאֶת שְׁכֶם בְּנוֹ הָרְגוּ — *And Chamor and Shechem his son they killed.* They searched and located them.

27. הָעִיר אֲשֶׁר טִמְּאוּ אֲחוֹתָם — *The city which had defiled their sister.* For Shechem would never have committed (this evil) if it had not been considered non-abhorrent (acceptable) to them and common practice for the lords to take any girl they desired without her consent, as wives or concubines, as we find, וַיִּקְחוּ לָהֶם נָשִׁים מִכֹּל אֲשֶׁר בָּחָרוּ, *And they took for themselves women, whoever they chose* (6:2).

30. לְהַבְאִישֵׁנִי — *Making me odious.* They will say we broke our word after they became circumcised.

31. הַכְזוֹנָה יַעֲשֶׂה אֶת אֲחוֹתֵנוּ — *Should he treat our sister as a harlot?* Is she a harlot who is not worthy to have her humiliation avenged, that the people of the land (treat her) in this manner? She is our sister, not a harlot, and we were right to avenge her humiliation. When the inhabitants of the land will consider all this they will not be inclined to attack us.

NOTES

25. וַיַּהַרְגוּ כָּל זָכָר — *They killed every male.* Their motive was impure. The only way Chamor and Shechem convinced them to do this act was by promising them that all the wealth of the Israelites would *be ours* (לָנוּ הֵם) (verse 23). Their greed eventually led to their downfall.

27. הָעִיר אֲשֶׁר טִמְּאוּ אֲחוֹתָם — *The city which had defiled their sister.* Shechem alone — not the city — had defiled Dinah! Why is the entire city to blame? The Torah tells us that they, *the city,* were all guilty, for they all accepted and condoned the immoral behavior of their lords.

31. הַכְזוֹנָה יַעֲשֶׂה אֶת אֲחוֹתֵנוּ — *Should he treat our sister as a harlot?* The brothers strongly affirmed the innocence of their sister. Shechem's act was a dastardly outrageous one and, as her brothers, they were justified in punishing him and his townspeople who were not innocents, having condoned this kind of behavior in their midst. As for the danger they exposed themselves to, they were convinced that after due deliberation and thought the inhabitants of the land would understand their need to avenge their sister's honor and would not harm them.

24 All the people who depart through the gate of his city listened to Hamor and his son Shechem, and all the males — all those who depart through the gate of his city — were circumcised.

25 And it came to pass on the third day, when they were in pain, that two of Jacob's sons, Simeon and Levi, Dinah's brothers, each took his sword and they came upon the city confidently, and killed every male. 26 And Hamor and Shechem his son they killed at the point of sword. Then they took Dinah from Shechem's house and left.

27 The sons of Jacob came upon the slain, and they plundered the city which had defiled their sister. 28 Their flocks, their cattle, their donkeys, whatever was in the town and whatever was in the field, they took. 29 All their wealth, all their children and wives they took captive and they plundered, as well as everything in the house.

30 Jacob said to Simeon and to Levi, "You have discomposed me, making me odious among the inhabitants of the land, among the Canaanite and among the Perizzite; I am few in number and should they band together and attack me, I will be annihilated — I and my household."

31 And they said, "Should he treat our sister like a harlot?"

35 *1 God said to Jacob, "Arise — go up to Beth-el and dwell there, and make an altar there to God Who appeared to you when you fled from Esau your brother." 2 So Jacob said to his household and to all who were with him, "Discard the alien gods that are in your midst; cleanse yourselves and change your clothes. 3 Then come, let us go up to Beth-el; I will make there an altar to God Who answered me in my time of distress, and was with me on the road that I traveled." 4 So they gave to Jacob*

XXXV

1. וְשֶׁב שָׁם — *And remain there* . . . to attune your mind spiritually before you build the altar, as our Sages tell us, "The pious men of old used to wait an hour before praying in order to concentrate their thoughts upon their Father in Heaven" (*Berachos* 30b).

וַעֲשֵׂה שָׁם מִזְבֵּחַ לָאֵל הַנִּרְאֶה אֵלֶיךָ בְּבָרְחֲךָ — *And make an altar there to God, Who appeared to you when you fled* . . . to give thanks (to God) for having fulfilled the promise made there. This is akin to the Sages' statement, (מְבָרֵךְ) בָּרוּךְ שֶׁעָשָׂה לִי נֵס בַּמָּקוֹם הַזֶּה, *He utters the benediction: "Blessed is He Who wrought a miracle for me in this place"* (*Berachos* 54a).

2. הָסִרוּ אֶת אֱלֹהֵי הַנֵּכָר — *Discard the alien gods* . . . which you took from Shechem. Even though the women of Shechem who worshiped them had renounced (nullified) them, and it was now permitted to derive benefit from them, as our Sages state, "A gentile can annul an idol, even if forced to do so" (*Avodah Zarah* 43a), nonetheless, remove them from your midst now that we are going to Beth El, so that any thought of idolatry be removed from your minds.

NOTES

XXXV

1. וְשֶׁב שָׁם — *And remain there.* The commandment of God to Jacob should have read simply, "Go to Beth El and build an altar." The phrase וְשֶׁב שָׁם, *and remain (settle down) there,* seems superfluous. Indeed the *Ramban* (initially) says that he does not know the significance of this command. The *Sforno* interprets it as a period of preparation, of contemplation, before one proceeds to pray or perform a religious act, such as the building of an altar.

2. הָסִרוּ אֶת אֱלֹהֵי הַנֵּכָר — *Discard the alien gods.* The *Sforno* mentions the *women of Shechem* because the males had all been killed.

אֶת כָּל־אֱלֹהֵי הַנֵּכָר אֲשֶׁר בְּיָדָם וְאֶת־הַנְּזָמִים אֲשֶׁר בְּאׇזְנֵיהֶם וַיִּטְמֹן
ה אֹתָם יַעֲקֹב תַּחַת הָאֵלָה אֲשֶׁר עִם־שְׁכֶם: וַיִּסָּעוּ וַיְהִי | חִתַּת אֱלֹהִים
ו עַל־הֶעָרִים אֲשֶׁר סְבִיבוֹתֵיהֶם וְלֹא רָדְפוּ אַחֲרֵי בְּנֵי יַעֲקֹב: וַיָּבֹא יַעֲקֹב
ז לוּזָה אֲשֶׁר בְּאֶרֶץ כְּנַעַן הִוא בֵּית־אֵל הוּא וְכׇל־הָעָם אֲשֶׁר־עִמּוֹ: וַיִּבֶן שָׁם
מִזְבֵּחַ וַיִּקְרָא לַמָּקוֹם אֵל בֵּית־אֵל כִּי שָׁם נִגְלוּ אֵלָיו הָאֱלֹהִים בְּבׇרְחוֹ
ח מִפְּנֵי אָחִיו: וַתָּמׇת דְּבֹרָה מֵינֶקֶת רִבְקָה וַתִּקָּבֵר מִתַּחַת לְבֵית־אֵל תַּחַת
הָאַלּוֹן וַיִּקְרָא שְׁמוֹ אַלּוֹן בָּכוּת:
ט־י וַיֵּרָא אֱלֹהִים אֶל־יַעֲקֹב עוֹד בְּבֹאוֹ מִפַּדַּן אֲרָם וַיְבָרֶךְ אֹתוֹ: וַיֹּאמֶר־לוֹ
אֱלֹהִים שִׁמְךָ יַעֲקֹב לֹא־יִקָּרֵא שִׁמְךָ עוֹד יַעֲקֹב כִּי אִם־יִשְׂרָאֵל יִהְיֶה שְׁמֶךָ
יא וַיִּקְרָא אֶת־שְׁמוֹ יִשְׂרָאֵל: וַיֹּאמֶר לוֹ אֱלֹהִים אֲנִי אֵל שַׁדַּי פְּרֵה וּרְבֵה

---

4. וַיִּטְמֹן אֹתָם יַעֲקֹב — *And Jacob buried them.* But he did not destroy them since they had been nullified and (halachically) it was permitted to derive benefit from them.

5. וַיִּסָּעוּ וַיְהִי חִתַּת אֱלֹהִים — *They set out, and there fell a Godly terror (on the cities).* When they left Shechem which was a fortified city they were in danger of being attacked along the way by the people of the surrounding cities, therefore it was necessary for God's terror to fall upon their enemies.

7. וַיִּקְרָא לַמָּקוֹם — *And named the place* . . . the inn where he lodged on his way to Haran, as it says, וַיִּפְגַּע בַּמָּקוֹם, *he encountered the place* (28:11, see the *Sforno's* comment there).

אֵל בֵּית אֵל — *El-beth-el* . . . the sanctuary of Beth-el.

8. אַלּוֹן בָּכוּת — *Allon-bachuth.* This caused the manifestation of the *Shechinah* (Divine Presence) to cease, as our Sages state, שֶׁאֵין הַשְּׁכִינָה שׁוֹרָה לֹא מִתּוֹךְ עַצְבוּת, *The Shechinah cannot rest amidst gloom (Shabbos* 30b).

9. וַיֵּרָא אֱלֹהִים — *And God appeared* . . . after the period of weeping had ended.

אֶל יַעֲקֹב עוֹד — *To Jacob again* . . . as He had appeared to him there when he went to Haran, as it says, *Who appeared to you when you fled* (v. 1).

בְּבֹאוֹ מִפַּדַּן אֲרָם — *When he came from Paddan-aram.* But in Paddan-aram God did not appear to him, though He did speak to him through an angel, as it states, *And an angel of God said to me in a dream* (31:11).

10. שִׁמְךָ יַעֲקֹב — *Your name is Jacob.* I now confirm this name (Jacob) indicating that you alone will survive the destruction of all other nations in the end of days, as it is said, כִּי אֶעֱשֶׂה כָלָה בְּכָל הַגּוֹיִם . . . וְאֹתְךָ לֹא אֶעֱשֶׂה כָלָה, *For I will make full end of all the nations* . . .

NOTES

4. וַיִּטְמֹן אֹתָם יַעֲקֹב — *And Jacob buried them.* The Talmud in tractate *Avodah Zarah* (43b and 51b) requires one to pulverize or scatter idols to the wind, or cast them into the sea. The reason Jacob only *buried* them is because strictly speaking even this was unnecessary, since these idols had been nullified and it was permitted to benefit from them. Nonetheless, Jacob buried them for he did not want his children and household to have any contact whatsoever with these idols.

9. בְּבֹאוֹ מִפַּדַּן אֲרָם — *When he came from Paddan Aram.* The verse quoted by the *Sforno* (31:11) states specifically *angel of God.* We must assume that 31:3 which states, וַיֹּאמֶר ה׳ אֶל יַעֲקֹב, *And* H*ASHEM said to Jacob,* also means through the medium of an angel, since God does not appear outside of *Eretz Yisrael.* The *Radak* interprets 31:3 in like manner.

10. שִׁמְךָ יַעֲקֹב — *Your name is Jacob.* Compare the *Sforno's* commentary to 25:26 and 32:29.

וַיִּקְרָא אֶת שְׁמוֹ יִשְׂרָאֵל — *Thus, He named him Israel.* The last two words of the previous verse are וַיְבָרֶךְ אֹתוֹ, *and He blessed him.* The *Sforno* apparently interprets this blessing as allowing Jacob to profit from his new name Israel *immediately,* so that he might benefit from this name even before the end of days, i.e., while still in *galus* (exile).

all the alien gods that were in their possession, as well as the rings that were
in their ears, and Jacob buried them underneath the terebinth near Shechem.
5 *They set out, and there fell a Godly terror on the cities which were around*
them, so that they did not pursue Jacob's sons.
6 *Thus Jacob came to Luz in the land of Canaan — it is Beth-el — he, and*
all the people who were with him. 7 *And he built an altar there and called*
the place El-beth-el, for it was there that God had been revealed to him
during his flight from his brother.
8 *Deborah, the wet-nurse of Rebecca, died, and she was buried below*
Beth-el, below the plateau; and he named it Allon-bachuth.
9 *And God appeared to Jacob again when he came from Paddan-aram,*
and He blessed him.
10 *Then God said to him, "Your name is Jacob. Your name shall not always*
be called Jacob, but Israel shall be your name." Thus He called his name
Israel. 11 *And God said to him, "I am El Shaddai. Be fruitful and multiply;*

---

but I will not make a full end of you (Jer. 46:28).

לֹא יִקָּרֵא שִׁמְךָ עוֹד יַעֲקֹב — *You shall not always be named Jacob.* When the implication of the name *Jacob* will be fulfilled, i.e., that you alone (of the nations) will remain at the end of days, as it says, הֶן עָם לְבָדָד יִשְׁכֹּן, *Lo, it is a people that shall dwell alone (Numbers* 23:9), then there will no longer be any need for this name, *Jacob.*

כִּי אִם יִשְׂרָאֵל יִהְיֶה שְׁמֶךָ — *But Israel shall be your name* ... for you will rule over the remnants of the nations, as it says, וְקַרְקַר כָּל בְּנֵי שֵׁת, *and break down all the sons of Seth (Numbers* 24:17).

וַיִּקְרָא אֶת שְׁמוֹ יִשְׂרָאֵל — *Thus, He named him Israel.* He blessed him that the implication of the name *Israel,* sovereignty, should commence (to a degree) *immediately,* to the extent that he might be able to withstand his enemies even in lands which are not his (i.e., in exile), as our Sages state, "Wherever they went, they became lords over their masters" (*Sanhedrin* 104a).

11. אֲנִי אֵל שַׁדַּי — *I am El Shaddai.* I swear by My Name, similar to, וְאָמַרְתִּי חַי אָנֹכִי לְעֹלָם, *And I say: As I live forever (Deut.* 32:40). This is the only place we find that God swore in His Name to Jacob.

פְּרֵה וּרְבֵה — *Be fruitful and multiply.* Do not be concerned that your children will be destroyed by the nations, nor that they will be unworthy. Therefore, do not cease from being fruitful and multiplying, as opposed to the advice of Rabbi Ishmael who said, "From the day that the evil kingdom came to power ... we ought by rights to accept upon ourselves not to marry and beget children, and the seed of Abraham our father would come to an end by itself" (*Bava Basra* 60b). (All) this is said because, 'I am *El Shaddai,* who does not need a prepared recipient. I shall do what I have said, regardless, even without a recipient prepared (for my blessing)."

NOTES

11. אֲנִי אֵל שַׁדַּי — *I am El Shaddai. Rashi* interprets this introductory statement, אֲנִי אֵל שַׁדַּי, *I am El Shaddai,* as implying, "I am *sufficient* to bless, for the blessings are Mine." The *Sforno,* however, explains this expression as denoting a Divine oath. This will explain *Exodus* 33:1 — *The land which I swore to Abraham, to Isaac and to Jacob.* This was the oath given to Jacob.

פְּרֵה וּרְבֵה — *Be fruitful and multiply.* According to the *Sforno, be fruitful and multiply* is not to be understood as a commandment, but as an exhortation and reassurance. He also is cognizant of the deeper meaning of this Divine Name, as indicating "I am sufficient" (שַׁדַּי = שֶׁאֲנִי דַּי). He interprets this to mean that God can give a blessing even without a proper recipient, for in His hand there is sufficient

ששי יב גּוֹי וּקְהַל גּוֹיִם יִהְיֶה מִמֶּךָּ וּמְלָכִים מֵחֲלָצֶיךָ יֵצֵאוּ׃ וְאֶת־הָאָרֶץ אֲשֶׁר נָתַתִּי
יג לְאַבְרָהָם וּלְיִצְחָק לְךָ אֶתְּנֶנָּה וּלְזַרְעֲךָ אַחֲרֶיךָ אֶתֵּן אֶת־הָאָרֶץ׃ וַיַּעַל
יד מֵעָלָיו אֱלֹהִים בַּמָּקוֹם אֲשֶׁר־דִּבֶּר אִתּוֹ׃ וַיַּצֵּב יַעֲקֹב מַצֵּבָה בַּמָּקוֹם אֲשֶׁר־
טו דִּבֶּר אִתּוֹ מַצֶּבֶת אָבֶן וַיַּסֵּךְ עָלֶיהָ נֶסֶךְ וַיִּצֹק עָלֶיהָ שָׁמֶן׃ וַיִּקְרָא יַעֲקֹב
טז אֶת־שֵׁם הַמָּקוֹם אֲשֶׁר דִּבֶּר אִתּוֹ שָׁם אֱלֹהִים בֵּית־אֵל׃ וַיִּסְעוּ מִבֵּית אֵל
יז וַיְהִי־עוֹד כִּבְרַת־הָאָרֶץ לָבוֹא אֶפְרָתָה וַתֵּלֶד רָחֵל וַתְּקַשׁ בְּלִדְתָּהּ׃ וַיְהִי
בְהַקְשֹׁתָהּ בְּלִדְתָּהּ וַתֹּאמֶר לָהּ הַמְיַלֶּדֶת אַל־תִּירְאִי כִּי־גַם־זֶה לָךְ בֵּן׃
יח וַיְהִי בְּצֵאת נַפְשָׁהּ כִּי מֵתָה וַתִּקְרָא שְׁמוֹ בֶּן־אוֹנִי וְאָבִיו קָרָא־לוֹ בִנְיָמִין׃
יט־כ וַתָּמָת רָחֵל וַתִּקָּבֵר בְּדֶרֶךְ אֶפְרָתָה הִוא בֵּית לָחֶם׃ וַיַּצֵּב יַעֲקֹב מַצֵּבָה
כא עַל־קְבֻרָתָהּ הִוא מַצֶּבֶת קְבֻרַת־רָחֵל עַד־הַיּוֹם׃ וַיִּסַּע יִשְׂרָאֵל וַיֵּט אָהֳלֹה
כב מֵהָלְאָה לְמִגְדַּל־עֵדֶר׃ וַיְהִי בִּשְׁכֹּן יִשְׂרָאֵל בָּאָרֶץ הַהִוא וַיֵּלֶךְ רְאוּבֵן
*פסקה באמצע פסוק וַיִּשְׁכַּב אֶת־בִּלְהָה פִּילֶגֶשׁ אָבִיו וַיִּשְׁמַע יִשְׂרָאֵל *
כג וַיִּהְיוּ בְנֵי־יַעֲקֹב שְׁנֵים עָשָׂר׃ בְּנֵי לֵאָה בְּכוֹר יַעֲקֹב רְאוּבֵן וְשִׁמְעוֹן וְלֵוִי

וּמְלָכִים מֵחֲלָצֶיךָ יֵצֵאוּ — *And kings shall issue forth from your loins* ... men, fit to be kings. There will be no need to appoint strangers as (Israel's) kings, as Edom did, i.e., Samlah of Masrekah, Saul of Rechovos and others (36:36,37).

12. וּלְזַרְעֲךָ אַחֲרֶיךָ אֶתֵּן אֶת הָאָרֶץ — *And to your offspring after you I will give the land.* In the end of days I will give your offspring the entire earth, not only *Eretz Yisrael*, as it says, *You will spread powerfully westward, eastward, northward and southward* (28:14); and as it is said, וְקַרְקַר כָּל בְּנֵי שֵׁת, *and break down all the sons of Seth* (*Numbers* 24:17).

13. בַּמָּקוֹם אֲשֶׁר דִּבֶּר אִתּוֹ — *In the place where He had spoken to him* ... when he left (home) to go to Haran, in the same inn that (God's) word was spoken; there *God appeared* (verse 9) and there He ascended, therefore (Jacob) set up a pillar in that self-same place.

14. וַיַּסֵּךְ עָלֶיהָ נֶסֶךְ — *And he poured a libation upon it* ... thereby completing the fulfillment of his oath, as he said, *"Then this stone which I have set up as a pillar shall become a House of God"* (28:22), for in this manner he prepared this place for the House of God. This is similar to David, when the angel appeared to him in the threshing floor of Aravnah (Arnan) the Jebusite (see *II Chronicles* 21:15-26).

17. אַל תִּירְאִי — *Have no fear* ... that your hard labor indicates it will be a girl, as our Sages tell us, חֶבְלֵי נְקֵבָה מְרוּבִּים מִשֶּׁל זָכָר, *The travail (of childbirth) is much greater when a girl (is born) than when a boy (is born)* (*Niddah* 31a).

NOTES

power to always give. Apparently the *Sforno* now interprets the phrase אֲנִי אֵל שַׁדַּי akin to *Rashi*, and also gives the added interpretation of "blessing" to the phrase פְּרֵה וּרְבֵה, *Be fruitful and multiply.*

12. וּלְזַרְעֲךָ אַחֲרֶיךָ אֶתֵּן אֶת הָאָרֶץ — *And to your offspring after you I will give the land.* The word הָאָרֶץ, *The land*, at the beginning of the verse refers to *Eretz Yisrael*. The same word at the end of the verse is not redundant. There it refers to the earth.

13-14. בַּמָּקוֹם אֲשֶׁר דִּבֶּר אִתּוֹ . . . וַיַּסֵּךְ עָלֶיהָ נֶסֶךְ — *In the place where He had spoken to him ... and he poured a libation upon it. Rashi* states that he does not know what the phrase, *In the place where He had spoken to him*, is meant to teach us. The *Sforno* interprets it to mean that God speaks to Jacob now, on his return, at the very site where He had spoken to him when he left home for Haran. When Jacob poured the libation on the pillar, he was completing the consecration of the מַצֵּבָה which he had begun so many years earlier. And since, according to the *Sforno*, *this place*, i.e., Beth-el-luz and Mt. Moriah, were merged into one at this time, this consecration was a preparation for the House of God (the Temple) which would one day be constructed on *this place*.

a nation and a congregation of nations shall descend from you, and kings shall issue from your loins. [12] *The land that I gave to Abraham and to Isaac, I will give to you; and to your offspring after you I will give the land."* [13] *Then God ascended from upon him in the place where He had spoken with him.*

[14] *Jacob had set up a pillar at the place where God had spoken with him — a pillar of stone — and he poured a libation upon it, and poured oil upon it.* [15] *Then Jacob called the name of the place where God had spoken with him Beth-el.*

[16] *They journeyed from Beth-el and there was still a stretch of land to go to Ephrath, when Rachel went into labor and had difficulty in her childbirth.*
[17] *And it was when she had difficulty in her labor that the midwife said to her, "Have no fear, for this one, too, is a son for you."* [18] *And it came to pass, as her soul was departing — for she died — that she called his name Ben Oni, but his father called him Benjamin.* [19] *Thus Rachel died, and was buried on the road to Ephrath, which is Bethlehem.* [20] *Jacob set up a monument over her grave; it is the monument of Rachel's grave until today.*

[21] *Israel journeyed on, and he pitched his tent beyond Migdal-eder.* [22] *And it came to pass, while Israel dwelt in that land, that Reuben went and lay with Bilhah, his father's concubine, and Israel heard.*

The sons of Jacob were twelve. [23] *The sons of Leah: Jacob's firstborn,*

כִּי גַם זֶה לָךְ בֵּן — *For this one, too, is a son for you.* Even though the pains are great, it is still a boy.

20. מַצֵּבָה עַל קְבֻרָתָהּ — *A monument over her grave.* Since her grave was on a public thoroughfare, he feared it might be disturbed or plundered.

22. וַיִּשְׁמַע יִשְׂרָאֵל וַיִּהְיוּ בְנֵי יַעֲקֹב שְׁנֵים עָשָׂר — *And Israel heard, and the sons of Jacob were twelve.* Though he was aware (of Reuben's deed) he did not remove him from the roster of his sons, for he was certain that (Reuben) had repented immediately. (As a result) he was not omitted from the roster of the sons of Jacob, who were destined to remain at the end of days and survive all the other nations.

23. בְּכוֹר יַעֲקֹב רְאוּבֵן — *Jacob's firstborn, Reuben.* Because he had repented, and repentance reaches God's Throne of Glory, he did not forfeit his birthright according to the law of heaven. He was not deprived (of his birthright as firstborn) until Jacob took it away from him in accordance with the law of man. This is similar to one who is deservant of excommunication but is not considered excommunicated until a leading scholar pronounces him as such, as our Sages teach us, "What is the source for שַׁמְתָּא, *excommunication?* It is written, אוֹרוּ מֵרוֹז, *Curse Meroz (Judges 5:23)*, (providing) this is concurred with by a prominent person, as it is written: אָמַר מַלְאַךְ ה׳, *Said the angel of God* (ibid.)" (*Moed Katan* 16a). And the latter authorities also concur with this decision.

NOTES

23. בְּכוֹר יַעֲקֹב רְאוּבֵן — *Jacob's firstborn, Reuben.* The Talmud in tractate *Shabbos* (55b) explains that Reuben had defended his mother Leah's honor. Upon the death of Rachel, Jacob had taken up residence in the tent of Bilhah, and Reuben strongly felt that this was improper, and so he "arose and transposed her couch." For this rash act, according to heavenly law (דִּינֵי שָׁמַיִם), he was not guilty of any overt transgression. His father, however, had the authority and right, according to temporal law (דִּינֵי אָדָם), to impose a ban upon him for this action. Jacob did so on his deathbed, when he referred to the incident, and removed the birthright from Reuben (see 49:4). Hence, in our verse, the Torah correctly states that Reuben was the firstborn in accordance with heavenly law, but nonetheless, Jacob was justified when he punished him later in accordance with the "law of man." The *Sforno* quotes the passage from tractate *Moed Katan* to prove that a prominent scholar (in our case, Jacob) has the power to pronounce a ban, and Reuben's demotion is considered to be, in a sense, a ban.

כד־כה וִיהוּדָה וְיִשָּׂשכָר וּזְבֻלוּן: בְּנֵי רָחֵל יוֹסֵף וּבִנְיָמִן: וּבְנֵי בִלְהָה שִׁפְחַת רָחֵל
כו דָּן וְנַפְתָּלִי: וּבְנֵי זִלְפָּה שִׁפְחַת לֵאָה גָּד וְאָשֵׁר אֵלֶּה בְּנֵי יַעֲקֹב אֲשֶׁר יֻלַּד־
כז לוֹ בְּפַדַּן אֲרָם: וַיָּבֹא יַעֲקֹב אֶל־יִצְחָק אָבִיו מַמְרֵא קִרְיַת הָאַרְבַּע הִוא
כח חֶבְרוֹן אֲשֶׁר־גָּר־שָׁם אַבְרָהָם וְיִצְחָק: וַיִּהְיוּ יְמֵי יִצְחָק מְאַת שָׁנָה וּשְׁמֹנִים
כט שָׁנָה: וַיִּגְוַע יִצְחָק וַיָּמָת וַיֵּאָסֶף אֶל־עַמָּיו זָקֵן וּשְׂבַע יָמִים וַיִּקְבְּרוּ אֹתוֹ
עֵשָׂו וְיַעֲקֹב בָּנָיו:

לו

א־ב וְאֵלֶּה תֹּלְדוֹת עֵשָׂו הוּא אֱדוֹם: עֵשָׂו לָקַח אֶת־נָשָׁיו מִבְּנוֹת כְּנָעַן אֶת־עָדָה
ג בַּת־אֵילוֹן הַחִתִּי וְאֶת־אָהֳלִיבָמָה בַּת־עֲנָה בַּת־צִבְעוֹן הַחִוִּי: וְאֶת־
ד בָּשְׂמַת בַּת־יִשְׁמָעֵאל אֲחוֹת נְבָיוֹת: וַתֵּלֶד עָדָה לְעֵשָׂו אֶת־אֱלִיפָז
ה וּבָשְׂמַת יָלְדָה אֶת־רְעוּאֵל: וְאָהֳלִיבָמָה יָלְדָה אֶת־°יעיש וְאֶת־יַעְלָם
ו וְאֶת־קֹרַח אֵלֶּה בְּנֵי עֵשָׂו אֲשֶׁר יֻלְּדוּ־לוֹ בְּאֶרֶץ כְּנָעַן: וַיִּקַּח עֵשָׂו אֶת־נָשָׁיו
וְאֶת־בָּנָיו וְאֶת־בְּנֹתָיו וְאֶת־כָּל־נַפְשׁוֹת בֵּיתוֹ וְאֶת־מִקְנֵהוּ וְאֶת־כָּל־
בְּהֶמְתּוֹ וְאֵת כָּל־קִנְיָנוֹ אֲשֶׁר רָכַשׁ בְּאֶרֶץ כְּנָעַן וַיֵּלֶךְ אֶל־אֶרֶץ מִפְּנֵי יַעֲקֹב
ז אָחִיו: כִּי־הָיָה רְכוּשָׁם רָב מִשֶּׁבֶת יַחְדָּו וְלֹא יָכְלָה אֶרֶץ מְגוּרֵיהֶם לָשֵׂאת
ח־ט אֹתָם מִפְּנֵי מִקְנֵיהֶם: וַיֵּשֶׁב עֵשָׂו בְּהַר שֵׂעִיר עֵשָׂו הוּא אֱדוֹם: וְאֵלֶּה
י תֹּלְדוֹת עֵשָׂו אֲבִי אֱדוֹם בְּהַר שֵׂעִיר: אֵלֶּה שְׁמוֹת בְּנֵי־עֵשָׂו אֱלִיפַז בֶּן־עָדָה
יא אֵשֶׁת עֵשָׂו רְעוּאֵל בֶּן־בָּשְׂמַת אֵשֶׁת עֵשָׂו: וַיִּהְיוּ בְּנֵי אֱלִיפָז תֵּימָן אוֹמָר
יב צְפוֹ וְגַעְתָּם וּקְנַז: וְתִמְנַע ׀ הָיְתָה פִילֶגֶשׁ לֶאֱלִיפַז בֶּן־עֵשָׂו וַתֵּלֶד לֶאֱלִיפַז
יג אֶת־עֲמָלֵק אֵלֶּה בְּנֵי עָדָה אֵשֶׁת עֵשָׂו: וְאֵלֶּה בְּנֵי רְעוּאֵל נַחַת וָזֶרַח שַׁמָּה
יד וּמִזָּה אֵלֶּה הָיוּ בְּנֵי בָשְׂמַת אֵשֶׁת עֵשָׂו: וְאֵלֶּה הָיוּ בְּנֵי אָהֳלִיבָמָה בַּת־עֲנָה
בַּת־צִבְעוֹן אֵשֶׁת עֵשָׂו וַתֵּלֶד לְעֵשָׂו אֶת־°יעיש וְאֶת־יַעְלָם וְאֶת־קֹרַח: °יְעוּשׁ ק׳

27. אֲשֶׁר גָּר שָׁם אַבְרָהָם וְיִצְחָק — *Where Abraham and Isaac dwelled.* The mention of the dwelling of the righteous in (a particular place) is of benefit to their children, for it creates an attitude of affection and good will among the inhabitants of that place. The reverse is true of the wicked of whom it is said, הָכִינוּ לְבָנָיו מַטְבֵּחַ בַּעֲוֹן אֲבוֹתָם בַּל יָקֻמוּ וְיָרְשׁוּ אָרֶץ, *Prepare slaughter for his children, for the iniquity of their fathers, that they rise not up and possess the earth (Isaiah* 14:21).

XXXVI

1. וְאֵלֶּה תֹּלְדוֹת — *And these are the chronicles.* These are the chronicles and happenings (of Esau) similar to, מַה יֵּלֶד יוֹם, *What a day may bring forth (Proverbs* 27:1).

עֵשָׂו הוּא אֱדוֹם — *Esau, who is Edom.* He was always (a person of) acquisitive greed consumed with desire, as we find on the day he (sold his birthright and) was called Edom. Since he was exhausted from his evil deeds he was not able to recognize the lentils to call them by name (only by color, אָדוֹם, *red*).

2. וְאֶת אָהֳלִיבָמָה בַּת עֲנָה — *Oholibamah daughter of Anah.* She was descended from the children of Seir, the Horites (see verse 20). It was through her that Esau went (to dwell)

NOTES

XXXVI

1. וְאֵלֶּה תֹּלְדוֹת — *And these are the chronicles.* The phrase תּוֹלְדוֹת has a variety of meanings, i.e., descendants, genealogies, chronicles, etc. In our verse the *Sforno* chooses the latter interpretation, as he does in 25:19 and 37:2.

עֵשָׂו הוּא אֱדוֹם — *Esau, who is Edom.* Regarding the name *Edom*, see the *Sforno's* commentary to 25:30.

*Reuben; Simeon; Levi; Judah; Issachar; and Zebulun. 24 The sons of Rachel:
Joseph and Benjamin. 25 The sons of Bilhah, maidservant of Rachel: Dan
and Naphtali. 26 And the sons of Zilpah, maidservant of Leah: Gad and
Asher — these are the sons of Jacob, who were born to him in Paddan Aram.*
*27 Jacob came to Isaac his father, at Mamre, Kiriath-arba; that is Hebron
where Abraham and Isaac sojourned. 28 Isaac's days were one hundred and
eighty years. 29 And Isaac expired and died, and he was gathered to his
people, old and fulfilled of days; his sons, Esau and Jacob, buried him.*

36 *1 And these are the descendants of Esau, he is Edom. 2 Esau had taken his
wives from among the Canaanite women: Adah, daughter of Elon the
Hittite; and Oholibamah, daughter of Anah, daughter of Zibeon the
Hivvite; 3 and Basemath, daughter of Ishmael, sister of Nebaioth.*
*4 Adah bore to Esau Eliphaz; Basemath bore Reuel; 5 and Oholibamah
bore Jeush, Jalam, and Korah; these are Esau's sons who were born to him
in the land of Canaan.*
*6 Esau took his wives, his sons, his daughters, and all the members of his
household — his livestock and all his animals, and all the wealth he had
acquired in the land of Canaan — and went to a land because of his brother
Jacob. 7 For their wealth was too abundant for them to dwell together, and
the land of their sojourns could not support them because of their livestock.
8 So Esau settled on Mount Seir; Esau, he is Edom.*
*9 And these are the descendants of Esau, ancestor of Edom, on Mount
Seir. 10 These are the names of Esau's sons: Eliphaz, son of Adah, Esau's
wife; Reuel, son of Basemath, Esau's wife.*
*11 The sons of Eliphaz were: Teman; Omar; Zepho; Gatam; and Kenaz.
12 And Timna was a concubine of Eliphaz, son of Esau, and she bore Amalek
to Eliphaz; these are the children of Adah, Esau's wife.*
*13 And these are the sons of Reuel: Nahath and Zerah; Shammah and
Mizzah — these were the children of Basemath, Esau's wife.*
*14 And these were the sons of Oholibamah, daughter of Anah, daughter
of Zibeon, Esau's wife: She bore to Esau Jeush, and Jalam, and Korah.*

---

in the land of Seir, as it says, *So Esau settled on Mount Seir* (verse 8). His children later destroyed the Hori, as it is written, כַּאֲשֶׁר עָשָׂה לִבְנֵי עֵשָׂו הַיֹּשְׁבִים בְּשֵׂעִיר אֲשֶׁר הִשְׁמִיד אֶת הַחֹרִי מִפְּנֵיהֶם, *As He did for the children of Esau, that dwell in Seir, when He destroyed the Hori from before them (Deut.* 2:22). Therefore (the Torah) continues and says ...

9. וְאֵלֶּה תֹּלְדוֹת עֵשָׂו אֲבִי אֱדוֹם בְּהַר שֵׂעִיר — *And these are the progeny of Esau, ancestor of Edom, on Mount Seir* ... (proceeding) to enumerate the chiefs, for his sons later conquered the land (of Seir); Timna became the concubine of Eliphaz and the descendants of Esau (born in Seir) became chiefs.

12. וְתִמְנַע הָיְתָה פִילֶגֶשׁ — *And Timna was a concubine*. Eliphaz was among the conquerors of the land (of Seir) and he took Timna, who was a sister of the (Hori) chieftains, as his concubine.

NOTES

2-20. וְאֵת אָהֳלִיבָמָה בַּת עֲנָה ... אֵלֶּה בְנֵי שֵׂעִיר — *Oholibamah daughter of Anah ... These are the sons of Seir*. The *Sforno* traces the conquests of Esau as follows: He first moved to the region of Seir, apparently after his marriage to Oholibamah who came from Seir, since she was the daughter of Anah the Hori (see verse 20). There he established himself in a small area called Edom, while the Hori

טו אֵלֶּה אַלּוּפֵי בְנֵי־עֵשָׂו בְּנֵי אֱלִיפַז בְּכוֹר עֵשָׂו אַלּוּף תֵּימָן אַלּוּף אוֹמָר
טז אַלּוּף צְפוֹ אַלּוּף קְנַז: אַלּוּף־קֹרַח אַלּוּף גַּעְתָּם אַלּוּף עֲמָלֵק אֵלֶּה אַלּוּפֵי
יז אֱלִיפַז בְּאֶרֶץ אֱדוֹם אֵלֶּה בְּנֵי עָדָה: וְאֵלֶּה בְּנֵי רְעוּאֵל בֶּן־עֵשָׂו אַלּוּף נַחַת
אַלּוּף זֶרַח אַלּוּף שַׁמָּה אַלּוּף מִזָּה אֵלֶּה אַלּוּפֵי רְעוּאֵל בְּאֶרֶץ אֱדוֹם אֵלֶּה
יח בְּנֵי בָשְׂמַת אֵשֶׁת עֵשָׂו: וְאֵלֶּה בְּנֵי אָהֳלִיבָמָה אֵשֶׁת עֵשָׂו אַלּוּף יְעוּשׁ אַלּוּף
יט יַעְלָם אַלּוּף קֹרַח אֵלֶּה אַלּוּפֵי אָהֳלִיבָמָה בַּת־עֲנָה אֵשֶׁת עֵשָׂו: אֵלֶּה בְנֵי־
שביעי כ עֵשָׂו וְאֵלֶּה אַלּוּפֵיהֶם הוּא אֱדוֹם: אֵלֶּה בְנֵי־שֵׂעִיר הַחֹרִי
כא יֹשְׁבֵי הָאָרֶץ לוֹטָן וְשׁוֹבָל וְצִבְעוֹן וַעֲנָה: וְדִשׁוֹן וְאֵצֶר וְדִישָׁן אֵלֶּה אַלּוּפֵי
כב הַחֹרִי בְּנֵי שֵׂעִיר בְּאֶרֶץ אֱדוֹם: וַיִּהְיוּ בְנֵי־לוֹטָן חֹרִי וְהֵימָם וַאֲחוֹת לוֹטָן
כג־כד תִּמְנָע: וְאֵלֶּה בְּנֵי שׁוֹבָל עַלְוָן וּמָנַחַת וְעֵיבָל שְׁפוֹ וְאוֹנָם: וְאֵלֶּה בְנֵי־צִבְעוֹן
וְאַיָּה וַעֲנָה הוּא עֲנָה אֲשֶׁר מָצָא אֶת־הַיֵּמִם בַּמִּדְבָּר בִּרְעֹתוֹ אֶת־הַחֲמֹרִים
כה־כו לְצִבְעוֹן אָבִיו: וְאֵלֶּה בְנֵי־עֲנָה דִּשֹׁן וְאָהֳלִיבָמָה בַּת־עֲנָה: וְאֵלֶּה בְּנֵי דִישָׁן
כז־כח חֶמְדָּן וְאֶשְׁבָּן וְיִתְרָן וּכְרָן: אֵלֶּה בְּנֵי־אֵצֶר בִּלְהָן וְזַעֲוָן וַעֲקָן: אֵלֶּה בְנֵי־
כט דִישָׁן עוּץ וַאֲרָן: אֵלֶּה אַלּוּפֵי הַחֹרִי אַלּוּף לוֹטָן אַלּוּף שׁוֹבָל אַלּוּף צִבְעוֹן
ל אַלּוּף עֲנָה: אַלּוּף דִּשֹׁן אַלּוּף אֵצֶר אַלּוּף דִּישָׁן אֵלֶּה אַלּוּפֵי הַחֹרִי
לְאַלֻּפֵיהֶם בְּאֶרֶץ שֵׂעִיר:
לא וְאֵלֶּה הַמְּלָכִים אֲשֶׁר מָלְכוּ בְּאֶרֶץ אֱדוֹם לִפְנֵי מְלָךְ־מֶלֶךְ לִבְנֵי יִשְׂרָאֵל:
לב־לג וַיִּמְלֹךְ בֶּאֱדוֹם בֶּלַע בֶּן־בְּעוֹר וְשֵׁם עִירוֹ דִּנְהָבָה: וַיָּמָת בָּלַע וַיִּמְלֹךְ
לד תַּחְתָּיו יוֹבָב בֶּן־זֶרַח מִבָּצְרָה: וַיָּמָת יוֹבָב וַיִּמְלֹךְ תַּחְתָּיו חֻשָׁם מֵאֶרֶץ
לה הַתֵּימָנִי: וַיָּמָת חֻשָׁם וַיִּמְלֹךְ תַּחְתָּיו הֲדַד בֶּן־בְּדַד הַמַּכֶּה אֶת־מִדְיָן בִּשְׂדֵה
לו־לז מוֹאָב וְשֵׁם עִירוֹ עֲוִית: וַיָּמָת הֲדָד וַיִּמְלֹךְ תַּחְתָּיו שַׂמְלָה מִמַּשְׂרֵקָה: וַיָּמָת
לח שַׂמְלָה וַיִּמְלֹךְ תַּחְתָּיו שָׁאוּל מֵרְחֹבוֹת הַנָּהָר: וַיָּמָת שָׁאוּל וַיִּמְלֹךְ תַּחְתָּיו

20. אֵלֶּה בְנֵי שֵׂעִיר הַחֹרִי — *These are the sons of Seir, the Hori.* (The Torah) records the names of these mighty men of repute to tell us that even so, the children of Esau were able to destroy them, for this was the will of the Almighty, as it says, כַּאֲשֶׁר עָשָׂה לִבְנֵי עֵשָׂו הַיֹּשְׁבִים בְּשֵׂעִיר, *As He did for the children of Esau that dwell in Seir (Deut.* 2:22).

31. וְאֵלֶּה הַמְּלָכִים — *Now these are the kings.* We are being told that they were constrained to appoint strangers as kings, for there were none among them worthy to reign; (also) they were unable to establish a dynasty (lit., a king, the son of a king).

לִפְנֵי מְלָךְ מֶלֶךְ — *Before a king reigned (over the children of Israel).* Before Moses reigned over (Israel) at the behest of God, the Blessed One, as it says, וַיְצַוֵּם אֶל בְּנֵי יִשְׂרָאֵל, *And gave them (Moses and Aaron) a charge to the children of Israel (Exodus* 6:13); similar to, וְצִוְּךָ לְנָגִיד, *And He will appoint you as ruler (over Israel) (I Samuel* 25:30). However, once a

NOTES

controlled the major area called Seir (see the *Sforno* to 32:4). The sons of Esau eventually destroyed the Hori, in spite of the latter's great strength and might, as indicated in verse 20 according to the *Sforno's* commentary. And with God's help (recorded in *Deut.* 2) the descendants of Esau took over Seir.

31. וְאֵלֶּה הַמְּלָכִים — *Now these are the kings.* See the *Sforno* on 35:11.

לִפְנֵי מְלָךְ מֶלֶךְ — *Before a king reigned (over the children of Israel).* The *Sforno* interprets the word צִוָּה as meaning *to appoint as a leader,* when used in a context such as the verse in *Exodus* 6:13

15 *These are the chiefs of the children of Esau — the descendants of Esau's firstborn Eliphaz: Chief Teman, Chief Omar, Chief Zepho, Chief Kenaz;*
16 *Chief Korah, Chief Gatam, Chief Amalek; these are the chiefs of Eliphaz in the land of Edom — these are the descendants of Adah.*

17 *And these are the descendants of Reuel, Esau's son: Chief Nahath, Chief Zerah, Chief Shammah, Chief Mizzah; these are the chiefs of Reuel in the land of Edom — these are the descendants of Basemath, Esau's wife.*

18 *And these are the descendants of Ohlibamah, Esau's wife: Chief Jeush, Chief Jalam, Chief Korah — these are the chiefs of Ohlibamah, daughter of*
Anah, Esau's wife. 19 *These are the children of Esau, and these are the chiefs; he is Edom.*

20 *These are the sons of Seir the Horite who were settled in the land: Lotah*
and Shobal and Zibeon and Anah, 21 *and Dishon and Ezer and Dishan — these are the chiefs of the Horite, the descendants of Seir in the land of Edom.*

22 *The sons of Lotan were: Hori and Hemam; Lotan's sister was Timna.*

23 *These are the sons of Shobal: Alvan and Manahath and Ebal; Shepho and Onam.*

24 *These are the sons of Zibeon: Aiah and Anah — the same Anah who discovered the mules in the desert while he was pasturing the donkeys for Zibeon, his father.*

25 *These are the children of Anah: Dishon and Oholibamah daughter of Anah.*

26 *These are the sons of Dishan: Hemdan and Eshban and Ithran and Cheran.*

27 *These are the sons of Ezer: Bilhan and Zaavan and Akan.*

28 *These are the sons of Dishan: Uz and Aran.*

29 *These are the chiefs of the Horite: Chief Lotan, Chief Shobal, Chief*
Zibeon, Chief Anah, 30 *Chief Dishon, Chief Etzer, Chief Dishan — these are the chiefs of the Horite, according to their chiefs, in the land of Seir.*

31 *Now these are the kings who reigned in the land of Edom before a king*
reigned over the Children of Israel: 32 *Bela, son of Beor, reigned in Edom, and*
the name of his city was Dinhabah. 33 *And Bela died, and Jobab son of Zerah,*
from Bozrah, reigned after him. 34 *And Jobab died and Husham, of the land*
of the Temanites, reigned after him. 35 *And Husham died, and Hadad son of*
Bedad, who defeated the Midianites in the field of Moab, reigned after him,
and the name of his city was Avith. 36 *And Hadad died, and Samlah of*
Masrekah reigned after him. 37 *And Samlah died, and Saul of Rehoboth*
nahar reigned after him. 38 *And Saul died, and Baal-hanan, son of Achbor,*

---

king reigned (over Israel), the kingdom of Esau ceased, and there were only chiefs, in keeping with, וּלְאֹם מִלְאֹם יֶאֱמָץ, *And one people shall be stronger than the other* (25:23).

NOTES

regarding Moses and Aaron; the verse in *Numbers* 27:23 regarding Joshua; and the verse in *I Samuel* 25:30 regarding David. The *Sforno* quotes the phrase וּלְאֹם מִלְאֹם (25:23), to explain why once Moses became a king over Israel, Esau no longer had kings reigning, only chieftains. *Rashi* on that verse states, "When one rises the other falls," i.e., Jacob and Esau cannot reign simultaneously. Since Moses was considered a king, Esau could no longer have a king ruling over his people.

לט בַּ֥עַל חָנָ֖ן בֶּן־עַכְבּֽוֹר׃ וַיָּ֜מָת בַּ֣עַל חָנָ֣ן בֶּן־עַכְבּ֗וֹר וַיִּמְלֹ֤ךְ תַּחְתָּיו֙ הֲדַ֔ר וְשֵׁ֥ם
מפטיר מ עִיר֖וֹ פָּ֑עוּ וְשֵׁ֣ם אִשְׁתּ֤וֹ מְהֵֽיטַבְאֵל֙ בַּת־מַטְרֵ֔ד בַּ֖ת מֵ֥י זָהָֽב׃ וְאֵ֨לֶּה שְׁמ֜וֹת
אַלּוּפֵ֤י עֵשָׂו֙ לְמִשְׁפְּחֹתָ֔ם לִמְקֹמֹתָ֖ם בִּשְׁמֹתָ֑ם אַלּ֥וּף תִּמְנָ֛ע אַלּ֥וּף עַֽלְוָ֖ה
מא־מב אַלּ֥וּף יְתֵֽת׃ אַלּ֧וּף אָהֳלִֽיבָמָ֛ה אַלּ֥וּף אֵלָ֖ה אַלּ֥וּף פִּינֹֽן׃ אַלּ֥וּף קְנַ֛ז אַלּ֥וּף
מג תֵּימָ֖ן אַלּ֥וּף מִבְצָֽר׃ אַלּ֥וּף מַגְדִּיאֵ֖ל אַלּ֣וּף עִירָ֑ם אֵ֣לֶּה ׀ אַלּוּפֵ֣י אֱד֗וֹם
לְמֹשְׁבֹתָם֙ בְּאֶ֣רֶץ אֲחֻזָּתָ֔ם ה֥וּא עֵשָׂ֖ו אֲבִ֥י אֱדֽוֹם׃

---

40. וְאֵלֶּה שְׁמוֹת אַלּוּפֵי עֵשָׂו לְמִשְׁפְּחֹתָם לִמְקֹמֹתָם בִּשְׁמֹתָם — *And these are the names of the chiefs of Esau by their families, by their regions, by their names. By their regions, by their*

reigned after him. [39] *Baal-hanan, son of Achbor, died, and Hadar reigned*
after him; the name of his city was Pau, and his wife's name was Mehetabel,
daughter of Matred, daughter of Me-zahab.
[40] *Now these are the names of the chiefs of Esau, by their families, by their*
regions, by their names: the chief of Timna; the chief of Alvah; the chief of
Jetheth; [41] *the chief of Oholibamah; the chief of Elah; the chief of Pinon;*
[42] *the chief of Kenaz; the chief of Teman; the chief of Mibzar;* [43] *the chief of*
Magdiel and the chief of Iram; these are the chiefs of Edom by their
settlements, in the land of their possession — he is Esau, father of Edom.

names, implies that they were not sufficiently important (distinguished) to be called by their names, only by their regions.

פרשת וישב

לז א־ב וַיֵּשֶׁב יַעֲקֹב בְּאֶרֶץ מְגוּרֵי אָבִיו בְּאֶרֶץ כְּנָעַן: אֵלֶּה ׀ תֹּלְדוֹת יַעֲקֹב יוֹסֵף
בֶּן־שְׁבַע־עֶשְׂרֵה שָׁנָה הָיָה רֹעֶה אֶת־אֶחָיו בַּצֹּאן וְהוּא נַעַר אֶת־בְּנֵי בִלְהָה
וְאֶת־בְּנֵי זִלְפָּה נְשֵׁי אָבִיו וַיָּבֵא יוֹסֵף אֶת־דִּבָּתָם רָעָה אֶל־אֲבִיהֶם:
ג וְיִשְׂרָאֵל אָהַב אֶת־יוֹסֵף מִכָּל־בָּנָיו כִּי־בֶן־זְקֻנִים הוּא לוֹ וְעָשָׂה לוֹ כְּתֹנֶת
ד פַּסִּים: וַיִּרְאוּ אֶחָיו כִּי־אֹתוֹ אָהַב אֲבִיהֶם מִכָּל־אֶחָיו וַיִּשְׂנְאוּ אֹתוֹ וְלֹא יָכְלוּ
ה־ו דַּבְּרוֹ לְשָׁלֹם: וַיַּחֲלֹם יוֹסֵף חֲלוֹם וַיַּגֵּד לְאֶחָיו וַיּוֹסִפוּ עוֹד שְׂנֹא אֹתוֹ: וַיֹּאמֶר
ז אֲלֵיהֶם שִׁמְעוּ־נָא הַחֲלוֹם הַזֶּה אֲשֶׁר חָלָמְתִּי: וְהִנֵּה אֲנַחְנוּ מְאַלְּמִים
אֲלֻמִּים בְּתוֹךְ הַשָּׂדֶה וְהִנֵּה קָמָה אֲלֻמָּתִי וְגַם־נִצָּבָה וְהִנֵּה תְסֻבֶּינָה
ח אֲלֻמֹּתֵיכֶם וַתִּשְׁתַּחֲוֶיןָ לַאֲלֻמָּתִי: וַיֹּאמְרוּ לוֹ אֶחָיו הֲמָלֹךְ תִּמְלֹךְ עָלֵינוּ
אִם־מָשׁוֹל תִּמְשֹׁל בָּנוּ וַיּוֹסִפוּ עוֹד שְׂנֹא אֹתוֹ עַל־חֲלֹמֹתָיו וְעַל־דְּבָרָיו:

XXXVII

1. וַיֵּשֶׁב יַעֲקֹב בְּאֶרֶץ מְגוּרֵי אָבִיו בְּאֶרֶץ כְּנָעַן — *And Jacob dwelt in the land of his father's sojournings, in the Land of Canaan.* He dwelt in that portion of the Land of Canaan where his father lived, as we find, *where Abraham and Isaac lived* (35:27).

2. אֵלֶּה תֹּלְדוֹת יַעֲקֹב — *These are the generations of Jacob.* These are the events which happened to him after he dwelt there (in Canaan). The events which occurred to him when he first left his father's house foreshadow our history during the first exile, while the events which occurred to him after he returned to his father's (home) foreshadow our history during the Second Temple and our subsequent exile — and redemption at the end of time.

הָיָה רֹעֶה אֶת אֶחָיו בַּצֹּאן — *Tending the sheep with his brethren.* He guided and instructed them in the technique of raising and tending sheep.

וְהוּא נַעַר — *He was a lad.* Because he was only a lad, he sinned by telling tales about his brothers, for he was inexperienced and could not foresee where this would lead; even though he was very intelligent and soon thereafter counseled the elders of Egypt, as we read, וּזְקֵנָיו יְחַכֵּם, *And teach his elders wisdom* (*Psalms* 105:22). This bears out what our Sages tell us, וְלֹא בְּדַרְדְּקֵי עֵצָה, *There is no counsel in the young* (*Shabbos* 89b).

וַיָּבֵא יוֹסֵף אֶת דִּבָּתָם רָעָה — *And Joseph brought evil report of them.* He accused them (his brothers) of neglecting the flocks and not caring for them properly; all this at a time when this enterprise represented the major source of their income and wealth.

NOTES

XXXVII

1. וַיֵּשֶׁב יַעֲקֹב בְּאֶרֶץ מְגוּרֵי אָבִיו בְּאֶרֶץ כְּנָעַן — *And Jacob dwelt in the land of his father's sojournings, in the Land of Canaan.* The Land of Canaan was comparatively large and the section where Jacob's father lived was also sizeable, hence אֶרֶץ כְּנָעַן and מְגוּרֵי אָבִיו does not necessarily mean that Jacob actually resided in the community of his fathers. The *Sforno* however interprets it so, based on 35:27. In his commentary there the *Sforno* points out that it is advantageous for a son and/or grandson of a prominent man to reside in his father's and grandfather's community where they have established a good name and were beloved to the people.

2. אֵלֶּה תֹּלְדוֹת יַעֲקֹב — *These are the generations of Jacob.* This is in keeping with the saying of our Sages, "Everything that happened to Jacob happened later to his children."

וְהוּא נַעַר — *He was a lad.* The *Sforno*, reflecting the attitude of our Sages, states that intelligence, and even wisdom, are independent of maturity, while the ability to offer counsel comes with the experience of age. Joseph possessed the former but lacked the latter.

וַיָּבֵא יוֹסֵף אֶת דִּבָּתָם רָעָה — *And Joseph brought evil report of them.* Unlike other commentators, the *Sforno* feels that the word דִּבָּה does not mean *evil tidings* in this case, rather informing and complaining.

PARASHAS VAYEISHEV

37 [1] *Jacob settled in the land of his father's sojournings, in the land of Canaan.*
[2] *These are the chronicles of Jacob: Joseph, at the age of seventeen, was a shepherd with his brothers by the flock, but he was a youth with the sons of Bilhah and the sons of Zilpah, his father's wives; and Joseph would bring evil reports about them to their father.* [3] *Now Israel loved Joseph more than all his sons since he was a child of his old age, and he made him a fine woolen tunic.* [4] *His brothers saw that it was he whom their father loved most of all his brothers so they hated him; and they could not speak to him peaceably.*

[5] *Joseph dreamt a dream which he told to his brothers, and they hated him even more.* [6] *He said to them, "Hear, if you please, this dream which I dreamt:* [7] *Behold! — we were binding sheaves in the middle of the field, when, behold! — my sheaf arose and remained standing; then behold! — your sheaves gathered around and bowed down to my sheaf."*

[8] *His brothers said to him, "Would you then reign over us? Would you then dominate us?" And they hated him even more — because of his dreams and because of his talk.*

---

3. וְעָשָׂה לוֹ כְּתֹנֶת פַּסִּים — *And he made him a coat of many colors* . . . as a sign that he will be the leader in the house and in the field, as we find, וְהִלְבַּשְׁתִּיו כֻּתָּנְתֶּךָ, *And I will clothe him with your robe (Isaiah 22:21)*, and as our Sages have said, 'The brothers are content that the eldest brother wear the finest clothes so that he be respected' (*Bava Kamma* 11b).

4. וַיִּרְאוּ אֶחָיו כִּי אֹתוֹ אָהַב אֲבִיהֶם — *And when his brothers saw that their father loved him.* Jacob erred in differentiating between his sons, in a manner that revealed to the brothers the love he felt (for Joseph) in his heart.

וְלֹא יָכְלוּ דַּבְּרוֹ לְשָׁלֹם — *And would not speak peaceably with him.* Even though the brothers found it necessary to speak with (Joseph) with regard to the household and flocks, since Joseph was in charge of them, at the direction of his father. (Nevertheless) they could not speak peaceably with him in friendship, as is customary among brothers.

5. וַיַּגֵּד לְאֶחָיו — *And he told it to his brothers.* In this, too, he acted with the inexperience of youth.

6. שִׁמְעוּ נָא הַחֲלוֹם הַזֶּה — *Hear, I pray you, this dream.* Not only did he tell them the dream but asked them to listen attentively and understand its significance. In this manner he added to their animosity as indicated in their response, '*Shall you indeed reign over us?*' (verse 8).

7. וְגַם נִצָּבָה — *And also stood upright.* This indicated that his rule would endure for a long time, as it did in fact, for eighty years, longer than the reign of any (Jewish) ruler recorded in the holy Scriptures.

8. עַל חֲלֹמֹתָיו — *For his dreams* . . . the detailed manner in which he related it, in a spirit of eager anticipation for its fulfillment.

NOTES

3. וְעָשָׂה לוֹ כְּתֹנֶת פַּסִּים — *And he made him a coat of many colors.* The coat of many colors, in itself, would not have upset the brothers. They could have had the same finery, if they so chose. It was what this cloak *represented* that angered them, namely the status and position of Joseph, their younger brother.

7. וְגַם נִצָּבָה — *And also stood upright.* The word נִצָּב has a special implication, that which stands firmly and well established. Since the phrase used by Joseph is not עוֹמֵד but נִצָּב, it has special significance.

8. עַל חֲלֹמֹתָיו וְעַל דְּבָרָיו — *For his dreams and for his words.* The verse uses two phrases — *his*

ט וַיַּחֲלֹם עוֹד חֲלוֹם אַחֵר וַיְסַפֵּר אֹתוֹ לְאֶחָיו וַיֹּאמֶר הִנֵּה חָלַמְתִּי חֲלוֹם עוֹד
י וְהִנֵּה הַשֶּׁמֶשׁ וְהַיָּרֵחַ וְאַחַד עָשָׂר כּוֹכָבִים מִשְׁתַּחֲוִים לִי: וַיְסַפֵּר אֶל־אָבִיו
וְאֶל־אֶחָיו וַיִּגְעַר־בּוֹ אָבִיו וַיֹּאמֶר לוֹ מָה הַחֲלוֹם הַזֶּה אֲשֶׁר חָלָמְתָּ הֲבוֹא
יא נָבוֹא אֲנִי וְאִמְּךָ וְאַחֶיךָ לְהִשְׁתַּחֲוֹת לְךָ אָרְצָה: וַיְקַנְאוּ־בוֹ אֶחָיו וְאָבִיו שָׁמַר
שני יב־יג אֶת־הַדָּבָר: *וַיֵּלְכוּ אֶחָיו לִרְעוֹת *אֶת־צֹאן אֲבִיהֶם בִּשְׁכֶם: וַיֹּאמֶר יִשְׂרָאֵל
אֶל־יוֹסֵף הֲלוֹא אַחֶיךָ רֹעִים בִּשְׁכֶם לְכָה וְאֶשְׁלָחֲךָ אֲלֵיהֶם וַיֹּאמֶר לוֹ
יד הִנֵּנִי: וַיֹּאמֶר לוֹ לֶךְ־נָא רְאֵה אֶת־שְׁלוֹם אַחֶיךָ וְאֶת־שְׁלוֹם הַצֹּאן וַהֲשִׁבֵנִי
טו דָּבָר וַיִּשְׁלָחֵהוּ מֵעֵמֶק חֶבְרוֹן וַיָּבֹא שְׁכֶמָה: וַיִּמְצָאֵהוּ אִישׁ וְהִנֵּה תֹעֶה
טז בַּשָּׂדֶה וַיִּשְׁאָלֵהוּ הָאִישׁ לֵאמֹר מַה־תְּבַקֵּשׁ: וַיֹּאמֶר אֶת־אַחַי אָנֹכִי מְבַקֵּשׁ
יז הַגִּידָה־נָּא לִי אֵיפֹה הֵם רֹעִים: וַיֹּאמֶר הָאִישׁ נָסְעוּ מִזֶּה כִּי שָׁמַעְתִּי אֹמְרִים
יח נֵלְכָה דֹּתָיְנָה וַיֵּלֶךְ יוֹסֵף אַחַר אֶחָיו וַיִּמְצָאֵם בְּדֹתָן: וַיִּרְאוּ אֹתוֹ מֵרָחֹק
יט וּבְטֶרֶם יִקְרַב אֲלֵיהֶם וַיִּתְנַכְּלוּ אֹתוֹ לַהֲמִיתוֹ: וַיֹּאמְרוּ אִישׁ אֶל־אָחִיו

וְעַל דְּבָרָיו — *And for his words* ... when he said to them, "*Hear, I pray you*" (verse 6), urging them to pay heed and grasp the significance of the dream.

10. מָה הַחֲלוֹם הַזֶּה — *What is this dream?* It is your evil thoughts (which) cause you to dream of ruling over us; your thoughts came while on your bed.

11. וַיְקַנְאוּ בוֹ אֶחָיו — *And his brothers envied him.* They believed that only because he was held in high esteem by his father did (Joseph) dare to tell such a dream to his father.

וְאָבִיו שָׁמַר — *But his father kept it in mind.* He was convinced that it was a true dream and he looked forward to its realization, as our Sages tell us, "One is jealous of all, except his son and his student" (*Sanhedrin* 105b).

13. הֲלוֹא אַחֶיךָ רֹעִים בִּשְׁכֶם — *Behold, your brothers are tending the flock in Shechem* ... and it is not too far to go there.

14. לֶךְ נָא רְאֵה — *Go now, please, and see.* Observe and judge (whether all is well) and do whatever is needed to be corrected, for had (Jacob) wanted only a report he could have sent one of his servants.

וַיִּשְׁלָחֵהוּ מֵעֵמֶק חֶבְרוֹן — *And he sent him from the vale of Hebron.* (Jacob) accompanied him to the vale.

15. תֹּעֶה בַּשָּׂדֶה — *Wandering in the field* ... walking hither and yon to find their pasture land.

מַה תְּבַקֵּשׁ — *What do you seek?* ... that you do not follow a single, straight path.

16. אֵיפֹה הֵם רֹעִים — *Where they are tending the flock?* ... in which part of this area.

17. נָסְעוּ מִזֶּה — *They have departed from here.* Without a doubt they have left this pasture land and there is no reason to continue your search in any part of this area.

NOTES

dreams and *his words.* The Hebrew word חֲלֹמֹתָיו is in the plural form — but Joseph only told them one dream! The answer given by the *Sforno* is that even though the dream was one, the details given by Joseph were elaborate. They objected not only to his expansive telling of the dream but also the manner (*his words*) where he insisted that they pay close attention to its implications.

10. מָה הַחֲלוֹם הַזֶּה — *What is this dream?* The expression, "your thoughts came while on your bed," is borrowed from *Daniel* 2:29. It is the basis of our Sages' saying, "A person dreams at night that which he thinks about during the day" (*Berachos* 55b).

17. אַחַר אֶחָיו — *After his brothers.* By going to Shechem Joseph has fulfilled the commandment

9 He dreamt another dream, and related it to his brothers. And he said,
"Look, I dreamt another dream: Behold! the sun, the moon, and eleven stars
were bowing down to me."
10 And he related it to his father and to his brothers; his father scolded him,
and said to him, "What is this dream that you have dreamt! Are we to come
— I and your mother and your brothers — to bow down to you to the
ground?" 11 So his brothers were jealous of him, but his father kept the
matter in mind.
12 Now, his brothers went to pasture their father's flock in Shechem.
13 And Israel said to Joseph, "Your brothers are pasturing in Shechem, are
they not? Come, I will send you to them." He said to him: "Here I am!"
14 And he said to him, "Go now, look into the welfare of your brothers and
the welfare of the flock, and bring me back word." So he sent him from the
depth of Hebron, and he arrived at Shechem.
15 A man discovered him, and behold! — he was blundering in the field; the
man asked him, saying, "What do you seek?" 16 And he said, "My brothers
do I seek; tell me, please, where they are pasturing." 17 The man said: "They
have journeyed on from here, for I heard them saying, 'Let us go to Dothan.' "
So Joseph went after his brothers and found them at Dothan.
18 They saw him from afar; and when he had not yet approached them
they conspired against him to kill him. 19 And they said to one another,

---

כִּי שָׁמַעְתִּי אֹמְרִים — *For I heard them say.* The reason I say that they have departed is not that I saw them leave, but because I heard them say, "נֵלְכָה דֹּתָיְנָה, *Let us go to Dothan.*"

אַחַר אֶחָיו — *After his brothers.* Even though he did not find them in Shechem, as his father had said, nonetheless he still exerted himself to find them so as to fulfill his father's will and desire.

18. וַיִּתְנַכְּלוּ אֹתוֹ לַהֲמִיתוֹ — *They were conspired against by him, that he slay (them).* The root נכל (*to beguile*) means to use one's wiles for an evil end, as we find, אֲשֶׁר נִכְּלוּ לָכֶם, *wherewith they have beguiled you* (*Numbers* 25:18). The brothers considered Joseph to be a נוֹכֵל (one who uses deceit and wiles to harm) even to the point of death. They reasoned, "He has not come in our interest, but only to find fault or transgression which he can report to our father so that he will curse us, or for which we will be punished by God; then he alone would remain blessed." The grammatical (Hebrew) form הִתְפָּעֵל (a reflexive verb) is applicable to thought and imagination (as well as action, i.e., that which has an impact upon one's designs and plans) as we find, אַתָּה מִתְנַקֵּשׁ בְּנַפְשִׁי, *You are setting a trap to harm my soul* (*I Samuel* 28:9). (The word) לַהֲמִיתוֹ, *to slay him,* means that he (Joseph) wishes to slay his brothers, as we find לַעֲשֹׂתְכֶם אֹתָם, *that* you *might do them* (*Deut.* 4:14), or לְעָבְרְךָ בִּבְרִית, *that* you *should enter into the covenant* (ibid. 29:11). We are then being told (by the Torah) that the brothers were convinced that Joseph was beguiling and deceiving them

NOTES

of כִּבּוּד אָב (respect for his father). He continues on, because he is anxious to fulfill this *mitzvah* in spirit as well as to the letter.

18. וַיִּתְנַכְּלוּ אֹתוֹ לַהֲמִיתוֹ — *They were conspired against by him, that he slay (them).* The *Sforno* interprets the three words, וַיִּתְנַכְּלוּ אֹתוֹ לַהֲמִיתוֹ, not in the traditional sense of *they conspired against him to slay him,* but the reverse, Joseph was conspiring to destroy them. Departing from his usual concise, succinct style, he expands on this theory by explaining the use of the הִתְפָּעֵל form (וַיִּתְנַכְּלוּ) and also shows that the word לַהֲמִיתוֹ need not mean *to kill him,* Joseph being the object, but can also mean that he will slay them. This interpretation the *Sforno* feels is correct since the brothers were righteous men, and it is inconceivable that

כ הִנֵּה בַּעַל הַחֲלֹמוֹת הַלָּזֶה בָּא: וְעַתָּה | לְכוּ וְנַהַרְגֵהוּ וְנַשְׁלִכֵהוּ בְּאַחַד הַבֹּרוֹת
כא וְאָמַרְנוּ חַיָּה רָעָה אֲכָלָתְהוּ וְנִרְאֶה מַה־יִּהְיוּ חֲלֹמֹתָיו: וַיִּשְׁמַע רְאוּבֵן
כב וַיַּצִּלֵהוּ מִיָּדָם וַיֹּאמֶר לֹא נַכֶּנּוּ נָפֶשׁ: וַיֹּאמֶר אֲלֵהֶם | רְאוּבֵן אַל־תִּשְׁפְּכוּ־דָם
הַשְׁלִיכוּ אֹתוֹ אֶל־הַבּוֹר הַזֶּה אֲשֶׁר בַּמִּדְבָּר וְיָד אַל־תִּשְׁלְחוּ־בוֹ לְמַעַן
שלישי כג הַצִּיל אֹתוֹ מִיָּדָם לַהֲשִׁיבוֹ אֶל־אָבִיו: וַיְהִי כַּאֲשֶׁר־בָּא יוֹסֵף אֶל־אֶחָיו
כד וַיַּפְשִׁיטוּ אֶת־יוֹסֵף אֶת־כֻּתָּנְתּוֹ אֶת־כְּתֹנֶת הַפַּסִּים אֲשֶׁר עָלָיו: וַיִּקָּחֻהוּ
כה וַיַּשְׁלִכוּ אֹתוֹ הַבֹּרָה וְהַבּוֹר רֵק אֵין בּוֹ מָיִם: וַיֵּשְׁבוּ לֶאֱכָל־לֶחֶם וַיִּשְׂאוּ
עֵינֵיהֶם וַיִּרְאוּ וְהִנֵּה אֹרְחַת יִשְׁמְעֵאלִים בָּאָה מִגִּלְעָד וּגְמַלֵּיהֶם נֹשְׂאִים
כו נְכֹאת וּצְרִי וָלֹט הוֹלְכִים לְהוֹרִיד מִצְרָיְמָה: וַיֹּאמֶר יְהוּדָה אֶל־אֶחָיו מַה־
כז בֶּצַע כִּי נַהֲרֹג אֶת־אָחִינוּ וְכִסִּינוּ אֶת־דָּמוֹ: לְכוּ וְנִמְכְּרֶנּוּ לַיִּשְׁמְעֵאלִים וְיָדֵנוּ

---

with the intent of destroying them in this world or in the world to come (or both), hence they felt justified in slaying (or selling) him to prevent him from slaying them, וְהַתּוֹרָה אָמְרָה הַבָּא לְהָרְגְךָ הַשְׁכֵּם לְהָרְגוֹ, *as the Torah teaches us, "He who comes to kill you, arise to slay him" (Sanhedrin 72a).*

(This we say) for they were all righteous men — so much so that their names are inscribed as a memorial before God (on the breastplate and *ephod* of the High Priest) — how then is it conceivable that they would kill or sell Joseph (without good reason) and subsequently not even regret their act? For even though they later say, *"We are guilty concerning our brother"* (42:21), they are not lamenting the sale or their intended slaying of him, only their cruelty and callousness in turning a deaf ear to his pleas.

19. הִנֵּה בַּעַל הַחֲלֹמוֹת הַלָּזֶה בָּא — *Behold, this dreamer comes.* He intentionally told us his dreams to provoke us to take revenge on him, so as to make us sin against God or our father (or both), that we might perish.

20. וְעַתָּה לְכוּ — *Come now therefore.* They encouraged one another to prepare to kill him.

וְאָמַרְנוּ חַיָּה רָעָה אֲכָלָתְהוּ — *And we will say an evil beast has devoured him* ... lest (our father) become angry and curse us.

וְנִרְאֶה מַה יִּהְיוּ חֲלֹמֹתָיו — *And we shall see what will become of his dreams.* The dreams he told us which foretold that he would be a ruler over us will now be proven false and they will be as naught, discredited and unfulfilled.

21. וַיַּצִּלֵהוּ מִיָּדָם — *And delivered him out of their hand* ... by preventing them from taking a rash irremediable step, which even the righteous man can be guilty of at times, as we find by Reuben and Bilhah, as (Jacob) says, פַּחַז כַּמַּיִם, *unstable (or hasty) as water* (49:4).

22. וְיָד אַל תִּשְׁלְחוּ בוֹ — *But lay no hand upon him.* To actually commit an act of cruelty, as it is written, מֵרְשָׁעִים יֵצֵא רֶשַׁע וְיָדִי לֹא תִהְיֶה בָּךְ, *Out of the wicked comes forth wickedness; but my hand shall not be upon you (I Samuel 24:13).*

NOTES

they would plot to kill Joseph, unless it was in self-defense. Obviously, the fear of the brothers that Joseph intended to harm them was unfounded.

22. וְיָד אַל תִּשְׁלְחוּ בוֹ — *But lay no hand upon him.* An overt act of violence is far graver than a passive one — such as casting him into the pit — even though he will be exposed to danger. The parallel brought by the *Sforno* is from the episode of David and Saul, where Saul was vulnerable and David could easily have slain him but desisted, for he did not want to do so in an overt manner. If evil is destined to befall a person, let it come through a רָשָׁע, *an evil man,* not through a צַדִּיק, *a righteous person.*

25. הוֹלְכִים לְהוֹרִיד מִצְרָיְמָה — *Going to carry it down to Egypt.* The story of the sale of Joseph recorded in the Torah is a bit confusing. What is

"Look! That dreamer is coming! [20] *So now, come and let us kill him, and throw him into one of the pits; and we will say, 'A wild beast devoured him.' Then we shall see what will become of his dreams."*

[21]*Reuben heard, and he rescued him from their hand; he said, "We will not strike him mortally!"* [22] *And Reuben said to them: "Shed no blood! Throw him into this pit in the wilderness, but lay no hand on him!" — intending to rescue him from their hand, to return him to his father.*

[23] *And so it was, when Joseph came to his brothers they stripped Joseph of his tunic, the fine woolen tunic that was on him.* [24] *Then they took him, and cast him into the pit; the pit was empty, no water was in it.*

[25] *They sat to eat food; they raised their eyes and they saw, behold! — a caravan of Ishmaelites was coming from Gilead, their camels bearing spices, balsam, and lotus — on their way to bring them down to Egypt.* [26] *Judah said to his brothers, "What gain will there be if we kill our brother and cover up his blood?* [27] *Come, let us sell him to the Ishmaelites —*

לְמַעַן הַצִּיל אֹתוֹ — *That he might deliver him . . .* to bring him up later (from the pit).

25. וַיֵּשְׁבוּ לֶאֱכָל לֶחֶם — *And they sat down to eat bread.* In their eyes they had done no wrong, nor committed any sin, which would have deterred them from sitting down to eat a meal, for a righteous person who feels he has done wrong refrains from eating, as we find when the Israelites slew the tribe of Benjamin, as it is written, וַיֵּשְׁבוּ שָׁם עַד הָעֶרֶב לִפְנֵי הָאֱלֹהִים וַיִּשְׂאוּ קוֹלָם וַיִּבְכּוּ בְּכִי גָדוֹל, וַיֹּאמְרוּ לָמָה ה׳ אֱלֹהֵי יִשְׂרָאֵל הָיְתָה זֹּאת בְּיִשְׂרָאֵל, *And they sat there till the evening, before God, and lifted up their voices and wept exceedingly. And they said, "O* HASHEM*, God of Israel, why is this come to pass in Israel?" (Judges* 21:2,3). Similarly we find by Darius, when he cast Daniel into the lions' den, as it is written, וּבָת טְוָת וְדַחֲוָן לָא הַנְעֵל קָדָמוֹהִי, *And (he) passed the night fasting, neither were diversions brought before him (Daniel* 6:19). The reason the brothers felt no remorse is because they considered Joseph to be a "pursuer" and the pursued is permitted to save himself, even if he must kill the pursuer, if there is no alternative.

הוֹלְכִים לְהוֹרִיד מִצְרָיְמָה — *Going to carry it down to Egypt.* They (the Ishmaelites) were the camel drivers, but not the owners of the merchandise, therefore their job was only to transport the merchandise (to Egypt) thereby concluding their task.

26. מַה בֶּצַע — *What profit is it?* What will we accomplish? Revenge must serve one of two ends (to satisfy one's desire to punish the wrongdoer or to serve as an example and deterrent). As for the satisfaction of revenge if we kill our own brother, it will recoil upon our own heads, for our hearts will grieve over his death and our cruelty towards him; and if we intend it to be a warning to other potential enemies not to harm us, how will it be so, seeing that we intend to conceal his death (and none will know)?

וְכִסִּינוּ אֶת דָּמוֹ — *And we will conceal his blood . . .* for our own honor and out of fear of our father.

27. לְכוּ וְנִמְכְּרֶנּוּ — *Come and let us sell him.* By so doing we will punish him measure for measure; because he wanted to rule over us, now he will become a slave.

NOTES

the role of the Ishmaelites and what is that of the Midianites? The *Sforno* explains that the Ishmaelites were only the camel drivers (the teamsters) while the Midianites were the merchants. The purchasers of Joseph were the Midianites, who subsequently sold him to Potiphar, while the Ishmaelites were only the intermediaries through whom the initial sale was made. The reason for this indirect transaction is explained by the *Sforno* in his commentary on verse 28.

כח אַל־תְּהִי־בוֹ כִּי־אָחִינוּ בְשָׂרֵנוּ הוּא וַיִּשְׁמְעוּ אֶחָיו: וַיַּעַבְרוּ אֲנָשִׁים מִדְיָנִים
סֹחֲרִים וַיִּמְשְׁכוּ וַיַּעֲלוּ אֶת־יוֹסֵף מִן־הַבּוֹר וַיִּמְכְּרוּ אֶת־יוֹסֵף לַיִּשְׁמְעֵאלִים
כט בְּעֶשְׂרִים כָּסֶף וַיָּבִיאוּ אֶת־יוֹסֵף מִצְרָיְמָה: וַיָּשָׁב רְאוּבֵן אֶל־הַבּוֹר וְהִנֵּה
ל אֵין־יוֹסֵף בַּבּוֹר וַיִּקְרַע אֶת־בְּגָדָיו: וַיָּשָׁב אֶל־אֶחָיו וַיֹּאמַר הַיֶּלֶד אֵינֶנּוּ וַאֲנִי
לא אָנָה אֲנִי־בָא: וַיִּקְחוּ אֶת־כְּתֹנֶת יוֹסֵף וַיִּשְׁחֲטוּ שְׂעִיר עִזִּים וַיִּטְבְּלוּ אֶת־
לב הַכֻּתֹּנֶת בַּדָּם: וַיְשַׁלְּחוּ אֶת־כְּתֹנֶת הַפַּסִּים וַיָּבִיאוּ אֶל־אֲבִיהֶם וַיֹּאמְרוּ זֹאת
לג מָצָאנוּ הַכֶּר־נָא הַכְּתֹנֶת בִּנְךָ הִוא אִם־לֹא: וַיַּכִּירָהּ וַיֹּאמֶר כְּתֹנֶת בְּנִי חַיָּה
לד רָעָה אֲכָלָתְהוּ טָרֹף טֹרַף יוֹסֵף: וַיִּקְרַע יַעֲקֹב שִׂמְלֹתָיו וַיָּשֶׂם שַׂק בְּמָתְנָיו
לה וַיִּתְאַבֵּל עַל־בְּנוֹ יָמִים רַבִּים: וַיָּקֻמוּ כָל־בָּנָיו וְכָל־בְּנֹתָיו לְנַחֲמוֹ וַיְמָאֵן
לו לְהִתְנַחֵם וַיֹּאמֶר כִּי־אֵרֵד אֶל־בְּנִי אָבֵל שְׁאֹלָה וַיֵּבְךְּ אֹתוֹ אָבִיו: וְהַמְּדָנִים
מָכְרוּ אֹתוֹ אֶל־מִצְרָיִם לְפוֹטִיפַר סְרִיס פַּרְעֹה שַׂר הַטַּבָּחִים:

לח רביעי א וַיְהִי בָּעֵת הַהִוא וַיֵּרֶד יְהוּדָה מֵאֵת אֶחָיו וַיֵּט עַד־אִישׁ עֲדֻלָּמִי וּשְׁמוֹ חִירָה:
ב-ג וַיַּרְא־שָׁם יְהוּדָה בַּת־אִישׁ כְּנַעֲנִי וּשְׁמוֹ שׁוּעַ וַיִּקָּחֶהָ וַיָּבֹא אֵלֶיהָ: וַתַּהַר
ד וַתֵּלֶד בֵּן וַיִּקְרָא אֶת־שְׁמוֹ עֵר: וַתַּהַר עוֹד וַתֵּלֶד בֵּן וַתִּקְרָא אֶת־שְׁמוֹ אוֹנָן:
ה וַתֹּסֶף עוֹד וַתֵּלֶד בֵּן וַתִּקְרָא אֶת־שְׁמוֹ שֵׁלָה וְהָיָה בִכְזִיב בְּלִדְתָּהּ אֹתוֹ:

---

28. מִדְיָנִים סֹחֲרִים — *Midianite merchantmen* ... the owners of the merchandise, being transported by the Ishmaelite camel drivers.

וַיִּמְכְּרוּ אֶת יוֹסֵף לַיִּשְׁמְעֵאלִים — *And sold Joseph to the Ishmaelites.* They sold him to the Ishmaelites (who, however, only acted as) intermediaries for the Midianites. They did not wish to deal directly with the merchantmen who came to sojourn in many towns and might recognize them, but dealt with the Ishmaelites who never remained in the towns (for any length of time), but merely passed through them. With them (the Ishmaelites) they (the brothers) concluded their deal. The purchasers were in reality the Midianites, as it says, *And the Midianites sold him to Egypt* (verse 36). A parallel occurred during the period of the Second Temple when Jews sold their own fellow Jews to the Romans during the time of the Hasmonean Kings; this caused the exile, just as the sale of Joseph by his brothers caused the exile of our forefathers to Egypt, as our Sages tell us *(Shabbos* 10b).

32. וַיְשַׁלְּחוּ אֶת כְּתֹנֶת הַפַּסִּים — *And they (cut) the coat of many colors.* They gashed (tore) it with a spear to make it appear torn by wild beasts.

34. וַיָּשֶׂם שַׂק בְּמָתְנָיו — *And put sackcloth upon his loins.* (He made a belt from) a strip of the woven material called שַׂק, *sackcloth* (usually made from goats' hair), which because of its thickness was used to make שַׂקִּים, *sacks.* (This was a common sign of mourning.)

NOTES

32. וַיְשַׁלְּחוּ אֶת כְּתֹנֶת הַפַּסִּים — *And they (cut) the coat of many colors.* In Hebrew, שֶׁלַח means a sword. The phrase וַיְשַׁלְּחוּ is therefore translated by the *Sforno* not as *sent,* but *gashed* or *cut,* to make it appear that a wild beast had torn the coat while attacking Joseph. See *Da'as Zekeinim* on this verse.

35. וַיְמָאֵן לְהִתְנַחֵם — *He refused to be comforted.* Jacob did not want to be comforted. By continuing to mourn and grieve for his son he kept alive the hope that Joseph was still alive, for it is ordained that a deceased person is ultimately forgotten (the intensity of the memory fades) and one can find comfort. That is why Jacob did not cease to grieve. *Rashi* gives a similar explanation.

וַיֵּבְךְּ אֹתוֹ אָבִיו — *And his father wept for him.* Isaac cried for his son Jacob, not only because of his personal loss, but because by continually mourning he was denied the opportunity and privilege of receiving the blessing of the Divine presence (שְׁכִינָה) which can only dwell where there is joy and happiness.

but let our hand not be upon him, for he is our brother, our own flesh." His
brothers agreed. [28] *Midianite men, traders, passed by; they drew Joseph up*
and lifted him out of the pit and sold Joseph to the Ishmaelites for twenty
pieces of silver; then they brought Joseph to Egypt. [29] *Reuben returned to*
the pit — and behold! — Joseph was not in the pit! So he rent his garments.
[30] *Returning to his brothers he said, "The boy is gone! And I — where can I*
go?" [31] *They took Joseph's tunic, slaughtered a goatling, and dipped the*
tunic in the blood. [32] *They dispatched the fine woolen tunic and they*
brought it to their father, and said, "We found this; identify, if you please:
Is it your son's tunic or not?" [33] *He recognized it and he said, "My son's*
tunic! A savage beast devoured him! Joseph has surely been torn to bits!"
[34] *Then Jacob rent his garments and placed sackcloth on his loins; he*
mourned for his son many days. [35] *All his sons and all his daughters arose*
to comfort him, but he refused to comfort himself, and said: "For I will go
down to the grave mourning for my son." And his father bewailed him.
[36] *Now the Medanites had sold him to Egypt, to Potiphar, a courtier of*
Pharaoh, the Chamberlain of the Butchers.

38 [1] *It was at that time that Judah went down from his brothers and turned*
away towards an Adullamite man whose name was Hirah. [2] *There*
Judah saw the daughter of a prominent merchant whose name was Shua;
he married her and consorted with her. [3] *She conceived and bore a son and*
he called his name Er. [4] *She conceived again and bore a son and she called*
his name Onan. [5] *And yet again and she bore a son; and called his name*
Shelah; and it was in Chezib when she bore him.

---

35. וַיְמָאֵן לְהִתְנַחֵם — *He refused to be comforted.* He refused to listen to words of comfort, for he did not want to remove (the sense and feeling of) worry from his heart.

וַיֹּאמֶר כִּי אֵרֵד אֶל בְּנִי אָבֵל שְׁאֹלָה — *He said, "I will go down to the grave, to my son, mourning."* He assumed lifelong mourning, because he blamed himself for having caused the calamity, since he was the one who sent Joseph to his brothers.

וַיֵּבְךְּ אֹתוֹ אָבִיו — *And his father wept for him.* Isaac wept that Jacob had assumed lifelong mourning, which would have the effect of keeping the Divine presence (*Shechinah*) away from him.

XXXVIII

1. וַיְהִי בָּעֵת הַהִוא — *And it came to pass at that time.* At the time Joseph was sold to Egypt due to Judah's counsel, (advising to) sell him and not (advising) to return him, thus bereaving his father, Judah was requited according to the fruits of his action (by) having two sons who would die (prematurely), and (thus) he would remain bereaved of both.

5. וְהָיָה בִכְזִיב — *And he was at Chezib.* She called him Shelah, a word denoting deceit and

NOTES

XXXVIII

1. וַיְהִי בָּעֵת הַהִוא — *And it came to pass at that time.* This chapter is linked to the concluding verse of the previous one, *And the Midianites sold him, etc.* Although this episode seems to interrupt the natural sequence, which is picked up later (chap. 39), it is placed here to teach us the great lesson of "measure for measure"; how consequences come forth from man's deeds. The sale of Joseph and the following tragic events in Judah's life are connected, as the *Sforno* so well explains, through the common theme of losing one's children.

5. וְהָיָה בִכְזִיב — *And he was at Chezib.* The Torah tells us that Judah was away when Shelah was

ו־ז וַיִּקַּח יְהוּדָה אִשָּׁה לְעֵר בְּכוֹרוֹ וּשְׁמָהּ תָּמָר: וַיְהִי עֵר בְּכוֹר יְהוּדָה רַע בְּעֵינֵי
ח יְהוָה וַיְמִתֵהוּ יְהוָה: וַיֹּאמֶר יְהוּדָה לְאוֹנָן בֹּא אֶל־אֵשֶׁת אָחִיךָ וְיַבֵּם אֹתָהּ
ט וְהָקֵם זֶרַע לְאָחִיךָ: וַיֵּדַע אוֹנָן כִּי לֹּא לוֹ יִהְיֶה הַזָּרַע וְהָיָה אִם־בָּא אֶל־
י אֵשֶׁת אָחִיו וְשִׁחֵת אַרְצָה לְבִלְתִּי נְתָן־זֶרַע לְאָחִיו: וַיֵּרַע בְּעֵינֵי יְהוָה אֲשֶׁר
יא עָשָׂה וַיָּמֶת גַּם־אֹתוֹ: וַיֹּאמֶר יְהוּדָה לְתָמָר כַּלָּתוֹ שְׁבִי אַלְמָנָה בֵית־אָבִיךְ
עַד־יִגְדַּל שֵׁלָה בְנִי כִּי אָמַר פֶּן־יָמוּת גַּם־הוּא כְּאֶחָיו וַתֵּלֶךְ תָּמָר וַתֵּשֶׁב
יב בֵּית אָבִיהָ: וַיִּרְבּוּ הַיָּמִים וַתָּמָת בַּת־שׁוּעַ אֵשֶׁת־יְהוּדָה וַיִּנָּחֶם יְהוּדָה וַיַּעַל
יג עַל־גֹּזְזֵי צֹאנוֹ הוּא וְחִירָה רֵעֵהוּ הָעֲדֻלָּמִי תִּמְנָתָה: וַיֻּגַּד לְתָמָר לֵאמֹר
יד הִנֵּה חָמִיךְ עֹלֶה תִמְנָתָה לָגֹז צֹאנוֹ: וַתָּסַר בִּגְדֵי אַלְמְנוּתָהּ מֵעָלֶיהָ
וַתְּכַס בַּצָּעִיף וַתִּתְעַלָּף וַתֵּשֶׁב בְּפֶתַח עֵינַיִם אֲשֶׁר עַל־דֶּרֶךְ תִּמְנָתָה כִּי
טו רָאֲתָה כִּי־גָדַל שֵׁלָה וְהִוא לֹא־נִתְּנָה לוֹ לְאִשָּׁה: וַיִּרְאֶהָ יְהוּדָה וַיַּחְשְׁבֶהָ
טז לְזוֹנָה כִּי כִסְּתָה פָּנֶיהָ: וַיֵּט אֵלֶיהָ אֶל־הַדֶּרֶךְ וַיֹּאמֶר הָבָה־נָּא אָבוֹא
אֵלַיִךְ כִּי לֹא יָדַע כִּי כַלָּתוֹ הִוא וַתֹּאמֶר מַה־תִּתֶּן־לִּי כִּי תָבוֹא אֵלָי:

---

disappointment, as we find, לֹא תַשְׁלֶה, *Do not deceive me* (*II Kings* 4:28), which is an unbecoming name. She did so because her husband was absent (in Chezib) when he was born, hence she was disappointed. (Judah) would not have agreed to such an unseemly name, had he been present.

7. וַיְהִי עֵר ... רַע בְּעֵינֵי ה׳ – *And Er ... was wicked in the sight of* HASHEM ... but not in the eyes of his fellow men.

9. כִּי לֹא לוֹ יִהְיֶה הַזָּרַע – *That the seed would not be his.* He knew that he would not gain exclusive credit for this *mitzvah,* since his (deceased) brother had wed her, and he (Onan) is only completing the *mitzvah* (of fathering a child).

לְבִלְתִּי נְתָן זֶרַע לְאָחִיו – *Lest he should give seed to his brother ...* so that his (deceased) brother should not realize, through him, the desired goal of his marriage.

11. שְׁבִי אַלְמָנָה – *Remain a widow.* Wait for a period of time, continuing your role as a widow, as we find, יָמִים רַבִּים תֵּשְׁבִי לִי, *You shall sit solitary for me many days* (*Hoshea* 3:3).

פֶּן יָמוּת גַּם הוּא כְּאֶחָיו – *Lest he also die as his brothers ...* lest he sin because of her beauty as his brother had done, and would die.

12. וַתָּמָת בַּת שׁוּעַ – *The daughter of Shua died.* Judah should have brought in his daughter-in-law to run his household in place of his wife, as Abraham had done, as it says, *And Isaac brought her into the tent of Sarah his mother* (24:67). Tamar, therefore, abandoned hope of ever remaining part of Judah's family.

NOTES

born. This seemingly gratuitous information is to explain how such an improper name was given to his son. It reflected his wife's feelings of frustration when she gave birth while her husband was away from her. The proof brought by the *Sforno* in support of his interpretation is from the story of the Shunamis and Elisha, where she bitterly remonstrates with the prophet for first granting her a child, only to have him taken from her.

7. וַיְהִי עֵר ... רַע בְּעֵינֵי ה׳ – *And Er ... was wicked in the sight of* HASHEM. The transgression of Er was a totally private one, known only to God. Hence it did not affect his standing and reputation amongst his fellow men.

9. כִּי לֹא לוֹ יִהְיֶה הַזָּרַע – *That the seed would not be his.* Onan was obviously a most selfish man. He could not bring himself to fulfill the *mitzvah* of "establishing a name for his brother," since the *zechus* (merit) would not be exclusively his.

11. שְׁבִי אַלְמָנָה – *Remain a widow.* The custom was for a widow who was not yet prepared to

6 *Judah took a wife for Er his firstborn; her name was Tamar.* 7 *But Er, Judah's firstborn, was evil in the eyes of* HASHEM, *and* HASHEM *caused him to die.* 8 *Then Judah said to Onan, "Consort with your brother's wife and enter into levirate marriage with her, and establish offspring for your brother."*
9 *But Onan knew that the seed would not be his; so it was, that whenever he would consort with his brother's wife, he would let it go to waste on the ground so as not to provide offspring for his brother.* 10 *What he did was evil in the eyes of* HASHEM, *and He caused him to die also.*
11 *Then Judah said to Tamar, his daughter-in-law, "Remain a widow in your father's house until my son Shelah grows up" — for he thought, "Lest he also die like his brothers." — So Tamar went and lived in her father's house.*
12 *Many days passed and Shua's daughter, the wife of Judah, died; when Judah was consoled, he went up to oversee his sheepshearers — he and his Adullamite friend, Hirah — to Timnah.*
13 *And Tamar was told, as follows, "Behold your father-in-law is coming up to Timnah to shear his sheep."* 14 *So she removed her widow's garb from upon her, covered herself with a veil, and wrapped herself up; she then sat by the crossroads which is on the road toward Timnah, for she saw that Shelah had grown, and she had not been given to him as a wife.*
15 *When Judah saw her, he thought her to be a harlot since she had covered her face.* 16 *So he detoured to her by the road and said, "Come, if you please, let me consort with you," for he did not know that she was his daughter-in-law.*
And she said, "What will you give me if you consort with me?"

---

14. בְּפֶתַח עֵינַיִם – *At the fork in the road* ... where two roads begin, for a road is called עַיִן, as we find עַל הָעַיִן בְּדֶרֶךְ שׁוּר, *By the road on the way to Shur* (16:7).

אֲשֶׁר עַל דֶּרֶךְ תִּמְנָתָה – *Which is on the way to Timnas.* It would then be impossible for Judah not to meet her as he returned from Timnas.

כִּי רָאֲתָה כִּי גָדַל שֵׁלָה – *For she saw that Shelah was grown up.* She reasoned that if Judah would see her without her widow's garments and ask her why she had removed them, she would tell him that the time had come to do so, since (Judah) had told her to wear them until Shelah grew up (verse 11) and now he had grown up.

16. כִּי לֹא יָדַע כִּי כַלָּתוֹ הִוא – *For he knew not that she was his daughter-in-law.* Even after he turned aside to her he did not recognize her, for had he recognized her he would have arranged for her to marry his son (Shelah). God's divine plan, however, was that she conceive from Judah, for he was more worthy than Shelah to father the ancestor of the *Mashiach* (Messiah).

מַה תִּתֶּן לִי – *What will you give me?* She began to speak so that he might recognize her (by her voice). She undoubtedly did not want any gift, her only desire being to have a

NOTES

remarry to live in seclusion. The expression *to sit* as a widow is used here and in *Hoshea* to indicate that her state of widowhood shall remain unchanged for a given period.

12. וַתָּמָת בַּת שׁוּעַ – *The daughter of Shua died.* The Hebrew term עֲקֶרֶת הַבַּיִת, *mainstay of the house*, is given to the woman (wife, daughter or daughter-in-law) who is in charge of the household. Tamar hoped to assume that role by becoming Shelah's wife after Judah's wife died. When this did not occur she began to devise an alternate plan to fulfill her desire to bring the Messiah into the world.

יז וַיֹּאמֶר אָנֹכִי אֲשַׁלַּח גְּדִי־עִזִּים מִן־הַצֹּאן וַתֹּאמֶר אִם־תִּתֵּן עֵרָבוֹן עַד
יח שָׁלְחֶךָ: וַיֹּאמֶר מָה הָעֵרָבוֹן אֲשֶׁר אֶתֶּן־לָּךְ וַתֹּאמֶר חֹתָמְךָ וּפְתִילֶךָ
יט וּמַטְּךָ אֲשֶׁר בְּיָדֶךָ וַיִּתֶּן־לָהּ וַיָּבֹא אֵלֶיהָ וַתַּהַר לוֹ: וַתָּקָם וַתֵּלֶךְ וַתָּסַר
כ צְעִיפָהּ מֵעָלֶיהָ וַתִּלְבַּשׁ בִּגְדֵי אַלְמְנוּתָהּ: וַיִּשְׁלַח יְהוּדָה אֶת־גְּדִי הָעִזִּים
כא בְּיַד רֵעֵהוּ הָעֲדֻלָּמִי לָקַחַת הָעֵרָבוֹן מִיַּד הָאִשָּׁה וְלֹא מְצָאָהּ: וַיִּשְׁאַל
אֶת־אַנְשֵׁי מְקֹמָהּ לֵאמֹר אַיֵּה הַקְּדֵשָׁה הִוא בָעֵינַיִם עַל־הַדָּרֶךְ וַיֹּאמְרוּ
כב לֹא־הָיְתָה בָזֶה קְדֵשָׁה: וַיָּשָׁב אֶל־יְהוּדָה וַיֹּאמֶר לֹא מְצָאתִיהָ וְגַם
כג אַנְשֵׁי הַמָּקוֹם אָמְרוּ לֹא־הָיְתָה בָזֶה קְדֵשָׁה: וַיֹּאמֶר יְהוּדָה תִּקַּח־לָהּ
כד פֶּן נִהְיֶה לָבוּז הִנֵּה שָׁלַחְתִּי הַגְּדִי הַזֶּה וְאַתָּה לֹא מְצָאתָהּ: וַיְהִי ׀
כְּמִשְׁלֹשׁ חֳדָשִׁים וַיֻּגַּד לִיהוּדָה לֵאמֹר זָנְתָה תָּמָר כַּלָּתֶךָ וְגַם הִנֵּה
כה הָרָה לִזְנוּנִים וַיֹּאמֶר יְהוּדָה הוֹצִיאוּהָ וְתִשָּׂרֵף: הִוא מוּצֵאת וְהִיא
שָׁלְחָה אֶל־חָמִיהָ לֵאמֹר לְאִישׁ אֲשֶׁר־אֵלֶּה לּוֹ אָנֹכִי הָרָה וַתֹּאמֶר
כו הַכֶּר־נָא לְמִי הַחֹתֶמֶת וְהַפְּתִילִים וְהַמַּטֶּה הָאֵלֶּה: וַיַּכֵּר יְהוּדָה וַיֹּאמֶר
צָדְקָה מִמֶּנִּי כִּי־עַל־כֵּן לֹא־נְתַתִּיהָ לְשֵׁלָה בְנִי וְלֹא־יָסַף עוֹד לְדַעְתָּהּ:
כז־כח וַיְהִי בְּעֵת לִדְתָּהּ וְהִנֵּה תְאוֹמִים בְּבִטְנָהּ: וַיְהִי בְלִדְתָּהּ וַיִּתֶּן־יָד וַתִּקַּח

---

child from (the house of) Judah. She therefore accepted the pledge, not for personal use but as proof; had he given her a gift she would not have accepted it. (The reason she accepted the pledge is) because she had no (other) proof to vindicate herself.

17. אם תתן ערבון – *If you will give me a pledge.* If you do so then I will do as you asked, *"Come, I pray, let me come in unto you"* (verse 16).

18. ופתילך – *Your cord* . . . that which is connected close to your body, i.e., your belt (girdle). She chose these items (signet, cord and staff) which symbolize power and authority as we find, אֱזָר נָא כְגֶבֶר חֲלָצֶיךָ, *Gird up now your loins like a man (Job* 38:3). She did this in order to contemplate the elevated stature of Judah and have a child with his (qualities).

19. וַתִּלְבַּשׁ בִּגְדֵי אַלְמְנוּתָהּ – *Then she put on the garments of her widowhood.* Because she had no further desire to marry, now that she was with child (from Judah).

22. וְגַם אַנְשֵׁי הַמָּקוֹם אָמְרוּ – *And the people of that place also said* . . . as though mocking you and shaming your honor.

23. הִנֵּה שָׁלַחְתִּי – *Behold I have sent.* I kept my word and did not break my promise.

24. וְגַם הִנֵּה הָרָה – *And behold she is with child.* And she has not (even) tried to prevent or conceal this shameful affront to your honor, as it is said (by our Sages), "A woman playing the harlot turns over (or uses an absorbent) to prevent conception" *(Yevamos* 35a).

25. הִיא מוּצֵאת וְהִיא שָׁלְחָה – *When she was brought forth, she sent (to her father-in-law).* She did not despair of defending and saving herself even as she was being taken out to be burnt, for her heart was strong as a lion.

NOTES

26. צָדְקָה מִמֶּנִּי – *She is more righteous than I.* This expression implies that there were two actions, one by Tamar and one by Judah, which were to be weighed and judged to determine which was the more righteous. Judah was fair enough to recognize that a person's intent and motivation is more important than one's action. A seemingly improper, even immoral act, if done for the sake of heaven, is superior to a *mitzvah* performed to assuage one's guilt feeling and satisfy one's ego. Tamar's motive was pure. Judah's was not.

17 *He replied, "I will send you a kid of the goats from the flock."*
And she said, "Provided you leave a pledge until you send it."
18 *And he said, "What pledge shall I give you?"*
She replied, "Your signet, your wrap, and your staff that is in your hand." And he gave them to her, and consorted with her, and she conceived by him.
19 *Then she arose, left, and removed her veil from upon her, and she put on her widow's garb.*
20 *Judah sent the kid of the goats through his friend the Adullamite to retrieve the pledge from the woman; but he did not find her.*
21 *He inquired of the people of her place, "Where is the prostitute, the one at the crossroads by the road?"*
And they said, "There was no prostitute here."
22 *So he returned to Judah and said, "I did not find her; even the local men said, 'There was no prostitute here.' "*
23 *So Judah said, "Let her keep them, lest we become a laughingstock; I really sent her this kid, but you could not find her."*
24 *And it was when about three months had passed, that Judah was told, "Your daughter-in-law has committed harlotry, and moreover, she has conceived by harlotry."*
Judah said, "Take her out and let her be burned!"
25 *As she was taken out, she sent word to her father-in-law, saying, "By the man to whom these belong I am with child." And she said, "Identify, if you please, whose are this seal, this wrap, and this staff."*
26 *Judah recognized; and he said, "She is right; it is from me, inasmuch as I did not give her to Shelah my son," and he was not intimate with her anymore.*
27 *And it came to pass at the time she gave birth that behold! There were twins in her womb.*
28 *And it happened that as she gave birth, one put out*

לְאִישׁ אֲשֶׁר אֵלֶּה לּוֹ – *By the man whose these are (am I with child).* Even though she was in mortal danger she would not shame him, as our Sages tell us, "It is better for a man that he should cast himself into a fiery furnace rather than that he should put his fellow to shame in public. Whence do we know this? From Tamar" (*Berachos* 43b).

26. צָדְקָה מִמֶּנִּי – *She is more righteous than I.* Even though she deceived me and I never recognized her, because I sent (her) the kid, nevertheless she was right to do what she did for it was for a (positive and) good purpose, acceptable by God. (Her purpose was) to have children (from him) not for personal (gain or) satisfaction, since we see that she returned immediately to her widow's status. (She was) more righteous than I was in keeping my word, since my intentions were (to maintain) my personal honor and to acquire my pledge, a false and deficient goal. (This is) as our Sages teach us, גְּדוֹלָה עֲבֵרָה לִשְׁמָהּ מִמִּצְוָה שֶׁלֹּא לִשְׁמָהּ, *A transgression performed with good intentions is better than a precept performed with evil intention* (*Nazir* 23b).

27. וְהִנֵּה תְאוֹמִים בְּבִטְנָהּ – *Behold twins were in her womb.* Before they were born it was perceived that they were twins; therefore the midwife tied a scarlet thread (on his hand) so as to identify the firstborn.

NOTES

27. וְהִנֵּה תְאוֹמִים בְּבִטְנָהּ – *Behold twins were in her womb.* The word בְּבִטְנָהּ, *in her womb,* indicates that this was known while they were still in the womb, i.e., before birth. Compare this to Rebecca in 25:24.

כט הַמְיַלֶּדֶת וַתִּקְשֹׁר עַל־יָדוֹ שָׁנִי לֵאמֹר זֶה יָצָא רִאשֹׁנָה: וַיְהִי | כְּמֵשִׁיב יָדוֹ
ל וְהִנֵּה יָצָא אָחִיו וַתֹּאמֶר מַה־פָּרַצְתָּ עָלֶיךָ פָּרֶץ וַיִּקְרָא שְׁמוֹ פָּרֶץ: וְאַחַר
לט חמישי א יָצָא אָחִיו אֲשֶׁר עַל־יָדוֹ הַשָּׁנִי וַיִּקְרָא שְׁמוֹ זָרַח: וְיוֹסֵף
הוּרַד מִצְרָיְמָה וַיִּקְנֵהוּ פּוֹטִיפַר סְרִיס פַּרְעֹה שַׂר הַטַּבָּחִים אִישׁ מִצְרִי
ב מִיַּד הַיִּשְׁמְעֵאלִים אֲשֶׁר הוֹרִדֻהוּ שָׁמָּה: וַיְהִי יהוה אֶת־יוֹסֵף וַיְהִי אִישׁ
ג מַצְלִיחַ וַיְהִי בְּבֵית אֲדֹנָיו הַמִּצְרִי: וַיַּרְא אֲדֹנָיו כִּי יהוה אִתּוֹ וְכֹל
ד אֲשֶׁר־הוּא עֹשֶׂה יהוה מַצְלִיחַ בְּיָדוֹ: וַיִּמְצָא יוֹסֵף חֵן בְּעֵינָיו וַיְשָׁרֶת אֹתוֹ
ה וַיַּפְקִדֵהוּ עַל־בֵּיתוֹ וְכָל־יֶשׁ־לוֹ נָתַן בְּיָדוֹ: וַיְהִי מֵאָז הִפְקִיד אֹתוֹ בְּבֵיתוֹ
וְעַל כָּל־אֲשֶׁר יֶשׁ־לוֹ וַיְבָרֶךְ יהוה אֶת־בֵּית הַמִּצְרִי בִּגְלַל יוֹסֵף וַיְהִי
ו בִּרְכַּת יהוה בְּכָל־אֲשֶׁר יֶשׁ־לוֹ בַּבַּיִת וּבַשָּׂדֶה: וַיַּעֲזֹב כָּל־אֲשֶׁר־לוֹ בְּיַד
יוֹסֵף וְלֹא־יָדַע אִתּוֹ מְאוּמָה כִּי אִם־הַלֶּחֶם אֲשֶׁר־הוּא אוֹכֵל וַיְהִי יוֹסֵף
ששי ז יְפֵה־תֹאַר וִיפֵה מַרְאֶה: וַיְהִי אַחַר הַדְּבָרִים הָאֵלֶּה וַתִּשָּׂא אֵשֶׁת־אֲדֹנָיו
ח אֶת־עֵינֶיהָ אֶל־יוֹסֵף וַתֹּאמֶר שִׁכְבָה עִמִּי: וַיְמָאֵן | וַיֹּאמֶר אֶל־אֵשֶׁת
אֲדֹנָיו הֵן אֲדֹנִי לֹא־יָדַע אִתִּי מַה־בַּבָּיִת וְכֹל אֲשֶׁר־יֶשׁ־לוֹ נָתַן בְּיָדִי:
ט אֵינֶנּוּ גָדוֹל בַּבַּיִת הַזֶּה מִמֶּנִּי וְלֹא־חָשַׂךְ מִמֶּנִּי מְאוּמָה כִּי אִם־אוֹתָךְ
בַּאֲשֶׁר אַתְּ־אִשְׁתּוֹ וְאֵיךְ אֶעֱשֶׂה הָרָעָה הַגְּדֹלָה הַזֹּאת וְחָטָאתִי לֵאלֹהִים:

---

29. וַיְהִי כְּמֵשִׁיב יָדוֹ – *And it came to pass, as he drew back his hand.* It was as though *he drew back his hand,* but it was not actually so, for it was not of his own volition but rather as a result of his brother pushing past him (that the first child) was forced back (entirely).

XXXIX

1. וְיוֹסֵף הוּרַד – *And Joseph was brought down.* At the same time that Judah departed from his brethren, and the events recorded above unfolded, Joseph was brought down (to Egypt).

מִיַּד הַיִּשְׁמְעֵאלִים – *Of the hand of the Ishmaelites . . .* the owners of the camels which bore the caravan, and acted as agents for the sale (on behalf of the Midianite merchants).

2. וַיְהִי ה׳ אֶת יוֹסֵף – *And God was with Joseph . . .* to save him from his enemies.

וַיְהִי אִישׁ מַצְלִיחַ – *And he was a prosperous man . . .* attaining whatever was required of him.

וַיְהִי בְּבֵית אֲדֹנָיו הַמִּצְרִי – *And he was in the house of his master the Egyptian . . .* prepared to serve him in his private chamber. The expression (here) of הָיָה (i.e., the word וַיְהִי from the root היה, *to be)* is to be understood as עָמַד, *standing* or *being (prepared),* as we find,

NOTES

XXXIX

1. וְיוֹסֵף הוּרַד — *And Joseph was brought down.* The Torah does not say, וַיּוֹרִדוּ אֶת יוֹסֵף, *And they took Joseph down,* which would have been the proper way to begin a new story. Rather it says, וְיוֹסֵף הוּרַד, the letter ו׳ in this case being a ו׳ הַחִדּוּשׁ — used not only to link (in the usual sense of "and") but to emphasize that two events took place at the same time. In our story the two events were Judah's departing from his brethren, who rejected him because of his role in selling Joseph, and Joseph's going down to Egypt.

2. וַיְהִי ה׳ אֶת יוֹסֵף וַיְהִי אִישׁ מַצְלִיחַ — *And God was with Joseph and he was a prosperous man.* The word וַיְהִי is repeated to teach us that Joseph was protected by God from his enemies and also blessed by God with success in all his endeavors.

a hand; the midwife took a crimson thread and tied it on his hand saying,
"This one emerged first!" [29] *And it was, as he drew back his hand, that be-*
hold! his brother emerged. And she said, "With what strength you asserted
yourself!" And he called his name Perez. [30] *Afterwards his brother on whose*
hand was the crimson thread came out; and he called his name Zerah.

39 [1] *And Joseph had been brought down to Egypt. Potiphar, a courtier of*
Pharaoh, the Chamberlain of the Butchers, a prominent Egyptian,
purchased him from the Ishmaelites who had brought him down there.
[2] *HASHEM was with Joseph, and he became a successful man; and he*
remained in the house of his Egyptian master. [3] *His master perceived that*
HASHEM was with him, and whatever he did HASHEM made succeed through
him. [4] *Joseph found favor in his eyes, and he attended him; he appointed him*
over his household, and whatever he had he placed in his custody.
[5] *And it happened, that from the time he appointed him in his house and*
over whatever he had, HASHEM blessed the Egyptian's house on Joseph's
account, so that HASHEM's blessing was in whatever he owned, in the house
and in the field. [6] *He left all that he had in Joseph's custody and with him*
present he concerned himself with nothing except for the bread he ate. Now
Joseph was handsome of form and handsome of appearance.
[7] *After these things, his master's wife cast her eyes upon Joseph and she*
said, "Lie with me." [8] *But he adamantly refused; he said to his master's wife,*
"Look — with me here, my master concerns himself about nothing in the
house, and whatever he has he placed in my custody. [9] *There is no one*
greater in this house than I, and he has denied me nothing but you, since you
are his wife; how then can I perpetrate this great evil and have sinned
against God!"

וְהָיָה שָׁם, *that it may be* (i.e., *stand) there (Deut.* 31:26); also, וַיִּהְיוּ שָׁם כַּאֲשֶׁר צִוַּנִי ה׳, *that they are there* (i.e., *they stand) as God commanded me* (ibid. 10:5).

4. וַיְשָׁרֶת אֹתוֹ – *And he ministered unto him* . . . in personal matters.

6. וַיַּעֲזֹב כָּל אֲשֶׁר לוֹ – *And he left all that he had* . . . without demanding an accounting.

וַיְהִי יוֹסֵף יְפֵה תֹאַר וִיפֵה מַרְאֶה – *And Joseph was of beautiful form, and fair to look upon* . . . after he was (entrusted with all of Potiphar's household possessions), in contrast to his early period of servitude when he had to do menial hard labor, as it says, הֲסִירוֹתִי מִסֵּבֶל שִׁכְמוֹ, *I removed his shoulder from the burden (Psalms* 81:7).

7. וַתִּשָּׂא אֵשֶׁת אֲדֹנָיו – *His master's wife cast her eyes* . . . because of his great beauty, as mentioned (in the previous verse).

9. כִּי אִם אוֹתָךְ בַּאֲשֶׁר אַתְּ אִשְׁתּוֹ – *But you, because you are his wife.* Only you, his wife, has he kept back from me.

הָרָעָה הַגְּדֹלָה הַזֹּאת – *This great wickedness.* (How can I do this) to repay evil for good.

NOTES

4. וַיְשָׁרֶת אֹתוֹ — *And he ministered to him.* When Joseph first came into the house of Potiphar, he was a lowly slave of the Hebrew race, loathed by the Egyptians. During that period his physical appearance must have been most unattractive. Only after his elevation to that of trusted steward does he have the wherewithal to eat properly and dress decently. Ironically, this good fortune is what precipitates his problems with Potiphar's wife and his subsequent imprisonment.

י וַיְהִי כְּדַבְּרָהּ אֶל־יוֹסֵף יוֹם | יוֹם וְלֹא־שָׁמַע אֵלֶיהָ לִשְׁכַּב אֶצְלָהּ לִהְיוֹת
יא עִמָּהּ: וַיְהִי כְּהַיּוֹם הַזֶּה וַיָּבֹא הַבַּיְתָה לַעֲשׂוֹת מְלַאכְתּוֹ וְאֵין אִישׁ מֵאַנְשֵׁי
יב הַבַּיִת שָׁם בַּבָּיִת: וַתִּתְפְּשֵׂהוּ בְּבִגְדוֹ לֵאמֹר שִׁכְבָה עִמִּי וַיַּעֲזֹב בִּגְדוֹ בְּיָדָהּ
יג־יד וַיָּנָס וַיֵּצֵא הַחוּצָה: וַיְהִי כִּרְאוֹתָהּ כִּי־עָזַב בִּגְדוֹ בְּיָדָהּ וַיָּנָס הַחוּצָה: וַתִּקְרָא
לְאַנְשֵׁי בֵיתָהּ וַתֹּאמֶר לָהֶם לֵאמֹר רְאוּ הֵבִיא לָנוּ אִישׁ עִבְרִי לְצַחֶק בָּנוּ
טו בָּא אֵלַי לִשְׁכַּב עִמִּי וָאֶקְרָא בְּקוֹל גָּדוֹל: וַיְהִי כְשָׁמְעוֹ כִּי־הֲרִימֹתִי קוֹלִי
טז וָאֶקְרָא וַיַּעֲזֹב בִּגְדוֹ אֶצְלִי וַיָּנָס וַיֵּצֵא הַחוּצָה: וַתַּנַּח בִּגְדוֹ אֶצְלָהּ עַד־בּוֹא
יז אֲדֹנָיו אֶל־בֵּיתוֹ: וַתְּדַבֵּר אֵלָיו כַּדְּבָרִים הָאֵלֶּה לֵאמֹר בָּא אֵלַי הָעֶבֶד
יח הָעִבְרִי אֲשֶׁר־הֵבֵאתָ לָּנוּ לְצַחֶק בִּי: וַיְהִי כַּהֲרִימִי קוֹלִי וָאֶקְרָא וַיַּעֲזֹב בִּגְדוֹ
יט אֶצְלִי וַיָּנָס הַחוּצָה: וַיְהִי כִשְׁמֹעַ אֲדֹנָיו אֶת־דִּבְרֵי אִשְׁתּוֹ אֲשֶׁר דִּבְּרָה אֵלָיו
כ לֵאמֹר כַּדְּבָרִים הָאֵלֶּה עָשָׂה לִי עַבְדֶּךָ וַיִּחַר אַפּוֹ: וַיִּקַּח אֲדֹנֵי יוֹסֵף אֹתוֹ
°אֲסִירֵי ק׳ וַיִּתְּנֵהוּ אֶל־בֵּית הַסֹּהַר מְקוֹם אֲשֶׁר־°אסורי הַמֶּלֶךְ אֲסוּרִים וַיְהִי־שָׁם
כא בְּבֵית הַסֹּהַר: וַיְהִי יהוה אֶת־יוֹסֵף וַיֵּט אֵלָיו חָסֶד וַיִּתֵּן חִנּוֹ בְּעֵינֵי שַׂר
כב בֵּית־הַסֹּהַר: וַיִּתֵּן שַׂר בֵּית־הַסֹּהַר בְּיַד־יוֹסֵף אֵת כָּל־הָאֲסִירִם אֲשֶׁר בְּבֵית
כג הַסֹּהַר וְאֵת כָּל־אֲשֶׁר עֹשִׂים שָׁם הוּא הָיָה עֹשֶׂה: אֵין | שַׂר בֵּית־הַסֹּהַר רֹאֶה
אֶת־כָּל־מְאוּמָה בְּיָדוֹ בַּאֲשֶׁר יהוה אִתּוֹ וַאֲשֶׁר־הוּא עֹשֶׂה יהוה מַצְלִיחַ:
מ שביעי א וַיְהִי אַחַר הַדְּבָרִים הָאֵלֶּה חָטְאוּ מַשְׁקֵה מֶלֶךְ־מִצְרַיִם וְהָאֹפֶה לַאֲדֹנֵיהֶם

10. לִהְיוֹת עִמָּהּ – *To be with her* ... alone (in the privacy of her chamber).

11. כְּהַיּוֹם הַזֶּה – *On a certain day* ... when she set her eyes (on him) and desired him.

וַיָּבֹא הַבַּיְתָה – *When he went into the house.* He entered *his* room, not knowing that she was there.

שָׁם בַּבָּיִת – *There within* ... in that room.

12. וַיָּנָס – *And fled* ... from the room, fearing that his evil inclination might prevail.

וַיֵּצֵא הַחוּצָה – *He went out.* Once outside the room he resumed his normal gait so as not to arouse curiosity and to deflect the question, "Why are you fleeing; who is pursuing you?" But she, seeing him flee, thought that he was still running and on being queried would tell all that had transpired — therefore ...

14. וַתִּקְרָא לְאַנְשֵׁי בֵיתָהּ – *She called to the men of her house* ... to protect herself. However, when she realized that once outside (Joseph) did not run, and that her household had also seen this, she was compelled to tell the truth, i.e., *He fled, and went out* (verse 15). Nevertheless, when she related the story to her husband who was not present at the time

NOTES

11. וַיָּבֹא הַבַּיְתָה — *When he went into the house.* The word בַּיִת in this verse does not mean *house* but *room.*

12-14. וַיָּנָס וַיֵּצֵא הַחוּצָה ... וַתִּקְרָא לְאַנְשֵׁי בֵיתָהּ — *And fled, he went out ... She called to the men of her house.* The *Sforno,* noting the subtle change in the language of these verses, gives this interpretation to the episode: When the Torah tells us of Joseph's actions it states וַיֵּצֵא הַחוּצָה, *he went out,* rather than וַיָּנָס, *he fled,* indicating that once he fled the room he purposely walked normally so as not to raise a hue and cry. Potiphar's wife, when she called her servants to tell them what happened, began with וַיָּנָס, *he fled,* but quickly changed it to וַיֵּצֵא הַחוּצָה, since they saw what happened. When she related the story to her husband, however, she used the phrase וַיָּנָס הַחוּצָה, *he fled outside;* the word וַיֵּצֵא no longer appears, for she wanted her charge and accusation to be buttressed by the guilty action and panicked flight of Joseph.

*[10] And so it was — just as she coaxed Joseph day after day, so he would
not listen to her to lie beside her, to be with her. [11] Then there was an oppor-
tune day when he entered the house to do his work — no man of the household staff being there in the house — [12] that she caught hold of him by his
garment, saying, "Lie with me!" But he left his garment in her hand, and
he fled, and went outside.*

*[13] When she saw that he had left his garment in her hand and fled outside,
[14] she called out to the men of her household and spoke to them saying, "Look!
He brought us a Hebrew man to sport with us! He came to lie with me but
I called out with a loud scream. [15] And when he heard that I raised my voice
and screamed, he left his garment beside me, fled, and went outside!"*

*[16] She kept his garment beside her until his master came home. [17] Then she
told him a similar account saying, "The Hebrew slave whom you brought to
us came to me to sport with me. [18] But it happened that when I raised my
voice and screamed, he left his garment beside me, and ran outside."*

*[19] And it was, when his master heard his wife's words which she spoke
to him, saying, "Your slave did things like these to me," his anger flared up.
[20] Then Joseph's master took him and placed him in the prison — the place
where the king's prisoners were confined — and he remained there in prison.*

*[21] HASHEM was with Joseph, and He endowed him with charisma, and He
put his favor in the eyes of the prison warden. [22] The prison warden placed
all inmates of the prison in Joseph's custody, and everything that was done
there, he would accomplish. [23] The prison warden did not scrutinize
anything that was in his charge inasmuch as HASHEM was with him; and
whatever he did HASHEM made successful.*

40 *[1] And it happened after these things that the cupbearer of the king of
Egypt and the baker transgressed against their master, against the*

(verse 18), she said, "וַיָּנָס הַחוּצָה, *he fled out,*" (after leaving the room he kept running), so as to avoid his pursuers. This she did to substantiate her false story (that she was victimized by Joseph).

לְצַחֶק בָּנוּ – *To mock us* . . . with his lewd and immoral ways, which in turn brought him to attempt to lie with me.

19. וַיִּחַר אַפּוֹ – *His wrath was kindled.* He was angry because she complained about his bringing a Hebrew into the house, not because of her accusations which he disbelieved. Nonetheless, he put Joseph in prison to demonstrate publicly that he did believe his wife (so as to defend her honor and reputation). Even in prison (Potiphar) utilized the services of Joseph, as we read: *And the captain of the guard (Potiphar) charged Joseph to be with them* (40:4).

XL

1. חָטְאוּ מַשְׁקֵה מֶלֶךְ מִצְרַיִם וְהָאֹפֶה – *The butler of the king of Egypt and his baker offended him* . . . the subordinates of the chief of the butlers and of the bakers.

NOTES

XL

1-13. חָטְאוּ מַשְׁקֵה מֶלֶךְ מִצְרַיִם וְהָאֹפֶה ... כַּמִּשְׁפָּט הָרִאשׁוֹן – *The butler of the king of Egypt and his baker offended him . . . after the former manner.* The *Sforno* examines these verses carefully and finds that at times the words מַשְׁקֶה, *butler,* and אֹפֶה, *baker,* are used; at others שַׂר הַמַּשְׁקִים, *chief butler,* and שַׂר הָאוֹפִים, *chief baker,* as well as the

ב לְמֶלֶךְ מִצְרָיִם: וַיִּקְצֹף פַּרְעֹה עַל שְׁנֵי סָרִיסָיו עַל שַׂר הַמַּשְׁקִים וְעַל שַׂר
ג הָאוֹפִים: וַיִּתֵּן אֹתָם בְּמִשְׁמַר בֵּית שַׂר הַטַּבָּחִים אֶל־בֵּית הַסֹּהַר מְקוֹם
ד אֲשֶׁר יוֹסֵף אָסוּר שָׁם: וַיִּפְקֹד שַׂר הַטַּבָּחִים אֶת־יוֹסֵף אִתָּם וַיְשָׁרֶת
ה אֹתָם וַיִּהְיוּ יָמִים בְּמִשְׁמָר: וַיַּחַלְמוּ חֲלוֹם שְׁנֵיהֶם אִישׁ חֲלֹמוֹ בְּלַיְלָה
אֶחָד אִישׁ כְּפִתְרוֹן חֲלֹמוֹ הַמַּשְׁקֶה וְהָאֹפֶה אֲשֶׁר לְמֶלֶךְ מִצְרַיִם אֲשֶׁר
ו אֲסוּרִים בְּבֵית הַסֹּהַר: וַיָּבֹא אֲלֵיהֶם יוֹסֵף בַּבֹּקֶר וַיַּרְא אֹתָם וְהִנָּם
ז זֹעֲפִים: וַיִּשְׁאַל אֶת־סְרִיסֵי פַרְעֹה אֲשֶׁר אִתּוֹ בְמִשְׁמַר בֵּית אֲדֹנָיו לֵאמֹר
ח מַדּוּעַ פְּנֵיכֶם רָעִים הַיּוֹם: וַיֹּאמְרוּ אֵלָיו חֲלוֹם חָלַמְנוּ וּפֹתֵר אֵין אֹתוֹ
ט וַיֹּאמֶר אֲלֵהֶם יוֹסֵף הֲלוֹא לֵאלֹהִים פִּתְרֹנִים סַפְּרוּ־נָא לִי: וַיְסַפֵּר
שַׂר־הַמַּשְׁקִים אֶת־חֲלֹמוֹ לְיוֹסֵף וַיֹּאמֶר לוֹ בַּחֲלוֹמִי וְהִנֵּה־גֶפֶן לְפָנָי:
י וּבַגֶּפֶן שְׁלֹשָׁה שָׂרִיגִם וְהִוא כְפֹרַחַת עָלְתָה נִצָּהּ הִבְשִׁילוּ אַשְׁכְּלֹתֶיהָ
יא עֲנָבִים: וְכוֹס פַּרְעֹה בְּיָדִי וָאֶקַּח אֶת־הָעֲנָבִים וָאֶשְׂחַט אֹתָם אֶל־כּוֹס
יב פַּרְעֹה וָאֶתֵּן אֶת־הַכּוֹס עַל־כַּף פַּרְעֹה: וַיֹּאמֶר לוֹ יוֹסֵף זֶה פִּתְרֹנוֹ
יג שְׁלֹשֶׁת הַשָּׂרִגִים שְׁלֹשֶׁת יָמִים הֵם: בְּעוֹד ׀ שְׁלֹשֶׁת יָמִים יִשָּׂא פַרְעֹה
אֶת־רֹאשֶׁךָ וַהֲשִׁיבְךָ עַל־כַּנֶּךָ וְנָתַתָּ כוֹס־פַּרְעֹה בְּיָדוֹ כַּמִּשְׁפָּט הָרִאשׁוֹן
יד אֲשֶׁר הָיִיתָ מַשְׁקֵהוּ: כִּי אִם־זְכַרְתַּנִי אִתְּךָ כַּאֲשֶׁר יִיטַב לָךְ וְעָשִׂיתָ־נָּא
טו עִמָּדִי חָסֶד וְהִזְכַּרְתַּנִי אֶל־פַּרְעֹה וְהוֹצֵאתַנִי מִן־הַבַּיִת הַזֶּה: כִּי־גֻנֹּב
גֻּנַּבְתִּי מֵאֶרֶץ הָעִבְרִים וְגַם־פֹּה לֹא־עָשִׂיתִי מְאוּמָה כִּי־שָׂמוּ אֹתִי בַּבּוֹר:

---

2. וַיִּקְצֹף פַּרְעֹה עַל שְׁנֵי סָרִיסָיו – *And Pharaoh was wroth against his two officers* ... for not properly overseeing their subordinates.

5. הַמַּשְׁקֶה וְהָאֹפֶה ... אֲשֶׁר אֲסוּרִים – *The butler and the baker ... who were imprisoned.* They dreamed as a butler and baker would, not as chiefs in positions of authority, for since they were incarcerated they were humbled and did not think as officers normally would.

7. סְרִיסֵי פַרְעֹה אֲשֶׁר אִתּוֹ בְמִשְׁמַר בֵּית אֲדֹנָיו – *Pharaoh's officers that were with him in the ward of his master's house.* Only because his master had appointed him to minister to their needs, as it states, *And the captain of the guard charged Joseph to be with them* (v.4), did he (have the temerity) to ask them why they were so sad.

8. הֲלוֹא לֵאלֹהִים פִּתְרֹנִים – *Do not interpretations belong to God?* Man has wisdom in interpreting dreams because he is formed in the image of God; therefore I may have it, too, even though I am a slave languishing in prison. Hence you may be wrong in saying, "*And there is none who can interpret it.*"

13. כַּמִּשְׁפָּט הָרִאשׁוֹן – *After the former manner* ... before you became the chief of the butlers.

אֲשֶׁר הָיִיתָ מַשְׁקֵהוּ – *When you were his butler* ... you yourself (directly). This (Pharaoh)

NOTES

phrase סְרִיסֵי פַּרְעֹה, *Pharaoh's officers.* He determines that the phrase מַשְׁקֶה or אֹפֶה means the vassal who does the actual act of *pouring the wine* or *baking;* the expression שַׂר הַמַּשְׁקִים or שַׂר הָאוֹפִים means chief butler or baker and סָרִיס is an officer of the king, implying a position of honor and respect. The initial offense was committed by the functionaries, not the chiefs; nevertheless the chiefs were held responsible. Hence in verse 1, the phrases used are מַשְׁקֶה and אֹפֶה, whereas in verse 2 it is סָרִיסָיו and שַׂר. In verse 5, even though we are speaking of the chiefs, the phrases used are מַשְׁקֶה and אֹפֶה, for the reason given in the *Sforno's* commentary. In verse 7, סְרִיסֵי is used again to

king of Egypt. 2 *Pharaoh was enraged at his two courtiers, the Chamberlain*
of the Cupbearers and the Chamberlain of the Bakers. 3 *And he placed*
them in the ward of the house of the Chamberlain of the Butchers, into the
prison, the place where Joseph was confined. 4 *The Chamberlain of the*
Butchers appointed Joseph to be with them, and he attended them and they remained in the ward for a period of days.

5 *The two of them dreamt a dream, each one had his dream on the same night, each one according to the interpretation of his dream — the cupbearer and the baker of the king of Egypt who were confined in the prison.*

6 *Joseph came to them in the morning. He saw them and behold! they were aggrieved.*

7 *And he asked Pharaoh's courtiers who were with him in the ward of his*
master's house, saying, "Why do you appear downcast today?" 8 *And they*
said to him, "We dreamt a dream, but there is no interpreter for it." So Joseph said to them, "Do not interpretations belong to God? Relate it to me, if you please."

9 *Then the Chamberlain of the Cupbearers recounted his dream to Joseph*
and said to him, "In my dream — behold! there was a grapevine in front of
me! 10 *On the grapevine were three tendrils; and it was as though it budded*
— its blossoms bloomed and its clusters ripened into grapes. 11 *And*
Pharaoh's cup was in my hand and I took the grapes, pressed them into Pharaoh's cup, and I placed the cup on Pharaoh's palm."

12 *Joseph said to him, "This is its interpretation: The three tendrils are*
three days. 13 *In another three days Pharaoh will lift up your head and will*
restore you to your post, and you will place Pharaoh's cup in his hand as
was the former practice when you were his cupbearer. 14 *If only you would*
think of me with yourself when he benefits you, and you will do me a kindness, if you please, and mention me to Pharaoh, then you would get me out
of this building. 15 *For indeed I was kidnaped from the land of the Hebrews,*
and even here I have done nothing for them to have put me in the pit."

---

will do to indicate to you that he is appeased, and looks upon you again with favor.

14. כִּי אִם זְכַרְתַּנִי אִתְּךָ – *But have me in your remembrance* . . . for the king will so cherish you, that if you will but remember (and mention me) . . .

כַּאֲשֶׁר יִיטַב לָךְ – *When it shall be well with you* . . . at an appropriate time . . .

וְהִזְכַּרְתַּנִי אֶל פַּרְעֹה – *And make mention of me to Pharaoh* . . . he knows me from the time I was in the house of the captain of the guards.

וְהוֹצֵאתַנִי – *And bring me out* . . . then surely you will win my release.

15. כִּי גֻנֹּב גֻּנַּבְתִּי . . . וְגַם פֹּה לֹא עָשִׂיתִי מְאוּמָה – *For indeed I was stolen* . . . *and here also have I done nothing.* You will assuredly procure my release for it can be proven that neither my state of slavery nor my imprisonment was justified.

NOTES

emphasize that were it not for the fact that Joseph had been given the responsibility by Potiphar to watch over them, he would never have had the temerity to speak so familiarly with them, or to ask them such a personal question. In verse 13, the phrase כְּמִשְׁפָּט הָרִאשׁוֹן, *after the former manner,* must mean that the chief butler, after being rehabilitated, would once again assume his original task of actually pouring the wine and serving it to Pharaoh.

טז וַיַּרְא שַׂר־הָאֹפִים כִּי טוֹב פָּתָר וַיֹּאמֶר אֶל־יוֹסֵף אַף־אֲנִי בַּחֲלוֹמִי וְהִנֵּה
יז שְׁלֹשָׁה סַלֵּי חֹרִי עַל־רֹאשִׁי: וּבַסַּל הָעֶלְיוֹן מִכֹּל מַאֲכַל פַּרְעֹה מַעֲשֵׂה
יח אֹפֶה וְהָעוֹף אֹכֵל אֹתָם מִן־הַסַּל מֵעַל רֹאשִׁי: וַיַּעַן יוֹסֵף וַיֹּאמֶר זֶה
יט פִּתְרֹנוֹ שְׁלֹשֶׁת הַסַּלִּים שְׁלֹשֶׁת יָמִים הֵם: בְּעוֹד ׀ שְׁלֹשֶׁת יָמִים יִשָּׂא
פַרְעֹה אֶת־רֹאשְׁךָ מֵעָלֶיךָ וְתָלָה אוֹתְךָ עַל־עֵץ וְאָכַל הָעוֹף אֶת־בְּשָׂרְךָ
מפטיר כ מֵעָלֶיךָ: וַיְהִי ׀ בַּיּוֹם הַשְּׁלִישִׁי יוֹם הֻלֶּדֶת אֶת־פַּרְעֹה וַיַּעַשׂ מִשְׁתֶּה
לְכָל־עֲבָדָיו וַיִּשָּׂא אֶת־רֹאשׁ ׀ שַׂר הַמַּשְׁקִים וְאֶת־רֹאשׁ שַׂר הָאֹפִים
כא בְּתוֹךְ עֲבָדָיו: וַיָּשֶׁב אֶת־שַׂר הַמַּשְׁקִים עַל־מַשְׁקֵהוּ וַיִּתֵּן הַכּוֹס עַל־כַּף
כב־כג פַּרְעֹה: וְאֵת שַׂר הָאֹפִים תָּלָה כַּאֲשֶׁר פָּתַר לָהֶם יוֹסֵף: וְלֹא־זָכַר
שַׂר־הַמַּשְׁקִים אֶת־יוֹסֵף וַיִּשְׁכָּחֵהוּ:

16. כִּי טוֹב פָּתָר — *That the interpretation was good* . . . and he hoped that Joseph would also interpret his dream for good, because the fulfillment of a dream depends on how it

NOTES

16. כי טוב פתר — *That the interpretation was good.* The expression, *as Joseph had interpreted,* implies that this was the cause for the eventual fate of the butler and baker. This then is the

16 *The Chamberlain of the Bakers saw that he had interpreted well, so he
said to Joseph, "I, too! In my dream — behold! three wicker baskets were on
my head.* 17 *And in the uppermost basket were all kinds of Pharaoh's food
— baker's handiwork — and the birds were eating them from the basket
above my head."*

18 *Joseph responded and said, "This is its interpretation: The three
baskets are three days.* 19 *In three days Pharaoh will lift your head from
you and hang you on a tree; birds will eat your flesh from you."*

20 *And it was on the third day, Pharaoh's birthday, that he made a feast
for all his servants and he counted the Chamberlain of the Cupbearers and
the Chamberlain of the Bakers among his servants.* 21 *He restored the
Chamberlain of the Cupbearers to his cupbearing and he placed the cup on
Pharaoh's palm.* 22 *But the Chamberlain of the Bakers he hung, just as
Joseph had interpreted to them.*

23 *Yet the Chamberlain of the Cupbearers did not remember Joseph, but
he forgot him.*

---

is interpreted, as our Sages tell us (*Berachos* 55b), and as the Torah later states, *As Joseph had interpreted to them* (verse 22).

NOTES

biblical source of our Sages' saying "All dreams follow the mouth," i.e., "The fulfillment of all dreams depends upon their interpretation" (*Berachos* 55b).

פרשת מקץ

מא

א־ב וַיְהִי מִקֵּץ שְׁנָתַיִם יָמִים וּפַרְעֹה חֹלֵם וְהִנֵּה עֹמֵד עַל־הַיְאֹר: וְהִנֵּה מִן־
הַיְאֹר עֹלֹת שֶׁבַע פָּרוֹת יְפוֹת מַרְאֶה וּבְרִיאֹת בָּשָׂר וַתִּרְעֶינָה בָּאָחוּ:
ג וְהִנֵּה שֶׁבַע פָּרוֹת אֲחֵרוֹת עֹלוֹת אַחֲרֵיהֶן מִן־הַיְאֹר רָעוֹת מַרְאֶה וְדַקּוֹת
ד בָּשָׂר וַתַּעֲמֹדְנָה אֵצֶל הַפָּרוֹת עַל־שְׂפַת הַיְאֹר: וַתֹּאכַלְנָה הַפָּרוֹת רָעוֹת
הַמַּרְאֶה וְדַקֹּת הַבָּשָׂר אֵת שֶׁבַע הַפָּרוֹת יְפֹת הַמַּרְאֶה וְהַבְּרִיאֹת וַיִּיקַץ
ה פַּרְעֹה: וַיִּישָׁן וַיַּחֲלֹם שֵׁנִית וְהִנֵּה | שֶׁבַע שִׁבֳּלִים עֹלוֹת בְּקָנֶה אֶחָד
ו בְּרִיאוֹת וְטֹבוֹת: וְהִנֵּה שֶׁבַע שִׁבֳּלִים דַּקּוֹת וּשְׁדוּפֹת קָדִים צֹמְחוֹת
ז אַחֲרֵיהֶן: וַתִּבְלַעְנָה הַשִּׁבֳּלִים הַדַּקּוֹת אֵת שֶׁבַע הַשִּׁבֳּלִים הַבְּרִיאוֹת
ח וְהַמְּלֵאוֹת וַיִּיקַץ פַּרְעֹה וְהִנֵּה חֲלוֹם: וַיְהִי בַבֹּקֶר וַתִּפָּעֶם רוּחוֹ וַיִּשְׁלַח
וַיִּקְרָא אֶת־כָּל־חַרְטֻמֵּי מִצְרַיִם וְאֶת־כָּל־חֲכָמֶיהָ וַיְסַפֵּר פַּרְעֹה לָהֶם
ט אֶת־חֲלֹמוֹ וְאֵין־פּוֹתֵר אוֹתָם לְפַרְעֹה: וַיְדַבֵּר שַׂר הַמַּשְׁקִים אֶת־פַּרְעֹה
י לֵאמֹר אֶת־חֲטָאַי אֲנִי מַזְכִּיר הַיּוֹם: פַּרְעֹה קָצַף עַל־עֲבָדָיו וַיִּתֵּן אֹתִי
יא בְּמִשְׁמַר בֵּית שַׂר הַטַּבָּחִים אֹתִי וְאֵת שַׂר הָאֹפִים: וַנַּחַלְמָה חֲלוֹם
יב בְּלַיְלָה אֶחָד אֲנִי וָהוּא אִישׁ כְּפִתְרוֹן חֲלֹמוֹ חָלָמְנוּ: וְשָׁם אִתָּנוּ נַעַר עִבְרִי
עֶבֶד לְשַׂר הַטַּבָּחִים וַנְּסַפֶּר־לוֹ וַיִּפְתָּר־לָנוּ אֶת־חֲלֹמֹתֵינוּ אִישׁ כַּחֲלֹמוֹ
יג פָּתָר: וַיְהִי כַּאֲשֶׁר פָּתַר־לָנוּ כֵּן הָיָה אֹתִי הֵשִׁיב עַל־כַּנִּי וְאֹתוֹ תָלָה:

XLI

1. וַיְהִי מִקֵּץ . . . וּפַרְעֹה חֹלֵם — *And it came to pass at the end of . . . that Pharaoh dreamed.* Among other dreams he had, which were without significance, he dreamed this also, that he was standing by the river, as our Sages say, כְּשֵׁם שֶׁאִי אֶפְשָׁר לְבַר בְּלֹא תֶבֶן, כָּךְ אִי אֶפְשָׁר לַחֲלוֹם בְּלֹא דְּבָרִים בְּטֵלִים, *Just as wheat cannot do without straw, so there cannot be a dream without nonsense (Berachos* 55b).

3. וַתַּעֲמֹדְנָה אֵצֶל הַפָּרוֹת — *And stood by the (other) cows.* They stood by them (for some time) before eating, symbolizing that for a period there would be both famine and plenty, as we find, *There was famine in all lands, but in all the land of Egypt there was plenty* (verse 54).

NOTES

XLI

1. וּפַרְעֹה חֹלֵם וְהִנֵּה עֹמֵד — *Pharaoh was dreaming and behold he was standing.* The verse does not state וַיַּחֲלוֹם פַּרְעֹה, *and Pharaoh dreamed,* rather וּפַרְעֹה חֹלֵם, *and Pharaoh was dreaming,* meaning that among his other dreams was this dream of the cattle and the corn. As our Sages teach us, only a very small percentage of our dreams are significant, and this is a very good example of a dream coming for the specific purpose of revealing future events. This is especially true when a dream does not reflect a person's thoughts and experiences of the day but occurs unexpectedly and suddenly. The word הִנֵּה, *behold,* appears twice; once in verse 1 regarding Pharaoh standing by the river and again in verse 2 regarding the cows. This word indicates suddenness, and tells us that Pharaoh was taken unawares since he had not been thinking of the river, and certainly not of the bizarre appearance of the kine. Hence he is convinced that the dream is pregnant with meaning. This thought is repeated by the *Sforno* again in verse 19, where he interprets the words *such as I never saw* to mean that Pharaoh had not seen such kine that day, which would have explained why he dreamed of them that night. It does not mean that he never saw such lean-fleshed kine before, as this phrase is usually explained.

3. וַתַּעֲמֹדְנָה אֵצֶל הַפָּרוֹת — *And stood by the (other) cows.* The fat-fleshed and lean-fleshed cattle standing side by side indicated that there would be a period of time when there would be both plenty and famine. This, the *Sforno* explains (based upon verse 54), refers to the time when the seven good

PARASHAS MIKEITZ

41 1 It happened at the end of two years to the day: Pharaoh was dreaming
that behold! — he was standing over the River, 2 *when behold! out of the*
River there emerged seven cows, of beautiful appearance and robust flesh,
and they were grazing in the marshland. 3 *Then behold! — seven other cows*
emerged after them out of the River — of ugly appearance and gaunt flesh;
and they stood next to the cows on the bank of the River. 4 *The cows of ugly*
appearance and gaunt flesh ate the seven cows of beautiful appearance and
robust, and Pharaoh awoke. 5 *He fell asleep and dreamt a second time, and*
behold! seven ears of grain were sprouting on a single stalk — healthy and
good. 6 *And behold! seven ears, thin, and scorched by the east wind, were*
growing after them. 7 *Then the seven thin ears swallowed up the seven*
healthy and full ears; Pharaoh awoke and behold! — it had been a dream.
8 *And it was in the morning: His spirit was agitated, so he sent and*
summoned all the necromancers of Egypt and all its wise men; Pharaoh
related his dream to them, but none could interpret them for Pharaoh.
9 *Then the Chamberlain of the Cupbearers spoke up before Pharaoh, "My*
transgressions do I mention today. 10 *Pharaoh had become incensed at his*
servants and placed me in the ward of the house of the Chamberlain of the
Butchers — me and the Chamberlain of the Bakers. 11 *We dreamt a dream*
on the same night, I and he; each of us according to the interpretation of his
dream did we dream. 12 *And there, with us, was a Hebrew youth, a slave of*
the Chamberlain of the Butchers; we related it to him, and he interpreted our
dreams for us; he interpreted for each in accordance with his dream. 13 *And*
it was that just as he interpreted for us so did it happen; me he restored to
my post and him he hanged."

7. וְהִנֵּה חֲלוֹם – *And, behold, it was a dream.* He felt it was all one dream, for when he dreamed the second dream he knew it was a continuation of the first, and so he explains later, when he says, "*And I saw in my dream*" (verse 22) (i.e., he said *dream,* not *dreams).*

8. וְאֵין פּוֹתֵר אוֹתָם – *There was none that could interpret them.* Because they (the magicians and wise men) thought that these were two (distinct and separate) dreams, therefore they erred in their interpretation. (The reason they were misled was because) the first part consisted of active, physical causes, i.e., the cattle that plough and the river that waters, whereas the second consisted of ultimate form and purpose, i.e., the ears of corn.

9. אֶת חֲטָאַי אֲנִי מַזְכִּיר – *I make mention of my faults.* I do not complain that you imprisoned me, for it was due to my own fault.

NOTES

years had concluded and the seven bad years had just begun. All other lands would feel the effects of the famine, while Egypt would still be insulated from hunger, as a result of its preparations during the good years.

7-8. וְהִנֵּה חֲלוֹם... וְאֵין פּוֹתֵר – *And, behold, it was a dream ... there was none that could interpret them.* Pharaoh knew that the two dreams were one. Joseph realized this after hearing the dreams, and his initial response to Pharaoh was, "The dream of Pharaoh is one." The necromancers and wise men failed to grasp this, for they were convinced that the two dreams were separate and distinct, since the first one dealt with the forces of productivity, the cause, i.e., the cattle that plough and the river that waters the plantings, while the second dealt with the result, i.e., the growing corn, which is the purpose and goal of the labor of the kine and the contribution of the water. This thought is repeated later by the *Sforno* in verse 24.

יד וַיִּשְׁלַח פַּרְעֹה וַיִּקְרָא אֶת־יוֹסֵף וַיְרִיצֻהוּ מִן־הַבּוֹר וַיְגַלַּח וַיְחַלֵּף שִׂמְלֹתָיו
טו וַיָּבֹא אֶל־פַּרְעֹה: וַיֹּאמֶר פַּרְעֹה אֶל־יוֹסֵף חֲלוֹם חָלַמְתִּי וּפֹתֵר אֵין אֹתוֹ שני
טז וַאֲנִי שָׁמַעְתִּי עָלֶיךָ לֵאמֹר תִּשְׁמַע חֲלוֹם לִפְתֹּר אֹתוֹ: וַיַּעַן יוֹסֵף אֶת־
יז פַּרְעֹה לֵאמֹר בִּלְעָדָי אֱלֹהִים יַעֲנֶה אֶת־שְׁלוֹם פַּרְעֹה: וַיְדַבֵּר פַּרְעֹה אֶל־
יח יוֹסֵף בַּחֲלֹמִי הִנְנִי עֹמֵד עַל־שְׂפַת הַיְאֹר: וְהִנֵּה מִן־הַיְאֹר עֹלֹת שֶׁבַע
יט פָּרוֹת בְּרִיאוֹת בָּשָׂר וִיפֹת תֹּאַר וַתִּרְעֶינָה בָּאָחוּ: וְהִנֵּה שֶׁבַע־פָּרוֹת
אֲחֵרוֹת עֹלוֹת אַחֲרֵיהֶן דַּלּוֹת וְרָעוֹת תֹּאַר מְאֹד וְרַקּוֹת בָּשָׂר לֹא־רָאִיתִי
כ כָהֵנָּה בְּכָל־אֶרֶץ מִצְרַיִם לָרֹעַ: וַתֹּאכַלְנָה הַפָּרוֹת הָרַקּוֹת וְהָרָעוֹת אֵת
כא שֶׁבַע הַפָּרוֹת הָרִאשֹׁנוֹת הַבְּרִיאֹת: וַתָּבֹאנָה אֶל־קִרְבֶּנָה וְלֹא נוֹדַע כִּי־
כב בָאוּ אֶל־קִרְבֶּנָה וּמַרְאֵיהֶן רַע כַּאֲשֶׁר בַּתְּחִלָּה וָאִיקָץ: וָאֵרֶא בַּחֲלֹמִי
כג וְהִנֵּה | שֶׁבַע שִׁבֳּלִים עֹלֹת בְּקָנֶה אֶחָד מְלֵאֹת וְטֹבוֹת: וְהִנֵּה שֶׁבַע שִׁבֳּלִים
כד צְנֻמוֹת דַּקּוֹת שְׁדֻפוֹת קָדִים צֹמְחוֹת אַחֲרֵיהֶם: וַתִּבְלַעְןָ הַשִּׁבֳּלִים הַדַּקֹּת
כה אֵת שֶׁבַע הַשִּׁבֳּלִים הַטֹּבוֹת וָאֹמַר אֶל־הַחַרְטֻמִּים וְאֵין מַגִּיד לִי: וַיֹּאמֶר
יוֹסֵף אֶל־פַּרְעֹה חֲלוֹם פַּרְעֹה אֶחָד הוּא אֵת אֲשֶׁר הָאֱלֹהִים עֹשֶׂה הִגִּיד
כו לְפַרְעֹה: שֶׁבַע פָּרֹת הַטֹּבֹת שֶׁבַע שָׁנִים הֵנָּה וְשֶׁבַע הַשִּׁבֳּלִים הַטֹּבֹת שֶׁבַע
כז שָׁנִים הֵנָּה חֲלוֹם אֶחָד הוּא: וְשֶׁבַע הַפָּרוֹת הָרַקּוֹת וְהָרָעֹת הָעֹלֹת
אַחֲרֵיהֶן שֶׁבַע שָׁנִים הֵנָּה וְשֶׁבַע הַשִּׁבֳּלִים הָרֵקוֹת שְׁדֻפוֹת הַקָּדִים יִהְיוּ

---

14. וַיְרִיצֻהוּ מִן הַבּוֹר – *They brought him hastily out of the dungeon.* The Divine salvation always comes hastily (unexpectedly), as it is written, כִּי קְרוֹבָה יְשׁוּעָתִי לָבוֹא, *For my salvation is near to come* (*Isaiah* 56:1), and also, לוּ עַמִּי שֹׁמֵעַ לִי . . . כִּמְעַט אוֹיְבֵיהֶם אַכְנִיעַ, *Oh, that My people would hearken unto me . . . I would soon subdue their enemies* (*Psalms* 81:14-15). And so it came to pass in the Egyptian bondage, as it says, כִּי גֹרְשׁוּ מִמִּצְרַיִם, *because they were thrust out of Egypt* (*Exodus* 12:39), as our Sages have told us, "Their dough had no time to rise, for the King of kings, the Almighty, revealed Himself to them and redeemed them" (*Passover Haggadah*). And so it shall be in the future, as it is written, וּפִתְאֹם יָבוֹא אֶל הֵיכָלוֹ הָאָדוֹן אֲשֶׁר אַתֶּם מְבַקְשִׁים, *And the Lord Whom you seek will suddenly come to His Temple* (*Malachi* 3:1).

וַיְחַלֵּף שִׂמְלֹתָיו – *And changed his clothes* . . . for it is not fitting to come to the gate of the king's palace wearing sackcloth. (Compare to *Esther* 4:2.)

15. תִּשְׁמַע חֲלוֹם לִפְתֹּר אֹתוֹ – *When you hear a dream you can interpret it.* You have a talent for interpretation, and understand the true meaning of a dream, interpreting it wisely, not merely guessing the truth by chance.

16. בִּלְעָדָי – *It is not in me.* Even though you say, "None can interpret it," as though I alone have this special talent, nonetheless I think that there are others besides me who can do so.

אֱלֹהִים יַעֲנֶה – *It is God who will respond.* He will cause me (teach me) to answer properly.

NOTES

14. וַיְרִיצֻהוּ מִן הַבּוֹר — *They brought him hastily out of the dungeon.* The sudden release of Joseph from the dungeon and his meteoric rise to greatness is a portent of the future destiny of *Klal Yisrael.* "The story of our ancestors is a sign for the children."

21. וְלֹא נוֹדַע כִּי בָאוּ אֶל קִרְבֶּנָה — *It could not be known that they had eaten them.* The verse quoted by the *Sforno* appears in the תּוֹכָחָה, *the admonition.* The quote from tractate *Yoma* explains why one can eat and still not be satisfied. This occurs when he has food only for today and knows not

14 So Pharaoh sent and summoned Joseph, and they rushed him from the dungeon. He shaved and changed his clothes, and he came to Pharaoh. 15 And Pharaoh said to Joseph, "I dreamt a dream, but no one can interpret it. Now I heard it said of you that you comprehend a dream to interpret it."

16 Joseph answered Pharaoh, saying, "That is beyond me; it is God Who will respond with Pharaoh's welfare."

17 Then Pharaoh said to Joseph, "In my dream, behold! — I was standing upon the bank of the River. 18 And behold, out of the River there emerged seven cows, of robust flesh and beautiful form, and they were grazing in the marshland. 19 Suddenly, seven other cows emerged after them — scrawny and of very inferior form and of emaciated flesh; I have never seen inferiority like theirs in all the land of Egypt. 20 And the emaciated and inferior cows ate up the first seven healthy cows. 21 They came inside them, but it was not apparent that they had come inside them, for their appearance remained as inferior as at first. Then I awoke. 22 I then saw in my dream: Behold! — seven ears of grain were sprouting on a single stalk — full and good. 23 And suddenly! — seven ears of grain, withered, thin and scorched by the east wind were growing after them. 24 Then the thin ears of grain swallowed up the seven good ears; I said this to the necromancers, but no one could explain it to me."

25 Joseph said to Pharaoh, "The dream of Pharaoh is a single one; what God is about to do, He has told to Pharaoh: 26 The seven good cows are seven years, and the good ears are seven years; it is a single dream. 27 Now, the seven emaciated and bad cows who emerged after them — they are seven years; as are the seven emaciated ears scorched by the east wind. There shall be

---

אֶת שְׁלוֹם פַּרְעֹה – *With Pharaoh's welfare* . . . an answer (interpretation) which will benefit Pharaoh, for "all dreams follow the mouth" (*Berachos* 55b).

19. לֹא רָאִיתִי כָהֵנָּה – *Such as I never saw.* Hence this cannot be a case of, *Your thoughts came upon your bed* (*Daniel* 2:29; see note to 37:10).

21. וְלֹא נוֹדַע כִּי בָאוּ אֶל קִרְבֶּנָה – *It could not be known that they had eaten them.* (This is) similar to, וַאֲכַלְתֶּם וְלֹא תִשְׂבָּעוּ, *And you shall eat and not be satisfied* (*Lev.* 26:26). As our Sages tell us, אֵינוֹ דוֹמֶה מִי שֶׁיֵּשׁ לוֹ פַּת בְּסַלּוֹ לְמִי שֶׁאֵין לוֹ פַּת בְּסַלּוֹ, *You cannot compare one who has bread in his basket with one who has no bread in his basket* (*Yoma* 74b).

24. וְאֵין מַגִּיד לִי – *But there was none to tell me.* He saw that they all thought there were two separate dreams, and interpreted accordingly, while he recognized that the two were one, as he said, *"And I saw in my dream"* (verse 22).

25. חֲלוֹם פַּרְעֹה אֶחָד הוּא – *The dream of Pharaoh is one* . . . and that is why the interpreters have erred.

אֵת אֲשֶׁר הָאֱלֹהִים עֹשֶׂה הִגִּיד לְפַרְעֹה – *What God is about to do, He has declared to Pharaoh* . . . therefore the necromancers did not know or understand it, for it is unknown to the spirits (who commune with the necromancers). But it has been declared to Pharaoh alone.

NOTES

where his bread will come from tomorrow, for just as a man who is blessed with bread feels so secure that he is never hungry, so one who is unsure cannot even enjoy what he has now. This is symbolized here by the lean-fleshed kine being unaffected after eating the fat-fleshed cattle.

25-28. אֵת אֲשֶׁר הָאֱלֹהִים עֹשֶׂה הִגִּיד לְפַרְעֹה. . . הֶרְאָה אֶת פַּרְעֹה — *What God is about to do, He has declared to Pharaoh . . . He has shown to Pharaoh.* The word הִגִּיד, *declared*, is used in one verse and הֶרְאָה, *shown*, in the other. The former refers to the foretelling of the famine, while the latter is

כח שֶׁבַע שְׁנֵי רָעָב׃ הוּא הַדָּבָר אֲשֶׁר דִּבַּרְתִּי אֶל־פַּרְעֹה אֲשֶׁר הָאֱלֹהִים
כט עֹשֶׂה הֶרְאָה אֶת־פַּרְעֹה׃ הִנֵּה שֶׁבַע שָׁנִים בָּאוֹת שָׂבָע גָּדוֹל בְּכָל־אֶרֶץ
ל מִצְרָיִם׃ וְקָמוּ שֶׁבַע שְׁנֵי רָעָב אַחֲרֵיהֶן וְנִשְׁכַּח כָּל־הַשָּׂבָע בְּאֶרֶץ מִצְרָיִם
לא וְכִלָּה הָרָעָב אֶת־הָאָרֶץ׃ וְלֹא־יִוָּדַע הַשָּׂבָע בָּאָרֶץ מִפְּנֵי הָרָעָב הַהוּא
לב אַחֲרֵי־כֵן כִּי־כָבֵד הוּא מְאֹד׃ וְעַל הִשָּׁנוֹת הַחֲלוֹם אֶל־פַּרְעֹה פַּעֲמָיִם
לג כִּי־נָכוֹן הַדָּבָר מֵעִם הָאֱלֹהִים וּמְמַהֵר הָאֱלֹהִים לַעֲשֹׂתוֹ׃ וְעַתָּה יֵרֶא
לד פַרְעֹה אִישׁ נָבוֹן וְחָכָם וִישִׁיתֵהוּ עַל־אֶרֶץ מִצְרָיִם׃ יַעֲשֶׂה פַרְעֹה וְיַפְקֵד
לה פְּקִדִים עַל־הָאָרֶץ וְחִמֵּשׁ אֶת־אֶרֶץ מִצְרַיִם בְּשֶׁבַע שְׁנֵי הַשָּׂבָע׃ וְיִקְבְּצוּ
אֶת־כָּל־אֹכֶל הַשָּׁנִים הַטֹּבוֹת הַבָּאֹת הָאֵלֶּה וְיִצְבְּרוּ־בָר תַּחַת
לו יַד־פַּרְעֹה אֹכֶל בֶּעָרִים וְשָׁמָרוּ׃ וְהָיָה הָאֹכֶל לְפִקָּדוֹן לָאָרֶץ לְשֶׁבַע
שְׁנֵי הָרָעָב אֲשֶׁר תִּהְיֶיןָ בְּאֶרֶץ מִצְרָיִם וְלֹא־תִכָּרֵת הָאָרֶץ בָּרָעָב׃
לז-לח וַיִּיטַב הַדָּבָר בְּעֵינֵי פַרְעֹה וּבְעֵינֵי כָּל־עֲבָדָיו׃ וַיֹּאמֶר פַּרְעֹה אֶל־עֲבָדָיו
לט הֲנִמְצָא כָזֶה אִישׁ אֲשֶׁר רוּחַ אֱלֹהִים בּוֹ׃ וַיֹּאמֶר פַּרְעֹה אֶל־יוֹסֵף שלישי
אַחֲרֵי הוֹדִיעַ אֱלֹהִים אוֹתְךָ אֶת־כָּל־זֹאת אֵין־נָבוֹן וְחָכָם כָּמוֹךָ׃
מ אַתָּה תִּהְיֶה עַל־בֵּיתִי וְעַל־פִּיךָ יִשַּׁק כָּל־עַמִּי רַק הַכִּסֵּא אֶגְדַּל מִמֶּךָּ׃
מא-מב וַיֹּאמֶר פַּרְעֹה אֶל־יוֹסֵף רְאֵה נָתַתִּי אֹתְךָ עַל כָּל־אֶרֶץ מִצְרָיִם׃ וַיָּסַר
פַּרְעֹה אֶת־טַבַּעְתּוֹ מֵעַל יָדוֹ וַיִּתֵּן אֹתָהּ עַל־יַד יוֹסֵף וַיַּלְבֵּשׁ אֹתוֹ
מג בִּגְדֵי־שֵׁשׁ וַיָּשֶׂם רְבִד הַזָּהָב עַל־צַוָּארוֹ׃ וַיַּרְכֵּב אֹתוֹ בְּמִרְכֶּבֶת
הַמִּשְׁנֶה אֲשֶׁר־לוֹ וַיִּקְרְאוּ לְפָנָיו אַבְרֵךְ וְנָתוֹן אֹתוֹ עַל כָּל־אֶרֶץ
מד מִצְרָיִם׃ וַיֹּאמֶר פַּרְעֹה אֶל־יוֹסֵף אֲנִי פַרְעֹה וּבִלְעָדֶיךָ לֹא־יָרִים אִישׁ

28. הוּא הַדָּבָר – *That is the thing* . . . the (impending) famine which has been told to you, so that the people shall not be decimated by the famine.

הֶרְאָה אֶת פַּרְעֹה – *He has shown to Pharaoh* . . . the years of plenty (as well), to tell (you) how to save your people during the famine years.

33. וְעַתָּה יֵרֶא פַרְעֹה – *Now therefore let Pharaoh seek out.* Since God informed you that there will be a famine to enable you to save your people, and He (even) showed you the (years of) plenty, informing you *how* you may save (them), it is proper that you do so and not sin against Him.

אִישׁ נָבוֹן וְחָכָם – *A man discerning and wise* . . . one who can plan, execute and administer a governmental project efficiently, that the king shall have no damage.

34. יַעֲשֶׂה פַרְעֹה וְיַפְקֵד – *Let Pharaoh do this and appoint.* And let this discerning man appoint overseers for each city who will accept his authority, so that there be a unified

NOTES

instructing Pharaoh what action to take to save his people. God is "telling" and "showing," revealing and teaching. Therefore when Joseph, in verse 33, told Pharaoh to appoint an administrator, he was not advising him, for that would be presumptuous. He was merely continuing to interpret the dream which he had been invited to do.

33. אִישׁ נָבוֹן וְחָכָם — *A man discerning and wise.* (a) The dual expression נָבוֹן, *discerning,* and חָכָם, *wise,* was used advisedly by Joseph, for this man must be both theoretician and manager. (b) The expression "that the king shall have no damage" is borrowed from *Daniel* 6:3.

34. יַעֲשֶׂה פַרְעֹה וְיַפְקֵד — *Let Pharaoh do this and appoint.* The verse from *Deuteronomy* quoted by the *Sforno* speaks of the Supreme Court in Jerusalem, be it the priests, the Levites, the king or the Sanhedrin, who are the final arbiters. And here

seven years of famine. [28] *It is this matter that I have spoken to Pharaoh: What God is about to do, He has shown to Pharaoh.*

[29] *Behold! — seven years are coming — a great abundance throughout all the land of Egypt.* [30] *Then seven years of famine will arise after them and all the abundance in the land of Egypt will be forgotten; the famine will ravage the land.* [31] *And the abundance will be unknown in the land in the face of the subsequent famine — for it will be terribly severe.* [32] *As for the repetition of the dream to Pharaoh — two times — it is because the matter stands ready before God, and God is hastening to accomplish it.*

[33] *Now let Pharaoh seek out a discerning and wise man and set him over the land of Egypt.* [34] *Let Pharaoh proceed and let him appoint overseers on the land, and he shall prepare the land of Egypt during the seven years of abundance.* [35] *And let them gather all the food of those approaching good years; let them amass fine grain under Pharaoh's authority for food in the cities, and safeguard it.* [36] *The food will be a reserve for the land against the seven years of famine which will befall the land of Egypt, so that the land will not perish in the famine."*

[37] *The matter appeared good in Pharaoh's eyes and in the eyes of all his servants.* [38] *Pharaoh said to his servants, "Could we find another like him — a man in whom is the spirit of God?"*

[39] *Then Pharaoh said to Joseph, "Since God has informed you of all this, there can be no one so discerning and wise as you.* [40] *You shall be in charge of my palace and by your command shall all my people be sustained; only by the throne shall I outrank you."*

[41] *Then Pharaoh said to Joseph, "See! I have placed you in charge of all the land of Egypt."* [42] *And Pharaoh removed his ring from his hand and put it on Joseph's hand. He then had him dressed in garments of fine linen and he placed a gold chain upon his neck.* [43] *He also had him ride in his second royal chariot and they proclaimed before him: "Avrech!" Thus, he appointed him over all the land of Egypt.*

[44] *Pharaoh said to Joseph, "I am Pharaoh. And without you no man may*

---

program and not a divided, fragmented one, as we find, וְקַמְתָּ וְעָלִיתָ אֶל הַמָּקוֹם, *And you shall arise and go up to the place* (*Deut.* 17:8).

37. וַיִּיטַב הַדָּבָר — *And the thing was good . . .* Joseph's advice and (suggested) plan.

41. רְאֵה נָתַתִּי אֹתְךָ עַל כָּל אֶרֶץ מִצְרָיִם — *See, I have set you over all the land of Egypt.* See that you do your best, for I have entrusted you with a great responsibility.

43. וַיִּקְרְאוּ לְפָנָיו אַבְרֵךְ — *And they cried before him, "Avrech" . . .* similar to הַבְרֵךְ, *let all bend the knee,* as it is customary to cry out to the people when the king passes by.

וְנָתוֹן אֹתוֹ עַל כָּל אֶרֶץ מִצְרָיִם — *And he set him over all the land of Egypt.* They all accepted his authority as is customary when a new king is coronated.

NOTES

too, there must be one central authority, else there will be anarchy and chaos.

37. וַיִּיטַב הַדָּבָר — *And the thing was good.* The phrase וַיִּיטַב הַדָּבָר, *And the thing was good,* does not refer to Joseph's interpretation of the dream. An interpretation is either accepted or not. It is not a matter of judgment and taste. Therefore the *Sforno* comments, "advice and plan," regarding the appointment of a governor, especially since it presents the opportunity for a new important government position.

מה אֶת־יָדֶ֛ו וְאֶת־רַגְל֖וֹ בְּכָל־אֶ֣רֶץ מִצְרָ֑יִם: וַיִּקְרָ֨א פַרְעֹ֤ה שֵׁם־יוֹסֵף֙ צָֽפְנַ֣ת
פַּעְנֵ֔חַ וַיִּתֶּן־ל֣וֹ אֶת־אָֽסְנַ֗ת בַּת־פּ֥וֹטִי פֶ֛רַע כֹּהֵ֥ן אֹ֖ן לְאִשָּׁ֑ה וַיֵּצֵ֥א יוֹסֵ֖ף
מו עַל־אֶ֥רֶץ מִצְרָֽיִם: וְיוֹסֵף֙ בֶּן־שְׁלֹשִׁ֣ים שָׁנָ֔ה בְּעָמְד֕וֹ לִפְנֵ֖י פַּרְעֹ֣ה
מז מֶֽלֶךְ־מִצְרָ֑יִם וַיֵּצֵ֤א יוֹסֵף֙ מִלִּפְנֵ֣י פַרְעֹ֔ה וַיַּֽעֲבֹ֖ר בְּכָל־אֶ֥רֶץ מִצְרָֽיִם: וַתַּ֣עַשׂ
מח הָאָ֔רֶץ בְּשֶׁ֖בַע שְׁנֵ֣י הַשָּׂבָ֑ע לִקְמָצִֽים: וַיִּקְבֹּ֞ץ אֶת־כָּל־אֹ֣כֶל | שֶׁ֣בַע שָׁנִ֗ים
אֲשֶׁ֤ר הָיוּ֙ בְּאֶ֣רֶץ מִצְרַ֔יִם וַיִּתֶּן־אֹ֖כֶל בֶּֽעָרִ֑ים אֹ֧כֶל שְׂדֵֽה־הָעִ֛יר אֲשֶׁ֥ר
מט סְבִיבֹתֶ֖יהָ נָתַ֥ן בְּתוֹכָֽהּ: וַיִּצְבֹּ֨ר יוֹסֵ֥ף בָּ֛ר כְּח֥וֹל הַיָּ֖ם הַרְבֵּ֣ה מְאֹ֑ד עַ֛ד
נ כִּי־חָדַ֥ל לִסְפֹּ֖ר כִּי־אֵ֥ין מִסְפָּֽר: וּלְיוֹסֵ֤ף יֻלַּד֙ שְׁנֵ֣י בָנִ֔ים בְּטֶ֥רֶם תָּב֖וֹא שְׁנַ֣ת
נא הָֽרָעָ֑ב אֲשֶׁ֤ר יָֽלְדָה־לּוֹ֙ אָֽסְנַ֔ת בַּת־פּ֥וֹטִי פֶ֖רַע כֹּהֵ֥ן אֽוֹן: וַיִּקְרָ֧א יוֹסֵ֛ף
אֶת־שֵׁ֥ם הַבְּכ֖וֹר מְנַשֶּׁ֑ה כִּֽי־נַשַּׁ֤נִי אֱלֹהִים֙ אֶת־כָּל־עֲמָלִ֔י וְאֵ֖ת כָּל־בֵּ֥ית
נב אָבִֽי: וְאֵ֛ת שֵׁ֥ם הַשֵּׁנִ֖י קָרָ֣א אֶפְרָ֑יִם כִּֽי־הִפְרַ֥נִי אֱלֹהִ֖ים בְּאֶ֥רֶץ עָנְיִֽי:
רביעי נג־נד *וַתִּכְלֶ֕ינָה שֶׁ֖בַע שְׁנֵ֣י הַשָּׂבָ֑ע אֲשֶׁ֥ר הָיָ֖ה בְּאֶ֥רֶץ מִצְרָֽיִם: וַתְּחִלֶּ֜ינָה שֶׁ֣בַע
שְׁנֵ֤י הָֽרָעָב֙ לָב֔וֹא כַּֽאֲשֶׁ֖ר אָמַ֣ר יוֹסֵ֑ף וַיְהִ֤י רָעָב֙ בְּכָל־הָ֣אֲרָצ֔וֹת וּבְכָל־
נה אֶ֥רֶץ מִצְרַ֖יִם הָ֣יָה לָ֑חֶם: וַתִּרְעַב֙ כָּל־אֶ֣רֶץ מִצְרַ֔יִם וַיִּצְעַ֥ק הָעָ֛ם אֶל־פַּרְעֹ֖ה
לַלָּ֑חֶם וַיֹּ֨אמֶר פַּרְעֹ֤ה לְכָל־מִצְרַ֨יִם֙ לְכ֣וּ אֶל־יוֹסֵ֔ף אֲשֶׁר־יֹאמַ֥ר לָכֶ֖ם
נו תַּֽעֲשֽׂוּ: וְהָֽרָעָ֣ב הָיָ֔ה עַ֖ל כָּל־פְּנֵ֣י הָאָ֑רֶץ וַיִּפְתַּ֨ח יוֹסֵ֜ף אֶת־כָּל־אֲשֶׁ֤ר בָּהֶם֙
נז וַיִּשְׁבֹּ֣ר לְמִצְרַ֔יִם וַיֶּֽחֱזַ֥ק הָֽרָעָ֖ב בְּאֶ֣רֶץ מִצְרָֽיִם: וְכָל־הָאָ֨רֶץ֙ בָּ֣אוּ מִצְרַ֔יְמָה
מב א לִשְׁבֹּ֖ר אֶל־יוֹסֵ֑ף כִּֽי־חָזַ֥ק הָֽרָעָ֖ב בְּכָל־הָאָֽרֶץ: וַיַּ֣רְא יַֽעֲקֹ֔ב כִּ֥י יֶשׁ־
ב שֶׁ֖בֶר בְּמִצְרָ֑יִם וַיֹּ֤אמֶר יַֽעֲקֹב֙ לְבָנָ֔יו לָ֖מָּה תִּתְרָאֽוּ: וַיֹּ֗אמֶר הִנֵּ֣ה שָׁמַ֔עְתִּי
כִּ֥י יֶשׁ־שֶׁ֖בֶר בְּמִצְרָ֑יִם רְדוּ־שָׁ֨מָּה֙ וְשִׁבְרוּ־לָ֣נוּ מִשָּׁ֔ם וְנִֽחְיֶ֖ה וְלֹ֥א נָמֽוּת:

---

45. וַיֵּצֵא יוֹסֵף עַל אֶרֶץ מִצְרָיִם — *And Joseph went out over the land of Egypt.* He left the presence of Pharaoh in an authoritative and stately manner, indicating that he was the governor of all Egypt.

46. וַיַּעֲבֹר בְּכָל אֶרֶץ מִצְרָיִם — *And went throughout the land of Egypt* . . . to attend to its affairs and make all necessary arrangements, as we find by Samuel, . . . וְסָבַב בֵּית אֵל וְהַמִּצְפָּה, *(He would set forth) and go to Beth-el . . . and Mitzpah (I Samuel 7:16).*

47. לִקְמָצִים — *In heaps.* Every ear of corn produced a handful.

49. כִּי אֵין מִסְפָּר — *For it was without number.* The quantities were beyond human calculation.

51. כִּי נַשַּׁנִי אֱלֹהִים — *For God has made me forget* . . . as it shall be regarding the future, as it is written, כִּי נִשְׁכְּחוּ הַצָּרוֹת הָרִאשֹׁנוֹת, *Because the former troubles are forgotten (Isaiah 65:16).*

56. וַיִּפְתַּח יוֹסֵף אֶת כָּל אֲשֶׁר בָּהֶם — *And Joseph opened all the storehouses* . . . to show them that there was enough to feed all of them.

וַיֶּחֱזַק הָרָעָב — *And the famine was sore* . . . in all kinds of food, besides bread.

NOTES

51. כִּי נַשַּׁנִי אֱלֹהִים — *For God has made me forget.* Joseph certainly did not forget his father Jacob and all that he had taught him. Indeed, the image of his father had prevented him from sinning with Potiphar's wife. Rather it must be understood in the manner that the quote from *Isaiah* implies: The memory of his travail and suffering had faded and was not as keen and painful as it once had been. This is also a portent for the future destiny of the Jewish people. They will also eventually forget the troubles of the past when they will be redeemed.

lift up his hand or foot in all the land of Egypt." 45 *Pharaoh called Joseph's*
name Zaphenath-paneah and he gave him Asenath daughter of Poti-phera,
Chief of On, for a wife. Thus, Joseph emerged in charge of the land of Egypt.
46 *Now Joseph was thirty years old when he stood before Pharaoh king of*
Egypt; Joseph left Pharaoh's presence and he passed through the entire land
of Egypt.

47 *The earth produced during the seven years of abundance by the*
handfuls. 48 *He gathered all food of the seven years that came to pass in*
Egypt, and he placed food in the cities; the food of the field around each city
he placed within it. 49 *Joseph amassed grain like the sand of the sea in great*
abundance until he ceased counting, for there was no number.

50 *Now to Joseph were born two sons — when the year of famine had not*
yet set in — whom Asenath daughter of Poti-phera, Chief of On, bore to him.
51 *Joseph called the name of the firstborn Manasseh for, "God has made me*
forget all my hardship and all my father's household." 52 *And the name of*
the second son he called Ephraim for, "God has made me fruitful in the land
of my suffering."

53 *The seven years of abundance that came to pass in the land of Egypt*
ended. 54 *And the seven years of famine began approaching just as Joseph*
had said. There was famine in all the lands, but in all the land of Egypt there
was bread.

55 *When all the land of Egypt hungered, the people cried out to Pharaoh*
for bread. So Pharaoh said to all of Egypt, "Go to Joseph. Whatever he tells
you, you should do." 56 *When the famine spread over all the face of the earth,*
Joseph opened all the containers and sold provisions to Egypt; and the
famine became severe in the land of Egypt. 57 *All the earth came to Egypt to*
Joseph to buy provisions, for the famine had become severe in all the earth.

42 1 *Jacob perceived that there were provisions in Egypt; so Jacob said to*
his sons, "Why do you make yourselves conspicuous?" 2 *And he*
said, "Behold, I have heard that there are provisions in Egypt; go down
there and purchase for us from there, that we may live and not die."

XLII

1. לָמָּה תִּתְרָאוּ — *Why do you look upon one another?* Why do you look at each other, each waiting for the other to go? As our Sages say: קִדְרָא דְּבֵי שֻׁתְּפֵי לָא חֲמִימָא וְלָא קְרִירָא, *A partners' pot is neither hot or cold* (*Eruvin* 3a), and נִתְרָאֶה פָנִים, *Let us look one another in the face* (*II Kings* 14:8), i.e., let us meet with one another.

2. וְנִחְיֶה — *That we may live . . .* not in plenty, but that we may have enough to keep us alive, and thus . . .

וְלֹא נָמוּת — *And not die.* From hunger.

NOTES

56. וַיִּפְתַּח יוֹסֵף — *And Joseph opened.* Joseph showed the people that there was plenty of food in the storehouses so as to prevent panic and food riots.

XLII

1. לָמָּה תִּתְרָאוּ — *Why do you look upon one another?* The reason that the partners' pot is "neither hot nor cold" is because each depends on the other to light the fire and keep it burning. Jacob chided his sons for failing to do anything about obtaining food from Egypt, each depending upon the other.

ג־ד וַיֵּרְדוּ אֲחֵי־יוֹסֵף עֲשָׂרָה לִשְׁבֹּר בָּר מִמִּצְרָיִם: וְאֶת־בִּנְיָמִין אֲחִי יוֹסֵף לֹא־
ה שָׁלַח יַעֲקֹב אֶת־אֶחָיו כִּי אָמַר פֶּן־יִקְרָאֶנּוּ אָסוֹן: וַיָּבֹאוּ בְּנֵי יִשְׂרָאֵל
ו לִשְׁבֹּר בְּתוֹךְ הַבָּאִים כִּי־הָיָה הָרָעָב בְּאֶרֶץ כְּנָעַן: וְיוֹסֵף הוּא הַשַּׁלִּיט עַל־
הָאָרֶץ הוּא הַמַּשְׁבִּיר לְכָל־עַם הָאָרֶץ וַיָּבֹאוּ אֲחֵי יוֹסֵף וַיִּשְׁתַּחֲווּ־לוֹ אַפַּיִם
ז אָרְצָה: וַיַּרְא יוֹסֵף אֶת־אֶחָיו וַיַּכִּרֵם וַיִּתְנַכֵּר אֲלֵיהֶם וַיְדַבֵּר אִתָּם קָשׁוֹת
ח וַיֹּאמֶר אֲלֵהֶם מֵאַיִן בָּאתֶם וַיֹּאמְרוּ מֵאֶרֶץ כְּנַעַן לִשְׁבָּר־אֹכֶל: וַיַּכֵּר יוֹסֵף
ט אֶת־אֶחָיו וְהֵם לֹא הִכִּרֻהוּ: וַיִּזְכֹּר יוֹסֵף אֵת הַחֲלֹמוֹת אֲשֶׁר חָלַם לָהֶם
י וַיֹּאמֶר אֲלֵהֶם מְרַגְּלִים אַתֶּם לִרְאוֹת אֶת־עֶרְוַת הָאָרֶץ בָּאתֶם: וַיֹּאמְרוּ
יא אֵלָיו לֹא אֲדֹנִי וַעֲבָדֶיךָ בָּאוּ לִשְׁבָּר־אֹכֶל: כֻּלָּנוּ בְּנֵי אִישׁ־אֶחָד נָחְנוּ
יב כֵּנִים אֲנַחְנוּ לֹא־הָיוּ עֲבָדֶיךָ מְרַגְּלִים: וַיֹּאמֶר אֲלֵהֶם לֹא כִּי־עֶרְוַת
יג הָאָרֶץ בָּאתֶם לִרְאוֹת: וַיֹּאמְרוּ שְׁנֵים עָשָׂר עֲבָדֶיךָ אַחִים | אֲנַחְנוּ בְּנֵי

3. וַיֵּרְדוּ אֲחֵי יוֹסֵף עֲשָׂרָה — *And Joseph's ten brothers went down.* The Egyptian authorities sold only to private households and not large quantities to individuals who might trade in the corn, as is customary in time of famine.

5. בְּתוֹךְ הַבָּאִים — *Among those that came.* They traveled in large companies as protection against bandits who would be particularly numerous because of the famine.

6. הוּא הַשַּׁלִּיט עַל הָאָרֶץ הוּא הַמַּשְׁבִּיר — *He was the governor over the land; it was he that sold.* Though he was the governor, he himself attended to the sales, not trusting his servants, for it involved large sums of money which belonged to Pharaoh, as it is written, *And Joseph brought the money into Pharaoh's house* (47:14); therefore he arranged that nothing should be sold without his seal or signature.

וַיָּבֹאוּ אֲחֵי יוֹסֵף וַיִּשְׁתַּחֲווּ לוֹ — *And Joseph's brothers came and bowed down to him.* Since Joseph was both governor and seller (of the corn) the brothers had to deal directly with him, and not through his servants.

7. וַיַּכִּרֵם — *And he knew them.* He recognized them (at first) as his brothers collectively, but not individually.

וַיִּתְנַכֵּר אֲלֵיהֶם — *But made himself strange with them.* He changed his manner, and did not speak humbly, as was his usual manner.

קָשׁוֹת — *(And spoke) roughly ...* lest they recognize him by his voice.

8. וַיַּכֵּר יוֹסֵף אֶת אֶחָיו — *And Joseph knew his brethren.* Afterward (he recognized them) individually.

9. וַיִּזְכֹּר יוֹסֵף אֵת הַחֲלֹמוֹת אֲשֶׁר חָלַם לָהֶם — *And Joseph remembered the dreams which he dreamed of them.* He remembered his dreams of them, that in the dream of the sheaves all bowed (to him) and that his sheaf stood upright, not falling. He therefore wanted them all to come and recognize him in order to fulfill, וְגַם נִצָּבָה, *and it stood* (37:7). (He did this) in

NOTES

3. וַיֵּרְדוּ אֲחֵי יוֹסֵף עֲשָׂרָה — *And Joseph's ten brothers went down.* Were it not for the restrictions placed upon the purchase of corn by Egypt, limiting a certain amount per person, there would be no reason for all ten brothers to come.

6. הוּא הַשַּׁלִּיט ... הוּא הַמַּשְׁבִּיר — *He was the governor ... it was he that sold.* The terms שַׁלִּיט and מַשְׁבִּיר refer to two separate and different roles, one was governor while the other was in charge of selling the provisions. Normally Joseph would have delegated the latter to his servants. The reason he did not do so was because he was concerned for the integrity of the coffers of Pharaoh. This dual role played by Joseph explains how his brothers came face to face with him, for under normal circumstances they would have dealt with an underling and would never have met their brother.

9. וַיִּזְכֹּר יוֹסֵף אֵת הַחֲלֹמוֹת — *And Joseph remem-*

3 So Joseph's brothers — ten of them — went down to buy grain from Egypt.
4 But Benjamin, Joseph's brother, Jacob did not send along with his brothers,
for he said, "Lest disaster befall him." 5 So the sons of Israel came to buy
provisions among the arrivals, for the famine was in the land of Canaan.
6 Now Joseph — he was the viceroy over the land, he was the provider to all the people of the land. Joseph's brothers came and they bowed to him, faces to the ground.

7 Joseph saw his brothers and he recognized them, but he acted like a stranger toward them and spoke with them harshly. He asked them, "From where do you come?" And they said, "From the land of Canaan to buy
food." 8 Joseph recognized his brothers, but they did not recognize him.

9 Joseph recalled the dreams that he dreamed about them, so he said to them, "You are spies! To see the land's nakedness have you come!"

10 They answered him, "Not so, my lord! For your servants have come to
buy food. 11 All of us, sons of one man are we; we are truthful people; your servants have never been spies."

12 And he said to them, "No! But the land's nakedness have you come to see."

13 And they replied, "We, your servants, are twelve brothers, the son of

---

order that he be a symbol of the future redeemer, as we find, יְרֵה וַיּוֹר, *"Shoot!" And he shot (II Kings* 13:17), as it says, וְנִקְבְּצוּ בְּנֵי יְהוּדָה וּבְנֵי יִשְׂרָאֵל יַחְדָּו וְשָׂמוּ לָהֶם רֹאשׁ אֶחָד, *And the children of Judah and the children of Israel shall be gathered together and they shall appoint themselves one head (Hosea* 2:2), and that (the symbolism of) וְגַם נִצָּבָה be fulfilled, as it says, מַלְכוּ דִּי לְעָלְמִין לָא תִתְחַבַּל, *A kingdom which shall never be destroyed (Daniel* 2:44).

לִרְאוֹת אֶת עֶרְוַת הָאָרֶץ בָּאתֶם — *To see the nakedness of the land did you come* ... to determine the quantity of our food stores if it be sufficient for our needs. You did not come simply to purchase for it is not customary for so many (ten) to come as one group.

11. כֻּלָּנוּ בְּנֵי אִישׁ אֶחָד נָחְנוּ — *We are all one man's sons.* If we are spies, spying on behalf of a foreign power, no king would choose ten men from one family! We are together, because we are indeed brothers.

כֵּנִים אֲנַחְנוּ — *We are upright men* ... in all our endeavors.

לֹא הָיוּ עֲבָדֶיךָ מְרַגְּלִים — *Your servants are no spies.* We never were, and there is no reason to suspect us now of being spies.

12. לֹא — *Nay.* It is not true that you are brothers.

כִּי עֶרְוַת הָאָרֶץ בָּאתֶם לִרְאוֹת — *But to see the nakedness of the land have you come.* You plotted to claim you are brothers, so as to mask your (true intentions) to see the nakedness of the land.

13. שְׁנֵים עָשָׂר עֲבָדֶיךָ אַחִים אֲנַחְנוּ בְּנֵי אִישׁ אֶחָד בְּאֶרֶץ כְּנָעַן — *We, your servants, are twelve brothers, the sons of one man in the Land of Canaan.* What we say can be ascertained, for

NOTES

bered the dreams. Joseph did not reveal himself immediately to his brothers for a variety of reasons, one of them being his conviction that the fulfillment of his dreams in their entirety was necessary to establish a precedent for the future complete and lasting redemption of Israel. He represented the model for the אַחֲרִית הַיָּמִים, *the end of days,* when Israel will be unified under one leader, never to be dispersed or destroyed (as the verses from *Hosea* and *Daniel* prophesy). Therefore Benjamin had to come down as well, to complete the number of eleven as shown in the dream of the sheaves, and eventually his father Jacob as well, to fulfill the second dream.

יד אִישׁ־אֶחָד בְּאֶרֶץ כְּנָעַן וְהִנֵּה הַקָּטֹן אֶת־אָבִינוּ הַיּוֹם וְהָאֶחָד אֵינֶנּוּ: וַיֹּאמֶר
טו אֲלֵהֶם יוֹסֵף הוּא אֲשֶׁר דִּבַּרְתִּי אֲלֵכֶם לֵאמֹר מְרַגְּלִים אַתֶּם: בְּזֹאת תִּבָּחֵנוּ
טז חֵי פַרְעֹה אִם־תֵּצְאוּ מִזֶּה כִּי אִם־בְּבוֹא אֲחִיכֶם הַקָּטֹן הֵנָּה: שִׁלְחוּ מִכֶּם
אֶחָד וְיִקַּח אֶת־אֲחִיכֶם וְאַתֶּם הֵאָסְרוּ וְיִבָּחֲנוּ דִּבְרֵיכֶם הַאֱמֶת אִתְּכֶם וְאִם־
יז לֹא חֵי פַרְעֹה כִּי מְרַגְּלִים אַתֶּם: וַיֶּאֱסֹף אֹתָם אֶל־מִשְׁמָר שְׁלֹשֶׁת יָמִים:
יח וַיֹּאמֶר אֲלֵהֶם יוֹסֵף בַּיּוֹם הַשְּׁלִישִׁי זֹאת עֲשׂוּ וִחְיוּ אֶת־הָאֱלֹהִים אֲנִי יָרֵא:
חמישי יט אִם־כֵּנִים אַתֶּם אֲחִיכֶם אֶחָד יֵאָסֵר בְּבֵית מִשְׁמַרְכֶם וְאַתֶּם לְכוּ הָבִיאוּ
כ שֶׁבֶר רַעֲבוֹן בָּתֵּיכֶם: וְאֶת־אֲחִיכֶם הַקָּטֹן תָּבִיאוּ אֵלַי וְיֵאָמְנוּ דִבְרֵיכֶם וְלֹא
כא תָמוּתוּ וַיַּעֲשׂוּ־כֵן: וַיֹּאמְרוּ אִישׁ אֶל־אָחִיו אֲבָל אֲשֵׁמִים | אֲנַחְנוּ עַל־אָחִינוּ
אֲשֶׁר רָאִינוּ צָרַת נַפְשׁוֹ בְּהִתְחַנְנוֹ אֵלֵינוּ וְלֹא שָׁמָעְנוּ עַל־כֵּן בָּאָה אֵלֵינוּ
כב הַצָּרָה הַזֹּאת: וַיַּעַן רְאוּבֵן אֹתָם לֵאמֹר הֲלוֹא אָמַרְתִּי אֲלֵיכֶם | לֵאמֹר אַל־
כג תֶּחֶטְאוּ בַיֶּלֶד וְלֹא שְׁמַעְתֶּם וְגַם־דָּמוֹ הִנֵּה נִדְרָשׁ: וְהֵם לֹא יָדְעוּ כִּי שֹׁמֵעַ
כד יוֹסֵף כִּי הַמֵּלִיץ בֵּינֹתָם: וַיִּסֹּב מֵעֲלֵיהֶם וַיֵּבְךְּ וַיָּשָׁב אֲלֵהֶם וַיְדַבֵּר אֲלֵהֶם
כה וַיִּקַּח מֵאִתָּם אֶת־שִׁמְעוֹן וַיֶּאֱסֹר אֹתוֹ לְעֵינֵיהֶם: וַיְצַו יוֹסֵף וַיְמַלְאוּ אֶת־
כְּלֵיהֶם בָּר וּלְהָשִׁיב כַּסְפֵּיהֶם אִישׁ אֶל־שַׂקּוֹ וְלָתֵת לָהֶם צֵדָה לַדָּרֶךְ
כו־כז וַיַּעַשׂ לָהֶם כֵּן: וַיִּשְׂאוּ אֶת־שִׁבְרָם עַל־חֲמֹרֵיהֶם וַיֵּלְכוּ מִשָּׁם: וַיִּפְתַּח
הָאֶחָד אֶת־שַׂקּוֹ לָתֵת מִסְפּוֹא לַחֲמֹרוֹ בַּמָּלוֹן וַיַּרְא אֶת־כַּסְפּוֹ וְהִנֵּה־
כח הוּא בְּפִי אַמְתַּחְתּוֹ: וַיֹּאמֶר אֶל־אֶחָיו הוּשַׁב כַּסְפִּי וְגַם הִנֵּה בְאַמְתַּחְתִּי
וַיֵּצֵא לִבָּם וַיֶּחֶרְדוּ אִישׁ אֶל־אָחִיו לֵאמֹר מַה־זֹּאת עָשָׂה אֱלֹהִים לָנוּ:

---

our father lives in Canaan, and it can be verified by him and our neighbors that we were twelve sons, but one is missing and the youngest is home attending to the household. All these details can be established as true, to your satisfaction.

14. הוּא אֲשֶׁר דִּבַּרְתִּי אֲלֵכֶם — *That is that which I spoke to you.* The one that you say is *not*, and you do not explain what happened to him, has probably gone back to reveal the information that you gathered or (perhaps) you plotted (all this) in order to spy, as I have said.

15. בְּזֹאת תִּבָּחֵנוּ — *Hereby, you shall be proved.* If you are not brothers, the younger one will not risk coming with you and thereby place himself unnecessarily (lit., "falsely") at risk of death which now faces you (lit., "together with you").

18. אֶת הָאֱלֹהִים אֲנִי יָרֵא — *For I fear God* . . . therefore, I will allow you to take home the provisions that you need.

20. וְלֹא תָמוּתוּ — *And you shall not die* . . . for even in Canaan I can have you put to death if you do not return.

21. בְּהִתְחַנְנוֹ אֵלֵינוּ וְלֹא שָׁמָעְנוּ — *When he besought us and we would not hear.* Because we were so callous toward our brother, and we should have had more compassion, even though we considered him a רוֹדֵף, *pursuer.* Now this ruler is treating us cruelly just as we did our brother (measure for measure).

22. הֲלוֹא אָמַרְתִּי אֲלֵיכֶם לֵאמֹר אַל תֶּחֶטְאוּ בַיֶּלֶד — *Didn't I speak and say to you, "Don't sin against the boy"?* He had no intention to kill you when he did what he did, even though

NOTES

21-28. בְּהִתְחַנְנוֹ אֵלֵינוּ . . . מַה זֹּאת עָשָׂה אֱלֹהִים לָנוּ — *When he besought us . . . What is this that God has done to us?* The brothers did not regret the sale of Joseph for they felt justified in their decision, based upon their conviction that he was a רוֹדֵף, *pursuer,* who according to *halachah* can even be killed in

one man in the land of Canaan. The youngest is now with our father and one is gone."

[14] *But Joseph said to them, "It is just as I have declared to you: 'You are spies!'* [15] *By this shall you be tested: By Pharaoh's life you will not leave here unless your youngest brother comes here.* [16] *Send one of you, and let him fetch your brother while you shall remain imprisoned, so that your words may be tested whether truth is with you; but if not, by Pharaoh's life — surely you are spies!"* [17] *Then he herded them into a ward for a three-day period.*

[18] *Joseph said to them on the third day, "Do this and live; I fear God:* [19] *If you are truthful people, let one of your brothers be imprisoned in your place of confinement while you go and bring provisions for the hunger of your households.* [20] *Then bring your youngest brother to me so your words will be verified and you will not die." And they did so.*

[21] *They then said to one another, "Indeed we are guilty concerning our brother inasmuch as we saw his heartfelt anguish when he pleaded with us and we paid no heed; that is why this anguish has come upon us."*

[22] *Reuben spoke up to them, saying, "Did I not speak to you saying, 'Do not sin against the boy,' but you would not listen! And his blood as well — behold! — is being avenged."*

[23] *Now they did not know that Joseph understood, for an interpreter was between them.* [24] *He turned away from them and wept; he returned to them and spoke to them; he took Simeon from them and imprisoned him before their eyes.*

[25] *Joseph commanded that they fill their vessels with grain, and to return their money, each one's to his sack, and to give them provisions for the journey. And so he did for them.* [26] *Then they loaded their purchase onto their donkeys and departed from there.*

[27] *When the one of them opened his sack to give feed to his donkey at the inn, he saw his money, and behold! — it was in the mouth of his sack.* [28] *So he said to his brothers, "My money has been returned and behold! it, too, is in my sack!" Their hearts sank, and they turned trembling one to another, saying, "What is this that God has done to us?"*

---

you thought so. What he did was due to his childish immaturity, not done with (malice). וְגַם דָּמוֹ הִנֵּה נִדְרָשׁ — *Therefore also behold, his blood is required.* Not only is the cruelty shown to him being repaid to you now, but *his blood* as well, for you slew him as well, even though he was innocent, since he must have died by now through (the) hard labor (imposed on him).

24. וַיֵּבְךְּ — *And he wept* . . . because of their distress.

25. וּלְהָשִׁיב כַּסְפֵּיהֶם — *And to restore their silver coins* (lit., *their monies*). The plural form (of the word כֶּסֶף which can mean either silver or money) does not apply to money but to (silver) coins.

28. מַה זֹּאת עָשָׂה אֱלֹהִים לָנוּ — *What is this that God has done to us?* . . . that He has caused

NOTES

self-defense. If anything, they felt that they were lenient with him by selling him rather than executing him as they had originally decided to do before being dissuaded by Judah. They did however admit their callousness and cruelty in turning a deaf ear to Joseph's pleas, and therefore felt that

כט וַיָּבֹאוּ אֶל־יַעֲקֹב אֲבִיהֶם אַרְצָה כְּנָעַן וַיַּגִּידוּ לוֹ אֵת כָּל־הַקֹּרֹת אֹתָם
ל לֵאמֹר: דִּבֶּר הָאִישׁ אֲדֹנֵי הָאָרֶץ אִתָּנוּ קָשׁוֹת וַיִּתֵּן אֹתָנוּ כִּמְרַגְּלִים
לא-לב אֶת־הָאָרֶץ: וַנֹּאמֶר אֵלָיו כֵּנִים אֲנָחְנוּ לֹא הָיִינוּ מְרַגְּלִים: שְׁנֵים־עָשָׂר
אֲנַחְנוּ אַחִים בְּנֵי אָבִינוּ הָאֶחָד אֵינֶנּוּ וְהַקָּטֹן הַיּוֹם אֶת־אָבִינוּ בְּאֶרֶץ
לג כְּנָעַן: וַיֹּאמֶר אֵלֵינוּ הָאִישׁ אֲדֹנֵי הָאָרֶץ בְּזֹאת אֵדַע כִּי כֵנִים אַתֶּם
לד אֲחִיכֶם הָאֶחָד הַנִּיחוּ אִתִּי וְאֶת־רַעֲבוֹן בָּתֵּיכֶם קְחוּ וָלֵכוּ: וְהָבִיאוּ
אֶת־אֲחִיכֶם הַקָּטֹן אֵלַי וְאֵדְעָה כִּי לֹא מְרַגְּלִים אַתֶּם כִּי כֵנִים אַתֶּם
לה אֶת־אֲחִיכֶם אֶתֵּן לָכֶם וְאֶת־הָאָרֶץ תִּסְחָרוּ: וַיְהִי הֵם מְרִיקִים שַׂקֵּיהֶם
וְהִנֵּה־אִישׁ צְרוֹר־כַּסְפּוֹ בְּשַׂקּוֹ וַיִּרְאוּ אֶת־צְרֹרוֹת כַּסְפֵּיהֶם הֵמָּה
לו וַאֲבִיהֶם וַיִּירָאוּ: וַיֹּאמֶר אֲלֵהֶם יַעֲקֹב אֲבִיהֶם אֹתִי שִׁכַּלְתֶּם יוֹסֵף אֵינֶנּוּ
לז וְשִׁמְעוֹן אֵינֶנּוּ וְאֶת־בִּנְיָמִן תִּקָּחוּ עָלַי הָיוּ כֻלָּנָה: וַיֹּאמֶר רְאוּבֵן אֶל־אָבִיו
לֵאמֹר אֶת־שְׁנֵי בָנַי תָּמִית אִם־לֹא אֲבִיאֶנּוּ אֵלֶיךָ תְּנָה אֹתוֹ עַל־יָדִי
לח וַאֲנִי אֲשִׁיבֶנּוּ אֵלֶיךָ: וַיֹּאמֶר לֹא־יֵרֵד בְּנִי עִמָּכֶם כִּי־אָחִיו מֵת וְהוּא
לְבַדּוֹ נִשְׁאָר וּקְרָאָהוּ אָסוֹן בַּדֶּרֶךְ אֲשֶׁר תֵּלְכוּ־בָהּ וְהוֹרַדְתֶּם אֶת־
מג א-ב שֵׂיבָתִי בְּיָגוֹן שְׁאוֹלָה: וְהָרָעָב כָּבֵד בָּאָרֶץ: וַיְהִי כַּאֲשֶׁר כִּלּוּ לֶאֱכֹל אֶת־
הַשֶּׁבֶר אֲשֶׁר הֵבִיאוּ מִמִּצְרָיִם וַיֹּאמֶר אֲלֵיהֶם אֲבִיהֶם שֻׁבוּ שִׁבְרוּ־לָנוּ
ג מְעַט־אֹכֶל: וַיֹּאמֶר אֵלָיו יְהוּדָה לֵאמֹר הָעֵד הֵעִד בָּנוּ הָאִישׁ לֵאמֹר
ד לֹא־תִרְאוּ פָנַי בִּלְתִּי אֲחִיכֶם אִתְּכֶם: אִם־יֶשְׁךָ מְשַׁלֵּחַ אֶת־אָחִינוּ
ה אִתָּנוּ נֵרְדָה וְנִשְׁבְּרָה לְךָ אֹכֶל: וְאִם־אֵינְךָ מְשַׁלֵּחַ לֹא נֵרֵד כִּי־הָאִישׁ
ו אָמַר אֵלֵינוּ לֹא־תִרְאוּ פָנַי בִּלְתִּי אֲחִיכֶם אִתְּכֶם: וַיֹּאמֶר יִשְׂרָאֵל
ז לָמָה הֲרֵעֹתֶם לִי לְהַגִּיד לָאִישׁ הַעוֹד לָכֶם אָח: וַיֹּאמְרוּ שָׁאוֹל שָׁאַל־
הָאִישׁ לָנוּ וּלְמוֹלַדְתֵּנוּ לֵאמֹר הַעוֹד אֲבִיכֶם חַי הֲיֵשׁ לָכֶם אָח וַנַּגֶּד־

---

this man, who claims to fear God, to use this pretext to enslave us, as it is written later, *and to take us for slaves* (43:18). This has come to pass to repay us, measure for measure, for selling our brother; even though we did it not because of wickedness, but because we believed him to be a רוֹדֵף, *pursuer*, and worthy even to be put to death, which we refrained from doing as a חֶסֶד, *kindness*, since he is our brother.

36. עָלַי הָיוּ כֻלָּנָה — *Upon me have all these things come.* Such things have happened to my children, but to none of yours. The reason must undoubtedly be on account of your quarrels. (Therefore I regard) you as the cause of my bereavement.

37. אֶת שְׁנֵי בָנַי תָּמִית — *You shall slay my two sons.* Curse my two sons that they should die if I do not bring him (Benjamin) back to you, as we find the curse of Rav to Shmuel, יְהֵא רַעֲנָא . . . דְּלָא לוּקְמוּ לֵיהּ בְּנֵי, וְכֵן הֲוָה, *"May no sons arise from him." And thus it was* (*Shabbos* 108a).

NOTES

their present plight and distress was a punishment from God for this transgression.

37. אֶת שְׁנֵי בָנַי תָּמִית — *You shall slay my two sons.* The *Sforno*, like many other commentators, wishes to avoid the literal meaning of תָּמִית, *to slay;* therefore he chooses to translate it as *curse.*

38. לֹא יֵרֵד בְּנִי — *My son shall not go down.* The phrase בְּנִי, *my son*, applied by Jacob to Benjamin is explained as referring to the only son left him from his beloved wife Rachel.

[29] They came to Jacob their father in the land of Canaan and they told him of all that had happened to them, saying: [30] "The man, the lord of the land, spoke harshly to us and considered us as if we were spying out the land. [31] But we said to him, 'We are truthful men: We have never been spies! [32] We are twelve brothers, sons of one father. One is gone and the youngest is now with our father in the land of Canaan.' [33] Then the man, the lord of the land, said to us, 'By this I will ascertain whether you are truthful people: One of your brothers, leave with me; and what is needed for the hunger of your households take and go. [34] And bring your youngest brother to me so I will know that you are not spies, but truthful people. I will restore your brother to you and you will be free to circulate about the land.' "

[35] Then, as they were emptying their sacks, behold! — every man's bundle of money was in his sack. When they and their father saw their bundles of money, they were terrified. [36] Their father Jacob said to them, "I am the one whom you bereaved! Joseph is gone, Simeon is gone, and now you would take away Benjamin? Upon me has it all fallen!"

[37] Then Reuben told his father, saying, "You may slay my two sons if I fail to bring him back to you. Put him in my care and I will return him to you."

[38] But he said, "My son shall not go down with you, for his brother is dead and he alone is left. Should disaster befall him on the journey which you shall take, then you will have brought down my hoariness in sorrow to the grave."

43 *[1] The famine was severe in the land. [2] When they had finished eating the provisions which they had brought from Egypt their father said to them, "Go back, buy us some food." [3] But Judah told him, saying, "The man sternly warned us saying, 'Do not see my face unless your brother is with you.' [4] If you are ready to send our brother with us, we will go down and buy you food. [5] But if you do not send, we will not go down, for the man said to us, 'Do not see my face unless your brother is with you.' "*

[6] Then Israel said, "Why did you treat me so ill by telling the man that you had another brother?"

[7] And they said, "The man persistently asked about us and our relatives saying, 'Is your father still alive? Have you a brother?' and we responded

38. לֹא יֵרֵד בְּנִי — *My son shall not go down.* He is the only one left of his mother who was the cornerstone of the house.

XLIII

2. שֻׁבוּ שִׁבְרוּ לָנוּ — *Go again, bring us (a little food).* (Jacob) disbelieved their story and thought that they only wanted an opportunity to kill Benjamin as they had Joseph, as he said to them, "אֹתִי שִׁכַּלְתֶּם, *You have bereaved me*" (42:36).

NOTES

XLIII

2. שֻׁבוּ שִׁבְרוּ לָנוּ — *Go again, bring us (a little food).* By using the expression שֻׁבוּ, *return*, Jacob is stressing and reiterating that only those who went the first time should now return — without Benjamin, for he does not trust them when it comes to the

לוֹ עַל־פִּי הַדְּבָרִים הָאֵלֶּה הֲיָדוֹעַ נֵדַע כִּי יֹאמַר הוֹרִידוּ אֶת־אֲחִיכֶם:
ח וַיֹּאמֶר יְהוּדָה אֶל־יִשְׂרָאֵל אָבִיו שִׁלְחָה הַנַּעַר אִתִּי וְנָקוּמָה וְנֵלֵכָה
ט וְנִחְיֶה וְלֹא נָמוּת גַּם־אֲנַחְנוּ גַם־אַתָּה גַּם־טַפֵּנוּ: אָנֹכִי אֶעֶרְבֶנּוּ מִיָּדִי
תְּבַקְשֶׁנּוּ אִם־לֹא הֲבִיאֹתִיו אֵלֶיךָ וְהִצַּגְתִּיו לְפָנֶיךָ וְחָטָאתִי לְךָ כָּל־
י־יא הַיָּמִים: כִּי לוּלֵא הִתְמַהְמָהְנוּ כִּי־עַתָּה שַׁבְנוּ זֶה פַעֲמָיִם: וַיֹּאמֶר אֲלֵהֶם
יִשְׂרָאֵל אֲבִיהֶם אִם־כֵּן ׀ אֵפוֹא זֹאת עֲשׂוּ קְחוּ מִזִּמְרַת הָאָרֶץ בִּכְלֵיכֶם
וְהוֹרִידוּ לָאִישׁ מִנְחָה מְעַט צֳרִי וּמְעַט דְּבַשׁ נְכֹאת וָלֹט בָּטְנִים
יב וּשְׁקֵדִים: וְכֶסֶף מִשְׁנֶה קְחוּ בְיֶדְכֶם וְאֶת־הַכֶּסֶף הַמּוּשָׁב בְּפִי אַמְתְּחֹתֵיכֶם
יג תָּשִׁיבוּ בְיֶדְכֶם אוּלַי מִשְׁגֶּה הוּא: וְאֶת־אֲחִיכֶם קָחוּ וְקוּמוּ שׁוּבוּ
יד אֶל־הָאִישׁ: וְאֵל שַׁדַּי יִתֵּן לָכֶם רַחֲמִים לִפְנֵי הָאִישׁ וְשִׁלַּח לָכֶם
טו אֶת־אֲחִיכֶם אַחֵר וְאֶת־בִּנְיָמִין וַאֲנִי כַּאֲשֶׁר שָׁכֹלְתִּי שָׁכָלְתִּי: וַיִּקְחוּ
הָאֲנָשִׁים אֶת־הַמִּנְחָה הַזֹּאת וּמִשְׁנֶה־כֶּסֶף לָקְחוּ בְיָדָם וְאֶת־בִּנְיָמִן
ששי טז וַיָּקֻמוּ וַיֵּרְדוּ מִצְרַיִם וַיַּעַמְדוּ לִפְנֵי יוֹסֵף: וַיַּרְא יוֹסֵף אִתָּם אֶת־בִּנְיָמִין
וַיֹּאמֶר לַאֲשֶׁר עַל־בֵּיתוֹ הָבֵא אֶת־הָאֲנָשִׁים הַבָּיְתָה וּטְבֹחַ טֶבַח וְהָכֵן

8. וְנִחְיֶה — *That we may live.* With food.

וְלֹא נָמוּת — *And not die* . . . in accordance with the words of the master of the land (Egypt) who said to us, *So shall your words be verified and you shall not die* (42:20).

10. כִּי לוּלֵא הִתְמַהְמָהְנוּ — *For had we not lingered.* The reason I accepted upon myself everlasting blame (lit., "eternal sin") if I didn't bring him back is because it is clear to me that had we not lingered from the time we told you the words of the man or from the time the (supply of) grain ended (and returned with Benjamin earlier . . .).

כִּי עַתָּה שַׁבְנוּ זֶה פַעֲמָיִם — *Surely we had now returned a second time* . . . for the ruler would have done no harm or deterred us, once he knew the truth (regarding the money) since he is a God-fearing man.

11. אִם כֵּן — *If it be so* . . . as you say that this man who contends with you is a God-fearing man.

אֵפוֹא — *So now (do this).* Perforce this is the proper thing to do.

קְחוּ מִזִּמְרַת הָאָרֶץ . . . מְעַט צֳרִי — *Take of the choice fruits . . . a little balm.* True, if one brings a gift to a greedy man, it must be of great quantity to satisfy his excessive desire, as was the manner of gift sent by Jacob to Esau. However, when a gift is brought to a generous, high-placed person who wants for naught, it is better to bring a smaller gift of high quality, a choice, rare item which he will appreciate. This was the kind of gift suggested by Jacob.

וְהוֹרִידוּ לָאִישׁ מִנְחָה — *Carry down a present to the man.* Before you present yourselves to

NOTES

children of Rachel.

8. וְנִחְיֶה וְלֹא נָמוּת — *That we may live and not die.* Once Judah said וְנִחְיֶה, *that we may live,* it is not necessary to add וְלֹא נָמוּת, *and not die.* The reason he added these words was to remind his father that the ruler of Egypt had warned them that if they failed to return with their youngest brother, he would pursue and find them even in Canaan and have them punished. See the *Sforno* to 42:20.

10. כִּי לוּלֵא הִתְמַהְמָהְנוּ כִּי עַתָּה שַׁבְנוּ זֶה פַעֲמָיִם — *For had we not lingered, surely we had now returned a second time.* Judah would never have jeopardized his share in the World to Come unless he was convinced that he could bring Benjamin back to his father unharmed. This certainty was based on his conviction that the individual they were deal-

to him according to these words; could we possibly have known that he would say, 'Bring your brother down'?"
8 Then Judah said to Israel his father, "Send the lad with me, and let us arise and go, so we will live and not die, we as well as you as well as our children.
9 I will personally guarantee him; of my own hand you can demand him. If I do not bring him back to you and stand him before you, then I will have sinned to you for all time.
10 For had we not delayed, by now we could have returned twice."
11 Israel their father said to them, "If it must be so, then do this: Take of the land's glory in your baggage and bring it down to the man as a tribute — a bit of balsam, a bit of honey, wax, lotus, pistachios, and almonds.
12 And take with you double the money, and the money that was returned in the mouth of your sacks return in your hands; perhaps it was an oversight.
13 Take your brother, and arise, return to the man.
14 And may Almighty God grant you mercy before the man that he may release to you your other brother as well as Benjamin. And as for me, as I have been bereaved, so I am bereaved."
15 So the men took this tribute and they took double money in their hand, as well as Benjamin. They set out and went down to Egypt and stood before Joseph.
16 Joseph saw Benjamin with them; so he said to the one in charge of his house, "Bring the men into the house. Have meat slaughtered, and prepare it,

---

him (make your offering), and you will determine from the manner in which he receives it whether he is favorably disposed toward you or not, as it is written, לוּ חָפֵץ ה׳ לַהֲמִיתֵנוּ, לֹא לָקַח מִיָּדֵנוּ עֹלָה וּמִנְחָה, *If HASHEM desired to kill us, He would not have received a burnt-offering or meal-offering at our hand (Judges* 13:23).

13. וְקוּמוּ שׁוּבוּ אֶל הָאִישׁ — *And arise, go again unto the man.* For in any event you will appease him to some extent by sending him this gift as it says, אֶבֶן חֵן הַשֹּׁחַד בְּעֵינֵי בְעָלָיו, אֶל כָּל אֲשֶׁר יִפְנֶה יַשְׂכִּיל, *A gift is as a precious stone in the eyes of him that has it, wherever he turns, he prospers (Proverbs* 17:8).

15. וַיַּעַמְדוּ לִפְנֵי יוֹסֵף — *And they stood before Joseph . . .* before they had presented the gift to him, hence they were afraid when *they were brought into Joseph's house* (see verse 18).

16. וַיֹּאמֶר לַאֲשֶׁר עַל בֵּיתוֹ — *He said to the steward of his house.* He did not want to speak to his brothers until all who were standing before him left, for he needed time (and privacy) for a lengthy discussion with them.

הָבֵא אֶת הָאֲנָשִׁים הַבָּיְתָה — *Bring the men into the house . . .* into the living quarters. They were as yet in the king's gate, or in the hall of justice.

NOTES

ing with was a God-fearing man, and once he knew the full story regarding the money, he would not detain them. The *Sforno* explains: "Had we not lingered" but had returned immediately after relating the story to you or as soon as our food ran out, then "we would have returned twice," literally. Judah was not exaggerating when he says פַּעֲמָיִם, *twice*. They would have made one trip shortly upon their first return and a second when their provisions began to run low.

11-15. וְהוֹרִידוּ לָאִישׁ מִנְחָה ... וַיַּעַמְדוּ לִפְנֵי יוֹסֵף — *Carry down a present to the man . . . And they stood before Joseph.* Jacob, in his perceptive wisdom of human behavior, advised his sons to send the gift to the ruler *prior* to their personal appearance, as he had done with Esau. They failed to do so, and "stand before Joseph" *before* the presentation of the gift; hence when they were summoned to his chambers they were afraid.

יז כִּי אִתִּי יֹאכְלוּ הָאֲנָשִׁים בַּצָּהֳרָיִם: וַיַּעַשׂ הָאִישׁ כַּאֲשֶׁר אָמַר יוֹסֵף וַיָּבֵא
יח הָאִישׁ אֶת־הָאֲנָשִׁים בֵּיתָה יוֹסֵף: וַיִּירְאוּ הָאֲנָשִׁים כִּי הוּבְאוּ בֵּית יוֹסֵף
וַיֹּאמְרוּ עַל־דְּבַר הַכֶּסֶף הַשָּׁב בְּאַמְתְּחֹתֵינוּ בַּתְּחִלָּה אֲנַחְנוּ מוּבָאִים
לְהִתְגֹּלֵל עָלֵינוּ וּלְהִתְנַפֵּל עָלֵינוּ וְלָקַחַת אֹתָנוּ לַעֲבָדִים וְאֶת־חֲמֹרֵינוּ:
יט־כ וַיִּגְּשׁוּ אֶל־הָאִישׁ אֲשֶׁר עַל־בֵּית יוֹסֵף וַיְדַבְּרוּ אֵלָיו פֶּתַח הַבָּיִת: וַיֹּאמְרוּ
כא בִּי אֲדֹנִי יָרֹד יָרַדְנוּ בַּתְּחִלָּה לִשְׁבָּר־אֹכֶל: וַיְהִי כִּי־בָאנוּ אֶל־הַמָּלוֹן
וַנִּפְתְּחָה אֶת־אַמְתְּחֹתֵינוּ וְהִנֵּה כֶסֶף־אִישׁ בְּפִי אַמְתַּחְתּוֹ כַּסְפֵּנוּ
כב בְּמִשְׁקָלוֹ וַנָּשֶׁב אֹתוֹ בְּיָדֵנוּ: וְכֶסֶף אַחֵר הוֹרַדְנוּ בְיָדֵנוּ לִשְׁבָּר־אֹכֶל לֹא
כג יָדַעְנוּ מִי־שָׂם כַּסְפֵּנוּ בְּאַמְתְּחֹתֵינוּ: וַיֹּאמֶר שָׁלוֹם לָכֶם אַל־תִּירָאוּ
אֱלֹהֵיכֶם וֵאלֹהֵי אֲבִיכֶם נָתַן לָכֶם מַטְמוֹן בְּאַמְתְּחֹתֵיכֶם כַּסְפְּכֶם בָּא
כד אֵלָי וַיּוֹצֵא אֲלֵהֶם אֶת־שִׁמְעוֹן: וַיָּבֵא הָאִישׁ אֶת־הָאֲנָשִׁים בֵּיתָה יוֹסֵף
כה וַיִּתֶּן־מַיִם וַיִּרְחֲצוּ רַגְלֵיהֶם וַיִּתֵּן מִסְפּוֹא לַחֲמֹרֵיהֶם: וַיָּכִינוּ אֶת־הַמִּנְחָה
כו עַד־בּוֹא יוֹסֵף בַּצָּהֳרָיִם כִּי שָׁמְעוּ כִּי־שָׁם יֹאכְלוּ לָחֶם: וַיָּבֹא יוֹסֵף הַבַּיְתָה
כז וַיָּבִיאוּ לוֹ אֶת־הַמִּנְחָה אֲשֶׁר־בְּיָדָם הַבָּיְתָה וַיִּשְׁתַּחֲווּ־לוֹ אָרְצָה: וַיִּשְׁאַל
לָהֶם לְשָׁלוֹם וַיֹּאמֶר הֲשָׁלוֹם אֲבִיכֶם הַזָּקֵן אֲשֶׁר אֲמַרְתֶּם הַעוֹדֶנּוּ חָי:
כח־כט וַיֹּאמְרוּ שָׁלוֹם לְעַבְדְּךָ לְאָבִינוּ עוֹדֶנּוּ חָי וַיִּקְּדוּ וַיִּשְׁתַּחֲוּ: וַיִּשָּׂא עֵינָיו
וַיַּרְא אֶת־בִּנְיָמִין אָחִיו בֶּן־אִמּוֹ וַיֹּאמֶר הֲזֶה אֲחִיכֶם הַקָּטֹן אֲשֶׁר
שביעי ל אֲמַרְתֶּם אֵלָי וַיֹּאמַר אֱלֹהִים יָחְנְךָ בְּנִי: וַיְמַהֵר יוֹסֵף כִּי־נִכְמְרוּ רַחֲמָיו
לא אֶל־אָחִיו וַיְבַקֵּשׁ לִבְכּוֹת וַיָּבֹא הַחַדְרָה וַיֵּבְךְּ שָׁמָּה: וַיִּרְחַץ פָּנָיו
לב וַיֵּצֵא וַיִּתְאַפַּק וַיֹּאמֶר שִׂימוּ לָחֶם: וַיָּשִׂימוּ לוֹ לְבַדּוֹ וְלָהֶם לְבַדָּם

כִּי אִתִּי יֹאכְלוּ — *For (the men) shall dine with me.* This was meant as a test. Joseph wished to see how they behaved with Benjamin, and whether they would display envy when he gave him larger portions than the rest.

21. כַּסְפֵּנוּ בְּמִשְׁקָלוֹ — *Our silver coins in full weight . . .* the same coins (with which we had paid); therefore we cannot think that other money had gotten into our sacks by mistake.

27. לְשָׁלוֹם — *Of their welfare* (lit., *peace*). Are you "at peace" regarding your physical health? Good health depends upon the harmony of opposing drives; this (peace) occurs when one drive does not overpower another.

אֲבִיכֶם הַזָּקֵן אֲשֶׁר אֲמַרְתֶּם — *(Is) your old father of whom you spoke (well)?* The health of an old person is precarious, as our Sages state, *The lips of older people slacken and their ears become hard of hearing (Shabbos* 152a).

28. שָׁלוֹם לְעַבְדְּךָ לְאָבִינוּ עוֹדֶנּוּ חָי — *Your servant, our father, is well, he is yet alive.* He is also well (as we are), i.e., at peace, and not "the peace of the dead" for he still lives.

וַיִּקְּדוּ וַיִּשְׁתַּחֲוּ — *And they bowed and made obeisance . . .* in recognition of his inquiry regarding their welfare (and their father's).

NOTES

27. לְשָׁלוֹם — *Of their welfare* (lit., *peace*). The *Sforno*, a physician, was aware that good health depends upon proper metabolism, which in turn means that the bodily functions are in perfect balance and harmony. Thus he explains the Torah's use of the word שָׁלוֹם, *peace*, in connection with the health of a person. If there is no conflict or tension within one's physical and mental being, one is "at peace" with himself, i.e., he enjoys good health.

for with me will these men dine at noon." [17] *The man did as Joseph said, and the man brought the men to Joseph's house.* [18] *But the men became frightened when they were brought to Joseph's house, and they said, "Because of the money replaced in our sacks originally are we being brought, so that a charge can be fabricated against us, that it crash down on us, and that we be taken as slaves along with our donkeys."*

[19] *They approached the man who was in charge of Joseph's house and spoke to him at the entrance of the house.* [20] *And they said, "If you please, my lord: We had indeed come down originally to buy food.* [21] *But it happened, when we arrived at the inn and opened our sacks, that behold! each one's money was in the mouth of his sack; it was our own money in its full amount, so we have brought it back in our hand.* [22] *We have also brought other money down in our hand to buy food; we do not know who put our money in our sacks."*

[23] *He replied, "Peace with you, fear not. Your God and the God of your father has put a hidden treasure in your sacks. Your payment had reached me." And he brought Simeon out to them.*

[24] *Then the man brought the men into Joseph's house. He provided water and they washed their feet, and he gave feed to their donkeys.* [25] *They prepared the tribute for when Joseph would come at noon, for they had heard that they were to eat a meal there.*

[26] *When Joseph came to the house they brought the tribute that was in their hands to him to the house, and they prostrated themselves to him toward the ground.* [27] *He inquired after their welfare, and he said, "Is your aged father of whom you spoke at peace? Is he still alive?"*

[28] *They replied, "Your servant our father is at peace; he still lives," and they bowed and prostrated themselves.*

[29] *Then he lifted up his eyes and saw his brother Benjamin, his mother's son, so he said, "Is this your 'little' brother of whom you spoke to me?" And he said, "God be gracious to you, my son."*

[30] *Then Joseph rushed because his compassion for his brother had been stirred and he wanted to weep; so he went into the room and wept there.* [31] *He washed his face and went out, fortified himself and said, "Serve food."* [32] *They served him separately and them separately and the*

29. אֱלֹהִים יָחְנְךָ בְּנִי — *God be gracious unto you, my son* . . . since you are the only one left of your mother, as it is written, *and he alone is left of his mother* (44:20), may God give you grace that your brothers, and also others, befriend you.

30. וַיֵּבְךְּ שָׁמָּה — *And he wept there.* He considered the grief of his father and brothers.

32. וַיָּשִׂימוּ לוֹ לְבַדּוֹ — *And they served for him separately* . . . that his brothers should not sense that he was (also) a Hebrew.

NOTES

30. וַיֵּבְךְּ שָׁמָּה — *And he wept there.* Both here and in 42:24 Joseph wept and in both cases the *Sforno* stresses that it was not because of self-pity but because he felt for his brothers and father. Small wonder that Joseph is referred to by our Sages as a צַדִּיק, *righteous man.*

וְלַמִּצְרִים הָאֹכְלִים אִתּוֹ לְבַדָּם כִּי לֹא יוּכְלוּן הַמִּצְרִים לֶאֱכֹל
לג אֶת־הָעִבְרִים לֶחֶם כִּי־תוֹעֵבָה הִוא לְמִצְרָיִם: וַיֵּשְׁבוּ לְפָנָיו הַבְּכֹר
לד כִּבְכֹרָתוֹ וְהַצָּעִיר כִּצְעִרָתוֹ וַיִּתְמְהוּ הָאֲנָשִׁים אִישׁ אֶל־רֵעֵהוּ: וַיִּשָּׂא
מַשְׂאֹת מֵאֵת פָּנָיו אֲלֵהֶם וַתֵּרֶב מַשְׂאַת בִּנְיָמִן מִמַּשְׂאֹת כֻּלָּם חָמֵשׁ
מד א יָדוֹת וַיִּשְׁתּוּ וַיִּשְׁכְּרוּ עִמּוֹ: וַיְצַו אֶת־אֲשֶׁר עַל־בֵּיתוֹ לֵאמֹר מַלֵּא
אֶת־אַמְתְּחֹת הָאֲנָשִׁים אֹכֶל כַּאֲשֶׁר יוּכְלוּן שְׂאֵת וְשִׂים כֶּסֶף־אִישׁ
ב בְּפִי אַמְתַּחְתּוֹ: וְאֶת־גְּבִיעִי גְּבִיעַ הַכֶּסֶף תָּשִׂים בְּפִי אַמְתַּחַת הַקָּטֹן
ג וְאֵת כֶּסֶף שִׁבְרוֹ וַיַּעַשׂ כִּדְבַר יוֹסֵף אֲשֶׁר דִּבֵּר: הַבֹּקֶר אוֹר וְהָאֲנָשִׁים
ד שֻׁלְּחוּ הֵמָּה וַחֲמֹרֵיהֶם: הֵם יָצְאוּ אֶת־הָעִיר לֹא הִרְחִיקוּ וְיוֹסֵף אָמַר
לַאֲשֶׁר עַל־בֵּיתוֹ קוּם רְדֹף אַחֲרֵי הָאֲנָשִׁים וְהִשַּׂגְתָּם וְאָמַרְתָּ
ה אֲלֵהֶם לָמָּה שִׁלַּמְתֶּם רָעָה תַּחַת טוֹבָה: הֲלוֹא זֶה אֲשֶׁר יִשְׁתֶּה
ו אֲדֹנִי בּוֹ וְהוּא נַחֵשׁ יְנַחֵשׁ בּוֹ הֲרֵעֹתֶם אֲשֶׁר עֲשִׂיתֶם: וַיַּשִּׂגֵם
ז וַיְדַבֵּר אֲלֵהֶם אֶת־הַדְּבָרִים הָאֵלֶּה: וַיֹּאמְרוּ אֵלָיו לָמָּה יְדַבֵּר אֲדֹנִי
ח כַּדְּבָרִים הָאֵלֶּה חָלִילָה לַעֲבָדֶיךָ מֵעֲשׂוֹת כַּדָּבָר הַזֶּה: הֵן כֶּסֶף אֲשֶׁר
מָצָאנוּ בְּפִי אַמְתְּחֹתֵינוּ הֱשִׁיבֹנוּ אֵלֶיךָ מֵאֶרֶץ כְּנָעַן וְאֵיךְ נִגְנֹב מִבֵּית
ט אֲדֹנֶיךָ כֶּסֶף אוֹ זָהָב: אֲשֶׁר יִמָּצֵא אִתּוֹ מֵעֲבָדֶיךָ וָמֵת וְגַם־אֲנַחְנוּ
י נִהְיֶה לַאדֹנִי לַעֲבָדִים: וַיֹּאמֶר גַּם־עַתָּה כְדִבְרֵיכֶם כֶּן־הוּא אֲשֶׁר יִמָּצֵא

כִּי לֹא יוּכְלוּן הַמִּצְרִים — *Because the Egyptians may not (eat bread with the Hebrews)* . . . therefore he did not eat with his brothers, nor did he or his brothers eat with the Egyptians.

34. וַתֵּרֶב מַשְׂאַת בִּנְיָמִן — *And Benjamin's portion was greater.* (Joseph did this) to see whether they would be jealous.

חָמֵשׁ יָדוֹת — *Five times as much.* For each portion he sent to two of them, as was the custom, he sent a similar one to Benjamin, to demonstrate his greater importance.

וַיִּשְׁכְּרוּ עִמּוֹ — *And they became intoxicated with him.* They were not accustomed to the great variety and volume of wine served at the royal table, and did not take heed not to drink all they wanted with the first goblet, as would be proper for those dining with princes, as it says, כִּי תֵשֵׁב לִלְחוֹם אֶת מוֹשֵׁל, בִּין תָּבִין אֶת אֲשֶׁר לְפָנֶיךָ, *When you sit to eat with a ruler, consider well that which is before you* (*Proverbs* 23:1).

XLIV

1. וְשִׂים כֶּסֶף אִישׁ בְּפִי אַמְתַּחְתּוֹ — *And put every man's money in his sack's mouth* . . . with their knowledge. Tell them this is reparation for their harsh treatment (on their first trip).

2. תָּשִׂים בְּפִי אַמְתַּחַת הַקָּטֹן — *Put it in the mouth of the youngest's sack.* His purpose was to see how they would commit themselves to save him.

NOTES

34. וַיִּשְׁכְּרוּ עִמּוֹ — *And they became intoxicated with him.* The Torah would not tell us something derogatory about the sons of Jacob, "the tribes of God." Therefore when we are told וַיִּשְׁכְּרוּ, *they became intoxicated*, the *Sforno* comments that we are being taught a lesson to be careful of our conduct when we find ourselves in a new and strange setting and to conduct ourselves with prudence.

XLIV

1. וְשִׂים כֶּסֶף אִישׁ — *And put every man's money.* It must have been with their knowledge, for when they searched the sacks and found the goblet they also found the money, yet no one was concerned. The reason must therefore be that this time the money was returned as a gesture of appeasement for their initial distress.

Egyptians who ate with him separately, for the Egyptians could not bear to eat food with the Hebrews, it being loathsome to Egyptians. 33 *They were seated before him, the firstborn according to his seniority and the youngest according to his youth. The men looked at one another in astonishment.*

34 *He had portions that had been set before him served to them, and Benjamin's portion was five times as much as the portion of any of them. They drank and became intoxicated with him.*

44 1 *Then he instructed the one in charge of his house, saying, "Fill the men's sacks with as much food as they can carry and put each man's money in the mouth of his sack.* 2 *And my goblet — the silver goblet — place in the mouth of the youngest one's sack along with the money of his purchase." And he followed Joseph's word exactly.*

3 *The day dawned and the men were sent off, they and their donkeys.* 4 *They had left the city, had not gone far, when Joseph said to the one in charge of his house, "Get up, chase after the men; when you overtake them, you are to say to them, 'Why do you repay evil for good?* 5 *Is it not the one from which my master drinks, and with which he regularly divines? You have done evil in how you acted!' "*

6 *He overtook them and spoke those words to them.* 7 *And they said to him, "Why does my lord say such things? It would be sacrilegious for your servants to do such a thing!* 8 *Here, look: The money that we found in the mouth of our sacks we brought back to you from the land of Canaan. How then could we have stolen from your master's house any silver or gold?* 9 *Anyone among your servants with whom it is found shall die, and we also will become slaves to my lord."*

10 *He replied, "What you say now is also correct. The one with whom it*

---

5. הֲלוֹא זֶה אֲשֶׁר יִשְׁתֶּה אֲדֹנִי בּוֹ — *Is this not that in which my lord drinks?* He spoke to them on the assumption that they were aware of everything.

7. לָמָּה יְדַבֵּר אֲדֹנִי כַּדְּבָרִים הָאֵלֶּה — *Why does my lord say such things?*. . . as though you suspect all of us.

10. גַּם עַתָּה כְדִבְרֵיכֶם כֶּן הוּא — *Now also let it be according to your words.* Even though justice demands exactly as you have stated, seeing that we are dealing with (the theft of) the king's goblet who rewarded you with only good by returning your money, nonetheless . . .

NOTES

2. תָּשִׂים בְּפִי אַמְתַּחַת הַקָּטֹן — *Put it in the mouth of the youngest's sack.* Joseph continually tested his brothers to determine their relationship with Benjamin. Had they learned a lesson in brotherly love from the episode of his sale into slavery and the subsequent grief and distress of their father? First he tested their jealousy — or lack of it — with the portions of food at his table. Now he wanted to know if they were prepared to deliver Benjamin from becoming a bondsman. *Teshuvah,* repentance, is measured by a man's behavior when he is given an opportunity to rectify his past sins by not repeating them under similar circumstances. They were jealous of Joseph — had this shortcoming been corrected? They sold him into slavery — would they now be willing to sacrifice all to save his brother from a similar fate?

5. הֲלוֹא זֶה אֲשֶׁר יִשְׁתֶּה אֲדֹנִי בּוֹ — *Is this not that in which my lord drinks?* The only word used is זֶה, *this,* not גָּבִיעַ, *goblet,* which indicates that when the steward spoke to the brothers he assumed that they knew to what זֶה referred.

יא אִתּוֹ יִהְיֶה־לִּי עָבֶד וְאַתֶּם תִּהְיוּ נְקִיִּם: וַיְמַהֲרוּ וַיּוֹרִדוּ אִישׁ אֶת־אַמְתַּחְתּוֹ
יב אָרְצָה וַיִּפְתְּחוּ אִישׁ אַמְתַּחְתּוֹ: וַיְחַפֵּשׂ בַּגָּדוֹל הֵחֵל וּבַקָּטֹן כִּלָּה וַיִּמָּצֵא
יג הַגָּבִיעַ בְּאַמְתַּחַת בִּנְיָמִן: וַיִּקְרְעוּ שִׂמְלֹתָם וַיַּעֲמֹס אִישׁ עַל־חֲמֹרוֹ וַיָּשֻׁבוּ
יד הָעִירָה: וַיָּבֹא יְהוּדָה וְאֶחָיו בֵּיתָה יוֹסֵף וְהוּא עוֹדֶנּוּ שָׁם וַיִּפְּלוּ לְפָנָיו מפטיר
טו אָרְצָה: וַיֹּאמֶר לָהֶם יוֹסֵף מָה־הַמַּעֲשֶׂה הַזֶּה אֲשֶׁר עֲשִׂיתֶם הֲלוֹא יְדַעְתֶּם
טז כִּי־נַחֵשׁ יְנַחֵשׁ אִישׁ אֲשֶׁר כָּמֹנִי: וַיֹּאמֶר יְהוּדָה מַה־נֹּאמַר לַאדֹנִי מַה־
נְּדַבֵּר וּמַה־נִּצְטַדָּק הָאֱלֹהִים מָצָא אֶת־עֲוֹן עֲבָדֶיךָ הִנֶּנּוּ עֲבָדִים לַאדֹנִי
יז גַּם־אֲנַחְנוּ גַּם אֲשֶׁר־נִמְצָא הַגָּבִיעַ בְּיָדוֹ: וַיֹּאמֶר חָלִילָה לִּי מֵעֲשׂוֹת זֹאת
הָאִישׁ אֲשֶׁר נִמְצָא הַגָּבִיעַ בְּיָדוֹ הוּא יִהְיֶה־לִּי עָבֶד וְאַתֶּם עֲלוּ לְשָׁלוֹם
אֶל־אֲבִיכֶם:

אֲשֶׁר יִמָּצֵא אִתּוֹ יִהְיֶה לִּי עָבֶד — *He with whom it is found shall be my slave* . . . and not all of you; nor shall he die, as the law would require.

וְאַתֶּם תִּהְיוּ נְקִיִּם — *And you shall be blameless* . . . (undeserving) of bondage or any other punishment.

15. מָה הַמַּעֲשֶׂה הַזֶּה — *What deed is this.* It was both wicked and foolish, for you should have known that it could not succeed.

16. מַה נֹּאמַר לַאדֹנִי — *What shall we say unto my lord?* . . . in answer to your question, *"What deed is this?"* For . . .

מַה נְּדַבֵּר — *What shall we speak?* . . . to refute (the accusation) and deny our involvement, even though we are innocent.

וּמַה נִּצְטַדָּק — *How shall we justify ourselves?* . . . and prove that this is all a trumped-up charge.

NOTES

16. מַה נֹּאמַר לַאדֹנִי מַה נְּדַבֵּר וּמַה נִּצְטַדָּק — *What shall we say unto my lord? What shall we speak? How shall we justify ourselves?* Three expressions are used – נֹאמַר, *say;* נְדַבֵּר, *speak;* and נִצְטַדָּק, *justify.* The *Sforno* explains Judah's statement thus: There is really nothing for us to say, nor is it of any use to "speak," i.e., to argue our case, for any proof of our innocence will be rejected, since we have been prejudged.

is found shall be my slave, but the rest of you shall be exonerated."
11 *Hurriedly, each one lowered his sack to the ground, and each one opened his sack.* 12 *He searched; he began with the oldest and ended with the youngest; and the goblet was found in Benjamin's sack.* 13 *They rent their garments. Each one reloaded his donkey and they returned to the city.*
14 *When Judah arrived with his brothers to Joseph's house, he was still there. They fell to the ground before him.* 15 *Joseph said to them, "What is this deed that you have done? Do you not realize that a man like me practices divination!"*
16 *So Judah said, "What can we say to my lord? How can we speak? And how can we justify ourselves? God has uncovered the sin of your servants. Here we are: We are ready to be slaves to my lord — both we and the one in whose hand the goblet was found."*
17 *But he replied, "It would be sacrilegious for me to do this. The man in whose possession the goblet was found, only he shall be my slave, and as for you — go up in peace to your father."*

הָאֱלֹהִים מָצָא אֶת עֲוֹן עֲבָדֶיךָ — *God has found out the iniquity of your servants.* We are not being punished for this "sin" for we are innocent. However, we sinned years ago in an entirely different matter and God has chosen to punish us through you, in the sense of, מֵרְשָׁעִים יֵצֵא רֶשַׁע, *From the wicked comes forth wickedness (I Samuel* 24:13). And as we find in the story of Lulainus and Pappas who said to Trajan, "We have deserved of the Omnipresent that we should die ... and He has many agents of death, leopards and lions who can attack and kill us, but He has chosen to punish us by your hand, and at some future time He will exact punishment of you for our blood" (*Taanis* 18b).

17. חָלִילָה לִּי מֵעֲשׂוֹת זֹאת — *Far be it from me that I should do so.* I do not wish to be the means of your being punished for a former sin, in the sense of, מֵרְשָׁעִים יֵצֵא רֶשַׁע, וְיָדִי לֹא תִהְיֶה בָּךְ, *From the wicked comes forth wickedness, but my hand shall not be upon you (I Samuel* 24:13). I will only punish and take as a slave the miscreant who sinned against me now.

NOTES

16-17. הָאֱלֹהִים מָצָא אֶת עֲוֹן עֲבָדֶיךָ ... חָלִילָה לִּי מֵעֲשׂוֹת זֹאת – *God has found out the iniquity of your servants ... Far be it from me that I should do so.* Judah put Joseph into the position of being used by God as the instrument of their punishment for an old heinous crime. Joseph, in turn, rejected this role since it implied that he was wicked. Rather he insisted that he was dealing only with the present transgression and punishing the guilty party leniently.

פרשת ויגש

יח וַיִּגַּשׁ אֵלָיו יְהוּדָה וַיֹּאמֶר בִּי אֲדֹנִי יְדַבֶּר־נָא עַבְדְּךָ דָבָר בְּאָזְנֵי אֲדֹנִי
יט וְאַל־יִחַר אַפְּךָ בְּעַבְדֶּךָ כִּי כָמוֹךָ כְּפַרְעֹה: אֲדֹנִי שָׁאַל אֶת־עֲבָדָיו לֵאמֹר
כ הֲיֵשׁ־לָכֶם אָב אוֹ־אָח: וַנֹּאמֶר אֶל־אֲדֹנִי יֶשׁ־לָנוּ אָב זָקֵן וְיֶלֶד זְקֻנִים
כא קָטָן וְאָחִיו מֵת וַיִּוָּתֵר הוּא לְבַדּוֹ לְאִמּוֹ וְאָבִיו אֲהֵבוֹ: וַתֹּאמֶר אֶל־
כב עֲבָדֶיךָ הוֹרִדֻהוּ אֵלָי וְאָשִׂימָה עֵינִי עָלָיו: וַנֹּאמֶר אֶל־אֲדֹנִי לֹא־יוּכַל
כג הַנַּעַר לַעֲזֹב אֶת־אָבִיו וְעָזַב אֶת־אָבִיו וָמֵת: וַתֹּאמֶר אֶל־עֲבָדֶיךָ אִם־
כד לֹא יֵרֵד אֲחִיכֶם הַקָּטֹן אִתְּכֶם לֹא תֹסִפוּן לִרְאוֹת פָּנָי: וַיְהִי כִּי עָלִינוּ
כה אֶל־עַבְדְּךָ אָבִי וַנַּגֶּד־לוֹ אֵת דִּבְרֵי אֲדֹנִי: וַיֹּאמֶר אָבִינוּ שֻׁבוּ שִׁבְרוּ־לָנוּ
כו מְעַט־אֹכֶל: וַנֹּאמֶר לֹא נוּכַל לָרֶדֶת אִם־יֵשׁ אָחִינוּ הַקָּטֹן אִתָּנוּ וְיָרַדְנוּ
כז כִּי־לֹא נוּכַל לִרְאוֹת פְּנֵי הָאִישׁ וְאָחִינוּ הַקָּטֹן אֵינֶנּוּ אִתָּנוּ: וַיֹּאמֶר עַבְדְּךָ
כח אָבִי אֵלֵינוּ אַתֶּם יְדַעְתֶּם כִּי שְׁנַיִם יָלְדָה־לִּי אִשְׁתִּי: וַיֵּצֵא הָאֶחָד מֵאִתִּי
כט וָאֹמַר אַךְ טָרֹף טֹרָף וְלֹא רְאִיתִיו עַד־הֵנָּה: וּלְקַחְתֶּם גַּם־אֶת־זֶה מֵעִם
ל פָּנַי וְקָרָהוּ אָסוֹן וְהוֹרַדְתֶּם אֶת־שֵׂיבָתִי בְּרָעָה שְׁאֹלָה: וְעַתָּה כְּבֹאִי אֶל־
לא עַבְדְּךָ אָבִי וְהַנַּעַר אֵינֶנּוּ אִתָּנוּ וְנַפְשׁוֹ קְשׁוּרָה בְנַפְשׁוֹ: וְהָיָה כִּרְאוֹתוֹ כִּי־ שני
אֵין הַנַּעַר וָמֵת וְהוֹרִידוּ עֲבָדֶיךָ אֶת־שֵׂיבַת עַבְדְּךָ אָבִינוּ בְּיָגוֹן שְׁאֹלָה:

18. יְדַבֶּר נָא עַבְדְּךָ דָבָר — *Let your servant, I pray, speak a word.* Since you said, *"Far be it from me that I should do so"* (v. 17), for you do not want damage or harm to come through you — even for the guilty — let me tell you the harm which you will inflict if you do this thing.

וְאַל יִחַר אַפְּךָ — *And let not your anger burn* . . . when I tell you that you are the cause of all this trouble.

כִּי כָמוֹךָ כְּפַרְעֹה — *For you are even as Pharaoh.* The harsh words I address to you are not meant as disrespect, for in my eyes you are as important and distinguished as Pharaoh, who is the king.

20. וְאָבִיו אֲהֵבוֹ — *And his father loves him* . . . more than the rest, and that is why he did not let him accompany us at first. For this reason he was not with us at that time; not as you thought, that our youngest brother was sent back to reveal the information gathered (see 42:14).

21. וְאָשִׂימָה עֵינִי עָלָיו — *That I may keep an eye* (lit., *set my eyes) upon him* . . . and there is no reason for his father to worry about sending him (for I will look after him).

22. לֹא יוּכַל הַנַּעַר לַעֲזֹב אֶת אָבִיו — *The lad cannot leave his father* . . . for if he is separated

NOTES

20. וְאָבִיו אֲהֵבוֹ — *And his father loves him* . . . When the brothers argued with Joseph regarding his accusation that they were spies, Joseph triumphantly cried out, "הוּא אֲשֶׁר דִּבַּרְתִּי אֲלֵכֶם, *That is it that I spoke unto you*" (42:14), which the *Sforno* interprets to mean that he claimed that the "missing one" or the "twelfth one" came and went to report their findings. Judah alluded to this now, saying that their youngest brother was not allowed to accompany them due to his father's great love for him and fear for his safety, not for subversive reasons.

22. וְעָזַב אֶת אָבִיו וָמֵת — *For if he should leave his father, he will die.* The word וָמֵת, *he will die,* at the conclusion of this verse is ambiguous. It can refer to Benjamin or to Jacob, and indeed the commentators differ as to who the subject is (*Rashi* and *Rashbam*). The *Sforno's* interpretation clarifies the verse: The first part refers to Benjamin and the second to Jacob. The word וָמֵת, *he will die,* could therefore refer to both; Benjamin would long for his father and pine away and die, causing his father in turn to die from grief.

PARASHAS VAYIGASH

18 *Then Judah approached him and said, "If you please, my lord, may*
your servant speak a word in my lord's ears and let not your anger
flare up at your servant — for you are like Pharaoh. 19 *My lord has asked*
his servants, saying, 'Have you a father or brother?' 20 *And we said to my*
lord, 'We have an old father and a young child of [his] old age; his brother
is dead, he alone is left from his mother, and his father loves him.' 21 *Then*
you said to your servants, 'Bring him down to me, and I will set my eye on
him.' 22 *We said to my lord, 'The youth cannot leave his father, for should*
he leave his father he will die.' 23 *But you said to your servants, 'If your*
youngest brother does not come down with you, you will not see my face
again!'

24 *"And it was, when we went up to your servant my father, we told him*
my lord's words; 25 *and our father said, 'Go back, buy us some food.'* 26 *We*
said, 'We cannot go down; only if our youngest brother is with us, then we
will go down, for we cannot see the man's face if our youngest brother is not
with us.' 27 *Then your servant my father said to us, 'You know that my wife*
bore me two [sons]. 28 *One has left me and I presumed: Alas, he has surely*
been torn to pieces, for I have not seen him since! 29 *So should you take this*
one, too, from my presence, and disaster befall him, then you will have
brought down my hoariness in evil to the grave.'

30 *"And now, if I come to your servant my father and the youth is not with*
us — since his soul is so bound up with his soul — 31 *it will happen that when*
he sees the youth is missing he will die, and your servants will have brought
down the hoariness of your servant our father in sorrow to the grave.

---

from his father he (Benjamin) will miss him so deeply that he will pine away and become ill, or even die.

וְעָזַב אֶת אָבִיו וָמֵת — *For if he should leave his father, he will die . . .* and consequently his father will, without question, die (as well).

23. אִם לֹא יֵרֵד — *If he would not come down.* Even though you heard our logical reasoned pleas, you decreed that we must perforce bring him down.

24. וַנַּגֶּד לוֹ אֵת דִּבְרֵי אֲדֹנִי — *We told him the words of my lord.* In spite of this he (Jacob) refused to send him (Benjamin) at that time.

25. שֻׁבוּ שִׁבְרוּ לָנוּ — *Go again, buy us (a little food).* Pressured by the famine, we forced him (Jacob) to send (Benjamin), even though he warned us that if we did not bring him back, we would be the cause of his death in sorrow.

30-31. וְעַתָּה כְּבֹאִי . . . וְהוֹרִידוּ עֲבָדֶיךָ — *Now therefore when I come . . . And your servants will bring down (our father with sorrow).* Since he warned us so strongly, he will disregard all that happened here, and it will be as if we had deliberately brought this misfortune upon him; similar to, בְּטֶרֶם תָּבוֹא הִשְׁמַעְתִּיךָ, פֶּן תֹּאמַר עָצְבִּי עָשָׂם, *Before it came to pass I announced it to you, lest you should say, "My idol has done them"* (*Isaiah* 48:5).

NOTES

23. אִם לֹא יֵרֵד — *If he would not come down.* You insisted, and that is why I say that you are the cause of this trouble which you claimed was not your intent (see *Sforno* verse 18).

30-31. וְעַתָּה כְּבֹאִי . . . וְהוֹרִידוּ עֲבָדֶיךָ — *Now therefore when I come . . . And your servants will bring down (our father with sorrow).* The proof brought from *Isaiah* is that when a person is forewarned, he

לב כִּי עַבְדְּךָ עָרַב אֶת־הַנַּעַר מֵעִם אָבִי לֵאמֹר אִם־לֹא אֲבִיאֶנּוּ אֵלֶיךָ
לג וְחָטָאתִי לְאָבִי כָּל־הַיָּמִים: וְעַתָּה יֵשֶׁב־נָא עַבְדְּךָ תַּחַת הַנַּעַר עֶבֶד
לד לַאדֹנִי וְהַנַּעַר יַעַל עִם־אֶחָיו: כִּי־אֵיךְ אֶעֱלֶה אֶל־אָבִי וְהַנַּעַר אֵינֶנּוּ אִתִּי
מה א פֶּן אֶרְאֶה בָרָע אֲשֶׁר יִמְצָא אֶת־אָבִי: וְלֹא־יָכֹל יוֹסֵף לְהִתְאַפֵּק לְכֹל
הַנִּצָּבִים עָלָיו וַיִּקְרָא הוֹצִיאוּ כָל־אִישׁ מֵעָלָי וְלֹא־עָמַד אִישׁ אִתּוֹ
ב בְּהִתְוַדַּע יוֹסֵף אֶל־אֶחָיו: וַיִּתֵּן אֶת־קֹלוֹ בִּבְכִי וַיִּשְׁמְעוּ מִצְרַיִם וַיִּשְׁמַע
ג בֵּית פַּרְעֹה: וַיֹּאמֶר יוֹסֵף אֶל־אֶחָיו אֲנִי יוֹסֵף הַעוֹד אָבִי חָי וְלֹא־יָכְלוּ
ד אֶחָיו לַעֲנוֹת אֹתוֹ כִּי נִבְהֲלוּ מִפָּנָיו: וַיֹּאמֶר יוֹסֵף אֶל־אֶחָיו גְּשׁוּ־נָא אֵלַי
ה וַיִּגָּשׁוּ וַיֹּאמֶר אֲנִי יוֹסֵף אֲחִיכֶם אֲשֶׁר־מְכַרְתֶּם אֹתִי מִצְרָיְמָה: וְעַתָּה | אַל־
תֵּעָצְבוּ וְאַל־יִחַר בְּעֵינֵיכֶם כִּי־מְכַרְתֶּם אֹתִי הֵנָּה כִּי לְמִחְיָה שְׁלָחַנִי
ו אֱלֹהִים לִפְנֵיכֶם: כִּי־זֶה שְׁנָתַיִם הָרָעָב בְּקֶרֶב הָאָרֶץ וְעוֹד חָמֵשׁ שָׁנִים
ז אֲשֶׁר אֵין־חָרִישׁ וְקָצִיר: וַיִּשְׁלָחֵנִי אֱלֹהִים לִפְנֵיכֶם לָשׂוּם לָכֶם שְׁאֵרִית
ח בָּאָרֶץ וּלְהַחֲיוֹת לָכֶם לִפְלֵיטָה גְּדֹלָה: וְעַתָּה לֹא־אַתֶּם שְׁלַחְתֶּם אֹתִי הֵנָּה שלישי
כִּי הָאֱלֹהִים וַיְשִׂימֵנִי לְאָב לְפַרְעֹה וּלְאָדוֹן לְכָל־בֵּיתוֹ וּמֹשֵׁל בְּכָל־אֶרֶץ
ט מִצְרָיִם: מַהֲרוּ וַעֲלוּ אֶל־אָבִי וַאֲמַרְתֶּם אֵלָיו כֹּה אָמַר בִּנְךָ יוֹסֵף שָׂמַנִי
י אֱלֹהִים לְאָדוֹן לְכָל־מִצְרָיִם רְדָה אֵלַי אַל־תַּעֲמֹד: וְיָשַׁבְתָּ בְאֶרֶץ־גֹּשֶׁן
וְהָיִיתָ קָרוֹב אֵלַי אַתָּה וּבָנֶיךָ וּבְנֵי בָנֶיךָ וְצֹאנְךָ וּבְקָרְךָ וְכָל־אֲשֶׁר־לָךְ:

---

32. כִּי עַבְדְּךָ עָרַב — *For your servant became surety.* He will die at once when he doesn't see (Benjamin returning with me), without even inquiring what happened to him, because since (I) became surety for him and did not bring him back, he will think that he is definitely dead, and that is why I could not fulfill my vow (to him).

33. וְעַתָּה יֵשֶׁב נָא עַבְדְּךָ תַּחַת הַנַּעַר — *Now therefore, let your servant, I pray, stay instead of the lad.* I beseech you to allow me to take his place, so that I can keep my promise and not sin against my father forever.

34. כִּי אֵיךְ אֶעֱלֶה — *For how shall I go up (to my father).* Even though I know he will be pained by my absence, it is preferable to my witnessing his death (over the loss of Benjamin).

XLV

1. לְהִתְאַפֵּק לְכֹל הַנִּצָּבִים עָלָיו — *Could not refrain himself before all those that stood by him* . . . to adequately control himself so as to be able to attend to all who were standing before him.

3. הַעוֹד אָבִי חָי — *Does my father yet live?* Is it possible that he has survived his sorrow and worry over me?

4. גְּשׁוּ נָא אֵלַי — *Come near to me* . . . so that those who hear my weeping will not hear about my sale.

NOTES

cannot attribute what happens to some other cause or reason, save that which he has been warned about.

32. כִּי עַבְדְּךָ עָרַב — *For your servant became surety.* Judah argued that before they will have an opportunity to reassure Jacob that Benjamin was still alive, Jacob would die, convinced that if Benjamin were alive Judah would have found a way to bring him back.

XLV

1. לְהִתְאַפֵּק לְכֹל הַנִּצָּבִים עָלָיו — *Could not refrain himself before all those that stood by him.* Joseph was so emotionally distraught by the anguished plea of Judah that he was incapable of continuing

32 *For your servant took responsibility for the youth from my father saying,*
'If I do not bring him back to you then I will be sinning to my father for all
time.' 33 *Now, therefore, please let your servant remain instead of the youth*
as a servant to my lord, and let the youth go up with his brothers. 34 *For how*
can I go up to my father if the youth is not with me, lest I see the evil that
will befall my father!"

45 1 *Now Joseph could not restrain himself in the presence of all who stood*
before him, so he called out, "Remove everyone from before me!"
Thus no one remained with him when Joseph made himself known to his
brothers.
2 *He cried in a loud voice. Egypt heard, and Pharaoh's household heard.*
3 *And Joseph said to his brothers, "I am Joseph. Is my father still alive?"*
But his brothers could not answer him because they were left disconcerted
before him.
4 *Then Joseph said to his brothers, "Come close to me, if you please," and*
they came close. And he said, "I am Joseph your brother — it is me, whom
you sold into Egypt. 5 *And now, be not distressed, nor reproach yourselves*
for having sold me here, for it was to be a provider that God sent me ahead
of you. 6 *For this has been two of the hunger years in the midst of the land,*
and there are yet five years in which there shall be neither plowing nor
harvest. 7 *Thus God has sent me ahead of you to insure your survival in the*
land and to sustain you for a momentous deliverance. 8 *And now: It was not*
you who sent me here, but God; He has made me father to Pharaoh, master
of his entire household, and ruler throughout the entire land of Egypt.
9 *Hurry — go up to my father and say to him, 'So said your son Joseph: "God*
has made me master of all Egypt. Come down to me; do not delay. 10 *You*
will reside in the land of Goshen and you will be near to me — you, your
sons, your grandchildren, your flock and your cattle, and all that is yours.

אֲשֶׁר מְכַרְתֶּם — *Whom you sold.* That I am aware of the incident is proof that I am Joseph, since no one else knew that I was your brother, including those who purchased me.

8. וְעַתָּה לֹא אַתֶּם שְׁלַחְתֶּם — *So now it was not you who sent me.* Now that you realize the Divine plan and purpose behind all this, a design which could not have been achieved without the earlier causes (of our conflicts), (then) undoubtedly those earlier causes were also the will of God (Who willed it so) in order to achieve (His) goal.

לְאָב לְפַרְעֹה — *A father to Pharaoh* . . . an advisor to the king.

וּלְאָדוֹן לְכָל בֵּיתוֹ — *And lord of all his house* . . . appointed over his house.

וּמֹשֵׁל בְּכָל אֶרֶץ מִצְרָיִם — *And ruler over all the land of Egypt* . . . to conduct matters of state.

9. מַהֲרוּ — *Hasten* . . . so that he (Jacob) spend no more time grieving.

NOTES

his audiences that day and therefore asked all to leave. The words לְכֹל הַנִּצָּבִים, *all those that stood,* is interpreted by the *Sforno* as referring to those who had appointments with Joseph, either for matters of state or their personal affairs.

4-12. אֲשֶׁר מְכַרְתֶּם . . . כִּי פִי הַמְדַבֵּר אֲלֵיכֶם — *Whom you sold . . . That it is my mouth that speaks to you.* Joseph realized that he must convince his brothers of his identity. His knowledge of the sale would not have been sufficient proof since it could have been related to him by another. That is why he stressed two points. One is the fact that no one involved in the sale knew that he was their

יא וְכִלְכַּלְתִּ֤י אֹֽתְךָ֙ שָׁ֔ם כִּי־ע֛וֹד חָמֵ֥שׁ שָׁנִ֖ים רָעָ֑ב פֶּן־תִּוָּרֵ֛שׁ אַתָּ֥ה וּבֵיתְךָ֖ וְכָל־
יב אֲשֶׁר־לָֽךְ׃ וְהִנֵּ֤ה עֵֽינֵיכֶם֙ רֹא֔וֹת וְעֵינֵ֖י אָחִ֣י בִנְיָמִ֑ין כִּי־פִ֖י הַֽמְדַבֵּ֥ר אֲלֵיכֶֽם׃
יג וְהִגַּדְתֶּ֣ם לְאָבִ֗י אֶת־כָּל־כְּבוֹדִי֙ בְּמִצְרַ֔יִם וְאֵ֖ת כָּל־אֲשֶׁ֣ר רְאִיתֶ֑ם וּמִֽהַרְתֶּ֛ם
יד וְהוֹרַדְתֶּ֥ם אֶת־אָבִ֖י הֵֽנָּה׃ וַיִּפֹּ֛ל עַל־צַוְּארֵ֥י בִנְיָמִֽן־אָחִ֖יו וַיֵּ֑בְךְּ וּבִנְיָמִ֕ן בָּכָ֖ה
טו עַל־צַוָּארָֽיו׃ וַיְנַשֵּׁ֥ק לְכָל־אֶחָ֖יו וַיֵּ֣בְךְּ עֲלֵהֶ֑ם וְאַ֣חֲרֵי כֵ֔ן דִּבְּר֥וּ אֶחָ֖יו אִתּֽוֹ׃
טז וְהַקֹּ֣ל נִשְׁמַ֗ע בֵּ֤ית פַּרְעֹה֙ לֵאמֹ֔ר בָּ֖אוּ אֲחֵ֣י יוֹסֵ֑ף וַיִּיטַב֙ בְּעֵינֵ֣י פַרְעֹ֔ה וּבְעֵינֵ֖י
יז עֲבָדָֽיו׃ וַיֹּ֤אמֶר פַּרְעֹה֙ אֶל־יוֹסֵ֔ף אֱמֹ֥ר אֶל־אַחֶ֖יךָ זֹ֣את עֲשׂ֑וּ טַֽעֲנוּ֙ אֶת־
יח בְּעִ֣ירְכֶ֔ם וּלְכוּ־בֹ֖אוּ אַ֥רְצָה כְּנָֽעַן׃ וּקְח֧וּ אֶת־אֲבִיכֶ֛ם וְאֶת־בָּתֵּיכֶ֖ם וּבֹ֣אוּ
רביעי יט אֵלָ֑י וְאֶתְּנָ֣ה לָכֶ֗ם אֶת־טוּב֙ אֶ֣רֶץ מִצְרַ֔יִם וְאִכְל֖וּ אֶת־חֵ֥לֶב הָאָֽרֶץ׃ וְאַתָּ֥ה
צֻוֵּ֖יתָה זֹ֣את עֲשׂ֑וּ קְחוּ־לָכֶם֩ מֵאֶ֨רֶץ מִצְרַ֜יִם עֲגָל֗וֹת לְטַפְּכֶם֙ וְלִנְשֵׁיכֶ֔ם
כ וּנְשָׂאתֶ֥ם אֶת־אֲבִיכֶ֖ם וּבָאתֶֽם׃ וְעֵ֣ינְכֶ֔ם אַל־תָּחֹ֖ס עַל־כְּלֵיכֶ֑ם כִּי־ט֛וּב כָּל־
כא אֶ֥רֶץ מִצְרַ֖יִם לָכֶ֥ם הֽוּא׃ וַיַּֽעֲשׂוּ־כֵן֙ בְּנֵ֣י יִשְׂרָאֵ֔ל וַיִּתֵּ֨ן לָהֶ֥ם יוֹסֵ֛ף עֲגָל֖וֹת עַל־
כב פִּ֣י פַרְעֹ֑ה וַיִּתֵּ֥ן לָהֶ֛ם צֵדָ֖ה לַדָּֽרֶךְ׃ לְכֻלָּ֥ם נָתַ֛ן לָאִ֖ישׁ חֲלִפ֣וֹת שְׂמָלֹ֑ת
כג וּלְבִנְיָמִ֤ן נָתַן֙ שְׁל֣שׁ מֵא֣וֹת כֶּ֔סֶף וְחָמֵ֖שׁ חֲלִפֹ֥ת שְׂמָלֹֽת׃ וּלְאָבִ֞יו שָׁלַ֤ח כְּזֹאת֙
עֲשָׂרָ֣ה חֲמֹרִ֔ים נֹשְׂאִ֖ים מִטּ֣וּב מִצְרָ֑יִם וְעֶ֣שֶׂר אֲתֹנֹ֡ת נֹֽשְׂאֹת֩ בָּ֨ר וָלֶ֧חֶם וּמָז֛וֹן
כד לְאָבִ֖יו לַדָּֽרֶךְ׃ וַיְשַׁלַּ֥ח אֶת־אֶחָ֖יו וַיֵּלֵ֑כוּ וַיֹּ֣אמֶר אֲלֵהֶ֔ם אַל־תִּרְגְּז֖וּ בַּדָּֽרֶךְ׃

11. פֶּן תִּוָּרֵשׁ — *Lest you come to poverty* . . . due to lack of pasture for the flocks, as indeed they later said, *"For there is no pasture for the flocks"* (47:4).

12. וְעֵינֵי אָחִי בִנְיָמִין — *And the eyes of my brother Benjamin* . . . who had no knowledge of my sale.

כִּי פִי הַמְדַבֵּר אֲלֵיכֶם — *That it is my mouth that speaks to you* . . . without an interpreter (as hitherto). Now consider, that at my sale there was no one who spoke our language (Hebrew) save us, for the purchasers were Ishmaelites and Midianites.

13. וּמִהַרְתֶּם וְהוֹרַדְתֶּם אֶת אָבִי הֵנָּה — *And you shall hasten and bring down my father here* . . . so that he may rejoice to see all this.

16. וַיִּיטַב בְּעֵינֵי פַרְעֹה — *And it pleased Pharaoh well.* Pharaoh thinks that now Joseph's care over (Egypt) will not be as that of a stranger but that of a citizen, dwelling in the land with his family and he would care (for them) wholeheartedly, (thus) benefiting the land and its people.

17. אֱמֹר אֶל אַחֶיךָ זֹאת עֲשׂוּ — *Say to your brethren, "This do."* (You should tell them) that this is your intent and desire that they take your father and families (and come down to Egypt).

19. וְאַתָּה צֻוֵּיתָה — *Now you are commanded.* And tell them also that you have been so commanded (by me).

NOTES

brother, and secondly, even the possibility of overhearing them speak of Joseph as their brother would not reveal his identity, since only they spoke the Hebrew language. All this the *Sforno* reads into the phrases, אֲחִיכֶם אֲשֶׁר מְכַרְתֶּם, *your brother whom you sold,* and כִּי פִי הַמְדַבֵּר אֲלֵיכֶם, *that it is my mouth that speaks to you,* in Hebrew (as *Rashi* states).

13. וּמִהַרְתֶּם וְהוֹרַדְתֶּם אֶת אָבִי הֵנָּה — *And you shall hasten and bring down my father here.* Even though he will hear the story from you, "one cannot compare hearing to seeing," therefore hasten to bring him down.

16. וַיִּיטַב בְּעֵינֵי פַרְעֹה — *And it pleased Pharaoh well.* Pharaoh was pleased, not because of the reunion of the brothers, but because once his family would join him Joseph would feel that he was an integral part of Egypt. His loyalty to Pharaoh and commitment to the welfare of the land would therefore become strengthened and enhanced.

[11] *And I will provide for you there — for there will be five more years of famine — so you do not become destitute, you, your household, and all that is yours." '*

[12] *"Behold! Your eyes see as do the eyes of my brother Benjamin that it is my mouth that is speaking to you.* [13] *Therefore, tell my father of all my glory in Egypt and all that you saw; but you must hurry, and bring my father down here."*

[14] *Then he fell upon his brother Benjamin's neck and wept; and Benjamin wept upon his neck.* [15] *He then kissed all his brothers and wept upon them; afterwards his brothers conversed with him.*

[16] *The news was heard in Pharaoh's palace saying, "Joseph's brothers have come!" And it was pleasing in the eyes of Pharaoh and in the eyes of his servants.* [17] *Pharaoh said to Joseph, "Say to your brothers, 'Do this: Load up your animals and go directly to the land of Canaan.* [18] *Bring your father and your households and come to me. I will give you the best of the land of Egypt and you will eat the fat of the land.'* [19] *And you are commanded [to say], 'Do this: Take for yourselves from the land of Egypt wagons for your small children and for your wives; transport your father and come.* [20] *And let your eyes not take pity on your belongings, for the best of all the land of Egypt — it is yours.' "*

[21] *The sons of Israel did so, and Joseph gave them wagons by Pharaoh's word, and he gave them provisions for the journey.* [22] *To each of them he gave changes of clothing; but to Benjamin he gave three hundred pieces of silver and five changes of clothing.* [23] *And to his father he sent the following: ten he-donkeys laden with the best of Egypt and ten she-donkeys laden with grain, bread, and food for his father for the journey.* [24] *And he sent off his brothers, and they went. He said to them, "Do not become agitated on the way."*

זֹאת עֲשׂוּ — *This do* — so that you realize this objective, and your father not refuse to come . . .

קְחוּ לָכֶם מֵאֶרֶץ מִצְרַיִם עֲגָלוֹת — *Take your wagons out of Egypt.* When Jacob will see the wagons prepared to transport them, he will have no excuse to refuse. This indeed was shown to be so later, where it says, *And he saw the wagons which Joseph had sent to carry him . . . And Israel said, "I will go and see him"* (vs. 27-28).

20. וְעֵינְכֶם אַל תָּחֹס עַל כְּלֵיכֶם — *Also regard not your stuff.* Do not delay on that account, because the ultimate loss would be greater in the value of the cattle sacrificed by your delay.

23. וּלְאָבִיו שָׁלַח כְּזֹאת — *And to his father he sent in like manner . . .* the same as Benjamin's gift, and in addition ten asses and ten she-asses. When there is a listing of many items, the letter *vav* appears at the end, similar to, יִשָּׂשכָר זְבוּלֻן וּבִנְיָמִן, *Issachar, Zebulun, and Benjamin* (*Exodus* 1:2).

24. וַיְשַׁלַּח אֶת אֶחָיו — *So he dismissed* (lit., *sent) his brothers.* He dismissed them and gave them permission, similar to, שַׁלְּחֵנִי כִּי עָלָה הַשָּׁחַר, *Let me go for the day breaks* (32:27), (also) שַׁלְּחוּנִי וְאֵלְכָה לַאדֹנִי, *Send me away so that I may go to my master* (24:56).

NOTES

23. וּלְאָבִיו שָׁלַח כְּזֹאת — *And to his father he sent in like manner.* The prefix ו׳ of וּלְאָבִיו, *"and" to his father,* connects this word to the end of the previous sentence, i.e., Joseph gave Benjamin three hundred shekels and five garments, which he also sent to his father — in addition to which he sent his father the gifts enumerated in this verse.

24. וַיְשַׁלַּח אֶת אֶחָיו — *So he dismissed* (lit., *sent) his brothers.* The word וַיְשַׁלַּח normally is trans-

כה-כו וַיַּעֲלוּ מִמִּצְרָיִם וַיָּבֹאוּ אֶרֶץ כְּנַעַן אֶל־יַעֲקֹב אֲבִיהֶם׃ וַיַּגִּדוּ לוֹ לֵאמֹר עוֹד
יוֹסֵף חַי וְכִי־הוּא מֹשֵׁל בְּכָל־אֶרֶץ מִצְרָיִם וַיָּפָג לִבּוֹ כִּי לֹא־הֶאֱמִין לָהֶם׃
כז וַיְדַבְּרוּ אֵלָיו אֵת כָּל־דִּבְרֵי יוֹסֵף אֲשֶׁר דִּבֶּר אֲלֵהֶם וַיַּרְא אֶת־הָעֲגָלוֹת
חמישי כח אֲשֶׁר־שָׁלַח יוֹסֵף לָשֵׂאת אֹתוֹ וַתְּחִי רוּחַ יַעֲקֹב אֲבִיהֶם׃ וַיֹּאמֶר יִשְׂרָאֵל רַב
מו א עוֹד־יוֹסֵף בְּנִי חָי אֵלְכָה וְאֶרְאֶנּוּ בְּטֶרֶם אָמוּת׃ וַיִּסַּע יִשְׂרָאֵל וְכָל־אֲשֶׁר־לוֹ
ב וַיָּבֹא בְּאֵרָה שָּׁבַע וַיִּזְבַּח זְבָחִים לֵאלֹהֵי אָבִיו יִצְחָק׃ וַיֹּאמֶר אֱלֹהִים ׀
ג לְיִשְׂרָאֵל בְּמַרְאֹת הַלַּיְלָה וַיֹּאמֶר יַעֲקֹב ׀ יַעֲקֹב וַיֹּאמֶר הִנֵּנִי׃ וַיֹּאמֶר אָנֹכִי
הָאֵל אֱלֹהֵי אָבִיךָ אַל־תִּירָא מֵרְדָה מִצְרַיְמָה כִּי־לְגוֹי גָּדוֹל אֲשִׂימְךָ שָׁם׃
ד אָנֹכִי אֵרֵד עִמְּךָ מִצְרַיְמָה וְאָנֹכִי אַעַלְךָ גַם־עָלֹה וְיוֹסֵף יָשִׁית יָדוֹ עַל־עֵינֶיךָ׃

26. וַיָּפָג לִבּוֹ – *And his heart fainted.* He fainted, his pulse rate dropped and his heartbeat slowed as happens when one faints. (This occurred) due to his concern caused by their mentioning Joseph.

כִּי לֹא הֶאֱמִין לָהֶם — *For he believed them not.* Therefore *the spirit of Jacob revived,* and his heartbeat did not fail when he later believed them, as happens (from) the shock of sudden joy which can even cause death, (because) the deceleration of his heart caused by his original concern, when he disbelieved them, (counterbalanced) its acceleration later (when he did believe them).

27. וַיְדַבְּרוּ אֵלָיו אֵת כָּל דִּבְרֵי יוֹסֵף — *And they told him all the words of Joseph.* (The words in v. 6) *And there are yet five years in which there will be neither plowing nor harvest,* so that the glad tiding was tempered by worry and concern.

וַתְּחִי רוּחַ יַעֲקֹב — *The spirit of Jacob revived.* He was healed from his fainting spell by gradually mitigating the joy with worry.

28. רַב . . . אֵלְכָה וְאֶרְאֶנּוּ — *It is enough . . . I will go and see him . . .* (only to see him), not to settle there as he requests.

XLVI

1. לֵאלֹהֵי אָבִיו יִצְחָק — *To the God of his father Isaac . . .* Who had said to Isaac, "*Go not down into Egypt*" (26:2).

2. וַיֹּאמֶר אֱלֹהִים לְיִשְׂרָאֵל — *And God said to Israel.* He spoke thus to him because he was "Israel," whose descendants would one day rule over their enemies.

3. אָנֹכִי הָאֵל אֱלֹהֵי אָבִיךָ — *I am God, the God of your father.* I, Who told your father, *Go not down into Egypt* (26:2), tell you . . .

NOTES

lated *and he sent.* In the context of this sentence, as is true in those verses quoted by the *Sforno,* it means granting permission to take one's leave.

26-27. וַיָּפָג לִבּוֹ כִּי לֹא הֶאֱמִין לָהֶם . . . וַתְּחִי רוּחַ יַעֲקֹב — *And his heart fainted, for he believed them not . . . The spirit of Jacob revived.* Careful examination of these two verses reveal what brings the *Sforno* to his unique interpretation. Jacob did not believe his sons, yet he fainted. After they convinced him, he revived. In the middle of these expressions — he "didn't believe" and "his spirit revived" — the brothers told their father *all* the words of Joseph. The *Sforno* feels that the sequence here is all important and occurred for Jacob's physical welfare. Extreme happiness and joy can be harmful, especially when one is taken unaware. To mingle concern with great *simchah* is beneficial, and to precede the inevitable acceleration of the heart with deceleration is prophylactic. Hence his fainting first prevented the shock of joy from harming him, and the information of five years more of famine tempered the intensity of the joy as well.

28. רַב . . . אֵלְכָה וְאֶרְאֶנּוּ — *It is enough . . . I will go and see him.* The word רַב is difficult to understand, and is explained in various ways by the commentators. The *Sforno* gives a simple interpretation. Jacob agreed *only* to go see his son, but did not agree to settle in Egypt. Hence the word רַב means: It is enough and sufficient that I go to see him.

[25] They went up from Egypt and came to the land of Canaan to Jacob their
father. [26] And they told him, saying, "Joseph is still alive," also that he is
ruler over all the land of Egypt; but his heart rejected it, for he could not
believe them. [27] However, when they related to him all the words that Joseph
had spoken to them, and he saw the wagons that Joseph had sent to
transport him, then the spirit of their father Jacob was revived.
[28] And Israel said, "How great! My son Joseph still lives! I shall go and see
him before I die."

46 *[1] So Israel set out with all that he had and he came to Beer-sheba where he*
slaughtered sacrifices to the God of his father Isaac.
[2] God spoke to Israel in night visions and He said, "Jacob, Jacob."
And he said, "Here I am."
[3] And He said, "I am the God — God of your father. Have no fear of
descending to Egypt, for I shall establish you as a great nation there. [4] I shall
descend with you to Egypt, and I shall also surely bring you up; and Joseph
shall place his hand on your eyes."

אַל תִּירָא מֵרְדָה מִצְרַיְמָה, כִּי לְגוֹי גָּדוֹל אֲשִׂימְךָ שָׁם — *Fear not to go down into Egypt, for I will make of you a great nation there.* If you remain here your children will intermarry and become absorbed by the Caananites, but in Egypt they will not be able to do so, *because the Egyptians may not eat bread with the Hebrews* (43:32); therefore they will be a separate, distinct people, as our Sages state, "The verse, וַיְהִי שָׁם לְגוֹי, *'And he became there a nation'* (*Deut.* 26:5), teaches us that they were distinctive there" (*Sifri*).

4. אַעַלְךָ גַם עָלֹה — *And I will also surely bring you up.* After I bring you up from there, I will raise you even higher than you were before going down there, as it is written, וּלְהַעֲלֹתוֹ מִן הָאָרֶץ הַהִוא אֶל אֶרֶץ טוֹבָה, *And to bring them up out of that land unto a good land* (*Exodus* 3:8).

יָשִׁית יָדוֹ עַל עֵינֶיךָ — *Shall put his hand upon your eyes.* You will not have to concern yourself with your affairs, for Joseph will look after everything you need, and you will

NOTES

XLVI

1. לֵאלֹהֵי אָבִיו יִצְחָק — *To the God of his father Isaac.* The question is obvious. Why didn't Jacob offer sacrifices to the God of his grandfather Abraham as well as his father Isaac? The commentators give a variety of answers. The *Sforno* ties together verses 1 and 3, explaining that since Jacob was mindful of Isaac's prohibition by God to leave Israel for Egypt, he had to be reassured by God that he was permitted to do so, and to placate his father, he brought a sacrifice to the *God of his father Isaac.*

2-5. וַיֹּאמֶר אֱלֹהִים לְיִשְׂרָאֵל . . . וַיִּשְׂאוּ בְנֵי יִשְׂרָאֵל — *And God said to Israel . . . And the sons of Israel carried.* These verses (2 and 5) present a strange mixture of the two names — Israel and Jacob. God spoke to *Israel*, but called him *Jacob* (v. 2). *Jacob* rose up from Beer-sheba, but the children of *Israel* carried their father *Jacob* (v. 5). The Sforno explains: *Israel* implies the power to confront one's enemies and prevail. *Jacob* represents both submission and ultimate victory over adversity, since עָקֵב means *heel* or the *end* (of time). Hence the names are used with great care. God spoke to *Israel*, to reassure him of his ability to deal with his adversaries as he went into exile, even though he would be enslaved there (i.e., Jacob). The sons had to appreciate their role as champions of Israel, strong and resolute, as they accompanied their father to Egypt, even though he was a *Jacob* in *Eretz Yisrael* — a luxury which he could afford in exile! And finally, the *Sforno* explains the use of the name Jacob (v. 5) to indicate that just as the joy of reuniting father and son would be complete — untouched by subsequent sorrow — so shall it be at the end of time for his descendants.

4. אַעַלְךָ גַם עָלֹה — *And I will also surely bring you up.* The word עָלֹה, *to bring up*, is repeated twice (אַעַלְךָ – עָלֹה) to teach us that first the children of Israel would be "brought up" from Egypt at the time of their deliverance, and secondly they would be brought up to *Eretz Yisrael*, which is a spiritual as well as a physical elevation.

ה וַיָּקָם יַעֲקֹב מִבְּאֵר שָׁבַע וַיִּשְׂאוּ בְנֵי־יִשְׂרָאֵל אֶת־יַעֲקֹב אֲבִיהֶם וְאֶת־
ו טַפָּם וְאֶת־נְשֵׁיהֶם בָּעֲגָלוֹת אֲשֶׁר־שָׁלַח פַּרְעֹה לָשֵׂאת אֹתוֹ: וַיִּקְחוּ אֶת־
מִקְנֵיהֶם וְאֶת־רְכוּשָׁם אֲשֶׁר רָכְשׁוּ בְּאֶרֶץ כְּנַעַן וַיָּבֹאוּ מִצְרָיְמָה יַעֲקֹב
ז וְכָל־זַרְעוֹ אִתּוֹ: בָּנָיו וּבְנֵי בָנָיו אִתּוֹ בְּנֹתָיו וּבְנוֹת בָּנָיו וְכָל־זַרְעוֹ הֵבִיא אִתּוֹ
ח מִצְרָיְמָה: וְאֵלֶּה שְׁמוֹת בְּנֵי־יִשְׂרָאֵל הַבָּאִים מִצְרַיְמָה יַעֲקֹב
ט־י וּבָנָיו בְּכֹר יַעֲקֹב רְאוּבֵן: וּבְנֵי רְאוּבֵן חֲנוֹךְ וּפַלּוּא וְחֶצְרֹן וְכַרְמִי: וּבְנֵי
יא שִׁמְעוֹן יְמוּאֵל וְיָמִין וְאֹהַד וְיָכִין וְצֹחַר וְשָׁאוּל בֶּן־הַכְּנַעֲנִית: וּבְנֵי לֵוִי גֵּרְשׁוֹן
יב קְהָת וּמְרָרִי: וּבְנֵי יְהוּדָה עֵר וְאוֹנָן וְשֵׁלָה וָפֶרֶץ וָזָרַח וַיָּמָת עֵר וְאוֹנָן בְּאֶרֶץ
יג כְּנַעַן וַיִּהְיוּ בְנֵי־פֶרֶץ חֶצְרֹן וְחָמוּל: וּבְנֵי יִשָּׂשכָר תּוֹלָע וּפֻוָּה וְיוֹב וְשִׁמְרֹן:
יד־טו וּבְנֵי זְבֻלוּן סֶרֶד וְאֵלוֹן וְיַחְלְאֵל: אֵלֶּה ׀ בְּנֵי לֵאָה אֲשֶׁר יָלְדָה לְיַעֲקֹב בְּפַדַּן
טז אֲרָם וְאֵת דִּינָה בִתּוֹ כָּל־נֶפֶשׁ בָּנָיו וּבְנוֹתָיו שְׁלֹשִׁים וְשָׁלֹשׁ: וּבְנֵי גָד צִפְיוֹן
יז וְחַגִּי שׁוּנִי וְאֶצְבֹּן עֵרִי וַאֲרוֹדִי וְאַרְאֵלִי: וּבְנֵי אָשֵׁר יִמְנָה וְיִשְׁוָה וְיִשְׁוִי
יח וּבְרִיעָה וְשֶׂרַח אֲחֹתָם וּבְנֵי בְרִיעָה חֶבֶר וּמַלְכִּיאֵל: אֵלֶּה בְּנֵי זִלְפָּה אֲשֶׁר־
יט נָתַן לָבָן לְלֵאָה בִתּוֹ וַתֵּלֶד אֶת־אֵלֶּה לְיַעֲקֹב שֵׁשׁ עֶשְׂרֵה נָפֶשׁ: בְּנֵי רָחֵל
כ אֵשֶׁת יַעֲקֹב יוֹסֵף וּבִנְיָמִן: וַיִּוָּלֵד לְיוֹסֵף בְּאֶרֶץ מִצְרַיִם אֲשֶׁר יָלְדָה־לּוֹ
כא אָסְנַת בַּת־פּוֹטִי פֶרַע כֹּהֵן אֹן אֶת־מְנַשֶּׁה וְאֶת־אֶפְרָיִם: וּבְנֵי בִנְיָמִן בֶּלַע
כב וָבֶכֶר וְאַשְׁבֵּל גֵּרָא וְנַעֲמָן אֵחִי וָרֹאשׁ מֻפִּים וְחֻפִּים וָאָרְדְּ: אֵלֶּה בְּנֵי רָחֵל
כג־כד אֲשֶׁר יֻלַּד לְיַעֲקֹב כָּל־נֶפֶשׁ אַרְבָּעָה עָשָׂר: וּבְנֵי־דָן חֻשִׁים: וּבְנֵי נַפְתָּלִי
כה יַחְצְאֵל וְגוּנִי וְיֵצֶר וְשִׁלֵּם: אֵלֶּה בְּנֵי בִלְהָה אֲשֶׁר־נָתַן לָבָן לְרָחֵל בִּתּוֹ
כו וַתֵּלֶד אֶת־אֵלֶּה לְיַעֲקֹב כָּל־נֶפֶשׁ שִׁבְעָה: כָּל־הַנֶּפֶשׁ הַבָּאָה לְיַעֲקֹב
כז מִצְרַיְמָה יֹצְאֵי יְרֵכוֹ מִלְּבַד נְשֵׁי בְנֵי־יַעֲקֹב כָּל־נֶפֶשׁ שִׁשִּׁים וָשֵׁשׁ: וּבְנֵי יוֹסֵף
אֲשֶׁר־יֻלַּד־לוֹ בְמִצְרַיִם נֶפֶשׁ שְׁנָיִם כָּל־הַנֶּפֶשׁ לְבֵית־יַעֲקֹב הַבָּאָה מִצְרַיְמָה

---

not find it necessary to deal with the Egyptians who are unworthy of your company.

5. וַיִּשְׂאוּ בְנֵי יִשְׂרָאֵל — *And the sons of Israel carried.* From now on they would have to be the people of *the sons of Israel,* striving with God and with men who rise against them, as they now go into a strange land.

אֶת יַעֲקֹב אֲבִיהֶם — *Jacob their father.* Going to a joy which would not be followed by any sorrow, following all the troubles of his life, teaches us what will occur at the end of days (when *Mashiach,* the Messiah, will come), as it is written, רָנּוּ לְיַעֲקֹב שִׂמְחָה, *Sing with gladness for Jacob (Jeremiah* 31:6).

8. וְאֵלֶּה שְׁמוֹת . . . יַעֲקֹב וּבָנָיו — *And these are the names . . . Jacob and his sons.* (Only Jacob and his sons) were worthy to be mentioned by name, as it is written, וְנָשָׂא אַהֲרֹן אֶת שְׁמוֹתָם לִפְנֵי ה׳, *And Aaron shall bear their names before* HASHEM (*Exodus* 28:12), but the rest of the seventy, although righteous, did not reach their height (stature).

19. בְּנֵי רָחֵל אֵשֶׁת יַעֲקֹב — *The sons of Rachel, Jacob's wife . . .* because she was the prime focus of his intentions and from her were born . . .

יוֹסֵף וּבִנְיָמִן — *Joseph and Benjamin . . .* who were the outstanding ones among the tribes,

NOTES

5. אֶת יַעֲקֹב אֲבִיהֶם — *Jacob their father.* The verse in *Jeremiah* also uses the terms "Jacob" and "Israel" (the conclusion of that sentence refers to שְׁאֵרִית יִשְׂרָאֵל, *the remnant of Israel).* The song of gladness,

5 *So Jacob arose from Beer-sheba; the sons of Israel transported Jacob their
father, as well as their young children and wives, in the wagons which
Pharaoh had sent to transport him.* 6 *They took their livestock and their
wealth which they had amassed in the land of Canaan and they came to
Egypt — Jacob and all his offspring with him.* 7 *His sons and grandsons with
him, his daughters and granddaughters and all his offspring he brought with
him to Egypt.*

8 *Now these are the names of the children of Israel who were coming to
Egypt — Jacob and his children: Jacob's firstborn, Reuben.*

9 *Reuben's sons: Hanoch, Pallu, Hezron, and Carmi.*

10 *Simeon's sons: Jemuel, Jamin, Ohad, Jachin, Zohar, and Shaul, son of
the Canaanite woman.*

11 *Levi's sons: Gershon, Kohath, and Merari.*

12 *Judah's sons: Er, Onan, Shelah, Perez, and Zerah; but Er and Onan had
died in the land of Canaan — and Perez's sons were Hezron and Hamul.*

13 *Issachar's sons: Tola, Puvah, Iov, and Shimron.*

14 *Zebulun's sons: Sered, Elon, and Jahleel.* 15 *These are the sons of Leah
whom she bore to Jacob in Paddan-aram, in addition to Dinah his daughter.
All the people — his sons and daughters — numbered thirty-three.*

16 *Gad's sons: Ziphion, Haggi, Shuni, Ezbon, Eri, Arodi, and Areli.*

17 *Asher's sons: Imnah, Ishvah, Ishvi, Beriah, and their sister Serah; and
Beriah's sons, Heber and Malchiel.* 18 *These are the sons of Zilpah whom Laban had given to Leah his daughter. These she bore to Jacob — sixteen people.*

19 *The sons of Rachel, Jacob's wife: Joseph and Benjamin.*

20 *To Joseph were born in the land of Egypt — whom Asenath daughter
of Poti-phera Chief of On bore to him — Manasseh and Ephraim.*

21 *Benjamin's sons: Bela, Becher, Ashbel, Gera, Naaman, Ehi, Rosh,
Muppim, Huppim, and Ard.* 22 *These are the sons of Rachel who were born
to Jacob — fourteen persons in all.*

23 *Dan's sons: Hushim.*

24 *Naphtali's sons: Jahzeel, Guni, Jezer, and Shillem.* 25 *These are the sons
of Bilhah whom Laban had given to Rachel his daughter. She bore these to
Jacob — seven people in all.*

26 *All the persons coming with Jacob to Egypt — his own descendants,
aside from the wives of Jacob's sons — sixty-six persons in all.*

27 *And Joseph's sons who were born to him in Egypt numbered two
persons. All the people of Jacob's household who came to Egypt — seventy.*

---

as our Sages tell us, רָאוּי הָיָה יוֹסֵף שֶׁיֵּצְאוּ מִמֶּנּוּ שְׁנֵים עָשָׂר שְׁבָטִים כְּיַעֲקֹב, *Joseph was worthy to have twelve tribes issue forth from him, as they did from Jacob (Sotah* 36b), and as they (also) tell us that Benjamin died (only) בְּעֶטְיוֹ שֶׁל נָחָשׁ, *through the serpent's machinations (Shabbos* 55b) (not on account of his sins), and so it is written, לִפְנֵי אֶפְרַיִם וּבִנְיָמִן וּמְנַשֶּׁה עוֹרְרָה אֶת גְּבוּרָתֶךָ, *Before Ephraim and Benjamin and Menasseh stir up Your might (and come to save us) (Psalms* 80:3).

NOTES

however, is for Jacob, which alludes to the "heel," i.e., the end of time. Following this joy there will be no sorrow, just as the joy of Jacob's reunion with Joseph was not marred by subsequent sorrow.

ששי
כח שִׁבְעִים: וְאֶת־יְהוּדָה שָׁלַח לְפָנָיו אֶל־יוֹסֵף לְהוֹרֹת לְפָנָיו
כט גֹּשְׁנָה וַיָּבֹאוּ אַרְצָה גֹּשֶׁן: וַיֶּאְסֹר יוֹסֵף מֶרְכַּבְתּוֹ וַיַּעַל לִקְרַאת־יִשְׂרָאֵל
ל אָבִיו גֹּשְׁנָה וַיֵּרָא אֵלָיו וַיִּפֹּל עַל־צַוָּארָיו וַיֵּבְךְּ עַל־צַוָּארָיו עוֹד: וַיֹּאמֶר
יִשְׂרָאֵל אֶל־יוֹסֵף אָמוּתָה הַפָּעַם אַחֲרֵי רְאוֹתִי אֶת־פָּנֶיךָ כִּי עוֹדְךָ חָי:
לא וַיֹּאמֶר יוֹסֵף אֶל־אֶחָיו וְאֶל־בֵּית אָבִיו אֶעֱלֶה וְאַגִּידָה לְפַרְעֹה וְאֹמְרָה
לב אֵלָיו אַחַי וּבֵית־אָבִי אֲשֶׁר בְּאֶרֶץ־כְּנַעַן בָּאוּ אֵלָי: וְהָאֲנָשִׁים רֹעֵי צֹאן כִּי־
לג אַנְשֵׁי מִקְנֶה הָיוּ וְצֹאנָם וּבְקָרָם וְכָל־אֲשֶׁר לָהֶם הֵבִיאוּ: וְהָיָה כִּי־יִקְרָא
לד לָכֶם פַּרְעֹה וְאָמַר מַה־מַּעֲשֵׂיכֶם: וַאֲמַרְתֶּם אַנְשֵׁי מִקְנֶה הָיוּ עֲבָדֶיךָ
מִנְּעוּרֵינוּ וְעַד־עַתָּה גַּם־אֲנַחְנוּ גַּם־אֲבֹתֵינוּ בַּעֲבוּר תֵּשְׁבוּ בְּאֶרֶץ גֹּשֶׁן כִּי־
מז
א תוֹעֲבַת מִצְרַיִם כָּל־רֹעֵה צֹאן: וַיָּבֹא יוֹסֵף וַיַּגֵּד לְפַרְעֹה וַיֹּאמֶר אָבִי וְאַחַי
ב וְצֹאנָם וּבְקָרָם וְכָל־אֲשֶׁר לָהֶם בָּאוּ מֵאֶרֶץ כְּנָעַן וְהִנָּם בְּאֶרֶץ גֹּשֶׁן: וּמִקְצֵה
ג אֶחָיו לָקַח חֲמִשָּׁה אֲנָשִׁים וַיַּצִּגֵם לִפְנֵי פַרְעֹה: וַיֹּאמֶר פַּרְעֹה אֶל־אֶחָיו מַה־
מַּעֲשֵׂיכֶם וַיֹּאמְרוּ אֶל־פַּרְעֹה רֹעֵה צֹאן עֲבָדֶיךָ גַּם־אֲנַחְנוּ גַּם־אֲבוֹתֵינוּ:
ד וַיֹּאמְרוּ אֶל־פַּרְעֹה לָגוּר בָּאָרֶץ בָּאנוּ כִּי־אֵין מִרְעֶה לַצֹּאן אֲשֶׁר לַעֲבָדֶיךָ
ה כִּי־כָבֵד הָרָעָב בְּאֶרֶץ כְּנָעַן וְעַתָּה יֵשְׁבוּ־נָא עֲבָדֶיךָ בְּאֶרֶץ גֹּשֶׁן: וַיֹּאמֶר
ו פַּרְעֹה אֶל־יוֹסֵף לֵאמֹר אָבִיךָ וְאַחֶיךָ בָּאוּ אֵלֶיךָ: אֶרֶץ מִצְרַיִם לְפָנֶיךָ הִוא
בְּמֵיטַב הָאָרֶץ הוֹשֵׁב אֶת־אָבִיךָ וְאֶת־אַחֶיךָ יֵשְׁבוּ בְּאֶרֶץ גֹּשֶׁן וְאִם־יָדַעְתָּ
ז וְיֶשׁ־בָּם אַנְשֵׁי־חַיִל וְשַׂמְתָּם שָׂרֵי מִקְנֶה עַל־אֲשֶׁר־לִי: וַיָּבֵא יוֹסֵף אֶת־
ח יַעֲקֹב אָבִיו וַיַּעֲמִדֵהוּ לִפְנֵי פַרְעֹה וַיְבָרֶךְ יַעֲקֹב אֶת־פַּרְעֹה: וַיֹּאמֶר פַּרְעֹה
ט אֶל־יַעֲקֹב כַּמָּה יְמֵי שְׁנֵי חַיֶּיךָ: וַיֹּאמֶר יַעֲקֹב אֶל־פַּרְעֹה יְמֵי שְׁנֵי מְגוּרַי

28. לְהוֹרֹת לְפָנָיו גֹּשְׁנָה — *To show the way before him unto Goshen* . . . so that Judah should prepare and establish a home in Goshen before the arrival of Jacob.

29. וַיֵּרָא אֵלָיו — *And he appeared before him* . . . from the midst of (the many) servants surrounding him, and he did not wait until his father (would) come to him in his chariot.

30. אָמוּתָה הַפָּעַם — *Now let me die.* I had other troubles in my life; salvation came, only to be followed by more sorrows. Now that this salvation has come, and I have seen your face, may it be God's will that I may die in this salvation before any fresh sorrow comes upon me.

31. אֶעֱלֶה וְאַגִּידָה — *I will go up and tell Pharaoh* . . . that your occupation is that of shepherds. I will not, however, ask of him to give you the land of Goshen (to live in and tend your flocks) so that he will believe (you) when you tell him what your occupation is. (In this way) he will not assume that you told him this in order that he give you that land.

XLVII

2. וּמִקְצֵה אֶחָיו לָקַח — *And from among his brothers he took* . . . so that Pharaoh should know from their words and manner that their exclusive occupation is the tending of sheep.

NOTES

XLVII

2. וּמִקְצֵה אֶחָיו לָקַח — *And from among his brothers he took.* Joseph was concerned lest Pharaoh believe that his brothers had various talents which the king would attempt to tap and use. Although he was able as viceroy to withstand the test and retain his faith and way of life, he was not sure that his brothers had the same strength of character. Far better that they retain their semi-isolated lifestyle as shepherds, living in Goshen. That is why he

28 He sent Judah ahead of him to Joseph, to prepare ahead of him in Goshen; and they arrived in the region of Goshen.

29 Joseph harnessed his chariot and went up to meet Israel his father in Goshen. He appeared before him, fell on his neck, and he wept on his neck excessively. 30 Then Israel said to Joseph, "Now I can die, after my having seen your face, because you are still alive."

31 And Joseph said to his brothers and to his father's household, "I will go up and tell Pharaoh, and I will say to him, 'My brothers and my father's household who were in the land of Canaan have come to me. 32 The men are shepherds, for they have been cattlemen; their flocks and cattle — and everything they own — they have brought.' 33 And it shall be, when Pharaoh summons you, and says, 'What is your occupation?' 34 Then you are to say, 'Your servants have been cattlemen from our youth till now, both we and our forefathers,' so that you may be able to settle on the region of Goshen, since all shepherds are abhorrent to Egyptians."

47 *1 Then Joseph came and told Pharaoh, and he said, "My father and my brothers, their flocks, their cattle, and everything they own, have arrived from the land of Canaan and they are now in the region of Goshen." 2 From the least of his brothers he took five men and presented them to Pharaoh. 3 Pharaoh said to his brothers, "What is your occupation?" They answered Pharaoh, "Your servants are shepherds — we as well as our forefathers." 4 And they said to Pharaoh, "We have come to sojourn in the land, since there is no grazing for your servants' flocks, for the famine is severe in the land of Canaan; now, if you please, allow your servants to dwell in the region of Goshen."*

5 And Pharaoh said to Joseph saying, "Your father and your brothers have come to you. 6 The land of Egypt is before you — in the best part of the land settle your father and your brothers; let them settle in the region of Goshen, and if you know that there are capable men among them, appoint them as chamberlains over the livestock that belongs to me."

7 Then Joseph brought Jacob, his father, and presented him to Pharaoh, and Jacob blessed Pharaoh. 8 Pharaoh said to Jacob, "How many are the days of the years of your life?"

9 Jacob answered Pharaoh, "The days of the years of my sojourns have

---

7. וַיְבָרֶךְ יַעֲקֹב — *And Jacob blessed (Pharaoh).* But he did not bow down to him as he entered nor as he left.

8. כַּמָּה יְמֵי שְׁנֵי חַיֶּיךָ — *How many are the days of the years of your life?* This was asked wonderingly, such old age as Jacob reached being rare in Egypt. And (since) Jacob looked older than his years (the wonder was even greater).

NOTES

presented his brothers to Pharaoh in a manner that would convince the king that they are "only" simple shepherds.

8. כַּמָּה יְמֵי שְׁנֵי חַיֶּיךָ — *How many are the days of the years of your life?* Because of his many trials and tribulations, Jacob appeared older than his years. Egyptians were not accustomed to seeing very old people, for apparently their lifespan was comparatively brief. The word כַּמָּה is interpreted by some not as *how many,* but as a term of exclamation and wonder.

שְׁלֹשִׁים וּמְאַת שָׁנָה מְעַט וְרָעִים הָיוּ יְמֵי שְׁנֵי חַיַּי וְלֹא הִשִּׂיגוּ אֶת־יְמֵי שְׁנֵי
י חַיֵּי אֲבֹתַי בִּימֵי מְגוּרֵיהֶם: וַיְבָרֶךְ יַעֲקֹב אֶת־פַּרְעֹה וַיֵּצֵא מִלִּפְנֵי פַרְעֹה:
שביעי יא וַיּוֹשֵׁב יוֹסֵף אֶת־אָבִיו וְאֶת־אֶחָיו וַיִּתֵּן לָהֶם אֲחֻזָּה בְּאֶרֶץ מִצְרַיִם בְּמֵיטַב
יב הָאָרֶץ בְּאֶרֶץ רַעְמְסֵס כַּאֲשֶׁר צִוָּה פַרְעֹה: וַיְכַלְכֵּל יוֹסֵף אֶת־אָבִיו וְאֶת־
יג אֶחָיו וְאֵת כָּל־בֵּית אָבִיו לֶחֶם לְפִי הַטָּף: וְלֶחֶם אֵין בְּכָל־הָאָרֶץ כִּי־כָבֵד
יד הָרָעָב מְאֹד וַתֵּלַהּ אֶרֶץ מִצְרַיִם וְאֶרֶץ כְּנַעַן מִפְּנֵי הָרָעָב: וַיְלַקֵּט יוֹסֵף אֶת־
כָּל־הַכֶּסֶף הַנִּמְצָא בְאֶרֶץ־מִצְרַיִם וּבְאֶרֶץ כְּנַעַן בַּשֶּׁבֶר אֲשֶׁר־הֵם שֹׁבְרִים
טו וַיָּבֵא יוֹסֵף אֶת־הַכֶּסֶף בֵּיתָה פַרְעֹה: וַיִּתֹּם הַכֶּסֶף מֵאֶרֶץ מִצְרַיִם וּמֵאֶרֶץ
כְּנַעַן וַיָּבֹאוּ כָל־מִצְרַיִם אֶל־יוֹסֵף לֵאמֹר הָבָה־לָּנוּ לֶחֶם וְלָמָּה נָמוּת נֶגְדֶּךָ
טז כִּי אָפֵס כָּסֶף: וַיֹּאמֶר יוֹסֵף הָבוּ מִקְנֵיכֶם וְאֶתְּנָה לָכֶם בְּמִקְנֵיכֶם אִם־
יז אָפֵס כָּסֶף: וַיָּבִיאוּ אֶת־מִקְנֵיהֶם אֶל־יוֹסֵף וַיִּתֵּן לָהֶם יוֹסֵף לֶחֶם בַּסּוּסִים
וּבְמִקְנֵה הַצֹּאן וּבְמִקְנֵה הַבָּקָר וּבַחֲמֹרִים וַיְנַהֲלֵם בַּלֶּחֶם בְּכָל־מִקְנֵהֶם
יח בַּשָּׁנָה הַהִוא: וַתִּתֹּם הַשָּׁנָה הַהִוא וַיָּבֹאוּ אֵלָיו בַּשָּׁנָה הַשֵּׁנִית וַיֹּאמְרוּ לוֹ
לֹא־נְכַחֵד מֵאֲדֹנִי כִּי אִם־תַּם הַכֶּסֶף וּמִקְנֵה הַבְּהֵמָה אֶל־אֲדֹנִי לֹא נִשְׁאַר
יט לִפְנֵי אֲדֹנִי בִּלְתִּי אִם־גְּוִיָּתֵנוּ וְאַדְמָתֵנוּ: לָמָּה נָמוּת לְעֵינֶיךָ גַּם־אֲנַחְנוּ
גַּם־אַדְמָתֵנוּ קְנֵה־אֹתָנוּ וְאֶת־אַדְמָתֵנוּ בַּלָּחֶם וְנִהְיֶה אֲנַחְנוּ וְאַדְמָתֵנוּ

---

9. מְעַט וְרָעִים הָיוּ יְמֵי שְׁנֵי חַיַּי — *Few and evil have been the days of the years of my life.* In response to your question, "How many are the days, etc.", the days of these years are "few and evil," filled with worries of livelihood and many troubles. In that sense these cannot even be called שְׁנֵי חַיִּים, *years of life.* However in regard to יְמֵי שְׁנֵי מְגוּרַי, *the days of the years of my sojourning,* they are one hundred and thirty.

וְלֹא הִשִּׂיגוּ אֶת יְמֵי שְׁנֵי חַיֵּי אֲבֹתַי בִּימֵי מְגוּרֵיהֶם — *And they have not attained unto the days of the years of the life of my fathers in the days of their sojournings.* Although my fathers were also strangers in foreign lands, they enjoyed a longer trouble-free period of actual "living" than I have. And (also) the years of my life have not reached the years of my fathers' lives in the days in their sojournings.

12. לֶחֶם לְפִי הַטָּף — *Bread, according to the want of (their) little ones . . .* only according to their essential needs. Although Joseph could have provided them with much more (it would not be fitting to do so), as our Sages state, "When the community is in trouble let not a man say, 'I will go to my house and I will eat and drink and all will be well with me' " (*Taanis* 11a).

14. וַיָּבֵא יוֹסֵף אֶת הַכֶּסֶף בֵּיתָה פַּרְעֹה — *And Joseph brought the money into Pharaoh's house.* He did not permit himself anything, despite the justification he could have found (being the one upon whom the) entire burden (of sustaining the country) fell.

17. וַיְנַהֲלֵם בַּלֶּחֶם — *He fed them with bread.* He gently led them, similar to, עָלוֹת יְנַהֵל, *And*

NOTES

9. מְעַט וְרָעִים הָיוּ יְמֵי שְׁנֵי חַיַּי — *Few and evil have been the days of the years of my life.* Jacob differentiated between the quantitative and qualitative years of his life. The total period of his sojourn on earth was one hundred and thirty years. Those years, however, in which he experienced pleasure and contentment, were but few.

17-18. בַּשָּׁנָה הַהִוא . . . בַּשָּׁנָה הַשֵּׁנִית — *For that year . . . The second year.* Unlike *Rashi* who interprets the phrase *that year* as referring to the first year of the famine and interprets *the second year* literally, the *Sforno* is of the opinion that the Torah is not *resuming* the story of the famine in verse 13, but *continuing* it, hence *that year* refers to the sixth year of

been a hundred and thirty years. Few and bad have been the days of the years of my life, and they have not reached the life spans of my forefathers in the days of their sojourns." [10] *Then Jacob blessed Pharaoh, and left Pharaoh's presence.*

[11] *So Joseph settled his father and his brothers and he gave them a possession in the land of Egypt in the best part of the land, in the region of Rameses, as Pharaoh had commanded.* [12] *Joseph sustained his father and his brothers and all of his father's household with food according to the children.*

[13] *Now there was no bread in all the earth for the famine was very severe; the land of Egypt and the land of Canaan became weary from hunger.* [14] *Joseph gathered all the money that was to be found in the land of Egypt and in the land of Canaan through the provisions that they were purchasing, and Joseph brought the money into Pharaoh's palace.* [15] *And when the money was exhausted from the land of Egypt and from the land of Canaan, all the Egyptians came to Joseph, saying, "Give us bread; why should we die in your presence? — for the money is gone!"*

[16] *And Joseph said, "Bring your livestock and I will provide for you in return for your livestock if the money is gone."* [17] *So they brought their livestock to Joseph, and Joseph gave them bread in return for the horses, for the flocks of sheep, for the herds of cattle, and for the donkeys; thus he provided them with bread for all their livestock during that year.*

[18] *And when that year ended, they came to him in the next year and said to him, "We will not withhold from my lord that with the money and flocks of cattle having been exhausted to my lord, nothing is left before my lord but our bodies and our land.* [19] *Why should we die before your eyes, both we and our land? Acquire us and our land for bread; and we — with our land —*

---

gently lead the lambkin (*Isaiah* 40:11), i.e., he gave them bread in small quantities, so as not to overeat, since it is not proper to do so in a time of famine, as (our Sages) say, "He who starves himself in years of famine escapes unnatural death" (*Taanis* 11a). As the learned men of medicine have taught us, overeating after a period of hunger leads to fatal illnesses.

בַּשָּׁנָה הַהִוא — *For that year* . . . after the money ran out, which was the sixth year of the famine.

18. בַּשָּׁנָה הַשֵּׁנִית — *The second year* . . . the second year after the money gave out which was the seventh year of the famine.

לֹא נְכַחֵד מֵאֲדֹנִי — *We will not hide from my lord* . . . that we still have cattle.

19. לָמָּה נָמוּת לְעֵינֶיךָ — *Wherefore should we die before your eyes?* For even if it be true, that our money is all spent and our cattle are by now all yours, it would not be right for you to allow us to die from hunger.

NOTES

the famine, when the money ran out, and the *second year* means the second year after the money was spent, which was the seventh of the famine. The reason for *Rashi's* interpretation is based on the statement of our Sages that the famine ceased when Jacob arrived in Egypt. Hence the first and second years must refer to the first two of the seven, for the last five were suspended thanks to Jacob.

19. לָמָּה נָמוּת לְעֵינֶיךָ – *Wherefore should we die before your eyes?* The argument of the people was that even though it was true that they no longer had any money or cattle, and therefore they could no longer purchase bread or seed, nonetheless they pleaded with Joseph that since he was aware of their circumstances, how could he permit them to perish?

כ עֲבָדִים לְפַרְעֹה וְתֶן־זֶרַע וְנִחְיֶה וְלֹא נָמוּת וְהָאֲדָמָה לֹא תֵשָׁם: וַיִּקֶן יוֹסֵף
אֶת־כָּל־אַדְמַת מִצְרַיִם לְפַרְעֹה כִּי־מָכְרוּ מִצְרַיִם אִישׁ שָׂדֵהוּ כִּי־חָזַק
כא עֲלֵהֶם הָרָעָב וַתְּהִי הָאָרֶץ לְפַרְעֹה: וְאֶת־הָעָם הֶעֱבִיר אֹתוֹ לֶעָרִים מִקְצֵה
כב גְבוּל־מִצְרַיִם וְעַד־קָצֵהוּ: רַק אַדְמַת הַכֹּהֲנִים לֹא קָנָה כִּי חֹק לַכֹּהֲנִים
מֵאֵת פַּרְעֹה וְאָכְלוּ אֶת־חֻקָּם אֲשֶׁר נָתַן לָהֶם פַּרְעֹה עַל־כֵּן לֹא מָכְרוּ
כג אֶת־אַדְמָתָם: וַיֹּאמֶר יוֹסֵף אֶל־הָעָם הֵן קָנִיתִי אֶתְכֶם הַיּוֹם וְאֶת־
כד אַדְמַתְכֶם לְפַרְעֹה הֵא־לָכֶם זֶרַע וּזְרַעְתֶּם אֶת־הָאֲדָמָה: וְהָיָה בַּתְּבוּאֹת
וּנְתַתֶּם חֲמִישִׁית לְפַרְעֹה וְאַרְבַּע הַיָּדֹת יִהְיֶה לָכֶם לְזֶרַע הַשָּׂדֶה
מפטיר כה וּלְאָכְלְכֶם וְלַאֲשֶׁר בְּבָתֵּיכֶם וְלֶאֱכֹל לְטַפְּכֶם: וַיֹּאמְרוּ הֶחֱיִתָנוּ נִמְצָא־חֵן
כו בְּעֵינֵי אֲדֹנִי וְהָיִינוּ עֲבָדִים לְפַרְעֹה: וַיָּשֶׂם אֹתָהּ יוֹסֵף לְחֹק עַד־הַיּוֹם הַזֶּה
עַל־אַדְמַת מִצְרַיִם לְפַרְעֹה לַחֹמֶשׁ רַק אַדְמַת הַכֹּהֲנִים לְבַדָּם לֹא הָיְתָה
כז לְפַרְעֹה: וַיֵּשֶׁב יִשְׂרָאֵל בְּאֶרֶץ מִצְרַיִם בְּאֶרֶץ גֹּשֶׁן וַיֵּאָחֲזוּ בָהּ וַיִּפְרוּ וַיִּרְבּוּ
מְאֹד:

21. הֶעֱבִיר אֹתוֹ לֶעָרִים — *He removed them city by city.* (Joseph) brought them with him to each parcel of land (so as to take legal possession on behalf of Pharaoh of the אַדְמַת מִצְרַיִם, *the land of Egypt* — v. 20) in their presence, with their acquiescence. He had them state explicitly, "לֵךְ חֲזֵק וּקְנֵי, *Go and perform an act of acquisition.*"

23. הֵן קָנִיתִי אֶתְכֶם הַיּוֹם וְאֶת אַדְמַתְכֶם לְפַרְעֹה — *Behold I have bought you this day and your land for Pharaoh* ... and therefore you are his bondmen and as such obligated to work the land. He in turn is responsible for your food and for seed to sow the land. Thus, according to law, all the produce will belong to Pharaoh.

הֵא לָכֶם זֶרַע וּזְרַעְתֶּם — *Here is seed for you, and you shall sow.* You are his bondmen, work ...

אֶת הָאֲדָמָה — *The land* ... which belongs to him (Pharaoh).

NOTES

21. הֶעֱבִיר אֹתוֹ לֶעָרִים — *He removed them city by city.* The *Sforno* explaines why it was necessary to bring the people with him in order to take possession of the land on behalf of Pharaoh. According to law, the transfer of land is executed by having the owner state publicly and openly to the purchaser, "לֵךְ חֲזֵק וּקְנֵי, *Go and perform an act of acquisition,*" and thereby you will take legal possession of this land. Joseph was determined that there be no irregularities in this transfer, or any question of illegality; hence he insisted that they go with him from city to city to finalize the sale.

23-24. הֵן קָנִיתִי אֶתְכֶם הַיּוֹם ... וּנְתַתֶּם חֲמִישִׁית לְפַרְעֹה וְאַרְבַּע הַיָּדֹת יִהְיֶה לָכֶם — *Behold I have bought you this day ... You shall give a fifth to Pharaoh and four parts shall be your own.* Joseph clearly and explicitly explained to the people the consequences

will become serfs to Pharaoh; and provide seed so that we may live and not die, and the land will not become desolate."

20 *Thus Joseph acquired all the land of Egypt for Pharaoh, for every Egyptian sold his field because the famine had overwhelmed them; and the land became Pharaoh's.*
21 *As for the nation, he resettled it by cities, from one end of Egypt's borders to the other.*
22 *Only the land of the priests he did not buy, since the priests had a stipend from Pharaoh, and they lived off their stipend that Pharaoh had given them; therefore they did not sell their land.*

23 *Joseph said to the people, "Look — I have acquired you this day with your land for Pharaoh; here is seed for you — sow the land.*
24 *At the ingathering of the harvests you will give a fifth to Pharaoh; the [other] four parts shall be yours — as seed for the field, and food for yourselves and for those in your household, and to feed your young ones."*

25 *And they said, "You have saved our lives; may we find favor in your eyes, my lord, and we will be serfs to Pharaoh."*

26 *So Joseph imposed it as a statute till this day regarding the land of Egypt: It was Pharaoh's for the fifth; only the priests' land alone did not become Pharaoh's.*

27 *Thus Israel settled in the land of Egypt in the region of Goshen; they acquired property in it and they were fruitful and multiplied greatly.*

---

24. וְהָיָה בַּתְּבוּאֹת — *And it shall come to pass at the ingathering ...* which is also his.

וּנְתַתֶּם חֲמִישִׁית לְפַרְעֹה — *You shall give a fifth to Pharaoh ...* because it is due to him, after he will have given you all that he is obligated to give.

וְאַרְבַּע הַיָּדֹת יִהְיֶה לָכֶם לְזֶרַע הַשָּׂדֶה — *And four parts shall be your own for seed of the field ...* which he is obligated to give to you as owner of the field.

וּלְאָכְלְכֶם — *And for your food ...* which he is also obligated to give to you. And so the law remained, that a fifth belongs to Pharaoh.

26. וַיָּשֶׂם אֹתָהּ יוֹסֵף לְחֹק — *And Joseph made it a statute.* After Joseph convinced (the populace) that this law was just, and not a new extortionist tax, it was entered into the legal code of Egypt.

NOTES

of their transferral of land to Pharaoh. From this time forward, Pharaoh was to be the legal owner not only of their land, but of themselves as well. They were obligated to work the fields on his behalf as he in turn was obligated to provide them with seed. They were entitled to four-fifths of the produce while Pharaoh would receive one-fifth.

26. וַיָּשֶׂם אֹתָהּ יוֹסֵף לְחֹק — *And Joseph made it a statute.* Joseph was not only careful to arrange the transferral of the land properly, as well as the sharecropper agreement between the people and Pharaoh, but he was also anxious that the people realize the voluntary nature of this transaction and arrangement. He felt that it was important not to perceive this plan as a harshly imposed exorbitant tax. Only then did he enter this arrangement into the legal code of Egypt.

פרשת ויחי

כח וַיְחִי יַעֲקֹב בְּאֶרֶץ מִצְרַיִם שְׁבַע עֶשְׂרֵה שָׁנָה וַיְהִי יְמֵי־יַעֲקֹב שְׁנֵי חַיָּיו שֶׁבַע
כט שָׁנִים וְאַרְבָּעִים וּמְאַת שָׁנָה: וַיִּקְרְבוּ יְמֵי־יִשְׂרָאֵל לָמוּת וַיִּקְרָא ׀ לִבְנוֹ
לְיוֹסֵף וַיֹּאמֶר לוֹ אִם־נָא מָצָאתִי חֵן בְּעֵינֶיךָ שִׂים־נָא יָדְךָ תַּחַת יְרֵכִי
ל וְעָשִׂיתָ עִמָּדִי חֶסֶד וֶאֱמֶת אַל־נָא תִקְבְּרֵנִי בְּמִצְרָיִם: וְשָׁכַבְתִּי עִם־אֲבֹתַי
וּנְשָׂאתַנִי מִמִּצְרַיִם וּקְבַרְתַּנִי בִּקְבֻרָתָם וַיֹּאמַר אָנֹכִי אֶעֱשֶׂה כִדְבָרֶךָ:
לא וַיֹּאמֶר הִשָּׁבְעָה לִי וַיִּשָּׁבַע לוֹ וַיִּשְׁתַּחוּ יִשְׂרָאֵל עַל־רֹאשׁ הַמִּטָּה:
מח א וַיְהִי אַחֲרֵי הַדְּבָרִים הָאֵלֶּה וַיֹּאמֶר לְיוֹסֵף הִנֵּה אָבִיךָ חֹלֶה וַיִּקַּח אֶת־שְׁנֵי
ב בָנָיו עִמּוֹ אֶת־מְנַשֶּׁה וְאֶת־אֶפְרָיִם: וַיַּגֵּד לְיַעֲקֹב וַיֹּאמֶר הִנֵּה בִּנְךָ יוֹסֵף
ג בָּא אֵלֶיךָ וַיִּתְחַזֵּק יִשְׂרָאֵל וַיֵּשֶׁב עַל־הַמִּטָּה: וַיֹּאמֶר יַעֲקֹב אֶל־יוֹסֵף אֵל
ד שַׁדַּי נִרְאָה־אֵלַי בְּלוּז בְּאֶרֶץ כְּנָעַן וַיְבָרֶךְ אֹתִי: וַיֹּאמֶר אֵלַי הִנְנִי מַפְרְךָ
וְהִרְבִּיתִךָ וּנְתַתִּיךָ לִקְהַל עַמִּים וְנָתַתִּי אֶת־הָאָרֶץ הַזֹּאת לְזַרְעֲךָ אַחֲרֶיךָ
ה אֲחֻזַּת עוֹלָם: וְעַתָּה שְׁנֵי־בָנֶיךָ הַנּוֹלָדִים לְךָ בְּאֶרֶץ מִצְרַיִם עַד־בֹּאִי אֵלֶיךָ

29. אַל נָא תִקְבְּרֵנִי בְּמִצְרָיִם — *Please do not bury me in Egypt.* Even in a coffin, similar to, *and he was put in a coffin in Egypt* (50:26), for if you will do so, even temporarily, they will not allow you to carry (my body) for (burial) in the cave (of Machpelah), for they will say that this (placing in the coffin) is sufficient considering that this was their custom.

30. וְשָׁכַבְתִּי עִם אֲבֹתַי — *When I will lie with my fathers.* The meaning of this phrase is the placing of the deceased on a bier for the purpose of eulogy. This phrase is therefore used in the Book of *Kings* regarding all kings, be they righteous or wicked, who died on their beds.

וּנְשָׂאתַנִי מִמִּצְרַיִם — *And you shall carry me out of Egypt.* If you will do this you will be permitted to carry me out of Egypt, for once the days of eulogy are completed the grief will subside, as we find, *And when the days of weeping for him were past* (50:4), and they will not prevent my body from being carried elsewhere.

אָנֹכִי אֶעֱשֶׂה כִדְבָרֶךָ — *I will do as you have said.* As far as I am concerned, I will do as you say with all my power.

31. הִשָּׁבְעָה לִי — *Swear unto me* . . . so that you will have a valid, strong excuse (to do as I ask) in case Pharaoh decides to forbid it.

וַיִּשְׁתַּחוּ יִשְׂרָאֵל — *And Israel bowed down* . . . in gratitude to God, that he was privileged to have this wish granted by his son, similar to, *And it came to pass when Abraham's servant heard their words, he bowed down to the earth unto God* (24:52).

NOTES

29. אַל נָא תִקְבְּרֵנִי בְּמִצְרָיִם – *Please do not bury me in Egypt.* Since the custom of the Egyptians was to inter royalty in a coffin and not to bury them in the ground, Jacob was afraid that once he would be placed in a coffin, the Egyptians, who considered him as king, would consider this act as one of permanent burial and not permit Joseph to transport his father to the Land of Canaan. He therefore asked his son not to place him into a coffin at all, but to transport his body directly to the Cave of Machpelah. Thus the phrase *do not bury me in Egypt* does not refer to interment in the earth of Egypt but to his being placed in a coffin in accordance with Egyptian custom.

30. וְשָׁכַבְתִּי עִם אֲבֹתַי — *When I will lie with my fathers.* The expression used by Jacob וְשָׁכַבְתִּי עִם אֲבֹתַי, *when I will lie with my fathers,* is interpreted by the *Sforno* as referring to the custom called אַשְׁכָּבָה, when the deceased would lie in state for a period of time, be eulogized and then interred. A similar expression is found in Scripture regarding the kings of Israel, וַיִּשְׁכַּב עִם אֲבֹתָיו, *and he did lie (slept) with his fathers* (*I Kings* 2:10) which also refers to אַשְׁכָּבָה. There is, however, another explanation for the expression *and he slept with his fathers*, meaning that one's soul returns to the abode of his ancestors in *Gan Eden* (Paradise). The former interpretation is applicable to all kings, be they

PARASHAS VAYECHI

28 *Jacob lived in the land of Egypt seventeen years; and the days of Jacob — the years of his life — were one hundred and forty-seven years.* 29 *The time approached for Israel to die, so he called for his son, for Joseph, and said to him, "Please — if I have found favor in your eyes, please place your hand under my thigh and do kindness and truth with me — please do not bury me in Egypt.* 30 *For I will lie down with my fathers and you shall transport me out of Egypt and bury me in their tomb."*

He said, "I personally will do as you have said."

31 *He replied, "Swear to me," and he swore to him; then Israel prostrated himself towards the head of the bed.*

48

1 *And it came to pass after these things that someone said to Joseph, "Behold! — your father is ill." So he took his two sons, Manasseh and Ephraim, with him.*

2 *Jacob was told, "Behold! — your son Joseph has come to you." So Israel exerted himself and sat up on the bed.*

3 *Jacob said to Joseph, "El Shaddai had appeared to me in Luz in the land of Canaan and He blessed me.* 4 *He said to me, 'Behold — I will make you fruitful and numerous; I will make you a congregation of nations, and I will give this land to your offspring after you as an eternal possession.'* 5 *And now, your two sons who were born to you in Egypt before my coming to you*

XLVIII

2. וַיֵּשֶׁב עַל הַמִּטָּה — *And sat upon the bed* ... to pay homage to Joseph's royal position, to the extent of his physical ability; we find the reverse (by Mordechai who refused to pay homage to Haman), וְלֹא קָם וְלֹא זָע מִמֶּנּוּ, *He stood not up nor moved for him (Esther* 5:9).

4. וּנְתַתִּיךָ לִקְהַל עַמִּים וְנָתַתִּי אֶת הָאָרֶץ — *I will make of you a company of peoples; and will give this Land (to your seed).* At the time this promise was made by God (35:11), all the tribes, save Benjamin, had been born, and since the promise of *the Land whereon you lie, to you will I give it, and to your seed* (28:13) was already made (when I left for Haran), the promise made (in Luz, upon my return) regarding a קְהַל עַמִּים, *a company of people,* had to refer to the inheritance of the Land. This in turn could only mean you and your sons, for you were all given to me together.

5. וְעַתָּה שְׁנֵי בָנֶיךָ הַנּוֹלָדִים לְךָ ... לִי הֵם — *And now your two sons who were born unto you (in Egypt) ... are mine.* For they alone were given to me, together with you, as we read, *I had not thought to see your face, and lo, God has let me see your seed also* (verse 11).

NOTES

righteous or wicked, while the latter only applies to righteous ones. In general the custom of lying in state was only practiced when the king died on his bed, not if he fell in battle or was assassinated.

31. הִשָּׁבְעָה לִי — *Swear unto me.* Jacob certainly trusted Joseph and his word was sufficient without any need to swear. The oath was given only for the purpose of being used by him in case Pharaoh would try to create difficulties. Indeed this proved to be of great importance, as we see later, *And Pharaoh said, "Go up and bury your father, as he made you swear"* (50:6).

וַיִּשְׁתַּחוּ יִשְׂרָאֵל — *And Israel bowed down.* Unlike other commentators who interpret the object of the phrase *and Israel bowed down* as referring to Joseph, the *Sforno* rejects this as being unfitting and interprets it to mean, "to God," bringing proof from Eliezer the servant of Abraham.

XLVIII

4-5. וּנְתַתִּיךָ לִקְהַל עַמִּים ... הַנּוֹלָדִים לְךָ ... לִי הֵם — *I will make of you a company of peoples ... who were born unto you ... are mine.* The terminology used by God when He speaks to Jacob upon his

ו מִצְרַיְמָה לִי־הֵם אֶפְרַיִם וּמְנַשֶּׁה כִּרְאוּבֵן וְשִׁמְעוֹן יִהְיוּ־לִי׃ וּמוֹלַדְתְּךָ
ז אֲשֶׁר־הוֹלַדְתָּ אַחֲרֵיהֶם לְךָ יִהְיוּ עַל שֵׁם אֲחֵיהֶם יִקָּרְאוּ בְּנַחֲלָתָם׃ וַאֲנִי ׀
בְּבֹאִי מִפַּדָּן מֵתָה עָלַי רָחֵל בְּאֶרֶץ כְּנַעַן בַּדֶּרֶךְ בְּעוֹד כִּבְרַת־אֶרֶץ לָבֹא
ח אֶפְרָתָה וָאֶקְבְּרֶהָ שָּׁם בְּדֶרֶךְ אֶפְרָת הִוא בֵּית לָחֶם׃ וַיַּרְא יִשְׂרָאֵל אֶת־
ט בְּנֵי יוֹסֵף וַיֹּאמֶר מִי־אֵלֶּה׃ וַיֹּאמֶר יוֹסֵף אֶל־אָבִיו בָּנַי הֵם אֲשֶׁר־נָתַן־לִי
י אֱלֹהִים בָּזֶה וַיֹּאמַר קָחֶם־נָא אֵלַי וַאֲבָרְכֵם׃ וְעֵינֵי יִשְׂרָאֵל כָּבְדוּ מִזֹּקֶן שני
יא לֹא יוּכַל לִרְאוֹת וַיַּגֵּשׁ אֹתָם אֵלָיו וַיִּשַּׁק לָהֶם וַיְחַבֵּק לָהֶם׃ וַיֹּאמֶר
יִשְׂרָאֵל אֶל־יוֹסֵף רְאֹה פָנֶיךָ לֹא פִלָּלְתִּי וְהִנֵּה הֶרְאָה אֹתִי אֱלֹהִים
יב גַּם אֶת־זַרְעֶךָ׃ וַיּוֹצֵא יוֹסֵף אֹתָם מֵעִם בִּרְכָּיו וַיִּשְׁתַּחוּ לְאַפָּיו אָרְצָה׃

6. וּמוֹלַדְתְּךָ אֲשֶׁר הוֹלַדְתָּ אַחֲרֵיהֶם — *And your issue which you begot after them . . .* namely, your grandchildren, who are properly called מוֹלַדְתְּךָ, *your issue.*

לְךָ יִהְיוּ — *Shall be yours.* They will be called "the house of Joseph" and be blessed with your blessings.

עַל שֵׁם אֲחֵיהֶם יִקָּרְאוּ בְּנַחֲלָתָם — *They shall be called after the name of their brethren in their inheritance.* The children of Menasseh will be called, each one like his brother, after the name of Menasseh to inherit with them in his share (of the Land) and so also each son of Ephraim will be considered (lit., "called") as his brother after the name of Ephraim to inherit together the share (in the Land) of Ephraim.

7. וַאֲנִי — *And as for me.* Do not think that when God said to me, "*I will make of you a company of peoples,*" the intent was that I would have more children, but my sins denied me (this privilege); this is not so, for . . .

בְּבֹאִי מִפַּדָּן — *When I came from Paddan . . .* and God appeared to me at that time.

מֵתָה עָלַי רָחֵל — *Rachel died unto me.* As our Sages say, אֵין אִשָּׁה מֵתָה אֶלָּא לְבַעְלָהּ, *The death of a woman is felt only by her husband (Sanhedrin 22b).*

בַּדֶּרֶךְ בְּעוֹד כִּבְרַת אֶרֶץ לָבֹא אֶפְרָתָה — *On the way, when there was still some way to come to Ephrath . . .* immediately, when I traveled from that place where God spoke to me and was still en route, before I came to Bethlehem.

וָאֶקְבְּרֶהָ שָּׁם בְּדֶרֶךְ אֶפְרָת — *And I buried her there in the way to Ephrath.* So intense was my grief that I had not the strength even to carry her to the cemetery in Bethlehem. From that moment on, all physical desire left me, and I no longer cohabited (with my wives).

NOTES

return from Paddan-aram is, *I am God Almighty . . . a nation and a company of nations shall be from you . . . and the Land . . . to you I will give it and to your seed* (35:11,12). The phrase *nation* refers to Benjamin, while the phrase *company of nations* alludes to Menasseh and Ephraim as Jacob understands it, for since Joseph was presumed dead by Jacob and now he is "returned to life" together with his sons as one, Jacob considers them as *his,* hence entitled to inherit equal portions in the land.

6. לְךָ יִהְיוּ עַל שֵׁם אֲחֵיהֶם יִקָּרְאוּ — *Shall be yours; they shall be called after the name of their brethren.* The wording in this verse presents certain difficulties. First Jacob says to Joseph, לְךָ יִהְיוּ, *shall be yours,* then he says they shall be called *after the name of their brethren.* The *Sforno* interprets the phrase וּמוֹלַדְתְּךָ, *and your issue,* as referring to his grandchildren, who will be called *the house of Joseph,* which explains *shall be yours,* but insofar as inheritance of the land is concerned they will only share in the portion already allocated to Menasseh and Ephraim.

7. מֵתָה עָלַי רָחֵל . . . וָאֶקְבְּרֶהָ שָּׁם — *Rachel died unto me . . . And I buried her there.* Jacob presents his case to Joseph so as to reassure him that the double portion granted to him is in keeping with God's promise regarding *a company of peoples.* He asserts that it could not have alluded to Jacob's own children, still unborn, since that particular revelation of God was followed immediately by the death of Rachel, which affected Jacob so profoundly that he no longer had marital relations; hence the

*in Egypt shall be mine; Ephraim and Manasseh shall be mine like Reuben
and Simeon.* 6 *But progeny born to you after them shall be yours; they will be
included under the name of their brothers with regard to their inheritance.* 7 *But as for me — when I came from Paddan, Rachel died on me in the
land of Canaan on the road, while there was still a stretch of land to go to
Ephrath; and I buried her there on the road to Ephrath, which is Bethlehem."*
8 *Then Israel saw Joseph's sons and he said, "Who are these?"*
9 *And Joseph said to his father, "They are my sons whom God has given
me here."*

He said, "Bring them to me, if you please, and I will bless them."
10 *Now Israel's eyes were heavy with age, he could not see; so he brought
them near him and he kissed them and hugged them.* 11 *Israel said to Joseph,
"I dared not accept the thought that I would see your face, and here God has
shown me even your offspring!"*
12 *Joseph then removed them from his knees and he prostrated himself
with his face toward the ground.*

---

8. וַיַּרְא יִשְׂרָאֵל אֶת בְּנֵי יוֹסֵף — *And Israel beheld Joseph's sons.* (His sight was good enough) to distinguish people but not to identify them.

9. בָּנַי הֵם אֲשֶׁר נָתַן לִי אֱלֹהִים בָּזֶה — *They are my sons whom God has given me here.* They are my sons, not my grandsons. They are those sons which God had given me while I was here alone (before your arrival, thereby meeting your condition of) *who were born unto you in Egypt before I came to you* (verse 5); (hence they are included in) your statement of לִי הֵם, *are mine.*

10. לֹא יוּכַל לִרְאוֹת — *So that he could not see.* He could not see them clearly, which was an impediment for his blessing to be effective; similar to, אֲשֶׁר תִּרְאֶנּוּ מִשָּׁם, *From whence you may see them (Numbers* 23:13), and to, וַיַּרְאֵהוּ ה׳ אֶת כָּל הָאָרֶץ, *And God showed him all the Land (Deut.* 34:1), so that (Moses) might bless it. Also we find by Elisha, וַיִּפֶן אַחֲרָיו וַיִּרְאֵם, *He looked behind him and saw them (II Kings* 2:24).

וַיִּשַּׁק לָהֶם וַיְחַבֵּק לָהֶם — *And he kissed them and embraced them* . . . so that his soul might cleave to them and his blessing take effect.

11. גַּם אֶת זַרְעֶךָ — *Your seed also* . . . and regarding them it is said קְהַל עַמִּים, *a company of peoples* (verse 4). Now this (blessing) was given in conjunction with the inheritance of the land, as it states above וַיְבָרֶךְ אוֹתִי, *(God) blessed me* (verse 3), therefore it is fitting that that blessing be given to them (and to Joseph) so (Jacob) blessed both Joseph and his sons (see verses 15-16).

12. מֵעִם בִּרְכָּיו — *From between his knees* . . . the knees of his father who was embracing them.

NOTES

company of peoples could only be fulfilled through one of his sons, namely, Joseph.

9. בָּנַי הֵם אֲשֶׁר נָתַן לִי אֱלֹהִים בָּזֶה – *They are my sons whom God has given me here.* Jacob had differentiated between those children born to Joseph before he came to Egypt, as well as any grandchildren of Joseph born afterwards. They would not be eligible to be considered as one of the tribes of Israel — as are Menasseh and Ephraim. Therefore when Jacob asks who these young men are, Joseph stresses that they are indeed his sons and qualify to receive a special blessing.

10. לֹא יוּכַל לִרְאוֹת – *So that he could not see.* The phrase *he could not see* in this verse cannot refer to his inability to recognize them, since their identity had already been established in the previous verse. Therefore the *Sforno* interprets it to mean that Jacob could not "connect" and relate to them through seeing, so he had to feel and touch them in order to have the blessing flow from him to the lads.

11. גַּם אֶת זַרְעֶךָ – *Your seed also.* See commentary and notes on verse 4.

יג וַיִּקַּח יוֹסֵף אֶת־שְׁנֵיהֶם אֶת־אֶפְרַיִם בִּימִינוֹ מִשְּׂמֹאל יִשְׂרָאֵל וְאֶת־מְנַשֶּׁה
יד בִשְׂמֹאלוֹ מִימִין יִשְׂרָאֵל וַיַּגֵּשׁ אֵלָיו: וַיִּשְׁלַח יִשְׂרָאֵל אֶת־יְמִינוֹ וַיָּשֶׁת
עַל־רֹאשׁ אֶפְרַיִם וְהוּא הַצָּעִיר וְאֶת־שְׂמֹאלוֹ עַל־רֹאשׁ מְנַשֶּׁה שִׂכֵּל
טו אֶת־יָדָיו כִּי מְנַשֶּׁה הַבְּכוֹר: וַיְבָרֶךְ אֶת־יוֹסֵף וַיֹּאמַר הָאֱלֹהִים אֲשֶׁר
הִתְהַלְּכוּ אֲבֹתַי לְפָנָיו אַבְרָהָם וְיִצְחָק הָאֱלֹהִים הָרֹעֶה אֹתִי
טז מֵעוֹדִי עַד־הַיּוֹם הַזֶּה: הַמַּלְאָךְ הַגֹּאֵל אֹתִי מִכָּל־רָע יְבָרֵךְ אֶת־הַנְּעָרִים
וְיִקָּרֵא בָהֶם שְׁמִי וְשֵׁם אֲבֹתַי אַבְרָהָם וְיִצְחָק וְיִדְגּוּ לָרֹב בְּקֶרֶב הָאָרֶץ:
שלישי יז וַיַּרְא יוֹסֵף כִּי־יָשִׁית אָבִיו יַד־יְמִינוֹ עַל־רֹאשׁ אֶפְרַיִם וַיֵּרַע בְּעֵינָיו
וַיִּתְמֹךְ יַד־אָבִיו לְהָסִיר אֹתָהּ מֵעַל רֹאשׁ־אֶפְרַיִם עַל־רֹאשׁ מְנַשֶּׁה:
יח וַיֹּאמֶר יוֹסֵף אֶל־אָבִיו לֹא־כֵן אָבִי כִּי־זֶה הַבְּכֹר שִׂים יְמִינְךָ עַל־רֹאשׁוֹ:
יט וַיְמָאֵן אָבִיו וַיֹּאמֶר יָדַעְתִּי בְנִי יָדַעְתִּי גַּם־הוּא יִהְיֶה־לְּעָם וְגַם־הוּא יִגְדָּל
כ וְאוּלָם אָחִיו הַקָּטֹן יִגְדַּל מִמֶּנּוּ וְזַרְעוֹ יִהְיֶה מְלֹא־הַגּוֹיִם: וַיְבָרְכֵם בַּיּוֹם
הַהוּא *לֵאמוֹר בְּךָ יְבָרֵךְ יִשְׂרָאֵל לֵאמֹר יְשִׂמְךָ אֱלֹהִים כְּאֶפְרַיִם
כא וְכִמְנַשֶּׁה וַיָּשֶׂם אֶת־אֶפְרַיִם לִפְנֵי מְנַשֶּׁה: וַיֹּאמֶר יִשְׂרָאֵל אֶל־יוֹסֵף הִנֵּה
כב אָנֹכִי מֵת וְהָיָה אֱלֹהִים עִמָּכֶם וְהֵשִׁיב אֶתְכֶם אֶל־אֶרֶץ אֲבֹתֵיכֶם: וַאֲנִי

14. שִׂכֵּל אֶת יָדָיו — *Guiding his hands wittingly*. He detected (their identity) through the sense of feeling, though he could not see.

15. וַיְבָרֶךְ אֶת יוֹסֵף — *And he blessed Joseph.* For this blessing (i.e., Joseph's) he did not have to see, kiss or embrace him. The Torah does not tell us what the blessing was.

וַיֹּאמַר — *And he said* ... after he blessed Joseph.

הָאֱלֹהִים אֲשֶׁר הִתְהַלְּכוּ אֲבֹתַי לְפָנָיו — *"The God before Whom my forefathers walked."* O God, in the merit of my forefathers who walked before You (bless them).

הָאֱלֹהִים הָרֹעֶה אֹתִי — *The God Who has been my shepherd.* You, Who always showed me kindness (bless them).

16. הַמַּלְאָךְ הַגֹּאֵל אֹתִי מִכָּל רָע יְבָרֵךְ — *The angel who has redeemed me from all evil, bless (the lads).* (O God,) do order *the angel who has redeemed me* to bless the lads, if they do not deserve to be blessed directly by You, without an intermediary.

וְיִקָּרֵא בָהֶם שְׁמִי וְשֵׁם אֲבֹתַי אַבְרָהָם וְיִצְחָק — *And let my name be named in them and the name of my forefathers Abraham and Isaac* ... but not Terach or Nachor, because righteous men are not called by their fathers' names when these are wicked, nor vice versa, as our Sages say, "A wicked man is called the son of a wicked man, even if he is actually the son of a righteous man" (*Sanhedrin* 52a), so that (this רָשָׁע) not be called by his righteous

NOTES

15. וַיְבָרֶךְ אֶת יוֹסֵף וַיֹּאמַר הָאֱלֹהִים ... — *And he blessed Joseph and he said, "The God..."* Since Jacob was linked to his son Joseph over the years with a profound and abiding love, there was no need, as there was with his grandchildren, to make physical contact with him before he blessed him. The *Sforno* is of the opinion that the phrase וַיְבָרֶךְ אֶת יוֹסֵף, *and he blessed Joseph*, is not connected to the וַיֹּאמַר, *and he said*, which follows, rather this word (וַיֹּאמַר) introduces the following phrase, *O God, etc.* The two expressions used by Jacob, i.e., *The God before Whom my forefathers walked* and *The God Who has been my shepherd*, are not redundant. The first is a request to consider the merits of his forefathers, therefore it is an earned reward he is asking for, whereas the second is in reference to himself which he acknowledges, with due modesty, is unearned, for God was his shepherd only out of kindness.

16. הַמַּלְאָךְ הַגֹּאֵל אֹתִי ... וְיִקָּרֵא בָהֶם שְׁמִי וְשֵׁם אֲבֹתַי — *The angel who has redeemed me ... And let my name be named in them and the name of my forefathers.* First Jacob asks God to bless his grand-

13 *Joseph took the two of them — Ephraim with his right [hand], to Israel's
left, and Manasseh with his left, to Israel's right — and he drew close to him.*
14 *But Israel extended his right hand and laid it on Ephraim's head though he
was the younger and his left hand on Manasseh's head. He maneuvered his
hands, for Manasseh was the firstborn.* 15 *He blessed Joseph and he said, "O
God before Whom my forefathers Abraham and Isaac walked — God Who
shepherds me from my inception until this day:* 16 *May the angel who
redeems me from all evil bless the lads, and may my name be declared upon
them, and the names of my forefathers Abraham and Isaac, and may they
proliferate abundantly like fish within the land."*

17 *Joseph saw that his father was placing his right hand on Ephraim's
head and it displeased him; so he supported his father's hand to remove it
from upon Ephraim's head to Manasseh's head.* 18 *And Joseph said to his
father, "Not so, Father, for this is the firstborn; place your right hand on his
head."*

19 *But his father refused, saying, "I know, my son, I know; he too will
become a people, and he too will become great; yet his younger brother shall
become greater than he, and his offspring['s fame] will fill the nations."* 20 *So
he blessed them that day, saying, "By you shall Israel bless saying, 'May
God make you like Ephraim and like Manasseh' " — and he put Ephraim
before Manasseh.*

21 *Then Israel said to Joseph, "Behold! — I am about to die; God will be
with you and will bring you back to the land of your fathers.* 22 *And as for me,*

---

father's name but be traced back to some wicked forebear. Hence his blessing was a prayer that they might be prepared to serve the Almighty so that they will be worthy to be called after Abraham and Isaac, in keeping with (the expression), יַחֵד לְבָבִי לְיִרְאָה שְׁמֶךָ, *Make one my heart, to fear Your name (Psalms* 86:11).

18. כִּי זֶה הַבְּכֹר שִׂים יְמִינְךָ עַל רֹאשׁוֹ — *For this is the firstborn; put your right hand upon his head.* Placing one's hand upon (the head) of the recipient of a blessing (or a charge) concentrates the thoughts and intent of the "giver" to the recipient, similar to, וַיִּסְמֹךְ אֶת יָדָיו עָלָיו, *And he laid his hands upon him (Numbers* 27:23). The power of the right hand is greater than the left, and it is (also) more effective to place the right hand on the right side, more so than the left hand on the left side.

21. הִנֵּה אָנֹכִי מֵת — *Behold I die.* I instruct you at the time of death, thereby confirming the gift I give to you.

וְהֵשִׁיב אֶתְכֶם אֶל אֶרֶץ — *And (He) will bring you back unto the Land . . .* and there my gift will become a reality (fulfilled).

NOTES

children *directly*, and if that be excessive, let it be through his guardian angel. Jacob prays that Ephraim and Menasseh be worthy, through their own piety, to be called after Abraham and Isaac. Even though our Sages have taught us that "fear of Heaven" cannot be granted by God, but must be formed and developed by the person on his own, nevertheless one *can* pray that the Almighty should assist him to withstand temptation and cleave to Him. To support this concept the *Sforno* correctly quotes David who also asks the assistance of God in bringing him to the level of יִרְאָה, *reverence* for God.

21. הִנֵּה אָנֹכִי מֵת — *Behold I die.* The *halachah* is that a person on his death bed (שְׁכִיב מְרַע) can effect a legal transfer by making a statement without the need for an act of selling or giving; nor must it be put in writing. That is why Jacob stresses that he is about to die, and as a שְׁכִיב מְרַע his gift of Shechem to Joseph is valid.

נָתַתִּי לְךָ שְׁכֶם אַחַד עַל־אַחֶיךָ אֲשֶׁר לָקַחְתִּי מִיַּד הָאֱמֹרִי בְּחַרְבִּי וּבְקַשְׁתִּי׃

מט

א וַיִּקְרָא יַעֲקֹב אֶל־בָּנָיו וַיֹּאמֶר הֵאָסְפוּ וְאַגִּידָה לָכֶם אֵת אֲשֶׁר־יִקְרָא אֶתְכֶם

ב בְּאַחֲרִית הַיָּמִים׃ הִקָּבְצוּ וְשִׁמְעוּ בְּנֵי יַעֲקֹב וְשִׁמְעוּ אֶל־יִשְׂרָאֵל אֲבִיכֶם׃

ג־ד רְאוּבֵן בְּכֹרִי אַתָּה כֹּחִי וְרֵאשִׁית אוֹנִי יֶתֶר שְׂאֵת וְיֶתֶר עָז׃ פַּחַז כַּמַּיִם אַל־
תּוֹתַר כִּי עָלִיתָ מִשְׁכְּבֵי אָבִיךָ אָז חִלַּלְתָּ יְצוּעִי עָלָה׃

ה־ו שִׁמְעוֹן וְלֵוִי אַחִים כְּלֵי חָמָס מְכֵרֹתֵיהֶם׃ בְּסֹדָם אַל־תָּבֹא נַפְשִׁי בִּקְהָלָם

---

22. וַאֲנִי נָתַתִּי לְךָ שְׁכֶם אַחַד עַל אַחֶיךָ אֲשֶׁר לָקַחְתִּי מִיַּד הָאֱמֹרִי — *I have given to you Shechem above your brethren, which I took out of the hand of the Amorite.* Do not think that I have (improperly) transferred the inheritance of all your brothers by giving you Shechem, for what I give (I am entitled to) since I took it from those who conducted themselves wickedly, akin to the Amorite. (Or) I took it from Esau who "says" much but does little beneficial, hence I bought the birthright from him, for had I not, your brothers would not have so large an inheritance in the Land (of Israel).

בְּחַרְבִּי וּבְקַשְׁתִּי — *With my sword and with my bow* . . . my wisdom and discernment which are referred to as the sword and bow of the righteous, as it is written: חֲגוֹר חַרְבְּךָ עַל יָרֵךְ גִּבּוֹר, *Gird your sword upon your thigh, O mighty one* (*Psalms* 45:4), which is explained by our Sages as referring to דִּבְרֵי תוֹרָה, *the words of Torah* (*Shabbos* 63a). The opposite is true (of the wicked), as it is written, שִׁנֵּיהֶם חֲנִית וְחִצִּים וּלְשׁוֹנָם חֶרֶב חַדָּה, *Whose teeth are spears and arrows, and their tongue a sharp sword* (*Psalms* 57:5), and also, וַיַּדְרְכוּ אֶת לְשׁוֹנָם קַשְׁתָּם שֶׁקֶר, *And they bend their tongue, their bow of falsehood* (*Jeremiah* 9:2).

XLIX

1. בְּאַחֲרִית הַיָּמִים — *In the end of days.* "The end of days" (refers to) the Messianic era which will mark the decline and fall of those nations who are enemies of God. (This will come to pass) when their measure (of evil) will be filled to overflowing, as it is said, כִּי אֶעֱשֶׂה כָלָה בְּכָל הַגּוֹיִם . . . וְאֹתְךָ לֹא אֶעֱשֶׂה כָלָה, *For I will make a full end of all the nations . . . but I will not make a full end of you* (*Jeremiah* 46:28). This is also what Balaam means when he says, בְּאַחֲרִית הַיָּמִים, *at the end of days* (*Numbers* 24:14). Proof can be found in what he later states, וְקַרְקַר כָּל בְּנֵי שֵׁת, *And break down all the sons of Seth* (ibid. v. 17). The prophets also refer to the Messianic Era when they use this phrase, וְהָיָה בְּאַחֲרִית הַיָּמִים יִהְיֶה הַר בֵּית ה׳ נָכוֹן בְּרֹאשׁ הֶהָרִים, *In the end of days it shall come to pass that the mountain of God's house shall be established as the top of the mountain* (*Micah* 4:1). And it is of this (same era) that Jacob speaks when he later says (verses 10-11), *Until Shiloh comes and unto*

NOTES

22. מִיַּד הָאֱמֹרִי בְּחַרְבִּי וּבְקַשְׁתִּי – *Which I took out of the hand of the Amorite with my sword and with my bow.* The *Sforno* gives two different interpretations to the word אֱמֹרִי. One is that it refers to Shechem and Chamor who conducted themselves in the devious manner of the Amorite. The second is that it refers to Esau, who used words to ensnare and mislead his father and others. The word אֱמֹרִי is related to אמר, *say*. Jacob, according to this latter interpretation, argues that Joseph's brothers should have no grievance against their father for giving a double portion to Joseph (whom he considers his בְּכוֹר, *firstborn*), for had Jacob not bought the birthright from Esau there would be far less land to divide between themselves. The point made here by the *Sforno* is that the words *sword* and *bow* are similes for wisdom, discernment and planning. The righteous man uses these gifts, which are developed through Torah, for positive ends, while the wicked person uses these same talents for evil ends.

XLIX

1. בְּאַחֲרִית הַיָּמִים – *In the end of days.* The *Sforno*, as do other commentators, interprets the words אַחֲרִית הַיָּמִים, *the end of days*, as referring to the time of *Mashiach*, the Messiah. His proof from Balaam's words are to be understood in the sense that mankind is called "sons of Seth" since they are descended from Seth, after the death of Cain and

I have given you Shechem — one portion more than your brothers, which I took from the hand of the Emorite with my sword and with my bow."

49

[1] *Then Jacob called for his sons and said, "Assemble yourselves and I will tell you what will befall you in the End of Days.* [2] *Gather yourselves and listen, O sons of Jacob, and listen to Israel your father.*

[3] *"Reuben, you are my firstborn, my strength and my initial vigor, foremost in rank and foremost in power.* [4] *Water-like impetuosity — you cannot be foremost, because you mounted your father's bed; then you desecrated Him Who ascended my couch.*

[5] *"Simeon and Levi are comrades, their weaponry is a stolen craft.* [6] *Into their conspiracy, may my soul not enter! With their congregation,*

---

him the obedience of the people be; binding his foal unto the vine.

2. וְשִׁמְעוּ אֶל יִשְׂרָאֵל אֲבִיכֶם — *And hearken unto Israel your father.* Accept the way which he has taught you all his life. Thereby you will be true "sons of Israel" and he in turn will be your father; you will strive with God and man (and prevail) and not forfeit the good (reward) which will be yours in the future.

4. פַּחַז כַּמַּיִם אַל תּוֹתַר — *Unstable as water, therefore you will not have (this) excellency.* You (Reuben, who are) unstable as water, will not be exalted over your brothers with an "excellency of dignity," i.e., priesthood and בְּכוֹרָה (the rights and privileges of the firstborn), even though you are רֵאשִׁית אוֹנִי, *the first fruits of my strength,* and entitled to these rights, as it says, . . . כִּי הוּא רֵאשִׁית אֹנוֹ, *for he is the first fruits of his strength, the right of the firstborn is his (Deut.* 21:17). Nor will you be exalted with "excellency of power," i.e., kingship, which is designated by (this term) "strength" as our Sages state, אֵין עוֹז אֶלָּא מַלְכוּת, *When the verse states "strength," it refers only to "kingship" (Bereishis Rabbah* 99:6). Kingship would also have been fitting for the firstborn, as it is written, וְאֶת הַמַּמְלָכָה נָתַן לִיהוֹרָם כִּי הוּא הַבְּכוֹר, *And the kingship he gave to Yehoram for he was the firstborn (II Chronicles* 21:3).

אָז חִלַּלְתָּ יְצוּעִי עָלָה — *Then you defiled it; he went up to my couch.* You defiled (desecrated) the honor of your father (or) the honor of the *Shechinah* (Divine Presence) which was wont to ascend my bed, and therefore your honor will be defiled and you will descend from your original status.

5. שִׁמְעוֹן וְלֵוִי אַחִים — *Simeon and Levi are brothers.* The honors which Reuben was entitled to (but forfeited) should have been theirs (Simeon and Levi) as next in seniority, however . . .

כְּלֵי חָמָס מְכֵרֹתֵיהֶם — *Weapons of violence (are) their kinship* . . . and it is not fitting for a king, who בְּמִשְׁפָּט יַעֲמִיד אָרֶץ, *with justice establishes the land (Proverbs* 29:4) (to use instruments of violence); therefore it is not fitting that the kingship be theirs.

NOTES

Abel, and *Mashiach* will rule over all mankind. The phrases used by Jacob in verses 10 and 11 also refer to *Mashiach,* who will come riding on a foal (ass) as a symbol of peace, and not a horse which is associated with war.

2. וְשִׁמְעוּ אֶל יִשְׂרָאֵל אֲבִיכֶם – *And hearken unto Israel your father.* The phrase, *hearken to Israel,* is not a repetition of, *hear you sons of Jacob.* The first phrase is to be understood in the literal sense, but the second one refers to the mission and purpose of "Israel," to strive with God and man, and to prevail.

5. שִׁמְעוֹן וְלֵוִי אַחִים – *Simeon and Levi are brothers.* The key word is אַחִים, *brothers.* As the brothers of Reuben, next to him in age, they should have succeeded to his rights and privileges, but were also found wanting — especially insofar as Jewish kingship is concerned. A king of Israel rules with justice and by right, not might and violence. Simeon and Levi's temperaments were such that they could not fit this required role.

ז אַל־תֵּחַד כְּבֹדִי כִּי בְאַפָּם הָרְגוּ אִישׁ וּבִרְצֹנָם עִקְּרוּ־שׁוֹר׃ אָרוּר אַפָּם כִּי
עָז וְעֶבְרָתָם כִּי קָשָׁתָה אֲחַלְּקֵם בְּיַעֲקֹב וַאֲפִיצֵם בְּיִשְׂרָאֵל׃
ח־ט יְהוּדָה אַתָּה יוֹדוּךָ אַחֶיךָ יָדְךָ בְּעֹרֶף אֹיְבֶיךָ יִשְׁתַּחֲווּ לְךָ בְּנֵי אָבִיךָ׃ גּוּר
י אַרְיֵה יְהוּדָה מִטֶּרֶף בְּנִי עָלִיתָ כָּרַע רָבַץ כְּאַרְיֵה וּכְלָבִיא מִי יְקִימֶנּוּ׃ לֹא־
יָסוּר שֵׁבֶט מִיהוּדָה וּמְחֹקֵק מִבֵּין רַגְלָיו עַד כִּי־יָבֹא שִׁילֹה וְלוֹ יִקְּהַת עַמִּים׃
יא אֹסְרִי לַגֶּפֶן עִירֹה וְלַשֹּׂרֵקָה בְּנִי אֲתֹנוֹ כִּבֵּס בַּיַּיִן לְבֻשׁוֹ וּבְדַם־עֲנָבִים סוּתֹה׃

---

7. אָרוּר אַפָּם — *Cursed be their anger.* Their anger will (perforce) be lessened through their lowly state and hard life, caused by the fact that they will be divided and scattered.

The priesthood, however, still remained with the firstborn until it was given to the Levites (in the merit of their loyalty to God) as it is written, בָּעֵת הַהִוא הִבְדִּיל ה׳ אֶת שֵׁבֶט הַלֵּוִי, *At that time the Lord separated the tribe of Levi (Deut.* 10:8).

8. יְהוּדָה אַתָּה יוֹדוּךָ אַחֶיךָ — *Judah, your brothers shall praise you.* You are worthy of kingship for one cannot find a blemish in you to disqualify you, as is the case with your (older) brothers; therefore (your brothers) shall accept you as king, because they shall praise you as worthy of ruling.

יָדְךָ בְּעֹרֶף אֹיְבֶיךָ — *Your hand shall be on the neck of your enemies.* They shall flee before you, similar to, וְנָתַתִּי אֶת כָּל אֹיְבֶיךָ אֵלֶיךָ עֹרֶף, *And I will make all your enemies turn their backs unto you (Exodus* 23:27).

יִשְׁתַּחֲווּ לְךָ בְּנֵי אָבִיךָ — *Your father's sons shall bow down before you.* You will reign over your father's sons but not over the nations, *until Shiloh comes* (verse 10), at which time you will rule not only over your father's sons but the nations as well, as it is written, *and unto him shall be the obedience of the peoples* (ibid.).

9. גּוּר אַרְיֵה יְהוּדָה — *Judah is a lion's whelp.* Though presently Judah is not yet a lion, for he is not yet a king, still he is like a גּוּר אַרְיֵה, *young lion,* ruling over his brothers, and ultimately will be a king, nonetheless ...

מִטֶּרֶף בְּנִי עָלִיתָ — *From the prey, my son, you are gone up.* You, my son Joseph, are gone up from the prey, i.e., (Judah was) not prepared to kill you in his anger, even though he (also) hated you, because ...

כָּרַע רָבַץ כְּאַרְיֵה — *He stooped down, he crouched as a lion.* He was like a lion that crouches but doesn't leap; he did not order his brothers to kill you.

וּכְלָבִיא מִי יְקִימֶנּוּ — *And as a lioness, who shall rise him up?* In the future, there will be a period when he shall crouch as a lioness in his homeland, none daring to frighten him away.

10. לֹא יָסוּר שֵׁבֶט מִיהוּדָה — *The scepter shall not depart from Judah ...* as long as there is kingship in Israel, as it says, וּכְלָבִיא מִי יְקִימֶנּוּ (verse 9). The scepter of kingship will not be removed from Judah in favor of another tribe of Israel, as it is written: וְחַסְדִּי לֹא יָסוּר מִמֶּנּוּ כַּאֲשֶׁר הֲסִרֹתִי מֵעִם שָׁאוּל אֲשֶׁר הֲסִרֹתִי מִלְּפָנֶיךָ, *But My mercy shall not depart from him,*

NOTES

7. אָרוּר אַפָּם – *Cursed be their anger.* Jacob does not curse his sons. The word אָרוּר in this case means *diminishment* or *reduction,* just as בְּרָכָה, *blessing,* denotes *increase* and *growth* (compare to 4:11). Their anger will be kept under control due to their difficult circumstances. The tribe of Simeon was destined to become itinerant teachers while the Levites had no portion in the Land and were dependent upon the gifts granted to them by the Torah.

8. יִשְׁתַּחֲווּ לְךָ בְּנֵי אָבִיךָ — *Your father's sons shall bow down before you.* Here again the *Sforno* weaves the theme of *Mashiach* into the blessings of Jacob. At the beginning of Israel's sojourn in *Eretz Yisrael,* the descendants of Judah will reign over their own people. At the "end of time," however, *Mashiach* will rule over the nations as well.

9. גּוּר אַרְיֵה יְהוּדָה ... כָּרַע רָבַץ כְּאַרְיֵה – *Judah is a lion's whelp ... He stooped down, he crouched as a*

do not join, O my honor! For in their rage they murdered people and at their whim they maimed an ox. [7] *Accursed is their rage for it is intense, and their wrath for it is harsh; I will separate them within Jacob, and I will disperse them in Israel.*

[8] *"Judah — you, your brothers shall acknowledge; your hand will be at your enemies' nape; your father's sons will prostrate themselves to you.*
[9] *A lion cub is Judah; from the prey, my son, you elevated yourself. He crouches, lies down like a lion, and like an awesome lion, who dares rouse him?* [10] *The scepter shall not depart from Judah nor a scholar from among his descendants until Shiloh arrives and his will be an assemblage of nations.* [11] *He will tie his donkey to the vine; to the vine branch his donkey's foal; he will launder his garments in wine and his robe in the blood of grapes.*

---

as I took it from Saul, whom I put away before you (*II Samuel* 7:15). However, when Judah fell, (conquered) by other nations (even though the scepter *was* removed) this is not called הֲסָרָה, *removal,* for this (word) is only (applicable to the) moving of an item (or power) from place to place (within a similar area or category). When, however, something is totally lost and no longer exists, the term הֲסָרָה cannot be used. (Since, at the time of the *churban,* destruction,) the scepter did not pass to another tribe of Israel, but was totally wrested from (Judah by the enemy, the prophecy of Jacob was not refuted).

וּמְחֹקֵק מִבֵּין רַגְלָיו — *Nor the ruler's staff from between his feet.* The judge who sits on the chair (throne) will be his descendant, and between (at) his feet will be the scribe, as was their custom.

עַד כִּי יָבֹא שִׁילֹה — *Until Shiloh does come.* The word *Shiloh* is derived from two roots: שול which means *sole,* and שלה which denotes שָׁלוֹם, *peace,* hence Shiloh means *peace at the end.* The prophecy (of Jacob) that Judah will be ruler and judge *only* among his brothers will be so *until Shiloh comes* (i.e., *Mashiach*) . . .

וְלוֹ יִקְּהַת עַמִּים — *And unto him shall be the obedience of the peoples.* But when *Mashiach* appears, and there will be שָׁלוֹם בַּסּוֹף, *peace at the end,* then his shall be the weakening of peoples, יִקְּהַת, similar to אִם קֵהָה הַבַּרְזֶל, *If the iron be blunt* (*Ecclesiastes* 10:10). Those who remain, weakened after the destruction of their kingdom, will be obedient (and subjugated) to Shiloh (*Mashiach*) as it says: וְקַרְקַר כָּל בְּנֵי שֵׁת, *And break down all the sons of Seth* (*Numbers* 24:17).

11. אֹסְרִי לַגֶּפֶן עִירֹה וְלַשֹּׂרֵקָה בְּנִי אֲתֹנוֹ כִּבֵּס בַּיַּיִן לְבֻשׁוֹ — *Binding his foal unto the vine and his ass's colt unto the choice vine, he washes his garment in wine.* The signs of the *Mashiach* are:

(a) He will appear on an עַיִר בֶּן אֲתֹנוֹת, *a colt, the foal of an ass* (*Zechariah* 9:9), as the

NOTES

lion. The final decision regarding Joseph's fate rested with Judah, who was acknowledged by his brothers as their leader. In this respect he was like a lion's whelp. It was not until later, in *Eretz Yisrael,* that he was destined to become a lion (i.e., a king). Nonetheless, even though he had the power to dispose of Joseph he declared, *"What profit is it, if we slay our brother?"* (37:26). So he is compared to a lion that crouches but does not leap.

10. וְלוֹ יִקְּהַת עַמִּים – *And unto him shall be the obedience of the peoples.* The *Sforno,* like the *Ramban* on this verse, connects the word יִקְּהַת, *obedience,* with the root meaning *to weaken,* thus the interpretation is "and his (*Mashiach's* — Shiloh's) shall be the weakening of peoples," i.e., the remnant of the nations who will survive the heavenly wrath and destruction will be subjugated by him. As in verse 1 the *Sforno* cites the words of Balaam to support this interpretation; the children of Seth (mankind) will be "broken down" by *Mashiach.*

11-12. אֹסְרִי לַגֶּפֶן עִירֹה . . . כִּבֵּס בַּיַּיִן לְבֻשׁוֹ . . . חַכְלִילִי עֵינַיִם מִיָּיִן – *Binding his foal unto the vine . . . He washes his garment in wine . . . His eyes shall be red with wine.* Consistent with his interpretation of

יב חַכְלִילִי עֵינַיִם מִיָּיִן וּלְבֶן־שִׁנַּיִם מֵחָלָב׃
יג זְבוּלֻן לְחוֹף יַמִּים יִשְׁכֹּן וְהוּא לְחוֹף אֳנִיֹּת וְיַרְכָתוֹ עַל־צִידֹן׃
יד־טו יִשָּׂשכָר חֲמֹר גָּרֶם רֹבֵץ בֵּין הַמִּשְׁפְּתָיִם׃ וַיַּרְא מְנֻחָה כִּי טוֹב וְאֶת־
טו הָאָרֶץ כִּי נָעֵמָה וַיֵּט שִׁכְמוֹ לִסְבֹּל וַיְהִי לְמַס־עֹבֵד׃　　דָּן

prophet says. He will not ride on a horse which is ready for battle (see *Proverbs* 21:31 — *a horse prepared for the day of battle)* because the war of the nations and the destruction of their kingdoms will have already been completed through the Almighty, and he *(Mashiach)* will be the king of peace.

(b) He will *bind the foal to a vine*, which is symbolic of his kingdom of peace dwelling in the midst of Israel, who are compared to the vine, as our Sages tell us, אוּמָה זוּ לְגֶפֶן נִמְשְׁלָה, *This nation (Israel) is compared to a vine (Chullin* 92a), and so the prophet also testifies: כִּי כֶרֶם ה׳ צְבָאוֹת בֵּית יִשְׂרָאֵל, *For the vineyard of* HASHEM, *Lord of Hosts, is the house of Israel (Isaiah* 5:7).

(c) The third of the signs (by which he will be recognized) is the tying of his ass to the choice vine, which means that he will cause his face to shine with favor upon the righteous ones of that generation — not upon the entire vineyard.

(d) The fourth of the signs will be his ability to *wash his garment* in blood, for his arrival will be preceded by the slaughter (of the nations), as we find, מַדּוּעַ אָדֹם לִלְבוּשֶׁךָ, *Wherefore is your apparel red? (Isaiah* 63:2), and, יָדִין בַּגּוֹיִם מָלֵא גְוִיּוֹת, *He will judge among the nations, He fills it with dead bodies (Psalms* 110:6).

12. חַכְלִילִי עֵינַיִם מִיָּיִן — *His eyes shall be red with wine.* The fifth sign will be the unusual abundance (of food) in the world, as it says: יְהִי פִסַּת בַּר בָּאָרֶץ בְּרֹאשׁ הָרִים יִרְעַשׁ כַּלְּבָנוֹן פִּרְיוֹ, *May he be as a rich cornfield in the land upon the top of the mountains, may his fruit rustle like Lebanon (Psalms* 72:16), and as our Sages tell us, "*Eretz Yisrael* is destined to bring forth cakes and woolen robes" *(Shabbos* 30b).

13. זְבוּלֻן לְחוֹף יַמִּים יִשְׁכֹּן — *Zebulun shall dwell at the shore of the sea . . .* in his Land, he dwelt at the shore for that was his inheritance. Zebulun is mentioned before Issachar (even though he is younger) because he occupied himself with commerce while Issachar studied Torah and one cannot study Torah unless his material wants are satisfied, as our Sages teach us, אִם אֵין קֶמַח אֵין תּוֹרָה, *Without flour there can be no Torah (Avos* 3:17). By Zebulun aiding Issachar the merit belongs to both. That is also why Moses in his blessing states: שְׂמַח זְבוּלֻן בְּצֵאתֶךָ וְיִשָּׂשכָר בְּאֹהָלֶיךָ, *Rejoice, Zebulun in your going out, and Issachar in your tents (Deut.* 33:18). This is also the Torah's purpose in commanding that gifts be given (by Israel) to the Priests and Levites, so that all shall support the scholars and teachers of Torah, i.e., the Priests and Levites, as it says יוֹרוּ מִשְׁפָּטֶיךָ לְיַעֲקֹב, *They shall teach Jacob your law (Deut.* 33:10), and thereby merit, together with them, eternal life, as our Sages teach us, כָּל יִשְׂרָאֵל יֵשׁ לָהֶם חֵלֶק לְעוֹלָם הַבָּא, *All Israel have a portion in the world to come (Sanhedrin* 90a).

NOTES

Shiloh as *Mashiach*, the *Sforno* interprets these verses as a series of signs by which he will be recognized. These include: the method by which he will appear; his dwelling in the midst of Israel with special favor shown to the righteous among them; the violent upheaval and destruction which will precede his arrival; and the blessing of material abundance which will follow upon his coming. The *Sforno* stresses that *Mashiach* is not a man of war, but of peace. The battles and annihilation will take place among the nations as part of a Divine plan, *preceding* the appearance of שִׁילֹה who is the embodiment of "peace at the end," as this name indicates.

13. זְבוּלֻן לְחוֹף יַמִּים יִשְׁכֹּן – *Zebulun shall dwell at the shore of the sea.* The *Sforno's* development of this verse mirrors the teachings of our Sages, that a partnership exists between the Torah scholar and the supporter of Torah. Both shall be equally rewarded, but the supporter is given precedence over the scholar since we see that Jacob blessed

12 *Red eyed from wine, and white toothed from milk.*
13 *"Zebulun shall settle by seashores. He shall be at the ship's harbor, and his last border will reach Zidon.*
14 *"Issachar is a strong-boned donkey; he rests between the boundaries.*
15 *He saw tranquility that it was good, and the land that it was pleasant, yet he bent his shoulder to bear and he became an indentured laborer.*

וְהוּא לְחוֹף אֳנִיֹּת — *And he shall be a shore for ships.* (This refers to Zebulun when he travels abroad), going to other shores to trade in various merchandise such as small fishes, purple (goods) and milk glass, which are found in the sea and sand, as the verse testifies, כִּי שֶׁפַע יַמִּים יִינָקוּ וּשְׂפֻנֵי טְמוּנֵי חוֹל, *For they shall suck the abundance of the seas, and the hidden treasures of the sand (Deut.* 33:19).

14. יִשָּׂשכָר חֲמֹר — *Issachar is a (large-boned) ass . . .* unsuited for war, as our Sages say: אִי סַפְרָא לָא סַיְיפָא, *If one is a scholar, he is not a robber* (lit., *a man of the sword) (Avodah Zarah* 17b).

גָּרֶם — *Large-boned.* Strong and firm-boned, as a result of which . . .

רֹבֵץ בֵּין הַמִּשְׁפְּתָיִם — *Crouching down between the sheepfolds.* When he takes his rest he does so while his burdens are still upon him (overflowing his flanks), for they are not removed until the task is done; now this can only be done by an ass that is extremely strong. In a similar fashion will Issachar carry the burdens of Torah study, worldly occupation and communal administration, as is fitting for a wise man who has attained perfection, intellectually and ethically.

15. וַיַּרְא מְנֻחָה כִּי טוֹב — *He saw a resting place that it was good.* He saw that peace of mind and fulfillment can be found in perfecting one's mental and spiritual potential, which is the ultimate good, as is written, וּמִצְאוּ מַרְגּוֹעַ לְנַפְשְׁכֶם, *And you shall find rest for your souls (Jeremiah* 6:16).

וְאֶת הָאָרֶץ כִּי נָעֵמָה — *And the land that it was pleasant.* He also saw that his portion of land (in *Eretz Yisrael*) was capable of sustaining him without difficulty and furnishing a livelihood without discomfort.

וַיֵּט שִׁכְמוֹ לִסְבֹּל — *And he bowed his shoulder to bear . . .* the double burden of Torah study and communal responsibility, as our Sages teach us, "A Torah scholar dwelling in a community should accept upon himself the responsibility of community affairs" *(Moed Katan* 6a).

וַיְהִי לְמַס עֹבֵד — *And became a servant under taskwork . . .* (whereupon) the rest of the community, which engaged only in worldly occupation (accepted to work for him and relieve him of that burden), as our Sages tell us, "His townspeople are commanded to do his work" *(Yoma* 72b).

NOTES

Zebulun before Issachar, even though the former was younger.

14. יִשָּׂשכָר חֲמֹר גָּרֶם רֹבֵץ בֵּין הַמִּשְׁפְּתָיִם — *Issachar is a large-boned ass, crouching down between the sheepfolds.* Compare to verse 11 where the *Sforno* posits that the horse symbolizes war, while the ass represents peace — which is the reason that *Mashiach* will arrive riding on "the foal of an ass." Here Issachar is also compared to חֲמוֹר, *an ass,* symbolizing peace, contentment and tranquility — the characteristics of the Torah scholar. The *Sforno's* philosophy, expressed in much of his writings, is that the אִישׁ שָׁלֵם — *complete man* — in the view of Torah, is one who combines Torah scholarship with דֶּרֶךְ אֶרֶץ, worldly occupation; מִדּוֹת, ethical excellence and the acceptance of communal responsibility. All these virtues Issachar possesses.

15. וַיַּרְא מְנֻחָה כִּי טוֹב וְאֶת הָאָרֶץ כִּי נָעֵמָה — *He saw a resting place that it was good, and the land that it was pleasant.* Careful review of this verse will clarify the profound interpretation of the *Sforno.* מְנוּחָה, *rest* and *tranquility,* is not to be understood in the negative sense i.e., inaction and non-exertion. The *Midrash* tells us that מְנוּחָה זוּ תּוֹרָה, *true tranquility results from the study of Torah.* This is the מְנוּחָה of the soul, and this is the real

יז יָדִין עַמּוֹ כְּאַחַד שִׁבְטֵי יִשְׂרָאֵל: יְהִי־דָן נָחָשׁ עֲלֵי־דֶרֶךְ שְׁפִיפֹן עֲלֵי־אֹרַח
חמישי יח־יט הַנֹּשֵׁךְ עִקְּבֵי־סוּס וַיִּפֹּל רֹכְבוֹ אָחוֹר: לִישׁוּעָתְךָ קִוִּיתִי יהוה: * גָּד
כ גְּדוּד יְגוּדֶנּוּ וְהוּא יָגֻד עָקֵב: מֵאָשֵׁר שְׁמֵנָה לַחְמוֹ וְהוּא
כא יִתֵּן מַעֲדַנֵּי־מֶלֶךְ: נַפְתָּלִי אַיָּלָה שְׁלֻחָה הַנֹּתֵן
כב אִמְרֵי־שָׁפֶר: בֵּן פֹּרָת יוֹסֵף בֵּן פֹּרָת עֲלֵי־עָיִן בָּנוֹת
כג־כד צָעֲדָה עֲלֵי־שׁוּר: וַיְמָרְרֻהוּ וָרֹבּוּ וַיִּשְׂטְמֻהוּ בַּעֲלֵי חִצִּים: וַתֵּשֶׁב בְּאֵיתָן
כה קַשְׁתּוֹ וַיָּפֹזּוּ זְרֹעֵי יָדָיו מִידֵי אֲבִיר יַעֲקֹב מִשָּׁם רֹעֶה אֶבֶן יִשְׂרָאֵל: מֵאֵל

---

17. יְהִי דָן נָחָשׁ — *Dan shall be a serpent . . .* a species of snake called צִפְעוֹנִי, *adder*, or חוּרְמוֹן, *chormon*, as called by Arab naturalists, which is most deadly — for one such serpent can kill many victims. Thus did Samson destroy many of his enemies swiftly by himself.

שְׁפִיפֹן — *A horned snake . . .* a long, thin snake, as our Sages tell us, כְּחוּט הַשַּׂעֲרָה הוּא וּשְׁפִיפוֹן שְׁמוֹ, *(Long and thin) like a single hair, and it is called sh'fifon (Yerushalmi Terumos* 8:5), and of this snake the experts tell us that he hides among the trees and attacks (his prey) like an arrow; so did Samson, who fought alone (without any army and suddenly attacked) whereupon he disappeared.

19. גָּד גְּדוּד יְגוּדֶנּוּ — *Gad, a troop shall troop upon him.* After telling us that Dan will fight like a serpent, (biting the horse's heels) and causing the horse and rider to fall, he now (foresees) that Gad will do battle by cutting down the rider and his horse, as we find, וְטָרַף זְרוֹעַ אַף קָדְקֹד, *And tears the arm, even the crown of the head (Deut.* 33:20).

וְהוּא יָגֻד עָקֵב — *And he shall cut down (their) heel.* When he cuts down the horse and rider it shall be from the rear, for (his enemy) will be fleeing from him, as we find, וְנָתַתִּי אֶת כָּל אֹיְבֶיךָ אֵלֶיךָ עֹרֶף, *And I will make all your enemies turn their backs unto you (Exodus* 23:27) (compare to verse 8).

22. בֵּן פֹּרָת יוֹסֵף — *Joseph is a fruitful vine.* Behold, Joseph is the son of a fruitful vine, the branch of a flowing vine which casts a protecting shade as does the vine, as it says: כָּסוּ הָרִים צִלָּהּ, *The mountains were covered with the shadow of it (Psalms* 80:11). So did (Joseph) protect his father and brothers in Egypt.

בֵּן פֹּרָת עֲלֵי עָיִן בָּנוֹת — *A fruitful vine by a fountain, whose branches* (lit., *daughters*). He was like the bough of a fruitful vine growing by a fountain, from which many branches grow . . .

צָעֲדָה עֲלֵי שׁוּר — *Run over the wall.* That vine which ran over the wall near the fountain (grew) in a manner in which beforehand it was not visible on the other side and (therefore

NOTES

meaning of שָׁלוֹם, *peace*, which concludes the priestly blessing, i.e., וְיָשֵׂם לְךָ שָׁלוֹם, *and grant you peace*, which the *Sforno* explains as "the tranquility of peace that is eternity" *(Numbers* 6:26). This is the way of life chosen by Issachar — pursuit of Torah coupled with communal responsibility.

As for his basic needs, even though Zebulun assisted him, Issachar apparently still tended to much of his own material requirements. The portion of land allocated to Issachar in *Eretz Yisrael* was fertile and productive, and hence did not require arduous labor. Still, in order to free Issachar from time-consuming worldly pursuits, the community of laymen lent him their assistance, a custom followed to this very day.

19. וְהוּא יָגֻד עָקֵב – *And he shall cut down (their) heel.* The verb גד means to cut, as we see in, לֹא תִתְגֹּדְדוּ, *You shall not cut yourselves (Deuteronomy* 14:1*)*. The *Sforno's* interpretation is based on this premise.

22. בֵּן פֹּרָת עֲלֵי עָיִן בָּנוֹת – *A fruitful vine by a fountain, whose branches . . .* The *Sforno* links the word בָּנוֹת, *branches* (lit., *daughter*), to the phrase above, i.e., *a fruitful vine by a fountain*, rather than with the subsequent one, i.e., "run over the wall." In this manner the imagery is quite clear and reasonable. The vine grows on one side of the wall producing new branches (Joseph and his sons), then suddenly appears on the other side becoming visible to others (Jacob and the brothers).

16 *"Dan will avenge his people, the tribes of Israel will be united as one.*
17 *Dan will be a serpent on the highway, a viper by the path, that bites a horse's heels so its rider falls backward.*
18 *For Your salvation do I long, O HASHEM!*
19 *"Gad will recruit a regiment and it will retreat on its heel.*
20 *"From Asher — his bread will have richness, and he will provide kingly delicacies.*
21 *"Naphtali is a hind let loose who delivers beautiful sayings.*
22 *"A charming son is Joseph, a charming son to the eye; each of the girls climbed heights to gaze.*
23 *They embittered him and became antagonists; the arrow-tongued men hated him.*
24 *But his bow was firmly emplaced and his arms were gilded, from the hands of the Mighty Power of Jacob — from there, he shepherded the stone of Israel.*
25 *[That was] from the God*

its existence) was unknown to those who lived there; so did Joseph and his sons suddenly make themselves known to Jacob and the brothers, as it is written: רְאֹה פָנֶיךָ לֹא פִלָּלְתִּי וְהִנֵּה הֶרְאָה אֹתִי אֱלֹהִים גַּם אֶת זַרְעֶךָ, *I had not thought to see your face; and lo, God has let me see your seed also* (48:11).

23. וַיְשַׂטְמֻהוּ בַּעֲלֵי חִצִּים — *The archers dealt bitterly with him.* Slanderers, as it is written, חֵץ שָׁחוּט לְשׁוֹנָם, *Their tongue is a sharpened arrow (Jeremiah* 9:7), among them being the chief butler (who when recalling Joseph to Pharaoh) says (slightingly), נַעַר עִבְרִי עֶבֶד, *a young man, a Hebrew, a slave* (41:12), as well as a number of Pharaoh's servants who disparaged Joseph by protesting, עֶבֶד שֶׁקָּנָה אוֹתוֹ רַבּוֹ בְּעֶשְׂרִים כֶּסֶף תַּמְלִיכֵהוּ עָלֵינוּ, *How can you appoint as your viceroy a slave, purchased by his master for twenty pieces of silver? (Sotah* 36b).

24. וַתֵּשֶׁב בְּאֵיתָן קַשְׁתּוֹ — *But his bow abode firm.* However his was a bow from which arrows were shot accurately to refute these slanderers, i.e., Pharaoh, who said (firmly) to his servants, הֲנִמְצָא כָזֶה אִישׁ אֲשֶׁר רוּחַ אֱלֹהִים בּוֹ, *Can we find such a one as this, a man in whom the spirit of God is?* (41:38), and אֵין נָבוֹן וְחָכָם כָּמוֹךָ, *There is none so discreet and wise as you* (41:39).

וַיָּפֹזּוּ זְרֹעֵי יָדָיו — *And the arms of his hands were made supple* ... when Pharaoh placed his ring on (Joseph's) finger.

מִידֵי אֲבִיר יַעֲקֹב — *By the hands of the Mighty One of Jacob.* This salvation and success was yours thanks to the intervention of the Mighty One of Jacob (God), Who insures the survival of His children among the nations unto the very end, as the name יַעֲקֹב, *Jacob,* implies, that his children will survive to the (end of time). So, also, He is the One Who saved you from the arrows of your enemies who dealt so bitterly with you.

מִשָּׁם — *From there* ... and it is ever from this source of God's goodness ...

רֹעֶה אֶבֶן יִשְׂרָאֵל — *The shepherd, the Stone of Israel.* He shepherds the remnant of Israel and

NOTES

23. וַיְשַׂטְמֻהוּ בַּעֲלֵי חִצִּים — *The archers dealt bitterly with him.* The *Sforno,* as do other commentators, rejects the interpretation that this refers to Joseph's brothers, for as the *Radak* states, 'Jacob would never denigrate his sons thus.' Therefore the word *archers* must refer to the chief butler and Pharaoh's servants.

24. וַתֵּשֶׁב בְּאֵיתָן קַשְׁתּוֹ — *But his bow abode firm.* The bow is Joseph's, the arrows are Pharaoh's. True, Pharaoh is the one who defends him, but were it not for Joseph's talents and wisdom, represented by the bow, Pharaoh's defense, represented by the arrows, could not be effective.

מִידֵי אֲבִיר יַעֲקֹב מִשָּׁם רֹעֶה אֶבֶן יִשְׂרָאֵל — *By the hands of the Mighty One of Jacob, from there the shepherd, the Stone of Israel.* As we find in other instances, the names "Jacob" and "Israel" are used in the same verse. In this particular case the reason

אָבִ֙יךָ֙ וְיַעְזְרֶ֔ךָּ וְאֵ֤ת שַׁדַּי֙ וִיבָ֣רְכֶ֔ךָּ בִּרְכֹ֤ת שָׁמַ֙יִם֙ מֵעָ֔ל בִּרְכֹ֥ת תְּה֖וֹם רֹבֶ֣צֶת
כו תָּ֑חַת בִּרְכֹ֥ת שָׁדַ֖יִם וָרָֽחַם׃ בִּרְכֹ֣ת אָבִ֗יךָ גָּֽבְרוּ֙ עַל־בִּרְכֹ֣ת הוֹרַ֔י עַד־
תַּאֲוַ֖ת גִּבְעֹ֣ת עוֹלָ֑ם תִּֽהְיֶ֙יןָ֙ לְרֹ֣אשׁ יוֹסֵ֔ף וּלְקָדְקֹ֖ד נְזִ֥יר אֶחָֽיו׃

insures their survival among the nations, be it as precious or non-precious stones, which (both) last many a year, similar to, הִתְגְּזֶרֶת אֶבֶן דִּי לָא בִידַיִן וּמְחָת לְצַלְמָא עַל רַגְלוֹהִי, *That a stone was cut out without hands, which smote the image upon its feet (Daniel* 2:34), referring to Israel who strive with God and man, as our Sages state, "Wherever they go they become princes to their masters" (*Sanhedrin* 104b).

25. מֵאֵל אָבִיךָ — *Even by the God of your father.* This (good fortune) befell you because He is the God of your father, Who assured me that after my seed will have fallen to the lowest level, they will be elevated, as it is written, וְהָיָה זַרְעֲךָ כַּעֲפַר הָאָרֶץ וּפָרַצְתָּ, *And your seed shall be as the dust of the earth, and you shall spread abroad* (28:14).

וְיַעְזְרֶךָּ — *Who shall help you . . .* that you shall fall no more.

וְאֵת שַׁדַּי — *And by the Almighty.* And from God Almighty, Who said to me, "*I am God Almighty, be fruitful and multiply; a nation and a company of nations shall be of you*" (35:11).

וִיבָרְכֶךָּ — *Who shall bless you . . .* Himself, without an intermediary. Unlike Menasseh and Ephraim who were blessed through הַמַּלְאָךְ הַגֹּאֵל, *The redeeming angel* (48:16), and Esau who was blessed by Isaac or (Israel) blessed by Moses; all these were blessed by man. (You however will be) blessed by the Almighty, in keeping with Isaac's statement to Jacob, וְאֵל שַׁדַּי יְבָרֵךְ אֹתְךָ, *And may God Almighty bless you* (28:3), and as was true of Israel before the sin of the spies when Moses said to them, וִיבָרֵךְ אֶתְכֶם כַּאֲשֶׁר דִּבֶּר לָכֶם, *And may He bless you as He has promised you (Deut.* 1:11).

בִּרְכֹת שָׁמַיִם מֵעָל — *With blessings of heaven above . . .* that the days of your life be complete.

בִּרְכֹת תְּהוֹם רֹבֶצֶת תָּחַת — *Blessings of the deep that crouches beneath . . .* the blessing of food and wealth.

בִּרְכֹת שָׁדַיִם וָרָחַם — *Blessings of the breasts and of the womb . . .* the blessing of children, the opposite of רֶחֶם מַשְׁכִּיל וְשָׁדַיִם צֹמְקִים, *A miscarrying womb and dry breasts (Hoshea* 9:14).

26. בִּרְכֹת אָבִיךָ — *The blessings of your father.* And may He bless you with the blessing He gave to (me), "וּפָרַצְתָּ יָמָּה וָקֵדְמָה וְצָפֹנָה וָנֶגְבָּה, *You shalt spread abroad to the west, and to the east, and to the north and to the south*" (28:14), which is a boundless, unlimited possession; and it is said, וְנִבְרְכוּ בְךָ כָּל מִשְׁפְּחֹת הָאֲדָמָה, *And in you shall all the families of the earth be blessed* (ibid.). This assures the future of Israel, of the שְׂרִידִים אֲשֶׁר ה׳ קֹרֵא, *The remnant called by God (Joel* 3:5), as it is said, כָּעֵת יֵאָמֵר לְיַעֲקֹב וּלְיִשְׂרָאֵל מַה פָּעַל אֵל, *Now it is said of Jacob and Israel, what has God wrought? (Numbers* 23:23), and it is written:

NOTES

given by the *Sforno* is that Jacob is used when the Torah speaks of the survival of his children and Israel is used when the reference is to their status and position. The "Mighty One of Jacob" insures our survival to the end of time, whereas the "stone of Israel" insures our prestige and honor among the nations even if we are not on the highest spiritual level, hence, non-precious stones . . .

25. מֵאֵל אָבִיךָ . . . וְאֵת שַׁדַּי — *Even by the God of your father . . . And by the Almighty.* God is called by two names in this blessing. He is *the God of your father* and *the Almighty.* The former, as the latter, refers to specific promises made when using these names. It was as "the God of your father (Jacob)" that He promised to elevate my descendants after they fall, at which time they will never fall again

of your father and He will help you, and with Shaddai — and He will bless you [with] blessings of heaven from above, blessings of the deep crouching below, blessings of the bosom and womb. 26 *The blessings of your father surpassed the blessings of my parents to the endless bounds of the world's hills. Let them be upon Joseph's head and upon the head of the exile from his brothers.*

וְאַתֶּם כֹּהֲנֵי ה׳ תִּקָּרֵאוּ, *You shall be named the priests of the Lord* (*Isaiah* 61:6); also אֲשֶׁר יַחֲזִיקוּ עֲשָׂרָה אֲנָשִׁים מִכֹּל לְשֹׁנוֹת הַגּוֹיִם ... בִּכְנַף אִישׁ יְהוּדִי לֵאמֹר, נֵלְכָה עִמָּכֶם כִּי שָׁמַעְנוּ אֱלֹהִים עִמָּכֶם, *Ten men, out of all the languages of the nations shall ... take hold of the skirt of a Jew saying, "We will go with you, for we have heard that God is with you"* (*Zechariah* 8:23).

גָּבְרוּ עַל בִּרְכֹת הוֹרַי — *Are mighty beyond the blessings of my progenitors.* I gave you (*my* blessings from God) for they are more mighty than those given by God to Abraham and Isaac.

עַד תַּאֲוַת גִּבְעֹת עוֹלָם — *Unto the utmost bound of the everlasting hills.* The blessing given to me will spread to the outermost boundaries of the earth, to both poles of the axis. These he calls *everlasting hills* because they are the farthest points from the center of the earth, i.e., as hills. This is the blessing of וּפָרַצְתָּ ... וְנִבְרְכוּ בְךָ, *You shall spread, ... in you shall be blessed* (28:14), a blessing which insures everlasting happiness and success for all mankind (through the people of Israel).

תִּהְיֶיןָ לְרֹאשׁ יוֹסֵף — *They shall be on the head of Joseph.* These blessings shall come from on High upon the head of Joseph without any intermediary. Moses also expresses this thought (regarding Joseph) when he says וּרְצוֹן שֹׁכְנִי סְנֶה, *And the good will of Him that dwelt in the bush*, i.e., God on High (Whose) blessings come from on High, followed by, תָּבוֹאתָה לְרֹאשׁ יוֹסֵף, *come upon the head of Joseph* (*Deut.* 33:16).

וּלְקָדְקֹד נְזִיר אֶחָיו — *And on the crown of the head of the prince among his brethren.* Since he was deemed worthy to be the prince among all his brothers, he is therefore also worthy to have God's blessings granted to him directly, without any intermediary. This is also true of his descendants whose superiority (among their brethren) brings them to positions of leadership, including מַלְכוּת, *kingship*, as it states, כְּדַבֵּר אֶפְרַיִם רְתֵת נָשָׂא הוּא בְּיִשְׂרָאֵל, *When Ephraim spoke there was trembling, He exalted himself in Israel* (*Hoshea* 13:1).

From Joseph came the first Judge (Joshua) and the king of the northern kingdom after the breakaway from the Davidic royal house (Jeroboam).

NOTES

(akin to נָפְלָה וְלֹא תֹסִיף, see *Isaiah* 24:20); and it was "the Almighty" that gave me the blessing of *a nation and company of nations*, which I have given in turn to you. Also, He will bless you (Joseph) directly without an intermediary, as befits one who is a צַדִּיק, *righteous man*.

26. בִּרְכֹת אָבִיךָ – *The blessings of your father.* The blessing given by God to Jacob was unique in the sense that he was promised that ultimately his children would spread and disseminate the word of God throughout the world. The expression וּפָרַצְתָּ, *You shalt spread abroad*, is not meant as geographic expansion but the spreading of Judaism's spiritual teachings to all mankind. Hence we are called "priests of HASHEM," for it is the duty of the כֹּהֵן, *priest*, to teach the Torah. This special blessing was not given to Abraham or Isaac, only to Jacob. He stresses in his blessing to Joseph that he is transferring this unique blessing to him and his children, since he is the prince among his own brothers, and even in later generations the first judge will be Joshua and the first king of the Northern Kingdom will be Jeroboam, both descendants of Ephraim. Because of this special merit, Joseph also is worthy that God bless him directly and not through an intermediary. Although Jacob has stated this in the previous verse he reiterates it here.

ששי כז־כח *בִּנְיָמִין זְאֵב יִטְרָף בַּבֹּקֶר יֹאכַל עַד וְלָעֶרֶב יְחַלֵּק שָׁלָל׃ כָּל־אֵלֶּה שִׁבְטֵי
יִשְׂרָאֵל שְׁנֵים עָשָׂר וְזֹאת אֲשֶׁר־דִּבֶּר לָהֶם אֲבִיהֶם וַיְבָרֶךְ אוֹתָם אִישׁ
כט אֲשֶׁר כְּבִרְכָתוֹ בֵּרַךְ אֹתָם׃ וַיְצַו אוֹתָם וַיֹּאמֶר אֲלֵהֶם אֲנִי נֶאֱסָף אֶל־עַמִּי
ל קִבְרוּ אֹתִי אֶל־אֲבֹתָי אֶל־הַמְּעָרָה אֲשֶׁר בִּשְׂדֵה עֶפְרוֹן הַחִתִּי׃ בַּמְּעָרָה
אֲשֶׁר בִּשְׂדֵה הַמַּכְפֵּלָה אֲשֶׁר־עַל־פְּנֵי מַמְרֵא בְּאֶרֶץ כְּנָעַן אֲשֶׁר קָנָה
לא אַבְרָהָם אֶת־הַשָּׂדֶה מֵאֵת עֶפְרֹן הַחִתִּי לַאֲחֻזַּת־קָבֶר׃ שָׁמָּה קָבְרוּ אֶת־
אַבְרָהָם וְאֵת שָׂרָה אִשְׁתּוֹ שָׁמָּה קָבְרוּ אֶת־יִצְחָק וְאֵת רִבְקָה אִשְׁתּוֹ
לב וְשָׁמָּה קָבַרְתִּי אֶת־לֵאָה׃ מִקְנֵה הַשָּׂדֶה וְהַמְּעָרָה אֲשֶׁר־בּוֹ מֵאֵת בְּנֵי־
לג חֵת׃ וַיְכַל יַעֲקֹב לְצַוֺּת אֶת־בָּנָיו וַיֶּאֱסֹף רַגְלָיו אֶל־הַמִּטָּה וַיִּגְוַע וַיֵּאָסֶף
נ א־ב אֶל־עַמָּיו׃ וַיִּפֹּל יוֹסֵף עַל־פְּנֵי אָבִיו וַיֵּבְךְּ עָלָיו וַיִּשַּׁק־לוֹ׃ וַיְצַו יוֹסֵף אֶת־
עֲבָדָיו אֶת־הָרֹפְאִים לַחֲנֹט אֶת־אָבִיו וַיַּחַנְטוּ הָרֹפְאִים אֶת־יִשְׂרָאֵל׃
ג וַיִּמְלְאוּ־לוֹ אַרְבָּעִים יוֹם כִּי כֵּן יִמְלְאוּ יְמֵי הַחֲנֻטִים וַיִּבְכּוּ אֹתוֹ מִצְרַיִם
ד שִׁבְעִים יוֹם׃ וַיַּעַבְרוּ יְמֵי בְכִיתוֹ וַיְדַבֵּר יוֹסֵף אֶל־בֵּית פַּרְעֹה לֵאמֹר אִם־

---

27. זְאֵב יִטְרָף — *A wolf that ravens.* The wolf attacks his prey at dawn or twilight when there is a minimum of light, as it is written, וְחַדּוּ מִזְּאֵבֵי עֶרֶב, *And more fierce than the wolves of the desert (Habbakuk* 1:8). So it shall be with Benjamin. The first king of Israel will be Saul (who is a descendant of Benjamin), when the sun of Jewish kingship first rises, and again at the conclusion of Jewish rulership in the days of Mordechai and Esther (who were also descended from Benjamin). Even though they were followed by the kingdom of the Second Temple, that period was comparatively brief, and included many years of subjugation as well.

28. כָּל אֵלֶּה שִׁבְטֵי יִשְׂרָאֵל שְׁנֵים עָשָׂר — *All these are the twelve tribes of Israel.* These who were mentioned and blessed by Jacob are the twelve authentic tribes; they are written on the breastplate and *ephod* as a remembrance before God; they were present at the time of the covenant at Mount Gerizim and Mount Ebal. For these twelve, Moses set up twelve pillars and Joshua twelve stones in the Jordan and at Gilgal, as did Elijah when he built the altar. Menasseh and Ephraim are not included in the number of the tribes, except in the dividing of the land, where Levi is excluded (and Joseph's portion is doubled on behalf of Menasseh and Ephraim).

וַיְבָרֶךְ אוֹתָם — *And he blessed them . . .* (an added blessing) to those already recorded above.

אִישׁ אֲשֶׁר כְּבִרְכָתוֹ בֵּרַךְ אֹתָם — *Every one according to his blessings he blessed them* — each according to his particular requirement; for Judah in the area of kingship, for Issachar regarding Torah, and for Levi pertaining to the *Avodah* (Sanctuary service).

NOTES

27. זְאֵב יִטְרָף — *A wolf that ravens.* To answer the obvious question as to how one can compare the leadership of Mordechai to the twilight of Jewish kingship in view of the ensuing period of the Second Temple (at which time there were periods during which they ruled, independent of foreign powers), the *Sforno* explains that since this period of Jewish history was brief and burdened with foreign rule, it is not considered as a period of authentic Jewish power and greatness.

28. כָּל אֵלֶּה שִׁבְטֵי יִשְׂרָאֵל שְׁנֵים עָשָׂר . . . וַיְבָרֶךְ אוֹתָם — *All these are the twelve tribes of Israel . . . And he blessed them.* The *Sforno* answers the question, "Why state *the twelve tribes of Israel;* isn't it self-evident?" Prior to these blessings given by Jacob to his sons, he stated, *"Ephraim and Menasseh even as Reuben and Simeon shall be mine."* That being the case, who are the twelve tribes? Or are there now thirteen? The Sages tell us that only in regard to inheritance of *Eretz Yisrael* will Ephraim and

27 *"Benjamin is a predatory wolf; in the morning he will devour prey and
in the evening he will distribute spoils."*
28 *All these are the tribes of Israel — twelve — and this is what their
father spoke to them and he blessed them; he blessed each according to his
appropriate blessing.*
29 *Then he instructed them; and he said to them, "I shall be gathered to
my people; bury me with my fathers in the cave that is in the field of
Ephron the Hittite.* 30 *In the cave that is in the field of Machpelah, which
faces Mamre, in the land of Canaan, which Abraham bought with the field
from Ephron the Hittite as a burial estate.* 31 *There they buried Abraham
and Sarah his wife; there they buried Isaac and Rebecca his wife; and there
I buried Leah.* 32 *Purchase of the field and the cave within it was from the
sons of Heth."*
33 *When Jacob finished instructing his sons, he drew his feet onto the bed;
he expired and was gathered to his people.*

50 1 *Then Joseph fell upon his father's face; he wept over him and kissed
him.* 2 *Joseph ordered his servants, the physicians, to embalm his
father; so the physicians embalmed Israel.*
3 *His forty-day term was completed, for such is the term of the
embalmed; and Egypt bewailed him for seventy days.* 4 *When his bewailing
period passed, Joseph spoke to Pharaoh's household, saying, "If*

---

30. אֲשֶׁר קָנָה אַבְרָהָם ... מֵאֵת עֶפְרֹן — *Which Abraham bought ... from Ephron.* Since they lived in another land for many years, Jacob told them the details regarding the purchase by Abraham from Ephron, and that his ancestors were already buried there, so that no one can challenge their rights.

L

2-3. וַיַּחַנְטוּ ... יִשְׂרָאֵל ... וַיִּבְכּוּ אֹתוֹ מִצְרַיִם — *They embalmed ... Israel ... The Egyptians wept for him.* They did so not only in Joseph's honor, or because they had been so ordered, but because he was 'Israel,' a worthy leader (in his own right); hence (they wept) as an act of homage.

4. וַיְדַבֵּר יוֹסֵף אֶל בֵּית פַּרְעֹה — *Joseph spoke unto the house of Pharaoh* ... because one is not allowed to enter the palace of the king while in mourning (lit., 'in sackcloth').

NOTES

Menasseh be reckoned as tribes, not insofar as any other privileges are concerned. Hence, when Jacob blesses his own sons, including Levi who has no share in *Eretz Yisrael*, the Torah stresses *these are the twelve tribes*, excluding Ephraim and Menasseh, who are not included in the twelve. The same is true later in Jewish history, when they stood at Mt. Grizim and Mt. Ebal, and at Gilgal, where they entered into a covenant with God. The tribes are twelve in number, "no more, no less."

The expression וַיְבָרֶךְ אוֹתָם, *And he blessed them*, is not repetitious, nor is it necessary to add, *Every one according to his blessings*, unless the Torah is adding the thought, as explained by the *Sforno*, that there were special blessings *added* by Jacob which fit the particular needs of those sons who were to play important roles of leadership, scholarship and service to God.

L

2-3. וַיַּחַנְטוּ ... אֶת יִשְׂרָאֵל ... וַיִּבְכּוּ אֹתוֹ — *They embalmed ... Israel ... wept for him.* The *Sforno* links the usage of the name Israel, rather than Jacob, to the mourning of the Egyptians. "Israel" denotes prestige and leadership qualities, virtues that the Egyptians recognized and appreciated in Jacob, and that is why their weeping was genuine.

4. וַיְדַבֵּר יוֹסֵף אֶל בֵּית פַּרְעֹה — *Joseph spoke unto the house of Pharaoh.* The phrase בֵּית פַּרְעֹה, *the house of Pharaoh*, implies that Joseph communicated

ה נָא מָצָאתִי חֵן בְּעֵינֵיכֶם דַּבְּרוּ־נָא בְּאָזְנֵי פַרְעֹה לֵאמֹר: אָבִי הִשְׁבִּיעַנִי
לֵאמֹר הִנֵּה אָנֹכִי מֵת בְּקִבְרִי אֲשֶׁר כָּרִיתִי לִי בְּאֶרֶץ כְּנַעַן שָׁמָּה תִּקְבְּרֵנִי
ו וְעַתָּה אֶעֱלֶה־נָּא וְאֶקְבְּרָה אֶת־אָבִי וְאָשׁוּבָה: וַיֹּאמֶר פַּרְעֹה עֲלֵה וּקְבֹר
ז אֶת־אָבִיךָ כַּאֲשֶׁר הִשְׁבִּיעֶךָ: וַיַּעַל יוֹסֵף לִקְבֹּר אֶת־אָבִיו וַיַּעֲלוּ אִתּוֹ
ח כָּל־עַבְדֵי פַרְעֹה זִקְנֵי בֵיתוֹ וְכֹל זִקְנֵי אֶרֶץ־מִצְרָיִם: וְכֹל בֵּית יוֹסֵף וְאֶחָיו
ט וּבֵית אָבִיו רַק טַפָּם וְצֹאנָם וּבְקָרָם עָזְבוּ בְּאֶרֶץ גֹּשֶׁן: וַיַּעַל עִמּוֹ גַּם־רֶכֶב
י גַּם־פָּרָשִׁים וַיְהִי הַמַּחֲנֶה כָּבֵד מְאֹד: וַיָּבֹאוּ עַד־גֹּרֶן הָאָטָד אֲשֶׁר בְּעֵבֶר
הַיַּרְדֵּן וַיִּסְפְּדוּ־שָׁם מִסְפֵּד גָּדוֹל וְכָבֵד מְאֹד וַיַּעַשׂ לְאָבִיו אֵבֶל שִׁבְעַת
יא יָמִים: וַיַּרְא יוֹשֵׁב הָאָרֶץ הַכְּנַעֲנִי אֶת־הָאֵבֶל בְּגֹרֶן הָאָטָד וַיֹּאמְרוּ
אֵבֶל־כָּבֵד זֶה לְמִצְרָיִם עַל־כֵּן קָרָא שְׁמָהּ אָבֵל מִצְרַיִם אֲשֶׁר בְּעֵבֶר
יב־יג הַיַּרְדֵּן: וַיַּעֲשׂוּ בָנָיו לוֹ כֵּן כַּאֲשֶׁר צִוָּם: וַיִּשְׂאוּ אֹתוֹ בָנָיו אַרְצָה כְּנַעַן
וַיִּקְבְּרוּ אֹתוֹ בִּמְעָרַת שְׂדֵה הַמַּכְפֵּלָה אֲשֶׁר קָנָה אַבְרָהָם אֶת־הַשָּׂדֶה
יד לַאֲחֻזַּת־קֶבֶר מֵאֵת עֶפְרֹן הַחִתִּי עַל־פְּנֵי מַמְרֵא: וַיָּשָׁב יוֹסֵף מִצְרַיְמָה
הוּא וְאֶחָיו וְכָל־הָעֹלִים אִתּוֹ לִקְבֹּר אֶת־אָבִיו אַחֲרֵי קָבְרוֹ אֶת־אָבִיו:
טו וַיִּרְאוּ אֲחֵי־יוֹסֵף כִּי־מֵת אֲבִיהֶם וַיֹּאמְרוּ לוּ יִשְׂטְמֵנוּ יוֹסֵף וְהָשֵׁב יָשִׁיב לָנוּ
טז אֵת כָּל־הָרָעָה אֲשֶׁר גָּמַלְנוּ אֹתוֹ: וַיְצַוּוּ אֶל־יוֹסֵף לֵאמֹר אָבִיךָ צִוָּה לִפְנֵי
יז מוֹתוֹ לֵאמֹר: כֹּה־תֹאמְרוּ לְיוֹסֵף אָנָּא שָׂא נָא פֶּשַׁע אַחֶיךָ וְחַטָּאתָם
כִּי־רָעָה גְמָלוּךָ וְעַתָּה שָׂא נָא לְפֶשַׁע עַבְדֵי אֱלֹהֵי אָבִיךָ וַיֵּבְךְּ יוֹסֵף
יח בְּדַבְּרָם אֵלָיו: וַיֵּלְכוּ גַּם־אֶחָיו וַיִּפְּלוּ לְפָנָיו וַיֹּאמְרוּ הִנֶּנּוּ לְךָ לַעֲבָדִים:

---

7. וַיַּעֲלוּ אִתּוֹ — *And with him went up* . . . of their own accord (not having been ordered by Joseph).

זִקְנֵי בֵיתוֹ וְכֹל זִקְנֵי אֶרֶץ מִצְרָיִם — *The elders of his house and the elders of the land of Egypt.* Because Jacob had been esteemed as a wise man in the eyes of the wise men of that generation. (*Elders* means "wise men") as it is written: וּזְקֵנָיו יְחַכֵּם, *And teach his elders wisdom (Psalms* 105:22).

9. גַּם רֶכֶב גַּם פָּרָשִׁים — *Also chariots and horsemen* . . . because the military chiefs regarded Jacob as a great warrior.

16. וַיְצַוּוּ אֶל יוֹסֵף — *And they (sent a message) to Joseph.* They sent (a message) through the servants of Jacob, or others, *regarding* Joseph, as we find, וַיְצַוֵּם אֶל בְּנֵי יִשְׂרָאֵל, *And gave them a charge unto the children of Israel (Exodus* 6:13).

לֵאמֹר אָבִיךָ צִוָּה — *Saying, "Your father did command."* He commanded us that we should say to you these words if we are concerned and apprehensive (lest you punish us), *but not in his name,* for he would never suspect you of doing us any harm.

NOTES

with officials of the government, not directly with Pharaoh. This is strange; since Joseph certainly had access to the king himself, why use intermediaries for such an important request? The answer must be that he could not enter the palace while in a state of mourning, since his clothes were probably rent and his appearance unkempt.

7-9. זִקְנֵי בֵיתוֹ וְכֹל זִקְנֵי אֶרֶץ מִצְרָיִם . . . גַּם רֶכֶב גַּם פָּרָשִׁים — *The elders of his house and the elders of the land of Egypt . . . Also chariots and horsemen.* Jacob was held in high regard for his great wisdom as well as for his military prowess. Hence both the wise men and the military chiefs paid him homage.

you please — if I have found favor in your eyes, speak now in the ears of
Pharaoh, saying: 5 *My father had adjured me, saying, 'Behold, I am about*
to die; in my grave, which I have hewn for myself in the land of Canaan —
there you are to bury me.' Now, I will go up if you please, and bury my
father; then I will return."
6 *And Pharaoh said, "Go up and bury your father as he adjured you."*
7 *So Joseph went up to bury his father, and with him went up all of*
Pharaoh's servants, the elders of his household, and all the elders of
the land of Egypt, 8 *and all of Joseph's household — his brothers, and*
his father's household; only their young children, their flocks, and their
cattle did they leave in the region of Goshen. 9 *And he brought up with*
him both chariots and horsemen; and the camp was very imposing. 10 *They*
came to Goren HaAtad, which is across the Jordan, and there they held
a very great and imposing eulogy; and he ordained a seven-day mourning
period for his father. 11 *When the Canaanite inhabitants of the land saw*
the mourning in Goren HaAtad, they said, "This is a grievous mourning
for Egypt." Therefore, it was named Avel Mizraim, which is across the
Jordan.
12 *His sons did for him exactly as he had instructed them.* 13 *His sons*
carried him to the land of Canaan and they buried him in the cave of the
Machpelah field, the field that Abraham had bought as a burial estate from
Ephron the Hittite, facing Mamre. 14 *Joseph returned to Egypt — he and his*
brothers, and all who had gone up with him to bury his father — after he
buried his father.
15 *Joseph's brothers perceived that their father was dead, and they said,*
"Perhaps Joseph will nurse hatred against us and then he will surely repay
us all the evil that we did him." 16 *So they instructed that Joseph be told,*
"Your father gave orders before his death, saying: 17 *'Thus shall you say to*
Joseph: "O please, kindly forgive the spiteful deed of your brothers and
their sin for they have done you evil" '; so now, please forgive the spiteful
deed of the servants of your father's God." And Joseph wept when they
spoke to him.
18 *His brothers themselves also went and flung themselves before him*
and said, "We are ready to be your slaves."

לִפְנֵי מותו — *Before his death.* (Since this happened right before he died) we had no opportunity to tell you about it until now.

17. וַיֵּבְךְּ יוֹסֵף — *And Joseph wept* ... when reminded of his father, and his love and confidence in him (that he would do no evil).

NOTES

16. וַיְצַוּוּ אֶל יוֹסֵף – *And they (sent a message) to Joseph.* The word וַיְצַוּוּ, *and they commanded,* cannot be understood literally, for how could the brothers command Joseph? The meaning must therefore be they instructed messengers to speak to Joseph; the word אֶל in this case does not mean *to* but *regarding* Joseph.

17. וַיֵּבְךְּ יוֹסֵף — *And Joseph wept.* The *Midrash* explains Joseph's weeping differently; he was distraught that his father suspected him of hatred toward his brothers. The *Sforno* rejects this interpretation and explains the weeping as tears of joy and relief that his father was confident he would not take revenge on his brothers.

יט־כ וַיֹּאמֶר אֲלֵהֶם יוֹסֵף אַל־תִּירָאוּ כִּי הֲתַחַת אֱלֹהִים אָנִי׃ וְאַתֶּם חֲשַׁבְתֶּם
עָלַי רָעָה אֱלֹהִים חֲשָׁבָהּ לְטֹבָה לְמַעַן עֲשֹׂה כַּיּוֹם הַזֶּה לְהַחֲיֹת עַם־רָב׃
שביעי כא וְעַתָּה אַל־תִּירָאוּ אָנֹכִי אֲכַלְכֵּל אֶתְכֶם וְאֶת־טַפְּכֶם וַיְנַחֵם אוֹתָם וַיְדַבֵּר
כב עַל־לִבָּם׃ וַיֵּשֶׁב יוֹסֵף בְּמִצְרַיִם הוּא וּבֵית אָבִיו וַיְחִי יוֹסֵף מֵאָה וָעֶשֶׂר
כג שָׁנִים׃ וַיַּרְא יוֹסֵף לְאֶפְרַיִם בְּנֵי שִׁלֵּשִׁים גַּם בְּנֵי מָכִיר בֶּן־מְנַשֶּׁה יֻלְּדוּ
כד עַל־בִּרְכֵּי יוֹסֵף׃ וַיֹּאמֶר יוֹסֵף אֶל־אֶחָיו אָנֹכִי מֵת וֵאלֹהִים פָּקֹד יִפְקֹד
אֶתְכֶם וְהֶעֱלָה אֶתְכֶם מִן־הָאָרֶץ הַזֹּאת אֶל־הָאָרֶץ אֲשֶׁר נִשְׁבַּע
כה לְאַבְרָהָם לְיִצְחָק וּלְיַעֲקֹב׃ וַיַּשְׁבַּע יוֹסֵף אֶת־בְּנֵי יִשְׂרָאֵל לֵאמֹר פָּקֹד
כו יִפְקֹד אֱלֹהִים אֶתְכֶם וְהַעֲלִתֶם אֶת־עַצְמֹתַי מִזֶּה׃ וַיָּמָת יוֹסֵף בֶּן־מֵאָה
וָעֶשֶׂר שָׁנִים וַיַּחַנְטוּ אֹתוֹ וַיִּישֶׂם בָּאָרוֹן בְּמִצְרָיִם׃

---

19. הֲתַחַת אֱלֹהִים אָנִי — *Am I in the place of God?* It is not for me to judge you, or to judge God's decrees. How can I punish His agents, for certainly you were God's agents, as we read, לֹא אַתֶּם שְׁלַחְתֶּם אֹתִי הֵנָּה כִּי הָאֱלֹהִים, *It was not you who sent me hither, but God* (45:8). This would be akin to בֵּית דִין הַמְּבַטֵּל דִּבְרֵי בֵּית דִּין חֲבֵירוֹ, *A court setting aside the decision of another court* (*Eduyos* 1:5).

20. וְאַתֶּם חֲשַׁבְתֶּם עָלַי רָעָה — *You meant evil against me.* Your act was in error, because you considered me to be a רוֹדֵף, *pursuer*, and had it been so, your act would have been justified.

NOTES

19. הֲתַחַת אֱלֹהִים אָנִי – *Am I in the place of God?* God's decision and decree is comparable to the *p'sak* (decision) of a religious court. The law is that a court cannot override the decision of the first court unless they are greater in number and wisdom. No man dare arrogate such authority to himself vis-a-vis the Almighty! Therefore Joseph reassures his brothers that he would never punish them for an act which God utilized for the fulfillment of His Divine plan.

[19] *But Joseph said to them, "Fear not, for am I instead of God?*
[20] *Although you intended me harm, God intended it for good: in order to accomplish — it is as clear as this day — that a vast people be kept alive.*
[21] *So now, fear not — I will sustain you and your young ones." Thus he comforted them and spoke to their heart.*

[22] *Joseph dwelt in Egypt — he and his father's household — and Joseph lived one hundred and ten years.* [23] *Joseph saw three generations through Ephraim; even the sons of Machir son of Manasseh were raised on Joseph's knees.*

[24] *Joseph said to his brothers, "I am about to die, but God will surely remember you and bring you up out of this land to the land that He swore to Abraham, to Isaac, and to Jacob."*

[25] *Then Joseph adjured the children of Israel saying, "When God will indeed remember you, then you must bring my bones up out of here."*

[26] *Joseph died at the age of one hundred and ten years; they embalmed him and he was placed in a coffin in Egypt.*

אֱלֹהִים חֲשָׁבָהּ לְטֹבָה — *God meant it for good.* He utilized this error for a good purpose.

26. וַיַּחַנְטוּ אֹתוֹ וַיִּישֶׂם בָּאָרוֹן — *And they embalmed him and he was put in a coffin.* His bones were placed in the same coffin in which he was embalmed. He was never buried in the earth, hence the coffin was known to future generations. Moses was able therefore to take it with him, as it is written, וַיִּקַּח מֹשֶׁה אֶת עַצְמוֹת יוֹסֵף, *And Moses took the bones of Joseph* (*Ex.* 13:19).

NOTES

26. וַיַּחַנְטוּ אֹתוֹ וַיִּישֶׂם בָּאָרוֹן – *And they embalmed him and he was put in a coffin.* The word בָּאָרוֹן, *in a coffin,* is vowelized with a קָמָץ (ָ) under the ב, not a שְׁוָא (ְ). This transforms it into a definite article, *the coffin.* This indicates that Joseph's bones were placed in the same coffin in which he was embalmed, and this coffin was known to future generations. This in turn enabled Moses to locate it at the time of the Exodus.

ספר שמות

Shemos / Exodus

Sforno's Introduction

In this second book it is related how the seed of Israel became enslaved in Egypt because of their violation of the covenant of the Patriarchs. As the Prophet Ezekiel states, וַיַּמְרוּ בִי וְלֹא אָבוּ לִשְׁמֹעַ אֵלַי, אִישׁ אֶת שִׁקּוּצֵי עֵינֵיהֶם לֹא הִשְׁלִיכוּ, וְאֶת גִּלּוּלֵי מִצְרַיִם לֹא עָזָבוּ, וָאֹמַר לִשְׁפֹּךְ חֲמָתִי עֲלֵיהֶם, לְכַלּוֹת אַפִּי בָּהֶם בְּתוֹךְ אֶרֶץ מִצְרָיִם, *And they rebelled against Me and chose not to listen to Me; they, each one (of them), did not cast away the detestable things of their eyes nor did they forsake the idols of Egypt; then I said I would pour out My fury upon them to spend My anger upon them in the land of Egypt* (*Ezekiel* 20:8). Thus were they enslaved with hard labor until a small number repented, prayed to God and a messenger did save them.[1]

The book then proceeds to relate how initially, when God chose to honor the Israelites, He spoke to them face to face and thus they were granted crowns of spiritual glory at Mount Horeb. They did, however, rebel against God and (were forced) to remove their crowns (*Exodus* 33:6), and the Divine Presence departed from them.[2]

The book then continues to tell us how in spite of all this God did not refrain from correcting their ways so that His presence (*Shechinah*) might dwell once again in their midst. He commanded that a Sanctuary be built, vessels be fashioned, and priests be invested in their sacred service; thus did the *Shechinah* return to their midst after their seemingly complete spiritual impairment and state of despair. Thus does this second book conclude.[3]

---

1. In the history of the Jewish people naught *occurs*, there are no accidental events — everything is the result of God's decrees and decisions, determining the destiny of Israel. The bondage in Egypt was not the result of political developments or military considerations; it was due to the straying of Israel from the path of righteousness and holiness as lived by the Patriarchs. Their subsequent liberation resulted from their repentance, which encompassed only a small percentage of the total Jewish people; as our Sages have taught us, only one-fifth were redeemed and left Egypt. The messenger refers to Moses.

2. This refers to the events immediately following the episode of the Golden Calf. The unique level of spiritual greatness realized by the Jews at the time of receiving the Torah was dissipated and God no longer appeared to Moses in the Camp of Israel — only outside the Camp. This indicated His displeasure with the Jews and demonstrated their fall from grace.

3. The second Tablets of Law represented a fresh opportunity granted to the Jews whereby they could regain once again their former spiritual status. This renewed elevated status was to be captured and concentrated in the *Mishkan* (Sanctuary) where God would cause His Divine Presence to dwell. Though Israel had fallen they were shown the way to return, and after transgression and rejection, fulfillment and hope became theirs once again.

פרשת שמות

א

א וְאֵלֶּה שְׁמוֹת בְּנֵי יִשְׂרָאֵל הַבָּאִים מִצְרָיְמָה אֵת יַעֲקֹב אִישׁ וּבֵיתוֹ בָּאוּ׃
ב־ד רְאוּבֵן שִׁמְעוֹן לֵוִי וִיהוּדָה׃ יִשָּׂשכָר זְבוּלֻן וּבִנְיָמִן׃ דָּן וְנַפְתָּלִי גָּד וְאָשֵׁר׃
ה־ו וַיְהִי כָּל־נֶפֶשׁ יֹצְאֵי יֶרֶךְ־יַעֲקֹב שִׁבְעִים נָפֶשׁ וְיוֹסֵף הָיָה בְמִצְרָיִם׃ וַיָּמָת
ז יוֹסֵף וְכָל־אֶחָיו וְכֹל הַדּוֹר הַהוּא׃ וּבְנֵי יִשְׂרָאֵל פָּרוּ וַיִּשְׁרְצוּ וַיִּרְבּוּ וַיַּעַצְמוּ
בִּמְאֹד מְאֹד וַתִּמָּלֵא הָאָרֶץ אֹתָם׃
ח־ט וַיָּקָם מֶלֶךְ־חָדָשׁ עַל־מִצְרָיִם אֲשֶׁר לֹא־יָדַע אֶת־יוֹסֵף׃ וַיֹּאמֶר אֶל־
י עַמּוֹ הִנֵּה עַם בְּנֵי יִשְׂרָאֵל רַב וְעָצוּם מִמֶּנּוּ׃ הָבָה נִתְחַכְּמָה לוֹ פֶּן־
יִרְבֶּה וְהָיָה כִּי־תִקְרֶאנָה מִלְחָמָה וְנוֹסַף גַּם־הוּא עַל־שֹׂנְאֵינוּ וְנִלְחַם־
יא בָּנוּ וְעָלָה מִן־הָאָרֶץ׃ וַיָּשִׂימוּ עָלָיו שָׂרֵי מִסִּים לְמַעַן עַנֹּתוֹ בְּסִבְלֹתָם

I

1. וְאֵלֶּה שְׁמוֹת — *These are the names.* Those who are mentioned here were worthy to be named for each was worthy of his name which indicates and reflects the stature and character of that man. These men were a beacon of light throughout their lifetime so that their generation did not become degraded. However, after their demise, even the righteous among their children were not equally important and worthy in the eyes of God and man.

6. וְכֹל הַדּוֹר הַהוּא — *And all that generation.* All seventy souls; that generation did not become (totally) degraded or demeaned all the days of their life.

7. פָּרוּ וַיִּשְׁרְצוּ — *Were fruitful and increased abundantly.* After the death of the original seventy souls, their descendants deviated from the ways of their fathers and followed the ways of creeping creatures, who pursue a path leading to the pit. (And therefore . . .)

8. וַיָּקָם מֶלֶךְ חָדָשׁ . . . אֲשֶׁר לֹא יָדַע אֶת יוֹסֵף — *There arose a new king . . . who knew not Joseph.* Although there certainly was a record of Joseph's accomplishments in the annals of the kings, especially regarding the law of the "Fifth" (*Gen.* 47:26) promulgated by him, nonetheless, the new king could not conceive that Joseph could have been a member of this same people so that Israel should be worthy of consideration on his account.

10. הָבָה נִתְחַכְּמָה לוֹ — *Come let us deal wisely with them.* To deal with them in a devious manner.

NOTES

I

1. וְאֵלֶּה שְׁמוֹת — *These are the names.* A man's name is important; it is an indication of his stature, an index to his very essence and character. This is reflected in the fact that the Torah considers him of sufficient worth to be recorded and mentioned. We find a similar approach in the *Sforno* in *Genesis* (46:8) and *Numbers* (1:2) where he also stresses the honored and valued role that names play in our Torah. Only certain names are carried by Aaron on his vestments before God. Those who are elevated from their brethren are alone considered worthy to have their names recorded. וָאֵדָעֲךָ בְּשֵׁם, *and I know you by name* (33:17), is a sign of favor.

6. וְכֹל הַדּוֹר הַהוּא — *And all that generation.* Although all the seventy souls are not considered important enough to be listed individually again here (the seventy are enumerated in *Genesis* 46:8-27), nonetheless a spirit of piety and sanctity permeated all of them and they remained steadfast in their unique way of life, unaffected by the alien environment.

7. פָּרוּ וַיִּשְׁרְצוּ — *Were fruitful and increased abundantly.* The *Sforno's* text reads שרצים שרצים — the first is to be vowelized שְׁרָצִים, *creeping creatures;* the second, שָׁרָצִים, *who run.* The *Sforno* allows himself a play on words: Those who behave as creeping creatures pursue a path which leads hastily to the pit.

The expression used by the *Sforno,* שָׁרָצִים לִבְאֵר שַׁחַת, *who pursue a path leading to the pit,* is taken from Tractate *Berachos* 28b.

8. וַיָּקָם מֶלֶךְ חָדָשׁ . . . אֲשֶׁר לֹא יָדַע אֶת יוֹסֵף — *There arose a new king . . . who knew not Joseph.* It is nigh impossible for any king of Egypt to have forgotten Joseph, or even to *act* unknowing. Such deceit is

PARASHAS SHEMOS

1 [1] *And these are the names of the Children of Israel who were coming to
Egypt; with Jacob, each man and his household came.* [2] *Reuben,
Simeon, Levi, and Judah;* [3] *Issachar, Zebulun, and Benjamin;* [4] *Dan and
Naphtali; Gad and Asher.* [5] *And all the persons who emerged from Jacob's
loins were seventy souls, and Joseph was in Egypt.* [6] *Joseph died, and all his
brothers and that entire generation.* [7] *The Children of Israel were fruitful,
teemed, increased, and became strong — very, very much so; and the land
became filled with them.*

[8] *A new king arose over Egypt, who did not know of Joseph.* [9] *He said to
his people, "Behold! the people, the Children of Israel are more numerous
and stronger than we.* [10] *Come, let us outsmart it lest it become numerous and
it may be that if a war will occur, it, too, may join our enemies, and wage war
against us and go up from the land."*

[11] *So they appointed taskmasters over it in order to afflict it with their*

וְעָלָה מִן הָאָרֶץ — *And get them up out of the land.* By their own volition; so it will not be necessary to drive them out by force, without reason, for this course would cause us to be a derision among our enemies. And this we shall do ...

פֶּן יִרְבֶּה וְהָיָה כִּי תִקְרֶאנָה מִלְחָמָה — *Lest they multiply and it come to pass when there befalls us any war.* When the evils and hardships of war befall us — (this abbreviated expression is) similar to וַתְּכַל דָּוִד הַמֶּלֶךְ, *and (the soul of) King David failed with longing (II Samuel* 13:39) (the word *soul* is understood and not specifically stated) ...

וְנוֹסַף גַּם הוּא עַל שֹׂנְאֵינוּ — *They also will join themselves to our enemies.* Since they are separated from us (and different from us) in that they are circumcised, speak a different language, and follow Hebrew customs in a manner that, לֹא יוּכְלוּן הַמִּצְרִים לֶאֱכֹל אֶת הָעִבְרִים לֶחֶם, *the Egyptians may not eat bread with the Hebrews (Genesis* 43:32), then they are without a doubt our enemies and their enmity will be revealed during the (strain and) duress of wartime.

11. לְמַעַן עַנֹּתוֹ — *To afflict them.* So that they (the Jews) shall voluntarily leave our land for another.

NOTES

unthinkable and would be unwise politically, since the law of granting one-fifth of all produce to Pharaoh was instituted by Joseph. The *Sforno,* consistent with his principle that evil befell the Jews due to their sinfulness, explains that this Pharaoh could not conceive that such a noble soul — Joseph — and such a base people — Israel — could be related. Hence gratitude and appreciation were uncalled for.

10. הָבָה נִתְחַכְּמָה לוֹ ... וְעָלָה מִן הָאָרֶץ — *Come let us deal wisely with them ... and get them up out of the land.* The original intention of the Egyptians was not to enslave the Hebrews but to make conditions unbearable for them, thereby compelling them to leave voluntarily. The Egyptians were sensitive to the opinion of other nations, hence they attempted in devious ways to rid themselves of this potential "fifth column" for they were convinced that a people so alien and strange as the Jews would certainly be disloyal in a time of national crisis.

The *Sforno* changes the sequence of the verse in his commentary. In the text, the phrase וְעָלָה מִן הָאָרֶץ, *and get them up out of the land,* appears after פֶּן יִרְבֶּה, *lest they multiply,* and וְנוֹסַף גַּם הוּא עַל שֹׂנְאֵינוּ, *they also will join themselves to our enemies.* The *Sforno,* however, comments on the former phrase before the latter phrases. The reason is because the *Sforno* wishes to explain the goal and purpose of Pharaoh's decree before stating the motivation. The goal was to force the Israelites to leave the land of their own volition, thereby ridding Egypt of an element which Pharaoh considered a threat to his kingdom. After interpreting the verse of *get them up out of the land,* he then explains the fear and apprehension which motivated Pharaoh's actions. These are reflected in the phrases of *lest they multiply,* and *they also will join themselves to our enemies.*

יב וַיִּבֶן עָרֵי מִסְכְּנוֹת לְפַרְעֹה אֶת־פִּתֹם וְאֶת־רַעַמְסֵס: וְכַאֲשֶׁר יְעַנּוּ אֹתוֹ כֵּן
יג יִרְבֶּה וְכֵן יִפְרֹץ וַיָּקֻצוּ מִפְּנֵי בְּנֵי יִשְׂרָאֵל: וַיַּעֲבִדוּ מִצְרַיִם אֶת־בְּנֵי יִשְׂרָאֵל
יד בְּפָרֶךְ: וַיְמָרְרוּ אֶת־חַיֵּיהֶם בַּעֲבֹדָה קָשָׁה בְּחֹמֶר וּבִלְבֵנִים וּבְכָל־עֲבֹדָה
טו בַּשָּׂדֶה אֵת כָּל־עֲבֹדָתָם אֲשֶׁר־עָבְדוּ בָהֶם בְּפָרֶךְ: וַיֹּאמֶר מֶלֶךְ מִצְרַיִם
טז לַמְיַלְּדֹת הָעִבְרִיֹּת אֲשֶׁר שֵׁם הָאַחַת שִׁפְרָה וְשֵׁם הַשֵּׁנִית פּוּעָה: וַיֹּאמֶר
בְּיַלֶּדְכֶן אֶת־הָעִבְרִיּוֹת וּרְאִיתֶן עַל־הָאָבְנָיִם אִם־בֵּן הוּא וַהֲמִתֶּן אֹתוֹ וְאִם־
יז בַּת הִוא וָחָיָה: וַתִּירֶאןָ הַמְיַלְּדֹת אֶת־הָאֱלֹהִים וְלֹא עָשׂוּ כַּאֲשֶׁר דִּבֶּר
שני יח אֲלֵיהֶן מֶלֶךְ מִצְרָיִם וַתְּחַיֶּיןָ אֶת־הַיְלָדִים: וַיִּקְרָא מֶלֶךְ־מִצְרַיִם לַמְיַלְּדֹת
יט וַיֹּאמֶר לָהֶן מַדּוּעַ עֲשִׂיתֶן הַדָּבָר הַזֶּה וַתְּחַיֶּיןָ אֶת־הַיְלָדִים: וַתֹּאמַרְןָ
הַמְיַלְּדֹת אֶל־פַּרְעֹה כִּי לֹא כַנָּשִׁים הַמִּצְרִיֹּת הָעִבְרִיֹּת כִּי־חָיוֹת הֵנָּה בְּטֶרֶם
כ תָּבוֹא אֲלֵהֶן הַמְיַלֶּדֶת וְיָלָדוּ: וַיֵּיטֶב אֱלֹהִים לַמְיַלְּדֹת וַיִּרֶב הָעָם וַיַּעַצְמוּ
כא־כב מְאֹד: וַיְהִי כִּי־יָרְאוּ הַמְיַלְּדֹת אֶת־הָאֱלֹהִים וַיַּעַשׂ לָהֶם בָּתִּים: וַיְצַו פַּרְעֹה
לְכָל־עַמּוֹ לֵאמֹר כָּל־הַבֵּן הַיִּלּוֹד הַיְאֹרָה תַּשְׁלִיכֻהוּ וְכָל־הַבַּת תְּחַיּוּן:
ב א־ב וַיֵּלֶךְ אִישׁ מִבֵּית לֵוִי וַיִּקַּח אֶת־בַּת־לֵוִי: וַתַּהַר הָאִשָּׁה וַתֵּלֶד בֵּן וַתֵּרֶא אֹתוֹ
ג כִּי־טוֹב הוּא וַתִּצְפְּנֵהוּ שְׁלֹשָׁה יְרָחִים: וְלֹא־יָכְלָה עוֹד הַצְּפִינוֹ וַתִּקַּח־לוֹ

וַיִּבֶן עָרֵי מִסְכְּנוֹת — *And they built store-cities.* But they accepted upon themselves the task of building these cities.

13. וַיַּעֲבִדוּ מִצְרַיִם — *And the Egyptians made (the Children of Israel) to serve.* When (the Egyptians) observed how the Jews degraded themselves and were willing to occupy themselves with such base labor they made them into slaves. All this resulted because the Jews continued to add חַטָּאת עַל חַטָּאת, *sin upon sin,* so they were deprived of reason and progressed מֵרָעָה אֶל רָעָה, *from evil to evil.*

14. וַיְמָרְרוּ אֶת חַיֵּיהֶם — *And they made their lives bitter.* As the Jews continued to sin in beliefs and practices, as the Prophet testifies: וַיַּמְרוּ בִי וְלֹא אָבוּ לִשְׁמֹעַ אֵלַי, אִישׁ אֶת שִׁקּוּצֵי עֵינֵיהֶם לֹא הִשְׁלִיכוּ, וְאֶת גִּלּוּלֵי מִצְרַיִם לֹא עָזָבוּ, וָאֹמַר לִשְׁפֹּךְ חֲמָתִי עֲלֵיהֶם, לְכַלּוֹת אַפִּי בָּהֶם בְּתוֹךְ אֶרֶץ מִצְרָיִם *But they rebelled against Me and would not hearken unto Me; they did not every man cast away the detestable things of their eyes, neither did they forsake the idols of Egypt; then I said I would pour out My fury upon them, to spend My anger upon them, in the midst of the land of Egypt* (*Ezekiel* 20:8), so did the hand of the oppressor increase in severity.

15. לַמְיַלְּדֹת הָעִבְרִיֹּת — *To the Hebrew midwives.* Certainly among such a large population there were more than two midwives. These, however, were the trusted ones in the capital city of Egypt, and after they betrayed the trust placed in them personally by the king, he no longer felt he could rely upon midwives in other places.

NOTES

11-13. לְמַעַן עַנֹּתוֹ . . . וַיַּעֲבִדוּ מִצְרַיִם — *To afflict them . . . And the Egyptians made (the Children of Israel) to serve.* Ironically, the Jews accepted upon themselves as a civic duty the building of these cities and voluntarily subjected themselves. This subjection resulted in their total subjugation. How did they permit themselves such folly? The *Sforno* answers that the transgressions of man cause reason to flee and wisdom to depart from him.

The expression *sin upon sin* is based on *Isaiah* 30:1; and *from evil to evil,* on *Jeremiah* 9:2.

14. וַיְמָרְרוּ אֶת חַיֵּיהֶם — *And they made their lives bitter.* God has many messengers — and the severity of oppression reflects the seriousness of Israel's spiritual decline. The *Sforno* interprets the sentence in *Ezekiel* as referring to the period when the Jews were in Egypt and departed from God's ways, thereby bringing upon themselves Divine wrath and punishment. *In the land of Egypt* does not refer to the Israelites' *subsequent* wickedness in pursuing Egyptian ways years later, as is understood by other commentaries.

burdens; it built storage cities for Pharaoh, Pithom and Raamses. [12] *But as much as they would afflict it, so it would increase and so it would spread out; and they became disgusted because of the Children of Israel.* [13] *The Egyptians enslaved the Children of Israel with crushing harshness.* [14] *They embittered their lives with hard work, with mortar and with bricks, and with every labor of the field; all their labors that they performed with them were with crushing harshness.*

[15] *The king of Egypt said to the Hebrew midwives, of whom the name of the first was Shifrah and the name of the second was Puah —* [16] *and he said, "When you deliver the Hebrew women, and you see them on the birthstool; if it is a son, you are to kill him, and if it is a daughter, she shall live."* [17] *But the midwives feared God and they did not do as the king of Egypt spoke to them, and they caused the boys to live.*

[18] *The king of Egypt summoned the midwives and said to them, "Why have you done this thing, that you have caused the boys to live!"*

[19] *The midwives said to Pharaoh, "Because the Hebrew women are unlike the Egyptian women, for they are experts; before the midwife comes to them, they have given birth."*

[20] *God benefited the midwives — and the people increased and became very strong.* [21] *And it was because the midwives feared God that He made them houses.*

[22] *Pharaoh commanded his entire people, saying, "Every son that will be born — into the River shall you throw him! And every daughter shall you keep alive!"*

2 [1] *A man went from the house of Levi and he took a daughter of Levi.* [2] *The woman conceived and gave birth to a son. She saw that he was good and she hid him for three months.* [3] *She could not hide him any longer, so she*

18. מַדּוּעַ עֲשִׂיתֶן — *Why have you done (this thing)?* You betrayed me, for when I made my request you did not refuse me and I trusted you to destroy the children, but my hope was frustrated.

וַתְּחַיֶּיןָ אֶת הַיְלָדִים — *And you have saved the children alive.* Not only did you fail to do as I commanded to destroy the infants, but you also counseled them (the women in childbirth) so as to preserve (the children).

19. כִּי חָיוֹת הֵנָּה — *For they are lively.* (The Jewish women are) skilled in childbirth and if we should attempt to act improperly through deed or word, they will immediately be aware of our intent and no longer will our services be solicited, and "it would not profit the king" to kill only one or two.

II

2. כִּי טוֹב הוּא — *That he was fair* (lit., *good*). "Fair," as we find, כִּי טֹבֹת הֵנָּה, *they were fair* (*Genesis* 6:2). She saw that he was unusually beautiful and she felt that this must be for some specific purpose of his Maker, for beauty of form indicates physical superiority and

NOTES

19. כִּי חָיוֹת הֵנָּה — *For they are lively.* The midwives argued that it would be far better for them to bide their time and gain the confidence of the other women. Then they would be able to comply with Pharaoh's request in a more successful manner.

II

2. כִּי טוֹב הוּא — *That he was a fair child.* The word טוֹב in the context of the sentence does not mean *good*, but *fair*. The *Sforno* cites as proof the expression used in *Genesis* regarding the beautiful

תֵּבַת גֹּמֶא וַתַּחְמְרָה בַחֵמָר וּבַזָּפֶת וַתָּשֶׂם בָּהּ אֶת־הַיֶּלֶד וַתָּשֶׂם בַּסּוּף עַל־
ד־ה שְׂפַת הַיְאֹר׃ וַתֵּתַצַּב אֲחֹתוֹ מֵרָחֹק לְדֵעָה מַה־יֵּעָשֶׂה לוֹ׃ וַתֵּרֶד בַּת־פַּרְעֹה
לִרְחֹץ עַל־הַיְאֹר וְנַעֲרֹתֶיהָ הֹלְכֹת עַל־יַד הַיְאֹר וַתֵּרֶא אֶת־הַתֵּבָה בְּתוֹךְ
ו הַסּוּף וַתִּשְׁלַח אֶת־אֲמָתָהּ וַתִּקָּחֶהָ׃ וַתִּפְתַּח וַתִּרְאֵהוּ אֶת־הַיֶּלֶד וְהִנֵּה־נַעַר
ז בֹּכֶה וַתַּחְמֹל עָלָיו וַתֹּאמֶר מִיַּלְדֵי הָעִבְרִים זֶה׃ וַתֹּאמֶר אֲחֹתוֹ אֶל־בַּת־
פַּרְעֹה הַאֵלֵךְ וְקָרָאתִי לָךְ אִשָּׁה מֵינֶקֶת מִן הָעִבְרִיֹּת וְתֵינִק לָךְ אֶת־
ח הַיָּלֶד׃ וַתֹּאמֶר־לָהּ בַּת־פַּרְעֹה לֵכִי וַתֵּלֶךְ הָעַלְמָה וַתִּקְרָא אֶת־אֵם הַיָּלֶד׃
ט וַתֹּאמֶר לָהּ בַּת־פַּרְעֹה הֵילִיכִי אֶת־הַיֶּלֶד הַזֶּה וְהֵינִקִהוּ לִי וַאֲנִי אֶתֵּן
י אֶת־שְׂכָרֵךְ וַתִּקַּח הָאִשָּׁה הַיֶּלֶד וַתְּנִיקֵהוּ׃ וַיִּגְדַּל הַיֶּלֶד וַתְּבִאֵהוּ לְבַת־
פַּרְעֹה וַיְהִי־לָהּ לְבֵן וַתִּקְרָא שְׁמוֹ מֹשֶׁה וַתֹּאמֶר כִּי מִן־הַמַּיִם מְשִׁיתִהוּ׃

---

perfection of one's imaginative powers.

3. וַתָּשֶׂם בַּסּוּף — *And she placed it in the bulrushes.* A place where the passersby would not be likely to observe her when she placed the basket there. Nonetheless, she chose a place in the reeds so as to transfer the royal decree of casting the child in the river to that of placing him into the reeds at the banks of the river.

4. לְדֵעָה מַה יֵּעָשֶׂה לוֹ — *To know what would be done to him.* She thought that some Egyptian would claim him as a foundling, for there were many foundlings in the land, without a doubt, since the land was filled with lewdness and immorality, as the Prophet testifies, וְזִרְמַת סוּסִים זִרְמָתָם, *their issue is like the issue of horses* (*Ezekiel* 23:20).

5. לִרְחֹץ עַל הַיְאֹר — *To bathe in the river.* In a royal room close to and overlooking the river, for without a doubt, since כְּבוּדָּה בַת מֶלֶךְ פְּנִימָה, *the king's daughter is all glorious within* (*Psalms* 45:14), she would not go down to the (open) river.

וְנַעֲרֹתֶיהָ הֹלְכֹת עַל יַד הַיְאֹר — *And her maidens* (i.e., her ladies-in-waiting) *walked along the riverside.* Therefore, she did not send one of them to fetch the basket since they were not with her.

וַתִּשְׁלַח אֶת אֲמָתָהּ — *And she sent her handmaiden (to fetch it).* The handmaiden who was attending her at her bath. All this happened by the will of God so that one of her ladies-in-waiting should not be sent to fetch (the child), since she might decide to cast the child into the river (of her own volition).

6. וַתִּפְתַּח וַתִּרְאֵהוּ — *And she opened it and saw (the child).* She saw that he was exceptionally beautiful and goodly.

NOTES

women who were coveted by the *B'nai Elohim*, where the word טֹבֹת is also used in the context of that episode, where it cannot mean *good*, but *fair*.

3. וַתָּשֶׂם בַּסּוּף — *And she placed it in the bulrushes.* Although a decree is issued by a temporal ruler, it is our belief that without the tacit acquiescence of God it would not have been decreed. Hence we must not defy it outright. We can, however, circumvent the decree, and this Yocheved did by placing the basket at the edge of the river in the reeds — thereby not actually defying the decree but observing, as it were, the spirit although not the letter of the law. The *Sforno,* in this manner, answers the obvious question: Why set the infant in such a comparatively hazardous place rather than a more secure one? But then the decree would have been flaunted outright — now it is partially observed. The Abarbanel gives a similar interpretation.

5. וַתִּשְׁלַח אֶת אֲמָתָהּ — *And she sent her handmaiden (to fetch it).* A lady-in-waiting is likely to use her own discretion and cast away the child without first consulting the princess. A mere handmaiden would never make her own decision but would always obey her mistress. The Divine pattern of God's intervention and concern is apparent in this initial episode of Moses's life.

6. וַתִּפְתַּח וַתִּרְאֵהוּ ... וַתֹּאמֶר מִיַּלְדֵי הָעִבְרִים זֶה — *And she opened it and saw (the child) . . . and she said, "This is one of the Hebrew children."* The unusual physical appearance of the child causes

took for him a wicker basket and smeared it with clay and pitch; she placed the child into it and placed it among the reeds at the bank of the River. 4 *His sister stationed herself at a distance to know what would be done with him.*
5 *Pharaoh's daughter went down to bathe by the River and her maidens walked along the River. She saw the basket among the reeds and she sent her maidservant and she took it.* 6 *She opened it and saw him, the child, and behold! a youth was crying. She took pity on him and said, "This is one of the Hebrew boys."*
7 *His sister said to Pharaoh's daughter, "Shall I go and summon for you a wet nurse from the Hebrew women, who will nurse the boy for you?"*
8 *The daughter of Pharaoh said, "Go." The girl went and summoned the boy's mother.* 9 *Pharaoh's daughter said to her, "Take this boy and nurse him for me, and I will give your pay." So the woman took the boy and nursed him.* 10 *The boy grew up and she brought him to the daughter of Pharaoh and he was a son to her. She called his name Moses, as she said, "For I drew him from the water."*

אֶת הַיֶּלֶד וְהִנֵּה נַעַר בֹּכֶה — *The child and behold a lad wept.* She saw that although he was a child, a lad was crying. A child from birth until growth and development is called יֶלֶד, as we find regarding Rehoboam, הַיְלָדִים אֲשֶׁר גָּדְלוּ אִתּוֹ, *the young men that were grown up with him* (*I Kings* 12:10); and also, יְלָדִים אֲשֶׁר אֵין בָּהֶם כָּל מאום, *youths in whom were no blemish* (*Daniel* 1:4), regarding Daniel and his friends. As soon as the young boy begins to awaken, develop and pursue activities leading to a specific goal, incomplete and unfinished as these actions may be, he is called נַעַר. For this reason every servant is called a lad or young boy (נַעַר), for the majority of his actions are imperfect in attaining the intended goal of his master. Now she (the daughter of Pharaoh) observed that although he was a *child*, recently born, nonetheless, *a lad wept*, i.e., his actions were, in a wondrous manner, far more advanced than any child his age.

וַתַּחְמֹל עָלָיו — *And she had compassion on him.* (She felt pity) that a child so fair, with such potential for perfection, be cast into the river.

וַתֹּאמֶר מִיַּלְדֵי הָעִבְרִים זֶה — *And she said, "This is one of the Hebrew children."* This cannot be a foundling born illegitimately who would be prepared to betray his benefactor, as it is said, יִלְדֵי פֶשַׁע זֶרַע שָׁקֶר, *children of transgression, seed of falsehood* (*Isaiah* 57:4).

7. מֵינֶקֶת מִן הָעִבְרִיֹּת — *A nurse of the Hebrew women.* So that the milk he nurses will be more befitting to his nature.

וְתֵינִק לָךְ אֶת הַיָּלֶד — *That she may nurse the child for you.* (He will be prepared) to serve you since his appearance and attributes are such that he is surely prepared to לִפְנֵי מְלָכִים יִתְיַצָּב, *stand before kings* (*Proverbs* 22:29).

10. וַתִּקְרָא שְׁמוֹ מֹשֶׁה — *And she called his name Moses.* He who rescues and draws forth others from trouble (and danger).

NOTES

Pharaoh's daughter to be attracted to him. She is motivated in her subsequent actions not only by pity, but by the consideration that he will be a welcome and valuable addition to the royal court. This reasoning could only be valid if he were not an illegitimate child, born from an act of immorality, for then his loyalty would ever be suspect, as we see from the verse in *Isaiah* which the *Sforno* quotes.

7. וְתֵינִק לָךְ אֶת הַיָּלֶד — *That she may nurse the child for you.* Since the Torah uses the phrase *for you*, it indicates that the retaining of a Hebrew woman to nurse the child would accrue to the benefit of Pharaoh's daughter, for in this manner the child's health would be more readily insured so he would be fit to be a member of the royal court.

10. וַתִּקְרָא שְׁמוֹ מֹשֶׁה — *And she called his name Moses.* The name given by Pharaoh's daughter to the rescued child should have been מָשׁוּי, *Mashui*,

שלישי יא וַיְהִי | בַּיָּמִים הָהֵם וַיִּגְדַּל מֹשֶׁה וַיֵּצֵא אֶל־אֶחָיו וַיַּרְא בְּסִבְלֹתָם וַיַּרְא אִישׁ
יב מִצְרִי מַכֶּה אִישׁ־עִבְרִי מֵאֶחָיו: וַיִּפֶן כֹּה וָכֹה וַיַּרְא כִּי אֵין אִישׁ וַיַּךְ אֶת־
יג הַמִּצְרִי וַיִּטְמְנֵהוּ בַּחוֹל: וַיֵּצֵא בַּיּוֹם הַשֵּׁנִי וְהִנֵּה שְׁנֵי־אֲנָשִׁים עִבְרִים נִצִּים
יד וַיֹּאמֶר לָרָשָׁע לָמָּה תַכֶּה רֵעֶךָ: וַיֹּאמֶר מִי שָׂמְךָ לְאִישׁ שַׂר וְשֹׁפֵט עָלֵינוּ
הַלְהָרְגֵנִי אַתָּה אֹמֵר כַּאֲשֶׁר הָרַגְתָּ אֶת־הַמִּצְרִי וַיִּירָא מֹשֶׁה וַיֹּאמַר אָכֵן
טו נוֹדַע הַדָּבָר: וַיִּשְׁמַע פַּרְעֹה אֶת־הַדָּבָר הַזֶּה וַיְבַקֵּשׁ לַהֲרֹג אֶת־מֹשֶׁה
טז וַיִּבְרַח מֹשֶׁה מִפְּנֵי פַרְעֹה וַיֵּשֶׁב בְּאֶרֶץ־מִדְיָן וַיֵּשֶׁב עַל־הַבְּאֵר: וּלְכֹהֵן מִדְיָן
שֶׁבַע בָּנוֹת וַתָּבֹאנָה וַתִּדְלֶנָה וַתְּמַלֶּאנָה אֶת־הָרְהָטִים לְהַשְׁקוֹת צֹאן
יז אֲבִיהֶן: וַיָּבֹאוּ הָרֹעִים וַיְגָרְשׁוּם וַיָּקָם מֹשֶׁה וַיּוֹשִׁעָן וַיַּשְׁקְ אֶת־צֹאנָם:
יח־יט וַתָּבֹאנָה אֶל־רְעוּאֵל אֲבִיהֶן וַיֹּאמֶר מַדּוּעַ מִהַרְתֶּן בֹּא הַיּוֹם: וַתֹּאמַרְןָ
אִישׁ מִצְרִי הִצִּילָנוּ מִיַּד הָרֹעִים וְגַם־דָּלֹה דָלָה לָנוּ וַיַּשְׁקְ אֶת־הַצֹּאן:
כ וַיֹּאמֶר אֶל־בְּנֹתָיו וְאַיּוֹ לָמָּה זֶּה עֲזַבְתֶּן אֶת־הָאִישׁ קִרְאֶן לוֹ וְיֹאכַל לָחֶם:
כא־כב וַיּוֹאֶל מֹשֶׁה לָשֶׁבֶת אֶת־הָאִישׁ וַיִּתֵּן אֶת־צִפֹּרָה בִתּוֹ לְמֹשֶׁה: וַתֵּלֶד בֵּן
וַיִּקְרָא אֶת־שְׁמוֹ גֵּרְשֹׁם כִּי אָמַר גֵּר הָיִיתִי בְּאֶרֶץ נָכְרִיָּה:

וַתֹּאמֶר כִּי מִן הַמַּיִם מְשִׁיתִהוּ — *And she said, "Because I drew him out of the water."* The reason I called him Moses is to indicate that he will save others. True, (at this moment) *I have drawn him from the water* where he was put, but this was all ordained by the *decree of the watchers* (based on *Daniel* 4:14) so that he (in turn) shall rescue others.

11. וַיַּרְא בְּסִבְלֹתָם — *And looked on their burdens.* He turned his attention to the sufferings of his brothers.

וַיַּרְא אִישׁ מִצְרִי מַכֶּה אִישׁ עִבְרִי מֵאֶחָיו — *And he saw an Egyptian smiting a Hebrew, one of his brethren.* And because of his sense of brotherhood he was aroused to avenge him.

13. וַיֹּאמֶר לָרָשָׁע — *And he said to the wicked one.* Because they were both his brothers he did not smite the guilty one but rather admonished him.

14. הַלְהָרְגֵנִי אַתָּה אֹמֵר — *Do you intend to kill me?* You are (apparently) seeking an excuse to kill me (as you did the Egyptian).

וַיִּירָא מֹשֶׁה — *And Moses feared.* He therefore sought to protect himself, and fled.

וַיֹּאמַר אָכֵן נוֹדַע הַדָּבָר — *And he said, "Surely the matter is known."* Since the informer made these remarks publicly he did not kill him, for it would serve no purpose once he had informed.

NOTES

implying one who is drawn forth, rather than מֹשֶׁה, *Moshe*, implying one who draws forth. The explanation is that he was called by a name reflecting his eventual role as *a rescuer*, a role played by Moses over a prolonged period, as opposed to *a rescued one*, which was a brief and isolated, although important, event in his life.

11. וַיַּרְא אִישׁ מִצְרִי מַכֶּה אִישׁ עִבְרִי מֵאֶחָיו — *And he saw an Egyptian smiting a Hebrew, one of his brethren.* When a brother was attacked by a stranger Moses reacted with alacrity to defend and punish. When two Israelites were involved he admonished (v. 13). When it was two strangers he neither punished nor admonished but defended the weak and oppressed (v. 17). These three episodes are recorded by the Torah to teach us what one's reaction should be to events which may seem similar but are not, for it all depends on the identity of those involved and the circumstances.

14. וַיֹּאמַר אָכֵן נוֹדַע הַדָּבָר — *And he said, "Surely the matter is known."* This explains the term, *the matter is known*, which is the reason for Moses's failure to react with the same degree of firm resolve as demonstrated in the previous episode. One's emotions must be controlled so as to resort to violence only if it will accomplish a reasonable end, not just to spend one's anger and frustration. Were it not for the futility of disposing of the informer, Moses would have been justified in killing him, for

11 *It happened in those days that Moses grew up and went out to his brethren and observed their burdens; and he saw an Egyptian man striking a Hebrew man, of his brethren.* 12 *He turned this way and that and saw that there was no man, so he struck down the Egyptian and hid him in the sand.*

13 *He went out the next day and behold! two Hebrew men were fighting. He said to the wicked one, "Why would you strike your fellow?"* 14 *He replied, "Who appointed you as a dignitary, a ruler, and a judge over us? Do you propose to murder me, as you murdered the Egyptian?" Moses was frightened and he thought, "Indeed, the matter is known!"* 15 *Pharaoh heard about this matter and sought to kill Moses; so Moses fled from before Pharaoh and settled in the land of Midian. He sat by a well.*

16 *The minister of Midian had seven daughters; they came and drew water and filled the troughs to water their father's sheep.* 17 *The shepherds came and drove them away. Moses got up and saved them and watered their sheep.* 18 *They came to Reuel their father. He said, "How could you come so quickly today?"* 19 *They replied, "An Egyptian man saved us from the shepherds, and he even drew water for us and watered the sheep."* 20 *He said to his daughters, "Then where is he? Why did you leave the man? Summon him and let him eat bread!"*

21 *Moses desired to dwell with the man; and he gave his daughter Zipporah to Moses.* 22 *She gave birth to a son and he named him Gershom, for he said, "I have been a stranger in a foreign land."*

---

15. וַיֵּשֶׁב בְּאֶרֶץ מִדְיָן — *And he dwelled in the land of Midian.* He chose to dwell for a time in Midian.

וַיֵּשֶׁב עַל הַבְּאֵר — *And he sat down by a well.* As he was passing through the land he chanced to stop at a well, as we find written, וַיִּפְגַּע בַּמָּקוֹם, *And he lighted upon the place (Genesis* 28:11), a certain place, as explained above.

17. וַיָּקָם מֹשֶׁה וַיּוֹשִׁעָן — *Moses arose and helped them.* Since both parties were strangers (non-Hebrews) he did not seek revenge nor did he bother to correct their conduct by admonishment; he only arose to save the oppressed from their oppressors.

20. לָמָּה זֶּה עֲזַבְתֶּן — *Why is it that you have left (the man)?* Since he is a guest and a kind man, it would have been proper to deal kindly with him and extend our hospitality to him.

21. לָשֶׁבֶת אֶת הָאִישׁ — *To dwell with the man.* To be a shepherd, similar to שְׁבָה עִמָּדִי, *dwell with me (Genesis* 29:19).

22. גֵּר הָיִיתִי בְּאֶרֶץ נָכְרִיָּה — *I have been a stranger in a strange land.* A stranger in a land which is not the land of my birth.

NOTES

the law is: *One is permitted to slay an informer before he informs (Rambam,* חובל ומזיק י׳ י״א).

15. וַיֵּשֶׁב בְּאֶרֶץ מִדְיָן וַיֵּשֶׁב עַל הַבְּאֵר — *And he dwelt in the land of Midian and he sat down by a well.* The first phrase וַיֵּשֶׁב, *and he dwelled,* is by choice, but the second one is through providence. Man is granted freedom of choice and action, but when there is need for Divine intervention in the course of human history, seemingly human events are guided by God. To rest at that particular well was ordained, as was the case with Jacob when he was fleeing from Esau.

21. לָשֶׁבֶת אֶת הָאִישׁ — *To dwell with the man.* The invitation extended by Jethro is not simply to dwell with him, but to assist him with his flocks, as was the case with Laban and Jacob, where the same phrase is used.

22. גֵּר הָיִיתִי בְּאֶרֶץ נָכְרִיָּה — *I have been a stranger in a strange land.* In Egypt, Moses was a stranger, yet he did live in the land of his birth. In Midian, he is both a stranger and one who lives in a land which is not his native land.

כג וַיְהִי בַיָּמִים הָרַבִּים הָהֵם וַיָּמָת מֶלֶךְ מִצְרַיִם וַיֵּאָנְחוּ בְנֵי־יִשְׂרָאֵל מִן־
כד הָעֲבֹדָה וַיִּזְעָקוּ וַתַּעַל שַׁוְעָתָם אֶל־הָאֱלֹהִים מִן־הָעֲבֹדָה׃ וַיִּשְׁמַע אֱלֹהִים
אֶת־נַאֲקָתָם וַיִּזְכֹּר אֱלֹהִים אֶת־בְּרִיתוֹ אֶת־אַבְרָהָם אֶת־יִצְחָק וְאֶת־
ג רביעי כה־א יַעֲקֹב׃ וַיַּרְא אֱלֹהִים אֶת־בְּנֵי יִשְׂרָאֵל וַיֵּדַע אֱלֹהִים׃ וּמֹשֶׁה
הָיָה רֹעֶה אֶת־צֹאן יִתְרוֹ חֹתְנוֹ כֹּהֵן מִדְיָן וַיִּנְהַג אֶת־הַצֹּאן אַחַר
ב הַמִּדְבָּר וַיָּבֹא אֶל־הַר הָאֱלֹהִים חֹרֵבָה׃ וַיֵּרָא מַלְאַךְ יהוה אֵלָיו
בְּלַבַּת־אֵשׁ מִתּוֹךְ הַסְּנֶה וַיַּרְא וְהִנֵּה הַסְּנֶה בֹּעֵר בָּאֵשׁ וְהַסְּנֶה אֵינֶנּוּ אֻכָּל׃

23. בַּיָּמִים הָרַבִּים הָהֵם — *In the course of those many days.* From the time Moses fled Egypt, as a young man, until Gershom was born, at which time he (Moses) was close to eighty, for Eliezer was born when Moses was en route to fulfill God's mission (*Exodus* 4:24), at which time Moses was eighty years old.

וַיָּמָת מֶלֶךְ מִצְרַיִם — *The king of Egypt died.* The king who was pursuing Moses died. He (Moses) therefore named his (second) son Eliezer for (only) then was he assured that he had been saved from the sword of Pharaoh.

וַיִּזְעָקוּ — *And they cried.* They cried with pained hearts because of their labors, similar to, הֵילִילִי שַׁעַר, זַעֲקִי עִיר, *Howl, O gate; cry, O city* (*Isaiah* 14:31).

וַתַּעַל שַׁוְעָתָם אֶל הָאֱלֹהִים מִן הָעֲבֹדָה — *And their cry came up to God from the bondage.* Not because of their repentance and prayers, but because God reacts zealously to the cruelty of oppressors, as we read, וְגַם רָאִיתִי אֶת הַלַּחַץ, *and I have also seen the oppression* (3:9).

24. וַיִּשְׁמַע אֱלֹהִים אֶת נַאֲקָתָם — *And God heard their groaning.* The prayer of the few righteous who prayed, as it is said, וַנִּצְעַק אֶל ה׳ וַיִּשְׁמַע קֹלֵנוּ, *and we cried unto* HASHEM, *and He heard our voice* (*Numbers* 20:16).

וַיִּזְכֹּר אֱלֹהִים אֶת בְּרִיתוֹ — *And God remembered His covenant.* As He said, וַהֲקִמֹתִי אֶת בְּרִיתִי בֵּינִי וּבֵינֶךָ וּבֵין זַרְעֲךָ אַחֲרֶיךָ ... לִהְיוֹת לְךָ לֵאלֹהִים וּלְזַרְעֲךָ אַחֲרֶיךָ, *and I will establish My covenant between Me and you and your seed after you (throughout their generations for an everlasting covenant) to be a God unto you and unto your seed after you* (*Genesis* 17:7). And this (God) does whenever we call upon Him, as it is testified to further, וְגַם אֲנִי שָׁמַעְתִּי אֶת נַאֲקַת בְּנֵי יִשְׂרָאֵל . . . וָאֶזְכֹּר אֶת בְּרִיתִי, *And I have heard the groaning of the Children of Israel . . . and I have remembered My covenant* (6:5).

25. וַיַּרְא אֱלֹהִים אֶת בְּנֵי יִשְׂרָאֵל — *And God saw the Children of Israel.* He extended His providence and no longer hid His face from them, similar to, כִּי רָאִיתִי אֶת עַמִּי, כִּי בָּאָה צַעֲקָתוֹ

NOTES

23. בַּיָּמִים הָרַבִּים הָהֵם וַיָּמָת מֶלֶךְ מִצְרַיִם — *In the course of those many days the king of Egypt died.* Moses called his first son Gershom and his second Eliezer, which means *God has saved me.* The reason he did not show his gratitude to God immediately, by naming his firstborn Eliezer, is because he could not be certain of his complete salvation until the death of the king that was pursuing him, and this occurred after the birth of his first child.

וַיִּזְעָקוּ וַתַּעַל שַׁוְעָתָם אֶל הָאֱלֹהִים מִן הָעֲבֹדָה — *And they cried, and their cry came up to God from the bondage.* The Israelites did not cry out to God because they regretted their transgressions and repented their sins, which was the real cause of their suffering. They cried, not due to any noble motivation, but simply because of their unbearable state of slavery. Nonetheless, God listened and reached a decision, to begin the process of liberation and salvation. The Israelites might cry out *from the bondage* which was incomplete, yet God determined to act because of their debilitating and destructive oppression. *From the bondage* is the cause of God's action, although the prayers of the Jews were sparse and their repentance, though stirring within them, was as yet non-existent.

25. וַיַּרְא אֱלֹהִים אֶת בְּנֵי יִשְׂרָאֵל וַיֵּדַע אֱלֹהִים — *And God saw the Children of Israel and God knew.* The Almighty is all-seeing and naught escapes Him. This does not mean, however, that God's attention and concern is ever present with His people. There

[23] *During those many days, it happened that the king of Egypt died, and the Children of Israel groaned because of the work and they cried out. Their outcry because of the work went up to God.* [24] *God heard their moaning, and God remembered His covenant with Abraham, with Isaac, and with Jacob.* [25] *God saw the Children of Israel; and God knew.*

3 [1] *Moses was shepherding the sheep of Jethro, his father-in-law, the priest of Midian; he guided the sheep far into the wilderness, and he arrived at the Mountain of God, toward Horeb.* [2] *An angel of* HASHEM *appeared to him in a blaze of fire from amid the bush. He saw and behold! the bush was burning in the fire but the bush was not consumed.*

אֵלָי, *I have seen the pain of My people, for their cries have come to Me (I Samuel* 9:16); and as is proven later when He says, רָאֹה רָאִיתִי אֶת עֳנִי עַמִּי אֲשֶׁר בְּמִצְרָיִם, *I have surely seen the affliction of My people that are in Egypt* (3:7).

וַיֵּדַע אֱלֹהִים — *And God knew.* He recognized the anguish of their hearts and that their prayers and cries were heartfelt, as we are later told, כִּי יָדַעְתִּי אֶת מַכְאֹבָיו, *for I know their pains* (3:7), the reverse of וַיְפַתּוּהוּ בְּפִיהֶם . . . וְלִבָּם לֹא נָכוֹן עִמּוֹ, *And they beguiled Him with their mouth . . . but their heart was not steadfast with Him (Psalms* 78:36-37).

III

1. וַיָּבֹא אֶל הַר הָאֱלֹהִים חֹרֵבָה — *And he came to the mountain of God, to Horeb.* He came alone, to seclude himself and pray (to God), similar to, וַיָּבֹא עַד חֶבְרוֹן, *and he came to Hebron (Numbers* 13:22).

2. וַיֵּרָא מַלְאַךְ ה׳ אֵלָיו — *And an angel of God appeared to him.* In a vision of prophecy. However, when angels appear in human form, not for the purpose of prophecy, as we find in the case of Abraham, Lot and Balaam, the phrase is not וַיֵּרָא, *he appeared,* but וַיַּרְא, *he saw;* as we find, וַיַּרְא וְהִנֵּה שְׁלֹשָׁה אֲנָשִׁים, *and behold, he saw three men (Genesis* 18:2); וַיַּרְא לוֹט, *and Lot saw (Genesis* 19:1); וַיַּרְא אֶת מַלְאַךְ ה׳ נִצָּב בַּדֶּרֶךְ, *and he (Balaam) saw the angel of God standing in the way (Numbers* 22:31).

וַיַּרְא וְהִנֵּה הַסְּנֶה בֹּעֵר בָּאֵשׁ — *And he looked and behold the bush is burning with fire.* בֹּעֵר means *burning.* This (vision) was a prophecy (clothed) in an enigma. The angel was in the midst of the bush and the fire was burning around the angel symbolizing that the

NOTES

are times when His face is hidden — when His providence is removed and at such moments in history Israel is abandoned to the mercies of others and the vicissitudes and forces of nature and man. It was at such a moment in Egypt that God *saw* Israel anew, His *hashgachah* (concern and supervision) was reactivated, and He *knew* that the initial cries of anguish had blossomed into sincere heartfelt prayer.

III

1. וַיָּבֹא . . . — *And he came . . .* The verse first tells us that Moses led the sheep into the wilderness (וַיִּנְהַג אֶת הַצֹּאן), then the word וַיָּבֹא is used, apparently introducing another action on his part. The *Sforno* therefore interprets this to mean that Moses used the solitude of the wilderness to commune with God. Proof is brought from Caleb who came (the same word וַיָּבֹא is used) to Hebron to seek guidance and pray at the gravesite of the Patriarchs, as our Sages tell us in Tractate *Sotah* 34b.

2. וַיֵּרָא מַלְאַךְ ה׳ אֵלָיו — *And an angel of God appeared to him.* In the three cases cited the angel of God appears, in human form, and since his coming is not to *reveal* the will or wish of God but rather to *fulfill* some mission or purpose, he is *seen* rather than *appears.* In the case of Abraham the angels came to assist him in fulfilling the *mitzvah* of hospitality and to tell him of the impending birth of Isaac; Lot was visited so as to be rescued; and Balaam saw the angel blocking his path. When, however, the angel of God is sent for the purpose of prophecy — as in this case — the correct phrase is *he appeared* rather than *he saw.*

וַיַּרְא וְהִנֵּה הַסְּנֶה בֹּעֵר בָּאֵשׁ — *And he looked and behold the bush is burning with fire.* The *Sforno*

ג וַיֹּאמֶר מֹשֶׁה אָסֻרָה־נָּא וְאֶרְאֶה אֶת־הַמַּרְאֶה הַגָּדֹל הַזֶּה מַדּוּעַ לֹא־
ד יִבְעַר הַסְּנֶה׃ וַיַּרְא יהוה כִּי סָר לִרְאוֹת וַיִּקְרָא אֵלָיו אֱלֹהִים מִתּוֹךְ
ה הַסְּנֶה וַיֹּאמֶר מֹשֶׁה מֹשֶׁה וַיֹּאמֶר הִנֵּנִי׃ וַיֹּאמֶר אַל־תִּקְרַב הֲלֹם שַׁל־
נְעָלֶיךָ מֵעַל רַגְלֶיךָ כִּי הַמָּקוֹם אֲשֶׁר אַתָּה עוֹמֵד עָלָיו אַדְמַת־קֹדֶשׁ
ו הוּא׃ וַיֹּאמֶר אָנֹכִי אֱלֹהֵי אָבִיךָ אֱלֹהֵי אַבְרָהָם אֱלֹהֵי יִצְחָק וֵאלֹהֵי יַעֲקֹב
ז וַיַּסְתֵּר מֹשֶׁה פָּנָיו כִּי יָרֵא מֵהַבִּיט אֶל־הָאֱלֹהִים׃ וַיֹּאמֶר יהוה
רָאֹה רָאִיתִי אֶת־עֳנִי עַמִּי אֲשֶׁר בְּמִצְרָיִם וְאֶת־צַעֲקָתָם שָׁמַעְתִּי מִפְּנֵי
ח נֹגְשָׂיו כִּי יָדַעְתִּי אֶת־מַכְאֹבָיו׃ וָאֵרֵד לְהַצִּילוֹ ׀ מִיַּד מִצְרַיִם וּלְהַעֲלֹתוֹ
מִן־הָאָרֶץ הַהִוא אֶל־אֶרֶץ טוֹבָה וּרְחָבָה אֶל־אֶרֶץ זָבַת חָלָב וּדְבָשׁ
ט אֶל־מְקוֹם הַכְּנַעֲנִי וְהַחִתִּי וְהָאֱמֹרִי וְהַפְּרִזִּי וְהַחִוִּי וְהַיְבוּסִי׃ וְעַתָּה

righteous Israelites, who are as Godly angels, were caught up in the midst of the bush, (which represented) the Egyptian people, who were as briers and thorns. The bush would burn with the anguished fire of the ten plagues but they would not be consumed in that distress, as indicated in the phrase, *and the bush is not consumed*, (meaning) it was not destroyed by the fire burning within it.

The prophetic power of Moses at this stage was not the same as it would become later — as is indicated in the phrase, כִּי יָרֵא מֵהַבִּיט אֶל הָאֱלֹהִים, *For he feared to look at God* (verse 6), as opposed to וּתְמֻנַת ה׳ יַבִּיט, *The image of God he did perceive (Numbers* 12:8). However, from the day of the giving of the Torah and onward, when God revealed Himself to all Israel, face to face, although they could not tolerate (this exalted experience), as it is written, לֹא אֹסֵף עוֹד לִשְׁמֹעַ אֶת קוֹל ה׳ אֱלֹהָי, *Let me not hear again the voice of* H*ASHEM*, *my God (Deut.* 18:16), (Moses) alone remained on that high level, as it is written, שׁוּבוּ לָכֶם לְאָהֳלֵיכֶם וְאַתָּה פֹּה עֲמֹד עִמָּדִי, *Return, you (the nation), to your tents; but as for you (Moses), stand here with Me (Deut.* 5:27-28); and as is written, וַיַּעֲמֹד הָעָם מֵרָחֹק וּמֹשֶׁה נִגַּשׁ, *And the people stood from afar but Moses approached (Exodus* 20:18). (From that moment) the prophecy of Moses was פָּנִים אֶל פָּנִים, *face to face (Exodus* 33:11), and וּמַרְאֶה וְלֹא בְחִידֹת, *manifestly, and not in dark speeches (Numbers* 12:8).

3. אָסֻרָה נָּא וְאֶרְאֶה — *I will turn aside now and see.* I will consider and see.

מַדּוּעַ לֹא יִבְעַר הַסְּנֶה — *Why the bush does not burn.* Why are the Egyptians not destroyed by the plagues; similar to, וְדָלְקוּ בָהֶם וַאֲכָלוּם, *And they shall kindle in them and devour them (Obadiah* 1:18).

4. וַיַּרְא ה׳ כִּי סָר לִרְאוֹת — *And* H*ASHEM saw that he turned aside to see.* To (study and) discern the matter.

וַיִּקְרָא אֵלָיו אֱלֹהִים — *And God called to him.* To inform him — as our Sages tell us, הַבָּא לִטַּהֵר מְסַיְּעִין אוֹתוֹ, *he who comes to be purified will be assisted from on High (Shabbos*

NOTES

makes two points here: (a) He interprets the symbolism of the bush in the following manner: The angel represents the righteous of Israel, caught up, as it were, in the midst of the burning bush, which symbolizes Egypt. The bush, which is not consumed, though enveloped in flames, is symbolic of Egypt ravaged by the ten plagues but not destroyed — for that is not the purpose of God's punishment, as is further developed in verse 7. (b) Prophecy through the medium of images and visions wrapped in enigmas and riddles is not the method God would use later in communicating with Moses. At this stage of Moses's calling, however, he was not yet prepared for direct, clear communication with the Almighty. From the moment of Sinai, however, when revelation occurred on the highest level of human experience, Moses alone remained on that exalted plane to which all were elevated momentarily. From that moment on he spoke to God — *face to face* — through a clear and vivid lens, and not through clouded visions and mysterious riddles.

[3] *Moses thought, "I will turn aside now and look at this great sight — why will the bush not be burned?"*

[4] *HASHEM saw that he turned aside to see; and God called out to him from amid the bush and said, "Moses, Moses," and he replied, "Here I am!"* [5] *He said, "Do not come closer to here, remove your shoes from your feet, for the place upon which you stand is holy ground."* [6] *And He said, "I am the God of your father, the God of Abraham, the God of Isaac, and the God of Jacob." Moses hid his face, for he was afraid to gaze toward God.*

[7] *HASHEM said, "I have indeed seen the affliction of My people that is in Egypt and I have heard its outcry because of its taskmasters, for I have known of its sufferings.* [8] *I shall descend to rescue it from the hand of Egypt and to bring it up from that land to a good and spacious land, to a land flowing with milk and honey, to the place of the Canaanite, the Hittite, the Amorite, the Perizzite, the Hivvite, and the Jebusite.* [9] *And now,*

104a), and as we find, וּמֹשֶׁה עָלָה אֶל הָאֱלֹהִים וַיִּקְרָא אֵלָיו ה׳ מִן הָהָר, *Moses went up to God, and HASHEM called to him from the mountain (Exodus* 19:3).

5. שַׁל נְעָלֶיךָ — *Take off your shoes.* Even in this place where you now stand.

7. רָאֹה רָאִיתִי אֶת עֳנִי עַמִּי — *I have surely seen the affliction of My people.* The righteous ones of this generation who sigh and bemoan the sins of their generation and their sufferings and who pray (to God). The angel of God who revealed himself in the bush symbolizes them.

The (double phrase) רָאֹה רָאִיתִי is meant as *"indeed" I have seen.* Whenever a phrase is repeated (as it is here), and as we find in the expression עָלֹה נַעֲלֶה, *ascend we shall ascend (Numbers* 13:30), or יָכוֹל נוּכַל, *able we will be able* (ibid.), or יָדַעְתִּי בְנִי יָדַעְתִּי, *I know, my son, I know (Genesis* 48:19), it is similar to (use of the word) אָמְנָם indicating that it is true in spite of evidence or claims to the contrary.

(The sense of the verse is:) Even though I have seen the affliction of My people in Egypt, demonstrated by the angel in the bush, and although I intend to punish their oppressors, as indicated by the fire in the bush, nonetheless they will not be utterly destroyed by the plagues, as indicated by the bush not being consumed. For the purpose of the plagues is not to destroy Egypt so that the Israelites can replace them, but to save the Israelites from their hand and establish them in another place. And this is the reason for . . .

8. וָאֵרֵד לְהַצִּילוֹ . . . וּלְהַעֲלֹתוֹ מִן הָאָרֶץ הַהִוא אֶל אֶרֶץ טוֹבָה — *And I have come down to save them from the land of Egypt to bring them up from this land to a good land . . .* i.e., I have revealed myself in this vision to save them and bring them up, not to destroy the Egyptians.

זָבַת חָלָב וּדְבָשׁ — *(A land) flowing with milk and honey.* (With) many cattle, plentiful food, pleasant and nutritious, as it is written, אֱכָל בְּנִי דְבַשׁ כִּי טוֹב וְנֹפֶת מָתוֹק, *My son, eat your honey for it is good and the honeycomb is sweet (Proverbs* 24:13).

9. וְעַתָּה — *And now.* Since all this is true (this always being the meaning of the word וְעַתָּה, *now),* the sense is: Since this is true, that I know their hurt and the anguish of their heart . . .

NOTES

בֹּעֵר — *Burned.* The root בער can either mean *removal* or *burn.* The *Sforno* stresses that the phrase בֹּעֵר in this instance must mean *is burning,* since *the bush is not* (totally) *consumed.*

4. וַיַּרְא ה׳ כִּי סָר לִרְאוֹת — *And HASHEM saw that he turned aside to see.* Man must take the first step in seeking out God. He must initiate, i.e., begin, then God will meet him. Only when Moses turned to observe and witness, did God call to him. At the time of the giving of the Torah, it was only after Moses went up to God that the Almighty called to him — here again man had to make the first move.

9. וְעַתָּה — *And now.* The *Sforno* explains the meaning of the word וְעַתָּה, *and now,* as indicating

הִנֵּה צַעֲקַת בְּנֵי־יִשְׂרָאֵל בָּאָה אֵלָי וְגַם־רָאִיתִי אֶת־הַלַּחַץ אֲשֶׁר מִצְרַיִם
י לֹחֲצִים אֹתָם: וְעַתָּה לְכָה וְאֶשְׁלָחֲךָ אֶל־פַּרְעֹה וְהוֹצֵא אֶת־עַמִּי בְנֵי־
יא יִשְׂרָאֵל מִמִּצְרָיִם: וַיֹּאמֶר מֹשֶׁה אֶל־הָאֱלֹהִים מִי אָנֹכִי כִּי אֵלֵךְ אֶל־פַּרְעֹה
יב וְכִי אוֹצִיא אֶת־בְּנֵי יִשְׂרָאֵל מִמִּצְרָיִם: וַיֹּאמֶר כִּי־אֶהְיֶה עִמָּךְ וְזֶה־לְּךָ הָאוֹת
כִּי אָנֹכִי שְׁלַחְתִּיךָ בְּהוֹצִיאֲךָ אֶת־הָעָם מִמִּצְרַיִם תַּעַבְדוּן אֶת־הָאֱלֹהִים עַל
יג הָהָר הַזֶּה: וַיֹּאמֶר מֹשֶׁה אֶל־הָאֱלֹהִים הִנֵּה אָנֹכִי בָא אֶל־בְּנֵי יִשְׂרָאֵל
וְאָמַרְתִּי לָהֶם אֱלֹהֵי אֲבוֹתֵיכֶם שְׁלָחַנִי אֲלֵיכֶם וְאָמְרוּ־לִי מַה־שְּׁמוֹ מָה
יד אֹמַר אֲלֵהֶם: וַיֹּאמֶר אֱלֹהִים אֶל־מֹשֶׁה אֶהְיֶה אֲשֶׁר אֶהְיֶה וַיֹּאמֶר כֹּה
טו תֹאמַר לִבְנֵי יִשְׂרָאֵל אֶהְיֶה שְׁלָחַנִי אֲלֵיכֶם: וַיֹּאמֶר עוֹד אֱלֹהִים אֶל־מֹשֶׁה
כֹּה־תֹאמַר אֶל־בְּנֵי יִשְׂרָאֵל יהוה אֱלֹהֵי אֲבֹתֵיכֶם אֱלֹהֵי אַבְרָהָם אֱלֹהֵי
יִצְחָק וֵאלֹהֵי יַעֲקֹב שְׁלָחַנִי אֲלֵיכֶם זֶה־שְּׁמִי לְעֹלָם וְזֶה זִכְרִי לְדֹר דֹּר:

הִנֵּה צַעֲקַת בְּנֵי יִשְׂרָאֵל בָּאָה אֵלָי — *The cry of the Children of Israel has come unto Me.* I have accepted their prayers for they have called to Me sincerely and not in the sense of, וַיְפַתּוּהוּ בְּפִיהֶם, *And they beguiled Him with their mouth* (*Psalms* 78:36).

וְגַם רָאִיתִי אֶת הַלַּחַץ — *Moreover I have seen the oppression.* And because the oppression is so great the oppressors are worthy of punishment; similar to, וְקֶצֶף גָּדוֹל אֲנִי קֹצֵף עַל הַגּוֹיִם הַשַּׁאֲנַנִּים אֲשֶׁר אֲנִי קָצַפְתִּי מְּעָט וְהֵמָּה עָזְרוּ לְרָעָה, *And I am very displeased with the nations that are at ease; for I was but a little displeased and they helped for evil* (*Zechariah* 1:15).

10. וְעַתָּה לְכָה וְאֶשְׁלָחֲךָ — *And now therefore come and I will send you (to Pharaoh).* To warn them before I punish them.

11. מִי אָנֹכִי כִּי אֵלֵךְ — *Who am I that I should go?* How will my warning carry weight?

וְכִי אוֹצִיא אֶת בְּנֵי יִשְׂרָאֵל — *And that I should bring forth the Children of Israel?* . . . that I shall be worthy to take forth Israel since they are at present unworthy (of liberation).

12. כִּי אֶהְיֶה עִמָּךְ וְזֶה לְּךָ הָאוֹת — *I will be with you and this shall be the sign.* You shall decree a thing and it shall be established for you wherever you will turn, and all will recognize that I sent you and will respect you and your words, as we find, גַּם הָאִישׁ מֹשֶׁה גָּדוֹל מְאֹד בְּאֶרֶץ מִצְרַיִם, *The man Moses was very great in the land of Egypt* (11:3).

בְּהוֹצִיאֲךָ אֶת הָעָם מִמִּצְרַיִם תַּעַבְדוּן אֶת הָאֱלֹהִים עַל הָהָר הַזֶּה — *When you will bring forth the people out of Egypt, you shall serve God upon this mountain.* Although they are not worthy, they are prepared to serve "God on the mountain," when you will "bring them

NOTES

something that is true — the reality of a given situation or condition. The sense of the verse according to him is: The reality of Israel's state and their bitter condition is known to Me and I am fully aware of their pain and suffering. However, My plan of action is not to punish the oppressor, but to save the Israelites and lead them forth from Egypt to another land (as the *Sforno* explained in verse 7).

וְגַם רָאִיתִי אֶת הַלַּחַץ — *Moreover I have seen the oppression.* The *Sforno* explains why the Egyptians were worthy of punishment though they were but the instruments of God in fulfilling the Divine plan revealed to Abraham when He said, *they will serve them and be afflicted by them* (*Genesis* 15:13). Their guilt lies in their excessive cruelty.

12. כִּי אֶהְיֶה עִמָּךְ וְזֶה לְּךָ הָאוֹת — *I will be with you and this shall be the sign.* God here answers Moses's first reservation, i.e., "What weight can my warning carry?" by reassuring him that his prestige and stature will grow and be recognized in time.

בְּהוֹצִיאֲךָ אֶת הָעָם מִמִּצְרַיִם תַּעַבְדוּן אֶת הָאֱלֹהִים עַל הָהָר הַזֶּה — *When you will bring forth the people out of Egypt, you shall serve God upon this mountain.* Moses was concerned, for since he felt incapable of liberating the Israelites by virtue of his own powers of leadership and personal powers, he could succeed only by virtue of the Jews' great merits, which he knew were woefully inadequate. He was therefore understandably dubious and pessimistic. God reassured him that one must not judge a people as

behold! the outcry of the Children of Israel has come to Me, and I have also seen the oppression with which the Egyptians oppress them. 10 *And now, go and I shall dispatch you to Pharaoh and you shall take My people the Children of Israel out of Egypt."*

11 *Moses replied to God, "Who am I that I should go to Pharaoh and that I should take the Children of Israel out of Egypt?"*

12 *And He said, "For I shall be with you — and this is your sign that I have sent you: When you take the people out of Egypt, you will serve God on this mountain."*

13 *Moses said to God, "Behold, when I come to the Children of Israel and say to them, 'The God of your forefathers has sent me to you,' and they say to me, 'What is His Name?' — what shall I say to them?"*

14 *HASHEM answered Moses, "I Shall Be As I Shall Be." And He said, "So shall you say to the Children of Israel, 'I Shall Be has sent me to you.' "*
15 *God said further to Moses, "So shall you say to the Children of Israel, 'HASHEM the God of your forefathers, the God of Abraham, the God of Isaac, and the God of Jacob has dispatched me to you. This is My Name forever, and this is My remembrance from generation to generation.'*

---

forth" from among these transgressors.

13. וְאָמְרוּ לִי מַה שְּׁמוֹ — *And they shall say to me, "What is His Name?"* A name reveals one's personal form (i.e., disposition), and the form is the cause of the unique function of that person. Therefore what they will say is: By which function emanating from Him, by which He can be called by name, did He send you to deliver us?

14. אֶהְיֶה אֲשֶׁר אֶהְיֶה — *I am that I am.* He Whose existence is constant and consistent, and Whose essence is His existence. From this (concept we are obliged to believe that) God loves (all) existence and detests all waste (loss or nihility) which is opposed to *what is,* as He says, כִּי לֹא אֶחְפֹּץ בְּמוֹת הַמֵּת, *For I do not desire the death of him who dies (Ezekiel* 18:32). And this impels (us to believe that) He loves justice and righteousness, for their objective is existence, while detesting injustice and brutality which cause destruction, loss and waste. Therefore He abhors the violence and brutality of the Egyptians directed against you.

15. וַיֹּאמֶר עוֹד אֱלֹהִים אֶל מֹשֶׁה כֹּה תֹאמַר אֶל בְּנֵי יִשְׂרָאֵל — *And God again said unto Moses, "Thus shall you say to the Children of Israel."* To the wise men of the generation.

ה' אֱלֹהֵי אֲבֹתֵיכֶם — *HASHEM, the God of your Fathers.* (Both as the God) Whose unique function is indicated by the special name (used to send Moses) and also as the God of your Fathers Who entered into a covenant with them and their children.

זֶה שְּׁמִי לְעֹלָם — *This is My Name forever.* The special (unique) Name Which is the original

NOTES

they *are,* especially when imprisoned in an environment that militates against their spiritual development. What is all-important is their willingness to listen, to learn and to serve if only granted the opportunity. Moses was assured by God that though unworthy they were not unprepared to hearken and obey. It was for this unrealized potential that they would be brought forth.

14. אֶהְיֶה אֲשֶׁר אֶהְיֶה — *I am that I am.* In response to Moses's question "What is God's name?" the answer is given by defining and describing the essential attribute by which God is known, for a name is that which sums up the essence and being of a person or object. That God "is" and "will be" denotes not only an element of timelessness but also a God, a Being that "is" in the sense of affirming and ratifying all that gives life, being and existence; in other words, all that serves a constructive end. Those forces which are destructive, that corrupt and destroy life and "being," are opposed to God and He to them; hence His fury is directed against the Egyptians who have unleashed forces of destruction and loss.

15. זֶה שְּׁמִי לְעֹלָם. . .זִכְרִי לְדֹר דֹּר — *This is My Name*

חמישי טז לֵךְ וְאָסַפְתָּ אֶת־זִקְנֵי יִשְׂרָאֵל וְאָמַרְתָּ אֲלֵהֶם יהוה אֱלֹהֵי אֲבֹתֵיכֶם נִרְאָה
אֵלַי אֱלֹהֵי אַבְרָהָם יִצְחָק וְיַעֲקֹב לֵאמֹר פָּקֹד פָּקַדְתִּי אֶתְכֶם וְאֶת־הֶעָשׂוּי
יז לָכֶם בְּמִצְרָיִם: וָאֹמַר אַעֲלֶה אֶתְכֶם מֵעֳנִי מִצְרַיִם אֶל־אֶרֶץ הַכְּנַעֲנִי וְהַחִתִּי
יח וְהָאֱמֹרִי וְהַפְּרִזִּי וְהַחִוִּי וְהַיְבוּסִי אֶל־אֶרֶץ זָבַת חָלָב וּדְבָשׁ: וְשָׁמְעוּ לְקֹלֶךָ
וּבָאתָ אַתָּה וְזִקְנֵי יִשְׂרָאֵל אֶל־מֶלֶךְ מִצְרַיִם וַאֲמַרְתֶּם אֵלָיו יהוה אֱלֹהֵי
הָעִבְרִיִּים נִקְרָה עָלֵינוּ וְעַתָּה נֵלְכָה־נָּא דֶּרֶךְ שְׁלֹשֶׁת יָמִים בַּמִּדְבָּר וְנִזְבְּחָה
יט לַיהוה אֱלֹהֵינוּ: וַאֲנִי יָדַעְתִּי כִּי לֹא־יִתֵּן אֶתְכֶם מֶלֶךְ מִצְרַיִם לַהֲלֹךְ וְלֹא בְּיָד
כ חֲזָקָה: וְשָׁלַחְתִּי אֶת־יָדִי וְהִכֵּיתִי אֶת־מִצְרַיִם בְּכֹל נִפְלְאֹתַי אֲשֶׁר אֶעֱשֶׂה
כא בְּקִרְבּוֹ וְאַחֲרֵי־כֵן יְשַׁלַּח אֶתְכֶם: וְנָתַתִּי אֶת־חֵן הָעָם־הַזֶּה בְּעֵינֵי מִצְרָיִם
כב וְהָיָה כִּי תֵלֵכוּן לֹא תֵלְכוּ רֵיקָם: וְשָׁאֲלָה אִשָּׁה מִשְּׁכֶנְתָּהּ וּמִגָּרַת בֵּיתָהּ
כְּלֵי־כֶסֶף וּכְלֵי זָהָב וּשְׂמָלֹת וְשַׂמְתֶּם עַל־בְּנֵיכֶם וְעַל־בְּנֹתֵיכֶם וְנִצַּלְתֶּם אֶת־
ד א מִצְרָיִם: וַיַּעַן מֹשֶׁה וַיֹּאמֶר וְהֵן לֹא־יַאֲמִינוּ לִי וְלֹא יִשְׁמְעוּ בְּקֹלִי כִּי יֹאמְרוּ
°מַה־זֶּה ק׳ ב לֹא־נִרְאָה אֵלֶיךָ יהוה: וַיֹּאמֶר אֵלָיו יהוה °מזה בְיָדֶךָ וַיֹּאמֶר מַטֶּה:

Name that manifests My being, eternity and (role of) originator — that is . . .

זִכְרִי לְדֹר דֹּר — *My memorial for every generation.* This is what the wise men of every generation have grasped, new and old alike, that there must perforce be an eternal unchanging "first cause."

16. פָּקֹד פָּקַדְתִּי אֶתְכֶם — *I have surely remembered you . . .* as descendants of the Patriarchs.

וְאֶת הֶעָשׂוּי לָכֶם בְּמִצְרָיִם — *And that which is done to you in Egypt.* Because (God) despises the cruelty and violence (demonstrated by the Egyptians).

18. וְשָׁמְעוּ לְקֹלֶךָ — *And they shall hearken to your voice.* All that you will command them.

אֱלֹהֵי הָעִבְרִיִּים — *The God of the Hebrews.* The God of those who adhere to the beliefs of Eber.

נִקְרָה עָלֵינוּ — *Has met with us.* At a time when it was not our intent to receive prophecy nor were we requesting aught from Him, (He met with us) and commanded us to sacrifice to fulfill His will.

19. כִּי לֹא יִתֵּן אֶתְכֶם מֶלֶךְ מִצְרַיִם לַהֲלֹךְ — *The king of Egypt will not give you leave to go.* He will not agree to do so.

וְלֹא בְּיָד חֲזָקָה — *Except by a mighty hand.* And I shall so ordain that he will not permit you to leave when My hand will be strengthened against him, for when each plague will cease I will harden his heart so that he will be unafraid of additional plagues.

20. וְהִכֵּיתִי אֶת מִצְרַיִם בְּכֹל נִפְלְאֹתַי — *And I will smite Egypt with all My wonders.* In a manner that all who hear will wonder (and marvel), and many will see and fear and perhaps some will repent.

NOTES

forever . . . my memorial for every generation. "To be remembered" means not to be forgotten or ignored. At no time in the history of mankind was God ever unknown or denied completely; hence His Name (being known) is ever His remembrance — *This is My Name forever,* because it is *My memorial for every generation.*

18. אֱלֹהֵי הָעִבְרִיִּים נִקְרָה עָלֵינוּ — *The God of the Hebrews has met with us.* The Israelites did not force the issue. God's appearance is neither contrived nor "coerced," it is entirely the will and volition of God; hence, they were not to be accused of initiating this troublesome demand. It was the command of the Almighty and they must obey.

20. וְהִכֵּיתִי אֶת מִצְרַיִם בְּכֹל נִפְלְאֹתַי — *And I will smite Egypt with all My wonders.* A "wonder" is an act which arouses wonder in the beholder. Its purpose is not to impress the witness but to awaken

[16] *Go and gather the elders of Israel and say to them, 'HASHEM, the God of your forefathers, has appeared to me, the God of Abraham, Isaac, and Jacob, saying, "I have surely remembered you and what is done to you in Egypt.' "*
[17] *And I have said, 'I shall bring you up from the affliction of Egypt to the land of the Canaanite, the Hittite, the Amorite, the Perizzite, the Hivvite, and the Jebusite, to a land flowing with milk and honey.'*

[18] *"They will heed your voice. You and the elders of Israel shall come to the king of Egypt and say to him, 'HASHEM, the God of the Hebrews, happened upon us. And now, please let us go on a three-day journey in the Wilderness, and we shall bring offerings to HASHEM, our God.'* [19] *I know that the king of Egypt will not allow you to go, except through a strong hand.* [20] *I shall stretch out My hand and I shall strike Egypt with all My wonders that I shall perform in its midst, and after that he will send you out.* [21] *I shall grant this people favor in the eyes of Egypt, so that it will happen that when you go, you will not go empty-handed.* [22] *Each woman shall request from her neighbor and from the one who lives in her house silver vessels, golden vessels, and garments; and you shall put them on your sons and daughters, and you shall empty out Egypt."*

4 [1] *Moses responded and said, "But they will not believe me and they will not heed my voice, for they will say, 'HASHEM did not appear to you.' "*
[2] *HASHEM said to him, "What is that in your hand?" and he said, "A staff."*

22. וְנִצַּלְתֶּם אֶת מִצְרָיִם — *And you shall empty Egypt.* Although you will receive everything from them as a loan, and be obligated to return (these articles to them), all this however will be corrected later according to law by their pursuing you to do battle against you and plunder your possessions. When they (the Egyptians) perished in battle, for God did battle for (Israel), then legally all the booty of the pursuer belonged to the pursued, measure for measure, as is the custom in every war.

IV

1. וְהֵן לֹא יַאֲמִינוּ לִי וְלֹא יִשְׁמְעוּ בְּקֹלִי — *They will not believe me nor listen to my voice.* When they realize that the king of Egypt will not permit them to leave.

כִּי יֹאמְרוּ לֹא נִרְאָה אֵלֶיךָ ה׳ — *For they will say, 'HASHEM did not appear to you.'* For כִּי הוּא אָמַר וַיֶּהִי, *He says and it becomes (Psalms 33:9).*

2. מַזֶּה בְיָדֶךָ — *What is this in your hand?* A rod is inanimate whereas a hand is alive, but

NOTES

and arouse him to react. It is not meant to evoke admiration, but awe and reverence which will bring man to repentance.

22. וְנִצַּלְתֶּם אֶת מִצְרָיִם — *And you shall empty Egypt.* The Jews were told to "borrow" items of value from their Egyptian neighbors, which certainly obligated them to return them to their owners. How then can we justify their appropriation of these valuables? The answer is given by the *Sforno*: The Egyptians, by pursuing the Israelites, intent upon destruction and plunder, would relinquish their rights of ownership, for now all would become the prize of war; and to the victor belongs the spoils.

V

1. וְהֵן לֹא יַאֲמִינוּ לִי וְלֹא יִשְׁמְעוּ בְּקֹלִי — *They will not believe me nor listen to my voice.* Moses did not mean that they would question the omnipotence of the Almighty when Pharaoh would refuse to send them forth. He meant that they would refuse to believe that he is God's true messenger, since they know that God decrees and it "is," whereas in this instance the will of God was frustrated and unfulfilled.

2. מַזֶּה בְיָדֶךָ — *What is this in your hand?* The *Sforno* interprets this question as God revealing His intention to show a double sign and wonder, one with his hand and one with what the hand is

ג וַיֹּאמֶר הַשְׁלִיכֵהוּ אַרְצָה וַיַּשְׁלִכֵהוּ אַרְצָה וַיְהִי לְנָחָשׁ וַיָּנָס מֹשֶׁה מִפָּנָיו:
ד וַיֹּאמֶר יהוה אֶל־מֹשֶׁה שְׁלַח יָדְךָ וֶאֱחֹז בִּזְנָבוֹ וַיִּשְׁלַח יָדוֹ וַיַּחֲזֶק בּוֹ וַיְהִי
ה לְמַטֶּה בְּכַפּוֹ: לְמַעַן יַאֲמִינוּ כִּי־נִרְאָה אֵלֶיךָ יהוה אֱלֹהֵי אֲבֹתָם אֱלֹהֵי
ו אַבְרָהָם אֱלֹהֵי יִצְחָק וֵאלֹהֵי יַעֲקֹב: וַיֹּאמֶר יהוה לוֹ עוֹד הָבֵא־נָא יָדְךָ
ז בְּחֵיקֶךָ וַיָּבֵא יָדוֹ בְּחֵיקוֹ וַיּוֹצִאָהּ וְהִנֵּה יָדוֹ מְצֹרַעַת כַּשָּׁלֶג: וַיֹּאמֶר הָשֵׁב
יָדְךָ אֶל־חֵיקֶךָ וַיָּשֶׁב יָדוֹ אֶל־חֵיקוֹ וַיּוֹצִאָהּ מֵחֵיקוֹ וְהִנֵּה־שָׁבָה כִּבְשָׂרוֹ:
ח וְהָיָה אִם־לֹא יַאֲמִינוּ לָךְ וְלֹא יִשְׁמְעוּ לְקֹל הָאֹת הָרִאשׁוֹן וְהֶאֱמִינוּ לְקֹל
ט הָאֹת הָאַחֲרוֹן: וְהָיָה אִם־לֹא יַאֲמִינוּ גַּם לִשְׁנֵי הָאֹתוֹת הָאֵלֶּה וְלֹא יִשְׁמְעוּן
לְקֹלֶךָ וְלָקַחְתָּ מִמֵּימֵי הַיְאֹר וְשָׁפַכְתָּ הַיַּבָּשָׁה וְהָיוּ הַמַּיִם אֲשֶׁר תִּקַּח מִן־
י הַיְאֹר וְהָיוּ לְדָם בַּיַּבָּשֶׁת: וַיֹּאמֶר מֹשֶׁה אֶל־יהוה בִּי אֲדֹנָי לֹא אִישׁ דְּבָרִים
אָנֹכִי גַּם מִתְּמוֹל גַּם מִשִּׁלְשֹׁם גַּם מֵאָז דַּבֶּרְךָ אֶל־עַבְדֶּךָ כִּי כְבַד־פֶּה
יא וּכְבַד לָשׁוֹן אָנֹכִי: וַיֹּאמֶר יהוה אֵלָיו מִי שָׂם פֶּה לָאָדָם אוֹ מִי־יָשׂוּם אִלֵּם
יב אוֹ חֵרֵשׁ אוֹ פִקֵּחַ אוֹ עִוֵּר הֲלֹא אָנֹכִי יהוה: וְעַתָּה לֵךְ וְאָנֹכִי אֶהְיֶה
יג עִם־פִּיךָ וְהוֹרֵיתִיךָ אֲשֶׁר תְּדַבֵּר: וַיֹּאמֶר בִּי אֲדֹנָי שְׁלַח־נָא בְּיַד־תִּשְׁלָח:

I (God), Who can destroy and bring to life, will cause the (living) hand to be as dead through leprosy, and grant life to the inanimate rod.

3. וַיָּנָס מֹשֶׁה מִפָּנָיו — *And Moses fled from it.* For this snake was a real one which pursued him, whereas the serpents made by Pharaoh's magicians through their secret arts had no real movement although they appeared as serpents. Sorcery cannot produce any authentic natural creatures, as our Sages taught us: "By God! they cannot create a camel (or any other creature)" (*Sanhedrin* 67b). Therefore (God) says, וְהַמַּטֶּה אֲשֶׁר נֶהְפַּךְ לְנָחָשׁ, *And the rod which was turned into a snake* (7:15), and not לְתַנִּין, *into a serpent.*

8. וְהֶאֱמִינוּ לְקֹל הָאֹת הָאַחֲרוֹן — *And they will believe the voice of the latter sign.* For it is far more unnatural to heal a particular limb of leprosy, which is strong (and white) as snow and undoubtedly akin to the death of that limb.

9. וְלָקַחְתָּ מִמֵּימֵי הַיְאֹר — *You shall take of the water of the river.* For a (primary) element (i.e., water) to be totally transformed into a composition without (benefit of) an intermediary is unimaginable.

10. לֹא אִישׁ דְּבָרִים אָנֹכִי — *I am not a man of words.* (I am) unskilled in the ways of

NOTES

holding, i.e., the rod. They are coupled because the opposing nature of the two signs — the living hand perishing and the inanimate rod becoming alive — manifest God's power to grant life and take it away. This is a most appropriate introduction to the drama of punishment and liberation that is about to unfold.

3. וַיָּנָס מֹשֶׁה מִפָּנָיו — *And Moses fled from it.* An examination of the phrases in 7:10 and 7:15 will reveal that in the presence of the magicians and wise men, Aaron transformed his rod לְתַנִּין, *into a serpent*, whereas when Moses was sent to warn Pharaoh regarding the first plague, the rod is referred to as that which turned into a נָחָשׁ, *a snake*! To resolve this incongruity the *Sforno* explains that in this episode the snake was real — hence Moses *fled;* whereas in the case of the sorcerers it was an illusion (and even if Aaron did create a נָחָשׁ the sorcerers felt it was only a תַּנִּין, and hence were unafraid) which also explains the lack of fear and fleeing there!

The quotation from *Sanhedrin* cited by the *Sforno* is to be understood thus: It is easier to "create" something large through sorcery than something very small, like a gnat. The Talmud therefore uses a camel as an example of the impotence of sorcerers, who can create illusions but never reality.

8. וְהֶאֱמִינוּ לְקֹל הָאֹת הָאַחֲרוֹן — *And they will believe the voice of the latter sign.* To heal is more impressive than turning a rod into a serpent.

[3] *He said, "Cast it on the ground," and he cast it on the ground and it became a snake. Moses fled from it.* [4] *HASHEM said to Moses, "Stretch out your hand and grasp its tail." He stretched out his hand and grasped it tightly, and it became a staff in his palm.* [5] *"So that they shall believe that HASHEM, the God of their forefathers, appeared to you, the God of Abraham, the God of Isaac, and the God of Jacob."* [6] *HASHEM said further to him, "Bring your hand to your bosom," and he brought his hand to his bosom; then he withdrew it and behold, his hand was leprous, like snow.* [7] *He said, "Return your hand to your bosom," and he returned his hand to his bosom; then he removed it from his bosom and behold, it reverted to be like his flesh.* [8] *"It shall be that if they do not believe you and do not heed the voice of the first sign, they will believe the voice of the latter sign.* [9] *And it shall be that if they do not believe even these two signs and do not heed your voice, then you shall take from the water of the River and pour it out on the dry land, and the water that you shall take from the River will become blood when it is on the dry land."*

[10] *Moses replied to HASHEM, "Please, my Lord, I am not a man of words, not since yesterday, nor since the day before yesterday, nor since You first spoke to Your servant, for I am heavy of mouth and heavy of speech."*

[11] *Then HASHEM said to him, "Who makes a mouth for man, or who makes one dumb or deaf, or sighted or blind? Is it not I, HASHEM?* [12] *So now, go! I shall be with your mouth and teach you what you should say."*

[13] *He replied, "Please, my Lord, send through whomever You will send!"*

---

eloquence and ordered speech, so as to speak (properly) before a king.

גַּם מִתְּמוֹל — *Neither yesterday* ... when I was a stranger in a strange land ...

גַּם מִשִּׁלְשֹׁם — *Nor heretofore* ... when I was in Pharaoh's palace.

גַּם מֵאָז דַּבֶּרְךָ אֶל עַבְדֶּךָ — *Nor since You have spoken to Your servant.* And even when my intellect and power of speech were exposed to the light of God, I did not attain the gift of learned speech.

כִּי כְבַד פֶּה וּכְבַד לָשׁוֹן אָנֹכִי — *For I am slow of speech and tongue.* This is so because my vessels of speech are unprepared, therefore I am incapable of learning how לָדַעַת לָעוּת אֶת יָעֵף דָּבָר, *to sustain with words him that is weary (Isaiah* 50:4).

11. מִי שָׂם פֶּה לָאָדָם — *Who has made man's mouth?* Who has given the natural preparation in the nature of man?

12. וְאָנֹכִי אֶהְיֶה עִם פִּיךָ — *I will be with your mouth* ... to prepare the vessels of speech.

וְהוֹרֵיתִיךָ — *And teach you* ... a skilled לְשׁוֹן לִמּוּדִים, *learned tongue (Isaiah* 50:4).

13. שְׁלַח נָא בְּיַד תִּשְׁלָח — *Send please by the hand of an agent* ... through one who is

NOTES

Therefore the impact and impression of the second sign will convince those who were unmoved by the first. This is an appropriate appreciation of healing powers by the *Sforno,* who was a physician.

9. וְלָקַחְתָּ מִמֵּימֵי הַיְאֹר — *You shall take of the water of the river.* Water, from the river, is a basic element of nature, while blood is composed of more than one part. To transform the former into the latter without any act or process is so unimaginable that it will certainly impress everyone, including those who were skeptical of the first two signs.

10. כִּי כְבַד פֶּה וּכְבַד לָשׁוֹן אָנֹכִי — *For I am slow of speech and tongue.* Though God grants blessing one must have the capacity to receive. Moses claimed that he had no vessel of an articulate tongue with which to receive God's blessing. God's answer to him was that the power to receive would also be granted to him (v. 11).

יד וַיִּחַר־אַף יְהוָה בְּמֹשֶׁה וַיֹּאמֶר הֲלֹא אַהֲרֹן אָחִיךָ הַלֵּוִי יָדַעְתִּי כִּי־דַבֵּר
טו יְדַבֵּר הוּא וְגַם הִנֵּה־הוּא יֹצֵא לִקְרָאתֶךָ וְרָאֲךָ וְשָׂמַח בְּלִבּוֹ: וְדִבַּרְתָּ אֵלָיו
וְשַׂמְתָּ אֶת־הַדְּבָרִים בְּפִיו וְאָנֹכִי אֶהְיֶה עִם־פִּיךָ וְעִם־פִּיהוּ וְהוֹרֵיתִי אֶתְכֶם
טז אֵת אֲשֶׁר תַּעֲשׂוּן: וְדִבֶּר־הוּא לְךָ אֶל־הָעָם וְהָיָה הוּא יִהְיֶה־לְּךָ לְפֶה
יז וְאַתָּה תִּהְיֶה־לּוֹ לֵאלֹהִים: וְאֶת־הַמַּטֶּה הַזֶּה תִּקַּח בְּיָדֶךָ אֲשֶׁר תַּעֲשֶׂה־בּוֹ
אֶת־הָאֹתֹת:
ששי יח וַיֵּלֶךְ מֹשֶׁה וַיָּשָׁב | אֶל־יֶתֶר חֹתְנוֹ וַיֹּאמֶר לוֹ אֵלְכָה־נָּא וְאָשׁוּבָה אֶל־אַחַי
אֲשֶׁר־בְּמִצְרַיִם וְאֶרְאֶה הַעוֹדָם חַיִּים וַיֹּאמֶר יִתְרוֹ לְמֹשֶׁה לֵךְ לְשָׁלוֹם:
יט וַיֹּאמֶר יְהוָה אֶל־מֹשֶׁה בְּמִדְיָן לֵךְ שֻׁב מִצְרָיִם כִּי־מֵתוּ כָּל־הָאֲנָשִׁים
כ הַמְבַקְשִׁים אֶת־נַפְשֶׁךָ: וַיִּקַּח מֹשֶׁה אֶת־אִשְׁתּוֹ וְאֶת־בָּנָיו וַיַּרְכִּבֵם עַל־
כא הַחֲמֹר וַיָּשָׁב אַרְצָה מִצְרָיִם וַיִּקַּח מֹשֶׁה אֶת־מַטֵּה הָאֱלֹהִים בְּיָדוֹ: וַיֹּאמֶר
יְהוָה אֶל־מֹשֶׁה בְּלֶכְתְּךָ לָשׁוּב מִצְרַיְמָה רְאֵה כָּל־הַמֹּפְתִים אֲשֶׁר־שַׂמְתִּי
בְיָדֶךָ וַעֲשִׂיתָם לִפְנֵי פַרְעֹה וַאֲנִי אֲחַזֵּק אֶת־לִבּוֹ וְלֹא יְשַׁלַּח אֶת־הָעָם:

(better) prepared to accomplish Your mission, and not a man such as I who will need Your (constant) support and guidance so that (in reality) You will be the one Who speaks.

14. הֲלֹא אַהֲרֹן אָחִיךָ הַלֵּוִי — *Is there not Aaron your brother, the Levite?* If the purpose was to send a man prepared to speak, then your brother Aaron, who is a Levite and without a doubt a wise person as are all his Levite brothers (would have been chosen).

יָדַעְתִּי כִּי דַבֵּר יְדַבֵּר הוּא — *I know that he can speak well* ... that he is, unassisted, an eloquent and skilled speaker.

וְגַם הִנֵּה הוּא יֹצֵא לִקְרָאתֶךָ — *And behold he comes to greet you.* Though he comes to greet you and honor you because of your superior position (status) nonetheless he will doubtless rejoice and be your spokesman with a full heart.

15. וְשַׂמְתָּ אֶת הַדְּבָרִים בְּפִיו וְאָנֹכִי אֶהְיֶה עִם פִּיךָ וְעִם פִּיהוּ — *And put the words in his mouth and I will be with your mouth and with his mouth.* Even though you will place the words in his mouth, that will not be sufficient. I must be with you so that your words will enter Pharaoh's heart so that he do you no harm nor drive you forth from his presence.

16. לֵאלֹהִים — *In God's stead.* To perform wonders at your behest.

17. וְאֶת הַמַּטֶּה הַזֶּה — *And this rod.* Although it is not taken from a significant tree I have hallowed it for you as a sign.

תִּקַּח בְּיָדֶךָ — *Take in your hand.* As the scepter of a ruler, for I have apppointed you to change the course of nature at your behest.

אֲשֶׁר תַּעֲשֶׂה בּוֹ אֶת הָאֹתֹת — *Wherewith you shall do the signs.* You will command the natural forces, in accordance with My behest, for this is your assignment and appointment.

18. אֵלְכָה נָּא וְאָשׁוּבָה — *Let me go and return.* In the interim my wife and sons will remain with you.

NOTES

13-14. שְׁלַח נָא בְּיַד תִּשְׁלָח ... הֲלֹא אַהֲרֹן אָחִיךָ הַלֵּוִי — יָדַעְתִּי כִּי דַבֵּר יְדַבֵּר הוּא וְגַם הִנֵּה הוּא יֹצֵא לִקְרָאתֶךָ — *Send please by the hand of an agent ... Is there not Aaron your brother, the Levite? I know that he can speak well. And behold he comes to greet you.* Moses' error lay in his assumption that the messenger had to have the skill and ability to fulfill this mission on his own, once direction and guidance had been given. The Almighty told him otherwise. That Aaron was capable and available was known to Him as well. If in spite of this Moses was called, it was precisely because God chose to use him as His instrument, and was not concerned with one's natural talents of speech. However, Moses's reluctance was so real that Aaron had to be co-opted to the leadership that was originally meant for Moses alone.

14 The wrath of HASHEM *burned against Moses and He said, "Is there not*
Aaron your brother, the Levite? I know that he will surely speak; moreover,
behold, he is going out to meet you and when he sees you he will rejoice in
his heart. *15 You shall speak to him and put the words in his mouth; and I*
shall be with your mouth and with his mouth, and teach you both what you
are to do. *16 He shall speak for you to the people; and it will be that he will*
be your mouth and you will be his leader. *17 And this staff you shall take in*
your hand, with which you shall perform the signs."
18 So Moses went and returned to Jether, his father-in-law, and said to
him, "Let me now go back to my brethren who are in Egypt, and see if they
are still alive." And Jethro said to Moses, "Go to peace."
19 HASHEM *said to Moses in Midian, "Go, return to Egypt, for all the*
people who seek your life have died."
20 So Moses took his wife and sons, mounted them on the donkey, and
returned to the land of Egypt; and Moses took the staff of God in his hand.
21 HASHEM *said to Moses, "When you go to return to Egypt, see all the*
wonders that I have put in your hand and perform them before Pharaoh;
but I shall strengthen his heart and he will not send out the people.

לֵךְ לְשָׁלוֹם — *Go in peace.* For I will do so.

19. כִּי מֵתוּ כָּל הָאֲנָשִׁים — *For all the men are dead.* The king and his servants who sought to kill you, as explained above when it says, וַיָּמָת מֶלֶךְ מִצְרַיִם, *And the king of Egypt died* (2:23).

20. וַיַּרְכִּבֵם עַל הַחֲמֹר — *And he seated them upon an ass* ... to bring them from the wilderness to his father-in-law's home in Midian.

וַיָּשָׁב אַרְצָה מִצְרָיִם — *And he returned to the land of Egypt* ... he alone, after he had sent them away.

21. בְּלֶכְתְּךָ לָשׁוּב מִצְרַיְמָה — *When you go to return to Egypt.* Whenever I will send you from your tent to Egypt, for his tent was pitched outside the city, as we read, כְּצֵאתִי אֶת הָעִיר אֶפְרֹשׂ כַּפַּי, *When I go forth from the city, I will lift up my hands* (9:29), and I will command you to return to Egypt to speak to Pharaoh.

רְאֵה כָּל הַמֹּפְתִים אֲשֶׁר שַׂמְתִּי בְיָדֶךָ — *See all the wonders.* Examine each time all the wonders that will be placed in your hands, to perform them in the manner and order which I shall command you.

וַעֲשִׂיתָם לִפְנֵי פַרְעֹה — *And do them before Pharaoh.* You will succeed to do them before Pharaoh providing you change nothing, for if one sins regarding the commandments of his Creator by adding or subtracting, he impairs the intent and it will fail, as was the case with the *waters of strife (Numbers* 20), and so we are instructed regarding fulfillment of the *mitzvos,* לֹא תֹסִפוּ וְלֹא תִגְרְעוּ, *You shall not add nor subtract (Deut.* 4:2).

וַאֲנִי אֲחַזֵּק אֶת לִבּוֹ — *And I will harden his heart.* The inability of Pharaoh to withstand the plagues would have doubtless caused him to send forth the people, (but) not because

NOTES

20. וַיָּשָׁב אַרְצָה מִצְרָיִם — *And he returned to the land of Egypt.* As the *Sforno* points out in this verse — as does *Rashi* — the Torah does not always present events in chronological order (אֵין מוּקְדָּם וּמְאוּחָר בַּתּוֹרָה).

21. בְּלֶכְתְּךָ לָשׁוּב. . . רְאֵה כָּל הַמֹּפְתִים — *When you go to return . . . see all the wonders.* The phrases *to return* and *all the wonders* are the key to the *Sforno's* interpretation of this sentence. God is not referring to his present return to Egypt, but to those periods of return during his future sojourn *outside* the city. The expression *see "all" the wonders* is explained as a word of caution to Moses to follow carefully the exact order of the mission entrusted to him.

וַאֲנִי אֲחַזֵּק אֶת לִבּוֹ — *And I will harden his heart.* Were Pharaoh to have submitted to God's will

כב־כג וְאָמַרְתָּ֖ אֶל־פַּרְעֹ֑ה כֹּ֚ה אָמַ֣ר יהו֔ה בְּנִ֥י בְכֹרִ֖י יִשְׂרָאֵ֑ל: וָאֹמַ֣ר אֵלֶ֗יךָ שַׁלַּ֤ח
כד אֶת־בְּנִי֙ וְיַעַבְדֵ֔נִי וַתְּמָאֵ֖ן לְשַׁלְּח֑וֹ הִנֵּ֣ה אָנֹכִ֣י הֹרֵ֔ג אֶת־בִּנְךָ֖ בְּכֹרֶֽךָ: וַיְהִ֥י
כה בַדֶּ֖רֶךְ בַּמָּל֑וֹן וַיִּפְגְּשֵׁ֣הוּ יהו֔ה וַיְבַקֵּ֖שׁ הֲמִיתֽוֹ: וַתִּקַּ֨ח צִפֹּרָ֜ה צֹ֗ר וַתִּכְרֹת֙
כו אֶת־עָרְלַ֣ת בְּנָ֔הּ וַתַּגַּ֖ע לְרַגְלָ֑יו וַתֹּ֕אמֶר כִּ֧י חֲתַן־דָּמִ֛ים אַתָּ֖ה לִֽי: וַיִּ֖רֶף מִמֶּ֑נּוּ
אָ֚ז אָֽמְרָ֔ה חֲתַ֥ן דָּמִ֖ים לַמּוּלֹֽת:
כז וַיֹּ֨אמֶר יהו֜ה אֶֽל־אַהֲרֹ֗ן לֵ֛ךְ לִקְרַ֥את מֹשֶׁ֖ה הַמִּדְבָּ֑רָה וַיֵּ֗לֶךְ וַֽיִּפְגְּשֵׁ֛הוּ בְּהַ֥ר

of his submission to God, the Blessed One, and (a desire) to do His will. Therefore God hardens his heart so as to strengthen him to be able to accept the plagues and not send them forth.

22. בְּנִי בְכֹרִי יִשְׂרָאֵל — *Israel, My firstborn son.* Even though at the end of days אֶהְפֹּךְ אֶל עַמִּים שָׂפָה בְרוּרָה, לִקְרוֹא כֻלָּם בְּשֵׁם ה׳ וּלְעָבְדוֹ שְׁכֶם אֶחָד, *I (God) will turn to the peoples a pure language that they may all call unto the Name of* HASHEM *to serve Him with one consent* (Zephaniah 3:9), nonetheless Israel will be honored above them all for he is My son, who serves (Me) as a son motivated by love, not as a slave who labors (motivated) by the love of money or the fear of punishment. He is My firstborn because he was the first to serve Me when all other people strayed from Me, as it says, כִּי כָל הָעַמִּים יֵלְכוּ אִישׁ בְּשֵׁם אֱלֹהָיו וַאֲנַחְנוּ נֵלֵךְ בְּשֵׁם ה׳ אֱלֹהֵינוּ לְעוֹלָם וָעֶד, *Let all the nations walk each one in the name of his god, but we will walk in the name of* HASHEM, *our God, forever* (Micah 4:5).

23. הִנֵּה אָנֹכִי הֹרֵג אֶת בִּנְךָ בְּכֹרֶךָ — *Behold I will slay your son, your firstborn.* In keeping with the Divine judgment of "measure for measure," as it says, וּכְאֹרַח אִישׁ יַמְצִאֶנּוּ, *And cause every man to find according to his ways* (Job 34:11). Indeed only the plague of the firstborn, of all the plagues, was visited upon Pharaoh as a punishment. The other plagues were meant to serve as signs and wonders for the purpose of bringing them to repentance, for (God) does not desire the death of any man. He did not close the door to true repentance, at all. Had they but had the wisdom to return to God, the Blessed One, from (a source) of love for His goodness or reverence for His greatness (they would have been spared), as our Sages state, "Transgressions are considered as merits" (Yoma 86b), or at the very least if they would have repented as servants, motivated by a fear of punishment. However, the plague of the firstborn and the drowning of Pharaoh and his army in the sea were Divine judgments — measure for measure.

24. וַיְהִי בַדֶּרֶךְ בַּמָּלוֹן — *And it came to pass on the way, at the lodging place.* On his way from the wilderness to Midian with his wife and sons. This episode took place after the completion of God's instructions to him regarding his mission.

NOTES

because he could not withstand the pressure of the plagues, it would have defeated God's purpose in visiting these plagues upon Egypt. The purpose was to bring Pharaoh to a recognition of God's might and kingship of the world, thereby causing him to submit willingly to God's rulership, not under duress. It is for this reason that God hardened his heart.

22. בְּנִי בְכֹרִי יִשְׂרָאֵל — *Israel, My firstborn son.* All people are considered the children of God. Israel, however, is worthy to be called His firstborn for two reasons: (a) They serve God from a motivation of love, not for any reward nor out of fear of punishment; and (b) when none recognized God, they did, and when all others forsook Him, Israel remained steadfast in their loyalty.

23. הִנֵּה אָנֹכִי הֹרֵג אֶת בִּנְךָ בְּכֹרֶךָ — *Behold I will slay your son, your firstborn.* The Egyptians decreed that all Jewish males be cast into the river. They were also responsible for the suffering and death of countless Jews, the firstborn of God. The retribution of drowning in the Red Sea and the plague of the firstborn are direct punishments, *measure for measure,* unlike the earlier plagues that were visited upon the Egyptians to awaken their reverence, in the hope that they might repent.

24. וַיִּפְגְּשֵׁהוּ ה׳ וַיְבַקֵּשׁ הֲמִיתוֹ — *And* HASHEM *met him, and he sought to slay him.* And he sought to slay him (Moses) refers not to God Who came to the circumcision, but to the angel of the covenant who sought to slay Moses for his laxity in delaying

22 *You shall say to Pharaoh, 'So said* HASHEM, *My firstborn son is Israel.* 23 *So I say to you, Send out My son that he may serve Me — but you have refused to send him out; behold, I shall kill your firstborn son.' "*

24 *It was on the way, in the lodging, that* HASHEM *encountered him and sought to kill him.* 25 *So Zipporah took a sharp stone and cut off the foreskin of her son and touched it to his feet; and she said, "You caused my bridegroom's bloodshed!"* 26 *So he released him; then she said, "A bridegroom's bloodshed was because of circumcision."*

27 HASHEM *said to Aaron, "Go to meet Moses, to the wilderness." So he went*

וַיִּפְגְּשֵׁהוּ ה׳ — *And* HASHEM *met him.* This happened because it was the day of his son's circumcision, at which time the Divine Presence *(Shechinah)* comes to be present at the *bris,* as we find, נִמֹּלוּ אִתּוֹ . . . וַיֵּרָא אֵלָיו ה׳, *They were circumcised with him . . . And God appeared to him (Genesis* 17:27-18:1). Perhaps this is the reason for the custom to prepare a chair of honor at a *bris.*

וַיְבַקֵּשׁ הֲמִיתוֹ — *And he sought to slay him.* The angel of the covenant, who sanctifies the infant being circumcised to serve God. He wanted to kill Moses for his laxity (in performing this *mitzvah).*

25. וַתֹּאמֶר כִּי חֲתַן דָּמִים אַתָּה לִי — *And she said, "A bridegroom of blood are you to me."* I did this because when you wed me and became my bridegroom, you made a condition that we would circumcise our children and draw forth the blood of the covenant. All this she said in defense of Moses, to (the angel) who wanted to slay him.

26. וַיִּרֶף מִמֶּנּוּ — *He let him alone . . .* but did not release him completely.

אָז אָמְרָה חֲתַן דָּמִים לַמּוּלֹת — *Then she said, "A bridegroom of blood," regarding the circumcision.* When you were my groom you said that we would draw the blood of the circumcision twice, i.e., the cutting of the foreskin and the exposing (of the glans).

27. לֵךְ לִקְרַאת מֹשֶׁה הַמִּדְבָּרָה — *Go into the wilderness to meet Moses . . .* as a disciple goes forth to greet his teacher, as it says, וְאַתָּה תִּהְיֶה לּוֹ לֵאלֹהִים, *And you shall be to him in God's stead* (4:16).

וַיִּפְגְּשֵׁהוּ בְּהַר הָאֱלֹהִים — *And he met him at the mountain of God . . .* when he returned from Midian to go to Egypt.

NOTES

the performance of the *mitzvah.* Regarding God's presence at a circumcision, see the *Sforno* to *Genesis* 18:1 and the notes.

25. וַתֹּאמֶר כִּי חֲתַן דָּמִים אַתָּה לִי — *And she said, "A bridegroom of blood are you to me."* Zipporah is defending Moses before the avenging angel. She explains that her groom (Moses) had insisted upon her agreement to circumcise their children. This was important since she was the daughter of Jethro, the Midianite priest, and the concept of drawing forth blood as a sign of the covenant was totally strange to her. The fact that Moses made this condition with her indicates that he was committed to this *mitzvah.* Therefore the *angel of the covenant* should spare Moses for his laxity in circumcising Eliezer, being that it was not due to a rejection of the covenant.

26. וַיִּרֶף מִמֶּנּוּ — *He let him alone.* The root רפה means to *weaken* one's hold, but not to release completely. The reason was because cutting the foreskin was not sufficient to fulfill the *mitzvah* until the glans is totally exposed (פְּרִיעָה). The angel, therefore, is not completely satisfied with Zipporah's cutting the foreskin (verse 25) until she reminded Moses to shed the blood doubly (לַמּוּלֹת), i.e., cutting (חֲתִיכָה) and exposing (פְּרִיעָה), for thus had he told her when they were first married. This basic law is established in the Talmud *(Sabbath* 137b): מָל וְלֹא פָרַע . . . כְּאִלּוּ לֹא מָל, *If one circumcises but does not expose (the glans), it is as though he did not circumcise.*

חֲתַן דָּמִים לַמּוּלֹת — *"A bridegroom of blood" regarding the circumcision.* This interpretation explains the plural מוּלֹת, *circumcisions.*

27. לֵךְ לִקְרַאת מֹשֶׁה הַמִּדְבָּרָה . . . וַיִּשַּׁק לוֹ — *Go into the wilderness to meet Moses . . . And he kissed him.* Aaron was older than Moses, still God told him to go and greet his younger brother. The

כח הָאֱלֹהִים וַיִּשַּׁק־לוֹ: וַיַּגֵּד מֹשֶׁה לְאַהֲרֹן אֵת כָּל־דִּבְרֵי יהוה אֲשֶׁר שְׁלָחוֹ
כט וְאֵת כָּל־הָאֹתֹת אֲשֶׁר צִוָּהוּ: וַיֵּלֶךְ מֹשֶׁה וְאַהֲרֹן וַיַּאַסְפוּ אֶת־כָּל־זִקְנֵי
ל בְּנֵי יִשְׂרָאֵל: וַיְדַבֵּר אַהֲרֹן אֵת כָּל־הַדְּבָרִים אֲשֶׁר־דִּבֶּר יהוה אֶל־מֹשֶׁה
לא וַיַּעַשׂ הָאֹתֹת לְעֵינֵי הָעָם: וַיַּאֲמֵן הָעָם וַיִּשְׁמְעוּ כִּי־פָקַד יהוה אֶת־בְּנֵי
ה שביעי א יִשְׂרָאֵל וְכִי רָאָה אֶת־עָנְיָם וַיִּקְּדוּ וַיִּשְׁתַּחֲוּוּ: וְאַחַר בָּאוּ מֹשֶׁה וְאַהֲרֹן
וַיֹּאמְרוּ אֶל־פַּרְעֹה כֹּה־אָמַר יהוה אֱלֹהֵי יִשְׂרָאֵל שַׁלַּח אֶת־עַמִּי וְיָחֹגּוּ
ב לִי בַּמִּדְבָּר: וַיֹּאמֶר פַּרְעֹה מִי יהוה אֲשֶׁר אֶשְׁמַע בְּקֹלוֹ לְשַׁלַּח אֶת־
ג יִשְׂרָאֵל לֹא יָדַעְתִּי אֶת־יהוה וְגַם אֶת־יִשְׂרָאֵל לֹא אֲשַׁלֵּחַ: וַיֹּאמְרוּ
אֱלֹהֵי הָעִבְרִים נִקְרָא עָלֵינוּ נֵלְכָה נָּא דֶּרֶךְ שְׁלֹשֶׁת יָמִים בַּמִּדְבָּר
ד וְנִזְבְּחָה לַיהוה אֱלֹהֵינוּ פֶּן־יִפְגָּעֵנוּ בַּדֶּבֶר אוֹ בֶחָרֶב: וַיֹּאמֶר אֲלֵהֶם מֶלֶךְ
מִצְרַיִם לָמָּה מֹשֶׁה וְאַהֲרֹן תַּפְרִיעוּ אֶת־הָעָם מִמַּעֲשָׂיו לְכוּ לְסִבְלֹתֵיכֶם:
ה־ו וַיֹּאמֶר פַּרְעֹה הֵן־רַבִּים עַתָּה עַם הָאָרֶץ וְהִשְׁבַּתֶּם אֹתָם מִסִּבְלֹתָם: וַיְצַו
ז פַּרְעֹה בַּיּוֹם הַהוּא אֶת־הַנֹּגְשִׂים בָּעָם וְאֶת־שֹׁטְרָיו לֵאמֹר: לֹא תֹאסִפוּן
לָתֵת תֶּבֶן לָעָם לִלְבֹּן הַלְּבֵנִים כִּתְמוֹל שִׁלְשֹׁם הֵם יֵלְכוּ וְקֹשְׁשׁוּ לָהֶם
ח תֶּבֶן: וְאֶת־מַתְכֹּנֶת הַלְּבֵנִים אֲשֶׁר הֵם עֹשִׂים תְּמוֹל שִׁלְשֹׁם תָּשִׂימוּ
עֲלֵיהֶם לֹא תִגְרְעוּ מִמֶּנּוּ כִּי־נִרְפִּים הֵם עַל־כֵּן הֵם צֹעֲקִים לֵאמֹר נֵלְכָה
ט נִזְבְּחָה לֵאלֹהֵינוּ: תִּכְבַּד הָעֲבֹדָה עַל־הָאֲנָשִׁים וְיַעֲשׂוּ־בָהּ וְאַל־יִשְׁעוּ
י בְּדִבְרֵי־שָׁקֶר: וַיֵּצְאוּ נֹגְשֵׂי הָעָם וְשֹׁטְרָיו וַיֹּאמְרוּ אֶל־הָעָם לֵאמֹר כֹּה
יא אָמַר פַּרְעֹה אֵינֶנִּי נֹתֵן לָכֶם תֶּבֶן: אַתֶּם לְכוּ קְחוּ לָכֶם תֶּבֶן מֵאֲשֶׁר
יב תִּמְצָאוּ כִּי אֵין נִגְרָע מֵעֲבֹדַתְכֶם דָּבָר: וַיָּפֶץ הָעָם בְּכָל־אֶרֶץ מִצְרָיִם
יג לְקֹשֵׁשׁ קַשׁ לַתֶּבֶן: וְהַנֹּגְשִׂים אָצִים לֵאמֹר כַּלּוּ מַעֲשֵׂיכֶם דְּבַר־יוֹם בְּיוֹמוֹ
יד כַּאֲשֶׁר בִּהְיוֹת הַתֶּבֶן: וַיֻּכּוּ שֹׁטְרֵי בְּנֵי יִשְׂרָאֵל אֲשֶׁר־שָׂמוּ עֲלֵהֶם נֹגְשֵׂי

וַיִּשַּׁק לוֹ — *And he kissed him* . . . as one kisses a holy object, similar to, וַיִּשָּׁקֵהוּ, וַיֹּאמֶר הֲלוֹא כִּי מְשָׁחֲךָ ה׳ עַל נַחֲלָתוֹ לְנָגִיד, *And he (Samuel) kissed him (Saul) and said, "Behold HASHEM has anointed you to be a prince over His inheritance"* (*I Samuel* 10:1).

V

2. לֹא יָדַעְתִּי אֶת ה׳ — *I know not HASHEM.* I do not know any Being that can bring another into being יֵשׁ מֵאַיִן, *ex nihilo* (from naught).

וְגַם אֶת יִשְׂרָאֵל לֹא אֲשַׁלֵּחַ — *And moreover I will not let Israel go.* And even if this be so, that there is such a Being, I will not send forth Israel on this account.

3. אֱלֹהֵי הָעִבְרִים — *The God of the Hebrews.* In answer to your question, "Who is He (God)?," He is the God of the Hebrews, who are well known as those who adhere to the

NOTES

Sforno explains that this was because Aaron's relationship to Moses was that of a disciple to a teacher, who must pay him respect. Consequently the kiss bestowed by Aaron upon Moses was not only one of a brother to a brother, but was also meant as a gesture of respect, i.e., akin to kissing a sacred object.

V

2. לֹא יָדַעְתִּי אֶת ה׳ — *I know not HASHEM.* In 3:14 it was established that God's name is derived from the concept of being and creating. Moses and Aaron doubtless explained this to Pharaoh who exclaimed that he could not recognize the existence of such a power.

and encountered him at the mountain of God, and he kissed him. 28 *Moses*
related to Aaron all the words of HASHEM, *that He had dispatched him, and*
all the signs that He had commanded him.
29 *Moses and Aaron went and gathered all the elders of the Children of*
Israel. 30 *Aaron spoke all the words that* HASHEM *had spoken to Moses; and*
he performed the signs in the sight of the people. 31 *And the people believed,*
and they heard that HASHEM *had remembered the Children of Israel and that*
He saw their affliction, and they bowed their heads and prostrated
themselves.

5 1 *Afterwards Moses and Aaron came and said to Pharaoh, "So said*
HASHEM, *the God of Israel, 'Send out My people that they may celebrate*
for Me in the wilderness.' "
2 *Pharaoh replied, "Who is* HASHEM *that I should heed His voice to send*
out Israel? I do not know HASHEM, *nor will I send out Israel!"* 3 *So they said,*
"The God of the Hebrews happened upon us. Let us now go for a three-day
journey in the wilderness and we shall bring offerings to HASHEM, *our God,*
lest he strike us dead with the plague or the sword." 4 *The king of Egypt said*
to them, "Moses and Aaron, why do you disturb the people from its work?
Go to your own burdens." 5 *And Pharaoh said, "Behold! the people of the land*
are now numerous, and you would have them cease from their burdens!"
6 *On that day Pharaoh ordered the taskmasters over the people and its*
foremen, saying, 7 *"You shall no longer give straw to the people to*
manufacture the bricks as yesterday and before yesterday; let them go and
gather straw for themselves. 8 *But the quota of bricks that they were making*
yesterday and before yesterday you shall impose upon them — do not reduce
it — for they are lazy; therefore they cry out saying, 'Let us go and bring
offerings to our God.' 9 *Let the work be heavier upon the men and let them*
engage in it; and let them not pay attention to false words."
10 *The taskmasters of the people and its foremen went out and spoke to*
the people, saying, "So said Pharaoh, I am not giving you straw. 11 *Go*
yourselves and take yourselves straw from whatever you find, for nothing
will be reduced from your work."
12 *So the people spread out through the entire land of Egypt to gather glean-*
ings for straw. 13 *The taskmasters pressed, saying, "Complete your work, the*
daily matter each day, as when there was straw!" 14 *The foremen of the*
Children of Israel, whom Pharaoh's taskmasters had appointed over them,

---

beliefs of Eber. And regarding your statement that you will not send them forth, it would be far better to listen to Him . . .

פֶּן יִפְגָּעֵנוּ — *Lest he fall upon us* . . . us and you (both will be affected).

5. הֵן רַבִּים עַתָּה עַם הָאָרֶץ — *Behold the people are now many.* For the intelligent ones will certainly not listen to you.

NOTES

5. הֵן רַבִּים עַתָּה עַם הָאָרֶץ — *Behold the people are now many.* Pharaoh lamented that the intelligent ones were few, while the *people of the land*, a euphemism for the ignorant ones, were many, and they would unfortunately listen to Moses, thereby causing idleness and unrest.

פַּרְעֹה לֵאמֹר מַדּוּעַ לֹא כִלִּיתֶם חָקְכֶם לִלְבֹּן כִּתְמוֹל שִׁלְשֹׁם גַּם־תְּמוֹל
טו גַּם־הַיּוֹם׃ וַיָּבֹאוּ שֹׁטְרֵי בְּנֵי יִשְׂרָאֵל וַיִּצְעֲקוּ אֶל־פַּרְעֹה לֵאמֹר לָמָּה
טז תַעֲשֶׂה כֹה לַעֲבָדֶיךָ׃ תֶּבֶן אֵין נִתָּן לַעֲבָדֶיךָ וּלְבֵנִים אֹמְרִים לָנוּ עֲשׂוּ
יז וְהִנֵּה עֲבָדֶיךָ מֻכִּים וְחָטָאת עַמֶּךָ׃ וַיֹּאמֶר נִרְפִּים אַתֶּם נִרְפִּים עַל־כֵּן
יח אַתֶּם אֹמְרִים נֵלְכָה נִזְבְּחָה לַיהוָה׃ וְעַתָּה לְכוּ עִבְדוּ וְתֶבֶן לֹא־יִנָּתֵן לָכֶם
יט וְתֹכֶן לְבֵנִים תִּתֵּנוּ׃ וַיִּרְאוּ שֹׁטְרֵי בְנֵי־יִשְׂרָאֵל אֹתָם בְּרָע לֵאמֹר לֹא־
כ תִגְרְעוּ מִלִּבְנֵיכֶם דְּבַר־יוֹם בְּיוֹמוֹ׃ וַיִּפְגְּעוּ אֶת־מֹשֶׁה וְאֶת־אַהֲרֹן נִצָּבִים
כא לִקְרָאתָם בְּצֵאתָם מֵאֵת פַּרְעֹה׃ וַיֹּאמְרוּ אֲלֵהֶם יֵרֶא יְהוָה עֲלֵיכֶם
וְיִשְׁפֹּט אֲשֶׁר הִבְאַשְׁתֶּם אֶת־רֵיחֵנוּ בְּעֵינֵי פַרְעֹה וּבְעֵינֵי עֲבָדָיו לָתֶת־
מפטיר כב חֶרֶב בְּיָדָם לְהָרְגֵנוּ׃ וַיָּשָׁב מֹשֶׁה אֶל־יְהוָה וַיֹּאמַר אֲדֹנָי לָמָה הֲרֵעֹתָה
כג לָעָם הַזֶּה לָמָּה זֶּה שְׁלַחְתָּנִי׃ וּמֵאָז בָּאתִי אֶל־פַּרְעֹה לְדַבֵּר בִּשְׁמֶךָ הֵרַע
ו א לָעָם הַזֶּה וְהַצֵּל לֹא־הִצַּלְתָּ אֶת־עַמֶּךָ׃ וַיֹּאמֶר יְהוָה אֶל־מֹשֶׁה עַתָּה
תִרְאֶה אֲשֶׁר אֶעֱשֶׂה לְפַרְעֹה כִּי בְיָד חֲזָקָה יְשַׁלְּחֵם וּבְיָד חֲזָקָה יְגָרְשֵׁם
מֵאַרְצוֹ׃

---

16. וְהִנֵּה עֲבָדֶיךָ מֻכִּים — *And behold your servants are beaten.* Behold, we the beaten ones, and the sinners who beat us, are all your people, therefore you should be concerned for both.

17. נִרְפִּים אַתֶּם נִרְפִּים — *You are idle.* You, the idle and lazy ones, are lax in your labors, therefore I have increased the work so as to stimulate you.

עַל כֵּן אַתֶּם אֹמְרִים נֵלְכָה נִזְבְּחָה — *Therefore you say, 'Let us go and sacrifice.'* This proves that you are idle, else why insist upon going to sacrifice if not to avoid your labors?

22. לָמָּה זֶּה שְׁלַחְתָּנִי — *Why have You sent me?* If they deserve to be punished, why has it been done through me?

23. וְהַצֵּל לֹא הִצַּלְתָּ — *Neither have You delivered* . . . the Jewish officers who are beaten.

NOTES

22. לָמָּה זֶּה שְׁלַחְתָּנִי — *Why have You sent me?* Our Sages teach us, "Merits are brought through meritorious ones and punishment through guilty ones" (*Sanhedrin* 8a, *Sabbath* 32a). Therefore Moses lamented that he was chosen as the instrument of God to bring pain and suffering.

were beaten, saying, "Why did you not complete your requirement to make bricks, as yesterday and before yesterday, even yesterday and even today?"

[15] *The foremen of the Children of Israel came and cried out to Pharaoh, saying, "Why do you this to your servants?* [16] *Straw is not given to your servants, yet they tell us, 'Make bricks!' Behold, your servants are being beaten, and it is a sin for your people."*

[17] *He said, "You are lazy, lazy! Therefore you say, 'Let us go and bring offerings to HASHEM.'* [18] *Now go to work. Straw will not be given to you, but you must provide the quota of bricks!"*

[19] *The foremen of the Children of Israel saw them in distress when they said, "Do not reduce your bricks, the daily matter each day."*

[20] *They encountered Moses and Aaron standing opposite them, as they left Pharaoh's presence.* [21] *They said to them, "May HASHEM look upon you and judge, for you have made our very scent abhorrent in the eyes of Pharaoh and the eyes of his servants, to place a sword in their hands to murder us!"*

[22] *Moses returned to HASHEM and said, "My Lord, why have You done evil to this people, why have You sent me?* [23] *From the time I came to Pharaoh to speak in Your Name he did evil to this people, but You did not rescue Your people."*

6 [1] *HASHEM said to Moses, "Now you will see what I shall do to Pharaoh, for through a strong hand will he send them out, and with a strong hand will he drive them from his land."*

VI

1. עַתָּה תִרְאֶה — *Now you shall see.* Now that you have seen the iniquity of Pharaoh, who is determined to keep Israel (under him) with his rod of anger, (so shall) you see . . .

כִּי בְיָד חֲזָקָה יְשַׁלְּחֵם — *By a strong hand shall he let them go.* He will strive with all his might to send them forth, pressured by the evil and sorrow (which will befall him).

וּבְיָד חֲזָקָה יְגָרְשֵׁם מֵאַרְצוֹ — *And by a strong hand he will drive them out of his land.* Whereas now Pharaoh has caused the Israelites to be dispersed throughout the land of Egypt (5:12), he will (later) strive to drive them out of his land so that not even one will remain.

NOTES

23. וְהַצֵּל לֹא הִצַּלְתָּ — *Neither have You delivered.* God had already told Moses that Pharaoh would not allow the Israelites to leave Egypt (3:19). Therefore Moses could not very well be upset that his demands for their liberation had been rejected by Pharaoh. What disturbed him was that as a result of his demands the Israelite officers were being beaten. For this reason he confronted God with the complaint that He had not delivered these righteous men from the hands of their oppressors.

פרשת וארא

ב-ג וַיְדַבֵּר אֱלֹהִים אֶל־מֹשֶׁה וַיֹּאמֶר אֵלָיו אֲנִי יהוה: וָאֵרָא אֶל־אַבְרָהָם אֶל־
ד יִצְחָק וְאֶל־יַעֲקֹב בְּאֵל שַׁדָּי וּשְׁמִי יהוה לֹא נוֹדַעְתִּי לָהֶם: וְגַם הֲקִמֹתִי
אֶת־בְּרִיתִי אִתָּם לָתֵת לָהֶם אֶת־אֶרֶץ כְּנָעַן אֵת אֶרֶץ מְגֻרֵיהֶם אֲשֶׁר־גָּרוּ
ה בָהּ: וְגַם ׀ אֲנִי שָׁמַעְתִּי אֶת־נַאֲקַת בְּנֵי יִשְׂרָאֵל אֲשֶׁר מִצְרַיִם מַעֲבִדִים
ו אֹתָם וָאֶזְכֹּר אֶת־בְּרִיתִי: לָכֵן אֱמֹר לִבְנֵי־יִשְׂרָאֵל אֲנִי יהוה וְהוֹצֵאתִי
אֶתְכֶם מִתַּחַת סִבְלֹת מִצְרַיִם וְהִצַּלְתִּי אֶתְכֶם מֵעֲבֹדָתָם וְגָאַלְתִּי
ז אֶתְכֶם בִּזְרוֹעַ נְטוּיָה וּבִשְׁפָטִים גְּדֹלִים: וְלָקַחְתִּי אֶתְכֶם לִי לְעָם וְהָיִיתִי
לָכֶם לֵאלֹהִים וִידַעְתֶּם כִּי אֲנִי יהוה אֱלֹהֵיכֶם הַמּוֹצִיא אֶתְכֶם מִתַּחַת
ח סִבְלוֹת מִצְרָיִם: וְהֵבֵאתִי אֶתְכֶם אֶל־הָאָרֶץ אֲשֶׁר נָשָׂאתִי אֶת־יָדִי

2. אֲנִי ה׳ — *I am HASHEM.* Not only the Creator, but He Who preserves existence, for existence has no substance or continuity except for that which emanates from Me, as it says, וְאַתָּה מְחַיֶּה אֶת כֻּלָּם, *And You preserve them all* (*Nehemiah* 9:6). From all this it follows that nothing can exist without His will.

3. וָאֵרָא — *And I appeared.* In a vision, which precedes (is lower than) prophecy, similar to, וַיֵּרָא אֵלָיו ה׳, *And HASHEM appeared to him* (*Genesis* 18:1).

בְּאֵל שַׁדָּי — *As God Almighty.* Which indicates Creator of all existence, as explained in *Lech Lecha* (*Genesis* 17:1) . . .

וּשְׁמִי ה׳ לֹא נוֹדַעְתִּי לָהֶם — *But My Name HASHEM I made not known to them.* The letter ב in the phrase בְּאֵל שַׁדָּי, *as God Almighty,* is to be incorporated in the word וּשְׁמִי, *and My Name.* (The phrase would then read,) וּבִשְׁמִי ה׳ לֹא נוֹדַעְתִּי לָהֶם, *But in My Name HASHEM I did not become known to them,* i.e., in that vision I did not make any changes in the laws of nature for them pertaining to any aspect which is unchanging. Therefore it is proper that I inform their descendants, since they did not receive (this information) from their fathers, so that I might establish them to Me as a people, and thus I will redeem them.

4. וְגַם הֲקִמֹתִי אֶת בְּרִיתִי — *And I have also established My covenant.* A second cause of their redemption is the covenant which I entered into with their fathers.

5. וְגַם אֲנִי שָׁמַעְתִּי — *And I have, moreover, heard.* The third cause of their redemption is that I have heard their groaning and prayers in their distress.

וָאֶזְכֹּר אֶת בְּרִיתִי — *And I have remembered My covenant.* And because of (all) this, they are worthy that I remember My covenant for them, similar to: וַיַּרְא בַּצַּר לָהֶם בְּשָׁמְעוֹ אֶת

NOTES

2. אֲנִי ה׳ — *I am HASHEM.* The Almighty is called by a variety of names, each depicting an attribute of the Divine. When Moses asks Him to reveal His Name (3:13), the cryptic answer given is, *"I am that I am"* (3:14). The *Sforno* there explains this four-letter Name (הַוָי״ה) as reflecting God's love of that which *is* and *exists*, since He is the Creator. In this verse, the statement אֲנִי ה׳, *I am HASHEM*, is explained by the *Sforno* as referring to God not only as Creator but also as the force which ensures the ongoing existence of all He originally created. Without this power emanating from Him naught would continue to exist. This statement is an introduction to that which is expanded upon in the next verse.

3. וָאֵרָא — *And I appeared.* See notes on *Genesis* 18:1 for clarification of the various levels of prophecy.

בְּאֵל שַׁדָּי — *As God Almighty.* See commentary of the *Sforno* and the explanatory notes on *Genesis* 17:1 regarding the name אֵל שַׁדָּי, *God Almighty.*

The name שַׁדָּי, *Almighty,* is derived from the expression *it is sufficient,* denoting that God set limitations on His creation in nature. In accordance with His will boundaries were established. This attribute of God was known to the Patriarchs and they in turn transmitted this knowledge to their children. However, the readiness of God to transform nature and involve Himself in the destiny of nations was never revealed to them. This manifesta-

PARASHAS VA'EIRA

2 *God spoke to Moses and said to him, "I am* HASHEM. 3 *I appeared to Abra-*
ham, to Isaac, and to Jacob as El Shaddai, but with My Name HASHEM
I did not make Myself known to them. 4 *Moreover, I established My cove-*
nant with them to give them the land of Canaan, the land of their sojourning,
in which they sojourned. 5 *Moreover, I have heard the groan of the Children*
of Israel whom Egypt enslaves and I have remembered My covenant.
6 *Therefore, say to the Children of Israel: 'I am* HASHEM, *and I shall take you*
out from under the burdens of Egypt; I shall rescue you from their service;
I shall redeem you with an outstretched arm and with great judgments. 7 *I*
shall take you to Me for a people and I shall be a God to you; and you shall
know that I am HASHEM *your God, Who takes you out from under the bur-*
dens of Egypt. 8 *I shall bring you to the land about which I raised My hand*

רִנָּתָם, וַיִּזְכֹּר לָהֶם בְּרִיתוֹ, *He looked upon their distress, when He heard their cry; and He remembered for them His covenant* (*Psalms* 106:44-45).

6. לָכֵן אֱמֹר לִבְנֵי יִשְׂרָאֵל אֲנִי יהוה — *Therefore, say to the Children of Israel, 'I am* HASHEM.' For the (aforementioned) three reasons, *say to the Children of Israel* that I, Who grant existence to all that exists, shall with this power bring them out by partially modifying nature.

וְהוֹצֵאתִי אֶתְכֶם מִתַּחַת סִבְלֹת מִצְרַיִם — *And I will bring you out from under the burdens of the Egyptians.* As soon as the plagues begin the bondage will subside.

וְהִצַּלְתִּי אֶתְכֶם — *And I will deliver you* . . . on the day you pass over the frontier at Raamses.

וְגָאַלְתִּי אֶתְכֶם — *And I will redeem you* . . . when the Egyptians drown in the sea, as (the Torah) testifies, וַיּוֹשַׁע ה' בַּיּוֹם הַהוּא, *And* HASHEM *saved Israel that day* (14:30), for after the demise of their oppressors they were no longer (in the category of) runaway slaves.

7. וְלָקַחְתִּי אֶתְכֶם לִי לְעָם — *And I will take you to Me for a people.* When you (will) stand at Mount Sinai.

וִידַעְתֶּם — *And you shall know.* Consider and recognize that all this will come to pass, similar to, וִידַעְתֶּם הַיּוֹם, כִּי לֹא אֶת בְּנֵיכֶם, *For you shall know this day, that it is not with your children . . .* (*Deut.* 11:2).

כִּי אֲנִי ה' אֱלֹהֵיכֶם הַמּוֹצִיא — *That I am* HASHEM, *your God, Who brought you out.* Since I am your God Who watches over you in a particular sense, and I am (the One) Who is involved in bringing you out, (then) without a doubt I will do all that I have said (promised).

8. וְהֵבֵאתִי אֶתְכֶם אֶל הָאָרֶץ — *And I will bring you into the land.* When you will consider (examine closely) all this, you will (then) be worthy that I bring you to the land and give it to you.

NOTES

tion of God's "finger in history," to use Rabbi S. R. Hirsch's felicitous term, and the changing of nature's laws, is expressed in the four-letter Name *HASHEM* (הֲוָיָ"ה). This attribute would now be demonstrated through the signs and wonders in Egypt, on behalf of the Children of Israel, and since this aspect of God was not known heretofore, God must now instruct Moses to teach it to Israel. It is through this manifestation of God as *HASHEM* that they will become His people and be delivered.

3-5. וּשְׁמִי ה' לֹא נוֹדַעְתִּי לָהֶם. וְגַם הֲקִמֹתִי אֶת בְּרִיתִי . . . וְגַם אֲנִי שָׁמַעְתִּי — *But My Name HASHEM I made not known to them. And I have also established My covenant . . . And I have, moreover, heard.* The *Sforno* interprets verses 3-5 as representing three reasons for God's redemption of Israel: (a) to reveal His control of nature's forces and concern for the destiny of His people; (b) to fulfill the covenant made with the Patriarchs; and (c) to respond to the prayers and cries of the Children of Israel.

6-8. וְהוֹצֵאתִי . . . וְהִצַּלְתִּי . . . וְגָאַלְתִּי . . . וְלָקַחְתִּי . . . וְהֵבֵאתִי — *And I will bring you out . . . and I will deliver you . . . and I will redeem you . . . and I will take you . . . and I will bring you . . .* Israel's deliver-

לָתֵת אֹתָהּ לְאַבְרָהָם לְיִצְחָק וּלְיַעֲקֹב וְנָתַתִּי אֹתָהּ לָכֶם מוֹרָשָׁה אֲנִי יְהוָה:
ט וַיְדַבֵּר מֹשֶׁה כֵּן אֶל־בְּנֵי יִשְׂרָאֵל וְלֹא שָׁמְעוּ אֶל־מֹשֶׁה מִקֹּצֶר רוּחַ
וּמֵעֲבֹדָה קָשָׁה:
י־יא וַיְדַבֵּר יְהוָה אֶל־מֹשֶׁה לֵּאמֹר: בֹּא דַבֵּר אֶל־פַּרְעֹה מֶלֶךְ מִצְרָיִם וִישַׁלַּח
יב אֶת־בְּנֵי־יִשְׂרָאֵל מֵאַרְצוֹ: וַיְדַבֵּר מֹשֶׁה לִפְנֵי יְהוָה לֵאמֹר הֵן בְּנֵי־יִשְׂרָאֵל
לֹא־שָׁמְעוּ אֵלַי וְאֵיךְ יִשְׁמָעֵנִי פַרְעֹה וַאֲנִי עֲרַל שְׂפָתָיִם:
יג וַיְדַבֵּר יְהוָה אֶל־מֹשֶׁה וְאֶל־אַהֲרֹן וַיְצַוֵּם אֶל־בְּנֵי יִשְׂרָאֵל וְאֶל־פַּרְעֹה מֶלֶךְ
שני יד מִצְרָיִם לְהוֹצִיא אֶת־בְּנֵי־יִשְׂרָאֵל מֵאֶרֶץ מִצְרָיִם: אֵלֶּה רָאשֵׁי
בֵית־אֲבֹתָם בְּנֵי רְאוּבֵן בְּכֹר יִשְׂרָאֵל חֲנוֹךְ וּפַלּוּא חֶצְרֹן וְכַרְמִי אֵלֶּה
טו מִשְׁפְּחֹת רְאוּבֵן: וּבְנֵי שִׁמְעוֹן יְמוּאֵל וְיָמִין וְאֹהַד וְיָכִין וְצֹחַר וְשָׁאוּל בֶּן־
טז הַכְּנַעֲנִית אֵלֶּה מִשְׁפְּחֹת שִׁמְעוֹן: וְאֵלֶּה שְׁמוֹת בְּנֵי־לֵוִי לְתֹלְדֹתָם גֵּרְשׁוֹן

9. וְלֹא שָׁמְעוּ אֶל מֹשֶׁה — *But they did not listen to Moses.* To consider all this in a manner which would (have caused them) to trust the salvation of God, the Blessed One, which would have been counted to them for righteousness, as it was for Abraham (*Genesis* 15:6). Therefore, the promise of *and I will give it to "you"* (v. 8) was not fulfilled, but (instead) was given to their children.

מִקֹּצֶר רוּחַ — *From impatience of spirit.* For their spirit prevented them from having faith in God, and they did not concentrate their mind (lit., "heart") to understand (the words of Moses).

וּמֵעֲבֹדָה קָשָׁה — *And from hard labor.* Were it not for the hard labor they would have considered and attended to the words of Moses and understood from his arguments that they should trust God.

12. הֵן בְּנֵי יִשְׂרָאֵל לֹא שָׁמְעוּ אֵלַי — *Behold the Children of Israel have not listened to me.* For he thought that (their refusal) was because they saw that from the time he came to speak to Pharaoh their condition had worsened and the messenger had not saved them. How much more so will Pharaoh, who does as he pleases and has even increased (the intensity of their labors), refuse to listen!

וַאֲנִי עֲרַל שְׂפָתָיִם — *And I am of "uncircumcised" lips.* For he thought that Aaron was only to be his associate (spokesman) for the initial message when they spoke to the people (of Israel).

13. וַיְצַוֵּם — *And He charged them.* He appointed them as leaders, similar to, וַיִּסְמֹךְ אֶת יָדָיו עָלָיו וַיְצַוֵּהוּ, *he (Moses) laid his hands upon him (Joshua) and charged him (Numbers 27:23)*, and וְצִוְּךָ לְנָגִיד, *has appointed you as a prince (I Samuel 25:30)*, and other such examples.

NOTES

ance and redemption shall come in separate phases. They will first find relief from their hard labor (וְהוֹצֵאתִי, *And I will bring you out*), then they will be delivered (וְהִצַּלְתִּי) when they cross the frontier of Egypt. The third phase is *redemption* (וְגָאַלְתִּי) when the Egyptians drown in the sea. At Mount Sinai, when the Torah will be given, Israel will be *taken as a people* (וְלָקַחְתִּי). The final step will be when God brings them to the land (וְהֵבֵאתִי). Only when they will appreciate and recognize God's role in their history and destiny will they be worthy to be brought to the Promised Land.

9. וְלֹא שָׁמְעוּ אֶל מֹשֶׁה — *But they did not listen to Moses.* Had Israel listened to Moses, this demonstration of faith would have been considered as a great merit and they would have been given the Land of Israel as promised in the previous verse. Since they failed to do so, they would not receive the land; their children, however, would.

12. וַאֲנִי עֲרַל שְׂפָתָיִם — *And I am of "uncircumcised" lips.* Moses, from the very start, protested that he could not speak clearly and God had therefore appointed Aaron as his spokesman (4:16). Seemingly this statement of Moses, *I am of uncircumcised lips*, is repetitious. The *Sforno* therefore explains that Moses was under the impression that Aaron had only been appointed to speak to the Children of Israel, not to Pharaoh. In this fashion the following

to give it to Abraham, Isaac, and Jacob; and I shall give it to you as a heritage — I am HASHEM.' "

9 *So Moses spoke accordingly to the Children of Israel; but they did not heed Moses, because of shortness of breath and hard work.*

10 *HASHEM spoke to Moses, saying,* 11 *"Come speak to Pharaoh, king of Egypt, that he send the Children of Israel from his land."*

12 *Moses spoke before HASHEM, saying, "Behold, the Children of Israel have not listened to me, so how will Pharaoh listen to me? And I have sealed lips!"*

13 *HASHEM spoke to Moses and Aaron and commanded them regarding the Children of Israel and regarding Pharaoh, king of Egypt, to take the Children of Israel out of the land of Egypt.*

14 *These were the heads of their fathers' houses: The sons of Reuben the firstborn of Israel: Hanoch and Pallu, Hezron and Carmi; these were the*
families of Reuben. 15 *The sons of Simeon: Jemuel, Jamin, Ohad, Jachin, and Zohar; and Shaul the son of a Canaanite woman; these were the families*
of Simeon. 16 *These were the sons of Levi in order of their birth: Gershon,*

אֶל בְּנֵי יִשְׂרָאֵל — *Over* (lit., *to*) *the Children of Israel.* Over the Children of Israel, similar to אֶל הֶהָרִים לֹא אָכָל, *And has not eaten upon the mountain (Ezekiel* 18:6).

וְאֶל פַּרְעֹה מֶלֶךְ מִצְרַיִם לְהוֹצִיא — *And over Pharaoh, king of Egypt, to bring out.* He appointed them as leaders over Pharaoh, the king of Egypt, regarding the bringing out of Israel from Egypt, in such a manner that Israel and also Pharaoh would perforce listen to Moses and Aaron who were appointed over them by God, the Blessed One.

14. אֵלֶּה רָאשֵׁי בֵית אֲבֹתָם — *These are the heads of their fathers' houses.* It was proper (justified) that these men be appointed leaders over Israel for they were the most distinguished (honored) of the entire nation. For (even though) ...

רְאוּבֵן בְּכֹר יִשְׂרָאֵל — *Reuben was the firstborn of Israel.* Except for his own children, who were included among the (original) seventy souls and who were now dead, none of their offspring were worthy to be mentioned by name, as it is explained when the verse states, וַיָּמָת יוֹסֵף וְכָל אֶחָיו, *And Joseph and all his brothers died ...* (1:6). And so it was regarding the children of Simeon. Levi, however, outlived them all and was able to rear his grandchildren (teaching them) to understand and (in turn) to teach (others), and so it was with Kehath and Amram, in such a manner that Moses, Aaron and Miriam came forth from them.

NOTES

verse also becomes clearer.

13. אֶל בְּנֵי יִשְׂרָאֵל — *Over the Children of Israel.* The word אֶל is to be understood not as *to* but *over* or *upon*, as we see in the verse from *Ezekiel* cited by the *Sforno.*

וְאֶל פַּרְעֹה מֶלֶךְ מִצְרַיִם לְהוֹצִיא — *And over Pharaoh, king of Egypt, to bring out.* God now appointed both Moses and Aaron as leaders over *both* Israel and Pharaoh, to the extent that regarding the deliverance of the Israelites, Pharaoh would be subservient to them. Hence, eventually he would listen to them, as would the Israelites.

14. אֵלֶּה רָאשֵׁי בֵית אֲבֹתָם — *These are the heads of their fathers' houses. Rashi* gives two reasons for inserting this genealogical table at this point, breaking the continuity of the narrative, which does not resume until verse 27. The flow of these verses is to be understood as follows: God appointed Moses and Aaron as leaders, though they are the descendants of Jacob's third son. Why were Reuben and Simeon denied leadership? The *Sforno* explains that although Reuben was the firstborn, only his four sons were worthy to be mentioned by name in the Torah, but none of the next generation. The same was true of Simeon. This indicates that the following generations were not on the same high level of importance and distinction as the previous generation. Levi's offspring however are mentioned by name through the fourth generation. The years of Levi, his son Kehath, and his grandson Amram are also recorded. The reason is to emphasize that the longevity of these men enabled them to educate and influence their grandsons, as well as their sons. The choice fruit of these spiritual plantings were Moses and

יז וְקָהָת וּמְרָרִי וּשְׁנֵי חַיֵּי לֵוִי שֶׁבַע וּשְׁלֹשִׁים וּמְאַת שָׁנָה: בְּנֵי גֵרְשׁוֹן לִבְנִי
יח וְשִׁמְעִי לְמִשְׁפְּחֹתָם: וּבְנֵי קְהָת עַמְרָם וְיִצְהָר וְחֶבְרוֹן וְעֻזִּיאֵל וּשְׁנֵי חַיֵּי
יט קְהָת שָׁלֹשׁ וּשְׁלֹשִׁים וּמְאַת שָׁנָה: וּבְנֵי מְרָרִי מַחְלִי וּמוּשִׁי אֵלֶּה מִשְׁפְּחֹת
כ הַלֵּוִי לְתֹלְדֹתָם: וַיִּקַּח עַמְרָם אֶת־יוֹכֶבֶד דֹּדָתוֹ לוֹ לְאִשָּׁה וַתֵּלֶד לוֹ אֶת־
כא אַהֲרֹן וְאֶת־מֹשֶׁה וּשְׁנֵי חַיֵּי עַמְרָם שֶׁבַע וּשְׁלֹשִׁים וּמְאַת שָׁנָה: וּבְנֵי יִצְהָר
כב־כג קֹרַח וָנֶפֶג וְזִכְרִי: וּבְנֵי עֻזִּיאֵל מִישָׁאֵל וְאֶלְצָפָן וְסִתְרִי: וַיִּקַּח אַהֲרֹן אֶת־
אֱלִישֶׁבַע בַּת־עַמִּינָדָב אֲחוֹת נַחְשׁוֹן לוֹ לְאִשָּׁה וַתֵּלֶד לוֹ אֶת־נָדָב וְאֶת־
כד אֲבִיהוּא אֶת־אֶלְעָזָר וְאֶת־אִיתָמָר: וּבְנֵי קֹרַח אַסִּיר וְאֶלְקָנָה וַאֲבִיאָסָף
כה אֵלֶּה מִשְׁפְּחֹת הַקָּרְחִי: וְאֶלְעָזָר בֶּן־אַהֲרֹן לָקַח־לוֹ מִבְּנוֹת פּוּטִיאֵל לוֹ
כו לְאִשָּׁה וַתֵּלֶד לוֹ אֶת־פִּינְחָס אֵלֶּה רָאשֵׁי אֲבוֹת הַלְוִיִּם לְמִשְׁפְּחֹתָם: הוּא
אַהֲרֹן וּמֹשֶׁה אֲשֶׁר אָמַר יהוה לָהֶם הוֹצִיאוּ אֶת־בְּנֵי יִשְׂרָאֵל מֵאֶרֶץ מִצְרַיִם
כז עַל־צִבְאֹתָם: הֵם הַמְדַבְּרִים אֶל־פַּרְעֹה מֶלֶךְ־מִצְרַיִם לְהוֹצִיא אֶת־בְּנֵי־
כח יִשְׂרָאֵל מִמִּצְרָיִם הוּא מֹשֶׁה וְאַהֲרֹן: וַיְהִי בְּיוֹם דִּבֶּר יהוה אֶל־מֹשֶׁה בְּאֶרֶץ
שלישי כט מִצְרָיִם: וַיְדַבֵּר יהוה אֶל־מֹשֶׁה לֵּאמֹר אֲנִי
ל יהוה דַּבֵּר אֶל־פַּרְעֹה מֶלֶךְ מִצְרַיִם אֵת כָּל־אֲשֶׁר אֲנִי דֹּבֵר אֵלֶיךָ: וַיֹּאמֶר
מֹשֶׁה לִפְנֵי יהוה הֵן אֲנִי עֲרַל שְׂפָתַיִם וְאֵיךְ יִשְׁמַע אֵלַי פַּרְעֹה:
ז א וַיֹּאמֶר יהוה אֶל־מֹשֶׁה רְאֵה נְתַתִּיךָ אֱלֹהִים לְפַרְעֹה וְאַהֲרֹן אָחִיךָ יִהְיֶה
ב נְבִיאֶךָ: אַתָּה תְדַבֵּר אֵת כָּל־אֲשֶׁר אֲצַוֶּךָּ וְאַהֲרֹן אָחִיךָ יְדַבֵּר אֶל־פַּרְעֹה
ג וְשִׁלַּח אֶת־בְּנֵי־יִשְׂרָאֵל מֵאַרְצוֹ: וַאֲנִי אַקְשֶׁה אֶת־לֵב פַּרְעֹה וְהִרְבֵּיתִי

23. וַיִּקַּח אַהֲרֹן . . . אֲחוֹת נַחְשׁוֹן — *And Aaron took . . . the daughter of Nachshon.* Who was the most important man of his generation, (thereby) giving birth to leaders of the generation, who were later chosen as priests; Elazar in turn took . . .

25. מִבְּנוֹת פּוּטִיאֵל — *Of the daughters of Putiel . . .* who was also important in his generation, and gave birth to . . .

פִּינְחָס — *Pinchas . . .* who merited the *covenant of peace (Numbers* 25:12).

אֵלֶּה רָאשֵׁי אֲבוֹת הַלְוִיִּם — *These are the heads of the fathers' houses of the Levites.* (Therefore) in this manner the aforementioned Moses and Aaron were *the heads of the fathers' houses of the Levites.*

26. הוּא אַהֲרֹן וּמֹשֶׁה — *These are that Aaron and Moses.* These were the most honored of the houses of their fathers, (therefore) they are the men who properly are the most worthy that God say to them . . .

הוֹצִיאוּ אֶת בְּנֵי יִשְׂרָאֵל — *Bring out the Children of Israel . . .* for they are deserving to have their words listened to by the Children of Israel.

NOTES

Aaron. This is the significance of the expression in verse 26, הוּא אַהֲרֹן וּמֹשֶׁה, *These are that Aaron and Moses*, as well as verse 27, *These are they who spoke to Pharaoh . . . these are Moses and Aaron.* They are the end result of the many years of education and guidance contributed by Levi, Kehath and Amram, and they are worthy to be chosen as leaders and spokesmen.

VII

3. וַאֲנִי אַקְשֶׁה — *And I will harden.* The hardening of Pharaoh's heart is for the purpose of counteracting the pressure of the plagues. Normally, one would crumble under the onslaught of such constant plagues and agree to whatever he was asked to do. This, however, was not God's intent, for then the submission would not be sincere nor would the

Kehath, and Merari; the years of Levi's life were a hundred and thirty-seven
years. 17 *The sons of Gershon: Livni and Shimei, according to their families.*
18 *The sons of Kehath: Amram, Izhar, Hebron, and Uzziel; the years of*
Kehath's life were a hundred and thirty-three years. 19 *The sons of Merari:*
Mahli and Mushi; these were the Levite families, in order of their birth.
20 *Amram took his aunt Jochebed as a wife, and she bore him Aaron and*
Moses; the years of Amram's life were a hundred and thirty-seven years.
21 *The sons of Izhar: Korah, Nepheg, and Zichri.* 22 *The sons of Uzziel:*
Mishael, Elzaphan, and Sithri. 23 *Aaron took Elisheba daughter of*
Amminadab, sister of Nahshon, as a wife; and she bore him Nadab and
Abihu, Elazar and Ithamar. 24 *The sons of Korah: Assir, Elkanah, and*
Abiassaph; these were the Korahite families. 25 *Elazar son of Aaron took for*
himself from the daughters of Putiel as a wife, and she bore to him Phineas;
these were the leaders of the fathers of the Levites, according to their
families. 26 *This was the Aaron and Moses to whom HASHEM said: "Take the*
Children of Israel out of Egypt according to their legions." 27 *They were the*
ones who spoke to Pharaoh, king of Egypt, to take the Children of Israel out
of the land of Egypt; this was the Moses and Aaron.

28 *It was on the day when HASHEM spoke to Moses in the land of Egypt.*
29 *HASHEM spoke to Moses, saying, "I am HASHEM. Speak to Pharaoh, king*
of Egypt, everything that I speak to you." 30 *Moses said before HASHEM,*
"Behold! I have sealed lips, so how shall Pharaoh heed me?"

7 1 *HASHEM said to Moses, "See, I have made you a master over Pharaoh,*
and Aaron your brother shall be your spokesman. 2 *You shall*
speak everything that I shall command you, and Aaron your brother
shall speak to Pharaoh, that he should send the Children of Israel
from his land. 3 *But I shall harden Pharaoh's heart and I shall multiply*

עַל צִבְאֹתָם — *According to their hosts* . . . the entire community together with its component sections.

27. הֵם הַמְדַבְּרִים — *These are they who spoke.* They were worthy to speak to Pharaoh and to be hearkened to by him.

28. וַיְהִי בְּיוֹם דִּבֶּר ה׳ אֶל מֹשֶׁה — *And it came to pass on the day when HASHEM spoke to Moses.* When God spoke to Moses and told him to speak to Pharaoh (v. 11), and Moses responded that Pharaoh would not listen to him, (whereupon) He appointed him and Aaron as leaders over Israel and Pharaoh, as mentioned above (v. 13); (the Torah now) explains that the intent was not to equate them (i.e., Moses and Aaron), but that . . .

VII

1. נְתַתִּיךָ אֱלֹהִים לְפַרְעֹה וְאַהֲרֹן אָחִיךָ יִהְיֶה נְבִיאֶךָ — *I have set you in God's stead to Pharaoh, and Aaron your brother shall be your prophet.* Moses will be as *Elohim* to Pharaoh, and Aaron will serve as an interpreter and expounder.

3. וַאֲנִי אַקְשֶׁה — *And I will harden.* Being that God desires the repentance of the wicked and not their death, as it says, חַי אָנִי, נְאֻם אֲדֹנָי אֱלֹהִים אִם אֶחְפֹּץ בְּמוֹת הָרָשָׁע, כִּי אִם בְּשׁוּב הָרָשָׁע מִדַּרְכּוֹ וְחָיָה, *As I live, says my Lord, HASHEM/ELOHIM, I do not desire the death of the wicked, but*

NOTES

Egyptians truly repent. By giving them strength to resist (hardening their hearts) their freedom of will was unimpaired; hence if they repented their evil ways, it would be a voluntary act. This, the *Sforno*

ד אֶת־אֹתֹתַי וְאֶת־מוֹפְתַי בְּאֶרֶץ מִצְרָיִם: וְלֹא־יִשְׁמַע אֲלֵכֶם פַּרְעֹה
וְנָתַתִּי אֶת־יָדִי בְּמִצְרָיִם וְהוֹצֵאתִי אֶת־צִבְאֹתַי אֶת־עַמִּי בְנֵי־יִשְׂרָאֵל
ה מֵאֶרֶץ מִצְרַיִם בִּשְׁפָטִים גְּדֹלִים: וְיָדְעוּ מִצְרַיִם כִּי־אֲנִי יהוה בִּנְטֹתִי
ו אֶת־יָדִי עַל־מִצְרָיִם וְהוֹצֵאתִי אֶת־בְּנֵי־יִשְׂרָאֵל מִתּוֹכָם: וַיַּעַשׂ מֹשֶׁה
ז וְאַהֲרֹן כַּאֲשֶׁר צִוָּה יהוה אֹתָם כֵּן עָשׂוּ: וּמֹשֶׁה בֶּן־שְׁמֹנִים שָׁנָה וְאַהֲרֹן
בֶּן־שָׁלֹשׁ וּשְׁמֹנִים שָׁנָה בְּדַבְּרָם אֶל־פַּרְעֹה:
רביעי ח־ט וַיֹּאמֶר יהוה אֶל־מֹשֶׁה וְאֶל־אַהֲרֹן לֵאמֹר: כִּי יְדַבֵּר אֲלֵכֶם פַּרְעֹה
לֵאמֹר תְּנוּ לָכֶם מוֹפֵת וְאָמַרְתָּ אֶל־אַהֲרֹן קַח אֶת־מַטְּךָ וְהַשְׁלֵךְ
י לִפְנֵי־פַרְעֹה יְהִי לְתַנִּין: וַיָּבֹא מֹשֶׁה וְאַהֲרֹן אֶל־פַּרְעֹה וַיַּעֲשׂוּ כֵן
כַּאֲשֶׁר צִוָּה יהוה וַיַּשְׁלֵךְ אַהֲרֹן אֶת־מַטֵּהוּ לִפְנֵי פַרְעֹה וְלִפְנֵי עֲבָדָיו
יא וַיְהִי לְתַנִּין: וַיִּקְרָא גַּם־פַּרְעֹה לַחֲכָמִים וְלַמְכַשְּׁפִים וַיַּעֲשׂוּ גַם־
יב הֵם חַרְטֻמֵּי מִצְרַיִם בְּלַהֲטֵיהֶם כֵּן: וַיַּשְׁלִיכוּ אִישׁ מַטֵּהוּ וַיִּהְיוּ

that the wicked turn from his way and live (*Ezekiel* 33:11). Therefore, the signs and wonders will be increased for the purpose of bringing the Egyptians to repentance, by demonstrating to them His greatness and kindness, through the signs and wonders, as it says, *For this cause I have made you stand to show you My power* (9:16). (Another reason was) so Israel would see and (be brought to) reverence, as it says, *That I might show My signs in their midst . . . that you may tell . . .* (10:1,2).

Without a doubt, were it not for the hardening of Pharaoh's heart he would have sent forth Israel, not because of repentance or submission to God, the Blessed One, (nor because) he regretted his rebellion, recognizing God's greatness and goodness — but because he could no longer abide the anguish of the plagues, as his (own) servants said, *Do you not know that Egypt is lost?* (10:7). Now this would not have been repentance. However, if Pharaoh would have (truly) wished to submit to God, the Blessed One, and return to Him in full repentance, there would have been no (Divine) deterrent at all. Now, God states, *and I will harden Pharaoh's heart*, granting him the strength to withstand the plagues, hence he will not send forth Israel because he fears the plagues, *but that I might show My signs in their midst* (10:1), through which they will perceive My greatness and goodness and repent to a degree, in sincerity. (And also) לְמַעַן תְּסַפֵּר, *that you may tell* (10:2), i.e., *you* Israel who see their anguish, (may tell) בְּאָזְנֵי בִנְךָ, *in the ears of your son* (ibid.), to tell (everyone) that all these things does God work with man (based on *Job* 33:29) so as to bring (man) to repentance, which will occur if they examine their deeds when misfortune befalls them.

4. וְלֹא יִשְׁמַע אֲלֵכֶם פַּרְעֹה — *But Pharaoh will not listen to you.* Neither before nor after the hardening (of his heart) even though he will see (witness) the increasing number of (lit., "many") signs and wonders, I will therefore bring judgments upon them, namely the plague

NOTES

explains, was the intent of the multiplicity of plagues (compare to 4:21).

Another reason for the many plagues was to impress the Israelites with God's might and His love for them, thereby bringing them to a state of awareness and reverence of God which in turn would motivate them to relate these wonders and God's providence to future generations (see 10:1-2).

4. וְלֹא יִשְׁמַע אֲלֵכֶם פַּרְעֹה — *But Pharaoh will not listen to you.* As explained in 4:23, all the plagues were meant to serve as a spur to repentance, not as punishment, except for the tenth one and the drowning of the Egyptians in the sea. Even then, the survival of some Egyptians was for the purpose of recognizing the true God, which is the first step to repentance.

7. וּמֹשֶׁה בֶּן שְׁמֹנִים שָׁנָה — *And Moses was eighty years old.* The terms שֵׂיבָה, *old age*, and גְּבוּרָה, *strength*, are used in *Pirkei Avos* 5:20: *Seventy to old age and eighty to strength.*

9. תְּנוּ לָכֶם מוֹפֵת — *Show a wonder for them.* When

My signs and My wonders in the land of Egypt. 4 *Pharaoh will not heed you,*
and I shall put My hand upon Egypt; and I shall take out My legions — My
people the Children of Israel — from the land of Egypt, with great judgments.
5 *And Egypt shall know that I am HASHEM, when I stretch out My hand over*
Egypt; and I shall take the Children of Israel out from among them."
6 *Moses and Aaron did as HASHEM commanded them; so they did.* 7 *Moses*
was eighty years old and Aaron was eighty-three years old when they spoke
to Pharaoh.
8 *HASHEM said to Moses and Aaron, saying:* 9 *"When Pharaoh speaks to*
you, saying, 'Provide a wonder for yourselves,' you shall say to Aaron, 'Take
your staff and cast it down before Pharaoh — it will become a snake!' "
10 *Moses came with Aaron to Pharaoh and they did so, as HASHEM had*
commanded; Aaron cast down his staff before Pharaoh and before his
servants, and it became a snake. 11 *Pharaoh, too, summoned his wise men*
and sorcerers, and they, too — the necromancers of Egypt — did so with
their incantations. 12 *Each one cast down his staff and they became*

---

of the firstborn and the drowning of Egypt in the Sea of Reeds. These two alone were in the category of punishment, measure for measure. The other plagues, however, were signs and wonders for the purpose of bringing them back (to God) through repentance, as it says: *In this you shall know that I am HASHEM* (v. 17); *To the end that you may know that I am HASHEM in the midst of the earth* (8:18); *That you may know that the earth is HASHEM's* (9:29); *That I might show these My signs in the midst of them . . . that you may tell . . . that you may know* (10:1-2), you, i.e., Israel and Egypt. Even when they were drowned the intent was to do it in such a way that the Egyptian survivors recognize and know Him, as it says, *and the Egyptians shall know that I am HASHEM* (v. 5).

6. וַיַּעַשׂ מֹשֶׁה וְאַהֲרֹן כַּאֲשֶׁר צִוָּה ה׳ אֹתָם — *And Moses and Aaron did as HASHEM commanded them.* Every directive (given to them) was observed in accordance with the commandment and its order, i.e., Moses first spoke as the messenger of God, the Blessed One, after which Aaron interpreted.

כֵּן עָשׂוּ — *So they did.* They neither added nor detracted.

7. וּמֹשֶׁה בֶּן שְׁמֹנִים שָׁנָה — *And Moses was eighty years old.* In spite of their advanced age they rose up with enthusiasm to (fulfill) the will of their Maker. Indeed, he who had reached the age of eighty, even in those days, had already passed the days of "gray hair" (old age) and reached (those of) "strength," as (Moses) attests to in his prayer, saying, יְמֵי שְׁנוֹתֵינוּ בָהֶם שִׁבְעִים שָׁנָה, וְאִם בִּגְבוּרֹת שְׁמוֹנִים שָׁנָה, *The days of our years are seventy years, or even by reason of strength, eighty years (Psalms* 90:10).

9. תְּנוּ לָכֶם מוֹפֵת — *Show a wonder for them.* A מוֹפֵת, *wonder*, comes to demonstrate the greatness of the sender, that it is proper to hearken to His voice. A אוֹת, *sign*, however, testifies to the authenticity of the messenger. That is why Moses performed "signs" in the presence of Israel, who did not doubt the greatness and ability of the Sender but questioned whether the messenger was authentic. Pharaoh, however, had (serious) doubts regarding the Sender — and even denied (His existence), as he said, לֹא יָדַעְתִּי אֶת ה׳, *I know not HASHEM* (5:2). (That is why) he asks for a "wonder," to authenticate the greatness of the Sender, in a manner which will demonstrate that He is worthy to be listened to. It is not unprecedented for the same object to be used as a sign and a wonder for different people.

NOTES

the *Sforno* states, "for the same object to be used as a sign and a wonder," he is referring to the rod which was used as a "sign" for Israel (4:30) and a 'wonder' for Pharaoh.

יג לְתַנִּינִם וַיִּבְלַע מַטֵּה־אַהֲרֹן אֶת־מַטֹּתָם: וַיֶּחֱזַק לֵב פַּרְעֹה וְלֹא שָׁמַע
יד אֲלֵהֶם כַּאֲשֶׁר דִּבֶּר יהוה: וַיֹּאמֶר יהוה אֶל־מֹשֶׁה כָּבֵד לֵב
טו פַּרְעֹה מֵאֵן לְשַׁלַּח הָעָם: לֵךְ אֶל־פַּרְעֹה בַּבֹּקֶר הִנֵּה יֹצֵא הַמַּיְמָה וְנִצַּבְתָּ
טז לִקְרָאתוֹ עַל־שְׂפַת הַיְאֹר וְהַמַּטֶּה אֲשֶׁר־נֶהְפַּךְ לְנָחָשׁ תִּקַּח בְּיָדֶךָ:
וְאָמַרְתָּ אֵלָיו יהוה אֱלֹהֵי הָעִבְרִים שְׁלָחַנִי אֵלֶיךָ לֵאמֹר שַׁלַּח אֶת־עַמִּי
יז וְיַעַבְדֻנִי בַּמִּדְבָּר וְהִנֵּה לֹא־שָׁמַעְתָּ עַד־כֹּה: כֹּה אָמַר יהוה בְּזֹאת תֵּדַע
כִּי אֲנִי יהוה הִנֵּה אָנֹכִי מַכֶּה | בַּמַּטֶּה אֲשֶׁר־בְּיָדִי עַל־הַמַּיִם אֲשֶׁר בַּיְאֹר
יח וְנֶהֶפְכוּ לְדָם: וְהַדָּגָה אֲשֶׁר־בַּיְאֹר תָּמוּת וּבָאַשׁ הַיְאֹר וְנִלְאוּ מִצְרַיִם
יט לִשְׁתּוֹת מַיִם מִן־הַיְאֹר: וַיֹּאמֶר יהוה אֶל־מֹשֶׁה אֱמֹר אֶל־אַהֲרֹן
קַח מַטְּךָ וּנְטֵה־יָדְךָ עַל־מֵימֵי מִצְרַיִם עַל־נַהֲרֹתָם | עַל־יְאֹרֵיהֶם וְעַל־
אַגְמֵיהֶם וְעַל כָּל־מִקְוֵה מֵימֵיהֶם וְיִהְיוּ־דָם וְהָיָה דָם בְּכָל־אֶרֶץ מִצְרַיִם
כ וּבָעֵצִים וּבָאֲבָנִים: וַיַּעֲשׂוּ־כֵן מֹשֶׁה וְאַהֲרֹן כַּאֲשֶׁר | צִוָּה יהוה וַיָּרֶם בַּמַּטֶּה
וַיַּךְ אֶת־הַמַּיִם אֲשֶׁר בַּיְאֹר לְעֵינֵי פַרְעֹה וּלְעֵינֵי עֲבָדָיו וַיֵּהָפְכוּ כָּל־הַמַּיִם
כא אֲשֶׁר־בַּיְאֹר לְדָם: וְהַדָּגָה אֲשֶׁר־בַּיְאֹר מֵתָה וַיִּבְאַשׁ הַיְאֹר וְלֹא־יָכְלוּ
כב מִצְרַיִם לִשְׁתּוֹת מַיִם מִן־הַיְאֹר וַיְהִי הַדָּם בְּכָל־אֶרֶץ מִצְרָיִם: וַיַּעֲשׂוּ־כֵן
חַרְטֻמֵּי מִצְרַיִם בְּלָטֵיהֶם וַיֶּחֱזַק לֵב־פַּרְעֹה וְלֹא־שָׁמַע אֲלֵהֶם כַּאֲשֶׁר דִּבֶּר
כג־כד יהוה: וַיִּפֶן פַּרְעֹה וַיָּבֹא אֶל־בֵּיתוֹ וְלֹא־שָׁת לִבּוֹ גַּם־לָזֹאת: וַיַּחְפְּרוּ
כָל־מִצְרַיִם סְבִיבֹת הַיְאֹר מַיִם לִשְׁתּוֹת כִּי לֹא יָכְלוּ לִשְׁתֹּת מִמֵּימֵי
כה הַיְאֹר: וַיִּמָּלֵא שִׁבְעַת יָמִים אַחֲרֵי הַכּוֹת־יהוה אֶת־הַיְאֹר:
כו וַיֹּאמֶר יהוה אֶל־מֹשֶׁה בֹּא אֶל־פַּרְעֹה וְאָמַרְתָּ אֵלָיו כֹּה אָמַר יהוה שַׁלַּח
כז אֶת־עַמִּי וְיַעַבְדֻנִי: וְאִם־מָאֵן אַתָּה לְשַׁלֵּחַ הִנֵּה אָנֹכִי נֹגֵף אֶת־כָּל־גְּבוּלְךָ

12. וַיִּהְיוּ לְתַנִּינִם — *And they became serpents.* With the appearance of serpents, but inert, without movement.

וַיִּבְלַע מַטֵּה אַהֲרֹן אֶת מַטֹּתָם — *And Aaron's rod swallowed up their rods.* To show that only God, the Blessed One, can grant living spirit (lit., "soul and spirit") whereas the sorcerers had no power to grant movement to their serpents.

14. כָּבֵד לֵב פַּרְעֹה — *Pharaoh's heart is stubborn.* Even though he has seen the difference between Your wonder and the deed of his sorcerers.

15. נֶהְפַּךְ לְנָחָשׁ — *Which turned to a snake.* In its movements (and actions) as well, as it says, וַיִּבְלַע, *and it swallowed* (v. 12); and above also, *And Moses fled from it* (4:3).

17. בְּזֹאת תֵּדַע כִּי אֲנִי ה׳ — *In this you shall know that I am HASHEM.* For I shall change the nature of a permanent (unchanging) thing in its totality, namely the river.

18. וְהַדָּגָה אֲשֶׁר בַּיְאֹר תָּמוּת — *And the fish that are in the river shall die.* There will be no

NOTES

12. וַיִּהְיוּ לְתַנִּינִם — *And they became serpents.* See 4:3, the *Sforno's* commentary.

17. בְּזֹאת תֵּדַע כִּי אֲנִי ה׳ — *In this you shall know that I am HASHEM.* The phrase בְּזֹאת, *in this,* implies that the transformation of the river into blood will be more effective in impressing the Egyptians than the wonder of the rod turning into a snake. Therefore the *Sforno* explains that to change the nature of an unchanging, permanent part of nature (בִּלְתִּי נִפְסָד), is a far greater feat than changing a rod (which is a perishable object) into a snake.

18. וְהַדָּגָה אֲשֶׁר בַּיְאֹר תָּמוּת — *And the fish that are in the river shall die.* The transformation of the water

snakes; and the staff of Aaron swallowed their staffs. [13] *The heart of Pharaoh was strong and he did not heed them, as HASHEM had spoken.*

[14] *HASHEM said to Moses, "Pharaoh's heart is stubborn, he refuses to send the people.* [15] *Go to Pharaoh in the morning — behold! he goes out to the water — and you shall stand opposite him at the River's bank, and the staff that was turned into a snake you shall take in your hand.* [16] *You shall say to him, 'HASHEM, the God of the Hebrews, has sent me to you, saying: Send out My people that they may serve Me in the Wilderness — but behold, you have not heeded up to now.'* [17] *So says HASHEM, 'Through this shall you know that I am HASHEM; behold, with the staff that is in my hand I shall strike the waters that are in the River, and they shall change to blood.* [18] *The fish-life that is in the water shall die and the River shall become foul. Egypt will grow weary of trying to drink water from the River.' "*

[19] *HASHEM said to Moses, "Say to Aaron, 'Take your staff and stretch out your hand over the waters of Egypt: over their rivers, over their canals, over their reservoirs, and over all their gatherings of water, and they shall become blood; there shall be blood throughout the land of Egypt, even in the wooden and stone vessels.' "*

[20] *Moses and Aaron did so, as HASHEM had commanded. He held the staff aloft and struck the water that was in the River in the presence of Pharaoh and in the presence of his servants, and all the water that was in the River changed to blood.* [21] *The fish-life that was in the River died and the River became foul; Egypt could not drink water from the River, and the blood was throughout the land of Egypt.* [22] *The necromancers of Egypt did the same by means of their incantations; so Pharaoh's heart was strong and he did not heed them, as HASHEM had spoken.* [23] *Pharaoh turned away and came to his palace. He did not take this to heart either.* [24] *All of the Egyptians dug roundabout the River for water to drink, for they could not drink from the waters of the River.* [25] *Seven days were completed after HASHEM struck the River.*

[26] *HASHEM said to Moses, "Come to Pharaoh and say to him, 'So said HASHEM: Send out My people that they may serve Me.* [27] *But if you refuse to send out, behold, I shall strike your entire boundary with*

---

form (essence) of water (combined) with the appearance of blood, rather it shall become the essence (form) as well as the appearance of blood; hence the fish will die.

וְנִלְאוּ מִצְרַיִם — *And the Egyptians will weary themselves* . . . digging around the river (in an attempt) to find water to drink, as it says, וַיַּחְפְּרוּ כָל מִצְרַיִם סְבִיבֹת הַיְאֹר, *And all the Egyptians dug round about the river* (v. 24).

23. וְלֹא שָׁת לִבּוֹ גַּם לָזֹאת — *Nor did he lay even this to his heart* . . . to understand the difference in this occurrence between the Divine act to that of the sorcerers. The act of God, the Blessed One, was a change in the nature of the river, which is (normally) unchanging, into the authentic nature of blood, causing the death of the fish. The act of the sorcerers (on the other hand) was a change in that (portion) which is impermanent (i.e., a portion of the water), and perhaps (it was only) conjuring.

NOTES

into blood was real, not an illusion, as we find in the story of Elisha and the Moabites (*II Kings* 3:22), where the sun shining on the water made it appear כַּדָּם, *as blood*. Here, however, the fish died, for the blood was real, unlike the sleight of hand of the sorcerers.

כח בַּצְפַרְדְּעִים: וְשָׁרַץ הַיְאֹר צְפַרְדְּעִים וְעָלוּ וּבָאוּ בְּבֵיתֶךָ וּבַחֲדַר מִשְׁכָּבְךָ
כט וְעַל־מִטָּתֶךָ וּבְבֵית עֲבָדֶיךָ וּבְעַמֶּךָ וּבְתַנּוּרֶיךָ וּבְמִשְׁאֲרוֹתֶיךָ: וּבְכָה וּבְעַמְּךָ
ח א וּבְכָל־עֲבָדֶיךָ יַעֲלוּ הַצְפַרְדְּעִים: וַיֹּאמֶר יהוה אֶל־מֹשֶׁה אֱמֹר אֶל־אַהֲרֹן נְטֵה
אֶת־יָדְךָ בְּמַטֶּךָ עַל־הַנְּהָרֹת עַל־הַיְאֹרִים וְעַל־הָאֲגַמִּים וְהַעַל אֶת־
ב הַצְפַרְדְּעִים עַל־אֶרֶץ מִצְרָיִם: וַיֵּט אַהֲרֹן אֶת־יָדוֹ עַל מֵימֵי מִצְרָיִם וַתַּעַל
ג הַצְפַרְדֵּעַ וַתְּכַס אֶת־אֶרֶץ מִצְרָיִם: וַיַּעֲשׂוּ־כֵן הַחַרְטֻמִּים בְּלָטֵיהֶם וַיַּעֲלוּ
ד אֶת־הַצְפַרְדְּעִים עַל־אֶרֶץ מִצְרָיִם: וַיִּקְרָא פַרְעֹה לְמֹשֶׁה וּלְאַהֲרֹן וַיֹּאמֶר
הַעְתִּירוּ אֶל־יהוה וְיָסֵר הַצְפַרְדְּעִים מִמֶּנִּי וּמֵעַמִּי וַאֲשַׁלְּחָה אֶת־הָעָם וְיִזְבְּחוּ
ה לַיהוה: וַיֹּאמֶר מֹשֶׁה לְפַרְעֹה הִתְפָּאֵר עָלַי לְמָתַי ׀ אַעְתִּיר לְךָ וְלַעֲבָדֶיךָ
ו וּלְעַמְּךָ לְהַכְרִית הַצְפַרְדְּעִים מִמְּךָ וּמִבָּתֶּיךָ רַק בַּיְאֹר תִּשָּׁאַרְנָה: וַיֹּאמֶר
ז לְמָחָר וַיֹּאמֶר כִּדְבָרְךָ לְמַעַן תֵּדַע כִּי־אֵין כַּיהוה אֱלֹהֵינוּ: וְסָרוּ הַצְפַרְדְּעִים חמישי
ח מִמְּךָ וּמִבָּתֶּיךָ וּמֵעֲבָדֶיךָ וּמֵעַמֶּךָ רַק בַּיְאֹר תִּשָּׁאַרְנָה: וַיֵּצֵא מֹשֶׁה וְאַהֲרֹן
מֵעִם פַּרְעֹה וַיִּצְעַק מֹשֶׁה אֶל־יהוה עַל־דְּבַר הַצְפַרְדְּעִים אֲשֶׁר־שָׂם לְפַרְעֹה:

VIII

3. וַיַּעֲלוּ אֶת הַצְפַרְדְּעִים — *And brought up crocodiles.* However, these (crocodiles) could not reproduce, for the (sorcerers) are incapable of producing a (living) authentically moving creature.

4. הַעְתִּירוּ אֶל ה׳ — *Entreat* HASHEM. For in this (case) he did take it to his heart and saw the superiority of God's act in comparison to the act of the sorcerers.

5. לְמָתַי אַעְתִּיר לְךָ — *Against what time shall I entreat for you?* So that you may recognize the great difference between the act of the sorcerers (as compared to) the act of God, as he says *against what time,* and also *and remain in the river only.* For indeed an act of sorcery lasts for a (specific) limited time after which nature returns to its strength, as soon as the sorcery ceases, for then the deterrent to the course of nature is removed, as our Sages say, "Why are they (magic or sorcery) called כְּשָׁפִים? For they deny the heavenly court" (*Sanhedrin* 67b). However, God, the Blessed One, commands nature to cease, change or function partially or fully, in a time (period) that He sets, and it will never disobey His word.

6. כִּדְבָרְךָ — *According to your word.* As you said, *"Take away the crocodiles from me and from my people"* (v. 4), but you did not request that they be totally destroyed.

לְמַעַן תֵּדַע כִּי אֵין כַּה׳ אֱלֹהֵינוּ — *That you may know there is none like* HASHEM *our God.* For there is no other power that can create a change in nature, except for a (limited) set time. Now

NOTES

VIII

3. וַיַּעֲלוּ אֶת הַצְפַרְדְּעִים — *And brought up the crocodiles.* Unlike most commentators, the *Sforno* is of the opinion that the צְפַרְדְּעִים were not frogs but crocodiles. See the *Sforno* to verse 6.

4. הַעְתִּירוּ אֶל ה׳ — *Entreat* HASHEM. In the previous chapter the *Sforno* discusses the difference between Aaron's snake and the magician's serpents, as well as that of the Divine plague of blood and the sorcerer's sleight of hand which seemingly duplicated this feat (see 7:12,14,15 and 23). Still Pharaoh was not moved to ask Moses and Aaron to entreat God on his behalf until this second plague. The reason is that the differentiation of the former signs were subtle and not as apparent. Here, however, we are dealing with living creatures (as opposed to the inanimate rod and water), and Pharaoh perceived that the crocodiles were not the same.

5. לְמָתַי אַעְתִּיר לְךָ — *Against what time shall I entreat for you?* Although Moses was challenging Pharaoh to set a specific time for the crocodiles to be removed, he was not doing so to impress Pharaoh with his powers or even those of the Almighty. The purpose was to teach Pharaoh the basic difference between God's control over nature, which is His creation, and the illusions created by the sorcerers.

frogs. [28] *The River shall swarm with frogs, and they shall ascend and come into your palace and your bedroom and your bed, and into the house of your servants and of your people, and into your ovens and into your kneading bowls.* [29] *And into you and your people and all your servants will the frogs ascend.' "*

8 [1] *HASHEM said to Moses, "Say to Aaron, 'Stretch out your hand with your staff over the rivers, over the canals, and over the reservoirs, and raise up the frogs over the land of Egypt.' "*

[2] *Aaron stretched out his hand over the waters of Egypt, and the frog-infestation ascended and covered the land of Egypt.* [3] *The necromancers did the same through their incantations, and they brought up the frogs upon the land of Egypt.*

[4] *Pharaoh summoned Moses and Aaron and said, "Entreat HASHEM that He remove the frogs from me and my people, and I shall send out the people that they may bring offerings to HASHEM."*

[5] *Moses said to Pharaoh, "Glorify yourself over me — for when should I entreat for you, for your servants, and for your people, to excise the frogs from you and from your houses? Only in the River shall they remain."* [6] *And he said, "For tomorrow." He said, "As you say — so that you will know that there is none like HASHEM, our God.* [7] *The frogs will depart from you and your houses, and from your servants and your people; only in the River shall they remain."*

[8] *Moses and Aaron left Pharaoh's presence; Moses cried out to HASHEM concerning the frogs that he had inflicted upon Pharaoh.*

---

these crocodiles in the river were a result of a change in the nature of the river, considering that they were crocodiles, different than all other creatures in that they move their upper jaw and ingest without defecating. Behold God, the Blessed One, will destroy those (that are in) your houses only (but the others will remain in the river).

7. וְסָרוּ הַצְפַרְדְּעִים — *And the crocodiles shall depart.* Not only will He destroy these but He will also decree that the remaining (ones) no longer come up to your houses.

מִמְּךָ וּמִבָּתֶּיךָ — *From you and from your houses.* However, not from the entire land, for indeed they will perish on the land and smell.

רַק בַּיְאֹר תִּשָּׁאַרְנָה — *They shall remain in the river only.* For generations, and will not come up on the land.

8. וַיִּצְעַק מֹשֶׁה אֶל ה׳ עַל דְּבַר הַצְפַרְדְּעִים אֲשֶׁר שָׂם לְפַרְעֹה — *And Moses cried to HASHEM concerning the crocodiles which He had brought upon Pharaoh.* That He remove those crocodiles alone, *which He had brought upon Pharaoh,* that they remain in the river. For this

NOTES

Even though they had the ability to temporarily suspend nature's course, only *Hashem* can command its *positive* order or institute changes which are permanent, or temporary, in accordance with His will. This is the reason Moses told Pharaoh to set the time, to underscore this fundamental lesson.

6. כִּדְבָרְךָ לְמַעַן תֵּדַע ... — *According to your word that you may know ...* There is a subtle change in Pharaoh's request and Moses's initial response. Pharaoh asks that the crocodiles be *removed* (v. 4), whereas Moses speaks of their *destruction* (v. 5). However, in this verse, Moses states כִּדְבָרְךָ, *according to your word,* i.e., as you originally requested, *removal* not *destruction.* Hence, although some will be destroyed, others will remain in the river. The *Sforno* is of the opinion that crocodiles only now took up their habitation in the Nile at the command of *Hashem.*

8. וַיִּצְעַק מֹשֶׁה אֶל ה׳ — *And Moses cried to HASHEM.* When man prays he cannot qualify his petition,

ט וַיַּעַשׂ יְהוָה כִּדְבַר מֹשֶׁה וַיָּמֻתוּ הַצְפַרְדְּעִים מִן־הַבָּתִּים מִן־הַחֲצֵרֹת
י־יא וּמִן־הַשָּׂדֹת: וַיִּצְבְּרוּ אֹתָם חֳמָרִם חֳמָרִם וַתִּבְאַשׁ הָאָרֶץ: וַיַּרְא פַּרְעֹה
כִּי הָיְתָה הָרְוָחָה וְהַכְבֵּד אֶת־לִבּוֹ וְלֹא שָׁמַע אֲלֵהֶם כַּאֲשֶׁר דִּבֶּר
יב יְהוָה: וַיֹּאמֶר יְהוָה אֶל־מֹשֶׁה אֱמֹר אֶל־אַהֲרֹן נְטֵה אֶת־מַטְּךָ
יג וְהַךְ אֶת־עֲפַר הָאָרֶץ וְהָיָה לְכִנִּם בְּכָל־אֶרֶץ מִצְרָיִם: וַיַּעֲשׂוּ־כֵן וַיֵּט אַהֲרֹן
אֶת־יָדוֹ בְמַטֵּהוּ וַיַּךְ אֶת־עֲפַר הָאָרֶץ וַתְּהִי הַכִּנָּם בָּאָדָם וּבַבְּהֵמָה כָּל־
יד עֲפַר הָאָרֶץ הָיָה כִנִּים בְּכָל־אֶרֶץ מִצְרָיִם: וַיַּעֲשׂוּ־כֵן הַחַרְטֻמִּים בְּלָטֵיהֶם
טו לְהוֹצִיא אֶת־הַכִּנִּים וְלֹא יָכֹלוּ וַתְּהִי הַכִּנָּם בָּאָדָם וּבַבְּהֵמָה: וַיֹּאמְרוּ
הַחַרְטֻמִּם אֶל־פַּרְעֹה אֶצְבַּע אֱלֹהִים הִוא וַיֶּחֱזַק לֵב־פַּרְעֹה וְלֹא־שָׁמַע
טז אֲלֵהֶם כַּאֲשֶׁר דִּבֶּר יְהוָה: וַיֹּאמֶר יְהוָה אֶל־מֹשֶׁה הַשְׁכֵּם
בַּבֹּקֶר וְהִתְיַצֵּב לִפְנֵי פַרְעֹה הִנֵּה יוֹצֵא הַמָּיְמָה וְאָמַרְתָּ אֵלָיו כֹּה אָמַר
יז יְהוָה שַׁלַּח עַמִּי וְיַעַבְדֻנִי: כִּי אִם־אֵינְךָ מְשַׁלֵּחַ אֶת־עַמִּי הִנְנִי מַשְׁלִיחַ בְּךָ
וּבַעֲבָדֶיךָ וּבְעַמְּךָ וּבְבָתֶּיךָ אֶת־הֶעָרֹב וּמָלְאוּ בָּתֵּי מִצְרַיִם אֶת־הֶעָרֹב וְגַם
יח הָאֲדָמָה אֲשֶׁר־הֵם עָלֶיהָ: וְהִפְלֵיתִי בַיּוֹם הַהוּא אֶת־אֶרֶץ גֹּשֶׁן אֲשֶׁר עַמִּי
עֹמֵד עָלֶיהָ לְבִלְתִּי הֱיוֹת־שָׁם עָרֹב לְמַעַן תֵּדַע כִּי אֲנִי יְהוָה בְּקֶרֶב הָאָרֶץ:
ששי יט־כ *וְשַׂמְתִּי פְדֻת בֵּין עַמִּי וּבֵין עַמֶּךָ לְמָחָר יִהְיֶה הָאֹת הַזֶּה: וַיַּעַשׂ יְהוָה כֵּן
וַיָּבֹא עָרֹב כָּבֵד בֵּיתָה פַרְעֹה וּבֵית עֲבָדָיו וּבְכָל־אֶרֶץ מִצְרַיִם תִּשָּׁחֵת
כא הָאָרֶץ מִפְּנֵי הֶעָרֹב: וַיִּקְרָא פַרְעֹה אֶל־מֹשֶׁה וּלְאַהֲרֹן וַיֹּאמֶר לְכוּ זִבְחוּ
כב לֵאלֹהֵיכֶם בָּאָרֶץ: וַיֹּאמֶר מֹשֶׁה לֹא נָכוֹן לַעֲשׂוֹת כֵּן כִּי תּוֹעֲבַת מִצְרַיִם
נִזְבַּח לַיהוָה אֱלֹהֵינוּ הֵן נִזְבַּח אֶת־תּוֹעֲבַת מִצְרַיִם לְעֵינֵיהֶם וְלֹא יִסְקְלֻנוּ:

(request) it was necessary to cry out in prayer, (since as the Sages teach,) "From Heaven, a half is not granted" (*Sanhedrin* 64a).

11. כִּי הָיְתָה הָרְוָחָה — *That there was respite.* Although the evil was not completely removed, for the stench remained in the land, and the crocodiles — which cause injury to this very day — remained in the river.

וְהַכְבֵּד אֶת לִבּוֹ — *He hardened his heart.* He strengthened (his resolve), overcoming his natural fear of the remaining crocodiles, (and he was prepared) to withstand the bad stench, so as not to listen to the voice of God, the Blessed One.

12. וְהַךְ אֶת עֲפַר הָאָרֶץ — *And smite the dust of the earth.* No warning was given to Pharaoh before this plague, nor the boils, nor darkness. The reason is that the nine plagues of דצ״ך באח״ב, עד״ש, (*blood, crocodiles, gnats; mixture, murrain, boils; hail, locusts, darkness*) alone were meant to be signs and wonders, (not so) the plague of the firstborn which was not meant to be a sign or wonder, but was a punishment, as explained above (4:23 and 7:4). Now the blood, crocodiles and gnats were signs in the two "heavy" elements (water and

NOTES

asking that it only be answered partially. This is the meaning of the saying of our Sages cited by the *Sforno.* Moses was confronted with this dilemma, since he was asking that only certain crocodiles be removed and brought back to the river. That is why he had to *cry out,* not just *entreat.*

12. וְהַךְ אֶת עֲפַר הָאָרֶץ — *And smite the dust of the earth.* A careful study of the first nine plagues will reveal that Pharaoh is given fair warning before each of the plagues except for numbers three, six and nine. A warning is very important when the purpose of the plague is to encourage repentance and not for punishment. This difficulty is answered by *Sforno,* based on the verse in *Job,* that the concept of הַתְרָאָה,

[9] *HASHEM carried out the word of Moses, and the frogs died — from the*
houses, from the courtyards, and from the fields. [10] *They piled them up into*
heaps and heaps, and the land stank.
[11] *Pharaoh saw that there had been a relief, and kept making his heart*
stubborn. He did not heed them, as HASHEM had spoken.
[12] *HASHEM said to Moses, "Say to Aaron, 'Stretch out your staff and strike*
the dust of the land; it shall become lice throughout the land of Egypt.'" [13] *So*
they did: Aaron stretched out his hand with his staff and struck the dust
of the land, and the lice-infestation was on man and beast; all the dust of the
land became lice, throughout the land of Egypt. [14] *The sorcerers did the same*
with their incantations to draw forth the lice, but they could not. And the
lice-infestation was on man and beast. [15] *The sorcerers said to Pharaoh, "It*
is a finger of God!" But Pharaoh's heart was strong and he did not heed them,
as HASHEM had spoken.
[16] *HASHEM said to Moses, "Arise early in the morning and station yourself*
before Pharaoh — behold, he goes out to the water — and you shall say to him,
'So said HASHEM: Send out My people that they may serve Me. [17] *For if you*
do not send out My people, behold, I shall incite against you, your servants,
your people, and your houses, the swarm of wild beasts; and the houses of
Egypt shall be filled with the swarm, and even the ground upon which they
are. [18] *And on that day I shall set apart the land of Goshen upon which My*
people stands, that there shall be no swarm there; so that you will know that
I am HASHEM in the midst of the land. [19] *I shall make a distinction between*
My people and your people — tomorrow this sign will come about.'"
[20] *HASHEM did so and a severe swarm of wild beasts came to the house of*
Pharaoh and the house of his servants; and throughout the land of Egypt the
land was being ruined because of the swarm.
[21] *Pharaoh summoned Moses and Aaron and said, "Go — bring offer-*
ings to your God in the land." [22] *Moses said, "It is not proper to do so,*
for we will offer the deity of Egypt to HASHEM, our God — behold, if we
were to slaughter the deity of Egypt in their sight, will they not stone us?

---

dust); mixture, murrain and boils were signs in living creatures; while hail, locusts and darkness were signs in the air (atmosphere). The first two in each (category) were (preceded) by a warning, while the third sign was sent without a warning, as it says, הֶן כָּל אֵלֶּה יִפְעַל אֵל, פַּעֲמַיִם שָׁלוֹשׁ עִם גָּבֶר, *All these things does God work, twice, yes thrice with a man* (Job 33:29).

14. וְלֹא יָכֹלוּ — *But they could not.* For it was impossible for them to bring into being anything which truly moved (alive).

17. וְגַם הָאֲדָמָה אֲשֶׁר הֵם עָלֶיהָ — *And also the ground on which they are.* The very ground on which the houses (of the Egyptians) stood would teem with serpents and other creatures which breed in the deep earth, in such a manner that they will not feel secure at night even in a locked house.

19. וְשַׂמְתִּי פְדֻת בֵּין עַמִּי וּבֵין עַמֶּךָ — *And I will put a division between my people and your people.* Even if some of *my people* come to the place where the mixtures are they will not be harmed; only *your people* will be harmed, in that selfsame place.

NOTES

warning, is called for only the first two times but not the third. Hence by dividing the plagues into three divisions there is no reason to warn whenever it is the third plague of that section. This explains the lack of

כג דֶּרֶךְ שְׁלֹשֶׁת יָמִים נֵלֵךְ בַּמִּדְבָּר וְזָבַחְנוּ לַיהוָה אֱלֹהֵינוּ כַּאֲשֶׁר יֹאמַר אֵלֵינוּ:
כד וַיֹּאמֶר פַּרְעֹה אָנֹכִי אֲשַׁלַּח אֶתְכֶם וּזְבַחְתֶּם לַיהוָה אֱלֹהֵיכֶם בַּמִּדְבָּר רַק
הַרְחֵק לֹא־תַרְחִיקוּ לָלֶכֶת הַעְתִּירוּ בַּעֲדִי: כה וַיֹּאמֶר מֹשֶׁה הִנֵּה אָנֹכִי יוֹצֵא
מֵעִמָּךְ וְהַעְתַּרְתִּי אֶל־יְהוָה וְסָר הֶעָרֹב מִפַּרְעֹה מֵעֲבָדָיו וּמֵעַמּוֹ מָחָר רַק אַל־
כו יֹסֵף פַּרְעֹה הָתֵל לְבִלְתִּי שַׁלַּח אֶת־הָעָם לִזְבֹּחַ לַיהוָה: וַיֵּצֵא מֹשֶׁה מֵעִם
כז פַּרְעֹה וַיֶּעְתַּר אֶל־יְהוָה: וַיַּעַשׂ יְהוָה כִּדְבַר מֹשֶׁה וַיָּסַר הֶעָרֹב מִפַּרְעֹה
כח מֵעֲבָדָיו וּמֵעַמּוֹ לֹא נִשְׁאַר אֶחָד: וַיַּכְבֵּד פַּרְעֹה אֶת־לִבּוֹ גַּם בַּפַּעַם הַזֹּאת
וְלֹא שִׁלַּח אֶת־הָעָם:

ט א וַיֹּאמֶר יְהוָה אֶל־מֹשֶׁה בֹּא אֶל־פַּרְעֹה וְדִבַּרְתָּ אֵלָיו כֹּה־אָמַר יְהוָה אֱלֹהֵי
ב הָעִבְרִים שַׁלַּח אֶת־עַמִּי וְיַעַבְדֻנִי: כִּי אִם־מָאֵן אַתָּה לְשַׁלֵּחַ וְעוֹדְךָ מַחֲזִיק בָּם:
ג הִנֵּה יַד־יְהוָה הוֹיָה בְּמִקְנְךָ אֲשֶׁר בַּשָּׂדֶה בַּסּוּסִים בַּחֲמֹרִים בַּגְּמַלִּים בַּבָּקָר
ד וּבַצֹּאן דֶּבֶר כָּבֵד מְאֹד: וְהִפְלָה יְהוָה בֵּין מִקְנֵה יִשְׂרָאֵל וּבֵין מִקְנֵה מִצְרָיִם
ה וְלֹא יָמוּת מִכָּל־לִבְנֵי יִשְׂרָאֵל דָּבָר: וַיָּשֶׂם יְהוָה מוֹעֵד לֵאמֹר מָחָר יַעֲשֶׂה
ו יְהוָה הַדָּבָר הַזֶּה בָּאָרֶץ: וַיַּעַשׂ יְהוָה אֶת־הַדָּבָר הַזֶּה מִמָּחֳרָת וַיָּמָת כֹּל מִקְנֵה
ז מִצְרָיִם וּמִמִּקְנֵה בְנֵי־יִשְׂרָאֵל לֹא־מֵת אֶחָד: וַיִּשְׁלַח פַּרְעֹה וְהִנֵּה לֹא־מֵת
מִמִּקְנֵה יִשְׂרָאֵל עַד־אֶחָד וַיִּכְבַּד לֵב פַּרְעֹה וְלֹא שִׁלַּח אֶת־הָעָם:
ח וַיֹּאמֶר יְהוָה אֶל־מֹשֶׁה וְאֶל־אַהֲרֹן קְחוּ לָכֶם מְלֹא חָפְנֵיכֶם פִּיחַ כִּבְשָׁן וּזְרָקוֹ
ט מֹשֶׁה הַשָּׁמַיְמָה לְעֵינֵי פַרְעֹה: וְהָיָה לְאָבָק עַל כָּל־אֶרֶץ מִצְרָיִם וְהָיָה עַל־
י הָאָדָם וְעַל־הַבְּהֵמָה לִשְׁחִין פֹּרֵחַ אֲבַעְבֻּעֹת בְּכָל־אֶרֶץ מִצְרָיִם: וַיִּקְחוּ אֶת־
פִּיחַ הַכִּבְשָׁן וַיַּעַמְדוּ לִפְנֵי פַרְעֹה וַיִּזְרֹק אֹתוֹ מֹשֶׁה הַשָּׁמַיְמָה וַיְהִי שְׁחִין
יא אֲבַעְבֻּעֹת פֹּרֵחַ בָּאָדָם וּבַבְּהֵמָה: וְלֹא־יָכְלוּ הַחַרְטֻמִּים לַעֲמֹד לִפְנֵי מֹשֶׁה
יב מִפְּנֵי הַשְּׁחִין כִּי־הָיָה הַשְּׁחִין בַּחַרְטֻמִּם וּבְכָל־מִצְרָיִם: וַיְחַזֵּק יְהוָה אֶת־לֵב

26. וַיֶּעְתַּר — *And entreated.* To remove the mixture at the time established (by Moses) and in the manner he designated to Pharaoh, as it says, *The mixture will depart* (v. 25), i.e., not to extirpate and cause to die, as it was with the crocodiles. This is indicated by the (expression), *And HASHEM did according to the word of Moses* (v. 27), regarding (both) the manner of removal and the time.

28. גַּם בַּפַּעַם הַזֹּאת — *This time also.* As he did by the (plague) of the crocodiles, even though he should have feared the mixture, who *did not die* but were only removed and could easily have been returned by God.

IX

7. וְהִנֵּה לֹא מֵת מִמִּקְנֵה יִשְׂרָאֵל עַד אֶחָד — *And behold there was not so much as one of the cattle of the Israelites dead.* Although this was a clear wonder, which could not be attributed to anyone (or anything) except God, the Blessed One, for there is none that can assure life, except He.

NOTES

warning for the third, sixth and ninth plagues.

28. גַּם בַּפַּעַם הַזֹּאת — *This time also.* The expression *this time also* must refer to a previous *similar* case. The *Sforno* connects this verse to verse 11, explaining in both instances that Pharaoh hardened his

heart even though the crocodiles and the mixture of wild beasts still existed and could quickly invade his land again.

IX

7. וְהִנֵּה לֹא מֵת מִמִּקְנֵה יִשְׂרָאֵל עַד אֶחָד — *And behold*

[23] *We will go on a three-day journey in the Wilderness, and bring offerings to HASHEM, our God, as He will tell us."*

[24] *Pharaoh said, "I will send you and you shall bring offerings to HASHEM, your God, in the Wilderness; only do not go far off — entreat for me!"*

[25] *Moses said, "Behold! I leave you and I shall entreat HASHEM — and the swarm will depart from Pharaoh, from his servants, and from his people — tomorrow. Only let Pharaoh not continue to mock, by not sending out the people to bring offerings to HASHEM."*

[26] *Moses left Pharaoh's presence and entreated HASHEM.* [27] *HASHEM did in accordance with Moses' word and He removed the swarm of wild beasts from Pharaoh, from his servants, and from his people — not one remained.* [28] *But Pharaoh made his heart stubborn even this time, and he did not send out the people.*

9 [1] *HASHEM said to Moses, "Come to Pharaoh and speak to him, 'So said HASHEM, the God of the Hebrews: Send out My people that they may serve Me.'* [2] *For if you refuse to send out, and you continue to grip them;* [3] *behold, the hand of HASHEM is on your livestock that are in the field, on the horses, on the donkeys, on the camels, on the cattle, and on the flock — a very severe epidemic.* [4] *HASHEM shall distinguish between the livestock of Israel and the livestock of Egypt, and not a thing that belongs to the Children of Israel will die.* [5] *HASHEM has set an appointed time, saying, 'Tomorrow HASHEM shall carry out this word in the land.' "*

[6] *HASHEM carried out this word the next day, and all the livestock of Egypt died, and of the livestock of the Children of Israel not one died.* [7] *Pharaoh sent and behold, of the livestock of Israel not even one had died — yet Pharaoh's heart became stubborn and he did not send out the people.*

[8] *HASHEM said to Moses and Aaron, "Take for yourselves handfuls of furnace soot, and let Moses hurl it heavenward before Pharaoh's eyes.* [9] *It will become dust over the entire land of Egypt, and it will become boils erupting into blisters on man and beast throughout the land of Egypt."* [10] *They took soot of the furnace, and stood before Pharaoh, and Moses threw it heavenward; and it became boils and blisters, erupting on man and beast.* [11] *The necromancers could not stand before Moses because of the boils, because the boils were on the necromancers and on all of Egypt.* [12] *HASHEM hardened the heart*

8. לְעֵינֵי פַרְעֹה — *In the sight of Pharaoh.* So that he may see that this plague was not caused by contamination of the air's quality or by the position of the heavenly bodies, (both of) which can at times bring about (such) a natural epidemic.

12. וַיְחַזֵּק ה' — *And HASHEM hardened.* For otherwise he doubtless would not have been able to withstand (this plague), similar to Job, וְגַע אֶל עַצְמוֹ וְאֶל בְּשָׂרוֹ, *And touch his bone and flesh* (*Job* 2:5).

NOTES

there was not so much as one of the cattle of the Israelites dead. The interpretation of the *Sforno* is to be understood as follows. Even if the murrain would not kill the cattle of the Israelites, nonetheless there could be other causes of death. The fact that not even one of the cattle of the Israelites died, of any cause, can only be attributed to the One Who controls life and death.

12. וַיְחַזֵּק ה' — *And HASHEM hardened.* The previous plagues, severe as they may have been, did not affect the physical being of Pharaoh and his servants. This plague of boils did, and as such should have brought Pharaoh to the point of surrender. That is why God had to harden Pharaoh's heart, for other-

יג פַּרְעֹה וְלֹא שָׁמַע אֲלֵהֶם כַּאֲשֶׁר דִּבֶּר יהוה אֶל־מֹשֶׁה׃ וַיֹּאמֶר
יהוה אֶל־מֹשֶׁה הַשְׁכֵּם בַּבֹּקֶר וְהִתְיַצֵּב לִפְנֵי פַרְעֹה וְאָמַרְתָּ אֵלָיו כֹּה־אָמַר
יד יהוה אֱלֹהֵי הָעִבְרִים שַׁלַּח אֶת־עַמִּי וְיַעַבְדֻנִי׃ כִּי ׀ בַּפַּעַם הַזֹּאת אֲנִי שֹׁלֵחַ
אֶת־כָּל־מַגֵּפֹתַי אֶל־לִבְּךָ וּבַעֲבָדֶיךָ וּבְעַמֶּךָ בַּעֲבוּר תֵּדַע כִּי אֵין כָּמֹנִי בְּכָל־
טו הָאָרֶץ׃ כִּי עַתָּה שָׁלַחְתִּי אֶת־יָדִי וָאַךְ אוֹתְךָ וְאֶת־עַמְּךָ בַּדָּבֶר וַתִּכָּחֵד מִן־
טז הָאָרֶץ׃ וְאוּלָם בַּעֲבוּר זֹאת הֶעֱמַדְתִּיךָ בַּעֲבוּר הַרְאֹתְךָ אֶת־כֹּחִי וּלְמַעַן
שביעי יז־יח סַפֵּר שְׁמִי בְּכָל־הָאָרֶץ׃ *עוֹדְךָ מִסְתּוֹלֵל בְּעַמִּי לְבִלְתִּי שַׁלְּחָם׃ הִנְנִי מַמְטִיר
כָּעֵת מָחָר בָּרָד כָּבֵד מְאֹד אֲשֶׁר לֹא־הָיָה כָמֹהוּ בְּמִצְרַיִם לְמִן־הַיּוֹם הִוָּסְדָה
יט וְעַד־עָתָּה׃ וְעַתָּה שְׁלַח הָעֵז אֶת־מִקְנְךָ וְאֵת כָּל־אֲשֶׁר לְךָ בַּשָּׂדֶה כָּל־
הָאָדָם וְהַבְּהֵמָה אֲשֶׁר־יִמָּצֵא בַשָּׂדֶה וְלֹא יֵאָסֵף הַבַּיְתָה וְיָרַד עֲלֵהֶם הַבָּרָד
כ וָמֵתוּ׃ הַיָּרֵא אֶת־דְּבַר יהוה מֵעַבְדֵי פַּרְעֹה הֵנִיס אֶת־עֲבָדָיו וְאֶת־מִקְנֵהוּ
כא אֶל־הַבָּתִּים׃ וַאֲשֶׁר לֹא־שָׂם לִבּוֹ אֶל־דְּבַר יהוה וַיַּעֲזֹב אֶת־עֲבָדָיו וְאֶת־
מִקְנֵהוּ בַּשָּׂדֶה׃
כב וַיֹּאמֶר יהוה אֶל־מֹשֶׁה נְטֵה אֶת־יָדְךָ עַל־הַשָּׁמַיִם וִיהִי בָרָד בְּכָל־אֶרֶץ מִצְרָיִם
כג עַל־הָאָדָם וְעַל־הַבְּהֵמָה וְעַל כָּל־עֵשֶׂב הַשָּׂדֶה בְּאֶרֶץ מִצְרָיִם׃ וַיֵּט מֹשֶׁה
אֶת־מַטֵּהוּ עַל־הַשָּׁמַיִם וַיהוה נָתַן קֹלֹת וּבָרָד וַתִּהֲלַךְ אֵשׁ אַרְצָה וַיַּמְטֵר

14. כִּי בַּפַּעַם הַזֹּאת — *For this time.* (This refers to) the third category of plagues affecting the air (atmosphere).

אֲנִי שֹׁלֵחַ אֶת כָּל מַגֵּפֹתַי אֶל לִבְּךָ וּבַעֲבָדֶיךָ וּבְעַמֶּךָ — *I will send all My plagues upon your person* (lit., *your heart*), *your servants and upon your people.* Each one of these plagues (i.e., hail, locust, darkness) which I will visit upon you will have a lasting effect (lit., "will remain in your hearts") even after they have been removed, for even later the prolonged damage will be felt. (In the case of hail and locust) there will be damage to vegetation and all food; and there will be physical illness (as an aftermath) from the plague of darkness which spoiled the climactic condition without a doubt. Also since *no man rose from his place*, doubtless serious illness resulted. The previous plagues, however, once they were removed left no protracted damage.

בַּעֲבוּר תֵּדַע כִּי אֵין כָּמֹנִי בְּכָל הָאָרֶץ — *That you may know that there is none like Me in all the earth.* When you will observe My power even in the atmosphere enveloping (the earth). However, His power in the upper regions was demonstrated to them at the Sea of Reeds through the angel of God, the pillar of cloud and the pillar of fire, for the existence of all these are supernatural.

16. בַּעֲבוּר הַרְאֹתְךָ אֶת כֹּחִי — *So that I might show you My power* . . . that you might repent, for כִּי לֹא אֶחְפֹּץ בְּמוֹת הַמֵּת, *I do not desire the death of him who dies* (*Ezekiel* 18:32).

NOTES

wise he could not have withstood this particular plague. The quotation from *Job* refers to Satan's statement that even righteous Job, if afflicted in his body, would rebel against God.

14. כִּי בַּפַּעַם הַזֹּאת . . . אֶל לִבְּךָ — *For this time . . . upon your person.* The expression *this time* does not refer to the seventh plague (hail) alone but to the third category, for they have a common characteristic, namely the lasting effect they will leave on the people and the produce which is their sustenance. The expression אֶל לִבְּךָ literally means *to your heart.* The *Sforno* feels that this expression is chosen deliberately to indicate that these three plagues were directed to the very heart of man's economic and physical condition.

19. וְעַתָּה שְׁלַח הָעֵז אֶת מִקְנְךָ — *Now therefore send, hasten in your cattle.* Pharaoh had demonstrated, during the plague of murrain, that he had no pity on the cattle of his people. Now, however, since the hail could kill human beings as well, he is cautioned to

of Pharaoh and he did not heed them, as HASHEM had spoken to Moses.
13 *HASHEM spoke to Moses, "Arise early in the morning and station your-*
self before Pharaoh; say to him, 'So said HASHEM, the God of the Hebrews:
Send out My people that they may serve Me. 14 *For this time I shall send all*
My plagues against your heart, and upon your servants, and your people,
so that you shall know that there is none like Me in all the world. 15 *For now*
I could have sent My hand and stricken you and your people with the
pestilence and you would have been obliterated from the earth. 16 *However,*
for this have I let you endure, in order to show you My strength and so that
My Name may be declared throughout the world.
17 *'You still tread upon My people, not to send them out.* 18 *Behold, at this*
time tomorrow I shall rain a very heavy hail, such as there has never been
in Egypt, from the day it was founded until now. 19 *And now send, gather*
in your livestock and everything you have in the field; all the people and
animals that are found in the field that are not gathered into the house — the
hail shall descend upon them and they shall die.' "
20 *Whoever among the servants of Pharaoh feared the word of HASHEM*
chased his servants and his livestock to the houses. 21 *And whoever did not*
take the word of God to heart — he left his servants and livestock in the field.
22 *HASHEM said to Moses, "Stretch out your hand toward heaven and there*
will be hail in the entire land of Egypt, on man and beast, and on all the grass
of the field in the land of Egypt."
23 *Moses stretched out his staff toward heaven, and HASHEM sent*
thunder and hail, and fire went earthward, and HASHEM rained hail

וּלְמַעַן סַפֵּר שְׁמִי — *And that My Name may be declared* . . . thereby turning many away from sin.

19. וְעַתָּה שְׁלַח הָעֵז אֶת מִקְנְךָ — *Now therefore send, hasten in your cattle* . . . so that your servants, who are with the cattle, will be saved, as our Sages say, חָבִיב אָדָם שֶׁנִּבְרָא בְּצֶלֶם, *Precious is man who was created in (God's) image (Avos* 3:18).

20. הַיָּרֵא אֶת דְּבַר ה׳ . . . הֵנִיס — *He that feared the word of HASHEM . . . made flee.* The reason I cautioned, *"Send and hasten"* (v. 19), is because I saw that at the plague of murrain, *he that feared the word of HASHEM (did) make flee.*

21. וַאֲשֶׁר לֹא שָׂם לִבּוֹ — *And he that regarded not.* But (he who regarded not) sinned.

וַיַּעֲזֹב אֶת עֲבָדָיו — *And left his servants* . . . In a manner that his sin caused him loss; therefore I am now warning so that the men in the field will not die.

23. וַתִּהֲלַךְ אֵשׁ אָרְצָה — *And fire ran down onto the earth.* The enflamed air came down to the earth through the forceful thrust (lit., "movement") of the hail which pressed upon it as it descended.

NOTES

take proper steps to protect human lives, in the hope that even Pharaoh will respect the value of man who was created in the Divine Image.

20-21. הַיָּרֵא אֶת דְּבַר ה׳ . . . הֵנִיס . . . וַאֲשֶׁר לֹא שָׂם לִבּוֹ — *He that feared the word of HASHEM . . . made flee . . . And he that regarded not.* Obviously there were those who took in their cattle during the plague of murrain thereby saving them. These were the Egyptians who feared the word of God. Otherwise there would be no cattle remaining following that plague. The sense of these verses is therefore as follows: Since I saw that there were those who believed the warning at the time of the murrain, I therefore am cautioning you now, before the hail, to do likewise especially since human life is now at stake.

23. וַתִּהֲלַךְ אֵשׁ אָרְצָה — *And fire ran down onto the earth.* Normally fire goes upward. In the case of the plague of hail, however, the fiery air was forced

כד יְהוָה בָּרָד עַל־אֶרֶץ מִצְרָיִם: וַיְהִי בָרָד וְאֵשׁ מִתְלַקַּחַת בְּתוֹךְ הַבָּרָד
כה כָּבֵד מְאֹד אֲשֶׁר לֹא־הָיָה כָמֹהוּ בְּכָל־אֶרֶץ מִצְרַיִם מֵאָז הָיְתָה לְגוֹי: וַיַּךְ
הַבָּרָד בְּכָל־אֶרֶץ מִצְרַיִם אֵת כָּל־אֲשֶׁר בַּשָּׂדֶה מֵאָדָם וְעַד־בְּהֵמָה וְאֵת
כו כָּל־עֵשֶׂב הַשָּׂדֶה הִכָּה הַבָּרָד וְאֶת־כָּל־עֵץ הַשָּׂדֶה שִׁבֵּר: רַק בְּאֶרֶץ גֹּשֶׁן
כז אֲשֶׁר־שָׁם בְּנֵי יִשְׂרָאֵל לֹא הָיָה בָּרָד: וַיִּשְׁלַח פַּרְעֹה וַיִּקְרָא לְמֹשֶׁה
וּלְאַהֲרֹן וַיֹּאמֶר אֲלֵהֶם חָטָאתִי הַפָּעַם יהוה הַצַּדִּיק וַאֲנִי וְעַמִּי הָרְשָׁעִים:
כח הַעְתִּירוּ אֶל־יהוה וְרַב מִהְיֹת קֹלֹת אֱלֹהִים וּבָרָד וַאֲשַׁלְּחָה אֶתְכֶם וְלֹא
כט תֹסִפוּן לַעֲמֹד: וַיֹּאמֶר אֵלָיו מֹשֶׁה כְּצֵאתִי אֶת־הָעִיר אֶפְרֹשׂ אֶת־כַּפַּי
אֶל־יְהוָה הַקֹּלוֹת יֶחְדָּלוּן וְהַבָּרָד לֹא יִהְיֶה־עוֹד לְמַעַן תֵּדַע כִּי לַיהוָה
ל הָאָרֶץ: וְאַתָּה וַעֲבָדֶיךָ יָדַעְתִּי כִּי טֶרֶם תִּירְאוּן מִפְּנֵי יְהוָה אֱלֹהִים:
לא־לב וְהַפִּשְׁתָּה וְהַשְּׂעֹרָה נֻכָּתָה כִּי הַשְּׂעֹרָה אָבִיב וְהַפִּשְׁתָּה גִּבְעֹל: וְהַחִטָּה
מפטיר לג וְהַכֻּסֶּמֶת לֹא נֻכּוּ כִּי אֲפִילֹת הֵנָּה: וַיֵּצֵא מֹשֶׁה מֵעִם פַּרְעֹה אֶת־הָעִיר
וַיִּפְרֹשׂ כַּפָּיו אֶל־יְהוָה וַיַּחְדְּלוּ הַקֹּלוֹת וְהַבָּרָד וּמָטָר לֹא־נִתַּךְ אָרְצָה:
לד וַיַּרְא פַּרְעֹה כִּי־חָדַל הַמָּטָר וְהַבָּרָד וְהַקֹּלֹת וַיֹּסֶף לַחֲטֹא וַיַּכְבֵּד לִבּוֹ
לה הוּא וַעֲבָדָיו: וַיֶּחֱזַק לֵב פַּרְעֹה וְלֹא שִׁלַּח אֶת־בְּנֵי יִשְׂרָאֵל כַּאֲשֶׁר דִּבֶּר
יְהוָה בְּיַד־מֹשֶׁה:

---

24. וְאֵשׁ מִתְלַקַּחַת בְּתוֹךְ הַבָּרָד — *And fire flashing up midst the hail.* The forceful thrust of the hail enflamed the atmosphere, causing thunder. The forceful movement was so great (intense) that it damaged the soft (pliable) as well as the hard (growths), as it says, *and the hail smote every herb of the field and broke every tree of the field* (v. 25).

29. כְּצֵאתִי אֶת הָעִיר — *As I go out of the city.* Even though you said, *"And let there be enough of these mighty thunderings and hail"* (v. 28), all this will not cease until I go out of the city.

הַקֹּלוֹת יֶחְדָּלוּן וְהַבָּרָד לֹא יִהְיֶה עוֹד לְמַעַן תֵּדַע כִּי לַה׳ הָאָרֶץ — *The thunders shall cease, neither shall there by any more hail, that you may know that the earth is* HASHEM's.* All this will occur simultaneously, as in a minute, which is contrary to the laws of nature. This will happen *that you may know . . .*, not because I think that you have repented, for indeed . . .

30. יָדַעְתִּי כִּי טֶרֶם תִּירְאוּן — *I know that you will not yet fear.* You still do not fear *(God).*

31. וְהַפִּשְׁתָּה וְהַשְּׂעֹרָה נֻכָּתָה — *And the flax and the barley were smitten.* Even though the flax and barley were smitten, which was a heavy loss for Egypt, as it says, וּבֹשׁוּ עֹבְדֵי פִשְׁתִּים, *And the workers of flax will be shamed (Isaiah* 19:9).

32. וְהַחִטָּה וְהַכֻּסֶּמֶת — *But the wheat and the spelt.* Come and see how great was the wickedness of Pharaoh and his servants, for even though the wheat and spelt were not smitten, and Moses prayed, and Pharaoh observed that the evil (decree) ceased through his prayers, for otherwise even the residue would have been destroyed, nonetheless Pharaoh and his servants continued to sin and willfully hardened their hearts.

NOTES

downward by the impact of the strong hail.

24. וְאֵשׁ מִתְלַקַּחַת בְּתוֹךְ הַבָּרָד — *And fire flashing up midst the hail.* Under normal circumstances the hail would not have damaged the soft, pliable plantings. However, in this case, the hail's force was so great that it affected both the hard and the soft, the pliable no different than the inflexible.

32. וְהַחִטָּה וְהַכֻּסֶּמֶת — *But the wheat and the spelt.* The *Sforno's* explanation answers the question of some commentators (the *Ramban* among them) as to the need for this verse. It comes to underscore the obdurate stand of Pharaoh who, in spite of the

upon the land of Egypt. 24 There was hail, and fire flaming amid the hail — very heavy such as had never been in the entire land of Egypt, from the time it became a nation. 25 The hail struck in the entire land of Egypt, everything that was in the field from man to beast; all the grass of the field the hail struck and every tree of the field it smashed. 26 Only in the land of Goshen, where the Children of Israel were, there was no hail.

27 Pharaoh sent and summoned Moses and Aaron and said to them, "This time I have sinned; HASHEM is the Righteous One, and I and my people are the wicked ones. 28 Entreat HASHEM — there has been an overabundance of Godly thunder and hail; I shall send you out and you shall not continue to remain."

29 Moses said to him, "When I leave the city I shall spread out my hands to HASHEM; the thunder will cease and the hail will no longer be, so that you shall know that the earth is HASHEM's. 30 And as for you and your servants, I know that you are not yet afraid of HASHEM, God." 31 The flax and the barley were struck, for the barley was ripe and the flax was in its stalk. 32 And the wheat and the spelt were not struck, for they ripen later.

33 Moses went out from Pharaoh, from the city, and he stretched out his hands to HASHEM; the thunder and hail ceased and rain did not reach the earth. 34 Pharaoh saw that the rain, the hail, and the thunder ceased, and he continued to sin; and he made his heart stubborn, he and his servants. 35 Pharaoh's heart became strong and he did not send out the Children of Israel, as HASHEM had spoken through Moses.

---

35. וַיֶּחֱזַק לֵב פַּרְעֹה — *And the heart of Pharaoh was hardened.* Not by himself but *as HASHEM had spoken by Moses,* before Aaron was associated with him, when he said, *"And I know that the king of Egypt will not permit you to go"* (3:19), meaning, he will not give you leave to go willingly, *except by a mighty hand* (ibid.). (Now) I do not want him to do so (motivated by) fear of My mighty hand (as a result of which) he will be unable to withstand (the pressures). And thus God acted; after (Pharaoh) continued to sin willfully and he himself hardened his heart contrary to his own nature, but (he was still) unsure whether he could (continue) to withstand, *then* (God) strengthened his heart in the manner that He had spoken to Moses, and (thereby) Pharaoh convinced himself that he would no longer be smitten.

NOTES

efficacy of Moses's prayers which salvaged the wheat and spelt, still continued to sin and refused to send forth the Israelites.

35. וַיֶּחֱזַק לֵב פַּרְעֹה — *And the heart of Pharaoh was hardened.* In the previous verse we are told that Pharaoh himself hardened his heart. Seemingly, this verse which speaks of God hardening his heart is either redundant or unnecessary, since Pharaoh was resisting God on his own! The *Sforno* explains that from the very beginning God had told Moses that Pharaoh's refusal to comply with the command of God would be buttressed by God Himself, for He did not want Pharaoh to succumb to the pressure of the plagues, but to repent of his own volition. This interpretation of the *Sforno* is repeated a number of times (see 3:19, 4:21 and 7:3). In our verse, the *Sforno* once again tells us that the hardening of Pharaoh's heart on his own (v. 34) was in danger of eroding, so God strengthened his resolve, as He had said He would do when He first spoke to Moses. All this is for the purpose of permitting Pharaoh to repent voluntarily and sincerely — being that the first nine plagues were visited upon Egypt for the sole purpose of bringing them to repentance.

פרשת בא

י א וַיֹּאמֶר יהוה אֶל־מֹשֶׁה בֹּא אֶל־פַּרְעֹה כִּי־אֲנִי הִכְבַּדְתִּי אֶת־לִבּוֹ וְאֶת־
ב לֵב עֲבָדָיו לְמַעַן שִׁתִי אֹתֹתַי אֵלֶּה בְּקִרְבּוֹ: וּלְמַעַן תְּסַפֵּר בְּאָזְנֵי בִנְךָ
וּבֶן־בִּנְךָ אֵת אֲשֶׁר הִתְעַלַּלְתִּי בְּמִצְרַיִם וְאֶת־אֹתֹתַי אֲשֶׁר־שַׂמְתִּי בָם
ג וִידַעְתֶּם כִּי־אֲנִי יהוה: וַיָּבֹא מֹשֶׁה וְאַהֲרֹן אֶל־פַּרְעֹה וַיֹּאמְרוּ אֵלָיו כֹּה־
אָמַר יהוה אֱלֹהֵי הָעִבְרִים עַד־מָתַי מֵאַנְתָּ לֵעָנֹת מִפָּנָי שַׁלַּח עַמִּי
ד וְיַעַבְדֻנִי: כִּי אִם־מָאֵן אַתָּה לְשַׁלֵּחַ אֶת־עַמִּי הִנְנִי מֵבִיא מָחָר אַרְבֶּה
ה בִּגְבֻלֶךָ: וְכִסָּה אֶת־עֵין הָאָרֶץ וְלֹא יוּכַל לִרְאֹת אֶת־הָאָרֶץ וְאָכַל | אֶת־
יֶתֶר הַפְּלֵטָה הַנִּשְׁאֶרֶת לָכֶם מִן־הַבָּרָד וְאָכַל אֶת־כָּל־הָעֵץ הַצֹּמֵחַ לָכֶם
ו מִן־הַשָּׂדֶה: וּמָלְאוּ בָתֶּיךָ וּבָתֵּי כָל־עֲבָדֶיךָ וּבָתֵּי כָל־מִצְרַיִם אֲשֶׁר לֹא־
רָאוּ אֲבֹתֶיךָ וַאֲבוֹת אֲבֹתֶיךָ מִיּוֹם הֱיוֹתָם עַל־הָאֲדָמָה עַד הַיּוֹם הַזֶּה וַיִּפֶן
ז וַיֵּצֵא מֵעִם פַּרְעֹה: וַיֹּאמְרוּ עַבְדֵי פַרְעֹה אֵלָיו עַד־מָתַי יִהְיֶה זֶה לָנוּ
לְמוֹקֵשׁ שַׁלַּח אֶת־הָאֲנָשִׁים וְיַעַבְדוּ אֶת־יהוה אֱלֹהֵיהֶם הֲטֶרֶם תֵּדַע כִּי
ח אָבְדָה מִצְרָיִם: וַיּוּשַׁב אֶת־מֹשֶׁה וְאֶת־אַהֲרֹן אֶל־פַּרְעֹה וַיֹּאמֶר אֲלֵהֶם
ט לְכוּ עִבְדוּ אֶת־יהוה אֱלֹהֵיכֶם מִי וָמִי הַהֹלְכִים: וַיֹּאמֶר מֹשֶׁה בִּנְעָרֵינוּ
וּבִזְקֵנֵינוּ נֵלֵךְ בְּבָנֵינוּ וּבִבְנוֹתֵנוּ בְּצֹאנֵנוּ וּבִבְקָרֵנוּ נֵלֵךְ כִּי חַג־יהוה לָנוּ:

X

1. כִּי אֲנִי הִכְבַּדְתִּי — *For I have hardened.* Although Moses had said, "*I know that as yet you do not fear*" (9:30), he thought that even though he (Pharaoh) did not humble himself before God, the Blessed One, (motivated) by reverence of His greatness, nonetheless he will listen because he would not be able to withstand the evil of the plagues. The reason he (Moses) thought so was because he saw that as a result of the plague (of hail) he said, ה' הַצַּדִּיק, *HASHEM is righteous* (9:27). However, when he saw that following all this he (still) did not hearken, Moses felt that the warnings were in vain, for even though he could not tolerate (the plagues), he would not listen. Therefore, God, the Blessed One, says to him, "Even though presently he himself also hardened his heart (9:34), (but) behold I already *hardened his heart* at the plague of boils. All this is (for the purpose) of increasing the signs in the midst of Egypt, so that some of them might repent, and (secondly) that Israel may tell (the story) to (future) generations and recognize My greatness and goodness." Therefore the warning is suitable even though Pharaoh will not listen.

לְמַעַן שִׁתִי אֹתֹתַי אֵלֶּה בְּקִרְבּוֹ — *That I might show these signs in their midst.* So that through them, the people will recognize My greatness and repent of their wickedness.

NOTES

X

1. כִּי אֲנִי הִכְבַּדְתִּי — *For I have hardened.* The difficulty of this verse is obvious. If God has hardened Pharaoh's heart, then what is the purpose of sending Moses to him? The *Sforno* resolves this difficulty by reviewing God's actions, Pharaoh's responses, and Moses's own statements during the previous two plagues, i.e., boils and hail. When Pharaoh said, "*God is right,*" during the plague of hail, Moses was convinced that the pressure of the plagues had finally broken down his resistance. However, when Pharaoh stubbornly continued to refuse to humble himself before God, Moses was frustrated and felt that any future warnings would be futile. God, however, reassured Moses that there is a purpose in coming to Pharaoh, for even though He had hardened Pharaoh's heart *before* the plague of hail, i.e., during that of boils which enabled Pharaoh to withstand the pressure of this last plague (i.e., hail), nonetheless there are two reasons for bringing additional plagues as signs and warnings. One is in

PARASHAS BO

10 [1] *HASHEM said to Moses, "Come to Pharaoh, for I have made his heart and the heart of his servants stubborn so that I can put these signs of Mine in his midst; [2] and so that you may relate in the ears of your son and your son's son that I made a mockery of Egypt and My signs that I placed among them — that you may know that I am HASHEM."*

[3] Moses and Aaron came to Pharaoh and said to him, "So said HASHEM, God of the Hebrews: Until when will you refuse to be humbled before Me? Send out My people that they may serve Me! [4] For if you refuse to send forth My people, behold, tomorrow I shall bring a locust-swarm into your border. [5] It will cover the surface of the earth so that one will not be able to see the earth; and it will consume the remaining residue that was left to you by the hail, and it will consume all the trees that grow for you from the field. [6] They will fill your houses, the houses of all your servants, and the houses of all Egypt, such as your fathers and your grandfathers have not seen from the day they came onto the earth until this day." And he turned and left Pharaoh's presence.

[7] Pharaoh's servants said to him, "How long will this be a snare for us? Send out the men that they may serve HASHEM, their God! Do you not yet know that Egypt is lost?"

[8] So Moses and Aaron were returned to Pharaoh and he said to them, "Go and serve HASHEM, your God; which ones are going?"

[9] Moses said, "With our youngsters and with our elders shall we go; with our sons and with our daughters, with our flock and with our cattle shall we go, because it is a festival of HASHEM for us."

---

2. וּלְמַעַן תְּסַפֵּר — *And that you may tell.* So that the generations of Israel shall know all these (events).

וִידַעְתֶּם — *That you may know.* You, your generations and the Egyptians.

3. עַד מָתַי מֵאַנְתָּ — *How long will you refuse?* Since you have not humbled yourself now, even after observing My mastery (lit., "ability") over the enveloping atmosphere (surrounding the earth, without which) you cannot live even for a moment, there is no hope that you will repent impelled by the force of any great plague; but perhaps you *will* repent from the force of their constancy over a long period. Therefore, it is proper to ask, "Until what time will the constancy of your refusal (match) the ongoing constancy of the plagues?"

5. וְאָכַל אֶת כָּל הָעֵץ — *And shall eat every tree . . .* i.e., destroy it, similar to וְהָיָה לֶאֱכֹל, *and they shall be devoured (Deut.* 31:17), and כִּי אָכַל אֶת יַעֲקֹב, *for they have devoured Jacob (Psalms* 79:7).

NOTES

the hope that some of Pharaoh's subjects will repent, even if he does not. The second is so that Israel will tell their children and children's children of God's greatness and goodness.

2. וִידַעְתֶּם — *That you may know.* The *Sforno* interprets the word *you* in the phrase *that you may know* as referring not only to the Israelites but to those sensitive Egyptians, who will be impressed and moved to repentance, as well.

3. עַד מָתַי מֵאַנְתָּ — *How long will you refuse?* No one plague had proven to be of sufficient strength to break Pharaoh's will. The cumulative effect of all the plagues, and their incessant impact would, however, take its toll. The only question was when. This is the question posed to Pharaoh by Moses and Aaron: *"How long will you refuse?"* The implication is that at some point God's endurance would outlast Pharaoh's persistence.

י וַיֹּאמֶר אֲלֵהֶם יְהִי כֵן יְהוָה עִמָּכֶם כַּאֲשֶׁר אֲשַׁלַּח אֶתְכֶם וְאֶת־טַפְּכֶם רְאוּ
יא כִּי רָעָה נֶגֶד פְּנֵיכֶם׃ לֹא כֵן לְכוּ נָא הַגְּבָרִים וְעִבְדוּ אֶת־יְהוָה כִּי אֹתָהּ
יב אַתֶּם מְבַקְשִׁים וַיְגָרֶשׁ אֹתָם מֵאֵת פְּנֵי פַרְעֹה׃ וַיֹּאמֶר יְהוָה שני
אֶל־מֹשֶׁה נְטֵה יָדְךָ עַל־אֶרֶץ מִצְרַיִם בָּאַרְבֶּה וְיַעַל עַל־אֶרֶץ מִצְרָיִם
יג וְיֹאכַל אֶת־כָּל־עֵשֶׂב הָאָרֶץ אֵת כָּל־אֲשֶׁר הִשְׁאִיר הַבָּרָד׃ וַיֵּט מֹשֶׁה
אֶת־מַטֵּהוּ עַל־אֶרֶץ מִצְרַיִם וַיהוָה נִהַג רוּחַ־קָדִים בָּאָרֶץ כָּל־הַיּוֹם הַהוּא
יד וְכָל־הַלָּיְלָה הַבֹּקֶר הָיָה וְרוּחַ הַקָּדִים נָשָׂא אֶת־הָאַרְבֶּה׃ וַיַּעַל הָאַרְבֶּה
עַל כָּל־אֶרֶץ מִצְרַיִם וַיָּנַח בְּכֹל גְּבוּל מִצְרָיִם כָּבֵד מְאֹד לְפָנָיו לֹא־הָיָה
טו כֵן אַרְבֶּה כָּמֹהוּ וְאַחֲרָיו לֹא יִהְיֶה־כֵּן׃ וַיְכַס אֶת־עֵין כָּל־הָאָרֶץ וַתֶּחְשַׁךְ
הָאָרֶץ וַיֹּאכַל אֶת־כָּל־עֵשֶׂב הָאָרֶץ וְאֵת כָּל־פְּרִי הָעֵץ אֲשֶׁר הוֹתִיר הַבָּרָד
טז וְלֹא־נוֹתַר כָּל־יֶרֶק בָּעֵץ וּבְעֵשֶׂב הַשָּׂדֶה בְּכָל־אֶרֶץ מִצְרָיִם׃ וַיְמַהֵר פַּרְעֹה
יז לִקְרֹא לְמֹשֶׁה וּלְאַהֲרֹן וַיֹּאמֶר חָטָאתִי לַיהוָה אֱלֹהֵיכֶם וְלָכֶם׃ וְעַתָּה שָׂא
נָא חַטָּאתִי אַךְ הַפַּעַם וְהַעְתִּירוּ לַיהוָה אֱלֹהֵיכֶם וְיָסֵר מֵעָלַי רַק אֶת־הַמָּוֶת
יח־יט הַזֶּה׃ וַיֵּצֵא מֵעִם פַּרְעֹה וַיֶּעְתַּר אֶל־יְהוָה׃ וַיַּהֲפֹךְ יְהוָה רוּחַ־יָם חָזָק מְאֹד
וַיִּשָּׂא אֶת־הָאַרְבֶּה וַיִּתְקָעֵהוּ יָמָּה סּוּף לֹא נִשְׁאַר אַרְבֶּה אֶחָד בְּכֹל גְּבוּל
כ מִצְרָיִם׃ וַיְחַזֵּק יְהוָה אֶת־לֵב פַּרְעֹה וְלֹא שִׁלַּח אֶת־בְּנֵי יִשְׂרָאֵל׃
כא וַיֹּאמֶר יְהוָה אֶל־מֹשֶׁה נְטֵה יָדְךָ עַל־הַשָּׁמַיִם וִיהִי חֹשֶׁךְ עַל־אֶרֶץ מִצְרָיִם
כב וְיָמֵשׁ חֹשֶׁךְ׃ וַיֵּט מֹשֶׁה אֶת־יָדוֹ עַל־הַשָּׁמָיִם וַיְהִי חֹשֶׁךְ־אֲפֵלָה בְּכָל־
כג אֶרֶץ מִצְרַיִם שְׁלֹשֶׁת יָמִים׃ לֹא־רָאוּ אִישׁ אֶת־אָחִיו וְלֹא־קָמוּ אִישׁ
כד מִתַּחְתָּיו שְׁלֹשֶׁת יָמִים וּלְכָל־בְּנֵי יִשְׂרָאֵל הָיָה אוֹר בְּמוֹשְׁבֹתָם׃ וַיִּקְרָא שלישי
פַרְעֹה אֶל־מֹשֶׁה וַיֹּאמֶר לְכוּ עִבְדוּ אֶת־יְהוָה רַק צֹאנְכֶם וּבְקַרְכֶם
כה יֻצָּג גַּם־טַפְּכֶם יֵלֵךְ עִמָּכֶם׃ וַיֹּאמֶר מֹשֶׁה גַּם־אַתָּה תִּתֵּן בְּיָדֵנוּ זְבָחִים

10. כַּאֲשֶׁר אֲשַׁלַּח אֶתְכֶם וְאֶת טַפְּכֶם — *As I will let you go and your little ones.* How much more so the cattle.

רְאוּ כִּי רָעָה נֶגֶד פְּנֵיכֶם — *See that evil is before your face.* See that with your actions you are headed to an evil (end) which you will (certainly) reach, similar to הוֹלֵךְ לָמוּת, *I am going to die* (*Genesis* 25:32), and רַגְלֶיהָ יֹרְדוֹת מָוֶת, *Her feet go down to death* (*Proverbs* 5:5), as our Sages say, "And they run to the destructive pit" (*Berachos* 28b).

12. עַל אֶרֶץ מִצְרַיִם בָּאַרְבֶּה — *Over the land of Egypt for the locusts.* Toward the direction of the locusts which is south, as though commanding the locusts to come, similar to, וְנָשָׂא נֵס לַגּוֹיִם מֵרָחוֹק, וְשָׁרַק לוֹ מִקְצֵה הָאָרֶץ, וְהִנֵּה מְהֵרָה קַל יָבוֹא, *And He will lift up a banner to the nations from afar, and will whistle to them from the ends of the earth and behold they shall come with speed swiftly* (*Isaiah* 5:26).

16. וַיְמַהֵר פַּרְעֹה — *And Pharaoh made haste.* Before the locust could consume the roots of the wheat and spelt and the rest of the herbage.

21. נְטֵה יָדְךָ עַל הַשָּׁמַיִם — *Stretch out your hand toward heaven.* To that part of the

NOTES

16. וַיְמַהֵר פַּרְעֹה — *And Pharaoh made haste.* The *Sforno* says "the roots of the wheat" because the produce itself was already consumed by the locusts. The only thing remaining were the roots.

21. נְטֵה יָדְךָ עַל הַשָּׁמַיִם — *Stretch out your hand toward heaven.* For the definition of שָׁמַיִם (heaven) see the *Sforno* on *Genesis* 1:7,8 and the explanatory notes there.

10 *He said to them, "So be HASHEM with you as I will send you forth with*
your children! Look — the evil intent is opposite your faces. 11 *Not so; let the*
men go now. Serve HASHEM, for that is what you seek!" And he drove them
out from Pharaoh's presence.
12 *HASHEM said to Moses, "Stretch out your hand over the land of Egypt for*
the locust-swarm, and it will ascend upon the land of Egypt and eat all the
grass of the land, everything that the hail had left." 13 *Moses stretched his*
staff over the land of Egypt, and HASHEM guided an east wind through the
land all that day and all the night. It became morning and the east wind
carried the locust-swarm. 14 *The locust-swarm ascended over the entire land*
of Egypt and it rested in the entire border of Egypt, very severely; before it
there was never a locust-swarm like it and after it there will not be its equal.
15 *It covered the surface of the entire land and the land was darkened; it ate*
all the grass of the land and all the fruit of the tree that the hail left over. No
greenery remained on the trees or the grass of the field in the entire land of
Egypt.
16 *Pharaoh hastened to summon Moses and Aaron and he said, "I have*
sinned to HASHEM, your God, and to you. 17 *And now, please forgive my sin*
just this time, and entreat HASHEM, your God, that He remove from me only
this death."
18 *He left Pharaoh and entreated HASHEM.* 19 *HASHEM turned back a very*
powerful west wind and it carried the locust-swarm and hurled it toward the
Sea of Reeds; not a single locust remained within the entire border of Egypt.
20 *But HASHEM strengthened the heart of Pharaoh, and he did not send out the*
Children of Israel.
21 *HASHEM said to Moses, "Stretch forth your hand toward the heavens, and*
there shall be darkness upon the land of Egypt, and the darkness will be tang-
ible." 22 *Moses stretched forth his hand toward the heavens and there was a*
thick darkness throughout the land of Egypt for a three-day period. 23 *No man*
could see his brother nor could anyone rise from his place for a three-day
period; but for all the Children of Israel there was light in their dwellings.
24 *Pharaoh summoned Moses and said, "Go — serve HASHEM, only your*
flock and cattle shall remain behind; even your children may go with you."
25 *Moses said, "Even you will place in our hands feast-offerings and*

---

atmosphere which is called heaven (שָׁמַיִם), as explained in *Genesis* (1:7).

וְיָמֵשׁ חֹשֶׁךְ — *And darkness will depart.* And the natural (normal) darkness of night will be removed. For indeed the darkness of night is atmosphere prepared to receive light. It is only dark due to the absence of light. This darkness, however, will be a substance that cannot receive light because of its great density (thickness), not because of the absence of light, and since it is not prepared to receive (light), therefore ...

23. לֹא רָאוּ אִישׁ אֶת אָחִיו — *They saw not one another.* For the light of a candle and torch was not sufficient (to illuminate this darkness).

NOTES

וְיָמֵשׁ חֹשֶׁךְ — *And darkness will depart.* The verb וְיָמֵשׁ is usually interpreted as meaning a darkness that was so intense and substantive it could be *felt.* The *Sforno,* however, interprets it as the *hiphil* of the root מוש, *to depart,* or *remove.* The meaning of the phrase is thus: The usual normal darkness of the night would depart and be replaced by a dense unique darkness which no light could penetrate.

כו וְעֹלֹ֖ת וְעָשִׂ֥ינוּ לַיהוָ֥ה אֱלֹהֵֽינוּ׃ וְגַם־מִקְנֵ֜נוּ יֵלֵ֣ךְ עִמָּ֗נוּ לֹ֤א תִשָּׁאֵר֙ פַּרְסָ֔ה כִּ֚י
מִמֶּ֣נּוּ נִקַּ֔ח לַעֲבֹ֖ד אֶת־יְהוָ֣ה אֱלֹהֵ֑ינוּ וַאֲנַ֣חְנוּ לֹֽא־נֵדַ֗ע מַה־נַּעֲבֹד֙ אֶת־יְהוָ֔ה
כז עַד־בֹּאֵ֖נוּ שָֽׁמָּה׃ וַיְחַזֵּ֥ק יְהוָ֖ה אֶת־לֵ֣ב פַּרְעֹ֑ה וְלֹ֥א אָבָ֖ה לְשַׁלְּחָֽם׃ וַיֹּאמֶר־ל֥וֹ
כח פַרְעֹ֖ה לֵ֣ךְ מֵעָלָ֑י הִשָּׁ֣מֶר לְךָ֗ אַל־תֹּ֙סֶף֙ רְא֣וֹת פָּנַ֔י כִּ֗י בְּי֛וֹם רְאֹתְךָ֥ פָנַ֖י
כט תָּמֽוּת׃ וַיֹּ֥אמֶר מֹשֶׁ֖ה כֵּ֣ן דִּבַּ֑רְתָּ לֹא־אֹסִ֥ף ע֖וֹד רְא֥וֹת פָּנֶֽיךָ׃

יא א וַיֹּ֨אמֶר יְהוָ֜ה אֶל־מֹשֶׁ֗ה ע֣וֹד נֶ֤גַע אֶחָד֙ אָבִ֤יא עַל־פַּרְעֹה֙ וְעַל־מִצְרַ֔יִם
ב אַֽחֲרֵי־כֵ֕ן יְשַׁלַּ֥ח אֶתְכֶ֖ם מִזֶּ֑ה כְּשַׁ֨לְּח֔וֹ כָּלָ֕ה גָּרֵ֛שׁ יְגָרֵ֥שׁ אֶתְכֶ֖ם מִזֶּֽה׃ דַּבֶּר־
נָ֖א בְּאָזְנֵ֣י הָעָ֑ם וְיִשְׁאֲל֞וּ אִ֣ישׁ ׀ מֵאֵ֣ת רֵעֵ֗הוּ וְאִשָּׁה֙ מֵאֵ֣ת רְעוּתָ֔הּ כְּלֵי־כֶ֖סֶף
ג וּכְלֵ֥י זָהָֽב׃ וַיִּתֵּ֧ן יְהוָ֛ה אֶת־חֵ֥ן הָעָ֖ם בְּעֵינֵ֣י מִצְרָ֑יִם גַּ֣ם ׀ הָאִ֣ישׁ מֹשֶׁ֗ה גָּד֤וֹל
ד מְאֹד֙ בְּאֶ֣רֶץ מִצְרַ֔יִם בְּעֵינֵ֥י עַבְדֵֽי־פַרְעֹ֖ה וּבְעֵינֵ֥י הָעָֽם׃ רביעי וַיֹּ֖אמֶר
ה מֹשֶׁ֑ה כֹּ֖ה אָמַ֣ר יְהוָ֑ה כַּחֲצֹ֣ת הַלַּ֔יְלָה אֲנִ֥י יוֹצֵ֖א בְּת֥וֹךְ מִצְרָֽיִם׃ וּמֵ֣ת כָּל־
בְּכוֹר֮ בְּאֶ֣רֶץ מִצְרַ֒יִם֒ מִבְּכ֤וֹר פַּרְעֹה֙ הַיֹּשֵׁ֣ב עַל־כִּסְא֔וֹ עַ֚ד בְּכ֣וֹר הַשִּׁפְחָ֔ה
ו אֲשֶׁ֖ר אַחַ֣ר הָרֵחָ֑יִם וְכֹ֖ל בְּכ֥וֹר בְּהֵמָֽה׃ וְהָֽיְתָ֛ה צְעָקָ֥ה גְדֹלָ֖ה בְּכָל־אֶ֣רֶץ
ז מִצְרָ֑יִם אֲשֶׁ֤ר כָּמֹ֙הוּ֙ לֹ֣א נִהְיָ֔תָה וְכָמֹ֖הוּ לֹ֥א תֹסִֽף׃ וּלְכֹ֣ל ׀ בְּנֵ֣י יִשְׂרָאֵ֗ל לֹ֤א

29. לֹא אֹסִף עוֹד רְאוֹת פָּנֶיךָ — *I will see your face no more.* For you shall die, similar to, לֹא תֹסִפוּ לִרְאֹתָם עוֹד עַד עוֹלָם, *You shall see them again no more forever* (14:13). When he summoned Moses and Aaron that night he did so only through his servants, as it says, וְיָרְדוּ כָל עֲבָדֶיךָ אֵלֶּה אֵלַי, *And all these, your servants, shall come down to me* (11:8).

XI

1. יְשַׁלַּח אֶתְכֶם מִזֶּה כְּשַׁלְּחוֹ — *He shall send you forth from here as he sent you forth (previously).* In the same manner that he willingly sent you and Aaron away, with his *rod of anger,* as it says, וַיְגָרֶשׁ אֹתָם מֵאֵת פְּנֵי פַרְעֹה, *and they were driven out from Pharaoh's presence* (10:11), in a similar manner he will now be forced to send you forth in anguish.

כָּלָה גָּרֵשׁ יְגָרֵשׁ אֶתְכֶם — *He shall surely thrust all of you out.* But the (previous) time he drove only the two of you out and it was only from his presence, now however he will drive all of you out of the entire place (i.e., Egypt). Indeed this is the measure of God's justice, that when a man stubbornly refuses to comply with the wishes of his Maker, he will (ultimately) do what he fled from doing, in distress and sorrow, against his will, as it says, תַּחַת אֲשֶׁר לֹא עָבַדְתָּ . . . וְעָבַדְתָּ אֶת אֹיְבֶיךָ, *because you did not serve HASHEM . . . therefore shall you serve your enemy* (*Deut.* 28:47,48), (and also) אִם לֹא כַּאֲשֶׁר דִּבַּרְתֶּם בְּאָזְנָי כֵּן אֶעֱשֶׂה לָכֶם, *As you have spoken in My ears, so will I do to you* (*Numbers* 14:28). As our Sages say: "He who abolishes (nullifies) the Torah when he is rich will eventually do so in poverty" (*Avos* 4:10).

2. דַּבֶּר נָא בְּאָזְנֵי הָעָם וְיִשְׁאֲלוּ — *Speak, I pray you, in the ears of the people and let them*

NOTES

XI

1. יְשַׁלַּח אֶתְכֶם מִזֶּה כְּשַׁלְּחוֹ כָּלָה גָּרֵשׁ — *He shall send you forth from here as he sent you forth (previously), he shall surely thrust.* The *Sforno* explains the word כְּשַׁלְּחוֹ, *as he sent,* as referring back to the time when Pharaoh drove Moses and Aaron out of his court. The phrase גָּרֵשׁ, *to cast* or *thrust out,* is used here, as well as in 10:11, indicating a parallel between these two cases. The sense of this verse then is as follows. On a previous occasion Pharaoh drove Moses and Aaron out of his presence by his own volition. Now he would thrust out all the Israelites from his land under Divine compulsion. The word כָּלָה, *everyone,* is connected to the concluding part of the verse, i.e., all will be thrust out.

The *Sforno* draws an important moral lesson from this verse. What man fails to do of his free will, he will eventually be forced by God to do under adverse circumstances.

5. מִבְּכוֹר פַּרְעֹה . . . עַד בְּכוֹר הַשִּׁפְחָה — *From the*

elevation-offerings, and we shall offer them to H*ASHEM*, *our God.* 26 *And our*
livestock, as well, will go with us — not a hoof will be left — for from it shall
we take to serve H*ASHEM*, *our God; and we will not know with what we are*
to serve H*ASHEM* *until our arrival there."*
27 H*ASHEM* *strengthened the heart of Pharaoh and he did not wish to send*
them out. 28 *Pharaoh said to him, "Go from me! Beware — do not see my face*
any more, for on the day you see my face you shall die!"
29 *Moses said, "You have spoken correctly. I shall never see your face*
again."

11 1 H*ASHEM said to Moses, "One more plague shall I bring upon Pharaoh*
and upon Egypt; after that he shall send you forth from here. When
he sends forth, it shall be complete — he shall drive you out of here. 2 *Please*
speak in the ears of the people: Let each man request of his fellow and each
woman from her fellow silver vessels and gold vessels." 3 H*ASHEM granted*
the people favor in the eyes of Egypt; moreover, the man Moses was very
great in the land of Egypt, in the eyes of the servants of Pharaoh and in the
eyes of the people.
4 *Moses said, "So said* H*ASHEM*, *'At about midnight I shall go out in the*
midst of Egypt. 5 *Every firstborn in the land of Egypt shall die, from the*
firstborn of Pharaoh who sits on his throne to the firstborn of the maidservant
who is behind the millstone and all the firstborn of beast. 6 *There shall be a*
great outcry in the entire land of Egypt, such as there has never been and
such as there shall never be again. 7 *But against all the Children of Israel, no*

---

ask (borrow). They (i.e., the Jews) should not worry lest they (i.e., the Egyptians) will be induced to pursue them because of the monetary (loss), for that (in itself) will be their salvation.

3. גַּם הָאִישׁ מֹשֶׁה גָּדוֹל מְאֹד — *Moreover, the man Moses was very great.* And in his honor they increased (the amount) loaned.

5. מִבְּכוֹר פַּרְעֹה ... עַד בְּכוֹר הַשִּׁפְחָה — *From the firstborn of Pharaoh even unto the firstborn of the maidservant.* From the most honored to the most base of all. (The expression used later however) מִבְּכֹר פַּרְעֹה . . . עַד בְּכוֹר הַשְּׁבִי, *From the firstborn of Pharaoh . . . to the firstborn of the captive* (12:29), implies from the most guilty in this matter (of slavery and hard labor) to the least guilty of all.

6. אֲשֶׁר כָּמֹהוּ לֹא נִהְיָתָה — *Such as there has been none like it.* That in such a night there was never such a cry, for considering that it was not a night of battle with enemy soldiers (invading) when indeed there is a great cry in the city, as we find, קוֹל צְעָקָה מִשַּׁעַר הַדָּגִים וִילָלָה מִן הַמִּשְׁנֶה וְשֶׁבֶר גָּדוֹל מֵהַגְּבָעוֹת, *The noise of a cry from the fish gate, and a wailing from the second quarter and a great crashing from the hills (Zephaniah* 1:10). But on a night such as this, when Egypt was at peace, there never was, nor would there be, a cry such as this.

NOTES

firstborn of Pharaoh even unto the firstborn of the maidservant. The parallel passage in 12:29 alters the latter part of the verse from *firstborn of the maidservant* to *firstborn of the captive.* The reason for this variation is explained by the *Sforno* in his interpretation of this verse.

6. אֲשֶׁר כָּמֹהוּ לֹא נִהְיָתָה — *Such as there has been none like it.* The Torah does not exaggerate. Certainly there can be circumstances which would cause an outcry equal to this one. However, during a time of peace as opposed to war, such a great cry never was and never will be.

יֶחֱרַץ־כֶּלֶב לְשֹׁנוֹ לְמֵאִישׁ וְעַד־בְּהֵמָה לְמַעַן תֵּדְעוּן אֲשֶׁר יַפְלֶה יהוה בֵּין
ח מִצְרַיִם וּבֵין יִשְׂרָאֵל: וְיָרְדוּ כָל־עֲבָדֶיךָ אֵלֶּה אֵלַי וְהִשְׁתַּחֲווּ־לִי לֵאמֹר צֵא
אַתָּה וְכָל־הָעָם אֲשֶׁר־בְּרַגְלֶיךָ וְאַחֲרֵי־כֵן אֵצֵא וַיֵּצֵא מֵעִם־פַּרְעֹה בָּחֳרִי־
ט אָף: וַיֹּאמֶר יהוה אֶל־מֹשֶׁה לֹא־יִשְׁמַע אֲלֵיכֶם פַּרְעֹה לְמַעַן
י רְבוֹת מוֹפְתַי בְּאֶרֶץ מִצְרָיִם: וּמֹשֶׁה וְאַהֲרֹן עָשׂוּ אֶת־כָּל־הַמֹּפְתִים הָאֵלֶּה
לִפְנֵי פַרְעֹה וַיְחַזֵּק יהוה אֶת־לֵב פַּרְעֹה וְלֹא־שִׁלַּח אֶת־בְּנֵי־יִשְׂרָאֵל
יב א מֵאַרְצוֹ: וַיֹּאמֶר יהוה אֶל־מֹשֶׁה וְאֶל־אַהֲרֹן בְּאֶרֶץ מִצְרַיִם
ב לֵאמֹר: הַחֹדֶשׁ הַזֶּה לָכֶם רֹאשׁ חֳדָשִׁים רִאשׁוֹן הוּא לָכֶם לְחָדְשֵׁי הַשָּׁנָה:
ג דַּבְּרוּ אֶל־כָּל־עֲדַת יִשְׂרָאֵל לֵאמֹר בֶּעָשֹׂר לַחֹדֶשׁ הַזֶּה וְיִקְחוּ לָהֶם אִישׁ
ד שֶׂה לְבֵית־אָבֹת שֶׂה לַבָּיִת: וְאִם־יִמְעַט הַבַּיִת מִהְיֹת מִשֶּׂה וְלָקַח הוּא
וּשְׁכֵנוֹ הַקָּרֹב אֶל־בֵּיתוֹ בְּמִכְסַת נְפָשֹׁת אִישׁ לְפִי אָכְלוֹ תָּכֹסּוּ עַל־הַשֶּׂה:
ה-ו שֶׂה תָמִים זָכָר בֶּן־שָׁנָה יִהְיֶה לָכֶם מִן־הַכְּבָשִׂים וּמִן־הָעִזִּים תִּקָּחוּ: וְהָיָה
לָכֶם לְמִשְׁמֶרֶת עַד אַרְבָּעָה עָשָׂר יוֹם לַחֹדֶשׁ הַזֶּה וְשָׁחֲטוּ אֹתוֹ כֹּל קְהַל
ז עֲדַת־יִשְׂרָאֵל בֵּין הָעַרְבָּיִם: וְלָקְחוּ מִן־הַדָּם וְנָתְנוּ עַל־שְׁתֵּי הַמְּזוּזֹת וְעַל־
ח הַמַּשְׁקוֹף עַל הַבָּתִּים אֲשֶׁר־יֹאכְלוּ אֹתוֹ בָּהֶם: וְאָכְלוּ אֶת־הַבָּשָׂר בַּלַּיְלָה

---

8. וְאַחֲרֵי כֵן אֵצֵא — *And after that I will go out.* I will not leave immediately when you ask me to go out, only *after that;* for I will wait until morning.

9-10. וַיֹּאמֶר ה׳ אֶל מֹשֶׁה לֹא יִשְׁמַע אֲלֵיכֶם פַּרְעֹה . . . וּמֹשֶׁה וְאַהֲרֹן עָשׂוּ וכו׳ — *And HASHEM said to Moses, "Pharaoh will not listen to you" . . . And Moses and Aaron performed . . .* Being that God, the Blessed One, said to Moses that the reason for the hardening of Pharaoh's heart was because God hardened his (Pharaoh's) spirit in order to increase His wonders so that the Egyptians and Israel would (come) to recognize His greatness and goodness, as it says, וִידַעְתֶּם כִּי אֲנִי ה׳, *That you may know that I am HASHEM* (10:2). And being that Moses and Aaron together occupied themselves in performing these wonders, so as to implement (lit., "complete") this intent (of God), therefore, now that God, the Blessed One, has decreed to punish Egypt and save Israel from that punishment, even though some of them were to an extent worthy (of punishment), and (also) to destroy the Egyptian gods so that the punishment could come to pass — and all this through the *Pesach* sacrifice, as it says: וְעָבַרְתִּי . . . וְהִכֵּיתִי . . . אֶעֱשֶׂה שְׁפָטִים . . . וּפָסַחְתִּי, *And I will go through . . . and will smite . . . and execute judgment . . . and I will pass over* (12:12,13). He wanted this commandment (i.e., which follows *this month,* etc. — 12:2) to be (given) through Moses and Aaron together, for just as they both attempted to bring Egypt to repentance and teach the Children of Israel, so shall they both merit to bring into reality the fruit of their efforts.

NOTES

9-10. לֹא יִשְׁמַע אֲלֵיכֶם פַּרְעֹה . . . וּמֹשֶׁה וְאַהֲרֹן עָשׂוּ וכו׳ — *Pharaoh will not listen to you . . . And Moses and Aaron performed . . .* The *Sforno* explains the reason for inserting verses 9 and 10 here, which repeat the reason for hardening Pharaoh's heart and also couples Aaron with Moses regarding the performance of the wonders. This concluding verse of chapter 11 explains the reason for including Aaron in the opening verses of the next chapter. Since Aaron was involved with his brother in performing the wonders, whose purpose was to teach and inspire, it is only fair and proper that he also be included as the moment of redemption arrives. *Let the one who guards the fig tree eat of its fruit (Proverbs 27:18).*

XII

2. הַחֹדֶשׁ הַזֶּה לָכֶם . . . רִאשׁוֹן הוּא לָכֶם — *This month shall be to you . . . It shall be the first . . . to you.* The word לָכֶם, *to you,* appears twice in this verse. The *Sforno* interprets the sense of the verse in a manner which explains the reason for this repetition. A

dog shall whet its tongue, against neither man nor beast, so that you shall know that HASHEM will have differentiated between Egypt and Israel.' [8] *Then all these servants of yours will come down to me and bow to me, saying, 'Leave — you and the entire people that follows you.' After that, I will leave!" And he left Pharaoh's presence in a burning anger.*

[9] *HASHEM said to Moses, "Pharaoh will not heed you, so that My wonders may be multiplied in the land of Egypt."* [10] *So Moses and Aaron performed all these wonders before Pharaoh, but HASHEM strengthened the heart of Pharaoh, and he did not send out the Children of Israel from his land.*

12 [1] *HASHEM said to Moses and Aaron in the land of Egypt, saying,* [2] *"This month shall be for you the beginning of the months, it shall be for you the first of the months of the year.*

[3] *"Speak to the entire assembly of Israel, saying: On the tenth of this month they shall take for themselves — each man — a lamb or kid for each father's house, a lamb or kid for the household.* [4] *But if the household is too small for a lamb or kid, then he and his neighbor who is near his house shall take according to the number of people; everyone according to what he eats shall be counted for the lamb or kid.* [5] *An unblemished lamb or kid, a male, within its first year shall it be for you; from the sheep or goats shall you take it.* [6] *It shall be yours for examination until the fourteenth day of this month; the entire congregation of the assembly of Israel shall slaughter it in the afternoon.* [7] *They shall take some of its blood and place it on the two doorposts and on the lintel of the houses in which they will eat it.* [8] *They shall eat the flesh on that night —*

XII

2. הַחֹדֶשׁ הַזֶּה לָכֶם רֹאשׁ חֳדָשִׁים — *This month shall be to you the beginning of months.* Henceforth the months (of the year) shall be yours, to do with them as you will. During the bondage, however, your days (time) did not belong to you but (were used) to work for others and fulfill their will, therefore . . .

רִאשׁוֹן הוּא לָכֶם לְחָדְשֵׁי הַשָּׁנָה — *It shall be the first month of the year to you.* For in (this month) your existence as a people of (free) choice began.

4. וּשְׁכֵנוֹ הַקָּרֹב אֶל בֵּיתוֹ — *And the neighbor closest to his house.* Even though there may be many Egyptians residing between the house of a Hebrew and the house of his friend, (nonetheless) that Hebrew is called his neighbor, for he is the nearest of all the Hebrews.

NOTES

slave has no time which he can call his own. He has no freedom of choice for he is totally subservient to his master who decides how his time shall be used and thereby controls his days and months. Therefore freedom would grant the Hebrew slaves mastery over their days and months, and they themselves would decide how to utilize their time. Hence, *this month is "to you."* It also represents the first month of a new era for the nation of Israel (indeed a new existence), which is also categorized as being *to you.* Therefore the word לָכֶם is repeated.

4. וּשְׁכֵנוֹ הַקָּרֹב אֶל בֵּיתוֹ — *And the neighbor closest to his house.* Normally the term *neighbor* refers to one who lives adjacent to, or in close proximity of, another resident or person. In this particular instance, however, the word קָרוֹב, *close*, qualifies the word שָׁכֵן, *neighbor.* Only a fellow Hebrew, who is a קָרוֹב, in the sense of being *close* to you in belief and practice, is a neighbor that can join with you in the *Pesach* sacrifice.

ט הַזֶּה צְלִי־אֵשׁ וּמַצּוֹת עַל־מְרֹרִים יֹאכְלֻהוּ: אַל־תֹּאכְלוּ מִמֶּנּוּ נָא וּבָשֵׁל
י מְבֻשָּׁל בַּמָּיִם כִּי אִם־צְלִי־אֵשׁ רֹאשׁוֹ עַל־כְּרָעָיו וְעַל־קִרְבּוֹ: וְלֹא־תוֹתִירוּ
יא מִמֶּנּוּ עַד־בֹּקֶר וְהַנֹּתָר מִמֶּנּוּ עַד־בֹּקֶר בָּאֵשׁ תִּשְׂרֹפוּ: וְכָכָה תֹּאכְלוּ
אֹתוֹ מָתְנֵיכֶם חֲגֻרִים נַעֲלֵיכֶם בְּרַגְלֵיכֶם וּמַקֶּלְכֶם בְּיֶדְכֶם וַאֲכַלְתֶּם
יב אֹתוֹ בְּחִפָּזוֹן פֶּסַח הוּא לַיהוָה: וְעָבַרְתִּי בְאֶרֶץ־מִצְרַיִם בַּלַּיְלָה הַזֶּה
וְהִכֵּיתִי כָל־בְּכוֹר בְּאֶרֶץ מִצְרַיִם מֵאָדָם וְעַד־בְּהֵמָה וּבְכָל־אֱלֹהֵי מִצְרַיִם
יג אֶעֱשֶׂה שְׁפָטִים אֲנִי יְהוָה: וְהָיָה הַדָּם לָכֶם לְאֹת עַל הַבָּתִּים אֲשֶׁר אַתֶּם
שָׁם וְרָאִיתִי אֶת־הַדָּם וּפָסַחְתִּי עֲלֵכֶם וְלֹא־יִהְיֶה בָכֶם נֶגֶף לְמַשְׁחִית
יד בְּהַכֹּתִי בְּאֶרֶץ מִצְרָיִם: וְהָיָה הַיּוֹם הַזֶּה לָכֶם לְזִכָּרוֹן וְחַגֹּתֶם אֹתוֹ חַג
טו לַיהוָה לְדֹרֹתֵיכֶם חֻקַּת עוֹלָם תְּחָגֻּהוּ: שִׁבְעַת יָמִים מַצּוֹת תֹּאכֵלוּ אַךְ
בַּיּוֹם הָרִאשׁוֹן תַּשְׁבִּיתוּ שְּׂאֹר מִבָּתֵּיכֶם כִּי ׀ כָּל־אֹכֵל חָמֵץ וְנִכְרְתָה
טז הַנֶּפֶשׁ הַהִוא מִיִּשְׂרָאֵל מִיּוֹם הָרִאשֹׁן עַד־יוֹם הַשְּׁבִעִי: וּבַיּוֹם הָרִאשׁוֹן
מִקְרָא־קֹדֶשׁ וּבַיּוֹם הַשְּׁבִיעִי מִקְרָא־קֹדֶשׁ יִהְיֶה לָכֶם כָּל־מְלָאכָה
לֹא־יֵעָשֶׂה בָהֶם אַךְ אֲשֶׁר יֵאָכֵל לְכָל־נֶפֶשׁ הוּא לְבַדּוֹ יֵעָשֶׂה לָכֶם:

11. מָתְנֵיכֶם חֲגֻרִים — *With your loins girded.* Prepared to travel, similar to וַיְשַׁנֵּס מָתְנָיו, *And he girded his loins (I Kings 18:46)*, to demonstrate implicit trust in God, the Blessed One, preparing themselves for the road while they were still in prison.

12. וְעָבַרְתִּי — *I will go through* ... to level a path for My anger, (something) which no messenger could do.

וְהִכֵּיתִי כָל בְּכוֹר — *And will smite all the firstborn.* I will differentiate between (lit., "examine") the "drop" of a firstborn and the "drop" of one who is not a firstborn.

וּבְכָל אֱלֹהֵי מִצְרַיִם אֶעֱשֶׂה שְׁפָטִים — *And against all the gods of Egypt I will execute judgment.* I will cast down the "princes on high" who now guide their (destiny) so that this punishment shall come to pass more (fully).

אֲנִי ה׳ — *I am* HASHEM. And all this cannot come to pass except through HASHEM, as it says, אֲנִי ה׳ — אֲנִי הוּא וְלֹא אַחֵר, *I am* HASHEM — *I am He and no other (Pesach Haggadah).* With this (statement, i.e., *I am* HASHEM) the reason is given for all the above, explaining why it was necessary for God Himself to do all the aforementioned, which He did not do with Sennacherib and others.

NOTES

12. וְעָבַרְתִּי . . . וְהִכֵּיתִי כָל בְּכוֹר — *I will go through ... And will smite all the firstborn.* The *Sforno* in his commentary on this verse explains why it was necessary for God Himself to smite the Egyptian firstborn, unlike other similar historic events when the enemy was also smitten, such as the time Sennacherib's army beleaguered Jerusalem. At that time a messenger sufficed while here, as the *Haggadah* stresses, *I and no other.* In *Psalms 78*, David describes the many miracles and acts of salvation enacted by God when the Israelites were in Egypt and after their deliverance. When he describes the plague of the firstborn he uses the expression, *He leveled* (יְפַלֵּס) *a path for His wrath* (ibid. v. 50). This refers to an exact, undeviating punishment which targets only those who are destined to die while guarding and protecting others. Our Rabbis have taught us that "Once the destroyer is given permission to destroy he does not differentiate between the innocent and the guilty." Therefore, to protect the Jewish firstborn, and even those Egyptians who were not really firstborn, it was imperative that God Himself exact this punishment. The word פַּלֵּס also means to balance, which is most appropriate in this context, for only God Himself could so perfectly and exactly focus this plague on those who were the chosen targets, while sparing the others.

וּבְכָל אֱלֹהֵי מִצְרַיִם אֶעֱשֶׂה שְׁפָטִים — *And against all the gods of Egypt I will execute judgment.* Our Sages teach us that every nation has a heavenly

roasted over the fire — and matzos; with bitter herbs shall they eat it.
9 *"You shall not eat it partially roasted or cooked in water; only roasted*
over fire — its head, its legs, with its innards. 10 *You shall not leave any of*
it until morning; any of it that is left until morning you shall burn in the fire.
11 *"So shall you eat it: your loins girded, your shoes on your feet, and your*
staff in your hand; you shall eat it in haste — it is a pesach-offering to
HASHEM.
12 *"I shall go through Egypt on this night, and I shall strike every*
firstborn in the land of Egypt, from man to beast; and against all the gods
of Egypt I shall mete out punishment — I am HASHEM. 13 *The blood shall be*
a sign for you upon the houses where you are; when I see the blood I shall
pass over you; there shall not be a plague of destruction upon you when I
strike in the land of Egypt.
14 *"This day shall become a remembrance for you and you shall celebrate*
it as a festival for HASHEM; for your generations, as an eternal decree shall
you celebrate it. 15 *For a seven-day period shall you eat matzos, but on the*
previous day you shall nullify the leaven from your homes; for anyone who
eats leavened food — that soul shall be cut off from Israel, from the first
day to the seventh day.
16 *"On the first day shall be a holy convocation and on the seventh day*
shall be a holy convocation for you, no work may be done on them, except
for what must be eaten for any person — only that may be done for you.

---

13. וְלֹא יִהְיֶה בָכֶם נֶגֶף לְמַשְׁחִית — *And there shall be no plague upon you to destroy you.* The plague will not affect you as a result of the destruction which I (will) visit upon Egypt. בְּהַכֹּתִי — *When I smite.* For in addition to the plague of the firstborn, He sent upon the people as a whole, עֶבְרָה וָזַעַם וְצָרָה מִשְׁלַחַת מַלְאֲכֵי רָעִים, *wrath, fury and anguish, a delegation of evil angels (Psalms* 78:49). Without the *skipping over* of Israel which God did in His mercy, they would not have been saved from the distress of the rest of Egypt, similar to, פֶּן תִּסָּפֶה בַּעֲוֺן הָעִיר, *lest you be swept away in the iniquity of the city (Genesis* 19:15). He (therefore) commanded them to place the blood as a sign so that they might be saved, all this for לְמַעַן שְׁמִי לְבִלְתִּי הֵחֵל, *the sake of My Name so it be not profaned* (based on *Ezekiel* 20:9) as it is said, וָאֹמַר לָךְ בְּדָמַיִךְ חֲיִי, *And I said to you, in your blood live* (ibid. 16:6).

NOTES

representative on high who guides the destiny of his people, in some mysterious manner. Before that nation can be punished, its heavenly prince or lord must first be cast down. This is what the *Sforno* refers to in his commentary.

13. וְלֹא יִהְיֶה בָכֶם נֶגֶף לְמַשְׁחִית בְּהַכֹּתִי — *And there shall be no plague upon you to destroy you when I smite.* Since God Himself would exact the punishment of the firstborn on this night, what danger could the Israelites be exposed to that they had to be confined to their houses and reassured that no plague will destroy them? The *Sforno* answers that in addition to the plague of the firstborn many other punishments were visited upon the Egyptians, as enumerated in *Psalms* 78. Exposure to these plagues would have endangered even the Israelites, akin to "woe to the wicked, woe to his neighbor" (*Succah* 56b); hence the need to remain indoors where the sign of the blood on the lintel and doorposts would guard them. From the *Sforno's* commentary on verse 23 we see that it was a messenger, not God Himself, who inflicted these additional punishments, therefore it was necessary for the Israelites to exercise caution, as explained above. The *Sforno* also implies that the Israelites, relying on their own merits, would not have been worthy to be saved but God rescued them for His Name's sake, as we find from time to time in Scriptures. Hence the verse in *Ezekiel* could also mean, בְּדָמַיִךְ, *the blood placed by you* on your doorposts and lintel were effective because of חֲיִי, *My life,* i.e., My Name.

יז וּשְׁמַרְתֶּם אֶת־הַמַּצּוֹת כִּי בְּעֶצֶם הַיּוֹם הַזֶּה הוֹצֵאתִי אֶת־צִבְאוֹתֵיכֶם
יח מֵאֶרֶץ מִצְרָיִם וּשְׁמַרְתֶּם אֶת־הַיּוֹם הַזֶּה לְדֹרֹתֵיכֶם חֻקַּת עוֹלָם: בָּרִאשֹׁן
בְּאַרְבָּעָה עָשָׂר יוֹם לַחֹדֶשׁ בָּעֶרֶב תֹּאכְלוּ מַצֹּת עַד יוֹם הָאֶחָד וְעֶשְׂרִים
יט לַחֹדֶשׁ בָּעָרֶב: שִׁבְעַת יָמִים שְׂאֹר לֹא יִמָּצֵא בְּבָתֵּיכֶם כִּי | כָּל־אֹכֵל
כ מַחְמֶצֶת וְנִכְרְתָה הַנֶּפֶשׁ הַהִוא מֵעֲדַת יִשְׂרָאֵל בַּגֵּר וּבְאֶזְרַח הָאָרֶץ: כָּל־
מַחְמֶצֶת לֹא תֹאכֵלוּ בְּכֹל מוֹשְׁבֹתֵיכֶם תֹּאכְלוּ מַצּוֹת:
חמישי כא וַיִּקְרָא מֹשֶׁה לְכָל־זִקְנֵי יִשְׂרָאֵל וַיֹּאמֶר אֲלֵהֶם מִשְׁכוּ וּקְחוּ לָכֶם צֹאן
כב לְמִשְׁפְּחֹתֵיכֶם וְשַׁחֲטוּ הַפָּסַח: וּלְקַחְתֶּם אֲגֻדַּת אֵזוֹב וּטְבַלְתֶּם בַּדָּם אֲשֶׁר־
בַּסַּף וְהִגַּעְתֶּם אֶל־הַמַּשְׁקוֹף וְאֶל־שְׁתֵּי הַמְּזוּזֹת מִן־הַדָּם אֲשֶׁר בַּסָּף וְאַתֶּם
כג לֹא תֵצְאוּ אִישׁ מִפֶּתַח־בֵּיתוֹ עַד־בֹּקֶר: וְעָבַר יהוה לִנְגֹּף אֶת־מִצְרַיִם
וְרָאָה אֶת־הַדָּם עַל־הַמַּשְׁקוֹף וְעַל שְׁתֵּי הַמְּזוּזֹת וּפָסַח יהוה עַל־הַפֶּתַח
כד וְלֹא יִתֵּן הַמַּשְׁחִית לָבֹא אֶל־בָּתֵּיכֶם לִנְגֹּף: וּשְׁמַרְתֶּם אֶת־הַדָּבָר הַזֶּה
כה לְחָק־לְךָ וּלְבָנֶיךָ עַד־עוֹלָם: וְהָיָה כִּי־תָבֹאוּ אֶל־הָאָרֶץ אֲשֶׁר יִתֵּן יהוה
כו לָכֶם כַּאֲשֶׁר דִּבֵּר וּשְׁמַרְתֶּם אֶת־הָעֲבֹדָה הַזֹּאת: וְהָיָה כִּי־יֹאמְרוּ אֲלֵיכֶם
כז בְּנֵיכֶם מָה הָעֲבֹדָה הַזֹּאת לָכֶם: וַאֲמַרְתֶּם זֶבַח־פֶּסַח הוּא לַיהוה אֲשֶׁר פָּסַח

---

17. וּשְׁמַרְתֶּם אֶת הַמַּצּוֹת — *You shall watch the matzos* (or, *observe the feast of matzos).* Which symbolizes the haste (by which it was made) without waiting for it to leaven.

כִּי בְּעֶצֶם הַיּוֹם הַזֶּה — *For in this selfsame day.* In this (one) day everyone was gathered (assembled) together, a (feat) which normally should have taken several days and nights.

הוֹצֵאתִי אֶת צִבְאוֹתֵיכֶם — *I brought forth your hosts.* Each group, as they were constituted, all together.

22. מִן הַדָּם אֲשֶׁר בַּסַּף — *From the blood that is in the basin.* For each sprinkling there shall be a dipping, as God commanded when He said, עַל שְׁתֵּי הַמְּזוּזֹת, *On the two doorposts* (verse 7), which is (to be done) first, followed by עַל הַמַּשְׁקוֹף, *on the lintel.* Now, this is only possible if there are three (separate) sprinklings, to indicate the three *yudin* (i.e., three letters י), as our Sages tell us, "The world to come was created with a *yud*" (*Menachos* 29b). This was also so before the sin of Adam and on the day of the giving of the Torah until the (Golden) Calf was made, כִּי בְּיָהּ ה׳ צוּר עוֹלָמִים, *For HASHEM, God, is an eternal Rock (Isaiah* 26:4), i.e., everlasting, for the (letter) *yud* indicates "eternal expansion." The upper *yud* indicates the existence of the One in His world, (ruling over) the (other) two eternal worlds.

NOTES

22. מִן הַדָּם אֲשֶׁר בַּסַּף — *From the blood that is in the basin.* The *Zohar* states that the three dots of blood placed by the Israelites on the lintel and the two doorposts are similar to three *yudin* which represent God's Name. In the Middle Ages God's name in holy books, including *Siddurim,* was represented by three *yudin,* not two, as the custom is today. The three *yudin* used centuries ago represented three Divine Names. There are those who say that the three *yudin* represent the first letters of the priestly benediction (יְבָרֶכְךָ, יָאֵר, יִשָּׂא). *Rashi* in Tractate *Menachos* 29b quotes the *Sefer Yetzirah* which states that at the time of Creation three drops were sprinkled from a letter of God's Name which in turn became water, fire and air. Three drops, as mentioned above, are similar to three dots or three *yudin.* Based upon all of the above we can understand the significance of the three *yudin* mentioned by the *Sforno* in this verse.

The *Sforno* also links these three *yudin* to three worlds that are or could have been everlasting: (a) the world to come; (b) this world from the time of creation to the time of the original sin; and (c) the world of Torah which began with the revelation at Sinai and lasted until the sin of the Golden Calf. The *yud* on the lintel represents God and the world to come. The drops on the doorpost represent what was and could have been eternal worlds. If Adam

17 *"You shall safeguard the matzos, for on this very day I will have taken
your legions out of the land of Egypt; you shall observe this day for your
generations as an eternal decree.* 18 *On the first day, on the fourteenth day
of the month in the evening shall you eat matzos, until the twenty-first day
of the month in the evening.*
19 *"For seven days, leaven may not be found in your houses, for anyone
who eats leavening — that soul shall be cut off from the assembly of Israel,
whether a convert or a native of the land.* 20 *You shall not eat any leavening;
in all your dwellings shall you eat matzos."*
21 *Moses called to all the elders of Israel and said to them, "Draw forth or
buy for yourselves one of the flock for your families, and slaughter the
pesach-offering.* 22 *You shall take a bundle of hyssop and dip it into the
blood that is in the basin, and touch the lintel and the two doorposts with
some of the blood that is in the basin, and as for you, you shall not leave the
entrance of the house until morning.* 23 *HASHEM will pass through to smite
Egypt, and He will see the blood that is on the lintel and the two doorposts;
and HASHEM will pass over the entrance and He will not permit the
destroyer to enter your homes to smite.* 24 *You shall observe this matter as
a decree for yourself and for your children forever.*
25 *"It shall be that when you come to the land that HASHEM will give
you, as He has spoken, you shall observe this service.* 26 *And it shall be
that when your children say to you, 'What is this service to you?'*
27 *You shall say, 'It is a pesach feast-offering to HASHEM, Who passed*

וְאַתֶּם לֹא תֵצְאוּ — *And none of you shall go out.* For the house will be marked by the blood; (therefore) וְאַתֶּם לֹא תֵצְאוּ, *and you shall not go out*, and only in this manner *He will pass over*, similar to, וְהִתְוִיתָ תָּו, *And set a mark (Ezekiel* 9:4).

23. לִנְגֹּף — *To smite* ... the Egyptian people with עֶבְרָה וָזַעַם וְצָרָה מִשְׁלַחַת מַלְאֲכֵי רָעִים, *wrath, fury and anguish and a delegation of evil messengers (Psalms* 78:49), for the (expression) נֶגֶף, *plague*, is used for every plague including those that are not fatal, as it says, וְנָגְפוּ אִשָּׁה הָרָה . . . וְלֹא יִהְיֶה אָסוֹן, *and hurt* (וְנָגְפוּ) *a woman with child . . . and yet no harm follow* (21:22).

הַמַּשְׁחִית — *The destroyer* . . . (who) destroys the Egyptian people, through *anger, fury*, etc.

26. מָה הָעֲבֹדָה הַזֹּאת לָכֶם — *What is this service to you?* . . . (since) it is not on a day of holy convocation, as are other sacrifices, nor is it in the time frame of other sacrifices, which are brought after the morning daily sacrifice and before the evening daily sacrifice. (Also) why shouldn't one offering suffice for all Israel, as is the case with other communal sacrifices?

27. זֶבַח פֶּסַח הוּא לַה׳ — *It is the sacrifice of HASHEM's Pesach.* This sacrifice is brought (to mark) the future passing over on the following midnight, and since one is not permitted

NOTES

had not sinned this, world would have enjoyed נִצְחִיּוּת, *eternity*, and had the Jews not sinned with the Golden Calf, the new world of Torah would have likewise been an everlasting one. These three perfect worlds are each represented by the letter *yud*, which is a simple, perfect dot and reflects "eternal expansion," as the *Sforno* puts it. The Talmud (*Menachos* 29b) explains that the letter *yud* was chosen to create the world to come because it is the smallest letter of the alphabet, and by the same token the truly righteous men in the world to come are few in numbers, as well as being humble in their demeanor, as suggested by the top of the *yud* which turns down a little.

26-27. מָה הָעֲבֹדָה הַזֹּאת לָכֶם . . . זֶבַח פֶּסַח הוּא לַה׳ — *What is this service to you . . . It is the sacrifice of HASHEM's Pesach.* Three inquiries are included in the question *"What is this service to you?"* (a) A

עַל־בָּתֵּי בְנֵי־יִשְׂרָאֵל בְּמִצְרַיִם בְּנָגְפּוֹ אֶת־מִצְרַיִם וְאֶת־בָּתֵּינוּ הִצִּיל וַיִּקֹּד
כח הָעָם וַיִּשְׁתַּחֲוּוּ׃ וַיֵּלְכוּ וַיַּעֲשׂוּ בְּנֵי יִשְׂרָאֵל כַּאֲשֶׁר צִוָּה יהוה אֶת־מֹשֶׁה
ששי כט וְאַהֲרֹן כֵּן עָשׂוּ׃ וַיְהִי ׀ בַּחֲצִי הַלַּיְלָה וַיהוה הִכָּה כָל־בְּכוֹר
בְּאֶרֶץ מִצְרַיִם מִבְּכֹר פַּרְעֹה הַיֹּשֵׁב עַל־כִּסְאוֹ עַד בְּכוֹר הַשְּׁבִי אֲשֶׁר בְּבֵית
ל הַבּוֹר וְכֹל בְּכוֹר בְּהֵמָה׃ וַיָּקָם פַּרְעֹה לַיְלָה הוּא וְכָל־עֲבָדָיו וְכָל־מִצְרַיִם
לא וַתְּהִי צְעָקָה גְדֹלָה בְּמִצְרָיִם כִּי־אֵין בַּיִת אֲשֶׁר אֵין־שָׁם מֵת׃ וַיִּקְרָא לְמֹשֶׁה
וּלְאַהֲרֹן לַיְלָה וַיֹּאמֶר קוּמוּ צְּאוּ מִתּוֹךְ עַמִּי גַּם־אַתֶּם גַּם־בְּנֵי יִשְׂרָאֵל וּלְכוּ
לב עִבְדוּ אֶת־יהוה כְּדַבֶּרְכֶם׃ גַּם־צֹאנְכֶם גַּם־בְּקַרְכֶם קְחוּ כַּאֲשֶׁר דִּבַּרְתֶּם
לג וָלֵכוּ וּבֵרַכְתֶּם גַּם־אֹתִי׃ וַתֶּחֱזַק מִצְרַיִם עַל־הָעָם לְמַהֵר לְשַׁלְּחָם מִן־
לד הָאָרֶץ כִּי אָמְרוּ כֻּלָּנוּ מֵתִים׃ וַיִּשָּׂא הָעָם אֶת־בְּצֵקוֹ טֶרֶם יֶחְמָץ מִשְׁאֲרֹתָם
לה צְרֻרֹת בְּשִׂמְלֹתָם עַל־שִׁכְמָם׃ וּבְנֵי־יִשְׂרָאֵל עָשׂוּ כִּדְבַר מֹשֶׁה וַיִּשְׁאֲלוּ
לו מִמִּצְרַיִם כְּלֵי־כֶסֶף וּכְלֵי זָהָב וּשְׂמָלֹת׃ וַיהוה נָתַן אֶת־חֵן הָעָם בְּעֵינֵי
מִצְרַיִם וַיַּשְׁאִלוּם וַיְנַצְּלוּ אֶת־מִצְרָיִם׃
לז וַיִּסְעוּ בְנֵי־יִשְׂרָאֵל מֵרַעְמְסֵס סֻכֹּתָה כְּשֵׁשׁ־מֵאוֹת אֶלֶף רַגְלִי הַגְּבָרִים לְבַד
לח־לט מִטָּף׃ וְגַם־עֵרֶב רַב עָלָה אִתָּם וְצֹאן וּבָקָר מִקְנֶה כָּבֵד מְאֹד׃ וַיֹּאפוּ אֶת־
הַבָּצֵק אֲשֶׁר הוֹצִיאוּ מִמִּצְרַיִם עֻגֹת מַצּוֹת כִּי לֹא חָמֵץ כִּי־גֹרְשׁוּ מִמִּצְרַיִם
מ וְלֹא יָכְלוּ לְהִתְמַהְמֵהַּ וְגַם־צֵדָה לֹא־עָשׂוּ לָהֶם׃ וּמוֹשַׁב בְּנֵי יִשְׂרָאֵל אֲשֶׁר
מא יָשְׁבוּ בְּמִצְרָיִם שְׁלֹשִׁים שָׁנָה וְאַרְבַּע מֵאוֹת שָׁנָה׃ וַיְהִי מִקֵּץ שְׁלֹשִׁים שָׁנָה
וְאַרְבַּע מֵאוֹת שָׁנָה וַיְהִי בְּעֶצֶם הַיּוֹם הַזֶּה יָצְאוּ כָּל־צִבְאוֹת יהוה מֵאֶרֶץ

---

to sacrifice at night we must offer it at a time which continues into the following night (i.e., toward evening). And each one must bring this sacrifice, for the miracle occurred with each individual as such, not to the community as a whole.

29. וַה׳ הִכָּה — *And HASHEM smote.* That is, Israel occupied themselves with the commandment of the *Pesach*, while God Himself, at the same time, smote the firstborn Egyptians, so as to redeem them (i.e., Israel).

38. וְצֹאן וּבָקָר — *And flocks and herds . . .* belonging to the mixed multitude that went up with them to dwell among them with all their possessions.

39. כִּי לֹא חָמֵץ — *For it was not leavened . . .* for it had not leavened, due to the brief time period which elapsed from the time they departed Raamses, which is in the land of Egypt, until they reached Succos, which is outside its boundary, as our Sages say, "For the dough

NOTES

sacrifice is usually brought on a day of holy convocation (מִקְרָא קֹדֶשׁ), see *Leviticus* 23:5; (b) no sacrifice is brought before or after the daily offering; and (c) a communal sacrifice can fulfill everyone's obligation. The *Pesach* sacrifice therefore puzzles the son who observes that each Israelite brings his own (or at least is a partner to the lamb); it is brought on the *eve* of the holiday, i.e., the fourteenth of Nissan, and it is brought toward evening, *after* the daily sacrifice. The three answers given in verse 27 are that since the miracle affected every individual Israelite it is proper that each one bring a sacrifice; and since the miracle of Passover occurred at night, were it not for the prohibition to bring sacrifices at night the *Pesach* would have been brought the night of the fifteenth of Nissan. We therefore bring it as close as possible to that time, which is toward the evening of the fourteenth, after the evening daily sacrifice.

29. וַה׳ הִכָּה – *And HASHEM smote.* The letter ו׳ is to be understood as a parallelism. The Israelites were occupied with the fulfillment of God's commandment while God was occupied with punishing the Egyptians — both at the same time. The latter act

over the houses of the Children of Israel in Egypt when He smote the
Egyptians, but He saved our households,' " and the people bowed their
heads and prostrated themselves. [28] *The Children of Israel went and did as*
HASHEM commanded Moses and Aaron, so did they do.
[29] *It was at midnight that HASHEM smote every firstborn in the land of*
Egypt, from the firstborn of Pharaoh sitting on his throne to the firstborn of
the captive who was in the dungeon, and every firstborn animal. [30] *Pharaoh*
rose up at midnight, he and all his servants and all Egypt, and there was a
great outcry in Egypt, for there was not a house where there was no corpse.
[31] *He called to Moses and Aaron at night and said, "Rise up, go out from*
among my people, even you, even the Children of Israel; go and serve
HASHEM as you have spoken! [32] *Take even your sheep and even your cattle,*
as you have spoken, and go — and bless me, as well!"
[33] *Egypt imposed itself strongly upon the people to hasten to send them*
out of the land, for they said, "We are all dying!"
[34] *The people picked up its dough before it could become leavened, their*
leftovers bound up in their garments upon their shoulders. [35] *The Children*
of Israel carried out the word of Moses; they requested from the Egyptians
silver vessels, gold vessels, and garments. [36] *HASHEM gave the people favor*
in the eyes of the Egyptians and they granted their request — so they
emptied Egypt.
[37] *The Children of Israel journeyed from Rameses to Succoth, about six*
hundred thousand men on foot, aside from children. [38] *Also a mixed multi-*
tude went up with them, and flock and cattle, very much livestock. [39] *They*
baked the dough that they took out of Egypt into unleavened cakes, for
they could not be leavened, for they were driven from Egypt for they could
not delay, nor had they made provisions for themselves. [40] *The habitation of*
the Children of Israel during which they dwelled in Egypt was four hun-
dred and thirty years. [41] *It was at the end of four hundred and thirty years,*
and it was on that very day that all the legions of HASHEM left the land of

of our forefathers did not have time to become leavened until the King of kings, the Holy One, Blessed is He, appeared and redeemed them" (*Pesach Haggadah*). For indeed when they were in Succos, beyond the boundary of Egypt, the pillars of cloud and fire revealed themselves, וַה׳ הֹלֵךְ לִפְנֵיהֶם, *and HASHEM went before them* (see 13:21).

40. אֲשֶׁר יָשְׁבוּ בְּמִצְרָיִם שְׁלֹשִׁים שָׁנָה וְאַרְבַּע מֵאוֹת שָׁנָה — *That they dwelled in Egypt was four hundred and thirty years.* The completion of 430 years (is reckoned) from the time Abraham our father was delivered from Ur Casdim to enter into the Covenant of the Parts, as it says, אֲנִי ה׳ אֲשֶׁר הוֹצֵאתִיךָ מֵאוּר כַּשְׂדִּים, *I am HASHEM Who brought you forth from Ur Casdim* (*Genesis* 15:7). This is stated in the *Seder Olam* (ch. 1), "Abraham our father was seventy years old at the Covenant of the Parts."

NOTES

can be considered a reward for the former one.

39. כִּי לֹא חָמֵץ — *For it was not leavened.* The heavenly presence, manifested in the pillars of cloud and fire, was not revealed in the unclean land of Egypt. Only when the Israelites crossed the border did the pillars of cloud and fire appear.

40. אֲשֶׁר יָשְׁבוּ בְּמִצְרָיִם שְׁלֹשִׁים שָׁנָה וְאַרְבַּע מֵאוֹת שָׁנָה — *That they dwelled in Egypt was four hundred and thirty years.* The number of years recorded in the Torah (430) during which Israel dwelled in Egypt must be calculated, according to the *Sforno* and other commentators, from the time that Abraham was seventy years old and entered into a covenant with God.

מב מִצְרָיִם: לֵיל שִׁמֻּרִים הוּא לַיהוָה לְהוֹצִיאָם מֵאֶרֶץ מִצְרָיִם הוּא־הַלַּיְלָה
הַזֶּה לַיהוָה שִׁמֻּרִים לְכָל־בְּנֵי יִשְׂרָאֵל לְדֹרֹתָם:
מג וַיֹּאמֶר יהוה אֶל־מֹשֶׁה וְאַהֲרֹן זֹאת חֻקַּת הַפָּסַח כָּל־בֶּן־נֵכָר לֹא־יֹאכַל
מד־מה בּוֹ: וְכָל־עֶבֶד אִישׁ מִקְנַת־כָּסֶף וּמַלְתָּה אֹתוֹ אָז יֹאכַל בּוֹ: תּוֹשָׁב וְשָׂכִיר
מו לֹא־יֹאכַל־בּוֹ: בְּבַיִת אֶחָד יֵאָכֵל לֹא־תוֹצִיא מִן־הַבַּיִת מִן־הַבָּשָׂר חוּצָה
מז־מח וְעֶצֶם לֹא תִשְׁבְּרוּ־בוֹ: כָּל־עֲדַת יִשְׂרָאֵל יַעֲשׂוּ אֹתוֹ: וְכִי־יָגוּר אִתְּךָ גֵּר
וְעָשָׂה פֶסַח לַיהוָה הִמּוֹל לוֹ כָל־זָכָר וְאָז יִקְרַב לַעֲשֹׂתוֹ וְהָיָה כְּאֶזְרַח
מט הָאָרֶץ וְכָל־עָרֵל לֹא־יֹאכַל בּוֹ: תּוֹרָה אַחַת יִהְיֶה לָאֶזְרָח וְלַגֵּר הַגָּר
נ בְּתוֹכְכֶם: וַיַּעֲשׂוּ כָּל־בְּנֵי יִשְׂרָאֵל כַּאֲשֶׁר צִוָּה יהוה אֶת־מֹשֶׁה וְאֶת־אַהֲרֹן
נא כֵּן עָשׂוּ: וַיְהִי בְּעֶצֶם הַיּוֹם הַזֶּה הוֹצִיא יהוה אֶת־בְּנֵי
יִשְׂרָאֵל מֵאֶרֶץ מִצְרַיִם עַל־צִבְאֹתָם:
יג שביעי א־ב וַיְדַבֵּר יהוה אֶל־מֹשֶׁה לֵּאמֹר: קַדֶּשׁ־לִי כָל־בְּכוֹר פֶּטֶר כָּל־רֶחֶם בִּבְנֵי
ג יִשְׂרָאֵל בָּאָדָם וּבַבְּהֵמָה לִי הוּא: וַיֹּאמֶר מֹשֶׁה אֶל־הָעָם זָכוֹר אֶת־הַיּוֹם
הַזֶּה אֲשֶׁר יְצָאתֶם מִמִּצְרַיִם מִבֵּית עֲבָדִים כִּי בְּחֹזֶק יָד הוֹצִיא יהוה
ד־ה אֶתְכֶם מִזֶּה וְלֹא יֵאָכֵל חָמֵץ: הַיּוֹם אַתֶּם יֹצְאִים בְּחֹדֶשׁ הָאָבִיב: וְהָיָה

---

42. לֵיל שִׁמֻּרִים הוּא לַה׳ לְהוֹצִיאָם — *It was a night of watching to HASHEM for bringing them out.* He looked forward to bringing them out, כִּי לֹא עִנָּה מִלִּבּוֹ, *He does not willingly afflict (Lamentations* 3:33), but He did not find Israel ready or worthy for redemption until that night, and it was for this He watched and waited, for He desires kindness as our Sages say, "The Holy One, Blessed is He, calculated the end" *(Pesach Haggadah).*

הוּא הַלַּיְלָה הַזֶּה לַה׳ שִׁמֻּרִים — *This same night is a night of watching unto HASHEM.* And just as He watched and looked forward to the redemption of Israel all the days of their exile in Egypt, so He watches and waits for the future redemption of Israel, as it says, וְלָכֵן יְחַכֶּה ה׳ לַחֲנַנְכֶם, *And therefore HASHEM will wait that He may be gracious to you (Isaiah* 30:18).

לְכָל בְּנֵי יִשְׂרָאֵל לְדֹרֹתָם — *For all the children of Israel throughout their generations.* As we are told, "In Nissan they were redeemed, and in Nissan they will eventually be redeemed" (*Rosh Hashanah* 11a).

43. זֹאת חֻקַּת הַפָּסַח — *This is the ordinance of the Passover.* For (future) generations, regarding those who may partake and regarding the proper place. However, the commandments enumerated above, except for these two, do not apply to future generations, as our Sages state, "The *Pesach* of generations does not require sprinkling on the lintel and the two doorposts, nor is it eaten in haste" (*Pesachim* 96a).

XIII

2. קַדֶּשׁ לִי כָל בְּכוֹר — *Sanctify unto Me all the firstborn.* They are all obligated to be redeemed similar to all other consecrated objects, in order that they be permitted to do

NOTES

42. הוּא הַלַּיְלָה הַזֶּה לַה׳ שִׁמֻּרִים — *This same night is a night of watching unto HASHEM.* The expression, הוּא הַלַּיְלָה הַזֶּה, *This same night,* is a cryptic one. What does it refer to? (See *Rashi.*) The *Sforno* explains that it is the promise of our future redemption which will also occur in Nissan. This also explains the concluding part of the verse, *throughout their generations.*

43. זֹאת חֻקַּת הַפָּסַח — *This is the ordinance of the Passover.* The word זֹאת, *this,* usually is meant to exclude. In this case it also comes to emphasize that only certain laws of the Egyptian Pesach will apply in the future — not all.

XIII

2. קַדֶּשׁ לִי כָל בְּכוֹר — *Sanctify unto Me all the first-*

Egypt. [42] *It is a night of anticipation for* HASHEM *to take them out of the land of Egypt, this was the night for* HASHEM; *a protection for all the Children of Israel for their generations.*

[43] HASHEM *said to Moses and Aaron, "This is the decree of the pesach-offering: no alienated person may eat from it.* [44] *Every slave of a man, who was bought for money, you shall circumcise him; then he may eat of it.* [45] *A sojourner and a hired laborer may not eat it.* [46] *In one house shall it be eaten; you shall not remove any of the meat from the house to the outside, and you shall not break a bone in it.* [47] *The entire assembly of Israel shall perform it.*

[48] *"When a proselyte sojourns among you he shall make the pesach-offering for* HASHEM; *each of his males shall be circumcised, and then he may draw near to perform it and he shall be like the native of the land; no uncircumcised male may eat of it.* [49] *One law shall there be for the native and the proselyte who lives among you."* [50] *All the Children of Israel did as* HASHEM *had commanded Moses and Aaron, so did they do.*

[51] *It happened on that very day:* HASHEM *took the Children of Israel out of the land of Egypt, in their legions.*

13 [1] HASHEM *spoke to Moses, saying,* [2] *"Sanctify to Me every firstborn, the first issue of every womb among the Children of Israel, of man and beast, is Mine."*

[3] *Moses said to the people, "Remember this day on which you departed from Egypt, from the house of bondage, for with a strong hand God removed you from here, and therefore chametz may not be eaten.* [4] *Today you are leaving, in the month of springtime.* [5] *And it shall come to pass*

---

secular work, for without redemption they are prohibited to occupy themselves with secular work, similar to, לֹא תַעֲבֹד בִּבְכֹר שׁוֹרֶךָ, *You shall do no work with the firstborn of your ox (Deut.* 15:19). Their redemption is according to the valuation of a one-month-old (as set) in the chapter of *Arachin* (valuations) *(Leviticus* 27:6), being that (one month) is the time for his redemption, as it says, וּפְדוּיָו מִבֶּן חֹדֶשׁ תִּפְדֶּה, *And their redemption money from a month old shall you redeem them (Numbers* 18:16).

4. הַיּוֹם אַתֶּם יֹצְאִים בְּחֹדֶשׁ הָאָבִיב — *This day you go forth in the month Aviv.* This year it happened that the lunar month of your exodus is the month of *Aviv*; therefore observe this day, and (when necessary) intercalate the year in such a manner that you always make this festival in the month of *Aviv*.

NOTES

born. Sanctity implies the exclusive right of use and labor by הֶקְדֵּשׁ, *the sacred domain.* Release can only be through redemption. The Torah establishes here the special sacred status of every Jewish firstborn because of their salvation and rescue by God when He smote the firstborn of the Egyptians and spared them. Although the amount of redemption money is not specified here, it is set at five *shekalim* in *Numbers* 18:16. (See the *Sforno's* commentary in verse 15 regarding the firstborn of Israel.)

4. הַיּוֹם אַתֶּם יֹצְאִים בְּחֹדֶשׁ הָאָבִיב — *This day you go forth in the month Aviv. Aviv* signifies the first ripening of the barley ears. The Torah stresses the word הַיּוֹם, *this day,* to indicate the importance of Pesach coinciding with the season of 'ripe ears.' The previous verse says, זָכוֹר, *remember this day,* while the verse in *Deuteronomy* (16:1) states שָׁמוֹר, *observe* or *guard,* the month of *Aviv*. Since ours is a lunar year, eleven days shorter than the solar year, it necessitates adjustment which is accomplished by inserting an extra month *(Adar Sheni)* seven times in every cycle of nineteen years. By doing so we both *remember* and *observe* the month of *Aviv* when God took us forth from Egypt. This

כִּי־יְבִיאֲךָ יהוה אֶל־אֶרֶץ הַכְּנַעֲנִי וְהַחִתִּי וְהָאֱמֹרִי וְהַחִוִּי וְהַיְבוּסִי אֲשֶׁר נִשְׁבַּע
לַאֲבֹתֶיךָ לָתֶת לָךְ אֶרֶץ זָבַת חָלָב וּדְבָשׁ וְעָבַדְתָּ אֶת־הָעֲבֹדָה הַזֹּאת בַּחֹדֶשׁ
ו־ז הַזֶּה: שִׁבְעַת יָמִים תֹּאכַל מַצֹּת וּבַיּוֹם הַשְּׁבִיעִי חַג לַיהוה: מַצּוֹת יֵאָכֵל אֵת
ח שִׁבְעַת הַיָּמִים וְלֹא־יֵרָאֶה לְךָ חָמֵץ וְלֹא־יֵרָאֶה לְךָ שְׂאֹר בְּכָל־גְּבֻלֶךָ: וְהִגַּדְתָּ
ט לְבִנְךָ בַּיּוֹם הַהוּא לֵאמֹר בַּעֲבוּר זֶה עָשָׂה יהוה לִי בְּצֵאתִי מִמִּצְרָיִם: וְהָיָה לְךָ
לְאוֹת עַל־יָדְךָ וּלְזִכָּרוֹן בֵּין עֵינֶיךָ לְמַעַן תִּהְיֶה תּוֹרַת יהוה בְּפִיךָ כִּי בְּיָד חֲזָקָה
י הוֹצִאֲךָ יהוה מִמִּצְרָיִם: וְשָׁמַרְתָּ אֶת־הַחֻקָּה הַזֹּאת לְמוֹעֲדָהּ מִיָּמִים יָמִימָה:
יא וְהָיָה כִּי־יְבִאֲךָ יהוה אֶל־אֶרֶץ הַכְּנַעֲנִי כַּאֲשֶׁר נִשְׁבַּע לְךָ וְלַאֲבֹתֶיךָ וּנְתָנָהּ לָךְ:
יב וְהַעֲבַרְתָּ כָל־פֶּטֶר־רֶחֶם לַיהוה וְכָל־פֶּטֶר | שֶׁגֶר בְּהֵמָה אֲשֶׁר יִהְיֶה לְךָ הַזְּכָרִים
יג לַיהוה: וְכָל־פֶּטֶר חֲמֹר תִּפְדֶּה בְשֶׂה וְאִם־לֹא תִפְדֶּה וַעֲרַפְתּוֹ וְכֹל בְּכוֹר אָדָם
מפטיר יד בְּבָנֶיךָ תִּפְדֶּה: וְהָיָה כִּי־יִשְׁאָלְךָ בִנְךָ מָחָר לֵאמֹר מַה־זֹּאת וְאָמַרְתָּ אֵלָיו
טו בְּחֹזֶק יָד הוֹצִיאָנוּ יהוה מִמִּצְרַיִם מִבֵּית עֲבָדִים: וַיְהִי כִּי־הִקְשָׁה פַרְעֹה לְשַׁלְּחֵנוּ
וַיַּהֲרֹג יהוה כָּל־בְּכוֹר בְּאֶרֶץ מִצְרַיִם מִבְּכֹר אָדָם וְעַד־בְּכוֹר בְּהֵמָה עַל־כֵּן אֲנִי
טז זֹבֵחַ לַיהוה כָּל־פֶּטֶר רֶחֶם הַזְּכָרִים וְכָל־בְּכוֹר בָּנַי אֶפְדֶּה: וְהָיָה לְאוֹת עַל־
יָדְכָה וּלְטוֹטָפֹת בֵּין עֵינֶיךָ כִּי בְּחֹזֶק יָד הוֹצִיאָנוּ יהוה מִמִּצְרָיִם:

---

9. כִּי בְּיָד חֲזָקָה הוֹצִאֲךָ — *For with a strong hand (HASHEM) brought you out* . . . when He changed the nature of the (normally) immutable (laws of nature), as it is said regarding the dividing of the waters of the Jordan, לְמַעַן דַּעַת כָּל עַמֵּי הָאָרֶץ אֶת יַד ה׳ כִּי חֲזָקָה הִיא, *So that all the people of the earth shall know that the hand of HASHEM is mighty* (*Joshua* 4:24).

14. מַה זֹּאת — *What is this?* (What is the reason for) the redemption of the firstborn of an ass, considering that it is an unclean animal and no sanctity of body can devolve on it? Also, (what is the reason for) breaking its neck if it is not redeemed?

בְּחֹזֶק יָד הוֹצִיאָנוּ ה׳ מִמִּצְרָיִם — *By strength of hand HASHEM brought us out from Egypt*. By the strong hand of the Egyptians, God brought us out, as it says, וַתֶּחֱזַק מִצְרַיִם עַל הָעָם, *And the Egyptians were urgent (strongly insistent) upon the people* (12:33), in such a manner that we could not carry our possessions on wagons, as was the Egyptian custom, (and) therefore we were forced to carry it on asses. Now, a miracle occurred and (these) asses were suddenly able to do so, therefore a certain sanctity devolved upon them, hence they became worthy of redemption.

15. וַיְהִי כִּי הִקְשָׁה פַרְעֹה — *And it came to pass when Pharaoh stubbornly (refused to let us go)*. And since Pharaoh strongly (refused) to send us forth, and he is likened to an ass, as it says, אֲשֶׁר בְּשַׂר חֲמוֹרִים בְּשָׂרָם, *Whose flesh is as the flesh of asses* (*Ezekiel* 23:20). Now

NOTES

is what the *Sforno* refers to in his commentary on this verse.

9. כִּי בְּיָד חֲזָקָה הוֹצִאֲךָ — *For with a strong hand (HASHEM) brought you out*. The phrase יָד חֲזָקָה, *strong hand*, used in relationship to God implies a change in the laws of nature, as we see from the verse in *Joshua*.

14. מַה זֹּאת . . . בְּחֹזֶק יָד הוֹצִיאָנוּ ה׳ מִמִּצְרָיִם — *What is this?... By strength of hand HASHEM brought us out from Egypt*. The *Sforno*, departing from the usual interpretation which attributes this question (*What is this?*) to the simple son, explains it as a legitimate, even learned, question. Since we never find the concept of קְדוּשַּׁת הַגּוּף, *sanctity of body*, applied to an unclean animal, why is there a degree of sanctity attached to the ass which is an unclean animal? The answer given by the Torah, בְּחֹזֶק יָד, *by a strong hand*, is interpreted by the *Sforno* as referring to the firm, insistent pressure by Egypt on the Israelites to leave quickly, thereby necessitating them to carry their considerable possessions on the backs of asses which normally could never accommodate such huge burdens. Since, miraculously,

when HASHEM *shall bring you to the land of the Canaanite, the Hittite, the*
Emorite, the Hivvite, and the Jebusite, which He swore to your forefathers
to give you — a land flowing with milk and honey — you shall perform this
service in this month. 6 *For a seven-day period shall you eat matzos, and on*
the seventh day there shall be a festival to HASHEM. 7 *Matzos shall be eaten*
throughout the seven-day period; no chametz may be seen in your posses-
sion, nor may leaven be seen in your possession in all your borders. 8 *And you*
shall tell your son on that day, saying, 'It is because of this that HASHEM
acted on my behalf when I left Egypt.' 9 *And it shall be for you a sign on your*
arm and a reminder between your eyes — so that HASHEM*'s Torah may be*
in your mouth — for with a strong hand HASHEM *removed you from Egypt.*
10 *You shall observe this decree at its designated time from year to year.*
11 *"It shall come to pass, when* HASHEM *will bring you to the land of the*
Canaanites, as He swore to you and your forefathers, and He will have given
it to you; 12 *then you shall set apart every first issue of the womb to* HASHEM,
and of every first issue that is dropped by livestock that belong to you, the
males are HASHEM*'s.* 13 *Every first-issue donkey you shall redeem with a*
lamb or kid; if you do not redeem it, you shall axe the back of its neck. And
you shall redeem every human firstborn among your sons. 14 *And it shall be*
when your son will ask you at some future time, 'What is this?' you shall say
to him, 'With a strong hand HASHEM *removed us from Egypt from the house*
of bondage. 15 *And it happened when Pharaoh stubbornly refused to send us*
out, that HASHEM *killed all the firstborn in the land of Egypt, from the*
firstborn of man to the firstborn of beast. Therefore I offer to HASHEM *all*
male first issue of the womb, and I shall redeem all the firstborn of my sons.
16 *And it shall be a sign upon your arm, and an ornament between your eyes,*
for with a strong hand HASHEM *removed us from Egypt.' "*

---

he could have redeemed himself and his people by sending out Israel, who are compared to a lamb, as it says, שֶׂה פְזוּרָה יִשְׂרָאֵל, *Israel is a scattered sheep (Jeremiah* 50:17), and also it says, וְאַתֵּנָה צֹאנִי, *You are my sheep (Ezekiel* 34:17).

וַיַּהֲרֹג ה׳ — *And* HASHEM *slew.* God slew those compared to the ass when they did not redeem themselves through the lamb.

כָּל בְּכוֹר בְּאֶרֶץ מִצְרַיִם — *All the firstborn in the land of Egypt.* And the firstborn of the Israelites were (also) worthy to be smitten with them, similar to, פֶּן תִּסָּפֶה בַּעֲוֹן הָעִיר, *Lest you be swept away in the iniquity of the city (Genesis* 19:15), but He saved them by sanctifying them to Himself in such a manner that the Israelite firstborn men were as Nazirites, or even higher, designated to serve God, the Blessed One, and prohibited to do common work ... *therefore I sacrifice the firstborns among the animals but all the firstborn of my sons I redeem,* so that they may be permitted to do secular work.

NOTES

they were able to accomplish this feat, their species took on a degree of sanctity, hence the requirement to redeem or dispose of the firstborn. (Similarly, the *Sforno* explains the question in verse 12:26, traditionally attributed to the wicked son, as also being a most incisive and proper one. See above.)

15. וַיְהִי כִּי הִקְשָׁה פַרְעֹה — *And it came to pass when Pharaoh stubbornly (refused to let us go).* The *Sforno* continues his interpretation of these verses to be understood as an answer to the question *"What is this?"* i.e., what is the significance of the ass and the lamb? He explains the symbolism thus: Pharaoh is compared to the ass while Israel is likened to the lamb. Pharaoh could have redeemed himself by sending forth the lamb (Israel), but since he failed to do so, Egypt's "neck" was broken.

פרשת בשלח

יז וַיְהִי בְּשַׁלַּח פַּרְעֹה אֶת־הָעָם וְלֹא־נָחָם אֱלֹהִים דֶּרֶךְ אֶרֶץ פְּלִשְׁתִּים כִּי
קָרוֹב הוּא כִּי | אָמַר אֱלֹהִים פֶּן־יִנָּחֵם הָעָם בִּרְאֹתָם מִלְחָמָה וְשָׁבוּ
יח מִצְרָיְמָה: וַיַּסֵּב אֱלֹהִים | אֶת־הָעָם דֶּרֶךְ הַמִּדְבָּר יַם־סוּף וַחֲמֻשִׁים עָלוּ
יט בְנֵי־יִשְׂרָאֵל מֵאֶרֶץ מִצְרָיִם: וַיִּקַּח מֹשֶׁה אֶת־עַצְמוֹת יוֹסֵף עִמּוֹ כִּי הַשְׁבֵּעַ
הִשְׁבִּיעַ אֶת־בְּנֵי יִשְׂרָאֵל לֵאמֹר פָּקֹד יִפְקֹד אֱלֹהִים אֶתְכֶם וְהַעֲלִיתֶם
כ אֶת־עַצְמֹתַי מִזֶּה אִתְּכֶם: וַיִּסְעוּ מִסֻּכֹּת וַיַּחֲנוּ בְאֵתָם בִּקְצֵה הַמִּדְבָּר:
כא וַיהוָה הֹלֵךְ לִפְנֵיהֶם יוֹמָם בְּעַמּוּד עָנָן לַנְחֹתָם הַדֶּרֶךְ וְלַיְלָה בְּעַמּוּד אֵשׁ
כב לְהָאִיר לָהֶם לָלֶכֶת יוֹמָם וָלָיְלָה: לֹא־יָמִישׁ עַמּוּד הֶעָנָן יוֹמָם וְעַמּוּד הָאֵשׁ
לָיְלָה לִפְנֵי הָעָם:

יד

א־ב וַיְדַבֵּר יְהוָה אֶל־מֹשֶׁה לֵּאמֹר: דַּבֵּר אֶל־בְּנֵי יִשְׂרָאֵל וְיָשֻׁבוּ וְיַחֲנוּ לִפְנֵי
ג פִּי הַחִירֹת בֵּין מִגְדֹּל וּבֵין הַיָּם לִפְנֵי בַּעַל צְפֹן נִכְחוֹ תַחֲנוּ עַל־הַיָּם: וְאָמַר
ד פַּרְעֹה לִבְנֵי יִשְׂרָאֵל נְבֻכִים הֵם בָּאָרֶץ סָגַר עֲלֵיהֶם הַמִּדְבָּר: וְחִזַּקְתִּי אֶת־

---

17. וְלֹא נָחָם אֱלֹהִים דֶּרֶךְ אֶרֶץ פְּלִשְׁתִּים — *God did not lead them by the way of the land of the Philistines.* Even though the Divine intention was to lead Israel to Mount Sinai to receive the Torah and from there to *Eretz Yisrael*, as it says, וְלָקַחְתִּי אֶתְכֶם לִי לְעָם . . . וְהֵבֵאתִי אֶתְכֶם אֶל הָאָרֶץ, *And I will take you to Me for a people . . . and I will bring you to the land* (6:7,8), nonetheless the *present* intention was to lead them to the Sea of Reeds (although) it was not the way to either of these (i.e., Mount Sinai or the Land of Israel). The purpose was to drown Pharaoh and his army there, similar to, וּמָשַׁכְתִּי אֵלֶיךָ אֶל נַחַל קִישׁוֹן אֶת סִיסְרָא, *And I will draw out to you to the wadi of Kishon, Sisera (Judges 4:7).*

Now the straightest and shortest route from Egypt to the Sea of Reeds was *by the way of the land of the Philistines* but God, the Blessed One, did not want to lead them on that way . . .

כִּי קָרוֹב הוּא — *Because it was near.* And since that road was near to Egypt many travelers frequented it coming and going from and to Egypt, hence . . .

בִּרְאֹתָם מִלְחָמָה — *When they see war.* When they (the Israelites) will hear (from these travelers) the news of Pharaoh's preparations to pursue them together with his army, they will without a doubt, due to their fear of war, regret and return to Egypt. Therefore He led them about by a way where no other man traveled.

18. דֶּרֶךְ הַמִּדְבָּר יַם סוּף — *By the way of the wilderness by the Sea of Reeds.* So they would travel by way of the wilderness, since no informers from Egypt would come (on that road); hence they will not be aware of Pharaoh's pursuit of them until he overtakes them, as it

NOTES

17-18. וְלֹא נָחָם אֱלֹהִים דֶּרֶךְ אֶרֶץ פְּלִשְׁתִּים כִּי קָרוֹב הוּא . . . בִּרְאֹתָם מִלְחָמָה . . . דֶּרֶךְ הַמִּדְבָּר יַם סוּף — *God did not lead them by the way of the land of the Philistines because it was near . . . When they see war . . . By the way of the wilderness by the Sea of Reeds.* Since God's intention was to entice Pharaoh to pursue the Israelites so that judgment might be executed upon him and the Egyptians at the Sea of Reeds, and that the miracle of the dividing of the waters take place, it would have been logical to lead the Israelites on a direct route to the sea through the land of the Philistines. The reason this was not done was because if a well-frequented route were used, travelers would have informed the Israelites of Pharaoh's pursuit, which in turn would have resulted in panic and an attempt to return to Egypt. By traveling along an unfrequented route the Israelites first became aware of Pharaoh's pursuit at a time when it was impossible for them to return. Their only option was to march forward, into the sea.

19. וַיִּקַּח מֹשֶׁה אֶת עַצְמוֹת יוֹסֵף עִמּוֹ — *And Moses took the bones of Joseph with him.* Since Joseph

PARASHAS BESHALACH

17 *It happened when Pharaoh sent out the people that God did not lead
them by way of the land of the Philistines, because it was near, for God
said, "Perhaps the people will reconsider when they see a war, and they
will return to Egypt."* 18 *So God turned the people toward the way of the
Wilderness to the Sea of Reeds. The Children of Israel were armed when
they went up from Egypt.* 19 *Moses took the bones of Joseph with him, for he
had firmly adjured the Children of Israel, saying, "God will surely
remember you, and you shall bring up my bones from here with you."*
20 *They journeyed from Succoth, and encamped in Etham, at the edge of
the Wilderness.* 21 *HASHEM went before them by day in a pillar of cloud to
lead them on the way, and by night in a pillar of fire to give them light, so
that they could travel day and night.* 22 *He did not remove the pillar of
cloud by day and the pillar of fire by night from before the people.*

14 1 *HASHEM spoke to Moses, saying,* 2 *"Speak to the Children of Israel
and let them turn back and encamp before Pi-hahiroth, between
Migdol and the sea, before Baal-zephon; you shall encamp opposite it, by
the sea.* 3 *Pharaoh will say of the Children of Israel, 'They are imprisoned
in the land, the Wilderness has locked them in.'* 4 *I shall strengthen the*

---

says; וַיִּשְׂאוּ בְנֵי יִשְׂרָאֵל אֶת עֵינֵיהֶם וְהִנֵּה מִצְרַיִם נֹסֵעַ אַחֲרֵיהֶם, *And the Children of Israel lifted up their eyes and behold the Egyptians were marching after them* (14:10), by which time they (no longer) could make amends by returning, for Pharaoh and his army would not accept them.

וַחֲמֻשִׁים עָלוּ בְנֵי יִשְׂרָאֵל — *And the Children of Israel went up armed.* All this had to be done, even though they were (well) armed, for with all their weapons they lacked the courage to fight with the Egyptians and escape, for they were inexperienced in all this (i.e., warfare).

19. וַיִּקַּח מֹשֶׁה אֶת עַצְמוֹת יוֹסֵף עִמּוֹ — *And Moses took the bones of Joseph with him* ... for he (Moses) was then the leader of the generation ...

כִּי הַשְׁבֵּעַ הִשְׁבִּיעַ אֶת בְּנֵי יִשְׂרָאֵל — *For he had strictly sworn the Children of Israel* ... and the obligation of the people (lit., "generation") rests on its leader.

21. וַה׳ הֹלֵךְ לִפְנֵיהֶם — *And HASHEM went before them* ... from the time they reached Succos which was across the border of Egypt, and entered the wilderness.

XIV

3. סָגַר עֲלֵיהֶם הַמִּדְבָּר — *The wilderness has shut them in.* Baal-Zephon has closed in the wilderness on them.

NOTES

had strictly sworn the Children of Israel to bring his coffin to *Eretz Yisrael*, why then did Moses alone feel the obligation to honor this pledge? The *Sforno's* answer is that the leader of a people must accept the responsibility for his generation's obligation.

21. וַה׳ הֹלֵךְ לִפְנֵיהֶם — *And HASHEM went before them.* The *Sforno* in 12:39 established that God did not reveal Himself to the Israelites in the unclean land of Egypt. Not until they came to Succos, which was across the border, did the pillars of cloud and fire appear. Similarly, in this verse he stresses that *HASHEM went before them* only when they had crossed the border of Egypt at Succos.

XIV

3-5. סָגַר עֲלֵיהֶם הַמִּדְבָּר ... וַיֵּהָפֵךְ לְבַב פַּרְעֹה — *The wilderness has shut them in ... And the heart of Pharaoh changed.* The *Mechilta* states that only Baal-Zephon of all the Egyptian idols was left intact and not destroyed by God (see 12:12). This

לֵב־פַּרְעֹה וְרָדַף אַחֲרֵיהֶם וְאִכָּבְדָה בְּפַרְעֹה וּבְכָל־חֵילוֹ וְיָדְעוּ מִצְרַיִם כִּי־
ה אֲנִי יהוה וַיַּעֲשׂוּ־כֵן: וַיֻּגַּד לְמֶלֶךְ מִצְרַיִם כִּי בָרַח הָעָם וַיֵּהָפֵךְ לְבַב פַּרְעֹה
וַעֲבָדָיו אֶל־הָעָם וַיֹּאמְרוּ מַה־זֹּאת עָשִׂינוּ כִּי־שִׁלַּחְנוּ אֶת־יִשְׂרָאֵל מֵעָבְדֵנוּ:
ו־ז וַיֶּאְסֹר אֶת־רִכְבּוֹ וְאֶת־עַמּוֹ לָקַח עִמּוֹ: וַיִּקַּח שֵׁשׁ־מֵאוֹת רֶכֶב בָּחוּר וְכֹל
ח רֶכֶב מִצְרָיִם וְשָׁלִשִׁם עַל־כֻּלּוֹ: וַיְחַזֵּק יהוה אֶת־לֵב פַּרְעֹה מֶלֶךְ מִצְרַיִם
ט וַיִּרְדֹּף אַחֲרֵי בְּנֵי יִשְׂרָאֵל וּבְנֵי יִשְׂרָאֵל יֹצְאִים בְּיָד רָמָה: וַיִּרְדְּפוּ מִצְרַיִם
אַחֲרֵיהֶם וַיַּשִּׂיגוּ אוֹתָם חֹנִים עַל־הַיָּם כָּל־סוּס רֶכֶב פַּרְעֹה וּפָרָשָׁיו וְחֵילוֹ
י עַל־פִּי הַחִירֹת לִפְנֵי בַּעַל צְפֹן: וּפַרְעֹה הִקְרִיב וַיִּשְׂאוּ בְנֵי־יִשְׂרָאֵל אֶת־
עֵינֵיהֶם וְהִנֵּה מִצְרַיִם ׀ נֹסֵעַ אַחֲרֵיהֶם וַיִּירְאוּ מְאֹד וַיִּצְעֲקוּ בְנֵי־יִשְׂרָאֵל אֶל־
יא יהוה: וַיֹּאמְרוּ אֶל־מֹשֶׁה הֲמִבְּלִי אֵין־קְבָרִים בְּמִצְרַיִם לְקַחְתָּנוּ לָמוּת
יב בַּמִּדְבָּר מַה־זֹּאת עָשִׂיתָ לָּנוּ לְהוֹצִיאָנוּ מִמִּצְרָיִם: הֲלֹא־זֶה הַדָּבָר אֲשֶׁר
דִּבַּרְנוּ אֵלֶיךָ בְמִצְרַיִם לֵאמֹר חֲדַל מִמֶּנּוּ וְנַעַבְדָה אֶת־מִצְרָיִם כִּי טוֹב לָנוּ
יג עֲבֹד אֶת־מִצְרַיִם מִמֻּתֵנוּ בַּמִּדְבָּר: וַיֹּאמֶר מֹשֶׁה אֶל־הָעָם אַל־תִּירָאוּ
הִתְיַצְּבוּ וּרְאוּ אֶת־יְשׁוּעַת יהוה אֲשֶׁר־יַעֲשֶׂה לָכֶם הַיּוֹם כִּי אֲשֶׁר רְאִיתֶם
יד אֶת־מִצְרַיִם הַיּוֹם לֹא תֹסִפוּ לִרְאֹתָם עוֹד עַד־עוֹלָם: יהוה יִלָּחֵם לָכֶם
וְאַתֶּם תַּחֲרִשׁוּן:
טו־טז וַיֹּאמֶר יהוה אֶל־מֹשֶׁה מַה־תִּצְעַק אֵלָי דַּבֵּר אֶל־בְּנֵי־יִשְׂרָאֵל וְיִסָּעוּ: וְאַתָּה

---

5. כִּי בָרַח הָעָם — *That the people had fled.* For they did not proceed in a direct route into the wilderness, as they had (originally) indicated when they said, דֶּרֶךְ שְׁלֹשֶׁת יָמִים נֵלֵךְ בַּמִּדְבָּר, *We will go three days' journey into the wilderness* (8:23), but turned back, akin to runaways who are confused, unsure of their direction.

וַיֵּהָפֵךְ לְבַב פַּרְעֹה — *And the heart of Pharaoh changed.* He thought that Baal-Zephon could withstand God, the Blessed One.

מַה זֹּאת עָשִׂינוּ כִּי שִׁלַּחְנוּ — *What is this we have done that we have sent forth?* We did not beseech Baal-Zephon who would have helped us and spared us the need to send (them forth).

6. וְאֶת עַמּוֹ לָקַח עִמּוֹ — *And took his people with him* . . . his choice horsemen and his army.

7. וְכֹל רֶכֶב מִצְרָיִם — *And all the chariots of Egypt* . . . the multitude.

וְשָׁלִשִׁם עַל כֻּלּוֹ — *And captains over all of them.* Also over the multitude who were not included among his people and army did he appoint captains learned in warfare, for indeed the strength of an army depends on the skill and strategy of its commanders.

8. וּבְנֵי יִשְׂרָאֵל יֹצְאִים בְּיָד רָמָה — *And the Children of Israel went out with a high hand.* Similar to יָדֵנוּ רָמָה, *our hand is exalted (Deut.* 32:27). They strove to vanquish Pharaoh

NOTES

was done to mislead Pharaoh into thinking that Baal-Zephon could measure up to God. This explains Pharaoh's delusion, as explained by the *Sforno* in verse 5, and his regret for not having beseeched this idol earlier.

6-7. וְאֶת עַמּוֹ לָקַח עִמּוֹ . . . וְכֹל רֶכֶב מִצְרַיִם וְשָׁלִשִׁם עַל כֻּלּוֹ — *And took his people with him . . . And all the chariots of Egypt, and captains over all of them.* The *Sforno* divides the Egyptian host into three categories: Pharaoh; his choice professional military men; and the Egyptian masses in their chariots. The latter, however, were untrained and needed the guidance and direction of skilled captains. This same division is alluded to by Moses in his song, which the *Sforno* (15:1, 6,8) refers to as the first, second and third "battles of Hashem."

8. וּבְנֵי יִשְׂרָאֵל יֹצְאִים בְּיָד רָמָה — *And the Children of Israel went out with a high hand.* The *Sforno*

heart of Pharaoh and he will pursue them, and I will be glorified through Pharaoh and his entire army, and Egypt will know that I am HASHEM." And so they did.

5 It was told to the king of Egypt that the people had fled; and the heart of Pharaoh and his servants became transformed regarding the people, and they said, "What is this that we have done that we have sent away Israel from serving us?"

6 He harnessed his chariot and attracted his people with him. 7 He took six hundred elite chariots and all the chariots of Egypt, with officers on them all. 8 HASHEM strengthened the heart of Pharaoh, king of Egypt, and he pursued the Children of Israel — and the Children of Israel were going out with an upraised arm.

9 Egypt pursued them and overtook them, encamped by the sea — all the horses and chariots of Pharaoh, and his horsemen and army — by Pi-hahiroth before Baal-zephon. 10 Pharaoh approached; the Children of Israel raised their eyes and behold! — Egypt was journeying after them, and they were very frightened; the Children of Israel cried out to HASHEM.
11 They said to Moses, "Were there no graves in Egypt that you took us to die in the Wilderness? What is this that you have done to us to take us out of Egypt? 12 Is this not the statement that we made to you in Egypt, saying, 'Let us be and we will serve Egypt'? — for it is better that we should serve Egypt than that we should die in the Wilderness!"

13 Moses said to the people, "Do not fear! Stand fast and see the salvation of HASHEM that He will perform for you today; for as you have seen Egypt today, you shall not see them ever again! 14 HASHEM shall do battle for you, and you shall remain silent."

15 HASHEM said to Moses, "Why do you cry out to Me? Speak to the Children of Israel and let them journey forth! 16 And you — lift up your

---

and his army who were not as numerous as they; however, this demonstrated their lack of military knowledge, for indeed they should have feared them, for though less in number they (the professional Egyptian army) were (superior) in military skill, and more to be feared than all the multitude of Egyptians who later traveled after them.

9. וַיִּרְדְּפוּ מִצְרַיִם אַחֲרֵיהֶם — *And the Egyptians pursued after them.* After those who went out with a high hand.

10. וּפַרְעֹה הִקְרִיב — *And Pharaoh drew close.* The assembled multitude of all the chariots of Egypt.

11. לְקַחְתָּנוּ לָמוּת בַּמִּדְבָּר — *You have taken us to die in the wilderness.* For even if Pharaoh and his army do not wage war against us, still they will stand before us to bar our way in obtaining any food, so we will die in the wilderness from hunger, (and) thirst and in nakedness, deprived of everything.

15. מַה תִּצְעַק אֵלָי — *Why do you cry out to Me?* For he was certainly included in וַיִּצְעֲקוּ בְנֵי יִשְׂרָאֵל אֶל ה׳, *and the Children of Israel cried out to* HASHEM (v. 10). However, the cry

NOTES

demonstrates his respect for the superiority of military skills over that of sheer numbers in his interpretation of this verse, as he does in the previous verse as well.

15. מַה תִּצְעַק אֵלָי דַּבֵּר אֶל בְּנֵי יִשְׂרָאֵל וְיִסָּעוּ — *Why do you cry out to Me? Speak to the Children of Israel, and they will go forward.* In verse 10 we are told that the Children of Israel cried out to *Hashem*, but

הָרֵם אֶת־מַטְּךָ וּנְטֵה אֶת־יָדְךָ עַל־הַיָּם וּבְקָעֵהוּ וְיָבֹאוּ בְנֵי־יִשְׂרָאֵל בְּתוֹךְ
יז הַיָּם בַּיַּבָּשָׁה: וַאֲנִי הִנְנִי מְחַזֵּק אֶת־לֵב מִצְרַיִם וְיָבֹאוּ אַחֲרֵיהֶם וְאִכָּבְדָה
יח בְּפַרְעֹה וּבְכָל־חֵילוֹ בְּרִכְבּוֹ וּבְפָרָשָׁיו: וְיָדְעוּ מִצְרַיִם כִּי־אֲנִי יהוה בְּהִכָּבְדִי
יט בְּפַרְעֹה בְּרִכְבּוֹ וּבְפָרָשָׁיו: וַיִּסַּע מַלְאַךְ הָאֱלֹהִים הַהֹלֵךְ לִפְנֵי מַחֲנֵה
יִשְׂרָאֵל וַיֵּלֶךְ מֵאַחֲרֵיהֶם וַיִּסַּע עַמּוּד הֶעָנָן מִפְּנֵיהֶם וַיַּעֲמֹד מֵאַחֲרֵיהֶם:
כ וַיָּבֹא בֵּין ׀ מַחֲנֵה מִצְרַיִם וּבֵין מַחֲנֵה יִשְׂרָאֵל וַיְהִי הֶעָנָן וְהַחֹשֶׁךְ וַיָּאֶר
כא אֶת־הַלָּיְלָה וְלֹא־קָרַב זֶה אֶל־זֶה כָּל־הַלָּיְלָה: וַיֵּט מֹשֶׁה אֶת־יָדוֹ עַל־
הַיָּם וַיּוֹלֶךְ יהוה ׀ אֶת־הַיָּם בְּרוּחַ קָדִים עַזָּה כָּל־הַלַּיְלָה וַיָּשֶׂם אֶת־
כב הַיָּם לֶחָרָבָה וַיִּבָּקְעוּ הַמָּיִם: וַיָּבֹאוּ בְנֵי־יִשְׂרָאֵל בְּתוֹךְ הַיָּם בַּיַּבָּשָׁה
כג וְהַמַּיִם לָהֶם חוֹמָה מִימִינָם וּמִשְּׂמֹאלָם: וַיִּרְדְּפוּ מִצְרַיִם וַיָּבֹאוּ אַחֲרֵיהֶם
כד כֹּל סוּס פַּרְעֹה רִכְבּוֹ וּפָרָשָׁיו אֶל־תּוֹךְ הַיָּם: וַיְהִי בְּאַשְׁמֹרֶת הַבֹּקֶר
וַיַּשְׁקֵף יהוה אֶל־מַחֲנֵה מִצְרַיִם בְּעַמּוּד אֵשׁ וְעָנָן וַיָּהָם אֵת מַחֲנֵה מִצְרָיִם:

---

of Moses was not motivated by fear of Pharaoh and his army, for he had already told Israel of the fall and death of the Egyptians, as it says, לֹא תֹסִפוּ לִרְאֹתָם עוֹד עַד עוֹלָם, *You shall never again see them forever* (v. 13), and ה׳ יִלָּחֵם לָכֶם, *HASHEM will fight for you* (v. 14). His cry was caused by the arrogance of the Jewish leaders who said, הֲמִבְּלִי אֵין קְבָרִים, *Are there not graves (in Egypt)*? (v. 11). He thought that because of this (defiance of him) the (people) would not listen to him to enter the sea. Therefore God says to him, *"Why do you cry out to Me?"* regarding this matter, for indeed you are distrustful of worthy ones. דַּבֵּר אֶל בְּנֵי יִשְׂרָאֵל וְיִסָּעוּ — *Speak to the Children of Israel, and they will go forward.* They will not disobey you.

16. הָרֵם אֶת מַטְּךָ — *Lift up your rod* ... to the east wind that it should dry the sea. וּנְטֵה אֶת יָדְךָ עַל הַיָּם — *And stretch out your hand over the sea* ... that the waters shall divide to one side and the other, similar to Elijah (*II Kings* 2:8).

18. וְיָדְעוּ מִצְרַיִם — *And the Egyptians shall know* ... those who remained in Egypt and who will return (repent) to Me, כִּי לֹא אֶחְפֹּץ בְּמוֹת הַמֵּת, *for I have no desire for the death of him who dies (Ezekiel* 18:32).

19. הַהֹלֵךְ לִפְנֵי מַחֲנֵה יִשְׂרָאֵל — *Who went before the camp of Israel* ... in the pillar of fire. וַיֵּלֶךְ מֵאַחֲרֵיהֶם — *And went behind them* ... to soften the deep (bed of the sea) which had hardened (lit., "frozen") before the Israelites when they crossed over, thereby transforming the sea bed into mud when the Egyptians passed through in pursuit. It was unnecessary at this time for the pillar of cloud before Israel to lead the way, for the path made by the

NOTES

Moses is not mentioned. Indeed he reassures them and allays their fears. Still in this verse God says to Moses, "Why do *you* cry out to Me?" The *Sforno* interprets the cry of Moses, which is implied in God's retort, as being far different than that of the Israelites. They are afraid of Pharaoh, while Moses is afraid that the people will not obey him to enter the sea, having been influenced and dissuaded by their leaders. God must therefore reassure him that they will follow. The expression וְיִסָּעוּ does not mean *and let them go forward*, as some commentators would have it, but *they "will" go forward.*

16. וּנְטֵה אֶת יָדְךָ עַל הַיָּם — *And stretch out your hand over the sea.* The *Sforno* uses the expression הֵנָּה וָהֵנָּה, *to one side and to the other*, based upon an expression used in the episode of Elijah and Elisha when they approached the Jordan River and Elijah took his mantle, rolled it up and struck the water whereupon *it divided to one side and the other.*

18. וְיָדְעוּ מִצְרַיִם — *And the Egyptians shall know.* Since all the Egyptians who pursued the Israelites perished, the only ones who could *know that I am HASHEM* were those who remained behind. They would be so impressed by the miracle that they would repent and recognize God.

staff and stretch out your arm over the sea and split it; and the Children of
Israel shall come into the midst of the sea on dry land. 17 *And I — behold! —*
I shall strengthen the heart of Egypt and they will come after them; and I
will be glorified through Pharaoh and through his entire army, through his
chariots and through his horsemen. 18 *Egypt will know that I am HASHEM,*
when I am glorified through Pharaoh, his chariots, and his horsemen."
19 *The angel of God who had been going in front of the Children of Israel*
moved and went behind them; and the pillar of cloud moved from in front
of them and went behind them. 20 *It came between the camp of Egypt and*
the camp of Israel and there were cloud and darkness — while it
illuminated the night — and one did not draw near the other all the night.
21 *Moses stretched out his hand over the sea, and HASHEM moved the sea*
with a strong east wind all the night, and He turned the sea to damp land
and the water split. 22 *The Children of Israel came within the sea on dry*
land; and the water was a wall for them, on their right and on their left.
23 *Egypt pursued and came after them — every horse of Pharaoh, his*
chariots, and his horsemen — into the midst of the sea. 24 *It happened at*
the morning watch that HASHEM looked down at the camp of Egypt
with a pillar of fire and cloud, and He confounded the camp of Egypt.

---

splitting of the sea directed them.

וַיַּעֲמֹד מֵאַחֲרֵיהֶם — *And stood behind them* ... behind the Israelites and behind the pillar of fire.

20. וַיָּבֹא — *And it came.* The angel came between the camp of Egypt and the camp of Israel to guide the two pillars.

וַיְהִי הֶעָנָן וְהַחֹשֶׁךְ — *And there was the cloud and the darkness.* The dark of night together with the cloud was behind Israel and the pillar of fire.

וַיָּאֶר אֶת הַלָּיְלָה — *And he gave light to the night.* (This refers to) the angel in the pillar of fire, for he removed the dark of night and there was no cloud separating between them (i.e., the Israelites) and the illuminating fire as there was on the Egyptian side.

וְלֹא קָרַב זֶה אֶל זֶה — *And the one did not come near the other.* For those who walk in darkness must perforce do so slowly not knowing what obstacles (lie before them).

21. וַיָּשֶׂם אֶת הַיָּם לֶחָרָבָה — *And made the sea into dry land.* The east wind hardened (lit., "froze") the mud of the sea floor.

וַיִּבָּקְעוּ הַמָּיִם — *And the waters were divided* ... by the stretching forth of Moses's hand at the command of his Creator.

22. בַּיַּבָּשָׁה — *Upon the dry ground.* For the deeps were congealed by the east wind and they covered over the hardened mud.

24. וַיַּשְׁקֵף ה׳ אֶל מַחֲנֵה מִצְרַיִם בְּעַמּוּד אֵשׁ וְעָנָן — *And HASHEM looked to the camp of Egypt through the pillar of fire and the cloud.* The two pillars that were going in the middle expanse between the camp of Egypt and the camp of Israel were brought close to the Egyptian camp.

וַיָּהָם — *And brought disease.* Through many kinds of ailments, similar to the Philistines.

NOTES

24. וַיָּהָם — *And brought disease.* The expression וַיָּהָם, translated by many as *and brought confusion,* is interpreted by the *Sforno* as the bringing upon them of many kinds of ailments. Since the plagues visited upon the Egyptians in their land were not in the form of ailments, except for שְׁחִין, *boils,* we

כה וַיָּסַר אֵת אֹפַן מַרְכְּבֹתָיו וַיְנַהֲגֵהוּ בִּכְבֵדֻת וַיֹּאמֶר מִצְרַיִם אָנוּסָה מִפְּנֵי
יִשְׂרָאֵל כִּי יהוה נִלְחָם לָהֶם בְּמִצְרָיִם:
רביעי כו וַיֹּאמֶר יהוה אֶל־מֹשֶׁה נְטֵה אֶת־יָדְךָ עַל־הַיָּם וְיָשֻׁבוּ הַמַּיִם עַל־מִצְרַיִם
כז עַל־רִכְבּוֹ וְעַל־פָּרָשָׁיו: וַיֵּט מֹשֶׁה אֶת־יָדוֹ עַל־הַיָּם וַיָּשָׁב הַיָּם לִפְנוֹת
בֹּקֶר לְאֵיתָנוֹ וּמִצְרַיִם נָסִים לִקְרָאתוֹ וַיְנַעֵר יהוה אֶת־מִצְרַיִם בְּתוֹךְ הַיָּם:
כח וַיָּשֻׁבוּ הַמַּיִם וַיְכַסּוּ אֶת־הָרֶכֶב וְאֶת־הַפָּרָשִׁים לְכֹל חֵיל פַּרְעֹה הַבָּאִים
כט אַחֲרֵיהֶם בַּיָּם לֹא־נִשְׁאַר בָּהֶם עַד־אֶחָד: וּבְנֵי יִשְׂרָאֵל הָלְכוּ בַיַּבָּשָׁה
ל בְּתוֹךְ הַיָּם וְהַמַּיִם לָהֶם חֹמָה מִימִינָם וּמִשְּׂמֹאלָם: וַיּוֹשַׁע יהוה בַּיּוֹם הַהוּא
אֶת־יִשְׂרָאֵל מִיַּד מִצְרָיִם וַיַּרְא יִשְׂרָאֵל אֶת־מִצְרַיִם מֵת עַל־שְׂפַת הַיָּם:
לא וַיַּרְא יִשְׂרָאֵל אֶת־הַיָּד הַגְּדֹלָה אֲשֶׁר עָשָׂה יהוה בְּמִצְרַיִם וַיִּירְאוּ הָעָם
אֶת־יהוה וַיַּאֲמִינוּ בַּיהוה וּבְמֹשֶׁה עַבְדּוֹ:

וַתְּהִי יַד ה׳ בָּעִיר מְהוּמָה גְּדוֹלָה מְאֹד, וַיַּךְ אֶת אַנְשֵׁי הָעִיר מִקָּטֹן וְעַד גָּדוֹל וַיִּשָּׂתְרוּ לָהֶם עְפֹלִים, *The hand of* Hashem *was against the city with great epidemic* (מְהוּמָה) *and He smote the people of the city, both small and big, and they were struck with swellings* (*I Samuel* 5:9). These ailments are (what is meant by) מַדְוֵי מִצְרַיִם הָרָעִים, *the evil diseases of Egypt* (*Deut.* 7:15), and that is הַיָּד הַגְּדֹלָה אֲשֶׁר עָשָׂה ה׳ בְּמִצְרַיִם, *the great hand which* Hashem *placed upon the Egyptians* (v. 31), which Israel saw and feared, as it says, אֲשֶׁר יָגֹרְתָּ מִפְּנֵיהֶם, *which you were in dread of* (*Deut.* 28:60). However, the plagues which are detailed in the Torah did not include any ailment except for boils, and indeed the Torah mentions (specifies) the boils (visited) upon Egypt and also mentions the *diseases of Egypt.*

25. וַיָּסַר אֵת אֹפַן — *And He took off the wheels ...* through the pillar of fire.

בִּכְבֵדֻת — *Heavily ...* because of the mud.

כִּי ה׳ נִלְחָם לָהֶם — *For* Hashem *is fighting for them.* And if we flee He will no longer fight with us.

27. לְאֵיתָנוֹ — *To its strength ...* with the return of the waves to the divided path, which had not occurred since it divided.

וּמִצְרַיִם נָסִים לִקְרָאתוֹ — *And the Egyptians fled towards it.* From the beginning of the morning watch, God's hand was upon them to confuse them and it was then they said, אָנוּסָה, *Let us flee,* and they fled till the morning by the way of the divided path, and at the time of the morning's appearance the sea returned to its strength carrying the waves to the (former) divided section which the Egyptians had then reached and thus they found themselves fleeing *toward* the water.

וַיְנַעֵר ה׳ אֶת מִצְרַיִם — *And* Hashem *shook out the Egyptians ...* the king and his people. He threw them out of the chariots to the floor of the sea, similar to, חָצְנִי נָעַרְתִּי, *Also I shook out my lap* (*Nehemiah* 5:13), and הִתְנַעֲרִי מֵעָפָר, *Shake yourself from the dust* (*Isaiah* 52:2).

NOTES

must conclude that the *evil diseases* mentioned in *Deut.* 7:15 refer to those brought upon them at the Sea of Reeds. This theory is buttressed by the verse in *Deut.* 28:60 where the Almighty refers to the *diseases of Egypt* and the fear of the Israelites, in the chapter of the תּוֹכֵחָה, *admonition.* He draws a parallel to the fear of the Israelites mentioned in verse 31 (וַיִּירְאוּ הָעָם). What was the cause of this fear considering that they had crossed over the sea safely? The answer must be that they dreaded the diseases inflicted on the Egyptians at the sea, lest it affect them as well. Indeed the expression וְדָבְקוּ בָּךְ, *and cleave unto you,* is used in the verse cited above (*Deut.* 28:60).

25 *He removed the wheels of their chariots and caused them to drive with difficulty. Egypt said, "I shall flee before Israel, for HASHEM is waging war for them against Egypt."*

26 *HASHEM said to Moses, "Stretch out your hand over the sea, and the water will go back upon Egypt, upon its chariots and upon its horsemen."*
27 *Moses stretched out his hand over the sea, and toward morning the water went back to its power as the Egyptians were fleeing toward it; and HASHEM churned Egypt in the midst of the sea.*
28 *The water came back and covered the chariots and the horsemen of the entire army of Pharaoh, who were coming behind them in the sea — there remained not a one of them.*
29 *The Children of Israel went on dry land in the midst of the sea; the water was a wall for them, on their right and on their left.*

30 *On that day, HASHEM saved Israel from the hand of Egypt, and Israel saw the Egyptians dead on the seashore.*
31 *Israel saw the great hand that HASHEM inflicted upon Egypt; and the people revered HASHEM, and they had faith in HASHEM and in Moses, His servant.*

---

28. וַיָּשֻׁבוּ הַמַּיִם — *And the waters returned* . . . by the accretion of the waves to the place of division.

וַיְכַסּוּ אֶת הָרֶכֶב — *And covered the chariots* . . . after the people who were in them were shaken out.

וְאֶת הַפָּרָשִׁים — *And the horsemen* . . . the riders on the horses.

לְכֹל חֵיל פַּרְעֹה הַבָּאִים אַחֲרֵיהֶם — *And all the hosts of Pharaoh that came after them* . . . the multitude of the Egyptian chariots and their riders who followed the horsemen into battle.

29. וּבְנֵי יִשְׂרָאֵל הָלְכוּ בַיַּבָּשָׁה — *And the Children of Israel walked on dry land* . . . while the Egyptians were drowning in the sea, since the sea did not return to its strength on the side where the Israelites were.

30. וַיּוֹשַׁע ה׳ בַּיּוֹם הַהוּא אֶת יִשְׂרָאֵל — *And HASHEM saved Israel that day* . . . through the death of those who oppressed them by bondage. They now became free men, for until their death (i.e., of their masters) the Israelites were considered runaway slaves.

31. הַיָּד הַגְּדֹלָה אֲשֶׁר עָשָׂה ה׳ בְּמִצְרַיִם — *The great work* (lit., *hand*) *which HASHEM did upon the Egyptians.* (These are) מַדְוֵי מִצְרַיִם הָרָעִים, *the evil diseases of Egypt* (*Deut.* 7:15), with which they were smitten on the sea.

וַיִּירְאוּ הָעָם — *And the people feared.* As it says, אֲשֶׁר יָגֹרְתָּ מִפְּנֵיהֶם, *which you were in dread of* (*Deut.* 28:60).

NOTES

29. וּבְנֵי יִשְׂרָאֵל הָלְכוּ בַיַּבָּשָׁה — *And the Children of Israel walked on dry land.* The prefix ו of וּבְנֵי יִשְׂרָאֵל, *'and' the Children of Israel*, is a ו׳ הַדְדִית, *reciprocal vav*, i.e., at the same moment that the Egyptians were drowning, the children of Israel were walking on dry land.

30. וַיּוֹשַׁע ה׳ בַּיּוֹם הַהוּא אֶת יִשְׂרָאֵל — *And HASHEM saved Israel that day.* A runaway slave is still considered to be in the possession of his master. He cannot be considered 'saved' from him unless his master is no longer alive. The term וַיּוֹשַׁע, *He saved*, or יְשׁוּעָה, *salvation*, is not used until now, even though the Israelites had fled Egypt. The reason given by the *Sforno* is because only when they see *the Egyptians dead on the seashore* are they truly saved.

31. הַיָּד הַגְּדֹלָה אֲשֶׁר עָשָׂה ה׳ בְּמִצְרַיִם וַיִּירְאוּ הָעָם — *The great hand which HASHEM did upon the Egyptians, and the people feared.* See notes on verse 24.

טו

א אָז יָשִׁיר־מֹשֶׁה וּבְנֵי יִשְׂרָאֵל אֶת־הַשִּׁירָה הַזֹּאת לַיהוָה וַיֹּאמְרוּ
לֵאמֹר אָשִׁירָה לַיהוָה כִּי־גָאֹה גָּאָה סוּס
ב וְרֹכְבוֹ רָמָה בַיָּם: עָזִּי וְזִמְרָת יָהּ וַיְהִי־לִי
לִישׁוּעָה זֶה אֵלִי וְאַנְוֵהוּ אֱלֹהֵי
ג אָבִי וַאֲרֹמְמֶנְהוּ: יהוה אִישׁ מִלְחָמָה יהוה
ד שְׁמוֹ: מַרְכְּבֹת פַּרְעֹה וְחֵילוֹ יָרָה בַיָּם וּמִבְחַר
ה שָׁלִשָׁיו טֻבְּעוּ בְיַם־סוּף: תְּהֹמֹת יְכַסְיֻמוּ יָרְדוּ בִמְצוֹלֹת
ו כְּמוֹ־אָבֶן: יְמִינְךָ יהוה נֶאְדָּרִי בַּכֹּחַ יְמִינְךָ

XV

1. אָז יָשִׁיר מֹשֶׁה — *Then Moses sang.* He determined (lit., "agreed") to sing.

כִּי גָאֹה גָּאָה — *For being exalted is He exalted.* To Him alone is the exaltation, (for) to Him (we) attribute the good which exists, not to Pharaoh, הַתַּנִּים הַגָּדוֹל . . . אָמַר לִי יְאֹרִי וַאֲנִי עֲשִׂיתִנִי, *the great crocodile . . . who has said, "My river is my own and I have made it for myself"* (*Ezekiel* 29:3).

סוּס וְרֹכְבוֹ רָמָה בַיָּם — *The horse and his rider He threw into the sea . . .* Pharaoh's horse and his rider, as it says, וְנִעֵר פַּרְעֹה וְחֵילוֹ בְיַם סוּף, *He overthrew Pharaoh and his army in the Sea of Reeds* (*Psalms* 136:15).

2. עָזִּי וְזִמְרָת יָהּ — *The strength and (praiseful) song of God.* The strength and song of the Holy One, Blessed is He (is reflected in), *He threw into the sea,* i.e., the horse and its rider (Pharaoh), thereby demonstrating His strength, that He is the King over all kings. Therefore, it is fitting that He be praised by the rescued through the sound of song, rejoicing that they are servants of the eternal King.

וַיְהִי לִי לִישׁוּעָה — *And He has become my salvation.* He who threw the enemy into the sea is my salvation, as it says: וְנוֹדְעָה יַד ה׳ אֶת עֲבָדָיו וְזָעַם אֶת אֹיְבָיו, *And the hand of* HASHEM *shall be known to His servants and His indignation toward His enemies* (*Isaiah* 66:14).

זֶה אֵלִי — *This is my God.* His is to be the everlasting and First Cause Who perforce is the causal (force) and from Whom flows the continuing, ongoing existence of all which is impermanent and transitory (lit., "perishable").

וְאַנְוֵהוּ — *And I will build a dwelling for Him.* I will build a habitation (the Holy Temple) for Him to dwell therein, and there I shall pray to Him alone and serve Him as is proper to (He) Who bestows good or evil, as it says, וְיִתְפַּלֵּל אֵלָיו, וְיֹאמַר הַצִּילֵנִי, כִּי אֵלִי אָתָּה, *And*

NOTES

XV

1. כִּי גָאֹה גָּאָה סוּס וְרֹכְבוֹ רָמָה בַיָּם — *For being exalted He is exalted, the horse and his rider He threw into the sea.* The *Sforno* interprets the song of praise to God as first being in recognition of His triumph over Pharaoh the king; secondly, over the army and its captains; and finally, over the multitude of Egypt and their chariots. Therefore he interprets the phrase *the horse and his rider* as referring to Pharaoh. The reason it is necessary to stress this victory over Pharaoh is because he had boastfully claimed to be a deity who possessed great power and was the great king to whom even other kings were subservient. The downfall of Pharaoh and the great miracle of the dividing of the waters established the supremacy of HASHEM and refuted the absurd claims of the king of Egypt. As the *Sforno* explains in the next verse, through His strength manifested at the Sea of Reeds, God demonstrated that He, and He alone, is the King of kings.

2. זֶה אֵלִי . . . אֱלֹהֵי אָבִי — *This is my God . . . the God of my fathers.* Consistent with his commentary in *Genesis* 1:1, the *Sforno* interprets the name אֵל as signifying the Eternal, everlasting One Who grants existence to all things. This power has now been demonstrated by God and as such Moses calls

15 [1] *Then Moses and the Children of Israel chose to sing this song to HASHEM, and they said the following:*

I shall sing to HASHEM for He is exalted above the arrogant, having hurled horse with its rider into the sea.

[2] *The might and vengeance of God was salvation for me. This is my God and I will build Him a Sanctuary; the God of my father and I will exalt Him.*

[3] *HASHEM is Master of war — His name is HASHEM.*

[4] *Pharaoh's chariots and army He threw in the sea, and the pick of his officers were mired in the Sea of Reeds.*

[5] *Deep waters covered them; they descended in the depths like stone.*

[6] *Your right hand, HASHEM, is glorified with strength; Your right hand,*

---

prays to Him and says, deliver me for You are my God (Isaiah 44:17), for indeed the intent of (all) service and prayer is to find favor.

אֱלֹהֵי אָבִי — *The God of my fathers* ... the God of Jacob who proclaimed by saying, אֵל אֱלֹהֵי יִשְׂרָאֵל, *El Elohai Israel* (God, the God of Israel) (*Genesis* 33:20), that He is awesome in His greatness and providence, which are the attributes of mercy and justice.

וַאֲרֹמְמֶנְהוּ — *And I will elevate Him* ... by bowing down (to Him) and humbling (myself) and by proclaiming to all that the intended purpose (of mankind) is to do His will, which (represents) the most exemplary of all purposes, being that מְרוֹמַם עַל כָּל בְּרָכָה וּתְהִלָּה, *He is exalted above all blessing and praise (Nehemiah* 9:5), similar to לַמְּדֵנִי לַעֲשׂוֹת רְצוֹנֶךָ כִּי אַתָּה אֱלֹהָי, *Teach me to do Your will for You are my God (Psalms* 143:10).

3. ה׳ אִישׁ מִלְחָמָה ה׳ שְׁמוֹ — *HASHEM is a man of war; HASHEM is His Name.* Even though He is a *man of war,* decimating the wicked with the attribute of justice, nonetheless *HASHEM is His Name,* (indicating) the attribute of mercy, for by this (action) He grants being and existence to His world by *removing the thorns from the vineyard (Bava Metzia* 83b), since they (the wicked) destroy the world.

4. מַרְכְּבֹת פַּרְעֹה וְחֵילוֹ — *Pharaoh's chariots and his host.* After telling of the loss of the horse and its rider, i.e., Pharaoh and his horse, for which they gave thanks to God, the Blessed One, they now tell of His battle against the army of Pharaoh and his chosen captains, who were the principal elements of the entire army.

6. יְמִינְךָ ה׳ נֶאְדָּרִי בַּכֹּחַ — *Your right hand, HASHEM, is glorious in power* ... not the right (hand) of Pharaoh's host and choice captains who rely on the arm of flesh. This thanks is given to God, the Blessed One, for this second phase of battle.

NOTES

Him אֵלִי, *My God,* and states his readiness to worship Him alone. The Name of God (אֵל) denotes the attribute of mercy, while אֱלֹהִים represents the attribute of justice. Both Names are used by Moses (אֵלִי-אֱלֹהָי), therefore the *Sforno* interprets אָבִי, *my father,* as referring to Jacob since he also proclaimed God as both אֵל and אֱלֹהֵי, for he recognized God's attributes of mercy and justice, accepting both in perfect faith and love. Perhaps this is why Jacob is the symbol of אֱמֶת, *truth,* for this attribute represents חֶסֶד שֶׁבִּגְבוּרָה, *kindness in strength,* which combines mercy and justice.

3. ה׳ אִישׁ מִלְחָמָה ה׳ שְׁמוֹ — *HASHEM is a man of war; HASHEM is His Name.* The Name HASHEM (also) represents the attribute of mercy. To use this Name associated with war may seem incongruous. The *Sforno,* however, explains that it is for the benefit of mankind that the wicked are destroyed, just as the clearing away of weeds and thorns benefits the field and its productivity. Hence, although He is a *man of war,* His Name is HASHEM, the Merciful One.

6. יְמִינְךָ ה׳ נֶאְדָּרִי בַּכֹּחַ — *Your right hand, HASHEM, is glorious in power.* As mentioned above (verses 1 and 14:6,7), Pharaoh's downfall represents the first battle while the destruction of the army and its choice captains is called the second phase of battle by the *Sforno.*

ז יְהוָה תִּרְעַץ אוֹיֵב: וּבְרֹב גְּאוֹנְךָ תַּהֲרֹס
ח קָמֶיךָ תְּשַׁלַּח חֲרֹנְךָ יֹאכְלֵמוֹ כַּקַּשׁ: וּבְרוּחַ
אַפֶּיךָ נֶעֶרְמוּ מַיִם נִצְּבוּ כְמוֹ־נֵד
ט נֹזְלִים קָפְאוּ תְהֹמֹת בְּלֶב־יָם: אָמַר
אוֹיֵב אֶרְדֹּף אַשִּׂיג אֲחַלֵּק שָׁלָל תִּמְלָאֵמוֹ
י נַפְשִׁי אָרִיק חַרְבִּי תּוֹרִישֵׁמוֹ יָדִי: נָשַׁפְתָּ
בְרוּחֲךָ כִּסָּמוֹ יָם צָלְלוּ כַּעוֹפֶרֶת בְּמַיִם
יא אַדִּירִים: מִי־כָמֹכָה בָּאֵלִם יהוה מִי
כָּמֹכָה נֶאְדָּר בַּקֹּדֶשׁ נוֹרָא תְהִלֹּת עֹשֵׂה
יב־יג פֶלֶא: נָטִיתָ יְמִינְךָ תִּבְלָעֵמוֹ אָרֶץ: נָחִיתָ
בְחַסְדְּךָ עַם־זוּ גָּאָלְתָּ נֵהַלְתָּ בְעָזְּךָ אֶל־נְוֵה

יְמִינְךָ ה׳ תִּרְעַץ אוֹיֵב — *Your right hand,* H*ASHEM, dashes the enemy to pieces.* May it be Thy will that it shall be so in the future that You dash in pieces every enemy of Israel, similar to כֵּן יֹאבְדוּ כָל אוֹיְבֶיךָ ה׳, *So let all Your enemies perish,* H*ASHEM* (*Judges* 5:31).

8. וּבְרוּחַ אַפֶּיךָ נֶעֶרְמוּ מַיִם — *And with the blast of Your nostrils the waters were piled up.* Now they tell of the third battle engaged in by God, the Blessed One, against the multitude of Egypt. And he says: Behold with the blast of Your nostrils the waters were divided and the waters became a pile and heap.

קָפְאוּ תְהֹמֹת — *The deeps were congealed.* (This means) the ground of the sea (became solid) in a manner which (allowed) the Israelites to cross over.

9. אָמַר אוֹיֵב אֶרְדֹּף — *The enemy said, "I will chase . . .* after them into the sea."

אַשִּׂיג אֲחַלֵּק שָׁלָל — *I will overtake, I will divide the spoil.* These were the multitude, all the chariots of Egypt who only came to rob the money of the Israelites.

10. נָשַׁפְתָּ בְרוּחֲךָ — *You blew with Your wind.* The same wind which congealed the sea bed so that a path for the redeemed was created (now is) blown to cover over the pursuers and destroy them.

אַדִּירִים — *Mighty (ones).* (The) princes and leaders of the people sank as lead in the water, (and) among them were שָׁלִשִׁים עַל כֻּלּוֹ, *the captains over all of them* (14:7), whom Pharaoh had appointed over all the Egyptian chariots.

11. מִי כָמֹכָה בָּאֵלִם ה׳ — *Who is like unto You,* H*ASHEM?* He gave praise to God, the Blessed One, for this third battle against the multitude of Egyptian chariots, saying, "Who is like unto You among the mighty who can change the nature of that which is permanent (unchanging) in its nature?"

נֶאְדָּר בַּקֹּדֶשׁ — *Glorious in holiness.* Behold, the holy that is absolute is that which never

NOTES

יְמִינְךָ ה׳ תִּרְעַץ אוֹיֵב — *Your right hand,* H*ASHEM, dashes the enemy into pieces.* The *Sforno* interprets the phrase *Your right hand,* etc., as a prayer that God should always destroy the enemies of Israel. He interprets the phrase יֹאחֲזֵמוֹ רָעַד in verse 15, תִּפֹּל עֲלֵיהֶם and עַד יַעֲבֹר in verse 16, and ה׳ יִמְלֹךְ וכו׳ in verse 18 in a similar fashion, i.e., as a prayer for the future.

8. וּבְרוּחַ אַפֶּיךָ . . . — *And with the blast of Your nostrils . . .* See notes on verse 6.

10. אַדִּירִים — *Mighty (ones).* Unlike some commentators who interpret the word אַדִּירִים, *mighty,* as an adjective describing the noun *water,* the *Sforno* explains it to mean the mighty leaders who sank as lead in the waters.

11. מִי כָמֹכָה בָּאֵלִם ה׳ . . . נֶאְדָּר בַּקֹּדֶשׁ — *Who is like unto You,* H*ASHEM . . . glorious in holiness.* The *Sforno's* belief, similar to that of the *Rambam,* is that this world and everything in nature is everlasting and unchanging. Hence the dividing of the

HASHEM, smashes the enemy.
7 *In Your abundant grandeur You shatter Your opponents; You send forth Your wrath, it consumes them like straw.*
8 *At a blast from Your nostrils the waters were heaped up; straight as a wall stood the running water, the deep waters congealed in the heart of the sea.*
9 *The enemy declared, "I will pursue, I will overtake, I will divide plunder; I will satisfy my lust with them. I will unsheathe my sword, my hand will impoverish them."*
10 *You blew with Your wind — the sea enshrouded them; the mighty sank like lead in water.*
11 *Who is like You among the heavenly powers, HASHEM! Who is like You, mighty in holiness, too awesome for praise, Doer of wonders!*
12 *You stretched out Your right hand — the earth swallowed them.*
13 *With Your kindness You guided this people that You redeemed; You led with Your might to Your holy abode.*

---

withers (nor loses its essence) as our Sages say, "The righteous whom the Holy One, Blessed is He, will resurrect will not return to dust, as it is written, הַנִּשְׁאָר . . . בִּירוּשָׁלַיִם קָדוֹשׁ יֵאָמֶר לוֹ, *He that remains . . . in Jerusalem shall be called holy* (*Isaiah* 4:3), as the holy exists forever, etc." (*Sanhedrin* 92a). Now, he says, there is none like God, the Blessed One, recognized as the mighty (one) King over all holy and eternal forces, therefore for Him alone it is proper to change the nature of all the permanent (unchanging) existing elements, since the eternal aspect of all that is everlasting cannot be without Him, Blessed is He.

נוֹרָא תְהִלֹּת — *Fearful in praises.* And he who recognizes the greatness of His praises will fear Him for Himself, not because he fears any punishment coming from Him.

עֹשֵׂה פֶלֶא — *Doing wonders.* Doing (wonders) which are (acknowledged to) transcend natural phenomena, such as the pillar of cloud and pillar of fire.

13. נָחִיתָ בְחַסְדְּךָ עַם זוּ גָּאָלְתָּ — *In loving-kindness You led this people that You redeemed.* From the time You redeemed them, which was when You took them forth from the borders of Egypt and they came to Succos, You began to show them the way, as it says, וַיִּסְעוּ מִסֻּכֹּת . . . וַה׳ הֹלֵךְ לִפְנֵיהֶם, *And they traveled from Succos . . . and HASHEM went before them* (13:20,21).

נֵהַלְתָּ בְעָזְּךָ — *You guided them in Your strength.* You guided them *gently* (see *Genesis* 33:14) on the dry land in the midst of the sea, as it says, מוֹלִיכָם בַּתְּהֹמוֹת, כַּסּוּס בַּמִּדְבָּר לֹא יִכָּשֵׁלוּ, *He Who led them through the deep, like a horse in the wilderness, that they should not stumble* (*Isaiah* 63:13).

אֶל נְוֵה קָדְשֶׁךָ — *To Your holy habitation.* On a direct (lit., "correct") way to come *to Your holy habitation* there to sanctify them in Your service.

NOTES

waters represents a radical change in nature, which manifests the might of God, Who alone can execute such a phenomena in a בִּלְתִּי נִפְסָד, *permanent unchanging,* part of nature. God alone can do so for He is eternal, the ultimate in holiness, which represents the absolute in permanence and the everlasting, and He is the Creator, granting existence to all, hence He can do with His creation as He wills. (There are those Sages who feel that every change in nature was ordained from the beginning of Creation and as such the permanence of nature's character was never affected.)

13. נֵהַלְתָּ בְעָזְּךָ — *You guided them in Your strength.* The expression לְנַהֵל, *to lead,* is interpreted by the *Sforno* as meaning *to lead gently,* based upon *Genesis* 33:14 where Jacob says, אֶתְנַהֲלָה לְאִטִּי, *I will journey on gently.* Therefore in our verse the phrase נֵהַלְתָּ בְעָזְּךָ means *You guided them "gently" in Your strength.* Similarly, the *Sforno* interprets the phrase in *Genesis* 47:17, וַיְנַהֲלֵם בַּלֶּחֶם, as *he gently led them with bread,* i.e., Joseph gave them bread in small quantities as was proper in a time of famine.

יד קָדְשֶֽׁךָ:   שָׁמְעוּ עַמִּים יִרְגָּזֽוּן   חִיל

טו אָחַז יֹשְׁבֵי פְּלָֽשֶׁת: אָז נִבְהֲלוּ אַלּוּפֵי

אֱדֹום   אֵילֵי מוֹאָב יֹאחֲזֵמוֹ רָעַד   נָמֹגוּ

טז כֹּל יֹשְׁבֵי כְנָֽעַן: תִּפֹּל עֲלֵיהֶם אֵימָֽתָה

וָפַחַד   בִּגְדֹל זְרוֹעֲךָ יִדְּמוּ כָּאָֽבֶן   עַד־

יַעֲבֹר עַמְּךָ יהוה   עַד־יַעֲבֹר עַם־זוּ

יז קָנִֽיתָ:   תְּבִאֵמוֹ וְתִטָּעֵמוֹ בְּהַר נַחֲלָֽתְךָ   מָכֹון

לְשִׁבְתְּךָ פָּעַלְתָּ יהוה   מִקְּדָשׁ אֲדֹנָי כּוֹנֲנוּ

יח-יט יָדֶֽיךָ:   יהוה | יִמְלֹךְ לְעֹלָם וָעֶד: כִּי

בָא סוּס פַּרְעֹה בְּרִכְבּוֹ וּבְפָרָשָׁיו בַּיָּם   וַיָּשֶׁב יהוה עֲלֵהֶם אֶת־מֵי

הַיָּם   וּבְנֵי יִשְׂרָאֵל הָלְכוּ בַיַּבָּשָׁה בְּתֹוךְ הַיָּם:

כ וַתִּקַּח מִרְיָם הַנְּבִיאָה אֲחוֹת אַהֲרֹן אֶת־הַתֹּף בְּיָדָהּ וַתֵּצֶאןָ כָל־הַנָּשִׁים

כא אַחֲרֶיהָ בְּתֻפִּים וּבִמְחֹלֹת: וַתַּעַן לָהֶם מִרְיָם שִׁירוּ לַיהוה כִּי־גָאֹה גָּאָה

כב סוּס וְרֹכְבוֹ רָמָה בַיָּם: וַיַּסַּע מֹשֶׁה אֶת־יִשְׂרָאֵל מִיַּם־סוּף

וַיֵּצְאוּ אֶל־מִדְבַּר־שׁוּר וַיֵּלְכוּ שְׁלֹשֶׁת־יָמִים בַּמִּדְבָּר וְלֹא־מָצְאוּ מָיִם:

כג וַיָּבֹאוּ מָרָתָה וְלֹא יָכְלוּ לִשְׁתֹּת מַיִם מִמָּרָה כִּי מָרִים הֵם עַל־כֵּן

---

15. אָז נִבְהֲלוּ אַלּוּפֵי אֱדֹום אֵילֵי מוֹאָב — *Then the chiefs of Edom were frightened; (may trembling take hold of) the mighty men of Moab.* When they observed all these miracles, even though they knew that Israel would not wage war against them, nonetheless they were frightened by what they saw.

יֹאחֲזֵמוֹ רָעַד — *May trembling take hold of them.* May it be Your will that they be seized by trembling so that they not rise up against us.

נָמֹגוּ כֹּל יֹשְׁבֵי כְנָֽעַן — *All the inhabitants of Canaan melted away.* For indeed the inhabitants of Canaan, when they heard of all these (events), without a doubt (their resolve) melted, for they knew the (Israelites) would go up against them and drive them out (of the land), as it says, וַנִּשְׁמַע וַיִּמַּס לְבָבֵנוּ וְלֹא קָמָה עוֹד רוּחַ בְּאִישׁ מִפְּנֵיכֶם, *And we heard, and our hearts melted, nor did there remain any more courage in any man because of you* (Joshua 2:11).

16. תִּפֹּל עֲלֵיהֶם אֵימָֽתָה וָפַחַד בִּגְדֹל זְרוֹעֲךָ — *May terror and dread fall upon them by the greatness of Your arm.* May it be Your will that *terror and dread fall upon them* in a manner which will (cause) them to flee from our presence (motivated) by fear of Your arm, similar to, אָנוּסָה מִפְּנֵי יִשְׂרָאֵל כִּי ה׳ נִלְחָם לָהֶם, *Let us flee from before Israel, for HASHEM fights for them* (14:25).

עַד יַעֲבֹר עַמְּךָ ה׳ — *Till Your people pass over.* And also may it be Your will that they will not rise up against us, when we go up to do battle with them, until we have crossed over the rivers Arnon and Jordan, for to do battle at the river crossing is difficult and we will

---

NOTES

15. אָז נִבְהֲלוּ אַלּוּפֵי אֱדֹום אֵילֵי מוֹאָב — *Then the chiefs of Edom were frightened; (may trembling take hold of) the mighty men of Moab.* Israel was prohibited to wage war against Edom and Moab (see *Deut.* 2:5 and 9).

יֹאחֲזֵמוֹ רָעַד — *May trembling take hold of.* See notes to verse 6.

17. תְּבִאֵמוֹ וְתִטָּעֵמוֹ — *Bring them in and plant them.* *Bring them in and plant them* is interpreted by the *Sforno* as a prayer uttered by Moses that Israel become firmly planted in the land; similar to a tree or plant which takes root and cannot easily be uprooted, so may Israel not be exiled from its land. Although God Himself did not construct the Temple,

14 *Peoples heard — they were agitated; terror gripped the dwellers of Philistia.*
15 *Then the chieftains of Edom were confounded, trembling gripped the powers of Moab, all the dwellers of Canaan dissolved.*
16 *May fear and terror befall them, at the greatness of Your arm may they be still as stone; until Your people passes through,* HASHEM *— until this people You have acquired passes through.*
17 *You will bring them and implant them on the mount of Your heritage, the foundation of Your dwelling-place that You,* HASHEM, *have made — the Sanctuary, my Lord, that Your hands established.*
18 HASHEM *shall reign for all eternity!*
19 *When Pharaoh's cavalry came with his chariots and horsemen into the sea and* HASHEM *turned back the waters of the sea upon them, the Children of Israel walked on the dry land amid the sea.*
20 *Miriam the prophetess, the sister of Aaron, took her drum in her hand and all the women went forth after her with drums and with dances.*
21 *Miriam spoke up to them, "Sing to* HASHEM *for He is exalted above the arrogant, having hurled horse with its rider into the sea."*
22 *Moses caused Israel to journey from the Sea of Reeds and they went out to the Wilderness of Shur; they went for a three-day period in the Wilderness, but they did not find water.* 23 *They came to Marah, but they could not drink the waters of Marah because they were bitter; therefore*

---

need a great miracle, one we may not be worthy of (receiving).

17. תְּבִאֵמוֹ וְתִטָּעֵמוֹ — *Bring them in and plant them* . . . that they not be exiled therefrom.

בְּהַר נַחֲלָתְךָ — *In the mountain of Your inheritance* . . . the mountain of the Temple of which it is said, בְּהַר ה׳ יֵרָאֶה, *On the mountain where* HASHEM *is seen (Genesis* 22:14).

מָכוֹן לְשִׁבְתְּךָ פָּעַלְתָּ ה׳ — *The place which You have made to dwell in* . . . as it says, פֹּה אֵשֵׁב כִּי אִוִּתִיהָ, *here will I dwell for I have desired it (Psalms* 132:14).

מִקְּדָשׁ ה׳ כּוֹנְנוּ יָדֶיךָ — *The Sanctuary,* HASHEM, *which Your hands established* . . . as it says, וְעָשׂוּ לִי מִקְדָּשׁ . . . כְּכֹל אֲשֶׁר אֲנִי מַרְאֶה אוֹתְךָ, *Let them make Me a sanctuary . . . according to all that I show you* (25:8,9), and David (also) said, הַכֹּל בִּכְתָב, מִיַּד ה׳ עָלַי הִשְׂכִּיל, כֹּל מַלְאֲכוֹת הַתַּבְנִית, *All is in writing, by the hand of* HASHEM *Who instructed me, all the works of this plan (I Chronicles* 28:19).

18. ה׳ יִמְלֹךְ לְעֹלָם וָעֶד — HASHEM *shall reign forever and ever.* May it be (Heaven's) will that He alone shall reign forever and ever — וְאֵין עִמּוֹ אֵל נֵכָר, *and no strange god be with Him (Deut.* 32:12).

19. כִּי בָא סוּס פַּרְעֹה — *For the horses of Pharaoh went.* The אָז יָשִׁיר, *then sang,* etc., occurred *when Pharaoh's horses went in with his chariots and horsemen into the sea,* and God, the Blessed One, drowned them while the Children of Israel were still walking *on the dry land in the midst of the sea.* Before they came out they began to sing.

NOTES

still the expression *which Your hands established* is valid since the Almighty prepared the plans and instructed them how to build it. The words כּוֹנְנוּ, *established,* and תַּבְנִית, *plan,* are closely related.

19. כִּי בָא סוּס פַּרְעֹה — *For the horses of Pharaoh went.* This concluding verse of the Song is understood by the *Sforno* (as well as the *Ramban)* as setting the time frame of the song which Moses and the Children of Israel sang. When Pharaoh's horse and his chariots and horsemen came into the sea and were drowned there, at that same time the Israelites were walking on dry land (see 14:19), and it was then (before they went out) that they began to sing.

כד־כה קָרָא־שְׁמָהּ מָרָה: וַיִּלֹּנוּ הָעָם עַל־מֹשֶׁה לֵּאמֹר מַה־נִּשְׁתֶּה: וַיִּצְעַק אֶל־
יהוה וַיּוֹרֵהוּ יהוה עֵץ וַיַּשְׁלֵךְ אֶל־הַמַּיִם וַיִּמְתְּקוּ הַמָּיִם שָׁם שָׂם לוֹ חֹק
כו וּמִשְׁפָּט וְשָׁם נִסָּהוּ: וַיֹּאמֶר אִם־שָׁמוֹעַ תִּשְׁמַע לְקוֹל ׀ יהוה אֱלֹהֶיךָ וְהַיָּשָׁר
בְּעֵינָיו תַּעֲשֶׂה וְהַאֲזַנְתָּ לְמִצְוֹתָיו וְשָׁמַרְתָּ כָּל־חֻקָּיו כָּל־הַמַּחֲלָה אֲשֶׁר־
חמישי כז שַׂמְתִּי בְמִצְרַיִם לֹא־אָשִׂים עָלֶיךָ כִּי אֲנִי יהוה רֹפְאֶךָ: וַיָּבֹאוּ
אֵילִמָה וְשָׁם שְׁתֵּים עֶשְׂרֵה עֵינֹת מַיִם וְשִׁבְעִים תְּמָרִים וַיַּחֲנוּ־שָׁם עַל־
טז א הַמָּיִם: וַיִּסְעוּ מֵאֵילִם וַיָּבֹאוּ כָּל־עֲדַת בְּנֵי־יִשְׂרָאֵל אֶל־מִדְבַּר־סִין אֲשֶׁר
בֵּין־אֵילִם וּבֵין סִינָי בַּחֲמִשָּׁה עָשָׂר יוֹם לַחֹדֶשׁ הַשֵּׁנִי לְצֵאתָם מֵאֶרֶץ
וַיִּלּוֹנוּ ק׳ ב מִצְרָיִם: °וילינו כָּל־עֲדַת בְּנֵי־יִשְׂרָאֵל עַל־מֹשֶׁה וְעַל־אַהֲרֹן בַּמִּדְבָּר:
ג וַיֹּאמְרוּ אֲלֵהֶם בְּנֵי יִשְׂרָאֵל מִי־יִתֵּן מוּתֵנוּ בְיַד־יהוה בְּאֶרֶץ מִצְרַיִם
בְּשִׁבְתֵּנוּ עַל־סִיר הַבָּשָׂר בְּאָכְלֵנוּ לֶחֶם לָשֹׂבַע כִּי־הוֹצֵאתֶם אֹתָנוּ אֶל־
ד הַמִּדְבָּר הַזֶּה לְהָמִית אֶת־כָּל־הַקָּהָל הַזֶּה בָּרָעָב: וַיֹּאמֶר
יהוה אֶל־מֹשֶׁה הִנְנִי מַמְטִיר לָכֶם לֶחֶם מִן־הַשָּׁמָיִם וְיָצָא הָעָם
ה וְלָקְטוּ דְּבַר־יוֹם בְּיוֹמוֹ לְמַעַן אֲנַסֶּנּוּ הֲיֵלֵךְ בְּתוֹרָתִי אִם־לֹא: וְהָיָה

---

25. וְשָׁם נִסָּהוּ — *And there He tested them* . . . whether they would accept the statute and ordinance which He had set for them, and not revert to their deviation. This test was (given) for indeed He said to Israel . . .

26. אִם שָׁמוֹעַ תִּשְׁמַע לְקוֹל ה׳ אֱלֹהֶיךָ — *If you will listen to the voice of* H*ASHEM*, *your God* . . . to accept upon yourselves the statute which He set before you, and from now onward, *do that which is right in His eyes and give ear*, etc., only then shall you escape *the diseases of Egypt*. However, if now you accept, (but) later you will betray (your pledge), then He shall doubtless visit upon you thus and thus. This is similar to what our Sages say, "A proselyte who comes to convert (to Judaism) . . . is told, 'Be advised that until now if you ate forbidden fat you would not be punished with כָּרֵת, *extirpation;* if you violated the Sabbath you would not be punished with stoning. Now, however, if you eat forbidden fat you will be punished with כָּרֵת, etc.' " (*Yevamos* 47a).

כִּי אֲנִי ה׳ רֹפְאֶךָ — *For I am* H*ASHEM Who heals you.* The reason you will be punished if you accept, but later betray (your promise), is because all My commandments are meant to heal your soul from the illness of false and corrupt desires and ideas, so you shall become holy to your God, as it says, וָאַבְדִּל אֶתְכֶם מִן הָעַמִּים לִהְיוֹת לִי, *I have set you apart from the peoples, that you should be Mine* (*Leviticus* 20:26). But if you deal treacherously, you will become ill and profane your soul, and it is fitting that one who *profanes the holiness of* H*ASHEM which he loved* (based on *Malachi* 2:11) be punished.

27. וְשָׁם שְׁתֵּים עֶשְׂרֵה עֵינֹת מַיִם — *And there were twelve springs of water there.* And despite all this . . .

NOTES

26. אִם שָׁמוֹעַ תִּשְׁמַע לְקוֹל ה׳ אֱלֹהֶיךָ . . . כִּי אֲנִי ה׳ רֹפְאֶךָ — *If you will listen to the voice of* H*ASHEM*, *your God* . . . *for I am* H*ASHEM Who heals you.* The Jewish people, chosen by God and delivered from Egypt, have been granted God's special protection and providence. This status carries with it responsibilities on their part. Their acceptance to listen and obey was for all time. If they betray the trust placed in them by God they must suffer the consequences of their sins. Their punishment, however, will not necessarily be one imposed on them in a physical manner. Deviation from the commandments will result in an illness of the spirit and a debilitation of the soul. God, as a good doctor, urges them to guard their uniqueness and to recognize that they have been set apart from other nations for the purpose of serving God. By so doing they will guarantee their spiritual health and well-being. This is the sense of the

they named it Marah. [24] *The people complained against Moses, saying, "What shall we drink?"*

[25] *He cried out to HASHEM, and HASHEM showed him a tree; he threw it into the water and the water became sweet. There He established for [the nation] a decree and an ordinance, and there He tested it.* [26] *He said, "If you hearken diligently to the voice of HASHEM, your God, and do what is just in His eyes, give ear to His commandments and observe all His decrees, then any of the diseases that I placed upon Egypt, I will not bring upon you, for I am HASHEM, your Healer."*

[27] *They arrived at Elim, where there were twelve springs of water and seventy date-palms; they encamped there by the water.*

16 [1] *They journeyed from Elim, and the entire assembly of the Children of Israel arrived at the Wilderness of Sin, which is between Elim and Sinai, on the fifteenth day of the second month from their departure from the land of Egypt.* [2] *The entire assembly of the Children of Israel complained against Moses and Aaron in the Wilderness.* [3] *The Children of Israel said to them, "If only we had died by the hand of HASHEM in the land of Egypt, as we sat by the pot of meat, when we ate bread to satiety, for you have taken us out to this Wilderness to kill this entire congregation by famine."*

[4] *HASHEM said to Moses, "Behold! — I shall rain down for you food from heaven; let the people go out and pick each day's portion on its day, so that I can test them, whether they will follow My teaching or not.* [5] *And it shall*

XVI

1. וַיִּסְעוּ מֵאֵילִם . . . אֶל מִדְבַּר סִין — *And they journeyed from Elim . . . to the wilderness of Sin;* similar to, לֶכְתֵּךְ אַחֲרַי בַּמִּדְבָּר, *When you went after Me in the wilderness (Jeremiah* 2:2).

3. מִי יִתֵּן מוּתֵנוּ . . . בְּשִׁבְתֵּנוּ עַל סִיר הַבָּשָׂר — *Would that we had died . . . when we sat by the pot of flesh.* If God, the Blessed One, desired our death it would have been better for us (had He) slain us there (in Egypt) where we were satiated; similar to, טוֹבִים הָיוּ חַלְלֵי חֶרֶב מֵחַלְלֵי רָעָב, *those slain with the sword are better than those slain with hunger (Lamentations* 4:9).

4. מַמְטִיר לָכֶם לֶחֶם . . . לְמַעַן אֲנַסֶּנּוּ הֲיֵלֵךְ בְּתוֹרָתִי — *(I) will cause to rain bread . . . that I may test them, whether they will walk in My Torah.* When they will have food without toil (lit., "pain") as our Sages say, לֹא נִתְּנָה תּוֹרָה לִדְרוֹשׁ אֶלָּא לְאוֹכְלֵי הַמָּן, *The (power of) interpretation of Torah was granted only to those who eat the manna (Mechilta).*

NOTES

Sforno's commentary on this vital verse.

27. וְשָׁם שְׁתֵּים עֶשְׂרֵה עֵינֹת מַיִם — *And there were twelve springs of water there.* The *Sforno* links this verse to the following one (16:1), explaining that the Israelites demonstrated great faith and trust in the Almighty by leaving the springs of water in Elim and following Moses into the wilderness at God's behest. Jeremiah calls this an act of *chesed,* loving-kindness, demonstrated by Israel to their God.

XVI

3. מִי יִתֵּן מוּתֵנוּ . . . בְּשִׁבְתֵּנוּ עַל סִיר הַבָּשָׂר — *Would that we had died . . . when we sat by the pot of flesh.* If they are going to die regardless, then why complain to Moses and God for taking them out of Egypt? The *Sforno,* basing himself on the verse in *Lamentations,* explains that although one may be destined to die, there are different degrees of suffering connected with the manner of one's death. Hunger is far worse than execution, therefore they would have preferred death at the hands of the Egyptians to their slow starvation in the wilderness.

4. מַמְטִיר לָכֶם לֶחֶם — *I will cause to rain bread.* The word לֶחֶם usually means *bread.* In this instance, however, it is to be interpreted as *food,* which included both the manna and the flesh of the quails.

4. לְמַעַן אֲנַסֶּנּוּ הֲיֵלֵךְ בְּתוֹרָתִי — *That I may test them, whether they will walk in My Torah.* The test

בַּיּוֹם הַשִּׁשִּׁי וְהֵכִינוּ אֵת אֲשֶׁר־יָבִיאוּ וְהָיָה מִשְׁנֶה עַל אֲשֶׁר־יִלְקְטוּ יוֹם ׀
ו יוֹם: וַיֹּאמֶר מֹשֶׁה וְאַהֲרֹן אֶל־כָּל־בְּנֵי יִשְׂרָאֵל עֶרֶב וִידַעְתֶּם כִּי יהוה
ז הוֹצִיא אֶתְכֶם מֵאֶרֶץ מִצְרָיִם: וּבֹקֶר וּרְאִיתֶם אֶת־כְּבוֹד יהוה בְּשָׁמְעוֹ
ח אֶת־תְּלֻנֹּתֵיכֶם עַל־יהוה וְנַחְנוּ מָה כִּי °תלונו עָלֵינוּ: וַיֹּאמֶר מֹשֶׁה בְּתֵת °תַּלִּינוּ ק׳
יהוה לָכֶם בָּעֶרֶב בָּשָׂר לֶאֱכֹל וְלֶחֶם בַּבֹּקֶר לִשְׂבֹּעַ בִּשְׁמֹעַ יהוה אֶת־
תְּלֻנֹּתֵיכֶם אֲשֶׁר־אַתֶּם מַלִּינִם עָלָיו וְנַחְנוּ מָה לֹא־עָלֵינוּ תְלֻנֹּתֵיכֶם כִּי
ט עַל־יהוה: וַיֹּאמֶר מֹשֶׁה אֶל־אַהֲרֹן אֱמֹר אֶל־כָּל־עֲדַת בְּנֵי יִשְׂרָאֵל קִרְבוּ
י לִפְנֵי יהוה כִּי שָׁמַע אֵת תְּלֻנֹּתֵיכֶם: וַיְהִי כְּדַבֵּר אַהֲרֹן אֶל־כָּל־עֲדַת בְּנֵי־
יִשְׂרָאֵל וַיִּפְנוּ אֶל־הַמִּדְבָּר וְהִנֵּה כְּבוֹד יהוה נִרְאָה בֶּעָנָן:
ששי יא־יב וַיְדַבֵּר יהוה אֶל־מֹשֶׁה לֵּאמֹר: שָׁמַעְתִּי אֶת־תְּלוּנֹּת בְּנֵי יִשְׂרָאֵל דַּבֵּר
אֲלֵהֶם לֵאמֹר בֵּין הָעַרְבַּיִם תֹּאכְלוּ בָשָׂר וּבַבֹּקֶר תִּשְׂבְּעוּ־לָחֶם וִידַעְתֶּם

---

5. וְהֵכִינוּ אֵת אֲשֶׁר יָבִיאוּ וְהָיָה מִשְׁנֶה — *And they shall prepare that which they bring in, and it shall be twice as much.* After they have prepared it (i.e., cooked it) it will (still) be double, for it will not diminish with cooking. (The reason) it says *prepare* is to alert them that they should eagerly get ready the delight of Sabbath (by preparing) savory food and that all their alacrity in this area shall be from the eve of the Sabbath.

6. עֶרֶב וִידַעְתֶּם — *At evening, and you shall know.* May it be the will (of Heaven) that (God's) promise to me to give you food will be in such a manner that He will give you your evening requirements at evening time, so that you may know that God, the Blessed One, has delivered you *totally* from the land of Egypt (including) their customs (as well). There you sat at the pots of flesh without a set time for meals, like animals; as our Sages say, "At first, Israel was compared to chickens that peck (constantly) in the rubbish, until Moses came and set (specific) times for meals" (*Yoma* 75b).

7. וּבֹקֶר — *And in the morning.* You will have your morning food.

וּרְאִיתֶם אֶת כְּבוֹד ה׳ — *Then you shall see the glory of* HASHEM. And so may it be the will (of Heaven) that you shall see the glory of *HASHEM* when He comes to establish these times (for food) in order that you will know that your murmurings are directed toward Him, and therefore He will appear to remove them from Himself.

8. וַיֹּאמֶר מֹשֶׁה בְּתֵת ה׳ לָכֶם — *And Moses said, "When* HASHEM *shall give you."* Moses said,

NOTES

mentioned in this verse is to be understood as one which challenged them to spend their time, effort and energy in the toil of Torah, since their material needs were being met by the Almighty.

5. וְהֵכִינוּ אֵת אֲשֶׁר יָבִיאוּ וְהָיָה מִשְׁנֶה — *And they shall prepare that which they bring in, and it shall be twice as much.* The *Sforno's* interpretation explains the sequence of this verse. *After* they prepare the manna there shall remain the full measure gathered, which on Sabbath eve was double the normal amount. He also explains why the word וְהֵכִינוּ, *prepare*, is used instead of וּבִשְּׁלוּ, *cook*. This teaches us the importance and significance of preparing for the Sabbath, as our Sages stress in the Talmud (*Sabbath* 117b; *Kiddushin* 41a; *Beitzah* 16a).

6. עֶרֶב וִידַעְתֶּם — *At evening, and you shall know.* The *Sforno* teaches us a most interesting and basic *halachah* regulating man's consumption of food. Established, set times for the intake of food differentiates the human from animals and fowl. By so doing man emphasizes that there are many more important pursuits in life than eating, or satisfying one's physical hunger.

7. וּרְאִיתֶם אֶת כְּבוֹד ה׳ — *Then you shall see the glory of* HASHEM. The *Sforno* implies that if man is sensitive to the fact that his sustenance comes from God, then he merits to see *the glory of* HASHEM every time he sits down to his morning and evening meal. This may well be the source of the Torah *hashkafah* (perspective) which views the Jewish table as an altar and the consuming of food (if done

be that on the sixth day when they prepare what they bring, it will be double what they pick every day."

6 Moses and Aaron said to all the Children of Israel, "In the evening, you shall know that HASHEM took you out of the land of Egypt. 7 And in the morning you will see the glory of HASHEM, that He has heard your complaints against HASHEM — for what are we that you should incite complaints against us?" — 8 and Moses said, "When, in the evening, HASHEM gives you meat to eat and bread to satiety in the morning, as HASHEM hears your complaints that you complain against Him — for what are we? — not against us are your complaints, but against HASHEM!"

9 Moses said to Aaron, "Say to the entire assembly of the Children of Israel, 'Approach the presence of HASHEM, for He has heard your complaints.' " 10 When Aaron spoke to the entire assembly of the Children of Israel, they turned to the Wilderness and behold! — the glory of HASHEM appeared in a cloud.

11 HASHEM spoke to Moses, saying, 12 "I have heard the complaints of the Children of Israel. Speak to them, saying, 'In the afternoon you shall eat meat and in the morning you shall be sated with bread, and you shall know

---

"When we prayed that *HASHEM* give you food in the evening so that you may know that God, the Blessed One, took you forth (from Egypt), we intended that He give you *in the evening flesh to eat,* but not (to the degree of) satiation as is the custom of the Egyptians who have no other interest than (to satisfy) their physical (needs). And (our intent also was) that in the morning He give you bread, (but) only to satisfy (your hunger) sufficient to fill you."

בְּשְׁמֹעַ ה׳ אֶת תְּלֻנֹּתֵיכֶם — *That HASHEM hears your murmurings.* (Moses continued,) "And as for our prayer that you shall see the glory of HASHEM, our intention is that He grant you this (flesh and bread) in a manner that He show you that your murmurings are (directed) to Him, and that He has heard your murmurings."

9. אֱמֹר אֶל כָּל עֲדַת — *Say unto all the congregation . . .* once he knew that his prayer was accepted, similar to Rabbi Chanina when he would pray on behalf of the sick — or even more so.

קִרְבוּ לִפְנֵי ה׳ — *Come near before HASHEM . . .* Who went before them in the pillar of cloud.

10. וַיִּפְנוּ אֶל הַמִּדְבָּר — *And they turned toward the wilderness . . .* for the (pillar of) cloud was traveling in the direction of the wilderness as they journeyed.

NOTES

properly) as a form of עֲבוֹדָה, *service of Hashem.*

8. וַיֹּאמֶר מֹשֶׁה בְּתֵת ה׳ לָכֶם — *And Moses said, "When HASHEM shall give you."* The sense of the verse, according to the *Sforno,* is: Although we interceded with God on your behalf to obtain meat and bread, we want you to understand how we, as opposed to others, view these blessings from God. While the Egyptians live to eat, we eat to live. Hence, even when we eat bread it is only for the purpose of satisfying our hunger.

Bread is a necessity while meat is a luxury. Therefore the word used regarding bread is לִשְׂבֹּעַ, *to the full,* but regarding meat the Torah states לֶאֱכֹל, *to eat,* implying that it should be partaken of sparingly. *Rashi* makes the same comment, based on the Talmud *(Chullin* 84a).

9. אֱמֹר אֶל כָּל עֲדַת — *Say unto all the congregation.* Moses, as a prophet and *tzaddik,* could sense whether his prayer had been accepted by God. Only after sensing its acceptance would he say to the people, with surety, that God had heard their request. The *Sforno* draws a parallel to the incident related in the Talmud *(Berachos* 34b) where Rabbi Chanina could tell from the fluency of his prayer on behalf of a sick person — or the lack of it — whether the patient would recover or not.

יג כִּי אֲנִי יְהוָה אֱלֹהֵיכֶם: וַיְהִי בָעֶרֶב וַתַּעַל הַשְּׂלָו וַתְּכַס אֶת־הַמַּחֲנֶה
יד וּבַבֹּקֶר הָיְתָה שִׁכְבַת הַטַּל סָבִיב לַמַּחֲנֶה: וַתַּעַל שִׁכְבַת הַטָּל וְהִנֵּה
טו עַל־פְּנֵי הַמִּדְבָּר דַּק מְחֻסְפָּס דַּק כַּכְּפֹר עַל־הָאָרֶץ: וַיִּרְאוּ בְנֵי־יִשְׂרָאֵל
וַיֹּאמְרוּ אִישׁ אֶל־אָחִיו מָן הוּא כִּי לֹא יָדְעוּ מַה־הוּא וַיֹּאמֶר מֹשֶׁה
טז אֲלֵהֶם הוּא הַלֶּחֶם אֲשֶׁר נָתַן יְהוָה לָכֶם לְאָכְלָה: זֶה הַדָּבָר אֲשֶׁר צִוָּה
יְהוָה לִקְטוּ מִמֶּנּוּ אִישׁ לְפִי אָכְלוֹ עֹמֶר לַגֻּלְגֹּלֶת מִסְפַּר נַפְשֹׁתֵיכֶם אִישׁ
יז לַאֲשֶׁר בְּאָהֳלוֹ תִּקָּחוּ: וַיַּעֲשׂוּ־כֵן בְּנֵי יִשְׂרָאֵל וַיִּלְקְטוּ הַמַּרְבֶּה וְהַמַּמְעִיט:
יח וַיָּמֹדּוּ בָעֹמֶר וְלֹא הֶעְדִּיף הַמַּרְבֶּה וְהַמַּמְעִיט לֹא הֶחְסִיר אִישׁ לְפִי־
יט אָכְלוֹ לָקָטוּ: וַיֹּאמֶר מֹשֶׁה אֲלֵהֶם אִישׁ אַל־יוֹתֵר מִמֶּנּוּ עַד־בֹּקֶר:
כ וְלֹא־שָׁמְעוּ אֶל־מֹשֶׁה וַיּוֹתִרוּ אֲנָשִׁים מִמֶּנּוּ עַד־בֹּקֶר וַיָּרֻם תּוֹלָעִים
כא וַיִּבְאַשׁ וַיִּקְצֹף עֲלֵהֶם מֹשֶׁה: וַיִּלְקְטוּ אֹתוֹ בַּבֹּקֶר בַּבֹּקֶר אִישׁ כְּפִי אָכְלוֹ
כב וְחַם הַשֶּׁמֶשׁ וְנָמָס: וַיְהִי ׀ בַּיּוֹם הַשִּׁשִּׁי לָקְטוּ לֶחֶם מִשְׁנֶה שְׁנֵי הָעֹמֶר
כג לָאֶחָד וַיָּבֹאוּ כָּל־נְשִׂיאֵי הָעֵדָה וַיַּגִּידוּ לְמֹשֶׁה: וַיֹּאמֶר אֲלֵהֶם הוּא
אֲשֶׁר דִּבֶּר יְהוָה שַׁבָּתוֹן שַׁבַּת־קֹדֶשׁ לַיהוָה מָחָר אֵת אֲשֶׁר־תֹּאפוּ אֵפוּ
וְאֵת אֲשֶׁר־תְּבַשְּׁלוּ בַּשֵּׁלוּ וְאֵת כָּל־הָעֹדֵף הַנִּיחוּ לָכֶם לְמִשְׁמֶרֶת
כד עַד־הַבֹּקֶר: וַיַּנִּיחוּ אֹתוֹ עַד־הַבֹּקֶר כַּאֲשֶׁר צִוָּה מֹשֶׁה וְלֹא הִבְאִישׁ וְרִמָּה
כה לֹא־הָיְתָה בּוֹ: וַיֹּאמֶר מֹשֶׁה אִכְלֻהוּ הַיּוֹם כִּי־שַׁבָּת הַיּוֹם לַיהוָה הַיּוֹם

14. וְהִנֵּה עַל פְּנֵי הַמִּדְבָּר דַּק — *And behold upon the face of the wilderness a fine* . . . a thing (plant) whose berry was fine, as it says, כִּזְרַע גַּד הוּא, *like coriander seed* (*Numbers* 11:7).

דַּק כַּכְּפֹר — *Fine as the frost.* As it lay (on the ground), it was also fine, i.e., one berry did not lie on (another) berry.

16. זֶה הַדָּבָר אֲשֶׁר צִוָּה ה׳ — *This is the thing which* HASHEM *has commanded* . . . when He said, וּבַבֹּקֶר תִּשְׂבְּעוּ לָחֶם, *And in the morning you shall be filled with bread* (v. 12).

לִקְטוּ מִמֶּנּוּ — *Gather of it* . . . every one as he desires, be it much or little.

אִישׁ לְפִי אָכְלוֹ עֹמֶר לַגֻּלְגֹּלֶת מִסְפַּר נַפְשֹׁתֵיכֶם אִישׁ לַאֲשֶׁר בְּאָהֳלוֹ תִּקָּחוּ — *Every man according to his eating, an omer a head, according to the number of your persons, each man for them that are in his tent, shall you take.* Regardless of how much you gather, whether a lot or a little, it shall always be for each one *according to his eating,* i.e., satisfying him who is accustomed to eat a lot, and not too much for him who is accustomed to eat a little. Also, whatever is gathered, be it much or a small amount, it will be (exactly) *an omer a head,* not more or less. Also, he who gathers for all his household will (find) an *omer* for each one, according to the number of persons in his tent.

20. וַיִּקְצֹף עֲלֵהֶם מֹשֶׁה — *And Moses was angry with them.* For indeed this did not occur (i.e., the manna did not spoil) because it was more than they needed, but it was done (i.e.,

NOTES

14. דַּק . . . דַּק כַּכְּפֹר — *Fine . . . fine as the frost.* The *Sforno's* interpretation explains the repetition of the word דַּק, *fine.* One refers to the composition of the berry, the second to its positioning on the ground.

16. אִישׁ לְפִי אָכְלוֹ עֹמֶר לַגֻּלְגֹּלֶת מִסְפַּר נַפְשֹׁתֵיכֶם אִישׁ לַאֲשֶׁר בְּאָהֳלוֹ תִּקָּחוּ — *Every man according to his eating, an omer a head, according to the number of your persons, each man for them that are in his tent, shall you take.* The *Sforno* explains the three expressions used in this verse: לְפִי אָכְלוֹ, *according to his eating;* עֹמֶר לַגֻּלְגֹּלֶת, *an omer a head;* and מִסְפַּר נַפְשֹׁתֵיכֶם, *the number of your persons.* The amount of manna will be determined by the number of members in one's household; it will always be an exact amount per person and will satisfy everyone's hunger.

that I am HASHEM, your God.' "

13 *It was toward evening that the quail ascended and covered the camp, and in the morning there was a layer of dew around the camp.* 14 *The layer of dew ascended and behold! — upon the surface of the Wilderness was something thin, exposed — thin as frost on the earth.* 15 *The Children of Israel saw and said to one another, "It is food!" — for they did not know what it was. Moses said to them, "This is the food that HASHEM has given you for eating.* 16 *This is the thing that HASHEM has commanded, 'Gather from it, for every man according to what he eats — an omer per person — according to the number of your people, everyone according to whomever is in his tent shall you take.'"*

17 *The Children of Israel did so and they gathered, whoever took more and whoever took less.* 18 *They measured in an omer and whoever took more had nothing extra and whoever took less was not lacking; everyone according to what he eats had they gathered.*

19 *Moses said to them, "No man may leave over from it until morning."* 20 *But they did not obey Moses and people left over from it until morning and it became infested with worms and it stank; and Moses became angry with them.* 21 *They gathered it morning by morning, every man according to what he eats, and when the sun grew hot it melted.*

22 *It happened on the sixth day that they gathered a double portion of food, two omers for each; and all the princes of the assembly came and told Moses.* 23 *He said to them, "This is what HASHEM had spoken; tomorrow is a rest day, a holy Sabbath to HASHEM. Bake what you wish to bake and cook what you wish to cook; and whatever is left over, put away for yourselves as a safekeeping until the morning.* 24 *They put it away until morning, as Moses had commanded; it did not stink and there was no infestation in it.*

25 *Moses said, "Eat it today, for today is a Sabbath for HASHEM; today you*

---

some manna was kept overnight) intentionally, to test (God or Moses).

21. בַּבֹּקֶר בַּבֹּקֶר — *Morning by morning.* Every morning, similar to, כְּדַבְּרָהּ אֶל יוֹסֵף יוֹם יוֹם, *as she spoke to Joseph day by day* (*Genesis* 39:10), and בַּבֹּקֶר בַּבֹּקֶר בְּהֵיטִיבוֹ אֶת הַנֵּרֹת, *Morning by morning when he dresses the lamps* (30:7).

וְחַם הַשֶּׁמֶשׁ וְנָמָס — *As the sun waxed hot it melted.* Therefore, they would gather it in the morning, so it should not melt in the heat of the sun.

23. אֵת אֲשֶׁר תֹּאפוּ אֵפוּ — *Bake that which you will bake.* That portion which you wish to bake in the oven, as it says, וְעָשׂוּ אֹתוֹ עֻגוֹת, *and make cakes of it* (*Numbers* 11:8), bake it now, on the eve of the Sabbath.

וְאֵת אֲשֶׁר תְּבַשְּׁלוּ בַּשֵּׁלוּ — *And cook that which you will cook . . .* similar to, וּבִשְּׁלוּ בַּפָּרוּר, *and cooked it in pots* (ibid.); cook it now (on the eve of the Sabbath).

25. אִכְלֻהוּ הַיּוֹם — *Eat it today.* At set times of this day.

כִּי שַׁבָּת הַיּוֹם לַה׳ — *For today is a Sabbath to HASHEM.* This entire day is Sabbath to God, and you are permitted to eat the manna left over from yesterday, this entire day. However, it will not be permitted after the Sabbath.

NOTES

25. אִכְלֻהוּ הַיּוֹם כִּי שַׁבָּת הַיּוֹם לַה׳ הַיּוֹם לֹא תִמְצָאֻהוּ בַּשָּׂדֶה — *Eat it today, for today is a Sabbath to HASHEM; today you shall not find it in the field.* The word הַיּוֹם (*today*) is mentioned three times in this verse to teach us three things: (1) that although the entire amount of manna was in one's hands from the eve of the Sabbath it should not be consumed at once but apportioned for

כו לֹא תִמְצָאֻהוּ בַּשָּׂדֶה: שֵׁשֶׁת יָמִים תִּלְקְטֻהוּ וּבַיּוֹם הַשְּׁבִיעִי שַׁבָּת

כז לֹא יִהְיֶה־בּֽוֹ: וַיְהִי בַּיּוֹם הַשְּׁבִיעִי יָצְאוּ מִן־הָעָם לִלְקֹט וְלֹא

כח מָצָֽאוּ: וַיֹּאמֶר יהוה אֶל־מֹשֶׁה עַד־אָנָה מֵאַנְתֶּם לִשְׁמֹר

כט מִצְוֺתַי וְתוֹרֹתָֽי: רְאוּ כִּֽי־יהוה נָתַן לָכֶם הַשַּׁבָּת עַל־כֵּן הוּא נֹתֵן לָכֶם

בַּיּוֹם הַשִּׁשִּׁי לֶחֶם יוֹמָיִם שְׁבוּ | אִישׁ תַּחְתָּיו אַל־יֵצֵא אִישׁ מִמְּקֹמוֹ בַּיּוֹם

ל-לא הַשְּׁבִיעִֽי: וַיִּשְׁבְּתוּ הָעָם בַּיּוֹם הַשְּׁבִעִֽי: וַיִּקְרְאוּ בֵית־יִשְׂרָאֵל אֶת־שְׁמוֹ מָן

לב וְהוּא כְּזֶרַע גַּד לָבָן וְטַעְמוֹ כְּצַפִּיחִת בִּדְבָֽשׁ: וַיֹּאמֶר מֹשֶׁה זֶה הַדָּבָר

אֲשֶׁר צִוָּה יהוה מְלֹא הָעֹמֶר מִמֶּנּוּ לְמִשְׁמֶרֶת לְדֹרֹתֵיכֶם לְמַעַן | יִרְאוּ

אֶת־הַלֶּחֶם אֲשֶׁר הֶאֱכַלְתִּי אֶתְכֶם בַּמִּדְבָּר בְּהוֹצִיאִי אֶתְכֶם מֵאֶרֶץ

לג מִצְרָֽיִם: וַיֹּאמֶר מֹשֶׁה אֶֽל־אַהֲרֹן קַח צִנְצֶנֶת אַחַת וְתֶן־שָׁמָּה

לד מְלֹֽא־הָעֹמֶר מָן וְהַנַּח אֹתוֹ לִפְנֵי יהוה לְמִשְׁמֶרֶת לְדֹרֹתֵיכֶֽם: כַּאֲשֶׁר צִוָּה

לה יהוה אֶל־מֹשֶׁה וַיַּנִּיחֵהוּ אַהֲרֹן לִפְנֵי הָעֵדֻת לְמִשְׁמָֽרֶת: וּבְנֵי יִשְׂרָאֵל

אָכְלוּ אֶת־הַמָּן אַרְבָּעִים שָׁנָה עַד־בֹּאָם אֶל־אֶרֶץ נוֹשָׁבֶת אֶת־הַמָּן

לו אָֽכְלוּ עַד־בֹּאָם אֶל־קְצֵה אֶרֶץ כְּנָֽעַן: וְהָעֹמֶר עֲשִׂרִית הָאֵיפָה הֽוּא:

הַיּוֹם לֹא תִמְצָאֻהוּ בַּשָּׂדֶה — *Today you shall not find it in the field.* On every Sabbath day, as today, *you shall not find it.*

27. יָצְאוּ מִן הָעָם — *There went out some of the people . . .* from the camp to a distant place, thinking they would find the (manna) there, for they (lit., ''their spirits'') did not believe God.

לִלְקֹט — *To gather.* Now this would have without a doubt been in violation of Sabbath (laws) were they to gather anything from its place of growth, as our Sages state, ''He who tears the cuscuta from thorns and thistles is guilty of עוֹקֵר, *tearing loose, detaching*'' (*Shabbos* 107b).

28. עַד אָנָה מֵאַנְתֶּם לִשְׁמֹר — *How long will you refuse to keep?* Behold the sin of (not) keeping is all inclusive (i.e., you are *all* responsible), for even though you did not go with them to gather, you caused them to do so by not instructing them in the laws of Sabbath and its affairs. You only said, ''שֵׁשֶׁת יָמִים תִּלְקְטֻהוּ, *Six days you shall gather it*,'' (v. 26) and not seven. In this they disobeyed you. You said, ''וּבַיּוֹם הַשְּׁבִיעִי שַׁבָּת לֹא יִהְיֶה בּוֹ,'' *But on the seventh day is the Sabbath, in it there shall be none'* (ibid.), and they did not believe you. But you did not teach them My commandments, that included in (the list of prohibited) work is the gathering of the manna, (and) that he who does so is guilty of תוֹלֵשׁ, *plucking or tearing,* and (also) the law of) bringing (carrying) from domain to domain, which is also among the prohibited labors (of Sabbath).

וְתוֹרֹתָי — *And My laws . . .* the subject of Sabbath, its reasons and the reward and punishment (connected to it), for without a doubt all who know this will be careful to rest (properly) on the Sabbath.

NOTES

specific meals; (2) that the food prepared on the eve of the Sabbath can be used the entire day of the Sabbath but not the next day; (3) that this order is to be followed every week on the Sabbath.

27. לִלְקֹט — *To gather.* The plucking or picking of מְחוּבָּר, *that which is attached to its natural source,* is prohibited on the Sabbath. The manna on the ground was considered attached, and as such had they found it and taken it, they would have

transgressed the law of labor on the Sabbath, since removing it from its source would be considered עוֹקֵר, *detaching* or *uprooting,* or תוֹלֵשׁ, *plucking* or *tearing.*

28. עַד אָנָה מֵאַנְתֶּם לִשְׁמֹר . . . וְתוֹרֹתָי — *How long will you refuse to keep . . . and My laws.* The Almighty included Moses in this chastisement. He did so because He held him responsible for not properly instructing the Israelites regarding the

shall not find it in the field. [26] *Six days shall you gather it, but the seventh day is a Sabbath, on it there will be none."* [27] *It happened on the seventh day that some of the people went out to gather, and they did not find.*

[28] *HASHEM said to Moses, "How long will you refuse to observe My commandments and My teachings?* [29] *See that HASHEM has given you the Sabbath; that is why He gives you on the sixth day a two-day portion of bread. Let every man remain in his place; let no man leave his place on the seventh day."* [30] *The people rested on the seventh day.*

[31] *The House of Israel called it manna. It was like coriander seed, it was white, and it tasted like a cake fried in honey.* [32] *Moses said, "This is the thing that HASHEM has commanded: A full omer of it shall be a safekeeping for your generations, so that they will see the food with which I fed you in the Wilderness when I took you out of Egypt."* [33] *Moses said to Aaron, "Take one jar and put a full omer of manna into it; place it before HASHEM for a safekeeping for your generations."* [34] *As HASHEM had commanded Moses, Aaron placed it before the Ark of Testimony for a safekeeping.* [35] *The Children of Israel ate the manna for forty years, until their arrival in an inhabited land; they ate the manna until their arrival at the border of the land of Canaan.* [36] *The omer is a tenth of an ephah.*

---

29. רְאוּ — *See.* Consider.

כִּי ה׳ נָתַן לָכֶם הַשַּׁבָּת — *That HASHEM has given you the Sabbath.* And this is not only a commandment but a gift which was not given to any other (people) but you, as our Sages say, מַתָּנָה טוֹבָה יֵשׁ לִי בְּבֵית גְּנָזַי וְשַׁבָּת שְׁמָהּ, וַאֲנִי מְבַקֵּשׁ לִיתְּנָהּ לְיִשְׂרָאֵל, *(God said) "I have a good gift in My treasure house, its name is Sabbath, and I wish to give it to Israel" (Shabbos* 10b). Also in the order of our prayers, וְלֹא נְתַתּוֹ . . . לְגוֹיֵי הָאֲרָצוֹת . . . וְגַם בִּמְנוּחָתוֹ לֹא יִשְׁכְּנוּ עֲרֵלִים, *And You . . . did not give it to the nations of the earth . . . and in its tranquility the uncircumcised do not rest (Amidah* for *Shacharis),* as it says, וְשָׁמְרוּ בְנֵי יִשְׂרָאֵל אֶת הַשַּׁבָּת לַעֲשׂוֹת אֶת הַשַּׁבָּת לְדֹרֹתָם, *The Children of Israel shall keep Sabbath to observe Sabbath throughout their generations* (31:16), and (through this observance) they will acquire the יוֹם שֶׁכֻּלּוֹ שַׁבָּת, *day that is entirely Sabbath (Tamid* 33b).

35. אָכְלוּ אֶת הַמָּן — *They ate the manna . . .* in place of bread made of wheat or other (grain), as it says, בִּלְתִּי אֶל הַמָּן עֵינֵינוּ, *We have naught but this manna to look to (Numbers* 11:6).

עַד בֹּאָם אֶל אֶרֶץ נוֹשָׁבֶת — *Until they came to a land inhabited . . .* to the land of Sichon and Og where they also ate the bread of the land.

אֶת הַמָּן אָכְלוּ עַד בֹּאָם אֶל קְצֵה אֶרֶץ כְּנָעַן — *They ate the manna until they came to the borders of the land of Canaan.* Together with the bread of the land, they (also) ate the manna after coming to the land of Sichon and Og, until they crossed over the Jordan, as it says, וַיֹּאכְלוּ מֵעֲבוּר הָאָרֶץ מִמָּחֳרַת הַפֶּסַח . . . וַיִּשְׁבֹּת הַמָּן מִמָּחֳרָת, *And they ate of the corn of the land on the morrow of the Pesach . . . and the manna ceased on the morrow (Joshua* 5:11,12).

NOTES

halachos (laws) of the Sabbath and also for not stressing sufficiently the importance and significance of the Sabbath, the unique role it plays in the eyes of Heaven and the reward and punishment attached to it. Had he done so the Israelites would have treated it with greater care and respect. This idea is also continued in the next verse.

35. אָכְלוּ אֶת הַמָּן . . . אֶת הַמָּן אָכְלוּ עַד בֹּאָם אֶל קְצֵה אֶרֶץ כְּנָעַן — *They ate the manna . . . They ate the manna until they came to the borders of the land of Canaan.* The *Sforno's* interpretation of this verse reconciles a number of difficulties. Until when did they eat the manna and exactly when did they supplement it with other produce of the land? Also

יז שביעי א וַיִּסְעוּ כָּל־עֲדַת בְּנֵי־יִשְׂרָאֵל מִמִּדְבַּר־סִין לְמַסְעֵיהֶם עַל־פִּי יְהוָה וַיַּחֲנוּ
ב בִּרְפִידִים וְאֵין מַיִם לִשְׁתֹּת הָעָם׃ וַיָּרֶב הָעָם עִם־מֹשֶׁה וַיֹּאמְרוּ תְּנוּ־לָנוּ
מַיִם וְנִשְׁתֶּה וַיֹּאמֶר לָהֶם מֹשֶׁה מַה־תְּרִיבוּן עִמָּדִי מַה־תְּנַסּוּן אֶת־יְהוָה׃
ג וַיִּצְמָא שָׁם הָעָם לַמַּיִם וַיָּלֶן הָעָם עַל־מֹשֶׁה וַיֹּאמֶר לָמָּה זֶּה הֶעֱלִיתָנוּ
ד מִמִּצְרַיִם לְהָמִית אֹתִי וְאֶת־בָּנַי וְאֶת־מִקְנַי בַּצָּמָא׃ וַיִּצְעַק מֹשֶׁה אֶל־
ה יְהוָה לֵאמֹר מָה אֶעֱשֶׂה לָעָם הַזֶּה עוֹד מְעַט וּסְקָלֻנִי׃ וַיֹּאמֶר יְהוָה אֶל־
מֹשֶׁה עֲבֹר לִפְנֵי הָעָם וְקַח אִתְּךָ מִזִּקְנֵי יִשְׂרָאֵל וּמַטְּךָ אֲשֶׁר הִכִּיתָ בּוֹ
ו אֶת־הַיְאֹר קַח בְּיָדְךָ וְהָלָכְתָּ׃ הִנְנִי עֹמֵד לְפָנֶיךָ שָּׁם ׀ עַל־הַצּוּר בְּחֹרֵב
וְהִכִּיתָ בַצּוּר וְיָצְאוּ מִמֶּנּוּ מַיִם וְשָׁתָה הָעָם וַיַּעַשׂ כֵּן מֹשֶׁה לְעֵינֵי זִקְנֵי
ז יִשְׂרָאֵל׃ וַיִּקְרָא שֵׁם הַמָּקוֹם מַסָּה וּמְרִיבָה עַל־רִיב ׀ בְּנֵי יִשְׂרָאֵל וְעַל
נַסֹּתָם אֶת־יְהוָה לֵאמֹר הֲיֵשׁ יְהוָה בְּקִרְבֵּנוּ אִם־אָיִן׃
ח־ט וַיָּבֹא עֲמָלֵק וַיִּלָּחֶם עִם־יִשְׂרָאֵל בִּרְפִידִם׃ וַיֹּאמֶר מֹשֶׁה אֶל־יְהוֹשֻׁעַ בְּחַר־
לָנוּ אֲנָשִׁים וְצֵא הִלָּחֵם בַּעֲמָלֵק מָחָר אָנֹכִי נִצָּב עַל־רֹאשׁ הַגִּבְעָה וּמַטֵּה
י הָאֱלֹהִים בְּיָדִי׃ וַיַּעַשׂ יְהוֹשֻׁעַ כַּאֲשֶׁר אָמַר־לוֹ מֹשֶׁה לְהִלָּחֵם בַּעֲמָלֵק

XVII

1. לִשְׁתֹּת הָעָם — *For the people to drink.* For the people to drink, similar to לְשֶׁבֶת אַבְרָם, *that Abram had dwelled (Genesis 16:3).*

2. מַה תְּרִיבוּן עִמָּדִי — *Why do you strive with me?* You certainly know that I am but commanded (by God) and perform (His will).

מַה תְּנַסּוּן אֶת ה׳ — *Why do you test* HASHEM? And if your strife with me is for the purpose of testing Him Who sent me, why do you do so for your own evil, for this testing is fraught with great danger, for if He is angered He will show His deeds to destroy you, and this test will result in dire consequences for you, as He says, "בְּחָנוּנִי, גַּם רָאוּ פָעֳלִי, *They tested me, even though they saw My deeds" (Psalms 95:9),* that is, (bringing) misfortune upon them.

5. עֲבֹר לִפְנֵי הָעָם — *Pass before the people.* And their murmurings will cease when they will see how you are exerting yourself to supply their need.

וּמַטְּךָ אֲשֶׁר הִכִּיתָ בּוֹ אֶת הַיְאֹר — *And your rod with which you smote the river.* And with that smiting the Egyptians wearied themselves to (find water to) drink. Now it will have the opposite effect.

NOTES

the verse repeats the phrase אָכְלוּ, *they ate,* regarding the manna but changes the order — first אָכְלוּ אֶת הַמָּן, *they ate the manna,* then אֶת הַמָּן אָכְלוּ, *the manna they ate.* The *Sforno* explains that during their wandering in the wilderness they ate the manna exclusively. When they came to the territory of Sichon and Og they *also* ate of the bread of the land. This combined diet continued until they crossed the Jordan when the manna ceased and they began to eat exclusively the produce of *Eretz Yisrael,* once חָדָשׁ, *new grain,* was permitted after the sixteenth day of Nissan.

XVII

1. לִשְׁתֹּת הָעָם — *For the people to drink.* The expression לִשְׁתֹּת הָעָם if translated literally would mean, *to drink the people,* which of course cannot be the intent of this phrase. The *Sforno* therefore explains that it is to be translated *for the people to drink,* similar to the expression in *Genesis,* לְשֶׁבֶת אַבְרָם, which is not to be translated literally but *that Abram had dwelled.*

2. מַה תְּרִיבוּן עִמָּדִי — *Why do you strive with me?* The verse is divided into two parts thereby obviating the question of redundancy. The sense of the verse is: Why argue with me since I am but a messenger? And if you mean to challenge God, then I warn you that you are exposing yourselves to grave punishment.

5. עֲבֹר לִפְנֵי הָעָם — *Pass before the people.* The *Sforno* is explaining why God tells Moses to *pass*

17 *[1] The entire assembly of the Children of Israel journeyed from the Wilderness of Sin to their journeys, according to the word of HASHEM. They
encamped in Rephidim and there was no water for the people to drink. [2] The
people contended with Moses and they said, "Give us water that we may
drink!" Moses said to them, "Why do you contend with me? Why do you
test HASHEM?" [3] The people thirsted there for water, and the people complained against Moses, and it said, "Why is this that you have brought us
up from Egypt to kill me and my children and my livestock through thirst?"
[4] Moses cried out to HASHEM, saying, "What shall I do for this people? A
bit more and they will stone me!"
[5] HASHEM said to Moses, "Pass before the people and take with you some
of the elders of Israel; and in your hand take your staff with which you
struck the River, and go. [6] Behold! — I shall stand before you by the rock in
Horeb; you shall strike the rock and water will come forth from it and the
people will drink. Moses did so in the sight of the elders of Israel. [7] He called
the place Massah U'Meribah, because of the contention of the Children of
Israel and because of their test of HASHEM, saying, "Is HASHEM among us or
not?"
[8] Amalek came and battled Israel in Rephidim. [9] Moses said to Joshua,
"Choose people for us and go do battle with Amalek; tomorrow I will
stand on top of the hill with the staff of God in my hand. [10] Joshua did
as Moses said to him, to do battle with Amalek; and Moses, Aaron, and*

וְהָלַכְתָּ — *And go* . . . from the camp to the rock.

6. וְהִכִּיתָ בַצּוּר . . . וְשָׁתָה הָעָם — *And you shall smite the rock . . . that the people may drink.* Thus they will appreciate (lit., "recognize") that the functions of the rod are not part of its nature, for natural (actions) are always consistent. Rather, its actions are according to (God's) will, which can accomplish contrasting (opposite) actions.

8. וַיָּבֹא עֲמָלֵק — *Then Amalek came* . . . on hearing of their strife and thirst, as it says, וְאַתָּה עָיֵף וְיָגֵעַ, *When you were faint and weary* (*Deut.* 25:18), similar to לֹא מַיִם עָיֵף תַּשְׁקֶה, *You have not given water to the weary to drink* (*Job* 22:7), and בְּאֶרֶץ עֲיֵפָה, *in a weary land* (*Isaiah* 32:2).

9. וּמַטֵּה הָאֱלֹהִים בְּיָדִי — *With the rod of God in my hand* . . . to signal to the people the time of his prayer so that they could direct their hearts and join him in prayer (as well), similar to the Alexandrian (Jews) in Egypt, who would wave scarves (in the synagogue, as signals) (*Succah* 51b).

NOTES

before the people. What will he accomplish by doing so? The answer is that he will demonstrate his active concern and involvement on their behalf, and in this manner reassure them.

8. וַיָּבֹא עֲמָלֵק — *Then Amalek came.* The verses cited by the *Sforno* from *Job* and *Isaiah* are to prove that the expression *weary* denotes a lack of water, be it regarding people or land. Hence the reason given for Amalek's attack, *you were faint and weary,* indicates that there is a link between the opening episode of this chapter which relates Israel's contention regarding the lack of water, and the concluding event which relates the attack of Amalek.

9. וּמַטֵּה הָאֱלֹהִים בְּיָדִי — *With the rod of God in my hand.* Since the battle between Israel and Amalek was one waged in a normal natural manner, and not a miraculous one, what need was there for the rod of God? The *Sforno* explains that it was used as a signal to Israel, letting them know when Moses prayed so that they could join with him. He compares this to the great synagogue in Alexandria which was immense and the only way the people knew that the reader had reached a point which required their response was to have a scarf waved to the congregation as a signal.

יא וּמֹשֶׁה אַהֲרֹן וְחוּר עָלוּ רֹאשׁ הַגִּבְעָה: וְהָיָה כַּאֲשֶׁר יָרִים מֹשֶׁה יָדוֹ וְגָבַר
יב יִשְׂרָאֵל וְכַאֲשֶׁר יָנִיחַ יָדוֹ וְגָבַר עֲמָלֵק: וִידֵי מֹשֶׁה כְּבֵדִים וַיִּקְחוּ־אֶבֶן
וַיָּשִׂימוּ תַחְתָּיו וַיֵּשֶׁב עָלֶיהָ וְאַהֲרֹן וְחוּר תָּמְכוּ בְיָדָיו מִזֶּה אֶחָד וּמִזֶּה
יג אֶחָד וַיְהִי יָדָיו אֱמוּנָה עַד־בֹּא הַשָּׁמֶשׁ: וַיַּחֲלֹשׁ יְהוֹשֻׁעַ אֶת־עֲמָלֵק
וְאֶת־עַמּוֹ לְפִי־חָרֶב:

מפטיר
יד וַיֹּאמֶר יהוה אֶל־מֹשֶׁה כְּתֹב זֹאת זִכָּרוֹן בַּסֵּפֶר וְשִׂים בְּאָזְנֵי יְהוֹשֻׁעַ
טו כִּי־מָחֹה אֶמְחֶה אֶת־זֵכֶר עֲמָלֵק מִתַּחַת הַשָּׁמָיִם: וַיִּבֶן מֹשֶׁה מִזְבֵּחַ
טז וַיִּקְרָא שְׁמוֹ יהוה ׀ נִסִּי: וַיֹּאמֶר כִּי־יָד עַל־כֵּס יָהּ מִלְחָמָה לַיהוה בַּעֲמָלֵק
מִדֹּר דֹּר:

---

13. אֶת עֲמָלֵק וְאֶת עַמּוֹ — *Amalek and his people* ... who were gathered together from another people to do battle (alongside Amalek).

14. כְּתֹב זֹאת זִכָּרוֹן בַּסֵּפֶר — *Write this for a memorial in the Book.* The section of זָכוֹר, *Zachor (Deut.* 25:17-19).

וְשִׂים בְּאָזְנֵי יְהוֹשֻׁעַ — *And place it in the ears of Joshua.* And place a memorial in the ears of Joshua. And this Moses did by building the altar through his prayer at that time and by stating, כִּי יָד עַל כֵּס יָהּ, *The hand upon the throne of* Y*AH* (i.e., H*ASHEM*) (v. 16).

מָחֹה אֶמְחֶה אֶת זֵכֶר עֲמָלֵק — *I will utterly blot out the remembrance of Amalek.* I will destroy their livestock as well, as it says, וְהַחֲרַמְתֶּם אֶת כָּל אֲשֶׁר לוֹ . . . מִשּׁוֹר וְעַד שֶׂה וכו׳, *And utterly destroy all that they have ... ox and sheep ... (I Samuel* 15:3).

15. וַיִּקְרָא שְׁמוֹ — *And called His Name.* (He) called (in) the Name of the Holy One, Blessed is He, in his prayer, similar to קָרָאתִי שִׁמְךָ ה׳, *I called upon Your Name,* H*ASHEM* (*Lamentations* 3:54).

NOTES

13. אֶת עֲמָלֵק וְאֶת עַמּוֹ — *Amalek and his people.* The phrase *his people* indicates soldiers who were not part of the Amalekites. These were foreign mercenaries in Amalek's army.

14. כְּתֹב זֹאת זִכָּרוֹן בַּסֵּפֶר וְשִׂים בְּאָזְנֵי יְהוֹשֻׁעַ — *Write this for a memorial in the book and place it in the ears of Joshua.* The *Sforno* is of the opinion that the first and second section of this verse are to be understood as separate statements. *Write this for a memorial in the Book* refers to *Parashas Zachor* found in the Book of *Deuteronomy* (see Tractate *Megillah* 7a). The command to *place it in the ears*

Hur ascended to the top of the hill. 11 *It happened that when Moses raised his hand Israel was stronger, and when he lowered his hand Amalek was stronger.* 12 *Moses' hands grew heavy, so they took a stone and put it under him and he sat on it, and Aaron and Hur supported his hands, one on this side and one on that side, and he remained with his hands in faithful prayer until sunset.* 13 *Joshua weakened Amalek and its people with the sword's blade.*

14 *HASHEM said to Moses, "Write this as a remembrance in the Book and recite it in the ears of Joshua, that I shall surely erase the memory of Amalek from under the heavens."* 15 *Moses built an altar and called its name "HASHEM is My Miracle";* 16 *and he said, "For the hand is on the throne of God: HASHEM maintains a war against Amalek, from generation to generation."*

ה׳ נִסִּי — *HASHEM Nissi. HASHEM* is my exalted (banner), similar to, נָתַתָּה לִּירֵאֶיךָ נֵּס לְהִתְנוֹסֵס, *You have given a banner to raise high, to those who fear You (Psalms* 60:6); i.e., God will raise me up and elevate me over those who rise up (against us), similar to, בְּשִׁמְךָ נָבוּס קָמֵינוּ, *through Your Name we will tread upon those who rise up against us* (ibid. 44:6), and וּבִשְׁמִי תָּרוּם קַרְנוֹ, *And in My Name shall his horn be exalted* (ibid. 89:25).

16. וַיֹּאמֶר כִּי יָד עַל כֵּס יָהּ — *And he said, "The hand upon the throne of YAH* (i.e., HASHEM)." (Moses) said: "The reason for this prayer of mine is because God, the Blessed One, has sworn that He will wage *war with Amalek from generation to generation,* therefore we are obligated to fight this battle in every generation." (This is) as our Sages say, "Israel was given three commandments when they entered the land: to appoint a king; to destroy the seed of Amalek; and to build the Holy Temple" *(Sanhedrin* 20b). Therefore I pray that He shall be my banner and raise me up over the enemy.

NOTES

of Joshua refers to the deeds and words of Moses at this time, i.e., the building of the altar and his prayer.

15. וַיִּקְרָא שְׁמוֹ ה׳ נִסִּי — *And called His Name HASHEM Nissi. Tosafos* in *Megillah* 18a is of the opinion that the verse means, *And he called the altar, HASHEM-is-my-banner.*

16. כִּי יָד עַל כֵּס יָהּ — *The hand upon the throne of YAH* (i.e., HASHEM). Israel was given the mission to wage war against Amalek and destroy them. God took an oath at this moment in history to wipe out Amalek *through* the Jewish people. Hence it is our obligation, but we can only succeed with the help of the Almighty. Therefore Moses asked that *HASHEM* be our banner, raising us on high over Amalek.

פרשת יתרו

יח א וַיִּשְׁמַע יִתְרוֹ כֹהֵן מִדְיָן חֹתֵן מֹשֶׁה אֵת כָּל־אֲשֶׁר עָשָׂה אֱלֹהִים לְמֹשֶׁה
ב וּלְיִשְׂרָאֵל עַמּוֹ כִּי־הוֹצִיא יהוה אֶת־יִשְׂרָאֵל מִמִּצְרָיִם: וַיִּקַּח יִתְרוֹ חֹתֵן
ג מֹשֶׁה אֶת־צִפֹּרָה אֵשֶׁת מֹשֶׁה אַחַר שִׁלּוּחֶיהָ: וְאֵת שְׁנֵי בָנֶיהָ אֲשֶׁר שֵׁם
ד הָאֶחָד גֵּרְשֹׁם כִּי אָמַר גֵּר הָיִיתִי בְּאֶרֶץ נָכְרִיָּה: וְשֵׁם הָאֶחָד אֱלִיעֶזֶר
ה כִּי־אֱלֹהֵי אָבִי בְּעֶזְרִי וַיַּצִּלֵנִי מֵחֶרֶב פַּרְעֹה: וַיָּבֹא יִתְרוֹ חֹתֵן מֹשֶׁה
וּבָנָיו וְאִשְׁתּוֹ אֶל־מֹשֶׁה אֶל־הַמִּדְבָּר אֲשֶׁר־הוּא חֹנֶה שָׁם הַר הָאֱלֹהִים:
ו וַיֹּאמֶר אֶל־מֹשֶׁה אֲנִי חֹתֶנְךָ יִתְרוֹ בָּא אֵלֶיךָ וְאִשְׁתְּךָ וּשְׁנֵי בָנֶיהָ עִמָּהּ:
ז וַיֵּצֵא מֹשֶׁה לִקְרַאת חֹתְנוֹ וַיִּשְׁתַּחוּ וַיִּשַּׁק־לוֹ וַיִּשְׁאֲלוּ אִישׁ־לְרֵעֵהוּ
ח לְשָׁלוֹם וַיָּבֹאוּ הָאֹהֱלָה: וַיְסַפֵּר מֹשֶׁה לְחֹתְנוֹ אֵת כָּל־אֲשֶׁר עָשָׂה יהוה

XVIII

1. וַיִּשְׁמַע יִתְרוֹ — *And Jethro heard.* The expression שְׁמִיעָה, *hearing,* is used regarding an event which is not occurring at the time that event is being related. If we are told of a current event then the expression רְאִיָּה, *seeing,* is used, be it far (away) or nearby, as we find, וַיַּרְא יַעֲקֹב כִּי יֶשׁ שֶׁבֶר בְּמִצְרָיִם, *Now Jacob saw that there was corn in Egypt* (*Genesis* 42:1), (or) וַיַּרְא בָּלָק, *And Balak saw* (*Numbers* 22:2), (or) וְרָאוּ כָּל עַמֵּי הָאָרֶץ, *And all the people of the earth shall see* (*Deut.* 28:10). Now, since the exodus of Israel from Egypt was then a current event, our Sages therefore say, "What did (Jethro) hear? The dividing of the waters of the Sea of Reeds and the war with Amalek" (*Zevachim* 116a), for these two events had already transpired. However, if we interpret כִּי הוֹצִיא ה׳ אֶת יִשְׂרָאֵל, (which literally means) *that HASHEM had brought Israel out*, as meaning כַּאֲשֶׁר הוֹצִיא, "*when*" *He brought them out*, then we may say that (Jethro) heard all that God, the Blessed One, had done when He took Israel out of Egypt, namely, the great plagues, signs and wonders, etc. Therefore he was moved to go himself to the wilderness and he did not send Moses' wife and children to him through an emissary, similar to the king of Babylonia who sent ambassadors to inquire of the wonder which was done in the land (*II Chronicles* 32:31), for he (himself) desired to seek out God.

2. אַחַר שִׁלּוּחֶיהָ — *After he had sent her* . . . after he (Jethro) had sent her to ascertain the place of his (Moses') encampment, and he was informed that they would not encamp until they reached *the Mount of God* where they would serve Him, as stated, תַּעַבְדוּן אֶת הָאֱלֹהִים עַל הָהָר הַזֶּה, *You shall serve God upon this mountain* (3:12). Therefore Jethro delayed his arrival until Moses and his people would be there.

NOTES

XVIII

1. וַיִּשְׁמַע יִתְרוֹ — *And Jethro heard.* (a) To reconcile the difficulty presented by the expression וַיִּשְׁמַע, *and he heard,* which is used in the Torah only regarding something which has already happened, our Sages explain that it refers to two events which had already transpired, namely the dividing of the waters and Amalek's attack. The *Sforno,* however, chooses to explain the verse differently by interpreting the phrase כִּי הוֹצִיא, which indicates the ongoing journey of the Israelites, as כַּאֲשֶׁר הוֹצִיא, *when He brought out*, indicating the past events which occurred at the time of Israel's deliverance.

(b) The *Sforno* also makes a second point regarding the difference between Jethro and the response of the Babylonian king at the time of Chizkiyahu the king of Judah. When Sennacherib, the king of Assyria, beleaguered Jerusalem only to have God smite Sennacherib's army, the king of Babylonia sent emissaries to inquire regarding this great wonder. He did not, however, come personally. Jethro, on the other hand, came himself, for he was not motivated by curiosity or by a wish to congratulate his son-in-law, but by a sincere desire to seek out God and convert to the Jewish faith.

2. אַחַר שִׁלּוּחֶיהָ — *After he had sent her.* Unlike other commentators who interpret the phrase

PARASHAS YISRO

18 [1] Jethro, the minister of Midian, the father-in-law of Moses, heard everything that God did to Moses and to Israel, His people — that HASHEM had taken Israel out of Egypt. [2] Jethro, the father-in-law of Moses, took Zipporah, the wife of Moses, after she had been sent away; [3] and her two sons: of whom the name of one was Gershom, for he had said, "I was a sojourner in a strange land"; [4] and the name of the other was Eliezer, for "the God of my father came to my aid, and He saved me from the sword of Pharaoh."

[5] Jethro, the father-in-law of Moses, came to Moses with his sons and wife, to the Wilderness where he was encamped, by the Mountain of God. [6] He said to Moses, "I, your father-in-law Jethro, have come to you, with your wife and her two sons with her."

[7] Moses went out to meet his father-in-law, and he prostrated himself and kissed him, and each inquired about the other's well-being; then they came to the tent. [8] Moses told his father-in-law everything that HASHEM had done

---

4. וַיַּצִּלֵנִי מֵחֶרֶב פַּרְעֹה — *And delivered me from the sword of Pharaoh . . .* at the time of Eliezer's birth the king of Egypt, who was pursuing Moses, had died, as it says, וַיְהִי בַיָּמִים הָרַבִּים הָהֵם וַיָּמָת מֶלֶךְ מִצְרַיִם, *And it came to pass in the course of those many days that the king of Egypt died* (2:23), hence he was (now) confident that he had been saved from Pharaoh's sword, for until his (i.e., Pharaoh's) death Moses could not feel safe from his sword wherever he might be found by Pharaoh, similar to, אִם יֶשׁ גּוֹי וּמַמְלָכָה אֲשֶׁר לֹא שָׁלַח אֲדֹנִי שָׁם . . . וְהִשְׁבִּיעַ אֶת הַמַּמְלָכָה וְאֶת הַגּוֹי, *there is no nation or kingdom where my lord has not sent to seek you . . . and he made the kingdom and nation swear (I Kings* 18:10).

6. אֲנִי חֹתֶנְךָ יִתְרוֹ — *I, your father-in-law Jethro.* He announced his coming beforehand as an ethical act so that (Moses) could prepare a place for them to dwell, as our Sages say, אַל תִּכָּנֵס לְבֵיתְךָ פִּתְאוֹם, כָּל שֶׁכֵּן לְבֵית חֲבֵרְךָ, *Do not enter your home suddenly (unannounced), how much more so the home of your friend (Pesachim* 112a).

7. וַיֵּצֵא מֹשֶׁה — *And Moses went out.* He did not refrain, because of his high position, to go out to meet the one who had helped him (lit., "done him a favor") in his time of distress, similar to, וְאֶת מַאֲמַר מָרְדֳּכַי אֶסְתֵּר עֹשָׂה, *For Esther carried out the bidding of Mordecai (Esther* 2:20), and also the (behavior) of Joseph with his brothers when he was a ruler. The reverse (i.e., ingratitude) is (also) found: וְלֹא זָכַר שַׂר הַמַּשְׁקִים אֶת יוֹסֵף, *And the wine steward did not remember Joseph (Genesis* 40:23).

8. אֵת כָּל אֲשֶׁר עָשָׂה ה׳ לְפַרְעֹה וּלְמִצְרַיִם עַל אוֹדֹת יִשְׂרָאֵל — *All that HASHEM had done to Pharaoh and to the Egyptians for Israel's sake . . .* as one who renders vengeance to the

NOTES

שִׁלּוּחֶיהָ as meaning the *sending away* of Zipporah by Moses, the *Sforno* explains it to mean the sending of Zipporah by her father to ascertain the plans of Moses and the Israelites so that he would be able to determine the most appropriate time and place for his visit.

4. וַיַּצִּלֵנִי מֵחֶרֶב פַּרְעֹה — *And delivered me from the sword of Pharaoh.* Eliezer is the second son born to Moses and Zipporah. The question is obvious. Why did Moses delay giving thanks to God for delivering him from the sword of Pharaoh and not give this name to his firstborn? The *Sforno's* answer is that not until the death of Pharaoh could Moses feel safe *from the sword of Pharaoh,* for when his first son was born Pharaoh was still alive.

7. וַיֵּצֵא מֹשֶׁה — *And Moses went out.* Moses, Esther and Joseph are all considered as royalty. None of them, however, stood on ceremony when the time came to welcome, greet or comply with the wishes of those who had either dealt kindly with them or whose relationship with them demanded respect and regard.

8. אֵת כָּל אֲשֶׁר עָשָׂה ה׳ לְפַרְעֹה וּלְמִצְרַיִם עַל אוֹדֹת יִשְׂרָאֵל — *All that HASHEM had done to Pharaoh and*

לְפַרְעֹה וּלְמִצְרַיִם עַל אוֹדֹת יִשְׂרָאֵל אֵת כָּל־הַתְּלָאָה אֲשֶׁר מְצָאָתַם
ט בַּדֶּרֶךְ וַיַּצִּלֵם יהוה: וַיִּחַדְּ יִתְרוֹ עַל כָּל־הַטּוֹבָה אֲשֶׁר־עָשָׂה יהוה לְיִשְׂרָאֵל
י אֲשֶׁר הִצִּילוֹ מִיַּד מִצְרָיִם: וַיֹּאמֶר יִתְרוֹ בָּרוּךְ יהוה אֲשֶׁר הִצִּיל אֶתְכֶם
מִיַּד מִצְרַיִם וּמִיַּד פַּרְעֹה אֲשֶׁר הִצִּיל אֶת־הָעָם מִתַּחַת יַד־מִצְרָיִם:
יא עַתָּה יָדַעְתִּי כִּי־גָדוֹל יהוה מִכָּל־הָאֱלֹהִים כִּי בַדָּבָר אֲשֶׁר זָדוּ עֲלֵיהֶם:
יב וַיִּקַּח יִתְרוֹ חֹתֵן מֹשֶׁה עֹלָה וּזְבָחִים לֵאלֹהִים וַיָּבֹא אַהֲרֹן וְכֹל ׀ זִקְנֵי
שני יג יִשְׂרָאֵל לֶאֱכָל־לֶחֶם עִם־חֹתֵן מֹשֶׁה לִפְנֵי הָאֱלֹהִים: וַיְהִי מִמָּחֳרָת וַיֵּשֶׁב
מֹשֶׁה לִשְׁפֹּט אֶת־הָעָם וַיַּעֲמֹד הָעָם עַל־מֹשֶׁה מִן־הַבֹּקֶר עַד־הָעָרֶב:

adversaries of his people, similar to, אָשִׁיב נָקָם לְצָרָי, *I will render vengeance to My adversaries* (*Deut.* 32:41). This was done by smiting their bodies at the sea as it says, יְשַׁלַּח בָּם חֲרוֹן אַפּוֹ עֶבְרָה וָזַעַם וְצָרָה מִשְׁלַחַת מַלְאֲכֵי רָעִים, *He cast upon them the fierceness of His anger, wrath and indignation and trouble, a delegation of evil messengers* (*Psalms* 78:49); He thereby demonstrated that He had chosen Israel as His treasure from among all the nations.

אֵת כָּל הַתְּלָאָה אֲשֶׁר מְצָאָתַם בַּדֶּרֶךְ — *All the travail that had come upon them by the way* . . . through hunger, thirst and the war against Amalek.

וַיַּצִּלֵם ה׳ — *And how* HASHEM *saved them.* Thereby He displayed His special Providence toward them. The cause of this perforce being their beliefs and deeds (which were) predisposed to serve Him with one accord.

9. וַיִּחַדְּ יִתְרוֹ עַל כָּל הַטּוֹבָה — *And Jethro rejoiced for all the goodness.* He did not rejoice over the destruction of Egypt, as would befit one who is zealous for the honor of His maker, similar to, יִשְׂמַח צַדִּיק כִּי חָזָה נָקָם, *The righteous shall rejoice when he sees vengeance* (*Psalms* 58:11). He rejoiced for the good that befell Israel as would one who feels compassion for the tears of the oppressed.

10. אֲשֶׁר הִצִּיל אֶתְכֶם — *Who delivered you* . . . Moses and Aaron.

מִיַּד מִצְרַיִם — *Out of the hand of the Egyptians* . . . when you did smite them.

וּמִיַּד פַּרְעֹה — *And out of the hand of Pharaoh* . . . when you came to warn him.

אֲשֶׁר הִצִּיל אֶת הָעָם — *Who had delivered the people* . . . who were in servitude.

11. כִּי בַדָּבָר אֲשֶׁר זָדוּ עֲלֵיהֶם — *For that they dealt presumptuously against them.* For He delivered the people by the same means that the Egyptians had planned against Israel, similar to, וְכִי יָזִד אִישׁ עַל רֵעֵהוּ, *And if a man comes presumptuously* (יָזִד) *upon his neighbor*

NOTES

to the Egyptians for Israel's sake. Moses stressed in his report to his father-in-law that God's actions were not only motivated by His abhorrence of Egypt's wickedness toward, and enslavement of, Israel in general, but also because of Israel's special status and God's love for them. What was done was *for Israel's sake*, not just to punish evil but to avenge the honor of His chosen children. Israel in turn was worthy of this special concern because they sincerely accepted God's sovereignty.

9. וַיִּחַדְּ יִתְרוֹ עַל כָּל הַטּוֹבָה — *And Jethro rejoiced for all the goodness.* Although the *Sforno* does not mention the comment of our Sages in *Sanhedrin* 94a (quoted here by *Rashi*) that Jethro felt pain for the punishment of his Egyptian brethren (hinted at in the choice of the word וַיִּחַדְּ), nonetheless it is inferred in his interpretation as well.

10. אֲשֶׁר הִצִּיל אֶתְכֶם מִיַּד מִצְרַיִם וּמִיַּד פַּרְעֹה אֲשֶׁר הִצִּיל אֶת הָעָם — *Who delivered you out of the hand of the Egyptians and out of the hand of Pharaoh, Who had delivered the people.* The *Sforno* interprets each part of this verse as applying to different subjects. Moses and Aaron had to confront Pharaoh and needed special Divine protection to enter and leave the palace unharmed. They also could have been held responsible by the people for their plight and attacked by them in their anger and anguish. The concluding section of the verse is

to Pharaoh and Egypt for Israel's sake — all the travail that had befallen them on the way — and that HASHEM had rescued them.

9 *Jethro rejoiced over all the good that HASHEM had done for Israel, that He had rescued it from Egypt.* 10 *Jethro said, "Blessed is HASHEM, Who has rescued you from the hand of Egypt and from the hand of Pharaoh, Who has rescued the people from under the hand of Egypt.* 11 *Now I know that HASHEM is the greatest of all the gods, for in the very matter in which [the Egyptians] had conspired against them . . . !"* 12 *Jethro, the father-in-law of Moses, took an elevation-offering and feast-offerings for God; and Aaron and all the elders of Israel came to eat bread with the father-in-law of Moses before God.*

13 *It was on the next day that Moses sat to judge the people, and the people stood by Moses from the morning until the evening.*

(21:14). This came to pass when He killed their firstborn just as the Egyptians killed the Israelite sons; He drowned them in the sea just as they drowned the children in the river. He killed the firstborn as a parallel to (lit., "opposed to"), בְּנִי בְכֹרִי יִשְׂרָאֵל . . . וַתְּמָאֵן לְשַׁלְּחוֹ, *Israel My son, My firstborn . . . and you have refused to let him go* (4:22-23). And He (also) hardened their hearts after they refused to listen of their own free will. Thus He displayed His greatness (and superiority) over all the gods (powers) for he (Jethro) could not find any nation whose deity (i.e., heavenly representative) could totally repay (punish) measure for measure, (although) he did think that he (the deity) could do so in one area which was specifically (exclusively) his.

12. עֹלָה וּזְבָחִים לֵאלֹהִים — *A burnt offering and sacrifices to God* . . . as a token of his acceptance of the Divine Sovereignty, similar to Naaman when he said: כִּי לוֹא יַעֲשֶׂה עוֹד עַבְדְּךָ עֹלָה וָזֶבַח לֵאלֹהִים אֲחֵרִים כִּי אִם לַה׳, *For your servant will henceforth offer neither burnt offering nor sacrifice to other gods, but to HASHEM* (*II Kings* 5:17).

לֶאֱכָל לֶחֶם עִם חֹתֵן מֹשֶׁה — *To eat bread with Moses' father-in-law* . . . to rejoice with him on the occasion of his entering under "God's wings," similar to, יִשְׂמַח יִשְׂרָאֵל בְּעֹשָׂיו, *Let Israel rejoice in Him Who made him* (*Psalms* 149:2).

לִפְנֵי הָאֱלֹהִים — *Before God.* (This means) before the altar on which these sacrifices were offred — either the altar which Moses built when Amalek was defeated (17:15) or a different altar whose construction is not mentioned (in the Torah). The eating of the sacrifice before the altar is similar to the eating (of sacrifices) behind the curtains (of the Sanctuary).

NOTES

self-explanatory, referring to Israel's bondage and their deliverance from slavery.

11. כִּי בַדָּבָר אֲשֶׁר זָדוּ עֲלֵיהֶם — *For that they dealt presumptuously against them.* The ancient pagans believed that a particular god had special power in a given area. When Jethro realized that *HASHEM* had punished the Egyptians in a variety of ways, each matching the criminal action taken against the Israelites — for example, the drowning in the Sea of Reeds as punishment for drowning Jewish infants and the slaying of the firstborn as punishment for slaying Jewish children, who are called God's firstborn — he appreciated the supremacy of *HASHEM,* whose powers are unlimited and whose ability to mete out punishment *measure for measure* proves His omnipotence.

12. עֹלָה וּזְבָחִים לֵאלֹהִים . . . לִפְנֵי הָאֱלֹהִים — *A burnt offering and sacrifices to God . . . before God.* The Torah is emphatic in its insistence upon monotheism which only permits the offering of sacrifices to God alone, *He that sacrifices to the gods, save unto HASHEM only, will be utterly destroyed* (22:19). Therefore the act of bringing sacrifices to God — an act performed by both Jethro and Naaman — is a manifestation of one's willingness to accept Him as one's exclusive Deity. Such a commitment deserves to be celebrated at a feast in which the leadership and Jethro participate, partaking of the sacrifice in front of the altar, which the Torah calls *before God.*

יד וַיַּרְא חֹתֵן מֹשֶׁה אֵת כָּל־אֲשֶׁר־הוּא עֹשֶׂה לָעָם וַיֹּאמֶר מָה־הַדָּבָר
הַזֶּה אֲשֶׁר אַתָּה עֹשֶׂה לָעָם מַדּוּעַ אַתָּה יוֹשֵׁב לְבַדֶּךָ וְכָל־הָעָם נִצָּב
טו עָלֶיךָ מִן־בֹּקֶר עַד־עָרֶב: וַיֹּאמֶר מֹשֶׁה לְחֹתְנוֹ כִּי־יָבֹא אֵלַי הָעָם לִדְרֹשׁ
טז אֱלֹהִים: כִּי־יִהְיֶה לָהֶם דָּבָר בָּא אֵלַי וְשָׁפַטְתִּי בֵּין אִישׁ וּבֵין רֵעֵהוּ
יז וְהוֹדַעְתִּי אֶת־חֻקֵּי הָאֱלֹהִים וְאֶת־תּוֹרֹתָיו: וַיֹּאמֶר חֹתֵן מֹשֶׁה אֵלָיו
יח לֹא־טוֹב הַדָּבָר אֲשֶׁר אַתָּה עֹשֶׂה: נָבֹל תִּבֹּל גַּם־אַתָּה גַּם־הָעָם הַזֶּה אֲשֶׁר
יט עִמָּךְ כִּי־כָבֵד מִמְּךָ הַדָּבָר לֹא־תוּכַל עֲשֹׂהוּ לְבַדֶּךָ: עַתָּה שְׁמַע בְּקֹלִי
אִיעָצְךָ וִיהִי אֱלֹהִים עִמָּךְ הֱיֵה אַתָּה לָעָם מוּל הָאֱלֹהִים וְהֵבֵאתָ אַתָּה
כ אֶת־הַדְּבָרִים אֶל־הָאֱלֹהִים: וְהִזְהַרְתָּה אֶתְהֶם אֶת־הַחֻקִּים וְאֶת־הַתּוֹרֹת
וְהוֹדַעְתָּ לָהֶם אֶת־הַדֶּרֶךְ יֵלְכוּ בָהּ וְאֶת־הַמַּעֲשֶׂה אֲשֶׁר יַעֲשׂוּן: וְאַתָּה
כא תֶחֱזֶה מִכָּל־הָעָם אַנְשֵׁי־חַיִל יִרְאֵי אֱלֹהִים אַנְשֵׁי אֱמֶת שֹׂנְאֵי בָצַע וְשַׂמְתָּ
עֲלֵהֶם שָׂרֵי אֲלָפִים שָׂרֵי מֵאוֹת שָׂרֵי חֲמִשִּׁים
כב וְשָׂרֵי עֲשָׂרֹת: וְשָׁפְטוּ אֶת־הָעָם בְּכָל־עֵת וְהָיָה כָּל־הַדָּבָר הַגָּדֹל
יָבִיאוּ אֵלֶיךָ וְכָל־הַדָּבָר הַקָּטֹן יִשְׁפְּטוּ־הֵם וְהָקֵל מֵעָלֶיךָ וְנָשְׂאוּ אִתָּךְ:

14. מַדּוּעַ אַתָּה יוֹשֵׁב לְבַדֶּךָ — *Why do you sit alone* ... (occupied with) public affairs?

וְכָל הָעָם — *And all the people* ... who need (you) for whatever reason, to submit their case before you, have to wait from morning to evening.

15. לִדְרֹשׁ אֱלֹהִים — *To inquire of God.* The princes and leaders of the generation who come regarding public business and order must come to me to inquire of God for *according to* HASHEM *they encamp* (and execute their tasks).

16. כִּי יִהְיֶה לָהֶם דָּבָר — *When they have a matter.* And when these heads who come to me regarding public business have a dispute.

בָּא אֵלַי וְשָׁפַטְתִּי בֵּין אִישׁ וּבֵין רֵעֵהוּ — *Come to me and I judge between a man and his neighbor.* Between these leaders (lit., "great men") of the generation who come to me regarding public business.

וְהוֹדַעְתִּי אֶת חֻקֵּי הָאֱלֹהִים וְאֶת תּוֹרֹתָיו — *And I inform them (of) the statutes of God and His laws.* (I inform) those leaders so that they might know, as it says, וַיָּשֻׁבוּ אֵלָיו אַהֲרֹן וְכָל הַנְּשִׂאִים בָּעֵדָה ... וְאַחֲרֵי כֵן נִגְּשׁוּ כָּל בְּנֵי יִשְׂרָאֵל, *And Aaron and all the rulers of the congregation returned to him ... and afterward all the Children of Israel drew close* (34:31-32); as our Sages tell us, כֵּיצַד סֵדֶר מִשְׁנָה, *How was the order of instruction (Eruvin* 54b). Now, because of these three reasons the people were forced to wait from morning to evening, (waiting) until the leaders leave so I can then turn to them and judge the poor people.

18. גַּם הָעָם הַזֶּה אֲשֶׁר עִמָּךְ — *And this people that is with you* ... your court.

לֹא תוּכַל עֲשֹׂהוּ לְבַדֶּךָ — *You are not able to do it alone* ... to hear all the business of the leaders, and to listen (also) to all who need speak to you regarding those matters which they cannot (resolve) without you.

NOTES

15. לִדְרֹשׁ אֱלֹהִים — *To inquire of God.* The three areas which occupied Moses, according to the *Sforno,* were public business (v. 15); disputes between the leaders regarding public policy (v.16); and teaching them God's laws and statutes (v. 16). The order of instruction (סֵדֶר הַמִּשְׁנָה) mentioned by the *Sforno* refers to Tractate *Eruvin* 54b where our Sages describe how Moses would learn Torah from the Almighty, then teach it to Aaron, then Aaron's sons, then the elders and finally the people. Jethro suggested that lower and higher courts be established so as to lighten Moses' load

14 *The father-in-law of Moses saw everything that he was doing to the people, and he said, "What is this thing that you do to the people? Why do you sit alone with all the people standing by you from morning to evening?"*

15 *Moses said to his father-in law, "Because the people come to me to seek God.* 16 *When they have a matter, one comes to me, and I judge between a man and his fellow, and I make known the decrees of God and His teachings."*

17 *The father-in-law of Moses said to him, "The thing that you do is not good.* 18 *You will surely become worn out — you as well as this people that is with you — for this matter is too hard for you, you will not be able to do it alone.* 19 *Now heed my voice, I shall advise you, and may God be with you. You be a representative to God, and you convey the matters to God.* 20 *You shall caution them regarding the decrees and the teachings, and you shall make known to them the path in which they should go and the deeds that they should do.* 21 *And you shall discern from among the entire people, men of accomplishment, God-fearing people, men of truth, people who despise money, and you shall appoint them leaders of thousands, leaders of hundreds, leaders of fifties, and leaders of tens.* 22 *They shall judge the people at all times, and they shall bring every major matter to you, and every minor matter they shall judge, and it will be eased for you, and they shall bear with you.*

---

19. הֱיֵה אַתָּה לָעָם מוּל הָאֱלֹהִים — *You be for the people before God* . . . to teach them the commandments and judgments which He commands, as an interpreter (intermediary) between them and God, the Blessed One.

וְהֵבֵאתָ אַתָּה אֶת הַדְּבָרִים אֶל הָאֱלֹהִים — *And you will bring these matters to God* . . . (the matters) which (you yourself) have not heard, such as, עִמְדוּ וְאֶשְׁמְעָה, *Stay, that I may hear (Numbers* 9:8), (also) וַיַּקְרֵב מֹשֶׁה אֶת מִשְׁפָּטָן לִפְנֵי ה׳, *and Moses brought their cause before* H*ashem* (ibid. 27:5).

21. וְאַתָּה תֶחֱזֶה מִכָּל הָעָם — *And you shall provide out of all the people.* You shall choose and appoint; (however) in these three areas (i.e., public affairs, dispute among the leaders, and teaching Torah to the leaders) you yourself will have to (be involved), and no one else will do. But regarding private legal decisions the rulers of thousands, the rulers of hundreds, etc., will suffice. Indeed when there will be four levels (of judges), one higher than the other, then the lesser one will judge first and if (the litigant) protests the court's decision he can appeal to a higher one, and (if necessary) from the second to the third and from the third to the fourth. In this manner there will be fewer coming to you for adjudication.

22. וְהָקֵל מֵעָלֶיךָ — *So it shall be made easier for you.* (There will be) many disputes which it will not be necessary to bring to you.

וְנָשְׂאוּ אִתָּךְ — *And bear the burden with you.* In that which you will have to do they will assist you, for example in teaching knowledge to the people after they have heard it from you, as mentioned in סֵדֶר מִשְׁנָה, *the order of study (Eruvin* 54b).

NOTES

while at the same time expediting the dispensing of justice.

19. וְהֵבֵאתָ אַתָּה אֶת הַדְּבָרִים אֶל הָאֱלֹהִים — *And you will bring these matters to God.* Jethro, wisely, appreciated that there might be matters which even Moses had not learned from God, in which case he would have to submit the question to Him, as happened in the case of those who were unclean and could not bring the *Pesach* lamb on time *(Numbers* 9:8); and also in the case of the inheritance of Zelaphchad who died leaving only daughters and no sons to inherit him (ibid. 27:5).

כג אִם אֶת־הַדָּבָר הַזֶּה תַּעֲשֶׂה וְצִוְּךָ אֱלֹהִים וְיָכָלְתָּ עֲמֹד וְגַם כָּל־הָעָם הַזֶּה
שלישי כד עַל־מְקֹמוֹ יָבֹא בְשָׁלוֹם: וַיִּשְׁמַע מֹשֶׁה לְקוֹל חֹתְנוֹ וַיַּעַשׂ כֹּל אֲשֶׁר אָמָר:
כה וַיִּבְחַר מֹשֶׁה אַנְשֵׁי־חַיִל מִכָּל־יִשְׂרָאֵל וַיִּתֵּן אֹתָם רָאשִׁים עַל־הָעָם שָׂרֵי
כו אֲלָפִים שָׂרֵי מֵאוֹת שָׂרֵי חֲמִשִּׁים וְשָׂרֵי עֲשָׂרֹת: וְשָׁפְטוּ אֶת־הָעָם
בְּכָל־עֵת אֶת־הַדָּבָר הַקָּשֶׁה יְבִיאוּן אֶל־מֹשֶׁה וְכָל־הַדָּבָר הַקָּטֹן יִשְׁפּוּטוּ
כז הֵם: וַיְשַׁלַּח מֹשֶׁה אֶת־חֹתְנוֹ וַיֵּלֶךְ לוֹ אֶל־אַרְצוֹ:
יט רביעי א בַּחֹדֶשׁ הַשְּׁלִישִׁי לְצֵאת בְּנֵי־יִשְׂרָאֵל מֵאֶרֶץ מִצְרָיִם בַּיּוֹם הַזֶּה בָּאוּ
ב מִדְבַּר סִינָי: וַיִּסְעוּ מֵרְפִידִים וַיָּבֹאוּ מִדְבַּר סִינַי וַיַּחֲנוּ בַּמִּדְבָּר וַיִּחַן־
ג שָׁם יִשְׂרָאֵל נֶגֶד הָהָר: וּמֹשֶׁה עָלָה אֶל־הָאֱלֹהִים וַיִּקְרָא אֵלָיו
יהוה מִן־הָהָר לֵאמֹר כֹּה תֹאמַר לְבֵית יַעֲקֹב וְתַגֵּיד לִבְנֵי יִשְׂרָאֵל:
ד אַתֶּם רְאִיתֶם אֲשֶׁר עָשִׂיתִי לְמִצְרָיִם וָאֶשָּׂא אֶתְכֶם עַל־כַּנְפֵי נְשָׁרִים

23. עַל מְקֹמוֹ יָבֹא בְשָׁלוֹם — *Shall go to their place in peace.* After the law will be clarified in so many courts of law every litigant will know that the decision is true and he will not continue to contend, as our Sages say, "When one leaves a court which has taken away his cloak, let him go forth singing on his way" (*Sanhedrin* 7a).

25. וַיִּבְחַר מֹשֶׁה אַנְשֵׁי חַיִל — *And Moses chose able men.* After seeking and not finding men who possessed all the qualities mentioned by Jethro (v. 21), he chose able men, well versed (in law) and diligent in determining the veracity of a matter and bringing it to a definite conclusion. (These were chosen over) those who feared God but were not able men, as our Sages say, "Even if a scholar is vengeful and bears malice like a serpent, gird him on your loins; whereas even if an *am haaretz* (an ignoramus) is pious, do not dwell in his vicinity" (*Shabbos* 63a).

27. וַיְשַׁלַּח מֹשֶׁה אֶת חֹתְנוֹ — *And Moses sent away his father-in-law.* He did not want to accompany Israel to the land, as he said, לֹא אֵלֵךְ כִּי אִם אֶל אַרְצִי וְאֶל מוֹלַדְתִּי אֵלֵךְ, *I will not go (with you), but I will depart to my own land and go to my birthplace* (*Numbers* 10:30). Perhaps this was due to his advanced age, as we find in the case of Barzilai who said, יָשָׁב נָא עַבְדְּךָ וְאָמֻת בְּעִירִי עִם קֶבֶר אָבִי וְאִמִּי, *Let your servant, I pray you, turn back that I may die in my own city and be buried in the grave of my father and mother* (*II Samuel* 19:38). The children of Jethro, however, did without a doubt go with Israel to the land, as it says, וּבְנֵי קֵינִי חֹתֵן מֹשֶׁה עָלוּ מֵעִיר הַתְּמָרִים אֶת בְּנֵי יְהוּדָה, *And the children of Keni, the father-in-law of Moses, went up from the city of palm trees with the children of Judah* (*Judges* 1:16), and regarding them Balaam said, אֵיתָן מוֹשָׁבֶךָ, *Firm be your dwelling place* (*Numbers* 24:21).

NOTES

23. עַל מְקֹמוֹ יָבֹא בְשָׁלוֹם — *Shall go to their place in peace.* The partners to a dispute can only find peace of mind if they are satisfied that justice has been done and that there has been no miscarriage of justice due to negligence or ignorance on the part of the court. The system devised by Jethro would hopefully satisfy the parties that the decision rendered was a fair and just one.

25. וַיִּבְחַר מֹשֶׁה אַנְשֵׁי חַיִל — *And Moses chose able men.* Jethro mentioned four qualifications as the criteria for choosing judges — *able men, who fear God, men of truth, who hate bribes* (18:21). Unfortunately Moses could not find any who met *all* of these qualifications. He therefore chose those who possessed the most important quality of all — ability. As the *Sforno* explains, it is vital that a judge be well versed in law, astute and capable of making a decision. These are the most important qualities a judge must possess. The saying of our Sages, cited by the *Sforno*, is most apt, since he interprets *able men* as meaning scholars who are knowledgeable and of strong character, though lacking some of the other qualities mentioned by Jethro.

23 *If you do this thing — and God shall command you — then you will be able to endure, and this entire people, as well, shall arrive at its destination in peace."*

24 *Moses heeded the voice of his father-in-law, and did everything that he had said.* 25 *Moses chose men of accomplishment from among all Israel and appointed them heads of the people, leaders of thousands, leaders of hundreds, leaders of fifties, and leaders of tens.* 26 *They judged the people at all times; the difficult thing they would bring to Moses and the minor thing they themselves would judge.*

27 *Moses sent off his father-in-law, and he went to his land.*

19 1 *In the third month from the Exodus of the Children of Israel from Egypt,*
on this day, they arrived at the Wilderness of Sinai. 2 *They journeyed*
from Rephidim and arrived at the Wilderness of Sinai and encamped in the
Wilderness; and Israel encamped there, opposite the mountain.
3 *Moses ascended to God, and* HASHEM *called to him from the mountain,*
saying, "So shall you say to the House of Jacob and relate to the Children of
Israel. 4 *'You have seen what I did to Egypt, and that I have borne you on*

XIX

1. בַּיּוֹם הַזֶּה — *The same day* . . . the first day of the month.

2. וַיִּסְעוּ מֵרְפִידִים וַיָּבֹאוּ מִדְבַּר סִינַי — *And they traveled from Rephidim and came to the wilderness of Sinai.* Their traveling from Rephidim was directed at their coming to the wilderness of Sinai where the Mount of God was located, because they knew that there they would worship (serve) Him, as it says, תַּעַבְדוּן אֶת הָאֱלֹהִים עַל הָהָר הַזֶּה, *You shall serve God upon this mountain* (3:12).

3. וּמֹשֶׁה עָלָה אֶל הָאֱלֹהִים — *And Moses went up to God.* The (verse) tells us that while Israel attended (lit., "set their face") to matters of encampment and its needs, Moses went up to prepare himself for the prophetic (spirit).

4. אַתֶּם רְאִיתֶם אֲשֶׁר עָשִׂיתִי לְמִצְרָיִם — *You have seen what I did to the Egyptians.* (You have seen) how I urged them to repent of their wickedness for I do not desire the death (of the wicked); but when they stiffened their neck, I was constrained to multiply my signs and wonders in their midst and to destroy them.

וָאֶשָּׂא אֶתְכֶם עַל כַּנְפֵי נְשָׁרִים — *And I carried you on eagles' wings* . . . on a road that no other person had traversed, like the eagle who takes his young ones high in the air where no

NOTES

XIX

2. וַיִּסְעוּ מֵרְפִידִים וַיָּבֹאוּ מִדְבַּר סִינַי — *And they traveled from Rephidim and came to the wilderness of Sinai.* We have already been told in verse 1 that *they came into the wilderness of Sinai;* why then is it necessary to repeat it again? The *Sforno's* answer is that the Torah is stressing that they traveled from Rephidim for the express purpose of reaching this destination, which was the Mount of God in the Sinai wilderness.

3. וּמֹשֶׁה עָלָה אֶל הָאֱלֹהִים — *And Moses went up to God.* The expression עָלָה, *went up,* is of special significance when used in the context of this verse. The *Rambam* in his *Guide* (1:10) states that the expression *to ascend* used here regarding Moses going up to God is to be understood thus, "When one directs his thoughts toward an exalted sublime object he is said *to have ascended.*" As for our verse he states, "In addition to the fact that he ascended to the top of the mountain upon which the light of HASHEM had descended," Moses also *ascended* in the sense explained above. This is the meaning of the *Sforno's* commentary when he states, "Moses went up to prepare himself for the prophetic spirit."

4. . . . אֲשֶׁר עָשִׂיתִי לְמִצְרָיִם וָאֶשָּׂא אֶתְכֶם — *What I did to the Egyptians, and I carried you . . .* God does not say, *"What I did for you."* Therefore the *Sforno* interprets the statement *what I did to the Egyp-*

ה וָאָבִא אֶתְכֶם אֵלָי: וְעַתָּה אִם־שָׁמוֹעַ תִּשְׁמְעוּ בְּקֹלִי וּשְׁמַרְתֶּם
ו אֶת־בְּרִיתִי וִהְיִיתֶם לִי סְגֻלָּה מִכָּל־הָעַמִּים כִּי־לִי כָּל־הָאָרֶץ: וְאַתֶּם
תִּהְיוּ־לִי מַמְלֶכֶת כֹּהֲנִים וְגוֹי קָדוֹשׁ אֵלֶּה הַדְּבָרִים אֲשֶׁר תְּדַבֵּר אֶל־בְּנֵי
חמישי ז יִשְׂרָאֵל: וַיָּבֹא מֹשֶׁה וַיִּקְרָא לְזִקְנֵי הָעָם וַיָּשֶׂם לִפְנֵיהֶם אֵת כָּל־הַדְּבָרִים
ח הָאֵלֶּה אֲשֶׁר צִוָּהוּ יהוה: וַיַּעֲנוּ כָל־הָעָם יַחְדָּו וַיֹּאמְרוּ כֹּל אֲשֶׁר־דִּבֶּר
ט יהוה נַעֲשֶׂה וַיָּשֶׁב מֹשֶׁה אֶת־דִּבְרֵי הָעָם אֶל־יהוה: וַיֹּאמֶר יהוה
אֶל־מֹשֶׁה הִנֵּה אָנֹכִי בָּא אֵלֶיךָ בְּעַב הֶעָנָן בַּעֲבוּר יִשְׁמַע הָעָם בְּדַבְּרִי
עִמָּךְ וְגַם־בְּךָ יַאֲמִינוּ לְעוֹלָם וַיַּגֵּד מֹשֶׁה אֶת־דִּבְרֵי הָעָם אֶל־יהוה:

---

other bird can fly. This was (done) to separate you from all the nations, and their pursuits, to be unto Me.

וָאָבִא אֶתְכֶם אֵלָי — *And brought you to Myself* . . . to the Mount of God which is predisposed to prophecy.

5. וְעַתָּה אִם שָׁמוֹעַ תִּשְׁמְעוּ בְּקֹלִי — *Now, therefore, if you will indeed hearken to My voice* . . . to accept upon yourselves Torah and commandments.

וּשְׁמַרְתֶּם אֶת בְּרִיתִי — *And keep My covenant.* The covenant which I will make when you accept (the Torah) — (meaning) the covenant entered into after they said, נַעֲשֶׂה וְנִשְׁמָע, *We will do and we will listen* (24:7), as it says, הִנֵּה דַם הַבְּרִית אֲשֶׁר כָּרַת ה׳ עִמָּכֶם עַל כָּל הַדְּבָרִים הָאֵלֶּה, *Behold the blood of the covenant which HASHEM had made with you in agreement with all these words* (24:8) — that I will not have to deal with you as I did with Egypt.

וִהְיִיתֶם לִי סְגֻלָּה מִכָּל הָעַמִּים — *You shall be My own treasure from among all peoples.* Although the entire human race is more precious to Me than all other inferior creatures (lit., "existent ones"), for he alone (i.e., man) among them represents My intention (purpose), as our Sages say, חָבִיב אָדָם שֶׁנִּבְרָא בְּצֶלֶם, *Precious is man who was created in the Image (Avos* 3:14), still you shall be to Me a treasure beyond all of them.

כִּי לִי כָּל הָאָרֶץ — *For all the earth is Mine.* And the difference between you and them is one of degree, for indeed *all the earth is Mine,* and the righteous of all people are without a doubt dear to Me.

6. וְאַתֶּם תִּהְיוּ לִי מַמְלֶכֶת כֹּהֲנִים — *And you shall be to Me a kingdom of priests.* In this fashion you will be the treasure of them all by being a *kingdom of priests* to understand and teach the entire human race that all shall call in the Name of HASHEM and serve Him *in one accord,* as shall (indeed) be the (role) of Israel in the future, as it says, וְאַתֶּם כֹּהֲנֵי ה׳

NOTES

tians as referring not to the plagues and punishment but the attempt by the Almighty to encourage them to repent.

וָאֶשָּׂא אֶתְכֶם עַל כַּנְפֵי נְשָׁרִים — *And I carried you on eagles' wings.* Unlike other commentators the *Sforno* does not interpret this statement as a protective act of God on behalf of Israel. Rather he interprets it to mean that God elevated Israel to a level unique among nations, taking them to a place inaccessible to all others, i.e., separating them from other nations and taking them unto Himself.

5. וּשְׁמַרְתֶּם אֶת בְּרִיתִי — *And keep My covenant.* There is a difference of opinion between the commentators as to which covenant the verse refers. The *Sforno,* as do others, submits that it refers to the covenant which was to be entered into *after* the revelation.

וִהְיִיתֶם לִי סְגֻלָּה מִכָּל הָעַמִּים — *You shall be My own treasure from among all peoples.* The *Sforno* interprets the words of the Almighty as implying that God's love is granted to all of mankind but Israel is His special treasure. This does not mean, however, that only they are precious to Him, rather that relatively speaking Israel is more precious in the eyes of God. This interpretation explains the meaning of the end of the verse *for all the earth is mine.* Every human being was created in the Image of God.

6. וְאַתֶּם תִּהְיוּ לִי מַמְלֶכֶת כֹּהֲנִים וְגוֹי קָדוֹשׁ — *And you shall be to Me a kingdom of priests and a holy*

the wings of eagles and brought you to Me. 5 *And now, if you hearken well to Me and observe My covenant, you shall be to Me the most beloved treasure of all peoples, for Mine is the entire world.* 6 *You shall be to Me a kingdom of ministers and a holy nation.' These are the words that you shall speak to the Children of Israel."*

7 *Moses came and summoned the elders of the people, and put before them all these words that HASHEM had commanded him.* 8 *The entire people responded together and said, "Everything that HASHEM has spoken we shall do!" Moses brought back the words of the people to HASHEM.*

9 *HASHEM said to Moses, "Behold! I come to you in the thickness of the cloud, so that the people will hear as I speak to you, and they will also believe in you forever." Moses related the words of the people to HASHEM.*

תִּקָּרֵאוּ, *But you shall be named priests of HASHEM* (*Isaiah* 61:6), and as it says, כִּי מִצִּיּוֹן תֵּצֵא תוֹרָה, *For out of Zion shall Torah go forth* (ibid. 2:3).

וְגוֹי קָדוֹשׁ — *And a holy nation.* A (nation) that shall never perish but exist forever among men, as it shall be in future time, as it says, וְהָיָה הַנִּשְׁאָר בְּצִיּוֹן וְהַנּוֹתָר בִּירוּשָׁלַםִ קָדוֹשׁ יֵאָמֶר, *And it shall come to pass that he who is left in Zion and he that remains in Jerusalem shall be called holy* (*Isaiah* 4:3), and our Sages say, מַה קָּדוֹשׁ לְעוֹלָם קַיָּים אַף הֵם לְעוֹלָם קַיָּימִים, *As the holy remains forever so shall they remain forever* (*Sanhedrin* 92a). Now this was indeed the intent of God, the Blessed One, when He gave the Torah, to grant them all the future good, had they not corrupted their ways through the (Golden) Calf as it says, וַיִּתְנַצְּלוּ בְנֵי יִשְׂרָאֵל אֶת עֶדְיָם מֵהַר חוֹרֵב, *And the Children of Israel stripped themselves of their ornaments from Mount Horeb onward* (33:6).

8. וַיָּשֶׁב מֹשֶׁה אֶת דִּבְרֵי הָעָם — *And Moses reported the words of the people.* He reported what he understood from their words, to Him Who had sent him; namely, he understood from their response that they would only do what God commanded (i.e., כֹּל אֲשֶׁר דִּבֶּר ה׳ נַעֲשֶׂה, *All that HASHEM has spoken we will do*).

9. בְּעַב הֶעָנָן — *In a thick cloud.* Although all the prophecies of Moses from the time of the giving of the Torah and beyond were through a "clear, bright lens" (and not through a "cloudy lens"), as it says, וּתְמֻנַת ה׳ יַבִּיט, *and the similitude of HASHEM he beholds* (*Numbers* 12:8); nonetheless, this particular prophecy was in a thick cloud.

בַּעֲבוּר יִשְׁמַע הָעָם . . . וְגַם בְּךָ יַאֲמִינוּ לְעוֹלָם — *That the people may hear . . . and may also believe you forever.* They will believe the possibility that your prophecy can be *face to face*, for indeed I will speak to them *face to face*, without (any medium) of a dream, as

NOTES

nation. Although all mankind is precious in the eyes of God, Israel is unique and special in two ways. First is their mission to teach mankind to recognize and serve God, as Abraham their father did from the very outset of his mission. This is the meaning of מַמְלֶכֶת כֹּהֲנִים, *a kingdom of priests*, for it is the responsibility of a priest to teach. The second difference between Israel and other people is that they are destined to be an eternal people. This characteristic of immortality is rooted in their being a holy nation, for our Sages have taught us that sanctity is the element which insures נִצְחִיּוּת, *everlasting existence.* (Compare to 15:11 — the *Sforno's* commentary on נֶאְדָּר בַּקֹּדֶשׁ.)

8-9. וַיָּשֶׁב מֹשֶׁה אֶת דִּבְרֵי הָעָם . . . בַּעֲבוּר יִשְׁמַע הָעָם . . . וְגַם בְּךָ יַאֲמִינוּ לְעוֹלָם וַיַּגֵּד מֹשֶׁה . . . — *And Moses reported the words of the people . . . that the people may hear . . . and may also believe you forever; And Moses told* . . . The *Rambam* in his *Guide* (2:45) writes of eleven degrees of prophecy. He stresses that "prophecy occurs in a vision or in a dream"; however Moses was the exception to whom God spoke "face to face," which the *Rambam* explains as "one presence to another presence without an intermediary" (1:37). Although the Torah tells us that this level of face to face was reached by Israel at Sinai (*Deut.* 5:4), the *Rambam* explains that only the voice of God reached Israel but not

י וַיֹּאמֶר יְהוָה אֶל־מֹשֶׁה לֵךְ אֶל־הָעָם וְקִדַּשְׁתָּם הַיּוֹם וּמָחָר וְכִבְּסוּ שִׂמְלֹתָם׃
יא וְהָיוּ נְכֹנִים לַיּוֹם הַשְּׁלִישִׁי כִּי ׀ בַּיּוֹם הַשְּׁלִשִׁי יֵרֵד יְהוָה לְעֵינֵי כָל־הָעָם עַל־
יב הַר סִינָי׃ וְהִגְבַּלְתָּ אֶת־הָעָם סָבִיב לֵאמֹר הִשָּׁמְרוּ לָכֶם עֲלוֹת בָּהָר וּנְגֹעַ
יג בְּקָצֵהוּ כָּל־הַנֹּגֵעַ בָּהָר מוֹת יוּמָת׃ לֹא־תִגַּע בּוֹ יָד כִּי־סָקוֹל יִסָּקֵל אוֹ־יָרֹה
יד יִיָּרֶה אִם־בְּהֵמָה אִם־אִישׁ לֹא יִחְיֶה בִּמְשֹׁךְ הַיֹּבֵל הֵמָּה יַעֲלוּ בָהָר׃ וַיֵּרֶד
טו מֹשֶׁה מִן־הָהָר אֶל־הָעָם וַיְקַדֵּשׁ אֶת־הָעָם וַיְכַבְּסוּ שִׂמְלֹתָם׃ וַיֹּאמֶר אֶל־
טז הָעָם הֱיוּ נְכֹנִים לִשְׁלֹשֶׁת יָמִים אַל־תִּגְּשׁוּ אֶל־אִשָּׁה׃ וַיְהִי בַיּוֹם הַשְּׁלִישִׁי
בִּהְיֹת הַבֹּקֶר וַיְהִי קֹלֹת וּבְרָקִים וְעָנָן כָּבֵד עַל־הָהָר וְקֹל שֹׁפָר חָזָק מְאֹד

it says, פָּנִים בְּפָנִים דִּבֶּר ה׳ עִמָּכֶם, *Face to face God spoke to you* (*Deut.* 5:4), implying that man can prophesy while in command of his senses, which they thought was impossible. *Now* they will also believe that your prophecy can be in such a manner, as it says, וְדִבֶּר ה׳ אֶל מֹשֶׁה פָּנִים אֶל פָּנִים, *And HASHEM spoke to Moses face to face* (33:11). Therefore it says, הַיּוֹם הַזֶּה רָאִינוּ כִּי יְדַבֵּר אֱלֹהִים אֶת הָאָדָם וָחָי, *We have seen this day that God does speak with man and he lives* (*Deut.* 5:21); for they never doubted the possibility of prophecy (as such), knowing that the Patriarchs, Moses, Aaron and Miriam had already prophesied, but until now no prophecy of any prophet was other than in a vision or dream as God, the Blessed One, explained, saying, בַּמַּרְאָה אֵלָיו אֶתְוַדָּע בַּחֲלוֹם אֲדַבֶּר בּוֹ, *I make Myself known to him in a vision, I do speak to him in a dream* (*Numbers* 12:6). However, the prophecy of Moses occurred while he still used his senses, and this they doubted, were it not that they themselves also prophesied in this manner, and thereby they will believe the words of Moses; and no other prophet will be able to rise up against them, for their (i.e., other prophets') prophecy will (never) be on this level.

וַיַּגֵּד מֹשֶׁה אֶת דִּבְרֵי הָעָם אֶל ה׳ — *And Moses told the words of the people to HASHEM.* When he heard the ordinance of his Maker (instituted) so that (the people) would believe in the kind of prophecy which was his, he sensed the doubts of the people (and therefore) told their words (to God), thinking that the reason they said, כֹּל אֲשֶׁר דִּבֶּר ה׳ נַעֲשֶׂה, *All that HASHEM has said we will do*, but did not say, כֵּן נַעֲשֶׂה, *so we shall do* (i.e., without mentioning God), was because they were doubtful whether Moses' prophecy was (actually) the words of *HASHEM* or (received) from an angel, and if they were to accept upon

NOTES

His speech (articulation) which only reached Moses (2:33). The *Sforno* does not elaborate to the extent that the *Rambam* does on this entire subject of prophecy, but he does establish the following points which are reflected in these two verses. The people of Israel always believed that there was communication between God and man. This was a part of their tradition from the time of the Patriarchs. However, they believed that this unique experience only occurred in a dream or vision where the prophet's senses were suspended and he went into a trance, transcending his physical being. Therefore they could not grasp the fact that God spoke to Moses in a different fashion, i.e., face to face, where man could be in full command of his senses, totally aware, comparable to *a man speaking to his friend* (*Exodus* 33:11). The only way to convince them that this was indeed the unique nature of God's communication with Moses was to have *them* experience this same level of prophecy themselves. This occurred at the time of the revelation at Sinai, thereby bringing them to an unequivocal faith in Moses (וְגַם בְּךָ יַאֲמִינוּ לְעוֹלָם). This also precluded the possibility of any other prophet (who could never reach this degree of prophecy) questioning the authenticity of the Torah given through Moses. However, until God granted this historic gift of prophecy to the people, and as yet their faith in Moses had not been fully established, their acceptance was also qualified. Hence they say *"All that God has spoken we will do,"* implying that if these commandments were to be given through an angel (i.e., on a lower level of prophecy), they would not accept them, for they feared that they would be vulnerable to his wrath if they deviated even slightly, as we see from the verse (23:21) quoted by the *Sforno*. This explains the meaning of verse 8 as well as the conclusion of

10 *HASHEM said to Moses, "Go to the people and sanctify them today and
tomorrow, and they shall wash their clothing.* 11 *Let them be prepared for the
third day, for on the third day HASHEM shall descend in the sight of the entire
people on Mount Sinai.* 12 *You shall set boundaries for the people roundabout,
saying, 'Beware of ascending the mountain or touching its edge; whoever
touches the mountain shall surely die.* 13 *A hand shall not touch it, for he shall
surely be stoned or thrown down; whether animal or person he shall not live;
upon an extended blast of the shofar, they may ascend the mountain.' "*
14 *Moses descended from the mountain to the people. He sanctified the
people and they washed their clothing.* 15 *He said to the people, "Be ready
after a three-day period; do not draw near a woman."*
16 *On the third day when it was morning, there was thunder and lightning
and a heavy cloud on the mountain, and the sound of the shofar was very*

---

themselves the words of an angel, he would examine carefully (their deeds) even (if they deviated) by a single hair and not forgive (the slightest deviation), as it says, כִּי לֹא יִשָּׂא לְפִשְׁעֲכֶם, *for he will not pardon your transgressions* (23:21), therefore they said that they would only do (fulfill) the words of *HASHEM* alone.

11. וְהָיוּ נְכֹנִים — *And be ready* . . . that your body be pure also, and ready for prophecy, not only the soul, since the level of this imminent prophecy will be *face to face*, while still in command of their senses. That is why a woman was prohibited to Moses from the time he reached that level, since all his prophecies from the time of the giving of the Torah and forward were *face to face*, as it says: לֵךְ אֱמֹר לָהֶם שׁוּבוּ לָכֶם לְאָהֳלֵיכֶם וְאַתָּה פֹּה עֲמֹד עִמָּדִי, *Go say to them, "Return to your tents," but as for you, stand here with Me (Deut.* 5:27,28), as our Sages have explained *(Shabbos* 87a).

12. הַנֹּגֵעַ בָּהָר מוֹת יוּמָת — *Whoever touches the mountain shall surely be put to death. Lest they break through to HASHEM to gaze, and many of them perish* (v. 21), and thereby mitigate the joy of God, the Blessed One, by defiling the place with their dead bodies. This will also impose a state of mourning on their relatives and (as a result) the Divine presence will not dwell upon them.

16. וַיְהִי קֹלֹת וּבְרָקִים — *And there was thunder and lightning* . . . similar to וְהִנֵּה . . . וְרוּחַ גְּדוֹלָה וְחָזָק . . . וְאַחַר הָרוּחַ רַעַשׁ . . . וְאַחַר הָרַעַשׁ אֵשׁ, *And behold . . . and a great and strong*

NOTES

verse 9, where we are told of Moses' report to God of the people's response. The sense of these verses would then be that Moses *reported the words of the people* (v. 8) and Moses *told the words of the people* (v. 9) prior to God's statement, *Lo, I came to you*, etc. (the first part of v. 9). God told Moses that by exposing the people themselves to the highest degree of prophecy they *would* believe.

11. וְהָיוּ נְכֹנִים — *And be ready.* Whereas all prophecies are through a vision or a dream, as mentioned above, the level of this prophecy at Sinai, as well as all of those experienced by Moses henceforth, were *face to face*, meaning that they were in full control of their feelings and senses, wide awake and aware, hence their *physical being* had to be holy and pure. This explains why they had to prepare themselves by sanctifying themselves and washing their garments. Now just as they had to abstain from marital relations during this preparatory period, so Moses had to continue this discipline even later since God would appear to him periodically without prior warning.

12. הַנֹּגֵעַ בָּהָר מוֹת יוּמָת — *Whoever touches the mountain shall surely be put to death.* Prophecy can only be experienced in a state of joy. We see that Elisha was unable to receive God's spirit until the minstrel played. Based on this the *Sforno* explains the importance of cautioning the people to distance themselves from the mountain, not only for the purpose of self-preservation, but also to prevent the exclusion of many Israelites from this great opportunity of experiencing the prophetic spirit as a result of their grief at the death of relatives, which would deny them the privilege of prophecy.

יז וַיֶּחֱרַד כָּל־הָעָם אֲשֶׁר בַּמַּחֲנֶה: וַיּוֹצֵא מֹשֶׁה אֶת־הָעָם לִקְרַאת הָאֱלֹהִים
יח מִן־הַמַּחֲנֶה וַיִּתְיַצְּבוּ בְּתַחְתִּית הָהָר: וְהַר סִינַי עָשַׁן כֻּלּוֹ מִפְּנֵי אֲשֶׁר יָרַד
יט עָלָיו יהוה בָּאֵשׁ וַיַּעַל עֲשָׁנוֹ כְּעֶשֶׁן הַכִּבְשָׁן וַיֶּחֱרַד כָּל־הָהָר מְאֹד: וַיְהִי
ששי כ קוֹל הַשֹּׁפָר הוֹלֵךְ וְחָזֵק מְאֹד מֹשֶׁה יְדַבֵּר וְהָאֱלֹהִים יַעֲנֶנּוּ בְקוֹל: וַיֵּרֶד יהוה
עַל־הַר סִינַי אֶל־רֹאשׁ הָהָר וַיִּקְרָא יהוה לְמֹשֶׁה אֶל־רֹאשׁ הָהָר וַיַּעַל
כא מֹשֶׁה: וַיֹּאמֶר יהוה אֶל־מֹשֶׁה רֵד הָעֵד בָּעָם פֶּן־יֶהֶרְסוּ אֶל־יהוה לִרְאוֹת
כב וְנָפַל מִמֶּנּוּ רָב: וְגַם הַכֹּהֲנִים הַנִּגָּשִׁים אֶל־יהוה יִתְקַדָּשׁוּ פֶּן־יִפְרֹץ בָּהֶם
כג יהוה: וַיֹּאמֶר מֹשֶׁה אֶל־יהוה לֹא־יוּכַל הָעָם לַעֲלֹת אֶל־הַר סִינָי כִּי־אַתָּה
כד הַעֵדֹתָה בָּנוּ לֵאמֹר הַגְבֵּל אֶת־הָהָר וְקִדַּשְׁתּוֹ: וַיֹּאמֶר אֵלָיו יהוה לֶךְ־רֵד
וְעָלִיתָ אַתָּה וְאַהֲרֹן עִמָּךְ וְהַכֹּהֲנִים וְהָעָם אַל־יֶהֶרְסוּ לַעֲלֹת אֶל־יהוה פֶּן־
כ כה־א יִפְרָץ־בָּם: וַיֵּרֶד מֹשֶׁה אֶל־הָעָם וַיֹּאמֶר אֲלֵהֶם: וַיְדַבֵּר
ב אֱלֹהִים אֵת כָּל־הַדְּבָרִים הָאֵלֶּה לֵאמֹר: אָנֹכִי
ג יהוה אֱלֹהֶיךָ אֲשֶׁר הוֹצֵאתִיךָ מֵאֶרֶץ מִצְרַיִם מִבֵּית עֲבָדִים: לֹא־יִהְיֶה

wind . . . and after the wind an earthquake . . . and after the earthquake a fire (I Kings 19:11,12), and so the (verse) testifies, saying, אֶרֶץ רָעָשָׁה אַף שָׁמַיִם נָטְפוּ, *the earth shook, the heavens also dripped (Psalms 68:9).*

17. לִקְרַאת הָאֱלֹהִים — *To meet God* . . . toward the heavenly household, who preceded the Holy One, Blessed is He, as it says later, וַיֵּרֶד ה׳ עַל הַר סִינַי, *And HASHEM came down on Mount Sinai* (v. 20).

21. רֵד הָעֵד בָּעָם פֶּן יֶהֶרְסוּ — *Go down, charge the people, lest they break through* . . . when I speak with them, (for) perhaps they will think that since they have ascended to the level of prophecy of *face to face*, as you have, they are then (also) permitted to ascend to your division (i.e., class).

23. וְקִדַּשְׁתּוֹ — *And sanctify it.* When You said to them, אִם בְּהֵמָה אִם אִישׁ לֹא יִחְיֶה, *Whether it be beast or man it shall not live* (v. 13), similar to אַדְמַת קֹדֶשׁ הוּא, *it is holy ground* (3:5).

24. לֶךְ רֵד — *Go, get you down* . . . now, while I speak, be together with them at the bottom of the mountain.

וְעָלִיתָ אַתָּה וְאַהֲרֹן — *And you shall come up, you and Aaron* . . . after the completion of the Ten Commandments and the chapter of *Mishpatim* (the Ordinances), as it says: וְאֶל מֹשֶׁה אָמַר עֲלֵה אֶל ה׳ אַתָּה וְאַהֲרֹן, *And to Moses He said, Come up to HASHEM, you and Aaron* (24:1).

25. וַיֹּאמֶר אֲלֵהֶם — *And told them* . . . the warning and the punishment (if they transgress), i.e., פֶּן יֶהֶרְסוּ . . . וְנָפַל מִמֶּנּוּ רָב, *Lest they break through . . . many of them shall perish* (v. 21).

XX

1. וַיְדַבֵּר אֱלֹהִים — *And God spoke.* After Moses' cautioning and warning, God spoke all

NOTES

17. לִקְרַאת הָאֱלֹהִים — *To meet God.* The royal entourage precedes the arrival of the king. The "heavenly household" (פַּמַלְיָא שֶׁל מַעְלָה) was the entourage of angels who came first, heralding the imminent arrival of God.

24. לֶךְ רֵד וְעָלִיתָ — *Go, get you down, and you shall come up.* Moses originally thought he was to be on the mountain when God spoke. According to the *Midrash* he wanted to be there, closer to God. God, however, told him to go down and be with the people when He proclaimed the Ten Commandments and the chapter of *Mishpatim.* Only after this was completed would Moses ascend the mountain once again.

XX

2. אָנֹכִי ה׳ אֱלֹהֶיךָ — *I am HASHEM your God.* The

powerful, and the entire people that was in the camp shuddered. [17] *Moses brought the people forth from the camp toward God, and they stood at the bottom of the mountain.* [18] *All of Mount Sinai was smoking because HASHEM had descended upon it in the fire; its smoke ascended like the smoke of the furnace, and the entire mountain shuddered exceedingly.* [19] *The sound of the shofar grew continually much stronger; Moses would speak and God would respond to him with a voice.*

[20] *HASHEM descended upon Mount Sinai to the top of the mountain; HASHEM summoned Moses to the top of the mountain, and Moses ascended.* [21] *HASHEM said to Moses, "Descend, warn the people, lest they break through to HASHEM to see, and a multitude of them will fall.* [22] *Even the Kohanim who approach HASHEM should be prepared, lest HASHEM burst forth against them."*

[23] *Moses said to HASHEM, "The people cannot ascend Mount Sinai, for You have warned us, saying, 'Bound the mountain and sanctify it.' "*

[24] *HASHEM said to him, "Go, descend. Then you shall ascend, and Aaron with you, but the Kohanim, and the people — they shall not break through to ascend to HASHEM, lest He burst forth against them."* [25] *Moses descended to the people and said [it] to them.*

20 [1] *God spoke all these statements, saying:*

[2] *I am HASHEM, your God, Who has taken you out of the land of Egypt, from the house of slavery.*

---

these words to them, as it says, אֶת הַדְּבָרִים הָאֵלֶּה דִּבֶּר ה׳ אֶל כָּל קְהַלְכֶם בָּהָר, *These words HASHEM spoke to all your assembly in the mount (Deut.* 5:19).

2. אָנֹכִי ה׳ אֱלֹהֶיךָ — *I am HASHEM your God.* I alone am *HASHEM* who grants existence; (I am) the Prime Cause known to you through tradition (lit., "receiving") and (logical) proof; and I confirm that you have accepted upon yourself (My sovereignty), to be your God, with (no need) for a mediator, therefore to Me alone shall you pray, and Me (alone) shall you serve (worship) without any mediator.

אֲשֶׁר הוֹצֵאתִיךָ מֵאֶרֶץ מִצְרַיִם — *Who brought you out of the land of Egypt . . .* through actions which were contrary to the (normal) laws of all "means," i.e., of nature and the constellations (of heaven). This (He did) when you accepted (His omnipotence) by stating, זֶה אֵלִי וְאַנְוֵהוּ, *This is my God and I will glorify Him* (15:2).

מִבֵּית עֲבָדִים — *Out of the house of bondage . . .* to remove all impediments (lit., "coercion") which (otherwise) would have prevented you from performing the commandments (of God) properly.

NOTES

first three words of the Ten Commandments are considered by the *Sforno* to be of prime importance, each signifying a fundamental attribute of the Almighty:

אָנֹכִי, *I*, emphasizes the oneness of God. He alone is the Master of the universe.

ה׳, *HASHEM*, denotes the concept taught by God to Moses when He said *I am that I am* (3:14). The *Sforno* comments on that verse that the implication of this name (the Tetragrammaton) is that God not only grants existence to all living things but also that He loves existence (life) and detests cruelty which destroys human existence. This idea was now pronounced by God at the beginning of the Ten Commandments.

אֱלֹהֶיךָ, *your God*, stresses the direct avenue of communication between God and His people without any need for intermediaries.

אֲשֶׁר הוֹצֵאתִיךָ מֵאֶרֶץ מִצְרַיִם — *Who brought you out of the land of Egypt.* Many commentators ask why God states, *"Who took you out of Egypt,"* rather than, *"Who created heaven and earth."* The

ד לְךָ אֱלֹהִים אֲחֵרִים עַל־פָּנָֽי׃ לֹֽא־תַֽעֲשֶׂה לְךָ פֶסֶל וְכָל־תְּמוּנָה אֲשֶׁר
בַּשָּׁמַיִם מִמַּעַל וַֽאֲשֶׁר בָּאָרֶץ מִתָּחַת וַֽאֲשֶׁר בַּמַּיִם מִתַּחַת לָאָֽרֶץ׃
ה לֹֽא־תִשְׁתַּחֲוֶה לָהֶם וְלֹא תָֽעָבְדֵם כִּי אָֽנֹכִי יהוה אֱלֹהֶיךָ אֵל קַנָּא פֹּקֵד
ו עֲוֺן אָבֹת עַל־בָּנִים עַל־שִׁלֵּשִׁים וְעַל־רִבֵּעִים לְשֹׂנְאָֽי׃ וְעֹשֶׂה חֶסֶד
ז לַֽאֲלָפִים לְאֹֽהֲבַי וּלְשֹֽׁמְרֵי מִצְוֺתָֽי׃ לֹא תִשָּׂא אֶת־שֵֽׁם־יהוה
אֱלֹהֶיךָ לַשָּׁוְא כִּי לֹא יְנַקֶּה יהוה אֵת אֲשֶׁר־יִשָּׂא אֶת־שְׁמוֹ לַשָּֽׁוְא׃

3. לֹא יִהְיֶה לְךָ אֱלֹהִים אֲחֵרִים — *You shall have no other gods.* Even though you accept My sovereignty, you shall serve none except Me, (even) as one serves the ministers (lit., "servant") of the king, akin to, אֶת ה׳ הָיוּ יְרֵאִים וְאֶת אֱלֹהֵיהֶם הָיוּ עֹבְדִים, *They feared* HASHEM *and served their own gods (II Kings* 17:33).

עַל פָּנָי — *Before Me* . . . for it is not permitted to show honor to (the king's) servants in his presence, and I am omnipresent, hence all places are equally (before Me).

4. לֹא תַעֲשֶׂה לְךָ פֶסֶל — *You shall not make a graven image* . . . even if not intended for idolatry (lit., "to be worshiped").

5. לֹא תִשְׁתַּחֲוֶה לָהֶם — *You shall not bow down to them* . . . to the objects found in the heavens and the earth.

אֵל קַנָּא — *A jealous God.* I resent that one who worships Me should worship another as well, for there is no (ground) for comparison between Me and another (object), therefore it is proper to be jealous for My honor, that it (not) be given to another who (or which) is unworthy.

פֹּקֵד עֲוֺן אָבֹת — *Remembering the iniquity of fathers.* The reason I practice forbearance to such an extent with some wicked (people) in this world is because I wait until their measure is full (and it is time) to destroy them even in this world; now I *remember* (or *visit*) *the iniquity of fathers* who have sinned . . .

עַל בָּנִים — *Upon the children.* (This is only so with those) who retain the (evil) deeds of their fathers, and add the כָל יֵצֶר מַחְשְׁבֹת לִבּוֹ, *imagination of the thoughts of their heart (Genesis* 6:5), proceeding from evil to evil in every generation, as it happened with Jeroboam.

עַל שִׁלֵּשִׁים — *Unto the third generation* . . . if they are more wicked than their fathers, as happened with the seed of Omri.

NOTES

Sforno explains that since the exodus from Egypt necessitated radical changes in nature, these phenomena proved God's omnipotence and also His role as Prime Cause and the Source of all existence. As such He demands of Israel that they accept Him alone as their God to the exclusion of all other deities, hence *you shall have no other gods.* Also their liberation from *the house of bondage* freed them to serve God and perform His commandments without the impediment of another master who would make demands on their time, energy and loyalty.

3. לֹא יִהְיֶה לְךָ אֱלֹהִים אֲחֵרִים עַל פָּנָי — *You shall have no other gods before Me.* The *Sforno* explains the second commandment in this sense: The acceptance of the sovereignty of a king precludes the worship of any of his ministers. This is especially true in the presence of the king, and since God is omnipresent it would always be in His presence.

5. פֹּקֵד עֲוֺן אָבֹת עַל בָּנִים עַל שִׁלֵּשִׁים וְעַל רִבֵּעִים — *Remembering the iniquity of fathers upon the children, unto the third generation and unto the fourth generation.* The *Sforno* cites as examples, in his interpretation of this verse, Jeroboam, Omri and Jehu. The former's punishment came in the second generation visited upon his son Nadav *(I Kings* 15:26). In the case of Omri the third generation was punished, i.e., in the reign of his grandson Jehoram son of Ahab, the royal house of Ahab was wiped out by Jehu *(II Kings* 9). As for Jehu himself,

[3] *You shall not recognize the gods of others in My presence.* [4] *You shall not make yourself a carved image nor any likeness of that which is in the heavens above or on the earth below or in the water beneath the earth.* [5] *You shall not prostrate yourself to them nor worship them, for I am* HASHEM, *your God — a jealous God, Who visits the sin of fathers upon children to the third and fourth generations, for My enemies;* [6] *but Who shows kindness for thousands [of generations] to those who love Me and observe My commandments.*

[7] *You shall not take the Name of* HASHEM, *your God, in vain, for* HASHEM *will not absolve anyone who takes His Name in vain.*

וְעַל רִבֵּעִים — *And unto the fourth generation.* This was the case with the offspring of Jehu, (who) did not add to the (wickedness) of their fathers, but who did reach the level of sin which had become the possession of (each) generation, (hence) there was no hope of repentance and they were liable for destruction, similar to כִּי לֹא שָׁלֵם עֲוֺן הָאֱמֹרִי, *for the iniquity of the Amorite is not yet full (Genesis* 15:16).

6. וְעֹשֶׂה חֶסֶד לַאֲלָפִים — *And showing mercy to the thousandth generation.* At times the cause for the extended (period) wherein I show kindness to thousands is because of the merit of a pious (lit., "one who loved Me") ancestor, and in his merit I show mercy to his offspring (for a number of generations).

7. לֹא תִשָּׂא — *You shall not take the Name.* (This refers to) שְׁבוּעַת הָאָלָה, *the oath of cursing,* similar to, וְנָשָׁא בוֹ אָלָה לְהַאֲלֹתוֹ, *And an oath be laid upon him to cause him to swear (I Kings* 8:31).

לַשָּׁוְא — *In vain.* There is no doubt that the curse and oath (is valid and) will take effect upon the one who swears in this fashion.

כִּי לֹא יְנַקֶּה ה׳ אֵת אֲשֶׁר יִשָּׂא אֶת שְׁמוֹ לַשָּׁוְא — *For* HASHEM *will not hold him guiltless who takes His Name in vain ...* for naught and when it is unnecessary. Even if one swears truthfully, God will not hold him guiltless from the curse and oath, how much more so if he swears falsely, for it is a dishonor (to God) if a man takes His Name except to substantiate a truth which otherwise could not be confirmed. However, an oath in His Name which is (utterly) false, i.e., if one states with an oath, "This is true, as God, the Blessed One, is true," behold he is an atheist and has desecrated His Name, for it is as though he said that God, the Blessed One, is not true, as it says: וְלֹא תִשָּׁבְעוּ בִשְׁמִי לַשָּׁקֶר וְחִלַּלְתָּ אֶת שֵׁם אֱלֹהֶיךָ, *And you shall not swear by My Name falsely, so that you profane the Name of your God (Lev.* 19:12).

NOTES

four generations of kings ruled until they in turn were deposed: Jehu, Jehoachaz, Joash and Jeroboam. When the latter's son Zechariah served as king for only six months, he was killed. Thus the statement that God visits the sins on the children, if they pursue the same path of wickedness as their forebears, is indeed *on children* (second generation), third and fourth generations. In each instance, punishment is executed only when God determines that the measure is full and there is no hope for repentance.

7. לֹא תִשָּׂא ... לַשָּׁוְא ... שְׁמוֹ לַשָּׁוְא — *You shall not take the Name ... in vain ... His Name in vain.* The word תִשָּׂא is ambiguous. To what is the commandment referring? By drawing a parallel to a similar word in *Kings,* וְנָשָׁא בוֹ, which specifies an *oath,* we learn that the phrase תִשָּׂא here also is speaking of swearing in God's Name. The first לַשָּׁוְא, *in vain,* refers to one who swears falsely, whereas the second refers to an unnecessary oath. The *Sforno* differentiates between one who swears falsely *in the Name of* HASHEM and one who links the truth of his testimony *directly* to the very essence of God's truth, for then he desecrates and profanes God. This explains the reason for the Torah's apparent repetition of this warning in *Leviticus.* The two are identical and we see this from the added words there, *profane the Name of God.*

ח־ט זָכוֹר אֶת־יוֹם הַשַּׁבָּת לְקַדְּשׁוֹ: שֵׁשֶׁת יָמִים תַּעֲבֹד וְעָשִׂיתָ כָּל־מְלַאכְתֶּךָ:
י וְיוֹם הַשְּׁבִיעִי שַׁבָּת לַיהוָה אֱלֹהֶיךָ לֹא־תַעֲשֶׂה כָל־מְלָאכָה אַתָּה | וּבִנְךָ
יא וּבִתֶּךָ עַבְדְּךָ וַאֲמָתְךָ וּבְהֶמְתֶּךָ וְגֵרְךָ אֲשֶׁר בִּשְׁעָרֶיךָ: כִּי שֵׁשֶׁת־יָמִים עָשָׂה
יהוָה אֶת־הַשָּׁמַיִם וְאֶת־הָאָרֶץ אֶת־הַיָּם וְאֶת־כָּל־אֲשֶׁר־בָּם וַיָּנַח בַּיּוֹם
יב הַשְּׁבִיעִי עַל־כֵּן בֵּרַךְ יהוָה אֶת־יוֹם הַשַּׁבָּת וַיְקַדְּשֵׁהוּ: כַּבֵּד
אֶת־אָבִיךָ וְאֶת־אִמֶּךָ לְמַעַן יַאֲרִכוּן יָמֶיךָ עַל הָאֲדָמָה אֲשֶׁר־יהוָה
יג אֱלֹהֶיךָ נֹתֵן לָךְ: לֹא תִרְצָח לֹא תִנְאָף לֹא תִגְנֹב לֹא־

---

8. זָכוֹר אֶת יוֹם הַשַּׁבָּת — *Remember the Sabbath day*. Be mindful and remember the Sabbath day constantly in all your dealings during the days of work, similar to, זָכוֹר אֵת אֲשֶׁר עָשָׂה לְךָ עֲמָלֵק, *Remember what Amalek did to you (Deut. 25:17)*; שָׁמוֹר אֶת חֹדֶשׁ הָאָבִיב, *Observe (guard) the month of Aviv (Deut. 16:1).*

לְקַדְּשׁוֹ — *To keep it holy*. This you shall do so that you be able to sanctify it. He cautions that a person should so order his affairs during the days of work in a manner that his mind be completely free of them on the Sabbath day.

9. שֵׁשֶׁת יָמִים תַּעֲבֹד — *Six days shall you labor*. In the works of earthly affairs (lit., "life of the hour") which are, without a doubt, (akin) to the labor of a slave, for the majority of these matters are those of man's sufferings (engendered) on behalf of עוֹלָם שֶׁאֵינוֹ שֶׁלּוֹ, *a world that is not his.*

וְעָשִׂיתָ כָּל מְלַאכְתֶּךָ — *And do all your work*. Necessary for your basic needs.

10. שַׁבָּת לַה׳ אֱלֹהֶיךָ — *A Sabbath unto* HASHEM, *your God* . . . (totally dedicated) to God; to study and teach, to observe and do, and to take delight in it sufficient to serve and honor the Blessed One, similar to (the saying of our Sages), "Wine and the aroma of spices made me bright" *(Yoma* 76b).

אַתָּה וּבִנְךָ וּבִתֶּךָ — *(Neither) you, nor your son, nor your daughter*. (This refers to) minor children who work at the behest of their father.

11. כִּי שֵׁשֶׁת יָמִים עָשָׂה ה׳ — *For in six days* HASHEM *made*. And the purpose of these (six days of Creation) was for man to be similar to his Creator as much as possible, which is in contemplation, study and freely chosen deeds, (all of which) will find favor in His presence.

NOTES

8. זָכוֹר אֶת יוֹם הַשַּׁבָּת לְקַדְּשׁוֹ — *Remember the Sabbath day to keep it holy*. The interpretation of the *Sforno* is based on the fact that זָכוֹר, *remember*, is an infinitive verb and as such is not limited in time. Therefore it implies that one should keep the Sabbath in mind during the week. The two verses cited are meant to demonstrate that the use of an infinitive verb is commonly used to indicate that one is exhorted to remember or observe continuously. The phrase *to keep it holy*, in turn, urges us to order our affairs during the week in such a manner that our mind be completely free of them on the Sabbath.

10. שַׁבָּת לַה׳ אֱלֹהֶיךָ — *A Sabbath unto* HASHEM, *your God*. The *Sforno* uses the expression כֻּלּוֹ לַה׳, *totally dedicated to God*, twice in his commentary: first in this verse on the phrase לַה׳ אֱלֹהֶיךָ, *unto* HASHEM *your God*, and again in verse 11 on the phrase וַיְקַדְּשֵׁהוּ *(and hallowed it)*. This presents a difficulty considering that the Talmud *(Pesachim* 68b) states, "All agree that on the Sabbath one should satisfy his physical needs" (i.e., eating, drinking, etc.). This would seem to contradict the *Sforno's* interpretation of these two phrases as implying exclusive involvement in spiritual and intellectual pursuits. One might answer, however, that since the prophet tells us to "*Call the Sabbath a delight* (עֹנֶג), *the holy day of* HASHEM *honorable* (מְכֻבָּד)" *(Isaiah* 58:13), therefore, when one engages in physical pleasures on the Sabbath motivated by the commandment to honor the Sabbath day, this is also considered as being לַה׳, *for* HASHEM*!*

12. לְמַעַן יַאֲרִכוּן יָמֶיךָ עַל הָאֲדָמָה — *That your days may be long upon the land*. The *Sforno* applies this promise *(that your days be long)* to the first five commandments, and following the interpretation of the Sages, explains that the length of days refers to the world to come where the term "long-lasting"

8 *Remember the Sabbath day to sanctify it.* 9 *Six days shall you work and accomplish all your work;* 10 *but the seventh day is Sabbath to* HASHEM, *your God; you shall not do any work — you, your son, your daughter, your slave, your maidservant, your animal, and your convert within your gates —* 11 *for in six days* HASHEM *made the heavens and the earth, the sea and all that is in them, and He rested on the seventh day. Therefore,* HASHEM *blessed the Sabbath day and sanctified it.*

12 *Honor your father and your mother, so that your days will be lengthened upon the land that* HASHEM, *your God, gives you.*

13 *You shall not kill; you shall not commit adultery; you shall not steal;*

וַיָּנַח בַּיּוֹם הַשְּׁבִיעִי — *And He rested on the seventh day.* For in it, all that was necessary to fulfill (God's) purpose and bring it to its goal was completed, and in (this) completion there is rest (tranquility).

עַל כֵּן בֵּרַךְ ה׳ אֶת יוֹם הַשַּׁבָּת — *Therefore* HASHEM *blessed the Sabbath day.* (He blessed it by granting man) a נְשָׁמָה יְתֵרָה, *added soul,* which is an expanded preparatory (spirit) for the service of God, the Blessed One.

וַיְקַדְּשֵׁהוּ — *And hallowed it* . . . that it be totally for God.

12. לְמַעַן יַאֲרִכוּן יָמֶיךָ — *That your days may be long.* These five commandments, if observed, will prolong your days, causing that your days be long (eternal life), i.e., without any natural or physical end, for the (concept) of width does not apply to these (days), as our Sages say, עוֹלָם שֶׁכֻּלּוֹ אָרוּךְ, *A world which is entirely "long" (lasting) (Kiddushin* 39b). For indeed these five commandments deal entirely with the honor of God, the Blessed One, and he who honors Him (by observing them) will inherit everlasting life. They are: that we (recognize) and know Him as the One Who brought into being (something) from nothing (*ex nihilo*); that He alone shall be your God and we will serve no other (deity), (and) we will not rebel against Him in thought, in speech, or deed, and we shall honor Him for He is our Father, our Maker.

עַל הָאֲדָמָה — *Upon the land.* By observing them (the first five commandments) you shall merit that the length of days which I have promised (lit., "said") shall be attained when dwelling on the land, i.e., you will not be exiled from it. However, the other five commandments, and they are: that we do not harm (lit., "injure") any man physically (lit., "his body"), his honor or his property, in deed, speech or thought, (all these) are warnings which protect (us) from punishment in this world and the world to come.

13. לֹא תִנְאָף — *You shall not commit adultery.* (This refers) primarily to a married woman, for it is the most common (offense) among sinners, but it also includes every prohibited intercourse.

NOTES

is applicable. *Length* implies eternity, whereas *width* is expansion, a concept applicable only to this world. The commandment to honor one's father and mother applies to God as well, Who is our Father. The commandments of אָנֹכִי, *I am* HASHEM *your God*, and לֹא יִהְיֶה, *You shall have no other*, are addressed to man's mind and thoughts (מַחְשָׁבָה); that of לֹא תִשָּׂא, *Thou shalt not take*, involves man's speech (דִּבּוּר); while לֹא תַעֲשֶׂה, *You shall not make*, and זָכוֹר, *Remember the Sabbath day*, involve deeds (מַעֲשֶׂה). By observing these commandments we honor God and are deserving of His blessing and protection on the soil of *Eretz Yisrael.*

The other five commandments deal with man's relationship to his fellow man. The prohibition against murder, adultery, and robbery are בְּמַעֲשֶׂה, *acts in deed;* the admonition not to bear false witness entails דִּבּוּר, *speech*, while the commandment not to covet involves מַחְשָׁבָה, *thought*. Thus the first and second parts of the Ten Commandments complement one another.

13. לֹא תִנְאָף — *You shall not commit adultery.* Although the prohibition of adultery applies primarily to a relationship with a married woman,

יד תַעֲנֶה בְרֵעֲךָ עֵד שָׁקֶר׃ לֹא תַחְמֹד
בֵּית רֵעֶךָ לֹא־תַחְמֹד אֵשֶׁת רֵעֶךָ וְעַבְדּוֹ וַאֲמָתוֹ
וְשׁוֹרוֹ וַחֲמֹרוֹ וְכֹל אֲשֶׁר לְרֵעֶךָ׃
שביעי טו וְכָל־הָעָם רֹאִים אֶת־הַקּוֹלֹת וְאֶת־הַלַּפִּידִם וְאֵת קוֹל הַשֹּׁפָר וְאֶת־הָהָר
טז עָשֵׁן וַיַּרְא הָעָם וַיָּנֻעוּ וַיַּעַמְדוּ מֵרָחֹק׃ וַיֹּאמְרוּ אֶל־מֹשֶׁה דַּבֵּר־אַתָּה
יז עִמָּנוּ וְנִשְׁמָעָה וְאַל־יְדַבֵּר עִמָּנוּ אֱלֹהִים פֶּן־נָמוּת׃ וַיֹּאמֶר מֹשֶׁה אֶל־
הָעָם אַל־תִּירָאוּ כִּי לְבַעֲבוּר נַסּוֹת אֶתְכֶם בָּא הָאֱלֹהִים וּבַעֲבוּר תִּהְיֶה
יח יִרְאָתוֹ עַל־פְּנֵיכֶם לְבִלְתִּי תֶחֱטָאוּ׃ וַיַּעֲמֹד הָעָם מֵרָחֹק וּמֹשֶׁה נִגַּשׁ
מפטיר יט אֶל־הָעֲרָפֶל אֲשֶׁר־שָׁם הָאֱלֹהִים׃ וַיֹּאמֶר יהוה אֶל־
מֹשֶׁה כֹּה תֹאמַר אֶל־בְּנֵי יִשְׂרָאֵל אַתֶּם רְאִיתֶם כִּי מִן־הַשָּׁמַיִם דִּבַּרְתִּי
כ עִמָּכֶם׃ לֹא תַעֲשׂוּן אִתִּי אֱלֹהֵי כֶסֶף וֵאלֹהֵי זָהָב לֹא תַעֲשׂוּ לָכֶם׃

לֹא תִגְנֹב — *You shall not steal.* This includes kidnapping, stealing property, stealing man's mind (i.e., deception), although the main warning applies to kidnapping, דָּבָר הַלָּמֵד מֵעִנְיָנוֹ, *an interpretation which is deduced from the text*, as our Sages say (*Sanhedrin* 86a).

לֹא תַעֲנֶה בְרֵעֲךָ עֵד שָׁקֶר — *Do not bear false witness against your neighbor.* Included in this (commandment) are talebearing and slander, although the main (warning) applies to testifying (falsely) in court.

14. לֹא תַחְמֹד — *You shall not covet.* You should consider everything (which is not yours) as something totally unattainable, for that which is unattainable (beyond one's reach) man's nature will not covet at all, similar to, וְלֹא יַחְמֹד אִישׁ אֶת אַרְצְךָ, *neither shall any man covet your land* (34:24), for covetousness causes (one) to steal, as we find by Achan, וָאֶחְמְדֵם וָאֶקָּחֵם, *then I coveted them and took them* (*Joshua* 7:21).

15. רֹאִים אֶת הַקּוֹלֹת — *Perceived the thunderings.* Comparable to וְלִבִּי רָאָה, *my heart has seen* (*Ecclesiastes* 1:16). They looked attentively at (considered) the thunderings and (realized) that they could not bear them, as it says, לֹא אֹסֵף לִשְׁמֹעַ אֶת קוֹל ה׳ אֱלֹהָי וְאֶת הָאֵשׁ הַגְּדֹלָה הַזֹּאת לֹא אֶרְאֶה עוֹד וְלֹא אָמוּת, *Let me not hear again the voice of* HASHEM *my God, neither let me see this great fire anymore, that I die not* (*Deut.* 18:16).

וַיַּרְא הָעָם — *And the people saw.* They considered what to do.

וַיָּנֻעוּ — *They reeled.* One who moves involuntarily to a place beyond his present one is called נָע, similar to וַיְנִעֵם בַּמִּדְבָּר, *and He made them wander to and fro in the wilderness* (*Numbers* 32:13); נוֹעַ תָּנוּעַ אֶרֶץ כַּשִּׁכּוֹר, *The earth shall reel to and fro like a drunkard* (*Isaiah* 24:20). As a result of this fear they involuntarily retreated from the area (where

NOTES

this commandment forbids all illicit relations between the sexes.

לֹא תִגְנֹב — *You shall not steal.* Our Sages, mindful of the verse in *Leviticus* 19:11, *You shall not steal*, explain that this verse in *Exodus* refers to kidnapping while the one in *Leviticus* refers to property. Their reasoning is based on the context of our chapter. Since the crimes of murder and adultery that immediately precede this commandment are punishable with death by a court, likewise that of stealing (לֹא תִגְנֹב) must involve a death penalty, hence it must be the act of stealing another person, i.e., kidnapping, since stealing property is not punishable by death.

14. לֹא תַחְמֹד — *You shall not covet.* The *Sforno* interprets the commandment, *You shall not covet*, which seemingly is an unrealistic demand made on frail man who is subject to desires and jealousies, to mean: What is another's should be considered as totally beyond your ken, utterly unavailable, akin to a princess beheld by a peasant, as other commentators put it. His proof from the verse which speaks of Israel going on their pilgrimage to Jerusalem during the festivals (34:24) is

you shall not bear false witness against your fellow.

14 *You shall not covet your fellow's house. You shall not covet your fellow's wife, his manservant, his maidservant, his ox, his donkey, nor anything that belongs to your fellow.*

15 *The entire people saw the thunder and the flames, the sound of the shofar and the smoking mountain; the people saw and trembled and stood from afar.* 16 *They said to Moses, "You speak to us and we shall hear; let God not speak to us lest we die."*

17 *Moses said to the people, "Do not fear, for in order to elevate you has God come; so that awe of Him shall be upon your faces, so that you shall not sin."* 18 *The people stood from afar and Moses approached the thick cloud where God was.*

19 *HASHEM said to Moses, "So shall you say to the Children of Israel, 'You have seen that I have spoken to you from heaven.* 20 *You shall not make [images of] what is with Me; gods of silver and gods of gold shall you not make for yourselves.*

---

they stood) to a place beyond (them).

17. לְבַעֲבוּר נַסּוֹת אֶתְכֶם — *To test you.* To accustom (familiarize) you to the prophecy which you have merited "face to face," similar to the case of Elijah whose prophecy (at that moment) was experienced while (he was) in command of his senses, as it says, וַיָּלֶט פָּנָיו בְּאַדַּרְתּוֹ וַיֵּצֵא וַיַּעֲמֹד פֶּתַח הַמְּעָרָה, *He wrapped his face in his mantle and went out and stood in the entrance of the cave (I Kings* 19:13), although it may not have been through a bright lens as was the case with Moses, our teacher, of whom it is said, אֲשֶׁר יְדָעוֹ ה׳ פָּנִים אֶל פָּנִים, *Whom HASHEM knew face to face (Deut.* 34:10).

בָּא הָאֱלֹהִים — *God is come . . .* (i.e.,) the heavenly household, as said above, לִקְרַאת הָאֱלֹהִים, *to meet God* (19:17).

וּבַעֲבוּר תִּהְיֶה יִרְאָתוֹ עַל פְּנֵיכֶם — *And that His fear may be before you.* (This is) similar to the reason given by Rabbi Yehoshua to the Caesar when he said, "You say that you cannot look (directly at the sun) which is but one of the servants standing before the Holy One, Blessed is He; how much more so the Divine Presence!" *(Chullin* 60a).

19. אַתֶּם רְאִיתֶם כִּי מִן הַשָּׁמַיִם דִּבַּרְתִּי עִמָּכֶם — *You have seen that I have talked with you from heaven,* similar to הַמַּגְבִּיהִי לָשָׁבֶת . . . הַמַּשְׁפִּילִי לִרְאוֹת, *Who is enthroned on high . . . Who lowers Himself to see (Psalms* 113:5,6).

20. לֹא תַעֲשׂוּן אִתִּי אֱלֹהֵי כֶסֶף — *You shall not make with Me gods of silver.* Now since you

NOTES

a most telling one. He interprets this assurance of God as meaning that the non-Jews will consider *Eretz Yisrael* as totally beyond their reach, a land which they can never aspire to own!

17. לְבַעֲבוּר נַסּוֹת אֶתְכֶם — *To test you.* The parallel drawn by the *Sforno* to Elijah refers to the time when Elijah had vanquished the prophets of Baal on Mt. Carmel only to find himself fleeing from the wrath of Jezebel into the wilderness. At that moment of despair God spoke to him in *a still small voice.* This revelation was on a higher level than any previous appearance or communication by God to Elijah. Even this great prophet could not gaze upon God's glory and had to cover his face. For all Israel to have reached this level at Sinai was indeed proof of their readiness to receive God. This unique encounter left a lasting imprint of יִרְאַת ה׳, *reverence of HASHEM,* upon them.

19. אַתֶּם רְאִיתֶם כִּי מִן הַשָּׁמַיִם דִּבַּרְתִּי עִמָּכֶם — *You have seen that I have talked with you from heaven.* In this verse God says that He spoke to Israel from heaven. In 10:20, the Torah tells us that *HASHEM descended onto Mt. Sinai.* This seeming contradiction is what the *Sforno* is addressing in his quotation from *Psalms.* Since God's presence is everywhere, and He is *the place of the world,* the concept of God *being* in a place is in itself a misleading one. He is above and below at the same time.

כא מִזְבַּח אֲדָמָה תַּעֲשֶׂה־לִּי וְזָבַחְתָּ עָלָיו אֶת־עֹלֹתֶיךָ וְאֶת־שְׁלָמֶיךָ אֶת־
צֹאנְךָ וְאֶת־בְּקָרֶךָ בְּכָל־הַמָּקוֹם אֲשֶׁר אַזְכִּיר אֶת־שְׁמִי אָבוֹא אֵלֶיךָ
כב וּבֵרַכְתִּיךָ: וְאִם־מִזְבַּח אֲבָנִים תַּעֲשֶׂה־לִּי לֹא־תִבְנֶה אֶתְהֶן גָּזִית כִּי
כג חַרְבְּךָ הֵנַפְתָּ עָלֶיהָ וַתְּחַלְלֶהָ: וְלֹא־תַעֲלֶה בְמַעֲלֹת עַל־מִזְבְּחִי אֲשֶׁר
לֹא־תִגָּלֶה עֶרְוָתְךָ עָלָיו:

---

saw that you need no intermediary to come close to Me, do not make *with Me* such (silver gods to serve as) intermediaries.

21. מִזְבַּח אֲדָמָה תַּעֲשֶׂה לִּי — *An altar of earth shall you make to Me.* It is also not necessary to make Temples of silver and gold and precious stones in order to bring Me close to you, but it is sufficient (to build) *an altar of earth.*

בְּכָל הַמָּקוֹם אֲשֶׁר אַזְכִּיר אֶת שְׁמִי — *In every place where I cause My Name to be mentioned.* (This means) which I shall choose as a meeting house to worship Me, similar to הַזְכִּירוּ כִּי נִשְׂגָּב שְׁמוֹ, *make mention that His Name is exalted (Isaiah* 12:4).

NOTES

20-23. לֹא תַעֲשׂוּן אִתִּי אֱלֹהֵי כֶסֶף ... מִזְבַּח אֲדָמָה תַּעֲשֶׂה לִּי ... וְלֹא תַעֲלֶה בְמַעֲלֹת — *You shall not make with Me gods of silver ... An altar of earth shall you make to Me ... Neither shall you go up by steps.* The thrust of these verses, as the *Sforno* sees it, is that God does not demand, or desire, any elaborate, ornate expensive expressions of reverence on the part of His people.

21 " *'An Altar of earth shall you make for Me, and you shall slaughter near it your elevation-offerings and your peace-offerings, your flock and your herd; wherever I permit My Name to be mentioned I shall come to you and bless you.* 22 *And when you make for Me an Altar of stones, do not build them hewn, for you will have raised your sword over it and desecrated it.*
23 *You shall not ascend My Altar on steps, so that your nakedness will not be uncovered upon it.' "*

אָבוֹא אֵלֶיךָ וּבֵרַכְתִּיךָ — *I will come to you and bless you.* You will not have to attract My providence through the medium of gold, silver or other (precious metals and stones), for indeed I *will come to you and bless you.*

22. לֹא תִבְנֶה אֶתְהֶן גָּזִית — *You shall not build it of hewn stone . . .* to beautify it.

23. וְלֹא תַעֲלֶה בְמַעֲלֹת — *Neither shall you go up by steps.* Although I will not impose upon you to fashion adornments to (bring Me to) dwell in your midst, nonetheless be careful not to treat My altar lightly (with levity).

NOTES

However, this does not mean that we are to take our obligations to, and service of, God lightly, which is the reason for the prohibition of installing steps to ascend the altar. By installing a ramp instead, the priest's garments will not be disturbed and he will not expose himself while ascending. God may be content with a simple unadorned altar but His honor, and our respect and reverence, are of paramount importance.

פרשת משפטים

כא

א־ב וְאֵלֶּה הַמִּשְׁפָּטִים אֲשֶׁר תָּשִׂים לִפְנֵיהֶם: כִּי תִקְנֶה עֶבֶד עִבְרִי שֵׁשׁ שָׁנִים
ג יַעֲבֹד וּבַשְּׁבִעִת יֵצֵא לַחָפְשִׁי חִנָּם: אִם־בְּגַפּוֹ יָבֹא בְּגַפּוֹ יֵצֵא אִם־בַּעַל
ד אִשָּׁה הוּא וְיָצְאָה אִשְׁתּוֹ עִמּוֹ: אִם־אֲדֹנָיו יִתֶּן־לוֹ אִשָּׁה וְיָלְדָה־לוֹ בָנִים
ה אוֹ בָנוֹת הָאִשָּׁה וִילָדֶיהָ תִּהְיֶה לַאדֹנֶיהָ וְהוּא יֵצֵא בְגַפּוֹ: וְאִם־אָמֹר
יֹאמַר הָעֶבֶד אָהַבְתִּי אֶת־אֲדֹנִי אֶת־אִשְׁתִּי וְאֶת־בָּנָי לֹא אֵצֵא חָפְשִׁי:
ו וְהִגִּישׁוֹ אֲדֹנָיו אֶל־הָאֱלֹהִים וְהִגִּישׁוֹ אֶל־הַדֶּלֶת אוֹ אֶל־הַמְּזוּזָה וְרָצַע
ז אֲדֹנָיו אֶת־אָזְנוֹ בַּמַּרְצֵעַ וַעֲבָדוֹ לְעֹלָם: וְכִי־יִמְכֹּר
ח אִישׁ אֶת־בִּתּוֹ לְאָמָה לֹא תֵצֵא כְּצֵאת הָעֲבָדִים: אִם־רָעָה בְּעֵינֵי אֲדֹנֶיהָ
אֲשֶׁר־°לֹא יְעָדָהּ וְהֶפְדָּהּ לְעַם נָכְרִי לֹא־יִמְשֹׁל לְמָכְרָהּ בְּבִגְדוֹ־בָהּ:
ט־י וְאִם־לִבְנוֹ יִיעָדֶנָּה כְּמִשְׁפַּט הַבָּנוֹת יַעֲשֶׂה־לָּהּ: אִם־אַחֶרֶת יִקַּח־לוֹ
יא שְׁאֵרָהּ כְּסוּתָהּ וְעֹנָתָהּ לֹא יִגְרָע: וְאִם־שְׁלָשׁ־אֵלֶּה לֹא יַעֲשֶׂה לָהּ וְיָצְאָה
יב חִנָּם אֵין כָּסֶף: מַכֵּה אִישׁ וָמֵת מוֹת יוּמָת:

XXI

1. וְאֵלֶּה הַמִּשְׁפָּטִים — *And these are the ordinances.* Behold, that in the previous chapter, the commandment (lit., "warning"), לֹא תַחְמֹד ... וְכֹל אֲשֶׁר לְרֵעֶךָ, *You shall not covet ... nor anything that is your neighbor's* (20:14) appears; (therefore) *and these are the ordinances* (follows), for through them men will know what is meant by *anything that is your neighbor's.*

אֲשֶׁר תָּשִׂים לִפְנֵיהֶם — *Which you shall set before them.* These do not consist of positive and negative commandments as the warnings of the previous chapter (did), rather when the occasion arises to judge, the legal decision shall be (determined) in the manner (set forth here).

7. לֹא תֵצֵא כְּצֵאת הָעֲבָדִים — *She shall not go out as the menservants do.* It is improper for a decent (lit., "kosher") man to purchase a Jewish girl as a bondwoman without her consent. Rather this purchase shall be with the view of marriage to himself or his son, and the purchase money will be considered as given to her father to wed her, since he is entitled to it, as our Sages have stated *(Kesubos* 46b).

8. אִם רָעָה בְּעֵינֵי אֲדֹנֶיהָ — *If she please not her master.* Even so, if she does not please him, he should not marry her, lest he come to despise her. Rather her father and master should attempt to let her be redeemed.

NOTES

XXI

1. וְאֵלֶּה הַמִּשְׁפָּטִים — *And these are the ordinances.* The law determines legal ownership. Without civil laws which define the parameters of possession one has no way of identifying the true ownership of any item or object. Hence, the prohibition against coveting that which belongs to my neighbor can only be properly understood and observed if I know what is legally his. That is why the concluding commandment of the Ten Commandments is followed by the chapter of מִשְׁפָּטִים, *Ordinances,* and the corpus of civil law. With this interpretation the *Sforno* explains the use of the prefix ו׳, *and,* in the first word of this chapter, וְאֵלֶּה, *and these,* for it links the end of *Yisro* with the beginning of *Mishpatim.*

אֲשֶׁר תָּשִׂים לִפְנֵיהֶם — *Which you shall set before them.* The *Sforno* explains the choice of the phrase אֲשֶׁר תָּשִׂים, *which you shall set,* as opposed to a seemingly more appropriate one such as תֹּאמַר, *state,* תְּדַבֵּר, *speak,* or תְּצַוֶּה, *command.* These phrases would be fitting if this chapter spoke of positive or negative commandments. This, however, is not the case, for the Torah is not dealing

PARASHAS MISHPATIM

21 [1] *And these are the ordinances that you shall place before them:*
[2] If you buy a Jewish bondsman, he shall work for six years; and in the
seventh he shall go free, for no charge. [3] If he shall arrive by himself, he shall
leave by himself; if he is the husband of a woman, his wife shall leave with
him. [4] If his master will give him a woman and she bears him sons or daugh-
ters, the wife and her children shall belong to her master, and he shall go out
by himself. [5] But if the bondsman shall say, "I love my master, my wife, and
my children — I shall not go free"; [6] then his master shall bring him to the
court and shall bring him to the door or to the doorpost, and his master shall
bore through his ear with the awl, and he shall serve him forever.
[7] If a man will sell his daughter as a bondswoman, she shall not leave like
the leavetaking of the slaves. [8] If she is displeasing in the eyes of her master,
who should have designated her for himself, he shall assist in her redemp-
tion; he shall not have the power to sell her to a strange man, for he had
betrayed her. [9] If he had designated her for his son, he shall deal with her
according to the rights of the young women. [10] If he shall take another in
addition to her, he shall not diminish her food, her clothing, or her marital
relationship. [11] If he does not perform these three for her, she shall leave free
of charge, without payment.
[12] One who strikes a man, so that he dies, shall surely be put to death.

לְעַם נָכְרִי לֹא יִמְשֹׁל לְמָכְרָהּ בְּבִגְדוֹ בָהּ — *To sell her to a strange people he shall have no power, seeing he has dealt deceitfully with her.* Her father dealt deceitfully with his daughter by selling her, as it says, הֲלוֹא נָכְרִיּוֹת נֶחְשַׁבְנוּ לוֹ כִּי מְכָרָנוּ, *Are we not accounted by him strangers? For he has sold us* (*Genesis* 31:15). After he (the father) has seen the actions (of the purchaser) which are alien to an Israelite, who bought a Jewish daughter not for the purpose of marriage, then he (her father) no longer has the power to sell her later to another person who (might) act as alien as did (the first one).

9. כְּמִשְׁפַּט הַבָּנוֹת יַעֲשֶׂה לָּהּ — *He shall deal with her after the manner of daughters.* (The subject is) his son. The (duties) are food, raiment and conjugal rights, even though he (the son) did not purchase her or betroth her.

10. לֹא יִגְרָע — *He shall not diminish.* He is not permitted to take other wives unless he can meet their needs in a manner that he not diminish that to which his first wife is entitled.

NOTES

here with obligatory injunctions. Rather we are being instructed how to deal justly with certain situations as they arise; hence the expression to *set before them* is a suitable one.

7-8. . . . לֹא תֵצֵא כְּצֵאת הָעֲבָדִים. אִם רָעָה בְּעֵינֵי אֲדֹנֶיהָ לְעַם נָכְרִי — *She shall not go out as the menservants do. If she please not her master . . . to a strange people.* The sense of these verses according to the *Sforno* is as follows. We consider it unseemly for a Jewish man to purchase a daughter of Israel as a bondwoman. It is improper, immodest, and degrading. Therefore the money paid by him to the father should be considered as being כֶּסֶף קִדּוּשִׁין, *betrothal money*, and she then becomes his wife or his son's. To do otherwise is alien to Jewish norms and is therefore called נָכְרִי, *strange*, by the Torah. Once she has been spurned by the purchaser and wronged by her father, the Torah prohibits a repetition of this injustice (v. 8).

9. כְּמִשְׁפַּט הַבָּנוֹת יַעֲשֶׂה לָּהּ — *He shall deal with her after the manner of daughters.* Our Sages derive the laws of marital obligations from this verse, which are included in the *Kesubah* (marriage contract) to this very day. They are: support, clothing, and conjugal rights.

10. לֹא יִגְרָע — *He shall not diminish.* The *Sforno* reflects the statement of our Sages (*Yevamos* 65a), "A man may marry a number of women, providing he can attend to their needs." (Compare the *Sforno's* comments to *Genesis* 29:18.)

יג וַאֲשֶׁר לֹא צָדָה וְהָאֱלֹהִים אִנָּה לְיָדוֹ וְשַׂמְתִּי לְךָ מָקוֹם אֲשֶׁר יָנוּס
יד שָׁמָּה: וְכִי־יָזִד אִישׁ עַל־רֵעֵהוּ לְהָרְגוֹ בְעָרְמָה מֵעִם מִזְבְּחִי
טו־טז תִּקָּחֶנּוּ לָמוּת: וּמַכֵּה אָבִיו וְאִמּוֹ מוֹת יוּמָת: וְגֹנֵב
יז אִישׁ וּמְכָרוֹ וְנִמְצָא בְיָדוֹ מוֹת יוּמָת: וּמְקַלֵּל אָבִיו וְאִמּוֹ
יח מוֹת יוּמָת: וְכִי־יְרִיבֻן אֲנָשִׁים וְהִכָּה־אִישׁ אֶת־רֵעֵהוּ בְּאֶבֶן
יט אוֹ בְאֶגְרֹף וְלֹא יָמוּת וְנָפַל לְמִשְׁכָּב: אִם־יָקוּם וְהִתְהַלֵּךְ בַּחוּץ
שני כ עַל־מִשְׁעַנְתּוֹ וְנִקָּה הַמַּכֶּה רַק שִׁבְתּוֹ יִתֵּן וְרַפֹּא יְרַפֵּא: וְכִי־
יַכֶּה אִישׁ אֶת־עַבְדּוֹ אוֹ אֶת־אֲמָתוֹ בַּשֵּׁבֶט וּמֵת תַּחַת יָדוֹ נָקֹם יִנָּקֵם:
כא־כב אַךְ אִם־יוֹם אוֹ יוֹמַיִם יַעֲמֹד לֹא יֻקַּם כִּי כַסְפּוֹ הוּא: וְכִי־
יִנָּצוּ אֲנָשִׁים וְנָגְפוּ אִשָּׁה הָרָה וְיָצְאוּ יְלָדֶיהָ וְלֹא יִהְיֶה אָסוֹן עָנוֹשׁ
כג יֵעָנֵשׁ כַּאֲשֶׁר יָשִׁית עָלָיו בַּעַל הָאִשָּׁה וְנָתַן בִּפְלִלִים: וְאִם־אָסוֹן יִהְיֶה
כד וְנָתַתָּה נֶפֶשׁ תַּחַת נָפֶשׁ: עַיִן תַּחַת עַיִן שֵׁן תַּחַת שֵׁן יָד תַּחַת יָד
כה רֶגֶל תַּחַת רָגֶל: כְּוִיָּה תַּחַת כְּוִיָּה פֶּצַע תַּחַת פָּצַע חַבּוּרָה תַּחַת
כו חַבּוּרָה: וְכִי־יַכֶּה אִישׁ אֶת־עֵין עַבְדּוֹ אוֹ־אֶת־עֵין אֲמָתוֹ
כז וְשִׁחֲתָהּ לַחָפְשִׁי יְשַׁלְּחֶנּוּ תַּחַת עֵינוֹ: וְאִם־שֵׁן עַבְדּוֹ אוֹ־שֵׁן אֲמָתוֹ יַפִּיל
לַחָפְשִׁי יְשַׁלְּחֶנּוּ תַּחַת שִׁנּוֹ:

---

13. וְהָאֱלֹהִים אִנָּה לְיָדוֹ — *But God caused it to come to his hand.* He was not guilty of negligence that this should have been caused (through him), but, מְגַלְגְּלִין חוֹבָה עַל יְדֵי חַיָּב, *punishment is brought about through a person of guilt* (*Sabbath* 32a), as it says, וְגַם רָשָׁע לְיוֹם רָעָה, *Even the wicked for the day of evil* (*Proverbs* 16:4).

וְשַׂמְתִּי לְךָ מָקוֹם אֲשֶׁר יָנוּס — *And I will appoint a place for you where he may flee . . .* to atone for his iniquity in exile.

14. מֵעִם מִזְבְּחִי — *From My Altar.* (This is so) even though the entire camp of the Levites was a place of refuge in the wilderness.

תִּקָּחֶנּוּ לָמוּת — *You shall take him, that he may die.* (This is) similar to, הַמְעָרַת פָּרִצִים הָיָה הַבַּיִת הַזֶּה, *Has this house become a den of robbers?* (*Jeremiah* 7:11).

20. נָקֹם יִנָּקֵם — *He shall surely be avenged.* The blood of the slave (shall be avenged), for the master is not permitted to smite (him) with such cruel blows, even though he does have

NOTES

13. וְהָאֱלֹהִים אִנָּה לְיָדוֹ — *But God caused it to come to his hand.* The first part of the verse from *Proverbs* reads: *HASHEM has made everything for His own purpose.* The Almighty uses many people as His messengers to exact justice. The Talmud in *Makkos* 10b (cited by *Rashi* on this verse) explains the expression, *caused it to come to his hand,* thus: Two people had committed murder in the past, one willfully, the other accidentally, but no witnesses were present. God brings them together at a given place and the latter falls upon the former, killing him accidentally in the presence of witnesses. In this manner the murderer is "executed" while the accidental killer goes into exile, which is his atonement and his punishment.

14. מֵעִם מִזְבְּחִי תִּקָּחֶנּוּ לָמוּת — *From My Altar you shall take him, that he may die.* The *Sforno* explains the use of the word מִזְבְּחִי (*My Altar*) in the sense of "*even* from the Altar" you shall take the killer, for he will not find sanctuary by entering the sacred precincts of the Sanctuary or Temple, even if he grasps the *horns of the Altar,* as we find by Joab (*I Kings* 2:28). The verse quoted by the *Sforno* (*Jeremiah* 7:11) is preceded by the words, *and come and stand before Me in this house . . . and say, "We are delivered."* The evildoers attempted to find sanctuary and deliverance from their transgressions by coming to the Temple, abusing its sanctity and perverting it to camouflage their wickedness. The prophet warned them that God

13 *But for one who had not lain in ambush and God had caused it to come to his hand, I shall provide you a place to which he shall flee.*

14 *If a man shall act intentionally against his fellow to kill him with guile — from My Altar shall you take him to die.*

15 *One who strikes his father or mother shall surely be put to death.*

16 *One who kidnaps a man and sells him, and he was found to have been in his power, shall surely be put to death.*

17 *One who curses his father or mother shall surely be put to death.*

18 *If men quarrel and one strikes his fellow with a stone or a fist, and he does not die but falls into bed:* 19 *If he gets up and goes about outside under his own power, the one who struck is absolved. Only for his lost time shall he pay, and he shall provide for healing.*

20 *If a man shall strike his slave or his maidservant with the rod and he shall die under his hand, he shall surely be avenged.* 21 *But if he will survive for a day or two, he shall not be avenged, for he is his property.*

22 *If men shall fight and they collide with a pregnant woman and she miscarries, but there will be no fatality, he shall surely be punished as the husband of the woman shall cause to be assessed against him, and he shall pay it by order of judges.* 23 *But if there shall be a fatality, then you shall award a life for a life;* 24 *an eye for an eye, a tooth for a tooth, a hand for a hand, a foot for a foot;* 25 *a burn for a burn, a wound for a wound, a bruise for a bruise.*

26 *If a man shall strike the eye of his slave or the eye of his maidservant and destroy it, he shall set him free in return for his eye.* 27 *And if he knocks out the tooth of his slave or the tooth of his maidservant, he shall set him free in return for his tooth.*

---

the right to smite him to correct him, as it says: בִּדְבָרִים לֹא יִוָּסֶר עָבֶד, *A slave will not be corrected by words (Proverbs* 29:19).

21. כִּי כַסְפּוֹ הוּא — *For he is his money.* And he has the right to discipline him, and at times the slave defies him causing the master to become so angered that he smites him excessively, as it says, אַךְ מְרִי יְבַקֶּשׁ רָע, *An evil man seeks only to be insolent (Proverbs* 17:11).

24. עַיִן תַּחַת עַיִן — *An eye for an eye.* This would have been the fitting (punishment) according to the strict law of measure for measure, but we have received a tradition that he should pay money, because our conjecture may be at fault (lit., "lacking"), and we may unwisely exceed the exact measure (in punishing) the guilty (one).

NOTES

would not permit His house to become a refuge for robbers and other sinners.

20. נָקֹם יִנָּקֵם — *He shall surely be avenged.* The Talmud *(Kesubos* 77a) applies this verse in *Proverbs* to every person, not only to a slave. Words alone do not suffice at all times to convince a person, and one must occasionally resort to physical persuasion.

24. עַיִן תַּחַת עַיִן — *An eye for an eye.* Our Sages have taught us that *an eye for an eye* means monetary compensation *(Bava Kama* 83b). The *Rambam (Mishneh Torah,* Laws of Injuries 1:3) states that the person who blinded the eye of another is *worthy* to have his eye blinded as well (measure for measure), but tradition teaches us not to do so. The reason given in the Talmud cited above is because this kind of punishment would not always be equitable and the Torah teaches us, מִשְׁפַּט אֶחָד יִהְיֶה לָכֶם, *You shall have one manner of law (Leviticus* 24:22). The *Sforno's* interpretation reflects all this.

כח וְכִי־יִגַּח שׁוֹר אֶת־אִישׁ אוֹ אֶת־אִשָּׁה וָמֵת סָקוֹל יִסָּקֵל הַשּׁוֹר וְלֹא יֵאָכֵל
כט אֶת־בְּשָׂרוֹ וּבַעַל הַשּׁוֹר נָקִי: וְאִם שׁוֹר נַגָּח הוּא מִתְּמֹל שִׁלְשֹׁם וְהוּעַד
בִּבְעָלָיו וְלֹא יִשְׁמְרֶנּוּ וְהֵמִית אִישׁ אוֹ אִשָּׁה הַשּׁוֹר יִסָּקֵל וְגַם־בְּעָלָיו
ל-לא יוּמָת: אִם־כֹּפֶר יוּשַׁת עָלָיו וְנָתַן פִּדְיֹן נַפְשׁוֹ כְּכֹל אֲשֶׁר־יוּשַׁת עָלָיו: אוֹ־בֵן
לב יִגָּח אוֹ־בַת יִגָּח כַּמִּשְׁפָּט הַזֶּה יֵעָשֶׂה לּוֹ: אִם־עֶבֶד יִגַּח הַשּׁוֹר אוֹ אָמָה
לג כֶּסֶף ׀ שְׁלֹשִׁים שְׁקָלִים יִתֵּן לַאדֹנָיו וְהַשּׁוֹר יִסָּקֵל: וְכִי־יִפְתַּח
אִישׁ בּוֹר אוֹ כִּי־יִכְרֶה אִישׁ בֹּר וְלֹא יְכַסֶּנּוּ וְנָפַל־שָׁמָּה שּׁוֹר אוֹ חֲמוֹר:
לד-לה בַּעַל הַבּוֹר יְשַׁלֵּם כֶּסֶף יָשִׁיב לִבְעָלָיו וְהַמֵּת יִהְיֶה־לּוֹ: וְכִי־
יִגֹּף שׁוֹר־אִישׁ אֶת־שׁוֹר רֵעֵהוּ וָמֵת וּמָכְרוּ אֶת־הַשּׁוֹר הַחַי וְחָצוּ
לו אֶת־כַּסְפּוֹ וְגַם אֶת־הַמֵּת יֶחֱצוּן: אוֹ נוֹדַע כִּי שׁוֹר נַגָּח הוּא מִתְּמוֹל
שִׁלְשֹׁם וְלֹא יִשְׁמְרֶנּוּ בְּעָלָיו שַׁלֵּם יְשַׁלֵּם שׁוֹר תַּחַת הַשּׁוֹר וְהַמֵּת יִהְיֶה־
לז לּוֹ: כִּי יִגְנֹב־אִישׁ שׁוֹר אוֹ־שֶׂה וּטְבָחוֹ אוֹ מְכָרוֹ חֲמִשָּׁה בָקָר
כב א יְשַׁלֵּם תַּחַת הַשּׁוֹר וְאַרְבַּע־צֹאן תַּחַת הַשֶּׂה: אִם־בַּמַּחְתֶּרֶת יִמָּצֵא הַגַּנָּב
ב וְהֻכָּה וָמֵת אֵין לוֹ דָּמִים: אִם־זָרְחָה הַשֶּׁמֶשׁ עָלָיו דָּמִים לוֹ שַׁלֵּם יְשַׁלֵּם
ג אִם־אֵין לוֹ וְנִמְכַּר בִּגְנֵבָתוֹ: אִם־הִמָּצֵא תִמָּצֵא בְיָדוֹ הַגְּנֵבָה מִשּׁוֹר
שלישי ד עַד־חֲמוֹר עַד־שֶׂה חַיִּים שְׁנַיִם יְשַׁלֵּם: כִּי יַבְעֶר־אִישׁ שָׂדֶה
אוֹ־כֶרֶם וְשִׁלַּח אֶת־בְּעִירֹה וּבִעֵר בִּשְׂדֵה אַחֵר מֵיטַב שָׂדֵהוּ וּמֵיטַב כַּרְמוֹ

29. וְגַם בְּעָלָיו יוּמָת — *And its owners also shall be put to death.* If there are no witnesses (whose evidence would) make them liable to pay a ransom (כֹּפֶר), they are (then) guilty according to the law of Heaven.

30. אִם כֹּפֶר יוּשַׁת עָלָיו — *If there be laid on him a ransom.* If witnesses testify in such a manner that the judges will impose a ransom on him.

32. כֶּסֶף שְׁלֹשִׁים שְׁקָלִים — *Thirty shekels of silver.* Which is the evaluation (redemption money) of a female (*Leviticus* 27:4), for a slave is similar to a woman in respect to the performance of *mitzvos*, as we find in tractate *Chagigah* in the first chapter (4a).

XXII

2. וְנִמְכַּר בִּגְנֵבָתוֹ — *Then he shall be sold for his theft.* Were it not for this (punishment) the majority of impoverished people would (resort) to thievery, (reasoning that) if they destroy or consume what they have stolen there is no way to force restitution, since they

NOTES

29-30. וְגַם בְּעָלָיו יוּמָת . . . אִם כֹּפֶר יוּשַׁת עָלָיו — *And its owners also shall be put to death . . . If there be laid on him a ransom.* The *Sforno* is in agreement with *Rashi*, based upon the Talmud (*Sanhedrin* 15b and 33), that one is not put to death when his ox kills. He is, however, morally responsible and therefore liable to Heavenly capital punishment. The *Sforno*, however, deviates from *Rashi* regarding the word אִם in the phrase אִם כֹּפֶר יוּשַׁת עָלָיו. Whereas *Rashi* interprets אִם in this case as meaning אֲשֶׁר, *which*, and not *if*, similar to his interpretation of אִם in 22:24, the *Sforno* explains it as meaning *if*, i.e., if there are witnesses then a ransom is imposed. The *Sforno* is consistent in his translation of אִם, for in 22:24, אִם כֶּסֶף תַּלְוֶה, *If you lend money*, he also explains how the word אִם can be translated as a supposition (*if*) and not an obligation. See his interpretation there.

32. כֶּסֶף שְׁלֹשִׁים שְׁקָלִים — *Thirty shekels of silver.* The *Sforno* explains the Torah's yardstick for a person's value. It is based on one's *mitzvah* obligations. Hence the compensation for a slave and the evaluation of a woman are the same, since their *mitzvah* obligations are equal.

28 *If an ox shall gore a man or woman and he shall die, the ox shall surely*
be stoned; its flesh may not be eaten and the owner of the ox shall be
innocent. 29 *But if it was an ox that gores habitually from yesterday and the*
day before yesterday, and its owners had been warned but did not guard it,
and it killed a man or woman, the ox shall be stoned and even its owners shall
die. 30 *When an atonement-payment shall be assessed against him, he shall*
pay as a redemption for his life whatever shall be assessed against him.
31 *Whether it gores a boy or it gores a girl, in accordance with this judgment*
shall be done to him. 32 *If the ox shall gore a slave or a maidservant, thirty*
silver shekels shall he give to his master, and the ox shall be stoned.

33 *If a man shall uncover a pit, or if a man shall dig a pit and not cover it,*
and an ox or a donkey fall into it, 34 *the owner of the pit shall make*
restitution. He shall return money to its owners, and the carcass shall be his.

35 *If one man's ox shall strike his fellow's ox which dies, they shall sell the*
living ox and divide its money, and the carcass, too, shall they divide. 36 *But*
if it becomes known that it was an ox that had gored habitually, from
yesterday and before yesterday, but its owner did not guard it, he shall
surely pay an ox in place of the ox, and the carcass shall be his.

37 *If a man shall steal an ox, or a sheep or goat, and slaughter it or sell it,*
he shall pay five cattle in place of the ox, and four sheep in place of the sheep.

22 1 *If the thief is discovered while tunneling in, and he is struck and dies,*
there is no blood-guilt on his account. 2 *If the sun shone upon him, there*
is blood-guilt on his account. He shall make restitution; if he has nothing, he
shall be sold for his theft. 3 *If the theft shall be found in his possession —*
whether a live ox or donkey or sheep or goat — he shall pay double.

4 *If a man permits livestock to devour a field or vineyard — whether he*
set loose his livestock or he grazed it in another's field — from the best of his
field and the best of his vineyard shall he pay.

---

are unable to pay. In this fashion וַתִּמָּלֵא הָאָרֶץ חָמָס, *the earth became filled with violence* (*Genesis* 6:11).

4. כִּי יַבְעֶר אִישׁ שָׂדֶה אוֹ כֶרֶם — *If a man causes a field or vineyard to be eaten* . . . i.e., in his own (field).

וּבִעֵר בִּשְׂדֵה אַחֵר — *And it feeds in another man's field* . . . even though the animal strayed on its own into the field of another.

מֵיטַב שָׂדֵהוּ וּמֵיטַב כַּרְמוֹ יְשַׁלֵּם — *Of the best of his own field and of the best of his own vineyard shall he pay* . . . for (the damage of) שֵׁן וְעַיִן, *tooth and eye,* are considered as forewarned (מוּעָד) when inflicted in the domain of the injured (wronged) party.

NOTES

XXII

4. כִּי יַבְעֶר אִישׁ שָׂדֶה . . . וּבִעֵר בִּשְׂדֵה אַחֵר מֵיטַב שָׂדֵהוּ . . . יְשַׁלֵּם — *If a man causes a field to be eaten . . . and it feeds in another man's field, of the best of his own field . . . shall he pay.* The *Sforno* interprets the first part of this verse as meaning that the owner of the animal originally put his animal in his *own* field to graze, however he did not properly guard it and prevent it from wandering into the adjacent fields of his neighbor; therefore he is liable to pay for damages incurred. This act of straying into another's property is a normal, common one and should have been anticipated by the owner of the animal even if there was no precedent. This is what we mean by the phrase מוּעָד, i.e., he is considered as being forewarned.

ה יְשַׁלֵּם׃ כִּי־תֵצֵא אֵשׁ וּמָצְאָה קֹצִים וְנֶאֱכַל גָּדִישׁ אוֹ הַקָּמָה אוֹ
ו הַשָּׂדֶה שַׁלֵּם יְשַׁלֵּם הַמַּבְעִר אֶת־הַבְּעֵרָה׃ כִּי־יִתֵּן אִישׁ אֶל־
רֵעֵהוּ כֶּסֶף אוֹ־כֵלִים לִשְׁמֹר וְגֻנַּב מִבֵּית הָאִישׁ אִם־יִמָּצֵא הַגַּנָּב יְשַׁלֵּם
ז שְׁנָיִם׃ אִם־לֹא יִמָּצֵא הַגַּנָּב וְנִקְרַב בַּעַל־הַבַּיִת אֶל־הָאֱלֹהִים אִם־לֹא
ח שָׁלַח יָדוֹ בִּמְלֶאכֶת רֵעֵהוּ׃ עַל־כָּל־דְּבַר־פֶּשַׁע עַל־שׁוֹר עַל־חֲמוֹר עַל־
שֶׂה עַל־שַׂלְמָה עַל־כָּל־אֲבֵדָה אֲשֶׁר יֹאמַר כִּי־הוּא זֶה עַד הָאֱלֹהִים יָבֹא
ט דְּבַר־שְׁנֵיהֶם אֲשֶׁר יַרְשִׁיעֻן אֱלֹהִים יְשַׁלֵּם שְׁנַיִם לְרֵעֵהוּ׃ כִּי־
יִתֵּן אִישׁ אֶל־רֵעֵהוּ חֲמוֹר אוֹ־שׁוֹר אוֹ־שֶׂה וְכָל־בְּהֵמָה לִשְׁמֹר וּמֵת
י אוֹ־נִשְׁבַּר אוֹ־נִשְׁבָּה אֵין רֹאֶה׃ שְׁבֻעַת יהוה תִּהְיֶה בֵּין שְׁנֵיהֶם אִם־לֹא
יא שָׁלַח יָדוֹ בִּמְלֶאכֶת רֵעֵהוּ וְלָקַח בְּעָלָיו וְלֹא יְשַׁלֵּם׃ וְאִם־גָּנֹב יִגָּנֵב מֵעִמּוֹ
יב יְשַׁלֵּם לִבְעָלָיו׃ אִם־טָרֹף יִטָּרֵף יְבִאֵהוּ עֵד הַטְּרֵפָה לֹא יְשַׁלֵּם׃
יג וְכִי־יִשְׁאַל אִישׁ מֵעִם רֵעֵהוּ וְנִשְׁבַּר אוֹ־מֵת בְּעָלָיו אֵין־עִמּוֹ שַׁלֵּם יְשַׁלֵּם׃
יד־טו אִם־בְּעָלָיו עִמּוֹ לֹא יְשַׁלֵּם אִם־שָׂכִיר הוּא בָּא בִּשְׂכָרוֹ׃ וְכִי־

6. כֶּסֶף אוֹ כֵלִים — *Money or vessels.* A rich man will (normally) guard these two things (immovable objects) without payment.

7. אִם לֹא שָׁלַח יָדוֹ — *If he has not sent forth his hand.* For if he did *send forth* (his hand) he is liable, even for accidental damages.

8. עַד הָאֱלֹהִים יָבֹא דְּבַר שְׁנֵיהֶם — *The cause of both parties shall come before the judges.* The plaintiff and defendant (must come before the judges for the purpose) of taking an oath, be they depositor and bailee (or) lender and borrower, (providing that the bailee or borrower) admitted partially.

אֲשֶׁר יֹאמַר כִּי הוּא זֶה — *Whereof one says, "This is it."* (This oath) also applies when the defendant says, "This is true, but not the rest of your claim"; and this is called "confessing to a partial claim" (מוֹדֶה בְּמִקְצָת).

אֲשֶׁר יַרְשִׁיעֻן אֱלֹהִים יְשַׁלֵּם שְׁנַיִם — *He whom the judges condemn shall pay double.* But if the judges condemn him (i.e., the bailee) of being a thief, for he claimed falsely that the object was stolen, then he must pay double, as does a thief.

NOTES

6. כֶּסֶף אוֹ כֵלִים — *Money or vessels.* There are four categories of שׁוֹמְרִים, *watchmen:* (1) One who does so without compensation (as a favor); (2) one who is paid; (3) one who leases, and (4) a borrower. Verses 6 through 13 discuss the various laws pertaining to these watchmen. The Torah does not specify which verses apply to category (1) and (2); however, our Sages teach us that verses 6-8 apply to one who watches as a favor whereas verses 9-12 refer to one who receives compensation for his efforts. The *Sforno* explains logically how our Sages reached this opinion. The former verses deal with inanimate objects which are easily guarded, hence it refers to one who watches without compensation. The *Sforno* adds that we are probably speaking of a well-to-do person who must guard his own possessions; therefore it is no great bother to include his friend's as well. Verse 9, however, speaks of livestock, which demands time and effort; therefore it logically refers to a watchman who is paid, and performs this service as part of his livelihood. (See the *Sforno's* commentary there.) *Tosafos* in tractate *Bava Metzia* (41b) uses the same reasoning as does the *Sforno* in his commentary on these verses.

7. אִם לֹא שָׁלַח יָדוֹ — *If he has not sent forth his hand.* If the watchman uses the item in his safekeeping for his own purpose, since he does so without permission he is considered to be a גַּזְלָן, *robber*, and as such is liable for any and every damage, even if it is accidental.

8. עַד הָאֱלֹהִים יָבֹא דְּבַר שְׁנֵיהֶם — *The cause of both parties shall come before the judges.* The Torah stresses דְּבַר שְׁנֵיהֶם, *the cause of "both" parties*, and the *Sforno* explains "plaintiff and defendant." This reflects the admonition of the *Mechilta* (23:1) that a judge should not accept the testimony of one

[5] *If a fire shall go forth and find thorns, and a stack of grain or a standing crop or a field is consumed, the one who kindled the fire shall make restitution.*

[6] *If a man shall give money or vessels to his fellow to safeguard, and it is stolen from the house of the man, if the thief is found he shall pay double.* [7] *If the thief is not found, then the householder shall approach the court that he had not laid his hand upon his fellow's property.* [8] *For every item of liability — whether an ox, a donkey, a sheep, or a garment — regarding any lost item about which he says, "This is it!" to the court shall come both their claims. Whomever the court finds guilty shall pay double to his fellow.*

[9] *If a man shall give his fellow a donkey or an ox or a sheep or any animal to safeguard, and it died or was broken or was looted, without an eyewitness;* [10] *an oath of* H*ASHEM* *shall be between them both that he did not lay his hand upon the property of his fellow; its owner shall accept it and he shall not pay.* [11] *If it shall be stolen from him, he shall pay to its owners.* [12] *If it shall be torn to death, he shall produce a witness; for a torn animal he does not pay.*

[13] *If a man shall borrow from his fellow and it shall become broken or shall die — provided its owner is not with him — he shall surely make restitution.* [14] *If its owner is with him, he shall not make restitution. If he was a renter, it came in return for his rental.*

---

9. חֲמוֹר אוֹ שׁוֹר אוֹ שֶׂה — *An ass, or an ox, or a sheep.* These are normally watched over by poorer people for compensation.

12. יְבִאֵהוּ עֵד — *Let him bring it for witness.* It has already been said that wherever (the Torah) says עֵד, *witness* (in the singular), it means two *(Sotah* 2a). The sense (of the verse) is therefore, *If it be torn in pieces* by a wild (lit., "evil") beast, which usually is an event seen by others, for אֲשֶׁר יִקָּרֵא עָלָיו מְלֹא רֹעִים, *a multitude of shepherds is called out against him (Isaiah* 31:4), hence let him bring the torn animal and a pair of witnesses to testify that this animal was torn by accident.

הַטְּרֵפָה לֹא יְשַׁלֵּם — *He shall not make good that which was torn . . .* by accident. But if beasts ate it due to his lack of guarding, then he must pay, as our Sages say, "One wolf is not considered an accident . . . two dogs are not considered accidental" *(Bava Metzia* 93b), and certainly a cat or marten or similar animals (where his intervention) could have saved (them).

14. אִם בְּעָלָיו עִמּוֹ — *If its owner is with him.* (If he is with him) in his work at the time of his borrowing.

לֹא יְשַׁלֵּם — *He shall not pay.* One who lends under such circumstances, which (reflects) a close relationship, intends to give a gift on the understanding of the return of same

NOTES

party in the absence of the other party. Both must be present.

אֲשֶׁר יֹאמַר כִּי הוּא זֶה — *Whereof one says, "This is it."* Our Sages interpret the expression *Whereof one says,* "כִּי הוּא זֶה, *This is it,*" as meaning a partial confession by the defendant. Only under such circumstances do we impose an oath upon the defendant. The *Sforno's* commentary explains how this principle of מוֹדֶה בְּמִקְצָת can reasonably be understood from the verse itself, "This is true (i.e., *part* of your claim) but not the rest of it."

12. יְבִאֵהוּ עֵד — *Let him bring it for witness.* The *Sforno* links this verse to verse 9. There the Torah states, אֵין רֹאֶה, *no man seeing it,* implying that the accident happened in a private place where there were no witnesses, hence the watchman must swear. In our case, however, the watchman was among other shepherds, for the Torah speaks not of death or hurt (as it does in verse 9) but of an attack by a beast which perforce is out in the open, therefore witnesses were available.

14. אִם בְּעָלָיו עִמּוֹ לֹא יְשַׁלֵּם — *If its owner is with him he shall not pay.* The *Sforno* explains why the law exempts a borrower from payment for loss

יְפַתֶּה אִישׁ בְּתוּלָה אֲשֶׁר לֹא־אֹרָשָׂה וְשָׁכַב עִמָּהּ מָהֹר יִמְהָרֶנָּה לּוֹ
טז לְאִשָּׁה׃ אִם־מָאֵן יְמָאֵן אָבִיהָ לְתִתָּהּ לוֹ כֶּסֶף יִשְׁקֹל כְּמֹהַר
יז־יח הַבְּתוּלֹת׃ מְכַשֵּׁפָה לֹא תְחַיֶּה׃ כָּל־שֹׁכֵב עִם־בְּהֵמָה מוֹת
יט־כ יוּמָת׃ זֹבֵחַ לָאֱלֹהִים יָחֳרָם בִּלְתִּי לַיהוָה לְבַדּוֹ׃ וְגֵר לֹא־
כא תוֹנֶה וְלֹא תִלְחָצֶנּוּ כִּי־גֵרִים הֱיִיתֶם בְּאֶרֶץ מִצְרָיִם׃ כָּל־אַלְמָנָה וְיָתוֹם
כב לֹא תְעַנּוּן׃ אִם־עַנֵּה תְעַנֶּה אֹתוֹ כִּי אִם־צָעֹק יִצְעַק אֵלַי שָׁמֹעַ אֶשְׁמַע
כג צַעֲקָתוֹ׃ וְחָרָה אַפִּי וְהָרַגְתִּי אֶתְכֶם בֶּחָרֶב וְהָיוּ נְשֵׁיכֶם אַלְמָנוֹת וּבְנֵיכֶם
יְתֹמִים׃
כד אִם־כֶּסֶף ׀ תַּלְוֶה אֶת־עַמִּי אֶת־הֶעָנִי עִמָּךְ לֹא־תִהְיֶה לוֹ כְּנֹשֶׁה
כה לֹא־תְשִׂימוּן עָלָיו נֶשֶׁךְ׃ אִם־חָבֹל תַּחְבֹּל שַׂלְמַת רֵעֶךָ עַד־בֹּא
כו הַשֶּׁמֶשׁ תְּשִׁיבֶנּוּ לוֹ׃ כִּי הִוא כְסוּתֹה לְבַדָּהּ הִוא שִׂמְלָתוֹ לְעֹרוֹ בַּמֶּה
רביעי כז יִשְׁכָּב וְהָיָה כִּי־יִצְעַק אֵלַי וְשָׁמַעְתִּי כִּי־חַנּוּן אָנִי׃ אֱלֹהִים

(מַתָּנָה עַל מְנָת לְהַחֲזִיר). Now since no condition was made he is not obligated to return it unless it still exists (i.e., it is in his possession). Even according to the opinion (of the Sage) who states that a gift given on condition of return obligates (the recipient) to compensate (even) for accidental loss, (that) is only because the proviso of *on condition* cancels out the gift, if the condition is not fulfilled. However, in our case, where it is a gift with the understanding of return, (but) with no condition (attached) which can nullify the gift if it is not returned, then as long as it is in the hands of the recipient (borrower) it is his, even if he does later return it, (therefore) he will not be held liable for aught that occurs even through negligence. Hence the transmitted (law) there (*Bava Metzia* 95a) that when the owner is with the borrower (lit., "guard") he is guiltless, even if negligent.

19. זֹבֵחַ לָאֱלֹהִים — *He that sacrifices to the gods.* To all the gods together, even though his intention is to include God, the Blessed One, as well.

יָחֳרָם — *Shall be destroyed* . . . (including) soul and body, for they (i.e., the gods) are accursed and (it is) prohibited to derive any benefit at all from them. To the extent that one accepts them as deities he (himself) becomes accursed as they are, as it says, וְהָיִיתָ חֵרֶם כָּמֹהוּ, *And be accursed like it (Deut.* 7:26).

בִּלְתִּי לַה׳ לְבַדּוֹ — *Save unto* HASHEM *only* . . . without the partnership of other gods.

21-22. לֹא תְעַנּוּן . . . אִם עַנֵּה תְעַנֶּה אֹתוֹ — *You shall not afflict . . . If you do afflict him.* (This law applies only) if when you afflict the orphan your intent is simply to afflict him; however, if you afflict him to instruct him and for his own good then it is an act of kindness.

22-23. שָׁמֹעַ אֶשְׁמַע צַעֲקָתוֹ. וְחָרָה אַפִּי — *I will surely hear his cry. And My wrath shall be*

NOTES

incurred by his negligence, if the lender is *with it,* i.e., employed by the borrower or is present and witnesses the accident. He suggests that the presence of the lender in the home or field of the borrower indicates a close friendship between them to such an extent that the status of the borrowed object is that of a gift, except that it is understood that it will be returned. As such, any mishap which occurs while it is in the possession of the borrower, who is in reality the recipient of a gift, does not obligate him to pay.

19. זֹבֵחַ לָאֱלֹהִים — *He that sacrifices to the gods.* See the *Sforno's* commentary on 34:23.

21-22. לֹא תְעַנּוּן . . . אִם עַנֵּה תְעַנֶּה אֹתוֹ — *You shall not afflict . . . If you do afflict him.* The *Sforno* explains that the first part of verse 22 qualifies the prohibition of לֹא תְעַנּוּן, *you shall not afflict* (v. 21). You transgress only if your motivation is to oppress the orphan, but if it is pure, i.e., to discipline and instruct him for his own good, it is proper.

22-23. שָׁמֹעַ אֶשְׁמַע צַעֲקָתוֹ. וְחָרָה אַפִּי — *I will surely*

*15 If a man shall seduce a virgin who was not betrothed and lie with her,
he shall provide her with a marriage contract as his wife. 16 If her father
refuses to give her to him, he shall weigh out silver according to the marriage
contract of the virgins.*
17 You shall not permit a sorceress to live.
18 Anyone who lies with an animal shall surely be put to death.
*19 One who brings offerings to the gods shall be destroyed — only to
HASHEM alone!*
*20 You shall not taunt or oppress a stranger, for you were strangers in the
land of Egypt. 21 You shall not cause pain to any widow or orphan. 22 If you
[dare to] cause him pain . . . ! — for if he shall cry out to Me, I shall surely
hear his outcry. 23 My wrath shall blaze and I shall kill you by the sword,
and your wives will be widows and your children orphans.*
*24 When you lend money to My people, to the poor person who is with you,
do not act toward him as a creditor; do not lay interest upon him. 25 If you
take your fellow's garment as security, until sunset shall you return it to
him. 26 For it alone is his clothing, it is his garment for his skin — in what
should he lie down? — so it will be that if he cries out to Me, I shall listen,
for I am compassionate.*

---

kindled. I will have compassion on the one who cries and be angry with the oppressor, similar to Israel in Egypt. And the punishment shall be measure for measure — he who willfully afflicts the widow and orphan shall cause the affliction of his own wife and children.

24. אִם כֶּסֶף תַּלְוֶה — *If you lend money.* If (the verse) which says: אֶפֶס כִּי לֹא יִהְיֶה בְּךָ אֶבְיוֹן, *Nevertheless there shall be no needy among you* (*Deut.* 15:4), will not be fulfilled in Israel, but (the verse) כִּי לֹא יֶחְדַּל אֶבְיוֹן, *For the poor shall never cease* (ibid. 11), will come to pass, then it will occur that you will lend.

26. וְשָׁמַעְתִּי כִּי חַנּוּן אָנִי — *I will hear for I am gracious.* Even though he is (not justified) to cry out that you (are guilty) of wrongdoing, considering that he does owe you (the money), nonetheless when he cries out to Me regarding his impoverished state which has caused his nakedness (resulting from) your action which deprived him of his garment, hence I will (feel constrained) to grant him some of the substance which I would normally have granted you, above and beyond your needs, for the purpose of lending and supporting (lit., "feeding") others.

NOTES

hear his cry. And My wrath shall be kindled. The comparison to Israel in Egypt drawn by the *Sforno* can be appreciated by consulting his commentary on 2:23 and 3:9.

24. אִם כֶּסֶף תַּלְוֶה — *If you lend money. Rashi* quotes the sage Rabbi Ishmael who states that although אִם usually means *if* and indicates an option, this אִם is not optional but mandatory, i.e., one is obligated to lend money to a person in need. The *Sforno*, however, teaches us how this verse can be translated literally. *If* (אִם) the promise that there will be no needy among us is not fulfilled and instead God's statement that *the poor shall never cease* comes to pass, then when you lend money do not take interest or press him unduly for repayment.

26. וְשָׁמַעְתִּי כִּי חַנּוּן אָנִי — *I will hear for I am gracious.* In verse 22, regarding the cry of the widow or orphan, God also says He will hear (אֶשְׁמַע), as it states here (וְשָׁמַעְתִּי), but the added phrase כִּי חַנּוּן אָנִי, *for I am gracious*, does not appear there. The reason is that in the case of the widow and orphan their cry is totally justified; hence the punishment of the oppressor is also based on justice, not compassion. Here, however, considering that the debtor owes the creditor and legally the latter is entitled to keep the pledge, there is no reason for God to listen to his complaint. Nonetheless, God does hearken to the cry of the poor man who has no cloak with which to cover himself, for

כח לֹא תְקַלֵּל וְנָשִׂיא בְעַמְּךָ לֹא תָאֹר: מְלֵאָתְךָ וְדִמְעֲךָ לֹא תְאַחֵר בְּכוֹר
כט בָּנֶיךָ תִּתֶּן־לִי: כֵּן־תַּעֲשֶׂה לְשֹׁרְךָ לְצֹאנֶךָ שִׁבְעַת יָמִים יִהְיֶה עִם־
ל אִמּוֹ בַּיּוֹם הַשְּׁמִינִי תִּתְּנוֹ־לִי: וְאַנְשֵׁי־קֹדֶשׁ תִּהְיוּן לִי וּבָשָׂר בַּשָּׂדֶה
כג א טְרֵפָה לֹא תֹאכֵלוּ לַכֶּלֶב תַּשְׁלִכוּן אֹתוֹ: לֹא תִשָּׂא
ב שֵׁמַע שָׁוְא אַל־תָּשֶׁת יָדְךָ עִם־רָשָׁע לִהְיֹת עֵד חָמָס: לֹא־תִהְיֶה
אַחֲרֵי־רַבִּים לְרָעֹת וְלֹא־תַעֲנֶה עַל־רִב לִנְטֹת אַחֲרֵי רַבִּים לְהַטֹּת:

27. אֱלֹהִים לֹא תְקַלֵּל — *You shall not blaspheme the judges.* Even if you think that the judge has miscarried justice do not curse him, for no person can find fault with himself.

וְנָשִׂיא בְעַמְּךָ לֹא תָאֹר — *And do not curse a ruler among your people.* For, indeed, the curse of a king and the evil which befalls him will in most cases cause great evil and harm to the community, as it says: יְרָא אֶת ה׳ בְּנִי וָמֶלֶךְ עִם שׁוֹנִים אַל תִּתְעָרָב, *My son, fear HASHEM and the king, and do not meddle with those who seek change (Proverbs* 24:21).

28. מְלֵאָתְךָ — *The fullness (of your harvest).* (This refers to) the offering of the corn, similar to מְלֵאֹת וְטֹבוֹת, *full and good (Genesis* 41:22).

וְדִמְעֲךָ — *And the outflow (of your presses).* (This is) the offerings of the wine and oil which flow.

בְּכוֹר בָּנֶיךָ תִּתֶּן לִי — *The firstborn of your sons you shall give to Me* . . . for all sacred service; (i.e.,) the service of the Sanctuary and the study of Torah, as the priests later functioned, as it says, כִּי שִׂפְתֵי כֹהֵן יִשְׁמְרוּ דַעַת וְתוֹרָה יְבַקְשׁוּ מִפִּיהוּ, *For the priest's lips should keep knowledge and they should seek Torah from his mouth (Malachi* 2:7).

29. כֵּן תַּעֲשֶׂה לְשֹׁרְךָ לְצֹאנֶךָ — *Likewise you shall do with your oxen and your sheep* . . . that you give to Me the firstborn once he no longer has the status of a נֵפֶל, *non-viable birth,* as our Sages say, "Any human being who lives thirty days is not a non-viable . . . an animal which lives eight days is not a non-viable" *(Shabbos* 135b).

30. וְאַנְשֵׁי קֹדֶשׁ תִּהְיוּן לִי — *And you shall be holy men to Me.* In this manner you will be holy men, if you separate the firstborn sons and the gifts (of firstborn animals) to My service; (for then) the firstborn will teach knowledge to the people, and וְהִתְקַדִּשְׁתֶּם וִהְיִיתֶם קְדֹשִׁים, *you will sanctify yourselves and you will be holy (Lev.* 11:44).

וּבָשָׂר בַּשָּׂדֶה טְרֵפָה — *And flesh that is torn off in the field* . . . even טְרֵפָה, *torn flesh,* which does not defile at all.

NOTES

God is gracious and merciful. The consequence of this act will be that God will transfer some of the creditor's blessing to the debtor.

27. וְנָשִׂיא בְעַמְּךָ לֹא תָאֹר — *And do not curse a ruler among your people.* The *Sforno* interprets the phrase בְעַמְּךָ to mean *among your people* in the sense of *affecting* the people. Undermining the authority of the ruler is harmful to the welfare of the community at large.

28. בְּכוֹר בָּנֶיךָ תִּתֶּן לִי — *The firstborn of your sons you shall give to Me.* Before the sin of the Golden Calf, the firstborn sons were designated to serve in the Sanctuary and teach Torah to the people. After the Jews transgressed but the Levites remained steadfast in their loyalty to God, the Levites replaced the firstborn in this role. The expression לִי, *to Me,* is used here in conjunction with the firstborn and is also used in conjunction with the Levites, וְהָיוּ לִי הַלְוִיִּם, *And the Levites shall be Mine (Numbers* 8:14). In both cases it means to serve.

30. וְאַנְשֵׁי קֹדֶשׁ תִּהְיוּן לִי — *And you shall be holy men to Me.* The *Sforno* explains the connection between the giving of the firstborn to God and the admonition to Israel to be holy men to Him. To attain holiness it is necessary to know God's commandments and study His Torah. Our Sages tell us that an ignorant man cannot be a pious man *(Avos* 2:5). Therefore, the people of Israel need teachers if they are to attain a level of holiness. Toward that end the firstborn were charged with the task of teaching the people knowledge of God, as the prophet proclaims.

וּבָשָׂר בַּשָּׂדֶה טְרֵפָה — *And flesh that is torn off in the field.* In addition to knowledge there must be

[27] *You shall not revile God, and you shall not curse a leader among your people.*

[28] *Do not delay your fullness-offering or your priestly heave-offering; the firstborn of your sons shall you present to Me.* [29] *So shall you do to your ox, to your flock; for a seven-day period shall it be with its mother, on the eighth day you may present it to Me.* [30] *People of holiness shall you be to Me; you shall not eat flesh of an animal that was torn in the field; to the dog shall you throw it.*

23 [1] *Do not accept a false report, do not extend your hand with the wicked to be a venal witness.* [2] *Do not be a follower of the majority for evil; and do not respond to a grievance by yielding to the majority to pervert [the law].*

XXIII

1. אַל תָּשֶׁת יָדְךָ עִם רָשָׁע — *Do not put your hand with a wicked (one)*... to be a co-signatory on a document with him, as (our Sages) say regarding the men of Jerusalem that they did not sign on a document unless they knew who their co-signatory was (*Sanhedrin* 23a).

לִהְיֹת עֵד חָמָס — *To be an unrighteous witness.* (If you do so,) then you will be (but) a single witness, since a wicked person is not fit to testify, and (as a result) the judge will withdraw all the money from the defendant through your testimony alone, which is contrary to law.

2. לֹא תִהְיֶה אַחֲרֵי רַבִּים לְרָעֹת — *You shall not follow a multitude to do evil*... (i.e.,) to tilt the scale toward guilt, in a capital case, where we do not judge (condemn) him by the majority of one judge alone.

וְלֹא תַעֲנֶה עַל רִב — *Do not respond regarding a controversy*... when your fellow judges ask your opinion.

לִנְטֹת אַחֲרֵי רַבִּים — *To lean toward the multitude.* Let not your answer be that it is fitting to tend toward the majority, if (for example) ten find (the defendant) innocent and eleven guilty.

לְהַטֹּת — *To bend* (the verdict). That through your word (lit., "mouth") the verdict will be decided toward guilt for then there will be twelve (voting) guilty. Instead voice your opinion and reasoning, and let it not suffice for you to say that it is proper to lean toward the opinion of the majority, without any reason other than that they outnumber those (who say) innocent, and (by your vote) a guilty verdict will be determined by a plurality of two.

NOTES

performance of *mitzvos*, such as abstaining from prohibited food and defilement, if one is to attain holiness. Although an animal that is a טְרֵפָה, *torn*, does not defile, nonetheless its flesh is prohibited; therefore God admonishes us not to eat it, for the eating of prohibited foods is a deterrent to holiness.

XXIII

1. לִהְיֹת עֵד חָמָס — *To be an unrighteous witness.* Whereas many commentators interpret the prohibition stated in this verse as meaning the support of a fictitious claim through false testimony, the *Sforno* is of the opinion that the Torah is not addressing itself to one who is himself a wicked person, rather to one who testifies truthfully, as does his fellow witness, who is a רָשָׁע, *a wicked person*, in the sense of being unqualified to serve as a witness. By so doing the honest witness becomes a party to the miscarrying of justice since his testimony stands alone and no case may be decided by one witness.

2. לֹא תִהְיֶה אַחֲרֵי רַבִּים לְרָעֹת וְלֹא תַעֲנֶה ... לִנְטֹת אַחֲרֵי רַבִּים לְהַטֹּת — *You shall not follow a multitude to do evil. Do not respond ... to lean toward the multitude so as to bend* (the verdict). The *Sforno* explains each section of this verse by interpreting its thrust as follows: Given the fact that a capital case cannot be decided by a majority of one (*Sanhedrin* 2a), the verse speaks of a case where one judge is undecided and is inclined to cast his vote on the side of the majority, because they are a majority, and not because he is convinced of the

ג־ד וְדָ֕ל לֹ֥א תֶהְדַּ֖ר בְּרִיבֽוֹ׃ כִּ֣י תִפְגַּ֞ע שׁ֧וֹר אֹֽיִבְךָ֛ א֥וֹ חֲמֹר֖וֹ תֹּעֶ֑ה
ה הָשֵׁ֥ב תְּשִׁיבֶ֖נּוּ לֽוֹ׃ כִּֽי־תִרְאֶ֞ה חֲמ֣וֹר שֹׂנַאֲךָ֗ רֹבֵץ֙ תַּ֣חַת מַשָּׂא֔וֹ
ו וְחָדַלְתָּ֖ מֵעֲזֹ֣ב ל֑וֹ עָזֹ֥ב תַּעֲזֹ֖ב עִמּֽוֹ׃ לֹ֥א תַטֶּ֛ה מִשְׁפַּ֥ט אֶבְיֹנְךָ֖ חמישי
ז בְּרִיבֽוֹ׃ מִדְּבַר־שֶׁ֖קֶר תִּרְחָ֑ק וְנָקִ֤י וְצַדִּיק֙ אַֽל־תַּהֲרֹ֔ג כִּ֥י לֹֽא־אַצְדִּ֖יק רָשָֽׁע׃
ח־ט וְשֹׁ֖חַד לֹ֣א תִקָּ֑ח כִּ֤י הַשֹּׁ֙חַד֙ יְעַוֵּ֣ר פִּקְחִ֔ים וִיסַלֵּ֖ף דִּבְרֵ֥י צַדִּיקִֽים׃ וְגֵ֖ר לֹ֣א
י תִלְחָ֑ץ וְאַתֶּ֗ם יְדַעְתֶּם֙ אֶת־נֶ֣פֶשׁ הַגֵּ֔ר כִּֽי־גֵרִ֥ים הֱיִיתֶ֖ם בְּאֶ֥רֶץ מִצְרָֽיִם׃ וְשֵׁ֥שׁ
יא שָׁנִ֖ים תִּזְרַ֣ע אֶת־אַרְצֶ֑ךָ וְאָסַפְתָּ֖ אֶת־תְּבוּאָתָֽהּ׃ וְהַשְּׁבִיעִ֞ת תִּשְׁמְטֶ֣נָּה
וּנְטַשְׁתָּ֗הּ וְאָֽכְלוּ֙ אֶבְיֹנֵ֣י עַמֶּ֔ךָ וְיִתְרָ֕ם תֹּאכַ֖ל חַיַּ֣ת הַשָּׂדֶ֑ה כֵּֽן־תַּעֲשֶׂ֥ה
יב לְכַרְמְךָ֖ לְזֵיתֶֽךָ׃ שֵׁ֤שֶׁת יָמִים֙ תַּעֲשֶׂ֣ה מַעֲשֶׂ֔יךָ וּבַיּ֥וֹם הַשְּׁבִיעִ֖י תִּשְׁבֹּ֑ת
יג לְמַ֣עַן יָנ֗וּחַ שֽׁוֹרְךָ֙ וַחֲמֹרֶ֔ךָ וְיִנָּפֵ֥שׁ בֶּן־אֲמָתְךָ֖ וְהַגֵּֽר׃ וּבְכֹ֛ל אֲשֶׁר־אָמַ֥רְתִּי
אֲלֵיכֶ֖ם תִּשָּׁמֵ֑רוּ וְשֵׁ֨ם אֱלֹהִ֤ים אֲחֵרִים֙ לֹ֣א תַזְכִּ֔ירוּ לֹ֥א יִשָּׁמַ֖ע עַל־פִּֽיךָ׃

6. לֹא תַטֶּה מִשְׁפַּט אֶבְיֹנְךָ בְּרִיבוֹ — *You shall not bend the judgment of your poor in his cause.* Do not be soft toward this one and harsh toward the (other) one at the time of judgment, while the litigants are presenting their claims. Likewise, do not (allow) one to stand and one to sit, or similar (disparate) situations.

7. מִדְּבַר שֶׁקֶר תִּרְחָק — *Keep far away from a false matter* . . . from every word or thing which can cause falsehood, as our Sages say, וֶהֱוֵי זָהִיר בִּדְבָרֶיךָ שֶׁמָּא מִתּוֹכָם יִלְמְדוּ לְשַׁקֵּר, *Be careful of your words, lest by them (your words) they will be led* (lit., *learn*) *to lie* (*Avos* 1:9).

11. תִּשְׁמְטֶנָּה — *You shall cause release.* (This refers to) release from debts (lit., "monies"), as it says, וְזֶה דְּבַר הַשְּׁמִטָּה שָׁמוֹט כָּל בַּעַל מַשֵּׁה יָדוֹ אֲשֶׁר יַשֶּׁה בְּרֵעֵהוּ, *And this is the manner of release, every creditor shall release that which he lent* (*Deut.* 15:2).

וּנְטַשְׁתָּהּ וְאָכְלוּ אֶבְיֹנֵי עַמֶּךָ — *Abandon it, that the poor of your people may eat.* Through the *shemittah* (release) of the soil, the poor will also be able to eat.

וְיִתְרָם — *And what they leave* . . . (i.e.,) what is left (behind) by the poor.

תֹּאכַל חַיַּת הַשָּׂדֶה — *The beast of the field shall eat.* Nevertheless, the poor have priority, as our Sages say, food fit for human consumption may not be fed to dogs (*Taanis* 20b).

12. תִּשְׁבֹּת — *You shall rest* . . . even from activities (lit., "things") which are not (technically) labor, but they are burdensome (troublesome) and of a secular (lit., "weekday") nature,

NOTES

merit of their decision. By so doing he will tilt the scales of justice, for now there will be a majority of two. However, he will have failed to meet his responsibility since his decision is not based on reasoning and judgment but by a desire to concur with the majority of his colleagues.

6. לֹא תַטֶּה מִשְׁפַּט אֶבְיֹנְךָ בְּרִיבוֹ — *You shall not bend the judgment of your poor in his cause.* This interpretation of the *Sforno* is based upon the Talmud, *Kesubos* 46a and *Shevuos* 30a.

7. מִדְּבַר שֶׁקֶר תִּרְחָק — *Keep far away from a false matter.* As in verse 1, the *Sforno* feels that the Torah is not addressing itself to an outright perjurer or liar. There is no need for the Torah to prohibit lying, which is self-understood. Rather this is a prohibition of causing or prompting a witness to lie through an injudicious word. That accounts for the phraseology of this verse. It does not say "Do not lie,' but, '*Keep far away from a false matter.*"

11. תִּשְׁמְטֶנָּה וּנְטַשְׁתָּהּ — *You shall cause release. Abandon it.* Two words are used in this verse, תִּשְׁמְטֶנָּה and וּנְטַשְׁתָּהּ. The *Sforno* explains that the first verb denotes the release from debts at the end of the *Shemittah* (Sabbatical) year, while the second prohibits agricultural labor and also permits others to enjoy the produce of the land, since private ownership is not recognized during the *Shemittah* year.

12. תִּשְׁבֹּת — *You shall rest.* The Talmud in tractate *Shabbos* (138a) tells us that even an act which is permitted on the Sabbath should not be done exactly as it is done on a weekday, in order to empha-

3 Do not glorify a destitute person in his grievance.
4 If you encounter an ox of your enemy or his donkey wandering, you shall return it to him repeatedly.
5 If you see the donkey of someone you hate crouching under its burden, would you refrain from helping him? — you shall help repeatedly with him.
6 Do not pervert the judgment of your destitute person in his grievance.
7 Distant yourself from a false word; do not execute the innocent or the
righteous, for I shall not exonerate the wicked. 8 Do not accept a bribe, for
the bribe will blind those who see and corrupt words that are just. 9 Do not
oppress a stranger; you know the feelings of a stranger, for you were
strangers in the land of Egypt. 10 Six years shall you sow your land and
gather in its produce. 11 And in the seventh, you shall leave it untended and
unharvested, and the destitute of your people shall eat, and the wildlife of the field shall eat what is left; so shall you do to your vineyard and your
olive grove. 12 Six days shall you accomplish your activities, and on the seventh day you shall desist, so that your ox and donkey may be content
and your maidservant's son and the sojourner may be refreshed. 13 Be
careful regarding everything I have said to you. The name of strange gods you shall not mention, nor shall your mouth cause it to be heard.

---

as it says, וְכִבַּדְתּוֹ מֵעֲשׂוֹת דְּרָכֶיךָ מִמְּצוֹא חֶפְצְךָ וְדַבֵּר דָּבָר, *And shall honor it not doing your own ways, nor pursuing your own business, nor speaking vain matters (Isaiah 58:13).*

לְמַעַן יָנוּחַ שׁוֹרְךָ וַחֲמֹרֶךָ — *That your ox and your ass may rest* . . . when you also will rest from such work.

וְיִנָּפֵשׁ בֶּן אֲמָתְךָ וְהַגֵּר — *And the son of your handmaid and the stranger may be refreshed.* And consequently your handmaid and the stranger will also be refreshed, the opposite of your condition in Egypt where you were enslaved and had no rest, as it says, תִּכְבַּד הָעֲבֹדָה עַל הָאֲנָשִׁים, *Let heavier work be laid on the men* (5:9). In this manner you will remember the exodus from Egypt, as it says in the (Ten) Commandments of *Mishneh Torah (Deuteronomy)*, וְזָכַרְתָּ כִּי עֶבֶד הָיִיתָ, *And you shall remember that you were a servant (Deut.* 5:15).

13. וּבְכֹל אֲשֶׁר אָמַרְתִּי אֲלֵיכֶם תִּשָּׁמֵרוּ וְשֵׁם אֱלֹהִים אֲחֵרִים לֹא תַזְכִּירוּ — *And all the things I have said to you take heed; and make no mention of other gods.* All other prohibitions which

NOTES

size that the Sabbath has sanctity, unlike the other days of the week. The verse from *Isaiah,* quoted by the *Sforno,* is interpreted by our Sages in tractate *Shabbos* (113a) as teaching us that our Sabbath garments should be distinctive and unlike our weekday clothes; that the way we walk on the Sabbath should be different than our gait during the week; and that our manner of speech on the Sabbath should also be different than it is on a weekday.

לְמַעַן יָנוּחַ שׁוֹרְךָ וַחֲמֹרֶךָ וְיִנָּפֵשׁ בֶּן אֲמָתְךָ וְהַגֵּר — *That your ox and your ass may rest, and the son of your handmaid and the stranger may be refreshed.* The *Sforno* links the master's abstention from work to his animals and servants. When he ceases from labor so do they. He also links the resting of one's servants to our deliverance from Egypt as we see from the Ten Commandments recorded in *Deuteronomy.* In the version of the Ten Commandments in *Exodus*, the reason given for the Sabbath is to recognize that God created the world in six days and rested on the seventh day. In *Deuteronomy* the reason given is to remember that we were slaves in Egypt. As the *Sforno* points out in his commentary there, the animal is enjoined from working, thereby freeing the servant from his labors, and the reason is to remind us that God took us forth from Egypt, where we were slaves. This explains the sense of the *Sforno's* explanation here as well.

13. וּבְכֹל אֲשֶׁר אָמַרְתִּי אֲלֵיכֶם תִּשָּׁמֵרוּ וְשֵׁם אֱלֹהִים אֲחֵרִים לֹא תַזְכִּירוּ לֹא יִשָּׁמַע עַל פִּיךָ — *And all the things I have said to you take heed; and make no mention of other gods; neither let it be heard out of your mouth.* The portion of *Mishpatim* (Ordinances) consists of ordinances, laws, and prohibitions culminating with this verse. The following verse deals with the three festivals followed in turn

יד־טו שָׁלֹשׁ רְגָלִים תָּחֹג לִי בַּשָּׁנָה: אֶת־חַג הַמַּצּוֹת תִּשְׁמֹר שִׁבְעַת יָמִים תֹּאכַל
מַצּוֹת כַּאֲשֶׁר צִוִּיתִךָ לְמוֹעֵד חֹדֶשׁ הָאָבִיב כִּי־בוֹ יָצָאתָ מִמִּצְרָיִם וְלֹא־
טז יֵרָאוּ פָנַי רֵיקָם: וְחַג הַקָּצִיר בִּכּוּרֵי מַעֲשֶׂיךָ אֲשֶׁר תִּזְרַע בַּשָּׂדֶה וְחַג הָאָסִף
יז בְּצֵאת הַשָּׁנָה בְּאָסְפְּךָ אֶת־מַעֲשֶׂיךָ מִן־הַשָּׂדֶה: שָׁלֹשׁ פְּעָמִים בַּשָּׁנָה
יח יֵרָאֶה כָּל־זְכוּרְךָ אֶל־פְּנֵי הָאָדֹן ׀ יהוה: לֹא־תִזְבַּח עַל־חָמֵץ דַּם־זִבְחִי
יט וְלֹא־יָלִין חֵלֶב־חַגִּי עַד־בֹּקֶר: רֵאשִׁית בִּכּוּרֵי אַדְמָתְךָ תָּבִיא בֵּית יהוה
אֱלֹהֶיךָ לֹא־תְבַשֵּׁל גְּדִי בַּחֲלֵב אִמּוֹ:
ששי כ הִנֵּה אָנֹכִי שֹׁלֵחַ מַלְאָךְ לְפָנֶיךָ לִשְׁמָרְךָ בַּדָּרֶךְ וְלַהֲבִיאֲךָ אֶל־הַמָּקוֹם אֲשֶׁר
כא הֲכִנֹתִי: הִשָּׁמֶר מִפָּנָיו וּשְׁמַע בְּקֹלוֹ אַל־תַּמֵּר בּוֹ כִּי לֹא יִשָּׂא לְפִשְׁעֲכֶם

I have commanded, you must take heed not to transgress, but it does not suffice regarding the prohibition against idolatry for one to (merely) refrain from transgressing; you must take care not to (even) mention its name.

לֹא יִשָּׁמַע עַל פִּיךָ — *Neither let it be heard out of your mouth.* It should not be mentioned, with your approval, even by others.

14. תָּחֹג לִי — *Keep a feast to Me.* (This is) similar to יִשְׂמַח יִשְׂרָאֵל בְּעֹשָׂיו, *Let Israel rejoice in his Maker (Psalms* 149:2), (which is) the opposite of וַיַּרְא אֶת הָעֵגֶל וּמְחֹלֹת, *and he saw the calf and the dancing* (32:19).

15. אֶת חַג הַמַּצּוֹת תִּשְׁמֹר — *The Festival of Matzos you shall keep.* (This is) similar to שָׁמוֹר אֶת חֹדֶשׁ הָאָבִיב וְעָשִׂיתָ פֶּסַח, *Observe the month of Aviv and keep the Pesach (Deut.* 16:1), as it states here, *at the time appointed in the month of Aviv.* Take care that *(Pesach)* be in the month of *Aviv*, by intercalating years and months, as we find in our tradition *(Rosh Hashanah* 21a).

16. בְּצֵאת הַשָּׁנָה — *At the end of the year.* When all of the produce has been gathered.

17. שָׁלֹשׁ פְּעָמִים בַּשָּׁנָה יֵרָאֶה כָּל זְכוּרְךָ — *Three times in the year all your males shall appear* ... to give thanks for their freedom, for the ripening of the fruit, the harvest and the ingathering, because all comes from Him.

אֶל פְּנֵי הָאָדֹן ה׳ — *Before the Lord* Hashem. The (term) אָדֹן, *Lord*, indicates He Who conducts the affairs of all perishable (transitory) things. Therefore the (verse) says that He is the Lord

NOTES

by narratives. The significance of positioning this prohibition at the conclusion of *Mishpatim* is to emphasize that whereas all other prohibitions are broken only when one does an action, the prohibition against idolatry is transgressed merely by mentioning the name of the idol and extends to the causing of others to mention the idol's name. According to the Talmudic Sage known as the father of Samuel *(Sanhedrin* 63b), this prohibits one from entering into partnership with a heathen, since a business dispute might ensue which would necessitate the taking of an oath by your partner, thereby causing the heathen to swear in the name of his god.

14. תָּחֹג לִי — *Keep a feast to Me.* This verse is the introduction to the observance of the three festivals. The *Sforno* is of the opinion that it introduces the theme and sets the tone of these holidays. He stresses the word לִי, *to Me*, indicating *to Me alone*, to counteract the tendency at that time in history for people to associate deities with one another and worship a variety of gods. The name אָדֹן, *Lord and Master*, used in verse 17 also is meant to stress our relationship to God as our exclusive master, and as such we come to pay Him — and Him alone — homage three times a year. *Ibn Ezra* gives a similar explanation.

15. אֶת חַג הַמַּצּוֹת תִּשְׁמֹר — *The Festival of Matzos you shall keep.* The *Sforno* explains that the phrase תִּשְׁמֹר, *keep*, is not meant as an admonition to keep the laws of *Pesach*, such as *chametz* and *matzah*, but should be understood as cautioning the court to be careful to arrange the calendar so as to insure that the holiday of *Pesach* shall fall in the time of *Aviv*, i.e., the season of ripe ears, which is springtime.

16. בְּצֵאת הַשָּׁנָה — *At the end of the year. The end of the year* means the end of the agricultural year.

[14] *Three pilgrimage festivals shall you celebrate for Me during the year.*
[15] *You shall observe the Festival of Matzos; seven days shall you eat matzos, as I have commanded you, at the appointed time of the month of springtime, for in it you left Egypt; you shall not be seen before Me empty-handed.*
[16] *And the Festival of the Harvest of the first fruits of your labor that you sow in the field; and the Festival of the Ingathering at the close of the year, when you gather in your work from the field.*
[17] *Three times during the year shall all your menfolk appear before the Lord, HASHEM.*
[18] *You shall not offer the blood of My feast-offering upon leavened bread; nor may the fat of My festive-offering remain overnight until morning.*
[19] *The choicest first fruit of your land shall you bring to the House of HASHEM, your God; you shall not cook a kid in the milk of its mother.*
[20] *Behold! I send an angel before you to protect you on the way, and to bring you to the place that I have made ready.*
[21] *Beware of him — hearken to his voice, do not rebel against him, for he will not forgive your willful sin*

---

of each one who appears before Him, and by appearing before Him they are akin to a servant who welcomes his master. Also He is the Lord of the soil as it says, כִּי לִי הָאָרֶץ כִּי גֵרִים וְתוֹשָׁבִים אַתֶּם עִמָּדִי, *for the land is Mine; for you are strangers and settlers with Me* (*Leviticus* 25:23); hence it is fitting that you thank Me for the ripening, the harvest, and the ingathering of the growth of the Land, therefore . . .

19. רֵאשִׁית בִּכּוּרֵי אַדְמָתְךָ — *The choicest first fruits of your Land.* The choicest of the first fruit, similar to וְרֵאשִׁית שְׁמָנִים יִמְשָׁחוּ, *and anoint themselves with chief* (רֵאשִׁית) *ointments* (*Amos* 6:6), and נְקֻבֵי רֵאשִׁית הַגּוֹיִם, *Who are named chief* (רֵאשִׁית) *of the nations* (ibid. 6:1). And these are the first fruit of the seven species, as we learn from tradition (*Bikkurim* 1:3).

לֹא תְבַשֵּׁל גְּדִי בַּחֲלֵב אִמּוֹ — *You shall not boil a kid in its mother's milk.* You shall not engage in such actions so as to increase your fruit, as was the way of idolaters. Rather, *the choicest first fruit of your Land you shall bring,* as it says, וְרֵאשִׁית כָּל בִּכּוּרֵי כֹל וְכָל תְּרוּמַת כֹּל . . . לְהָנִיחַ בְּרָכָה אֶל בֵּיתֶךָ, *The first of all the first fruits of all things, and every offering . . . to cause a blessing to rest in your house* (*Ezekiel* 44:30).

21. הִשָּׁמֶר מִפָּנָיו — *Take heed of him.* Do not profane his honor; similar to the (angel who appeared) to Joshua (and commanded him), שַׁל נַעַלְךָ מֵעַל רַגְלֶךָ, *Take your shoe off your foot* (*Joshua* 5:15).

וּשְׁמַע בְּקֹלוֹ — *And listen to his voice . . .* to go in his footsteps, as opposed to what they said, "אָנָה אֲנַחְנוּ עֹלִים, *Whither are we going up?*" (*Deut.* 1:28).

אַל תַּמֵּר בּוֹ כִּי לֹא יִשָּׂא לְפִשְׁעֲכֶם — *Be not rebellious against him; for he will not pardon your*

NOTES

17-19. שָׁלֹשׁ פְּעָמִים בַּשָּׁנָה יֵרָאֶה כָּל זְכוּרְךָ אֶל פְּנֵי הָאָדֹן ה׳ . . . רֵאשִׁית בִּכּוּרֵי אַדְמָתְךָ . . . לֹא תְבַשֵּׁל גְּדִי בַּחֲלֵב אִמּוֹ — *Three times in the year all your males shall appear before the Lord HASHEM . . . The choicest first fruits of your Land . . . you shall not boil a kid in its mother's milk.* See note on verse 14. The *Sforno* explains the close relationship between God and the earth's blessings which is acknowledged by Israel at these three festivals that are linked to the Land, marking as they do the various seasons of the year and the cycle of ripening harvest and ingathering. It therefore follows logically that in verse 19 Israel is urged to offer their first, choicest fruit to God, demonstrating their gratitude to Him and acknowledging that the blessings of the Land come from Him alone. This realization in turn will deter them from engaging in heathen practices, such as the boiling of a kid in its mother's milk, which were followed by the idolaters to propitiate their gods in the hope of increasing their fruit. This explains the continuity of verse 19 and its connection to verse 17. See the *Sforno's* commentary on 34:18 where this thought is developed by him.

21. אַל תַּמֵּר בּוֹ כִּי לֹא יִשָּׂא לְפִשְׁעֲכֶם — *Be not rebellious against him; for he will not pardon your transgressions.* The reason for the angel's inability

כב כִּי שְׁמִי בְּקִרְבּוֹ: כִּי אִם־שָׁמוֹעַ תִּשְׁמַע בְּקֹלוֹ וְעָשִׂיתָ כֹּל אֲשֶׁר אֲדַבֵּר
כג וְאָיַבְתִּי אֶת־אֹיְבֶיךָ וְצַרְתִּי אֶת־צֹרְרֶיךָ: כִּי־יֵלֵךְ מַלְאָכִי לְפָנֶיךָ וֶהֱבִיאֲךָ
כד אֶל־הָאֱמֹרִי וְהַחִתִּי וְהַפְּרִזִּי וְהַכְּנַעֲנִי הַחִוִּי וְהַיְבוּסִי וְהִכְחַדְתִּיו: לֹא־
תִשְׁתַּחֲוֶה לֵאלֹהֵיהֶם וְלֹא תָעָבְדֵם וְלֹא תַעֲשֶׂה כְּמַעֲשֵׂיהֶם כִּי הָרֵס
כה תְּהָרְסֵם וְשַׁבֵּר תְּשַׁבֵּר מַצֵּבֹתֵיהֶם: וַעֲבַדְתֶּם אֵת יהוה אֱלֹהֵיכֶם וּבֵרַךְ
כו אֶת־לַחְמְךָ וְאֶת־מֵימֶיךָ וַהֲסִרֹתִי מַחֲלָה מִקִּרְבֶּךָ: לֹא תִהְיֶה שביעי
כז מְשַׁכֵּלָה וַעֲקָרָה בְּאַרְצֶךָ אֶת־מִסְפַּר יָמֶיךָ אֲמַלֵּא: אֶת־אֵימָתִי אֲשַׁלַּח
לְפָנֶיךָ וְהַמֹּתִי אֶת־כָּל־הָעָם אֲשֶׁר תָּבֹא בָּהֶם וְנָתַתִּי אֶת־כָּל־אֹיְבֶיךָ
כח אֵלֶיךָ עֹרֶף: וְשָׁלַחְתִּי אֶת־הַצִּרְעָה לְפָנֶיךָ וְגֵרְשָׁה אֶת־הַחִוִּי אֶת־הַכְּנַעֲנִי
כט וְאֶת־הַחִתִּי מִלְּפָנֶיךָ: לֹא אֲגָרְשֶׁנּוּ מִפָּנֶיךָ בְּשָׁנָה אֶחָת פֶּן־תִּהְיֶה הָאָרֶץ
ל שְׁמָמָה וְרַבָּה עָלֶיךָ חַיַּת הַשָּׂדֶה: מְעַט מְעַט אֲגָרְשֶׁנּוּ מִפָּנֶיךָ עַד אֲשֶׁר
לא תִּפְרֶה וְנָחַלְתָּ אֶת־הָאָרֶץ: וְשַׁתִּי אֶת־גְּבֻלְךָ מִיַּם־סוּף וְעַד־יָם פְּלִשְׁתִּים

---

transgressions. (Even) if (but) one man will sin (the) many will be punished as was the case with Achan, as it says, הֲלוֹא עָכָן בֶּן זֶרַח מָעַל מַעַל בַּחֵרֶם וְעַל כָּל עֲדַת יִשְׂרָאֵל הָיָה קָצֶף וְהוּא אִישׁ אֶחָד לֹא גָוַע בַּעֲוֹנוֹ, *Did not Achan the son of Zerach commit a trespass in regard to the devoted property, and wrath fell on all the congregation of Israel, and that man did not perish alone in his iniquity?* (*Joshua* 22:20).

כִּי שְׁמִי בְּקִרְבּוֹ — *For My Name is in him.* And he does not have the power to pardon (the desecration of) My honor.

22. כִּי אִם שָׁמוֹעַ תִּשְׁמַע בְּקֹלוֹ . . . וְאָיַבְתִּי אֶת אֹיְבֶיךָ — *But if you shall indeed hearken to his voice . . . I will be an enemy to your enemies.* And I will have no pity on them, in keeping with My attribute of goodness, as opposed to, וַאֲנִי לֹא אָחוּס עַל נִינְוֵה, *"And should I not have pity on Nineveh?"* (*Jonah* 4:11).

23. כִּי יֵלֵךְ מַלְאָכִי לְפָנֶיךָ — *For My angel shall go before you.* He will not forgive the transgressions of the enemy.

24. לֹא תִשְׁתַּחֲוֶה לֵאלֹהֵיהֶם — *You shall not bow down to their gods.* Do not act as Amazyahu did after he conquered Seir — וַיָּבֵא אֶת אֱלֹהֵי בְּנֵי שֵׂעִיר . . . וְלִפְנֵיהֶם יִשְׁתַּחֲוֶה, *And he brought the gods of the children of Seir . . . and prostrated himself before them* (*II Chronicles* 25:14). Perhaps he wanted to appease them that they should not be angry with him for having killed their worshipers.

25. וַעֲבַדְתֶּם אֵת ה׳ אֱלֹהֵיכֶם — *And you shall serve* HASHEM, *your God.* And in this manner (i.e., by overthrowing their gods) you shall serve Him, for after the nations and their idols will be destroyed, (as well as) the places where they did worship, you will no longer have anyone to instigate and seduce you away from My service.

וּבֵרַךְ אֶת לַחְמְךָ — *And He will bless your bread.* It will nourish you and the abundance

NOTES

to forgive Israel if they transgress is because God's Name is in him. Since the angel's very being and essence emanates from God, to defy him is to rebel against God, and the angel has no power to pardon the desecration of God's honor. Now just as the angel cannot pardon the transgressions of Israel, he also cannot forgive those of Israel's enemies. This is the meaning of verse 23, as the *Sforno* explains in his commentary on that verse.

24. לֹא תִשְׁתַּחֲוֶה לֵאלֹהֵיהֶם — *You shall not bow down to their gods.* The allure of, and respect for, עֲבוֹדָה זָרָה, *idol worship,* was so strong and pervasive in ancient times that even after victory Amazyahu feared the consequence of his conquest and the retribution of the gods of Seir! The *Sforno* cites this incident to explain the imperative need for Israel to utterly eradicate the gods of the nations, to *overthrow them and break them in*

— for My Name is within him. [22] *For if you hearken to his voice and carry out all that I shall speak, then I shall be the enemy of your enemies and persecute your persecutors.* [23] *For My angel shall go before you and bring you to the Amorite, the Hittite, the Perizzite, the Canaanite, the Hivvite, and the Jebusite, and I will annihilate them.* [24] *Do not prostrate yourself to their gods, do not worship them, and do not act according to their practices; rather, you shall tear them apart, and you shall smash their pillars.* [25] *You shall worship* HASHEM, *your God, and He shall bless your bread and your water, and I shall remove illness from your midst.*

[26] *There shall be no woman who loses her young or is infertile in your land; I shall fill the number of your days.* [27] *I shall send My fear before you and I shall confound the entire people among whom you shall come; and I shall make all your enemies turn their back to you.* [28] *I shall send the hornet-swarm before you and it will drive away the Hivvite, the Canaanite and the Hittite before you.* [29] *I shall not drive them away from you in a single year, lest the Land become desolate and the wildlife of the field multiply against you.* [30] *Little by little shall I drive them away from you, until you become fruitful and make the Land your heritage.*

[31] *I shall set your border from the Sea of Reeds to the Sea of the Philistines,*

(thereof) will not be the cause of (any) ailments.

וַהֲסִרֹתִי מַחֲלָה מִקִּרְבֶּךָ — *And I will take sickness away from your midst.* (This refers to sickness) caused by the climate or the order (of the planets).

26. לֹא תִהְיֶה מְשַׁכֵּלָה וַעֲקָרָה — *None shall miscarry or be barren.* In this manner you will be able to teach your children.

אֶת מִסְפַּר יָמֶיךָ אֲמַלֵּא — *The number of your days I will fulfill.* You will live to the (full) measure of oil which is in your *lamp of God* (the soul of man), i.e., the vitality (or *natural force)* rooted (in man) from birth. The reverse of this mostly occurs when man dies from (various) illnesses before his basic vitality has ceased. This occurs due to wrong choices (made in life) or due to fate (lit., "the order of the planets") and the elements (lit., "foundations"). Now when a man's number of days are fulfilled he will in most cases see children born to his children and will be able to teach them, as it says, וְהוֹדַעְתָּם לְבָנֶיךָ וְלִבְנֵי בָנֶיךָ, *Make them known to your children and children's children (Deut.* 4:9). (In this fashion) the affairs of (new) generations will be remedied in the lifetime of their elders, as we are told happened with Levi, Kehath, and Amram (see *Sforno* on 6:14).

27. וְהַמֹּתִי — *And will discomfit . . .* as it happened with the Egyptians (who said), "אָנוּסָה מִפְּנֵי יִשְׂרָאֵל כִּי ה׳ נִלְחָם לָהֶם, *Let us flee from Israel, for* HASHEM *fights for them"* (14:25).

וְנָתַתִּי אֶת כָּל אֹיְבֶיךָ אֵלֶיךָ עֹרֶף — *And I will make all your enemies turn their backs to you.* Because of the terror and tumult which (God) designated when He said, *"I will send My terror before you"* (beginning of this verse).

NOTES

pieces. Otherwise Israel will be vulnerable to the instigation and seduction of the idolaters, as the *Sforno* states in the next verse.

26. אֶת מִסְפַּר יָמֶיךָ אֲמַלֵּא — *The number of your days I will fulfill.* The *Sforno's* choice of language to describe man's source of life as oil to the lamp is based on, *the soul of man is the lamp of* HASHEM (*Proverbs* 20:27). The expression "natural force" or vitality is taken from *Deuteronomy* 34:7, *his natural force did not abate,* regarding Moses. The *Sforno* already developed the idea of long life affording one the opportunity to influence later generations in his commentary on 6:14. See the note there.

וּמִמִּדְבָּר עַד־הַנָּהָר כִּי ׀ אֶתֵּן בְּיֶדְכֶם אֵת יֹשְׁבֵי הָאָרֶץ וְגֵרַשְׁתָּמוֹ מִפָּנֶיךָ׃
לב-לג לֹא־תִכְרֹת לָהֶם וְלֵאלֹהֵיהֶם בְּרִית׃ לֹא יֵשְׁבוּ בְּאַרְצְךָ פֶּן־יַחֲטִיאוּ אֹתְךָ
לִי כִּי תַעֲבֹד אֶת־אֱלֹהֵיהֶם כִּי־יִהְיֶה לְךָ לְמוֹקֵשׁ׃
כד א וְאֶל־מֹשֶׁה אָמַר עֲלֵה אֶל־יהוה אַתָּה וְאַהֲרֹן נָדָב וַאֲבִיהוּא וְשִׁבְעִים
ב מִזִּקְנֵי יִשְׂרָאֵל וְהִשְׁתַּחֲוִיתֶם מֵרָחֹק׃ וְנִגַּשׁ מֹשֶׁה לְבַדּוֹ אֶל־יהוה וְהֵם לֹא
ג יִגָּשׁוּ וְהָעָם לֹא יַעֲלוּ עִמּוֹ׃ וַיָּבֹא מֹשֶׁה וַיְסַפֵּר לָעָם אֵת כָּל־דִּבְרֵי יהוה
וְאֵת כָּל־הַמִּשְׁפָּטִים וַיַּעַן כָּל־הָעָם קוֹל אֶחָד וַיֹּאמְרוּ כָּל־הַדְּבָרִים
ד אֲשֶׁר־דִּבֶּר יהוה נַעֲשֶׂה׃ וַיִּכְתֹּב מֹשֶׁה אֵת כָּל־דִּבְרֵי יהוה וַיַּשְׁכֵּם בַּבֹּקֶר
וַיִּבֶן מִזְבֵּחַ תַּחַת הָהָר וּשְׁתֵּים עֶשְׂרֵה מַצֵּבָה לִשְׁנֵים עָשָׂר שִׁבְטֵי יִשְׂרָאֵל׃
ה וַיִּשְׁלַח אֶת־נַעֲרֵי בְּנֵי יִשְׂרָאֵל וַיַּעֲלוּ עֹלֹת וַיִּזְבְּחוּ זְבָחִים שְׁלָמִים לַיהוה
ו פָּרִים׃ וַיִּקַּח מֹשֶׁה חֲצִי הַדָּם וַיָּשֶׂם בָּאַגָּנֹת וַחֲצִי הַדָּם זָרַק עַל־הַמִּזְבֵּחַ׃
ז וַיִּקַּח סֵפֶר הַבְּרִית וַיִּקְרָא בְּאָזְנֵי הָעָם וַיֹּאמְרוּ כֹּל אֲשֶׁר־דִּבֶּר יהוה נַעֲשֶׂה
ח וְנִשְׁמָע׃ וַיִּקַּח מֹשֶׁה אֶת־הַדָּם וַיִּזְרֹק עַל־הָעָם וַיֹּאמֶר הִנֵּה דַם־הַבְּרִית

---

31. כִּי אֶתֵּן בְּיֶדְכֶם אֵת יֹשְׁבֵי הָאָרֶץ וְגֵרַשְׁתָּמוֹ — *For I will deliver the inhabitants of the Land into your hand and you shall drive them out.* The matter is in your hand, and you must not be indolent (neglectful) regarding it, as Joshua testified to them (Israel) saying, עַד אָנָה אַתֶּם מִתְרַפִּים לָבוֹא לָרֶשֶׁת אֶת הָאָרֶץ אֲשֶׁר נָתַן לָכֶם ה׳ אֱלֹהֵי אֲבוֹתֵיכֶם, *How long will you be remiss in going to possess the Land which* HASHEM, *the God of your fathers, has given to you?*' (*Joshua* 18:3).

33. לֹא יֵשְׁבוּ בְּאַרְצְךָ — *They shall not dwell in your Land.* In that portion of the Land which you will conquer and dwell in, they shall not dwell. (However) they did the opposite as the verse testifies saying, וַיֵּשֶׁב הַכְּנַעֲנִי בְּקִרְבּוֹ בְּגָזֶר ... וַיֵּשֶׁב ... בְּקֶרֶב הַכְּנַעֲנִי יֹשְׁבֵי הָאָרֶץ, *but the Canaanites dwelt in Gezer among them ... But dwelt ... among the Canaanites the inhabitants of the land* (*Judges* 1:29,32).

כִּי יִהְיֶה לְךָ לְמוֹקֵשׁ — *For they will be a snare unto you.* They will cause you to serve their gods.

XXIV

1. וְאֶל מֹשֶׁה אָמַר עֲלֵה — *And to Moses He said, "Come up."* After He concluded saying, כֹּה תֹאמַר אֶל בְּנֵי יִשְׂרָאֵל אַתֶּם רְאִיתֶם״, *Thus shall you say to the Children of Israel, 'You have seen'* " (20:19), and (after God) explained to them that they needed no intermediary to reach Him (see 20:20), and (also) that an earthen altar is sufficient (20:21), together with the observance of His commandments which He explained in the (Ten) Commandments and the chapter of *Mishpatim,* (now) all this was said and commanded to the congregation of Israel; (but) *to Moses He said, "Come up,"* as He had ordained before the giving of the Torah, as He said, "לֵךְ רֵד וְעָלִיתָ אַתָּה וְאַהֲרֹן עִמָּךְ, *Go, get you down and you shall come up, you and Aaron with you*" (19:24).

NOTES

31. כִּי אֶתֵּן בְּיֶדְכֶם אֵת יֹשְׁבֵי הָאָרֶץ וְגֵרַשְׁתָּמוֹ — *For I will deliver the inhabitants of the Land into your hand and you shall drive them out.* God will do His part but you must do yours. He will give the inhabitants of the Land into Israel's hand but they must in turn drive them out. The matter is in their hand to act and they must not squander that opportunity.

XXIV

1. וְאֶל מֹשֶׁה אָמַר עֲלֵה — *And to Moses He said, "Come up."* The commentators disagree as to the time this chapter was spoken to Moses. The *Sforno* explains that it belongs to the order and sequence of events as recorded in these chapters. The narrative is now resuming what was said by God before

and from the Wilderness until the River, for I shall deliver the inhabitants of the Land into your hand and you shall drive them away from before you. 32 You shall not seal a covenant with them or their gods. 33 They shall not dwell in your Land lest they cause you to sin against Me, that you will worship their gods, for it will be a trap for you.

24 *1 To Moses He said, "Go up to HASHEM, you, Aaron, Nadab and Abihu, and seventy of the elders of Israel, and you shall prostrate yourselves from a distance. 2 And Moses alone shall approach HASHEM, but they shall not approach, and the people shall not go up with him."*

3 Moses came and told the people all the words of HASHEM and all the ordinances, and the entire people responded with one voice and they said, "All the words that HASHEM has spoken, we will do."

4 Moses wrote all the words of HASHEM. He arose early in the morning and built an altar at the foot of the mountain, and twelve pillars for the twelve tribes of Israel. 5 He sent the youths of the Children of Israel and they brought up elevation-offerings, and they slaughtered bulls to HASHEM as feast peace-offerings to HASHEM. 6 Moses took half the blood and placed it in basins, and half the blood he threw upon the altar. 7 He took the Book of the Covenant and read it in earshot of the people, and they said, "Everything that HASHEM has said, we will do and we will obey!" 8 Moses took the blood and threw it upon the people, and he said, "Behold the blood of the covenant

---

3. וַיָּבֹא מֹשֶׁה וַיְסַפֵּר לָעָם אֵת כָּל דִּבְרֵי ה׳ — *And Moses came and told the people all the words of HASHEM.* From the beginning of כֹּה תֹאמַר, *Thus shall you say* (19:3), until וְאֵלֶּה הַמִּשְׁפָּטִים, *And these are the ordinances* (21:1).

וְאֵת כָּל הַמִּשְׁפָּטִים — *And all the ordinances.* From the beginning of וְאֵלֶּה הַמִּשְׁפָּטִים, *And these are the ordinances* (21:1) until וְאֶל מֹשֶׁה אָמַר, *And to Moses He said* (v. 1).

6. וַחֲצִי הַדָּם זָרַק עַל הַמִּזְבֵּחַ — *And half of the blood he dashed against the altar.* He considered the altar as the emissary of God, the Blessed One, (for the purpose of) entering into the covenant, therefore it received half the blood. The other half was sprinkled on the people who were entering into the covenant.

7. סֵפֶר הַבְּרִית — *The Book of the Covenant.* The book in which he had written the words of *HASHEM*, and the ordinances, based upon which they would enter into the covenant, as it states above, וַיִּכְתֹּב מֹשֶׁה, *And Moses wrote* (v. 4).

וַיִּקְרָא בְּאָזְנֵי הָעָם — *And read in the hearing of the people . . .* so that they would know what they were accepting upon themselves, and not be misled.

נַעֲשֶׂה וְנִשְׁמָע — *We will do, and we will listen.* We *will do* toward the end (purpose) of *listening* to His voice, akin to servants who serve the master without a motivation to receive reward, similar to, עֹשֵׂי דְבָרוֹ לִשְׁמֹעַ בְּקוֹל דְּבָרוֹ, *Who perform His bidding, hearkening to the voice of His word* (*Psalms* 103:20).

NOTES

He gave the Torah. The time had now come to implement that original plan.

6. וַחֲצִי הַדָּם זָרַק עַל הַמִּזְבֵּחַ — *And half of the blood he dashed against the altar.* It was customary to sprinkle the blood of the sacrifice, brought to mark the entering into a covenant, on the two parties to that covenant. In this case the altar represents God and, Israel, of course, the party of the second part.

7. נַעֲשֶׂה וְנִשְׁמָע — *We will do, and we will listen.* The *Sforno* is paraphrasing the Mishnah in *Avos* 1:3, "Be not like servants who serve their master with the thought of reward; rather be like servants who serve their master without thought of reward."

ט אֲשֶׁר כָּרַת יהוה עִמָּכֶם עַל כָּל־הַדְּבָרִים הָאֵלֶּה׃ וַיַּעַל מֹשֶׁה וְאַהֲרֹן נָדָב
י וַאֲבִיהוּא וְשִׁבְעִים מִזִּקְנֵי יִשְׂרָאֵל׃ וַיִּרְאוּ אֵת אֱלֹהֵי יִשְׂרָאֵל וְתַחַת רַגְלָיו
יא כְּמַעֲשֵׂה לִבְנַת הַסַּפִּיר וּכְעֶצֶם הַשָּׁמַיִם לָטֹהַר׃ וְאֶל־אֲצִילֵי בְּנֵי יִשְׂרָאֵל
יב לֹא שָׁלַח יָדוֹ וַיֶּחֱזוּ אֶת־הָאֱלֹהִים וַיֹּאכְלוּ וַיִּשְׁתּוּ׃ וַיֹּאמֶר
יהוה אֶל־מֹשֶׁה עֲלֵה אֵלַי הָהָרָה וֶהְיֵה־שָׁם וְאֶתְּנָה לְךָ אֶת־לֻחֹת הָאֶבֶן
יג וְהַתּוֹרָה וְהַמִּצְוָה אֲשֶׁר כָּתַבְתִּי לְהוֹרֹתָם׃ וַיָּקָם מֹשֶׁה וִיהוֹשֻׁעַ מְשָׁרְתוֹ

---

9. וַיַּעַל מֹשֶׁה וְאַהֲרֹן — *And Moses and Aaron went up*. After he fulfilled the commandment of God, the Blessed One, who said, "כֹּה תֹאמַר אֶל בְּנֵי יִשְׂרָאֵל, *Thus shall you say to the Children of Israel*" (20:19), he then fulfilled what was later commanded to him, when (God) said, "עֲלֵה אֶל ה׳ אַתָּה וְאַהֲרֹן, *Come up to HASHEM, you and Aaron*" (v. 1).

10. וְתַחַת רַגְלָיו — *And under His feet* . . . upon the earth, which is the lowest of all, as it says, וְהָאָרֶץ הֲדֹם רַגְלָי, *And the earth is My footstool* (*Isaiah* 66:1).

כְּמַעֲשֵׂה לִבְנַת הַסַּפִּיר — *A work of the whiteness of sapphire stone*. An object lacking all the forms of intelligence and prepared to receive them, similar to the white sapphire which is deficient of all color. This (refers to) the substance of man's intelligent (soul) which lacks all knowledge but is prepared to receive it through free inquiry (contemplation directed by his choice).

וּכְעֶצֶם הַשָּׁמַיִם לָטֹהַר — *And like the very substance of heaven's clarity*. And they apprehended that this substance (i.e., man's soul) was separated from the matter of man and more pure than it, just as the substance of heaven, which is the spirit (soul) of the wheel, when uncombined with the material of the wheel or its body at all (is) purer and clearer than it. (Thus) this substance is as that of the heaven and its spirit (soul), insofar as purity and clearness from the material is concerned.

11. וְאֶל אֲצִילֵי בְּנֵי יִשְׂרָאֵל לֹא שָׁלַח יָדוֹ — *And upon the nobles of the Children of Israel He did not send forth His hand* . . . to suspend their senses so that they might prophesy, as is the case with other prophets when *the hand of HASHEM* is upon them, as it says of Ezekiel, וַתִּפֹּל עָלַי שָׁם יַד ה׳, *the hand of HASHEM fell there upon me (Ezekiel* 8:1), for then the functioning of one's senses ceases, as it occurred to Saul when he prophesied, as it says, וַיִּפְשַׁט גַּם הוּא בְּגָדָיו וַיִּתְנַבֵּא גַּם הוּא לִפְנֵי שְׁמוּאֵל וַיִּפֹּל עָרֹם כָּל הַיּוֹם הַהוּא וְכָל הַלָּיְלָה, *And he also stripped off his clothes and he himself also prophesied before Samuel, and lay down naked all that day and all that night (I Samuel* 19:24). However, to these nobles He did not send forth His hand to

NOTES

10. כְּמַעֲשֵׂה לִבְנַת הַסַּפִּיר וּכְעֶצֶם הַשָּׁמַיִם לָטֹהַר — *A work of the whiteness of sapphire stone and like the very substance of heaven's clarity*. The *Rambam* in his *Guide* (I:28) explains that the word *whiteness* in this verse signifies "transparency and not a white color." He explains that "a transparent body receives all colors in succession because it lacks a color of its own." We can now understand the commentary here of the *Sforno*. The *object* referred to here is man's spirit of the intellect which begins as a clear substance lacking knowledge, just as the sapphire lacks color. Therefore it is prepared to *receive*, just as a transparent body can receive all colors. Hence Moses, Aaron, and the elders of Israel apprehended God through a prophet's vision. They also comprehended that their intellect and soul was superior and purer than their material being just as the essence (soul) of heaven is purer and more clear than the matter of heaven. This is the meaning of the latter part of the verse, *and like the very substance of heaven's clarity*, i.e., their "human intellectual spirit" (נֶפֶשׁ אֱנוֹשִׁית שִׂכְלִית) was separate from man's physical nature and superior to it, similar to נֶפֶשׁ הַגַּלְגַּל, *the spirit of the wheel*, which is separate from the wheel's material. This the verse calls *the substance of heaven's clarity*.

11. וְאֶל אֲצִילֵי בְּנֵי יִשְׂרָאֵל לֹא שָׁלַח יָדוֹ וַיֶּחֱזוּ אֶת הָאֱלֹהִים וַיֹּאכְלוּ וַיִּשְׁתּוּ — *And upon the nobles of the Children of Israel He did not send forth His hand, and they beheld God and they ate and drank*. The *Sforno* established in 19:9 that Israel reached an unusual level of prophecy at Sinai. Whereas all prophetic visions involve a suspension of man's

that HASHEM *sealed with you concerning all these matters."*

9 *Moses, Aaron, Nadab and Abihu, and seventy of the elders of Israel ascended.* 10 *They saw the God of Israel, and under His feet was the likeness of sapphire brickwork, and it was like the essence of the heaven in purity.* 11 *Against the great men of the Children of Israel, He did not stretch out His hand — they gazed at God, yet they ate and drank.*

12 HASHEM *said to Moses, "Ascend to Me to the mountain and remain there, and I shall give you the stone Tablets and the teaching and the commandment that I have written, to teach them."* 13 *Moses stood up with Joshua, his servant;*

---

suspend their senses in order for them to apprehend (grasp) what they then saw.

וַיֶּחֱזוּ אֶת הָאֱלֹהִים — *And they beheld God . . .* in a prophetic vision.

וַיֹּאכְלוּ וַיִּשְׁתּוּ — *And they ate and drank.* They made a feast afterward, without changing their senses, and this they did to rejoice in their (spiritual) attainment.

12. עֲלֵה אֵלַי הָהָרָה — *Come up to Me onto the mount.* To the top of the mountain. After he had come nearer than the others who came up with him, as it says, וְנִגַּשׁ מֹשֶׁה לְבַדּוֹ, *And Moses alone shall come near* (v. 2), he still did not ascend to the top of the mountain. The elders (however) did apprehend the great vision at that site (position). (Now) He says to Moses to go up to the top of the mountain where the *appearance of the glory of* HASHEM was (present), as it is written: וּמַרְאֵה כְּבוֹד ה׳ כְּאֵשׁ אֹכֶלֶת בְּרֹאשׁ הָהָר, *And the appearance of the glory of* HASHEM *was like a devouring fire on the top of the mountain* (v. 17). This also (occurred) at the giving of the Torah, where it says, וַיִּקְרָא ה׳ לְמֹשֶׁה אֶל רֹאשׁ הָהָר, *And* HASHEM *called Moses to the top of the mountain* (19:20).

וֶהְיֵה שָׁם — *And be there.* Remain there for a long period of time, similar to, וַיִּהְיוּ שָׁם כַּאֲשֶׁר צִוַּנִי ה׳, *And there they are, as* HASHEM *commanded me (Deut.* 10:5).

וְהַתּוֹרָה — *And the Torah.* The theoretical part of it.

וְהַמִּצְוָה — *And the commandment.* The practical, active part of it.

אֲשֶׁר כָּתַבְתִּי — *Which I have written.* Had they not sinned with the (Golden) Calf, the entire Torah would have been given to them, written (lit., "signed") by the Creator, the Blessed One, similar to the tablets, as (the verse) testifies, saying, וְאָתָה מֵרִבְבֹת קֹדֶשׁ מִימִינוֹ אֵשׁ דָּת לָמוֹ, *And He came from the myriads holy, at His right hand was a fiery law unto them (Deut.* 33:2). Once they sinned with the Calf they did not merit it, but (instead) Moses wrote it at His behest as it says later, כְּתָב לְךָ אֶת הַדְּבָרִים הָאֵלֶּה, *Write you these words* (34:27). Our teacher Moses brought (down) the tablets only (for the purpose) of breaking them in view (of the people), so as to break their straying hearts, that they might return and repent.

לְהוֹרֹתָם — *That you may teach them.* I will give them to you so that you may teach them, for although all is written, as our Sages say, "Is there anything in the Prophets or Writings which

NOTES

senses, the highest form of prophecy such as that of Moses and of the Children of Israel at Sinai did not. The nobles in the episode related here were also able to experience a prophetic vision (וַיֶּחֱזוּ אֶת הָאֱלֹהִים) without taking leave of their physical senses. This explains the concluding part of the verse which states, *they ate and drank.* The Torah tells us that since their physical senses were not affected there was no need for a transition from the spiritual to the physical. Immediately after *beholding God,* they were able to *eat and drink!*

12. אֲשֶׁר כָּתַבְתִּי — *Which I have written.* Since it is not recorded that God wrote down the תּוֹרָה וּמִצְוָה, *law and commandment, Rashi* explains that these are implicit in the Ten Commandments which He did write, thereby clarifying the statement *which I have written.* The *Sforno,* however, interprets this phrase in the sense that *everything* was written originally in heaven and would have been given to Israel in its totality were it not for the sin of the Golden Calf. Ultimately the Torah was written by Moses at God's behest.

לְהוֹרֹתָם — *That you may teach them.* The word לְהוֹרֹתָם *(to teach them)* implies that Torah was

יד וַיַּעַל מֹשֶׁה אֶל־הַר הָאֱלֹהִים: וְאֶל־הַזְּקֵנִים אָמַר שְׁבוּ־לָנוּ בָזֶה עַד אֲשֶׁר־
טו נָשׁוּב אֲלֵיכֶם וְהִנֵּה אַהֲרֹן וְחוּר עִמָּכֶם מִי־בַעַל דְּבָרִים יִגַּשׁ אֲלֵהֶם: וַיַּעַל
מפטיר טז מֹשֶׁה אֶל־הָהָר וַיְכַס הֶעָנָן אֶת־הָהָר: וַיִּשְׁכֹּן כְּבוֹד־יהוה עַל־הַר סִינַי וַיְכַסֵּהוּ
יז הֶעָנָן שֵׁשֶׁת יָמִים וַיִּקְרָא אֶל־מֹשֶׁה בַּיּוֹם הַשְּׁבִיעִי מִתּוֹךְ הֶעָנָן: וּמַרְאֵה
יח כְּבוֹד יהוה כְּאֵשׁ אֹכֶלֶת בְּרֹאשׁ הָהָר לְעֵינֵי בְּנֵי יִשְׂרָאֵל: וַיָּבֹא מֹשֶׁה בְּתוֹךְ
הֶעָנָן וַיַּעַל אֶל־הָהָר וַיְהִי מֹשֶׁה בָּהָר אַרְבָּעִים יוֹם וְאַרְבָּעִים לָיְלָה:

---

is not intimated by Moses in the Torah?" (*Taanis* 9a), and as some of our Sages say, רוֹב בִּכְתָב, וּמִעוּט בְּעַל פֶּה, *The major part is written, (only) a minor part is oral* (*Gittin* 60b), (yet) behold that the allusions (implications) which are found in it, be it theoretical or in deed, cannot be understood by the majority of Israel save through a righteous teacher. Therefore the opinion of the other Sages who say, רוֹב בְּעַל פֶּה וּמִעוּט בִּכְתָב, *The major part (of Torah) is oral, and a minor part written* (ibid.), is also correct.

14. וְאֶל הַזְּקֵנִים אָמַר — *And to the elders he said . . .* when he left them, to go up to the top of the mount, as God, the Blessed One, had commanded him, saying, "עֲלֵה אֵלַי הָהָרָה, *Come up to Me unto the mount*" (v. 12).

18. וַיְהִי מֹשֶׁה בָּהָר — *And Moses was in the mount.* Every time he went up there, from this time forward, (he was there) forty days and forty nights equal to the days of the forming of an embryo, (thereby) acquiring there a more honored (elevated) existence, (making him) worthy to listen (learn) from the mouth of the Teacher, (an experience) which no other person attained, as the (Torah) testifies, saying, כִּי קָרַן עוֹר פָּנָיו בְּדַבְּרוֹ אִתּוֹ, *the skin of his face sent forth beams while He talked with him* (34:29). (Now) their sin impaired this (lofty spiritual level) at the end of the first forty days, when they were worthy to grasp (attain) it, as it says, לֶךְ רֵד כִּי שִׁחֵת עַמְּךָ, *Go, get you down for your people have dealt corruptly* (32:7). During the "middle" (forty days) which according to tradition were (marked) by (Divine) anger, they did not merit to enjoy the rays of glory, which were attained during the "last" forty days, during which time (Moses) was commanded regarding the work of the Sanctuary, as it is explained (in the verse) saying, וְאֶל הָאָרֹן תִּתֵּן אֶת הָעֵדֻת אֲשֶׁר אֶתֵּן אֵלֶיךָ, *And in the Ark you shall put the testimony that I shall give you* (25:21). Now this was not realized with the first Tablets which never rested in any ark, only the broken pieces without the "testimony," as our Sages say, לוּחוֹת נִשְׁבְּרוּ וְאוֹתִיּוֹת פּוֹרְחוֹת, *the Tablets broke and the letters flew away* (*Pesachim* 87b). This itself is explained when He said, "וְעָשׂוּ לִי מִקְדָּשׁ וְשָׁכַנְתִּי בְּתוֹכָם, *They shall make Me a Sanctuary that I may dwell in their midst*" (25:8), (that is) not as He had designated prior to

NOTES

taught orally by Moses to Israel. The *Sforno* explains that although the written Torah (תּוֹרָה שֶׁבִּכְתָב) is precisely that, written, still one cannot possibly understand it without exposition by a righteous teacher. The Talmudic selection (*Gittin* 60b) which he cites is of particular interest. Rabbi Elazar is of the opinion that the major part of Torah was given in writing, basing his opinion on a verse in *Hoshea* (8:12). Rabbi Yochanan insists that the major part of Torah was transmitted orally, basing his opinion on *Exodus* (34:27). The *Sforno* reconciles the two opinions suggesting that indeed the written Torah *contains* the major elements of God's laws but it can only be understood through the interpretation, explanation, and exposition of a master teacher.

18. וַיְהִי מֹשֶׁה בָּהָר — *And Moses was in the mount.* The *Sforno* interprets the phrase *And Moses was in the mount* as referring to each of the three forty-day periods which he spent with God. The first was from the seventh (or sixth) of Sivan until the 17th of Tammuz, when he descended and broke the Tablets of law. The second was from the 19th of Tammuz, until Rosh Chodesh Elul. The third was from Rosh Chodesh Elul until Yom Kippur. The first and third were periods of grace, but the second was one of disfavor and anger because of the Golden Calf. Now the episode of the Calf occurred at the end of the first forty-day period; hence it is strange that two *sidros* (portions), *Terumah* and *Tetzaveh*, separate the last verse of *Mishpatim*, which relates the ascent of Moses to the mountain,

and Moses ascended to the Mountain of God. 14 *To the elders he said, "Wait
for us here until we return to you. Behold! Aaron and Hur are with you;
whoever has a grievance should approach them."*
15 *Moses ascended the mountain, and the cloud covered the mountain.*
16 *The glory of* HASHEM *rested upon Mount Sinai, and the cloud covered it
for a six-day period. He called to Moses on the seventh day from the midst
of the cloud.* 17 *The appearance of the glory of* HASHEM *was like a
consuming fire on the mountaintop before the eyes of the Children of Israel.*
18 *Moses arrived in the midst of the cloud and ascended the mountain; and
Moses was on the mountain for forty days and forty nights.*

---

this, when He said, "מִזְבַּח אֲדָמָה תַּעֲשֶׂה לִּי . . . בְּכָל הַמָּקוֹם אֲשֶׁר אַזְכִּיר אֶת שְׁמִי אָבוֹא אֵלֶיךָ, *An altar of earth you shall make for Me . . . in every place where I cause My Name to be mentioned I will come to you*" (20:21). Now however they will need priests, which is explained when He says, "וְאַתָּה הַקְרֵב אֵלֶיךָ אֶת אַהֲרֹן אָחִיךָ, *And you (shall) bring near to you Aaron your brother*" (28:1). Behold that the tribe of Levi was not chosen to serve until *after* the incident of the Calf, as is proven by the verse, בָּעֵת הַהִוא הִבְדִּיל ה׳ אֶת שֵׁבֶט הַלֵּוִי . . . לְשָׁרְתוֹ וּלְבָרֵךְ בִּשְׁמוֹ, *At that time* HASHEM *separated the tribe of Levi . . . to serve Him and to bless in His Name (Deut.* 10:8).

Therefore (the Torah now) says that every time Moses went up to the mount he remained there forty days and forty nights, and the time he attained this end purpose was the last time of them all, when he was commanded regarding the work of the Sanctuary. Now after (the Torah) completes (the story of) the work of the Sanctuary, the priestly vestments, the incense and the oil of anointment, (then) it explains that at the end of the first (forty days) God, the Blessed One, gave (us) the first Tablets, and He, the Blessed One, did not cause any delay, for כִּי לֹא עִנָּה מִלִּבּוֹ, *He did not willingly afflict (Lamentations* 3:33), rather it was Israel that corrupted their affairs as it says, כִּי שִׁחֵת עַמְּךָ, *your people have dealt corruptly* (32:7). During the "middle" (forty days) according to the tradition of our Rabbis, of blessed memory, the chapter, רְאֵה אַתָּה אֹמֵר אֵלַי, *See, You say to me*, etc. (33:12), and פְּסָל לְךָ, *Hew thee out*, etc. (34:1) (took place). And in the "third" (forty days) the entire event related in (34:28), וַיְהִי שָׁם עִם ה׳ אַרְבָּעִים יוֹם וְאַרְבָּעִים לַיְלָה . . . וַיִּכְתֹּב עַל הַלֻּחֹת, *And he was there with* HASHEM *forty days and forty nights . . . and he wrote upon the Tablets* (occurred) and he descended with the rays of glory (shining from his face) and commanded them regarding the work of the Sanctuary.

NOTES

and the *sidrah* of *Ki Sisa* which relates the story of the Calf and the breaking of the Tablets. The *Sforno* resolves this difficulty in his commentary on this verse. He first explains the significance of the number forty as representing the time it takes for an embryo to develop. Each time Moses spent this period of time with God he was reborn, as it were. The special privilege he enjoyed of studying Torah with God Himself resulted in the *rays of light* which shone forth from his face and this in turn would have radiated out to the people upon his descent, had they not sinned. After the forty days and nights of entreating God to forgive Israel for the sin of the Calf, Moses ascended the mountain to spend the third, and last, period during which he was given the second Tablets and told to build a Sanctuary. Now since he was told to place the tablets in the Ark, this proves that the commandment to construct the Sanctuary (which included the Ark) had to be during the last forty-day period since the first Tablets were broken and only later were the שִׁבְרֵי לוּחוֹת, *broken fragments*, placed in the Ark alongside the second (whole) Tablets, for which the Ark was made. Another proof that the order to build the Sanctuary was given after the sin of the Calf is the fact that whereas originally God said that He would come to the people *wherever they mentioned His Name*, i.e., without need of a special place or any intermediary, now however there was need for a Sanctuary, and for the tribe of Levi to serve as intermediary as a consequence of the sin. All this being the case, the *sidros* dealing with the Sanctuary, the priesthood, etc. (namely תְּרוּמָה and תְּצַוֶּה), follow *Mishpatim* which concludes with the *last* forty days and nights to complete the story, after which the Torah tells us (in כִּי תִשָּׂא) why there was a need for the second Tablets, the Sanctuary and the priesthood.

פרשת תרומה

כה א־ב וַיְדַבֵּר יהוה אֶל־מֹשֶׁה לֵּאמֹר: דַּבֵּר אֶל־בְּנֵי יִשְׂרָאֵל וְיִקְחוּ־לִי תְּרוּמָה
ג מֵאֵת כָּל־אִישׁ אֲשֶׁר יִדְּבֶנּוּ לִבּוֹ תִּקְחוּ אֶת־תְּרוּמָתִי: וְזֹאת הַתְּרוּמָה
ד אֲשֶׁר תִּקְחוּ מֵאִתָּם זָהָב וָכֶסֶף וּנְחֹשֶׁת: וּתְכֵלֶת וְאַרְגָּמָן וְתוֹלַעַת
ה שָׁנִי וְשֵׁשׁ וְעִזִּים: וְעֹרֹת אֵילִם מְאָדָּמִים וְעֹרֹת תְּחָשִׁים וַעֲצֵי שִׁטִּים:
ו־ז שֶׁמֶן לַמָּאֹר בְּשָׂמִים לְשֶׁמֶן הַמִּשְׁחָה וְלִקְטֹרֶת הַסַּמִּים: אַבְנֵי־שֹׁהַם
ח־ט וְאַבְנֵי מִלֻּאִים לָאֵפֹד וְלַחֹשֶׁן: וְעָשׂוּ לִי מִקְדָּשׁ וְשָׁכַנְתִּי בְּתוֹכָם: כְּכֹל
אֲשֶׁר אֲנִי מַרְאֶה אוֹתְךָ אֵת תַּבְנִית הַמִּשְׁכָּן וְאֵת תַּבְנִית כָּל־כֵּלָיו וְכֵן

XXV

2. דַּבֵּר אֶל בְּנֵי יִשְׂרָאֵל וְיִקְחוּ לִי תְּרוּמָה — *Speak to the Children of Israel that they take for Me an offering.* Tell the Israelites that I want officers to collect offerings for Me. Moses did so when he descended the mountain, as it says, וְאַחֲרֵי כֵן נִגְּשׁוּ כָּל בְּנֵי יִשְׂרָאֵל וַיְצַוֵּם אֵת כָּל אֲשֶׁר דִּבֶּר ה׳ אִתּוֹ בְּהַר סִינָי, *And afterward all the Children of Israel drew close and he commanded them all that HASHEM had spoken with him on Mount Sinai* (34:32), and afterward, וַיֹּאמֶר מֹשֶׁה אֶל כָּל עֲדַת בְּנֵי יִשְׂרָאֵל, *And Moses spoke to all the congregation of the Children of Israel* (i.e., the *Sanhedrin*), ״קְחוּ מֵאִתְּכֶם תְּרוּמָה, *Take from among you an offering''* (35:4,5). In this manner he commanded them to collect (for the Sanctuary) but Israel did not wait for the *Sanhedrin* to collect but immediately left Moses' presence and brought more than enough (36:5). Therefore naught remained for the princes, who had thought to collect, to do except (to bring) the (precious) stones and the oil which the Israelites had not yet brought.

מֵאֵת כָּל אִישׁ — *Of every man.* He commanded that they should not collect forcibly, similar to the placing of a lien for (matters of) *tzedakah* (charity) *(Bava Basra* 8b). Rather they are to collect only from voluntary contributors.

3. וְזֹאת הַתְּרוּמָה — *And this is the offering.* He commanded that they should not accept any items of monetary value such as fruit, pearls or precious stones which were not the stones (required for the) *ephod* and *choshen* (breastplate). But they should accept offerings which could themselves be used for the work of the Sanctuary, which are the thirteen items specified (in the following verses).

8-9. וְשָׁכַנְתִּי בְּתוֹכָם ... כְּכֹל אֲשֶׁר אֲנִי מַרְאֶה אוֹתְךָ — *That I may dwell among them ... According to all that I show you.* I will dwell among them to accept their prayer and worship, in the same manner that *I show you* My Divine Presence on the mountain (and

NOTES

XXV

2. דַּבֵּר אֶל בְּנֵי יִשְׂרָאֵל וְיִקְחוּ לִי תְּרוּמָה — *Speak to the Children of Israel that they take for Me an offering.* This chapter relates what God commanded Moses regarding the Sanctuary and the offerings brought for its construction, while he was still with God on the mountaintop. The implementation of this commandment regarding the contributions took place when Moses descended, as recorded in 34:32 and 35:4. The *Sforno* indicates that the two phrases בְּנֵי יִשְׂרָאֵל, *Children of Israel* (34:32), and עֲדַת בְּנֵי יִשְׂרָאֵל, *the congregation of the Children of Israel* (35:4), are meant to differentiate between the people and their leaders — whom he refers to as the *Sanhedrin.* He also interprets the expression *speak to the Children of Israel* in the sense of informing them that they will be asked by the officers to contribute to the Sanctuary, while the leaders were to be told to appoint officers for this purpose, which is the meaning of *that they take for Me an offering.* The people, however, did not wait and brought their gifts with alacrity. As a result the leaders had no need to appoint officers to collect and the only thing remaining for them to do was to bring the precious stones and the oil.

3. וְזֹאת הַתְּרוּמָה — *And this is the offering.* Moses was given three commandments: (a) to have officers appointed to collect the offerings; (b) to do so

PARASHAS TERUMAH

25 [1] *HASHEM spoke to Moses, saying:* [2] *Speak to the Children of Israel and let them take for Me a portion, from every man whose heart motivates him you shall take My portion.*

[3] *This is the portion that you shall take from them: gold, silver, and copper;* [4] *and turquoise, purple, and scarlet wool; linen and goat hair;* [5] *red-dyed ram skins, tachash skins, acacia wood;* [6] *oil for illumination, spices for the anointment oil and the aromatic incense;* [7] *shoham stones and stones for the settings, for the Ephod and the Breastplate.*

[8] *They shall make a Sanctuary for Me — so that I may dwell among them —* [9] *like everything that I show you, the form of the Tabernacle and the form of all its vessels; and so shall you do.*

---

this will be) on the Ark cover between the two Cherubim with the תַּבְנִית הַמִּשְׁכָּן, *pattern of the Sanctuary,* and with the pattern of all its furnishings (vessels). For indeed the pattern of the Sanctuary indicates the Cherubim who are (as the) שְׂרָפִים עֹמְדִים מִמַּעַל לוֹ, *Serafim who stood above Him (Isaiah* 6:2), which is beheld by the Prophets, some in the Holy and some in the Holy of Holies. (Now) they (the Cherubim) are on two sets (of the curtains) coupled together by clasps, to become as one in the service of their Creator. And so it is proper that it be in Israel; all the holy ones shall be coupled (linked) to the multitude to instruct and teach them. In the Holy of Holies the Torah (tablets of law) was placed in a receptacle (lit., "body") overlaid with gold within and without (and) as our Sages say, regarding this: כָּל תַּלְמִיד חָכָם שֶׁאֵין תּוֹכוֹ כְּבָרוֹ אֵינוֹ תַּלְמִיד חָכָם, *A Torah scholar whose inner being is not as his outer one is not considered a Torah scholar (Yoma* 72b). On that receptacle (lit., "body") which is the Ark a cover was placed, which was all gold indicating the *image of God,* which is not coupled with it at all. And so the Cherubim with פְּנֵיהֶם אִישׁ אֶל אָחִיו, *their faces one to another* (v. 20), symbolize the transmitting and receiving of the powers of understanding which comes through looking into the Torah, as it says, אֶל הַכַּפֹּרֶת יִהְיוּ פְּנֵי הַכְּרֻבִים, *toward the Ark cover shall the faces of the Cherubim be* (ibid.), and thus they spread their wings on high, as it says, אֹרַח חַיִּים לְמַעְלָה לְמַשְׂכִּיל, *the way of life for the wise leads upward (Proverbs* 15:24), and thus God will bethink Himself of us, as it says: וְאֶל זֶה אַבִּיט, *but to this man will I look (Isaiah* 66:2).

NOTES

on a purely voluntary basis — there was to be no coercion; and (c) to collect only the thirteen items enumerated in verses 3-7.

8-9. וְשָׁכַנְתִּי בְּתוֹכָם ... כְּכֹל אֲשֶׁר אֲנִי מַרְאֶה אוֹתְךָ — *That I may dwell among them ... According to all that I show you.* The sense of the *Sforno's* interpretation of these verses is as follows: Cherubim are found in two places in the Sanctuary — over the Ark cover and woven into the curtains which comprised the walls of the Sanctuary. The former was located in the Holy of Holies while the latter was only designated as "Holy." Now the Jewish people are called a holy people (19:6), while the Torah scholars and men of the spirit are considered "Holy of Holies." The curtains clasped together symbolize the need for Torah scholars to be connected to the multitude and instruct them in God's ways. On an even higher level, symbolized by the Cherubim in the Holy of Holies, there will be the select few who will transmit and receive the profound wisdom and mysteries of God by plumbing the depths of Torah. This is indicated by the Cherubim facing one another while at the same time looking down at the Ark which contains the testimony of law. God in turn will turn His attention and concern to them. (See the note on verse 20 for further elaboration.) The *Sforno* refers to the Ark as גוּף, *body,* for it symbolizes the physical being of the Torah scholar. Just as the Ark was made of acacia wood and gold — actually three boxes, two of gold and one of wood, fitted into one another — so the body of a holy person, although physical, must be pure on the outside and the inside. The Ark cover, however, was totally made of gold for it represents the *image of God* (and in man, the soul); hence it was not attached to the Ark but separate from it. The concluding words of

י תַּעֲשׂוּ: וְעָשׂוּ אֲרוֹן עֲצֵי שִׁטִּים אַמָּתַיִם וָחֵצִי אָרְכּוֹ וְאַמָּה
יא וָחֵצִי רָחְבּוֹ וְאַמָּה וָחֵצִי קֹמָתוֹ: וְצִפִּיתָ אֹתוֹ זָהָב טָהוֹר מִבַּיִת וּמִחוּץ תְּצַפֶּנּוּ
יב וְעָשִׂיתָ עָלָיו זֵר זָהָב סָבִיב: וְיָצַקְתָּ לּוֹ אַרְבַּע טַבְּעֹת זָהָב וְנָתַתָּה עַל
אַרְבַּע פַּעֲמֹתָיו וּשְׁתֵּי טַבָּעֹת עַל־צַלְעוֹ הָאֶחָת וּשְׁתֵּי טַבָּעֹת עַל־צַלְעוֹ
יג־יד הַשֵּׁנִית: וְעָשִׂיתָ בַדֵּי עֲצֵי שִׁטִּים וְצִפִּיתָ אֹתָם זָהָב: וְהֵבֵאתָ אֶת־הַבַּדִּים
טו בַּטַּבָּעֹת עַל צַלְעֹת הָאָרֹן לָשֵׂאת אֶת־הָאָרֹן בָּהֶם: בְּטַבְּעֹת הָאָרֹן יִהְיוּ
טז הַבַּדִּים לֹא יָסֻרוּ מִמֶּנּוּ: וְנָתַתָּ אֶל־הָאָרֹן אֵת הָעֵדֻת אֲשֶׁר אֶתֵּן אֵלֶיךָ:
שני יז־יח וְעָשִׂיתָ כַפֹּרֶת זָהָב טָהוֹר אַמָּתַיִם וָחֵצִי אָרְכָּהּ וְאַמָּה וָחֵצִי רָחְבָּהּ: וְעָשִׂיתָ
יט שְׁנַיִם כְּרֻבִים זָהָב מִקְשָׁה תַּעֲשֶׂה אֹתָם מִשְּׁנֵי קְצוֹת הַכַּפֹּרֶת: וַעֲשֵׂה כְּרוּב
אֶחָד מִקָּצָה מִזֶּה וּכְרוּב־אֶחָד מִקָּצָה מִזֶּה מִן־הַכַּפֹּרֶת תַּעֲשׂוּ אֶת־
כ הַכְּרֻבִים עַל־שְׁנֵי קְצוֹתָיו: וְהָיוּ הַכְּרֻבִים פֹּרְשֵׂי כְנָפַיִם לְמַעְלָה סֹכְכִים

וְכֵן תַּעֲשׂוּ — *And so shall you make it* . . . you (yourself), so that I shall dwell in your midst to speak with you and receive the prayers and service of Israel, not as it was before the (Golden) Calf, as it says, בְּכָל הַמָּקוֹם . . . אָבוֹא אֵלֶיךָ, *in every place . . . I will come to you* (20:21).

12. פַּעֲמֹתָיו — *Feet* . . . the corners of its bottom rim.

וּשְׁתֵּי טַבָּעֹת עַל צַלְעוֹ הָאֶחָת — *And two rings shall be on the one side of it.* The long side (length) is called צֶלַע. He therefore commanded that the four (rings) should be placed on the four corners of the bottom (rim) and He also commanded that it not be placed on the narrow side (the breadth) but on the long side called צְלָעוֹת, two of them on one side and two of them on the second.

16. וְנָתַתָּ אֶל הָאָרֹן — *And you shall put into the Ark.* He had to explain its purpose since this was a furnishing which was not fit for any sacrificial service.

20. וְהָיוּ הַכְּרֻבִים פֹּרְשֵׂי כְנָפַיִם — *And the Cherubim shall spread out their wings.* The prophets have already explained that in their prophetic visions angels appeared to them in the form of Cherubim, with the face of a human and with wings. All this (comes to) teach the nature of the intellects separated from matter (i.e., angels) whose entire movement

NOTES

verse 9, *and so shall you make it,* is interpreted by the *Sforno* as implying a rebuke. Until the sin of the Golden Calf there was no need for a Sanctuary, since God was prepared to come wherever Israel would cause *His Name to be mentioned.* However, after the sin it was necessary to designate a specific, limited place for the Divine Presence to dwell.

12. וּשְׁתֵּי טַבָּעֹת עַל צַלְעוֹ הָאֶחָת — *And two rings shall be on the one side of it.* The *Sforno* disagrees with *Rashi* (and other commentators) regarding the positioning of the rings on the Ark. He is of the opinion that they were to be placed at the corners of the bottom rim — not at the top near the Ark cover, and they were to be placed along the length, not the width, for the word צֶלַע, used here by the Torah as opposed to צַד, means length.

16. וְנָתַתָּ אֶל הָאָרֹן — *And you shall put into the Ark.* Pagan worship was well known to the Israelites, hence they could relate to various furnishings and vessels of the Sanctuary since there were counterparts among the heathens. The Ark, however, was completely new and unique. What was the purpose of this box? This is what the *Sforno* means when he states that it was necessary to explain the purpose of the Ark, being that it did not fit any service known to them in that culture and time period.

20. וְהָיוּ הַכְּרֻבִים פֹּרְשֵׂי כְנָפַיִם — *And the Cherubim shall spread out their wings.* The *Sforno* in his commentary on verses 8-9 explains the symbolism of the Cherubim and their lesson for man as our responsibility to understand God's ways through Torah and to transmit this knowledge to others as well. In this verse he elaborates on the significance of the Cherubim and interprets the imagery of *two,* rather than one, and what is meant by their wings being *spread out on high.* The *Rambam* in his *Guide* (I:49) says, "The angels are not endowed

10 *They shall make an Ark of acacia wood, two and a half cubits its length; a cubit and a half its width; and a cubit and a half its height.* 11 *You shall cover it with pure gold, from within and from without shall you cover it, and you shall make on it a gold crown all around.* 12 *You shall cast for it four rings of gold and place them on its four corners, two rings on its one side and two rings on its second side.* 13 *You shall make staves of acacia wood and cover them with gold;* 14 *and insert the staves in the rings on the sides of the Ark, with which to carry the Ark.* 15 *The staves shall remain in the rings of the Ark; they may not be removed from it.* 16 *You shall place in the Ark the Testimonial-tablets that I shall give you.*

17 *You shall make a Cover of pure gold, two and a half cubits its length; and a cubit and a half its width.* 18 *You shall make two Cherubim of gold — hammered out shall you make them — from both ends of the Cover.* 19 *You shall make one Cherub from the end at one side and one Cherub from the end at the other; from the Cover shall you make the Cherubim at its two ends.* 20 *The Cherubim shall be with wings spread upward, sheltering*

---

is in an upward direction, toward God — to understand and know Him. Each of these "intellects separated from matter" according to its ability. Now by the statement, וְהָיוּ הַכְּרֻבִים פֹּרְשֵׂי כְנָפַיִם, *And the Cherubim shall spread out their wings,* we are being taught that the human intellect is one that (also) has the potential to reach a second (level) of perfection, which can be attained through principles (of truth and apprehension) and the removal of (one's physical) matter, so as to understand and know one's Creator to the extent possible, by examining (lit., "gazing at") the wonders in the Torah which clearly show His wondrous acts and merciful ways. For indeed the essence and form of a thing is made known to us through its deeds (actions) and this occurs to human understanding when one grasps (lit., "understands") the existence of the Creator as much as he possibly can (through His ways), as it says, הוֹדִעֵנִי נָא אֶת דְּרָכֶךָ וְאֵדָעֲךָ לְמַעַן אֶמְצָא חֵן בְּעֵינֶיךָ, *Show me now Your ways that I may know You to the end that I may find grace in Your eyes* (33:13). (This the verse indicates by) saying that the Cherubim shall *spread out their wings on high.* Now (our Sages) have said (*Yoma* 54a) that the Cherubim were male and female, indicating the action of delivering (or giving) the general principles (of truth and apprehension) removed (from the physical) which is akin to the action of the male who conveys, (as well as) indicating receiving these (principles) which are removed from (the mundane), akin to the function of the female. And the (verse also) says, וּפְנֵיהֶם אִישׁ אֶל אָחִיו, *with their*

NOTES

with bodies but are intellects separate from matter." Based on this concept the *Sforno* explains that man, as well, can attain a higher understanding of God if he also could to a certain extent transcend his physical being and *remove his matter* as it were, thereby also becoming separate from matter, i.e., pure intellect, although still less than an angel. The *Rambam* explains the imagery of the wings thus: The act of flying represents the ability to soar to the heights as well as swiftness of movement. All this requires wings and it is in this sense that the concept of wings is linked to angels and to the Cherubim in particular. This explains the *Sforno's* opening comment that Cherubim have *the face of a human and wings.* A human being can also aspire to develop his spiritual and intellectual potential so as to soar to greater heights of apprehension and understanding of God. Now this can only be realized by examining God's ways, as we see from Moses that to *know God* can only be through the medium of knowing His ways, i.e., understanding the way of God as manifested through His attributive qualifications, as the *Rambam* puts it in the *Guide* (I:54): "The apprehension of God's actions is an apprehension of His attributes with respect to which He is known" (ibid.). These actions are called מִדּוֹת, *characteristics,* by our Sages, hence the י"ג מִדּוֹת, *thirteen characteristics,* which are revealed to Moses. To know God's ways through His actions

בְּכַנְפֵיהֶם֙ עַל־הַכַּפֹּ֔רֶת וּפְנֵיהֶ֖ם אִ֣ישׁ אֶל־אָחִ֑יו אֶל־הַכַּפֹּ֔רֶת יִהְי֖וּ פְּנֵ֥י
כא הַכְּרֻבִֽים׃ וְנָתַתָּ֧ אֶת־הַכַּפֹּ֛רֶת עַל־הָאָרֹ֖ן מִלְמָ֑עְלָה וְאֶל־הָ֣אָרֹ֔ן תִּתֵּן֙
כב אֶת־הָ֣עֵדֻ֔ת אֲשֶׁ֥ר אֶתֵּ֖ן אֵלֶֽיךָ׃ וְנוֹעַדְתִּ֣י לְךָ֮ שָׁם֒ וְדִבַּרְתִּ֨י אִתְּךָ֜ מֵעַ֣ל
הַכַּפֹּ֗רֶת מִבֵּין֙ שְׁנֵ֣י הַכְּרֻבִ֔ים אֲשֶׁ֖ר עַל־אֲר֣וֹן הָעֵדֻ֑ת אֵ֣ת כָּל־אֲשֶׁ֧ר אֲצַוֶּ֛ה
אוֹתְךָ֖ אֶל־בְּנֵ֥י יִשְׂרָאֵֽל׃
כג וְעָשִׂ֥יתָ שֻׁלְחָ֖ן עֲצֵ֣י שִׁטִּ֑ים אַמָּתַ֤יִם אָרְכּוֹ֙ וְאַמָּ֣ה רָחְבּ֔וֹ וְאַמָּ֥ה וָחֵ֖צִי קֹמָתֽוֹ׃
כד־כה וְצִפִּיתָ֥ אֹת֖וֹ זָהָ֣ב טָה֑וֹר וְעָשִׂ֥יתָ לּ֛וֹ זֵ֥ר זָהָ֖ב סָבִֽיב׃ וְעָשִׂ֨יתָ לּ֥וֹ מִסְגֶּ֛רֶת טֹ֖פַח
כו סָבִ֑יב וְעָשִׂ֧יתָ זֵר־זָהָ֛ב לְמִסְגַּרְתּ֖וֹ סָבִֽיב׃ וְעָשִׂ֣יתָ לּ֔וֹ אַרְבַּ֖ע טַבְּעֹ֣ת זָהָ֑ב

---

faces one to another, for the process of giving these general principles and disseminating them (require one) to consider and concentrate toward the action of receiving these general principles that are removed from matter, (since) through them one attains the intended perfection. And it (then) says, אֶל הַכַּפֹּרֶת יִהְיוּ פְּנֵי הַכְּרֻבִים, *toward the Ark cover shall the faces of the Cherubim be.*

21. וְנָתַתָּ אֶת הַכַּפֹּרֶת עַל הָאָרֹן מִלְמָעְלָה וְאֶל הָאָרֹן תִּתֵּן אֶת הָעֵדֻת אֲשֶׁר אֶתֵּן אֵלֶיךָ — *And you shall put the Ark cover on the Ark above and in the Ark you shall put the testimony that I will give you.* For indeed the application (lit., "gazing") of the intellect and the giving (delivering) of the general principles from which matter has been removed, as well as the receiving (of same), said receiving (being such) that it becomes his possession; behold, all this can (only) be through the medium of analysis and active preparation. Therefore all this can (only) be attained by examining (studying) the testimony which is in the Ark upon which is the Ark cover, for indeed in the testimony, which is the Ten Commandments, are found the general principles (of Torah), the theoretical and active (deeds) portions (parts), and so He designated ...

22. וְנוֹעַדְתִּי לְךָ שָׁם וְדִבַּרְתִּי אִתְּךָ — *And there I shall meet with you and I will speak with you.* For through this the Divine Presence came to rest (among them) and will dwell in

NOTES

can only be achieved through His Torah which is why the Cherubim gaze at the Ark cover, to teach man this truth, which is the key to wisdom, for in the Torah are recorded "His wondrous acts and merciful ways" as the *Sforno* states.

The *Sforno* also emphasizes that the statement of the Sages regarding the two Cherubim as being male and female is meant to teach us the importance of two forces in grasping God's ways and transmitting this understanding to others. The male represents the power of giving, delivering, conveying while the female receives, just as it is in the physical union which results in a new life. So the ultimate truth and wisdom of Torah is drawn forth from the Torah and absorbed by the recipient. Hence the imagery is complete — the Cherubim face one another, spread out their wings and face the Ark cover.

21. וְנָתַתָּ אֶת הַכַּפֹּרֶת עַל הָאָרֹן מִלְמָעְלָה וְאֶל הָאָרֹן תִּתֵּן אֶת הָעֵדֻת אֲשֶׁר אֶתֵּן אֵלֶיךָ — *And you shall put the Ark cover on the Ark above, and in the Ark you shall put the testimony that I will give you.* The *Sforno*, reflecting the opinion of the *Rambam*, explains that man can only hope to attain a true understanding of God and Torah through intellectual in-depth analysis of God's existence and His ways, and preparation to accept His will and translate it into action. This in turn can only be realized through the study of Torah which will refine his character and grant him clarity of thought, resulting in purity of action. All this the Cherubim symbolize facing the Ark cover — כַּפֹּרֶת — which is on top of the Ark housing the Ten Commandments. The Ten Commandments, in turn, represent the totality of Torah — the theoretical-analytical as well as the action-deed aspect of Torah, as the *Sforno* explains in his commentary to chapter 20.

22. וְנוֹעַדְתִּי לְךָ שָׁם וְדִבַּרְתִּי אִתְּךָ — *And there I shall meet with you and I will speak with you.* The result of all that is described in the previous verses is that the Divine Presence (שְׁכִינָה) will come to rest in the Sanctuary between the Cherubim above the Ark cover. The *Sforno* carries this idea over to the study of the מַעֲשֵׂה מֶרְכָּבָה, *Work of the Chariot,* by a select group of wise men who attained the heights of Torah knowledge and were worthy of pursuing

the Cover with their wings with their faces toward one another; toward the Cover shall be the faces of the Cherubim. 21 *You shall place the Cover on the Ark from above, and into the Ark shall you place the Testimonial-tablets that I shall give you.* 22 *It is there that I will set My meetings with you, and I shall speak with you from atop the Cover, from between the two Cherubim that are on the Ark of the Testimonial-tablets, everything that I shall command you to the Children of Israel.*

23 *You shall make a Table of acacia wood, two cubits its length, a cubit its width, and a cubit and a half its height.* 24 *You shall cover it with pure gold and you shall make for it a gold crown all around.* 25 *You shall make for it a molding of one handbreadth all around, and you shall make a gold crown on the molding all around.* 26 *You shall make for it four rings of gold*

every place where the wise men of the generation are found, whose purpose is to understand and know Him, as it is attested to by saying, וְשָׁכַנְתִּי בְּתוֹכָם כְּכֹל אֲשֶׁר אֲנִי מַרְאֶה אוֹתְךָ, *That I may dwell among them according to all that I show you,* to which He adds and says, וְכֵן תַּעֲשׂוּ, *and so shall you make it* (verses 8-9). Our Sages have testified that it happened to them when they were expounding the "Work of the Chariot" as the Sages say, "You are expounding the Work of the Chariot and the Divine Presence (שְׁכִינָה) is with us and the ministering angels accompany us, etc." (*Chagigah* 14b).

23. וְעָשִׂיתָ שֻׁלְחָן — *And you shall make a table.* After (telling us) the work of the Ark, which was in the likeness of a throne for the Divine Presence, as it says, וְנוֹעַדְתִּי לְךָ שָׁם, *And there I will meet with you* (v. 22), (he) now commands regarding the table and menorah, in accordance with the custom of princes, as we find with the Shunamis when she said, וְנָשִׂים לוֹ שָׁם מִטָּה וְשֻׁלְחָן וְכִסֵּא וּמְנוֹרָה, *and let us set for him there a bed, table, chair and candlestick (II Kings* 4:10). Since the crown of the table represents the crown of kingship, as our Sages say (*Yoma* 72b), (and) the king's responsibilities (lit., "affairs") in conducting matters of state are twofold; one being in the area of justice and the affairs of state, (while) the second is to defend the state from all enemies and oppressors, as it says, וּשְׁפָטָנוּ מַלְכֵּנוּ וְיָצָא לְפָנֵינוּ וְנִלְחַם אֶת מִלְחֲמֹתֵינוּ, *that our king may judge us and go out before us and fight our battles (I Samuel* 8:20), (therefore) two crowns were placed on the table, one for the table itself indicating the livelihood and order of the state and its affairs and the second for the border (rim) indicating a (protective) border for it (the state) against all harm and to *still the enemy and avenger (Psalms* 8:3).

NOTES

this esoteric wisdom. He proves this from the selection cited from the Talmud (*Chagigah* 14b) where Rabban Yochanan ben Zakkai says that the Divine Presence was present at the time Rabbi Elazar ben Arach expounded on the "Work of the Chariot," for through his mastery of the truth of Torah he was able to bring God into their midst, similar to God's "meeting" with Moses and speaking to him in the Sanctuary. The expression וְכֵן תַּעֲשׂוּ, *and so you shall do* (v. 9), is interpreted by the *Sforno* as encouraging those who have the capacity to pursue the knowledge of God to do so, as did the Sages of the Talmud mentioned above.

23. וְעָשִׂיתָ שֻׁלְחָן — *And you shall make a table.* The word זֵר, *crown,* appears twice in conjunction with the table — in verse 24 and verse 25. *Rashi* is of the opinion that there was only one crown and that verse 25 clarifies verse 24. The *Sforno,* however, interprets these verses literally and explains that one crown was for the table itself whereas the second one was for the border or rim, indicating the twofold responsibility of the king, domestic tranquility and national security. That the table represents kingship is based upon the Talmud (*Yoma* 72b) where our Sages tell us that there were three crowns in the furnishings of the Sanctuary — on the Ark, on the table and on the golden altar. The crown of the golden altar represents the crown of priesthood; the table represents שֻׁלְחַן מְלָכִים, *the royal table* (and its crown is thus the crown of kingship); while the crown on the Ark represents the crown of Torah.

כז וְנָתַתָּ אֶת־הַטַּבָּעֹת עַל אַרְבַּע הַפֵּאֹת אֲשֶׁר לְאַרְבַּע רַגְלָיו: לְעֻמַּת
כח הַמִּסְגֶּרֶת תִּהְיֶיןָ הַטַּבָּעֹת לְבָתִּים לְבַדִּים לָשֵׂאת אֶת־הַשֻּׁלְחָן: וְעָשִׂיתָ
אֶת־הַבַּדִּים עֲצֵי שִׁטִּים וְצִפִּיתָ אֹתָם זָהָב וְנִשָּׂא־בָם אֶת־הַשֻּׁלְחָן:
כט וְעָשִׂיתָ קְּעָרֹתָיו וְכַפֹּתָיו וּקְשׂוֹתָיו וּמְנַקִּיֹּתָיו אֲשֶׁר יֻסַּךְ בָּהֵן זָהָב טָהוֹר
ל תַּעֲשֶׂה אֹתָם: וְנָתַתָּ עַל־הַשֻּׁלְחָן לֶחֶם פָּנִים לְפָנַי תָּמִיד:
לא וְעָשִׂיתָ מְנֹרַת זָהָב טָהוֹר מִקְשָׁה תֵּיעָשֶׂה הַמְּנוֹרָה יְרֵכָהּ וְקָנָהּ גְּבִיעֶיהָ
לב כַּפְתֹּרֶיהָ וּפְרָחֶיהָ מִמֶּנָּה יִהְיוּ: וְשִׁשָּׁה קָנִים יֹצְאִים מִצִּדֶּיהָ שְׁלֹשָׁה | קְנֵי
לג מְנֹרָה מִצִּדָּהּ הָאֶחָד וּשְׁלֹשָׁה קְנֵי מְנֹרָה מִצִּדָּהּ הַשֵּׁנִי: שְׁלֹשָׁה גְבִעִים
מְשֻׁקָּדִים בַּקָּנֶה הָאֶחָד כַּפְתֹּר וָפֶרַח וּשְׁלֹשָׁה גְבִעִים מְשֻׁקָּדִים בַּקָּנֶה
לד הָאֶחָד כַּפְתֹּר וָפָרַח כֵּן לְשֵׁשֶׁת הַקָּנִים הַיֹּצְאִים מִן־הַמְּנֹרָה: וּבַמְּנֹרָה
לה אַרְבָּעָה גְבִעִים מְשֻׁקָּדִים כַּפְתֹּרֶיהָ וּפְרָחֶיהָ: וְכַפְתֹּר תַּחַת שְׁנֵי הַקָּנִים
מִמֶּנָּה וְכַפְתֹּר תַּחַת שְׁנֵי הַקָּנִים מִמֶּנָּה וְכַפְתֹּר תַּחַת־שְׁנֵי הַקָּנִים מִמֶּנָּה
לו לְשֵׁשֶׁת הַקָּנִים הַיֹּצְאִים מִן־הַמְּנֹרָה: כַּפְתֹּרֵיהֶם וּקְנֹתָם מִמֶּנָּה יִהְיוּ
לז כֻּלָּהּ מִקְשָׁה אַחַת זָהָב טָהוֹר: וְעָשִׂיתָ אֶת־נֵרֹתֶיהָ שִׁבְעָה וְהֶעֱלָה
לח-לט אֶת־נֵרֹתֶיהָ וְהֵאִיר עַל־עֵבֶר פָּנֶיהָ: וּמַלְקָחֶיהָ וּמַחְתֹּתֶיהָ זָהָב טָהוֹר: כִּכַּר
מ זָהָב טָהוֹר יַעֲשֶׂה אֹתָהּ אֵת כָּל־הַכֵּלִים הָאֵלֶּה: וּרְאֵה וַעֲשֵׂה בְּתַבְנִיתָם
כו שלישי א אֲשֶׁר־אַתָּה מָרְאֶה בָּהָר: וְאֶת־הַמִּשְׁכָּן תַּעֲשֶׂה עֶשֶׂר
יְרִיעֹת שֵׁשׁ מָשְׁזָר וּתְכֵלֶת וְאַרְגָּמָן וְתֹלַעַת שָׁנִי כְּרֻבִים מַעֲשֵׂה חֹשֵׁב

---

29. קְעָרֹתָיו וְכַפֹּתָיו — *The pans and spoons thereof.* Which were well known at that time, used (in conjunction) with the table of kings.

31. וְעָשִׂיתָ מְנֹרַת זָהָב טָהוֹר — *And you shall make a menorah of pure gold.* After ordering the two crowns, which are the crown of Torah through the Ark and the crown of kingship through the table, He now orders (arranges) the menorah all beaten out of one piece, and the light of its candles (are also) one, as He says . . .

37. וְהֵאִיר עַל עֵבֶר פָּנֶיהָ — *To give light over against it.* The light of the right candles (wicks) and left candles will be directed toward the center, and it is proper that it be so; that the light of the intellect in the part of (Torah) which is theory (analysis) and also the light in the active part (of Torah, i.e., deeds) turn and face the Divine light, to serve Him in one accord, for then all will illuminate as designated regarding the menorah, when He said: בְּהַעֲלֹתְךָ אֶת הַנֵּרֹת אֶל מוּל פְּנֵי הַמְּנוֹרָה יָאִירוּ שִׁבְעַת הַנֵּרוֹת . . . וְזֶה מַעֲשֵׂה הַמְּנֹרָה מִקְשָׁה, *When you light the lamps the seven lamps shall give light over against the central candlestick . . . and this was the work of the candlestick, (it should be) beaten (out of one piece) (Numbers* 8:2, 4). When all the light is directed *to one* — (similar to the fact that

NOTES

31-37. וְעָשִׂיתָ מְנֹרַת זָהָב טָהוֹר . . . וְהֵאִיר עַל עֵבֶר פָּנֶיהָ — *And you shall make a menorah of pure gold . . . To give light over against it.* The commentary of the *Sforno* here and his commentary on *Numbers* 8:2,4 complement one another and clarify his explanation of the menorah and the arrangement of its wicks, as well as the significance of the candlestick being beaten out of one piece of gold. The central theme of the menorah is unity — the unity of Israel and, of course, that of God. There are three lights on either side of the central candlestick which represent the different parts of Torah (the theoretical and the practical) as well as the two segments of Israel, i.e., those who occupy themselves exclusively with the spiritual and those who involve themselves with the temporal, as the *Sforno* explains in *Numbers* 8:2. By bending the wicks, from the left and right to the center which represents the Divine light, we are taught that all segments of Israel and all areas of Torah are to be

and place the rings upon the four corners of its four legs. 27 *The rings shall*
be opposite the molding as housings for the staves, to carry the Table. 28 *You*
shall make the staves of acacia wood and cover them with gold, and the
Table shall be carried through them. 29 *You shall make its dishes, its spoons,*
its shelving-tubes, and its pillars, with which it shall be covered; of pure
gold shall you make them. 30 *On the Table shall you place show-bread*
before Me, always.
31 *You shall make a Menorah of pure gold, hammered out shall the*
Menorah be made, its base, its shaft, its cups, its knobs, and its blossoms
shall be [hammered] from it. 32 *Six branches shall emerge from its sides,*
three branches of the Menorah from its one side and three branches of the
Menorah from its second side; 33 *three cups engraved like almonds on the*
one branch, a knob and a flower; and three cups engraved like almonds on
the next branch, a knob and a flower — so for the six branches that emerge
from the Menorah. 34 *And on the Menorah shall be four cups, engraved like*
almonds, its knobs and its flowers. 35 *A knob shall be under two of the*
branches from it, a knob under two of the branches from it, and a knob
under two of the branches from it — for the six branches emerging from the
Menorah. 36 *Their knobs and branches shall be of it; all of it a single*
hammered piece of pure gold. 37 *You shall make its lamps seven; he shall*
kindle its lamps so as to give light toward its face. 38 *Its tongs and its spoons*
shall be of pure gold. 39 *Of a talent of pure gold shall he make it, with all*
these vessels. 40 *See and make, according to their form that you are shown*
on the mountain.

26 1 *You shall make the Tabernacle of ten curtains — twisted linen with tur-*
quoise, purple, and scarlet wool — with a woven design of cherubim

---

the menorah was) beaten out of one solid piece (piece of gold) — which teaches us (the lesson of) unity, then the light will be seen as shining from the great light.

XXVI

1. וְאֶת הַמִּשְׁכָּן תַּעֲשֶׂה — *And you shall make the mishkan.* He called the curtains by the name *mishkan* (sanctuary or tabernacle) because within them were the chair (i.e., Ark), table, and menorah for the Divine Presence to dwell. They (the curtains) were made with Cherubim similar to שְׂרָפִים עֹמְדִים מִמַּעַל לוֹ, *Seraphim stood above Him (Isaiah* 6:2), and to, וְכָל צְבָא הַשָּׁמַיִם עֹמֵד עָלָיו מִימִינוֹ וּמִשְּׂמֹאלוֹ, *all the hosts of heaven standing by Him on His right and on His left (I Kings* 22:19), seen by the prophets in visions of prophecy.

NOTES

united together and directed to a common purpose, i.e., to serve the Almighty with one accord. This is also the significance of the menorah itself being hammered out of one piece. In this manner the light of Torah and of Israel shall shine forth, emanating from the one great source of light — Almighty God.

XXVI

1. וְאֶת הַמִּשְׁכָּן תַּעֲשֶׂה — *And you shall make the mishkan.* The *Sforno* explains why the curtains are called *mishkan,* a term normally reserved for the Sanctuary. Since they veil off the area in which the Ark (chair), table and candlestick are housed, they are referred to by this name.

The *Sforno* uses the term *chair* for the Ark, as he explained above (25:23), because it represents the throne of the Divine Presence since God comes and speaks from between the Cherubim over the Ark cover.

ב תַּעֲשֶׂה אֹתָם: אֹרֶךְ | הַיְרִיעָה הָאַחַת שְׁמֹנֶה וְעֶשְׂרִים בָּאַמָּה וְרֹחַב אַרְבַּע
ג בָּאַמָּה הַיְרִיעָה הָאֶחָת מִדָּה אַחַת לְכָל־הַיְרִיעֹת: חֲמֵשׁ הַיְרִיעֹת תִּהְיֶיןָ
ד חֹבְרֹת אִשָּׁה אֶל־אֲחֹתָהּ וְחָמֵשׁ יְרִיעֹת חֹבְרֹת אִשָּׁה אֶל־אֲחֹתָהּ: וְעָשִׂיתָ
לֻלְאֹת תְּכֵלֶת עַל שְׂפַת הַיְרִיעָה הָאֶחָת מִקָּצָה בַּחֹבָרֶת וְכֵן תַּעֲשֶׂה
ה בִּשְׂפַת הַיְרִיעָה הַקִּיצוֹנָה בַּמַּחְבֶּרֶת הַשֵּׁנִית: חֲמִשִּׁים לֻלָאֹת תַּעֲשֶׂה
בַּיְרִיעָה הָאֶחָת וַחֲמִשִּׁים לֻלָאֹת תַּעֲשֶׂה בִּקְצֵה הַיְרִיעָה אֲשֶׁר בַּמַּחְבֶּרֶת
ו הַשֵּׁנִית מַקְבִּילֹת הַלֻּלָאֹת אִשָּׁה אֶל־אֲחֹתָהּ: וְעָשִׂיתָ חֲמִשִּׁים קַרְסֵי זָהָב
וְחִבַּרְתָּ אֶת־הַיְרִיעֹת אִשָּׁה אֶל־אֲחֹתָהּ בַּקְּרָסִים וְהָיָה הַמִּשְׁכָּן אֶחָד:
ז וְעָשִׂיתָ יְרִיעֹת עִזִּים לְאֹהֶל עַל־הַמִּשְׁכָּן עַשְׁתֵּי־עֶשְׂרֵה יְרִיעֹת תַּעֲשֶׂה
ח אֹתָם: אֹרֶךְ | הַיְרִיעָה הָאַחַת שְׁלֹשִׁים בָּאַמָּה וְרֹחַב אַרְבַּע בָּאַמָּה הַיְרִיעָה
ט הָאֶחָת מִדָּה אַחַת לְעַשְׁתֵּי עֶשְׂרֵה יְרִיעֹת: וְחִבַּרְתָּ אֶת־חֲמֵשׁ הַיְרִיעֹת
לְבָד וְאֶת־שֵׁשׁ הַיְרִיעֹת לְבָד וְכָפַלְתָּ אֶת־הַיְרִיעָה הַשִּׁשִּׁית אֶל־מוּל פְּנֵי
י הָאֹהֶל: וְעָשִׂיתָ חֲמִשִּׁים לֻלָאֹת עַל שְׂפַת הַיְרִיעָה הָאֶחָת הַקִּיצֹנָה
יא בַּחֹבָרֶת וַחֲמִשִּׁים לֻלָאֹת עַל שְׂפַת הַיְרִיעָה הַחֹבֶרֶת הַשֵּׁנִית: וְעָשִׂיתָ
קַרְסֵי נְחֹשֶׁת חֲמִשִּׁים וְהֵבֵאתָ אֶת־הַקְּרָסִים בַּלֻּלָאֹת וְחִבַּרְתָּ אֶת־הָאֹהֶל
יב וְהָיָה אֶחָד: וְסֶרַח הָעֹדֵף בִּירִיעֹת הָאֹהֶל חֲצִי הַיְרִיעָה הָעֹדֶפֶת תִּסְרַח
יג עַל אֲחֹרֵי הַמִּשְׁכָּן: וְהָאַמָּה מִזֶּה וְהָאַמָּה מִזֶּה בָּעֹדֵף בְּאֹרֶךְ יְרִיעֹת הָאֹהֶל
יד יִהְיֶה סָרוּחַ עַל־צִדֵּי הַמִּשְׁכָּן מִזֶּה וּמִזֶּה לְכַסֹּתוֹ: וְעָשִׂיתָ מִכְסֶה לָאֹהֶל
עֹרֹת אֵילִם מְאָדָּמִים וּמִכְסֵה עֹרֹת תְּחָשִׁים מִלְמָעְלָה:
רביעי טו־טז וְעָשִׂיתָ אֶת־הַקְּרָשִׁים לַמִּשְׁכָּן עֲצֵי שִׁטִּים עֹמְדִים: עֶשֶׂר אַמּוֹת אֹרֶךְ
יז הַקָּרֶשׁ וְאַמָּה וַחֲצִי הָאַמָּה רֹחַב הַקֶּרֶשׁ הָאֶחָד: שְׁתֵּי יָדוֹת לַקֶּרֶשׁ
הָאֶחָד מְשֻׁלָּבֹת אִשָּׁה אֶל־אֲחֹתָהּ כֵּן תַּעֲשֶׂה לְכֹל קַרְשֵׁי הַמִּשְׁכָּן:

---

3. חֲמֵשׁ הַיְרִיעֹת תִּהְיֶיןָ חֹבְרֹת — *Five curtains shall be coupled together.* The work of each one of them should be directed (matched) to that of its mate in the work of their images (pictures). (All) this is (meant) to separate between the curtains of the Holy and the curtains of the Holy of Holies, for although all the work of the (woven images of the) Cherubim indicate (symbolize) "intellects separated from matter" (i.e., angels), *given from one shepherd* (based on *Koheles* 11:11), nonetheless they are not on an equal level.

6. וְהָיָה הַמִּשְׁכָּן אֶחָד — *And the mishkan shall be one.* For although the various levels are not equal (in importance), nonetheless they are (all) arranged in one order to do the will of their Creator, as it says, וְקָרָא זֶה אֶל זֶה וְאָמַר קָדוֹשׁ, *And one cried to the other and said, "Holy, etc."* (*Isaiah* 6:3).

NOTES

3. חֲמֵשׁ הַיְרִיעֹת תִּהְיֶיןָ חֹבְרֹת — *Five curtains shall be coupled together.* The word *coupled* does not only mean sewn together by a needle, as *Rashi* comments, but also to align the figures of the Cherubim, which were as the figures of a lion and eagle, with one another on the two sections. The *Sforno*, in keeping with his interpretation of the Cherubim as representing categories of angels, explains that the curtains enclosing the Holy are not equal in sanctity to those enclosing the Holy of Holies, even though these angels all emanate from the one God. As he points out in verse 6, they are not equal in rank yet they all serve God as one unit.

7. לְאֹהֶל עַל הַמִּשְׁכָּן — *For a tent over the mishkan.* Although the *mishkan* curtains could be considered אֹהֶל, *a tent*, nevertheless, the Torah uses this

shall you make them. [2] The length of a single curtain twenty-eight cubits, and the width four cubits for each curtain, the same measure for all the curtains. [3] Five curtains shall be attached to one another, and five curtains attached to one another. [4] You shall make loops of turquoise wool at the edge of the single curtain at the end of one set, and you shall make the same on the edge of the outermost curtain on the second set. [5] Fifty loops shall you make on the first curtain and fifty loops shall you make on the end of the curtain that is on the second set; the loops shall correspond to one another. [6] You shall make fifty hooks of gold, and you shall attach the curtains to one another with the hooks, so that the Tabernacle shall become one.

[7] You shall make curtains of goat hair for a Tent over the Tabernacle; eleven curtains shall you make them. [8] The length of a single curtain thirty cubits, and the width of a single curtain four cubits; the same measure for the eleven curtains. [9] You shall attach five of the curtains separately and six of the curtains separately, and you shall fold the sixth curtain over the front of the Tent. [10] You shall make fifty loops on the edge of the first curtain at the end of one set, and fifty loops on the edge of the curtain of the second set. [11] You shall make fifty hooks of copper; you shall bring the hooks into the loops and attach the Tent, so that it shall become one. [12] As for the extra overhang of the curtains of the Tent — half of the extra curtain shall hang over the back of the Tabernacle. [13] And the cubit on one side and the cubit on the other side, that are extra in the length of the curtains of the Tent, shall hang over the sides of the Tabernacle on one side and the other, to cover it.

[14] You shall make a Cover for the Tent of red-dyed ram skins, and a Cover of tachash skins above.

[15] You shall make the planks of the Tabernacle of acacia wood, standing erect. [16] Ten cubits the length of each plank, and a cubit and a half the width of each plank. [17] Each plank should have two tenons, parallel to one another — so shall you do for all the planks of the Tabernacle.

7. לְאֹהֶל עַל הַמִּשְׁכָּן — *For a tent over the mishkan.* For the *mishkan* (itself) was not meant to serve as a tent but (for the purpose) that the Cherubim should envelop the chair, table, and candlestick.

9. וְחִבַּרְתָּ אֶת חֲמֵשׁ הַיְרִיעֹת לְבָד — *And you shall couple five curtains by themselves.* For in the (curtains known as the) tent there is also a difference between the level of some and the level of others, similar to the movers of the spheres who are called אֹהֶל, *tent*, as it says, לַשֶּׁמֶשׁ שָׂם אֹהֶל בָּהֶם, *In them He has set a tent for the sun (Psalms* 19:5).

15. עֲצֵי שִׁטִּים עֹמְדִים — *Acacia wood standing up.* (They should be standing vertically and) not lying (horizontally) one on the other as building planks.

NOTES

term only in conjunction with the goats'-hair curtains. The *Sforno* explains that since the curtains of linen and wool had the Cherubim woven into them their purpose was not to serve as a *tent* to protect the vessels and furnishings; hence the term *a tent* is reserved for the curtains which covered them.

9. וְחִבַּרְתָּ אֶת חֲמֵשׁ הַיְרִיעֹת לְבָד — *And you shall couple five curtains by themselves.* Whenever two sections are coupled together it indicates that although similar they are not the same. The goats'-hair curtains, although not as sacred as the inner curtains which have the design of Cherubim on them, nonetheless also represent Divine levels which are diverse, hence they were made in sections and coupled together.

יח וְעָשִׂ֜יתָ אֶת־הַקְּרָשִׁ֤ים לַמִּשְׁכָּן֙ עֶשְׂרִ֣ים קֶ֔רֶשׁ לִפְאַ֖ת נֶ֥גְבָּה תֵימָֽנָה׃
יט וְאַרְבָּעִ֣ים אַדְנֵי־כֶ֗סֶף תַּעֲשֶׂ֔ה תַּ֖חַת עֶשְׂרִ֣ים הַקָּ֑רֶשׁ שְׁנֵ֣י אֲדָנִ֗ים תַּֽחַת־הַקֶּ֤רֶשׁ הָֽאֶחָד֙ לִשְׁתֵּ֣י יְדֹתָ֔יו וּשְׁנֵ֣י אֲדָנִ֗ים תַּֽחַת־הַקֶּ֥רֶשׁ הָֽאֶחָ֖ד לִשְׁתֵּ֥י יְדֹתָֽיו׃
כ-כא וּלְצֶ֧לַע הַמִּשְׁכָּ֛ן הַשֵּׁנִ֖ית לִפְאַ֣ת צָפ֑וֹן עֶשְׂרִ֖ים קָֽרֶשׁ׃ וְאַרְבָּעִ֥ים אַדְנֵיהֶ֖ם כָּ֑סֶף
כב שְׁנֵ֣י אֲדָנִ֗ים תַּ֚חַת הַקֶּ֣רֶשׁ הָֽאֶחָ֔ד וּשְׁנֵ֣י אֲדָנִ֗ים תַּ֖חַת הַקֶּ֥רֶשׁ הָֽאֶחָֽד׃ וּלְיַרְכְּתֵ֧י
כג הַמִּשְׁכָּ֛ן יָ֖מָּה תַּעֲשֶׂ֣ה שִׁשָּׁ֣ה קְרָשִֽׁים׃ וּשְׁנֵ֣י קְרָשִׁ֗ים תַּעֲשֶׂ֛ה לִמְקֻצְעֹ֥ת הַמִּשְׁכָּ֖ן
כד בַּיַּרְכָתָֽיִם׃ וְיִֽהְי֣וּ תֹֽאֲמִם֮ מִלְּמַטָּה֒ וְיַחְדָּ֗ו יִהְי֤וּ תַמִּים֙ עַל־רֹאשׁ֔וֹ אֶל־הַטַּבַּ֖עַת
כה הָֽאֶחָ֑ת כֵּ֚ן יִהְיֶ֣ה לִשְׁנֵיהֶ֔ם לִשְׁנֵ֥י הַמִּקְצֹעֹ֖ת יִֽהְיֽוּ׃ וְהָיוּ֙ שְׁמֹנָ֣ה קְרָשִׁ֔ים וְאַדְנֵיהֶ֣ם כֶּ֔סֶף שִׁשָּׁ֥ה עָשָׂ֖ר אֲדָנִ֑ים שְׁנֵ֣י אֲדָנִ֗ים תַּ֚חַת הַקֶּ֣רֶשׁ הָֽאֶחָ֔ד וּשְׁנֵ֣י
כו אֲדָנִ֔ים תַּ֖חַת הַקֶּ֥רֶשׁ הָֽאֶחָֽד׃ וְעָשִׂ֥יתָ בְרִיחִ֖ם עֲצֵ֣י שִׁטִּ֑ים חֲמִשָּׁ֕ה לְקַרְשֵׁ֥י
כז צֶֽלַע־הַמִּשְׁכָּ֖ן הָֽאֶחָֽד׃ וַחֲמִשָּׁ֣ה בְרִיחִ֔ם לְקַרְשֵׁ֖י צֶ֣לַע־הַמִּשְׁכָּ֣ן הַשֵּׁנִ֑ית
כח וַחֲמִשָּׁ֣ה בְרִיחִ֗ם לְקַרְשֵׁי֙ צֶ֣לַע הַמִּשְׁכָּ֔ן לַיַּרְכָתַ֖יִם יָֽמָּה׃ וְהַבְּרִ֥יחַ הַתִּיכֹ֖ן
כט בְּת֣וֹךְ הַקְּרָשִׁ֑ים מַבְרִ֕חַ מִן־הַקָּצֶ֖ה אֶל־הַקָּצֶֽה׃ וְאֶת־הַקְּרָשִׁ֞ים תְּצַפֶּ֣ה זָהָ֗ב וְאֶת־טַבְּעֹֽתֵיהֶם֙ תַּעֲשֶׂ֣ה זָהָ֔ב בָּתִּ֖ים לַבְּרִיחִ֑ם וְצִפִּיתָ֥ אֶת־הַבְּרִיחִ֖ם זָהָֽב׃
ל-לא חמישי וַהֲקֵֽמֹתָ֖ אֶת־הַמִּשְׁכָּ֑ן כְּמִ֨שְׁפָּט֔וֹ אֲשֶׁ֥ר הׇרְאֵ֖יתָ בָּהָֽר׃ וְעָשִׂ֣יתָ פָרֹ֗כֶת תְּכֵ֧לֶת וְאַרְגָּמָ֛ן וְתוֹלַ֥עַת שָׁנִ֖י וְשֵׁ֣שׁ מָשְׁזָ֑ר מַעֲשֵׂ֥ה חֹשֵׁ֛ב יַעֲשֶׂ֥ה אֹתָ֖הּ
לב כְּרֻבִֽים׃ וְנָתַתָּ֣ה אֹתָ֗הּ עַל־אַרְבָּעָה֙ עַמּוּדֵ֣י שִׁטִּ֔ים מְצֻפִּ֣ים זָהָ֗ב וָוֵיהֶ֖ם זָהָ֑ב
לג עַל־אַרְבָּעָ֖ה אַדְנֵי־כָֽסֶף׃ וְנָתַתָּ֣ה אֶת־הַפָּרֹ֘כֶת֮ תַּ֣חַת הַקְּרָסִים֒ וְהֵבֵאתָ֣ שָׁ֗מָּה מִבֵּ֣ית לַפָּרֹ֔כֶת אֵ֖ת אֲר֣וֹן הָֽעֵד֑וּת וְהִבְדִּילָ֤ה הַפָּרֹ֙כֶת֙ לָכֶ֔ם בֵּ֣ין הַקֹּ֔דֶשׁ
לד וּבֵ֖ין קֹ֥דֶשׁ הַקֳּדָשִֽׁים׃ וְנָתַתָּ֙ אֶת־הַכַּפֹּ֔רֶת עַ֖ל אֲר֣וֹן הָֽעֵדֻ֑ת בְּקֹ֖דֶשׁ הַקֳּדָשִֽׁים׃
לה וְשַׂמְתָּ֤ אֶת־הַשֻּׁלְחָן֙ מִח֣וּץ לַפָּרֹ֔כֶת וְאֶת־הַמְּנֹרָה֙ נֹ֣כַח הַשֻּׁלְחָ֔ן עַ֛ל צֶ֥לַע הַמִּשְׁכָּ֖ן תֵּימָ֑נָה וְהַ֨שֻּׁלְחָ֔ן תִּתֵּ֖ן עַל־צֶ֥לַע צָפֽוֹן׃ וְעָשִׂ֤יתָ מָסָךְ֙ לְפֶ֣תַח הָאֹ֔הֶל
לו תְּכֵ֧לֶת וְאַרְגָּמָ֛ן וְתוֹלַ֥עַת שָׁנִ֖י וְשֵׁ֣שׁ מָשְׁזָ֑ר מַעֲשֵׂ֖ה רֹקֵֽם׃ וְעָשִׂ֣יתָ לַמָּסָ֗ךְ
לז חֲמִשָּׁה֙ עַמּוּדֵ֣י שִׁטִּ֔ים וְצִפִּיתָ֤ אֹתָם֙ זָהָ֔ב וָוֵיהֶ֖ם זָהָ֑ב וְיָצַקְתָּ֣ לָהֶ֔ם חֲמִשָּׁ֖ה אַדְנֵ֥י

---

24. אֶל־הַטַּבַּ֖עַת הָֽאֶחָ֑ת — *Unto one ring.* To that ring which was in the thickness of the corner board, which was even (parallel) in its placement to the width of the side boards. In that thickness there was one ring above lined up to the rings of the side boards on top, and one ring on the thickness below lined up to the rings of the side boards beneath. The bars entered the rings set in the thickness of the corner board and the side boards above and below, thereby joining together the west wall with the north and south (walls).

29. וְאֶת־טַבְּעֹֽתֵיהֶם — *And their rings.* For all regular bars are inserted into rings unless the opposite is stated, as it is explained regarding the middle bar, as it says, בְּתוֹךְ הַקְּרָשִׁים, *in the midst of the boards* (v. 28), that it should be inserted in the thickness of the boards, not in the rings.

NOTES

24. אֶל־הַטַּבַּעַת הָֽאֶחָת — *Unto one ring.* The *Sforno* explains that the side sections of the *Mishkan*, i.e., the north and south sides, were joined together by inserting the bars into the rings set on the northwest and southwest corner. These were inserted into the incisions made in the thickness of the

north and south boards respectively and the top of the board which was in the west row adjacent to it.

29. וְאֶת־טַבְּעֹֽתֵיהֶם — *And their rings.* Although the Torah did not mention the rings before, but since the bars have already been described, and the

[18] *You shall make planks for the Tabernacle, twenty planks for the south*
side. [19] *You shall make forty silver sockets under the twenty planks; two*
sockets under one plank for its two tenons, and two sockets under the next
plank for its two tenons. [20] *For the second wall of the Tabernacle on the north*
side — twenty planks. [21] *Their forty silver sockets: two sockets under one*
plank and two sockets under the next plank. [22] *For the back of the Tabernacle*
on the west, you shall make six planks. [23] *You shall make two planks for the*
corners of the Tabernacle, in the back. [24] *They shall be even at the bottom, and*
together shall they match at its top, for a single ring, so shall it be for them
both, for the two corners shall they be. [25] *There shall be eight planks and their*
silver sockets, sixteen sockets — two sockets under one plank and two sockets
under the next plank.

[26] *You shall make bars of acacia wood; five for the planks of one side of the*
Tabernacle, [27] *and five bars for the planks of the second wall of the Tab-*
ernacle, and five bars for the planks of the Tabernacle wall at the back, on the
west. [28] *The middle bar inside the planks shall extend from end to end.*

[29] *You shall cover the planks with gold, and its rings shall you make of gold*
as housing for the bars, and you shall cover the bars with gold. [30] *You shall*
erect the Tabernacle according to its manner, as you will have been shown on
the mountain.

[31] *You shall make a Partition of turquoise, purple, and scarlet wool, and*
linen, twisted; he shall make it with a woven design of cherubim. [32] *You shall*
place it upon four pillars of acacia wood, plated with gold with hooks of gold,
upon four silver sockets. [33] *You shall put the Partition under the hooks. You*
shall bring there, inside the Partition, the Ark of the Testimonial-tablets, and
the Partition shall separate for you between the Holy and the Holy of Holies.

[34] *You shall put the Cover upon the Ark of the Testimonial-tablets in the*
Holy of Holies. [35] *You shall place the Table outside the Partition, and the*
Menorah opposite the Table on the south side of the Tabernacle, and the Table
you shall place on the north side.

[36] *You shall make a Screen for the entrance of the Tent, of turquoise, purple,*
and scarlet wool, and twisted linen; the work of an embroiderer. [37] *You shall*
make for the Screen five pillars of acacia wood and cover them with gold, and
their hooks shall be gold; and you shall cast for them five sockets of copper.

---

35. וְשַׂמְתָּ אֶת הַשֻּׁלְחָן מִחוּץ לַפָּרֹכֶת — *And you shall set the table outside* (i.e., *in front*) *of the curtain.* After he arranged the seat inside, he arranged the table and menorah in front of it beyond the curtain, (for) they are put there to honor the One Who sits on the chair. The menorah is placed to the right and the table to the left, as it says, אֹרֶךְ יָמִים בִּימִינָהּ בִּשְׂמאוֹלָהּ עֹשֶׁר וְכָבוֹד, *Length of days is in her right hand and in her left hand are riches and honor* (*Proverbs* 3:16).

NOTES

ordinary bar is one that is inserted in rings, it is appropriate to use the possessive form "*their*" *rings.*

35. וְשַׂמְתָּ אֶת הַשֻּׁלְחָן מִחוּץ לַפָּרֹכֶת — *And you shall set the table outside (i.e., in front) of the curtain.* The menorah's light represents Torah, and the table represents riches. Following the idea expressed in the verse quoted from *Proverbs*, he who pursues Torah will merit long life for *it is our life and the length of our days* while he who lives a proper, decent life of *mitzvos* and supports Torah will be granted riches and honor. Hence the menorah is placed on the right and the table on the left, in keeping with the wording of the verse in *Proverbs.*

כז א ששי נְחֹשֶׁת׃ וְעָשִׂיתָ אֶת־הַמִּזְבֵּחַ עֲצֵי שִׁטִּים חָמֵשׁ אַמּוֹת אֹרֶךְ
ב וְחָמֵשׁ אַמּוֹת רֹחַב רָבוּעַ יִהְיֶה הַמִּזְבֵּחַ וְשָׁלֹשׁ אַמּוֹת קֹמָתוֹ׃ וְעָשִׂיתָ קַרְנֹתָיו
ג עַל אַרְבַּע פִּנֹּתָיו מִמֶּנּוּ תִּהְיֶיןָ קַרְנֹתָיו וְצִפִּיתָ אֹתוֹ נְחֹשֶׁת׃ וְעָשִׂיתָ סִּירֹתָיו
לְדַשְּׁנוֹ וְיָעָיו וּמִזְרְקֹתָיו וּמִזְלְגֹתָיו וּמַחְתֹּתָיו לְכָל־כֵּלָיו תַּעֲשֶׂה נְחֹשֶׁת׃
ד וְעָשִׂיתָ לּוֹ מִכְבָּר מַעֲשֵׂה רֶשֶׁת נְחֹשֶׁת וְעָשִׂיתָ עַל־הָרֶשֶׁת אַרְבַּע טַבְּעֹת
ה נְחֹשֶׁת עַל אַרְבַּע קְצוֹתָיו׃ וְנָתַתָּה אֹתָהּ תַּחַת כַּרְכֹּב הַמִּזְבֵּחַ מִלְּמָטָּה
ו וְהָיְתָה הָרֶשֶׁת עַד חֲצִי הַמִּזְבֵּחַ׃ וְעָשִׂיתָ בַדִּים לַמִּזְבֵּחַ בַּדֵּי עֲצֵי שִׁטִּים וְצִפִּיתָ
ז אֹתָם נְחֹשֶׁת׃ וְהוּבָא אֶת־בַּדָּיו בַּטַּבָּעֹת וְהָיוּ הַבַּדִּים עַל־שְׁתֵּי צַלְעֹת
ח הַמִּזְבֵּחַ בִּשְׂאֵת אֹתוֹ׃ נְבוּב לֻחֹת תַּעֲשֶׂה אֹתוֹ כַּאֲשֶׁר הֶרְאָה אֹתְךָ בָּהָר כֵּן
ט שביעי יַעֲשׂוּ׃ וְעָשִׂיתָ אֵת חֲצַר הַמִּשְׁכָּן לִפְאַת נֶגֶב־תֵּימָנָה קְלָעִים לֶחָצֵר
י שֵׁשׁ מָשְׁזָר מֵאָה בָאַמָּה אֹרֶךְ לַפֵּאָה הָאֶחָת׃ וְעַמֻּדָיו עֶשְׂרִים וְאַדְנֵיהֶם
יא עֶשְׂרִים נְחֹשֶׁת וָוֵי הָעַמֻּדִים וַחֲשֻׁקֵיהֶם כָּסֶף׃ וְכֵן לִפְאַת צָפוֹן בָּאֹרֶךְ קְלָעִים
מֵאָה אֹרֶךְ וְעַמֻּדָו עֶשְׂרִים וְאַדְנֵיהֶם עֶשְׂרִים נְחֹשֶׁת וָוֵי הָעַמֻּדִים וַחֲשֻׁקֵיהֶם
יב כָּסֶף׃ וְרֹחַב הֶחָצֵר לִפְאַת־יָם קְלָעִים חֲמִשִּׁים אַמָּה עַמֻּדֵיהֶם עֲשָׂרָה
יג־יד וְאַדְנֵיהֶם עֲשָׂרָה׃ וְרֹחַב הֶחָצֵר לִפְאַת קֵדְמָה מִזְרָחָה חֲמִשִּׁים אַמָּה׃ וַחֲמֵשׁ
טו עֶשְׂרֵה אַמָּה קְלָעִים לַכָּתֵף עַמֻּדֵיהֶם שְׁלֹשָׁה וְאַדְנֵיהֶם שְׁלֹשָׁה׃ וְלַכָּתֵף
טז הַשֵּׁנִית חֲמֵשׁ עֶשְׂרֵה קְלָעִים עַמֻּדֵיהֶם שְׁלֹשָׁה וְאַדְנֵיהֶם שְׁלֹשָׁה׃ וּלְשַׁעַר
הֶחָצֵר מָסָךְ ׀ עֶשְׂרִים אַמָּה תְּכֵלֶת וְאַרְגָּמָן וְתוֹלַעַת שָׁנִי וְשֵׁשׁ מָשְׁזָר מַעֲשֵׂה
יז מפטיר רֹקֵם עַמֻּדֵיהֶם אַרְבָּעָה וְאַדְנֵיהֶם אַרְבָּעָה׃ כָּל־עַמּוּדֵי הֶחָצֵר סָבִיב מְחֻשָּׁקִים
יח כֶּסֶף וָוֵיהֶם כָּסֶף וְאַדְנֵיהֶם נְחֹשֶׁת׃ אֹרֶךְ הֶחָצֵר מֵאָה בָאַמָּה וְרֹחַב ׀ חֲמִשִּׁים
יט בַּחֲמִשִּׁים וְקֹמָה חָמֵשׁ אַמּוֹת שֵׁשׁ מָשְׁזָר וְאַדְנֵיהֶם נְחֹשֶׁת׃ לְכֹל כְּלֵי הַמִּשְׁכָּן
בְּכֹל עֲבֹדָתוֹ וְכָל־יְתֵדֹתָיו וְכָל־יִתְדֹת הֶחָצֵר נְחֹשֶׁת׃

XXVII

2. קַרְנֹתָיו — *The horns of it . . .* (well) known (as part of) every altar, and the same (is true) when he says, *its shovels and its basins* (v. 3).

5. כַּרְכֹּב הַמִּזְבֵּחַ — *The ledge of the altar.* Which is customary for all wooden vessels, as our Sages say, "The following wooden articles are regarded as unfinished, whatever still requires to be smoothed . . . or trimmed wood (כַּרְכֹּב)" (*Chullin* 25a).

8. נְבוּב לֻחֹת — *Hollow (with) planks...* similar to a box which has no bottom or cover.

כַּאֲשֶׁר הֶרְאָה אֹתְךָ בָּהָר — *As it was shown to you in the mount.* That the hollow space is to be filled with earth when they encamp, and on that earth אֵשׁ תָּמִיד תּוּקַד, *fire shall be kept burning continually (Leviticus* 6:6).

9-10. מֵאָה בָאַמָּה . . . וְעַמֻּדָיו עֶשְׂרִים — *A hundred cubits . . . and its pillars twenty.* The

NOTES

XXVII

2. קַרְנֹתָיו — *The horns of it.* The verse assumes that one knows what is meant by the *horns, shovels,* and *basins* of an altar since they were commonly used by others in their religious services.

9-10. מֵאָה בָאַמָּה . . . וְעַמֻּדָיו עֶשְׂרִים — *A hundred cubits . . . and its pillars twenty.* The *Sforno* interprets the plan of the Tabernacle courtyard as follows: The last pillar on the west side, in the southwest corner, also served as the first support of the curtains on the south side and the first pillar on the south side was distanced five cubits from that corner. The last pillar at the southeast corner also served the curtains on the east side, therefore the

27 [1] *You shall make the Altar of acacia wood, five cubits in length and five
cubits in width — the Altar shall be square — and three cubits its height.
[2] You shall make its horns on its four corners, from it shall its horns be; and
you shall cover it with copper. [3] You shall make its pots to clear its ashes, its
shovels, its basins, its forks, and its fire-pans; you shall make all its vessels
of copper. [4] You shall make for it a netting of copper meshwork and make
upon the meshwork four copper rings at its four edges. [5] You shall place it
under the surrounding border of the Altar from below, and the meshwork
shall go to the midpoint of the Altar. [6] You shall make staves for the Altar,
staves of acacia wood, and you shall plate them with copper. [7] Its staves shall
be brought into the rings, and the staves shall be on two sides of the Altar
when it is carried. [8] Hollow, of boards, shall you make it; as you were shown
on the mountain, so shall they do.*

*[9] You shall make the Courtyard of the Tabernacle: On the south side the
lace-hangings of the Courtyard, of twisted linen, a hundred cubits long for one
side; [10] and its pillars twenty and their sockets twenty, of copper, the hooks
of the pillars and their bands silver. [11] So, too, for the north side in length,
lace-hangings a hundred long: its pillars twenty; and their sockets twenty, of
copper; the hooks of the pillars and their bands, silver. [12] The width of the
Courtyard on the west side, lace-hangings of fifty cubits, their pillars ten; and
their sockets ten. [13] The width of the Courtyard on the eastern side, fifty
cubits; [14] and fifteen cubits of lace-hangings on a shoulder, their pillars three;
and their sockets three. [15] And the second shoulder, fifteen of lace-hangings;
their pillars three; and their sockets three. [16] At the gate of the Courtyard, a
Screen of twenty cubits: turquoise, purple, and scarlet wool, and twisted
linen, work of an embroiderer, their pillars four; and their sockets four.*

*[17] All the pillars of the Courtyard, all around, banded with silver; their
hooks of silver, and their sockets of copper. [18] The length of the Courtyard a
hundred cubits; the width fifty by fifty; and the height five cubits of twisted
linen; and their sockets of copper. [19] All the vessels of the Tabernacle for all
its labor, all its pegs and all the pegs of the Courtyard — copper.*

---

space between them including the pillar was five (cubits). However, the twenty pillars on the north and the twenty pillars on the south did not start one across the other on a straight line. Rather the beginning of one side extended the equivalent of one space from the beginning of the opposite side, and the eastern and western pillars began the equivalent of one space away from the extended corner.

וַחֲשֻׁקֵיהֶם — *And their fillets.* Circles which encircled the pillar in its middle for beauty.

19. לְכֹל כְּלֵי הַמִּשְׁכָּן בְּכֹל עֲבֹדָתוֹ — *All the instruments of the Mishkan in all its service.* The tools needed for its service, such as hammers and mallets and other (such tools) which were needed when it was dismantled and erected.

NOTES

first of the three pillars on the east side was drawn in five cubits from that corner. The pillar in the northeast corner served the north-side curtains as well so that the first of the twenty pillars on the north began five cubits in from the northeast corner, finishing at the northwest corner, where the first pillar of the west side began five cubits southward from that corner.

19. לְכֹל כְּלֵי הַמִּשְׁכָּן בְּכֹל עֲבֹדָתוֹ — *All the instruments of the Mishkan in all its service.* The expression *all the instruments* implies instruments which were not mentioned above. Hence it must refer to tools needed to erect and dismantle the *Mishkan* in their travels.

פרשת תצוה

כ וְאַתָּה תְּצַוֶּה ׀ אֶת־בְּנֵי יִשְׂרָאֵל וְיִקְחוּ אֵלֶיךָ שֶׁמֶן זַיִת זָךְ כָּתִית לַמָּאוֹר
כא לְהַעֲלֹת נֵר תָּמִיד: בְּאֹהֶל מוֹעֵד מִחוּץ לַפָּרֹכֶת אֲשֶׁר עַל־הָעֵדֻת יַעֲרֹךְ
אֹתוֹ אַהֲרֹן וּבָנָיו מֵעֶרֶב עַד־בֹּקֶר לִפְנֵי יהוה חֻקַּת עוֹלָם לְדֹרֹתָם מֵאֵת
כח א בְּנֵי יִשְׂרָאֵל: וְאַתָּה הַקְרֵב אֵלֶיךָ אֶת־אַהֲרֹן אָחִיךָ וְאֶת־
בָּנָיו אִתּוֹ מִתּוֹךְ בְּנֵי יִשְׂרָאֵל לְכַהֲנוֹ־לִי אַהֲרֹן נָדָב וַאֲבִיהוּא אֶלְעָזָר
ב וְאִיתָמָר בְּנֵי אַהֲרֹן: וְעָשִׂיתָ בִגְדֵי־קֹדֶשׁ לְאַהֲרֹן אָחִיךָ לְכָבוֹד וּלְתִפְאָרֶת:
ג וְאַתָּה תְּדַבֵּר אֶל־כָּל־חַכְמֵי־לֵב אֲשֶׁר מִלֵּאתִיו רוּחַ חָכְמָה וְעָשׂוּ אֶת־
ד בִּגְדֵי אַהֲרֹן לְקַדְּשׁוֹ לְכַהֲנוֹ־לִי: וְאֵלֶּה הַבְּגָדִים אֲשֶׁר יַעֲשׂוּ חֹשֶׁן וְאֵפוֹד
וּמְעִיל וּכְתֹנֶת תַּשְׁבֵּץ מִצְנֶפֶת וְאַבְנֵט וְעָשׂוּ בִגְדֵי־קֹדֶשׁ לְאַהֲרֹן אָחִיךָ
ה וּלְבָנָיו לְכַהֲנוֹ־לִי: וְהֵם יִקְחוּ אֶת־הַזָּהָב וְאֶת־הַתְּכֵלֶת וְאֶת־הָאַרְגָּמָן
וְאֶת־תּוֹלַעַת הַשָּׁנִי וְאֶת־הַשֵּׁשׁ:
ו וְעָשׂוּ אֶת־הָאֵפֹד זָהָב תְּכֵלֶת וְאַרְגָּמָן תּוֹלַעַת שָׁנִי וְשֵׁשׁ מָשְׁזָר מַעֲשֵׂה
ז־ח חֹשֵׁב: שְׁתֵּי כְתֵפֹת חֹבְרֹת יִהְיֶה־לּוֹ אֶל־שְׁנֵי קְצוֹתָיו וְחֻבָּר: וְחֵשֶׁב אֲפֻדָּתוֹ

---

20. וְאַתָּה תְּצַוֶּה — *And you shall command.* Behold that until now when it states וְעָשִׂיתָ, *and you shall do,* it is to be understood that it should be done through others, i.e., that he (Moses) should command the artisans to do (certain tasks). Therefore regarding these three commandments which God commanded, He said, "וְאַתָּה, *and you,*" to tell him (Moses) that he should do it himself. He shall command Israel regarding the making of the oil; he shall bring near to himself (appoint) Aaron and his sons; and he shall speak to all the wise-hearted (workers).

וְיִקְחוּ אֵלֶיךָ — *That they bring to you . . .* when needed; namely, when the oil for the light contributed now to the Sanctuary will be consumed. They are not to think that the commandment to kindle the lamp is only a temporary one involving only this oil (now) offered.

XXVIII

2. לְכָבוֹד — *For honor . . .* for the honor of God, the Blessed One, since they are holy garments for His service.

וּלְתִפְאָרֶת — *And for beauty (glory).* That he be a "teaching priest" (based on *II Chronicles* 15:3) held in reverence by all them round about him *(Psalms* 89:8), (for) they are his disciples, engraved on his heart and shoulders.

3. וְאַתָּה תְּדַבֵּר אֶל כָּל חַכְמֵי לֵב — *And you shall speak to all that are wise hearted . . .* that they do all that is mentioned above (i.e., the various labors of the Sanctuary).

NOTES

20. וְאַתָּה תְּצַוֶּה — *And you shall command.* The word וְאַתָּה, *and you,* precedes the command regarding the oil in this verse, as well as the one regarding Aaron (28:1), and that of the wise-hearted workers (28:3). This implies that Moses himself was to attend to these three matters.

XXVIII

2. לְכָבוֹד וּלְתִפְאָרֶת — *For honor and for beauty (glory).* The garments of the priest serve a twofold purpose. Primarily they are for the honor of God, not for the honor of the priest. However, they are also meant to lend dignity to the office of the High Priest so that the people, who are all meant to be his pupils, will revere and respect him. In a subtle manner the *Sforno* indicates that reverence for a teacher is motivated not only by the inherent respect students have for their teacher but also by the concern the teacher shows for them. This is symbolized by the names of the tribes which the

PARASHAS TETZAVEH

20 Now you shall command the Children of Israel that they shall take for
you pure, pressed olive oil for illumination, to kindle the lamp
continually. 21 In the Tent of Meeting, outside the Partition that is near the
Testimonial-tablets, Aaron and his sons shall arrange it from evening until
morning, before HASHEM, an eternal decree for their generations, from the
Children of Israel.

28 *1 Bring near to yourself Aaron your brother, and his sons with him, from*
among the Children of Israel — Aaron, Nadab and Abihu, Elazar and
Ithamar, the sons of Aaron — to minister to Me. 2 You shall make vestments
of sanctity for Aaron your brother, for glory and splendor. 3 And you shall
speak to all the wise-hearted people whom I have invested with a spirit of
wisdom, and they shall make the vestments of Aaron, to sanctify him to
minister to Me. 4 These are the vestments that they shall make: a
Breastplate, an Ephod, a Robe, a Tunic of a box-like knit, a Turban, and a
Sash. They shall make vestments of sanctity for Aaron your brother and
his sons, to minister to Me. 5 They shall take the gold, the turquoise, purple,
and scarlet wool, and the linen.

6 They shall make the Ephod of gold; turquoise, purple, and scarlet wool,
and twisted linen, with a woven design. 7 It shall have two shoulder straps
attached to its two ends, and it shall be attached. 8 The belt with which it is

---

וְעָשׂוּ אֶת בִּגְדֵי אַהֲרֹן — *That they make Aaron's garments.* And they shall also make Aaron's garments.

לְקַדְּשׁוֹ — *To sanctify him.* Toward that purpose shall they make the garments.

5. וְהֵם יִקְחוּ אֶת הַזָּהָב — *And they shall take the gold.* Just as they have (proper) intent at the time of their labor so they should have (proper) intent when they take the gold.

6. הָאֵפֹד — *Ephod* ... a garment (covering) from a person's hips and down. The upper border (was) made like a belt of skillful work, and with it the wearer of the *ephod* girds the robe, as it says, וַיַּחְגֹּר אֹתוֹ בְּחֵשֶׁב הָאֵפֹד, וַיֶּאְפֹּד לוֹ בּוֹ, *and he girded him with the skillfully woven band of the ephod, and bound it to him with it (Leviticus* 8:7).

7. שְׁתֵּי כְתֵפֹת חֹבְרֹת — *Two shoulder pieces joined* ... matched in the work of their images (pictures or designs).

אֶל שְׁנֵי קְצוֹתָיו — *To the two ends* ... to the two extremities of its width.

וְחֻבָּר — *That it may be joined together.* The *ephod* shall be joined with the shoulder pieces in a manner that it be matched in its work with that of the shoulder pieces (straps).

NOTES

High Priest carries engraved on his heart (the breastplate, see verse 21) and his shoulders (the onyx stones, see verse 12).

3-5. וְאַתָּה תְּדַבֵּר אֶל כָּל חַכְמֵי לֵב ... וְעָשׂוּ אֶת בִּגְדֵי אַהֲרֹן לְקַדְּשׁוֹ ... וְהֵם יִקְחוּ אֶת הַזָּהָב — *And you shall speak to all that are wise hearted ... that they make Aaron's garments to sanctify him ... And they shall take the gold.* When one fulfills a sacred task his intent is most important. Therefore when the craftsmen receive the gold from the contributors it must be with the express intent of using it for the priestly vestments, and when they make the garments they must have in mind at all times that with these garments the priest will be consecrated to the service of God. Compare the *Sforno's* commentary on verse 21 regarding the stones.

7. שְׁתֵּי כְתֵפֹת חֹבְרֹת ... וְחֻבָּר — *Two shoulder pieces joined ... that it may be joined together.* The *Sforno* interprets the words חֹבְרֹת and וְחֻבָּר as *joined* in the sense of *matched.* Compare to the *Sforno* in 26:3 regarding the curtains of the Sanctuary where the same phrase is used by the Torah.

אֲשֶׁר עָלָיו כְּמַעֲשֵׂהוּ מִמֶּנּוּ יִהְיֶה זָהָב תְּכֵלֶת וְאַרְגָּמָן וְתוֹלַעַת שָׁנִי וְשֵׁשׁ
ט מָשְׁזָר׃ וְלָקַחְתָּ אֶת־שְׁתֵּי אַבְנֵי־שֹׁהַם וּפִתַּחְתָּ עֲלֵיהֶם שְׁמוֹת בְּנֵי
י יִשְׂרָאֵל׃ שִׁשָּׁה מִשְּׁמֹתָם עַל הָאֶבֶן הָאֶחָת וְאֶת־שְׁמוֹת הַשִּׁשָּׁה הַנּוֹתָרִים
יא עַל־הָאֶבֶן הַשֵּׁנִית כְּתוֹלְדֹתָם׃ מַעֲשֵׂה חָרַשׁ אֶבֶן פִּתּוּחֵי חֹתָם תְּפַתַּח
אֶת־שְׁתֵּי הָאֲבָנִים עַל־שְׁמֹת בְּנֵי יִשְׂרָאֵל מֻסַבֹּת מִשְׁבְּצוֹת זָהָב
יב תַּעֲשֶׂה אֹתָם׃ וְשַׂמְתָּ אֶת־שְׁתֵּי הָאֲבָנִים עַל כִּתְפֹת הָאֵפֹד אַבְנֵי זִכָּרֹן
לִבְנֵי יִשְׂרָאֵל וְנָשָׂא אַהֲרֹן אֶת־שְׁמוֹתָם לִפְנֵי יהוה עַל־שְׁתֵּי כְתֵפָיו
שני יג־יד לְזִכָּרֹן׃ וְעָשִׂיתָ מִשְׁבְּצֹת זָהָב׃ וּשְׁתֵּי שַׁרְשְׁרֹת זָהָב
טָהוֹר מִגְבָּלֹת תַּעֲשֶׂה אֹתָם מַעֲשֵׂה עֲבֹת וְנָתַתָּה אֶת־שַׁרְשְׁרֹת הָעֲבֹתֹת
טו עַל־הַמִּשְׁבְּצֹת׃ וְעָשִׂיתָ חֹשֶׁן מִשְׁפָּט מַעֲשֵׂה חֹשֵׁב
כְּמַעֲשֵׂה אֵפֹד תַּעֲשֶׂנּוּ זָהָב תְּכֵלֶת וְאַרְגָּמָן וְתוֹלַעַת שָׁנִי וְשֵׁשׁ מָשְׁזָר
טז־יז תַּעֲשֶׂה אֹתוֹ׃ רָבוּעַ יִהְיֶה כָּפוּל זֶרֶת אָרְכּוֹ וְזֶרֶת רָחְבּוֹ׃ וּמִלֵּאתָ בוֹ
מִלֻּאַת אֶבֶן אַרְבָּעָה טוּרִים אָבֶן טוּר אֹדֶם פִּטְדָה וּבָרֶקֶת הַטּוּר הָאֶחָד׃
יח־יט וְהַטּוּר הַשֵּׁנִי נֹפֶךְ סַפִּיר וְיָהֲלֹם׃ וְהַטּוּר הַשְּׁלִישִׁי לֶשֶׁם שְׁבוֹ וְאַחְלָמָה׃
כ וְהַטּוּר הָרְבִיעִי תַּרְשִׁישׁ וְשֹׁהַם וְיָשְׁפֵה מְשֻׁבָּצִים זָהָב יִהְיוּ בְּמִלּוּאֹתָם׃
כא וְהָאֲבָנִים תִּהְיֶיןָ עַל־שְׁמֹת בְּנֵי־יִשְׂרָאֵל שְׁתֵּים עֶשְׂרֵה עַל־שְׁמֹתָם
כב פִּתּוּחֵי חוֹתָם אִישׁ עַל־שְׁמוֹ תִּהְיֶיןָ לִשְׁנֵי עָשָׂר שָׁבֶט׃ וְעָשִׂיתָ עַל־הַחֹשֶׁן
כג שַׁרְשֹׁת גַּבְלֻת מַעֲשֵׂה עֲבֹת זָהָב טָהוֹר׃ וְעָשִׂיתָ עַל־הַחֹשֶׁן שְׁתֵּי טַבְּעוֹת
כד זָהָב וְנָתַתָּ אֶת־שְׁתֵּי הַטַּבָּעוֹת עַל־שְׁנֵי קְצוֹת הַחֹשֶׁן׃ וְנָתַתָּה אֶת־
כה שְׁתֵּי עֲבֹתֹת הַזָּהָב עַל־שְׁתֵּי הַטַּבָּעֹת אֶל־קְצוֹת הַחֹשֶׁן׃ וְאֵת שְׁתֵּי
קְצוֹת שְׁתֵּי הָעֲבֹתֹת תִּתֵּן עַל־שְׁתֵּי הַמִּשְׁבְּצוֹת וְנָתַתָּה עַל־כִּתְפוֹת
כו הָאֵפֹד אֶל־מוּל פָּנָיו׃ וְעָשִׂיתָ שְׁתֵּי טַבְּעוֹת זָהָב וְשַׂמְתָּ אֹתָם עַל־
כז שְׁנֵי קְצוֹת הַחֹשֶׁן עַל־שְׂפָתוֹ אֲשֶׁר אֶל־עֵבֶר הָאֵפוֹד בָּיְתָה׃ וְעָשִׂיתָ
שְׁתֵּי טַבְּעוֹת זָהָב וְנָתַתָּה אֹתָם עַל־שְׁתֵּי כִתְפוֹת הָאֵפוֹד מִלְּמַטָּה

12. עַל שְׁתֵּי כְתֵפָיו לְזִכָּרֹן — *Upon his two shoulders for a memorial* . . . to attain mercy for Israel in their merit.

14. מִגְבָּלֹת — *Of plaited thread* . . . matched (lined up) exactly from the end of the shoulder pieces to the end of the breastplate.

21. וְהָאֲבָנִים תִּהְיֶיןָ עַל שְׁמֹת בְּנֵי יִשְׂרָאֵל — *And the stones shall be according to the names of the sons of Israel.* When the donors sanctify them, let their sanctification be specifically for the purpose of writing the names of the tribes upon them.

שְׁתֵּים עֶשְׂרֵה עַל שְׁמֹתָם — *Twelve, according to their names.* And they shall be twelve in keeping with their names, neither less nor more.

NOTES

12. עַל שְׁתֵּי כְתֵפָיו לְזִכָּרֹן — *Upon his two shoulders for a memorial.* The Almighty need not be reminded of aught; *"There is no forgetfulness before Your throne of glory"* (from *Mussaf* of Rosh Hashanah). The phrase לְזִכָּרֹן, *for a memorial,* therefore cannot mean as a memorial to God, but to awaken His compassion in merit of the names of Israel inscribed on the onyx stones carried on the High Priest's shoulders. Compare the *Sforno's* commentary on *Genesis* 9:16.

21. שְׁתֵּים עֶשְׂרֵה עַל שְׁמֹתָם — *Twelve, according to their names.* The *Sforno* explains why God had to state specifically, *"twelve, according to their*

emplaced, which is on it, shall be of the same workmanship, it shall be made
of it, of gold; turquoise, purple, and scarlet wool, and twisted linen. 9 *You shall*
take the two shoham stones and engrave upon them the names of the sons
of Israel; 10 *six of their names on one stone, and the names of the six remaining*
ones on the second stone, according to the order of their birth. 11 *With a*
jeweler's handiwork, engraved like a signet ring, shall you engrave the two
stones with the names of the sons of Israel; encircled with gold settings shall
you make them. 12 *You shall place both stones on the shoulder straps of the*
Ephod, remembrance stones for the Children of Israel. Aaron shall carry their
names before HASHEM *on both his shoulders as a remembrance.*

13 *You shall make settings of gold;* 14 *and two chains of pure gold — make*
them at the edges, of braided craftsmanship — and place the braided chains
on the settings.

15 *You shall make a Breastplate of Judgment of a woven design, like the*
craftsmanship of the Ephod shall you make it, of gold; turquoise, purple,
and scarlet wool; and linen — twisted together — shall you make it.
16 *Square shall it be, folded, its length a half-cubit and its width a half-cubit.*
17 *You shall fill it with stone mounting, four rows of stone: a row of odem,*
pitdah, and barekes — the one row; 18 *the second row: nophech, sapir, and*
yahalom; 19 *the third row: leshem, shevo, and achlamah;* 20 *and the fourth*
row: tarshish, shoham, and yashfeh; set in gold shall they be in their
mountings. 21 *The stones shall be according to the names of the sons of Israel,*
twelve according to their names, engraved like a signet ring, each according
to its name shall they be, for the twelve tribes.

22 *For the Breastplate you shall make chains at the edges, of braided*
craftsmanship, of pure gold. 23 *For the Breastplate you shall make two*
rings of gold, and you shall place the two rings on the two ends of the
Breastplate. 24 *You shall place the two golden ropes on the two rings, at*
the ends of the Breastplate. 25 *And the two ends of the two ropes, you*
shall place on the two settings, which you shall place on the shoulder
straps of the Ephod, toward its front. 26 *You shall make two rings of gold*
and place them on the two ends of the Breastplate at its bottom, on its
inner side, toward the Ephod. 27 *You shall make two rings of gold and*
place them at the bottom of the two shoulder straps of the Ephod

---

פִּתּוּחֵי חוֹתָם אִישׁ עַל שְׁמוֹ — *Like the engravings of a signet, every one according to his name.* Also the engraver shall engrave the name on the stone of each one and neither change the stone nor the (original) intent from this to that.

22. גַּבְלֻת — *Plaited (chains).* Not chains which can be made longer or shorter.

NOTES

names," since it already states *the names of the sons of Israel.* The verse stresses the number twelve to emphasize that although Menasseh and Ephraim had been designated by Jacob as being *his,* akin to Reuben and Simeon, this was only regarding the dividing of the Land of Israel, where Levi receives no portion. As for all other areas, including the engraving of the name on the breastplate, only the original twelve sons of Jacob shall appear. Hence the *Sforno* states, 'neither less nor more.' See the commentary of the *Sforno* on *Genesis* 49:28.

פִּתּוּחֵי חוֹתָם אִישׁ עַל שְׁמוֹ — *Like the engravings of a signet, every one according to his name.* Since each stone was designated for a specific tribe and the donor sanctified it for that tribe they could not be interchanged. This is the meaning of the concluding part of this verse, *every one according to his name.*

כח מִמּוּל פָּנָיו לְעֻמַּת מַחְבַּרְתּוֹ מִמַּעַל לְחֵשֶׁב הָאֵפוֹד: וְיִרְכְּסוּ אֶת־הַחֹשֶׁן
מִטַּבְּעֹתָו אֶל־טַבְּעֹת הָאֵפוֹד בִּפְתִיל תְּכֵלֶת לִהְיוֹת עַל־חֵשֶׁב הָאֵפוֹד
כט וְלֹא־יִזַּח הַחֹשֶׁן מֵעַל הָאֵפוֹד: וְנָשָׂא אַהֲרֹן אֶת־שְׁמוֹת בְּנֵי־יִשְׂרָאֵל בְּחֹשֶׁן
ל הַמִּשְׁפָּט עַל־לִבּוֹ בְּבֹאוֹ אֶל־הַקֹּדֶשׁ לְזִכָּרֹן לִפְנֵי־יְהוָה תָּמִיד: וְנָתַתָּ
אֶל־חֹשֶׁן הַמִּשְׁפָּט אֶת־הָאוּרִים וְאֶת־הַתֻּמִּים וְהָיוּ עַל־לֵב אַהֲרֹן בְּבֹאוֹ
לִפְנֵי יְהוָה וְנָשָׂא אַהֲרֹן אֶת־מִשְׁפַּט בְּנֵי־יִשְׂרָאֵל עַל־לִבּוֹ לִפְנֵי יְהוָה
שלישי לא-לב תָּמִיד: וְעָשִׂיתָ אֶת־מְעִיל הָאֵפוֹד כְּלִיל תְּכֵלֶת: וְהָיָה פִי־
רֹאשׁוֹ בְּתוֹכוֹ שָׂפָה יִהְיֶה לְפִיו סָבִיב מַעֲשֵׂה אֹרֵג כְּפִי תַחְרָא יִהְיֶה־לּוֹ לֹא
לג יִקָּרֵעַ: וְעָשִׂיתָ עַל־שׁוּלָיו רִמֹּנֵי תְּכֵלֶת וְאַרְגָּמָן וְתוֹלַעַת שָׁנִי עַל־שׁוּלָיו
לד סָבִיב וּפַעֲמֹנֵי זָהָב בְּתוֹכָם סָבִיב: פַּעֲמֹן זָהָב וְרִמּוֹן פַּעֲמֹן זָהָב וְרִמּוֹן עַל־
לה שׁוּלֵי הַמְּעִיל סָבִיב: וְהָיָה עַל־אַהֲרֹן לְשָׁרֵת וְנִשְׁמַע קוֹלוֹ בְּבֹאוֹ אֶל־
לו הַקֹּדֶשׁ לִפְנֵי יְהוָה וּבְצֵאתוֹ וְלֹא יָמוּת: וְעָשִׂיתָ צִּיץ זָהָב טָהוֹר
לז וּפִתַּחְתָּ עָלָיו פִּתּוּחֵי חֹתָם קֹדֶשׁ לַיהוָה: וְשַׂמְתָּ אֹתוֹ עַל־פְּתִיל תְּכֵלֶת
לח וְהָיָה עַל־הַמִּצְנָפֶת אֶל־מוּל פְּנֵי־הַמִּצְנֶפֶת יִהְיֶה: וְהָיָה עַל־מֵצַח אַהֲרֹן
וְנָשָׂא אַהֲרֹן אֶת־עֲוֺן הַקֳּדָשִׁים אֲשֶׁר יַקְדִּישׁוּ בְּנֵי יִשְׂרָאֵל לְכָל־מַתְּנֹת
לט קָדְשֵׁיהֶם וְהָיָה עַל־מִצְחוֹ תָּמִיד לְרָצוֹן לָהֶם לִפְנֵי יְהוָה: וְשִׁבַּצְתָּ הַכְּתֹנֶת
מ שֵׁשׁ וְעָשִׂיתָ מִצְנֶפֶת שֵׁשׁ וְאַבְנֵט תַּעֲשֶׂה מַעֲשֵׂה רֹקֵם: וְלִבְנֵי אַהֲרֹן תַּעֲשֶׂה
כֻתֳּנֹת וְעָשִׂיתָ לָהֶם אַבְנֵטִים וּמִגְבָּעוֹת תַּעֲשֶׂה לָהֶם לְכָבוֹד וּלְתִפְאָרֶת:
מא וְהִלְבַּשְׁתָּ אֹתָם אֶת־אַהֲרֹן אָחִיךָ וְאֶת־בָּנָיו אִתּוֹ וּמָשַׁחְתָּ אֹתָם וּמִלֵּאתָ
מב אֶת־יָדָם וְקִדַּשְׁתָּ אֹתָם וְכִהֲנוּ־לִי: וַעֲשֵׂה לָהֶם מִכְנְסֵי־בָד לְכַסּוֹת בְּשַׂר
מג עֶרְוָה מִמָּתְנַיִם וְעַד־יְרֵכַיִם יִהְיוּ: וְהָיוּ עַל־אַהֲרֹן וְעַל־בָּנָיו בְּבֹאָם | אֶל־
אֹהֶל מוֹעֵד אוֹ בְגִשְׁתָּם אֶל־הַמִּזְבֵּחַ לְשָׁרֵת בַּקֹּדֶשׁ וְלֹא־יִשְׂאוּ עָוֺן וָמֵתוּ
כט רביעי א חֻקַּת עוֹלָם לוֹ וּלְזַרְעוֹ אַחֲרָיו: וְזֶה הַדָּבָר אֲשֶׁר תַּעֲשֶׂה לָהֶם
לְקַדֵּשׁ אֹתָם לְכַהֵן לִי לְקַח פַּר אֶחָד בֶּן־בָּקָר וְאֵילִם שְׁנַיִם תְּמִימִם:

27. מִמּוּל פָּנָיו — *In the forepart thereof* . . . (underneath) but not (actually) in the forepart. לְעֻמַּת מַחְבַּרְתּוֹ — *Close by the coupling.* Across the coupling, in a straight line opposite the place where the shoulder pieces join the *ephod.*

29. לְזִכָּרֹן לִפְנֵי ה׳ תָּמִיד — *For a memorial before* HASHEM *continually.* That God may remember their merits and be mindful of their children that (there be) peace in their merit.

30. מִשְׁפַּט בְּנֵי יִשְׂרָאֵל עַל לִבּוֹ — *The judgment of the Children of Israel on his heart* . . . that he may pray for them that they be found meritorious in judgment.

32. לֹא יִקָּרֵעַ — *That it be not split.* The neck opening shall not open lengthwise in the front but shall be round. The phrase יִקָּרֵעַ is used to (indicate) something which is open lengthwise, similar to, וְקָרַע לוֹ חַלּוֹנָי, *and he cuts him out windows* (*Jeremiah* 22:14), for the windows were constructed long and narrow.

NOTES

29. לְזִכָּרֹן — *For a memorial.* See the note on verse 12.

30. מִשְׁפַּט בְּנֵי יִשְׂרָאֵל עַל לִבּוֹ — *The judgment of the Children of Israel on his heart.* The *Sforno* is referring to the judgment of Heaven. The High Priest prays that his people be vindicated when judged from on High.

32. לֹא יִקָּרֵעַ — *That it be not split.* According to

toward its front, opposite its seam, above the belt of the Ephod. [28] *They shall attach the Breastplate from its rings to the rings of the Ephod with a turquoise woolen cord so that it will remain above the belt of the Ephod, and the Breastplate will not be loosened from upon the Ephod.* [29] *Aaron shall bear the names of the sons of Israel on the Breastplate of Judgment on his heart when he enters the Sanctuary, as a constant remembrance before HASHEM.* [30] *Into the Breastplate of Judgment shall you place the Urim and the Tumim, and they shall be on Aaron's heart when he comes before HASHEM; and Aaron shall bear the judgment of the Children of Israel on his heart constantly before HASHEM.*

[31] *You shall make the Robe of the Ephod entirely of turquoise wool.* [32] *Its head-opening shall be folded over within it, its opening shall have a border all around of weaver's work — it shall be for it like the opening of a coat of mail — it may not be torn.* [33] *You shall make on its hem pomegranates of turquoise, purple, and scarlet wool, on its hem all around, and gold bells between them, all around;* [34] *a gold bell and a pomegranate, a gold bell and a pomegranate on the hem of the robe, all around.* [35] *It must be on Aaron in order to minister. Its sound shall be heard when he enters the Sanctuary before HASHEM and when he leaves, so that he not die.*

[36] *You shall make a Head-plate of pure gold, and you shall engrave upon it, engraved like a signet ring, "HOLY TO HASHEM."* [37] *You shall place it on a cord of turquoise wool and it shall be on the Turban, opposite the front of the Turban shall it be.* [38] *It shall be on Aaron's forehead so that Aaron shall bring forgiveness for a sin regarding the sacred offerings that the Children of Israel consecrate for any gifts of their sacred offerings; and it shall be on his forehead always, to bring them favor before HASHEM.*

[39] *You shall make a linen Tunic of a box-like knit. You shall make a linen Turban and you shall make a Sash of embroiderer's work.*

[40] *For the sons of Aaron you shall make Tunics and make them Sashes; and you shall make them Headdresses for glory and splendor.* [41] *With them you shall dress Aaron your brother and his sons with him. You shall anoint them, inaugurate them and sanctify them, and they shall minister to Me.* [42] *You shall make them linen breeches to cover the flesh of nakedness, from the hips to the thighs shall they be.* [43] *They shall be on Aaron and his sons when they enter the Tent of Meeting or when they approach the Altar to serve in holiness, and they should not bear a sin and die; it is an eternal decree for him and his offspring after him.*

29
[1] *This is the matter that you shall do for them to sanctify them to minister for Me: Take one young bull and two rams, unblemished;*

---

41. וּמִלֵּאתָ אֶת יָדָם — *And fill their hands.* Perfect (complete) them in a way that they be complete and worthy to serve (in the) sacred service.

NOTES

the *Sforno's* interpretation the word יִקָּרֵעַ is not used in its usual sense of *torn*. Rather the Torah is describing the design of the neck opening, that it be round, and not an opening which is cut lengthwise. He supports this interpretation from a similar expression in *Jeremiah* where the meaning is clearly an opening that was *long*, not *torn*.

ב וְלֶחֶם מַצּוֹת וְחַלֹּת מַצֹּת בְּלוּלֹת בַּשֶּׁמֶן וּרְקִיקֵי מַצּוֹת מְשֻׁחִים בַּשָּׁמֶן
ג סֹלֶת חִטִּים תַּעֲשֶׂה אֹתָם: וְנָתַתָּ אוֹתָם עַל־סַל אֶחָד וְהִקְרַבְתָּ אֹתָם
ד בַּסָּל וְאֶת־הַפָּר וְאֵת שְׁנֵי הָאֵילִם: וְאֶת־אַהֲרֹן וְאֶת־בָּנָיו תַּקְרִיב אֶל־
ה פֶּתַח אֹהֶל מוֹעֵד וְרָחַצְתָּ אֹתָם בַּמָּיִם: וְלָקַחְתָּ אֶת־הַבְּגָדִים וְהִלְבַּשְׁתָּ
אֶת־אַהֲרֹן אֶת־הַכֻּתֹּנֶת וְאֵת מְעִיל הָאֵפֹד וְאֶת־הָאֵפֹד וְאֶת־הַחֹשֶׁן
ו וְאָפַדְתָּ לוֹ בְּחֵשֶׁב הָאֵפֹד: וְשַׂמְתָּ הַמִּצְנֶפֶת עַל־רֹאשׁוֹ וְנָתַתָּ אֶת־נֵזֶר
ז הַקֹּדֶשׁ עַל־הַמִּצְנָפֶת: וְלָקַחְתָּ אֶת־שֶׁמֶן הַמִּשְׁחָה וְיָצַקְתָּ עַל־רֹאשׁוֹ
ח־ט וּמָשַׁחְתָּ אֹתוֹ: וְאֶת־בָּנָיו תַּקְרִיב וְהִלְבַּשְׁתָּם כֻּתֳּנֹת: וְחָגַרְתָּ אֹתָם אַבְנֵט
אַהֲרֹן וּבָנָיו וְחָבַשְׁתָּ לָהֶם מִגְבָּעֹת וְהָיְתָה לָהֶם כְּהֻנָּה לְחֻקַּת עוֹלָם
י וּמִלֵּאתָ יַד־אַהֲרֹן וְיַד־בָּנָיו: וְהִקְרַבְתָּ אֶת־הַפָּר לִפְנֵי אֹהֶל מוֹעֵד וְסָמַךְ
יא אַהֲרֹן וּבָנָיו אֶת־יְדֵיהֶם עַל־רֹאשׁ הַפָּר: וְשָׁחַטְתָּ אֶת־הַפָּר לִפְנֵי יְהוָה
יב פֶּתַח אֹהֶל מוֹעֵד: וְלָקַחְתָּ מִדַּם הַפָּר וְנָתַתָּה עַל־קַרְנֹת הַמִּזְבֵּחַ
יג בְּאֶצְבָּעֶךָ וְאֶת־כָּל־הַדָּם תִּשְׁפֹּךְ אֶל־יְסוֹד הַמִּזְבֵּחַ: וְלָקַחְתָּ אֶת־כָּל־
הַחֵלֶב הַמְכַסֶּה אֶת־הַקֶּרֶב וְאֵת הַיֹּתֶרֶת עַל־הַכָּבֵד וְאֵת שְׁתֵּי הַכְּלָיֹת
יד וְאֶת־הַחֵלֶב אֲשֶׁר עֲלֵיהֶן וְהִקְטַרְתָּ הַמִּזְבֵּחָה: וְאֶת־בְּשַׂר הַפָּר וְאֶת־עֹרוֹ
טו וְאֶת־פִּרְשׁוֹ תִּשְׂרֹף בָּאֵשׁ מִחוּץ לַמַּחֲנֶה חַטָּאת הוּא: וְאֶת־הָאַיִל הָאֶחָד
טז תִּקָּח וְסָמְכוּ אַהֲרֹן וּבָנָיו אֶת־יְדֵיהֶם עַל־רֹאשׁ הָאָיִל: וְשָׁחַטְתָּ אֶת־
יז הָאָיִל וְלָקַחְתָּ אֶת־דָּמוֹ וְזָרַקְתָּ עַל־הַמִּזְבֵּחַ סָבִיב: וְאֶת־הָאַיִל תְּנַתֵּחַ
יח לִנְתָחָיו וְרָחַצְתָּ קִרְבּוֹ וּכְרָעָיו וְנָתַתָּ עַל־נְתָחָיו וְעַל־רֹאשׁוֹ: וְהִקְטַרְתָּ
חמישי יט אֶת־כָּל־הָאַיִל הַמִּזְבֵּחָה עֹלָה הוּא לַיהוָה רֵיחַ נִיחוֹחַ אִשֶּׁה לַיהוָה הוּא:
כ וְלָקַחְתָּ אֵת הָאַיִל הַשֵּׁנִי וְסָמַךְ אַהֲרֹן וּבָנָיו אֶת־יְדֵיהֶם עַל־רֹאשׁ הָאָיִל:
וְשָׁחַטְתָּ אֶת־הָאַיִל וְלָקַחְתָּ מִדָּמוֹ וְנָתַתָּה עַל־תְּנוּךְ אֹזֶן אַהֲרֹן וְעַל־
תְּנוּךְ אֹזֶן בָּנָיו הַיְמָנִית וְעַל־בֹּהֶן יָדָם הַיְמָנִית וְעַל־בֹּהֶן רַגְלָם הַיְמָנִית
כא וְזָרַקְתָּ אֶת־הַדָּם עַל־הַמִּזְבֵּחַ סָבִיב: וְלָקַחְתָּ מִן־הַדָּם אֲשֶׁר עַל־הַמִּזְבֵּחַ
וּמִשֶּׁמֶן הַמִּשְׁחָה וְהִזֵּיתָ עַל־אַהֲרֹן וְעַל־בְּגָדָיו וְעַל־בָּנָיו וְעַל־בִּגְדֵי בָנָיו
כב אִתּוֹ וְקָדַשׁ הוּא וּבְגָדָיו וּבָנָיו וּבִגְדֵי בָנָיו אִתּוֹ: וְלָקַחְתָּ מִן־הָאַיִל הַחֵלֶב
וְהָאַלְיָה וְאֶת־הַחֵלֶב ׀ הַמְכַסֶּה אֶת־הַקֶּרֶב וְאֵת יֹתֶרֶת הַכָּבֵד וְאֵת ׀ שְׁתֵּי
כג הַכְּלָיֹת וְאֶת־הַחֵלֶב אֲשֶׁר עֲלֵיהֶן וְאֵת שׁוֹק הַיָּמִין כִּי אֵיל מִלֻּאִים הוּא:

XXIX

22. כִּי אֵיל מִלֻּאִים הוּא — *For it is a ram of consecration.* Therefore the right shoulder of this (sacrifice) was given onto the altar, which was not (the case) with other sacrifices, because the right shoulder of an animal corresponds to the right hand of a person, and therefore it was proper that the shoulder of the sacrifice on the altar be symbolic of a hand,

NOTES

XXIX

22. כִּי אֵיל מִלֻּאִים הוּא — *For it is a ram of consecration. Rashi* in his commentary on this verse states, "We do not find that burning is prescribed for the right shoulder ... except in this case alone." He also interprets the word מִלֻּאִים, *consecration,* as having the literal meaning of *full,* synonymous with שְׁלָמִים, *peace offering* and שְׁלֵמוּת, *completeness.* The *Sforno* extends this interpretation to explain why the right shoulder was brought onto

2 with unleavened breads, unleavened loaves mixed with oil, and unleavened wafers smeared with oil; of fine wheat flour shall you make them. 3 You
shall place them in a single basket and bring them near in the basket, with
the bull and the two rams. 4 Aaron and his sons you shall bring near to the
entrance of the Tent of Meeting, and you shall immerse them in the water.
5 You shall take the vestments and dress Aaron with the Tunic, the Robe of
the Ephod, the Ephod, and the Breastplate, and you shall girdle him with the
belt of the Ephod. 6 You shall place the Turban on his head and place the
crown of sanctity over the Turban. 7 You shall take the anointment oil and
pour it on his head, and anoint him.

8 You shall cause his sons to come near, and dress them in Tunics. 9 You
shall girdle them with a Sash — Aaron and his sons — and you shall wrap
the Headdresses on them. The priesthood shall be an eternal duty for them,
and you shall inaugurate Aaron and his sons.

10 You shall bring the bull near before the Tent of Meeting; Aaron and his
sons shall lean their hands upon the head of the bull. 11 You shall slaughter
the bull before HASHEM, before the entrance of the Tent of Meeting. 12 You
shall take some blood of the bull and place it with your finger on the horns
of the Altar, and you shall pour all the blood on the base of the Altar. 13 You
shall take all the fat that covers the innards, the diaphragm with the liver,
the two kidneys and the fat that is upon them; and you shall cause them to
go up in smoke upon the Altar. 14 The flesh of the bull, its hide, and its waste
you shall burn in fire outside the camp — it is a sin-offering.

15 You shall take the first ram. Aaron and his sons shall lean their hands
on the head of the ram. 16 You shall slaughter the ram, and take its blood and
throw it on the Altar all around. 17 You shall cut the ram into its pieces; wash
its innards and feet, and place [them] with its pieces and its head. 18 You shall
cause the entire ram to go up in smoke upon the Altar — it is an elevation-
offering to HASHEM; it is a satisfying aroma, a fire-offering to HASHEM.

19 You shall take the second ram. Aaron and his sons shall lean their hands
on the head of the ram. 20 You shall slaughter the ram. You shall take some
of its blood and place it on the middle part of the ear of Aaron and on the
middle part of the ear of his sons — the right one — and on the thumb of their
right hand and the big toe of their right foot, and you shall throw the blood
upon the Altar, all around. 21 You shall take some of the blood that is on the
Altar and some of the anointment oil and sprinkle on Aaron and on his vestments, and on his sons and the vestments of his sons with him; he and his
vestments, and his sons and his sons' vestments with him, shall become holy.

22 From the ram you shall take the fat, the tail, the fat that covers
the innards, the diaphragm with the liver, the two kidneys and the fat
that is on them, and the right thigh — it is a ram of perfection —

---

to consecrate the right hand of the priest who offered it, for indeed the service of the priest was (exclusively) with the right hand as our Sages say, "Wherever 'finger' and

NOTES

the altar in this instance. It was done to symbolize the consecration of the priest's right hand which he uses exclusively during his service at the altar and the Temple service. The *Sforno's* interpreta-

כג וְכִכַּר לֶחֶם אַחַת וַחַלַּת לֶחֶם שֶׁמֶן אַחַת וְרָקִיק אֶחָד מִסַּל הַמַּצּוֹת אֲשֶׁר
כד לִפְנֵי יהוה: וְשַׂמְתָּ הַכֹּל עַל כַּפֵּי אַהֲרֹן וְעַל כַּפֵּי בָנָיו וְהֵנַפְתָּ אֹתָם תְּנוּפָה
כה לִפְנֵי יהוה: וְלָקַחְתָּ אֹתָם מִיָּדָם וְהִקְטַרְתָּ הַמִּזְבֵּחָה עַל־הָעֹלָה לְרֵיחַ נִיחוֹחַ
כו לִפְנֵי יהוה אִשֶּׁה הוּא לַיהוה: וְלָקַחְתָּ אֶת־הֶחָזֶה מֵאֵיל הַמִּלֻּאִים אֲשֶׁר
כז לְאַהֲרֹן וְהֵנַפְתָּ אֹתוֹ תְּנוּפָה לִפְנֵי יהוה וְהָיָה לְךָ לְמָנָה: וְקִדַּשְׁתָּ אֵת ׀ חֲזֵה
הַתְּנוּפָה וְאֵת שׁוֹק הַתְּרוּמָה אֲשֶׁר הוּנַף וַאֲשֶׁר הוּרָם מֵאֵיל הַמִּלֻּאִים
כח מֵאֲשֶׁר לְאַהֲרֹן וּמֵאֲשֶׁר לְבָנָיו: וְהָיָה לְאַהֲרֹן וּלְבָנָיו לְחָק־עוֹלָם מֵאֵת בְּנֵי
יִשְׂרָאֵל כִּי תְרוּמָה הוּא וּתְרוּמָה יִהְיֶה מֵאֵת בְּנֵי־יִשְׂרָאֵל מִזִּבְחֵי שַׁלְמֵיהֶם
כט תְּרוּמָתָם לַיהוה: וּבִגְדֵי הַקֹּדֶשׁ אֲשֶׁר לְאַהֲרֹן יִהְיוּ לְבָנָיו אַחֲרָיו לְמָשְׁחָה
ל בָהֶם וּלְמַלֵּא־בָם אֶת־יָדָם: שִׁבְעַת יָמִים יִלְבָּשָׁם הַכֹּהֵן תַּחְתָּיו מִבָּנָיו
לא אֲשֶׁר יָבֹא אֶל־אֹהֶל מוֹעֵד לְשָׁרֵת בַּקֹּדֶשׁ: וְאֵת אֵיל הַמִּלֻּאִים תִּקָּח
לב וּבִשַּׁלְתָּ אֶת־בְּשָׂרוֹ בְּמָקֹם קָדֹשׁ: וְאָכַל אַהֲרֹן וּבָנָיו אֶת־בְּשַׂר הָאַיִל
לג וְאֶת־הַלֶּחֶם אֲשֶׁר בַּסָּל פֶּתַח אֹהֶל מוֹעֵד: וְאָכְלוּ אֹתָם אֲשֶׁר כֻּפַּר בָּהֶם
לד לְמַלֵּא אֶת־יָדָם לְקַדֵּשׁ אֹתָם וְזָר לֹא־יֹאכַל כִּי־קֹדֶשׁ הֵם: וְאִם־יִוָּתֵר
מִבְּשַׂר הַמִּלֻּאִים וּמִן־הַלֶּחֶם עַד־הַבֹּקֶר וְשָׂרַפְתָּ אֶת־הַנּוֹתָר בָּאֵשׁ לֹא
לה יֵאָכֵל כִּי־קֹדֶשׁ הוּא: וְעָשִׂיתָ לְאַהֲרֹן וּלְבָנָיו כָּכָה כְּכֹל אֲשֶׁר־צִוִּיתִי אֹתָכָה
לו שִׁבְעַת יָמִים תְּמַלֵּא יָדָם: וּפַר חַטָּאת תַּעֲשֶׂה לַיּוֹם עַל־הַכִּפֻּרִים וְחִטֵּאתָ
לז עַל־הַמִּזְבֵּחַ בְּכַפֶּרְךָ עָלָיו וּמָשַׁחְתָּ אֹתוֹ לְקַדְּשׁוֹ: שִׁבְעַת יָמִים תְּכַפֵּר
עַל־הַמִּזְבֵּחַ וְקִדַּשְׁתָּ אֹתוֹ וְהָיָה הַמִּזְבֵּחַ קֹדֶשׁ קָדָשִׁים כָּל־הַנֹּגֵעַ בַּמִּזְבֵּחַ
לח יִקְדָּשׁ: וְזֶה אֲשֶׁר תַּעֲשֶׂה עַל־הַמִּזְבֵּחַ כְּבָשִׂים בְּנֵי־שָׁנָה שְׁנַיִם לַיּוֹם ששי
לט תָּמִיד: אֶת־הַכֶּבֶשׂ הָאֶחָד תַּעֲשֶׂה בַבֹּקֶר וְאֵת הַכֶּבֶשׂ הַשֵּׁנִי תַּעֲשֶׂה בֵּין
מ הָעַרְבָּיִם: וְעִשָּׂרֹן סֹלֶת בָּלוּל בְּשֶׁמֶן כָּתִית רֶבַע הַהִין וְנֵסֶךְ רְבִיעִת הַהִין
מא יָיִן לַכֶּבֶשׂ הָאֶחָד: וְאֵת הַכֶּבֶשׂ הַשֵּׁנִי תַּעֲשֶׂה בֵּין הָעַרְבָּיִם כְּמִנְחַת הַבֹּקֶר
מב וּכְנִסְכָּהּ תַּעֲשֶׂה־לָּהּ לְרֵיחַ נִיחֹחַ אִשֶּׁה לַיהוה: עֹלַת תָּמִיד לְדֹרֹתֵיכֶם
פֶּתַח אֹהֶל־מוֹעֵד לִפְנֵי יהוה אֲשֶׁר אִוָּעֵד לָכֶם שָׁמָּה לְדַבֵּר אֵלֶיךָ שָׁם:

'priesthood' is said (in the Torah) it means only the right one" *(Menachos* 10a).

24. וְהֵנַפְתָּ אֹתָם — *And you shall wave them.* Behold the תְּנוּפָה (whatever is waved) applies to the priest's portion to indicate that they receive (lit., "merit") it from the שֻׁלְחַן גָּבֹהַּ, *table of the Exalted One.* Now here (in our case) the portion which was elevated onto the altar was also waved, because it (included) the right shoulder which was fitting for the priest (i.e., belonged to him by right) for it came up onto the altar to consecrate him (lit., "to fill his hand").

29. וּלְמַלֵּא בָם אֶת יָדָם — *And to be consecrated (lit., to fill their hand) in them.* But his children (successors) will not have to bring the sacrifices of consecration written here (in this chapter).

NOTES

tion also clarifies the use of the word כִּי, *because.* The Torah is explaining why this offering requires the burning of the right shoulder. It is *because* this ram is brought to complete the consecration of the priest who serves with his right hand.

24. וְהֵנַפְתָּ אֹתָם — *And you shall wave them.* The ritual of "waving" a sacred object horizontally and vertically is usually interpreted as indicating that the four corners of the earth, the heaven above, and the earth below all belong to God. The *Sforno,* however, explains that when the portion of a sacri-

23 one cake of bread, one oily loaf, and one wafer from the basket of
unleavened loaves that is before HASHEM. 24 You shall place it all on the
palms of Aaron and on the palms of his sons, and you shall wave them as
a waving before HASHEM. 25 You shall take them from their hands and cause
it to go up in smoke on the Altar, on the elevation-offering, as a satisfying
aroma before HASHEM; it is a fire-offering to HASHEM. 26 You shall take the
breast of the inauguration ram that is Aaron's, and you shall wave it as a
waving before HASHEM. Then it shall be your portion. 27 You shall sanctify
the breast of the waving and the thigh of the raising-up, that was waved and
that was raised up, from the inauguration ram that was for Aaron and for
his sons. 28 It shall be for Aaron and his sons as an eternal portion from the
Children of Israel, for it is a portion and it shall remain a portion from the
Children of Israel from their peace-offering feasts, their portion to HASHEM.
29 The holy vestments of Aaron shall belong to his sons after him to become
elevated through them, to become inaugurated through them. 30 For a seven-
day period, the Kohen who succeeds him from his sons, who shall enter the
Tent of Meeting to serve in the Sanctuary, shall don them.
31 You shall take the inauguration ram and cook its flesh in a holy place.
32 Aaron and his sons shall eat the flesh of the ram and the bread that is in
the basket before the entrance of the Tent of Meeting. 33 They — who received
atonement through them — shall eat them, to inaugurate them, to sanctify
them; an alien shall not eat for they are holy. 34 If anything shall be left over
from the flesh of the inauguration-offering or from the bread until the morn-
ing, you shall burn the leftover in the fire. It may not be eaten, for it is holy.
35 You shall do thus for Aaron and his sons, like everything that I have
commanded you; for a seven-day period shall you inaugurate them. 36 A bull
sin-offering shall you make for each day for the atonements; you shall
purify the Altar by bringing atonement for it and you shall anoint it to
sanctify it. 37 For a seven-day period shall you bring atonement for the Altar
and sanctify it. The Altar shall be holy of holies; whatever touches the Altar
shall become sanctified.
38 This is what you shall offer upon the Altar: two sheep within their first
year every day, continually. 39 You shall offer the one sheep in the morning,
and the second sheep shall you offer in the afternoon; 40 and a tenth-ephah
of fine flour mixed with a quarter-hin of beaten oil, and a libation of a
quarter-hin of wine for each sheep. 41 You shall offer the second sheep in the
afternoon, like the meal-offering of the morning and its libation shall you
offer for it, for a satisfying aroma, a fire-offering to HASHEM; 42 as a continual
elevation-offering for your generations, before the entrance of the Tent of
Meeting, before HASHEM; where I shall set My meeting with you to speak to
you there.

NOTES

fice which was given to a priest was waved, it came to teach that he was given it not as his due but from God's table, granted to him by God. Since this right shoulder belonged to the priest it had to be waved.

29. וּלְמַלֵּא בָם אֶת יָדָם — *And to be consecrated in them.* Only Aaron had to be invested into the office of the High Priesthood through the medium of these sacrifices and the placing of the blood on his ear lobe, thumb, and large toe. Henceforth the successors to this position would be consecrated by putting on the eight garments.

מג־מד וְנֹעַדְתִּ֥י שָׁ֖מָּה לִבְנֵ֣י יִשְׂרָאֵ֑ל וְנִקְדַּ֖שׁ בִּכְבֹדִֽי׃ וְקִדַּשְׁתִּ֛י אֶת־אֹ֥הֶל מוֹעֵ֖ד
מה וְאֶת־הַמִּזְבֵּ֑חַ וְאֶת־אַהֲרֹ֧ן וְאֶת־בָּנָ֛יו אֲקַדֵּ֖שׁ לְכַהֵ֥ן לִֽי׃ וְשָׁ֣כַנְתִּ֔י בְּת֖וֹךְ בְּנֵ֣י
מו יִשְׂרָאֵ֑ל וְהָיִ֥יתִי לָהֶ֖ם לֵאלֹהִֽים׃ וְיָֽדְע֗וּ כִּ֣י אֲנִ֤י יהוה֙ אֱלֹ֣הֵיהֶ֔ם אֲשֶׁ֨ר
הוֹצֵ֧אתִי אֹתָ֛ם מֵאֶ֥רֶץ מִצְרַ֖יִם לְשָׁכְנִ֣י בְתוֹכָ֑ם אֲנִ֖י יהוה אֱלֹהֵיהֶֽם׃

ל　שביעי　א־ב וְעָשִׂ֥יתָ מִזְבֵּ֖חַ מִקְטַ֣ר קְטֹ֑רֶת עֲצֵ֥י שִׁטִּ֖ים תַּעֲשֶׂ֥ה אֹתֽוֹ׃ אַמָּ֨ה אָרְכּ֜וֹ וְאַמָּ֤ה
ג רָחְבּוֹ֙ רָב֣וּעַ יִהְיֶ֔ה וְאַמָּתַ֖יִם קֹמָת֑וֹ מִמֶּ֖נּוּ קַרְנֹתָֽיו׃ וְצִפִּיתָ֨ אֹת֜וֹ זָהָ֣ב טָה֗וֹר
אֶת־גַּגּ֧וֹ וְאֶת־קִירֹתָ֛יו סָבִ֖יב וְאֶת־קַרְנֹתָ֑יו וְעָשִׂ֥יתָ לּ֛וֹ זֵ֥ר זָהָ֖ב סָבִֽיב׃
ד וּשְׁתֵּי֩ טַבְּעֹ֨ת זָהָ֜ב תַּעֲשֶׂה־לּ֣וֹ ׀ מִתַּ֣חַת לְזֵר֗וֹ עַ֚ל שְׁתֵּ֣י צַלְעֹתָ֔יו תַּעֲשֶׂ֖ה
ה עַל־שְׁנֵ֣י צִדָּ֑יו וְהָיָה֙ לְבָתִּ֣ים לְבַדִּ֔ים לָשֵׂ֥את אֹת֖וֹ בָּהֵֽמָּה׃ וְעָשִׂ֥יתָ
ו אֶת־הַבַּדִּ֖ים עֲצֵ֣י שִׁטִּ֑ים וְצִפִּיתָ֥ אֹתָ֖ם זָהָֽב׃ וְנָתַתָּ֤ה אֹתוֹ֙ לִפְנֵ֣י הַפָּרֹ֔כֶת
אֲשֶׁ֖ר עַל־אֲרֹ֣ן הָעֵדֻ֑ת לִפְנֵ֣י הַכַּפֹּ֗רֶת אֲשֶׁר֙ עַל־הָ֣עֵדֻ֔ת אֲשֶׁ֛ר אִוָּעֵ֥ד לְךָ֖
ז שָֽׁמָּה׃ וְהִקְטִ֥יר עָלָ֛יו אַהֲרֹ֖ן קְטֹ֣רֶת סַמִּ֑ים בַּבֹּ֣קֶר בַּבֹּ֗קֶר בְּהֵיטִיב֛וֹ
ח　מפטיר אֶת־הַנֵּרֹ֖ת יַקְטִירֶֽנָּה׃ וּבְהַעֲלֹ֨ת אַהֲרֹ֧ן אֶת־הַנֵּרֹ֛ת בֵּ֥ין הָעַרְבַּ֖יִם יַקְטִירֶ֑נָּה
ט קְטֹ֧רֶת תָּמִ֛יד לִפְנֵ֥י יהוה לְדֹרֹתֵיכֶֽם׃ לֹא־תַעֲל֥וּ עָלָ֛יו קְטֹ֥רֶת זָרָ֖ה וְעֹלָ֣ה
י וּמִנְחָ֑ה וְנֵ֕סֶךְ לֹ֥א תִסְּכ֖וּ עָלָֽיו׃ וְכִפֶּ֤ר אַהֲרֹן֙ עַל־קַרְנֹתָ֔יו אַחַ֖ת בַּשָּׁנָ֑ה מִדַּ֞ם
חַטַּ֣את הַכִּפֻּרִ֗ים אַחַ֤ת בַּשָּׁנָה֙ יְכַפֵּ֤ר עָלָיו֙ לְדֹרֹ֣תֵיכֶ֔ם קֹֽדֶשׁ־קָֽדָשִׁ֥ים ה֖וּא
לַֽיהוָֽה׃

45. וְשָׁכַנְתִּי בְּתוֹךְ בְּנֵי יִשְׂרָאֵל — *And I will dwell among the Children of Israel . . .* to accept their service with favor and to hearken to their prayers.

וְהָיִיתִי לָהֶם לֵאלֹהִים — *And I will be their God.* To direct their affairs without an intermediary. And they will not need fear the heavenly signs, for they will be more honored before Me than the heavens whose conduct (movement) is directed through (the angels) that move them. And as a result (of all this) their eternity is ensured.

XXX

1. מִזְבֵּחַ מִקְטַר קְטֹרֶת — *An altar to burn incense upon.* A small amount of fire will be sufficient for the incense alone and (therefore) it need not be hollow, filled with earth, as was necessary for the altar of the burnt-offering (where) a continual fire had to be made on the earth. But the fire on this altar (burnt) on its overlay which was of gold and since the fire was small it did not burn the block of the altar which was of wood. Now this altar is not mentioned with the other furnishings in *Parashas Terumah* for its intent (purpose) was not to cause God, the Blessed One, to dwell in our midst, as was the case with the other furnishings as it says, וְשָׁכַנְתִּי בְּתוֹכָם כְּכֹל אֲשֶׁר אֲנִי מַרְאֶה אוֹתְךָ אֵת תַּבְנִית הַמִּשְׁכָּן וְאֵת תַּבְנִית

NOTES

45. וְהָיִיתִי לָהֶם לֵאלֹהִים — *And I will be their God.* God is eternal (נִצְחִי). Israel's destiny and fate is linked to Him. Hence, that which is connected to the Eternal is also granted eternity.

XXX

1. מִזְבֵּחַ מִקְטַר קְטֹרֶת — *An altar to burn incense upon.* In the previous *sidrah (Terumah)* the various furnishings of the Sanctuary were discussed — the Ark, table, menorah, altar — whereas the golden altar is not included among these furnishings. Instead it is introduced at the end of the chapter regarding the priestly vestments. The *Sforno* explains this seeming discrepancy by explaining the unique role played by the golden altar as opposed to the outer altar upon which animal sacrifices

[43] I shall set My meeting there with the Children of Israel, and it shall be sanctified with My glory. [44] I shall sanctify the Tent of Meeting and the Altar; and Aaron and his sons shall I sanctify to minister to Me. [45] I shall rest My Presence among the Children of Israel, and I shall be their God. [46] They shall know that I am HASHEM, their God, Who took them out of the land of Egypt to rest My Presence among them. I am HASHEM, their God.

30 *[1] You shall make an Altar on which to bring incense up in smoke, of acacia wood shall you make it. [2] Its length a cubit; and its width a cubit — it shall be square — and its height two cubits; from it shall its horns be. [3] You shall cover it with pure gold, its roof and its walls all around, and its horns, and you shall make for it a gold crown, all around. [4] You shall make for it two gold rings under its crown on its two corners, you shall make on its two sides; and it shall be housings for the staves, with which to carry it. [5] You shall make the staves of acacia wood and cover them with gold. [6] You shall place it before the Partition that is by the Ark of the Testimonial-tablets, in front of the Cover that is on the Testimonial-tablets, where I shall set My meetings with you. [7] Upon it shall Aaron bring the spice incense up in smoke, every morning, when he cleans the lamps he shall bring it up in smoke. [8] And when Aaron kindles the lamps in the afternoon he shall bring it up in smoke, continual incense before HASHEM, for your generations. [9] You shall not bring upon it alien incense, or an elevation-offering or meal-offering; nor may you pour a libation upon it. [10] Aaron shall bring atonement upon its horns once a year, from the blood of the sin-offering of the atonements, once a year, shall he bring atonement upon it for your generations; it is holy of holies to HASHEM.*

כָּל כֵּלָיו, *that I may dwell among them; according to all that I show you the pattern of the Tabernacle and the pattern of all its furniture* (25:8,9). Nor was it meant to bring down the appearance of His glory (honor) in the House as was the case of the sacrifices as it says, וְנֹעַדְתִּי שָׁמָּה לִבְנֵי יִשְׂרָאֵל, *and there I will meet with the Children of Israel* (29:43); and so Moses our Teacher attested saying, "זֶה הַדָּבָר אֲשֶׁר צִוָּה ה׳ תַּעֲשׂוּ וְיֵרָא אֲלֵיכֶם כְּבוֹד ה׳, *This is the thing which HASHEM commanded that you should do, that the glory of HASHEM may appear to you" (Leviticus* 9:6). But the purpose of this altar was to honor God, the Blessed One, after He comes to accept with favor the service of His people (through) the morning and evening sacrifices, and to welcome His presence with the offering of incense, similar to, הָבוּ לַה׳ כְּבוֹד שְׁמוֹ שְׂאוּ מִנְחָה וּבֹאוּ לְפָנָיו, *Ascribe to HASHEM the glory of His Name, bring an offering and come before Him (I Chronicles* 16:29).

4. שְׁתֵּי צַלְעֹתָיו — *The two ribs.* Its upper corners.

שְׁנֵי צִדָּיו — *Two sides.* The sides of its width.

NOTES

were brought. The goal and purpose of sacrifices was a twofold one; to bring about God's dwelling in the Sanctuary and to bring down His glory so that He meet with the Children of Israel. All this is tied in with the various furnishings and vessels as well. The golden altar, however, is only used for incense and its purpose is to honor God. This is the reason that this command is separated from the other furnishings discussed above. The *Tanchuma* puts it very well, "The incense offering does not come to expiate sin or transgression or guilt. It comes only to bring *simchah* (joy and happiness)."

פרשת כי תשא

יא־יב וַיְדַבֵּר יְהוָה אֶל־מֹשֶׁה לֵּאמֹר: כִּי תִשָּׂא אֶת־רֹאשׁ בְּנֵי־יִשְׂרָאֵל
לִפְקֻדֵיהֶם וְנָתְנוּ אִישׁ כֹּפֶר נַפְשׁוֹ לַיהוָה בִּפְקֹד אֹתָם וְלֹא־יִהְיֶה בָהֶם
יג נֶגֶף בִּפְקֹד אֹתָם: זֶה ׀ יִתְּנוּ כָּל־הָעֹבֵר עַל־הַפְּקֻדִים מַחֲצִית הַשֶּׁקֶל
יד בְּשֶׁקֶל הַקֹּדֶשׁ עֶשְׂרִים גֵּרָה הַשֶּׁקֶל מַחֲצִית הַשֶּׁקֶל תְּרוּמָה לַיהוָה: כֹּל
טו הָעֹבֵר עַל־הַפְּקֻדִים מִבֶּן עֶשְׂרִים שָׁנָה וָמָעְלָה יִתֵּן תְּרוּמַת יְהוָה: הֶעָשִׁיר
לֹא־יַרְבֶּה וְהַדַּל לֹא יַמְעִיט מִמַּחֲצִית הַשָּׁקֶל לָתֵת אֶת־תְּרוּמַת יְהוָה
טז לְכַפֵּר עַל־נַפְשֹׁתֵיכֶם: וְלָקַחְתָּ אֶת־כֶּסֶף הַכִּפֻּרִים מֵאֵת בְּנֵי יִשְׂרָאֵל
וְנָתַתָּ אֹתוֹ עַל־עֲבֹדַת אֹהֶל מוֹעֵד וְהָיָה לִבְנֵי יִשְׂרָאֵל לְזִכָּרוֹן לִפְנֵי יְהוָה
לְכַפֵּר עַל־נַפְשֹׁתֵיכֶם:

יז־יח וַיְדַבֵּר יְהוָה אֶל־מֹשֶׁה לֵּאמֹר: וְעָשִׂיתָ כִּיּוֹר נְחֹשֶׁת וְכַנּוֹ נְחֹשֶׁת לְרָחְצָה
יט וְנָתַתָּ אֹתוֹ בֵּין־אֹהֶל מוֹעֵד וּבֵין הַמִּזְבֵּחַ וְנָתַתָּ שָׁמָּה מָיִם: וְרָחֲצוּ אַהֲרֹן
כ וּבָנָיו מִמֶּנּוּ אֶת־יְדֵיהֶם וְאֶת־רַגְלֵיהֶם: בְּבֹאָם אֶל־אֹהֶל מוֹעֵד יִרְחֲצוּ־
מַיִם וְלֹא יָמֻתוּ אוֹ בְגִשְׁתָּם אֶל־הַמִּזְבֵּחַ לְשָׁרֵת לְהַקְטִיר אִשֶּׁה לַיהוָה:
כא וְרָחֲצוּ יְדֵיהֶם וְרַגְלֵיהֶם וְלֹא יָמֻתוּ וְהָיְתָה לָהֶם חָק־עוֹלָם לוֹ וּלְזַרְעוֹ
לְדֹרֹתָם:

כב־כג וַיְדַבֵּר יְהוָה אֶל־מֹשֶׁה לֵּאמֹר: וְאַתָּה קַח־לְךָ בְּשָׂמִים רֹאשׁ מָר־דְּרוֹר
חֲמֵשׁ מֵאוֹת וְקִנְּמָן־בֶּשֶׂם מַחֲצִיתוֹ חֲמִשִּׁים וּמָאתָיִם וּקְנֵה־בֹשֶׂם
כד חֲמִשִּׁים וּמָאתָיִם: וְקִדָּה חֲמֵשׁ מֵאוֹת בְּשֶׁקֶל הַקֹּדֶשׁ וְשֶׁמֶן זַיִת הִין:

---

12. וְנָתְנוּ אִישׁ כֹּפֶר נַפְשׁוֹ — *Every man shall give ransom for his soul.* Since the need to count men of the human (race) is due to the changes (of circumstances) which occur in his personality, (both) positive and negative (lit., "existence and loss") and this is caused by their sins, as our Sages say, אֵין מִיתָה בְּלֹא חֵטְא, *There is no death without sin* (*Shabbos* 55a), therefore every counting (census) causes iniquities to be recalled, therefore it is fitting that each one give a ransom for his soul in honor of God, the Blessed One, and *He being merciful atones iniquity* (based on *Psalms* 78:38), as it says, לְכַפֵּר עַל נַפְשֹׁתֵיכֶם, *to make atonement for your souls* (v. 15) and hence it says . . .

15. הֶעָשִׁיר לֹא יַרְבֶּה וְהַדַּל לֹא יַמְעִיט — *The rich shall not give more and the poor shall not give less.* For in this לֹא נִכַּר שׁוֹעַ לִפְנֵי דָל, *the rich is not regarded more than the poor* (*Job* 34:19).

18. וְעָשִׂיתָ כִּיּוֹר — *And you shall make a laver.* This vessel is also not mentioned above together with the other vessels (and furnishings) for its purpose (lit., "intent") was not to

NOTES

12-15. וְנָתְנוּ אִישׁ כֹּפֶר נַפְשׁוֹ . . . לֹא יַרְבֶּה . . . לֹא יַמְעִיט — *Every man shall give ransom for his soul . . . shall not give more . . . shall not give less.* In Torah perspective, counting (a census) of people plays a most significant role. The *Sforno*, at the beginning of *Exodus*, comments regarding the *name* of an individual which he explains reveals the essential personality of that person. Here he tells us that counting is not to be considered simply as a way of determining the quantity of a people but it also is an index to their quality. Each time God ordered a census — when they left Egypt; after the sin of the Golden Calf and now when He is prepared to "dwell" in the Sanctuary — it indicates, to a degree, a change in their status due to their actions. Hence it is akin to a close examination which may reveal many blemishes and shortcomings. Therefore they are told to bring a "ransom" for their souls which need an atonement. This being the case the amount collected (half-shekel) is uniform,

PARASHAS KI SISA

11 *HASHEM spoke to Moses, saying:* 12 *"When you take a census of the
Children of Israel according to their numbers, every man shall give
HASHEM an atonement for his soul when counting them, so that there will not
be a plague among them when counting them.* 13 *This shall they give —
everyone who passes through the census — a half shekel of the sacred
shekel, the shekel is twenty geras, half a shekel as a portion to HASHEM.*
14 *Everyone who passes through the census, from twenty years of age and
up, shall give the portion of HASHEM.* 15 *The wealthy shall not increase and
the destitute shall not decrease from half a shekel — to give the portion of
HASHEM, to atone for your souls.* 16 *You shall take the silver of the
atonements from the Children of Israel and give it for the work of the Tent
of Meeting; and it shall be a remembrance before HASHEM for the Children
of Israel, to atone for your souls."*
17 *HASHEM spoke to Moses, saying:* 18 *"You shall make a copper Laver and
its base of copper, for washing; place it between the Tent of Meeting and the
Altar, and put water there.* 19 *From it, Aaron and his sons shall wash their
hands together with their feet.* 20 *Whenever they come to the Tent of
Meeting, they shall wash with water and not die, or when they approach the
Altar to serve, to raise up in smoke a fire-offering to HASHEM.* 21 *They shall
wash their hands and feet and not die. It shall be for them an eternal decree,
for him and his offspring for their generations."*
22 *HASHEM spoke to Moses, saying:* 23 *"Now you, take for yourself choice
spices: five hundred shekel-weights of pure myrrh; fragrant cinnamon, half
of which shall be two hundred fifty; two hundred fifty of fragrant cane;*
24 *five hundred of cassia — in the sacred shekel-weight, and a hin of olive oil.*

---

cause the Divine Presence to dwell in the Sanctuary, as was the intent of those vessels as explained above. But the intent (of the laver) was to prepare the priests for their service.

24. וְשֶׁמֶן זַיִת הִין — *And of olive oil a hin.* Without a doubt this quantity of oil was not sufficient to smear the quantity of all those spices, but they cooked the oil with the water in which the spices had been boiled or they floated it (the oil) on the water in which (the spices) had been steeped until the water evaporated (lit., "ended") through the cooking or through the minimal heat of the water, while the oil remained, as in the art of a compounder. The dispute between our Sages (*Horayos* 11b) is regarding this (question): whether it was sufficient to cook it (the oil) with the water in which the roots had been boiled or to float it (the oil) on the water in which they were steeped and melt them through minimal heat.

NOTES

for certainly in this regard there is no difference between rich and poor.

18. וְעָשִׂיתָ כִּיּוֹר — *And you shall make a laver.* Compare to the *Sforno's* commentary on verse 1, regarding the altar of incense.

24. וְשֶׁמֶן זַיִת הִין — *And of olive oil a hin.* The Talmud (*Horayos* 11b) relates a dispute between R' Meir and R' Yehudah regarding this oil of anointment. The former is of the opinion that the roots (of the various spices) were boiled in the oil to give it fragrance. The latter disagrees for he argues that the amount of oil was insufficient to even *smear* the roots, let alone to be boiled with them and not cook out. He therefore is of the opinion (according to *Rashi*) that the spices were steeped in water, the oil then poured over them and left thus until the oil absorbed the scent, after which they skimmed off the oil. The *Sforno* however interprets the argument of R' Meir and

כה וְעָשִׂיתָ אֹתוֹ שֶׁמֶן מִשְׁחַת־קֹדֶשׁ רֹקַח מִרְקַחַת מַעֲשֵׂה רֹקֵחַ שֶׁמֶן מִשְׁחַת־
כו־כז קֹדֶשׁ יִהְיֶה: וּמָשַׁחְתָּ בוֹ אֶת־אֹהֶל מוֹעֵד וְאֵת אֲרוֹן הָעֵדֻת: וְאֶת־
הַשֻּׁלְחָן וְאֶת־כָּל־כֵּלָיו וְאֶת־הַמְּנֹרָה וְאֶת־כֵּלֶיהָ וְאֵת מִזְבַּח הַקְּטֹרֶת:
כח־כט וְאֶת־מִזְבַּח הָעֹלָה וְאֶת־כָּל־כֵּלָיו וְאֶת־הַכִּיֹּר וְאֶת־כַּנּוֹ: וְקִדַּשְׁתָּ אֹתָם
ל וְהָיוּ קֹדֶשׁ קָדָשִׁים כָּל־הַנֹּגֵעַ בָּהֶם יִקְדָּשׁ: וְאֶת־אַהֲרֹן וְאֶת־בָּנָיו תִּמְשָׁח
לא וְקִדַּשְׁתָּ אֹתָם לְכַהֵן לִי: וְאֶל־בְּנֵי יִשְׂרָאֵל תְּדַבֵּר לֵאמֹר שֶׁמֶן מִשְׁחַת־
לב קֹדֶשׁ יִהְיֶה זֶה לִי לְדֹרֹתֵיכֶם: עַל־בְּשַׂר אָדָם לֹא יִיסָךְ וּבְמַתְכֻּנְתּוֹ לֹא
לג תַעֲשׂוּ כָּמֹהוּ קֹדֶשׁ הוּא קֹדֶשׁ יִהְיֶה לָכֶם: אִישׁ אֲשֶׁר יִרְקַח כָּמֹהוּ וַאֲשֶׁר
לד יִתֵּן מִמֶּנּוּ עַל־זָר וְנִכְרַת מֵעַמָּיו: וַיֹּאמֶר יהוה אֶל־
מֹשֶׁה קַח־לְךָ סַמִּים נָטָף | וּשְׁחֵלֶת וְחֶלְבְּנָה סַמִּים וּלְבֹנָה זַכָּה בַּד בְּבַד
לה יִהְיֶה: וְעָשִׂיתָ אֹתָהּ קְטֹרֶת רֹקַח מַעֲשֵׂה רוֹקֵחַ מְמֻלָּח טָהוֹר קֹדֶשׁ:
לו וְשָׁחַקְתָּ מִמֶּנָּה הָדֵק וְנָתַתָּה מִמֶּנָּה לִפְנֵי הָעֵדֻת בְּאֹהֶל מוֹעֵד אֲשֶׁר אִוָּעֵד
לז לְךָ שָׁמָּה קֹדֶשׁ קָדָשִׁים תִּהְיֶה לָכֶם: וְהַקְּטֹרֶת אֲשֶׁר תַּעֲשֶׂה בְּמַתְכֻּנְתָּהּ
לח לֹא תַעֲשׂוּ לָכֶם קֹדֶשׁ תִּהְיֶה לְךָ לַיהוה: אִישׁ אֲשֶׁר־יַעֲשֶׂה כָמוֹהָ לְהָרִיחַ
לא א־ב בָּהּ וְנִכְרַת מֵעַמָּיו: וַיְדַבֵּר יהוה אֶל־מֹשֶׁה לֵּאמֹר: רְאֵה
ג קָרָאתִי בְשֵׁם בְּצַלְאֵל בֶּן־אוּרִי בֶן־חוּר לְמַטֵּה יְהוּדָה: וָאֲמַלֵּא אֹתוֹ

25. רֹקַח מִרְקַחַת — *A perfume compounded . . .* (i.e.,) a compound which was compounded. The oil was compounded in the compounded water.

31. יִהְיֶה זֶה לִי לְדֹרֹתֵיכֶם — *Unto Me throughout your generations.* It will not be diminished (lit., "deteriorate").

34. קַח לְךָ סַמִּים — *Take for yourself sweet spices.* Those mentioned by the anointing oil; they are myrrh, calamus, cinnamon and cassia. With these (bring) stacte, onycha and galbanum and with them aromatics which are able (lit., "known") to prepare the aforementioned spices, as for example the perfumers know that corn ears (are used) to prepare *rhubarbiro,* and rocksalt to prepare *agrico* and (other) similar (mixtures). Our Sages (*Kerisos* 6a) had a tradition that spikenard, saffron and costus were used to prepare the spices mentioned above.

וּלְבֹנָה זַכָּה — *Pure frankincense.* Which needed no other preparation (fixing); and so these are the eleven spices which our Sages enumerate for the compounding of the incense (*Kerisos* 6a).

35. רֹקַח — *A compound.* Each of these spices shall absorb from one another, and from

NOTES

R' Yehudah differently in order to justify the position of R' Meir, who also understood that a *hin* of oil could not suffice to even smear the roots. Hence he interprets R' Meir's position as meaning that the oil was boiled in the *water* in which the roots of the spices had originally been cooked. R' Yehudah, on the other hand, is of the opinion that the oil was floated on the top of the water in which the roots had been steeped, and after evaporation of the water, fragrant oil remained.

31. יִהְיֶה זֶה לִי לְדֹרֹתֵיכֶם — *Unto Me throughout your generations.* The phrase לְדֹרֹתֵיכֶם does not mean that the oil of anointment is to be made in each generation. Rather it is to be interpreted as miraculously remaining for all generations. This is based on the Talmud (ibid.).

34. קַח לְךָ סַמִּים — *Take for yourself sweet spices.* The word סַמִּים, *spices* or *aromatics*, appears twice in this verse. Both are not specified. The *Sforno* therefore interprets the first phrase as referring to the spices enumerated in verses 23-24 and the second as referring to spices, well known at that time to those skilled in the art of compounding, as useful in the preparation of the spices specified in

25 *Of it you shall make oil of sacred anointment, a blended compound, the*
handiwork of a perfumer; it shall remain oil of sacred anointment. 26 *With it*
you shall anoint the Tent of Meeting and the Ark of Testimonial-tablets; 27 *the*
Table and all its utensils, the Menorah and its utensils, and the Incense Altar;
28 *the Elevation-offering Altar and all its utensils; and the Laver and its base.*
29 *You shall sanctify them and they shall remain holy of holies; whatever*
touches them shall become holy.
30 *"You shall anoint Aaron and his sons and sanctify them to minister to Me.*
31 *"You shall speak to the Children of Israel, saying: 'This shall remain for*
Me oil of sacred anointment for your generations. 32 *It shall not be smeared on*
human flesh and you shall not duplicate it in its formulation; it is holy, it shall
remain holy for you. 33 *Anyone who shall compound its like or who shall put*
it upon an alien shall be cut off from his people.' "
34 *HASHEM said to Moses: "Take yourself spices — stacte, onycha and*
galbanum — spices and pure frankincense: these shall all be of equal weight.
35 *You shall make it into a spice-compound, the handiwork of a perfumer,*
thoroughly mixed, pure and holy. 36 *You shall grind some of it finely and place*
some of it before the Testimonial-tablets in the Tent of Meeting, where I shall
designate a time to meet you; it shall remain holy of holies to you. 37 *The*
incense that you shall make — in its proportion you shall not make for
yourselves; it shall remain holy to you, for HASHEM. 38 *Whoever makes its like*
to smell it shall be cut off from his people."

31 1 *HASHEM spoke to Moses, saying:* 2 *"See, I have called by the name:*
Bezalel son of Uri, son of Hur, of the tribe of Judah. 3 *I have filled him*

---

all (together) one composition will be made.

מַעֲשֵׂה רוֹקֵחַ — *After the art of the compounder.* Each of these spices was to be pounded (crushed) befitting it, for it was not proper that each one of these spices be crushed in a single (similar) manner.

מְמֻלָּח — *Mixed together.* The spices were to be well mixed together so that none of them (remain) separate.

טָהוֹר — *Pure . . .* (i.e.,) clean of all refuse. This was necessary (to caution us) because the incense was made from the original perfume, but for the oil of anointment this (warning) was unnecessary because there were no particles of spices mixed in with the oil at all.

XXXI

2. רְאֵה קָרָאתִי בְשֵׁם — *See, I have called by name.* See and understand that I call him for good reasons (lit., "not for nothing") for it is of major import in sacred work that it be done

NOTES

this verse. The eleven spices alluded to by the *Sforno* which comprised the incense offered on the golden altar were: balm, onycha, galbanum, frankincense, myrrh, cassia, spikenard, saffron, costus, aromatic bark and cinnamon.

35. מְמֻלָּח — *Mixed together.* The word מְמֻלָּח has (incorrectly) been translated seasoned with salt. In reality, as *Rashi* and *Onkelos* translate, it means *mixed together.* This is also the interpretation of the *Sforno.*

טָהוֹר — *Pure.* The word טָהוֹר usually means *ritually pure.* In the context of this verse it means free from impurity.

XXXI

2. רְאֵה קָרָאתִי בְשֵׁם — *See, I have called by name.* The Talmud (*Berachos* 55a) states that there are

ד רוּחַ אֱלֹהִים בְּחָכְמָה וּבִתְבוּנָה וּבְדַעַת וּבְכָל־מְלָאכָה: לַחְשֹׁב מַחֲשָׁבֹת
ה לַעֲשׂוֹת בַּזָּהָב וּבַכֶּסֶף וּבַנְּחֹשֶׁת: וּבַחֲרֹשֶׁת אֶבֶן לְמַלֹּאת וּבַחֲרֹשֶׁת עֵץ
ו לַעֲשׂוֹת בְּכָל־מְלָאכָה: וַאֲנִי הִנֵּה נָתַתִּי אִתּוֹ אֵת אָהֳלִיאָב בֶּן־אֲחִיסָמָךְ
לְמַטֵּה־דָן וּבְלֵב כָּל־חֲכַם־לֵב נָתַתִּי חָכְמָה וְעָשׂוּ אֵת כָּל־אֲשֶׁר צִוִּיתִךָ:
ז אֵת | אֹהֶל מוֹעֵד וְאֶת־הָאָרֹן לָעֵדֻת וְאֶת־הַכַּפֹּרֶת אֲשֶׁר עָלָיו וְאֵת
ח כָּל־כְּלֵי הָאֹהֶל: וְאֶת־הַשֻּׁלְחָן וְאֶת־כֵּלָיו וְאֶת־הַמְּנֹרָה הַטְּהֹרָה וְאֶת־
ט כָּל־כֵּלֶיהָ וְאֵת מִזְבַּח הַקְּטֹרֶת: וְאֶת־מִזְבַּח הָעֹלָה וְאֶת־כָּל־כֵּלָיו וְאֶת־
י הַכִּיּוֹר וְאֶת־כַּנּוֹ: וְאֵת בִּגְדֵי הַשְּׂרָד וְאֶת־בִּגְדֵי הַקֹּדֶשׁ לְאַהֲרֹן הַכֹּהֵן
יא וְאֶת־בִּגְדֵי בָנָיו לְכַהֵן: וְאֵת שֶׁמֶן הַמִּשְׁחָה וְאֶת־קְטֹרֶת הַסַּמִּים לַקֹּדֶשׁ
כְּכֹל אֲשֶׁר־צִוִּיתִךָ יַעֲשׂוּ:
יב־יג וַיֹּאמֶר יהוה אֶל־מֹשֶׁה לֵּאמֹר: וְאַתָּה דַּבֵּר אֶל־בְּנֵי יִשְׂרָאֵל לֵאמֹר אַךְ
אֶת־שַׁבְּתֹתַי תִּשְׁמֹרוּ כִּי אוֹת הִוא בֵּינִי וּבֵינֵיכֶם לְדֹרֹתֵיכֶם לָדַעַת כִּי
יד אֲנִי יהוה מְקַדִּשְׁכֶם: וּשְׁמַרְתֶּם אֶת־הַשַּׁבָּת כִּי קֹדֶשׁ הִוא לָכֶם מְחַלְלֶיהָ
מוֹת יוּמָת כִּי כָּל־הָעֹשֶׂה בָהּ מְלָאכָה וְנִכְרְתָה הַנֶּפֶשׁ הַהִוא מִקֶּרֶב עַמֶּיהָ:
טו שֵׁשֶׁת יָמִים יֵעָשֶׂה מְלָאכָה וּבַיּוֹם הַשְּׁבִיעִי שַׁבַּת שַׁבָּתוֹן קֹדֶשׁ לַיהוה

---

by one chosen of God who has proper intent in his actions to attain the commanded purpose (and end).

13. אַךְ אֶת שַׁבְּתֹתַי תִּשְׁמֹרוּ — *However, you shall keep My Sabbaths.* Although I have commanded you regarding the work of the Sanctuary, nonetheless *you shall keep My Sabbaths* and do not override them for the sake of (the *Mishkan).*

כִּי אוֹת הִוא בֵּינִי וּבֵינֵיכֶם — *For it is a sign between Me and you.* And if you desecrate (lit., "spoil") this sign there is no purpose in making a Sanctuary for Me to dwell in your midst.

14. וּשְׁמַרְתֶּם אֶת הַשַּׁבָּת — *You shall keep the Sabbath.* And also for another reason it is proper that you not override the Sabbath for the building of the Sanctuary . . .

כִּי קֹדֶשׁ הִוא לָכֶם — *For it is holy unto you . . .* being a positive commandment (מִצְוַת עֲשֵׂה).

מְחַלְלֶיהָ מוֹת יוּמָת — *Every one that profanes it shall be put to death.* (This refers to) the negative commandment (לֹא תַעֲשֶׂה), and it is not proper to override a positive and negative commandment which carries a death penalty, to fulfill the positive commandment of building the Sanctuary.

כִּי כָּל הָעֹשֶׂה בָהּ מְלָאכָה וְנִכְרְתָה הַנֶּפֶשׁ הַהִוא — *For whoever does any work on it, that soul*

NOTES

three things which God Himself announces (מַכְרִיז עֲלֵיהֶם), and they are: hunger; plenty (prosperity); and the designation of a good leader. The Talmud brings as proof to the last statement the appointment of Bezalel. This is the thrust of the *Sforno's* comment as well. God told Moses to observe and appreciate that He had chosen the right man for the task of designing and constructing the *Mishkan,* for not only did Bezalel have the necessary skills but he also understood the symbolism of every object designed.

13-15. אַךְ אֶת שַׁבְּתֹתַי תִּשְׁמֹרוּ . . . וּשְׁמַרְתֶּם אֶת הַשַּׁבָּת . . . שֵׁשֶׁת יָמִים יֵעָשֶׂה מְלָאכָה — *However, you shall keep My Sabbaths . . . You shall keep the Sabbath . . . Six days shall work be done.* God gives four reasons for not overriding the Sabbath for the sake of building the *Mishkan:* (a) since the Sabbath is a sign of the covenant between God and Israel, if you desecrate the sign you defeat the purpose of the Sanctuary; (b) the only reason one might think he is permitted to override the Sabbath is because the building of the Sanctuary is a מִצְוַת עֲשֵׂה, *positive commandment,* but no עֲשֵׂה can set aside an עֲשֵׂה and לֹא תַעֲשֶׂה (positive and negative commandments which apply to one commandment), and the Sabbath is such a מִצְוָה; (c) since the

with a Godly spirit, with wisdom, insight, and knowledge, and with every craft; 4 *to weave designs, to work with gold, silver, and copper;* 5 *stone-cutting for setting, and wood-carving — to perform every craft.*

6 *"And I, behold, I have assigned with him Oholiab son of Ahisamach of the tribe of Dan, and I have endowed the heart of every wise-hearted person with wisdom, and they shall make all that I have commanded you:* 7 *the Tent of Meeting, the Ark of the Testimonial-tablets and the Cover that is upon it, and all the utensils of the Tent;* 8 *the Table and its utensils, the pure Menorah and all its utensils, and the Incense Altar;* 9 *the Elevation-offering Altar and all its utensils, the Laver and its base;* 10 *the knit vestments, the sacred vestments of Aaron the Kohen and the vestments of his sons, to minister;* 11 *the anointment oil and the incense-spices of the Sanctuary. Like everything that I have commanded you shall you make."*

12 *HASHEM said to Moses, saying:* 13 *"You shall speak to the Children of Israel, saying: 'However, you must observe My Sabbaths, for it is a sign between Me and you for your generations, to know that I am HASHEM, Who makes you holy.* 14 *You shall observe the Sabbath, for it is holy to you; its desecrators shall be put to death, for whoever does work on it, that soul shall be cut off from among its people.* 15 *For six days work may be done and the seventh day is a day of complete rest, it is sacred to HASHEM;*

---

shall be cut off. Also it is fitting (proper) not to override the Sabbath, for its profanation is punished greatly, in that the soul of the profaner is cut off (from his people), because by so doing he denies the creation (lit., "newness") of the world, and he has no portion in the Sanctuary nor in He Who dwells therein.

מִקֶּרֶב עַמֶּיהָ — *From among his people . . .* from the (spiritual) level of the national souls which are of (similar) quality — for eternal life.

15. שֵׁשֶׁת יָמִים יֵעָשֶׂה מְלָאכָה — *Six days shall work be done.* Behold in the six days of labor you can do the work of the Sanctuary, therefore it is not proper to override the Sabbath for it, (since) there is no *mitzvah* (commandment) which overrides the Sabbath unless it has a set, permanent time, which coincides with the Sabbath, such as Divine service (i.e., the daily and Sabbath sacrifice) and circumcision. But when it is possible to fulfill the commandment on another day, it never overrides the Sabbath.

שַׁבַּת שַׁבָּתוֹן — *A Sabbath of complete rest.* Behold even that which is not included (technically) in the general (list) of (prohibited) labors is prohibited as it says, וּבַיּוֹם הַשְּׁבִיעִי תִּשְׁבֹּת, *on the seventh day you shall rest* (23:12). This is (so) in order that it be *holy to HASHEM,* that a person should give up completely his temporal affairs and occupy himself with the affairs of eternal life in honor of his Maker.

NOTES

profaning of the Sabbath is so serious that it causes the sinner to be cut off from his people, then he would consequently have no share in the Sanctuary anyway, hence the commandment of building such a place is nullified and consequently there is no force of a *mitzvah* to override the Sabbath; (d) the only precedent for another commandment overriding the Sabbath is when we deal with one that must be performed at a specific time, which coincides with the Sabbath as well, such as circumcision (on the eighth day) and sacrifices that have a set time (such as the daily sacrifice, Sabbath offerings and the *Pesach* lamb), but this does not apply in the case of constructing the Sanctuary, since the six days of the week would suffice.

15. שַׁבַּת שַׁבָּתוֹן — *A Sabbath of complete rest.* *Rashi* comments on the phrase מְחַלְלֶיהָ (verse 14): "Whoever treats it as חול, *ordinary, secular,* insofar as its sanctity is concerned." This is the intent of the *Sforno* in his commentary on this verse as

טז כָּל־הָעֹשֶׂה מְלָאכָה בְּיוֹם הַשַּׁבָּת מוֹת יוּמָת: וְשָׁמְרוּ בְנֵי־יִשְׂרָאֵל
יז אֶת־הַשַּׁבָּת לַעֲשׂוֹת אֶת־הַשַּׁבָּת לְדֹרֹתָם בְּרִית עוֹלָם: בֵּינִי וּבֵין בְּנֵי
יִשְׂרָאֵל אוֹת הִוא לְעֹלָם כִּי־שֵׁשֶׁת יָמִים עָשָׂה יהוה אֶת־הַשָּׁמַיִם
שני יח וְאֶת־הָאָרֶץ וּבַיּוֹם הַשְּׁבִיעִי שָׁבַת וַיִּנָּפַשׁ: וַיִּתֵּן אֶל־מֹשֶׁה
כְּכַלֹּתוֹ לְדַבֵּר אִתּוֹ בְּהַר סִינַי שְׁנֵי לֻחֹת הָעֵדֻת לֻחֹת אֶבֶן כְּתֻבִים
לב א בְּאֶצְבַּע אֱלֹהִים: וַיַּרְא הָעָם כִּי־בֹשֵׁשׁ מֹשֶׁה לָרֶדֶת מִן־הָהָר וַיִּקָּהֵל הָעָם
עַל־אַהֲרֹן וַיֹּאמְרוּ אֵלָיו קוּם ׀ עֲשֵׂה־לָנוּ אֱלֹהִים אֲשֶׁר יֵלְכוּ לְפָנֵינוּ
כִּי־זֶה ׀ מֹשֶׁה הָאִישׁ אֲשֶׁר הֶעֱלָנוּ מֵאֶרֶץ מִצְרַיִם לֹא יָדַעְנוּ מֶה־הָיָה לוֹ:
ב וַיֹּאמֶר אֲלֵהֶם אַהֲרֹן פָּרְקוּ נִזְמֵי הַזָּהָב אֲשֶׁר בְּאָזְנֵי נְשֵׁיכֶם בְּנֵיכֶם
ג וּבְנֹתֵיכֶם וְהָבִיאוּ אֵלָי: וַיִּתְפָּרְקוּ כָּל־הָעָם אֶת־נִזְמֵי הַזָּהָב אֲשֶׁר
ד בְּאָזְנֵיהֶם וַיָּבִיאוּ אֶל־אַהֲרֹן: וַיִּקַּח מִיָּדָם וַיָּצַר אֹתוֹ בַּחֶרֶט וַיַּעֲשֵׂהוּ
עֵגֶל מַסֵּכָה וַיֹּאמְרוּ אֵלֶּה אֱלֹהֶיךָ יִשְׂרָאֵל אֲשֶׁר הֶעֱלוּךָ מֵאֶרֶץ מִצְרָיִם:

כָּל הָעֹשֶׂה מְלָאכָה . . . יוּמָת — *Whosoever does any work . . . shall be put to death.* Therefore the law is that he who nullifies this intent by doing work shall be put to death.

16. וְשָׁמְרוּ בְנֵי יִשְׂרָאֵל אֶת הַשַּׁבָּת — *The Children of Israel shall keep the Sabbath.* In this world (so as) to observe the Sabbath in the day which (will be) wholly Sabbath.

17. וּבַיּוֹם הַשְּׁבִיעִי שָׁבַת — *And the seventh day He ceased.* On it the work was complete and in completion there is tranquility.

וַיִּנָּפַשׁ — *And rested.* Therefore the seventh (day) became the "owner" of an additional soul, which is an added preparation to attain what God, the Blessed One, intended for him (man) regarding the completeness of this world when He said, "נַעֲשֶׂה אָדָם בְּצַלְמֵנוּ כִּדְמוּתֵנוּ, *Let us make man in Our image, after Our likeness*" (*Genesis* 1:26).

18. וַיִּתֵּן אֶל מֹשֶׁה כְּכַלֹּתוֹ — *And He gave to Moses, when He ended (speaking).* After relating to us the good which was attained each time at the conclusion of Moses' stay on the mountain forty days, (the Torah) explains the reason why the goal which God, the Blessed One, ordained when the Torah was given, when He said, "*And you shall be to Me a kingdom of priests and a holy people*" (19:6), (and also) when He said, "*An earthen altar make unto Me . . . in every place . . . I will come to you*" (20:21), was not realized. (Instead) they were constrained to make a Sanctuary. (Now) we are told that (all) this happened because of the evil choice (made) by Israel, for indeed after the first forty days the tablets (which were) the work of God were given to sanctify everyone (to be) priests

NOTES

well, but he links it to the expression שַׁבַּת שַׁבָּתוֹן, *A Sabbath of complete rest*, which is followed by, קֹדֶשׁ לַה׳, *holy to* HASHEM.

16. וְשָׁמְרוּ בְנֵי יִשְׂרָאֵל אֶת הַשַּׁבָּת – *The Children of Israel shall keep the Sabbath.* The *Sforno's* commentary explains the order and sequence of the verse. Israel is enjoined to keep the Sabbath, לַעֲשׂוֹת אֶת הַשַּׁבָּת, *so as to make the Sabbath;* seemingly this latter phrase being a reason for the former injunction. The explanation is that by keeping the Sabbath in this life they will merit to observe the "day" which is wholly Sabbath, namely in the world to come.

17. וּבַיּוֹם הַשְּׁבִיעִי שָׁבַת וַיִּנָּפַשׁ — *And the seventh day He ceased and rested.* There are two phrases in this verse which if translated literally are seemingly anthropomorphic, as ascribing human attributes to the Deity. They are שָׁבַת, *He ceased*, and וַיִּנָּפַשׁ, *He rested. Rashi* and other commentators attempt to interpret these phrases in a manner which would not attribute to God, Who created the world through His word and Who "neither faints nor grows weary," the need to rest or refresh Himself. The *Sforno* in his interpretation of this verse anticipates this problem and explains the verse thus: When God completed His work of

whoever does work on the Sabbath day shall be put to death.'
16 *"The Children of Israel shall observe the Sabbath, to make the Sabbath an eternal covenant for their generations.*
17 *Between Me and the Children of Israel it is a sign forever that in a six-day period* HASHEM *made heaven and earth, and on the seventh day He rested and was refreshed."*
18 *When He finished speaking to him on Mount Sinai, He gave Moses the two Tablets of Testimony, stone tablets inscribed by the finger of God.*

32
1 *The people saw that Moses had delayed in descending the mountain, and the people gathered around Aaron and said to him, "Rise up, make for us gods that will go before us, for this man Moses who brought us up from the land of Egypt — we do not know what became of him!"*
2 *Aaron said to them, "Remove the rings of gold that are in the ears of your wives, sons, and daughters, and bring them to me."*
3 *The entire people removed the gold rings that were in their ears, and brought them to Aaron.*
4 *He took it from their hands and bound it up in a cloth, and fashioned it into a molten calf. They said, "This is your god, O Israel, which brought you up from the land of Egypt."*

---

and a holy nation according to the good words He had spoken. (But) they rebelled and corrupted their ways and fell from their exalted level, as (the Torah) testifies, saying, וַיִּתְנַצְּלוּ בְנֵי יִשְׂרָאֵל אֶת עֶדְיָם מֵהַר חוֹרֵב, *And the Children of Israel stripped themselves of their ornaments (crowns) from Mount Horeb* (33:6).

שְׁנֵי לֻחֹת הָעֵדֻת — *Two tablets of the testimony.* Those which were designated when He said, *"And I will give you the tablets of stone"* (24:2), but before He gave (them) the Torah and commandments which He wrote as He (had) designated, they began the act of the (Golden) Calf, and (He) said to Moses, לֶךְ רֵד כִּי שִׁחֵת עַמְּךָ, *Get you down for your people have dealt corruptly* (32:7).

XXXII

4. אֵלֶּה אֱלֹהֶיךָ יִשְׂרָאֵל — *This is your god, O Israel.* These will be for you "gods" to whom you shall pray for all your needs, and you will worship (serve) them to attain your desires.

NOTES

creation it brought tranquility, for completion of any task brings with it a great sense of peace and serenity. This is the sense of the word שָׁבַת. (See the *Sforno* on 20:11.) As for the phrase וַיִּנָּפַשׁ, the *Sforno* explains it to mean that the Sabbath was given to expand man's soul (נֶפֶשׁ), and indeed to grant an added dimension to it (נֶפֶשׁ יְתֵרָה), so that he be better prepared to realize the purpose meant for him and to reach the goal of serving God by perfecting his Divine image and likeness. Hence the word וַיִּנָּפַשׁ pertains to the נֶפֶשׁ of man, not of God.

18. וַיִּתֵּן אֶל מֹשֶׁה כְּכַלֹּתוֹ — *And He gave to Moses, when He ended (speaking).* For the explanation of the *Sforno's* commentary on this verse see his commentary on 24:18 and the explanatory notes on that verse.

XXXII

4. אֵלֶּה אֱלֹהֶיךָ יִשְׂרָאֵל — *This is your god, O Israel.* The *Sforno* uses language mirroring phrases he used in 20:2 in his interpretation of the first commandment of God on Mount Sinai. Thus he underscores how diametrically opposed the Golden Calf episode is to that of the Revelation. There God commanded them to pray only to Him and worship only Him, while here the leaders of the mixed multitude urged Israel to worship the Golden Calf. Even if their intent was that the calf be an intermediary, this was in contradiction to the word אֱלֹהֶיךָ, *your God,* which the *Sforno* explains to mean 'without any need of an intermediary."

ה וַיַּרְא אַהֲרֹן וַיִּבֶן מִזְבֵּחַ לְפָנָיו וַיִּקְרָא אַהֲרֹן וַיֹּאמַר חַג לַיהוָה מָחָר:
ו וַיַּשְׁכִּימוּ מִמָּחֳרָת וַיַּעֲלוּ עֹלֹת וַיַּגִּשׁוּ שְׁלָמִים וַיֵּשֶׁב הָעָם לֶאֱכֹל וְשָׁתוֹ
וַיָּקֻמוּ לְצַחֵק:
ז וַיְדַבֵּר יְהוָה אֶל־מֹשֶׁה לֶךְ־רֵד כִּי שִׁחֵת עַמְּךָ אֲשֶׁר הֶעֱלֵיתָ מֵאֶרֶץ
ח מִצְרָיִם: סָרוּ מַהֵר מִן־הַדֶּרֶךְ אֲשֶׁר צִוִּיתִם עָשׂוּ לָהֶם עֵגֶל מַסֵּכָה
וַיִּשְׁתַּחֲווּ־לוֹ וַיִּזְבְּחוּ־לוֹ וַיֹּאמְרוּ אֵלֶּה אֱלֹהֶיךָ יִשְׂרָאֵל אֲשֶׁר הֶעֱלוּךָ
ט מֵאֶרֶץ מִצְרָיִם: וַיֹּאמֶר יְהוָה אֶל־מֹשֶׁה רָאִיתִי אֶת־הָעָם הַזֶּה וְהִנֵּה עַם־
י קְשֵׁה־עֹרֶף הוּא: וְעַתָּה הַנִּיחָה לִּי וְיִחַר־אַפִּי בָהֶם וַאֲכַלֵּם וְאֶעֱשֶׂה אוֹתְךָ
יא לְגוֹי גָּדוֹל: וַיְחַל מֹשֶׁה אֶת־פְּנֵי יְהוָה אֱלֹהָיו וַיֹּאמֶר לָמָה יְהוָה יֶחֱרֶה אַפְּךָ
יב בְּעַמֶּךָ אֲשֶׁר הוֹצֵאתָ מֵאֶרֶץ מִצְרַיִם בְּכֹחַ גָּדוֹל וּבְיָד חֲזָקָה: לָמָּה יֹאמְרוּ
מִצְרַיִם לֵאמֹר בְּרָעָה הוֹצִיאָם לַהֲרֹג אֹתָם בֶּהָרִים וּלְכַלֹּתָם מֵעַל פְּנֵי
יג הָאֲדָמָה שׁוּב מֵחֲרוֹן אַפֶּךָ וְהִנָּחֵם עַל־הָרָעָה לְעַמֶּךָ: זְכֹר לְאַבְרָהָם
לְיִצְחָק וּלְיִשְׂרָאֵל עֲבָדֶיךָ אֲשֶׁר נִשְׁבַּעְתָּ לָהֶם בָּךְ וַתְּדַבֵּר אֲלֵהֶם אַרְבֶּה
אֶת־זַרְעֲכֶם כְּכוֹכְבֵי הַשָּׁמָיִם וְכָל־הָאָרֶץ הַזֹּאת אֲשֶׁר אָמַרְתִּי אֶתֵּן
יד לְזַרְעֲכֶם וְנָחֲלוּ לְעֹלָם: וַיִּנָּחֶם יְהוָה עַל־הָרָעָה אֲשֶׁר דִּבֶּר לַעֲשׂוֹת לְעַמּוֹ:
טו וַיִּפֶן וַיֵּרֶד מֹשֶׁה מִן־הָהָר וּשְׁנֵי לֻחֹת הָעֵדֻת בְּיָדוֹ לֻחֹת כְּתֻבִים
טז מִשְּׁנֵי עֶבְרֵיהֶם מִזֶּה וּמִזֶּה הֵם כְּתֻבִים: וְהַלֻּחֹת מַעֲשֵׂה אֱלֹהִים הֵמָּה

5. חַג לַה׳ מָחָר — *Tomorrow shall be a feast to* Hashem. And do not mingle His happiness with another god.

8. סָרוּ מַהֵר — *They have turned aside quickly.* Before I completed giving you what I designated to give, namely, הַתּוֹרָה וְהַמִּצְוָה אֲשֶׁר כָּתַבְתִּי, *the Torah and the commandments which I have written* (24:12).

9. וְהִנֵּה עַם קְשֵׁה עֹרֶף הוּא — *And behold it is a stiff-necked people.* Their neck is (like) an iron sinew and they will not turn to listen to the words of any righteous teacher in any manner; (hence) there is no hope that they will repent.

11. לָמָה ה׳ יֶחֱרֶה אַפְּךָ בְּעַמֶּךָ — Hashem, *why are You so angry with Your people?* (This refers to) those that did not sin with the calf.

13. וְכָל הָאָרֶץ הַזֹּאת אֲשֶׁר אָמַרְתִּי אֶתֵּן לְזַרְעֲכֶם וְנָחֲלוּ — *And all this land that I have spoken of I will give to your seed and they shall inherit it.* (Moses spoke of) the fourth generation, as it says, וְדוֹר רְבִיעִי יָשׁוּבוּ הֵנָּה, *And in the fourth generation they shall come back here*

NOTES

5. חַג לַה׳ מָחָר — *Tomorrow shall be a feast to* Hashem. Just as Israel was enjoined from communicating with God through an intermediary, so were they forbidden to serve other gods *together* with Hashem (the second commandment — לֹא יִהְיֶה לְךָ). Aaron, hoping to avoid a confrontation while stalling for time, pleaded with the people to delay their service of the calf, appealing to them not to join their worship of the calf with that of *God's feast* which he declared for the morrow.

8. סָרוּ מַהֵר — *They have turned aside quickly.* The *Sforno* interprets the word מַהֵר, *quickly*, as meaning a hasty act which precluded God's implementation of His original plan. Since the Ten Commandments had already been inscribed, it can only refer to the Torah and *mitzvos* which had as yet not been written.

9. וְהִנֵּה עַם קְשֵׁה עֹרֶף הוּא — *And behold it is a stiff-necked people.* As the *Sforno* says later (verse 30), in knowledge (recognition) of one's sins lies the beginning of repentance. Conversely, if one refuses to listen to admonition and is blind to his shortcomings, there is scant chance that he will

5 *Aaron saw and built an altar before him. Aaron called out and said, "A*
festival for HASHEM *tomorrow!"*
6 *They arose early the next day and offered up elevation-offerings and*
brought peace-offerings. The people sat to eat and drink, and they got up to
revel.
7 HASHEM *spoke to Moses: "Go, descend — for your people that you*
brought up from Egypt has become corrupt. 8 *They have strayed quickly*
from the way that I have commanded them. They have made themselves a
molten calf, prostrated themselves to it and sacrificed to it, and they said,
'This is your god, O Israel, which brought you up from the land of Egypt.'
" 9 HASHEM *said to Moses, "I have seen this people, and behold! it is a*
stiff-necked people. 10 *And now, desist from Me. Let My anger flare up*
against them and I shall annihilate them; and I shall make you a great
nation."
11 *Moses pleaded before* HASHEM, *his God, and said, "Why,* HASHEM,
should Your anger flare up against Your people, whom You have taken out
of the land of Egypt, with great power and a strong hand? 12 *Why should*
Egypt say the following: 'With evil intent did He take them out, to kill them
in the mountains and to annihilate them from the face of the earth'?
Relent from Your flaring anger and reconsider regarding the evil against
Your people. 13 *Remember for the sake of Abraham, Isaac, and Israel, Your*
servants, to whom You swore by Yourself, and You told them, 'I shall
increase your offspring like the stars of heaven, and this entire land of
which I spoke, I shall give to your offspring and it shall be their heritage
forever.' "
14 HASHEM *reconsidered regarding the evil that He declared He would do*
to His people.
15 *Moses turned and descended from the mountain, with the two Tablets*
of the Testimony in his hand, Tablets inscribed on both their sides; they were
inscribed on one side and the other. 16 *The Tablets were God's handiwork,*

(*Genesis* 15:16). (He said, "This promise was to include all of Israel) but it will now not be fulfilled except through my seed alone."

15. וּשְׁנֵי לֻחֹת הָעֵדֻת בְּיָדוֹ — *With the two tablets of the testimony in his hand.* For he thought that when he returned to them they would repent; and if not, he would break them (the tablets) in their sight that *their eyes might fail* (based on *Lamentations* 4:17 and *Psalms* 69:4) so that they would repent.

NOTES

repent. This is the meaning of the *Sforno's* interpretation of a *stiff-necked people.*

11. לָמָה ה׳ יֶחֱרֶה אַפְּךָ בְּעַמֶּךָ — HASHEM, *why are You so angry with Your people?* This interpretation is called for, else Moses' question is without merit. The Children of Israel have sinned in a grievous manner, and God is understandably angry; why then this question? The answer is that Moses is referring to the many who did not transgress. Moses himself eventually grasped the answer, as we see in verse 25, when he realized that although they did not actively sin, nonetheless they were guilty of apathy and they failed to protest against, and oppose, the actions of the sinners.

15. וּשְׁנֵי לֻחֹת הָעֵדֻת בְּיָדוֹ — *With the two tablets of the testimony in his hand.* The *Sforno* explains the reason for bringing down the tablets. Since Israel had sinned and were not worthy to receive them, why not leave them in heaven? The answer is that if they repent *at once* he will give the tablets to them, and if not, the shattering of the tablets will hopefully shock them into repentance.

יז וְהַ֨מִּכְתָּ֔ב מִכְתַּ֥ב אֱלֹהִ֖ים ה֑וּא חָר֥וּת עַל־הַלֻּחֹֽת: וַיִּשְׁמַ֧ע יְהוֹשֻׁ֛עַ אֶת־ק֥וֹל

יח הָעָ֖ם בְּרֵעֹ֑ה וַיֹּ֨אמֶר֙ אֶל־מֹשֶׁ֔ה ק֥וֹל מִלְחָמָ֖ה בַּֽמַּחֲנֶֽה: וַיֹּ֗אמֶר אֵ֥ין קוֹל֙

יט עֲנ֣וֹת גְּבוּרָ֔ה וְאֵ֥ין ק֖וֹל עֲנ֣וֹת חֲלוּשָׁ֑ה ק֣וֹל עַנּ֔וֹת אָנֹכִ֖י שֹׁמֵֽעַ: וַֽיְהִ֗י כַּֽאֲשֶׁ֤ר

קָרַב֙ אֶל־הַֽמַּחֲנֶ֔ה וַיַּ֥רְא אֶת־הָעֵ֖גֶל וּמְחֹלֹ֑ת וַיִּֽחַר־אַ֣ף מֹשֶׁ֗ה וַיַּשְׁלֵ֤ךְ מִיָּדָו֙

כ אֶת־הַלֻּחֹ֔ת וַיְשַׁבֵּ֥ר אֹתָ֖ם תַּ֥חַת הָהָֽר: וַיִּקַּ֞ח אֶת־הָעֵ֣גֶל אֲשֶׁ֣ר עָשׂ֗וּ וַיִּשְׂרֹ֤ף

בָּאֵשׁ֙ וַיִּטְחַ֣ן עַ֣ד אֲשֶׁר־דָּ֔ק וַיִּ֙זֶר֙ עַל־פְּנֵ֣י הַמַּ֔יִם וַיַּ֖שְׁקְ אֶת־בְּנֵ֥י יִשְׂרָאֵֽל:

כא וַיֹּ֤אמֶר מֹשֶׁה֙ אֶֽל־אַהֲרֹ֔ן מֶֽה־עָשָׂ֥ה לְךָ֖ הָעָ֣ם הַזֶּ֑ה כִּֽי־הֵבֵ֥אתָ עָלָ֖יו חֲטָאָ֥ה

כב גְדֹלָֽה: וַיֹּ֣אמֶר אַהֲרֹ֔ן אַל־יִ֥חַר אַ֖ף אֲדֹנִ֑י אַתָּה֙ יָדַ֣עְתָּ אֶת־הָעָ֔ם כִּ֥י בְרָ֖ע

כג הֽוּא: וַיֹּ֣אמְרוּ לִ֔י עֲשֵׂה־לָ֣נוּ אֱלֹהִ֔ים אֲשֶׁ֥ר יֵֽלְכ֖וּ לְפָנֵ֑ינוּ כִּי־זֶ֣ה | מֹשֶׁ֣ה

כד הָאִ֗ישׁ אֲשֶׁ֤ר הֶֽעֱלָ֨נוּ֙ מֵאֶ֣רֶץ מִצְרַ֔יִם לֹ֥א יָדַ֖עְנוּ מֶה־הָ֥יָה לֽוֹ: וָֽאֹמַ֤ר לָהֶם֙

לְמִ֣י זָהָ֔ב הִתְפָּרָ֖קוּ וַיִּתְּנוּ־לִ֑י וָֽאַשְׁלִכֵ֣הוּ בָאֵ֔שׁ וַיֵּצֵ֖א הָעֵ֥גֶל הַזֶּֽה:

כה וַיַּ֤רְא מֹשֶׁה֙ אֶת־הָעָ֔ם כִּ֥י פָרֻ֖עַ ה֑וּא כִּֽי־פְרָעֹ֣ה אַהֲרֹ֔ן לְשִׁמְצָ֖ה בְּקָֽמֵיהֶֽם:

---

19. וַיַּרְא אֶת־הָעֵגֶל וּמְחֹלֹת וַיִּחַר אַף מֹשֶׁה — *And he saw the calf and the dancing, and Moses'
anger was kindled.* When he saw that they were happy in their disgrace, similar to, כִּי
רָעָתֵכִי אָז תַּעֲלֹזִי, *When you do evil then you rejoice (Jeremiah* 11:15), this angered him and
he despaired that he would be able to repair the crooked in a manner that they would
return to their perfection and be worthy (to receive) those tablets.

21. כִּי הֵבֵאתָ עָלָיו חֲטָאָה גְדֹלָה — *That you have brought a great sin upon them.* They
rejoiced in their disgrace with dance because you fixed a feast for them on the morrow,
and that is more evil than the transgression and rebellion in making the calf; for this he
had to ask mercy even more so (than he did on the mountain — verses 11-13), as it says,
אַתֶּם חֲטָאתֶם חֲטָאָה גְדֹלָה, *You have sinned a great sin* (verse 30), and also in his prayer he
said, "אָנָּא חָטָא הָעָם הַזֶּה חֲטָאָה גְדֹלָה, *This people has sinned a great sin"* (v. 31). Also in
the order of the thirteen attributes he mentions *iniquity, transgression and sin* (34:7), and
also in his prayer there, וְסָלַחְתָּ לַעֲוֹנֵנוּ וּלְחַטָּאתֵנוּ, *and pardon our iniquity and our sin* (ibid.
9). Therefore he said (to Aaron), "Although they gathered against you and compelled you
to make the calf for them, what did they do to you that you (felt it) necessary to fix a feast
for them on the morrow? For that was the cause of the dancing which they (did do) to
rejoice with the calf — (and this) was worse than the making of it!"

22. כִּי בְרָע הוּא — *That they are set on evil.* They were already inclined to evil, (for they
were) attached (joined) to the idolatry of Egypt.

24. וָאֹמַר לָהֶם לְמִי זָהָב — *And I said to them, "Who has gold?"* I diverted (lit., "placed")
them to the infeasible, for there was no ready gold (at hand).

NOTES

19. וַיַּרְא אֶת־הָעֵגֶל וּמְחֹלֹת וַיִּחַר אַף מֹשֶׁה — *And he
saw the calf and the dancing, and Moses' anger
was kindled.* One may excuse man for transgressing by rationalizing that he did so in a moment of
weakness or passion. However when that is the
case, the sinner is contrite after he has sinned. To
rejoice, however, is an indication that he is happy
in his deviate act; hence there is little hope that he
will repent. When Moses saw the dancing he
despaired of their eventual penitence and therefore he broke the tablets, for they were not worthy
to receive them.

21. כִּי הֵבֵאתָ עָלָיו חֲטָאָה גְדֹלָה — *That you have
brought a great sin upon them.* Extending his
interpretation on verse 19, regarding the happiness demonstrated by the sinners in their new god,
the *Sforno* explains that this was the thrust of
Moses' admonition of his brother. Moses felt that
the declaration by Aaron of a *feast to God on the
morrow* sanctioned the making of the calf, thereby
precipitating their celebration. It is this rejoicing
with idolatry which is called *a great sin*, more
serious than the actual making of the calf. In his
commentary on 34:7 the *Sforno* explains the word

and the script was the script of God, engraved on the Tablets.
17 *Joshua heard the sound of the people in its shouting, and he said to Moses, "The sound of battle is in the camp!"*
18 *He said, "Not a sound shouting strength nor a sound shouting weakness; a sound of distress do I hear!"*
19 *It happened as he drew near the camp and saw the calf and the dances, that Moses' anger flared up. He threw down the Tablets from his hands and shattered them at the foot of the mountain.*
20 *He took the calf that they had made and burned it in fire. He ground it to a fine powder and sprinkled it over the water. He made the Children of Israel drink.*
21 *Moses said to Aaron, "What did this people do to you that you brought a grievous sin upon it?"*
22 *Aaron said, "Let not my master's anger flare up. You know that the people is disposed toward evil.*
23 *They said to me, 'Make us a god that will go before us, for this man Moses who brought us up from the land of Egypt — we do not know what became of him.'*
24 *So I said to them, 'Who has gold?' They removed it and gave it to me. I threw it into the fire, and this calf emerged."*
25 *Moses saw the people, that it was exposed, for Aaron had exposed them to disgrace among those who rise up against them.*

הִתְפָּרָקוּ וַיִּתְּנוּ לִי — *They removed it and gave it to me.* And they contributed the gold quickly.

וָאַשְׁלִכֵהוּ בָאֵשׁ — *And I cast it into the fire.* I attempted to delay the matter, so I threw the gold into the fire without using any of the goldsmith's devices necessary to melt (and refine) the gold.

וַיֵּצֵא הָעֵגֶל הַזֶּה — *And there came out this calf.* Without my (overt) act, and they did not wait for me to do as they had said (requested); for indeed when it says, וַיַּעֲשֵׂהוּ עֵגֶל מַסֵּכָה, *And make it into a molten calf* (v. 4), it does not refer to Aaron but it means whosoever did make it, similar to, וְסָמַךְ אֶת יָדוֹ . . . וְשָׁחַט, *and he shall lay his hand . . . and he shall slaughter (Leviticus* 3:8) which means: *He who brings the offering shall lay, etc., the one who slaughters shall kill, etc.* and so (the Torah) attests, saying, אֲשֶׁר עָשׂוּ אֶת הָעֵגֶל אֲשֶׁר עָשָׂה אַהֲרֹן, *Who made the calf which Aaron made* (v. 35), i.e., they made the calf from which Aaron had done his work; the fashioning and casting the gold into the fire.

25. כִּי פָרֻעַ הוּא — *That they were uncovered.* The inclination (lit., "heart") of the (people) to evil was revealed and made known through this (i.e., the calf).

כִּי פְרָעֹה אַהֲרֹן — *For Aaron had uncovered them.* He had revealed that there were no righteous men among them, for if there had been righteous ones there to help Aaron when (the people) gathered against him, Aaron would not have made the calf at all.

NOTES

חֲטָאָה, *sin,* as meaning "additional angering (of God)" which is engendered by rejoicing in one's transgression and iniquity.

24. וָאַשְׁלִכֵהוּ בָאֵשׁ — *And I cast it into the fire.* Aaron attempted to mitigate his involvement in the making of the calf. In verse 4 the Torah tells us that Aaron did *fashion the gold with a graving tool* and cast it into the fire. However, the Torah does not tell us specifically who the subject is of *and made it into a molten calf,* the word וַיַּעֲשֵׂהוּ being indefinite. The *Sforno* feels that verse 35 casts some light on the identity of those who actually made the Golden Calf; they were men *other* than Aaron who did so with the consent of the people, as he states in his interpretation of that verse.

25. כִּי פְרָעֹה אַהֲרֹן — *For Aaron had uncovered them.* As *Rashi* points out the word פָּרֻעַ means to *uncover* (as we find by the *sotah* whose hair is uncovered). However, whereas *Rashi* explains it to mean that the people's shame and disgrace were

כו וַיַּעֲמֹד מֹשֶׁה בְּשַׁעַר הַמַּחֲנֶה וַיֹּאמֶר מִי לַיהוָה אֵלָי וַיֵּאָסְפוּ אֵלָיו כָּל־בְּנֵי
כז לֵוִי: וַיֹּאמֶר לָהֶם כֹּה־אָמַר יהוה אֱלֹהֵי יִשְׂרָאֵל שִׂימוּ אִישׁ־חַרְבּוֹ
עַל־יְרֵכוֹ עִבְרוּ וָשׁוּבוּ מִשַּׁעַר לָשַׁעַר בַּמַּחֲנֶה וְהִרְגוּ אִישׁ־אֶת־אָחִיו
כח וְאִישׁ אֶת־רֵעֵהוּ וְאִישׁ אֶת־קְרֹבוֹ: וַיַּעֲשׂוּ בְנֵי־לֵוִי כִּדְבַר מֹשֶׁה וַיִּפֹּל
כט מִן־הָעָם בַּיּוֹם הַהוּא כִּשְׁלֹשֶׁת אַלְפֵי אִישׁ: וַיֹּאמֶר מֹשֶׁה מִלְאוּ
יֶדְכֶם הַיּוֹם לַיהוָה כִּי אִישׁ בִּבְנוֹ וּבְאָחִיו וְלָתֵת עֲלֵיכֶם הַיּוֹם בְּרָכָה:
ל וַיְהִי מִמָּחֳרָת וַיֹּאמֶר מֹשֶׁה אֶל־הָעָם אַתֶּם חֲטָאתֶם חֲטָאָה גְדֹלָה
לא וְעַתָּה אֶעֱלֶה אֶל־יהוה אוּלַי אֲכַפְּרָה בְּעַד חַטַּאתְכֶם: וַיָּשָׁב מֹשֶׁה
אֶל־יהוה וַיֹּאמַר *אָנָּא חָטָא הָעָם הַזֶּה חֲטָאָה גְדֹלָה וַיַּעֲשׂוּ לָהֶם אֱלֹהֵי
לב זָהָב: וְעַתָּה אִם־תִּשָּׂא חַטָּאתָם וְאִם־אַיִן מְחֵנִי נָא מִסִּפְרְךָ אֲשֶׁר
לג כָּתָבְתָּ: וַיֹּאמֶר יהוה אֶל־מֹשֶׁה מִי אֲשֶׁר חָטָא־לִי אֶמְחֶנּוּ מִסִּפְרִי:

לְשִׁמְצָה בְּקָמֵיהֶם — *For a derision among their adversaries.* (They will now be) an ignominy among their enemies, who will (now) say of them that they are not loyal to their covenant and there is not even one among them who does good; nor did they show favor to a prophet or leader in their midst. This (will be said) for although not all, or even the majority of them, rose up against Aaron still they will all be derided because they did not protest against those who did.

27. עִבְרוּ וָשׁוּבוּ מִשַּׁעַר לָשַׁעַר — *Go to and fro from gate to gate.* This will atone for the non-sinners who did not protest against (and prevent) those who did sin. This (atonement shall be) since just as they did not protest against the sinners, so they will (now) not protest against (or prevent) those who kill them!

29. מִלְאוּ יֶדְכֶם הַיּוֹם לַה׳ — *Consecrate* (lit., *fill*) *your hands today to* HASHEM. Attain perfection (completeness) for your hands today that they be prepared to serve Him in His holy House (Temple).

כִּי אִישׁ בִּבְנוֹ — *For every man "through" his son.* For each one of you already became holy to God through his son by circumcising (him) in the wilderness!

וּבְאָחִיו — *And against his brothers* . . . by killing (him) today and thereby *consecrate your hands* by proper (good) intent and complete your preparation in the service of God.

וְלָתֵת עֲלֵיכֶם הַיּוֹם בְּרָכָה — *That He may also bestow upon you a blessing today.* And also

NOTES

revealed, the *Sforno* explains it as revealing that there were no righteous men among Israel prepared to rise to Aaron's defense. This lack of support for Aaron would be derided by the enemies of Israel.

27. עִבְרוּ וָשׁוּבוּ מִשַּׁעַר לָשַׁעַר — *Go to and fro from gate to gate.* To counteract the sin of apathy and the failure to protest the evil action of a large number of their brethren, it was necessary to balance that inaction with a willingness to support the Levites' punishment of the sinners, if only by not interfering with them. That is why this punishment had to be carried out publicly and openly — not stealthily. Hence they were told to *go to and fro from gate to gate.* The phrase *gate* in the Torah implies *in the open.*

29. מִלְאוּ יֶדְכֶם הַיּוֹם לַה׳ — *Consecrate* (lit., *fill your hands*) *yourselves today to* HASHEM. The expression מִלְאוּ יֶדְכֶם means to prepare one's self to fulfill a certain charge, to devote one's energies and talents to some purpose. This same expression was used above (28:41) regarding the consecration of the priests. Here it is used for the Levites who through their willingness to avenge the honor of *Hashem* will also become consecrated to God's service — replacing the firstborn who had heretofore been entrusted with that responsibility. By responding to Moses' call of *Whosoever is on* HASHEM*'s side let him come to me* (v. 26), the tribe of Levi prepared themselves for the service of *Hashem* and were blessed by Him. The verses from *Deut.* 33:9-11 refer to the episode related here.

26 *Moses stood at the gateway of the camp, and said, "Whoever is for*
HASHEM, join me!" — and all the Levites gathered around him. 27 *He said to*
them, "So said HASHEM the God of Israel, 'Every man, put his sword on his
thigh and pass back and forth from gate to gate in the camp. Let every man
kill his brother, every man his fellow, and every man his near one.' "
28 *The Levites did as Moses said, and about three thousand men of the*
people fell that day. 29 *Moses said, "Dedicate yourselves this day to HASHEM*
— for each has opposed his son and his brother — that He may bestow upon
you a blessing, this day."
30 *On the next day, Moses said to the people, "You have committed a*
grievous sin! And now I shall ascend to HASHEM — perhaps I can win
atonement in the face of your sin." 31 *Moses returned to HASHEM and said, "I*
implore! This people has committed a grievous sin and made themselves a
god of gold. 32 *And now if You would but forgive their sin! — but if not, erase*
me now from Your book that You have written."
33 *HASHEM said to Moses, "Whoever has sinned against Me, I shall erase*

---

consecrate your hands in a manner that *Hashem*, the Blessed One, give you *a blessing today* by making as your aim the keeping of His judgment and covenant, as it says, כִּי שָׁמְרוּ אִמְרָתֶךָ וּבְרִיתְךָ יִנְצֹרוּ, יוֹרוּ מִשְׁפָּטֶיךָ . . . בָּרֵךְ ה׳ חֵילוֹ וּפֹעַל יָדָיו תִּרְצֶה, *For they have observed Your word and keep Your covenant. They shall teach Your ordinances . . . Bless, HASHEM, his substance and accept the work of his hands* (*Deut.* 33:9-11).

30. אַתֶּם חֲטָאתֶם חֲטָאָה גְדֹלָה — *You have sinned a great sin.* Recognize the greatness of your sin for indeed through such knowledge there will doubtless be repentance, as it says, כִּי פְשָׁעַי אֲנִי אֵדָע, *for I acknowledge my transgressions* (*Psalms* 51:5), and as it says, אַךְ דְּעִי עֲוֹנֵךְ, *only acknowledge your iniquity* (*Jeremiah* 3:13).

32. אִם תִּשָּׂא חַטָּאתָם וְאִם אַיִן מְחֵנִי נָא מִסִּפְרְךָ — *If You will forgive their sin — and if not blot me, I pray You, out of Your book.* Whether You agree to forgive their sins or You do not agree to forgive, blot out my merits from Your book and add it to their account so that they will merit forgiveness.

33. מִי אֲשֶׁר חָטָא לִי אֶמְחֶנּוּ מִסִּפְרִי — *Whosoever has sinned against Me, him will I blot out of My book.* Who is there that sinned against Me, that I should erase his merits from My book so that he shall merit forgiveness for sins — this never ever happened! For the law before Me (Divine judgment) is the reverse; indeed each one must bear punishment for his iniquity, and will receive reward for his merits, for אֵין מִצְוָה מְכַבָּה עֲבֵירָה, *a mitzvah cannot*

NOTES

See the *Sforno* 28:41.

כִּי אִישׁ בִּבְנוֹ — *For every man "through" his son.* When the command is given in verse 27 to *slay every man his brother* it is interpreted to mean a half-brother who is from the same mother but a different father; hence, a non-Levite since *all* the sons of Levi were loyal to God. However, the phrase אִישׁ בִּבְנוֹ, *every man his son*, is most difficult to comprehend, for is not his son also a Levite? The *Sforno* answers this question in a most original manner. This is not to be understood as being part of the order to slay, but refers to the fact that the tribe of Levi had already established their credentials of sanctity, self-sacrifice and loyalty to God, since they were the only tribe that circumcised their sons in the wilderness. The sense of this phrase is: Because each man had circumcised his son he is worthy to be chosen to serve God, be it to exterminate the wicked or to serve Him in the Temple.

32-33. אִם תִּשָּׂא חַטָּאתָם וְאִם אַיִן מְחֵנִי נָא מִסִּפְרְךָ . . . מִי אֲשֶׁר חָטָא לִי אֶמְחֶנּוּ מִסִּפְרִי — *If You will forgive their sin — and if not blot me, I pray You, out of Your book . . . Whosoever has sinned against Me, him will I blot out of My book.* Moses did not ask God to erase him from His book if Israel is not forgiven. Rather he suggested that his merits be *transferred* to the credit of Israel in the hope that

לד וְעַתָּה לֵךְ ׀ נְחֵה אֶת־הָעָם אֶל אֲשֶׁר־דִּבַּרְתִּי לָךְ הִנֵּה מַלְאָכִי יֵלֵךְ לְפָנֶיךָ
לה וּבְיוֹם פָּקְדִי וּפָקַדְתִּי עֲלֵהֶם חַטָּאתָם: וַיִּגֹּף יהוה אֶת־הָעָם עַל אֲשֶׁר עָשׂוּ
לג א אֶת־הָעֵגֶל אֲשֶׁר עָשָׂה אַהֲרֹן: וַיְדַבֵּר יהוה אֶל־מֹשֶׁה
לֵךְ עֲלֵה מִזֶּה אַתָּה וְהָעָם אֲשֶׁר הֶעֱלִיתָ מֵאֶרֶץ מִצְרָיִם אֶל־הָאָרֶץ אֲשֶׁר
ב נִשְׁבַּעְתִּי לְאַבְרָהָם לְיִצְחָק וּלְיַעֲקֹב לֵאמֹר לְזַרְעֲךָ אֶתְּנֶנָּה: וְשָׁלַחְתִּי
לְפָנֶיךָ מַלְאָךְ וְגֵרַשְׁתִּי אֶת־הַכְּנַעֲנִי הָאֱמֹרִי וְהַחִתִּי וְהַפְּרִזִּי הַחִוִּי
ג וְהַיְבוּסִי: אֶל־אֶרֶץ זָבַת חָלָב וּדְבָשׁ כִּי לֹא אֶעֱלֶה בְּקִרְבְּךָ כִּי עַם־
ד קְשֵׁה־עֹרֶף אַתָּה פֶּן־אֲכֶלְךָ בַּדָּרֶךְ: וַיִּשְׁמַע הָעָם אֶת־הַדָּבָר הָרָע הַזֶּה
ה וַיִּתְאַבָּלוּ וְלֹא־שָׁתוּ אִישׁ עֶדְיוֹ עָלָיו: וַיֹּאמֶר יהוה אֶל־מֹשֶׁה אֱמֹר אֶל־
בְּנֵי־יִשְׂרָאֵל אַתֶּם עַם־קְשֵׁה־עֹרֶף רֶגַע אֶחָד אֶעֱלֶה בְקִרְבְּךָ וְכִלִּיתִיךָ

---

extinguish a transgression (*Sotah* 21a); how much more so will I not add *your* merits to *their* account!

34. אֶל אֲשֶׁר דִּבַּרְתִּי לָךְ — *To (the place) of which I have spoken to you.* When I said: אַעֲלֶה אֶתְכֶם מֵעֳנִי מִצְרַיִם, *I will bring you up out of the affliction of Egypt* (3:17), אֶל אֶרֶץ טוֹבָה, *unto a good land* (3:8).

וּבְיוֹם פָּקְדִי — *In the day when I visit* . . . when they will continue to sin, as (for example) the sin of the spies.

וּפָקַדְתִּי עֲלֵהֶם חַטָּאתָם — *I will visit their sin upon them* . . . this sin — and I will no longer continue to forgive it, similar to, וְאִם רָעָה תִמָּצֵא בוֹ וָמֵת, *but if wickedness shall be found in him, he shall die (I Kings* 1:52). And so He indicated when He said there (the episode of the spies), עַד אָנָה יְנַאֲצֻנִי הָעָם הַזֶּה, *How long will this people despise Me? (Numbers* 14:11); for after they have persisted in their foolishness they are certain to continue their guilty ways, as our Sages state, "When a man transgresses and repeats his offense it becomes (as if it were) permitted to him" (*Yoma* 86b).

35. עַל אֲשֶׁר עָשׂוּ אֶת הָעֵגֶל אֲשֶׁר עָשָׂה אַהֲרֹן — *Because they made the calf which Aaron made.* With their consent, the one who made the molten calf brought it forth into actuality (from) that object which Aaron had made when he fashioned it and threw it in the fire, as he (Aaron) attested, saying, "וַיֵּצֵא הָעֵגֶל הַזֶּה, *and there came out this calf*" (v. 24).

NOTES

this would tilt the scales in their favor and they would be forgiven. God answered that when a person is judged from on High he cannot cancel out his transgressions with his merits (*mitzvos*) but each side of his ledger is independent of the other, i.e., he is rewarded for his *mitzvos* and punished for his sins; how much more so is this true of one person's merits (Moses') and another's sins (Israel's).

34. וּפָקַדְתִּי עֲלֵהֶם חַטָּאתָם — *I will visit their sin upon them.* Our Sages interpret this verse as meaning that "no punishment comes upon Israel in which there is not a part of payment for the sin of the Golden Calf" (*Sanhedrin* 102a). The *Sforno* however interprets the verse thus: Whenever they will sin against Me in a similar vein, i.e., questioning God or the credibility of Moses such as we find in the incident of the spies (*Numbers* 14), I will have to conclude that they will continue to do so on and on. Therefore I will be constrained to punish them at that time for this sin as well. Indeed at that time God decreed that they would not enter the Land of Israel, a punishment not only for the episode of the spies but for the sin of the calf as well.

XXXIII

2. וְשָׁלַחְתִּי לְפָנֶיךָ מַלְאָךְ — *And I will send an angel before you.* The *Sforno* in his commentary on verses 12 and 16 states that the mission of this angel began with the entrance of Israel into the Land. His role was a military one for the purpose of expelling the seven nations from Canaan. Therefore the *Sforno* identifies this angel as the *captain of the host of* HASHEM who appeared to Joshua as Israel began the conquest of the Land.

3. כִּי לֹא אֶעֱלֶה בְּקִרְבְּךָ פֶּן אֲכֶלְךָ בַּדָּרֶךְ — *For I will not go up in your midst lest I consume you on the way.*

from My book. 34 *Now, go and lead the people to where I have told you.*
Behold! My angel shall go before you, and on the day that I make My account,
I shall bring their sin to account against them."
35 *Then* HASHEM *struck the people with a plague, because they had made*
the calf that Aaron had made.

33 1 *HASHEM spoke to Moses, "Go, ascend from here, you and the people whom*
you brought up from the land of Egypt, to the land about which I swore
to Abraham, Isaac, and Jacob, saying, 'I shall give it to your offspring.' 2 *I shall*
send an angel ahead of you, and I shall drive out the Canaanite, the Amorite,
the Hittite, the Perizzite, the Hivvite, and the Jebusite — 3 *to a land that flows*
with milk and honey, because I shall not ascend among you, for you are a
stiff-necked people, lest I annihilate you on the way."
4 *The people heard this bad tiding and they became grief-stricken, and no*
one donned his jewelry.
5 HASHEM *said to Moses, "Say to the Children of Israel, 'You are a stiff-*
necked people. If I ascend among you, I may annihilate you in an instant.

XXXIII

2. וְשָׁלַחְתִּי לְפָנֶיךָ מַלְאָךְ — *And I will send an angel before you.* The *captain of the host of* HASHEM who appeared to Joshua (*Joshua* 5:14).

3. אֶל אֶרֶץ זָבַת חָלָב וּדְבָשׁ — *To a land flowing with milk and honey.* Go up from this place which is dry and desolate and (hence) you are dependent upon miracles for your sustenance of which you are unworthy, and go to a land flowing with milk and honey where you can sustain (yourselves) without (need) for miracles.

כִּי לֹא אֶעֱלֶה בְּקִרְבְּךָ — *For I will not go up in your midst.* Therefore I say, *Go up from here, you and the people* (v. 1) and do not wait to camp or journey according to *Hashem's* word (command).

פֶּן אֲכֶלְךָ בַּדָּרֶךְ — *Lest I consume you on the way.* Because when I dwell in your midst the punishment for your iniquities is far greater.

5. רֶגַע אֶחָד אֶעֱלֶה בְקִרְבְּךָ וְכִלִּיתִיךָ — *If I go up into your midst for one moment I shall consume you.* You mourn My saying, "*I will not go up in your midst,*' but that is for your good, for if I were to go up in your midst, I would consume you, since you are "a stiff-necked people" that does not attend (lit., "turn") to the voice of teachers, even though you *are* prepared (to reach) perfection, with the spiritual preparation you attained standing at Mount Sinai.

NOTES

Not only the existence of Israel, but their itinerary in the wilderness was totally in the hands of God. Their food and water were provided by Him miraculously and their travel schedule was determined by God. *At the commandment of* HASHEM *the Children of Israel journeyed and at the commandment of* HASHEM *they encamped (Numbers* 9:18). This intimate relationship of God with Israel in the wilderness, though beneficial, was also fraught with a certain danger. When the Almighty is constantly present and directly involved, any transgression becomes magnified and the people are more vulnerable to God's wrath. Hence God told Moses that as a result of the sin of the Golden Calf, He would remove Himself from their midst for they were no longer worthy to be sustained miraculously by God nor to have their movements directed by Him. Although this is meant as retribution for their transgression it also is for their own benefit, since their vulnerability to God's anger would now be lessened and they would also go to the Land of Israel where they would live a normal, natural life, earning their own livelihood and determining their own destiny. This was God's intent at this point, but the sin of the spies prolonged their wandering in the wilderness for many more years.

ו וְעַתָּה הוֹרֵד עֶדְיְךָ מֵעָלֶיךָ וְאֵדְעָה מָה אֶעֱשֶׂה־לָּךְ: וַיִּתְנַצְּלוּ בְנֵי־יִשְׂרָאֵל
ז אֶת־עֶדְיָם מֵהַר חוֹרֵב: וּמֹשֶׁה יִקַּח אֶת־הָאֹהֶל וְנָטָה־לוֹ ׀ מִחוּץ לַמַּחֲנֶה
הַרְחֵק מִן־הַמַּחֲנֶה וְקָרָא לוֹ אֹהֶל מוֹעֵד וְהָיָה כָּל־מְבַקֵּשׁ יהוה יֵצֵא
ח אֶל־אֹהֶל מוֹעֵד אֲשֶׁר מִחוּץ לַמַּחֲנֶה: וְהָיָה כְּצֵאת מֹשֶׁה אֶל־הָאֹהֶל
יָקוּמוּ כָּל־הָעָם וְנִצְּבוּ אִישׁ פֶּתַח אָהֳלוֹ וְהִבִּיטוּ אַחֲרֵי מֹשֶׁה עַד־בֹּאוֹ
ט הָאֹהֱלָה: וְהָיָה כְּבֹא מֹשֶׁה הָאֹהֱלָה יֵרֵד עַמּוּד הֶעָנָן וְעָמַד פֶּתַח הָאֹהֶל
י וְדִבֶּר עִם־מֹשֶׁה: וְרָאָה כָל־הָעָם אֶת־עַמּוּד הֶעָנָן עֹמֵד פֶּתַח הָאֹהֶל וְקָם
יא כָּל־הָעָם וְהִשְׁתַּחֲווּ אִישׁ פֶּתַח אָהֳלוֹ: וְדִבֶּר יהוה אֶל־מֹשֶׁה פָּנִים
אֶל־פָּנִים כַּאֲשֶׁר יְדַבֵּר אִישׁ אֶל־רֵעֵהוּ וְשָׁב אֶל־הַמַּחֲנֶה וּמְשָׁרְתוֹ
יְהוֹשֻׁעַ בִּן־נוּן נַעַר לֹא יָמִישׁ מִתּוֹךְ הָאֹהֶל:
שלישי יב וַיֹּאמֶר מֹשֶׁה אֶל־יהוה רְאֵה אַתָּה אֹמֵר אֵלַי הַעַל אֶת־הָעָם הַזֶּה וְאַתָּה
לֹא הוֹדַעְתַּנִי אֵת אֲשֶׁר־תִּשְׁלַח עִמִּי וְאַתָּה אָמַרְתָּ יְדַעְתִּיךָ בְשֵׁם וְגַם־

וְעַתָּה הוֹרֵד עֶדְיְךָ מֵעָלֶיךָ — *Now take off your ornaments from yourself* ... i.e., that spiritual preparation given to you at that honored (glorious) station (i.e., when you received the Torah), remove it from yourselves, for God, the Blessed One, once He has given a gift, will not recall it from the recipient without his acquiescence, as our Sages say, "We have learned, once He has given, He will not take back" (*Taanis* 25a).

וְאֵדְעָה מָה אֶעֱשֶׂה לָּךְ — *That I may know what to do to you.* For then you will not deserve to (receive) such a severe punishment.

7. וְקָרָא לוֹ אֹהֶל מוֹעֵד — *And he called it the Tent of Meeting.* To let it be known that God, the Blessed One, met with him there and not in the Israelite camp.

11. פָּנִים אֶל פָּנִים — *Face to face.* Not, נֹפֵל וּגְלוּי עֵינָיִם, *fallen down, yet with opened eyes* (*Numbers* 24:4), but while in control of his senses.

כַּאֲשֶׁר יְדַבֵּר אִישׁ אֶל רֵעֵהוּ — *As a man speaks to his friend* ... and not through riddles.

לֹא יָמִישׁ מִתּוֹךְ הָאֹהֶל — *Departed not out of the tent.* To prevent any Israelite from entering since they were all under rebuke then, and that place (the Tent) was predisposed to the resting of the Divine Presence, similar to, אַל תִּקְרַב הֲלֹם, *do not approach near here* (*Exodus* 3:5), which was said to Moses since he was not sufficiently (spiritually) prepared at that time (to approach) that place.

12. רְאֵה — *See.* Watch (over us) and do not conceal Your face from us regarding this.

NOTES

5. וְעַתָּה הוֹרֵד עֶדְיְךָ מֵעָלֶיךָ — *Now take off your ornaments from yourself.* The *Sforno* continues his commentary on verse 3 in this verse. Israel was told to appreciate that God's departure from the camp was for their own benefit, as was the demand that they remove their ornaments. A person and a people are judged by different standards; the greater one's superiority the more stringent the judgment. The *Sforno* interprets the word עֲד as a "spiritual *ornament*," namely the special gift of spiritual apprehension of God granted to Israel at Sinai. As such, their punishment for iniquity would be extremely severe. Hence they were told to divest themselves of this unique gift and thereby they would be judged more leniently. The *Sforno* stresses that *they* had to remove this ornament themselves, for once God gives a gift, He does not take it back on His own.

11. פָּנִים אֶל פָּנִים — *Face to face.* See the *Sforno's* commentary 19:9 where he states that all of Israel merited to reach this special level of prophecy at Sinai, and were able to apprehend and comprehend God without suspending their senses. See notes there. Even Balaam, whom our Sages compare to Moses insofar as his prophetic powers were concerned, was only able to see a vision of the Almighty while in a trance, or in a dream through a medium (see *Rashi* verse 17). The expression *face*

And now remove your jewelry from yourself, and I shall know what I shall do to you.' " 6 *So the Children of Israel were stripped of their jewelry from Mount Horeb.*

7 *Moses would take the Tent and pitch it outside the camp, far from the camp, and call it Tent of Meeting. So it was that whoever sought* HASHEM *would go out to the Tent of Meeting, which was outside the camp.* 8 *Whenever Moses would go out to the Tent, the entire people would stand up and remain standing, everyone at the entrance of his tent, and they would gaze after Moses until he arrived at the Tent.* 9 *When Moses would arrive at the Tent, a pillar of cloud would descend and stand at the entrance of the Tent, and He would speak with Moses.* 10 *The entire people would see the pillar of cloud standing at the entrance of the Tent, and the entire people would rise and prostrate themselves, everyone at the entrance of his tent.* 11 HASHEM *would speak to Moses face to face, as a man would speak with his fellow; then he would return to the camp. His servant, Joshua son of Nun, a lad, would not depart from within the tent.*

12 *Moses said to* HASHEM, *"See, You say to me, 'Take this people onward,' but You did not inform me whom You will send with me; and You had said, 'I shall know you by name, and you have also found*

אַתָּה אֹמֵר אֵלַי הַעַל אֶת הָעָם הַזֶּה — *You say to me, 'Bring up this people'* ... when You said to me, לֵךְ עֲלֵה מִזֶּה אַתָּה וְהָעָם, *Depart, go up from here, you and the people* (v. 1).

וְאַתָּה לֹא הוֹדַעְתַּנִי אֵת אֲשֶׁר תִּשְׁלַח עִמִּי — *And You have not let me know whom You will send with me.* When You said, וְשָׁלַחְתִּי לְפָנֶיךָ מַלְאָךְ וְגֵרַשְׁתִּי, *and I will send an angel before you and I will drive out, etc.* (v. 2), it was understood (as applying) to the time when we shall enter the Land, but en route we will have neither Your Presence nor (that of) an angel.

וְאַתָּה אָמַרְתָּ יְדַעְתִּיךָ בְשֵׁם — *And You said, I know you by name.* And perforce when You placed upon me (the task) to lead them (Israel) on the way, it did not mean (that You were) abandoning them, similar to, וָאֹמַר לֹא אֶרְעֶה אֶתְכֶם הַמֵּתָה תָמוּת וְהַנִּכְחֶדֶת תִּכָּחֵד, *Then I said, I will not be your shepherd; that which dies, let it die; and that which is to be cut off, let it be cut off (Zechariah* 11:9), but You desired that I be the messenger who goes before the camp of Israel.

NOTES

to face is explained by the *Rambam* in his *Guide* (I:37) as "a presence to another presence without an intermediary."

לֹא יָמִישׁ מִתּוֹךְ הָאֹהֶל — *Departed not out of the tent.* The *Sforno* is referring to the middle forty days (see his commentary to 24:18) when he says, 'they were all under rebuke then.'

12. אַתָּה אֹמֵר אֵלַי . . . אֵת אֲשֶׁר תִּשְׁלַח עִמִּי — *You say to me ... whom You will send with me.* Moses realized that since the angel appointed by God (v. 2) will not assume his responsibilities until they enter the Land of Israel, hence in the absence of the *Shechinah* (Divine Presence), he (i.e., Moses) is to serve as the מַלְאָךְ, *messenger*, during this interim period. As such he feels it necessary to comprehend God more fully, else how can he function as His messenger? The *Rambam* in his *Guide* (I:54) explains that Moses made two requests. 'One... to let him know His essence and true reality. The second request ... was that He should let him know His attributes.' This latter request was granted (see v. 19) but the former was not (see v. 20), according to the *Rambam*. The *Sforno*, however, interprets the two requests differently (see v. 13). As for God's answer see the *Sforno* on verses 19, 20 and 23. Also see the *Sforno* on 25:20 and the Notes there for clarification of וְאֵדָעֲךָ, *that I may know You*, and the finding of favor and grace in God's sight through knowledge of Him.

יג מָצָאתָ חֵן בְּעֵינָי: וְעַתָּה אִם־נָא מָצָאתִי חֵן בְּעֵינֶיךָ הוֹדִעֵנִי נָא אֶת־
יד דְּרָכֶךָ וְאֵדָעֲךָ לְמַעַן אֶמְצָא־חֵן בְּעֵינֶיךָ וּרְאֵה כִּי עַמְּךָ הַגּוֹי הַזֶּה: וַיֹּאמַר
טו פָּנַי יֵלֵכוּ וַהֲנִחֹתִי לָךְ: וַיֹּאמֶר אֵלָיו אִם־אֵין פָּנֶיךָ הֹלְכִים אַל־תַּעֲלֵנוּ
טז מִזֶּה: וּבַמֶּה ׀ יִוָּדַע אֵפוֹא כִּי־מָצָאתִי חֵן בְּעֵינֶיךָ אֲנִי וְעַמֶּךָ הֲלוֹא
בְּלֶכְתְּךָ עִמָּנוּ וְנִפְלֵינוּ אֲנִי וְעַמְּךָ מִכָּל־הָעָם אֲשֶׁר עַל־פְּנֵי הָאֲדָמָה:
רביעי יז וַיֹּאמֶר יהוה אֶל־מֹשֶׁה גַּם אֶת־הַדָּבָר הַזֶּה אֲשֶׁר דִּבַּרְתָּ אֶעֱשֶׂה כִּי־
יח־יט מָצָאתָ חֵן בְּעֵינַי וָאֵדָעֲךָ בְּשֵׁם: וַיֹּאמַר הַרְאֵנִי נָא אֶת־כְּבֹדֶךָ: וַיֹּאמֶר
אֲנִי אַעֲבִיר כָּל־טוּבִי עַל־פָּנֶיךָ וְקָרָאתִי בְשֵׁם יהוה לְפָנֶיךָ וְחַנֹּתִי אֶת־

13. וְעַתָּה — *Now, therefore.* And since You have agreed that I should be the (מַלְאָךְ) messenger . . .

הוֹדִעֵנִי נָא אֶת דְּרָכֶךָ — *Show me now Your ways.* Show me (inform me) two of Your wondrous ways: one, how through Your knowledge alone You grant existence to all existence, as is demonstrated in fact; second, (given) Your unimpeachable knowledge of the future, how can there be in the nature (of man) the possible (freedom of) choice?

וְאֵדָעֲךָ — *That I may know You.* For indeed through knowledge of actions (manifestation) there is some knowledge of the form from which these manifestations (actions) emanate.

לְמַעַן אֶמְצָא חֵן בְּעֵינֶיךָ — *That I may find grace in Your sight.* For this I will find grace and good favor in the sight of God, as it says, כִּי אִם בְּזֹאת יִתְהַלֵּל הַמִּתְהַלֵּל הַשְׂכֵּל וְיָדֹעַ אוֹתִי . . . כִּי בְאֵלֶּה חָפַצְתִּי, *But let him that glories glory in this, that he understands and knows Me . . . for in these things I delight (Jeremiah 9:23).*

וּרְאֵה כִּי עַמְּךָ הַגּוֹי הַזֶּה — *And consider that this nation is Your people.* For Your Name is known in their midst, and not among the nations, as it says, נוֹדָע בִּיהוּדָה אֱלֹהִים בְּיִשְׂרָאֵל גָּדוֹל שְׁמוֹ, *In Judah, God is known, His name is great in Israel (Psalms 76:2).* And therefore it is improper that You withhold from me that which I requested, because of their sins, as our Sages say, "Thirty of them were worthy that the Divine Presence come to rest upon them as (it did) for Moses our Teacher" *(Bava Basra* 134a).

14. פָּנַי יֵלֵכוּ — *My presence shall go with you.* As you journey to *Eretz Yisrael,* My presence shall go before you but not in your midst.

וַהֲנִחֹתִי לָךְ — *And I will give you rest.* I will give you rest from all your enemies about you, in such a manner that you will bring them to the Land securely.

15. אִם אֵין פָּנֶיךָ הֹלְכִים — *If Your presence does not go.* Now, while we are still encamped. If Your presence, which You removed, does not accompany us to dwell in our midst . . .

אַל תַּעֲלֵנוּ מִזֶּה — *Carry us not up from here.* Then it would be better for us to dwell in the

NOTES

13. וּרְאֵה כִּי עַמְּךָ הַגּוֹי הַזֶּה — *And consider that this nation is Your people.* The Talmud *(Bava Basra* 134a) relates that the Elder Hillel had eighty pupils of whom thirty were so outstanding that they were worthy to have the Divine Presence rest on them, but since their generation had sinned, this misconduct prevented it from coming to pass. Moses, however, argued that the sin of the people should not prevent God from granting his request, in spite of their transgression, since God's existence and might was only recognized by Israel among all the nations.

14-15. פָּנַי יֵלֵכוּ . . . אַל תַּעֲלֵנוּ מִזֶּה — *My presence shall go with you . . . Carry us not up from here.* God responded favorably to Moses' request, but only partially. He would go *before* them to prepare the way to *Eretz Yisrael* but He would not be *in* their midst. Moses was not satisfied, for if Israel would enter the Land without God's presence they would not remain there permanently. Unfortunately history proved him to be right.

16. הֲלוֹא בְּלֶכְתְּךָ עִמָּנוּ וְנִפְלֵינוּ — *Is it not if You go up with us so that we be distinguished?* The *Sforno*

favor in My eyes.' 13 *And now, if I have indeed found favor in Your eyes,
make Your way known to me, so that I may comprehend Your 'you have
found favor in My eyes.' But see that this nation is Your people."*
14 *He said, "My Presence will go and provide you rest."*
15 *He said to Him, "If Your Presence does not go along, do not bring us
forward from here.* 16 *How, then, will it be known that I have found favor in
Your eyes — I and Your people — unless You accompany us, and I and Your
people will be made distinct from every people on the face of the earth!"*
17 *HASHEM said to Moses, "Even this thing of which you spoke I shall do,
for you have found favor in My eyes, and I have known you by name."*
18 *He said, "Show me now Your glory."*
19 *He said, "I shall make all My goodness pass before you, and I shall
call out with the Name HASHEM before you; I shall show favor when I*

---

wilderness than to enter the Land without your *Shechinah* (Divine Presence), for in such a manner we will, without a doubt, be exiled from it quickly.

16. וּבַמֶּה יִוָּדַע אֵפוֹא — *For with what shall it be known.* Although we will enter the Land, for the angel will drive out the nations, (but) how will it be known that this was a Divine act? In every war it is customary for one nation to overpower another nation and at times expel them.

הֲלוֹא בְּלֶכְתְּךָ עִמָּנוּ וְנִפְלֵינוּ — *Is it not if You go up with us so that we be distinguished?* Similar to, נָחִיתָ בְחַסְדְּךָ עַם זוּ גָּאָלְתָּ נֵהַלְתָּ בְעָזְּךָ . . . שָׁמְעוּ עַמִּים יִרְגָּזוּן, *With kindness You led this people that You redeemed; You have guided them in Your strength . . . The peoples have heard, they tremble* (15:13,14). For when the nations see that You are with us we shall be in their eyes more wonderful and singular in virtue than all other nations, and they will not strive to rise up against us, as Rahab attested when she said, כִּי שָׁמַעְנוּ אֵת אֲשֶׁר הוֹבִישׁ ה׳ אֶת מֵי יַם סוּף . . . וְלֹא קָמָה עוֹד רוּחַ בְּאִישׁ מִפְּנֵיכֶם כִּי ה׳ אֱלֹהֵיכֶם הוּא אֱלֹהִים בַּשָּׁמַיִם מִמַּעַל וְעַל הָאָרֶץ מִתָּחַת, *For we have heard how HASHEM dried up the waters of the Sea of Reeds . . . neither did there remain any more courage in any man because of you; for HASHEM your God is the God of heaven above and on the earth beneath* (*Joshua* 2:10,11).

18. אֶת כְּבֹדֶךָ — *Your glory . . .* (i.e.,) how all existence draws its existence from Yours, considering the great disparity between them (and You) as it says, מְלֹא כָל הָאָרֶץ כְּבוֹדוֹ, *the whole earth is full of His glory* (*Isaiah* 6:3).

19. אֲנִי אַעֲבִיר כָּל טוּבִי עַל פָּנֶיךָ — *I will make all My goodness pass before you.* This (answer) will not be withheld because I am not gracious, for indeed, *I will pass all My goodness before you.*

וְקָרָאתִי בְשֵׁם ה׳ לְפָנֶיךָ — *And I will proclaim the Name of HASHEM before you.* Behold he who calls in the Name of *HASHEM* is one who makes known and teaches the existence of God, the Blessed One, and His ways of goodness. He therefore says, *I will make all My goodness pass before you* in such a manner that were your faculties of discernment

NOTES

underscores that our distinction as a people, which all the nations recognize, lies in the fact that our power and strength is not our own, but emanates from God alone. Otherwise we are no different than other nations and our unique role in the history of man is forfeit. This is the thrust of Moses' argument that God relent and bring Israel into the Land Himself.

19-20. אֲנִי אַעֲבִיר כָּל טוּבִי עַל פָּנֶיךָ . . . וְרִחַמְתִּי אֶת אֲשֶׁר אֲרַחֵם . . . וַיֹּאמֶר לֹא תוּכַל לִרְאֹת — *I will make all My goodness pass before you . . . And I will show mercy to whom I will show mercy . . . And He said, "You cannot see."* The sense of the *Sforno's* interpretation of this verse is as follows: God, being gracious, was prepared to comply with the request of Moses — to make *His ways* known to

כ אֲשֶׁר אָחֹן וְרִחַמְתִּי אֶת־אֲשֶׁר אֲרַחֵם: וַיֹּאמֶר לֹא תוּכַל לִרְאֹת אֶת־פָּנָי
כא כִּי לֹא־יִרְאַנִי הָאָדָם וָחָי: וַיֹּאמֶר יהוה הִנֵּה מָקוֹם אִתִּי וְנִצַּבְתָּ עַל־
כב הַצּוּר: וְהָיָה בַּעֲבֹר כְּבֹדִי וְשַׂמְתִּיךָ בְּנִקְרַת הַצּוּר וְשַׂכֹּתִי כַפִּי עָלֶיךָ עַד־
כג עָבְרִי: וַהֲסִרֹתִי אֶת־כַּפִּי וְרָאִיתָ אֶת־אֲחֹרָי וּפָנַי לֹא יֵרָאוּ:
לד חמישי א וַיֹּאמֶר יהוה אֶל־מֹשֶׁה פְּסָל־לְךָ שְׁנֵי־לֻחֹת אֲבָנִים כָּרִאשֹׁנִים וְכָתַבְתִּי
עַל־הַלֻּחֹת אֶת־הַדְּבָרִים אֲשֶׁר הָיוּ עַל־הַלֻּחֹת הָרִאשֹׁנִים אֲשֶׁר שִׁבַּרְתָּ:
ב וֶהְיֵה נָכוֹן לַבֹּקֶר וְעָלִיתָ בַבֹּקֶר אֶל־הַר סִינַי וְנִצַּבְתָּ לִי שָׁם עַל־רֹאשׁ
ג הָהָר: וְאִישׁ לֹא־יַעֲלֶה עִמָּךְ וְגַם־אִישׁ אַל־יֵרָא בְּכָל־הָהָר גַּם־הַצֹּאן
ד וְהַבָּקָר אַל־יִרְעוּ אֶל־מוּל הָהָר הַהוּא: וַיִּפְסֹל שְׁנֵי־לֻחֹת אֲבָנִים
כָּרִאשֹׁנִים וַיַּשְׁכֵּם מֹשֶׁה בַבֹּקֶר וַיַּעַל אֶל־הַר סִינַי כַּאֲשֶׁר צִוָּה יהוה אֹתוֹ
ה וַיִּקַּח בְּיָדוֹ שְׁנֵי לֻחֹת אֲבָנִים: וַיֵּרֶד יהוה בֶּעָנָן וַיִּתְיַצֵּב עִמּוֹ שָׁם וַיִּקְרָא
ו בְשֵׁם יהוה: וַיַּעֲבֹר יהוה ׀ עַל־פָּנָיו וַיִּקְרָא יהוה ׀ יהוה אֵל רַחוּם וְחַנּוּן

(understanding) sufficient in this (area) you would attain all you desire (— but they are not!). Nonetheless, I will teach you a bit of My ways of goodness, for your benefit, and with this knowledge you will gain some knowledge of My essence (being) as it says, *and stood with Him there and proclaimed the Name of HASHEM* (34:5).

וְחַנֹּתִי אֶת אֲשֶׁר אָחֹן — *And I will be gracious to whom I will be gracious.* I will grant to you that grace which I am wont to give all who find favor in My eyes, which is with an abundant flow, without parsimony or miserliness.

וְרִחַמְתִּי אֶת אֲשֶׁר אֲרַחֵם — *And I will show mercy to whom I will show mercy.* I will have mercy on you that you shall not perish from the lightning flash of My glory, as it is My wont to show mercy to all who are proper and worthy of this (privilege), as it says, וְשַׂכֹּתִי כַפִּי עָלֶיךָ עַד עָבְרִי, *and I will cover you with My hand until I have passed by* (v. 22).

20. וַיֹּאמֶר לֹא תוּכַל לִרְאֹת — *And He said, "You cannot see."* This will not be impossible (lit., "denied you") because of any lack in My manifestation but due to a deficiency in your (ability to) receive, for you will be unable to receive the outpouring of the Light.

21. הִנֵּה מָקוֹם אִתִּי — *Behold there is a place by Me.* A place ready for the vision of God, as our Sages say regarding the cave wherein Moses and Elijah stood. (This cave) is one of the ten things created on the sixth day at twilight (בֵּין הַשְּׁמָשׁוֹת) (*Pesachim* 54a).

NOTES

him. However, the limitations of man, including even a Moses, are such that he is not able to grasp *all* that God is willing to reveal. Nonetheless, through the manifestation of His deeds, man can comprehend a bit of God's being and essence. When God agreed to reveal Himself to Moses (albeit minimally) there was also a need for mercy, since the intensity of the Divine light is so great that a human being is endangered by it, hence there was a need for God's "protective hand."

21. הִנֵּה מָקוֹם אִתִּי — *Behold there is a place by Me.* The Sages in *Avos* (5:9) list certain things created on the eve of the Sabbath בֵּין הַשְּׁמָשׁוֹת, *at twilight.* That list does not mention the cave where Moses and Elijah both stood to catch a glimpse of the Almighty. However, in Tractate *Pesachim* 54a this cave is included among the ten things created at that time.

23. וְרָאִיתָ אֶת אֲחֹרָי וּפָנַי לֹא יֵרָאוּ — *And you shall see My back, but My face shall not be seen.* The *Rambam* in his *Guide* (I:21,38) interprets the phrase פָּנָי *(My face)* as meaning a certain apprehension of God which Moses requested but which was not granted. Rather he was shown a relatively "inferior" apprehension, which is designated as אֲחֹרָי *(My back).* The *Rambam* also interprets *back* as meaning that which follows from God's will, "all things created by Me." The *Sforno* combines these two interpretations of the *Rambam,* interpreting אֲחֹרָי as referring to the actions of God which manifest His being but are not to be understood as His essence, which is far superior. This

choose to show favor, and I shall show mercy when I choose to show mercy."

[20] *He said, "You will not be able to see My face, for no human can see My face and live."* [21] *HASHEM said, "Behold! there is a place near Me; you may stand on the rock.* [22] *When My glory passes by, I shall place you in a cleft of the rock; I shall shield you with My hand until I have passed.* [23] *Then I shall remove My hand and you will see My back, but My face may not be seen."*

34 [1] *HASHEM said to Moses, "Carve for yourself two stone Tablets like the first ones, and I shall inscribe on the Tablets the words that were on the first Tablets, which you shattered.* [2] *Be prepared in the morning; ascend Mount Sinai in the morning and stand by Me there on the mountaintop.* [3] *No man may ascend with you nor may anyone be seen on the entire mountain. Even the flock and the cattle may not graze facing that mountain."*

[4] *So he carved out two stone Tablets like the first ones. Moses arose early in the morning and ascended to Mount Sinai, as HASHEM had commanded him, and he took two stone Tablets in his hand.*

[5] *HASHEM descended in a cloud and stood with him there, and He called out with the Name HASHEM.* [6] *HASHEM passed before him and proclaimed: HASHEM, HASHEM, God, Compassionate and Gracious, Slow*

---

23. וְרָאִיתָ אֶת אֲחֹרָי — *And you shall see My back.* You will see the action (manifestation) of that which is lower (inferior) to Me.

וּפָנַי לֹא יֵרָאוּ — *But My face shall not be seen.* But none, beside Me, shall see how the existence of everything draws its existence from My existence, as you requested.

XXXIV

5. וַיִּתְיַצֵּב עִמּוֹ שָׁם — *And stood with Him there.* Moses stood with God, the Blessed One, as He had said to him, וְנִצַּבְתָּ לִי שָׁם, *and stand there with Me* (v. 2).

וַיִּקְרָא — *And proclaimed.* God, the Blessed One (proclaimed).

בְשֵׁם ה׳ — *In the Name of HASHEM* . . . a proclamation making known the Divine actions (attributes).

6. וַיִּקְרָא — *And proclaimed.* God, The Blessed One (proclaimed).

ה׳ ה׳ — *HASHEM, HASHEM.* He is the Cause, Who made of "nothing something" *(ex nihilo)* and He sustains the existence of all that exists, for there is no preservation of any existence except for that which flows (emanates) from His existence.

NOTES

concept is also found in the *Guide* (I:53) where the *Rambam* states, "Every attribute (of God) is an attribute of His action and not an attribute of His essence." The *Sforno*, however, interprets the expression פָּנִים *(face)* as referring to God's existence from which all existence emanates, and this no man can hope to comprehend.

XXXIV

5. וַיִּתְיַצֵּב עִמּוֹ שָׁם — *And stood with Him there.* Although God is the subject of the verbs וַיֵּרֶד, *and He descended*, and וַיִּקְרָא, *and He proclaimed* or *called*, the subject of וַיִּתְיַצֵּב, *and he stood*, is Moses. The reason for the *Sforno's* interpretation is that the word is identical to that in verse 2 where God specifically commanded Moses to *stand* on the top of the mountain.

6. וַיִּקְרָא ה׳ ה׳ — *And proclaimed, "HASHEM, HASHEM."* The Sages tell us that these verses (6-7) comprise the י״ג מִדּוֹת, *thirteen attributes of God.* Each of His names represents a different aspect of His Being as do the various descriptive terms of

*נ׳ רבתי

ז אֶ֥רֶךְ אַפַּ֖יִם וְרַב־חֶ֥סֶד וֶאֱמֶֽת׃ נֹצֵ֥ר חֶ֙סֶד֙ לָאֲלָפִ֔ים נֹשֵׂ֥א עָוֺ֛ן וָפֶ֖שַׁע
וְחַטָּאָ֑ה וְנַקֵּה֙ לֹ֣א יְנַקֶּ֔ה פֹּקֵ֣ד ׀ עֲוֺ֣ן אָב֗וֹת עַל־בָּנִים֙ וְעַל־בְּנֵ֣י
ח בָנִ֔ים עַל־שִׁלֵּשִׁ֖ים וְעַל־רִבֵּעִֽים׃ וַיְמַהֵ֖ר מֹשֶׁ֑ה וַיִּקֹּ֥ד אַ֖רְצָה וַיִּשְׁתָּֽחוּ׃

אֵל — *God* . . . capable of all actions which are according to His will, (this being) the opposite of actions which extend from a natural force which do so out of necessity, not due to free choice.

רַחוּם — *Merciful* . . . to those who are guilty, lightening their punishment when they call out to Him, as it says, פְּנֵי ה׳ בְּעֹשֵׂי רָע . . . צָעֲקוּ וַה׳ שָׁמֵעַ, *The face of HASHEM is against those who do evil . . . they cry out and HASHEM hears* (*Psalms* 34:17,18). And He (also) sees the affliction of the oppressed, as (we find), *Moreover I have seen the oppression* (3:9).

וְחַנּוּן — *And gracious.* He is gracious and good to (i.e., rewards) those who beseech Him even though they are not (fully) deserving.

אֶרֶךְ אַפַּיִם — *Long suffering* . . . to the righteous and to the wicked so that they might repent (*Bava Kamma* 50b).

וְרַב חֶסֶד — *And abundant in loving-kindness.* Tilting (the scale) toward loving-kindness when one is judged, as our Sages say, "He forgives the very first (sin) and that is (His) attribute" (*Rosh Hashanah* 17a).

וֶאֱמֶת — *And truth.* And abundant truth. He is long-suffering but collects His due (*Midrash Bereishis Rabbah* 67:4), as our Sages say, "The sin itself is not forgiven" (*Rosh Hashanah* 17a), and as it says, אֲשֶׁר לֹא יִשָּׂא פָנִים, *Who regards not persons* (*Deut.* 10:17); "Abraham cannot save Ishmael nor can Isaac save Esau" (*Sanhedrin* 104a); וְלֹא יִקַּח שֹׁחַד, *nor takes bribe* (*Deut.* 10:17); "A mitzvah does not extinguish a transgression" (*Sotah* 21a).

7. נֹצֵר חֶסֶד לָאֲלָפִים — *Keeping mercy (kindness) to the thousands.* He guards (keeps) the merit of fathers for the sons, to do good for the sons because of their fathers.

נֹשֵׂא עָוֺן — *Forgiving iniquity* . . . (a sin committed) with premeditation.

NOTES

His actions, such as merciful, gracious, etc. The *Sforno* explains each of these names and terms in his commentary on these two verses. The repetition of *HASHEM, HASHEM,* is explained in a different vein than that of *Rashi* (quoting the Talmud, *Rosh Hashanah* 17) who states "the attribute of mercy applies before a man sins and after he sins." The *Sforno* explains the dual usage as indicating two aspects of God's omnipotence — one as the Creator *ex nihilo* and secondly as the One Who grants, in an ongoing fashion, existence to all He has created.

אֵל — *God.* Regarding the name אֵל, *God,* the *Sforno* departs from *Rashi's* interpretation that this name is also one of mercy and compassion. The *Sforno,* as do some other commentators, interprets it as indicating God's infinite power whose every action represents His freedom of will, whereas the natural forces He created function according to the ways ordained by the Almighty at the time of creation, be it the sun, moon, planets, etc., which cannot choose to function or to cease operating.

רַחוּם וְחַנּוּן — *Merciful and gracious.* Mercy (רַחוּם) indicates a disposition to forgive or forbear. Hence it is applicable to one who has sinned and is guilty. He will be punished but God's attribute of mercy will lighten the punishment. The phrase חַנּוּן implies *grace,* the freely given unmerited favor of God; hence it relates to one who is not fully guilty yet not fully deserving of forbearance either.

אֶרֶךְ אַפַּיִם — *Long suffering.* The Hebrew term אַפַּיִם is in the plural, implying that God's patience and forbearance is extended to two categories of people. One is the righteous, who are also in need of this attribute, the second being the wicked — for both are in need of repentance.

וְרַב חֶסֶד וֶאֱמֶת — *And abundant in loving-kindness and truth.* The Talmud (*Rosh Hashanah* 17a) cited by the *Sforno* refers to a בֵּינוֹנִי, *an average person,* whose actions are half *mitzvos* and half transgressions. By removing the first sin from the scale of justice, God causes the scale to tilt in the merit of that individual. However, if the sins still outweigh the merits, then that first sin is placed back on the scale. This is the meaning of וֶאֱמֶת, *and truth,* for the initial transgression is only *set aside* but not *cancelled.* Coupled with God's loving-kindness is

to Anger, and Abundant in Kindness and Truth; [7] *Preserver of Kindness for thousands of generations, Forgiver of Iniquity, Willful Sin, and Error, and Who Cleanses — but does not cleanse completely, recalling the iniquity of parents upon children and grandchildren, to the third and fourth generations.*
[8] *Moses hastened to bow his head toward the ground and prostrate himself.*

וָפֶשַׁע — *And transgression* ... (a sin committed) as rebellion against the kingdom (of heaven).

וְחַטָּאָה — *And sin* ... provocation added to rebellion, similar to כִּי רָעָתֵכִי אָז תַּעֲלֹזִי, *When you do evil then you rejoice (Jeremiah* 11:15). However, the forgiveness of one is not similar to the other, without a doubt; therefore these attributes are enumerated separately.

וְנַקֵּה לֹא יְנַקֶּה — *And clear, He will not clear.* Although He will clear those who repent (from a motivation of) love, which is the repentance that "reaches to the throne of glory" *(Yoma* 86a), as our Sages state, "iniquities are considered as merits" *(Yoma* 86b), and of whom is said, חָיוֹ יִחְיֶה, *he shall surely live (Ezekiel* 33:15), nonetheless *He will not clear* even those who repent, if their repentance (is motivated) only by fear of punishment, as our Sages say, "sins of premeditation are considered as sins committed in error" (ibid.), as it is written: כִּי כָשַׁלְתָּ בַּעֲוֹנֶךָ, *for you have stumbled in your iniquity (Hosea* 14:2).

פֹּקֵד עֲוֹן אָבוֹת עַל בָּנִים — *Visiting the iniquity of the fathers upon the children.* He waits to destroy the wicked of the land until their measure is full. (Now) this fullness comes when their iniquity reaches a level of evil where there is no hope of repentance. This occurs most often when their wickedness persists over successive generations.

עַל שִׁלֵּשִׁים — *Unto the third (generation)* ... if the later generation is more wicked than their fathers, similar to, וַיַּקְשׁוּ אֶת עָרְפָּם, הֵרֵעוּ מֵאֲבוֹתָם, *but stiffened their neck, they did worse than their fathers (Jeremiah* 7:26).

וְעַל רִבֵּעִים — *And unto the fourth (generation).* If they do not add, but persist (in doing evil).

8. וַיְמַהֵר מֹשֶׁה — *And Moses made haste.* An added (dimension of) submissiveness; for indeed (when one) hastens to bow down it indicates the great (importance) of the one to whom he is bowing, as our Sages say, "When Rav Sheshes bowed (at מוֹדִים), he bowed like a stick" *(Berachos* 12b).

NOTES

His insistence that justice be done. The two are delicately balanced by Him in His infinite wisdom.

7. נֹשֵׂא עָוֹן וָפֶשַׁע וְחַטָּאָה — *Forgiving iniquity and transgression and sin. Rashi,* basing himself on the Talmud *(Yoma* 36), distinguishes between עָוֹן and פֶּשַׁע — the former being a premeditated sin, while the latter implies a sin committed with malice aforethought to rebel against God. The word חַטָּאָה, however, is not translated by *Rashi.* The *Sforno,* consistent with his commentary on the sin of the Golden Calf (32:21), interprets this phrase to mean the sin added to iniquity and transgression by rejoicing, rather than regretting one's sinful actions.

וְנַקֵּה לֹא יְנַקֶּה — *And clear, He will not clear.* The Talmud addresses itself to the seeming self-contradictory nature of the phrase — *clear, not clear* — and explains that it depends on the action of the sinner as to whether he repents or not. The *Sforno* elaborates on this interpretation and comments that even if one repents, his motivation is a determining factor. תְּשׁוּבָה מֵאַהֲבָה, *repentance motivated by love,* transforms sins into merits while תְּשׁוּבָה מִיִּרְאָה, *repentance motivated by fear,* can only transform iniquities into שׁוֹגֵג, as though they were non-premeditated; hence the punishment will be lighter.

פֹּקֵד עֲוֹן אָבוֹת עַל בָּנִים ... עַל שִׁלֵּשִׁים וְעַל רִבֵּעִים — *Visiting the iniquity of the fathers upon the children ... unto the third (generation) and unto the fourth (generation).* God does not punish the sinner immediately. He waits patiently in the hope that he will repent. When that hope proves to be false, God will still wait until the third or fourth generation to exact retribution. If the descendants add to the wickedness of their ancestors, the third generation will be punished; if they only persist but do not add, God will wait until the fourth generation.

8. וַיְמַהֵר מֹשֶׁה — *And Moses made haste.* A stick descends quickly in one fell swoop. Compare this *Sforno* to *Genesis* 18:2 and 24:20.

ט וַיֹּאמֶר אִם־נָא מָצָאתִי חֵן בְּעֵינֶיךָ אֲדֹנָי יֵלֶךְ־נָא אֲדֹנָי בְּקִרְבֵּנוּ כִּי
י עַם־קְשֵׁה־עֹרֶף הוּא וְסָלַחְתָּ לַעֲוֺנֵנוּ וּלְחַטָּאתֵנוּ וּנְחַלְתָּנוּ: וַיֹּאמֶר הִנֵּה (ששי)
אָנֹכִי כֹּרֵת בְּרִית נֶגֶד כָּל־עַמְּךָ אֶעֱשֶׂה נִפְלָאֹת אֲשֶׁר לֹא־נִבְרְאוּ
בְכָל־הָאָרֶץ וּבְכָל־הַגּוֹיִם וְרָאָה כָל־הָעָם אֲשֶׁר־אַתָּה בְקִרְבּוֹ אֶת־
יא מַעֲשֵׂה יהוה כִּי־נוֹרָא הוּא אֲשֶׁר אֲנִי עֹשֶׂה עִמָּךְ: *שְׁמָר־לְךָ אֵת (*בראש עמוד בי״ה שמ״ו סימן)
אֲשֶׁר אָנֹכִי מְצַוְּךָ הַיּוֹם הִנְנִי גֹרֵשׁ מִפָּנֶיךָ אֶת־הָאֱמֹרִי וְהַכְּנַעֲנִי וְהַחִתִּי
יב וְהַפְּרִזִּי וְהַחִוִּי וְהַיְבוּסִי: הִשָּׁמֶר לְךָ פֶּן־תִּכְרֹת בְּרִית לְיוֹשֵׁב הָאָרֶץ
יג אֲשֶׁר אַתָּה בָּא עָלֶיהָ פֶּן־יִהְיֶה לְמוֹקֵשׁ בְּקִרְבֶּךָ: כִּי אֶת־מִזְבְּחֹתָם
יד תִּתֹּצוּן וְאֶת־מַצֵּבֹתָם תְּשַׁבֵּרוּן וְאֶת־אֲשֵׁרָיו תִּכְרֹתוּן: כִּי לֹא
טו תִשְׁתַּחֲוֶה לְאֵל *אַחֵר כִּי יהוה קַנָּא שְׁמוֹ אֵל קַנָּא הוּא: פֶּן־תִּכְרֹת (*ר' רבתי)
בְּרִית לְיוֹשֵׁב הָאָרֶץ וְזָנוּ ׀ אַחֲרֵי אֱלֹהֵיהֶם וְזָבְחוּ לֵאלֹהֵיהֶם וְקָרָא
טז לְךָ וְאָכַלְתָּ מִזִּבְחוֹ: וְלָקַחְתָּ מִבְּנֹתָיו לְבָנֶיךָ וְזָנוּ בְנֹתָיו אַחֲרֵי
יז אֱלֹהֵיהֶן וְהִזְנוּ אֶת־בָּנֶיךָ אַחֲרֵי אֱלֹהֵיהֶן: אֱלֹהֵי מַסֵּכָה לֹא תַעֲשֶׂה־לָּךְ:

9. כִּי עַם קְשֵׁה עֹרֶף הוּא — *For it is a stiff-necked people.* And they will certainly sin, and even though by accompanying us the iniquity of the generation will be greater, as You said, "רֶגַע אֶחָד אֶעֱלֶה בְקִרְבְּךָ וְכִלִּיתִיךָ, *If I go up in your midst for one moment I shall consume you*" (33:5), nonetheless it is better for us that You accompany us ...

וְסָלַחְתָּ לַעֲוֺנֵנוּ — *And pardon our iniquity* ... for pardon is Yours and we can hope to (receive) Your forgiveness. But let not an angel accompany us, even though the sin of rebellion against him will be lesser; still, there is (also) no hope of pardon with him, as You (Yourself) said, כִּי לֹא יִשָּׂא לְפִשְׁעֲכֶם, *For he will not pardon your transgression* (23:21).

10. הִנֵּה אָנֹכִי כֹּרֵת בְּרִית — *Behold I make a covenant.* To be in your midst, as (our Sages) said, "They were exiled to Babylonia and the *Shechinah* (Divine Presence) was with them; when they were exiled to Elam the *Shechinah* was with them; they were exiled to Edom and the *Shechinah* was with them" (*Megillah* 29a).

נֶגֶד כָּל עַמְּךָ אֶעֱשֶׂה נִפְלָאֹת — *Before all your people I will do marvels.* When they will pray invoking (lit., "through") these attributes.

וְרָאָה כָל הָעָם אֲשֶׁר אַתָּה בְקִרְבּוֹ — *And all the people, in whose midst you are, shall see.* However, the awesome work of God in the presence of all the people will only be in the sight of those people in whose midst you (Moses) are, (they alone) will see the *works of* HASHEM.

אֲשֶׁר אֲנִי עֹשֶׂה עִמָּךְ — *That I do with you* ... in your merit, as it says, כִּי מָצָאתָ חֵן בְּעֵינַי וָאֵדָעֲךָ בְּשֵׁם, *For you have found grace in My sight and I know you by name* (33:17).

11. שְׁמָר לְךָ אֵת אֲשֶׁר אָנֹכִי מְצַוְּךָ הַיּוֹם — *Observe, you, that which I am commanding you this day.* I not only warn you not to *change your glory for that which does not profit* (*Jeremiah* 2:11), but I also caution you not to allow others to worship (any god) except Me.

NOTES

9. כִּי עַם קְשֵׁה עֹרֶף הוּא — *For it is a stiff-necked people.* Although Israel will be more vulnerable if God accompanies them, still the advantage of God's presence and His power of forgiveness outweigh the drawbacks. As *Rashi* points out, the word כִּי in the context of this verse is the reason for Moses' request — i.e., precisely *because* they are stiff-necked they need Your presence.

10. וְרָאָה כָל הָעָם אֲשֶׁר אַתָּה בְקִרְבּוֹ . . . אֲשֶׁר אֲנִי עֹשֶׂה עִמָּךְ — *And all the people, in whose midst you are, shall see ... that I do with you.* Although God will always answer Israel when they invoke the י״ג מִדּוֹת (as we do in our prayers to this very day), the awesome wonders will only be witnessed by Israel in the generation of Moses, for they were performed only in his merit.

9 He said, "If I have now found favor in Your eyes, my Lord, let my Lord go
among us — for it is a stiff-necked people, and You shall forgive our iniquity
and error, and make us Your heritage."
10 He said, "Behold! I seal a covenant: Before your entire people I shall
make distinctions such as have never been created in the entire world and
among all the nations; and the entire people among whom you are will see
the work of HASHEM — which is awesome — that I am about to do with you.
11 "Beware of what I command you today: Behold I drive out before you
the Amorite, the Canaanite, the Hittite, the Perizzite, the Hivvite, and the
Jebusite. 12 Be vigilant lest you seal a covenant with the inhabitant of the land
to which you come, lest it be a snare among you. 13 Rather you shall break
apart their altars, smash their pillars, and cut down its sacred trees. 14 For
you shall not prostrate yourselves to an alien god, for the very Name of
HASHEM is 'Jealous One,' He is a jealous God. 15 Lest you seal a covenant with
the inhabitant of the land and stray after their gods, slaughter to their gods,
and he invite you and you eat from his slaughter. 16 And you take their
daughters for your sons, and their daughters stray after their gods and
entice your sons to stray after their gods!
17 "You shall not make yourselves molten gods.

---

14. כִּי לֹא תִשְׁתַּחֲוֶה לְאֵל אַחֵר — *For you shall bow down to no other god.* Therefore you shall break down his altar and show him no favor for you shall honor no other god but Me.

כִּי ה' קַנָּא שְׁמוֹ — *For HASHEM's Name is Jealous.* Because His Name indicates a category of an Existent which is inapplicable to any other existent save Him, therefore . . .

אֵל קַנָּא הוּא — *A jealous God is He . . .* (Who) will punish anyone who serves another (god) together with Him.

15. פֶּן תִּכְרֹת בְּרִית — *Lest you make a covenant.* And the reason I said (that) you shall not make a covenant with the inhabitants of the land is because if you are (joined) with him in a covenant you will be misled (to follow) another god, in one of two ways: If he invites you to eat of his sacrifice, you will serve his god together with him, so as to satisfy his desire; (or) you will do it because of love for women, as occurred at Peor (*Numbers* 22:5).

17. אֱלֹהֵי מַסֵּכָה — *Molten gods.* These (refer to) talismen which were made at certain known hours in conjunction with certain stars. They were made molten so that the various parts of those symbols should (combine) together at that moment. Those who made them thought that they would attain their (desired) material and bodily needs (through them). Now perhaps one might think that this (practice) was not a rebellion against God, the Blessed One, since the participant did not accept it upon himself as a god, but (nonetheless) this is indeed contrary to His will, for He does not want His worshipers to turn for help to any god but Him, as it says, וַאֲנַחְנוּ לֹא נֵדַע מַה נַּעֲשֶׂה כִּי עָלֶיךָ עֵינֵינוּ, *We know not what to do, but our eyes are upon You* (*II Chronicles* 20:12).

NOTES

11. שְׁמָר לְךָ אֵת אֲשֶׁר אָנֹכִי מְצַוְּךָ הַיּוֹם — *Observe, you, that which I am commanding you this day.* Although God had already prohibited the bowing down to other gods (23:24), the admonition here is not redundant for it adds the warning of not allowing others to do so as well.

17. אֱלֹהֵי מַסֵּכָה — *Molten gods.* A talisman was an object engraved with magical symbols purported to bring luck or protection to its bearer. As the *Sforno* explains, this prohibition was necessary, although God had already cautioned them not to worship other gods, because these objects were not considered deities. Nonetheless they are forbidden for the reason given by the *Sforno*.

יח אֶת־חַג הַמַּצּוֹת תִּשְׁמֹר שִׁבְעַת יָמִים תֹּאכַל מַצּוֹת אֲשֶׁר צִוִּיתִךָ לְמוֹעֵד
יט חֹדֶשׁ הָאָבִיב כִּי בְּחֹדֶשׁ הָאָבִיב יָצָאתָ מִמִּצְרָיִם: כָּל־פֶּטֶר רֶחֶם לִי
כ וְכָל־מִקְנְךָ תִּזָּכָר פֶּטֶר שׁוֹר וָשֶׂה: וּפֶטֶר חֲמוֹר תִּפְדֶּה בְשֶׂה וְאִם־לֹא
כא תִפְדֶּה וַעֲרַפְתּוֹ כֹּל בְּכוֹר בָּנֶיךָ תִּפְדֶּה וְלֹא־יֵרָאוּ פָנַי רֵיקָם: שֵׁשֶׁת
כב יָמִים תַּעֲבֹד וּבַיּוֹם הַשְּׁבִיעִי תִּשְׁבֹּת בֶּחָרִישׁ וּבַקָּצִיר תִּשְׁבֹּת: וְחַג שָׁבֻעֹת
כג תַּעֲשֶׂה לְךָ בִּכּוּרֵי קְצִיר חִטִּים וְחַג הָאָסִיף תְּקוּפַת הַשָּׁנָה: שָׁלֹשׁ פְּעָמִים
בַּשָּׁנָה יֵרָאֶה כָּל־זְכוּרְךָ אֶת־פְּנֵי הָאָדֹן ׀ יהוה אֱלֹהֵי יִשְׂרָאֵל: כִּי־אוֹרִישׁ

18. אֶת חַג הַמַּצּוֹת תִּשְׁמֹר — *The Feast of Matzos you shall keep.* After mentioning the prohibition of molten gods, through whom their makers thought to attain their temporal needs (lit., "life of the hour"), (the Torah) makes mention of those commandments from which various imagined success will result: the ripening, the harvest, the ingathering and matters of possessions. These are arranged in this chapter according to the order that they were (first) given to Israel. The first of them is the Feast of Matzos, at the time appointed in the month of *Aviv* when the ripening is blessed. Second is the subject of the firstborn, through whom the flocks are blessed, and this commandment was after the Feast of Matzos immediately after the exodus from Egypt. Third is the commandment of the Sabbath which was given at Marah and through it the days of work are blessed, as it says, שֵׁשֶׁת יָמִים תַּעֲשֶׂה מַעֲשֶׂיךָ, *Six days you shall do your work* (23:12). Together with it (the Torah) speaks of the seventh year which blesses the years, as it says, וְשֵׁשׁ שָׁנִים תִּזְרַע, *And six years you shall sow* (23:10). Fourth is the Feast of Harvest (Shavuos) wherein *the appointed weeks of the harvest are kept for us* (based on *Jeremiah* 5:24). Fifth is the Feast of Ingathering (Succos) through which the ingathering is blessed, as it says, כְּבִרְכַּת ה׳ אֱלֹהֶיךָ אֲשֶׁר נָתַן לָךְ, *according to the blessing of* HASHEM *your God which He has given you (Deut.* 16:17). After all these commandments (the Torah) mentions a commandment which is common to the three festivals, namely, יֵרָאֶה כָּל זְכוּרְךָ, *all your males shall appear* (v. 23). Afterward commandments special to the Feast of Matzos are mentioned: לֹא תִשְׁחַט עַל חָמֵץ, *You shall not offer on chometz, etc.*; and וְלֹא יָלִין, *You shall not leave etc.* (v. 25). Afterward (the Torah) mentions a special *mitzvah* which is mainly connected to the Feast of Harvest, i.e., רֵאשִׁית בִּכּוּרֵי אַדְמָתְךָ, *the choicest first fruits of your land, etc.* (v. 26), as our Sages say, "From *Atzereth* (Shavuos) until the Feast (Succos) one brings and reads" *(Bikkurim* 1:6). Later (the Torah) mentions a commandment which in the majority of cases is especially linked to Succos, i.e., לֹא תְבַשֵּׁל גְּדִי בַּחֲלֵב אִמּוֹ, *You shall not boil a kid in its mother's milk*, for that is the season of the kids, as some of our Sages say, "On the first day of Tishrei is the Rosh Hashanah of tithing animals" (*Mishnah, Rosh Hashanah* 1:1).

19. כָּל פֶּטֶר רֶחֶם לִי — *All that opens the womb is Mine.* Among man, clean animals and some unclean ones, but they shall be so in various ways, therefore it says . . .

וְכָל מִקְנְךָ תִּזָּכָר פֶּטֶר שׁוֹר וָשֶׂה — *And of all your cattle you shall sanctify the males, the firstlings of ox and sheep.* That is . . . the firstling of an ox and sheep תִּזָּכָר, it shall be *remembered* as a part of the sacrifices called אַזְכָּרָה, *a remembrance*, as it says, אַךְ בְּכוֹר שׁוֹר

NOTES

18-26. אֶת חַג הַמַּצּוֹת תִּשְׁמֹר . . . לֹא תְבַשֵּׁל גְּדִי . . . — *The Feast of Matzos you shall keep . . . You shall not boil a kid . . .* The sequence of these verses is difficult to comprehend. The three festivals are separated by commandments regarding firstlings, the Sabbath and the Sabbatical year, after which we find the verses regarding the commandment to come up to the Temple three times a year, followed by the laws of the *Pesach* lamb and the first fruits, culminating with the prohibition of mixing milk and meat! The *Sforno* in his commentary on these verses clarifies the sequence.

18 "You shall observe the Festival of Matzos: For a seven-day period you shall eat matzos, as I commanded you, at the appointed time in the month of spring, for in the month of spring you went forth from Egypt.
19 "Every first issue of a womb is Mine; as well as any of your livestock that produces a male, the first issue of cattle or sheep. 20 The first issue of a donkey you shall redeem with a lamb or kid, and if you do not redeem it you shall axe the back of its neck. You shall redeem every firstborn of your sons. They shall not appear before Me emptyhanded.
21 "Six days shall you work and on the seventh day you shall desist; you shall desist from plowing and harvesting. 22 You shall make the Festival of Weeks with the first offering of the wheat harvest; and the Festival of the Harvest shall be at the changing of the year. 23 Three times a year all your males shall appear before the Lord HASHEM, the God of Israel.

אוֹ בְכוֹר כֶּשֶׂב אוֹ בְכוֹר עֵז לֹא תִפְדֶּה קֹדֶשׁ הֵם אֶת דָּמָם תִּזְרֹק... וְאֶת חֶלְבָּם תַּקְטִיר, *But the firstling of an ox or the firstling of a sheep or the firstling of a goat you shall not redeem; they are holy, you shall dash their blood ... and their fat burn* (*Numbers* 18:17).

20. וּפֶטֶר חֲמוֹר תִּפְדֶּה בְשֶׂה ... כֹּל בְּכוֹר בָּנֶיךָ תִּפְדֶּה — *And the firstling of an ass you shall redeem with a lamb ... All the firstborn of your sons you shall redeem.* The redemption (being) the established valuation (five *shekels* — see *Numbers* 18:16).

21. שֵׁשֶׁת יָמִים תַּעֲבֹד וּבַיּוֹם הַשְּׁבִיעִי תִּשְׁבֹּת — *Six days you shall work, but on the seventh day you shall rest.* You shall succeed in your six days of work when you rest on the seventh.

בֶּחָרִישׁ וּבַקָּצִיר תִּשְׁבֹּת — *In plowing time and in harvest you shall rest.* Also when you will rest once every seven years from plowing and harvest, which is the Sabbath of years that is also called שַׁבָּת לַה׳, *a Sabbath to HASHEM* (*Leviticus* 25:2), then you will be successful in your plowing and harvest (the other six years) as it says, שֵׁשׁ שָׁנִים תִּזְרַע שָׂדֶךָ וְאָסַפְתָּ אֶת תְּבוּאָתָהּ, *Six years you shall sow your field ... and gather its produce* (ibid. v. 3).

23. יֵרָאֶה כָּל זְכוּרְךָ — *All your males shall appear* ... to give thanks for all the good which emanates from Him to you in (all) natural matters (in His role as) *Lord of Israel*, and for that which emanates from Him for eternal life as the *God of Israel.*

אֶת פְּנֵי הָאָדֹן ה׳ — *Before the Lord, HASHEM* ... Who arranges all your affairs in the natural (material) realm, similar to, וּלְאָדוֹן לְכָל בֵּיתוֹ, *And master of all his house* (*Genesis* 45:8).

אֱלֹהֵי יִשְׂרָאֵל — *God of Israel* ... Who arranges (controls) the affairs of Israel in spiritual matters which transcend nature, which do not apply except to that which is separated (from matter) and (hence) called *Elohim*, similar to זֹבֵחַ לָאֱלֹהִים יָחֳרָם, *He who sacrifices to the gods shall be utterly destroyed* (22:19), and (also) to אֱלָהִין דִּי מְדָרְהוֹן עִם בִּשְׂרָא לָא אִיתוֹהִי, *the gods whose dwelling is not with flesh* (*Daniel* 2:11). It is for this (reason) that it is said of the demons, לֹא אֱלֹהַּ, *no-gods* (*Deut.* 32:17), for they are material beings who are mortal like man, as our Sages have mentioned (*Chagigah* 16a). Expert judges are also called *Elohim* (22:27), for they occasionally judge in an extrasensory (fashion) similar to Solomon of

NOTES

23. אֶת פְּנֵי הָאָדֹן ה׳ אֱלֹהֵי יִשְׂרָאֵל — *Before the Lord, HASHEM, God of Israel.* Two expressions are used in this verse — אָדוֹן which means master or lord, and אֱלֹהֵי, *God*, of Israel. The *Sforno* interprets the former appellation (אָדוֹן) as indicating the role of God as our Master guiding the material and physical affairs of Israel, while the latter name (אֱלֹהֵי) indicates God's role in guiding the spiritual (and historical) destiny of Israel. See the *Sforno* on *Genesis* 1:1 and the note there for an explanation of the term אֱלֹהִים and its application to judges and heavenly forces. When Israel went up to the Temple three times a year, it was to pay homage to God in His dual role as אָדוֹן and as אֱלֹהֵי יִשְׂרָאֵל.

כד גּוֹיִם מִפָּנֶיךָ וְהִרְחַבְתִּי אֶת־גְּבֻלֶךָ וְלֹא־יַחְמֹד אִישׁ אֶת־אַרְצְךָ בַּעֲלֹתְךָ
לֵרָאוֹת אֶת־פְּנֵי יהוה אֱלֹהֶיךָ שָׁלֹשׁ פְּעָמִים בַּשָּׁנָה: לֹא־תִשְׁחַט
כה־כו עַל־חָמֵץ דַּם־זִבְחִי וְלֹא־יָלִין לַבֹּקֶר זֶבַח חַג הַפָּסַח: רֵאשִׁית בִּכּוּרֵי
אַדְמָתְךָ תָּבִיא בֵּית יהוה אֱלֹהֶיךָ לֹא־תְבַשֵּׁל גְּדִי בַּחֲלֵב אִמּוֹ:
שביעי כז וַיֹּאמֶר יהוה אֶל־מֹשֶׁה כְּתָב־לְךָ אֶת־הַדְּבָרִים הָאֵלֶּה כִּי עַל־פִּי ׀
כח הַדְּבָרִים הָאֵלֶּה כָּרַתִּי אִתְּךָ בְּרִית וְאֶת־יִשְׂרָאֵל: וַיְהִי־שָׁם עִם־יהוה
אַרְבָּעִים יוֹם וְאַרְבָּעִים לַיְלָה לֶחֶם לֹא אָכַל וּמַיִם לֹא שָׁתָה וַיִּכְתֹּב
כט עַל־הַלֻּחֹת אֵת דִּבְרֵי הַבְּרִית עֲשֶׂרֶת הַדְּבָרִים: וַיְהִי בְּרֶדֶת מֹשֶׁה מֵהַר
סִינַי וּשְׁנֵי לֻחֹת הָעֵדֻת בְּיַד־מֹשֶׁה בְּרִדְתּוֹ מִן־הָהָר וּמֹשֶׁה לֹא־יָדַע כִּי
ל קָרַן עוֹר פָּנָיו בְּדַבְּרוֹ אִתּוֹ: וַיַּרְא אַהֲרֹן וְכָל־בְּנֵי יִשְׂרָאֵל אֶת־מֹשֶׁה
לא וְהִנֵּה קָרַן עוֹר פָּנָיו וַיִּירְאוּ מִגֶּשֶׁת אֵלָיו: וַיִּקְרָא אֲלֵהֶם מֹשֶׁה וַיָּשֻׁבוּ אֵלָיו
לב אַהֲרֹן וְכָל־הַנְּשִׂאִים בָּעֵדָה וַיְדַבֵּר מֹשֶׁה אֲלֵהֶם: וְאַחֲרֵי־כֵן נִגְּשׁוּ כָּל־בְּנֵי
מפטיר לג יִשְׂרָאֵל וַיְצַוֵּם אֵת כָּל־אֲשֶׁר דִּבֶּר יהוה אִתּוֹ בְּהַר סִינָי: וַיְכַל מֹשֶׁה
לד מִדַּבֵּר אִתָּם וַיִּתֵּן עַל־פָּנָיו מַסְוֶה: וּבְבֹא מֹשֶׁה לִפְנֵי יהוה לְדַבֵּר אִתּוֹ
יָסִיר אֶת־הַמַּסְוֶה עַד־צֵאתוֹ וְיָצָא וְדִבֶּר אֶל־בְּנֵי יִשְׂרָאֵל אֵת אֲשֶׁר
לה יְצֻוֶּה: וְרָאוּ בְנֵי־יִשְׂרָאֵל אֶת־פְּנֵי מֹשֶׁה כִּי קָרַן עוֹר פְּנֵי מֹשֶׁה וְהֵשִׁיב
מֹשֶׁה אֶת־הַמַּסְוֶה עַל־פָּנָיו עַד־בֹּאוֹ לְדַבֵּר אִתּוֹ:

---

whom it is said, כִּי חָכְמַת אֱלֹהִים בְּקִרְבּוֹ לַעֲשׂוֹת מִשְׁפָּט, *The wisdom of God was in him to do judgment* (*I Kings* 3:28), and as it says, וְלֹא לְמַרְאֵה עֵינָיו יִשְׁפּוֹט וְלֹא לְמִשְׁמַע אָזְנָיו יוֹכִיחַ, *and he shall not judge after the sight of his eyes, neither decide after the hearing of his ears* (*Isaiah* 11:3). This is why God, the Blessed One, is called אֱלֹהֵי הָאֱלֹהִים, *God of gods* (*Deut.* 10:17), Who arranges those affairs which are not in the natural realm but they are separated from matter; (and also) אֲדֹנֵי הָאֲדֹנִים, *the Lord of lords* (ibid.), Who arranges the matters of nature, which are the heavenly causes (phenomena) — therefore (the Torah) says . . .

26. רֵאשִׁית בִּכּוּרֵי אַדְמָתְךָ תָּבִיא — *The choicest first fruits of your Land you shall bring.* And through this you will attain success with (your) fruit, as it says: וְרֵאשִׁית כָּל בִּכּוּרֵי כֹל . . . תִּתְּנוּ לַכֹּהֵן לְהָנִיחַ בְּרָכָה אֶל בֵּיתֶךָ, *And the first of all the first fruits of all things . . . you shall give to the priest that he may cause a blessing to rest in your house* (*Ezekiel* 44:30).

. . . לֹא תְבַשֵּׁל גְּדִי — *You shall not boil a kid . . .* As was the way of the heathens (lit., "strange sons") who thought they would attain prosperity in their fruit or flocks, by means of this practice.

27. כְּתָב לְךָ אֶת הַדְּבָרִים הָאֵלֶּה — *Write yourself these words.* Although before the sin of the calf I intended to give you אֶת לֻחֹת הָאֶבֶן וְהַתּוֹרָה וְהַמִּצְוָה אֲשֶׁר כָּתַבְתִּי, *the tablets of law, and the Torah and the commandment which I have written* (24:12), now that they sinned and you hewed out for yourself the tablets — (upon which) I will write — I will not give

NOTES

27. כְּתָב לְךָ אֶת הַדְּבָרִים הָאֵלֶּה — *Write yourself these words.* God's original intention was to write the Ten Commandments, the law and the commandments *Himself*, but after they sinned with the Golden Calf and consequently were no longer worthy of this special honor, Moses is charged with the task of writing all this.

28. וַיְהִי שָׁם עִם ה׳ — *And he was there with* HASHEM. The third and final time. See 24:18.

33. וַיְכַל מֹשֶׁה מִדַּבֵּר אִתָּם — *And when Moses had done speaking with them (he placed a veil over his face).* Moses' face was not covered by the veil while speaking to God nor when he spoke to the

24 *For I shall banish nations before you and broaden your boundary; no man will covet your land when you go up to appear before* HASHEM, *your God, three times a year.*
25 *"You shall not slaughter My blood-offering while in the possession of leavened food, nor may the feast-offering of the Pesach festival be left over-*
night until morning. 26 *The first of your land's early produce you shall bring to the Temple of* HASHEM, *your God. Do not cook a kid in its mother's milk."*
27 HASHEM *said to Moses, "Write these words for yourself, for according*
to these words have I sealed a covenant with you and Israel." 28 *He*
remained there with HASHEM *for forty days and forty nights — he did not eat bread and he did not drink water — and He wrote on the Tablets the words of the covenant, the Ten Commandments.*
29 *When Moses descended from Mount Sinai — with the two Tablets of the Testimony in the hand of Moses as he descended from the mountain — Moses did not know that the skin of his face had become radiant when He*
had spoken to him. 30 *Aaron and all the Children of Israel saw Moses, and behold! — the skin of his face had become radiant; and they feared to*
approach him. 31 *Moses called to them, and Aaron and all the leaders of the*
assembly returned to him, and Moses would speak to them. 32 *After that, all the Children of Israel would approach; he would command them regarding everything that* HASHEM *had spoken to him on Mount Sinai.*
33 *Moses finished speaking with them and placed a mask on his face.*
34 *When Moses would come before* HASHEM *to speak with Him, he would remove the mask until his departure; then he would leave and tell the*
Children of Israel whatever he had been commanded. 35 *When the Children of Israel saw Moses' face, that Moses' face had become radiant, Moses put the mask back on his face, until he came to speak with Him.*

---

you (now) the Torah and the commandment which I wrote, but you will have to write it yourself.

28. וַיְהִי שָׁם עִם ה׳ — *And he was there with* HASHEM . . . for the last time.

32. וַיְצַוֵּם אֵת כָּל אֲשֶׁר דִּבֶּר ה׳ אִתּוֹ — *And he commanded them all that* HASHEM *had spoken with him* . . . the work of the Sanctuary, its appointments and the offering of the *beka* (half-*shekel*) for each person (lit., "per head").

33. וַיְכַל מֹשֶׁה מִדַּבֵּר אִתָּם — *And when Moses had done speaking with them.* But when he still spoke to them it was without the veil, similar to, וְהָיוּ עֵינֶיךָ רֹאוֹת אֶת מוֹרֶיךָ, *your eyes shall see your teachers (Isaiah* 30:20), and as our Sages say: "And if I saw his face I would be even sharper" *(Eruvin* 13b).

NOTES

people, communicating the message of God to them. Although his face sent forth rays of heavenly light, and the people after the sin were not really worthy to gaze at this radiance, nonetheless Moses did not cover his face, for Torah can best be transmitted when students see the face of their teacher. The *Maharsha* in *Eruvin* 13b explains that when a student sees the subtle expressions on his teacher's face he can more readily understand him. The Talmud there relates that Rav was a student of R' Meir. In those days students sat in a circle with some sitting in front of their teacher while others sat behind him. Rav is quoted as saying, "I am sharper than others because I studied under R' Meir, but I was seated behind him. Had I been seated in front and been privileged to see his face I would be even sharper." The *Sforno* cites this statement to prove his point that Moses showed his face to the people while instructing them.

פרשת ויקהל

לה
א וַיַּקְהֵ֣ל מֹשֶׁ֗ה אֶֽת־כָּל־עֲדַ֛ת בְּנֵ֥י יִשְׂרָאֵ֖ל וַיֹּ֣אמֶר אֲלֵהֶ֑ם אֵ֚לֶּה הַדְּבָרִ֔ים
ב אֲשֶׁר־צִוָּ֥ה יהוה לַעֲשֹׂ֥ת אֹתָֽם׃ שֵׁ֣שֶׁת יָמִים֮ תֵּעָשֶׂ֣ה מְלָאכָה֒ וּבַיּ֣וֹם
הַשְּׁבִיעִ֗י יִהְיֶ֨ה לָכֶ֥ם קֹ֛דֶשׁ שַׁבַּ֥ת שַׁבָּת֖וֹן לַֽיהוה כָּל־הָעֹשֶׂ֥ה ב֛וֹ מְלָאכָ֖ה
ג יוּמָֽת׃ לֹא־תְבַעֲר֣וּ אֵ֔שׁ בְּכֹ֖ל מֹשְׁבֹֽתֵיכֶ֑ם בְּי֖וֹם הַשַּׁבָּֽת׃
ד וַיֹּ֣אמֶר מֹשֶׁ֔ה אֶל־כָּל־עֲדַ֥ת בְּנֵֽי־יִשְׂרָאֵ֖ל לֵאמֹ֑ר זֶ֣ה הַדָּבָ֔ר אֲשֶׁר־צִוָּ֥ה
ה יהוה לֵאמֹֽר׃ קְח֨וּ מֵאִתְּכֶ֤ם תְּרוּמָה֙ לַֽיהוה כֹּ֚ל נְדִ֣יב לִבּ֔וֹ יְבִיאֶ֕הָ אֵ֖ת
ו תְּרוּמַ֣ת יהוה זָהָ֥ב וָכֶ֖סֶף וּנְחֹֽשֶׁת׃ וּתְכֵ֧לֶת וְאַרְגָּמָ֛ן וְתוֹלַ֥עַת שָׁנִ֖י
ז־ח וְשֵׁ֥שׁ וְעִזִּֽים׃ וְעֹרֹ֨ת אֵילִ֧ם מְאָדָּמִ֛ים וְעֹרֹ֥ת תְּחָשִׁ֖ים וַעֲצֵ֥י שִׁטִּֽים׃ וְשֶׁ֖מֶן
ט לַמָּא֑וֹר וּבְשָׂמִים֙ לְשֶׁ֣מֶן הַמִּשְׁחָ֔ה וְלִקְטֹ֖רֶת הַסַּמִּֽים׃ וְאַבְנֵי־שֹׁ֔הַם וְאַבְנֵ֖י
י מִלֻּאִ֑ים לָאֵפ֖וֹד וְלַחֹֽשֶׁן׃ וְכָל־חֲכַם־לֵ֖ב בָּכֶ֑ם יָבֹ֣אוּ וְיַעֲשׂ֔וּ אֵ֥ת כָּל־
יא אֲשֶׁ֥ר צִוָּ֖ה יהוה׃ אֶ֨ת־הַמִּשְׁכָּ֔ן אֶת־אָהֳל֖וֹ וְאֶת־מִכְסֵ֑הוּ אֶת־קְרָסָיו֙
יב וְאֶת־קְרָשָׁ֔יו אֶת־בְּרִיחָ֕ו אֶת־עַמֻּדָ֖יו וְאֶת־אֲדָנָֽיו׃ אֶת־הָאָרֹ֥ן וְאֶת־בַּדָּ֖יו
יג אֶת־הַכַּפֹּ֑רֶת וְאֵ֖ת פָּרֹ֥כֶת הַמָּסָֽךְ׃ אֶת־הַשֻּׁלְחָ֥ן וְאֶת־בַּדָּ֖יו וְאֶת־כָּל־
יד כֵּלָ֑יו וְאֵ֖ת לֶ֥חֶם הַפָּנִֽים׃ וְאֶת־מְנֹרַ֥ת הַמָּא֛וֹר וְאֶת־כֵּלֶ֖יהָ וְאֶת־נֵרֹתֶ֑יהָ
טו וְאֵ֖ת שֶׁ֥מֶן הַמָּאֽוֹר׃ וְאֶת־מִזְבַּ֤ח הַקְּטֹ֙רֶת֙ וְאֶת־בַּדָּ֔יו וְאֵת֙ שֶׁ֣מֶן הַמִּשְׁחָ֔ה
טז וְאֵ֖ת קְטֹ֣רֶת הַסַּמִּ֑ים וְאֶת־מָסַ֥ךְ הַפֶּ֖תַח לְפֶ֥תַח הַמִּשְׁכָּֽן׃ אֵ֣ת ׀ מִזְבַּ֣ח
הָעֹלָ֗ה וְאֶת־מִכְבַּ֤ר הַנְּחֹ֙שֶׁת֙ אֲשֶׁר־ל֔וֹ אֶת־בַּדָּ֖יו וְאֶת־כָּל־כֵּלָ֑יו אֶת־
יז הַכִּיֹּ֖ר וְאֶת־כַּנּֽוֹ׃ אֵ֚ת קַלְעֵ֣י הֶֽחָצֵ֔ר אֶת־עַמֻּדָ֖יו וְאֶת־אֲדָנֶ֑יהָ וְאֵ֕ת מָסַ֖ךְ

XXXV

1. אֵלֶּה הַדְּבָרִים אֲשֶׁר צִוָּה ה׳ — *These are the words which Hashem has commanded.* That which I said above when I commanded you all that God had spoken with me on the mountain of Sinai (34:32), they are the things which He commanded to do (only) on weekdays.

2. וּבַיּוֹם הַשְּׁבִיעִי יִהְיֶה לָכֶם קֹדֶשׁ — *On the seventh day there shall be to you a holy [day].* And you shall not do (any work) even the work of the Sanctuary.

כָּל הָעֹשֶׂה בוֹ מְלָאכָה יוּמָת — *Whosoever does any work therein shall be put to death.* Even though it is the work of a *mitzvah* (commanded by God).

3. לֹא תְבַעֲרוּ אֵשׁ — *You shall kindle no fire.* Even though kindling a fire in itself is in most instances destructive (damaging), nonetheless since (fire) is the medium (means) for all, or most, works — it is prohibited on the Sabbath.

NOTES

XXXV

1. אֵלֶּה הַדְּבָרִים אֲשֶׁר צִוָּה ה׳ — *These are the words which Hashem has commanded.* The *Sforno* links this verse to the following one which speaks of the Sabbath and the prohibition of doing any work — including that of constructing the *Mishkan* — on the Sabbath. The sense of the verse is: When Moses came down from Sinai he commanded Israel concerning the Tabernacle and the half-*shekel*, as the *Sforno* explained above (34:32). Now he tells them that these labors and contributions shall only be done and collected during the six days of the week, but not on the Sabbath, even though it is a *mitzvah*.

3. לֹא תְבַעֲרוּ אֵשׁ — *You shall kindle no fire.* There are thirty-nine prohibited labors on the Sabbath. There are different reasons given in the Talmud (*Sanhedrin* 35) as to why the Torah here chooses to specify only one, namely that of kindling a fire. The *Sforno's* answer is according to R' Shimon

PARASHAS VAYAKHEL

35 *1 Moses assembled the entire assembly of the Children of Israel and said
to them: "These are the things that HASHEM commanded, to do them:
2 " 'On six days, work may be done, but the seventh day shall be holy for
you, a day of complete rest for HASHEM; whoever does work on it shall be put
to death. 3 You shall not kindle fire in any of your dwellings on the Sabbath
day.' "
4 Moses said to the entire assembly of the Children of Israel, saying: "This
is the word that HASHEM has commanded, saying: 5 'Take from yourselves
a portion for HASHEM, everyone whose heart motivates him shall bring it, as
the gift for HASHEM: gold, silver, copper; 6 turquoise, purple, and scarlet
wool; linen, goat hair; 7 red-dyed ram skins, tachash skins, acacia wood; 8 oil
for illumination, spices for the anointment oil and the aromatic incense;
9 shoham stones and stones for the settings, for the Ephod and the
Breastplate.'
10 " 'Every wise-hearted person among you shall come and make
everything that HASHEM has commanded: 11 the Tabernacle, its Tent, and its
Cover, its hooks, its planks, its bars, its pillars, and its sockets; 12 the Ark and
its staves, the Cover, the Partition-curtain; 13 the Table, its staves, and all its
utensils, and the show-bread; 14 the Menorah of illumination, its utensils,
and its lamps, and oil for the illumination; 15 the Incense Altar and its staves,
the anointment oil and the incense spices, and the entrance-screen for
the entrance of the Tabernacle; 16 the Elevation-offering Altar and the
copper netting for it, its staves, and all its utensils, the Laver and its base;
17 the curtains of the Courtyard, its pillars, and its sockets, and the screen*

---

5. קְחוּ מֵאִתְּכֶם — *Take from among you.* You shall choose men who will accept from you offerings to God.

כֹּל נְדִיב לִבּוֹ — *Whosoever is of a willing heart.* The officers shall not collect with force.

יְבִיאֶהָ אֵת תְּרוּמַת ה׳ — *Let him bring it with HASHEM's offering.* He shall bring the offering (together) with *HASHEM's offering* which is not a (voluntary) offering, (namely) the offering of בֶּקַע לַגֻּלְגֹּלֶת, *a half-shekel a head* (38:26).

11. אֶת הַמִּשְׁכָּן אֶת אָהֳלוֹ — *The Mishkan, its tent.* That which he had already explained to Israel when he said, וַיְצַוֵּם אֵת כָּל אֲשֶׁר דִּבֶּר ה׳ אִתּוֹ בְּהַר סִינָי, *And he commanded them all that HASHEM had spoken with him in Mount Sinai* (34:32).

NOTES

(*Shabbos* 106a). Whereas מְקַלְקֵל, *a destructive, damaging act*, on the Sabbath is normally non-punishable, if it serves a constructive purpose one is liable. As the *Sforno* explains, in conjunction with the construction of the Sanctuary most work required fire, hence it was no longer מְקַלְקֵל but of a positive nature and therefore prohibited.

5. קְחוּ מֵאִתְּכֶם — *Take from among you.* The expression קְחוּ, *take*, in this verse, similar to that of וְיִקְחוּ in 25:2, is difficult to understand. Would not the word תְּנוּ, *give*, and וְיִתְּנוּ have been more appropriate? The *Sforno*, however, both here and in *Parashas Terumah*, explains the choice of this word as meaning to appoint officers who will *take* (i.e., accept) the offerings from the people.

יְבִיאֶהָ אֵת תְּרוּמַת ה׳ — *Let him bring it with HASHEM's offering.* The word אֵת in this verse means *with.* Therefore the *Sforno* explains that together with the free-will offerings of gold, silver and brass, the officers were to collect the mandatory half-*shekel* from each Israelite. This explains the repetition of the word תְּרוּמָה in this verse; one applies to the contribution and the other to the tax.

יח שַׁעַר הֶחָצֵר: אֶת־יִתְדֹת הַמִּשְׁכָּן וְאֶת־יִתְדֹת הֶחָצֵר וְאֶת־מֵיתְרֵיהֶם:
יט אֶת־בִּגְדֵי הַשְּׂרָד לְשָׁרֵת בַּקֹּדֶשׁ אֶת־בִּגְדֵי הַקֹּדֶשׁ לְאַהֲרֹן הַכֹּהֵן
שני כ־כא וְאֶת־בִּגְדֵי בָנָיו לְכַהֵן: וַיֵּצְאוּ כָּל־עֲדַת בְּנֵי־יִשְׂרָאֵל מִלִּפְנֵי מֹשֶׁה: וַיָּבֹאוּ
כָּל־אִישׁ אֲשֶׁר־נְשָׂאוֹ לִבּוֹ וְכֹל אֲשֶׁר נָדְבָה רוּחוֹ אֹתוֹ הֵבִיאוּ
אֶת־תְּרוּמַת יהוה לִמְלֶאכֶת אֹהֶל מוֹעֵד וּלְכָל־עֲבֹדָתוֹ וּלְבִגְדֵי הַקֹּדֶשׁ:
כב וַיָּבֹאוּ הָאֲנָשִׁים עַל־הַנָּשִׁים כֹּל | נְדִיב לֵב הֵבִיאוּ חָח וָנֶזֶם וְטַבַּעַת וְכוּמָז
כג כָּל־כְּלִי זָהָב וְכָל־אִישׁ אֲשֶׁר הֵנִיף תְּנוּפַת זָהָב לַיהוה: וְכָל־אִישׁ
אֲשֶׁר־נִמְצָא אִתּוֹ תְּכֵלֶת וְאַרְגָּמָן וְתוֹלַעַת שָׁנִי וְשֵׁשׁ וְעִזִּים וְעֹרֹת אֵילִם
כד מְאָדָּמִים וְעֹרֹת תְּחָשִׁים הֵבִיאוּ: כָּל־מֵרִים תְּרוּמַת כֶּסֶף וּנְחֹשֶׁת הֵבִיאוּ
אֵת תְּרוּמַת יהוה וְכֹל אֲשֶׁר נִמְצָא אִתּוֹ עֲצֵי שִׁטִּים לְכָל־מְלֶאכֶת
כה הָעֲבֹדָה הֵבִיאוּ: וְכָל־אִשָּׁה חַכְמַת־לֵב בְּיָדֶיהָ טָווּ וַיָּבִיאוּ מַטְוֶה
כו אֶת־הַתְּכֵלֶת וְאֶת־הָאַרְגָּמָן אֶת־תּוֹלַעַת הַשָּׁנִי וְאֶת־הַשֵּׁשׁ: וְכָל־הַנָּשִׁים
כז אֲשֶׁר נָשָׂא לִבָּן אֹתָנָה בְּחָכְמָה טָווּ אֶת־הָעִזִּים: וְהַנְּשִׂאִם הֵבִיאוּ אֵת
כח אַבְנֵי הַשֹּׁהַם וְאֵת אַבְנֵי הַמִּלֻּאִים לָאֵפוֹד וְלַחֹשֶׁן: וְאֶת־הַבֹּשֶׂם
כט וְאֶת־הַשָּׁמֶן לְמָאוֹר וּלְשֶׁמֶן הַמִּשְׁחָה וְלִקְטֹרֶת הַסַּמִּים: כָּל־אִישׁ וְאִשָּׁה
אֲשֶׁר נָדַב לִבָּם אֹתָם לְהָבִיא לְכָל־הַמְּלָאכָה אֲשֶׁר צִוָּה יהוה לַעֲשׂוֹת
בְּיַד־מֹשֶׁה הֵבִיאוּ בְנֵי־יִשְׂרָאֵל נְדָבָה לַיהוה:
שלישי [שני] ל וַיֹּאמֶר מֹשֶׁה אֶל־בְּנֵי יִשְׂרָאֵל רְאוּ קָרָא יהוה בְּשֵׁם בְּצַלְאֵל בֶּן־אוּרִי
לא בֶן־חוּר לְמַטֵּה יְהוּדָה: וַיְמַלֵּא אֹתוֹ רוּחַ אֱלֹהִים בְּחָכְמָה בִּתְבוּנָה וּבְדַעַת
לב וּבְכָל־מְלָאכָה: וְלַחְשֹׁב מַחֲשָׁבֹת לַעֲשֹׂת בַּזָּהָב וּבַכֶּסֶף וּבַנְּחֹשֶׁת:
לג וּבַחֲרֹשֶׁת אֶבֶן לְמַלֹּאת וּבַחֲרֹשֶׁת עֵץ לַעֲשׂוֹת בְּכָל־מְלֶאכֶת מַחֲשָׁבֶת:
לד וּלְהוֹרֹת נָתַן בְּלִבּוֹ הוּא וְאָהֳלִיאָב בֶּן־אֲחִיסָמָךְ לְמַטֵּה־דָן:

---

22. וַיָּבֹאוּ הָאֲנָשִׁים עַל הַנָּשִׁים — *And the men came with the women.* (Together) with the contributing women came their men (husbands) to confirm their offerings, so that the officers would accept them, since we do not accept (contributions) from women except for small (insignificant) things.

וְכָל אִישׁ אֲשֶׁר הֵנִיף תְּנוּפַת זָהָב — *And every man that brought a waving (offering) of gold.* And together with the women who contributed gold jewelry, men also who offered (gifts) of gold, similar to that which our Sages say, "A row which was all silver — silver; which was all gold — gold. They were not mingled" (*Pesachim* 64a).

NOTES

22. וַיָּבֹאוּ הָאֲנָשִׁים עַל הַנָּשִׁים . . . וְכָל אִישׁ אֲשֶׁר הֵנִיף תְּנוּפַת זָהָב — *And the men came with the women . . . And every man that brought a waving (offering) of gold.* The Talmud (*Bava Kama* 119a) states that since what a woman owns belongs to her husband, she can only contribute a small amount of her funds or possessions to charity or any religious cause for we assume that in such a case her husband will not object. When these women were moved to contribute their golden ornaments to the *Mishkan*, it was necessary for their husbands to accompany them and inform the officers that it was with their consent. In this manner the *Sforno* explains the reason why the men came with the women. He also explains the concluding part of this verse as meaning that since those men who brought gold were in the minority, since it was unusual for them to have gold trinkets or jewelry, they came together with the women so as to join those who were contributing that particular precious metal. We see from the selection of the Mishnah cited by the *Sforno* that when the *Pesach*

of the gate of the Courtyard; 18 *the pegs of the Tabernacle, the pegs of the*
Courtyard, and their cords; 19 *the knit vestments to serve in the Sanctuary,*
the sacred vestments for Aaron the Kohen and the vestments of his sons to minister.' "

20 *The entire assembly of the Children of Israel left Moses' presence.*

21 *Every man whose heart inspired him came; and everyone whose spirit motivated him brought the portion of HASHEM for the work of the Tent of Meeting, for all its labor and for the sacred vestments.*

22 *The men came with the women; everyone whose heart motivated him*
brought bracelets, nose-rings, rings, body ornaments — all sorts of gold
ornaments — every man who raised up an offering of gold to HASHEM.
23 *Every man with whom was found turquoise, purple, and scarlet wool,*
linen, and goat hair, red-dyed ram skins, and tachash skins brought them.
24 *Every man who separated a portion of silver or copper brought it as a*
portion for HASHEM; and everyone with whom there was acacia wood for
any work of the labor brought it. 25 *Every wise-hearted woman spun with her*
hands; and they brought the spun yarn of turquoise, purple, and scarlet
wool, and the linen. 26 *All the women whose hearts inspired them with*
wisdom spun the goat hair. 27 *The leaders brought the shoham stones and the*
stones for the settings for the Ephod and the Breastplate; 28 *the spice and the*
oil, for illumination and for the anointment oil and the incense spices.
29 *Every man and woman whose heart motivated them to bring for any of*
the work that HASHEM had commanded to make, through Moses — the
Children of Israel brought a free-willed offering to HASHEM.

30 *Moses said to the Children of Israel, "See, HASHEM has proclaimed by*
name, Bezalel son of Uri son of Hur, of the tribe of Judah. 31 *He filled him with*
Godly spirit, with wisdom, insight, and knowledge, and with every craft —
32 *to weave designs, to work with gold, silver, and copper;* 33 *stone-cutting for*
setting, and wood-carving — to perform every craft of design. 34 *He gave him*
the ability to teach, him and Oholiab, son of Ahisamach, of the tribe of Dan.

---

26. טָווּ אֶת הָעִזִּים — *Spun the goats' hair . . .* (while it was still) on the goats, as our Sages tell us (*Shabbos* 99a), so that there be added gloss to the spun hair, because many removed (items) are diminished somewhat in quality when they are detached from their place of growth (origin), as it happens with bee honey, cassia (a variety of cinnamon), milk and others.

NOTES

sacrifice (קָרְבַּן פֶּסַח) was brought, the row of priests with gold receptacles was separate from those who stood with silver receptacles (*Pesachim* 64a). This was done for aesthetic reasons; hence the same was true when the Israelites lined up to bring their offerings to the work of the *Mishkan*. The *Ramban* also comments that there were few men who brought gold, and that is why the expression תְּנוּפָה, *waving*, is used, indicating that the officers would wave it so the people should see the generous contribution of that particular donor!

26. טָווּ אֶת הָעִזִּים — *Spun the goats' hair.* The previous verse states, *all the women that were wise hearted*, whereas this verse uses the expression *whose heart stirred them up*. Also the expression טָווּ אֶת הָעִזִּים literally translated means *spun the goats;* the word *hair* is not specifically written. For these reasons *Rashi*, quoting the Talmud, comments that the spinning was done while the hair was still on the living animal, which required extraordinary skill. The *Sforno* adds that this was done so that none of the gloss should be lost in the process.

לה מְלֵּא אֹתָם חָכְמַת־לֵב לַעֲשׂוֹת כָּל־מְלֶאכֶת חָרָשׁ ׀ וְחֹשֵׁב וְרֹקֵם
בַּתְּכֵלֶת וּבָאַרְגָּמָן בְּתוֹלַעַת הַשָּׁנִי וּבַשֵּׁשׁ וְאֹרֵג עֹשֵׂי כָּל־מְלָאכָה
לו א וְחֹשְׁבֵי מַחֲשָׁבֹת: וְעָשָׂה בְצַלְאֵל וְאָהֳלִיאָב וְכֹל ׀ אִישׁ חֲכַם־לֵב אֲשֶׁר
נָתַן יהוה חָכְמָה וּתְבוּנָה בָּהֵמָּה לָדַעַת לַעֲשֹׂת אֶת־כָּל־מְלֶאכֶת עֲבֹדַת
ב הַקֹּדֶשׁ לְכֹל אֲשֶׁר־צִוָּה יהוה: וַיִּקְרָא מֹשֶׁה אֶל־בְּצַלְאֵל וְאֶל־אָהֳלִיאָב
וְאֶל כָּל־אִישׁ חֲכַם־לֵב אֲשֶׁר נָתַן יהוה חָכְמָה בְּלִבּוֹ כֹּל אֲשֶׁר נְשָׂאוֹ
ג לִבּוֹ לְקָרְבָה אֶל־הַמְּלָאכָה לַעֲשֹׂת אֹתָהּ: וַיִּקְחוּ מִלִּפְנֵי מֹשֶׁה אֵת
כָּל־הַתְּרוּמָה אֲשֶׁר הֵבִיאוּ בְּנֵי יִשְׂרָאֵל לִמְלֶאכֶת עֲבֹדַת הַקֹּדֶשׁ לַעֲשֹׂת
ד אֹתָהּ וְהֵם הֵבִיאוּ אֵלָיו עוֹד נְדָבָה בַּבֹּקֶר בַּבֹּקֶר: וַיָּבֹאוּ כָּל־הַחֲכָמִים
הָעֹשִׂים אֵת כָּל־מְלֶאכֶת הַקֹּדֶשׁ אִישׁ־אִישׁ מִמְּלַאכְתּוֹ אֲשֶׁר־הֵמָּה
ה עֹשִׂים: וַיֹּאמְרוּ אֶל־מֹשֶׁה לֵּאמֹר מַרְבִּים הָעָם לְהָבִיא מִדֵּי הָעֲבֹדָה
ו לַמְּלָאכָה אֲשֶׁר־צִוָּה יהוה לַעֲשֹׂת אֹתָהּ: וַיְצַו מֹשֶׁה וַיַּעֲבִירוּ קוֹל בַּמַּחֲנֶה
לֵאמֹר אִישׁ וְאִשָּׁה אַל־יַעֲשׂוּ־עוֹד מְלָאכָה לִתְרוּמַת הַקֹּדֶשׁ וַיִּכָּלֵא
ז הָעָם מֵהָבִיא: וְהַמְּלָאכָה הָיְתָה דַיָּם לְכָל־הַמְּלָאכָה לַעֲשׂוֹת אֹתָהּ
רביעי ח וְהוֹתֵר: וַיַּעֲשׂוּ כָל־חֲכַם־לֵב בְּעֹשֵׂי הַמְּלָאכָה אֶת־
הַמִּשְׁכָּן עֶשֶׂר יְרִיעֹת שֵׁשׁ מָשְׁזָר וּתְכֵלֶת וְאַרְגָּמָן וְתוֹלַעַת שָׁנִי כְּרֻבִים

XXXVI

4. אִישׁ אִישׁ מִמְּלַאכְתּוֹ — *Every man from his work.* The (Torah) relates the trustworthiness of each craftsman and the generosity of Israel regarding all that was necessary for each of the works.

5. לַמְּלָאכָה אֲשֶׁר צִוָּה ה׳ לַעֲשֹׂת אֹתָהּ — *For the work which HASHEM commanded to make.* Behold, the contribution of the people is more than what is required for the work which God commanded to make, i.e., without additions or subtractions, for He gave exact measures (requirements) for the *Mishkan* and its furnishings, (and one is) neither to add nor diminish them, unlike the structures of Solomon and Herod (Hordos).

6. אַל יַעֲשׂוּ עוֹד מְלָאכָה לִתְרוּמַת הַקֹּדֶשׁ — *Let none make any more work for the offering of the Sanctuary.* He did not announce that they should not bring voluntary contributions, but he announced that they should not do any more work, such as the spinning work, as it says, וַיָּבִיאוּ מַטְוֶה, *and brought that which they had spun* (35:25), and the preparation work of the wood, as it says, עֲצֵי שִׁטִּים לְכָל מְלֶאכֶת הָעֲבֹדָה הֵבִיאוּ, *acacia wood for any work of the service did they bring* (35:24), and the preparation of the hides, and other (similar work).

NOTES

XXXVI

5-7. לַמְּלָאכָה אֲשֶׁר צִוָּה ה׳ לַעֲשֹׂת אֹתָהּ . . . אַל יַעֲשׂוּ עוֹד מְלָאכָה לִתְרוּמַת הַקֹּדֶשׁ . . . וְהַמְּלָאכָה הָיְתָה דַיָּם . . . וְהוֹתֵר — *For the work which HASHEM commanded to make . . . Let none make any more work for the offering of the Sanctuary . . . And the work was sufficient . . . and too much.* The *Sforno* explains these three verses in the following manner. Insofar as contributions were concerned there was no objection to the people bringing as much as they wanted. This, however, would in no way change the number of component parts of the *Mishkan,* nor the qualitative manner in which they would be constructed or fashioned, since God had given exact instructions regarding the dimensions and measurements of the structure, the furnishings and vessels. Therefore the announcement was not to do any more work. It was not to cease bringing contributions of gold, silver, brass or other materials. The *Sforno* explains verse 7 which seemingly contradicts itself, by first stating דַיָּם, *sufficient,* and then וְהוֹתֵר, *too much,* by pointing out that only by bringing a bit more than needed was the material sufficient for the worker who did not

[35] *He filled them with a wise heart to do every craft of the carver, weaver
of designs, and embroiderer — with the turquoise, purple, and scarlet wool,
and the linen — and the weaver; the artisans of every craft and makers of
designs.*

36 [1] *Bezalel shall carry out — with Oholiab and every wise-hearted man
within whom* HASHEM *had endowed wisdom and insight to know and
to do all the work for the labor of the Sanctuary — everything that* HASHEM
had commanded. [2] *Moses summoned Bezalel, Oholiab, and every wise-
hearted man whose heart* HASHEM *endowed with wisdom, everyone whose
heart inspired him, to approach the work, to do it.* [3] *From Moses' presence
they took the entire gift that the Children of Israel had brought for the work
for the labor of the Sanctuary, to do it. But they continued to bring him
free-willed gifts morning after morning.*

[4] *All the wise people came — those performing all the sacred work, each
of them from his work that they were doing —* [5] *and they said to Moses, as
follows, "The people are bringing more than enough for the labor of the
work that* HASHEM *has commanded to perform."*

[6] *Moses commanded that they proclaim throughout the camp, saying,
"Man and woman shall not do more work toward the gift for the
Sanctuary!" And the people were restrained from bringing.* [7] *But the work
had been enough for all the work, to do it — and there was extra.*

[8] *The wise-hearted among those doing the work made the Tabernacle:
ten curtains of linen, twisted with turquoise, purple, and scarlet wool; they*

---

7. וְהַמְּלָאכָה הָיְתָה דַיָּם — *And the work was sufficient.* The work (i.e., material) of the donors in all that they contributed was sufficient for the workers of the *Mishkan.*

לְכָל הַמְּלָאכָה — *For all the work . . .* (i.e.,) for every aspect of work that was (required) to do it.

לַעֲשׂוֹת אֹתָהּ וְהוֹתֵר — *To make it, and too much.* To do that work and to leave over, in such a manner that they did not have to stint in the method of their workmanship due to any concern that material may be lacking.

8. וַיַּעֲשׂוּ כָל חֲכַם לֵב בְּעֹשֵׂי הַמְּלָאכָה — *And every wise-hearted man among them who did the work.* The wiser ones among them made the *mishkan* (curtains) which was *the work of skillful workers* (26:1) having different figures on their two sides, as our Sages mention (*Yoma* 72b). Now these curtains were not as thick as the *paroches* (the curtain separating the Holy of Holies from the Holy). The (Torah) repeats in this chapter all that was (already) said in (the form) of a command in *Parashas Terumah,* (in order) to tell us that they made everything with the intent to do the will of Him Who commanded and toward (His) goal (purpose). The Ark, which was singular among the furnishings, was made by

NOTES

have to stint or worry that he would not have enough to complete his work.

8. וַיַּעֲשׂוּ כָל חֲכַם לֵב בְּעֹשֵׂי הַמְּלָאכָה — *And every wise-hearted man among them who did the work.* The *Sforno* explains that although both the *mishkan*-curtains and the *paroches* required skillful workmanship the former was more demanding and was executed by wiser ones, for it was made of finer, more delicate material than the veil.

The curtains had figures of cherubim woven into them, the figure of a lion on the one side and an eagle on the other (*Rashi* 26:1). This is referred to as מַעֲשֵׂה חֹשֵׁב, *skillful work.* This same phrase is used regarding the *paroches* in verse 31 of that chapter.

ט מַעֲשֵׂה חֹשֵׁב עָשָׂה אֹתָם: אֹרֶךְ הַיְרִיעָה הָאַחַת שְׁמֹנֶה וְעֶשְׂרִים בָּאַמָּה וְרֹחַב

י אַרְבַּע בָּאַמָּה הַיְרִיעָה הָאֶחָת מִדָּה אַחַת לְכָל-הַיְרִיעֹת: וַיְחַבֵּר אֶת-חֲמֵשׁ

יא הַיְרִיעֹת אַחַת אֶל-אֶחָת וְחָמֵשׁ יְרִיעֹת חִבַּר אַחַת אֶל-אֶחָת: וַיַּעַשׂ לֻלְאֹת

תְּכֵלֶת עַל שְׂפַת הַיְרִיעָה הָאֶחָת מִקָּצָה בַּמַּחְבָּרֶת כֵּן עָשָׂה בִּשְׂפַת הַיְרִיעָה

יב הַקִּיצוֹנָה בַּמַּחְבֶּרֶת הַשֵּׁנִית: חֲמִשִּׁים לֻלָאֹת עָשָׂה בַּיְרִיעָה הָאֶחָת וַחֲמִשִּׁים

לֻלָאֹת עָשָׂה בִּקְצֵה הַיְרִיעָה אֲשֶׁר בַּמַּחְבֶּרֶת הַשֵּׁנִית מַקְבִּילֹת הַלֻּלָאֹת אַחַת

יג אֶל-אֶחָת: וַיַּעַשׂ חֲמִשִּׁים קַרְסֵי זָהָב וַיְחַבֵּר אֶת-הַיְרִיעֹת אַחַת אֶל-אַחַת

בַּקְּרָסִים וַיְהִי הַמִּשְׁכָּן אֶחָד:

יד-טו וַיַּעַשׂ יְרִיעֹת עִזִּים לְאֹהֶל עַל-הַמִּשְׁכָּן עַשְׁתֵּי-עֶשְׂרֵה יְרִיעֹת עָשָׂה אֹתָם: אֹרֶךְ

הַיְרִיעָה הָאַחַת שְׁלֹשִׁים בָּאַמָּה וְאַרְבַּע אַמּוֹת רֹחַב הַיְרִיעָה הָאֶחָת מִדָּה

טז אַחַת לְעַשְׁתֵּי עֶשְׂרֵה יְרִיעֹת: וַיְחַבֵּר אֶת-חֲמֵשׁ הַיְרִיעֹת לְבָד וְאֶת-שֵׁשׁ

יז הַיְרִיעֹת לְבָד: וַיַּעַשׂ לֻלָאֹת חֲמִשִּׁים עַל שְׂפַת הַיְרִיעָה הַקִּיצֹנָה בַּמַּחְבָּרֶת

יח וַחֲמִשִּׁים לֻלָאֹת עָשָׂה עַל-שְׂפַת הַיְרִיעָה הַחֹבֶרֶת הַשֵּׁנִית: וַיַּעַשׂ קַרְסֵי נְחֹשֶׁת

יט חֲמִשִּׁים לְחַבֵּר אֶת-הָאֹהֶל לִהְיֹת אֶחָד: וַיַּעַשׂ מִכְסֶה לָאֹהֶל עֹרֹת אֵילִם

כ מְאָדָּמִים וּמִכְסֵה עֹרֹת תְּחָשִׁים מִלְמָעְלָה: וַיַּעַשׂ אֶת-הַקְּרָשִׁים   חמישי

כא לַמִּשְׁכָּן עֲצֵי שִׁטִּים עֹמְדִים: עֶשֶׂר אַמֹּת אֹרֶךְ הַקָּרֶשׁ וְאַמָּה וַחֲצִי הָאַמָּה רֹחַב

כב הַקֶּרֶשׁ הָאֶחָד: שְׁתֵּי יָדֹת לַקֶּרֶשׁ הָאֶחָד מְשֻׁלָּבֹת אַחַת אֶל-אֶחָת כֵּן עָשָׂה

כג לְכֹל קַרְשֵׁי הַמִּשְׁכָּן: וַיַּעַשׂ אֶת-הַקְּרָשִׁים לַמִּשְׁכָּן עֶשְׂרִים קְרָשִׁים לִפְאַת נֶגֶב

כד תֵּימָנָה: וְאַרְבָּעִים אַדְנֵי-כֶסֶף עָשָׂה תַּחַת עֶשְׂרִים הַקְּרָשִׁים שְׁנֵי אֲדָנִים

תַּחַת-הַקֶּרֶשׁ הָאֶחָד לִשְׁתֵּי יְדֹתָיו וּשְׁנֵי אֲדָנִים תַּחַת-הַקֶּרֶשׁ הָאֶחָד לִשְׁתֵּי

כה-כו יְדֹתָיו: וּלְצֶלַע הַמִּשְׁכָּן הַשֵּׁנִית לִפְאַת צָפוֹן עָשָׂה עֶשְׂרִים קְרָשִׁים: וְאַרְבָּעִים

אַדְנֵיהֶם כָּסֶף שְׁנֵי אֲדָנִים תַּחַת הַקֶּרֶשׁ הָאֶחָד וּשְׁנֵי אֲדָנִים תַּחַת הַקֶּרֶשׁ

כז-כח הָאֶחָד: וּלְיַרְכְּתֵי הַמִּשְׁכָּן יָמָּה עָשָׂה שִׁשָּׁה קְרָשִׁים: וּשְׁנֵי קְרָשִׁים עָשָׂה

כט לִמְקֻצְעֹת הַמִּשְׁכָּן בַּיַּרְכָתָיִם: וְהָיוּ תוֹאֲמִם מִלְּמַטָּה וְיַחְדָּו יִהְיוּ תַמִּים

אֶל-רֹאשׁוֹ אֶל-הַטַּבַּעַת הָאֶחָת כֵּן עָשָׂה לִשְׁנֵיהֶם לִשְׁנֵי הַמִּקְצֹעֹת: וְהָיוּ

ל שְׁמֹנָה קְרָשִׁים וְאַדְנֵיהֶם כֶּסֶף שִׁשָּׁה עָשָׂר אֲדָנִים שְׁנֵי אֲדָנִים שְׁנֵי אֲדָנִים תַּחַת

לא הַקֶּרֶשׁ הָאֶחָד: וַיַּעַשׂ בְּרִיחֵי עֲצֵי שִׁטִּים חֲמִשָּׁה לְקַרְשֵׁי צֶלַע-הַמִּשְׁכָּן הָאֶחָת:

לב וַחֲמִשָּׁה בְרִיחִם לְקַרְשֵׁי צֶלַע-הַמִּשְׁכָּן הַשֵּׁנִית וַחֲמִשָּׁה בְרִיחִם לְקַרְשֵׁי הַמִּשְׁכָּן

לג לַיַּרְכָתַיִם יָמָּה: וַיַּעַשׂ אֶת-הַבְּרִיחַ הַתִּיכֹן לִבְרֹחַ בְּתוֹךְ הַקְּרָשִׁים מִן-הַקָּצֶה

לד אֶל-הַקָּצֶה: וְאֶת-הַקְּרָשִׁים צִפָּה זָהָב וְאֶת-טַבְּעֹתָם עָשָׂה זָהָב בָּתִּים לַבְּרִיחִם

לה וַיְצַף אֶת-הַבְּרִיחִם זָהָב: וַיַּעַשׂ אֶת-הַפָּרֹכֶת תְּכֵלֶת וְאַרְגָּמָן וְתוֹלַעַת שָׁנִי

לו וְשֵׁשׁ מָשְׁזָר מַעֲשֵׂה חֹשֵׁב עָשָׂה אֹתָהּ כְּרֻבִים: וַיַּעַשׂ לָהּ אַרְבָּעָה עַמּוּדֵי שִׁטִּים

וַיְצַפֵּם זָהָב וָוֵיהֶם זָהָב וַיִּצֹק לָהֶם אַרְבָּעָה אַדְנֵי-כָסֶף: וַיַּעַשׂ מָסָךְ לְפֶתַח

לז

לח הָאֹהֶל תְּכֵלֶת וְאַרְגָּמָן וְתוֹלַעַת שָׁנִי וְשֵׁשׁ מָשְׁזָר מַעֲשֵׂה רֹקֵם: וְאֶת-עַמּוּדָיו

חֲמִשָּׁה וְאֶת-וָוֵיהֶם וְצִפָּה רָאשֵׁיהֶם וַחֲשֻׁקֵיהֶם זָהָב וְאַדְנֵיהֶם חֲמִשָּׁה נְחֹשֶׁת:

Bezalel who was the greatest (craftsman) of them all, as our Sages say, "Bezalel knew how to combine (or join) the letters with which heaven and earth were created" (*Berachos* 55a).

made them with a woven design of cherubs. 9 The length of each curtain was
twenty-eight cubits, and the width of each curtain was four cubits, the same
measure for all the curtains. 10 He attached five curtains to one another, and
five curtains he attached to one another. 11 He made loops of turquoise wool
on the edge of a single curtain at the end of one set; so he did at the edge of
the outermost curtain on the second set. 12 He made fifty loops on the one
curtain and he made fifty loops at the end of the curtain that was on the
second set, the loops corresponding to one another. 13 He made fifty clasps of
gold and attached the curtains to one another with the clasps — so the
Tabernacle became one.

14 He made curtains of goat hair for a Tent over the Tabernacle; he made
them eleven curtains. 15 The length of each curtain was thirty cubits, and the
width of each curtain was four cubits; the same measure for the eleven
curtains. 16 He attached five curtains separately and six curtains separately.
17 He made fifty loops on the edge of the outermost curtain of the set, and he
made fifty loops on the edge of the curtain of the second set. 18 He made fifty
clasps of copper to attach the Tent so that it would become one.

19 He made a Cover for the Tent of red-dyed ram hides, and a Cover of
tachash hides on top.

20 He made the planks for the Tabernacle of acacia wood, standing erect.
21 Ten cubits was the height of the plank, and a cubit and a half was the width
of each plank. 22 Each plank shall have two tenons, parallel to one another,
so he did for all the planks of the Tabernacle. 23 He made the planks for the
Tabernacle, twenty planks for the south side. 24 He made forty silver sockets
under the twenty planks, two sockets under one plank for its two tenons, and
two sockets under the next plank for its two tenons. 25 And for the second wall
of the Tabernacle on its north side, he made twenty planks. 26 Their forty
sockets of silver, two sockets under one plank and two sockets under the next
plank. 27 For the back of the Tabernacle on the west, he made six planks. 28 He
made two planks for the corners of the Tabernacle, in the back. 29 They were
even at the bottom and together they were matching at the top, to a single
ring, so he did to them both, at the two corners. 30 There were eight planks and
their silver sockets, sixteen sockets, two sockets, two sockets, under each
plank. 31 He made bars of acacia wood, five for the planks of one side of the
Tabernacle; 32 and five bars for the planks of the second side, and five bars
for the planks of the Tabernacle at the back, on the west. 33 He made the
middle bar to extend within the planks from end to end.

34 He covered the planks with gold and made their rings of gold as housings
for the bars, and he covered the bars with gold.

35 He made the Partition of turquoise, purple, and scarlet wool, and linen,
twisted; he made it with a woven design of cherubs. 36 He made for it four
pillars of acacia wood and plated them with gold, their hooks were gold; and
he cast for them four sockets of silver.

37 For the entrance of the Tent he made a Screen of turquoise, purple, and
scarlet wool, and linen, twisted; work of an embroiderer. 38 Its pillars were
five, with their hooks, and he plated their tops and their bands with gold; and
their sockets were five, of copper.

לז

א וַיַּעַשׂ בְּצַלְאֵל אֶת־הָאָרֹן עֲצֵי שִׁטִּים אַמָּתַיִם וָחֵצִי אָרְכּוֹ וְאַמָּה וָחֵצִי רָחְבּוֹ
ב וְאַמָּה וָחֵצִי קֹמָתוֹ׃ וַיְצַפֵּהוּ זָהָב טָהוֹר מִבַּיִת וּמִחוּץ וַיַּעַשׂ לוֹ זֵר זָהָב סָבִיב׃
ג וַיִּצֹק לוֹ אַרְבַּע טַבְּעֹת זָהָב עַל אַרְבַּע פַּעֲמֹתָיו וּשְׁתֵּי טַבָּעֹת עַל־צַלְעוֹ הָאֶחָת
ד וּשְׁתֵּי טַבָּעֹת עַל־צַלְעוֹ הַשֵּׁנִית׃ וַיַּעַשׂ בַּדֵּי עֲצֵי שִׁטִּים וַיְצַף אֹתָם זָהָב׃ וַיָּבֵא
ה־ו אֶת־הַבַּדִּים בַּטַּבָּעֹת עַל צַלְעֹת הָאָרֹן לָשֵׂאת אֶת־הָאָרֹן׃ וַיַּעַשׂ כַּפֹּרֶת זָהָב
ז טָהוֹר אַמָּתַיִם וָחֵצִי אָרְכָּהּ וְאַמָּה וָחֵצִי רָחְבָּהּ׃ וַיַּעַשׂ שְׁנֵי כְרֻבִים זָהָב מִקְשָׁה
ח עָשָׂה אֹתָם מִשְּׁנֵי קְצוֹת הַכַּפֹּרֶת׃ כְּרוּב־אֶחָד מִקָּצָה מִזֶּה וּכְרוּב־אֶחָד מִקָּצָה
ט מִזֶּה מִן־הַכַּפֹּרֶת עָשָׂה אֶת־הַכְּרֻבִים מִשְּׁנֵי °קצוותו׃ וַיִּהְיוּ הַכְּרֻבִים פֹּרְשֵׂי °קְצוֹתָיו ק׳
כְנָפַיִם לְמַעְלָה סֹכְכִים בְּכַנְפֵיהֶם עַל־הַכַּפֹּרֶת וּפְנֵיהֶם אִישׁ אֶל־אָחִיו אֶל־
הַכַּפֹּרֶת הָיוּ פְּנֵי הַכְּרֻבִים׃

י וַיַּעַשׂ אֶת־הַשֻּׁלְחָן עֲצֵי שִׁטִּים אַמָּתַיִם אָרְכּוֹ וְאַמָּה רָחְבּוֹ וְאַמָּה וָחֵצִי קֹמָתוֹ׃
יא־יב וַיְצַף אֹתוֹ זָהָב טָהוֹר וַיַּעַשׂ לוֹ זֵר זָהָב סָבִיב׃ וַיַּעַשׂ לוֹ מִסְגֶּרֶת טֹפַח סָבִיב
יג וַיַּעַשׂ זֵר־זָהָב לְמִסְגַּרְתּוֹ סָבִיב׃ וַיִּצֹק לוֹ אַרְבַּע טַבְּעֹת זָהָב וַיִּתֵּן אֶת־הַטַּבָּעֹת
יד עַל אַרְבַּע הַפֵּאֹת אֲשֶׁר לְאַרְבַּע רַגְלָיו׃ לְעֻמַּת הַמִּסְגֶּרֶת הָיוּ הַטַּבָּעֹת בָּתִּים
טו לַבַּדִּים לָשֵׂאת אֶת־הַשֻּׁלְחָן׃ וַיַּעַשׂ אֶת־הַבַּדִּים עֲצֵי שִׁטִּים וַיְצַף אֹתָם זָהָב
טז לָשֵׂאת אֶת־הַשֻּׁלְחָן׃ וַיַּעַשׂ אֶת־הַכֵּלִים ׀ אֲשֶׁר עַל־הַשֻּׁלְחָן אֶת־קְעָרֹתָיו
וְאֶת־כַּפֹּתָיו וְאֵת מְנַקִּיֹּתָיו וְאֶת־הַקְּשָׂוֹת אֲשֶׁר יֻסַּךְ בָּהֵן זָהָב טָהוֹר׃
ששי [שלישי] יז וַיַּעַשׂ אֶת־הַמְּנֹרָה זָהָב טָהוֹר מִקְשָׁה עָשָׂה אֶת־הַמְּנֹרָה יְרֵכָהּ וְקָנָהּ גְּבִיעֶיהָ
יח כַּפְתֹּרֶיהָ וּפְרָחֶיהָ מִמֶּנָּה הָיוּ׃ וְשִׁשָּׁה קָנִים יֹצְאִים מִצִּדֶּיהָ שְׁלֹשָׁה ׀ קְנֵי מְנֹרָה
יט מִצִּדָּהּ הָאֶחָד וּשְׁלֹשָׁה קְנֵי מְנֹרָה מִצִּדָּהּ הַשֵּׁנִי׃ שְׁלֹשָׁה גְבִעִים מְשֻׁקָּדִים בַּקָּנֶה
הָאֶחָד כַּפְתֹּר וָפֶרַח וּשְׁלֹשָׁה גְבִעִים מְשֻׁקָּדִים בְּקָנֶה אֶחָד כַּפְתֹּר וָפָרַח כֵּן
כ לְשֵׁשֶׁת הַקָּנִים הַיֹּצְאִים מִן־הַמְּנֹרָה׃ וּבַמְּנֹרָה אַרְבָּעָה גְבִעִים מְשֻׁקָּדִים
כא כַּפְתֹּרֶיהָ וּפְרָחֶיהָ׃ וְכַפְתֹּר תַּחַת שְׁנֵי הַקָּנִים מִמֶּנָּה וְכַפְתֹּר תַּחַת שְׁנֵי הַקָּנִים
מִמֶּנָּה וְכַפְתֹּר תַּחַת־שְׁנֵי הַקָּנִים מִמֶּנָּה לְשֵׁשֶׁת הַקָּנִים הַיֹּצְאִים מִמֶּנָּה׃
כב־כג כַּפְתֹּרֵיהֶם וּקְנֹתָם מִמֶּנָּה הָיוּ כֻּלָּהּ מִקְשָׁה אַחַת זָהָב טָהוֹר׃ וַיַּעַשׂ אֶת־נֵרֹתֶיהָ
כד שִׁבְעָה וּמַלְקָחֶיהָ וּמַחְתֹּתֶיהָ זָהָב טָהוֹר׃ כִּכָּר זָהָב טָהוֹר עָשָׂה אֹתָהּ וְאֵת
כָּל־כֵּלֶיהָ׃

כה וַיַּעַשׂ אֶת־מִזְבַּח הַקְּטֹרֶת עֲצֵי שִׁטִּים אַמָּה אָרְכּוֹ וְאַמָּה רָחְבּוֹ רָבוּעַ וְאַמָּתַיִם
כו קֹמָתוֹ מִמֶּנּוּ הָיוּ קַרְנֹתָיו׃ וַיְצַף אֹתוֹ זָהָב טָהוֹר אֶת־גַּגּוֹ וְאֶת־קִירֹתָיו סָבִיב
כז וְאֶת־קַרְנֹתָיו וַיַּעַשׂ לוֹ זֵר זָהָב סָבִיב׃ וּשְׁתֵּי טַבְּעֹת זָהָב עָשָׂה־לוֹ ׀ מִתַּחַת לְזֵרוֹ
כח עַל שְׁתֵּי צַלְעֹתָיו עַל שְׁנֵי צִדָּיו לְבָתִּים לְבַדִּים לָשֵׂאת אֹתוֹ בָּהֶם׃ וַיַּעַשׂ
כט אֶת־הַבַּדִּים עֲצֵי שִׁטִּים וַיְצַף אֹתָם זָהָב׃ וַיַּעַשׂ אֶת־שֶׁמֶן הַמִּשְׁחָה קֹדֶשׁ

XXXVII

29. וַיַּעַשׂ אֶת שֶׁמֶן הַמִּשְׁחָה קֹדֶשׁ — *And he made the anointing oil holy.* With the intent that

NOTES

XXXVII

29. וַיַּעַשׂ אֶת שֶׁמֶן הַמִּשְׁחָה קֹדֶשׁ וְאֶת קְטֹרֶת הַסַּמִּים טָהוֹר — *And he made the anointing oil holy and the pure incense of the sweet spices.* See the *Sforno* on 30:31 and 30:35 and the explanatory notes on those verses.

37 1 *Bezalel made the Ark of acacia wood, two and a half cubits its length; a
cubit and a half its width; and a cubit and a half its height.* 2 *He covered
it with pure gold, within and without, and he made for it a gold crown all
around.* 3 *He cast for them four rings of gold on its four corners; two rings on
its one side and two rings on its second side.* 4 *He made staves of acacia wood
and covered them with gold.* 5 *He inserted the staves in the rings on the sides
of the Ark, to carry the Ark.*

6 *He made a Cover of pure gold, two and a half cubits its length, and a cubit
and a half its width.* 7 *He made two Cherubs of gold — hammered out did he
make them — from the two ends of the Cover:* 8 *one Cherub from the end at
one side and one Cherub from the end at the other; from the Cover did he
make the Cherubs, from its two ends.* 9 *The Cherubs were with wings spread
upward sheltering the Cover with their wings, with their faces toward one
another; toward the Cover were the faces of the Cherubs.*

10 *He made the Table of acacia wood; two cubits its length; a cubit its
width; and a cubit and a half its height.* 11 *He covered it with pure gold and
made for it a gold crown all around.* 12 *He made for it a molding of one
handbreadth all around, and he made a gold crown for its molding all around.*
13 *He cast for it four rings of gold and placed the rings on the four corners of
its four legs.* 14 *The rings were opposite the molding as housings for the staves,
to carry the Table.* 15 *He made the staves of acacia wood and covered them
with gold, to carry the Table.* 16 *He made the utensils that were on the Table,
its dishes, its spoons, its pillars, and its shelving-tubes, with which it was
covered, of pure gold.*

17 *He made the Menorah of pure gold, hammered out did he make the
Menorah, its base and its shaft, its cups, its knobs, and its flowers were from
it.* 18 *Six branches emerged from its sides, three branches of the Menorah from
its side and three branches of the Menorah from its second side;* 19 *three cups
engraved like almonds on one branch, a knob and a flower; and three cups
engraved like almonds, a knob and a flower on the next branch — so for the
six branches that emerge from the Menorah.* 20 *And on the Menorah were four
cups, engraved like almonds, its knobs and its blossoms.* 21 *A knob was under
two of the branches from it, a knob was under two of the branches from it, and
a knob was under two of the branches from it — for the six branches emerging
from it.* 22 *Their knobs and branches were of it, all of a single hammered piece
of pure gold.* 23 *He made its lamps seven, and its tongs and spoons of pure
gold.* 24 *Of a talent of pure gold did he make it and all its utensils.*

25 *He made the Incense Altar of acacia wood; a cubit its length, and a
cubit its width — square — and two cubits its height, from it were its
horns.* 26 *He covered it with pure gold, its roof and its walls all around and
its horns, and he made for it a gold crown all around.* 27 *He made for it
two gold rings under its crown on its two corners, on its two sides, as
housings for staves, with which to carry it.* 28 *He made the staves of acacia
wood, and covered them with gold.* 29 *He made the anointment oil, holy;*

---

it should not be impaired, as it says, קֹדֶשׁ יִהְיֶה זֶה לִי לְדֹרֹתֵיכֶם, *it shall be holy to Me throughout your generations* (30:31).

לח שביעי א וְאֶת־קְטֹרֶת הַסַּמִּים טָהוֹר מַעֲשֵׂה רֹקֵחַ׃ וַיַּעַשׂ אֶת־מִזְבַּח
[רביעי] הָעֹלָה עֲצֵי שִׁטִּים חָמֵשׁ אַמּוֹת אָרְכּוֹ וְחָמֵשׁ־אַמּוֹת רָחְבּוֹ רָבוּעַ וְשָׁלֹשׁ
ב אַמּוֹת קֹמָתוֹ׃ וַיַּעַשׂ קַרְנֹתָיו עַל אַרְבַּע פִּנֹּתָיו מִמֶּנּוּ הָיוּ קַרְנֹתָיו וַיְצַף
ג אֹתוֹ נְחֹשֶׁת׃ וַיַּעַשׂ אֶת־כָּל־כְּלֵי הַמִּזְבֵּחַ אֶת־הַסִּירֹת וְאֶת־הַיָּעִים
וְאֶת־הַמִּזְרָקֹת אֶת־הַמִּזְלָגֹת וְאֶת־הַמַּחְתֹּת כָּל־כֵּלָיו עָשָׂה נְחֹשֶׁת׃
ד וַיַּעַשׂ לַמִּזְבֵּחַ מִכְבָּר מַעֲשֵׂה רֶשֶׁת נְחֹשֶׁת תַּחַת כַּרְכֻּבּוֹ מִלְּמַטָּה
ה עַד־חֶצְיוֹ׃ וַיִּצֹק אַרְבַּע טַבָּעֹת בְּאַרְבַּע הַקְּצָוֺת לְמִכְבַּר הַנְּחֹשֶׁת בָּתִּים
ו־ז לַבַּדִּים׃ וַיַּעַשׂ אֶת־הַבַּדִּים עֲצֵי שִׁטִּים וַיְצַף אֹתָם נְחֹשֶׁת׃ וַיָּבֵא
אֶת־הַבַּדִּים בַּטַּבָּעֹת עַל צַלְעֹת הַמִּזְבֵּחַ לָשֵׂאת אֹתוֹ בָּהֶם נְבוּב לֻחֹת
ח עָשָׂה אֹתוֹ׃ וַיַּעַשׂ אֵת הַכִּיּוֹר נְחֹשֶׁת וְאֵת כַּנּוֹ נְחֹשֶׁת
ט בְּמַרְאֹת הַצֹּבְאֹת אֲשֶׁר צָבְאוּ פֶּתַח אֹהֶל מוֹעֵד׃ וַיַּעַשׂ
אֶת־הֶחָצֵר לִפְאַת ׀ נֶגֶב תֵּימָנָה קַלְעֵי הֶחָצֵר שֵׁשׁ מָשְׁזָר מֵאָה בָּאַמָּה׃
י עַמּוּדֵיהֶם עֶשְׂרִים וְאַדְנֵיהֶם עֶשְׂרִים נְחֹשֶׁת וָוֵי הָעַמּוּדִים וַחֲשֻׁקֵיהֶם כָּסֶף׃
יא וְלִפְאַת צָפוֹן מֵאָה בָאַמָּה עַמּוּדֵיהֶם עֶשְׂרִים וְאַדְנֵיהֶם עֶשְׂרִים נְחֹשֶׁת וָוֵי
יב הָעַמּוּדִים וַחֲשֻׁקֵיהֶם כָּסֶף׃ וְלִפְאַת־יָם קְלָעִים חֲמִשִּׁים בָּאַמָּה עַמּוּדֵיהֶם
יג עֲשָׂרָה וְאַדְנֵיהֶם עֲשָׂרָה וָוֵי הָעַמֻּדִים וַחֲשׁוּקֵיהֶם כָּסֶף׃ וְלִפְאַת קֵדְמָה
יד מִזְרָחָה חֲמִשִּׁים אַמָּה׃ קְלָעִים חֲמֵשׁ־עֶשְׂרֵה אַמָּה אֶל־הַכָּתֵף עַמּוּדֵיהֶם
טו שְׁלֹשָׁה וְאַדְנֵיהֶם שְׁלֹשָׁה׃ וְלַכָּתֵף הַשֵּׁנִית מִזֶּה וּמִזֶּה לְשַׁעַר הֶחָצֵר
טז קְלָעִים חֲמֵשׁ עֶשְׂרֵה אַמָּה עַמֻּדֵיהֶם שְׁלֹשָׁה וְאַדְנֵיהֶם שְׁלֹשָׁה׃ כָּל־קַלְעֵי
יז הֶחָצֵר סָבִיב שֵׁשׁ מָשְׁזָר׃ וְהָאֲדָנִים לָעַמֻּדִים נְחֹשֶׁת וָוֵי הָעַמּוּדִים
וַחֲשׁוּקֵיהֶם כֶּסֶף וְצִפּוּי רָאשֵׁיהֶם כָּסֶף וְהֵם מְחֻשָּׁקִים כֶּסֶף כֹּל עַמֻּדֵי
מפטיר יח הֶחָצֵר׃ וּמָסַךְ שַׁעַר הֶחָצֵר מַעֲשֵׂה רֹקֵם תְּכֵלֶת וְאַרְגָּמָן וְתוֹלַעַת שָׁנִי
וְשֵׁשׁ מָשְׁזָר וְעֶשְׂרִים אַמָּה אֹרֶךְ וְקוֹמָה בְרֹחַב חָמֵשׁ אַמּוֹת לְעֻמַּת
יט קַלְעֵי הֶחָצֵר׃ וְעַמֻּדֵיהֶם אַרְבָּעָה וְאַדְנֵיהֶם אַרְבָּעָה נְחֹשֶׁת וָוֵיהֶם כֶּסֶף
כ וְצִפּוּי רָאשֵׁיהֶם וַחֲשֻׁקֵיהֶם כָּסֶף׃ וְכָל־הַיְתֵדֹת לַמִּשְׁכָּן וְלֶחָצֵר סָבִיב
נְחֹשֶׁת׃

וְאֵת קְטֹרֶת הַסַּמִּים טָהוֹר — *And the pure incense of the sweet spices.* Spices cleansed of waste as it says, מְמֻלָּח טָהוֹר, *mixed together, pure* (30:35).

XXXVIII

8. בְּמַרְאֹת הַצֹּבְאֹת — *Of the mirrors of the serving women.* Which were not included in the brass of the offering, as explained in *Parashas Pekudei*, where it says, וַיַּעַשׂ בָּהּ, *and he made with it, etc.* (38:30), but does not mention the laver and the base among those made of it (brass).

NOTES

XXXVIII

8. בְּמַרְאֹת הַצֹּבְאֹת אֲשֶׁר צָבְאוּ . . . — *Of the mirrors of the serving women who did service* . . . In the next *parashah* (38:29) the Torah gives us an exact count of the brass offering and continues with an accounting of the items made from the brass (verses 30 and 31). The laver and its stand, however, which were also made of brass, are not included. The *Sforno* explains that the reason for

and the incense spices, pure; a perfumer's handiwork.

[1] *He made the Elevation-offering Altar of acacia wood; five cubits its
length, and five cubits its width — square — and three cubits its
height.* [2] *He made its horns on its four corners, from it were its horns, and he
covered it with copper.* [3] *He made all the utensils of the Altar — the pots, the
shovels, the basins, the forks, and the fire-pans — he made all its utensils of
copper.* [4] *He made for the Altar a netting of copper meshwork, below its
surrounding border downwards until its midpoint.* [5] *He cast four rings on
the four edges of the copper netting, as housings for the staves.* [6] *He made
the staves of acacia wood and covered them with copper.* [7] *He inserted the
staves in the rings on the sides of the Altar, with which to carry it; hollow,
of boards, did he make it.*

[8] *He made the Laver of copper and its base of copper, from the mirrors of
the legions who massed at the entrance of the Tent of Meeting.*

[9] *He made the Courtyard: On the south side, the lace-hangings of the
Courtyard, of twisted linen, a hundred cubits.* [10] *Their pillars twenty, and
their sockets twenty, of copper; the hooks of the pillars and their bands of
silver.* [11] *On the north side, a hundred cubits, their pillars twenty and their
sockets twenty, of copper; the hooks of the pillars and their bands of silver.*
[12] *On the west side, lace-hangings of fifty cubits; their pillars ten and their
sockets ten; the hooks of the pillars and their bands of silver.* [13] *And on the
eastern side, fifty cubits;* [14] *fifteen-cubit lace-hangings at the shoulder,
their pillars three and their sockets three;* [15] *and at the second shoulder —
on either side of the gate of the Courtyard — fifteen-cubit lace-hangings;
their pillars three and their sockets three.* [16] *All the lace-hangings of the
Courtyard all around were of twisted linen.* [17] *The sockets of the pillars
were copper, the hooks of the pillars and their bands were silver, and the
plating of their tops were silver. They were banded with silver, all the
pillars of the Courtyard.*

[18] *The Screen of the gate of the Courtyard was embroiderer's work, of
turquoise, purple, and scarlet wool, and twisted linen; twenty cubits in
length and the height, in width, was five cubits, corresponding to the
lace-hangings of the courtyard.* [19] *Their pillars four and their sockets four,
of copper; their hooks silver, and the plating of their tops and their bands
silver.* [20] *All the pegs of the Tabernacle and the Courtyard all around were
copper.*

אֲשֶׁר צָבְאוּ פֶּתַח אֹהֶל מוֹעֵד — *Who did service at the door of the tent of meeting.* To hearken to the words of the living God, as it says, וְהָיָה כָּל מְבַקֵּשׁ ה׳ יֵצֵא אֶל אֹהֶל מוֹעֵד, *and every one who sought HASHEM went out to the tent of meeting* (33:7). Now these women rejected their ornaments, and sanctified their mirrors, (thereby) demonstrating that they no longer needed them.

NOTES

this omission is that the brass for the laver was not taken from the general brass offerings, but from the mirrors of those women who parted with them and offered them to the *Mishkan*. By so doing they demonstrated their willingness to give up these beauty aids, which they considered of relatively little value, and instead committed them to the service of God.

פרשת פקודי

כא אֵלֶּה פְקוּדֵי הַמִּשְׁכָּן מִשְׁכַּן הָעֵדֻת אֲשֶׁר פֻּקַּד עַל־פִּי מֹשֶׁה עֲבֹדַת
כב הַלְוִיִּם בְּיַד אִיתָמָר בֶּן־אַהֲרֹן הַכֹּהֵן: וּבְצַלְאֵל בֶּן־אוּרִי בֶן־חוּר לְמַטֵּה
כג יְהוּדָה עָשָׂה אֵת כָּל־אֲשֶׁר־צִוָּה יהוה אֶת־מֹשֶׁה: וְאִתּוֹ אָהֳלִיאָב בֶּן־
אֲחִיסָמָךְ לְמַטֵּה־דָן חָרָשׁ וְחֹשֵׁב וְרֹקֵם בַּתְּכֵלֶת וּבָאַרְגָּמָן וּבְתוֹלַעַת
כד הַשָּׁנִי וּבַשֵּׁשׁ: כָּל־הַזָּהָב הֶעָשׂוּי לַמְּלָאכָה בְּכֹל
מְלֶאכֶת הַקֹּדֶשׁ וַיְהִי ׀ זְהַב הַתְּנוּפָה תֵּשַׁע וְעֶשְׂרִים כִּכָּר וּשְׁבַע
כה מֵאוֹת וּשְׁלֹשִׁים שֶׁקֶל בְּשֶׁקֶל הַקֹּדֶשׁ: וְכֶסֶף פְּקוּדֵי הָעֵדָה מְאַת כִּכָּר

21. אֵלֶּה פְקוּדֵי הַמִּשְׁכָּן — *These are the accounts of the Mishkan.* Each part of the *Mishkan,* written above, were those counted of which are said, . . . וּבְשֵׁמֹת תִּפְקְדוּ אֶת כְּלֵי מִשְׁמֶרֶת מַשָּׂאָם, בְּיַד אִיתָמָר, *and by name you shall appoint the furnishings (articles) of the charge of their burden . . . under the hand of Ithamar* (*Numbers* 4:32-33). This is because each one of them (the articles counted) was worthy to be considered as important and to be called by its private (individual) name, not only part of a generic group (category). This is certainly justified (regarding) each one of the holy vessels which were carried by the children of Kehath, and therefore they did not deteriorate, as our Sages say, "Perhaps you will say their hope of restoration is gone and their expectation is frustrated, so it is written, *Acacia wood standing up* (26:15), (this means) which stand forever and ever" (*Yoma* 72a).

They also did not fall into the hands of the enemy, as opposed to what happened to the Temple of Solomon and its articles (furnishings and vessels) as it is explained (regarding) the destruction of the First Temple at the hands of Nebuchadnezzar, (where) none of the articles of the *Mishkan* of our teacher Moses are mentioned (*II Kings* 25:13-17).

מִשְׁכַּן הָעֵדֻת — *The Tabernacle of the testimony.* The (Torah) tells us the virtues of this *Mishkan,* by which (reason) it was worthy to be everlasting and not to fall into the hands of the enemy: first, because it was מִשְׁכַּן הָעֵדֻת, *the Tabernacle of the testimony,* where the tablets of testimony were (deposited); second, אֲשֶׁר פֻּקַּד עַל פִּי מֹשֶׁה, *as they were rendered according to the commandment of Moses;* third, because it was through עֲבוֹדַת הַלְוִיִּם בְּיַד אִיתָמָר, *the service of the Levites by the hand of Ithamar,* for indeed the charge of all the parts of the *Mishkan* were in the hands of Ithamar; fourth . . .

22. וּבְצַלְאֵל בֶּן אוּרִי בֶן חוּר לְמַטֵּה יְהוּדָה עָשָׂה . . . — *And Bezalel the son of Uri, the son of Hur of the tribe of Judah made . . .* the leaders of the craftsmen of the *Mishkan's* work and its

NOTES

21. אֵלֶּה פְקוּדֵי הַמִּשְׁכָּן מִשְׁכַּן הָעֵדֻת — *These are the accounts of the Mishkan, the Tabernacle of the testimony.* The *Sforno* established at the beginning of this Book which is called שְׁמוֹת, *Names,* that any person called by name in the Torah is worthy to be recorded by that name. The same is true of the articles of the Sanctuary, be it the component parts or the furnishings and vessels therein. These are all accounted for here in *Parashas Pekudei.* However, it is in the Book of *Numbers* that the Torah emphasizes the significance of all these parts and vessels by stating, *by "name" you shall appoint, etc.* It is for this reason that the *Sforno* cites *Numbers* 4:32 in his commentary here. Now that which is holy and of great import does not deteriorate or decay but is everlasting. Nor does it pass into the possession of any other people save Israel. This was the unique character of "the *Mishkan* of our teacher Moses," as the *Sforno* puts it. He gives four reasons for the special role played by this Sanctuary in our history, and its superiority to all the other Temples, enjoying God's special providence: (a) the לוחות הַבְּרִית, *tablets of the covenant,* were deposited in the Ark, testifying to God's covenant with Israel; (b) only this Sanctuary was constructed by Moses, the master of all prophets, of whom the Torah tells us, *there has not arisen a prophet since in Israel like unto Moses,* and therefore it was worthy of the Almighty's protection; (c) the fact that the service of the Levites in this *Mishkan* was in the hands of Ithamar, Aaron's son, who was an outstanding

PARASHAS PEKUDEI

[21] *These are the reckonings of the Tabernacle, the Tabernacle of Testimony, which were reckoned at Moses' bidding. The labor of the Levites was under the authority of Issamar, son of Aaron the Kohen.*
[22] *Bezalel, son of Uri son of Hur, of the tribe of Judah, did everything that*
HASHEM commanded Moses. [23] *With him was Oholiab, son of Ahisamach, of the tribe of Dan, a carver, weaver, and embroiderer, with turquoise, purple, and scarlet wool, and with linen.*

[24] *All the gold that was used for the work — for all the holy work — the offered-up gold was twenty-nine talents and seven hundred thirty shekels, in the sacred shekel.*

[25] *The silver of the census of the community was a hundred talents, one*

---

articles were noblemen (noble lineage) and the righteous ones of the generation, and therefore the Divine Presence rested on the work of their hands, and it did not fall into the hands of their enemies. But the Temple of Solomon (was built by) workers of the nations of the world (*I Kings* 7:13), and although the Divine Presence did rest there its sections deteriorated and it was necessary לְחַזֵּק בֶּדֶק הַבָּיִת, *to repair the breaches of the house* (*II Kings* 22:5), and eventually it all fell into the hands of the enemy. But the Second Temple, which did not meet even one of these conditions (and) the Divine Presence did not come to rest in it at all, fell into the hand of the enemy for indeed the Second Temple was not *the Mishkan of the testimony* since there were no tablets of testimony in it (at all) and it was Koresh [Cyrus] who charged (that it be built) (*Ezra* 1:2), and (also) there were no sons of Levi there, as Ezra attested when he said, וָאָבִינָה בָעָם וּבַכֹּהֲנִים וּמִבְּנֵי לֵוִי לֹא מָצָאתִי שָׁם, *and I inspected the people and the priests but found there none of the sons of Levi* (*Ezra* 8:15), and among those who occupied themselves with the building were Zidonites and Zorites, as is explained in the Book of *Ezra* (3:7).

24. כָּל הַזָּהָב — *All the gold.* (The Torah) attests to, and defines the (quantity) of gold, silver and brass included in the work of the *Mishkan*, which was a very small amount compared to the riches of the First Temple, as explained in the Book of *Kings* (*I Kings* 6; 20:35 and 7; 48-50), and even more so were the riches of Herod's temple. Nevertheless the appearance of God's glory was more constantly (found) in the *Mishkan* of Moses than in the First Temple, and was not present at all in the Second Temple. This teaches us that it is not the amount of riches and the size of the structure which causes the Divine Presence to dwell in Israel, but God desires those who fear Him, and their deeds, in order to dwell in their midst.

NOTES

man of piety and integrity, also contributed to the elevated status of this particular Sanctuary; and (d) the fact that Bezalel was the architect and builder of the *Mishkan* helped to insure its everlasting nature, for the *Mishkan* mirrors the creation of heaven and earth and Bezalel had been blessed with special wisdom and the ability to reflect God's creative powers.

The *Sforno* adds that not only Bezalel, but all who occupied themselves with the construction of the *Mishkan*, were men of stature, sincerity and piety, as compared to the First and Second Temples which were built by workmen of various peoples, and also did not possess — in some cases — the other factors which gave this *Mishkan* its special status.

24. כָּל הַזָּהָב — *All the gold.* The *Sforno* is of the opinion that there must be some vital reason for the Torah to enumerate the quantities of precious metal collected and used in the *Mishkan* of Moses. This is to be understood as telling us how insignificant they were in comparison to the Temples of Solomon and Herod. Nevertheless the *Shechinah* appeared more often in this humbler structure. The Torah, thereby, is teaching us a great moral lesson. It is not the amount of gold one lavishes upon a holy temple which draws the Divine Presence to it, but the obedience of the people to God's will.

כו וְאֶ֜לֶף וּשְׁבַ֤ע מֵאוֹת֙ וַחֲמִשָּׁ֣ה וְשִׁבְעִ֔ים שֶׁ֖קֶל בְּשֶׁ֥קֶל הַקֹּֽדֶשׁ: בֶּ֚קַע
לַגֻּלְגֹּ֣לֶת מַחֲצִ֣ית הַשֶּׁ֗קֶל בְּשֶׁ֙קֶל֙ הַקֹּ֔דֶשׁ לְכֹ֞ל הָעֹבֵ֣ר עַל־הַפְּקֻדִ֗ים מִבֶּ֨ן
עֶשְׂרִ֤ים שָׁנָה֙ וָמַ֔עְלָה לְשֵׁשׁ־מֵא֥וֹת אֶ֖לֶף וּשְׁלֹ֣שֶׁת אֲלָפִ֑ים וַחֲמֵ֥שׁ מֵא֖וֹת
כז וַחֲמִשִּֽׁים: וַיְהִ֗י מְאַת֙ כִּכַּ֣ר הַכֶּ֔סֶף לָצֶ֗קֶת אֵ֚ת אַדְנֵ֣י הַקֹּ֔דֶשׁ וְאֵ֖ת אַדְנֵ֣י
כח הַפָּרֹ֑כֶת מְאַ֧ת אֲדָנִ֛ים לִמְאַ֥ת הַכִּכָּ֖ר כִּכָּ֥ר לָֽאָדֶן: וְאֶת־הָאֶ֜לֶף וּשְׁבַ֣ע
הַמֵּא֗וֹת וַחֲמִשָּׁ֤ה וְשִׁבְעִים֙ עָשָׂ֥ה וָוִ֖ים לָֽעַמּוּדִ֑ים וְצִפָּ֥ה רָֽאשֵׁיהֶ֖ם וְחִשַּׁ֥ק
כט־ל אֹתָֽם: וּנְחֹ֥שֶׁת הַתְּנוּפָ֖ה שִׁבְעִ֣ים כִּכָּ֑ר וְאַלְפַּ֥יִם וְאַרְבַּע־מֵא֖וֹת שָֽׁקֶל: וַיַּ֣עַשׂ
בָּ֗הּ אֶת־אַדְנֵי֙ פֶּ֚תַח אֹ֣הֶל מוֹעֵ֔ד וְאֵת֙ מִזְבַּ֣ח הַנְּחֹ֔שֶׁת וְאֶת־מִכְבַּ֥ר
לא הַנְּחֹ֖שֶׁת אֲשֶׁר־ל֑וֹ וְאֵ֖ת כָּל־כְּלֵ֥י הַמִּזְבֵּֽחַ: וְאֶת־אַדְנֵ֤י הֶֽחָצֵר֙ סָבִ֔יב וְאֶת־
אַדְנֵ֖י שַׁ֣עַר הֶֽחָצֵ֑ר וְאֵ֨ת כָּל־יִתְדֹ֧ת הַמִּשְׁכָּ֛ן וְאֶת־כָּל־יִתְדֹ֥ת הֶֽחָצֵ֖ר סָבִֽיב:

לט

א וּמִן־הַתְּכֵ֤לֶת וְהָֽאַרְגָּמָן֙ וְתוֹלַ֣עַת הַשָּׁנִ֔י עָשׂ֥וּ בִגְדֵי־שְׂרָ֖ד לְשָׁרֵ֣ת בַּקֹּ֑דֶשׁ
וַֽיַּעֲשׂ֞וּ אֶת־בִּגְדֵ֤י הַקֹּ֙דֶשׁ֙ אֲשֶׁ֣ר לְאַֽהֲרֹ֔ן כַּֽאֲשֶׁ֛ר צִוָּ֥ה יְהֹוָ֖ה אֶת־מֹשֶֽׁה:
שני [חמישי] ב־ג וַיַּ֖עַשׂ אֶת־הָֽאֵפֹ֑ד זָהָ֗ב תְּכֵ֧לֶת וְאַרְגָּמָ֛ן וְתוֹלַ֥עַת שָׁנִ֖י וְשֵׁ֥שׁ מָשְׁזָֽר: וַֽיְרַקְּע֞וּ
אֶת־פַּחֵ֣י הַזָּהָב֮ וְקִצֵּ֣ץ פְּתִילִם֒ לַֽעֲשׂ֗וֹת בְּת֤וֹךְ הַתְּכֵ֙לֶת֙ וּבְת֣וֹךְ הָֽאַרְגָּמָ֔ן
ד וּבְת֛וֹךְ תּוֹלַ֥עַת הַשָּׁנִ֖י וּבְת֣וֹךְ הַשֵּׁ֑שׁ מַֽעֲשֵׂ֖ה חֹשֵֽׁב: כְּתֵפֹ֥ת עָֽשׂוּ־ל֖וֹ חֹֽבְרֹ֑ת
ה עַל־שְׁנֵ֥י °קצוותו חֻבָּֽר: וְחֵ֣שֶׁב אֲפֻדָּת֗וֹ אֲשֶׁ֣ר עָלָ֜יו מִמֶּ֤נּוּ הוּא֙ כְּמַֽעֲשֵׂ֔הוּ °קצוותיו ק
זָהָ֗ב תְּכֵ֧לֶת וְאַרְגָּמָ֛ן וְתוֹלַ֥עַת שָׁנִ֖י וְשֵׁ֣שׁ מָשְׁזָ֑ר כַּֽאֲשֶׁ֛ר צִוָּ֥ה יְהֹוָ֖ה אֶת־
ו מֹשֶֽׁה: וַֽיַּֽעֲשׂוּ֙ אֶת־אַבְנֵ֣י הַשֹּׁ֔הַם מֻֽסַבֹּ֖ת מִשְׁבְּצֹ֣ת זָהָ֑ב
ז מְפֻתָּחֹת֙ פִּתּוּחֵ֣י חוֹתָ֔ם עַל־שְׁמ֖וֹת בְּנֵ֣י יִשְׂרָאֵֽל: וַיָּ֣שֶׂם אֹתָ֗ם עַ֚ל כִּתְפֹ֣ת
הָֽאֵפֹ֔ד אַבְנֵ֥י זִכָּר֖וֹן לִבְנֵ֣י יִשְׂרָאֵ֑ל כַּֽאֲשֶׁ֛ר צִוָּ֥ה יְהֹוָ֖ה אֶת־מֹשֶֽׁה:
ח וַיַּ֧עַשׂ אֶת־הַחֹ֛שֶׁן מַֽעֲשֵׂ֥ה חֹשֵׁ֖ב כְּמַֽעֲשֵׂ֣ה אֵפֹ֑ד זָהָ֗ב תְּכֵ֧לֶת וְאַרְגָּמָ֛ן
ט וְתוֹלַ֥עַת שָׁנִ֖י וְשֵׁ֥שׁ מָשְׁזָֽר: רָב֧וּעַ הָיָ֛ה כָּפ֖וּל עָשׂ֣וּ אֶת־הַחֹ֑שֶׁן זֶ֧רֶת אָרְכּ֛וֹ
י וְזֶ֥רֶת רָחְבּ֖וֹ כָּפֽוּל: וַיְמַלְאוּ־ב֔וֹ אַרְבָּעָ֖ה ט֣וּרֵי אָ֑בֶן ט֗וּר אֹ֤דֶם פִּטְדָה֙
יא־יב וּבָרֶ֔קֶת הַטּ֖וּר הָֽאֶחָֽד: וְהַטּ֖וּר הַשֵּׁנִ֑י נֹ֥פֶךְ סַפִּ֖יר וְיָֽהֲלֹֽם: וְהַטּ֖וּר הַשְּׁלִישִׁ֑י
יג לֶ֥שֶׁם שְׁב֖וֹ וְאַחְלָֽמָה: וְהַטּוּר֙ הָֽרְבִיעִ֔י תַּרְשִׁ֥ישׁ שֹׁ֖הַם וְיָֽשְׁפֵ֑ה מֽוּסַבֹּ֛ת
יד מִשְׁבְּצֹ֥ת זָהָ֖ב בְּמִלֻּֽאֹתָֽם: וְ֠הָֽאֲבָנִ֠ים עַל־שְׁמֹ֨ת בְּנֵֽי־יִשְׂרָאֵ֥ל הֵ֛נָּה שְׁתֵּ֥ים
עֶשְׂרֵ֖ה עַל־שְׁמֹתָ֑ם פִּתּוּחֵ֤י חֹתָם֙ אִ֣ישׁ עַל־שְׁמ֔וֹ לִשְׁנֵ֥ים עָשָׂ֖ר שָֽׁבֶט:

XXXIX

1. בִּגְדֵי שְׂרָד — *Crocheted garments.* Garments (covers) which had no precise images (on them) except for a crocheted design; (they were) of sufficient (size) to cover the vessels.

3. וַיְרַקְּעוּ אֶת פַּחֵי הַזָּהָב — *And they beat the gold into thin plates.* The donors who contributed the gold for the priestly garments beat (it) into thin plates, preparing it for the craftsmen to make into threads.

וְקִצֵּץ פְּתִילִם — *And he cut threads.* The craftsman cut threads from the beaten (gold) plates

NOTES

XXXIX

3. וַיְרַקְּעוּ אֶת פַּחֵי הַזָּהָב וְקִצֵּץ פְּתִילִם — *And they beat the gold into thin plates and he cut threads.* The phrase וַיְרַקְּעוּ, *and they beat,* is in the plural,

whereas the verb וְקִצֵּץ, *and he cut,* is in the singular. The *Sforno* explains the former as referring to the numerous donors who contributed the gold. Their responsibility was to prepare the gold by

thousand seven hundred seventy-five shekels, in the sacred shekel; 26 *a*
beka for every head, a half-shekel in the sacred shekel for everyone who
passed through the census takers, from twenty years of age and up, for the
six hundred three thousand, five hundred fifty. 27 *The hundred talents of*
silver were to cast the sockets of the Sanctuary and the sockets of the
Partition; a hundred sockets for a hundred talents, a talent per socket.
28 *And from the one thousand seven hundred seventy-five he made hooks*
for the pillars, covered their tops and banded them.

29 *The offered-up copper was seventy talents and two thousand four*
hundred shekels. 30 *With it he made the sockets of the entrance to the Tent*
of Meeting, the Copper Altar, the copper meshwork that was on it, and all
the vessels of the Altar; 31 *the sockets of the Courtyard all around, the*
sockets of the gate of the Courtyard, all the pegs of the Tabernacle, and all
the pegs of the Courtyard, all around.

39 1 *From the turquoise, purple, and scarlet wool they made knit vestments*
to serve in the Sanctuary, and they made the holy vestments for Aaron,
as HASHEM *had commanded Moses.*

2 *He made the Ephod of gold, turquoise, purple, and scarlet wool, and*
twisted linen. 3 *They hammered out the thin sheets of gold and cut threads*
to work the weaver's craft into the turquoise, into the purple, and into the
scarlet wool, and into the linen. 4 *They made attached shoulder straps for it,*
attached to its two ends. 5 *The belt with which it was emplaced, which was*
on it, was made from it, of the same workmanship, of gold, turquoise, pur-
ple, and scarlet wool, and linen, twisted, as HASHEM *had commanded Moses.*

6 *They made the shoham stones, encircled with gold settings, engraved*
like the engraving of a signet ring, according to the names of the sons of
Israel. 7 *He placed them on the shoulder straps of the Ephod as remem-*
brance stones for the sons of Israel, as HASHEM *had commanded Moses.*

8 *He made the Breastplate of a weaver's craft, like the workmanship of*
the Ephod, of gold, turquoise, purple, and scarlet wool, and linen, twisted. 9 *It*
was square, folded over did they make the Breastplate; its length was a
half-cubit and its width was a half-cubit, folded over. 10 *They filled it with*
four rows of stones: a row of odem, pitdah, and barekes — one row; 11 *the*
second row: nofech, sapir, and yahalom; 12 *the third row: leshem, shevo, and*
achlamah; 13 *the fourth row: tarshish, shoham, and yashfeh; encircled with*
gold settings in their mountings. 14 *The stones were according to the names*
of the sons of Israel, twelve according to their names, like the engraving of
a signet ring, each man according to his name, for the twelve tribes.

---

which had been contributed.

5. כַּאֲשֶׁר צִוָּה ה׳ אֶת מֹשֶׁה — *As* HASHEM *commanded Moses.* The intent of the craftsmen, in their work, was to fulfill the will of God, the Blessed One, in accordance with His command to Moses.

NOTES

beating it into plates. The latter task of cutting it into threads was that of each craftsman; hence it is written in the singular.

5. כַּאֲשֶׁר צִוָּה ה׳ אֶת מֹשֶׁה — *As* HASHEM *commanded Moses.* Compare to the *Sforno's* commentary 36:8.

טו-טז וַיַּעֲשׂוּ עַל־הַחֹשֶׁן שַׁרְשְׁרֹת גַּבְלֻת מַעֲשֵׂה עֲבֹת זָהָב טָהוֹר: וַיַּעֲשׂוּ שְׁתֵּי
מִשְׁבְּצֹת זָהָב וּשְׁתֵּי טַבְּעֹת זָהָב וַיִּתְּנוּ אֶת־שְׁתֵּי הַטַּבָּעֹת עַל־שְׁנֵי קְצוֹת
יז הַחֹשֶׁן: וַיִּתְּנוּ שְׁתֵּי הָעֲבֹתֹת הַזָּהָב עַל־שְׁתֵּי הַטַּבָּעֹת עַל־קְצוֹת הַחֹשֶׁן:
יח וְאֵת שְׁתֵּי קְצוֹת שְׁתֵּי הָעֲבֹתֹת נָתְנוּ עַל־שְׁתֵּי הַמִּשְׁבְּצֹת וַיִּתְּנֻם
יט עַל־כִּתְפֹת הָאֵפֹד אֶל־מוּל פָּנָיו: וַיַּעֲשׂוּ שְׁתֵּי טַבְּעֹת זָהָב וַיָּשִׂימוּ
כ עַל־שְׁנֵי קְצוֹת הַחֹשֶׁן עַל־שְׂפָתוֹ אֲשֶׁר אֶל־עֵבֶר הָאֵפֹד בָּיְתָה: וַיַּעֲשׂוּ
שְׁתֵּי טַבְּעֹת זָהָב וַיִּתְּנֻם עַל־שְׁתֵּי כִתְפֹת הָאֵפֹד מִלְּמַטָּה מִמּוּל פָּנָיו
כא לְעֻמַּת מַחְבַּרְתּוֹ מִמַּעַל לְחֵשֶׁב הָאֵפֹד: וַיִּרְכְּסוּ אֶת־הַחֹשֶׁן מִטַּבְּעֹתָיו
אֶל־טַבְּעֹת הָאֵפֹד בִּפְתִיל תְּכֵלֶת לִהְיֹת עַל־חֵשֶׁב הָאֵפֹד וְלֹא־יִזַּח
הַחֹשֶׁן מֵעַל הָאֵפֹד כַּאֲשֶׁר צִוָּה יהוה אֶת־מֹשֶׁה:
שלישי כב-כג וַיַּעַשׂ אֶת־מְעִיל הָאֵפֹד מַעֲשֵׂה אֹרֵג כְּלִיל תְּכֵלֶת: וּפִי־הַמְּעִיל בְּתוֹכוֹ
[ששי] כד כְּפִי תַחְרָא שָׂפָה לְפִיו סָבִיב לֹא יִקָּרֵעַ: וַיַּעֲשׂוּ עַל־שׁוּלֵי הַמְּעִיל רִמּוֹנֵי
כה תְּכֵלֶת וְאַרְגָּמָן וְתוֹלַעַת שָׁנִי מָשְׁזָר: וַיַּעֲשׂוּ פַעֲמֹנֵי זָהָב טָהוֹר וַיִּתְּנוּ
אֶת־הַפַּעֲמֹנִים בְּתוֹךְ הָרִמֹּנִים עַל־שׁוּלֵי הַמְּעִיל סָבִיב בְּתוֹךְ הָרִמֹּנִים:
כו פַּעֲמֹן וְרִמֹּן פַּעֲמֹן וְרִמֹּן עַל־שׁוּלֵי הַמְּעִיל סָבִיב לְשָׁרֵת כַּאֲשֶׁר צִוָּה יהוה
כז אֶת־מֹשֶׁה: וַיַּעֲשׂוּ אֶת־הַכָּתְנֹת שֵׁשׁ מַעֲשֵׂה אֹרֵג לְאַהֲרֹן
כח וּלְבָנָיו: וְאֵת הַמִּצְנֶפֶת שֵׁשׁ וְאֶת־פַּאֲרֵי הַמִּגְבָּעֹת שֵׁשׁ וְאֶת־מִכְנְסֵי הַבָּד
כט שֵׁשׁ מָשְׁזָר: וְאֶת־הָאַבְנֵט שֵׁשׁ מָשְׁזָר וּתְכֵלֶת וְאַרְגָּמָן וְתוֹלַעַת שָׁנִי
ל מַעֲשֵׂה רֹקֵם כַּאֲשֶׁר צִוָּה יהוה אֶת־מֹשֶׁה: וַיַּעֲשׂוּ אֶת־צִיץ
נֵזֶר־הַקֹּדֶשׁ זָהָב טָהוֹר וַיִּכְתְּבוּ עָלָיו מִכְתַּב פִּתּוּחֵי חוֹתָם קֹדֶשׁ לַיהוה:
לא וַיִּתְּנוּ עָלָיו פְּתִיל תְּכֵלֶת לָתֵת עַל־הַמִּצְנֶפֶת מִלְמָעְלָה כַּאֲשֶׁר צִוָּה יהוה
לב אֶת־מֹשֶׁה: וַתֵּכֶל כָּל־עֲבֹדַת מִשְׁכַּן אֹהֶל מוֹעֵד וַיַּעֲשׂוּ
בְּנֵי יִשְׂרָאֵל כְּכֹל אֲשֶׁר צִוָּה יהוה אֶת־מֹשֶׁה כֵּן עָשׂוּ:
רביעי לג וַיָּבִיאוּ אֶת־הַמִּשְׁכָּן אֶל־מֹשֶׁה אֶת־הָאֹהֶל וְאֶת־כָּל־כֵּלָיו קְרָסָיו קְרָשָׁיו
לד בְּרִיחָו וְעַמֻּדָיו וַאֲדָנָיו: וְאֶת־מִכְסֵה עוֹרֹת הָאֵילִם הַמְאָדָּמִים וְאֶת־
לה מִכְסֵה עֹרֹת הַתְּחָשִׁים וְאֵת פָּרֹכֶת הַמָּסָךְ: אֶת־אֲרוֹן הָעֵדֻת וְאֶת־בַּדָּיו
לו-לז וְאֵת הַכַּפֹּרֶת: אֶת־הַשֻּׁלְחָן אֶת־כָּל־כֵּלָיו וְאֵת לֶחֶם הַפָּנִים: אֶת־הַמְּנֹרָה
הַטְּהֹרָה אֶת־נֵרֹתֶיהָ נֵרֹת הַמַּעֲרָכָה וְאֶת־כָּל־כֵּלֶיהָ וְאֵת שֶׁמֶן הַמָּאוֹר:

---

32. וַתֵּכֶל . . . וַיַּעֲשׂוּ בְּנֵי יִשְׂרָאֵל — *Thus was finished . . . and the Children of Israel did.* The entire, complete work (project) was done by all of Israel; some of them contributed money while some did the work, (motivated) by the generosity of their heart to fulfill the will of their Maker.

וְכֵן עָשׂוּ — *So they did* . . . not less, not more.

33. וַיָּבִיאוּ אֶת הַמִּשְׁכָּן — *And they brought the mishkan* . . . the curtains, the work of the skillful workmen (26:1).

NOTES

33. וַיָּבִיאוּ אֶת הַמִּשְׁכָּן . . . וְאֶת כָּל כֵּלָיו — *And they brought the mishkan . . . and all its furniture.* The *Sforno,* commenting on 26:1, states that the curtains are called the *mishkan* because within the area enclosed by them are the sacred vessels. Similarly in this verse he translates the word מִשְׁכָּן as

15 For the Breastplate they made chains at the edges, of braided
craftsmanship, of pure gold. 16 They made two gold settings and two gold
rings, and they placed the two rings on the two ends of the Breastplate.
17 They placed the two gold ropes on the two rings, on the ends of the
Breastplate. 18 The two ends of the two ropes they placed on the two settings,
and placed them on the shoulder straps of the Ephod, toward its front.
19 They made two gold rings and placed them on the two ends of the
Breastplate, at its edge, which is on its inner side, toward the Ephod. 20 They
made two gold rings and placed them at the bottom of the two shoulder
straps, toward the front, opposite its seam, above the belt of the Ephod.
21 They attached the Breastplate from its rings to the rings of the Ephod with
a turquoise woolen cord, so that it would remain above the belt of the Ephod,
and the Breastplate would not be loosened from above the Ephod, as HASHEM
had commanded Moses.

22 They made the Robe of the Ephod of a weaver's craft, entirely of
turquoise wool. 23 Its head-opening was folded over within, like the opening
of a coat of mail; its opening had a border all around, so that it would not
tear. 24 On the Robe's hem they made pomegranates of turquoise, purple,
and scarlet wool, twisted. 25 They made bells of pure gold, and they placed
the bells amid the pomegranates on the hem of the Robe, all around, amid
the pomegranates. 26 A bell and a pomegranate, a bell and a pomegranate on
the hem of the Robe all around, to minister, as HASHEM *commanded Moses.*

27 They made the Tunics of linen, of a weaver's craft, for Aaron and his
sons; 28 and the Turban of linen, and the splendid headdresses of linen, and
the linen Breeches of twisted linen; 29 the Sash of twisted linen, turquoise,
purple, and scarlet wool, of an embroiderer's work, as HASHEM *had*
commanded Moses.

30 They made the Head-plate, the holy crown, of pure gold, and they
*inscribed on it with script like that of a signet ring, "*HOLY TO HASHEM.*"*
31 They placed on it a cord of turquoise wool, to put over the Turban from
above, as HASHEM *commanded Moses.*

32 All the work of the Tabernacle, the Tent of Meeting, was completed, and
the Children of Israel had done everything that HASHEM *commanded Moses,*
so did they do.

33 They brought the Tabernacle to Moses, the Tent and all its utensils: its
hooks, its planks, its bars, its pillars, and its sockets; 34 the Cover of red-dyed
ram hides, and the Cover of tachash skins, and the Partition-curtain; 35 the
Ark of Testimony and its staves, and the Cover; 36 the Table and all its
utensils, and the show-bread; 37 the pure Menorah, its lamps — the lamps
of the prescribed order — and all its utensils, and the oil of illumination;

אֶת הָאֹהֶל — *The tent* . . . the curtains of goats' hair (26:7).

וְאֶת כָּל כֵּלָיו — *And all its furniture* . . . of the *Mishkan;* for the clasps, boards, bars, pillars, and the sockets were the furnishings of the *Mishkan.*

NOTES

meaning the curtains. The concluding part of the verse, וְאֶת כָּל כֵּלָיו, *and all its furniture*, refers to the *Mishkan*, i.e., the Tabernacle, not the curtains, for these are all integral parts of the Tabernacle.

לח וְאֵת מִזְבַּח הַזָּהָב וְאֵת שֶׁמֶן הַמִּשְׁחָה וְאֵת קְטֹרֶת הַסַּמִּים וְאֵת מָסַךְ פֶּתַח
לט הָאֹהֶל: אֵת | מִזְבַּח הַנְּחֹשֶׁת וְאֶת־מִכְבַּר הַנְּחֹשֶׁת אֲשֶׁר־לוֹ אֶת־בַּדָּיו
מ וְאֶת־כָּל־כֵּלָיו אֶת־הַכִּיֹּר וְאֶת־כַּנּוֹ: אֵת קַלְעֵי הֶחָצֵר אֶת־עַמֻּדֶיהָ וְאֶת־
אֲדָנֶיהָ וְאֶת־הַמָּסָךְ לְשַׁעַר הֶחָצֵר אֶת־מֵיתָרָיו וִיתֵדֹתֶיהָ וְאֵת כָּל־כְּלֵי
מא עֲבֹדַת הַמִּשְׁכָּן לְאֹהֶל מוֹעֵד: אֶת־בִּגְדֵי הַשְּׂרָד לְשָׁרֵת בַּקֹּדֶשׁ אֶת־בִּגְדֵי
מב הַקֹּדֶשׁ לְאַהֲרֹן הַכֹּהֵן וְאֶת־בִּגְדֵי בָנָיו לְכַהֵן: כְּכֹל אֲשֶׁר־צִוָּה יהוה אֶת־
מג מֹשֶׁה כֵּן עָשׂוּ בְּנֵי יִשְׂרָאֵל אֵת כָּל־הָעֲבֹדָה: וַיַּרְא מֹשֶׁה אֶת־כָּל־
הַמְּלָאכָה וְהִנֵּה עָשׂוּ אֹתָהּ כַּאֲשֶׁר צִוָּה יהוה כֵּן עָשׂוּ וַיְבָרֶךְ אֹתָם מֹשֶׁה:
מ חמישי א־ב וַיְדַבֵּר יהוה אֶל־מֹשֶׁה לֵּאמֹר: בְּיוֹם־הַחֹדֶשׁ הָרִאשׁוֹן בְּאֶחָד לַחֹדֶשׁ תָּקִים
[שביעי] ג אֶת־מִשְׁכַּן אֹהֶל מוֹעֵד: וְשַׂמְתָּ שָׁם אֵת אֲרוֹן הָעֵדוּת וְסַכֹּתָ עַל־הָאָרֹן
ד אֶת־הַפָּרֹכֶת: וְהֵבֵאתָ אֶת־הַשֻּׁלְחָן וְעָרַכְתָּ אֶת־עֶרְכּוֹ וְהֵבֵאתָ אֶת־
ה הַמְּנֹרָה וְהַעֲלֵיתָ אֶת־נֵרֹתֶיהָ: וְנָתַתָּה אֶת־מִזְבַּח הַזָּהָב לִקְטֹרֶת לִפְנֵי
ו אֲרוֹן הָעֵדֻת וְשַׂמְתָּ אֶת־מָסַךְ הַפֶּתַח לַמִּשְׁכָּן: וְנָתַתָּה אֵת מִזְבַּח הָעֹלָה
ז לִפְנֵי פֶּתַח מִשְׁכַּן אֹהֶל־מוֹעֵד: וְנָתַתָּ אֶת־הַכִּיֹּר בֵּין־אֹהֶל מוֹעֵד וּבֵין
ח הַמִּזְבֵּחַ וְנָתַתָּ שָׁם מָיִם: וְשַׂמְתָּ אֶת־הֶחָצֵר סָבִיב וְנָתַתָּ אֶת־מָסַךְ שַׁעַר
ט הֶחָצֵר: וְלָקַחְתָּ אֶת־שֶׁמֶן הַמִּשְׁחָה וּמָשַׁחְתָּ אֶת־הַמִּשְׁכָּן וְאֶת־כָּל־אֲשֶׁר־
י בּוֹ וְקִדַּשְׁתָּ אֹתוֹ וְאֶת־כָּל־כֵּלָיו וְהָיָה קֹדֶשׁ: וּמָשַׁחְתָּ אֶת־מִזְבַּח הָעֹלָה
יא וְאֶת־כָּל־כֵּלָיו וְקִדַּשְׁתָּ אֶת־הַמִּזְבֵּחַ וְהָיָה הַמִּזְבֵּחַ קֹדֶשׁ קָדָשִׁים: וּמָשַׁחְתָּ
יב אֶת־הַכִּיֹּר וְאֶת־כַּנּוֹ וְקִדַּשְׁתָּ אֹתוֹ: וְהִקְרַבְתָּ אֶת־אַהֲרֹן וְאֶת־בָּנָיו
יג אֶל־פֶּתַח אֹהֶל מוֹעֵד וְרָחַצְתָּ אֹתָם בַּמָּיִם: וְהִלְבַּשְׁתָּ אֶת־אַהֲרֹן אֵת בִּגְדֵי
יד הַקֹּדֶשׁ וּמָשַׁחְתָּ אֹתוֹ וְקִדַּשְׁתָּ אֹתוֹ וְכִהֵן לִי: וְאֶת־בָּנָיו תַּקְרִיב וְהִלְבַּשְׁתָּ
טו אֹתָם כֻּתֳּנֹת: וּמָשַׁחְתָּ אֹתָם כַּאֲשֶׁר מָשַׁחְתָּ אֶת־אֲבִיהֶם וְכִהֲנוּ לִי וְהָיְתָה
טז לִהְיֹת לָהֶם מָשְׁחָתָם לִכְהֻנַּת עוֹלָם לְדֹרֹתָם: וַיַּעַשׂ מֹשֶׁה
יז כְּכֹל אֲשֶׁר צִוָּה יהוה אֹתוֹ כֵּן עָשָׂה: וַיְהִי בַּחֹדֶשׁ הָרִאשׁוֹן
יח בַּשָּׁנָה הַשֵּׁנִית בְּאֶחָד לַחֹדֶשׁ הוּקַם הַמִּשְׁכָּן: וַיָּקֶם מֹשֶׁה אֶת־הַמִּשְׁכָּן
וַיִּתֵּן אֶת־אֲדָנָיו וַיָּשֶׂם אֶת־קְרָשָׁיו וַיִּתֵּן אֶת־בְּרִיחָיו וַיָּקֶם אֶת־עַמּוּדָיו:

42. כְּכֹל אֲשֶׁר צִוָּה ה׳ אֶת מֹשֶׁה כֵּן עָשׂוּ בְּנֵי יִשְׂרָאֵל אֵת כָּל הָעֲבֹדָה — *According to all that HASHEM commanded Moses, so the Children of Israel did all the work.* In the order that God later commanded Moses (to follow) when erecting the *Mishkan* (40:2-15).

43. כֵּן עָשׂוּ — *So they had done it.* In that same order itself did the craftsmen make (the various articles) and (in that same order) those who brought them did bring them.

XL

18. וַיָּקֶם מֹשֶׁה אֶת הַמִּשְׁכָּן — *And Moses raised up the mishkan.* The ten curtains, the work

NOTES

42-43. כְּכֹל אֲשֶׁר צִוָּה ה׳ אֶת מֹשֶׁה כֵּן עָשׂוּ בְּנֵי יִשְׂרָאֵל אֵת כָּל הָעֲבֹדָה ... כֵּן עָשׂוּ — *According to all that HASHEM commanded Moses, so the Children of Israel did all the work ... So they had done it.* The fashioning of every part of the Tabernacle, the sequence of bringing every item to Moses, and the order in which he put it together all followed an exact order, as commanded by God to Moses. This is what the *Sforno* stresses in his commentary on these two verses.

38 *The Gold Altar, the anointment oil, and the incense spices; and the*
Partition of the entrance of the Tent; 39 *the Copper Altar and its copper*
meshwork, its staves, and all its utensils, the Laver and its base; 40 *the*
curtains of the Courtyard, its pillars and its sockets, the Partition of the gate
of the Courtyard, its ropes and its pegs, and all the utensils for the service
of the Tabernacle of the Tent of Meeting; 41 *the knitted vestments to serve*
in the Sanctuary, the sacred vestments of Aaron the Kohen, and the
vestments of his sons to minister.

42 *Like everything that* HASHEM *commanded Moses, so did the Children of*
Israel perform all the labor. 43 *Moses saw the entire work, and behold! —*
they had done it as HASHEM *had commanded, so had they done! And Moses*
blessed them.

40 1 HASHEM *spoke to Moses, saying:* 2 *"On the day of the first new moon, on*
the first of the month, you shall erect the Tabernacle, the Tent of Meet-
ing. 3 *There you shall place the Ark of Testimony and screen the Ark with the*
Partition. 4 *You shall bring the Table and prepare its setting, bring the*
Menorah and kindle its lamps. 5 *You shall place the Gold Altar for incense in*
front of the Ark of Testimony, and emplace the Curtain of the entrance of the
Tabernacle. 6 *You shall place the Elevation-offering Altar in front of the*
entrance of the Tabernacle, the Tent of Meeting. 7 *You shall place the Laver*
between the Tent of Meeting and the Altar, and you shall put water there.
8 *You shall emplace the Courtyard all around, and emplace the Curtain at the*
gate of the Courtyard. 9 *You shall take the anointment oil and anoint the*
Tabernacle and everything that is in it, sanctify it and all its utensils, and it
shall become holy. 10 *You shall anoint the Elevation-offering Altar and all its*
utensils; you shall sanctify the Altar, and the Altar shall become holy of
holies. 11 *You shall anoint the Laver and its stand, and sanctify it.*

12 *"You shall bring Aaron and his sons near to the entrance of the Tent of*
Meeting, and immerse them in water. 13 *You shall dress Aaron in the sacred*
vestments and anoint him; you shall sanctify him and he shall minister to
Me. 14 *And his sons you shall bring near and dress them in tunics.* 15 *You shall*
anoint them as you had anointed their father and they shall minister to Me,
and so it shall be that their anointment shall be for eternal priesthood for their
generations." 16 *Moses did according to everything that* HASHEM *com-*
manded him, so he did.

17 *It was in the first month of the second year on the first of the month that*
the Tabernacle was erected. 18 *Moses erected the Tabernacle; he put down its*
sockets and emplaced its planks and inserted its bars, and erected its pillars.

of the skillful workmen, which is called *mishkan,* were raised up before the erection of the boards — either by men holding them or in a miraculous way, as our Sages tell us (*Menachos* 99a). And in this order they were made and brought to Moses. For indeed these

NOTES

XL

18. וַיָּקֶם מֹשֶׁה אֶת הַמִּשְׁכָּן — *And Moses raised up the mishkan.* As mentioned above Moses erected the *Mishkan* in a precise exact order. As these verses clearly state (18-19) he first raised up the curtains (which are called "the *mishkan*" as explained in 26:1 and 39:33) followed by the laying of the sockets, the setting up of the boards (which

יט וַיִּפְרֹשׂ אֶת־הָאֹהֶל עַל־הַמִּשְׁכָּן וַיָּשֶׂם אֶת־מִכְסֵה הָאֹהֶל עָלָיו מִלְמָעְלָה
כ כַּאֲשֶׁר צִוָּה יהוה אֶת־מֹשֶׁה: וַיִּקַּח וַיִּתֵּן אֶת־הָעֵדֻת אֶל־
הָאָרֹן וַיָּשֶׂם אֶת־הַבַּדִּים עַל־הָאָרֹן וַיִּתֵּן אֶת־הַכַּפֹּרֶת עַל־הָאָרֹן
כא מִלְמָעְלָה: וַיָּבֵא אֶת־הָאָרֹן אֶל־הַמִּשְׁכָּן וַיָּשֶׂם אֵת פָּרֹכֶת הַמָּסָךְ וַיָּסֶךְ עַל
כב אֲרוֹן הָעֵדוּת כַּאֲשֶׁר צִוָּה יהוה אֶת־מֹשֶׁה: וַיִּתֵּן אֶת־הַשֻּׁלְחָן
כג בְּאֹהֶל מוֹעֵד עַל יֶרֶךְ הַמִּשְׁכָּן צָפֹנָה מִחוּץ לַפָּרֹכֶת: וַיַּעֲרֹךְ עָלָיו עֵרֶךְ לֶחֶם
כד לִפְנֵי יהוה כַּאֲשֶׁר צִוָּה יהוה אֶת־מֹשֶׁה: וַיָּשֶׂם אֶת־הַמְּנֹרָה
כה בְּאֹהֶל מוֹעֵד נֹכַח הַשֻּׁלְחָן עַל יֶרֶךְ הַמִּשְׁכָּן נֶגְבָּה: וַיַּעַל הַנֵּרֹת לִפְנֵי יהוה
כו כַּאֲשֶׁר צִוָּה יהוה אֶת־מֹשֶׁה: וַיָּשֶׂם אֶת־מִזְבַּח הַזָּהָב בְּאֹהֶל
כז מוֹעֵד לִפְנֵי הַפָּרֹכֶת: וַיַּקְטֵר עָלָיו קְטֹרֶת סַמִּים כַּאֲשֶׁר צִוָּה יהוה אֶת־
שביעי כח-כט מֹשֶׁה: וַיָּשֶׂם אֶת־מָסַךְ הַפֶּתַח לַמִּשְׁכָּן: וְאֵת מִזְבַּח הָעֹלָה שָׂם
פֶּתַח מִשְׁכַּן אֹהֶל־מוֹעֵד וַיַּעַל עָלָיו אֶת־הָעֹלָה וְאֶת־הַמִּנְחָה כַּאֲשֶׁר צִוָּה
ל יהוה אֶת־מֹשֶׁה: וַיָּשֶׂם אֶת־הַכִּיֹּר בֵּין־אֹהֶל מוֹעֵד וּבֵין
לא הַמִּזְבֵּחַ וַיִּתֵּן שָׁמָּה מַיִם לְרָחְצָה: וְרָחֲצוּ מִמֶּנּוּ מֹשֶׁה וְאַהֲרֹן וּבָנָיו
לב אֶת־יְדֵיהֶם וְאֶת־רַגְלֵיהֶם: בְּבֹאָם אֶל־אֹהֶל מוֹעֵד וּבְקָרְבָתָם אֶל־הַמִּזְבֵּחַ
לג יִרְחָצוּ כַּאֲשֶׁר צִוָּה יהוה אֶת־מֹשֶׁה: וַיָּקֶם אֶת־הֶחָצֵר סָבִיב
לַמִּשְׁכָּן וְלַמִּזְבֵּחַ וַיִּתֵּן אֶת־מָסַךְ שַׁעַר הֶחָצֵר וַיְכַל מֹשֶׁה אֶת־הַמְּלָאכָה:
מפטיר לד-לה וַיְכַס הֶעָנָן אֶת־אֹהֶל מוֹעֵד וּכְבוֹד יהוה מָלֵא אֶת־הַמִּשְׁכָּן: וְלֹא־יָכֹל מֹשֶׁה
לָבוֹא אֶל־אֹהֶל מוֹעֵד כִּי־שָׁכַן עָלָיו הֶעָנָן וּכְבוֹד יהוה מָלֵא אֶת־
לו הַמִּשְׁכָּן: וּבְהֵעָלוֹת הֶעָנָן מֵעַל הַמִּשְׁכָּן יִסְעוּ בְּנֵי יִשְׂרָאֵל בְּכֹל מַסְעֵיהֶם:
לז-לח וְאִם־לֹא יֵעָלֶה הֶעָנָן וְלֹא יִסְעוּ עַד־יוֹם הֵעָלֹתוֹ: כִּי עֲנַן יהוה עַל־הַמִּשְׁכָּן
יוֹמָם וְאֵשׁ תִּהְיֶה לַיְלָה בּוֹ לְעֵינֵי כָל־בֵּית־יִשְׂרָאֵל בְּכָל־מַסְעֵיהֶם:

---

ten curtains comprise the principal (part) of the *Mishkan's* structure. The other (items) which were part of that structure, (such as) the sockets, boards, bars, pillars and the tent, were only (for the purpose) of supporting and covering the *mishkan* curtains.

33-34. וַיְכַל מֹשֶׁה ... וַיְכַס הֶעָנָן — *And Moses finished ... and the cloud covered.* Immediately after Moses finished the work necessary to cause the Divine Presence to dwell, which is the work of the raising and the labors therein, the cloud covered and the *Shechinah* dwelled (therein).

מָלֵא אֶת הַמִּשְׁכָּן — *Filled the Mishkan.* (God's glory) revealed itself in every part of the

NOTES

were on the inside of the curtains), the placing of the bars and the spreading of the tent over the Tabernacle. Now the question is, how did the curtains hang prior to the erecting of the boards since they had no support whatsoever? This is what the *Sforno* means when he states that either "men (the Levites) held them" in place, or they remained suspended "in a miraculous way." The selection from the Talmud *(Menachos* 99a) cited by the *Sforno* discusses the principle that in the realm of the sacred מַעֲלִין וְלֹא מוֹרִידִין, *one always elevates but never debases.* The proof brought to the prohibition of debasing something sacred is from the order in which Moses erected the *Mishkan. Rashi* explains that since Moses began by raising up the curtains, they could not be allowed to fall while he was putting up the boards for this would constitute debasement of the most sacred part of the *Mishkan,* namely the curtains which are also called the *mishkan,* as explained above! Hence the curtains must have remained in their elevated position, one way or another, as the *Sforno* states, while the sockets, boards and bars were being put into place.

19 He spread the Tent over the Tabernacle and put the Cover of the Tent on it from above, as HASHEM had commanded Moses.

20 He took and placed the Testimony into the Ark and inserted the staves on the Ark, and he placed the Cover on the Ark from above. 21 He brought the Ark into the Tabernacle and emplaced the Partition sheltering the Ark of Testimony, as HASHEM had commanded Moses.

22 He put the Table in the Tent of Meeting on the north side of the Tabernacle, outside the Partition. 23 He prepared on it the setting of bread before HASHEM, as HASHEM had commanded Moses.

24 He placed the Menorah in the Tent of Meeting, opposite the Table, on the south side of the Tabernacle. 25 He kindled the lamps before HASHEM, as HASHEM had commanded Moses.

26 He placed the Gold Altar in the Tent of Meeting, in front of the Partition. 27 Upon it he caused incense spices to go up in smoke, as HASHEM had commanded Moses.

28 He emplaced the Curtain of the entrance of the Tabernacle. 29 He placed the Elevation-offering Altar at the entrance of the Tent of Meeting, and brought up upon it the elevation-offering and the meal-offering, as HASHEM had commanded Moses.

30 He emplaced the Laver between the Tent of Meeting and the Altar, and there he put water for washing. 31 Moses, Aaron, and his sons washed their hands and feet from it. 32 When they came to the Tent of Meeting and when they approached the Altar they would wash, as HASHEM had commanded Moses.

33 He erected the Courtyard all around the Tabernacle and the Altar, and he emplaced the curtain of the gate of the Courtyard. So Moses completed the work.

34 The cloud covered the Tent of Meeting, and the glory of HASHEM filled the Tabernacle. 35 Moses could not enter the Tent of Meeting, for the cloud rested upon it, and the glory of HASHEM filled the Tabernacle. 36 When the cloud was raised up from upon the Tabernacle, the Children of Israel would embark on all their journeys. 37 If the cloud did not rise up, they would not embark, until the day it rose up. 38 For the cloud of HASHEM would be on the Tabernacle by day, and fire would be on it at night, before the eyes of all of the House of Israel throughout their journeys.

Mishkan (Tabernacle) but not outside of it at all.

35. אֶל אֹהֶל מוֹעֵד — *Into the tent of meeting.* Within the curtains outside the *paroches*.

36. וּבְהֵעָלוֹת הֶעָנָן — *And whenever the cloud went up.* The *Shechinah* was so (firmly) established in the *Mishkan* that it did not depart at all from there until Israel had to journey. (Now) this was not so in Shiloh, nor in the First Temple nor in the Second Temple. But even more than this will be (manifested) in the Third Temple (may it be built and established speedily in our days), as it says: וַאֲנִי אֶהְיֶה לָּהּ נְאֻם ה׳ חוֹמַת אֵשׁ סָבִיב וּלְכָבוֹד אֶהְיֶה בְתוֹכָהּ, *"For I," says HASHEM, "will be to her a wall of fire roundabout, and will be the glory in the midst of her"* (*Zechariah* 2:9).

NOTES

36. וּבְהֵעָלוֹת הֶעָנָן — *And whenever the cloud went up.* The prophet Zechariah saw a man in his vision measuring Jerusalem, who said to the prophet that the city *will be inhabited like unwalled towns because of the multitude of men* in it. The verse quoted by the *Sforno* follows this statement of the man in Zechariah's vision. Based on this verse the *Sforno* states that God's presence in Jerusalem at the time of redemption will be even more pervasive than it was in the time of the *Mishkan* of Moses.

ספר ויקרא

Vayikra / Leviticus

Sforno's Introduction

In this third book we are told how various sacrifices were ordered so as to secure (God's) Presence in their midst. Among them were sin-offerings, guilt-offerings and communal-drink offerings to eliminate the evil (consequences) of communal and private transgressions (*Parshiyos Vayikra-Tzav*). We are then cautioned regarding various defilements caused by reproduction, by ethical and moral (errors), through (prohibited) food and by contact, carrying and resting beneath the same roof (*Parshiyos Tazria-Metzora*). (Then follows) the order of the festivals (and) holy convocations for the purpose of gathering (the people) together on special days in the service of God, the Blessed One (*Parashas Emor*). (Next follows) the order of the *Shemittah* (Sabbatical year) and the *Yovel* (Jubilee) through which (Israel) will merit to inherit God's land, which has been prepared for His service (*Parashas Behar*) and in which He designated (all) material things necessary for temporal life (lit. life of the hour) so that they might support themselves painlessly, and that their hearts be unencumbered, enabling them to serve Him — as it says, וַיִּתֵּן לָהֶם אַרְצוֹת גּוֹיִם וַעֲמַל לְאֻמִּים יִירָשׁוּ. בַּעֲבוּר יִשְׁמְרוּ חֻקָּיו, *And He gave them the lands of the nations and they inherited the toil of nations, that they might observe His statutes* (*Psalms* 105:44-45). Regarding all this, He imposed an oath upon them after they nullified His first covenant through their sin (of the Golden Calf), and at the end of the curses we are told of the redemption of Israel after (their) despair (*Parashas Bechukosai*), and thus the third book concludes.

פרשת ויקרא

א *א׳ זעירא א־ב וַיִּקְרָ֖א* אֶל־מֹשֶׁ֑ה וַיְדַבֵּ֤ר יהוה֙ אֵלָ֔יו מֵאֹ֥הֶל מוֹעֵ֖ד לֵאמֹֽר׃ דַּבֵּ֞ר אֶל־בְּנֵ֤י
יִשְׂרָאֵל֙ וְאָמַרְתָּ֣ אֲלֵהֶ֔ם אָדָ֗ם כִּֽי־יַקְרִ֥יב מִכֶּ֛ם קָרְבָּ֖ן לַֽיהוה מִן־הַבְּהֵמָ֔ה

I

1. וַיִּקְרָא אֶל מֹשֶׁה — *And He called to Moses.* Constantly from the midst of the cloud, similar to (the experience at) Mt. Sinai, as it says, וַיִּקְרָא אֶל מֹשֶׁה בַּיּוֹם הַשְּׁבִיעִי מִתּוֹךְ הֶעָנָן, *He called to Moses, on the seventh day, out of the midst of the cloud* (*Exodus* 24:16), for he (Moses) would never enter there without permission.

מֵאֹהֶל מוֹעֵד — *Out of the Tent of Meeting.* Moses did not enter the Tent of Meeting then, while the glory (of God) was there, which was on the day Moses completed erecting the *Mishkan*, at which time the glory descended to sanctify the place and its servants, as it says, וְנֹעַדְתִּי שָׁמָּה לִבְנֵי יִשְׂרָאֵל וְנִקְדַּשׁ בִּכְבֹדִי. וְקִדַּשְׁתִּי אֶת אֹהֶל מוֹעֵד וְאֶת הַמִּזְבֵּחַ וְאֶת אַהֲרֹן וְאֶת בָּנָיו, *And there I will meet with the Children of Israel and* (*the Tent*) *shall be sanctified by My glory. And I will sanctify the Tent of Meeting and the Altar; also Aaron and his sons* (*Exodus* 29:43,44). And so He did in Solomon's Temple as it says, וְלֹא יָכְלוּ הַכֹּהֲנִים לַעֲמֹד לְשָׁרֵת מִפְּנֵי הֶעָנָן, כִּי מָלֵא כְבוֹד ה׳ אֶת בֵּית ה׳, *The Kohanim could not stand to minister because of the cloud, for the glory of* HASHEM *filled the house of* HASHEM (*I Kings* 8:11), and thus He sanctified the place, as it says, הִקְדַּשְׁתִּי אֶת הַבַּיִת הַזֶּה אֲשֶׁר בָּנִתָה, *I have hallowed this house which you have built* (ibid. 9:3). From that first day forward, however, Moses entered the Tent of Meeting outside the veil and the word (of God) came to him from above the Ark cover, as it says, וּבְבֹא מֹשֶׁה אֶל אֹהֶל מוֹעֵד לְדַבֵּר אִתּוֹ וַיִּשְׁמַע אֶת הַקּוֹל מִדַּבֵּר אֵלָיו מֵעַל הַכַּפֹּרֶת, *And when Moses went into the Tent of Meeting that He might speak with him, then he heard the Voice speaking to him from above the Ark cover* (*Numbers* 7:89).

2. אָדָם כִּי יַקְרִיב מִכֶּם — *When any man of you brings an offering* . . . when he sacrifices himself (lit., from yourself) through confession and submission, akin to, וּנְשַׁלְּמָה פָרִים שְׂפָתֵינוּ, *So we will offer the words of our lips instead of calves* (*Hosea* 14:3) and as it says,

NOTES

I

1. וַיִּקְרָא אֶל מֹשֶׁה . . . מֵאֹהֶל מוֹעֵד — *And He called to Moses . . . out of the Tent of Meeting.* The Book of *Exodus* ends with a description of the cloud covering the אֹהֶל מוֹעֵד, *Tent of Meeting*, and the glory of God filling the *Mishkan* in such a manner that Moses could not enter, but remained standing outside. Therefore, God had to call to him *from* the אֹהֶל מוֹעֵד, the meaning of the verse being *And He called from the Tent of Meeting to Moses and spoke to him* (as the *Rashbam* explains). Now this only happened on the day that the *Mishkan* was completed. After that first day, as the *Sforno* explains, Moses could enter the Tent, and God would speak to him from the other side of the veil from above the Ark cover. However, the cloud of glory hovered over the Tent at all times when they were encamped in the wilderness, and God would *always* call to Moses from the midst of the cloud, as both the *Sforno* and *Rashi* explain, based on the *Sifra*. The phenomenon of the intensity of the cloud coming to rest on the first day after completion of the *Mishkan*, as well as on the day Solomon's Temple was inaugurated, is explained by the *Sforno* as a Divine act of sanctification of the holy place and the *Kohanim*, as explicitly stated in *Exodus* 29:43,44 and in *I Kings* 9:3.

2. אָדָם כִּי יַקְרִיב מִכֶּם — *When any man of you brings an offering.* The phrase מִכֶּם means *"from you,"* i.e., from yourself. When one brings a sacrifice it is symbolic of offering himself to God in the sense of submitting his will to the will of God. By doing so, he manifests repentance for any actions which were in defiance of God's will. This interpretation is not in conflict with the Sages' exclusion of the apostate from the privilege of bringing sacrifices, for an apostate cannot meet these requirements and comply with the true purpose and motivation which must underlie all offerings, as already explained.

מִן הַבְּהֵמָה — *Of the cattle.* The term בְּהֵמָה is an all-inclusive generic one, as the *Sforno* proves from the verse in *Deuteronomy*, since a hart and a deer

PARASHAS VAYIKRA

1 [1] He called to Moses, and HASHEM spoke to him from the Tent of Meeting, saying: [2] Speak to the Children of Israel and say to them: When a man among you brings an offering to HASHEM: from animals —

זִבְחֵי אֱלֹהִים רוּחַ נִשְׁבָּרָה, *The sacrifices of God are a broken spirit* (*Psalms* 51:19), for He has no desire for fools who bring offerings without a (sense) of prior submission (to God), and our Sages have already said, "מִכֶּם, *From you,* and not all of you, to exclude the apostate" (*Chullin* 8a).

מִן הַבְּהֵמָה — *Of the cattle.* If he sacrifices an animal it shall be only from the species of herd or flock but not from the species of beasts, even though they are included in (the term) בְּהֵמָה, *animal,* as it says, זֹאת הַבְּהֵמָה אֲשֶׁר תֹּאכֵלוּ . . . אַיָּל וּצְבִי, *These are the animals which you may eat . . . the hart and the deer* (*Deut.* 14:4,5). Now the intent of these chapters is to explain the categories of *those who bring* sacrifices, of those (animals) that can be offered, the types of sacrifices and the reason for (various) offerings. He (first) explains that free-will offerings are accepted from every man, even from heathens (lit., the nations) as is explained later on, when (the Torah) says, *Neither from the hand of a foreigner shall you offer the bread of your God of any of these, because their corruption is in them, there is a blemish in them* (22:25). Now behold that apostates (מְשׁוּמָּדִים) are worse than heathens, especially those who are idolaters or desecrate the Sabbath in public. (The Torah then) explains that the species of sacrifices are herd and flock among the cattle, turtledoves and young pigeons from the fowl, and fine flour, oil and frankincense (for a meal offering). (The Torah then) explains the types of sacrifices, among them burnt offerings, peace offerings and meal offerings which can at times be brought as a free-will offering, and (others) among them are sin offerings and guilt offerings which are only brought if obligated to do so. From this (i.e., the above) the affair of Cain can be clarified (explained) when it says, וְאֶל קַיִן וְאֶל מִנְחָתוֹ לֹא שָׁעָה, *But to Cain and to his offering He did not turn* (*Genesis* 4:5), for he was of the class of heretics, as the end of the story shows (lit., whose conclusion proves the beginning), from whom offerings are not accepted, and (also) his offering was from a kind not fitting for sacrifice. Also by Noah (we find) when it says,

NOTES

are חַיּוֹת, *beasts,* yet are included in the general class of בְּהֵמָה, *animals.* Nonetheless, the Torah, by specifying בָּקָר, *herd,* and צֹאן, *flock,* disqualifies חַיּוֹת from the Altar.

Three areas are covered in these chapters. The first is the מַקְרִיב, *he who brings the offering,* i.e., his qualifications. The second are the species of animals and birds that are acceptable and the third are the types of sacrifices, which vary in accordance with the purpose for which they are offered. The *Sforno,* commenting on the first three chapters of *Leviticus,* makes the following points:

(a) The reason God did not accept Cain's offering is because he was not qualified to bring a sacrifice since he proved to be a heretic after the murder of his brother, as reflected in his answers to God (see *Genesis* 4:9 and the *Sforno* there). The second reason for God's rejection was the fact that Cain's offering was unworthy and not fitting to be brought to God (see the *Sforno, Genesis* 4:5).

(b) After the Flood Noah brought sacrifices from *all* the clean animals and birds, including those which the Torah here does not consider acceptable for the purpose of קָרְבָּן, *sacrifice.* The *Sforno* interprets the verse (*Genesis* 8:21), *smelled the pleasing aroma,* as applying only to those animals and fowl which were acceptable as offerings. It is interesting to note that the *Sforno* comments there that God accepted *all* of Noah's sacrifices since at that time (before the giving of the Torah) all clean animals and birds were acceptable and only after the giving of the Torah were some qualified and others not. It is possible that the *Sforno* here retreats from his original opinion or perhaps the text there is incorrect and should read as it does here, *Those that were fitting to be accepted for a pleasing aroma.*

(c) Being that there are restrictions regarding both the one who brings the offering and the types of animals and fowl offered, the verses cited by the *Sforno* from *Psalms* and *Isaiah* become clear and understandable. God is not rejecting sacrifices out of hand, as some latter-day critics would have it; He is rejecting only those which do not meet His standards.

ג מִן־הַבָּקָר וּמִן־הַצֹּאן תַּקְרִיבוּ אֶת־קָרְבַּנְכֶם: אִם־עֹלָה קָרְבָּנוֹ מִן־הַבָּקָר
זָכָר תָּמִים יַקְרִיבֶנּוּ אֶל־פֶּתַח אֹהֶל מוֹעֵד יַקְרִיב אֹתוֹ לִרְצֹנוֹ לִפְנֵי יהוה:
ד־ה וְסָמַךְ יָדוֹ עַל רֹאשׁ הָעֹלָה וְנִרְצָה לוֹ לְכַפֵּר עָלָיו: וְשָׁחַט אֶת־בֶּן הַבָּקָר
לִפְנֵי יהוה וְהִקְרִיבוּ בְּנֵי אַהֲרֹן הַכֹּהֲנִים אֶת־הַדָּם וְזָרְקוּ אֶת־הַדָּם
ו עַל־הַמִּזְבֵּחַ סָבִיב אֲשֶׁר־פֶּתַח אֹהֶל מוֹעֵד: וְהִפְשִׁיט אֶת־הָעֹלָה וְנִתַּח
ז אֹתָהּ לִנְתָחֶיהָ: וְנָתְנוּ בְּנֵי אַהֲרֹן הַכֹּהֵן אֵשׁ עַל־הַמִּזְבֵּחַ וְעָרְכוּ עֵצִים
ח עַל־הָאֵשׁ: וְעָרְכוּ בְּנֵי אַהֲרֹן הַכֹּהֲנִים אֵת הַנְּתָחִים אֶת־הָרֹאשׁ וְאֶת־
ט הַפָּדֶר עַל־הָעֵצִים אֲשֶׁר עַל־הָאֵשׁ אֲשֶׁר עַל־הַמִּזְבֵּחַ: וְקִרְבּוֹ וּכְרָעָיו
יִרְחַץ בַּמָּיִם וְהִקְטִיר הַכֹּהֵן אֶת־הַכֹּל הַמִּזְבֵּחָה עֹלָה אִשֵּׁה רֵיחַ־נִיחוֹחַ
י לַיהוה: וְאִם־מִן־הַצֹּאן קָרְבָּנוֹ מִן־הַכְּשָׂבִים אוֹ מִן־הָעִזִּים
יא לְעֹלָה זָכָר תָּמִים יַקְרִיבֶנּוּ: וְשָׁחַט אֹתוֹ עַל יֶרֶךְ הַמִּזְבֵּחַ צָפֹנָה לִפְנֵי יהוה
יב וְזָרְקוּ בְּנֵי אַהֲרֹן הַכֹּהֲנִים אֶת־דָּמוֹ עַל־הַמִּזְבֵּחַ סָבִיב: וְנִתַּח אֹתוֹ לִנְתָחָיו
וְאֶת־רֹאשׁוֹ וְאֶת־פִּדְרוֹ וְעָרַךְ הַכֹּהֵן אֹתָם עַל־הָעֵצִים אֲשֶׁר עַל־הָאֵשׁ
יג אֲשֶׁר עַל־הַמִּזְבֵּחַ: וְהַקֶּרֶב וְהַכְּרָעַיִם יִרְחַץ בַּמָּיִם וְהִקְרִיב הַכֹּהֵן אֶת־הַכֹּל
וְהִקְטִיר הַמִּזְבֵּחָה עֹלָה הוּא אִשֵּׁה רֵיחַ נִיחֹחַ לַיהוה:
שני יד וְאִם מִן־הָעוֹף עֹלָה קָרְבָּנוֹ לַיהוה וְהִקְרִיב מִן־הַתֹּרִים אוֹ מִן־בְּנֵי הַיּוֹנָה
טו אֶת־קָרְבָּנוֹ: וְהִקְרִיבוֹ הַכֹּהֵן אֶל־הַמִּזְבֵּחַ וּמָלַק אֶת־רֹאשׁוֹ וְהִקְטִיר

וַיָּרַח ה׳ אֶת רֵיחַ הַנִּיחֹחַ, *And* HASHEM *smelled the pleasing aroma* (*Genesis* 8:21), meaning that He (God) accepted those parts of his offerings which were fitting to be a pleasing aroma, being that they were from the species fitting to be sacrificed, but He did not accept all his offerings which were מִכֹּל הַבְּהֵמָה הַטְּהֹרָה וּמִכֹּל הָעוֹף הַטָּהוֹר, *of every tahor* (i.e., kosher) *animal and of every tahor* (i.e., kosher) *bird* (ibid. v. 20). We can (now) also understand what is meant by the statement, זֶבַח וּמִנְחָה לֹא חָפַצְתָּ אָזְנַיִם כָּרִיתָ לִּי, *You do not desire sacrifice nor meal offering, You have opened my ears* (*Psalms* 40:7), and when it states, לָמָּה לִּי רֹב זִבְחֵיכֶם, *To what purpose is the multitude of your sacrifices?* (*Isaiah* 1:11), and many more such (verses) in holy books, for indeed it is proper that he who brings the offering be a man acceptable to do so, choosing from the species fitting for sacrifice, which are suitable for attaining the purpose for which he brought the offering. He should lay his hand on the sacrifice, as though he was falling down and praying (to God) that his iniquity be on the head of the sacrifice, similar to the scapegoat (16:21), and thus he will manifest the submissive thoughts of repentance which are in his heart.

4. וְנִרְצָה לוֹ לְכַפֵּר עָלָיו — *And it shall be accepted for him to make atonement for him.* Now being that the kinds of sin (are varied), some being only in the thoughts of (man's) heart, while some are also in deed, (therefore) to atone for the thoughts of the heart, it is proper that those parts of the sacrifice which are burnt, namely the עוֹלָה, *burnt offering,* the אֵימוּרִים, *limbs of the sacrifice which are burnt,* and the מַזְכֶּרֶת הַמִּנְחָה, *the memorial of the meal offerings,* be consumed by the flames of the Altar. (However) to atone for (sinful) deeds, it is proper that certain parts of the sacrifice be given to the *Kohanim,* the servants of God who occupy themselves with His service, as a symbolic exchange of the

NOTES

4. וְנִרְצָה לוֹ לְכַפֵּר עָלָיו — *And it shall be accepted for him to make atonement for him.* The ceremony of *semichah,* in which the person who brings the offering lays his hands on its head, is explained by

from the cattle or from the flock shall you bring your offering.
[3] *If one's offering is an elevation-offering from the cattle, he shall offer*
an unblemished male; he shall bring it to the entrance of the Tent of
Meeting, voluntarily, before HASHEM. [4] *He shall lean his hand upon the*
head of the elevation-offering; and it shall become acceptable for him, to
atone for him. [5] *He shall slaughter the bull before* HASHEM; *the sons of*
Aaron, the Kohanim, shall bring the blood and throw the blood on the Altar,
all around — which is at the entrance of the Tent of Meeting. [6] *He shall skin*
the elevation-offering and cut it into its pieces. [7] *The sons of Aaron the*
Kohen shall place fire on the Altar, and arrange wood on the fire. [8] *The sons*
of Aaron, the Kohanim, shall arrange the pieces, the head and the fats, on
the wood that is on the fire, that is on the Altar. [9] *He shall wash its innards*
and its feet with water; and the Kohen shall cause it all to go up in smoke
on the Altar — an elevation-offering, a fire-offering, a satisfying aroma to
HASHEM.
[10] *And if one's offering is from the flock, from the sheep or from the*
goats, for an elevation-offering: He shall offer an unblemished male. [11] *He*
shall slaughter it at the northern side of the Altar before HASHEM; *and the*
sons of Aaron, the Kohanim, shall throw its blood on the Altar, all around.
[12] *He shall cut it into its pieces, its head, and its fats. The Kohen shall*
arrange them on the wood that is on the fire that is on the Altar. [13] *He shall*
wash the innards and the feet in water; the Kohen shall bring it all and
cause it to go up in smoke on the Altar — it is an elevation-offering, a
fire-offering, a satisfying aroma to HASHEM.
[14] *If one's offering to* HASHEM *is an elevation-offering of fowl, he shall*
bring his offering from turtledoves or from young doves. [15] *The Kohen*
shall bring it to the Altar, nip its head, and cause it to go up in smoke

---

limbs of the sinner which were used for evildoing, as it says, *He has given it to you to bear the iniquity of the congregation, to make atonement for them* (10:17). And so our Sages say that "the *Kohanim* eat (from the sacrifice) and the owners gain atonement" (*Pesachim* 59b). Now being that the evil acts which are fitting to be atoned for through a sacrifice are of two categories, some connected with serious iniquities such as (those) which incur the penalty of *kares, excision,* while some are lighter than those but do (cause) desecration of the holy, then behold, for the first (type) of sin, a sin offering is suitable, to cleanse (purge) the soul defiled by a sin incurring *kares,* as it says, וְנִכְרְתָה הַנֶּפֶשׁ הַהִוא, *that soul shall be cut off* (*Exodus* 31:14); and (as for) the second type, a guilt offering is suitable to remove the desecration of which he is guilty. This (shall be) through (his) submission as manifested through the sacrifice, coupled with repentance; and there is one law for both of them (i.e., sin offering and guilt offering). However, peace offerings associate the owners with the servants of God *to serve Him in one accord* (based on *Zephaniah* 3:9). Now being that sinners are of divergent degrees, some of them more prone to stumble into sin, (while) others are further removed from it and it is rare that they (will sin), therefore (the Torah) addresses itself to them in different ways and their sacrifices are (also) diverse, and thus regarding the anointed *Kohen,* because he is unlikely to slip into sin, it says . . .

NOTES

the *Sforno* as being not only symbolic of the transference of his sin to the animal but also a manifestation of his submission to God and a sign of his desire to repent.

טז הַמִּזְבֵּחָה וְנִמְצָה דָמוֹ עַל קִיר הַמִּזְבֵּחַ: וְהֵסִיר אֶת־מֻרְאָתוֹ בְּנֹצָתָהּ
יז וְהִשְׁלִיךְ אֹתָהּ אֵצֶל הַמִּזְבֵּחַ קֵדְמָה אֶל־מְקוֹם הַדָּשֶׁן: וְשִׁסַּע אֹתוֹ
בִכְנָפָיו לֹא יַבְדִּיל וְהִקְטִיר אֹתוֹ הַכֹּהֵן הַמִּזְבֵּחָה עַל־הָעֵצִים אֲשֶׁר
ב א עַל־הָאֵשׁ עֹלָה הוּא אִשֵּׁה רֵיחַ נִיחֹחַ לַיהוָה: וְנֶפֶשׁ
כִּי־תַקְרִיב קָרְבַּן מִנְחָה לַיהוָה סֹלֶת יִהְיֶה קָרְבָּנוֹ וְיָצַק עָלֶיהָ שֶׁמֶן
ב וְנָתַן עָלֶיהָ לְבֹנָה: וֶהֱבִיאָהּ אֶל־בְּנֵי אַהֲרֹן הַכֹּהֲנִים וְקָמַץ מִשָּׁם
מְלֹא קֻמְצוֹ מִסָּלְתָּהּ וּמִשַּׁמְנָהּ עַל כָּל־לְבֹנָתָהּ וְהִקְטִיר הַכֹּהֵן
ג אֶת־אַזְכָּרָתָהּ הַמִּזְבֵּחָה אִשֵּׁה רֵיחַ נִיחֹחַ לַיהוָה: וְהַנּוֹתֶרֶת מִן־הַמִּנְחָה
ד לְאַהֲרֹן וּלְבָנָיו קֹדֶשׁ קָדָשִׁים מֵאִשֵּׁי יהוה: וְכִי תַקְרִב
קָרְבַּן מִנְחָה מַאֲפֵה תַנּוּר סֹלֶת חַלּוֹת מַצֹּת בְּלוּלֹת בַּשֶּׁמֶן וּרְקִיקֵי
ה מַצּוֹת מְשֻׁחִים בַּשָּׁמֶן: וְאִם־מִנְחָה עַל־הַמַּחֲבַת קָרְבָּנֶךָ
ו סֹלֶת בְּלוּלָה בַשֶּׁמֶן מַצָּה תִהְיֶה: פָּתוֹת אֹתָהּ פִּתִּים וְיָצַקְתָּ עָלֶיהָ
שלישי ז שָׁמֶן מִנְחָה הִוא: וְאִם־מִנְחַת מַרְחֶשֶׁת קָרְבָּנֶךָ סֹלֶת
ח בַּשֶּׁמֶן תֵּעָשֶׂה: וְהֵבֵאתָ אֶת־הַמִּנְחָה אֲשֶׁר יֵעָשֶׂה מֵאֵלֶּה לַיהוָה
ט וְהִקְרִיבָהּ אֶל־הַכֹּהֵן וְהִגִּישָׁהּ אֶל־הַמִּזְבֵּחַ: וְהֵרִים הַכֹּהֵן מִן־הַמִּנְחָה
י אֶת־אַזְכָּרָתָהּ וְהִקְטִיר הַמִּזְבֵּחָה אִשֵּׁה רֵיחַ נִיחֹחַ לַיהוָה: וְהַנּוֹתֶרֶת
יא מִן־הַמִּנְחָה לְאַהֲרֹן וּלְבָנָיו קֹדֶשׁ קָדָשִׁים מֵאִשֵּׁי יהוה: כָּל־הַמִּנְחָה
אֲשֶׁר תַּקְרִיבוּ לַיהוָה לֹא תֵעָשֶׂה חָמֵץ כִּי כָל־שְׂאֹר וְכָל־דְּבַשׁ
יב לֹא־תַקְטִירוּ מִמֶּנּוּ אִשֶּׁה לַיהוָה: קָרְבַּן רֵאשִׁית תַּקְרִיבוּ אֹתָם לַיהוָה
יג וְאֶל־הַמִּזְבֵּחַ לֹא־יַעֲלוּ לְרֵיחַ נִיחֹחַ: וְכָל־קָרְבַּן מִנְחָתְךָ בַּמֶּלַח תִּמְלָח
וְלֹא תַשְׁבִּית מֶלַח בְּרִית אֱלֹהֶיךָ מֵעַל מִנְחָתֶךָ עַל כָּל־קָרְבָּנְךָ
יד תַּקְרִיב מֶלַח: וְאִם־תַּקְרִיב מִנְחַת בִּכּוּרִים לַיהוָה
טו אָבִיב קָלוּי בָּאֵשׁ גֶּרֶשׂ כַּרְמֶל תַּקְרִיב אֵת מִנְחַת בִּכּוּרֶיךָ: וְנָתַתָּ
טז עָלֶיהָ שֶׁמֶן וְשַׂמְתָּ עָלֶיהָ לְבֹנָה מִנְחָה הִוא: וְהִקְטִיר הַכֹּהֵן
אֶת־אַזְכָּרָתָהּ מִגִּרְשָׂהּ וּמִשַּׁמְנָהּ עַל כָּל־לְבֹנָתָהּ אִשֶּׁה לַיהוָה:
ג רביעי א וְאִם־זֶבַח שְׁלָמִים קָרְבָּנוֹ אִם מִן־הַבָּקָר הוּא מַקְרִיב אִם־זָכָר
ב אִם־נְקֵבָה תָּמִים יַקְרִיבֶנּוּ לִפְנֵי יהוה: וְסָמַךְ יָדוֹ עַל־רֹאשׁ קָרְבָּנוֹ
וּשְׁחָטוֹ פֶּתַח אֹהֶל מוֹעֵד וְזָרְקוּ בְּנֵי אַהֲרֹן הַכֹּהֲנִים אֶת־הַדָּם
ג עַל־הַמִּזְבֵּחַ סָבִיב: וְהִקְרִיב מִזֶּבַח הַשְּׁלָמִים אִשֶּׁה לַיהוָה אֶת־
ד הַחֵלֶב הַמְכַסֶּה אֶת־הַקֶּרֶב וְאֵת כָּל־הַחֵלֶב אֲשֶׁר עַל־הַקֶּרֶב: וְאֵת
שְׁתֵּי הַכְּלָיֹת וְאֶת־הַחֵלֶב אֲשֶׁר עֲלֵהֶן אֲשֶׁר עַל־הַכְּסָלִים וְאֶת־
ה הַיֹּתֶרֶת עַל־הַכָּבֵד עַל־הַכְּלָיוֹת יְסִירֶנָּה: וְהִקְטִירוּ אֹתוֹ בְנֵי־אַהֲרֹן
הַמִּזְבֵּחָה עַל־הָעֹלָה אֲשֶׁר עַל־הָעֵצִים אֲשֶׁר עַל־הָאֵשׁ אִשֵּׁה רֵיחַ נִיחֹחַ
לַיהוָה:

on the Altar, having pressed out its blood on the Altar's wall. 16 He shall remove
its crop with its feathers, and he shall throw it near the Altar toward the east, to
the place of the ashes. 17 He shall split it — with its feathers — he need not sever
it; the Kohen shall cause it to go up in smoke on the Altar, on the wood that is on
the fire — it is an elevation-offering, a fire-offering, a satisfying aroma to HASHEM.

2 1 When a person offers a meal-offering to HASHEM, his offering shall be of fine
flour; he shall pour oil upon it and place frankincense upon it. 2 He shall
bring it to the sons of Aaron, the Kohanim, one of whom shall scoop his threefingersful from it, from its fine flour and from its oil, as well as all its frankincense;
and the Kohen shall cause its memorial portion to go up in smoke upon the Altar
— a fire-offering, a satisfying aroma to HASHEM. 3 The remnant of the meal-
offering is for Aaron and his sons; most holy, from the fire-offerings of HASHEM.
4 When you offer a meal-offering that is baked in an oven, it shall be of fine
flour: unleavened loaves mixed with oil, or unleavened wafers smeared with oil.
5 If your offering is a meal-offering on the pan, it shall be of fine flour mixed
with oil, it shall be unleavened. 6 You shall break it into pieces and pour oil upon
it — it is a meal-offering.
7 If your offering is a meal-offering in a deep pan, it shall be made of fine flour
with oil. 8 You shall present to HASHEM the meal-offering that will be prepared
from these; he shall bring it to the Kohen who shall bring it close to the Altar.
9 The Kohen shall lift up its memorial portion from the meal-offering and cause
it to go up in smoke on the Altar — a fire-offering, a satisfying aroma to HASHEM.
10 The remnant of the meal-offering is for Aaron and his sons — most holy, from
the fire-offerings of HASHEM.
11 Any meal-offering that you offer to HASHEM shall not be prepared leavened,
for you shall not cause to go up in smoke from any leavening or fruit-honey as
a fire-offering to HASHEM. 12 You shall offer them as a first-fruit offering to
HASHEM, but they may not go up upon the Altar for a satisfying aroma.
13 You shall salt your every meal-offering with salt; you may not discontinue
the salt of your God's covenant from upon your meal-offering — on your every
offering shall you offer salt.
14 When you bring a meal-offering of the first grain to HASHEM: from ripe ears,
parched over fire, ground from plump kernels, shall you offer the meal-offering
of your first grain. 15 You shall put oil on it and place frankincense on it — a
meal-offering. 16 The Kohen shall cause its memorial portion to go up in smoke —
from its flour and its oil, as well as its frankincense — a fire-offering to HASHEM.

3 1 If his offering is a feast peace-offering, if he offers it from the cattle — whether
male or female — unblemished shall he offer it before HASHEM. 2 He shall lean
his hand upon the head of his offering and slaughter it at the entrance of the Tent
of Meeting; the sons of Aaron, the Kohanim, shall throw the blood upon the Altar,
all around. 3 From the feast peace-offering he shall offer as a fire-offering to
HASHEM: the fat that covers the innards, and all the fat that is upon the innards;
4 and the two kidneys with the fat that is upon them, that is upon the flanks, and
he shall remove the diaphragm with the liver, with the kidneys. 5 The sons of
Aaron shall cause it to go up in smoke on the Altar, besides the elevation-offering
that is on the wood that is on the fire — a fire-offering, a satisfying aroma to
HASHEM.

ו וְאִם־מִן־הַצֹּאן קָרְבָּנוֹ לְזֶבַח שְׁלָמִים לַיהוָה זָכָר אוֹ נְקֵבָה תָּמִים
ז יַקְרִיבֶנּוּ: אִם־כֶּשֶׂב הוּא־מַקְרִיב אֶת־קָרְבָּנוֹ וְהִקְרִיב אֹתוֹ לִפְנֵי יהוָה:
ח וְסָמַךְ אֶת־יָדוֹ עַל־רֹאשׁ קָרְבָּנוֹ וְשָׁחַט אֹתוֹ לִפְנֵי אֹהֶל מוֹעֵד וְזָרְקוּ בְּנֵי
ט אַהֲרֹן אֶת־דָּמוֹ עַל־הַמִּזְבֵּחַ סָבִיב: וְהִקְרִיב מִזֶּבַח הַשְּׁלָמִים אִשֶּׁה לַיהוָה
חֶלְבּוֹ הָאַלְיָה תְמִימָה לְעֻמַּת הֶעָצֶה יְסִירֶנָּה וְאֶת־הַחֵלֶב הַמְכַסֶּה
י אֶת־הַקֶּרֶב וְאֵת כָּל־הַחֵלֶב אֲשֶׁר עַל־הַקֶּרֶב: וְאֵת שְׁתֵּי הַכְּלָיֹת
וְאֶת־הַחֵלֶב אֲשֶׁר עֲלֵהֶן אֲשֶׁר עַל־הַכְּסָלִים וְאֶת־הַיֹּתֶרֶת עַל־הַכָּבֵד
יא עַל־הַכְּלָיֹת יְסִירֶנָּה: וְהִקְטִירוֹ הַכֹּהֵן הַמִּזְבֵּחָה לֶחֶם אִשֶּׁה לַיהוָה:
יב-יג וְאִם־עֵז קָרְבָּנוֹ וְהִקְרִיבוֹ לִפְנֵי יהוָה: וְסָמַךְ אֶת־יָדוֹ עַל־רֹאשׁוֹ וְשָׁחַט
אֹתוֹ לִפְנֵי אֹהֶל מוֹעֵד וְזָרְקוּ בְּנֵי אַהֲרֹן אֶת־דָּמוֹ עַל־הַמִּזְבֵּחַ סָבִיב:
יד וְהִקְרִיב מִמֶּנּוּ קָרְבָּנוֹ אִשֶּׁה לַיהוָה אֶת־הַחֵלֶב הַמְכַסֶּה אֶת־הַקֶּרֶב וְאֵת
טו כָּל־הַחֵלֶב אֲשֶׁר עַל־הַקֶּרֶב: וְאֵת שְׁתֵּי הַכְּלָיֹת וְאֶת־הַחֵלֶב אֲשֶׁר עֲלֵהֶן
אֲשֶׁר עַל־הַכְּסָלִים וְאֶת־הַיֹּתֶרֶת עַל־הַכָּבֵד עַל־הַכְּלָיֹת יְסִירֶנָּה:
טז-יז וְהִקְטִירָם הַכֹּהֵן הַמִּזְבֵּחָה לֶחֶם אִשֶּׁה לְרֵיחַ נִיחֹחַ כָּל־חֵלֶב לַיהוָה: חֻקַּת
עוֹלָם לְדֹרֹתֵיכֶם בְּכֹל מוֹשְׁבֹתֵיכֶם כָּל־חֵלֶב וְכָל־דָּם לֹא תֹאכֵלוּ:
ד חמישי א-ב וַיְדַבֵּר יהוָה אֶל־מֹשֶׁה לֵּאמֹר: דַּבֵּר אֶל־בְּנֵי יִשְׂרָאֵל לֵאמֹר נֶפֶשׁ
כִּי־תֶחֱטָא בִשְׁגָגָה מִכֹּל מִצְוֹת יהוָה אֲשֶׁר לֹא תֵעָשֶׂינָה וְעָשָׂה מֵאַחַת
ג מֵהֵנָּה: אִם הַכֹּהֵן הַמָּשִׁיחַ יֶחֱטָא לְאַשְׁמַת הָעָם וְהִקְרִיב עַל חַטָּאתוֹ
ד אֲשֶׁר חָטָא פַּר בֶּן־בָּקָר תָּמִים לַיהוָה לְחַטָּאת: וְהֵבִיא אֶת־הַפָּר
אֶל־פֶּתַח אֹהֶל מוֹעֵד לִפְנֵי יהוָה וְסָמַךְ אֶת־יָדוֹ עַל־רֹאשׁ הַפָּר וְשָׁחַט
ה אֶת־הַפָּר לִפְנֵי יהוָה: וְלָקַח הַכֹּהֵן הַמָּשִׁיחַ מִדַּם הַפָּר וְהֵבִיא אֹתוֹ
ו אֶל־אֹהֶל מוֹעֵד: וְטָבַל הַכֹּהֵן אֶת־אֶצְבָּעוֹ בַּדָּם וְהִזָּה מִן־הַדָּם שֶׁבַע
ז פְּעָמִים לִפְנֵי יהוָה אֶת־פְּנֵי פָּרֹכֶת הַקֹּדֶשׁ: וְנָתַן הַכֹּהֵן מִן־הַדָּם
עַל־קַרְנוֹת מִזְבַּח קְטֹרֶת הַסַּמִּים לִפְנֵי יהוָה אֲשֶׁר בְּאֹהֶל מוֹעֵד וְאֵת ׀
כָּל־דַּם הַפָּר יִשְׁפֹּךְ אֶל־יְסוֹד מִזְבַּח הָעֹלָה אֲשֶׁר־פֶּתַח אֹהֶל מוֹעֵד:
ח וְאֶת־כָּל־חֵלֶב פַּר הַחַטָּאת יָרִים מִמֶּנּוּ אֶת־הַחֵלֶב הַמְכַסֶּה עַל־הַקֶּרֶב

IV

3. אִם הַכֹּהֵן הַמָּשִׁיחַ יֶחֱטָא לְאַשְׁמַת הָעָם — *If the anointed Kohen shall sin (due) to the guilt of the people.* That is to say, he will not sin (even) inadvertently except for *the people that ensnare* (based on *Job* 34:30), as (our Sages) say, "He who prays and makes a mistake, it is a bad omen for himself; and if he is the messenger of the congregation (ש״ץ), it is a bad omen for those who sent him" (*Berachos* 34b). (Now) his offering is burnt but the *Kohen* gets no part of it, and therefore the phrase וְאָשֵׁם, *and he is guilty,* is not written in this instance as it is written regarding all other sinners, for when it states וְאָשֵׁם it indicates an

NOTES

IV

3. אִם הַכֹּהֵן הַמָּשִׁיחַ יֶחֱטָא לְאַשְׁמַת הָעָם — *If the anointed Kohen shall sin (due) to the guilt of the people.* The *Sforno* interprets the phrase אָשֵׁם, *guilty,* as implying the need for repentance. In this fashion, he explains the reason for the Torah's inclusion or exclusion of this phrase in subsequent verses. See 4:3,21,22,27. The *Sforno* is of the

[6] *If his offering to HASHEM is a feast peace-offering from the flock — male or female — unblemished shall he offer it.* [7] *If he offers a sheep as his offering, he shall bring it before HASHEM.* [8] *He shall lean his hands upon the head of his offering and slaughter it before the Tent of Meeting; and the sons of Aaron shall throw its blood upon the Altar, all around.* [9] *From the feast peace-offering he shall offer as a fire-offering to HASHEM its choicest part — the entire tail — he shall remove it above the kidneys; and the fat that covers the innards and all the fat that is upon the innards;* [10] *and the two kidneys and the fat that is upon them, that is upon the flanks; and he shall remove the diaphragm with the liver, with the kidneys.* [11] *The Kohen shall cause it to go up in smoke on the Altar; it is the food of the fire — for HASHEM.*

[12] *If his offering is a goat, he shall bring it before HASHEM.* [13] *He shall lean his hand upon its head and slaughter it before the Tent of Meeting; and the sons of Aaron shall throw its blood upon the Altar, all around.* [14] *He shall bring his offering from it as a fire-offering to HASHEM: the fat that covers the innards and all the fat that is upon the innards;* [15] *and the two kidneys and the fat that is upon them, that is upon the flanks; and he shall remove the diaphragm with the liver, with the kidneys.* [16] *The Kohen shall cause them to go up in smoke on the Altar — the food of the fire for a satisfying aroma, all the choice parts for HASHEM.* [17] *An eternal decree for your generations in all your dwelling places; you may not consume any fat or any blood.*

4 [1] *HASHEM spoke to Moses, saying:* [2] *Speak to the Children of Israel, saying: When a person will sin unintentionally from among all the commandments of HASHEM that may not be done, and he commits one of them.*

[3] *If the anointed Kohen will sin, bringing guilt upon the people; for his sin that he committed he shall offer a young bull, unblemished, to HASHEM as a sin-offering.* [4] *He shall bring the bull to the entrance of the Tent of Meeting before HASHEM; he shall lean his hand upon the head of the bull, and he shall slaughter the bull before HASHEM.* [5] *The anointed Kohen shall take from the blood of the bull and bring it to the Tent of Meeting.* [6] *The Kohen shall dip his forefinger into the blood; he shall sprinkle some of the blood seven times before HASHEM toward the Curtain of the Holy.* [7] *The Kohen shall put some of the blood on the horns of the Altar where incense is caused to go up in smoke before HASHEM, which is in the Tent of Meeting; and all the [remaining] blood of the bull he shall pour onto the base of the Elevation-offering Altar, which is at the entrance of the Tent of Meeting.* [8] *He shall separate all the fats of the sin-offering bull from it: the fat that covers the innards*

---

admonition to repent, but this is not applicable to the anointed *Kohen* for he did not sin on his own (lit., from his heart) whatsoever, but it happened *due to the guilt of the people.* (Now) regarding the inadvertent sin of the Sanhedrin (court), which is also a far-removed (occurrence), it says . . .

NOTES

opinion that the *Kohen Gadol*, High Priest (the anointed one), as the representative of the people, is himself above suspicion, but he may sin without intent because of their sins. Therefore, it is not he who is guilty and must repent, but the people. This explains the absence of the word וְאָשֵׁם, *and he is guilty*, from this portion, as explained above.

ט וְאֵת֙ כָּל־הַחֵ֔לֶב אֲשֶׁ֖ר עַל־הַקֶּ֑רֶב וְאֵת֙ שְׁתֵּ֣י הַכְּלָיֹ֔ת וְאֶת־הַחֵ֙לֶב֙ אֲשֶׁ֣ר
עֲלֵיהֶ֔ן אֲשֶׁ֖ר עַל־הַכְּסָלִ֑ים וְאֶת־הַיֹּתֶ֙רֶת֙ עַל־הַכָּבֵ֔ד עַל־הַכְּלָיֹ֖ות יְסִירֶֽנָּה:

י כַּאֲשֶׁ֣ר יוּרַ֔ם מִשֹּׁ֖ור זֶ֣בַח הַשְּׁלָמִ֑ים וְהִקְטִירָם֙ הַכֹּהֵ֔ן עַ֖ל מִזְבַּ֥ח הָעֹלָֽה:

יא וְאֶת־ע֤וֹר הַפָּר֙ וְאֶת־כָּל־בְּשָׂר֔וֹ עַל־רֹאשׁ֖וֹ וְעַל־כְּרָעָ֑יו וְקִרְבּ֖וֹ וּפִרְשֽׁוֹ:

יב וְהוֹצִ֣יא אֶת־כָּל־הַ֠פָּר אֶל־מִח֨וּץ לַֽמַּחֲנֶ֜ה אֶל־מָק֤וֹם טָהוֹר֙ אֶל־שֶׁ֣פֶךְ
הַדֶּ֔שֶׁן וְשָׂרַ֥ף אֹת֛וֹ עַל־עֵצִ֖ים בָּאֵ֑שׁ עַל־שֶׁ֥פֶךְ הַדֶּ֖שֶׁן יִשָּׂרֵֽף:

יג וְאִ֞ם כָּל־עֲדַ֣ת יִשְׂרָאֵ֗ל יִשְׁגּוּ֙ וְנֶעְלַ֣ם דָּבָ֔ר מֵעֵינֵ֖י הַקָּהָ֑ל וְ֠עָשׂוּ אַחַ֨ת
יד מִכָּל־מִצְוֹ֧ת יְהֹוָ֛ה אֲשֶׁ֥ר לֹא־תֵעָשֶׂ֖ינָה וְאָשֵֽׁמוּ: וְנֽוֹדְעָה֙ הַֽחַטָּ֔את אֲשֶׁ֣ר
חָטְא֣וּ עָלֶ֔יהָ וְהִקְרִ֣יבוּ הַקָּהָ֗ל פַּ֣ר בֶּן־בָּקָר֮ לְחַטָּאת֒ וְהֵבִ֣יאוּ אֹת֔וֹ לִפְנֵ֖י אֹ֥הֶל
טו מוֹעֵֽד: וְ֠סָמְכ֨וּ זִקְנֵ֤י הָֽעֵדָה֙ אֶת־יְדֵיהֶ֔ם עַל־רֹ֥אשׁ הַפָּ֖ר לִפְנֵ֣י יְהֹוָ֑ה וְשָׁחַ֥ט
טז אֶת־הַפָּ֖ר לִפְנֵ֥י יְהֹוָֽה: וְהֵבִ֛יא הַכֹּהֵ֥ן הַמָּשִׁ֖יחַ מִדַּ֣ם הַפָּ֑ר אֶל־אֹ֖הֶל מוֹעֵֽד:
יז וְטָבַ֧ל הַכֹּהֵ֛ן אֶצְבָּע֖וֹ מִן־הַדָּ֑ם וְהִזָּ֞ה שֶׁ֤בַע פְּעָמִים֙ לִפְנֵ֣י יְהֹוָ֔ה אֵ֖ת פְּנֵ֥י
יח הַפָּרֹֽכֶת: וּמִן־הַדָּ֞ם יִתֵּ֣ן ׀ עַל־קַרְנֹ֣ת הַמִּזְבֵּ֗חַ אֲשֶׁר֙ לִפְנֵ֣י יְהֹוָ֔ה אֲשֶׁ֖ר בְּאֹ֣הֶל
מוֹעֵ֑ד וְאֵ֣ת כָּל־הַדָּ֗ם יִשְׁפֹּךְ֙ אֶל־יְסוֹד֙ מִזְבַּ֣ח הָעֹלָ֔ה אֲשֶׁר־פֶּ֖תַח אֹ֥הֶל
יט־כ מוֹעֵֽד: וְאֵ֥ת כָּל־חֶלְבּ֖וֹ יָרִ֣ים מִמֶּ֑נּוּ וְהִקְטִ֖יר הַמִּזְבֵּֽחָה: וְעָשָׂ֣ה לַפָּ֔ר כַּֽאֲשֶׁ֤ר
כא עָשָׂה֙ לְפַ֣ר הַֽחַטָּ֔את כֵּ֖ן יַֽעֲשֶׂה־לּ֑וֹ וְכִפֶּ֧ר עֲלֵהֶ֛ם הַכֹּהֵ֖ן וְנִסְלַ֥ח לָהֶֽם: וְהוֹצִ֣יא
אֶת־הַפָּ֗ר אֶל־מִחוּץ֙ לַֽמַּחֲנֶ֔ה וְשָׂרַ֣ף אֹת֔וֹ כַּֽאֲשֶׁ֣ר שָׂרַ֔ף אֵ֖ת הַפָּ֣ר הָֽרִאשׁ֑וֹן
חַטַּ֥את הַקָּהָ֖ל הֽוּא:

כב אֲשֶׁ֥ר נָשִׂ֖יא יֶֽחֱטָ֑א וְעָשָׂ֡ה אַחַ֣ת מִכָּל־מִצְוֹת֩ יְהֹוָ֨ה אֱלֹהָ֜יו אֲשֶׁ֥ר לֹֽא־
כג תֵעָשֶׂ֛ינָה בִּשְׁגָגָ֖ה וְאָשֵֽׁם: אֽוֹ־הוֹדַ֤ע אֵלָיו֙ חַטָּאת֔וֹ אֲשֶׁ֥ר חָטָ֖א בָּ֑הּ וְהֵבִ֧יא
כד אֶת־קָרְבָּנ֛וֹ שְׂעִ֥יר עִזִּ֖ים זָכָ֣ר תָּמִ֑ים וְסָמַ֤ךְ יָדוֹ֙ עַל־רֹ֣אשׁ הַשָּׂעִ֔יר וְשָׁחַ֣ט
כה אֹת֗וֹ בִּמְק֛וֹם אֲשֶׁר־יִשְׁחַ֥ט אֶת־הָֽעֹלָ֖ה לִפְנֵ֣י יְהֹוָ֑ה חַטָּ֖את הֽוּא: וְלָקַ֨ח הַכֹּהֵ֜ן
מִדַּ֤ם הַֽחַטָּאת֙ בְּאֶצְבָּע֔וֹ וְנָתַ֕ן עַל־קַרְנֹ֖ת מִזְבַּ֣ח הָֽעֹלָ֑ה וְאֶת־דָּמ֣וֹ יִשְׁפֹּ֔ךְ

---

13. יִשְׁגּוּ וְנֶעְלַם דָּבָר מֵעֵינֵי הַקָּהָל — *Shall err, the thing being hidden from the eyes of the assembly.* For being that they are the eyes of the assembly (the public) who should see for others, they themselves did not look (observe) well, and of them it is also said (וְאָשֵׁמוּ, *and are guilty*).

21. חַטַּאת הַקָּהָל הוּא — *It is the sin offering for the assembly.* For this does not occur except for the iniquity of the generation as well. However, here (v. 13) (the Torah) writes וְאָשֵׁמוּ, *and are guilty,* to caution them to repent before the offering is brought. Their sin offering is also burnt and due to the severity of both (the sins of the anointed *Kohen* and of the Sanhedrin), the blood (of their sacrifices) was brought to the inner sanctuary. Now regarding the transgression of the king it says . . .

NOTES

13. יִשְׁגּוּ וְנֶעְלַם דָּבָר מֵעֵינֵי הַקָּהָל — *Shall err, the thing being hidden from the eyes of the assembly.* The Sanhedrin, unlike the *Kohen Gadol,* are considered to be an integral part of the people. When they err there is direct personal involvement and responsibility; hence both they and the people are guilty (וְאָשֵׁמוּ).

22. אֲשֶׁר נָשִׂיא יֶחֱטָא — *When a ruler sins.* נָשִׂיא refers to the king. It is not unusual for a man of power and wealth to sin, hence he must repent (וְאָשֵׁם). However, as a king, others need not accuse him. He will be big enough to acknowledge his own sin. There will be occasions, however, when he will be unaware and at such times it should be

and all the fat that is upon the innards; [9] *and the two kidneys and the fat*
that is upon them, which is upon the flanks; and he shall remove the
diaphragm with the liver, with the kidneys — [10] *just as it would be removed*
from the feast peace-offering bull; and the Kohen shall cause them to go up
in smoke on the Elevation-offering Altar. [11] *But the hide of the bull and all*
its flesh with its head and with its feet, and its innards and its waste —
[12] *the entire bull shall he remove to the outside of the camp, to a pure place,*
to where the ash is poured, and he shall burn it on wood in fire; on the place
where the ash is poured shall it be burned.

[13] *If the entire assembly of Israel shall err, and a matter became obscured*
from the eyes of the congregation; and they commit one from among all the
commandments of HASHEM that may not be done, and they become guilty;
[14] *when the sin regarding which they committed becomes known, the*
congregation shall offer a young bull as a sin-offering, and they shall bring
it before the Tent of Meeting. [15] *The elders of the assembly shall lean their*
hands upon the head of the bull before HASHEM, and someone shall
slaughter the bull before HASHEM. [16] *The anointed Kohen shall bring part of*
the bull's blood to the Tent of Meeting. [17] *The Kohen shall dip his finger*
from the blood; and he shall sprinkle seven times before HASHEM, toward
the Curtain. [18] *He shall put some of the blood upon the horns of the Altar*
that is before HASHEM, which is in the Tent of Meeting; and all the
remaining blood he shall pour onto the base of the Elevation-offering Altar,
which is at the entrance of the Tent of Meeting. [19] *He shall separate all its*
fats from it and cause it to go up in smoke on the Altar. [20] *He shall do to the*
bull as he had done to the sin-offering bull, so shall he do to it; thus shall the
Kohen provide them atonement and it shall be forgiven them. [21] *He shall*
remove the bull to the outside of the camp and burn it, as he had burned the
first bull; it is a sin-offering of the congregation.

[22] *When a ruler sins, and commits one from among all the command-*
ments of HASHEM that may not be done — unintentionally — and becomes
guilty: [23] *If the sin that he committed becomes known to him, he shall bring*
his offering, a male goat, unblemished. [24] *He shall lean his hand on the head*
of the goat and he shall slaughter it in the place he would slaughter the
elevation-offering before HASHEM; it is a sin-offering. [25] *The Kohen shall*
take from the blood of the sin-offering with his forefinger and place it
upon the horns of the Elevation-offering Altar; and he shall pour its blood

---

22. אֲשֶׁר נָשִׂיא יֶחֱטָא — *When a ruler sins.* For, indeed, this event is prone (to happen) that he sins, as it says, וַיִּשְׁמַן יְשֻׁרוּן וַיִּבְעָט, *But Yeshurun waxed fat and kicked* (*Deut.* 32:15), and here it says, וְאָשֵׁם, *and is guilty,* i.e., he himself will acknowledge his sin.

23. אוֹ הוֹדַע אֵלָיו — *Or it is made known to him* ... through others. The (long vowel) *cholam* (וֹ) in the word הוֹדַע is in place of the *shuruk* (ֻ). It then says regarding the common people ...

NOTES

made known to him.

23. אוֹ הוֹדַע אֵלָיו — *Or it is made known to him.* The *Sforno* explains that the word הוֹדַע spelled with the long vowel *cholam* (וֹ) should be read as though it is written with a *shuruk* (ֻ), i.e., הֻדַע, for then the conjugation would be in הָפְעַל which is the *passive* of הִפְעִיל, *the causative*. The meaning would then be *it is made known to him.*

כו אֶל־יְס֖וֹד מִזְבַּ֥ח הָעֹלָֽה׃ וְאֶת־כָּל־חֶלְבּוֹ֙ יַקְטִ֣יר הַמִּזְבֵּ֔חָה כְּחֵ֖לֶב זֶ֣בַח
הַשְּׁלָמִ֑ים וְכִפֶּ֨ר עָלָ֧יו הַכֹּהֵ֛ן מֵחַטָּאת֖וֹ וְנִסְלַ֥ח לֽוֹ׃
כז וְאִם־נֶ֧פֶשׁ אַחַ֛ת תֶּחֱטָ֥א בִשְׁגָגָ֖ה מֵעַ֣ם הָאָ֑רֶץ בַּעֲשֹׂתָ֨הּ אַחַ֜ת מִמִּצְוֺ֧ת ששי
כח יְהוָ֛ה אֲשֶׁ֥ר לֹא־תֵעָשֶׂ֖ינָה וְאָשֵֽׁם׃ א֚וֹ הוֹדַ֣ע אֵלָ֔יו חַטָּאת֖וֹ אֲשֶׁ֣ר חָטָ֑א
וְהֵבִ֣יא קָרְבָּנ֗וֹ שְׂעִירַ֤ת עִזִּים֙ תְּמִימָ֣ה נְקֵבָ֔ה עַל־חַטָּאת֖וֹ אֲשֶׁ֥ר חָטָֽא׃
כט וְסָמַךְ֙ אֶת־יָד֔וֹ עַ֖ל רֹ֣אשׁ הַֽחַטָּ֑את וְשָׁחַט֙ אֶת־הַ֣חַטָּ֔את בִּמְק֖וֹם הָעֹלָֽה׃
ל וְלָקַ֨ח הַכֹּהֵ֤ן מִדָּמָהּ֙ בְּאֶצְבָּע֔וֹ וְנָתַ֕ן עַל־קַֽרְנֹ֖ת מִזְבַּ֣ח הָעֹלָ֑ה וְאֶת־כָּל־
לא דָּמָ֣הּ יִשְׁפֹּ֔ךְ אֶל־יְס֖וֹד הַמִּזְבֵּֽחַ׃ וְאֶת־כָּל־חֶלְבָּ֣הּ יָסִ֗יר כַּאֲשֶׁ֨ר הוּסַ֣ר חֵלֶב֮
מֵעַ֣ל זֶ֣בַח הַשְּׁלָמִים֒ וְהִקְטִ֤יר הַכֹּהֵן֙ הַמִּזְבֵּ֔חָה לְרֵ֥יחַ נִיחֹ֖חַ לַיהוָ֑ה וְכִפֶּ֥ר
עָלָ֛יו הַכֹּהֵ֖ן וְנִסְלַ֥ח לֽוֹ׃

לב-לג וְאִם־כֶּ֛בֶשׂ יָבִ֥יא קָרְבָּנ֖וֹ לְחַטָּ֑את נְקֵבָ֥ה תְמִימָ֖ה יְבִיאֶֽנָּה׃ וְסָמַךְ֙ אֶת־יָד֔וֹ
עַ֖ל רֹ֣אשׁ הַֽחַטָּ֑את וְשָׁחַ֤ט אֹתָהּ֙ לְחַטָּ֔את בִּמְק֕וֹם אֲשֶׁ֥ר יִשְׁחַ֖ט
לד אֶת־הָעֹלָֽה׃ וְלָקַ֨ח הַכֹּהֵ֜ן מִדַּ֤ם הַֽחַטָּאת֙ בְּאֶצְבָּע֔וֹ וְנָתַ֕ן עַל־קַֽרְנֹ֖ת מִזְבַּ֣ח
לה הָעֹלָ֑ה וְאֶת־כָּל־דָּמָ֣הּ יִשְׁפֹּ֔ךְ אֶל־יְס֖וֹד הַמִּזְבֵּֽחַ׃ וְאֶת־כָּל־חֶלְבָּ֣הּ יָסִ֗יר
כַּאֲשֶׁ֨ר יוּסַ֥ר חֵֽלֶב־הַכֶּשֶׂב֮ מִזֶּ֣בַח הַשְּׁלָמִים֒ וְהִקְטִ֨יר הַכֹּהֵ֤ן אֹתָם֙
הַמִּזְבֵּ֔חָה עַ֖ל אִשֵּׁ֣י יְהוָ֑ה וְכִפֶּ֨ר עָלָ֧יו הַכֹּהֵ֛ן עַל־חַטָּאת֥וֹ אֲשֶׁר־חָטָ֖א
וְנִסְלַ֥ח לֽוֹ׃

ה
א וְנֶ֣פֶשׁ כִּֽי־תֶחֱטָ֗א וְשָֽׁמְעָה֙ ק֣וֹל אָלָ֔ה וְה֣וּא עֵ֔ד א֥וֹ רָאָ֖ה א֣וֹ יָדָ֑ע אִם־
ב ל֥וֹא יַגִּ֖יד וְנָשָׂ֥א עֲוֺנֽוֹ׃ אוֹ֮ נֶ֣פֶשׁ אֲשֶׁ֣ר תִּגַּע֮ בְּכָל־דָּבָ֣ר טָמֵא֒ א֣וֹ בְנִבְלַ֞ת
חַיָּ֣ה טְמֵאָ֗ה א֚וֹ בְּנִבְלַת֙ בְּהֵמָ֣ה טְמֵאָ֔ה א֕וֹ בְּנִבְלַ֖ת שֶׁ֣רֶץ טָמֵ֑א
ג וְנֶעְלַ֣ם מִמֶּ֔נּוּ וְה֥וּא טָמֵ֖א וְאָשֵֽׁם׃ א֣וֹ כִ֤י יִגַּע֙ בְּטֻמְאַ֣ת אָדָ֔ם לְכֹל֙
ד טֻמְאָת֔וֹ אֲשֶׁ֥ר יִטְמָ֖א בָּ֑הּ וְנֶעְלַ֣ם מִמֶּ֔נּוּ וְה֥וּא יָדַ֖ע וְאָשֵֽׁם׃ א֣וֹ נֶ֡פֶשׁ כִּ֣י
תִשָּׁבַע֩ לְבַטֵּ֨א בִשְׂפָתַ֜יִם לְהָרַ֣ע ׀ א֣וֹ לְהֵיטִ֗יב לְכֹל֩ אֲשֶׁ֨ר יְבַטֵּ֧א
ה הָאָדָ֛ם בִּשְׁבֻעָ֖ה וְנֶעְלַ֣ם מִמֶּ֑נּוּ וְהוּא־יָדַ֥ע וְאָשֵׁ֖ם לְאַחַ֥ת מֵאֵֽלֶּה׃ וְהָיָ֥ה
ו כִֽי־יֶאְשַׁ֖ם לְאַחַ֣ת מֵאֵ֑לֶּה וְהִ֨תְוַדָּ֔ה אֲשֶׁ֥ר חָטָ֖א עָלֶֽיהָ׃ וְהֵבִ֣יא אֶת־
אֲשָׁמ֣וֹ לַיהוָ֡ה עַ֣ל חַטָּאתוֹ֩ אֲשֶׁ֨ר חָטָ֜א נְקֵבָ֨ה מִן־הַצֹּ֥אן כִּשְׂבָּ֛ה
ז אֽוֹ־שְׂעִירַ֥ת עִזִּ֖ים לְחַטָּ֑את וְכִפֶּ֥ר עָלָ֛יו הַכֹּהֵ֖ן מֵחַטָּאתֽוֹ׃ וְאִם־לֹ֨א
תַגִּ֣יעַ יָדוֹ֮ דֵּ֣י שֶׂה֒ וְהֵבִ֨יא אֶת־אֲשָׁמ֜וֹ אֲשֶׁ֣ר חָטָ֗א שְׁתֵּ֥י תֹרִ֛ים אֽוֹ־שְׁנֵ֥י
ח בְנֵי־יוֹנָ֖ה לַיהוָ֑ה אֶחָ֥ד לְחַטָּ֖את וְאֶחָ֥ד לְעֹלָֽה׃ וְהֵבִ֤יא אֹתָם֙ אֶל־הַכֹּהֵ֔ן
וְהִקְרִ֛יב אֶת־אֲשֶׁ֥ר לַֽחַטָּ֖את רִֽאשׁוֹנָ֑ה וּמָלַ֧ק אֶת־רֹאשׁ֛וֹ מִמּ֥וּל עָרְפּ֖וֹ
ט וְלֹ֥א יַבְדִּֽיל׃ וְהִזָּ֞ה מִדַּ֤ם הַֽחַטָּאת֙ עַל־קִ֣יר הַמִּזְבֵּ֔חַ וְהַנִּשְׁאָ֣ר בַּדָּ֔ם יִמָּצֵ֖ה
י אֶל־יְס֣וֹד הַמִּזְבֵּ֑חַ חַטָּ֖את הֽוּא׃ וְאֶת־הַשֵּׁנִ֛י יַעֲשֶׂ֥ה עֹלָ֖ה כַּמִּשְׁפָּ֑ט

27. וְאִם נֶפֶשׁ אַחַת תֶּחֱטָא בִשְׁגָגָה מֵעַם הָאָרֶץ — *And if any one of the common people sin through error*. For it is a likely possibility that one of the common people will sin. Now here, and regarding the sin of the ruler it says וְאָשֵׁם, *and is guilty*, which is an admonition to repent prior to the (bringing of the) sacrifice. In both of these (cases) and by all guilt offerings, a portion is given to the *Kohanim*, for the eating of the *Kohanim* is beneficial for the atonement of the sinners.

upon the base of the Elevation-offering Altar. 26 And he shall cause all its fats
to go up in smoke on the Altar, like the fats of the feast peace-offering; thus shall
the Kohen provide him atonement for his sin, and it shall be forgiven him.
27 If an individual person from among the people of the land shall sin unintentionally, by committing one of the commandments of HASHEM that may not
be done, and he becomes guilty: 28 If the sin that he committed becomes known
to him, he shall bring as his offering a she-goat, unblemished, for the sin that he
committed. 29 He shall lean his hands upon the head of the sin-offering; and he
shall slaughter the sin-offering in the place of the elevation-offering. 30 The
Kohen shall take from its blood with his forefinger and place it on the horns of
the Elevation-offering Altar; and he shall pour all of its [remaining] blood upon
the base of the Altar. 31 He shall remove all of its fat, as the fat had been removed
from upon the feast peace-offering, and the Kohen shall cause it to go up in
smoke on the Altar as a satisfying aroma to HASHEM; and the Kohen shall
provide him atonement, and it shall be forgiven him.
32 If he shall bring a sheep as his offering for a sin-offering, he shall bring a
female, unblemished. 33 He shall lean his hand upon the head of the sin-offering;
he shall slaughter it for a sin-offering in the place where he would slaughter the
elevation-offering. 34 The Kohen shall take from the blood of the sin-offering
with his forefinger and place it upon the horns of the Elevation-offering Altar;
and he shall pour all its [remaining] blood upon the base of the Altar. 35 And he
shall remove all its fat as the fat would be removed from the feast peace-offering
sheep, and the Kohen shall cause them to go up in smoke on the Altar, on the
fires of HASHEM; and the Kohen shall provide him atonement for his sin that he
committed, and it shall be forgiven him.

5 1 If a person will sin: If he accepted a demand for an oath, and he is a witness
— either he saw or he knew — if he does not testify, he shall bear his inquity;
2 or if a person will have touched any contaminated object — whether the
contaminating carcass of a beast, the contaminating carcass of an animal, or the
contaminating carcass of a creeping animal — but it was concealed from him,
and he is contaminated and became guilty; 3 or if he will touch a human
contamination in any manner of its contamination through which he can
become contaminated but it was concealed from him — and then he knew — and
he became guilty; 4 or if a person will swear, expressing with his lips to do harm
or to do good, anything that a person will express in an oath, but it was concealed
from him, and then he knew — and he became guilty regarding one of these
matters. 5 When one shall become guilty regarding one of these matters, he shall
confess what he had sinned. 6 He shall bring as his guilt-offering to HASHEM, for
his sin that he committed, a female from the flock — a sheep or a goat — for a
sin-offering; and the Kohen shall provide him atonement for his sin.
7 But if his means are insufficient for a sheep or goat, then he shall bring as
his guilt-offering for that which he sinned: two turtledoves or two young doves
to HASHEM, one for a sin-offering and one for an elevation-offering. 8 He shall
bring them to the Kohen, who shall offer first the one that is for a sin-offering;
he shall nip its head at its nape, but not separate it. 9 He shall sprinkle from
the blood of the sin-offering upon the wall of the Altar, and the remainder of
the blood he shall press out toward the base of the Altar; it is a sin-offering.
10 And he shall make the second one an elevation-offering according to [its] law;

שביעי
יא וְכִפֶּר עָלָיו הַכֹּהֵן מֵחַטָּאתוֹ אֲשֶׁר־חָטָא וְנִסְלַח לוֹ׃ וְאִם־לֹא תַשִּׂיג
יָדוֹ לִשְׁתֵּי תֹרִים אוֹ לִשְׁנֵי בְנֵי־יוֹנָה וְהֵבִיא אֶת־קָרְבָּנוֹ אֲשֶׁר חָטָא עֲשִׂירִת
הָאֵפָה סֹלֶת לְחַטָּאת לֹא־יָשִׂים עָלֶיהָ שֶׁמֶן וְלֹא־יִתֵּן עָלֶיהָ לְבֹנָה כִּי חַטָּאת
יב הִוא׃ וֶהֱבִיאָהּ אֶל־הַכֹּהֵן וְקָמַץ הַכֹּהֵן ׀ מִמֶּנָּה מְלוֹא קֻמְצוֹ אֶת־אַזְכָּרָתָהּ
יג וְהִקְטִיר הַמִּזְבֵּחָה עַל אִשֵּׁי יְהוָה חַטָּאת הִוא׃ וְכִפֶּר עָלָיו הַכֹּהֵן עַל־חַטָּאתוֹ
יד אֲשֶׁר־חָטָא מֵאַחַת מֵאֵלֶּה וְנִסְלַח לוֹ וְהָיְתָה לַכֹּהֵן כַּמִּנְחָה׃ וַיְדַבֵּר
טו יְהוָה אֶל־מֹשֶׁה לֵּאמֹר׃ נֶפֶשׁ כִּי־תִמְעֹל מַעַל וְחָטְאָה בִּשְׁגָגָה מִקָּדְשֵׁי יְהוָה
וְהֵבִיא אֶת־אֲשָׁמוֹ לַיהוָה אַיִל תָּמִים מִן־הַצֹּאן בְּעֶרְכְּךָ כֶּסֶף־שְׁקָלִים בְּשֶׁקֶל־
טז הַקֹּדֶשׁ לְאָשָׁם׃ וְאֵת אֲשֶׁר חָטָא מִן־הַקֹּדֶשׁ יְשַׁלֵּם וְאֶת־חֲמִישִׁתוֹ יוֹסֵף עָלָיו
וְנָתַן אֹתוֹ לַכֹּהֵן וְהַכֹּהֵן יְכַפֵּר עָלָיו בְּאֵיל הָאָשָׁם וְנִסְלַח לוֹ׃
יז וְאִם־נֶפֶשׁ כִּי תֶחֱטָא וְעָשְׂתָה אַחַת מִכָּל־מִצְוֹת יְהוָה אֲשֶׁר לֹא תֵעָשֶׂינָה
יח וְלֹא־יָדַע וְאָשֵׁם וְנָשָׂא עֲוֺנוֹ׃ וְהֵבִיא אַיִל תָּמִים מִן־הַצֹּאן בְּעֶרְכְּךָ לְאָשָׁם
אֶל־הַכֹּהֵן וְכִפֶּר עָלָיו הַכֹּהֵן עַל שִׁגְגָתוֹ אֲשֶׁר־שָׁגָג וְהוּא לֹא־יָדַע וְנִסְלַח לוֹ׃
יט אָשָׁם הוּא אָשֹׁם אָשַׁם לַיהוָה׃
כ־כא וַיְדַבֵּר יְהוָה אֶל־מֹשֶׁה לֵּאמֹר׃ נֶפֶשׁ כִּי תֶחֱטָא וּמָעֲלָה מַעַל בַּיהוָה וְכִחֵשׁ
כב בַּעֲמִיתוֹ בְּפִקָּדוֹן אוֹ־בִתְשׂוּמֶת יָד אוֹ בְגָזֵל אוֹ עָשַׁק אֶת־עֲמִיתוֹ׃ אוֹ־מָצָא
אֲבֵדָה וְכִחֶשׁ בָּהּ וְנִשְׁבַּע עַל־שָׁקֶר עַל־אַחַת מִכֹּל אֲשֶׁר־יַעֲשֶׂה הָאָדָם לַחֲטֹא
כג בָהֵנָּה׃ וְהָיָה כִּי־יֶחֱטָא וְאָשֵׁם וְהֵשִׁיב אֶת־הַגְּזֵלָה אֲשֶׁר גָּזָל אוֹ אֶת־הָעֹשֶׁק
מפטיר
כד אֲשֶׁר עָשָׁק אוֹ אֶת־הַפִּקָּדוֹן אֲשֶׁר הָפְקַד אִתּוֹ אוֹ אֶת־הָאֲבֵדָה אֲשֶׁר מָצָא׃ אוֹ
מִכֹּל אֲשֶׁר־יִשָּׁבַע עָלָיו לַשֶּׁקֶר וְשִׁלַּם אֹתוֹ בְּרֹאשׁוֹ וַחֲמִשִׁתָיו יֹסֵף עָלָיו לַאֲשֶׁר
כה הוּא לוֹ יִתְּנֶנּוּ בְּיוֹם אַשְׁמָתוֹ׃ וְאֶת־אֲשָׁמוֹ יָבִיא לַיהוָה אַיִל תָּמִים מִן־הַצֹּאן
כו בְּעֶרְכְּךָ לְאָשָׁם אֶל־הַכֹּהֵן׃ וְכִפֶּר עָלָיו הַכֹּהֵן לִפְנֵי יְהוָה וְנִסְלַח לוֹ עַל־אַחַת
מִכֹּל אֲשֶׁר־יַעֲשֶׂה לְאַשְׁמָה בָהּ׃

V

17. וְאָשֵׁם וְנָשָׂא עֲוֹנוֹ — *He is guilty and shall bear his iniquity.* Our Sages know from tradition that this (verse) speaks of an אָשָׁם תָּלוּי, *guilt offering for a doubtful transgression.* He is not certain if he sinned or not, and regarding this it says, *And he shall bear his iniquity,* i.e., in accordance with what is fitting for him, whether he sinned inadvertently or (perhaps) did not lapse into sin (at all). But his transgression was that he was not careful and slipped into doubt; according to his iniquity he shall bear the punishment.

19. אָשָׁם הוּא — *It is a guilt offering.* Although at times this sacrifice (אָשָׁם תָּלוּי) may be brought and (in reality) he never stumbled into that sin, let him not think that he is bringing a secular (animal) to the courtyard (of the Temple) for indeed it is nonetheless a guilt offering, even though he did not stumble in that sin of which he is in doubt. The reason is because . . .

NOTES

V

19. אָשָׁם הוּא אָשֹׁם אָשַׁם לַה׳ — *It is a guilt offering; he is certainly guilty to* H*ASHEM.* The *Sforno* explains the difficult wording of this verse in the following manner. One can be guilty of *actually* violating a precept of the Torah or one can be guilty of conducting himself in such a careless manner that he is unaware of his actions and cannot determine whether or not he transgressed. The latter heedless action requires atonement no less than the former overt act of transgression.

23-25. וְהֵשִׁיב אֶת הַגְּזֵלָה . . . וְאֶת אֲשָׁמוֹ יָבִיא — *And he shall restore that which he took . . . and he shall bring his guilt offering.* Man will not be forgiven

and the Kohen shall provide him atonement for his sin that he committed, and it shall be forgiven him.

[11] *But if his means are insufficient for two turtledoves or for two young doves, then he shall bring, as his guilt-offering for that which he sinned, a tenth-ephah of fine flour for a sin-offering; he shall not place oil on it nor shall he put frankincense on it, for it is a sin-offering.* [12] *He shall bring it to the Kohen, and the Kohen shall scoop his threefingersful as its memorial portion and cause it to go up in smoke on the Altar, on the fires of HASHEM; it is a sin-offering.* [13] *The Kohen shall provide him atonement for the sin that he committed regarding any of these, and it will be forgiven him; and it shall belong to the Kohen, like the meal-offering.*

[14] *HASHEM spoke to Moses, saying:* [15] *If a person commits treachery and sins unintentionally against HASHEM's holies, he shall bring his guilt-offering to HASHEM, an unblemished ram from the flock, with a value of silver shekels, according to the sacred shekel, for a guilt-offering.* [16] *For what he has deprived the Sanctuary he shall make restitution, and add a fifth to it, and give it to the Kohen; then the Kohen shall provide him atonement with the ram of the guilt-offering and it shall be forgiven him.*

[17] *If a person will sin and will commit one of all the commandments of HASHEM that may not be done, but did not know and became guilty, he shall bear his iniquity;* [18] *he shall bring an unblemished ram from the flock, of the proper value, as a guilt-offering — to the Kohen; and the Kohen shall provide him atonement for the inadvertence that he committed unintentionally and he did not know, and it shall be forgiven him.* [19] *It is a guilt-offering; he has become guilty before HASHEM.*

[20] *HASHEM spoke to Moses, saying:* [21] *If a person will sin and commit a treachery against HASHEM by lying to his comrade regarding a pledge or a loan or a robbery; or by defrauding his comrade;* [22] *or he found a lost item and denied it — and he swore falsely about any of all the things that a person can do and sin thereby —* [23] *so it shall be that when he will sin and become guilty, he shall return the robbed item that he robbed, or the proceeds of his fraud, or the pledge that was left with him, or the lost item that he found,* [24] *or anything about which he had sworn falsely — he shall repay its principal and add its fifth to it; he shall give it to its owner on the day he admits his guilt.* [25] *And he shall bring his guilt-offering to HASHEM — an unblemished ram from the flock, of the proper value, as a guilt-offering — to the Kohen.* [26] *The Kohen shall provide him atonement before HASHEM, and it shall be forgiven him for any of all the things he might do to incur guilt.*

אָשׁוֹם אָשַׁם לַה׳ — *He is certainly guilty to HASHEM* . . . when he wasn't careful in this matter until (he reached a point) that he was in doubt.

23-25. וְהֵשִׁיב אֶת הַגְּזֵלָה . . . וְאֶת אֲשָׁמוֹ יָבִיא — *And he shall restore that which he took . . . and he shall bring his guilt offering.* The sacrifice cannot atone unless he first recompenses (appeases) the injured party before he brings the offering, as our Sages say, "If one brings his guilt offering before he repays what he stole, he has not fulfilled his obligation" (*Bava Kama* 110a).

NOTES

by God for the sin committed against Him until he has rid himself of ill-begotten (stolen) gains and compensated his victim. This is similar to the last Mishnah in *Yoma* which states that Yom Kippur will not atone for man's sins against God unless one has first appeased those whom he has harmed.

פרשת צו

ו א־ב וַיְדַבֵּר יהוה אֶל־מֹשֶׁה לֵּאמֹר: צַו אֶת־אַהֲרֹן וְאֶת־בָּנָיו לֵאמֹר זֹאת תּוֹרַת
*מ׳ זעירא הָעֹלָה הִוא הָעֹלָה עַל *מוֹקְדָה עַל־הַמִּזְבֵּחַ כָּל־הַלַּיְלָה עַד־הַבֹּקֶר וְאֵשׁ
ג הַמִּזְבֵּחַ תּוּקַד בּוֹ: וְלָבַשׁ הַכֹּהֵן מִדּוֹ בַד וּמִכְנְסֵי־בַד יִלְבַּשׁ עַל־בְּשָׂרוֹ
וְהֵרִים אֶת־הַדֶּשֶׁן אֲשֶׁר תֹּאכַל הָאֵשׁ אֶת־הָעֹלָה עַל־הַמִּזְבֵּחַ וְשָׂמוֹ
ד אֵצֶל הַמִּזְבֵּחַ: וּפָשַׁט אֶת־בְּגָדָיו וְלָבַשׁ בְּגָדִים אֲחֵרִים וְהוֹצִיא אֶת־
ה הַדֶּשֶׁן אֶל־מִחוּץ לַמַּחֲנֶה אֶל־מָקוֹם טָהוֹר: וְהָאֵשׁ עַל־הַמִּזְבֵּחַ תּוּקַד־
בּוֹ לֹא תִכְבֶּה וּבִעֵר עָלֶיהָ הַכֹּהֵן עֵצִים בַּבֹּקֶר בַּבֹּקֶר וְעָרַךְ עָלֶיהָ
ו הָעֹלָה וְהִקְטִיר עָלֶיהָ חֶלְבֵי הַשְּׁלָמִים: אֵשׁ תָּמִיד תּוּקַד עַל־הַמִּזְבֵּחַ
ז לֹא תִכְבֶּה: וְזֹאת תּוֹרַת הַמִּנְחָה הַקְרֵב אֹתָהּ בְּנֵי־אַהֲרֹן
ח לִפְנֵי יהוה אֶל־פְּנֵי הַמִּזְבֵּחַ: וְהֵרִים מִמֶּנּוּ בְּקֻמְצוֹ מִסֹּלֶת הַמִּנְחָה וּמִשַּׁמְנָהּ
וְאֵת כָּל־הַלְּבֹנָה אֲשֶׁר עַל־הַמִּנְחָה וְהִקְטִיר הַמִּזְבֵּחַ רֵיחַ נִיחֹחַ אַזְכָּרָתָהּ
ט לַיהוה: וְהַנּוֹתֶרֶת מִמֶּנָּה יֹאכְלוּ אַהֲרֹן וּבָנָיו מַצּוֹת תֵּאָכֵל בְּמָקוֹם קָדֹשׁ
י בַּחֲצַר אֹהֶל־מוֹעֵד יֹאכְלוּהָ: לֹא תֵאָפֶה חָמֵץ חֶלְקָם נָתַתִּי אֹתָהּ מֵאִשָּׁי
יא קֹדֶשׁ קָדָשִׁים הִוא כַּחַטָּאת וְכָאָשָׁם: כָּל־זָכָר בִּבְנֵי אַהֲרֹן יֹאכְלֶנָּה
חָק־עוֹלָם לְדֹרֹתֵיכֶם מֵאִשֵּׁי יהוה כֹּל אֲשֶׁר־יִגַּע בָּהֶם יִקְדָּשׁ:

VI

2. צַו אֶת אַהֲרֹן ... זֹאת תּוֹרַת הָעֹלָה הִוא הָעֹלָה — *Command Aaron ... this is the law of the burnt offering, it is that which goes up.* After telling (us) the work of the sacrifices, (the Torah) now states the laws applicable to each one of them, (including) their analytical aspects. Without a doubt, there are great differences among "the children of the living God" (based on *Hosea* 2:1) in their works and intents, similar to the differences in the various kinds of sacrifices. (The Torah) makes mention that the entire burnt offering is brought on the Altar as a sweet savor (to God); however (only) part of it *goes up* in the flame of the Altar, (and of that part) it is said that it truly is הָעוֹלָה, "*the*" *olah*. And part of it is *beside the Altar* (v. 3), namely the דֶּשֶׁן, *ashes*, which still retain some moisture in such a manner that the fire can burn within them together with the authentic (central) part of the *olah*, as it says ...

3. הַדֶּשֶׁן אֲשֶׁר תֹּאכַל הָאֵשׁ אֶת הָעֹלָה — *The ashes of the burnt offering which the fire consumed.* And some of it is totally ashes which are brought out ...

4. אֶל מִחוּץ לַמַּחֲנֶה אֶל מָקוֹם טָהוֹר — *Outside the camp to a clean place.* (With the *Kohen* wearing) inferior garments, nonetheless it is brought to a *clean place.*

NOTES

VI

2-4. הוּא הָעֹלָה ... הַדֶּשֶׁן אֲשֶׁר תֹּאכַל הָאֵשׁ אֶת הָעֹלָה ... אֶל מִחוּץ לַמַּחֲנֶה אֶל מָקוֹם טָהוֹר — *It is that which goes up ... the ashes of the burnt offering which the fire consumed ... outside the camp to a clean place.* The *Sforno* explains that there are three parts of the burnt offering (עוֹלָה), the disposition of which are indicated in these verses. The principal part is that which is totally consumed and goes up, hence the term עוֹלָה (lit., going up). The second part consists of the ashes which still retain some fat of the animal and are burnt together with the first part. Thus the words אֶת הָעוֹלָה (v. 3) are to be translated *with* the *olah*. The third part consists of the ashes carried out of the camp by the *Kohen* after he changed his priestly garments for clothes of inferior quality, since he would be occupied with a non-holy duty. Nonetheless, the ashes are still treated with respect and placed in a מָקוֹם טָהוֹר, *clean place*, as we find in chapter 4:12, *A clean place, where the ashes are poured out* (שֶׁפֶךְ הַדֶּשֶׁן).

7. תּוֹרַת הַמִּנְחָה ... לִפְנֵי ה׳ אֶל פְּנֵי הַמִּזְבֵּחַ — *The law of the meal offering ... before* HASHEM *in front of the Altar.* The מִנְחָה, *meal offering*, is eaten by the

PARASHAS TZAV

6 1 *HASHEM spoke to Moses, saying:* 2 *Command Aaron and his sons,*
saying: This is the law of the elevation-offering: It is the elevation-
offering [that stays] on the flame, on the Altar, all night until the morning,
and the fire of the Altar should be kept aflame on it. 3 *The Kohen shall don*
his fitted linen Tunic, and he shall don linen breeches on his flesh; he shall
separate the ash of what the fire consumed of the elevation-offering on the
Altar, and place it next to the Altar. 4 *He shall remove his garments and don*
other garments, and he shall remove the ash to the outside of the camp, to
a pure place. 5 *The fire on the Altar shall be kept burning on it, it shall not*
be extinguished; and the Kohen shall kindle wood upon it every morning;
he shall prepare the elevation-offering upon it and shall cause the fats of the
peace-offerings to go up in smoke upon it. 6 *A permanent fire shall remain*
aflame on the Altar; it shall not be extinguished.
7 *This is the law of the meal-offering: The sons of Aaron shall bring it*
before HASHEM, *to the front of the Altar.* 8 *He shall separate from it with his*
threefingersful some of the fine flour of the meal-offering and some of its oil,
and all the frankincense that is on the meal-offering; and he shall cause
them to go up in smoke on the Altar for a satisfying aroma — its memorial
portion unto HASHEM. 9 *Aaron and his sons shall eat what is left of it; it shall*
be eaten unleavened in a holy place, in the Courtyard of the Tent of Meeting
shall they eat it. 10 *It shall not be baked leavened, I have presented it as their*
share from My fire-offerings; it is most holy, like the sin-offering and like
the guilt-offering. 11 *Every male of the children of Aaron shall eat it, an*
eternal portion for your generations, from the fire-offerings of HASHEM;
whatever touches them shall become holy.

7. תּוֹרַת הַמִּנְחָה . . . לִפְנֵי ה׳ אֶל פְּנֵי הַמִּזְבֵּחַ — *The law of the meal offering . . . before* HASHEM *in front of the Altar.* (The Torah) then makes mention of the law of the meal offering and states that all of it be brought close *before* HASHEM *in front of the Altar,* for to God, the Blessed One, alone does the person making the offering bring his entire sacrifice, and the *Kohanim* "receive their (portion) from the heavenly (lit., higher) table" (*Beitzah* 21a) while a small part of the total is chosen (to be offered as) a *sweet savor* (v. 8). The priestly portion also atones and (hence) is also prevented from becoming leavened similar to the Divine portion. (And we also are taught that) the meal offering of the *Kohen* is offered totally to (the One) on High, not just a small part thereof, as is (true) regarding the meal offerings of the masses.

NOTES

Kohen. However, a קֹמֶץ, *handful,* is brought on the Altar as a רֵיחַ נִיחֹחַ, *sweet savor,* to God. The *Sforno* explains that although the *major* part of the offering is consumed by the *Kohanim* and not by the fire of the Altar, initially, the entire meal offering is brought close to the Altar to indicate that the *Kohen's* portion is not given to him directly but, as it were, by God from His table. This concept is clearly stated in verse 10. Therefore, the portion eaten by the *Kohanim* must be unleavened since all that is related to offerings on the Altar must be מַצָּה and the *Kohen's* share is granted to him from God's table. As mentioned above (4:27), the eating of the sacrifice by the *Kohanim* is considered part of the atonement. The reason that the *Kohen's* own meal offering is wholly burnt on the Altar, and not eaten by him, as is the case regarding the מִנְחָה of the Israelite, is explained by the *Rambam* in his *Guide* [and brought here (v. 10) by the *Ramban*]. Were the *Kohen* to eat his own meal offering, since only a handful is brought on the altar, it would be considered as though he had offered naught; hence he must bring it all on the Altar to be consumed there by the holy fire.

שני יב־יג וַיְדַבֵּר יְהוָה אֶל־מֹשֶׁה לֵּאמֹר: זֶה קָרְבַּן אַהֲרֹן וּבָנָיו אֲשֶׁר־יַקְרִיבוּ לַיהוָה
בְּיוֹם הִמָּשַׁח אֹתוֹ עֲשִׂירִת הָאֵפָה סֹלֶת מִנְחָה תָּמִיד מַחֲצִיתָהּ בַּבֹּקֶר
יד וּמַחֲצִיתָהּ בָּעָרֶב: עַל־מַחֲבַת בַּשֶּׁמֶן תֵּעָשֶׂה מֻרְבֶּכֶת תְּבִיאֶנָּה תֻּפִינֵי
טו מִנְחַת פִּתִּים תַּקְרִיב רֵיחַ־נִיחֹחַ לַיהוָה: וְהַכֹּהֵן הַמָּשִׁיחַ תַּחְתָּיו מִבָּנָיו
טז יַעֲשֶׂה אֹתָהּ חָק־עוֹלָם לַיהוָה כָּלִיל תָּקְטָר: וְכָל־מִנְחַת כֹּהֵן כָּלִיל תִּהְיֶה
לֹא תֵאָכֵל:
יז־יח וַיְדַבֵּר יְהוָה אֶל־מֹשֶׁה לֵּאמֹר: דַּבֵּר אֶל־אַהֲרֹן וְאֶל־בָּנָיו לֵאמֹר זֹאת
תּוֹרַת הַחַטָּאת בִּמְקוֹם אֲשֶׁר תִּשָּׁחֵט הָעֹלָה תִּשָּׁחֵט הַחַטָּאת לִפְנֵי יְהוָה
יט קֹדֶשׁ קָדָשִׁים הִוא: הַכֹּהֵן הַמְחַטֵּא אֹתָהּ יֹאכְלֶנָּה בְּמָקוֹם קָדֹשׁ תֵּאָכֵל
כ בַּחֲצַר אֹהֶל מוֹעֵד: כֹּל אֲשֶׁר־יִגַּע בִּבְשָׂרָהּ יִקְדָּשׁ וַאֲשֶׁר יִזֶּה מִדָּמָהּ
כא עַל־הַבֶּגֶד אֲשֶׁר יִזֶּה עָלֶיהָ תְּכַבֵּס בְּמָקוֹם קָדֹשׁ: וּכְלִי־חֶרֶשׂ אֲשֶׁר
כב תְּבֻשַּׁל־בּוֹ יִשָּׁבֵר וְאִם־בִּכְלִי נְחֹשֶׁת בֻּשָּׁלָה וּמֹרַק וְשֻׁטַּף בַּמָּיִם: כָּל־זָכָר
כג בַּכֹּהֲנִים יֹאכַל אֹתָהּ קֹדֶשׁ קָדָשִׁים הִוא: וְכָל־חַטָּאת אֲשֶׁר יוּבָא מִדָּמָהּ
אֶל־אֹהֶל מוֹעֵד לְכַפֵּר בַּקֹּדֶשׁ לֹא תֵאָכֵל בָּאֵשׁ תִּשָּׂרֵף:
ז א־ב וְזֹאת תּוֹרַת הָאָשָׁם קֹדֶשׁ קָדָשִׁים הוּא: בִּמְקוֹם אֲשֶׁר יִשְׁחֲטוּ אֶת־הָעֹלָה
ג יִשְׁחֲטוּ אֶת־הָאָשָׁם וְאֶת־דָּמוֹ יִזְרֹק עַל־הַמִּזְבֵּחַ סָבִיב: וְאֵת כָּל־חֶלְבּוֹ
ד יַקְרִיב מִמֶּנּוּ אֵת הָאַלְיָה וְאֶת־הַחֵלֶב הַמְכַסֶּה אֶת־הַקֶּרֶב: וְאֵת שְׁתֵּי
הַכְּלָיֹת וְאֶת־הַחֵלֶב אֲשֶׁר עֲלֵיהֶן אֲשֶׁר עַל־הַכְּסָלִים וְאֶת־הַיֹּתֶרֶת
ה עַל־הַכָּבֵד עַל־הַכְּלָיֹת יְסִירֶנָּה: וְהִקְטִיר אֹתָם הַכֹּהֵן הַמִּזְבֵּחָה אִשֶּׁה
ו לַיהוָה אָשָׁם הוּא: כָּל־זָכָר בַּכֹּהֲנִים יֹאכְלֶנּוּ בְּמָקוֹם קָדוֹשׁ יֵאָכֵל קֹדֶשׁ
ז קָדָשִׁים הוּא: כַּחַטָּאת כָּאָשָׁם תּוֹרָה אַחַת לָהֶם הַכֹּהֵן אֲשֶׁר יְכַפֶּר־בּוֹ לוֹ
ח יִהְיֶה: וְהַכֹּהֵן הַמַּקְרִיב אֶת־עֹלַת אִישׁ עוֹר הָעֹלָה אֲשֶׁר הִקְרִיב לַכֹּהֵן לוֹ
ט יִהְיֶה: וְכָל־מִנְחָה אֲשֶׁר תֵּאָפֶה בַּתַּנּוּר וְכָל־נַעֲשָׂה בַמַּרְחֶשֶׁת וְעַל־
י מַחֲבַת לַכֹּהֵן הַמַּקְרִיב אֹתָהּ לוֹ תִהְיֶה: וְכָל־מִנְחָה בְלוּלָה־בַשֶּׁמֶן וַחֲרֵבָה
לְכָל־בְּנֵי אַהֲרֹן תִּהְיֶה אִישׁ כְּאָחִיו:

18. וזאת תורת החטאת — *This is the law of the sin offering.* (The Torah then) makes mention of the law of the sin offering, stating in regard to that (particular) sin offering that due to the severity of the sin (for which it is brought), it cannot atone unless its blood is brought into the inner sanctuary. Unlike other sin offerings, it does not (attain) atonement through the eating of the *Kohanim*, but by being burnt.

VII

1. וְזֹאת תּוֹרַת הָאָשָׁם — *And this is the law of the guilt offering.* Although the guilt offering is not brought (to atone) for a sin punishable by excision (כָּרֵת), as is (true of) a sin offering, nonetheless, since his sin is a trespass against the holy, one law shall apply to them (see v. 7). (The Torah then) says . . .

NOTES

18. זאת תורת החטאת — *This is the law of the sin offering.* The *Sforno* is referring to the sin offerings of the anointed *Kohen* and the Sanhedrin, brought when they sin through an error in judgment, as well as to the bull and goat brought on Yom Kippur, the flesh of which must not be eaten but burnt as the Torah states explicitly in verse 23.

*12 HASHEM spoke to Moses, saying: 13 This is the offering of Aaron and his
sons, which each shall offer to HASHEM on the day he is inaugurated: a
tenth-ephah of fine flour as a continual meal-offering; half of it in the
morning and half of it in the afternoon. 14 It should be made on a pan with
oil, scalded shall you bring it; a repeatedly baked meal-offering, broken into
pieces, you shall offer it as a satisfying aroma to HASHEM. 15 The Kohen from
among his sons who is anointed in his place shall perform it; it is an eternal
decree for HASHEM; it shall be caused to go up in smoke in its entirety.
16 Every meal-offering of a Kohen is to be entirely [caused to go up in smoke];
it shall not be eaten.*

*17 HASHEM spoke to Moses, saying: 18 Speak to Aaron and his sons, saying:
This is the law of the sin-offering; in the place where the elevation-offering
is slaughtered shall the sin-offering be slaughtered, before HASHEM — it is
most holy. 19 The Kohen who performs its sin-offering service shall eat it; it
shall be eaten in a holy place: in the Courtyard of the Tent of Meeting.*

*20 Whatever touches its flesh becomes holy; and if its blood is sprinkled
upon a garment, whatever it has been sprinkled upon you shall wash in a
holy place. 21 An earthenware vessel in which it was cooked shall be broken;
but if it was cooked in a copper vessel, that should be purged and rinsed in
water. 22 Every male among the Kohanim may eat it; it is most holy. 23 Any
sin-offering from which some blood has been brought to the Tent of Meeting,
to effect atonement within the Holy, shall not be eaten; it shall be burned in
fire.*

7 *1 This is the teaching of the guilt-offering; it is most holy. 2 In the place
where they shall slaughter the elevation-offering shall they slaughter
the guilt-offering; and he shall throw its blood upon the Altar, all around.
3 All of its fat shall he offer of it; the tail and the fat that covers the innards;
4 and the two kidneys and the fat that covers them, which is on the flanks;
and he shall remove the diaphragm as well as the liver, as well as the
kidneys. 5 The Kohen shall cause them to go up in smoke on the Altar, a
fire-offering to HASHEM; it is a guilt-offering.*

*6 Every male among the Kohanim may eat it; it shall be eaten in a holy
place, it is most holy. 7 Like the sin-offering is the guilt-offering, there is one
law for them; it shall belong to a Kohen who performs its atonement service.
8 And the Kohen who offers a person's elevation-offering — the hide of the
elevation-offering that he offered shall belong to that Kohen, it shall be his.*

*9 Any meal-offering that is baked in the oven and any that is made in a
deep pan or upon a shallow pan — it shall belong to the Kohen who offers
it; it shall be his. 10 And any meal-offering that is mixed with oil or that is
dry, it shall belong to all the sons of Aaron, every man alike.*

NOTES

VII

1. וְזֹאת תּוֹרַת הָאָשָׁם — *And this is the law of the guilt offering.* The five cases where the Torah imposes the obligation to bring a guilt offering (אָשָׁם) is discussed in chapter 5. In this chapter (v. 7), the Torah equates the sin offering and the guilt offering (כַּחַטָּאת כָּאָשָׁם תּוֹרָה אַחַת) regarding the laws regulating the eating of the flesh, the place where it can be eaten, and the status of purity of the *Kohen*.

שלישי יא־יב וְזֹאת תּוֹרַת זֶבַח הַשְּׁלָמִים אֲשֶׁר יַקְרִיב לַיהוָה: אִם עַל־תּוֹדָה יַקְרִיבֶנּוּ
וְהִקְרִיב | עַל־זֶבַח הַתּוֹדָה חַלּוֹת מַצּוֹת בְּלוּלֹת בַּשֶּׁמֶן וּרְקִיקֵי מַצּוֹת
יג מְשֻׁחִים בַּשָּׁמֶן וְסֹלֶת מֻרְבֶּכֶת חַלֹּת בְּלוּלֹת בַּשָּׁמֶן: עַל־חַלֹּת לֶחֶם חָמֵץ
יד יַקְרִיב קָרְבָּנוֹ עַל־זֶבַח תּוֹדַת שְׁלָמָיו: וְהִקְרִיב מִמֶּנּוּ אֶחָד מִכָּל־קָרְבָּן
טו תְּרוּמָה לַיהוָה לַכֹּהֵן הַזֹּרֵק אֶת־דַּם הַשְּׁלָמִים לוֹ יִהְיֶה: וּבְשַׂר זֶבַח תּוֹדַת
טז שְׁלָמָיו בְּיוֹם קָרְבָּנוֹ יֵאָכֵל לֹא־יַנִּיחַ מִמֶּנּוּ עַד־בֹּקֶר: וְאִם־נֶדֶר | אוֹ נְדָבָה
זֶבַח קָרְבָּנוֹ בְּיוֹם הַקְרִיבוֹ אֶת־זִבְחוֹ יֵאָכֵל וּמִמָּחֳרָת וְהַנּוֹתָר מִמֶּנּוּ
יז־יח יֵאָכֵל: וְהַנּוֹתָר מִבְּשַׂר הַזָּבַח בַּיּוֹם הַשְּׁלִישִׁי בָּאֵשׁ יִשָּׂרֵף: וְאִם הֵאָכֹל
יֵאָכֵל מִבְּשַׂר־זֶבַח שְׁלָמָיו בַּיּוֹם הַשְּׁלִישִׁי לֹא יֵרָצֶה הַמַּקְרִיב אֹתוֹ לֹא
יט יֵחָשֵׁב לוֹ פִּגּוּל יִהְיֶה וְהַנֶּפֶשׁ הָאֹכֶלֶת מִמֶּנּוּ עֲוֺנָהּ תִּשָּׂא: וְהַבָּשָׂר אֲשֶׁר
יִגַּע בְּכָל־טָמֵא לֹא יֵאָכֵל בָּאֵשׁ יִשָּׂרֵף וְהַבָּשָׂר כָּל־טָהוֹר יֹאכַל בָּשָׂר:
כ וְהַנֶּפֶשׁ אֲשֶׁר־תֹּאכַל בָּשָׂר מִזֶּבַח הַשְּׁלָמִים אֲשֶׁר לַיהוָה וְטֻמְאָתוֹ עָלָיו
כא וְנִכְרְתָה הַנֶּפֶשׁ הַהִוא מֵעַמֶּיהָ: וְנֶפֶשׁ כִּי־תִגַּע בְּכָל־טָמֵא בְּטֻמְאַת אָדָם
אוֹ | בִּבְהֵמָה טְמֵאָה אוֹ בְּכָל־שֶׁקֶץ טָמֵא וְאָכַל מִבְּשַׂר־זֶבַח הַשְּׁלָמִים
כב אֲשֶׁר לַיהוָה וְנִכְרְתָה הַנֶּפֶשׁ הַהִוא מֵעַמֶּיהָ: וַיְדַבֵּר יְהוָה אֶל־מֹשֶׁה
כג לֵּאמֹר: דַּבֵּר אֶל־בְּנֵי יִשְׂרָאֵל לֵאמֹר כָּל־חֵלֶב שׁוֹר וְכֶשֶׂב וָעֵז לֹא
כד תֹאכֵלוּ: וְחֵלֶב נְבֵלָה וְחֵלֶב טְרֵפָה יֵעָשֶׂה לְכָל־מְלָאכָה וְאָכֹל לֹא
כה תֹאכְלֻהוּ: כִּי כָּל־אֹכֵל חֵלֶב מִן־הַבְּהֵמָה אֲשֶׁר יַקְרִיב מִמֶּנָּה אִשֶּׁה
כו לַיהוָה וְנִכְרְתָה הַנֶּפֶשׁ הָאֹכֶלֶת מֵעַמֶּיהָ: וְכָל־דָּם לֹא תֹאכְלוּ בְּכֹל
כז מוֹשְׁבֹתֵיכֶם לָעוֹף וְלַבְּהֵמָה: כָּל־נֶפֶשׁ אֲשֶׁר־תֹּאכַל כָּל־דָּם וְנִכְרְתָה
הַנֶּפֶשׁ הַהִוא מֵעַמֶּיהָ:
כח־כט וַיְדַבֵּר יְהוָה אֶל־מֹשֶׁה לֵּאמֹר: דַּבֵּר אֶל־בְּנֵי יִשְׂרָאֵל לֵאמֹר הַמַּקְרִיב

---

11. וְזֹאת תּוֹרַת זֶבַח הַשְּׁלָמִים — *And this is the law of the sacrifice of peace offerings.* (The Torah) tells us that even though all peace offerings are (in the category of) קָדָשִׁים קַלִּים, (sacrifices belonging to) *a lesser level of sanctity,* nonetheless, there are differences among them. (For example) if one is brought as a תּוֹדָה, a *thanksgiving offering,* then bread is to be brought with it, including leavened loaves, for indeed, the cause of the danger (which he experienced and was delivered from) for which he is now thanking God was the "leaven in the dough." Nonetheless, those cakes which are unleavened outnumber them (i.e., the leavened ones). Now, through the many cakes and the increased number of those who eat, the miracle will become well known. All of the תּוֹדָה must be eaten in the time limitation of קָדְשֵׁי קָדָשִׁים, *holy of holies,* namely for a day and a night (v. 15). However, when one brings regular peace offerings other than a תּוֹדָה, the time (in which it must be consumed) is two days and one night (v. 16).

NOTES

11. וְזֹאת תּוֹרַת זֶבַח הַשְּׁלָמִים — *And this is the law of the sacrifice of peace offerings.* As mentioned above (note 6:7), nothing leavened is brought on the Altar, except on some infrequent occasions. One of these exceptions are the ten loaves of leavened bread brought in conjunction with the thanksgiving offering. The *Sforno* explains that this exception is to symbolize what our Sages call שְׂאוֹר שֶׁבְּעִסָּה, *the leaven in the dough* (*Berachos* 17a). *Rashi* there states that this expression refers to the evil inclination in the heart of man. Now a תּוֹדָה, *thanksgiving sacrifice,* is brought by one delivered from peril. The very fact that he was exposed to danger indicates that he was vulnerable

11 *This is the law of the feast peace-offering that one will offer to* H*ASHEM:*
12 *If he shall offer it for a thanksgiving-offering, he shall offer with the feast thanksgiving-offering unleavened loaves mixed with oil, unleavened wafers smeared with oil, and loaves of scalded fine flour mixed with oil.*
13 *With loaves of leavened bread shall he bring his offering, with his feast thanksgiving peace-offering.* 14 *From it he shall offer one from each as an offering, a portion to* H*ASHEM; it shall belong to the Kohen who throws the blood of the peace-offering.* 15 *And the flesh of his feast thanksgiving peace-offering must be eaten on the day of its offering; he shall not leave any of it until morning.*

16 *If his feast-offering is for a vow or a donation, it must be eaten on the day he offered his feast-offering; and on the next day, what is left over may be eaten.* 17 *What is left over from the flesh of the feast-offering shall be burned in the fire on the third day.* 18 *And if some of the flesh of his feast thanksgiving peace-offering was intended to be eaten on the third day, it is not acceptable, the one who offers it may not intend this — it remains rejected; and the soul that eats it shall bear its iniquity.*

19 *The flesh that touches any contaminated thing may not be eaten, it shall be burned in fire; but of the [uncontaminated] flesh, any uncontaminated person may eat the flesh.* 20 *A person who eats flesh from the feast peace-offering that is* H*ASHEM's while his contamination is upon him, that soul will be cut off from its people.* 21 *If a person touches any contamination — whether human contamination or a contaminated animal [carcass] or any contaminated detestable [carcass] — and he eats from the flesh of a feast peace-offering that is* H*ASHEM's, then that soul will be cut off from its people.*

22 H*ASHEM spoke to Moses, saying:* 23 *Speak to the Children of Israel, saying: Any fat of oxen, sheep, or goats — you shall not eat.* 24 *The fat of an animal that died and the fat of an animal that had been torn to death may be put to any use; but you shall not eat it.* 25 *For anyone who eats the fat of animal species from which one may bring a fire-offering to* H*ASHEM — the soul that eats will be cut off from its people.* 26 *You shall not consume any blood, in any of your dwelling places, whether from fowl or from animals.*
27 *Any person who consumes any blood — that soul will be cut off from its people.*

28 H*ASHEM spoke to Moses, saying:* 29 *Speak to the Children of Israel,*

Now, since they are all קָדָשִׁים קַלִּים, it is prohibited to be eaten by one who is *tamei*, unclean, and also prohibited to be eaten if the flesh is *tamei*. The punishment of excision, however, applies only to a *tamei* person who eats the *tahor*, flesh of an offering, for he who is *tamei*, and approaches to eat from the holy which is *tahor*, has desecrated the holy (vs. 19-21).

NOTES

due to his spiritual shortcomings. However, God in His mercy saved him. This is symbolized by the loaves of leavened bread (see the *Sforno* on 23:17).

The *Sforno* explains why the punishment for one who eats unclean sanctified flesh is lighter than the punishment imposed on an unclean person who consumes clean holy meat. The reason is that the latter is guilty of חִלּוּל הַקּוֹדֶשׁ, *desecration of the holy*, which is not so in the case of the former.

ל אֶת־זֶבַח שְׁלָמָיו לַיהוָה יָבִיא אֶת־קָרְבָּנוֹ לַיהוָה מִזֶּבַח שְׁלָמָיו: יָדָיו
תְּבִיאֶינָה אֵת אִשֵּׁי יְהוָה אֶת־הַחֵלֶב עַל־הֶחָזֶה יְבִיאֶנּוּ אֵת הֶחָזֶה לְהָנִיף
לא אֹתוֹ תְּנוּפָה לִפְנֵי יְהוָה: וְהִקְטִיר הַכֹּהֵן אֶת־הַחֵלֶב הַמִּזְבֵּחָה וְהָיָה הֶחָזֶה
לב לְאַהֲרֹן וּלְבָנָיו: וְאֵת שׁוֹק הַיָּמִין תִּתְּנוּ תְרוּמָה לַכֹּהֵן מִזִּבְחֵי שַׁלְמֵיכֶם:
לג הַמַּקְרִיב אֶת־דַּם הַשְּׁלָמִים וְאֶת־הַחֵלֶב מִבְּנֵי אַהֲרֹן לוֹ תִהְיֶה שׁוֹק
לד הַיָּמִין לְמָנָה: כִּי אֶת־חֲזֵה הַתְּנוּפָה וְאֵת | שׁוֹק הַתְּרוּמָה לָקַחְתִּי מֵאֵת
בְּנֵי־יִשְׂרָאֵל מִזִּבְחֵי שַׁלְמֵיהֶם וָאֶתֵּן אֹתָם לְאַהֲרֹן הַכֹּהֵן וּלְבָנָיו לְחָק־
לה עוֹלָם מֵאֵת בְּנֵי יִשְׂרָאֵל: זֹאת מִשְׁחַת אַהֲרֹן וּמִשְׁחַת בָּנָיו מֵאִשֵּׁי יְהוָה
לו בְּיוֹם הִקְרִיב אֹתָם לְכַהֵן לַיהוָה: אֲשֶׁר צִוָּה יְהוָה לָתֵת לָהֶם בְּיוֹם מָשְׁחוֹ
לז אֹתָם מֵאֵת בְּנֵי יִשְׂרָאֵל חֻקַּת עוֹלָם לְדֹרֹתָם: זֹאת הַתּוֹרָה לָעֹלָה
לח לַמִּנְחָה וְלַחַטָּאת וְלָאָשָׁם וְלַמִּלּוּאִים וּלְזֶבַח הַשְּׁלָמִים: אֲשֶׁר צִוָּה יְהוָה
אֶת־מֹשֶׁה בְּהַר סִינָי בְּיוֹם צַוֹּתוֹ אֶת־בְּנֵי יִשְׂרָאֵל לְהַקְרִיב אֶת־
קָרְבְּנֵיהֶם לַיהוָה בְּמִדְבַּר סִינָי:
ח רביעי א־ב וַיְדַבֵּר יְהוָה אֶל־מֹשֶׁה לֵּאמֹר: קַח אֶת־אַהֲרֹן וְאֶת־בָּנָיו אִתּוֹ וְאֵת
הַבְּגָדִים וְאֵת שֶׁמֶן הַמִּשְׁחָה וְאֵת | פַּר הַחַטָּאת וְאֵת שְׁנֵי הָאֵילִים וְאֵת
ג־ד סַל הַמַּצּוֹת: וְאֵת כָּל־הָעֵדָה הַקְהֵל אֶל־פֶּתַח אֹהֶל מוֹעֵד: וַיַּעַשׂ מֹשֶׁה
ה כַּאֲשֶׁר צִוָּה יְהוָה אֹתוֹ וַתִּקָּהֵל הָעֵדָה אֶל־פֶּתַח אֹהֶל מוֹעֵד: וַיֹּאמֶר
ו מֹשֶׁה אֶל־הָעֵדָה זֶה הַדָּבָר אֲשֶׁר־צִוָּה יְהוָה לַעֲשׂוֹת: וַיַּקְרֵב מֹשֶׁה אֶת־
ז אַהֲרֹן וְאֶת־בָּנָיו וַיִּרְחַץ אֹתָם בַּמָּיִם: וַיִּתֵּן עָלָיו אֶת־הַכֻּתֹּנֶת וַיַּחְגֹּר אֹתוֹ

30. יָדָיו תְּבִיאֶינָה אֵת אִשֵּׁי ה׳ — *His own hands shall bring the fire-offerings of* HASHEM. Being that the rest belongs to the owners, the act of waving (by the owners) will indicate that they are giving everything, the fat and breast, to God, while the *Kohanim receive their portion from the Higher Table.*

אֶת הֶחָזֶה לְהָנִיף אֹתוֹ — *That the breast may be waved.* Even though the fat is placed on the breast when it is waved, nonetheless, the principle purpose of waving is to demonstrate that the breast is offered on High, whereas it is already known that the fat belongs to God, for it is offered on the altar.

32. וְאֵת שׁוֹק הַיָּמִין תִּתְּנוּ תְרוּמָה לַכֹּהֵן — *And the right thigh you shall give as an offering to the Kohen*... from the portion of the owners, (as though) they are greeting the servants (of the king) with a gift in honor of the king.

VIII

2. וְאֵת פַּר הַחַטָּאת וְאֵת שְׁנֵי הָאֵילִים — *And the bull of the sin offering and the two rams.* The bull of the sin offering precedes (the burnt offering) as our Sages say, "Every sin offering precedes the burnt offering brought with it" (*Pesachim* 59a), because until the sin is expiated, the burnt offering serves no purpose at all, as it says עוֹלָה וַחֲטָאָה לֹא שָׁאָלְתָּ, *burnt offering and sin offering You have not required* (*Psalms* 40:7). Now, his sin offering

NOTES

30. יָדָיו תְּבִיאֶינָה אֵת אִשֵּׁי ה׳ — *His own hands shall bring the offerings of* HASHEM. See 6:7 regarding the *Kohen's* portion coming from the *Higher Table* of God.

32. וְאֵת שׁוֹק הַיָּמִין תִּתְּנוּ תְרוּמָה לַכֹּהֵן — *And the right thigh you shall give as an offering to the Kohen.* The right shoulder is not given to the *Kohanim* from "God's table," rather it is an offer-

saying: When one brings his feast peace-offering to HASHEM, he shall deliver
his offering to HASHEM from his feast peace-offering. 30 *With his own hands*
shall he bring the fire-offerings of HASHEM: the fat atop the breast shall he
bring; the breast, in order to wave it as a wave-service before HASHEM. 31 *The*
Kohen shall cause the fat to go up in smoke on the Altar; and the breast shall
be for Aaron and his sons. 32 *You shall give the right thigh as a raised-up gift*
to the Kohen, from your feast peace-offerings. 33 *Anyone from among the*
sons of Aaron who shall offer the blood of the peace-offering and the fat —
the right thigh shall be his as a portion. 34 *For the breast of the waving and*
the thigh of the raising-up have I taken from the Children of Israel, from
their feast peace-offering, and I have given them to Aaron the Kohen and
his sons as an eternal stipend from the Children of Israel.

35 *This is the anointment [portion] of Aaron and the anointment [portion]*
gift of his sons from the fire-offerings of HASHEM, on the day He brought
them near to minister to HASHEM; 36 *that HASHEM commanded to be given*
them on the day He anointed them from among the Children of Israel; it is
an eternal decree for their generations.

37 *This is the law of the elevation-offering, the meal-offering, the*
sin-offering, and the guilt-offering; and the inauguration-offerings, and the
feast peace-offering; 38 *which HASHEM commanded Moses on Mount Sinai,*
on the day He commanded the Children of Israel to bring their offerings to
HASHEM, in the Wilderness of Sinai.

8 1 *HASHEM spoke to Moses, saying:* 2 *Take Aaron and his sons with him,*
and the garments and the oil of anointment, and the bull of the
sin-offering, and the two rams, and the basket of matzos. 3 *Gather the entire*
assembly to the entrance of the Tent of Meeting. 4 *Moses did as HASHEM*
commanded him; and the assembly was gathered to the entrance of the Tent
of Meeting. 5 *Moses said to the assembly: "This is the thing that HASHEM*
commanded to be done." 6 *Moses brought Aaron and his sons forward and*
he immersed them in water. 7 *He placed the Tunic upon him and girdled him*

---

after his anointment was a bull in accordance with the rule (regarding) the anointed *Kohen* (subsequent to his installation — 4:3). But the blood was not brought into the inner sanctum because his sin was not on such a level of evil as to necessitate it, as is necessary with the (erroneous) decision of the anointed *Kohen* and the (erroneous) verdict of a court, (or) the bull and goat of Yom Kippur which come to atone for the impurity of the Sanctuary and (to expiate) sins, iniquities, and transgressions, as explained in chapter 16.

NOTES

ing (תְּרוּמָה) given to them by the owners as a gesture of respect to the servants of the king.

VIII

2. וְאֵת פַּר הַחַטָּאת וְאֵת שְׁנֵי הָאֵילִים — *And the bull of the sin offering and the two rams.* To bring the blood of a sacrifice into the קֹדֶשׁ, *the holy*, is an indication of the severity of the sin which the sacrifice is meant to expiate. Since Aaron was now anointed as *Kohen Gadol*, his sin offering (for his role in the sin of the Golden Calf) conformed with the ritual of the sacrifice brought by the anointed *Kohen* (4:3) except for the sprinkling of the blood in front of the veil of the Sanctuary (4:6). The *Sforno* is of the opinion that Aaron's involvement in the Golden Calf was minimal (see *Sforno* on *Exodus* 32:24); hence, the procedure here did not include bringing the blood of his bull into *the holy*, as is the case of those transgressions mentioned by the *Sforno*, which were of a more serious nature.

בָּאַבְנֵט וַיַּלְבֵּשׁ אֹתוֹ אֶת־הַמְּעִיל וַיִּתֵּן עָלָיו אֶת־הָאֵפֹד וַיַּחְגֹּר אֹתוֹ
ח *חצי התורה בפסוקים בְּחֵשֶׁב הָאֵפֹד וַיֶּאְפֹּד לוֹ בּוֹ: * וַיָּשֶׂם עָלָיו אֶת־הַחֹשֶׁן וַיִּתֵּן אֶל־הַחֹשֶׁן
ט אֶת־הָאוּרִים וְאֶת־הַתֻּמִּים: וַיָּשֶׂם אֶת־הַמִּצְנֶפֶת עַל־רֹאשׁוֹ וַיָּשֶׂם
עַל־הַמִּצְנֶפֶת אֶל־מוּל פָּנָיו אֵת צִיץ הַזָּהָב נֵזֶר הַקֹּדֶשׁ כַּאֲשֶׁר צִוָּה יהוה
י אֶת־מֹשֶׁה: וַיִּקַּח מֹשֶׁה אֶת־שֶׁמֶן הַמִּשְׁחָה וַיִּמְשַׁח אֶת־הַמִּשְׁכָּן
יא וְאֶת־כָּל־אֲשֶׁר־בּוֹ וַיְקַדֵּשׁ אֹתָם: וַיַּז מִמֶּנּוּ עַל־הַמִּזְבֵּחַ שֶׁבַע פְּעָמִים
יב וַיִּמְשַׁח אֶת־הַמִּזְבֵּחַ וְאֶת־כָּל־כֵּלָיו וְאֶת־הַכִּיֹּר וְאֶת־כַּנּוֹ לְקַדְּשָׁם: וַיִּצֹק
יג מִשֶּׁמֶן הַמִּשְׁחָה עַל רֹאשׁ אַהֲרֹן וַיִּמְשַׁח אֹתוֹ לְקַדְּשׁוֹ: וַיַּקְרֵב מֹשֶׁה
אֶת־בְּנֵי אַהֲרֹן וַיַּלְבִּשֵׁם כֻּתֳּנֹת וַיַּחְגֹּר אֹתָם אַבְנֵט וַיַּחֲבֹשׁ לָהֶם מִגְבָּעוֹת
חמישי יד כַּאֲשֶׁר צִוָּה יהוה אֶת־מֹשֶׁה: וַיַּגֵּשׁ אֵת פַּר הַחַטָּאת וַיִּסְמֹךְ אַהֲרֹן
טו וּבָנָיו אֶת־יְדֵיהֶם עַל־רֹאשׁ פַּר הַחַטָּאת: וַיִּשְׁחָט וַיִּקַּח מֹשֶׁה אֶת־הַדָּם
וַיִּתֵּן עַל־קַרְנוֹת הַמִּזְבֵּחַ סָבִיב בְּאֶצְבָּעוֹ וַיְחַטֵּא אֶת־הַמִּזְבֵּחַ וְאֶת־
טז הַדָּם יָצַק אֶל־יְסוֹד הַמִּזְבֵּחַ וַיְקַדְּשֵׁהוּ לְכַפֵּר עָלָיו: וַיִּקַּח אֶת־כָּל־הַחֵלֶב
אֲשֶׁר עַל־הַקֶּרֶב וְאֵת יֹתֶרֶת הַכָּבֵד וְאֶת־שְׁתֵּי הַכְּלָיֹת וְאֶת־חֶלְבְּהֶן
יז וַיַּקְטֵר מֹשֶׁה הַמִּזְבֵּחָה: וְאֶת־הַפָּר וְאֶת־עֹרוֹ וְאֶת־בְּשָׂרוֹ וְאֶת־פִּרְשׁוֹ
יח שָׂרַף בָּאֵשׁ מִחוּץ לַמַּחֲנֶה כַּאֲשֶׁר צִוָּה יהוה אֶת־מֹשֶׁה: וַיַּקְרֵב אֵת
יט אֵיל הָעֹלָה וַיִּסְמְכוּ אַהֲרֹן וּבָנָיו אֶת־יְדֵיהֶם עַל־רֹאשׁ הָאָיִל: וַיִּשְׁחָט
כ וַיִּזְרֹק מֹשֶׁה אֶת־הַדָּם עַל־הַמִּזְבֵּחַ סָבִיב: וְאֶת־הָאַיִל נִתַּח לִנְתָחָיו
כא וַיַּקְטֵר מֹשֶׁה אֶת־הָרֹאשׁ וְאֶת־הַנְּתָחִים וְאֶת־הַפָּדֶר: וְאֶת־הַקֶּרֶב
וְאֶת־הַכְּרָעַיִם רָחַץ בַּמָּיִם וַיַּקְטֵר מֹשֶׁה אֶת־כָּל־הָאַיִל הַמִּזְבֵּחָה עֹלָה
ששי כב הוּא לְרֵיחַ־נִיחֹחַ אִשֶּׁה הוּא לַיהוה כַּאֲשֶׁר צִוָּה יהוה אֶת־מֹשֶׁה: וַיַּקְרֵב
אֶת־הָאַיִל הַשֵּׁנִי אֵיל הַמִּלֻּאִים וַיִּסְמְכוּ אַהֲרֹן וּבָנָיו אֶת־יְדֵיהֶם
כג עַל־רֹאשׁ הָאָיִל: וַיִּשְׁחָט | וַיִּקַּח מֹשֶׁה מִדָּמוֹ וַיִּתֵּן עַל־תְּנוּךְ אֹזֶן־אַהֲרֹן
כד הַיְמָנִית וְעַל־בֹּהֶן יָדוֹ הַיְמָנִית וְעַל־בֹּהֶן רַגְלוֹ הַיְמָנִית: וַיַּקְרֵב אֶת־בְּנֵי
אַהֲרֹן וַיִּתֵּן מֹשֶׁה מִן־הַדָּם עַל־תְּנוּךְ אָזְנָם הַיְמָנִית וְעַל־בֹּהֶן יָדָם
הַיְמָנִית וְעַל־בֹּהֶן רַגְלָם הַיְמָנִית וַיִּזְרֹק מֹשֶׁה אֶת־הַדָּם עַל־הַמִּזְבֵּחַ
כה סָבִיב: וַיִּקַּח אֶת־הַחֵלֶב וְאֶת־הָאַלְיָה וְאֶת־כָּל־הַחֵלֶב אֲשֶׁר עַל־הַקֶּרֶב
וְאֵת יֹתֶרֶת הַכָּבֵד וְאֶת־שְׁתֵּי הַכְּלָיֹת וְאֶת־חֶלְבְּהֶן וְאֵת שׁוֹק הַיָּמִין:

---

18. וַיַּקְרֵב אֵת אֵיל הָעֹלָה — *And the ram of the burnt offering was presented.* The burnt offering preceded the ram of consecration because the burnt offering also came for some expiation, as it says, *And it shall be accepted for him to make atonement for him* (1:4). After the atonement was complete, they became worthy to "fill their hand" and perfect it for the service (of God).

NOTES

18. וַיַּקְרֵב אֵת אֵיל הָעֹלָה — *And the ram of the burnt offering was presented.* The first of the two rams brought for the ceremony of induction was meant to atone for sins committed by Aaron and his sons other than that of the Golden Calf. Therefore, it preceded the offering of the second ram which was the ram of consecration. Only after expiation from sin could Aaron and his sons be fully (מָלֵא) and completely (שָׁלֵם) inducted into the priestly office (see *Rashi* on v. 22).

with the Sash; he dressed him in the Robe and placed the Ephod on him; he girdled him with the belt of the Ephod and adorned him with it. 8 *He placed the Breastplate upon him; and in the Breastplate he placed the Urim and the Tumim.* 9 *He put the Turban upon his head; and upon the Turban, toward his face, he placed the golden Head-plate, the sacred diadem, as HASHEM had commanded Moses.*

10 *Moses took the oil of anointment and anointed the Tabernacle and everything within it; thus he sanctified them.* 11 *He sprinkled from it seven times upon the Altar; he anointed the Altar and all its utensils, and the laver and its base, in order to sanctify them.* 12 *He poured from the oil of anointment upon Aaron's head, and he anointed him to sanctify him.*
13 *Moses brought the sons of Aaron forward, he dressed them in Tunics and girdled [each of] them with a Sash and wrapped the Headdresses upon them, as HASHEM had commanded Moses.*

14 *He brought forward the sin-offering bull; Aaron and his sons leaned their hands upon the head of the sin-offering bull.* 15 *He slaughtered it, and Moses took the blood and placed it on the horns of the Altar, all around, with his forefinger, and he purified the Altar; he poured the [remaining] blood upon the base of the Altar and he sanctified it to provide atonement for it.*

16 *Then he took all the fat that is upon the innards, and the diaphragm of the liver, and the two kidneys with their fat; and Moses caused them to go up in smoke on the Altar.* 17 *And the bull, with its hide, flesh and waste, he burned in fire outside the camp, as HASHEM had commanded Moses.* 18 *Then he brought near the ram for the elevation-offering, and Aaron and his sons leaned their hands upon the head of the ram.* 19 *He slaughtered it, and Moses threw its blood upon the Altar, all around.* 20 *He cut the ram into its parts; Moses caused the head, the parts, and the fats to go up in smoke.* 21 *He washed the innards and the feet with water; Moses caused the entire ram to go up in smoke on the Altar — it was an elevation-offering, for a satisfying aroma; it was a fire-offering to HASHEM, as HASHEM had commanded Moses.*

22 *Then he brought near the second ram, the inauguration ram, and Aaron and his sons leaned their hands upon the head of the ram.* 23 *He slaughtered it, and Moses took some of its blood and placed it upon the middle part of Aaron's right ear, upon the thumb of his right hand, and upon the big toe of his right foot.* 24 *He brought the sons of Aaron forward, and Moses put some of the blood upon the middle part of their right ear, upon the thumb of their right hand and upon the big toe of their right foot; and Moses threw the [remaining] blood upon the Altar, all around.* 25 *He took the fat, and the tail, and all the fat that was upon the innards, and the diaphragm of the liver, and the two kidneys and their fat, and the right thigh.*

25. וְאֵת שׁוֹק הַיָּמִין — *And the right thigh.* Behold, from all peace offerings the right thigh belongs to the *Kohanim* (7:32), but from the *nazir's* peace offering the thigh and arm, i.e.,

NOTES

25. וְאֵת שׁוֹק הַיָּמִין — *And the right thigh.* The *Sforno* explains the significance and symbolism of the thigh of the peace offerings given to the *Kohen,* and the additional gift of the arm from the peace offering of the *nazir,* in the following manner. The thigh is connected to the foot while the

כו וּמִסַּל הַמַּצּוֹת אֲשֶׁר ׀ לִפְנֵי יהוה לָקַח חַלַּת מַצָּה אַחַת וְחַלַּת לֶחֶם שֶׁמֶן
כז אַחַת וְרָקִיק אֶחָד וַיָּשֶׂם עַל־הַחֲלָבִים וְעַל שׁוֹק הַיָּמִין: וַיִּתֵּן אֶת־הַכֹּל
כח עַל כַּפֵּי אַהֲרֹן וְעַל כַּפֵּי בָנָיו וַיָּנֶף אֹתָם תְּנוּפָה לִפְנֵי יהוה: וַיִּקַּח מֹשֶׁה
אֹתָם מֵעַל כַּפֵּיהֶם וַיַּקְטֵר הַמִּזְבֵּחָה עַל־הָעֹלָה מִלֻּאִים הֵם לְרֵיחַ נִיחֹחַ
כט אִשֶּׁה הוּא לַיהוה: וַיִּקַּח מֹשֶׁה אֶת־הֶחָזֶה וַיְנִיפֵהוּ תְנוּפָה לִפְנֵי יהוה
שביעי ל מֵאֵיל הַמִּלֻּאִים לְמֹשֶׁה הָיָה לְמָנָה כַּאֲשֶׁר צִוָּה יהוה אֶת־מֹשֶׁה: וַיִּקַּח
מֹשֶׁה מִשֶּׁמֶן הַמִּשְׁחָה וּמִן־הַדָּם אֲשֶׁר עַל־הַמִּזְבֵּחַ וַיַּז עַל־אַהֲרֹן
עַל־בְּגָדָיו וְעַל־בָּנָיו וְעַל־בִּגְדֵי בָנָיו אִתּוֹ וַיְקַדֵּשׁ אֶת־אַהֲרֹן אֶת־בְּגָדָיו
לא וְאֶת־בָּנָיו וְאֶת־בִּגְדֵי בָנָיו אִתּוֹ: וַיֹּאמֶר מֹשֶׁה אֶל־אַהֲרֹן וְאֶל־בָּנָיו בַּשְּׁלוּ
אֶת־הַבָּשָׂר פֶּתַח אֹהֶל מוֹעֵד וְשָׁם תֹּאכְלוּ אֹתוֹ וְאֶת־הַלֶּחֶם אֲשֶׁר בְּסַל
לב הַמִּלֻּאִים כַּאֲשֶׁר צִוֵּיתִי לֵאמֹר אַהֲרֹן וּבָנָיו יֹאכְלֻהוּ: וְהַנּוֹתָר בַּבָּשָׂר
מפטיר לג וּבַלָּחֶם בָּאֵשׁ תִּשְׂרֹפוּ: וּמִפֶּתַח אֹהֶל מוֹעֵד לֹא תֵצְאוּ שִׁבְעַת יָמִים עַד
לד יוֹם מְלֹאת יְמֵי מִלֻּאֵיכֶם כִּי שִׁבְעַת יָמִים יְמַלֵּא אֶת־יֶדְכֶם: כַּאֲשֶׁר עָשָׂה
לה בַּיּוֹם הַזֶּה צִוָּה יהוה לַעֲשֹׂת לְכַפֵּר עֲלֵיכֶם: וּפֶתַח אֹהֶל מוֹעֵד תֵּשְׁבוּ
יוֹמָם וָלַיְלָה שִׁבְעַת יָמִים וּשְׁמַרְתֶּם אֶת־מִשְׁמֶרֶת יהוה וְלֹא תָמוּתוּ
לו כִּי־כֵן צֻוֵּיתִי: וַיַּעַשׂ אַהֲרֹן וּבָנָיו אֵת כָּל־הַדְּבָרִים אֲשֶׁר־צִוָּה יהוה
בְּיַד־מֹשֶׁה:

---

the foot and hand, are given to the *Kohen* (*Numbers* 6:19,20). (However), the thigh of the consecration ram was put on the Altar (25-28). For indeed, when an Israelite (lit., "stranger") brings his sacrifice, he generally gives the thigh, together with the foot, to the *Kohen*, who can enter beyond the partition allowable to the Israelite who is bringing the sacrifice. The *nazir* also gives the arm, meaning the hand, as though he were transmitting

NOTES

arm is connected to the hand. Since the *Kohen* can enter where the Israelite who brings the peace offering cannot, he is entitled to the thigh (foot). The *nazir* adds the arm (hand) to indicate that heretofore his actions and deeds were restricted by his vow, i.e., given over to קֹדֶשׁ, the holy — but now the hand is once again in his domain and control. Since the consecration sacrifice is unique, symbolizing the preparation of the *Kohen* to minister in the Sanctuary, the thigh (foot) was rightfully placed on the Altar.

*26 And from the basket of matzos that was before HASHEM he took one
matzah loaf, one oily bread loaf, and one wafer, and placed them on the fats
and on the right thigh. 27 He put it all on Aaron's palms and on the palms
of his sons; and he waved them as a wave-service before HASHEM. 28 Then
Moses took them from on their palms and caused them to go up in smoke on
the Altar after the elevation-offering; they were inauguration offerings, for
a satisfying aroma; it was a fire-offering to HASHEM. 29 Moses took the
breast and waved it as a wave-service before HASHEM; from the ram of the
dedication it was a portion for Moses, as HASHEM had commanded Moses.*

*30 Moses took from the oil of anointment and some of the blood that was
on the Altar, and he sprinkled it upon Aaron and his vestments, and upon
his sons and upon the vestments of his sons who were with him; thus he
sanctified Aaron and his vestments, and his sons, and the vestments of his
sons with him.*

*31 Moses said to Aaron and to his sons: Cook the flesh at the entrance of
the Tent of the Meeting and there you shall eat it and the bread that is in the
basket of the inauguration-offerings, as I have been commanded, saying:
"Aaron and his sons shall eat it." 32 And whatever is left over of the flesh
and of the bread, you shall burn in the fire. 33 You shall not leave the
entrance of the Tent of the Meeting for seven days, until the day when your
days of inauguration are completed; for you shall be inaugurated for a
seven-day period.*

*34 As he did on this day, so HASHEM had commanded to be done to
provide atonement for you. 35 At the entrance of the Tent of Meeting shall
you dwell day and night for a seven-day period, and you shall protect
HASHEM's charge so that you will not die; for so have I been commanded.*

*36 Aaron and his sons carried out all the matters that HASHEM
commanded through Moses.*

---

to the *Kohen* the work of his hands which until now were kept (reserved) for God. However, (since) the consecration (ram) is a preparatory offering for the *Kohen* with which to enter within, (therefore) the thigh was placed on the Altar.

35. יוֹמָם וָלַיְלָה — *Day and night* ... because the curtains were not dismantled, as explained above.

NOTES

35. יוֹמָם וָלַיְלָה — *Day and night*. The curtains are called *mishkan* (see *Sforno — Exodus* 40:18). They remained in place during the seven days of consecration, even though the other parts of the Sanctuary were erected and dismantled during that period (*Yerushalmi Yoma* 1:1). The *Sforno* explains how the *Kohanim* were able to abide at the door of the Tent of Meeting during these seven days. They were able to do so since the curtains remained in place and were not dismantled.

פרשת שמיני

ט א־ב וַיְהִי בַּיּוֹם הַשְּׁמִינִי קָרָא מֹשֶׁה לְאַהֲרֹן וּלְבָנָיו וּלְזִקְנֵי יִשְׂרָאֵל: וַיֹּאמֶר
אֶל־אַהֲרֹן קַח־לְךָ עֵגֶל בֶּן־בָּקָר לְחַטָּאת וְאַיִל לְעֹלָה תְּמִימִם וְהַקְרֵב
ג לִפְנֵי יהוה: וְאֶל־בְּנֵי יִשְׂרָאֵל תְּדַבֵּר לֵאמֹר קְחוּ שְׂעִיר־עִזִּים לְחַטָּאת
ד וְעֵגֶל וָכֶבֶשׂ בְּנֵי־שָׁנָה תְּמִימִם לְעֹלָה: וְשׁוֹר וָאַיִל לִשְׁלָמִים לִזְבֹּחַ לִפְנֵי
ה יהוה וּמִנְחָה בְּלוּלָה בַשָּׁמֶן כִּי הַיּוֹם יהוה נִרְאָה אֲלֵיכֶם: וַיִּקְחוּ אֵת אֲשֶׁר
צִוָּה מֹשֶׁה אֶל־פְּנֵי אֹהֶל מוֹעֵד וַיִּקְרְבוּ כָּל־הָעֵדָה וַיַּעַמְדוּ לִפְנֵי יהוה:
ו וַיֹּאמֶר מֹשֶׁה זֶה הַדָּבָר אֲשֶׁר־צִוָּה יהוה תַּעֲשׂוּ וְיֵרָא אֲלֵיכֶם כְּבוֹד יהוה:
ז וַיֹּאמֶר מֹשֶׁה אֶל־אַהֲרֹן קְרַב אֶל־הַמִּזְבֵּחַ וַעֲשֵׂה אֶת־חַטָּאתְךָ
וְאֶת־עֹלָתֶךָ וְכַפֵּר בַּעַדְךָ וּבְעַד הָעָם וַעֲשֵׂה אֶת־קָרְבַּן הָעָם וְכַפֵּר בַּעֲדָם
ח כַּאֲשֶׁר צִוָּה יהוה: וַיִּקְרַב אַהֲרֹן אֶל־הַמִּזְבֵּחַ וַיִּשְׁחַט אֶת־עֵגֶל הַחַטָּאת
ט אֲשֶׁר־לוֹ: וַיַּקְרִבוּ בְּנֵי אַהֲרֹן אֶת־הַדָּם אֵלָיו וַיִּטְבֹּל אֶצְבָּעוֹ בַּדָּם וַיִּתֵּן
י עַל־קַרְנוֹת הַמִּזְבֵּחַ וְאֶת־הַדָּם יָצַק אֶל־יְסוֹד הַמִּזְבֵּחַ: וְאֶת־הַחֵלֶב
וְאֶת־הַכְּלָיֹת וְאֶת־הַיֹּתֶרֶת מִן־הַכָּבֵד מִן־הַחַטָּאת הִקְטִיר הַמִּזְבֵּחָה
יא כַּאֲשֶׁר צִוָּה יהוה אֶת־מֹשֶׁה: וְאֶת־הַבָּשָׂר וְאֶת־הָעוֹר שָׂרַף בָּאֵשׁ מִחוּץ
יב לַמַּחֲנֶה: וַיִּשְׁחַט אֶת־הָעֹלָה וַיַּמְצִאוּ בְּנֵי אַהֲרֹן אֵלָיו אֶת־הַדָּם וַיִּזְרְקֵהוּ
יג עַל־הַמִּזְבֵּחַ סָבִיב: וְאֶת־הָעֹלָה הִמְצִיאוּ אֵלָיו לִנְתָחֶיהָ וְאֶת־הָרֹאשׁ
יד וַיַּקְטֵר עַל־הַמִּזְבֵּחַ: וַיִּרְחַץ אֶת־הַקֶּרֶב וְאֶת־הַכְּרָעָיִם וַיַּקְטֵר עַל־הָעֹלָה
טו הַמִּזְבֵּחָה: וַיַּקְרֵב אֵת קָרְבַּן הָעָם וַיִּקַּח אֶת־שְׂעִיר הַחַטָּאת אֲשֶׁר לָעָם
שני טז־יז וַיִּשְׁחָטֵהוּ וַיְחַטְּאֵהוּ כָּרִאשׁוֹן: וַיַּקְרֵב אֶת־הָעֹלָה וַיַּעֲשֶׂהָ כַּמִּשְׁפָּט: וַיַּקְרֵב
אֶת־הַמִּנְחָה וַיְמַלֵּא כַפּוֹ מִמֶּנָּה וַיַּקְטֵר עַל־הַמִּזְבֵּחַ מִלְּבַד עֹלַת הַבֹּקֶר:

IX

4. כִּי הַיּוֹם ה׳ נִרְאָה אֲלֵיכֶם — *For today* HASHEM *appeared unto you.* He already appeared in the work of your hands, as it says, וּכְבוֹד ה׳ מָלֵא אֶת הַמִּשְׁכָּן, *And the glory of* HASHEM *filled the Mishkan* (*Exodus* 40:34), therefore it is fitting that you honor Him with this offering (in recognition of) the revelation of His Divine Presence (*Shechinah*).

6. זֶה הַדָּבָר אֲשֶׁר צִוָּה ה׳ תַּעֲשׂוּ — *This is the thing which* HASHEM *has commanded that you do* ... to lay your hands on the communal sin offering and burnt offering.

וְיֵרָא אֲלֵיכֶם כְּבוֹד ה׳ — *That the glory of* HASHEM *may appear to you.* Besides (in addition to) the revelation of the Divine Presence in the *Mishkan*, as it says, *And the glory of* HASHEM *appeared to all the people* (v. 23).

12. וַיַּמְצִאוּ ... אֵלָיו — *And* (*they*) *delivered ... to him* ... to be trained (in the method) by

NOTES

IX

4. ה׳ נִרְאָה אֲלֵיכֶם — HASHEM *appeared unto you.* The *Sforno* interprets the word נִרְאָה in the past tense, i.e., He already appeared to you; therefore it is fitting that you bring this offering in recognition of His revelation at the time that the *Mishkan* was completed.

6. זֶה הַדָּבָר אֲשֶׁר צִוָּה ה׳ תַּעֲשׂוּ — *This is the thing which* HASHEM *has commanded that you do.* Since the glory of God had already filled the Sanctuary, the act of *laying the hands* (סְמִיכָה) at this time will merit an additional revelation of God's glory, as the Torah indeed records in verse 23. The *Sforno* explains the obscure phrase, זֶה הַדָּבָר, *this is the thing*, as referring to the ritual of סְמִיכָה.

12. וַיַּמְצִאוּ ... אֵלָיו — *And* (*they*) *delivered ... to him.* The purpose of having Aaron's sons participate in the service of the burnt offering as well as the

PARASHAS SHEMINI

9 1 *It was on the eighth day, Moses summoned Aaron and his sons, and the elders
of Israel. 2 *He said to Aaron: Take yourself a young bull for a sin-offering and*
a ram for an elevation-offering — unblemished; and offer [them] before HASHEM.
3 *And to the Children of Israel speak as follows: Take a he-goat for a sin-offer-*
ing, and a calf and a sheep in their first year — unblemished — for an elevation-
offering. 4 *And a bull and a ram for a peace-offering to slaughter before HASHEM,*
and a meal-offering mixed with oil; for today HASHEM appears to you.
5 *They took what Moses had commanded to the front of the Tent of Meeting;*
and the entire assembly approached and stood before HASHEM. 6 *Moses said:*
This is the thing that HASHEM has commanded you to do; then the glory of
HASHEM will appear to you.
7 *Moses said to Aaron: Come near to the Altar and perform the service of your*
sin-offering and your elevation-offering and provide atonement for yourself
and for the people; then perform the service of the people's offering and provide
atonement for them, as HASHEM has commanded.
8 *Aaron came near to the Altar, and slaughtered the sin-offering calf that was*
his. 9 *The sons of Aaron brought the blood to him. He dipped his finger into the*
blood and placed it upon the horns of the Altar, and he poured the [remaining]
blood upon the foundation of the Altar. 10 *And the fats, and the kidneys, and the*
diaphragm with the liver of the sin-offering, he caused to go up in smoke on the
Altar, as HASHEM had commanded Moses. 11 *And the flesh and the hide he*
burned in fire outside the camp. 12 *He slaughtered the elevation-offering; the*
sons of Aaron presented the blood to him and he threw it upon the Altar, all
around. 13 *They presented the elevation-offering to him in its pieces with the*
head; and he caused it to go up in smoke on the Altar. 14 *He washed the innards*
and the feet, and caused them to go up in smoke on the elevation-offering on the
Altar.
15 *He brought near the offering of the people: He took the sin-offering goat that*
was for the people, and slaughtered it and performed the sin-offering service, as
for the first one. 16 *He brought near the elevation-offering and performed its ser-*
vice according to the law. 17 *He brought near the meal-offering, filled his palm*
from it, and caused it to go up in smoke on the Altar; aside from the morning

---

occupying themselves in their father's sacrifice.

15. כָּרִאשֹׁן — *As the first.* It was burnt, although it was an "outer" sin offering.

16. כַּמִּשְׁפָּט — *According to the ordinance.* The sons of Aaron sprinkled (the blood), prepared (the wood on the Altar) and burnt (the sacrifice).

17. מִלְּבַד עֹלַת הַבֹּקֶר — *Besides the burnt offering of the morning* ... besides the meal offering of the (daily) morning burnt offering.

NOTES

peace offering (v. 18) was to teach and train them in these functions which they as *Kohanim* would be charged with in the future.

15. כָּרִאשֹׁן — *As the first.* As *Rashi* points out, although those sin offerings whose blood was sprinkled on the outer altar were not burnt, and the *Kohanim* were entitled to eat the flesh, this sin offering and the one of the consecration ceremony as well *were* burnt. These were exceptions to the rule and the *Sforno* explains the verse accordingly.

17. עֹלַת הַבֹּקֶר — *The burnt offering of the morning.* The *Sforno*, following the commentary of the *Ramban*, interprets the words עֹלַת הַבֹּקֶר as referring to the *meal offering* of the daily morning sacrifice.

יח וַיִּשְׁחַט אֶת־הַשּׁוֹר וְאֶת־הָאַיִל זֶבַח הַשְּׁלָמִים אֲשֶׁר לָעָם וַיַּמְצִאוּ בְּנֵי
יט אַהֲרֹן אֶת־הַדָּם אֵלָיו וַיִּזְרְקֵהוּ עַל־הַמִּזְבֵּחַ סָבִיב: וְאֶת־הַחֲלָבִים
כ מִן־הַשּׁוֹר וּמִן־הָאַיִל הָאַלְיָה וְהַמְכַסֶּה וְהַכְּלָיֹת וְיֹתֶרֶת הַכָּבֵד: וַיָּשִׂימוּ
כא אֶת־הַחֲלָבִים עַל־הֶחָזוֹת וַיַּקְטֵר הַחֲלָבִים הַמִּזְבֵּחָה: וְאֵת הֶחָזוֹת וְאֵת
כב שׁוֹק הַיָּמִין הֵנִיף אַהֲרֹן תְּנוּפָה לִפְנֵי יהוה כַּאֲשֶׁר צִוָּה מֹשֶׁה: וַיִּשָּׂא אַהֲרֹן
אֶת־יָדָו אֶל־הָעָם וַיְבָרְכֵם וַיֵּרֶד מֵעֲשֹׂת הַחַטָּאת וְהָעֹלָה וְהַשְּׁלָמִים:
כג וַיָּבֹא מֹשֶׁה וְאַהֲרֹן אֶל־אֹהֶל מוֹעֵד וַיֵּצְאוּ וַיְבָרְכוּ אֶת־הָעָם וַיֵּרָא
שלישי כד כְבוֹד־יהוה אֶל־כָּל־הָעָם: וַתֵּצֵא אֵשׁ מִלִּפְנֵי יהוה וַתֹּאכַל עַל־הַמִּזְבֵּחַ
י א אֶת־הָעֹלָה וְאֶת־הַחֲלָבִים וַיַּרְא כָּל־הָעָם וַיָּרֹנּוּ וַיִּפְּלוּ עַל־פְּנֵיהֶם: וַיִּקְחוּ
בְנֵי־אַהֲרֹן נָדָב וַאֲבִיהוּא אִישׁ מַחְתָּתוֹ וַיִּתְּנוּ בָהֵן אֵשׁ וַיָּשִׂימוּ עָלֶיהָ
ב קְטֹרֶת וַיַּקְרִיבוּ לִפְנֵי יהוה אֵשׁ זָרָה אֲשֶׁר לֹא צִוָּה אֹתָם: וַתֵּצֵא אֵשׁ
ג מִלִּפְנֵי יהוה וַתֹּאכַל אוֹתָם וַיָּמֻתוּ לִפְנֵי יהוה: וַיֹּאמֶר מֹשֶׁה אֶל־אַהֲרֹן
הוּא אֲשֶׁר־דִּבֶּר יהוה ׀ לֵאמֹר בִּקְרֹבַי אֶקָּדֵשׁ וְעַל־פְּנֵי כָל־הָעָם אֶכָּבֵד
ד וַיִּדֹּם אַהֲרֹן: וַיִּקְרָא מֹשֶׁה אֶל־מִישָׁאֵל וְאֶל אֶלְצָפָן בְּנֵי עֻזִּיאֵל דֹּד
אַהֲרֹן וַיֹּאמֶר אֲלֵהֶם *קִרְבוּ שְׂאוּ אֶת־אֲחֵיכֶם מֵאֵת פְּנֵי־הַקֹּדֶשׁ
ה אֶל־מִחוּץ לַמַּחֲנֶה: וַיִּקְרְבוּ וַיִּשָּׂאֻם בְּכֻתֳּנֹתָם אֶל־מִחוּץ לַמַּחֲנֶה כַּאֲשֶׁר
ו דִּבֶּר מֹשֶׁה: וַיֹּאמֶר מֹשֶׁה אֶל־אַהֲרֹן וּלְאֶלְעָזָר וּלְאִיתָמָר ׀ בָּנָיו
רָאשֵׁיכֶם אַל־תִּפְרָעוּ ׀ וּבִגְדֵיכֶם לֹא־תִפְרֹמוּ וְלֹא תָמֻתוּ וְעַל כָּל־הָעֵדָה
יִקְצֹף וַאֲחֵיכֶם כָּל־בֵּית יִשְׂרָאֵל יִבְכּוּ אֶת־הַשְּׂרֵפָה אֲשֶׁר שָׂרַף יהוה:

*הקורא יטעים הגרשיים קודם התלישא

18. וַיַּמְצִאוּ — *And* (*they*) *delivered to him.* They were also trained in (the method) of the communal peace offerings.

X

1. וַיִּקְחוּ בְנֵי אַהֲרֹן ... אִישׁ מַחְתָּתוֹ — *And the sons of Aaron* (*took*) ... *each of them his censer.* They were under the impression that (just) as the incense came after the daily offering whereby the *Shechinah* manifested itself, as it says, עֹלַת תָּמִיד לְדֹרֹתֵיכֶם פֶּתַח אֹהֶל מוֹעֵד לִפְנֵי ה' אֲשֶׁר אִוָּעֵד לָכֶם שָׁמָּה, *It shall be a continual burnt offering throughout your generations at the door of the Tent of Meeting before* HASHEM, *where I will meet with you* (*Exodus* 29:42), so it would be proper to burn additional incense now that the Divine Glory had been revealed to all the people and the fire had descended, therefore they offered it ...

לִפְנֵי ה' — *Before* HASHEM ... on the inner Altar, of which (the Torah) said, לֹא תַעֲלוּ עָלָיו קְטֹרֶת זָרָה, *You shall offer no strange incense on it* (*Exodus* 30:9). Now even if it was the proper thing to do had they (but) been commanded to do so, (nevertheless) they sinned by doing it presently (since) ...

אֲשֶׁר לֹא צִוָּה אֹתָם — *Which He had not commanded them* ... as our Sages say, "They decided the law in the presence of Moses their teacher" (*Eruvin* 63a).

NOTES

X

1. וַיִּקְחוּ בְנֵי אַהֲרֹן ... אִישׁ מַחְתָּתוֹ — *And the sons of Aaron* (*took*) ... *each of them his censer.* The *Sforno* explains what prompted Nadav and Avihu to bring the incense at this particular time. However, their reasoning was faulty and they erred for two reasons. Firstly, no incense may be brought on the inner Altar except at those times specified by the Torah, and secondly, even if one were to argue that this day was different, as indeed it was, for we see that certain ordinary regulations were not operative the day of the consecration, nonetheless they were not empowered to determine the law in the presence of their teacher Moses.

elevation-offering. 18 *He slaughtered the bull and the ram — the people's feast peace-offering; the sons of Aaron presented the blood to him, and he threw it upon the Altar, all around.* 19 *As for the fats from the bull and from the ram, and the tail, the covering fats, the kidneys, and the diaphragm with the liver,* 20 *they placed the fats upon the breasts, and caused the fats to go up in smoke on the Altar.* 21 *Aaron had lifted up the breasts and the right thigh as a wave-service before HASHEM, as Moses had commanded.*

22 *Aaron raised his hands toward the people and blessed them; then he descended from having performed the sin-offering, the elevation-offering, and the peace-offering.* 23 *Moses and Aaron came to the Tent of Meeting, and they went out and they blessed the people — and the glory of HASHEM appeared to the entire people!*

24 *A fire went forth from before HASHEM and consumed upon the Altar the elevation-offering and the fats; the people saw and sang glad song and fell upon their faces.*

10 1 *The sons of Aaron, Nadab and Abihu, each took his fire pan, they put fire in them and placed incense upon it; and they brought before HASHEM an alien fire that He had not commanded them.* 2 *A fire came forth from before HASHEM and consumed them, and they died before HASHEM.*

3 *Moses said to Aaron: Of this did HASHEM speak, saying: "I will be sanctified through those who are nearest Me, thus I will be honored before the entire people"; and Aaron was silent.*

4 *Moses summoned Mishael and Elzaphan, sons of Aaron's uncle Uzziel, and said to them, "Approach, carry your brothers out of the Sanctuary to the outside of the camp."* 5 *They approached and carried them by their Tunics to the outside of the camp, as Moses had spoken.*

6 *Moses said to Aaron and to his sons Elazar and Ithamar, "Do not leave your heads unshorn and do not rend your garments that you not die and He become wrathful with the entire assembly; and your brethren the entire House of Israel shall bewail the conflagration that HASHEM ignited.*

---

3. וַיִּדֹּם אַהֲרֹן — *And Aaron was silent* . . . comforting himself (in the thought) that God was sanctified through their death.

5. בְּכֻתֳּנֹתָם אֶל מִחוּץ לַמַּחֲנֶה — *In their shirts out of the camp.* They were not concerned about removing their holy (priestly) tunics, since they were already *tamei.*

6. רָאשֵׁיכֶם אַל תִּפְרָעוּ — *Let not the hair of your heads grow (long).* Although the deceased were relatives for whom an ordinary *Kohen* could defile himself (21:2), (the law) for them was more stringent because they were anointed (that day) as it says, *For the anointing oil of HASHEM is upon you* (v. 7).

כָּל בֵּית יִשְׂרָאֵל יִבְכּוּ — *The whole house of Israel will bewail* . . . that two great pious men are now lacking (from Israel), and therefore *honor of the dead* (based on *Sanhedrin* 46b) will not be denied.

NOTES

3. וַיִּדֹּם אַהֲרֹן — *And Aaron was silent.* See *Rashi's* commentary on this verse where the concept of קִדּוּשׁ ה׳, *sanctification of God's Name,* mentioned by the *Sforno,* is elaborated upon.

6. רָאשֵׁיכֶם אַל תִּפְרָעוּ . . . כָּל בֵּית יִשְׂרָאֵל יִבְכּוּ — *Let not the hair of your heads grow (long) . . . The whole house of Israel will bewail.* Since they were anointed that day, they had the status of a *Kohen Gadol,*

ז וּמִפֶּתַח אֹהֶל מוֹעֵד לֹא תֵצְאוּ פֶּן־תָּמֻתוּ כִּי־שֶׁמֶן מִשְׁחַת יהוה עֲלֵיכֶם
וַיַּעֲשׂוּ כִּדְבַר מֹשֶׁה:
ח־ט וַיְדַבֵּר יהוה אֶל־אַהֲרֹן לֵאמֹר: יַיִן וְשֵׁכָר אַל־תֵּשְׁתְּ | אַתָּה | וּבָנֶיךָ אִתָּךְ
י בְּבֹאֲכֶם אֶל־אֹהֶל מוֹעֵד וְלֹא תָמֻתוּ חֻקַּת עוֹלָם לְדֹרֹתֵיכֶם: וּלְהַבְדִּיל
יא בֵּין הַקֹּדֶשׁ וּבֵין הַחֹל וּבֵין הַטָּמֵא וּבֵין הַטָּהוֹר: וּלְהוֹרֹת אֶת־בְּנֵי יִשְׂרָאֵל
אֵת כָּל־הַחֻקִּים אֲשֶׁר דִּבֶּר יהוה אֲלֵיהֶם בְּיַד־מֹשֶׁה:
רביעי יב וַיְדַבֵּר מֹשֶׁה אֶל־אַהֲרֹן וְאֶל אֶלְעָזָר וְאֶל־אִיתָמָר | בָּנָיו הַנּוֹתָרִים קְחוּ
אֶת־הַמִּנְחָה הַנּוֹתֶרֶת מֵאִשֵּׁי יהוה וְאִכְלוּהָ מַצּוֹת אֵצֶל הַמִּזְבֵּחַ כִּי קֹדֶשׁ
יג קָדָשִׁים הִוא: וַאֲכַלְתֶּם אֹתָהּ בְּמָקוֹם קָדוֹשׁ כִּי חָקְךָ וְחָק־בָּנֶיךָ הִוא
יד מֵאִשֵּׁי יהוה כִּי־כֵן צֻוֵּיתִי: וְאֵת חֲזֵה הַתְּנוּפָה וְאֵת | שׁוֹק הַתְּרוּמָה
תֹּאכְלוּ בְּמָקוֹם טָהוֹר אַתָּה וּבָנֶיךָ וּבְנֹתֶיךָ אִתָּךְ כִּי־חָקְךָ וְחָק־בָּנֶיךָ נִתְּנוּ
טו מִזִּבְחֵי שַׁלְמֵי בְּנֵי יִשְׂרָאֵל: שׁוֹק הַתְּרוּמָה וַחֲזֵה הַתְּנוּפָה עַל אִשֵּׁי
הַחֲלָבִים יָבִיאוּ לְהָנִיף תְּנוּפָה לִפְנֵי יהוה וְהָיָה לְךָ וּלְבָנֶיךָ אִתְּךָ
חמישי טז לְחָק־עוֹלָם כַּאֲשֶׁר צִוָּה יהוה: וְאֵת | שְׂעִיר הַחַטָּאת דָּרֹשׁ * דָּרַשׁ מֹשֶׁה
*חצי התורה בתיבות דרש מכא ודרש מכא וְהִנֵּה שֹׂרָף וַיִּקְצֹף עַל־אֶלְעָזָר וְעַל־אִיתָמָר בְּנֵי אַהֲרֹן הַנּוֹתָרִם לֵאמֹר:
יז מַדּוּעַ לֹא־אֲכַלְתֶּם אֶת־הַחַטָּאת בִּמְקוֹם הַקֹּדֶשׁ כִּי קֹדֶשׁ קָדָשִׁים הִוא
יח וְאֹתָהּ | נָתַן לָכֶם לָשֵׂאת אֶת־עֲוֺן הָעֵדָה לְכַפֵּר עֲלֵיהֶם לִפְנֵי יהוה: הֵן
לֹא־הוּבָא אֶת־דָּמָהּ אֶל־הַקֹּדֶשׁ פְּנִימָה אָכוֹל תֹּאכְלוּ אֹתָהּ בַּקֹּדֶשׁ
יט כַּאֲשֶׁר צִוֵּיתִי: וַיְדַבֵּר אַהֲרֹן אֶל־מֹשֶׁה הֵן הַיּוֹם הִקְרִיבוּ אֶת־חַטָּאתָם

10-11. וּלְהַבְדִּיל... וּלְהוֹרֹת — *And that you may differentiate ... and that you may teach* ... because יַיִן וְתִירוֹשׁ יִקַּח לֵב, *Wine and new wine take away the heart* (*Hosea* 4:11), as it says, אַל לַמְלָכִים שְׁתוֹ יָיִן וּלְרוֹזְנִים אֵי שֵׁכָר פֶּן יִשְׁתֶּה וְיִשְׁכַּח מְחֻקָּק, *It is not for kings to drink wine, nor for princes to say, where is strong drink? Lest he drink and forget the decree* (*Proverbs* 31:4,5).

15. יָבִיאוּ לְהָנִיף... וְהָיָה לְךָ וּלְבָנֶיךָ — *They shall bring to wave ... and it shall be yours and your sons.* You shall not acquire them till after the waving; then you will acquire them from the *Higher Table.*

16. וְאֵת שְׂעִיר הַחַטָּאת — *And the goat of the sin offering* ... that goat which was for an everlasting statute, namely, the "goat of the New Moon," a holy (sacrifice) for future generations.

17. וְאֹתָהּ נָתַן לָכֶם לָשֵׂאת אֶת עֲוֺן הָעֵדָה — *And He has given it to you to bear the iniquity*

NOTES

and as such were not permitted to defile themselves or manifest mourning for a brother. However, lest we think that their abstinence from involvement with their deceased brothers be viewed as a denial of כְּבוֹד הַמֵּת, *honor of the dead,* the Torah tells us that *all* of Israel will mourn for these great men, thereby granting them the proper respect.

15. יָבִיאוּ לְהָנִיף — *They shall bring to wave.* The act of הֲנָפָה, *waving,* qualifies the *Kohen* to partake of the offering. The expression מִשֻּׁלְחַן גָּבוֹהַּ זָכוּ, *to merit acquisition from the Higher Table* (i.e., of God), is used throughout the Talmud to indicate that the *Kohanim* do not receive their portion *directly* from the owner of the sacrifice, but are like sons or servants who take their portion from the table of their Father and King.

16-19. וְאֵת שְׂעִיר הַחַטָּאת ... וְאֹתָהּ נָתַן לָכֶם לָשֵׂאת אֶת עֲוֺן הָעֵדָה ... הֵן הַיּוֹם הִקְרִיבוּ — *And the goat of the sin offering ... and He has given it to you to bear the iniquity of the congregation ... if this day they had offered.* The discussion between Moses

[7] Do not leave the entrance of the Tent of Meeting lest you die, for the oil of HASHEM's anointment is upon you"; and they carried out Moses' bidding.

[8] HASHEM spoke to Aaron saying: [9] Do not drink intoxicating wine, you and your sons with you, when you come to the Tent of Meeting, that you not die — this is an eternal decree for your generations. [10] In order to distinguish between the sacred and the profane, and between the contaminated and the pure, [11] and to teach the Children of Israel all the decrees that HASHEM had spoken to them through Moses.

[12] Moses spoke to Aaron and to Elazar and Ithamar, his remaining sons, "Take the meal-offering that is left from the fire-offerings of HASHEM, and eat it unleavened near the Altar; for it is the most holy. [13] You shall eat it in a holy place, for it is your portion and the portion of your sons from the fire-offerings of HASHEM, for so have I been commanded. [14] And the breast of the waving and the thigh of the raising-up you shall eat in a pure place, you and your sons and daughters with you; for they have been given as your portion and the portion of your sons from the feast peace-offerings of the Children of Israel. [15] They are to bring the thigh of the raising-up and the breast of the waving upon the fire-offering fats to wave as a wave-service before HASHEM; and it shall be for you and your sons with you for an eternal decree, as HASHEM has commanded."

[16] Moses inquired insistently about the he-goat of the sin-offering, for behold, it had been burned! — and he was wrathful with Elazar and Ithamar, Aaron's remaining sons, saying: [17] "Why did you not eat the sin-offering in a holy place, for it is most holy; and He gave it to you to gain forgiveness for the sin of the assembly and to atone for them before HASHEM? [18] Behold, its blood was not brought into the Sanctuary within; you should have eaten it in the Holy, as I had commanded!"

[19] Aaron spoke to Moses: "Was it they who this day offered their sin-

---

of the congregation. Although it was given to you, you had no permission to burn it because it was given to you to eat (in order) *to bear the iniquity of the congregation.*

19. הֵן הַיּוֹם הִקְרִיבוּ — *If this day they had offered.* This is similar to, הֵן יְשַׁלַּח אִישׁ אֶת אִשְׁתּוֹ, *If a man send away his wife* (*Jeremiah* 3:1); הֵן יִשָּׂא אִישׁ בְּשַׂר קֹדֶשׁ, *If one carries consecrated meat* (*Chaggai* 2:12). His reasoning was: If the situation were such that they were sacrificing their obligatory sin offering and their freewill burnt offering, even though these sacrifices are not permanent communal holy offerings, and we were to have eaten the sin offering today while in a state of *aninus*, mourning, would it have been pleasing in the sight of God that in a state of *aninus* we should (also) eat a sacrifice which is obligatory upon all generations? It is well known that if a *Kohen* who is an *onein* eats

NOTES

and Aaron is explained by the *Sforno* as follows. The eighth day (from which this Torah portion takes its name) was *Rosh Chodesh* (the New Moon of) Nissan. The sin offering which the *Kohanim* had burned was that of the New Moon sacrifice which Moses felt had to be eaten if it was to serve its purpose of atonement. Aaron, however, argued that an *onen* (a mourner from the time of his relative's death until nightfall following the burial), in which category they all were, may not partake of any sacrifice, especially a communal one which is incumbent upon Israel to offer for all time. Even if an exception was made by Moses regarding the meal offering of consecration, this dispensation could not apply to the sin offering of the New Moon which is an obligation for all generations, unlike that meal offering which was only קָדְשֵׁי שָׁעָה, *a one-time transitory offering.* Therefore,

וְאֶת־עֹלָתָם לִפְנֵי יהוה וַתִּקְרֶאנָה אֹתִי כָּאֵלֶּה וְאָכַלְתִּי חַטָּאת הַיּוֹם הַיִּיטַב
כ בְּעֵינֵי יהוה: וַיִּשְׁמַע מֹשֶׁה וַיִּיטַב בְּעֵינָיו:
יא ששי א־ב וַיְדַבֵּר יהוה אֶל־מֹשֶׁה וְאֶל־אַהֲרֹן לֵאמֹר אֲלֵהֶם: דַּבְּרוּ אֶל־בְּנֵי יִשְׂרָאֵל
ג לֵאמֹר זֹאת הַחַיָּה אֲשֶׁר תֹּאכְלוּ מִכָּל־הַבְּהֵמָה אֲשֶׁר עַל־הָאָרֶץ: כֹּל ׀
מַפְרֶסֶת פַּרְסָה וְשֹׁסַעַת שֶׁסַע פְּרָסֹת מַעֲלַת גֵּרָה בַּבְּהֵמָה אֹתָהּ תֹּאכֵלוּ:
ד אַךְ אֶת־זֶה לֹא תֹאכְלוּ מִמַּעֲלֵי הַגֵּרָה וּמִמַּפְרִסֵי הַפַּרְסָה אֶת־הַגָּמָל כִּי־
ה מַעֲלֵה גֵרָה הוּא וּפַרְסָה אֵינֶנּוּ מַפְרִיס טָמֵא הוּא לָכֶם: וְאֶת־הַשָּׁפָן כִּי־מַעֲלֵה
ו גֵרָה הוּא וּפַרְסָה לֹא יַפְרִיס טָמֵא הוּא לָכֶם: וְאֶת־הָאַרְנֶבֶת כִּי־מַעֲלַת גֵּרָה
ז הִוא וּפַרְסָה לֹא הִפְרִיסָה טְמֵאָה הִוא לָכֶם: וְאֶת־הַחֲזִיר כִּי־מַפְרִיס פַּרְסָה
ח הוּא וְשֹׁסַע שֶׁסַע פַּרְסָה וְהוּא גֵּרָה לֹא־יִגָּר טָמֵא הוּא לָכֶם: מִבְּשָׂרָם לֹא
ט תֹאכֵלוּ וּבְנִבְלָתָם לֹא תִגָּעוּ טְמֵאִים הֵם לָכֶם: אֶת־זֶה תֹּאכְלוּ מִכֹּל
אֲשֶׁר בַּמָּיִם כֹּל אֲשֶׁר־לוֹ סְנַפִּיר וְקַשְׂקֶשֶׂת בַּמַּיִם בַּיַּמִּים וּבַנְּחָלִים אֹתָם

an offering with knowledge and intent, it cannot atone, as it says regarding קָדָשִׁים קַלִּים (*the lesser holy*), לֹא אָכַלְתִּי בְאֹנִי מִמֶּנּוּ, *I have not eaten thereof in my mourning* (*Deut.* 26:14). Although you commanded us to eat the meal offering which is of transitory sanctity, even in a state of mourning, it does not follow that this ruling also applies in the case of permanent sacrifices.

20. וַיִּיטַב בְּעֵינָיו — *It was pleasing in his eyes.* He rejoiced in the good reasoning of his brother and his sons who understood and taught (decided the law) so well.

XI

2. זֹאת הַחַיָּה אֲשֶׁר תֹּאכְלוּ — *These are the living things which you may eat.* Behold, after Israel removed their spiritual crowns (ornaments) which they had attained at the time of the giving of the Torah, and through which they were deemed worthy that the Divine Presence dwell in their midst without (the need for) any intermediary, as it says, בְּכָל הַמָּקוֹם אֲשֶׁר אַזְכִּיר אֶת שְׁמִי אָבוֹא אֵלֶיךָ וּבֵרַכְתִּיךָ, *In every place where I cause My Name to be mentioned I will come to you and bless you* (*Exodus* 20:21), and which shall be in the future (end of days), as it says, *And I will set My Mishkan among you, and My soul shall not abhor you* (26:11), God, the Blessed One, afterward refused to have His Presence dwell among them at all, as it says, כִּי לֹא אֶעֱלֶה בְּקִרְבְּךָ, *For I will not go up in the midst of you* (*Exodus* 33:3). Moses our Teacher (however) achieved through his prayer some amelioration that the Divine Presence would abide among them through the medium of the *Mishkan* (Sanctuary), its furnishings, attendants (servants) and sacrifices, and they merited and attained (the level of) *And the glory of HASHEM appeared unto all the people* (9:23) and to the fire descending from heaven (9:24). Therefore, (God) considered (the need)

NOTES

they were justified in burning the sin offering, given their state of *aninus* (mourning). Moses accepted Aaron's reasoning and was pleased to see the clarity and logic of his brother's thinking which was not beclouded by the tragic death of his two sons.

XI

2. זֹאת הַחַיָּה אֲשֶׁר תֹּאכְלוּ — *These are the living things which you may eat.* God's original intent was to dwell in the midst of the Jewish people without the medium of a Sanctuary or any other form of intermediary between Israel and God. Were it not for the sin of the Golden Calf this would have come to pass and Israel, as a holy nation, would never have withered or perished but would have been everlasting (see notes to the *Sforno* on *Exodus* 19:6). After this grand plan was thwarted, God originally refused to cause His Presence to dwell in the midst of Israel until Moses prevailed upon Him through his prayers to dwell

offering and their elevation-offering before HASHEM? Now that such things befell me — were I to eat this day's sin-offering, would HASHEM approve?"
[20] *Moses heard and he approved.*

11 [1] *HASHEM spoke to Moses and to Aaron, saying to them.* [2] *Speak to the Children of Israel, saying: These are the creatures that you may eat from among all the animals that are upon the earth.* [3] *Everything among the animals that has a split hoof, which is completely separated into double hooves, and that brings up its cud — that one you may eat.* [4] *But this is what you shall not eat from among those that bring up their cud or that have split hooves: the camel, for it brings up its cud, but its hoof is not split — it is unclean to you;* [5] *and the hyrax, for it brings up its cud, but its hoof is not split — it is unclean to you;* [6] *and the hare, for it brings up its cud, but its hoof is not split — it is unclean to you;* [7] *and the pig, for its hoof is split and its hoof is completely separated, but it does not chew its cud — it is unclean to you.* [8] *You shall not eat of their flesh nor shall you touch their carcass — they are unclean to you.*
[9] *This may you eat from everything that is in the water: everything that has fins and scales in the water, in the seas, and in the streams, those*

to remedy their temperament that it be predisposed to be illuminated with the light of everlasting life. This (was to be done) through the regulation (lit., repair) of food and (laws regarding) the reproductive system. (The Torah) prohibits foods which defile (man's) (moral) characteristics and (mental) powers, as it says, *And you shall be defiled through them* (11:43), and as it says, *You shall not make yourselves detestable* (v. 43), and as it says, *Neither shall you defile yourselves with any manner of swarming things, because I am HASHEM that brought you up out of the land of Egypt to be your God; you shall therefore be holy* (vs. 44-45), namely, everlasting, comparable to the Creator, Blessed be He, as it says, *for I am holy* (ibid.). And (He) prohibited a *niddah* (menstruant), a *zavah* (one who has an issue) and a *yoledes* (woman who gave birth) so as to sanctify the seed (of Israel) and purify it from all *tumah*, uncleanness, as it says, *You shall separate the Children of Israel from their tumah that they die not in their tumah when they defile My Mishkan that is in the midst of them* (15:31). And (the Torah) makes mention of (utilizes) the term *tumah* regarding the carcass of a non-kosher animal and beast (vs. 26-28) and regarding the eight swarming things (vs. 29-38) and regarding the carcass of a kosher animal (vs. 39-40) because each of these has (laws of) *tumah* through contact and some through carrying. However, (regarding) those which only defile the soul, and do not make one *tamei* through contact at all, such as fish, fowl, locusts and other crawling things, the term used is שִׁקּוּץ, *detestable*, as it says, *They are a detestable thing to you* (vs. 10-13), and *Is a detestable thing, it shall not be eaten* (v. 41) and *For they are a detestable thing* (v. 42).

NOTES

in the Sanctuary. Our Sages teach us that the laws enumerated in this portion of the Torah (*Shemini*) and those which follow (*Tazria-Metzora*) serve to refine and purify the collective soul and character of Israel, thereby preparing them to receive the *Shechinah*, Divine Presence. The laws of *Kashrus* and the laws of *Niddah*, as well as the laws of purity and uncleanness, are all meant to sanctify the people of Israel, thereby bringing them to a level of holiness which reflects the Holy One Himself. This is the thrust of the *Sforno's* commentary on this verse, and verses 43-44. The *Sforno* then proceeds to explain the difference between the expressions טָמֵא, unclean, and שֶׁקֶץ, *detestable*. He submits that only that which can convey defilement through contact or carrying is referred to as טָמֵא while that which is prohibited but does not physically defile is referred to as שֶׁקֶץ.

י תֹּאכֵלוּ: וְכֹל אֲשֶׁר אֵין־לוֹ סְנַפִּיר וְקַשְׂקֶשֶׂת בַּיַּמִּים וּבַנְּחָלִים מִכֹּל
יא שֶׁרֶץ הַמַּיִם וּמִכֹּל נֶפֶשׁ הַחַיָּה אֲשֶׁר בַּמָּיִם שֶׁקֶץ הֵם לָכֶם: וְשֶׁקֶץ יִהְיוּ
יב לָכֶם מִבְּשָׂרָם לֹא תֹאכֵלוּ וְאֶת־נִבְלָתָם תְּשַׁקֵּצוּ: כֹּל אֲשֶׁר אֵין־לוֹ
יג סְנַפִּיר וְקַשְׂקֶשֶׂת בַּמָּיִם שֶׁקֶץ הוּא לָכֶם: וְאֶת־אֵלֶּה תְּשַׁקְּצוּ מִן־הָעוֹף
לֹא יֵאָכְלוּ שֶׁקֶץ הֵם אֶת־הַנֶּשֶׁר וְאֶת־הַפֶּרֶס וְאֵת הָעָזְנִיָּה:
יד־טו־טז וְאֶת־הַדָּאָה וְאֶת־הָאַיָּה לְמִינָהּ: אֵת כָּל־עֹרֵב לְמִינוֹ: וְאֵת בַּת הַיַּעֲנָה
יז וְאֶת־הַתַּחְמָס וְאֶת־הַשָּׁחַף וְאֶת־הַנֵּץ לְמִינֵהוּ: וְאֶת־הַכּוֹס וְאֶת־
יח הַשָּׁלָךְ וְאֶת־הַיַּנְשׁוּף: וְאֶת־הַתִּנְשֶׁמֶת וְאֶת־הַקָּאָת וְאֶת־הָרָחָם:
יט־כ וְאֵת הַחֲסִידָה הָאֲנָפָה לְמִינָהּ וְאֶת־הַדּוּכִיפַת וְאֶת־הָעֲטַלֵּף: כֹּל
כא שֶׁרֶץ הָעוֹף הַהֹלֵךְ עַל־אַרְבַּע שֶׁקֶץ הוּא לָכֶם: אַךְ אֶת־זֶה תֹּאכְלוּ
מִכֹּל שֶׁרֶץ הָעוֹף הַהֹלֵךְ עַל־אַרְבַּע אֲשֶׁר־°לא כְרָעַיִם מִמַּעַל °לוֹ ק׳
כב לְרַגְלָיו לְנַתֵּר בָּהֵן עַל־הָאָרֶץ: אֶת־אֵלֶּה מֵהֶם תֹּאכֵלוּ אֶת־הָאַרְבֶּה
לְמִינוֹ וְאֶת־הַסָּלְעָם לְמִינֵהוּ וְאֶת־הַחַרְגֹּל לְמִינֵהוּ וְאֶת־הֶחָגָב
כג לְמִינֵהוּ: וְכֹל שֶׁרֶץ הָעוֹף אֲשֶׁר־לוֹ אַרְבַּע רַגְלָיִם שֶׁקֶץ הוּא לָכֶם:
כד־כה וּלְאֵלֶּה תִּטַּמָּאוּ כָּל־הַנֹּגֵעַ בְּנִבְלָתָם יִטְמָא עַד־הָעָרֶב: וְכָל־הַנֹּשֵׂא
כו מִנִּבְלָתָם יְכַבֵּס בְּגָדָיו וְטָמֵא עַד־הָעָרֶב: לְכָל־הַבְּהֵמָה אֲשֶׁר הִוא
מַפְרֶסֶת פַּרְסָה וְשֶׁסַע ׀ אֵינֶנָּה שֹׁסַעַת וְגֵרָה אֵינֶנָּה מַעֲלָה טְמֵאִים הֵם
כז לָכֶם כָּל־הַנֹּגֵעַ בָּהֶם יִטְמָא: וְכֹל ׀ הוֹלֵךְ עַל־כַּפָּיו בְּכָל־הַחַיָּה הַהֹלֶכֶת
עַל־אַרְבַּע טְמֵאִים הֵם לָכֶם כָּל־הַנֹּגֵעַ בְּנִבְלָתָם יִטְמָא עַד־הָעָרֶב:
כח וְהַנֹּשֵׂא אֶת־נִבְלָתָם יְכַבֵּס בְּגָדָיו וְטָמֵא עַד־הָעָרֶב טְמֵאִים הֵמָּה לָכֶם:
כט וְזֶה לָכֶם הַטָּמֵא בַּשֶּׁרֶץ הַשֹּׁרֵץ עַל־הָאָרֶץ
ל הַחֹלֶד וְהָעַכְבָּר וְהַצָּב לְמִינֵהוּ: וְהָאֲנָקָה וְהַכֹּחַ וְהַלְּטָאָה וְהַחֹמֶט
לא וְהַתִּנְשָׁמֶת: אֵלֶּה הַטְּמֵאִים לָכֶם בְּכָל־הַשָּׁרֶץ כָּל־הַנֹּגֵעַ בָּהֶם בְּמֹתָם
לב יִטְמָא עַד־הָעָרֶב: וְכֹל אֲשֶׁר־יִפֹּל עָלָיו מֵהֶם ׀ בְּמֹתָם יִטְמָא
מִכָּל־כְּלִי־עֵץ אוֹ בֶגֶד אוֹ־עוֹר אוֹ שָׂק כָּל־כְּלִי אֲשֶׁר־יֵעָשֶׂה מְלָאכָה
לג בָּהֶם בַּמַּיִם יוּבָא וְטָמֵא עַד־הָעֶרֶב וְטָהֵר: וְכָל־כְּלִי־חֶרֶשׂ אֲשֶׁר־ שביעי
יִפֹּל מֵהֶם אֶל־תּוֹכוֹ כֹּל אֲשֶׁר בְּתוֹכוֹ יִטְמָא וְאֹתוֹ תִשְׁבֹּרוּ:
לד מִכָּל־הָאֹכֶל אֲשֶׁר יֵאָכֵל אֲשֶׁר יָבוֹא עָלָיו מַיִם יִטְמָא וְכָל־מַשְׁקֶה
לה אֲשֶׁר יִשָּׁתֶה בְּכָל־כְּלִי יִטְמָא: וְכֹל אֲשֶׁר־יִפֹּל מִנִּבְלָתָם ׀ עָלָיו
לו יִטְמָא תַּנּוּר וְכִירַיִם יֻתָּץ טְמֵאִים הֵם וּטְמֵאִים יִהְיוּ לָכֶם: אַךְ מַעְיָן
לז וּבוֹר מִקְוֵה־מַיִם יִהְיֶה טָהוֹר וְנֹגֵעַ בְּנִבְלָתָם יִטְמָא: וְכִי יִפֹּל
לח מִנִּבְלָתָם עַל־כָּל־זֶרַע זֵרוּעַ אֲשֶׁר יִזָּרֵעַ טָהוֹר הוּא: וְכִי יֻתַּן־מַיִם
לט עַל־זֶרַע וְנָפַל מִנִּבְלָתָם עָלָיו טָמֵא הוּא לָכֶם: וְכִי
יָמוּת מִן־הַבְּהֵמָה אֲשֶׁר־הִיא לָכֶם לְאָכְלָה הַנֹּגֵעַ בְּנִבְלָתָהּ יִטְמָא

may you eat. 10 And everything that does not have fins and scales in the seas and in
the streams — from all that teems in the water, and from all living creatures in the
water — they are an abomination to you. 11 And they shall remain an abomination
to you; you shall not eat of their flesh and you shall abominate their carcass.
12 Everything that does not have fins and scales in the water — it is an abomination
to you.

13 These shall you abominate from among the birds, they may not be eaten — they
are an abomination: the nesher, the peres, the ozniah; 14 the daah and the ayah
according to its kind; 15 every orev according to its kind; 16 the bas hayaanah, the
tachmos, the shachaf, and the netz according to its kind; 17 the kos, the shalach, and
the yanshuf; 18 the tinshemes, the kaas, and the racham; 19 the chasidah, the
anafah according to its kind, the duchifas, and the atalef.

20 Every flying teeming creature that walks on four legs — it is an abomination to
you. 21 Only this may you eat from among all flying teeming creatures that walk on
four legs: one that has jumping legs above its legs, with which to spring upon the
earth. 22 You may eat these from among them: the arbeh according to its kind; the
sal'am according to its kind, the chargol according to its kind, and the chagav
according to its kind. 23 Every flying teeming thing that has four legs — it is an
abomination to you.

24 You become contaminated through the following — anyone who touches their
carcass becomes contaminated until evening; 25 and anyone who carries their
carcass shall immerse his clothing and be contaminated until evening — 26 every
animal that has split hooves that are not completely split, or does not chew its cud,
they are contaminated to you; whoever touches them becomes contaminated.
27 And every one that walks on its paws, among all animals that walk on four legs,
they are contaminated to you; whoever touches their carcass shall be
contaminated until evening. 28 One who carries their carcass shall immerse his
clothing and be contaminated until evening; they are contaminated to you.

29 These are the contaminated ones among the teeming animals that teem upon
the earth: the choled, the achbar, and the tzav according to its variety; 30 the
anakah, the koach, and the letaah; and the chomet and the tinshemes. 31 Only these
are contaminated to you among all the teeming animals; anyone who touches them
when they are dead shall be contaminated until evening; 32 and when they are
dead, anything upon which part of them will fall shall become contaminated,
whether it is a wooden utensil, a garment, leather, or sackcloth — any utensil with
which work is done — shall be brought into the water, and remain contaminated
until evening, and then become cleansed.

33 Any earthenware utensil into whose interior one of them will fall, everything
in it shall become contaminated — and you shall break it — 34 of any food that is
edible, upon which water comes, shall become contaminated; and any beverage
that can be drunk, in any vessel, shall become contaminated. 35 Anything upon
which part of their carcass may fall shall be contaminated — an oven or a stove
shall be smashed — they are contaminated and they shall remain contaminated to
you — 36 only a spring or a cistern, a gathering of water, shall remain pure — but one
who touches their carcass shall become contaminated. 37 And if its carcass will fall
upon any edible seed that has been planted, it remains pure. 38 But if water had been
placed upon a seed and then their carcass falls upon it, it is contaminated to you.

39 If an animal that you may eat has died, one who touches its carcass shall

מ עַד־הָעָרֶב: וְהָאֹכֵל מִנִּבְלָתָהּ יְכַבֵּס בְּגָדָיו וְטָמֵא עַד־הָעָרֶב וְהַנֹּשֵׂא
מא אֶת־נִבְלָתָהּ יְכַבֵּס בְּגָדָיו וְטָמֵא עַד־הָעָרֶב: וְכָל־הַשֶּׁרֶץ הַשֹּׁרֵץ
מב עַל־הָאָרֶץ שֶׁקֶץ הוּא לֹא יֵאָכֵל: כֹּל הוֹלֵךְ עַל־*גָּחוֹן וְכֹל | הוֹלֵךְ — *יו׳ דגחון רבתי
עַל־אַרְבַּע עַד כָּל־מַרְבֵּה רַגְלַיִם לְכָל־הַשֶּׁרֶץ הַשֹּׁרֵץ עַל־הָאָרֶץ לֹא — והיא חצי התורה באותיות
מג תֹאכְלוּם כִּי־שֶׁקֶץ הֵם: אַל־תְּשַׁקְּצוּ אֶת־נַפְשֹׁתֵיכֶם בְּכָל־הַשֶּׁרֶץ הַשֹּׁרֵץ
מד וְלֹא תִטַּמְּאוּ בָּהֶם וְנִטְמֵתֶם בָּם: כִּי אֲנִי יהוה אֱלֹהֵיכֶם וְהִתְקַדִּשְׁתֶּם
וִהְיִיתֶם קְדֹשִׁים כִּי קָדוֹשׁ אָנִי וְלֹא תְטַמְּאוּ אֶת־נַפְשֹׁתֵיכֶם בְּכָל־הַשֶּׁרֶץ
מה הָרֹמֵשׂ עַל־הָאָרֶץ: כִּי | אֲנִי יהוה הַמַּעֲלֶה אֶתְכֶם מֵאֶרֶץ מִצְרַיִם לִהְיֹת — מפטיר
מו לָכֶם לֵאלֹהִים וִהְיִיתֶם קְדֹשִׁים כִּי קָדוֹשׁ אָנִי: זֹאת תּוֹרַת הַבְּהֵמָה וְהָעוֹף
וְכֹל נֶפֶשׁ הַחַיָּה הָרֹמֶשֶׂת בַּמָּיִם וּלְכָל־נֶפֶשׁ הַשֹּׁרֶצֶת עַל־הָאָרֶץ:
מז לְהַבְדִּיל בֵּין הַטָּמֵא וּבֵין הַטָּהֹר וּבֵין הַחַיָּה הַנֶּאֱכֶלֶת וּבֵין הַחַיָּה אֲשֶׁר
לֹא תֵאָכֵל:

43-44. וְלֹא תִטַּמְּאוּ בָּהֶם וְנִטְמֵתֶם בָּם... כִּי אֲנִי ה׳ אֱלֹהֵיכֶם וְהִתְקַדִּשְׁתֶּם — *You shall not make yourselves tamei through them that you shall become tamei thereby ... For I am HASHEM your God; sanctify yourselves.* Do not make yourselves unclean through them in a manner (that will result in) your becoming unclean and vacuous. This will occur if you eat them; for since *I am your God* I desire that you sanctify yourselves and prepare yourselves for holiness.

וִהְיִיתֶם קְדֹשִׁים כִּי קָדוֹשׁ אָנִי — *And be holy, for I am holy* ... in order that you be holy and everlasting by acknowledging your Creator and walking in His ways. Now this I desire so that you shall become similar to Me, *for I am holy.* All this you will realize when you sanctify yourselves and take care (not to partake) of prohibited foods, as (our Sages) say,

NOTES

44. וִהְיִיתֶם קְדֹשִׁים — *And be holy.* The concept that holiness insures the everlasting nature of Israel was developed by the *Sforno* in *Exodus* 15:11 and 19:6. See his commentary and notes there which elucidate his commentary here.

45. כִּי אֲנִי ה׳ הַמַּעֲלֶה אֶתְכֶם מֵאֶרֶץ מִצְרַיִם לִהְיֹת לָכֶם לֵאלֹהִים — *For I am HASHEM Who brought you up*

become contaminated until evening. [40] *And one who eats from its carcass shall immerse his clothing and remain contaminated until evening; and one who carries its carcass shall immerse his clothing and remain contaminated until evening.*

[41] *Every teeming creature that teems upon the ground — it is an abomination, it shall not be eaten.* [42] *Everything that creeps on its belly, and everything that walks on four legs, up to those with numerous legs, among all the teeming things that teem upon the earth, you may not eat them, for they are an abomination.* [43] *Do not make yourselves abominable by means of any teeming thing; do not contaminate yourselves through them lest you become contaminated through them.*

[44] *For I am* Hashem *your God — you are to sanctify yourselves and you shall become holy, for I am holy; and you shall not contaminate yourselves through any teeming thing that creeps on the earth.* [45] *For I am* Hashem *Who elevates you from the land of Egypt to be a God unto you; you shall be holy, for I am holy.*

[46] *This is the law of the animal, the bird, every living creature that swarms in the water, and for every creature that teems on the ground;* [47] *to distinguish between the contaminated and the pure, and between the creature that may be eaten and the creature that may not be eaten.*

"A man sanctifies himself a little, and he is sanctified (by God) in great measure" (*Yoma* 39a).

45. כִּי אֲנִי ה׳ הַמַּעֲלֶה אֶתְכֶם מֵאֶרֶץ מִצְרַיִם לִהְיֹת לָכֶם לֵאלֹהִים — *For I am* Hashem *Who brought you up out of the land of Egypt to be your God.* And it is proper that you make this effort to sanctify (yourselves) and to be holy so as to fulfill My desire, for indeed, My intent in bringing you out from the land of Egypt was that you attain this (degree of holiness), that I shall be a God to you without any intermediary, and you (in turn) shall be holy and everlasting, resembling Me in characteristics (conduct) and concepts, *for I am holy.*

46. זֹאת תּוֹרַת הַבְּהֵמָה וְהָעוֹף — *This is the law of the beast and of the fowl.* This is the purpose and reason for the food prohibitions enumerated (mentioned) above.

NOTES

out of the land of Egypt to be your God. Since God wishes us to be holy, thereby "imitating him," He gave us the laws of food and of purity which help us lead holy lives. That was His intention in bringing us out of Egypt. Redemption was for the purpose of becoming a *holy nation.*

פרשת תזריע

יב

א-ב וַיְדַבֵּ֥ר יהו֖ה אֶל־מֹשֶׁ֥ה לֵּאמֹֽר: דַּבֵּ֞ר אֶל־בְּנֵ֤י יִשְׂרָאֵל֙ לֵאמֹ֔ר אִשָּׁה֙ כִּ֣י

ג תַזְרִ֔יעַ וְיָלְדָ֖ה זָכָ֑ר וְטָֽמְאָה֙ שִׁבְעַ֣ת יָמִ֔ים כִּימֵ֛י נִדַּ֥ת דְּוֺתָ֖הּ תִּטְמָֽא: וּבַיּ֖וֹם

ד הַשְּׁמִינִ֑י יִמּ֖וֹל בְּשַׂ֥ר עָרְלָתֽוֹ: וּשְׁלֹשִׁ֥ים יוֹם֙ וּשְׁלֹ֣שֶׁת יָמִ֔ים תֵּשֵׁ֖ב בִּדְמֵ֣י

טׇהֳרָ֑ה בְּכׇל־קֹ֣דֶשׁ לֹֽא־תִגָּ֗ע וְאֶל־הַמִּקְדָּשׁ֙ לֹ֣א תָבֹ֔א עַד־מְלֹ֖את יְמֵ֥י

ה טׇהֳרָֽהּ: וְאִם־נְקֵבָ֣ה תֵלֵ֔ד וְטָֽמְאָ֥ה שְׁבֻעַ֖יִם כְּנִדָּתָ֑הּ וְשִׁשִּׁ֥ים יוֹם֙ וְשֵׁ֣שֶׁת

ו יָמִ֔ים תֵּשֵׁ֖ב עַל־דְּמֵ֥י טׇהֳרָֽה: וּבִמְלֹ֣את ׀ יְמֵ֣י טׇהֳרָ֗הּ לְבֵן֙ א֣וֹ לְבַ֔ת תָּבִ֞יא

כֶּ֤בֶשׂ בֶּן־שְׁנָתוֹ֙ לְעֹלָ֔ה וּבֶן־יוֹנָ֥ה אוֹ־תֹ֖ר לְחַטָּ֑את אֶל־פֶּ֥תַח אֹֽהֶל־מוֹעֵ֖ד

ז אֶל־הַכֹּהֵֽן: וְהִקְרִיב֞וֹ לִפְנֵ֤י יהוה֙ וְכִפֶּ֣ר עָלֶ֔יהָ וְטָֽהֲרָ֖ה מִמְּקֹ֣ר דָּמֶ֑יהָ זֹ֤את

ח תּוֹרַת֙ הַיֹּלֶ֔דֶת לַזָּכָ֖ר א֥וֹ לַנְּקֵבָֽה: וְאִם־לֹ֨א תִמְצָ֣א יָדָהּ֮ דֵּ֣י שֶׂה֒ וְלָֽקְחָ֣ה

שְׁתֵּֽי־תֹרִ֗ים א֤וֹ שְׁנֵי֙ בְּנֵ֣י יוֹנָ֔ה אֶחָ֥ד לְעֹלָ֖ה וְאֶחָ֣ד לְחַטָּ֑את וְכִפֶּ֥ר עָלֶ֛יהָ

הַכֹּהֵ֖ן וְטָהֵֽרָה:

XII

2. אִשָּׁה כִּי תַזְרִיעַ וְיָלְדָה זָכָר — *If a woman caused fructification of seed and gives birth to a male.* (Our Sages) have said, "If a woman emits seed first she bears a male" (*Niddah* 31a). This means that the seed of the woman, which is the liquid emitted by her at times during intercourse, plays no role in the formation of the male fetus at all; rather her (uterine) blood is worked upon and jells in the seed of the male. When (however) her liquid seed enters her jelled blood, there is an excess of liquid (seed) and the child will be female.

כִּימֵי נִדַּת דְּוֺתָהּ — *As the days of the niddos (impurity) of the sickness.* Because in the initial seven days, the *niddah* blood, which has not yet degenerated nor lost its form of *tumah* is stimulated.

3. וּבַיּוֹם הַשְּׁמִינִי יִמּוֹל — *And on the eighth day there shall be circumcised.* For then the unclean *niddah* blood from which the child received his nourishment in the womb of his mother, has been consumed (lit., digested), and the child is now (sufficiently) pure to enter the holy covenant.

NOTES

XII

2. אִשָּׁה כִּי תַזְרִיעַ וְיָלְדָה זָכָר — *If a woman caused fructification of seed and gives birth to a male.* The saying of our Sages, quoted by the *Sforno,* is based upon their interpretation of this verse. If a woman emits seed (תַזְרִיעַ) first, then the result will be that she will give birth to a male child (וְיָלְדָה זָכָר). The *Sforno,* who was a doctor, explains the reason for this as follows: At the time of ovulation, the woman releases her seed which loses a degree of potency as it jells in the seed of the male, being more dominant since it is released later than hers. However, if she ovulates after the male has emitted his seed, her liquid seed is dominant and will result in the conception of a female.

Recent medical research has established that the acid in the vaginal canal can destroy the male Y chromosome, resulting in the male X chromosome impregnating the egg whereby the offspring will be a female. However, at the time of ovulation, the alkaline which is secreted by the female neutralizes the acid, thereby permitting the Y chromosome to come into play and impregnate the woman, resulting in a male offspring. This bears out the statement of our Sages that if the woman emits her seed first (i.e., ovulates and thereby ejects alkaline), the chances of a male child being conceived are far greater. [I am indebted to Dr. Fred Rosner and Rabbi David Cohen for their assistance in the preparation of this note.]

כִּימֵי נִדַּת דְּוֺתָהּ — *As the days of the niddos (impurity) of the sickness.* The *Sforno* explains the reason for the seven-day period of impurity. Being that the impure blood is still viable, the woman remains *tamei.* This also explains the reason for the twofold expression וְטָֽמְאָה, *and she shall be in an impure condition,* and תִּטְמָא which has the same meaning and is seemingly redundant. How-

PARASHAS TAZRIA

12
[1] HASHEM *spoke to Moses, saying:* [2] *Speak to the Children of Israel, saying:When a woman conceives and gives birth to a male, she shall be contaminated for a seven-day period, as during the days of her separation infirmity shall she be contaminated.* [3] *On the eighth day, the flesh of his foreskin shall be circumcised.* [4] *For thirty-three days she shall remain in blood of purity; she may not touch anything sacred and she may not enter the Sanctuary, until the completion of her days of purity.* [5] *If she gives birth to a female, she shall be contaminated for two weeks, as during her separation; and for sixty-six days she shall remain in blood of purity.*

[6] *Upon the completion of the days of her purity for a son or for a daughter, she shall bring a sheep within its first year for an elevation-offering, and a young dove or a turtledove for a sin-offering, to the entrance of the Tent of Meeting, to the Kohen.* [7] *He shall offer it before* HASHEM *and atone for her, and she becomes purified from the source of her blood; this is the law of one who gives birth to a male or to a female.* [8] *But if she cannot afford a sheep, then she shall take two turtledoves or two young doves, one for an elevation-offering and one for a sin-offering; and the Kohen shall provide atonement for her and she shall become purified.*

4. בִּדְמֵי טָהֳרָה — *In the blood of purification.* Because the *niddah* blood is not from her present menstrual period, but from those periods which preceded her pregnancy, (and they) already degenerated and no longer have the form of the blood (from) those periods of *tumah.*

5. שְׁבֻעַיִם — *Two weeks.* For the aftereffects (of birth) are increased (prolonged) with the birth of a female.

8. וְכִפֶּר עָלֶיהָ — *Shall make atonement for her.* Because all the days that her unclean (blood) flows, her thoughts are concentrated on the reproductive organs and their functioning, (hence) she is not worthy (prepared or geared) to (enter) the Temple or (come into contact) with its sacred objects — until she brings her atonement (offering) and turns (her thoughts) to the holy.

NOTES

ever, the meaning of these two expressions is: She is in an impure state (וְטָמְאָה) for seven days because her blood has as yet not been purified, and therefore תִּטְמָא — she remains in an impure state since her condition has not changed.

3. וּבַיּוֹם הַשְּׁמִינִי יִמּוֹל — *And on the eighth day there shall be circumcised.* The *Sforno* explains why the Torah finds it necessary to mention *bris milah, the covenant of circumcision,* in this *parashah* which deals with the ritual laws pertaining to the woman, not the child! His answer is that the nature of the mother's blood, which is the subject of this chapter, also has an effect upon the status and readiness of the child. Only after the impure blood from which the child received his nourishment in the womb has been eliminated is he fit to enter the holy covenant of circumcision.

4. בִּדְמֵי טָהֳרָה — *In the blood of purification.* The *Sforno* explains the reason for this law that any blood seen by the woman during the thirty-three-day period after the birth of a male child is considered טָהוֹר, *clean, pure.* See *Rashi.* [This passage does not reflect the *halachah* in practice today.]

8. וְכִפֶּר עָלֶיהָ — *Shall make atonement for her.* The *Sforno* explains the reason for this waiting period before the woman can bring her sacrifices and once again qualify to enter the Temple precincts and come into contact with the sacred. Although she is physically ready and ritually clean, mentally she is not yet geared to concentrate on the holy. Since the sacred demands כַּוָּנָה, *intent,* she must wait until her thoughts are sufficiently predisposed to focus on the non-physical, namely, the spiritual and the holy.

יג
א־ב וַיְדַבֵּר יהוה אֶל־מֹשֶׁה וְאֶל־אַהֲרֹן לֵאמֹר: אָדָם כִּי־יִהְיֶה בְעוֹר־בְּשָׂרוֹ
שְׂאֵת אוֹ־סַפַּחַת אוֹ בַהֶרֶת וְהָיָה בְעוֹר־בְּשָׂרוֹ לְנֶגַע צָרָעַת וְהוּבָא אֶל־
ג אַהֲרֹן הַכֹּהֵן אוֹ אֶל־אַחַד מִבָּנָיו הַכֹּהֲנִים: וְרָאָה הַכֹּהֵן אֶת־הַנֶּגַע בְּעוֹר־
הַבָּשָׂר וְשֵׂעָר בַּנֶּגַע הָפַךְ לָבָן וּמַרְאֵה הַנֶּגַע עָמֹק מֵעוֹר בְּשָׂרוֹ נֶגַע צָרַעַת
ד הוּא וְרָאָהוּ הַכֹּהֵן וְטִמֵּא אֹתוֹ: וְאִם־בַּהֶרֶת לְבָנָה הִוא בְּעוֹר בְּשָׂרוֹ
ה׳ רפה וְעָמֹק אֵין־מַרְאֶהָ מִן־הָעוֹר וּשְׂעָרָה לֹא־הָפַךְ לָבָן וְהִסְגִּיר הַכֹּהֵן אֶת־
ה הַנֶּגַע שִׁבְעַת יָמִים: וְרָאָהוּ הַכֹּהֵן בַּיּוֹם הַשְּׁבִיעִי וְהִנֵּה הַנֶּגַע עָמַד בְּעֵינָיו

XIII

2. אָדָם כִּי יִהְיֶה בְעוֹר בְּשָׂרוֹ — *When a man shall have in the skin of his flesh.* Now this happens most frequently if the seed does not become purified from the unclean blood (lit., blood of *niddos*).

שְׂאֵת אוֹ סַפַּחַת אוֹ בַהֶרֶת — *A rising or a scab or a bright spot.* These are all types of leprosy and their appearance is white, as tradition teaches us. Among them there is no variety of leprosy discussed by doctors (today), except for the *morphia albaram* (white mole) and the scall. Indeed, (regarding) other types of severe leprosy of which they (the doctors) have told us, (such as) cancerous spreading over the entire body, which tend (in color) toward red and black, the Torah does not (declare) them *tamei* at all. For only these four appearances (of leprosy) of which our Sages tell us — namely a *rising*, and its sub-species, a *bright spot*, and its sub-species — come as an admonition for iniquity, as (our Sages) state, "Any person who has one of these four appearances (of leprosy), it is naught but an altar of atonement" (*Berachos* 5b). But other types of leprosy which the doctors speak of are not (considered) as an altar of atonement among our people, (but are a result) of ultimate debasement, God forbid, as are the other evil diseases of Egypt (*Deut.* 7:15) or they are due to (improper) deviations in (one's) eating and drinking habits (lit., behavior) and other (similar aberrations); (but) these are not (considered) *tamei* at all.

וְהוּבָא — *Then he shall be brought.* (Regarding) one who goes to a place to be worked upon (i.e., to receive the act of another) the term בָּא, *come*, is not used; rather it is termed מוּבָא, *to be brought*, similar to, לִרְקָמוֹת תּוּבַל לַמֶּלֶךְ . . . רֵעוֹתֶיהָ מוּבָאוֹת לָךְ, *She shall be brought to the king . . . her companions shall be brought to you* (*Psalms* 45:15), (also) וְהִגִּישׁוֹ אֲדֹנָיו, *Then his master shall bring him* (*Exodus* 21:6), (also) וְהֵבִיא הָאִישׁ אֶת אִשְׁתּוֹ, *Then shall the man bring his wife* (*Numbers* 5:15). The reverse (being) וְנִגְּשׁוּ אֶל הַמִּשְׁפָּט, *And they "come" unto judgment* (*Deut.* 25:1), (and) וְנִקְרַב בַּעַל הַבַּיִת, *The master of the house "shall come" near*

NOTES

XIII

2. אָדָם כִּי יִהְיֶה בְעוֹר בְּשָׂרוֹ — *When a man shall have in the skin of his flesh.* The *Sforno* is explaining the link between the previous chapter, which discusses the status of the woman who has given birth, with this chapter which deals with various נְגָעִים, *afflictions.*

שְׂאֵת אוֹ סַפַּחַת אוֹ בַהֶרֶת — *A rising or a scab or a bright spot.* The *Sforno* explains that the afflictions of leprosy which make a person *tamei*, unclean, are not connected with those afflictions which may be far more severe physically (in nature) than the four which our Sages have listed as causing *tumah*, uncleanness. One must not confuse *tumah* with physical illness. They are separate, distinct and unrelated. *Tumah* is caused only by those afflictions which the Torah has ordained. As the *Sforno* will explain later, these four types of leprosy are visited upon man, as are the afflictions of garments and houses, for the purpose of alerting him to his shortcomings in the hope that he will repent and improve his behavior. That is why the Sages refer to them as "an altar of atonement," for through the suffering experienced by the victim, he will repent and God will forgive him.

וְהוּבָא — *Then he shall be brought.* The word וְהוּבָא is interpreted by the *Sforno* as being in the *huphal* form — the passive recipient of the causative *hiphil*. The afflicted person does not "come" on his own volition to the *Kohen* — he is brought. How-

13
[1] *Hashem spoke to Moses and to Aaron, saying:* [2] *If a person will have on
the skin of his flesh a s'eis, or a sapachas, or a baheres, and it will become a tzaraas affliction on the skin of his flesh, he shall be brought to Aaron
the Kohen, or to one of his sons the Kohanim.* [3] *The Kohen shall look at the
affliction on the skin of his flesh: If hair in the affliction has changed to white,
and the affliction's appearance is deeper than the skin of the flesh — it is a
tzaraas affliction; the Kohen shall look at it and declare him contaminated.*
[4] *If it is a white baheres on the skin of his flesh, and its appearance is not
deeper than the skin, and its hair has not changed to white, then the Kohen
shall quarantine the affliction for a seven-day period.* [5] *The Kohen shall look
at it on the seventh day, and behold! — the affliction retained its color,*

(*Exodus* 22:7) (and) עַד הָאֱלֹהִים יָבֹא דְּבַר שְׁנֵיהֶם, *The cause of both parties "shall come" before the judges* (ibid. 8).

3. נֶגַע צָרַעַת הוּא — *It is an affliction of leprosy.* Behold, at times (the Torah) says, נֶגַע צָרַעַת הוּא, *It is an affliction of leprosy*, and at other times, צָרַעַת הִיא, *It is leprosy* (v. 8), and at times, צָרַעַת נוֹשֶׁנֶת הִוא, *It is an old leprosy* (v. 11), and at times נֶגַע הוּא, *It is an affliction* (v. 22). (The reason for this) is that leprosy, as is true of other illnesses, has periods of inception, of increase and of completeness and when the ailment is cured, (it is preceded by) a period of recession. The inception is called נֶגַע, *affliction*; when it worsens it is called נֶגַע צָרַעַת, *affliction of leprosy*; when full blown it is called צָרַעַת, *leprosy*; when it becomes established (lit., old) it is called צָרַעַת נוֹשֶׁנֶת, *an old leprosy*, and when it recedes it is said נִרְפָּא הַנֶּגַע, *the affliction is healed* (14:48), and נִרְפָּא הַנֶּתֶק, *the scall is healed* (v. 37). Now since this kind of ailment (is inflicted) as a punishment, as our Sages say, "It is only an altar of atonement" (*Berachos* 5b), a time of isolation is given to arouse him to repent, as it says, וַיִּגֶל אָזְנָם לַמּוּסָר וַיֹּאמֶר כִּי יְשׁוּבוּן מֵאָוֶן, *He opens also their ear to discipline and commands that they return from iniquity* (*Job* 36:10).

4. וְעָמֹק אֵין מַרְאֶהָ מִן הָעוֹר — *And the appearance thereof is not deeper than the skin.* Although (our Sages) said, "Every white color is deep, just as anything illuminated by the sun is deeper than the shadow" (*Shevuos* 6b); nonetheless, since the skin is also, to an extent, part of the white, (hence) not every white (affliction) is deeper than it (the skin) unless it is a whiter shade than the skin. (The result is) that the whiteness of the skin relative to it (the affliction) will be as that of the shadow to the sunlight.

5. וְרָאָהוּ הַכֹּהֵן — *And the Kohen shall look on him.* It is an enactment of Scriptures (גְּזֵרַת

NOTES

ever, he is brought for his own benefit, to be cleansed and purified. The examples cited by the *Sforno* all refer to instances where a person is brought by another, unwillingly in certain cases such as the Hebrew slave and the wife suspected of infidelity, but ultimately for their own good as in the case of the leper. The *Sforno* points out that when the Torah speaks of one who comes voluntarily, and not necessarily for his own benefit, the verb used is not in the *hiphil* or the *huphal* but in the *kal* or *niphal*, i.e., ונקרב ונגשו, יבא.

3. נֶגַע צָרַעַת הוּא — *It is an affliction of leprosy.* The *Sforno* amplifies the thought developed in v. 2 that the period of הֶסְגֵּר, when the afflicted person is "shut up" and isolated from society, is for the purpose of contemplation and self-examination, which brings him eventually to תְּשׁוּבָה, *repentance.*

4. וְעָמֹק אֵין מַרְאֶהָ מִן הָעוֹר — *And the appearance thereof is not deeper than the skin.* The *Sforno* resolves the seeming discrepancy between verses 3 and 4. *Rashi*, commenting on verse 4, says: "I do not know the meaning of this." He refers to the fact that in verse 3 he had stated that the white spot is *always* deeper in appearance than the surrounding skin, therefore he cannot understand why verse 4 speaks of an instance of the white spot *not* being deeper in appearance than the skin. The *Sforno*, however, explains that it depends upon the relative shades of whiteness between the skin and the נֶגַע, *affliction.* Only if the skin is darker will the white spot appear deeper but if the skin also takes on the white hue of the affliction, then the נֶגַע will not appear deeper than the skin.

5. וְרָאָהוּ הַכֹּהֵן — *And the Kohen shall look on him.*

שני ו לֹא־פָשָׂה הַנֶּגַע בָּעוֹר וְהִסְגִּירוֹ הַכֹּהֵן שִׁבְעַת יָמִים שֵׁנִית: וְרָאָה הַכֹּהֵן
אֹתוֹ בַּיּוֹם הַשְּׁבִיעִי שֵׁנִית וְהִנֵּה כֵּהָה הַנֶּגַע וְלֹא־פָשָׂה הַנֶּגַע בָּעוֹר וְטִהֲרוֹ
ז הַכֹּהֵן מִסְפַּחַת הִוא וְכִבֶּס בְּגָדָיו וְטָהֵר: וְאִם־פָּשֹׂה תִפְשֶׂה הַמִּסְפַּחַת
ח בָּעוֹר אַחֲרֵי הֵרָאֹתוֹ אֶל־הַכֹּהֵן לְטָהֳרָתוֹ וְנִרְאָה שֵׁנִית אֶל־הַכֹּהֵן: וְרָאָה
הַכֹּהֵן וְהִנֵּה פָּשְׂתָה הַמִּסְפַּחַת בָּעוֹר וְטִמְּאוֹ הַכֹּהֵן צָרַעַת הִוא:
ט־י נֶגַע צָרַעַת כִּי תִהְיֶה בְּאָדָם וְהוּבָא אֶל־הַכֹּהֵן: וְרָאָה הַכֹּהֵן וְהִנֵּה
שְׂאֵת־לְבָנָה בָּעוֹר וְהִיא הָפְכָה שֵׂעָר לָבָן וּמִחְיַת בָּשָׂר חַי בַּשְׂאֵת:
יא צָרַעַת נוֹשֶׁנֶת הִוא בְּעוֹר בְּשָׂרוֹ וְטִמְּאוֹ הַכֹּהֵן לֹא יַסְגִּרֶנּוּ כִּי טָמֵא הוּא:
יב וְאִם־פָּרוֹחַ תִּפְרַח הַצָּרַעַת בָּעוֹר וְכִסְּתָה הַצָּרַעַת אֵת כָּל־עוֹר הַנֶּגַע
יג מֵרֹאשׁוֹ וְעַד־רַגְלָיו לְכָל־מַרְאֵה עֵינֵי הַכֹּהֵן: וְרָאָה הַכֹּהֵן וְהִנֵּה כִסְּתָה
יד הַצָּרַעַת אֶת־כָּל־בְּשָׂרוֹ וְטִהַר אֶת־הַנָּגַע כֻּלּוֹ הָפַךְ לָבָן טָהוֹר הוּא: וּבְיוֹם
טו הֵרָאוֹת בּוֹ בָּשָׂר חַי יִטְמָא: וְרָאָה הַכֹּהֵן אֶת־הַבָּשָׂר הַחַי וְטִמְּאוֹ הַבָּשָׂר
טז הַחַי טָמֵא הוּא צָרַעַת הוּא: אוֹ כִי יָשׁוּב הַבָּשָׂר הַחַי וְנֶהְפַּךְ לְלָבָן וּבָא
יז אֶל־הַכֹּהֵן: וְרָאָהוּ הַכֹּהֵן וְהִנֵּה נֶהְפַּךְ הַנֶּגַע לְלָבָן וְטִהַר הַכֹּהֵן אֶת־הַנֶּגַע
טָהוֹר הוּא:
שלישי יח־יט וּבָשָׂר כִּי־יִהְיֶה בוֹ־בְעֹרוֹ שְׁחִין וְנִרְפָּא: וְהָיָה בִּמְקוֹם הַשְּׁחִין שְׂאֵת לְבָנָה
כ אוֹ בַהֶרֶת לְבָנָה אֲדַמְדָּמֶת וְנִרְאָה אֶל־הַכֹּהֵן: וְרָאָה הַכֹּהֵן וְהִנֵּה
מַרְאֶהָ שָׁפָל מִן־הָעוֹר וּשְׂעָרָהּ הָפַךְ לָבָן וְטִמְּאוֹ הַכֹּהֵן נֶגַע־צָרַעַת
כא הִוא בַּשְּׁחִין פָּרָחָה: וְאִם ׀ יִרְאֶנָּה הַכֹּהֵן וְהִנֵּה אֵין־בָּהּ שֵׂעָר לָבָן
כב וּשְׁפָלָה אֵינֶנָּה מִן־הָעוֹר וְהִיא כֵהָה וְהִסְגִּירוֹ הַכֹּהֵן שִׁבְעַת יָמִים: וְאִם־
כג פָּשֹׂה תִפְשֶׂה בָּעוֹר וְטִמֵּא הַכֹּהֵן אֹתוֹ נֶגַע הִוא: וְאִם־תַּחְתֶּיהָ תַּעֲמֹד
רביעי [שני] כד הַבַּהֶרֶת לֹא פָשָׂתָה צָרֶבֶת הַשְּׁחִין הִוא וְטִהֲרוֹ הַכֹּהֵן: אוֹ
בָשָׂר כִּי־יִהְיֶה בְעֹרוֹ מִכְוַת־אֵשׁ וְהָיְתָה מִחְיַת הַמִּכְוָה בַּהֶרֶת לְבָנָה
כה אֲדַמְדֶּמֶת אוֹ לְבָנָה: וְרָאָה אֹתָהּ הַכֹּהֵן וְהִנֵּה נֶהְפַּךְ שֵׂעָר לָבָן בַּבַּהֶרֶת

הַכָּתוּב) that the (declaration) of uncleanness and purification of afflictions be pronounced only by the mouth of a *Kohen* (*Sifra*) — כִּי שִׂפְתֵי כֹהֵן יִשְׁמְרוּ דַעַת, *For the Kohen's lips should keep knowledge* (*Malachi* 2:7) — and they will instruct the afflicted one to examine his deeds, and he will pray for himself and the *Kohen* will also pray on his behalf. Additionally, since all afflictions (are decided) by their "mouths," they will gain expertise regarding the (various) levels of appearance, (thereby being able) to differentiate between one affliction and another.

19. וְהָיָה בִּמְקוֹם הַשְּׁחִין שְׂאֵת לְבָנָה — *And in the place of the boil there is a white rising.* That place is not judged by the (same) signs as the skin mentioned above (nor) the place of the *burning by fire* either (v. 24), for indeed, the natural skin destroyed by the boil or burn

NOTES

The *Sforno* gives two reasons for empowering the *Kohen* to determine whether the afflicted person is *tamei* or *tahor*. Firstly, as mentioned above, since leprosy is visited upon the person to awaken him to examine his ways and redirect them, the most suitable person to assist him through prayer and instruction is the *Kohen*, who is charged to be the teacher of the people of Israel. Secondly, since the *Kohen* gains experience through constant practice, he becomes the expert who can distinguish between different appearances and thereby determine the status of each case.

*and the affliction did not spread on the skin, then the Kohen shall quarantine
it for a second seven-day period. 6 The Kohen shall look at it again on the
seventh day, and behold! — if the affliction has dimmed and the affliction
has not spread on the skin, then the Kohen shall declare him pure, it is a
mispachas; he shall immerse his garments and become pure. 7 But if the
mispachas should spread on the skin after it had been shown to the Kohen
for its purification, it should be shown to the Kohen again. 8 The Kohen shall
look, and behold! — the mispachas has spread on the skin; the Kohen shall
declare him contaminated; it is tzaraas.*

*9 If a tzaraas affliction will be in a person, he shall be brought to the Kohen.
10 The Kohen shall look, and behold! — it is a white s'eis on the skin, and it
has changed hair to white, or there is healthy, live flesh within the s'eis: 11 It
is an old tzaraas in the skin of his flesh and the Kohen shall declare him
contaminated; he shall not quarantine it for it is contaminated.*

*12 If the tzaraas will erupt on the skin, and the tzaraas will cover the entire
skin of the affliction from his head to his feet, wherever the eyes of the Kohen
can see — 13 the Kohen shall look, and behold! — the affliction has covered
his entire flesh, then he shall declare the affliction to be pure; having turned
completely white, it is pure. 14 On the day healthy flesh appears in it, it shall
be contaminated. 15 The Kohen shall look at the healthy flesh and declare
him contaminated; the healthy flesh is contaminated, it is tzaraas. 16 But if
the healthy flesh changes again and turns white, he shall come to the Kohen.
17 The Kohen shall look at it, and behold! — the affliction has changed to
white, the Kohen shall declare the affliction pure; it is pure.*

*18 If flesh will have had an inflammation on its skin, and it will have
healed, 19 and on the place of the inflammation there will be a white s'eis or
a white baheres, streaked with red; it shall be shown to the Kohen. 20 The
Kohen shall look, and behold! — its appearance is lower than the skin, and
its hair has turned white: The Kohen shall declare him contaminated; it is
a tzaraas affliction that erupted on the inflammation. 21 But if the Kohen
looks at it, and behold! — there is no white hair in it, and it is not lower than
the skin, and it is dim, the Kohen shall quarantine it for a seven-day period.
22 If it spreads on the skin, the Kohen shall declare him contaminated; it is
an affliction. 23 But if the baheres remains in its place without spreading, it
is the scarring of the inflammation; the Kohen shall declare him pure.*

*24 If a person will have a burn from fire on his skin, and the healed skin
of the burn is a white baheres that is streaked with red or is all white,
25 the Kohen shall look, and behold! — hair has turned white in the baheres,*

---

cannot be restored as it was originally. Instead, in its place something similar to skin develops, but the skin (itself) is not renewed, as (our Sages) tell us (*Niddah* 55a) and as the doctors have related (to us).

NOTES

19. וְהָיָה בִּמְקוֹם הַשְּׁחִין שְׂאֵת לְבָנָה — *And in the place of the boil there is a white rising.* The *Sforno* explains why the law concerning a *white rising* (שְׂאֵת) in the place of a boil, or a *bright spot* (בַּהֶרֶת) in a place burnt by fire, is different than when these appearances occur in normal skin. The new skin which grows in these areas is not the same as the original, as our Sages tell us in Tractate *Niddah*; therefore the regulation and ordinances are also not similar.

ומראה עמק מן־העור צרעת הוא במכוה פרחה וטמא אתו הכהן נגע
כו צרעת הוא: ואם | יראנה הכהן והנה אין־בבהרת שער לבן ושפלה
כז איננה מן־העור והוא כהה והסגירו הכהן שבעת ימים: וראהו הכהן
ביום השביעי אם־פשה תפשה בעור וטמא הכהן אתו נגע צרעת הוא:
כח ואם־תחתיה תעמד הבהרת לא־פשתה בעור והוא כהה שאת המכוה
הוא וטהרו הכהן כי־צרבת המכוה הוא:
חמישי כט־ל ואיש או אשה כי־יהיה בו נגע בראש או בזקן: וראה הכהן את־הנגע
והנה מראהו עמק מן־העור ובו שער צהב דק וטמא אתו הכהן
לא נתק הוא צרעת הראש או הזקן הוא: וכי־יראה הכהן את־נגע הנתק
והנה אין־מראהו עמק מן־העור ושער שחר אין בו והסגיר הכהן
לב את־נגע הנתק שבעת ימים: וראה הכהן את־הנגע ביום השביעי והנה
לא־פשה הנתק ולא־היה בו שער צהב ומראה הנתק אין עמק
ג' רבתי לג מן־העור: והתגלח ואת־הנתק לא יגלח והסגיר הכהן את־הנתק
לד שבעת ימים שנית: וראה הכהן את־הנתק ביום השביעי והנה
לא־פשה הנתק בעור ומראהו איננו עמק מן־העור וטהר אתו הכהן
לה־לו וכבס בגדיו וטהר: ואם־פשה יפשה הנתק בעור אחרי טהרתו: וראהו
הכהן והנה פשה הנתק בעור לא־יבקר הכהן לשער הצהב טמא
לז הוא: ואם־בעיניו עמד הנתק ושער שחר צמח־בו נרפא הנתק טהור
לח הוא וטהרו הכהן: ואיש או־אשה כי־יהיה בעור־
לט בשרם בהרת בהרת לבנת: וראה הכהן והנה בעור־בשרם בהרת
ששי [שלישי] מ כהות לבנת בהק הוא פרח בעור טהור הוא: ואיש
מא כי ימרט ראשו קרח הוא טהור הוא: ואם מפאת פניו ימרט ראשו
מב גבח הוא טהור הוא: וכי־יהיה בקרחת או בגבחת נגע לבן אדמדם
מג צרעת פרחת הוא בקרחתו או בגבחתו: וראה אתו הכהן והנה
שאת־הנגע לבנה אדמדמת בקרחתו או בגבחתו כמראה צרעת
מד עור בשר: איש־צרוע הוא טמא הוא טמא יטמאנו הכהן בראשו
מה נגעו: והצרוע אשר־בו הנגע בגדיו יהיו פרמים וראשו יהיה פרוע
מו ועל־שפם יעטה וטמא | טמא יקרא: כל־ימי אשר הנגע בו יטמא

30. נֶתֶק הוא — *It is a scall.* If in the area of hair there be a place from which the hair fell out due to infection (lit., power of illness), and not due to (the action of) man or because of a drug, and even though there is no (aberrant) appearance, as our Sages have taught us [this is considered a נֶתֶק, *scall*]. This condition is also considered to be a form of leprosy by the doctors. (The Torah) therefore says that even though there are unclean appearances or spreading in the area of the scall, (a condition) which otherwise would have (established) a definitive decision (of uncleanness) were it not in the area of the hair, (in our case) the black hair in the area of hair overrides (lit., saves) the appearance of *white* and spreading (which usually denotes uncleanness).

39. כֵּהוֹת לְבָנֹת — *Dull white . . .* a degree lesser (in whiteness) than that of the membrane surrounding the egg, of which our Sages have taught.

and its appearance is deeper than the skin, it is tzaraas that erupted on the
burn, the Kohen shall declare him contaminated; it is a tzaraas affliction.
26 And if the Kohen looks at it and behold! — there is no white hair in the
baheres, and it is not lower than the skin, and it is dim, the Kohen shall
quarantine him for a seven-day period. 27 The Kohen shall look at it on the
seventh day: If it has spread on the skin, the Kohen shall declare him
contaminated; it is a tzaraas affliction. 28 But if the baheres remains in its
place, not spreading on the skin, and it is dim, it is a s'eis of the burn; the
Kohen shall declare him pure, for it is the scarring of the inflammation.

29 A man or a woman in whom there will be an affliction, on the scalp or
in the beard: 30 The Kohen shall look at the affliction, and behold! — its
appearance is deeper than the skin, and within it is weak, golden hair; the
Kohen shall declare him contaminated; it is a nesek, a tzaraas of the head
or the beard.

31 But if the Kohen looks at the nesek affliction, and behold! — its
appearance is not deeper than the skin, but there is no dark hair within it,
the Kohen shall quarantine the nesek affliction for seven days. 32 The Kohen
shall look at the affliction on the seventh day and behold! — the nesek had
not spread and no golden hair was in it, and the appearance of the nesek is
not deeper than the skin — 33 then he shall shave himself, but he shall not
shave the nesek; and the Kohen shall quarantine the nesek for a second
seven-day period. 34 The Kohen shall look at the nesek on the seventh day,
and behold! — the nesek had not spread on the skin, and its appearance is
not deeper than the skin; the Kohen shall declare him pure, and he shall
immerse his clothing and he is pure.

35 But if the nesek shall spread on the skin after he has been declared pure,
36 the Kohen shall look at it, and behold! — the nesek has spread on the skin:
The Kohen need not examine it for a golden hair, it is contaminated. 37 But
if the nesek has retained its appearance, and dark hair has sprouted in it,
the nesek has healed — it is pure; the Kohen shall declare it pure.

38 If a man or woman has spots in the skin of their flesh, white spots, 39 the
Kohen shall look, and behold! — on the skin of their flesh are dim white spots,
it is a bohak that has erupted on the skin, it is pure.

40 If the hair of a man's head falls out: He is bald at the back of the head,
he is pure. 41 And if his hair falls out toward the front of his head, he is
frontally bald, he is pure. 42 And if in the posterior or frontal baldness there
shall be a white affliction streaked with red: It is an eruption of tzaraas on
his posterior or frontal baldness. 43 The Kohen shall look at it, and behold! —
there is a s'eis affliction that is white streaked with red, in his posterior or
frontal baldness, like the appearance of tzaraas on the skin of the flesh. 44 He
is a person with tzaraas, he is contaminated; the Kohen shall declare him
contaminated; his affliction is upon his head.

45 And the person with tzaraas in whom there is the affliction — his
garments shall be rent, the hair of his head shall be unshorn, and he shall
cloak himself up to his lips; he is to call out: "Contaminated, contaminated!"
46 All the days that the affliction is upon him he shall remain contaminated;

מז טָמֵא הוּא בָּדָד יֵשֵׁב מִחוּץ לַמַּחֲנֶה מוֹשָׁבוֹ: וְהַבֶּגֶד כִּי־יִהְיֶה בוֹ נֶגַע
מח צָרָעַת בְּבֶגֶד צֶמֶר אוֹ בְּבֶגֶד פִּשְׁתִּים: אוֹ בִשְׁתִי אוֹ בְעֵרֶב לַפִּשְׁתִּים וְלַצָּמֶר

47. וְהַבֶּגֶד כִּי יִהְיֶה בוֹ נֶגַע צָרָעַת — *And when an affliction of leprosy is in a garment.* There is no doubt that this (phenomena) cannot possibly be a natural one, for these strange colors (appearances) cannot occur in a garment except through (1) the work (of the dyer) using various colors, by some error which happened with the color dyes intentionally or unintentionally; or (2) the dyer's (lit., workman's) performance; or (3) the (chemical) reaction in the garment being colored. Now we have a tradition that these laws of נִגְעֵי בְּגָדִים, *afflictions of garments*, do not apply except to white, uncolored garments. In truth, the Torah is attesting that at times this wonder (phenomenon) will occur in garments and in houses so as to awaken (open) the ear of the owners to their transgressions, as (our Sages) tell us regarding שְׁבִיעִית, *the Sabbatical year*, as they say, "Come and see the far-reaching results of violating the laws of the seventh year. A man who trades in seventh-year produce must eventually sell his movables ... if he disregards this, he eventually sells his estates" (*Kiddushin* 20a). All this is because of God's compassion for His people.

Also (our Sages) received a tradition that the garments of gentiles do not become *tamei* through (these) afflictions (*Negaim* 11:1). This is so, for in truth the human species represents the ultimate purpose intended (by the Creator) in all existence, particularly among mortal beings, for he alone among all (creatures) is predisposed to be like the Creator in intellect and deed, as He, the Blessed One, testifies saying, בְּצַלְמֵנוּ כִּדְמוּתֵנוּ, *In our image after our likeness* (*Genesis* 1:26). Now this is justly so regarding all humans (who possess) human reason, which is called "the image of God," and (who possess) the power of free will which is called "God's likeness," for among all creation man alone possesses free will. When (man) is aroused to reflect upon the existence of his Creator, His greatness and goodness, in Whom there is abundant kindness and truth, through (which) He performs righteousness and justice; and after perceiving and recognizing (all) this he will walk in His ways, making His will as his own (will). Behold, in this manner he becomes, without a doubt, like unto his Creator more so than all other creatures, and this is the ultimate purpose intended from the Creator Who brought (all) into existence as it says, וְצַדִּיק יְסוֹד עוֹלָם, *And the righteous one is the foundation of the world* (*Proverbs* 10:25). (But) when a deceived heart turned man aside from this (path) for he listened (instead) to the power of physical temptations in all, or some, of his actions, (causing him) to be lax in (fulfilling) the will of his Maker or to rebel against Him, then his punishment was everlasting or transitory according to Divine judgment as it says, כִּי לֹא אַצְדִּיק רָשָׁע, *For I will not justify*

NOTES

47. וְהַבֶּגֶד כִּי יִהְיֶה בוֹ נֶגַע צָרָעַת — *And when an affliction of leprosy is in a garment.* The *Sforno*, in his lengthy commentary on this section dealing with נִגְעֵי בְגָדִים, *afflictions of garments*, including as well the chapter (14:34-53) which discusses נִגְעֵי בָתִּים, *afflictions of houses*, makes the following points:

(1) Since the discolorations mentioned in verse 49, namely green and red, can only appear in a garment for one of the three reasons listed by the *Sforno*, and since the laws regarding the affliction of garments only apply to a white neutral garment, then it is impossible for this discoloration to happen naturally.

(2) It therefore follows that this phenomenon is heaven sent for the purpose of alerting the owner of the garment or house to take stock and repent for his sins, as the *Rambam* states (*Hilchos Tumas Tzaraas* 16:10), "These changes stated (in the Torah) regarding garments and houses ... are not according to the natural order of the world, but they are a sign and wonder for Israel, cautioning them to abstain from the evil tongue."

(3) The fact that these laws do not apply to gentiles serves as a springboard for the *Sforno* to stress once again, as he already did at the beginning of *Genesis*, that man is indeed the crown of creation chosen to imitate God through his power of reason and freedom of choice. However, the bulk of mankind did not realize this awesome

he is contaminated. He shall dwell in isolation; his dwelling shall be outside the camp.

47 *If there shall be a tzaraas affliction in a garment, in a woolen garment or a linen garment,* 48 *or in the warp or the woof of the linen or the wool;*

---

the wicked (*Exodus* 23:7). Now when this occurs to man, who sins in error, he will suffer pain (or loss) in his possessions or physical being, according to Divine wisdom, to alert his ear, as it says, וַיִּגֶל אָזְנָם לַמּוּסָר, *He opens also their ear to discipline* (*Job* 36:10). However, those who slumber and are not awakened at all to know any of these things, these being the gentiles and the majority of the Israelite nation save an elite few, (hence) they, without a doubt, are under the control (lit., conduct) of nature and the heavenly forces, which are superior to these human beings, similar to other living creatures who are not subject to God's providence individually but only in terms of their species, for through them (i.e., the species as a whole) the intent of their Creator, Blessed is He, is fulfilled. And He chose the Israelite nation as it says, בְּךָ בָּחַר ה' אֱלֹהֶיךָ לִהְיוֹת לוֹ לְעַם סְגֻלָּה, *HASHEM, your God has chosen you to be His own treasure* (*Deut.* 7:6), and this (He did) because the hopeful intent of (God) the Blessed One was more likely (to be realized) among the men of this nation than among other men, for the existence of God and His unity was known partially and accepted among all (of Israel) from their ancestors, as it says, נוֹדָע בִּיהוּדָה אֱלֹהִים בְּיִשְׂרָאֵל גָּדוֹל שְׁמוֹ, *In Judah is God known, His name is great in Israel* (*Psalms* 76:2). He (therefore) wrote and taught them the Torah, which is the intellectual (analytical) portion, and the commandment which is the section of deeds, as He testifies saying, וְהַתּוֹרָה וְהַמִּצְוָה אֲשֶׁר כָּתַבְתִּי לְהוֹרֹתָם, *And the Torah and the commandment which I have written that you may teach them* (*Exodus* 24:12). He (then) warned that if they deviate from this path, He will awaken their ears through suffering, as it says, אִם שָׁמוֹעַ תִּשְׁמַע . . . כָּל הַמַּחֲלָה אֲשֶׁר שַׂמְתִּי בְמִצְרַיִם לֹא אָשִׂים עָלֶיךָ, *If you will hearken . . . I will put none of the diseases upon you which I have put upon Egypt* (*Exodus* 15:26), and in His compassion for them (at such a time) when the majority of them will be viewed favorably before Him, He resolved to alert a select few among them, first through afflictions of garments, regarding which we have a tradition that the garments of gentiles do not become defiled through these afflictions, and when this does not suffice to alert them, (then He shall visit) afflictions on their houses, and (in this case) also, no affliction of leprosy can come naturally at all. Therefore, it is appropriate that the garments and houses of gentiles are not defiled by these afflictions, as our Sages have received from tradition. But when (subsequent) generations did not attain the proper level which would make them worthy of this compassion, there is no (longer) any memory of these early (phenomena) of the affliction of houses, bringing some Sages to state that they never ever happened!

NOTES

responsibility except for the people of Israel. Even among them only a relatively small number attained the level of excellence which God had ordained for them, and even they must be reminded, when they falter and deviate, to mend their ways and return to God. One of the methods used by God to awaken them from their periodic slumber is that of נְגָעִים, *afflictions*. It therefore is understandable that these laws would not apply to gentiles, for נְגָעִים are a miraculous lesson reserved only for those who understand their ultimate purpose and act accordingly.

(4) Based upon the above, the *Sforno* explains that the visiting of these afflictions upon Israel is motivated by God's compassion for them and His desire that they repent and accept their historic mission to be a holy people. The special providence enjoyed by Israel is manifested by His ongoing attention and concern which, ironically, also carries with it these special reminders. It is precisely because Israel reached a high level of holiness that their sins create such vulnerability. Once Israel descended from that exalted plateau, they no longer were worthy to be singled out for such direct, wondrous Divine reminders as נְגָעִים. That is why we do not witness these phenomena today, nor have we heard of them for many generations.

מט אֹ֥ו בָע֖וֹר אֹ֥ו בְּכׇל־מְלֶ֥אכֶת עֽוֹר׃ וְהָיָ֨ה הַנֶּ֜גַע יְרַקְרַ֣ק ׀ א֣וֹ אֲדַמְדָּ֗ם בַּבֶּ֡גֶד
א֣וֹ בָע֞וֹר אֽוֹ־בַשְּׁתִ֤י אֽוֹ־בָעֵ֙רֶב֙ א֣וֹ בְכׇל־כְּלִי־ע֔וֹר נֶ֥גַע צָרַ֖עַת ה֑וּא וְהׇרְאָ֖ה
נ אֶת־הַכֹּהֵֽן׃ וְרָאָ֥ה הַכֹּהֵ֖ן אֶת־הַנָּ֑גַע וְהִסְגִּ֥יר אֶת־הַנֶּ֖גַע שִׁבְעַ֥ת יָמִֽים׃
נא וְרָאָ֨ה אֶת־הַנֶּ֜גַע בַּיּ֣וֹם הַשְּׁבִיעִ֗י כִּֽי־פָשָׂ֤ה הַנֶּ֙גַע֙ בַּ֠בֶּ֠גֶד אֽוֹ־בַשְּׁתִ֤י
אֽוֹ־בָעֵ֙רֶב֙ א֣וֹ בָע֔וֹר לְכֹ֛ל אֲשֶׁר־יֵעָשֶׂ֥ה הָע֖וֹר לִמְלָאכָ֑ה צָרַ֧עַת מַמְאֶ֛רֶת
נב הַנֶּ֖גַע טָמֵ֥א הֽוּא׃ וְשָׂרַ֨ף אֶת־הַבֶּ֜גֶד א֣וֹ אֶת־הַשְּׁתִ֣י ׀ א֣וֹ אֶת־הָעֵ֗רֶב בַּצֶּ֙מֶר֙
א֣וֹ בַפִּשְׁתִּ֔ים א֚וֹ אֶת־כׇּל־כְּלִ֣י הָע֔וֹר אֲשֶׁר־יִהְיֶ֥ה ב֖וֹ הַנָּ֑גַע כִּֽי־צָרַ֤עַת
נג מַמְאֶ֙רֶת֙ הִ֔וא בָּאֵ֖שׁ תִּשָּׂרֵֽף׃ וְאִם֙ יִרְאֶ֣ה הַכֹּהֵ֔ן וְהִנֵּה֙ לֹֽא־פָשָׂ֣ה הַנֶּ֔גַע
נד בַּבֶּ֕גֶד א֥וֹ בַשְּׁתִ֖י א֣וֹ בָעֵ֑רֶב א֖וֹ בְּכׇל־כְּלִי־עֽוֹר׃ וְצִוָּה֙ הַכֹּהֵ֔ן וְכִ֨בְּס֔וּ אֵ֥ת
שביעי [רביעי] נה אֲשֶׁר־בּ֖וֹ הַנָּ֑גַע וְהִסְגִּיר֥וֹ שִׁבְעַת־יָמִ֖ים שֵׁנִֽית׃ וְרָאָ֨ה הַכֹּהֵ֜ן אַחֲרֵ֣י ׀ הֻכַּבֵּ֣ס
אֶת־הַנֶּ֗גַע וְ֠הִנֵּ֠ה לֹֽא־הָפַ֨ךְ הַנֶּ֤גַע אֶת־עֵינוֹ֙ וְהַנֶּ֣גַע לֹא־פָשָׂ֔ה טָמֵ֣א ה֔וּא
נו בָּאֵ֖שׁ תִּשְׂרְפֶ֑נּוּ פְּחֶ֣תֶת הִ֔וא בְּקָֽרַחְתּ֖וֹ א֥וֹ בְגַבַּחְתּֽוֹ׃ וְאִם֙ רָאָ֣ה הַכֹּהֵ֔ן וְהִנֵּה֙
כֵּהָ֣ה הַנֶּ֔גַע אַחֲרֵ֖י הֻכַּבֵּ֣ס אֹת֑וֹ וְקָרַ֣ע אֹת֗וֹ מִן־הַבֶּ֙גֶד֙ א֣וֹ מִן־הָע֔וֹר א֥וֹ
מפטיר נז מִן־הַשְּׁתִ֖י א֥וֹ מִן־הָעֵֽרֶב׃ וְאִם־תֵּרָאֶ֨ה ע֜וֹד בַּ֠בֶּ֠גֶד אֽוֹ־בַשְּׁתִ֤י אֽוֹ־בָעֵ֙רֶב֙ א֣וֹ
נח בְכׇל־כְּלִי־ע֔וֹר פֹּרַ֖חַת הִ֑וא בָּאֵ֣שׁ תִּשְׂרְפֶ֔נּוּ אֵ֥ת אֲשֶׁר־בּ֖וֹ הַנָּֽגַע׃ וְהַבֶּ֡גֶד
אֽוֹ־הַשְּׁתִ֨י אֽוֹ־הָעֵ֜רֶב אֽוֹ־כׇל־כְּלִ֤י הָעוֹר֙ אֲשֶׁ֣ר תְּכַבֵּ֔ס וְסָ֥ר מֵהֶ֖ם הַנָּ֑גַע
נט וְכֻבַּ֥ס שֵׁנִ֖ית וְטָהֵֽר׃ זֹ֡את תּוֹרַ֣ת נֶֽגַע־צָרַ֩עַת֩ בֶּ֨גֶד הַצֶּ֜מֶר ׀ א֣וֹ הַפִּשְׁתִּ֗ים א֤וֹ
הַשְּׁתִי֙ א֣וֹ הָעֵ֔רֶב א֖וֹ כׇּל־כְּלִי־ע֑וֹר לְטַהֲר֖וֹ א֥וֹ לְטַמְּאֽוֹ׃

or in leather or in anything fashioned of leather; [49] and the affliction shall be deep green or deep red, in the garment or the leather, or the warp or the woof, or in any leather utensil: It is a tzaraas affliction, and it shall be shown to the Kohen. [50] The Kohen shall look at the affliction; and he shall quarantine the affliction for a seven-day period. [51] He shall look at the affliction on the seventh day: If the affliction has spread in the garment or in the warp or in the woof or in the leather — for whatever purpose the leather has been fashioned — the affliction is a malignant tzaraas; it is contaminated. [52] He shall burn the garment, or the warp or the woof, of the wool or of the linen, or any leather utensil in which the affliction may be; for it is a malignant tzaraas, it shall be burned in fire.

[53] But if the Kohen shall look, and behold! — the affliction had not spread in the garment, or the warp or the woof; or in any leather utensil, [54] the Kohen shall command; and they shall wash the area of the affliction; and he shall quarantine it for a second seven-day period. [55] The Kohen shall look after the affliction has been washed, and behold! — the affliction has not changed its color and the affliction has not spread, it is contaminated, you shall burn it in fire; it is a penetrating affliction in his worn garment or in his new garment. [56] But if the Kohen shall look, and behold! — the affliction grew dimmer after it was washed, he shall rip it from the garment or from the leather, or from the warp or from the woof. [57] If it appears again in the garment or in the warp or in the woof, or in any leather utensil, it is an eruption; you shall burn in fire that which contains the affliction. [58] But if the garment or the warp or the woof or any leather utensil had been washed and then the affliction left them, it shall be immersed again and it shall become pure.

[59] This is the law of the tzaraas affliction, a garment of wool or linen, or the warp or the woof, or any leather utensil; to declare it pure or to declare it contaminated.

פרשת מצורע

יד א-ב וַיְדַבֵּר יְהוָה אֶל־מֹשֶׁה לֵּאמֹר: זֹאת תִּהְיֶה תּוֹרַת הַמְּצֹרָע בְּיוֹם טָהֳרָתוֹ
ג וְהוּבָא אֶל־הַכֹּהֵן: וְיָצָא הַכֹּהֵן אֶל־מִחוּץ לַמַּחֲנֶה וְרָאָה הַכֹּהֵן וְהִנֵּה נִרְפָּא
ד נֶגַע־הַצָּרַעַת מִן־הַצָּרוּעַ: וְצִוָּה הַכֹּהֵן וְלָקַח לַמִּטַּהֵר שְׁתֵּי־צִפֳּרִים חַיּוֹת
ה טְהֹרוֹת וְעֵץ אֶרֶז וּשְׁנִי תוֹלַעַת וְאֵזֹב: וְצִוָּה הַכֹּהֵן וְשָׁחַט אֶת־הַצִּפּוֹר הָאֶחָת
ו אֶל־כְּלִי־חֶרֶשׂ עַל־מַיִם חַיִּים: אֶת־הַצִּפֹּר הַחַיָּה יִקַּח אֹתָהּ וְאֶת־עֵץ הָאֶרֶז
וְאֶת־שְׁנִי הַתּוֹלַעַת וְאֶת־הָאֵזֹב וְטָבַל אוֹתָם וְאֵת | הַצִּפֹּר הַחַיָּה בְּדַם
ז הַצִּפֹּר הַשְּׁחֻטָה עַל הַמַּיִם הַחַיִּים: וְהִזָּה עַל הַמִּטַּהֵר מִן־הַצָּרַעַת שֶׁבַע
ח פְּעָמִים וְטִהֲרוֹ וְשִׁלַּח אֶת־הַצִּפֹּר הַחַיָּה עַל־פְּנֵי הַשָּׂדֶה: וְכִבֶּס הַמִּטַּהֵר
אֶת־בְּגָדָיו וְגִלַּח אֶת־כָּל־שְׂעָרוֹ וְרָחַץ בַּמַּיִם וְטָהֵר וְאַחַר יָבוֹא אֶל־הַמַּחֲנֶה
ט וְיָשַׁב מִחוּץ לְאָהֳלוֹ שִׁבְעַת יָמִים: וְהָיָה בַיּוֹם הַשְּׁבִיעִי יְגַלַּח אֶת־כָּל־שְׂעָרוֹ
אֶת־רֹאשׁוֹ וְאֶת־זְקָנוֹ וְאֵת גַּבֹּת עֵינָיו וְאֶת־כָּל־שְׂעָרוֹ יְגַלֵּחַ וְכִבֶּס אֶת־
י בְּגָדָיו וְרָחַץ אֶת־בְּשָׂרוֹ בַּמַּיִם וְטָהֵר: וּבַיּוֹם הַשְּׁמִינִי יִקַּח שְׁנֵי־כְבָשִׂים
תְּמִימִם וְכַבְשָׂה אַחַת בַּת־שְׁנָתָהּ תְּמִימָה וּשְׁלֹשָׁה עֶשְׂרֹנִים סֹלֶת מִנְחָה
יא בְּלוּלָה בַשֶּׁמֶן וְלֹג אֶחָד שָׁמֶן: וְהֶעֱמִיד הַכֹּהֵן הַמְטַהֵר אֵת הָאִישׁ הַמִּטַּהֵר
יב וְאֹתָם לִפְנֵי יְהוָה פֶּתַח אֹהֶל מוֹעֵד: וְלָקַח הַכֹּהֵן אֶת־הַכֶּבֶשׂ הָאֶחָד
וְהִקְרִיב אֹתוֹ לְאָשָׁם וְאֶת־לֹג הַשָּׁמֶן וְהֵנִיף אֹתָם תְּנוּפָה לִפְנֵי יְהוָה:

XIV

2. וְהוּבָא אֶל הַכֹּהֵן — *He shall be brought to the Kohen* . . . to a nearby place outside the camp, where the *Kohen* can go to see him in a dignified manner, and without excessive exertion.

7. וְטִהֲרוֹ — *And pronounce him clean* . . . from the (regulations) of rent clothing and the loose hair (of the leper) (13:45).

8. וְרָחַץ בַּמַּיִם וְטָהֵר — *And he shall bathe himself in water and he shall be clean* . . . from the (restriction) of *"Outside the camp shall be his dwelling"* (13:46).

9. וְרָחַץ אֶת בְּשָׂרוֹ בַּמַּיִם וְטָהֵר — *And he shall bathe his flesh in water and he shall be clean* . . . from the (restriction) of *"But he shall dwell outside his tent"* (v. 8).

12. וְהִקְרִיב אֹתוֹ לְאָשָׁם — *And offer it as a guilt offering.* As already explained, the guilt offering is brought when one misappropriates holy things, just as the sin offering is brought for (a sin which is) punishable by excision. Now, (our Sages) have said that צָרַעַת, *leprosy*, (comes as a punishment) for evil talk and for haughtiness, both of which are (akin

NOTES

XIV

2. וְהוּבָא אֶל הַכֹּהֵן — *He shall be brought to the Kohen.* In the previous chapter (13:2), the expression וְהוּבָא, *and he shall be brought*, is also used, but whereas there it means literally *he shall be brought to Aaron* (within the camp), here it cannot mean that the מְצֹרָע, *leper*, is brought to the *Kohen into* the camp, since he is still prohibited to enter therein. The *Sforno*, therefore, interprets the phrase וְהוּבָא in this instance to mean that he will be brought to a place *near* the camp, and the *Kohen* will go out to examine him, as it clearly states in the next verse (3).

7. וְטִהֲרוֹ — *And pronounce him clean.* The leper is cleansed in stages. First, the regulations of *rent clothing* and *loose hair* are waived. The second step is permission to come back into the camp. Third, he may enter his tent and will not be restricted to dwell outside. Finally, he is allowed to enter the environs of the Holy and partake of קָדָשִׁים, *sacred meat*, once he has brought his offerings. These four stages are indicated by the four expressions of

PARASHAS METZORA

14
[1] *HASHEM spoke to Moses, saying: [2] This shall be the law of the metzora
on the day of his purification: He shall be brought to the Kohen. [3] The
Kohen shall go forth to the outside of the camp; the Kohen shall look, and
behold! — the tzaraas affliction had been healed from the metzora. [4] The
Kohen shall command; and for the person being purified there shall be taken
two live, clean birds, cedarwood, crimson thread, and hyssop. [5] The Kohen
shall command; and the one bird shall be slaughtered into an earthenware
vessel over spring water. [6] As for the live bird: He shall take it with the
cedarwood and the crimson thread and the hyssop, and he shall dip them and
the live bird into the blood of the bird that was slaughtered over the spring
water. [7] Then he shall sprinkle seven times upon the person being purified
from the tzaraas; he shall purify him, and he shall set the live bird free upon
the open field. [8] The person being purified shall immerse his clothing, shave
off all his hair, and immerse himself in the water and become pure. Thereafter
he may enter the camp; but he shall dwell outside of his tent for seven days.*
*[9] On the seventh day he shall shave off all his hair — his head, his beard,
his eyebrows, and all his hair shall he shave off; he shall immerse his clothing
and immerse his flesh in water, and become pure.*
*[10] On the eighth day, he shall take two unblemished male lambs and one
unblemished ewe in its first year, three tenth-ephah of fine flour mixed with
oil, and one log of oil. [11] The Kohen who purifies shall place the person being
purified along with them before HASHEM at the entrance of the Tent of
Meeting. [12] The Kohen shall take the one lamb and bring it near for a guilt-
offering, with the log of oil; and he shall wave them as a wave-service before
HASHEM.*

---

to) misappropriation of the holy, for indeed, evil talk is principally spoken in secret, as one who "seeks deeply to hide counsel from HASHEM" (based on *Isaiah* 29:15), as (our Sages) said, "When anyone commits a transgression in secret, it is as though he has thrust aside the feet of the Divine Presence" (*Chagigah* 16a). And as for one who is haughty it says, גְּבַהּ עֵינַיִם וּרְחַב לֵבָב אֹתוֹ לֹא אוּכָל, *He that has a haughty look and a proud heart I will not tolerate* (*Psalms* 101:5). "The Holy One, Blessed is He, says, 'This one steals My raiment. He and I cannot abide in one world' " (*Sotah* 5a). And the Scriptures have already told us of Uzziyahu, saying, וּכְחֶזְקָתוֹ גָּבַהּ לִבּוֹ עַד לְהַשְׁחִית וַיִּמְעַל בַּה׳ אֱלֹהָיו . . . וְהַצָּרַעַת זָרְחָה בְמִצְחוֹ, *But when he was strong his heart was lifted up to his destruction; for he trespassed against HASHEM his God . . . the leprosy broke out on his forehead* (*II Chronicles* 26:16, 19).

NOTES

טָהֳרָה, *cleansing*, which appear in verses 7 (וְטִהֲרוֹ), 8, 9 and 20 (וְטָהֵר).

12. וְהִקְרִיב אֹתוֹ לְאָשָׁם — *And offer it as a guilt offering*. The *Sforno* already explained (1:2) that an אָשָׁם, *guilt offering*, is brought to make amends for the unlawful use of sacred property (מְעִילָה). He now points out that our Sages have taught us that leprosy comes as a punishment for evil talk and for haughtiness. The former is considered a form of מְעִילָה, for by slandering his fellow secretly one acts as though God is unaware of his transgression and thus he encroaches on the Almighty's omniscience. As for the latter sin, he misappropriates God's exclusive right to גֵּאוּת, *majesty*, which is related to גַּאֲוָה, *pride*. Here again, he intrudes on God's domain. In both cases he is guilty of trespassing which obligates him to bring a guilt offering. The *Sforno* demonstrates the link between haughtiness and מְעִילָה by citing the episode of King Uzziyahu who, in his arrogance, entered the Temple to burn incense upon the Altar although he was not a *Kohen*. The verse in *Chronicles* refers to this act as מְעִילָה and he was punished for it with leprosy.

שני יג וְשָׁחַט אֶת־הַכֶּבֶשׂ בִּמְקוֹם אֲשֶׁר יִשְׁחַט אֶת־הַחַטָּאת וְאֶת־הָעֹלָה
בִּמְקוֹם הַקֹּדֶשׁ כִּי כַּחַטָּאת הָאָשָׁם הוּא לַכֹּהֵן קֹדֶשׁ קָדָשִׁים הוּא׃
יד וְלָקַח הַכֹּהֵן מִדַּם הָאָשָׁם וְנָתַן הַכֹּהֵן עַל־תְּנוּךְ אֹזֶן הַמִּטַּהֵר הַיְמָנִית
טו וְעַל־בֹּהֶן יָדוֹ הַיְמָנִית וְעַל־בֹּהֶן רַגְלוֹ הַיְמָנִית׃ וְלָקַח הַכֹּהֵן מִלֹּג
טז הַשָּׁמֶן וְיָצַק עַל־כַּף הַכֹּהֵן הַשְּׂמָאלִית׃ וְטָבַל הַכֹּהֵן אֶת־אֶצְבָּעוֹ
הַיְמָנִית מִן־הַשֶּׁמֶן אֲשֶׁר עַל־כַּפּוֹ הַשְּׂמָאלִית וְהִזָּה מִן־הַשֶּׁמֶן בְּאֶצְבָּעוֹ
יז שֶׁבַע פְּעָמִים לִפְנֵי יהוה׃ וּמִיֶּתֶר הַשֶּׁמֶן אֲשֶׁר עַל־כַּפּוֹ יִתֵּן הַכֹּהֵן
עַל־תְּנוּךְ אֹזֶן הַמִּטַּהֵר הַיְמָנִית וְעַל־בֹּהֶן יָדוֹ הַיְמָנִית וְעַל־בֹּהֶן רַגְלוֹ
יח הַיְמָנִית עַל דַּם הָאָשָׁם׃ וְהַנּוֹתָר בַּשֶּׁמֶן אֲשֶׁר עַל־כַּף הַכֹּהֵן יִתֵּן
יט עַל־רֹאשׁ הַמִּטַּהֵר וְכִפֶּר עָלָיו הַכֹּהֵן לִפְנֵי יהוה׃ וְעָשָׂה הַכֹּהֵן
אֶת־הַחַטָּאת וְכִפֶּר עַל־הַמִּטַּהֵר מִטֻּמְאָתוֹ וְאַחַר יִשְׁחַט אֶת־הָעֹלָה׃
כ וְהֶעֱלָה הַכֹּהֵן אֶת־הָעֹלָה וְאֶת־הַמִּנְחָה הַמִּזְבֵּחָה וְכִפֶּר עָלָיו הַכֹּהֵן
שלישי [חמישי] כא וְטָהֵר׃ וְאִם־דַּל הוּא וְאֵין יָדוֹ מַשֶּׂגֶת וְלָקַח כֶּבֶשׂ
אֶחָד אָשָׁם לִתְנוּפָה לְכַפֵּר עָלָיו וְעִשָּׂרוֹן סֹלֶת אֶחָד בָּלוּל בַּשֶּׁמֶן
כב לְמִנְחָה וְלֹג שָׁמֶן׃ וּשְׁתֵּי תֹרִים אוֹ שְׁנֵי בְּנֵי יוֹנָה אֲשֶׁר תַּשִּׂיג יָדוֹ
כג וְהָיָה אֶחָד חַטָּאת וְהָאֶחָד עֹלָה׃ וְהֵבִיא אֹתָם בַּיּוֹם הַשְּׁמִינִי לְטָהֳרָתוֹ
כד אֶל־הַכֹּהֵן אֶל־פֶּתַח אֹהֶל־מוֹעֵד לִפְנֵי יהוה׃ וְלָקַח הַכֹּהֵן אֶת־כֶּבֶשׂ
כה הָאָשָׁם וְאֶת־לֹג הַשָּׁמֶן וְהֵנִיף אֹתָם הַכֹּהֵן תְּנוּפָה לִפְנֵי יהוה׃ וְשָׁחַט
אֶת־כֶּבֶשׂ הָאָשָׁם וְלָקַח הַכֹּהֵן מִדַּם הָאָשָׁם וְנָתַן עַל־תְּנוּךְ
אֹזֶן־הַמִּטַּהֵר הַיְמָנִית וְעַל־בֹּהֶן יָדוֹ הַיְמָנִית וְעַל־בֹּהֶן רַגְלוֹ הַיְמָנִית׃
כו-כז וּמִן־הַשֶּׁמֶן יִצֹק הַכֹּהֵן עַל־כַּף הַכֹּהֵן הַשְּׂמָאלִית׃ וְהִזָּה הַכֹּהֵן בְּאֶצְבָּעוֹ
הַיְמָנִית מִן־הַשֶּׁמֶן אֲשֶׁר עַל־כַּפּוֹ הַשְּׂמָאלִית שֶׁבַע פְּעָמִים לִפְנֵי
כח יהוה׃ וְנָתַן הַכֹּהֵן מִן־הַשֶּׁמֶן ׀ אֲשֶׁר עַל־כַּפּוֹ עַל־תְּנוּךְ אֹזֶן הַמִּטַּהֵר
הַיְמָנִית וְעַל־בֹּהֶן יָדוֹ הַיְמָנִית וְעַל־בֹּהֶן רַגְלוֹ הַיְמָנִית עַל־מְקוֹם
כט דַּם הָאָשָׁם׃ וְהַנּוֹתָר מִן־הַשֶּׁמֶן אֲשֶׁר עַל־כַּף הַכֹּהֵן יִתֵּן עַל־רֹאשׁ
ל הַמִּטַּהֵר לְכַפֵּר עָלָיו לִפְנֵי יהוה׃ וְעָשָׂה אֶת־הָאֶחָד מִן־הַתֹּרִים אוֹ
לא מִן־בְּנֵי הַיּוֹנָה מֵאֲשֶׁר תַּשִּׂיג יָדוֹ׃ אֵת אֲשֶׁר־תַּשִּׂיג יָדוֹ אֶת־הָאֶחָד
חַטָּאת וְאֶת־הָאֶחָד עֹלָה עַל־הַמִּנְחָה וְכִפֶּר הַכֹּהֵן עַל הַמִּטַּהֵר
לב לִפְנֵי יהוה׃ זֹאת תּוֹרַת אֲשֶׁר־בּוֹ נֶגַע צָרָעַת אֲשֶׁר לֹא־תַשִּׂיג יָדוֹ
בְּטָהֳרָתוֹ׃
שביעי [ששי] לג-לד וַיְדַבֵּר יהוה אֶל־מֹשֶׁה וְאֶל־אַהֲרֹן לֵאמֹר׃ כִּי תָבֹאוּ אֶל־אֶרֶץ כְּנַעַן

---

20. וְכִפֶּר עָלָיו הַכֹּהֵן וְטָהֵר — *And the Kohen shall make atonement for him and he shall be clean* . . . for (the purpose of) eating sacred things (קָדָשִׁים) and to enter the Holy, as our Sages have said, "Once he brings his offerings (lit., his atonements) he may partake of the Holy (flesh)" (*Negaim* 14:3).

13 He shall slaughter the lamb in the place where he would slaughter the
sin-offering and the elevation-offering, in the holy place; for the guilt-
offering is like the sin-offering, it is the Kohen's, it is most holy. 14 The Kohen
shall take from the blood of the guilt-offering, and the Kohen shall place it
on the middle part of the right ear of the person being purified and on the
thumb of his right hand and the big toe of his right foot. 15 The Kohen shall
take from the log of oil and he shall pour it upon the Kohen's left palm.
16 The Kohen shall dip his right forefinger into the oil that is in his left palm;
and he shall sprinkle from the oil with his finger seven times before
HASHEM. 17 Some of the oil remaining on his palm, the Kohen shall put on the
middle part of the right ear of the man being purified, on the thumb of his
right hand and on the big toe of his right foot; on the blood of the guilt-
offering. 18 And the rest of the oil that is on the Kohen's palm, he shall place
upon the head of the person being purified; and the Kohen shall provide him
atonement before HASHEM. 19 The Kohen shall perform the sin-offering
service and provide atonement for the person being purified from his
contamination; after that he shall slaughter the elevation-offering. 20 The
Kohen shall bring the elevation-offering and the meal-offering up to the
Altar; and the Kohen shall provide him atonement, and he becomes pure.

21 If he is poor and his means are not sufficient, then he shall take one
male lamb as a guilt-offering for a wave-service to provide atonement for
him; and one tenth-ephah of fine flour mixed with oil for a meal-offering,
and a log of oil. 22 And two turtledoves or two young doves — for whichever
his means are sufficient — one shall be a sin-offering and one an elevation-
offering. 23 He shall bring them to the Kohen, on the eighth day of his
purification, to the entrance of the Tent of Meeting, before HASHEM. 24 The
Kohen shall take the guilt-offering lamb and the log of oil; and the Kohen
shall wave them as a wave-service before HASHEM. 25 He shall slaughter the
guilt-offering lamb and the Kohen shall take some of the guilt-offering's
blood and place it on the middle part of the right ear of the man being
purified and on the thumb of his right hand and on the big toe of his right
foot. 26 From the oil, the Kohen shall pour upon the Kohen's left palm. 27 The
Kohen shall sprinkle with his right forefinger some of the oil that is in his
left palm seven times before HASHEM. 28 The Kohen shall place some of the
oil that is on his palm upon the middle of the right ear of the person being
purified, on the thumb of his right hand and on the big toe of his right foot
— on the place of the guilt-offering's blood. 29 And the rest of the oil that is
on the Kohen's palm, he shall place upon the head of the person being
purified; to provide him atonement before HASHEM.

30 He shall then perform the service of one of the turtledoves or of the
young doves, for whichever his means are sufficient. 31 Of whichever his
means are sufficient — one is a sin-offering and one is an elevation-offering
— along with the meal-offering; and the Kohen shall provide atonement for
the one being purified, before HASHEM. 32 This is the law of one in whom
there is a tzaraas affliction — whose means are not sufficient — for his
purification.

33 HASHEM spoke to Moses and Aaron, saying: 34 When you arrive in the

אשר אני נתן לכם לאחזה ונתתי נגע צרעת בבית ארץ אחזתכם:
לה־לו ובא אשר־לו הבית והגיד לכהן לאמר כנגע נראה לי בבית: וצוה
הכהן ופנו את־הבית בטרם יבא הכהן לראות את־הנגע ולא יטמא
לז כל־אשר בבית ואחר כן יבא הכהן לראות את־הבית: וראה
את־הנגע והנה הנגע בקירת הבית שקערורת ירקרקת או אדמדמת
לח ומראיהן שפל מן־הקיר: ויצא הכהן מן־הבית אל־פתח הבית והסגיר
לט את־הבית שבעת ימים: ושב הכהן ביום השביעי וראה והנה פשה
מ הנגע בקירת הבית: וצוה הכהן וחלצו את־האבנים אשר בהן הנגע
מא והשליכו אתהן אל־מחוץ לעיר אל־מקום טמא: ואת־הבית יקצע
מבית סביב ושפכו את־העפר אשר הקצו אל־מחוץ לעיר אל־מקום
מב טמא: ולקחו אבנים אחרות והביאו אל־תחת האבנים ועפר אחר יקח
מג וטח את־הבית: ואם־ישוב הנגע ופרח בבית אחר חלץ את־האבנים
מד ואחרי הקצות את־הבית ואחרי הטוח: ובא הכהן וראה והנה פשה
מה הנגע בבית צרעת ממארת הוא בבית טמא הוא: ונתץ את־הבית
את־אבניו ואת־עציו ואת כל־עפר הבית והוציא אל־מחוץ לעיר
מו אל־מקום טמא: והבא אל־הבית כל־ימי הסגיר אתו יטמא
מז עד־הערב: והשכב בבית יכבס את־בגדיו והאכל בבית יכבס
מח את־בגדיו: ואם־בא יבא הכהן וראה והנה לא־פשה הנגע בבית
מט אחרי הטח את־הבית וטהר הכהן את־הבית כי נרפא הנגע: ולקח
נ לחטא את־הבית שתי צפרים ועץ ארז ושני תולעת ואזב: ושחט
נא את־הצפר האחת אל־כלי־חרש על־מים חיים: ולקח את־עץ־
הארז ואת־האזב ואת | שני התולעת ואת הצפר החיה וטבל אתם
בדם הצפר השחוטה ובמים החיים והזה אל־הבית שבע פעמים: וחטא
נב את־הבית בדם הצפור ובמים החיים ובצפר החיה ובעץ
נג הארז ובאזב ובשני התולעת: ושלח את־הצפר החיה אל־מחוץ לעיר

---

36. ופנו את הבית בטרם יבא הכהן — *And they shall empty the house before the Kohen comes.* But he shall not come before this (is done). In the interim, there will be time for the owners to pray and repent (as well as) time for the *Kohen's* prayers. The period of "shutting up" is given for this (purpose, as well) (13:3). In the *Midrash* (*Vayikra Rabbah, Metzora*), it is said that all this alludes to the first destruction (of the Holy Temple), its remedy (restoration) in the Second (Temple), and its demolishment in the second destruc-

NOTES

36. ופנו את הבית בטרם יבא הכהן — *And they shall empty the house before the Kohen comes.* Consistent with his commentary in the previous chapter (13:47), the *Sforno* explains that the purpose of נגעי בתים, *afflictions of a house,* is to arouse the owner to examine his conduct and repent his sins, therefore an opportunity is given to him to do so *before* the *Kohen* comes to pronounce the house *tamei,* unclean.

The Midrash cited by the *Sforno* interprets this *parashah* in a symbolic manner as alluding to the destruction of the First Temple, the construction and subsequent destruction of the Second Temple and the eventual rebuilding of the Third Temple. *The house in the land of your possession* (v. 34) introduces the theme of the Temple, the House of God. *He that owns the house* (v. 35) refers to God. The dismantling of the house (vs. 40-41) symbol-

land of Canaan that I give you as a possession, and I will place a tzaraas
affliction upon a house in the land of your possession; 35 the one to whom the
house belongs shall come and declare to the Kohen, saying: Something like
an affliction has appeared to me in the house. 36 The Kohen shall command;
and they shall clear the house before the Kohen comes to look at the
affliction, so that everything in the house should not become contaminated;
and afterward shall the Kohen come to look at the house. 37 He shall look at
the affliction and behold! — the affliction is in the walls of the house,
depressed, deep greens or deep reds; and their appearance is lower than the
wall. 38 The Kohen shall exit from the house to the entrance of the house; and
he shall quarantine the house for a seven-day period. 39 The Kohen shall
return on the seventh day; he shall look and behold! — the affliction had
spread in the walls of the house. 40 The Kohen shall command, and they shall
remove the stones that contain the affliction, and they shall cast them
outside the city onto a contaminated place. 41 And the house shall be scraped
on the inside, all around; the mortar that they have scraped they are to pour
outside the city onto a contaminated place. 42 They shall take other stones
and bring them in place of the stones; and they shall take other mortar and
plaster the house.

43 If the affliction returns and erupts in the house after he has removed the
stones, after he has scraped the house and after plastering; 44 then the Kohen
shall come and look, and behold! — the affliction had spread in the house:
It is a malignant tzaraas in the house, it is contaminated. 45 He shall demolish
the house — its stones, its timber, and all the mortar of the house; they shall
take it to the outside of the city, to a contaminated place. 46 Anyone who
comes into the house during all the days he had quarantined it shall be contaminated until evening. 47 But one who reclines in the house shall immerse
his garments; and one who eats in the house shall immerse his garments.

48 If the Kohen is to come and look and behold! — the affliction has not
spread in the house after the plastering of the house; then the Kohen shall
declare the house to be pure, for the affliction has healed. 49 To purify the
house, he shall take two birds, cedarwood, crimson thread, and hyssop. 50 He
shall slaughter the one bird into an earthenware vessel over fresh water.
51 He shall take the cedarwood, the hyssop, the crimson thread, and the live
bird, and he shall dip them into the blood of the slaughtered bird and into the
fresh water; and he shall sprinkle upon the house seven times. 52 He shall
cleanse the house with the blood of the bird and with the fresh water; and
with the live bird, with the cedarwood, with the hyssop, and with the
crimson thread. 53 He shall set the live bird free toward the outside of the city

---

tion, and its purification through the third construction, may it be built and established speedily in our days, Amen.

NOTES

izes the destruction of the Temple and *casting them . . . outside the city* (v. 40) indicates the exile of Israel. Taking other stones and rebuilding the house (v. 42) symbolizes the rebuilding of the Temple when the people return from Babylonia, but verse 45 indicates that the house will once again be destroyed. The expression *So shall he make atonement for the house and it shall be clean* (v. 53) alludes to the Third Temple which shall be everlasting.

חמישי נד אֶל־פְּנֵי הַשָּׂדֶה וְכִפֶּר עַל־הַבַּיִת וְטָהֵר: זֹאת הַתּוֹרָה לְכָל־נֶגַע הַצָּרַעַת
נה־נז וְלַנָּתֶק: וּלְצָרַעַת הַבֶּגֶד וְלַבָּיִת: וְלַשְׂאֵת וְלַסַּפַּחַת וְלַבֶּהָרֶת: לְהוֹרֹת
בְּיוֹם הַטָּמֵא וּבְיוֹם הַטָּהֹר זֹאת תּוֹרַת הַצָּרָעַת:
טו א־ב וַיְדַבֵּר יהוה אֶל־מֹשֶׁה וְאֶל־אַהֲרֹן לֵאמֹר: דַּבְּרוּ אֶל־בְּנֵי יִשְׂרָאֵל
ג וַאֲמַרְתֶּם אֲלֵהֶם אִישׁ אִישׁ כִּי יִהְיֶה זָב מִבְּשָׂרוֹ זוֹבוֹ טָמֵא הוּא: וְזֹאת
תִּהְיֶה טֻמְאָתוֹ בְּזוֹבוֹ רָר בְּשָׂרוֹ אֶת־זוֹבוֹ אוֹ־הֶחְתִּים בְּשָׂרוֹ מִזּוֹבוֹ
ד טֻמְאָתוֹ הִוא: כָּל־הַמִּשְׁכָּב אֲשֶׁר יִשְׁכַּב עָלָיו הַזָּב יִטְמָא וְכָל־הַכְּלִי
ה אֲשֶׁר־יֵשֵׁב עָלָיו יִטְמָא: וְאִישׁ אֲשֶׁר יִגַּע בְּמִשְׁכָּבוֹ יְכַבֵּס בְּגָדָיו
ו וְרָחַץ בַּמַּיִם וְטָמֵא עַד־הָעָרֶב: וְהַיֹּשֵׁב עַל־הַכְּלִי אֲשֶׁר־יֵשֵׁב עָלָיו הַזָּב

---

54. זאת הַתּוֹרָה — *This is the law.* He who comes to instruct regarding the afflictions must know how to differentiate between two kinds (of afflictions), even though they are of one class, as it says, וּבֵין נֶגַע לָנֶגַע, *Between affliction and affliction* (*Deut.* 17:8).

לְכָל נֶגַע הַצָּרַעַת וְלַנָּתֶק — *For all manner of affliction of leprosy and for a scall.* Although they are both a leprosy on the skin of man, nonetheless, they are different in that the scall is judged not by its appearance, but by that hair which falls out and by black hair (Chapter 13). All other types of leprosy are (however) always judged through appearance.

55. וּלְצָרַעַת הַבֶּגֶד וְלַבָּיִת — *And for the leprosy of a garment and for a house.* Although they are similar regarding their green or red appearance, and both are (afflicted) in an unnatural manner (see *Sforno* 13:47), nonetheless, they are differentiated in the following fashion: If (the affliction) in the garment has spread by the end of the first week, the (garment) must be burnt in its entirety (13:51,52), but (if the affliction) has spread in a house by the end of the first week, the stones are taken out, scraped and plastered and a (further) week is granted (to determine whether the affliction will return or not) (vs. 39-42).

56. וְלַשְׂאֵת וְלַסַּפַּחַת וְלַבֶּהָרֶת — *And for a rising, and for a scab and for a bright spot.* Although they are similar (in many ways) — each one is white, they have similar laws and they (can be) combined (to effect the needed size) — as (our Sages) have received the tradition, nonetheless, he who comes to instruct regarding (these) afflictions must be expert in the different degrees of whiteness and their location. For (whereas) the place of a boil and a burn is judged by mixed appearances, a scab and a hairy area are not judged by appearance at all.

57. זאת תּוֹרַת הַצָּרָעַת — *This is the law of leprosy.* One must not be extra strict in pronouncing *tamei* other afflictions of the skin and flesh, even though there are many more types of leprosy among us, as it says, אַל תּוֹסְףְּ עַל דְּבָרָיו, *Add not to His words* (*Proverbs* 30:6). For indeed, even with all their severity we cannot apply the laws of leprosy to them at all, just as the (Torah) pronounces him *tahor*, clean, when the afflicted

NOTES

54-56. זאת הַתּוֹרָה . . . הַצָּרַעַת וְלַנָּתֶק: וּלְצָרַעַת הַבֶּגֶד וְלַבָּיִת: וְלַשְׂאֵת — *This is the law . . . of leprosy and for a scall. And for the leprosy of a garment and for a house. And for a rising.* The phrase זאת הַתּוֹרָה, the introductory phrase of these three verses, is interpreted by the *Sforno* as emphasizing the need for the *Kohen* to be expert in these laws because there are so many subtle variations of *halachah* and differentiations between one affliction and another, as he explains in his commentary. The combining of certain afflictions in the same verse is explained by the *Sforno* as the listing of afflictions which possess similarities, yet are different. For example, *leprosy and scall* (v. 54), *leprosy of a garment and a house* (v. 55), and *a rising, a scab and a bright spot* (v. 56) have common characteristics but there is diversity in their laws. For the *Kohen* to know how to decide these questions, he must possess great expertise.

upon the open field; thus he shall provide atonement for the house, and it shall become purified.

54 *This is the law for every tzaraas affliction and the nesek;* 55 *and tzaraas of the garment and of the house;* 56 *and of the s'eis, of the sapachas, and of the baheres;* 57 *to rule on which day it is contaminated and on which day it is purified; this is the law of tzaraas.*

15

1 *HASHEM spoke to Moses and Aaron, saying:* 2 *Speak to the Children of Israel and say to them: Any man who will have a discharge from his flesh, his discharge is contaminated.* 3 *Thus shall be his contamination when he discharges: whether his flesh runs with his discharge or it becomes stopped up because of his discharge, that is his contamination.* 4 *Any bedding upon which the person with the discharge will recline shall be contaminated, and any vessel upon which he will sit shall become contaminated.* 5 *A person who will touch his bedding shall immerse his garments and immerse himself in the water, and he remains contaminated until the evening.* 6 *And one who sits upon a vessel upon which the man with the discharge will sit, shall*

---

skin turns entirely white (13:13) for the leprosy has crossed utterly over the boundary of *tumah* to (a level of) evil, similar to *tamei* (holy meat) which is burnt and (thereby) its form is obliterated.

XV

2. זָב מִבְּשָׂרוֹ — *An issue from his flesh.* (We) have learned from tradition that *from his flesh* (implies) "not due to an accident," meaning that the issue's flow is caused by *his flesh,* which is an euphemism for the male organ or reproductive system, but not by any other cause which aroused the emission. (Our Sages) here explained that this issue (looks like) the white of an addled egg. Now, when this occurs *from his flesh,* caused solely by an ailment of the reproductive organ, behold, this indicates a weakness and lack in its assimilative ability which usually happens because of overindulgence in sexual intercourse and his preoccupation (with these matters), as a result of which the folly of his lewd sinfulness does not cease. Therefore, it is fitting that he count seven clean (days) (v. 13) in which to erase his preoccupation from his heart, (after which) he immerses himself, (thereby removing) his (state of) *tumah* and finds atonement through sin and burnt offerings (vs. 14-15) for his deeds and thoughts.

NOTES

57. זֹאת תּוֹרַת הַצָּרָעַת — *This is the law of leprosy.* The *Sforno* in the previous chapter (13:2) explained that it is not the severity of the physical ailment which determines the cleanness or *tumah* of the affliction. Since it is a גְּזֵרַת הַכָּתוּב, *a Scriptural decree,* only those ordained by God as being *tamei* are considered to be so. Therefore, it follows that only those enumerated by the Torah in these chapters are deemed צָרַעַת, *leprosy*. Thus, the laws of leprosy cannot be understood logically by man. One cannot, with pure reason, grasp why a white spot causes *tumah* whereas the *total* spreading of white over one's skin is deemed *tahor*! The *Sforno* does, however, suggest a reason. When holy meat (קָדָשִׁים) becomes *tamei,* and is burnt, the ashes are no longer considered as being *tamei,* nor do they have the stringencies of holy meat for the form has been changed. So too, with the affliction; when it covers the entire body it is as though the skin has been consumed and thereby transformed.

XV

2. זָב מִבְּשָׂרוֹ — *An issue from his flesh.* The *Sforno* explains that זִיבָה, *an abnormal issue,* which some interpret to mean gonorrhea, is caused by impure thoughts and unbridled sexual indulgence. Therefore, two sacrifices must be brought by the זָב when he is ready for atonement. One is the חַטָּאת, *sin offering,* which atones for overt sinful acts, while the second is the עוֹלָה, *burnt offering,* which atones for man's thoughts, as the *Sforno* explained above (1:2).

ז יְכַבֵּס בְּגָדָיו וְרָחַץ בַּמַּיִם וְטָמֵא עַד־הָעָרֶב: וְהַנֹּגֵעַ בִּבְשַׂר הַזָּב יְכַבֵּס
ח בְּגָדָיו וְרָחַץ בַּמַּיִם וְטָמֵא עַד־הָעָרֶב: וְכִי־יָרֹק הַזָּב בַּטָּהוֹר וְכִבֶּס בְּגָדָיו
ט וְרָחַץ בַּמַּיִם וְטָמֵא עַד־הָעָרֶב: וְכָל־הַמֶּרְכָּב אֲשֶׁר יִרְכַּב עָלָיו הַזָּב
י יִטְמָא: וְכָל־הַנֹּגֵעַ בְּכֹל אֲשֶׁר יִהְיֶה תַחְתָּיו יִטְמָא עַד־הָעָרֶב וְהַנּוֹשֵׂא
יא אוֹתָם יְכַבֵּס בְּגָדָיו וְרָחַץ בַּמַּיִם וְטָמֵא עַד־הָעָרֶב: וְכֹל אֲשֶׁר יִגַּע־בּוֹ הַזָּב
וְיָדָיו לֹא־שָׁטַף בַּמָּיִם וְכִבֶּס בְּגָדָיו וְרָחַץ בַּמַּיִם וְטָמֵא עַד־הָעָרֶב:
יב וּכְלִי־חֶרֶשׂ אֲשֶׁר־יִגַּע־בּוֹ הַזָּב יִשָּׁבֵר וְכָל־כְּלִי־עֵץ יִשָּׁטֵף בַּמָּיִם:
יג וְכִי־יִטְהַר הַזָּב מִזּוֹבוֹ וְסָפַר לוֹ שִׁבְעַת יָמִים לְטָהֳרָתוֹ וְכִבֶּס בְּגָדָיו וְרָחַץ
יד בְּשָׂרוֹ בְּמַיִם חַיִּים וְטָהֵר: וּבַיּוֹם הַשְּׁמִינִי יִקַּח־לוֹ שְׁתֵּי תֹרִים אוֹ שְׁנֵי בְּנֵי
טו יוֹנָה וּבָא ׀ לִפְנֵי יהוה אֶל־פֶּתַח אֹהֶל מוֹעֵד וּנְתָנָם אֶל־הַכֹּהֵן: וְעָשָׂה
אֹתָם הַכֹּהֵן אֶחָד חַטָּאת וְהָאֶחָד עֹלָה וְכִפֶּר עָלָיו הַכֹּהֵן לִפְנֵי יהוה
ששי [שביעי] טז מִזּוֹבוֹ: וְאִישׁ כִּי־תֵצֵא מִמֶּנּוּ שִׁכְבַת־זָרַע וְרָחַץ בַּמַּיִם
יז אֶת־כָּל־בְּשָׂרוֹ וְטָמֵא עַד־הָעָרֶב: וְכָל־בֶּגֶד וְכָל־עוֹר אֲשֶׁר־יִהְיֶה עָלָיו
יח שִׁכְבַת־זָרַע וְכֻבַּס בַּמַּיִם וְטָמֵא עַד־הָעָרֶב: וְאִשָּׁה אֲשֶׁר יִשְׁכַּב אִישׁ
אֹתָהּ שִׁכְבַת־זָרַע וְרָחֲצוּ בַמַּיִם וְטָמְאוּ עַד־הָעָרֶב:
יט וְאִשָּׁה כִּי־תִהְיֶה זָבָה דָּם יִהְיֶה זֹבָהּ בִּבְשָׂרָהּ שִׁבְעַת יָמִים תִּהְיֶה בְנִדָּתָהּ
כ וְכָל־הַנֹּגֵעַ בָּהּ יִטְמָא עַד־הָעָרֶב: וְכֹל אֲשֶׁר תִּשְׁכַּב עָלָיו בְּנִדָּתָהּ יִטְמָא
כא וְכֹל אֲשֶׁר־תֵּשֵׁב עָלָיו יִטְמָא: וְכָל־הַנֹּגֵעַ בְּמִשְׁכָּבָהּ יְכַבֵּס בְּגָדָיו וְרָחַץ
כב בַּמַּיִם וְטָמֵא עַד־הָעָרֶב: וְכָל־הַנֹּגֵעַ בְּכָל־כְּלִי אֲשֶׁר־תֵּשֵׁב עָלָיו יְכַבֵּס
כג בְּגָדָיו וְרָחַץ בַּמַּיִם וְטָמֵא עַד־הָעָרֶב: וְאִם עַל־הַמִּשְׁכָּב הוּא אוֹ

---

18. וְאִשָּׁה אֲשֶׁר יִשְׁכַּב אִישׁ אֹתָהּ — *The woman also with whom a man shall lie carnally.* It is not written אִישׁ כִּי יִשְׁכַּב אֶת אִשָּׁה, *If a man lies with a woman,* for (the Torah) attests that a woman does not become unclean from any issue unless it is red or from a seminal emission, as does a man. However the *tumah* of a woman through semen only results when a man lies with her, even though (the semen) is in (her) concealed chamber.

19. וְאִשָּׁה כִּי תִהְיֶה זָבָה דָּם — *And if a woman have an issue of blood.* (The Torah) teaches the laws of a נִדָּה, *menstruant*, and a זָבָה, *woman that has a flow many days*, imposing (the obligation) upon a זָבָה (to bring) a sin and a burnt offering. Thus (the Torah) testifies that this does not (normally) occur with the daughters of His people, except to alert them (lit., awaken their ear) to the "early rebellion" in deed and in thought, for it is, in actuality, (merely) an extension of the punishment with which Eve was punished for her deed and thought, included in His saying, הַרְבָּה אַרְבֶּה עִצְּבוֹנֵךְ, *I will greatly multiply your pain* (*Genesis* 3:16). Therefore, it is fitting that she count seven clean days until a spirit of repentance and purity "pours over her," and then she will immerse herself and achieve

NOTES

18. וְאִשָּׁה אֲשֶׁר יִשְׁכַּב אִישׁ אֹתָהּ — *The woman also with whom a man shall lie carnally.* A woman becomes טְמֵאָה, *unclean,* in one of two ways: if blood flows from her, or through semen (שִׁכְבַת זֶרַע) which has entered her body through sexual intercourse. The latter law, however, is difficult to understand since there is a principle that טוּמְאַת בֵּית הַסְּתָרִים, *tumah in a concealed region,* does not render her unclean. The Talmud (*Niddah* 41b) therefore states that, in this case, it is a Scriptural ordinance (גְּזֵרַת הַכָּתוּב). The *Sforno* explains that our Sages understanding of this *halachah* is derived from the phraseology of our verse — i.e., אִשָּׁה אֲשֶׁר יִשְׁכַּב אִישׁ אֹתָהּ, rather than אִישׁ כִּי יִשְׁכַּב.

immerse his garments and immerse himself in the water, and he remains contaminated until the evening. 7 *One who touches the flesh of the man with the discharge shall immerse his garments and immerse himself in the water, and he remains contaminated until the evening.* 8 *If the person with the discharge will spit upon a pure person, he shall immerse his garments and immerse himself in the water, and he remains contaminated until the evening.* 9 *Any riding equipment upon which the person with the discharge will ride shall become contaminated.* 10 *And whoever touches anything that will be beneath him shall become contaminated until evening; and whoever carries them shall immerse his garments and immerse himself in the water, and he remains contaminated until the evening.* 11 *Whomever the man with the discharge touches without having rinsed his hands in the water shall immerse his garments and immerse himself in the water, and he remains contaminated until the evening.* 12 *Pottery that the man with the discharge will touch shall be broken; and any wooden utensil shall be rinsed in water.*

13 *When the man with the discharge ceases his discharge, he shall count for himself seven days from his cessation, immerse his garments and immerse his flesh in spring water, and become purified.* 14 *On the eighth day he shall take for himself two turtledoves or two young doves; he shall come before* HASHEM *to the entrance of the Tent of Meeting, and give them to the Kohen.* 15 *The Kohen shall make them one as a sin-offering and one as an elevation-offering — thus the Kohen shall provide him atonement before* HASHEM *from his discharge.*

16 *A man from whom there is a discharge of semen shall immerse his entire flesh in the water and remain contaminated until evening.* 17 *Any garment or anything of leather, upon which there shall be semen, shall be immersed in the water and remain contaminated until evening.* 18 *A woman with whom a man will have carnal relations, they shall immerse themselves in the water and remain contaminated until evening.*

19 *When a woman has a discharge — her discharge from her flesh being blood — she shall be in her state of separation for a seven-day period and anyone who touches her shall remain contaminated until the evening.* 20 *Anything upon which she may recline during her state of separation shall become contaminated; and anything upon which she sits shall become contaminated.* 21 *Anyone who touches her bedding shall immerse his garments and immerse himself in the water, and he remains contaminated until evening.* 22 *Anyone who touches any utensil upon which she will sit shall immerse his garments and immerse himself in the water, and he remains contaminated until evening.* 23 *Or if someone is upon the bedding or*

atonement for (her) misdeeds through the sin offering, and from her (evil) thoughts through the burnt offering.

NOTES

19. וְאִשָּׁה כִּי תִהְיֶה זָבָה דָּם — *And if a woman have an issue of blood.* The *Sforno* in his commentary on *Genesis* 3:16 interprets עִצְּבוֹנֵךְ, *your pain,* as referring to menstruation. זִיבָה, *an abnormal flow,* is, in his opinion, an extension (in terms of the pain endured) of this "early" punishment of Eve. Hence, when a woman is thus afflicted it is meant to spur her to repentance, as is the case with all afflictions; such as leprosy of the body, garments, and houses. She also must bring a sin and a burnt offering for the reasons given in verse 2 (see the note there), and in verse 32 (see the *Sforno's* commentary).

כד עַל־הַכְּלִי אֲשֶׁר־הִוא יֹשֶׁבֶת־עָלָיו בְּנָגְעוֹ־בוֹ יִטְמָא עַד־הָעָרֶב׃ וְאִם
שָׁכֹב יִשְׁכַּב אִישׁ אֹתָהּ וּתְהִי נִדָּתָהּ עָלָיו וְטָמֵא שִׁבְעַת יָמִים
כה וְכָל־הַמִּשְׁכָּב אֲשֶׁר־יִשְׁכַּב עָלָיו יִטְמָא׃ וְאִשָּׁה כִּי־יָזוּב
זוֹב דָּמָהּ יָמִים רַבִּים בְּלֹא עֶת־נִדָּתָהּ אוֹ כִי־תָזוּב עַל־נִדָּתָהּ כָּל־יְמֵי זוֹב
כו טֻמְאָתָהּ כִּימֵי נִדָּתָהּ תִּהְיֶה טְמֵאָה הִוא׃ כָּל־הַמִּשְׁכָּב אֲשֶׁר־תִּשְׁכַּב
עָלָיו כָּל־יְמֵי זוֹבָהּ כְּמִשְׁכַּב נִדָּתָהּ יִהְיֶה־לָּהּ וְכָל־הַכְּלִי אֲשֶׁר תֵּשֵׁב עָלָיו
כז טָמֵא יִהְיֶה כְּטֻמְאַת נִדָּתָהּ׃ וְכָל־הַנּוֹגֵעַ בָּם יִטְמָא וְכִבֶּס בְּגָדָיו וְרָחַץ
כח בַּמַּיִם וְטָמֵא עַד־הָעָרֶב׃ וְאִם־טָהֲרָה מִזּוֹבָהּ וְסָפְרָה לָּהּ שִׁבְעַת יָמִים
שביעי כט וְאַחַר תִּטְהָר׃ וּבַיּוֹם הַשְּׁמִינִי תִּקַּח־לָהּ שְׁתֵּי תֹרִים אוֹ שְׁנֵי בְּנֵי יוֹנָה
ל וְהֵבִיאָה אוֹתָם אֶל־הַכֹּהֵן אֶל־פֶּתַח אֹהֶל מוֹעֵד׃ וְעָשָׂה הַכֹּהֵן
אֶת־הָאֶחָד חַטָּאת וְאֶת־הָאֶחָד עֹלָה וְכִפֶּר עָלֶיהָ הַכֹּהֵן לִפְנֵי יהוה מִזּוֹב
מפטיר לא טֻמְאָתָהּ׃ וְהִזַּרְתֶּם אֶת־בְּנֵי־יִשְׂרָאֵל מִטֻּמְאָתָם וְלֹא יָמֻתוּ בְּטֻמְאָתָם
לב בְּטַמְּאָם אֶת־מִשְׁכָּנִי אֲשֶׁר בְּתוֹכָם׃ זֹאת תּוֹרַת הַזָּב וַאֲשֶׁר תֵּצֵא מִמֶּנּוּ
לג שִׁכְבַת־זֶרַע לְטָמְאָה־בָהּ׃ וְהַדָּוָה בְּנִדָּתָהּ וְהַזָּב אֶת־זוֹבוֹ לַזָּכָר וְלַנְּקֵבָה
וּלְאִישׁ אֲשֶׁר יִשְׁכַּב עִם־טְמֵאָה׃

---

32. זֹאת תּוֹרַת הַזָּב — *This is the law of one who has an issue.* This is what is proper to reflect upon in all these (laws): Firstly, since a זָב is obligated to bring a sin offering (and burnt offering), it indicates that they are brought (to atone for) for that which is sinful, both in deed and in thought.

וַאֲשֶׁר תֵּצֵא מִמֶּנּוּ שִׁכְבַת זֶרַע לְטָמְאָה בָהּ — *And of one from whom the flow of seed issues forth so that he is unclean thereby.* (And secondly), because the reason for the *tumah* resulting from a nocturnal emission is that the intent of the one who emitted it was *to become tamei thereby,* (which was caused by) the "instigation of the serpent" (based on *Bava Basra* 17a), and not for the perpetuation of the species; otherwise, there would be no *tumah* (connected) with semen just as there is no *tumah* in excrement and urine.

33. וְהַדָּוָה בְּנִדָּתָהּ — *And of she who is sick with her menstruation.* The term דְּוֹתָהּ, *her sickness* (12:2), implies that this is (due) to sin, and therefore she becomes *tamei.*

NOTES

32. זֹאת תּוֹרַת הַזָּב — *This is the law of one who has an issue.* The *Sforno* interprets this phrase in the context of the *learning* of certain lessons. One lesson is elucidated through the reason for the bringing of two offerings, as explained above (to expiate the evil act and thought). The second lies in the fact that the only emission from the human body which makes a man unclean (and a woman as

the utensil upon which she is sitting, when he touches it, he becomes contaminated until evening. [24] *If a man lies with her, then her state of separation will be upon him and he becomes contaminated for a seven-day period; any bedding upon which he may recline shall become contaminated.*

[25] *If a woman's blood flows for many days outside of her period of separation, or if she has a flow after her separation, all the days of her contaminated flow shall be like the days of her separation; she is contaminated.* [26] *Any bedding upon which she may lie throughout the days of her flow shall be to her like the bedding of her state of separation; any vessel upon which she may sit shall be contaminated, like the contamination of her state of separation.* [27] *Anyone who touches them shall become contaminated; he shall immerse his garments and immerse himself in the water, and he remains contaminated until evening.* [28] *If she ceases her flow, she must count seven days for herself, and afterwards she can be purified.*

[29] *On the eighth day she shall take for herself two turtledoves or two young doves; she shall bring them to the Kohen, to the entrance of the Tent of Meeting.* [30] *The Kohen shall make one a a sin-offering and one an elevation-offering; the Kohen shall provide atonement for her before HASHEM from her contaminating flow.*

[31] *You shall separate the Children of Israel from their contamination; and they shall not die as a result of their contamination if they contaminate My Tabernacle that is among them.* [32] *This is the teaching concerning the man with a discharge, and from whom there is a seminal discharge, through which he becomes contaminated;* [33] *and concerning a woman who suffers through her separation, and concerning a person who has his flow, whether male or female, and concerning a man who lies with a contaminated woman.*

וְהַזָּב — *And of those who have an issue* . . . and to consider the matter of a *zav*, which is to alert one (lit., awaken the ear) to the sin which preceded it.

אֶת זוֹבוֹ לַזָּכָר וְלַנְּקֵבָה — *The issue of a man and of a woman.* And (in connection) with this, it is fitting to discern the differences (in law) regarding the issue of a man and the issue of a woman, for the issue of a woman is only *tamei* if it is red, (whereas) the issue of a man is only *tamei* if it is *not* red.

וּלְאִישׁ אֲשֶׁר יִשְׁכַּב עִם טְמֵאָה — *And of the man that lies with her that is unclean.* It is also proper to consider that regarding a man who lies with an unclean (woman), (the Torah) says, *and her niddos shall be upon him* (v. 24), whereas this is not said of a clean woman who lies with a *zav*, because (the Torah) is teaching us that a male is more impaired by lying with a "sick woman" (i.e., נִדָּה) than a woman is impaired by lying with a "sick man" (i.e., זָב), as we find from experience regarding leprous women and similar cases.

NOTES

well under certain circumstances) is semen. The reason for this is that this emission, although involuntary, is connected to impure thoughts; yet is not for reproductive purposes. The Torah exhorts us to contemplate the laws discussed in this chapter so that we may better understand their significance and better appreciate the different levels of *tumah*, as well as the importance of examining our thoughts and deeds which cause these abnormal ailments.

פרשת אחרי

טז א וַיְדַבֵּר יהוה אֶל־מֹשֶׁה אַחֲרֵי מוֹת שְׁנֵי בְּנֵי אַהֲרֹן בְּקָרְבָתָם לִפְנֵי־יהוה
ב וַיָּמֻתוּ: וַיֹּאמֶר יהוה אֶל־מֹשֶׁה דַּבֵּר אֶל־אַהֲרֹן אָחִיךָ וְאַל־יָבֹא בְכָל־עֵת
אֶל־הַקֹּדֶשׁ מִבֵּית לַפָּרֹכֶת אֶל־פְּנֵי הַכַּפֹּרֶת אֲשֶׁר עַל־הָאָרֹן וְלֹא יָמוּת
ג כִּי בֶּעָנָן אֵרָאֶה עַל־הַכַּפֹּרֶת: בְּזֹאת יָבֹא אַהֲרֹן אֶל־הַקֹּדֶשׁ בְּפַר בֶּן־בָּקָר
ד לְחַטָּאת וְאַיִל לְעֹלָה: כְּתֹנֶת־בַּד קֹדֶשׁ יִלְבָּשׁ וּמִכְנְסֵי־בַד יִהְיוּ עַל־בְּשָׂרוֹ
וּבְאַבְנֵט בַּד יַחְגֹּר וּבְמִצְנֶפֶת בַּד יִצְנֹף בִּגְדֵי־קֹדֶשׁ הֵם וְרָחַץ בַּמַּיִם אֶת־
ה בְּשָׂרוֹ וּלְבֵשָׁם: וּמֵאֵת עֲדַת בְּנֵי יִשְׂרָאֵל יִקַּח שְׁנֵי־שְׂעִירֵי עִזִּים לְחַטָּאת
ו וְאַיִל אֶחָד לְעֹלָה: וְהִקְרִיב אַהֲרֹן אֶת־פַּר הַחַטָּאת אֲשֶׁר־לוֹ וְכִפֶּר בַּעֲדוֹ
ז וּבְעַד בֵּיתוֹ: וְלָקַח אֶת־שְׁנֵי הַשְּׂעִירִם וְהֶעֱמִיד אֹתָם לִפְנֵי יהוה פֶּתַח אֹהֶל
ח מוֹעֵד: וְנָתַן אַהֲרֹן עַל־שְׁנֵי הַשְּׂעִירִם גֹּרָלוֹת גּוֹרָל אֶחָד לַיהוה וְגוֹרָל אֶחָד

XVI

1. וַיְדַבֵּר ה׳ אֶל מֹשֶׁה אַחֲרֵי מוֹת — *And HASHEM spoke to Moses after the death.* Behold, the word וַיְדַבֵּר, *and he spoke,* in the holy tongue does not usually introduce a particular statement but refers to a general course of communication. Therefore, the expression וַיְדַבֵּר, *and he spoke,* is usually followed by the word וַיֹּאמֶר, which indicates a particular statement. Hence, the sense of the verse is, *And HASHEM spoke to Moses after the death,* (v. 1) ... *and said to him, "Speak to Aaron your brother"* (v. 2). But because v. 1 speaks at length about the death of Aaron's sons which is a particular subject, (the Torah) does not simply state *and said to him* (in v. 2) but repeats the name of God, the Blessed One, Who is the speaker, and Moses, who is the listener.

However, according to some of our Sages, of blessed memory, these (two verses) represent two statements. The sense of the verses (will then be) *And HASHEM spoke to Moses and said, "Speak to Aaron ... that he come not ... that he die not."* And (secondly) *after the death of the two sons of Aaron,* He said to Moses, *"Speak to Aaron ... that he come not,"* that he should not enter (the Holy) except when he is so commanded *"that he die not,"* as his sons did when they persisted in offering incense beyond that which had been commanded. This (second statement) is meant to put him on guard more so than the first (statement).

2. כִּי בֶּעָנָן אֵרָאֶה — *For I will appear in a cloud ...* to speak with Moses in this generation, and in other generations to call those who are prepared for prophecy, similar to Samuel,

NOTES

XVI

1-2. וַיְדַבֵּר ה׳ אֶל מֹשֶׁה — *And HASHEM spoke to Moses.* Although verse 1 begins וַיְדַבֵּר ה׳, *And HASHEM spoke,* verse 2 nevertheless begins וַיֹּאמֶר ה׳, *And HASHEM said,* a seeming repetition. The *Sforno* explains that the two are not redundant. The former phrase refers to God's general communication with a prophet whereas the latter phrase refers to the exact nature of that communication. There is, however, a difficulty regarding these two verses since the Torah could have simply written in verse 2, ... וַיֹּאמֶר, דַּבֵּר, *And He said, 'Speak ...'* Why was it necessary to repeat the Name of God and the name of Moses? The *Sforno* answers that since there is an interruption in verse 1 where the Torah tells us about the death of Aaron's sons and the circumstances surrounding that incident, the Torah finds it necessary to repeat, once again, the name of the communicator (God) and the name of the recipient of that communication (Moses). The *Sforno* also suggests another interpretation of these two verses, as does *Rashi,* based on the *Sifra* that there were two orders and commandments which Moses was told to give to Aaron. The first was simply to warn Aaron not to enter the Holy (i.e., the Sanctuary) at will, but only at specifically ordained times, lest he die. The second was to underscore the peril of doing so by telling him that this was indeed the cause of his sons' death, thereby putting Aaron on guard. See *Rashi* who brings the

PARASHAS ACHAREI

16 [1] *HASHEM spoke to Moses after the death of Aaron's two sons, when*
they approached before HASHEM, and they died. [2] *And HASHEM said*
to Moses: Speak to Aaron, your brother — he shall not come at all times into
the Sanctuary, within the Curtain, in front of the Cover that is upon the
Ark, so that he should not die; for in a cloud will I appear upon the
Ark-cover. [3] *With this shall Aaron come into the Sanctuary: with a young*
bull for a sin-offering and a ram for an elevation-offering. [4] *He shall don a*
sacred linen Tunic; linen breeches shall be upon his flesh, he shall gird
himself with a linen Sash, and cover his head with a linen Turban; they are
sacred vestments — he shall immerse himself in water and then don them.
[5] *From the assembly of the Children of Israel he shall take two he-goats for*
a sin-offering and one ram for an elevation-offering.
[6] *Aaron shall bring near his own sin-offering bull, and provide atonement*
for himself and for his household. [7] *He shall take the two he-goats and*
stand them before HASHEM, at the entrance of the Tent of Meeting. [8] *Aaron*
shall place lots upon the two he-goats: one lot "for HASHEM" and one lot

---

about whom (the Torah) says, וּשְׁמוּאֵל שֹׁכֵב בְּהֵיכַל ה׳ אֲשֶׁר שָׁם אֲרוֹן אֱלֹהִים, וַיִּקְרָא ה׳ אֶל שְׁמוּאֵל, *And Samuel was lying in the Temple of HASHEM, where the Ark of God was and HASHEM called to Samuel* (*I Samuel* 3:3,4).

3. בְּזֹאת יָבֹא . . . בְּפַר בֶּן בָּקָר — *With this (Aaron) shall come . . . with a young bull.* (He shall come) with the sanctification of the bull as a sin offering and a ram as a burnt offering and the wearing of the linen (garments), which have no color, nor artificial design. For, indeed, the *Kohen Gadol* must not postpone his entrance to the inner (room) until after the sacrifice of the burnt offering, but must enter to burn the incense immediately after the slaughtering of the sin offering.

4. בִּגְדֵי קֹדֶשׁ הֵם — *They are holy garments.* In similar garments do angels appear to the prophets, for they (also) appear in linen garments.

5. שְׁנֵי שְׂעִירֵי עִזִּים לְחַטָּאת — *Two he-goats for a sin offering.* The first (goat) is to (atone) for sins committed in connection with the Sanctuary, and the (second) is sent away (to expiate) the other sins of the community which, due to the excess of its *tumah,* is not fit to be sacrificed and (even) defiles the one through whom it is sent.

8. גֹּרָלוֹת — *Lots.* Because the lot, particularly through the hand of His pious one, is

NOTES

words of Rabbi Elazar ben Azariah and the parable used by him regarding this second statement.

3. בְּזֹאת יָבֹא — *With this (Aaron) shall come.* The word בְּזֹאת, *with this,* is ambiguous. The *Midrash* offers numerous interpretations as to its meaning. The *Sforno* explains that it simply means that with *these* offerings (sin and burnt offerings) and *this* wearing of simple, unadorned, white linen garments, the *Kohen Gadol* is deemed worthy to enter the Holy of Holies to offer the incense in honor of God. (See the *Sforno's* commentary on verse 12.) Since the Torah tells us (vs. 23-24) that the linen garments were removed *before* the burnt offering was brought, the *Sforno* stresses that his entrance into the inner sanctum must have perforce preceded the burnt offering.

4. בִּגְדֵי קֹדֶשׁ הֵם — *They are holy garments.* The first part of this verse already stated that the linen tunic was *holy* (כְּתֹנֶת בַּד קֹדֶשׁ); hence what is the purpose of repeating the phrase קֹדֶשׁ הֵם, *they are holy*? The *Sforno* explains that the Torah is telling us that white linen garments in general are holy, being that angels appear in prophetic visions wearing these same kinds of garments (See *Ezekiel* 9:3 and *Daniel* 12:6).

8. גֹּרָלוֹת — *Lots.* The expression "pious one" used by the *Sforno* is based on *Deut.* 33:8, referring there specifically to Aaron, and in general to the tribe of

ט לַעֲזָאזֵל: וְהִקְרִיב אַהֲרֹן אֶת־הַשָּׂעִיר אֲשֶׁר עָלָה עָלָיו הַגּוֹרָל לַיהוָה
י וְעָשָׂהוּ חַטָּאת: וְהַשָּׂעִיר אֲשֶׁר עָלָה עָלָיו הַגּוֹרָל לַעֲזָאזֵל יָעֳמַד־חַי
יא לִפְנֵי יהוָה לְכַפֵּר עָלָיו לְשַׁלַּח אֹתוֹ לַעֲזָאזֵל הַמִּדְבָּרָה: וְהִקְרִיב אַהֲרֹן
אֶת־פַּר הַחַטָּאת אֲשֶׁר־לוֹ וְכִפֶּר בַּעֲדוֹ וּבְעַד בֵּיתוֹ וְשָׁחַט אֶת־פַּר
יב הַחַטָּאת אֲשֶׁר־לוֹ: וְלָקַח מְלֹא־הַמַּחְתָּה גַּחֲלֵי־אֵשׁ מֵעַל הַמִּזְבֵּחַ
מִלִּפְנֵי יהוָה וּמְלֹא חָפְנָיו קְטֹרֶת סַמִּים דַּקָּה וְהֵבִיא מִבֵּית לַפָּרֹכֶת:
יג וְנָתַן אֶת־הַקְּטֹרֶת עַל־הָאֵשׁ לִפְנֵי יהוָה וְכִסָּה ׀ עֲנַן הַקְּטֹרֶת
יד אֶת־הַכַּפֹּרֶת אֲשֶׁר עַל־הָעֵדוּת וְלֹא יָמוּת: וְלָקַח מִדַּם הַפָּר וְהִזָּה
בְאֶצְבָּעוֹ עַל־פְּנֵי הַכַּפֹּרֶת קֵדְמָה וְלִפְנֵי הַכַּפֹּרֶת יַזֶּה שֶׁבַע־פְּעָמִים
טו מִן־הַדָּם בְּאֶצְבָּעוֹ: וְשָׁחַט אֶת־שְׂעִיר הַחַטָּאת אֲשֶׁר לָעָם וְהֵבִיא
אֶת־דָּמוֹ אֶל־מִבֵּית לַפָּרֹכֶת וְעָשָׂה אֶת־דָּמוֹ כַּאֲשֶׁר עָשָׂה לְדַם הַפָּר
טז וְהִזָּה אֹתוֹ עַל־הַכַּפֹּרֶת וְלִפְנֵי הַכַּפֹּרֶת: וְכִפֶּר עַל־הַקֹּדֶשׁ מִטֻּמְאֹת
בְּנֵי יִשְׂרָאֵל וּמִפִּשְׁעֵיהֶם לְכָל־חַטֹּאתָם וְכֵן יַעֲשֶׂה לְאֹהֶל מוֹעֵד הַשֹּׁכֵן
יז אִתָּם בְּתוֹךְ טֻמְאֹתָם: וְכָל־אָדָם לֹא־יִהְיֶה ׀ בְּאֹהֶל מוֹעֵד בְּבֹאוֹ לְכַפֵּר
בַּקֹּדֶשׁ עַד־צֵאתוֹ וְכִפֶּר בַּעֲדוֹ וּבְעַד בֵּיתוֹ וּבְעַד כָּל־קְהַל יִשְׂרָאֵל:
יח וְיָצָא אֶל־הַמִּזְבֵּחַ אֲשֶׁר לִפְנֵי־יהוָה וְכִפֶּר עָלָיו וְלָקַח מִדַּם הַפָּר וּמִדַּם שני
יט הַשָּׂעִיר וְנָתַן עַל־קַרְנוֹת הַמִּזְבֵּחַ סָבִיב: וְהִזָּה עָלָיו מִן־הַדָּם בְּאֶצְבָּעוֹ
כ שֶׁבַע פְּעָמִים וְטִהֲרוֹ וְקִדְּשׁוֹ מִטֻּמְאֹת בְּנֵי יִשְׂרָאֵל: וְכִלָּה מִכַּפֵּר אֶת־
כא הַקֹּדֶשׁ וְאֶת־אֹהֶל מוֹעֵד וְאֶת־הַמִּזְבֵּחַ וְהִקְרִיב אֶת־הַשָּׂעִיר הֶחָי: וְסָמַךְ
אַהֲרֹן אֶת־שְׁתֵּי יָדָו עַל־רֹאשׁ הַשָּׂעִיר הַחַי וְהִתְוַדָּה עָלָיו אֶת־כָּל־

considered as if the one who casts it is seeking the word of God, as it says, בַּחֵיק יוּטַל אֶת הַגּוֹרָל וּמֵה׳ כָּל מִשְׁפָּטוֹ, *The lot is cast into the lap, but the whole of its decision is from HASHEM* (*Proverbs* 16:33).

9. וְעָשָׂהוּ חַטָּאת — *And make it a sin offering.* The lot designates (makes) the goat as a sin offering, as (our Sages) say, "It is the lot that makes the sin offering, not the calling of the Name which makes it a sin offering" (*Yoma* 40b).

11. וְכִפֶּר בַּעֲדוֹ — *And shall make atonement for himself.* We know from tradition that the two atonements for himself (v. 6 and here) are atonements achieved through the words of confession. Therefore, they precede the slaughter of the sin offering.

12. וְלָקַח מְלֹא הַמַּחְתָּה — *And he shall take a censer full.* For immediately after the sin offering has been slaughtered and he has confessed and his iniquity has been removed, he is prepared to be illuminated by the light of the King's countenance. Now, behold, the King will appear to all who are prepared (to receive) His light, as it says, *For in a cloud I*

NOTES

Levi. The *Sforno*, in his commentary on that verse, calls the tribe of Levi, שֵׁבֶט הֶחָסִיד, *the pious tribe.* Since we believe that nothing happens by chance (see *Sforno, Genesis* 24:14), the *Sforno* explains that a lot cast by a pious, righteous man is akin to seeking out God's decision.

9. וְעָשָׂהוּ חַטָּאת — *And make it a sin offering.* The expression וְעָשָׂהוּ is usually translated *and offer him.* The *Sforno* stresses that the correct translation should be *and make him.* The lot actually converts that particular goat into a חַטָּאת, *sin offering.*

12. וְלָקַח מְלֹא הַמַּחְתָּה — *And he shall take a censer full.* The portion dealing with the incense altar (*Exodus* 30) follows the portion dealing with the daily sacrifices, indicating that whenever God

"for Azazel." [9] *Aaron shall bring near the he-goat designated by lot for HASHEM, and make it a sin-offering.* [10] *And the he-goat designated by lot for Azazel shall be stood alive before HASHEM, to provide atonement through it, to send it to Azazel to the Wilderness.* [11] *Aaron shall bring near his own sin-offering bull and he shall provide atonement for himself and for his household; then he shall slaughter his own sin-offering bull.*

[12] *He shall take a shovelful of fiery coals from atop the Altar that is before HASHEM, and his cupped handsful of finely ground incense-spices, and bring it within the Curtain.* [13] *He shall place the incense upon the fire before HASHEM — so that the cloud of the incense shall blanket the Ark-cover that is atop the [Tablets of the] Testimony — so that he shall not die.* [14] *He shall take some of the blood of the bull and sprinkle with his forefinger upon the eastern front of the Ark-cover; and in front of the Ark-cover he shall sprinkle seven times from the blood with his forefinger.* [15] *He shall slaughter the sin-offering he-goat of the people, and bring its blood within the Curtain; he shall do with its blood as he had done with the blood of the bull, and sprinkle it upon the Ark-cover and in front of the Ark-cover.* [16] *Thus shall he provide atonement upon the Sanctuary for the contaminations of the Children of Israel, even for their rebellious sins among all their sins; and so shall he do for the Tent of Meeting that dwells with them amid their contamination.* [17] *Any person shall not be in the Tent of Meeting when he comes to provide atonement in the Sanctuary until his departure; he shall provide atonement for himself, for his household, and for the entire congregation of Israel.*

[18] *He shall go out to the Altar that is before HASHEM, and make atonement upon it: He shall take some blood of the bull and some blood of the he-goat and place it on the horns of the Altar all around.* [19] *He shall sprinkle upon it from the blood with his forefinger seven times; thus shall he cleanse it and sanctify it from the contaminations of the Children of Israel.*

[20] *When he is finished atoning for the Sanctuary, the Tent of Meeting, and the Altar, he shall bring the living he-goat near.* [21] *Aaron shall lean his two hands upon the head of the living he-goat and confess upon it all the*

---

will appear (v. 2). And it is proper to honor Him with incense, which is the case after the daily sacrifices (have been offered) as it says, עֹלַת תָּמִיד לְדֹרֹתֵיכֶם פֶּתַח אֹהֶל מוֹעֵד לִפְנֵי ה׳ אֲשֶׁר אִוָּעֵד לָכֶם שָׁמָּה, *It shall be a continual burnt offering throughout your generations at the door of the Tent of Meeting before HASHEM where I will meet with you* (Exodus 29:42). And this was the error of the sons of Aaron who offered (incense) *which He had not commanded them* (10:1).

15. הַחַטָּאת אֲשֶׁר לָעָם — *The sin offering that is for the people.* (This took place) after he completed his own atonement through his sin offering, similar to הִתְקוֹשְׁשׁוּ וָקוֹשׁוּ, *Gather yourselves together, and assemble together* (Zephaniah 2:1); with (all) this, the countenance of the King will appear.

NOTES

appears, whether on Yom Kippur or on an ordinary weekday, it is proper to offer incense in His honor.

15. הַחַטָּאת אֲשֶׁר לָעָם — *The sin offering that is for the people.* The *Sforno* cites the verse from *Zephaniah* because of the commentary of our Sages on that phrase, "Chastise yourself (first) and afterward chastise others" (*Sanhedrin* 18a).

עֲוֺנֹת בְּנֵי יִשְׂרָאֵל וְאֶת־כׇּל־פִּשְׁעֵיהֶם לְכׇל־חַטֹּאתָם וְנָתַן אֹתָם
כב עַל־רֹאשׁ הַשָּׂעִיר וְשִׁלַּח בְּיַד־אִישׁ עִתִּי הַמִּדְבָּרָה: וְנָשָׂא הַשָּׂעִיר עָלָיו
כג אֶת־כׇּל־עֲוֺנֹתָם אֶל־אֶרֶץ גְּזֵרָה וְשִׁלַּח אֶת־הַשָּׂעִיר בַּמִּדְבָּר: וּבָא אַהֲרֹן
אֶל־אֹהֶל מוֹעֵד וּפָשַׁט אֶת־בִּגְדֵי הַבָּד אֲשֶׁר לָבַשׁ בְּבֹאוֹ אֶל־הַקֹּדֶשׁ
כד וְהִנִּיחָם שָׁם: וְרָחַץ אֶת־בְּשָׂרוֹ בַמַּיִם בְּמָקוֹם קָדוֹשׁ וְלָבַשׁ אֶת־בְּגָדָיו
שלישי [שני] כה וְיָצָא וְעָשָׂה אֶת־עֹלָתוֹ וְאֶת־עֹלַת הָעָם וְכִפֶּר בַּעֲדוֹ וּבְעַד הָעָם: וְאֵת
כו חֵלֶב הַחַטָּאת יַקְטִיר הַמִּזְבֵּחָה: וְהַמְשַׁלֵּחַ אֶת־הַשָּׂעִיר לַעֲזָאזֵל יְכַבֵּס
כז בְּגָדָיו וְרָחַץ אֶת־בְּשָׂרוֹ בַּמָּיִם וְאַחֲרֵי־כֵן יָבוֹא אֶל־הַמַּחֲנֶה: וְאֵת פַּר
הַחַטָּאת וְאֵת ׀ שְׂעִיר הַחַטָּאת אֲשֶׁר הוּבָא אֶת־דָּמָם לְכַפֵּר בַּקֹּדֶשׁ
יוֹצִיא אֶל־מִחוּץ לַמַּחֲנֶה וְשָׂרְפוּ בָאֵשׁ אֶת־עֹרֹתָם וְאֶת־בְּשָׂרָם
כח וְאֶת־פִּרְשָׁם: וְהַשֹּׂרֵף אֹתָם יְכַבֵּס בְּגָדָיו וְרָחַץ אֶת־בְּשָׂרוֹ בַּמָּיִם
כט וְאַחֲרֵי־כֵן יָבוֹא אֶל־הַמַּחֲנֶה: וְהָיְתָה לָכֶם לְחֻקַּת עוֹלָם בַּחֹדֶשׁ הַשְּׁבִיעִי
בֶּעָשׂוֹר לַחֹדֶשׁ תְּעַנּוּ אֶת־נַפְשֹׁתֵיכֶם וְכׇל־מְלָאכָה לֹא תַעֲשׂוּ הָאֶזְרָח
ל וְהַגֵּר הַגָּר בְּתוֹכְכֶם: כִּי־בַיּוֹם הַזֶּה יְכַפֵּר עֲלֵיכֶם לְטַהֵר אֶתְכֶם מִכֹּל
לא חַטֹּאתֵיכֶם לִפְנֵי יהוה תִּטְהָרוּ: שַׁבַּת שַׁבָּתוֹן הִיא לָכֶם וְעִנִּיתֶם
לב אֶת־נַפְשֹׁתֵיכֶם חֻקַּת עוֹלָם: וְכִפֶּר הַכֹּהֵן אֲשֶׁר־יִמְשַׁח אֹתוֹ וַאֲשֶׁר
יְמַלֵּא אֶת־יָדוֹ לְכַהֵן תַּחַת אָבִיו וְלָבַשׁ אֶת־בִּגְדֵי הַבָּד בִּגְדֵי הַקֹּדֶשׁ:

---

23. וְהִנִּיחָם שָׁם — *And shall leave them there.* For he has offered them before God and thus they became sanctified with an extra sanctity; (therefore), it is not proper that they (be used), even by the *Kohen Gadol*, after this exalted hour has passed.

24. וְרָחַץ אֶת בְּשָׂרוֹ — *And he shall bathe his flesh . . .* after placing his hands on the goat sent (to the wilderness).

וְעָשָׂה אֶת עֹלָתוֹ — *And offer his burnt offering. . .* after he has atoned for himself through his sin offering, and for the people through the two sin offerings, the goat sent away (also) being called *sin offering,* as it says, *two he-goats for a sin offering* (v. 5). And both of them precede the burnt offering of the people, according to the rule that every sin offering precedes a burnt offering, as we know from tradition.

וְכִפֶּר בַּעֲדוֹ וּבְעַד הָעָם — *And make atonement for himself and for the people . . .* atonement for the evil thoughts of the heart as is fitting for those that are נְקִי כַפַּיִם וּבַר לֵבָב, *clean of hands and pure of heart* (*Psalms* 24:4), and this is (accomplished) through the burnt offering.

29. לְחֻקַּת עוֹלָם — *A statute forever.* Even when there is a Sanctuary for the service (of Yom Kippur), nonetheless, you must also observe (the laws of) rest and affliction.

NOTES

23. וְהִנִּיחָם שָׁם — *And shall leave them there.* The garments used on Yom Kippur were not to be used again, even on a subsequent Yom Kippur, as *Rashi* comments. The *Sforno* explains the reason for this law. Once used, they became holy to God for that specific service at that specific time; hence, they may no longer be used.

24. וְרָחַץ אֶת בְּשָׂרוֹ — *And he shall bathe his flesh.* The *Sforno* in verse 5 stated that the goat sent away to the wilderness carried with it excessive *tumah*, so much so that he who brought it there became *tamei.* Therefore, since the *Kohen Gadol* had *laid his hands on the head of this goat* (v. 21), it was necessary for him to bathe his flesh before bringing his burnt offering.

29. לְחֻקַּת עוֹלָם — *A statute forever.* This term appears here and in verses 31 and 34. The *Sforno* explains that each comes to teach us a different

iniquities of the Children of Israel, and all their rebellious sins among all their sins, and place them upon the head of the he-goat, and send it with a designated man to the desert. [22] *The he-goat will bear upon itself all their iniquities to an uninhabited land, and he should send the he-goat to the desert.*

[23] *Aaron shall come to the Tent of Meeting — he shall remove the linen vestments that he had worn when he entered the Sanctuary, and he shall leave them there.* [24] *He shall immerse himself in the water in a sacred place and don his vestments; he shall go out and perform his own elevation-offering and the elevation-offering of the people, and shall provide atonement for himself and for the people.*

[25] *And the fat of the sin-offering he shall cause to go up in smoke upon the Altar.* [26] *The one who dispatched the he-goat to Azazel shall immerse his clothing and immerse himself in the water; thereafter he may enter the camp.* [27] *The sin-offering bull and the sin-offering he-goat, whose blood had been brought to provide atonement in the Sanctuary, someone shall remove to the outside of the camp; and they shall burn in fire their hides, their flesh, and their dung.* [28] *The one who burns them shall immerse his clothing and immerse himself in the water; thereafter he may enter the camp.*

[29] *This shall remain for you an eternal decree: In the seventh month, on the tenth of the month, you shall afflict yourselves and you shall not do any work, neither the native nor the proselyte who dwells among you.* [30] *For on this day he shall provide atonement for you to cleanse you; from all your sins before HASHEM shall you be cleansed.*

[31] *It is a Sabbath of complete rest for you, and you shall afflict yourselves; an eternal decree.* [32] *The Kohen, who has been anointed or who has been given the authority to serve in place of his father, shall provide atonement; he shall don the linen vestments, the sacred vestments.*

---

30. כִּי בַיּוֹם הַזֶּה יְכַפֵּר — *For on this day shall atonement be made.* The reason that you will also need, in addition (to the service), rest (from labor) and affliction (of the soul) is because the *Kohen* through his service can merely atone, the purpose of this atonement being to mitigate the sin and prepare (the sinner) to receive forgiveness.

לִפְנֵי ה׳ תִּטְהָרוּ — *You shall be clean before HASHEM.* But the attainment of (spiritual) purification and complete forgiveness can only be *before HASHEM*, through confession and repentance, for He alone knows their sincerity — and therefore . . .

31. שַׁבַּת שַׁבָּתוֹן הִיא לָכֶם — *It is a Sabbath of Sabbaths unto you . . .* the reverse of הֵן בְּיוֹם צֹמְכֶם תִּמְצְאוּ חֵפֶץ, *Behold, on the day of your fast you pursue your business* (*Isaiah* 58:3).

חֻקַּת עוֹלָם — *A statute forever.* Even when the Temple no longer stands, you must (still) observe (the Sabbath of) rest and affliction (fasting).

32. וַאֲשֶׁר יְמַלֵּא אֶת יָדוֹ . . . וְלָבַשׁ — *And who shall be consecrated . . . and shall put on.* Even

NOTES

lesson. The first refers to a time when Israel had a Temple service but nonetheless were obligated to refrain from labor and fast on Yom Kippur. The second teaches us that these laws apply even when there is no Temple. The third comes to tell us that Yom Kippur itself has the power to atone even when the Temple is destroyed and there is no עֲבוֹדַת יוֹם הַכִּפּוּרִים, *service of Yom Kippur.*

31. שַׁבַּת שַׁבָּתוֹן — *Sabbath of Sabbaths.* The *Sforno* interprets the phrase שַׁבַּת שַׁבָּתוֹן as meaning *absolute;* total rest, abstinence from labor and all material pursuits, as opposed to the kind of fast which Isaiah criticized because it was only ceremonial and in no way affected their behavior.

32. וַאֲשֶׁר יְמַלֵּא אֶת יָדוֹ . . . וְלָבַשׁ — *And who shall be consecrated . . . and shall put on.* There are two

לג וְכִפֶּר֙ אֶת־מִקְדַּ֣שׁ הַקֹּ֔דֶשׁ וְאֶת־אֹ֧הֶל מוֹעֵ֛ד וְאֶת־הַמִּזְבֵּ֖חַ יְכַפֵּ֑ר וְעַ֧ל
לד הַכֹּהֲנִ֛ים וְעַל־כָּל־עַ֥ם הַקָּהָ֖ל יְכַפֵּֽר׃ וְהָֽיְתָה־זֹּ֨את לָכֶ֜ם לְחֻקַּ֣ת עוֹלָ֗ם לְכַפֵּ֞ר
עַל־בְּנֵ֤י יִשְׂרָאֵל֙ מִכָּל־חַטֹּאתָ֔ם אַחַ֖ת בַּשָּׁנָ֑ה וַיַּ֕עַשׂ כַּאֲשֶׁ֛ר צִוָּ֥ה יְהוָ֖ה
אֶת־מֹשֶֽׁה׃

יז רביעי א־ב וַיְדַבֵּ֥ר יְהוָ֖ה אֶל־מֹשֶׁ֥ה לֵּאמֹֽר׃ דַּבֵּ֨ר אֶֽל־אַהֲרֹ֜ן וְאֶל־בָּנָ֗יו וְאֶל֙ כָּל־בְּנֵ֣י
ג יִשְׂרָאֵ֔ל וְאָמַרְתָּ֖ אֲלֵיהֶ֑ם זֶ֣ה הַדָּבָ֔ר אֲשֶׁר־צִוָּ֥ה יְהוָ֖ה לֵאמֹֽר׃ אִ֥ישׁ אִישׁ֙
מִבֵּ֣ית יִשְׂרָאֵ֔ל אֲשֶׁ֨ר יִשְׁחַ֜ט שׁ֥וֹר אוֹ־כֶ֛שֶׂב אוֹ־עֵ֖ז בַּֽמַּחֲנֶ֑ה א֚וֹ אֲשֶׁ֣ר יִשְׁחָ֔ט
ד מִח֖וּץ לַֽמַּחֲנֶֽה׃ וְאֶל־פֶּ֜תַח אֹ֣הֶל מוֹעֵד֮ לֹ֣א הֱבִיאוֹ֒ לְהַקְרִ֤יב קָרְבָּן֙ לַֽיהוָ֔ה
לִפְנֵ֖י מִשְׁכַּ֣ן יְהוָ֑ה דָּ֣ם יֵחָשֵׁ֞ב לָאִ֤ישׁ הַהוּא֙ דָּ֣ם שָׁפָ֔ךְ וְנִכְרַ֛ת הָאִ֥ישׁ הַה֖וּא
ה מִקֶּ֥רֶב עַמּֽוֹ׃ לְמַעַן֩ אֲשֶׁ֨ר יָבִ֜יאוּ בְּנֵ֣י יִשְׂרָאֵ֗ל אֶת־זִבְחֵיהֶם֮ אֲשֶׁ֣ר הֵ֣ם זֹבְחִים֒
עַל־פְּנֵ֣י הַשָּׂדֶה֒ וֶהֱבִיאֻ֣ם לַֽיהוָ֗ה אֶל־פֶּ֛תַח אֹ֥הֶל מוֹעֵ֖ד אֶל־הַכֹּהֵ֑ן וְזָ֨בְח֜וּ זִבְחֵ֧י
ו שְׁלָמִ֛ים לַֽיהוָ֖ה אוֹתָֽם׃ וְזָרַ֨ק הַכֹּהֵ֤ן אֶת־הַדָּם֙ עַל־מִזְבַּ֣ח יְהוָ֔ה פֶּ֖תַח אֹ֣הֶל
ז מוֹעֵ֑ד וְהִקְטִ֣יר הַחֵ֔לֶב לְרֵ֥יחַ נִיחֹ֖חַ לַֽיהוָֽה׃ וְלֹא־יִזְבְּח֥וּ עוֹד֙ אֶת־זִבְחֵיהֶ֔ם
לַשְּׂעִירִ֕ם אֲשֶׁ֛ר הֵ֥ם זֹנִ֖ים אַחֲרֵיהֶ֑ם חֻקַּ֥ת עוֹלָ֛ם תִּֽהְיֶה־זֹּ֥את לָהֶ֖ם לְדֹרֹתָֽם׃

(a *Kohen Gadol* who is only distinguished by) a greater number of official garments can also atone.

34. וְהָיְתָה זֹּאת לָכֶם לְחֻקַּת עוֹלָם — *And this shall be an everlasting statute to you* . . . that the day itself atone, even though there is no Temple or service, as (our Sages) say, "Repentance suspends punishment and Yom Kippur atones" (*Yoma* 86a).

XVII

2. זֶה הַדָּבָר — *This is the thing.* When (God) said, *Thus shall you separate the Children of Israel from their tumah* (15:31), He was also warning that they be separated from the *tumah* of the spirit of impurity and the demons.

4. דָּם יֵחָשֵׁב לָאִישׁ הַהוּא — *Blood shall be imputed to that man.* (The rule here) is as it was prior to the Flood, when they were not permitted to slaughter any living creature for human consumption.

7. חֻקַּת עוֹלָם תִּהְיֶה זֹּאת — *This shall be a statute forever.* That they may not sacrifice unto

NOTES

ways a *Kohen Gadol* is invested into his office. One is through anointment with the oil of anointing (שֶׁמֶן הַמִּשְׁחָה), and the second is by clothing him in eight garments as compared to the four worn by ordinary *Kohanim*. This is called מְרוּבֶּה בְּגָדִים. In the days of King Josiah, the flask of anointing oil was concealed (*Horayos* 12a) and subsequently a *Kohen Gadol* was consecrated by putting the additional priestly garments on him. The verse here teaches us that regardless of the method, the *Kohen Gadol* can function in his office on Yom Kippur and attain atonement for Israel.

XVII

2. זֶה הַדָּבָר — *This is the thing.* The *Sforno* explains this phrase as referring back to the concluding section of chapter 15 (end of *parashas Metzora*) where Moses is urged to separate Israel from *tumah*. Now the Torah tells us that just as we are to separate ourselves from the *tumah* of the body, so is Israel to reject the רוּחַ הַטּוּמְאָה, *spirit of tumah,* engendered by demons.

4. דָּם יֵחָשֵׁב לָאִישׁ הַהוּא — *Blood shall be imputed to that man.* From the time of Creation until the Flood, man was not permitted to slaughter any living creature and eat its flesh. Such slaughter was tantamount to shedding blood. However, after the Flood, God permitted the flesh of animals to Noah and his children, provided they did not violate other laws ordained by God in the process of slaughtering. If they were to do so, then it would be as if they had shed blood unnecessarily. The *Sforno* explains that this is the meaning of the words *blood shall be imputed to that man.*

33 *He shall bring atonement upon the Holy of Holies, and he shall bring atonement upon the Tent of Meeting and the Altar; and upon the Kohanim and upon all the people of the congregation shall he bring atonement.* 34 *This shall be to you an eternal decree to bring atonement upon the Children of Israel for all their sins once a year; and [Aaron] did as HASHEM commanded Moses.*

17

1 *HASHEM spoke to Moses, saying:* 2 *Speak to Aaron and to his sons and to all the Children of Israel, and say to them: This is the matter that HASHEM has commanded, saying:* 3 *Any man from the House of Israel who will slaughter a bull, a sheep, or a goat in the camp, or who will slaughter it outside the camp,* 4 *and he has not brought it to the entrance of the Tent of Meeting to bring it as an offering to HASHEM before the Tabernacle of HASHEM — it shall be considered as bloodshed for that man, he has shed blood, and that man shall be cut off from his people.* 5 *So that the Children of Israel will bring their feast-offerings that they have been slaughtering on the open field, and they shall bring them to HASHEM to the entrance of the Tent of Meeting to the Kohen; and they shall slaughter them as feast peace-offerings to HASHEM.* 6 *The Kohen shall throw the blood upon the Altar of HASHEM, at the entrance of the Tent of Meeting; and he shall cause the fats to go up in smoke for a satisfying aroma to HASHEM.* 7 *They shall no longer slaughter their offerings to the demons after whom they stray; this shall be an eternal decree to them for their generations.*

---

the satyrs (demons), even though they do not accept them in any way as gods, but (only) desire their companionship so that the demons will be their servants and assist them in their affairs or as messengers to (be sent to) a distant land, as (the Sages) make mention regarding יוֹסֵף שֵׁידָא, *Joseph the Demon* (*Eruvin* 43a), and the demon that frequented the house of Rav Ashi (*Chullin* 105b).

However, regarding the demons, whose creation is not mentioned (in the Torah), it is proper to study (consider) them. Our Sages, of blessed memory, called them מַזִּיקִים, *injurers*, and mention (the fact) that they eat, drink, reproduce and die (*Chagigah* 16a). Still and all, they can see but are not visible! Now this cannot properly be (understood) unless they are composed of an (extremely) fine substance which is invisible. And since they eat and drink, their food perforce must be of a substance composed of (something) extremely fine which is assimilated into the organism consuming it. Now there are no compositions known to us more refined than the "vapor" of blood from which the spirit, which carries the life force, exists. This force being carried is the soul of life through which (every creature) lives, and since this force cannot be without this "carrier," at times it is

NOTES

7. חֻקַּת עוֹלָם תִּהְיֶה זֹּאת — *This shall be a statute forever.* Our Sages treated the existence of שֵׁדִים, *demons,* as a fact of life. Apparently, at the time when the Torah was given people attempted to court the demons' favor and fraternize with them, "so that they (would) come to him and let him know future events" (*Guide* 3:46). Maimonides tells us further that the Sabians believed that these demons, whom they called *jinn,* assumed the form of goats, and that blood was their only food. Hence, "whoever ate it (blood) fraternized with the *jinn*" by gathering at a pool of blood. The *Sforno* has a similar approach in his commentary on this verse while adding that these demons, once befriended, could also serve as messengers and assistants to those who knew how to attract them. The Torah, however, admonishes Israel not to *sacrifice to the* שְׂעִירִים, i.e., the שֵׁדִים, *demons,* who, as mentioned above, took on the form of goats (שָׂעִיר in Hebrew means "goat"). The *Sforno* proceeds to link this prohibition to that of blood, which follows (vs. 10-14). Since blood was the food of the demons, those who desired their friendship would provide it for them and join with them in

חמישי [שלישי] ח וַאֲלֵהֶם תֹּאמַר אִישׁ אִישׁ מִבֵּית יִשְׂרָאֵל וּמִן־הַגֵּר אֲשֶׁר־יָגוּר בְּתוֹכָם
ט אֲשֶׁר־יַעֲלֶה עֹלָה אוֹ־זָבַח: וְאֶל־פֶּתַח אֹהֶל מוֹעֵד לֹא יְבִיאֶנּוּ לַעֲשׂוֹת
י אֹתוֹ לַיהוָה וְנִכְרַת הָאִישׁ הַהוּא מֵעַמָּיו: וְאִישׁ אִישׁ מִבֵּית יִשְׂרָאֵל
וּמִן־הַגֵּר הַגָּר בְּתוֹכָם אֲשֶׁר יֹאכַל כָּל־דָּם וְנָתַתִּי פָנַי בַּנֶּפֶשׁ הָאֹכֶלֶת
יא אֶת־הַדָּם וְהִכְרַתִּי אֹתָהּ מִקֶּרֶב עַמָּהּ: כִּי־נֶפֶשׁ הַבָּשָׂר בַּדָּם הִוא וַאֲנִי
נְתַתִּיו לָכֶם עַל־הַמִּזְבֵּחַ לְכַפֵּר עַל־נַפְשֹׁתֵיכֶם כִּי־הַדָּם הוּא בַּנֶּפֶשׁ
יב יְכַפֵּר: עַל־כֵּן אָמַרְתִּי לִבְנֵי יִשְׂרָאֵל כָּל־נֶפֶשׁ מִכֶּם לֹא־תֹאכַל דָּם וְהַגֵּר
יג הַגָּר בְּתוֹכְכֶם לֹא־יֹאכַל דָּם: וְאִישׁ אִישׁ מִבְּנֵי יִשְׂרָאֵל וּמִן־הַגֵּר הַגָּר
בְּתוֹכָם אֲשֶׁר יָצוּד צֵיד חַיָּה אוֹ־עוֹף אֲשֶׁר יֵאָכֵל וְשָׁפַךְ אֶת־דָּמוֹ וְכִסָּהוּ
יד בֶּעָפָר: כִּי־נֶפֶשׁ כָּל־בָּשָׂר דָּמוֹ בְנַפְשׁוֹ הוּא וָאֹמַר לִבְנֵי יִשְׂרָאֵל דַּם
כָּל־בָּשָׂר לֹא תֹאכֵלוּ כִּי נֶפֶשׁ כָּל־בָּשָׂר דָּמוֹ הִוא כָּל־אֹכְלָיו יִכָּרֵת:

called נֶפֶשׁ, *life*, as it says, כִּי הַדָּם הוּא הַנָּפֶשׁ, *For the blood is the life* (*Deut.* 12:23). Being that this (i.e., blood) is the food of demons, consequently he who offers them blood, which is (the source) of their substance and which they are powerless to take (on their own), as our Sages say, "We have no permission to take anything which is closed, sealed, measured or counted" (*Chullin* 105b), (he) will gain their love, and he who eats it (blood) will acquire a temperament which tends toward their nature and (therefore) they will long for his company. Now since many desired the companionship of demons and their love, so that (the demons) would assist them in acquiring futile pleasures (which are sweet, but without practical benefit) — the identical desire which was attained by the eating from the tree of knowledge — (hence) they would bring blood as an offering to the demons and eat it (themselves) in order to join together with them. Some would eat (the blood) adjacent to a pool of blood, where they believed that the satyrs danced, so as to attract their love and fraternize with them. When God, the Blessed One, sanctified us and distanced His people as much as possible from pursuing futile pleasures, He distanced them from the demons and their company, since they are, in truth, "injurers" as our Sages named them. He (also) prohibited blood (which He made) punishable by כָּרֵת, *excision*, similar to the penalty of death (imposed on man) for partaking of the tree of knowledge (*Genesis* 2:17) and gave as the reason for this, *For the life of the flesh is in the blood* (v. 10), because the force which is the living spirit is carried in the mistlike delicate part of the blood, and that mistlike part, which is also called נֶפֶשׁ, *life*, is essentially found in all blood. He then additionally states, *And I have given it to you upon the Altar* (v. 11), (and) I have not chosen it (the blood) to atone because it is beloved to Me, but rather because it is, to a certain extent, נֶפֶשׁ, *life*, (therefore) it atones for the נֶפֶשׁ (of the one who brings the offering) similar to the burning

NOTES

partaking of the blood. In order to dissuade Israel from this practice, the Torah forbids blood to them totally, except for the blood brought to the Altar of God, and also blood used for a special purpose such as the consecration of the *Kohanim*. The reason why God commands Israel to offer blood on the Altar is because it represents the life force (the נֶפֶשׁ) of man, and just as the limbs of the animal are offered on the Altar symbolizing those of the מַקְרִיב, *he who brings the sacrifice*, so too, the blood of the animal fulfills the same symbolic purpose. The *Sforno* also offers a reason for blood being the food of the demons. According to our Sages, demons live, breed, and die — hence they need sustenance. We are also told that they are invisible. To explain this phenomenon, the *Sforno* discusses the property of blood in light of 16th-century medical knowledge. What he terms אֵיד הַדָּם (based on the word אֵד in *Genesis* 2:6), *the vapor of the blood*, must refer to oxygen which is conveyed to the tissues by hemoglobin — the red blood corpuscles. Since oxygen is a gaseous substance it is the least substantial of all compositions known to man; in other words it is mistlike (אֵד), made up of

[8] *And to them you shall say: Any man of the House of Israel and of the proselyte who shall dwell among you who will offer up an elevation-offering or a feast-offering,* [9] *and he will not bring it to the entrance of the Tent of Meeting to perform its service to* HASHEM *— that man shall be cut off from his people.*

[10] *Any man of the House of Israel and of the proselyte who dwells among them who will consume any blood — I shall concentrate My attention upon the soul consuming the blood, and I will cut it off from its people.* [11] *For the soul of the flesh is in the blood and I have assigned it for you upon the Altar to provide atonement for your souls; for it is the blood that atones for the soul.* [12] *Therefore I have said to the Children of Israel: "Any person among you may not consume blood; and the proselyte who dwells among you may not consume blood."*

[13] *Any man of the Children of Israel and of the proselyte who dwells among them who will trap a beast or bird that may be eaten, he shall pour out its blood and cover it with earth.* [14] *For the life of any creature — its blood represents its life, so I say to the Children of Israel, "You shall not consume the blood of any creature; for the life of any creature is its blood, whoever consumes it will be cut off."*

(on the Altar) of the various limbs of the sacrifices which atones for the limbs of the one who is making the sacrifice (see the *Sforno* on 1:2).

13. אֲשֶׁר יָצוּד צֵיד — *That takes in hunting.* The places (where animals) are usually hunted are deserted and predisposed to be frequented by demons, as it says, וְשָׁכְנוּ שָׁם בְּנוֹת יַעֲנָה וּשְׂעִירִים יְרַקְּדוּ שָׁם, *And ostriches shall dwell there and satyrs dance there* (*Isaiah* 13:21). (Therefore), He prohibited (us) to leave blood exposed, and commanded (us) to cover it with dirt to forestall the tendency of demons to frequent (that place), and He said ...

14. כִּי נֶפֶשׁ כָּל בָּשָׂר דָּמוֹ בְנַפְשׁוֹ הוּא — *As for the life of all flesh, its blood is with the life thereof.* Because the *life* (נֶפֶשׁ) of (every) living creature is *its blood* — i.e., the mistlike substances of blood with the life force carried in it (בְּנַפְשׁוֹ), for indeed this fine vaporlike (part) of the blood carries the force of life, and being the thinnest and most insubstantial of all material things, it (therefore qualifies) without a doubt to be the food (sustenance) of demons and those who seek their company.

וָאֹמַר לִבְנֵי יִשְׂרָאֵל — *Therefore, I said to the Children of Israel.* And besides this (i.e., the reason given above), even though I permitted (blood) to the sons of Noah, I prohibited it to Israel (as stated) above in *parashas Tzav* (7:26) because (when) the soul of life (blood) is (ingested) into one's body (lit., his life), the (nature) of the one fed by it returns to its animalistic nature.

NOTES

minute particles (דַק), and invisible, but life giving! Hence, the demons who subsist on the oxygen component of the blood are also invisible, for "we are what we eat." Based on this premise, the *Sforno* explains the word נֶפֶשׁ used by the Torah in conjunction with blood as referring to the oxygen carried by the blood, which is indeed the supporter of life. Although oxygen was not recognized as a separate element in the *Sforno's* time, nonetheless he knew there was such an element within the blood, carried by it, as we see from his commentary here. For further commentary of the *Sforno* on שֵׁדִים, see his כַּוָּנוֹת הַתּוֹרָה כ״ב.

14. כִּי נֶפֶשׁ כָּל בָּשָׂר דָּמוֹ בְנַפְשׁוֹ הוּא — *As for the life of all flesh, its blood is with the life thereof.* See notes on verse 7 for clarification of the *Sforno's* commentary. The *Sforno* gives two reasons for the prohibition of blood. One is to prevent Israel from associating with the demons, as explained above. Second, by consuming the blood of the animal, man will take on the characteristics of the animal since blood is the essence of the animal's life force.

טו וְכָל־נֶפֶשׁ אֲשֶׁר תֹּאכַל נְבֵלָה וּטְרֵפָה בָּאֶזְרָח וּבַגֵּר וְכִבֶּס בְּגָדָיו וְרָחַץ
טז בַּמַּיִם וְטָמֵא עַד־הָעֶרֶב וְטָהֵר: וְאִם לֹא יְכַבֵּס וּבְשָׂרוֹ לֹא יִרְחָץ וְנָשָׂא
עֲוֺנוֹ:
יח א־ב וַיְדַבֵּר יהוה אֶל־מֹשֶׁה לֵּאמֹר: דַּבֵּר אֶל־בְּנֵי יִשְׂרָאֵל וְאָמַרְתָּ אֲלֵהֶם אֲנִי
ג יהוה אֱלֹהֵיכֶם: כְּמַעֲשֵׂה אֶרֶץ־מִצְרַיִם אֲשֶׁר יְשַׁבְתֶּם־בָּהּ לֹא תַעֲשׂוּ
וּכְמַעֲשֵׂה אֶרֶץ־כְּנַעַן אֲשֶׁר אֲנִי מֵבִיא אֶתְכֶם שָׁמָּה לֹא תַעֲשׂוּ
ד וּבְחֻקֹּתֵיהֶם לֹא תֵלֵכוּ: אֶת־מִשְׁפָּטַי תַּעֲשׂוּ וְאֶת־חֻקֹּתַי תִּשְׁמְרוּ לָלֶכֶת
ה בָּהֶם אֲנִי יהוה אֱלֹהֵיכֶם: וּשְׁמַרְתֶּם אֶת־חֻקֹּתַי וְאֶת־מִשְׁפָּטַי אֲשֶׁר יַעֲשֶׂה
ששי ו אֹתָם הָאָדָם וָחַי בָּהֶם אֲנִי יהוה: אִישׁ אִישׁ אֶל־כָּל־שְׁאֵר בְּשָׂרוֹ
ז לֹא תִקְרְבוּ לְגַלּוֹת עֶרְוָה אֲנִי יהוה: עֶרְוַת אָבִיךָ וְעֶרְוַת אִמְּךָ

15. וְכָל נֶפֶשׁ אֲשֶׁר תֹּאכַל נְבֵלָה וּטְרֵפָה — *And every soul (i.e., individual) that eats that which dies of itself or that which is torn by beasts.* After writing of the prohibition of blood which attracts the company of demons, (the Torah) now speaks of the eating of that which dies of itself (נְבֵלָה) and of that which is torn by beasts (טְרֵפָה), for this predisposes (a person) for a spirit of *tumah* to dwell upon him, as (our Sages) say, "The verse וְדֹרֵשׁ אֶל הַמֵּתִים, *One who consults the dead* (*Deut.* 18:11), refers to one who starves himself and spends the night in a cemetery so that an unclean spirit may rest upon him" (*Sanhedrin* 65b).

16. וְנָשָׂא עֲוֹנוֹ — *Then he shall bear his iniquity* ... according to (the severity) of his sin of *tumah;* whether he ate holy things, merely touched them or defiled *tahor* non-holy things.

XVIII

6. אִישׁ אִישׁ אֶל כָּל שְׁאֵר בְּשָׂרוֹ לֹא תִקְרְבוּ — *None of you shall approach to any one that is near of kin to him.* Behold, that (regarding) the offspring of relatives, since the active and passive (parties) are close (to each other) in temperament, it would properly (follow) that (these children) be more worthy and compatible, as happened with the birth of Moses, Aaron and Miriam (born of) Amram and his aunt Yocheved, and as (our Sages) said in regard to marrying a sister's daughter (*Yevamos* 62b). Now, this assumption would be so if the active and passive parties were to have as their sole intent the fulfillment of their Creator's will. However, this rarely occurs, for indeed, what happens with all human beings, or the majority of them in these (matters), is only the desire to (find) pleasure (in

NOTES

15. וְכָל נֶפֶשׁ אֲשֶׁר תֹּאכַל נְבֵלָה וּטְרֵפָה — *And every soul that eats that which dies of itself or that which is torn by beasts.* The *Sforno* explains that after issuing a prohibition against blood, the Torah now forbids נְבֵלָה וּטְרֵפָה which, if partaken of, convey a spirit of *tumah.*

16. וְנָשָׂא עֲוֹנוֹ — *Then he shall bear his iniquity.* The expression *he shall bear his iniquity* is indefinite. The *Sforno* explains it to mean that the severity of the punishment depends on the extent of his transgression. To eat holy things in a state of *tumah* is a more serious infraction than touching them, and to defile non-holy things which are *tahor* is a lesser sin than the former two infractions.

XVIII

6. אִישׁ אִישׁ אֶל כָּל שְׁאֵר בְּשָׂרוֹ לֹא תִקְרְבוּ — *None of you shall approach to any one that is near of kin to him.* The *Sforno* explains the prohibition of marriage between שְׁאֵר בָּשָׂר, *near of kin,* in a similar vein to that of the *Rambam* in his *Guide* (3:49). The *Rambam* states, "All illicit unions with (related) females have one thing in common ... they are easily accessible to him ... and if it were possible to marry them ... most people would have ... fornicated with them." However, since the Torah forbids them, "their thoughts are turned away from them." The *Sforno,* however, includes a most unique point in his commentary on this chapter of

15 *Any person who will eat a [bird] that died or was torn — the native or the proselyte — he shall immerse his garments and immerse himself in the water; he shall remain contaminated until evening and then become pure.*
16 *But if he does not immerse [his garments] and does not immerse his flesh, he shall bear his iniquity.*

18

1 *HASHEM spoke to Moses, saying:* 2 *Speak to the Children of Israel and say to them: I am HASHEM, your God.* 3 *Do not perform the practice of the land of Egypt in which you dwelled; and do not perform the practice of the land of Canaan to which I bring you, and do not follow their traditions.*
4 *Carry out My laws and safeguard My decrees to follow them; I am HASHEM, your God.* 5 *You shall observe My decrees and My laws, which man shall carry out and by which he shall live — I am HASHEM.*
6 *Any man shall not approach his close relative to uncover nakedness; I am HASHEM.*
7 *The nakedness of your father and the nakedness of your mother you*

---

the act of intimacy), as it says, הֵן בְּעָווֹן חוֹלָלְתִּי וּבְחֵטְא יֶחֱמַתְנִי אִמִּי, *Behold I was shaped in iniquity and in sin did my mother conceive me* (*Psalms* 51:7). Now being that relatives are very accessible, and the (lewd) thoughts and pleasure in this matter are very great, hence if they would both think that their union was not prohibited, these thoughts would increase and their (sexual) union would be only (for the purpose) of pleasure. Thereby, they would fornicate and desist from reproducing and the earth would be filled with lewdness. Therefore it states . . .

לְגַלּוֹת עֶרְוָה — *To uncover their nakedness . . .* because, in the majority of these cases, the intimate relationship (lit., uncovering of nakedness) is intended only to attain pleasure. Therefore, the Torah prohibited unions among relatives of common ancestry (lit., common offspring), including relatives (who are) of the same line on one level. These levels of relationship are enumerated by the Torah as they apply to the male, and a wife is considered as her husband (regarding these regulations). Therefore, (the Torah) prohibited a sister of one's father since she is on the first level with the father but permitted the daughter of one's brother (a niece) since she is on a second level (in relationship) to him. (The Torah) forbade the wife of one's father, the wife of a brother, and the wife of an uncle even after the husband is deceased, although they are in no manner related, because they are considered as being on the same level as their husbands. In this manner the prohibition of all other relatives can (also) be understood.

NOTES

consanguineous unions. Contrary to the opinion of some that children born of such unions would be defective, the *Sforno* suggests the opposite. He is of the opinion that children born to parents who are similar in temperament and who come from a common ancestry may well be exceptional and even superior! He cites as proof the fact that Moses, Aaron, and Miriam — all great personalities — were the offspring of Amram and Yocheved. The latter, who was Amram's aunt, was permitted to him prior to the giving of the Torah. Similarly, the Talmud lauds one who marries his sister's daughter, noting that he is deserving of the blessing which appears in *Isaiah* (58:9), *Then shall you call and HASHEM will answer*. *Tosfos* explains that this is because they are especially suited for one another, precisely because of their close relationship. The *Sforno*, however, qualifies this as being so only if one marries "for the sake of heaven." Since in most cases this is not so, for their attraction is not a spiritual but a physical one, the Torah prohibited these unions for the reason given by the *Sforno* and the *Rambam* in his *Guide*. The Torah alludes to this base motivation by using the expression *to uncover their nakedness* throughout the chapter, rather than a more delicate phrase.

ח לֹא תְגַלֵּה אִמְּךָ הִוא לֹא תְגַלֶּה עֶרְוָתָהּ: עֶרְוַת אֵשֶׁת־אָבִיךָ לֹא
ט תְגַלֵּה עֶרְוַת אָבִיךָ הִוא: עֶרְוַת אֲחוֹתְךָ בַת־אָבִיךָ אוֹ בַת־אִמֶּךָ
י מוֹלֶדֶת בַּיִת אוֹ מוֹלֶדֶת חוּץ לֹא תְגַלֶּה עֶרְוָתָן: עֶרְוַת בַּת־בִּנְךָ
יא אוֹ בַת־בִּתְּךָ לֹא תְגַלֶּה עֶרְוָתָן כִּי עֶרְוָתְךָ הֵנָּה: עֶרְוַת בַּת־אֵשֶׁת
יב אָבִיךָ מוֹלֶדֶת אָבִיךָ אֲחוֹתְךָ הִוא לֹא תְגַלֶּה עֶרְוָתָהּ: עֶרְוַת
יג אֲחוֹת־אָבִיךָ לֹא תְגַלֵּה שְׁאֵר אָבִיךָ הִוא: עֶרְוַת אֲחוֹת־אִמְּךָ לֹא
יד תְגַלֵּה כִּי־שְׁאֵר אִמְּךָ הִוא: עֶרְוַת אֲחִי־אָבִיךָ לֹא תְגַלֵּה אֶל־
טו אִשְׁתּוֹ לֹא תִקְרָב דֹּדָתְךָ הִוא: עֶרְוַת כַּלָּתְךָ לֹא תְגַלֵּה אֵשֶׁת
טז בִּנְךָ הִוא לֹא תְגַלֶּה עֶרְוָתָהּ: עֶרְוַת אֵשֶׁת־אָחִיךָ לֹא תְגַלֵּה
יז עֶרְוַת אָחִיךָ הִוא: עֶרְוַת אִשָּׁה וּבִתָּהּ לֹא תְגַלֵּה אֶת־בַּת־
בְּנָהּ וְאֶת־בַּת־בִּתָּהּ לֹא תִקַּח לְגַלּוֹת עֶרְוָתָהּ שַׁאֲרָה הֵנָּה זִמָּה הִוא:
יח וְאִשָּׁה אֶל־אֲחֹתָהּ לֹא תִקָּח לִצְרֹר לְגַלּוֹת עֶרְוָתָהּ עָלֶיהָ בְּחַיֶּיהָ:
יט־כ וְאֶל־אִשָּׁה בְּנִדַּת טֻמְאָתָהּ לֹא תִקְרַב לְגַלּוֹת עֶרְוָתָהּ: וְאֶל־אֵשֶׁת
כא עֲמִיתְךָ לֹא־תִתֵּן שְׁכָבְתְּךָ לְזָרַע לְטָמְאָה־בָהּ: וּמִזַּרְעֲךָ לֹא־תִתֵּן
שביעי [רביעי] כב לְהַעֲבִיר לַמֹּלֶךְ וְלֹא תְחַלֵּל אֶת־שֵׁם אֱלֹהֶיךָ אֲנִי יהוה: וְאֶת־זָכָר לֹא
כג תִשְׁכַּב מִשְׁכְּבֵי אִשָּׁה תּוֹעֵבָה הִוא: וּבְכָל־בְּהֵמָה לֹא־תִתֵּן שְׁכָבְתְּךָ
לְטָמְאָה־בָהּ וְאִשָּׁה לֹא־תַעֲמֹד לִפְנֵי בְהֵמָה לְרִבְעָהּ תֶּבֶל הוּא:

17. זִמָּה הִוא — *It is lewdness* ... a union resulting only from sinful thoughts.

18. לֹא תִקָּח לִצְרֹר — *You shall not take to be a rival to her.* (The Torah) says that were it not for this (problem of rivalry), the sister of one's wife would not be forbidden since she is not the offspring of this woman (the wife) and the woman herself is permitted. However, she is prohibited so that they shall not become rivals. Therefore, (the Torah) only forbids her during the lifetime of her sister, unlike other forbidden relatives (who are permanently forbidden).

21. וּמִזַּרְעֲךָ לֹא תִתֵּן לְהַעֲבִיר לַמֹּלֶךְ וְלֹא תְחַלֵּל אֶת שֵׁם אֱלֹהֶיךָ — *And you shall not give any of your seed to set them apart to Molech and you shall not profane the Name of your God.* For indeed, when you offer other living creatures (i.e., animals) to God, the Blessed One, and you offer your son to the Molech, then behold it would appear that the Molech is superior to Him — God forbid!

אֲנִי ה׳ — *I am HASHEM.* Unchanging — and I vowed to be your God when I said to Abraham, לִהְיוֹת לְךָ לֵאלֹהִים וּלְזַרְעֲךָ אַחֲרֶיךָ, *To be a God to you and to your seed after you* (*Genesis* 17:7). Now since He speaks (i.e., commands) concerning prohibited relatives so as to prepare the seed (of Israel) that they be worthy that (God's) great Name dwell upon

NOTES

21. וּמִזַּרְעֲךָ לֹא תִתֵּן לְהַעֲבִיר לַמֹּלֶךְ וְלֹא תְחַלֵּל אֶת שֵׁם אֱלֹהֶיךָ אֲנִי ה׳ — *And you shall not give any of your seed to set them apart to Molech and you shall not profane the Name of your God, I am HASHEM.* To serve the Molech is obviously an act of עֲבוֹדָה זָרָה, *idolatry.* Why then does the Torah have to give the added reason, *you shall not profane the Name of your God*? It is also necessary to understand the concluding phrase, *I am HASHEM.* The *Sforno* explains both of these additions in the following manner: When one worships the Molech he is guilty of a most serious offense, for not only does he serve a strange god but he also denigrates and desecrates God's Holy Name by acknowledging the superiority of the Molech. This is manifested by the offering of his son to the Molech, whereas when he worships God, he "only" sacrifices animals! This is a חִלּוּל הַשֵּׁם, *profanation of the Name*

shall not uncover; she is your mother, you shall not uncover her nakedness.
8 The nakedness of your father's wife you shall not uncover; it is your
father's shame.
9 The nakedness of your sister — whether your father's daughter or your
mother's daughter, whether born to one who may remain in the home or
born to one who must remain outside of it — you shall not uncover their
nakedness.
10 The nakedness of your son's daughter or your daughter's daughter —
you shall not uncover their nakedness; for they are your own shame.
11 The nakedness of your father's wife's daughter who was born to your
father — she is your sister; you shall not uncover her nakedness.
12 The nakedness of your father's sister you shall not uncover; she is your
father's flesh.
13 The nakedness of your mother's sister you shall not uncover; for she is
your mother's flesh.
14 The nakedness of your father's brother you shall not uncover; do not
approach his wife, she is your aunt.
15 The nakedness of your daughter-in-law you shall not uncover; she is
your son's wife, you shall not uncover her nakedness.
16 The nakedness of your brother's wife you shall not uncover; it is your
brother's shame.
17 The nakedness of a woman and her daughter you shall not uncover;
you shall not take her son's daughter or her daughter's daughter to uncover
her nakedness — they are close relatives, it is a depraved plot.
18 You shall
not take a woman in addition to her sister, to make them rivals, to uncover
the nakedness of one upon the other in her lifetime.
19 You shall not approach a woman in her time of unclean separation, to
uncover her nakedness.
20 You shall not lie carnally with your neighbor's
wife, to contaminate yourself with her.
21 You shall not present any of your children to pass through for Molech,
and do not profane the Name of your God — I am HASHEM.
22 You shall not lie with a man as one lies with a woman, it is an
abomination.
23 Do not lie with any animal to be contaminated with it; a
woman shall not stand before an animal for mating, it is a perversion.

---

them, (therefore) He speaks of the Molech whose worshipers thought that by serving him they would prepare their other seed for (the blessing) of success. (That is why the Torah) says that by serving him (the Molech), there will be desecration of God and (that will) cause the Divine Presence to abandon their other children (lit., seed).

NOTES

of God. Secondly, by serving the Molech, one accomplishes precisely the reverse of his intention. Those who offered one of their offspring to the Molech did so in the false hope that the Molech would bless their other children. This was of course patently false. Were Israel to serve God, as they were commanded to do, and keep Abraham's covenant with Him, they and their children would receive blessings from on High. However, by deserting God and following the Molech, they deny themselves the Divine blessing which is granted through God's presence in their midst, a presence which is removed when Israel deviates from God's laws. This is why the verse concludes with the phrase, *"I am God,"* to underscore that only from Him do blessings for his children emanate.

כד אַל־תִּטַּמְּאוּ בְּכָל־אֵלֶּה כִּי בְכָל־אֵלֶּה נִטְמְאוּ הַגּוֹיִם אֲשֶׁר־אֲנִי מְשַׁלֵּחַ
כה מִפְּנֵיכֶם: וַתִּטְמָא הָאָרֶץ וָאֶפְקֹד עֲוֹנָהּ עָלֶיהָ וַתָּקִא הָאָרֶץ אֶת־יֹשְׁבֶיהָ:
כו וּשְׁמַרְתֶּם אַתֶּם אֶת־חֻקֹּתַי וְאֶת־מִשְׁפָּטַי וְלֹא תַעֲשׂוּ מִכֹּל הַתּוֹעֵבֹת
כז הָאֵלֶּה הָאֶזְרָח וְהַגֵּר הַגָּר בְּתוֹכְכֶם: כִּי אֶת־כָּל־הַתּוֹעֵבֹת הָאֵל עָשׂוּ
מפטיר כח אַנְשֵׁי־הָאָרֶץ אֲשֶׁר לִפְנֵיכֶם וַתִּטְמָא הָאָרֶץ: וְלֹא־תָקִיא הָאָרֶץ אֶתְכֶם
כט בְּטַמַּאֲכֶם אֹתָהּ כַּאֲשֶׁר קָאָה אֶת־הַגּוֹי אֲשֶׁר לִפְנֵיכֶם: כִּי כָּל־אֲשֶׁר
יַעֲשֶׂה מִכֹּל הַתּוֹעֵבֹת הָאֵלֶּה וְנִכְרְתוּ הַנְּפָשׁוֹת הָעֹשֹׂת מִקֶּרֶב עַמָּם:
ל וּשְׁמַרְתֶּם אֶת־מִשְׁמַרְתִּי לְבִלְתִּי עֲשׂוֹת מֵחֻקּוֹת הַתּוֹעֵבֹת אֲשֶׁר נַעֲשׂוּ
לִפְנֵיכֶם וְלֹא תִטַּמְּאוּ בָּהֶם אֲנִי יהוה אֱלֹהֵיכֶם:

24. אַל תִּטַּמְּאוּ בְּכָל אֵלֶּה — *Do not defile yourselves in any of these things* . . . even to draw nigh to uncover nakedness.

כִּי בְכָל אֵלֶּה נִטְמְאוּ הַגּוֹיִם — *For in all these the nations defiled themselves* . . . for the beginning of these nations' transgressions in (the area) of prohibited unions was not in the actual uncovering of nakedness, but only in the coming close (to the forbidden partner).

25. וַתִּטְמָא הָאָרֶץ — *And the land was defiled.* Drawing nigh resulted in the defilement of the land through actual uncovering of nakedness.

26. וּשְׁמַרְתֶּם אַתֶּם אֶת חֻקֹּתַי — *You shall therefore keep My statutes* . . . that you shall not draw nigh to uncover any (forbidden) nakedness.

וְאֶת מִשְׁפָּטַי — *And My ordinances* . . . to punish the sinners.

וְלֹא תַעֲשׂוּ מִכֹּל הַתּוֹעֵבֹת — *And you shall not do any of these abominations* And in this manner you will not commit even one of these abominable statutes.

27. כִּי אֶת כָּל הַתּוֹעֵבֹת הָאֵל עָשׂוּ אַנְשֵׁי הָאָרֶץ — *For all these abominations have the men of the land done.* For the nations that did not guard themselves from drawing nigh (to these immoralities) and who did not inflict punishment upon those who sinned by uncovering prohibited nakedness, (eventually) they did all (these) abominations, for they proceeded

NOTES

24-28. אַל תִּטַּמְּאוּ בְּכָל אֵלֶּה . . . וַתִּטְמָא הָאָרֶץ . . . וּשְׁמַרְתֶּם אַתֶּם אֶת חֻקֹּתַי . . . וְלֹא תָקִיא הָאָרֶץ אֶתְכֶם . . . כַּאֲשֶׁר קָאָה אֶת הַגּוֹי — *Do not defile yourselves in any of these things . . . And the land was defiled . . . You shall therefore keep My statutes . . . That the land not vomit you out . . . as it vomited out the nation.* The *Sforno,* sensitive to the subtle differences within the terminology used by the Torah in these verses, explains their progression as follows: One does not usually violate the prohibition of incest immediately. The first step is one of close association which starts a trend that culminates in ultimate iniquity. The Torah therefore cautions Israel to erect a protective moral fence so as to avoid an initial transgression. This is referred to by the indefinite term אֵלֶּה, *these things* (v. 24). The failure to do so leads inevitably to the land casting out its sinful inhabitants. Had the original inhabitants imposed stern and prompt punishments, thereby not permitting the early, less severe transgressions to proceed and proliferate, the progression of abominations would not have reached a point where the inhabitants would have to be expelled from the Land of Canaan. This, as the *Sforno* sees it, is the burden of admonition given to Israel in these five verses.

24 *Do not become contaminated through any of these; for through all of these the nations that I expel before you became contaminated.* 25 *The Land became contaminated and I recalled its iniquity upon it; and the Land disgorged its inhabitants.* 26 *But you shall safeguard My decrees and My judgments, and not commit any of these abominations — the native or the proselyte who lives among you.* 27 *For the inhabitants of the Land who are before you committed all these abominations, and the Land became contaminated.* 28 *Let not the Land disgorge you for having contaminated it, as it disgorged the nation that was before you.* 29 *For if anyone commits any of these abominations, the people doing so will be cut off from among their people.*

30 *You shall safeguard My charge not to do any of the abominable traditions that were done before you and not contaminate yourselves through them; I am HASHEM, your God.*

---

from evil to evil. And so shall you also (transgress) if you do not observe all these statutes and ordinances; therefore keep them!

28. וְלֹא תָקִיא הָאָרֶץ אֶתְכֶם . . . כַּאֲשֶׁר קָאָה אֶת הַגּוֹי — *That the land not vomit you out . . . as it vomited out the nation.* And in this manner the land will not vomit you out in the same evil way that it now vomits out the (other) nations.

29. כִּי כָּל אֲשֶׁר יַעֲשֶׂה מִכֹּל הַתּוֹעֵבֹת הָאֵלֶּה וְנִכְרְתוּ הַנְּפָשׁוֹת — *For whosoever shall do any of these abominations, these souls shall be cut off.* The reason that the land will vomit you out in this evil fashion if you do *even* one of these (sins) is because each one of these sins alone is worthy to be punished with excision.

30. וּשְׁמַרְתֶּם אֶת מִשְׁמַרְתִּי לְבִלְתִּי עֲשׂוֹת מֵחֻקּוֹת הַתּוֹעֵבֹת — *And you shall keep My charge that you not do any of these abominable statutes.* Also observe the commandments I commanded to serve as a safeguard and a fence so that you do not stumble over all these (sins), such as: prohibited foods; the *tumah* of *niddah; zavah; yoledes* (a woman who gives birth); and similar cases (of *tumah*). For in this manner *you will not make yourselves tamei therein.*

NOTES

29. כִּי כָּל אֲשֶׁר יַעֲשֶׂה מִכֹּל הַתּוֹעֵבֹת הָאֵלֶּה וְנִכְרְתוּ הַנְּפָשׁוֹת — *For whosoever shall do any of these abominations, these souls shall be cut off.* The *Sforno* interprets the expression מִכֹּל הַתּוֹעֵבֹת to mean *any "one" of these abominations.* The reason why merely one infraction carries with it the punishment of כָּרֵת, *excision*, is because of the severity of immoral sexual acts.

30. וּשְׁמַרְתֶּם אֶת מִשְׁמַרְתִּי — *And you shall keep My charge.* The *Sforno* interprets מִשְׁמַרְתִּי, *My charge*, as including more than just the laws of prohibited marriage relationships listed in this chapter. To insure a life of restraint, purity, and sanctity, one must discipline himself in this total area as well as in all other aspects of his life. Hence, this warning to keep God's charge through self-discipline is all-inclusive. It ranges from the laws of *niddah* to the dietary laws; from the laws of a יוֹלֶדֶת (a woman after childbirth) to that of a זָבָה (a woman who has an abnormal flow). Only by training oneself, and establishing a pattern of discipline in these varied areas, will Israel be able to observe the laws enumerated in the *parashah* of עֲרָיוֹת, *prohibited marriages.* This verse is not an additional admonition. Rather, it is one of assurance. By keeping the charge, they will assuredly not follow (לְבִלְתִּי עֲשׂוֹת) the abominable customs of the nations whom they are displacing.

פרשת קדושים

יט א־ב וַיְדַבֵּר יְהוָה אֶל־מֹשֶׁה לֵּאמֹר: דַּבֵּר אֶל־כָּל־עֲדַת בְּנֵי־יִשְׂרָאֵל וְאָמַרְתָּ
ג אֲלֵהֶם קְדֹשִׁים תִּהְיוּ כִּי קָדוֹשׁ אֲנִי יְהוָה אֱלֹהֵיכֶם: אִישׁ אִמּוֹ וְאָבִיו
ד תִּירָאוּ וְאֶת־שַׁבְּתֹתַי תִּשְׁמֹרוּ אֲנִי יְהוָה אֱלֹהֵיכֶם: אַל־תִּפְנוּ אֶל־
ה הָאֱלִילִם וֵאלֹהֵי מַסֵּכָה לֹא תַעֲשׂוּ לָכֶם אֲנִי יְהוָה אֱלֹהֵיכֶם: וְכִי תִזְבְּחוּ
ו זֶבַח שְׁלָמִים לַיהוָה לִרְצֹנְכֶם תִּזְבָּחֻהוּ: בְּיוֹם זִבְחֲכֶם יֵאָכֵל וּמִמָּחֳרָת
ז וְהַנּוֹתָר עַד־יוֹם הַשְּׁלִישִׁי בָּאֵשׁ יִשָּׂרֵף: וְאִם הֵאָכֹל יֵאָכֵל בַּיּוֹם הַשְּׁלִישִׁי
ח פִּגּוּל הוּא לֹא יֵרָצֶה: וְאֹכְלָיו עֲוֹנוֹ יִשָּׂא כִּי־אֶת־קֹדֶשׁ יְהוָה חִלֵּל
ט וְנִכְרְתָה הַנֶּפֶשׁ הַהִוא מֵעַמֶּיהָ: וּבְקֻצְרְכֶם אֶת־קְצִיר אַרְצְכֶם לֹא תְכַלֶּה

XIX

2. דַּבֵּר אֶל כָּל עֲדַת . . . קְדֹשִׁים תִּהְיוּ — *Speak unto all the congregation . . . you shall be holy.* After (God) had caused His Divine Presence to abide in the midst of Israel, so as to sanctify them for everlasting life, as was (His) intent when He said, וְאַתֶּם תִּהְיוּ לִי מַמְלֶכֶת כֹּהֲנִים וְגוֹי קָדוֹשׁ, *And you shall be unto Me a kingdom of Kohanim and a holy nation* (*Exodus* 19:6), and when He said, *For I am HASHEM that brought you up out of the land of Egypt to be your God; you shall therefore be holy* (11:45); and (after) He separated them from the defilement of (prohibited) food (ch. 11) and the *tamei* seed of a *niddah* (ch. 15) and the afflictions which emanate from her; and from the *tumah* of the זָבָה (a woman who has an issue); and the defilement of sins, as it says, *From all your sins shall you be clean before HASHEM* (16:30) and from the company of demons, and the spirit of *tumah* and from the *tumah* of prohibited unions (עֲרָיוֹת) as it says, *Defile not yourselves in any of these things* (18:24) — (after all this) He now says that the intent (purpose) of all these warnings is that they be holy. This is in order that they may imitate their Creator as much as possible, as was the original intent when man was created, as it says, נַעֲשֶׂה אָדָם בְּצַלְמֵנוּ כִּדְמוּתֵנוּ, *Let us make man in our image, after our likeness* (*Genesis* 1:26). This he now explains saying . . .

כִּי קָדוֹשׁ אֲנִי ה׳ אֱלֹהֵיכֶם — *For I HASHEM your God am holy.* And it is fitting that you be like Me, as much as possible in mind and in deed. Now to attain this identification (with God), He explains that we must observe the commandments which are written on the First Tablet (of the Ten Commandments), for their entire purpose is to (attain) eternal life, as explained at their conclusion where it says, לְמַעַן יַאֲרִכוּן יָמֶיךָ, *that your days may be long* (*Exodus* 20:12), as was explained there. (The Torah) begins now to explain the subject of honoring one's father and mother, saying . . .

3. אִישׁ אִמּוֹ וְאָבִיו תִּירָאוּ — *You shall fear, every man, his mother and his father.* This teaches (us) that the honoring of them shall not be in an arrogant manner, even though one honors them by supplying them with food, drink, and clothing, as (our Sages) mention, saying, 'One can give his father pheasant to eat, yet drive him out of the world

NOTES

XIX

2. דַּבֵּר אֶל כָּל עֲדַת . . . קְדֹשִׁים תִּהְיוּ — *Speak unto all the congregation . . . you shall be holy. Rashi,* quoting the *Sifra,* states that this section of the Torah (*parashas Kedoshim*) contains "most of the fundamental teachings of the Torah." The *Sforno,* however, explains that the Torah is now summing up the purpose of all the laws presented in the portions of *Shemini, Tazria, Metzora and Acharei* (chs. 9-18), that purpose being to attain a state of קְדוּשָּׁה, *holiness,* as a people and as individuals. He also interprets the opening verses of this chapter (vs. 3-7) as mirroring the basic ideas of the first five commandments of the Ten Commandments — in reverse order — starting with the fifth commandment (honor your father and mother) and concluding with the first commandment, אָנֹכִי (*I am HASHEM your God*). Verses

PARASHAS KEDOSHIM

19 1 *HASHEM spoke to Moses, saying:* 2 *Speak to the entire assembly of the*
Children of Israel and say to them: You shall be holy, for holy am I,
HASHEM, your God.
3 *Every man: Your mother and father shall you revere and My Sabbaths*
shall you observe — I am HASHEM, your God. 4 *Do not turn to the idols, and*
molten gods shall you not make for yourselves — I am HASHEM, your God.
5 *When you slaughter a feast peace-offering to HASHEM, you shall*
slaughter it to find favor for yourselves. 6 *On the day of your slaughter*
shall it be eaten and on the next day, and whatever remains until the third
day shall be burned in fire. 7 *But if it shall be eaten on the third day, it is*
rejected — it shall not be accepted. 8 *Each of those who eat it will bear his*
iniquity, for what is sacred to HASHEM has he desecrated; and that soul will
be cut off from its people.
9 *When you reap the harvest of your land, you shall not complete your*

(make him desperate)" (*Kiddushin* 31a), but (rather) his honoring them shall be as one who honors revered people who are superior to himself. Following this, (the Torah) explains the subject of Shabbos, saying . . .

וְאֶת שַׁבְּתֹתַי תִּשְׁמֹרוּ — *And you shall keep My Sabbaths.* It is not the Sabbath of Creation (i.e., the seventh day of every week) alone in regard to which (the Torah) cautions, but regarding every kind of Sabbath, namely the Sabbath of Creation and the Sabbath of the Land (i.e., the Sabbatical Year) with the nullification of monetary (debts), all of which testify to the (Divine) origin of the world (lit., the new "beginning" of the world, i.e., that is created by God), as He says later . . .

4. אַל תִּפְנוּ אֶל הָאֱלִילִם — *Turn not to the idols (nonentities).* (The Torah) explains that when (He) warned and said, לֹא תַעֲשֶׂה לְךָ פֶסֶל, *You shall not make for yourself a graven image* (*Exodus* 20:4), this was not only a prohibition to accept it as a god but it forbade (us) to honor them or to make talismen at specific hours to attain illusionary material success or other (similar) things through them.

5. וְכִי תִזְבְּחוּ — *And when you offer.* (The Torah) explains that when He said, אָנֹכִי ה׳ אֱלֹהֶיךָ, *I am HASHEM your God* (*Exodus* 20:2), (it was meant) that they should accept only Him as a God, as they accepted Him when they left Egypt when they said, זֶה אֵלִי וְאַנְוֵהוּ אֱלֹהֵי אָבִי וַאֲרֹמְמֶנְהוּ, *This is my God and I will glorify Him, my father's God and I will exalt Him* (*Exodus* 15:2). Not only did they say that they would observe His commandments and exalt Him, as it is fitting for one accepted as king, and that they would pray to Him alone (for assistance) in all their troubles, but they are (now) cautioned to be very concerned for His honor in such a manner that His holy things are not profaned even in thought.

9-10. וּבְקֻצְרְכֶם . . . לֶעָנִי וְלַגֵּר תַּעֲזֹב אֹתָם — *And when you reap . . . you shall leave them for the poor and the stranger.* (The Torah) explains that since we have accepted Him as God,

NOTES

5-7 are interpreted by the *Sforno* as amplifying the first commandment of אָנֹכִי. To accept God is to honor Him and refrain from profaning קֹדֶשׁ, *holy things*, even in thought (i.e., פִּגּוּל). Verses 3 and 4 amplify the second, third, fourth, and fifth commandments. To reject other gods means also rejecting talismen even though one doesn't actually worship them (v.4). To keep שַׁבָּת, *the Sabbath*, includes festivals and the Sabbatical year (v. 3). To honor parents, one must not merely meet their material needs, but respect and revere them as well (v. 3).

For clarification of many of the thoughts expressed by the *Sforno* on this verse, see the *Sforno* and notes on *Genesis* 1:26, *Exodus* 20:12 regarding length of days, *Leviticus* 11:2 and 45 and 13:47.

י פְּאַת שָׂדְךָ לִקְצֹר וְלֶקֶט קְצִירְךָ לֹא תְלַקֵּט: וְכַרְמְךָ לֹא תְעוֹלֵל וּפֶרֶט
יא כַּרְמְךָ לֹא תְלַקֵּט לֶעָנִי וְלַגֵּר תַּעֲזֹב אֹתָם אֲנִי יהוה אֱלֹהֵיכֶם: לֹא
יב תִּגְנֹבוּ וְלֹא־תְכַחֲשׁוּ וְלֹא־תְשַׁקְּרוּ אִישׁ בַּעֲמִיתוֹ: וְלֹא־תִשָּׁבְעוּ בִשְׁמִי
יג לַשָּׁקֶר וְחִלַּלְתָּ אֶת־שֵׁם אֱלֹהֶיךָ אֲנִי יהוה: לֹא־תַעֲשֹׁק אֶת־רֵעֲךָ וְלֹא
יד תִגְזֹל לֹא־תָלִין פְּעֻלַּת שָׂכִיר אִתְּךָ עַד־בֹּקֶר: לֹא־תְקַלֵּל חֵרֵשׁ וְלִפְנֵי
שני [חמישי] טו עִוֵּר לֹא תִתֵּן מִכְשֹׁל וְיָרֵאתָ מֵּאֱלֹהֶיךָ אֲנִי יהוה: לֹא־תַעֲשׂוּ עָוֶל
בַּמִּשְׁפָּט לֹא־תִשָּׂא פְנֵי־דָל וְלֹא תֶהְדַּר פְּנֵי גָדוֹל בְּצֶדֶק תִּשְׁפֹּט
טז עֲמִיתֶךָ: לֹא־תֵלֵךְ רָכִיל בְּעַמֶּיךָ לֹא תַעֲמֹד עַל־דַּם רֵעֶךָ אֲנִי יהוה:
יז לֹא־תִשְׂנָא אֶת־אָחִיךָ בִּלְבָבֶךָ הוֹכֵחַ תּוֹכִיחַ אֶת־עֲמִיתֶךָ וְלֹא־תִשָּׂא
יח עָלָיו חֵטְא: לֹא־תִקֹּם וְלֹא־תִטֹּר אֶת־בְּנֵי עַמֶּךָ וְאָהַבְתָּ לְרֵעֲךָ
יט כָּמוֹךָ אֲנִי יהוה: אֶת־חֻקֹּתַי תִּשְׁמֹרוּ בְּהֶמְתְּךָ לֹא־תַרְבִּיעַ כִּלְאַיִם
שָׂדְךָ לֹא־תִזְרַע כִּלְאָיִם וּבֶגֶד כִּלְאַיִם שַׁעַטְנֵז לֹא יַעֲלֶה עָלֶיךָ:

---

it is proper that we walk in His ways, to do righteousness and justice, and among the (various) categories of righteousness are gleanings, forgotten sheaves and the corner of the field mentioned in this chapter. And this is explained by His saying . . .

אֲנִי ה׳ אֱלֹהֵיכֶם — *I am HASHEM your God.* That is to say: Since I am your God and all My ways are kindness and truth, (hence) it is fitting that you observe these categories of righteousness which are desirable before Me Afterwards, (the Torah) continues to explain categories of justice, some of which (deal) with individuals comprising the populace, some (with matters) between the judge and the populace, while others (pertain to matters) regarding the leaders of the people. In the category regarding individuals of the populace, (the Torah) cautions against one man harming another in matters of money, which is to say . . .

11. לֹא תִּגְנֹבוּ וְלֹא תְכַחֲשׁוּ וְלֹא תְשַׁקְּרוּ — *You shall not steal, neither shall you deal falsely nor lie.* All this refers to money, and similarly when it says . . .

12. וְלֹא תִשָּׁבְעוּ בִשְׁמִי לַשָּׁקֶר — *And you shall not swear by My Name falsely* . . . so as to be acquitted from a monetary obligation. Therefore (the verse) adds and states . . .

וְחִלַּלְתָּ אֶת שֵׁם אֱלֹהֶיךָ — *And profane the Name of your God.* That is to say: Besides harming your friend by acquitting yourself falsely, behold, you (also) profane the name of your God. Following this, (the Torah) cautions (us) not to harm him by debasing his honor; this is stated by saying . . .

14. לֹא תְקַלֵּל חֵרֵשׁ — *You shall not curse the deaf.* After which (the Torah) warns us not to cause a person harm, stating, וְלִפְנֵי עִוֵּר לֹא תִתֵּן מִכְשֹׁל, *Do not put a stumbling block before the blind,* (meaning that) although you do not harm him directly (lit., with your hands), still you can cause him damage. After (all this), He explains that area of justice which concerns the relationship between the judges and the populace, stating . . .

15. לֹא תַעֲשׂוּ עָוֶל בַּמִּשְׁפָּט — *You shall do no unrighteousness in judgment.* Do not be lenient toward one (party) and harsh with the other (*Kesuvos* 46a), (or) make one stand while the other sits (*Shevuos* 30a), and (situations) similar to these. After this, the (Torah)

NOTES

15. לֹא תַעֲשׂוּ עָוֶל בַּמִּשְׁפָּט — *You shall do no unrighteousness in judgment. Unrighteousness in judgment* (עָוֶל בַּמִּשְׁפָּט) is not to be understood literally. Rather, it is an admonition to refrain from treating the parties in a dispute in a disparate fashion, thereby showing partiality. The *Sforno* interprets verse 16 as referring to men in power who can influence a ruler in such a way that their talebearing can lead to bloodshed. That is why he cites the episode of Doeg, Saul, and David, and why he

reaping to the corner of your field, and the gleanings of your harvest you shall not take. 10 *You shall not pick the undeveloped twigs of your vineyard; and the fallen fruit of your vineyard you shall not gather; for the poor and the proselyte shall you leave them — I am* HASHEM, *your God.*

11 *You shall not steal, you shall not deny falsely, and you shall not lie to one another.* 12 *You shall not swear falsely by My Name, thereby desecrating the Name of your God — I am* HASHEM. 13 *You shall not cheat your fellow and you shall not rob; a worker's wage shall not remain with you overnight until morning.* 14 *You shall not curse the deaf, and you shall not place a stumbling block before the blind; you shall fear your God — I am* HASHEM.

15 *You shall not commit a perversion of justice; you shall not favor the poor and you shall not honor the great; with righteousness shall you judge your fellow.*

16 *You shall not be a gossipmonger among your people, you shall not stand aside while your fellow's blood is shed — I am* HASHEM. 17 *You shall not hate your brother in your heart; you shall reprove your fellow and do not bear a sin because of him.* 18 *You shall not take revenge and you shall not bear a grudge against the members of your people; you shall love your fellow as yourself — I am* HASHEM.

19 *You shall observe My decrees: you shall not mate your animal into another species, you shall not plant your field with mixed seed; and a garment that is a mixture of combined fibers shall not come upon you.*

---

relates the portion (of laws) pertaining to judges and leaders of the people which involve hatred and talebearing to the king; similar to the episode of Doeg and his comrades who informed on David to Saul, resulting in (Saul's) bearing a grudge, seeking vengeance and attempting to have (David) killed, as the prophet attests saying, אַנְשֵׁי רָכִיל הָיוּ בָךְ לְמַעַן שְׁפָךְ דָּם, *In your midst were men of slander for the purpose of shedding blood* (Ezekiel 22:9). He then teaches (us) a great principle regarding these (admonitions) by saying . . .

18. וְאָהַבְתָּ לְרֵעֲךָ כָּמוֹךָ — *And you shall love your neighbor as yourself.* You should desire for your neighbor that which you would desire (lit., love) for yourself, were you in his position.

Now being that included in one's reverence of God, the Blessed One, is the keeping of the statutes, for indeed those who observe them in order not to sin against Him do so because they have come to recognize His greatness and goodness, and know that He did not command (anything) except that which is worthy and good, (hence) it is not proper to disobey His word, even though the reason for the commandment is not known; (therefore), He says . . .

19. אֶת חֻקֹּתַי תִּשְׁמֹרוּ — *You shall keep My statutes.* (The Torah) mentions statutes

NOTES

quotes the verse from *Ezekiel.* This explains the continuity of verse 16 — *do not bear tales* and *do not stand idly by the blood of your neighbor.*

18. וְאָהַבְתָּ לְרֵעֲךָ כָּמוֹךָ — *And you shall love your neighbor as yourself.* The *Sforno*, among many other commentators, does not translate the phrase וְאָהַבְתָּ לְרֵעֲךָ כָּמוֹךָ to mean *love your neighbor "as" yourself,* for then the Torah would have written אֶת רֵעֲךָ. In general, this is an unrealistic expectation. Rather, man is being told to love and to treat his fellowman as he would desire others to treat him. This is precisely what Hillel meant when he said to the non-Jew who wished to convert, "What is hateful to you, do it not to your friend" (*Shabbos* 31a); however, since he was speaking to a non-Jew he expressed it in the negative sense.

19-20. אֶת חֻקֹּתַי תִּשְׁמֹרוּ . . . כִּי לֹא חֻפָּשָׁה — *You shall keep My statutes . . . Because she was not free.*

כ וְאִישׁ כִּי־יִשְׁכַּב אֶת־אִשָּׁה שִׁכְבַת־זֶרַע וְהִוא שִׁפְחָה נֶחֱרֶפֶת לְאִישׁ
וְהׇפְדֵּה לֹא נִפְדָּתָה אוֹ חֻפְשָׁה לֹא נִתַּן־לָהּ בִּקֹּרֶת תִּהְיֶה לֹא יוּמְתוּ
כא כִּי־לֹא חֻפָּשָׁה׃ וְהֵבִיא אֶת־אֲשָׁמוֹ לַיהוָה אֶל־פֶּתַח אֹהֶל מוֹעֵד אֵיל
כב אָשָׁם׃ וְכִפֶּר עָלָיו הַכֹּהֵן בְּאֵיל הָאָשָׁם לִפְנֵי יהוה עַל־חַטָּאתוֹ אֲשֶׁר
חָטָא וְנִסְלַח לוֹ מֵחַטָּאתוֹ אֲשֶׁר חָטָא׃
שלישי כג וְכִי־תָבֹאוּ אֶל־הָאָרֶץ וּנְטַעְתֶּם כׇּל־עֵץ מַאֲכָל וַעֲרַלְתֶּם עׇרְלָתוֹ
כד אֶת־פִּרְיוֹ שָׁלֹשׁ שָׁנִים יִהְיֶה לָכֶם עֲרֵלִים לֹא יֵאָכֵל׃ וּבַשָּׁנָה הָרְבִיעִת
כה יִהְיֶה כׇּל־פִּרְיוֹ קֹדֶשׁ הִלּוּלִים לַיהוָה׃ וּבַשָּׁנָה הַחֲמִישִׁת תֹּאכְלוּ אֶת־
כו פִּרְיוֹ לְהוֹסִיף לָכֶם תְּבוּאָתוֹ אֲנִי יהוה אֱלֹהֵיכֶם׃ לֹא תֹאכְלוּ עַל־הַדָּם
כז לֹא תְנַחֲשׁוּ וְלֹא תְעוֹנֵנוּ׃ לֹא תַקִּפוּ פְּאַת רֹאשְׁכֶם וְלֹא תַשְׁחִית
כח אֵת פְּאַת זְקָנֶךָ׃ וְשֶׂרֶט לָנֶפֶשׁ לֹא תִתְּנוּ בִּבְשַׂרְכֶם וּכְתֹבֶת קַעֲקַע
כט לֹא תִתְּנוּ בָּכֶם אֲנִי יהוה׃ אַל־תְּחַלֵּל אֶת־בִּתְּךָ לְהַזְנוֹתָהּ וְלֹא־
ל תִזְנֶה הָאָרֶץ וּמָלְאָה הָאָרֶץ זִמָּה׃ אֶת־שַׁבְּתֹתַי תִּשְׁמֹרוּ וּמִקְדָּשִׁי תִּירָאוּ

regarding the work of animals, agricultural labor, clothing, breeding, food and drink, and foretelling the future, for all these were representative of their lifestyle at that time. Many of these statutes are prohibitions meant to eliminate practices which are contrary to the nature of things as intended and ordered by God, the Exalted One. However, regarding a שִׁפְחָה חֲרוּפָה, *a designated bondwoman* (v.20), although it is also a statute, considering that *she* receives lashes whereas *he* does not, and also in that *he* brings an offering even for an intentional transgression (מֵזִיד) and that both these laws (lashes only for the woman and bringing a sacrifice for מֵזִיד) are not found regarding any other *mitzvos* in the Torah (hence it is certainly a חֹק), nonetheless, some explanation is given for this statute (in the next verse) where it says . . .

20. כִּי לֹא חֻפָּשָׁה — *Because she was not free.* The sin (of the perpetrator) is (relatively) light because the act of betrothal (of this bondwoman) is not totally valid and the principal aspect of the sin committed lies in his being intimate with one who is partially a bondwoman (חֲצִי שִׁפְחָה), thereby profaning the sanctity of God. Now, being that this deed on the human level represents an impairment of the honor of the man (the active participant) and not of the honor of the woman (the passive participant), we must assume that she enticed him and therefore she deserves to receive the lashes. (As for the bringing of a guilt offering) this intentional trangression (מֵזִיד), whereby he so foolishly profaned himself, borders on an unintentional act, שׁוֹגֵג; hence he brings a guilt offering for profaning the holy.

26. לֹא תֹאכְלוּ עַל הַדָּם לֹא תְנַחֲשׁוּ וְלֹא תְעוֹנֵנוּ — *You shall not eat with the blood, neither shall you practice divination nor soothsaying.* All these methods (were practiced) among

NOTES

Statutes are laws commanded by God which defy logical explanation and must be accepted on faith. However, the *Sforno* feels that not all חֻקִּים are equal. Some appear more understandable than others since their purpose is to maintain the balance and order of nature ordained by God, the Creator. However, some not only seem to lack rationale but contain seemingly contradictory elements. One such example is שִׁפְחָה חֲרוּפָה, *a designated bondwoman,* as the *Sforno* explains. Paradoxically, in this instance, the Torah *does* indicate some reason for the statute. The guilt of the maidservant lies in the fact that, having nothing to lose in regard to her reputation, she feels she may as well be the seductress; hence she is punished. The man, on the other hand, is a prisoner of passion and closer to שׁוֹגֵג, *unintentional transgression,* than to מֵזִיד, *intentional;* therefore, he can atone with a sacrifice.

20 *If a man lies carnally with a woman, and she is a slavewoman who has been designated for another man, and who has not been redeemed, or freedom has not been granted her; there shall be an investigation — they shall not be put to death, for she has not been freed.* 21 *He shall bring his guilt-offering to* HASHEM, *to the entrance of the Tent of the Meeting, a ram guilt-offering.* 22 *The Kohen shall provide him atonement with the ram guilt-offering before* HASHEM *for the sin that he had committed; and the sin that he had committed shall be forgiven him.*

23 *When you shall come to the land and you shall plant any food tree, you shall treat its fruit as forbidden; for three years they shall be forbidden to you, they shall not be eaten.* 24 *In the fourth year, all its fruit shall be sanctified to laud* HASHEM. 25 *And in the fifth year you may eat its fruit — so that it will increase its crop for you — I am* HASHEM, *your God.*

26 *You shall not eat over the blood; you shall not indulge in sorcery and you shall not believe in lucky times.* 27 *You shall not round off the edge of your scalp and you shall not destroy the edge of your beard.* 28 *You shall not make a cut in your flesh for the dead, and a tattoo shall you not place upon yourselves — I am* HASHEM.

29 *Do not profane your daughter to make her a harlot, lest the land become lewd, and the land become filled with depravity.*

30 *My Sabbaths shall you observe and My Sanctuary shall you revere —*

---

them to predict the future (in the process of) turning aside from the spirit of *taharah* and prophecy to the way of the spirit of *tumah*. And being that the ways of revering and honoring God (include) the prohibition of physically profaning His people whom He hallowed to serve Him, (the Torah) says . . .

27-29. לֹא תַקִּפוּ . . . אַל תְּחַלֵּל אֶת בִּתְּךָ — *You shall not round . . . do not profane your daughter*. And He commanded that we are not to profane (our bodies) by rounding the corners of the head as is the practice of fools, drunkards or heathen priests and (also) not to shave the beard, as our Sages say, "The beard is the dignity (beauty) of the face" (*Shabbos* 152a), nor to *make a cutting in the flesh* (v. 28), thereby attaching excessive importance to man's death, and mourning excessively over it. (He also prohibited us) *to imprint any marks on the body* (tattooing) so as not to have any sign on our flesh other than the sign of the covenant (בְּרִית מִילָה), and to make one's daughter a harlot (v. 29) even though she be unmarried, for it profanes her and her father, similar to *If she profanes herself by playing the harlot, she profanes her father* (21:9). (Now), after warning (us) regarding those things which are a profanation, He commands (us) to honor the holy days, places and people — saying . . .

30. אֶת שַׁבְּתֹתַי תִּשְׁמֹרוּ — *You shall keep My Sabbaths* . . . which means the Shabbos and all the holy convocations.

NOTES

26. לֹא תֹאכְלוּ עַל הַדָּם — *You shall not eat with the blood*. See the *Sforno* and the notes on 17:7 regarding the link between blood and the demons who were courted by people in the hope of having future events revealed to them.

27-28. לֹא תַקִּפוּ — *You shall not round*. The *Sforno* explains that the concept of קְדוּשָׁה, *sanctity*, extends to the care of one's body which must be treated with respect and dignity. One way this is manifested is through one's refraining from imprinting any permanent mark on his body. The one notable exception is that of the בְּרִית מִילָה which demonstrates the Jew's identification with his God and his people.

30. אֶת שַׁבְּתֹתַי תִּשְׁמֹרוּ — *You shall keep My Sabbaths*. The term שַׁבְּתֹתַי, *My Sabbaths*, is in the

לא אֲנִי יהוה: אַל־תִּפְנוּ אֶל־הָאֹבֹת וְאֶל־הַיִּדְּעֹנִים אַל־תְּבַקְשׁוּ לְטָמְאָה
לב בָהֶם אֲנִי יהוה אֱלֹהֵיכֶם: מִפְּנֵי שֵׂיבָה תָּקוּם וְהָדַרְתָּ פְּנֵי זָקֵן וְיָרֵאתָ
רביעי [ששי] לג מֵּאֱלֹהֶיךָ אֲנִי יהוה: וְכִי־יָגוּר אִתְּךָ גֵּר בְּאַרְצְכֶם לֹא תוֹנוּ
לד אֹתוֹ: כְּאֶזְרָח מִכֶּם יִהְיֶה לָכֶם הַגֵּר ׀ הַגָּר אִתְּכֶם וְאָהַבְתָּ לוֹ כָּמוֹךָ כִּי־
לה גֵרִים הֱיִיתֶם בְּאֶרֶץ מִצְרָיִם אֲנִי יהוה אֱלֹהֵיכֶם: לֹא־תַעֲשׂוּ עָוֶל בַּמִּשְׁפָּט
לו בַּמִּדָּה בַּמִּשְׁקָל וּבַמְּשׂוּרָה: מֹאזְנֵי צֶדֶק אַבְנֵי־צֶדֶק אֵיפַת צֶדֶק וְהִין צֶדֶק
יִהְיֶה לָכֶם אֲנִי יהוה אֱלֹהֵיכֶם אֲשֶׁר־הוֹצֵאתִי אֶתְכֶם מֵאֶרֶץ מִצְרָיִם:
לז וּשְׁמַרְתֶּם אֶת־כָּל־חֻקֹּתַי וְאֶת־כָּל־מִשְׁפָּטַי וַעֲשִׂיתֶם אֹתָם אֲנִי יהוה:
כ חמישי א־ב וַיְדַבֵּר יהוה אֶל־מֹשֶׁה לֵּאמֹר: וְאֶל־בְּנֵי יִשְׂרָאֵל תֹּאמַר אִישׁ אִישׁ מִבְּנֵי
יִשְׂרָאֵל וּמִן־הַגֵּר ׀ הַגָּר בְּיִשְׂרָאֵל אֲשֶׁר יִתֵּן מִזַּרְעוֹ לַמֹּלֶךְ מוֹת יוּמָת

וּמִקְדָּשִׁי תִּירָאוּ — *And revere My Sanctuary* ... which means every place hallowed for Torah, prayer and service (of God). (Now) being that inquiring of the אֹבֹת (a form of necromancy) among the nations was (considered) as a divine search, (appealing) to the dead on behalf of the living, (the Torah) states ...

31. אַל תִּפְנוּ אֶל הָאֹבֹת — *Do not turn to the "ovos."* Do not turn toward them, but show them (lit., give them) the back of your neck and not your face. Needless to say, do not honor them.

אַל תְּבַקְשׁוּ לְטָמְאָה בָהֶם — *Do not seek them out to be defiled by them.* Do not seek them out in order to be defiled through them, but you may seek them to know their nature so as to teach, as (our Sages say) (*Shabbos* 75a), "Do not learn (these subjects) in order to perform them, but you may learn them to understand and to teach."

32. מִפְּנֵי שֵׂיבָה תָּקוּם — *You shall rise up before the hoary head.* But you shall honor the "holy ones of the Most High" (based on *Daniel* 7:18) of whom most are hoary heads, as it says, עֲטֶרֶת תִּפְאֶרֶת שֵׂיבָה בְּדֶרֶךְ צְדָקָה תִּמָּצֵא, *The hoary head is a crown of glory, it is found in the way of righteousness* (*Proverbs* 16:31).

וְהָדַרְתָּ פְּנֵי זָקֵן — *And honor the face of the elder.* These are the Torah scholars (lit., who hold the Torah), as our Rabbis, of blessed memory, say, "A *zaken* is none other than one who has acquired wisdom" (*Kiddushin* 32b). After cautioning (us) regarding the honor of the holy ones, (the Torah) warns us not to shame the lowly ones, saying ...

33. וְכִי יָגוּר אִתְּךָ גֵּר ... לֹא תוֹנוּ אֹתוֹ — *And if a stranger sojourn with you ... you shall not do him wrong* ... even by vexing him with words ... (the Torah) then additionally says...

35. לֹא תַעֲשׂוּ עָוֶל בַּמִּשְׁפָּט בַּמִּדָּה בַּמִּשְׁקָל וּבַמְּשׂוּרָה — *You shall do no unrighteousness concerning judgment in land measurement, in weight or in measure.* Being that אוֹנָאָה (*wrongdoing* — misleading a person) also includes money matters, namely, liquid and dry measures and weights, (the Torah) cautions against general wrongdoing toward the native and the stranger.

37. וּשְׁמַרְתֶּם אֶת כָּל חֻקֹּתַי וְאֶת כָּל מִשְׁפָּטַי — *And you shall observe all My statutes and all My ordinances.* Analyze them and recognize that they are worthy.

NOTES

plural, therefore the *Sforno* interprets it as including, in addition to Shabbos, festivals and the *Shemittah* (seventh year) as well. (See verse 3.) And just as *My Sabbaths* is all-inclusive, so does the term מִקְדָּשִׁי, *My Sanctuary*, include every holy place designated for prayer and Torah study, which must be treated with reverence.

32. מִפְּנֵי שֵׂיבָה תָּקוּם — *You shall rise up before the hoary head.* Whereas the status of שֵׂיבָה is deter-

I am HASHEM. [31] *Do not turn to [the sorcery of] the Ovos and Yid'onim; do not seek to be contaminated through them — I am* HASHEM, *your God.*

[32] *In the presence of an old person shall you rise and you shall honor the presence of a sage and you shall revere your God — I am* HASHEM.

[33] *When a proselyte dwells among you in your land, do not taunt him.* [34] *The proselyte who dwells with you shall be like a native among you, and you shall love him like yourself, for you were aliens in the land of Egypt — I am* HASHEM, *your God.*

[35] *You shall not commit a perversion in justice, in measures of length, weight, or volume.* [36] *You shall have correct scales, correct weights, correct dry measures, and correct liquid measures — I am* HASHEM, *your God, Who brought you forth from the land of Egypt.* [37] *You shall observe all My decrees and all My ordinances, and you shall perform them — I am* HASHEM.

20 [1] HASHEM *spoke to Moses, saying:* [2] *Say to the Children of Israel: Any man from the Children of Israel and from the proselyte who lives with Israel, who shall give of his seed to Molech, shall be put to death;*

וַעֲשִׂיתֶם אֹתָם — *And do them.* And in this way (i.e., through studying them and recognizing their great worth), you will do them.

אֲנִי ה' — *I am* HASHEM. (The Torah) explains that it is proper to keep the statutes and ordinances without adding (to) or diminishing (them) because, indeed, the works of God and His commandments are the ultimate in perfection, and עָלָיו אֵין לְהוֹסִיף וּמִמֶּנּוּ אֵין לִגְרוֹעַ, *Nothing can be added to it nor anything taken from it* (Koheles 3:14).

XX

2. אֲשֶׁר יִתֵּן מִזַּרְעוֹ לַמֹּלֶךְ — *That gives of his seed to Molech.* After explaining the Godly intent to sanctify Israel so that they shall be like Him as much as possible, and (after) teaching them the way through which the intended goal of God, the Exalted One, shall be attained, and (after) cautioning against acting contrary (to these teachings), He now speaks of the punishment (of those who) become *tamei* with one of three types of *tumah* which are the antithesis of the aforementioned holiness. The first is *tumah* in the area of דֵּעוֹת (philosophical opinions) such as that of the Molech which is said *to defile My sanctuary* (v. 3) and that of *ovos* and familiar spirits of which it was said earlier, *Seek them not out to be defiled by them* (19:31). The second is *tumah* regarding one's seed (i.e., offspring), which is עֲרָיוֹת (prohibited sexual relations) of which (the Torah) stated above, *Defile not yourselves in any of these things, for in all these the nations are defiled . . . and the land was defiled* (18:24,25). And the third *tumah* is (contracted through the consumption) of prohibited foods, of which it is said at the conclusion of this chapter, *Which I have set apart for you to consider tamei* (v. 25). However, in *parashas Emor*, (the

NOTES

mined by age, that of a זָקֵן is established by Torah scholarship, regardless of one's chronological age.

37. וּשְׁמַרְתֶּם אֶת כָּל חֻקֹּתַי . . . וַעֲשִׂיתֶם אֹתָם — *And you shall observe all My statutes . . . and do them.* The *Sforno* explains that וַעֲשִׂיתֶם and וּשְׁמַרְתֶּם are not redundant. The former does not refer to *observance* but to study and analysis, which leads to *keeping* and *doing*.

XX

2. אֲשֶׁר יִתֵּן מִזַּרְעוֹ לַמֹּלֶךְ . . . — *That gives of his seed to Molech.* The *Sforno* explains the concluding section of *parashas Kedoshim* in the following manner. The numerous laws set forth in this portion of the Torah are meant to refine and sanctify the Jewish people. The antithesis of קְדוּשָׁה, *holiness*, is טוּמְאָה, *impurity*. The *Sforno* calls our

ג עַם הָאָרֶץ יִרְגְּמֻהוּ בָאָבֶן: וַאֲנִי אֶתֵּן אֶת־פָּנַי בָּאִישׁ הַהוּא וְהִכְרַתִּי אֹתוֹ
מִקֶּרֶב עַמּוֹ כִּי מִזַּרְעוֹ נָתַן לַמֹּלֶךְ לְמַעַן טַמֵּא אֶת־מִקְדָּשִׁי וּלְחַלֵּל
ד אֶת־שֵׁם קָדְשִׁי: וְאִם הַעְלֵם יַעְלִימוּ עַם הָאָרֶץ אֶת־עֵינֵיהֶם מִן־הָאִישׁ
ה הַהוּא בְּתִתּוֹ מִזַּרְעוֹ לַמֹּלֶךְ לְבִלְתִּי הָמִית אֹתוֹ: וְשַׂמְתִּי אֲנִי אֶת־פָּנַי
בָּאִישׁ הַהוּא וּבְמִשְׁפַּחְתּוֹ וְהִכְרַתִּי אֹתוֹ וְאֵת | כָּל־הַזֹּנִים אַחֲרָיו לִזְנוֹת
ו אַחֲרֵי הַמֹּלֶךְ מִקֶּרֶב עַמָּם: וְהַנֶּפֶשׁ אֲשֶׁר תִּפְנֶה אֶל־הָאֹבֹת וְאֶל־
הַיִּדְּעֹנִים לִזְנֹת אַחֲרֵיהֶם וְנָתַתִּי אֶת־פָּנַי בַּנֶּפֶשׁ הַהִוא וְהִכְרַתִּי אֹתוֹ
ז מִקֶּרֶב עַמּוֹ: וְהִתְקַדִּשְׁתֶּם וִהְיִיתֶם קְדֹשִׁים כִּי אֲנִי יְהוָה אֱלֹהֵיכֶם:
ששי [שביעי] ח־ט וּשְׁמַרְתֶּם אֶת־חֻקֹּתַי וַעֲשִׂיתֶם אֹתָם אֲנִי יְהוָה מְקַדִּשְׁכֶם: כִּי־אִישׁ אִישׁ
אֲשֶׁר יְקַלֵּל אֶת־אָבִיו וְאֶת־אִמּוֹ מוֹת יוּמָת אָבִיו וְאִמּוֹ קִלֵּל דָּמָיו בּוֹ:

Torah) speaks of the *tumah* (caused) by a dead person, the profanation of (one's) seed, of blemishes (how they relate to the laws of *Kohanim* and of sacrifices) and of מְעִילָה (*trespass* — forbidden enjoyment of the holy), topics which pertain only to holy items and persons. Now (the Torah) begins to speak of Molech, saying —

עַם הָאָרֶץ יִרְגְּמֻהוּ בָאָבֶן — *The people of the land shall stone him with stones.* Thus the populace shall do in their zealousness (to defend) the honor of their Creator. This shall be when there are witnesses and a warning.

3. וַאֲנִי אֶתֵּן אֶת פָּנַי בָּאִישׁ הַהוּא — *I will set My face against that man . . .* if he does not repent of his wickedness, and in this manner his death will not be an atonement.

וְהִכְרַתִּי אֹתוֹ — *And I will cut him off.* This must perforce be understood as an allusion to the World to Come, for after he is stoned he can no longer be cut off from This World.

לְמַעַן טַמֵּא אֶת מִקְדָּשִׁי — *To defile My Sanctuary.* (This caused) the *Shechinah* (Divine Presence) to depart from Israel, (therefore) it is fitting that they stone him.

וּלְחַלֵּל אֶת שֵׁם קָדְשִׁי — *And to profane My holy Name.* Therefore, I will set My face against him, though it (the Molech) is not an (actual) idol.

5. וּבְמִשְׁפַּחְתּוֹ — *And against his family.* For the people of the land would not have hidden their eyes (to this evil) except for fear of his family who support him.

7. וְהִתְקַדִּשְׁתֶּם — *Sanctify yourselves . . .* by separating yourselves from sexual immorality.

וִהְיִיתֶם קְדֹשִׁים — *And you shall be holy . . .* that your offspring (lit., seed) be predisposed

NOTES

attention to the fact that the term טוּמְאָה is used in connection with laws regulating food, sexual relationships, and the occult. This is the common denominator of the subjects which comprise the concluding section of *Kedoshim*. They all represent the opposite of the ideal which the Torah demands of us, i.e., *you shall be holy*.

3. וַאֲנִי אֶתֵּן אֶת פָּנַי בָּאִישׁ הַהוּא — *I will set My face against that man.* The *Sforno* teaches us two important concepts in his commentary on this verse. One is that a person's death is a כַּפָּרָה, *atonement*, only if he repents beforehand and the second is that the term כָּרֵת, *excision*, in this case alludes not to עוֹלָם הַזֶּה, *This World*, but to עוֹלָם הַבָּא, *the World to Come*.

לְמַעַן טַמֵּא אֶת מִקְדָּשִׁי וּלְחַלֵּל — *To defile My Sanctuary and to profane.* Giving one's seed to the Molech is an act which both defiles and desecrates. It defiles by causing the *Shechinah* to depart, leaving a spiritual vacuum which is filled by טוּמְאָה. By offering one's child to the Molech, a man profanes God's Name, even though he does not accept the Molech as a god.

5. וּבְמִשְׁפַּחְתּוֹ — *And against his family.* To punish the family of the sinner seems contrary to the teaching that *each man shall die for his own sin* (אִישׁ בְּחֶטְאוֹ יָמוּת). The *Sforno* explains, however, that the family shares in the blame for supporting the sinner and shielding him.

7. וְהִתְקַדִּשְׁתֶּם — *Sanctify yourselves.* Unlike *Rashi*, who interprets וְהִתְקַדִּשְׁתֶּם as referring to rejection of idolatry, the *Sforno* applies it to rejection

the people of the land shall pelt him with stones. [3] *I shall concentrate My attention upon that man, and I shall cut him off from among his people, for he had given from his offspring to Molech in order to defile My Sanctuary and to desecrate My holy Name.* [4] *But if the people of the land avert their eyes from that man when he gives from his offspring to Molech, not to put him to death —* [5] *then I shall concentrate My attention upon that man and upon his family; I will cut off from among their people, him and all who stray after him to stray after the Molech.* [6] *And the person who shall turn to the sorcery of the Ovos and the Yid'onim to stray after them — I shall concentrate My attention upon that person and cut him off from among his people.*

[7] *You shall sanctify yourselves and you will be holy, for I am* H*ASHEM*, *your God.*

[8] *You shall observe My decrees and perform them — I am* H*ASHEM*, *Who sanctifies you.* [9] *For any man who will curse his father or mother shall be put to death; his father or his mother has he cursed, his blood is upon himself.*

---

for the *Shechinah* to dwell in their midst, as (our Sages) say, "The *Shechinah* only dwells upon families of distinguished ancestry in Israel" (*Kiddushin* 70b).

כִּי אֲנִי ה׳ אֱלֹהֵיכֶם — *For I am* H*ASHEM your God* ... who said to Abraham, לִהְיוֹת לְךָ לֵאלֹהִים וּלְזַרְעֲךָ אַחֲרֶיךָ, *To be a God to you and to your seed after you* (*Genesis* 17:7), i.e., (only) to seed descended from your ancestral line, as (our Sages) explained (*Midrash Bamidbar Rabbah* 12:4).

8. וּשְׁמַרְתֶּם אֶת חֻקֹּתַי וַעֲשִׂיתֶם אֹתָם — *And keep My statutes and do them.* In this manner, namely, that you sanctify yourselves through separation from forbidden unions, you will thereby *keep* and *do them* for (future) generations. (But) if you do not sanctify yourselves, your descendants will undoubtedly also rebel (against these laws) since they will have been born in sin, as we find in הֵן בְּעָווֹן חוֹלָלְתִּי, *Behold, I was shaped in iniquity* (*Psalms* 51:7).

אֲנִי ה׳ מְקַדִּשְׁכֶם — *I am* H*ASHEM Who sanctifies you.* For, in truth, I have prohibited (these) forbidden unions (to you) to sanctify you to my service.

9. כִּי אִישׁ אִישׁ אֲשֶׁר יְקַלֵּל אֶת אָבִיו וְאֶת אִמּוֹ — *For any man there be that curses his father or his mother.* As an indication (lit., sign) that I am extremely exacting regarding the sanctity of your offspring is the fact that I ordained capital punishment (lit., death sentence by the court) for whosoever curses his parents. Now this occurs, in most cases, when there is a flaw in one's offspring, for then he is not predisposed to that which is written, שְׁמַע בְּנִי מוּסַר אָבִיךָ, *My son, hear the instruction of your father* (*Proverbs* 1:8). And a man such as this will (also) not keep the statutes and ordinances, for he will utterly refuse to accept them from his father and mother.

NOTES

of immorality. For only through proper moral conduct is Israel fit for the *Shechinah* to dwell in its midst. Their children, in turn, by perpetuating this way of life, are thereby worthy to have God as their God and also to have the *Shechinah* abide with them. The *Sforno's* commentary on the following verse (8) continues this theme.

8-9. וּשְׁמַרְתֶּם אֶת חֻקֹּתַי וַעֲשִׂיתֶם אֹתָם ... כִּי אִישׁ אִישׁ אֲשֶׁר יְקַלֵּל אֶת אָבִיו וְאֶת אִמּוֹ — *And keep My statutes and do them ... For any man there be that curses his father or his mother.* The *Sforno* points out the link connecting the chastity of family life, the obligation of children to have respect for parental authority, and the observance of God's commandments. Only when the people of Israel exercise discipline and thereby safeguard the nobility of their moral character will they merit offspring who will honor and obey their parents and accept their instruction which, in turn, will shape them into servants of God.

י וְאִישׁ אֲשֶׁר יִנְאַף אֶת־אֵשֶׁת אִישׁ אֲשֶׁר יִנְאַף אֶת־אֵשֶׁת רֵעֵהוּ מוֹת־
יא יוּמַת הַנֹּאֵף וְהַנֹּאָפֶת: וְאִישׁ אֲשֶׁר יִשְׁכַּב אֶת־אֵשֶׁת אָבִיו עֶרְוַת אָבִיו
יב גִּלָּה מוֹת־יוּמְתוּ שְׁנֵיהֶם דְּמֵיהֶם בָּם: וְאִישׁ אֲשֶׁר יִשְׁכַּב אֶת־כַּלָּתוֹ מוֹת
יג יוּמְתוּ שְׁנֵיהֶם תֶּבֶל עָשׂוּ דְּמֵיהֶם בָּם: וְאִישׁ אֲשֶׁר יִשְׁכַּב אֶת־זָכָר מִשְׁכְּבֵי
יד אִשָּׁה תּוֹעֵבָה עָשׂוּ שְׁנֵיהֶם מוֹת יוּמָתוּ דְּמֵיהֶם בָּם: וְאִישׁ אֲשֶׁר יִקַּח
אֶת־אִשָּׁה וְאֶת־אִמָּהּ זִמָּה הִוא בָּאֵשׁ יִשְׂרְפוּ אֹתוֹ וְאֶתְהֶן וְלֹא־תִהְיֶה
טו זִמָּה בְּתוֹכְכֶם: וְאִישׁ אֲשֶׁר יִתֵּן שְׁכָבְתּוֹ בִּבְהֵמָה מוֹת יוּמָת וְאֶת־הַבְּהֵמָה
טז תַּהֲרֹגוּ: וְאִשָּׁה אֲשֶׁר תִּקְרַב אֶל־כָּל־בְּהֵמָה לְרִבְעָה אֹתָהּ וְהָרַגְתָּ
יז אֶת־הָאִשָּׁה וְאֶת־הַבְּהֵמָה מוֹת יוּמָתוּ דְּמֵיהֶם בָּם: וְאִישׁ אֲשֶׁר־יִקַּח
אֶת־אֲחֹתוֹ בַּת־אָבִיו אוֹ־בַת־אִמּוֹ וְרָאָה אֶת־עֶרְוָתָהּ וְהִיא תִרְאֶה
אֶת־עֶרְוָתוֹ חֶסֶד הוּא וְנִכְרְתוּ לְעֵינֵי בְּנֵי עַמָּם עֶרְוַת אֲחֹתוֹ גִּלָּה עֲוֺנוֹ
יח יִשָּׂא: וְאִישׁ אֲשֶׁר־יִשְׁכַּב אֶת־אִשָּׁה דָּוָה וְגִלָּה אֶת־עֶרְוָתָהּ אֶת־מְקֹרָהּ
יט הֶעֱרָה וְהִוא גִּלְּתָה אֶת־מְקוֹר דָּמֶיהָ וְנִכְרְתוּ שְׁנֵיהֶם מִקֶּרֶב עַמָּם: וְעֶרְוַת
אֲחוֹת אִמְּךָ וַאֲחוֹת אָבִיךָ לֹא תְגַלֵּה כִּי אֶת־שְׁאֵרוֹ הֶעֱרָה עֲוֺנָם יִשָּׂאוּ:
כ וְאִישׁ אֲשֶׁר יִשְׁכַּב אֶת־דֹּדָתוֹ עֶרְוַת דֹּדוֹ גִּלָּה חֶטְאָם יִשָּׂאוּ עֲרִירִים יָמֻתוּ:
כא וְאִישׁ אֲשֶׁר יִקַּח אֶת־אֵשֶׁת אָחִיו נִדָּה הִוא עֶרְוַת אָחִיו גִּלָּה עֲרִירִים יִהְיוּ:
כב וּשְׁמַרְתֶּם אֶת־כָּל־חֻקֹּתַי וְאֶת־כָּל־מִשְׁפָּטַי וַעֲשִׂיתֶם אֹתָם וְלֹא־תָקִיא
שביעי כג אֶתְכֶם הָאָרֶץ אֲשֶׁר אֲנִי מֵבִיא אֶתְכֶם שָׁמָּה לָשֶׁבֶת בָּהּ: וְלֹא תֵלְכוּ
בְּחֻקֹּת הַגּוֹי אֲשֶׁר־אֲנִי מְשַׁלֵּחַ מִפְּנֵיכֶם כִּי אֶת־כָּל־אֵלֶּה עָשׂוּ וָאָקֻץ בָּם:
כד וָאֹמַר לָכֶם אַתֶּם תִּירְשׁוּ אֶת־אַדְמָתָם וַאֲנִי אֶתְּנֶנָּה לָכֶם לָרֶשֶׁת אֹתָהּ
אֶרֶץ זָבַת חָלָב וּדְבָשׁ אֲנִי יהוה אֱלֹהֵיכֶם אֲשֶׁר־הִבְדַּלְתִּי אֶתְכֶם
מפטיר כה מִן־הָעַמִּים: וְהִבְדַּלְתֶּם בֵּין־הַבְּהֵמָה הַטְּהֹרָה לַטְּמֵאָה וּבֵין־הָעוֹף הַטָּמֵא
לַטָּהֹר וְלֹא־תְשַׁקְּצוּ אֶת־נַפְשֹׁתֵיכֶם בַּבְּהֵמָה וּבָעוֹף וּבְכֹל אֲשֶׁר תִּרְמֹשׂ
כו הָאֲדָמָה אֲשֶׁר־הִבְדַּלְתִּי לָכֶם לְטַמֵּא: וִהְיִיתֶם לִי קְדֹשִׁים כִּי קָדוֹשׁ אֲנִי
כז יהוה וָאַבְדִּל אֶתְכֶם מִן־הָעַמִּים לִהְיוֹת לִי: וְאִישׁ אוֹ־אִשָּׁה כִּי־יִהְיֶה בָהֶם
אוֹב אוֹ יִדְּעֹנִי מוֹת יוּמָתוּ בָּאֶבֶן יִרְגְּמוּ אֹתָם דְּמֵיהֶם בָּם:

---

25. וְלֹא תְשַׁקְּצוּ אֶת נַפְשֹׁתֵיכֶם בַּבְּהֵמָה וּבָעוֹף וּבְכֹל אֲשֶׁר תִּרְמֹשׂ הָאֲדָמָה — *And you shall not make your souls detestable by beast, or by fowl, or by anything which creeps on the ground . . .* from the species which are unclean (i.e., non-kosher) which I have set apart for you from the ones that are clean (i.e., kosher).

לְטַמֵּא — *To make you unclean.* The manner in which the detestable (species) shall make the soul unclean is exclusively by eating them, not merely by touching or carrying them.

27. וְאִישׁ אוֹ אִשָּׁה כִּי יִהְיֶה בָהֶם אוֹב אוֹ יִדְּעֹנִי — *A man or a woman that divines by a necromancy or a familiar spirit.* Since the intent of all these (commandments) is to sanctify Israel, hence, he who veers from this (through utilization of) a necromancy or a familiar spirit, a practice which is entirely steeped in the spirit of *tumah*, the very opposite

NOTES

25. לְטַמֵּא — *To make you unclean.* The *Sforno* explains that *tumah* can be contracted not only by touching a דָּבָר טָמֵא but also by ingesting it.

*10 A man who will commit adultery with a man's wife, who will commit
adultery with his fellow's wife; the adulterer and the adulteress shall be put
to death.*
*11 A man who shall lie with his father's wife will have uncovered his father's
shame; the two of them shall be put to death, their blood is upon themselves.*
*12 A man who shall lie with his daughter-in-law, the two of them shall be
put to death; they have committed a perversion, their blood is upon
themselves.*
*13 A man who lies with a man as one lies with a woman, they have both done
an abomination; they shall be put to death, their blood is upon themselves.*
*14 A man who shall take a woman and her mother, it is a depraved plot; they
shall burn him and them in fire, and there shall not be depravity among you.*
*15 A man who shall lie with an animal shall be put to death; and you shall
kill the animal. 16 And a woman who approaches any animal for it to mate with
her, you shall kill the woman and the animal; they shall be put to death, their
blood is upon them.*
*17 A man who shall take his sister, the daughter of his father or the daughter
of his mother, and he shall see her nakedness and she shall see his nakedness,
it is a disgrace and they shall be cut off in the sight of the members of their
people; he will have uncovered the nakedness of his sister, he shall bear his
iniquity.*
*18 A man who shall lie with a woman in her affliction and has uncovered
her nakedness, he will have bared her source and she has bared the source of
her blood; the two of them will be cut off from the midst of their people.*
*19 The nakedness of your mother's sister or your father's sister shall you not
uncover, for that is baring one's own flesh; they shall bear their iniquity. 20 And
a man who shall lie with his aunt will have uncovered the nakedness of his
aunt; they shall bear their sin, they shall die childless. 21 A man who shall take
his brother's wife, it is loathsome; he will have uncovered his brother's shame,
they shall be childless.*
*22 You shall observe all My decrees and all My ordinances and perform
them; then the Land to which I bring you to dwell will not disgorge you. 23 Do
not follow the traditions of the nation that I expel from before you, for they
did all of these and I was disgusted with them. 24 So I said to you: You shall
inherit their land, and I will give it to you to inherit it, a land flowing with milk
and honey — I am* H*ASHEM*, *your God, Who has separated you from the
peoples.*
*25 You shall distinguish between the clean animal and the unclean, and
between the clean bird and the unclean; and you shall not render your souls
abominable through such animals and birds, and through anything that creeps
on the ground, which I have set apart for you to render unclean.*
26 You shall be holy for Me, for I H*ASHEM am holy; and I have separated you
from the peoples to be Mine. 27 Any man or woman in whom there shall be the
sorcery of Ov or of Yid'oni, they shall be put to death; they shall pelt them
with stones, their blood is upon themselves.*

of (God's) intent, (that man) undoubtedly deserves to be stoned.

פרשת אמור

כא א וַיֹּאמֶר יהוה אֶל־מֹשֶׁה אֱמֹר אֶל־הַכֹּהֲנִים בְּנֵי אַהֲרֹן וְאָמַרְתָּ אֲלֵהֶם
ב לְנֶפֶשׁ לֹא־יִטַּמָּא בְּעַמָּיו: כִּי אִם־לִשְׁאֵרוֹ הַקָּרֹב אֵלָיו לְאִמּוֹ וּלְאָבִיו
ג וְלִבְנוֹ וּלְבִתּוֹ וּלְאָחִיו: וְלַאֲחֹתוֹ הַבְּתוּלָה הַקְּרוֹבָה אֵלָיו אֲשֶׁר לֹא־
ד־ה הָיְתָה לְאִישׁ לָהּ יִטַּמָּא: לֹא יִטַּמָּא בַּעַל בְּעַמָּיו לְהֵחַלּוֹ: לֹא־
°יקרחה קָרְחָה בְּרֹאשָׁם וּפְאַת זְקָנָם לֹא יְגַלֵּחוּ וּבִבְשָׂרָם לֹא יִשְׂרְטוּ °יִקְרְחוּ ק׳
ו שָׂרָטֶת: קְדֹשִׁים יִהְיוּ לֵאלֹהֵיהֶם וְלֹא יְחַלְּלוּ שֵׁם אֱלֹהֵיהֶם כִּי אֶת־
ז אִשֵּׁי יהוה לֶחֶם אֱלֹהֵיהֶם הֵם מַקְרִיבִם וְהָיוּ קֹדֶשׁ: אִשָּׁה זֹנָה וַחֲלָלָה
לֹא יִקָּחוּ וְאִשָּׁה גְּרוּשָׁה מֵאִישָׁהּ לֹא יִקָּחוּ כִּי־קָדֹשׁ הוּא לֵאלֹהָיו:

XXI

1. אֱמֹר אֶל הַכֹּהֲנִים — *Speak to the Kohanim* . . . regarding that which was said above, to understand and to teach (the laws of) the various types of *tumos* and to differentiate between those animals and birds which are clean (i.e., kosher) and those which are unclean (i.e., non-kosher). Now this (role) is most appropriate for the *Kohanim,* as it says, *To differentiate between the holy and the profane, and between the tamei and the tahor, and that you may teach* (10:10 and 11).

וְאָמַרְתָּ אֲלֵהֶם — *And you shall say to them* . . . that they must also exercise caution, in addition to these (laws), (to distance themselves) from *tumah* contracted through contact with the dead and the profanation of their offspring, these being higher levels of holiness for *Kohanim* alone.

לְנֶפֶשׁ לֹא יִטַּמָּא בְּעַמָּיו — *He shall not defile himself for the dead among his people.* No *Kohen* shall defile himself for a dead (person) among his people; (implying) any dead person from among the populace who is not related to him, but is only *from his people.*

4. לֹא יִטַּמָּא בַּעַל בְּעַמָּיו לְהֵחַלּוֹ — *He shall not defile himself, being a chief among his people, to profane himself.* The reason that a *Kohen* should not defile himself except for a relative is because a *Kohen* is indeed a chief among his people, (whose task is) to learn (lit., understand) and to teach, כִּי שִׂפְתֵי כֹהֵן יִשְׁמְרוּ דַעַת וְתוֹרָה יְבַקְשׁוּ מִפִּיהוּ, *for the Kohen's lips should*

NOTES

XXI

1. אֱמֹר אֶל הַכֹּהֲנִים . . . וְאָמַרְתָּ אֲלֵהֶם — *Speak to the Kohanim . . . and you shall say to them.* The repetition of the verb *say* (אֱמֹר־וְאָמַרְתָּ) is explained by our Sages (*Yevamos* 114a) as emphasizing the responsibility of adult *Kohanim* to teach and caution their young sons to observe these laws. The *Sforno,* however, interprets the first verb (אֱמֹר) as referring to the concluding section of the previous *parashah* (קְדוֹשִׁים). The laws of *tumah* and the differences between animals and birds which are kosher and non-kosher mentioned there are to be mastered by the *Kohanim* whose mission it is to be the scholars, teachers, and arbiters of Torah law. The second verb (וְאָמַרְתָּ) is an admonition that they are to guard their sanctity as *Kohanim* and observe an added dimension of *taharah* by refraining from defilement through contact with those dead who are non-relatives, and through certain marital restrictions.

4. לֹא יִטַּמָּא בַּעַל בְּעַמָּיו לְהֵחַלּוֹ — *He shall not defile himself, being a chief among his people, to profane himself.* The expression בַּעַל בְּעַמָּיו is interpreted by the *Sifra* (and so quoted by *Rashi*) to mean that a *Kohen* who is married to a woman halachically unfit for him may not defile himself with her corpse, providing she has others to bury her and therefore is not a מֵת מִצְוָה (a dead person who has no one to bury him or her; hence it becomes a *mitzvah* to do so). The term בַּעַל, according to this interpretation, means "husband." The *Sforno,* however, interprets this word (בַּעַל) as *master* or *chief,* namely a leader among his people (בְּעַמָּיו). Hence the Torah, in this verse, is giving a *reason* for the prohibition of a *Kohen* to defile himself through involvement with a corpse. Were the burial and eulogy meant to honor the living, as some of our Sages assert (יְקָרָא דְחַיֵּי), the *Kohen* would be permitted to take part. However, the final decision in the Talmud is that it is to honor

PARASHAS EMOR

21 1 *HASHEM said to Moses: Say to the Kohanim, the sons of Aaron, and tell*
them: Each of you shall not contaminate himself to a [dead] person
among his people; 2 *except for the relative who is closest to him, to his*
mother and to his father, to his son, to his daughter, and to his brother; 3 *and*
to his virgin sister who is close to him, who has not been wed to a man; to
her shall he contaminate himself. 4 *A husband among his people shall not*
contaminate himself to one who desecrates him.
5 *They shall not make a bald spot on their heads, and they shall not shave*
an edge of their beard; and in their flesh they shall not cut a gash. 6 *They*
shall be holy to their God and they shall not desecrate the Name of their
God; for the fire-offerings of HASHEM, the food of their God, they offer, so
they must remain holy.
7 *They shall not marry a woman who is a harlot or has been desecrated,*
and they shall not marry a woman who has been divorced by her husband;
for each one is holy to his God.

---

preserve knowledge, and they should seek Torah from his mouth (*Malachi* 2:7); (therefore,) it is proper that such a man conduct himself as a prince "so that his words will be listened to" (based on *Gittin* 52b). It is improper for him to profane his readiness toward the (service) of the Sanctuary and its holy things for the purpose of honoring the dead who are not his relatives, as (our Sages), of blessed memory, say that the burial of, and eulogy for, a dead person is יְקָרָא דִשְׁכְבֵי, *in honor of the dead* (*Sanhedrin* 47a). However, for one's relatives, (the Torah) permitted (the *Kohen*) to defile himself, for their honor is also his.

5. לֹא יִקְרְחוּ — *They shall not make baldness.* Although I have permitted them to defile themselves with their dead relatives for their own honor, I have not permitted them to mourn excessively so as to increase honor for their dead through "baldness" and "cuttings," as our Sages state, "As the case there (applies to baldness made) for the dead, so here too it applies to the dead" (*Makkos* 20a).

6. וְלֹא יְחַלְּלוּ שֵׁם אֱלֹהֵיהֶם — *And not profane the name of their God.* Although all these (acts) are for his (i.e., the priest's) honor, he has no permission to forgo God's honor, for indeed, the intent (of the Torah) in honoring the *Kohanim* is for (the purpose of enhancing) the honor of God, the Blessed One; hence, by forgoing their own honor they thereby profane His Name.

7. כִּי קָדֹשׁ הוּא לֵאלֹהָיו — *For he is holy to his God.* All the offspring of the priesthood, who

NOTES

the dead (יְקָרָא דִשְׁכְבֵי); therefore, the *Kohen's* main concern must be to uphold the dignity due his station of leadership. Occupying himself with a corpse would only serve to impede his ability to do so. Only if it is on behalf of a close relative do we consider his involvement as an extension of his own honor and it would therefore be permitted since the prohibition is transcended by the honor given to the *Kohen* himself.

5-6. לֹא יִקְרְחוּ ... וְלֹא יְחַלְּלוּ שֵׁם אֱלֹהֵיהֶם ... — *They shall not make baldness ... and not profane the name of their God.* Since the Torah makes an exception for a *Kohen* in the case of the burial of a relative because he enhances his own honor, one might think that *all* restrictive laws of mourning are waived, including those which prohibit קָרְחָה (tearing out one's hair in grief) and שָׂרֶטֶת (making a cutting in one's flesh); therefore, the Torah must specifically state that it is forbidden to do so. This comment of the *Sforno* also explains the need for reiterating this dual prohibition for the *Kohanim*, inasmuch as the law applies equally to *all* Israel (see *Deut.* 14:1). The Torah then proceeds to explain the reason for this prohibition. Although it may be honorable for the *Kohen* to perform these acts, nonetheless he is forbidden since by doing so he profanes the name of God, who confers this special honor upon the *Kohanim*.

ח וְקִדַּשְׁתּוֹ כִּי אֶת־לֶחֶם אֱלֹהֶיךָ הוּא מַקְרִיב קָדֹשׁ יִהְיֶה־לָּךְ כִּי קָדוֹשׁ אֲנִי
ט יהוה מְקַדִּשְׁכֶם: וּבַת אִישׁ כֹּהֵן כִּי תֵחֵל לִזְנוֹת אֶת־אָבִיהָ הִיא מְחַלֶּלֶת
י בָּאֵשׁ תִּשָּׂרֵף: וְהַכֹּהֵן הַגָּדוֹל מֵאֶחָיו אֲשֶׁר־יוּצַק עַל־רֹאשׁוֹ ׀
שֶׁמֶן הַמִּשְׁחָה וּמִלֵּא אֶת־יָדוֹ לִלְבֹּשׁ אֶת־הַבְּגָדִים אֶת־רֹאשׁוֹ לֹא יִפְרָע
יא וּבְגָדָיו לֹא יִפְרֹם: וְעַל כָּל־נַפְשֹׁת מֵת לֹא יָבֹא לְאָבִיו וּלְאִמּוֹ לֹא יִטַּמָּא:
יב וּמִן־הַמִּקְדָּשׁ לֹא יֵצֵא וְלֹא יְחַלֵּל אֵת מִקְדַּשׁ אֱלֹהָיו כִּי נֵזֶר שֶׁמֶן מִשְׁחַת
יג־יד אֱלֹהָיו עָלָיו אֲנִי יהוה: וְהוּא אִשָּׁה בִבְתוּלֶיהָ יִקָּח: אַלְמָנָה וּגְרוּשָׁה
וַחֲלָלָה זֹנָה אֶת־אֵלֶּה לֹא יִקָּח כִּי אִם־בְּתוּלָה מֵעַמָּיו יִקַּח אִשָּׁה:
שני טו־טז וְלֹא־יְחַלֵּל זַרְעוֹ בְּעַמָּיו כִּי אֲנִי יהוה מְקַדְּשׁוֹ: וַיְדַבֵּר יהוה
יז אֶל־מֹשֶׁה לֵּאמֹר: דַּבֵּר אֶל־אַהֲרֹן לֵאמֹר אִישׁ מִזַּרְעֲךָ לְדֹרֹתָם אֲשֶׁר
יח יִהְיֶה בוֹ מוּם לֹא יִקְרַב לְהַקְרִיב לֶחֶם אֱלֹהָיו: כִּי כָל־אִישׁ אֲשֶׁר־בּוֹ מוּם
יט לֹא יִקְרָב אִישׁ עִוֵּר אוֹ פִסֵּחַ אוֹ חָרֻם אוֹ שָׂרוּעַ: אוֹ אִישׁ אֲשֶׁר־יִהְיֶה בוֹ
כ שֶׁבֶר רָגֶל אוֹ שֶׁבֶר יָד: אוֹ־גִבֵּן אוֹ־דַק אוֹ תְּבַלֻּל בְּעֵינוֹ אוֹ גָרָב אוֹ יַלֶּפֶת
כא אוֹ מְרוֹחַ אָשֶׁךְ: כָּל־אִישׁ אֲשֶׁר־בּוֹ מוּם מִזֶּרַע אַהֲרֹן הַכֹּהֵן לֹא יִגַּשׁ
כב לְהַקְרִיב אֶת־אִשֵּׁי יהוה מוּם בּוֹ אֵת לֶחֶם אֱלֹהָיו לֹא יִגַּשׁ לְהַקְרִיב: לֶחֶם
כג אֱלֹהָיו מִקָּדְשֵׁי הַקֳּדָשִׁים וּמִן־הַקֳּדָשִׁים יֹאכֵל: אַךְ אֶל־הַפָּרֹכֶת לֹא יָבֹא
וְאֶל־הַמִּזְבֵּחַ לֹא יִגַּשׁ כִּי־מוּם בּוֹ וְלֹא יְחַלֵּל אֶת־מִקְדָּשַׁי כִּי אֲנִי יהוה
כד מְקַדְּשָׁם: וַיְדַבֵּר מֹשֶׁה אֶל־אַהֲרֹן וְאֶל־בָּנָיו וְאֶל־כָּל־בְּנֵי יִשְׂרָאֵל:
כב א־ב וַיְדַבֵּר יהוה אֶל־מֹשֶׁה לֵּאמֹר: דַּבֵּר אֶל־אַהֲרֹן וְאֶל־בָּנָיו וְיִנָּזְרוּ מִקָּדְשֵׁי
בְנֵי־יִשְׂרָאֵל וְלֹא יְחַלְּלוּ אֶת־שֵׁם קָדְשִׁי אֲשֶׁר הֵם מַקְדִּשִׁים לִי אֲנִי יהוה:

---

are (in the category of) *chief among his people*, are sanctified to their God, and if a *Kohen* marries one of these women, he profanes his honor and his offspring, for they (the children) will not be worthy of that holiness.

12. וּמִן הַמִּקְדָּשׁ לֹא יֵצֵא — *He shall not go out of the Sanctuary* . . . on behalf of the dead person.

וְלֹא יְחַלֵּל אֵת מִקְדַּשׁ אֱלֹהָיו — *Nor profane the Sanctuary of his God* . . . (for) thereby he will demonstrate that he esteems the honor of the dead more than the honor of the Sanctuary and the holy which has been (entrusted) to him.

18. כִּי כָל אִישׁ אֲשֶׁר בּוֹ מוּם לֹא יִקְרָב — *For any man that has a blemish shall not approach* . . . to stand to serve in the Name of God, similar to כִּי אֵין לָבוֹא אֶל שַׁעַר הַמֶּלֶךְ בִּלְבוּשׁ שָׂק, *No one may enter the king's gate clothed with sackcloth* (*Esther* 4:2).

אִישׁ עִוֵּר — *A blind man.* These are blemishes from birth, due to a physical deficiency or the imaginative powers (of the parents).

19. שֶׁבֶר רָגֶל — *A broken foot.* These are blemishes which are caused by external

NOTES

12. וְלֹא יְחַלֵּל אֵת מִקְדַּשׁ אֱלֹהָיו — *Nor profane the Sanctuary of his God.* The *Kohen Gadol*, in addition to his dignified station as a *Kohen*, is also the guardian of the Sanctuary. As such, he cannot abandon his special charge and defile himself, even on behalf of his father or mother, for the reason given by the *Sforno*.

18-20. אִישׁ עִוֵּר . . . שֶׁבֶר רָגֶל . . . אוֹ גִבֵּן — *A blind man . . . a broken foot . . . Or one whose eyebrows overhang his eyes.* The *Sforno* explains that there are three categories of blemishes which disqualify a *Kohen*. The first is congenital, the second category is the result of an accident, while the third relates to physical deformities resulting from illnesses subse-

[8] You shall sanctify him, for he offers the food of your God; he shall remain
holy to you, for holy am I, HASHEM, Who sanctifies you. [9] If the daughter of
a Kohen will be desecrated through adultery, she desecrates her father — she
shall be consumed by the fire.
[10] The Kohen who is exalted above his brethren — upon whose head the
anointment oil has been poured or who has been inaugurated to don the
vestments — shall not leave his head unshorn and shall not rend his
garments. [11] He shall not come near any dead person; he shall not
contaminate himself to his father or his mother. [12] He shall not leave the
Sanctuary and he shall not desecrate the Sanctuary of his God; for a crown
— the oil of his God's anointment — is upon him; I am HASHEM. [13] He shall
marry a woman in her virginity. [14] A widow, a divorcee, a desecrated woman,
a harlot — he shall not marry these; only a virgin of his people shall he take
as a wife. [15] Thus shall he not desecrate his offspring among his people; for
I am HASHEM Who sanctifies him.
[16] HASHEM spoke to Moses, saying: [17] Speak to Aaron, saying: Any man of
your offspring throughout their generations in whom there will be a blemish
shall not come near to offer the food of his God. [18] For any man in whom there
is a blemish shall not approach: a man who is blind or lame or whose nose has
no bridge, or who has one limb longer than the other; [19] or in whom there will
be a broken leg or a broken arm; [20] or who has abnormally long eyebrows, or
a membrane on his eye, or a blemish in his eye, or a dry skin eruption, or a
moist skin eruption, or has crushed testicles. [21] Any man from among the
offspring of Aaron the Kohen who has a blemish shall not approach to offer
the fire-offerings of HASHEM; he has a blemish — the food of his God he shall
not approach to offer.
[22] The food of his God from the most holy and from the holy may he eat.
[23] But he shall not come to the Curtain, and he shall not approach the Altar,
for he has a blemish; and he shall not desecrate My sacred offerings, for I am
HASHEM, Who sanctifies them. [24] Moses spoke to Aaron and to his sons, and
to all the Children of Israel.

22 *[1] HASHEM spoke to Moses, saying: [2] Speak to Aaron and his sons, that they*
shall withdraw from the holies of the Children of Israel — that which
they sanctify to Me — so as not to desecrate My holy Name, I am HASHEM.

---

happenings (mishaps).

20. אוֹ גִבֵּן — *Or one whose eyebrows overhang his eyes.* These are blemishes which are caused through deficiences in the body's chemical makeup.

XXII

2. וְיִנָּזְרוּ מִקָּדְשֵׁי בְנֵי יִשְׂרָאֵל — *That they separate themselves from the holy things of the Children of Israel.* Let them not think that on account of their exalted status, the holy

NOTES

quent to birth.

XXII

2. וְיִנָּזְרוּ מִקָּדְשֵׁי בְנֵי יִשְׂרָאֵל וְלֹא יְחַלְּלוּ אֶת שֵׁם קָדְשִׁי . . . — *That they separate themselves from the holy things of the Children of Israel and that they do not profane My holy Name . . .* The Talmud (*Moed Katan* 16a) differentiates between a ban imposed by a teacher and one imposed by a disciple. In the

ג אֱמֹר אֲלֵהֶם לְדֹרֹתֵיכֶם כָּל־אִישׁ | אֲשֶׁר־יִקְרַב מִכָּל־זַרְעֲכֶם אֶל־
הַקֳּדָשִׁים אֲשֶׁר יַקְדִּישׁוּ בְנֵי־יִשְׂרָאֵל לַיהוה וְטֻמְאָתוֹ עָלָיו וְנִכְרְתָה
ד הַנֶּפֶשׁ הַהִוא מִלְּפָנַי אֲנִי יהוה: אִישׁ אִישׁ מִזֶּרַע אַהֲרֹן וְהוּא צָרוּעַ אוֹ זָב
בַּקֳּדָשִׁים לֹא יֹאכַל עַד אֲשֶׁר יִטְהָר וְהַנֹּגֵעַ בְּכָל־טְמֵא־נֶפֶשׁ אוֹ אִישׁ
ה אֲשֶׁר־תֵּצֵא מִמֶּנּוּ שִׁכְבַת־זָרַע: אוֹ־אִישׁ אֲשֶׁר יִגַּע בְּכָל־שֶׁרֶץ אֲשֶׁר
ו יִטְמָא־לוֹ אוֹ בְאָדָם אֲשֶׁר יִטְמָא־לוֹ לְכֹל טֻמְאָתוֹ: נֶפֶשׁ אֲשֶׁר תִּגַּע־בּוֹ
וְטָמְאָה עַד־הָעָרֶב וְלֹא יֹאכַל מִן־הַקֳּדָשִׁים כִּי אִם־רָחַץ בְּשָׂרוֹ בַּמָּיִם:
ז־ח וּבָא הַשֶּׁמֶשׁ וְטָהֵר וְאַחַר יֹאכַל מִן־הַקֳּדָשִׁים כִּי לַחְמוֹ הוּא: נְבֵלָה וּטְרֵפָה
ט לֹא יֹאכַל לְטָמְאָה־בָהּ אֲנִי יהוה: וְשָׁמְרוּ אֶת־מִשְׁמַרְתִּי וְלֹא־יִשְׂאוּ עָלָיו
י חֵטְא וּמֵתוּ בוֹ כִּי יְחַלְּלֻהוּ אֲנִי יהוה מְקַדְּשָׁם: וְכָל־זָר לֹא־יֹאכַל קֹדֶשׁ
יא תּוֹשַׁב כֹּהֵן וְשָׂכִיר לֹא־יֹאכַל קֹדֶשׁ: וְכֹהֵן כִּי־יִקְנֶה נֶפֶשׁ קִנְיַן כַּסְפּוֹ הוּא
יב יֹאכַל בּוֹ וִילִיד בֵּיתוֹ הֵם יֹאכְלוּ בְלַחְמוֹ: וּבַת־כֹּהֵן כִּי תִהְיֶה לְאִישׁ זָר
יג הִוא בִּתְרוּמַת הַקֳּדָשִׁים לֹא תֹאכֵל: וּבַת־כֹּהֵן כִּי תִהְיֶה אַלְמָנָה וּגְרוּשָׁה
וְזֶרַע אֵין לָהּ וְשָׁבָה אֶל־בֵּית אָבִיהָ כִּנְעוּרֶיהָ מִלֶּחֶם אָבִיהָ תֹּאכֵל
יד וְכָל־זָר לֹא־יֹאכַל בּוֹ: וְאִישׁ כִּי־יֹאכַל קֹדֶשׁ בִּשְׁגָגָה וְיָסַף חֲמִשִׁיתוֹ עָלָיו
טו וְנָתַן לַכֹּהֵן אֶת־הַקֹּדֶשׁ: וְלֹא יְחַלְּלוּ אֶת־קָדְשֵׁי בְּנֵי יִשְׂרָאֵל אֵת
טז אֲשֶׁר־יָרִימוּ לַיהוה: וְהִשִּׂיאוּ אוֹתָם עֲוֺן אַשְׁמָה בְּאָכְלָם אֶת־קָדְשֵׁיהֶם כִּי
אֲנִי יהוה מְקַדְּשָׁם:
שלישי יז־יח וַיְדַבֵּר יהוה אֶל־מֹשֶׁה לֵּאמֹר: דַּבֵּר אֶל־אַהֲרֹן וְאֶל־בָּנָיו וְאֶל כָּל־בְּנֵי

---

things of the people may be considered as profane (חולין) to them, similar to "one excommunicated by the disciple need not be treated as such by the teacher" (*Moed Kattan* 16a).

וְלֹא יְחַלְּלוּ אֶת שֵׁם קָדְשִׁי אֲשֶׁר הֵם מַקְדִּשִׁים לִי — *And that they do not profane My holy Name which they sanctify unto Me ...* that they do not profane the name of holiness which Israel sanctified to Me by declaring it holy.

7. כִּי לַחְמוֹ הוּא — *Because it is his bread.* He need not wait for his atonement before eating his bread, as our Sages said, "When the sun sets, he eats *terumah* (heave offering)" (*Pesachim* 35a).

9. אֲנִי ה׳ מְקַדְּשָׁם — *I am HASHEM Who sanctifies them.* Since Israel sanctified (these holy things) I (also) sanctified them, therefore, it is fitting that those *Kohanim* who profane them be punished.

16. וְהִשִּׂיאוּ אוֹתָם עֲוֺן אַשְׁמָה — *And so cause them to bear the iniquity of guilt.* They themselves, when they sanctified the holy things, brought about their own guilt at such

NOTES

former case, the ban must be respected by the disciple as well, whereas in the latter case, although the ban is in effect, the teacher is not obligated to honor it. From this *halachah*, we learn that there are degrees of stringency in law which one might mistakenly assume can be likened to degrees of sanctity. Just as the disciple's ban doesn't carry enough authority so as to be binding on his teacher since the teacher is superior to him, so too, the status of holiness declared by an Israelite over an animal or object should not be binding upon the *Kohen*, since the Israelite is inferior to him. Therefore, the Torah stresses that this analogy is incorrect and the sanctity of all things is binding on the *Kohen* as well. The reason for this is because the act of sanctification by Israel is sanctioned by God Who hallows these things Himself, and therefore must be honored by the *Kohen* as well. See the *Sforno's* commentary on verses 9 and 16. Also see *Rashi* who interprets this verse differently.

3 *Say to them: Throughout your generations, any man from among any of
your offspring who shall come near the holies that the Children of Israel
may sanctify to HASHEM with his contamination upon him — that person
shall be cut off from before Me, I am HASHEM.* 4 *Any man from the offspring
of Aaron who is a metzora or a zav shall not eat from the holies until he
becomes purified; and one who touches anyone contaminated by a corpse,
or a man from whom there is a seminal emission;* 5 *or a man who touches any
swarming thing through which he can become contaminated, or a person
through whom he can become contaminated, whatever his contamination.*
6 *The person who touches it shall be contaminated until evening; he shall not
eat from the holies unless he has immersed his body in the water.* 7 *After the
sun has set he shall become purified; thereafter he may eat from the holies,
for it is his food.* 8 *He shall not eat from a carcass or from a torn animal, to
be contaminated through it — I am HASHEM.*

9 *They shall protect My charge and not bear a sin thereby and die because
of it, for they will have desecrated it — I am HASHEM, Who sanctifies them.*

10 *No layman shall eat of the holy; one who resides with a Kohen or his
laborer shall not eat of the holy.* 11 *If a Kohen shall acquire a person, an
acquisition of his money, he may eat of it; and someone born in his home —
they may eat of his food.* 12 *If a Kohen's daughter shall be married to a
layman, she may not eat of the separated holies.* 13 *And a Kohen's daughter
who will become a widow or a divorcee, and not have offspring, she may
return to her father's home, as in her youth, she may eat from her father's
food; but no layman may eat of it.* 14 *If a man will eat of the holy
inadvertently, he shall add its fifth to it and shall repay the holy to the
Kohen.* 15 *They shall not desecrate the holies of the Children of Israel, which
they set aside to HASHEM;* 16 *and they will cause themselves to bear the sin
of guilt when they eat their holies — for I am HASHEM Who sanctifies them.*

17 *HASHEM spoke to Moses, saying:* 18 *Speak to Aaron and to his sons and*

---

time that they would trespass and have enjoyment from it — and we do not (apply the principle), הַפֶּה שֶׁאָסַר הוּא הַפֶּה שֶׁהִתִּיר, *The mouth which prohibited is the mouth which (now) permits* (*Demai* 6:11), the reason for this being . . .

כִּי אֲנִי ה׳ מְקַדְּשָׁם — *For I am HASHEM Who sanctifies them* . . . since they sanctified this thing, I God likewise sanctified it, and they have no power to rescind its sanctity.

NOTES

7. כִּי לַחְמוֹ הוּא — *Because it is his bread.* The Torah is explaining why the *Kohen* who was *tamei* and immersed himself need only wait until sunset to eat his *terumah,* even though he has not yet brought his offerings. The reason is *because it is his bread* and he depends upon it for his basic sustenance.

16. וְהִשִּׂיאוּ אוֹתָם עֲוֹן אַשְׁמָה . . . כִּי אֲנִי ה׳ מְקַדְּשָׁם — *And so cause them to bear the iniquity of guilt . . . for I am HASHEM Who sanctifies them.* There is a fundamental principle in *halachah* that one who establishes (creates) an אִיסוּר, *prohibition*, is empowered to remove it as well. For example, if a woman declares that she is married and subsequently states that she received a divorce, if there is no other evidence, her testimony is accepted, for "the mouth which prohibited is the mouth which now permits." This, however, is not the case regarding הֶקְדֵּשׁ, *sanctifying an object*. Although the one who sanctified transformed a secular object (חוּלִין) into a holy one, nonetheless, that same person is not empowered to declare it חוּלִין once again. The reason is because, as mentioned above (verse 2), God has joined in the act of sanctification, thereby removing the power of the מַקְדִּישׁ (he who sanctified it originally) to change it back to its original status.

יִשְׂרָאֵ֗ל וְאָמַרְתָּ֣ אֲלֵהֶ֔ם אִ֣ישׁ אִישׁ֩ מִבֵּ֨ית יִשְׂרָאֵ֜ל וּמִן־הַגֵּ֣ר בְּיִשְׂרָאֵ֗ל
אֲשֶׁ֨ר יַקְרִ֤יב קָרְבָּנוֹ֙ לְכָל־נִדְרֵיהֶם֙ וּלְכָל־נִדְבוֹתָ֔ם אֲשֶׁר־יַקְרִ֥יבוּ לַיהוָ֖ה
יט־כ לְעֹלָֽה: לִֽרְצֹנְכֶ֑ם תָּמִ֣ים זָכָ֔ר בַּבָּקָ֕ר בַּכְּשָׂבִ֖ים וּבָֽעִזִּֽים: כֹּ֛ל אֲשֶׁר־בּ֥וֹ מ֖וּם
כא לֹ֣א תַקְרִ֑יבוּ כִּי־לֹ֥א לְרָצ֖וֹן יִֽהְיֶ֥ה לָכֶֽם: וְאִ֗ישׁ כִּֽי־יַקְרִ֞יב זֶֽבַח־שְׁלָמִים֙
לַֽיהוָ֔ה לְפַלֵּא־נֶ֙דֶר֙ א֣וֹ לִנְדָבָ֔ה בַּבָּקָ֖ר א֣וֹ בַצֹּ֑אן תָּמִ֤ים יִֽהְיֶה֙ לְרָצ֔וֹן כָּל־
כב מ֖וּם לֹ֥א יִֽהְיֶה־בּֽוֹ: עַוֶּ֩רֶת֩ א֨וֹ שָׁב֜וּר אֽוֹ־חָר֣וּץ אֽוֹ־יַבֶּ֗לֶת א֤וֹ גָרָב֙ א֣וֹ יַלֶּ֔פֶת
לֹֽא־תַקְרִ֥יבוּ אֵ֖לֶּה לַֽיהוָ֑ה וְאִשֶּׁ֗ה לֹֽא־תִתְּנ֥וּ מֵהֶ֛ם עַל־הַמִּזְבֵּ֖חַ לַֽיהוָֽה:
כג־כד וְשׁ֣וֹר וָשֶׂ֗ה שָׂר֤וּעַ וְקָלוּט֙ נְדָבָ֣ה תַּֽעֲשֶׂ֣ה אֹת֔וֹ וּלְנֵ֖דֶר לֹ֣א יֵֽרָצֶ֑ה: וּמָע֤וּךְ
כה וְכָתוּת֙ וְנָת֣וּק וְכָר֔וּת לֹ֥א תַקְרִ֖יבוּ לַֽיהוָ֑ה וּבְאַרְצְכֶ֖ם לֹ֥א תַֽעֲשֽׂוּ: וּמִיַּ֣ד
בֶּן־נֵכָ֗ר לֹ֥א תַקְרִ֛יבוּ אֶת־לֶ֥חֶם אֱלֹֽהֵיכֶ֖ם מִכָּל־אֵ֑לֶּה כִּ֣י מָשְׁחָתָ֤ם בָּהֶם֙

---

18. אֲשֶׁר יַקְרִיב קָרְבָּנוֹ — *That brings his offering.* After (the Torah) tells us of the *Kohanim* who offer (the sacrifices) and their sanctity, it now speaks of the conditions (regulating) the offerings, saying ...

לְכָל נִדְרֵיהֶם וּלְכָל נִדְבוֹתָם — *Whether it be any of their vows, or any of their free-will offerings.* Although they are free-will offerings, hence one might think that whatever he contributes, even a blemished animal, is acceptable since that which he gives is not obligatory, as (indeed) some Israelites thought, and the prophet (therefore) had to show them their error, saying, וְכִי תַגִּשׁוּן עִוֵּר לִזְבֹּחַ אֵין רָע וְכִי תַגִּישׁוּ פִּסֵּחַ וְחֹלֶה אֵין רָע הַקְרִיבֵהוּ נָא לְפֶחָתֶךָ, *And if you offer the blind for sacrifice, is it not evil? And if you offer a lame or sick animal, is that not evil? Offer it now to your governor* (Malachi 1:8).

19. לִרְצֹנְכֶם — *That you may be accepted* ... as an offering which will be acceptable on your behalf, and not for (the purpose of) *repair of the House* (the Sanctuary) (בֶּדֶק הַבַּיִת).

תָּמִים זָכָר — *A male without blemish.* It (the sacrifice) must be perfect (without blemish), for *the Rock, His work is perfect* (Deut. 32:4); (therefore) He desires perfection. This (the Torah) explains, saying ...

20. כֹּל אֲשֶׁר בּוֹ מוּם לֹא תַקְרִיבוּ כִּי לֹא לְרָצוֹן יִהְיֶה לָכֶם — *But whatsoever has a blemish you shall not bring, for it shall not be acceptable for you.* This is similar to הֲיִרְצְךָ אוֹ הֲיִשָּׂא פָנֶיךָ, *Will he be pleased with you or will he show you favor* (Malachi 1:8). After (the Torah) cautions us regarding a burnt offering, which is (in the category of) קָדְשֵׁי קָדָשִׁים, *sacrifices of major sanctity*, and which must be a male and without blemish, it is explained that these restrictions are only obligatory regarding cattle and sheep, as our Sages say, "The law requiring an unblemished male (for a burnt offering) only applies to animals, not to fowl" (*Kiddushin* 24b). (The Torah now) says ...

NOTES

18. לְכָל נִדְרֵיהֶם וּלְכָל נִדְבוֹתָם — *Whether it be any of their vows, or any of their free-will offerings.* The *Sforno's* commentary clarifies the verse in *Malachi.* How could any Israelite think that it would be proper to bring a blind or lame animal as an offering to God, as alluded to by the prophet in cautioning them against such a practice? The answer given by the *Sforno* is that since it is a free-will offering (נְדָבָה), and not an *obligatory offering* (חוֹבָה), one might think that any animal is acceptable. That is why the prophet concludes, *Offer it now to your governor; will he be pleased?*

19-23. תָּמִים זָכָר ... נְדָבָה תַּעֲשֶׂה אֹתוֹ — *A male without blemish ... You may make it a free-will offering.* A blemish-free animal of the proper sex (a male in the case of a burnt offering) may be brought as an offering on the Altar. One which is blemished, although not qualified to be offered to God on the Altar (whether the blemish occurred before or after its sanctification), may, however, be designated as קְדוּשַׁת דָּמִים, *sanctified for its monetary value.* This is the case even if blemished excessively.

The *Sforno* proceeds to explain the reason for

to all the Children of Israel and say to them: Any man of the House of Israel and of the proselytes among Israel who will bring his offering for any of their vows or their free-will offerings that they will bring to HASHEM *for an elevation-offering;* 19 *to be favorable for you: [it must be] unblemished, male, from the cattle, the flock, or the goats.* 20 *Any in which there is a blemish you shall not offer, for it will not be favorable for you.* 21 *And a man who will bring a feast peace-offering to* HASHEM *because of an articulated vow or as a free-will offering from the cattle or the flock, it shall be unblemished to find favor, there shall not be any blemish in it.* 22 *One that is blind or broken or with a split eyelid or a wart or a dry skin eruption or a moist skin eruption —you shall not offer these to* HASHEM, *and you shall not place any of them as a fire-offering on the Altar for* HASHEM. 23 *A bull or sheep that has one limb longer than the other or unsplit hooves — you may make it a donation, but it is not acceptable for a vow-offering.* 24 *One whose testicles are squeezed, crushed, torn, or cut, you shall not offer to* HASHEM, *nor shall you do these in your Land.* 25 *From the hand of a stranger you may not offer the food of your God from any of these, for their corruption is in them,*

---

21. וְאִישׁ כִּי יַקְרִיב זֶבַח שְׁלָמִים לַה׳ — *And whosoever brings a sacrifice of peace offerings to* HASHEM. (The Torah) states that although these are (in the category of) קָדָשִׁים קַלִּים, *sacrifices of lesser sanctity,* and they do not require a male animal, as explained above when it stated, *whether male or female* (3:1); nonetheless, they may not have a blemish. (The Torah) explains the reason for this by stating, *You shall not offer these to* HASHEM (v. 22), i.e., it is improper to offer a blemished animal to God, the Blessed One. (The Torah) then adds a second reason, saying, *Nor make from them an offering by fire upon the Altar to* HASHEM (ibid.), (meaning) if the blemish developed after the owners sanctified it, one is not to offer the אֵימוּרִים, *ordained parts,* on the Altar, for it is not fitting that there be a blemish, which is despised by Him, in (any) offering.

23. נְדָבָה תַּעֲשֶׂה אֹתוֹ — *You may make it a free-will offering.* Although these are blemishes which are extremely visible, and one might think that these animals are unsuitable even for *repair of the House* (בֶּדֶק הַבַּיִת), (the Torah) says that they *are* fit for contribution towards בֶּדֶק הַבַּיִת, as tradition teaches us, since the Altar has no share in them, and their sanctity is only in terms of their monetary value (קְדוּשַּׁת דָּמִים), i.e., they are to be sold and thereby they become profane (חוּלִּין).

24. וּמָעוּךְ וְכָתוּת — *That which has its stones bruised or crushed.* After telling us of accidental blemishes, which affect only קָדָשִׁים, *sanctified animals,* making them prohibited to be offered on the Altar, and of the prohibition to impose any blemish on them after they have been sanctified, (the Torah) now speaks of artificial blemishes which are prohibited to be inflicted even on a profane animal.

25. וּמִיַּד בֶּן נֵכָר לֹא תַקְרִיבוּ — *Neither from the hand of a foreigner shall you offer.* Although we accept vows and free-will offerings from them, we are not (permitted) to accept blemished animals from them, even those castrated which, in their opinion, are

NOTES

the Torah's insistence upon תְּמִימוּת, *perfection*, in an offering. Since God is perfect, one cannot offer any animal to Him which is less than perfect. This explains the disqualification of a סָרִיס, *an emasculated animal*, whose blemish is concealed but is incapable of fulfilling its primary purpose as a living creature of God, i.e., to reproduce its own kind. As the *Sforno* points out (in these verses and verse 27 as well), the criteria for selecting an offering to be brought to a human king is not the same as that offered to God on the Altar in His Sanctuary. The standards and rationale are totally different.

כו מ֣וּם בָּ֔ם לֹ֥א יֵרָצ֖וּ לָכֶֽם׃ וַיְדַבֵּ֥ר יְהוָ֖ה אֶל־מֹשֶׁ֥ה לֵּאמֹֽר׃
כז שׁ֣וֹר אוֹ־כֶ֤שֶׂב אוֹ־עֵז֙ כִּ֣י יִוָּלֵ֔ד וְהָיָ֛ה שִׁבְעַ֥ת יָמִ֖ים תַּ֣חַת אִמּ֑וֹ וּמִיּ֤וֹם
כח הַשְּׁמִינִי֙ וָהָ֔לְאָה יֵרָצֶ֕ה לְקָרְבַּ֥ן אִשֶּׁ֖ה לַיהוָֽה׃ וְשׁ֖וֹר אוֹ־שֶׂ֑ה אֹת֣וֹ וְאֶת־בְּנ֔וֹ
כט לֹ֥א תִשְׁחֲט֖וּ בְּי֥וֹם אֶחָֽד׃ וְכִֽי־תִזְבְּח֥וּ זֶֽבַח־תּוֹדָ֖ה לַיהוָ֑ה לִֽרְצֹנְכֶ֖ם תִּזְבָּֽחוּ׃
ל-לא בַּיּ֤וֹם הַהוּא֙ יֵאָכֵ֔ל לֹֽא־תוֹתִ֥ירוּ מִמֶּ֖נּוּ עַד־בֹּ֑קֶר אֲנִ֖י יְהוָֽה׃ וּשְׁמַרְתֶּם֙
לב מִצְוֺתַ֔י וַעֲשִׂיתֶ֖ם אֹתָ֑ם אֲנִ֖י יְהוָֽה׃ וְלֹ֤א תְחַלְּלוּ֙ אֶת־שֵׁ֣ם קָדְשִׁ֔י וְנִ֨קְדַּשְׁתִּ֔י
לג בְּת֖וֹךְ בְּנֵ֣י יִשְׂרָאֵ֑ל אֲנִ֥י יְהוָ֖ה מְקַדִּשְׁכֶֽם׃ הַמּוֹצִ֤יא אֶתְכֶם֙ מֵאֶ֣רֶץ מִצְרַ֔יִם
לִהְי֥וֹת לָכֶ֖ם לֵאלֹהִ֑ים אֲנִ֖י יְהוָֽה׃

כג רביעי א-ב וַיְדַבֵּ֥ר יְהוָ֖ה אֶל־מֹשֶׁ֥ה לֵּאמֹֽר׃ דַּבֵּ֞ר אֶל־בְּנֵ֤י יִשְׂרָאֵל֙ וְאָמַרְתָּ֣ אֲלֵהֶ֔ם
מוֹעֲדֵ֣י יְהוָ֔ה אֲשֶׁר־תִּקְרְא֥וּ אֹתָ֖ם מִקְרָאֵ֣י קֹ֑דֶשׁ אֵ֥לֶּה הֵ֖ם מוֹעֲדָֽי׃

---

better (superior), and hence there is no deficiency of הַקְרִיבֵהוּ נָא לְפֶחָתֶךָ, *Would you offer it to your governor?* (*Malachi* 1:8). Now the reason why a castrated animal is not fit for the Altar is "because their impairment is in them." Even though it is a concealed blemish, it impairs (lit., corrupts) their intended שְׁלֵימוּת, *completeness,* which is the capacity to reproduce in their likeness.

27. שׁוֹר אוֹ כֶשֶׂב — *A bull or a sheep.* After mentioning the various types of blemishes which invalidate קָדָשִׁים, *sanctified animals,* from being offered on the Altar, even though at times the perfect (animal) may be worth a *sela* while the blemished one, because of its size and fat, is worth two; and at times the blemish may even be considered an advantage, as when brought as a gift to a human king; (still, it is invalid as a sacrifice to God) because הַצּוּר תָּמִים פָּעֳלוֹ, *the Rock His work is perfect* (*Deut.* 32:4). He desires the perfection and completeness of the offering and of the one who offers it; the offering must possess its natural completeness and the one who offers it must possess Divine completeness, to be like his Creator as much as it is possible. (Now the Torah) says similarly, regarding the limits of time which God established, that one is not permitted to add or subtract from them. (The Torah) mentions the prohibition of מְחוּסַר זְמַן (sacrificing an animal without waiting the minimum period from birth), the prohibition of slaughtering אוֹתוֹ וְאֶת בְּנוֹ, *it and its young,* on the same day and the prohibition against intending to eat the sacrifices חוּץ לִזְמַנּוֹ, *beyond the allotted time,* which includes even קָדָשִׁים קַלִּים, *sacrifices of lesser sanctity.* (The Torah) then mentions the thanksgiving offering, for even though it is included in (the category) of peace offerings, its time limit (for consumption) is only one day and one night, not two days and one night as is true of other peace offerings.

29-30. לִרְצֹנְכֶם תִּזְבָּחוּ ... בַּיּוֹם הַהוּא יֵאָכֵל — *You shall sacrifice it, that you may be accepted ... On the same day it shall be eaten.* It must be your will and intention at the time you bring the sacrifice that it be eaten that day, and this is because ...

אֲנִי ה׳ — *I am* HASHEM. I perform My deeds with perfection and set a limit to completeness without tolerating anything more or less.

NOTES

27-30. שׁוֹר אוֹ כֶשֶׂב ... לִרְצֹנְכֶם תִּזְבָּחוּ ... בַּיּוֹם הַהוּא יֵאָכֵל — *A bull or a sheep ... you shall sacrifice it, that you may be accepted ... On the same day it shall be eaten.* The Torah sets time limits regarding sacrifices just as it establishes rules regarding blemishes which disqualify either the *Kohen* who officiates or the animal brought to God. The *Sforno* explains that the time factor regulates the minimum age of the animal (v. 27); the offering of an animal and its young on the same day (v. 28); the intent in the mind of the *Kohen* who brings the קָרְבָּן as to when the sacrifice will be eaten (v. 29), which also explains why the תּוֹדָה, *the thanksgiving offering,* is singled out; and finally (v. 30) the law of נוֹתָר (the meat of a sacrifice *remaining* past the allotted time).

a blemish is in them, they will not find favor for you.
[26] *HASHEM spoke to Moses, saying:* [27] *When an ox or a sheep or a goat is*
born, it shall remain under its mother for seven days; and from the eighth
day on, it is acceptable for a fire-offering to HASHEM. [28] *But an ox or a sheep*
or goat, you may not slaughter it and its offspring on the same day. [29] *When*
you slaughter a feast thanksgiving-offering to HASHEM, you shall slaughter
it to gain favor for yourselves. [30] *It must be eaten on that same day, you*
shall not leave any of it until morning; I am HASHEM. [31] *You shall observe*
My commandments and perform them; I am HASHEM. [32] *You shall not*
desecrate My holy Name, rather I should be sanctified among the Children
of Israel; I am HASHEM Who sanctifies you, [33] *Who took you out of the land*
of Egypt to be a God unto you; I am HASHEM.

23 [1] *HASHEM spoke to Moses, saying:* [2] *Speak to the Children of Israel*
and say to them: HASHEM's appointed festivals that you are to
designate as holy convocations — these are My appointed festivals.

---

32. וְלֹא תְחַלְּלוּ אֶת שֵׁם קָדְשִׁי — *And you shall not profane My holy Name.* Since you see the completeness of My work, therefore, you who are sanctified to walk in My ways, *do not profane My holy Name* through faulty and disgraceful deeds, similar to, וַיָּבוֹא אֶל הַגּוֹיִם אֲשֶׁר בָּאוּ שָׁם וַיְחַלְּלוּ אֶת שֵׁם קָדְשִׁי, *And when they came to the nations, into which they came, they profaned My holy Name* (*Ezekiel* 36:20).

וְנִקְדַּשְׁתִּי בְּתוֹךְ בְּנֵי יִשְׂרָאֵל — *And I will be sanctified among the Children of Israel* ... to perform wonders for them as I vowed, saying, הִנֵּה אָנֹכִי כֹּרֵת בְּרִית נֶגֶד כָּל עַמְּךָ אֶעֱשֶׂה נִפְלָאֹת, *Behold I make a covenant, before all your people I will do marvels* (*Exodus* 34:10); the reason for this is (because) indeed — אֲנִי ה׳ מְקַדִּשְׁכֶם, *I am HASHEM Who sanctifies you.*

33. הַמּוֹצִיא אֶתְכֶם מֵאֶרֶץ מִצְרַיִם לִהְיוֹת לָכֶם לֵאלֹהִים — *Who brought you out of the land of Egypt to be your God* ... to lead you without any intermediary, as is the rule with those "separated from corporeality" (i.e., angels), providing you walk in My holy ways, as it says, אֶל דֶּרֶךְ הַגּוֹיִם אַל תִּלְמָדוּ וּמֵאֹתוֹת הַשָּׁמַיִם אַל תֵּחָתּוּ, *Learn not the way of the nations and be not dismayed at the signs of heaven* (*Jeremiah* 10:2).

אֲנִי ה׳ — *I am HASHEM* ... (Who is) unchangeable, and I will act towards you as in the past as long as your sins do not create a barrier between you and your God, as it says, כִּימֵי צֵאתְךָ מֵאֶרֶץ מִצְרָיִם אַרְאֶנּוּ נִפְלָאוֹת, *As in the days of your coming out of the land of Egypt I will show him marvelous things* (*Micah* 7:15).

XXIII

2. מוֹעֲדֵי ה׳ אֲשֶׁר תִּקְרְאוּ אֹתָם מִקְרָאֵי קֹדֶשׁ — *The appointed seasons of HASHEM which you shall proclaim to be holy convocations.* After (the Torah) speaks regarding the offerings

NOTES

32-33. וְלֹא תְחַלְּלוּ ... וְנִקְדַּשְׁתִּי בְּתוֹךְ בְּנֵי יִשְׂרָאֵל — הַמּוֹצִיא אֶתְכֶם מֵאֶרֶץ מִצְרַיִם לִהְיוֹת לָכֶם לֵאלֹהִים — *And you shall not profane ... and I will be sanctified among the Children of Israel ... Who brought you out of the land of Egypt to be your God.* The Almighty becomes sanctified in the eyes of mankind when He manifests His power and might on behalf of His people. He did so at the time of the Exodus and has promised to do so in the future as well, providing that Israel is worthy and fulfills its mission to be a holy people. The expression "separated from corporeality" refers to those who never perish and are everlasting. The *Sforno* in *Genesis* 17:7 explains the special relationship between God and Abraham's descendants, which is a direct one without need for an intermediary, as he explains in this verse as well. See the *Sforno's* commentary there and the notes.

XXIII

2. מוֹעֲדֵי ה׳ ... מִקְרָאֵי קֹדֶשׁ אֵלֶּה הֵם מוֹעֲדָי — *The appointed seasons of HASHEM ... holy convocations,*

ג שֵׁשֶׁת יָמִים תֵּעָשֶׂה מְלָאכָה וּבַיּוֹם הַשְּׁבִיעִי שַׁבַּת שַׁבָּתוֹן מִקְרָא־קֹדֶשׁ
כָּל־מְלָאכָה לֹא תַעֲשׂוּ שַׁבָּת הִוא לַיהוָה בְּכֹל מוֹשְׁבֹתֵיכֶם:
ד אֵלֶּה מוֹעֲדֵי יהוה מִקְרָאֵי קֹדֶשׁ אֲשֶׁר־תִּקְרְאוּ אֹתָם בְּמוֹעֲדָם:
ה בַּחֹדֶשׁ הָרִאשׁוֹן בְּאַרְבָּעָה עָשָׂר לַחֹדֶשׁ בֵּין הָעַרְבָּיִם פֶּסַח לַיהוָה:

and those who bring these offerings, the purpose of which is to cause the Divine Presence to dwell in Israel, as it says, עֹלַת תָּמִיד לְדֹרֹתֵיכֶם פֶּתַח אֹהֶל מוֹעֵד לִפְנֵי ה׳ אֲשֶׁר אִוָּעֵד לָכֶם שָׁמָּה, *A continual burnt-offering throughout your generations at the door of the Tent of Meeting before HASHEM, where I will meet with you* (*Exodus* 29:42), it now speaks of the appointed seasons wherein one's intent should be to cease from doing common work, some of which involve a total abstention such as Shabbos and Yom Kippur, and to occupy (oneself) during all of them with Torah and holy concerns, as it says, ... שֵׁשֶׁת יָמִים תַּעֲבֹד וְיוֹם הַשְּׁבִיעִי שַׁבָּת לַה׳ אֱלֹהֶיךָ, *Six days shall you labor . . . but the seventh day is a Sabbath to HASHEM your God* (*Exodus* 20:9,10), (when) you shall rest from your work and your occupation shall be totally with God your God. During some (of these festivals), you shall rest only from servile work, as it is true of (all) other appointed seasons.

Now their intent (and purpose) is that, through the rejoicing on the day (itself) when Israel will rejoice with its Maker, (the festival shall be spent) at least partially in (pursuing) holy concerns, as (our Sages) say, "(Divide the) *Yom Tov* — half is for God and half is for you" (*Pesachim* 68b), and in this manner, undoubtedly, the Divine Presence will dwell in Israel, as it states, אֱלֹהִים נִצָּב בַּעֲדַת אֵל, *God stands in the congregation of El (God)* (*Psalms* 82:1). (Therefore the Torah) mentions those appointed seasons which you will proclaim as *holy convocations*, meaning a gathering of the people for holy concerns — for a gathering of the people is called מִקְרָא, *an assembly*, similar to חֹדֶשׁ וְשַׁבָּת קְרֹא מִקְרָא, *New Moons, and Sabbaths and the calling of assemblies* (*Isaiah* 1:13), and also, עַל כָּל מְכוֹן הַר צִיּוֹן וְעַל מִקְרָאֶהָ, *Upon every dwelling place of Mt. Zion and upon her assemblies* (ibid. 4:5) ...

אֵלֶּה הֵם מוֹעֲדָי — *These are My appointed seasons.* These are the appointed seasons which I desire. However, when you do not proclaim them as *holy convocations*, but as mundane gatherings devoted to the transitory pleasures of man, then they will not be (considered) מוֹעֲדָי, "*My*" appointed seasons; rather they will be (in the category of) וּמוֹעֲדֵיכֶם שָׂנְאָה נַפְשִׁי, *Your appointed feasts My soul hates* (ibid. 1:14).

3. שַׁבָּת הִוא לַה׳ בְּכֹל מוֹשְׁבֹתֵיכֶם — *It is a Sabbath to HASHEM in all your dwelling places.* He who formed light and created darkness (based on *Isaiah* 45:7) determines (fixes) them (the Sabbaths) for *all your dwelling places*, even though the beginning of the day and the night changes in accordance with the time span (of day and night) in a particular

NOTES

these are My appointed seasons. The *Sforno* explains the link between the previous chapter, which speaks of offerings, and this chapter which discusses the various festivals. Both represent that which causes God's presence to dwell in the midst of Israel. Although the prohibition of labor on the Sabbath is not identical to that of the festivals, the latter being less stringent insofar as אוֹכֶל נֶפֶשׁ, work connected with food preparation, is concerned, nonetheless, in both cases the cessation of labor is for the purpose of assembling Israel together to occupy themselves with Torah study and holy activities. Only in this manner will these appointed seasons be worthy to be called מוֹעֲדָי, "*My*" *appointed seasons;* otherwise they are totally man's and rejected by God (See *Rambam, Mishneh Torah, Hilchos Yom Tov* 6:18-20).

3. שַׁבָּת הִוא לַה׳ בְּכֹל מוֹשְׁבֹתֵיכֶם — *It is a Sabbath to HASHEM in all your dwelling places.* As the *Sforno* explained in *Genesis* 1:4-5, the terms *day* and *night* as we understand them were not applicable during the six days of creation; therefore, the beginning and end of the first Sabbath were also perforce unique. However, once the laws of nature regulating the spheres and their movements were established, the times of the beginning and end of Shabbos would be determined by local conditions

3 *For six days labor may be done, and the seventh day is a day of complete rest, a holy convocation, you shall not do any work; it is a Sabbath for HASHEM in all your dwelling places.*

4 *These are the appointed festivals of HASHEM, the holy convocations, which you shall designate in their appropriate time.* 5 *In the first month on the fourteenth of the month in the afternoon is the time of the pesach-offering*

---

geographical region. Whereas the first Sabbath was measured according to some special singular time span (of day and night), nonetheless, the beginning and end of the Sabbath in each region (is determined) for its inhabitants according to the (local) beginning of the day and the night in that region.

4. אֵלֶּה מוֹעֲדֵי ה׳ — *These are the appointed seasons of HASHEM.* After (the Torah) speaks of the Sabbath whose time is already fixed, as (our Sages) say, "It is the Sabbath whose time is fixed" (*Pesachim* 117b), (the Torah) now begins the subject of the appointed seasons whose appointed time (is determined) by the proclamation of the court, as we have it from tradition, אַתֶּם אֲפִילוּ שׁוֹגְגִין אַתֶּם אֲפִילוּ מְזִידִין אַתֶּם אֲפִילוּ מוּטְעִין, *By you, even if (you err) unintentionally; by you, even if (you err) with intention; by you, even if you are mistaken* (*Rosh Hashanah* 25a).

5. בֵּין הָעַרְבָּיִם פֶּסַח לַה׳ — *At dusk is HASHEM's Pesach.* (The Torah) mentions the subject of the *Pesach* (i.e., the sacrifice of the *Pesach* lamb on the 14th day of Nissan) even though that day is not a *holy convocation,* because it is the cause of changes in the times of the appointed seasons. For, indeed, it is (God's intent) that the time of the sacrifice of the *Pesach* (lamb) for all generations shall coincide with the time of the sacrifice when (the original) "passing over" took place exactly at that midnight. This is the reason that the court is empowered to decide intercalations and (other) calculations, as explained (by the Torah) saying, שָׁמוֹר אֶת חֹדֶשׁ הָאָבִיב וְעָשִׂיתָ פֶּסַח לַה׳ אֱלֹהֶיךָ כִּי בְּחֹדֶשׁ הָאָבִיב הוֹצִיאֲךָ ה׳ אֱלֹהֶיךָ מִמִּצְרַיִם לָיְלָה, *Observe the month of Aviv and keep the Pesach unto HASHEM your God; for in the month of Aviv, HASHEM your God brought you forth out of Egypt by night* (*Deut.* 16:1). Tradition dictates that (the court) shall so fix the calendar that the New Moon of *Pesach* shall fall in the *Aviv*.

NOTES

of longitude and latitude. This is the meaning of *"in all your dwelling places."*

4. אֵלֶּה מוֹעֲדֵי ה׳ — *These are the appointed seasons of HASHEM.* The commentators give various explanations for the repetition of the phrase אֵלֶּה מוֹעֲדֵי ה׳, *these are the appointed seasons,* in this verse, since practically the identical phrase appears in verse 2 (אֵלֶּה הֵם מוֹעֲדָי) The *Sforno* explains it by emphasizing the concluding portion of the verse — *which "you" shall proclaim.* The Sabbath, which is commanded in the previous verse, is set by heaven, whereas *these appointed seasons* are set by the Sanhedrin (the Supreme Religious Court) who are empowered to determine the day of ראשׁ חֹדֶשׁ, *the New Moon.* See *Rashi's* commentary on this verse.

5. בֵּין הָעַרְבָּיִם פֶּסַח לַה׳ — *At dusk is HASHEM's Pesach.* The *Sforno* explains why the Torah begins the *parashas Hamoadim* (the chapter of the festivals) with the *Pesach* lamb sacrificed on the fourteenth day of Nissan (*erev Pesach*), although the fourteenth is not, itself, a *Yom Tov* (festival). Nonetheless, as the *Sforno* points out, it is a pivotal date affecting all the מוֹעֲדִים. Since Israel's is a lunar year, it is inevitable that the festivals will fall in different seasons with the passing of time. To solve this problem, an extra month is inserted seven times in every cycle of nineteen years. The authority to intercalate the year is based on the verse in *Deut.* 16:1 where the Torah commands Israel to observe the festival of *Pesach* in the season when the ears become ripe (*Aviv*). The *Sforno* explains that the reason we are careful to adjust the calendar so as to bring the lunar and solar years into alignment is not only because of seasonal fluctuation but also for the purpose of having the *Pesach* sacrifice offered at a time which coincides with the "passing over" by God when He punished Egypt with the plague of the first-born, namely on the fourteenth of Nissan. Hence, it is proper to begin this section of the festivals with the *Pesach* sacrifice brought on the fourteenth day of the first month, considering that all calendar calculations are determined by that particular date.

ו וּבַחֲמִשָּׁה עָשָׂר יוֹם לַחֹדֶשׁ הַזֶּה חַג הַמַּצּוֹת לַיהוָה שִׁבְעַת יָמִים מַצּוֹת
ז תֹּאכֵלוּ: בַּיּוֹם הָרִאשׁוֹן מִקְרָא־קֹדֶשׁ יִהְיֶה לָכֶם כָּל־מְלֶאכֶת עֲבֹדָה לֹא
ח תַעֲשׂוּ: וְהִקְרַבְתֶּם אִשֶּׁה לַיהוָה שִׁבְעַת יָמִים בַּיּוֹם הַשְּׁבִיעִי מִקְרָא־קֹדֶשׁ
כָּל־מְלֶאכֶת עֲבֹדָה לֹא תַעֲשׂוּ:
ט־י וַיְדַבֵּר יהוה אֶל־מֹשֶׁה לֵּאמֹר: דַּבֵּר אֶל־בְּנֵי יִשְׂרָאֵל וְאָמַרְתָּ אֲלֵהֶם
כִּי־תָבֹאוּ אֶל־הָאָרֶץ אֲשֶׁר אֲנִי נֹתֵן לָכֶם וּקְצַרְתֶּם אֶת־קְצִירָהּ וַהֲבֵאתֶם
יא אֶת־עֹמֶר רֵאשִׁית קְצִירְכֶם אֶל־הַכֹּהֵן: וְהֵנִיף אֶת־הָעֹמֶר לִפְנֵי יהוה
יב לִרְצֹנְכֶם מִמָּחֳרַת הַשַּׁבָּת יְנִיפֶנּוּ הַכֹּהֵן: וַעֲשִׂיתֶם בְּיוֹם הֲנִיפְכֶם אֶת־
יג הָעֹמֶר כֶּבֶשׂ תָּמִים בֶּן־שְׁנָתוֹ לְעֹלָה לַיהוָה: וּמִנְחָתוֹ שְׁנֵי עֶשְׂרֹנִים סֹלֶת
יד בְּלוּלָה בַשֶּׁמֶן אִשֶּׁה לַיהוָה רֵיחַ נִיחֹחַ וְנִסְכֹּה יַיִן רְבִיעִת הַהִין: וְלֶחֶם
וְקָלִי וְכַרְמֶל לֹא תֹאכְלוּ עַד־עֶצֶם הַיּוֹם הַזֶּה עַד הֲבִיאֲכֶם אֶת־קָרְבַּן
טו אֱלֹהֵיכֶם חֻקַּת עוֹלָם לְדֹרֹתֵיכֶם בְּכֹל מֹשְׁבֹתֵיכֶם: וּסְפַרְתֶּם

8. וְהִקְרַבְתֶּם אִשֶּׁה לַה׳ שִׁבְעַת יָמִים — *And you shall bring an offering made by fire to* H*ASHEM for seven days.* (This comes) to tell us that חוֹל הַמּוֹעֵד, *the intermediate days of the festival*, are not completely חוֹל, *profane*, i.e., regular weekdays, for since a communal offering is offered at that time in addition to the daily offering, as on a day of holy assembly, undoubtedly, it is considered part of the festival. (The Torah), however, does not explain here the subject of *Mussafim*, the additional offerings, for that is not its intent presently, just as it does not explain that subject by the other festivals. In a similar manner, (the Torah) writes, *And you shall bring for seven days*, regarding the festival of Succos (verse 36), to indicate the holiness of the intermediate days. As for Rosh Hashanah, אִשֶּׁה לַה׳, *an offering made by fire*, is also mentioned, to teach us that there is an extra מוּסָף besides that of the New Moon, as it says, מִלְּבַד עֹלַת הַחֹדֶשׁ וּמִנְחָתָהּ, *Beside the burnt-offering of the New Moon and the meal-offering thereof* (Numbers 29:6). However, (in the sections of) Shabbos, the festival of Shavuos and Yom Kippur, the subject of *Mussafim* is not mentioned at all, for that which is written regarding Yom Kippur, *And you shall bring an offering made by fire to* H*ASHEM* (v. 27), refers (not to *Mussaf* but) to the burnt-offerings and sin-offerings of the *Kohen Gadol* and of the congregation as explained in *parashas Acharei Mos.*

(The Torah) introduces Shabbos, the *Pesach* (sacrifice) and the Festival of Matzos (unleavened bread) with one all-inclusive דִבּוּר, *statement*, (וַיְדַבֵּר ה׳ — verse 1) because

NOTES

8. וְהִקְרַבְתֶּם אִשֶּׁה לַה׳ שִׁבְעַת יָמִים — *And you shall bring an offering made by fire to* H*ASHEM for seven days.* On a festival, a קָרְבָּן מוּסָף, *additional sacrifice*, is offered besides the קָרְבָּן תָּמִיד, *daily offering*. The laws of *Mussafim* are recorded in the Book of *Numbers, parashas Pinchas.* The *Sforno* states that the only reason this sacrifice is mentioned here in *Emor* is to explain the significance of the intermediate days of Pesach and Succos. Since each of these days requires a קָרְבָּן מוּסָף, this indicates that they have festival status. There is a different reason for the קָרְבָּן מוּסָף being mentioned in conjunction with Rosh Hashanah. Since Rosh Hashanah is also ראש חֹדֶשׁ, *the New Moon*, it is necessary for the Torah to teach us that, in addition to the regular New Moon sacrifice, an additional offering is brought to mark Rosh Hashanah. As for Yom Kippur, the אִשֶּׁה לַה׳ does not refer to the *Mussaf* offering but to the sin and burnt offerings of the *Kohen Gadol* and of the people, peculiar to that day.

The expression וַיְדַבֵּר ה׳ אֶל מֹשֶׁה, *And* H*ASHEM spoke to Moses*, appears as an introductory phrase in verses 1,9,23,26 and 33. Following the first וַיְדַבֵּר, the Torah discusses the Sabbath, the *Pesach* sacrifice and the festival of Pesach. The phrase is then repeated to introduce the festivals of Shavuos, Rosh Hashanah, Yom Kippur and Succos. The *Sforno* explains the grouping of the first three (Sabbath, the *Pesach* sacrifice and Pesach festival)

to HASHEM. [6] *And on the fifteenth day of this month is the Festival of Matzos to* HASHEM; *you shall eat matzos for a seven-day period.* [7] *On the first day there shall be a holy convocation for you; you shall do no laborious work.* [8] *You shall bring a fire-offering to* HASHEM *for a seven-day period; on the seventh day shall be a holy convocation; you shall do no laborious work.*

[9] HASHEM *spoke to Moses, saying:* [10] *Speak to the Children of Israel and say to them: When you shall enter the Land that I give you and you reap its harvest, you shall bring an Omer from your first harvest to the Kohen.* [11] *He shall wave the Omer before* HASHEM *to gain favor for you; on the morrow of the rest day the Kohen shall wave it.* [12] *On the day you wave the Omer, you shall perform the service of an unblemished lamb in its first year as an elevation-offering to* HASHEM. [13] *Its meal-offering shall be two tenth-ephah of fine flour mixed with oil, a fire-offering to* HASHEM, *a satisfying aroma; and its libation shall be wine, a quarter-hin.* [14] *You shall not eat bread or roasted kernels or plump kernels until this very day, until you bring the offering of your God; it is an eternal decree for your generations in all your dwelling places.*

the three of them were commanded prior to the giving of the Torah, but for each of the other *appointed seasons,* (lit.) (the Torah) allocates a separate דִּבּוּר for each festival (vs. 9,23,26,33).

Now (the Torah) introduces the statement (regarding) the festival of Shavuos with the *Omer* because that is when the harvest of the *Omer* begins, and with the counting of the weeks, both of which relate to the festival that is called *the harvest festival* and the Feast of Weeks, at which time thanks is given to God, the Blessed One, for *the appointed weeks of the harvest which He kept for us* (based on *Jeremiah* 5:24). For indeed, the purpose of the festivals is (to occupy oneself with) prayer and thanksgiving, just as the appointed season of the month of *Aviv* is (for the purpose) of praying to God for the ripening of the ears and to give thanks for our freedom. And being that the success of the harvest depends on the climate of the season from the time of ripening until the harvest, as it says, שְׁבֻעֹת חֻקֹּת קָצִיר יִשְׁמָר לָנוּ, *The appointed weeks of the harvest He keeps for us* (*Jeremiah* 5:24), (therefore) the *Omer* is a thanksgiving for the *Aviv,* as though one is offering the first fruits of the field to the owner. The offering which accompanies it (verses 12,13) serves as a prayer for the future, and the counting is a remembrance of prayer each day, (while) the harvest festival is (an occasion for giving) thanks for the good harvest, (and) the festival of ingathering (Succos) is for the goodness of the ingathering.

14. בְּכֹל מֹשְׁבֹתֵיכֶם — *In all your dwellings.* The prohibition of חָדָשׁ, *new grain,* (is still in effect) until the sixteenth day of Nissan even though the sacrifice (of the *Omer*) and the Temple are no more.

NOTES

as having in common the fact that they all preceded Sinai; the others, however, were commanded at Sinai and are therefore discussed independently.

The *Omer,* which is a measure equal to a tenth of an *ephah,* was brought on the sixteenth day of Nissan. The festival of Shavuos, or the חַג הַקָּצִיר, the *harvest festival,* is celebrated seven weeks later. The *Sforno* explains why the Torah begins the discussion of Shavuos with the commandments regarding the *Omer,* the animal offering and *Sefirah,* the counting of the weeks. The observance of every festival is for the purpose of thanksgiving on the past and prayer for the future, hence the prerequisite for the harvest is the bringing of the *Omer* which is our manner of giving thanks for the *Aviv,* namely the ripening of the barley which is reaped at that time. In the same vein, the animal offering is a prayer for the future while the counting is meant to remind Israel to pray for God's providence daily during these seven critical weeks leading up to the wheat harvest.

14. בְּכֹל מֹשְׁבֹתֵיכֶם — *In all your dwellings.* This phrase appears again in verses 21 and 31. In all

לָכֶם מִמָּחֳרַת הַשַּׁבָּת מִיּוֹם הֲבִיאֲכֶם אֶת־עֹמֶר הַתְּנוּפָה שֶׁבַע שַׁבָּתוֹת
טז תְּמִימֹת תִּהְיֶינָה׃ עַד מִמָּחֳרַת הַשַּׁבָּת הַשְּׁבִיעִת תִּסְפְּרוּ חֲמִשִּׁים יוֹם
יז וְהִקְרַבְתֶּם מִנְחָה חֲדָשָׁה לַיהוָה׃ מִמּוֹשְׁבֹתֵיכֶם תָּבִיאוּ ׀ לֶחֶם תְּנוּפָה (*א' דגושה)
שְׁתַּיִם שְׁנֵי עֶשְׂרֹנִים סֹלֶת תִּהְיֶינָה חָמֵץ תֵּאָפֶינָה בִּכּוּרִים לַיהוָה׃
יח וְהִקְרַבְתֶּם עַל־הַלֶּחֶם שִׁבְעַת כְּבָשִׂים תְּמִימִם בְּנֵי שָׁנָה וּפַר בֶּן־בָּקָר אֶחָד
וְאֵילִם שְׁנָיִם יִהְיוּ עֹלָה לַיהוָה וּמִנְחָתָם וְנִסְכֵּיהֶם אִשֵּׁה רֵיחַ־נִיחֹחַ לַיהוָה׃
יט וַעֲשִׂיתֶם שְׂעִיר־עִזִּים אֶחָד לְחַטָּאת וּשְׁנֵי כְבָשִׂים בְּנֵי שָׁנָה לְזֶבַח שְׁלָמִים׃
כ וְהֵנִיף הַכֹּהֵן ׀ אֹתָם עַל לֶחֶם הַבִּכֻּרִים תְּנוּפָה לִפְנֵי יְהוָה עַל־שְׁנֵי כְּבָשִׂים
כא קֹדֶשׁ יִהְיוּ לַיהוָה לַכֹּהֵן׃ וּקְרָאתֶם בְּעֶצֶם ׀ הַיּוֹם הַזֶּה מִקְרָא־קֹדֶשׁ יִהְיֶה
לָכֶם כָּל־מְלֶאכֶת עֲבֹדָה לֹא תַעֲשׂוּ חֻקַּת עוֹלָם בְּכָל־מוֹשְׁבֹתֵיכֶם
כב לְדֹרֹתֵיכֶם׃ וּבְקֻצְרְכֶם אֶת־קְצִיר אַרְצְכֶם לֹא־תְכַלֶּה פְּאַת שָׂדְךָ בְּקֻצְרֶךָ
וְלֶקֶט קְצִירְךָ לֹא תְלַקֵּט לֶעָנִי וְלַגֵּר תַּעֲזֹב אֹתָם אֲנִי יְהוָה אֱלֹהֵיכֶם׃
חמישי כג־כד וַיְדַבֵּר יְהוָה אֶל־מֹשֶׁה לֵּאמֹר׃ דַּבֵּר אֶל־בְּנֵי יִשְׂרָאֵל לֵאמֹר בַּחֹדֶשׁ
הַשְּׁבִיעִי בְּאֶחָד לַחֹדֶשׁ יִהְיֶה לָכֶם שַׁבָּתוֹן זִכְרוֹן תְּרוּעָה מִקְרָא־קֹדֶשׁ׃

---

17. חָמֵץ תֵּאָפֶינָה בִּכּוּרִים לַה׳ — *They shall be baked with leaven, as first fruits to* HASHEM. The *Omer* was the first fruit of barley, whereas (these loaves) are the first fruits of the wheat harvest, and for this reason the festival is called יוֹם הַבִּכּוּרִים, *the Day of the first-fruits*, as it says, וּבְיוֹם הַבִּכּוּרִים בְּהַקְרִיבְכֶם מִנְחָה חֲדָשָׁה, *Also in the day of the first-fruits when you bring a new meal offering* (*Numbers* 28:26); and (the Torah) states, לַה׳, *to* HASHEM, because from that time onward, the חָדָשׁ is permitted to be brought as an offering (to God).

Now, being that (these loaves) are the means of giving thanks for *the appointed weeks of the harvest* (*Jeremiah* 5:24) at which time the grain is endangered, (therefore) the two loaves, brought with the he-lambs (offered as) a peace-offering, are leavened, similar to the שַׁלְמֵי תוֹדָה, *thanksgiving peace-offering,* (which is offered) *with loaves of leavened bread* (7:13).

21. חֻקַּת עוֹלָם בְּכָל מוֹשְׁבֹתֵיכֶם — *A statute forever in all your dwellings.* Although no sacrifices are brought in your dwellings that are in exile (outside *Eretz Yisrael*), the concepts of *Sefirah* (counting) and the (holding of) a holy convocation shall not cease.

22. וּבְקֻצְרְכֶם — *And when you reap.* After giving thanks for the success of the harvest,

NOTES

three cases, it comes to teach us that certain laws apply even when circumstances have changed. For example, חָדָשׁ, *new grain*, is prohibited until the sixteenth day of Nissan even subsequent to the Temple's destruction when the *Omer* sacrifice could no longer be offered. The second case (v. 21) deals with the *mitzvah* of *Sefiras HaOmer*, the Counting of the *Omer*, and the observance of Shavuos as a *Yom Tov*. Both are operative even when the two loaves cannot be brought to the Temple. The third case is that of Yom Kippur (v. 31). The Torah tells us that work is prohibited on the tenth day of Tishrei even when the service of Yom Kippur cannot be held in the Temple. Hence, the expression *in all your dwellings* teaches us that changing circumstances and locales do not effect these laws, prohibitions, and *mitzvos*.

17. חָמֵץ תֵּאָפֶינָה בִּכּוּרִים לַה׳ — *They shall be baked with leaven, as first fruits to* HASHEM. The Torah tells us that כָּל שְׂאֹר וְכָל דְּבַשׁ לֹא תַקְטִירוּ מִמֶּנּוּ אִשֶּׁה לַה׳, *You shall burn no leaven or honey as a smoke offering to* HASHEM (*Leviticus* 2:11). The two loaves brought on Shavuos are an exception to this rule, as is the תּוֹדָה, *thanksgiving offering*, when leavened cakes are brought together with unleavened cakes and wafers (7:12-13). The *Sforno* suggests that the reason leavened bread is offered on this *Yom Tov* is because it is the means by which Israel gives thanks to the Almighty for protecting the

15 *You shall count for yourselves — from the morrow of the rest day, from the day when you bring the Omer of the waving — seven weeks, they shall be complete.*
16 *Until the morrow of the seventh week you shall count, fifty days; and you shall offer a new meal-offering to* HASHEM.
17 *From your dwelling places you shall bring bread that shall be waved, two loaves made of two tenth-ephah, they shall be fine flour, they shall be baked leavened; first-offerings to* HASHEM.
18 *With the bread you shall offer seven unblemished lambs in their first year, one young bull, and two rams; they shall be an elevation-offering to* HASHEM, *with their meal-offering and their libations — a fire-offering, a satisfying aroma to* HASHEM.
19 *You shall make one he-goat as a sin-offering, and two lambs in their first year as feast peace-offerings.*
20 *The Kohen shall wave them upon the first-offering breads as a wave-service before* HASHEM *— upon the two sheep — they shall be holy, for* HASHEM *and for the Kohen.*
21 *You shall convoke on this very day — there shall a holy convocation for yourselves — you shall do no laborious work; it is an eternal decree in your dwelling places for your generations.*

22 *When you reap the harvest of your land, you shall not remove completely the corners of your field as you reap and you shall not gather the gleanings of your harvest; for the poor and the proselyte shall you leave them; I am* HASHEM, *your God.*

23 HASHEM *spoke to Moses, saying:*
24 *Speak to the Children of Israel, saying: In the seventh month, on the first of the month, there shall be a rest day for you, a remembrance with shofar blasts, a holy convocation.*

(the Torah) cautions (us) regarding those commandments which will preserve the wealth attained thereby, i.e., by commanding (us) regarding לֶקֶט, *the gleanings* and פֵּאָה, *the corner* of the field, as (our Sages) say, "To salt (preserve) wealth, deduct from it; and others say, (do acts of) kindness" (*Kesubos* 66b).

אֲנִי ה׳ אֱלֹהֵיכֶם — *I am* HASHEM *your God.* The God of the harvesters and the God of those poor who collect from the gleanings and corners of the field, and I shall be good to those who are good to them, (motivated to) do My will.

24. זִכְרוֹן תְּרוּעָה — *A memorial of a blast of horns.* A memorial of the trumpet-signal for the king (based on *Numbers* 23:21) by which the people rejoice in their king, as it says, הַרְנִינוּ לֵאלֹהִים עוּזֵּנוּ הָרִיעוּ, *Sing aloud to God our strength, make a joyful noise* (הָרִיעוּ) (*Psalms* 81:2). This is (done) because He sits on the throne of justice, as we know from tradition (*Rosh Hashanah* 8b), (and) as it says, תִּקְעוּ בַחֹדֶשׁ שׁוֹפָר בַּכֶּסֶה לְיוֹם חַגֵּנוּ כִּי חֹק

NOTES

grain during the critical period from Pesach until this time. (See notes on verse 8.)

21. חֻקַּת עוֹלָם בְּכָל מוֹשְׁבֹתֵיכֶם — *A statute forever in all your dwellings.* See note on verse 14.

22. וּבְקֻצְרְכֶם — *And when you reap.* It is difficult to understand why the commandments regarding gifts to the poor are inserted in this section of the festivals, especially since they already appeared in chapter 19:9. While various answers are given by the commentators (see *Rashi*), the *Sforno* offers this explanation. Since the offerings on Shavuos are brought in order to give thanks to God for the blessings of the harvest, the Torah now teaches us how to insure and conserve that blessing. It is through acts of righteousness and kindness and through sharing our bounty with the less fortunate that we can preserve our wealth. As our Sages say in the aphorism cited by the *Sforno*, just as salt preserves food, so do acts of kindness and sharing one's bounty preserve one's possessions.

24. זִכְרוֹן תְּרוּעָה — *A memorial of a blast of horns.* The *Sforno* interprets the word תְּרוּעָה, *blast*, (as in trumpet-signal) as indicating the role played by

כה-כו כָּל־מְלֶאכֶת עֲבֹדָה לֹא תַעֲשׂוּ וְהִקְרַבְתֶּם אִשֶּׁה לַיהוָה: וַיְדַבֵּר
כז יְהוָה אֶל־מֹשֶׁה לֵּאמֹר: אַךְ בֶּעָשׂוֹר לַחֹדֶשׁ הַשְּׁבִיעִי הַזֶּה יוֹם הַכִּפֻּרִים
הוּא מִקְרָא־קֹדֶשׁ יִהְיֶה לָכֶם וְעִנִּיתֶם אֶת־נַפְשֹׁתֵיכֶם וְהִקְרַבְתֶּם אִשֶּׁה
כח לַיהוָה: וְכָל־מְלָאכָה לֹא תַעֲשׂוּ בְּעֶצֶם הַיּוֹם הַזֶּה כִּי יוֹם כִּפֻּרִים
כט הוּא לְכַפֵּר עֲלֵיכֶם לִפְנֵי יְהוָה אֱלֹהֵיכֶם: כִּי כָל־הַנֶּפֶשׁ אֲשֶׁר
ל לֹא־תְעֻנֶּה בְּעֶצֶם הַיּוֹם הַזֶּה וְנִכְרְתָה מֵעַמֶּיהָ: וְכָל־הַנֶּפֶשׁ
אֲשֶׁר תַּעֲשֶׂה כָּל־מְלָאכָה בְּעֶצֶם הַיּוֹם הַזֶּה וְהַאֲבַדְתִּי אֶת־הַנֶּפֶשׁ הַהִוא
לא מִקֶּרֶב עַמָּהּ: כָּל־מְלָאכָה לֹא תַעֲשׂוּ חֻקַּת עוֹלָם לְדֹרֹתֵיכֶם בְּכֹל
לב מֹשְׁבֹתֵיכֶם: שַׁבַּת שַׁבָּתוֹן הוּא לָכֶם וְעִנִּיתֶם אֶת־נַפְשֹׁתֵיכֶם בְּתִשְׁעָה
לַחֹדֶשׁ בָּעֶרֶב מֵעֶרֶב עַד־עֶרֶב תִּשְׁבְּתוּ שַׁבַּתְּכֶם:
ששי לג-לד וַיְדַבֵּר יְהוָה אֶל־מֹשֶׁה לֵּאמֹר: דַּבֵּר אֶל־בְּנֵי יִשְׂרָאֵל לֵאמֹר בַּחֲמִשָּׁה
עָשָׂר יוֹם לַחֹדֶשׁ הַשְּׁבִיעִי הַזֶּה חַג הַסֻּכּוֹת שִׁבְעַת יָמִים לַיהוָה:
לה-לו בַּיּוֹם הָרִאשׁוֹן מִקְרָא־קֹדֶשׁ כָּל־מְלֶאכֶת עֲבֹדָה לֹא תַעֲשׂוּ: שִׁבְעַת
יָמִים תַּקְרִיבוּ אִשֶּׁה לַיהוָה בַּיּוֹם הַשְּׁמִינִי מִקְרָא־קֹדֶשׁ יִהְיֶה לָכֶם
וְהִקְרַבְתֶּם אִשֶּׁה לַיהוָה עֲצֶרֶת הִוא כָּל־מְלֶאכֶת עֲבֹדָה לֹא תַעֲשׂוּ:

לְיִשְׂרָאֵל הוּא מִשְׁפָּט לֵאלֹהֵי יַעֲקֹב, *Blow a shofar at the New Moon, at the full moon of our festival day; for this is a statute for Israel, an ordinance of the God of Jacob* (*Psalms* 81:4,5). It is (therefore) fitting that we rejoice more so at this time when He is our King who will lean towards (being) kindly and judging us favorably, as it says, כִּי ה׳ שֹׁפְטֵנוּ ה׳ מְחֹקְקֵנוּ ה׳ מַלְכֵּנוּ הוּא יוֹשִׁיעֵנוּ, *For HASHEM is our Judge, HASHEM is our Ruler, HASHEM is our King, He will save us* (*Isaiah* 33:22).

27. אַךְ בֶּעָשׂוֹר לַחֹדֶשׁ הַשְּׁבִיעִי — *Nonetheless on the tenth day of the seventh month.* Although on all other holy convocations it is proper to rejoice and to enjoy food and drink, as it says, אִכְלוּ מַשְׁמַנִּים וּשְׁתוּ מַמְתַקִּים וְשִׁלְחוּ מָנוֹת לְאֵין נָכוֹן לוֹ כִּי קָדוֹשׁ הַיּוֹם לַאֲדֹנֵינוּ, *Eat fat (meat), and drink sweet beverages and send portions to those for whom nothing is prepared, for this day is holy to our Master* (*Nechemiah* 8:10), nonetheless, the tenth day is a day of atonement (wherein one) shall confess and (every) man shall bemoan his sins (based on *Lamentations* 3:39), (therefore) it is not a day of joy and pleasure but a day of affliction, as it says . . .

וְעִנִּיתֶם אֶת נַפְשֹׁתֵיכֶם וְהִקְרַבְתֶּם אִשֶּׁה — *And you shall afflict your souls; and you shall bring an offering made by fire.* This אִשֶּׁה consists of the offerings of the *Kohen Gadol* and the offerings of the congregation, which are brought for atonement.

28. וְכָל מְלָאכָה לֹא תַעֲשׂוּ . . . כִּי יוֹם כִּפֻּרִים הוּא — *And you shall do no manner of work . . . for it is a day of atonement.* Because it is fitting on this day to turn away from other

NOTES

God on the Day of Judgment. This function of God as King is one which causes Israel to rejoice, for He shall surely judge His children with compassion and love.

27. אַךְ בֶּעָשׂוֹר לַחֹדֶשׁ הַשְּׁבִיעִי — *Nonetheless on the tenth day of the seventh month.* The word אַךְ lends itself to various interpretations. *Rashi* interprets it in a restrictive sense. The *Ramban* translates it as *surely*. The *Sforno*, however, explains it to mean אַף עַל פִּי, *although*, i.e., although all festivals have the common characteristics of מִשְׁתֶּה וְשִׂמְחָה, *feasting and rejoicing*, Yom Kippur is the exception to this rule since the stress is on confession and affliction. Regarding the *Sforno's* explanation of the אִשֶּׁה לַה׳, *offering made by fire*, see the note on verse 8.

28. וְכָל מְלָאכָה לֹא תַעֲשׂוּ . . . כִּי יוֹם כִּפֻּרִים הוּא — *And you shall do no manner of work . . . for it is a*

25 *You shall not do any laborious work, and you shall offer a fire-offering to*
HASHEM.
26 *HASHEM spoke to Moses, saying:* 27 *But on the tenth day of this month*
it is the Day of Atonement; there shall be a holy convocation for you, and
you shall afflict yourselves; you shall offer a fire-offering to HASHEM. 28 *You*
shall not do any work on this very day, for it is the Day of Atonement to pro-
vide you atonement before HASHEM, your God. 29 *For any soul who will not*
be afflicted on this very day will be cut off from its people. 30 *And any soul*
who will do any work on this very day, I will destroy that soul from among
its people. 31 *You shall not do any work; it is an eternal decree throughout*
your generations in all your dwelling places. 32 *It is a day of complete rest*
for you and you shall afflict yourselves; on the ninth of the month in the
evening — from evening to evening — shall you rest on your rest day.
33 *HASHEM spoke to Moses, saying:* 34 *Speak to the Children of Israel,*
saying: On the fifteenth day of this seventh month is the Festival of Succos,
a seven-day period for HASHEM. 35 *On the first day is a holy convocation, you*
shall not do any laborious work. 36 *For a seven-day period you shall offer a*
fire-offering to HASHEM; on the eighth day there shall be a holy convocation
for you and you shall offer a fire-offering to HASHEM, it is an assembly, you
shall not do any laborious work.

---

pursuits and to concentrate on attaining forgiveness and atonement, as opposed to, הֵן בְּיוֹם צֹמְכֶם תִּמְצְאוּ חֵפֶץ וְכָל עַצְּבֵיכֶם תִּנְגֹּשׂוּ, *Behold, on the day of your fast you pursue your business and exact all your payments* (*Isaiah* 58:3). Now since most who sin by not afflicting themselves do so only because of their physical appetites, while the majority of those who sin by doing work do so to be provocative; (therefore, the Torah) imposes the punishment of כָּרֵת, *excision,* upon one who does not afflict (his soul) (verse 29) while imposing the punishment of destruction of the soul upon one who works (v. 30).

31. בְּכֹל מוֹשְׁבֹתֵיכֶם — *In all your dwellings.* Although atonement is no longer attained through the Altar, it is (still) an obligation of the day, as (indeed) it is, in (our) Exile.

36. עֲצֶרֶת הִוא — *It is a day of solemn assembly* (lit., *restraint*). The concept of עֲצִירָה, *restraint,* is not only in order to rest from ordinary labor, but it is also a warning to spend some time in holy places, serving God, the Blessed One, through Torah or prayer or Divine service, similar to, וְשָׁם אִישׁ מֵעַבְדֵי שָׁאוּל בַּיּוֹם הַהוּא נֶעְצָר לִפְנֵי ה׳, *Now a certain man of the servants of Saul was there that day detained before HASHEM* (*I Samuel* 21:8), and it is also said, קַדְּשׁוּ צוֹם קִרְאוּ עֲצָרָה, *Sanctify a fast, call a solemn assembly* (עֲצָרָה) (*Joel* 1:14), and in this manner Yehu said, קַדְּשׁוּ עֲצָרָה לַבַּעַל, *Sanctify a solemn assembly for the Baal* (*II Kings* 10:20).

(The Torah) therefore says that this day following the festival of Succos, wherein the

NOTES

day of atonement. The *Sforno* explains why the punishment for eating on Yom Kippur is a lesser one than that imposed for working. The former, he submits, is caused by human weakness, i.e., by man's difficulty in controlling his physical cravings. The latter, however, is a case of לְהַכְעִיס, *an intent to anger* God. When one sits idle, his inborn desires do not tempt him to get up and begin working. Thus, one who works on Yom Kippur does so in blatant defiance of God's will. For this rebellion, he is liable to a far harsher punishment.

31. בְּכֹל מוֹשְׁבֹתֵיכֶם — *In all your dwellings.* See note on verse 14.

36. עֲצֶרֶת הִוא — *It is a day of solemn assembly.* Three festival days are called עֲצֶרֶת: the seventh day of Pesach, the eighth day of Succos, and Shavuos. The latter is only called as such by our Sages, not by the Torah. The *Sforno* explains the reason for calling these three festivals עֲצֶרֶת,

לז אֵלֶּה מוֹעֲדֵי יהוה אֲשֶׁר־תִּקְרְאוּ אֹתָם מִקְרָאֵי קֹדֶשׁ לְהַקְרִיב אִשֶּׁה
לח לַיהוה עֹלָה וּמִנְחָה זֶבַח וּנְסָכִים דְּבַר־יוֹם בְּיוֹמוֹ: מִלְּבַד שַׁבְּתֹת יהוה
וּמִלְּבַד מַתְּנוֹתֵיכֶם וּמִלְּבַד כָּל־נִדְרֵיכֶם וּמִלְּבַד כָּל־נִדְבֹתֵיכֶם אֲשֶׁר
לט תִּתְּנוּ לַיהוה: אַךְ בַּחֲמִשָּׁה עָשָׂר יוֹם לַחֹדֶשׁ הַשְּׁבִיעִי בְּאָסְפְּכֶם
אֶת־תְּבוּאַת הָאָרֶץ תָּחֹגּוּ אֶת־חַג־יהוה שִׁבְעַת יָמִים בַּיּוֹם הָרִאשׁוֹן
מ שַׁבָּתוֹן וּבַיּוֹם הַשְּׁמִינִי שַׁבָּתוֹן: וּלְקַחְתֶּם לָכֶם בַּיּוֹם הָרִאשׁוֹן פְּרִי עֵץ
הָדָר כַּפֹּת תְּמָרִים וַעֲנַף עֵץ־עָבֹת וְעַרְבֵי־נָחַל וּשְׂמַחְתֶּם לִפְנֵי יהוה
מא אֱלֹהֵיכֶם שִׁבְעַת יָמִים: וְחַגֹּתֶם אֹתוֹ חַג לַיהוה שִׁבְעַת יָמִים בַּשָּׁנָה חֻקַּת
מב עוֹלָם לְדֹרֹתֵיכֶם בַּחֹדֶשׁ הַשְּׁבִיעִי תָּחֹגּוּ אֹתוֹ: בַּסֻּכֹּת תֵּשְׁבוּ שִׁבְעַת יָמִים
מג כָּל־הָאֶזְרָח בְּיִשְׂרָאֵל יֵשְׁבוּ בַּסֻּכֹּת: לְמַעַן יֵדְעוּ דֹרֹתֵיכֶם כִּי בַסֻּכּוֹת
הוֹשַׁבְתִּי אֶת־בְּנֵי יִשְׂרָאֵל בְּהוֹצִיאִי אוֹתָם מֵאֶרֶץ מִצְרָיִם אֲנִי יהוה
מד אֱלֹהֵיכֶם: וַיְדַבֵּר מֹשֶׁה אֶת־מֹעֲדֵי יהוה אֶל־בְּנֵי יִשְׂרָאֵל:

כד שביעי א־ב וַיְדַבֵּר יהוה אֶל־מֹשֶׁה לֵּאמֹר: צַו אֶת־בְּנֵי יִשְׂרָאֵל וְיִקְחוּ אֵלֶיךָ שֶׁמֶן זַיִת

joy of all the festivals reaches its climax, is to be sanctified as a day of solemn assembly, to remain (i.e., spend time) in the holy places, and that his (Israel's) joy be that of rejoicing with the Torah and good deeds as it says, יִשְׂמַח יִשְׂרָאֵל בְּעֹשָׂיו, *Let Israel rejoice in Him who made him* (*Psalms* 149:2). This is similar to, וַיְהִי כִּי הִקִּיפוּ יְמֵי הַמִּשְׁתֶּה וַיִּשְׁלַח אִיּוֹב וַיְקַדְּשֵׁם וְהִשְׁכִּים בַּבֹּקֶר וְהֶעֱלָה עֹלוֹת מִסְפַּר כֻּלָּם כִּי אָמַר אִיּוֹב אוּלַי חָטְאוּ בָנַי, *And when the days of their feasting were completed, Job sent and sanctified them, and rose up early in the morning and offered burnt offerings according to their complete number, for Job said, "It may be that my sons have sinned ..."* (*Job* 1:5), all this due to the previous rejoicing.

Now, being that on the seventh day of Pesach Israel stood together with Moses to sing to God, the Blessed One, as it says, אָז יָשִׁיר מֹשֶׁה וּבְנֵי יִשְׂרָאֵל, *Then sang Moses and the Children of Israel* (*Exodus* 15:1); therefore, that day was hallowed to be עֲצֶרֶת לַה׳, *an assembly to God*, even though the salvation did not occur at the beginning of the day (i.e., the preceding night). This is explained in מִשְׁנֵה תוֹרָה (*Deuteronomy*) where it says, וּבַיּוֹם הַשְּׁבִיעִי עֲצֶרֶת לַה׳ אֱלֹהֶיךָ לֹא תַעֲשֶׂה מְלָאכָה, *And on the seventh day shall be a solemn assembly to HASHEM your God; you shall do no work therein* (*Deut.* 16:8).

And since the fiftieth day after the Exodus from Egypt was the day the Torah was given, at which time Israel remained together in the service of God, the Blessed One, (therefore) our Sages of blessed memory called it עֲצֶרֶת (remaining in a certain place) (*Pesachim* 68b). The Torah, however, does not mention this name (עֲצֶרֶת) at all, because Israel impaired the goal (lit., attainment) of that solemn assembly, and וַיִּתְנַצְּלוּ אֶת עֶדְיָם מֵהַר חוֹרֵב, *removed their ornaments from Mt. Horeb* (*Exodus* 33:6).

39. אַךְ בַּחֲמִשָּׁה עָשָׂר יוֹם — *However, on the fifteenth day*. After (God) mentions the regula-

NOTES

which implies being detained for the purpose of a solemn assembly. On Shemini Atzeres, Israel gathers to rejoice with the Torah and the performance of good deeds, as a culmination of the week of rejoicing which preceded it, as the *Sforno* explains. On the seventh day of Pesach, Israel joined Moses in singing to God in gratitude for their deliverance from the Egyptians at the Sea of Reeds, and on Shavuos, the people gathered together to receive the Torah. The reason, however, that the Torah itself refrains from calling Shavuos by the name עֲצֶרֶת is because Israel sinned with the Golden Calf and forfeited their special status as מַמְלֶכֶת כֹּהֲנִים וְגוֹי קָדוֹשׁ, *a kingdom of Kohanim and holy nation*. Regarding the seventh day of Pesach, the *Sforno* points out that although the actual miracle did not occur until morning, as it says in *Exodus* 14:27, nonetheless, the significance of the observance of this day begins the night before as is true of the Sabbath and all festivals.

37 *These are the appointed festivals of HASHEM that you shall proclaim as
holy convocations, to offer a fire-offering to HASHEM: an elevation-offering
and its meal-offering, a feast-offering and its libation, each day's
requirement on its day.* 38 *Aside from HASHEM's Sabbaths, and aside from
your gifts, aside from all your vows, and aside from all your free-will
offerings, which you will present to HASHEM.*
39 *But on the fifteenth day of the seventh month, when you gather in the
crop of the Land, you shall celebrate HASHEM's festival for a seven-day
period; the first day is a rest day and the eighth day is a rest day.* 40 *You
shall take for yourselves on the first day the fruit of a citron tree, the
branches of date palms, twigs of a plaited tree, and brook willows; and you
shall rejoice before HASHEM, your God, for a seven-day period.* 41 *You shall
celebrate it as a festival for HASHEM, a seven-day period in the year, an
eternal decree for your generations; in the seventh month shall you
celebrate it.* 42 *You shall dwell in booths for a seven-day period; every
native in Israel shall dwell in booths.* 43 *So that your generations will know
that I caused the Children of Israel to dwell in booths when I took them
from the land of Egypt; I am HASHEM, your God.*
44 *And Moses declared the appointed festivals of HASHEM to the Children
of Israel.*

24 1 *HASHEM spoke to Moses, saying:* 2 *Command the Children of Israel
that they take to you clear olive oil, pressed for lighting, to kindle a*

tions common to all the festivals, namely that all are *holy convocations* and require an additional offering, as it says, *These are the appointed seasons of HASHEM which you shall proclaim to be holy convocations, to bring an offering made by fire* (v. 37), He now says, *However, on the fifteenth day, etc.*, telling us that the festival of Succos is distinguished from the other appointed seasons (in a number of ways). The first is in that the eighth day (i.e., the day following Succos) is a holy assembly, as it says, *And on the eighth day shall be a solemn rest* (v.39) (שַׁבָּתוֹן), as distinct from the days of the week and the days of the Festival of Matzos and the months and years, where the seventh is holy instead of the eighth. Secondly, this festival requires a change of residence (i.e., dwelling in booths) as it says, *You shall dwell in booths* (v. 42), and thirdly, (there is) the waving of the four species, as it says, *And you shall take to yourself on the first day the fruit of goodly trees* (v. 40).

43. אֲנִי ה׳ אֱלֹהֵיכֶם — *I am HASHEM your God.* He explains that all these (festivals) are for the purpose intended by Him, the Blessed One, i.e., for our benefit because He is our God Who does not remove His watchful eye from us.

XXIV

2. צַו אֶת בְּנֵי יִשְׂרָאֵל וְיִקְחוּ אֵלֶיךָ שֶׁמֶן — *Command the Children of Israel to bring you oil.* After the oil which was contributed at the time of the building of the Sanctuary was

NOTES

39. אַךְ בַּחֲמִשָּׁה עָשָׂר יוֹם — *However, on the fifteenth day.* The *Sforno* interprets the word אַךְ in this verse (unlike his translation of this word in verse 27) as meaning *however.* The sense of the verse is: The various festivals enumerated above have two things in common; they are *holy convocations* and require a מוּסָף, *additional offering.* However, the festival of Succos is different in three ways: in the manner of dwelling, in the added *mitzvah* of the four species and the designation of the eighth day as a day of solemn assembly.

XXIV

2. צַו אֶת בְּנֵי יִשְׂרָאֵל וְיִקְחוּ אֵלֶיךָ שֶׁמֶן — *Command the Children of Israel to bring you oil.* The Children

ג זֶ֗ךְ כָּתִ֛ית לַמָּא֖וֹר לְהַעֲלֹ֥ת נֵ֖ר תָּמִֽיד: מִח֜וּץ לְפָרֹ֤כֶת הָֽעֵדֻת֙ בְּאֹ֣הֶל מוֹעֵ֗ד יַעֲרֹךְ֩ אֹת֨וֹ אַהֲרֹ֜ן מֵעֶ֧רֶב עַד־בֹּ֛קֶר לִפְנֵ֥י יהו֖ה תָּמִ֑יד חֻקַּ֥ת עוֹלָ֖ם ד לְדֹרֹתֵיכֶֽם: עַ֚ל הַמְּנֹרָ֣ה הַטְּהֹרָ֔ה יַעֲרֹ֖ךְ אֶת־הַנֵּר֑וֹת לִפְנֵ֥י יהו֖ה תָּמִֽיד:

ה וְלָֽקַחְתָּ֣ סֹ֔לֶת וְאָֽפִיתָ֣ אֹתָ֔הּ שְׁתֵּ֥ים עֶשְׂרֵ֖ה חַלּ֑וֹת שְׁנֵי֙ עֶשְׂרֹנִ֔ים יִהְיֶ֖ה הַֽחַלָּ֥ה ו הָֽאֶחָֽת: וְשַׂמְתָּ֥ אוֹתָ֛ם שְׁתַּ֥יִם מַֽעֲרָכ֖וֹת שֵׁ֣שׁ הַמַּֽעֲרָ֑כֶת עַ֛ל הַשֻּׁלְחָ֥ן הַטָּהֹ֖ר ז לִפְנֵ֥י יהוֽה: וְנָֽתַתָּ֥ עַל־הַמַּֽעֲרֶ֖כֶת לְבֹנָ֣ה זַכָּ֑ה וְהָֽיְתָ֤ה לַלֶּ֨חֶם֙ לְאַזְכָּרָ֔ה אִשֶּׁ֖ה ח לַֽיהוֽה: בְּי֨וֹם הַשַּׁבָּ֜ת בְּי֣וֹם הַשַּׁבָּ֗ת יַֽעַרְכֶ֛נּוּ לִפְנֵ֥י יהו֖ה תָּמִ֑יד מֵאֵ֥ת ט בְּנֵֽי־יִשְׂרָאֵ֖ל בְּרִ֥ית עוֹלָֽם: וְהָֽיְתָה֙ לְאַֽהֲרֹ֣ן וּלְבָנָ֔יו וַֽאֲכָלֻ֖הוּ בְּמָק֣וֹם קָדֹ֑שׁ י כִּ֡י קֹ֩דֶשׁ֩ קָֽדָשִׁ֨ים ה֥וּא ל֛וֹ מֵֽאִשֵּׁ֥י יהו֖ה חָק־עוֹלָֽם: וַיֵּצֵא֙ בֶּן־אִשָּׁ֣ה יִשְׂרְאֵלִ֔ית וְהוּא֙ בֶּן־אִ֣ישׁ מִצְרִ֔י בְּת֖וֹךְ בְּנֵ֣י יִשְׂרָאֵ֑ל וַיִּנָּצוּ֙ בַּֽמַּֽחֲנֶ֔ה יא בֶּ֚ן הַיִּשְׂרְאֵלִ֔ית וְאִ֖ישׁ הַיִּשְׂרְאֵלִֽי: וַ֠יִּקֹּ֠ב בֶּן־הָֽאִשָּׁ֨ה הַיִּשְׂרְאֵלִ֤ית אֶת־הַשֵּׁם֙ וַיְקַלֵּ֔ל וַיָּבִ֥יאוּ אֹת֖וֹ אֶל־מֹשֶׁ֑ה וְשֵׁ֥ם אִמּ֛וֹ שְׁלֹמִ֥ית בַּת־דִּבְרִ֖י יב לְמַטֵּה־דָֽן: וַיַּנִּיחֻ֖הוּ בַּמִּשְׁמָ֑ר לִפְרֹ֥שׁ לָהֶ֖ם עַל־פִּ֥י יהוֽה:

יג־יד וַיְדַבֵּ֥ר יהו֖ה אֶל־מֹשֶׁ֥ה לֵּאמֹֽר: הוֹצֵ֣א אֶת־הַֽמְקַלֵּ֗ל אֶל־מִחוּץ֙ לַֽמַּֽחֲנֶ֔ה וְסָֽמְכ֧וּ כָל־הַשֹּֽׁמְעִ֛ים אֶת־יְדֵיהֶ֖ם עַל־רֹאשׁ֑וֹ וְרָֽגְמ֥וּ אֹת֖וֹ טו כָּל־הָֽעֵדָֽה: וְאֶל־בְּנֵ֥י יִשְׂרָאֵ֖ל תְּדַבֵּ֣ר לֵאמֹ֑ר אִ֥ישׁ אִ֛ישׁ כִּֽי־יְקַלֵּ֥ל אֱלֹהָ֖יו טז וְנָשָׂ֥א חֶטְאֽוֹ: וְנֹקֵ֤ב שֵֽׁם־יהוה֙ מ֣וֹת יוּמָ֔ת רָג֥וֹם יִרְגְּמוּ־ב֖וֹ כָּל־הָֽעֵדָ֑ה

depleted, (God) commanded them to bring it for all generations.

3. יַעֲרֹךְ אֹתוֹ אַהֲרֹן — *Shall Aaron arrange.* Though the kindling of the lamps and the burning of the incense of the daily (i.e., continual) sacrifice could be performed by an ordinary *Kohen* in future generations as (our Sages) received (this law) from tradition, nonetheless, Aaron's name is mentioned in conjunction with both acts. (This is) because during all the days (that Israel was in) the wilderness, the status of the Sanctuary on a daily basis was akin to that of Yom Kippur in future generations of which it says, *For I appear in the cloud upon the Ark cover* (16:2), and during the period of the wilderness it says, כִּי עֲנַן ה' עַל הַמִּשְׁכָּן, יוֹמָם וְאֵשׁ תִּהְיֶה לַיְלָה בּוֹ, *For the cloud of HASHEM was upon the Sanctuary by day and there was fire therein by night* (*Exodus* 40:38). Therefore, it was fitting for the act of the burning of the incense and the kindling of the lamps, which were performed within (the Holy), to be done by the *Kohen Gadol*, as it was done on Yom Kippur in future generations.

5. וְלָקַחְתָּ סֹלֶת — *And you shall take fine flour.* It seems (to me) that this also was said after the appropriation (of flour) for the showbread, offered at the time of the Sanctuary's

NOTES

of Israel were commanded to bring pure olive oil for the light when the Sanctuary's construction was completed, as recorded in *Exodus* 27:20. *Rashi* explains that the verse in *Exodus* is referring to the eventual issue of this command at some future date, while the *actual* command regarding the lamps appears here. The *Sforno*, however, explains these two verses thus: When the Sanctuary was completed, a certain amount of oil was contributed. At that time, Moses was told that when the original oil would be depleted, he was to command the Children of Israel to bring addi-

tional oil. This was necessary to be said by God lest Moses think that the kindling of the menorah was only a *mitzvah* at that time (see the *Sforno* on *Exodus* 27:20). In our verse, the time had come to command Israel to bring new oil since the original supply had been exhausted.

3. יַעֲרֹךְ אֹתוֹ אַהֲרֹן — *Shall Aaron ararnge.* The *Sforno* explains why the Torah specifies Aaron, the *Kohen Gadol*, as being the one to arrange the lamps, since a כֹּהֵן הֶדְיוֹט, *an ordinary priest,* is also qualified to do so. The same question can be asked on the verse in *Exodus* 30:7 regarding the קְטֹרֶת,

continual lamp. 3 *Outside the Curtain of the Testimony, in the Tent of Meeting, Aaron shall arrange it, from evening to morning, before* H*ASHEM*, *continually; an eternal decree for your generations.* 4 *On the pure Menorah shall he arrange the lamps, before* H*ASHEM*, *continually.*

5 *You shall take fine flour and bake it into twelve loaves; each loaf shall be two tenth-ephah.* 6 *You shall place them in two stacks, six in each stack, upon the pure Table, before* H*ASHEM*. 7 *You shall put pure frankincense on each stack and it shall be a remembrance for the bread, a fire-offering for* H*ASHEM*. 8 *Each and every Sabbath he shall arrange them before* H*ASHEM* *continually, from the Children of Israel as an eternal covenant.* 9 *It shall belong to Aaron and his sons, and they shall eat it in a holy place; for it is most holy for him, from the fire-offerings of* H*ASHEM*, *an eternal decree.*

10 *The son of an Israelite woman went out — and he was the son of an Egyptian man — among the Children of Israel; they fought in the camp, the son of the Israelite woman and an Israelite man.* 11 *The son of the Israelite woman pronounced the Name and blasphemed — so they brought him to Moses; the name of his mother was Shelomis daughter of Divri, of the tribe of Dan.* 12 *They placed him under guard to clarify for themselves through* H*ASHEM*.

13 H*ASHEM* *spoke to Moses, saying:* 14 *Remove the blasphemer to the outside of the camp, and all those who heard shall lean their hands upon his head: The entire assembly shall stone him.* 15 *And to the Children of Israel you shall speak, saying: Any man who will blaspheme his God shall bear his sin;* 16 *and one who pronounces blasphemously the Name of* H*ASHEM* *shall be put to death, the entire assembly shall surely stone him;*

---

completion, was exhausted (lit., completed), as explained in the narrative of וַיָּבִיאוּ אֶת הַמִּשְׁכָּן אֶל מֹשֶׁה, *and they brought the Sanctuary to Moses* (*Exodus* 39:33).

10. וְהוּא בֶּן אִישׁ מִצְרִי — *And he was the son of an Egyptian man . . .* and therefore he was impudent and blessed (an euphemism for cursed) "the Name" (of God), for an Israelite would not be "that unrestrained (lawless)," (based on *Sanhedrin* 60a).

15. כִּי יְקַלֵּל אֱלֹהָיו — *Whosoever curses his God . . .* and transgresses the prohibition of אֱלֹהִים לֹא תְקַלֵּל, *You shall not curse (revile) the judges* (*Exodus* 22:27) [אֱלֹהִים meaning *judges*].

וְנָשָׂא חֶטְאוֹ — *Shall bear his sin.* He shall bear a punishment fitting (the status of) the one who curses, and he who is cursed, providing if he does not curse with God's Name, or if he only insults and degrades (the judges), as the *Targum* (*Onkelos*) translates, "You shall not curse the judges."

16. וְנֹקֵב שֵׁם ה׳ מוֹת יוּמָת — *And he that blasphemes the Name of* H*ASHEM* *shall surely be*

NOTES

burning of the incense, where Aaron is also specifically mentioned as being in charge. The answer of the *Sforno* is that during the years when Israel was in the wilderness, the daily status of the Sanctuary was equal to its status on Yom Kippur after Israel came into *Eretz Yisrael*, in that the cloud of glory was continuously present. Later, this was only true on Yom Kippur. Hence, these rituals (arranging the lamps and burning the incense) were only performed by the *Kohen Gadol* during their sojourn in the wilderness, for only he was permitted to perform these services on Yom Kippur.

5. וְלָקַחְתָּ סֹלֶת — *And you shall take fine flour.* Compare the *Sforno's* commentary here to his commentary on verse 2 and the notes there.

15-16. כִּי יְקַלֵּל אֱלֹהָיו וְנָשָׂא חֶטְאוֹ: וְנֹקֵב שֵׁם ה׳ מוֹת יוּמָת . . . כַּגֵּר כָּאֶזְרָח — *Whosoever curses his God*

יז כַּגֵּר כָּאֶזְרָח בְּנָקְבוֹ שֵׁם יוּמָת: וְאִישׁ כִּי יַכֶּה כָּל־נֶפֶשׁ אָדָם מוֹת יוּמָת:
יח־יט וּמַכֵּה נֶפֶשׁ־בְּהֵמָה יְשַׁלְּמֶנָּה נֶפֶשׁ תַּחַת נָפֶשׁ: וְאִישׁ כִּי־יִתֵּן מוּם בַּעֲמִיתוֹ
כ כַּאֲשֶׁר עָשָׂה כֵּן יֵעָשֶׂה לּוֹ: שֶׁבֶר תַּחַת שֶׁבֶר עַיִן תַּחַת עַיִן שֵׁן תַּחַת שֵׁן
מפטיר כא כַּאֲשֶׁר יִתֵּן מוּם בָּאָדָם כֵּן יִנָּתֶן בּוֹ: וּמַכֵּה בְהֵמָה יְשַׁלְּמֶנָּה וּמַכֵּה אָדָם
כב יוּמָת: מִשְׁפַּט אֶחָד יִהְיֶה לָכֶם כַּגֵּר כָּאֶזְרָח יִהְיֶה כִּי אֲנִי יהוה אֱלֹהֵיכֶם:
כג וַיְדַבֵּר מֹשֶׁה אֶל־בְּנֵי יִשְׂרָאֵל וַיּוֹצִיאוּ אֶת־הַמְקַלֵּל אֶל־מִחוּץ לַמַּחֲנֶה
וַיִּרְגְּמוּ אֹתוֹ אָבֶן וּבְנֵי־יִשְׂרָאֵל עָשׂוּ כַּאֲשֶׁר צִוָּה יהוה אֶת־מֹשֶׁה:

---

put to death. But the punishment for one who blasphemes the Name of God shall not be the same as for one who curses other אֱלֹהִים, *judges*, nor shall it be from the same category of punishment, even though their number is great (i.e., he cursed many judges); (rather) it shall be the death penalty.

כַּגֵּר כָּאֶזְרָח — *As well for the stranger as for the homeborn* (*citizen*). This punishment now being given to this blasphemer is not because he is a stranger (i.e., the son of an Egyptian), for a native (Israelite) would be equal to him in this instance, were he to blaspheme the Name.

17. וְאִישׁ כִּי יַכֶּה כָּל נֶפֶשׁ אָדָם — *And a man that smites any person mortally.* Being that blasphemy among some (heathen) nations is treated most lightly, as it says, וְהִתְקַצַּף וְקִלֵּל בְּמַלְכּוֹ וּבֵאלֹהָיו, *They shall become angry and curse their king and their god* (*Isaiah* 8:21), and as (our Sages) say, "If one hears God's Name pronounced by a heathen (in a blasphemous manner) he is not obligated to rent his garment, for were (the law) so, one's garment would be totally rent" (*Sanhedrin* 60a), hence, considering this, it would appear that the words of the blasphemer should be considered null and void since every curse is as naught relative to the existence of God, the Blessed One. (The Torah, however,) explains the reason (for the severe punishment exacted) thus: When the "subject" (really the object) of an evil act varies, even though the act is the same, the punishment (for that act) varies (also) according to the standing of the particular subject so that the punishment for a sin in certain cases will be physical punishment or capital punishment, whereas in other cases where the subject is inferior, the punishment is monetary compensation. (The Torah proceeds) to give three examples (lit., proofs): Firstly, regarding killing; if one murders a man, he receives the death penalty whereas if he kills his friend's animal, he is only liable to monetary payment. Secondly, regarding injury; if one injures (another) person it would

NOTES

shall bear his sin. And he that blasphemes the Name of HASHEM *shall surely be put to death . . . as well for the stranger as for the homeborn* (*citizen*). The *Sforno* in his commentary on *Genesis* 1:1 explains that the word אֱלֹהִים, at times, means *judges*. He also interprets the phrase אֱלֹהִים לֹא תְקַלֵּל as meaning *you shall not curse the judges* (*Exodus* 22:27). The meaning, therefore, of these two verses is: He who reviles a judge, or even a number of judges, shall be punished in accordance with the laws of damages which cover בֹּשֶׁת (the shaming or embarrassing of another person). The Talmud teaches us that these damages are determined according to the status of both the מְבַיֵּישׁ וּמִתְבַּיֵּישׁ, *the one who shames and the one embarrassed* (*Bava Kamma* 83b). This is the meaning of the ambiguous term *he shall bear his sin*, for the Torah cannot be exact or precise in this kind of case. However, if one blasphemes God, Who is (also) called אֱלֹהִים (God), his punishment is far more severe. He shall be put to death, whether he is a native Israelite or a proselyte.

17. וְאִישׁ כִּי יַכֶּה כָּל נֶפֶשׁ אָדָם — *And a man that smites any person mortally.* The *Sforno* explains the linkage and continuity of verses 15-21 which, at first reading, is most difficult to comprehend. What connection is there between the laws of murder and damages with cursing and blasphemy? The *Sforno*, however, explains the meaning of these verses as follows: Although the heathens treated blasphemy most lightly, the Torah demands the death penalty for this grave sin. This is not because a man's curse in any way diminishes

proselyte and native alike, when he blasphemes the Name, he shall be put to death.

[17] *And a man — if he strikes mortally any human life, he shall be put to death.* [18] *And a man who strikes mortally an animal life shall make restitution, a life for a life.* [19] *And if a man inflicts a wound in his fellow, as he did, so shall be done to him:* [20] *a break for a break, an eye for an eye, a tooth for a tooth; just as he will have inflicted a wound on a person, so shall be inflicted upon him.* [21] *One who strikes an animal shall make restitution, and one who strikes a person shall be put to death.* [22] *There shall be one law for you, it shall be for proselyte and native alike, for I, HASHEM, am your God.*

[23] *Moses spoke to the Children of Israel, and they took the blasphemer to the outside of the camp, and they stoned him to death; and the Children of Israel did as HASHEM had commanded Moses.*

---

have been proper to punish him physically were it not for our inability to measure precisely (the degree of punishment), as our Sages learn from tradition (*Bava Kamma* 84a); therefore, it is necessary to (substitute) monetary punishment. The payment, however, is considerable since one is obligated to pay five items (damages, suffering, medical costs, forced unemployment and shame), as (our Sages) learned from tradition. (However,) if one injures an animal, minimal monetary payment shall be his punishment. The third (proof) is in the case of inflicting injury on a person. If one injures his father or his mother, he is liable to capital punishment, whereas when one injures another man he is obligated to compensate (him) monetarily, and certainly if one inflicts injury on an animal, his punishment is quite minimal. (The Torah) does not mention the cursing of a father or mother because it is dissimilar to this curse (blasphemy) which is a totally ineffective statement, unlike the cursing of (one's) father.

22. כַּגֵּר כָּאֶזְרָח יִהְיֶה — *As well for the stranger as for the homeborn it shall be . . .* because *I am HASHEM your God,* the God of the stranger and the God of the citizen (as it says), וְלֹא נִכַּר שׁוֹעַ לִפְנֵי דָל, *Nor regards the rich more than the poor* (*Job* 34:19).

23. וּבְנֵי יִשְׂרָאֵל עָשׂוּ כַּאֲשֶׁר צִוָּה ה׳ אֶת מֹשֶׁה — *And the Children of Israel did as HASHEM commanded Moses.* They did not stone him due to hatred because he was a stranger who quarreled with a citizen, but they did so to fulfill the commandment (of God).

NOTES

God's honor, but since the object of his blasphemy is God, this sinful act is extremely serious and is therefore punishable by death. The Torah then proceeds to show how a similar injurious act calls for the imposition of different degrees of punishment, depending upon the one towards whom that action is directed. For example, whether one kills a man or an animal, the means (i.e., the act of violence) and the end are the same, but a different punishment is imposed in each case, as is true when one injures a man as opposed to an animal. Parenthetically, the *Sforno* explains that the *lex talionis* (an eye for an eye, etc.) was interpreted by our Sages as meaning monetary compensation because it would be impossible to inflict *exactly* the same degree of physical damage upon the perpetrator as that suffered by the victim, and the consequences could also be far different, depending upon the person's physical condition. The *Sforno* also explains why cursing one's parent is omitted here. It is precisely because these verses speak of blasphemy regarding God that the Torah does not choose to discuss the cursing of one's parents, so as to differentiate between the two.

22. כַּגֵּר כָּאֶזְרָח יִהְיֶה — *As well for the stranger as for the homeborn it shall be . . .* Although the nature of the punishment varies with different sinful acts, the law itself applies equally to the citizen and the stranger.

23. וּבְנֵי יִשְׂרָאֵל עָשׂוּ כַּאֲשֶׁר צִוָּה ה׳ אֶת מֹשֶׁה — *And the Children of Israel did as HASHEM commanded Moses.* The Torah stresses the motivation of the people when they executed the sinner. It was not inspired by hatred but by a desire to carry out the law.

פרשת בהר

כה א־ב וַיְדַבֵּר יהוה אֶל־מֹשֶׁה בְּהַר סִינַי לֵאמֹר: דַּבֵּר אֶל־בְּנֵי יִשְׂרָאֵל וְאָמַרְתָּ
אֲלֵהֶם כִּי תָבֹאוּ אֶל־הָאָרֶץ אֲשֶׁר אֲנִי נֹתֵן לָכֶם וְשָׁבְתָה הָאָרֶץ שַׁבָּת
ג לַיהוה: שֵׁשׁ שָׁנִים תִּזְרַע שָׂדֶךָ וְשֵׁשׁ שָׁנִים תִּזְמֹר כַּרְמֶךָ וְאָסַפְתָּ
ד אֶת־תְּבוּאָתָהּ: וּבַשָּׁנָה הַשְּׁבִיעִת שַׁבַּת שַׁבָּתוֹן יִהְיֶה לָאָרֶץ שַׁבָּת
ה לַיהוה שָׂדְךָ לֹא תִזְרָע וְכַרְמְךָ לֹא תִזְמֹר: אֵת סְפִיחַ קְצִירְךָ לֹא
תִקְצוֹר וְאֶת־עִנְּבֵי נְזִירֶךָ לֹא תִבְצֹר שְׁנַת שַׁבָּתוֹן יִהְיֶה לָאָרֶץ:
ו וְהָיְתָה שַׁבַּת הָאָרֶץ לָכֶם לְאָכְלָה לְךָ וּלְעַבְדְּךָ וְלַאֲמָתֶךָ וְלִשְׂכִירְךָ
ז וּלְתוֹשָׁבְךָ הַגָּרִים עִמָּךְ: וְלִבְהֶמְתְּךָ וְלַחַיָּה אֲשֶׁר בְּאַרְצֶךָ תִּהְיֶה
ח כָל־תְּבוּאָתָהּ לֶאֱכֹל: וְסָפַרְתָּ לְךָ שֶׁבַע שַׁבְּתֹת שָׁנִים שֶׁבַע

XXV

1. וַיְדַבֵּר ה׳ אֶל מֹשֶׁה בְּהַר סִינַי — *And HASHEM spoke to Moses on Mount Sinai.* Consider that the Torah does not mention the place where any commandment was given unless something unique (lit., new) occurred at that place. However, (here the verse) explains that when God, the Exalted One, said at Sinai, וְהַשְּׁבִיעִת תִּשְׁמְטֶנָּה וּנְטַשְׁתָּהּ וְאָכְלוּ אֶבְיֹנֵי עַמֶּךָ וְיִתְרָם וכו׳, *But the seventh year you shall let it rest and lie fallow, that the poor of your people may eat; and what they leave,* etc. (*Exodus* 23:11), He explained to Moses all the laws of the Seventh Year which were set forth (lit., said) here. This is to teach (us) and to make us understand that likewise, with all other *mitzvos,* although there is little written regarding some of them, the explanation (however) is broad and well explained, as our Sages say, "What connection is there between the *Shemittah* (Sabbatical year) and Mt. Sinai? (It comes to teach us) that just as (this law of) *Shemittah* was told to us at Sinai with its general rules, minute details and explanations, so all the commandments were told (to us) at Sinai with their general rules, minute details and explanations" (*Sifra*).

Now, Moses our Teacher mentions this chapter here because he thought that they would immediately enter the Land, as he stated (lit., testified) saying, נֹסְעִים אֲנַחְנוּ אֶל הַמָּקוֹם, *We are journeying to the place* (*Numbers* 10:29). He (therefore) is particularly careful to emphasize the resting of the Land, for if they were to transgress in the matter of this observance they would be exiled from it, as the (Torah) testifies, saying, *Then shall the land appease* (the wrath of God) *for the neglect of her Sabbaths* (*Leviticus* 26:34), and so it is (also) testified to at the end of *Chronicles,* where it says, עַד רָצְתָה הָאָרֶץ אֶת שַׁבְּתוֹתֶיהָ, *Until the Land had been appeased (paid) for her Sabbaths* (*II Chronicles* 36:21).

NOTES

XXV

1. וַיְדַבֵּר ה׳ אֶל מֹשֶׁה בְּהַר סִינַי — *And HASHEM spoke to Moses on Mount Sinai.* Similar to *Rashi* in his commentary on this verse based upon the *Sifra,* the *Sforno* explains why the Torah specifies the location where God spoke to Moses. תּוֹרָה שֶׁבִּכְתָב, the *Written Torah,* is presented in somewhat of a shorthand fashion. It is the תּוֹרָה שֶׁבְּעַל פֶּה, the *Oral Torah,* which elaborates upon the *Written Torah,* filling in the missing pieces, so to speak, of what is implied in its brief, succinct words. Hence, what was done regarding the detailed laws of the Sabbatical year is true of all other commandments as well.

The *Sforno* adds an additional point beyond that which was mentioned in *Rashi's* commentary. He states that the reason Moses placed this chapter toward the end of *Leviticus,* which is the concluding section that discusses the commandments given to Moses at Mt. Sinai (see 27:34), is because he believed that Israel was on the threshold of entering the Land. Moses understood that the way in which to insure their continued stay in *Eretz Yisrael* was to observe the laws of the Sabbatical year, as is indicated in the verses in *Leviticus* and *Chronicles* quoted by the *Sforno.*

2. כִּי תָבֹאוּ אֶל הָאָרֶץ — *When you come into the land.* The area mentioned by the *Sforno* refers to the land first conquered by the Israelites after crossing the

PARASHAS BEHAR

25 [1] *HASHEM spoke to Moses on Mount Sinai, saying: [2] Speak to the
Children of Israel and say to them: When you come into the land that
I give you, the land shall observe a Sabbath rest for HASHEM. [3] For six years
you may sow your field and for six years you may prune your vineyard;
and you may gather in its crop. [4] But the seventh year shall be a complete
rest for the land, a Sabbath for HASHEM; your field you shall not sow and
your vineyard you shall not prune. [5] The aftergrowth of your harvest you
shall not reap and the grapes you had set aside for yourself you shall not
pick; it shall be a year of rest for the land. [6] The Sabbath produce of the land
shall be yours to eat, for you, for your slave, and for your maidservant; and
for your laborer and for your resident who dwell with you. [7] And for your
animal and for the beast that is in your land shall all its crop be to eat.
[8] You shall count for yourself seven cycles of sabbatical years, seven*

---

2. כִּי תָבֹאוּ אֶל הָאָרֶץ — *When you come into the land . . .* to גְּלִיל הַגּוֹיִם, *the district of nations* (based on *Isaiah* 8:23).

וְשָׁבְתָה הָאָרֶץ — *And the land shall rest . . .* those lands which are prepared for agricultural work.

שַׁבָּת לַה׳ — *A Sabbath to HASHEM.* The entire year, which shall be devoid of agricultural work, will (instead) be one devoted to His service, as was the intent of the Sabbath of *Bereishis* (*Genesis*) as it says, שַׁבָּת לַה׳ אֱלֹהֶיךָ, *A Sabbath to HASHEM your God* (*Exodus* 20:10).

3. שֵׁשׁ שָׁנִים תִּזְרַע שָׂדֶךָ — *Six years shall you sow your field.* You will then be able to plant the same field for six consecutive years, unlike the usual practice of agricultural labor which is to allow (a field) to lie fallow one year and plant it the next year, as mentioned by our Sages (*Bava Basra* 36b).

וְאָסַפְתָּ אֶת תְּבוּאָתָהּ — *And gather in its produce . . .* unlike the usual tendency of agricultural labor whereby if the same portion (field) is planted in consecutive years it loses its productivity (lit., no longer gives of its strength).

4. שַׁבַּת שַׁבָּתוֹן יִהְיֶה לָאָרֶץ — *A Sabbath of Sabbaths shall it be to the Land . . .* including, as well, all agricultural preparations such as besmearing the saplings, and smearing (with oil) and piercing unripe figs and other fruits, as mentioned by our Sages (*Avodah Zarah* 50b).

שַׁבָּת לַה׳ — *A Sabbath to HASHEM.* Landworkers, who will rest during that year, will also be awakened (aroused) to seek God in some manner.

NOTES

Jordan River. The land on the east bank of the river (עֵבֶר הַיַּרְדֵּן — *Trans-Jordan*) is only Rabbinically obligated to observe the laws of the Sabbatical year and not by Torah law (see *Rambam, Mishneh Torah, Shemittah VeYovel* 4:28). The phrase הָאָרֶץ, *"the" land*, using the definite article, comes to teach this law.

שַׁבָּת לַה׳ — *A Sabbath to HASHEM.* The expression שַׁבָּת לַה׳ is used here, and again in verse 4. Here it is a general statement teaching us that the Sabbatical year is meant to be utilized to seek out and serve God, similar to the purpose of the weekly Sabbath. In verse 4, it is repeated to emphasize that even the simple land laborer whose Torah knowledge is minimal will also be afforded the opportunity to seek God on his own simple level.

3. שֵׁשׁ שָׁנִים תִּזְרַע שָׂדֶךָ — *Six years shall you sow your field.* The Torah assures Israel that if the laws of *Shemittah* are kept, the fields will not lose their productivity even though they will be sown for six consecutive years rather than alternately, as was common agricultural practice.

4. שַׁבַּת שַׁבָּתוֹן — *A Sabbath of Sabbaths.* The expression שַׁבַּת שַׁבָּתוֹן, which is translated *a Sabbath of Sabbaths* or *a Sabbath of solemn rest*, is used here to indicate *absolute* rest, i.e., cessation of all agricultural work and commercial use of the produce yielded by the fields.

שְׁנִים שֶׁבַע פְּעָמִים וְהָיוּ לְךָ יְמֵי שֶׁבַע שַׁבְּתֹת הַשָּׁנִים תֵּשַׁע וְאַרְבָּעִים שָׁנָה:
ט וְהַעֲבַרְתָּ שׁוֹפַר תְּרוּעָה בַּחֹדֶשׁ הַשְּׁבִעִי בֶּעָשׂוֹר לַחֹדֶשׁ בְּיוֹם הַכִּפֻּרִים
י תַּעֲבִירוּ שׁוֹפָר בְּכָל־אַרְצְכֶם: וְקִדַּשְׁתֶּם אֵת שְׁנַת הַחֲמִשִּׁים שָׁנָה וּקְרָאתֶם
דְּרוֹר בָּאָרֶץ לְכָל־יֹשְׁבֶיהָ יוֹבֵל הִוא תִּהְיֶה לָכֶם וְשַׁבְתֶּם אִישׁ אֶל־אֲחֻזָּתוֹ
יא וְאִישׁ אֶל־מִשְׁפַּחְתּוֹ תָּשֻׁבוּ: יוֹבֵל הִוא שְׁנַת הַחֲמִשִּׁים שָׁנָה תִּהְיֶה לָכֶם לֹא
יב תִזְרָעוּ וְלֹא תִקְצְרוּ אֶת־סְפִיחֶיהָ וְלֹא תִבְצְרוּ אֶת־נְזִרֶיהָ: כִּי יוֹבֵל הִוא
יג קֹדֶשׁ תִּהְיֶה לָכֶם מִן־הַשָּׂדֶה תֹּאכְלוּ אֶת־תְּבוּאָתָהּ: בִּשְׁנַת הַיּוֹבֵל הַזֹּאת
יד תָּשֻׁבוּ אִישׁ אֶל־אֲחֻזָּתוֹ: וְכִי־תִמְכְּרוּ מִמְכָּר לַעֲמִיתֶךָ אוֹ קָנֹה מִיַּד עֲמִיתֶךָ שני
טו אַל־תּוֹנוּ אִישׁ אֶת־אָחִיו: בְּמִסְפַּר שָׁנִים אַחַר הַיּוֹבֵל תִּקְנֶה מֵאֵת עֲמִיתֶךָ

8. וְהָיוּ לְךָ יְמֵי שֶׁבַע שַׁבְּתֹת הַשָּׁנִים — *And there shall be to you the days of seven Sabbaths of years.* For (determining) the Jubilee, you shall not count years according to the calculation of twelve lunar months per year, but rather include the regular as well as the intercalated (months) as ordained by the Sages, so that it (may) correspond to forty-nine solar years, as this undoubtedly is (also how we determine) the Sabbatical year which is linked to ploughing and sowing, as explained in (the portion of the Torah) pertaining to it.

9. שׁוֹפַר תְּרוּעָה — *The blast of the shofar . . .* (as a sign) of joy for the emancipation of the slaves and the return of fields to their (original) owners.

10. יוֹבֵל הִוא תִּהְיֶה לָכֶם — *It shall be a Jubilee to you.* You shall also be free from the servitude of the nations, as opposed to אַתֶּם לֹא שְׁמַעְתֶּם אֵלַי לִקְרֹא דְּרוֹר אִישׁ לְאָחִיו וְאִישׁ לְרֵעֵהוּ הִנְנִי קֹרֵא לָכֶם דְּרוֹר נְאֻם ה׳ אֶל הַחֶרֶב אֶל הַדֶּבֶר וְאֶל הָרָעָב, *"You have not hearkened to Me to proclaim liberty every man to his brother and every man to his neighbor; behold, I proclaim for you liberty," says God, "to the sword, to the pestilence and to the famine"* (*Jeremiah* 34:17).

11. יוֹבֵל הִוא שְׁנַת הַחֲמִשִּׁים שָׁנָה תִּהְיֶה לָכֶם — *A Jubilee shall the fiftieth year be to you.* Just as the land was liberated from the hands of the buyer, so shall it not be controlled by the returning owners, i.e., they shall not make use of it during that year in the (usual) manner of owners.

12. קֹדֶשׁ תִּהְיֶה לָכֶם מִן הַשָּׂדֶה תֹּאכְלוּ — *It shall be holy to you; you shall eat from the field.* Although I have prohibited the owners to use the (field) for sowing and reaping as well as for the gathering of (its) fruit which is done in other years, as it says, *Neither reap that which grows of itself nor gather the grapes* (v. 11); (nonetheless,) I did not prohibit the

NOTES

8. וְהָיוּ לְךָ יְמֵי שֶׁבַע שַׁבְּתֹת הַשָּׁנִים — *And there shall be to you the days of seven Sabbaths of years.* The word *year* and *years* is repeated four times in this verse. This is meant to teach us that only after forty-nine complete years of solar months, and not twelve lunar months, shall the fiftieth year mark the Jubilee. The seven cycles of seven years must reflect the seasons of planting and harvesting; hence they are determined by the solar calendar, not the lunar one. The extra months of the intercalated years must therefore be included in the calculations.

10. יוֹבֵל הוּא תִּהְיֶה לָכֶם — *It shall be a Jubilee to you.* This phrase seems to be superfluous. The proclamation of liberty has been mentioned; the return of each man to his possession and to his family is also specifically noted. Hence, what is the meaning of this phrase? The *Sforno*, quoting from *Jeremiah*, explains that it refers to the national independence of Israel who will be free from onslaught of war and the ravages of famine and pestilence.

11. יוֹבֵל הִוא שְׁנַת הַחֲמִשִּׁים שָׁנָה תִּהְיֶה לָכֶם — *A Jubilee shall the fiftieth year be to you.* The *Sforno* explains why the phrase, יוֹבֵל הִוא . . . לָכֶם, *It shall be a Jubilee . . . to you,* which appears in the previous verse as well, is not superfluous or repetitious. The land which was liberated from the purchaser and returned to the original owner shall also be liberated from *his* mastery and control. Thus, the *Sforno's* interpretation is buttressed by

years seven times; the years of the seven cycles of sabbatical years shall be for you forty-nine years.
[9] *You shall sound a broken blast on the shofar, in the seventh month, on the tenth of the month; on the Day of Atonement you shall sound the shofar throughout your land.*
[10] *You shall sanctify the fiftieth year and proclaim freedom throughout the land for all its inhabitants; it shall be the Jubilee Year for you, you shall return each man to his ancestral heritage and you shall return each man to his family.*
[11] *It shall be a Jubilee Year for you — this fiftieth year — you shall not sow, you shall not harvest its aftergrowth and you shall not pick what was set aside of it for yourself.*
[12] *For it is a Jubilee Year, it shall be holy to you; from the field you may eat its crop.*
[13] *In this Jubilee Year you shall return each man to his ancestral heritage.*

[14] *When you make a sale to your fellow or make a purchase from the hand of your fellow, do not aggrieve one another.*
[15] *According to the number of years after the Jubilee Year shall you buy from your fellow;*

---

eating of the fruit by the owners. They are permitted to partake like everyone else, just as in the Sabbatical year.

13. תָּשֻׁבוּ אִישׁ אֶל אֲחֻזָּתוֹ — *Every man shall return to his possession.* The returning owner is permitted to take possession of (the land) and use it to build houses, dovecotes, sheep enclosures and other (structures), but not for agricultural work (of the field) and guarding its fruit.

14. וְכִי תִמְכְּרוּ — *And if you sell.* There shall be no kind of deceit in any transaction (lit., sale), as (our Sages) state, "One must not pick out the refuse from the top of the bin, because its only purpose is to deceive the eye" (*Bava Metzia* 60a).

אוֹ קָנֹה — *Or buy* . . . when the seller is not aware of the value of the article, even though it was in his possession (lit., hand) and he had time to show it to a merchant or his relative.

אַל תּוֹנוּ — *Do not deceive.* Although (our Sages) taught us that deceit does not apply to land (*Kesubos* 99b), nonetheless . . .

15. בְּמִסְפַּר שָׁנִים . . . תִּקְנֶה — *According to the number of the years . . . you shall buy.* There must not be any deceit regarding the number of the years (till the Jubilee), as (our Sages) say, "Any (fraud) in measure, weight or number, even if less than the standard of אוֹנָאָה, *deceit*, one can withdraw" (*Bava Metzia* 56b).

NOTES

the concluding portion of this verse, *you shall not sow, neither reap . . . nor gather, etc.* Consequently there are two consecutive rest years, the forty-ninth, which is *Shemittah* and the fiftieth, which is the Jubilee.

12. קֹדֶשׁ תִּהְיֶה לָכֶם מִן הַשָּׂדֶה תֹּאכְלוּ — *It shall be holy to you; you shall eat from the field.* The *Sforno* interprets this verse to mean: Although the produce of this year has a status of "holiness," nonetheless, it may be eaten by the owners, and others as well.

13. תָּשֻׁבוּ אִישׁ אֶל אֲחֻזָּתוֹ — *Every man shall return to his possession.* Since, as explained in verse 11, the original owner is not permitted to use the land for agricultural purposes during the Jubilee year, then in what way does he *return to his possession*? The answer given by the *Sforno* is that he will *return to his possession* in the sense that he will be able to build various types of structures there.

14. וְכִי תִמְכְּרוּ . . . אוֹ קָנֹה . . . אַל תּוֹנוּ — *And if you sell . . . or buy . . . do not deceive.* The law cited by the *Sforno* from *Bava Metzia* 60a prohibits the seller to pick out the refuse from the top of the bin and mix it in with the grain beneath, for this is patently deceptive. By the same token, the Torah cautions the buyer not to take unfair advantage of the seller's lack of knowledge regarding the true value of the article he is selling.

15. בְּמִסְפַּר שָׁנִים . . . תִּקְנֶה — *According to the number of the years . . . you shall buy.* The *Sforno* links this verse with the preceding one. At the

טז בְּמִסְפַּ֣ר שָׁנֵ֣י־תְבוּאֹ֔ת יִמְכָּר־לָֽךְ: לְפִ֣י | רֹ֣ב הַשָּׁנִ֗ים תַּרְבֶּה֙ מִקְנָת֔וֹ וּלְפִי֙

יז מְעֹ֣ט הַשָּׁנִ֔ים תַּמְעִ֖יט מִקְנָת֑וֹ כִּ֚י מִסְפַּ֣ר תְּבוּאֹ֔ת ה֥וּא מֹכֵ֖ר לָֽךְ: וְלֹ֤א

יח תוֹנוּ֙ אִ֣ישׁ אֶת־עֲמִית֔וֹ וְיָרֵ֖אתָ מֵֽאֱלֹהֶ֑יךָ כִּ֛י אֲנִ֥י יהו֖ה אֱלֹֽהֵיכֶֽם: וַעֲשִׂיתֶם֙

אֶת־חֻקֹּתַ֗י וְאֶת־מִשְׁפָּטַ֛י תִּשְׁמְר֖וּ וַעֲשִׂיתֶ֣ם אֹתָ֑ם וִֽישַׁבְתֶּ֥ם עַל־הָאָ֖רֶץ

שלישי [שני] יט לָבֶֽטַח: וְנָתְנָ֤ה הָאָ֨רֶץ֙ פִּרְיָ֔הּ וַאֲכַלְתֶּ֖ם לָשֹׂ֑בַע וִֽישַׁבְתֶּ֥ם לָבֶ֖טַח עָלֶֽיהָ:

כ וְכִ֣י תֹאמְר֔וּ מַה־נֹּאכַ֖ל בַּשָּׁנָ֣ה הַשְּׁבִיעִ֑ת הֵ֚ן לֹ֣א נִזְרָ֔ע וְלֹ֥א נֶאֱסֹ֖ף אֶת־

כא תְּבוּאָתֵֽנוּ: וְצִוִּ֤יתִי אֶת־בִּרְכָתִי֙ לָכֶ֔ם בַּשָּׁנָ֖ה הַשִּׁשִּׁ֑ית וְעָשָׂת֙ אֶת־

כב הַתְּבוּאָ֔ה לִשְׁלֹ֖שׁ הַשָּׁנִֽים: וּזְרַעְתֶּ֗ם אֵ֚ת הַשָּׁנָ֣ה הַשְּׁמִינִ֔ת וַאֲכַלְתֶּ֖ם

מִן־הַתְּבוּאָ֣ה יָשָׁ֑ן עַ֣ד | הַשָּׁנָ֣ה הַתְּשִׁיעִ֗ת עַד־בּוֹא֙ תְּבֽוּאָתָ֔הּ תֹּאכְל֖וּ יָשָֽׁן:

אַחַר הַיּוֹבֵל תִּקְנֶה — *After the Jubilee you shall buy.* For it is improper to buy land during the Jubilee year in a manner which will, at times, result in depriving the returning owners any time (to possess it), and hence it will be as though they never returned to their possession at all.

שְׁנֵי תְבוּאֹת — *Years of the crops . . .* but not years of blast or drought, as is the case (lit., law) with leasing or tenancy (of land).

16. תַּרְבֶּה מִקְנָתוֹ — *You shall increase the price thereof.* You shall buy it for a higher (price) than one would pay for leasing it on a yearly basis, because, indeed, when one buys it many years prior to the Jubilee, during that time he can construct there sheep enclosures, dovecotes and similar (structures), besides (using its) produce.

תַּמְעִיט מִקְנָתוֹ — *You shall diminish its price.* You shall not buy according to the calculation of one who leases, and certainly not of a short-term buyer (lit., a few years), the reason being . . .

כִּי מִסְפַּר תְּבוּאֹת הוּא מֹכֵר לָךְ — *For according to the amount of produce he sells it to you . . .* because when you buy it for a few years you can only use it for its produce, and may not (plant) that which impoverishes the land, (that is) in a manner which does not permit the field to regain its strength (productivity) when it reverts to its owner, as (our Sages) say, "If a man leases a field for but a few years, he must not sow it with flax" (*Bava Metzia* 109a).

17. וְלֹא תוֹנוּ — *And you shall not wrong . . .* even through speech, (or) misleading (lit., stealth of mind) information or improper advice, although there is no money at stake.

כִּי אֲנִי ה' אֱלֹהֵיכֶם — *For I am* HASHEM *your God.* The God of the buyer and the God of the seller and I object to the wronging of either of them.

NOTES

conclusion of verse 14, he comments that although the law of אוֹנָאָה, *overreaching*, does not apply to fields or land (קַרְקַע), nonetheless, the Torah admonishes one, upon establishing the sale price of his field, to take into consideration the amount of years left till the Jubilee. The reason, he explains, is because we are dealing with the amount of time that the buyer can enjoy the use of the field, and that which is numbered or measured (דָּבָר שֶׁבְּמִנְיָן) is, without exception, covered by the law of (וּבְמִדָּה) אוֹנָאָה, *overreaching*. Therefore, if the buyer is unaware of the number of years until the Jubilee, this knowledge must be shared with him.

אַחַר הַיּוֹבֵל תִּקְנֶה — *After the Jubilee you shall buy.* Were the Torah merely telling us here to set a fair

price for the field by calculating the number of years that the field will remain in the hands of the buyer, it would have stated עַד, *until*, not אַחַר, *after*. The choice of the word אַחַר implies that one should only purchase land *after* the Jubilee, not during it, for the reason given by the *Sforno*.

16. תַּרְבֶּה מִקְנָתוֹ . . . תַּמְעִיט מִקְנָתוֹ — *You shall increase the price thereof . . . you shall diminish its price.* Increasing or diminishing the price is not to be understood only as reflecting the number of years that the buyer will be able to use the field. It also is to be understood relative to the amount normally paid for leasing a similar field. Purchase, as compared to leasing, makes for less restrictions while offering greater opportunity for the buyer if

according to the number of crop-years shall he sell to you. [16] *According to the greater number of years shall you increase its price, and according to the lesser number of years shall you decrease its price; for he is selling you the number of crops.*

[17] *Each of you shall not aggrieve his fellow, and you shall fear your God; for I am* HASHEM, *your God.*

[18] *You shall perform My decrees, and observe My ordinances and perform them; then you shall dwell securely on the land.*

[19] *The land will give its fruit and you will eat your fill; you will dwell securely upon it.* [20] *If you will say: What will we eat in the seventh year? — behold! we will not sow and not gather in our crops!* [21] *I will ordain My blessing for you in the sixth year and it will yield a crop sufficient for the three-year period.* [22] *You will sow in the eighth year, but you will eat from the old crop; until the ninth year, until the arrival of its crop, you will eat the old.*

---

18. וַעֲשִׂיתֶם אֶת חֻקֹּתַי — *And you shall do My statutes* ... in the matter of the Sabbatical year and the Jubilee.

וְאֶת מִשְׁפָּטַי תִּשְׁמְרוּ — *And keep My ordinances* ... (in the) matter of selling and buying according to the number (of years till) the Jubilee, and similar matters, that there be no deceit.

וִישַׁבְתֶּם עַל הָאָרֶץ לָבֶטַח — *And you shall dwell in the land in safety* ... so that you won't be exiled from it, as opposed to *And the land shall be paid her Sabbaths* (26:43), and to בַּעֲוֹן בִּצְעוֹ קָצַפְתִּי, *For the iniquity of his unjust gain I was angered* (*Isaiah* 57:17).

19. וַאֲכַלְתֶּם לָשֹׂבַע — *And you shall eat until you are satiated.* The fruits' nutritional value shall be plentiful, similar to the measures (of manna) which sufficed for adult and child alike, as (our Sages) state, "One eats a little and it is blessed in his intestines" (*Sifra*), (so that) the produce of the sixth year will suffice also for the seventh.

וִישַׁבְתֶּם לָבֶטַח עָלֶיהָ — *And dwell therein in safety.* You will not bear the shame of hunger among the nations for you will not have to travel to their lands to buy produce.

20. וְכִי תֹאמְרוּ מַה נֹּאכַל — *And if you shall say, "What shall we eat?"* Now, if you will doubt this assurance and will not trust (the promise) that the small (amount of food) will satisfy qualitatively ...

21. וְעָשָׂת אֶת הַתְּבוּאָה — *And it shall bring forth grain* ... in such a manner as to satisfy (your) eye from what it sees, and (you) shall see that the quantity is sufficient.

NOTES

it is bought for a long period, and greater restrictions with lesser opportunity if purchased for a shorter period. All this must be taken into consideration when the purchase price is set.

18. וַעֲשִׂיתֶם אֶת חֻקֹּתַי וְאֶת מִשְׁפָּטַי תִּשְׁמְרוּ — *And you shall do My statutes and keep My ordinances.* A חֹק, *statute,* is a law enacted by God which is not always understood by man's limited reasoning. A מִשְׁפָּט, *ordinance,* is that which appears logical and reasonable. Hence, the *Sforno* interprets the phrase *My statutes* as referring to the laws of *Shemittah* and Jubilee, whereas *My ordinances* refer to the prohibition against אוֹנָאָה, *deceit.*

18-19. וִישַׁבְתֶּם עַל הָאָרֶץ לָבֶטַח ... וִישַׁבְתֶּם לָבֶטַח עָלֶיהָ — *And you shall dwell in the land in safety ... and dwell therein in safety.* The assurance that Israel shall dwell on its land in safety (לָבֶטַח) as a reward for observing the aforementioned laws is repeated twice in these two verses. The *Sforno* explains that the first refers to national security while the second is a promise of economic stability.

20-21. וְכִי תֹאמְרוּ מַה נֹּאכַל ... וְעָשָׂת אֶת הַתְּבוּאָה — *And if you shall say, "What shall we eat ...?" ... and it shall bring forth grain.* To the person of faith, God's assurance that the earth will yield enough produce to nourish Israel for the sixth, seventh and eighth years is sufficient. However, if one lacks faith in the Almighty, asking, "What shall we eat?", it is necessary to *show* him that there is enough to satisfy his needs. God will grant him the ability to see that the seemingly small quantity contains a lot!

כג וְהָאָרֶץ לֹא תִמָּכֵר לִצְמִתֻת כִּי־לִי הָאָרֶץ כִּי־גֵרִים וְתוֹשָׁבִים אַתֶּם
*רביעי כד־כה עִמָּדִי: וּבְכֹל אֶרֶץ אֲחֻזַּתְכֶם גְּאֻלָּה תִּתְּנוּ לָאָרֶץ: *כִּי־יָמוּךְ
אָחִיךָ וּמָכַר מֵאֲחֻזָּתוֹ וּבָא גֹאֲלוֹ הַקָּרֹב אֵלָיו וְגָאַל אֵת מִמְכַּר אָחִיו:
כו־כז וְאִישׁ כִּי לֹא יִהְיֶה־לּוֹ גֹּאֵל וְהִשִּׂיגָה יָדוֹ וּמָצָא כְּדֵי גְאֻלָּתוֹ: וְחִשַּׁב
אֶת־שְׁנֵי מִמְכָּרוֹ וְהֵשִׁיב אֶת־הָעֹדֵף לָאִישׁ אֲשֶׁר מָכַר־לוֹ וְשָׁב לַאֲחֻזָּתוֹ:
כח וְאִם לֹא־מָצְאָה יָדוֹ דֵּי הָשִׁיב לוֹ וְהָיָה מִמְכָּרוֹ בְּיַד הַקֹּנֶה אֹתוֹ עַד שְׁנַת
חמישי [שלישי] כט הַיּוֹבֵל וְיָצָא בַּיֹּבֵל וְשָׁב לַאֲחֻזָּתוֹ: וְאִישׁ כִּי־יִמְכֹּר בֵּית־
מוֹשַׁב עִיר חוֹמָה וְהָיְתָה גְּאֻלָּתוֹ עַד־תֹּם שְׁנַת מִמְכָּרוֹ יָמִים תִּהְיֶה
ל גְאֻלָּתוֹ: וְאִם לֹא־יִגָּאֵל עַד־מְלֹאת לוֹ שָׁנָה תְמִימָה וְקָם הַבַּיִת אֲשֶׁר־
°לוֹ ק׳ בָּעִיר אֲשֶׁר־°לֹא חֹמָה לַצְּמִיתֻת לַקֹּנֶה אֹתוֹ לְדֹרֹתָיו לֹא יֵצֵא בַּיֹּבֵל:
לא וּבָתֵּי הַחֲצֵרִים אֲשֶׁר אֵין־לָהֶם חֹמָה סָבִיב עַל־שְׂדֵה הָאָרֶץ יֵחָשֵׁב גְּאֻלָּה
לב תִּהְיֶה־לּוֹ וּבַיֹּבֵל יֵצֵא: וְעָרֵי הַלְוִיִּם בָּתֵּי עָרֵי אֲחֻזָּתָם גְּאֻלַּת עוֹלָם תִּהְיֶה
לג לַלְוִיִּם: וַאֲשֶׁר יִגְאַל מִן־הַלְוִיִּם וְיָצָא מִמְכַּר־בַּיִת וְעִיר אֲחֻזָּתוֹ בַּיֹּבֵל כִּי
לד בָתֵּי עָרֵי הַלְוִיִּם הִוא אֲחֻזָּתָם בְּתוֹךְ בְּנֵי יִשְׂרָאֵל: וּשְׂדֵה מִגְרַשׁ עָרֵיהֶם
לה לֹא יִמָּכֵר כִּי־אֲחֻזַּת עוֹלָם הוּא לָהֶם: וְכִי־יָמוּךְ אָחִיךָ
לו וּמָטָה יָדוֹ עִמָּךְ וְהֶחֱזַקְתָּ בּוֹ גֵּר וְתוֹשָׁב וָחַי עִמָּךְ: אַל־תִּקַּח מֵאִתּוֹ
לז נֶשֶׁךְ וְתַרְבִּית וְיָרֵאתָ מֵאֱלֹהֶיךָ וְחֵי אָחִיךָ עִמָּךְ: אֶת־כַּסְפְּךָ לֹא־תִתֵּן
לח לוֹ בְּנֶשֶׁךְ וּבְמַרְבִּית לֹא־תִתֵּן אָכְלֶךָ: אֲנִי יהוה אֱלֹהֵיכֶם אֲשֶׁר־
הוֹצֵאתִי אֶתְכֶם מֵאֶרֶץ מִצְרָיִם לָתֵת לָכֶם אֶת־אֶרֶץ כְּנַעַן לִהְיוֹת לָכֶם
ששי [רביעי] לט לֵאלֹהִים: וְכִי־יָמוּךְ אָחִיךָ עִמָּךְ וְנִמְכַּר־לָךְ לֹא־תַעֲבֹד בּוֹ
מ עֲבֹדַת עָבֶד: כְּשָׂכִיר כְּתוֹשָׁב יִהְיֶה עִמָּךְ עַד־שְׁנַת הַיֹּבֵל יַעֲבֹד עִמָּךְ:

23. וְהָאָרֶץ לֹא תִמָּכֵר לִצְמִתֻת — *And the land shall not be sold in perpetuity* . . . i.e., land that is cultivated.

כִּי לִי הָאָרֶץ — *For the Land is Mine.* This region (i.e., *Eretz Yisrael*) is the land of God. כִּי גֵרִים וְתוֹשָׁבִים אַתֶּם עִמָּדִי — *For you are strangers and settlers with Me* . . . in that region, for it is not included in the general principle of וְהָאָרֶץ נָתַן לִבְנֵי אָדָם, *But the earth He has given to mankind* (*Psalms* 115:16).

24. וּבְכֹל אֶרֶץ אֲחֻזַּתְכֶם גְּאֻלָּה תִּתְּנוּ לָאָרֶץ — *And in all the land of your possession you shall grant redemption to the land.* However, outside the Land (of Israel) the laws of the Sabbatical year and the Jubilee do not apply.

35. וְהֶחֱזַקְתָּ בּוֹ — *Then you shall uphold him* . . . to support him.

36. אַל תִּקַּח מֵאִתּוֹ — *Do not take interest from him* . . . because the proper way to support him is to lend him (money) without interest or increase.

וְחֵי אָחִיךָ עִמָּךְ — *That your brother may live with you.* And you shall do this when you

NOTES

23. וְהָאָרֶץ לֹא תִמָּכֵר לִצְמִתֻת כִּי לִי הָאָרֶץ — *And the land shall not be sold in perpetuity, for the land is Mine.* The phrase הָאָרֶץ, *the land,* appears twice in this verse. The *Sforno* explains the first as meaning cultivated land which is not to be sold in perpetuity. The second refers to the unique status of *Eretz Yisrael.* Unlike other lands which God apportioned to various nations (*He set the borders of the people — Deut.* 32:8), the Land of Israel was not given to Israel unconditionally. They are *strangers and settlers* with God, Who is the true owner and master of the land called *Eretz Yisrael.* Therefore the

*23 The land shall not be sold in perpetuity, for the land is Mine; for you
are sojourners and residents with Me. 24 In the entire land of your ancestral
heritage you shall provide redemption for the land. 25 If your brother
becomes impoverished and sells part of his ancestral heritage, his redeemer
who is closest to him shall come and redeem his brother's sale. 26 If a man
will have no redeemer, but his means suffice and he acquires enough for its
redemption, 27 then he shall reckon the years of his sale and return the
remainder to the man to whom he had sold it; and he shall return to his ancestral heritage. 28 But if he does not acquire sufficient means to repay him,
then his sale shall remain in possession of its purchaser until the Jubilee
Year; in the Jubilee Year, it shall leave and return to his ancestral heritage.*

*29 If a man shall sell a residence house in a walled city, its redemption can
take place until the end of the year of its sale; its period of redemption shall
be a year. 30 But if it is not redeemed until its full year has elapsed, then the
home that is in a city that has a wall shall pass in perpetuity to the one who
purchased it, for his generations; it shall not go out in the Jubilee Year.
31 But homes in the open towns, which have no surrounding wall, shall be
considered like the land's open field; it shall have redemption, and shall go
out in the Jubilee Year. 32 As for the cities of the Levites, the homes in the
cities of their ancestral heritage, the Levites shall have an eternal right of
redemption. 33 And what one will buy from the Levites — a home that has
been sold or the city of its ancestral heritage — shall go out in the Jubilee
year; for the homes of the Levite cities, that is their ancestral heritage
among the Children of Israel! 34 But the fields of the open land of their cities
may not be sold; for it is an eternal heritage for them.*

*35 If your brother becomes impoverished and his means falter in your
proximity, you shall strengthen him — proselyte or resident — so that he
can live with you. 36 Do not take from him interest and increase; and you
shall fear your God — and let your brother live with you. 37 Do not give him
your money for interest, and do not give your food for increase. 38 I am
HASHEM, your God, Who took you out of the land of Egypt, to give you the
land of Canaan, to be God unto you.*

*39 If your brother becomes impoverished with you and is sold to you;
you shall not work him with slave labor. 40 Like a laborer or a resident
shall he be with you; until the Jubilee Year shall he work with you.*

---

have sufficient (means) for your own livelihood while (still) lending him, as (our Sages) say, "Your life takes precedence over the life of your friend" (*Bava Metzia* 62a).

38. לִהְיוֹת לָכֶם לֵאלֹהִים — *To be your God* . . . that His intended purpose be attained by all, and therefore it is proper that you organize your social and political order in such a manner that everyone can live together and assist each other so as to fulfill (God's) intent.

40. כְּשָׂכִיר כְּתוֹשָׁב יִהְיֶה עִמָּךְ — *As a hired servant and as a settler he shall be with you.*

NOTES

laws of the Sabbatical year and the Jubilee apply only to the Land of Israel itself and not to חוּץ לָאָרֶץ, *outside the Land*, as the *Sforno* explains in verse 24.

38. לִהְיוֹת לָכֶם לֵאלֹהִים — *To be your God.* The preceding verses appear in the singular form. This verse, however, appears in the plural form to indicate that only when all Jews feel responsible for one another can these laws be fulfilled and God's purpose in creating man realized.

40. כְּשָׂכִיר כְּתוֹשָׁב יִהְיֶה עִמָּךְ — *As a hired servant*

מא וְיָצָא מֵעִמָּךְ הוּא וּבָנָיו עִמּוֹ וְשָׁב אֶל־מִשְׁפַּחְתּוֹ וְאֶל־אֲחֻזַּת אֲבֹתָיו יָשׁוּב׃
מב כִּי־עֲבָדַי הֵם אֲשֶׁר־הוֹצֵאתִי אֹתָם מֵאֶרֶץ מִצְרָיִם לֹא יִמָּכְרוּ מִמְכֶּרֶת
מג־מד עָבֶד׃ לֹא־תִרְדֶּה בוֹ בְּפָרֶךְ וְיָרֵאתָ מֵאֱלֹהֶיךָ׃ וְעַבְדְּךָ וַאֲמָתְךָ אֲשֶׁר
מה יִהְיוּ־לָךְ מֵאֵת הַגּוֹיִם אֲשֶׁר סְבִיבֹתֵיכֶם מֵהֶם תִּקְנוּ עֶבֶד וְאָמָה׃ וְגַם מִבְּנֵי
הַתּוֹשָׁבִים הַגָּרִים עִמָּכֶם מֵהֶם תִּקְנוּ וּמִמִּשְׁפַּחְתָּם אֲשֶׁר עִמָּכֶם אֲשֶׁר
מו הוֹלִידוּ בְּאַרְצְכֶם וְהָיוּ לָכֶם לַאֲחֻזָּה׃ וְהִתְנַחַלְתֶּם אֹתָם לִבְנֵיכֶם אַחֲרֵיכֶם
*ב' טעמים לָרֶשֶׁת אֲחֻזָּה לְעֹלָם בָּהֶם תַּעֲבֹדוּ *וּבְאַחֵיכֶם בְּנֵי־יִשְׂרָאֵל אִישׁ בְּאָחִיו
שביעי מז לֹא־תִרְדֶּה בּוֹ בְּפָרֶךְ׃ וְכִי תַשִּׂיג יַד גֵּר וְתוֹשָׁב עִמָּךְ וּמָךְ אָחִיךָ
מח עִמּוֹ וְנִמְכַּר לְגֵר תּוֹשָׁב עִמָּךְ אוֹ לְעֵקֶר מִשְׁפַּחַת גֵּר׃ אַחֲרֵי נִמְכַּר גְּאֻלָּה
מט תִּהְיֶה־לּוֹ אֶחָד מֵאֶחָיו יִגְאָלֶנּוּ׃ אוֹ־דֹדוֹ אוֹ בֶן־דֹּדוֹ יִגְאָלֶנּוּ אוֹ־מִשְּׁאֵר
נ בְּשָׂרוֹ מִמִּשְׁפַּחְתּוֹ יִגְאָלֶנּוּ אוֹ־הִשִּׂיגָה יָדוֹ וְנִגְאָל׃ וְחִשַּׁב עִם־קֹנֵהוּ מִשְּׁנַת
הִמָּכְרוֹ לוֹ עַד שְׁנַת הַיֹּבֵל וְהָיָה כֶּסֶף מִמְכָּרוֹ בְּמִסְפַּר שָׁנִים כִּימֵי שָׂכִיר
נא יִהְיֶה עִמּוֹ׃ אִם־עוֹד רַבּוֹת בַּשָּׁנִים לְפִיהֶן יָשִׁיב גְּאֻלָּתוֹ מִכֶּסֶף מִקְנָתוֹ׃
נב וְאִם־מְעַט נִשְׁאַר בַּשָּׁנִים עַד־שְׁנַת הַיֹּבֵל וְחִשַּׁב־לוֹ כְּפִי שָׁנָיו יָשִׁיב אֶת־
נג־נד גְּאֻלָּתוֹ׃ כִּשְׂכִיר שָׁנָה בְּשָׁנָה יִהְיֶה עִמּוֹ לֹא־יִרְדֶּנּוּ בְּפֶרֶךְ לְעֵינֶיךָ׃ וְאִם־לֹא
מפטיר נה יִגָּאֵל בְּאֵלֶּה וְיָצָא בִּשְׁנַת הַיֹּבֵל הוּא וּבָנָיו עִמּוֹ׃ כִּי־לִי בְנֵי־יִשְׂרָאֵל
עֲבָדִים עֲבָדַי הֵם אֲשֶׁר־הוֹצֵאתִי אוֹתָם מֵאֶרֶץ מִצְרָיִם אֲנִי יְהוָה אֱלֹהֵיכֶם׃

He who is purchased for six years will have the status of a servant hired annually, and he who is purchased (for the time period) until the Jubilee will have the status of a servant who has settled with you (in your employ) for many years.

42. כִּי עֲבָדַי הֵם — *For they are My servants.* Although this person went and took a master upon himself (and) is (therefore) deserving of total servitude, nonetheless, since he is My servant, it is not in his hand to sell himself as an absolute slave.

48. אַחֲרֵי נִמְכַּר גְּאֻלָּה תִּהְיֶה לּוֹ — *After he is sold, he may be redeemed.* (Our Sages) have explained, "Lest you say, 'since he went and became an acolyte in the service of idolatry, I will cast a stone after the fallen,' the Torah says, *After he is sold, he may be redeemed*" (*Kiddushin* 20b).

50. וְחִשַּׁב עִם קוֹנֵהוּ — *And he shall reckon with the one who bought him.* Though the gentile buyer in your control (lit., under your hand) bought (this Israelite) improperly, (nonetheless) you shall not withdraw and release him (i.e., without payment).

51. אִם עוֹד רַבּוֹת בַּשָּׁנִים — *If there be yet many years.* Without a doubt, after the slave has been in his master's house for a lengthy period, his work will be more valuable than it was when he first entered his service. Therefore, (the Torah) tells (us) that even though there is yet a long time until the end of his sale, and there is no question that his work in the future (years) will improve even more if he serves out the entire time, nonetheless, (we)

NOTES

and as a settler he shall be with you. A שָׂכִיר is one who is employed for a short period while a תּוֹשָׁב is one who is hired for many years.

42. כִּי עֲבָדַי הֵם — *For they are My servants.* This statement is an explanation of verses 40-41. No Israelite can sell himself permanently since he is the servant of God. Therefore, his servitude ceases on the Jubilee and he *returns to his own family.*

51-52. אִם עוֹד רַבּוֹת בַּשָּׁנִים ... וְאִם מְעַט נִשְׁאַר — *If there be yet many years . . . And if there remain but few.* The principle established in the Talmud (*Kid-*

41 *Then he shall leave you, he and his children with him; he shall return to his family, and to his ancestral heritage shall he return.* 42 *For they are My servants, whom I have taken out of the land of Egypt; they shall not be sold in the manner of a slave.* 43 *You shall not subjugate him through hard labor — you shall fear your God.*

44 *Your slave or your maidservant whom you may own, from the gentiles who surround you, from among them you may purchase a slave or a maidservant.* 45 *Also from among the children of the residents who live with you, from them you may purchase, from their family that is with you, whom they begot in your land; and they shall remain yours as an ancestral heritage.* 46 *You shall hold them as a heritage for your children after you to inherit as a possession, you shall work with them forever; but with your brethren, the Children of Israel — a man with his brother — you shall not subjugate him through hard labor.*

47 *If the means of a sojourner who resides with you shall become sufficient, and your brother becomes impoverished with him, and he is sold to an alien who resides with you, or to an idol of a sojourner's family;*
48 *after he has been sold, he shall have a redemption; one of his brothers shall redeem him;* 49 *or his uncle, or his cousin shall redeem him, or a relative from his family shall redeem him; or if his own means become sufficient, he shall be redeemed.* 50 *He shall make a reckoning with his purchaser from the year he was sold to him until the Jubilee Year; the money of his purchase shall be divided by the number of years, he shall be regarded with him like the years of a laborer.* 51 *If there are yet many years, he shall repay his redemption accordingly from the money of his purchase.*
52 *And if there are few years left until the Jubilee Year, he shall reckon that with him; according to his years shall he repay his redemption.* 53 *He shall be with him like a laborer hired by the year; he shall not subjugate him through hard labor in your sight.*

54 *If he has not been redeemed by these means, then he shall go out in the Jubilee Year, he and his children with him.*

55 *For the Children of Israel are servants to Me, they are My servants, whom I have taken out of the land of Egypt — I am* HASHEM, *your God.*

---

deduct from the cost of the sale according to the (original) cost when he was sold, as (the Sages) state, "If his value increases, then (his redemption shall be) from the money he was bought for" (*Kiddushin* 20b).

52. וְאִם מְעַט נִשְׁאַר — *And if there remain but few . . .* in such a manner that the hire for the work of the good years which have passed exceeds the expected value according to the sale price, then one deducts that which is appropriate for the labor of the years which passed, as (the Sages) say there, "If his value decreases, then (we reckon) according to his years" (ibid.).

NOTES

dushin 20b) is as follows: Although a slave's work is more valuable to his master after several years since he has gained experience, nonetheless, when the slave is redeemed one gives back the price paid minus the years worked. Conversely, if the slave's value has depreciated with time due to advanced age, one only pays the estimated value of the remaining years. The *Sforno's* explanation is to be understood based upon this principle. Accordingly, the phrase רַבּוֹת בַּשָּׁנִים, *many years*, implies increased value, while the phrase מְעַט בַּשָּׁנִים, *few years*, implies diminished value. In each case the Torah is lenient with the Israelite slave, making his redemption less difficult.

כו א לֹא־תַעֲשׂוּ לָכֶם אֱלִילִם וּפֶסֶל וּמַצֵּבָה לֹא־תָקִימוּ לָכֶם וְאֶבֶן מַשְׂכִּית
לֹא תִתְּנוּ בְּאַרְצְכֶם לְהִשְׁתַּחֲוֹת עָלֶיהָ כִּי אֲנִי יהוה אֱלֹהֵיכֶם:
ב אֶת־שַׁבְּתֹתַי תִּשְׁמֹרוּ וּמִקְדָּשִׁי תִּירָאוּ אֲנִי יהוה:

XXVI

1. לֹא תַעֲשׂוּ לָכֶם — *You shall not make for yourselves.* Although you will be subjected to the nations, similar to the one who sold himself to the gentiles, (nonetheless) do not exchange your honor for that which does not profit (based on *Jeremiah* 2:11). This (is said) so that they should not err, as (our Sages) mention that many did err at the time of the exile and said to the prophets, "If a master sells his slave or a husband divorces his wife, has one a claim upon the other?" (*Sanhedrin* 105a). This is so because even after subjugation (to the nations), you are My servants, as (our Sages) tell us that the prophets answered them, saying: "דָּוִד עַבְדִּי, *David My servant* (*II Samuel* 3:18) and נְבֻכַדְנֶאצַּר ... עַבְדִּי, *Nebuchadnezzar My servant* (*Jeremiah* 43:10) ... When a servant acquires property — to whom does the servant belong and to whom the property?" (ibid.).

NOTES

XXVI

1. לֹא תַעֲשׂוּ לָכֶם ... כִּי אֲנִי ה׳ אֱלֹהֵיכֶם — *You shall not make for yourselves ... for I am HASHEM your God.* The *Sforno* explains the connection between this verse and the previous chapter. The concluding portion of chapter 25 speaks of an Israelite slave who sold himself to one who ministers to עֲבוֹדָה זָרָה, *idolatry,* in a heathen temple, and becomes his helper. Nonetheless, as explained in verse 48, he must not be rejected but should be redeemed. The Torah, in our verse, speaks of the people of Israel in exile among the nations who in despair may argue that it matters not whether they remain loyal to their faith or accept the religion of their masters. Hence, they are admonished not to make idols nor bow down to existing ones, for God is still their Master and they are still His servants. Nebuchadnezzar, the king of Babylonia, is called God's servant, not in a complimentary sense but to stress that even though he has conquered Israel,

26 [1] *You shall not make idols for yourselves, and you shall not erect for yourselves a statue or a pillar, and in your land you shall not emplace a flooring stone upon which to prostrate oneself — for I am* HASHEM, *your God.* [2] *My Sabbaths shall you observe and My Sanctuary shall you revere — I am* HASHEM.

כִּי אֲנִי ה' אֱלֹהֵיכֶם — *For I am* HASHEM *your God.* Even in the period of your servitude as it says, *And yet for all that . . . I will not reject them . . . for I am* HASHEM *their God* (v. 44).

2. אֶת שַׁבְּתֹתַי תִּשְׁמֹרוּ — *You shall keep My Sabbaths* . . . in the period of servitude as well, even though the quietude (of the Sabbath) is a remembrance of freedom.

וּמִקְדָּשִׁי תִּירָאוּ — *And revere My Sanctuary.* (This refers to) those sanctified places in exile, namely Houses of Assembly (synagogues) and Houses of Study, even though the Temple is destroyed, as it says, וָאֱהִי לָהֶם לְמִקְדָּשׁ מְעַט, *And I shall be to them as a little sanctuary* (*Ezekiel* 11:16). And (in regard to this) (the Sages) say, "these are Houses of Assembly (for prayer) and Houses of Study" (*Megillah* 29a).

NOTES

they are not his, for what a servant owns belongs to his master, and so the people of Israel still belong to God as His servants. As such, He still retains His claim over them. The verse therefore concludes, *I am* HASHEM *your God*, emphasizing this point, and the *Sforno* links this statement to verse 44 where the Torah explicitly states that, in spite of having driven Israel into exile, God has not rejected them and is still their God. Just as the Israelite sold to the heathen priest can still be redeemed, so the people of Israel, though in exile, shall be redeemed.

2. אֶת שַׁבְּתֹתַי תִּשְׁמֹרוּ וּמִקְדָּשִׁי תִּירָאוּ — *You shall keep My Sabbaths and revere My Sanctuary.* This verse continues the theme of Israel in exile among the nations. Although they are no longer free and are subjugated to others, they are commanded to continue to keep the Sabbath, and although their Holy Temple is destroyed, the Houses of Prayer and Study in exile are miniature sanctuaries wherein God still dwells in their midst.

פרשת בחקתי

ג־ד אִם־בְּחֻקֹּתַי תֵּלֵכוּ וְאֶת־מִצְוֺתַי תִּשְׁמְרוּ וַעֲשִׂיתֶם אֹתָם: וְנָתַתִּי גִשְׁמֵיכֶם
ה בְּעִתָּם וְנָתְנָה הָאָרֶץ יְבוּלָהּ וְעֵץ הַשָּׂדֶה יִתֵּן פִּרְיוֹ: וְהִשִּׂיג לָכֶם דַּיִשׁ
אֶת־בָּצִיר וּבָצִיר יַשִּׂיג אֶת־זָרַע וַאֲכַלְתֶּם לַחְמְכֶם לָשֹׂבַע וִישַׁבְתֶּם לָבֶטַח
שני ו בְּאַרְצְכֶם: וְנָתַתִּי שָׁלוֹם בָּאָרֶץ וּשְׁכַבְתֶּם וְאֵין מַחֲרִיד וְהִשְׁבַּתִּי חַיָּה רָעָה
ז מִן־הָאָרֶץ וְחֶרֶב לֹא־תַעֲבֹר בְּאַרְצְכֶם: וּרְדַפְתֶּם אֶת־אֹיְבֵיכֶם וְנָפְלוּ
ח לִפְנֵיכֶם לֶחָרֶב: וְרָדְפוּ מִכֶּם חֲמִשָּׁה מֵאָה וּמֵאָה מִכֶּם רְבָבָה יִרְדֹּפוּ וְנָפְלוּ
ט אֹיְבֵיכֶם לִפְנֵיכֶם לֶחָרֶב: וּפָנִיתִי אֲלֵיכֶם וְהִפְרֵיתִי אֶתְכֶם וְהִרְבֵּיתִי אֶתְכֶם
*שלישי [חמישי] י וַהֲקִימֹתִי אֶת־בְּרִיתִי אִתְּכֶם: *וַאֲכַלְתֶּם יָשָׁן נוֹשָׁן וְיָשָׁן מִפְּנֵי חָדָשׁ תּוֹצִיאוּ:

---

3. אִם בְּחֻקֹּתַי תֵּלֵכוּ — *If you walk in My statutes.* Statutes are decrees of the king by which man should conduct the endeavors of his life, and such conduct is called "walking," as it says, *And you shall not walk in their statutes* (18:3), and also, *And My statutes you shall keep to walk therein* (18:4), and also בְּחֻקּוֹת הַחַיִּים הָלַךְ, *Walk in the statutes of life* (*Ezekiel* 33:15).

וְאֶת מִצְוֺתַי תִּשְׁמְרוּ — *And keep My commandments.* Behold, the keeping of commandments (denotes) scrupulous care in the manner that they are done and in their intent, (which comes about through) proper reflection as (our Sages) say, " 'To keep' implies (the need for) constant repetition (מִשְׁנָה)" (*Sifre* on *Deut.* 12:28). (The Torah) is therefore saying: If you conduct (yourselves) in the ways of God, the Blessed One, which are incorporated into the pragmatical portion of His Torah, and you will reflect upon the commandments so as to know the manner in which they are done and their purpose, you will thereby fully (realize) His intent so that you may make yourselves in His image and likeness.

וַעֲשִׂיתֶם אֹתָם — *And do them.* Then you shall acquire this perfection in such a manner that you shall do them (i.e., the *mitzvos*) as good laborers (who do so) willingly; not as those who are commanded and do (so) out of a sense of fear (though) the doer is inspired somewhat. (Rather), you shall do (them) out of a sense of love, desiring to fulfill the will of God, the Blessed One, as (our Sages) say, עֲשֵׂה רְצוֹנוֹ כִּרְצוֹנְךָ, *Do His will as if it were your will* (*Avos* 2:4).

7. וּרְדַפְתֶּם אֶת אֹיְבֵיכֶם — *And you shall pursue your enemies* ... beyond your borders.

וְנָפְלוּ לִפְנֵיכֶם לֶחָרֶב — *And they shall fall before you by the sword* ... without your waging war, as it says, כִּי בָאֵשׁ ה׳ נִשְׁפָּט וּבְחַרְבּוֹ אֶת כָּל בָּשָׂר וְרַבּוּ חַלְלֵי ה׳, *For by fire will* HASHEM *contend, and by His sword with all flesh, and the slain of* HASHEM *shall be many* (*Isaiah* 66:16).

NOTES

3. אִם בְּחֻקֹּתַי תֵּלֵכוּ וְאֶת מִצְוֺתַי תִּשְׁמְרוּ וַעֲשִׂיתֶם אֹתָם — *If you walk in My statutes and keep My commandments and do them.* This verse uses three different verbs — *to walk, to keep* and *to do.* The *Sforno* explains the first as referring to man's behavior and conduct, the second is applicable both to one's understanding of and obedience to God's commandments, while the third is not meant as an admonition (*to do the commandments*), but is to be understood as an *assurance* that if one obeys the first two (*walking in the statutes* and *keeping the commandments*), then he shall do God's will with enthusiasm and love.

7. וּרְדַפְתֶּם אֶת אֹיְבֵיכֶם וְנָפְלוּ לִפְנֵיכֶם לֶחָרֶב — *And you shall pursue your enemies and they shall fall before you by the sword.* (a) The previous verse states that there will be *peace in the land* and that *no sword shall pass through the land.* How is it relevant to say that we shall *pursue the enemy?* The *Sforno* explains that this pursuit shall be *beyond* the borders. (b) The *Sforno's* commentary on the latter part of this verse is unlike that of *Rashi* who explains it to mean, "each man by the sword of his companion." Rather, it is to be understood as God intervening, thereby obviating the need for Israel to wage war themselves.

PARASHAS BECHUKOSAI

3 *If you will follow My decrees and observe My commandments and perform them;* 4 *then I will provide your rains in their time, and the land will give its produce and the tree of the field will give its fruit.* 5 *Your threshing will last until the vintage, and the vintage will last until the sowing; you will eat your bread to satiety and you will dwell securely in your land.*

6 *I will provide peace in the land, and you will lie down with none to frighten you; I will cause wild beasts to withdraw from the land, and a sword will not cross your land.* 7 *You will pursue your enemies; and they will fall before you by the sword.* 8 *Five of you will pursue a hundred, and a hundred of you will pursue ten thousand; and your enemies will fall before you by the sword.* 9 *I will turn My attention to you, I will make you fruitful and increase you; and I will establish My covenant with you.*

10 *You will eat very old grain and remove the old to make way for the new.*

---

9. וּפָנִיתִי אֲלֵיכֶם — *And I will turn unto you* . . . after the destruction of the nations, as it says, כִּי אֶעֱשֶׂה כָלָה בְּכָל הַגּוֹיִם . . . וְאֹתְךָ לֹא אֶעֱשֶׂה כָלָה, *For I will make a full end of all the nations . . . but I will not make a full end of you* (*Jeremiah* 46:28).

וַהֲקִימֹתִי אֶת בְּרִיתִי — *And I will establish My covenant* . . . that covenant wherein I said, לִהְיוֹת לְךָ לֵאלֹהִים וּלְזַרְעֲךָ אַחֲרֶיךָ, *to be a God unto you and to your seed after you* (*Genesis* 17:7).

אִתְּכֶם — *With you.* I shall fulfill it with you, in your (own) merit, besides the fact that I will remember for you the covenant of the Fathers, as it says, וְכָרַתִּי לָהֶם בְּרִית שָׁלוֹם בְּרִית עוֹלָם יִהְיֶה אוֹתָם, *I will make a covenant of peace with them, it shall be an everlasting covenant with them* (*Ezekiel* 37:26), and as it says, וּבְרִית שְׁלוֹמִי לֹא תָמוּט, *Neither shall My covenant of peace be removed* (*Isaiah* 54:10).

10. וַאֲכַלְתֶּם יָשָׁן נוֹשָׁן — *And you shall eat old store long kept.* After the nations will be diminished, (including) *their* (lit., *your*) *plowmen and vinedressers* (based on *Isaiah* 61:5), the annual corn will (last) for years in order that the few (laborers) from the remnant of the nations will be able to serve you by gathering the produce and other (goods) so that you shall be sustained without suffering, similar to, יְהִי פִסַּת בַּר בָּאָרֶץ בְּרֹאשׁ הָרִים יִרְעַשׁ כַּלְּבָנוֹן פִּרְיוֹ, *May he be as a rich cornfield in the land upon the top of the mountains; may his fruit rustle like Lebanon* (*Psalms* 72:16), and as (our Sages) say, "*Eretz Yisrael is destined to bring forth cakes and woolen robes*" (*Shabbos* 30b).

וְיָשָׁן מִפְּנֵי חָדָשׁ תּוֹצִיאוּ — *And you shall bring forth the old from before the new.* You will have sufficient (produce) from the old (store) for your needs, although you will supply sustenance from the old (crop) to those who escape from the nations, as it says,

NOTES

9. וַהֲקִימֹתִי אֶת בְּרִיתִי אִתְּכֶם — *And I will establish My covenant with you. Rashi* explains the phrase *My covenant* as referring to a new covenant which, unlike the original one, will never be nullified. The *Sforno,* however, interprets it to mean the original covenant made between the Almighty and Abraham which was never abrogated! And since the Torah here stresses אִתְּכֶם, *with you,* we are being told that this covenant will be fulfilled in our own merit, as well as in the merit of our forefathers.

10. וַאֲכַלְתֶּם יָשָׁן נוֹשָׁן וְיָשָׁן מִפְּנֵי חָדָשׁ תּוֹצִיאוּ — *And you shall eat old store long kept and you shall bring forth the old from before the new.* The *Sforno* interprets this *parashah* as referring to the *end of days,* the Messianic age. At that time, only a remnant will remain from among the nations and they will be dependent upon Israel for their sustenance. They will also serve Israel as necessary laborers. Now according to Torah law, one is not permitted to export life's necessities such as flour, oil or wine from *Eretz Yisrael* to other lands unless

יא־יב וְנָתַתִּי מִשְׁכָּנִי בְּתוֹכְכֶם וְלֹא־תִגְעַל נַפְשִׁי אֶתְכֶם׃ וְהִתְהַלַּכְתִּי בְּתוֹכְכֶם
יג וְהָיִיתִי לָכֶם לֵאלֹהִים וְאַתֶּם תִּהְיוּ־לִי לְעָם׃ אֲנִי יהוה אֱלֹהֵיכֶם אֲשֶׁר
הוֹצֵאתִי אֶתְכֶם מֵאֶרֶץ מִצְרַיִם מִהְיֹת לָהֶם עֲבָדִים וָאֶשְׁבֹּר מֹטֹת עֻלְּכֶם
וָאוֹלֵךְ אֶתְכֶם קוֹמְמִיּוּת׃
יד־טו וְאִם־לֹא תִשְׁמְעוּ לִי וְלֹא תַעֲשׂוּ אֵת כָּל־הַמִּצְוֹת הָאֵלֶּה׃ וְאִם־בְּחֻקֹּתַי
תִּמְאָסוּ וְאִם אֶת־מִשְׁפָּטַי תִּגְעַל נַפְשְׁכֶם לְבִלְתִּי עֲשׂוֹת אֶת־כָּל־מִצְוֹתַי

כִּי הַגּוֹי וְהַמַּמְלָכָה אֲשֶׁר לֹא יַעַבְדוּךְ יֹאבֵדוּ, *For that nation and kingdom that will not serve you shall perish* (*Isaiah* 60:12). Now the reason that you will export (even) items which are life's necessities from your land to the nations is because the new (harvest) will have come and you will (therefore) have no need to worry for lack — as (our Sages) say, "One must not carry out of *Eretz Yisrael* things which are life's necessities such as wine, oil and flour" (*Bava Basra* 90b).

11. וְנָתַתִּי מִשְׁכָּנִי בְּתוֹכְכֶם — *And I will set My Sanctuary* (*Presence*) *among you.* My Divine Presence (שְׁכִינָה) will dwell in your midst, wherever you shall be, as was intended before the (sin of the) Golden Calf when (*God*) said, בְּכָל הַמָּקוֹם אֲשֶׁר אַזְכִּיר אֶת שְׁמִי אָבוֹא אֵלֶיךָ, *In every place where I cause My Name to be mentioned I will come to you* (*Exodus* 20:21).

וְלֹא תִגְעַל נַפְשִׁי אֶתְכֶם — *And My soul will not abhor you.* Never — as it says, לֹא יוֹסִיף לְהַגְלוֹתֵךְ, *He will not exile you again* (*Lamentations* 4:22), and as it says, כֵּן נִשְׁבַּעְתִּי מִקְּצֹף עָלַיִךְ וּמִגְּעָר בָּךְ, *So have I sworn that I would not be angry with you, nor rebuke you* (*Isaiah* 54:9).

12. וְהִתְהַלַּכְתִּי בְּתוֹכְכֶם — *And I will walk among you.* The term מִתְהַלֵּךְ (*to walk* — in the reflexive form) signifies walking from place to place (lit., hither and yon), not only to one place. The (verse) therefore states, *I will walk among you,* because the Divine glory will not only descend into one place which was (the case) in the *Mishkan* and the Holy Temple, as it says, וְעָשׂוּ לִי מִקְדָּשׁ וְשָׁכַנְתִּי בְּתוֹכָם, *And let them make Me a Sanctuary that I may dwell among them* (*Exodus* 25:8). (This means to say) that only in that place and in that manner shall I dwell among them; and this is explained when He said, אֲשֶׁר אִוָּעֵד לְךָ שָׁמָּה, *Where I will meet with you* (ibid. 30:6), (and also) וְנֹעַדְתִּי שָׁמָּה לִבְנֵי יִשְׂרָאֵל, *And there I will meet with the Children of Israel* (ibid. 29:43). Rather, I will walk among you and My glory will be seen wherever you will be, for indeed, wherever the righteous of (each) generation are to be found, that (place) is קְדֹשׁ מִשְׁכְּנֵי עֶלְיוֹן, *the holiest dwelling place of the Most High* (*Psalms* 46:5), where His (original) intent is fulfilled as it says, הַשָּׁמַיִם כִּסְאִי וְהָאָרֶץ הֲדֹם רַגְלָי . . . וְאֶל זֶה אַבִּיט אֶל עָנִי וּנְכֵה רוּחַ וְחָרֵד עַל דְּבָרִי, *The heaven is My throne and the earth is*

NOTES

they are in surplus. The *Sforno* interprets this verse to mean that even earlier harvests will provide this surplus food supply for many years, and that since the new crops will grow and be harvested while the old store is not yet exhausted, Israel will be able to feed other nations from their granaries.

11-12. וְנָתַתִּי מִשְׁכָּנִי בְּתוֹכְכֶם . . . וְהִתְהַלַּכְתִּי בְּתוֹכְכֶם וְהָיִיתִי לָכֶם לֵאלֹהִים — *And I will set My Sanctuary* (*Presence*) *among you . . . and I will walk among you and I will be unto you as God.* The original intent of God was that all mankind should reach the level of צֶלֶם אֱלֹהִים, *the image of God,* which was frustrated when Adam and Eve sinned. When the Torah was given at Sinai, God's purpose was to communicate with all Israel in a prophetic manner, similar to His communication with Moses (see the *Sforno's* commentary, on *Exodus* 19:9). The sin of the Golden Calf, however, thwarted this plan and the Divine Presence limited itself to the Sanctuary alone. In the end of days, the original plan — that God will dwell actually in our very midst — will come to pass, and this chapter speaks of that time. Hence, according to the explanation of the *Sforno,* the phrase וְנָתַתִּי מִשְׁכָּנִי בְּתוֹכְכֶם does not refer to the Holy Temple as *Rashi* states, but it means that the Divine Presence will dwell in the *midst of Israel.* וְהִתְהַלַּכְתִּי בְּתוֹכְכֶם, *And I will walk among you,* means that the Divine glory will radiate everywhere and not just confine itself to the Sanctuary. The phrase וְהָיִיתִי לָכֶם לֵאלֹהִים, *And I will be unto*

11 *I will place My Sanctuary among you; and My Spirit will not reject you.*
12 *I will walk among you, I will be God unto you and you will be a people unto Me.* 13 *I am HASHEM, your God, Who took you out of the land of Egypt from being their slaves; I broke the staves of your yoke and I led you erect.*
14 *But if you will not listen to Me and will not perform all of these commandments;* 15 *if you consider My decrees loathsome, and if your being rejects My ordinances, so as not to perform all My commandments,*

My footstool . . . but to this (man) will I look, to him who is poor and of contrite spirit and trembles at My word (*Isaiah* 66:1,2).

וְהָיִיתִי לָכֶם לֵאלֹהִים — *And I will be unto you as God.* I will be God exclusively for you and you will have no other God or leader besides Me. Therefore, the everlasting nature of your existence will emanate from Me with no intermediary, as is the case of all separate (entities) who are everlasting; for you will then be (a people) in My image and likeness, as was the (original) intent in the creation of man and in the giving of the Torah. This is (the meaning) of the statement, וְלָקַחְתִּי אֶתְכֶם לִי לְעָם וְהָיִיתִי לָכֶם לֵאלֹהִים, *And I will take you to Me for a people, and I will be to you as God* (*Exodus* 6:7). For through the giving of the Torah, had they not become corrupted, the intent would have been to establish them on the level of Messianic days and of the World to Come which (is indicated) without a doubt as an objective in this portion (*Bechukosai*). However, in the portion of *Nitzavim* (*Deut.* 29:12), the intent stated there is that He will establish them (Israel) as a people so that He shall be (their) God, but it was not destined to come to pass at that time. However, the continuous functioning of the Sanctuary, (of which the Torah) says, וְשָׁכַנְתִּי בְּתוֹךְ בְּנֵי יִשְׂרָאֵל וְהָיִיתִי לָהֶם לֵאלֹהִים, *And I will dwell among the Children of Israel and will be their God* (*Exodus* 29:45), (does appear) as an objective in this chapter. In other passages (of the Torah), however, the expressions used are, *To be unto you as God* and *You shall be unto Me as a people*, that is, their exclusive desire shall be to do My will and to serve Me *with one consent* (based on *Zephaniah* 3:9), as it befits every people to (conduct themselves) toward their king in truth.

13. קוֹמְמִיּוּת — *Upright.* The reverse of, אָמְרוּ לְנַפְשֵׁךְ שְׁחִי וְנַעֲבֹרָה וַתָּשִׂימִי כָאָרֶץ גֵּוֵךְ, *have said to your soul, "Bow down that we may go over, and you have laid your back as the ground"* (*Isaiah* 51:23).

14. וְאִם לֹא תִשְׁמְעוּ לִי — *But if you will not hearken to Me* . . . to walk in My statutes, as explained above.

וְלֹא תַעֲשׂוּ אֵת כָּל הַמִּצְוֹת הָאֵלֶּה — *And will not do all these commandments.* Since you will not walk in My statutes, then you will not do *all* the commandments, rather you will only do those which are favorable in your eyes.

15. וְאִם בְּחֻקֹּתַי תִּמְאָסוּ — *And if you shall reject My statutes* . . . not only to nullify them but to reject (despise) them.

וְאִם אֶת מִשְׁפָּטַי תִּגְעַל נַפְשְׁכֶם — *And if your soul abhor My ordinances.* You will abhor them,

NOTES

you as God, is to be understood as the direct relationship of God with Israel, with no need for any intermediary. This, in turn, will insure their everlasting existence as a people.

The *Sforno*, however, draws a distinction between various verses where the expression *To be unto you as God* is used. In some instances, it refers to the *end of days*, as is the case in this chapter, and is therefore interpreted to mean a special direct relationship, while in others (such as *Nitzavim*) it refers to the relationship of a nation to its king, namely one of subservience, discipline and respect.

14. וְאִם לֹא תִשְׁמְעוּ לִי וְלֹא תַעֲשׂוּ — *But if you will not hearken to Me and will not do.* The *Sforno* reconciles the apparent redundancy of this verse (*not hearken* and *not do*) by explaining that if one rejects the statutes (which are not readily understood), then he shall ultimately become selective and perform only those commandments which appeal to him.

טו לְהַפְרְכֶם אֶת־בְּרִיתִי: אַף־אֲנִי אֶעֱשֶׂה־זֹּאת לָכֶם וְהִפְקַדְתִּי עֲלֵיכֶם
בֶּהָלָה אֶת־הַשַּׁחֶפֶת וְאֶת־הַקַּדַּחַת מְכַלּוֹת עֵינַיִם וּמְדִיבֹת נָפֶשׁ וּזְרַעְתֶּם
יז לָרִיק זַרְעֲכֶם וַאֲכָלֻהוּ אֹיְבֵיכֶם: וְנָתַתִּי פָנַי בָּכֶם וְנִגַּפְתֶּם לִפְנֵי אֹיְבֵיכֶם
יח וְרָדוּ בָכֶם שֹׂנְאֵיכֶם וְנַסְתֶּם וְאֵין־רֹדֵף אֶתְכֶם: וְאִם־עַד־אֵלֶּה לֹא תִשְׁמְעוּ
יט לִי וְיָסַפְתִּי לְיַסְּרָה אֶתְכֶם שֶׁבַע עַל־חַטֹּאתֵיכֶם: וְשָׁבַרְתִּי אֶת־גְּאוֹן עֻזְּכֶם
כ וְנָתַתִּי אֶת־שְׁמֵיכֶם כַּבַּרְזֶל וְאֶת־אַרְצְכֶם כַּנְּחֻשָׁה: וְתַם לָרִיק כֹּחֲכֶם
כא וְלֹא־תִתֵּן אַרְצְכֶם אֶת־יְבוּלָהּ וְעֵץ הָאָרֶץ לֹא יִתֵּן פִּרְיוֹ: וְאִם־תֵּלְכוּ עִמִּי
קֶרִי וְלֹא תֹאבוּ לִשְׁמֹעַ לִי וְיָסַפְתִּי עֲלֵיכֶם מַכָּה שֶׁבַע כְּחַטֹּאתֵיכֶם:
כב וְהִשְׁלַחְתִּי בָכֶם אֶת־חַיַּת הַשָּׂדֶה וְשִׁכְּלָה אֶתְכֶם וְהִכְרִיתָה אֶת־
כג בְּהֶמְתְּכֶם וְהִמְעִיטָה אֶתְכֶם וְנָשַׁמּוּ דַּרְכֵיכֶם: וְאִם־בְּאֵלֶּה לֹא תִוָּסְרוּ לִי
כד וַהֲלַכְתֶּם עִמִּי קֶרִי: וְהָלַכְתִּי אַף־אֲנִי עִמָּכֶם בְּקֶרִי וְהִכֵּיתִי אֶתְכֶם גַּם־אָנִי
כה שֶׁבַע עַל־חַטֹּאתֵיכֶם: וְהֵבֵאתִי עֲלֵיכֶם חֶרֶב נֹקֶמֶת נְקַם־בְּרִית וְנֶאֱסַפְתֶּם
כו אֶל־עָרֵיכֶם וְשִׁלַּחְתִּי דֶבֶר בְּתוֹכְכֶם וְנִתַּתֶּם בְּיַד־אוֹיֵב: בְּשִׁבְרִי לָכֶם
מַטֵּה־לֶחֶם וְאָפוּ עֶשֶׂר נָשִׁים לַחְמְכֶם בְּתַנּוּר אֶחָד וְהֵשִׁיבוּ לַחְמְכֶם

similar to one who intentionally causes (himself) to vomit, for it is not logical (lit., customary) to abhor them (i.e., the ordinances) since they are reasonable and proper.

לְבִלְתִּי עֲשׂוֹת אֶת כָּל מִצְוֹתַי — *So that you will not do all My commandments.* This abhorrence of the ordinances is (motivated) only for the purpose of casting off the yoke of all the commandments from yourselves, as (our Sages) said, "Israel knew that the idols were non-entities but they engaged in idolatry only that they might satisfy (lit., permit to themselves) in public their immoral sexual desires" (*Sanhedrin* 63b), and the prophet also attests (to this) when he says, לֹא יִתְּנוּ מַעַלְלֵיהֶם לָשׁוּב אֶל אֱלֹהֵיהֶם כִּי רוּחַ זְנוּנִים בְּקִרְבָּם, *Their actions will not allow them to return to their God for the spirit of harlotry is within them* (*Hosea* 5:4).

לְהַפְרְכֶם אֶת בְּרִיתִי — *To break My covenant . . .* so as to be like the other nations who reign in this world without any yoke of Torah and *mitzvos* (commandments), as it says, וְהָעֹלָה עַל רוּחֲכֶם הָיוֹ לֹא תִהְיֶה אֲשֶׁר אַתֶּם אֹמְרִים נִהְיֶה כַגּוֹיִם כְּמִשְׁפְּחוֹת הָאֲרָצוֹת לְשָׁרֵת עֵץ וָאָבֶן, *And that which enters your mind shall not be of any consequence at all; in that you say we will be as the nations, as the families of the lands, to serve wood and stone* (*Ezekiel* 20:32).

16. אַף אֲנִי אֶעֱשֶׂה זֹּאת לָכֶם — *I also will do this unto you.* I will do what you thought to do, namely, the covenant will be abrogated and nullified by Me as well, as I said that (only) when you will be a people to Me will I be a God to you, without any intermediary.

וְהִפְקַדְתִּי עֲלֵיכֶם בֶּהָלָה — *I will appoint terror over you.* I will appoint over you officials of terror, similar to, וּלְאֵלֶּה אָמַר בְּאָזְנַי עִבְרוּ בָעִיר אַחֲרָיו וְהַכּוּ אַל תָּחֹס עֵינְכֶם וְאַל תַּחְמֹלוּ, *And to these He said in my hearing, go through the city after him and smite; let not your eye spare, neither have pity* (*Ezekiel* 9:5).

NOTES

15. וְאִם בְּחֻקֹּתַי תִּמְאָסוּ וְאִם אֶת מִשְׁפָּטַי תִּגְעַל נַפְשְׁכֶם לְבִלְתִּי עֲשׂוֹת — *And if you shall reject My statutes and if your soul abhor My ordinances so that you will not do.* The motivation to reject a חֹק, *statute,* is perhaps understandable but to *abhor* a מִשְׁפָּט, *ordinance,* which is logical and reasonable, is beyond comprehension. The *Sforno* therefore explains that the answer lies in the Torah's choice of the word גָעַל, *abhor,* which is not based upon reason but is willful repudiation, similar to self-induced regurgitation. Now this is done in order to live a life of licentiousness and to indulge one's most base desires and appetites without any restraints or inhibitions, as the *Sforno* cites from the words of the Prophets and our Sages.

so that you annul My covenant —
16 *then I will do the same to you; I will assign upon you panic, swelling lesions, and burning fever, which cause eyes to long and souls to suffer; you will sow your seeds in vain, for your enemies will eat it.*
17 *I will turn My attention against you, you will be struck down before enemies; those who hate you will subjugate you — you will flee with no one pursuing you.*
18 *If despite this you do not heed Me, then I shall punish you further, seven ways for your sins.*
19 *I will break the pride of your might; I will make your heaven like iron and your land like copper.*
20 *Your strength will be spent in vain; your land will not give its produce and the tree of the land will not give its fruit.*
21 *If you behave casually with Me and refuse to heed Me, then I shall lay a further blow upon you — seven ways, like your sins.*
22 *I will incite the wildlife of the field against you and it will leave you bereft of your children, decimate your livestock, and diminish you; and your roads will become desolate.*
23 *If despite these you will not be chastised toward Me, and you behave casually with Me,*
24 *then I, too, will behave toward you with casualness; and I will strike you, even I, seven ways for your sins.*
25 *I will bring upon you a sword, avenging the vengeance of a covenant, you will be gathered into your cities; then I will send a pestilence among you and you will be delivered into the hand of your enemy.*
26 *When I break for you the staff of bread, ten women will bake your bread in one oven, and they will bring back your bread*

וַאֲכָלֻהוּ אֹיְבֵיכֶם — *For your enemies shall eat it* . . . as it came to pass in the days of the Judges, as it says, וְהָיָה אִם זָרַע יִשְׂרָאֵל וְעָלָה מִדְיָן וַעֲמָלֵק וּבְנֵי קֶדֶם, *When Israel had sown, the Midianites came up and the Amalekites and the children of the east* (*Judges* 6:3).

19. וְשָׁבַרְתִּי אֶת גְּאוֹן עֻזְּכֶם — *And I will break the pride of your powers.* (This refers to) the destruction of the Sanctuary at Shiloh, as it says, וַיִּתֵּן לַשְּׁבִי עֻזּוֹ, *And delivered His strength into captivity* (*Psalms* 78:61).

25. וְהֵבֵאתִי עֲלֵיכֶם חֶרֶב — *And I will bring a sword upon you* . . . as occurred in the days of the kings of Israel, as it says, כִּי יָדַעְתִּי אֵת אֲשֶׁר תַּעֲשֶׂה לִבְנֵי יִשְׂרָאֵל רָעָה מִבְצְרֵיהֶם תְּשַׁלַּח בָּאֵשׁ וּבַחֻרֵיהֶם בַּחֶרֶב תַּהֲרֹג, *Because I know the evil that you will do to the Children of Israel; you will set their strongholds on fire and you will slay their young men with the sword* (*II Kings* 8:12).

נֹקֶמֶת נְקַם בְּרִית — *That shall execute the vengeance of the covenant* . . . executing that vengeance which is written in the Book of the Covenant (i.e., the Torah), as (our Sages) state, "Although the Sanhedrin ceased, the judgment of the four forms of capital punishment has not ceased" (*Kesubos* 30a).

וְנִתַּתֶּם בְּיַד אוֹיֵב — *And you shall be delivered into the hand of the enemy* . . . as was the case with the Ten Tribes (who were delivered) into the hand of the king of Assyria.

NOTES

16-33. אַף אֲנִי אֶעֱשֶׂה זֹּאת לָכֶם — *I also will do this unto you* . . . that which you planned to do is what I shall, in turn, do, i.e., I will abrogate the covenant.

Beginning with this verse, the *Sforno* interprets the dire predictions and promises (recorded through verse 33) as referring to specific historic periods and events. For example, וַאֲכָלֻהוּ אֹיְבֵיכֶם, *For your enemies shall eat* (*your plantings*), refers to the period following the era of Deborah, while verses 19 and 25 refer to the destruction of the Sanctuary in Shiloh, the period of the Northern Kingdom (מַלְכוּת יִשְׂרָאֵל) and the exile of the Ten Tribes. Verses 31 through 33 refer to the fate of the Southern Kingdom (מַלְכוּת יְהוּדָה), including the destruction of the Holy Temple in Jerusalem and the flight of the Jews to Egypt where the sword of

כז בְּמִשְׁקָל וַאֲכַלְתֶּם וְלֹא תִשְׂבָּעוּ: וְאִם־בְּזֹאת לֹא
כח תִשְׁמְעוּ לִי וַהֲלַכְתֶּם עִמִּי בְּקֶרִי: וְהָלַכְתִּי עִמָּכֶם בַּחֲמַת־קֶרִי וְיִסַּרְתִּי
כט אֶתְכֶם אַף־אָנִי שֶׁבַע עַל־חַטֹּאתֵיכֶם: וַאֲכַלְתֶּם בְּשַׂר בְּנֵיכֶם וּבְשַׂר
ל בְּנֹתֵיכֶם תֹּאכֵלוּ: וְהִשְׁמַדְתִּי אֶת־בָּמֹתֵיכֶם וְהִכְרַתִּי אֶת־חַמָּנֵיכֶם וְנָתַתִּי
לא אֶת־פִּגְרֵיכֶם עַל־פִּגְרֵי גִּלּוּלֵיכֶם וְגָעֲלָה נַפְשִׁי אֶתְכֶם: וְנָתַתִּי אֶת־עָרֵיכֶם
לב חָרְבָּה וַהֲשִׁמּוֹתִי אֶת־מִקְדְּשֵׁיכֶם וְלֹא אָרִיחַ בְּרֵיחַ נִיחֹחֲכֶם: וַהֲשִׁמֹּתִי
לג אֲנִי אֶת־הָאָרֶץ וְשָׁמְמוּ עָלֶיהָ אֹיְבֵיכֶם הַיֹּשְׁבִים בָּהּ: וְאֶתְכֶם אֱזָרֶה
בַגּוֹיִם וַהֲרִיקֹתִי אַחֲרֵיכֶם חָרֶב וְהָיְתָה אַרְצְכֶם שְׁמָמָה וְעָרֵיכֶם יִהְיוּ
לד חָרְבָּה: אָז תִּרְצֶה הָאָרֶץ אֶת־שַׁבְּתֹתֶיהָ כֹּל יְמֵי הָשַּׁ*מָּה וְאַתֶּם בְּאֶרֶץ *ש׳ דגושה
לה אֹיְבֵיכֶם אָז תִּשְׁבַּת הָאָרֶץ וְהִרְצָת אֶת־שַׁבְּתֹתֶיהָ: כָּל־יְמֵי הָשַּׁ*מָּה *ש׳ דגושה
תִּשְׁבֹּת אֵת אֲשֶׁר לֹא־שָׁבְתָה בְּשַׁבְּתֹתֵיכֶם בְּשִׁבְתְּכֶם עָלֶיהָ:
לו וְהַנִּשְׁאָרִים בָּכֶם וְהֵבֵאתִי מֹרֶךְ בִּלְבָבָם בְּאַרְצֹת אֹיְבֵיהֶם וְרָדַף אֹתָם
לז קוֹל עָלֶה נִדָּף וְנָסוּ מְנֻסַת־חֶרֶב וְנָפְלוּ וְאֵין רֹדֵף: וְכָשְׁלוּ אִישׁ־בְּאָחִיו
כְּמִפְּנֵי־חֶרֶב וְרֹדֵף אָיִן וְלֹא־תִהְיֶה לָכֶם תְּקוּמָה לִפְנֵי אֹיְבֵיכֶם:
לח־לט וַאֲבַדְתֶּם בַּגּוֹיִם וְאָכְלָה אֶתְכֶם אֶרֶץ אֹיְבֵיכֶם: וְהַנִּשְׁאָרִים בָּכֶם יִמַּקּוּ
מ בַּעֲוֹנָם בְּאַרְצֹת אֹיְבֵיכֶם וְאַף בַּעֲוֹנֹת אֲבֹתָם אִתָּם יִמָּקּוּ: וְהִתְוַדּוּ
אֶת־עֲוֹנָם וְאֶת־עֲוֹן אֲבֹתָם בְּמַעֲלָם אֲשֶׁר מָעֲלוּ־בִי וְאַף אֲשֶׁר־הָלְכוּ
מא עִמִּי בְּקֶרִי: אַף־אֲנִי אֵלֵךְ עִמָּם בְּקֶרִי וְהֵבֵאתִי אֹתָם בְּאֶרֶץ אֹיְבֵיהֶם

30. וְנָתַתִּי אֶת פִּגְרֵיכֶם עַל פִּגְרֵי גִלּוּלֵיכֶם — *And cast your carcasses upon the carcasses of your idols.* (This refers to) when the city was besieged, as we are told regarding Elijah the Righteous One who found a child languishing with hunger, and when he said to him, "Recite 'Hear O Israel' and you shall live," (the child) retorted, 'Be silent, and don't mention the name of God.' " He then brought forth his idol from his bosom, kissed it and fell dead upon it (see *Sanhedrin* 63b).

31. וְנָתַתִּי אֶת עָרֵיכֶם חָרְבָּה — *And I will make your cities a waste* . . . through the king of Babylonia and his lords.

וַהֲשִׁמּוֹתִי אֶת מִקְדְּשֵׁיכֶם — *And bring your sanctuaries to desolation* . . . through Nebuzradan. וְלֹא אָרִיחַ בְּרֵיחַ נִיחֹחֲכֶם — *And I will not smell the savor of your sweet odors.* Even though the sons of Zadok the Kohen were then (functioning as) *Kohanim* in (the Temple), whose sacrifices, without a doubt, had the savor of sweet odors, nonetheless, they were not acceptable due to the guilt of the people.

33. וְאֶתְכֶם אֱזָרֶה בַגּוֹיִם — *And I will scatter you among the nations* . . . when they go down to Egypt after the destruction (of the Temple). (See *II Kings* 25:26.)

וַהֲרִיקֹתִי אַחֲרֵיכֶם חָרֶב — *And I will draw out the sword after you.* The sword of Nebuchadnezzar (will overtake you) in Egypt, as it says, הַחֶרֶב אֲשֶׁר אַתֶּם יְרֵאִים מִמֶּנָּה שָׁם תַּשִּׂיג אֶתְכֶם בְּאֶרֶץ מִצְרָיִם, *The sword of which you are afraid shall overtake you there in*

NOTES

Nebuchadnezzar, king of Babylonia, overtook them.

34. אָז תִּרְצֶה הָאָרֶץ אֶת שַׁבְּתֹתֶיהָ — *Then shall the land be appeased (be paid) her Sabbaths.* Because the people failed to allow the land to lie fallow during the Sabbatical and Jubilee years, the land will demand its due and remain desolate for those same number of years before the people can return to *Eretz Yisrael* from Babylonia.

by weight; you will eat and not be sated.
27 *If despite this you will not heed Me, and you behave toward Me with*
casualness, 28 *I will behave toward you with a fury of casualness; I will*
chastise you, even I, seven ways for your sins. 29 *You will eat the flesh of*
your sons; and the flesh of your daughters will you eat. 30 *I will destroy*
your lofty buildings and decimate your sun-idols, I will cast your carcasses
upon the carcasses of your idols, and My Spirit will reject you. 31 *I will lay*
your cities in ruin and I will make your sanctuaries desolate; I will not
savor your satisfying aromas. 32 *I will make the land desolate; and your*
foes who dwell upon it will be desolate. 33 *And you, I will scatter among the*
nations, I will unsheathe the sword after you; your land will be desolate
and your cities will be a ruin.
34 *Then the land will be appeased for its sabbaticals during all the years*
of its desolation, while you are in the land of your foes; then the land will
rest and it will appease for its sabbaticals. 35 *All the years of its desolation*
it will rest, whatever it did not rest during your sabbaticals when you
dwelled upon her.
36 *The survivors among you — I will bring weakness into their hearts in*
the lands of their foes; the sound of a rustling leaf will pursue them, they
will flee as one flees the sword, and they will fall, but without a pursuer.
37 *They will stumble over one another as in flight from the sword, but there*
is no pursuer; you will not have the power to withstand your foes. 38 *You*
will become lost among the nations; the land of your foes will devour you.
39 *Because of their iniquity, your remnant will disintegrate in the lands of*
your foes; and because the iniquities of their forefathers are with them as
well, they will disintegrate.
40 *Then they will confess their sin and the sin of their forefathers, for*
the treachery with which they betrayed Me, and also for having be-
haved toward Me with casualness. 41 *I, too, will behave toward them*
with casualness and I will bring them into the land of their enemies —

---

the land of Egypt (*Jeremiah* 42:16).

34. אָז תִּרְצֶה הָאָרֶץ — *Then shall the land be appeased* (*be paid*) . . . will be paid and will be remitted.

אֶת שַׁבְּתֹתֶיהָ — *Her Sabbaths.* (This refers to) Sabbatical years and Jubilees, as it is explained when it says, עַד רָצְתָה הָאָרֶץ אֶת שַׁבְּתוֹתֶיהָ כָּל יְמֵי הָשַּׁמָּה שָׁבָתָה לְמַלֹּאת שִׁבְעִים שָׁנָה, *Until the land had been paid her Sabbaths; for as long as she lay desolate she kept the Sabbath to fulfill seventy years* (*II Chronicles* 36:21).

40. וְהִתְוַדּוּ אֶת עֲוֹנָם — *And they shall confess their iniquity.* (This means) a number of them such as Daniel, Ezra and others.

41. וְהֵבֵאתִי אֹתָם בְּאֶרֶץ אֹיְבֵיהֶם — *And bring them into the land of their enemies.* When the exiles returned to the Land of Israel at the command of Cyrus the Persian king, the land was under the rule of the nations, as it says, וְהָאָרֶץ אֲשֶׁר נָתַתָּה לַאֲבֹתֵינוּ לֶאֱכֹל אֶת פִּרְיָהּ וְאֶת

NOTES

41. וְהֵבֵאתִי אֹתָם בְּאֶרֶץ אֹיְבֵיהֶם — *And bring them into the land of their enemies.* Unlike other commentators, the *Sforno* interprets this verse as applying to Israel's *return* to the Land of Israel, not their exile *from* it to the land of their enemies. The difficulty, however, is in the word בְּאֶרֶץ, *into the*

מב אוֹ־אָז יִכָּנַע לְבָבָם הֶעָרֵל וְאָז יִרְצוּ אֶת־עֲוֹנָם: וְזָכַרְתִּי אֶת־בְּרִיתִי
יַעֲקוֹב וְאַף אֶת־בְּרִיתִי יִצְחָק וְאַף אֶת־בְּרִיתִי אַבְרָהָם אֶזְכֹּר וְהָאָרֶץ *מלא ו'
מג אֶזְכֹּר: וְהָאָרֶץ תֵּעָזֵב מֵהֶם וְתִרֶץ אֶת־שַׁבְּתֹתֶיהָ בָּהְשַׁמָּה מֵהֶם וְהֵם יִרְצוּ
מד אֶת־עֲוֹנָם יַעַן וּבְיַעַן בְּמִשְׁפָּטַי מָאָסוּ וְאֶת־חֻקֹּתַי גָּעֲלָה נַפְשָׁם: וְאַף
גַּם־זֹאת בִּהְיוֹתָם בְּאֶרֶץ אֹיְבֵיהֶם לֹא־מְאַסְתִּים וְלֹא־גְעַלְתִּים לְכַלֹּתָם
מה לְהָפֵר בְּרִיתִי אִתָּם כִּי אֲנִי יהוה אֱלֹהֵיהֶם: וְזָכַרְתִּי לָהֶם בְּרִית רִאשֹׁנִים
אֲשֶׁר הוֹצֵאתִי־אֹתָם מֵאֶרֶץ מִצְרַיִם לְעֵינֵי הַגּוֹיִם לִהְיוֹת לָהֶם לֵאלֹהִים
מו אֲנִי יהוה: אֵלֶּה הַחֻקִּים וְהַמִּשְׁפָּטִים וְהַתּוֹרֹת אֲשֶׁר נָתַן יהוה בֵּינוֹ וּבֵין
בְּנֵי יִשְׂרָאֵל בְּהַר סִינַי בְּיַד־מֹשֶׁה:

כז רביעי [ששי]
א-ב וַיְדַבֵּר יהוה אֶל־מֹשֶׁה לֵּאמֹר: דַּבֵּר אֶל־בְּנֵי יִשְׂרָאֵל וְאָמַרְתָּ אֲלֵהֶם
ג אִישׁ כִּי יַפְלִא נֶדֶר בְּעֶרְכְּךָ נְפָשֹׁת לַיהוה: וְהָיָה עֶרְכְּךָ הַזָּכָר מִבֶּן
עֶשְׂרִים שָׁנָה וְעַד בֶּן־שִׁשִּׁים שָׁנָה וְהָיָה עֶרְכְּךָ חֲמִשִּׁים שֶׁקֶל כֶּסֶף בְּשֶׁקֶל
ד-ה הַקֹּדֶשׁ: וְאִם־נְקֵבָה הִוא וְהָיָה עֶרְכְּךָ שְׁלֹשִׁים שָׁקֶל: וְאִם מִבֶּן־
חָמֵשׁ שָׁנִים וְעַד בֶּן־עֶשְׂרִים שָׁנָה וְהָיָה עֶרְכְּךָ הַזָּכָר עֶשְׂרִים שְׁקָלִים
ו וְלַנְּקֵבָה עֲשֶׂרֶת שְׁקָלִים: וְאִם מִבֶּן־חֹדֶשׁ וְעַד בֶּן־חָמֵשׁ שָׁנִים וְהָיָה
עֶרְכְּךָ הַזָּכָר חֲמִשָּׁה שְׁקָלִים כָּסֶף וְלַנְּקֵבָה עֶרְכְּךָ שְׁלֹשֶׁת שְׁקָלִים
ז כָּסֶף: וְאִם מִבֶּן־שִׁשִּׁים שָׁנָה וָמַעְלָה אִם־זָכָר וְהָיָה עֶרְכְּךָ חֲמִשָּׁה
ח עָשָׂר שָׁקֶל וְלַנְּקֵבָה עֲשָׂרָה שְׁקָלִים: וְאִם־מָךְ הוּא מֵעֶרְכֶּךָ וְהֶעֱמִידוֹ

טוּבָהּ הִנֵּה אֲנַחְנוּ עֲבָדִים עָלֶיהָ. וּתְבוּאָתָהּ מַרְבָּה לַמְּלָכִים אֲשֶׁר נָתַתָּה עָלֵינוּ בְּחַטֹּאותֵינוּ, *And as for the land that You gave to our fathers to eat its fruit and the good thereof, behold we are servants on it. And it yields much produce to the kings whom You have set over us because of our sins* (*Nehemiah* 9:36-37).

42. וְזָכַרְתִּי אֶת בְּרִיתִי — *And I will remember My covenant* ... with the building of the Second Temple.

43. וְהָאָרֶץ תֵּעָזֵב מֵהֶם — *For the land shall lie forsaken without them* ... when destroyed.

45. וְזָכַרְתִּי לָהֶם — *And I shall remember for their sake* ... when I gather the exiles.

אֲשֶׁר הוֹצֵאתִי ... לִהְיוֹת לָהֶם לֵאלֹהִים — *Whom I brought forth ... to be a God to them.* (For) I brought them forth to be their God, as it says, וְאַתֶּם תִּהְיוּ לִי מַמְלֶכֶת כֹּהֲנִים וְגוֹי קָדוֹשׁ, *And you shall be unto Me a kingdom of Kohanim and a holy nation* (*Exodus* 19:6). And what they then destroyed shall be reestablished after the ingathering of the exiles in the days of Messiah and the World to Come.

אֲנִי ה׳ — *I am* HASHEM ... Who does not change (based on *Malachi* 3:6). The impairment (deterioration) was due to them alone, (but) I will fulfill my (original) intent when their

NOTES

land, rather than מֵאֶרֶץ, *from the land*. The *Sforno* resolves this difficulty by explaining that even after their return to *Eretz Yisrael* in the time of Cyrus, they were not free but were still subjected to alien rule.

42-45. וְזָכַרְתִּי אֶת בְּרִיתִי ... וְהָאָרֶץ תֵּעָזֵב מֵהֶם ... וְזָכַרְתִּי לָהֶם ... לִהְיוֹת לָהֶם לֵאלֹהִים — *And I will remember My covenant ... for the land shall lie forsaken without them ... and I shall remember for their sake ... to be a God to them.* The *Sforno*, consistent with his running commentary on this chapter, interprets these verses as representing the culmination of the Jewish people's journey through history. They shall return to the land, rebuild the Temple, be exiled once again but ulti-

perhaps then their unfeeling heart will be humbled and then they will gain
appeasement for their sin. 42 *I will remember My covenant with Jacob and*
also My covenant with Isaac, and also My covenant with Abraham will I
remember, and I will remember the Land. 43 *The Land will be bereft of them;*
and it will be appeased for its sabbaticals having become desolate of them;
and they must gain appeasement for their iniquity; because they were
revolted by My ordinances and because their spirit rejected My decrees.
44 *But despite all this, while they will be in the land of their enemies, I will*
not have been revolted by them nor will I have rejected them to obliterate
them, to annul My covenant with them — for I am HASHEM*, their God.* 45 *I*
will remember for them the covenant of the ancients, those whom I have
taken out of the land of Egypt before the eyes of the nations, to be God unto
them — I am HASHEM.
46 *These are the decrees, the ordinances, and the teachings that* HASHEM
gave, between Himself and the Children of Israel, at Mount Sinai, through
Moses.

27 1 HASHEM *spoke to Moses, saying:* 2 *Speak to the Children of Israel and*
say to them: If a man articulates a vow to HASHEM *regarding a valua-*
tion of living beings, 3 *the valuation of a male shall be: for someone twenty*
years to sixty years of age, the valuation shall be fifty silver shekels, of the
sacred shekel. 4 *If she is female, the valuation shall be thirty shekels.* 5 *And*
if from five to twenty years of age, the valuation of a male shall be twenty
shekels and of a female ten shekels. 6 *And if from one month to five years*
of age, the valuation of a male shall be five silver shekels; and for a female,
the valuation shall be three silver shekels. 7 *And if from sixty years and up,*
if for a male, the valuation shall be fifteen shekels; and for a female, ten she-
kels. 8 *But if he is too poor for the valuation, then he should cause him to stand*

---

impairment will be removed at the end of days (lit., in the future time).

46. אֵלֶּה הַחֻקִּים — *These are the statutes.* All the commandments given (lit., said) before the beginning of the portion of *Bechukosai* (fall into the categories of) the statutes, ordinances and laws upon which the covenant was made with the blessings and curses. This is the covenant mentioned when (the Torah) says, מִלְּבַד הַבְּרִית אֲשֶׁר כָּרַת אִתָּם בְּחֹרֵב, *Beside the covenant which He made with them in Horeb* (Deuteronomy 28:69).

בֵּינוֹ וּבֵין בְּנֵי יִשְׂרָאֵל — *Between Him and the Children of Israel.* The Exalted One vowed (to fulfill) the blessings when they would so merit, and they accepted the curses upon themselves in the event that they would not hearken. However, (the laws of) human valuation and those of sanctification of houses and fields and of a firstling and bans and the animal tithe (chapter 27) were all said (i.e., commanded) *after* this covenant (was made) even though they were also said on Mount Sinai, as it says . . .

NOTES

mately they will return to the Land of Israel in the Messianic time and the end of days when they will finally bring to fruition the original plan of God for mankind in general, and the people of Israel in particular.

46. אֵלֶּה הַחֻקִּים — *These are the statutes.* The *Sforno* explains that *the statutes, ordinances and laws* mentioned in this verse refer to all the laws preceding this chapter, which are all part of the covenant between God and Israel. However, the laws of the next chapter (27) are not part of the covenant even though they were also commanded on Mount Sinai as were the preceding ones.

לִפְנֵי הַכֹּהֵן וְהֶעֱרִיךְ אֹתוֹ הַכֹּהֵן עַל־פִּי אֲשֶׁר תַּשִּׂיג יַד הַנֹּדֵר יַעֲרִיכֶנּוּ
ט הַכֹּהֵן׃ וְאִם־בְּהֵמָה אֲשֶׁר יַקְרִיבוּ מִמֶּנָּה קָרְבָּן לַיהוָה כֹּל
י אֲשֶׁר יִתֵּן מִמֶּנּוּ לַיהוָה יִהְיֶה־קֹּדֶשׁ׃ לֹא יַחֲלִיפֶנּוּ וְלֹא־יָמִיר אֹתוֹ טוֹב
בְּרָע אוֹ־רַע בְּטוֹב וְאִם־הָמֵר יָמִיר בְּהֵמָה בִּבְהֵמָה וְהָיָה־הוּא וּתְמוּרָתוֹ
יא יִהְיֶה־קֹּדֶשׁ׃ וְאִם כָּל־בְּהֵמָה טְמֵאָה אֲשֶׁר לֹא־יַקְרִיבוּ מִמֶּנָּה קָרְבָּן
יב לַיהוָה וְהֶעֱמִיד אֶת־הַבְּהֵמָה לִפְנֵי הַכֹּהֵן׃ וְהֶעֱרִיךְ הַכֹּהֵן אֹתָהּ בֵּין טוֹב
יג וּבֵין רָע כְּעֶרְכְּךָ הַכֹּהֵן כֵּן יִהְיֶה׃ וְאִם־גָּאֹל יִגְאָלֶנָּה וְיָסַף חֲמִישִׁתוֹ
יד עַל־עֶרְכֶּךָ׃ וְאִישׁ כִּי־יַקְדִּשׁ אֶת־בֵּיתוֹ קֹדֶשׁ לַיהוָה וְהֶעֱרִיכוֹ הַכֹּהֵן בֵּין
טו טוֹב וּבֵין רָע כַּאֲשֶׁר יַעֲרִיךְ אֹתוֹ הַכֹּהֵן כֵּן יָקוּם׃ וְאִם־הַמַּקְדִּישׁ יִגְאַל
חמישי [שביעי] טז אֶת־בֵּיתוֹ וְיָסַף חֲמִישִׁית כֶּסֶף־עֶרְכְּךָ עָלָיו וְהָיָה לוֹ׃ וְאִם ׀ מִשְּׂדֵה אֲחֻזָּתוֹ
יַקְדִּישׁ אִישׁ לַיהוָה וְהָיָה עֶרְכְּךָ לְפִי זַרְעוֹ זֶרַע חֹמֶר שְׂעֹרִים בַּחֲמִשִּׁים
יז־יח שֶׁקֶל כָּסֶף׃ אִם־מִשְּׁנַת הַיֹּבֵל יַקְדִּישׁ שָׂדֵהוּ כְּעֶרְכְּךָ יָקוּם׃ וְאִם־אַחַר
הַיֹּבֵל יַקְדִּישׁ שָׂדֵהוּ וְחִשַּׁב־לוֹ הַכֹּהֵן אֶת־הַכֶּסֶף עַל־פִּי הַשָּׁנִים הַנּוֹתָרֹת
יט עַד שְׁנַת הַיֹּבֵל וְנִגְרַע מֵעֶרְכֶּךָ׃ וְאִם־גָּאֹל יִגְאַל אֶת־הַשָּׂדֶה הַמַּקְדִּישׁ
כ אֹתוֹ וְיָסַף חֲמִשִׁית כֶּסֶף־עֶרְכְּךָ עָלָיו וְקָם לוֹ׃ וְאִם־לֹא יִגְאַל אֶת־הַשָּׂדֶה
כא וְאִם־מָכַר אֶת־הַשָּׂדֶה לְאִישׁ אַחֵר לֹא־יִגָּאֵל עוֹד׃ וְהָיָה הַשָּׂדֶה בְּצֵאתוֹ
ששי כב בַיֹּבֵל קֹדֶשׁ לַיהוָה כִּשְׂדֵה הַחֵרֶם לַכֹּהֵן תִּהְיֶה אֲחֻזָּתוֹ׃ וְאִם אֶת־שְׂדֵה
כג מִקְנָתוֹ אֲשֶׁר לֹא מִשְּׂדֵה אֲחֻזָּתוֹ יַקְדִּישׁ לַיהוָה׃ וְחִשַּׁב־לוֹ הַכֹּהֵן אֵת
מִכְסַת הָעֶרְכְּךָ עַד שְׁנַת הַיֹּבֵל וְנָתַן אֶת־הָעֶרְכְּךָ בַּיּוֹם הַהוּא קֹדֶשׁ
כד לַיהוָה׃ בִּשְׁנַת הַיּוֹבֵל יָשׁוּב הַשָּׂדֶה לַאֲשֶׁר קָנָהוּ מֵאִתּוֹ לַאֲשֶׁר־לוֹ אֲחֻזַּת
כה הָאָרֶץ׃ וְכָל־עֶרְכְּךָ יִהְיֶה בְּשֶׁקֶל הַקֹּדֶשׁ עֶשְׂרִים גֵּרָה יִהְיֶה הַשָּׁקֶל׃
כו אַךְ־בְּכוֹר אֲשֶׁר יְבֻכַּר לַיהוָה בִּבְהֵמָה לֹא־יַקְדִּישׁ אִישׁ אֹתוֹ אִם־שׁוֹר
כז אִם־שֶׂה לַיהוָה הוּא׃ וְאִם בַּבְּהֵמָה הַטְּמֵאָה וּפָדָה בְעֶרְכֶּךָ וְיָסַף חֲמִשִׁתוֹ
כח עָלָיו וְאִם־לֹא יִגָּאֵל וְנִמְכַּר בְּעֶרְכֶּךָ׃ אַךְ כָּל־חֵרֶם אֲשֶׁר יַחֲרִם אִישׁ
לַיהוָה מִכָּל־אֲשֶׁר־לוֹ מֵאָדָם וּבְהֵמָה וּמִשְּׂדֵה אֲחֻזָּתוֹ לֹא יִמָּכֵר וְלֹא
שביעי כט יִגָּאֵל כָּל־חֵרֶם קֹדֶשׁ־קָדָשִׁים הוּא לַיהוָה׃ כָּל־חֵרֶם אֲשֶׁר יָחֳרַם
ל מִן־הָאָדָם לֹא יִפָּדֶה מוֹת יוּמָת׃ וְכָל־מַעְשַׂר הָאָרֶץ מִזֶּרַע הָאָרֶץ מִפְּרִי
לא הָעֵץ לַיהוָה הוּא קֹדֶשׁ לַיהוָה׃ וְאִם־גָּאֹל יִגְאַל אִישׁ מִמַּעַשְׂרוֹ חֲמִשִׁיתוֹ
מפטיר לב יֹסֵף עָלָיו׃ וְכָל־מַעְשַׂר בָּקָר וָצֹאן כֹּל אֲשֶׁר־יַעֲבֹר תַּחַת הַשָּׁבֶט הָעֲשִׂירִי
לג יִהְיֶה־קֹּדֶשׁ לַיהוָה׃ לֹא יְבַקֵּר בֵּין־טוֹב לָרַע וְלֹא יְמִירֶנּוּ וְאִם־הָמֵר
לד יְמִירֶנּוּ וְהָיָה־הוּא וּתְמוּרָתוֹ יִהְיֶה־קֹּדֶשׁ לֹא יִגָּאֵל׃ אֵלֶּה הַמִּצְוֹת אֲשֶׁר
צִוָּה יהוה אֶת־מֹשֶׁה אֶל־בְּנֵי יִשְׂרָאֵל בְּהַר סִינָי׃

XXVII

34. אֵלֶּה הַמִּצְוֹת אֲשֶׁר צִוָּה ה׳ אֶת מֹשֶׁה אֶל בְּנֵי יִשְׂרָאֵל בְּהַר סִינָי — *These are the commandments which HASHEM commanded Moses to the Children of Israel on Mount Sinai.* But they were not given as (part of the) covenant between Him and the Children of Israel.

before the Kohen, and the Kohen should evaluate him; according to what the person
making the vow can afford should the Kohen evaluate him.

9 If it is the kind of animal that one can bring as an offering to HASHEM, whatever
part of it he may give to HASHEM shall be holy. 10 He shall not exchange it nor
substitute it, whether good for bad or bad for good; but if he does substitute one
animal for another animal, then it and its substitute shall be holy. 11 And if it is any
disqualified animal from which they may not bring an offering to HASHEM, then he
shall stand the animal before the Kohen. 12 The Kohen shall evaluate it, whether
good or bad; like the Kohen's valuation so shall it be. 13 If he redeems it, he must add
a fifth to the valuation.

14 If a man consecrates his house to be holy to HASHEM, the Kohen shall evaluate
it, whether good or bad; as the Kohen shall evaluate it, so shall it remain. 15 If the
one who sanctified it will redeem his house, he shall add a fifth of the money-
valuation to it, and it shall be his.

16 If a man consecrates a field from his ancestral heritage to HASHEM, the
valuation shall be according to its seeding: an area seeded by a chomer of barley for
fifty silver shekels. 17 If he consecrates his field from the Jubilee Year, it shall
remain at its valuation. 18 And if he consecrates his field after the Jubilee, the Kohen
shall calculate the money for him according to the remaining years until the Jubilee
Year, and it shall be subtracted from its valuation. 19 If the one who consecrated the
field will redeem it, he shall add a fifth of the money-valuation to it, and it shall be
his. 20 But if he does not redeem the field, or if he had sold the field to another man
— it cannot be redeemed anymore. 21 Then, when the field goes out in the Jubilee,
it will be holy to HASHEM, like a segregated field; his ancestral heritage shall become
the Kohen's.

22 But if he will consecrate to HASHEM a field that he acquired, that is not of the
field of his ancestral heritage, 23 then the Kohen shall calculate for him the sum of
the valuation until the Jubilee Year; and he shall pay the valuation of that day, it
is holy to HASHEM. 24 In the Jubilee Year the field shall return to the one from whom
he acquired it; whose ancestral heritage of the land it was. 25 Every valuation shall
be in the sacred shekel; that shekel shall be twenty gera.

26 However, a firstborn that will become a firstling for HASHEM among livestock,
a man shall not consecrate it; whether it is of oxen or of the flock, it is HASHEM's.
27 If among the unclean animals, he shall redeem it according to the valuation and
add a fifth to it; and if it is not redeemed it shall be sold for its valuation.

28 However, any segregated property that a man will segregate for the sake of
HASHEM, from anything that is his — whether human, animal, or the field of his
ancestral heritage — may not be sold and may not be redeemed, any segregated
item may be most holy to HASHEM.

29 Any condemned person who has been banned from mankind shall not be
redeemed; he shall be put to death.

30 Any tithe of the land, of the seed of the land, of the fruit of the tree, belongs to
HASHEM; it is holy to HASHEM. 31 If a person shall redeem some of his tithe, he shall
add his fifth to it.

32 Any tithe of cattle or of the flock, any that passes under the staff, the tenth one
shall be holy to HASHEM. 33 He shall not distinguish between good and bad and he
should not substitute for it; and if he does substitute for it, then it and its substitute
shall be holy, it may not be redeemed.

34 These are the commandments that HASHEM commanded Moses to the Children
of Israel on Mount Sinai.

ספר במדבר
Bamidbar / Numbers

Sforno's Introduction

In this fourth book it is related how, (because) He desired (to bestow) kindness (upon Israel), He arranged their flags similar to (the arrangement of) the (Divine) chariot as seen in the vision of His prophets, the intent being that just as they encamped so would they journey, thereby entering the Land immediately without need to resort to weapons.[1] Now to merit this, He arranged the charge of the *Kohanim* and Levites,[2] separated all those who were *tamei* from their camps,[3] and set down the laws (lit. "the subject") of the *sotah* (a woman suspected of infidelity) and the *nazir*,[4] in order to remove all bastardy (from their midst) and to sanctify a number of their sons as *nazirim*. Through all this, they became worthy (to receive) the Priestly Blessings.[5]

And therefore, (the Torah) makes mention of the merits of Israel by which they became worthy to enter the Land in this manner (i.e., without opposition). These are the dedication of the Altar;[6] their efforts towards the *taharah* of the Levites [7] and the (preparation of the) *Pesach*,[8] and their (willingness) to follow Him in the wilderness.

He (then) commanded (regarding) the trumpets (which alerted) the camps to journey, to battle and for other (purposes).[9] He then led them on three journeys in the great and awesome wilderness until Kadesh Barnea. (However) they, in the manner of (fallible) mortals, transgressed His covenant and behaved treacherously in the episode of the spies,[10] thereby subverting their (own) interests. It was therefore decreed that they perish in the wilderness and that their children would go into exile for (many) generations at the ordained time.[11] As a result (of this sin), their children encircled the lands of the nations for forty years and did not enter the land without a struggle.

The third part (of this book) relates that, in spite of all this, the mercy of God did not cease in arranging the affairs of His children as much as possible, and He commanded regarding the libations (נְסָכִים) of an offering made by an individual, and the (separation of) *challah*, and the goat (sacrifice) to atone for

1. See the *Sforno's* commentary on 1:2.
2. Chapter 4.
3. 5:1-4.
4. 5:11-31; 6:1-21.
5. 6:22-27.
6. Chapter 7.
7. 8:5-14.
8. 9:1-8.
9. 10:1-10.
10. Chapter 13.
11. See the *Sforno's* commentary on 14:28.

idolatry,[12] all this instituted from (the time of) the (episode of) the spies and beyond.[13] He (also) sanctified them unto Himself through the commandment of *tzitzis.*[14] In spite of all this, Korach and his congregation did not hesitate to rebel against His honored leaders.[15] Indeed, they transgressed and were punished, (but) He had compassion on the rest of the masses and mended the breach, as symbolized by the firepans and the rod[16] and the priestly gifts[17] so that they should not revert to their reckless ways (lit., "foolishness").

(The Torah) then mentions the *taharah* process of one rendered *tamei* through contact with a dead person, by means of water (mixed with the ashes of the Red Cow).[18] (Now) when they entered that portion of the land of the Emorites which is identified with Sichon and Og, He also gave them the order of dividing the land on the other side of the Jordan and beyond.[19] All this (took place) after the despair of their fathers, due to the impairment of the spies. Thus the fourth book concludes.

12. 15:1-31.
13. See the *Sforno's* commentary there.
14. 15:37-41.
15. Chapter 16 — (Korach).
16. Chapter 17.
17. 18:8-20.
18. Chapter 19 — (Chukas).
19. *Parashios Pinchas, Mattos, Maasei.*

פרשת במדבר

א

א וַיְדַבֵּר יהוה אֶל־מֹשֶׁה בְּמִדְבַּר סִינַי בְּאֹהֶל מוֹעֵד בְּאֶחָד °לַחֹדֶשׁ הַשֵּׁנִי
ב בַּשָּׁנָה הַשֵּׁנִית לְצֵאתָם מֵאֶרֶץ מִצְרַיִם לֵאמֹר: שְׂאוּ אֶת־רֹאשׁ כָּל־עֲדַת
בְּנֵי־יִשְׂרָאֵל לְמִשְׁפְּחֹתָם לְבֵית אֲבֹתָם בְּמִסְפַּר שֵׁמוֹת כָּל־זָכָר
ג לְגֻלְגְּלֹתָם: מִבֶּן עֶשְׂרִים שָׁנָה וָמַעְלָה כָּל־יֹצֵא צָבָא בְּיִשְׂרָאֵל תִּפְקְדוּ
ד אֹתָם לְצִבְאֹתָם אַתָּה וְאַהֲרֹן: וְאִתְּכֶם יִהְיוּ אִישׁ אִישׁ לַמַּטֶּה אִישׁ רֹאשׁ
ה לְבֵית־אֲבֹתָיו הוּא: וְאֵלֶּה שְׁמוֹת הָאֲנָשִׁים אֲשֶׁר יַעַמְדוּ אִתְּכֶם לִרְאוּבֵן
ו־ז אֱלִיצוּר בֶּן־שְׁדֵיאוּר: לְשִׁמְעוֹן שְׁלֻמִיאֵל בֶּן־צוּרִישַׁדָּי: לִיהוּדָה נַחְשׁוֹן
ח־י בֶּן־עַמִּינָדָב: לְיִשָּׂשכָר נְתַנְאֵל בֶּן־צוּעָר: לִזְבוּלֻן אֱלִיאָב בֶּן־חֵלֹן: לִבְנֵי
יוֹסֵף לְאֶפְרַיִם אֱלִישָׁמָע בֶּן־עַמִּיהוּד לִמְנַשֶּׁה גַּמְלִיאֵל בֶּן־פְּדָהצוּר:
יא־יג לְבִנְיָמִן אֲבִידָן בֶּן־גִּדְעֹנִי: לְדָן אֲחִיעֶזֶר בֶּן־עַמִּישַׁדָּי: לְאָשֵׁר פַּגְעִיאֵל
יד־טז בֶּן־עָכְרָן: לְגָד אֶלְיָסָף בֶּן־דְּעוּאֵל: לְנַפְתָּלִי אֲחִירַע בֶּן־עֵינָן: אֵלֶּה
יז °קְרִיאֵי הָעֵדָה נְשִׂיאֵי מַטּוֹת אֲבוֹתָם רָאשֵׁי אַלְפֵי יִשְׂרָאֵל הֵם: וַיִּקַּח
יח מֹשֶׁה וְאַהֲרֹן אֵת הָאֲנָשִׁים הָאֵלֶּה אֲשֶׁר נִקְּבוּ בְּשֵׁמוֹת: וְאֵת כָּל־הָעֵדָה
הִקְהִילוּ בְּאֶחָד לַחֹדֶשׁ הַשֵּׁנִי וַיִּתְיַלְדוּ עַל־מִשְׁפְּחֹתָם לְבֵית אֲבֹתָם
יט בְּמִסְפַּר שֵׁמוֹת מִבֶּן עֶשְׂרִים שָׁנָה וָמַעְלָה לְגֻלְגְּלֹתָם: כַּאֲשֶׁר צִוָּה יהוה

°קְרוּאֵי ק׳

I

1. וַיְדַבֵּר ה׳ אֶל מֹשֶׁה — *And HASHEM spoke to Moses.*

2. שְׂאוּ אֶת רֹאשׁ — *Take you the sum ...* to organize them so that they might enter the Land immediately, each man according to his standard (i.e., flag or banner), without having to wage war. Rather, the nations will depart (voluntarily), as the (Torah) testifies in regard to some who did when it says, כַּעֲזוּבַת הַחֹרֶשׁ וְהָאָמִיר אֲשֶׁר עָזְבוּ מִפְּנֵי בְּנֵי יִשְׂרָאֵל, *Which were forsaken from before the Children of Israel after the manner of woods and lofty forests* (*Isaiah* 17:9). Perhaps these were the families of the Girgoshi of whom (our Sages) say that they arose and left of their own volition (see *Rashi, Exodus* 33:2). (However) because of the impairment of the Spies, the seven nations increased their evil (ways) for forty years and it was (therefore) necessary to destroy them.

בְּמִסְפַּר שֵׁמוֹת — *According to the number of names* ... for at that time every one of that generation was designated by his name which indicated and reflected stature and character, similar to, וָאֵדָעֲךָ בְשֵׁם, *And I know you by name* (*Exodus* 33:17). It was not so regarding (the people of) the generation which entered the Land, and therefore, they were

NOTES

I

2. שְׂאוּ אֶת רֹאשׁ — *Take you the sum.* The *Sforno* is of the opinion, stated here as well as in his commentary later in this Book (9:1 and 10:35), that had the Israelites not sinned in the episode of the spies (*parashas Shlach*) they would have entered the Promised Land much earlier in the course of their journey, without having to wage war, and would not have been compelled to wander in the wilderness for close to forty years. The seven nations would have forsaken the land on their own, as indeed one of them (the Girgoshi) did, as *Rashi* tells us in *Exodus* 33:2 where only six of the seven nations are mentioned because one had already left voluntarily. However, since the Israelites sinned, the inhabitants of the land intensified their evil ways during the forty years of Israel's wanderings, thereby necessitating a prolonged war of conquest by Joshua and the Israelite army. The original intent of taking the census and organizing the tribes under their individual ensigns was not for military purposes, but rather to

PARASHAS BAMIDBAR

1 *1 HASHEM spoke to Moses in the Wilderness of Sinai, in the Tent of
Meeting, on the first of the second month, in the second year after
their exodus from the land of Egypt, saying:*
*2 "Take a census of the entire assembly of the Children of Israel according
to their families, according to their fathers' household, by number of the
names, every male according to their head count. 3 From twenty years of age
and up — everyone who goes out to the legion in Israel — you shall count
them according to their legions, you and Aaron. 4 And with you shall be one
man from each tribe; a man who is a leader of his father's household.*
*5 "These are the names of the men who shall stand with you: For Reuben,
Elizur son of Shedeur. 6 For Simeon, Shelumiel son of Zurishaddai. 7 For
Judah, Nachshon son of Amminadab. 8 For Issachar, Nethanel son of Zuar.
9 For Zebulun, Eliab son of Helon. 10 For the children of Joseph — for
Ephraim, Elishama son of Ammihud; for Manasseh, Gamaliel son of
Pedahzur. 11 For Benjamin, Abidan son of Gideoni. 12 For Dan, Ahiezer son of
Ammishaddai. 13 For Asher, Pagiel son of Ochran. 14 For Gad, Eliasaph son
of Deuel. 15 For Naphtali, Ahira son of Enan."*
*16 These were the ones summoned by the assembly, the leaders of their
fathers' tribes, they are the heads of Israel's thousands. 17 Moses and Aaron
took these men who had been designated by [their] names.*
*18 They gathered together the entire assembly on the first of the second
month, and they established their genealogy according to their families,
according to their fathers' household, by number of the names, from twenty
years of age and up, according to their head count. 19 As HASHEM had*

not counted by the number of names. Only the heads of families were mentioned and the number of men (chapter 26). This tells us that the (original) intent was that these selfsame men should live to inherit the Land, without exception.

4. אִישׁ רֹאשׁ לְבֵית אֲבֹתָיו — *Every one head of his father's house.* The reason that they should be with you is because each one is the head of his father's house and will (therefore) be knowledgeable regarding the lineage of each individual.

18. וַיִּתְיַלְדוּ עַל מִשְׁפְּחֹתָם — *And they declared their pedigrees according to their families* ... because the purpose of this census was to enable the army to go out to war; hence, the intent was to protect their pedigree since the merit of their fathers would assist them (see *Kiddushin* 76b). Thus (our Sages) have stated, "We make no investigation of one who was recorded among the king's list of officers" (*Kiddushin* 76a), and this is in accordance with the statement, "The Divine Presence rests only upon families of pure birth in Israel" (*Kiddushin* 70b).

NOTES

lead them to *Eretz Yisrael* in an organized and dignified manner. The verse from Isaiah cited by the *Sforno* alludes to the nature of the conquest, when cities were forsaken in the manner of woods and forests which are uninhabited.

בְּמִסְפַּר שֵׁמוֹת — *According to the number of names.* The significance of names is established by the *Sforno* in his commentary on *Exodus* 1:1.

18. וַיִּתְיַלְדוּ עַל מִשְׁפְּחֹתָם — *And they declared their pedigrees according to their families* ... Although the original and primary purpose of the census was to lead them into the Land in an orderly fashion, as explained above, nonetheless it was also for the purpose of organizing them into a disciplined, efficient army. As such, their יִחוּס, *lineage,* was an extremely important factor, for in the merit of their familial purity God would protect them.

כ אֶת־מֹשֶׁה וַיִּפְקְדֵם בְּמִדְבַּר סִינָי׃ וַיִּהְיוּ בְנֵי־רְאוּבֵן בְּכֹר
יִשְׂרָאֵל תּוֹלְדֹתָם לְמִשְׁפְּחֹתָם לְבֵית אֲבֹתָם בְּמִסְפַּר שֵׁמוֹת לְגֻלְגְּלֹתָם
כא כָּל־זָכָר מִבֶּן עֶשְׂרִים שָׁנָה וָמַעְלָה כֹּל יֹצֵא צָבָא׃ פְּקֻדֵיהֶם לְמַטֵּה רְאוּבֵן
שִׁשָּׁה וְאַרְבָּעִים אֶלֶף וַחֲמֵשׁ מֵאוֹת׃
כב לִבְנֵי שִׁמְעוֹן תּוֹלְדֹתָם לְמִשְׁפְּחֹתָם לְבֵית אֲבֹתָם פְּקֻדָיו בְּמִסְפַּר שֵׁמוֹת
כג לְגֻלְגְּלֹתָם כָּל־זָכָר מִבֶּן עֶשְׂרִים שָׁנָה וָמַעְלָה כֹּל יֹצֵא צָבָא׃ פְּקֻדֵיהֶם
לְמַטֵּה שִׁמְעוֹן תִּשְׁעָה וַחֲמִשִּׁים אֶלֶף וּשְׁלֹשׁ מֵאוֹת׃
כד לִבְנֵי גָד תּוֹלְדֹתָם לְמִשְׁפְּחֹתָם לְבֵית אֲבֹתָם בְּמִסְפַּר שֵׁמוֹת מִבֶּן
כה עֶשְׂרִים שָׁנָה וָמַעְלָה כֹּל יֹצֵא צָבָא׃ פְּקֻדֵיהֶם לְמַטֵּה גָד חֲמִשָּׁה
וְאַרְבָּעִים אֶלֶף וְשֵׁשׁ מֵאוֹת וַחֲמִשִּׁים׃
כו לִבְנֵי יְהוּדָה תּוֹלְדֹתָם לְמִשְׁפְּחֹתָם לְבֵית אֲבֹתָם בְּמִסְפַּר שְׁמֹת מִבֶּן
כז עֶשְׂרִים שָׁנָה וָמַעְלָה כֹּל יֹצֵא צָבָא׃ פְּקֻדֵיהֶם לְמַטֵּה יְהוּדָה אַרְבָּעָה
וְשִׁבְעִים אֶלֶף וְשֵׁשׁ מֵאוֹת׃
כח לִבְנֵי יִשָּׂשכָר תּוֹלְדֹתָם לְמִשְׁפְּחֹתָם לְבֵית אֲבֹתָם בְּמִסְפַּר שְׁמֹת מִבֶּן
כט עֶשְׂרִים שָׁנָה וָמַעְלָה כֹּל יֹצֵא צָבָא׃ פְּקֻדֵיהֶם לְמַטֵּה יִשָּׂשכָר אַרְבָּעָה
וַחֲמִשִּׁים אֶלֶף וְאַרְבַּע מֵאוֹת׃
ל לִבְנֵי זְבוּלֻן תּוֹלְדֹתָם לְמִשְׁפְּחֹתָם לְבֵית אֲבֹתָם בְּמִסְפַּר שְׁמֹת מִבֶּן
לא עֶשְׂרִים שָׁנָה וָמַעְלָה כֹּל יֹצֵא צָבָא׃ פְּקֻדֵיהֶם לְמַטֵּה זְבוּלֻן שִׁבְעָה
וַחֲמִשִּׁים אֶלֶף וְאַרְבַּע מֵאוֹת׃
לב לִבְנֵי יוֹסֵף לִבְנֵי אֶפְרַיִם תּוֹלְדֹתָם לְמִשְׁפְּחֹתָם לְבֵית אֲבֹתָם בְּמִסְפַּר
לג שְׁמֹת מִבֶּן עֶשְׂרִים שָׁנָה וָמַעְלָה כֹּל יֹצֵא צָבָא׃ פְּקֻדֵיהֶם לְמַטֵּה אֶפְרָיִם
אַרְבָּעִים אֶלֶף וַחֲמֵשׁ מֵאוֹת׃
לד לִבְנֵי מְנַשֶּׁה תּוֹלְדֹתָם לְמִשְׁפְּחֹתָם לְבֵית אֲבֹתָם בְּמִסְפַּר שֵׁמוֹת מִבֶּן
לה עֶשְׂרִים שָׁנָה וָמַעְלָה כֹּל יֹצֵא צָבָא׃ פְּקֻדֵיהֶם לְמַטֵּה מְנַשֶּׁה שְׁנַיִם
וּשְׁלֹשִׁים אֶלֶף וּמָאתָיִם׃
לו לִבְנֵי בִנְיָמִן תּוֹלְדֹתָם לְמִשְׁפְּחֹתָם לְבֵית אֲבֹתָם בְּמִסְפַּר שְׁמֹת מִבֶּן
לז עֶשְׂרִים שָׁנָה וָמַעְלָה כֹּל יֹצֵא צָבָא׃ פְּקֻדֵיהֶם לְמַטֵּה בִנְיָמִן חֲמִשָּׁה
וּשְׁלֹשִׁים אֶלֶף וְאַרְבַּע מֵאוֹת׃
לח לִבְנֵי דָן תּוֹלְדֹתָם לְמִשְׁפְּחֹתָם לְבֵית אֲבֹתָם בְּמִסְפַּר שְׁמֹת מִבֶּן עֶשְׂרִים
לט שָׁנָה וָמַעְלָה כֹּל יֹצֵא צָבָא׃ פְּקֻדֵיהֶם לְמַטֵּה דָן שְׁנַיִם וְשִׁשִּׁים אֶלֶף וּשְׁבַע
מֵאוֹת׃

---

20. בְּכֹר יִשְׂרָאֵל — *Israel's firstborn.* For he (Reuben) did not fall from his elevated status according to the law of heaven because he repented, as we find, וַיִּהְיוּ בְנֵי יַעֲקֹב שְׁנֵים עָשָׂר, בְּנֵי לֵאָה בְּכוֹר יַעֲקֹב רְאוּבֵן, *And the sons of Jacob were twelve; the sons of Leah, Jacob's firstborn, Reuben* (*Genesis* 35:22, 23); even though he fell from this status according to the

NOTES

20. בְּכֹר יִשְׂרָאֵל — *Israel's firstborn.* See *Genesis* 35:23, the *Sforno's* commentary on that verse and the explanatory note.

commanded Moses, he counted them in the Wilderness of Sinai.
[20] *These were the sons of Reuben, firstborn of Israel, their offspring*
according to their families, according to their fathers' household, by number
of the names according to their head count, every male from twenty years
of age and up, everyone who goes out to the legion.
[21] *Their count, for the tribe*
of Reuben: forty-six thousand, five hundred.
[22] *For the sons of Simeon, their offspring according to their families,*
according to their fathers' household, its numbers, by number of the names
according to their head count, every male from twenty years of age and up,
everyone who goes out to the legion.
[23] *Their count, for the tribe of Simeon:*
fifty-nine thousand, three hundred.
[24] *For the sons of Gad, their offspring according to their families,*
according to their fathers' household, by number of the names, every male
from twenty years of age and up, everyone who goes out to the legion.
[25] *Their count, for the tribe of Gad: forty-five thousand, six hundred and*
fifty.
[26] *For the sons of Judah, their offspring according to their families,*
according to their fathers' household, by number of the names, every male
from twenty years of age and up, everyone who goes out to the legion.
[27] *Their count, for the tribe of Judah: seventy-four thousand, six hundred.*
[28] *For the sons of Issachar, their offspring according to their families,*
according to their fathers' household, by number of the names, every male
from twenty years of age and up, everyone who goes out to the legion.
[29] *Their count, for the tribe of Issachar: fifty-four thousand, four hundred.*
[30] *For the sons of Zebulun, their offspring according to their families,*
according to their fathers' household, by number of the names, every male
from twenty years of age and up, everyone who goes out to the legion.
[31] *Their count, for the tribe of Zebulun: fifty-seven thousand, four hundred.*
[32] *For the sons of Joseph: for the sons of Ephraim, their offspring*
according to their families, according to their fathers' household, by number
of the names, every male from twenty years of age and up, everyone who
goes out to the legion.
[33] *Their count, for the tribe of Ephraim: forty thousand,*
five hundred.
[34] *For the sons of Manasseh, their offspring according to their families,*
according to their fathers' household, by number of the names, every male
from twenty years of age and up, everyone who goes out to the legion.
[35] *Their count, for the tribe of Manasseh: thirty-two thousand, two hundred.*
[36] *For the sons of Benjamin, their offspring according to their families,*
according to their fathers' household, by number of the names, every male
from twenty years of age and up, everyone who goes out to the legion.
[37] *Their count, for the tribe of Benjamin: thirty-five thousand, four hundred.*
[38] *For the sons of Dan, their offspring according to their families,*
according to their fathers' household, by number of the names, every male
from twenty years of age and up, everyone who goes out to the legion.
[39] *Their count, for the tribe of Dan: sixty-two thousand, seven hundred.*

---

law (i.e., perspective) of man.

מ לִבְנֵי אָשֵׁר תּוֹלְדֹתָם לְמִשְׁפְּחֹתָם לְבֵית אֲבֹתָם בְּמִסְפַּר שֵׁמֹת מִבֶּן
מא עֶשְׂרִים שָׁנָה וָמַעְלָה כֹּל יֹצֵא צָבָא׃ פְּקֻדֵיהֶם לְמַטֵּה אָשֵׁר אֶחָד
וְאַרְבָּעִים אֶלֶף וַחֲמֵשׁ מֵאוֹת׃
מב בְּנֵי נַפְתָּלִי תּוֹלְדֹתָם לְמִשְׁפְּחֹתָם לְבֵית אֲבֹתָם בְּמִסְפַּר שֵׁמֹת מִבֶּן
מג עֶשְׂרִים שָׁנָה וָמַעְלָה כֹּל יֹצֵא צָבָא׃ פְּקֻדֵיהֶם לְמַטֵּה נַפְתָּלִי שְׁלֹשָׁה
וַחֲמִשִּׁים אֶלֶף וְאַרְבַּע מֵאוֹת׃
מד אֵלֶּה הַפְּקֻדִים אֲשֶׁר פָּקַד מֹשֶׁה וְאַהֲרֹן וּנְשִׂיאֵי יִשְׂרָאֵל שְׁנֵים עָשָׂר אִישׁ
מה אִישׁ־אֶחָד לְבֵית־אֲבֹתָיו הָיוּ׃ וַיִּהְיוּ כָּל־פְּקוּדֵי בְנֵי־יִשְׂרָאֵל לְבֵית
מו אֲבֹתָם מִבֶּן עֶשְׂרִים שָׁנָה וָמַעְלָה כָּל־יֹצֵא צָבָא בְּיִשְׂרָאֵל׃ וַיִּהְיוּ
כָּל־הַפְּקֻדִים שֵׁשׁ־מֵאוֹת אֶלֶף וּשְׁלֹשֶׁת אֲלָפִים וַחֲמֵשׁ מֵאוֹת וַחֲמִשִּׁים׃
מז וְהַלְוִיִּם לְמַטֵּה אֲבֹתָם לֹא הָתְפָּקְדוּ בְּתוֹכָם׃
מח־מט וַיְדַבֵּר יְהוָה אֶל־מֹשֶׁה לֵּאמֹר׃ אַךְ אֶת־מַטֵּה לֵוִי לֹא תִפְקֹד וְאֶת־
נ רֹאשָׁם לֹא תִשָּׂא בְּתוֹךְ בְּנֵי יִשְׂרָאֵל׃ וְאַתָּה הַפְקֵד אֶת־הַלְוִיִּם
עַל־מִשְׁכַּן הָעֵדֻת וְעַל כָּל־כֵּלָיו וְעַל כָּל־אֲשֶׁר־לוֹ הֵמָּה יִשְׂאוּ
נא אֶת־הַמִּשְׁכָּן וְאֶת־כָּל־כֵּלָיו וְהֵם יְשָׁרְתֻהוּ וְסָבִיב לַמִּשְׁכָּן יַחֲנוּ׃ וּבִנְסֹעַ
הַמִּשְׁכָּן יוֹרִידוּ אֹתוֹ הַלְוִיִּם וּבַחֲנֹת הַמִּשְׁכָּן יָקִימוּ אֹתוֹ הַלְוִיִּם וְהַזָּר
נב הַקָּרֵב יוּמָת׃ וְחָנוּ בְּנֵי יִשְׂרָאֵל אִישׁ עַל־מַחֲנֵהוּ וְאִישׁ עַל־דִּגְלוֹ
נג לְצִבְאֹתָם׃ וְהַלְוִיִּם יַחֲנוּ סָבִיב לְמִשְׁכַּן הָעֵדֻת וְלֹא־יִהְיֶה קֶצֶף עַל־עֲדַת

44. אֵלֶּה הַפְּקֻדִים — *These are those that were numbered.* Each one of these was counted by Moses and Aaron.

45. וַיִּהְיוּ כָּל פְּקוּדֵי . . . כָּל יֹצֵא צָבָא בְּיִשְׂרָאֵל — *And all those that were numbered . . . all that were able to go forth to war in Israel . . .* not including those over sixty years of age who no longer went forth to war, as (our Sages) mention regarding Yair the son of Menashe and others (*Bava Basra* 121b). Now, without them, the total was that which is written later (in the following verse).

47. לֹא הָתְפָּקְדוּ בְּתוֹכָם — *Were not numbered among them.* They were not numbered by the census takers nor did they count themselves, for they did not prepare themselves, as did the others, by gathering (in order to establish their) lineage. Now this was *before* God, the Blessed One, said to Moses, *Nevertheless, the tribe of Levi you shall not number* (v. 49), because they waited to see what God would command them (to do) since the tribe of Levi was not mentioned with the other tribes when He said, *And with you there shall be a man from every tribe* (v. 4).

49. אַךְ אֶת מַטֵּה לֵוִי — *Nevertheless the tribe of Levi.* Even though I said, *Take you the sum of all the congregation of the Children of Israel* (v. 2), and the Levites are included among them to be counted as well, nonetheless, they are separated from the rest of the people of

NOTES

47. לֹא הָתְפָּקְדוּ בְּתוֹכָם — *Were not numbered among them.* The expression הָתְפָּקְדוּ, *numbered*, is written in the הִתְפַּעֵל (reflexive form), suggesting that they themselves (the Levites) were the ones doing the act of counting, as well as being the referents. The *Sforno*, therefore, explains that they were neither counted by the census takers nor did they gather and prepare themselves for a count as did the others. Since the tribe of Levi was not included when God told Moses to take a representative from each tribe with whom to take the census, the Levites realized that their counting was to be different — and separate — from that of the rest of Israel.

[40] *For the sons of Asher, their offspring according to their families,*
according to their fathers' household, by numbers of the names, every male
from twenty years of age and up, everyone who goes out to the legion.
[41] *Their count, for the tribe of Asher: forty-one thousand, five hundred.*
[42] *The sons of Naphtali, their offspring according to their families,*
according to their fathers' household, by number of the names, every male
from twenty years of age and up, everyone who goes out to the legion.
[43] *Their count, for the tribe of Naftali: fifty-three thousand, four hundred.*
[44] *These are the countings that Moses, Aaron, and the leaders of Israel*
counted — twelve men, one man for his father's household, were they —
[45] *these were all the countings of the Children of Israel, according to their*
fathers' households, from twenty years of age and up, everyone who goes
out to the legion in Israel: [46] *All their countings were six hundred and three*
thousand, five hundred and fifty.
[47] *The Levites according to their fathers' tribe were not counted among*
them.
[48] *HASHEM spoke to Moses, saying,* [49] *"But you shall not count the tribe of*
Levi, and you shall not take a census of them among the Children of Israel.
[50] *You shall appoint the Levites over the Tabernacle of the Testimony, over*
all of its utensils and everything that belongs to it. They shall carry the
Tabernacle and all its utensils and they shall minister to it; and they shall
encamp around the Tabernacle. [51] *When the Tabernacle journeys, the*
Levites shall take it down, and when the Tabernacle encamps, the Levites
shall erect it, and an alien who approaches shall die. [52] *The Children of*
Israel shall encamp, every man at his camp and every man at his banner,
according to their legions. [53] *The Levites shall encamp around the Taber-*
nacle of the Testimony so that there shall be no wrath upon the assembly of

---

Israel (in two ways): Firstly, regarding the count, that the counting of their men (is different), and (also in that) their sum total shall not be included with the rest of the people.

לֹא תִפְקֹד — *You shall not number.* The counting of their individuals shall not be from twenty years old and higher, as was the case with the counting of the rest of the people.

וְאֶת רֹאשָׁם לֹא תִשָּׂא — *Neither shall you take their sum.* When you take the total count of all the tribes (of Israel), the total of the tribe of Levi shall not be included (with them).

50. וְאַתָּה הַפְקֵד — *And you shall appoint.* Secondly, they shall be separated from the rest of the people regarding their appointments, for only they shall be assigned the sacred appointments.

53. וְהַלְוִיִּם יַחֲנוּ סָבִיב לְמִשְׁכַּן — *But the Levites shall pitch round about the Sanctuary.* Thirdly, they shall be separated from the rest of the people in their encampment, for they

NOTES

49-53. אַךְ אֶת מַטֵּה לֵוִי לֹא תִפְקֹד . . . וְאַתָּה הַפְקֵד . . . וְהַלְוִיִּם יַחֲנוּ סָבִיב לְמִשְׁכַּן — *Nevertheless, the tribe of Levi you shall not number . . . And you shall appoint . . . But the Levites shall pitch round about the Sanctuary.* The Levites were distinct from the rest of the Israelites in three ways. Since they were counted from the age of thirty days rather than twenty years, their total number was not included in the sum total of all the tribes. Secondly, they alone were charged with the sacred service connected with the Sanctuary, and thirdly, they alone encamped around the Sanctuary, unlike the other tribes who encamped as distinct units under their individual banners. The reason for this differentiation and separation was because they were exempt from military service, for their mission was to serve in the Sanctuary.

נד בְּנֵי יִשְׂרָאֵל וְשָׁמְרוּ הַלְוִיִּם אֶת־מִשְׁמֶרֶת מִשְׁכַּן הָעֵדוּת: וַיַּעֲשׂוּ בְּנֵי
יִשְׂרָאֵל כְּכֹל אֲשֶׁר צִוָּה יהוה אֶת־מֹשֶׁה כֵּן עָשׂוּ:
ב שלישי א-ב וַיְדַבֵּר יהוה אֶל־מֹשֶׁה וְאֶל־אַהֲרֹן לֵאמֹר: אִישׁ עַל־דִּגְלוֹ בְאֹתֹת לְבֵית
ג אֲבֹתָם יַחֲנוּ בְּנֵי יִשְׂרָאֵל מִנֶּגֶד סָבִיב לְאֹהֶל־מוֹעֵד יַחֲנוּ: וְהַחֹנִים קֵדְמָה
מִזְרָחָה דֶּגֶל מַחֲנֵה יְהוּדָה לְצִבְאֹתָם וְנָשִׂיא לִבְנֵי יְהוּדָה נַחְשׁוֹן בֶּן־
ד-ה עַמִּינָדָב: וּצְבָאוֹ וּפְקֻדֵיהֶם אַרְבָּעָה וְשִׁבְעִים אֶלֶף וְשֵׁשׁ מֵאוֹת: וְהַחֹנִים
ו עָלָיו מַטֵּה יִשָּׂשכָר וְנָשִׂיא לִבְנֵי יִשָּׂשכָר נְתַנְאֵל בֶּן־צוּעָר: וּצְבָאוֹ וּפְקֻדָיו
ז אַרְבָּעָה וַחֲמִשִּׁים אֶלֶף וְאַרְבַּע מֵאוֹת: מַטֵּה זְבוּלֻן וְנָשִׂיא לִבְנֵי זְבוּלֻן
ח-ט אֱלִיאָב בֶּן־חֵלֹן: וּצְבָאוֹ וּפְקֻדָיו שִׁבְעָה וַחֲמִשִּׁים אֶלֶף וְאַרְבַּע מֵאוֹת: כָּל־
הַפְּקֻדִים לְמַחֲנֵה יְהוּדָה מְאַת אֶלֶף וּשְׁמֹנִים אֶלֶף וְשֵׁשֶׁת־אֲלָפִים וְאַרְבַּע־
י מֵאוֹת לְצִבְאֹתָם רִאשֹׁנָה יִסָּעוּ: דֶּגֶל מַחֲנֵה רְאוּבֵן תֵּימָנָה
יא לְצִבְאֹתָם וְנָשִׂיא לִבְנֵי רְאוּבֵן אֱלִיצוּר בֶּן־שְׁדֵיאוּר: וּצְבָאוֹ וּפְקֻדָיו שִׁשָּׁה
יב וְאַרְבָּעִים אֶלֶף וַחֲמֵשׁ מֵאוֹת: וְהַחוֹנִם עָלָיו מַטֵּה שִׁמְעוֹן וְנָשִׂיא לִבְנֵי
יג שִׁמְעוֹן שְׁלֻמִיאֵל בֶּן־צוּרִישַׁדָּי: וּצְבָאוֹ וּפְקֻדֵיהֶם תִּשְׁעָה וַחֲמִשִּׁים אֶלֶף
יד-טו וּשְׁלֹשׁ מֵאוֹת: וּמַטֵּה גָּד וְנָשִׂיא לִבְנֵי גָד אֶלְיָסָף בֶּן־רְעוּאֵל: וּצְבָאוֹ
טז וּפְקֻדֵיהֶם חֲמִשָּׁה וְאַרְבָּעִים אֶלֶף וְשֵׁשׁ מֵאוֹת וַחֲמִשִּׁים: כָּל־הַפְּקֻדִים
לְמַחֲנֵה רְאוּבֵן מְאַת אֶלֶף וְאֶחָד וַחֲמִשִּׁים אֶלֶף וְאַרְבַּע־מֵאוֹת וַחֲמִשִּׁים
יז לְצִבְאֹתָם וּשְׁנִיִּם יִסָּעוּ: וְנָסַע אֹהֶל־מוֹעֵד מַחֲנֵה הַלְוִיִּם בְּתוֹךְ
יח הַמַּחֲנֹת כַּאֲשֶׁר יַחֲנוּ כֵּן יִסָּעוּ אִישׁ עַל־יָדוֹ לְדִגְלֵיהֶם: דֶּגֶל
מַחֲנֵה אֶפְרַיִם לְצִבְאֹתָם יָמָּה וְנָשִׂיא לִבְנֵי אֶפְרַיִם אֱלִישָׁמָע בֶּן־עַמִּיהוּד:

alone shall encamp round about the Sanctuary, while the others shall encamp each one with his own standard.

II

17. וְנָסַע אֹהֶל מוֹעֵד . . . בְּתוֹךְ הַמַּחֲנֹת — *Then the Tent of Meeting traveled . . . in the midst of the camps . . .* between the two aforementioned standards (Judah and Reuben).

כַּאֲשֶׁר יַחֲנוּ — *As they encamped.* So that when half of all the standards arrive, the Sanctuary will be completely standing in their midst, for immediately following the standard of Reuben traveled the Kehathites who carried the holy (articles) which are the central (feature) of the (Tent of) Meeting, as it says, וְנוֹעַדְתִּי לְךָ שָׁם וְדִבַּרְתִּי אִתְּךָ מֵעַל הַכַּפֹּרֶת, *And there I will meet with you and I will speak with you from above the Ark cover* (*Exodus* 25:22).

NOTES

II

17. וְנָסַע אֹהֶל מוֹעֵד . . . בְּתוֹךְ הַמַּחֲנֹת — *Then the Tent of Meeting traveled . . . in the midst of the camps.* It would seem from *Rashi's* commentary on this verse that he is of the opinion that after the camps of Judah and Reuben had set off, the Tent of Meeting with the Levites immediately began to move, followed by the remaining two camps (see the *Sifsai Chachomim* on this *Rashi*). The *Sforno*, however, is of the opinion that immediately following Judah's departure, the Tent of Meeting with the Levites followed, *after which* the camp of Reuben set out. In chapter 10, verse 17, *Rashi* also seems to accept this interpretation (although he does not state so clearly). He states there that the encampment broke up in the following order: After the departure of the division of Judah, Aaron and his sons went into the Tabernacle and covered the Ark and all the other holy vessels which were in the charge of the Kehathites. Then the Gershonites and the Merarites dismantled the *Mishkan*, loaded it on the wagons, and started off behind

the Children of Israel, and the Levites shall safeguard the watch of the Tabernacle of the Testimony."

54 The Children of Israel did everything that HASHEM commanded Moses, so did they do.

2 *1 HASHEM spoke to Moses and Aaron, saying, 2 "The Children of Israel shall encamp, each man by his banner according to the insignias of their fathers' household, at a distance surrounding the Tent of Meeting shall they encamp. 3 Those who encamp to the front, at the east, shall be the banner of the camp of Judah according to their legions — and the leader of the children of Judah is Nachshon son of Amminadab — 4 its legion and their count are seventy-four thousand, six hundred. 5 Those encamping near him are: the tribe of Issachar — and the leader of the children of Issachar is Nethanel son of Zuar — 6 its legion and their count are fifty-four thousand, four hundred; 7 the tribe of Zebulun — and the leader of the tribe of Zebulun is Eliab son of Helon — 8 its legion and their count are fifty-seven thousand, four hundred. 9 All those counted for the camp of Judah are one hundred and eighty-six thousand, four hundred, according to their legions; they shall be the first to journey.*

10 "The banner of the camp of Reuben shall be to the south, according to their legions — and the leader of the children of Reuben is Elizur son of Shedeur — 11 its legion and their count are forty-six thousand, five hundred. 12 Those encamping near him are: the tribe of Simeon — and the leader of the tribe of Simeon is Shelumiel son of Zurishaddai — 13 its legion and their count are fifty-nine thousand, three hundred; 14 and the tribe of Gad — and the leader of the children of Gad is Eliasaph son of Reuel — 15 its legion and their count are forty-five thousand, six hundred and fifty. 16 All those counted for the camp of Reuben are one hundred and fifty-one thousand, four hundred and fifty, according to their legions, they shall be the second to journey.

17 "The Tent of Meeting, the camp of the Levites, shall journey in the middle of the camps; as they encamp so shall they journey, everyone at his place according to their banners.

18 "The banner of the camp of Ephraim according to their legions shall be to the west — and the leader of the children of Ephraim is Elishama son of

---

כַּאֲשֶׁר יַחֲנוּ כֵּן יִסָּעוּ — *As they encamp, so they shall journey* . . . and therefore, the entire (*Mishkan*) was in the midst of all the camps, even when they journeyed.

NOTES

Judah. Next came the division of Reuben and after them the Kehathites with the holy objects. All this is clearly stated in chapter 10 verses 17 and 21. The *Sforno's* interpretation of our verse is consistent with the order written in *Behaaloscha.*

כַּאֲשֶׁר יַחֲנוּ — *As they encamp.* The Kehathites were charged with carrying the Ark (3:31). The *Sforno*, therefore, refers to their arrival at the encampment as representing עיקר אהל מועד (the central, important feature of the Tent of Meeting), for God spoke to Moses above the Ark cover. Now, since they followed immediately after the section of Reuben which was the second group after Judah, one half of all the camps were now in place, with the Tabernacle set up in the middle by the Gershonites and Merarites when the Kehathites arrived with the ark. (See *Rashi* on 10:21 for a fuller description of the sequence followed during Israel's journeying and encamping.)

יט-כ וּצְבָאוֹ וּפְקֻדֵיהֶם אַרְבָּעִים אֶלֶף וַחֲמֵשׁ מֵאוֹת: וְעָלָיו מַטֵּה מְנַשֶּׁה
כא וְנָשִׂיא לִבְנֵי מְנַשֶּׁה גַּמְלִיאֵל בֶּן־פְּדָהצוּר: וּצְבָאוֹ וּפְקֻדֵיהֶם שְׁנַיִם
כב וּשְׁלֹשִׁים אֶלֶף וּמָאתָיִם: וּמַטֵּה בִּנְיָמִן וְנָשִׂיא לִבְנֵי בִנְיָמִן אֲבִידָן בֶּן־
כג-כד גִּדְעֹנִי: וּצְבָאוֹ וּפְקֻדֵיהֶם חֲמִשָּׁה וּשְׁלֹשִׁים אֶלֶף וְאַרְבַּע מֵאוֹת: כָּל־
הַפְּקֻדִים לְמַחֲנֵה אֶפְרַיִם מְאַת אֶלֶף וּשְׁמֹנַת־אֲלָפִים וּמֵאָה לְצִבְאֹתָם
כה וּשְׁלִשִׁים יִסָּעוּ: דֶּגֶל מַחֲנֵה דָן צָפֹנָה לְצִבְאֹתָם וְנָשִׂיא
כו לִבְנֵי דָן אֲחִיעֶזֶר בֶּן־עַמִּישַׁדָּי: וּצְבָאוֹ וּפְקֻדֵיהֶם שְׁנַיִם וְשִׁשִּׁים אֶלֶף וּשְׁבַע
כז מֵאוֹת: וְהַחֹנִים עָלָיו מַטֵּה אָשֵׁר וְנָשִׂיא לִבְנֵי אָשֵׁר פַּגְעִיאֵל בֶּן־עָכְרָן:
כח-כט וּצְבָאוֹ וּפְקֻדֵיהֶם אֶחָד וְאַרְבָּעִים אֶלֶף וַחֲמֵשׁ מֵאוֹת: וּמַטֵּה נַפְתָּלִי
ל וְנָשִׂיא לִבְנֵי נַפְתָּלִי אֲחִירַע בֶּן־עֵינָן: וּצְבָאוֹ וּפְקֻדֵיהֶם שְׁלֹשָׁה וַחֲמִשִּׁים
לא אֶלֶף וְאַרְבַּע מֵאוֹת: כָּל־הַפְּקֻדִים לְמַחֲנֵה דָן מְאַת אֶלֶף וְשִׁבְעָה
וַחֲמִשִּׁים אֶלֶף וְשֵׁשׁ מֵאוֹת לָאַחֲרֹנָה יִסְעוּ לְדִגְלֵיהֶם:
לב אֵלֶּה פְּקוּדֵי בְנֵי־יִשְׂרָאֵל לְבֵית אֲבֹתָם כָּל־פְּקוּדֵי הַמַּחֲנֹת לְצִבְאֹתָם
לג שֵׁשׁ־מֵאוֹת אֶלֶף וּשְׁלֹשֶׁת אֲלָפִים וַחֲמֵשׁ מֵאוֹת וַחֲמִשִּׁים: וְהַלְוִיִּם לֹא
לד הָתְפָּקְדוּ בְּתוֹךְ בְּנֵי יִשְׂרָאֵל כַּאֲשֶׁר צִוָּה יהוה אֶת־מֹשֶׁה: וַיַּעֲשׂוּ בְּנֵי
יִשְׂרָאֵל כְּכֹל אֲשֶׁר־צִוָּה יהוה אֶת־מֹשֶׁה כֵּן־חָנוּ לְדִגְלֵיהֶם וְכֵן נָסָעוּ אִישׁ
לְמִשְׁפְּחֹתָיו עַל־בֵּית אֲבֹתָיו:
ג רביעי א וְאֵלֶּה תּוֹלְדֹת אַהֲרֹן וּמֹשֶׁה בְּיוֹם דִּבֶּר יהוה אֶת־מֹשֶׁה בְּהַר סִינָי:
ב-ג וְאֵלֶּה שְׁמוֹת בְּנֵי־אַהֲרֹן הַבְּכֹר | נָדָב וַאֲבִיהוּא אֶלְעָזָר וְאִיתָמָר: אֵלֶּה
ד שְׁמוֹת בְּנֵי אַהֲרֹן הַכֹּהֲנִים הַמְּשֻׁחִים אֲשֶׁר־מִלֵּא יָדָם לְכַהֵן: וַיָּמָת
נָדָב וַאֲבִיהוּא לִפְנֵי יהוה בְּהַקְרִבָם אֵשׁ זָרָה לִפְנֵי יהוה בְּמִדְבַּר סִינַי

---

33. וְהַלְוִיִּם לֹא הָתְפָּקְדוּ — *But the Levites were not numbered* . . . in the sum total of all the other tribes, as well.

כַּאֲשֶׁר צִוָּה ה' אֶת מֹשֶׁה — *As* HASHEM *commanded Moses.* As He said, *Neither shall you take their sum among the Children of Israel* (1:49).

III

1. וְאֵלֶּה תּוֹלְדֹת אַהֲרֹן וּמֹשֶׁה בְּיוֹם דִּבֶּר ה' אֶת מֹשֶׁה — *Now these are the generations of Aaron and Moses on the day that* HASHEM *spoke to Moses.* At the time that (God) separated the tribe of Levi, some to carry (the Tabernacle) and some to serve Him and bless His name, (at that time) Nadav and Avihu were among them.

2. וְאֵלֶּה שְׁמוֹת בְּנֵי אַהֲרֹן — *And these are the names of the sons of Aaron.* Each one of them was important in his own right besides (the fact that) he was the son of Aaron.

NOTES

III

2. וְאֵלֶּה שְׁמוֹת — *And these are the names.* The *Sforno* explains why the expression *These are the names* is repeated twice — in this verse and in verse 3; it is to emphasize the importance of each son in his own right, not only as the son of an illustrious father. For the significance of a "name," see 1:2 above and the beginning of the Book of *Exodus.*

3. הַכֹּהֲנִים הַמְּשֻׁחִים — *The Kohanim that were anointed.* The son of a *Kohen* inherits the status of priesthood from his father, provided he was born after his father already attained that status himself. The sons of Aaron required anointing to be

Ammihud — 19 its legion and their count are forty thousand, five hundred.
20 Those [encamping] near him are: the tribe of Manasseh — and the leader
of the children of Manasseh is Gamaliel son of Pedahzur — 21 its legion and
their count are thirty-two thousand, two hundred; 22 and the tribe of Benja-
min — and the leader of the children of Benjamin is Abidan son of Gideoni
— 23 its legion and their count are thirty-five thousand, four hundred. 24 All
those count for the camp of Ephraim are one hundred and eight thousand,
one hundred, according to their legions; they shall be the third to journey.
25 "The banner of the camp of Dan shall be to the north, according to their
legions — and the leader of the children of Dan is Ahiezer son of Ammi-
shaddai — 26 its legion and their count are sixty-two thousand, seven hun-
dred. 27 Those encamping near him are: the tribe of Asher — and the leader
of the children of Asher is Pagiel son of Ochran — 28 its legion and their
count are forty-one thousand, five hundred; 29 and the tribe of Naphtali —
and the leader of the children of Naphtali is Ahira son of Enan — 30 its
legion and their count are fifty-three thousand, four hundred. 31 All those
counted for the camp of Dan are one hundred and fifty-seven thousand, six
hundred; they shall be the last to journey according to their banners."
32 These are the countings of the Children of Israel according to their
fathers' households; all the countings of the camps according to their
legions, six hundred and three thousand, five hundred and fifty.
33 The Levites were not counted among the Children of Israel, as HASHEM
had commanded Moses. 34 The Children of Israel did everything that
HASHEM *had commanded Moses — so they encamped according to their*
banners and so they journeyed; every man according to his families, by his
father's household.

3 *1 These are the offspring of Aaron and Moses on the day* HASHEM *spoke*
with Moses at Mount Sinai: 2 These are the names of the sons of
Aaron, the firstborn was Nadab, and Abihu, Elazar, and Ithamar. 3 These
were the names of the sons of Aaron, the anointed Kohanim, whom he
inaugurated to minister. 4 Nadab and Abihu died before HASHEM *when*
they offered an alien fire before HASHEM *in the Wilderness of Sinai,*

---

3. הַכֹּהֲנִים הַמְּשֻׁחִים — *The Kohanim that were anointed* ... unlike future generations when a כֹּהֵן הֶדְיוֹט, *an ordinary priest,* was never anointed during the lifetime of the *Kohen Gadol* — the reason being ...

אֲשֶׁר מִלֵּא יָדָם לְכַהֵן — *Whom he consecrated to minister in the Kohen's office* ... for at that time they required the anointing, without which they would never have become *Kohanim* at all since they were born before Aaron was chosen to function as a *Kohen,* as was the case (also) with Pinchas before he killed Zimri (see 25:13).

4. בְּהַקְרִבָם אֵשׁ זָרָה — *When they offered strange fire.* This was the only (sin) they had committed.

NOTES

consecrated as *Kohanim* since they were born before Aaron had been designated as the *Kohen Gadol*. This was also the case with Pinchas to whom God gave *the covenant of eternal priesthood* (25:13) for, as *Rashi* explains there, "He was born before his father (Elazar) was designated as a *Kohen*"; hence, he could not attain priesthood through his lineage alone.

וּבָנִים לֹא־הָיוּ לָהֶם וַיְכַהֵן אֶלְעָזָר וְאִיתָמָר עַל־פְּנֵי אַהֲרֹן אֲבִיהֶם:
ה־ו וַיְדַבֵּר יהוה אֶל־מֹשֶׁה לֵּאמֹר: הַקְרֵב אֶת־מַטֵּה לֵוִי וְהַעֲמַדְתָּ אֹתוֹ לִפְנֵי
ז אַהֲרֹן הַכֹּהֵן וְשֵׁרְתוּ אֹתוֹ: וְשָׁמְרוּ אֶת־מִשְׁמַרְתּוֹ וְאֶת־מִשְׁמֶרֶת כָּל־הָעֵדָה
ח לִפְנֵי אֹהֶל מוֹעֵד לַעֲבֹד אֶת־עֲבֹדַת הַמִּשְׁכָּן: וְשָׁמְרוּ אֶת־כָּל־כְּלֵי אֹהֶל
ט מוֹעֵד וְאֶת־מִשְׁמֶרֶת בְּנֵי יִשְׂרָאֵל לַעֲבֹד אֶת־עֲבֹדַת הַמִּשְׁכָּן: וְנָתַתָּה
אֶת־הַלְוִיִּם לְאַהֲרֹן וּלְבָנָיו נְתוּנִם נְתוּנִם הֵמָּה לוֹ מֵאֵת בְּנֵי יִשְׂרָאֵל:
י וְאֶת־אַהֲרֹן וְאֶת־בָּנָיו תִּפְקֹד וְשָׁמְרוּ אֶת־כְּהֻנָּתָם וְהַזָּר הַקָּרֵב יוּמָת:
יא־יב וַיְדַבֵּר יהוה אֶל־מֹשֶׁה לֵּאמֹר: וַאֲנִי הִנֵּה לָקַחְתִּי אֶת־הַלְוִיִּם מִתּוֹךְ בְּנֵי
יג יִשְׂרָאֵל תַּחַת כָּל־בְּכוֹר פֶּטֶר רֶחֶם מִבְּנֵי יִשְׂרָאֵל וְהָיוּ לִי הַלְוִיִּם: כִּי לִי
כָּל־בְּכוֹר בְּיוֹם הַכֹּתִי כָל־בְּכוֹר בְּאֶרֶץ מִצְרַיִם הִקְדַּשְׁתִּי לִי כָל־בְּכוֹר

וּבָנִים לֹא הָיוּ לָהֶם — *And they had no children.* For if they would have had children to succeed them, they (the offspring) would have inherited the prominent positions fitting for their fathers.

וַיְכַהֵן אֶלְעָזָר וְאִיתָמָר — *And Elazar and Ithamar ministered in the Kohen's office.* They were appointed to exercise authority in the Sanctuary by the command of God, the Blessed One.

עַל פְּנֵי אַהֲרֹן אֲבִיהֶם — *In the presence of Aaron their father.* During Aaron's lifetime, his sons were anointed, two of whom died and two of whom gained authority; yet (all this took place) without his sanction even though he was the *Kohen Gadol*. Now this would not continue throughout the generations, for (there would come a time that) there would be no anointing of an ordinary *Kohen*, nor any appointment during the lifetime of the *Kohen Gadol* without his authorization.

6. וְשֵׁרְתוּ אֹתוֹ — *That they may minister unto him.* For the entire guardianship (of the Sanctuary) is vested in him, as it says, *You and your sons and your father's house with you shall bear the iniquity (i.e., responsibility) of the Sanctuary, and you and your sons with you shall bear the iniquity (i.e., responsibility) of your priesthood* (18:1). Therefore, the work of the Levites (was) to serve the *Kohen Gadol* in the area incumbent upon him, i.e., to guard the Sanctuary and its vessels, while the guarding of the priesthood, that no stranger should draw close, was incumbent only upon Aaron and his sons.

7. וְאֶת מִשְׁמֶרֶת כָּל הָעֵדָה לִפְנֵי אֹהֶל מוֹעֵד לַעֲבֹד אֶת עֲבֹדַת הַמִּשְׁכָּן — *And the charge of the whole congregation before the Tent of Meeting to do the service of the Sanctuary . . .* to minister to the needs of the (Divine) service, which would have been the privilege of the members of the Sanhedrin, were it not for the sin of the Golden Calf.

NOTES

4. וּבָנִים לֹא הָיוּ לָהֶם — *And they had no children.* The *Sforno* explains the parenthetical insertion of the phrase *and they had no children* as the reason for Elazar and Ithamar succeeding to the priesthood following the death of their older brothers. If Nadav and Avihu would have had children, those children would have inherited their father's positions rather than Elazar and Ithamar.

עַל פְּנֵי אַהֲרֹן אֲבִיהֶם — *In the presence of Aaron their father.* The addition of this phrase is to be understood, as *Rashi* comments, in the sense of "in his lifetime." The Torah stresses this to teach us that only at that period in Jewish history was this so, i.e., that children attained positions of authority in the priesthood even while the *Kohen Gadol* was alive, yet without his sanction. In later generations, this would not be the case, as the *Sforno* explains.

6. וְשֵׁרְתוּ אֹתוֹ — *That they may minister unto him.* The *Sforno* draws a subtle distinction between the guardianship of the Sanctuary and its vessels, to which role the Levites were assigned to assist the *Kohen Gadol* (whose primary responsibility this was), and that of preventing any זָר, non-*Kohen*, from "drawing close," i.e., assuming the role reserved for the *Kohanim* alone, which is the *sole* responsibility of the *Kohanim* and did not require the Levites' intervention.

and they had no children; but Elazar and Ithamar ministered during the lifetime of Aaron, their father.

[5] *HASHEM spoke to Moses, saying,* [6] *"Bring near the tribe of Levi and have it stand before Aaron the Kohen, and they shall serve him.* [7] *They shall safeguard his charge and the charge of the entire assembly before the Tent of Meeting, to perform the service of the Tabernacle.* [8] *They shall safeguard all the utensils of the Tent of Meeting and the charge of the Children of Israel, to perform the service of the Tabernacle.* [9] *You shall present the Levites to Aaron and his sons — presented, presented are they to him — from the Children of Israel.* [10] *You shall appoint Aaron and his sons and they shall safeguard their priesthood; an alien who approaches will die."*

[11] *HASHEM spoke to Moses, saying,* [12] *"Behold! I have taken the Levites from among the Children of Israel, in place of every firstborn, the first issue of every womb among the Children of Israel, and the Levites shall be Mine.* [13] *For every firstborn is Mine: On the day I struck down every firstborn in the land of Egypt I sanctified every firstborn in Israel for Myself,*

---

8. מִשְׁמֶרֶת בְּנֵי יִשְׂרָאֵל לַעֲבֹד אֶת עֲבֹדַת הַמִּשְׁכָּן — *The charge of the Children of Israel to do the service of the Sanctuary* ... to carry (the components of the *Mishkan*) and to sing (chant) which was (originally) the privilege of all Israel.

9. נְתוּנִם נְתוּנִם הֵמָּה לוֹ — *They are given, they are given to him.* All their (involvement with the Divine service) shall be exclusively according (to the instruction) of Aaron and his sons exclusively.

מֵאֵת בְּנֵי יִשְׂרָאֵל — *From the Children of Israel* ... who are obligated to give them the first tithe in exchange for their (participation in the Divine) service.

10. וְשָׁמְרוּ אֶת כְּהֻנָּתָם — *And they shall guard their priesthood* ... regarding everything (associated) with the Altar and (the service) within the veil, that the Levites shall not draw nigh (to participate or enter).

וְהַזָּר הַקָּרֵב — *And the stranger (i.e., non-Levite or non-Kohen) that draws nigh* ... to the service of the Levites or the priesthood.

12. תַּחַת כָּל בְּכוֹר — *Instead of every firstborn* ... as a redemption.

וְהָיוּ לִי הַלְוִיִּם — *And the Levites shall be mine* ... for (My) service.

13. כִּי לִי כָּל בְּכוֹר — *For all the firstborn are Mine.* Originally, the service (of God) was done by the firstborn.

בְּיוֹם הַכֹּתִי כָל בְּכוֹר בְּאֶרֶץ מִצְרַיִם הִקְדַּשְׁתִּי לִי כָל בְּכוֹר בְּיִשְׂרָאֵל — *On the day that I smote all*

NOTES

7. וְאֶת מִשְׁמֶרֶת כָּל הָעֵדָה לִפְנֵי אֹהֶל מוֹעֵד לַעֲבֹד אֶת עֲבֹדַת הַמִּשְׁכָּן — *And the charge of the whole congregation before the Tent of Meeting to do the service of the Sanctuary.* The phrase עֵדָה, *congregation*, in Biblical usage refers to the Sanhedrin. The *Sforno*, therefore, explains this verse as implying that, were it not for the sin of the Golden Calf, the members of the Sanhedrin would have been worthy to perform certain aspects of the service of the *Mishkan*, which are now assumed by the Levites.

9. נְתוּנִם נְתוּנִם הֵמָּה לוֹ מֵאֵת בְּנֵי יִשְׂרָאֵל — *They are given, they are given to him from the Children of Israel.* The *Sforno's* interpretation is similar to that of *Rashi's* commentary on verse 8, except that *Rashi* understands מֵאֵת בְּנֵי יִשְׂרָאֵל as meaning the Levites were chosen and separated from the midst of Israel while the *Sforno* interprets this phrase as meaning that Israel is obligated to support the Levites in exchange for their ministration, which was originally meant to be performed by the entire people.

For a fuller understanding of the *Sforno's* interpretation of the phrase נְתוּנִם נְתוּנִם, *they are given, they are given*, see his commentary on 8:16-19.

13. בְּיוֹם הַכֹּתִי כָל בְּכוֹר בְּאֶרֶץ מִצְרַיִם הִקְדַּשְׁתִּי לִי כָל בְּכוֹר בְּיִשְׂרָאֵל — *On the day that I smote all the*

בְּיִשְׂרָאֵל מֵאָדָם עַד־בְּהֵמָה לִי יִהְיוּ אֲנִי יְהוָה׃
חמישי יד־טו וַיְדַבֵּר יְהוָה אֶל־מֹשֶׁה בְּמִדְבַּר סִינַי לֵאמֹר׃ פְּקֹד אֶת־בְּנֵי לֵוִי לְבֵית
טז אֲבֹתָם לְמִשְׁפְּחֹתָם כָּל־זָכָר מִבֶּן־חֹדֶשׁ וָמַעְלָה תִּפְקְדֵם׃ וַיִּפְקֹד אֹתָם
יז מֹשֶׁה עַל־פִּי יְהוָה כַּאֲשֶׁר צֻוָּה׃ וַיִּהְיוּ־אֵלֶּה בְנֵי־לֵוִי בִּשְׁמֹתָם גֵּרְשׁוֹן וּקְהָת
יח־יט וּמְרָרִי׃ וְאֵלֶּה שְׁמוֹת בְּנֵי־גֵרְשׁוֹן לְמִשְׁפְּחֹתָם לִבְנִי וְשִׁמְעִי׃ וּבְנֵי קְהָת
כ לְמִשְׁפְּחֹתָם עַמְרָם וְיִצְהָר חֶבְרוֹן וְעֻזִּיאֵל׃ וּבְנֵי מְרָרִי לְמִשְׁפְּחֹתָם מַחְלִי
כא וּמוּשִׁי אֵלֶּה הֵם מִשְׁפְּחֹת הַלֵּוִי לְבֵית אֲבֹתָם׃ לְגֵרְשׁוֹן מִשְׁפַּחַת הַלִּבְנִי
כב וּמִשְׁפַּחַת הַשִּׁמְעִי אֵלֶּה הֵם מִשְׁפְּחֹת הַגֵּרְשֻׁנִּי׃ פְּקֻדֵיהֶם בְּמִסְפַּר כָּל־זָכָר
כג מִבֶּן־חֹדֶשׁ וָמָעְלָה פְּקֻדֵיהֶם שִׁבְעַת אֲלָפִים וַחֲמֵשׁ מֵאוֹת׃ מִשְׁפְּחֹת
כד הַגֵּרְשֻׁנִּי אַחֲרֵי הַמִּשְׁכָּן יַחֲנוּ יָמָּה׃ וּנְשִׂיא בֵית־אָב לַגֵּרְשֻׁנִּי אֶלְיָסָף בֶּן־
כה לָאֵל׃ וּמִשְׁמֶרֶת בְּנֵי־גֵרְשׁוֹן בְּאֹהֶל מוֹעֵד הַמִּשְׁכָּן וְהָאֹהֶל מִכְסֵהוּ וּמָסַךְ
כו פֶּתַח אֹהֶל מוֹעֵד׃ וְקַלְעֵי הֶחָצֵר וְאֶת־מָסַךְ פֶּתַח הֶחָצֵר אֲשֶׁר עַל־הַמִּשְׁכָּן
כז וְעַל־הַמִּזְבֵּחַ סָבִיב וְאֵת מֵיתָרָיו לְכֹל עֲבֹדָתוֹ׃ וְלִקְהָת
מִשְׁפַּחַת הָעַמְרָמִי וּמִשְׁפַּחַת הַיִּצְהָרִי וּמִשְׁפַּחַת הַחֶבְרֹנִי וּמִשְׁפַּחַת
כח הָעָזִּיאֵלִי אֵלֶּה הֵם מִשְׁפְּחֹת הַקְּהָתִי׃ בְּמִסְפַּר כָּל־זָכָר מִבֶּן־חֹדֶשׁ וָמָעְלָה
כט שְׁמֹנַת אֲלָפִים וְשֵׁשׁ מֵאוֹת שֹׁמְרֵי מִשְׁמֶרֶת הַקֹּדֶשׁ׃ מִשְׁפְּחֹת בְּנֵי־קְהָת
ל יַחֲנוּ עַל יֶרֶךְ הַמִּשְׁכָּן תֵּימָנָה׃ וּנְשִׂיא בֵית־אָב לְמִשְׁפְּחֹת הַקְּהָתִי אֱלִיצָפָן

---

the firstborn in the land of Egypt, I sanctified unto Me all the firstborn in Israel. Indeed, (at the time) of the smiting of the firstborn, the firstborn (of Israel) also deserved to be punished for the sins of that generation being that they were the most honored (members of the community); and they were not worthy of being saved from the plague visited on the community, similar to פֶּן תִּסָּפֶה בַּעֲוֹן הָעִיר, *Lest you be swept away in the iniquity of the city* (*Genesis* 19:15). But I saved them by sanctifying them unto Me; thus they are prohibited from engaging in ordinary (secular) labor, as is the law regarding sacred animals who may not be sheared or worked with. (Now) in order for them to be permitted to occupy (themselves in secular pursuits) redemption is necessary, as is the rule with all sacred objects (or animals) which are transformed into profane (objects), as it says, וְכֹל בְּכוֹר אָדָם בְּבָנֶיךָ תִּפְדֶּה, *And all the firstborn of man among your sons, you shall redeem* (*Exodus* 13:13). However, they were not absolved from (God's) service as a result of this redemption; only now that they sinned (with the Golden Calf), I rejected them and

NOTES

firstborn in the land of Egypt, I sanctified unto Me all the firstborn in Israel. Originally, the firstborn son of each family was charged with the responsibility of spiritual leadership which included *avodah*, the service of God. See *Rashi* on *Genesis* 25:31 regarding the sale of the birthright by Esau to Jacob. As such, they were also responsible for the behavior of the members of their family, and hence were held accountable for the sins of their generation. Consequently, because of their special status, even the Jewish firstborn were vulnerable during the plague of the firstborn in Egypt. Only by sanctifying them at that time were they saved by God, as the *Sforno* explains here and elaborates in his commentary on 8:17. Once sanctified however, they were not permitted to occupy themselves with non-sacred labor and therefore needed פִּדְיוֹן, *redemption*, as is the case with all *kodesh*, holy articles, as explained in *Exodus* 13:13. After the sin of the Golden Calf, the firstborn were relieved of their duties in the service of God, and this privilege was transferred to the Levites, who had remained steadfast in their loyalty to God at that time. The law of redemption, however, was unaffected, since their status of *kedushah* still remained. See the notes on 8:17 as well as the *Sforno's* commentary and the notes on *Exodus* 13:2.

from man to beast; they shall be Mine — I am HASHEM."
14 HASHEM spoke to Moses in the Wilderness of Sinai, saying, 15 "Count the sons of Levi according to their fathers' household, according to their families, every male from one month of age and up shall you count them." 16 Moses counted them according to the word of HASHEM, as he had been commanded.
17 These were the sons of Levi, by their names: Gershon, Kohath, and Merari. 18 These were the names of the sons of Gershon according to their families: Libni and Shimei. 19 The sons of Kohath according to their families were Amram and Izhar, Hebron and Uzziel. 20 The sons of Merari according to their families were Mahli and Mushi. These were the families of the Levites, according to their fathers' household.
21 Gershon had the family of the Libnites and the family of the Shimeites; these were the Gershonite families. 22 Their count according to the number of every male, from one month of age and up: their count was seven thousand, five hundred. 23 The Gershonite families would encamp behind the Tabernacle, to the west. 24 The leader of the father's household of the Gershonites was Eliasaph son of Lael. 25 The charge of the sons of Gershon in the Tent of Meeting was the Tabernacle, the Tent, its Cover, the Screen of the entrance of the Tent of Meeting; 26 the curtains of the Courtyard, the Screen of the entrance of the Courtyard that surrounded the Tabernacle and the Altar, and its ropes — for all its labor.
27 Kohath had the family of the Amramites, the family of the Izharites, the family of the Hebronites, and the family of the Uzzielites; these were the Kohathite families. 28 The number of every male from one month of age and up was eight thousand, six hundred; the guardians of the charge of the sanctity. 29 The families of the children of Kohath would encamp on the side of the Tabernacle, to the south. 30 The leader of the father's household of the Kohathite families was Elizaphan son of Uzziel.

redeemed them by taking the Levites in their place.

מֵאָדָם עַד בְּהֵמָה לִי יִהְיוּ — *Both man and animal they shall be Mine* . . . both now and in the future — man for redemption and animals for sacrifice.

אֲנִי ה' — *I am HASHEM.* I did not change (based on *Malachi* 3:6), when I rejected the firstborn, for this change did not originate with Me but with them when they sinned. And so (also) the reason that I wanted the Levites to redeem the firstborn in this generation (only) and not in the future is because in this generation they are of sufficient worth to (redeem them) but they will not be so in the future.

NOTES

אֲנִי ה' — *I am HASHEM.* The expression אֲנִי ה', *I am HASHEM,* at the conclusion of this verse requires explanation since there is no commandment given in this verse. It is to be understood, therefore, as an explanatory statement regarding the firstborn and the Levites. It is meant to stress the fact that although God, Who is unchanging, originally chose the firstborn to be His servants, a change in *their* status took place as a result of their participation in the sin of the Golden Calf. The *Sforno* also points out that Hashem determined that only in this generation were the Levites considered worthy to redeem the firstborn, but not in later generations. This is a second reason for the phrase אֲנִי ה' used at the conclusion of the verse .Although the *Sforno* does not give a reason for this decision, we can surmise that since the Levites of that generation responded to the call of Moses in the aftermath of the sin of the Golden Calf, they were deemed worthy not only to *replace* the firstborn in the service of God, but also to *redeem* them.

לא בֶּן־עֻזִּיאֵל: וּמִשְׁמַרְתָּם הָאָרֹן וְהַשֻּׁלְחָן וְהַמְּנֹרָה וְהַמִּזְבְּחֹת וּכְלֵי הַקֹּדֶשׁ
לב אֲשֶׁר יְשָׁרְתוּ בָּהֶם וְהַמָּסָךְ וְכֹל עֲבֹדָתוֹ: וּנְשִׂיא נְשִׂיאֵי הַלֵּוִי אֶלְעָזָר
לג בֶּן־אַהֲרֹן הַכֹּהֵן פְּקֻדַּת שֹׁמְרֵי מִשְׁמֶרֶת הַקֹּדֶשׁ: לִמְרָרִי מִשְׁפַּחַת
לד הַמַּחְלִי וּמִשְׁפַּחַת הַמּוּשִׁי אֵלֶּה הֵם מִשְׁפְּחֹת מְרָרִי: וּפְקֻדֵיהֶם בְּמִסְפַּר
לה כָּל־זָכָר מִבֶּן־חֹדֶשׁ וָמָעְלָה שֵׁשֶׁת אֲלָפִים וּמָאתָיִם: וּנְשִׂיא בֵית־אָב
לְמִשְׁפְּחֹת מְרָרִי צוּרִיאֵל בֶּן־אֲבִיחָיִל עַל יֶרֶךְ הַמִּשְׁכָּן יַחֲנוּ צָפֹנָה:
לו וּפְקֻדַּת מִשְׁמֶרֶת בְּנֵי מְרָרִי קַרְשֵׁי הַמִּשְׁכָּן וּבְרִיחָיו וְעַמֻּדָיו וַאֲדָנָיו
לז וְכָל־כֵּלָיו וְכֹל עֲבֹדָתוֹ: וְעַמֻּדֵי הֶחָצֵר סָבִיב וְאַדְנֵיהֶם וִיתֵדֹתָם
לח וּמֵיתְרֵיהֶם: וְהַחֹנִים לִפְנֵי הַמִּשְׁכָּן קֵדְמָה לִפְנֵי אֹהֶל־מוֹעֵד | מִזְרָחָה
מֹשֶׁה | וְאַהֲרֹן וּבָנָיו שֹׁמְרִים מִשְׁמֶרֶת הַמִּקְדָּשׁ לְמִשְׁמֶרֶת בְּנֵי יִשְׂרָאֵל
*נקוד על ואהרן לט וְהַזָּר הַקָּרֵב יוּמָת: כָּל־פְּקוּדֵי הַלְוִיִּם אֲשֶׁר פָּקַד מֹשֶׁה *וְאַהֲרֹן עַל־
פִּי יהוה לְמִשְׁפְּחֹתָם כָּל־זָכָר מִבֶּן־חֹדֶשׁ וָמַעְלָה שְׁנַיִם וְעֶשְׂרִים
ששי מ אָלֶף: וַיֹּאמֶר יהוה אֶל־מֹשֶׁה פְּקֹד כָּל־בְּכֹר זָכָר לִבְנֵי
מא יִשְׂרָאֵל מִבֶּן־חֹדֶשׁ וָמָעְלָה וְשָׂא אֵת מִסְפַּר שְׁמֹתָם: וְלָקַחְתָּ אֶת־
הַלְוִיִּם לִי אֲנִי יהוה תַּחַת כָּל־בְּכֹר בִּבְנֵי יִשְׂרָאֵל וְאֵת בֶּהֱמַת הַלְוִיִּם
מב תַּחַת כָּל־בְּכוֹר בְּבֶהֱמַת בְּנֵי יִשְׂרָאֵל: וַיִּפְקֹד מֹשֶׁה כַּאֲשֶׁר צִוָּה יהוה
מג אֹתוֹ אֶת־כָּל־בְּכֹר בִּבְנֵי יִשְׂרָאֵל: וַיְהִי כָל־בְּכוֹר זָכָר בְּמִסְפַּר שֵׁמֹת
מִבֶּן־חֹדֶשׁ וָמַעְלָה לִפְקֻדֵיהֶם שְׁנַיִם וְעֶשְׂרִים אֶלֶף שְׁלֹשָׁה וְשִׁבְעִים
וּמָאתָיִם:
מד-מה וַיְדַבֵּר יהוה אֶל־מֹשֶׁה לֵּאמֹר: קַח אֶת־הַלְוִיִּם תַּחַת כָּל־בְּכוֹר בִּבְנֵי
יִשְׂרָאֵל וְאֶת־בֶּהֱמַת הַלְוִיִּם תַּחַת בְּהֶמְתָּם וְהָיוּ־לִי הַלְוִיִּם אֲנִי יהוה:
מו וְאֵת פְּדוּיֵי הַשְּׁלֹשָׁה וְהַשִּׁבְעִים וְהַמָּאתָיִם הָעֹדְפִים עַל־הַלְוִיִּם מִבְּכוֹר
מז בְּנֵי יִשְׂרָאֵל: וְלָקַחְתָּ חֲמֵשֶׁת חֲמֵשֶׁת שְׁקָלִים לַגֻּלְגֹּלֶת בְּשֶׁקֶל הַקֹּדֶשׁ
מח תִּקָּח עֶשְׂרִים גֵּרָה הַשָּׁקֶל: וְנָתַתָּה הַכֶּסֶף לְאַהֲרֹן וּלְבָנָיו פְּדוּיֵי הָעֹדְפִים
מט בָּהֶם: וַיִּקַּח מֹשֶׁה אֵת כֶּסֶף הַפִּדְיוֹם מֵאֵת הָעֹדְפִים עַל פְּדוּיֵי הַלְוִיִּם:
נ מֵאֵת בְּכוֹר בְּנֵי יִשְׂרָאֵל לָקַח אֶת־הַכָּסֶף חֲמִשָּׁה וְשִׁשִּׁים וּשְׁלֹשׁ מֵאוֹת
נא וָאֶלֶף בְּשֶׁקֶל הַקֹּדֶשׁ: וַיִּתֵּן מֹשֶׁה אֶת־כֶּסֶף הַפְּדֻיִם לְאַהֲרֹן וּלְבָנָיו
עַל־פִּי יהוה כַּאֲשֶׁר צִוָּה יהוה אֶת־מֹשֶׁה:
ד שביעי א-ב וַיְדַבֵּר יהוה אֶל־מֹשֶׁה וְאֶל־אַהֲרֹן לֵאמֹר: נָשֹׂא אֶת־רֹאשׁ בְּנֵי קְהָת
ג מִתּוֹךְ בְּנֵי לֵוִי לְמִשְׁפְּחֹתָם לְבֵית אֲבֹתָם: מִבֶּן שְׁלֹשִׁים שָׁנָה וָמַעְלָה
וְעַד בֶּן־חֲמִשִּׁים שָׁנָה כָּל־בָּא לַצָּבָא לַעֲשׂוֹת מְלָאכָה בְּאֹהֶל מוֹעֵד:
ד-ה זֹאת עֲבֹדַת בְּנֵי־קְהָת בְּאֹהֶל מוֹעֵד קֹדֶשׁ הַקֳּדָשִׁים: וּבָא אַהֲרֹן וּבָנָיו
בִּנְסֹעַ הַמַּחֲנֶה וְהוֹרִדוּ אֵת פָּרֹכֶת הַמָּסָךְ וְכִסּוּ־בָהּ אֵת אֲרֹן הָעֵדֻת:

IV

5. בִּנְסֹעַ הַמַּחֲנֶה — *When the camp journeys* ... after the (Divine) cloud removes itself, because prior to that it is prohibited to enter (the Holy of Holies).

31 Their charge was the Ark, the Table, the Menorah, the Altars and the sacred
utensils with which they would minister, the Partition and all its accessories.

32 The leader of the Levite leaders was Elazar son of Aaron the Kohen, the
assignment of the guardians of the charge of the sanctity.

33 Merari had the family of the Mahlites and the family of the Mushites; these
were the Merarite families. 34 Their count according to the number of every male
from one month of age and up was six thousand, two hundred. 35 The leader of
the father's household of the Merarite families was Zuriel son of Abihail; they
would encamp on the side of the Tabernacle, to the north. 36 The assignment of
the charge of the sons of Merari was the planks of the Tabernacle, its bars, its
pillars, its sockets and all its utensils, and all its accessories. 37 The pillars of the
Courtyard all around and their sockets, their pegs and their ropes.

38 Those who encamped before the Tabernacle to the front, before the Tent of
Meeting to the east, were Moses and Aaron and his sons, guardians of the charge
of the Sanctuary, for the charge of the Children of Israel; any alien who
approaches shall die.

39 All the countings of the Levites, which Moses and Aaron counted by the
word of HASHEM according to their families, every male from one month of age
and up, were twenty-two thousand.

40 HASHEM said to Moses, "Count every firstborn male of the Children of Israel
from one month of age and up, and take a census of their names. 41 You shall take
the Levites for Me — I, HASHEM — in place of every firstborn of the Children of
Israel, and the livestock of the Levites in place of every firstborn of the animals
of the Children of Israel." 42 Moses counted — as HASHEM had commanded him
— every firstborn of the Children of Israel. 43 Every firstborn male according to
the number of their names, from one month of age and up, according to their
numbers, was twenty-two thousand, two hundred and seventy-three."

44 HASHEM spoke to Moses, saying, 45 "Take the Levites in place of every
firstborn of the Children of Israel, and the livestock of the Levites in place of their
livestock, and the Levites shall be Mine, I am HASHEM. 46 And as for the
redemptions of the two hundred and seventy-three of the firstborn of the
Children of Israel who are in excess of the Levites; 47 you shall take five shekels
each according to the head count, in the sacred shekel shall you take; the shekel
is twenty geras. 48 You shall give the money to Aaron and his sons, as
redemptions of the additional ones among them."

49 Moses took the money of the redemption from those who were in excess of
the redemptions of the Levites; 50 from the firstborn of the Children of Israel he
took the money: one thousand, three hundred and sixty-five in the sacred
shekels. 51 Moses gave the money of the redemptions to Aaron and his sons
according to the word of HASHEM, as HASHEM had commanded Moses.

4 1 HASHEM spoke to Moses and Aaron, saying: 2 "Take a census of the sons of
Kohath from among the sons of Levi, according to their families, according
to their fathers' households; 3 from thirty years of age and up, until fifty years
of age, everyone who comes to the legion to perform work in the Tent of Meeting.

4 "This is the work of the sons of Kohath in the Tent of Meeting: the most
holy. 5 When the camp is to journey, Aaron and his sons shall come and
take down the Partition-curtain and cover the Ark of the Testimony with it.

ו וְנָתְנוּ עָלָיו כְּסוּי עוֹר תַּחַשׁ וּפָרְשׂוּ בֶגֶד־כְּלִיל תְּכֵלֶת מִלְמָעְלָה וְשָׂמוּ
ז בַּדָּיו׃ וְעַל ׀ שֻׁלְחַן הַפָּנִים יִפְרְשׂוּ בֶּגֶד תְּכֵלֶת וְנָתְנוּ עָלָיו אֶת־הַקְּעָרֹת
וְאֶת־הַכַּפֹּת וְאֶת־הַמְּנַקִּיֹּת וְאֵת קְשׂוֹת הַנָּסֶךְ וְלֶחֶם הַתָּמִיד עָלָיו יִהְיֶה׃
ח וּפָרְשׂוּ עֲלֵיהֶם בֶּגֶד תּוֹלַעַת שָׁנִי וְכִסּוּ אֹתוֹ בְּמִכְסֵה עוֹר תָּחַשׁ וְשָׂמוּ
ט אֶת־בַּדָּיו׃ וְלָקְחוּ ׀ בֶּגֶד תְּכֵלֶת וְכִסּוּ אֶת־מְנֹרַת הַמָּאוֹר וְאֶת־נֵרֹתֶיהָ
וְאֶת־מַלְקָחֶיהָ וְאֶת־מַחְתֹּתֶיהָ וְאֵת כָּל־כְּלֵי שַׁמְנָהּ אֲשֶׁר יְשָׁרְתוּ־לָהּ
י בָּהֶם׃ וְנָתְנוּ אֹתָהּ וְאֶת־כָּל־כֵּלֶיהָ אֶל־מִכְסֵה עוֹר תָּחַשׁ וְנָתְנוּ
יא עַל־הַמּוֹט׃ וְעַל ׀ מִזְבַּח הַזָּהָב יִפְרְשׂוּ בֶּגֶד תְּכֵלֶת וְכִסּוּ אֹתוֹ בְּמִכְסֵה עוֹר
יב תָּחַשׁ וְשָׂמוּ אֶת־בַּדָּיו׃ וְלָקְחוּ אֶת־כָּל־כְּלֵי הַשָּׁרֵת אֲשֶׁר יְשָׁרְתוּ־בָם
בַּקֹּדֶשׁ וְנָתְנוּ אֶל־בֶּגֶד תְּכֵלֶת וְכִסּוּ אוֹתָם בְּמִכְסֵה עוֹר תָּחַשׁ וְנָתְנוּ
יג־יד עַל־הַמּוֹט׃ וְדִשְּׁנוּ אֶת־הַמִּזְבֵּחַ וּפָרְשׂוּ עָלָיו בֶּגֶד אַרְגָּמָן׃ וְנָתְנוּ עָלָיו
אֶת־כָּל־כֵּלָיו אֲשֶׁר יְשָׁרְתוּ עָלָיו בָּהֶם אֶת־הַמַּחְתֹּת אֶת־הַמִּזְלָגֹת
וְאֶת־הַיָּעִים וְאֶת־הַמִּזְרָקֹת כֹּל כְּלֵי הַמִּזְבֵּחַ וּפָרְשׂוּ עָלָיו כְּסוּי עוֹר תַּחַשׁ
טו וְשָׂמוּ בַדָּיו׃ וְכִלָּה אַהֲרֹן־וּבָנָיו לְכַסֹּת אֶת־הַקֹּדֶשׁ וְאֶת־כָּל־כְּלֵי הַקֹּדֶשׁ
בִּנְסֹעַ הַמַּחֲנֶה וְאַחֲרֵי־כֵן יָבֹאוּ בְנֵי־קְהָת לָשֵׂאת וְלֹא־יִגְּעוּ אֶל־הַקֹּדֶשׁ
טז וָמֵתוּ אֵלֶּה מַשָּׂא בְנֵי־קְהָת בְּאֹהֶל מוֹעֵד׃ וּפְקֻדַּת אֶלְעָזָר ׀ בֶּן־אַהֲרֹן
הַכֹּהֵן שֶׁמֶן הַמָּאוֹר וּקְטֹרֶת הַסַּמִּים וּמִנְחַת הַתָּמִיד וְשֶׁמֶן הַמִּשְׁחָה פְּקֻדַּת
כָּל־הַמִּשְׁכָּן וְכָל־אֲשֶׁר־בּוֹ בְּקֹדֶשׁ וּבְכֵלָיו׃
מפטיר יז־יח וַיְדַבֵּר יהוה אֶל־מֹשֶׁה וְאֶל־אַהֲרֹן לֵאמֹר׃ אַל־תַּכְרִיתוּ אֶת־שֵׁבֶט
יט מִשְׁפְּחֹת הַקְּהָתִי מִתּוֹךְ הַלְוִיִּם׃ וְזֹאת ׀ עֲשׂוּ לָהֶם וְחָיוּ וְלֹא יָמֻתוּ
בְּגִשְׁתָּם אֶת־קֹדֶשׁ הַקֳּדָשִׁים אַהֲרֹן וּבָנָיו יָבֹאוּ וְשָׂמוּ אוֹתָם אִישׁ אִישׁ
כ עַל־עֲבֹדָתוֹ וְאֶל־מַשָּׂאוֹ׃ וְלֹא־יָבֹאוּ לִרְאוֹת כְּבַלַּע אֶת־הַקֹּדֶשׁ וָמֵתוּ׃

---

10. וְנָתְנוּ עַל הַמּוֹט — *And shall put it upon a bar* ... and (only) then shall the Levites be allowed to carry (them).

16. וּפְקֻדַּת אֶלְעָזָר — *And the charge of Elazar* ... to command which (articles of the Sanctuary) each one should carry.

פְּקֻדַּת כָּל הַמִּשְׁכָּן — *And the charge of the entire Sanctuary.* During the time of their journeying and encampment, his charge was to command them (i.e., the Kehathites) regarding the erection, dismantling and setting up (of the items entrusted to them) in their proper places.

18. אַל תַּכְרִיתוּ — *Do not cause to be cut off.* Do not (simply) put down the objects (to be carried) in such a way that the one who takes them first will merit (to carry them), for in this manner it may happen that one will push another (in their eagerness to carry the holy objects) and thereby profane the Holy. This (in turn) will cause their being "cut off," as

NOTES

IV

18-20. אַל תַּכְרִיתוּ ... וְשָׂמוּ אוֹתָם אִישׁ אִישׁ עַל עֲבֹדָתוֹ ... וְאֶל מַשָּׂאוֹ. וְלֹא יָבֹאוּ לִרְאוֹת ... — *Do not cause to be cut off ... and appoint each one of them to his service and to his burden. But they shall not enter to observe ...* The Torah tells us that specific assignments were given by Elazar to the Kehathites as to which articles they were to carry since it was not permitted for them to do so on a "first come first serve" basis. The *Sforno* explains the reason for this strictness by citing the Mishnah in tractate *Yoma* (22a and 23a) where we are told that the *Kohanim* originally would race up the ramp to the top of the Altar for the privilege of removing the ashes. Once, in his zeal to be first, one *Kohen* pushed his colleague off the ramp and he broke his leg. On

6 They shall place upon it a tachash-hide covering, and spread a cloth entirely
of turquoise wool over it, and adjust its staves. 7 Upon the Table of the show-
bread they shall spread a cloth of turquoise wool and place upon it the dishes,
the spoons, the pillars, and the shelving-tubes; and the constant bread shall
remain on it. 8 They shall spread over it a cloth of scarlet wool and cover it with
a cover of tachash hide, and emplace its staves. 9 They shall take a cloth of
turquoise wool and cover the Menorah of illumination, and its lamps, and its
tongs, and its spoons, and all the vessels of its oil, with which they minister to
it. 10 They shall place it and all its utensils into a cover of tachash-hide, and
place it on the pole. 11 Upon the Gold Altar they shall spread a cloth of turquoise
wool, and cover it with a covering of tachash-hide, and emplace its staves.
12 They shall take all the utensils of service with which they serve in the
Sanctuary and place them on a cloth of turquoise wool, and cover them with
a covering of tachash-hide, and place them on the pole. 13 They shall clear the
ash from the Altar and spread a cloth of purple wool over it, 14 they shall place
upon it all the utensils with which they minister upon it: the fire-pans, the
forks, the shovels, and the basins — all the utensils of the Altar — and spread
over it a covering of tachash hide, and emplace its staves.

15 "Aaron and his sons shall finish covering the holy and all the holy utensils
when the camp journeys, and then the sons of Kohath shall come to carry, so
that they not touch the Sanctuary and die. These are the burden of the sons of
Kohath in the Tent of Meeting.

16 "The charge of Elazar son of Aaron the Kohen is the oil of illumination, the
incense spices, the meal-offering of the continual offering, and the anointment
oil — the charge of the entire Tabernacle and everything in it — of the
Sanctuary and its utensils."

17 HASHEM spoke to Moses and Aaron, saying: 18 "Do not let the tribe of the
Kohathite families be cut off from among the Levites. 19 Thus shall you do for
them so that they shall live and not die: when they approach the Holy of Holies,
Aaron and his sons shall come and assign them, every man to his work and his
burden. 20 But they shall not come and look as the holy is inserted, lest they die."

(our Sages) tell us that this occurred with the "offering of the ashes" (see *Yoma* 22, 23).

19. וְשָׂמוּ אוֹתָם אִישׁ אִישׁ עַל עֲבֹדָתוֹ וְאֶל מַשָּׂאוֹ — *And appoint each one of them to his service and to his burden.* And it shall not be that those who arrive earlier shall merit (to choose), but each one must wait to be commanded and then he shall act.

20. וְלֹא יָבֹאוּ לִרְאוֹת — *But they shall not enter to observe.* In this manner, they will not enter to observe when the *Kohen* covers the sacred articles (in such a manner) as to be able to precede the others, and (thereby) they will (avoid the pitfall of) conducting themselves in a frivolous fashion, bringing upon themselves the death penalty.

NOTES

another occasion, two *Kohanim* reached the top together and one stabbed the other. After these incidents, a lottery was instituted so as to eliminate such dangerous competition. In a similar vein, in order to protect the Levites from being "cut off" (i.e., exposed to danger) due to frivolous conduct in the Sanctuary, the Torah ordained that all assignments were to be given by Elazar in an orderly fashion. Since there was nothing to be gained by being there first, the Kehathites would not be tempted to enter the Holy of Holies while the *Kohanim* were covering the holy objects and preparing them to be carried. In this manner they would avoid wrongdoing and its consequent punishment.

פרשת נשא

כא־כב וַיְדַבֵּר יְהוָה אֶל־מֹשֶׁה לֵּאמֹר: נָשֹׂא אֶת־רֹאשׁ בְּנֵי גֵרְשׁוֹן גַּם־הֵם לְבֵית
כג אֲבֹתָם לְמִשְׁפְּחֹתָם: מִבֶּן שְׁלֹשִׁים שָׁנָה וָמַעְלָה עַד בֶּן־חֲמִשִּׁים שָׁנָה
כד תִּפְקֹד אוֹתָם כָּל־הַבָּא לִצְבֹא צָבָא לַעֲבֹד עֲבֹדָה בְּאֹהֶל מוֹעֵד: זֹאת
כה עֲבֹדַת מִשְׁפְּחֹת הַגֵּרְשֻׁנִּי לַעֲבֹד וּלְמַשָּׂא: וְנָשְׂאוּ אֶת־יְרִיעֹת הַמִּשְׁכָּן
וְאֶת־אֹהֶל מוֹעֵד מִכְסֵהוּ וּמִכְסֵה הַתַּחַשׁ אֲשֶׁר־עָלָיו מִלְמָעְלָה וְאֶת־
כו מָסַךְ פֶּתַח אֹהֶל מוֹעֵד: וְאֵת קַלְעֵי הֶחָצֵר וְאֶת־מָסַךְ ׀ פֶּתַח ׀ שַׁעַר
הֶחָצֵר אֲשֶׁר עַל־הַמִּשְׁכָּן וְעַל־הַמִּזְבֵּחַ סָבִיב וְאֵת מֵיתְרֵיהֶם וְאֶת־כָּל־
כז כְּלֵי עֲבֹדָתָם וְאֵת כָּל־אֲשֶׁר יֵעָשֶׂה לָהֶם וְעָבָדוּ: עַל־פִּי אַהֲרֹן וּבָנָיו
תִּהְיֶה כָּל־עֲבֹדַת בְּנֵי הַגֵּרְשֻׁנִּי לְכָל־מַשָּׂאָם וּלְכֹל עֲבֹדָתָם וּפְקַדְתֶּם
כח עֲלֵהֶם בְּמִשְׁמֶרֶת אֵת כָּל־מַשָּׂאָם: זֹאת עֲבֹדַת מִשְׁפְּחֹת בְּנֵי הַגֵּרְשֻׁנִּי
כט בְּאֹהֶל מוֹעֵד וּמִשְׁמַרְתָּם בְּיַד אִיתָמָר בֶּן־אַהֲרֹן הַכֹּהֵן: בְּנֵי
ל מְרָרִי לְמִשְׁפְּחֹתָם לְבֵית־אֲבֹתָם תִּפְקֹד אֹתָם: מִבֶּן שְׁלֹשִׁים שָׁנָה
וָמַעְלָה וְעַד בֶּן־חֲמִשִּׁים שָׁנָה תִּפְקְדֵם כָּל־הַבָּא לַצָּבָא לַעֲבֹד
לא אֶת־עֲבֹדַת אֹהֶל מוֹעֵד: וְזֹאת מִשְׁמֶרֶת מַשָּׂאָם לְכָל־עֲבֹדָתָם בְּאֹהֶל
לב מוֹעֵד קַרְשֵׁי הַמִּשְׁכָּן וּבְרִיחָיו וְעַמּוּדָיו וַאֲדָנָיו: וְעַמּוּדֵי הֶחָצֵר סָבִיב
וְאַדְנֵיהֶם וִיתֵדֹתָם וּמֵיתְרֵיהֶם לְכָל־כְּלֵיהֶם וּלְכֹל עֲבֹדָתָם וּבְשֵׁמֹת
לג תִּפְקְדוּ אֶת־כְּלֵי מִשְׁמֶרֶת מַשָּׂאָם: זֹאת עֲבֹדַת מִשְׁפְּחֹת בְּנֵי מְרָרִי
לד לְכָל־עֲבֹדָתָם בְּאֹהֶל מוֹעֵד בְּיַד אִיתָמָר בֶּן־אַהֲרֹן הַכֹּהֵן: וַיִּפְקֹד
מֹשֶׁה וְאַהֲרֹן וּנְשִׂיאֵי הָעֵדָה אֶת־בְּנֵי הַקְּהָתִי לְמִשְׁפְּחֹתָם וּלְבֵית
לה אֲבֹתָם: מִבֶּן שְׁלֹשִׁים שָׁנָה וָמַעְלָה וְעַד בֶּן־חֲמִשִּׁים שָׁנָה כָּל־הַבָּא
לו לַצָּבָא לַעֲבֹדָה בְּאֹהֶל מוֹעֵד: וַיִּהְיוּ פְקֻדֵיהֶם לְמִשְׁפְּחֹתָם אַלְפַּיִם שְׁבַע
לז מֵאוֹת וַחֲמִשִּׁים: אֵלֶּה פְקוּדֵי מִשְׁפְּחֹת הַקְּהָתִי כָּל־הָעֹבֵד בְּאֹהֶל מוֹעֵד
שני לח אֲשֶׁר פָּקַד מֹשֶׁה וְאַהֲרֹן עַל־פִּי יְהוָה בְּיַד־מֹשֶׁה: וּפְקוּדֵי
לט בְּנֵי גֵרְשׁוֹן לְמִשְׁפְּחוֹתָם וּלְבֵית אֲבֹתָם: מִבֶּן שְׁלֹשִׁים שָׁנָה וָמַעְלָה

24. לַעֲבֹד וּלְמַשָּׂא — *In serving and in bearing burdens.* "Serving" (refers to) when they are encamped and "bearing burdens" to when they are on a journey. Now, since the Torah stated above (3:25), *And the charge of the sons of Gershon in the Tent of Meeting,* in reference to their charge at the time (Israel) encamped, (therefore) it states here that all the work in their charge at the time of encampment, was also in their charge when (carrying) burdens at the time of journeying.

26. וְעָבָדוּ — *Therein shall they serve.* At the time of encampment, their charge shall be over all these vessels and (also) over all the implements *concerning that which is to be done to them* and for them in order to do the work, such as pliers and mallets to set in the pegs

NOTES

24. לַעֲבֹד וּלְמַשָּׂא — *In serving and in bearing burdens.* The *Sforno* explains throughout this section (vs. 24-49) that the assignment of the Levites was a two-fold one: to carry the various parts of the Tabernacle when the Israelites journeyed, which the Torah refers to as מַשָּׂא, *burden;* and also to assume responsibility for these same parts, vessels and instruments when they encamped, which the Torah refers to as עֲבוֹדָה, *serving.*

PARASHAS NASSO

21 HASHEM spoke to Moses, saying, 22 "Take a census of the sons of
Gershon, as well, according to their fathers' household, according to
their families. 23 *From thirty years of age and up, until fifty years of age shall*
you count them, everyone who comes to join the legion to perform work in
the Tent of Meeting. 24 *This is the work of the Gershonite families: to work*
and to carry. 25 *They shall carry the curtains of the Tabernacle and the Tent*
of Meeting, its Cover and the tachash cover that is over it from above. And
the Screen of the entrance of the Tent of Meeting, 26 *the lace-hangings of the*
Courtyard and the Screen of the entrance of the gate of the Courtyard that
were around the Courtyard and the Altar, their ropes and all the utensils of
their service, and everything that is made for them, and they shall serve.
27 *According to the word of Aaron and his sons shall be all the work of the*
sons of Gershonites, their entire burden and their entire work; you shall
appoint their entire burden as their charge. 28 *This is the work of the sons of*
the Gershonites in the Tent of Meeting; and their charge shall be under the
authority of Ithamar, the son of Aaron the Kohen.
29 *"The sons of Merari — according to their families, according to their*
fathers' household shall you count them. 30 *From thirty years of age and up,*
until fifty years of age shall you count them, everyone who comes to the
legion to perform the work of the Tent of Meeting. 31 *This is the charge of*
their burden for all of their work in the Tent of Meeting: the planks of the
Tabernacle, its bars, its pillars, and its sockets; 32 *the pillars of the Courtyard*
all around and their sockets, their pegs and their ropes for all of their utensils
and for all of their work. You shall appoint them by name to the utensils they
are to carry on their watch. 33 *This is the work of the families of the sons of*
Merari according to all their work in the Tent of Meeting, under the
authority of Ithamar, son of Aaron the Kohen."
34 *Moses and Aaron and the leaders of the assembly counted the sons of*
the Kohathites, according to their families, according to their fathers'
household. 35 *From thirty years of age and up, until fifty years of age,*
everyone who comes to the legion for the work in the Tent of Meeting. 36 *Their*
countings according to their families were two thousand, seven hundred and
fifty. 37 *These are the countings of the Kohathite families, all who work in*
the Tent of Meeting, whom Moses and Aaron counted, at the word of
HASHEM, under the authority of Moses.
38 *The count of the sons of Gershon according to their families, and*
according to their fathers' household; 39 *from thirty years of age and up,*

---

and to extract them.

27. לְכָל מַשָּׂאָם — *In all their burden . . .* when they journey.

וּלְכֹל עֲבֹדָתָם — *And in all their service . . .* when they encamp.

NOTES

26. וְעָבָדוּ — *Therein shall they serve.* The phrase וְעָבָדוּ is translated by the *Sforno* as meaning "in order to do their work." Hence, it applies to the implements such as those necessary to drive in the pegs and remove them. Compare this to the *Sforno's* commentary on *Exodus* 27:19.

מ וְעַד בֶּן־חֲמִשִּׁים שָׁנָה כָּל־הַבָּא לַצָּבָא לַעֲבֹדָה בְּאֹהֶל מוֹעֵד: וַיִּהְיוּ
מא פְּקֻדֵיהֶם לְמִשְׁפְּחֹתָם לְבֵית אֲבֹתָם אַלְפַּיִם וְשֵׁשׁ מֵאוֹת וּשְׁלֹשִׁים: אֵלֶּה
פְקוּדֵי מִשְׁפְּחֹת בְּנֵי גֵרְשׁוֹן כָּל־הָעֹבֵד בְּאֹהֶל מוֹעֵד אֲשֶׁר פָּקַד מֹשֶׁה
מב וְאַהֲרֹן עַל־פִּי יהוה: וּפְקוּדֵי מִשְׁפְּחֹת בְּנֵי מְרָרִי לְמִשְׁפְּחֹתָם לְבֵית
מג אֲבֹתָם: מִבֶּן שְׁלֹשִׁים שָׁנָה וָמַעְלָה וְעַד בֶּן־חֲמִשִּׁים שָׁנָה כָּל־הַבָּא לַצָּבָא
מד לַעֲבֹדָה בְּאֹהֶל מוֹעֵד: וַיִּהְיוּ פְקֻדֵיהֶם לְמִשְׁפְּחֹתָם שְׁלֹשֶׁת אֲלָפִים
מה וּמָאתָיִם: אֵלֶּה פְקוּדֵי מִשְׁפְּחֹת בְּנֵי מְרָרִי אֲשֶׁר פָּקַד מֹשֶׁה וְאַהֲרֹן עַל־פִּי
מו יהוה בְּיַד־מֹשֶׁה: כָּל־הַפְּקֻדִים אֲשֶׁר פָּקַד מֹשֶׁה וְאַהֲרֹן וּנְשִׂיאֵי יִשְׂרָאֵל
מז אֶת־הַלְוִיִּם לְמִשְׁפְּחֹתָם וּלְבֵית אֲבֹתָם: מִבֶּן שְׁלֹשִׁים שָׁנָה וָמַעְלָה וְעַד
בֶּן־חֲמִשִּׁים שָׁנָה כָּל־הַבָּא לַעֲבֹד עֲבֹדַת עֲבֹדָה וַעֲבֹדַת מַשָּׂא בְּאֹהֶל
מח-מט מוֹעֵד: וַיִּהְיוּ פְּקֻדֵיהֶם שְׁמֹנַת אֲלָפִים וַחֲמֵשׁ מֵאוֹת וּשְׁמֹנִים: עַל־פִּי יהוה
פָּקַד אוֹתָם בְּיַד־מֹשֶׁה אִישׁ אִישׁ עַל־עֲבֹדָתוֹ וְעַל־מַשָּׂאוֹ וּפְקֻדָיו
אֲשֶׁר־צִוָּה יהוה אֶת־מֹשֶׁה:
ה שלישי א-ב וַיְדַבֵּר יהוה אֶל־מֹשֶׁה לֵּאמֹר: צַו אֶת־בְּנֵי יִשְׂרָאֵל וִישַׁלְּחוּ מִן־הַמַּחֲנֶה
ג כָּל־צָרוּעַ וְכָל־זָב וְכֹל טָמֵא לָנָפֶשׁ: מִזָּכָר עַד־נְקֵבָה תְּשַׁלֵּחוּ אֶל־מִחוּץ
לַמַּחֲנֶה תְּשַׁלְּחוּם וְלֹא יְטַמְּאוּ אֶת־מַחֲנֵיהֶם אֲשֶׁר אֲנִי שֹׁכֵן בְּתוֹכָם:
ד וַיַּעֲשׂוּ־כֵן בְּנֵי יִשְׂרָאֵל וַיְשַׁלְּחוּ אוֹתָם אֶל־מִחוּץ לַמַּחֲנֶה כַּאֲשֶׁר דִּבֶּר
יהוה אֶל־מֹשֶׁה כֵּן עָשׂוּ בְּנֵי יִשְׂרָאֵל:
ה-ו וַיְדַבֵּר יהוה אֶל־מֹשֶׁה לֵּאמֹר: דַּבֵּר אֶל־בְּנֵי יִשְׂרָאֵל אִישׁ אוֹ־אִשָּׁה כִּי
יַעֲשׂוּ מִכָּל־חַטֹּאת הָאָדָם לִמְעֹל מַעַל בַּיהוה וְאָשְׁמָה הַנֶּפֶשׁ הַהִוא:
ז וְהִתְוַדּוּ אֶת־חַטָּאתָם אֲשֶׁר עָשׂוּ וְהֵשִׁיב אֶת־אֲשָׁמוֹ בְּרֹאשׁוֹ וַחֲמִישִׁתוֹ
ח יֹסֵף עָלָיו וְנָתַן לַאֲשֶׁר אָשַׁם לוֹ: וְאִם־אֵין לָאִישׁ גֹּאֵל לְהָשִׁיב הָאָשָׁם אֵלָיו
הָאָשָׁם הַמּוּשָׁב לַיהוה לַכֹּהֵן מִלְּבַד אֵיל הַכִּפֻּרִים אֲשֶׁר יְכַפֶּר־בּוֹ עָלָיו:

---

49. אִישׁ אִישׁ עַל עֲבֹדָתוֹ וְעַל מַשָּׂאוֹ וּפְקֻדָיו — *Every one to his service and to his burden and to his appointment.* He appointed every one of them to the service he was to do at the time of encampment and *to his burden* at the time of journeying, so that each would know the weight of his burden; and he would also know פְּקֻדָיו, *his appointment*, i.e., he shall know the names of all the vessels (and implements) which he will carry, (for) these were designated by name as it says, *And by name you shall appoint the instruments of the charge of their burden* (v. 32).

V

6. לִמְעֹל מַעַל בַּה׳ — *To commit a trespass against HASHEM.* Tradition teaches that this verse refers to robbery of a proselyte, for indeed, if one robs him he profanes the Name

NOTES

49. אִישׁ אִישׁ עַל עֲבֹדָתוֹ וְעַל מַשָּׂאוֹ וּפְקֻדָיו — *Every one to his service and to his burden and to his appointment.* The phrase וּפְקֻדָיו is translated by other commentators to mean 'their number,' referring to the count of the Levites. The *Sforno*, however, is of the opinion that it applies to the articles and instruments which were in the Levites' charge. Just as a medical practitioner must be able to identify every bone, muscle, and tendon in the human body by name for the purpose of diagnosis and treatment, so were the Levites instructed and trained to identify every item of the *Mishkan* in their charge by name. They were also instructed to have intimate knowledge of the weight of their respective burdens so as to know how many men and wagons should be assigned for transport.

until fifty years of age, everyone who comes to the legion for the work in the Tent of Meeting. [40] *Their countings according to their families, according to their fathers' household were two thousand, six hundred and thirty.* [41] *These are the countings of the families of the sons of Gershon, all who work in the Tent of Meeting, whom Moses and Aaron counted, at the word of* HASHEM.

[42] *The count of the families of the sons of Merari, according to their families, according to their fathers' household;* [43] *from thirty years of age and up, until fifty years of age, everyone who comes to the legion, for the work in the Tent of Meeting.* [44] *Their countings according to their families were three thousand, two hundred.* [45] *These were the countings of the families of the sons of Merari, whom Moses and Aaron counted, at the word of* HASHEM*, through Moses.*

[46] *All those counted of the Levites, whom Moses and Aaron and the leaders of Israel counted, according to their families and according to their fathers' household;* [47] *from thirty years of age and up, until fifty years of age, everyone who comes to perform the work of service and the work of burden in the Tent of Sanctuary.* [48] *Their countings were eight thousand, five hundred and eighty.* [49] *He counted them at the word of* HASHEM*, through Moses, every man over his work and over his burden; and his count [was] as* HASHEM *had commanded Moses.*

5

[1] HASHEM *spoke to Moses, saying,* [2] *"Command the Children of Israel that they shall expel from the camp everyone with tzaraas, everyone who has had a zav-emission, and everyone contaminated by a human corpse.* [3] *Male and female alike shall you expel, to the outside of the camp shall you expel them, so that they should not contaminate their camps, among which I dwell."* [4] *The Children of Israel did so: They expelled them to the outside of the camp, as* HASHEM *had spoken to Moses — so did the Children of Israel do.*

[5] HASHEM *spoke to Moses, saying,* [6] *"Speak to the Children of Israel: A man or woman who commits any of man's sins, by committing treachery toward* HASHEM*, and that person shall become guilty —* [7] *they shall confess their sin that they committed; he shall make restitution for his guilt in its principal amount and add its fifth to it, and give it to the one to whom he is indebted.* [8] *If the man has no kinsman to whom the debt can be returned, the returned debt is for* HASHEM*, for the Kohen, aside from the ram of atonement with which he shall provide him atonement.*

---

of his God in the eyes of the proselyte who came to find protection under His wings. Therefore, he is called "one who trespasses against the sacred" and is required to bring a guilt offering, as is the law regarding all who trespass against Him.

8. הָאָשָׁם הַמּוּשָׁב לַה' — *The restitution for guilt which is made shall be to* HASHEM. Because when the owner is no longer alive, it is proper to return the stolen goods to the master of

NOTES

V

8. הָאָשָׁם הַמּוּשָׁב לַה' — *The restitution for guilt which is made shall be to* HASHEM. The Talmud in *Bava Basra* states that one should not accept a פִּקָּדוֹן, *a pledge,* from a slave because there is a probability that it was stolen. However, if one did

ט־י וְכָל־תְּרוּמָה לְכָל־קָדְשֵׁי בְנֵי־יִשְׂרָאֵל אֲשֶׁר־יַקְרִיבוּ לַכֹּהֵן לוֹ יִהְיֶה: וְאִישׁ
אֶת־קֳדָשָׁיו לוֹ יִהְיוּ אִישׁ אֲשֶׁר־יִתֵּן לַכֹּהֵן לוֹ יִהְיֶה:
רביעי יא־יב וַיְדַבֵּר יהוה אֶל־מֹשֶׁה לֵּאמֹר: דַּבֵּר אֶל־בְּנֵי יִשְׂרָאֵל וְאָמַרְתָּ אֲלֵהֶם אִישׁ
יג אִישׁ כִּי־תִשְׂטֶה אִשְׁתּוֹ וּמָעֲלָה בוֹ מָעַל: וְשָׁכַב אִישׁ אֹתָהּ שִׁכְבַת־זֶרַע
וְנֶעְלַם מֵעֵינֵי אִישָׁהּ וְנִסְתְּרָה וְהִיא נִטְמָאָה וְעֵד אֵין בָּהּ וְהִוא לֹא
יד נִתְפָּשָׂה: וְעָבַר עָלָיו רוּחַ־קִנְאָה וְקִנֵּא אֶת־אִשְׁתּוֹ וְהִוא נִטְמָאָה אוֹ־עָבַר
טו עָלָיו רוּחַ־קִנְאָה וְקִנֵּא אֶת־אִשְׁתּוֹ וְהִיא לֹא נִטְמָאָה: וְהֵבִיא הָאִישׁ
אֶת־אִשְׁתּוֹ אֶל־הַכֹּהֵן וְהֵבִיא אֶת־קָרְבָּנָהּ עָלֶיהָ עֲשִׂירִת הָאֵיפָה קֶמַח
שְׂעֹרִים לֹא־יִצֹק עָלָיו שֶׁמֶן וְלֹא־יִתֵּן עָלָיו לְבֹנָה כִּי־מִנְחַת קְנָאֹת הוּא

the owner — who (in this instance) is God, the Blessed One, as our Sages stated, "If the slave died, it shall be returned to his master" (*Bava Basra* 51b).

9. וְכָל תְּרוּמָה — *And every heave-offering.* Tradition has it that the offering mentioned here refers to בִּכּוּרִים, *the first fruits,* which are offered to God, the Blessed One, as is the custom to offer the first fruits to the owner of the field, as it says, הִגַּדְתִּי הַיּוֹם לַה׳ אֱלֹהֶיךָ, כִּי בָאתִי אֶל הָאָרֶץ אֲשֶׁר נִשְׁבַּע ה׳, *I profess this day to HASHEM your God that I have come to the land which HASHEM swore* (*Deut.* 26:3). The (Torah) here tells us that just as the stolen property of the proselyte being returned to God is given to the *Kohen* of the מִשְׁמָר, *the watch,* so also are the first fruits, which are offered to God, the Blessed One, given to the *Kohen* of the watch.

10. וְאִישׁ אֶת קֳדָשָׁיו לוֹ יִהְיוּ — *And every man's holy things shall be his* . . . but regarding other holy things, namely heave-offerings and tithes, even though they are sanctified to God, they do not belong to any specific *Kohen*, but rather to the *Kohen* to whom the owner chooses to give it.

אִישׁ אֲשֶׁר יִתֵּן לַכֹּהֵן — *Whatsoever any man gives to the Kohen.* But when any owner gives a holy thing to the *Kohen*, it is no longer in the category of "his holy thing" but . . .

לוֹ יִהְיֶה — *It shall be his.* (It belongs) to the *Kohen* who received it, and neither the owner or the other *Kohanim* can expropriate it from him.

12. כִּי תִשְׂטֶה אִשְׁתּוֹ — *If his wife goes aside.* (She) deviates from the path of modesty.

וּמָעֲלָה בוֹ מָעַל — *And acts deceitfully against him.* She profaned *the holiness of HASHEM which He loves* (*Malachi* 2:11) inherent in marriage by embracing and kissing (a man) other than her husband and similar acts (of immorality).

NOTES

accept it then he should return it to the slave. If the slave dies then he returns it to his master. And so in our case, where an Israelite has stolen something from a proselyte who subsequently died, it shall be returned to the *Kohanim* who represent God, who is considered the "Master" of the deceased owner (i.e., the proselyte).

8-10. הָאָשָׁם הַמּוּשָׁב לַה׳ . . . וְכָל תְּרוּמָה . . . וְאִישׁ אֶת קֳדָשָׁיו לוֹ יִהְיוּ — *The restitution for guilt which is made shall be to HASHEM . . . And every heave-offering . . . And every man's holy things shall be his.* The *Sforno* explains the reason for the juxtaposition of verses 8-10. Seemingly, there is no link between the law of returning a stolen article to the *Kohen* (v. 8), the bringing of the first fruits to the Temple (v. 9) and the offerings of תְּרוּמָה, *heave-offering,* and מַעֲשֵׂר, *tithe* (v. 10). The *Sforno*, however, explains the linkage thus: Just as the stolen item is returned to the *Kohanim* of that particular watch (מִשְׁמָר), so shall the first fruits be brought to them. However, other offerings, such as תְּרוּמָה and מַעֲשֵׂר can be given to any *Kohen* or Levite whom the owner chooses.

12. וּמָעֲלָה בוֹ מָעַל — *And acts deceitfully against him.* The expression מְעִילָה, *trespass,* is applicable to one's actions vis-a-vis God. Why then does the Torah use this particular phrase regarding a woman who is unfaithful to her husband? The *Sforno* explains that this particular expression was chosen to underscore the seriousness of her action

[9] *And every portion from any of the holies that the Children of Israel bring to the Kohen shall be his.* [10] *A man's holies shall be his, and what a man gives to the Kohen shall be his."*

[11] *HASHEM spoke to Moses, saying,* [12] *"Speak to the Children of Israel and say to them: Any man whose wife shall go astray and commit treachery against him;* [13] *and a man could have lain with her carnally, but it was hidden from the eyes of her husband, and she became secluded and could have been defiled — but there was no witness against her — and she had not been forced;* [14] *and a spirit of jealousy had passed over him and he had warned his wife, and she had become defiled, or a spirit of jealousy had passed over him and he had warned his wife and she had not become defiled.* [15] *The man shall bring his wife to the Kohen and he shall bring her offering for her, a tenth-ephah of barley flour; he shall not pour oil over it and shall not put frankincense upon it, for it is a meal-offering of jealousies,*

---

13. וְשָׁכַב אִישׁ אֹתָהּ — *And a man lie with her.* For this is the way of the evil inclination to proceed from evil to evil.

וְנֶעְלַם מֵעֵינֵי אִישָׁהּ — *And it be hid from the eyes of the husband.* Although all these incidents preceded (the husband's awareness), it can (still) come about that the matter will be hidden from the eyes of her husband, as though his eyes are dimmed and unseeing, for if he knows and is silent the waters will not examine the woman to determine her guilt at all, as (our Sages) explain (*Sifre*).

וְנִסְתְּרָה — *And she be hidden* . . . after all this, and it (then) becomes known to her husband.

14. וְעָבַר עָלָיו רוּחַ קִנְאָה — *And the spirit of jealousy comes over him* . . . a pure spirit (prompting him) to warn her, since he knows that she deviated from the path of modesty.

וְקִנֵּא אֶת אִשְׁתּוֹ — *And he is jealous of his wife.* He warned her and said, "Do not meet secretly with this man."

אוֹ עָבַר עָלָיו רוּחַ קִנְאָה — *Or if the spirit of jealousy comes upon him.* A spirit which is foolish, without reasonable cause for him to be jealous.

וְהִיא לֹא נִטְמָאָה — *And she is not defiled.* However, she did disregard (lit., transgress) his warning and hid (secretly with that man) nonetheless . . .

15. וְהֵבִיא הָאִישׁ אֶת אִשְׁתּוֹ — *Then shall the man bring his wife.* And we shall not say that since he took no action and was silent despite the fact that his wife had deviated from the path of modesty and had acted deceitfully against him, hence, it is an indication of his evil heart, and even though (the truth of the matter is that) it was hidden from his eyes that a man laid with her, we shall pay no heed to his jealousy. Similarly, if he is jealous without cause, we will not say that his jealousy is a meaningless thing and ignore it, but we will blot out the scroll and bring (the offering) as it is written in this chapter.

NOTES

which is, in reality, not only a trespass against her husband, but also against God. This is an example of how a sinful act can be a violation of trust between man and man as well as between man and God. The expression *the holiness ... which He loves* refers to the holiness of matrimony.

14-15. וְעָבַר עָלָיו רוּחַ קִנְאָה . . . אוֹ עָבַר עָלָיו רוּחַ קִנְאָה . . . וְהֵבִיא הָאִישׁ אֶת אִשְׁתּוֹ — *And the spirit of jealousy comes over him . . . or if the spirit of jealousy comes upon him . . . Then shall the man bring his wife.* The *Sforno* explains the sequence of these verses in the following manner. The water of bitterness which the *sotah*, the suspected woman, must drink consists of water and ink erased from a special scroll containing the curses (including God's Name). The *Kohen* can only perform an act extreme as that of blotting out God's Name under specially prescribed circumstances. The Torah is teaching us in these verses that even when we might argue that the husband was lax in his concern regarding

טז־יז מִנְחַת זִכָּרוֹן מַזְכֶּרֶת עָוֺן: וְהִקְרִיב אֹתָהּ הַכֹּהֵן וְהֶעֱמִדָהּ לִפְנֵי יהוה: וְלָקַח
הַכֹּהֵן מַיִם קְדֹשִׁים בִּכְלִי־חָרֶשׂ וּמִן־הֶעָפָר אֲשֶׁר יִהְיֶה בְּקַרְקַע הַמִּשְׁכָּן
יח יִקַּח הַכֹּהֵן וְנָתַן אֶל־הַמָּיִם: וְהֶעֱמִיד הַכֹּהֵן אֶת־הָאִשָּׁה לִפְנֵי יהוה וּפָרַע
אֶת־רֹאשׁ הָאִשָּׁה וְנָתַן עַל־כַּפֶּיהָ אֵת מִנְחַת הַזִּכָּרוֹן מִנְחַת קְנָאֹת הִוא
יט וּבְיַד הַכֹּהֵן יִהְיוּ מֵי הַמָּרִים הַמְאָרְרִים: וְהִשְׁבִּיעַ אֹתָהּ הַכֹּהֵן וְאָמַר
אֶל־הָאִשָּׁה אִם־לֹא שָׁכַב אִישׁ אֹתָךְ וְאִם־לֹא שָׂטִית טֻמְאָה תַּחַת
כ אִישֵׁךְ הִנָּקִי מִמֵּי הַמָּרִים הַמְאָרְרִים הָאֵלֶּה: וְאַתְּ כִּי שָׂטִית תַּחַת אִישֵׁךְ
כא וְכִי נִטְמֵאת וַיִּתֵּן אִישׁ בָּךְ אֶת־שְׁכָבְתּוֹ מִבַּלְעֲדֵי אִישֵׁךְ: וְהִשְׁבִּיעַ הַכֹּהֵן
אֶת־הָאִשָּׁה בִּשְׁבֻעַת הָאָלָה וְאָמַר הַכֹּהֵן לָאִשָּׁה יִתֵּן יהוה אוֹתָךְ לְאָלָה
וְלִשְׁבֻעָה בְּתוֹךְ עַמֵּךְ בְּתֵת יהוה אֶת־יְרֵכֵךְ נֹפֶלֶת וְאֶת־בִּטְנֵךְ צָבָה:
כב וּבָאוּ הַמַּיִם הַמְאָרְרִים הָאֵלֶּה בְּמֵעַיִךְ לַצְבּוֹת בֶּטֶן וְלַנְפִּל יָרֵךְ וְאָמְרָה
כג הָאִשָּׁה אָמֵן | אָמֵן: וְכָתַב אֶת־הָאָלֹת הָאֵלֶּה הַכֹּהֵן בַּסֵּפֶר וּמָחָה אֶל־מֵי
כד הַמָּרִים: וְהִשְׁקָה אֶת־הָאִשָּׁה אֶת־מֵי הַמָּרִים הַמְאָרְרִים וּבָאוּ בָהּ הַמַּיִם
כה הַמְאָרְרִים לְמָרִים: וְלָקַח הַכֹּהֵן מִיַּד הָאִשָּׁה אֵת מִנְחַת הַקְּנָאֹת וְהֵנִיף
כו אֶת־הַמִּנְחָה לִפְנֵי יהוה וְהִקְרִיב אֹתָהּ אֶל־הַמִּזְבֵּחַ: וְקָמַץ הַכֹּהֵן
מִן־הַמִּנְחָה אֶת־אַזְכָּרָתָהּ וְהִקְטִיר הַמִּזְבֵּחָה וְאַחַר יַשְׁקֶה אֶת־הָאִשָּׁה
כז אֶת־הַמָּיִם: וְהִשְׁקָהּ אֶת־הַמַּיִם וְהָיְתָה אִם־נִטְמְאָה וַתִּמְעֹל מַעַל
בְּאִישָׁהּ וּבָאוּ בָהּ הַמַּיִם הַמְאָרְרִים לְמָרִים וְצָבְתָה בִטְנָהּ וְנָפְלָה יְרֵכָהּ

---

19. וְהִשְׁבִּיעַ — *He shall cause* (*her*) *to swear.* He shall tell her to accept the oath and the curse upon herself with this condition.

אם לא שָׁכַב איש — *If no man have lain* . . . now (presently).

וְאִם לֹא שָׂטִית טֻמְאָה — *And if you have not gone aside to defilement* . . . on other occasions.

הִנָּקִי — *You will be free.* Because it was already stated, כִּי לֹא יְנַקֶּה ה׳ אֵת אֲשֶׁר יִשָּׂא אֶת שְׁמוֹ לַשָּׁוְא, *For* HASHEM *will not hold him guiltless that takes His Name in vain* (*Exodus* 20:7), (which is interpreted) to mean that even a person who swears truthfully but unnecessarily, as for example, one who swears regarding a known true fact is not held guiltless of that oath. Therefore, it would be proper that you who caused this matter to be in doubt, thereby obligating yourself to swear, should not be held guiltless even if you swear truthfully. Nonetheless, accept these curses on the condition that you will be free of them if you have not gone aside.

NOTES

his wife's behavior or conversely that his jealousy is unfounded, nonetheless we proceed with the ceremony, providing the woman had been warned not to conceal herself (in private) with a particular man and had disregarded that warning.

19. הִנָּקִי — *You will be free.* The Torah teaches us that the severity of taking an oath in the Name of God is so great that even if one swears truthfully, but unnecessarily, he is liable to punishment. Hence, the suspected woman (סוֹטָה) would be reluctant to accept the oath and its attendant curse, even though she is innocent of infidelity, since she is responsible for the administering of the oath in God's Name and the blotting out of His Name written in the scroll. The Torah therefore reassures her that she will be held guiltless (clean) if she is indeed innocent of the charge of infidelity. Although the *sotah* is not guilty of an overt immoral act, still by secluding herself with a strange man, she defied her husband and ultimately caused an oath to be administered, and the Name of God in the scroll to be blotted out. Why then is she not punished? The answer is given by the *Sforno* in his commentary on verse 28 in this chapter where he states that God recognizes and appreciates human

a meal-offering of remembrance, a reminder of iniquity.
16 *"The Kohen shall bring her near and have her stand before* HASHEM.
17 *The Kohen shall take sacred water in an earthenware vessel, and the Kohen shall take from the earth that is on the floor of the Tabernacle and put it in the water.* 18 *The Kohen shall have the woman stand before* HASHEM *and uncover the woman's head, and upon her hands he shall put the meal-offering of remembrance — it is a meal-offering of jealousies, and in the hand of the Kohen shall be the bitter waters that cause a curse.*
19 *"The Kohen shall adjure her and say to the woman, 'If a man has not lain with you, and you have not strayed in defilement with someone other than your husband, then you shall be innocent of these bitter waters that cause curse.* 20 *But if you have strayed with someone other than your husband, and if you have become defiled, and a man other than your husband has lain with you — !'*
21 *"The Kohen shall adjure the woman with the oath of the curse, and the Kohen shall say to the woman, 'May* HASHEM *render you as a curse and as an oath amid your people, when* HASHEM *causes your thigh to collapse and your stomach to distend.* 22 *These waters that cause curse shall enter your innards to cause stomach to distend and thigh to collapse!' And the woman shall respond, 'Amen, amen.'*
23 *"The Kohen shall inscribe these curses on a scroll and erase it into the bitter waters.* 24 *When he shall cause the woman to drink the bitter waters that cause curse, and the bitter waters that cause curse shall come into her.*
25 *"The Kohen shall take the meal-offering of jealousies from the hand of the woman; he shall wave the meal-offering before* HASHEM, *and he shall offer it on the Altar.* 26 *The Kohen shall scoop up from the meal-offering its remembrance and cause it to go up in smoke on the Altar; after which he shall cause the woman to drink the water.* 27 *He shall cause her to drink the water, and it shall be that if she had become defiled and had committed treachery against her husband, the waters that cause curse shall come into her for bitterness, and her stomach shall be distended and her thigh shall collapse,*

---

20. וְאַתְּ — *And you* . . . also accept upon yourself . . .

כִּי שָׂטִית תַּחַת אִישֵׁךְ וְכִי נִטְמֵאת — *Have gone aside, being under your husband, and if you have been defiled* . . . that the oath (curse) will take effect because you went aside and became defiled and for no other reason, and being that the cause is removed and is not valid, the words of the oath (curse) will not take effect.

22. אָמֵן אָמֵן — *Amen, amen.* I accept the two conditions which you stated, (namely) that if I did not go aside I shall be clear, and if I did go aside the curse will take effect.

NOTES

frailty which causes a person to commit foolish acts, and therefore He is willing to make an exception in this particular case, considering that it will preserve a marriage.

20. כִּי שָׂטִית תַּחַת אִישֵׁךְ וְכִי נִטְמֵאת — *Have gone aside, being under your husband, and if you have been defiled.* The woman must also be reassured that the oath and curse apply exclusively to the charge of infidelity and not to other transgressions. The sin of infidelity, however, is all inclusive, be it the act she is suspected of now which has brought her to the Temple, or acts of infidelity perpetrated on other occasions — as mentioned in verse 19 and as indicated in the repetition of the word "Amen" in verse 22. (See tractate *Sotah* 18b.)

כח וְהָיְתָה הָאִשָּׁה לְאָלָה בְּקֶרֶב עַמָּהּ: וְאִם־לֹא נִטְמְאָה הָאִשָּׁה וּטְהֹרָה
כט הִוא וְנִקְּתָה וְנִזְרְעָה זָרַע: זֹאת תּוֹרַת הַקְּנָאֹת אֲשֶׁר תִּשְׂטֶה אִשָּׁה תַּחַת
ל אִישָׁהּ וְנִטְמָאָה: אוֹ אִישׁ אֲשֶׁר תַּעֲבֹר עָלָיו רוּחַ קִנְאָה וְקִנֵּא אֶת־אִשְׁתּוֹ
וְהֶעֱמִיד אֶת־הָאִשָּׁה לִפְנֵי יהוה וְעָשָׂה לָהּ הַכֹּהֵן אֵת כָּל־הַתּוֹרָה הַזֹּאת:
לא וְנִקָּה הָאִישׁ מֵעָוֺן וְהָאִשָּׁה הַהִוא תִּשָּׂא אֶת־עֲוֺנָהּ:
ו א־ב וַיְדַבֵּר יהוה אֶל־מֹשֶׁה לֵּאמֹר: דַּבֵּר אֶל־בְּנֵי יִשְׂרָאֵל וְאָמַרְתָּ אֲלֵהֶם אִישׁ
ג אוֹ־אִשָּׁה כִּי יַפְלִא לִנְדֹּר נֶדֶר נָזִיר לְהַזִּיר לַיהוה: מִיַּיִן וְשֵׁכָר יַזִּיר חֹמֶץ
יַיִן וְחֹמֶץ שֵׁכָר לֹא יִשְׁתֶּה וְכָל־מִשְׁרַת עֲנָבִים לֹא יִשְׁתֶּה וַעֲנָבִים לַחִים
ד וִיבֵשִׁים לֹא יֹאכֵל: כֹּל יְמֵי נִזְרוֹ מִכֹּל אֲשֶׁר יֵעָשֶׂה מִגֶּפֶן הַיַּיִן מֵחַרְצַנִּים

28. וְנִקְּתָה — *She shall be cleared* ... from the punishment of the oath which she caused, even though it states, כִּי לֹא יְנַקֶּה ה׳, *For HASHEM will not hold him guiltless;* nonetheless, in this case God, the Blessed One, wanted the woman to be cleared כִּי הוּא יָדַע יִצְרֵנוּ, *for He knows our nature* (*Psalms* 103:14).

29. זֹאת תּוֹרַת הַקְּנָאֹת — *This is the law of jealousy* ... a jealousy which is justified, and a jealousy which is not justified. This (the Torah) explains by stating ...

אֲשֶׁר תִּשְׂטֶה אִשָּׁה תַּחַת אִישָׁהּ וְנִטְמָאָה — *When a woman, being under her husband, goes aside and is defiled.* Now this refers to justified jealousy. The (Torah) then additionally states ...

30. אוֹ אִישׁ אֲשֶׁר תַּעֲבֹר עָלָיו רוּחַ קִנְאָה — *Or when the spirit of jealousy comes upon a man* ... without proper cause.

וְקִנֵּא אֶת אִשְׁתּוֹ — *And he is jealous over his wife.* He warns her not to hide (meet secretly), nonetheless ...

וְעָשָׂה לָהּ הַכֹּהֵן אֵת כָּל הַתּוֹרָה הַזֹּאת — *And the Kohen shall execute upon her all this law* ... and he will not be concerned about blotting out the scroll.

31. וְנִקָּה הָאִישׁ מֵעָוֺן — *And the man shall be clear from iniquity* ... even though he suspected an innocent (lit., kosher) woman, because she caused this by violating his warning and (thereby) creating (a situation of) circumstantial evidence, as (our Sages) say, "David did not pay heed to slander; he saw self-evident things in him," regarding Mephiboshes (*Shabbos* 56a).

וְהָאִשָּׁה הַהִוא תִּשָּׂא אֶת עֲוֺנָהּ — *And that woman shall bear her iniquity.* If she was defiled

NOTES

28. וְנִקְּתָה — *She shall be cleared.* See note on verse 19.

29-30. זֹאת תּוֹרַת הַקְּנָאֹת אֲשֶׁר תִּשְׂטֶה אִשָּׁה תַּחַת אִישָׁהּ וְנִטְמָאָה. אוֹ אִישׁ אֲשֶׁר תַּעֲבֹר עָלָיו רוּחַ קִנְאָה — *This is the law of jealousy when a woman, being under her husband, goes aside and is defiled. Or when the spirit of jealousy comes upon a man.* The word הַקְּנָאֹת, *jealousy,* is written in the plural. The *Sforno* interprets it to mean two kinds of jealousy — one justified and the other unjustified. The former is indicated by the expression *when a woman ... goes aside and is defiled* while the latter is indicated by the opening phrase of verse 30 — *Or when the spirit of jealousy comes upon a man.* Nonetheless, in both instances, it is incumbent upon the *Kohen* to follow the formula of the Torah even though it involves the blotting out of God's Name in the scroll.

31. וְנִקָּה הָאִישׁ מֵעָוֺן וְהָאִשָּׁה הַהִוא תִּשָּׂא אֶת עֲוֺנָהּ — *And the man shall be clear from iniquity and that woman shall bear her iniquity.* The Torah teaches us that the husband shall be held blameless whereas the woman shall be considered guilty, even when she is proven innocent! The *Sforno* explains this anomaly in the following manner: By defying her husband and closeting herself with a particular man, she is guilty of brazenness and hence is held up to shame. He, in turn, confronted by her defiant action is left with no other choice than to bring her to the *Kohen,* who will give her the water to drink so as to resolve this matter.

The selection from tractate *Shabbos* cited by the

and the woman shall become a curse amid her people. [28] *But if the woman had not become defiled, and she is pure, then she shall be proven innocent and she shall bear seed.*

[29] *"This is the law of the jealousies, when a woman shall go astray with someone other than her husband and become defiled;* [30] *or of a man over whom passes a spirit of jealousy and he warns his wife, and he causes his wife to stand before HASHEM, then the Kohen shall carry out for her this entire law.* [31] *The man will be innocent of iniquity, but that woman shall bear her iniquity."*

6 [1] *HASHEM spoke to Moses, saying,* [2] *"Speak to the Children of Israel and say to them: A man or woman who shall dissociate himself by taking a Nazirite vow of abstinence for the sake of HASHEM;* [3] *from new or aged wine shall he abstain, and he shall not drink vinegar of wine or vinegar of aged wine; anything in which grapes have been steeped shall he not drink, and fresh and dried grapes shall he not eat.* [4] *All the days of his abstinence, anything made from wine grapes, even the pips*

she will die, and if she was not defiled she will be degraded in public for impudently violating her husband's warning and hiding herself (secretly with another man).

VI

2. כִּי יַפְלִא — *If he pronounce (a vow).* He separates himself from the vanities and pleasures of man.

לִנְדֹּר נֶדֶר נָזִיר — *Uttering a vow of a nazir* . . . to be removed and separated from the normal pleasures.

לְהַזִּיר לַה' — *To consecrate himself to HASHEM* . . . to separate himself from all these (pleasures) in order to be totally (committed) to God; to occupy himself in His Torah, to walk in His ways and to cleave to Him.

3. מִיַּיִן וְשֵׁכָר יַזִּיר — *He shall abstain from wine and strong drink* (alternatively: *new wine and old wine*). He must not afflict himself by fasting for that would diminish his heavenly work, as we find in the words (of our Sages) (*Taanis* 11b), nor should he torture his body with 'flagellation of the abstemious' (*Sotah* 20a), as is the custom of hypocrites and idolatrous *Kohanim*. Rather, he shall separate himself (abstain) from wine, for in that manner he will considerably reduce licentiousness and subdue his (evil) inclination, but he will not weaken his strength through this (abstinence) at all.

NOTES

Sforno relates the strange behavior of Mephiboshes, the son of Saul, when David returned to his throne after Absalom's revolt failed. David detected that Mephiboshes was not very pleased with the failure of Absalom to overthrow him. Just as David perceived from Mephiboshes' garb and behavior his true attitude and feelings, so the husband of the *sotah* can detect his wife's rebellious nature from her conduct even when she is technically innocent of infidelity.

VI

3. מִיַּיִן וְשֵׁכָר יַזִּיר — *He shall abstain from wine and strong drink.* Although a *nazir* separates himself from certain physical pleasures and refrains from certain behaviors which would impair his state of holiness, the *Sforno* emphasizes that he is not permitted to deny himself more than the Torah has bidden and certainly not to impose afflictions upon himself which are prohibited by the Torah. The Talmud in tractate *Taanis*, which the *Sforno* alludes to, states that "a scholar is not permitted to fast (beyond the prescribed fasts) because it diminishes his heavenly service." The other selection cited by the *Sforno* is from tractate *Sotah* where our Sages reject and criticize the practice of those who inflict physical pain upon themselves as a religious act.

ה וְעַד־זָג לֹא יֹאכֵל: כָּל־יְמֵי נֶדֶר נִזְרוֹ תַּעַר לֹא־יַעֲבֹר עַל־רֹאשׁוֹ
עַד־מְלֹאת הַיָּמִם אֲשֶׁר־יַזִּיר לַיהוה קָדֹשׁ יִהְיֶה גַּדֵּל פֶּרַע שְׂעַר רֹאשׁוֹ:
ו־ז כָּל־יְמֵי הַזִּירוֹ לַיהוה עַל־נֶפֶשׁ מֵת לֹא יָבֹא: לְאָבִיו וּלְאִמּוֹ לְאָחִיו
ח וּלְאַחֹתוֹ לֹא־יִטַּמָּא לָהֶם בְּמֹתָם כִּי נֵזֶר אֱלֹהָיו עַל־רֹאשׁוֹ: כֹּל יְמֵי נִזְרוֹ
ט קָדֹשׁ הוּא לַיהוה: וְכִי־יָמוּת מֵת עָלָיו בְּפֶתַע פִּתְאֹם וְטִמֵּא רֹאשׁ
י נִזְרוֹ וְגִלַּח רֹאשׁוֹ בְּיוֹם טָהֳרָתוֹ בַּיּוֹם הַשְּׁבִיעִי יְגַלְּחֶנּוּ: וּבַיּוֹם הַשְּׁמִינִי
יָבִא שְׁתֵּי תֹרִים אוֹ שְׁנֵי בְּנֵי יוֹנָה אֶל־הַכֹּהֵן אֶל־פֶּתַח אֹהֶל מוֹעֵד:
יא וְעָשָׂה הַכֹּהֵן אֶחָד לְחַטָּאת וְאֶחָד לְעֹלָה וְכִפֶּר עָלָיו מֵאֲשֶׁר חָטָא
יב עַל־הַנָּפֶשׁ וְקִדַּשׁ אֶת־רֹאשׁוֹ בַּיּוֹם הַהוּא: וְהִזִּיר לַיהוה אֶת־יְמֵי נִזְרוֹ
וְהֵבִיא כֶּבֶשׂ בֶּן־שְׁנָתוֹ לְאָשָׁם וְהַיָּמִים הָרִאשֹׁנִים יִפְּלוּ כִּי טָמֵא נִזְרוֹ:
יג וְזֹאת תּוֹרַת הַנָּזִיר בְּיוֹם מְלֹאת יְמֵי נִזְרוֹ יָבִיא אֹתוֹ אֶל־פֶּתַח
יד אֹהֶל מוֹעֵד: וְהִקְרִיב אֶת־קָרְבָּנוֹ לַיהוה כֶּבֶשׂ בֶּן־שְׁנָתוֹ תָמִים אֶחָד
לְעֹלָה וְכַבְשָׂה אַחַת בַּת־שְׁנָתָהּ תְּמִימָה לְחַטָּאת וְאַיִל־אֶחָד תָּמִים
טו לִשְׁלָמִים: וְסַל מַצּוֹת סֹלֶת חַלֹּת בְּלוּלֹת בַּשֶּׁמֶן וּרְקִיקֵי מַצּוֹת
טז מְשֻׁחִים בַּשָּׁמֶן וּמִנְחָתָם וְנִסְכֵּיהֶם: וְהִקְרִיב הַכֹּהֵן לִפְנֵי יהוה וְעָשָׂה
יז אֶת־חַטָּאתוֹ וְאֶת־עֹלָתוֹ: וְאֶת־הָאַיִל יַעֲשֶׂה זֶבַח שְׁלָמִים לַיהוה עַל סַל
יח הַמַּצּוֹת וְעָשָׂה הַכֹּהֵן אֶת־מִנְחָתוֹ וְאֶת־נִסְכּוֹ: וְגִלַּח הַנָּזִיר פֶּתַח אֹהֶל
מוֹעֵד אֶת־רֹאשׁ נִזְרוֹ וְלָקַח אֶת־שְׂעַר רֹאשׁ נִזְרוֹ וְנָתַן עַל־הָאֵשׁ
יט אֲשֶׁר־תַּחַת זֶבַח הַשְּׁלָמִים: וְלָקַח הַכֹּהֵן אֶת־הַזְּרֹעַ בְּשֵׁלָה מִן־הָאַיִל

---

5. תַּעַר לֹא יַעֲבֹר עַל רֹאשׁוֹ — *No razor shall come upon his head.* And thereby he will divert all thoughts of beauty and the arranging of (his) hair.

קָדֹשׁ יִהְיֶה — *He shall be holy* . . . separated from material desires.

6. עַל נֶפֶשׁ מֵת לֹא יָבֹא — *He shall not come near a dead body.* He shall not desecrate his holiness by occupying himself with honoring the dead, as is also the case with the *Kohen Gadol.*

8. קדש הוא לה׳ — *He is holy to* HASHEM. He will merit to be illuminated by the light of life, to be prepared to understand and to instruct (others), as is fitting for the holy ones of the generation. It is to this, it seems (to me), that Elkanah referred when he said, אַךְ יָקֵם ה׳ אֶת דְּבָרוֹ, *But let* HASHEM *establish his word* (*I Samuel* 1:23), meaning "I agree to vow that he be a *nazir* and ask of God, the Blessed One, no other thing for the child than that His word be established and that he be holy to God."

13. יָבִיא אֹתוֹ — *He shall bring it.* (Our Sages) have already explained (the word *it*) as meaning "he shall bring himself" (*Sifre*). This is (to be understood as follows): For indeed,

NOTES

8. קדש הוא לה׳ — *He is holy to* HASHEM. The *Sforno* interprets the expression קדש הוא לה׳, *He is holy to* HASHEM, in the sense of a Divine promise and assurance. He suggests that this was the intent of Samuel's father, Elkanah, when he permitted his son to be dedicated to God's service at a tender age. His only stipulation was that the assurance given by God in this chapter of the *nazir* be fullfilled.

13. יָבִיא אֹתוֹ — *He shall bring it. Rashi* explains the expression יָבִיא אֹתוֹ, *He shall bring it,* as meaning "he shall bring himself," based upon the interpretation of our Sages. The *Sforno* interprets this phrase in the same manner, citing three cases where the Torah tells us that the person whose status is about to be affected or changed, whether a leper, a *sotah* or a slave, is brought to one who is

or skin, he shall not eat. 5 *All the days of his Nazirite vow, a razor shall not*
pass over his head; until the completion of the days that he will be a
Nazirite for the sake of HASHEM, *holy shall he be, the growth of hair on his*
head shall grow. 6 *All the days of his abstinence for the sake of* HASHEM *he*
shall not come near a dead person. 7 *To his father or to his mother, to his*
brother or to his sister — he shall not contaminate himself to them upon
their death, for the crown of his God is upon his head. 8 *All the days of his*
abstinence he is holy to HASHEM.

9 *"If a person should die near him with quick suddenness and conta-*
minate his Nazirite head, he shall shave his head on the day he becomes
purified; on the seventh day shall he shave it. 10 *On the eighth day he shall*
bring two turtledoves or two young doves to the Kohen, to the entrance of
the Tent of Meeting. 11 *The Kohen shall make one as a sin-offering and one*
as an elevation-offering, and he shall provide him atonement for having
sinned regarding the person; and he shall sanctify his head on that day.
12 *He shall dedicate to* HASHEM *the days of his abstinence, and he shall bring*
a sheep in its first year for a guilt-offering; the first days shall fall aside, for
his abstinence had been contaminated.

13 *"This shall be the law of the Nazirite: on the day his abstinence is*
completed, he shall bring himself to the entrance of the Tent of Meeting.
14 *He shall bring his offering to* HASHEM: *one unblemished sheep in its first*
year as an elevation-offering, one unblemished ewe in its first year as a
sin-offering, and one unblemished ram as a peace-offering; 15 *a basket of*
unleavened loaves: loaves of fine flour mixed with oil and unleavened
wafers smeared with oil; and their meal-offerings and their libations. 16 *The*
Kohen shall approach before HASHEM *and perform the service of his*
sin-offering and his elevation-offering. 17 *He shall make the ram a feast*
peace-offering for HASHEM *with the basket of unleavened loaves, and the*
Kohen shall make its meal-offering and its libation. 18 *At the entrance of the*
Tent of Meeting the Nazir shall shave his Nazirite head; he shall take the
hair of his Nazirite head and put it on the fire that is under the feast
peace-offering. 19 *The Kohen shall take the cooked upper foreleg of the ram*

(regarding) whoever draws nigh to one who initiates a new action affecting him, it (always) says that he is *brought* to the one superior to him who changes (his status), similar to, "He who is imprisoned cannot free himself" (*Berachos* 5b). Therefore, regarding the *tumah* and *taharah* of a leper it is written, וְהוּבָא אֶל הַכֹּהֵן, *And he is "brought" to the Kohen* (*Leviticus* 14:2), and regarding a *sotah*, וְהֵבִיא הָאִישׁ אֶת אִשְׁתּוֹ אֶל הַכֹּהֵן, *And then shall the man "bring" his wife to the Kohen* (5:15), and also regarding a slave, וְהִגִּישׁוֹ אֲדֹנָיו אֶל הָאֱלֹהִים, *Then his master shall 'bring' him to the judges* (*Exodus* 21:6). However, regarding the *nazir* who, through the act of shaving (his hair), was renewed and changed into a different man — there is no one more honored (esteemed) than he in this regard; rather he shall bring himself (to the Temple).

NOTES

in a position to exercise authority over him. In these three cases, the person in authority, i.e., the *Kohen*, the husband or the master, actively brings or receives the passive party, i.e., the leper, *sotah* or slave. In the case of the *nazir*, however, *he* himself is capable of bringing about the termination of his present status and is thus an active, not a passive, party.

וְחַלַּת מַצָּה אַחַת מִן־הַסַּל וּרְקִיק מַצָּה אֶחָד וְנָתַן עַל־כַּפֵּי הַנָּזִיר אַחַר
כ הִתְגַּלְּחוֹ אֶת־נִזְרוֹ: וְהֵנִיף אוֹתָם הַכֹּהֵן | תְּנוּפָה לִפְנֵי יהוה קֹדֶשׁ הוּא
כא לַכֹּהֵן עַל חֲזֵה הַתְּנוּפָה וְעַל שׁוֹק הַתְּרוּמָה וְאַחַר יִשְׁתֶּה הַנָּזִיר יָיִן: זֹאת
תּוֹרַת הַנָּזִיר אֲשֶׁר יִדֹּר קָרְבָּנוֹ לַיהוה עַל־נִזְרוֹ מִלְּבַד אֲשֶׁר־תַּשִּׂיג יָדוֹ
כְּפִי נִדְרוֹ אֲשֶׁר יִדֹּר כֵּן יַעֲשֶׂה עַל תּוֹרַת נִזְרוֹ:
כב-כג וַיְדַבֵּר יהוה אֶל־מֹשֶׁה לֵּאמֹר: דַּבֵּר אֶל־אַהֲרֹן וְאֶל־בָּנָיו לֵאמֹר כֹּה
כד-כה תְבָרְכוּ אֶת־בְּנֵי יִשְׂרָאֵל אָמוֹר לָהֶם: יְבָרֶכְךָ יהוה וְיִשְׁמְרֶךָ: יָאֵר
כו יהוה | פָּנָיו אֵלֶיךָ וִיחֻנֶּךָּ: יִשָּׂא יהוה | פָּנָיו אֵלֶיךָ וְיָשֵׂם לְךָ
ז חמישי כז-א שָׁלוֹם: וְשָׂמוּ אֶת־שְׁמִי עַל־בְּנֵי יִשְׂרָאֵל וַאֲנִי אֲבָרְכֵם: וַיְהִי
בְּיוֹם כַּלּוֹת מֹשֶׁה לְהָקִים אֶת־הַמִּשְׁכָּן וַיִּמְשַׁח אֹתוֹ וַיְקַדֵּשׁ אֹתוֹ
וְאֶת־כָּל־כֵּלָיו וְאֶת־הַמִּזְבֵּחַ וְאֶת־כָּל־כֵּלָיו וַיִּמְשָׁחֵם וַיְקַדֵּשׁ אֹתָם:
ב וַיַּקְרִיבוּ נְשִׂיאֵי יִשְׂרָאֵל רָאשֵׁי בֵּית אֲבֹתָם הֵם נְשִׂיאֵי הַמַּטֹּת הֵם
ג הָעֹמְדִים עַל־הַפְּקֻדִים: וַיָּבִיאוּ אֶת־קָרְבָּנָם לִפְנֵי יהוה שֵׁשׁ־עֶגְלֹת צָב
וּשְׁנֵי עָשָׂר בָּקָר עֲגָלָה עַל־שְׁנֵי הַנְּשִׂאִים וְשׁוֹר לְאֶחָד וַיַּקְרִיבוּ אוֹתָם
ד-ה לִפְנֵי הַמִּשְׁכָּן: וַיֹּאמֶר יהוה אֶל־מֹשֶׁה לֵּאמֹר: קַח מֵאִתָּם וְהָיוּ לַעֲבֹד
אֶת־עֲבֹדַת אֹהֶל מוֹעֵד וְנָתַתָּה אוֹתָם אֶל־הַלְוִיִּם אִישׁ כְּפִי עֲבֹדָתוֹ:

24. יְבָרֶכְךָ — *May (Hashem) bless you* . . . with wealth and property, for אִם אֵין קֶמַח אֵין תּוֹרָה, *if there is no flour there is no Torah* (*Avos* 3:21).

וְיִשְׁמְרֶךָ — *And guard you* . . . from robbers.

25. יָאֵר ה׳ — *May HASHEM shine* (*illuminate*). May He open your eyes through the light of His countenance to see wonders from His Torah and His deeds, after you have attained your needs through His blessings.

26. יִשָּׂא ה׳ פָּנָיו אֵלֶיךָ — *May HASHEM lift up His countenance upon you* . . . to (merit) eternal life, similar to, כִּי עִמְּךָ מְקוֹר חַיִּים בְּאוֹרְךָ נִרְאֶה אוֹר, *For with You is the fountain of life; in Your light do we see light* (*Psalms* 36:10), and so (our Sages) say, "The righteous will sit with their crowns on their heads enjoying the brightness of the Divine Presence" (*Berachos* 17a).

וְיָשֵׂם לְךָ שָׁלוֹם — *And give you peace* . . . the tranquility of peace which is everlasting, unadulterated by punishment, as is fitting for every perfect (complete) (person who merits) eternal life.

VII

1. וְאֶת הַמִּזְבֵּחַ וְאֶת כָּל כֵּלָיו — *And the altar and all the vessels thereof* . . . to set up the Altar and all the vessels thereof (i.e., of the Tabernacle), each one in its (proper) place.

NOTES

VII

2. הֵם נְשִׂיאֵי הַמַּטֹּת הֵם הָעֹמְדִים עַל הַפְּקֻדִים — *These were the princes of the tribes, these are they that were over them when they were numbered.* The Torah tells us that these princes made offerings on behalf of their tribes for two reasons — they were נְשִׂיאִים, *princes,* and they also joined Moses and Aaron when the census was taken (*Bamidbar* 1:4). Consistent with his commentary on that verse, the *Sforno* explains that since each leader recognized the shortcomings of his people, he was able to bring the appropriate sacrifices to atone for those particular sins, and since they were princes they were willing to do so for each felt responsible for his respective tribe.

3. עֲגָלָה עַל שְׁנֵי הַנְּשִׂאִים — *A wagon for every two of the princes.* The princes were certainly wealthy enough so that each one could bring his

and one unleavened loaf from the basket and one unleavened wafer, and place them on the hands of the Nazirite after he has shaved his Nazirite hair. 20 *The Kohen shall wave them as a wave-service before HASHEM; it shall be holy for the Kohen, aside from the breast of the waving and the thigh of the raising-up — afterward the Nazirite may drink wine.*

21 *"This is the law of the Nazirite who shall pledge his offering to HASHEM for his abstinence — aside from what he can afford, according to his vow that he shall pledge, so shall he do in addition to the law of his abstinence."*

22 *HASHEM spoke to Moses, saying,* 23 *"Speak to Aaron and his sons, saying: So shall you bless the Children of Israel, saying to them:* 24 *'May HASHEM bless you and safeguard you.* 25 *May HASHEM illuminate His countenance for you and be gracious to you.* 26 *May HASHEM lift His countenance to you and establish peace for you.'* 27 *Let them place My Name upon the Children of Israel, and I shall bless them."*

7 1 *It was on the day that Moses finished erecting the Tabernacle that he anointed it, sanctified it and all its utensils, and the Altar and all its utensils, and he had anointed and sanctified them.* 2 *The leaders of Israel, the heads of their fathers' household, brought offerings; they were the leaders of the tribes, they were those who stand at the countings.* 3 *They brought their offering before HASHEM: six covered wagons and twelve oxen — a wagon for each two leaders and an ox for each — and they brought them before the Tabernacle.* 4 *HASHEM said to Moses, saying,* 5 *"Take from them, and they shall be to perform the work of the Tent of Meeting; you shall give them to the Levites, each man according to his work."*

וַיִּמְשָׁחֵם וַיְקַדֵּשׁ אֹתָם — *And he anointed them and sanctified them . . .* after setting up each of them properly.

2. הֵם נְשִׂיאֵי הַמַּטֹּת הֵם הָעֹמְדִים עַל הַפְּקֻדִים — *These were the princes of the tribes, these are they that were over them when they were numbered.* And as such, each one of them brought an offering for his tribe and its members because inasmuch as they stood over (i.e., supervised) those who were numbered, each of them sensed that some members of his tribe were suspect of sin, and as princes they agreed to stand in the breach and offer sacrifices to atone on their behalf.

3. עֲגָלָה עַל שְׁנֵי הַנְּשִׂאִים — *A wagon for every two of the princes . . .* as an indication of the brotherhood (existing) between them, through which they would be worthy that the Divine Presence dwell between them, as it says, וַיְהִי בִישֻׁרוּן מֶלֶךְ בְּהִתְאַסֵּף רָאשֵׁי עָם יַחַד, *And there was a king in Jeshurun when the heads of the people were gathered (Deuteronomy* 33:5), as opposed to, חָלַק לִבָּם עַתָּה יֶאְשָׁמוּ, *Their heart is divided; now shall they bear their guilt* (*Hosea* 10:2).

5. קַח מֵאִתָּם — *Take it from them . . .* for Moses thought that the burden of all the Levites was to be carried on their shoulders, as was the case of the Kehathites and their burden.

NOTES

own wagon. The reason that two shared one wagon was to demonstrate the unity which reigned in their midst, as the *Sforno* explains. The Sanctuary is called מִשְׁכָּן, indicating that the שְׁכִינָה, *the Divine Presence*, dwells therein, and tradition teaches us that it only dwells in the midst of unity but departs when there is strife and friction in Israel.

ו־ז וַיִּקַּח מֹשֶׁה אֶת־הָעֲגָלֹת וְאֶת־הַבָּקָר וַיִּתֵּן אוֹתָם אֶל־הַלְוִיִּם: אֵת ׀
שְׁתֵּי הָעֲגָלוֹת וְאֵת אַרְבַּעַת הַבָּקָר נָתַן לִבְנֵי גֵרְשׁוֹן כְּפִי עֲבֹדָתָם:
ח וְאֵת ׀ אַרְבַּע הָעֲגָלֹת וְאֵת שְׁמֹנַת הַבָּקָר נָתַן לִבְנֵי מְרָרִי כְּפִי עֲבֹדָתָם
ט בְּיַד אִיתָמָר בֶּן־אַהֲרֹן הַכֹּהֵן: וְלִבְנֵי קְהָת לֹא נָתָן כִּי־עֲבֹדַת הַקֹּדֶשׁ
י עֲלֵהֶם בַּכָּתֵף יִשָּׂאוּ: וַיַּקְרִיבוּ הַנְּשִׂאִים אֵת חֲנֻכַּת הַמִּזְבֵּחַ בְּיוֹם הִמָּשַׁח
יא אֹתוֹ וַיַּקְרִיבוּ הַנְּשִׂיאִם אֶת־קָרְבָּנָם לִפְנֵי הַמִּזְבֵּחַ: וַיֹּאמֶר יהוה אֶל־מֹשֶׁה
נָשִׂיא אֶחָד לַיּוֹם נָשִׂיא אֶחָד לַיּוֹם יַקְרִיבוּ אֶת־קָרְבָּנָם לַחֲנֻכַּת
יב הַמִּזְבֵּחַ: וַיְהִי הַמַּקְרִיב בַּיּוֹם הָרִאשׁוֹן אֶת־קָרְבָּנוֹ נַחְשׁוֹן
יג בֶּן־עַמִּינָדָב לְמַטֵּה יְהוּדָה: וְקָרְבָּנוֹ קַעֲרַת־כֶּסֶף אַחַת שְׁלֹשִׁים וּמֵאָה
מִשְׁקָלָהּ מִזְרָק אֶחָד כֶּסֶף שִׁבְעִים שֶׁקֶל בְּשֶׁקֶל הַקֹּדֶשׁ שְׁנֵיהֶם ׀ מְלֵאִים
יד סֹלֶת בְּלוּלָה בַשֶּׁמֶן לְמִנְחָה: כַּף אַחַת עֲשָׂרָה זָהָב מְלֵאָה קְטֹרֶת:
טו־טז פַּר אֶחָד בֶּן־בָּקָר אַיִל אֶחָד כֶּבֶשׂ־אֶחָד בֶּן־שְׁנָתוֹ לְעֹלָה: שְׂעִיר־עִזִּים
יז אֶחָד לְחַטָּאת: וּלְזֶבַח הַשְּׁלָמִים בָּקָר שְׁנַיִם אֵילִם חֲמִשָּׁה עַתֻּדִים
חֲמִשָּׁה כְּבָשִׂים בְּנֵי־שָׁנָה חֲמִשָּׁה זֶה קָרְבַּן נַחְשׁוֹן בֶּן־עַמִּינָדָב:
יח־יט בַּיּוֹם הַשֵּׁנִי הִקְרִיב נְתַנְאֵל בֶּן־צוּעָר נְשִׂיא יִשָּׂשכָר: הִקְרִב אֶת־
קָרְבָּנוֹ קַעֲרַת־כֶּסֶף אַחַת שְׁלֹשִׁים וּמֵאָה מִשְׁקָלָהּ מִזְרָק אֶחָד
כֶּסֶף שִׁבְעִים שֶׁקֶל בְּשֶׁקֶל הַקֹּדֶשׁ שְׁנֵיהֶם ׀ מְלֵאִים סֹלֶת בְּלוּלָה
כ־כא בַשֶּׁמֶן לְמִנְחָה: כַּף אַחַת עֲשָׂרָה זָהָב מְלֵאָה קְטֹרֶת: פַּר אֶחָד בֶּן־
כב בָּקָר אַיִל אֶחָד כֶּבֶשׂ־אֶחָד בֶּן־שְׁנָתוֹ לְעֹלָה: שְׂעִיר־עִזִּים אֶחָד

9. וְלִבְנֵי קְהָת לֹא נָתָן כִּי עֲבֹדַת הַקֹּדֶשׁ עֲלֵהֶם — *But to the sons of Kehath he gave none because the service of the holy things belonged to them.* Not the service of the Tent (of Meeting) but the service of the holy. Now behold, God, the Blessed One, said regarding the wagons that they were (to be used) for the service of the Tent of Meeting, which was the burden of the sons of Gershon and the sons of Merari. The burden of the sons of Kehath, however, had no item whatsoever (pertaining) to the structure of the Tent of Meeting, but their burden was (that of) the holy vessels housed in it which is called מִקְדָּשׁ (Sanctuary) as it says, *And the Kehathites, the bearers of the Sanctuary, set forward* (10:21).

10. וַיַּקְרִיבוּ הַנְּשִׂאִים אֵת חֲנֻכַּת הַמִּזְבֵּחַ — *And the princes brought the dedication offerings of the Altar.* They sanctified it.

וַיַּקְרִיבוּ הַנְּשִׂיאִם אֶת קָרְבָּנָם לִפְנֵי הַמִּזְבֵּחַ — *And the princes brought their offerings before the altar.* After they sanctified the offerings, they brought them near before the Altar.

13-17. וְקָרְבָּנוֹ קַעֲרַת כֶּסֶף אַחַת — *And his offering was one silver dish.* Behold, each one of

NOTES

9. וְלִבְנֵי קְהָת לֹא נָתָן כִּי עֲבֹדַת הַקֹּדֶשׁ עֲלֵהֶם — *But to the sons of Kehath he gave none because the service of the holy things belonged to them.* The Kehathites were not in charge of any part of the Tabernacle itself. They were responsible solely for the holy objects, such as the Ark, table, etc. These are called מִקְדָּשׁ, *Sanctuary.* Therefore, it was not fitting to place any of these sacred items on a wagon. They were to be carried on the shoulders of the Kehathites as a sign of respect.

10. וַיַּקְרִיבוּ הַנְּשִׂאִים אֵת חֲנֻכַּת הַמִּזְבֵּחַ ... וַיַּקְרִיבוּ הַנְּשִׂיאִם אֶת קָרְבָּנָם לִפְנֵי הַמִּזְבֵּחַ — *And the princes brought the dedication offerings of the Altar ... and the princes brought their offerings before the Altar.* The word וַיַּקְרִיבוּ, *and brought,* is repeated twice in this verse. The *Sforno* explains that the princes first sanctified their offerings, after which each brought his to the Altar. *Rashi* gives a different answer to explain the difficulty presented by this repetition.

6 So Moses took the wagons and the oxen and gave them to the Levites.
7 Two of the wagons and four of the oxen he presented to the sons of
Gershon, in accordance with their work. 8 And four of the wagons and eight
of the oxen he gave to the sons of Merari, in accordance with their work,
under the authority of Ithamar, son of Aaron the Kohen. 9 And to the sons
of Kohath he did not give; since the sacred service was upon them, they
carried on the shoulder. 10 Then the leaders brought forward offerings for
the dedication of the Altar on the day it was anointed, and the leaders
brought their offering before the Altar.

11 HASHEM said to Moses, "One leader each day, one leader each day shall
they bring their offering for the dedication of the Altar."

12 The one who brought his offering on the first day was Nachshon son of
Amminadab, of the tribe of Judah. 13 His offering was: one silver bowl, its
weight a hundred and thirty [shekels]; and one silver basin of seventy
shekels in the sacred shekel; both of them filled with fine flour mixed with
oil for a meal-offering; 14 one gold ladle of ten [shekels] filled with incense;
15 one young bull, one ram, one sheep in its first year for an elevation-offer-
ing; 16 one he-goat for a sin-offering; 17 and for a feast peace-offering: two
cattle, five rams, five he-goats, five sheep in their first year — this is the
offering of Nachshon son of Amminadab.

18 On the second day, Nethanel son of Zuar offered, the leader of
Issachar. 19 He brought his offering: one silver bowl, its weight a hundred
and thirty [shekels]; and one silver basin of seventy shekels in the sacred
shekel; both of them filled with fine flour mixed with oil for a meal-offering;
20 one gold ladle of ten [shekels] filled with incense; 21 one young bull, one
ram, one sheep in its first year for an elevation-offering; 22 one he-goat

---

them brought every kind of offering, and these were: burnt offering, meal offering, sin offering, peace offering and incense, to dedicate the Altar, and those who serve it, through these various kinds of offerings — except for the guilt offering, because the sin and guilt offerings have one law. (Now) the Torah relates the offering of each (prince) separately to teach us that each of them had intent to atone for the specific transgressions of his tribe which he was aware of. (Now) this (intent was incorporated) into each specific offering so as to make it acceptable for them before God. (Each prince) laid (his hand on the head of the animal) and stood there on behalf of his tribe, as was the case with the מַעֲמָדוֹת (public representatives) and the public sacrifices (*Taanis* 26a).

NOTES

13-17. וְקָרְבָּנוֹ קַעֲרַת כֶּסֶף אַחַת — *And his offering was one silver dish.* The Torah records the detailed offering of each prince, even though they were all precisely the same. The *Sforno* explains the reason for this lengthy and seemingly unnecessary repetition.

The citing of the Mishnah in *Taanis* by *Sforno* is most appropriate. The קָרְבַּן תָּמִיד, *daily sacrifice,* was offered on behalf of all Israel. However, it was incumbent upon the person who brought a sacrifice to be present at the time his sacrifice was offered in the Temple. Now this was not the case regarding the public daily sacrifice. Therefore, the Early Prophets (David and Samuel) instituted 24 מִשְׁמָרוֹת, *watches,* of *Kohanim* and 24 מַעֲמָדוֹת, *posts* (of public representatives), some of whom stood by when the daily sacrifice was offered, while those who were a distance from Jerusalem gathered in the synagogues of their communities to fast and pray and read from the Torah. In this manner it was considered as though all Israel was present during the offering of the daily sacrifice. The *Sforno* indicates that the origin of this custom had its roots in the dedication of the Altar, where the princes brought sacrifices on behalf of their tribe and served as אַנְשֵׁי מַעֲמָד, *public representatives.*

כג לְחַטָּאת: וּלְזֶבַח הַשְּׁלָמִים בָּקָר שְׁנַיִם אֵילִם חֲמִשָּׁה עַתֻּדִים חֲמִשָּׁה
כְּבָשִׂים בְּנֵי־שָׁנָה חֲמִשָּׁה זֶה קָרְבַּן נְתַנְאֵל בֶּן־צוּעָר:
כד-כה בַּיּוֹם הַשְּׁלִישִׁי נָשִׂיא לִבְנֵי זְבוּלֻן אֱלִיאָב בֶּן־חֵלֹן: קָרְבָּנוֹ קַעֲרַת־כֶּסֶף
אַחַת שְׁלֹשִׁים וּמֵאָה מִשְׁקָלָהּ מִזְרָק אֶחָד כֶּסֶף שִׁבְעִים שֶׁקֶל בְּשֶׁקֶל
כו הַקֹּדֶשׁ שְׁנֵיהֶם ׀ מְלֵאִים סֹלֶת בְּלוּלָה בַשֶּׁמֶן לְמִנְחָה: כַּף אַחַת עֲשָׂרָה
כז זָהָב מְלֵאָה קְטֹרֶת: פַּר אֶחָד בֶּן־בָּקָר אַיִל אֶחָד כֶּבֶשׂ־אֶחָד בֶּן־שְׁנָתוֹ
כח-כט לְעֹלָה: שְׂעִיר־עִזִּים אֶחָד לְחַטָּאת: וּלְזֶבַח הַשְּׁלָמִים בָּקָר שְׁנַיִם אֵילִם
חֲמִשָּׁה עַתֻּדִים חֲמִשָּׁה כְּבָשִׂים בְּנֵי־שָׁנָה חֲמִשָּׁה זֶה קָרְבַּן אֱלִיאָב
בֶּן־חֵלֹן:

ל-לא בַּיּוֹם הָרְבִיעִי נָשִׂיא לִבְנֵי רְאוּבֵן אֱלִיצוּר בֶּן־שְׁדֵיאוּר: קָרְבָּנוֹ
קַעֲרַת־כֶּסֶף אַחַת שְׁלֹשִׁים וּמֵאָה מִשְׁקָלָהּ מִזְרָק אֶחָד כֶּסֶף שִׁבְעִים
לב שֶׁקֶל בְּשֶׁקֶל הַקֹּדֶשׁ שְׁנֵיהֶם ׀ מְלֵאִים סֹלֶת בְּלוּלָה בַשֶּׁמֶן לְמִנְחָה: כַּף
לג אַחַת עֲשָׂרָה זָהָב מְלֵאָה קְטֹרֶת: פַּר אֶחָד בֶּן־בָּקָר אַיִל אֶחָד
לד-לה כֶּבֶשׂ־אֶחָד בֶּן־שְׁנָתוֹ לְעֹלָה: שְׂעִיר־עִזִּים אֶחָד לְחַטָּאת: וּלְזֶבַח
הַשְּׁלָמִים בָּקָר שְׁנַיִם אֵילִם חֲמִשָּׁה עַתֻּדִים חֲמִשָּׁה כְּבָשִׂים בְּנֵי־שָׁנָה
חֲמִשָּׁה זֶה קָרְבַּן אֱלִיצוּר בֶּן־שְׁדֵיאוּר:

לו-לז בַּיּוֹם הַחֲמִישִׁי נָשִׂיא לִבְנֵי שִׁמְעוֹן שְׁלֻמִיאֵל בֶּן־צוּרִישַׁדָּי: קָרְבָּנוֹ
קַעֲרַת־כֶּסֶף אַחַת שְׁלֹשִׁים וּמֵאָה מִשְׁקָלָהּ מִזְרָק אֶחָד כֶּסֶף שִׁבְעִים
לח שֶׁקֶל בְּשֶׁקֶל הַקֹּדֶשׁ שְׁנֵיהֶם ׀ מְלֵאִים סֹלֶת בְּלוּלָה בַשֶּׁמֶן לְמִנְחָה: כַּף
לט אַחַת עֲשָׂרָה זָהָב מְלֵאָה קְטֹרֶת: פַּר אֶחָד בֶּן־בָּקָר אַיִל אֶחָד
מ-מא כֶּבֶשׂ־אֶחָד בֶּן־שְׁנָתוֹ לְעֹלָה: שְׂעִיר־עִזִּים אֶחָד לְחַטָּאת: וּלְזֶבַח
הַשְּׁלָמִים בָּקָר שְׁנַיִם אֵילִם חֲמִשָּׁה עַתֻּדִים חֲמִשָּׁה כְּבָשִׂים בְּנֵי־שָׁנָה
חֲמִשָּׁה זֶה קָרְבַּן שְׁלֻמִיאֵל בֶּן־צוּרִישַׁדָּי:

ששי מב-מג בַּיּוֹם הַשִּׁשִּׁי נָשִׂיא לִבְנֵי גָד אֶלְיָסָף בֶּן־דְּעוּאֵל: קָרְבָּנוֹ קַעֲרַת־כֶּסֶף
אַחַת שְׁלֹשִׁים וּמֵאָה מִשְׁקָלָהּ מִזְרָק אֶחָד כֶּסֶף שִׁבְעִים שֶׁקֶל בְּשֶׁקֶל
מד הַקֹּדֶשׁ שְׁנֵיהֶם ׀ מְלֵאִים סֹלֶת בְּלוּלָה בַשֶּׁמֶן לְמִנְחָה: כַּף אַחַת עֲשָׂרָה
מה זָהָב מְלֵאָה קְטֹרֶת: פַּר אֶחָד בֶּן־בָּקָר אַיִל אֶחָד כֶּבֶשׂ־אֶחָד בֶּן־שְׁנָתוֹ
מו-מז לְעֹלָה: שְׂעִיר־עִזִּים אֶחָד לְחַטָּאת: וּלְזֶבַח הַשְּׁלָמִים בָּקָר שְׁנַיִם אֵילִם
חֲמִשָּׁה עַתֻּדִים חֲמִשָּׁה כְּבָשִׂים בְּנֵי־שָׁנָה חֲמִשָּׁה זֶה קָרְבַּן אֶלְיָסָף
בֶּן־דְּעוּאֵל:

מח-מט בַּיּוֹם הַשְּׁבִיעִי נָשִׂיא לִבְנֵי אֶפְרָיִם אֱלִישָׁמָע בֶּן־עַמִּיהוּד: קָרְבָּנוֹ
קַעֲרַת־כֶּסֶף אַחַת שְׁלֹשִׁים וּמֵאָה מִשְׁקָלָהּ מִזְרָק אֶחָד כֶּסֶף שִׁבְעִים
נ שֶׁקֶל בְּשֶׁקֶל הַקֹּדֶשׁ שְׁנֵיהֶם ׀ מְלֵאִים סֹלֶת בְּלוּלָה בַשֶּׁמֶן לְמִנְחָה: כַּף
נא אַחַת עֲשָׂרָה זָהָב מְלֵאָה קְטֹרֶת: פַּר אֶחָד בֶּן־בָּקָר אַיִל אֶחָד
נב-נג כֶּבֶשׂ־אֶחָד בֶּן־שְׁנָתוֹ לְעֹלָה: שְׂעִיר־עִזִּים אֶחָד לְחַטָּאת: וּלְזֶבַח
הַשְּׁלָמִים בָּקָר שְׁנַיִם אֵילִם חֲמִשָּׁה עַתֻּדִים חֲמִשָּׁה כְּבָשִׂים בְּנֵי־שָׁנָה
חֲמִשָּׁה זֶה קָרְבַּן אֱלִישָׁמָע בֶּן־עַמִּיהוּד:

for a sin-offering; 23 and for a feast peace-offering: two cattle, five rams,
five he-goats, five sheep in their first year — this is the offering of Nethanel
son of Zuar.
24 On the third day, the leader of the children of Zebulun, Eliab son of
Helon. 25 His offering was: one silver bowl, its weight a hundred and thirty
[shekels]; and one silver basin of seventy shekels in the sacred shekel; both
of them filled with fine flour mixed with oil for a meal-offering; 26 one gold
ladle of ten [shekels] filled with incense; 27 one young bull, one ram, one
sheep in its first year for an elevation-offering; 28 one he-goat for a sin-offering; 29 and for a feast peace-offering: two cattle, five rams, five he-goats,
five sheep in their first year — this is the offering of Eliab son of Helon.
30 On the fourth day, the leader of the children of Reuben, Elizur son of
Shedeur. 31 His offering was: one silver bowl, its weight a hundred and thirty
[shekels]; and one silver basin of seventy shekels in the sacred shekel; both
of them filled with fine flour mixed with oil for a meal-offering; 32 one gold
ladle of ten [shekels] filled with incense; 33 one young bull, one ram, one
sheep in its first year for an elevation-offering; 34 one he-goat for a sin-offering; 35 and for a feast peace-offering: two cattle, five rams, five he-goats,
five sheep in their first year — this is the offering of Elizur son of Shedeur.
36 On the fifth day, the leader of the children of Simeon, Shelumiel son of
Zurishaddai. 37 His offering was: one silver bowl, its weight a hundred and
thirty [shekels]; and one silver basin of seventy shekels in the sacred shekel;
both of them filled with fine flour mixed with oil for a meal-offering; 38 one
gold ladle of ten [shekels] filled with incense; 39 one young bull, one ram, one
sheep in its first year for an elevation-offering; 40 one he-goat for a
sin-offering; 41 and for a feast peace-offering: two cattle, five rams, five
he-goats, five sheep in their first year — this is the offering of Shelumiel son
of Zurishaddai.
42 On the sixth day, the leader of the children of Gad, Eliasaph son of
Deuel. 43 His offering was: one silver bowl, its weight a hundred and thirty
[shekels]; and one silver basin of seventy shekels in the sacred shekel; both
of them filled with fine flour mixed with oil for a meal-offering; 44 one gold
ladle of ten [shekels] filled with incense; 45 one young bull, one ram, one
sheep in its first year for an elevation-offering; 46 one he-goat for a
sin-offering; 47 and for a feast peace-offering: two cattle, five rams, five
he-goats, five sheep in their first year — this is the offering of Eliasaph son
of Deuel.
48 On the seventh day, the leader of the children of Ephraim, Elishama son
of Ammihud. 49 His offering was: one silver bowl, its weight a hundred and
thirty [shekels]; and one silver basin of seventy shekels in the sacred shekel;
both of them filled with fine flour mixed with oil for a meal-offering; 50 one
gold ladle of ten [shekels] filled with incense; 51 one young bull, one ram, one
sheep in its first year for an elevation-offering; 52 one he-goat for a
sin-offering; 53 and for a feast peace-offering: two cattle, five rams, five
he-goats, five sheep in their first year — this is the offering of Elishama son
of Ammihud.

נד־נה בַּיּוֹם֙ הַשְּׁמִינִ֔י נָשִׂ֖יא לִבְנֵ֣י מְנַשֶּׁ֑ה גַּמְלִיאֵ֖ל בֶּן־פְּדָהצֽוּר׃ קָרְבָּנ֞וֹ
קַעֲרַת־כֶּ֣סֶף אַחַ֗ת שְׁלֹשִׁ֣ים וּמֵאָה֮ מִשְׁקָלָהּ֒ מִזְרָ֤ק אֶחָד֙ כֶּ֔סֶף שִׁבְעִ֥ים
נו שֶׁ֖קֶל בְּשֶׁ֣קֶל הַקֹּ֑דֶשׁ שְׁנֵיהֶ֣ם ׀ מְלֵאִ֗ים סֹ֛לֶת בְּלוּלָ֥ה בַשֶּׁ֖מֶן לְמִנְחָֽה׃ כַּ֥ף
נז אַחַ֛ת עֲשָׂרָ֥ה זָהָ֖ב מְלֵאָ֥ה קְטֹֽרֶת׃ פַּ֣ר אֶחָ֞ד בֶּן־בָּקָ֗ר אַ֧יִל אֶחָ֛ד
נח־נט כֶּֽבֶשׂ־אֶחָ֥ד בֶּן־שְׁנָת֖וֹ לְעֹלָֽה׃ שְׂעִֽיר־עִזִּ֥ים אֶחָ֖ד לְחַטָּֽאת׃ וּלְזֶ֣בַח
הַשְּׁלָמִים֮ בָּקָ֣ר שְׁנַ֒יִם֒ אֵילִ֤ם חֲמִשָּׁה֙ עַתֻּדִ֣ים חֲמִשָּׁ֔ה כְּבָשִׂ֥ים בְּנֵי־שָׁנָ֖ה
חֲמִשָּׁ֑ה זֶ֛ה קָרְבַּ֥ן גַּמְלִיאֵ֖ל בֶּן־פְּדָהצֽוּר׃

ס־סא בַּיּוֹם֙ הַתְּשִׁיעִ֔י נָשִׂ֖יא לִבְנֵ֣י בִנְיָמִ֑ן אֲבִידָ֖ן בֶּן־גִּדְעֹנִֽי׃ קָרְבָּנ֞וֹ קַעֲרַת־כֶּ֣סֶף
אַחַ֗ת שְׁלֹשִׁ֣ים וּמֵאָה֮ מִשְׁקָלָהּ֒ מִזְרָ֤ק אֶחָד֙ כֶּ֔סֶף שִׁבְעִ֥ים שֶׁ֖קֶל בְּשֶׁ֣קֶל
סב הַקֹּ֑דֶשׁ שְׁנֵיהֶ֣ם ׀ מְלֵאִ֗ים סֹ֛לֶת בְּלוּלָ֥ה בַשֶּׁ֖מֶן לְמִנְחָֽה׃ כַּ֥ף אַחַ֛ת עֲשָׂרָ֥ה
סג זָהָ֖ב מְלֵאָ֥ה קְטֹֽרֶת׃ פַּ֣ר אֶחָ֞ד בֶּן־בָּקָ֗ר אַ֧יִל אֶחָ֛ד כֶּֽבֶשׂ־אֶחָ֥ד בֶּן־שְׁנָת֖וֹ
סד־סה לְעֹלָֽה׃ שְׂעִֽיר־עִזִּ֥ים אֶחָ֖ד לְחַטָּֽאת׃ וּלְזֶ֣בַח הַשְּׁלָמִים֮ בָּקָ֣ר שְׁנַ֒יִם֒ אֵילִ֤ם
חֲמִשָּׁה֙ עַתֻּדִ֣ים חֲמִשָּׁ֔ה כְּבָשִׂ֥ים בְּנֵי־שָׁנָ֖ה חֲמִשָּׁ֑ה זֶ֛ה קָרְבַּ֥ן אֲבִידָ֖ן
בֶּן־גִּדְעֹנִֽי׃

סו־סז בַּיּוֹם֙ הָעֲשִׂירִ֔י נָשִׂ֖יא לִבְנֵ֣י דָ֑ן אֲחִיעֶ֖זֶר בֶּן־עַמִּישַׁדָּֽי׃ קָרְבָּנ֞וֹ קַעֲרַת־כֶּ֣סֶף
אַחַ֗ת שְׁלֹשִׁ֣ים וּמֵאָה֮ מִשְׁקָלָהּ֒ מִזְרָ֤ק אֶחָד֙ כֶּ֔סֶף שִׁבְעִ֥ים שֶׁ֖קֶל בְּשֶׁ֣קֶל
סח הַקֹּ֑דֶשׁ שְׁנֵיהֶ֣ם ׀ מְלֵאִ֗ים סֹ֛לֶת בְּלוּלָ֥ה בַשֶּׁ֖מֶן לְמִנְחָֽה׃ כַּ֥ף אַחַ֛ת עֲשָׂרָ֥ה
סט זָהָ֖ב מְלֵאָ֥ה קְטֹֽרֶת׃ פַּ֣ר אֶחָ֞ד בֶּן־בָּקָ֗ר אַ֧יִל אֶחָ֛ד כֶּֽבֶשׂ־אֶחָ֥ד בֶּן־שְׁנָת֖וֹ
ע־עא לְעֹלָֽה׃ שְׂעִֽיר־עִזִּ֥ים אֶחָ֖ד לְחַטָּֽאת׃ וּלְזֶ֣בַח הַשְּׁלָמִים֮ בָּקָ֣ר שְׁנַ֒יִם֒ אֵילִ֤ם
חֲמִשָּׁה֙ עַתֻּדִ֣ים חֲמִשָּׁ֔ה כְּבָשִׂ֥ים בְּנֵי־שָׁנָ֖ה חֲמִשָּׁ֑ה זֶ֛ה קָרְבַּ֥ן אֲחִיעֶ֖זֶר
בֶּן־עַמִּישַׁדָּֽי׃

שביעי עב־עג בְּיוֹם֙ עַשְׁתֵּ֣י עָשָׂ֣ר י֔וֹם נָשִׂ֖יא לִבְנֵ֣י אָשֵׁ֑ר פַּגְעִיאֵ֖ל בֶּן־עָכְרָֽן׃ קָרְבָּנ֞וֹ
קַעֲרַת־כֶּ֣סֶף אַחַ֗ת שְׁלֹשִׁ֣ים וּמֵאָה֮ מִשְׁקָלָהּ֒ מִזְרָ֤ק אֶחָד֙ כֶּ֔סֶף שִׁבְעִ֥ים
עד שֶׁ֖קֶל בְּשֶׁ֣קֶל הַקֹּ֑דֶשׁ שְׁנֵיהֶ֣ם ׀ מְלֵאִ֗ים סֹ֛לֶת בְּלוּלָ֥ה בַשֶּׁ֖מֶן לְמִנְחָֽה׃ כַּ֥ף
עה אַחַ֛ת עֲשָׂרָ֥ה זָהָ֖ב מְלֵאָ֥ה קְטֹֽרֶת׃ פַּ֣ר אֶחָ֞ד בֶּן־בָּקָ֗ר אַ֧יִל אֶחָ֛ד
עו־עז כֶּֽבֶשׂ־אֶחָ֥ד בֶּן־שְׁנָת֖וֹ לְעֹלָֽה׃ שְׂעִֽיר־עִזִּ֥ים אֶחָ֖ד לְחַטָּֽאת׃ וּלְזֶ֣בַח
הַשְּׁלָמִים֮ בָּקָ֣ר שְׁנַ֒יִם֒ אֵילִ֤ם חֲמִשָּׁה֙ עַתֻּדִ֣ים חֲמִשָּׁ֔ה כְּבָשִׂ֥ים בְּנֵי־שָׁנָ֖ה
חֲמִשָּׁ֑ה זֶ֛ה קָרְבַּ֥ן פַּגְעִיאֵ֖ל בֶּן־עָכְרָֽן׃

עח־עט בְּיוֹם֙ שְׁנֵ֣ים עָשָׂ֣ר י֔וֹם נָשִׂ֖יא לִבְנֵ֣י נַפְתָּלִ֑י אֲחִירַ֖ע בֶּן־עֵינָֽן׃ קָרְבָּנ֞וֹ
קַעֲרַת־כֶּ֣סֶף אַחַ֗ת שְׁלֹשִׁ֣ים וּמֵאָה֮ מִשְׁקָלָהּ֒ מִזְרָ֤ק אֶחָד֙ כֶּ֔סֶף שִׁבְעִ֥ים
פ שֶׁ֖קֶל בְּשֶׁ֣קֶל הַקֹּ֑דֶשׁ שְׁנֵיהֶ֣ם ׀ מְלֵאִ֗ים סֹ֛לֶת בְּלוּלָ֥ה בַשֶּׁ֖מֶן לְמִנְחָֽה׃ כַּ֥ף
פא אַחַ֛ת עֲשָׂרָ֥ה זָהָ֖ב מְלֵאָ֥ה קְטֹֽרֶת׃ פַּ֣ר אֶחָ֞ד בֶּן־בָּקָ֗ר אַ֧יִל אֶחָ֛ד
פב־פג כֶּֽבֶשׂ־אֶחָ֥ד בֶּן־שְׁנָת֖וֹ לְעֹלָֽה׃ שְׂעִֽיר־עִזִּ֥ים אֶחָ֖ד לְחַטָּֽאת׃ וּלְזֶ֣בַח
הַשְּׁלָמִים֮ בָּקָ֣ר שְׁנַ֒יִם֒ אֵילִ֤ם חֲמִשָּׁה֙ עַתֻּדִ֣ים חֲמִשָּׁ֔ה כְּבָשִׂ֥ים בְּנֵי־שָׁנָ֖ה
חֲמִשָּׁ֑ה זֶ֛ה קָרְבַּ֥ן אֲחִירַ֖ע בֶּן־עֵינָֽן׃

54 On the eighth day, the leader of the children of Manasseh, Gamaliel
son of Pedahzur. 55 His offering was: one silver bowl, its weight a hundred
and thirty [shekels]; and one silver basin of seventy shekels in the sacred
shekel; both of them filled with fine flour mixed with oil for a
meal-offering; 56 one gold ladle of ten [shekels] filled with incense; 57 one
young bull, one ram, one sheep in its first year for an elevation-offering;
58 one he-goat for a sin-offering; 59 and for a feast peace-offering: two
cattle, five rams, five he-goats, five sheep in their first year — this is the
offering of Gamaliel son of Pedahzur.

60 On the ninth day, the leader of the children of Benjamin, Abidan son of
Gideoni. 61 His offering was: one silver bowl, its weight a hundred and
thirty [shekels]; and one silver basin of seventy shekels in the sacred
shekel; both of them filled with fine flour mixed with oil for a
meal-offering; 62 one gold ladle of ten [shekels] filled with incense; 63 one
young bull, one ram, one sheep in its first year for an elevation-offering;
64 one he-goat for a sin-offering; 65 and for a feast peace-offering: two
cattle, five rams, five he-goats, five sheep in their first year — this is the
offering of Abidan son of Gideoni.

66 On the tenth day, the leader of the children of Dan, Ahiezer son of
Ammishaddai. 67 His offering was: one silver bowl, its weight a hundred
and thirty [shekels]; and one silver basin of seventy shekels in the sacred
shekel; both of them filled with fine flour mixed with oil for a
meal-offering; 68 one gold ladle of ten [shekels] filled with incense; 69 one
young bull, one ram, one sheep in its first year for an elevation-offering;
70 one he-goat for a sin-offering; 71 and for a feast peace-offering: two
cattle, five rams, five he-goats, five sheep in their first year — this is the
offering of Ahiezer son of Ammishaddai.

72 On the eleventh day, the leader of the children of Asher, Pagiel son of
Ochran. 73 His offering was: one silver bowl, its weight a hundred and
thirty [shekels]; and one silver basin of seventy shekels in the sacred
shekel; both of them filled with fine flour mixed with oil for a
meal-offering; 74 one gold ladle of ten [shekels] filled with incense; 75 one
young bull, one ram, one sheep in its first year for an elevation-offering;
76 one he-goat for a sin-offering; 77 and for a feast peace-offering: two
cattle, five rams, five he-goats, five sheep in their first year — this is the
offering of Pagiel son of Ochran.

78 On the twelfth day, the leader of the children of Naftali, Ahira son of
Enan. 79 His offering was: one silver bowl, its weight a hundred and thirty
[shekels]; and one silver basin of seventy shekels in the sacred shekel; both
of them filled with fine flour mixed with oil for a meal-offering; 80 one gold
ladle of ten [shekels] filled with incense; 81 one young bull, one ram, one
sheep in its first year for an elevation-offering; 82 one he-goat for a
sin-offering; 83 and for a feast peace-offering: two cattle, five rams, five
he-goats, five sheep in their first year — this is the offering of Ahira son of
Enan.

פד זֹאת ׀ חֲנֻכַּת הַמִּזְבֵּ֫חַ בְּיוֹם הִמָּשַׁח אֹתוֹ מֵאֵת נְשִׂיאֵ֥י יִשְׂרָאֵ֖ל קַעֲרֹ֣ת כֶּ֗סֶף

פה שְׁתֵּ֣ים עֶשְׂרֵ֗ה מִזְרְקֵי־כֶ֙סֶף֙ שְׁנֵ֣ים עָשָׂ֔ר כַּפּ֥וֹת זָהָ֖ב שְׁתֵּ֣ים עֶשְׂרֵ֑ה: שְׁלֹשִׁ֣ים

וּמֵאָ֣ה הַקְּעָרָ֣ה הָאַחַ֗ת כֶּ֔סֶף וְשִׁבְעִ֖ים הַמִּזְרָ֣ק הָאֶחָ֑ד כֹּ֚ל כֶּ֣סֶף הַכֵּלִ֔ים

פו אַלְפַּ֥יִם וְאַרְבַּע־מֵא֖וֹת בְּשֶׁ֣קֶל הַקֹּ֑דֶשׁ: כַּפּ֨וֹת זָהָ֤ב שְׁתֵּים־עֶשְׂרֵה֙ מְלֵאֹ֣ת

קְטֹ֗רֶת עֲשָׂרָ֧ה עֲשָׂרָ֛ה הַכַּ֖ף בְּשֶׁ֣קֶל הַקֹּ֑דֶשׁ כָּל־זְהַ֥ב הַכַּפּ֖וֹת עֶשְׂרִ֥ים

פז וּמֵאָֽה: כָּל־הַבָּקָ֞ר לָעֹלָ֗ה שְׁנֵ֧ים עָשָׂ֣ר פָּרִ֗ים אֵילִ֤ם עָשָׂר֙ שְׁנֵים־עָשָׂר֙ כְּבָשִׂ֤ים   מפטיר

פח בְּנֵֽי־שָׁנָה֙ שְׁנֵ֣ים עָשָׂ֔ר וּמִנְחָתָ֑ם וּשְׂעִירֵ֥י עִזִּ֛ים עָשָׂ֖ר שְׁנֵ֥ים עָשָׂ֖ר לְחַטָּֽאת: וְכֹ֣ל

בְּקַ֣ר ׀ זֶ֣בַח הַשְּׁלָמִ֗ים עֶשְׂרִ֣ים וְאַרְבָּעָה֙ פָּרִ֔ים אֵילִ֥ם שִׁשִּׁ֖ים עַתֻּדִ֣ים שִׁשִּׁ֑ים

פט כְּבָשִׂ֥ים בְּנֵֽי־שָׁנָ֖ה שִׁשִּׁ֑ים זֹ֚את חֲנֻכַּ֣ת הַמִּזְבֵּ֔חַ אַחֲרֵ֖י הִמָּשַׁ֥ח אֹתֽוֹ: וּבְבֹ֨א

מֹשֶׁ֜ה אֶל־אֹ֣הֶל מוֹעֵד֮ לְדַבֵּ֣ר אִתּוֹ֒ וַיִּשְׁמַ֣ע אֶת־הַקּ֗וֹל מִדַּבֵּ֤ר אֵלָיו֙ מֵעַ֣ל

הַכַּפֹּ֗רֶת אֲשֶׁר֙ עַל־אֲרֹ֣ן הָעֵדֻ֔ת מִבֵּ֖ין שְׁנֵ֣י הַכְּרֻבִ֑ים וַיְדַבֵּ֖ר אֵלָֽיו:

---

84. זֹאת חֲנֻכַּת הַמִּזְבֵּחַ — *This was the dedication-offering of the Altar.* Behold, the dedication of the altar at that time was, in general, a small event compared to the dedication of the First Temple (of Solomon) with its many vessels, its riches and abundance of sacrifices.

89. וּבְבֹא משֶׁה אֶל אֹהֶל מוֹעֵד לְדַבֵּר אִתּוֹ וַיִּשְׁמַע אֶת הַקּוֹל — *And when Moses went into the Tent of Meeting that he might speak with Him, then he heard the Voice.* And even though the event was very small in comparison to the dedication of (the Temple of) Solomon, nonetheless, when Moses went into the Tent of Meeting he heard the same Voice that he had heard prior to the act of the Golden Calf. This did not occur in (the time) of the First Temple and certainly not (in the period) of the Second Temple, for no prophet

NOTES

84-89. זֹאת חֲנֻכַּת הַמִּזְבֵּחַ ... וּבְבֹא מֹשֶׁה אֶל אֹהֶל מוֹעֵד לְדַבֵּר אתו אֶת הַקּוֹל ... — *This was the dedication-offering of the Altar ... And when Moses went into the Tent of Meeting that he might speak with Him, then he heard the Voice.* The *Sforno* explains the reason for placing this seemingly unrelated verse (89) at the conclusion of the section dealing with the dedication of the Altar. He explains that the Torah is teaching us that although the offerings brought in honor of the dedication in the wilderness were insignificant compared to those brought at the dedication of Solomon's Temple, nonetheless this dedication

was far superior because Moses heard the Voice of God, a phenomenon not experienced at the time of the dedication of the First and Second Temples in Jerusalem.

89. מִדַּבֵּר אֵלָיו — *Speaking to him.* The word מִדַּבֵּר, *speaking,* as *Rashi* points out is similar to מִתְדַּבֵּר (in the *hitpael* form), implying that "he heard the Voice speaking to itself." The *Sforno* expands upon this, explaining that God, as it were, "makes known to Himself" (not directly to His prophet) and that the Voice heard by Moses was an overflow of God's words which are received by each

84 *This was the dedication of the Altar, on the day it was anointed, from the leaders of Israel: twelve silver bowls, twelve silver basins, twelve gold ladles;* 85 *each bowl was one hundred and thirty silver [shekels] and each basin was seventy; all the silver of the vessels was two thousand, four hundred in the sacred shekel.* 86 *Twelve gold ladles filled with incense, each ladle was ten of the sacred shekels; all the gold of the ladles was one hundred and twenty [shekels].* 87 *All the livestock for the elevation-offering: twelve bulls, twelve rams, twelve sheep in their first year, and their meal-offerings; and twelve he-goats for a sin-offering.* 88 *All the livestock for the feast peace-offering: twenty-four bulls, sixty rams, sixty he-goats, sixty sheep in their first year — this was the dedication of the Altar after it was anointed.*

89 *When Moses arrived at the Tent of Meeting to speak with Him, he heard the Voice speaking to him from atop the Cover that was upon the Ark of the Testimony, from between the two Cherubim, and He spoke to him.*

went into the Temple to prophesize in such a manner that he would attain prophecy at once. (Now) this was because this dedication (of the Sanctuary) was acceptable (to God), as were those who made the offerings, and as was Moses who was the shepherd.

מִדַּבֵּר אֵלָיו — *Speaking to him* . . . to Himself, because כֹּל פָּעַל ה׳ לַמַּעֲנֵהוּ, *HASHEM has made everything for His own purpose* (*Proverbs* 16:4), making known (elucidating) to Himself and thus imparting knowledge and (granting) goodness to others through the generosity of His influence which is without parsimony. Now this action (of God) will become apparent (i.e., have effect) on the recipient according to (the extent of) his preparation (to hear it — i.e., the Voice). With this, (the Torah) explains the manner of every "saying" (דִּבּוּר) which is stated in the Torah whenever it says *And HASHEM spoke.*

NOTES

prophet according to his own personal powers of perception and understanding. The *Rambam* states in his *Guide* (1:68) that regarding the Almighty, the intellect (שֵׂכֶל), concept (מוּשְׂכָּל) and intelligence (מַשְׂכִּיל) are one. "God is an intellect which is always in action . . . He comprehends constantly; consequently He and the things comprehended are one and the same thing." This idea is what the *Sforno* is alluding to when he says, וּבְהַשְׂכִּילוֹ אֶת עַצְמוֹ (elucidating to Himself), i.e., He is always (as the *Guide* puts it) the intellect (דֵּעָה), the intelligence (יוֹדֵעַ), and the concept (יָדוּעַ). The *Rambam* states this principle in *Mishnah Torah* (*Yesodai Hatorah* 2:10) as well. "Our knowledge and ourselves are separate. But as for the Creator, Blessed is He, His knowledge and His life are One . . . He is One in every aspect . . . God is the One Who knows (יוֹדֵעַ), is known (יָדוּעַ) and is the knowledge (דֵּעָה) of Himself. This is beyond the power of speech to express, beyond the capacity of the ear to hear and of the human mind to apprehend clearly." The *Sforno* also uses this principle as the basis of his statement that the "knowledge and goodness" of God are given to man through the generosity of His influence, and it was given to Moses in a far greater measure than to any other human being.

פרשת בהעלותך

ח א־ב וַיְדַבֵּר יהוה אֶל־מֹשֶׁה לֵּאמֹר: דַּבֵּר אֶל־אַהֲרֹן וְאָמַרְתָּ אֵלָיו בְּהַעֲלֹתְךָ
ג אֶת־הַנֵּרֹת אֶל־מוּל פְּנֵי הַמְּנוֹרָה יָאִירוּ שִׁבְעַת הַנֵּרוֹת: וַיַּעַשׂ כֵּן אַהֲרֹן
ד אֶל־מוּל פְּנֵי הַמְּנוֹרָה הֶעֱלָה נֵרֹתֶיהָ כַּאֲשֶׁר צִוָּה יהוה אֶת־מֹשֶׁה: וְזֶה
מַעֲשֵׂה הַמְּנֹרָה מִקְשָׁה זָהָב עַד־יְרֵכָהּ עַד־פִּרְחָהּ מִקְשָׁה הִוא כַּמַּרְאֶה
אֲשֶׁר הֶרְאָה יהוה אֶת־מֹשֶׁה כֵּן עָשָׂה אֶת־הַמְּנֹרָה:
ה־ו וַיְדַבֵּר יהוה אֶל־מֹשֶׁה לֵּאמֹר: קַח אֶת־הַלְוִיִּם מִתּוֹךְ בְּנֵי יִשְׂרָאֵל
ז וְטִהַרְתָּ אֹתָם: וְכֹה־תַעֲשֶׂה לָהֶם לְטַהֲרָם הַזֵּה עֲלֵיהֶם מֵי חַטָּאת
ח וְהֶעֱבִירוּ תַעַר עַל־כָּל־בְּשָׂרָם וְכִבְּסוּ בִגְדֵיהֶם וְהִטֶּהָרוּ: וְלָקְחוּ פַּר
בֶּן־בָּקָר וּמִנְחָתוֹ סֹלֶת בְּלוּלָה בַשָּׁמֶן וּפַר־שֵׁנִי בֶן־בָּקָר תִּקַּח לְחַטָּאת:
ט וְהִקְרַבְתָּ אֶת־הַלְוִיִּם לִפְנֵי אֹהֶל מוֹעֵד וְהִקְהַלְתָּ אֶת־כָּל־עֲדַת בְּנֵי
י יִשְׂרָאֵל: וְהִקְרַבְתָּ אֶת־הַלְוִיִּם לִפְנֵי יהוה וְסָמְכוּ בְנֵי־יִשְׂרָאֵל אֶת־יְדֵיהֶם
יא עַל־הַלְוִיִּם: וְהֵנִיף אַהֲרֹן אֶת־הַלְוִיִּם תְּנוּפָה לִפְנֵי יהוה מֵאֵת בְּנֵי
יב יִשְׂרָאֵל וְהָיוּ לַעֲבֹד אֶת־עֲבֹדַת יהוה: וְהַלְוִיִּם יִסְמְכוּ אֶת־יְדֵיהֶם עַל
רֹאשׁ הַפָּרִים וַעֲשֵׂה אֶת־הָאֶחָד חַטָּאת וְאֶת־הָאֶחָד עֹלָה לַיהוה לְכַפֵּר
יג עַל־הַלְוִיִּם: וְהַעֲמַדְתָּ אֶת־הַלְוִיִּם לִפְנֵי אַהֲרֹן וְלִפְנֵי בָנָיו וְהֵנַפְתָּ אֹתָם
יד תְּנוּפָה לַיהוה: וְהִבְדַּלְתָּ אֶת־הַלְוִיִּם מִתּוֹךְ בְּנֵי יִשְׂרָאֵל וְהָיוּ לִי הַלְוִיִּם:

VIII

2. בְּהַעֲלֹתְךָ אֶת הַנֵּרֹת — *When you light the lamps* . . . when you kindle the six lamps.

אֶל מוּל פְּנֵי הַמְּנוֹרָה — *Over against the central candlestick* . . . which is the central shaft; that is, when you turn the wick (lit., flame) of each of the six lamps toward the center shaft, then . . .

יָאִירוּ שִׁבְעַת הַנֵּרוֹת — *The seven lamps shall give light.* All seven (lamps) will illuminate and shed the Divine light upon Israel, (and in this manner) teach them that the light of the right (lamps) and the light of the left (lamps) must turn toward the light of the central shaft, which is the principal part of the menorah. And so it is fitting (to be) the intention of those who turn to the right, i.e., who occupy themselves with (activities of) eternal life and those who turn to the left, i.e., who occupy themselves with (activities of) temporal life, yet assist (the ones on) the right, as it says, "If not for the leaves, the grapes could not exist" (*Chullin* 92a). All shall have as their purpose the fulfillment of the will of God, the Blessed

NOTES

VIII

2. בְּהַעֲלֹתְךָ אֶת הַנֵּרֹת אֶל מוּל פְּנֵי הַמְּנוֹרָה יָאִירוּ שִׁבְעַת הַנֵּרוֹת — *When you light the lamps over against the central candlestick, the seven lamps shall give light.* The Book of *Proverbs* (3:16) states regarding wisdom, *Length of days is in her right hand, in her left hand are riches and honor.* The Talmud in tractate *Shabbos* 63a interprets this verse to mean that those who pursue the study of Torah motivated by a desire to master the wisdom which God shared with us therein, devoting their efforts and energies to the realm of the spirit, are called מְיַימְּנִים — "those who go to the right hand" — and are promised length of days. Those, however, who are called מַשְׂמְאִילִים — "those who go to the left hand" — i.e., who occupy themselves with worldly affairs, but who nonetheless lend their support to the students of Torah, shall be blessed with "riches and honor." This latter group is referred to by our Sages as the "leaves" that protect the "grapes," the "grapes" referring to the Torah scholars. The Talmud in tractate *Chullin* 92a states, "Let the grapes (the scholars) pray for the leaves (the untutored), for the grapes could not exist if not for the leaves."

The *Sforno* incorporates both of these Talmudic concepts in his commentary on this verse. The

PARASHAS BEHA'ALOSCHA

8 1 *HASHEM spoke to Moses, saying,* 2 *"Speak to Aaron and say to him:
When you kindle the lamps, toward the face of the Menorah shall the
seven lamps cast light."*
3 *Aaron did so; toward the face of the Menorah he kindled its lamps, as
HASHEM had commanded Moses.* 4 *This is the workmanship of the Menorah,
hammered-out gold, from its base to its flower it is hammered out; according to the vision that HASHEM showed Moses, so did he make the Menorah.*
5 *HASHEM spoke to Moses, saying,* 6 *"Take the Levites from among the
Children of Israel and purify them.* 7 *So shall you do to them to purify them:
Sprinkle upon them water of purification, and let them pass a razor over
their entire flesh, and let them immerse their garments, and they shall
become pure.* 8 *They shall take a young bull and its meal-offering, fine flour
mixed with oil, and a second young bull shall you take as a sin-offering.*
9 *You shall bring the Levites before the Tent of Meeting, and you shall
gather together the entire assembly of the Children of Israel.* 10 *You shall
bring the Levites before HASHEM, and the Children of Israel shall lean their
hands upon the Levites.* 11 *Aaron shall wave the Levites as a wave-service
before HASHEM from the Children of Israel, and they shall remain to
perform the service of HASHEM.* 12 *The Levites shall lean their hands upon
the head of the bulls; you shall make one a sin-offering and one an
elevation-offering to HASHEM, to provide atonement for the Levites.* 13 *You
shall stand the Levites before Aaron and before his sons, and wave them as
a wave-offering before HASHEM.* 14 *So shall you separate the Levites from
among the Children of Israel, and the Levites shall remain Mine.*

One, in such a manner that through all of them His intent will be realized, and together they shall exalt His Name, as they accepted upon themselves (at Sinai), to which (the Torah) attests saying, וַיַּעֲנוּ כָל הָעָם יַחְדָּו וַיֹּאמְרוּ כֹּל אֲשֶׁר דִּבֶּר ה׳ נַעֲשֶׂה, *And all the people answered together and said, "All that HASHEM has spoken we will do"* (Exodus 19:8) — meaning that together we will fulfill His intent.

4. וְזֶה מַעֲשֵׂה הַמְּנֹרָה מִקְשָׁה — *And this was the work of the menorah, (it should be) beaten (out of one piece).* And this intended purpose (תַּכְלִית) of lighting the lamps *over against the central candlestick* is also the reason for the obligation of making the menorah of *beaten work*, for it thereby teaches (the need for) unity, which is the intended purpose (of the menorah) itself.

14. וְהִבְדַּלְתָּ אֶת הַלְוִיִּם — *And you shall separate the Levites.* You shall separate the encampment of the Levites who lived at that time (in the wilderness).

NOTES

central shaft of the menorah represents the Divine light. The three wicks on the right represent the Torah scholars while the three on the left represent the supporters of Torah. Both are necessary, and together they exalt God's Name, and when they are unified they are able to effectuate the intent of God in His giving the Torah to the people of Israel.

See the *Sforno's* commentary on *Exodus* 25:37 and the explanatory notes on verses 31-37 there for a different interpretation of the right and left wicks. However, both there and in verse 4, the *Sforno* stresses the symbolism of מִקְשָׁה (beaten out of one piece) which teaches the need for unity among all segments of Israel and among the students and supporters of Torah.

14. וְהִבְדַּלְתָּ אֶת הַלְוִיִּם . . . וְהָיוּ לִי הַלְוִיִּם — *And you shall separate the Levites . . . and the Levites shall be Mine.* The *Sforno* explains that there is no redundancy in this verse regarding the special

שני טו וְאַחֲרֵי־כֵן יָבֹאוּ הַלְוִיִּם לַעֲבֹד אֶת־אֹהֶל מוֹעֵד וְטִהַרְתָּ אֹתָם וְהֵנַפְתָּ
טז אֹתָם תְּנוּפָה: כִּי נְתֻנִים נְתֻנִים הֵמָּה לִי מִתּוֹךְ בְּנֵי יִשְׂרָאֵל תַּחַת
יז פִּטְרַת כָּל־רֶחֶם בְּכוֹר כֹּל מִבְּנֵי יִשְׂרָאֵל לָקַחְתִּי אֹתָם לִי: כִּי לִי
כָל־בְּכוֹר בִּבְנֵי יִשְׂרָאֵל בָּאָדָם וּבַבְּהֵמָה בְּיוֹם הַכֹּתִי כָל־בְּכוֹר
יח בְּאֶרֶץ מִצְרַיִם הִקְדַּשְׁתִּי אֹתָם לִי: וָאֶקַּח אֶת־הַלְוִיִּם תַּחַת כָּל־בְּכוֹר
יט בִּבְנֵי יִשְׂרָאֵל: וָאֶתְּנָה אֶת־הַלְוִיִּם נְתֻנִים | לְאַהֲרֹן וּלְבָנָיו מִתּוֹךְ בְּנֵי
יִשְׂרָאֵל לַעֲבֹד אֶת־עֲבֹדַת בְּנֵי־יִשְׂרָאֵל בְּאֹהֶל מוֹעֵד וּלְכַפֵּר עַל־בְּנֵי
יִשְׂרָאֵל וְלֹא יִהְיֶה בִּבְנֵי יִשְׂרָאֵל נֶגֶף בְּגֶשֶׁת בְּנֵי־יִשְׂרָאֵל אֶל־הַקֹּדֶשׁ:

וְהָיוּ לִי הַלְוִיִּם — *And the Levites shall be Mine.* They and their offspring shall be prepared to serve Me.

15. וְאַחֲרֵי כֵן יָבֹאוּ הַלְוִיִּם — *And after that shall the Levites go in . . .* who are of the present (in this generation).

16. כִּי נְתֻנִים נְתֻנִים הֵמָּה לִי — *For they are given, they are given unto Me. They are given,* (voluntarily offering) themselves, for they gave themselves over to My service, as the (verse) attests saying, מִי לַה׳ אֵלָי וַיֵּאָסְפוּ אֵלָיו כָּל בְּנֵי לֵוִי, *Whoever is on* HASHEM*'s side let him come to me. And all the sons of Levi gathered themselves together to him* (*Exodus* 32:26). And they are also *given . . .*

מִתּוֹךְ בְּנֵי יִשְׂרָאֵל — *From among the Children of Israel . . .* who will give the Levites their sustenance through the first tithe in exchange for their (Divine) service so that My service be done through all of them.

תַּחַת פִּטְרַת כָּל רֶחֶם — *Instead of all that open the womb . . .* for (originally) the service was incumbent upon them (i.e., the firstborn).

17. כִּי לִי כָל בְּכוֹר — *For all the firstborn are Mine.* Originally, the (Divine) service was (the responsibility) of the firstborn because they are the most honored in their household and to them (belonged) the rights of the service.

בְּיוֹם הַכֹּתִי כָל בְּכוֹר . . . הִקְדַּשְׁתִּי אֹתָם — *On the day that I smote all the firstborn . . . I sanctified them.* However, the reason that I made it necessary for them (to have) redemption is because on the day that I smote (the Egyptian firstborn) I sanctified them for Myself in that they should not occupy themselves with any ordinary labor at all, just as I prohibited shearing or working with a firstborn animal. And this I did in order to save them through the law (relating to) a sacred (object), for they were not (really) worthy to

NOTES

status of the Levites. The first part of the verse refers to the Levites of that generation, while the latter part refers to the appointment of the Levites for all time.

16. כִּי נְתֻנִים נְתֻנִים הֵמָּה לִי — *For they are given, they are given unto Me.* The word נְתֻנִים, *they are given,* is repeated twice in this verse, and also in 3:9. The *Sforno* explains that the first נְתֻנִים refers to the voluntary giving of the Levites by themselves to His service when they responded to the cry of Moses at the time of the sin of the Golden Calf. The second נְתֻנִים refers to the giving of the tithes by the Israelites as compensation for the Levites' service. The latter interpretation is given above in 3:9 as well. However, the first expression *they are given* there refers to the Levites' acceptance of direction by the *Kohanim*, to whom they were *given* as subordinates.

17. כִּי לִי כָל בְּכוֹר . . . בְּיוֹם הַכֹּתִי כָל בְּכוֹר . . . הִקְדַּשְׁתִּי אֹתָם — *For all the firstborn are Mine . . . on the day that I smote all the firstborn . . . I sanctified them.* The role of the firstborn from earliest times, their sanctification in Egypt and the need for their redemption are intertwined. Because of their role of leadership, they bear the responsibility for the behavior — and hence the sins — of all. Therefore, by right they should have been included in the smiting of the firstborn in Egypt. However, by

15 *"Thereafter the Levites shall come to serve the Tent of Meeting; you shall purify them and you shall wave them as a wave-service.* 16 *For presented, presented are they to Me from among the Children of Israel; in place of the first issue of every womb, the firstborn of everyone of the Children of Israel, have I taken them to Myself.* 17 *For every firstborn of the Children of Israel became Mine, of man and livestock; on the day I struck every firstborn in the land of Egypt I sanctified them for Myself.* 18 *I took the Levites in place of every firstborn among the Children of Israel.* 19 *Then I assigned the Levites to be presented to Aaron and his sons from among the Children of Israel to perform the service of the Children of Israel in the Tent of Meeting and to provide atonement for the Children of Israel, so that there will not be a plague among the Children of Israel when the Children of Israel approach the Sanctuary."*

---

be saved from the plague of the *messengers of evil* (based on *Psalms* 78:49) since they were the (most) honored among the people and the onus (lit., prisoner's band) of everyone was resting upon them. (Therefore) I said that they are to be redeemed so that they will thereby become non-holy and hence permitted to do ordinary labor.

18. וָאֶקַּח אֶת הַלְוִיִּם תַּחַת כָּל בְּכוֹר — *And I have taken the Levites instead of all the firstborn* ... only in that generation, as explained above (3:45).

19. וָאֶתְּנָה אֶת הַלְוִיִּם — *And I have given the Levites.* Since they gave of themselves (voluntarily) to My service, (therefore) I have given them to Aaron and his sons for My service.

לַעֲבֹד אֶת עֲבֹדַת בְּנֵי יִשְׂרָאֵל בְּאֹהֶל מוֹעֵד — *To do the service of the Children of Israel in the Tent of Meeting* ... to perform that service which was (originally) fitting for their firstborn.

וּלְכַפֵּר עַל בְּנֵי יִשְׂרָאֵל — *And to make atonement for the Children of Israel.* By receiving the tithes from the Israelites so that they will be able to serve God, the Blessed One, they will atone for Israel, all of who caused the rejection of their firstborn, through the (sin) of the calf.

וְלֹא יִהְיֶה בִּבְנֵי יִשְׂרָאֵל נֶגֶף — *That there be no plague among the Children of Israel* ... Among the Levites and the rest of Israel.

בְּגֶשֶׁת בְּנֵי יִשְׂרָאֵל אֶל הַקֹּדֶשׁ — *Through the Children of Israel coming nigh to the holy.* For then the strangers (i.e., the Israelites) who draw nigh will sin, and the Levites who permit the strangers to come nigh (will also sin) and all of them will be guilty, as it says, *That they die not, neither they, nor you* (18:3)

NOTES

sanctifying them God granted them immunity from annihilation as "objects of holiness" (הֶקְדֵּשׁ). This, in turn, meant that they were not permitted to occupy themselves with any common (i.e., non-holy) labor or endeavors (חולין); hence, they had to be ultimately redeemed, thereby permitting them to do common labor.

18. וָאֶקַּח אֶת הַלְוִיִּם תַּחַת כָּל בְּכוֹר — *And I have taken the Levites instead of all the firstborn.* In that generation, the Levites redeemed the firstborn. Later, as in our time, it is done with five *shekalim.*

19. וָאֶתְּנָה אֶת הַלְוִיִּם ... לַעֲבֹד אֶת עֲבֹדַת בְּנֵי יִשְׂרָאֵל בְּאֹהֶל מוֹעֵד — *And I have given the Levites ... to do the service of the Children of Israel in the Tent of Meeting.* See the *Sforno's* commentary and the notes on verse 16 above. The meaning of this verse is: Being that the Levites voluntarily gave themselves to Me and My service, I have now given them over to the *Kohanim*, whom they shall serve — a service which originally was meant to be fulfilled by the firstborn.

כ וַיַּעַשׂ מֹשֶׁה וְאַהֲרֹן וְכָל־עֲדַת בְּנֵי־יִשְׂרָאֵל לַלְוִיִּם כְּכֹל אֲשֶׁר־צִוָּה יְהוָה
כא אֶת־מֹשֶׁה לַלְוִיִּם כֵּן־עָשׂוּ לָהֶם בְּנֵי יִשְׂרָאֵל: וַיִּתְחַטְּאוּ הַלְוִיִּם וַיְכַבְּסוּ
בִּגְדֵיהֶם וַיָּנֶף אַהֲרֹן אֹתָם תְּנוּפָה לִפְנֵי יְהוָה וַיְכַפֵּר עֲלֵיהֶם אַהֲרֹן לְטַהֲרָם:
כב וְאַחֲרֵי־כֵן בָּאוּ הַלְוִיִּם לַעֲבֹד אֶת־עֲבֹדָתָם בְּאֹהֶל מוֹעֵד לִפְנֵי אַהֲרֹן וְלִפְנֵי
כג בָנָיו כַּאֲשֶׁר צִוָּה יְהוָה אֶת־מֹשֶׁה עַל־הַלְוִיִּם כֵּן עָשׂוּ לָהֶם: וַיְדַבֵּר
כד יְהוָה אֶל־מֹשֶׁה לֵּאמֹר: זֹאת אֲשֶׁר לַלְוִיִּם מִבֶּן חָמֵשׁ וְעֶשְׂרִים שָׁנָה וָמַעְלָה
כה יָבוֹא לִצְבֹא צָבָא בַּעֲבֹדַת אֹהֶל מוֹעֵד: וּמִבֶּן חֲמִשִּׁים שָׁנָה יָשׁוּב מִצְּבָא
כו הָעֲבֹדָה וְלֹא יַעֲבֹד עוֹד: וְשֵׁרֵת אֶת־אֶחָיו בְּאֹהֶל מוֹעֵד לִשְׁמֹר מִשְׁמֶרֶת
וַעֲבֹדָה לֹא יַעֲבֹד כָּכָה תַּעֲשֶׂה לַלְוִיִּם בְּמִשְׁמְרֹתָם:
ט שלישי א וַיְדַבֵּר יְהוָה אֶל־מֹשֶׁה בְמִדְבַּר־סִינַי בַּשָּׁנָה הַשֵּׁנִית לְצֵאתָם מֵאֶרֶץ
ב מִצְרַיִם בַּחֹדֶשׁ הָרִאשׁוֹן לֵאמֹר: וְיַעֲשׂוּ בְנֵי־יִשְׂרָאֵל אֶת־הַפָּסַח בְּמוֹעֲדוֹ:

---

20. וַיַּעַשׂ מֹשֶׁה וְאַהֲרֹן וְכָל עֲדַת בְּנֵי יִשְׂרָאֵל לַלְוִיִּם — *Thus did Moses and Aaron and all the congregation of the Children of Israel to the Levites.* On behalf of the Levites they lent their assistance in the matter of the shaving of their hair, the washing of their clothes and the offering.

כְּכֹל אֲשֶׁר צִוָּה ה׳ אֶת מֹשֶׁה לַלְוִיִּם — *According to all that* HASHEM *commanded Moses regarding the Levites* ... as He had commanded Moses to command the Levites that they shall do.

כֵּן עָשׂוּ לָהֶם בְּנֵי יִשְׂרָאֵל — *So did the Children of Israel unto them.* Israel eagerly did this on their behalf so that the will of their Master be done.

22. כַּאֲשֶׁר צִוָּה ה׳ אֶת מֹשֶׁה עַל הַלְוִיִּם — *As* HASHEM *had commanded Moses concerning the Levites* ... above (chapter 4) where He commanded that their watches were to serve, (to carry) burdens and sing according to (the instructions of) Aaron and his sons — so did Aaron and his sons set them in order in their watches.

IX

1. בַּחֹדֶשׁ הָרִאשׁוֹן — *In the first month.* After he counted the men for the army and set in order the standards and those who carried the Tabernacle so as to bring them into the Land, and he made *tahor* the camp of the *tameim*, as it says, וְהָיָה מַחֲנֶיךָ קָדוֹשׁ, *therefore shall your camp be holy* (*Deut.* 23:15), and (after he eliminated) illegitimate offspring through the matter (i.e., law) of the *sotah* so that the Divine Presence might dwell in the midst of their hosts — the Scripture (text) then relates four good (meritorious) acts which

NOTES

IX

1. בַּחֹדֶשׁ הָרִאשׁוֹן — *In the first month.* The *Sforno* in the general introduction to his commentary on the Torah mentions among the many criticisms leveled by those who question the paramount, central role that Torah plays in Judaism the lack of chronological order of the events recorded therein. These chapters in the Book of *Numbers* would seem to be a target for these criticisms since the opening chapter of the book is set in the *second* month of the second year after the Exodus from Egypt, while the ninth chapter records God's words to Moses in the *first* month! The *Sforno* reconciles this seeming anomaly, explaining that the Torah, at times, deviates from the chronological order in favor of a different order which contains a purposeful lesson. The original intent of God was to bring the Israelites into the Land of Israel soon after their departure from Egypt, and have them occupy the Land without recourse to war. Hence, at the beginning of this book (בְּמִדְבַּר), which sets out to tell us the story of the Israelites' journey and entrance into the Land, the Torah tells us first of the preparatory arrangements leading to this goal. The camps were organized, assignments were given to the *Kohanim* and Levites, the camp of Israel was cleansed of *tumah* — all vital aspects of this preparation. These events, although occur-

[20] *Moses, Aaron, and the entire assembly of the Children of Israel did to the*
Levites according to everything that HASHEM *had commanded Moses about*
the Levites, so did the Children of Israel do to them. [21] *The Levites purified*
themselves and immersed their garments; and Aaron waved them as a
wave-service before HASHEM, *and Aaron provided atonement for them to*
purify them. [22] *Afterwards the Levites came to perform their service in the*
Tent of Meeting, before Aaron and before his sons, as HASHEM *had*
commanded Moses concerning the Levites; so they did for them.
[23] HASHEM *spoke to Moses, saying,* [24] *This shall apply to the Levites: From*
twenty-five years of age and up, he shall join the legion of the service of the
Tent of Meeting. [25] *From fifty years age, he shall withdraw from the legion of*
work and no longer work. [26] *He shall minister with his brethren in the Tent of*
Meeting to safeguard the charge, but work shall he not perform. So shall you
do to the Levites concerning their charge."

9 [1] HASHEM *spoke to Moses, in the Wilderness of Sinai, in the second year*
from their exodus from the land of Egypt, in the first month, saying:
[2] *"The Children of Israel shall make the pesach-offering in its appointed time.*

Israel performed through which they would have merited to enter the Land immediately without a struggle, had it not been for (the sin of) the Spies, as Moses our Teacher attested when he said to Chovev, *We are journeying to the place* (10:29). First, (the Torah) relates the dedication of the Altar (7:1-8); second, their zealousness in the matter of the dedication of the Levites (8:5-26); third, their zealousness in (bringing) the *Pesach* offering (9:1-14); and fourth, (their) following God, the Blessed One, in the wilderness, even though the cloud would travel (lit., ascend) at unknown (unscheduled) times. At times, (they would travel) after a lengthy period and other times after short periods, in a manner that their encampment and journeying was most difficult for them (9:17-23). Now, in making all this known, (the Torah) relates it according to their degree of acceptance (רָצוֹן) before Him, not according to the (sequence) of time (i.e., chronologically). Therefore, (the Torah) relates here the matter of the dedication of the Altar, and the (induction of) the Levites and the (bringing) of the *Pesach* which (all) occurred in the first month (even though the events recorded in) the beginning of the Book (of *Numbers*) (occurred in the) second month, and the matter of their encampments and journeying by the order of God (began) from the day they left Egypt. It is regarding (cases) like these that (our Sages) say, אֵין מוּקְדָּם וּמְאוּחָר בַּתּוֹרָה, *There is no chronological order in the Torah* (*Pesachim* 6b), this being so when the intent is to (teach us) something (through the order of the text), beside the time sequence of the events related.

2. וְיַעֲשׂוּ בְנֵי יִשְׂרָאֵל אֶת הַפָּסַח — *Let the Children of Israel make the Pesach.* Besides (the offerings) which they made (i.e., offered) on the eighth day of מִלּוּאִים (the ceremony of

NOTES

ring later in time, are recorded first since they are of primary importance for they contain instructions and commandments given by the Almighty. However, there were also other acts performed by the people of Israel which were instrumental in qualifying them to be worthy of God's Providence in bringing them into the Land of Israel in a miraculous manner, i.e., through a bloodless conquest! These were four in number and are recorded in the order of their importance, not in the order of their occurrence. They are: the dedication of the Altar, the induction of the Levites, the offering of the *Pesach* sacrifice and the loyal adherence to the cloud which signaled when to journey and when to encamp. Here then is a case in point of what our Sages mean when they state, אֵין מוּקְדָּם וּמְאוּחָר בַּתּוֹרָה, *There is no chronological order in the Torah.*

2. וְיַעֲשׂוּ בְנֵי יִשְׂרָאֵל אֶת הַפָּסַח — *Let the Children of Israel make the Pesach.* Since the word וְיַעֲשׂוּ

ג בְּאַרְבָּעָה עָשָׂר־יוֹם בַּחֹדֶשׁ הַזֶּה בֵּין הָעַרְבַּיִם תַּעֲשׂוּ אֹתוֹ בְּמֹעֲדוֹ כְּכָל־
ד חֻקֹּתָיו וּכְכָל־מִשְׁפָּטָיו תַּעֲשׂוּ אֹתוֹ: וַיְדַבֵּר מֹשֶׁה אֶל־בְּנֵי יִשְׂרָאֵל לַעֲשֹׂת
ה הַפָּסַח: וַיַּעֲשׂוּ אֶת־הַפֶּסַח בָּרִאשׁוֹן בְּאַרְבָּעָה עָשָׂר יוֹם לַחֹדֶשׁ בֵּין
הָעַרְבַּיִם בְּמִדְבַּר סִינָי כְּכֹל אֲשֶׁר צִוָּה יהוה אֶת־מֹשֶׁה כֵּן עָשׂוּ בְּנֵי
ו יִשְׂרָאֵל: וַיְהִי אֲנָשִׁים אֲשֶׁר הָיוּ טְמֵאִים לְנֶפֶשׁ אָדָם וְלֹא־יָכְלוּ לַעֲשֹׂת־
ז הַפֶּסַח בַּיּוֹם הַהוּא וַיִּקְרְבוּ לִפְנֵי מֹשֶׁה וְלִפְנֵי אַהֲרֹן בַּיּוֹם הַהוּא: וַיֹּאמְרוּ
הָאֲנָשִׁים הָהֵמָּה אֵלָיו אֲנַחְנוּ טְמֵאִים לְנֶפֶשׁ אָדָם לָמָּה נִגָּרַע לְבִלְתִּי
ח הַקְרִיב אֶת־קָרְבַּן יהוה בְּמֹעֲדוֹ בְּתוֹךְ בְּנֵי יִשְׂרָאֵל: וַיֹּאמֶר אֲלֵהֶם מֹשֶׁה
עִמְדוּ וְאֶשְׁמְעָה מַה־יְצַוֶּה יהוה לָכֶם:
ט־י וַיְדַבֵּר יהוה אֶל־מֹשֶׁה לֵּאמֹר: דַּבֵּר אֶל־בְּנֵי יִשְׂרָאֵל לֵאמֹר אִישׁ אִישׁ
כִּי־יִהְיֶה טָמֵא | לָנֶפֶשׁ אוֹ בְדֶרֶךְ רְחֹקָה לָכֶם אוֹ לְדֹרֹתֵיכֶם וְעָשָׂה פֶסַח　　* נקוד על ה
יא לַיהוה: בַּחֹדֶשׁ הַשֵּׁנִי בְּאַרְבָּעָה עָשָׂר יוֹם בֵּין הָעַרְבַּיִם יַעֲשׂוּ אֹתוֹ עַל־
יב מַצּוֹת וּמְרֹרִים יֹאכְלֻהוּ: לֹא־יַשְׁאִירוּ מִמֶּנּוּ עַד־בֹּקֶר וְעֶצֶם לֹא יִשְׁבְּרוּ־בוֹ
יג כְּכָל־חֻקַּת הַפֶּסַח יַעֲשׂוּ אֹתוֹ: וְהָאִישׁ אֲשֶׁר־הוּא טָהוֹר וּבְדֶרֶךְ לֹא־הָיָה
וְחָדַל לַעֲשׂוֹת הַפֶּסַח וְנִכְרְתָה הַנֶּפֶשׁ הַהִוא מֵעַמֶּיהָ כִּי | קָרְבַּן יהוה לֹא
יד הִקְרִיב בְּמֹעֲדוֹ חֶטְאוֹ יִשָּׂא הָאִישׁ הַהוּא: וְכִי־יָגוּר אִתְּכֶם גֵּר וְעָשָׂה פֶסַח
לַיהוה כְּחֻקַּת הַפֶּסַח וּכְמִשְׁפָּטוֹ כֵּן יַעֲשֶׂה חֻקָּה אַחַת יִהְיֶה לָכֶם וְלַגֵּר
טו וּלְאֶזְרַח הָאָרֶץ: 　　　וּבְיוֹם הָקִים אֶת־הַמִּשְׁכָּן כִּסָּה הֶעָנָן אֶת־　　רביעי
הַמִּשְׁכָּן לְאֹהֶל הָעֵדֻת וּבָעֶרֶב יִהְיֶה עַל־הַמִּשְׁכָּן כְּמַרְאֵה־אֵשׁ עַד־בֹּקֶר:
טז־יז כֵּן יִהְיֶה תָמִיד הֶעָנָן יְכַסֶּנּוּ וּמַרְאֵה־אֵשׁ לָיְלָה: וּלְפִי הֵעָלֹת הֶעָנָן מֵעַל
הָאֹהֶל וְאַחֲרֵי כֵן יִסְעוּ בְּנֵי יִשְׂרָאֵל וּבִמְקוֹם אֲשֶׁר יִשְׁכָּן־שָׁם הֶעָנָן שָׁם

inducting the *Kohanim*) and the dedication (ceremony) of the princes, let them also make (i.e., offer) the *Pesach*. They shall not be exempt from offering it because of their rejoicing in the commandments which they kept, as happened at the time of the building of the First Temple, (concerning which) our Sages tell us (*Moed Katan* 9a) that Solomon nullified Yom Kippur because of the rejoicing in the dedication of the Temple.

7. אֲנַחְנוּ טְמֵאִים לְנֶפֶשׁ אָדָם לָמָּה נִגָּרַע — *We are tamei by the dead body of a man; why are we to be kept back?* Since our *tumah* (affects our ability to perform) a commandment, why should that "lead to a transgression"? (Based on *Avos* 4:2).

בְּמֹעֲדוֹ — *In its appointed season.* (Hence) it is a "passing commandment."

NOTES

begins with the prefix *vav*, which links this verse to previous events, the *Sforno* connects it to the other sacrifices and offerings mentioned above, i.e., the offerings brought on the eighth day of מִלּוּאִים and those brought by the princes (7:10).

The reason it was necessary for God to tell Moses to command the Children of Israel to bring the *Pesach* lamb is discussed by a number of the commentators (*Rashi*, *Ramban*, and *Ibn Ezra*). The *Sforno* explains that Israel had to be told that their rejoicing in the dedication of the Sanctuary and the Altar did not exempt them from the *mitzvah* of the קָרְבַּן פֶּסַח, *Pesach offering*, as was the case regarding Yom Kippur when King Solomon dedicated the Holy Temple in Jerusalem. The Talmud (*Moed Katan* 9a) tells us that the fourteen days of rejoicing in conjunction with this dedication included Yom Kippur, which was not observed that year as a day of fasting in deference to the rejoicing associated with the dedication of the Temple (*I Kings* 8:65).

7. אֲנַחְנוּ טְמֵאִים לְנֶפֶשׁ אָדָם לָמָּה נִגָּרַע . . . בְּמֹעֲדוֹ . . . — *We are tamei by the dead body of a man; why*

3 On the fourteenth day of this month in the afternoon shall you make it, in its appointed time; according to all its decrees and laws shall you make it."
4 Moses spoke to the Children of Israel to make the pesach-offering.
5 They made the pesach-offering in the first [month], on the fourteenth day of the month, in the afternoon, in the Wilderness of Sinai; according to everything that HASHEM had commanded Moses, so the Children of Israel did.
6 There were men who had been contaminated by a human corpse and could not make the pesach-offering on that day; so they approached Moses and Aaron on that day.
7 Those men said to him, "We are contaminated through a human corpse; why should we be diminished by not offering HASHEM's offering in its appointed time among the Children of Israel?"
8 Moses said to them, "Stand and I will hear what HASHEM will command you."
9 HASHEM spoke to Moses, saying,
10 "Speak to the Children of Israel, saying: If any man will become contaminated through a human corpse or on a distant road, whether you or your generations, he shall make the pesach-offering for HASHEM,
11 in the second month, on the fourteenth day, in the afternoon, shall he make it; with matzos and bitter herbs shall he eat it.
12 They shall not leave over from it until morning nor shall they break a bone of it; like all the decrees of the pesach-offering shall they make it.
13 But a man who is pure and was not on the road and had refrained from making the pesach-offering, that soul shall be cut off from its people, for he had not offered HASHEM's offering in its appointed time; that man will bear his sin.
14 When a convert shall dwell with you, he shall make a pesach-offering to HASHEM; according to the decree of the pesach-offering and its law, so shall he do; one decree shall be for you, for the proselyte and the native of the Land."
15 On the day the Tabernacle was set up, the cloud covered the Tabernacle that was a tent for the Testimony, and in the evening there would be upon the Tabernacle like a fiery appearance until morning.
16 So it would always be: The cloud would cover it, and an appearance of fire at night.
17 And whenever the cloud was lifted from atop the Tent, afterwards the Children of Israel would journey, and in the place where the cloud would rest, there

14. חֻקָּה אַחַת יִהְיֶה לָכֶם — *You shall have one statute* ... here in the wilderness.

וְלַגֵּר וּלְאֶזְרַח הָאָרֶץ — *For the stranger and for the one that is born in the Land* ... in the Land of Israel.

17. וְאַחֲרֵי כֵן יִסְעוּ — *Then after that they journeyed.* After it (the cloud) ascended, they traveled to that side (direction) where the cloud moved.

NOTES

are we to be kept back ... in its appointed season. The Mishnah in *Avos* (4:2) *states that one mitzvah leads to another mitzvah and one sin to another sin.* Therefore, these men who, according to tradition, were carrying the coffin of Joseph wondered how the performance of such a *mitzvah* could result in the deprivation of another *mitzvah*, especially since the latter could only be performed at an appointed time, and once the time passed could not be retrieved. Perhaps they felt that just as communal *tumah* (טוּמְאָה בְּצִבּוּר) is set aside in order to perform the commandment of the *Pesach* offering, so should *tumah* caused by the performance of a *mitzvah* be set aside, thereby permitting them to participate in the offering of the *Pesach* sacrifice.

יח יַחֲנוּ בְּנֵי יִשְׂרָאֵל: עַל־פִּי יהוֹה יִסְעוּ בְּנֵי יִשְׂרָאֵל וְעַל־פִּי יהוָה יַחֲנוּ
יט כָּל־יְמֵי אֲשֶׁר יִשְׁכֹּן הֶעָנָן עַל־הַמִּשְׁכָּן יַחֲנוּ: וּבְהַאֲרִיךְ הֶעָנָן עַל־הַמִּשְׁכָּן
כ יָמִים רַבִּים וְשָׁמְרוּ בְנֵי־יִשְׂרָאֵל אֶת־מִשְׁמֶרֶת יהוֹה וְלֹא יִסָּעוּ: וְיֵשׁ אֲשֶׁר
יִהְיֶה הֶעָנָן יָמִים מִסְפָּר עַל־הַמִּשְׁכָּן עַל־פִּי יהוָה יַחֲנוּ וְעַל־פִּי יהוָה יִסָּעוּ:
כא וְיֵשׁ אֲשֶׁר יִהְיֶה הֶעָנָן מֵעֶרֶב עַד־בֹּקֶר וְנַעֲלָה הֶעָנָן בַּבֹּקֶר וְנָסָעוּ אוֹ יוֹמָם
כב וָלַיְלָה וְנַעֲלָה הֶעָנָן וְנָסָעוּ: אוֹ־יֹמַיִם אוֹ־חֹדֶשׁ אוֹ־יָמִים בְּהַאֲרִיךְ הֶעָנָן
עַל־הַמִּשְׁכָּן לִשְׁכֹּן עָלָיו יַחֲנוּ בְנֵי־יִשְׂרָאֵל וְלֹא יִסָּעוּ וּבְהֵעָלֹתוֹ יִסָּעוּ:
כג עַל־פִּי יהוֹה יַחֲנוּ וְעַל־פִּי יהוֹה יִסָּעוּ אֶת־מִשְׁמֶרֶת יהוֹה שָׁמָרוּ עַל־פִּי
יהוָה בְּיַד־מֹשֶׁה:
י א־ב וַיְדַבֵּר יהוָה אֶל־מֹשֶׁה לֵּאמֹר: עֲשֵׂה לְךָ שְׁתֵּי חֲצוֹצְרֹת כֶּסֶף
מִקְשָׁה תַּעֲשֶׂה אֹתָם וְהָיוּ לְךָ לְמִקְרָא הָעֵדָה וּלְמַסַּע אֶת־הַמַּחֲנוֹת:

וּבִמְקוֹם אֲשֶׁר יִשְׁכָּן שָׁם הֶעָנָן שָׁם יַחֲנוּ — *And in the place where the cloud abode, there they encamped.* The (Torah) relates the merit of Israel concerning their traveling after Him in the wilderness. The first (point of praise) is that they encamped in the place where the cloud stopped, even though it was a place of waste, a howling wilderness (based on *Deut* 32:10).

19. וְשָׁמְרוּ בְנֵי יִשְׂרָאֵל אֶת מִשְׁמֶרֶת ה' — *And the Children of Israel kept the charge of* HASHEM. Secondly, the (Torah) relates that they waited for a long time, even though the place (of their encampment) was very poor.

וְלֹא יִסָּעוּ — *And did not journey* . . . to scout out a better place for themselves to camp.

20. וְיֵשׁ אֲשֶׁר יִהְיֶה הֶעָנָן יָמִים מִסְפָּר — *And sometimes the cloud was a few days.* Thirdly, the (Torah) relates that, at times, their encampment was in a place pleasant for themselves and their cattle, and the cloud rested there (only) for a few days, but nonetheless . . .

עַל פִּי ה' יַחֲנוּ — *At the commandment of* HASHEM *they encamped* . . . and not because of their love for that place.

וְעַל פִּי ה' יִסָּעוּ — *And at the commandment of* HASHEM *they journeyed* . . . although they were leaving that good place.

21. וְיֵשׁ אֲשֶׁר יִהְיֶה הֶעָנָן מֵעֶרֶב עַד בֹּקֶר — *And sometimes the cloud was (fixed) from evening until morning.* Fourth, the (Torah) relates that, at times, the encampment of the cloud was for an undetermined period, in a manner that it was only for a night, which was insufficient preparatory time (to attend) to the needs of encamping and journeying. However, with all this we are told that no journey began at night.

NOTES

17-23. וּבִמְקוֹם אֲשֶׁר יִשְׁכָּן שָׁם הֶעָנָן שָׁם יַחֲנוּ . . . וְשָׁמְרוּ בְנֵי יִשְׂרָאֵל אֶת מִשְׁמֶרֶת ה' וְלֹא יִסָּעוּ. וְיֵשׁ אֲשֶׁר יִהְיֶה הֶעָנָן יָמִים מִסְפָּר . . . עַל פִּי ה' יַחֲנוּ וְעַל פִּי ה' יִסָּעוּ — *And in the place where the cloud abode, there they encamped . . . and the Children of Israel kept the charge of HASHEM and did not journey. And sometimes the cloud was a few days . . . and at the commandment of HASHEM they encamped and at the commandment of HASHEM they journeyed.* These verses which relate in detail the journeying of the Israelites in the wilderness come to tell us of Israel's implicit trust in the Almighty. They followed the cloud faithfully and unquestioningly, halting wherever it stopped even if the place was desolate and dangerous. If they encamped in a pleasant and fertile area it was only because God so commanded, and not because they derived pleasure from the congenial surroundings. And even if they were content and happy in a particular location, they left as soon as the cloud moved on. The period of time was irrelevant; whether they had not yet established themselves or had been settled there for some time, they always broke camp and followed the cloud. Such was the total commitment of that generation to the dictates and direction of God.

the Children of Israel would encamp. [18] *According to the word of* HASHEM *would the Children of Israel journey, and according to the word of* HASHEM *would they encamp; all the days that the cloud would rest upon the Tabernacle they would encamp.* [19] *When the cloud lingered upon the Tabernacle many days, the Children of Israel would maintain the charge of* HASHEM *and would not journey.* [20] *Sometimes the cloud would be upon the Tabernacle for a number of days; according to the word of* HASHEM *would they encamp and according to the word of* HASHEM *would they journey.*
[21] *And sometimes the cloud would remain from evening until morning, and the cloud would be lifted in the morning and they would journey; or for a day and a night, and the cloud would be lifted and they would journey.*
[22] *Or for two days, or a month, or a year, when the cloud would linger over the Tabernacle, resting upon it, the Children of Israel would encamp and would not journey, but when it was lifted they would journey.* [23] *According to the word of* HASHEM *would they encamp, and according to the word of* HASHEM *would they journey; the charge of* HASHEM *would they safeguard, according to the word of* HASHEM *through Moses.*

10 [1] *H*ASHEM *spoke to Moses, saying,* [2] *"Make for yourself two silver trumpets — make them hammered out, and they shall be yours for the summoning of the assembly and to cause the camps to journey.*

22. אוֹ יֹמַיִם אוֹ חֹדֶשׁ אוֹ יָמִים — *Whether it were two days, a month, or a year.* Fifth, (the Torah) relates that sometimes they had no opportunity to set in order their affairs and that of their cattle, while at other (times) they had already prepared and set in order (their affairs) and they had to depart immediately and break camp (lit., 'dismantle their preparations").

23. עַל פִּי ה׳ יַחֲנוּ — *At the commandment of* HASHEM *they encamped . . .* even for a short period, when they were unable to attain (the proper) ordering of their affairs.

וְעַל פִּי ה׳ יִסָּעוּ — *And at the commandment of* HASHEM *they journeyed . . .* when the cloud was taken up (from over the Tent), even after a lengthy period, after all their affairs and needs had already been set in order.

X

2. עֲשֵׂה לְךָ שְׁתֵּי חֲצוֹצְרֹת כֶּסֶף — *Make for yourself two trumpets of silver.* Since the intent now was to travel and enter the Land immediately, He commanded that trumpets (be made) for *the trumpet signal for the king is among them* (23:21); (this referred to) when the Sanctuary traveled, and when the Holy traveled and when they went forth to battle, as it says, *And when you go to war in your land against the adversary that oppresses you then you shall sound an alarm with the trumpets* (v. 9).

וְהָיוּ לְךָ לְמִקְרָא הָעֵדָה — *And they shall be for you for the calling of the congregation . . .* because the calling of the congregation and the princes (was) . . .

NOTES

X

2. עֲשֵׂה לְךָ שְׁתֵּי חֲצוֹצְרֹת כֶּסֶף . . . וְהָיוּ לְךָ לְמִקְרָא הָעֵדָה — *Make for yourself two trumpets of silver . . . and they shall be for you for the calling of the congregation.* The signals sounded on the two trumpets of silver, as the *Sforno* explains, are linked to the kingdom of heaven and the King of Kings. The verse cited from *parashas Balak* (23:21) demonstrates that the תְּרוּעָה, *alarm,* is one which heralds the King of the Universe. Hence, it was sounded when the various parts of the Sanctuary set forth on their journey, carried by the sons of Gershon

ג־ד וְתָקְעוּ בָּהֵן וְנוֹעֲדוּ אֵלֶיךָ כָּל־הָעֵדָה אֶל־פֶּתַח אֹהֶל מוֹעֵד: וְאִם־בְּאַחַת
ה יִתְקָעוּ וְנוֹעֲדוּ אֵלֶיךָ הַנְּשִׂיאִים רָאשֵׁי אַלְפֵי יִשְׂרָאֵל: וּתְקַעְתֶּם תְּרוּעָה
ו וְנָסְעוּ הַמַּחֲנוֹת הַחֹנִים קֵדְמָה: וּתְקַעְתֶּם תְּרוּעָה שֵׁנִית וְנָסְעוּ הַמַּחֲנוֹת
ז הַחֹנִים תֵּימָנָה תְּרוּעָה יִתְקְעוּ לְמַסְעֵיהֶם: וּבְהַקְהִיל אֶת־הַקָּהָל תִּתְקְעוּ
ח וְלֹא תָרִיעוּ: וּבְנֵי אַהֲרֹן הַכֹּהֲנִים יִתְקְעוּ בַּחֲצֹצְרוֹת וְהָיוּ לָכֶם לְחֻקַּת
ט עוֹלָם לְדֹרֹתֵיכֶם: וְכִי־תָבֹאוּ מִלְחָמָה בְּאַרְצְכֶם עַל־הַצַּר הַצֹּרֵר אֶתְכֶם
וַהֲרֵעֹתֶם בַּחֲצֹצְרֹת וְנִזְכַּרְתֶּם לִפְנֵי יהוה אֱלֹהֵיכֶם וְנוֹשַׁעְתֶּם מֵאֹיְבֵיכֶם:
י וּבְיוֹם שִׂמְחַתְכֶם וּבְמוֹעֲדֵיכֶם וּבְרָאשֵׁי חָדְשֵׁכֶם וּתְקַעְתֶּם בַּחֲצֹצְרֹת עַל
עֹלֹתֵיכֶם וְעַל זִבְחֵי שַׁלְמֵיכֶם וְהָיוּ לָכֶם לְזִכָּרוֹן לִפְנֵי אֱלֹהֵיכֶם אֲנִי יהוה
אֱלֹהֵיכֶם:
חמישי יא וַיְהִי בַּשָּׁנָה הַשֵּׁנִית בַּחֹדֶשׁ הַשֵּׁנִי בְּעֶשְׂרִים בַּחֹדֶשׁ נַעֲלָה הֶעָנָן מֵעַל
יב מִשְׁכַּן הָעֵדֻת: וַיִּסְעוּ בְנֵי־יִשְׂרָאֵל לְמַסְעֵיהֶם מִמִּדְבַּר סִינָי וַיִּשְׁכֹּן הֶעָנָן
יג־יד בְּמִדְבַּר פָּארָן: וַיִּסְעוּ בָּרִאשֹׁנָה עַל־פִּי יהוה בְּיַד־מֹשֶׁה: וַיִּסַּע דֶּגֶל
מַחֲנֵה בְנֵי־יְהוּדָה בָּרִאשֹׁנָה לְצִבְאֹתָם וְעַל־צְבָאוֹ נַחְשׁוֹן בֶּן־עַמִּינָדָב:

3. אֶל פֶּתַח אֹהֶל מוֹעֵד — *At the door of the Tent of Meeting.* In the presence of (lit., before) God, He wanted that call to be (through) the trumpets which were in honor of the King.

5. וּתְקַעְתֶּם תְּרוּעָה וְנָסְעוּ הַמַּחֲנוֹת הַחֹנִים קֵדְמָה — *And when you blow an alarm, the camps that lie on the eastern side shall journey.* For together with them, the bearers of the Sanctuary did journey.

6. וּתְקַעְתֶּם תְּרוּעָה שֵׁנִית וְנָסְעוּ הַמַּחֲנוֹת הַחֹנִים תֵּימָנָה — *And when you blow an alarm the second time, the camps that lie to the southern side shall journey ...* for together with them journeyed the bearers of the holy (vessels and furnishings).

תְּרוּעָה יִתְקְעוּ לְמַסְעֵיהֶם — *They shall blow an alarm for their journeys ...* for in their journeying there is (both) a תְּקִיעָה (blast) and a תְּרוּעָה (alarm). (Now) this is because the alarm is for the traveling of the Holy, while the blast (sounded) with it was meant (as a signal) for them to gather together for their travels, similar to the calling of the congregation and the princes, which was through a blast without an alarm (v. 7).

11. בַּחֹדֶשׁ הַשֵּׁנִי בְּעֶשְׂרִים בַּחֹדֶשׁ — *In the second month on the twentieth day of the month.* After the *tameim* had offered the second *Pesach* lamb on the fourteenth day of the month, the trumpets were made with which the congregation and princes were called to Moses,

NOTES

and Merari, as well as the "Holy" vessels and furnishings, i.e., the Ark, table, golden Altar and its implements, carried by the sons of Kehath, for the trumpets are meant to be used exclusively for the sacred. As the *Sforno* points out in his commentary on the verse in *Balak* mentioned above, the blast of the trumpets is also a sign of שִׂמְחָה, *joy*, for Israel rejoiced in its King whenever the Sanctuary traveled. The trumpets were also sounded to rally the people to the defense of *Eretz Yisrael*, for this land is the *holy* land, and also to call the congregation and princes to *the door of the Tent of Meeting* in the wilderness, because that gathering was for the sake of the King, as the *Sforno* explains in his commentary on verse 3.

5. וּתְקַעְתֶּם תְּרוּעָה וְנָסְעוּ הַמַּחֲנוֹת הַחֹנִים קֵדְמָה — *And when you blow an alarm, the camps that lie on the eastern side shall journey.* The תְּרוּעָה was sounded twice. The first was to signal the departure of the eastern camps of Judah, Issachar and Zevulun with whom the Gershonites and Merarites, carrying the Sanctuary (i.e., the boards, curtains, etc.), traveled. The second blast was for the southern contingent of Reuben, Simeon and Gad accompanied by the Kehathites, bearing the holy vessels and furnishings. The *Sforno*, unlike other commentators such as the *Ramban*, is of the opinion that the other two camps (western and northern) did not need, nor did they have, a special alarm to signal their departure. The reason may

*3 When they sound a long blast with them, the entire assembly shall assem-
ble to you, to the entrance of the Tent of Meeting. 4 If they sound a long blast
with one, the leaders shall assemble to you, the heads of Israel's thousands.
5 When you sound short blasts, the camps resting to the east shall journey.
6 When you sound short blasts a second time, the camps resting to the south
shall journey; short blasts shall they sound for their journeys. 7 When you
gather together the congregation, you shall sound a long blast, but not a short
blast. 8 The sons of Aaron, the Kohanim, shall sound the trumpets, and it
shall be for you an eternal decree for your generations.*

9 "When you go to wage war in your Land against an enemy who oppresses you, you shall sound short blasts of the trumpets, and you shall be recalled before HASHEM, your God, and you shall be saved from your foes.

10 "On a day of your gladness, and on your festivals, and on your new moons, you shall sound the trumpets over your elevation-offerings and over your feast peace-offerings; and they shall be a remembrance for you before your God; I am HASHEM, your God."

*11 It was in the second year, in the second month, on the twentieth of the
month, the cloud was lifted from upon the Tabernacle of the Testimony.
12 The Children of Israel journeyed on their journeys from the Wilderness of
Sinai, and the cloud rested in the Wilderness of Paran.*

*13 They journeyed for the first time at the bidding of HASHEM through
Moses. 14 The banner of the camp of the children of Judah journeyed first according to their legions, and over its legion was Nahshon son of Amminadab;*

---

who informed them regarding the order of their journeys through the (medium of the) trumpets and the order of the (use of these) trumpets in the Holy and when (going) to battle. And thus the cloud ascended (signaling them) to move forward to Kadesh Barnea, which was the first city in *Eretz Yisrael* they would reach on that road, the road (which went through) the great and dreadful wilderness as it says, וַנִּסַּע מֵחֹרֵב וַנֵּלֶךְ אֵת כָּל הַמִּדְבָּר הַגָּדוֹל וְהַנּוֹרָא . . . וַנָּבֹא עַד קָדֵשׁ בַּרְנֵעַ, *And we journeyed from Horeb and went through all that great and dreadful wilderness . . . and we came to Kadesh Barnea (Deut.* 1:19).

NOTES

have been because these camps did not have any items of sanctity traveling with them. The *Ibn Ezra* offers another reason for the absence of a trumpet sound in conjunction with these last two camps. Since the sons of Aaron were given the task of blowing the trumpets (v. 8), and the *Kohanim* had all departed with the first two camps, there was no one available who was permitted to sound the trumpets!

6. תְּרוּעָה יִתְקְעוּ לְמַסְעֵיהֶם — *They shall blow an alarm for their journeys.* There were two kinds of notes sounded by the trumpets. One was תְּקִיעָה (a simple straight blowing), and the second, תְּרוּעָה (an alarm). Now the Torah established that the former was to be used for the gathering of the congregation or the princes (vs. 3 and 4) whereas the latter was to signal the journeying of the *Mishkan* and its sacred vessels. This explains why the breaking of camp and the signal to depart combined both the תְּקִיעָה and תְּרוּעָה, for as the *Sforno* points out, this included a calling together of the people, as well as the dismantling and transporting of the Sanctuary and its contents.

11. בַּחֹדֶשׁ הַשֵּׁנִי בְּעֶשְׂרִים בַּחֹדֶשׁ — *In the second month on the twentieth day of the month.* The narrative now returns to a chronological order of events. The twentieth day of the second month in the second year sets the scene, following all that has been recorded in the first part of this book. All necessary preparations to enter *Eretz Yisrael* had been made: the census, the banners, the purification of the camp of Israel, the consecration of the Levites, the dedication of the Altar, the offering of the *Pesach* sacrifice (first and second) and the fashioning of the trumpets. Israel was now ready to enter the Land and so Moses invited his father-in-law and his family to join them.

טו־טז וְעַל־צְבָא מַטֵּה בְּנֵי יִשָּׂשכָר נְתַנְאֵל בֶּן־צוּעָר׃ וְעַל־צְבָא מַטֵּה בְּנֵי זְבוּלֻן
יז אֱלִיאָב בֶּן־חֵלֹן׃ וְהוּרַד הַמִּשְׁכָּן וְנָסְעוּ בְנֵי־גֵרְשׁוֹן וּבְנֵי מְרָרִי נֹשְׂאֵי
יח הַמִּשְׁכָּן׃ וְנָסַע דֶּגֶל מַחֲנֵה רְאוּבֵן לְצִבְאֹתָם וְעַל־צְבָאוֹ אֱלִיצוּר בֶּן־
יט־כ שְׁדֵיאוּר׃ וְעַל־צְבָא מַטֵּה בְּנֵי שִׁמְעוֹן שְׁלֻמִיאֵל בֶּן־צוּרִישַׁדָּי׃ וְעַל־צְבָא
כא מַטֵּה בְנֵי־גָד אֶלְיָסָף בֶּן־דְּעוּאֵל׃ וְנָסְעוּ הַקְּהָתִים נֹשְׂאֵי הַמִּקְדָּשׁ וְהֵקִימוּ
כב אֶת־הַמִּשְׁכָּן עַד־בֹּאָם׃ וְנָסַע דֶּגֶל מַחֲנֵה בְנֵי־אֶפְרַיִם לְצִבְאֹתָם וְעַל־
כג צְבָאוֹ אֱלִישָׁמָע בֶּן־עַמִּיהוּד׃ וְעַל־צְבָא מַטֵּה בְּנֵי מְנַשֶּׁה גַּמְלִיאֵל
כד־כה בֶּן־פְּדָהצוּר׃ וְעַל־צְבָא מַטֵּה בְּנֵי בִנְיָמִן אֲבִידָן בֶּן־גִּדְעוֹנִי׃ וְנָסַע דֶּגֶל
מַחֲנֵה בְנֵי־דָן מְאַסֵּף לְכָל־הַמַּחֲנֹת לְצִבְאֹתָם וְעַל־צְבָאוֹ אֲחִיעֶזֶר
כו־כז בֶּן־עַמִּישַׁדָּי׃ וְעַל־צְבָא מַטֵּה בְּנֵי אָשֵׁר פַּגְעִיאֵל בֶּן־עָכְרָן׃ וְעַל־צְבָא
כח מַטֵּה בְּנֵי נַפְתָּלִי אֲחִירַע בֶּן־עֵינָן׃ אֵלֶּה מַסְעֵי בְנֵי־יִשְׂרָאֵל לְצִבְאֹתָם
כט וַיִּסָּעוּ׃ וַיֹּאמֶר מֹשֶׁה לְחֹבָב בֶּן־רְעוּאֵל הַמִּדְיָנִי חֹתֵן
מֹשֶׁה נֹסְעִים ׀ אֲנַחְנוּ אֶל־הַמָּקוֹם אֲשֶׁר אָמַר יהוה אֹתוֹ אֶתֵּן לָכֶם
ל לְכָה אִתָּנוּ וְהֵטַבְנוּ לָךְ כִּי־יהוה דִּבֶּר־טוֹב עַל־יִשְׂרָאֵל׃ וַיֹּאמֶר אֵלָיו
לא לֹא אֵלֵךְ כִּי אִם־אֶל־אַרְצִי וְאֶל־מוֹלַדְתִּי אֵלֵךְ׃ וַיֹּאמֶר אַל־נָא תַּעֲזֹב
לב אֹתָנוּ כִּי ׀ עַל־כֵּן יָדַעְתָּ חֲנֹתֵנוּ בַּמִּדְבָּר וְהָיִיתָ לָּנוּ לְעֵינָיִם׃ וְהָיָה
כִּי־תֵלֵךְ עִמָּנוּ וְהָיָה ׀ הַטּוֹב הַהוּא אֲשֶׁר יֵיטִיב יהוה עִמָּנוּ וְהֵטַבְנוּ
לג לָךְ׃ וַיִּסְעוּ מֵהַר יהוה דֶּרֶךְ שְׁלֹשֶׁת יָמִים וַאֲרוֹן בְּרִית־יהוה נֹסֵעַ לִפְנֵיהֶם

---

30. כִּי אִם אֶל אַרְצִי וְאֶל מוֹלַדְתִּי אֵלֵךְ — *But I will depart to my own land and to my birthplace* . . . for in my advanced age I will not be able to tolerate the climate and food of another country.

31. אַל נָא תַּעֲזֹב אֹתָנוּ — *Please do not leave us.* At least let your sons come with us.

כִּי עַל כֵּן יָדַעְתָּ חֲנֹתֵנוּ בַּמִּדְבָּר — *Seeing that you know how we are to encamp in the wilderness.* For if your children will also leave us, you will profane God in the eyes of the nations who will say, "If Jethro had observed an authentic presence of Godliness (in the camp of Israel) he and his children would not have left them." And in this (matter), Moses, Jethro and his sons agreed, for indeed Jethro returned to his land, as it says, וַיְשַׁלַּח מֹשֶׁה אֶת חֹתְנוֹ וַיֵּלֶךְ לוֹ אֶל אַרְצוֹ, *And Moses sent away his father-in-law and he went his way into his own land (Exodus* 18:27), while his children, without a doubt, went with the Israelites, as the Book of *Judges* attests saying, וּבְנֵי קֵינִי חֹתֵן מֹשֶׁה עָלוּ מֵעִיר הַתְּמָרִים אֶת בְּנֵי יְהוּדָה, *And the children of the Keni, Moses' father-in-law, went up out of the city of palm trees with the children of Judah (Judges* 1:16).

33. דֶּרֶךְ שְׁלֹשֶׁת יָמִים — *Three days' journey* . . . to *Eretz Yisrael*. Because indeed, in three (phased) journeys they arrived opposite Kadesh Barnea in the wilderness of Paran from

NOTES

31. אַל נָא תַּעֲזֹב אֹתָנוּ כִּי עַל כֵּן יָדַעְתָּ חֲנֹתֵנוּ בַּמִּדְבָּר — *Please do not leave us seeing that you know how we are to encamp in the wilderness.* The *Sforno* explains why Moses insisted that Jethro not forsake them. The original decision of Jethro to leave Midian, when he heard of all the miracles wrought by the Almighty during Israel's Exodus from Egypt, and to join the camp of Israel must have had a profound impact upon the people of his time and place who respected his position and reputation. By leaving now and rejecting the invitation of Moses, he would cast aspersion upon the Israelite camp. Moses, therefore, pleads with him that even though Jethro himself is too old to change his abode and adjust to a new land, still and all, by allowing his chil-

15 *over the legion of the tribe of the children of Issachar was Nethanel son
of Zuar;* 16 *and over the legion of the tribe of Zebulun was Eliab son of
Helon.*
17 *The Tabernacle was taken down, then journeyed the sons of Gershon
and the sons of Merari, the bearers of the Tabernacle.*
18 *Then journeyed the banner of the camp of Reuben according to their
legions; and over its legion was Elizur son of Shedeur;* 19 *over the legion of
the tribe of the children of Simeon was Shelumiel son of Zurishaddai;* 20 *and
over the legion of the tribe of the children of Gad was Eliasaph son of Deuel.*
21 *Then journeyed the Kohathites, bearers of the sanctuary; and they would
erect the Tabernacle before their arrival.*
22 *Then journeyed the banner of the camp of Ephraim according to their
legions, and over its legion was Elishama son of Ammihud;* 23 *over the
legion of the tribe of the children of Manasseh was Gamaliel son of
Pedahzur;* 24 *and over the legion of the tribe of the children of Benjamin was
Abidan son of Gideoni.*
25 *Then journeyed the banner of the camp of the children of Dan, the rear
guard of all the camps, according to their legions, and over its legion was
Ahiezer son of Ammishaddai;* 26 *over the legion of the tribe of the children
of Asher was Pagiel son of Ochran;* 27 *and over the legion of the tribe of the
children of Naphtali was Ahira son of Enan.* 28 *These were the journeys of
the Children of Israel according to their legions, and they journeyed.*
29 *Moses said to Hobab son of Reuel, the Midianite, the father-in-law of
Moses, "We are journeying to the place of which* HASHEM *has said, 'I shall
give it to you.' Go with us and we shall treat you well, for* HASHEM *has
spoken of good for Israel."* 30 *He said to him, "I shall not go; only to my land
and my family shall I go."* 31 *He said, "Please do not forsake us, inasmuch
as you know our encampments in the Wilderness, and you have been as
eyes for us.* 32 *And it shall be that if you come with us, then with the
goodness with which* HASHEM *will benefit us, we will do good to you."*
33 *They journeyed from the Mountain of* HASHEM *a three-day distance, and the Ark of the covenant of* HASHEM *journeyed before them*

---

whence they sent forth the spies as Moses our Teacher explained, when he said, וַתִּקְרְבוּן אֵלַי כֻּלְּכֶם וַתֹּאמְרוּ נִשְׁלְחָה אֲנָשִׁים, *And you came near unto me every one of you and said, "Let us send men before us"* (*Deut.* 1:22), and this was the place of their encampment in the wilderness of Paran mentioned here (in this *sedrah*) saying, *and afterward the people journeyed from Chazeros and pitched in the wilderness of Paran* (12:16) and it was there that the spies returned as it says, *And they returned ... and they came ... to the wilderness of Paran to Kadesh* (13:25-26). Now that place was called Rismah, as it says, *and they journeyed from Chazeros and pitched in Rismah* (33:18), and there (in that chapter) three journeys are mentioned from the wilderness of Sinai until there and they are: Kivros Hataaveh, and Chazeros and Rismah — for the affair of "Taverah" (11:3) occurred en route, and not when they were encamped.

NOTES

dren to accompany the Israelites into the Promised Land, the honor of Israel would be safeguarded. Jethro and his sons agreed to this proposal as the *Sforno* proves from the Book of *Judges.* (See also the *Sforno's* commentary to *Exodus* 18:27.)

לד דֶּרֶךְ שְׁלֹשֶׁת יָמִים לָתוּר לָהֶם מְנוּחָה: וַעֲנַן יהוה עֲלֵיהֶם יוֹמָם בְּנָסְעָם
ששי לה מִן־הַמַּחֲנֶה: נ וַיְהִי בִּנְסֹעַ הָאָרֹן וַיֹּאמֶר מֹשֶׁה קוּמָה | יהוה וְיָפֻצוּ
לו אֹיְבֶיךָ וְיָנֻסוּ מְשַׂנְאֶיךָ מִפָּנֶיךָ: וּבְנֻחֹה יֹאמַר שׁוּבָה יהוה רִבְבוֹת אַלְפֵי
יִשְׂרָאֵל: נ

יא א וַיְהִי הָעָם כְּמִתְאֹנְנִים רַע בְּאָזְנֵי יהוה וַיִּשְׁמַע יהוה וַיִּחַר אַפּוֹ וַתִּבְעַר־
ב בָּם אֵשׁ יהוה וַתֹּאכַל בִּקְצֵה הַמַּחֲנֶה: וַיִּצְעַק הָעָם אֶל־מֹשֶׁה וַיִּתְפַּלֵּל
ג מֹשֶׁה אֶל־יהוה וַתִּשְׁקַע הָאֵשׁ: וַיִּקְרָא שֵׁם־הַמָּקוֹם הַהוּא תַּבְעֵרָה
ד כִּי־בָעֲרָה בָם אֵשׁ יהוה: וְהָאסַפְסֻף אֲשֶׁר בְּקִרְבּוֹ הִתְאַוּוּ תַּאֲוָה

וַאֲרוֹן בְּרִית ה׳ נֹסֵעַ לִפְנֵיהֶם דֶּרֶךְ שְׁלֹשֶׁת יָמִים — *And the Ark of the covenant of HASHEM went before them on the three days' journey.* During the three days that they traveled those three journeys by the way of הַמִּדְבָּר הַגָּדוֹל וְהַנּוֹרָא, *the great and dreadful wilderness (Deut.* 1:19), the Ark *went before them* to secure the way from serpents and scorpions and other (dangerous creatures). However, on all other journeys the Ark traveled *in the midst of the camps* (2:17), similar to the other carryings of the Kehathites (i.e., who carried the Ark on their shoulders).

לָתוּר לָהֶם מְנוּחָה — *To seek out a resting place for them* ... a secure (safe) camping place in the dreadful wilderness.

34. וַעֲנַן ה׳ עֲלֵיהֶם יוֹמָם — *And the cloud of HASHEM was over them by day.* It did not go *before* them, as it did during other journeys, for it was sufficient then for the Ark to prepare the way as it traveled before them. But (the cloud) did hover over them by day during the time they traveled.

35. וַיְהִי בִּנְסֹעַ הָאָרֹן — *And it came to pass when the Ark set forward* ... to go and enter into *Eretz Yisrael.*

קוּמָה ה׳ וְיָפֻצוּ אֹיְבֶיךָ — *Rise up, HASHEM, and let Your enemies be scattered.* Because indeed, had they not sent the spies they would have entered (the Land of Israel) without (recourse to) war, for the nations would have fled כַּעֲזוּבַת הַחֹרֶשׁ וְהָאָמִיר אֲשֶׁר עָזְבוּ מִפְּנֵי בְּנֵי יִשְׂרָאֵל, *as the forsaken portion of the thicket and the uppermost branch which they left because of the Children of Israel (Isaiah* 17:9).

NOTES

33. וַאֲרוֹן בְּרִית ה׳ נֹסֵעַ לִפְנֵיהֶם — *And the Ark of the covenant of HASHEM went before them.* The Kehathites were charged with the task of carrying the Holy Ark on their shoulders and were therefore not given wagons, as were the Gershonites and Merarites. In chapter 2, where the Torah discusses the order of the camps in their journeying, we are told that the Kehathites traveled בְּתוֹךְ הַמַּחֲנֹת, *in the midst of the camps,* i.e., between the groupings of Judah and Reuben (v. 17). However, during the three days' journey from the "mountain of God," the Ark of the covenant went miraculously before the Israelites on its own, without being carried by the Kehathites. As *Rashi* explains in his commentary on this verse, "They traveled three days' journey in one day because God wished to bring them into the Land immediately." It was for this reason that the Ark preceded the Israelites on its own and was not carried by the Levites.

33-36. דֶּרֶךְ שְׁלֹשֶׁת יָמִים וַאֲרוֹן בְּרִית ה׳ נֹסֵעַ לִפְנֵיהֶם ... קוּמָה ה׳ וְיָפֻצוּ אֹיְבֶיךָ וְיָנֻסוּ מְשַׂנְאֶיךָ ... שׁוּבָה ה׳ רִבְבוֹת אַלְפֵי יִשְׂרָאֵל — *Three days' journey and theArk of the covenant of HASHEM went before them ... Rise up, HASHEM, and let Your enemies be scattered and let them that hate You flee ... Return, HASHEM, unto the ten thousand thousands of Israel.* The *Sforno*, as is his wont, explains these verses according to their plain meaning as opposed to the interpretation of other commentators and the Midrashic exegesis of our Sages. He explains these verses thus: Israel was supposed to enter *Eretz Yisrael* in a period of three days, had they not insisted on sending the spies and subsequently believing their defeatist and despairing report. The Ark, during this special period, went before them (v. 33) while the cloud hovered over them. Verses 35-36 are, according to him and contrary to other interpretations, inserted in their correct

a three-day distance to search out for them a resting place. [34] *The cloud of HASHEM was over them by day when they journeyed from the camp.*

[35] *When the Ark would journey, Moses said, "Arise, HASHEM, and let Your foes be scattered, let those who hate You flee from before You."* [36] *And when it rested, he would say, "Reside tranquilly, O, HASHEM, among the myriad thousands of Israel."*

11 [1] *The people took to seeking complaints; it was evil in the ears of HASHEM, and HASHEM heard and His wrath flared, and a fire of HASHEM burned against them, and it consumed at the edge of the camp.* [2] *The people cried out to Moses; Moses prayed to HASHEM, and the fire died down.* [3] *He named that place Taberah, for the fire of HASHEM had burned against them.*

[4] *The rabble that was among them cultivated a craving, and the Children*

וְיָנֻסוּ מְשַׂנְאֶיךָ מִפָּנֶיךָ — *And let them that hate You flee before You* ... lest Israel come to annihilate them.

36. שׁוּבָה — *Return* (or "*abide*"). Let Your tranquility abide here among us, similar to זֹאת מְנוּחָתִי עֲדֵי עַד, *This is My resting place forever* (*Psalms* 132:14), and although You will reveal Your Divine Presence before Israel to evict their enemies, (nonetheless) the resting place of Your Divine Presence will (abide) in our midst.

ה׳ רִבְבוֹת אַלְפֵי יִשְׂרָאֵל — *HASHEM, unto the ten thousand thousands of Israel.* Similar to, "HASHEM of the hosts of the thousands of Israel," as (our Sages) say, "The term hosts (צְבָאוֹת) only refers to the name hosts of Israel" (*Shevuos* 35b). And (the verse) says *ten thousand thousands*, similar to, רִבֹּתַיִם אַלְפֵי, *twice ten thousand, thousands* (*Psalms* 68:18), for perhaps Israel at that time reached that number, with men, women and children (all included).

XI

1. כְּמִתְאֹנְנִים — *As murmurers* ... regarding the travail of the road; not that they truly complained in their hearts, for they had no worthwhile reason to murmur. (Rather), they murmured with their words to test (God).

2. וַתִּשְׁקַע הָאֵשׁ — *And the fire sank down* (*abated*) ... contrary to the nature of fire, so that they might recognize that it was a supernatural wonder, and that it was not a natural fire that had then occurred due to some natural cause.

NOTES

place. They follow logically the sequence of the previous verses. Since the Israelites were about to enter the Promised Land, Moses uttered a prayer that God rise up so that His and Israel's enemies be scattered, for the *Sforno* has already explained that it would not have been necessary for Israel to wage war since the Almighty Himself would have driven out the nations from Canaan. Then the Israelites would have entered to possess the Land and God's presence would have come to rest in their midst.

XI

1. כְּמִתְאֹנְנִים — *As murmurers.* The phrase used by the Torah regarding the murmuring and complaining of the people (כְּמִתְאֹנְנִים) is qualified by the preposition *kaf* (כ״ף הַדִּמְיוֹן), meaning "as" or "like." The *Sforno* therefore interprets it to mean that the people were not expressing their real feelings; it was not a sincere, true outpouring of criticism for there was no basis for them to do so. Hence, it must be understood in the sense of a test of God and Moses by certain elements among the people of Israel, as we see in chapter 78 of *Psalms* from which the *Sforno* quotes at length in his commentary on this chapter. *Ibn Ezra*, indeed, renders the phrase מִתְאֹנְנִים as "they that uttered words of wickedness," since it was not a legitimate complaint.

2. וַתִּשְׁקַע הָאֵשׁ — *And the fire sank down (abated).* Fire normally goes up — here it sank down. This demonstrated that it was not a natural occurrence but a heavenly retribution, as it is indeed identified in verse 3, "the fire of God."

ה וַיָּשֻׁבוּ וַיִּבְכּוּ גַּם בְּנֵי יִשְׂרָאֵל וַיֹּאמְרוּ מִי יַאֲכִלֵנוּ בָּשָׂר: זָכַרְנוּ אֶת־הַדָּגָה
אֲשֶׁר־נֹאכַל בְּמִצְרַיִם חִנָּם אֵת הַקִּשֻּׁאִים וְאֵת הָאֲבַטִּחִים וְאֶת־הֶחָצִיר
ו וְאֶת־הַבְּצָלִים וְאֶת־הַשּׁוּמִים: וְעַתָּה נַפְשֵׁנוּ יְבֵשָׁה אֵין כֹּל בִּלְתִּי
ז־ח אֶל־הַמָּן עֵינֵינוּ: וְהַמָּן כִּזְרַע־גַּד הוּא וְעֵינוֹ כְּעֵין הַבְּדֹלַח: שָׁטוּ הָעָם
וְלָקְטוּ וְטָחֲנוּ בָרֵחַיִם אוֹ דָכוּ בַּמְּדֹכָה וּבִשְּׁלוּ בַּפָּרוּר וְעָשׂוּ אֹתוֹ עֻגוֹת
ט וְהָיָה טַעְמוֹ כְּטַעַם לְשַׁד הַשָּׁמֶן: וּבְרֶדֶת הַטַּל עַל־הַמַּחֲנֶה לָיְלָה יֵרֵד הַמָּן
י עָלָיו: וַיִּשְׁמַע מֹשֶׁה אֶת־הָעָם בֹּכֶה לְמִשְׁפְּחֹתָיו אִישׁ לְפֶתַח אָהֳלוֹ
יא וַיִּחַר־אַף יהוה מְאֹד וּבְעֵינֵי מֹשֶׁה רָע: וַיֹּאמֶר מֹשֶׁה אֶל־יהוה לָמָה
הֲרֵעֹתָ לְעַבְדֶּךָ וְלָמָּה לֹא־*מָצָתִי חֵן בְּעֵינֶיךָ לָשׂוּם אֶת־מַשָּׂא כָּל־הָעָם *חסר א
יב הַזֶּה עָלָי: הֶאָנֹכִי הָרִיתִי אֵת כָּל־הָעָם הַזֶּה אִם־אָנֹכִי יְלִדְתִּיהוּ
כִּי־תֹאמַר אֵלַי שָׂאֵהוּ בְחֵיקֶךָ כַּאֲשֶׁר יִשָּׂא הָאֹמֵן אֶת־הַיֹּנֵק עַל הָאֲדָמָה
יג אֲשֶׁר נִשְׁבַּעְתָּ לַאֲבֹתָיו: מֵאַיִן לִי בָּשָׂר לָתֵת לְכָל־הָעָם הַזֶּה כִּי־יִבְכּוּ
יד עָלַי לֵאמֹר תְּנָה־לָּנוּ בָשָׂר וְנֹאכֵלָה: לֹא־אוּכַל אָנֹכִי לְבַדִּי לָשֵׂאת
טו אֶת־כָּל־הָעָם הַזֶּה כִּי כָבֵד מִמֶּנִּי: וְאִם־כָּכָה | אַתְּ־עֹשֶׂה לִּי הָרְגֵנִי נָא
הָרֹג אִם־מָצָאתִי חֵן בְּעֵינֶיךָ וְאַל־אֶרְאֶה בְּרָעָתִי:

---

4. וַיָּשֻׁבוּ וַיִּבְכּוּ — *And* (*the Children of Israel*) *wept again.* They continued to act as murmurers (in order) to test (God), and now they cried for having left Egypt, as though they rejected the value (i.e., privilege) of having the Divine Presence amongst them, as (the Torah) testifies (v. 20), saying, *because you have rejected* HASHEM *Who is among you, and you have wept before Him saying, "Why is this that we have come forth from Egypt?"*

מִי יַאֲכִלֵנוּ בָּשָׂר — *Who shall give us flesh to eat?* (This was in order) to test אִם יָכִין שְׁאֵר לְעַמּוֹ, *Can He supply meat for his people?* (*Psalms* 78:20), as the psalmist attested when he said, וַיְנַסּוּ אֵל בִּלְבָבָם לִשְׁאָל אֹכֶל לְנַפְשָׁם, *They tested God in their hearts by requesting food for their craving* (ibid. 18).

11. לָמָה הֲרֵעֹתָ לְעַבְדֶּךָ — *Why have You done evil to Your servant?* ... by sending me, against my will, to bring this people out of Egypt.

וְלָמָּה לֹא מָצָתִי חֵן בְּעֵינֶיךָ — *And why have I not found favor in Your eyes* ... when I said, שְׁלַח נָא בְּיַד תִּשְׁלָח, *Send please by the hand of an agent* (*Exodus* 4:13).

לָשׂוּם אֶת מַשָּׂא כָּל הָעָם הַזֶּה עָלָי — *That You put the burden of all this people upon me.* And this You did in order to place the burden of all of them upon me, as though You had no leader other than myself, to at least share with me, that it might benefit them.

NOTES

4. וַיָּשֻׁבוּ וַיִּבְכּוּ . . . מִי יַאֲכִלֵנוּ בָּשָׂר — *And* (*the Children of Israel*) *wept again ... Who shall give us meat to eat?* Although the Torah clearly states that the cause of this second complaint, accompanied by weeping, was their inadequate diet, the *Sforno* explains that there were two other motivations implicit in this complaint. One was their regret for having left Egypt, ignoring the fact that their leaving that spiritually contaminated land resulted in having the Divine Presence in their midst which was impossible in the land of Egypt. (See the *Sforno* on *Exodus* 13:21 and *Rashi* on *Exodus* 9:29.) The second was to test God once again to see if He was capable of providing them with meat in the desolate wilderness. Indeed, the *Sifre* states that "they were looking for a pretext to remove themselves from God."

11-12. לָמָה הֲרֵעֹתָ לְעַבְדֶּךָ וְלָמָּה לֹא מָצָתִי חֵן בְּעֵינֶיךָ לָשׂוּם אֶת מַשָּׂא כָּל הָעָם הַזֶּה עָלָי. הֶאָנֹכִי הָרִיתִי — *Why have You done evil to Your servant? And why have I not found favor in Your eyes that You put the burden of all this people upon me? Have I conceived ...?* At the end of this *sedrah*, Moses is depicted by the Torah as being "very meek above all men upon the face of the earth" (12:3) This great

of Israel also wept once more, and said, "Who will feed us meat? [5] *We
remember the fish that we ate in Egypt free of charge; and the cucumbers,
melons, leeks, onions, and garlic.* [6] *But now, our life is parched, there is
nothing; we have nothing to anticipate but the manna!"*
[7] *Now the manna was like coriander seed and its color was like the color
of b'dolach.* [8] *The people would stroll and gather it, and grind it in a mill or
pound it in a mortar and cook it in a pot or make it into cakes, and it tasted
like the taste of dough kneaded with oil.* [9] *When the dew descended upon
the camp at night, the manna would descend upon it.*
[10] *Moses heard the people weeping in their family groups, each one at the
entrance of his tent, and the wrath of HASHEM flared greatly; and in the
eyes of Moses it was bad.*
[11] *Moses said to HASHEM, "Why have You done evil to Your servant; why
have I not found favor in Your eyes, that You place the burden of this entire
people upon me?* [12] *Did I conceive this entire people or did I give birth to it,
that You say to me, 'Carry them in your bosom, as a nurse carries a
suckling, to the Land that You swore to its forefathers?* [13] *Where shall I get
meat to give to this entire people when they weep to me, saying, 'Give us
meat that we may eat'?* [14] *I alone cannot carry this entire nation, for it is too
heavy for me!* [15] *And if this is how You deal with me, then kill me now, if
I have found favor in Your eyes, and let me not see my evil!"*

---

12. הֶאָנֹכִי הָרִיתִי — *Have I conceived.* Behold, a father can lead his sons even though they (the father and the sons) have diverse opinions, and this is because they all consider him as one who loves them and who attempts with all his might to benefit them. But these (people) have no trust in me at all, and are suspicious (of me), testing (me) to see what I can do for them.

13. מֵאַיִן לִי בָּשָׂר — *Whence should I have meat.* Behold, without a doubt they (know) that I have no meat to give them, and therefore when they weep to me and say *give us meat* as if it were in my power (to do so), and (as though) through their weeping I will fulfill their desires, this is only (done) to test my leadership by Your command, to (see) what I can attain from You for them.

14. לֹא אוּכַל אָנֹכִי לְבַדִּי — *I am not able alone.* You must join others with me in whom this people will trust.

15. וְאִם כָּכָה אַתְּ עֹשֶׂה לִּי — *And if You treat me thus.* And if You, the Perfect One, withhold perfection of leadership which is fitting to come from You, and (instead You) lead them *thus,* (i.e.,) in a way that is lacking, akin to the leadership of a female, (and all this) for my sake and my honor, and You do not join others with me so as not to mar my honor ...

NOTES

humility is manifested in these verses. Moses is convinced that he is unequal to the task of leadership given to him by God. The discontent displayed by Israel is not their fault, rather it is due to their lack of trust in him, which he feels is justified. When he uses the expression *"Have I conceived, etc.,"* he is not disclaiming any relationship with them, nor is he demonstrating insensitivity to their plight. Rather, he is reiterating his perception of his shortcomings and inability to evoke Israel's trust.

15. וְאִם כָּכָה אַתְּ עֹשֶׂה לִּי הָרְגֵנִי נָא הָרֹג . . . וְאַל אֶרְאֶה בְּרָעָתִי — *And if You treat me thus, kill me, I pray You ... and let me not see my evil.* The Hebrew word *You* is written in the feminine form (אַתְּ) instead of the masculine (אַתָּה). *Rashi* explains this as an indication that Moses' strength weakened to become like that of a woman. The difficulty with this explanation is obvious. The term אַתְּ refers to God, not to Moses! The *Sforno*, therefore, explains the word אַתְּ as reflecting a diminishment in the

טז וַיֹּאמֶר יהוה אֶל־מֹשֶׁה אֶסְפָה־לִּי שִׁבְעִים אִישׁ מִזִּקְנֵי יִשְׂרָאֵל אֲשֶׁר
יָדַעְתָּ כִּי־הֵם זִקְנֵי הָעָם וְשֹׁטְרָיו וְלָקַחְתָּ אֹתָם אֶל־אֹהֶל מוֹעֵד וְהִתְיַצְּבוּ
יז שָׁם עִמָּךְ: וְיָרַדְתִּי וְדִבַּרְתִּי עִמְּךָ שָׁם וְאָצַלְתִּי מִן־הָרוּחַ אֲשֶׁר עָלֶיךָ
וְשַׂמְתִּי עֲלֵיהֶם וְנָשְׂאוּ אִתְּךָ בְּמַשָּׂא הָעָם וְלֹא־תִשָּׂא אַתָּה לְבַדֶּךָ:
יח וְאֶל־הָעָם תֹּאמַר הִתְקַדְּשׁוּ לְמָחָר וַאֲכַלְתֶּם בָּשָׂר כִּי בְּכִיתֶם בְּאָזְנֵי
יהוה לֵאמֹר מִי יַאֲכִלֵנוּ בָּשָׂר כִּי־טוֹב לָנוּ בְּמִצְרָיִם וְנָתַן יהוה לָכֶם בָּשָׂר
יט וַאֲכַלְתֶּם: לֹא יוֹם אֶחָד תֹּאכְלוּן וְלֹא יוֹמָיִם וְלֹא | חֲמִשָּׁה יָמִים וְלֹא
כ עֲשָׂרָה יָמִים וְלֹא עֶשְׂרִים יוֹם: עַד | חֹדֶשׁ יָמִים עַד אֲשֶׁר־יֵצֵא מֵאַפְּכֶם
וְהָיָה לָכֶם לְזָרָא יַעַן כִּי־מְאַסְתֶּם אֶת־יהוה אֲשֶׁר בְּקִרְבְּכֶם וַתִּבְכּוּ
כא לְפָנָיו לֵאמֹר לָמָּה זֶּה יָצָאנוּ מִמִּצְרָיִם: וַיֹּאמֶר מֹשֶׁה שֵׁשׁ־מֵאוֹת אֶלֶף
רַגְלִי הָעָם אֲשֶׁר אָנֹכִי בְּקִרְבּוֹ וְאַתָּה אָמַרְתָּ בָּשָׂר אֶתֵּן לָהֶם וְאָכְלוּ
כב חֹדֶשׁ יָמִים: הֲצֹאן וּבָקָר יִשָּׁחֵט לָהֶם וּמָצָא לָהֶם אִם אֶת־כָּל־דְּגֵי הַיָּם
יֵאָסֵף לָהֶם וּמָצָא לָהֶם:
כג וַיֹּאמֶר יהוה אֶל־מֹשֶׁה הֲיַד יהוה תִּקְצָר עַתָּה תִרְאֶה הֲיִקְרְךָ
כד דְבָרִי אִם־לֹא: וַיֵּצֵא מֹשֶׁה וַיְדַבֵּר אֶל־הָעָם אֵת דִּבְרֵי יהוה וַיֶּאֱסֹף

הָרְגֵנִי נָא הָרֹג אִם מָצָאתִי חֵן בְּעֵינֶיךָ — *Kill me, I pray You, if I have found favor in Your eyes* . . . so that You will be able to appoint others, through whom the leadership of the people will be perfect (complete), as (our Sages) state regarding Samuel, that he died before his time so that the kingship of the House of David might be established (*Taanis* 5b).

וְאַל אֶרְאֶה בְּרָעָתִי — *And let me not see my evil* . . . the evil of diminished leadership on my account, because that would be more difficult for me (to accept) than death!

17. וְנָשְׂאוּ אִתְּךָ — *And they shall carry* (*the burden of the people*) *with you.* Since they will also be established (accepted) as prophets, the people will trust your leadership when they see that the elders are with you and concur in your actions.

20. וְהָיָה לָכֶם לְזָרָא — *And it shall be loathsome to you.* For you will eat of it until the excess will cause sickness, as (the verse) testifies, וּבַחוּרֵי יִשְׂרָאֵל הִכְרִיעַ, *And the young men of Israel He bent over* (*Psalms* 78:31) — (i.e., in pain).

לָמָּה זֶּה יָצָאנוּ מִמִּצְרָיִם — *Why is this that we came forth from Egypt?* For there we had a variety of many foods, not only the manna.

21. שֵׁשׁ מֵאוֹת אֶלֶף רַגְלִי — *Six hundred thousand men on foot.* And much meat will be necessary to satisfy them.

וְאַתָּה אָמַרְתָּ בָּשָׂר אֶתֵּן לָהֶם וְאָכְלוּ חֹדֶשׁ יָמִים — *And yet You have said, I will give them meat that they may eat a whole month.* And therefore, the meat you give them must be of a very large amount as it says, וַיַּמְטֵר עֲלֵיהֶם כֶּעָפָר שְׁאֵר וּכְחוֹל יַמִּים עוֹף כָּנָף, *He rained upon*

NOTES

flow of God's blessing of leadership qualities to Moses, similar to the weaker strength of a female as compared to a male. Moses is convinced that this is also due to his shortcoming, and the only reason God does not appoint others to augment — or even replace — his leadership is because of God's concern for his (Moses') honor. Hence, he pleads with God not to deprive Israel of strong leadership, even if it means that he will be removed before his time — as was the prophet Samuel.

22. הֲצֹאן וּבָקָר יִשָּׁחֵט לָהֶם וּמָצָא לָהֶם — *If flocks and herds are slain for them, will they suffice for them?* Moses does not understand how Israel will be cured of their lustful desires unless God removes their desire and appetite, thereby denying them freedom

16 *HASHEM said to Moses, "Gather to Me seventy men from the elders of
Israel, whom you know to be the elders of the people and its officers; take
them to the Tent of Meeting and have them stand there with you.*
17 *I will
descend and speak with you there, and I will increase some of the spirit
that is upon you and place it upon them, and they shall bear the burden of
the people with you, and you shall not bear alone.*
18 *"To the people you shall say, 'Prepare yourselves for tomorrow and
you shall eat meat, for you have wept in the ears of HASHEM, saying: Who
will feed us meat? for it was better for us in Egypt! So HASHEM will give you
meat and you will eat.*
19 *Not for one day shall you eat, nor two days, nor
five days, nor ten days, and nor twenty days.*
20 *Until an entire month of
days, until it comes out of your nose, and becomes nauseating to you,
because you have rejected HASHEM Who is in your midst, and you have
wept before Him, saying: Why did we leave Egypt?' "*
21 *Moses said, "Six hundred thousand footmen are the people in whose
midst I am, yet You say I shall give them meat, and they shall eat for a
month of days!*
22 *Can sheep and cattle be slaughtered for them and suffice
for them? Or if all the fish of the sea will be gathered for them, would it
suffice for them?"*
23 *HASHEM said to Moses, "Is the hand of HASHEM limited? Now you will
see whether My word comes to pass or not!"*
24 *Moses left and spoke the words of HASHEM to the people; and he*

---

them meat like dust, and winged birds like the sands of the seas (*Psalms* 78:27); (still) nonetheless . . .

22. הַצֹּאן וּבָקָר יִשָּׁחֵט לָהֶם וּמָצָא לָהֶם — *If flocks and herds are slain for them, will they suffice for them?* How will this suffice to remove their complaints since they are only requesting meat in order to test (God), as it says, וַיְנַסּוּ אֵל בִּלְבָבָם, *And they tested God in their hearts* (*Psalms* 78:18)? Surely, without a doubt, just as they tested (You) with this (request), so they will test (You) with (requests for) other food without end — and You will not remove their free will, as (our Sages) say, הַכֹּל בִּידֵי שָׁמַיִם חוּץ מִיִּרְאַת שָׁמָיִם, *Everything is in the hands of Heaven except the fear of Heaven* (*Berachos* 33b).

23. הֲיַד ה׳ תִּקְצָר — *Will the hand of HASHEM be too short?*. . . to find a way by which they (themselves) will find all lustful food abhorrent, as it says *until it come out of your nostrils* (v. 20).

עַתָּה תִרְאֶה הֲיִקְרְךָ דְבָרִי אִם לֹא — *Now you shall see whether My word shall come to pass or not.* You will see this happen, that they will eat the meat motivated by their desire for pleasure until it comes out of their nostrils, and (then) they will reject it — (all this) without My removing their free will at all; for indeed (then) they will be able to repent out of love and fear if they so desire, as it says, יָדַעְתִּי כִּי כֹל תּוּכָל וְלֹא יִבָּצֵר מִמְּךָ מְזִמָּה, *I know that You can do everything and that no purpose of Yours can be thwarted* (*Job* 42:2).

NOTES

of will and choice — something He would never do. Hence, how will this failing of Israel be resolved? Certainly not by indulging them, for that will only encourage them to make more demands.

23. הֲיַד ה׳ תִּקְצָר עַתָּה תִרְאֶה הֲיִקְרְךָ דְבָרִי אִם לֹא — *Will the hand of HASHEM be too short? Now you shall see whether My word shall come to pass or not.* God reassures Moses that they themselves, of their own free will, will overindulge to the point of disgust with their own satiety and this will cure them of their lustful desires for a variety of foods other than the manna. When this occurs they will repent their evil ways.

כה שִׁבְעִים אִישׁ מִזִּקְנֵי הָעָם וַיַּעֲמֵד אֹתָם סְבִיבֹת הָאֹהֶל: וַיֵּרֶד יְהוָה ׀ בֶּעָנָן
וַיְדַבֵּר אֵלָיו וַיָּאצֶל מִן־הָרוּחַ אֲשֶׁר עָלָיו וַיִּתֵּן עַל־שִׁבְעִים אִישׁ הַזְּקֵנִים
כו וַיְהִי כְּנוֹחַ עֲלֵיהֶם הָרוּחַ וַיִּתְנַבְּאוּ וְלֹא יָסָפוּ: וַיִּשָּׁאֲרוּ שְׁנֵי־אֲנָשִׁים ׀
בַּמַּחֲנֶה שֵׁם הָאֶחָד ׀ אֶלְדָּד וְשֵׁם הַשֵּׁנִי מֵידָד וַתָּנַח עֲלֵהֶם הָרוּחַ וְהֵמָּה
כז בַּכְּתֻבִים וְלֹא יָצְאוּ הָאֹהֱלָה וַיִּתְנַבְּאוּ בַּמַּחֲנֶה: וַיָּרָץ הַנַּעַר וַיַּגֵּד לְמֹשֶׁה
כח וַיֹּאמַר אֶלְדָּד וּמֵידָד מִתְנַבְּאִים בַּמַּחֲנֶה: וַיַּעַן יְהוֹשֻׁעַ בִּן־נוּן מְשָׁרֵת
כט מֹשֶׁה מִבְּחֻרָיו וַיֹּאמַר אֲדֹנִי מֹשֶׁה כְּלָאֵם: וַיֹּאמֶר לוֹ מֹשֶׁה הַמְקַנֵּא אַתָּה
ל (שביעי) לִי וּמִי יִתֵּן כָּל־עַם יְהוָה נְבִיאִים כִּי־יִתֵּן יְהוָה אֶת־רוּחוֹ עֲלֵיהֶם: וַיֵּאָסֵף
לא מֹשֶׁה אֶל־הַמַּחֲנֶה הוּא וְזִקְנֵי יִשְׂרָאֵל: וְרוּחַ נָסַע ׀ מֵאֵת יְהוָה וַיָּגָז שַׂלְוִים
מִן־הַיָּם וַיִּטֹּשׁ עַל־הַמַּחֲנֶה כְּדֶרֶךְ יוֹם כֹּה וּכְדֶרֶךְ יוֹם כֹּה סְבִיבוֹת הַמַּחֲנֶה
לב וּכְאַמָּתַיִם עַל־פְּנֵי הָאָרֶץ: וַיָּקָם הָעָם כָּל־הַיּוֹם הַהוּא וְכָל־הַלַּיְלָה וְכֹל ׀
יוֹם הַמָּחֳרָת וַיַּאַסְפוּ אֶת־הַשְּׂלָו הַמַּמְעִיט אָסַף עֲשָׂרָה חֳמָרִים וַיִּשְׁטְחוּ
לג לָהֶם שָׁטוֹחַ סְבִיבוֹת הַמַּחֲנֶה: הַבָּשָׂר עוֹדֶנּוּ בֵּין שִׁנֵּיהֶם טֶרֶם יִכָּרֵת וְאַף
לד יְהוָה חָרָה בָעָם וַיַּךְ יְהוָה בָּעָם מַכָּה רַבָּה מְאֹד: וַיִּקְרָא אֶת־שֵׁם־הַמָּקוֹם
לה הַהוּא קִבְרוֹת הַתַּאֲוָה כִּי־שָׁם קָבְרוּ אֶת־הָעָם הַמִּתְאַוִּים: מִקִּבְרוֹת
הַתַּאֲוָה נָסְעוּ הָעָם חֲצֵרוֹת וַיִּהְיוּ בַּחֲצֵרוֹת:

---

28. אֲדֹנִי מֹשֶׁה כְּלָאֵם — *My master Moses, shut them in* . . . for he (Joshua) thought that the (reason) they did not present themselves at the Tent was to show that they could prophesize without accepting the spirit of Moses our Teacher (upon themselves).

29. כִּי יִתֵּן ה׳ אֶת רוּחוֹ עֲלֵיהֶם — *That HASHEM would put His spirit upon them* . . . without receiving the spirit through me.

31. מִן הַיָּם — *From the sea* . . . from the (direction) of the Sea of Reeds which was southward from their location. And this (was so) because the quails passed over the sea from the southern extremity (i.e., direction).

32. הַמַּמְעִיט אָסַף עֲשָׂרָה חֳמָרִים — *He that gathered least gathered ten heaps* . . . for they were all desirous to eat a large amount of them.

33. הַבָּשָׂר עוֹדֶנּוּ בֵּין שִׁנֵּיהֶם — *While the meat was yet between their teeth.* (And) they had as yet not reached the limit where they would reject it.

טֶרֶם יִכָּרֵת — *Before it was cut off* . . . for the time of a full month, which was set by God (v. 20), had not yet been reached.

וַיַּךְ ה׳ בָּעָם — *And HASHEM smote the people* . . . (referring to) those who lusted, who had

NOTES

28-29. אֲדֹנִי מֹשֶׁה כְּלָאֵם . . . כִּי יִתֵּן ה׳ אֶת רוּחוֹ עֲלֵיהֶם — *My master Moses, shut them in . . . that HASHEM would put His spirit upon them.* Joshua is jealous for Moses' honor and feels that Eldad and Medad were arrogant in not presenting themselves to Moses at the Tent, as though to declare that the spirit of prophecy could rest on them without the intervention and assistance of Moses. However, Moses dismisses the complaint of Joshua and expresses his hope that God would rest His spirit directly upon all who are worthy to receive the spirit of prophecy, without need for any mediator.

31. מִן הַיָּם — *From the sea.* The term יָם, when used to denote direction, always means west, since the sea lies westward of *Eretz Yisrael.* In this case, however, the *Sforno* explains that it refers to the Sea of Reeds (not the Mediterranean) which lies to the south, since these quails breed in the south.

33. וַיַּךְ ה׳ בָּעָם — *And HASHEM smote the people.* The *Sforno* explains that there were two groupings and each was punished in a different manner. One consisted of those who demanded meat because

gathered seventy men from among the elders of the people and had them stand around the Tent.

[25] *HASHEM descended in a cloud and spoke to him, and He increased some of the spirit that was upon him and gave it to the seventy men, the elders; when the spirit rested upon them, they prophesied, but did not do so again.*

[26] *Two men remained behind in the camp, the name of one was Eldad and the name of the second was Medad, and the spirit rested upon them; they had been among the recorded ones, but they had not gone out to the Tent, and they prophesied in the camp.* [27] *The youth ran and told Moses, and he said, "Eldad and Medad are prophesying in the camp."*

[28] *Joshua son of Nun, the servant of Moses since his youth, spoke up and said, "My lord Moses, incarcerate them!"*

[29] *Moses said to him, "Are you being zealous for my sake? Would that the entire people of HASHEM could be prophets, if HASHEM would but place His spirit upon them!"*

[30] *Moses was brought into the camp, he and the elders of Israel.* [31] *A wind went forth from HASHEM and blew quail from the sea and spread them over the camp, a day's journey this way and a day's journey that way, all around the camp, and two cubits above the face of the earth.* [32] *The people rose up all that day and all the night and all the next day and gathered up the quail — the one with the least gathered in ten chomers — and they spread them out all around the camp.* [33] *The meat was still between their teeth, not yet chewed, when the wrath of HASHEM flared against the people, and HASHEM struck a very mighty blow against the people.* [34] *He named that place Kibroth-hattaavah, because there they buried the people who had been craving.*

[35] *From Kibroth-hattaavah the people journeyed to Hazeroth, and they remained in Hazeroth.*

---

asked for meat in order to test (God) and were afflicted (at once) through their testing — because the (time period) of *and they shall eat a whole month* was (only) said regarding those who cried, and did not lust (or test) but who said, *Why is this that we came forth from Egypt?* (v. 20). Now they (i.e., the criers) (eventually) cried in (their state) of illness, as it says, *and it shall be loathsome to you* (ibid.).

35. וַיִּהְיוּ בַּחֲצֵרוֹת — *And they stayed in Chazeros.* They remained there for a period of time, similar to, וַיִּהְיוּ שָׁם . . . כְּעֶשֶׂר שָׁנִים, *and remained there . . . about ten years* (*Ruth* 1:2, 4) (and) וַיִּהְיוּ שָׁם כַּאֲשֶׁר צִוַּנִי ה׳, *and remained there as HASHEM commanded me* (*Deut.* 10:5). (The Torah) states that at that time when they tarried there (in Chazeros), the (incident) of Miriam speaking against Moses occurred, and since the Tent of Meeting was then standing, God, the Blessed One, ordered them (i.e., Moses, Miriam and Aaron) to leave their tents and (present themselves) at the Tent of Meeting.

NOTES

they wanted to test God. They were smitten immediately as a punishment for their arrogant, blasphemous lack of faith. The other group consisted of those who wept and lamented at the thought of having left Egypt. They were punished at the end of a month when the meat of the quails came out of their nostrils and it became so loathsome to them that they fell ill, as God had promised (v. 20).

35. וַיִּהְיוּ בַּחֲצֵרוֹת — *And they stayed in Chazeros.* The *Sforno* understands this phrase as being an introduction to the following chapter, for the reason they stayed in Chazeros was because of the incident of Miriam (12:15,16).

יב
א וַתְּדַבֵּר מִרְיָם וְאַהֲרֹן בְּמֹשֶׁה עַל־אֹדוֹת הָאִשָּׁה הַכֻּשִׁית אֲשֶׁר לָקָח
ב כִּי־אִשָּׁה כֻשִׁית לָקָח׃ וַיֹּאמְרוּ הֲרַק אַךְ־בְּמֹשֶׁה דִּבֶּר יהוה הֲלֹא גַּם־בָּנוּ
ג דִבֵּר וַיִּשְׁמַע יהוה׃ וְהָאִישׁ מֹשֶׁה עָנָו מְאֹד מִכֹּל הָאָדָם אֲשֶׁר עַל־פְּנֵי
ד הָאֲדָמָה׃ וַיֹּאמֶר יהוה פִּתְאֹם אֶל־מֹשֶׁה וְאֶל־אַהֲרֹן
ה וְאֶל־מִרְיָם צְאוּ שְׁלָשְׁתְּכֶם אֶל־אֹהֶל מוֹעֵד וַיֵּצְאוּ שְׁלָשְׁתָּם׃ וַיֵּרֶד יהוה
בְּעַמּוּד עָנָן וַיַּעֲמֹד פֶּתַח הָאֹהֶל וַיִּקְרָא אַהֲרֹן וּמִרְיָם וַיֵּצְאוּ שְׁנֵיהֶם׃
ו וַיֹּאמֶר שִׁמְעוּ־נָא דְבָרָי אִם־יִהְיֶה נְבִיאֲכֶם יהוה בַּמַּרְאָה אֵלָיו אֶתְוַדָּע
ז־ח בַּחֲלוֹם אֲדַבֶּר־בּוֹ׃ לֹא־כֵן עַבְדִּי מֹשֶׁה בְּכָל־בֵּיתִי נֶאֱמָן הוּא׃ פֶּה
אֶל־פֶּה אֲדַבֶּר־בּוֹ וּמַרְאֶה וְלֹא בְחִידֹת וּתְמֻנַת יהוה יַבִּיט וּמַדּוּעַ לֹא

XII

2. הֲרַק אַךְ בְּמֹשֶׁה דִּבֶּר ה׳ — *Has* HASHEM *indeed spoken only to Moses?* Indeed, has Moses alone merited this (status), that the word of God is directed exclusively to him, in addition to the (gift of) prophecy which he merited together with the multitude of Israel at the giving of the Torah?

וַיִּשְׁמַע ה׳ — *And* HASHEM *heard it.* As (our Sages) say, "A rabbinical student is different, because the Holy One, Blessed is He, avenges his honor" (*Berachos* 19a).

4. צְאוּ שְׁלָשְׁתְּכֶם — *Go out, you three.* He wanted Moses to know the goodness of God, the Blessed One, Who was scrupulous regarding his (Moses') honor.

6. אִם יִהְיֶה נְבִיאֲכֶם — *If there be a prophet among you.* If Moses were a prophet on the level which you imagined when you said, *Has He not spoken also to us?* (v. 2) . . .

ה׳ בַּמַּרְאָה אֵלָיו אֶתְוַדָּע — *I,* HASHEM, *will make Myself known to him in a vision.* I would not make Myself known, or reveal Myself to him with this (particular) Divine Name, but (rather) in a vision (מַרְאָה, in the feminine form) — not in a waking state — as was the case with Isaiah when he said, וָאֶרְאֶה אֶת ה׳ יֹשֵׁב עַל כִּסֵּא רָם וְנִשָּׂא, *I saw* HASHEM *sitting upon a throne, high and exalted* (*Isaiah* 6:1), and also (in the case) of Michayahu (who said,) רָאִיתִי אֶת ה׳ יֹשֵׁב עַל כִּסְאוֹ, *I saw* HASHEM *sitting on His throne* (*I Kings* 22:19). (Now) all this was, without a doubt, in a prophetic vision and not in a waking state. (Regarding) Balaam also, even though the (Divine) Word came to him in a waking state, it was not

NOTES

XII

2. הֲרַק אַךְ בְּמֹשֶׁה דִּבֶּר ה׳ — *Has* HASHEM *indeed spoken only to Moses?* The words אַךְ and רַק both mean "only"; why then is it necessary to use here two terms of מִיעוּט, *limitation?* The *Sforno* explains that Miriam and Aaron were challenging the exclusive character of Moses' prophetic powers: Is he the "only" (רַק) one who has merited this level of prophecy? We have also reached this status (אַךְ), where God speaks to us "alone."

וַיִּשְׁמַע ה׳ — *And* HASHEM *heard it.* The Talmudic quote cited by the *Sforno* is meant to explain the significance of this expression. Certainly, God hears and knows all. Therefore, this phrase must mean that He reacted vigorously, defending the honor of Moses. This is in keeping with the statement of our Sages who tell us that if one makes a derogatory remark about a scholar after his death, God avenges his insult.

4. צְאוּ שְׁלָשְׁתְּכֶם — *Go out, you three.* The *Sforno* explains why all three were summoned since God only wanted to speak to Miriam and Aaron.

6-8. . . . ה׳ בַּמַּרְאָה אֵלָיו אֶתְוַדָּע . . . לֹא כֵן עַבְדִּי מֹשֶׁה . . . פֶּה אֶל פֶּה אֲדַבֶּר בּוֹ וּמַרְאֶה וְלֹא בְחִידֹת וּתְמֻנַת ה׳ יַבִּיט וּמַדּוּעַ לֹא יְרֵאתֶם . . . — *I,* HASHEM, *will make Myself known to him in a vision . . . My servant Moses is not so . . . With him do I speak mouth to mouth in a manifest vision and not in riddles, and the similitude of* HASHEM *he beholds; wherefore then were you not afraid?* . . . The phrase מַרְאָה, *vision,* appears in verse 6 in the feminine form as opposed to מַרְאֶה, used in verse 8, which is the masculine form. The feminine form is a weaker one and denotes a certain deficiency. (See chapter 11:15, the *Sforno's* commentary there, as well as the notes.) Hence, the word מַרְאָה signifies a lesser kind of prophecy than that of מַרְאֶה. There is also a profound difference whether God communicates with a prophet

12 [1] *Miriam and Aaron spoke against Moses regarding the Cushite woman he had married, for he had married a Cushite woman.* [2] *They said, "Was it only to Moses that* HASHEM *spoke? Did He not speak to us, as well?" And* HASHEM *heard.* [3] *Now the man Moses was exceedingly humble, more than any person on the face of the earth!*

[4] HASHEM *said suddenly to Moses, to Aaron, and to Miriam, "You three, go out to the Tent of Meeting." And the three of them went out.* [5] HASHEM *descended in a pillar of cloud and stood at the entrance to the Tent, and He summoned Aaron and Miriam; the two of them went out.* [6] *He said, "Hear now My words. If there shall be prophets among you, in a vision shall I,* HASHEM, *make Myself known to him; in a dream shall I speak with him.* [7] *Not so is My servant Moses; in My entire house he is the trusted one.* [8] *Mouth to mouth do I speak to him, in a clear vision and not in riddles, at the image of* HASHEM *does he gaze. Why did you not*

---

through the special Name (i.e., the Tetragrammaton), as he thought when he said, *Perhaps* HASHEM *will come to meet me* (23:3), for indeed, this was never accomplished, but it says regarding him, *and God met Balaam* (23:4).

7. לֹא כֵן עַבְדִּי מֹשֶׁה — *My servant Moses is not so.* The (Divine) Word to him is through the special Name (the Tetragrammaton) in a waking state. (Now) this he explains, saying . . .

8. פֶּה אֶל פֶּה אֲדַבֶּר בּוֹ — *With him do I speak mouth to mouth.* His prophecy is without the dulling (lit., the slumbering) of his senses.

וּמַרְאֶה — *In a manifest vision . . .* (written) in the masculine form, which our Sages called אַסְפַּקְלַרְיָה הַמְּאִירָה, *a transparent glass* (*Yevamos* 49b).

וְלֹא בְחִידֹת — *And not in riddles.* (Moses perceived) the (Divine) Word clearly defined without a riddle, unlike Zechariah and other (prophets) who saw riddles and (of Zechariah it is related) parables, and the angel said to him, הֲלוֹא יָדַעְתָּ מָה הֵמָּה אֵלֶּה וָאֹמַר לֹא אֲדֹנִי, *Do you not know what these are? And I said, "No, my Lord"* (*Zechariah* 4:5), and the angel had to explain the parable to him. And there were (prophets) among them who saw the parables and did understand them, similar to, הֵיטַבְתָּ לִרְאוֹת, *You have seen well* (*Jeremiah* 1:12), and Balaam (of whom) it says, *and he took up his parable*, because first he told the parable he had seen and later he explained it.

וּתְמֻנַת ה׳ יַבִּיט — *And the similitude of* HASHEM *he beholds.* And all this he grasps through God's revelation to him with the special Name, unlike Balaam who only grasped (G-d's

NOTES

through His particular Name (שֵׁם הֲוָיָ׳ — the Tetragrammaton) or through the Name of אֱלֹהִים (God). Finally, save for a number of exceptions, God speaks to his prophets in visions and parables when the prophet is not in a waking state and in command of his senses; nor is he always capable of grasping the meaning of the parable revealed to him. The exception to these rules was Moses with whom God spoke *mouth to mouth*, i.e., while Moses was in total command of his senses — in a waking state, and *not in riddles*, i.e., it was a sharp, clear and defined communication. Also, the word of God always came to Moses through the particular Name of the Tetragrammaton (שֵׁם הֲוָיָ׳) which denotes a special relationship between the Almighty and the prophet. Even Balaam (whom our Sages compare partially to Moses) who was privileged to hear the Word of God in a waking state never reached the level of receiving prophecy through the particular special Name of God, nor in the form of a מַרְאֶה (in the masculine form), which our Sages explain to mean as the clarity of a transparent glass (אַסְפַּקְלַרְיָה הַמְּאִירָה). Also, all Balaam's prophecies were through the medium of a מָשָׁל, *parable*. Only Moses merited clarity of vision, communication with God in a waking state and the privilege of revelation through His special Name. This is the sense of the *Sforno's* commentary on verses 6, 7 and 8. (See the *Sforno's* commentary on *Exodus* 19:9 and the notes.)

ט־י יְרֵאתֶם לְדַבֵּר בְּעַבְדִּי בְמֹשֶׁה: וַיִּחַר־אַף יהוה בָּם וַיֵּלַךְ: וְהֶעָנָן סָר מֵעַל
הָאֹהֶל וְהִנֵּה מִרְיָם מְצֹרַעַת כַּשָּׁלֶג וַיִּפֶן אַהֲרֹן אֶל־מִרְיָם וְהִנֵּה מְצֹרָעַת:
יא וַיֹּאמֶר אַהֲרֹן אֶל־מֹשֶׁה בִּי אֲדֹנִי אַל־נָא תָשֵׁת עָלֵינוּ חַטָּאת אֲשֶׁר
יב נוֹאַלְנוּ וַאֲשֶׁר חָטָאנוּ: אַל־נָא תְהִי כַּמֵּת אֲשֶׁר בְּצֵאתוֹ מֵרֶחֶם אִמּוֹ
יג וַיֵּאָכֵל חֲצִי בְשָׂרוֹ: וַיִּצְעַק מֹשֶׁה אֶל־יהוה לֵאמֹר אֵל נָא רְפָא נָא לָהּ:
מפטיר יד וַיֹּאמֶר יהוה אֶל־מֹשֶׁה וְאָבִיהָ יָרֹק יָרַק בְּפָנֶיהָ הֲלֹא תִכָּלֵם שִׁבְעַת יָמִים
טו תִּסָּגֵר שִׁבְעַת יָמִים מִחוּץ לַמַּחֲנֶה וְאַחַר תֵּאָסֵף: וַתִּסָּגֵר מִרְיָם מִחוּץ
טז לַמַּחֲנֶה שִׁבְעַת יָמִים וְהָעָם לֹא נָסַע עַד הֵאָסֵף מִרְיָם: וְאַחַר נָסְעוּ הָעָם
מֵחֲצֵרוֹת וַיַּחֲנוּ בְּמִדְבַּר פָּארָן:

message) through the (medium) of the parable and his perception was only through the name of "Elohim," not the special Name (the Tetragrammaton).

וּמַדּוּעַ לֹא יְרֵאתֶם — *Wherefore then were you not afraid?* It is therefore inescapable that this can only be (attributed) to the evil of the heart, for if you (truly) thought (i.e., understood) that I am cognizant of his deeds, then you (must have) thought that I was in error and I desire evil men, which is the opposite of what you should have thought, because I would never have granted him this exalted (position) were he not worthy. Therefore, you should have been afraid to speak thus against such a man. And if perhaps you thought that I (really) am not cognizant of his actions and that you know him better than I do and that I (incorrectly) thought he is worthy of this (status) and (in reality) he is not, then all the more so do you consider God to be in error, (and) as (our Sages) say, "This (statement) is even worse than the previous one" (*Sifre*).

9. וַיִּחַר אַף ה׳ בָּם — *And the anger of HASHEM was kindled against them*... (because) they did not humble themselves immediately, as did David when he said to Nathan (the prophet), חָטָאתִי, *I have sinned* (*II Samuel* 12:13).

9-10. וַיֵּלַךְ... וְהֶעָנָן סָר — *And He departed*... *And the cloud was removed*... indicating, as it were, a distancing of the leper, so that they should send her outside the camp to shame her.

12. אַל נָא תְהִי כַּמֵּת אֲשֶׁר בְּצֵאתוֹ מֵרֶחֶם אִמּוֹ וַיֵּאָכֵל חֲצִי בְשָׂרוֹ — *Please do not be as a dead fetus of whom the flesh is half consumed when he comes out of his mother's womb.* Behold, when a dead fetus is delivered from his mother's womb in such a manner that half his flesh is consumed and impaired, even though it may appear that he becomes more complete through (his) birth by leaving (the womb) and entering a place of complete life, (as compared) to his previous (state) when he was in his mother's womb; nonetheless, (in a sense) he becomes more deficient since half his flesh is consumed through that birth. So,

NOTES

וּמַדּוּעַ לֹא יְרֵאתֶם — *Wherefore then were you not afraid?* The Almighty rebukes Miriam and Aaron for questioning either His judgement or His omniscience. "If I was aware of Moses' shortcomings," the Almighty argues, "then I had no right to designate him as the teacher and leader of Israel, and if I was not aware, then it means that I am not all-knowing, and that would be a far more serious accusation on your part." (See *Rashi's* commentary on this verse.)

9. וַיִּחַר אַף ה׳ בָּם — *And the anger of HASHEM was kindled against them.* The *Sforno* interprets God's anger as being precipitated by a new action — or inaction — on the part of Miriam and Aaron *following* His words of admonition and rebuke. He therefore explains that this anger was evoked through their failure to humble themselves promptly, as David did when he was admonished for his transgression.

12. אַל נָא תְהִי כַּמֵּת אֲשֶׁר בְּצֵאתוֹ מֵרֶחֶם אִמּוֹ וַיֵּאָכֵל חֲצִי בְשָׂרוֹ — *Please do not be as a dead fetus of whom the flesh is half consumed when he comes out of his mother's womb.* To understand the *Sforno's* commentary on this verse, one must preface it with *Rashi's* explanation. A brother and sister are considered as one flesh. If Moses will not intervene to

fear to speak against My servant Moses?"

9 *The wrath of* HASHEM *flared up against them, and He left.*

10 *The cloud had departed from atop the Tent, and behold! Miriam was afflicted with tzaraas, like snow! Aaron turned to Miriam and behold! she was afflicted with tzaraas.*

11 *Aaron said to Moses, "I beg you, my lord, do not cast a sin upon us, for we have been foolish and we have sinned.* 12 *Let her not be like a corpse, like one who leaves his mother's womb with half his flesh having been consumed!"*

13 *Moses cried out to* HASHEM*, saying, "Please,* HASHEM*, heal her now."*

14 HASHEM *said to Moses, "Were her father to spit in her face, would she not be humiliated for seven days? Let her be quarantined outside the camp for seven days, and then she may be brought in."* 15 *So Miriam was quarantined outside the camp for seven days, and the people did not journey until Miriam was brought in.* 16 *Then the people journeyed from Hazeroth, and they encamped in the Wilderness of Paran.*

---

you who will leave this wilderness and enter the Chosen Land, thereby (establishing) a better dwelling place for yourself, (still) I pray you, do not be as that dead (fetus) by leaving over half your flesh in the wilderness.

13. אֵל נָא רְפָא נָא לָהּ — *Heal her now, O God, I beseech You.* Please, I ask (of You), cure her now so that we will not have to shame her by sending her outside the camp.

14. הֲלֹא תִכָּלֵם — *She would be shamed.* She is worthy to (suffer) this shame.

15. וְהָעָם לֹא נָסַע — *And the people did not journey.* Even though the cloud was removed from above the Tent, and it is written, וּבְהֵעָלוֹת הֶעָנָן מֵעַל הַמִּשְׁכָּן יִסְעוּ בְּנֵי יִשְׂרָאֵל בְּכֹל מַסְעֵיהֶם, *And whenever the cloud went up from above the Sanctuary the Children of Israel traveled throughout all their journeys* (*Exodus* 40:36), nonetheless (at that time) they did not journey, for they realized that (the cloud) went up then only (in order) to distance the leper (i.e., Miriam).

16. וַיַּחֲנוּ בְּמִדְבַּר פָּארָן — *And they encamped in the wilderness of Paran* . . . in a place in the wilderness which had no name at all but was across from and close to Kadesh Barnea, in order to arrange their affairs so as to enter therein, for this was the first city of *Eretz Yisrael* which they encountered on that road as (the Torah) attests, saying, וַנָּבֹא עַד קָדֵשׁ בַּרְנֵעַ וָאֹמַר אֲלֵכֶם בָּאתֶם עַד הַר הָאֱמֹרִי אֲשֶׁר ה׳ אֱלֹהֵינוּ נֹתֵן לָנוּ . . . עֲלֵה רֵשׁ וכו׳, *And we came to Kadesh Barnea, and I said to you, "You have come to the hill country of the Emorites, which* HASHEM *our God gives to us . . . go up, take possession"* (*Deut.* 19-21). And that place was called "Rismah," as explained in *Maasei* (33:18).

NOTES

help his afflicted sister Miriam, then he will be affected as well, for it will be as though half of his own flesh is consumed. The *Sforno*, however, adds a new and different interpretation to the meaning of רֶחֶם, *womb*. He considers it symbolic of the wilderness in which Israel (and Moses) now find themselves. Leaving the wilderness and entering the Land of Israel is comparable to the fetus leaving the mother's womb and entering the real world. However, if Miriam will not be healed and perforce remain behind, then it would be like a dead fetus whose flesh is consumed in the process of birth, for Moses would be leaving part of himself (as a brother) behind in the process of Israel's "birth" — i.e., their departure from the wilderness and entry into the Promised Land.

15. וְהָעָם לֹא נָסַע — *And the people did not journey.* In verse 10, the *Sforno* explained that the removal of the cloud, which represents the Divine Glory of God, was an indication that Miriam was to leave the camp of Israel for a period of time. Although normally the removal of the cloud was a signal to journey, in this case it was only meant to indicate that the leper (Miriam) be distanced from the camp, as the *Sforno* explains.

פרשת שלח

יג א־ב וַיְדַבֵּר יְהוָה אֶל־מֹשֶׁה לֵּאמֹר: שְׁלַח־לְךָ אֲנָשִׁים וְיָתֻרוּ אֶת־אֶרֶץ כְּנַעַן
אֲשֶׁר־אֲנִי נֹתֵן לִבְנֵי יִשְׂרָאֵל אִישׁ אֶחָד אִישׁ אֶחָד לְמַטֵּה אֲבֹתָיו תִּשְׁלָחוּ
ג כֹּל נָשִׂיא בָהֶם: וַיִּשְׁלַח אֹתָם מֹשֶׁה מִמִּדְבַּר פָּארָן עַל־פִּי יְהוָה כֻּלָּם
ד אֲנָשִׁים רָאשֵׁי בְנֵי־יִשְׂרָאֵל הֵמָּה: וְאֵלֶּה שְׁמוֹתָם לְמַטֵּה רְאוּבֵן שַׁמּוּעַ
ה־ו בֶּן־זַכּוּר: לְמַטֵּה שִׁמְעוֹן שָׁפָט בֶּן־חוֹרִי: לְמַטֵּה יְהוּדָה כָּלֵב בֶּן־יְפֻנֶּה:
ז־ט לְמַטֵּה יִשָּׂשכָר יִגְאָל בֶּן־יוֹסֵף: לְמַטֵּה אֶפְרָיִם הוֹשֵׁעַ בִּן־נוּן: לְמַטֵּה בִנְיָמִן
י־יא פַּלְטִי בֶּן־רָפוּא: לְמַטֵּה זְבוּלֻן גַּדִּיאֵל בֶּן־סוֹדִי: לְמַטֵּה יוֹסֵף לְמַטֵּה מְנַשֶּׁה
יב־יג גַּדִּי בֶּן־סוּסִי: לְמַטֵּה דָן עַמִּיאֵל בֶּן־גְּמַלִּי: לְמַטֵּה אָשֵׁר סְתוּר בֶּן־מִיכָאֵל:
יד־טז לְמַטֵּה נַפְתָּלִי נַחְבִּי בֶּן־וָפְסִי: לְמַטֵּה גָד גְּאוּאֵל בֶּן־מָכִי: אֵלֶּה שְׁמוֹת
הָאֲנָשִׁים אֲשֶׁר־שָׁלַח מֹשֶׁה לָתוּר אֶת־הָאָרֶץ וַיִּקְרָא מֹשֶׁה לְהוֹשֵׁעַ
יז בִּן־נוּן יְהוֹשֻׁעַ: וַיִּשְׁלַח אֹתָם מֹשֶׁה לָתוּר אֶת־אֶרֶץ כְּנָעַן וַיֹּאמֶר אֲלֵהֶם

XIII

2. שְׁלַח לְךָ אֲנָשִׁים — *Send out men for yourself.* Do not permit them to send (men of their own choice), which they intended to do when they said, נִשְׁלְחָה אֲנָשִׁים לְפָנֵינוּ, *we would send men before us* (*Deut.* 1:22), lest they send common men who will not appreciate how praiseworthy the Land is and will disparage it in such a manner that Israel will think that God has misled (them), and (therefore) they will not repent, as they (partially) did, (however) later when they said, חָטָאנוּ לַה׳, *We have sinned against* HASHEM (*Deut.* 1:41). Now, the spies whom Moses sent, although they acted wickedly in turning away the heart of the people due to their (own) lack of faith in Almighty God, nonetheless, they recognized and related the goodness of the Land when they said, *and it is also a (land) which flows with milk and honey* (13:27), which (the Torah) attests (to) saying, וַיִּקְחוּ בְיָדָם מִפְּרִי הָאָרֶץ . . . וַיֹּאמְרוּ טוֹבָה הָאָרֶץ, *And they took in their hands from the fruit of the Land . . . and they said, "The Land is good"* (*Deut.* 1:25) — but they (also) said that it was impossible to conquer. And when Israel realized their sin in not trusting the salvation of God, the Exalted One, and His (ability to be) victorious after having (performed) such wonders for them, they repented and said, חָטָאנוּ לַה׳ אֲנַחְנוּ נַעֲלֶה וְנִלְחַמְנוּ, *We have sinned against* HASHEM, *we will go up and do battle* (*Deut.* 1:41), and they prayed (to Him) as it says, וַתָּשֻׁבוּ וַתִּבְכּוּ לִפְנֵי ה׳, *You returned and wept before* HASHEM (ibid. verse 45); however, God, the Blessed One, did not accept their prayers because of the desecration of God's Name which they committed, (a transgression) which cannot be atoned for except

NOTES

XIII

2. שְׁלַח לְךָ אֲנָשִׁים — *Send out men for yourself.* The question as to whether Moses was agreeable to sending the spies, and whether God gave His approval, is one that *Rashi* addresses both here and in the Book of *Deuteronomy* (1:22,23). The *Sforno* is of the opinion that God advised Moses to send men of his own choosing who would appreciate the qualities of the Land of Israel. And indeed, they did — for with all their criticism and ambivalence, they did not fail to praise the Land and its fruits. Thanks to this measure of honesty, the Children of Israel eventually repented. Now, we have been taught that there is nothing which stands in the way of repentance. Nonetheless, God did not accept the repentance of Israel following the sin of the spies. The *Sforno* offers two reasons for this exception to the rule. One is, that only death can atone for the sin of חִלּוּל הַשֵּׁם, *the desecration of God's Name*, which this rejection of the Land of Israel and of God's powers reflected. Secondly, as the *Sforno* explained more fully in *Exodus* 32:34, the sin of the spies preceded by that of the Golden Calf represents an established pattern of habitual transgression; repentance in such a case is of no avail, for "when a man transgresses and repeats his offense it becomes as if it were permitted to him" (*Yoma* 86b). The *Sforno* in *Deut.* 1:45 gives an

PARASHAS SHELACH

17 [1] HASHEM spoke to Moses, saying, [2] "Send forth men, if you please, and let them spy out the Land of Canaan that I give to the Children of Israel; one man each from his father's tribe shall you send, every one a leader among them." [3] Moses sent them forth from the Wilderness of Paran at HASHEM's command; they were all distinguished men; heads of the Children of Israel were they.

[4] These are their names: For the tribe of Reuben, Shammua son of Zaccur. [5] For the tribe of Simeon, Shaphat son of Hori. [6] For the tribe of Judah, Caleb son of Jephunneh. [7] For the tribe of Issachar, Yigal son of Joseph. [8] For the tribe of Ephraim, Hoshea son of Nun. [9] For the tribe of Benjamin, Palti son of Raphu. [10] For the tribe of Zebulun, Gaddiel son of Sodi. [11] For the tribe of Joseph for the tribe of Manasseh, Gaddi son of Susi. [12] For the tribe of Dan, Ammiel son of Gemalli. [13] For the tribe of Asher, Sethur son of Michael. [14] For the tribe of Naphtali, Nahbi son of Vophsi. [15] For the tribe of Gad, Geuel son of Machi.

[16] These are the names of the men whom Moses sent to spy out the Land. Moses called Hoshea son of Nun "Joshua."

[17] Moses sent them to spy out the Land of Canaan, and he said to them,

---

through death, similar to that which the Torah attests to, saying, וּבְיוֹם פָּקְדִי וּפָקַדְתִּי עֲלֵהֶם חַטָּאתָם, *In the day when I visit, I will visit their sin upon them* (*Exodus* 32:34).

כֹּל נָשִׂיא בָהֶם — *Each a prince among them* ... those who were the most outstanding in their (respective) tribes, (so as) to (be able to) recognize the quality of the Land.

3. כֻּלָּם אֲנָשִׁים — *They were, all of them, men* ... men of strength, similar to הֲלוֹא אִישׁ אַתָּה, *Are you not a valiant man* (*I Samuel* 26:15), and also וְחָזַקְתָּ וְהָיִיתָ לְאִישׁ, *Be strong and show yourself a man* (*I Kings* 2:2).

4. וְאֵלֶּה שְׁמוֹתָם — *And these were their names.* They were all men of importance, each a man whose name (reflected) his elevated role. (The Torah) mentions them according to their age and not according to the order of the tribes nor the order of the flags, because at that time they were all equal in stature, particularly insofar as the nature of the assignment was concerned.

16. וַיִּקְרָא מֹשֶׁה לְהוֹשֵׁעַ בִּן נוּן יְהוֹשֻׁעַ — *And Moses called Hoshea the son of Nun "Joshua."* (The verse) states that he was known in his tribe as a man of strength by the name Hoshea (הוֹשֵׁעַ). (Now) the (reason) he is called (by the name) Joshua (יְהוֹשֻׁעַ) above (11:28) is because Moses our Teacher called him thus as (a mark) of honor, and (also) to pray for him that he be saved (from the plot of the spies) and that he should save others.

NOTES

additional reason for God's rejection of their repentance.

4. וְאֵלֶּה שְׁמוֹתָם — *And these were their names.* The *Sforno* disagrees with the *Ramban* who states that they are listed according to their superior qualities of wisdom and leadership. As the *Sforno* says, they were all equal in importance, hence the order must be according to age.

16. וַיִּקְרָא מֹשֶׁה לְהוֹשֵׁעַ בִּן נוּן יְהוֹשֻׁעַ — *And Moses called Hoshea the son of Nun "Joshua."* The name Joshua was not initially given to Hoshea now for we find this name used above in chapter 11:28. Still, the Torah tells us here that his name was Hoshea. The *Sforno* explains that within his tribe (Ephraim) he was called Hoshea. Moses, however, added the letter *yud*, for two reasons. Originally, it was meant as a mark of honor, and subsequently (as *Rashi* also explains) it served as a prayer that he be saved from the plot of the spies. Since the name יְהוֹשֻׁעַ is "*piel*" (the grammatical intensive form), the *Sforno* interprets it to mean that not only should *he* be saved, but he should also save others.

יח עֲלוּ זֶה בַּנֶּגֶב וַעֲלִיתֶם אֶת־הָהָר׃ וּרְאִיתֶם אֶת־הָאָרֶץ מַה־הִוא וְאֶת־הָעָם
יט הַיֹּשֵׁב עָלֶיהָ הֶחָזָק הוּא הֲרָפֶה הַמְעַט הוּא אִם־רָב׃ וּמָה הָאָרֶץ אֲשֶׁר־
הוּא יֹשֵׁב בָּהּ הֲטוֹבָה הִוא אִם־רָעָה וּמָה הֶעָרִים אֲשֶׁר־הוּא יוֹשֵׁב בָּהֵנָּה
כ הַבְּמַחֲנִים אִם בְּמִבְצָרִים׃ וּמָה הָאָרֶץ הַשְּׁמֵנָה הִוא אִם־רָזָה הֲיֵשׁ־בָּהּ עֵץ
אִם־אַיִן וְהִתְחַזַּקְתֶּם וּלְקַחְתֶּם מִפְּרִי הָאָרֶץ וְהַיָּמִים יְמֵי בִּכּוּרֵי עֲנָבִים׃
שני כא־כב וַיַּעֲלוּ וַיָּתֻרוּ אֶת־הָאָרֶץ מִמִּדְבַּר־צִן עַד־רְחֹב לְבֹא חֲמָת׃ וַיַּעֲלוּ בַנֶּגֶב
וַיָּבֹא עַד־חֶבְרוֹן וְשָׁם אֲחִימַן שֵׁשַׁי וְתַלְמַי יְלִידֵי הָעֲנָק וְחֶבְרוֹן שֶׁבַע
כג שָׁנִים נִבְנְתָה לִפְנֵי צֹעַן מִצְרָיִם׃ וַיָּבֹאוּ עַד־נַחַל אֶשְׁכֹּל וַיִּכְרְתוּ מִשָּׁם
זְמוֹרָה וְאֶשְׁכּוֹל עֲנָבִים אֶחָד וַיִּשָּׂאֻהוּ בַמּוֹט בִּשְׁנָיִם וּמִן־הָרִמֹּנִים וּמִן־
כד הַתְּאֵנִים׃ לַמָּקוֹם הַהוּא קָרָא נַחַל אֶשְׁכּוֹל עַל אֹדוֹת הָאֶשְׁכּוֹל אֲשֶׁר־
כה־כו כָּרְתוּ מִשָּׁם בְּנֵי יִשְׂרָאֵל׃ וַיָּשֻׁבוּ מִתּוּר הָאָרֶץ מִקֵּץ אַרְבָּעִים יוֹם׃ וַיֵּלְכוּ
וַיָּבֹאוּ אֶל־מֹשֶׁה וְאֶל־אַהֲרֹן וְאֶל־כָּל־עֲדַת בְּנֵי־יִשְׂרָאֵל אֶל־מִדְבַּר
פָּארָן קָדֵשָׁה וַיָּשִׁיבוּ אֹתָם דָּבָר וְאֶת־כָּל־הָעֵדָה וַיַּרְאוּם אֶת־פְּרִי הָאָרֶץ׃

---

17. עֲלוּ זֶה בַּנֶּגֶב — *Go up here in the south* ... from this side, where we are (located) presently, for you will find it good (easy) to enter (here), and there is no need for us to circle around to another place.

18. וּרְאִיתֶם אֶת הָאָרֶץ מַה הִוא — *And see the Land, what it is like* ... whether the Land is settled with many (fortified) as well as open cities.

וְאֶת הָעָם הַיֹּשֵׁב עָלֶיהָ — *And the people that dwell therein* ... to know (determine) if the living conditions are good, as the wise men of medicine have taught regarding the choice of residence, that one should observe the inhabitants of the Land as to whether they are strong, wholesome and healthy or the reverse. And one should also look to see if they are many or a few, for a great number of people and their well-being (lit., strength) indicates whether the climate and produce of the Land are good, while the opposite denotes the reverse.

19. הֲטוֹבָה הִוא — *Is it good* ... with plentiful, good water, as it says, כִּי ה׳ אֱלֹהֶיךָ מְבִיאֲךָ אֶל אֶרֶץ טוֹבָה אֶרֶץ נַחֲלֵי מָיִם, *For* HASHEM *your God is bringing you into a good land, a land full of brooks of water* (*Deut.* 8:7).

הַבְּמַחֲנִים — *Whether open cities* ... whether they dwell in open cities securely, with no fear of war.

אִם בְּמִבְצָרִים — *Or in fortified ones* ... (or) if they dwell in fortified cities because of fear of war, similar to, חָדְלוּ פְרָזוֹן בְּיִשְׂרָאֵל חָדֵלּוּ, *The inhabitants of open cities ceased* (*Judges* 5:7).

20. הַשְּׁמֵנָה הִוא — *Whether fat* ... with riches and possessions, as it says, אֲשֶׁר לֹא בְמִסְכֵּנֻת תֹּאכַל בָּהּ לֶחֶם, *In which you will not eat bread in parsimony* (*Deut.* 8:9).

NOTES

20. וְהִתְחַזַּקְתֶּם וּלְקַחְתֶּם מִפְּרִי הָאָרֶץ — *And take courage and take some of the fruit of the land.* The term חֲזָקָה means to perform an act for the purpose of taking possession, and by taking of the fruits, they performed such an act, this being the meaning of וְהִתְחַזַּקְתֶּם. Hence, the *Sforno* says that Moses had to encourage them not to be afraid since they were thereby acquiring the ownership of the Land, an act which normally would evoke strong opposition on the part of its inhabitants.

וְהַיָּמִים יְמֵי בִּכּוּרֵי עֲנָבִים — *And the time was the season of the ripening of the first grapes.* The *Sforno* explains why it is necessary for the Torah to tell us precisely the season of the year. Since they were instructed to bring back all the species of *Eretz Yisrael* which are cited as being exceptionally praiseworthy, there was an element of risk involved. When the grapes first ripen, the other fruits are not as yet ready. Still, Moses was confident that the people would recognize the superior

"Ascend here in the south and climb the mountain. [18] *See the Land — how is it? and the people that dwells in it — is it strong or weak? is it few or numerous?* [19] *And how is the Land in which it dwells — is it good or is it bad? And how are the cities in which it dwells — are they open or are they fortified?* [20] *And how is the land — is it fertile or is it lean? are there trees in it or not? You shall strengthen yourselves and take from the fruit of the Land." The days were the season of the first ripe grapes.*

[21] *They ascended and spied out the Land, from the Wilderness of Zin to the expanse at the approach to Hamath.* [22] *They ascended in the south and he arrived at Hebron, where there were Ahiman, Sheshai, and Talmai, the offspring of the giant. Hebron had been built seven years before Zoan of Egypt.* [23] *They arrived at the Valley of Eshcol and cut from there a vine with one cluster of grapes, and bore it on a double pole, and of the pomegranates and of the figs.* [24] *They named that place the Valley of Eshcol because of the cluster that the Children of Israel cut from there.*

[25] *They returned from spying out the Land at the end of forty days.* [26] *They went and came to Moses and to Aaron and to the entire assembly of the Children of Israel, to the Wilderness of Paran at Kadesh, and brought back the report to them and the entire assembly, and they showed them the fruit of the Land.*

הֲיֵשׁ בָּהּ עֵץ — *Are there trees there . . .* vines, figs and pomegranates, oil-producing olives and honey (from dates), (fruits) for which (the Land) was praised (see *Deut.* 8:8).

וְהִתְחַזַּקְתֶּם וּלְקַחְתֶּם מִפְּרִי הָאָרֶץ — *And take courage and take some of the fruit of the Land* . . . to take (legal) possession of it (i.e., the Land), and do not fear that they will consider you spies.

וְהַיָּמִים יְמֵי בִּכּוּרֵי עֲנָבִים — *And the time was the season of the ripening of the first grapes.* And although the fruit with which the Land was praised was not as yet fully ripened (lit., perfected), nonetheless, Moses our Teacher was confident that the size and taste of the fruit, even at that time, would suffice to attest to the goodness and praiseworthiness of the Land.

22. וַיָּבֹא עַד חֶבְרוֹן — *And he came to Hebron.* He (Caleb) alone (came) to seclude himself and pray at the graves of the Patriarchs (based on *Sotah* 34b).

24. עַל אֹדוֹת הָאֶשְׁכּוֹל אֲשֶׁר כָּרְתוּ מִשָּׁם בְּנֵי יִשְׂרָאֵל — *On account of the cluster of grapes which the Children of Israel cut down there.* The Canaanites were astonished that this grape cluster, which the Children of Israel cut, was considered by them to be so novel and wondrous, for there were many such clusters in the Land as large, or larger, than this (particular) one. To them, i.e., the Canaanites, the inhabitants of the land, this was nothing wondrous at all; hence their wonderment [resulted] in their calling the place *The brook of Eshkol.*

26. אֶל מִדְבַּר פָּארָן קָדֵשָׁה — *Unto the wilderness of Paran to Kadesh . . .* to that portion of the wilderness which was across from Kadesh Barnea.

NOTES

quality of these fruits even at an unripe stage.

22. וַיָּבֹא עַד חֶבְרוֹן — *And he came to Hebron.* This commentary of the *Sforno* is not found in many editions. Compare to *Rashi* here and to the *Sforno* on *Exodus* 3:1.

24. עַל אֹדוֹת הָאֶשְׁכּוֹל — *On account of the cluster of grapes.* The name נַחַל אֶשְׁכּוֹל, *the brook of the grape cluster,* was given by the Canaanites — not the Children of Israel.

26. אֶל מִדְבַּר פָּארָן קָדֵשָׁה — *Unto the wilderness of Paran to Kadesh.* See the commentary of the *Sforno* on chapter 12:16.

כז וַיְסַפְּרוּ־לוֹ וַיֹּאמְרוּ בָּאנוּ אֶל־הָאָרֶץ אֲשֶׁר שְׁלַחְתָּנוּ וְגַם זָבַת חָלָב וּדְבַשׁ
כח הִוא וְזֶה־פִּרְיָהּ: אֶפֶס כִּי־עַז הָעָם הַיֹּשֵׁב בָּאָרֶץ וְהֶעָרִים בְּצֻרוֹת גְּדֹלֹת
כט מְאֹד וְגַם־יְלִדֵי הָעֲנָק רָאִינוּ שָׁם: עֲמָלֵק יוֹשֵׁב בְּאֶרֶץ הַנֶּגֶב וְהַחִתִּי
ל וְהַיְבוּסִי וְהָאֱמֹרִי יוֹשֵׁב בָּהָר וְהַכְּנַעֲנִי יֹשֵׁב עַל־הַיָּם וְעַל יַד הַיַּרְדֵּן: וַיַּהַס*   *במסורה ס׳ רבתי
כָּלֵב אֶת־הָעָם אֶל־מֹשֶׁה וַיֹּאמֶר עָלֹה נַעֲלֶה וְיָרַשְׁנוּ אֹתָהּ כִּי־יָכוֹל
לא נוּכַל לָהּ: וְהָאֲנָשִׁים אֲשֶׁר־עָלוּ עִמּוֹ אָמְרוּ לֹא נוּכַל לַעֲלוֹת אֶל־הָעָם
לב כִּי־חָזָק הוּא מִמֶּנּוּ: וַיֹּצִיאוּ דִּבַּת הָאָרֶץ אֲשֶׁר תָּרוּ אֹתָהּ אֶל־בְּנֵי יִשְׂרָאֵל
לֵאמֹר הָאָרֶץ אֲשֶׁר עָבַרְנוּ בָהּ לָתוּר אֹתָהּ אֶרֶץ אֹכֶלֶת יוֹשְׁבֶיהָ הִוא
לג וְכָל־הָעָם אֲשֶׁר־רָאִינוּ בְתוֹכָהּ אַנְשֵׁי מִדּוֹת: וְשָׁם רָאִינוּ אֶת־הַנְּפִילִים
יד א בְּנֵי עֲנָק מִן־הַנְּפִלִים וַנְּהִי בְעֵינֵינוּ כַּחֲגָבִים וְכֵן הָיִינוּ בְּעֵינֵיהֶם: וַתִּשָּׂא
ב כָּל־הָעֵדָה וַיִּתְּנוּ אֶת־קוֹלָם וַיִּבְכּוּ הָעָם בַּלַּיְלָה הַהוּא: וַיִּלֹּנוּ עַל־מֹשֶׁה
וְעַל־אַהֲרֹן כֹּל בְּנֵי יִשְׂרָאֵל וַיֹּאמְרוּ אֲלֵהֶם כָּל־הָעֵדָה לוּ־מַתְנוּ בְּאֶרֶץ

---

27. וְגַם זָבַת חָלָב וּדְבַשׁ הִוא — *And indeed, it flows with milk and honey.* Not only is it *good* (see verse 19) but it also flows with milk and honey; i.e., it produces, without great effort, much cattle who give plentiful milk, and it produces much honey and royal delights (based on *Genesis* 49:20).

28. אֶפֶס כִּי עַז הָעָם — *But the people are too strong.* But it is impossible to conquer it because the people are fierce, and the cities are fortified, and the inhabitants of the Land are our enemies; the children of Amalek will also do battle against us so that we should not come nigh to their borders.

30. וַיַּהַס כָּלֵב אֶת הָעָם — *Then Caleb stilled the people.* He silenced the people who had already begun to lift up their voices, as (indeed) they later did — as it is said, *And the whole congregation lifted up their voice* (14:1).

אֶל מֹשֶׁה — *Toward Moses.* (He urged them) to listen to what Moses would answer. Perhaps it was then that Moses said what is attested to later when he said, וָאֹמַר אֲלֵכֶם לֹא תַעַרְצוּן וְלֹא תִירְאוּן מֵהֶם, *And I said to you: "Do not be dismayed and do not fear them"* (*Deut.* 1:29), and Caleb strengthened (supported) his words, by stating . . .

עָלֹה נַעֲלֶה — *We will indeed go up.* It is proper for us to go up, for they will not rise up against us to prevent our going up.

וְיָרַשְׁנוּ אֹתָהּ כִּי יָכוֹל נוּכַל לָהּ — *And take possession of it for we are truly able to do so . . .* for after we go up there they will flee from our presence, because all the inhabitants of Canaan have already *melted away* (based on *Exodus* 15:15).

NOTES

30. וַיַּהַס כָּלֵב אֶת הָעָם אֶל מֹשֶׁה — *Then Caleb stilled the people toward Moses.* The expression וַיַּהַס, *and he stilled,* is applicable only when there are those who are speaking or complaining. This, however, is not mentioned until the beginning of the next chapter (14:1). The *Sforno* therefore explains that at first some did begin to complain, and later the *whole congregation* followed suit. Caleb attempted to silence those who had already begun to raise their voices — but to no avail. Unlike *Rashi*, who bases his interpretation upon the Midrash, the *Sforno* explains the verse to mean that Caleb urged the people to listen to the words of Moses (which are not recorded here but in *parashas Devarim*), and he also made a personal plea to the people.

31. לֹא נוּכַל לַעֲלוֹת — *We are not able to go up.* The *Sforno* explains that their despair and lack of faith precipitated the eventual debacle. Their hopelessness was father to the reality. The *Sforno* expresses this same idea in his commentary on 14:37.

33. בְּנֵי עֲנָק מִן הַנְּפִלִים — *The sons of Anak of the Nephilim.* The word *nephilim* is usually translated "giants." It is first mentioned in *Genesis* 6:4. The

[27] They reported to him and said, "We arrived at the Land to which you sent us, and indeed it flows with milk and honey, and this is its fruit. [28] But — the people that dwells in the Land is powerful, the cities are very greatly fortified, and we also saw there the offspring of the giant. [29] Amalek dwells in the area of the south; the Hittite, the Jebusite, and the Emorite dwell on the mountain; and the Canaanite dwells by the Sea and on the bank of the Jordan."

[30] Caleb silenced the people toward Moses and said, "We shall surely ascend and conquer it, for we can surely do it!"

[31] But the men who had ascended with him said, "We cannot ascend to that people for it is too strong for us!" [32] They brought forth to the Children of Israel an evil report on the Land that they had spied out, saying, "The Land through which we have passed, to spy it out, is a land that devours its inhabitants! All the people that we saw in it were huge! [33] There we saw the Nephilim, the sons of the giant from among the Nephilim; we were like grasshoppers in our eyes, and so we were in their eyes!"

14 *[1] The entire assembly raised up and issued its voice; the people wept that night. [2] All the Children of Israel murmured against Moses and Aaron, and the entire assembly said to them, "If only we had died in the land of*

---

31. לֹא נוּכַל לַעֲלוֹת — *We are not able to go up . . .* for they will rise up against us and not allow us to go up, as (indeed) it occured after the sin, as it says *and the Amalekites and the Canaanites came down* (14:45).

32. אֶרֶץ אֹכֶלֶת יוֹשְׁבֶיהָ — *A land that consumes its inhabitants.* Even though the people who dwell in it (the Land) are strong, it is not due to the praiseworthiness (i.e., quality) of the Land, but it is because only the strong survive, for they are strong by nature, while the others perish because of the poor climate.

33. בְּנֵי עֲנָק — *The sons of Anak . . .* from (their) father's side.

מִן הַנְּפִלִים — *Of the Nephilim . . .* from (their) mother's side.

וְכֵן הָיִינוּ בְעֵינֵיהֶם — *And so were we in their eyes . . .* like grasshoppers, or even inferior to them. Therefore, they did not rise up against us for we were not sufficiently important, and it was contemptible in their eyes to do us harm (similar to *Megillas Esther* 3:6).

XIV

2. וַיִּלֹּנוּ עַל מֹשֶׁה וְעַל אַהֲרֹן — *And they murmured against Moses and Aaron.* For they were the messengers of God, the Blessed One, sent to bring them forth from Egypt and to save them from all fear of death in the wilderness. (But now) they said that all this was done (in order to) deliver them into the hands of the Emorites.

NOTES

Abarbanel, however, explains the phrase differently. In Hebrew, the word נֹפֶל means an aborted or premature infant. Being that the (human) mother was of average size while the (Anak) father was of giant proportions, the infant could not be carried to term — hence נֹפֶל, or נְפִלִים in the plural. The *Sforno,* following this interpretation, interprets *sons of Anak* as referring to the lineage of their fathers, and *from the Nephilim* as referring to the lineage of the mother — who occasionally did give birth to these huge offspring.

XIV

2. וַיִּלֹּנוּ עַל מֹשֶׁה וְעַל אַהֲרֹן — *And they murmured against Moses and Aaron.* The question is: Why did the people turn against Moses and Aaron, since they themselves claimed it was the Almighty who hated them and was determined to hand them over to the Emorites? The *Sforno* explains that in keeping with the Talmudic dictum that שְׁלוּחוֹ שֶׁל אָדָם כְּמוֹתוֹ, *a messenger of a person is considered to be as him,* Moses and Aaron as the messengers of God were fair target for their murmurings.

ג מִצְרַיִם אוֹ בַּמִּדְבָּר הַזֶּה לוּ־מָתְנוּ: וְלָמָה יְהוָה מֵבִיא אֹתָנוּ אֶל־הָאָרֶץ
הַזֹּאת לִנְפֹּל בַּחֶרֶב נָשֵׁינוּ וְטַפֵּנוּ יִהְיוּ לָבַז הֲלוֹא טוֹב לָנוּ שׁוּב מִצְרָיְמָה:
ד־ה וַיֹּאמְרוּ אִישׁ אֶל־אָחִיו נִתְּנָה רֹאשׁ וְנָשׁוּבָה מִצְרָיְמָה: וַיִּפֹּל מֹשֶׁה וְאַהֲרֹן
ו עַל־פְּנֵיהֶם לִפְנֵי כָּל־קְהַל עֲדַת בְּנֵי יִשְׂרָאֵל: וִיהוֹשֻׁעַ בִּן־נוּן וְכָלֵב בֶּן־
ז יְפֻנֶּה מִן־הַתָּרִים אֶת־הָאָרֶץ קָרְעוּ בִּגְדֵיהֶם: וַיֹּאמְרוּ אֶל־כָּל־עֲדַת בְּנֵי־
יִשְׂרָאֵל לֵאמֹר הָאָרֶץ אֲשֶׁר עָבַרְנוּ בָהּ לָתוּר אֹתָהּ טוֹבָה הָאָרֶץ מְאֹד
שלישי ח מְאֹד: אִם־חָפֵץ בָּנוּ יְהוָה וְהֵבִיא אֹתָנוּ אֶל־הָאָרֶץ הַזֹּאת וּנְתָנָהּ לָנוּ אֶרֶץ
ט אֲשֶׁר־הִוא זָבַת חָלָב וּדְבָשׁ: אַךְ בַּיהוָה אַל־תִּמְרֹדוּ וְאַתֶּם אַל־תִּירְאוּ
אֶת־עַם הָאָרֶץ כִּי לַחְמֵנוּ הֵם סָר צִלָּם מֵעֲלֵיהֶם וַיהוָה אִתָּנוּ אַל־תִּירָאֻם:

3. וְלָמָה ה׳ מֵבִיא אֹתָנוּ — *And why does* HASHEM *bring us.* How have we sinned against Him that He now attempts, through you, to bring us to this (state)? For they thought that all this had occurred by His design, (motivated by) His hatred for them on account of their idolatry in Egypt, or some other reason — as (the Torah) testifies, saying, וַתֵּאמְרוּ בְּשִׂנְאַת ה׳ אֹתָנוּ הוֹצִיאָנוּ מֵאֶרֶץ מִצְרָיִם לָתֵת אֹתָנוּ בְּיַד הָאֱמֹרִי לְהַשְׁמִידֵנוּ, *And you said, "Because* HASHEM *hates us He brought us out of the land of Egypt to deliver us into the hand of the Emorites, to destroy us"* (*Deut.* 1:27).

5. וַיִּפֹּל מֹשֶׁה וְאַהֲרֹן עַל פְּנֵיהֶם — *And Moses and Aaron fell on their faces . . .* when they saw (that this was) מְעֻוָּת לֹא יוּכַל לִתְקֹן, *something crooked which cannot be made straight* (*Ecclesiastes* 1:15), similar to (the episode of) the Sanhedrin who pressed their faces into the ground when they did not know what to do because of their fear of the king (*Sanhedrin* 19b).

7. הָאָרֶץ אֲשֶׁר עָבַרְנוּ בָהּ לָתוּר אֹתָהּ — *The Land through which we have passed to spy it out . . .* to spy out the place and its inhabitants, as it says, *And see the Land, what it is; and the people that dwell therein* (13:18).

טוֹבָה הָאָרֶץ — *The Land is good.* Behold, regarding *the land, what it is,* we testify that it is a place that is exceedingly good, with no blemish, and not as our colleagues testified (when) they said that although it *flows with milk and honey* (13:27), (nonetheless), it *consumes its inhabitants* (13:32). And regarding *the people that dwell therein,* we testify that *they are our bread* (verse 9) and they will not dare oppose us, contrary to the testimony of our colleagues who said *the people are too strong* (13:28).

8. אִם חָפֵץ בָּנוּ ה׳ — *If* HASHEM *desires us.* However, the exceeding goodness (of this place) is conditional upon HASHEM's delight in us, as it says, אֶרֶץ אֲשֶׁר ה׳ אֱלֹהֶיךָ דֹּרֵשׁ אֹתָהּ . . . וְהָיָה אִם שָׁמֹעַ תִּשְׁמְעוּ, *A land which* HASHEM *your God seeks . . . and it shall come to pass if you*

NOTES

5. וַיִּפֹּל מֹשֶׁה וְאַהֲרֹן עַל פְּנֵיהֶם — *And Moses and Aaron fell on their faces.* The *Sforno* explains the reaction of Moses and Aaron as manifesting their sense of inadequacy and despair, similar to the episode related in the Talmud regarding Shimon ben Shetach and King Yanai. The slave of the king had committed murder and Shimon urged the Sanhedrin to bring him to justice, but they were afraid of the king and did nothing. Rather, they "pressed their faces into the ground" as Moses and Aaron did in the case at hand. The *Sforno* implies that Moses and Aaron were immobilized by the report of the spies and unable to stand up to the people.

7-9. טוֹבָה הָאָרֶץ . . . אִם חָפֵץ בָּנוּ ה׳ . . . וְאַתֶּם אַל תִּירְאוּ אֶת עַם הָאָרֶץ — *The Land is good . . . If* HASHEM *desires us . . . And you should not fear the people of the Land.* The meaning of these verses, according to the *Sforno,* is as follows: Caleb and Joshua first address themselves to the original purpose of their mission, following which they refute the claims of the other spies. Regarding the Land itself, they insist that it is exceedingly good, and as for the inhabitants, they will not put up any resistance. The former they submit in order to refute the false claim that *Eretz Yisrael* is a land which *consumes its inhabitants,* and the latter

Egypt, or if only we had died in this Wilderness! [3] *Why is HASHEM bringing us to this Land to die by the sword? Our wives and young children will be taken captive! Is it not better for us to return to Egypt?"*

[4] *So they said to one another, "Let us appoint a leader and let us return to Egypt!"*

[5] *Moses and Aaron fell on their faces before the entire congregation of the assembly of the Children of Israel.*

[6] *Joshua son of Nun and Caleb son of Jephunneh, of the spies of the Land, tore their garments.* [7] *They spoke to the entire assembly of the Children of Israel, saying, "The Land that we passed through, to spy it out — the Land is very, very good!* [8] *If HASHEM desires us, He will bring us to this Land and give it to us, a Land that flows with milk and honey.* [9] *But do not rebel against HASHEM! You should not fear the people of the Land, for they are our bread. Their protection has departed from them; HASHEM is with us. Do not fear them!"*

---

hearken (*Deut.* 11:12,13).

וְהֵבִיא אֹתָנוּ אֶל הָאָרֶץ הַזֹּאת — *Then He will bring us into this land* . . . contrary to what our colleagues have testified saying, *We are not able to go up against the people* (13:31), for indeed the inhabitants of the Land will not rise up against us at all, as it says, יִדְּמוּ כָּאָבֶן עַד יַעֲבֹר עַמְּךָ ה׳, *They shall be still as a stone, till Your people pass over, HASHEM* (*Exodus* 15:16). And so it was, for they (the inhabitants) erected no barriers nor made any preparations to prevent the people (of Israel) from going up against them.

וּנְתָנָהּ לָנוּ — *And give it to us* . . . for we saw that there did not arise any spirit in any man to oppose us, and that their intention was to flee.

אֶרֶץ אֲשֶׁר הִוא זָבַת חָלָב וּדְבָשׁ — *A land which flows with milk and honey* . . . (the Land) itself, (on its own), without the labor of those who work the earth, similar to the forests as we find, וְכָל הָאָרֶץ בָּאוּ בַיָּעַר וַיְהִי דְבַשׁ עַל פְּנֵי הַשָּׂדֶה, *And all the people came to the wood and behold, there was a stream of honey on the ground* (*I Samuel* 14:25), and this would have been impossible if the Land or its climate had some blemish.

9. אַךְ בַּה׳ אַל תִּמְרֹדוּ — *Only rebel not against HASHEM*. However, if you want the Land to be on this level of goodness, then do not rebel against God, as it says, וְהָיָה אִם שָׁמֹעַ תִּשְׁמְעוּ . . . וְנָתַתִּי מְטַר אַרְצְכֶם בְּעִתּוֹ . . . וְאָסַפְתָּ, *And it shall come to pass if you will continually hearken . . . then I will send rain to your land in its proper time . . . that you may gather* (*Deut.* 11:13, 14).

וְאַתֶּם אַל תִּירְאוּ אֶת עַם הָאָרֶץ — *And you should not fear the people of the Land*. Behold, if you do not rebel, then God will bring us (into the Land) and you, have no fear . . .

כִּי לַחְמֵנוּ הֵם — *For they are our bread*. Because we observed that they have no intention to rise up against us at all, just as bread does not rise up against those who eat it, as Rahab testified when she said, וְלֹא קָמָה עוֹד רוּחַ בְּאִישׁ מִפְּנֵיכֶם, *Neither did there remain any more courage in any man because of you* (*Joshua* 2:11).

סָר צִלָּם מֵעֲלֵיהֶם — *Their defense is departed from them*. And we saw that they have

NOTES

they underscore in order to give the Israelites courage and strengthen their trust in God. They stress, however, that their triumphant entry into the Land, as well as the blessings of the Land, depend completely upon their finding favor in God's eyes, which can only be possible if they do not rebel against Him.

9. סָר צִלָּם מֵעֲלֵיהֶם — *Their defense is departed from them*. The *Ramban* and *Ibn Ezra* both inter-

י וַיֹּאמְרוּ כָּל־הָעֵדָה לִרְגּוֹם אֹתָם בָּאֲבָנִים וּכְבוֹד יהוה נִרְאָה בְּאֹהֶל מוֹעֵד
אֶל־כָּל־בְּנֵי יִשְׂרָאֵל׃
יא וַיֹּאמֶר יהוה אֶל־מֹשֶׁה עַד־אָנָה יְנַאֲצֻנִי הָעָם הַזֶּה וְעַד־אָנָה לֹא־יַאֲמִינוּ
יב בִי בְּכֹל הָאֹתוֹת אֲשֶׁר עָשִׂיתִי בְּקִרְבּוֹ׃ אַכֶּנּוּ בַדֶּבֶר וְאוֹרִשֶׁנּוּ וְאֶעֱשֶׂה
יג אֹתְךָ לְגוֹי־גָּדוֹל וְעָצוּם מִמֶּנּוּ׃ וַיֹּאמֶר מֹשֶׁה אֶל־יהוה וְשָׁמְעוּ מִצְרַיִם
יד כִּי־הֶעֱלִיתָ בְכֹחֲךָ אֶת־הָעָם הַזֶּה מִקִּרְבּוֹ׃ וְאָמְרוּ אֶל־יוֹשֵׁב הָאָרֶץ הַזֹּאת
שָׁמְעוּ כִּי־אַתָּה יהוה בְּקֶרֶב הָעָם הַזֶּה אֲשֶׁר־עַיִן בְּעַיִן נִרְאָה ׀ אַתָּה יהוה
וַעֲנָנְךָ עֹמֵד עֲלֵהֶם וּבְעַמֻּד עָנָן אַתָּה הֹלֵךְ לִפְנֵיהֶם יוֹמָם וּבְעַמּוּד אֵשׁ
טו לָיְלָה׃ וְהֵמַתָּה אֶת־הָעָם הַזֶּה כְּאִישׁ אֶחָד וְאָמְרוּ הַגּוֹיִם אֲשֶׁר־שָׁמְעוּ אֶת־
טז שִׁמְעֲךָ לֵאמֹר׃ מִבִּלְתִּי יְכֹלֶת יהוה לְהָבִיא אֶת־הָעָם הַזֶּה אֶל־הָאָרֶץ
יז אֲשֶׁר־נִשְׁבַּע לָהֶם וַיִּשְׁחָטֵם בַּמִּדְבָּר׃ וְעַתָּה יִגְדַּל־נָא כֹּחַ אֲדֹנָי כַּאֲשֶׁר

agreed to abandon every shield and buckler so as to hasten their flight from our presence, similar to, כָּל הַדֶּרֶךְ מְלֵאָה בְגָדִים וְכֵלִים אֲשֶׁר הִשְׁלִיכוּ אֲרָם בְּחָפְזָם, *All the way was full of garments and vessels which Aram had cast away in their haste* (*II Kings* 7:15).

11. עַד אָנָה יְנַאֲצֻנִי — *How far shall (this people) provoke Me?* To what extent of contempt shall I tolerate their contempt of Me?

וְעַד אָנָה לֹא יַאֲמִינוּ בִי — *And to what extent will they not believe in Me?* And to what extent must I perform wonders before they will trust Me and rely upon My word?

12. אַכֶּנּוּ בַדֶּבֶר — *I will smite them with pestilence . . .* similar to, וְגַם יַד ה׳ הָיְתָה בָּם לְהֻמָּם מִקֶּרֶב הַמַּחֲנֶה עַד תֻּמָּם, *And also the hand of HASHEM was against them to destroy them from the midst of the camp until they were spent* (*Deut.* 2:15).

וְאוֹרִשֶׁנּוּ — *And they will inherit them.* I will cause them to *leave over their possessions to others* (based on *Psalms* 49:11) and they (the others) will inherit them, similar to "the dead were heirs to the living" (*Bava Basra* 117a) regarding the division of the Land. Thereby He fulfilled (His) vow to those who came out of Egypt, when He said, וְנָתַתִּי אֹתָהּ לָכֶם מוֹרָשָׁה, *And I will give it to you as a heritage* (*Exodus* 6:8).

13. וְשָׁמְעוּ מִצְרַיִם — *When the Egyptians hear.* Moses thought that when God, the Blessed One, said, *I will smite them with pestilence,* the intent was to smite all of them immediately, and so he was moved to ask what will happen to His Great Name, and he said,

NOTES

pret צִלָּם (lit., their shadow) in the sense of a person's defense, comparing a warrior's weapons to a protective shadow. *Ibn Ezra* writes, "If the mighty warrior has no shield with which to protect himself and serve as a shadow for him, his heart is afraid." The *Sforno* follows their method of interpretation in his commentary as well.

11. עַד אָנָה יְנַאֲצֻנִי . . . וְעַד אָנָה לֹא יַאֲמִינוּ בִי — *How far shall (this people) provoke Me? And to what extent will they not believe in Me?* The Hebrew phrase אָנָה is interpreted by *Rashi* to mean "how long"; not "how far." The former refers to time while the latter denotes place. (See the *Sifsei Chachamim* on *Rashi* here.) The *Sforno* prefers the latter interpretation — עַד אֵיזֶה גְבוּל (lit., to what boundary) meaning, how far can My patience be tried and to what outer limits of wonders must I extend Myself in order to evoke Israel's trust in Me?

12. וְאוֹרִשֶׁנּוּ — *And they will inherit them. Rashi* explains the word וְאוֹרִשֶׁנּוּ as meaning "a cutting off or driving out." He interprets the phrase יוֹרִשֶׁנָּה in verse 24 in a similar manner. The *Sforno*, however, interprets both of these phrases as meaning "inheritance" or "bequeathing," i.e., in the sense of יְרוּשָׁה. The Sages in tractate *Bava Basra* (117a) disagree regarding the division of *Eretz Yisrael* among the tribes of Israel. Rabbi Josiah states that the Land was divided according to those who came out of Egypt (לְיוֹצְאֵי מִצְרַיִם נִתְחַלְּקָה הָאָרֶץ), i.e., it was divided according to the number of men that left Egypt, and not according to the number that entered Canaan. Rabbi Jonathan is of the opinion

10 *But the entire assembly said to pelt them with stones — and the glory
of HASHEM appeared in the Tent of Meeting to all the Children of Israel.*
11 *HASHEM said to Moses, "How long will this people provoke Me, and
how long will they not have faith in Me, despite all the signs that I have performed in their midst?* 12 *I will smite them with the plague and annihilate
them, and I shall make you a greater and more powerful nation than they."*
13 *Moses said to HASHEM, "Then Egypt — from whose midst You brought
up this nation with Your power — will hear,* 14 *and they will say about
the inhabitants of this Land, 'They have heard that You, HASHEM, are in
the midst of this people — that You, HASHEM, appeared eye to eye and
Your cloud stands over them, and that in a pillar of cloud You go before
them by day and in a pillar of fire at night —* 15 *yet You killed this people
like a single man!' Then the nations that heard of Your fame will say,*
16 *'Because HASHEM lacked the ability to bring this people to the Land
that He had sworn to give them, He slaughtered them in the Wilderness.'*
17 *And now — may the strength of my Lord be magnified as You have*

"Behold, the Egyptians will immediately hear that You killed these (people) suddenly, and they will say that You did so because You *were not able* (verse 16) to (overcome) the inhabitants of this land (Canaan). This (they will say) because, indeed, they saw that *You brought up this people from their midst in Your might,* and (also) *they have heard that You, HASHEM, are in the midst of this people* (verse 14); (hence) they will not think that their downfall was due to Your leaving them because of their iniquities."

14. אֲשֶׁר עַיִן בְּעַיִן נִרְאָה אַתָּה ה׳ — *That face to face* (lit., *eye to eye*), *You, HASHEM, were seen* . . . the eye of Your Providence (supervision) over them, has already been seen in its reality (by Israel).

וַעֲנָנְךָ עֹמֵד עֲלֵהֶם — *And Your cloud stands over them* . . . in the present, as it says, כִּי עֲנַן ה׳ עַל הַמִּשְׁכָּן יוֹמָם וְאֵשׁ תִּהְיֶה לַיְלָה בּוֹ לְעֵינֵי כָל בֵּית יִשְׂרָאֵל בְּכָל מַסְעֵיהֶם, *For the cloud of HASHEM was on the Sanctuary by day, and a fire was on it by night, before the eyes of all the house of Israel throughout all their journeys* (Exodus 40:38).

17. יִגְדַּל נָא כֹּחַ ה׳ — *Let the power of HASHEM be great* . . . so as to conquer (overcome) the attribute of justice.

NOTES

that the Land was divided according to those who entered it, and not according to the number of those who came out of Egypt (לְבָאֵי הָאָרֶץ נִתְחַלְּקָה הָאָרֶץ). Explaining his opinion, Rabbi Jonathan adds, "this manner of inheritance is different from all others . . . for in the case of all others, the living are heirs to the dead, but in this case, the dead were heirs to the living." The meaning of this cryptic statement is that those who entered the Land received shares according to their numbers, but these shares were considered to belong to the fathers who came out of Egypt (even though they were dead), and then in turn reverted to and were "inherited" by the sons. Hence, although the generation that left Egypt was destined to die out, nonetheless, they would still inherit the Land through their children. In this manner, God's promise to the people of Israel in Egypt that *I shall give it to you as a heritage* (*Exodus* 6:8) was still fulfilled even though that generation did not actually enter the Land.

13-14. וְשָׁמְעוּ מִצְרַיִם . . . אֲשֶׁר עַיִן בְּעַיִן נִרְאָה אַתָּה ה׳ . . . וַעֲנָנְךָ עֹמֵד עֲלֵהֶם — *When the Egyptians hear . . . That face to face* (lit., *eye to eye*), *You, HASHEM, were seen and Your cloud stands over them.* The meaning of these verses according to the *Sforno* is as follows: The Egyptians had witnessed the greatness and might of the Almighty in Egypt and the Exodus of the Israelites through His Omnipotence. They had also heard of God's Presence in the midst of Israel and were unaware of any reason for Him to abandon them. Were He to slay them all at one time, the reason could only be because He was unable to overcome the inhabitants of Canaan and bring the Israelites into the Land. This, in turn, would cause His great Name to be desecrated.

17. יִגְדַּל נָא כֹּחַ ה׳ — *Let the power of HASHEM be great.* "HASHEM" represents the attribute of mercy.

יח דִּבַּרְתָּ לֵאמֹר: יְהוָה אֶרֶךְ אַפַּיִם וְרַב־חֶסֶד נֹשֵׂא עָוֹן וָפָשַׁע וְנַקֵּה לֹא יְנַקֶּה

יט פֹּקֵד עֲוֹן אָבוֹת עַל־בָּנִים עַל־שִׁלֵּשִׁים וְעַל־רִבֵּעִים: סְלַח־נָא לַעֲוֹן הָעָם

כ הַזֶּה כְּגֹדֶל חַסְדֶּךָ וְכַאֲשֶׁר נָשָׂאתָה לָעָם הַזֶּה מִמִּצְרַיִם וְעַד־הֵנָּה: וַיֹּאמֶר

כא יְהוָה סָלַחְתִּי כִּדְבָרֶךָ: וְאוּלָם חַי־אָנִי וְיִמָּלֵא כְבוֹד־יְהוָה אֶת־כָּל־הָאָרֶץ:

כב כִּי כָל־הָאֲנָשִׁים הָרֹאִים אֶת־כְּבֹדִי וְאֶת־אֹתֹתַי אֲשֶׁר־עָשִׂיתִי בְמִצְרַיִם

כג וּבַמִּדְבָּר וַיְנַסּוּ אֹתִי זֶה עֶשֶׂר פְּעָמִים וְלֹא שָׁמְעוּ בְּקוֹלִי: אִם־יִרְאוּ

כד אֶת־הָאָרֶץ אֲשֶׁר נִשְׁבַּעְתִּי לַאֲבֹתָם וְכָל־מְנַאֲצַי לֹא יִרְאוּהָ: וְעַבְדִּי כָלֵב

עֵקֶב הָיְתָה רוּחַ אַחֶרֶת עִמּוֹ וַיְמַלֵּא אַחֲרָי וַהֲבִיאֹתִיו אֶל־הָאָרֶץ

כה אֲשֶׁר־בָּא שָׁמָּה וְזַרְעוֹ יוֹרִשֶׁנָּה: וְהָעֲמָלֵקִי וְהַכְּנַעֲנִי יוֹשֵׁב בָּעֵמֶק מָחָר פְּנוּ

וּסְעוּ לָכֶם הַמִּדְבָּר דֶּרֶךְ יַם־סוּף:

רביעי　כו־כז וַיְדַבֵּר יְהוָה אֶל־מֹשֶׁה וְאֶל־אַהֲרֹן לֵאמֹר: עַד־מָתַי לָעֵדָה הָרָעָה הַזֹּאת

אֲשֶׁר הֵמָּה מַלִּינִים עָלָי אֶת־תְּלֻנּוֹת בְּנֵי יִשְׂרָאֵל אֲשֶׁר הֵמָּה מַלִּינִים עָלַי

---

18. פֹּקֵד עֲוֹן אָבוֹת עַל בָּנִים — *Visiting the iniquity of the fathers upon the children.* He is long suffering (containing His anger) until the fourth generation. If they (the children) hold fast to the (evil) deeds of their fathers and even increase (their) wickedness, then their measure becomes full in the third generation and the hope for their repentance is lost and He exacts payment (i.e., punishment) from them. If they hold fast to the (evil) ways of their fathers, but do not increase in their wicked ways, then (God) waits until the fourth generation, and then their measure will be full, for there is no hope that they will repent, and they will perish.

20. סָלַחְתִּי כִּדְבָרֶךָ — *I have pardoned according to your word.* When I said, *I will smite them with pestilence,* I had already forgiven them in the manner which you are (now) saying, because My intent was not to put them to death all together. Rather, (it was) to have them die gradually in the wilderness, and that no man among them would enter the Land.

21. וְאוּלָם חַי אָנִי וְיִמָּלֵא כְבוֹד ה׳ אֶת כָּל הָאָרֶץ — *However, as surely as I live and as the whole earth will be full of the glory of HASHEM.* However, I swear that as it is true that I live and that all the earth will be filled with My glory, so it will be true that all the men who are twenty years (and older) . . .

23. אִם יִרְאוּ אֶת הָאָרֶץ — *Shall surely not see the Land.* They will *not* see the Land, in keeping with (the general principle) that every expression אִם, *if,* when not followed by a double תְּנַאי, *condition,* (is a negative). (This is) similar to, אִם מִחוּט וְעַד שְׂרוֹךְ נַעַל וְאִם אֶקַּח

NOTES

Moses asks God to strengthen that attribute to the point where it will overcome and override the attribute of justice (God).

18. פֹּקֵד עֲוֹן אָבוֹת עַל בָּנִים — *Visiting the iniquity of the fathers upon the children.* See the *Sforno* on *Exodus* 20:5 and the notes.

20. סָלַחְתִּי כִּדְבָרֶךָ — *I have pardoned according to your word.* The expression סָלַחְתִּי, *I have forgiven*, is in the past tense. The *Sforno* explains this to mean that God was not responding to the argument of Moses. Rather, Moses had misunderstood God's statement of אַכֶּנּוּ בַדֶּבֶר, *I will smite them with pestilence,* for he thought it would take place at once, but God now tells him that the Divine plan, in any event, was to bring about the death of the present generation over a period of many years. Hence, כִּדְבָרֶךָ, *according to your word,* does not mean as *Rashi* says, "because of what you have said." The *Sforno's* view is that it means that your request, not to slay all of them immediately, was My original intent. Hence, God does not "change His mind" — for He is unchanging.

23. וְכָל מְנַאֲצַי לֹא יִרְאוּהָ — *And all those who angered Me shall not see it.* Since God had already decreed that this generation would not merit to *see the Land,* why then is it necessary to add the words, *And all those who angered Me shall not see it?* The *Sforno* explains that this latter phrase refers to

spoken, saying, [18] *'HASHEM, Slow to Anger, Abundant in Kindness, Forgiver of Iniquity and Willful Sin, and Who cleanses — but does not cleanse completely, recalling the iniquity of parents upon children to the third and fourth generations' —* [19] *forgive now the iniquity of this people according to the greatness of Your kindness and as You have forgiven this people from Egypt until now."*

[20] *And HASHEM said, "I have forgiven because of your words.* [21] *But as I live — and the glory of HASHEM shall fill the entire world —* [22] *that all the men who have seen My glory and My signs that I performed in Egypt and in the Wilderness, and have tested Me these ten times and have not heeded My voice,* [23] *if they will see the Land that I have sworn to give their forefathers! — and all who anger Me shall not see it.* [24] *But My servant Caleb, because a different spirit was with him and he followed Me wholeheartedly, I shall bring him to the Land to which he came, and his offspring shall possess it.* [25] *The Amalekite and the Canaanite dwell in the valley — tomorrow, turn and journey toward the Wilderness in the direction of the Sea of Reeds."*

[26] *HASHEM spoke to Moses and Aaron, saying,* [27] *"How long for this evil assembly that provokes complaints against Me!? I have heard the complaints of the Children of Israel whom they provoke against Me.*

מִכָּל אֲשֶׁר לָךְ, *I will not take so much as a thread or a shoelace, and I will not take anything that is yours* (*Genesis* 14:23), and חַי ה׳ אִם יוּמָת, *As HASHEM lives, he will not be slain* (*I Samuel* 19:6) and other similar verses.

וְכָל מְנַאֲצַי לֹא יִרְאוּהָ — *And all those who angered Me shall not see it* . . . and also, their children who are not (included) in this decree since they have not yet reached the age of twenty, all who will anger Me in the future will not see it (the Land), as happened with those who died (as a result) of the episode of Korach (chapter 16), the matter of Pe'or (chapter 25) and the fiery serpents (chapter 21).

24. וְזַרְעוֹ יוֹרִשֶׁנָּה — *And his seed shall inherit it.* He shall bequeath it to his seed unlike the rest of the generation of the wilderness, for although their children inherited from them (their fathers), they (the original members of that wilderness generation) were not the bequeathers. Rather, God, the Blessed One, bequeathed an arrangement in accordance with His commandment to the distributors of the Land, as (the Torah) attests, saying, וְאוֹרִשֶׁנּוּ, *And they will inherit them* (verse 12).

27. עַד מָתַי לָעֵדָה הָרָעָה הַזֹּאת — *How long shall this evil congregation.* Although I have pardoned in accordance with your words (request), and will be forbearing so as not to slay them immediately, nor all at one time; nonetheless, I have not forgiven the congregation of the spies (themselves).

אֲשֶׁר הֵמָּה מַלִּינִים עָלָי — *That keeps murmuring against Me* . . . for they caused others to

NOTES

those who were under twenty years of age at the time of the decree and therefore not included in this decree, but because they were guilty of other transgressions (such as joining the congregation of Korach, etc.) they would also not merit to see the land.

24. וְזַרְעוֹ יוֹרִשֶׁנָּה — *And his seed shall inherit it.* As in verse 12, the *Sforno* differs from *Rashi* who interprets the word יוֹרִשֶׁנָּה to mean "drive them out." *Sforno* interprets it to mean "he will bequeath it"; i.e., Caleb alone, of the generation that went forth from Egypt, will merit to bequeath his portion of the Land to his children, unlike the others who never actually possessed their share in the Land. See verse 12 above and the note there. The *Sforno* apparently finds *Rashi's* explanation difficult since Caleb himself, and not his offspring, drove out the children of Anak from Hebron and its environs (see *Joshua* 14-15).

27. אֲשֶׁר הֵמָּה מַלִּינִים עָלָי — *That keeps murmuring against Me.* Although repentance is always

כח שָׁמָעְתִּי: אֱמֹר אֲלֵהֶם חַי־אָנִי נְאֻם־יְהוָה אִם־לֹא כַּאֲשֶׁר דִּבַּרְתֶּם בְּאָזְנָי
כט כֵּן אֶעֱשֶׂה לָכֶם: בַּמִּדְבָּר הַזֶּה יִפְּלוּ פִגְרֵיכֶם וְכָל־פְּקֻדֵיכֶם לְכָל־מִסְפַּרְכֶם
ל מִבֶּן עֶשְׂרִים שָׁנָה וָמָעְלָה אֲשֶׁר הֲלִינֹתֶם עָלָי: אִם־אַתֶּם תָּבֹאוּ אֶל־
הָאָרֶץ אֲשֶׁר נָשָׂאתִי אֶת־יָדִי לְשַׁכֵּן אֶתְכֶם בָּהּ כִּי אִם־כָּלֵב בֶּן־יְפֻנֶּה
לא וִיהוֹשֻׁעַ בִּן־נוּן: וְטַפְּכֶם אֲשֶׁר אֲמַרְתֶּם לָבַז יִהְיֶה וְהֵבֵיאתִי אֹתָם וְיָדְעוּ
לב אֶת־הָאָרֶץ אֲשֶׁר מְאַסְתֶּם בָּהּ: וּפִגְרֵיכֶם אַתֶּם יִפְּלוּ בַּמִּדְבָּר הַזֶּה:
לג °וּבְנֵיכֶם יִהְיוּ רֹעִים בַּמִּדְבָּר אַרְבָּעִים שָׁנָה וְנָשְׂאוּ אֶת־זְנוּתֵיכֶם עַד־תֹּם
לד פִּגְרֵיכֶם בַּמִּדְבָּר: בְּמִסְפַּר הַיָּמִים אֲשֶׁר־תַּרְתֶּם אֶת־הָאָרֶץ אַרְבָּעִים יוֹם
יוֹם לַשָּׁנָה יוֹם לַשָּׁנָה תִּשְׂאוּ אֶת־עֲוֹנֹתֵיכֶם אַרְבָּעִים שָׁנָה וִידַעְתֶּם אֶת־
לה תְּנוּאָתִי: אֲנִי יְהוָה דִּבַּרְתִּי אִם־לֹא | זֹאת אֶעֱשֶׂה לְכָל־הָעֵדָה הָרָעָה
לו הַזֹּאת הַנּוֹעָדִים עָלָי בַּמִּדְבָּר הַזֶּה יִתַּמּוּ וְשָׁם יָמֻתוּ: וְהָאֲנָשִׁים אֲשֶׁר־שָׁלַח
מֹשֶׁה לָתוּר אֶת־הָאָרֶץ וַיָּשֻׁבוּ °וילונו עָלָיו אֶת־כָּל־הָעֵדָה לְהוֹצִיא דִבָּה　　°וַיַּלִּינוּ ק׳

sin, and (the responsibility for) the sin of the multitude lies with them; hence, I shall not practice forbearance with them at all. And because of this *murmuring of the Children of Israel which they*, i.e., the spies, *keep murmuring against Me, have I heard*, and I (now) set My face (against them) to punish them — therefore ...

28. אֱמֹר אֲלֵהֶם חַי אָנִי נְאֻם ה׳ אִם לֹא — *Say unto them: As I live, says HASHEM, as you have (spoken)*. (These are) two negatives in place of a positive. This means to say, that indeed, (it shall be) *as you have spoken in My ears* when you said, *or would we had died in this wilderness* (verse 2), and when you said, *our wives and children will become a prey* (verse 3), and also when the spies said, *a land that consumes its inhabitants* (13:32) — all this will be fulfilled with you!

כֵּן אֶעֱשֶׂה לָכֶם — *So I will do to you* ... at various (different) times. And to this He swore, as the psalmist attests, saying, וַיִּשָּׂא יָדוֹ לָהֶם לְהַפִּיל אוֹתָם בַּמִּדְבָּר. וּלְהַפִּיל זַרְעָם בַּגּוֹיִם, *And He lifted up His hand against them to throw them down in the wilderness. And to throw down their descendants among the nations* (*Psalms* 106:26, 27), and also Ezekiel (who) says, גַּם אֲנִי נָשָׂאתִי אֶת יָדִי לָהֶם בַּמִּדְבָּר לְהָפִיץ אֹתָם בַּגּוֹיִם, *I lifted up my hand to them also in the wilderness, to scatter them among the nations* (*Ezekiel* 20:23).

33. וְנָשְׂאוּ אֶת זְנוּתֵיכֶם — *And will bear your defections* ... for you rebelled against Me when you said, *Let us appoint a chief etc.* (verse 4).

NOTES

accepted, nonetheless, there are times when one is not assisted from Heaven and this assistance is vital in bringing a person to this end. The *Sforno* interprets this verse as indicating God's determination to prevent the spies from repenting because they were guilty of causing others to sin as well, and our Sages teach us, "One who influences the masses to sin will not be given the means to achieve repentance" (*Avos* 5:21).

34. יוֹם לַשָּׁנָה — *A day for a year*. The *Sforno* overcomes the difficulty presented by the expression יוֹם לַשָּׁנָה, *a day for a year*, which would have been better expressed in the reverse שָׁנָה לַיּוֹם, *a year for a day*, by applying the statement of our Sages in tractate *Taanis* 30b to these two words. There, we are told that during the 40-year trek in the wilderness, on the Ninth of Av, the day marking the return of the spies and the consequent "mourning" of the Children of Israel, every person dug a grave and went to sleep in it. The next morning, those who were still alive arose, while those who died during the night were buried. With this Talmudic interpretation, the *Sforno* explains the expression, יוֹם לַשָּׁנָה, as meaning that on a specific day each year they shall pay for their sin. This will also clarify the reason for the repetition of the phrase יוֹם לַשָּׁנָה — since this occurred each year for forty years.

תְּנוּאָתִי — *My removal*. Although the phrase תְּנוּאָתִי means *My removal* or turning away, and

[28] Say to them: As I live — the words of HASHEM — if I shall not do to you as you have spoken in My ears. [29] In this Wilderness shall your carcasses drop; all of you who were counted in any of your numberings, from twenty years of age and above, whom you provoked against Me; [30] if you shall come to the Land about which I have raised My hand in an oath to settle you there, except for Caleb son of Jephunneh and Joshua son of Nun. [31] And your young children of whom you said they will be taken captive, I shall bring them; they shall know the Land that you have despised. [32] But your carcasses shall drop in this Wilderness. [33] Your children will roam in the Wilderness for forty years and bear your guilt, until the last of your carcasses in the Wilderness. [34] Like the number of the days that you spied out the Land, forty days, a day for a year, a day for a year, shall you bear your iniquities — forty years — and you shall comprehend straying from Me. [35] I HASHEM have spoken — if I shall not do this to this entire evil assembly that gathers against Me! In this Wilderness shall they cease to be, and there shall they die!"

[36] But as for the men whom Moses sent to spy out the Land, and who returned and provoked the entire assembly against him by spreading a report

34. בְּמִסְפַּר הַיָּמִים — *According to the number of days . . .* that they (the spies) prolonged (their visit), in keeping with your (i.e., the people of Israel's) command, to determine whether it is possible to conquer it (the Land).

יוֹם לַשָּׁנָה — *A day for a year . . .* the Ninth Day of Av, each year, as explained in the last chapter of tractate *Taanis* (30b).

תְּנוּאָתִי — *My removal.* You will recognize how bad it is to nullify My intent, by turning away from it, as it says, *and you will fall by the sword because you turned back from following HASHEM* (verse 43).

36. וְהָאֲנָשִׁים אֲשֶׁר שָׁלַח מֹשֶׁה — *And the men whom Moses had sent . . .* who were loyal to him and then became his enemies.

וַיָּשֻׁבוּ וַיַּלִּינוּ עָלָיו אֶת כָּל הָעֵדָה — *And who, when they returned, caused all the congregation to murmur against him.* (The word עֵדָה) refers to the Sanhedrin and the leaders of the people (who reacted) when they (the spies) said, *for they are stronger than we* (13:31). Now this was done to submit an evil report against the Land, for while the elders were occupied in their murmuring, they (the spies) in turn could submit an evil report against the Land to the multitude. This they could not have done in the presence of the elders who knew and (would) recognize their falsehood.

NOTES

according to the *Sforno's* commentary, the Torah should have written תְּנוּאָתֵיכֶם, *Your turning away,* nonetheless, the Torah's choice of expression can be explained thus: When a man turns away from God, the Almighty turns away from him. Your removal, God says, has caused תְּנוּאָתִי, *My removal,* and the withdrawal of My protection from Israel.

36. וַיָּשֻׁבוּ וַיַּלִּינוּ עָלָיו אֶת כָּל הָעֵדָה — *And who, when they returned, caused all the congregation to murmur against him.* The *Sforno* divides the verse into two parts. The first part states that the spies initially incited the leaders of the people, i.e., the Sanhedrin, who are called עֵדָה ("congregation" — a term of importance), by telling them their misgivings regarding the inhabitants of the Land who, in their opinion, were too mighty to be conquered. This judgment even the Sanhedrin could accept. The spies then spoke against the Land itself to the masses, deprecating its character and worth — a qualitative judgment which the Sanhedrin would never have accepted. But these leaders were so occupied with murmuring among themselves regarding the might of the inhabitants of Canaan that they were not even present to refute the spies when they spread calumnies about the Land to the multitude.

לז עַל־הָאָרֶץ: וַיָּמֻ֙תוּ֙ הָֽאֲנָשִׁ֔ים מֽוֹצִאֵ֥י דִבַּת־הָאָ֖רֶץ רָעָ֑ה בַּמַּגֵּפָ֖ה לִפְנֵ֥י
לח יהוֹה: וִֽיהוֹשֻׁ֣עַ בִּן־נ֗וּן וְכָלֵב֙ בֶּן־יְפֻנֶּ֔ה חָי֕וּ מִן־הָֽאֲנָשִׁ֣ים הָהֵ֔ם הַהֹֽלְכִ֖ים
לט לָת֣וּר אֶת־הָאָֽרֶץ: וַיְדַבֵּ֤ר מֹשֶׁה֙ אֶת־הַדְּבָרִ֣ים הָאֵ֔לֶּה אֶל־כָּל־בְּנֵ֣י
מ יִשְׂרָאֵ֑ל וַיִּֽתְאַבְּל֥וּ הָעָ֖ם מְאֹֽד: וַיַּשְׁכִּ֣מוּ בַבֹּ֔קֶר וַיַּעֲל֥וּ אֶל־רֹאשׁ־הָהָ֖ר
מא לֵאמֹ֑ר הִנֶּ֗נּוּ וְעָלִ֛ינוּ אֶל־הַמָּק֛וֹם אֲשֶׁר־אָמַ֥ר יהוֹ֖ה כִּ֥י חָטָֽאנוּ: וַיֹּ֣אמֶר
מב מֹשֶׁ֗ה לָ֤מָּה זֶּה֙ אַתֶּ֣ם עֹֽבְרִ֔ים אֶת־פִּ֣י יהוֹ֑ה וְהִ֖וא לֹ֣א תִצְלָ֑ח: אַֽל־תַּעֲל֗וּ
מג כִּ֣י אֵ֤ין יהוֹה֙ בְּקִרְבְּכֶ֔ם וְלֹ֥א תִּנָּ֣גְפ֔וּ לִפְנֵ֖י אֹֽיְבֵיכֶֽם: כִּ֩י הָֽעֲמָלֵקִ֨י וְהַכְּנַעֲנִ֥י
שָׁ֣ם לִפְנֵיכֶ֗ם וּנְפַלְתֶּ֖ם בֶּחָ֑רֶב כִּֽי־עַל־כֵּ֤ן שַׁבְתֶּם֙ מֵאַֽחֲרֵ֣י יהוֹ֔ה וְלֹֽא־יִהְיֶ֥ה
מד יהוֹ֖ה עִמָּכֶֽם: וַיַּעְפִּ֕לוּ לַֽעֲל֖וֹת אֶל־רֹ֣אשׁ הָהָ֑ר וַֽאֲר֤וֹן בְּרִֽית־יהוֹה֙ וּמֹשֶׁ֔ה
מה לֹא־מָ֖שׁוּ מִקֶּ֥רֶב הַֽמַּחֲנֶֽה: וַיֵּ֤רֶד הָֽעֲמָלֵקִי֙ וְהַֽכְּנַעֲנִ֔י הַיֹּשֵׁ֖ב בָּהָ֣ר הַה֑וּא
     וַיַּכּ֥וּם וַֽיַּכְּת֖וּם עַד־הַֽחָרְמָֽה:

טו א־ב וַיְדַבֵּ֥ר יהוֹ֖ה אֶל־מֹשֶׁ֥ה לֵּאמֹֽר: דַּבֵּר֙ אֶל־בְּנֵ֣י יִשְׂרָאֵ֔ל וְאָֽמַרְתָּ֖ אֲלֵהֶ֑ם
ג כִּ֣י תָבֹ֗אוּ אֶל־אֶ֙רֶץ֙ מֽוֹשְׁבֹ֣תֵיכֶ֔ם אֲשֶׁ֥ר אֲנִ֖י נֹתֵ֣ן לָכֶֽם: וַֽעֲשִׂיתֶ֨ם אִשֶּׁ֤ה
     לַֽיהוֹה֙ עֹלָ֣ה אֽוֹ־זֶ֔בַח לְפַלֵּא־נֶ֙דֶר֙ א֣וֹ בִנְדָבָ֔ה א֖וֹ בְּמֹֽעֲדֵיכֶ֑ם לַֽעֲשׂ֞וֹת רֵ֤יחַ
ד נִיחֹ֙חַ֙ לַֽיהוֹ֔ה מִן־הַבָּקָ֖ר א֥וֹ מִן־הַצֹּֽאן: וְהִקְרִ֛יב הַמַּקְרִ֥יב קָרְבָּנ֖וֹ לַֽיהוֹ֑ה
ה מִנְחָה֙ סֹ֣לֶת עִשָּׂר֔וֹן בָּל֕וּל בִּרְבִעִ֥ית הַהִ֖ין שָֽׁמֶן: וְיַ֙יִן֙ לַנֶּ֔סֶךְ רְבִיעִ֥ית הַהִ֖ין

---

37. וַיָּמֻתוּ הָאֲנָשִׁים מוֹצִאֵי דִבַּת הָאָרֶץ רָעָה בַּמַּגֵּפָה — *And these men who had brought up the evil report of the Land died by the plague* . . . by the same plague which they said would occur in the land which *consumes its inhabitants* (13:32). Behold, the effect of the climate of the land (in which they now were) became loathsome to them and they died immediately.

41. לָמָּה זֶה אַתֶּם עֹבְרִים אֶת פִּי ה' וְהִוא לֹא תִצְלָח — *Why do you transgress the order of* HASHEM, *(being that) it will not succeed?* Because, in this manner, you will be considered sinners, not (seeking to satisfy your) desire or for your own pleasure, but rather (in order) to anger (me).

44. וַיַּעְפִּלוּ — *And they persisted.* They hardened their hearts, similar to, וַיֶּחֱזַק לֵב פַּרְעֹה וְלֹא שָׁמַע אֲלֵהֶם, *The heart of Pharaoh was hardened and he did not listen to them* (*Exodus* 7:13).

45. וַיֵּרֶד הָעֲמָלֵקִי — *And the Amalekites came down* . . . and did not permit them to go up.

XV

3-4. רֵיחַ נִיחֹחַ לַה' . . . וְהִקְרִיב הַמַּקְרִיב — *A sweet savor to* HASHEM . . . *And he who brings the offering shall bring.* Behold, until (the sin of) the Golden Calf, an offering was *a*

NOTES

37. וַיָּמֻתוּ הָאֲנָשִׁים מוֹצִאֵי דִבַּת הָאָרֶץ רָעָה בַּמַּגֵּפָה — *And these men who had brought up the evil report of the Land died by the plague.* The *Sforno* explains the cause of the plague in keeping with the principle of מִדָּה כְּנֶגֶד מִדָּה, *measure for measure.*

41. לָמָּה זֶה אַתֶּם עֹבְרִים אֶת פִּי ה' וְהִוא לֹא תִצְלָח — *Why do you transgress the order of* HASHEM, *(being that) it will not succeed?* Once Moses told them

that their efforts to go up the mountain were doomed to failure, their insistence upon doing so became לְהַכְעִיס, utterly provocative — and the punishment in such cases is swift and harsh.

44. וַיַּעְפִּלוּ — *And they persisted.* See *Rashi* who, indeed, interprets the root of the word וַיַּעְפִּלוּ as an expression of חוֹזֶק, *insolent force,* characterizing the nature of Israel's persistence. The *Sforno* follows his view.

against the Land — [37] *the people who spread the evil report about the Land died in a plague before HASHEM.* [38] *But Joshua son of Nun and Caleb son of Jephunneh lived from among those men who were going to spy out the Land.*

[39] *Moses spoke these words to all of the Children of Israel, and the people mourned exceedingly.*

[40] *They awoke early in the morning and ascended toward the mountaintop saying, "We are ready, and we shall ascend to the place of which HASHEM has spoken, for we have sinned!"*

[41] *Moses said, "Why do you transgress the word of HASHEM? It will not succeed.* [42] *Do not ascend, for HASHEM is not in your midst! And do not be smitten before your enemies.* [43] *For the Amalekite and the Canaanite are there before you, and you will fall by the sword, because you have turned away from HASHEM, and HASHEM will not be with you."*

[44] *But they defiantly ascended to the mountaintop, while the Ark of HASHEM's covenant and Moses did not move from the midst of the camp.* [45] *The Amalekite and the Canaanite who dwelled on that mountain descended; they struck them and pounded them until Hormah.*

15

[1] *HASHEM spoke to Moses, saying,* [2] *"Speak to the Children of Israel and say to them: When you will come to the Land of your dwelling places that I give you,* [3] *and you perform a fire-offering to HASHEM — an elevation-offering or a feast-offering because of an articulated vow or as a free-will offering, or on your festivals, to produce a satisfying aroma to HASHEM, from the cattle or from the flock —* [4] *the one who brings his offering to HASHEM shall bring a meal-offering of a tenth[-ephah] fine flour, mixed with a quarter-hin of oil;* [5] *and a quarter-hin of wine for a libation*

---

satisfying aroma (to God) even without a meal-offering and drink-offering, similar to (the offerings brought by) Abel, Noah and Abraham, and similar to וַיִּשְׁלַח אֶת נַעֲרֵי בְּנֵי יִשְׂרָאֵל וַיַּעֲלוּ עֹלֹת וַיִּזְבְּחוּ זְבָחִים שְׁלָמִים לַה׳ פָּרִים, *And he sent the young men of the Children of Israel and they offered burnt offerings and sacrificed peace-offerings of oxen to HASHEM* (*Exodus* 24:5), i.e., without (bringing) these (מְנָחוֹת and נְסָכִים). (However) when they sinned with the Golden Calf, (the Torah) required that a meal-offering and drink-offering (be brought) with the daily burnt offering, which is a communal offering; and from the time they sinned (in the incident of) the spies, a meal-offering and drink-offering were also needed to qualify (לְהַכְשִׁיר) an individual offering.

NOTES

XV

3-4. רֵיחַ נִיחֹחַ לַה׳ ... וְהִקְרִיב הַמַּקְרִיב — *A sweet savor to HASHEM ... And he who brings the offering shall bring.* The obligation to bring מְנָחוֹת וּנְסָכִים, *meal-offerings and libations,* as an accompaniment to the קָרְבַּן תָּמִיד, *daily communal offering,* was already ordained in *Exodus* 29 and in regard to the קָרְבַּן מוּסָף, *additional offering,* it is mentioned later in *Numbers* 28. In our present chapter, Israel is commanded to bring נְסָכִים with every קָרְבַּן יָחִיד, *individual offering,* as well. The *Sforno* explains that there were three periods in which the law regarding offerings differed. Originally, no נְסָכִים were necessary. After the sin of the Golden Calf, they were commanded to bring them with communal offerings, andfollowing the sin of the spies it was incumbent upon every individual who brought an offering to do so as well. As a result of these sins, it was necessary to compensate for them by adding a new dimension of devotion to God in order to make the offerings more acceptable — "a sweet savor to God." This interpretation explains why this particular commandment appears here, following the episode of the spies.

ו תַּעֲשֶׂה עַל־הָעֹלָה אוֹ לַזָּבַח לַכֶּבֶשׂ הָאֶחָד: אוֹ לָאַיִל תַּעֲשֶׂה מִנְחָה
ז סֹלֶת שְׁנֵי עֶשְׂרֹנִים בְּלוּלָה בַשֶּׁמֶן שְׁלִשִׁית הַהִין: וְיַיִן לַנֶּסֶךְ שְׁלִשִׁית הַהִין
חמישי ח תַּקְרִיב רֵיחַ־נִיחֹחַ לַיהוָה: וְכִי־תַעֲשֶׂה בֶן־בָּקָר עֹלָה אוֹ־זָבַח לְפַלֵּא־נֶדֶר
ט אוֹ־שְׁלָמִים לַיהוָה: וְהִקְרִיב עַל־בֶּן־הַבָּקָר מִנְחָה סֹלֶת שְׁלֹשָׁה עֶשְׂרֹנִים
י בָּלוּל בַּשֶּׁמֶן חֲצִי הַהִין: וְיַיִן תַּקְרִיב לַנֶּסֶךְ חֲצִי הַהִין אִשֵּׁה רֵיחַ־נִיחֹחַ
יא לַיהוָה: כָּכָה יֵעָשֶׂה לַשּׁוֹר הָאֶחָד אוֹ לָאַיִל הָאֶחָד אוֹ־לַשֶּׂה בַכְּבָשִׂים אוֹ
יב בָעִזִּים: כַּמִּסְפָּר אֲשֶׁר תַּעֲשׂוּ כָּכָה תַּעֲשׂוּ לָאֶחָד כְּמִסְפָּרָם: כָּל־הָאֶזְרָח
יג יַעֲשֶׂה־כָּכָה אֶת־אֵלֶּה לְהַקְרִיב אִשֵּׁה רֵיחַ־נִיחֹחַ לַיהוָה: וְכִי־יָגוּר אִתְּכֶם
יד גֵּר אוֹ אֲשֶׁר־בְּתוֹכְכֶם לְדֹרֹתֵיכֶם וְעָשָׂה אִשֵּׁה רֵיחַ־נִיחֹחַ לַיהוָה כַּאֲשֶׁר
טו תַּעֲשׂוּ כֵּן יַעֲשֶׂה: הַקָּהָל חֻקָּה אַחַת לָכֶם וְלַגֵּר הַגָּר חֻקַּת עוֹלָם
טז לְדֹרֹתֵיכֶם כָּכֶם כַּגֵּר יִהְיֶה לִפְנֵי יהוָה: תּוֹרָה אַחַת וּמִשְׁפָּט אֶחָד יִהְיֶה
לָכֶם וְלַגֵּר הַגָּר אִתְּכֶם:
ששי יז־יח וַיְדַבֵּר יהוָה אֶל־מֹשֶׁה לֵּאמֹר: דַּבֵּר אֶל־בְּנֵי יִשְׂרָאֵל וְאָמַרְתָּ אֲלֵהֶם
יט בְּבֹאֲכֶם אֶל־הָאָרֶץ אֲשֶׁר אֲנִי מֵבִיא אֶתְכֶם שָׁמָּה: וְהָיָה בַּאֲכָלְכֶם
כ מִלֶּחֶם הָאָרֶץ תָּרִימוּ תְרוּמָה לַיהוָה: רֵאשִׁית עֲרִסֹתֵכֶם חַלָּה תָּרִימוּ
כא תְרוּמָה כִּתְרוּמַת גֹּרֶן כֵּן תָּרִימוּ אֹתָהּ: מֵרֵאשִׁית עֲרִסֹתֵיכֶם תִּתְּנוּ
כב לַיהוָה תְּרוּמָה לְדֹרֹתֵיכֶם: וְכִי תִשְׁגּוּ וְלֹא תַעֲשׂוּ אֵת
כג כָּל־הַמִּצְוֺת הָאֵלֶּה אֲשֶׁר־דִּבֶּר יהוָה אֶל־מֹשֶׁה: אֵת כָּל־אֲשֶׁר צִוָּה יהוָה
כד אֲלֵיכֶם בְּיַד־מֹשֶׁה מִן־הַיּוֹם אֲשֶׁר צִוָּה יהוָה וָהָלְאָה לְדֹרֹתֵיכֶם: וְהָיָה
אִם מֵעֵינֵי הָעֵדָה נֶעֶשְׂתָה לִשְׁגָגָה וְעָשׂוּ כָל־הָעֵדָה פַּר בֶּן־בָּקָר אֶחָד

20. חַלָּה תָּרִימוּ תְרוּמָה — *You shall set apart challah as a heave-offering.* Following the sin of the spies, (the Torah) also instituted (the *mitzvah*) of *challah,* so that they would be worthy that a blessing come to rest in their homes, as it says, וְרֵאשִׁית עֲרִיסוֹתֵיכֶם תִּתְּנוּ לַכֹּהֵן לְהָנִיחַ בְּרָכָה אֶל בֵּיתֶךָ, *You shall give to the Kohen the first of your dough that he may cause a blessing to rest on your house* (*Ezekiel* 44:30), and (as we find) regarding Elijah, עֲשִׂי לִי מִשָּׁם עֻגָה קְטַנָּה בָרִאשֹׁנָה וְהוֹצֵאת לִי . . . כִּי כֹה אָמַר ה׳ . . . כַּד הַקֶּמַח לֹא תִכְלָה, *Make me a little cake of it first and bring it to me . . . for thus says HASHEM . . . the jar of flour shall not be spent* (*I Kings* 17:13, 14).

22. וְכִי תִשְׁגּוּ — *And if you err.* It has already been explained according to tradition, that this verse refers to the inadvertent transgression of idolatry (*Horayos* 8a). Now this (will happen) since it was decreed that *their descendants would be thrown down among the nations* (based on *Psalms* 106:27); therefore, it will not be unusual for them to err regarding idolatry when they return to their land.

NOTES

20. חַלָּה תָּרִימוּ תְרוּמָה — *You shall set apart challah as a heave-offering.* Just as in verse 4, the *Sforno* gives the reason for the Torah's inclusion of a particular commandment in this chapter.

22. וְכִי תִשְׁגּוּ וְלֹא תַעֲשׂוּ אֵת כָּל הַמִּצְוֹת הָאֵלֶּה אֲשֶׁר דִּבֶּר ה׳ אֶל מֹשֶׁה — *And if you err and do not observe all these commandments which HASHEM has spoken to Moses.* The *Sforno* explains why this grave sin of idolatry is written in this particular *parashah.* In the previous chapter (14:28), the *Sforno* cites the verse from *Psalms* (106:27) where the sin of the spies and the subsequent retribution (death in the wilderness) is linked to the punishment of exile, when their seed will be "cast among the nations." In the Diaspora, it is difficult for the Jew

shall you prepare for the elevation-offering or the feast-offering for each sheep. [6] *Or for a ram — you shall prepare a meal-offering, two tenth[-ephah] fine flour mixed with a third-hin of oil;* [7] *and a third-hin of wine for a libation shall you bring as a satisfying aroma to* HASHEM. [8] *When you prepare a young bull as an elevation-offering or feast-offering, because of an articulated vow, or a peace-offering to* HASHEM, [9] *one shall bring with the young bull a meal-offering: three tenth[-ephah] fine flour mixed with a half-hin of oil.* [10] *You shall bring a half-hin of wine for a libation, a fire-offering, a satisfying aroma to* HASHEM.

[11] *"So shall be done for each bull or for each ram, or for a lamb or kid among the sheep or goats.* [12] *According to the number that you prepare, so shall you do for each one, according to their number.* [13] *Every native shall do so with them, to bring a fire-offering, a satisfying aroma to* HASHEM.

[14] *"When a proselyte sojourns with you or one who is among you throughout your generations and he shall prepare a fire-offering, a satisfying aroma to* HASHEM *— as you do, so shall he do.* [15] *For the congregation — the same decree shall be for you and for the proselyte who sojourns, an eternal decree for your generations; like you like the proselyte shall it be before* HASHEM. [16] *One teaching and one judgment shall be for you and for the proselyte who sojourns among you."*

[17] HASHEM *spoke to Moses, saying,* [18] *"Speak to the Children of Israel and say to them: When you come to the Land to which I bring you,* [19] *it shall be that when you will eat of the bread of the Land, you shall set aside a portion for* HASHEM. [20] *As the first of your kneading you shall set aside a loaf as a portion, like the portion of the threshing-floor, so shall you set it aside.* [21] *From the first of your kneading shall you give a portion to* HASHEM, *for your generations.*

[22] *"If you err and do not perform all of these commandments, which* HASHEM *has spoken to Moses,* [23] *everything that* HASHEM *commanded you through Moses, from the day that* HASHEM *commanded and onward, throughout your generations.* [24] *If because of the eyes of the assembly it was done unintentionally, the entire assembly shall prepare one young bull*

וְלֹא תַעֲשׂוּ אֵת כָּל הַמִּצְוֺת הָאֵלֶּה אֲשֶׁר דִּבֶּר ה׳ אֶל מֹשֶׁה — *And do not observe all these commandments which* HASHEM *has spoken to Moses.* Since you will err regarding idolatry, hence even though you will (technically) perform all the acts of the commandments you will not be doing those *commandments which God spoke to Moses,* because He, the Blessed One, prefaced all (the commandments) with knowledge (recognition) of His Godliness, as it says, אָנֹכִי ה׳ אֱלֹהֶיךָ, *I am* HASHEM, *your God* (*Exodus* 20:2), and so (our Sages) have stated, "He who accepts idolatry is as one who denies the entire Torah" (*Sifre*).

NOTES

not to be influenced by the culture and beliefs of his host country. Hence, the law concerning idolatry follows the chapter of the spies.

The *Sforno* also explains why the non-observance of *all* the commandments of God will result if one is guilty of idolatry — even בְּשׁוֹגֵג (with no outright intent). A person can *perform* the *mitzvos* and still be deemed as one who has failed to do God's wish (רְצוֹן ה׳). Without recognizing a מְצַוֶּה, *one who commands,* there can be no מִצְוָה, *commandment.* The act of idolatry is a denial of God, and without a total unadulterated belief in the One God, performance of the *mitzvos* is meaningless. See *Rashi* here and in verse 23.

לְעֹלָה לְרֵיחַ נִיחֹחַ לַיהוה וּמִנְחָתוֹ וְנִסְכּוֹ כַּמִּשְׁפָּט וּשְׂעִיר־עִזִּים אֶחָד
כה לְחַטָּת: וְכִפֶּר הַכֹּהֵן עַל־כָּל־עֲדַת בְּנֵי יִשְׂרָאֵל וְנִסְלַח לָהֶם כִּי־שְׁגָגָה
הִוא וְהֵם הֵבִיאוּ אֶת־קָרְבָּנָם אִשֶּׁה לַיהוה וְחַטָּאתָם לִפְנֵי יהוה עַל־
כו שִׁגְגָתָם: וְנִסְלַח לְכָל־עֲדַת בְּנֵי יִשְׂרָאֵל וְלַגֵּר הַגָּר בְּתוֹכָם כִּי לְכָל־הָעָם
שביעי כז בִּשְׁגָגָה: וְאִם־נֶפֶשׁ אַחַת תֶּחֱטָא בִשְׁגָגָה וְהִקְרִיבָה עֵז
יה׳ רפה כח בַּת־שְׁנָתָהּ לְחַטָּאת: וְכִפֶּר הַכֹּהֵן עַל־הַנֶּפֶשׁ הַשֹּׁגֶגֶת בְּחֶטְאָה בִשְׁגָגָה
כט לִפְנֵי יהוה לְכַפֵּר עָלָיו וְנִסְלַח לוֹ: הָאֶזְרָח בִּבְנֵי יִשְׂרָאֵל וְלַגֵּר הַגָּר
ל בְּתוֹכָם תּוֹרָה אַחַת יִהְיֶה לָכֶם לָעֹשֶׂה בִּשְׁגָגָה: וְהַנֶּפֶשׁ אֲשֶׁר־תַּעֲשֶׂה ׀
בְּיָד רָמָה מִן־הָאֶזְרָח וּמִן־הַגֵּר אֶת־יהוה הוּא מְגַדֵּף וְנִכְרְתָה הַנֶּפֶשׁ
לא הַהִוא מִקֶּרֶב עַמָּהּ: כִּי דְבַר־יהוה בָּזָה וְאֶת־מִצְוָתוֹ הֵפַר הִכָּרֵת ׀ תִּכָּרֵת
יה׳ רפה הַנֶּפֶשׁ הַהִוא עֲוֺנָה בָהּ:
לב וַיִּהְיוּ בְנֵי־יִשְׂרָאֵל בַּמִּדְבָּר וַיִּמְצְאוּ אִישׁ מְקֹשֵׁשׁ עֵצִים בְּיוֹם הַשַּׁבָּת:
לג וַיַּקְרִיבוּ אֹתוֹ הַמֹּצְאִים אֹתוֹ מְקֹשֵׁשׁ עֵצִים אֶל־מֹשֶׁה וְאֶל־אַהֲרֹן
לד וְאֶל כָּל־הָעֵדָה: וַיַּנִּיחוּ אֹתוֹ בַּמִּשְׁמָר כִּי לֹא פֹרַשׁ מַה־יֵּעָשֶׂה
לה לוֹ: וַיֹּאמֶר יהוה אֶל־מֹשֶׁה מוֹת יוּמַת הָאִישׁ רָגוֹם אֹתוֹ
לו בָאֲבָנִים כָּל־הָעֵדָה מִחוּץ לַמַּחֲנֶה: וַיֹּצִיאוּ אֹתוֹ כָּל־הָעֵדָה אֶל־מִחוּץ
לַמַּחֲנֶה וַיִּרְגְּמוּ אֹתוֹ בָּאֲבָנִים וַיָּמֹת כַּאֲשֶׁר צִוָּה יהוה אֶת־מֹשֶׁה:
מפטיר לז־לח וַיֹּאמֶר יהוה אֶל־מֹשֶׁה לֵּאמֹר: דַּבֵּר אֶל־בְּנֵי יִשְׂרָאֵל וְאָמַרְתָּ אֲלֵהֶם
וְעָשׂוּ לָהֶם צִיצִת עַל־כַּנְפֵי בִגְדֵיהֶם לְדֹרֹתָם וְנָתְנוּ עַל־צִיצִת הַכָּנָף
לט פְּתִיל תְּכֵלֶת: וְהָיָה לָכֶם לְצִיצִת וּרְאִיתֶם אֹתוֹ וּזְכַרְתֶּם אֶת־כָּל־
מִצְוֺת יהוה וַעֲשִׂיתֶם אֹתָם וְלֹא־תָתֻרוּ אַחֲרֵי לְבַבְכֶם וְאַחֲרֵי עֵינֵיכֶם

30. אֶת ה׳ הוּא מְגַדֵּף — *He has blasphemed* HASHEM ... and he shall not be granted atonement in this world until he dies, even if he repents out of a fear of punishment. Therefore, the repentance of Israel in regard to (the sin of) the spies was to no avail, as it says, וַתָּשֻׁבוּ וַתִּבְכּוּ לִפְנֵי ה׳ וְלֹא שָׁמַע ה׳ בְּקֹלְכֶם, *And you returned and wept before* HASHEM, *but* HASHEM *did not hearken to your voice* (*Deut.* 1:45)

39. וּרְאִיתֶם אֹתוֹ וּזְכַרְתֶּם אֶת כָּל מִצְוֹת — *And you will see it and remember all the commandments of* HASHEM. You will remember that you are servants of God, the Blessed One, (and that) you accepted His commandments with an oath and a curse. This (shall be) when you see the *tzitzis* which are as the seal of the king (imprinted) on his servants. And thus you will cease to turn ...

אַחֲרֵי לְבַבְכֶם — *After your heart* ... to attain the caprice of your heart in terms of wealth and honor, even if it be through robbery.

NOTES

30. אֶת ה׳ הוּא מְגַדֵּף — *He has blasphemed* HASHEM. See note on 14:27 regarding repentance. One who blasphemes can only gain atonement through death. The Talmud (*Yoma* 86a) states that if one is guilty of חִלּוּל הַשֵּׁם (the profaning of God's Name), only death can atone for that sin. See *Rambam, Mishneh Torah, Laws of Teshuvah* 1:4. The *Sforno*, however, indicates that if one repents, motivated by אַהֲבָה (love, i.e., of God) rather than יִרְאָה (fear of punishment), his repentance will be accepted. Apparently the regret and repentance of the Children of Israel recorded in *Deut.* 1:45 was not in the category of תְּשׁוּבָה מֵאַהֲבָה, *repentance motivated by love.* See the

as an elevation-offering for a satisfying aroma to HASHEM, and its
meal-offering and its libation according to the rule, and one he-goat as a
sin-offering. 25 The Kohen shall atone for the entire assembly of the
Children of Israel and it shall be forgiven them, for it was unintentional, and they have brought their offering, a fire-offering to HASHEM,
and their sin-offering before HASHEM for their unintentional sin. 26 And
it shall be forgiven to the entire assembly of Israel and to the proselyte
who sojourns among them, for it happened to the entire people unintentionally.

27 "If one person sins unintentionally, he shall offer a she-goat within its
first year as a sin-offering. 28 The Kohen shall atone for the erring person
when he sins unintentionally before HASHEM, to atone for him; and it shall
be forgiven him. 29 The native among the Children of Israel and the
proselyte who sojourns among them — there shall be a single teaching for
them, for one who does unintentionally.

30 "A person who shall act high-handedly, whether native or proselyte,
he blasphemed HASHEM! — that person shall be cut off from among his
people, 31 for he scorned the word of HASHEM and broke His commandment;
that person will surely be cut off, his sin is upon him."

32 The Children of Israel were in the Wilderness and they found a man
gathering wood on the Sabbath day. 33 Those who found him gathering
wood brought him to Moses and Aaron, and to the entire assembly. 34 They
placed him in custody, for it had not been clarified what should be done to
him.

35 HASHEM said to Moses: "The man shall be put to death; the entire
assembly shall pelt him with stones outside of the camp."

36 The entire assembly removed him to the outside of the camp; they
pelted him with stones and he died, as HASHEM had commanded Moses.

37 HASHEM said to Moses, saying: 38 "Speak to the Children of Israel and
say to them that they shall make themselves tzitzis on the corners of their
garments, throughout their generations. And they shall place upon the tzitzis of each corner a thread of turquoise wool. 39 It shall constitute tzitzis for
you, that you may see it and remember all the commandments of HASHEM
and perform them; and not explore after your heart and after your eyes

---

וְאַחֲרֵי עֵינֵיכֶם — *And after your eyes* ... to attain the desires of that which you have laid your eyes upon.

אֲשֶׁר אַתֶּם זֹנִים אַחֲרֵיהֶם — *(In pursuit of) that by which you have been led astray.* You turn your intelligent soul away from the ways of eternal life, to the ways of death and destruction.

NOTES

Sforno's commentary there.

39. אַחֲרֵי לְבַבְכֶם וְאַחֲרֵי עֵינֵיכֶם אֲשֶׁר אַתֶּם זֹנִים אַחֲרֵיהֶם — *After your heart and after your eyes (in pursuit of) that by which you have been led astray.* The *Sforno* submits that the heart is greedy, propelling man to pursue and satisfy his desired goals even through dishonest, illegal means, while man's eyes are lustful and bring him to partake of forbidden pleasures. Both of these "agents of the evil inclination" lead man astray, causing him to deviate from the right path to a deceitful, devious and destructive one.

מ אֲשֶׁר־אַתֶּם זֹנִים אַחֲרֵיהֶם: לְמַעַן תִּזְכְּרוּ וַעֲשִׂיתֶם אֶת־כָּל־מִצְוֺתָי
מא וִהְיִיתֶם קְדֹשִׁים לֵאלֹהֵיכֶם: אֲנִי יְהוָה אֱלֹהֵיכֶם אֲשֶׁר הוֹצֵאתִי אֶתְכֶם
מֵאֶרֶץ מִצְרַיִם לִהְיוֹת לָכֶם לֵאלֹהִים אֲנִי יְהוָה אֱלֹהֵיכֶם:

40. לְמַעַן תִּזְכְּרוּ — *In order that you may remember* . . . in order that you may be free of vain thoughts, and thereby remember the wonders of Torah and through them recognize the greatness of God and His kindness.

וַעֲשִׂיתֶם אֶת כָּל מִצְוֹתָי — *And do all My commandments* . . . and thus you will do all My commandments out of love and awe (reverence).

וִהְיִיתֶם קְדֹשִׁים לֵאלֹהֵיכֶם — *And be holy to your God* . . . and thus you will be holy before Him, (leading you to) eternal life, as He intended when He said, וְאַתֶּם תִּהְיוּ לִי מַמְלֶכֶת כֹּהֲנִים וְגוֹי קָדוֹשׁ, *And you shall be unto Me a kingdom of Kohanim and a holy nation* (*Exodus* 19:6).

NOTES

40-41. וַעֲשִׂיתֶם אֶת כָּל מִצְוֹתָי וִהְיִיתֶם קְדֹשִׁים לֵאלֹהֵיכֶם . . . אֲנִי ה׳ אֱלֹהֵיכֶם — *And do all My commandments and be holy to your God . . . I am* H*ASHEM your God.* The sense of these verses, according to the *Sforno*, is as follows: God's intention was to grant the people of Israel eternal existence. This was to be effectuated through two means, which the *Sforno* explained above in *Genesis* 17:7 and *Exodus* 19:6. One way was by creating them in such a manner that their existence as a

after which you stray. [40] *So that you may remember and perform all My commandments and be holy to your God.* [41] *I am HASHEM, your God, Who has removed you from the land of Egypt to be a God unto you; I am HASHEM your God."*

---

41. אֲנִי ה׳ אֱלֹהֵיכֶם אֲשֶׁר הוֹצֵאתִי אֶתְכֶם — *I am HASHEM your God Who brought you out. I am HASHEM,* in the sense that I am *your God* Whom you recognize as the One Who is the First Cause and Who is worthy to be served and to Whom prayer should be directed.

הוֹצֵאתִי אֶתְכֶם מֵאֶרֶץ מִצְרַיִם — *Who brought you out of the land of Egypt.* (This I did) so that you shall merit that I be *your God,* (and thus) your ongoing existence will flow from Me, without need for any intermediary. Such existence is unchanging and will in no manner deteriorate, as is true regarding the existence of all everlasting matter.

אֲנִי ה׳ אֱלֹהֵיכֶם — *I am HASHEM your God.* I now command you (to perform) this commandment for this purpose, in order that you may merit this intended (end) — as He said, *and be holy unto your God* (verse 40).

NOTES

people emanates directly from Him and not through any heavenly intermediary, as is the case with other nations. The second medium was by sanctifying them, because sanctity ensures eternity. The *tzitzis* (fringes) remind Israel of their mission and purpose in the world, and it was in order to fulfill this role that they were delivered from Egypt.

פרשת קרח

טז

א וַיִּקַּח קֹרַח בֶּן־יִצְהָר בֶּן־קְהָת בֶּן־לֵוִי וְדָתָן וַאֲבִירָם בְּנֵי אֱלִיאָב וְאוֹן
ב בֶּן־פֶּלֶת בְּנֵי רְאוּבֵן׃ וַיָּקֻמוּ לִפְנֵי מֹשֶׁה וַאֲנָשִׁים מִבְּנֵי־יִשְׂרָאֵל חֲמִשִּׁים
ג וּמָאתָיִם נְשִׂיאֵי עֵדָה קְרִאֵי מוֹעֵד אַנְשֵׁי־שֵׁם׃ וַיִּקָּהֲלוּ עַל־מֹשֶׁה
וְעַל־אַהֲרֹן וַיֹּאמְרוּ אֲלֵהֶם רַב־לָכֶם כִּי כָל־הָעֵדָה כֻּלָּם קְדֹשִׁים וּבְתוֹכָם
ד יהוה וּמַדּוּעַ תִּתְנַשְּׂאוּ עַל־קְהַל יהוה׃ וַיִּשְׁמַע מֹשֶׁה וַיִּפֹּל עַל־פָּנָיו׃
ה וַיְדַבֵּר אֶל־קֹרַח וְאֶל־כָּל־עֲדָתוֹ לֵאמֹר בֹּקֶר וְיֹדַע יהוה אֶת־אֲשֶׁר־לוֹ
ו וְאֶת־הַקָּדוֹשׁ וְהִקְרִיב אֵלָיו וְאֵת אֲשֶׁר יִבְחַר־בּוֹ יַקְרִיב אֵלָיו׃ זֹאת עֲשׂוּ
ז קְחוּ־לָכֶם מַחְתּוֹת קֹרַח וְכָל־עֲדָתוֹ׃ וּתְנוּ־בָהֵן ׀ אֵשׁ וְשִׂימוּ עֲלֵיהֶן ׀
קְטֹרֶת לִפְנֵי יהוה מָחָר וְהָיָה הָאִישׁ אֲשֶׁר־יִבְחַר יהוה הוּא הַקָּדוֹשׁ
ח־ט רַב־לָכֶם בְּנֵי לֵוִי׃ וַיֹּאמֶר מֹשֶׁה אֶל־קֹרַח שִׁמְעוּ־נָא בְּנֵי לֵוִי׃ הַמְעַט

XVI

1-2. וַיִּקַּח קֹרַח — *Now, Korach took.* The sense and sequence of the verse is as though it said: And Korach, Dathan and Abiram and On the son of Peleth took two hundred and fifty men who were princes of the congregation and they rose up in the face of Moses with certain of the Children of Israel, after which . . .

3. וַיִּקָּהֲלוּ עַל מֹשֶׁה וְעַל אַהֲרֹן — *And they assembled themselves together against Moses and against Aaron.* Korach, Dathan and Abiram assembled together to complain against Moses and Aaron in the presence of the two hundred and fifty princes of the congregation who had gone there, at the advice of these complainers, at a time when *certain of the Children of Israel* had come (to Moses and Aaron) for judgment (i.e., adjudication). (Now) these two hundred and fifty men gathered there as though they were innocently coming to stand there with Moses. (This was done) so that when Korach, Dathan and Aviram would later assemble against Moses and Aaron, they (the 250) would agree, as one, with the demands of those assembling, in the presence of certain of the Children of Israel who were (also) present there. (Now) they (i.e., Korach et al.) chose a time when a multitude would be there so as to publicize (the event) and to spread (their complaints) throughout the camp in order to increase the number of those who would rise up with them.

כִּי כָל הָעֵדָה — *Being that all the congregation* . . . each and every one of them.

כֻּלָּם קְדֹשִׁים — *Are all holy.* From the sole of the foot unto the head (based on *Isaiah* 1:6),

NOTES

XVI

1-3. וַיִּקַּח קֹרַח . . . וַיִּקָּהֲלוּ עַל מֹשֶׁה וְעַל אַהֲרֹן — *Now, Korach took . . . And they assembled themselves together against Moses and against Aaron.* The *Sforno* construes the verb *took* (וַיִּקַּח) as an antecedent of אֲנָשִׁים מִבְּנֵי יִשְׂרָאֵל, *certain of the Children of Israel,* and also of חֲמִשִּׁים וּמָאתָיִם נְשִׂיאֵי עֵדָה, *two hundred and fifty princes of the congregation.* As the *Sforno* explains, the challenge to Moses' authority and Aaron's priesthood was carefully planned. When Korach and his cohorts would appear to rise up against Moses, the princes would be present, together with those who had come to Moses for a decision of law. In this manner, their complaints would be heard and joined in by others, and the fire of rebellion would quickly spread throughout the camp.

3. כֻּלָּם קְדֹשִׁים — *Are all holy.* The *Sforno* interprets the word כֻּלָּם, *are all,* in a literal sense, referring to the total being of each Israelite, for hadn't God stated (in the *parashah* of *tzitzis*) that everyone is holy? And the *parashah* of *tzitzis* was commanded to all Israel! Hence, by what right does Moses strip the firstborn of their right to serve and arrogate this honor to himself, his brother Aaron and Aaron's sons?

5-7. וַיְדַבֵּר אֶל קֹרַח וְאֶל כָּל עֲדָתוֹ . . . אֶת אֲשֶׁר לוֹ וְאֶת הַקָּדוֹשׁ וְהִקְרִיב אֵלָיו וְאֵת אֲשֶׁר יִבְחַר בּוֹ יַקְרִיב אֵלָיו . . . הוּא הַקָּדוֹשׁ — *And he spoke to Korach*

PARASHAS KORACH

16 [1] *Korah son of Izhar son of Kohath son of Levi separated himself, with*
Dathan and Abiram, sons of Eliab, and On son of Peleth, the offspring
of Reuben. [2] *They stood before Moses with two hundred and fifty men from*
the Children of Israel, leaders of the assembly, those summoned for
meeting, men of renown. [3] *They gathered together against Moses and*
against Aaron and said to them, "It is too much for you! For the entire
assembly — all of them — are holy and HASHEM is among them; why do you
exalt yourselves over the congregation of HASHEM?"
[4] *Moses heard and fell on his face.*
[5] *He spoke to Korah and to his entire assembly, saying, "In the morning*
God will make known the one who is His own and the holy one, and He will
draw him close to Himself, and whomever He will choose, He will draw
close to Himself. [6] *Do this: Take for yourselves fire-pans — Korah and his*
entire assembly — [7] *and put fire in them and place incense upon them*
before HASHEM tomorrow. Then the man whom HASHEM will choose — he is
the holy one. It is too much for you, O offspring of Levi!"
[8] *Moses said to Korah, "Hear now, O offspring of Levi:* [9] *Is it not enough*

---

as it says, *And you shall be holy unto your God* (15:40).

וּמַדּוּעַ תִּתְנַשְּׂאוּ — *Why then do you lift yourselves up* ... in the area of sanctity by prohibiting the firstborn from (officiating) at the service, (while) Moses already served as a *Kohen* during the seven days of consecration, and Aaron and his sons (have been designated) as *Kohanim* forever?

5. וַיְדַבֵּר אֶל קֹרַח וְאֶל כָּל עֲדָתוֹ — *And he spoke to Korach and to all his company.* He informed them that he was aware of their stratagem and the plot of their congregation.

אֶת אֲשֶׁר לוֹ — *Who are His* . . . who (truly) speak on behalf of God, the Blessed One's, honor.

וְאֶת הַקָּדוֹשׁ וְהִקְרִיב אֵלָיו — *And who is holy to come near unto Him* . . . and He will notify (us) who the holy one is that is worthy to offer sacrifices unto Him.

וְאֵת אֲשֶׁר יִבְחַר בּוֹ יַקְרִיב אֵלָיו — *And whom He shall choose to come near unto Him.* He alone will God draw near to Him from the midst of the destruction which will befall the others, as it says, *separate yourselves from among this congregation* (v. 21).

7. הוּא הַקָּדוֹשׁ — *He shall be holy.* He alone, for only one shall merit this (role). This was said so that they would be afraid, repent and not be lost, for (God) does not desire the death (of the wicked) (based on *Ezekiel* 18:32.)

רַב לָכֶם בְּנֵי לֵוִי — *You want too much, sons of Levi.* You, *the men that belong to Korach* (v. 32), take too much upon yourselves, for God will be angry with you all the more, being that you have already been chosen for His service.

NOTES

and to all his company . . . who are His and who is holy to come near unto Him and whom He shall choose to come near unto Him . . . He shall be holy. The *Sforno* divides the statement of Moses to Korach and his company into three parts. First, he tells them that he is fully cognizant of their evil plot. Secondly, the Almighty will let them know, in no uncertain terms, who truly speaks in His behalf and is competent to offer sacrifices on the Altar. Finally, he cautions them that they are courting danger, for the only survivor from the destruction which will befall them will be the one who is worthy. Moses was hopeful that they would heed his warning and repent. The *Sforno* is of the opinion that this is another example of God not wanting to punish the wicked. Rather, His greatest desire is for the transgressor to do *teshuvah.*

מִכֶּם כִּי־הִבְדִּיל° אֱלֹהֵי יִשְׂרָאֵל אֶתְכֶם מֵעֲדַת יִשְׂרָאֵל לְהַקְרִיב אֶתְכֶם
אֵלָיו לַעֲבֹד אֶת־עֲבֹדַת מִשְׁכַּן יהוה וְלַעֲמֹד לִפְנֵי הָעֵדָה לְשָׁרְתָם:
י־יא וַיַּקְרֵב אֹתְךָ וְאֶת־כָּל־אַחֶיךָ בְנֵי־לֵוִי אִתָּךְ וּבִקַּשְׁתֶּם גַּם־כְּהֻנָּה: לָכֵן
°תַּלִּינוּ ק׳ אַתָּה וְכָל־עֲדָתְךָ הַנֹּעָדִים עַל־יהוה וְאַהֲרֹן מַה־הוּא כִּי °תלונו עָלָיו:
יב וַיִּשְׁלַח מֹשֶׁה לִקְרֹא לְדָתָן וְלַאֲבִירָם בְּנֵי אֱלִיאָב וַיֹּאמְרוּ לֹא נַעֲלֶה:
יג הַמְעַט כִּי הֶעֱלִיתָנוּ מֵאֶרֶץ זָבַת חָלָב וּדְבַשׁ לַהֲמִיתֵנוּ בַּמִּדְבָּר
שני יד כִּי־תִשְׂתָּרֵר עָלֵינוּ גַּם־הִשְׂתָּרֵר: אַף לֹא אֶל־אֶרֶץ זָבַת חָלָב וּדְבַשׁ
הֲבִיאֹתָנוּ וַתִּתֶּן־לָנוּ נַחֲלַת שָׂדֶה וָכָרֶם הַעֵינֵי הָאֲנָשִׁים הָהֵם תְּנַקֵּר
טו לֹא נַעֲלֶה: וַיִּחַר לְמֹשֶׁה מְאֹד וַיֹּאמֶר אֶל־יהוה אַל־תֵּפֶן אֶל־
מִנְחָתָם לֹא° חֲמוֹר אֶחָד מֵהֶם נָשָׂאתִי וְלֹא הֲרֵעֹתִי אֶת־אַחַד מֵהֶם:

---

9. וְלַעֲמֹד לִפְנֵי הָעֵדָה לְשָׁרְתָם — *And to stand before the congregation to minister to them* . . . to serve God, the Exalted One, through song, and (serving in) His Sanctuary through the labor of carrying and other (labors). Now, He wanted you to perform this service *before the congregation* so as to inform them of their shortcoming, disqualifying them from serving, and that you have been chosen in their stead.

11. לָכֵן אַתָּה וְכָל עֲדָתְךָ הַנֹּעָדִים עַל ה׳ — *Therefore, you and all your congregation that are gathered against* HASHEM. . . I say to you, that it is עַל ה׳, *against* HASHEM! Let it be known that I cast my burden upon HASHEM (based on *Psalms* 55:23) and He will (no doubt) repay you for His insult, but I will not rise up against you at all.

14. אַף לֹא אֶל אֶרֶץ . . . וַתִּתֶּן לָנוּ — *Moreover, you have not brought us to a land . . .* (*nor*) *given us*. Not only have you perpetrated evil against us by taking us out of a land flowing with milk and honey and bringing us into the wilderness, but you also jest with us — for you have not brought us to the Land into which you said (you would bring us) and still you speak (to us) as though you have given us "an inheritance of fields and vineyards," by commanding us those commandments which are connected (only) to the Land, when you said, לֹא תְכַלֶּה פְּאַת שָׂדְךָ . . . וּפֶרֶט כַּרְמְךָ לֹא תְלַקֵּט, *You shall not wholly reap the corner of your field . . . nor shall you gather the fallen fruit of your vineyard* (*Leviticus* 19:9, 10), as though it was already ours and we have fields and vineyards in it!

הַעֵינֵי הָאֲנָשִׁים הָהֵם תְּנַקֵּר — *Will you put out the eyes of these men?* Do you think you can put out our eyes (i.e., blindfold us) in such a manner that we will not discern your scheme?

15. אַל תֵּפֶן אֶל מִנְחָתָם — *Turn not to their offering*. Do not accept any kind of offering which they will bring to atone for themselves — the reverse of יָרַח מִנְחָה, *Let Him accept*

NOTES

9. וְלַעֲמֹד לִפְנֵי הָעֵדָה לְשָׁרְתָם — *And to stand before the congregation to minister to them*. Moses appeals to the Levites to be reasonable. Why do they join the others in claiming that all are holy and why do they demand the rights of the holy service on behalf of the firstborn? They know full well that they were chosen after the sin of the Golden Calf to replace the firstborn — and this was done openly ("before the congregation"); not in a secret manner.

11. לָכֵן אַתָּה וְכָל עֲדָתְךָ הַנֹּעָדִים עַל ה׳ — *Therefore, you and all your congregation that are gathered upon* HASHEM. The expression עַל ה׳ is not interpreted by the *Sforno* as meaning *against* HASHEM but in the sense of *upon* HASHEM, similar to the expression used in *Psalms* 55:23 — הַשְׁלֵךְ עַל ה׳ יְהָבְךָ וכו׳, *Cast your burden upon* HASHEM *and He will sustain you etc.* Hence, Moses is saying that he will do naught to punish them, for he is confident that God will exact retribution for their rebellion against the one who was chosen by the Almighty.

14. אַף לֹא אֶל אֶרֶץ . . . וַתִּתֶּן לָנוּ . . . הַעֵינֵי הָאֲנָשִׁים הָהֵם תְּנַקֵּר — *Moreover, you have not brought us to a land . . .* (*nor*) *given us . . . will you put out the eyes of these men?* The *Sforno* explains the sense of the verse in a manner which clarifies the (seemingly)

for you that the God of Israel has segregated you from the assembly of Israel to draw you near to Himself, to perform the service of the Tabernacle of HASHEM, *and to stand before the assembly to minister to them?* 10 *And He drew you near, and all your brethren, the offspring of Levi, with you — yet you seek priesthood, as well!* 11 *Therefore, you and your entire assembly that are joining together are against* HASHEM! *And as for Aaron — what is he that you protest against him?"*

12 *Moses sent forth to summon Dathan and Abiram, the sons of Eliab, but they said, "We shall not go up!* 13 *Is it not enough that you have brought us up from a land flowing with milk and honey to cause us to die in the Wilderness, yet you seek to dominate us, even to dominate further?*
14 *Moreover, you did not bring us to a land flowing with milk and honey nor give us a heritage of field and vineyard! Even if you would gouge out the eyes of those men, we shall not go up!"*

15 *This distressed Moses greatly, and he said to* HASHEM, *"Do not turn to their gift-offering! I have not taken even a single donkey of theirs, nor have I wronged even one of them."*

---

an offering (*I Samuel* 26:19). This is because I do not forgive my insult and You cannot pardon them without this (exculpation), as (our Sages) said, "Sins committed between man and his fellow man are not atoned for on Yom Kippur unless he appeases his fellow" (*Yoma* 85b), and so Jeremiah says, ... כִּי כָרוּ שׁוּחָה לְנַפְשִׁי זְכֹר עָמְדִי לְפָנֶיךָ לְדַבֵּר עֲלֵיהֶם טוֹבָה ... אַל תְּכַפֵּר עַל עֲוֹנָם וְחַטָּאתָם מִלְּפָנֶיךָ אַל תֶּמְחִי, *For they have dug a pit for my soul. Remember that I stood before You to speak good for them ... forgive not their iniquity, neither blot out their sin from Your sight* (*Jeremiah* 18:20,23).

לֹא חֲמוֹר אֶחָד מֵהֶם נָשָׂאתִי — *I have not taken one ass from them.* I did not benefit from them even as a common man would benefit from his friend, for I did not even borrow an ass from them. Hence, my rulership over them was totally for their benefit and to attend to their affairs; not for mine or for my pleasure, as is the custom of those who are in a position of authority. Their criticism of my leadership is therefore only due to their ingratitude.

וְלֹא הֲרֵעֹתִי אֶת אַחַד מֵהֶם — *Neither have I hurt one of them.* Even the enmity caused by a guilty verdict in court is not applicable to me, for it never happened that they should appear before me for a decision of law in a manner that I should declare them culpable.

NOTES

awkward lack of continuity in the phraseology of this verse. The first part is a simple complaint that Moses has not kept his promise to bring them into *Eretz Yisrael.* The second part is a more serious grievance, for Moses has added insult to injury by speaking to them as though they had already inherited the Land and were already obligated to give gifts to the poor from fields and vineyards which were nonexistent! Surely this is a case of mockery on the part of Moses, which Korach and his company refused to accept with equanimity.

15. אַל תֵּפֶן אֶל מִנְחָתָם לֹא חֲמוֹר אֶחָד מֵהֶם נָשָׂאתִי וְלֹא הֲרֵעֹתִי אֶת אַחַד מֵהֶם — *Turn not to their offering; I have not taken one ass from them, neither have I hurt one of them.* The *Sforno* explains why Moses asked God not to accept their act of repentance. Surely, the power of acceptance or rejection is not in his domain but in the hands of the Almighty. But in truth, a sin committed against one's fellowman may be forgiven by God, but it is not completely exculpated until the injured party is appeased, and Moses states that he is not prepared to forgive his insult, just as we find in the case of Jeremiah. The reason for Moses' anger and adamant refusal to forgive them is, as he explains, because of their profound ingratitude. The *Sforno* interprets the words of Moses as referring to his judicial decisions, for how could we presume that Moses would ever "hurt" anyone.

טז וַיֹּאמֶר מֹשֶׁה אֶל־קֹרַח אַתָּה וְכָל־עֲדָתְךָ הֱיוּ לִפְנֵי יהוה אַתָּה וָהֵם
יז וְאַהֲרֹן מָחָר׃ וּקְחוּ ׀ אִישׁ מַחְתָּתוֹ וּנְתַתֶּם עֲלֵיהֶם קְטֹרֶת וְהִקְרַבְתֶּם לִפְנֵי
יהוה אִישׁ מַחְתָּתוֹ חֲמִשִּׁים וּמָאתַיִם מַחְתֹּת וְאַתָּה וְאַהֲרֹן אִישׁ מַחְתָּתוֹ׃
יח וַיִּקְחוּ אִישׁ מַחְתָּתוֹ וַיִּתְּנוּ עֲלֵיהֶם אֵשׁ וַיָּשִׂימוּ עֲלֵיהֶם קְטֹרֶת וַיַּעַמְדוּ
יט פֶּתַח אֹהֶל מוֹעֵד וּמֹשֶׁה וְאַהֲרֹן׃ וַיַּקְהֵל עֲלֵיהֶם קֹרַח אֶת־כָּל־הָעֵדָה
שלישי כ אֶל־פֶּתַח אֹהֶל מוֹעֵד וַיֵּרָא כְבוֹד־יהוה אֶל־כָּל־הָעֵדָה׃ וַיְדַבֵּר
כא יהוה אֶל־מֹשֶׁה וְאֶל־אַהֲרֹן לֵאמֹר׃ הִבָּדְלוּ מִתּוֹךְ הָעֵדָה הַזֹּאת וַאֲכַלֶּה
כב אֹתָם כְּרָגַע׃ וַיִּפְּלוּ עַל־פְּנֵיהֶם וַיֹּאמְרוּ אֵל אֱלֹהֵי הָרוּחֹת לְכָל־
כג בָּשָׂר הָאִישׁ אֶחָד יֶחֱטָא וְעַל כָּל־הָעֵדָה תִּקְצֹף׃ וַיְדַבֵּר יהוה
כד אֶל־מֹשֶׁה לֵּאמֹר׃ דַּבֵּר אֶל־הָעֵדָה לֵאמֹר הֵעָלוּ מִסָּבִיב לְמִשְׁכַּן־קֹרַח
כה דָּתָן וַאֲבִירָם׃ וַיָּקָם מֹשֶׁה וַיֵּלֶךְ אֶל־דָּתָן וַאֲבִירָם וַיֵּלְכוּ אַחֲרָיו זִקְנֵי
כו יִשְׂרָאֵל׃ וַיְדַבֵּר אֶל־הָעֵדָה לֵאמֹר סוּרוּ נָא מֵעַל אָהֳלֵי הָאֲנָשִׁים
הָרְשָׁעִים הָאֵלֶּה וְאַל־תִּגְּעוּ בְּכָל־אֲשֶׁר לָהֶם פֶּן־תִּסָּפוּ בְּכָל־חַטֹּאתָם׃
כז וַיֵּעָלוּ מֵעַל מִשְׁכַּן־קֹרַח דָּתָן וַאֲבִירָם מִסָּבִיב וְדָתָן וַאֲבִירָם יָצְאוּ
כח נִצָּבִים פֶּתַח אָהֳלֵיהֶם וּנְשֵׁיהֶם וּבְנֵיהֶם וְטַפָּם׃ וַיֹּאמֶר מֹשֶׁה בְּזֹאת תֵּדְעוּן
כִּי־יהוה שְׁלָחַנִי לַעֲשׂוֹת אֵת כָּל־הַמַּעֲשִׂים הָאֵלֶּה כִּי־לֹא מִלִּבִּי׃
כט אִם־כְּמוֹת כָּל־הָאָדָם יְמֻתוּן אֵלֶּה וּפְקֻדַּת כָּל־הָאָדָם יִפָּקֵד עֲלֵיהֶם
ל לֹא יהוה שְׁלָחָנִי׃ וְאִם־בְּרִיאָה יִבְרָא יהוה וּפָצְתָה הָאֲדָמָה אֶת־פִּיהָ
וּבָלְעָה אֹתָם וְאֶת־כָּל־אֲשֶׁר לָהֶם וְיָרְדוּ חַיִּים שְׁאֹלָה וִידַעְתֶּם כִּי נִאֲצוּ
לא הָאֲנָשִׁים הָאֵלֶּה אֶת־יהוה׃ וַיְהִי כְּכַלֹּתוֹ לְדַבֵּר אֵת כָּל־הַדְּבָרִים הָאֵלֶּה
לב וַתִּבָּקַע הָאֲדָמָה אֲשֶׁר תַּחְתֵּיהֶם׃ וַתִּפְתַּח הָאָרֶץ אֶת־פִּיהָ וַתִּבְלַע
אֹתָם וְאֶת־בָּתֵּיהֶם וְאֵת כָּל־הָאָדָם אֲשֶׁר לְקֹרַח וְאֵת כָּל־הָרְכוּשׁ׃

16. אַתָּה וְכָל עֲדָתְךָ הֱיוּ לִפְנֵי ה׳ — *You and all your congregation are to be before* HASHEM. You are summoned to judgment before Him.

21. הִבָּדְלוּ — *Separate yourselves* ... so that your merit shall not shield them, similar to יְמַלֵּט אִי נָקִי, *He delivers the one who is not innocent* (Job 22:30).

22. הָאִישׁ אֶחָד יֶחֱטָא — *Shall one man sin* ... since he (alone) caused the congregation to assemble against us, as it says, *and Korach assembled all the congregation against them* (v. 19).

24. דַּבֵּר אֶל הָעֵדָה לֵאמֹר הֵעָלוּ מִסָּבִיב — *Speak to the congregation saying: Get up from around.* He explained that when it says *separate yourselves from the congregation* (v. 21), it only referred to the congregation of Korach.

26. פֶּן תִּסָּפוּ — *Lest you be swept away* ... for you are not worthy to be saved if you will be with them when they are smitten.

NOTES

21. הִבָּדְלוּ — *Separate yourselves.* The verse from *Job* cited by the *Sforno* proves that the guilty can be saved by the righteous, for as the *Metzudos David* interprets the verse, the meaning is: God delivers those who are not innocent in the merit of those *whose hands are pure* (וְנִמְלַט בְּבֹר כַּפֶּיךָ). Therefore, Moses and Aaron are told to separate themselves from these sinners, for otherwise their presence will protect them from punishment. On the other hand, those who may not be guilty of rebellion, but are also not deemed righteous, would nonetheless be vulnerable to destruction were they

[16] *Moses said to Korah, "You and your entire assembly, be before HASHEM — you, they, and Aaron — tomorrow.* [17] *Let each man take his fire-pan and you shall place incense on them and you shall bring before HASHEM each man with his fire-pan — two hundred and fifty fire-pans; and you and Aaron, each man with his fire-pan."*

[18] *So they took — each man his fire-pan — and they placed fire on them and put incense on them; and they stood at the entrance of the Tent of Meeting, with Moses and Aaron.* [19] *Korah gathered the entire assembly to the entrance of the Tent of Meeting, and the glory of HASHEM appeared to the entire assembly.*

[20] *HASHEM spoke to Moses and Aaron, saying,* [21] *"Separate yourselves from amid this assembly, and I shall destroy them in an instant!"*

[22] *They fell on their faces and said, "O God, God of the spirits of all flesh, shall one man sin, and You be angry with the entire assembly?"*

[23] *HASHEM spoke to Moses saying,* [24] *"Speak to the assembly, saying, 'Get yourselves up from all around the dwelling places of Korah, Dathan, and Abiram.' "*

[25] *So Moses stood up and went to Dathan and Abiram, and the elders of Israel followed him.* [26] *He spoke to the assembly, saying, "Turn away now from near the tents of these wicked men, and do not touch anything of theirs, lest you perish because of all their sins."* [27] *So they got themselves up from near the dwelling of Korah, Dathan, and Abiram, from all around. Dathan and Abiram went out erect at the entrance of their tents, with their wives, children, and infants.*

[28] *Moses said, "Through this shall you know that HASHEM sent me to perform all these acts, that it was not from my heart.* [29] *If these die like the death of all men, and the destiny of all men is visited upon them, then it is not HASHEM Who has sent me.* [30] *But if HASHEM will create a phenomenon, and the earth opens its mouth and swallows them and all that is theirs, and they will descend alive to the pit — then you shall know that these men have provoked HASHEM!"*

[31] *When he finished speaking all these words, the ground that was under them split open.* [32] *The earth opened its mouth and swallowed them and their households, and all the people who were with Korah, and the entire wealth.*

---

30. וִידַעְתֶּם כִּי נִאֲצוּ — *Then you will know that (these men) have derided (God)* . . . and they are not worthy to receive the (normal) honor given the dead, i.e., to be buried with the rest of the people.

32. וַתִּפְתַּח הָאָרֶץ אֶת פִּיהָ — *And the earth opened its mouth.* The cleft widened to (encompass) the place of their homes.

וְאֵת כָּל הָאָדָם אֲשֶׁר לְקֹרַח — *And all the men that belonged to Korach* . . . and all those who joined with Korach in his controversy. Therefore, his sons did not die for they were not drawn after him in this (matter).

וְאֵת כָּל הָרְכוּשׁ — *And all their possessions* . . . so they shall gain no merit from the fact that

NOTES

to remain in the vicinity of Korach, for we have a principle, "Woe to the wicked, and woe to his neighbor." Hence, they are told to distance themselves *lest they be swept away* (v. 26).

לג וַיֵּרְדוּ הֵם וְכָל־אֲשֶׁר לָהֶם חַיִּים שְׁאֹלָה וַתְּכַס עֲלֵיהֶם הָאָרֶץ וַיֹּאבְדוּ
לד מִתּוֹךְ הַקָּהָל: וְכָל־יִשְׂרָאֵל אֲשֶׁר סְבִיבֹתֵיהֶם נָסוּ לְקֹלָם כִּי אָמְרוּ פֶּן־
לה תִּבְלָעֵנוּ הָאָרֶץ: וְאֵשׁ יָצְאָה מֵאֵת יהוה וַתֹּאכַל אֵת הַחֲמִשִּׁים וּמָאתַיִם
יז א־ב אִישׁ מַקְרִיבֵי הַקְּטֹרֶת: וַיְדַבֵּר יהוה אֶל־מֹשֶׁה לֵּאמֹר: אֱמֹר
אֶל־אֶלְעָזָר בֶּן־אַהֲרֹן הַכֹּהֵן וְיָרֵם אֶת־הַמַּחְתֹּת מִבֵּין הַשְּׂרֵפָה וְאֶת־
ג הָאֵשׁ זְרֵה־הָלְאָה כִּי קָדֵשׁוּ: אֵת מַחְתּוֹת הַחַטָּאִים הָאֵלֶּה בְּנַפְשֹׁתָם
וְעָשׂוּ אֹתָם רִקֻּעֵי פַחִים צִפּוּי לַמִּזְבֵּחַ כִּי־הִקְרִיבֻם לִפְנֵי־יהוה וַיִּקְדָּשׁוּ
ד וְיִהְיוּ לְאוֹת לִבְנֵי יִשְׂרָאֵל: וַיִּקַּח אֶלְעָזָר הַכֹּהֵן אֵת מַחְתּוֹת הַנְּחֹשֶׁת
ה אֲשֶׁר הִקְרִיבוּ הַשְּׂרֻפִים וַיְרַקְּעוּם צִפּוּי לַמִּזְבֵּחַ: זִכָּרוֹן לִבְנֵי יִשְׂרָאֵל לְמַעַן
אֲשֶׁר לֹא־יִקְרַב אִישׁ זָר אֲשֶׁר לֹא מִזֶּרַע אַהֲרֹן הוּא לְהַקְטִיר קְטֹרֶת
לִפְנֵי יהוה וְלֹא־יִהְיֶה כְקֹרַח וְכַעֲדָתוֹ כַּאֲשֶׁר דִּבֶּר יהוה בְּיַד־מֹשֶׁה לוֹ:
ו וַיִּלֹּנוּ כָּל־עֲדַת בְּנֵי־יִשְׂרָאֵל מִמָּחֳרָת עַל־מֹשֶׁה וְעַל־אַהֲרֹן לֵאמֹר
ז אַתֶּם הֲמִתֶּם אֶת־עַם יהוה: וַיְהִי בְּהִקָּהֵל הָעֵדָה עַל־מֹשֶׁה וְעַל־אַהֲרֹן
ח וַיִּפְנוּ אֶל־אֹהֶל מוֹעֵד וְהִנֵּה כִסָּהוּ הֶעָנָן וַיֵּרָא כְּבוֹד יהוה: וַיָּבֹא מֹשֶׁה
רביעי ט וְאַהֲרֹן אֶל־פְּנֵי אֹהֶל מוֹעֵד: וַיְדַבֵּר יהוה אֶל־מֹשֶׁה לֵּאמֹר:
י הֵרֹמּוּ מִתּוֹךְ הָעֵדָה הַזֹּאת וַאֲכַלֶּה אֹתָם כְּרָגַע וַיִּפְּלוּ עַל־פְּנֵיהֶם:

---

righteous men might derive benefit from their toil, similar to, "if a sela (coin) fell out of his lap and a poor man found it and used it to purchase food" (*Sifra* cited in *Rashi, Leviticus* 5:17).

33. וַתְּכַס עֲלֵיהֶם הָאָרֶץ — *And the earth closed upon them.* (The verse) tells us that this opening (of the earth) was unlike the openings caused by an earthquake which does not close immediately. In this instance, however, it closed at once, similar to one who opens his mouth to swallow something and closes it after swallowing.

XVII

2. וְאֶת הָאֵשׁ זְרֵה הָלְאָה — *And scatter the fire yonder* . . . but not in the place where the ashes are (normally) poured out (שֶׁפֶךְ הַדֶּשֶׁן) [see *Leviticus* 4:12] because this was an alien (lit. strange) incense.

כִּי קָדֵשׁוּ — *For they have become holy* . . . and it is not fitting to allow them to lie in disgrace.

NOTES

32. וְאֵת כָּל הָרְכוּשׁ — *And all their possessions.* The *Sforno* explains the reason for the "swallowing up" of all their possessions. Were these possessions salvaged and enjoyed by others who were righteous men, then Korach and his company would have gained merit thereby, even though it was not given directly and willingly, for as *Rashi* tells us in *Leviticus* 5:17 that just as one is punished for sinning in error, so he is rewarded for doing good unintentionally.

33. וַתְּכַס עֲלֵיהֶם הָאָרֶץ — *And the earth closed upon them.* The *Sforno* emphasizes that this was indeed a *new thing* (v. 30), for the manner in which it happened was unlike that which occurs in an ordinary earthquake.

XVII

2-3. וְאֶת הָאֵשׁ זְרֵה הָלְאָה כִּי קָדֵשׁוּ . . . כִּי הִקְרִיבֻם לִפְנֵי ה׳ וַיִּקְדָּשׁוּ . . . — *And scatter the fire yonder for they have become holy . . . for they were offered before* HASHEM *and became holy* . . . The שֶׁפֶךְ הַדֶּשֶׁן was a special place outside the three camps when the Israelites were in the wilderness, and outside Jerusalem at the time when the Holy Temple stood. The ashes of certain sacrifices were poured out there. The *Sforno* explains that the fire in the censers of those who challenged Aaron was not to be scattered in that special place since only that which was acceptable and hence sacred could be poured out on the שֶׁפֶךְ הַדֶּשֶׁן. The fire pans of these men, however, were to be treated with care and

[33] They and all that was theirs descended alive to the pit; the earth covered them over and they were lost from among the congregation. [34] All Israel that was around them fled at their sound, for they said, "Lest the earth swallow us!"

[35] A flame came forth from HASHEM and consumed the two hundred and fifty men who were offering the incense.

16 *[1] HASHEM spoke to Moses, saying, [2] "Say to Elazar son of Aaron the Kohen and let him pick up the fire-pans from amid the fire — and he should throw away the flame — for they have become holy. [3] As for the fire-pans of these sinners against their souls — they shall make them hammered-out sheets as a covering for the Altar, for they offered them before HASHEM, so they became holy; they shall be for a sign to the Children of Israel." [4] Elazar the Kohen took the copper fire-pans that the consumed ones had offered and hammered them out as a covering for the Altar, [5] as a reminder to the Children of Israel, so that no alien who is not of the offspring of Aaron shall draw near to bring up the smoke of incense before HASHEM, that he not be like Korah and his assembly, as HASHEM spoke about him through Moses.*

[6] The entire assembly of the Children of Israel complained on the morrow against Moses and Aaron, saying, "You have killed the people of HASHEM!" [7] And it was when the assembly gathered against Moses and Aaron, they turned to the Tent of Meeting and behold! the cloud had covered it, and the glory of HASHEM appeared. [8] Moses and Aaron came before the Tent of Meeting.

[9] HASHEM spoke to Moses, saying, [10] "Remove yourselves from among this assembly and I shall destroy them in an instant!" They fell on their faces.

3. כִּי הִקְרִיבֻם לִפְנֵי ה׳ וַיִּקְדָּשׁוּ — *For they were offered before HASHEM and became holy . . .* for they were sanctified as vessels of service (to be used) for other Divine service besides this defective one, and thus they are worthy to be used as a covering in the holy.

6. אַתֶּם הֲמִתֶּם — *You have killed . . .* because you told them to be tested through the (burning) of the incense which is only fitting to be burnt by one who offers the daily burnt-offering. You should have tested them with sacrifices that are fitting to be brought by many *Kohanim* together.

NOTES

respect and used *for a covering of the Altar* since they were holy. Some commentators say that this was so because the offering was made at the behest of Moses, while others say it was so because these men sincerely believed that it would be acceptable to God. The *Sforno*, however, explains that they were holy because they were meant to be used for Divine service other than this improper one.

6. אַתֶּם הֲמִתֶּם — *You have killed.* The difficulty posed by this accusation, *you have killed*, is obvious. The punishment was meted out by Heaven, not by Moses! The *Sforno* explains that they were angry at Moses for suggesting a test which exposed them to imminent danger, since bringing the incense was done by only one person who is therefore more vulnerable than he who participates in a service in which many are involved. The wording of the *Sforno* however is puzzling. He states that the burning of the incense is done only by "one who offers the daily burnt offering." The Mishnayos in *Yoma* (chapter 2) discuss the lots drawn each morning to determine which *Kohanim* shall participate in the service. Regarding the incense it states that anyone who never had that privilege before is eligible (*Mishnah* 4). However, that privilege has no connection with the offering of the daily sacrifice which involved quite a number of *Kohanim*. Perhaps the text should be emended to read "by one who offers the incense alone."

יא וַיֹּאמֶר מֹשֶׁה אֶל־אַהֲרֹן קַח אֶת־הַמַּחְתָּה וְתֶן־עָלֶיהָ אֵשׁ מֵעַל הַמִּזְבֵּחַ
וְשִׂים קְטֹרֶת וְהוֹלֵךְ מְהֵרָה אֶל־הָעֵדָה וְכַפֵּר עֲלֵיהֶם כִּי־יָצָא הַקֶּצֶף
יב מִלִּפְנֵי יהוה הֵחֵל הַנָּגֶף: וַיִּקַּח אַהֲרֹן כַּאֲשֶׁר ׀ דִּבֶּר מֹשֶׁה וַיָּרָץ אֶל־תּוֹךְ
יג הַקָּהָל וְהִנֵּה הֵחֵל הַנֶּגֶף בָּעָם וַיִּתֵּן אֶת־הַקְּטֹרֶת וַיְכַפֵּר עַל־הָעָם: וַיַּעֲמֹד
יד בֵּין־הַמֵּתִים וּבֵין הַחַיִּים וַתֵּעָצַר הַמַּגֵּפָה: וַיִּהְיוּ הַמֵּתִים בַּמַּגֵּפָה אַרְבָּעָה
טו עָשָׂר אֶלֶף וּשְׁבַע מֵאוֹת מִלְּבַד הַמֵּתִים עַל־דְּבַר־קֹרַח: וַיָּשָׁב אַהֲרֹן
אֶל־מֹשֶׁה אֶל־פֶּתַח אֹהֶל מוֹעֵד וְהַמַּגֵּפָה נֶעֱצָרָה:

חמישי טז־יז וַיְדַבֵּר יהוה אֶל־מֹשֶׁה לֵּאמֹר: דַּבֵּר ׀ אֶל־בְּנֵי יִשְׂרָאֵל וְקַח מֵאִתָּם
מַטֶּה מַטֶּה לְבֵית אָב מֵאֵת כָּל־נְשִׂיאֵהֶם לְבֵית אֲבֹתָם שְׁנֵים עָשָׂר
יח מַטּוֹת אִישׁ אֶת־שְׁמוֹ תִּכְתֹּב עַל־מַטֵּהוּ: וְאֵת שֵׁם אַהֲרֹן תִּכְתֹּב
יט עַל־מַטֵּה לֵוִי כִּי מַטֶּה אֶחָד לְרֹאשׁ בֵּית אֲבוֹתָם: וְהִנַּחְתָּם בְּאֹהֶל מוֹעֵד
*חצי הספר כ לִפְנֵי הָעֵדוּת אֲשֶׁר אִוָּעֵד לָכֶם שָׁמָּה: * וְהָיָה הָאִישׁ אֲשֶׁר אֶבְחַר־בּוֹ
מַטֵּהוּ יִפְרָח וַהֲשִׁכֹּתִי מֵעָלַי אֶת־תְּלֻנּוֹת בְּנֵי יִשְׂרָאֵל אֲשֶׁר הֵם מַלִּינִם
כא עֲלֵיכֶם: וַיְדַבֵּר מֹשֶׁה אֶל־בְּנֵי יִשְׂרָאֵל וַיִּתְּנוּ אֵלָיו ׀ כָּל־נְשִׂיאֵיהֶם מַטֶּה
לְנָשִׂיא אֶחָד מַטֶּה לְנָשִׂיא אֶחָד לְבֵית אֲבֹתָם שְׁנֵים עָשָׂר מַטּוֹת וּמַטֵּה
כב אַהֲרֹן בְּתוֹךְ מַטּוֹתָם: וַיַּנַּח מֹשֶׁה אֶת־הַמַּטֹּת לִפְנֵי יהוה בְּאֹהֶל הָעֵדֻת:
כג וַיְהִי מִמָּחֳרָת וַיָּבֹא מֹשֶׁה אֶל־אֹהֶל הָעֵדוּת וְהִנֵּה פָּרַח מַטֵּה־אַהֲרֹן
כד לְבֵית לֵוִי וַיֹּצֵא פֶרַח וַיָּצֵץ צִיץ וַיִּגְמֹל שְׁקֵדִים: וַיֹּצֵא מֹשֶׁה
אֶת־כָּל־הַמַּטֹּת מִלִּפְנֵי יהוה אֶל־כָּל־בְּנֵי יִשְׂרָאֵל וַיִּרְאוּ וַיִּקְחוּ אִישׁ
מַטֵּהוּ:

ששי כה וַיֹּאמֶר יהוה אֶל־מֹשֶׁה הָשֵׁב אֶת־מַטֵּה אַהֲרֹן לִפְנֵי הָעֵדוּת לְמִשְׁמֶרֶת
כו לְאוֹת לִבְנֵי־מֶרִי וּתְכַל תְּלוּנֹּתָם מֵעָלַי וְלֹא יָמֻתוּ: וַיַּעַשׂ מֹשֶׁה כַּאֲשֶׁר
צִוָּה יהוה אֹתוֹ כֵּן עָשָׂה:

---

13. וַיַּעֲמֹד בֵּין הַמֵּתִים וּבֵין הַחַיִּים — *And he stood between the dead and the living . . .* after he stood there, he remained (there) to protect the sick ones that they should not die; the reverse of (the command to) *separate yourselves from among this congregation* (16:21).

וַתֵּעָצַר הַמַּגֵּפָה — *And the pestilence was stopped.* No one else became ill due to the illness (caused by) the pestilence.

15. וְהַמַּגֵּפָה נֶעֱצָרָה — *And the pestilence was stopped.* Those stricken by the plague were healed.

NOTES

13. . . . וַיַּעֲמֹד בֵּין הַמֵּתִים וּבֵין הַחַיִּים — *And he stood between the dead and the living.* Previously, God had told Moses and Aaron not to stand in the proximity of the rebels for their presence would protect them, which was contrary to God's wishes (16:21). Here, however, in the absence of such an order, Aaron chooses to remain in the midst of the afflicted so as to protect them from the consequences of their accusation — *you have killed the people of HASHEM* (v. 16).

15. וְהַמַּגֵּפָה נֶעֱצָרָה — *And the pestilence was stopped.* The phrase *and the pestilence (plague) was stopped* appears in verse 13 as well, but in a different sequence. In verse 13, it is written וַתֵּעָצַר הַמַּגֵּפָה, whereas in this verse the wording is וְהַמַּגֵּפָה נֶעֱצָרָה. The *Sforno's* interpretation of these two verses is a reconciliation of this variance. In verse 13, it refers to a complete cessation of the plague, i.e., no one became ill any longer. Hence the verb precedes the noun to indicate that the plague

*11 Moses said to Aaron, "Take the fire-pan and put on it fire from upon
the Altar and place incense — and go quickly to the assembly and provide
atonement for them, for the fury has gone out from the presence of
HASHEM; the plague has begun!"
12 Aaron took as Moses had spoken and ran to the midst of the
congregation, and behold! the plague had begun among the people. He
placed the incense and provided atonement for the people. 13 He stood
between the dead and the living, and the plague was checked. 14 Those
who died in the plague were fourteen thousand, seven hundred, aside
from those who died because of the affair of Korah. 15 Aaron returned to
Moses at the entrance of the Tent of Assembly, and the plague had been
checked.
16 HASHEM spoke to Moses, saying: 17 "Speak to the Children of Israel and
take from them one staff for each father's house, from all their leaders
according to their fathers' house, twelve staffs; each man's name shall
you inscribe on his staff. 18 And the name of Aaron shall you inscribe on
the staff of Levi, for there shall be one staff for the head of their fathers'
house. 19 You shall lay them in the Tent of Meeting before the Testimony,
where I meet with you. 20 It shall be that the man whom I shall choose —
his staff will blossom; thus I shall cause to subside from upon Me the
complaints of the Children of Israel, which they complain against you."
21 Moses spoke to the Children of Israel, and all their leaders gave him a
staff for each leader, a staff for each leader, according to their fathers'
house, twelve staffs; and Aaron's staff was among their staffs. 22 Moses
laid their staffs before HASHEM in the Tent of the Testimony. 23 On the next
day, Moses came to the Tent of the Testimony and behold! the staff of
Aaron of the house of Levi had blossomed; it brought forth a blossom,
sprouted a bud and almonds ripened. 24 Moses brought out all the staffs
from before HASHEM to all the Children of Israel; they saw and they took,
each man his staff.
25 HASHEM said to Moses: "Bring back the staff of Aaron before the
Testimony as a safekeeping, as a sign for rebellious ones; let their
complaints cease from Me that they not die." 26 Moses did as HASHEM had
commanded him, so he did.*

24. וַיִּרְאוּ וַיִּקְחוּ אִישׁ מַטֵּהוּ — *And they looked, and every man took his rod* . . . to identify the markings of their rods in their homes, for perhaps they were interchanged.

25. וּתְכַל תְּלוּנֹּתָם — *That there may be an end to their murmurings.* This token and sign shall put an end to their murmurings so that they will not continue to complain.

NOTES

totally ceased, וַתֵּעָצַר הַמַּגֵּפָה — the plague was stopped. In this verse, the noun precedes the verb to indicate that although the victims had been stricken, they were now healed; the meaning is that the *effect* of the plague was stayed and the victims were healed.

24. וַיִּרְאוּ וַיִּקְחוּ אִישׁ מַטֵּהוּ — *And they looked, and every man took his rod.* The rods were taken home for careful examination; why else would they be "taken" at all?

25. וּתְכַל תְּלוּנֹּתָם — *That there may be an end to their murmurings.* Whenever someone in the future might question the right of Aaron to serve as *Kohen Gadol,* he would be shown the blossoming rod as proof of his being Divinely chosen.

כז־כח וַיֹּאמְרוּ בְּנֵי יִשְׂרָאֵל אֶל־מֹשֶׁה לֵאמֹר הֵן גָּוַעְנוּ אָבַדְנוּ כֻּלָּנוּ אָבָדְנוּ: כֹּל
יח א הַקָּרֵב | הַקָּרֵב אֶל־מִשְׁכַּן יהוה יָמוּת הַאִם תַּמְנוּ לִגְוֹעַ: וַיֹּאמֶר
יהוה אֶל־אַהֲרֹן אַתָּה וּבָנֶיךָ וּבֵית־אָבִיךָ אִתָּךְ תִּשְׂאוּ אֶת־עֲוֹן הַמִּקְדָּשׁ
ב וְאַתָּה וּבָנֶיךָ אִתָּךְ תִּשְׂאוּ אֶת־עֲוֹן כְּהֻנַּתְכֶם: וְגַם אֶת־אַחֶיךָ מַטֵּה לֵוִי
שֵׁבֶט אָבִיךָ הַקְרֵב אִתָּךְ וְיִלָּווּ עָלֶיךָ וִישָׁרְתוּךָ וְאַתָּה וּבָנֶיךָ אִתָּךְ לִפְנֵי
ג אֹהֶל הָעֵדֻת: וְשָׁמְרוּ מִשְׁמַרְתְּךָ וּמִשְׁמֶרֶת כָּל־הָאֹהֶל אַךְ אֶל־כְּלֵי
ד הַקֹּדֶשׁ וְאֶל־הַמִּזְבֵּחַ לֹא יִקְרָבוּ וְלֹא־יָמֻתוּ גַם־הֵם גַּם־אַתֶּם: וְנִלְווּ עָלֶיךָ
וְשָׁמְרוּ אֶת־מִשְׁמֶרֶת אֹהֶל מוֹעֵד לְכֹל עֲבֹדַת הָאֹהֶל וְזָר לֹא־יִקְרַב
ה אֲלֵיכֶם: וּשְׁמַרְתֶּם אֵת מִשְׁמֶרֶת הַקֹּדֶשׁ וְאֵת מִשְׁמֶרֶת הַמִּזְבֵּחַ וְלֹא־
ו יִהְיֶה עוֹד קֶצֶף עַל־בְּנֵי יִשְׂרָאֵל: וַאֲנִי הִנֵּה לָקַחְתִּי אֶת־אֲחֵיכֶם הַלְוִיִּם
מִתּוֹךְ בְּנֵי יִשְׂרָאֵל לָכֶם מַתָּנָה נְתֻנִים לַיהוה לַעֲבֹד אֶת־עֲבֹדַת אֹהֶל
ז מוֹעֵד: וְאַתָּה וּבָנֶיךָ אִתְּךָ תִּשְׁמְרוּ אֶת־כְּהֻנַּתְכֶם לְכָל־דְּבַר הַמִּזְבֵּחַ
וּלְמִבֵּית לַפָּרֹכֶת וַעֲבַדְתֶּם עֲבֹדַת מַתָּנָה אֶתֵּן אֶת־כְּהֻנַּתְכֶם וְהַזָּר הַקָּרֵב
יוּמָת:

XVIII

1. אַתָּה וּבָנֶיךָ וּבֵית אָבִיךָ אִתָּךְ תִּשְׂאוּ אֶת עֲוֹן הַמִּקְדָּשׁ — *You and your sons and your father's house with you shall bear the iniquity of the Sanctuary* ... that no *tamei* person or stranger enter within its confines, for this (responsibility) rests on all of you and if one enters through your negligence (lit. lack of effort), you will bear his iniquity.

וְאַתָּה וּבָנֶיךָ אִתָּךְ תִּשְׂאוּ אֶת עֲוֹן כְּהֻנַּתְכֶם — *And you and your sons with you shall bear the iniquity of your priesthood.* You alone (i.e., the *Kohanim*) are (responsible) to prevent any stranger from participating in the priestly service.

2. וִישָׁרְתוּךָ — *And minister to you* ... only in regard to that which is in your charge and the charge of your sons.

וְאַתָּה וּבָנֶיךָ אִתָּךְ לִפְנֵי אֹהֶל הָעֵדֻת — *And you and your sons with you before the tent of testimony.* The order shall be thus: You and your sons shall keep the charge in front of the Holy of Holies which is the tent of the Ark where the tablets of testimony are located.

3. וְשָׁמְרוּ מִשְׁמַרְתְּךָ וּמִשְׁמֶרֶת כָּל הָאֹהֶל — *And they shall keep your charge and the charge of all the tent.* And the Levites shall keep your charge which is (outside) the Holy of Holies and the charge of the rest of the Sanctuary which is outside the boards of the Sanctuary.

אַךְ אֶל כְּלֵי הַקֹּדֶשׁ — *Only* (*they shall not come nigh to*) *the holy furnishings* ... which are within the Sanctuary, namely the menorah, the table and the golden Altar.

NOTES

XVIII

1. אַתָּה וּבָנֶיךָ וּבֵית אָבִיךָ אִתָּךְ תִּשְׂאוּ אֶת עֲוֹן הַמִּקְדָּשׁ . . . — *You and your sons and your father's house with you shall bear the iniquity of the Sanctuary.* It is the responsibility of both the *Kohanim* and the Kehathites to prevent any stranger from entering the Sanctuary or touching the holy objects. The phrase *your father's house* refers to the sons of Kehath who were Levites. All precautions, however, in connection with the priesthood are the exclusive responsibility of the *Kohanim*.

2. וִישָׁרְתוּךָ — *And minister to you.* The Levites were charged with ministering to the needs of the *Kohanim* in the domain of the sacred service, and not to their personal needs.

3-5. וְשָׁמְרוּ מִשְׁמַרְתְּךָ וּמִשְׁמֶרֶת כָּל הָאֹהֶל . . . וּשְׁמַרְתֶּם אֵת מִשְׁמֶרֶת הַקֹּדֶשׁ — *And they shall keep your*

[27] *The Children of Israel said to Moses, saying, "Behold! we perish, we are lost, we are all lost.* [28] *Everyone who approaches closer to the Tabernacle of* HASHEM *will die. Will we ever stop perishing?"*

18

[1] *HASHEM said to Aaron, "You, your sons, and your father's household with you shall bear the iniquity of the Sanctuary; and you and your sons with you shall bear the iniquity of your priesthood.* [2] *Also your brethren the tribe of Levi, the tribe of your father, shall you draw near with you, and they shall be joined to you and minister to you. You and your sons with you shall be before the Tent of the Testimony.* [3] *They shall safeguard your charge and the charge of the entire tent — but to the holy vessels and to the Altar they shall not approach, that they not die — they as well as you.* [4] *They shall be joined to you and safeguard the charge of the Tent of Meeting for the entire service of the Tent, and an alien shall not approach you.* [5] *You shall safeguard the charge of the Holy and the charge of the Altar, and there shall be no more wrath against the Children of Israel.* [6] *And I — behold! I have taken your brethren the Levites from among the Children of Israel; to you they are presented as a gift for* HASHEM, *to perform the service of the Tent of Meeting.* [7] *You and your sons with you shall safeguard your priesthood regarding every matter of the Altar and within the Curtain, and you shall serve; I have presented your priesthood as a service that is a gift, and any alien who approaches shall die."*

וְאֶל הַמִּזְבֵּחַ — *And unto the altar* . . . the outer altar which is the altar of the burnt offering — even though it is outside the boards.

4. וְשָׁמְרוּ אֶת מִשְׁמֶרֶת אֹהֶל מוֹעֵד — *And keep the charge of the Tent of Meeting* . . . within the curtains, which is the entire courtyard.

5. וּשְׁמַרְתֶּם אֵת מִשְׁמֶרֶת הַקֹּדֶשׁ — *And you shall keep the charge of the holy things.* And you, the *Kohanim*, shall keep the charge of the Sanctuary within the boards.

6. לָכֶם מַתָּנָה נְתֻנִים לַה' — *For you, they are given as a gift to* HASHEM. They will be obligated to serve, by Your command, all the needs of the Tent of Meeting.

7. תִּשְׁמְרוּ אֶת כְּהֻנַּתְכֶם — *Shall guard your priesthood* . . . that no stranger shall come nigh to the priestly service, as it occurred with Uziyahu (*II Chronicles* 26:16).

וַעֲבַדְתֶּם — *And you shall serve.* And likewise you shall prevent any stranger from the service in which you (alone) serve. Now this (warning) is necessary because, indeed . . .

עֲבֹדַת מַתָּנָה אֶתֵּן אֶת כְּהֻנַּתְכֶם — *I give you the priesthood as a service of gift.* The service of the priesthood which is imposed only upon you, is given and placed as a gift of honor and superiority in the eyes of all men. Therefore, all will desire it; hence you must guard it well.

NOTES

charge and the charge of all the tent . . . And you shall keep the charge of the holy things. The *Sforno* explains that the guarding of the Holy is a joint endeavor of the *Kohanim* and the Levites, with precise parameters; "the *Kohanim* on the inside, the Levites on the outside" as the *Sifri* puts it.

7. עֲבֹדַת מַתָּנָה אֶתֵּן אֶת כְּהֻנַּתְכֶם — *I give you the priesthood as a service of gift.* The *Sforno* interprets the expression עֲבֹדַת מַתָּנָה as a gift so precious in the eyes of others that they will be tempted to usurp the privilege, as did King Uziyahu who attempted to offer קְטֹרֶת, *incense*, on the golden Altar. It was therefore imperative that they exercise caution not to permit others to participate in the priestly service in which they would be interested.

ח וַיְדַבֵּר יְהוָה אֶל־אַהֲרֹן וַאֲנִי הִנֵּה נָתַתִּי לְךָ אֶת־מִשְׁמֶרֶת תְּרוּמֹתָי
ט לְכָל־קָדְשֵׁי בְנֵי־יִשְׂרָאֵל לְךָ נְתַתִּים לְמָשְׁחָה וּלְבָנֶיךָ לְחָק־עוֹלָם: זֶה
יִהְיֶה לְךָ מִקֹּדֶשׁ הַקֳּדָשִׁים מִן־הָאֵשׁ כָּל־קָרְבָּנָם לְכָל־מִנְחָתָם
וּלְכָל־חַטָּאתָם וּלְכָל־אֲשָׁמָם אֲשֶׁר יָשִׁיבוּ לִי קֹדֶשׁ קָדָשִׁים לְךָ הוּא
י וּלְבָנֶיךָ: בְּקֹדֶשׁ הַקֳּדָשִׁים תֹּאכְלֶנּוּ כָּל־זָכָר יֹאכַל אֹתוֹ קֹדֶשׁ יִהְיֶה־לָּךְ:
יא וְזֶה־לְּךָ תְּרוּמַת מַתָּנָם לְכָל־תְּנוּפֹת בְּנֵי יִשְׂרָאֵל לְךָ נְתַתִּים וּלְבָנֶיךָ
יב וְלִבְנֹתֶיךָ אִתְּךָ לְחָק־עוֹלָם כָּל־טָהוֹר בְּבֵיתְךָ יֹאכַל אֹתוֹ: כֹּל חֵלֶב
יִצְהָר וְכָל־חֵלֶב תִּירוֹשׁ וְדָגָן רֵאשִׁיתָם אֲשֶׁר־יִתְּנוּ לַיהוָה לְךָ נְתַתִּים:
יג בִּכּוּרֵי כָּל־אֲשֶׁר בְּאַרְצָם אֲשֶׁר־יָבִיאוּ לַיהוָה לְךָ יִהְיֶה כָּל־טָהוֹר בְּבֵיתְךָ
יד־טו יֹאכְלֶנּוּ: כָּל־חֵרֶם בְּיִשְׂרָאֵל לְךָ יִהְיֶה: כָּל־פֶּטֶר רֶחֶם לְכָל־בָּשָׂר
אֲשֶׁר־יַקְרִיבוּ לַיהוָה בָּאָדָם וּבַבְּהֵמָה יִהְיֶה־לָּךְ אַךְ | פָּדֹה תִפְדֶּה אֵת
טז בְּכוֹר הָאָדָם וְאֵת בְּכוֹר־הַבְּהֵמָה הַטְּמֵאָה תִּפְדֶּה: וּפְדוּיָו מִבֶּן־חֹדֶשׁ
תִּפְדֶּה בְּעֶרְכְּךָ כֶּסֶף חֲמֵשֶׁת שְׁקָלִים בְּשֶׁקֶל הַקֹּדֶשׁ עֶשְׂרִים גֵּרָה הוּא:
יז אַךְ בְּכוֹר־שׁוֹר אוֹ־בְכוֹר כֶּשֶׂב אוֹ־בְכוֹר עֵז לֹא תִפְדֶּה קֹדֶשׁ הֵם אֶת־
דָּמָם תִּזְרֹק עַל־הַמִּזְבֵּחַ וְאֶת־חֶלְבָּם תַּקְטִיר אִשֶּׁה לְרֵיחַ נִיחֹחַ לַיהוָה:
יח־יט וּבְשָׂרָם יִהְיֶה־לָּךְ כַּחֲזֵה הַתְּנוּפָה וּכְשׁוֹק הַיָּמִין לְךָ יִהְיֶה: כֹּל | תְּרוּמֹת
הַקֳּדָשִׁים אֲשֶׁר יָרִימוּ בְנֵי־יִשְׂרָאֵל לַיהוָה נָתַתִּי לְךָ וּלְבָנֶיךָ וְלִבְנֹתֶיךָ
אִתְּךָ לְחָק־עוֹלָם בְּרִית מֶלַח עוֹלָם הִוא לִפְנֵי יְהוָה לְךָ וּלְזַרְעֲךָ אִתָּךְ:
כ וַיֹּאמֶר יְהוָה אֶל־אַהֲרֹן בְּאַרְצָם לֹא תִנְחָל וְחֵלֶק לֹא־יִהְיֶה לְךָ בְּתוֹכָם
שביעי כא אֲנִי חֶלְקְךָ וְנַחֲלָתְךָ בְּתוֹךְ בְּנֵי יִשְׂרָאֵל: וְלִבְנֵי
לֵוִי הִנֵּה נָתַתִּי כָּל־מַעֲשֵׂר בְּיִשְׂרָאֵל לְנַחֲלָה חֵלֶף עֲבֹדָתָם אֲשֶׁר־
כב הֵם עֹבְדִים אֶת־עֲבֹדַת אֹהֶל מוֹעֵד: וְלֹא־יִקְרְבוּ עוֹד בְּנֵי יִשְׂרָאֵל
כג אֶל־אֹהֶל מוֹעֵד לָשֵׂאת חֵטְא לָמוּת: וְעָבַד הַלֵּוִי הוּא אֶת־עֲבֹדַת
אֹהֶל מוֹעֵד וְהֵם יִשְׂאוּ עֲוֹנָם חֻקַּת עוֹלָם לְדֹרֹתֵיכֶם וּבְתוֹךְ בְּנֵי
כד יִשְׂרָאֵל לֹא יִנְחֲלוּ נַחֲלָה: כִּי אֶת־מַעְשַׂר בְּנֵי־יִשְׂרָאֵל אֲשֶׁר יָרִימוּ

8. וַאֲנִי הִנֵּה נָתַתִּי לְךָ — *And I, behold, have given you.* You shall keep the charge of the holy things as I commanded you, and I (in turn) give you the priestly gifts written in this chapter.

9. מִן הָאֵשׁ — *(Reserved) from the fire.* The entire (offering) is given (to the One) on High, and the *Kohanim* have no part in it until after the (sacrifice) has been burnt (on the Altar), for they (only) receive from the "elevated table" (i.e., the Altar), therefore ...

10. בְּקֹדֶשׁ הַקֳּדָשִׁים תֹּאכְלֶנּוּ — *In a most holy place shall you eat it* ... within the curtains.

11. תְּרוּמַת מַתָּנָם — *The heave-offering of their gift* ... that which is given by the "owners" (the ones who bring the offering) to the *Kohanim* from the holy of "lesser degree" (קָדָשִׁים קַלִּים), in which the owners have a portion.

NOTES

9. מִן הָאֵשׁ — *(Reserved) from the fire.* The portion received by the *Kohen* from קָדְשֵׁי קָדָשִׁים (most holy offerings) is not given to him *directly*, as is the case of קָדָשִׁים קַלִּים (offerings of a "lesser" degree of holiness) where the owner gives it directly to the *Kohen*. In the first case, it is *from the fire,* meaning

8 *HASHEM spoke to Aaron: And I — behold! I have given you the
safeguard of My heave-offerings, of all the sanctities of the Children of
Israel; I have given them to you for distinction and to your sons as an
eternal portion.* 9 *This shall be yours from the most holy, from the fire: their
every offering, their every meal-offering, their every sin-offering, their
every guilt-offering, that which they return to Me — as most holy it shall be
yours and your sons.* 10 *In the most holy shall you eat it, every male may eat
it, it shall be holy for you.* 11 *And this shall be yours: what is set aside from
their gift, from all the wavings of the Children of Israel, have I presented
them to you and to your sons and daughters with you as an eternal portion;
every pure person in your household may eat it.* 12 *All the best of your oil
and the best of your wine and grain, their first, which they give to HASHEM,
to you have I given them.* 13 *The first fruits of everything that is in their
land, which they bring to HASHEM, shall be yours, every pure person in your
household may eat it.* 14 *Every segregated property in Israel shall be yours.*

15 *Every first issue of a womb of any flesh that they offer to HASHEM,
whether man or beast, shall be yours; but you shall surely redeem the
firstborn of man, and the firstborn of an impure beast shall you redeem.*
16 *Those that are to be redeemed — from one month shall you redeem
according to the valuation, five silver shekels by the sacred shekel; it is
twenty gera.* 17 *But the firstborn of a cow or the firstborn of a sheep or the
firstborn of a goat you shall not redeem; they are holy; their blood shall you
throw upon the Altar and their fat shall you cause to go up in smoke, a
fire-offering, a satisfying aroma to HASHEM.* 18 *Their flesh shall be yours;
like the breast of the waving and the right foreleg shall it be yours.*

19 *Everything that is separated from the sanctities that the Children of
Israel raise up to HASHEM have I given to you and your sons and daughters
with you as an eternal portion; it is an eternal salt-like covenant before
HASHEM, for you and your offspring with you."*

20 *HASHEM said to Aaron, "In their Land you shall have no heritage, and
a share shall you not have among them; I am your share and your heritage
among the Children of Israel.*

21 *"To the sons of Levi, behold! I have given every tithe in Israel as a heritage in exchange for the service that they perform, the service of the Tent
of Meeting —* 22 *so that the Children of Israel shall not again approach the
Tent of Meeting to bear a sin to die.* 23 *The Levite himself shall perform the
service of the Tent of Meeting, and they shall bear their iniquity, an eternal
decree for your generations; and among the Children of Israel they shall not
inherit a heritage.* 24 *For the tithe of the Children of Israel that they raise up*

19. כֹּל תְּרוּמֹת הַקֳּדָשִׁים — *All the heave-offerings of the holy things* . . . such as that which is lifted from the breads of the thanksgiving offering, and the two loaves and *challah* (from the dough).

NOTES

that the Altar is entitled to everything, except that God grants the *Kohanim* a portion from "His Table." It therefore follows that this meat can only be eaten in the most holy place, unlike the priestly gifts which are of a lesser degree of holiness that they may be eaten elsewhere.

לַיהוה֙ תְּרוּמָ֔ה נָתַ֥תִּי לַלְוִיִּ֖ם לְנַחֲלָ֑ה עַל־כֵּן֙ אָמַ֣רְתִּי לָהֶ֔ם בְּתוֹךְ֙ בְּנֵ֣י יִשְׂרָאֵ֔ל לֹ֥א יִנְחֲל֖וּ נַחֲלָֽה:

כה-כו וַיְדַבֵּ֥ר יהו֖ה אֶל־מֹשֶׁ֥ה לֵּאמֹֽר: וְאֶל־הַלְוִיִּ֞ם תְּדַבֵּר֙ וְאָמַרְתָּ֣ אֲלֵהֶ֔ם כִּי־תִקְח֣וּ מֵאֵ֣ת בְּנֵֽי־יִשְׂרָאֵ֗ל אֶת־הַמַּעֲשֵׂר֙ אֲשֶׁ֨ר נָתַ֧תִּי לָכֶ֛ם מֵֽאִתָּ֖ם

כז בְּנַחֲלַתְכֶ֑ם וַהֲרֵמֹתֶ֤ם מִמֶּ֨נּוּ֙ תְּרוּמַ֣ת יהו֔ה מַעֲשֵׂ֖ר מִן־הַֽמַּעֲשֵֽׂר: וְנֶחְשַׁ֤ב

כח לָכֶם֙ תְּרֽוּמַתְכֶ֔ם כַּדָּגָן֙ מִן־הַגֹּ֔רֶן וְכַֽמְלֵאָ֖ה מִן־הַיָּ֑קֶב: כֵּ֣ן תָּרִ֤ימוּ גַם־אַתֶּם֙ תְּרוּמַ֣ת יהו֔ה מִכֹּל֙ מַעְשְׂרֹ֣תֵיכֶ֔ם אֲשֶׁ֣ר תִּקְח֔וּ מֵאֵ֖ת בְּנֵ֣י יִשְׂרָאֵ֑ל וּנְתַתֶּ֤ם

כט מִמֶּ֨נּוּ֙ אֶת־תְּרוּמַ֣ת יהו֔ה לְאַהֲרֹ֖ן הַכֹּהֵֽן: מִכֹּל֙ מַתְּנֹ֣תֵיכֶ֔ם תָּרִ֨ימוּ֙ אֵ֖ת

ל כָּל־תְּרוּמַ֣ת יהו֑ה מִכָּל־חֶלְבּ֔וֹ אֶת־מִקְדְּשׁ֖וֹ מִמֶּֽנּוּ: וְאָמַרְתָּ֣ אֲלֵהֶ֔ם בַּהֲרִֽימְכֶ֤ם אֶת־חֶלְבּוֹ֙ מִמֶּ֔נּוּ וְנֶחְשַׁב֙ לַלְוִיִּ֔ם כִּתְבוּאַ֥ת גֹּ֖רֶן וְכִתְבוּאַ֥ת יָֽקֶב:

לא וַאֲכַלְתֶּ֤ם אֹתוֹ֙ בְּכָל־מָק֔וֹם אַתֶּ֖ם וּבֵֽיתְכֶ֑ם כִּי־שָׂכָ֥ר הוּא֙ לָכֶ֔ם חֵ֖לֶף

לב עֲבֹדַתְכֶ֖ם בְּאֹ֣הֶל מוֹעֵֽד: וְלֹֽא־תִשְׂא֤וּ עָלָיו֙ חֵ֔טְא בַּהֲרִֽימְכֶ֥ם אֶת־חֶלְבּ֖וֹ מִמֶּ֑נּוּ וְאֶת־קָדְשֵׁ֧י בְנֵֽי־יִשְׂרָאֵ֛ל לֹ֥א תְחַלְּל֖וּ וְלֹ֥א תָמֽוּתוּ:

מפטיר

---

27. וְנֶחְשַׁב לָכֶם תְּרוּמַתְכֶם — *And your offering which you set apart shall be reckoned to you . . .* to cause a blessing to rest on your household, even though it is measured, and (our Sages) have said, "If he first measured the grain and recited the benediction, his prayer is

NOTES

27. . . . . וְנֶחְשַׁב לָכֶם תְּרוּמַתְכֶם — *And your offering which you set apart shall be reckoned to you.* The expression "and your offering (i.e., the heave-offering of the Levite's tithe) shall be reckoned as the corn of the threshing floor etc." is difficult to

understand. The *Sforno* offers this explanation. Just as the gift of the Israelite to the *Kohen* brings heavenly blessing to his household and his possessions, so shall the heave-offering from the Levite's tithe bring a blessing to his household, even

to HASHEM as a gift have I given to the Levites as a heritage; therefore have
I said to them: Among the Children of Israel they shall not inherit a
heritage."
25 HASHEM spoke to Moses, saying, 26 "To the Levites shall you speak and
you shall say to them, When you accept from the Children of Israel the
tithe that I have given you from them as your heritage, you shall raise up
from it a gift to HASHEM, a tithe from the tithe. 27 Your gift shall be reckoned
for you like grain from the threshing-floor and like the ripeness of the vat.
28 So shall you, too, raise up the gift of HASHEM from all your tithes that you
accept from the Children of Israel, and you shall give from it a gift of
HASHEM to Aaron the Kohen. 29 From all your gifts you shall raise up every
gift of HASHEM, from all its best part, its sacred part from it.
30 "You shall say to them: 'When you have raised up its best from it, it
shall be considered for the Levites like the produce of the threshing-floor
and the produce of the vat. 31 You may eat it everywhere, you and your
household, for it is a wage for you in exchange for your service in the Tent
of Meeting. 32 You shall not bear a sin because of it when you raise up its
best from it; and the sanctities of the Children of Israel you shall not
desecrate, so that you shall not die.' "

---

in vain" (*Taanis* 8b); nonetheless, the offering set apart from the tithe (the tithe of the tithe) shall bring a good blessing in the rest of the tithe, which is considered as *chullin* (non-holy) in the hands of the Levite.

NOTES

though (unlike the *terumah* of the Israelite) it is measured, and there is a principle that a blessing does not dwell on that which is "measured, weighed or counted." Since the offering of the Levite to the *Kohen* is precise — a tenth from his tenth — one might think that this would prevent the effectiveness of the blessing. Therefore, the Torah reassures the Levite that he shall enjoy the same blessing as that enjoyed by the Israelite who gives from the corn and the wine press.

פרשת חקת

יט א־ב וַיְדַבֵּר יהוה אֶל־מֹשֶׁה וְאֶל־אַהֲרֹן לֵאמֹר: זֹאת חֻקַּת הַתּוֹרָה אֲשֶׁר־צִוָּה
יהוה לֵאמֹר דַּבֵּר ׀ אֶל־בְּנֵי יִשְׂרָאֵל וְיִקְחוּ אֵלֶיךָ פָרָה
אֲדֻמָּה תְּמִימָה אֲשֶׁר אֵין־בָּהּ מוּם אֲשֶׁר לֹא־עָלָה עָלֶיהָ עֹל:

XIX

2. זאת חֻקַּת הַתּוֹרָה אֲשֶׁר צִוָּה ה׳ — *This is the statute of the Torah which* HASHEM *has commanded ...* when He said, *Sprinkle water of purifying upon them* (8:7).

Now behold, our Sages have stated, "The term *statute* (חוק) is (used) to imply that it is an enactment before Me and you have no right to question it" (*Yoma* 67b), and regarding this Solomon said, אָמַרְתִּי אֶחְכָּמָה וְהִיא רְחוֹקָה מִמֶּנִּי, *I said, "I will be wise, but it was far from me"* (*Ecclesiastes* 7:23). The major enigma of this (statute) is that (the red cow) makes *tamei* those who are *tahor* while making *tahor* those who are *tamei*. However, as we (examine) and discern the totality of this commandment, *a word secretly came to me and we received a whisper of it* (based on *Job* 4:12). (Now) this is because we found initially that all who occupy themselves with it (i.e, the red cow) from the time of its burning and beyond become *tamei* — namely, the one who burns it and he who casts in the cedarwood, hyssop and scarlet thread as it burns, as well as he who gathers, touches and carries (its ashes). However, he who sprinkles and he who sanctifies remain *tahor*. Secondly, a cardinal rule of the cow is that it must be perfectly red, and the prophet has explained that sin is compared to red, saying, אִם יִהְיוּ חֲטָאֵיכֶם כַּשָּׁנִים כַּשֶּׁלֶג יַלְבִּינוּ, *Though your sins be like scarlet they shall be as white as snow* (*Isaiah* 1:18), and our Sages therefore said that they would "tie a strip of red wool atop the Temple entrance (on Yom Kippur); if it became white they rejoiced, and if not they were sad" (*Yoma* 67a).

Third, it is proper to consider that since כָּל אִמְרַת אֱלוֹהַּ צְרוּפָה, *every word of God is proven* (*Proverbs* 30:5), then without a doubt, they (are meant) to bring (lit., straighten) all (man's) deeds to the middle path, for either extreme is to be rejected, as it says, וְנֶעְקַשׁ דְּרָכַיִם יִפּוֹל בְּאֶחָת, *He who takes crooked paths shall fall suddenly* (*Proverbs* 28:18).

Fourth, it is fitting to consider that there is no better way to straighten the crooked and bring it back to the middle path than to (first) bend it to the extreme, as is (true) of bodily ailments, as it says, חַבֻּרוֹת פֶּצַע תַּמְרוּק בְּרָע, *Sharp wounds cleanse away evil* (*Proverbs*

NOTES

XIX

2. זאת חֻקַּת הַתּוֹרָה — *This is the statute of the Torah.* The *Sforno* explains the red cow ritual allegorically. The color of the cow, as well as the scarlet thread, symbolizes sin, while the cedarwood and hyssop represent pride and humility respectively. Sin, in general, and these two traits in particular, mirror extremes in man's behavior. The golden path is the middle path, eschewing both extremes, as the *Rambam* explains in *Hilchos Daos* (1:3-5). However, when one sins, thereby in effect going to an extreme, he can only correct this deviation by bending to the opposite extreme and eventually he will return to the desired middle. When a Jew sins he defiles his soul and impairs the Divine image which is housed in his body, this body being comparable to God's Sanctuary. Now just as one becomes *tamei* when he comes into contact with a dead person or enters a tent where a dead person lies, so does this likewise happen when he defiles himself by transgressing God's Torah. The degree, however, of his impurity varies. When he deviates at times from the norm, the *Sforno* refers to him as one who only draws nigh to the vanities of this world, but if he becomes immersed in the pursuit of material and physical pleasures, he is guilty of sullying his sacred Jewish soul. As a member of *Klal Yisrael*, he also contaminates the climate of the society of which he is a part. Such a serious infraction requires sincere repentance so as to rehabilitate and purify him.

מֵי חַטָּאת, *the waters of purification*, sprinkled on the one who became *tamei* through a dead body, defines the means of *taharah*, purification, for the sinner as well. This water, which combines extreme elements, i.e., the ashes of the red cow symbolizing sin, and water which is the ultimate in purity, as well as the cedar representing pride,

PARASHAS CHUKAS

19 [1] HASHEM spoke to Moses and to Aaron, saying: [2] This is the decree of the Torah, which HASHEM has commanded, saying: Speak to the Children of Israel, and they shall take to you a completely red cow, which is without blemish, and upon which a yoke has not come.

20:30), although inclining to the extreme is in itself to be rejected, and could be destructive to one who is in the middle path, similar to a laxative medication which is beneficial for the ill person and harmful to a healthy person.

Fifth, it is important to consider that the purification effected by the ashes of the cow is applicable only to *tumah* caused by a dead person and to no other kind of *tumah*. Now, it is known that Torah and Mitzvos are (commandments) giving life to those who find them and occupy themselves with them, as it says, כִּי הוּא חַיֵּיכֶם, *For it is your life* (*Deut.* 32:47), and he who turns away from them (to pursue) the vanity of the transitory (lit., perishable) is (in danger) of dying or is altogether dead, as (our Sages) state, "The wicked even in their lifetime are called dead" (*Berachos* 18b).

Sixth, it is fitting to consider that which our Sages told us, that the cedarwood symbolizes pride (or arrogance) and the hyssop symbolizes the opposite (i.e., humility), and since the scarlet thread is combined with them, it symbolizes (lit., teaches) that both (traits) are sinful, as (the Sages) said, "He (the scholar) in whom there is pride deserves excommunication, as well as the one in whom there is no pride" (*Sotah* 5a), especially regarding one who must exercise leadership on behalf of the people. And indeed, our Sages have told us that Saul was punished because he was not particular about his honor (*Yoma* 22b), as it says, וַיִּבְזֻהוּ וְלֹא הֵבִיאוּ לוֹ מִנְחָה וַיְהִי כְּמַחֲרִישׁ, *And they despised him and did not bring him presents, but he held his peace* (*I Samuel* 10:27). And the prophet also chastened him when he said, הֲלוֹא אִם קָטֹן אַתָּה בְּעֵינֶיךָ רֹאשׁ שִׁבְטֵי יִשְׂרָאֵל אָתָּה, *Although you are little in your own sight, you are the head of the tribes of Israel* (ibid. 15:17).

Therefore, let us say that although this commandment is a statute and we must not criticize it nor question (lit., doubt) whether it is proper or not, for "every word of God is proven" and doubtless there is some sublime reason (for this *mitzvah*) known to the King Who commanded it, and perhaps also to Moses our Teacher and those who are like him

NOTES

and the hyssop symbolizing humility, will serve to instruct him of the danger of extremes and thereby bring him back to the golden middle path.

Those occupied in preparing the water of purification, who are themselves not *tamei*, take on this state of impurity for they represent those who are not in need of purification; hence for them the extreme is harmful — unlike the recipient of the water who has already gone to one extreme, and by being lead to the other is ultimately brought back to the middle. The one who sprinkles and sanctifies, however, does not become *tamei* since he represents the wise teacher of Torah who instructs the sinner in the ways of repentance.

The *Sforno* skillfully draws from Scripture, the Talmud and medical science to prove that red and scarlet represent sin; that both pride and humility carried to the extreme are faulty and injurious, and that which is harmful to a healthy person is beneficial to a sick person. In this manner he is able to resolve the anomaly that the red cow is מְטַהֵר טְמֵאִים וּמְטַמֵּא טְהוֹרִים, i.e., *purifies the unclean and defiles the clean.*

The reason that the sprinkling of the מֵי חַטָּאת is used only to make *tahor* a טְמֵא מֵת (one who is defiled by contact with the dead) is linked to the severe punishment imposed by the Torah upon one who is *tamei* in such a manner and enters the Holy. In similar fashion, one who becomes "impure" through sin defiles himself and must purge his sins through the living waters of Torah and through repentance. The *Sforno* teaches that this is the subtle meaning of the introductory phrase זֹאת חֻקַּת הַתּוֹרָה, *This is the statute of the Torah.*

אֲשֶׁר צִוָּה ה׳ — *Which HASHEM has commanded.* The expression *which HASHEM has commanded* implies that God had already instructed Moses regarding the מֵי חַטָּאת, *purifying waters.* The *Sforno* explains that this refers to the *taharah*, purification, of the Levites at the time of their consecration, recorded above in *parashas Beha'aloscha* (8:7).

ג וּנְתַתֶּם אֹתָהּ אֶל־אֶלְעָזָר הַכֹּהֵן וְהוֹצִיא אֹתָהּ אֶל־מִחוּץ לַמַּחֲנֶה וְשָׁחַט
ד אֹתָהּ לְפָנָיו: וְלָקַח אֶלְעָזָר הַכֹּהֵן מִדָּמָהּ בְּאֶצְבָּעוֹ וְהִזָּה אֶל־נֹכַח פְּנֵי
ה אֹהֶל־מוֹעֵד מִדָּמָהּ שֶׁבַע פְּעָמִים: וְשָׂרַף אֶת־הַפָּרָה לְעֵינָיו אֶת־עֹרָהּ
ו וְאֶת־בְּשָׂרָהּ וְאֶת־דָּמָהּ עַל־פִּרְשָׁהּ יִשְׂרֹף: וְלָקַח הַכֹּהֵן עֵץ אֶרֶז וְאֵזוֹב
ז וּשְׁנִי תוֹלָעַת וְהִשְׁלִיךְ אֶל־תּוֹךְ שְׂרֵפַת הַפָּרָה: וְכִבֶּס בְּגָדָיו הַכֹּהֵן וְרָחַץ
ח בְּשָׂרוֹ בַּמַּיִם וְאַחַר יָבֹא אֶל־הַמַּחֲנֶה וְטָמֵא הַכֹּהֵן עַד־הָעָרֶב: וְהַשֹּׂרֵף
ט אֹתָהּ יְכַבֵּס בְּגָדָיו בַּמַּיִם וְרָחַץ בְּשָׂרוֹ בַּמָּיִם וְטָמֵא עַד הָעָרֶב: וְאָסַף ׀
אִישׁ טָהוֹר אֵת אֵפֶר הַפָּרָה וְהִנִּיחַ מִחוּץ לַמַּחֲנֶה בְּמָקוֹם טָהוֹר וְהָיְתָה
י לַעֲדַת בְּנֵי־יִשְׂרָאֵל לְמִשְׁמֶרֶת לְמֵי נִדָּה חַטָּאת הִוא: וְכִבֶּס הָאֹסֵף
אֶת־אֵפֶר הַפָּרָה אֶת־בְּגָדָיו וְטָמֵא עַד־הָעָרֶב וְהָיְתָה לִבְנֵי יִשְׂרָאֵל וְלַגֵּר
יא הַגָּר בְּתוֹכָם לְחֻקַּת עוֹלָם: הַנֹּגֵעַ בְּמֵת לְכָל־נֶפֶשׁ אָדָם וְטָמֵא שִׁבְעַת
יב יָמִים: הוּא יִתְחַטָּא־בוֹ בַּיּוֹם הַשְּׁלִישִׁי וּבַיּוֹם הַשְּׁבִיעִי יִטְהָר וְאִם־לֹא
יג יִתְחַטָּא בַּיּוֹם הַשְּׁלִישִׁי וּבַיּוֹם הַשְּׁבִיעִי לֹא יִטְהָר: כָּל־הַנֹּגֵעַ בְּמֵת בְּנֶפֶשׁ
הָאָדָם אֲשֶׁר־יָמוּת וְלֹא יִתְחַטָּא אֶת־מִשְׁכַּן יהוה טִמֵּא וְנִכְרְתָה הַנֶּפֶשׁ
הַהִוא מִיִּשְׂרָאֵל כִּי מֵי נִדָּה לֹא־זֹרַק עָלָיו טָמֵא יִהְיֶה עוֹד טֻמְאָתוֹ בוֹ:
יד זֹאת הַתּוֹרָה אָדָם כִּי־יָמוּת בְּאֹהֶל כָּל־הַבָּא אֶל־הָאֹהֶל וְכָל־אֲשֶׁר
טו בָּאֹהֶל יִטְמָא שִׁבְעַת יָמִים: וְכֹל כְּלִי פָתוּחַ אֲשֶׁר אֵין־צָמִיד פָּתִיל עָלָיו
טז טָמֵא הוּא: וְכֹל אֲשֶׁר־יִגַּע עַל־פְּנֵי הַשָּׂדֶה בַּחֲלַל־חֶרֶב אוֹ בְמֵת אוֹ־
יז בְעֶצֶם אָדָם אוֹ בְקָבֶר יִטְמָא שִׁבְעַת יָמִים: וְלָקְחוּ לַטָּמֵא מֵעֲפַר שְׂרֵפַת
יח הַחַטָּאת וְנָתַן עָלָיו מַיִם חַיִּים אֶל־כֶּלִי: וְלָקַח אֵזוֹב וְטָבַל בַּמַּיִם אִישׁ   שני
טָהוֹר וְהִזָּה עַל־הָאֹהֶל וְעַל־כָּל־הַכֵּלִים וְעַל־הַנְּפָשׁוֹת אֲשֶׁר הָיוּ־שָׁם

— it contains an allusion to the way of repentance necessary for every sinner, (which is) to incline to the opposite extreme of his (evil) deeds, which defile the purity of every (man's) heart, in order to attain the middle path and (thereby) become purified. Now this course, although good and purifying for the sinner, is discreditable and bad and defiling for those whose hearts are pure, as our Sages state (regarding the *nazir*), "Against which soul did he sin? It must refer to the fact that he denied himself wine" (*Taanis* 11a).

However, the (cleansing) waters (of the red cow) composed of ashes and water, which are two extremes from which combination there evolves a middle path, teaches us that through this middle path the sinner shall be corrected and this is called *taharah*, as it says, מִכֹּל חַטֹּאתֵיכֶם לִפְנֵי ה׳ תִּטְהָרוּ, *From all your sins you shall become tahor before* HASHEM (*Leviticus* 16:30). Now, it is fitting to consider that the Almighty decreed that one who comes into contact with a dead person, as well as one who enters the tent (of a dead person), makes *tamei* the Sanctuary of God (if he enters it), and this (teaches us) that indeed, whoever draws nigh to the vanities of the perishable aspects (of this world), without a doubt, will defile the pure heart which is the sanctuary of God's temple called צֶלֶם אֱלֹהִים, *the image of God*, and this impurity is characterized as an error of omission. (However), when one enters the tent of a dead person, similar to, שֹׁכְנֵי בָתֵּי חֹמֶר, *those who dwell in houses of clay* (*Job* 4:19), meaning those who have naught in life save their bodies and who are immersed in the pursuit of the transitory experiences of this world, and whose steps (lit., feet) lead them to death — such a person, without a doubt, defiles the aforementioned מִקְדַּשׁ ה׳, *God's Temple*, by which the people (of Israel) and each

3 You shall give it to Elazar the Kohen; he shall take it to the outside of the
camp and someone shall slaughter it in his presence. 4 Elazar the Kohen shall
take some of its blood with his forefinger, and sprinkle some of its blood
toward the Tent of Meeting seven times. 5 Someone shall burn the cow before
his eyes — its hide, and its flesh, and its blood, with its dung, shall he burn.
6 The Kohen shall take cedarwood, hyssop, and crimson thread, and he shall
throw them into the burning of the cow.

7 The Kohen shall immerse his clothing and immerse himself in water, and
afterwards he may enter the camp; and the Kohen shall remain conta-
minated until evening. 8 The one who burns it shall immerse his clothing and
immerse himself in water; and he shall remain contaminated until evening.
9 A pure man shall gather the ash of the cow and place it outside the camp
in a pure place. For the assembly of Israel it shall remain as a safekeeping,
for water of sprinkling; it is for purification. 10 The one who gathered the ash
of the cow shall immerse his clothing and remain contaminated until
evening. It shall be for the Children of Israel and for the proselyte who
dwells among them as an eternal decree.

11 Whoever touches the corpse of any human being shall be contaminated
for seven days. 12 He shall purify himself with it on the third day and on the
seventh day become pure; but if he will not purify himself on the third day,
then on the seventh day he will not become pure. 13 Whoever touches the
dead body of a human being who will have died and will not have purified
himself — if he shall have contaminated the Tabernacle of HASHEM, *that*
person shall be cut off from Israel; because the water of sprinkling has not
been thrown upon him, he shall remain contaminated; his contamination is
still upon him.

14 This is the teaching regarding a man who would die in a tent: Anything
that enters the tent and anything that is in the tent shall be contaminated
for seven days. 15 Any open vessel that has no cover fastened to it is conta-
minated. 16 On the open field: Anyone who touches one slain by the sword,
or one that died, or a human bone, or a grave, shall be contaminated for seven
days. 17 They shall take for the contaminated person some of the ashes of
the burning of the purification [animal], and put upon it spring water in
a vessel. 18 A pure man shall take hyssop and dip it in the water, and
sprinkle upon the tent, upon all the vessels, upon the people who were there,

---

individual is meant to be sanctified to God, as it says, וְלִהְיֹתְךָ עַם קָדֹשׁ לַה׳ אֱלֹהֶיךָ, *And that you may be a holy people to* HASHEM *your God* (*Deut.* 26:19). In this case, he defiles himself (in a positive manner) which is considered an error of commission, and all this is contrary to the intent (of God). For these (reasons), it is fitting that only the dead body of an Israelite can cause *tumah* in a tent, because only his physical matter (i.e., body) is chosen and prepared above all others to serve God, the Blessed One, and only he (the Israelite) sins against his honored soul. However, the wise men who instruct the sinners in the way of repentance, who are akin to the one who sprinkles the water and to the one who sanctifies, are not susceptible to any *tumah*.

And thus in the detailed observance of this commandment, as it is written (in the Torah) and as (taught in) tradition, there is an indication of all these (interpretations) which are part of the intention (and purpose) of Torah, without a doubt.

יט וְעַל־הַנֹּגֵעַ בַּעֶצֶם אוֹ בֶחָלָל אוֹ בַמֵּת אוֹ בַקָּבֶר׃ וְהִזָּה הַטָּהֹר עַל־הַטָּמֵא
בַּיּוֹם הַשְּׁלִישִׁי וּבַיּוֹם הַשְּׁבִיעִי וְחִטְּאוֹ בַּיּוֹם הַשְּׁבִיעִי וְכִבֶּס בְּגָדָיו וְרָחַץ
כ בַּמַּיִם וְטָהֵר בָּעָרֶב׃ וְאִישׁ אֲשֶׁר־יִטְמָא וְלֹא יִתְחַטָּא וְנִכְרְתָה הַנֶּפֶשׁ
הַהִוא מִתּוֹךְ הַקָּהָל כִּי אֶת־מִקְדַּשׁ יהוה טִמֵּא מֵי נִדָּה לֹא־זֹרַק עָלָיו
כא טָמֵא הוּא׃ וְהָיְתָה לָהֶם לְחֻקַּת עוֹלָם וּמַזֵּה מֵי־הַנִּדָּה יְכַבֵּס בְּגָדָיו וְהַנֹּגֵעַ
כב בְּמֵי הַנִּדָּה יִטְמָא עַד־הָעָרֶב׃ וְכֹל אֲשֶׁר־יִגַּע־בּוֹ הַטָּמֵא יִטְמָא וְהַנֶּפֶשׁ
הַנֹּגַעַת תִּטְמָא עַד־הָעָרֶב׃

כ *ב׳ טעמים א וַיָּבֹאוּ בְנֵי־יִשְׂרָאֵל כָּל־הָעֵדָה מִדְבַּר־צִן בַּחֹדֶשׁ הָרִאשׁוֹן וַיֵּשֶׁב הָעָם
ב בְּקָדֵשׁ וַתָּמָת שָׁם מִרְיָם וַתִּקָּבֵר שָׁם׃ וְלֹא־הָיָה מַיִם לָעֵדָה וַיִּקָּהֲלוּ
ג עַל־מֹשֶׁה וְעַל־אַהֲרֹן׃ וַיָּרֶב הָעָם עִם־מֹשֶׁה וַיֹּאמְרוּ לֵאמֹר וְלוּ גָוַעְנוּ
ד בִּגְוַע אַחֵינוּ לִפְנֵי יהוה׃ וְלָמָה הֲבֵאתֶם אֶת־קְהַל יהוה אֶל־הַמִּדְבָּר הַזֶּה
ה לָמוּת שָׁם אֲנַחְנוּ וּבְעִירֵנוּ׃ וְלָמָה הֶעֱלִיתֻנוּ מִמִּצְרַיִם לְהָבִיא אֹתָנוּ
אֶל־הַמָּקוֹם הָרָע הַזֶּה לֹא | מְקוֹם זֶרַע וּתְאֵנָה וְגֶפֶן וְרִמּוֹן וּמַיִם אַיִן
ו לִשְׁתּוֹת׃ וַיָּבֹא מֹשֶׁה וְאַהֲרֹן מִפְּנֵי הַקָּהָל אֶל־פֶּתַח אֹהֶל מוֹעֵד וַיִּפְּלוּ
עַל־פְּנֵיהֶם וַיֵּרָא כְבוֹד־יהוה אֲלֵיהֶם׃
שלישי [שני] ז־ח וַיְדַבֵּר יהוה אֶל־מֹשֶׁה לֵּאמֹר׃ קַח אֶת־הַמַּטֶּה וְהַקְהֵל אֶת־הָעֵדָה אַתָּה
וְאַהֲרֹן אָחִיךָ וְדִבַּרְתֶּם אֶל־הַסֶּלַע לְעֵינֵיהֶם וְנָתַן מֵימָיו וְהוֹצֵאתָ לָהֶם

XX

3. וַיָּרֶב הָעָם עִם מֹשֶׁה — *And the people strove with Moses* ... Behold, their strife with Moses was in their saying ...

4. וְלָמָה הֲבֵאתֶם אֶת קְהַל ה׳ אֶל הַמִּדְבָּר הַזֶּה — *And why have you brought the assembly of HASHEM into this wilderness?* However, they also (did strive) with God, the Blessed One, (as well) as the (Torah) attests to by saying, *Where the Children of Israel strove with HASHEM* (v. 13), and this (striving with God) was (also manifest) in their saying *and wherefore have you made us come up out of Egypt* (v. 5).

8. קַח אֶת הַמַּטֶּה ... וְדִבַּרְתֶּם אֶל הַסֶּלַע — *Take the rod ... and speak unto the rock.* There are many opinions as to the nature of the sin of "the waters of Meribah" (strife), and many are in doubt as to what the sin of Moses and Aaron was that the (Torah) does write of them, *you believed not* (v. 12), *you trespassed* (*desecrated*) (*Deut.* 32:51) and *you rebelled* (v. 24). Now, if it was the intent of God, the Blessed One, that they should only *speak* to the rock, then what was the purpose of taking the rod, and if the sin was that Moses hit the rock in the absence of any such command of the One Who sent him, then what was Aaron's sin?

NOTES

XX

3-4. וַיָּרֶב הָעָם עִם מֹשֶׁה ... וְלָמָה הֲבֵאתֶם אֶת קְהַל ה׳ ... אֶל הַמִּדְבָּר הַזֶּה — *And the people strove with Moses ... And why have you brought the assembly of HASHEM into this wilderness?* ... Although the verse states that they only strove with Moses for leading them into the wilderness, the *Sforno* explains that they also were critical of God for bringing them forth from Egypt, as we clearly see in verse 13. The *Sforno* explains this point further in his commentary on verse 8.

8. קַח אֶת הַמַּטֶּה ... וְדִבַּרְתֶּם אֶל הַסֶּלַע — *Take the rod ... and speak unto the rock.* At Rephidim, the Almighty commanded Moses to smite the rock with his rod and bring forth water (*Exodus* 17:6). At Meribah, Moses and Aaron were told to speak to the rock. Still, Moses was also commanded to "take the rod," which puzzles the *Sforno*. If they

and upon the one who touched the bone, or the slain one, or the one that
died, or the grave. 19 *The pure person shall sprinkle upon the contaminated*
person on the third day and on the seventh day, and shall purify him on the
seventh day; then he shall immerse his clothing and immerse himself in
water and become purified in the evening. 20 *But a man who becomes*
contaminated and does not purify himself, that person shall be cut off from
the midst of the congregation, if he shall have contaminated the Sanctuary
of HASHEM; *because the water of sprinkling has not been thrown upon him,*
he is contaminated.
21 *This shall be for them an eternal decree. And the one who sprinkles the*
water of sprinkling shall immerse his clothing, and one who touches water
of sprinkling shall be contaminated until evening. 22 *Anything that the*
contaminated one may touch shall become contaminated, and the person
who touches him shall become contaminated until evening.

20 1 *The Children of Israel, the whole assembly, arrived at the Wilderness*
of Zin in the first month and the people settled in Kadesh. Miriam
died there and she was buried there. 2 *There was no water for the assembly,*
and they gathered against Moses and Aaron. 3 *The people quarreled with*
Moses and spoke up saying, "If only we had perished as our brethren
perished before HASHEM! 4 *Why have you brought the congregation of*
HASHEM *to this wilderness to die there, we and our animals?* 5 *And why did*
you have us ascend from Egypt to bring us to this evil place? -- not a place
of seed, or fig, or grape, or pomegranate; and there is no water to drink!"
6 *Moses and Aaron went from the presence of the congregation to the*
entrance of the Tent of Meeting and fell on their faces. The glory of HASHEM
appeared to them.
7 HASHEM *spoke to Moses, saying,* 8 *"Take the staff and gather together*
the assembly, you and Aaron your brother, and speak to the rock before
their eyes that it shall give its waters. You shall bring forth for them

---

However, if we consider the matter of the strife it is fitting that we realize that God's command was (given) in such a fashion that they (i.e., Israel) recognize the evil of their strife and confess their sin and repent so that they be healed, for *He does not desire the death* (*of the wicked*) [based on *Ezekiel* 18:32]. And thus we will understand that it was this that Moses and Aaron overlooked, i.e., the intent of God, the Holy One, and for this He punished them. For, indeed, the strife with Moses was in their saying that his leadership was imperfect, being that he brought them to the worst part of the wilderness, while their strife with God, the Blessed One, was in their saying that He took them forth from a good, settled land to a (barren) wilderness. Now to make known to them their

NOTES

were meant only to speak to it, then what need was there for the rod? Secondly, why was it proper to smite the rock at Rephidim, whereas here the water was to be drawn forth through speech?

The *Sforno* explains that there are three kinds of miracles. The first is one that manifests itself through seemingly natural channels. This can result from the prayers of the righteous. The second transforms the laws of nature to a certain degree, yet is still within the realm of the natural. This can only be achieved by God but is done through His servants who cause it to happen by way of some action — which is in keeping with a specific directive of God. The third — and highest — type of miracle is one which completely transcends nature. This is done through the speech of His

ט מַ֙יִם֙ מִן־הַסֶּ֔לַע וְהִשְׁקִיתָ֥ אֶת־הָעֵדָ֖ה וְאֶת־בְּעִירָֽם׃ וַיִּקַּ֥ח מֹשֶׁ֛ה אֶת־
י הַמַּטֶּ֖ה מִלִּפְנֵ֣י יְהוָ֑ה כַּאֲשֶׁ֖ר צִוָּֽהוּ׃ וַיַּקְהִ֜לוּ מֹשֶׁ֧ה וְאַהֲרֹ֛ן אֶת־הַקָּהָ֖ל
אֶל־פְּנֵ֣י הַסָּ֑לַע וַיֹּ֣אמֶר לָהֶ֗ם שִׁמְעוּ־נָא֙ הַמֹּרִ֔ים הֲמִן־הַסֶּ֣לַע הַזֶּ֔ה נוֹצִ֥יא
יא לָכֶ֖ם מָֽיִם׃ וַיָּ֨רֶם מֹשֶׁ֜ה אֶת־יָד֗וֹ וַיַּ֧ךְ אֶת־הַסֶּ֛לַע בְּמַטֵּ֖הוּ פַּעֲמָ֑יִם וַיֵּצְאוּ֙
יב מַ֣יִם רַבִּ֔ים וַתֵּ֥שְׁתְּ הָעֵדָ֖ה וּבְעִירָֽם׃ וַיֹּ֣אמֶר יְהוָה֮ אֶל־מֹשֶׁ֣ה
וְאֶל־אַהֲרֹן֒ יַ֚עַן לֹא־הֶאֱמַנְתֶּ֣ם בִּ֔י לְהַ֨קְדִּישֵׁ֔נִי לְעֵינֵ֖י בְּנֵ֣י יִשְׂרָאֵ֑ל לָכֵ֗ן לֹ֤א

wickedness, it was necessary that this miracle (should) inform them that the messenger was functioning (lit., leading them) with perfection and that He who sent him did it for their benefit and not to harm them whatsoever.

Now there are three kinds of miracles related in Holy Scriptures, each (taking place) in one of three ways: One is a hidden miracle, such as rainfall or when one is delivered from illness or travail. This type of miracle can be attained by the righteous through their prayers, similar to, וַיִּתְפַּלֵּל אַבְרָהָם אֶל הָאֱלֹהִים וַיִּרְפָּא אֱלֹהִים אֶת אֲבִימֶלֶךְ וְאֶת אִשְׁתּוֹ וְאַמְהֹתָיו וַיֵּלֵדוּ, *And Abraham prayed to God and God healed Abimelech and his wife and his maidservants and they gave birth* (*Genesis* 20:17); also *And Moses prayed for the people* (21:7). The second is a revealed miracle, which nature cannot achieve in that (particular) manner but it can be brought about after a period of time through much movement. This type of miracle is wrought by God, the Blessed One, through His servants, preceded by certain actions ordered by Him such as הַשְׁלִיכֵהוּ אַרְצָה, *Cast it on the ground* (*Exodus* 4:3), and הָרֵם אֶת מַטְּךָ, *Lift up your rod* (ibid. 14:16), or וְהִכִּיתָ בַצּוּר, *And you shall smite the rock* (ibid. 17:6), and יְרֵה וַיּוֹר, *"Shoot!" and he shot* (*II Kings* 13:17), and other (such examples).

The third kind of miracle is one that nature can, in no way, achieve and this type (of miracle) God, the Exalted One, achieves with His servants only through speech alone, which is an intellectual act and more distinguished than other physical movements, as was the case when the earth opened its mouth, as it says, *And it came to pass when he finished speaking . . . that the ground did cleave asunder* (16:31). And when the sun stood still for Joshua, it says, אָז יְדַבֵּר יְהוֹשֻׁעַ, *And then Joshua spoke* (*Joshua* 10:12). Now, behold that regarding this episode of Meribah, it was imperative to remove the evil complaints of Israel (in such a manner) that the miracle wrought would clarify the excellence of the King Who dispatched (Moses) and His ways of goodness while (also) clarifying the excellence of the messenger and *his* goodness, that he was prepared to achieve good for his people (on behalf of) the King. Now, the excellence of the One Who sends is elucidated through the third type of miracle, which nature cannot achieve at all in any fashion or at any time, while the excellence of the messenger is (demonstrated) through the second kind of miracle, which is achieved through the appropriate movements of the messenger. Therefore, God, the Blessed One, commanded that the rock be transformed into (a source) of water, as it says, *that it give forth its water*, meaning that the water will come forth

NOTES

servant, for speech is an act more intellectual than physical; hence it represents an action, on the part of God, which is supernatural.

As mentioned above, the Children of Israel had challenged both the motivation of God in taking them out of Egypt as well as the authenticity of Moses' leadership. The purpose of this miracle was to establish the beneficence and goodness of God and the legitimacy of His messengers — Moses and Aaron. To establish the former, the third category of miracle was called for; namely, to do it through speech and transform the stone into water — a totally radical change in nature. To establish the credibility of Moses, it was sufficient to perform a miracle of the second kind, which was to bring the water from the rock to the tents of the people, as was the accepted case during their travels in the wilderness (see *Rashi*, Chapter 21:18). For this latter purpose, the rod was necessary. However, Moses and Aaron felt that Israel was not

water from the rock and give drink to the assembly and to their animals."
9 *Moses took the staff from before HASHEM, as He had commanded him.*
10 *Moses and Aaron gathered the congregation before the rock and he said to them, "Listen now, O rebels, shall we bring forth water for you from this rock?"*
11 *Then Moses raised his arm and struck the rock with his staff twice; abundant water came forth and the assembly and their animals drank.*
12 *HASHEM said to Moses and to Aaron, "Because you did not believe in Me to sanctify Me in the eyes of the Children of Israel, therefore you will not*

---

from the rock itself, and not be drawn to it from another place. Now this would have been impossible unless the rock changed its form from "rock" to "water," as (the verse) later testifies to by saying, הַמּוֹצִיא לְךָ מַיִם מִצּוּר הַחַלָּמִישׁ, *Who brought forth for you water out of the rock of flint* (*Deut.* 8:15); because if the water would have been brought there miraculously from a different source it would make no difference whether it (gushed forth) from a rock of flint or from anything else!

Now this type of miracle cannot be effectuated by nature through any means or at any time. (Therefore) He commanded that it be done through the speech of His servants, as it says, *and speak unto the rock*, so that Israel shall realize that this miracle is of the third kind, as we have said (above) — namely, that the water was not being drawn from another place, and thus they will recognize (lit., know) the greatness and goodness of the מְשַׁלֵּחַ (Sender) and consider that although He brought them forth from Egypt to a wilderness it was not detrimental to them at all since He was with them and since He was capable of transforming the wilderness into a *pond of water*, (an act) which cannot be achieved through nature; hence, "if He is here, all are here" (based on *Succah* 53a) and as it is written, הֲמִדְבָּר הָיִיתִי לְיִשְׂרָאֵל, *Have I been a wilderness to Israel* (*Jeremiah* 2:31)? With all this, He (also) commanded that after the rock would change over to water, Moses was to bring forth this water with his rod to their tribes, as it says, *with the scepter and with their staves* (21:18), and for this kind of miracle He said, *Take the rod . . . and bring forth to them water from the rock.* (Now) behold, Moses and Aaron agreed to perform the second category of miracle, and to bring the water to the rock from another (existing) place as they did in Rephidim, as it says, וְהִכִּיתָ בַצּוּר וְיָצְאוּ מִמֶּנּוּ מַיִם, *And you shall smite the rock and water shall come out of it* (*Exodus* 17:6), because they did not trust that God, the Blessed One, would fulfill His word to perform the third type of miracle for Israel, for they thought that Israel were rebels and hence unworthy of God's goodness. Therefore, they performed the second kind of miracle with the rod, which proclaimed the excellence of the messenger, but did not follow the third way by which Israel would have been told of the excellence and goodness of the Sender. Therefore, it is written regarding them . . .

12. לֹא הֶאֱמַנְתֶּם בִּי — *You did not believe in Me.* This means: You had no confidence that I would fulfill that which I had said; (and) מְעַלְתֶּם בִּי, *You trespassed against Me* (*Deut.* 32:51), for you desecrated My honor and did not show those who were striving (against us) their foolishness, and (also) *You rebelled against My word* (v. 24) by not observing My commandment.

NOTES

worthy of the highest form of miracle, namely to have God transform the rock into a *direct* source of new water through their speech. Therefore, they smote the rock in order to bring water from an existing well or spring, as had been done at Rephidim. Hence, they were guilty of non-belief, of מְעִילָה, *trespass*, as well as rebellion, as explained by the *Sforno* in verse 12.

12. לֹא הֶאֱמַנְתֶּם בִּי — *You did not believe in Me.* God had told Moses and Aaron that He was prepared to perform a miracle of the third kind. Moses and Aaron (1) did not believe Him; (2) were guilty of מְעִילָה (trespass or unlawful use of sacred property) for they failed to properly utilize their God-given power of teaching to relate to the people God's willingness to care for them in spite

יג תָּבִיאוּ אֶת־הַקָּהָל הַזֶּה אֶל־הָאָרֶץ אֲשֶׁר־נָתַתִּי לָהֶם׃ הֵמָּה מֵי מְרִיבָה
יד אֲשֶׁר־רָבוּ בְנֵי־יִשְׂרָאֵל אֶת־יהוה וַיִּקָּדֵשׁ בָּם׃ וַיִּשְׁלַח מֹשֶׁה רביעי
מַלְאָכִים מִקָּדֵשׁ אֶל־מֶלֶךְ אֱדוֹם כֹּה אָמַר אָחִיךָ יִשְׂרָאֵל אַתָּה יָדַעְתָּ אֵת
טו כָּל־הַתְּלָאָה אֲשֶׁר מְצָאָתְנוּ׃ וַיֵּרְדוּ אֲבֹתֵינוּ מִצְרַיְמָה וַנֵּשֶׁב בְּמִצְרַיִם יָמִים
טז רַבִּים וַיָּרֵעוּ לָנוּ מִצְרַיִם וְלַאֲבֹתֵינוּ׃ וַנִּצְעַק אֶל־יהוה וַיִּשְׁמַע קֹלֵנוּ וַיִּשְׁלַח
יז מַלְאָךְ וַיֹּצִאֵנוּ מִמִּצְרָיִם וְהִנֵּה אֲנַחְנוּ בְקָדֵשׁ עִיר קְצֵה גְבוּלֶךָ׃ נַעְבְּרָה־נָּא
בְאַרְצֶךָ לֹא נַעֲבֹר בְּשָׂדֶה וּבְכֶרֶם וְלֹא נִשְׁתֶּה מֵי בְאֵר דֶּרֶךְ הַמֶּלֶךְ נֵלֵךְ
יח לֹא נִטֶּה יָמִין וּשְׂמֹאול עַד אֲשֶׁר־נַעֲבֹר גְּבֻלֶךָ׃ וַיֹּאמֶר אֵלָיו אֱדוֹם לֹא יתיר ו׳
יט תַעֲבֹר בִּי פֶּן־בַּחֶרֶב אֵצֵא לִקְרָאתֶךָ׃ וַיֹּאמְרוּ אֵלָיו בְּנֵי־יִשְׂרָאֵל בַּמְסִלָּה
נַעֲלֶה וְאִם־מֵימֶיךָ נִשְׁתֶּה אֲנִי וּמִקְנַי וְנָתַתִּי מִכְרָם רַק אֵין־דָּבָר בְּרַגְלַי
כ אֶעֱבֹרָה׃ וַיֹּאמֶר לֹא תַעֲבֹר וַיֵּצֵא אֱדוֹם לִקְרָאתוֹ בְּעַם כָּבֵד וּבְיָד חֲזָקָה׃
כא וַיְמָאֵן ׀ אֱדוֹם נְתֹן אֶת־יִשְׂרָאֵל עֲבֹר בִּגְבֻלוֹ וַיֵּט יִשְׂרָאֵל מֵעָלָיו׃
כב־כג וַיִּסְעוּ מִקָּדֵשׁ וַיָּבֹאוּ בְנֵי־יִשְׂרָאֵל כָּל־הָעֵדָה הֹר הָהָר׃ וַיֹּאמֶר יהוה אֶל־ חמישי
כד מֹשֶׁה וְאֶל־אַהֲרֹן בְּהֹר הָהָר עַל־גְּבוּל אֶרֶץ־אֱדוֹם לֵאמֹר׃ יֵאָסֵף אַהֲרֹן [שלישי]
אֶל־עַמָּיו כִּי לֹא יָבֹא אֶל־הָאָרֶץ אֲשֶׁר נָתַתִּי לִבְנֵי יִשְׂרָאֵל עַל אֲשֶׁר־
כה מְרִיתֶם אֶת־פִּי לְמֵי מְרִיבָה׃ קַח אֶת־אַהֲרֹן וְאֶת־אֶלְעָזָר בְּנוֹ וְהַעַל
כו אֹתָם הֹר הָהָר׃ וְהַפְשֵׁט אֶת־אַהֲרֹן אֶת־בְּגָדָיו וְהִלְבַּשְׁתָּם אֶת־אֶלְעָזָר בְּנוֹ

13. וַיִּקָּדֵשׁ בָּם — *And He was sanctified in them* . . . with those very same waters He was later sanctified at the episode of the valley of Arnon, when Israel was shown that these waters were supernatural, as their song indicates when they said, *And from Nachliel Bamos* (21:19), for the water went upward, higher than their source, which is contrary to the nature of water.

17. דֶּרֶךְ הַמֶּלֶךְ — *The King's highway.* We will travel on the road which the King shall command us (to traverse), as is the custom of every king who grants passage to the army of his friends (lit., "those with whom he has peaceful relations"), sending a scout with them so that the soldiers will do no damage to the inhabitants of the land as they pass through.

18. פֶּן בַּחֶרֶב אֵצֵא לִקְרָאתֶךָ — *Lest I come out with the sword to meet you* . . . for the masses of the Edomites are bloodthirsty men, and for any minor reason (such as that) caused by an argument or similar incident between the inhabitants and those passing through, the inhabitants will be roused to take up their swords against those passing through.

19. בַּמְסִלָּה נַעֲלֶה — *We will go up by the highway.* Behold, this is possible to occur were we to pass through the cities, but we will only travel on the highway, and there will be no cause to arouse your people to take up arms (lit., sword) against us.

NOTES

of their unworthiness; and (3) they did not observe the direct commandment of God to speak to the rock, which was a rebellious act. In this manner, the *Sforno* explains all three expressions used in the Torah — "lack of belief" (in this verse), "trespass" (*Deut.* 32:51) and "rebellion" (in verse 24).

13. וַיִּקָּדֵשׁ בָּם — *And He was sanctified in them.* Since Moses and Aaron had not obeyed God's command, how then was *He sanctified* through this well? The *Sforno* explains that the supernatural character of these waters was eventually recognized by Israel in the valley of Arnon, as recorded in 21:16 — *that is the well etc.* — and those waters defied the laws of nature by rising higher than their source.

18-20. . . . בַּמְסִלָּה נַעֲלֶה . . . פֶּן בַּחֶרֶב אֵצֵא לִקְרָאתֶךָ . . . אֶעֱבֹרָה . . . וַיֵּצֵא אֱדוֹם לִקְרָאתוֹ — *Lest I come out with the sword to meet you* . . . *we will go up by the*

bring this congregation to the Land that I have given them." [13] *They are the waters of strife, where the Children of Israel contended with* HASHEM, *and He was sanctified through them.*

[14] *Moses sent emissaries from Kadesh to the king of Edom: "So said your brother Israel: You know all the hardship that has befallen us.* [15] *Our forefathers descended to Egypt and we dwelled in Egypt many years, and the Egyptians did evil to us and to our forefathers.* [16] *We cried out to* HASHEM *and He heard our voice; He sent an emissary and took us out of Egypt. Now behold! we are in Kadesh, a city at the edge of your border.* [17] *Let us pass through your land; we shall not pass through field or vineyard, and we shall not drink well water; on the king's road shall we travel — we shall not veer right or left — until we pass through your border."*

[18] *The king of Edom said to him, "You shall not pass through me — lest I come against you with the sword!"*

[19] *The Children of Israel said to him, "We shall go up on the highway, and if we drink your water — I or my flock — I shall pay their price. Only nothing will happen; let me pass through on foot."*

[20] *He said, "You shall not pass through!" Then Edom went out against him with a massive throng and a strong hand.* [21] *So Edom refused to permit Israel to pass through his border, and Israel turned away from near him.*

[22] *They journeyed from Kadesh and the Children of Israel arrived — the entire assembly — at Mount Hor.* [23] HASHEM *said to Moses and Aaron at Mount Hor by the border of the land of Edom, saying,* [24] *"Aaron shall be gathered to his people, for he shall not enter the Land that I have given to the Children of Israel, because you defied My word at the waters of strife.* [25] *Take Aaron and Elazar his son and bring them up to Mount Hor.* [26] *Strip Aaron of his vestments and dress Elazar his son in them;*

רַק אֵין דָּבָר בְּרַגְלַי — *There is no reason (to object) on my account.* We have naught with us which will instigate a quarrel.

אֶעֱבֹרָה — *Let us pass* . . . for since you refuse to let us pass only because of what you have said, then behold, we can pass, for there is no reason to be concerned at all.

20. וַיֵּצֵא אֱדוֹם לִקְרָאתוֹ — *And Edom came out against him* . . . to the boundary.

26. וְהַפְשֵׁט אֶת אַהֲרֹן אֶת בְּגָדָיו — *And remove Aaron's garments from him* . . . those garments which are reserved for the *Kohen Gadol* (alone) more so than those used by a common *Kohen*.

וְהִלְבַּשְׁתָּם אֶת אֶלְעָזָר — *And put them upon Elazar* . . . who was (already) wearing the four

NOTES

highway . . . let us pass . . . and Edom came out against him. The discussion between Israel and Edom presents certain difficulties. Considering that Israel courteously asked permission of the king, why was the response such a threatening, militant one? Secondly, the phraseology is strange; the word פֶּן, *lest*, should have read כִּי, *because*. And finally, once they were refused why did they keep pressing for permission? The *Sforno* resolves these difficulties by explaining the sense of these verses thus: The king stated that he would be amenable to follow protocol and permit Israel passage; however, he could not be responsible for the actions of his people. Israel, however, argued that they would only travel on the outskirts of the inhabited areas and therefore not incite the populace. The king then showed his true colors and marshaled his forces on the border, thereby demonstrating his enmity toward his "cousins."

26. וְהַפְשֵׁט אֶת אַהֲרֹן אֶת בְּגָדָיו וְהִלְבַּשְׁתָּם אֶת אֶלְעָזָר . . . — *And remove Aaron's garments from him and*

כז וְאַהֲרֹן יֵאָסֵף וּמֵת שָׁם׃ וַיַּעַשׂ מֹשֶׁה כַּאֲשֶׁר צִוָּה יהוה וַיַּעֲלוּ אֶל־הֹר הָהָר
כח לְעֵינֵי כָּל־הָעֵדָה׃ וַיַּפְשֵׁט מֹשֶׁה אֶת־אַהֲרֹן אֶת־בְּגָדָיו וַיַּלְבֵּשׁ אֹתָם אֶת־
אֶלְעָזָר בְּנוֹ וַיָּמָת אַהֲרֹן שָׁם בְּרֹאשׁ הָהָר וַיֵּרֶד מֹשֶׁה וְאֶלְעָזָר מִן־הָהָר׃
כט וַיִּרְאוּ כָּל־הָעֵדָה כִּי גָוַע אַהֲרֹן וַיִּבְכּוּ אֶת־אַהֲרֹן שְׁלֹשִׁים יוֹם כֹּל בֵּית
כא
א יִשְׂרָאֵל׃ וַיִּשְׁמַע הַכְּנַעֲנִי מֶלֶךְ־עֲרָד יֹשֵׁב הַנֶּגֶב כִּי בָּא
ב יִשְׂרָאֵל דֶּרֶךְ הָאֲתָרִים וַיִּלָּחֶם בְּיִשְׂרָאֵל וַיִּשְׁבְּ | מִמֶּנּוּ שֶׁבִי׃ וַיִּדַּר יִשְׂרָאֵל
נֶדֶר לַיהוה וַיֹּאמַר אִם־נָתֹן תִּתֵּן אֶת־הָעָם הַזֶּה בְּיָדִי וְהַחֲרַמְתִּי אֶת־
ג עָרֵיהֶם׃ וַיִּשְׁמַע יהוה בְּקוֹל יִשְׂרָאֵל וַיִּתֵּן אֶת־הַכְּנַעֲנִי וַיַּחֲרֵם אֶתְהֶם
וְאֶת־עָרֵיהֶם וַיִּקְרָא שֵׁם־הַמָּקוֹם חָרְמָה׃
ד וַיִּסְעוּ מֵהֹר הָהָר דֶּרֶךְ יַם־סוּף לִסְבֹב אֶת־אֶרֶץ אֱדוֹם וַתִּקְצַר נֶפֶשׁ־הָעָם
ה בַּדָּרֶךְ׃ וַיְדַבֵּר הָעָם בֵּאלֹהִים וּבְמֹשֶׁה לָמָה הֶעֱלִיתֻנוּ מִמִּצְרַיִם לָמוּת
ו בַּמִּדְבָּר כִּי אֵין לֶחֶם וְאֵין מַיִם וְנַפְשֵׁנוּ קָצָה בַּלֶּחֶם הַקְּלֹקֵל׃ וַיְשַׁלַּח יהוה
בָּעָם אֵת הַנְּחָשִׁים הַשְּׂרָפִים וַיְנַשְּׁכוּ אֶת־הָעָם וַיָּמָת עַם־רָב מִיִּשְׂרָאֵל׃
ז וַיָּבֹא הָעָם אֶל־מֹשֶׁה וַיֹּאמְרוּ חָטָאנוּ כִּי־דִבַּרְנוּ בַיהוה וָבָךְ הִתְפַּלֵּל אֶל־
ח יהוה וְיָסֵר מֵעָלֵינוּ אֶת־הַנָּחָשׁ וַיִּתְפַּלֵּל מֹשֶׁה בְּעַד הָעָם׃ וַיֹּאמֶר יהוה אֶל־
מֹשֶׁה עֲשֵׂה לְךָ שָׂרָף וְשִׂים אֹתוֹ עַל־נֵס וְהָיָה כָּל־הַנָּשׁוּךְ וְרָאָה אֹתוֹ וָחָי׃
ט וַיַּעַשׂ מֹשֶׁה נְחַשׁ נְחֹשֶׁת וַיְשִׂמֵהוּ עַל־הַנֵּס וְהָיָה אִם־נָשַׁךְ הַנָּחָשׁ אֶת־
ששי י־יא אִישׁ וְהִבִּיט אֶל־נְחַשׁ הַנְּחֹשֶׁת וָחָי׃ וַיִּסְעוּ בְּנֵי יִשְׂרָאֵל וַיַּחֲנוּ בְּאֹבֹת׃ וַיִּסְעוּ

---

garments of a common *Kohen*. Hence, Aaron remained clothed in the four garments of a common *Kohen*, the linen garments, as was his garb when he entered the Holy of Holies (lit., "all the way within"), and similar to the appearance of God's angels (when they are seen by) His servants.

XXI

1. וַיִּשְׁבְּ מִמֶּנּוּ שֶׁבִי — *And took from them a prisoner* ... (but) no one was killed.

3. וַיַּחֲרֵם אֶתְהֶם וְאֶת עָרֵיהֶם — *And they utterly destroyed them and their cities.* They vowed to utterly destroy them when they entered the Land, and so they did, as explained in the Book of *Judges* 1:17.

NOTES

put them upon Elazar ... The *Sforno* explains (similar to *Rashi*) that Moses only removed the four special garments of the *Kohen Gadol* from Aaron, which were then transferred to Elazar. Aaron remained clothed with the four linen garments of the כֹּהֵן הֶדְיוֹט, *the common priest*, which was most fitting. The reason for this was that he was now going to meet his Maker, an act which was akin to his entering the holy of Holies on Yom Kippur, at which time the *Kohen Gadol* removed his gold-embroidered garments, ornaments and vestments, entering only in his white linen clothing. The *Sforno* adds that, indeed, the angels, the messengers of God, always appeared garbed as such in visions to the prophets — hence, it was appropriate for Aaron to leave this world and enter the next dressed in these four garments.

XXI

3. וַיַּחֲרֵם אֶתְהֶם וְאֶת עָרֵיהֶם — *And they utterly destroyed them and their cities.* The word חֵרֶם means "to destroy," and also means to dedicate something to a sacred purpose, as *Rashi* explains in his commentary on this verse. However, the vow of the Israelites could not be fulfilled at that time since they were on the east bank of the Jordan while the Canaanites and King Arad were on the west side. The *Sforno*, therefore, explains (as does the *Ramban*) that this vow was taken with the intent of fulfilling it later, when Israel would enter the Land. The Book of *Judges*, indeed, records that they destroyed the Canaanites and called the city (of Arad) Chormah. The Torah relates here what eventually happened.

Aaron shall be gathered in and die there."
27 Moses did as HASHEM commanded, and they ascended Mount Hor
before the eyes of the entire assembly. 28 Moses stripped Aaron's garments
from him and dressed Elazar his son in them; then Aaron died there on
Mount Hor, and Moses and Elazar descended from the mountain. 29 When
the entire assembly saw that Aaron had perished, they wept for Aaron
thirty days, the entire House of Israel.

21 *1 The Canaanite king of Arad, who dwelled in the south, heard that*
Israel had come by the route of the spies, and he warred against Israel
and took a captive from it. 2 Israel made a vow to HASHEM and said, "If He
will deliver this people into my hand, I will consecrate their cities."
3 HASHEM heard the voice of Israel, and He delivered the Canaanite, and it
consecrated them and their cities. It named the place Hormah.
4 They journeyed from Mount Hor by way of the Sea of Reeds to go
around the land of Edom, and the spirit of the people grew short on the way.
5 The people spoke against God and Moses: "Why did you bring us up from
Egypt to die in this Wilderness, for there is no food and no water, and our
soul is disgusted with the insubstantial food?"
6 God sent the fiery serpents against the people and they bit the people.
A large multitude of Israel died. 7 The people came to Moses and said, "We
have sinned, for we have spoken against HASHEM and against you! Pray to
HASHEM that He remove from us the serpent." Moses prayed for the people.
8 HASHEM said to Moses, "Make yourself a fiery [serpent] and place it on
a pole, and it will be that anyone who was bitten will look at it and live."
9 Moses made a serpent of copper and placed it on the pole; so it was that
if the serpent bit a man, he would stare at the copper serpent and live.
10 The Children of Israel journeyed and encamped at Oboth. 11 They

8. עֲשֵׂה לְךָ שָׂרָף — *Make for yourself a fiery serpent.* The serpent is to be (fashioned) from a material which implies "burning" (i.e., such as brass) so that they would concentrate on the burning vapor (exhalation) of the serpent's mouth, this being akin to their iniquity and its resultant retribution, and thus they will repent.

9. נְחַשׁ נְחֹשֶׁת — *A serpent of brass.* After he (Moses) understood the intent of his Creator, he agreed to make it of brass and not of gold, so as to remind them (Israel) of their iniquity through (the medium) of the appearance of the material, its name and its form. (This was to teach them) that they had acted as serpents, through the vapor of their mouths, when they spoke against God, His action and His servant.

NOTES

8-9. עֲשֵׂה לְךָ שָׂרָף ... נְחַשׁ נְחֹשֶׁת ... — *Make for yourself a fiery serpent ... a serpent of brass.* The Children of Israel were guilty of לָשׁוֹן הָרָע, *slander,* a transgression traditionally attributed to the serpent. Slander consumes the victim — it "burns" — as these fiery serpents burned and consumed the Israelites. The fashioning of a brass serpent and placing it on a banner aroused the Israelites to examine their sin of slander, thereby bringing them to repentance. This was the purpose served by the *serpent of brass.* It was a means toward an end, not some magical cure. Moses originally thought to make it of gold, because any artifact commanded to be fashioned by God deserves to be made of the most expensive material — similar to the vessels of the Sanctuary. In this case, however, the intention was to underscore the link between נְחֹשֶׁת, *brass* forged through fire, and נָחָשׁ, *a serpent,* whose venom burns and destroys, as does slander. This is a play on words which is most instructive.

מֵאֹבֹת וַיַּחֲנוּ בְּעִיֵּי הָעֲבָרִים בַּמִּדְבָּר אֲשֶׁר עַל־פְּנֵי מוֹאָב מִמִּזְרַח
יב־יג הַשָּׁמֶשׁ׃ מִשָּׁם נָסָעוּ וַיַּחֲנוּ בְּנַחַל זָרֶד׃ מִשָּׁם נָסָעוּ וַיַּחֲנוּ מֵעֵבֶר אַרְנוֹן
אֲשֶׁר בַּמִּדְבָּר הַיֹּצֵא מִגְּבֻל הָאֱמֹרִי כִּי אַרְנוֹן גְּבוּל מוֹאָב בֵּין מוֹאָב וּבֵין
יד הָאֱמֹרִי׃ עַל־כֵּן יֵאָמַר בְּסֵפֶר מִלְחֲמֹת יהוה אֶת־וָהֵב בְּסוּפָה וְאֶת־
טו הַנְּחָלִים אַרְנוֹן׃ וְאֶשֶׁד הַנְּחָלִים אֲשֶׁר נָטָה לְשֶׁבֶת עָר וְנִשְׁעַן לִגְבוּל
טז מוֹאָב׃ וּמִשָּׁם בְּאֵרָה הִוא הַבְּאֵר אֲשֶׁר אָמַר יהוה לְמֹשֶׁה אֱסֹף אֶת־
יז הָעָם וְאֶתְּנָה לָהֶם מָיִם׃ אָז יָשִׁיר יִשְׂרָאֵל אֶת־
יח הַשִּׁירָה הַזֹּאת עֲלִי בְאֵר עֱנוּ־לָהּ׃ בְּאֵר חֲפָרוּהָ שָׂרִים כָּרוּהָ נְדִיבֵי הָעָם

13. מֵעֵבֶר אַרְנוֹן ... הַיֹּצֵא — *On the other side of the Arnon ... that goes out* ... in that portion of the Arnon, and the wilderness that goes out.

כִּי אַרְנוֹן גְּבוּל מוֹאָב — *For Arnon is the border of Moab* ... because the border of Moab was (situated) only in that portion which met that of the Emorites, but in the portion where (Israel) entered, Moab had no border (whatsoever).

14. בְּסֵפֶר מִלְחֲמֹת ה׳ אֶת וָהֵב בְּסוּפָה — *In the Book of the Wars of HASHEM, Vaheb and Suphah* ... it will be told of God to (future) generations, together with the (accounts of) His other wars, regarding *Vaheb and Suphah and the brooks of Arnon.* Behold, that part of Arnon where Israel passed through in peace and Sichon at that time did not rise up against them — that this was granted to them *through Suphah* (i.e., a storm wind) in the valley of Arnon where God, the Blessed One, stirred up a storm and caused a pouring forth of many waters which prevented Sichon from coming out to rise up against them.

15. וְאֶשֶׁד הַנְּחָלִים — *And the discharge of the brooks.* That Book will also tell about the event of the pouring forth of those brooks *that incline to Shebes-ar and lean upon the border of Moab.* (These waters) reached into the city called *Ar,* across from which the Israelites were, but nonetheless (the waters) did not spread to the place where Israel stood, rather it *leaned up* and pressed up *to the border of Moab.*

16. וּמִשָּׁם בְּאֵרָה — *And from there to Be'er* (*the well*) ... And from there, that pouring forth of the brooks inclined to the place of the well, whereof ...

אָמַר ה׳ לְמֹשֶׁה, אֱסֹף אֶת הָעָם — *HASHEM said to Moses, 'Gather the people together.'* We find that the place of that well, which (enabled it) to deepen in such a way that it could not (normally) elevate itself, was much lower than the place where Israel was now standing at the time of the Song, and since that well came up with them to the high (area) of the

NOTES

14-15. בְּסֵפֶר מִלְחֲמֹת ה׳ אֶת וָהֵב בְּסוּפָה ... וְאֶשֶׁד הַנְּחָלִים ... — *In the Book of the Wars of HASHEM, Vaheb and Suphah ... And the discharge of the brooks* ... When Israel encamped on the other side of Arnon, they were not attacked by the Emorites. This verse explains the reason for this inaction. The word וָהֵב (Vaheb) means *to give* (as *Rashi* states); the word סוּפָה (Suphah) means *storm.* The sense of the verse is: God gave (or granted) Israel peace by preventing Sichon from attacking them through a fierce storm wind and the gushing forth of the brook waters. These strong currents of water reached the city of Ar in the vicinity of the Israelites, yet did not engulf them. Miraculously, the waters did not spread out but "leaned up," and hence did not inundate the camp of Israel.

16. וּמִשָּׁם בְּאֵרָה — *And from there to Be'er* (*the well*). As mentioned above, the rock to which Moses was commanded to speak was transformed into water but did not possess the properties or nature of water. Water always descends, but this supernatural water had the power to *ascend.* When the Israelites beheld this phenomena, they burst into a song of praise, "Spring up, O well."

17. עֲלִי בְאֵר — *Spring up, O well.* The *Sforno* is of the opinion that the expression *The Book of the Wars of HASHEM* refers to the destruction of the Emorites who were hiding in caves above the valley through which Israel was marching with the intent of killing them with arrows and stone missiles. As our Sages tell us (and so does *Rashi* in

journeyed from Oboth and encamped in the desolate passes in the wilderness facing Moab, towards the rising sun. [12] *From there they journeyed and encamped in the valley of Zered.* [13] *From there they journeyed and encamped on the other side of Arnon, which is in the wilderness that juts out from the border of the Amorite; for Arnon is the border of Moab, between Moab and the Amorite.* [14] *Therefore it is said in the Book of the Wars of HASHEM:*
"The gift of [the Sea of] Reeds and the rivers of Arnon;
[15] *the outpouring of the rivers when it veered to dwell at Ar, and leaned against the border of Moab.*
[16] *And from there to the well — of which HASHEM said to Moses, 'Assemble the people and I shall give them water.' "*
[17] *Then Israel sang this song: "Come up, O well, announce it!*
[18] *Well that the princes dug, that the nobles of the people excavated,*

---

other side of Arnon, from whence the brooks poured down, they (then) saw that God, the Blessed One, had given power to those waters to rise upward — and therefore they began their song, and said . . .

17. עֲלִי בְאֵר — *Spring up, O well.* It appears to me that the war with the Ammonites at that time, as our Sages tell us (in *tractate Berachos* 54b), is alluded to in the expression, *The Book of the Wars of HASHEM* (v. 14). (Now) Scripture does not elaborate (lit., explain) the details of the miracles (regarding the well) so as to protect (lit., because of) the honor of Moses and Aaron, for indeed these (miracles) were only necessary to demonstrate to Israel that which was proper for Moses and Aaron to have told them had their actions been complete and in keeping with the command of God, the Blessed One. And this (lesson) was that they should know that the waters brought forth from the rock were not natural waters brought there in a wondrous way from some spring or river, but rather they were supernatural, for the rock had been transformed into a pond of water through the will of its Creator in such a manner that it did not possess the nature of other waters whose movement inclines toward the center, and therefore it went up with them to a place higher than its source — and all the more so since it brought up the limbs of the dead in the course of their movement, as our Sages tell us (ibid.). And therefore, Moses our Teacher does not participate in this song, for its theme was to explain how his action was deficient in (fulfilling) the will of his Creator, may He be Blessed, Who completed it, as it says, *And He was sanctified in them* (20:13) (i.e.,) by demonstrating that these waters had power contrary to the nature of other waters, as already explained (20:8).

18. בְּאֵר חֲפָרוּהָ שָׂרִים — *The well which the princes dug . . .* for this well was not full, as would be (a well) which flowed from a high place.

NOTES

his commentary on verse 15), the mountain opposite the caves had projections which moved miraculously across to this mountain, penetrated the caves and crushed the ambushers to death. This event is alluded to in the phrase *The Wars of HASHEM.* However, the miracle regarding the well where God transformed the rock into a *pond of water* (אֲגַם מָיִם) is alluded to in the song of Israel (*Spring up, O well*) in celebration of the supernatural character of these waters and their ability to flow upward. The *Sforno* points out that Moses did not join in this song (as opposed to the Song of the Sea) because it reflects the deficiency in his faith and his disobedience of God's command, manifested when he smote the rock instead of speaking to it. Had he done so he would have sanctified God's Name. Since he did not, God Himself had to demonstrate the miraculous nature of this well by causing it to go up with Israel to a place higher than its source, and by bringing up the blood and limbs of the Emorites from the valley. Therefore, Moses sadly had no part in the sanctification of God through these waters and it was appropriate that he not share in the song.

יט בִּמְחֹקֵק בְּמִשְׁעֲנֹתָם וּמִמִּדְבָּר מַתָּנָה: וּמִמַּתָּנָה נַחֲלִיאֵל וּמִנַּחֲלִיאֵל
כ בָּמוֹת: וּמִבָּמוֹת הַגַּיְא אֲשֶׁר בִּשְׂדֵה מוֹאָב רֹאשׁ הַפִּסְגָּה וְנִשְׁקָפָה עַל־פְּנֵי
הַיְשִׁימֹן:
שביעי [רביעי] כא־כב וַיִּשְׁלַח יִשְׂרָאֵל מַלְאָכִים אֶל־סִיחֹן מֶלֶךְ־הָאֱמֹרִי לֵאמֹר: אֶעְבְּרָה
בְאַרְצֶךָ לֹא נִטֶּה בְּשָׂדֶה וּבְכֶרֶם לֹא נִשְׁתֶּה מֵי בְאֵר בְּדֶרֶךְ הַמֶּלֶךְ
כג נֵלֵךְ עַד אֲשֶׁר־נַעֲבֹר גְּבֻלֶךָ: וְלֹא־נָתַן סִיחֹן אֶת־יִשְׂרָאֵל עֲבֹר בִּגְבֻלוֹ
וַיֶּאֱסֹף סִיחֹן אֶת־כָּל־עַמּוֹ וַיֵּצֵא לִקְרַאת יִשְׂרָאֵל הַמִּדְבָּרָה וַיָּבֹא
כד יָהְצָה וַיִּלָּחֶם בְּיִשְׂרָאֵל: וַיַּכֵּהוּ יִשְׂרָאֵל לְפִי־חָרֶב וַיִּירַשׁ אֶת־אַרְצוֹ
כה מֵאַרְנֹן עַד־יַבֹּק עַד־בְּנֵי עַמּוֹן כִּי עַז גְּבוּל בְּנֵי עַמּוֹן: וַיִּקַּח יִשְׂרָאֵל
אֵת כָּל־הֶעָרִים הָאֵלֶּה וַיֵּשֶׁב יִשְׂרָאֵל בְּכָל־עָרֵי הָאֱמֹרִי בְּחֶשְׁבּוֹן
כו וּבְכָל־בְּנֹתֶיהָ: כִּי חֶשְׁבּוֹן עִיר סִיחֹן מֶלֶךְ הָאֱמֹרִי הִוא וְהוּא נִלְחַם
כז בְּמֶלֶךְ מוֹאָב הָרִאשׁוֹן וַיִּקַּח אֶת־כָּל־אַרְצוֹ מִיָּדוֹ עַד־אַרְנֹן: עַל־כֵּן
כח יֹאמְרוּ הַמֹּשְׁלִים בֹּאוּ חֶשְׁבּוֹן תִּבָּנֶה וְתִכּוֹנֵן עִיר סִיחוֹן: כִּי־אֵשׁ יָצְאָה
מֵחֶשְׁבּוֹן לֶהָבָה מִקִּרְיַת סִיחֹן אָכְלָה עָר מוֹאָב בַּעֲלֵי בָּמוֹת אַרְנֹן:
כט אוֹי־לְךָ מוֹאָב אָבַדְתָּ עַם־כְּמוֹשׁ נָתַן בָּנָיו פְּלֵיטִם וּבְנֹתָיו בַּשְּׁבִית
ל לְמֶלֶךְ אֱמֹרִי סִיחוֹן: וַנִּירָם אָבַד חֶשְׁבּוֹן עַד־דִּיבֹן וַנַּשִּׁים עַד־נֹפַח *אֲשֶׁר *נקוד על ר'
לא־לב עַד־מֵידְבָא: וַיֵּשֶׁב יִשְׂרָאֵל בְּאֶרֶץ הָאֱמֹרִי: וַיִּשְׁלַח מֹשֶׁה לְרַגֵּל אֶת־יַעְזֵר

וּמִמִּדְבָּר מַתָּנָה — *And from the wilderness to Mattanah* . . . and thus it was revealed (lit., explained) that the existence (of the water) was given (by God) (directly) from that rock in the wilderness.

19. וּמִמַּתָּנָה נַחֲלִיאֵל — *And from Mattanah to Nachliel* . . . and with (all this), it did not increase or diminish as it went up and came down, as would have occurred (lit., been fitting) according to the nature of water if it had flowed from another place.

25. בְּכָל עָרֵי הָאֱמֹרִי בְּחֶשְׁבּוֹן וּבְכָל בְּנֹתֶיהָ — *In all the cities of the Emorites, in Cheshbon, and in all the towns thereof.* All the towns conquered by Sichon, together with all the other towns of his kingdom, were (considered as) daughter-cities of Cheshbon which was the (principal) city from (days of) yore, similar to (the expression), וְנָתַתִּי אֶתְהֶן לָךְ לְבָנוֹת, *And I will give them to you as daughter-cities* (*Ezekiel* 16:61).

26. כִּי חֶשְׁבּוֹן עִיר סִיחֹן מֶלֶךְ הָאֱמֹרִי הִוא — *For Cheshbon was the city of Sichon, the king of the Emorites.* The reason we stated that all the cities of the Emorites were daughter-cities of Cheshbon is because Cheshbon was the principal city of the kingdom of Sichon, king of the Emorites, prior to the conquest of the cities of the Moabites.

NOTES

18-19. בְּאֵר חֲפָרוּהָ שָׂרִים . . . וּמִמִּדְבָּר מַתָּנָה. וּמִמַּתָּנָה נַחֲלִיאֵל — *The well which the princes dug . . . and from the wilderness to Mattanah. And from Mattanah to Nachliel.* The *Sforno* in his commentary on these verses is strengthening his interpretation regarding the nature of the waters of the well given in verses 20:8 and 21:16, 17.

26-31. כִּי חֶשְׁבּוֹן עִיר סִיחֹן מֶלֶךְ הָאֱמֹרִי הִוא . . . בֹּאוּ חֶשְׁבּוֹן . . . וַנִּירָם אָבַד חֶשְׁבּוֹן . . . וַיֵּשֶׁב יִשְׂרָאֵל בְּאֶרֶץ הָאֱמֹרִי — *For Cheshbon was the city of Sichon, the king of the Emorites . . . come into Cheshbon . . . And their dominion and Cheshbon were destroyed . . . Thus Israel dwelt in the land of the Emorites.* The Israelites were prohibited by God from waging war against Moab and Ammon and taking their land away from them (*Deut.* 2:19). They were not enjoined from doing so to the Emorites. These verses come to tell us that many Moabite towns were first conquered by Sichon, the Emorite king,

through a lawgiver, with their staff. A gift from the Wilderness —
[19] the gift went to the valley, and from the valley to the heights,
[20] and from the heights to the valley in the field of Moab, at the top of the
peak, overlooking the surface of the wilderness."
[21] Israel sent emissaries to Sihon, king of the Amorite, saying, [22] "Let me
pass through your land; we shall not turn off to field or vineyard; we shall not drink well water; on the king's road shall we travel, until we pass through your border."
[23] But Sihon did not permit Israel to pass through his border, and Sihon
assembled his entire people and went out against Israel to the Wilderness. He arrived at Jahaz and waged war against Israel. [24] Israel smote him with
the edge of the sword and took possession of his land, from Arnon to Jabbok to the children of Ammon — for the border of the children of Ammon was powerful. [25] Israel took all these cities, and Israel settled in all the Amorite
cities, in Heshbon and all its suburbs. [26] For Heshbon — it was the city of
Sihon, king of the Amorite; and he had warred against the first king of Moab and took all his land from his control, until Arnon. [27] Regarding this
the poets would say:
"Come to Heshbon — let it be built and established as the city of Sihon.
[28] For a fire has come forth from Heshbon a flame from the city of Sihon.
It consumed Ar of Moab, the masters of Arnon's heights.
[29] Woe to you, O Moab, you are lost, O people of Chemosh! He made your
sons fugitives and your daughters captives of the king of the Amorite, Sihon.
[30] Their sovereignty over Heshbon was lost, it was removed from Dibon,
and we laid waste to Nophah, which reaches up to Medeba."
[31] Israel settled in the land of the Amorites. [32] Moses sent to spy out Jazer

---

27. עַל כֵּן יֹאמְרוּ הַמֹּשְׁלִים — *Wherefore those who speak in parables say . . .* Those who tell the meaning of parables which they saw in a visionary dream, as did Balaam, when it says, *And he took up his parable* (23:7).

בֹּאוּ חֶשְׁבּוֹן — *Come into Cheshbon.* You, the inhabitants of the Moabite towns, come to Cheshbon and submit to Sichon, for he shall be victorious and rule over you.

30. וַנִּירָם אָבַד חֶשְׁבּוֹן — *And their dominion and Cheshbon were destroyed.* The dominion (נִיר) and kingdom of Sichon, his fire and his flame (see v. 28), namely the military officers (of Sichon), shall perish. Because after they (the מוֹשְׁלִים) told (parables of) Sichon's victories, they also told of the loss of his kingdom through the Israelites.

31. וַיֵּשֶׁב יִשְׂרָאֵל בְּאֶרֶץ הָאֱמֹרִי — *Thus Israel dwelt in the land of the Emorites.* All this is related to explain that Israel did not dwell in the land of Moab, but (rather) they dwelt in the land of the Emorites, as Yiftach explains, saying, לֹא לָקַח יִשְׂרָאֵל אֶת אֶרֶץ מוֹאָב וְאֶת אֶרֶץ בְּנֵי עַמּוֹן, *Israel did not take away the land of Moab nor the land of the children of Ammon* (*Judges* 11:15).

NOTES

and were subsequently taken from him by Israel. This was permitted since these towns were now his and were no longer considered part of Moab or Ammon. It is precisely this argument which Yiftach used when he spoke to the Ammonites, as recorded in *Judges* 11. The *haftarah* of *parashas Chukas* is taken from this chapter in the Book of *Judges* for this reason.

°וַיּ֖וֹרֶשׁ ק׳ לג וַֽיִּלְכְּד֖וּ בְּנֹתֶ֑יהָ °ויירש אֶת־הָאֱמֹרִ֥י אֲשֶׁר־שָֽׁם׃ וַיִּפְנוּ֙ וַֽיַּעֲל֔וּ דֶּ֖רֶךְ הַבָּשָׁ֑ן
וַיֵּצֵ֣א עוֹג֩ מֶֽלֶךְ־הַבָּשָׁ֨ן לִקְרָאתָ֜ם ה֧וּא וְכָל־עַמּ֛וֹ לַמִּלְחָמָ֖ה אֶדְרֶֽעִי׃
מפטיר לד וַיֹּ֨אמֶר יְהוָ֤ה אֶל־מֹשֶׁה֙ אַל־תִּירָ֣א אֹת֔וֹ כִּ֣י בְיָדְךָ֞ נָתַ֧תִּי אֹת֛וֹ
וְאֶת־כָּל־עַמּ֖וֹ וְאֶת־אַרְצ֑וֹ וְעָשִׂ֣יתָ לּ֔וֹ כַּאֲשֶׁ֣ר עָשִׂ֗יתָ לְסִיחֹן֙ מֶ֣לֶךְ הָאֱמֹרִ֔י
לה אֲשֶׁ֥ר יוֹשֵׁ֖ב בְּחֶשְׁבּֽוֹן׃ וַיַּכּ֨וּ אֹת֤וֹ וְאֶת־בָּנָיו֙ וְאֶת־כָּל־עַמּ֔וֹ עַד־בִּלְתִּ֥י
כב א הִשְׁאִֽיר־ל֖וֹ שָׂרִ֑יד וַיִּֽירְשׁ֖וּ אֶת־אַרְצֽוֹ׃ וַיִּסְע֖וּ בְּנֵ֣י יִשְׂרָאֵ֑ל וַֽיַּחֲנוּ֙ בְּעַרְב֣וֹת
מוֹאָ֔ב מֵעֵ֖בֶר לְיַרְדֵּ֥ן יְרֵחֽוֹ׃

32. וַיִּלְכְּדוּ בְּנֹתֶיהָ — *And they conquered its towns.* The spies sent by Moses took the daughter-cities of Jazer.

וַיּוֹרֶשׁ — *And drove out.* Moses later drove out the Emorites from Jazer.

*and they conquered its suburbs; and he drove away the Amorites that were
there.* [33] *They turned and ascended by way of Bashan; Og, king of Bashan,
went out against them, he and his entire people, to do battle at Edrei.*
[34] *HASHEM said to Moses, "Do not fear him, for into your hand have I given
him, his entire people, and his land; you shall do to him as you did to Sihon,
king of the Amorites, who dwells in Heshbon."* [35] *They smote him, his sons,
and all his people, until there was no survivor left of him, and they took
possession of his land.*

22

[1] *The Children of Israel journeyed and encamped in the plains of Moab,
on the bank of the Jordan, opposite Jericho.*

NOTES

32. וַיִּלְכְּדוּ בְּנֹתֶיהָ וַיּוֹרֶשׁ — *And they conquered its towns and drove out. They* refers to those who were sent by Moses to spy out Jazer, whereas the expression *and drove out* is singular, implying that Moses was the one who drove out the Emorites from Jazer.

פרשת בלק

ב־ג וַיַּרְא בָּלָק בֶּן־צִפּוֹר אֵת כָּל־אֲשֶׁר־עָשָׂה יִשְׂרָאֵל לָאֱמֹרִי: וַיָּגָר מוֹאָב
ד מִפְּנֵי הָעָם מְאֹד כִּי רַב־הוּא וַיָּקָץ מוֹאָב מִפְּנֵי בְּנֵי יִשְׂרָאֵל: וַיֹּאמֶר מוֹאָב
אֶל־זִקְנֵי מִדְיָן עַתָּה יְלַחֲכוּ הַקָּהָל אֶת־כָּל־סְבִיבֹתֵינוּ כִּלְחֹךְ הַשּׁוֹר אֵת
ה יֶרֶק הַשָּׂדֶה וּבָלָק בֶּן־צִפּוֹר מֶלֶךְ לְמוֹאָב בָּעֵת הַהִוא: וַיִּשְׁלַח מַלְאָכִים
אֶל־בִּלְעָם בֶּן־בְּעוֹר פְּתוֹרָה אֲשֶׁר עַל־הַנָּהָר אֶרֶץ בְּנֵי־עַמּוֹ לִקְרֹא־לוֹ
לֵאמֹר הִנֵּה עַם יָצָא מִמִּצְרַיִם הִנֵּה כִסָּה אֶת־עֵין הָאָרֶץ וְהוּא יֹשֵׁב מִמֻּלִי:
ו וְעַתָּה לְכָה־נָּא אָרָה־לִּי אֶת־הָעָם הַזֶּה כִּי־עָצוּם הוּא מִמֶּנִּי אוּלַי אוּכַל
נַכֶּה־בּוֹ וַאֲגָרְשֶׁנּוּ מִן־הָאָרֶץ כִּי יָדַעְתִּי אֵת אֲשֶׁר־תְּבָרֵךְ מְבֹרָךְ וַאֲשֶׁר
ז תָּאֹר יוּאָר: וַיֵּלְכוּ זִקְנֵי מוֹאָב וְזִקְנֵי מִדְיָן וּקְסָמִים בְּיָדָם וַיָּבֹאוּ אֶל־
ח בִּלְעָם וַיְדַבְּרוּ אֵלָיו דִּבְרֵי בָלָק: וַיֹּאמֶר אֲלֵיהֶם לִינוּ פֹה הַלַּיְלָה וַהֲשִׁבֹתִי
אֶתְכֶם דָּבָר כַּאֲשֶׁר יְדַבֵּר יהוה אֵלָי וַיֵּשְׁבוּ שָׂרֵי־מוֹאָב עִם־בִּלְעָם:

XXII

2. וַיַּרְא בָּלָק — *And Balak saw.* (Balak was) a man famed for his military knowledge (prowess) as it says, וְעַתָּה הֲטוֹב טוֹב אַתָּה מִבָּלָק בֶּן צִפּוֹר מֶלֶךְ מוֹאָב, *And now, are you better than Balak the son of Zippor, king of Moab? (Judges 11:25).* (Still) he observed that when Israel asked permission to pass through the land of Sichon and he refused, they destroyed him; and they (i.e., Moab) saw that this victory was accomplished without a normal stratagem of war.

3. וַיָּגָר מוֹאָב — *And Moab was afraid.* (This refers to) the mighty ones (leaders) of Moab who did not permit Israel to pass (through their land), as Yiftach stated, וְגַם אֶל מֶלֶךְ מוֹאָב שָׁלַח וְלֹא אָבָה, *And in like manner they sent to the king of Moab, but he would not consent (Judges 11:17).*

כִּי רַב הוּא — *Because they were many* . . . (and) not due to their stratagem of battle.

וַיָּקָץ מוֹאָב — *And Moab was seized with dread.* The masses of Moab were *weary of life* (based on *Genesis* 27:46) because of the Children of Israel who plundered them.

4. עַתָּה — *Now* . . . that they have conquered the lands of Sichon and Og.

יְלַחֲכוּ הַקָּהָל אֶת כָּל סְבִיבֹתֵינוּ — *This multitude will lick up all that is around about us* . . . to expand and secure their borders.

וּבָלָק בֶּן צִפּוֹר — *And Balak the son of Zippor* . . . who was known for his strength and as a man of war.

מֶלֶךְ לְמוֹאָב בָּעֵת הַהִוא — *Was king of Moab at that time* . . . and yet, he had no heart to fight the Israelites, as it says, הֲרוֹב רָב עִם יִשְׂרָאֵל אִם נִלְחֹם נִלְחַם בָּם, *Did he ever strive against*

NOTES

XXII

2. וַיַּרְא בָּלָק — *And Balak saw.* See the *Sforno's* commentary on *Exodus* 18:1 where he explains the difference between the expressions וַיַּרְא, *and he saw*, and וַיִּשְׁמַע, *and he heard.*

3. וַיָּגָר מוֹאָב . . . וַיָּקָץ מוֹאָב — *And Moab was afraid . . . and Moab was seized with dread.* The first part of the verse refers to the leadership of Moab who were *afraid.* The second part refers to the people of Moab who were *seized with dread.* In this manner, the *Sforno* explains that these expressions are not redundant.

4-6. וּבָלָק . . . מֶלֶךְ לְמוֹאָב . . . אוּלַי אוּכַל נַכֶּה בּוֹ — *And Balak . . . was King of Moab . . . perhaps I shall prevail that we may smite them.* The *Sforno* explains here, as he does in verse 2, that although Balak was a famous warrior, he was unwilling to confront Israel in battle even though, as king, he had the authority to do so. The reason, therefore, had to be his conviction that Israel was protected

PARASHAS BALAK

2 *Balak son of Zippor saw all that Israel had done to the Amorite.* 3 *Moab
became very frightened of the people, because it was numerous, and
Moab was disgusted in the face of the Children of Israel.* 4 *Moab said to the
elders of Midian, "Now the congregation will lick up our entire
surroundings, as an ox licks up the greenery of the field." Balak son of
Zippor was king of Moab at that time.*

5 *He sent messengers to Balaam son of Beor to Pethor, which is by the
River of the land of the members of his people, to summon him, saying,
"Behold! a people has come out of Egypt, behold! it has covered the surface
of the earth and it sits opposite me.* 6 *So now — please come and curse this
people for me, for it is too powerful for me; perhaps I will be able to strike
it and drive it away from the land. For I know that whomever you bless is
blessed and whomever you curse is accursed."*

7 *The elders of Moab and the elders of Midian went with charms in their
hand; they came to Balaam and spoke to him the words of Balak.* 8 *He said
to them, "Spend the night here and I shall give you a response, as* Hashem
shall speak to me." So the officers of Moab stayed with Balaam.

Israel or did he ever fight against them? (*Judges* 11:25). And Joshua who said, וַיָּקָם בָּלָק בֶּן צִפּוֹר מֶלֶךְ מוֹאָב וַיִּלָּחֶם בְּיִשְׂרָאֵל, *Then Balak the son of Zippor, King of Moab arose and warred against Israel* (*Joshua* 24:9), was referring to his hiring of Balaam to curse (them) as he explains saying, וַיִּשְׁלַח וַיִּקְרָא לְבִלְעָם, *And he sent and called Balaam* (ibid.).

6. אוּלַי אוּכַל — *Perhaps I shall prevail* . . . after you curse them.

נַכֶּה בּוֹ — *That we may smite them.* I [will smite] through battle, and you, through a curse.

אֲשֶׁר תְּבָרֵךְ מְבֹרָךְ — *The one whom you bless is blessed.* Behold, his power was not in blessing but in cursing, by reminding (God) of (man's) iniquity or by anticipating the time (of God's anger), as our Sages say (*Berachos* 7a). Therefore, he (Balak) did not ask him for a blessing to be victorious, or that he might be able to stand up to them; but he said, *I know that he whom you bless is blessed*, for Balaam's honor, to demonstrate that he does not consider him to be one who only does damage.

7. וּקְסָמִים בְּיָדָם — *With all kinds of divination in their hand* . . . the implements of magic, for Balaam was a diviner who knew how to anticipate the time, as it says, וְאֶת בִּלְעָם בֶּן בְּעוֹר הַקּוֹסֵם הָרְגוּ בְנֵי יִשְׂרָאֵל בַּחֶרֶב אֶל חַלְלֵיהֶם, *And Balaam the son of Be'or, the soothsayer, did the Children of Israel slay with the sword among those that were slain* (*Joshua* 13:22).

8. כַּאֲשֶׁר יְדַבֵּר ה׳ אֵלָי — *As* Hashem *may speak to me* . . . because I will prepare myself for prophecy.

NOTES

by God and that his only hope was to engage Balaam to utilize his powers for cursing this people, thereby weakening them and making them vulnerable. Thereby, he would be able to do battle against them, having a greater chance for victory.

6. אֲשֶׁר תְּבָרֵךְ מְבֹרָךְ — *The one whom you bless is blessed.* The *Sforno* explains why Balak didn't ask Balaam to bless *him* rather than curse Israel. Balaam only had the power to curse but not to bless. Balak's statement that whomsoever Balaam *blesses is blessed* was only said to flatter him. According to our Sages, Balaam's power to curse lay in his ability to determine the exact moment when God's wrath was kindled, at which time he would invoke the Divine anger on his chosen target.

7. וּקְסָמִים בְּיָדָם — *With all kinds of divination in their hand.* See note on verse 6 regarding the importance of Balaam's ability to anticipate the time when God was angry.

ט־י וַיָּבֹא אֱלֹהִים אֶל־בִּלְעָם וַיֹּאמֶר מִי הָאֲנָשִׁים הָאֵלֶּה עִמָּךְ: וַיֹּאמֶר בִּלְעָם
יא אֶל־הָאֱלֹהִים בָּלָק בֶּן־צִפֹּר מֶלֶךְ מוֹאָב שָׁלַח אֵלָי: הִנֵּה הָעָם הַיֹּצֵא
מִמִּצְרַיִם וַיְכַס אֶת־עֵין הָאָרֶץ עַתָּה לְכָה קָבָה־לִּי אֹתוֹ אוּלַי אוּכַל
יב לְהִלָּחֶם בּוֹ וְגֵרַשְׁתִּיו: וַיֹּאמֶר אֱלֹהִים אֶל־בִּלְעָם לֹא תֵלֵךְ עִמָּהֶם לֹא
יג תָאֹר אֶת־הָעָם כִּי בָרוּךְ הוּא: וַיָּקָם בִּלְעָם בַּבֹּקֶר וַיֹּאמֶר אֶל־שָׂרֵי בָלָק שני [חמישי]
יד לְכוּ אֶל־אַרְצְכֶם כִּי מֵאֵן יהוה לְתִתִּי לַהֲלֹךְ עִמָּכֶם: וַיָּקוּמוּ שָׂרֵי מוֹאָב
טו וַיָּבֹאוּ אֶל־בָּלָק וַיֹּאמְרוּ מֵאֵן בִּלְעָם הֲלֹךְ עִמָּנוּ: וַיֹּסֶף עוֹד בָּלָק שְׁלֹחַ
טז שָׂרִים רַבִּים וְנִכְבָּדִים מֵאֵלֶּה: וַיָּבֹאוּ אֶל־בִּלְעָם וַיֹּאמְרוּ לוֹ כֹּה אָמַר בָּלָק
יז בֶּן־צִפּוֹר אַל־נָא תִמָּנַע מֵהֲלֹךְ אֵלָי: כִּי־כַבֵּד אֲכַבֶּדְךָ מְאֹד וְכֹל אֲשֶׁר־
יח תֹּאמַר אֵלַי אֶעֱשֶׂה וּלְכָה־נָּא קָבָה־לִּי אֵת הָעָם הַזֶּה: וַיַּעַן בִּלְעָם וַיֹּאמֶר
אֶל־עַבְדֵי בָלָק אִם־יִתֶּן־לִי בָלָק מְלֹא בֵיתוֹ כֶּסֶף וְזָהָב לֹא אוּכַל לַעֲבֹר
יט אֶת־פִּי יהוה *אֱלֹהָי לַעֲשׂוֹת קְטַנָּה אוֹ גְדוֹלָה: וְעַתָּה שְׁבוּ נָא בָזֶה גַּם־ *קמץ בז"ק באות ה'
כ אַתֶּם הַלָּיְלָה וְאֵדְעָה מַה־יֹּסֵף יהוה דַּבֵּר עִמִּי: וַיָּבֹא אֱלֹהִים | אֶל־בִּלְעָם
לַיְלָה וַיֹּאמֶר לוֹ אִם־לִקְרֹא לְךָ בָּאוּ הָאֲנָשִׁים קוּם לֵךְ אִתָּם וְאַךְ
כא אֶת־הַדָּבָר אֲשֶׁר־אֲדַבֵּר אֵלֶיךָ אֹתוֹ תַעֲשֶׂה: וַיָּקָם בִּלְעָם בַּבֹּקֶר וַיַּחֲבֹשׁ שלישי
כב אֶת־אֲתֹנוֹ וַיֵּלֶךְ עִם־שָׂרֵי מוֹאָב: וַיִּחַר־אַף אֱלֹהִים כִּי־הוֹלֵךְ הוּא וַיִּתְיַצֵּב
מַלְאַךְ יהוה בַּדֶּרֶךְ לְשָׂטָן לוֹ וְהוּא רֹכֵב עַל־אֲתֹנוֹ וּשְׁנֵי נְעָרָיו עִמּוֹ:

---

9. מִי הָאֲנָשִׁים הָאֵלֶּה עִמָּךְ — *Who are these men with you?* What are their (dealings) with you that you have prepared yourself for prophecy on their behalf so as to know what to do for them? Are they here with you to inquire regarding the future and (therefore) you wish to know the future so as to be able to tell it to them? Or are they here with you to attain some (desired) specific purpose through your curse, and your intention now is to ask (My) permission as to whether you can fulfill their desire?

12. לֹא תֵלֵךְ עִמָּהֶם — *You shall not go with them.* You shall not go even though you will not curse them, so that you shall not look at them with an evil eye, as our Sages tell us, "He cast his eyes upon him and he became a heap of bones" (*Berachos* 58a).

20. אִם לִקְרֹא לְךָ בָּאוּ הָאֲנָשִׁים — *If the men have come to call you* . . . if they have only come to you for consultation, (the phrase לִקְרֹא being) similar to, קְרוּאֵי הָעֵדָה, *the elect of the congregation*, and similar to, וָאֶקְרָאֶה לְךָ לְהוֹדִיעֵנִי מָה אֶעֱשֶׂה, *I have called you that you may make known to me what I shall do* (*I Samuel* 28:15).

קוּם לֵךְ אִתָּם — *Rise up, go with them* . . . to caution them not to sin.

NOTES

9. מִי הָאֲנָשִׁים הָאֵלֶּה עִמָּךְ — *Who are these men with you?* Superficially, this question suggested to Balaam that God was not all-knowing. Indeed, this is the explanation of this question given by *Rashi*, quoting the *Tanchuma*. In *Genesis* 3:9, *Rashi* gives a different explanation, namely that God at times puts a seemingly superfluous question to a person in order to initiate a conversation. The *Sforno*, however, gives a most plausible reason for the question, *Who are these men?* The Almighty is not asking their identity. Rather, He is asking Balaam what his motivation is in contacting Him at this time. Have these men come to find out what the future holds in store for them, or is their purpose to retain Balaam's services to curse Israel?

12. לֹא תֵלֵךְ עִמָּהֶם — *You shall not go with them.* God prohibits Balaam from going with these men (לֹא תֵלֵךְ) and also from uttering any curse (לֹא תָאֹר). The *Sforno* explains that Balaam was prohibited from going even if he would not curse, for his evil gaze would suffice to bring harm upon Israel. Such was the evil power of Balaam! To prove that casting an evil glance upon a person can destroy him,

[9] God came to Balaam and said, "Who are these men with you?"
[10] Balaam said to God, "Balak son of Zippor, king of Moab, sent to me:
[11] 'Behold! the people coming out of Egypt has covered the surface of the
earth. Now go and curse it for me; perhaps I will be able to make war
against it and drive it away.' "
[12] God said to Balaam, "You shall not go with them! You shall not curse
the people, for it is blessed!"
[13] Balaam arose in the morning and said to the officers of Balak, "Go to
your land, for HASHEM refuses to let me go with you."
[14] The officers of Moab arose and came to Balak and said, "Balaam
refused to go with us."
[15] Balak kept on sending officers — more, and higher ranking than these.
[16] They came to Balaam and said to him, "So said Balak son of Zippor, 'Do
not refrain from going to me, [17] for I shall honor you greatly, and everything
that you say to me I shall do; so go now and curse this people for me.' "
[18] Balaam answered and said to the servants of Balak, "If Balak will give
me his houseful of silver and gold, I cannot transgress the word of HASHEM,
my God, to do anything small or great. [19] And now, you, too, stay here for
the night, and I will know what more HASHEM will speak with me."
[20] HASHEM came to Balaam at night and said to him, "If the men came
to summon you, arise and go with them, but only the thing that I shall
speak to you — that shall you do."
[21] Balaam arose in the morning and saddled his she-donkey and
went with the officers of Moab. [22] God's wrath flared because he was
going, and an angel of HASHEM stood on the road to impede him. He
was riding on his she-donkey and his two young men were with him.

22. כִּי הוֹלֵךְ הוּא — *Because he was going* . . . for it was not a case of others leading him, similar to, וַיָּקָם וַיֵּלֶךְ אַחֲרֶיהָ, *And he arose and followed her* (*II Kings* 4:30); rather he went as an interested party, and as one who was attempting to defy the will of God, the Blessed One, because they had not come for consultation at all.

לְשָׂטָן לוֹ — *For an adversary against him.* The phrase הַשִּׂטְנָה, *hindering,* implies opposition to an action, similar to, וַיָּרִיבוּ גַּם עָלֶיהָ וַיִּקְרָא שְׁמָהּ שִׂטְנָה, *And they strove for that* (*well*) *also and they called its name* שִׂטְנָה, *enmity* (*Genesis* 26:21). Now, the angel came out to oppose Balaam so that his way would not be a smooth one (lit., "prepared before him"); so that he might divine, as was his wont, and not force the issue. All this was (done) so that he should not sin and thereby be destroyed (i.e., punished).

וְהוּא רֹכֵב עַל אֲתֹנוֹ וּשְׁנֵי נְעָרָיו עִמּוֹ — *Now he was riding on his ass and his two servants were with him.* Therefore, he did not see the angel, as our Sages say, "To three, it (the evil spirit)

NOTES

the *Sforno* cites the story of R' Shesheth, who cast his eye on a Sadducean who had treated him disrespectfully, and as a result became a heap of bones.

20. אִם לִקְרֹא לְךָ בָּאוּ הָאֲנָשִׁים — *If the men have come to call you.* God did not change His mind. He granted permission to Balaam to accompany these men for only one purpose, namely to admonish and advise them and caution them, thereby cautioning them not to sin.

22. לְשָׂטָן לוֹ — *For an adversary against him.* The *Sforno* explains the phrase לְשָׂטָן לוֹ as meaning "hindrance" or "opposition," exercised here by God for the person's good. Man's freedom of choice is never denied him, but often there are signs from heaven which will hopefully cause him to reconsider his ways. Since Balaam was sensitive to these omens, the obstacles placed in his path might influence him to reconsider his evil decision.

כג וַתֵּרֶא הָאָתוֹן אֶת־מַלְאַךְ יהוה נִצָּב בַּדֶּרֶךְ וְחַרְבּוֹ שְׁלוּפָה בְּיָדוֹ וַתֵּט
הָאָתוֹן מִן־הַדֶּרֶךְ וַתֵּלֶךְ בַּשָּׂדֶה וַיַּךְ בִּלְעָם אֶת־הָאָתוֹן לְהַטֹּתָהּ הַדָּרֶךְ:
כד־כה וַיַּעֲמֹד מַלְאַךְ יהוה בְּמִשְׁעוֹל הַכְּרָמִים גָּדֵר מִזֶּה וְגָדֵר מִזֶּה: וַתֵּרֶא הָאָתוֹן
אֶת־מַלְאַךְ יהוה וַתִּלָּחֵץ אֶל־הַקִּיר וַתִּלְחַץ אֶת־רֶגֶל בִּלְעָם אֶל־הַקִּיר
כו וַיֹּסֶף לְהַכֹּתָהּ: וַיּוֹסֶף מַלְאַךְ־יהוה עֲבוֹר וַיַּעֲמֹד בְּמָקוֹם צָר אֲשֶׁר אֵין־
כז דֶּרֶךְ לִנְטוֹת יָמִין וּשְׂמֹאול: וַתֵּרֶא הָאָתוֹן אֶת־מַלְאַךְ יהוה וַתִּרְבַּץ תַּחַת *יתיר ו'
כח בִּלְעָם וַיִּחַר־אַף בִּלְעָם וַיַּךְ אֶת־הָאָתוֹן בַּמַּקֵּל: וַיִּפְתַּח יהוה אֶת־פִּי
הָאָתוֹן וַתֹּאמֶר לְבִלְעָם מֶה־עָשִׂיתִי לְךָ כִּי הִכִּיתַנִי זֶה שָׁלֹשׁ רְגָלִים:
כט וַיֹּאמֶר בִּלְעָם לָאָתוֹן כִּי הִתְעַלַּלְתְּ בִּי לוּ יֶשׁ־חֶרֶב בְּיָדִי כִּי עַתָּה הֲרַגְתִּיךְ:
ל וַתֹּאמֶר הָאָתוֹן אֶל־בִּלְעָם הֲלוֹא אָנֹכִי אֲתֹנְךָ אֲשֶׁר־רָכַבְתָּ עָלַי מֵעוֹדְךָ
לא עַד־הַיּוֹם הַזֶּה הַהַסְכֵּן הִסְכַּנְתִּי לַעֲשׂוֹת לְךָ כֹּה וַיֹּאמֶר לֹא: וַיְגַל יהוה
אֶת־עֵינֵי בִלְעָם וַיַּרְא אֶת־מַלְאַךְ יהוה נִצָּב בַּדֶּרֶךְ וְחַרְבּוֹ שְׁלֻפָה בְּיָדוֹ
לב וַיִּקֹּד וַיִּשְׁתַּחוּ לְאַפָּיו: וַיֹּאמֶר אֵלָיו מַלְאַךְ יהוה עַל־מָה הִכִּיתָ אֶת־
אֲתֹנְךָ זֶה שָׁלוֹשׁ רְגָלִים הִנֵּה אָנֹכִי יָצָאתִי לְשָׂטָן כִּי־יָרַט הַדֶּרֶךְ
לג לְנֶגְדִּי: וַתִּרְאַנִי הָאָתוֹן וַתֵּט לְפָנַי זֶה שָׁלֹשׁ רְגָלִים אוּלַי נָטְתָה מִפָּנַי

---

will not show itself or do harm' (*Berachos* 43b).

23. וַתֵּלֶךְ בַּשָּׂדֶה — *And went into the field.* Hence, he left his two servants and the lords of Moab behind and therefore they were not aware of the episode with the ass.

28. וַיִּפְתַּח ה' אֶת פִּי הָאָתוֹן — *And* HASHEM *opened the mouth of the ass.* He gave her the power of speech, similar to, ה' שְׂפָתַי תִּפְתָּח, HASHEM, *open my lips* (*Psalms* 51:17). All this occurred so that Balaam should be aroused to repent and be reminded that וּמֵה' מַעֲנֵה לָשׁוֹן, *from* HASHEM *come the utterances of the tongue* (*Proverbs* 16:1), even to one who is unprepared; how much more so that (God) can remove (this power) according to His will from one who is prepared. (Now) all this (happened) so that a man such as he not be destroyed.

30. הַהַסְכֵּן הִסְכַּנְתִּי — *Was I ever wont to do so . . .* and it would have been fitting for you to consider that since this happened to you outside the manner of my normal behavior, it is to indicate that you will not succeed — for even though there is no (validity) to divination, there is (validity) to a sign (based on *Chullin* 95b).

32. עַל מָה הִכִּיתָ אֶת אֲתֹנְךָ — *Wherefore have you smitten your ass.* Since you saw these signs, you should have realized (concluded) that your mission (lit., "journey") is unacceptable and will not succeed.

זֶה שָׁלוֹשׁ רְגָלִים — *These three times . . .* and how did you "stiffen your neck" three times (in an attempt) to force the issue?

NOTES

וּשְׁנֵי נְעָרָיו עִמּוֹ — *And his two servants were with him.* Although the saying of our Sages cited by the *Sforno* speaks of "evil spirits," while in our case it is an angel who stands in Balaam's path, the comparison is apt. Man is not able to see any noncorporeal being when three people are present, whether that being is good or evil.

28. וַיִּפְתַּח ה' אֶת פִּי הָאָתוֹן — *And* HASHEM *opened the mouth of the ass.* In this verse, as well as in verses 22 and 32, the *Sforno* is of the opinion that God was concerned for Balaam's welfare and did not want him to bring calamity on himself. Apparently, Balaam was a man of great spiritual powers which were sadly mischanneled, but nonetheless, it would have been tragic for such a person to be destroyed despite the fact that such great potential was squandered.

30. הַהַסְכֵּן הִסְכַּנְתִּי — *Was I ever wont to do so.* The Talmudic saying cited by the *Sforno* states that although we are not permitted to divine, we should

23 *The she-donkey saw the angel of* HASHEM *standing on the road with his
sword drawn in his hand, so the she-donkey turned away from the road and
went into the field; then Balaam struck the she-donkey to turn it back onto
the road.* 24 *The angel of* HASHEM *stood in the path of the vineyards, a fence
on this side and a fence on that side.* 25 *The she-donkey saw the angel of*
HASHEM *and pressed against the wall, and it pressed Balaam's leg against
the wall — and he continued to strike it.* 26 *The angel of* HASHEM *went
further and stood in a narrow place, where there was no room to turn right
or left.* 27 *The she-donkey saw the angel of* HASHEM *and crouched beneath
Balaam. Balaam's anger flared and he struck the she-donkey with the staff.*
28 HASHEM *opened the mouth of the she-donkey and it said to Balaam,
"What have I done to you that you struck me these three times?"*
29 *Balaam said to the she-donkey, "Because you mocked me! If only there
were a sword in my hand I would now have killed you!"*
30 *The she-donkey said to Balaam, "Am I not your she-donkey that you
have ridden all your life until this day? Have I been accustomed to do such
a thing to you?"*
He said, "No."
31 *Then* HASHEM *uncovered Balaam's eyes and he saw the angel of*
HASHEM *standing on the road with his sword drawn in his hand. He bowed
his head and prostrated himself on his face.*
32 *The angel of* HASHEM *said to him, "For what reason did you strike
your she-donkey these three times? Behold! I went out to impede, for
you hastened on a road to oppose me.* 33 *The she-donkey saw me and
turned away from me these three times. Had it not turned away from me,*

הִנֵּה אָנֹכִי יָצָאתִי לְשָׂטָן — *Behold, I went out as an adversary.* Behold, I did whatever was possible to obstruct your journey in this manner for your own good.

כִּי יָרַט הַדֶּרֶךְ לְנֶגְדִּי — *Because your way trembles before me.* The word יָרַט comes from וְרֶטֶט הֶחֱזִיקָה, *And fear* (רֶטֶט) *has gripped her* (*Jeremiah* 49:24), just as וַתָּרִץ אֶת גֻּלְגָּלְתּוֹ, *And crushed* (וַתָּרִץ) *his skull* (*Judges* 9:53), is derived from רָצַץ. (The angel) then says: Behold, I have come forth to hinder you, and this hindrance was by causing the way before me "to tremble," similar to, לֹא רָאוּ אֶת הַמַּרְאָה אֲבָל חֲרָדָה גְדֹלָה נָפְלָה עֲלֵיהֶם, *They did not see the vision but a great trembling fell upon them* (*Daniel* 10:7), (but) all this did not suffice to frighten you because you have hardened your heart.

33. וַתִּרְאַנִי הָאָתוֹן וַתֵּט לְפָנַי — *And the ass saw me and turned aside before me.* And with all this, you experienced the turning aside of the ass from me three times; how could you not pay attention to this (strange behavior)?

אוּלַי נָטְתָה מִפָּנַי — *Perhaps she had turned aside from me.* You should have considered that perhaps she turned aside before *me*, for you already knew that God, the Blessed One, has before Him those who advocate good regarding Israel.

NOTES

pay attention to a sign which may have validity. For example, if one's business prospers after moving into a house, or after marrying a woman or after the birth of a child, it is a sign that his success is now insured from heaven. The reverse is also true. Balaam should therefore have paid attention to the strange behavior of his she-ass and considered it as a sign of God's displeasure, as the *Sforno* explains in verse 32.

33. אוּלַי נָטְתָה מִפָּנַי — *Perhaps she had turned aside from me.* We find reference made in our

לד כִּי עַתָּה גַּם־אֹתְכָה הָרַגְתִּי וְאוֹתָהּ הֶחֱיֵיתִי: וַיֹּאמֶר בִּלְעָם אֶל־מַלְאַךְ
יהוה חָטָאתִי כִּי לֹא יָדַעְתִּי כִּי אַתָּה נִצָּב לִקְרָאתִי בַּדָּרֶךְ וְעַתָּה אִם־
לה רַע בְּעֵינֶיךָ אָשׁוּבָה לִּי: וַיֹּאמֶר מַלְאַךְ יהוה אֶל־בִּלְעָם לֵךְ עִם־הָאֲנָשִׁים
וְאֶפֶס אֶת־הַדָּבָר אֲשֶׁר־אֲדַבֵּר אֵלֶיךָ אֹתוֹ תְדַבֵּר וַיֵּלֶךְ בִּלְעָם עִם־
לו שָׂרֵי בָלָק: וַיִּשְׁמַע בָּלָק כִּי־בָא בִלְעָם וַיֵּצֵא לִקְרָאתוֹ אֶל־עִיר מוֹאָב
לז אֲשֶׁר עַל־גְּבוּל אַרְנֹן אֲשֶׁר בִּקְצֵה הַגְּבוּל: וַיֹּאמֶר בָּלָק אֶל־בִּלְעָם הֲלֹא
שָׁלֹחַ שָׁלַחְתִּי אֵלֶיךָ לִקְרֹא־לָךְ לָמָּה לֹא־הָלַכְתָּ אֵלָי הַאֻמְנָם לֹא אוּכַל
לח כַּבְּדֶךָ: וַיֹּאמֶר בִּלְעָם אֶל־בָּלָק הִנֵּה־בָאתִי אֵלֶיךָ עַתָּה הֲיָכֹל אוּכַל דַּבֵּר
רביעי [ששי] לט מְאוּמָה הַדָּבָר אֲשֶׁר יָשִׂים אֱלֹהִים בְּפִי אֹתוֹ אֲדַבֵּר: וַיֵּלֶךְ בִּלְעָם
מ עִם־בָּלָק וַיָּבֹאוּ קִרְיַת חֻצוֹת: וַיִּזְבַּח בָּלָק בָּקָר וָצֹאן וַיְשַׁלַּח לְבִלְעָם
מא וְלַשָּׂרִים אֲשֶׁר אִתּוֹ: וַיְהִי בַבֹּקֶר וַיִּקַּח בָּלָק אֶת־בִּלְעָם
כג א וַיַּעֲלֵהוּ בָּמוֹת בָּעַל וַיַּרְא מִשָּׁם קְצֵה הָעָם: וַיֹּאמֶר בִּלְעָם אֶל־בָּלָק
בְּנֵה־לִי בָזֶה שִׁבְעָה מִזְבְּחֹת וְהָכֵן לִי בָּזֶה שִׁבְעָה פָרִים וְשִׁבְעָה אֵילִים:

כִּי עַתָּה גַּם אֹתְכָה הָרַגְתִּי וְאוֹתָהּ הֶחֱיֵיתִי — *Surely now I would have slain you and saved her alive.* The reason that I said *wherefore have you smitten your ass* (v. 32) in an accusatory manner is because now, indeed, *to you it was shown that you might know* (based on *Deut.* 4:35) that even if I would slay you and spare her (the she-ass) in such a manner that you would (clearly) recognize that this (entire episode) was not a chance happening at all, nonetheless, you would not have refrained from going. Hence, you are as one who hands himself over to death (in order) to transgress the will of his Maker — and there is no greater apostate than such (a person).

34. חָטָאתִי — *I have sinned* . . . by stiffening my neck (i.e., by being so stubborn).

כִּי לֹא יָדַעְתִּי — *For I knew not* . . . and I should have been more sensitive to it.

וְעַתָּה אִם רַע בְּעֵינֶיךָ — *Now, therefore, if it displeases you* . . . for perhaps you are the angel who is the advocate on behalf of Israel.

אָשׁוּבָה לִּי — *I will return* . . . so as not to do anything against your will, even though God, the Blessed One, gave me permission (to go).

35. לֵךְ עִם הָאֲנָשִׁים — *Go with the men.* Do not go as a בַּעַל דָּבָר, *an interested party*, but as one who goes with them at their request so that you shall not be destroyed.

וְאֶפֶס אֶת הַדָּבָר — *But only the words* . . . and with all (this), I am not apprehensive that you will do anything contrary to my will, for indeed, you will not be able to do except that which I will say to you.

36. וַיֵּצֵא לִקְרָאתוֹ — *And he went out to meet him* . . . to honor him, for he knew that he had an "arrogant spirit," which our Rabbis attest to (*Avos* 5:18).

NOTES

prayers to angels who are מְלִיצֵי יֹשֶׁר — advocates on behalf of Israel. The *Sforno* is referring to such a מֵלִיץ both here and in verse 34.

36. וַיֵּצֵא לִקְרָאתוֹ — *And he went out to meet him.* The Mishnah in *Avos* 5:18 teaches us that Balaam possessed three characteristics; an evil eye, a haughty temperament and an insatiable spirit. The *Sforno* refers to these vices in his commentary on this verse and in verse 40. He paraphrases the Mishnah, substituting *arrogant spirit* for *haughty temperament* and *eye of pride* for *insatiable spirit.*

38. הַדָּבָר אֲשֶׁר יָשִׂים אֱלֹהִים בְּפִי — *The word that God puts in my mouth.* The *Rambam* in his *Guide* (2:45) lists different degrees of prophecy. He describes the effect of the prophetic spirit upon a person as "another force which has come upon him and has made him speak." He writes that it was this kind of רוּחַ הַקֹּדֶשׁ, *holy spirit*, that

I would now even have killed you and let it live!"
34 *Balaam said to the angel of HASHEM, " I have sinned, for I did not know that you were standing opposite me on the road. And now, if it is evil in your eyes, I shall return."*
35 *The angel of HASHEM said to Balaam, "Go with the men, but only the word that I shall speak to you — that shall you speak." So Balaam went with the officers of Balak.*
36 *Balak heard that Balaam had come, so he went out toward him to the city of Moab, which is on the border of Arnon, which is at the edge of the border.*
37 *Balak said to Balaam, "Did I not urgently send to you to summon you? Why did you not go to me? Am I not capable of honoring you?"*
38 *Balaam said to Balak, "Behold! now I have come to you — am I empowered to say anything? Whatever word God puts into my mouth, that shall I speak!"*
39 *Balaam went with Balak and they came to Kiriath-huzoth.*
40 *Balak slaughtered cattle and sheep and sent to Balaam and to the officers who were with him.*
41 *And it was in the morning: Balak took Balaam and brought him up to the heights of Baal, and from there he saw the edge of the people.*

23
1 *Balaam said to Balak, "Build for me here seven altars and prepare for me here seven bulls and seven rams."*

---

38. הִנֵּה בָאתִי אֵלֶיךָ — *Behold, I have come to you.* Although I would have come to you (initially) in accordance with your request (lit., "word"), how could I be of any benefit to you? And this is so now, as well.

הֲיָכֹל אוּכַל דַּבֵּר מְאוּמָה — *Am I able to speak anything at all?* Can I speak in the manner of one who speaks of his own will?

הַדָּבָר אֲשֶׁר יָשִׂים אֱלֹהִים בְּפִי אֹתוֹ אֲדַבֵּר — *The word that God puts in my mouth, that shall I speak* . . . similar to, רוּחַ ה׳ דִּבֶּר בִּי, *The spirit of HASHEM spoke in me* (*II Samuel* 23:2), and in this manner I shall not (really) be the speaker.

40. וַיְשַׁלַּח לְבִלְעָם — *And sent to Balaam* . . . as a gift of honor besides his (regular) meal, so as to satisfy his "eye of pride."

41. וַיַּרְא מִשָּׁם קְצֵה הָעָם — *And he saw from there the utmost part of the people* . . . so as to cast his (evil) eye upon them, similar to, וַיִּפֶן אַחֲרָיו וַיִּרְאֵם וַיְקַלְלֵם, *And he turned back and looked at them and cursed them* (*II Kings* 2:24), as opposed to, וַיַּרְאֵהוּ ה׳ אֶת כָּל הָאָרֶץ, *And HASHEM showed him all the land* (*Deut.* 34:1), so that he (Moses) should bless it before his death.

XXIII

1. בְּנֵה לִי בָזֶה — *Build me here.* A place from which I can see them (the Israelites).

NOTES

descended on David, who described this experience when he said, "The spirit of HASHEM spoke through me and His word was upon my tongue." This is the verse which the *Sforno* quotes regarding Balaam. The *Rambam*, indeed, proceeds to tell us that "the powers of Balaam, when he was righteous, also belonged to this kind (i.e., degree) of prophecy" (ibid.). According to the *Sforno* and the *Rambam*, this is the meaning of *The word that God puts in my mouth, that shall I speak.*

41. וַיַּרְא מִשָּׁם — *And he saw from there.* To bless or curse effectively, one must see the object of his blessing or his curse. The *Sforno* explains this in *Genesis* 48:10 regarding Jacob when he wanted to bless Ephraim and Menasseh. When Elisha cursed those who taunted him, it states that "he turned and *saw* them." Balaam also *sees* the people of Israel from a high vantage point. Moses, the אוֹהֵב יִשְׂרָאֵל, *lover of Israel*, and אוֹהֵב אֶרֶץ יִשְׂרָאֵל, *lover of the Land of Israel*, is shown the Land before he dies so that his blessing shall be a complete, effective and lasting one. Balaam's power of prophecy is compared to Moses', but he used his gift for evil while Moses used his for good.

ב וַיַּ֣עַשׂ בָּלָ֔ק כַּאֲשֶׁ֖ר דִּבֶּ֣ר בִּלְעָ֑ם וַיַּ֧עַל בָּלָ֛ק וּבִלְעָ֖ם פָּ֥ר וָאַ֖יִל בַּמִּזְבֵּֽחַ:
ג וַיֹּ֨אמֶר בִּלְעָ֜ם לְבָלָ֗ק הִתְיַצֵּב֮ עַל־עֹלָתֶ֒ךָ֒ וְאֵֽלְכָ֗ה אוּלַ֞י יִקָּרֵ֤ה יהוה֙
לִקְרָאתִ֔י וּדְבַ֥ר מַה־יַּרְאֵ֖נִי וְהִגַּ֣דְתִּי לָ֑ךְ וַיֵּ֖לֶךְ שֶֽׁפִי: ד וַיִּקָּ֥ר אֱלֹהִ֖ים אֶל־
בִּלְעָ֑ם וַיֹּ֣אמֶר אֵלָ֗יו אֶת־שִׁבְעַ֤ת הַֽמִּזְבְּחֹת֙ עָרַ֔כְתִּי וָאַ֛עַל פָּ֥ר וָאַ֖יִל
ה בַּמִּזְבֵּֽחַ: וַיָּ֨שֶׂם יהו֤ה דָּבָר֙ בְּפִ֣י בִלְעָ֔ם וַיֹּ֖אמֶר שׁ֣וּב אֶל־בָּלָ֑ק וְכֹ֥ה תְדַבֵּֽר:
ו־ז וַיָּ֣שׇׁב אֵלָ֔יו וְהִנֵּ֥ה נִצָּ֖ב עַל־עֹֽלָת֑וֹ ה֖וּא וְכׇל־שָׂרֵ֥י מוֹאָֽב: וַיִּשָּׂ֥א מְשָׁל֖וֹ
וַיֹּאמַ֑ר מִן־אֲ֠רָ֠ם יַנְחֵ֨נִי בָלָ֤ק מֶֽלֶךְ־מוֹאָב֙ מֵֽהַרְרֵי־קֶ֔דֶם לְכָ֤ה אָֽרָה־לִּ֣י
ח יַעֲקֹ֔ב וּלְכָ֖ה זֹעֲמָ֥ה יִשְׂרָאֵֽל: מָ֣ה אֶקֹּ֔ב לֹ֥א קַבֹּ֖ה אֵ֑ל וּמָ֣ה אֶזְעֹ֔ם לֹ֥א זָעַ֖ם
ט יהוֽה: כִּֽי־מֵרֹ֤אשׁ צֻרִים֙ אֶרְאֶ֔נּוּ וּמִגְּבָע֖וֹת אֲשׁוּרֶ֑נּוּ הֶן־עָם֙ לְבָדָ֣ד יִשְׁכֹּ֔ן
י וּבַגּוֹיִ֖ם לֹ֥א יִתְחַשָּֽׁב: מִ֤י מָנָה֙ עֲפַ֣ר יַעֲקֹ֔ב וּמִסְפָּ֖ר אֶת־רֹ֣בַע יִשְׂרָאֵ֑ל תָּמֹ֤ת
יא נַפְשִׁי֙ מ֣וֹת יְשָׁרִ֔ים וּתְהִ֥י אַחֲרִיתִ֖י כָּמֹֽהוּ: וַיֹּ֤אמֶר בָּלָק֙ אֶל־בִּלְעָ֔ם מֶ֥ה
יב עָשִׂ֖יתָ לִ֑י לָקֹ֤ב אֹֽיְבַי֙ לְקַחְתִּ֔יךָ וְהִנֵּ֖ה בֵּרַ֥כְתָּ בָרֵֽךְ: וַיַּ֖עַן וַיֹּאמַ֑ר הֲלֹ֗א אֵ֚ת
יג אֲשֶׁ֨ר יָשִׂ֤ים יהוה֙ בְּפִ֔י אֹת֥וֹ אֶשְׁמֹ֖ר לְדַבֵּֽר: וַיֹּ֨אמֶר אֵלָ֜יו בָּלָ֗ק לְךָ־נָּ֤א אִתִּי֙
אֶל־מָק֣וֹם אַחֵ֔ר אֲשֶׁ֥ר תִּרְאֶ֖נּוּ מִשָּׁ֑ם אֶ֤פֶס קָצֵ֨הוּ֙ תִרְאֶ֔ה וְכֻלּ֖וֹ לֹ֣א תִרְאֶ֑ה

חמישי

---

3. הִתְיַצֵּב עַל עֹלָתֶךָ — *Stand by your burnt-offering . . . so as to have (proper) intent when* every part of it is offered (lit., elevated), akin to, כִּי הַדָּם הוּא בַּנֶּפֶשׁ יְכַפֵּר, *for it is the blood that makes atonement for (man's) life (Leviticus 17:11).*

אוּלַי יִקָּרֵה ה׳ לִקְרָאתִי — *Perhaps HASHEM will come to meet me.* Perhaps in my solitude — even though I will not attain a (prophetic) level of (spiritual) elevation (and merit) to be *in the light of the King's countenance* (based on *Proverbs* 16:15) as was the case with Moses, as it says, *in all My house, he is the faithful one* (12:7) — (nonetheless,) it may happen that God will come to meet me as it occurred with Moses at the beginning of his prophetic (experience) before he was elevated to the perfection which he (ultimately) attained, as it says, וַיַּרְא ה׳ כִּי סָר לִרְאוֹת וַיִּקְרָא אֵלָיו אֱלֹהִים, *And HASHEM saw that he turned aside to see, and God called to him* (Exodus 3:4).

7. וַיִּשָּׂא מְשָׁלוֹ — *And he took up his parable.* He stated the parable which he had seen in his prophetic vision.

וַיֹּאמַר מִן אֲרָם — *And he said: From Aram.* After he related the parable, he interpreted its content and said that the meaning (lit., teaching) of the parable was that Balak brought him from Aram, etc.

9. הֶן עָם לְבָדָד יִשְׁכֹּן — *They are a nation that will dwell alone.* They alone will inhabit the earth at the end of "the matter" (i.e., "the end of time"), as it says, ה׳ בָּדָד יַנְחֶנּוּ, *HASHEM alone did lead him* (Deut. 32:12); (hence,) how can I annihilate them?

NOTES

XXIII

3. הִתְיַצֵּב עַל עֹלָתֶךָ — *Stand by your burnt-offering.* When a man brings an animal offering to God, he should consider the sacrifice of its parts and the blood offered on the Altar as representing his own limbs and blood. This is the significance of the verse from *Leviticus*, quoted by the *Sforno*, to explain why Balaam instructed Balak to *stand by his offering* and associate himself with the sacrifice — its various parts and the blood — so that his wish might be granted.

אוּלַי יִקָּרֶה ה׳ לִקְרָאתִי — *Perhaps HASHEM will come to meet me.* The *Sforno*, in his commentary on *Exodus* 3:2, explains at great length the gradual progress of Moses in the realm of prophecy. The least of these prophetic levels was experienced by him at the time of the "burning bush," which was his initial encounter with an angel of God. Balaam here expresses the hope that he might merit that God meet him at least on that level.

7. וַיִּשָּׂא מְשָׁלוֹ — *And he took up his parable.* The parable which Balaam related is not recorded in the

2 *Balak did as Balaam had spoken, and Balak and Balaam brought up a bull and a ram on each altar.* 3 *Balaam said to Balak, "Stand by your burnt-offering while I go; perhaps* HASHEM *will happen toward me and show me something that I can tell you." He went alone.*

4 *God happened upon Balaam and he said to Him, "I have prepared the seven altars and brought up a bull and ram on each altar."*

5 HASHEM *put an utterance in Balaam's mouth, and said, "Go back to Balak, and thus shall you say."*

6 *He returned to him and behold! he was standing by his burnt-offering, he and all the officers of Moab.* 7 *He declaimed his parable and said:*

"From Aram, Balak, king of Moab, led me, from the mountains of the east, 'Come curse Jacob for me, come bring anger upon Israel.'

8 *"How can I curse? — God has not cursed. How can I anger? — God is not angry.*

9 *"For from its origins, I see it rock-like, and from hills do I see it. Behold! it is a nation that will dwell in solitude and not be reckoned among the nations.*

10 *"Who has counted the dust of Jacob or numbered a quarter of Israel? May my soul die the death of the upright, and may my end be like his!"*

11 *Balak said to Balaam, "What have you done to me! To curse my enemy have I brought you — but behold! you have even blessed!"*

12 *He spoke up and said, "Is it not so that whatever* HASHEM *puts in my mouth, that I must take heed to speak?"*

13 *Balak said to him, "Go now with me to a different place from which you will see them; however, you will see its edge but not see all of it —*

10. תָּמֹת נַפְשִׁי מוֹת יְשָׁרִים — *Let me die that death of the righteous.* Wouldst that my living spirit die now, providing however, that my death be that of the righteous — that (my soul) merit eternal life.

וּתְהִי אַחֲרִיתִי כָּמֹהוּ — *And let my end be like his.* Only let my end and my offspring (lit., the offspring of my bowels) be like (those of) Israel because, indeed, a man's children and offspring are called אַחֲרִיתוֹ, *his posterity*, similar to, יְהִי אַחֲרִיתוֹ לְהַכְרִית, *Let his posterity be cut off* (*Psalms* 109:13), and also, וְלֹא לְאַחֲרִיתוֹ, *And not to his posterity* (*Daniel* 11:4).

12. הֲלֹא אֵת אֲשֶׁר יָשִׂים ה׳ בְּפִי — *Must I not (take heed to speak) that which* HASHEM *has put in my mouth* . . . and you already know that He is the God of Israel, and will not speak aught but good regarding Israel.

13. אֲשֶׁר תִּרְאֶנּוּ מִשָּׁם — *From whence you may see them* . . . and you will be able to cast your eye upon them for evil.

אֶפֶס קָצֵהוּ תִרְאֶה וְכֻלּוֹ לֹא תִרְאֶה — *You shall see but part of them and shall not see them all.* Do not (however) cast your (evil) eye upon all of them, for you will not be able to attain

NOTES

Torah, only its interpretation as explained by Balaam, i.e., *From Aram Balak brought me, etc.*

9. הֶן עָם לְבָדָד יִשְׁכֹּן — *They are a nation that will dwell alone.* The *Sforno* does not interpret the word הֶן as meaning *Behold*, followed by the observation that Israel is a nation that dwells alone, i.e., separate and distinct from other people. Rather, he interprets the sense of the verse as follows: הֶן, *they*, alone will remain at the end of time (אַחֲרִית הַיָּמִים), for all other nations will be destroyed, as the prophet states, *For I shall make an end to all the nations* (*Jeremiah* 46). See his commentary on *Genesis* 49:1 where he elaborates on this theme, and on *Deut.* 32:12 where he quotes the aforementioned verse from *Jeremiah*.

13. אֶפֶס קָצֵהוּ תִרְאֶה — *You shall see but part of them.* Balak is a pragmatist. He knows that God will never permit Israel to be totally destroyed;

יד וקבנו-לי משם: ויקחהו שדה צפים אל-ראש הפסגה ויבן שבעה
טו מזבחת ויעל פר ואיל במזבח: ויאמר אל-בלק התיצב כה על-עלתך
טז ואנכי אקרה כה: ויקר יהוה אל-בלעם וישם דבר בפיו ויאמר שוב אל-
יז בלק וכה תדבר: ויבא אליו והנו נצב על-עלתו ושרי מואב אתו ויאמר
יח לו בלק מה-דבר יהוה: וישא משלו ויאמר קום בלק ושמע האזינה עדי
יט בנו צפר: לא איש אל ויכזב ובן-אדם ויתנחם ההוא אמר ולא יעשה
כ-כא ודבר ולא יקימנה: הנה ברך לקחתי וברך ולא אשיבנה: לא-הביט
און ביעקב ולא-ראה עמל בישראל יהוה אלהיו עמו ותרועת מלך בו:
כב-כג אל מוציאם ממצרים כתועפת ראם לו: כי לא-נחש ביעקב ולא-
כד קסם בישראל כעת יאמר ליעקב ולישראל מה-פעל אל: הן-עם
כלביא יקום וכארי יתנשא לא ישכב עד-יאכל טרף ודם-חללים
כה ישתה: ויאמר בלק אל-בלעם גם-קב לא תקבנו גם-ברך לא תברכנו:

---

your intended (goal) at all, as it says, כי אעשה כלה בכל הגוים... ואתך לא אעשה כלה, *for I will make a full end of all the nations . . . but I will not make a full end of you* (*Jeremiah* 46:28).

20. וברך — *And when He has blessed* . . . and He has already blessed!

21. ותרועת מלך בו — *The trumpet-signal for the king is among them.* When the camps journey, they sound the תרועה, *trumpet-signal,* as an expression of joy and rejoicing in their God, for the Sanctuary travels (with them).

22. כתועפת ראם לו — *Like the lofty horns of the wild-ox.* (This refers) to the people of Israel who do not devour and eat like a lion, but they push with their horn like a *wild-ox,* for their intent is to expel the nations and to bring themselves into the Land without (resorting) to the slaughter of the nations, as it says, תגרש גוים ותטעה, *You have cast out nations and planted it* (*Psalms* 80:9), for He does not desire the death (of the wicked). And so our Sages said, ". . . Joshua sent three letters (to the inhabitants of Canaan): Whoever wishes to leave, let him leave; whoever wishes to make peace, let him make peace; whoever wants to do battle let him do so" (*Jerusalem Talmud, Tractate Sheveis* 6:1). However, they stiffened their necks and did battle, forcing (Israel) to destroy them. Thus, they (Israel) did not deal with them (the nations) at all as a lion who devours, but dealt with them as a wild-ox who either pushes out or conquers, yet does not consume at all.

23. כי לא נחש ביעקב — *For there is not enchantment with Jacob* . . . and the reason He brought Israel forth from Egypt and cast out the nations on their behalf and gave them *the lofty horns of the wild-ox* was because they are דור דרשו, *the generation of those who seek Him* (*Psalms* 24:6), and they do not seek after enchantment, as it says, כי הגוים האלה

NOTES

hence, if Balaam is overanxious and curses them all, none shall be affected. Balak therefore cautions him to concentrate only on part of the people (קצהו); otherwise he will end with "nothing" (אפס).

21. ותרועת מלך בו — *The trumpet-signal for the king is among them.* The תרועה, *trumpet-signal,* is symbolic of the Kingship of heaven. *HASHEM his God is with him* is attested to by the presence of the משכן, *Sanctuary,* in their midst; hence, they are secure and happy.

22. כתועפת ראם לו — *Like the lofty horns of the wild-ox.* At the very beginning of the Book of *Numbers,* the *Sforno* explains that the original intent of God was to bring Israel into the Land without recourse to war. The reason for the eventual need to destroy the inhabitants of the land of Canaan was due to the sin of the spies which extended the Canaanite stay in the land. During this time, their conduct became totally corrupt, thereby sealing their doom. Here, however, the *Sforno* gives a different reason for

and you will curse it for me from there." [14] *He took him to the field of the lookouts, to the summit of the height, and he built seven altars and brought up a bull and a ram on each altar.* [15] *He said to Balak, "Stand here by your burnt-offering, and I will be happened upon here."*

[16] *HASHEM happened upon Balaam and put an utterance in his mouth; and said, "Go back to Balak and so shall you say."*

[17] *He came to him and — behold! he was standing by his burnt-offering and the officers of Moab were with him. Balak said to him, "What did HASHEM speak?"*

[18] *He declaimed his parable and said: "Stand erect, O Balak, and hear; give ear to me, O son of Zippor.*

[19] *"God is not a man that He should be deceitful, nor a son of man that He should relent.*

Would He say and not do, or speak and not confirm?

[20] *"Behold! to bless have I received — He has blessed, and I shall not contradict it.*

[21] *"He perceived no iniquity in Jacob, and saw no perversity in Israel. HASHEM his God is with him, and the friendship of the King is in him.*

[22] *"It is God Who brought them out of Egypt according to the power of His loftiness,*

[23] *for there is no divination in Jacob and no sorcery in Israel. Even now it is said to Jacob and Israel what God has wrought.*

[24] *Behold! the people will arise like a lion cub and raise itself like a lion; it will not lie down until it consumes prey, and drinks the blood of the slain."*

[25] *Balak said to Balaam, "Neither shall you curse them at all, nor shall you bless them at all!"*

...אֶל מְעֹנְנִים וְאֶל קֹסְמִים יִשְׁמָעוּ וְאַתָּה לֹא כֵן, *For these nations . . . hearken unto soothsayers and diviners, but you are not so* (Deut. 18:14).

כָּעֵת — *Now* (*lit., this time*) . . . at a time when they want to know the future . . .

יֵאָמֵר לְיַעֲקֹב וּלְיִשְׂרָאֵל מַה פָּעַל אֵל — *It will be said to Jacob and Israel what God has wrought.* It shall be told to them through prophecy or through some prophet what God, the Blessed One, has decreed. It shall not be told to them what the signs of heaven indicate (lit., teach) or how the constellations will work because they are not under those constellations.

24. כְּלָבִיא יָקוּם — *That rises up as a lioness* . . . to battle with those who have not waged war against them at all.

עַד יֹאכַל טֶרֶף — *Until he eats of the prey.* They will eat and consume those nations who are now their prey as it says, *For they are our bread* (14:9).

NOTES

the need to resort to physical destruction of the inhabitants. It resulted from the refusal of the nations residing in Canaan to accept the offer of Joshua to leave unharmed or to make peace. Nonetheless, the simile of Balaam is correct; Israel is compared to a רְאֵם, *wild-ox*, and not to a lion, for their original intent was not to devour their enemies but merely to drive them out of the land.

23. כִּי לֹא נַחַשׁ בְּיַעֲקֹב — *For there is not enchantment with Jacob.* The interpretation of the *Sforno* regarding God's communication with Israel through prophets is similar to *Rashi's* explanation. However, he adds the thought that the destiny of Israel is not dictated by the stars, nor is their fate determined by the "signs of heaven," as our Sages teach us, אֵין מַזָּל לְיִשְׂרָאֵל, *Israel is not subject to planetary influences* (*Nedarim* 32a).

כו וַיַּעַן בִּלְעָם וַיֹּאמֶר אֶל־בָּלָק הֲלֹא דִּבַּרְתִּי אֵלֶיךָ לֵאמֹר כֹּל אֲשֶׁר־יְדַבֵּר
ששי [שביעי] כז יְהוָה אֹתוֹ אֶעֱשֶׂה: וַיֹּאמֶר בָּלָק אֶל־בִּלְעָם לְכָה־נָּא אֶקָּחֲךָ אֶל־מָקוֹם
כח אַחֵר אוּלַי יִישַׁר בְּעֵינֵי הָאֱלֹהִים וְקַבֹּתוֹ לִי מִשָּׁם: וַיִּקַּח בָּלָק אֶת־בִּלְעָם
כט רֹאשׁ הַפְּעוֹר הַנִּשְׁקָף עַל־פְּנֵי הַיְשִׁימֹן: וַיֹּאמֶר בִּלְעָם אֶל־בָּלָק בְּנֵה־
ל לִי בָזֶה שִׁבְעָה מִזְבְּחֹת וְהָכֵן לִי בָּזֶה שִׁבְעָה פָרִים וְשִׁבְעָה אֵילִים: וַיַּעַשׂ
כד א בָּלָק כַּאֲשֶׁר אָמַר בִּלְעָם וַיַּעַל פַּר וָאַיִל בַּמִּזְבֵּחַ: וַיַּרְא בִּלְעָם כִּי טוֹב
בְּעֵינֵי יְהוָה לְבָרֵךְ אֶת־יִשְׂרָאֵל וְלֹא־הָלַךְ כְּפַעַם־בְּפַעַם לִקְרַאת נְחָשִׁים
ב וַיָּשֶׁת אֶל־הַמִּדְבָּר פָּנָיו: וַיִּשָּׂא בִלְעָם אֶת־עֵינָיו וַיַּרְא אֶת־יִשְׂרָאֵל
ג שֹׁכֵן לִשְׁבָטָיו וַתְּהִי עָלָיו רוּחַ אֱלֹהִים: וַיִּשָּׂא מְשָׁלוֹ וַיֹּאמַר נְאֻם בִּלְעָם
ד בְּנוֹ בְעֹר וּנְאֻם הַגֶּבֶר שְׁתֻם הָעָיִן: נְאֻם שֹׁמֵעַ אִמְרֵי־אֵל אֲשֶׁר מַחֲזֵה
ה שַׁדַּי יֶחֱזֶה נֹפֵל וּגְלוּי עֵינָיִם: מַה־טֹּבוּ אֹהָלֶיךָ יַעֲקֹב מִשְׁכְּנֹתֶיךָ יִשְׂרָאֵל:
ו כִּנְחָלִים נִטָּיוּ כְּגַנֹּת עֲלֵי נָהָר כַּאֲהָלִים נָטַע יְהוָה כַּאֲרָזִים עֲלֵי־מָיִם:

---

27. אוּלַי יִישַׁר בְּעֵינֵי הָאֱלֹהִים וְקַבֹּתוֹ לִי מִשָּׁם — *Perhaps it will please God that you may curse for me there . . .* because it may be that particular part (of Israel) which is more vulnerable to curses.

XXIV

1. לִקְרַאת נְחָשִׁים — *To seek for enchantments.* He ceased attempting to anticipate the time which might be appropriate for curses to take effect upon them because he realized (lit., "saw") *that it was good in the eyes of God to bless Israel,* and (therefore) there was no hope for him to curse them.

וַיָּשֶׁת אֶל הַמִּדְבָּר פָּנָיו — *And he set his face toward the desert . . .* to bless them with limited blessings which contain (the element) of damage within them, as our Sages say, "Better the curse which Achiya the Shiloni cursed Israel than the blessing of Balaam" (*Taanis* 20a).

5. מַה טֹּבוּ אֹהָלֶיךָ יַעֲקֹב — *How goodly are your tents, O Jacob.* (This refers to) Houses of Study, similar to, יֹשֵׁב אֹהָלִים, *Dwelling in tents* (*Genesis* 25:27), and to, וְיִשְׁכֹּן בְּאָהֳלֵי שֵׁם, *And he shall dwell in the tents of Shem* (*Genesis* 9:27), as well as, וְהָיָה כָּל מְבַקֵּשׁ ה׳ יֵצֵא אֶל אֹהֶל מוֹעֵד, *Every one that sought* H*ASHEM* *went out to the Tent of Meeting* (*Exodus* 33:7).

מִשְׁכְּנֹתֶיךָ יִשְׂרָאֵל — *Your dwellings, O Israel.* (This refers to) Houses of Assembly (prayer) and the Sanctuary of God, which are designated for His Name to dwell there and to accept the prayers of worshipers.

Now he said, *how goodly etc.*, for not only do they benefit those who are occupied therein, but they also bring good to the entire nation, as the name "Jacob" indicates,

NOTES

27. וְקַבֹּתוֹ לִי מִשָּׁם — *That you may curse for me there.* Since Balak has been frustrated in his plan to curse Israel time after time, what does he expect to accomplish by bringing Balaam to another place? The *Sforno* explains that Balak realized that the people of Israel as a whole was impervious to any curse, but he reasoned that sections of the camp of Israel, which could be seen from another place, might be vulnerable.

XXIV

1. וַיָּשֶׁת אֶל הַמִּדְבָּר פָּנָיו — *And he set his face toward the desert.* The blessings of Balaam were uttered with a lack of sincerity because Balaam was, in truth, an enemy of Israel. Our Sages tell us that hidden within each blessing was a curse. The *Sforno* interprets the expression אֶל הַמִּדְבָּר, *toward the desert,* as implying something which is barren and desolate, and symbolically the antithesis of a blessing; hence, any blessing he would pronounce would contain an element of curse within it, even though superficially it was a blessing. The saying of our Sages in tractate *Taanis,* cited by the *Sforno,* is most apt. The Talmud interprets the verse in *Proverbs* 27:6, *Faithful are the wounds of a friend, but the kisses of an enemy are deceptive,* as refer-

[26] *Balaam answered and said to Balak, "Have I not spoken to you, saying, 'Whatever* HASHEM *shall speak, that I shall do'?"*

[27] *Balak said to Balaam, "Go, now, I shall take you to a different place, perhaps it will be proper in God's eyes that you will curse them for me from there."* [28] *Balak took Balaam to the summit of the height that overlooks the face of the wasteland.*

[29] *Balaam said to Balak, "Build for me here seven altars and prepare for me here seven bulls and seven rams."* [30] *Balak did as Balaam said, and he brought up a bull and a ram on each altar.*

24

[1] *Balaam saw that it was good in God's eyes to bless Israel, so he did not go as every other time toward divinations, but he set his face toward the Wilderness.* [2] *Balaam raised his eyes and saw Israel dwelling according to its tribes, and the spirit of God was upon him.* [3] *He declaimed his parable and said:*

"The words of Balaam son of Beor, the words of the man with the open eye;

[4] *"the words of the one who hears the sayings of God, who sees the vision of Shaddai, while fallen and with uncovered eyes:*

[5] *"How goodly are your tents, O Jacob, your dwelling places, O Israel;*

[6] *"stretching out like brooks, like gardens by a river, like aloes planted by* HASHEM, *like cedars by water.*

---

namely that they shall remain at the end after all others (will disappear), and they shall never cease (to exist), as the name "Israel" indicates, i.e., that they will strive with *Elohim* and with man (and be victorious).

6. כִּנְחָלִים נִטָּיוּ — *As streams winding their way.* For indeed, Houses of Prayer and Houses of Study are to the masses of Israel as streams which make their way into the fields to water them, and those who dwell in these tents and comprehend the Torah draw and give to drink of their Torah to the masses — and so also are those who pray . . .

כְּגַנֹּת עֲלֵי נָהָר — *As gardens by the riverside* . . . who do not cease to produce fruit, as our Sages say, "A covenant has been made with the 13 Attributes of Mercy that they will not be turned away empty-handed" (*Rosh Hashanah* 17b).

NOTES

ring to Achiya the Shiloni who admonished Israel but did so out of love, and to Balaam who blessed them but did so in a spirit of animosity.

5. מַה טֹּבוּ אֹהָלֶיךָ יַעֲקֹב מִשְׁכְּנֹתֶיךָ יִשְׂרָאֵל — *How goodly are your tents, O Jacob, your dwellings, O Israel. Rashi* interprets *tents* as referring to the private tents of Israel, but the *Sforno* is of the opinion that the phrase אֹהֶל, *tent,* be it here or in the various verses cited by him, means the tent of study, while the word מִשְׁכָּן, *dwelling place,* refers to a place of prayer or the Sanctuary. He also explains why the name *Jacob* is associated with אֹהֶל (tent), while the name *Israel* is linked to מִשְׁכָּן (dwelling). The *Sforno* established in his commentary on *Genesis* 32:29, and again in *Genesis* 49:24, that the name *Jacob* indicates that the Jewish people shall remain at the "end" of time, while *Israel* is indicative of their superior rank as a nation who will prevail over their adversaries, be they "heavenly" or earthly. Hence, the choice of these names in this verse are most fitting. Through the study of Torah, they will guarantee their survival, and through prayer they will earn God's support and His Providence.

6. כְּגַנֹּת עֲלֵי נָהָר — *As gardens by the river side.* The *Sforno* explains the comparison of those who pray to a garden which produces fruit as referring to the prayer of the י״ג מִדּוֹת הָרַחֲמִים (the Thirteen Attributes of Mercy) recorded in *Exodus* 34:6-7. According to our Sages, God revealed this prayer to Moses and promised him that whenever the Children of Israel would recite this prayer, He would have mercy upon them and forgive them. This תְּפִלָּה is an integral part of our *Selichos* prayers.

ז יִזַּל־מַיִם מִדָּלְיָו וְזַרְעוֹ בְּמַיִם רַבִּים וְיָרֹם מֵאֲגַג מַלְכּוֹ וְתִנַּשֵּׂא מַלְכֻתוֹ׃
ח אֵל מוֹצִיאוֹ מִמִּצְרַיִם כְּתוֹעֲפֹת רְאֵם לוֹ יֹאכַל גּוֹיִם צָרָיו וְעַצְמֹתֵיהֶם
ט יְגָרֵם וְחִצָּיו יִמְחָץ׃ כָּרַע שָׁכַב כַּאֲרִי וּכְלָבִיא מִי יְקִימֶנּוּ מְבָרְכֶיךָ *בָרוּךְ *הב׳ רפה
י וְאֹרְרֶיךָ אָרוּר׃ וַיִּחַר־אַף בָּלָק אֶל־בִּלְעָם וַיִּסְפֹּק אֶת־כַּפָּיו וַיֹּאמֶר בָּלָק
אֶל־בִּלְעָם לָקֹב אֹיְבַי קְרָאתִיךָ וְהִנֵּה בֵּרַכְתָּ בָרֵךְ זֶה שָׁלֹשׁ פְּעָמִים׃
יא וְעַתָּה בְּרַח־לְךָ אֶל־מְקוֹמֶךָ אָמַרְתִּי כַּבֵּד אֲכַבֶּדְךָ וְהִנֵּה מְנָעֲךָ יהוה
יב מִכָּבוֹד׃ וַיֹּאמֶר בִּלְעָם אֶל־בָּלָק הֲלֹא גַּם אֶל־מַלְאָכֶיךָ אֲשֶׁר־שָׁלַחְתָּ
יג אֵלַי דִּבַּרְתִּי לֵאמֹר׃ אִם־יִתֶּן־לִי בָלָק מְלֹא בֵיתוֹ כֶּסֶף וְזָהָב לֹא אוּכַל
לַעֲבֹר אֶת־פִּי יהוה לַעֲשׂוֹת טוֹבָה אוֹ רָעָה מִלִּבִּי אֲשֶׁר־יְדַבֵּר יהוה אֹתוֹ
יד אֲדַבֵּר׃ וְעַתָּה הִנְנִי הוֹלֵךְ לְעַמִּי לְכָה אִיעָצְךָ אֲשֶׁר יַעֲשֶׂה הָעָם הַזֶּה שביעי
טו לְעַמְּךָ בְּאַחֲרִית הַיָּמִים׃ וַיִּשָּׂא מְשָׁלוֹ וַיֹּאמַר נְאֻם בִּלְעָם בְּנוֹ בְעֹר וּנְאֻם
טז הַגֶּבֶר שְׁתֻם הָעָיִן׃ נְאֻם שֹׁמֵעַ אִמְרֵי־אֵל וְיֹדֵעַ דַּעַת עֶלְיוֹן מַחֲזֵה שַׁדַּי
יז יֶחֱזֶה נֹפֵל וּגְלוּי עֵינָיִם׃ אֶרְאֶנּוּ וְלֹא עַתָּה אֲשׁוּרֶנּוּ וְלֹא קָרוֹב דָּרַךְ כּוֹכָב
מִיַּעֲקֹב וְקָם שֵׁבֶט מִיִּשְׂרָאֵל וּמָחַץ פַּאֲתֵי מוֹאָב וְקַרְקַר כָּל־בְּנֵי־שֵׁת׃

---

8. יֹאכַל גּוֹיִם צָרָיו — *He shall devour the nations that are his adversaries* . . . in the distant future, as it says, וְנָקָם יָשִׁיב לְצָרָיו, *and renders vengeance to his adversaries* (*Deut.* 32:43).

וְחִצָּיו יִמְחָץ — *And pierce them through with his arrows* . . . as it says, אַשְׁכִּיר חִצַּי מִדָּם, *I will make my arrows drunk with blood* (*Deut.* 32:42).

9. מְבָרְכֶיךָ בָרוּךְ — *Blessed be he who blesses you* . . . as was the case with Abraham, for indeed, the remnant of Israel will (attain) the level of Abraham our father, as it says, כִּי יָשׁוּב ה׳ לָשׂוּשׂ עָלֶיךָ לְטוֹב כַּאֲשֶׁר שָׂשׂ עַל אֲבֹתֶיךָ, *For* H*ASHEM will again rejoice over you for good as He rejoiced over your fathers* (*Deut.* 30:9).

10. וַיִּסְפֹּק אֶת כַּפָּיו — *And he clapped his hands together.* For he despaired of attaining his desire since he (Balaam) had cursed those who curse (Israel).

11. בְּרַח לְךָ — *Flee, you.* בְּרִיחָה, *fleeing,* wherever it is mentioned (in Scriptures) does not mean *fleeing* from a pursuer, but (it means rather) to leave a place (motivated) by fear of future harm.

12. הֲלֹא גַּם אֶל מַלְאָכֶיךָ — *Did I not also* (*speak so*) *to your messengers.* There is no reason (lit., it is not fitting) for you to wonder why I did not fulfill your wish in the hope of receiving honor, for I told the messengers whom you sent to say to me, *For I will promote you unto very great honor* (22:17), that it was not in my hand (to fulfill your request).

14. לְכָה אִיעָצְךָ — *Come and I will advise you* . . . the counsel being that of sending women (to mislead Israel) as it is explained (later in the Torah) when it says, *Behold these caused the Children of Israel, through the counsel of Balaam* (*to break faith etc.*) (31:16).

NOTES

10. וַיִּסְפֹּק אֶת כַּפָּיו — *And he clapped his hands together.* Once Balaam proclaimed that anyone who cursed Israel would themselves be cursed (v. 9), it was inconceivable that he would now curse them, so Balak despairs completely of attaining his goal and proceeds to dismiss Balaam.

11. בְּרַח לְךָ — *Flee, you.* See the *Sforno's* commentary on *Genesis* 31:21, where he explains the difference between the words בְּרִיחָה and נִיסָה, both of which mean "flight."

14. לְכָה אִיעָצְךָ — *Come and I will advise you.* The advice given by Balaam to Balak was to have the daughters of Moab seduce the men of Israel and through harlotry entice them to practice idolatry. All this is recorded in the next chapter (25), while in *Mattos* (31:16) the Torah tells us explicitly that

7 *"Water shall flow from his wells, and his seed shall be by abundant waters. His king shall be exalted over Agag, and his kingdom shall be upraised.*
8 *"It is God Who took him out of Egypt according to the power of His loftiness. He will consume the nations that oppress him and crush their bones, and his arrows shall pierce them.*
9 *"He crouched and lay down like a lion, and, like a lion cub — who can stand him up? Those who bless you are blessed and those who curse you are accursed."*
10 *Balak's anger flared against Balaam and he clapped his hands. Balak said to Balaam, "To curse my enemies did I summon you, and behold! you have continually blessed them these three times!*
11 *Now, flee to your place. I said I would honor you, but — behold! HASHEM has withheld you from honor."*
12 *Balaam said to Balak, "Did I not speak to your emissaries whom you sent to me, saying,*
13 *'If Balak were to give me his houseful of silver and gold, I cannot transgress the word of HASHEM to do good or bad on my own. Whatever HASHEM speaks, that shall I speak.'*
14 *And now, behold! I go to my people. Come, I shall advise you what this people will do to your people in the End of Days."*
15 *He declaimed his parable and said:*
"The words of Balaam son of Beor, the words of the man with the open eye.
16 *"The words of one who hears the sayings of God, and knows the knowledge of the Supreme One, who sees the vision of Shaddai, while fallen and with uncovered eyes.*
17 *"I shall see him, but not now, I shall look at him, but it is not near. A star has issued from Jacob and a scepter-bearer has risen from Israel, and he shall pierce the nobles of Moab and undermine the children of Seth.*

אֲשֶׁר יַעֲשֶׂה הָעָם הַזֶּה לְעַמְּךָ בְּאַחֲרִית הַיָּמִים — *What this people shall do to your people in the end of days . . .* because, indeed, the evil *which this people shall do to your people* will not happen in your day, and you have nothing to fear. But it shall only (come to pass) *in the end of days* as it says, *And shall smite the corners of Moab* (v. 17), and as it says, אֱדוֹם וּמוֹאָב מִשְׁלוֹחַ יָדָם, *They shall lay their hand upon Edom and Moab* (*Isaiah* 11:14).

17. אֶרְאֶנּוּ — *I see him . . .* that which this people shall do to your people.

דָּרַךְ כּוֹכָב — *There shall step forth a star from Jacob . . .* corporeal and everlasting, as it says, וּמַצְדִּיקֵי הָרַבִּים כַּכּוֹכָבִים לְעוֹלָם וָעֶד, *And they who turn many to righteousness are like the stars forever and ever* (*Daniel* 12:3).

וּמָחַץ פַּאֲתֵי מוֹאָב — *And shall smite the corners of Moab* — Although all the nations will be destroyed through the breath of God, as it says, כִּי אֶעֱשֶׂה כָלָה בְּכָל הַגּוֹיִם, *For I will make a full end of all the nations* (*Jeremiah* 30:11), Edom's and Moab's downfall (lit., "revenge") will be through the hand of Israel because these two nations were always his enemies and evil neighbors.

NOTES

this plan was Balaam's, who knew that the God of Israel detests immorality and idolatry.

17. דָּרַךְ כּוֹכָב — *There shall step forth a star from Jacob. Rashi* explains that the *star from Jacob* refers to the Messiah. The *Sforno* explains that the Messiah will be a man (a physical being), yet one who shall be everlasting, which he bases on the verse in *Daniel.* The verse here compares the Messiah to a *star,* as does the verse in *Daniel.* Just as the

יח־יט וְהָיָה אֱדוֹם יְרֵשָׁה וְהָיָה יְרֵשָׁה שֵׂעִיר אֹיְבָיו וְיִשְׂרָאֵל עֹשֶׂה חָיִל: וְיֵרְדְּ
כ מִיַּעֲקֹב וְהֶאֱבִיד שָׂרִיד מֵעִיר: וַיַּרְא אֶת־עֲמָלֵק וַיִּשָּׂא מְשָׁלוֹ וַיֹּאמַר
כא רֵאשִׁית גּוֹיִם עֲמָלֵק וְאַחֲרִיתוֹ עֲדֵי אֹבֵד: וַיַּרְא אֶת־הַקֵּינִי וַיִּשָּׂא מְשָׁלוֹ
כב וַיֹּאמַר אֵיתָן מוֹשָׁבֶךָ וְשִׂים בַּסֶּלַע קִנֶּךָ: כִּי אִם־יִהְיֶה לְבָעֵר קָיִן עַד־מָה
כג־כד אַשּׁוּר תִּשְׁבֶּךָּ: וַיִּשָּׂא מְשָׁלוֹ וַיֹּאמַר אוֹי מִי יִחְיֶה מִשֻּׂמוֹ אֵל: וְצִים מִיַּד
כה כִּתִּים וְעִנּוּ אַשּׁוּר וְעִנּוּ־עֵבֶר וְגַם־הוּא עֲדֵי אֹבֵד: וַיָּקָם בִּלְעָם וַיֵּלֶךְ וַיָּשָׁב
לִמְקֹמוֹ וְגַם־בָּלָק הָלַךְ לְדַרְכּוֹ:

כה א־ב וַיֵּשֶׁב יִשְׂרָאֵל בַּשִּׁטִּים וַיָּחֶל הָעָם לִזְנוֹת אֶל־בְּנוֹת מוֹאָב: וַתִּקְרֶאןָ לָעָם

18. וְהָיָה אֱדוֹם יְרֵשָׁה — *And Edom shall be a possession . . .* (a possession) for the beasts and birds of the wilderness, as it says, וִירֵשׁוּהָ קָאַת וְקִפּוֹד, *But the pelican and bittern shall possess it* (*Isaiah* 34:11).

וְהָיָה יְרֵשָׁה שֵׂעִיר — *Seir also shall be a possession . . .* (a possession) for Israel, since it is a part of the Kenite, the Kenizzite and the Kadmonite (*Genesis* 15:19).

אֹיְבָיו — *His enemies . . .* and the reason that the avenging of Moab and Edom shall be greater than that of other nations is because they were the perpetual enemies of Israel.

וְיִשְׂרָאֵל עֹשֶׂה חָיִל — *And Israel shall do valiantly . . .* and then Israel shall be able to do valiantly, as it says, וּלְאֹם מִלְאֹם יֶאֱמָץ, *And the one people shall be stronger than the other people* (*Genesis* 25:23).

19. וְיֵרְדְּ מִיַּעֲקֹב — *And out of Jacob shall come he that shall have dominion.* Each one of his descendants shall rule among the nations, as it says, וְהָיָה הַנִּכְשָׁל בָּהֶם בַּיּוֹם הַהוּא כְּדָוִיד, *And he that stumbles among them on that day shall be as David* (*Zechariah* 12:8), and as it says, וְהָיָה שְׁאֵרִית יַעֲקֹב בַּגּוֹיִם בְּקֶרֶב עַמִּים רַבִּים כְּאַרְיֵה בְּבַהֲמוֹת יַעַר כִּכְפִיר בְּעֶדְרֵי צֹאן, *And the remnant of Jacob shall be among the nations, in the midst of many peoples, as a lion among the beasts of the forest, as a young lion among the flocks of sheep* (*Michah* 5:7).

וְהֶאֱבִיד שָׂרִיד מֵעִיר — *And shall destroy the remnant from the city . . .* as it says, וְרָמַס וְטָרַף וְאֵין מַצִּיל תָּרֹם יָדְךָ עַל צָרֶיךָ וְכָל אֹיְבֶיךָ יִכָּרֵתוּ, *And tread down and tear and there is none to deliver. Let your hand be lifted up above your adversaries and let all your enemies be cut off* (ibid. vs. 7-8).

20. עֲדֵי אֹבֵד — *Shall come to destruction.* Although the sovereignty of all nations shall be eliminated in the future, as it says, וּשְׁאָר חֵיוָתָא הֶעְדִּיו שָׁלְטָנְהוֹן, *And as for the rest of the nations (lit., beasts), their dominion was taken away* (*Daniel* 7:12), nonetheless, the nations will not be totally destroyed except for these two nations, and they are Amalek who began

NOTES

stars are forever, so shall be the Messiah.

17-20. וּמָחַץ פַּאֲתֵי מוֹאָב . . . עֲדֵי אֹבֵד — *And shall smite the corners of Moab . . . shall come to destruction.* The *Sforno's* commentary on these verses does not appear in the מִקְרָאוֹת גְּדוֹלוֹת — the standard edition of the Bible, which includes numerous commentaries including that of the *Sforno.* We have, however, translated his commentary on these verses, taken from various manuscripts and published in the Mosad Harav Kook edition 5740. We assume that the censor removed the commentary on these verses because it was considered too harsh an indictment of the Christian world's treatment of the Jews, and depicts too vividly the revenge that Israel will take of them at the end of time. One can surmise that the censor knew that Edom is synonymous with Rome, and in these verses the Torah singles out Edom (Rome) as the eternal enemy of the Jewish people, who will eventually be subdued and conquered by Israel and become its possession (v. 18).

18. וְהָיָה אֱדוֹם יְרֵשָׁה וְהָיָה יְרֵשָׁה שֵׂעִיר — *And Edom shall be a possession, Seir also shall be a possession.* Since Edom and Seir are one and the same, the word *possession* seems to be repetitious. The *Sforno,* however, explains that the first part of the verse refers to its desolation, while the second part refers to the annexation of its land by Israel.

18 "Edom shall be a conquest and Seir shall be the conquest of his enemies — and Israel will attain success.
19 "One from Jacob shall rule and destroy the remnant of the city."
20 He saw Amalek and declaimed his parable and said: "Amalek is the first among nations, but its end will be eternal destruction."
21 He saw the Kenite and declaimed his parable and said: "Strong is your dwelling, and set in a rock is your nest.
22 "For if the Kenite should be laid waste, till where can Assyria take you captive?"
23 He declaimed his parable and said: "Who will survive when He imposes these!
24 "Big ships from the coast of Kittim will afflict Assyria and afflict the other bank — but it, too, will be forever destroyed."
25 Then Balaam rose up and went and returned to his place, and Balak also went on his way.

25 1 Israel settled in the Shittim and the people began to commit harlotry with the daughters of Moab. 2 They invited the people to the feasts of

to battle against Israel, and the Kuthim who completed the destruction of Israel, as it says, *And he also shall come to destruction* (v. 24).

21. אֵיתָן מוֹשָׁבֶךָ — *Your dwelling place is strong.* You dwelt with Israel in a land which was אֵיתָן, namely in the wilderness, in a land which was unplanted.

וְשִׂים בַּסֶּלַע קִנֶּךָ — *And set your nest in the rock.* Hence, because of this, at the time that they (Israel) will be elevated and strong, your nest shall (also) be with them, as our Sages say, "He who lives with you in your poverty shall be settled among you in your wealth" (*Yevamos* 24b).

23. אוֹי מִי יִחְיֶה — *Alas, who shall live* . . . similar to, "Let him (the Messiah) come but let me not see him" (*Sanhedrin* 98b).

XXV

1. וַיָּחֶל הָעָם לִזְנוֹת — *And the people began to commit harlotry.* At the beginning, they did

NOTES

וְיִשְׂרָאֵל עֹשֶׂה חָיִל — *And Israel shall do valiantly. Rashi* explains the phrase *and the one people shall be stronger than the other people* (*Gen.* 25:23) to mean that when one rises the other must fall, relating to the historic conflict between Esau (Edom) and Jacob. The *Sforno* correctly quotes that verse here to explain the link between *and Edom shall be a possession* with *Israel shall do valiantly.* Only when Esau falls shall Israel do valiantly and be victorious over all its enemies.

19. וְיֵרְדְּ מִיַּעֲקֹב — *And out of Jacob shall come he that shall have dominion.* The word וְיֵרְדְּ (and he shall have dominion) is in the singular, hence it must refer to every descendant of Jacob, regardless of how mighty or weak he may appear to be.

20. עֲדֵי אֹבֵד — *Shall come to destruction.* Amalek is also a descendant of Esau. Here again, the *Sforno* emphasizes the eventual total destruction of Esau-Edom.

21. אֵיתָן מוֹשָׁבֶךָ — *Your dwelling place is strong.* The Kenites were the descendants of Jethro, who joined the Israelites in the wilderness and faithfully remained with Israel, sharing their travails and difficulties, even though Jethro himself ultimately returned to his homeland. Therefore, they were given a share in the Land of Israel which was only fitting and proper, as the *Sforno* points out citing the saying of our Sages that he who remains loyal to you in your time of need is entitled to share in your eventual success.

23. אוֹי מִי יִחְיֶה — *Alas, who shall live.* The preceding verses speak of the Messianic period. According to tradition, that period will be a most difficult and painful one, so much so that Ulla said he does not want to be present when the Messiah will arrive! Balaam therefore exclaims, "Woe, who would want to live during that difficult time?" This, according to the *Sforno,* is the sense of אוֹי מִי יִחְיֶה.

ג לְזִבְחֵי אֱלֹהֵיהֶן וַיֹּאכַל הָעָם וַיִּשְׁתַּחֲווּ לֵאלֹהֵיהֶן: וַיִּצָּמֶד יִשְׂרָאֵל לְבַעַל
ד פְּעוֹר וַיִּחַר־אַף־יהוה בְּיִשְׂרָאֵל: וַיֹּאמֶר יהוה אֶל־מֹשֶׁה קַח אֶת־כָּל־
רָאשֵׁי הָעָם וְהוֹקַע אוֹתָם לַיהוה נֶגֶד הַשָּׁמֶשׁ וְיָשֹׁב חֲרוֹן אַף־יהוה
ה מִיִּשְׂרָאֵל: וַיֹּאמֶר מֹשֶׁה אֶל־שֹׁפְטֵי יִשְׂרָאֵל הִרְגוּ אִישׁ אֲנָשָׁיו הַנִּצְמָדִים
ו לְבַעַל פְּעוֹר: וְהִנֵּה אִישׁ מִבְּנֵי יִשְׂרָאֵל בָּא וַיַּקְרֵב אֶל־אֶחָיו
אֶת־הַמִּדְיָנִית לְעֵינֵי מֹשֶׁה וּלְעֵינֵי כָּל־עֲדַת בְּנֵי־יִשְׂרָאֵל וְהֵמָּה בֹכִים
מפטיר ז פֶּתַח אֹהֶל מוֹעֵד: וַיַּרְא פִּינְחָס בֶּן־אֶלְעָזָר בֶּן־אַהֲרֹן הַכֹּהֵן וַיָּקָם מִתּוֹךְ
ח הָעֵדָה וַיִּקַּח רֹמַח בְּיָדוֹ: וַיָּבֹא אַחַר אִישׁ־יִשְׂרָאֵל אֶל־הַקֻּבָּה וַיִּדְקֹר
אֶת־שְׁנֵיהֶם אֵת אִישׁ יִשְׂרָאֵל וְאֶת־הָאִשָּׁה אֶל־קֳבָתָהּ וַתֵּעָצַר הַמַּגֵּפָה
ט מֵעַל בְּנֵי יִשְׂרָאֵל: וַיִּהְיוּ הַמֵּתִים בַּמַּגֵּפָה אַרְבָּעָה וְעֶשְׂרִים אָלֶף:

---

not worship idols at all but (their sole intent was to) commit harlotry; however, they were led to idolatry (lit., it happened to them) as the Torah cautioned (lit., attested) when it prohibited intermarriage with the nations, as it says, וְקָרָא לְךָ וְאָכַלְתָּ מִזִּבְחוֹ. וְלָקַחְתָּ מִבְּנֹתָיו . . . וְזָנוּ בְנֹתָיו . . . וְהִזְנוּ אֶת בָּנֶיךָ אַחֲרֵי אֱלֹהֵיהֶן . . ., *And they will call you to eat of their sacrifice. And you will take of their daughters . . . and their daughters will go astray . . . and make your sons go astray after their gods* (Exodus 34:15-16).

2. וַיֹּאכַל הָעָם וַיִּשְׁתַּחֲווּ לֵאלֹהֵיהֶן — *And the people ate and bowed down to their gods.* For this is the way of the evil inclination, to lead one from evil to evil, as our Sages have testified (*Shabbos* 105b).

NOTES

XXV

2. וַיֹּאכַל . . . וַיִּשְׁתַּחֲווּ — *And the people ate and bowed down.* The *Sforno* explains that Israel's transgression developed gradually. It began with harlotry, followed by the eating of pagan sacrifices, and culminated in Israel's bowing down to idols. This is reflected in the saying of our Sages in tractate *Shabbos* 105b: *Such are the wiles of the evil inclination; today he says to him, "Do this," tomorrow he tells him, "Do that," until he bids him, "Go and serve idols."*

4. נֶגֶד הַשָּׁמֶשׁ — *In the face of the sun.* The masses were not guilty of harlotry or idolatry. However, they were guilty of apathy, having witnessed these grave transgressions and failed to object or intervene. Their atonement, in turn, would be

their gods; the people ate and prostrated themselves to their gods. [3] *Israel became attached to Baal-peor, and the wrath of* HASHEM *flared up against Israel.*

[4] HASHEM *said to Moses, "Take all the leaders of the people. Hang them before Hashem against the sun — and the flaring wrath of* HASHEM *will withdraw from Israel."*

[5] *Moses said to the judges of Israel, "Let each man kill his men who were attached to Baal-peor."*

[6] *Behold! a man of the Children of Israel came and brought a Midianite woman near to his brothers in the sight of Moses and in the sight of the entire assembly of the Children of Israel; and they were weeping at the entrance of the Tent of Meeting.*

[7] *Phineas son of Elazar son of Aaron the Kohen saw, and he stood up from amid the assembly and took a spear in his hand.* [8] *He followed the Israelite man into the tent and pierced them both, the Israelite man and the woman into her stomach — and the plague was halted from the Children of Israel.* [9] *Those who died in the plague were twenty-four thousand.*

---

4. נֶגֶד הַשָּׁמֶשׁ — *In the face of the sun . . .* so that the people will see the execution of those who worshipped the idols and they will not protest (prevent) and thus they will find atonement for not protesting against these sinners.

8. וַתֵּעָצַר הַמַּגֵּפָה — *And the plague was stayed . . .* (the plague or decree) which God, the Exalted One, had already decreed when He said, *Neither shall any of them that angered Me see it* (14:23).

NOTES

attained by permitting the culprits to be hung in public without protest or intervention. The *Sforno* gives a similar explanation in *Exodus* 32:27 regarding the punishment meted out to those who were guilty of worshiping the Golden Calf.

8. וַתֵּעָצַר הַמַּגֵּפָה — *And the plague was stayed.* The *Sforno's* interpretation of the word הַמַּגֵּפָה, *the plague,* written with the definite article "ה," is to be understood according to his commentary in chapter 14:23. There he explains that the decree of the Almighty regarding those who would not merit to enter the Land extended beyond the generation of the spies, and included those who would be guilty of other transgressions as well, such as the congregation of Korach; those who worshiped Baal Peor and those who were killed by the fiery serpents. *The plague* cited here refers to God's decree in *Parashas Shelach* where He said, *Neither shall any who angered Me see it.* It was that plague which now ceased, for all the episodes mentioned above had already occurred and no other sins would merit such radical punishment.

פרשת פינחס

*י' זעירא י-יא וַיְדַבֵּר יהוה אֶל־מֹשֶׁה לֵּאמֹר: פִּינְחָס בֶּן־אֶלְעָזָר בֶּן־אַהֲרֹן הַכֹּהֵן הֵשִׁיב
אֶת־חֲמָתִי מֵעַל בְּנֵי־יִשְׂרָאֵל בְּקַנְאוֹ אֶת־קִנְאָתִי בְּתוֹכָם וְלֹא־כִלִּיתִי
*ו' קטיעא יב אֶת־בְּנֵי־יִשְׂרָאֵל בְּקִנְאָתִי: לָכֵן אֱמֹר הִנְנִי נֹתֵן לוֹ אֶת־בְּרִיתִי שָׁלוֹם:
יג וְהָיְתָה לּוֹ וּלְזַרְעוֹ אַחֲרָיו בְּרִית כְּהֻנַּת עוֹלָם תַּחַת אֲשֶׁר קִנֵּא לֵאלֹהָיו
יד וַיְכַפֵּר עַל־בְּנֵי יִשְׂרָאֵל: וְשֵׁם אִישׁ יִשְׂרָאֵל הַמֻּכֶּה אֲשֶׁר הֻכָּה אֶת־
טו הַמִּדְיָנִית זִמְרִי בֶּן־סָלוּא נְשִׂיא בֵית־אָב לַשִּׁמְעֹנִי: וְשֵׁם הָאִשָּׁה הַמֻּכָּה
הַמִּדְיָנִית כָּזְבִּי בַת־צוּר רֹאשׁ אֻמּוֹת בֵּית־אָב בְּמִדְיָן הוּא:
טז-יח וַיְדַבֵּר יהוה אֶל־מֹשֶׁה לֵּאמֹר: צָרוֹר אֶת־הַמִּדְיָנִים וְהִכִּיתֶם אוֹתָם: כִּי
צֹרְרִים הֵם לָכֶם בְּנִכְלֵיהֶם אֲשֶׁר־נִכְּלוּ לָכֶם עַל־דְּבַר פְּעוֹר וְעַל־דְּבַר
כו א כָּזְבִּי בַת־נְשִׂיא מִדְיָן אֲחֹתָם הַמֻּכָּה בְיוֹם־הַמַּגֵּפָה עַל־דְּבַר־פְּעוֹר: וַיְהִי
*פסקא באמצע פסוק אַחֲרֵי הַמַּגֵּפָה
ב וַיֹּאמֶר יהוה אֶל־מֹשֶׁה וְאֶל אֶלְעָזָר בֶּן־אַהֲרֹן הַכֹּהֵן לֵאמֹר: שְׂאוּ אֶת־
רֹאשׁ | כָּל־עֲדַת בְּנֵי־יִשְׂרָאֵל מִבֶּן עֶשְׂרִים שָׁנָה וָמַעְלָה לְבֵית אֲבֹתָם

11. בְּקַנְאוֹ אֶת קִנְאָתִי בְּתוֹכָם — *He was zealous for My sake in their midst.* He avenged (My honor) in the sight of all, so that (although) they (Israel) saw this (despicable act) against which they did not protest, they (still) would find atonement for not having protested against Pinchas, and thereby *he turned My wrath away* from them.

12. אֶת בְּרִיתִי שָׁלוֹם — *My covenant of peace* . . . from the angel of death, similar to עֹשֶׂה שָׁלוֹם בִּמְרוֹמָיו, *He who makes peace in His heights* (*Job* 25:2). Because, indeed, all diminishment (of life) is caused only (as a result) of opposing conflicting (forces). Now, this (blessing of peace) was fulfilled with Pinchas [Phinehas] who lived much longer than all his contemporaries (lit., the men of his generation), to such an extent that he (even) served (as the *Kohen*) in the Sanctuary of Shiloh at the time (of the episode) of the concubine in Givah (*Judges* 20:28) which, doubtless, occurred after the death of Joshua and the death of הַזְּקֵנִים אֲשֶׁר הֶאֱרִיכוּ יָמִים אַחֲרֵי יְהוֹשֻׁעַ, *the elders who outlived Joshua* (*Joshua* 24:31). And certainly (this is the case) if (Pinchas) lived in the time of Yiftach who wrote to the King of Ammon, בְּשֶׁבֶת יִשְׂרָאֵל בְּחֶשְׁבּוֹן וּבִבְנוֹתֶיהָ . . . שְׁלֹשׁ מֵאוֹת שָׁנָה, *While Israel dwelt in Cheshbon and its hamlets . . . for three hundred years* (*Judges* 11:26), and our Sages have (also) related to us that Pinchas did not want to go to Yiftach to absolve him from his vow. And this (i.e., Pinchas' longevity) is certainly true according to (the Sage) who says that

NOTES

11. בְּקַנְאוֹ אֶת קִנְאָתִי בְּתוֹכָם — *He was zealous for My sake in their midst.* See the *Sforno's* commentary on verse 4 and the note thereon.

12. אֶת בְּרִיתִי שָׁלוֹם — *My covenant of peace.* Angels, although they represent opposing forces and are diverse in their mission and purpose, are still able to exist in peace with one another. We learn this from the verse in *Job* cited by the *Sforno* in his commentary on this verse. The angel of death, however, represents the ultimate force of negation, deprivation and loss which results from opposing, conflicting forces (הִתְנַגְּדוּת הַהֲפָכִים). In other words, the angel of death is the only angel who cannot coexist in peace with the other angels on High. Pinchas, who is the personification of peace, possesses the antidote to death and consequently merits longevity, and perhaps even eternal life. The *Sforno* cites various verses to confirm Pinchas' longevity, as well as the opinion of one Sage that Pinchas and Elijah are the same person which would mean that he still lives and exists (חַי וְקַיָּם).

The episode of the concubine in Givah is recorded in the Book of *Judges* as is that of Yiftach. The former tragic event involved the tribe of Benjamin against whom all of the other tribes did battle after receiving an affirmative answer from the Urim and Tummim (אוּרִים וְתֻמִּים) through

PARASHAS PINCHAS

[10] *HASHEM spoke to Moses, saying:* [11] *Phineas, son of Elazar, son of Aaron the Kohen, turned back My wrath from upon the Children of Israel, when he zealously avenged Me among them, so I did not consume the Children of Israel in My vengeance.* [12] *Therefore, say: Behold! I give him My covenant of peace.* [13] *And it shall be for him and his offspring after him a covenant of eternal priesthood, because he took vengeance for his God, and he atoned for the Children of Israel.*

[14] *The name of the slain Israelite man who was slain with the Midianitess was Zimri son of Salu, leader of a father's house of the Simeonites.* [15] *And the name of the slain Midianite woman was Cozbi daughter of Zur, who was head of the peoples of a father's house in Midian.*

[16] *HASHEM spoke to Moses, saying:* [17] *Harass the Midianites and smite them;* [18] *for they harassed you through their conspiracy that they conspired against you in the matter of Peor, and in the matter of Cozbi, daughter of a leader of Midian, their sister, who was slain on the day of the plague, in the matter of Peor.*

26

[1] *It was after the plague — HASHEM spoke to Moses and to Elazar son of Aaron the Kohen, saying:* [2] *Take a census of the entire assembly of the Children of Israel, from twenty and above, according to their father's houses,*

Elijah and Pinchas are one (and the same) for he (Elijah) still lives and exists.

13. תַּחַת אֲשֶׁר קִנֵּא לֵאלֹהָיו — *Because he was zealous for his God* . . . and since he fought My battle, I shall save him from strife (caused by) any opposition, and he shall have peace.

וַיְכַפֵּר עַל בְּנֵי יִשְׂרָאֵל — *And made atonement for the Children of Israel* . . . by avenging (God's honor) publicly in order that they find atonement for failing to protest against the sinners, and therefore he is worthy (to be granted) an everlasting priesthood through which he will atone for them.

14. וְשֵׁם אִישׁ יִשְׂרָאֵל הַמֻּכֶּה — *The name of the man of Israel who was slain.* And this (reward is given) because he atoned for them in a manner which demanded a willingness to expose oneself to danger by publicly killing a (Jewish) prince and a (heathen) princess.

NOTES

Pinchas. The latter episode is that of Yiftach's daughter who was the first to come out of her father's house upon his return from his victory over Ammon. He had vowed to sacrifice the first one who came forth to greet him, and according to the Midrash, Pinchas refused to go and absolve him from this vow. Since these two events occurred hundreds of years after the conquest of the land, Pinchas, perforce, was a very old man at that time. The tradition that Pinchas and Elijah were one and the same is brought by *Rashi* in tractate *Bava Metzia* (114b) regarding Rabbah bar Abuhu who met Elijah in a cemetery and asked him a halachic question, after which he expressed his amazement that a *Kohen* should be in a cemetery. *Rashi* explains that since according to tradition Elijah and Pinchas were one and the same, perforce Elijah (Pinchas) was a *Kohen*.

13. וַיְכַפֵּר עַל בְּנֵי יִשְׂרָאֵל — *And made atonement for the Children of Israel.* The mission of a *Kohen* is to perform the service of God at the Altar through which he atones for the sins of the Children of Israel. It is therefore most fitting that Pinchas, who atoned for Israel's transgressions at the risk of his own life, should be granted the covenant of everlasting priesthood.

14. וְשֵׁם אִישׁ יִשְׂרָאֵל הַמֻּכֶּה — *The name of the man of Israel who was slain.* The Torah does not reveal the name of sinners unless it serves an educational purpose. The *Sforno*, similar to *Rashi*, explains that the reason the Torah records the name of Zimri, prince of the tribe of Simeon, as well as informing us that the woman was a Midianite princess, is to underscore the willingness of Pinchas to defend God's honor, even at the risk of his own life.

ג כָּל־יֹצֵא צָבָא בְּיִשְׂרָאֵל: וַיְדַבֵּר מֹשֶׁה וְאֶלְעָזָר הַכֹּהֵן אֹתָם בְּעַרְבֹת
ד מוֹאָב עַל־יַרְדֵּן יְרֵחוֹ לֵאמֹר: מִבֶּן עֶשְׂרִים שָׁנָה וָמָעְלָה כַּאֲשֶׁר° צִוָּה יהוה
שני ה אֶת־מֹשֶׁה וּבְנֵי יִשְׂרָאֵל הַיֹּצְאִים מֵאֶרֶץ מִצְרָיִם: רְאוּבֵן בְּכוֹר יִשְׂרָאֵל
ו בְּנֵי רְאוּבֵן חֲנוֹךְ מִשְׁפַּחַת הַחֲנֹכִי לְפַלּוּא מִשְׁפַּחַת הַפַּלֻּאִי: לְחֶצְרֹן
ז מִשְׁפַּחַת הַחֶצְרוֹנִי לְכַרְמִי מִשְׁפַּחַת הַכַּרְמִי: אֵלֶּה מִשְׁפְּחֹת הָרְאוּבֵנִי
ח וַיִּהְיוּ פְקֻדֵיהֶם שְׁלֹשָׁה וְאַרְבָּעִים אֶלֶף וּשְׁבַע מֵאוֹת וּשְׁלֹשִׁים: וּבְנֵי פַלּוּא
ט אֱלִיאָב: וּבְנֵי אֱלִיאָב נְמוּאֵל וְדָתָן וַאֲבִירָם הוּא־דָתָן וַאֲבִירָם °קרואי
הָעֵדָה אֲשֶׁר הִצּוּ עַל־מֹשֶׁה וְעַל־אַהֲרֹן בַּעֲדַת־קֹרַח בְּהַצֹּתָם עַל־יהוה: °קְרִיאֵי ק׳
י וַתִּפְתַּח הָאָרֶץ אֶת־פִּיהָ וַתִּבְלַע אֹתָם וְאֶת־קֹרַח בְּמוֹת הָעֵדָה בַּאֲכֹל
יא הָאֵשׁ אֵת חֲמִשִּׁים וּמָאתַיִם אִישׁ וַיִּהְיוּ לְנֵס: וּבְנֵי־קֹרַח לֹא־מֵתוּ: בְּנֵי
יב שִׁמְעוֹן לְמִשְׁפְּחֹתָם לִנְמוּאֵל מִשְׁפַּחַת
יג הַנְּמוּאֵלִי לְיָמִין מִשְׁפַּחַת הַיָּמִינִי לְיָכִין מִשְׁפַּחַת הַיָּכִינִי: לְזֶרַח מִשְׁפַּחַת
יד הַזַּרְחִי לְשָׁאוּל מִשְׁפַּחַת הַשָּׁאוּלִי: אֵלֶּה מִשְׁפְּחֹת הַשִּׁמְעֹנִי שְׁנַיִם
טו וְעֶשְׂרִים אֶלֶף וּמָאתָיִם: בְּנֵי גָד לְמִשְׁפְּחֹתָם לִצְפוֹן
טז מִשְׁפַּחַת הַצְּפוֹנִי לְחַגִּי מִשְׁפַּחַת הַחַגִּי לְשׁוּנִי מִשְׁפַּחַת הַשּׁוּנִי: לְאָזְנִי
יז מִשְׁפַּחַת הָאָזְנִי לְעֵרִי מִשְׁפַּחַת הָעֵרִי: לַאֲרוֹד מִשְׁפַּחַת הָאֲרוֹדִי
יח לְאַרְאֵלִי מִשְׁפַּחַת הָאַרְאֵלִי: אֵלֶּה מִשְׁפְּחֹת בְּנֵי־גָד לִפְקֻדֵיהֶם אַרְבָּעִים
יט אֶלֶף וַחֲמֵשׁ מֵאוֹת: בְּנֵי יְהוּדָה עֵר וְאוֹנָן וַיָּמָת עֵר
כ וְאוֹנָן בְּאֶרֶץ כְּנָעַן: וַיִּהְיוּ בְנֵי־יְהוּדָה לְמִשְׁפְּחֹתָם לְשֵׁלָה מִשְׁפַּחַת הַשֵּׁלָנִי
כא לְפֶרֶץ מִשְׁפַּחַת הַפַּרְצִי לְזֶרַח מִשְׁפַּחַת הַזַּרְחִי: וַיִּהְיוּ בְנֵי־פֶרֶץ לְחֶצְרֹן
כב מִשְׁפַּחַת הַחֶצְרֹנִי לְחָמוּל מִשְׁפַּחַת הֶחָמוּלִי: אֵלֶּה מִשְׁפְּחֹת יְהוּדָה
כג לִפְקֻדֵיהֶם שִׁשָּׁה וְשִׁבְעִים אֶלֶף וַחֲמֵשׁ מֵאוֹת: בְּנֵי יִשָּׂשכָר לְמִשְׁפְּחֹתָם
כד תּוֹלָע מִשְׁפַּחַת הַתּוֹלָעִי לְפֻוָּה מִשְׁפַּחַת הַפּוּנִי: לְיָשׁוּב מִשְׁפַּחַת הַיָּשֻׁבִי
כה לְשִׁמְרֹן מִשְׁפַּחַת הַשִּׁמְרֹנִי: אֵלֶּה מִשְׁפְּחֹת יִשָּׂשכָר לִפְקֻדֵיהֶם אַרְבָּעָה
כו וְשִׁשִּׁים אֶלֶף וּשְׁלֹשׁ מֵאוֹת: בְּנֵי זְבוּלֻן לְמִשְׁפְּחֹתָם
לְסֶרֶד מִשְׁפַּחַת הַסַּרְדִּי לְאֵלוֹן מִשְׁפַּחַת הָאֵלֹנִי לְיַחְלְאֵל מִשְׁפַּחַת
כז הַיַּחְלְאֵלִי: אֵלֶּה מִשְׁפְּחֹת הַזְּבוּלֹנִי לִפְקֻדֵיהֶם שִׁשִּׁים אֶלֶף וַחֲמֵשׁ
כח-כט מֵאוֹת: בְּנֵי יוֹסֵף לְמִשְׁפְּחֹתָם מְנַשֶּׁה וְאֶפְרָיִם: בְּנֵי מְנַשֶּׁה
לְמָכִיר מִשְׁפַּחַת הַמָּכִירִי וּמָכִיר הוֹלִיד אֶת־גִּלְעָד לְגִלְעָד מִשְׁפַּחַת
ל הַגִּלְעָדִי: אֵלֶּה בְּנֵי גִלְעָד אִיעֶזֶר מִשְׁפַּחַת הָאִיעֶזְרִי לְחֵלֶק מִשְׁפַּחַת
לא-לב הַחֶלְקִי: וְאַשְׂרִיאֵל מִשְׁפַּחַת הָאַשְׂרִאֵלִי וְשֶׁכֶם מִשְׁפַּחַת הַשִּׁכְמִי: וּשְׁמִידָע

XXVI

3-4. לֵאמֹר מִבֶּן עֶשְׂרִים שָׁנָה וָמָעְלָה — *Saying,* (*Take the sum of the people*) *from twenty years old and upwards.* Moses and Elazar said to Israel that they should relate and report all individuals who were twenty years of age.

כַּאֲשֶׁר צִוָּה ה׳ אֶת מֹשֶׁה וּבְנֵי יִשְׂרָאֵל הַיֹּצְאִים מֵאֶרֶץ מִצְרָיִם — *As* HASHEM *commanded Moses*

all who go out to the legion in Israel.
[3] Moses and Elazar the Kohen spoke to them in the plains of Moab, by the
Jordan near Jericho, saying: [4] "From twenty years of age and above, as
HASHEM had commanded Moses and the Children of Israel, who were
coming out of the land of Egypt."
[5] Reuben the firstborn of Israel — the sons of Reuben: of Hanoch, the
Hanochite family; of Pallu, the Palluite family; [6] of Hezron, the Hezronite
family; of Carmi, the Carmite family. [7] These are the families of the
Reubenites; their count was forty-three thousand, seven hundred and
thirty.[8] The sons of Pallu: Eliab. [9] And the sons of Eliab: Nemuel and
Dathan and Abiram, the same Dathan and Abiram who were summoned
by the assembly, who contended against Moses and Aaron among the
assembly of Korah, when they contended against HASHEM. [10] Then the
earth opened its mouth and swallowed them and Korah with the death of
the assembly, when the fire consumed two hundred and fifty men — and
they became a sign. [11] But the sons of Korah did not die.
[12] The sons of Simeon according to their families: of Nemuel, the Nemu-
elite family; of Jamin, the Jaminite family; of Jachin, the Jachinite family;
[13] of Zerah, the Zerahite family; of Shaul, the Shaulite family. [14] These are
the families of the Simeonites: twenty-two thousand, two hundred.
[15] The sons of Gad according to their families: of Zephon, the Zephonite
family; of Haggi, the Haggite family; of Shuni, the Shunite family; [16] of
Ozni, the Oznite family; of Eri, the Erite family; [17] of Arod, the Arodite
family; of Areli, the Arelite family. [18] These are the families of the sons of
Gad according to their count forty thousand, five hundred.
[19] The sons of Judah, Er and Onan; Er and Onan died in the land of
Canaan. [20] The sons of Judah according to their families were: of Shelah,
the Shelanite family; of Perez, the Perezite family; of Zerah, the Zerahite
family. [21] The sons of Peretz were: of Hezron, the Hezronite family; of
Hamul, the Hamulite family. [22] These are the families of Judah according to
their count: seventy-six thousand, five hundred.
[23] The sons of Issachar according to their families were: Tola, the Tolaite
family; of Puvah, the Punite family; [24] of Jashub, the Jashubite family; of
Shimron, the Shimronite family. [25] These are the families of Issachar
according to their count: sixty-four thousand, three hundred.
[26] The sons of Zebulun according to their families: of Sered, the Seredite
family; of Elon, the Elonite family; of Jahleel, the Jahleelite family. [27] These
are the families of the Zebulunites according to their count: sixty thousand,
five hundred.
[28] The sons of Joseph according to their families: Manasseh and Ephraim.
[29] The sons of Manasseh: of Machir, the Machirite family, and Machir
begat Gilead; of Gilead, the Gileadite family. [30] These are the sons of Gilead:
of Iezer, the Iezerite family; of Helek, the Helekite family; [31] of Asriel,
the Asrielite family; of Shechem, the Shechemite family; [32] of Shemida,

---

and the Children of Israel who went forth out of the land of Egypt . . . as He said at that time: *after their families, by the house of their fathers* (1:2).

לג מִשְׁפַּחַת הַשְּׁמִידָעִי וְחֵפֶר מִשְׁפַּחַת הַחֶפְרִי: וּצְלָפְחָד בֶּן־חֵפֶר לֹא־הָיוּ
לוֹ בָּנִים כִּי אִם־בָּנוֹת וְשֵׁם בְּנוֹת צְלָפְחָד מַחְלָה וְנֹעָה חָגְלָה מִלְכָּה
לד וְתִרְצָה: אֵלֶּה מִשְׁפְּחֹת מְנַשֶּׁה וּפְקֻדֵיהֶם שְׁנַיִם וַחֲמִשִּׁים אֶלֶף וּשְׁבַע
לה מֵאוֹת: אֵלֶּה בְנֵי־אֶפְרַיִם לְמִשְׁפְּחֹתָם לְשׁוּתֶלַח
מִשְׁפַּחַת הַשֻּׁתַלְחִי לְבֶכֶר מִשְׁפַּחַת הַבַּכְרִי לְתַחַן מִשְׁפַּחַת הַתַּחֲנִי:
לו־לז וְאֵלֶּה בְּנֵי שׁוּתָלַח לְעֵרָן מִשְׁפַּחַת הָעֵרָנִי: אֵלֶּה מִשְׁפְּחֹת בְּנֵי־אֶפְרַיִם
לִפְקֻדֵיהֶם שְׁנַיִם וּשְׁלֹשִׁים אֶלֶף וַחֲמֵשׁ מֵאוֹת אֵלֶּה בְנֵי־יוֹסֵף
לח לְמִשְׁפְּחֹתָם: בְּנֵי בִנְיָמִן לְמִשְׁפְּחֹתָם לְבֶלַע מִשְׁפַּחַת הַבַּלְעִי
לט לְאַשְׁבֵּל מִשְׁפַּחַת הָאַשְׁבֵּלִי לַאֲחִירָם מִשְׁפַּחַת הָאֲחִירָמִי: לִשְׁפוּפָם
מ מִשְׁפַּחַת הַשּׁוּפָמִי לְחוּפָם מִשְׁפַּחַת הַחוּפָמִי: וַיִּהְיוּ בְנֵי־בֶלַע אַרְדְּ וְנַעֲמָן
מא מִשְׁפַּחַת הָאַרְדִּי לְנַעֲמָן מִשְׁפַּחַת הַנַּעֲמִי: אֵלֶּה בְנֵי־בִנְיָמִן לְמִשְׁפְּחֹתָם
מב וּפְקֻדֵיהֶם חֲמִשָּׁה וְאַרְבָּעִים אֶלֶף וְשֵׁשׁ מֵאוֹת: אֵלֶּה
בְנֵי־דָן לְמִשְׁפְּחֹתָם לְשׁוּחָם מִשְׁפַּחַת הַשּׁוּחָמִי אֵלֶּה מִשְׁפְּחֹת דָּן
מג לְמִשְׁפְּחֹתָם: כָּל־מִשְׁפְּחֹת הַשּׁוּחָמִי לִפְקֻדֵיהֶם אַרְבָּעָה וְשִׁשִּׁים אֶלֶף
מד וְאַרְבַּע מֵאוֹת: בְּנֵי אָשֵׁר לְמִשְׁפְּחֹתָם לְיִמְנָה מִשְׁפַּחַת
מה הַיִּמְנָה לְיִשְׁוִי מִשְׁפַּחַת הַיִּשְׁוִי לִבְרִיעָה מִשְׁפַּחַת הַבְּרִיעִי: לִבְנֵי בְרִיעָה
מו לְחֶבֶר מִשְׁפַּחַת הַחֶבְרִי לְמַלְכִּיאֵל מִשְׁפַּחַת הַמַּלְכִּיאֵלִי: וְשֵׁם בַּת־אָשֵׁר
מז שָׂרַח: אֵלֶּה מִשְׁפְּחֹת בְּנֵי־אָשֵׁר לִפְקֻדֵיהֶם שְׁלֹשָׁה וַחֲמִשִּׁים אֶלֶף וְאַרְבַּע
מח מֵאוֹת: בְּנֵי נַפְתָּלִי לְמִשְׁפְּחֹתָם לְיַחְצְאֵל מִשְׁפַּחַת
מט הַיַּחְצְאֵלִי לְגוּנִי מִשְׁפַּחַת הַגּוּנִי: לְיֵצֶר מִשְׁפַּחַת הַיִּצְרִי לְשִׁלֵּם מִשְׁפַּחַת
נ הַשִּׁלֵּמִי: אֵלֶּה מִשְׁפְּחֹת נַפְתָּלִי לְמִשְׁפְּחֹתָם וּפְקֻדֵיהֶם חֲמִשָּׁה וְאַרְבָּעִים
נא אֶלֶף וְאַרְבַּע מֵאוֹת: אֵלֶּה פְּקוּדֵי בְּנֵי יִשְׂרָאֵל שֵׁשׁ־מֵאוֹת אֶלֶף וָאָלֶף
שְׁבַע מֵאוֹת וּשְׁלֹשִׁים:
נב־נג וַיְדַבֵּר יהוה אֶל־מֹשֶׁה לֵּאמֹר: לָאֵלֶּה תֵּחָלֵק הָאָרֶץ בְּנַחֲלָה בְּמִסְפַּר שלישי
נד שֵׁמוֹת: לָרַב תַּרְבֶּה נַחֲלָתוֹ וְלַמְעַט תַּמְעִיט נַחֲלָתוֹ אִישׁ לְפִי פְקֻדָיו יֻתַּן

54. לָרַב תַּרְבֶּה נַחֲלָתוֹ — *To the numerous you shall increase the inheritance.* (This increase refers to) the quantity of the land (allotted) because the land was divided into twelve portions equal in value, although unequal quantitatively. Rather, a *kor* of inferior quality (was given) as the equivalent of a good piece of land sufficient to sow a *seah.* Now, the tribe that was numerous took a portion larger in area while the tribe that was lesser took a smaller portion in quantity but in value it was equal to the larger portion, as it says, *to the numerous you shall increase the inheritance* (33:54). In this manner, Menasseh and Ephraim received two portions because of Joseph's birthright as a firstborn, as it says, נָתַתִּי לְךָ שְׁכֶם אַחַד עַל אַחֶיךָ, *I have given you one portion, Shechem, above your brothers*

NOTES

XXVI

54. לָרַב תַּרְבֶּה נַחֲלָתוֹ — *To the numerous you shall increase the inheritance. Rashi's* commentary on this verse explains that, in addition to giving a larger portion to the tribe that had a numerous population, the fertility and value of the soil also had to be considered, and thus an inferior piece of land sufficient to sow a *kor* (a measure mentioned in the Mishnah and Talmud) was regarded as the equivalent of a good piece of land sufficient to

the Shemidaite family; of Hepher, the Hepherite family. 33 *Zelophehad son*
of Hepher had no sons, only daughters; and the names of Zelophehad's
daughters: Mahlah, Noah, Hoglah, Milcah, and Tirzah. 34 *These are the*
families of Manasseh, and their count: fifty-two thousand, seven hundred.
35 *These are the sons of Ephraim according to their families: of Shuthelah,*
the Shuthelahite family; of Becher, the Becherite family; of Tahan, the
Tahanite family 36 *And these are the sons of Shuthelah: of Eran, the Eranite*
family. 37 *These are the families of the sons of Ephraim according to their*
count: thirty-two thousand, five hundred. These are the sons of Joseph
according to their families.
38 *The sons of Benjamin according to their families: of Bela, the Belaite*
family; of Ashbel, the Ashbelite family; of Ahiram, the Ahiramite family;
39 *of Shephupham, the Shephuphamite family; of Hupham, the Huphamite*
family. 40 *And the sons of Bela were Ard and Naaman: the Ardite family;*
of Naaman, the Naamanite family. 41 *These are the sons of Benjamin ac-*
cording to their families, and their count: forty-five thousand, six hundred.
42 *These are the sons of Dan according to their families: of Shuham, the*
Shuhamite family. These are the families of Dan according to their
families. 43 *All the Shuhamite families according to their count: sixty-four*
thousand, four hundred.
44 *The sons of Asher according to their families: of Imnah, the Imnite*
family; of Ishvi, the Ishvite family; of Beriah, the Beriite family; 45 *of the*
sons of Beriah: of Heber, the Heberite family; of Malchiel, the Malchielite
family. 46 *The name of Asher's daughter: Serah.* 47 *These are the families of*
the sons of Asher according to their count: fifty-three thousand, four
hundred.
48 *The sons of Naphtali according to their families: of Jahzeel, the Jahzeel-*
ite family; of Guni, the Gunite family; 49 *of Jezer, the Jezerite family; of*
Shillem, the Shillemite family. 50 *These are the families of Naphtali accord-*
ing to their families, and their count: forty-five thousand, four hundred.
51 *These are the countings of the sons of Israel: six hundred and one*
thousand, seven hundred and thirty.
52 *HASHEM spoke to Moses, saying:* 53 *To these shall the Land be divided*
as an inheritance, according to the number of names. 54 *For the numerous one*
you shall increase its inheritance, and for the fewer one you shall lessen its
inheritance; each one according to his count shall his inheritance be given.

(*Genesis* 48:22), and so it is explained in *I Chronicles* 5:1, וּבְחַלְּלוֹ יְצוּעֵי אָבִיו נִתְּנָה בְּכֹרָתוֹ לִבְנֵי יוֹסֵף בֶּן יִשְׂרָאֵל, *But since he defiled his father's bed, his birthright was given to the sons of Joseph, the son of Israel.* Now, to Simeon, who was the least numerous of all the tribes when they entered the Land, was given the smallest portion in quantity (but) very valuable, and since there was no continuous concentrated tract of land of sufficient value

NOTES

plant a *seah*, which is the 30th part of a *kor*. The *Ramban* interprets this verse to mean that each family should receive an allotment proportionate to the number of its members. While each tribe was given an equal share of the land, that share was subdivided among its families, each family receiving a portion according to its number.

The *Sforno*, while following the lead of *Rashi* in his commentary, adds two important points. He explains that since quantity and quality were both

נה נַחֲלָתֽוֹ: אַךְ־בְּגוֹרָ֗ל יֵחָלֵ֖ק אֶת־הָאָ֑רֶץ לִשְׁמ֥וֹת מַטּוֹת־אֲבֹתָ֖ם יִנְחָֽלוּ:

נו-נז עַל־פִּי֙ הַגּוֹרָ֔ל תֵּחָלֵ֖ק נַחֲלָת֑וֹ בֵּ֥ין רַ֖ב לִמְעָֽט: וְאֵ֙לֶּה֙ פְּקוּדֵ֣י הַלֵּוִ֜י לְמִשְׁפְּחֹתָ֗ם לְגֵרְשׁ֞וֹן מִשְׁפַּ֤חַת הַגֵּֽרְשֻׁנִּי֙ לִקְהָ֔ת מִשְׁפַּ֖חַת הַקְּהָתִ֑י

נח לִמְרָרִ֕י מִשְׁפַּ֖חַת הַמְּרָרִֽי: אֵ֣לֶּה | מִשְׁפְּחֹ֣ת לֵוִ֗י מִשְׁפַּ֤חַת הַלִּבְנִי֙ מִשְׁפַּ֣חַת הַחֶבְרֹנִ֔י מִשְׁפַּ֥חַת הַמַּחְלִ֖י מִשְׁפַּ֣חַת הַמּוּשִׁ֑י מִשְׁפַּ֖חַת הַקָּרְחִ֑י וּקְהָ֖ת הוֹלִ֥ד

נט אֶת־עַמְרָֽם: וְשֵׁ֣ם | אֵ֣שֶׁת עַמְרָ֗ם יוֹכֶ֙בֶד֙ בַּת־לֵוִ֔י אֲשֶׁ֨ר יָֽלְדָ֥ה אֹתָ֛הּ לְלֵוִ֖י

ס בְּמִצְרָ֑יִם וַתֵּ֣לֶד לְעַמְרָ֗ם אֶת־אַהֲרֹן֙ וְאֶת־מֹשֶׁ֔ה וְאֵ֖ת מִרְיָ֥ם אֲחֹתָֽם: וַיִּוָּלֵ֣ד

סא לְאַהֲרֹ֔ן אֶת־נָדָ֖ב וְאֶת־אֲבִיה֑וּא אֶת־אֶלְעָזָ֖ר וְאֶת־אִֽיתָמָֽר: וַיָּ֥מָת נָדָ֖ב

סב וַֽאֲבִיה֗וּא בְּהַקְרִיבָ֥ם אֵשׁ־זָרָ֖ה לִפְנֵ֥י יהוֹֽה: וַיִּֽהְי֣וּ פְקֻֽדֵיהֶ֗ם שְׁלֹשָׁ֤ה וְעֶשְׂרִים֙ אֶ֔לֶף כָּל־זָכָ֖ר מִבֶּן־חֹ֣דֶשׁ וָמָ֑עְלָה כִּ֣י | לֹ֣א הָתְפָּֽקְד֗וּ בְּתוֹךְ֙ בְּנֵ֣י יִשְׂרָאֵ֔ל כִּ֣י

סג לֹא־נִתַּ֤ן לָהֶם֙ נַֽחֲלָ֔ה בְּת֖וֹךְ בְּנֵ֥י יִשְׂרָאֵֽל: אֵ֚לֶּה פְּקוּדֵ֣י מֹשֶׁ֔ה וְאֶלְעָזָ֖ר הַכֹּהֵ֑ן אֲשֶׁ֣ר פָּֽקְד֗וּ אֶת־בְּנֵ֣י יִשְׂרָאֵ֔ל בְּעַרְבֹ֖ת מוֹאָ֑ב עַ֖ל יַרְדֵּ֥ן יְרֵחֽוֹ:

סד וּבְאֵ֙לֶּה֙ לֹא־הָ֣יָה אִ֔ישׁ מִפְּקוּדֵ֣י מֹשֶׁ֔ה וְאַֽהֲרֹ֖ן הַכֹּהֵ֑ן אֲשֶׁ֥ר פָּֽקְד֛וּ אֶת־בְּנֵֽי־

סה יִשְׂרָאֵ֖ל בְּמִדְבַּ֥ר סִינָֽי: כִּֽי־אָמַ֤ר יהוֹה֙ לָהֶ֔ם מ֥וֹת יָמֻ֖תוּ בַּמִּדְבָּ֑ר וְלֹא־נוֹתַ֤ר

כז

א מֵהֶם֙ אִ֔ישׁ כִּ֚י אִם־כָּלֵ֣ב בֶּן־יְפֻנֶּ֔ה וִֽיהוֹשֻׁ֖עַ בִּן־נֽוּן: וַתִּקְרַ֜בְנָה בְּנ֣וֹת צְלָפְחָ֗ד בֶּן־חֵ֤פֶר בֶּן־גִּלְעָד֙ בֶּן־מָכִ֣יר בֶּן־מְנַשֶּׁ֔ה לְמִשְׁפְּחֹ֖ת מְנַשֶּׁ֣ה בֶן־יוֹסֵ֑ף וְאֵ֙לֶּה֙ שְׁמ֣וֹת בְּנֹתָ֔יו מַחְלָ֣ה נֹעָ֔ה וְחָגְלָ֥ה וּמִלְכָּ֖ה וְתִרְצָֽה:

ב וַֽתַּעֲמֹ֜דְנָה לִפְנֵ֣י מֹשֶׁ֗ה וְלִפְנֵי֙ אֶלְעָזָ֣ר הַכֹּהֵ֔ן וְלִפְנֵ֥י הַנְּשִׂיאִ֖ם וְכָל־הָֽעֵדָ֑ה

ג פֶּ֥תַח אֹֽהֶל־מוֹעֵ֖ד לֵאמֹֽר: אָבִ֘ינוּ֮ מֵ֣ת בַּמִּדְבָּר֒ וְה֨וּא לֹֽא־הָיָ֜ה בְּת֣וֹךְ הָֽעֵדָ֗ה הַנּֽוֹעָדִ֛ים עַל־יהוֹה֖ בַּֽעֲדַת־קֹ֑רַח כִּֽי־בְחֶטְא֣וֹ מֵ֔ת וּבָנִ֖ים לֹא־הָ֥יוּ לֽוֹ:

---

for Simeon's share, his portion was chosen from a number of places in the land of Judah, as it says, מֵחֶבֶל בְּנֵי יְהוּדָה נַחֲלַת בְּנֵי שִׁמְעוֹן, *Out of the portion of the children of Judah was the inheritance of the children of Simeon* (Joshua 19:9), and thus was fulfilled regarding the tribe of Simeon (the prophecy of Jacob), אֲחַלְּקֵם בְּיַעֲקֹב, *I will divide them in Jacob* (Genesis 49:7).

55. אַךְ בְּגוֹרָל — *Notwithstanding, by lot.* Although the (land was) divided into larger and smaller portions according to the needs of the tribes and their size, (nonetheless) no portion was given to a tribe except *according to the lot*, and thus each tribe received its portion according to God.

56. עַל פִּי הַגּוֹרָל תֵּחָלֵק נַחֲלָתוֹ — *According to the lot shall the possession be divided . . .* and when the tribe allotted portions according to the number (of individuals) in each family,

NOTES

taken into account, one can now understand the advantage gained by Menasseh and Ephraim in being considered as two tribes. For one could well ask, even if they were but one tribe, would they not receive land according to their total numbers? However, once we are told that the value of the land is a determinant, the advantage of receiving a portion as a distinct separate tribe becomes apparent. The second point made by the *Sforno* is regarding Simeon. Jacob, in his blessing (*parashas Vayechi*), had said אֲחַלְּקֵם בְּיַעֲקֹב, *I will divide them*

in Jacob — and וַאֲפִיצֵם בְּיִשְׂרָאֵל, *and I will scatter them in Israel* (Genesis 49:7). The *Sforno* explains that this prophecy was fulfilled, not by denying them a permanent portion in the Land (which was never the intent of Jacob), but by giving them land of superior quality since they were few numerically. Perforce, this had to involve different areas since there was not sufficient contiguous good land to meet the quota of land to which Simeon was entitled, thereby realizing the prophecy of his father.

[55] Only by lot shall the Land be divided, according to the names of their fathers' tribes shall they inherit. [56] According to the lot shall one's inheritance be divided, between the numerous and the few.

[57] These are the countings of the Levites, according to their families: of Gershon, the Gershonite family; of Kohath, the Kohathite family; of Merari, the Merarite family. [58] These are the Levite families: the Libnite family; the Hebronite family; the Mahlite family; the Mushite family; the Korahite family; and Kohath begat Amram. [59] The name of Amram's wife was Jocheved, daughter of Levi, who was born to Levi in Egypt; and she bore to Amram Aaron, Moses, and their sister Miriam. [60] To Aaron were born Nadab and Abihu, Elazar and Ithamar. [61] Nadab and Abihu died when they brought an alien fire before HASHEM. [62] Their counts were twenty-three thousand, every male from one month of age and above, for they did not count themselves among the Children of Israel, for an inheritance was not given them among the Children of Israel.

[63] These are the ones counted by Moses and Elazar the Kohen, who counted the Children of Israel in the plains of Moab, by the Jordan, near Jericho. [64] And of these, there was no man of those counted by Moses and Aaron the Kohen, who counted the Children of Israel in the Wilderness of Sinai. [65] For HASHEM had said of them, "They will surely die in the Wilderness," and not a man was left of them, except for Caleb son of Jephunneh, and Joshua son of Nun.

27 *[1] The daughters of Zelophehad, son of Hepher, son of Gilead, son of Machir, son of Manasseh, of the family of Manasseh son of Joseph drew near — and these are the names of his daughters: Mahlah, Noah, Hoglah, Milcah, and Tirzah — [2] and they stood before Moses, before Elazar the Kohen, and before the leaders and the entire assembly at the entrance to the Tent of Meeting, saying: [3] "Our father died in the Wilderness, but he was not among the assembly that was gathering against HASHEM in the assembly of Korah, but he died of his own sin; and he had no son.*

---

it was also given *according to the lot.*

XXVII

3. וְהוּא לֹא הָיָה — *And he was not.* (He was not) a member of Korach's congregation whose sentence was that all their possessions (lit., money) be condemned (חֵרֶם), for Moses our Teacher did condemn it when he said, סוּרוּ נָא מֵעַל אָהֳלֵי הָאֲנָשִׁים הָרְשָׁעִים הָאֵלֶּה וְאַל תִּגְּעוּ בְּכָל אֲשֶׁר לָהֶם פֶּן תִּסָּפוּ, *Depart, I pray you, from the tents of these wicked men, and touch nothing of theirs, lest you be swept away* (16:26); and they were also judged so by Heavenly law, as it says, וְאֵת כָּל הָרְכוּשׁ, *and all their goods* (16:32).

כִּי בְחֶטְאוֹ מֵת — *But he died in his own sin.* The sole punishment for his sin was that he

NOTES

55. אַךְ בְּגוֹרָל — *Notwithstanding, by lot.* The *Sforno* here reflects the statement of our Sages in *Bava Basra* 122a that although the portions of the land were assigned according to the size of each tribe, nonetheless, it was done through lots, and these lots fell according to רוּחַ הַקֹּדֶשׁ, *the Holy Spirit.* See *Rashi* here who gives a fuller explanation of how these lots fell.

XXVII

3. וְהוּא לֹא הָיָה . . . כִּי בְחֶטְאוֹ מֵת — *And he was not . . . but he died in his own sin.* The Talmud in

ד לָמָּה יִגָּרַע שֵׁם־אָבִינוּ מִתּוֹךְ מִשְׁפַּחְתּוֹ כִּי אֵין לוֹ בֵּן תְּנָה־לָּנוּ אֲחֻזָּה
ה בְּתוֹךְ אֲחֵי אָבִינוּ: וַיַּקְרֵב מֹשֶׁה אֶת־מִשְׁפָּטָן לִפְנֵי יְהוָה: נ׳ רבתי
ו־ז וַיֹּאמֶר יְהוָה אֶל־מֹשֶׁה לֵּאמֹר: כֵּן בְּנוֹת צְלָפְחָד דֹּבְרֹת נָתֹן תִּתֵּן לָהֶם רביעי
אֲחֻזַּת נַחֲלָה בְּתוֹךְ אֲחֵי אֲבִיהֶם וְהַעֲבַרְתָּ אֶת־נַחֲלַת אֲבִיהֶן לָהֶן:
ח וְאֶל־בְּנֵי יִשְׂרָאֵל תְּדַבֵּר לֵאמֹר אִישׁ כִּי־יָמוּת וּבֵן אֵין לוֹ וְהַעֲבַרְתֶּם
ט־י אֶת־נַחֲלָתוֹ לְבִתּוֹ: וְאִם־אֵין לוֹ בַּת וּנְתַתֶּם אֶת־נַחֲלָתוֹ לְאֶחָיו: וְאִם־אֵין
יא לוֹ אַחִים וּנְתַתֶּם אֶת־נַחֲלָתוֹ לַאֲחֵי אָבִיו: וְאִם־אֵין אַחִים לְאָבִיו וּנְתַתֶּם
אֶת־נַחֲלָתוֹ לִשְׁאֵרוֹ הַקָּרֹב אֵלָיו מִמִּשְׁפַּחְתּוֹ וְיָרַשׁ אֹתָהּ וְהָיְתָה לִבְנֵי
יִשְׂרָאֵל לְחֻקַּת מִשְׁפָּט כַּאֲשֶׁר צִוָּה יְהוָה אֶת־מֹשֶׁה:
יב וַיֹּאמֶר יְהוָה אֶל־מֹשֶׁה עֲלֵה אֶל־הַר הָעֲבָרִים הַזֶּה וּרְאֵה אֶת־הָאָרֶץ
יג אֲשֶׁר נָתַתִּי לִבְנֵי יִשְׂרָאֵל: וְרָאִיתָה אֹתָהּ וְנֶאֱסַפְתָּ אֶל־עַמֶּיךָ גַּם־אָתָּה
יד כַּאֲשֶׁר נֶאֱסַף אַהֲרֹן אָחִיךָ: כַּאֲשֶׁר מְרִיתֶם פִּי בְּמִדְבַּר־צִן בִּמְרִיבַת
הָעֵדָה לְהַקְדִּישֵׁנִי בַמַּיִם לְעֵינֵיהֶם הֵם מֵי־מְרִיבַת קָדֵשׁ מִדְבַּר־
טו־טז צִן: וַיְדַבֵּר מֹשֶׁה אֶל־יְהוָה לֵאמֹר: יִפְקֹד יְהוָה אֱלֹהֵי
יז הָרוּחֹת לְכָל־בָּשָׂר אִישׁ עַל־הָעֵדָה: אֲשֶׁר־יֵצֵא לִפְנֵיהֶם וַאֲשֶׁר יָבֹא
לִפְנֵיהֶם וַאֲשֶׁר יוֹצִיאֵם וַאֲשֶׁר יְבִיאֵם וְלֹא תִהְיֶה עֲדַת יְהוָה כַּצֹּאן
יח אֲשֶׁר אֵין־לָהֶם רֹעֶה: וַיֹּאמֶר יְהוָה אֶל־מֹשֶׁה קַח־לְךָ אֶת־יְהוֹשֻׁעַ בִּן־נוּן
יט אִישׁ אֲשֶׁר־רוּחַ בּוֹ וְסָמַכְתָּ אֶת־יָדְךָ עָלָיו: וְהַעֲמַדְתָּ אֹתוֹ לִפְנֵי
כ אֶלְעָזָר הַכֹּהֵן וְלִפְנֵי כָּל־הָעֵדָה וְצִוִּיתָה אֹתוֹ לְעֵינֵיהֶם: וְנָתַתָּה
כא מֵהוֹדְךָ עָלָיו לְמַעַן יִשְׁמְעוּ כָּל־עֲדַת בְּנֵי יִשְׂרָאֵל: וְלִפְנֵי אֶלְעָזָר הַכֹּהֵן

would die, but not that his possessions would be denied his heirs.

17. אֲשֶׁר יֵצֵא לִפְנֵיהֶם — *Who may go out before them* . . . in military affairs. וַאֲשֶׁר יוֹצִיאֵם — *Who may lead them out* . . . in administering national affairs.

18. אִישׁ אֲשֶׁר רוּחַ בּוֹ — *A man in whom is spirit* . . . who is prepared to receive *the light of the living king's countenance* (based on *Proverbs* 16:15), similar to, וּבְלֵב כָּל חֲכַם לֵב נָתַתִּי חָכְמָה, *And in the hearts of all that are wise-hearted I have put wisdom* (*Exodus* 31:6).

19. וְצִוִּיתָה אֹתוֹ לְעֵינֵיהֶם — *And appoint him in their sight.* Appoint him as a ruler over them in their presence so that they shall accept him and listen to him. The phrase צִוּוּי applies to appointment, similar to וְצִוְּךָ לְנָגִיד, *And appoint you as ruler* (*I Samuel* 25:30), and to וּלְמִן הַיּוֹם אֲשֶׁר צִוִּיתִי שֹׁפְטִים, *And as since the time that I appointed judges* (*II Samuel* 7:11).

NOTES

tractate *Bava Basra* 118b states that "the murmurers and the company of Korach did not receive a share in the land." The daughters of Zelaphchad told Moses that their father was not among the company of Korach and therefore, it was not reasonable that his share in the Land should be forfeited due to a different sin which he did commit. According to tradition, he was the man who picked up wood on Shabbos (15:32).

The *Sforno*, as does the *Ramban*, interprets the phrase וְאַל תִּגְּעוּ, *touch nothing* (16:26), as meaning that all the possessions of Korach's group were to be considered as חֵרֶם, a word which means "*set apart*," be it because the item is hallowed or condemned. Now, this admonition of Moses only applied to the possessions of Korach and his company which were at hand, and not necessarily to their share in the Land of Israel. The *Sforno* therefore adds that they were also judged בְּדִינֵי שָׁמַיִם, *through Heavenly justice*, which caused them to forfeit their portion in the Land. He bases this upon the phrase כָּל הָרְכוּשׁ, *all their goods* or substance (16:32), which is all inclusive and includes their share in *Eretz Yisrael*.

4 *Why should the name of our father be omitted from among his family because he had no son? Give us a possession among our father's brothers."*
5 *And Moses brought their claim before* HASHEM.
6 HASHEM *said to Moses, saying,* 7 *"The daughters of Zelophehad speak properly. You shall surely give them a possession of inheritance among the brothers of their father, and you shall cause the inheritance of their father to pass over to them.* 8 *And to the Children of Israel you shall speak, saying: If a man will die and he has no son, you shall cause his inheritance to pass over to his daughter.* 9 *If he has no daughter, you shall give his inheritance to his brothers.* 10 *If he has no brothers, you shall give his inheritance to the brothers of his father.* 11 *If there are no brothers of his father, you shall give his inheritance to the relative who is closest to him of his family, and he shall inherit it. This shall be for the Children of Israel as a decree of justice, as* HASHEM *commanded Moses."*
12 HASHEM *said to Moses, "Go up to this mountain of Abarim and see the Land that I have given to the Children of Israel.* 13 *You shall see it and you shall be gathered unto your people, you, too, as Aaron your brother was gathered in;* 14 *because you rebelled against My word in the Wilderness of Zin, in the assembly's strife, to sanctify Me at the water before their eyes. They were the waters of strife at Kadesh, in the Wilderness of Zin."*
15 *Moses spoke to* HASHEM, *saying,* 16 *"May* HASHEM, *God of the spirits of all flesh, appoint a man over the assembly,* 17 *who shall go out before them and come in before them, who shall take them out and bring them in; and let the assembly of* HASHEM *not be like sheep that have no shepherd."*
18 HASHEM *said to Moses, "Take to yourself Joshua son of Nun, a man in whom there is spirit, and lean your hand upon him.* 19 *You shall stand him before Elazar the Kohen and before the entire assembly, and command him before their eyes.* 20 *You shall place some of your majesty upon him, so that the entire assembly of Israel will pay heed.* 21 *Before Elazar the Kohen*

---

20. וְנָתַתָּה מֵהוֹדְךָ עָלָיו — *And you shall put* (*some*) *of your honor upon him.* (This refers to) the glory of kingship (majesty). Give him some authority in your lifetime so that they (Israel) will begin (at once) to conduct themselves (toward him) with honor.

לְמַעַן יִשְׁמְעוּ — *So that they shall hearken* . . . and the reason for appointing him in their sight and granting him honor in your lifetime is so that the entire congregation, namely the Sanhedrin (courts) and the elders of the people, shall hearken to his voice.

NOTES

18. אִישׁ אֲשֶׁר רוּחַ בּוֹ — *A man in whom is spirit.* The Talmud in tractate *Berachos* 55a says, "The Holy One, Blessed is He, gives wisdom only to one who already has wisdom." R' Abbahu derived this concept from *Exodus* 31:6, which is quoted by the *Sforno* in his commentary on this verse. In other words, God's light and inspiration demands a vessel which is capable of receiving it. That is why God assures Moses that Joshua is indeed such a man — one in whom there is spirit and hence, he will be able to receive additional spirit and wisdom.

19. וְצִוִּיתָה אֹתוֹ לְעֵינֵיהֶם — *And appoint him in their sight.* The *Sforno* explains that the term וְצִוִּיתָה in the context of this verse does not mean *"to command,"* but *"to appoint."* He brings proof from the verses in *Samuel.* See the commentary of the *Sforno* in *Exodus* 6:13 regarding Moses and Aaron where he gives a similar explanation.

20. וְנָתַתָּה מֵהוֹדְךָ עָלָיו — *And you shall put* (*some*) *of your honor upon him.* God impresses upon Moses the importance of establishing Joshua's credentials during his own lifetime, because it is only natural that the elders and judges will be slow in accepting the successor of their Master and

יַעֲמֹד וְשָׁאַל לוֹ בְּמִשְׁפַּט הָאוּרִים לִפְנֵי יְהוָה עַל־פִּיו יֵצְאוּ וְעַל־פִּיו יָבֹאוּ
כב הוּא וְכָל־בְּנֵי־יִשְׂרָאֵל אִתּוֹ וְכָל־הָעֵדָה: וַיַּעַשׂ מֹשֶׁה כַּאֲשֶׁר צִוָּה יְהוָה
אֹתוֹ וַיִּקַּח אֶת־יְהוֹשֻׁעַ וַיַּעֲמִדֵהוּ לִפְנֵי אֶלְעָזָר הַכֹּהֵן וְלִפְנֵי כָּל־הָעֵדָה:
כג וַיִּסְמֹךְ אֶת־יָדָיו עָלָיו וַיְצַוֵּהוּ כַּאֲשֶׁר דִּבֶּר יְהוָה בְּיַד־מֹשֶׁה:
כח חמישי א־ב וַיְדַבֵּר יְהוָה אֶל־מֹשֶׁה לֵּאמֹר: צַו אֶת־בְּנֵי יִשְׂרָאֵל וְאָמַרְתָּ אֲלֵהֶם אֶת־
ג קָרְבָּנִי לַחְמִי לְאִשַּׁי רֵיחַ נִיחֹחִי תִּשְׁמְרוּ לְהַקְרִיב לִי בְּמוֹעֲדוֹ: וְאָמַרְתָּ
לָהֶם זֶה הָאִשֶּׁה אֲשֶׁר תַּקְרִיבוּ לַיהוָה כְּבָשִׂים בְּנֵי־שָׁנָה תְמִימִם שְׁנַיִם
ד לַיּוֹם עֹלָה תָמִיד: אֶת־הַכֶּבֶשׂ אֶחָד תַּעֲשֶׂה בַבֹּקֶר וְאֵת הַכֶּבֶשׂ הַשֵּׁנִי
ה תַּעֲשֶׂה בֵּין הָעַרְבָּיִם: וַעֲשִׂירִית הָאֵיפָה סֹלֶת לְמִנְחָה בְּלוּלָה בְּשֶׁמֶן
ו כָּתִית רְבִיעִת הַהִין: עֹלַת תָּמִיד הָעֲשֻׂיָה בְּהַר סִינַי לְרֵיחַ נִיחֹחַ אִשֶּׁה
ז לַיהוָה: וְנִסְכּוֹ רְבִיעִת הַהִין לַכֶּבֶשׂ הָאֶחָד בַּקֹּדֶשׁ הַסֵּךְ נֶסֶךְ שֵׁכָר לַיהוָה:
ח וְאֵת הַכֶּבֶשׂ הַשֵּׁנִי תַּעֲשֶׂה בֵּין הָעַרְבָּיִם כְּמִנְחַת הַבֹּקֶר וּכְנִסְכּוֹ תַּעֲשֶׂה
אִשֵּׁה רֵיחַ נִיחֹחַ לַיהוָה:
ט וּבְיוֹם הַשַּׁבָּת שְׁנֵי־כְבָשִׂים בְּנֵי־שָׁנָה תְּמִימִם וּשְׁנֵי עֶשְׂרֹנִים סֹלֶת מִנְחָה
י בְּלוּלָה בַשֶּׁמֶן וְנִסְכּוֹ: עֹלַת שַׁבַּת בְּשַׁבַּתּוֹ עַל־עֹלַת הַתָּמִיד וְנִסְכָּהּ:
יא וּבְרָאשֵׁי חָדְשֵׁיכֶם תַּקְרִיבוּ עֹלָה לַיהוָה פָּרִים בְּנֵי־בָקָר שְׁנַיִם וְאַיִל אֶחָד
יב כְּבָשִׂים בְּנֵי־שָׁנָה שִׁבְעָה תְּמִימִם: וּשְׁלֹשָׁה עֶשְׂרֹנִים סֹלֶת מִנְחָה בְּלוּלָה

XXVIII

6. עֹלַת תָּמִיד הָעֲשֻׂיָה בְּהַר סִינַי — *A continual burnt-offering which was offered on Mt. Sinai* . . . (offered) prior to (the sin of) the Golden Calf, at which time it did not necessitate נְסָכִים, *drink offerings.*

8. כְּמִנְחַת הַבֹּקֶר וּכְנִסְכּוֹ תַּעֲשֶׂה אִשֵּׁה רֵיחַ נִיחֹחַ — *As the meal-offering of the morning and as the drink-offering thereof, you shall present it, a burnt-offering, a sweet savor.* Even though, on that very (same) day, you already brought the *morning* burnt-offering, identical to this second one (i.e., the evening offering), nonetheless this second one will also be (acceptable as) *a sweet savor.*

11. וּבְרָאשֵׁי חָדְשֵׁיכֶם — *And on your New Moons.* Behold, it was a custom among the Israelites to observe Rosh Chodesh (the New Moon) as a semi-holy day (festival), as (the verse) testifies saying, אֲשֶׁר נִסְתַּרְתָּ שָׁם בְּיוֹם הַמַּעֲשֶׂה, *Where you hid yourself on the day of the deed* (*I Samuel* 20:19), which implies that Rosh Chodesh was not a day of labor to them. Therefore, (this day) is associated with Israel, as it says, "*your* New Moons," (an expression) not found regarding (other) festivals. It is not written regarding Shabbos, "*your* Sabbaths"

NOTES

Teacher. By sharing some of his authority in his lifetime and by honoring Joshua in their presence, Moses will strengthen the hand and establish the authority of his disciple.

XXVIII

6. עֹלַת תָּמִיד הָעֲשֻׂיָה בְּהַר סִינַי — *A continual burnt-offering which was offered on Mt. Sinai. Rashi* on verse 4 comments, "Although this מִצְוָה has already been stated (in תְּצַוֶּה — *Exodus* 29:38), that instruction (to offer a morning and evening sacrifice of a lamb) was intended for the יְמֵי הַמִּלּוּאִים, *days of installation*, but here the command is for all generations." The *Sforno* gives a different explanation for the repetition, by commenting that although prior to the sin of the Golden Calf the daily sacrifice was indeed brought, it did not include a drink-offering. After that transgression, the drink-offering was added, and that is the reason for the Torah repeating the instruction here in פָּרָשַׁת פִּינְחָס. Indeed, the verse which follows states, *and the drink-offering thereof shall be etc.* (verse 7), which

shall he stand, who shall inquire for him of the judgment of the Urim before HASHEM; at his word shall they go out and at his word shall they come in, he and all the Children of Israel with him, and the entire assembly.
22 *Moses did as HASHEM had commanded him. He took Joshua and stood him before Elazar the Kohen and before the entire assembly.*
23 *He leaned his hands upon him and commanded him, as HASHEM had spoken through Moses.*

28
1 *HASHEM spoke to Moses, saying:*
2 *Command the Children of Israel and say to them: My offering, My food for My fires, My satisfying aroma, shall you be scrupulous to offer to Me in its appointed time.*
3 *And you shall say to them: This is the fire-offering that you are to offer to HASHEM: male lambs in their first year, unblemished, two a day, as a continual elevation-offering.*
4 *The one lamb shall you make in the morning and the second lamb shall you make in the afternoon,*
5 *with a tenth-ephah of fine flour as a meal-offering, mixed with a quarter-hin of crushed oil.*
6 *It is the continual elevation-offering that was done at Mount Sinai, for a satisfying aroma, a fire-offering to HASHEM.*
7 *And its libation is a quarter-hin for the one lamb, to be poured on the holy [Altar], an intoxicating libation for HASHEM.*
8 *The second lamb you shall make in the afternoon; like the meal-offering of the morning and like its libation shall you make, a fire-offering for a satisfying aroma to HASHEM.*
9 *And on the Sabbath day: two male lambs in their first year, unblemished, two tenth-ephah of fine flour for a meal offering, mixed with oil, and its libation.*
10 *The elevation-offering of each Sabbath on its own Sabbath, in addition to the continual elevation-offering and its libation.*
11 *On your New Moons, you shall bring an elevation-offering to HASHEM: two young bulls, one ram, seven male lambs in their first year, unblemished.*
12 *And three tenth-ephah of fine flour for a meal-offering mixed*

(שַׁבַּתְּכֶם), nor (regarding the *bikurim*), "In the day of *your* first fruits" (בִּכּוּרֵיכֶם), nor (regarding Succos), "In the day of *your* booths" (סֻכּוֹתֵיכֶם). Now, the reason for this custom (to observe Rosh Chodesh) is because, to a certain extent, the fate (lit., success) of Israel in this world is similar to that of the moon which has no light of its own whatsoever save that which it receives from another (luminary). This is so because prior to the (sin of the) Golden Calf (they were destined to be in a state of) חָרוּת עַל הַלֻּחֹת, *engraved on the Tablets*

NOTES

supports the *Sforno's* interpretation.

8. כְּמִנְחַת הַבֹּקֶר וּכְנִסְכּוֹ תַּעֲשֶׂה אִשֵּׁה רֵיחַ נִיחֹחַ — *As the meal-offering of the morning and as the drink-offering thereof, you shall present it, a burnt-offering, a sweet savor.* Although the evening sacrifice was identical to that of the morning, hence seemingly a duplication, still it is pleasing to God. As the Sifri quoted by *Rashi* on this verse states, "רֵיחַ נִיחֹחַ — it causes satisfaction to Me, that I commanded and My will was obeyed."

11. וּבְרָאשֵׁי חָדְשֵׁיכֶם — *And on your New Moons.* The *Sforno,* citing the episode of David and Jonathan, supports his contention that Rosh Chodesh was a semi-holiday when labor was not performed. The verse preceding the one quoted by him states, "And Jonathan said to him, 'Tomorrow is (Rosh) Chodesh' ", after which he refers to the day when David hid from Saul as יוֹם הַמַּעֲשֶׂה, *the day of deed,* i.e., a workday, implying that Rosh Chodesh would not be a day of work.

The *Sforno* proceeds to explain why the New Moon is the only festival in this chapter referred to as *your* Rosh Chodesh, indicating a special link between this day and the people of Israel. The moon has no light of its own, for it reflects the light

בְּשֶׁמֶן לַפָּר הָאֶחָד וּשְׁנֵי עֶשְׂרֹנִים סֹלֶת מִנְחָה בְּלוּלָה בַשֶּׁמֶן לָאַיִל
יג הָאֶחָד: וְעִשָּׂרֹן עִשָּׂרוֹן סֹלֶת מִנְחָה בְּלוּלָה בַשֶּׁמֶן לַכֶּבֶשׂ הָאֶחָד עֹלָה
יד רֵיחַ נִיחֹחַ אִשֶּׁה לַיהוָה: וְנִסְכֵּיהֶם חֲצִי הַהִין יִהְיֶה לַפָּר וּשְׁלִישִׁת הַהִין
לָאַיִל וּרְבִיעִת הַהִין לַכֶּבֶשׂ יָיִן זֹאת עֹלַת חֹדֶשׁ בְּחָדְשׁוֹ לְחָדְשֵׁי
טו הַשָּׁנָה: וּשְׂעִיר עִזִּים אֶחָד לְחַטָּאת לַיהוָה עַל־עֹלַת הַתָּמִיד יֵעָשֶׂה
ששי טז וְנִסְכּוֹ: וּבַחֹדֶשׁ הָרִאשׁוֹן בְּאַרְבָּעָה עָשָׂר יוֹם לַחֹדֶשׁ פֶּסַח
יז לַיהוָה: וּבַחֲמִשָּׁה עָשָׂר יוֹם לַחֹדֶשׁ הַזֶּה חָג שִׁבְעַת יָמִים מַצּוֹת יֵאָכֵל:
יח־יט בַּיּוֹם הָרִאשׁוֹן מִקְרָא־קֹדֶשׁ כָּל־מְלֶאכֶת עֲבֹדָה לֹא תַעֲשׂוּ: וְהִקְרַבְתֶּם
אִשֶּׁה עֹלָה לַיהוָה פָּרִים בְּנֵי־בָקָר שְׁנַיִם וְאַיִל אֶחָד וְשִׁבְעָה כְבָשִׂים בְּנֵי
כ שָׁנָה תְּמִימִם יִהְיוּ לָכֶם: וּמִנְחָתָם סֹלֶת בְּלוּלָה בַשָּׁמֶן שְׁלֹשָׁה עֶשְׂרֹנִים
כא לַפָּר וּשְׁנֵי עֶשְׂרֹנִים לָאַיִל תַּעֲשׂוּ: עִשָּׂרוֹן עִשָּׂרוֹן תַּעֲשֶׂה לַכֶּבֶשׂ הָאֶחָד
כב־כג לְשִׁבְעַת הַכְּבָשִׂים: וּשְׂעִיר חַטָּאת אֶחָד לְכַפֵּר עֲלֵיכֶם: מִלְּבַד עֹלַת
כד הַבֹּקֶר אֲשֶׁר לְעֹלַת הַתָּמִיד תַּעֲשׂוּ אֶת־אֵלֶּה: כָּאֵלֶּה תַּעֲשׂוּ לַיּוֹם
שִׁבְעַת יָמִים לֶחֶם אִשֵּׁה רֵיחַ־נִיחֹחַ לַיהוָה עַל־עוֹלַת הַתָּמִיד יֵעָשֶׂה
כה וְנִסְכּוֹ: וּבַיּוֹם הַשְּׁבִיעִי מִקְרָא־קֹדֶשׁ יִהְיֶה לָכֶם כָּל־מְלֶאכֶת עֲבֹדָה לֹא

(*Exodus* 32:16), (interpreted to mean) freedom (חֵרוּת) from the subjugation of (world) kingdoms forever. However, when they sinned with the Golden Calf, (their) crown of kingship was stripped (from them for the time being) and they were not able to employ it continually as do other nations, but it (i.e., kingship) was theirs periodically according to (the extent of) the overflow of Divine Light upon them. Without it (i.e., this light), they walked in darkness and there was no light unto them (based on *Isaiah* 50:10), as is the case of the moon when it does not receive the light (reflection) of the sun — because אֵין מַזָּל לְיִשְׂרָאֵל, *Israel is not subject to the influence of the planets* (*Shabbos* 156a), and they possess no light of their own whatsoever except the light of God, the Blessed One, when they are acceptable (to Him). And therefore, the prophets refer to God, the Blessed One, as the *Light of Israel*, saying, וְהָיָה אוֹר יִשְׂרָאֵל לְאֵשׁ, *And the Light of Israel shall be for a fire* (*Isaiah* 10:17), and so it is attested to when it is said, ה׳ אוֹרִי וְיִשְׁעִי, *HASHEM is my light and my salvation* (*Psalms* 27:1). Now, when (Israel's) sins separated them (from God) as it says, כִּי אִם עֲוֹנֹתֵיכֶם הָיוּ מַבְדִּלִים בֵּינֵכֶם לְבֵין אֱלֹהֵיכֶם וְחַטֹּאותֵיכֶם הִסְתִּירוּ פָנִים מִכֶּם מִשְּׁמוֹעַ, *But your iniquities have separated between you and your God, and your sins have hid His face from you that He will not hear* (*Isaiah* 59:2), they then walked in darkness, bewildered and driven among the nations, and this, without a doubt, caused a profanation of God's Name, בֶּאֱמֹר לָהֶם עַם ה׳ אֵלֶּה, *that it was said of them, these are the people of HASHEM* (*Ezekiel* 36:20), and consequently, to some extent, it lead to the condition of בְּכָל צָרָתָם לוֹ צָר, *In all*

NOTES

of the sun. Israel also has no other source of light than that of the אוֹר ה׳, *the light of God* (as we see in *Psalms* 36:10, *by Your light shall we see light*). That light, however, depends upon their conduct and behavior which, if sinful, dims or obscures the light of God, casting them into a state of darkness. The destiny of Israel is totally determined by the degree of their relationship to God. When they obey God's commandments and conduct their lives in accordance with Torah, they sanctify His Name, and are thereby worthy of His Providence, but when they transgress and defect, they bring about חִלּוּל הַשֵּׁם, *desecration of God's Name*, causing Him to turn away from them.

Every Rosh Chodesh, the moon is reborn and reflects the light of the sun. This is symbolic of Israel's rebirth as well, when they once again find the light of God by atoning for their sins. Not only do they atone for themselves through the sin

with oil, for each bull; and two tenth-ephah of fine flour mixed with oil, for the one ram; [13] *and a tenth-ephah of fine flour for a meal-offering, mixed with oil, for each lamb — an elevation-offering, a satisfying aroma, a fire-offering to* HASHEM. [14] *And their libations: a half-hin for each bull, a third-hin for the ram, a quarter-hin for each lamb — of wine. This is the elevation offering of each month in its own month for the months of the year.* [15] *And one male of the goats for a sin-offering to* HASHEM. *In addition to the continual elevation-offering shall it be made, and its libation.*

[16] *In the first month, on the fourteenth day of the month, shall be a pesach-offering to* HASHEM. [17] *The fifteenth day of this month is a festival; for a seven-day period matzos shall be eaten.* [18] *On the first day is a holy convocation; you shall not do any laborious work.* [19] *You shall offer a fire-offering, an elevation-offering to* HASHEM: *two young bulls, one ram, seven male lambs within their first year, unblemished shall they be for you.* [20] *And their meal-offering: fine flour mixed with oil; you shall make three tenth-ephah for each bull and two tenth-ephah for the ram.* [21] *One tenth-ephah shall you make for each lamb of the seven lambs.* [22] *And one he-goat for a sin-offering, to provide you atonement.* [23] *Aside from the elevation-offering of the morning that is for the continual elevation-offering shall you make these.* [24] *Like these shall you make each day of the seven-day period: food, a fire-offering, a satisfying aroma to* HASHEM; *in addition to the continual elevation-offering shall it be made, and its libation.* [25] *The seventh day shall be a holy convocation for you; you shall not do any laborious work.*

---

their affliction He was afflicted (*Isaiah* 63:9), as our Sages say, "The spoiler (שׁוֹדֵד) is come, as it were, upon Me and upon you" (*Gittin* 58a). Now the sin offering of Rosh Chodesh is meant to be an atonement for Israel who cause the diminishment or prevention of the Divine Light (from shining on them), as our Sages state (in the *siddur*) saying, וּשְׂעִירֵי חַטָּאת לְכַפֵּר בַּעֲדָם זִכָּרוֹן לְכֻלָּם יִהְיוּ וּתְשׁוּעַת נַפְשָׁם מִיַּד שׂוֹנֵא, *and goats of sin-offering to atone on their behalf. They would serve as a remembrance for them all and a salvation for their soul from the hand of the enemy*, and through this atonement there will be, to an extent, salvation for (their sin) of profanation of God's Name. Therefore (our Sages) said it is for this reason (the Torah) says regarding the goat offering of Rosh Chodesh, חַטָּאת לַה׳, *a sin offering for* HASHEM (v. 15), because this atonement effects the sanctification of His Blessed Name; and this was (also) their intent when they said, "The Holy One, Blessed is He, said, 'Bring an atonement for Me for making the moon smaller' " (*Chullin* 60b). This (in essence) means, "Bring an atonement for Me so that you may be able to attain Sanctification of My Name which was profaned among the nations as a result of My making the 'moon' smaller when I exiled Israel and concealed My face from them."

NOTES

offering of Rosh Chodesh, but in a sense, they also atone for God, Who sent them into exile thereby causing the desecration of God's Name. The *Sforno* is interpreting the statement of our Sages in Tractate *Chullin* 60b regarding the diminishment of "the moon" as meaning the diminishment of Israel's sacred status, by their being sent into *galus* by God. This is radically different than the explanation of other commentators. His interpretation of the phrase חַטָּאת לַה׳, *a sin offering for God*, is also different than theirs, since they explain it literally as meaning "for God," i.e., to atone for His unfair treatment of the moon at the time of Creation. The *Sforno*, however, interprets חַטָּאת לַה׳ as a sin offering brought to atone for God's banishment of Israel, which was the prime cause of the desecration of His Holy Name. For this act, He also, as it were, needs atonement.

כו תַּעֲשׂוּ: וּבְיוֹם הַבִּכּוּרִים בְּהַקְרִיבְכֶם מִנְחָה חֲדָשָׁה לַיהוה
יב' טעמים בְּשָׁבֻעֹתֵיכֶם מִקְרָא־קֹדֶשׁ יִהְיֶה לָכֶם כָּל־מְלֶאכֶת עֲבֹדָה לֹא תַעֲשׂוּ:
כז וְהִקְרַבְתֶּם עוֹלָה לְרֵיחַ נִיחֹחַ לַיהוה פָּרִים בְּנֵי־בָקָר שְׁנַיִם אַיִל אֶחָד
כח שִׁבְעָה כְבָשִׂים בְּנֵי שָׁנָה: וּמִנְחָתָם סֹלֶת בְּלוּלָה בַשָּׁמֶן שְׁלֹשָׁה עֶשְׂרֹנִים
כט לַפָּר הָאֶחָד שְׁנֵי עֶשְׂרֹנִים לָאַיִל הָאֶחָד: עִשָּׂרוֹן עִשָּׂרוֹן לַכֶּבֶשׂ הָאֶחָד
ל-לא לְשִׁבְעַת הַכְּבָשִׂים: שְׂעִיר עִזִּים אֶחָד לְכַפֵּר עֲלֵיכֶם: מִלְּבַד עֹלַת
הַתָּמִיד וּמִנְחָתוֹ תַּעֲשׂוּ תְּמִימִם יִהְיוּ־לָכֶם וְנִסְכֵּיהֶם:

כט

א וּבַחֹדֶשׁ הַשְּׁבִיעִי בְּאֶחָד לַחֹדֶשׁ מִקְרָא־קֹדֶשׁ יִהְיֶה לָכֶם כָּל־מְלֶאכֶת
ב עֲבֹדָה לֹא תַעֲשׂוּ יוֹם תְּרוּעָה יִהְיֶה לָכֶם: וַעֲשִׂיתֶם עֹלָה לְרֵיחַ נִיחֹחַ
לַיהוה פַּר בֶּן־בָּקָר אֶחָד אַיִל אֶחָד כְּבָשִׂים בְּנֵי־שָׁנָה שִׁבְעָה תְּמִימִם:
ג וּמִנְחָתָם סֹלֶת בְּלוּלָה בַשָּׁמֶן שְׁלֹשָׁה עֶשְׂרֹנִים לַפָּר שְׁנֵי עֶשְׂרֹנִים לָאָיִל:
ד-ה וְעִשָּׂרוֹן אֶחָד לַכֶּבֶשׂ הָאֶחָד לְשִׁבְעַת הַכְּבָשִׂים: וּשְׂעִיר־עִזִּים אֶחָד
ו חַטָּאת לְכַפֵּר עֲלֵיכֶם: מִלְּבַד עֹלַת הַחֹדֶשׁ וּמִנְחָתָהּ וְעֹלַת הַתָּמִיד
ז וּמִנְחָתָהּ וְנִסְכֵּיהֶם כְּמִשְׁפָּטָם לְרֵיחַ נִיחֹחַ אִשֶּׁה לַיהוה: וּבֶעָשׂוֹר
לַחֹדֶשׁ הַשְּׁבִיעִי הַזֶּה מִקְרָא־קֹדֶשׁ יִהְיֶה לָכֶם וְעִנִּיתֶם אֶת־נַפְשֹׁתֵיכֶם
ח כָּל־מְלָאכָה לֹא תַעֲשׂוּ: וְהִקְרַבְתֶּם עֹלָה לַיהוה רֵיחַ נִיחֹחַ פַּר בֶּן־
בָּקָר אֶחָד אַיִל אֶחָד כְּבָשִׂים בְּנֵי־שָׁנָה שִׁבְעָה תְּמִימִם יִהְיוּ לָכֶם:
ט וּמִנְחָתָם סֹלֶת בְּלוּלָה בַשָּׁמֶן שְׁלֹשָׁה עֶשְׂרֹנִים לַפָּר שְׁנֵי עֶשְׂרֹנִים
י לָאַיִל הָאֶחָד: עִשָּׂרוֹן עִשָּׂרוֹן לַכֶּבֶשׂ הָאֶחָד לְשִׁבְעַת הַכְּבָשִׂים:
יא שְׂעִיר־עִזִּים אֶחָד חַטָּאת מִלְּבַד חַטַּאת הַכִּפֻּרִים וְעֹלַת הַתָּמִיד וּמִנְחָתָהּ
יב וְנִסְכֵּיהֶם: וּבַחֲמִשָּׁה עָשָׂר יוֹם לַחֹדֶשׁ הַשְּׁבִיעִי מִקְרָא־קֹדֶשׁ שביעי
יִהְיֶה לָכֶם כָּל־מְלֶאכֶת עֲבֹדָה לֹא תַעֲשׂוּ וְחַגֹּתֶם חַג לַיהוה שִׁבְעַת
יג יָמִים: וְהִקְרַבְתֶּם עֹלָה אִשֵּׁה רֵיחַ נִיחֹחַ לַיהוה פָּרִים בְּנֵי־בָקָר שְׁלֹשָׁה
יד עָשָׂר אֵילִם שְׁנָיִם כְּבָשִׂים בְּנֵי־שָׁנָה אַרְבָּעָה עָשָׂר תְּמִימִם יִהְיוּ: וּמִנְחָתָם
סֹלֶת בְּלוּלָה בַשָּׁמֶן שְׁלֹשָׁה עֶשְׂרֹנִים לַפָּר הָאֶחָד לִשְׁלֹשָׁה עָשָׂר פָּרִים
טו שְׁנֵי עֶשְׂרֹנִים לָאַיִל הָאֶחָד לִשְׁנֵי הָאֵילִם: וְעִשָּׂרוֹן עִשָּׂרוֹן לַכֶּבֶשׂ *נקוד על ו' בתרא של עשרון
טז הָאֶחָד לְאַרְבָּעָה עָשָׂר כְּבָשִׂים: וּשְׂעִיר־עִזִּים אֶחָד חַטָּאת מִלְּבַד עֹלַת
יז הַתָּמִיד מִנְחָתָהּ וְנִסְכָּהּ: וּבַיּוֹם הַשֵּׁנִי פָּרִים בְּנֵי־בָקָר שְׁנֵים
יח עָשָׂר אֵילִם שְׁנָיִם כְּבָשִׂים בְּנֵי־שָׁנָה אַרְבָּעָה עָשָׂר תְּמִימִם: וּמִנְחָתָם

26. בְּשָׁבֻעֹתֵיכֶם — *On account of your weeks* ... because of שְׁבֻעֹת חֻקּוֹת קָצִיר, *the appointed weeks of the harvest* (*Jeremiah* 5:24), which I kept for you. The meaning of the letter ב in the word בְּשָׁבֻעֹתֵיכֶם is the same as (the ב) in בַּנֶּפֶשׁ יְכַפֵּר, *That makes an atonement for the soul* (*Leviticus* 17:11), and בְּדַם עֲשָׂהאֵל, *for the blood of Asa'el* (*II Samuel* 3:27), and בַּלֶּחֶם נִשְׂכָּרוּ, *have hired themselves out for bread* (*I Samuel* 2:5).

NOTES

26. בְּשָׁבֻעֹתֵיכֶם — *On account of your weeks.* On the holiday of Shevuos, two loaves of wheat bread were brought from the new harvest. This 50th day follows the counting of the forty-nine days since Pesach and marks the completion of the seven weeks. Hence, the phrase בְּשָׁבֻעֹתֵיכֶם cannot mean *"on" your feast of weeks* since it was already after the weeks *were out*. The sense of this expression

26 On the day of the first-fruits, when you offer a new meal-offering to
HASHEM on your Festival of Weeks, it shall be a holy convocation to you;
you shall not do any laborious work. 27 You shall offer an elevation-offering
for a satisfying aroma to HASHEM: two young bulls, one ram, seven lambs
within their first year. 28 And their meal-offering: fine flour mixed with oil
— three tenth-ephah for each bull; two tenth-ephah for the one ram; 29 one
tenth-ephah for each lamb of the seven lambs. 30 One male of the goats to
atone for you. 31 Aside from the continual elevation-offering and its
meal-offering shall you offer [them] — unblemished shall they be for you —
and their libations.

29 1 In the seventh month, on the first day of the month, there shall be a holy
convocation for you; you shall do no laborious work, it shall be a day of
shofar-sounding for you. 2 You shall make an elevation-offering for a
satisfying aroma to HASHEM: one young bull, one ram, seven male lambs in
their first year, unblemished. 3 And their meal-offering: fine flour mixed
with oil — three tenth-ephah for the bull; two tenth-ephah for the ram;
4 and one tenth-ephah for each lamb of the seven lambs. 5 One male of the
goats for a sin-offering to provide you atonement. 6 Aside from the
elevation-offering of the New Moon and its meal-offering, the continual
elevation-offering and its meal-offering, and their libations according to
their law — for a satisfying aroma, a fire-offering to HASHEM.
7 On the tenth day of this seventh month there shall be a holy
convocation for you and you shall afflict yourselves; you shall not do any
work. 8 You shall offer an elevation-offering to HASHEM for a satisfying
aroma — one young bull, one ram, seven male lambs in their first year; they
shall be unblemished for you. 9 And their meal-offering: fine flour mixed
with oil — three tenth-ephah for the bull; two tenth-ephah for the one ram;
10 and one tenth-ephah for each lamb of the seven lambs. 11 One male of the
goats for a sin-offering, aside from the sin-offering of the atonement and
the continual elevation-offering, with its meal-offering, and their libations.
12 On the fifteenth day of the seventh month, there shall be a holy
convocation for you; you shall do no laborious work; you shall celebrate a
festival to HASHEM for a seven-day period. 13 You shall offer an
elevation-offering, a fire-offering, a satisfying aroma to HASHEM: thirteen
young bulls, two rams, fourteen male lambs in their first year; they shall be
unblemished. 14 And their meal-offering: fine flour mixed with oil — three
tenth-ephah for each bull of the thirteen bulls; two tenth-ephah for each
ram of the two rams; 15 and one tenth-ephah for each lamb of the fourteen
lambs. 16 One male of the goats for a sin-offering, aside from the continual
elevation-offering with its meal-offering and its libation.
17 And on the second day: twelve young bulls, two rams, fourteen male
lambs within their first year, unblemished. 18 And their meal-offerings

NOTES

must perforce be, as the *Sforno* explains, you shall bring this offering of two loaves in recognition of God's blessing granted to you during these seven weeks which brought you to this harvest. The prefix has a variety of meanings. In this verse, it means "for" (or "on account of"), as it does in the verses cited by the *Sforno* in support of his interpretation.

יט וְנִסְכֵּיהֶם לַפָּרִים לָאֵילִם וְלַכְּבָשִׂים בְּמִסְפָּרָם כַּמִּשְׁפָּט: וּשְׂעִיר־עִזִּים
כ אֶחָד חַטָּאת מִלְּבַד עֹלַת הַתָּמִיד וּמִנְחָתָהּ וְנִסְכֵּיהֶם: וּבַיּוֹם
הַשְּׁלִישִׁי פָּרִים עַשְׁתֵּי־עָשָׂר אֵילִם שְׁנָיִם כְּבָשִׂים בְּנֵי־שָׁנָה אַרְבָּעָה
כא עָשָׂר תְּמִימִם: וּמִנְחָתָם וְנִסְכֵּיהֶם לַפָּרִים לָאֵילִם וְלַכְּבָשִׂים בְּמִסְפָּרָם
כב כַּמִּשְׁפָּט: וּשְׂעִיר חַטָּאת אֶחָד מִלְּבַד עֹלַת הַתָּמִיד וּמִנְחָתָהּ
כג וְנִסְכָּהּ: וּבַיּוֹם הָרְבִיעִי פָּרִים עֲשָׂרָה אֵילִם שְׁנָיִם כְּבָשִׂים בְּנֵי־
כד שָׁנָה אַרְבָּעָה עָשָׂר תְּמִימִם: מִנְחָתָם וְנִסְכֵּיהֶם לַפָּרִים לָאֵילִם וְלַכְּבָשִׂים
כה בְּמִסְפָּרָם כַּמִּשְׁפָּט: וּשְׂעִיר־עִזִּים אֶחָד חַטָּאת מִלְּבַד עֹלַת הַתָּמִיד
כו מִנְחָתָהּ וְנִסְכָּהּ: וּבַיּוֹם הַחֲמִישִׁי פָּרִים תִּשְׁעָה אֵילִם שְׁנָיִם
כז כְּבָשִׂים בְּנֵי־שָׁנָה אַרְבָּעָה עָשָׂר תְּמִימִם: וּמִנְחָתָם וְנִסְכֵּיהֶם לַפָּרִים
כח לָאֵילִם וְלַכְּבָשִׂים בְּמִסְפָּרָם כַּמִּשְׁפָּט: וּשְׂעִיר חַטָּאת אֶחָד מִלְּבַד עֹלַת
כט הַתָּמִיד וּמִנְחָתָהּ וְנִסְכָּהּ: וּבַיּוֹם הַשִּׁשִּׁי פָּרִים שְׁמֹנָה אֵילִם
ל שְׁנָיִם כְּבָשִׂים בְּנֵי־שָׁנָה אַרְבָּעָה עָשָׂר תְּמִימִם: וּמִנְחָתָם וְנִסְכֵּיהֶם
לא לַפָּרִים לָאֵילִם וְלַכְּבָשִׂים בְּמִסְפָּרָם כַּמִּשְׁפָּט: וּשְׂעִיר חַטָּאת אֶחָד
לב מִלְּבַד עֹלַת הַתָּמִיד מִנְחָתָהּ וּנְסָכֶיהָ: וּבַיּוֹם הַשְּׁבִיעִי פָּרִים
לג שִׁבְעָה אֵילִם שְׁנָיִם כְּבָשִׂים בְּנֵי־שָׁנָה אַרְבָּעָה עָשָׂר תְּמִימִם: וּמִנְחָתָם
לד וְנִסְכֵּהֶם לַפָּרִים לָאֵילִם וְלַכְּבָשִׂים בְּמִסְפָּרָם כְּמִשְׁפָּטָם: וּשְׂעִיר חַטָּאת
מפטיר לה אֶחָד מִלְּבַד עֹלַת הַתָּמִיד מִנְחָתָהּ וְנִסְכָּהּ: בַּיּוֹם הַשְּׁמִינִי
לו עֲצֶרֶת תִּהְיֶה לָכֶם כָּל־מְלֶאכֶת עֲבֹדָה לֹא תַעֲשׂוּ: וְהִקְרַבְתֶּם עֹלָה אִשֵּׁה
רֵיחַ נִיחֹחַ לַיהוָה פַּר אֶחָד אַיִל אֶחָד כְּבָשִׂים בְּנֵי־שָׁנָה שִׁבְעָה תְּמִימִם:
לז מִנְחָתָם וְנִסְכֵּיהֶם לַפָּר לָאַיִל וְלַכְּבָשִׂים בְּמִסְפָּרָם כַּמִּשְׁפָּט: וּשְׂעִיר
לח-לט חַטָּאת אֶחָד מִלְּבַד עֹלַת הַתָּמִיד וּמִנְחָתָהּ וְנִסְכָּהּ: אֵלֶּה תַּעֲשׂוּ לַיהוָה
בְּמוֹעֲדֵיכֶם לְבַד מִנִּדְרֵיכֶם וְנִדְבֹתֵיכֶם לְעֹלֹתֵיכֶם וּלְמִנְחֹתֵיכֶם
ל א וּלְנִסְכֵּיכֶם וּלְשַׁלְמֵיכֶם: וַיֹּאמֶר מֹשֶׁה אֶל־בְּנֵי יִשְׂרָאֵל כְּכֹל אֲשֶׁר־צִוָּה
יְהוָה אֶת־מֹשֶׁה:

XXIX

35. עֲצֶרֶת תִּהְיֶה לָכֶם — *You shall have a solemn assembly* ... as explained in (the commentary on) *Parashas Emor* (*Leviticus* 23:36).

and their libations for the bulls, the rams, and the lambs, in their proper
numbers, as required. 19 One male of the goats for a sin-offering; aside from
the continual elevation-offering, its meal-offering and their libations.
20 And on the third day: eleven bulls, two rams, fourteen male lambs
within their first year, unblemished. 21 And their meal-offering and their
libations for the bulls, the rams, and the lambs, in their proper numbers, as
required. 22 One he-goat for a sin-offering; aside from the continual
elevation-offering, its meal-offering and its libation.
23 And on the fourth day: ten bulls, two rams, fourteen male lambs within
their first year, unblemished. 24 And their meal-offering and their libations
for the bulls, the rams, and the lambs, in their proper numbers, as required.
25 One male of the goats for a sin-offering; aside from the continual
elevation-offering, its meal-offering and its libation.
26 And on the fifth day: nine bulls, two rams, fourteen male lambs within
their first year, unblemished. 27 And their meal-offering and their libations
for the bulls, the rams, and the lambs, in their proper numbers, as required.
28 One he-goat for a sin-offering; aside from the continual elevation-offering, its meal-offering and its libation.
29 And on the sixth day: eight bulls, two rams, fourteen male lambs
within their first year, unblemished. 30 And their meal-offering and their
libations for the bulls, the rams, and the lambs, in their proper numbers, as
required. 31 One he-goat for a sin-offering; aside from the continual
elevation-offering, its meal-offering and its libations.
32 And on the seventh day: seven bulls, two rams, fourteen lambs within
their first year, unblemished. 33 And their meal-offering and their libations
for the bulls, the rams, and the lambs, in their proper numbers, in their
requirements. 34 One he-goat for a sin-offering; aside from the continual
elevation-offering, its meal-offering and its libation.
35 The eighth day shall be a restriction for you; you shall not do any
laborious work. 36 You shall offer an elevation-offering, a fire-offering, a
satisfying aroma to HASHEM; one bull, one ram, seven lambs within their
first year, unblemished. 37 Their meal-offering and libations for the bull, the
ram, and the lambs shall be in their proper numbers, as required. 38 One
he-goat for a sin-offering; aside from the continual elevation-offering, its
meal-offering and its libation.
39 These are what you shall make for HASHEM on your appointed
festivals, aside from your vows and your free-will offerings for your
elevation-offerings, your meal-offerings, your libations, and your peace-
offerings.

30 1 Moses said to the Children of Israel according to everything that
HASHEM had commanded Moses.

פרשת מטות

ב וַיְדַבֵּר מֹשֶׁה אֶל־רָאשֵׁי הַמַּטּוֹת לִבְנֵי יִשְׂרָאֵל לֵאמֹר זֶה הַדָּבָר אֲשֶׁר צִוָּה
ג יהוה: אִישׁ כִּי־יִדֹּר נֶדֶר לַיהוה אוֹ־הִשָּׁבַע שְׁבֻעָה לֶאְסֹר אִסָּר עַל־נַפְשׁוֹ
ד לֹא יַחֵל דְּבָרוֹ כְּכָל־הַיֹּצֵא מִפִּיו יַעֲשֶׂה: וְאִשָּׁה כִּי־תִדֹּר נֶדֶר לַיהוה
ה וְאָסְרָה אִסָּר בְּבֵית אָבִיהָ בִּנְעֻרֶיהָ: וְשָׁמַע אָבִיהָ אֶת־נִדְרָהּ וֶאֱסָרָהּ אֲשֶׁר
אָסְרָה עַל־נַפְשָׁהּ וְהֶחֱרִישׁ לָהּ אָבִיהָ וְקָמוּ כָּל־נְדָרֶיהָ וְכָל־אִסָּר אֲשֶׁר־
ו אָסְרָה עַל־נַפְשָׁהּ יָקוּם: וְאִם־הֵנִיא אָבִיהָ אֹתָהּ בְּיוֹם שָׁמְעוֹ כָּל־נְדָרֶיהָ
וֶאֱסָרֶיהָ אֲשֶׁר־אָסְרָה עַל־נַפְשָׁהּ לֹא יָקוּם וַיהוה יִסְלַח־לָהּ כִּי־הֵנִיא
ז אָבִיהָ אֹתָהּ: וְאִם־הָיוֹ תִהְיֶה לְאִישׁ וּנְדָרֶיהָ עָלֶיהָ אוֹ מִבְטָא שְׂפָתֶיהָ אֲשֶׁר
ח אָסְרָה עַל־נַפְשָׁהּ: וְשָׁמַע אִישָׁהּ בְּיוֹם שָׁמְעוֹ וְהֶחֱרִישׁ לָהּ וְקָמוּ נְדָרֶיהָ
ט וֶאֱסָרֶהָ אֲשֶׁר־אָסְרָה עַל־נַפְשָׁהּ יָקֻמוּ: וְאִם בְּיוֹם שְׁמֹעַ אִישָׁהּ יָנִיא אוֹתָהּ
וְהֵפֵר אֶת־נִדְרָהּ אֲשֶׁר עָלֶיהָ וְאֵת מִבְטָא שְׂפָתֶיהָ אֲשֶׁר אָסְרָה עַל־נַפְשָׁהּ
י וַיהוה יִסְלַח־לָהּ: וְנֵדֶר אַלְמָנָה וּגְרוּשָׁה כֹּל אֲשֶׁר־אָסְרָה עַל־נַפְשָׁהּ יָקוּם
יא־יב עָלֶיהָ: וְאִם־בֵּית אִישָׁהּ נָדָרָה אוֹ־אָסְרָה אִסָּר עַל־נַפְשָׁהּ בִּשְׁבֻעָה: וְשָׁמַע
אִישָׁהּ וְהֶחֱרִשׁ לָהּ לֹא הֵנִיא אֹתָהּ וְקָמוּ כָּל־נְדָרֶיהָ וְכָל־אִסָּר אֲשֶׁר־
יג אָסְרָה עַל־נַפְשָׁהּ יָקוּם: וְאִם־הָפֵר יָפֵר אֹתָם | אִישָׁהּ בְּיוֹם שָׁמְעוֹ כָּל־
מוֹצָא שְׂפָתֶיהָ לִנְדָרֶיהָ וּלְאִסַּר נַפְשָׁהּ לֹא יָקוּם אִישָׁהּ הֲפֵרָם וַיהוה
יד יִסְלַח־לָהּ: כָּל־נֵדֶר וְכָל־שְׁבֻעַת אִסָּר לְעַנֹּת נָפֶשׁ אִישָׁהּ יְקִימֶנּוּ וְאִישָׁהּ
טו יְפֵרֶנּוּ: וְאִם־הַחֲרֵשׁ יַחֲרִישׁ לָהּ אִישָׁהּ מִיּוֹם אֶל־יוֹם וְהֵקִים אֶת־כָּל־נְדָרֶיהָ
אוֹ אֶת־כָּל־אֱסָרֶיהָ אֲשֶׁר עָלֶיהָ הֵקִים אֹתָם כִּי־הֶחֱרִשׁ לָהּ בְּיוֹם שָׁמְעוֹ:

XXX

2. זֶה הַדָּבָר אֲשֶׁר צִוָּה ה׳ — *This is the thing which HASHEM has commanded.* When He said at Mt. Sinai, וְלֹא תִשָּׁבְעוּ בִשְׁמִי לַשָּׁקֶר וְחִלַּלְתָּ, *And you shall not swear by My name falsely, so that you profane* (*Leviticus* 19:12), the intent was that when a man takes a vow or swears an oath, "he shall not profane (break) his word," because when he profanes his word, he (also) profanes God. However, a woman who is not independent (lit., in her own control) will not have profaned (her vow) if he who has the power (i.e., her father or husband) declares it null and void.

6. וַה׳ יִסְלַח לָהּ — *And HASHEM will forgive her* . . . for taking a vow which she is unable to fulfill.

כִּי הֵנִיא אָבִיהָ אֹתָהּ — *Because her father disallowed her* . . . and (since) she did not know

NOTES

XXX

2. זֶה הַדָּבָר אֲשֶׁר צִוָּה ה׳ — *This is the thing which HASHEM has commanded.* The expression, זֶה הַדָּבָר אֲשֶׁר צִוָּה ה׳, *This is the thing which HASHEM has commanded*, normally is used regarding a commandment which one is obligated to fulfill immediately. For example, in *Exodus* 16:16 it is used regarding the manna and in *Exodus* 35:4 regarding the collection of offerings for the Sanctuary. This, however, cannot be the meaning in the context of our *parshah* which deals with vows and oaths. The *Sforno*, therefore, explains that זֶה הַדָּבָר וכו׳ refers to the verse in *Leviticus* 19:12 where we have already been cautioned not to profane the Name of God by swearing falsely. This admonition is now carried over to פָּרָשַׁת נְדָרִים, *the section dealing with vows*. Hence, the phrase זֶה הַדָּבָר serves as a link to the verse in *Leviticus* cited by the *Sforno*. A similar interpretation of this expression can also be found in the *Sforno's* commentary on *Leviticus* 17:2.

PARASHAS MATTOS

2 *Moses spoke to the heads of the tribes of the Children of Israel, saying:
This is the thing that HASHEM has commanded:* 3 *If a man takes a
vow to HASHEM or swears an oath to establish a prohibition upon himself, he
shall not desecrate his word; according to whatever comes from his mouth
shall he do.*
4 *But if a woman will take a vow to HASHEM or establish a prohibition in
her father's home in her youth;* 5 *and her father heard of her vow or the
prohibition that she established upon herself, and her father was silent about
her, then all her vows shall stand, and any prohibition that she established
upon herself shall stand.* 6 *But if her father restrained her on the day of his
hearing, all her vows or prohibitions that she established upon herself shall
not stand; and HASHEM will forgive her, for her father had restrained her.*
7 *If she shall be married to a man and her vows were upon her, or an
utterance of her lips by which she had prohibited something upon herself,*
8 *and her husband heard, and on the day he heard he was silent about her
— then her vows shall stand and her prohibition that she established upon
herself shall stand.* 9 *But if on the day of her husband's hearing he shall
restrain her and he shall revoke the vow that is upon her or the utterance
of her lips by which she had prohibited something upon herself — then
HASHEM will forgive her.*
10 *The vow of a widow or a divorcee — anything she had prohibited upon
herself — shall remain upon her.*
11 *But if she vowed in her husband's home, or she established a prohibition upon herself through an oath,* 12 *and her husband heard about it
and was silent about her — he did not restrain her — then all her vows
shall stand and any prohibition she established upon herself shall stand.*
13 *But if her husband shall revoke them on the day of his hearing, anything that came out of her mouth regarding her oaths or the prohibition
upon herself shall not stand; her husband had revoked them and HASHEM
will forgive her.* 14 *Any vow and any oath-prohibition to cause personal
affliction, her husband may let it stand and her husband may revoke it.*
15 *If her husband shall be silent about her from day to day — he will have
let stand all her vows; or all the prohibitions that are upon her, he will
have let them stand, for he was silent about her on the day of his hearing.*

---

her father's opinion when she took the vow, (hence) she intended to fulfill it (at the time).

15. וְאִם הַחֲרֵשׁ יַחֲרִישׁ לָהּ אִישָׁהּ — *But if her husband keeps silent.* Silence on the part of one who has the power to protest is tantamount to admission (consent), for regarding he who is silent (it is as though) he agrees with the action.

NOTES

6. וַה׳ יִסְלַח לָהּ כִּי הֵנִיא אָבִיהָ אֹתָהּ — *And HASHEM will forgive her because her father disallowed her.* Although she may have acted improperly by taking a vow which she had no power to fulfill, nonetheless since she assumed that her father would agree with her, she honestly intended to keep her word. Therefore, God will forgive her.

15. וְאִם הַחֲרֵשׁ יַחֲרִישׁ לָהּ אִישָׁהּ — *But if her husband keeps silent.* The *Sforno* bases his commentary of this verse on the Talmudic dictum, שְׁתִיקָה כְּהוֹדָאָה, *Silence is like admission,* mentioned in tractate *Bava Metzia* 37b and elsewhere throughout the Talmud. If one who had the power to do so does not protest and is silent, it is considered as a sign of

טז-יז וְאִם־הָפֵר יָפֵר אֹתָם אַחֲרֵי שָׁמְעוֹ וְנָשָׂא אֶת־עֲוֺנָהּ: אֵלֶּה הַחֻקִּים אֲשֶׁר צִוָּה
יהוה אֶת־מֹשֶׁה בֵּין אִישׁ לְאִשְׁתּוֹ בֵּין־אָב לְבִתּוֹ בִּנְעֻרֶיהָ בֵּית אָבִיהָ:
לא שני א-ב וַיְדַבֵּר יהוה אֶל־מֹשֶׁה לֵּאמֹר: נְקֹם נִקְמַת בְּנֵי יִשְׂרָאֵל מֵאֵת הַמִּדְיָנִים
ג אַחַר תֵּאָסֵף אֶל־עַמֶּיךָ: וַיְדַבֵּר מֹשֶׁה אֶל־הָעָם לֵאמֹר הֵחָלְצוּ מֵאִתְּכֶם
ד אֲנָשִׁים לַצָּבָא וְיִהְיוּ עַל־מִדְיָן לָתֵת נִקְמַת־יהוה בְּמִדְיָן: אֶלֶף לַמַּטֶּה
ה אֶלֶף לַמַּטֶּה לְכֹל מַטּוֹת יִשְׂרָאֵל תִּשְׁלְחוּ לַצָּבָא: וַיִּמָּסְרוּ מֵאַלְפֵי יִשְׂרָאֵל
ו אֶלֶף לַמַּטֶּה שְׁנֵים־עָשָׂר אֶלֶף חֲלוּצֵי צָבָא: וַיִּשְׁלַח אֹתָם מֹשֶׁה אֶלֶף
לַמַּטֶּה לַצָּבָא אֹתָם וְאֶת־פִּינְחָס בֶּן־אֶלְעָזָר הַכֹּהֵן לַצָּבָא וּכְלֵי הַקֹּדֶשׁ
ז וַחֲצֹצְרוֹת הַתְּרוּעָה בְּיָדוֹ: וַיִּצְבְּאוּ עַל־מִדְיָן כַּאֲשֶׁר צִוָּה יהוה אֶת־מֹשֶׁה
ח וַיַּהַרְגוּ כָּל־זָכָר: וְאֶת־מַלְכֵי מִדְיָן הָרְגוּ עַל־חַלְלֵיהֶם אֶת־אֱוִי וְאֶת־רֶקֶם
וְאֶת־צוּר וְאֶת־חוּר וְאֶת־רֶבַע חֲמֵשֶׁת מַלְכֵי מִדְיָן וְאֵת בִּלְעָם בֶּן־בְּעוֹר
ט הָרְגוּ בֶּחָרֶב: וַיִּשְׁבּוּ בְנֵי־יִשְׂרָאֵל אֶת־נְשֵׁי מִדְיָן וְאֶת־טַפָּם וְאֵת
י כָּל־בְּהֶמְתָּם וְאֶת־כָּל־מִקְנֵהֶם וְאֶת־כָּל־חֵילָם בָּזָזוּ: וְאֵת כָּל־עָרֵיהֶם
יא בְּמוֹשְׁבֹתָם וְאֵת כָּל־טִירֹתָם שָׂרְפוּ בָּאֵשׁ: וַיִּקְחוּ אֶת־כָּל־הַשָּׁלָל וְאֵת
יב כָּל־הַמַּלְקוֹחַ בָּאָדָם וּבַבְּהֵמָה: וַיָּבִאוּ אֶל־מֹשֶׁה וְאֶל־אֶלְעָזָר הַכֹּהֵן וְאֶל־
עֲדַת בְּנֵי־יִשְׂרָאֵל אֶת־הַשְּׁבִי וְאֶת־הַמַּלְקוֹחַ וְאֶת־הַשָּׁלָל אֶל־הַמַּחֲנֶה
יג שלישי [שני] אֶל־עַרְבֹת מוֹאָב אֲשֶׁר עַל־יַרְדֵּן יְרֵחוֹ: וַיֵּצְאוּ מֹשֶׁה וְאֶלְעָזָר הַכֹּהֵן
יד וְכָל־נְשִׂיאֵי הָעֵדָה לִקְרָאתָם אֶל־מִחוּץ לַמַּחֲנֶה: וַיִּקְצֹף מֹשֶׁה עַל פְּקוּדֵי

---

16. וְאִם הָפֵר יָפֵר אֹתָם אַחֲרֵי שָׁמְעוֹ — *But if he shall make them null and void after he heard them* ... after the day he has heard them, at which time he cannot regret or nullify.

וְנָשָׂא אֶת עֲוֺנָהּ — *Then he shall bear her iniquity* ... as is the law regarding anyone who forces another to transgress, or who misleads and instructs (someone) falsely.

XXXI

5. וַיִּמָּסְרוּ — *So there were delivered* ... unto Moses, from each tribe.

NOTES

acquiescence. Hence, since her husband has the authority to protest and does not, it is regarded as his having tacitly consented to her vow. This concept of one's failure to protest being regarded as approval is based on an episode recorded in a mishnah in tractate *Shabbos* 54b. The mishnah relates that R' Elazar ben Azariah's cow used to go out on the Sabbath with a thong between its horn, against the consent of the Rabbis. The Talmud explains that the cow did not actually belong to him but to a neighbor. However, since he did not protest it was considered as his! We learn from this that silence on the part of one who has the power to protest is tantamount to agreement.

The *Sforno* also expresses this idea in his commentary (*Exodus* 32) regarding the culpability of those Israelites who did not participate actively in the sin of the Golden Calf but nonetheless were silent. Conversely, they were forgiven for this sin of omission when they were silent and did not interfere at the time punishment was meted out to the sinners. Similarly, in the episode of Baal Peor, non-protest at the time the sinners were executed atoned for the silence of those who failed to object when the sin was first perpetrated (see 25:4, 11).

16. וְאִם הָפֵר יָפֵר ... וְנָשָׂא אֶת עֲוֺנָהּ — *But if he shall make them null and void ... then he shall bear her iniquity.* The Torah considers the husband responsible for his wife's broken vow since he forced her to break it or he misled her into believing that her vow was nullified. The *Sforno* explains that the transfer of her iniquity upon him is justified, because we assume that the active transgressor would not have sinned were it not for the intervention of the one who forced or misled. See *Rashi's* commentary on this verse which gives a similar explanation.

16 *But if he shall revoke them after his having heard, he shall bear her iniquity.*

17 *These are the decrees that God commanded Moses, between a man and his wife, between a father and his daughter in her youth, in her father's house.*

31

1 *HASHEM spoke to Moses, saying,* 2 *"Take vengeance for the Children of Israel against the Midianites; afterward you will be gathered unto your people."*

3 *Moses spoke to the people, saying, "Arm men from among yourselves for the legion that they may be against Midian to inflict HASHEM's vengeance against Midian.* 4 *A thousand from a tribe, a thousand from a tribe, for all the tribes of Israel shall you send to the legion."*

5 *So there were delivered from the thousands of the Children of Israel, a thousand from each tribe, twelve thousand armed for the legion.* 6 *Moses sent them — a thousand from each tribe for the legion — them and Phineas son of Elazar the Kohen to the legion, and the sacred vessels and the trumpets for sounding in his hand.* 7 *They massed against Midian, as HASHEM had commanded Moses, and they killed every male.* 8 *They killed the kings of Midian along with their slain ones: Evi, Rekem, Zur, Hur, and Reba, the five kings of Midian; and Balaam son of Beor they slew with the sword.* 9 *The Children of Israel took captive the women of Midian and their young children; and all their cattle and flocks and all their wealth they took as spoils.* 10 *All the cities of their habitations and all their palaces they burned in fire.* 11 *They took all the booty and all the captives of people and animals.* 12 *They brought to Moses, to Elazar the Kohen, and to the assembly of the Children of Israel the captives, the animals, and the booty to the camp, at the plains of Moab, which was by the Jordan near Jericho.*

13 *Moses, Elazar the Kohen, and all the leaders of the assembly went out to meet them outside the camp.* 14 *Moses was angry with the commanders*

---

6. וַיִּשְׁלַח אֹתָם מֹשֶׁה אֶלֶף לַמַּטֶּה לַצָּבָא — *And Moses sent them, a thousand of every tribe, to war.* He sent one thousand from each tribe, to gather together for war.

אֹתָם וְאֶת פִּינְחָס — *Them and Pinchas . . .* and after they had gathered, he sent them out all together, and with them he sent Pinchas.

לַצָּבָא וּכְלֵי הַקֹּדֶשׁ וַחֲצֹצְרוֹת הַתְּרוּעָה בְּיָדוֹ — *To the war, with the holy vessels and the trumpets for the alarm in his hand.* He sent him to the war, as the leader and anointed *Kohen* of battle, as well (as entrusting) the holy vessels and trumpets of alarm to him (that they) be under his control.

NOTES

XXXI

5. וַיִּמָּסְרוּ — *So there were delivered.* The Torah states that they *were delivered,* but does not tell us who they were. The *Sforno,* therefore, explains that each tribe sent a thousand men to Moses, who organized them into a fighting force.

6. וַיִּשְׁלַח אֹתָם מֹשֶׁה אֶלֶף לַמַּטֶּה לַצָּבָא . . . לַצָּבָא וּכְלֵי הַקֹּדֶשׁ . . . בְּיָדוֹ — *And Moses sent them, a thousand of every tribe, to war . . . to the war, with the holy vessels . . . in his hand.* The word לַצָּבָא, *to war,* appears twice in this verse. The *Sforno* explains that the first time it refers to the gathering together of the soldiers in the camp, while the second refers to Pinchas who was sent together with the holy Ark and trumpets to act as the כֹּהֵן מְשִׁיחַ מִלְחָמָה, *the anointed Kohen of battle,* as taught in *Deut.* 20:2.

טו הֶחָיִל שָׂרֵי הָאֲלָפִים וְשָׂרֵי הַמֵּאוֹת הַבָּאִים מִצְּבָא הַמִּלְחָמָה: וַיֹּאמֶר
טז אֲלֵיהֶם מֹשֶׁה הַחִיִּיתֶם כָּל־נְקֵבָה: הֵן הֵנָּה הָיוּ לִבְנֵי יִשְׂרָאֵל בִּדְבַר בִּלְעָם
יז לִמְסָר־מַעַל בַּיהוָה עַל־דְּבַר־פְּעוֹר וַתְּהִי הַמַּגֵּפָה בַּעֲדַת יהוָה: וְעַתָּה
יח הִרְגוּ כָל־זָכָר בַּטָּף וְכָל־אִשָּׁה יֹדַעַת אִישׁ לְמִשְׁכַּב זָכָר הֲרֹגוּ: וְכֹל הַטַּף
יט בַּנָּשִׁים אֲשֶׁר לֹא־יָדְעוּ מִשְׁכַּב זָכָר הַחֲיוּ לָכֶם: וְאַתֶּם חֲנוּ מִחוּץ לַמַּחֲנֶה
שִׁבְעַת יָמִים כֹּל הֹרֵג נֶפֶשׁ וְכֹל ׀ נֹגֵעַ בֶּחָלָל תִּתְחַטְּאוּ בַּיּוֹם הַשְּׁלִישִׁי
כ וּבַיּוֹם הַשְּׁבִיעִי אַתֶּם וּשְׁבִיכֶם: וְכָל־בֶּגֶד וְכָל־כְּלִי־עוֹר וְכָל־מַעֲשֵׂה עִזִּים
כא וְכָל־כְּלִי־עֵץ תִּתְחַטָּאוּ: וַיֹּאמֶר אֶלְעָזָר הַכֹּהֵן אֶל־אַנְשֵׁי
הַצָּבָא הַבָּאִים לַמִּלְחָמָה זֹאת חֻקַּת הַתּוֹרָה אֲשֶׁר־צִוָּה יהוָה אֶת־מֹשֶׁה:
כב אַךְ אֶת־הַזָּהָב וְאֶת־הַכָּסֶף אֶת־הַנְּחֹשֶׁת אֶת־הַבַּרְזֶל אֶת־הַבְּדִיל וְאֶת־
כג הָעֹפָרֶת: כָּל־דָּבָר אֲשֶׁר־יָבֹא בָאֵשׁ תַּעֲבִירוּ בָאֵשׁ וְטָהֵר אַךְ בְּמֵי נִדָּה
כד יִתְחַטָּא וְכֹל אֲשֶׁר לֹא־יָבֹא בָּאֵשׁ תַּעֲבִירוּ בַמָּיִם: וְכִבַּסְתֶּם בִּגְדֵיכֶם בַּיּוֹם
רביעי כה הַשְּׁבִיעִי וּטְהַרְתֶּם וְאַחַר תָּבֹאוּ אֶל־הַמַּחֲנֶה: וַיֹּאמֶר
כו יהוָה אֶל־מֹשֶׁה לֵּאמֹר: שָׂא אֵת רֹאשׁ מַלְקוֹחַ הַשְּׁבִי בָּאָדָם וּבַבְּהֵמָה
כז אַתָּה וְאֶלְעָזָר הַכֹּהֵן וְרָאשֵׁי אֲבוֹת הָעֵדָה: וְחָצִיתָ אֶת־הַמַּלְקוֹחַ בֵּין
כח תֹּפְשֵׂי הַמִּלְחָמָה הַיֹּצְאִים לַצָּבָא וּבֵין כָּל־הָעֵדָה: וַהֲרֵמֹתָ מֶכֶס לַיהוָה
מֵאֵת אַנְשֵׁי הַמִּלְחָמָה הַיֹּצְאִים לַצָּבָא אֶחָד נֶפֶשׁ מֵחֲמֵשׁ הַמֵּאוֹת
כט מִן־הָאָדָם וּמִן־הַבָּקָר וּמִן־הַחֲמֹרִים וּמִן־הַצֹּאן: מִמַּחֲצִיתָם תִּקָּחוּ וְנָתַתָּה
ל לְאֶלְעָזָר הַכֹּהֵן תְּרוּמַת יהוָה: וּמִמַּחֲצִת בְּנֵי־יִשְׂרָאֵל תִּקַּח ׀ אֶחָד ׀ אָחֻז
מִן־הַחֲמִשִּׁים מִן־הָאָדָם מִן־הַבָּקָר מִן־הַחֲמֹרִים וּמִן־הַצֹּאן מִכָּל־הַבְּהֵמָה

15. הַחִיִּיתֶם כָּל נְקֵבָה — *Have you kept alive all the females?* Although in regard to battle with all nations except for the seven nations, it is written, רַק הַנָּשִׁים וְהַטַּף וְהַבְּהֵמָה וְכֹל אֲשֶׁר יִהְיֶה בָעִיר כָּל שְׁלָלָהּ תָּבֹז לָךְ, *But the women and the little ones and the animals, and all that is in the city, even all the spoil, shall you take for a prey* (Deut. 20:14), (still) you should, at the least, not have permitted those women to live whom you recognized as being the ones who were the cause of your (moral) stumbling at the suggestion of Balaam.

17. הִרְגוּ כָל זָכָר בַּטָּף — *Kill every male among the young ones.* Although they are not fit for sexual congress; this was done for the purpose of revenge, that there shall not remain sons or son's son (נִין וָנֶכֶד) to Midian.

21. זֹאת חֻקַּת הַתּוֹרָה — *This is the statute of the law.* That which Moses told you regarding the purification (procedure) on the third and seventh day is a law (called) חֻקַּת הַתּוֹרָה, *the statute of the Torah,* of the red cow which makes *tahor* from *tumah* caused by death.

22. אַךְ אֶת הַזָּהָב — *But the gold . . .* but regarding metal vessels, besides *taharah,* it is necessary to purge them (i.e., הַגְעָלָה).

23. וְטָהֵר — *And shall be clean . . .* (cleansed) of the abhorrent (forbidden food) of the idolaters.

NOTES

22-23. אַךְ אֶת הַזָּהָב . . . וְטָהֵר אַךְ בְּמֵי נִדָּה יִתְחַטָּא — *But the gold . . . and shall be clean; nevertheless it shall be made tahor with the water of sprinkling.* The phrase אַךְ, *but,* implies מִעוּט, *exclusion.* Although purification of these vessels from the defilement caused by a corpse was completed, they still had to be cleansed from the forbidden food which they had absorbed. Some metal vessels can be cleansed by immersion in hot water (הַגְעָלָה) while others must be purged by fire (לִבּוּן). The

of the army, the officers of the thousands and the officers of the hundreds,
who came from the legion of the battle.
15 Moses said to them, "Did you let every female live? 16 Behold! — they
caused the Children of Israel, by the word of Balaam, to commit a betrayal
against HASHEM regarding the matter of Peor; and the plague occurred in the
assembly of HASHEM. 17 So now, kill every male among the young children,
and every woman fit to know a man by lying with a male, you shall kill.
18 But all the young children among the women who have not known lying
with a male, you may keep alive for yourselves. 19 And as for you, encamp
outside the camp for a seven-day period; whoever killed a person or touched
a corpse shall purify yourselves on the third day and on the seventh day —
you and your captives. 20 And every garment, every vessel of hide,
everything made of goat's hair, and every vessel of wood, you shall purify."
21 Elazar the Kohen said to the men of the legion who came to the battle,
"This is the decree of the Torah, which HASHEM commanded Moses: 22 Only
the gold and the silver, the copper, the iron, the tin, and the lead —
23 everything that comes into the fire — you shall pass through the fire and
it will be purified; but it must be purified with the water of sprinkling; and
everything that would not come in the fire, you shall pass through the water.
24 You shall immerse your garments on the seventh day and become
purified; afterward you may enter the camp.
25 HASHEM said to Moses, saying: 26 Calculate the total of the captured
spoils, of people and animals, you, Elazar the Kohen, and the heads of the
fathers of the assembly. 27 Divide the spoils in half, between those who
undertook the battle, who go out to the legion, and the entire assembly. 28 You
shall raise up a tribute to HASHEM from the men of war who go out to the
legion, one living being of five hundred, from the people, from the cattle,
from the donkeys, and from the flock. 29 You shall take it from their half and
give it to Elazar the Kohen, as a portion of HASHEM. 30 And from the half of
the Children of Israel you shall take one drawn from fifty, from the people,
from the cattle, from the donkeys, from the flock — from all the animals —

אַךְ בְּמֵי נִדָּה יִתְחַטָּא — *Nevertheless it shall be made tahor with the water of sprinkling.* For it still does not become ritually *tahor* with purging by fire (לִבּוּן) even though it now appears as new.

27. וְחָצִיתָ אֶת הַמַּלְקוֹחַ — *And divide the prey into two parts.* Since this battle was one of vengeance (in retaliation) for what had been done to all of them, (God) wanted the promise of וְאָכַלְתָּ אֶת שְׁלַל אֹיְבֶיךָ, *And you shall eat the booty of your enemies* (*Deut.* 20:14), to be fulfilled, similar to that of David and the booty of Amalek, of which it says, הִנֵּה לָכֶם בְּרָכָה מִשְּׁלַל אֹיְבֵי ה׳, *Behold, a present (blessing) for you of the spoil of the enemies of HASHEM* (*I Samuel* 30:26).

NOTES

Sforno incorporates these laws in his commentary, adding that even when purged by fire the vessel requires ritual purification although it appears new.

27. וְחָצִיתָ אֶת הַמַּלְקוֹחַ — *And divide the prey into two parts.* The *Sforno* tells us why those who did not participate in the war received a portion of the booty. He explains that since the nefarious plot of Balaam and Balak was aimed at the undermining of all the Children of Israel, it was only proper that the prey and booty realized from this war of vengeance be shared with all who were the intended victims of Moab and Midian.

לא וְנָתַתָּ֞ה אֹתָ֣ם לַלְוִיִּ֗ם שֹֽׁמְרֵי֙ מִשְׁמֶ֣רֶת מִשְׁכַּ֣ן יהו֔ה וַיַּ֣עַשׂ מֹשֶׁ֣ה וְאֶלְעָזָ֣ר

לב הַכֹּהֵ֔ן כַּֽאֲשֶׁ֛ר צִוָּ֥ה יהו֖ה אֶת־מֹשֶֽׁה: וַיְהִי֙ הַמַּלְק֔וֹחַ יֶ֣תֶר הַבָּ֔ז אֲשֶׁ֥ר בָּֽזְז֖וּ עַ֣ם

לג הַצָּבָ֑א צֹ֗אן שֵֽׁשׁ־מֵא֥וֹת אֶ֛לֶף וְשִׁבְעִ֥ים אֶ֖לֶף וַֽחֲמֵ֥שֶׁת אֲלָפִֽים: וּבָקָ֕ר שְׁנַ֥יִם

לד-לה וְשִׁבְעִ֖ים אָֽלֶף: וַֽחֲמֹרִ֕ים אֶחָ֥ד וְשִׁשִּׁ֖ים אָֽלֶף: וְנֶ֣פֶשׁ אָדָ֔ם מִן־הַנָּשִׁים֙ אֲשֶׁר־

לו לֹא־יָֽדְע֖וּ מִשְׁכַּ֣ב זָכָ֑ר כָּל־נֶ֕פֶשׁ שְׁנַ֥יִם וּשְׁלֹשִׁ֖ים אָֽלֶף: וַתְּהִי֙ הַֽמֶּֽחֱצָ֔ה חֵ֕לֶק

הַיֹּֽצְאִ֖ים בַּצָּבָ֑א מִסְפַּ֣ר הַצֹּ֗אן שְׁלֹשׁ־מֵא֥וֹת אֶ֛לֶף וּשְׁלֹשִׁ֥ים אֶ֖לֶף וְשִׁבְעַ֥ת

לז אֲלָפִ֖ים וַֽחֲמֵ֣שׁ מֵאֽוֹת: וַיְהִ֛י הַמֶּ֥כֶס לַיהו֖ה מִן־הַצֹּ֑אן שֵׁ֥שׁ מֵא֖וֹת חָמֵ֥שׁ

לח וְשִׁבְעִֽים: וְהַ֨בָּקָ֔ר שִׁשָּׁ֥ה וּשְׁלֹשִׁ֖ים אָ֑לֶף וּמִכְסָ֥ם לַיהו֖ה שְׁנַ֥יִם וְשִׁבְעִֽים:

לט-מ וַֽחֲמֹרִ֕ים שְׁלֹשִׁ֥ים אֶ֖לֶף וַֽחֲמֵ֣שׁ מֵא֑וֹת וּמִכְסָ֥ם לַיהו֖ה אֶחָ֥ד וְשִׁשִּֽׁים: וְנֶ֣פֶשׁ

מא אָדָ֗ם שִׁשָּׁ֤ה עָשָׂר֙ אֶ֔לֶף וּמִכְסָם֙ לַֽיהו֔ה שְׁנַ֥יִם וּשְׁלֹשִׁ֖ים נָ֑פֶשׁ וַיִּתֵּ֣ן מֹשֶׁ֗ה

אֶת־מֶ֨כֶס֙ תְּרוּמַ֣ת יהו֔ה לְאֶלְעָזָ֖ר הַכֹּהֵ֑ן כַּֽאֲשֶׁ֛ר צִוָּ֥ה יהו֖ה אֶת־מֹשֶֽׁה:

חמישי מב-מג וּמִמַּֽחֲצִ֖ית בְּנֵ֣י יִשְׂרָאֵ֑ל אֲשֶׁר֙ חָצָ֣ה מֹשֶׁ֔ה מִן־הָֽאֲנָשִׁ֖ים הַצֹּֽבְאִֽים: וַתְּהִ֛י

מֶֽחֱצַ֥ת הָֽעֵדָ֖ה מִן־הַצֹּ֑אן שְׁלֹשׁ־מֵא֥וֹת אֶ֛לֶף וּשְׁלֹשִׁ֥ים אֶ֖לֶף שִׁבְעַ֥ת אֲלָפִ֖ים

מד-מה וַֽחֲמֵ֥שׁ מֵאֽוֹת: וּבָקָ֕ר שִׁשָּׁ֥ה וּשְׁלֹשִׁ֖ים אָֽלֶף: וַֽחֲמֹרִ֕ים שְׁלֹשִׁ֥ים אֶ֖לֶף וַֽחֲמֵ֥שׁ

מו-מז מֵאֽוֹת: וְנֶ֣פֶשׁ אָדָ֔ם שִׁשָּׁ֥ה עָשָׂ֖ר אָ֑לֶף: וַיִּקַּ֨ח מֹשֶׁ֜ה מִמַּֽחֲצִ֣ת בְּנֵֽי־

יִשְׂרָאֵ֗ל אֶת־הָֽאָחֻ֤ז אֶחָד֙ מִן־הַֽחֲמִשִּׁ֔ים מִן־הָֽאָדָ֖ם וּמִן־הַבְּהֵמָ֑ה וַיִּתֵּ֨ן אֹתָ֜ם

מח לַלְוִיִּ֗ם שֹֽׁמְרֵי֙ מִשְׁמֶ֙רֶת֙ מִשְׁכַּ֣ן יהו֔ה כַּֽאֲשֶׁ֛ר צִוָּ֥ה יהו֖ה אֶת־מֹשֶֽׁה: וַֽיִּקְרְבוּ֙

אֶל־מֹשֶׁ֔ה הַפְּקֻדִ֕ים אֲשֶׁ֖ר לְאַלְפֵ֣י הַצָּבָ֑א שָׂרֵ֥י הָֽאֲלָפִ֖ים וְשָׂרֵ֥י הַמֵּאֽוֹת:

מט וַיֹּֽאמְרוּ֙ אֶל־מֹשֶׁ֔ה עֲבָדֶ֣יךָ נָֽשְׂא֗וּ אֶת־רֹ֛אשׁ אַנְשֵׁ֥י הַמִּלְחָמָ֖ה אֲשֶׁ֣ר בְּיָדֵ֑נוּ

נ וְלֹֽא־נִפְקַ֥ד מִמֶּ֖נּוּ אִֽישׁ: וַנַּקְרֵ֞ב אֶת־קָרְבַּ֣ן יהו֗ה אִישׁ֩ אֲשֶׁ֨ר מָצָ֤א כְלִֽי־זָהָב֙

נא אֶצְעָדָ֣ה וְצָמִ֔יד טַבַּ֖עַת עָגִ֣יל וְכוּמָ֑ז לְכַפֵּ֥ר עַל־נַפְשֹׁתֵ֖ינוּ לִפְנֵ֥י יהוֽה: וַיִּקַּ֨ח

נב מֹשֶׁ֜ה וְאֶלְעָזָ֤ר הַכֹּהֵן֙ אֶת־הַזָּהָ֣ב מֵֽאִתָּ֑ם כֹּ֖ל כְּלִ֥י מַֽעֲשֶֽׂה: וַיְהִ֣י ׀ כָּל־זְהַ֣ב

הַתְּרוּמָ֗ה אֲשֶׁ֤ר הֵרִ֨ימוּ֙ לַֽיהו֔ה שִׁשָּׁ֨ה עָשָׂ֥ר אֶ֛לֶף שְׁבַע־מֵא֥וֹת וַֽחֲמִשִּׁ֖ים

נג שָׁ֑קֶל מֵאֵת֙ שָׂרֵ֣י הָֽאֲלָפִ֔ים וּמֵאֵ֖ת שָׂרֵ֣י הַמֵּאֽוֹת: אַנְשֵׁי֙ הַצָּבָ֔א בָּֽזְז֖וּ אִ֥ישׁ

נד לֽוֹ: וַיִּקַּ֨ח מֹשֶׁ֜ה וְאֶלְעָזָ֤ר הַכֹּהֵן֙ אֶת־הַזָּהָ֔ב מֵאֵ֛ת שָׂרֵ֥י הָֽאֲלָפִ֖ים וְהַמֵּא֑וֹת

וַיָּבִ֤אוּ אֹתוֹ֙ אֶל־אֹ֣הֶל מוֹעֵ֔ד זִכָּר֥וֹן לִבְנֵֽי־יִשְׂרָאֵ֖ל לִפְנֵ֥י יהוֽה:

---

32. יֶ֣תֶר הַבָּ֔ז אֲשֶׁ֥ר בָּֽזְז֖וּ עַ֣ם הַצָּבָ֑א — *Over and above the booty which the men of war plundered*... because the men of war took the property of the houses (entered by them) for themselves.

50. לְכַפֵּ֥ר עַל־נַפְשֹׁתֵ֖ינוּ — *To atone for our souls*... (as an expiation) for the episode of Peor, because we did not protest against the sinners.

51. וַיִּקַּ֨ח מֹשֶׁ֜ה — *And Moses took.* He accepted (the gold) from them and weighed it.

כָּל־כְּלִ֥י מַֽעֲשֶֽׂה — *All articles made for use.* Every kind of article which was used as a

NOTES

50. לְכַפֵּ֥ר עַל־נַפְשֹׁתֵ֖ינוּ — *To atone for our souls.* The Talmud (*Shabbos* 64a) explains that although these soldiers had not sinned overtly, they were guilty of lustful thoughts which required atonement. The *Sforno* offers another explanation consistent with his interpretation of verses 4 and 11 in

chapter 25, as well as *Exodus* 32:27. Their failure to protest the action of the wicked men who sinned at Pe'or necessitated atonement.

51-54. וַיִּקַּ֨ח מֹשֶׁ֜ה ... כָּל־כְּלִ֥י מַֽעֲשֶֽׂה ... וַיִּקַּ֨ח מֹשֶׁ֜ה ... זִכָּר֥וֹן לִבְנֵ֣י יִשְׂרָאֵ֖ל — *And Moses took ... all articles*

and you shall give them to the Levites, the guardians of the charge of HASHEM's Tabernacle.

[31] *Moses and Elazar the Kohen did as HASHEM had commanded Moses.*
[32] *The animal booty, beyond the spoils that the people of the legion looted:*
the flock, six hundred and seventy-five thousand; [33] *and cattle, seventy-*
two thousand; [34] *and donkeys, sixty-one thousand;* [35] *and human beings,*
the women who had not known lying with a male, all the souls, thirty-two
thousand. [36] *The half, which was the share of those who went out to the*
legion, was: the count of the flock, three hundred and thirty-seven
thousand, five hundred — [37] *the tribute of HASHEM from the flock, six*
hundred and seventy-five; [38] *and the cattle, thirty-six thousand — and their*
tribute to HASHEM, seventy-two; [39] *and the donkeys, thirty thousand, five*
hundred — and their tribute to HASHEM, sixty-one; [40] *and the human beings,*
sixteen thousand — and their tribute to HASHEM, thirty-two people. [41] *Moses*
gave the tribute that was raised up for HASHEM to Elazar the Kohen, as
HASHEM had commanded Moses.

[42] *From the half of the Children of Israel that Moses had divided from the*
men of the legions, [43] *the half of the assembly was: of the flock, three*
hundred and thirty-seven thousand, five hundred — [44] *and the cattle,*
thirty-six thousand; [45] *and the donkeys, thirty thousand five hundred;*
[46] *and the human beings, sixteen thousand.* [47] *Moses took from the half of*
the Children of Israel the one drawn from the fifty, from the people and the
animals, and gave them to the Levites, the guardians of the charge of
HASHEM's Tabernacle, as HASHEM had commanded Moses.

[48] *The commanders of the thousands in the legions, the officers of the*
thousands and the officers of the hundreds, approached Moses. [49] *They said*
to Moses, "Your servants took a census of the men of war under our
command, and not a man of us is missing. [50] *So we have brought an offering*
for HASHEM: what any man found of gold vessels, anklet and bracelet, ring,
earring, and clasp, to atone for our souls before HASHEM." [51] *Moses and*
Elazar the Kohen took the gold from them, every fashioned vessel. [52] *All the*
gold that was raised up, which they set apart for HASHEM, was sixteen
thousand, seven hundred and fifty shekel, from the officers of the thous-
ands and the officers of the hundreds. [53] *As for the men of the legion, each*
man looted for himself. [54] *Moses and Elazar the Kohen took the gold from the*
officers of the thousands and the hundreds and brought it to the Tent of
Meeting, a remembrance for the Children of Israel before HASHEM.

---

woman's ornament at the episode of Peor.

54. וַיִּקַּח מֹשֶׁה — *And Moses took.* After he weighed them, he brought them to the Tent of Meeting.

זִכָּרוֹן לִבְנֵי יִשְׂרָאֵל — *As a remembrance to the Children of Israel . . .* as an atonement for the iniquity of Peor.

NOTES

made for use . . . And Moses took . . . as a remembrance to the Children of Israel. The *Sforno* explains the repetition of the verb וַיִּקַּח, *took,* in these two verses. The first refers to his accepting the ornaments of gold which he then weighed. The second refers to his subsequent act of bringing them into the Tent of Meeting. The phrase זִכָּרוֹן, *remembrance,* is also used in *Exodus* 30:16 as an

לב ששי א וּמִקְנֶה | רַב הָיָה לִבְנֵי רְאוּבֵן וְלִבְנֵי־גָד עָצוּם מְאֹד וַיִּרְאוּ אֶת־אֶרֶץ יַעְזֵר
[שלישי] ב וְאֶת־אֶרֶץ גִּלְעָד וְהִנֵּה הַמָּקוֹם מְקוֹם מִקְנֶה׃ וַיָּבֹאוּ בְנֵי־גָד וּבְנֵי רְאוּבֵן
ג וַיֹּאמְרוּ אֶל־מֹשֶׁה וְאֶל־אֶלְעָזָר הַכֹּהֵן וְאֶל־נְשִׂיאֵי הָעֵדָה לֵאמֹר׃ עֲטָרוֹת
ד וְדִיבֹן וְיַעְזֵר וְנִמְרָה וְחֶשְׁבּוֹן וְאֶלְעָלֵה וּשְׂבָם וּנְבוֹ וּבְעֹן׃ הָאָרֶץ אֲשֶׁר הִכָּה
ה יְהוָה לִפְנֵי עֲדַת יִשְׂרָאֵל אֶרֶץ מִקְנֶה הִוא וְלַעֲבָדֶיךָ מִקְנֶה׃ וַיֹּאמְרוּ
אִם־מָצָאנוּ חֵן בְּעֵינֶיךָ יֻתַּן אֶת־הָאָרֶץ הַזֹּאת לַעֲבָדֶיךָ לַאֲחֻזָּה אַל־
ו תַּעֲבִרֵנוּ אֶת־הַיַּרְדֵּן׃ וַיֹּאמֶר מֹשֶׁה לִבְנֵי־גָד וְלִבְנֵי רְאוּבֵן הַאַחֵיכֶם יָבֹאוּ
°תְּנִיאוּן ק׳ ז לַמִּלְחָמָה וְאַתֶּם תֵּשְׁבוּ פֹה׃ וְלָמָּה °תנואון אֶת־לֵב בְּנֵי יִשְׂרָאֵל מֵעֲבֹר
ח אֶל־הָאָרֶץ אֲשֶׁר־נָתַן לָהֶם יְהוָה׃ כֹּה עָשׂוּ אֲבֹתֵיכֶם בְּשָׁלְחִי אֹתָם מִקָּדֵשׁ
ט בַּרְנֵעַ לִרְאוֹת אֶת־הָאָרֶץ׃ וַיַּעֲלוּ עַד־נַחַל אֶשְׁכּוֹל וַיִּרְאוּ אֶת־הָאָרֶץ
וַיָּנִיאוּ אֶת־לֵב בְּנֵי יִשְׂרָאֵל לְבִלְתִּי־בֹא אֶל־הָאָרֶץ אֲשֶׁר־נָתַן לָהֶם יְהוָה׃
י־יא וַיִּחַר־אַף יְהוָה בַּיּוֹם הַהוּא וַיִּשָּׁבַע לֵאמֹר׃ אִם־יִרְאוּ הָאֲנָשִׁים הָעֹלִים
מִמִּצְרַיִם מִבֶּן עֶשְׂרִים שָׁנָה וָמַעְלָה אֵת הָאֲדָמָה אֲשֶׁר נִשְׁבַּעְתִּי לְאַבְרָהָם
יב לְיִצְחָק וּלְיַעֲקֹב כִּי לֹא־מִלְאוּ אַחֲרָי׃ בִּלְתִּי כָּלֵב בֶּן־יְפֻנֶּה הַקְּנִזִּי וִיהוֹשֻׁעַ
יג בִּן־נוּן כִּי מִלְאוּ אַחֲרֵי יְהוָה׃ וַיִּחַר־אַף יְהוָה בְּיִשְׂרָאֵל וַיְנִעֵם בַּמִּדְבָּר
יד אַרְבָּעִים שָׁנָה עַד־תֹּם כָּל־הַדּוֹר הָעֹשֶׂה הָרַע בְּעֵינֵי יְהוָה׃ וְהִנֵּה קַמְתֶּם
תַּחַת אֲבֹתֵיכֶם תַּרְבּוּת אֲנָשִׁים חַטָּאִים לִסְפּוֹת עוֹד עַל חֲרוֹן אַף־יְהוָה
טו אֶל־יִשְׂרָאֵל׃ כִּי תְשׁוּבֻן מֵאַחֲרָיו וְיָסַף עוֹד לְהַנִּיחוֹ בַּמִּדְבָּר וְשִׁחַתֶּם
טז לְכָל־הָעָם הַזֶּה׃ וַיִּגְּשׁוּ אֵלָיו וַיֹּאמְרוּ גִּדְרֹת צֹאן נִבְנֶה לְמִקְנֵנוּ
יז פֹּה וְעָרִים לְטַפֵּנוּ׃ וַאֲנַחְנוּ נֵחָלֵץ חֻשִׁים לִפְנֵי בְּנֵי יִשְׂרָאֵל עַד אֲשֶׁר אִם־
יח הֲבִיאֹנֻם אֶל־מְקוֹמָם וְיָשַׁב טַפֵּנוּ בְּעָרֵי הַמִּבְצָר מִפְּנֵי יֹשְׁבֵי הָאָרֶץ׃ לֹא
יט נָשׁוּב אֶל־בָּתֵּינוּ עַד הִתְנַחֵל בְּנֵי יִשְׂרָאֵל אִישׁ נַחֲלָתוֹ׃ כִּי לֹא נִנְחַל אִתָּם
מֵעֵבֶר לַיַּרְדֵּן וָהָלְאָה כִּי בָאָה נַחֲלָתֵנוּ אֵלֵינוּ מֵעֵבֶר הַיַּרְדֵּן מִזְרָחָה׃

XXXII

3. עֲטָרוֹת וְדִיבֹן — *Ataroth and Dibon.* Each one of these lands, by itself, was land (fit) for cattle.

6. הַאַחֵיכֶם יָבֹאוּ לַמִּלְחָמָה — *Shall your brothers go to war?* Do you actually think that your brothers will be willing to go to war, so as to conquer (the land)?

וְאַתֶּם תֵּשְׁבוּ פֹה — *And you shall sit here . . .* in (the land) which has already been conquered! There is no doubt that you cannot presume that this will be accepted; (therefore) this (proposal) can only serve to turn away the hearts of your brothers.

7. וְלָמָּה תְנִיאוּן — *And wherefore will you turn away the heart?* You certainly know how those who discouraged (others) in the previous generation were punished.

NOTES

expression of atonement. When man remembers his sins and also remembers God, Whom he "forgot" in the passion of the moment, he finds atonement.

XXXII

3. עֲטָרוֹת וְדִיבֹן — *Ataroth and Dibon.* The expression אֶרֶץ מִקְנֶה, *a land for cattle,* in the next verse is written in the singular because it refers to each of the individual lands enumerated here, i.e., Ataroth, Dibon, etc. That is what the *Sforno* alludes to in his commentary on this verse. The phrase הָאָרֶץ אֲשֶׁר הִכָּה ה׳, *the land which* H*ASHEM smote* (v. 4), is to be understood parenthetically. The Torah tells us that these were the same lands which Israel had conquered, with God's help, from Sichon and Og.

32
*[1] The children of Reuben and the children of Gad had abundant
livestock — very great. They saw the land of Jazer and the land of
Gilead, and behold! — it was a place for livestock. [2] The children of Gad
and the children of Reuben came and said to Moses, to Elazar the Kohen,
and to the leaders of the assembly, saying, [3] "Ataroth, and Dibon, and
Jazer, and Nimrah, and Heshbon, and Elealeh, and Sebam, and Nebo, and
Beon — [4] the land that HASHEM smote before the assembly of Israel — it is
a land for livestock, and your servants have livestock."*
*[5] They said, "If we have found favor in your eyes, let this land be given
to your servants as a heritage; do not bring us across the Jordan."*
*[6] Moses said to the children of Gad and the children of Reuben, "Shall
your brothers go out to battle while you settle here? [7] Why do you dissuade
the heart of the Children of Israel from crossing to the Land that HASHEM
has given them? [8] This is what your fathers did, when I sent them from
Kadesh-barnea to see the Land. [9] They went up to the valley of Eshcol and
saw the Land and they dissuaded the heart of the Children of Israel, not to
come to the Land that HASHEM has given them. [10] The wrath of HASHEM
burned on that day, and He swore saying, [11] 'If these men who came up
from Egypt — from the age of twenty years and above — will see the
ground that I swore to Abraham, to Isaac, and to Jacob. . . for they have not
followed Me fully, [12] except for Caleb son of Jephunneh, the Kenizzite, and
Joshua son of Nun, for they followed HASHEM fully.' [13] The wrath of
HASHEM burned against Israel and He made them wander in the
Wilderness for forty years, until the generation that did evil in the eyes of
HASHEM was consumed. [14] Behold! — you have risen up in place of your
fathers, a society of sinful people, to add more to the burning wrath of
HASHEM against Israel. [15] For if you will turn away from after Him, He will
again let it rest in the Wilderness, and you will destroy this entire people."*
*[16] They approached him and said, "Pens for the flock shall we build here
for our livestock and cities for our small children. [17] We shall arm ourselves
swiftly in the vanguard of the Children of Israel until we will have brought
them to their place, and our small children will dwell in the fortified cities
before the inhabitants of the land. [18] We shall not return to our homes until
the Children of Israel will have inherited — every man his inheritance —
[19] for we shall not inherit with them across the Jordan and beyond, for our
inheritance has come to us on the east bank of the Jordan."*

---

17. עַד אֲשֶׁר אִם הֲבִיאֹנֻם — *Until we have brought them.* (The meaning of עַד is) "while as yet" they have not been brought, similar to, עַד לֹא עָשָׂה אֶרֶץ וְחוּצוֹת, *While as yet he had not made the earth or the fields* (*Mishlei* 8:26), (and also) עַד אִם כִּלּוּ לִשְׁתּוֹת, *While as yet they had not finished drinking* (*Genesis* 24:19).

NOTES

6. הַאַחֵיכֶם יָבֹאוּ לַמִּלְחָמָה וְאַתֶּם תֵּשְׁבוּ פֹה — *Shall your brothers go to war and you shall sit here?* The *Sforno* explains the verse thus: Moses argues that it was inconceivable that the land on the east side of the Jordan, which was conquered by *all* Israel, should be given to a *few* tribes who would then remain there in peace while the rest of Israel would have to wage war to conquer the west side of the Jordan — the Land of Canaan. Now since this is obvious, what then could be the purpose of the demand of the children of Gad and Reuben? It had to be for the purpose of discouraging Israel from crossing the Jordan, as the spies had attempted to do a generation earlier.

שביעי [רביעי] כ וַיֹּאמֶר אֲלֵיהֶם מֹשֶׁה אִם־תַּעֲשׂוּן אֶת־הַדָּבָר הַזֶּה אִם־תֵּחָלְצוּ לִפְנֵי יהוה
כא לַמִּלְחָמָה: וְעָבַר לָכֶם כָּל־חָלוּץ אֶת־הַיַּרְדֵּן לִפְנֵי יהוה עַד הוֹרִישׁוֹ אֶת־
כב אֹיְבָיו מִפָּנָיו: וְנִכְבְּשָׁה הָאָרֶץ לִפְנֵי יהוה וְאַחַר תָּשֻׁבוּ וִהְיִיתֶם נְקִיִּם מֵיהוה
כג וּמִיִּשְׂרָאֵל וְהָיְתָה הָאָרֶץ הַזֹּאת לָכֶם לַאֲחֻזָּה לִפְנֵי יהוה: וְאִם־לֹא תַעֲשׂוּן
כד כֵּן הִנֵּה חֲטָאתֶם לַיהוה וּדְעוּ חַטַּאתְכֶם אֲשֶׁר תִּמְצָא אֶתְכֶם: בְּנוּ־לָכֶם עָרִים
כה לְטַפְּכֶם וּגְדֵרֹת לְצֹנַאֲכֶם וְהַיֹּצֵא מִפִּיכֶם תַּעֲשׂוּ: וַיֹּאמֶר בְּנֵי־גָד וּבְנֵי רְאוּבֵן
כו אֶל־מֹשֶׁה לֵאמֹר עֲבָדֶיךָ יַעֲשׂוּ כַּאֲשֶׁר אֲדֹנִי מְצַוֶּה: טַפֵּנוּ נָשֵׁינוּ מִקְנֵנוּ
כז וְכָל־בְּהֶמְתֵּנוּ יִהְיוּ־שָׁם בְּעָרֵי הַגִּלְעָד: וַעֲבָדֶיךָ יַעַבְרוּ כָּל־חֲלוּץ צָבָא לִפְנֵי
כח יהוה לַמִּלְחָמָה כַּאֲשֶׁר אֲדֹנִי דֹּבֵר: וַיְצַו לָהֶם מֹשֶׁה אֵת אֶלְעָזָר הַכֹּהֵן וְאֵת
כט יְהוֹשֻׁעַ בִּן־נוּן וְאֶת־רָאשֵׁי אֲבוֹת הַמַּטּוֹת לִבְנֵי יִשְׂרָאֵל: וַיֹּאמֶר מֹשֶׁה אֲלֵהֶם
אִם־יַעַבְרוּ בְנֵי־גָד וּבְנֵי־רְאוּבֵן ׀ אִתְּכֶם אֶת־הַיַּרְדֵּן כָּל־חָלוּץ לַמִּלְחָמָה
לִפְנֵי יהוה וְנִכְבְּשָׁה הָאָרֶץ לִפְנֵיכֶם וּנְתַתֶּם לָהֶם אֶת־אֶרֶץ הַגִּלְעָד לַאֲחֻזָּה:
ל־לא וְאִם־לֹא יַעַבְרוּ חֲלוּצִים אִתְּכֶם וְנֹאחֲזוּ בְתֹכְכֶם בְּאֶרֶץ כְּנָעַן: וַיַּעֲנוּ בְנֵי־גָד
לב וּבְנֵי רְאוּבֵן לֵאמֹר אֵת אֲשֶׁר דִּבֶּר יהוה אֶל־עֲבָדֶיךָ כֵּן נַעֲשֶׂה: נַחְנוּ נַעֲבֹר
לג חֲלוּצִים לִפְנֵי יהוה אֶרֶץ כְּנָעַן וְאִתָּנוּ אֲחֻזַּת נַחֲלָתֵנוּ מֵעֵבֶר לַיַּרְדֵּן: וַיִּתֵּן
לָהֶם ׀ מֹשֶׁה לִבְנֵי־גָד וְלִבְנֵי רְאוּבֵן וְלַחֲצִי ׀ שֵׁבֶט ׀ מְנַשֶּׁה בֶן־יוֹסֵף
אֶת־מַמְלֶכֶת סִיחֹן מֶלֶךְ הָאֱמֹרִי וְאֶת־מַמְלֶכֶת עוֹג מֶלֶךְ הַבָּשָׁן הָאָרֶץ
לד לְעָרֶיהָ בִּגְבֻלֹת עָרֵי הָאָרֶץ סָבִיב: וַיִּבְנוּ בְנֵי־גָד אֶת־דִּיבֹן וְאֶת־עֲטָרֹת וְאֵת
לה־לו עֲרֹעֵר: וְאֶת־עַטְרֹת שׁוֹפָן וְאֶת־יַעְזֵר וְיָגְבְּהָה: וְאֶת־בֵּית נִמְרָה וְאֶת־בֵּית
לז הָרָן עָרֵי מִבְצָר וְגִדְרֹת צֹאן: וּבְנֵי רְאוּבֵן בָּנוּ אֶת־חֶשְׁבּוֹן וְאֶת־אֶלְעָלֵא וְאֵת
לח קִרְיָתָיִם: וְאֶת־נְבוֹ וְאֶת־בַּעַל מְעוֹן מוּסַבֹּת שֵׁם וְאֶת־שִׂבְמָה וַיִּקְרְאוּ בְשֵׁמֹת
לט אֶת־שְׁמוֹת הֶעָרִים אֲשֶׁר בָּנוּ: וַיֵּלְכוּ בְּנֵי מָכִיר בֶּן־מְנַשֶּׁה גִּלְעָדָה וַיִּלְכְּדֻהָ
מפטיר מ וַיּוֹרֶשׁ אֶת־הָאֱמֹרִי אֲשֶׁר־בָּהּ: וַיִּתֵּן מֹשֶׁה אֶת־הַגִּלְעָד לְמָכִיר בֶּן־מְנַשֶּׁה
מא וַיֵּשֶׁב בָּהּ: וְיָאִיר בֶּן־מְנַשֶּׁה הָלַךְ וַיִּלְכֹּד אֶת־חַוֹּתֵיהֶם וַיִּקְרָא אֶתְהֶן חַוֺּת
ה' רפה מב יָאִיר: וְנֹבַח הָלַךְ וַיִּלְכֹּד אֶת־קְנָת וְאֶת־בְּנֹתֶיהָ וַיִּקְרָא לָה נֹבַח בִּשְׁמוֹ:

23. הִנֵּה חֲטָאתֶם לַה׳ — *Behold, you have sinned against* HASHEM. In this event, you will reveal at a later time that you have sinned now, (because) you will reveal (lit., make known) that your intent was to perpetrate evil.

25. עֲבָדֶיךָ יַעֲשׂוּ — *Your servants will do.* (We accept) this part of what you say (and agree) to cross over as armed men.

28. וַיְצַו לָהֶם מֹשֶׁה — *So Moses gave charge concerning them.* He commanded (Elazar and Joshua) not to give them the lands of Sichon and Og until after they returned from the conquest of the land (i.e., Canaan) as it states, וְנִכְבְּשָׁה הָאָרֶץ . . . וְאַחַר תָּשֻׁבוּ . . . וְהָיְתָה הָאָרֶץ הַזֹּאת לָכֶם, *And the land be conquered . . . and you return afterward . . . and this land shall be unto you* (v. 22), but not before that. But they did not accept this, and they said, נַחְנוּ נַעֲבֹר חֲלוּצִים . . . וְאִתָּנוּ אֲחֻזַּת נַחֲלָתֵנוּ, *We will pass over armed . . . and the possession of our*

NOTES

28. וַיְצַו לָהֶם מֹשֶׁה — *So Moses gave charge concerning them.* Moses stipulated that these two and a half tribes (Gad, Reuben and half of Menasseh) should not receive title to the land on the east side of the Jordan, even after they joined their brothers in battle, until the task was

[20] Moses said to them, "If you do this thing, if you arm yourselves before HASHEM for the battle, [21] and every armed man among you shall cross the Jordan before HASHEM, until He drives out His enemies before Him, [22] and the Land shall be conquered before HASHEM, and then you shall return — then you shall be vindicated from HASHEM and from Israel, and this Land shall be a heritage for you before HASHEM. [23] But if you do not do so, behold! — you will have sinned to HASHEM; know your sin that will encounter you. [24] Build for yourselves cities for your small children and pens for your flock, and what has come from your mouth shall you do."

[25] The children of Gad and the children of Reuben said to Moses, saying, "Your servants shall do as my lord commands. [26] Our small children, our wives, our livestock, and all our animals will be there in the cities of the Gilead. [27] And your servants shall cross over — every armed person of the legion — before HASHEM, to do battle, as my lord speaks."

[28] Concerning them, Moses commanded Elazar the Kohen, Joshua son of Nun, and the heads of the fathers of the tribes of Israel. [29] Moses said to them, "If the children of Gad and children of Reuben will cross the Jordan with you — everyone armed for battle before HASHEM, and the Land is conquered before you — you shall give them the land of Gilead as a heritage. [30] But if they do not cross over, armed, with you, then they will take [their] heritage among you in the land of Canaan."

[31] The children of Gad and the children of Reuben spoke up, saying, "As HASHEM has spoken to your servants, so shall we do. [32] We shall cross over, armed, before HASHEM to the land of Canaan, and ours shall be the heritage of our inheritance across the Jordan."

[33] So Moses gave to them — to the children of Gad, and the children of Reuben, and half the tribe of Manasseh son of Joseph — the kingdom of Sihon king of the Amorite, and the kingdom of Og king of the Bashan; the land with its cities in the boundaries, and the cities of the surrounding land.

[34] The children of Gad built Dibon, and Ataroth, and Aroer; [35] and Atroth-shophan, and Jazer, and Jogbehah; [36] and Beth-nimrah, and Beth-haran — fortified cities and pens for the flock. [37] The children of Reuben built Heshbon, and Elealeh, and Kiriathaim; [38] and Nebo and Baal-meon with altered names, and Sibmah; and they called [them] by [other] names [instead of] the names of the cities that they built. [39] The children of Machir son of Manasseh went to Gilead and occupied it, and drove out the Amorite who were in it. [40] Moses gave the Gilead to Machir son of Manasseh and he settled in it. [41] Jair son of Manasseh went and occupied their villages, and called them Havvoth-jair. [42] Nobah went and occupied Kenath and her suburbs, and called it Nobah, after his name.

---

inheritance shall remain with us (v. 32), i.e., it shall be in our possession at the time we cross the Jordan!

33. וַיִּתֵּן לָהֶם מֹשֶׁה — *And Moses gave unto them.* Moses agreed with them in order not to enter into a dispute.

NOTES

finished and they returned home. They, however, refused to accept this condition. They were willing to join the army and fight alongside their brothers, but they demanded to take possession of the lands of the Emorites and Bashan — now!

פרשת מסעי

לג א אֵלֶּה מַסְעֵי בְנֵי־יִשְׂרָאֵל אֲשֶׁר יָצְאוּ מֵאֶרֶץ מִצְרַיִם לְצִבְאֹתָם בְּיַד־מֹשֶׁה
ב וְאַהֲרֹן: וַיִּכְתֹּב מֹשֶׁה אֶת־מוֹצָאֵיהֶם לְמַסְעֵיהֶם עַל־פִּי יְהוָה וְאֵלֶּה
ג מַסְעֵיהֶם לְמוֹצָאֵיהֶם: וַיִּסְעוּ מֵרַעְמְסֵס בַּחֹדֶשׁ הָרִאשׁוֹן בַּחֲמִשָּׁה עָשָׂר
יוֹם לַחֹדֶשׁ הָרִאשׁוֹן מִמָּחֳרַת הַפֶּסַח יָצְאוּ בְנֵי־יִשְׂרָאֵל בְּיָד רָמָה לְעֵינֵי
ד כָּל־מִצְרָיִם: וּמִצְרַיִם מְקַבְּרִים אֵת אֲשֶׁר הִכָּה יְהוָה בָּהֶם כָּל־בְּכוֹר
ה וּבֵאלֹהֵיהֶם עָשָׂה יְהוָה שְׁפָטִים: וַיִּסְעוּ בְנֵי־יִשְׂרָאֵל מֵרַעְמְסֵס וַיַּחֲנוּ
ו־ז בְּסֻכֹּת: וַיִּסְעוּ מִסֻּכֹּת וַיַּחֲנוּ בְאֵתָם אֲשֶׁר בִּקְצֵה הַמִּדְבָּר: וַיִּסְעוּ מֵאֵתָם
ח וַיָּשָׁב עַל־פִּי הַחִירֹת אֲשֶׁר עַל־פְּנֵי בַּעַל צְפוֹן וַיַּחֲנוּ לִפְנֵי מִגְדֹּל: וַיִּסְעוּ
מִפְּנֵי הַחִירֹת וַיַּעַבְרוּ בְתוֹךְ־הַיָּם הַמִּדְבָּרָה וַיֵּלְכוּ דֶּרֶךְ שְׁלֹשֶׁת יָמִים
ט בְּמִדְבַּר אֵתָם וַיַּחֲנוּ בְּמָרָה: וַיִּסְעוּ מִמָּרָה וַיָּבֹאוּ אֵילִמָה וּבְאֵילִם שְׁתֵּים
י עֶשְׂרֵה עֵינֹת מַיִם וְשִׁבְעִים תְּמָרִים וַיַּחֲנוּ־שָׁם: וַיִּסְעוּ מֵאֵילִם וַיַּחֲנוּ
יא־יב עַל־יַם־סוּף: *וַיִּסְעוּ מִיַּם־סוּף וַיַּחֲנוּ בְּמִדְבַּר־סִין: וַיִּסְעוּ מִמִּדְבַּר־סִין *שני
יג־יד וַיַּחֲנוּ בְּדָפְקָה: וַיִּסְעוּ מִדָּפְקָה וַיַּחֲנוּ בְּאָלוּשׁ: וַיִּסְעוּ מֵאָלוּשׁ וַיַּחֲנוּ
טו בִּרְפִידִם וְלֹא־הָיָה שָׁם מַיִם לָעָם לִשְׁתּוֹת: וַיִּסְעוּ מֵרְפִידִם וַיַּחֲנוּ בְּמִדְבַּר
טז־יז סִינָי: וַיִּסְעוּ מִמִּדְבַּר סִינָי וַיַּחֲנוּ בְּקִבְרֹת הַתַּאֲוָה: וַיִּסְעוּ מִקִּבְרֹת
יח־יט הַתַּאֲוָה וַיַּחֲנוּ בַּחֲצֵרֹת: וַיִּסְעוּ מֵחֲצֵרֹת וַיַּחֲנוּ בְּרִתְמָה: וַיִּסְעוּ מֵרִתְמָה
כ־כא וַיַּחֲנוּ בְּרִמֹּן פָּרֶץ: וַיִּסְעוּ מֵרִמֹּן פָּרֶץ וַיַּחֲנוּ בְּלִבְנָה: וַיִּסְעוּ מִלִּבְנָה
כב־כג וַיַּחֲנוּ בְּרִסָּה: וַיִּסְעוּ מֵרִסָּה וַיַּחֲנוּ בִּקְהֵלָתָה: וַיִּסְעוּ מִקְּהֵלָתָה וַיַּחֲנוּ
כד־כה בְּהַר־שָׁפֶר: וַיִּסְעוּ מֵהַר־שָׁפֶר וַיַּחֲנוּ בַּחֲרָדָה: וַיִּסְעוּ מֵחֲרָדָה וַיַּחֲנוּ
כו־כז בְּמַקְהֵלֹת: וַיִּסְעוּ מִמַּקְהֵלֹת וַיַּחֲנוּ בְּתָחַת: וַיִּסְעוּ מִתָּחַת וַיַּחֲנוּ בְּתָרַח:

XXXIII

1. אֵלֶּה מַסְעֵי — *These are the journeys.* God, Blessed is He, wanted the journeys of the Israelites to be written (in order to) make known their merit in their following Him in the wilderness, *in a land that was not sown* (based on *Jeremiah* 2:2), and in this manner they deserved to enter the land.

2. וַיִּכְתֹּב מֹשֶׁה — *And Moses wrote.* He wrote down their destination and the place of their departure, for sometimes the place they headed for was exceedingly bad and the place from which they departed was good . . .

וְאֵלֶּה מַסְעֵיהֶם לְמוֹצָאֵיהֶם — *And these are their journeys according to their departures . . .* and sometimes the reverse happened (i.e., they departed from a bad place and traveled to a good one). He also wrote down the details of their journeys which entailed going from

NOTES

XXXIII

1. אֵלֶּה מַסְעֵי — *These are the journeys.* The reason for recording Israel's stations in the wilderness has preoccupied the commentators of the Torah. *Rashi* explains that the purpose was to publicize the lovingkindness of God Who in forty years kept the various stations down to only forty-two. The *Rambam* in his Guide (3:50) explains the necessity to enumerate the stations of the Israelites in the wilderness so that later generations will know that these places were uninhabited and did not contain any natural resources, and thus they will appreciate that the forty years of Israel's existence in the wilderness was a miraculous one. He also adds another reason, namely, to instruct us that all their journeys were planned and ordered by God, and not disorganized and haphazard.

The *Sforno,* however, submits a different reason

PARASHAS MASEI

33 1 *These are the journeys of the Children of Israel, who went forth from
the land of Egypt according to their legions, under the hand of Moses
and Aaron.* 2 *Moses wrote their goings forth according to their journeys at
the bidding of HASHEM, and these were their journeys according to their
goings forth:* 3 *They journeyed from Rameses in the first month, on the
fifteenth day of the first month — on the day after the pesach-offering —
the Children of Israel went forth with an upraised hand, before the eyes of
all Egypt.* 4 *And the Egyptians were burying those whom HASHEM had
struck, every firstborn; and on their gods HASHEM had inflicted punishments.* 5 *The Children of Israel journeyed from Rameses and encamped in
Succoth.* 6 *They journeyed from Succoth and encamped in Etham, which is
on the edge of the Wilderness.* 7 *They journeyed from Etham and it turned
back to Pi-Hahiroth, which is before Baal-zephon, and they encamped
before Migdol.* 8 *They journeyed from before Hahiroth and passed through
the midst of the Sea toward the Wilderness; they went on a three-day trip
in the Wilderness of Etham, and they encamped in Marah.* 9 *They journeyed
from Marah and arrived at Elim; in Elim were twelve springs of water and
seventy date palms, and they encamped there.* 10 *They journeyed from Elim
and encamped by the Sea of Reeds.* 11 *They journeyed from the Sea of Reeds
and encamped in the Wilderness of Sin.* 12 *They journeyed from the
Wilderness of Sin and encamped in Dophkah.* 13 *They journeyed from
Dophkah and encamped in Alush.* 14 *They journeyed from Alush and
encamped in Rephidim, and there was no water there for the people to drink.*
15 *They journeyed from Rephidim and they encamped in the Wilderness of
Sinai.* 16 *They journeyed from the Wilderness of Sinai and encamped in
Kibroth Hattaavah.* 17 *They journeyed from Kibroth-Hattaavah and
encamped in Hazeroth.* 18 *They journeyed from Hazeroth and encamped in
Rithmah.* 19 *They journeyed from Rithmah and encamped in Rimmon-
perez.* 20 *They journeyed from Rimmon-perez and encamped in Libnah.*
21 *They journeyed from Libnah and encamped in Rissah.* 22 *They journeyed
from Rissah and encamped in Kehelathah.* 23 *They journeyed from Kehelathah and encamped in Mount Shepher.* 24 *They journeyed from Mount
Shepher and encamped in Haradah.* 25 *They journeyed from Haradah
and encamped in Makheloth.* 26 *They journeyed from Makheloth and encamped in Tahath.* 27 *They journeyed from Tahath and encamped in Terah.*

---

place to place without prior notice, which was very difficult. Nonetheless, they did not refrain (from journeying), and therefore it is written of each one of them that they journeyed from a certain place and encamped in (another) certain place, to indicate that the journeying and the encampment were (both) difficult.

NOTES

for the Torah's recording of these journeys. It is to teach us Israel's faith in God and their readiness to travel at His behest, regardless of any difficulty or their lack of understanding the decision to leave a given place and proceed to another. Because of this willingness to obey God and follow Him, they merited to eventually enter the Promised Land.

2. וְאֵלֶּה מַסְעֵיהֶם לְמוֹצָאֵיהֶם — *And these are their journeys according to their departures.* Compare the *Sforno's* commentary here to his commentary in chapter 9, verses 19-23 and the notes there.

כח-ל וַיִּסְעוּ מִתָּרַח וַיַּחֲנוּ בְּמִתְקָה: וַיִּסְעוּ מִמִּתְקָה וַיַּחֲנוּ בְּחַשְׁמֹנָה: וַיִּסְעוּ
לא-לב מֵחַשְׁמֹנָה וַיַּחֲנוּ בְּמֹסֵרוֹת: וַיִּסְעוּ מִמֹּסֵרוֹת וַיַּחֲנוּ בִּבְנֵי יַעֲקָן: וַיִּסְעוּ
לג-לד מִבְּנֵי יַעֲקָן וַיַּחֲנוּ בְּחֹר הַגִּדְגָּד: וַיִּסְעוּ מֵחֹר הַגִּדְגָּד וַיַּחֲנוּ בְּיָטְבָתָה: וַיִּסְעוּ
לה-לו מִיָּטְבָתָה וַיַּחֲנוּ בְּעַבְרֹנָה: וַיִּסְעוּ מֵעַבְרֹנָה וַיַּחֲנוּ בְּעֶצְיֹן גָּבֶר: וַיִּסְעוּ
לז מֵעֶצְיֹן גָּבֶר וַיַּחֲנוּ בְמִדְבַּר־צִן הִוא קָדֵשׁ: וַיִּסְעוּ מִקָּדֵשׁ וַיַּחֲנוּ בְּהֹר הָהָר
לח בִּקְצֵה אֶרֶץ אֱדוֹם: וַיַּעַל אַהֲרֹן הַכֹּהֵן אֶל־הֹר הָהָר עַל־פִּי יְהוָה וַיָּמָת
שָׁם בִּשְׁנַת הָאַרְבָּעִים לְצֵאת בְּנֵי־יִשְׂרָאֵל מֵאֶרֶץ מִצְרַיִם בַּחֹדֶשׁ הַחֲמִישִׁי
לט בְּאֶחָד לַחֹדֶשׁ: וְאַהֲרֹן בֶּן־שָׁלֹשׁ וְעֶשְׂרִים וּמְאַת שָׁנָה בְּמֹתוֹ בְּהֹר
מ הָהָר: וַיִּשְׁמַע הַכְּנַעֲנִי מֶלֶךְ עֲרָד וְהוּא־יֹשֵׁב בַּנֶּגֶב בְּאֶרֶץ כְּנַעַן
מא-מב בְּבֹא בְּנֵי יִשְׂרָאֵל: וַיִּסְעוּ מֵהֹר הָהָר וַיַּחֲנוּ בְּצַלְמֹנָה: וַיִּסְעוּ מִצַּלְמֹנָה וַיַּחֲנוּ
מג-מד בְּפוּנֹן: וַיִּסְעוּ מִפּוּנֹן וַיַּחֲנוּ בְּאֹבֹת: וַיִּסְעוּ מֵאֹבֹת וַיַּחֲנוּ בְּעִיֵּי הָעֲבָרִים בִּגְבוּל
מה-מו מוֹאָב: וַיִּסְעוּ מֵעִיִּים וַיַּחֲנוּ בְּדִיבֹן גָּד: וַיִּסְעוּ מִדִּיבֹן גָּד וַיַּחֲנוּ בְּעַלְמֹן
מז-מח דִּבְלָתָיְמָה: וַיִּסְעוּ מֵעַלְמֹן דִּבְלָתָיְמָה וַיַּחֲנוּ בְּהָרֵי הָעֲבָרִים לִפְנֵי נְבוֹ: וַיִּסְעוּ
מט מֵהָרֵי הָעֲבָרִים וַיַּחֲנוּ בְּעַרְבֹת מוֹאָב עַל יַרְדֵּן יְרֵחוֹ: וַיַּחֲנוּ עַל־הַיַּרְדֵּן מִבֵּית
שלישי [חמישי] נ הַיְשִׁמֹת עַד אָבֵל הַשִּׁטִּים בְּעַרְבֹת מוֹאָב: וַיְדַבֵּר יְהוָה אֶל־
נא מֹשֶׁה בְּעַרְבֹת מוֹאָב עַל־יַרְדֵּן יְרֵחוֹ לֵאמֹר: דַּבֵּר אֶל־בְּנֵי יִשְׂרָאֵל וְאָמַרְתָּ
נב אֲלֵהֶם כִּי אַתֶּם עֹבְרִים אֶת־הַיַּרְדֵּן אֶל־אֶרֶץ כְּנָעַן: וְהוֹרַשְׁתֶּם אֶת־כָּל־
יֹשְׁבֵי הָאָרֶץ מִפְּנֵיכֶם וְאִבַּדְתֶּם אֵת כָּל־מַשְׂכִּיֹּתָם וְאֵת כָּל־צַלְמֵי מַסֵּכֹתָם
נג תְּאַבֵּדוּ וְאֵת כָּל־בָּמוֹתָם תַּשְׁמִידוּ: וְהוֹרַשְׁתֶּם אֶת־הָאָרֶץ וִישַׁבְתֶּם־בָּהּ כִּי
נד לָכֶם נָתַתִּי אֶת־הָאָרֶץ לָרֶשֶׁת אֹתָהּ: וְהִתְנַחַלְתֶּם אֶת־הָאָרֶץ בְּגוֹרָל
לְמִשְׁפְּחֹתֵיכֶם לָרַב תַּרְבּוּ אֶת־נַחֲלָתוֹ וְלַמְעַט תַּמְעִיט אֶת־נַחֲלָתוֹ אֶל
נה אֲשֶׁר־יֵצֵא לוֹ שָׁמָּה הַגּוֹרָל לוֹ יִהְיֶה לְמַטּוֹת אֲבֹתֵיכֶם תִּתְנֶחָלוּ: וְאִם־לֹא
תוֹרִישׁוּ אֶת־יֹשְׁבֵי הָאָרֶץ מִפְּנֵיכֶם וְהָיָה אֲשֶׁר תּוֹתִירוּ מֵהֶם לְשִׂכִּים
בְּעֵינֵיכֶם וְלִצְנִינִם בְּצִדֵּיכֶם וְצָרְרוּ אֶתְכֶם עַל־הָאָרֶץ אֲשֶׁר אַתֶּם יֹשְׁבִים
נו בָּהּ: וְהָיָה כַּאֲשֶׁר דִּמִּיתִי לַעֲשׂוֹת לָהֶם אֶעֱשֶׂה לָכֶם:

---

40. וַיִּשְׁמַע הַכְּנַעֲנִי — *And the Canaanite heard.* This was also a merit for them because they did not say as their fathers had, *"Let us make a leader and return to Egypt"* (14:4), even when faced by war, but they made a vow to God and fulfilled it (see 21:2,3).

53. וְהוֹרַשְׁתֶּם אֶת הָאָרֶץ — *And you shall bequeath the land.* If you remove the inhabitants of the land, then you will merit to have your children inhabit the land. (However) if you do not rid (the land) of them, although you may conquer the land you will not merit to bequeath it to your children.

NOTES

40. וַיִּשְׁמַע הַכְּנַעֲנִי — *And the Canaanite heard. Rashi* comments that the news heard by the Canaanites was that of Aaron's death which resulted in the departure of the clouds of glory. Emboldened by this, they attacked the Israelites who did battle against them, as recorded in chapter 21, verses 1-3. The *Sforno* comments that this brave act on the part of Israel demonstrated that this generation possessed great courage and faith which was lacking in the previous one at the time of the spies.

53. וְהוֹרַשְׁתֶּם אֶת הָאָרֶץ — *And you shall bequeath the land.* The expression וְהוֹרַשְׁתֶּם appears also in the previous verse. The *Sforno* interprets the former one as meaning *to dispossess* or *drive out,* while the present one means *to inherit and be-*

*28 They journeyed from Terah and encamped in Mithkah. 29 They journeyed
from Mithkah and encamped in Hashmonah. 30 They journeyed from
Hashmonah and encamped in Moseroth. 31 They journeyed from Moseroth
and encamped in Bene-jaakan. 32 They journeyed from Bene-jaakan and
encamped in Hor-haggidgad. 33 They journeyed from Hor-haggidgad and
encamped in Jotbathah. 34 They journeyed from Jotbathah and encamped in
Abronah. 35 They journeyed from Abronah and encamped in Ezion-geber.
36 They journeyed from Ezion-geber and encamped in the Wilderness of Zin,
which is Kadesh. 37 They journeyed from Kadesh and encamped in Mount
Hor, at the edge of the land of Edom. 38 Then Aaron the Kohen went up to
Mount Hor at the word of HASHEM and died there, in the fortieth year after
the Children of Israel went forth from the land of Egypt, in the fifth month
on the first of the month. 39 Aaron was one hundred and twenty-three years
old at his death on Mount Hor.*

*40 The Canaanite king of Arad heard — he was dwelling in the south of the
land of Canaan — of the approach of the Children of Israel. 41 They
journeyed from Mount Hor and encamped in Zalmonah. 42 They journeyed
from Zalmonah and encamped in Punon. 43 They journeyed from Punon and
encamped in Oboth. 44 They journeyed from Oboth and encamped in the
ruins of the passes, at the border of Moab. 45 They journeyed from the ruins
and encamped in Dibon-gad. 46 They journeyed from Dibon-gad and
encamped in Almon-diblathaimah. 47 They journeyed from Almon-diblathaimah and encamped in the mountains of the passes before Nebo. 48 They
journeyed from the mountains of the passes and encamped in the plains of
Moab by the Jordan, at Jericho. 49 They encamped by the Jordan, from
Beth-jeshimoth until the plains of Shittim, in the plains of Moab.*

*50 HASHEM spoke to Moses in the plains of Moab, by the Jordan, at Jericho,
saying: 51 Speak to the Children of Israel and say to them: When you cross
the Jordan to the land of Canaan, 52 you shall drive out all the inhabitants
of the Land before you; and you shall destroy all their prostration stones; all
their molten images shall you destroy; and all their high places shall you
demolish. 53 You shall possess the Land and you shall settle in it, for to you
have I given the Land to possess it. 54 You shall give the Land as an
inheritance by lot to your families; to the many you shall increase its
inheritance and to the few shall you decrease its inheritance; wherever its
lot shall fall, his shall it be, according to the tribes of your fathers shall you
inherit. 55 But if you do not drive out the inhabitants of the Land before you,
those of them whom you leave shall be pins in your eyes and thorns in your
sides, and they will harass you upon the Land in which you dwell. 56 And it
shall be that what I had meant to do to them, I shall do to you.*

---

56. וְהָיָה כַּאֲשֶׁר דִּמִּיתִי לַעֲשׂוֹת לָהֶם אֶעֱשֶׂה לָכֶם — *And it shall come to pass that as I thought to do unto them, so will I do unto you . . .* for undoubtedly, you will go astray after their gods.

NOTES

queath as a possession. He therefore explains that one is contingent on the other. Only if Israel will drive out the present inhabitants and rid the land of idolatry will they merit to inherit and bequeath the land to future generations. See *Rashi* who interprets this verse in a similar fashion, stating, "If you drive them out of the land only then shall you dwell in it and be able to remain in it."

לד

א־ב וַיְדַבֵּר יְהוָה אֶל־מֹשֶׁה לֵּאמֹר: צַו אֶת־בְּנֵי יִשְׂרָאֵל וְאָמַרְתָּ אֲלֵהֶם
כִּי־אַתֶּם בָּאִים אֶל־הָאָרֶץ כְּנָעַן זֹאת הָאָרֶץ אֲשֶׁר תִּפֹּל לָכֶם בְּנַחֲלָה
ג אֶרֶץ כְּנַעַן לִגְבֻלֹתֶיהָ: וְהָיָה לָכֶם פְּאַת־נֶגֶב מִמִּדְבַּר־צִן עַל־יְדֵי אֱדוֹם
ד וְהָיָה לָכֶם גְּבוּל נֶגֶב מִקְצֵה יָם־הַמֶּלַח קֵדְמָה: וְנָסַב לָכֶם הַגְּבוּל מִנֶּגֶב
°וְהָיוּ ק׳ לְמַעֲלֵה עַקְרַבִּים וְעָבַר צִנָה °והיה תּוֹצְאֹתָיו מִנֶּגֶב לְקָדֵשׁ בַּרְנֵעַ וְיָצָא
ה חֲצַר־אַדָּר וְעָבַר עַצְמֹנָה: וְנָסַב הַגְּבוּל מֵעַצְמוֹן נַחְלָה מִצְרָיִם וְהָיוּ
ו תוֹצְאֹתָיו הַיָּמָּה: וּגְבוּל יָם וְהָיָה לָכֶם הַיָּם הַגָּדוֹל וּגְבוּל זֶה־יִהְיֶה לָכֶם
ז גְּבוּל יָם: וְזֶה־יִהְיֶה לָכֶם גְּבוּל צָפוֹן מִן־הַיָּם הַגָּדֹל תְּתָאוּ לָכֶם הֹר הָהָר:
ח־ט מֵהֹר הָהָר תְּתָאוּ לְבֹא חֲמָת וְהָיוּ תּוֹצְאֹת הַגְּבֻל צְדָדָה: וְיָצָא הַגְּבֻל
י זִפְרֹנָה וְהָיוּ תוֹצְאֹתָיו חֲצַר עֵינָן זֶה־יִהְיֶה לָכֶם גְּבוּל צָפוֹן: וְהִתְאַוִּיתֶם
יא לָכֶם לִגְבוּל קֵדְמָה מֵחֲצַר עֵינָן שְׁפָמָה: וְיָרַד הַגְּבֻל מִשְּׁפָם הָרִבְלָה
יב מִקֶּדֶם לָעַיִן וְיָרַד הַגְּבֻל וּמָחָה עַל־כֶּתֶף יָם־כִּנֶּרֶת קֵדְמָה: וְיָרַד הַגְּבוּל
הַיַּרְדֵּנָה וְהָיוּ תוֹצְאֹתָיו יָם הַמֶּלַח זֹאת תִּהְיֶה לָכֶם הָאָרֶץ לִגְבֻלֹתֶיהָ
יג סָבִיב: וַיְצַו מֹשֶׁה אֶת־בְּנֵי יִשְׂרָאֵל לֵאמֹר זֹאת הָאָרֶץ אֲשֶׁר תִּתְנַחֲלוּ
יד אֹתָהּ בְּגוֹרָל אֲשֶׁר צִוָּה יְהוָה לָתֵת לְתִשְׁעַת הַמַּטּוֹת וַחֲצִי הַמַּטֶּה: כִּי
לָקְחוּ מַטֵּה בְנֵי הָראוּבֵנִי לְבֵית אֲבֹתָם וּמַטֵּה בְנֵי־הַגָּדִי לְבֵית אֲבֹתָם
טו וַחֲצִי מַטֵּה מְנַשֶּׁה לָקְחוּ נַחֲלָתָם: שְׁנֵי הַמַּטּוֹת וַחֲצִי הַמַּטֶּה לָקְחוּ נַחֲלָתָם
מֵעֵבֶר לְיַרְדֵּן יְרֵחוֹ קֵדְמָה מִזְרָחָה:
רביעי [ששי] טז־יז וַיְדַבֵּר יְהוָה אֶל־מֹשֶׁה לֵּאמֹר: אֵלֶּה שְׁמוֹת הָאֲנָשִׁים אֲשֶׁר־יִנְחֲלוּ לָכֶם
יח אֶת־הָאָרֶץ אֶלְעָזָר הַכֹּהֵן וִיהוֹשֻׁעַ בִּן־נוּן: וְנָשִׂיא אֶחָד נָשִׂיא אֶחָד מִמַּטֶּה
יט תִּקְחוּ לִנְחֹל אֶת־הָאָרֶץ: וְאֵלֶּה שְׁמוֹת הָאֲנָשִׁים לְמַטֵּה יְהוּדָה כָּלֵב
כ־כא בֶּן־יְפֻנֶּה: וּלְמַטֵּה בְּנֵי שִׁמְעוֹן שְׁמוּאֵל בֶּן־עַמִּיהוּד: לְמַטֵּה בִנְיָמִן אֱלִידָד
כב־כג בֶּן־כִּסְלוֹן: וּלְמַטֵּה בְנֵי־דָן נָשִׂיא בֻּקִּי בֶּן־יָגְלִי: לִבְנֵי יוֹסֵף לְמַטֵּה
כד בְנֵי־מְנַשֶּׁה נָשִׂיא חַנִּיאֵל בֶּן־אֵפֹד: וּלְמַטֵּה בְנֵי־אֶפְרַיִם נָשִׂיא קְמוּאֵל

XXXIV

2. זאת הָאָרֶץ אֲשֶׁר תִּפֹּל לָכֶם בְּנַחֲלָה — *This shall be the land that shall fall to you for an inheritance.* It will fall to you by lot (even) before you will completely conquer it; the expression "to fall" (or "to cast") is fitting (to be used) regarding a lot, similar to וְעַל לְבוּשִׁי יַפִּילוּ גוֹרָל, *And cast lots for my clothing* (*Psalms* 22:19), and to הִפִּיל פּוּר הוּא הַגּוֹרָל, *He cast a pur, that is the lot* (*Esther* 3:7). (The verse) says זֹאת, *this,* because that which they conquered outside the land did not require (casting of) a lot to be divided. Therefore, Moses divided the land of Sichon and Og without casting lots, as we see in the Book of *Joshua.*

NOTES

XXXIV

2. זאת הָאָרֶץ אֲשֶׁר תִּפֹּל לָכֶם בְּנַחֲלָה — *This shall be the land that shall fall to you for an inheritance.* The *Sforno,* as does *Rashi* in his commentary on this verse, explains that the expression אֲשֶׁר תִּפֹּל, *that shall fall,* applies to the casting of lots which determined which area fell to each tribe. Our Sages explain that the lot itself cried out saying, "I, the lot, have come up for such and such district and for such and such tribe" (*Bava Basra* 122a). As *Rashi* states in *parashas Pinchas* (26:54), "The lot fell by the utterance of the Holy Spirit (רוּחַ הַקֹּדֶשׁ)." Based upon this, the *Sforno* explains the significance of the phrase זֹאת הָאָרֶץ, *this shall be the land.* The word זֹאת, *this,* is meant to exclude the land conquered by the Israelites on the east side of the

34 1 HASHEM spoke to Moses, saying: 2 Command the Children of Israel and
say to them: Since you come to the land of Canaan, this is the land
that shall fall to you as an inheritance, the land of Canaan according to its
borders. 3 Your southern side shall be from the Wilderness of Zin at the side
of Edom, and your southern border shall be from the edge of the Salt Sea to
the east. 4 The border shall go around south of Maaleh-akrabbim, and shall
pass toward Zin; and its outskirts shall be south of Kadesh-barnea; then it
shall go out to Hazar-addar and pass to Azmon. 5 The border shall go
around from Azmon to the stream of Egypt, and its outskirts shall be
toward the Sea. 6 The western border: It shall be for you the Great Sea and
the district; this shall be for you the western border.
7 This shall be for you the northern border: from the Great Sea you shall
turn to Mount Hor. 8 From Mount Hor you shall turn to the approach to
Hamath, and the outskirts of the border shall be toward Zedad. 9 The
border shall go forth toward Zifron and its outskirts shall be Hazar-enan;
this shall be for you the northern border. 10 You shall draw yourselves as the
eastern border from Hazar-enan to Shefam. 11 The border shall descend
from Shefam to Riblah, east of Ain; the border shall descend and extend to
the bank of the Kinnereth Sea to the east. 12 The border shall descend to the
Jordan, and its outskirts shall be the Salt Sea; this shall be the Land for you,
according to its borders all around.
13 Moses commanded the Children of Israel, saying: This is the Land that
you shall divide as an inheritance by lot, which HASHEM has commanded to
give to the nine-and-a-half tribes. 14 For the tribe of the children of Reuben
have taken according to their fathers' house, and the tribe of the children of
Gad according to their fathers' house, and half the tribe of Manasseh have
taken their inheritance. 15 Two-and-a-half tribes have taken their inheritance on the bank of the Jordan by Jericho, eastward toward the sunrise.
16 HASHEM spoke to Moses, saying, 17 These are names of the men who are
to take possession of the Land for you: Elazar the Kohen and Joshua son of
Nun, 18 and one leader from each tribe shall you take to possess the Land.
19 These are the names of the men: for the tribe of Judah, Caleb son of
Jephunneh; 20 and for the tribe of the children of Simeon, Shemuel son of
Ammihud; 21 for the tribe of Benjamin, Elidad son of Chislon; 22 and for the
tribe of the children of Dan, as leader, Bukki son of Jogli; 23 for the children
of Joseph, for the tribe of the children of Manasseh, as leader, Hanniel son
of Ephod; 24 and for the tribe of the children of Ephraim, as leader, Kemuel

This is because the lands of Sichon and Og did not possess the sanctity of *Eretz Yisrael*, as it says, וְאַךְ אִם טְמֵאָה אֶרֶץ אֲחֻזַּתְכֶם, *Nevertheless, if the land of your possession be tamei* (*Joshua* 22:19), and was therefore unworthy (to be divided) by lot, which was directed by the Holy Spirit.

NOTES

Jordan which lacked the sanctity of *Eretz Yisrael*. As such, the lot which was guided by the Holy Spirit in *Eretz Yisrael* was not operative there; hence Moses had the right to divide the land as he saw fit. To support this, the *Sforno* cites the Book of *Joshua*, referring to chapter 13, verse 8, where it is written regarding the inheritance of Gad, Reuven and Menasseh on the east bank of the Jordan, אֲשֶׁר נָתַן לָהֶם מֹשֶׁה, *which Moses gave to them.*

כה-כו בֶּן־שִׁפְטָן: וּלְמַטֵּה בְנֵי־זְבוּלֻן נָשִׂיא אֱלִיצָפָן בֶּן־פַּרְנָךְ: וּלְמַטֵּה בְנֵי־
כז יִשָּׂשכָר נָשִׂיא פַּלְטִיאֵל בֶּן־עַזָּן: וּלְמַטֵּה בְנֵי־אָשֵׁר נָשִׂיא אֲחִיהוּד בֶּן־
כח-כט שְׁלֹמִי: וּלְמַטֵּה בְנֵי־נַפְתָּלִי נָשִׂיא פְּדַהְאֵל בֶּן־עַמִּיהוּד: אֵלֶּה אֲשֶׁר צִוָּה
יְהוָה לְנַחֵל אֶת־בְּנֵי־יִשְׂרָאֵל בְּאֶרֶץ כְּנָעַן:

לה חמישי א-ב וַיְדַבֵּר יְהוָה אֶל־מֹשֶׁה בְּעַרְבֹת מוֹאָב עַל־יַרְדֵּן יְרֵחוֹ לֵאמֹר: צַו אֶת־בְּנֵי
יִשְׂרָאֵל וְנָתְנוּ לַלְוִיִּם מִנַּחֲלַת אֲחֻזָּתָם עָרִים לָשָׁבֶת וּמִגְרָשׁ לֶעָרִים
ג סְבִיבֹתֵיהֶם תִּתְּנוּ לַלְוִיִּם: וְהָיוּ הֶעָרִים לָהֶם לָשָׁבֶת וּמִגְרְשֵׁיהֶם יִהְיוּ
ד לִבְהֶמְתָּם וְלִרְכֻשָׁם וּלְכֹל חַיָּתָם: וּמִגְרְשֵׁי הֶעָרִים אֲשֶׁר תִּתְּנוּ לַלְוִיִּם
ה מִקִּיר הָעִיר וָחוּצָה אֶלֶף אַמָּה סָבִיב: וּמַדֹּתֶם מִחוּץ לָעִיר אֶת־פְּאַת־
קֵדְמָה אַלְפַּיִם בָּאַמָּה וְאֶת־פְּאַת־נֶגֶב אַלְפַּיִם בָּאַמָּה וְאֶת־פְּאַת־יָם ׀
אַלְפַּיִם בָּאַמָּה וְאֵת פְּאַת צָפוֹן אַלְפַּיִם בָּאַמָּה וְהָעִיר בַּתָּוֶךְ זֶה יִהְיֶה לָהֶם
ו מִגְרְשֵׁי הֶעָרִים: וְאֵת הֶעָרִים אֲשֶׁר תִּתְּנוּ לַלְוִיִּם אֵת שֵׁשׁ־עָרֵי הַמִּקְלָט
אֲשֶׁר תִּתְּנוּ לָנֻס שָׁמָּה הָרֹצֵחַ וַעֲלֵיהֶם תִּתְּנוּ אַרְבָּעִים וּשְׁתַּיִם עִיר:
ז כָּל־הֶעָרִים אֲשֶׁר תִּתְּנוּ לַלְוִיִּם אַרְבָּעִים וּשְׁמֹנֶה עִיר אֶתְהֶן וְאֶת־
ח מִגְרְשֵׁיהֶן: וְהֶעָרִים אֲשֶׁר תִּתְּנוּ מֵאֲחֻזַּת בְּנֵי־יִשְׂרָאֵל מֵאֵת הָרַב תַּרְבּוּ
וּמֵאֵת הַמְעַט תַּמְעִיטוּ אִישׁ כְּפִי נַחֲלָתוֹ אֲשֶׁר יִנְחָלוּ יִתֵּן מֵעָרָיו לַלְוִיִּם:
ששי [שביעי] ט-י וַיְדַבֵּר יְהוָה אֶל־מֹשֶׁה לֵּאמֹר: דַּבֵּר אֶל־בְּנֵי יִשְׂרָאֵל וְאָמַרְתָּ אֲלֵהֶם כִּי
יא אַתֶּם עֹבְרִים אֶת־הַיַּרְדֵּן אַרְצָה כְּנָעַן: וְהִקְרִיתֶם לָכֶם עָרִים עָרֵי מִקְלָט
יב תִּהְיֶינָה לָכֶם וְנָס שָׁמָּה רֹצֵחַ מַכֵּה־נֶפֶשׁ בִּשְׁגָגָה: וְהָיוּ לָכֶם הֶעָרִים לְמִקְלָט
יג מִגֹּאֵל וְלֹא יָמוּת הָרֹצֵחַ עַד־עָמְדוֹ לִפְנֵי הָעֵדָה לַמִּשְׁפָּט: וְהֶעָרִים אֲשֶׁר
יד תִּתֵּנוּ שֵׁשׁ־עָרֵי מִקְלָט תִּהְיֶינָה לָכֶם: אֵת ׀ שְׁלֹשׁ הֶעָרִים תִּתְּנוּ מֵעֵבֶר
טו לַיַּרְדֵּן וְאֵת שְׁלֹשׁ הֶעָרִים תִּתְּנוּ בְּאֶרֶץ כְּנָעַן עָרֵי מִקְלָט תִּהְיֶינָה: לִבְנֵי
יִשְׂרָאֵל וְלַגֵּר וְלַתּוֹשָׁב בְּתוֹכָם תִּהְיֶינָה שֵׁשׁ־הֶעָרִים הָאֵלֶּה לְמִקְלָט לָנוּס
טז שָׁמָּה כָּל־מַכֵּה־נֶפֶשׁ בִּשְׁגָגָה: וְאִם־בִּכְלִי בַרְזֶל ׀ הִכָּהוּ וַיָּמֹת רֹצֵחַ הוּא
יז מוֹת יוּמַת הָרֹצֵחַ: וְאִם בְּאֶבֶן יָד אֲשֶׁר־יָמוּת בָּהּ הִכָּהוּ וַיָּמֹת רֹצֵחַ הוּא
יח מוֹת יוּמַת הָרֹצֵחַ: אוֹ בִּכְלִי עֵץ־יָד אֲשֶׁר־יָמוּת בּוֹ הִכָּהוּ וַיָּמֹת רֹצֵחַ הוּא
יט מוֹת יוּמַת הָרֹצֵחַ: גֹּאֵל הַדָּם הוּא יָמִית אֶת־הָרֹצֵחַ בְּפִגְעוֹ־בוֹ הוּא יְמִתֶנּוּ:

XXXV

3. לִבְהֶמְתָּם — *For their animals . . .* for riding and (to carry) burdens.

וְלִרְכֻשָׁם — *And for their goods.* Cattle and sheep.

וּלְכֹל חַיָּתָם — *And for all their amenities of life . . .* such as beehives, dovecotes and other such items.

8. מֵאֵת הָרַב תַּרְבּוּ — *From those that have much you shall take more.* Because (the division

NOTES

XXXV

8. מֵאֵת הָרַב תַּרְבּוּ — *From those that have much you shall take more.* The *Sforno* explained in his commentary on 26:54 that the twelve portions of land divided among the tribes were not equal in area but were equal in value. In order that the land given by the Israelites to the Levites for cities and open space (מִגְרָשׁ) be equitable, the Torah commands that it not be in proportion to the size of the tribe but to the value of that particular city and open space.

*son of Shiftan; 25 and for the tribe of the children of Zebulun, as leader, Eliza-
phan son of Parnach; 26 and for the tribe of the children of Issachar, as leader, Paltiel son of Azzan; 27 and for the tribe of the children of Asher, as leader,
Ahihud son of Shelomi; 28 and for the tribe of the children of Naphtali, as
leader, Pedahel son of Ammihud. 29 These are the ones whom HASHEM commanded to apportion to the Children of Israel in the land of Canaan.*

35 *1 HASHEM spoke to Moses in the plains of Moab, by the Jordan, at Jericho,
saying: 2 Command the Children of Israel that they shall give to the
Levites, from the heritage of their possession, cities for dwelling, and open
space for the cities all around them shall you give to the Levites. 3 The cities
shall be theirs for dwelling, and their open space shall be for their animals,
for their wealth, and for all their needs. 4 The open spaces of the cities that
you shall give to the Levites, from the wall of the city outward: a thousand
cubits all around. 5 You shall measure from outside the city on the eastern
side two thousand cubits; on the southern side two thousand cubits; on the
western side two thousand cubits; and on the northern side two thousand
cubits, with the city in the middle; this shall be for them the open spaces of
the cities. 6 The cities that you shall give to the Levites: the six cities of refuge
that you shall provide for a murderer to flee there, and in addition to them
you shall give forty-two cities. 7 All the cities that you shall give to the
Levites: forty-eight cities, them and their open spaces. 8 The cities that you
shall give from the possession of the Children of Israel, from the many you
shall increase and from the few you shall decrease, each according to his
inheritance that they shall inherit shall he give of his cities to the Levites.*

*9 HASHEM spoke to Moses, saying: 10 Speak to the Children of Israel and
say to them: When you cross the Jordan to the land of Canaan, 11 you shall
designate cities for yourselves, cities of refuge shall they be for you, and a
murderer shall flee there — one who takes a life unintentionally. 12 The cities
shall be for you a refuge from the avenger, so that the murderer will not die
until he stands before the assembly for judgment. 13 As to the cities that you
shall designate, there shall be six cities of refuge for you. 14 Three cities shall
you designate on the other side of the Jordan, and three cities shall you
designate in the land of Canaan; they shall be cities of refuge. 15 For the
Children of Israel and the proselyte and resident among them shall these six
cities be a refuge, for anyone who kills a person unintentionally to flee there.*

*16 If he had struck him with an iron implement and he died, he is a mur-
derer; the murderer shall surely be put to death. 17 Or if with a hand-sized
stone by which one could die did he strike him, and he died, he is a murderer;
the murderer shall surely be put to death. 18 Or if he struck him with a hand-
sized wood implement through which one could die, and he died, he is a
murderer; the murderer shall surely be put to death. 19 The avenger of the
blood, he shall kill the murderer; when he encounters him, he shall kill him.*

---

of land) was according to value, hence, the smaller portion (given to the Levites) by the tribe which had less was equal in value to the larger portion given to the Levites by the tribe which received more in quantity (see 26:54).

כ-כא וְאִם־בְּשִׂנְאָה יֶהְדָּפֶנּוּ אוֹ־הִשְׁלִיךְ עָלָיו בִּצְדִיָּה וַיָּמֹת: אוֹ בְאֵיבָה הִכָּהוּ
בְיָדוֹ וַיָּמֹת מוֹת־יוּמַת הַמַּכֶּה רֹצֵחַ הוּא גֹּאֵל הַדָּם יָמִית אֶת־הָרֹצֵחַ
כב בְּפִגְעוֹ־בוֹ: וְאִם־בְּפֶתַע בְּלֹא־אֵיבָה הֲדָפוֹ אוֹ־הִשְׁלִיךְ עָלָיו כָּל־כְּלִי בְּלֹא
כג צְדִיָּה: אוֹ בְכָל־אֶבֶן אֲשֶׁר־יָמוּת בָּהּ בְּלֹא רְאוֹת וַיַּפֵּל עָלָיו וַיָּמֹת וְהוּא
כד לֹא־אוֹיֵב לוֹ וְלֹא מְבַקֵּשׁ רָעָתוֹ: וְשָׁפְטוּ הָעֵדָה בֵּין הַמַּכֶּה וּבֵין גֹּאֵל הַדָּם
כה עַל הַמִּשְׁפָּטִים הָאֵלֶּה: וְהִצִּילוּ הָעֵדָה אֶת־הָרֹצֵחַ מִיַּד גֹּאֵל הַדָּם וְהֵשִׁיבוּ
אֹתוֹ הָעֵדָה אֶל־עִיר מִקְלָטוֹ אֲשֶׁר־נָס שָׁמָּה וְיָשַׁב בָּהּ עַד־מוֹת הַכֹּהֵן
כו הַגָּדֹל אֲשֶׁר־מָשַׁח אֹתוֹ בְּשֶׁמֶן הַקֹּדֶשׁ: וְאִם־יָצֹא יֵצֵא הָרֹצֵחַ אֶת־גְּבוּל
כז עִיר מִקְלָטוֹ אֲשֶׁר יָנוּס שָׁמָּה: וּמָצָא אֹתוֹ גֹּאֵל הַדָּם מִחוּץ לִגְבוּל עִיר
כח מִקְלָטוֹ וְרָצַח גֹּאֵל הַדָּם אֶת־הָרֹצֵחַ אֵין לוֹ דָּם: כִּי בְעִיר מִקְלָטוֹ יֵשֵׁב
עַד־מוֹת הַכֹּהֵן הַגָּדֹל וְאַחֲרֵי מוֹת הַכֹּהֵן הַגָּדֹל יָשׁוּב הָרֹצֵחַ אֶל־אֶרֶץ
כט אֲחֻזָּתוֹ: וְהָיוּ אֵלֶּה לָכֶם לְחֻקַּת מִשְׁפָּט לְדֹרֹתֵיכֶם בְּכֹל מוֹשְׁבֹתֵיכֶם:
ל כָּל־מַכֵּה־נֶפֶשׁ לְפִי עֵדִים יִרְצַח אֶת־הָרֹצֵחַ וְעֵד אֶחָד לֹא־יַעֲנֶה בְנֶפֶשׁ
לא לָמוּת: וְלֹא־תִקְחוּ כֹפֶר לְנֶפֶשׁ רֹצֵחַ אֲשֶׁר־הוּא רָשָׁע לָמוּת כִּי־מוֹת יוּמָת:
לב וְלֹא־תִקְחוּ כֹפֶר לָנוּס אֶל־עִיר מִקְלָטוֹ לָשׁוּב לָשֶׁבֶת בָּאָרֶץ עַד־מוֹת
לג הַכֹּהֵן: וְלֹא־תַחֲנִיפוּ אֶת־הָאָרֶץ אֲשֶׁר אַתֶּם בָּהּ כִּי הַדָּם הוּא יַחֲנִיף
אֶת־הָאָרֶץ וְלָאָרֶץ לֹא־יְכֻפַּר לַדָּם אֲשֶׁר שֻׁפַּךְ־בָּהּ כִּי־אִם בְּדַם שֹׁפְכוֹ:
לד וְלֹא תְטַמֵּא אֶת־הָאָרֶץ אֲשֶׁר אַתֶּם יֹשְׁבִים בָּהּ אֲשֶׁר אֲנִי שֹׁכֵן בְּתוֹכָהּ
כִּי אֲנִי יהוה שֹׁכֵן בְּתוֹךְ בְּנֵי יִשְׂרָאֵל:

לו שביעי א וַיִּקְרְבוּ רָאשֵׁי הָאָבוֹת לְמִשְׁפַּחַת בְּנֵי־גִלְעָד בֶּן־מָכִיר בֶּן־מְנַשֶּׁה
מִמִּשְׁפְּחֹת בְּנֵי יוֹסֵף וַיְדַבְּרוּ לִפְנֵי מֹשֶׁה וְלִפְנֵי הַנְּשִׂאִים רָאשֵׁי אָבוֹת לִבְנֵי
ב יִשְׂרָאֵל: וַיֹּאמְרוּ אֶת־אֲדֹנִי צִוָּה יהוה לָתֵת אֶת־הָאָרֶץ בְּנַחֲלָה בְּגוֹרָל

---

25. עַד מוֹת הַכֹּהֵן הַגָּדֹל — *Until the death of the Kohen Gadol.* It has already been explained that גָלוּת (exile to a city of refuge) is the punishment for one who kills in error. Now being that there are different kinds of unintentional sins (שׁוֹגֵג), which are disparate because some are closer to being considered accidental (אוֹנֵס) while others are closer to being considered intentional (מֵזִיד), therefore there are varying periods of exile for one who kills unintentionally. For some, the unintentional act (of killing) is (punished by exile) for a brief period before the *Kohen* dies, while some murderers die in exile before the death of the *Kohen*. This occurs (according to) the judgment of God, Blessed is He, the One Who knows and is a witness (based on *Jeremiah* 29:23), Who punishes the unintentional sinner according to the degree of his error, as it says, וְהָאֱלֹהִים אִנָּה לְיָדוֹ, *but God caused it to come to hand* (*Exodus* 21:13).

NOTES

25. עַד מוֹת הַכֹּהֵן הַגָּדֹל — *Until the death of the Kohen Gadol.* The Torah teaches us in the Book of *Exodus* (21:13) that whenever an unpremeditated murder occurs, it is nonetheless considered predestined, as the verse states וְהָאֱלֹהִים אִנָּה לְיָדוֹ, *but God caused it to come to hand.* Nonetheless, there are degrees of fault involved even when the act is in error and not premeditated (שׁוֹגֵג). At times, it is due to gross negligence which is akin to an intentional act (מֵזִיד), whereas on other occasions it is almost an unavoidable accident (אוֹנֵס). Now since the punishment for all of these acts is the same, namely גָּלוּת (exile to a city of refuge), it seems unjust. The *Sforno*, therefore, explains that since the murderer is freed when the *Kohen Gadol* dies, the *length* of his stay in exile will vary considerably. Since the manslaughter is preordained by God, He in His infinite wisdom will arrange it to happen relative to the timing of the

20 *If he pushed him out of hatred or hurled upon him from ambush, and he*
died; 21 *or in enmity struck him with his hand and he died, the assailant*
shall surely be put to death, he is a murderer; the avenger of the blood shall
kill the murderer when he encounters him.

22 *But if with suddenness, without enmity, did he push him, or he hurled*
any implement upon him without ambush; 23 *or with any stone through*
which one could die, without having seen, and caused it to fall upon him
and he died — but he was not his enemy and did not seek his harm — 24 *then*
the assembly shall judge between the assailant and the avenger of the
blood, according to these laws. 25 *The assembly shall rescue the murderer*
from the hand of the avenger of the blood, and the assembly shall return
him to his city of refuge where he had fled; he shall dwell in it until the
death of the Kohen Gadol, whom one had anointed with the sacred oil.
26 *But if the murderer will ever leave the border of the city of refuge to*
which he had fled, 27 *and the avenger of the blood shall find him outside of*
the border of his city of refuge, and the avenger of the blood will kill the
murderer — he has no blood-guilt. 28 *For he must dwell in his city of refuge*
until the death of the Kohen Gadol, and after the death of the Kohen Gadol
the murderer shall return to the land of his possession.

29 *These shall be for you a decree of justice for your generations, in all*
your dwelling places. 30 *Whoever smites a person, according to the*
testimony of witnesses shall one kill the murderer, but a single witness shall
not testify against a person regarding death.

31 *You shall not accept ransom for the life of a murderer who is worthy of*
death, for he shall surely be put to death. 32 *You shall not accept ransom for*
one who fled to his city of refuge to return to dwell in the land, before the
death of the Kohen.

33 *You shall not bring guilt upon the land in which you are, for the blood*
will bring guilt upon the Land; the Land will not have atonement for the
blood that was spilled in it, except through the blood of the one who spilled
it. 34 *You shall not contaminate the Land in which you dwell, in whose midst*
I rest, for I am HASHEM *Who rests among the Children of Israel.*

36 1 *The heads of the fathers of the family of the children of Gilead,*
son of Machir son of Manasseh, of the families of the children
of Joseph, approached and spoke before Moses and before the leaders,
the heads of the fathers of the Children of Israel. 2 *They said, "*HASHEM
has commanded my master to give the Land as an inheritance by lot

XXXVI

2. בְּנַחֲלָה בְּגוֹרָל — *For inheritance by lot.* If any tribe would have a portion within the area of a fellow (tribe), then the lot cast would not be correct regarding the boundaries of the diminished tribe. Also regarding the (tribe) which received this addition, the (lot) will not

NOTES

eventual death of the *Kohen Gadol,* and thus the length of the murderer's imprisonment will be determined by the degree of his negligence.

XXXVI

2. בְּנַחֲלָה בְּגוֹרָל — *For inheritance by lot.* As the *Sforno* explains this verse, the thrust of the com-

לִבְנֵי יִשְׂרָאֵל וַאדֹנִי צֻוָּה בַיהוה לָתֵת אֶת־נַחֲלַת צְלָפְחָד אָחִינוּ לִבְנֹתָיו:
ג וְהָיוּ לְאֶחָד מִבְּנֵי שִׁבְטֵי בְנֵי־יִשְׂרָאֵל לְנָשִׁים וְנִגְרְעָה נַחֲלָתָן מִנַּחֲלַת
אֲבֹתֵינוּ וְנוֹסַף עַל נַחֲלַת הַמַּטֶּה אֲשֶׁר תִּהְיֶינָה לָהֶם וּמִגֹּרַל נַחֲלָתֵנוּ יִגָּרֵעַ:
ד וְאִם־יִהְיֶה הַיֹּבֵל לִבְנֵי יִשְׂרָאֵל וְנוֹסְפָה נַחֲלָתָן עַל נַחֲלַת הַמַּטֶּה אֲשֶׁר
ה תִּהְיֶינָה לָהֶם וּמִנַּחֲלַת מַטֵּה אֲבֹתֵינוּ יִגָּרַע נַחֲלָתָן: וַיְצַו מֹשֶׁה אֶת־בְּנֵי
ו יִשְׂרָאֵל עַל־פִּי יהוה לֵאמֹר כֵּן מַטֵּה בְנֵי־יוֹסֵף דֹּבְרִים: זֶה הַדָּבָר
אֲשֶׁר־צִוָּה יהוה לִבְנוֹת צְלָפְחָד לֵאמֹר לַטּוֹב בְּעֵינֵיהֶם תִּהְיֶינָה לְנָשִׁים
ז אַךְ לְמִשְׁפַּחַת מַטֵּה אֲבִיהֶם תִּהְיֶינָה לְנָשִׁים: וְלֹא־תִסֹּב נַחֲלָה לִבְנֵי
יִשְׂרָאֵל מִמַּטֶּה אֶל־מַטֶּה כִּי אִישׁ בְּנַחֲלַת מַטֵּה אֲבֹתָיו יִדְבְּקוּ בְּנֵי
ח יִשְׂרָאֵל: וְכָל־בַּת יֹרֶשֶׁת נַחֲלָה מִמַּטּוֹת בְּנֵי יִשְׂרָאֵל לְאֶחָד מִמִּשְׁפַּחַת
מַטֵּה אָבִיהָ תִּהְיֶה לְאִשָּׁה לְמַעַן יִירְשׁוּ בְּנֵי יִשְׂרָאֵל אִישׁ נַחֲלַת אֲבֹתָיו:
ט וְלֹא־תִסֹּב נַחֲלָה מִמַּטֶּה לְמַטֶּה אַחֵר כִּי־אִישׁ בְּנַחֲלָתוֹ יִדְבְּקוּ מַטּוֹת בְּנֵי
מפטיר י־יא יִשְׂרָאֵל: כַּאֲשֶׁר צִוָּה יהוה אֶת־מֹשֶׁה כֵּן עָשׂוּ בְּנוֹת צְלָפְחָד: וַתִּהְיֶינָה
מַחְלָה תִרְצָה וְחָגְלָה וּמִלְכָּה וְנֹעָה בְּנוֹת צְלָפְחָד לִבְנֵי דֹדֵיהֶן לְנָשִׁים:
יב מִמִּשְׁפְּחֹת בְּנֵי־מְנַשֶּׁה בֶן־יוֹסֵף הָיוּ לְנָשִׁים וַתְּהִי נַחֲלָתָן עַל־מַטֵּה
יג מִשְׁפַּחַת אֲבִיהֶן: אֵלֶּה הַמִּצְוֹת וְהַמִּשְׁפָּטִים אֲשֶׁר צִוָּה יהוה בְּיַד־מֹשֶׁה
אֶל־בְּנֵי יִשְׂרָאֵל בְּעַרְבֹת מוֹאָב עַל יַרְדֵּן יְרֵחוֹ:

---

be correct unless that portion, which belongs to his fellow tribe, is added to his area.

4. וְאִם יִהְיֶה הַיֹּבֵל . . . יִגָּרַע נַחֲלָתָן — *And when the Jubilee shall be . . . their inheritance will be taken away.* Also, since the entire land was not conquered immediately as it says, מְעַט מְעַט אֲגָרְשֶׁנּוּ מִפָּנֶיךָ, *Little by little I will drive them out before you* (Exodus 23:30), and each tribe had to conquer its portion; therefore, although an individual may sell his portion to a member of another tribe, that seller would not refrain from striving, together with his tribe, to conquer (the land), being that it would return to him at the Jubilee. However, the members of the tribe will not attempt to conquer the portion of the daughters (who marry outside the tribe) which will not return at the Jubilee, or they will permit the inhabitants of the land to remain there since it now belongs to another tribe, and thus the conquest of their inheritance will be subtracted from the allotted (portion) of our father's tribe.

NOTES

plaint submitted by the heads of the children of Gilead, son of Machir, was that if the daughters of Zelaphchad were to marry men from a different tribe (other than Menasseh), the allocation of land in Eretz Yisrael by the casting of lots would be frustrated because the land they inherited from their father would eventually be passed on to their children whose tribal relationship would be that of their father — who was a member of another tribe. Since the lot cast was directed by the Holy Spirit, as mentioned above, such a deviation could not be tolerated. This explains why the complainants stressed the fact that it was an *inheritance by lot*.

4. וְאִם יִהְיֶה הַיֹּבֵל . . . יִגָּרַע נַחֲלָתָן — *And when the Jubilee shall be . . . their inheritance will be taken away.* This verse seems to be repetitious, since it has already been established that the concern of the heads of the family of Gilead was that their inheritance would be diminished. The *Sforno*, however, explains that there was an added concern. Since the conquest of *Eretz Yisrael* was not completed when Israel initially entered the land, it behooved each tribe to complete that conquest over a period of time — on their own. Now, if certain parts of their family's inheritance were transferred to another tribe, then there would be no motivation for their fellow tribesmen, who belonged to other families within the tribe of Menasseh, to assist them in the completion of the task of conquering those areas, since these areas no longer belonged to their tribe. The result would be a diminishment of their family's share.

to the Children of Israel, and My master has been commanded by HASHEM to give the inheritance of Zelophehad our brother to his daughters. [3] *If they become wives of one of the sons of the tribes of the Children of Israel, then their inheritance will be subtracted from the inheritance of our fathers and be added to the inheritance of the tribe into which they will marry, and it will be subtracted from the lot of our inheritance.* [4] *And when the Jubilee will arrive for the Children of Israel, their inheritance will be added to the inheritance of the tribe into which they will marry; and from the inheritance of the tribe of our fathers will their inheritance be subtracted."*

[5] *Moses commanded the Children of Israel according to the word of HASHEM, saying, "Correctly does the tribe of the children of Joseph speak.* [6] *This is the word that HASHEM has commanded regarding the daughters of Zelophehad, saying: Let them be wives to whomever is good in their eyes, but only to the family of their father's tribe shall they become wives.* [7] *An inheritance of the Children of Israel shall not make rounds from tribe to tribe; rather the Children of Israel shall cleave every man to the inheritance of the tribe of his fathers.* [8] *Every daughter who inherits an inheritance of the tribes of the Children of Israel shall become the wife of someone from a family of her father's tribe, so that everyone of the Children of Israel will inherit the inheritance of his fathers.* [9] *An inheritance shall not make rounds from a tribe to another tribe, for the tribes of the Children of Israel shall cleave every man to his own inheritance."*

[10] *As HASHEM commanded Moses, so did the daughters of Zelophehad do.* [11] *Mahlah, Tirzah, Hoglah, Milcah, and Noah, the daughters of Zelophehad, became wives to sons of their uncles.* [12] *[To cousins] from the families of the children of Manasseh son of Joseph did they become wives, and their inheritance remained with the tribe of the family of their father.*

[13] *These are the commandments and the ordinances that HASHEM commanded through Moses to the Children of Israel in the Plains of Moab, at the Jordan, by Jericho.*

---

10. כֵּן עָשׂוּ בְּנוֹת צְלָפְחָד — *So did the daughters of Zelaphchad.* Their (sole) intent was to fulfill the will of their Maker, *as HASHEM had commanded Moses;* not because they desired to marry these men.

12. מִמִּשְׁפְּחֹת בְּנֵי מְנַשֶּׁה — *Of the families of the sons of Menasseh.* Since they saw that it was the intent of God, the Exalted One, not to remove the inheritance (from tribe to tribe), they chose their cousins (as husbands) from among all the families (within the tribe) because they were the closest, even though they were given permission to choose whomsoever they wished from their tribe.

וַתְּהִי נַחֲלָתָן עַל מַטֵּה מִשְׁפַּחַת אֲבִיהֶן — *And their inheritance remained in the tribe of the family of their father . . .* and thus there was no removal of inheritance whatsoever, even from family to family (within the tribe of Menasseh).

NOTES

12. מִמִּשְׁפְּחֹת בְּנֵי מְנַשֶּׁה — *Of the families of the sons of Menasseh.* Although each tribe was allocated an equal share of land, that share was subdivided among its families. This being the case, were the daughters of Zelaphchad to have married within the tribe but not within their family, although it would have satisfied the law now promulgated, it would have meant subtracting their share of land from the family unit. Sensing this, they decided to marry their cousins, who were their closest relatives within the family of their father.

ספר דברים

Devarim / Deuteronomy

Sforno's Introduction

When the ruling King spoke and decreed that Moses, the shepherd of His sheep, would not enter the Land due to the transgression of His people, then before the removal of his "shadow" (i.e., protective shield) from them, he began to explain the Torah after he prefaced (this explanation) by telling and reminding them why this was necessary, i.e., because they were to enter the Land without him, due to their foolishness and sins.[1] When he completed this (reminder), he set aside the cities (of refuge)[2] and began to explain and caution them regarding the commandments in whose merit (i.e., by observing them) they would have longevity in the land of their inheritance.[3] (He also explained) those commandments which they are obligated to do when they enter the Land, such as the writing on the stones[4] and the Covenant of Mt. Gerizim[5] and others which are meant as signs for (all) generations that they not deal treacherously. He also gave them the order of the oath[6] that was to be administered, since they had nullified the Covenant of Horeb through the sin of the spies. (He also) testified regarding them, telling them what the future would bring to them in exile, as well as the future redemption which would come after total despair.[7] And he prayed on their behalf and blessed them by casting his eye for good on their Land. And he told of the coming of the redeemer and their future happiness — all this in his blessing given before he died.[8] And thus, the Torah is completed, with the testimony at its conclusion that no other man ever reached the level of prophecy attained by Moses[9] through whom the true Torah was given, (a Torah) to which naught can be added nor subtracted.

Thus, (in this book) we are told of the Divine lovingkindness which granted Moses prophetic powers (lit., prophetic preparedness), more than that which is (conceivably) possible in the nature of man, in order to grant the true Torah through him, (a Torah) which is unchanging, to which naught can be added or subtracted [10] through any other prophet, as our Sages state, שְׁאֵין נָבִיא רַשָּׁאִי לְחַדֵּשׁ דָּבָר מֵעַתָּה, *A prophet may henceforth* (i.e., after Moses) *make no*

1. *Parashas Devarim.*
2. *Deut.* 4:41.
3. *Deut.* 4:44 and 5:30.
4. *Deut.* 27:2.
5. *Deut.* 11:29.
6. *Deut.* 27:15.
7. *Deut.* chapter 30.
8. *Parashas VeZos HaBerachah.*
9. *Deut.* 34:10.
10. *Deut.* 4:2.

innovations (*Shabbos* 104b), and this is what the prophet taught when he said, ה׳ אֲשֶׁר עָשָׂה אֶת מֹשֶׁה וְאֶת אַהֲרֹן, *HASHEM Who made Moses and Aaron* (*I Samuel* 12:6), because, indeed, through Moses He gave a level (lit., the wherewithal) of prophecy which surpasses all (such) possible powers in the nature of man, and also with Aaron (He granted) the priesthood so that his seed would be sanctified through it forever.

פרשת דברים

א

א אֵ֣לֶּה הַדְּבָרִ֗ים אֲשֶׁ֨ר דִּבֶּ֤ר מֹשֶׁה֙ אֶל־כָּל־יִשְׂרָאֵ֔ל בְּעֵ֖בֶר הַיַּרְדֵּ֑ן בַּמִּדְבָּ֡ר
ב בָּֽעֲרָבָה֩ מ֨וֹל ס֜וּף בֵּֽין־פָּארָ֧ן וּבֵֽין־תֹּ֛פֶל וְלָבָ֥ן וַחֲצֵרֹ֖ת וְדִ֥י זָהָֽב: אַחַ֨ד עָשָׂ֥ר
ג י֜וֹם מֵֽחֹרֵ֗ב דֶּ֛רֶךְ הַר־שֵׂעִ֖יר עַ֣ד קָדֵ֣שׁ בַּרְנֵ֑עַ: וַיְהִי֙ בְּאַרְבָּעִ֣ים שָׁנָ֔ה בְּעַשְׁתֵּֽי־
עָשָׂ֥ר חֹ֛דֶשׁ בְּאֶחָ֥ד לַחֹ֖דֶשׁ דִּבֶּ֤ר מֹשֶׁה֙ אֶל־בְּנֵ֣י יִשְׂרָאֵ֔ל כְּכֹ֛ל אֲשֶׁ֨ר צִוָּ֧ה
ד יְהֹוָ֛ה אֹת֖וֹ אֲלֵהֶֽם: אַֽחֲרֵ֣י הַכֹּת֗וֹ אֵ֚ת סִיחֹן֙ מֶ֣לֶךְ הָֽאֱמֹרִ֔י אֲשֶׁ֥ר יוֹשֵׁ֖ב
ה בְּחֶשְׁבּ֑וֹן וְאֵ֗ת ע֚וֹג מֶ֣לֶךְ הַבָּשָׁ֔ן אֲשֶׁר־יוֹשֵׁ֥ב בְּעַשְׁתָּרֹ֖ת בְּאֶדְרֶֽעִי: בְּעֵ֥בֶר
ו הַיַּרְדֵּ֖ן בְּאֶ֣רֶץ מוֹאָ֑ב הוֹאִ֣יל מֹשֶׁ֔ה בֵּאֵ֛ר אֶת־הַתּוֹרָ֥ה הַזֹּ֖את לֵאמֹֽר: יְהֹוָ֧ה
אֱלֹהֵ֛ינוּ דִּבֶּ֥ר אֵלֵ֖ינוּ בְּחֹרֵ֣ב לֵאמֹ֑ר רַב־לָכֶ֥ם שֶׁ֖בֶת בָּהָ֥ר הַזֶּֽה:
ז פְּנ֣וּ | וּסְע֣וּ לָכֶ֗ם וּבֹ֚אוּ הַ֣ר הָֽאֱמֹרִי֮ וְאֶל־כָּל־שְׁכֵנָיו֒ בָּֽעֲרָבָ֥ה בָהָ֛ר וּבַשְּׁפֵלָ֥ה
וּבַנֶּ֖גֶב וּבְח֣וֹף הַיָּ֑ם אֶ֣רֶץ הַֽכְּנַֽעֲנִי֙ וְהַלְּבָנ֔וֹן עַד־הַנָּהָ֥ר הַגָּדֹ֖ל נְהַר־פְּרָֽת:

I

1. אֵלֶּה הַדְּבָרִים אֲשֶׁר דִּבֶּר מֹשֶׁה אֶל כָּל יִשְׂרָאֵל — *These are the words which Moses spoke to all Israel.* (The verse) says that in every place [which is] mentioned here, these being places where they (Israel) deviated from the path (of proper behavior), and by the decree of God, the Exalted One, they wandered about in the wilderness because of the sin of the spies, Moses said these words to all Israel which are now mentioned, namely:

2. אַחַד עָשָׂר יוֹם מֵחֹרֵב — *It is eleven days journey from Horeb.* The entire thirty-eight years they wandered in the wilderness hither and fro, not following a direct route to a specific place — and whenever they reached a (specific) place, they would wander (again) and retrace their steps or go off on a side (route), but never (travel) in a straight direct path. Moses would then say to them: "See what you have caused, for it is but *a journey of eleven days from Horeb to Kadesh Barnea by way of Mount Seir* which is the shortest route (followed) by travelers, and God, the Blessed One, brought you to Kadesh Barnea in three days through the great and awful wilderness, but because of your transgressions you wandered all this time." All this he told them (time and again) so that they might remember and return to God.

3. וַיְהִי בְּאַרְבָּעִים שָׁנָה — *And it came to pass in the fortieth year.* After the (older generation) had already died in the wilderness, *Moses spoke to the Children of Israel,*

NOTES

I

1. אֵלֶּה הַדְּבָרִים — *These are the words.* According to the *Sifri,* as quoted in *Rashi* in his commentary on this verse, the places mentioned in this *pasuk* are all "places where they angered God." This is what the *Sforno* refers to as places where Israel deviated from the path of God and were guilty of misconduct. In each of these places, as they sinned, Moses spoke these words to them, i.e., *it is eleven days journey from Horeb to Kadesh Barnea,* to remind them that due to the sin of the spies they were punished and condemned to wander thirty-eight years in the wilderness. As the *Sforno* explains in the next verse, Moses did this in the hope that they would be encouraged to repent, for this was the real purpose of his reminding them of their sins and

admonishing them. Hence, it was not simply a case of reproach but for the purpose of urging them to do *teshuvah;* to repent and mend their ways.

3. וַיְהִי בְּאַרְבָּעִים שָׁנָה — *And it came to pass in the fortieth year.* The *Sforno* explains why the Torah tells us that it came to pass in the 40th year that Moses spoke these words to Israel. He says it was necessary after four decades to instruct the new generation in the teachings of Torah, since the older generation had all died out and the obligation to observe the commandments was now theirs.

4. אַחֲרֵי הַכֹּתוֹ — *After he had smitten.* The *Sforno* explains the reason for the Torah's telling us that this occurred after Moses had smitten Sichon and Og. Following that victory, the Israelites were able to settle down in peace, and were not forced to wan-

1

PARASHAS DEVARIM

1 *These are the words that Moses spoke to all Israel, on the other side of the Jordan, concerning the Wilderness, concerning the Arabah, opposite the Sea of Reeds, between Paran and Tophel, and Laban, and Hazeroth, and Di-zahab;* 2 *eleven days from Horeb, by way of Mount Seir to Kadesh-barnea.* 3 *It was in the fortieth year, in the eleventh month, on the first of the month, when Moses spoke to the Children of Israel, according to everything that* HASHEM *commanded him to them,* 4 *after he had smitten Sihon, king of the Amorites, who dwelt in Heshbon, and Og, king of Bashan, who dwelt in Ashtaroth, in Edrei.* 5 *On the other side of the Jordan in the land of Moab, Moses began explaining this Torah, saying:*

6 HASHEM, *our God, spoke to us in Horeb, saying: Enough of your dwelling by this mountain.* 7 *Turn yourselves around and journey, and come to the Amorite mountain and all its neighbors, in the Arabah, on the mountain, and in the lowland, and in the south, and at the seacoast; the land of the Canaanite and the Lebanon, until the great river, the Euphrates River.*

---

namely to those who were to enter the Land, *according to all that God had given him as a commandment to them* — he reviewed with them the entire Torah which had been given till now.

4. אַחֲרֵי הַכֹּתוֹ — *After he had smitten . . .* and this he did after (Israel) had attained a degree of tranquility in a settled land.

5. בְּעֵבֶר הַיַּרְדֵּן בְּאֶרֶץ מוֹאָב הוֹאִיל מֹשֶׁה בֵּאֵר — *Beyond the Jordan in the land of Moab, Moses began to explain.* After they no longer wandered and roved, for the encampment in the plains of Moab was (at the end) of their final journey, and since (Moses), after his beseeching (God), despaired of attaining (his request) to cross over, (therefore) he now began to explain (those areas of Torah) which he thought might be unclear (lit., doubtful) after his death. This explanation began when he later said ה׳ אֱלֹהֵינוּ כָּרַת עִמָּנוּ בְּרִית בְּחֹרֵב, HASHEM, *our God, made a covenant with us in Horeb* (5:2).

לֵאמֹר — *Saying.* Before he began this exposition, wherein he elaborated and cautioned (them) regarding a number of the commandments, he said to Israel that the reason they needed (these words of) explanation and caution at this time was because they were crossing over without him and (therefore) he would not be able to caution them at the appropriate time nor resolve every doubt which might arise. He related how they stumbled through their wicked choices and iniquities (resulting) in his not being able to cross over with them. (This he did) so that they should be careful in the future and not corrupt their ways (lit., affairs).

NOTES

der. This newly found tranquility created an atmosphere in which the people were able to listen, concentrate and absorb the teachings of their master.

5. הוֹאִיל מֹשֶׁה בֵּאֵר — *Moses began to explain.* Once Moses is convinced that he will not be permitted to accompany Israel into the Promised Land, he decides (and desires) to expound the Torah, and he attempts to anticipate and resolve all future questions in regard to the law since he will not be present to address these problems when they ultimately arise. This interpretation of the *Sforno* is based on the *Rambam's* introduction to his commentary on the Mishnah. The *Rambam* there states, "In the fortieth year, in the eleventh month, on Rosh Chodesh Shevat, he (Moses) gathered the people and said to them, 'The time of my death has arrived. If there be among you one who heard a *halachah* (law) and has forgotten it, let him come and ask me and I shall explain it . . .' as it is written, 'Moses began to explain.' " The *Rambam,* in turn, is expounding upon the *Sifri,* and indeed he quotes from it in his introduction.

ח רְאֵה נָתַתִּי לִפְנֵיכֶם אֶת־הָאָרֶץ בֹּאוּ וּרְשׁוּ אֶת־הָאָרֶץ אֲשֶׁר נִשְׁבַּע יְהוָה
לַאֲבֹתֵיכֶם לְאַבְרָהָם לְיִצְחָק וּלְיַעֲקֹב לָתֵת לָהֶם וּלְזַרְעָם אַחֲרֵיהֶם:
ט־י וָאֹמַר אֲלֵכֶם בָּעֵת הַהִוא לֵאמֹר לֹא־אוּכַל לְבַדִּי שְׂאֵת אֶתְכֶם: יְהוָה
שני יא אֱלֹהֵיכֶם הִרְבָּה אֶתְכֶם וְהִנְּכֶם הַיּוֹם כְּכוֹכְבֵי הַשָּׁמַיִם לָרֹב: יְהוָה אֱלֹהֵי
אֲבוֹתֵכֶם יֹסֵף עֲלֵיכֶם כָּכֶם אֶלֶף פְּעָמִים וִיבָרֵךְ אֶתְכֶם כַּאֲשֶׁר דִּבֶּר לָכֶם:
יב־יג אֵיכָה אֶשָּׂא לְבַדִּי טָרְחֲכֶם וּמַשַּׂאֲכֶם וְרִיבְכֶם: הָבוּ לָכֶם אֲנָשִׁים חֲכָמִים
יד וּנְבֹנִים וִידֻעִים לְשִׁבְטֵיכֶם וַאֲשִׂימֵם בְּרָאשֵׁיכֶם: וַתַּעֲנוּ אֹתִי וַתֹּאמְרוּ טוֹב־
טו הַדָּבָר אֲשֶׁר־דִּבַּרְתָּ לַעֲשׂוֹת: וָאֶקַּח אֶת־רָאשֵׁי שִׁבְטֵיכֶם אֲנָשִׁים חֲכָמִים
וִידֻעִים וָאֶתֵּן אוֹתָם רָאשִׁים עֲלֵיכֶם שָׂרֵי אֲלָפִים וְשָׂרֵי מֵאוֹת וְשָׂרֵי חֲמִשִּׁים
טז וְשָׂרֵי עֲשָׂרֹת וְשֹׁטְרִים לְשִׁבְטֵיכֶם: וָאֲצַוֶּה אֶת־שֹׁפְטֵיכֶם בָּעֵת הַהִוא לֵאמֹר
יז שָׁמֹעַ בֵּין־אֲחֵיכֶם וּשְׁפַטְתֶּם צֶדֶק בֵּין־אִישׁ וּבֵין־אָחִיו וּבֵין גֵּרוֹ: לֹא־
תַכִּירוּ פָנִים בַּמִּשְׁפָּט כַּקָּטֹן כַּגָּדֹל תִּשְׁמָעוּן לֹא תָגוּרוּ מִפְּנֵי־אִישׁ כִּי
הַמִּשְׁפָּט לֵאלֹהִים הוּא וְהַדָּבָר אֲשֶׁר יִקְשֶׁה מִכֶּם תַּקְרִבוּן אֵלַי וּשְׁמַעְתִּיו:
יח־יט וָאֲצַוֶּה אֶתְכֶם בָּעֵת הַהִוא אֵת כָּל־הַדְּבָרִים אֲשֶׁר תַּעֲשׂוּן: וַנִּסַּע מֵחֹרֵב
וַנֵּלֶךְ אֵת כָּל־הַמִּדְבָּר הַגָּדוֹל וְהַנּוֹרָא הַהוּא אֲשֶׁר רְאִיתֶם דֶּרֶךְ הַר
כ הָאֱמֹרִי כַּאֲשֶׁר צִוָּה יְהוָה אֱלֹהֵינוּ אֹתָנוּ וַנָּבֹא עַד קָדֵשׁ בַּרְנֵעַ: וָאֹמַר
כא אֲלֵכֶם בָּאתֶם עַד־הַר הָאֱמֹרִי אֲשֶׁר־יְהוָה אֱלֹהֵינוּ נֹתֵן לָנוּ: רְאֵה נָתַן יְהוָה
אֱלֹהֶיךָ לְפָנֶיךָ אֶת־הָאָרֶץ עֲלֵה רֵשׁ כַּאֲשֶׁר דִּבֶּר יְהוָה אֱלֹהֵי אֲבֹתֶיךָ

8. רְאֵה נָתַתִּי לִפְנֵיכֶם אֶת הָאָרֶץ — *Behold, I have set before you the land . . .* (namely) the inhabitants of the land; for they will *melt away before you* (based on *Joshua* 2:9), and will not rise up.

בֹּאוּ וּרְשׁוּ אֶת הָאָרֶץ — *Come and possess the land . . .* (namely) the (geographical) area of these nations, because due to their fears, they (the inhabitants) will turn and flee or die; (all this) without doing battle.

12. טָרְחֲכֶם — *Your cumbrance . . .* quarrels which do not involve monetary claims.

וּמַשַּׂאֲכֶם — *And your burden . . .* in (providing) for the needs of the public.

וְרִיבְכֶם — *And your strife . . .* in matters of law and monetary claims. Now this he related to them to remind them of their transgression, that even though he had told them the good tiding that they would enter the Land without a battle, and that this would be a great accomplishment, bringing honor far greater than all their possessions and affairs (here) in the wilderness, (nonetheless,) they did not cease to strive with one another, so that it became necessary to appoint various levels of judges to the extent that every ten of them

NOTES

8. נָתַתִּי לִפְנֵיכֶם אֶת הָאָרֶץ בֹּאוּ וּרְשׁוּ אֶת הָאָרֶץ — *I have set before you the land; come and possess the land.* The *Sforno* explains the word אֶרֶץ, *land,* in the first part of the verse as meaning "inhabitants of the land" while אֶרֶץ in the second part refers literally to the land itself. In this manner, there is no redundancy in the verse.

12. טָרְחֲכֶם וּמַשַּׂאֲכֶם וְרִיבְכֶם — *Your cumbrance and your burden and your strife.* The *Sforno's* commentary on this verse explains the seeming parenthetical nature of verses 12 through 18. Since Moses is relating the command of God to go up and conquer the Land, which is frustrated by their insistence upon sending spies, it is difficult to understand the insertion of these verses which speak of Israel's quarrels, contentions and strife resulting in the appointment of judges. The *Sforno,* however, shows the link between the command to enter the Land and the failure of the Israelites to appreciate how insignificant were their cumbrances and

*8 See! I have given the Land before you; come and possess the Land that
HASHEM swore to your forefathers, to Abraham, to Isaac, and to Jacob, to give
them and their children after them.*
*9 I said to you at that time, saying, "I cannot carry you alone. 10 HASHEM,
your God, has multiplied you and behold! you are like the stars of heaven in
abundance. 11 May HASHEM, the God of your forefathers, add to you a
thousand times yourselves, and bless you as He has spoken of you. 12 How
can I alone carry your contentiousness, your burdens, and your quarrels?
13 Provide for yourselves distinguished men, who are wise, understanding,
and well known to your tribes, and I shall appoint them as your heads."*
*14 You answered me and said, "The thing that you have proposed to do is
good."*
*15 So I took the heads of your tribes, distinguished men, who were wise and
well known, and I appointed them as heads over you, leaders of thousands,
leaders of hundreds, leaders of fifties, and leaders of tens, and officers for
your tribes. 16 I instructed your judges at that time, saying, "Listen among
your brethren and judge righteously between a man and his brother or his
litigant. 17 You shall not show favoritism in judgment, small and great alike
shall you hear; you shall not tremble before any man, for the judgment is
God's; any matter that is too difficult for you, you shall bring to me and I shall
hear it." 18 I commanded you at that time all the things that you should do.*
*19 We journeyed from Horeb and we went through that entire great and
awesome Wilderness that you saw, by way of the Amorite mountain, as
HASHEM, our God, commanded us, and we came until Kadesh-barnea. 20 Then
I said to you, "You have come until the Amorite mountain that HASHEM,
our God, gives us. 21 See — HASHEM, your God, has placed the Land before
you; go up and possess, as HASHEM, God of your forefathers, has spoken*

---

needed a private judge. (Now,) this could only be due to the evil in their heart.

19. וַנֵּלֶךְ אֵת כָּל הַמִּדְבָּר הַגָּדוֹל וְהַנּוֹרָא — *And we went through all that great and dreadful wilderness.* A path which no man had traversed because of its many serpents and scorpions and their monstrous size, as it says, נָחָשׁ שָׂרָף וְעַקְרָב, *serpents, fiery serpents and scorpions* (8:15). Our Sages have indeed told us that there were "serpents like beams and scorpions (as large) as bows" (*Sifre*). All this, God, the Blessed One, did to shorten the way for them so that they could enter the Land at once, *before their pots could feel the thorns* (based on *Psalms* 58:10) and increase their transgression. But all this was insufficient for, in the interim, they sinned through the "murmurers" (*Numbers* 11:1) and with "lusting" (ibid. 11:4) and finally, with the "spies" (ibid. 13).

21. עֲלֵה רֵשׁ — *Go up, take possession.* For no man will stand before you.

NOTES

quarrels in view of the great gift of *Eretz Yisrael* which awaits them.

19. וַנֵּלֶךְ אֵת כָּל הַמִּדְבָּר הַגָּדוֹל וְהַנּוֹרָא — *And we went through all that great and dreadful wilderness.* The *Sforno* explains that God led Israel through that part of the wilderness which men normally never traversed due to the terrible conditions which prevailed there. This He did so as to shorten their way, in the hope that by reducing their difficult stay in the desert, it would diminish the opportunity to rebel against Moses and God. Unfortunately, this proved to be of no avail. The expression used by the *Sforno*, בְּטֶרֶם יָבִינוּ סִירֹתֵיהֶם אָטָד, "before their pots could feel the thorns," symbolizes an uncertain state wherein one is in imminent danger of harm befalling him.

שלישי
כב לָךְ אַל־תִּירָא וְאַל־תֵּחָת: וַתִּקְרְבוּן אֵלַי כֻּלְּכֶם וַתֹּאמְרוּ נִשְׁלְחָה אֲנָשִׁים
לְפָנֵינוּ וְיַחְפְּרוּ־לָנוּ אֶת־הָאָרֶץ וְיָשִׁבוּ אֹתָנוּ דָּבָר אֶת־הַדֶּרֶךְ אֲשֶׁר נַעֲלֶה־
כג בָּהּ וְאֵת הֶעָרִים אֲשֶׁר נָבֹא אֲלֵיהֶן: וַיִּיטַב בְּעֵינַי הַדָּבָר וָאֶקַּח מִכֶּם שְׁנֵים
כד עָשָׂר אֲנָשִׁים אִישׁ אֶחָד לַשָּׁבֶט: וַיִּפְנוּ וַיַּעֲלוּ הָהָרָה וַיָּבֹאוּ עַד־נַחַל
כה אֶשְׁכֹּל וַיְרַגְּלוּ אֹתָהּ: וַיִּקְחוּ בְיָדָם מִפְּרִי הָאָרֶץ וַיּוֹרִדוּ אֵלֵינוּ וַיָּשִׁבוּ אֹתָנוּ
כו דָבָר וַיֹּאמְרוּ טוֹבָה הָאָרֶץ אֲשֶׁר־יְהוָה אֱלֹהֵינוּ נֹתֵן לָנוּ: וְלֹא אֲבִיתֶם
כז לַעֲלֹת וַתַּמְרוּ אֶת־פִּי יְהוָה אֱלֹהֵיכֶם: וַתֵּרָגְנוּ בְאָהֳלֵיכֶם וַתֹּאמְרוּ
בְּשִׂנְאַת יְהוָה אֹתָנוּ הוֹצִיאָנוּ מֵאֶרֶץ מִצְרָיִם לָתֵת אֹתָנוּ בְּיַד הָאֱמֹרִי
כח לְהַשְׁמִידֵנוּ: אָנָה | אֲנַחְנוּ עֹלִים אַחֵינוּ הֵמַסּוּ אֶת־לְבָבֵנוּ לֵאמֹר עַם גָּדוֹל
כט וָרָם מִמֶּנּוּ עָרִים גְּדֹלֹת וּבְצוּרֹת בַּשָּׁמָיִם וְגַם־בְּנֵי עֲנָקִים רָאִינוּ שָׁם: וָאֹמַר
ל אֲלֵכֶם לֹא־תַעַרְצוּן וְלֹא־תִירְאוּן מֵהֶם: יְהוָה אֱלֹהֵיכֶם הַהֹלֵךְ לִפְנֵיכֶם
לא הוּא יִלָּחֵם לָכֶם כְּכֹל אֲשֶׁר עָשָׂה אִתְּכֶם בְּמִצְרַיִם לְעֵינֵיכֶם: וּבַמִּדְבָּר
אֲשֶׁר רָאִיתָ אֲשֶׁר נְשָׂאֲךָ יְהוָה אֱלֹהֶיךָ כַּאֲשֶׁר יִשָּׂא־אִישׁ אֶת־בְּנוֹ

---

22. וַתִּקְרְבוּן אֵלַי כֻּלְּכֶם — *And you came near to me, every one of you.* Even though you had leaders who were appointed over you to attend to public needs, yet you all came. נִשְׁלְחָה אֲנָשִׁים — *Let us send men.* We will choose men and send them (to spy out the Land). (However) God, the Exalted One, did not agree to this, and said to Moses, שְׁלַח לְךָ, *You send* (*Numbers* 13:2), i.e., he (Moses) was to choose the men, not they, lest they choose common men who will compound their wickedness. Therefore, Moses chose כֻּלָּם אֲנָשִׁים, *All of them men* (ibid. 13:3), and among them Joshua and Caleb; and even the wicked ones among them, although they acted in an evil manner when they said that it is impossible to conquer it (the Land), still they did not brazenly state that the Land was bad. Rather, they spoke well of it and in such a manner that eventually (the people) repented, as it says, וַתַּעֲנוּ וַתֹּאמְרוּ אֵלַי, חָטָאנוּ לַה׳ . . . וַתָּשֻׁבוּ וַתִּבְכּוּ לִפְנֵי ה׳, *Then you answered and said to me: We have sinned against* HASHEM (1:41) . . . *And you returned and wept before* HASHEM (1:45).

23. וַיִּיטַב בְּעֵינַי הַדָּבָר — *And the thing pleased me well* . . . because I thought you did not doubt the word of God, the Blessed One, that the Land was good and that you would conquer it, but you wished to select that portion which would be best for you (to settle) now, as you said, וְאֵת הֶעָרִים אֲשֶׁר נָבֹא אֲלֵיהֶן, *And the cities unto which we shall come* (1:22). And this (you wished to do) because you knew that you would not conquer the entire (land) in one year, as it says, לֹא אֲגָרְשֶׁנּוּ מִפָּנֶיךָ בְּשָׁנָה אֶחָת, *I will not drive them out from before you in one year* (*Exodus* 23:29).

NOTES

22. וַתִּקְרְבוּן אֵלַי כֻּלְּכֶם — *And you came near to me, every one of you.* The *Sforno* interprets this statement of Moses as one that is critical of Israel's behavior when they approached him en masse. Since they had representatives, it would have been more seemly for these leaders to come and suggest to Moses that he send spies, rather than for all of them to descend upon him with their request.

נִשְׁלְחָה אֲנָשִׁים — *Let us send men.* God did not object as such to sending the spies, but He insisted that Moses be the one to choose them. By selecting men of stature, who were basically decent and pious, there was a better chance that this mission would be beneficial. Although unfortunately this did not materialize, still, the inherent honesty and stature of the spies did not permit them to deny the excellent character of the Land, and as a result there was no total rejection. Consequently, there was subsequent regret on the part of many for losing faith in God and Moses, and they later wept and repented.

23. וַיִּיטַב בְּעֵינַי הַדָּבָר — *And the thing pleased me well.* The *Sforno* links this verse to verse 26. At first, Moses thought that the intention of Israel

to you. Do not fear and do not lose resolve."

22 *All of you approached me and said, "Let us send men ahead of us and let them spy out the Land, and bring word back to us: the road on which we should ascend and the cities to which we should come."*

23 *The idea was good in my eyes, so I took from you twelve men, one man for each tribe.* 24 *They turned and ascended the mountain and came until the Valley of Eshcol, and spied it out.* 25 *They took in their hands from the fruit of the Land and brought it down to us; they brought back word to us and said, "Good is the Land that HASHEM, our God, gives us!"*

26 *But you did not wish to ascend, and you rebelled against the word of HASHEM, your God.* 27 *You slandered in your tents and said, "Because of HASHEM's hatred for us did He take us out of the land of Egypt, to deliver us into the hand of the Amorite to destroy us.* 28 *To where shall we ascend? Our brothers have melted our hearts, saying, 'A people greater and taller than we, cities great and fortified to the heavens, and even children of giants have we seen there!'"*

29 *Then I said to you, "Do not be broken and do not fear them!* 30 *HASHEM, your God, Who goes before you — He shall make war for you, like everything He did for you in Egypt, before your eyes.* 31 *And in the Wilderness, as you have seen, that HASHEM, your God, bore you, as a man carries his son,*

---

24. וַיָּבֹאוּ עַד נַחַל אֶשְׁכֹּל — *And came to the valley of Eshkol.* As it says, עֲלוּ זֶה בַּנֶּגֶב, *Go up here in the south* (*Numbers* 13:17), this being the side where Israel was (then situated), next to Kadesh Barnea, which is in the south of *Eretz Yisrael* as explained (regarding) the boundaries of the land (*Numbers* 34:4).

25. וַיֹּאמְרוּ טוֹבָה הָאָרֶץ — *And said: "The Land is good."* Even the wicked ones admitted that it was good, as they said, וְגַם זָבַת חָלָב וּדְבַשׁ הִוא, *and surely it flows with milk and honey* (*Numbers* 13:27).

26. וְלֹא אֲבִיתֶם לַעֲלֹת — *Yet, you would not go up.* You revealed your wickedness, (demonstrating) that this mission was not to select that part of the land which would benefit you most (during this initial period) as I had thought and you had indicated. Rather, your intent in sending (the spies) was to determine if you would be able to conquer it. This you did because you did not believe that God could give it to you. Hence, when the spies told you that the people were (very) strong, *you would not go up.*

27. בְּשִׂנְאַת ה׳ אֹתָנוּ — *Because HASHEM hated us . . .* because we worshiped Egyptian gods.

לָתֵת אֹתָנוּ בְּיַד הָאֱמֹרִי — *To deliver us into the hands of the Emorites.* For, although He is able to conquer the Emorites and kill them, (nonetheless) He will deliver us into their hands in revenge (for our sin).

31. אֲשֶׁר נְשָׂאֲךָ ה׳ אֱלֹהֶיךָ — *That HASHEM your God bore you . . .* (through this) *great and dreadful wilderness* (v. 19), and if He wanted to exact vengeance of you, He would have abandoned you in the hands of the serpents and scorpions of the wilderness.

NOTES

was good and proper. Since the total conquest of *Eretz Yisrael* would take a considerable amount of time, it was fitting to find the best place to establish a foothold in the Land which would serve as a base for their eventual total conquest. Later, however, he realized that this was not their true intention, for they became convinced that God would not simply *give* them the Land but it would be necessary for *them* to conquer it. Hence, it was now necessary to determine if the Land could be invaded and the people defeated in battle. The spies' report established that this was not the case,

לב בְּכָל־הַדֶּ֙רֶךְ֙ אֲשֶׁ֣ר הֲלַכְתֶּ֔ם עַד־בֹּאֲכֶ֖ם עַד־הַמָּק֣וֹם הַזֶּ֑ה וּבַדָּבָ֖ר הַזֶּ֔ה

לג אֵֽינְכֶ֣ם מַאֲמִינִ֔ם בַּֽיהֹוָ֖ה אֱלֹֽהֵיכֶֽם: הַהֹלֵ֨ךְ לִפְנֵיכֶ֜ם בַּדֶּ֗רֶךְ לָת֥וּר לָכֶ֛ם מָק֖וֹם לַֽחֲנֹֽתְכֶ֑ם בָּאֵ֣שׁ ׀ לַ֗יְלָה לַרְאֹֽתְכֶ֤ם בַּדֶּ֙רֶךְ֙ אֲשֶׁ֣ר תֵּֽלְכוּ־בָ֔הּ וּבֶֽעָנָ֖ן יוֹמָֽם:

לד-לה וַיִּשְׁמַ֥ע יְהֹוָ֖ה אֶת־ק֣וֹל דִּבְרֵיכֶ֑ם וַיִּקְצֹ֖ף וַיִּשָּׁבַ֥ע לֵאמֹֽר: אִם־יִרְאֶ֥ה אִישׁ֙ בָּֽאֲנָשִׁ֣ים הָאֵ֔לֶּה הַדּ֥וֹר הָרָ֖ע הַזֶּ֑ה אֵ֚ת הָאָ֣רֶץ הַטּוֹבָ֔ה אֲשֶׁ֣ר נִשְׁבַּ֔עְתִּי לָתֵ֖ת

לו לַֽאֲבֹֽתֵיכֶֽם: זֽוּלָתִ֞י כָּלֵ֤ב בֶּן־יְפֻנֶּה֙ ה֣וּא יִרְאֶ֔נָּה וְלֽוֹ־אֶתֵּ֧ן אֶת־הָאָ֛רֶץ אֲשֶׁ֥ר

לז דָּֽרַךְ־בָּ֖הּ וּלְבָנָ֑יו יַ֕עַן אֲשֶׁ֥ר מִלֵּ֖א אַֽחֲרֵ֥י יְהֹוָֽה: גַּם־בִּי֙ הִתְאַנַּ֣ף יְהֹוָ֔ה בִּגְלַלְכֶ֖ם

לח לֵאמֹ֑ר גַּם־אַתָּ֖ה לֹֽא־תָבֹ֥א שָֽׁם: יְהוֹשֻׁ֤עַ בִּן־נוּן֙ הָֽעֹמֵ֣ד לְפָנֶ֔יךָ ה֖וּא יָ֣בֹא

רביעי לט שָׁ֑מָּה אֹת֣וֹ חַזֵּ֔ק כִּי־ה֖וּא יַנְחִלֶ֥נָּה אֶת־יִשְׂרָאֵֽל: וְטַפְּכֶם֩ אֲשֶׁ֙ר אֲמַרְתֶּ֜ם לָבַ֣ז יִֽהְיֶ֗ה וּבְנֵיכֶ֡ם אֲשֶׁר֩ לֹא־יָֽדְע֙וּ הַיּוֹם֙ ט֣וֹב וָרָ֔ע הֵ֖מָּה יָבֹ֣אוּ שָׁ֑מָּה

מ וְלָהֶ֣ם אֶתְּנֶ֔נָּה וְהֵ֖ם יִֽירָשֽׁוּהָ: וְאַתֶּ֖ם פְּנ֣וּ לָכֶ֑ם וּסְע֥וּ הַמִּדְבָּ֖רָה דֶּ֥רֶךְ יַם־סֽוּף:

מא וַתַּֽעֲנ֣וּ ׀ וַתֹּֽאמְר֣וּ אֵלַ֗י חָטָ֘אנוּ֮ לַֽיהֹוָה֒ אֲנַ֣חְנוּ נַֽעֲלֶ֗ה וְנִלְחַ֔מְנוּ כְּכֹ֥ל אֲשֶׁר־ צִוָּ֖נוּ יְהֹוָ֣ה אֱלֹהֵ֑ינוּ וַתַּחְגְּר֗וּ אִ֚ישׁ אֶת־כְּלֵ֣י מִלְחַמְתּ֔וֹ וַתָּהִ֖ינוּ לַֽעֲלֹ֥ת הָהָֽרָה:

מב וַיֹּ֨אמֶר יְהֹוָ֜ה אֵלַ֗י אֱמֹ֤ר לָהֶם֙ לֹ֤א תַֽעֲלוּ֙ וְלֹֽא־תִלָּ֣חֲמ֔וּ כִּ֥י אֵינֶ֖נִּי בְּקִרְבְּכֶ֑ם

מג וְלֹ֙א תִּנָּ֣גְפ֔וּ לִפְנֵ֖י אֹֽיְבֵיכֶֽם: וָֽאֲדַבֵּ֤ר אֲלֵיכֶם֙ וְלֹ֣א שְׁמַעְתֶּ֔ם וַתַּמְר֙וּ אֶת־פִּ֣י

---

33. לָתוּר לָכֶם מָקוֹם לַחֲנֹתְכֶם — *To seek out a place for you to encamp . . .* in that wilderness, as it says, לָתוּר לָהֶם מְנוּחָה, *to seek out a resting place for them* (*Numbers* 10:33). Now, all this teaches His love and compassion for you.

34. אֶת קוֹל דִּבְרֵיכֶם — *The voice of your words.* The voice of unfounded (unjustified) weeping.

37. גַּם בִּי הִתְאַנַּף ה׳ בִּגְלַלְכֶם — *HASHEM was also angry with me for your sakes.* And this happened so as to fulfill (the decree of) בְּכִיָּה לְדוֹרוֹת, *weeping for generations,* as He had designated when He said, אִם לֹא כַּאֲשֶׁר דִּבַּרְתֶּם בְּאָזְנָי כֵּן אֶעֱשֶׂה לָכֶם, *Surely as you have spoken in My ears, so will I do to you* (*Numbers* 14:28), the speaking *in His ears* (referring to) when they said, נָשֵׁינוּ וְטַפֵּנוּ יִהְיוּ לָבַז, *Our wives and our little ones will be a prey* (ibid. 14:3). At this point, (Moses) related the event of his death, even though it would not occur until thirty-eight years later; (still) he incorporated it in the words of the Holy One, Blessed is He, spoken in the second year after they departed from Egypt, for it was then that He said, אִם יִרְאֶה אִישׁ בָּאֲנָשִׁים הָאֵלֶּה, *If any one of these men shall see* (v. 35), and He also said, וְטַפְּכֶם אֲשֶׁר אֲמַרְתֶּם לָבַז יִהְיֶה, *And your little ones that you said would be a prey* (v. 39). The intent (of His words) was that (indeed,) at the end they *would* be a prey, as the Psalmist (i.e., David) explained when he said, וַיִּשָּׂא יָדוֹ לָהֶם לְהַפִּיל אוֹתָם בַּמִּדְבָּר. וּלְהַפִּיל זַרְעָם בַּגּוֹיִם וּלְזָרוֹתָם בָּאֲרָצוֹת, *He swore concerning them that He would overthrow them in the wilderness; and that He would cast out their seed among the nations and scatter them*

NOTES

for the inhabitants were too strong and their cities well fortified. Had Israel retained their faith in God, this report would have had no bearing on their entering the Land, but they had lost their trust in the Almighty, and as a result they doomed their generation to perish in the wilderness.

34. אֶת קוֹל דִּבְרֵיכֶם — *The voice of your words.* The *Sforno* notes that the expression קוֹל, *voice,* is added to the phrase דִּבְרֵיכֶם, *your words.* By listening to

the *voice,* one can detect the true meaning of another's *words.* Although they cried, and the "gates of tears are always open" (*Berachos* 32b), in this case it was meaningless, since their tears were unjustified; hence their words were unacceptable.

37. גַּם בִּי הִתְאַנַּף ה׳ בִּגְלַלְכֶם — *HASHEM was also angry with me for your sakes.* The explanation of the *Sforno's* commentary on this verse is as follows: Although the sin of the spies and God's de-

on the entire way that you traveled, until you arrived at this place. 32 *Yet in*
this matter you do not believe in HASHEM, *your God,* 33 *Who goes before you*
on the way to seek out for you a place for you to encamp, with fire by night
to show you the road that you should travel and with a cloud by day!"
34 HASHEM *heard the sound of your words, and He was incensed and He*
swore, saying, 35 *"If even a man of these people, this evil generation, shall see*
the good Land that I swore to give to your forefathers. 36 *Except for Caleb son*
of Jephunneh: He shall see it, and to him shall I give the Land on which he
walked, and to his children, because he followed HASHEM *wholeheartedly."*
37 *With me, as well,* HASHEM *became angry because of you, saying: You,*
too, shall not come there. 38 *Joshua son of Nun, who stands before you, he shall*
come there; strengthen him, for he shall cause Israel to inherit it. 39 *And as*
for your small children, of whom you said, "They will be taken captive," and
your children who did not know good from evil this day — they will come
there; to them shall I give it and they shall possess it. 40 *And as for you, turn*
yourselves around and journey to the Wilderness, toward the Sea of Reeds.
41 *Then you spoke up and said to me, "We have sinned to* HASHEM! *We*
shall go up and do battle according to everything that HASHEM, *our God, has*
commanded us!" Every man of you girded his weapons of war, and you were
ready to ascend the mountain!
42 HASHEM *said to me: Tell them, "Do not ascend and do not do battle, for*
I am not among you; so that you not be struck down before your enemies."
43 *So I spoke to you, but you did not listen. You rebelled against the word*

---

in the lands (*Psalms* 106:26,27), and so also Ezekiel testified when he said — גַּם אֲנִי נָשָׂאתִי אֶת יָדִי לָהֶם בַּמִּדְבָּר לְהָפִיץ אֹתָם בַּגּוֹיִם, *And I did also swear concerning them in the wilderness to scatter them among the nations* (*Ezekiel* 20:23). Now, by telling them his personal fate and incorporating it in the words of the Holy One, Blessed is He, he informed them that his being prevented from entering the Land with them would cause the severity of the decree, regarding their little ones becoming a prey for generations, to be increased, and this is what the singer (David) attests to when he says: וַיַּקְצִיפוּ עַל מֵי מְרִיבָה וַיֵּרַע לְמֹשֶׁה בַּעֲבוּרָם ... לֹא הִשְׁמִידוּ אֶת הָעַמִּים ... וַיִּתְעָרְבוּ בַגּוֹיִם ... וַיִּחַר אַף ה׳ בְּעַמּוֹ, *They angered Him also at the waters of Meribah, and it went ill with Moses because of them ... they did not destroy the peoples ... but mingled themselves with the nations ... therefore, the wrath of* HASHEM *was kindled against His people* (*Psalms* 106: 32,34,35,40).

NOTES

cree took place in the second year after the Exodus, while the death of Moses occurred thirty-eight years later, the two are interwoven. When the Israelites lamented that their "little ones would be a prey," it was a self-imposed punishment, although it was one that would not be implemented until many years later when they would be exiled from their land. Now, had Moses entered *Eretz Yisrael* with them, there would have been no exile, which ironically would have been disastrous for Israel because when they ultimately sinned, God's wrath would have been poured out upon them and they would ח״ו have been annihilated. Since Moses did not accompany them into the Land, the wrath of heaven was deflected upon "the trees and rocks," and although Israel was exiled, they still survived. In exile, the ominous prediction regarding their children, which God had sworn to fulfill (see the *Sforno* on *Numbers* 14:28 where he quotes the same verses from *Psalms* and *Ezekiel* cited here), was indeed fulfilled but the people of Israel endured. Hence, the fact that Moses did not enter *Eretz Yisrael* was ultimately for the benefit of Israel, which is stated explicitly in chapter 3, verse 26, *and God was angry with me for your sake.* See the *Sforno's* commentary on that verse. This explains why Moses mentions God's anger with him when he reviews the sin of the spies and God's response to it.

מד יְהוָה וַתָּזִדוּ וַתַּעֲלוּ הָהָרָה: וַיֵּצֵא הָאֱמֹרִי הַיֹּשֵׁב בָּהָר הַהוּא לִקְרַאתְכֶם
וַיִּרְדְּפוּ אֶתְכֶם כַּאֲשֶׁר תַּעֲשֶׂינָה הַדְּבֹרִים וַיַּכְּתוּ אֶתְכֶם בְּשֵׂעִיר עַד־
מה חָרְמָה: וַתָּשֻׁבוּ וַתִּבְכּוּ לִפְנֵי יְהוָה וְלֹא־שָׁמַע יְהוָה בְּקֹלְכֶם וְלֹא הֶאֱזִין
ב מו-א אֲלֵיכֶם: וַתֵּשְׁבוּ בְקָדֵשׁ יָמִים רַבִּים כַּיָּמִים אֲשֶׁר יְשַׁבְתֶּם: וַנֵּפֶן וַנִּסַּע
הַמִּדְבָּרָה דֶּרֶךְ יַם־סוּף כַּאֲשֶׁר דִּבֶּר יְהוָה אֵלָי וַנָּסָב אֶת־הַר־שֵׂעִיר יָמִים
חמישי ב-ג רַבִּים: וַיֹּאמֶר יְהוָה אֵלַי לֵאמֹר: רַב־לָכֶם סֹב אֶת־הָהָר
ד הַזֶּה פְּנוּ לָכֶם צָפֹנָה: וְאֶת־הָעָם צַו לֵאמֹר אַתֶּם עֹבְרִים בִּגְבוּל אֲחֵיכֶם
ה בְּנֵי־עֵשָׂו הַיֹּשְׁבִים בְּשֵׂעִיר וְיִירְאוּ מִכֶּם וְנִשְׁמַרְתֶּם מְאֹד: אַל־תִּתְגָּרוּ בָם
כִּי לֹא־אֶתֵּן לָכֶם מֵאַרְצָם עַד מִדְרַךְ כַּף־רָגֶל כִּי־יְרֻשָּׁה לְעֵשָׂו נָתַתִּי
ו אֶת־הַר שֵׂעִיר: אֹכֶל תִּשְׁבְּרוּ מֵאִתָּם בַּכֶּסֶף וַאֲכַלְתֶּם וְגַם־מַיִם תִּכְרוּ
ז מֵאִתָּם בַּכֶּסֶף וּשְׁתִיתֶם: כִּי יְהוָה אֱלֹהֶיךָ בֵּרַכְךָ בְּכֹל מַעֲשֵׂה יָדֶךָ יָדַע
לֶכְתְּךָ אֶת־הַמִּדְבָּר הַגָּדֹל הַזֶּה זֶה | אַרְבָּעִים שָׁנָה יְהוָה אֱלֹהֶיךָ עִמָּךְ לֹא
ח חָסַרְתָּ דָּבָר: וַנַּעֲבֹר מֵאֵת אַחֵינוּ בְנֵי־עֵשָׂו הַיֹּשְׁבִים בְּשֵׂעִיר מִדֶּרֶךְ
*פסקא באמצע פסוק הָעֲרָבָה מֵאֵילַת וּמֵעֶצְיֹן גָּבֶר * וַנֵּפֶן וַנַּעֲבֹר דֶּרֶךְ מִדְבַּר מוֹאָב:

45. וְלֹא שָׁמַע ה׳ בְּקֹלְכֶם — *But* HASHEM *did not hearken to your voice* . . . due to the desecration of the Name (חִלּוּל הַשֵּׁם) which they had committed, (a sin) for which repentance is insufficient and which can only be purged through death. Also, this was a decree accompanied by an oath, since Moses and Joshua and Caleb had (all) urged them (lit., awakened them) to repent but they only did so later because they feared punishment. Therefore, their repentance did not suffice to eliminate the punishment decreed in this world, similar to the (episodes) of Cain, and Saul with the Amalekites, and that of Eli's sons.

וְלֹא הֶאֱזִין אֲלֵיכֶם — *Nor gave ear to you* . . . to postpone (the implementation) or even to cancel the decree regarding the children after the death of the fathers. And thus he admonished them that their repentance was not complete (i.e., sincere), and therefore they accomplished nothing, even with their tears.

NOTES

45. וְלֹא שָׁמַע ה׳ בְּקֹלְכֶם — *But* HASHEM *did not hearken to your voice*. The *Sforno* offers two reasons for God's rejection of Israel's repentance. The first is that the sin of חִלּוּל הַשֵּׁם, *the profaning of God's name*, cannot be expiated through repentance. Only death can remove this sin and complete the process of repentance, purging and cleansing, as our Sages teach us in tractate *Yoma* 86a. The second reason is because God had sworn to punish them for the sin of the spies, and our Sages in tractate *Rosh Hashanah* teach us that a decree from on High that is accompanied by an oath "cannot be torn asunder" (18a). As mentioned above, the decree denying this generation the right to enter the Land was one to which the Almighty swore (*Numbers* 14:28). The reason for this adamant stand on the part of God was due to their refusal to repent of their own volition. Their subsequent willingness to do so was unacceptable since it was only due to pressure and fear of punishment. The *Sforno* cites three other examples of repentance which were blemished and inadequate: first, that of Cain, who said *my sin is too great to be forgiven*, for he himself realized that he waited too long to voice his regret (see the *Sforno's* commentary in *Genesis* 4:13). The second is that of Saul after he returned from the campaign against Amalek but failed to fulfill his mission completely and as a result his kingship was stripped from him. Although he said, *I have sinned for I have transgressed*, and asked for pardon, his plea was rejected, for here also it was motivated by fear of punishment and was not sufficiently sincere (*I Samuel* 15:24,25). Finally, that of the house of Eli is cited by the *Sforno* where God swore that *the iniquity of the house of Eli will not be purged with sacrifice or offering* (*I Samuel* 3:14) for reasons similar to those explained above.

וְלֹא הֶאֱזִין אֲלֵיכֶם — *Nor gave ear to you*. The *Sforno's* interpretation resolves the seeming repetitive nature of the phraseology in this verse. וְלֹא שָׁמַע ה׳, HASHEM *did not hearken*, refers to their repentance, while וְלֹא הֶאֱזִין, *nor gave ear*, refers to God's refusal to postpone the punishment of this generation or

of HASHEM, and you were willful and climbed the mountain. [44] *The Amorite*
who dwell on that mountain went out against you and pursued you as the
bees would do; they struck you in Seir until Hormah. [45] *Then you retreated*
and wept before HASHEM, but HASHEM did not listen to your voice and He did
not hearken to you. [46] *You dwelt in Kadesh for many days, as many days as*
you dwelt.

2 [1] *We turned and journeyed to the Wilderness toward the Sea of Reeds,*
as HASHEM spoke to me, and we circled Mount Seir for many days.
[2] *HASHEM said to me, saying:* [3] *Enough of your circling this mountain; turn*
yourselves northward. [4] *You shall command the people, saying, "You are*
passing through the boundary of your brothers the children of Esau, who
dwell in Seir; they will fear you, but you should be very careful. [5] *You shall*
not provoke them, for I shall not give you of their land even the right to set
foot, for as an inheritance to the children of Esau have I given Mount Seir.
[6] *You shall purchase food from them for money so that you may eat; also*
water shall you buy from them for money so that you may drink. [7] *For*
HASHEM, your God, has blessed you in all your handiwork; He knew your way
in this great Wilderness; this forty-year period HASHEM, your God, was with
you; you did not lack a thing." [8] *So we passed from our brothers, the children*
of Esau who dwell in Seir, from the way of the Arabah, from Elath and from
Ezion-geber and we turned and passed on the way of the Moabite desert.

II

7. יָדַע לֶכְתְּךָ — *He has known your walking.* He supplied you with all the necessities (of life). The expression יָדַע, *He has known,* is similar to, וַיֵּדַע אֱלֹהִים, *And God knew* (*took cognizance*) (*Exodus* 2:25); יְדַעְתִּיךָ בְשֵׁם, *I have known you by name* (ibid. 33:12); אֲשֶׁר יְדָעוֹ ה׳ פָּנִים אֶל פָּנִים, *Whom HASHEM knew face to face* (34:10); מָה אָדָם וַתֵּדָעֵהוּ, *What is man that you recognize him?* (*Psalms* 144:3), and many other such (expressions). This expression (*known*) is said of God, the Exalted One, because all actions (of God), the Blessed One, are effected by Divine knowledge.

לֹא חָסַרְתָּ דָּבָר — *You have lacked nothing.* Hence, they will realize that you are not buying necessary things, but your purchases are motivated (solely) by brotherly feelings, so that they might have benefit (from you). Another reason is that they will come to your (camp) and observe the deeds of God and His wonders.

NOTES

to commute the sentence for the next generation.

II

7. יָדַע לֶכְתְּךָ — *He has known your walking.* The *Rambam* in his *Mishneh Torah* (*Hilchos Yesodai HaTorah* 2:10) discusses the concept of God's knowledge. He explains that unlike man whose being and knowledge are separate, since his knowledge is gained from outside himself, God is "He Who knows, is known and is the knowledge (of Himself), all these being One." This is what the *Sforno* is referring to when he states that the verb *known* is used in the sense that Divine action is effected by Divine knowledge. See the *Sforno's* commentary on *Numbers* 7:89 and the notes there.

לֹא חָסַרְתָּ דָּבָר — *You have lacked nothing.* The previous verse (v. 6) speaks of purchasing food and water from the children of Esau in Seir, followed by this verse which seemingly precludes the necessity to do so, since God had provided Israel with all their needs. The *Sforno* explains that Israel was told to buy food and drink from Esau, not because they were in need of them, but in order that their 'brothers' might benefit from their presence and be assured of Israel's good will toward them. An additional reason is that through this contact the inhabitants of Seir would be afforded the opportunity of witnessing the wonders of God manifested in the camp of Israel.

ט וַיֹּאמֶר יְהוָה אֵלַי אַל־תָּצַר אֶת־מוֹאָב וְאַל־תִּתְגָּר בָּם מִלְחָמָה כִּי לֹא־
י אֶתֵּן לְךָ מֵאַרְצוֹ יְרֻשָּׁה כִּי לִבְנֵי־לוֹט נָתַתִּי אֶת־עָר יְרֻשָּׁה: הָאֵמִים לְפָנִים
יא יָשְׁבוּ בָהּ עַם גָּדוֹל וְרַב וָרָם כַּעֲנָקִים: רְפָאִים יֵחָשְׁבוּ אַף־הֵם כָּעֲנָקִים
יב וְהַמֹּאָבִים יִקְרְאוּ לָהֶם אֵמִים: וּבְשֵׂעִיר יָשְׁבוּ הַחֹרִים לְפָנִים וּבְנֵי עֵשָׂו
יִירָשׁוּם וַיַּשְׁמִידוּם מִפְּנֵיהֶם וַיֵּשְׁבוּ תַּחְתָּם כַּאֲשֶׁר עָשָׂה יִשְׂרָאֵל לְאֶרֶץ
יג יְרֻשָּׁתוֹ אֲשֶׁר־נָתַן יְהוָה לָהֶם: עַתָּה קֻמוּ וְעִבְרוּ לָכֶם אֶת־נַחַל זָרֶד וַנַּעֲבֹר
יד אֶת־נַחַל זָרֶד: וְהַיָּמִים אֲשֶׁר־הָלַכְנוּ ׀ מִקָּדֵשׁ בַּרְנֵעַ עַד אֲשֶׁר־עָבַרְנוּ אֶת־
נַחַל זֶרֶד שְׁלֹשִׁים וּשְׁמֹנֶה שָׁנָה עַד־תֹּם כָּל־הַדּוֹר אַנְשֵׁי הַמִּלְחָמָה מִקֶּרֶב
טו הַמַּחֲנֶה כַּאֲשֶׁר נִשְׁבַּע יְהוָה לָהֶם: וְגַם יַד־יְהוָה הָיְתָה בָּם לְהֻמָּם מִקֶּרֶב
טז הַמַּחֲנֶה עַד תֻּמָּם: וַיְהִי כַאֲשֶׁר־תַּמּוּ כָּל־אַנְשֵׁי הַמִּלְחָמָה לָמוּת מִקֶּרֶב
יז-יח הָעָם: וַיְדַבֵּר יְהוָה אֵלַי לֵאמֹר: אַתָּה עֹבֵר הַיּוֹם אֶת־גְּבוּל
יט מוֹאָב אֶת־עָר: וְקָרַבְתָּ מוּל בְּנֵי עַמּוֹן אַל־תְּצֻרֵם וְאַל־תִּתְגָּר בָּם כִּי לֹא־
כ אֶתֵּן מֵאֶרֶץ בְּנֵי־עַמּוֹן לְךָ יְרֻשָּׁה כִּי לִבְנֵי־לוֹט נְתַתִּיהָ יְרֻשָּׁה: אֶרֶץ־
רְפָאִים תֵּחָשֵׁב אַף־הִוא רְפָאִים יָשְׁבוּ־בָהּ לְפָנִים וְהָעַמֹּנִים יִקְרְאוּ לָהֶם
כא זַמְזֻמִּים: עַם גָּדוֹל וְרַב וָרָם כַּעֲנָקִים וַיַּשְׁמִידֵם יְהוָה מִפְּנֵיהֶם וַיִּירָשֻׁם
כב וַיֵּשְׁבוּ תַחְתָּם: כַּאֲשֶׁר עָשָׂה לִבְנֵי עֵשָׂו הַיֹּשְׁבִים בְּשֵׂעִיר אֲשֶׁר הִשְׁמִיד
כג אֶת־הַחֹרִי מִפְּנֵיהֶם וַיִּירָשֻׁם וַיֵּשְׁבוּ תַחְתָּם עַד הַיּוֹם הַזֶּה: וְהָעַוִּים הַיֹּשְׁבִים

---

10. הָאֵמִים לְפָנִים — *The Emim (dwelt there) aforetime.* Because the children of Lot were definitely not the heirs of Abraham according to law, (it is necessary) to state that God also gave them their land as He did to the children of Esau. The proof (lies in the fact) that they both conquered the land (given to them) in a manner contrary to the natural laws (lit., "custom") of the world.

12. וַיַּשְׁמִידוּם — *And they destroyed them.* Esau and Moab (both) destroyed and laid waste more territory than they needed for their own settlement, in order to destroy all those who dwelt there previously and deter them from rising up and reclaiming the land. Both Moab and Esau did not settle the entire (original) area of the Horites and the Emim whom they had destroyed. Now being that Mt. Seir reached the border of Moab, near which there was no settlement of the children of Esau, and likewise the border of Moab reached the wilderness next to which there was no settlement of the children of Moab; therefore (it was necessary to) say that, nonetheless, they (the Israelites) were not to cross over the borders of either one of these lands.

כַּאֲשֶׁר עָשָׂה יִשְׂרָאֵל — *As Israel did ...* at the time when the Torah was written, having already conquered the great and mighty kings Sichon and Og in a brief period, contrary to the natural laws of the world.

NOTES

10-22. הָאֵמִים לְפָנִים ... וַיַּשְׁמִידוּם ... כַּאֲשֶׁר עָשָׂה יִשְׂרָאֵל ... אֶרֶץ רְפָאִים ... כַּאֲשֶׁר עָשָׂה לִבְנֵי עֵשָׂו — *The Emim (dwelt there) aforetime ... and they destroyed them ... as Israel did ... a land of Rephaim ... As He did for the children of Esau.* Land given to a people by God belongs to them by Divine right, and therefore the Israelites were not permitted to wage war against them so as to conquer their territory. The Torah tells us that the children of Esau and the children of Lot (Moab and Ammon) were given Seir, Ar and part of the Rephaim's territory respectively. The conquest of these lands, inhabited by such mighty people as the Emim, Horites and Zamzumim, by the children of Esau and Lot attests to the fact that it was Divinely ordained, just as the conquest of Canaan by the Israelites was a fulfillment of God's promise to Abraham.

*9 HASHEM said to me: You shall not distress Moab and you shall not
provoke war with them, for I shall not give you an inheritance from their
land, for to the children of Lot have I given Ar as an inheritance. 10 The Emim
dwelled there previously, a great and populous people, and tall as the giants.
11 They, too, were considered Rephaim, like the giants; and the Moabites
called them Emim. 12 And in Seir the Horites dwelled previously, and the
children of Esau drove them away from before themselves and dwelled in
their place, as Israel did to the Land of its inheritance, which HASHEM gave
them. 13 Now, rise up and get yourselves across Zered Brook — so we crossed
Zered Brook.*

*14 The days that we traveled from Kadesh-barnea until we crossed Zered
Brook were thirty-eight years, until the end of the entire generation, the men
of war, from the midst of the camp, as HASHEM swore to them. 15 Even the
hand of HASHEM was on them to confound them from amid the camp, until
their end. 16 So it was that the men of war finished dying from amidst the
people . . .*

*17 HASHEM spoke to me, saying: 18 This day you shall cross the border of
Moab, at Ar, 19 and you shall approach opposite the children of Ammon; you
shall not distress them and you shall not provoke them, for I shall not give
any of the land of the children of Ammon to you as an inheritance, for to the
children of Lot have I given it as an inheritance. 20 It, too, is considered the
land of the Rephaim; the Rephaim dwelled in it previously, and the
Ammonites called them Zamzumim. 21 A great and populous people, and
tall as giants, and HASHEM destroyed them before them, and they drove them
out and dwelled in their place, 22 just as he did for the children of Esau who
dwell in Seir, who destroyed the Horite before them; they drove them out
and dwelled in their place until this day. 23 As for the Avvim who dwell*

---

13. עַתָּה קֻמוּ — *Now rise up.* Now since it is prohibited for you to pass over the border of these two (peoples), קֻמוּ וְעִבְרוּ לָכֶם אֶת נַחַל זָרֶד, *Rise up and bring yourselves over the brook of Zered* (which is beyond the boundary of both these nations), and from there you will be able to pass outside the borders of both until you (reach) the Jordan.

20. אֶרֶץ רְפָאִים תֵּחָשֵׁב אַף הִוא — *That also is considered a land of Rephaim* . . . and without a doubt, the children of Ammon were not capable of destroying them, but God, the Blessed One, did it for them . . .

22. כַּאֲשֶׁר עָשָׂה לִבְנֵי עֵשָׂו — *As He did for the children of Esau.* He drove out the inhabitants because they were dwelling in the land of Seir.

23. וְהָעַוִּים הַיֹּשְׁבִים בַּחֲצֵרִים עַד עַזָּה — *And the Avim that dwelt in villages as far as Gaza.* Although they were the children of Esau or the children of the Philistines to whom Abraham had sworn (that he would do them no harm), still, Israel did not refrain from conquering their land. The reason for this was because Israel did not find the land in their possession, since the Caphtorim, who came out of Caphtor seeking a place to settle (lit., "to find rest"), were then the majority of its inhabitants having destroyed the Avim. It was from the hands of these Caphtorim that Israel conquered the land.

NOTES

23. וְהָעַוִּים הַיֹּשְׁבִים בַּחֲצֵרִים עַד עַזָּה — *And the Avim that dwelt in villages as far as Gaza.* Although the Israelites were forbidden to expropriate any land which belonged to Esau, Moab or Ammon, as

בַּחֲצֵרִים עַד־עַזָּה כַּפְתֹּרִים הַיֹּצְאִים מִכַּפְתֹּר הִשְׁמִידֻם וַיֵּשְׁבוּ תַחְתָּם׃
כד קוּמוּ *סְּעוּ וְעִבְרוּ אֶת־נַחַל אַרְנֹן רְאֵה נָתַתִּי בְיָדְךָ אֶת־סִיחֹן מֶלֶךְ־חֶשְׁבּוֹן *ס׳ דגושה
כה הָאֱמֹרִי וְאֶת־אַרְצוֹ הָחֵל רָשׁ וְהִתְגָּר בּוֹ מִלְחָמָה׃ הַיּוֹם הַזֶּה אָחֵל תֵּת
פַּחְדְּךָ וְיִרְאָתְךָ עַל־פְּנֵי הָעַמִּים תַּחַת כָּל־הַשָּׁמָיִם אֲשֶׁר יִשְׁמְעוּן שִׁמְעֲךָ
כו וְרָגְזוּ וְחָלוּ מִפָּנֶיךָ׃ וָאֶשְׁלַח מַלְאָכִים מִמִּדְבַּר קְדֵמוֹת אֶל־סִיחוֹן מֶלֶךְ
כז חֶשְׁבּוֹן דִּבְרֵי שָׁלוֹם לֵאמֹר׃ אֶעְבְּרָה בְאַרְצֶךָ בַּדֶּרֶךְ בַּדֶּרֶךְ אֵלֵךְ לֹא
כח אָסוּר יָמִין וּשְׂמֹ*אול׃ אֹכֶל בַּכֶּסֶף תַּשְׁבִּרֵנִי וְאָכַלְתִּי וּמַיִם בַּכֶּסֶף תִּתֶּן־לִי *מלא ו׳
כט וְשָׁתִיתִי רַק אֶעְבְּרָה בְרַגְלָי׃ כַּאֲשֶׁר עָשׂוּ־לִי בְּנֵי עֵשָׂו הַיֹּשְׁבִים בְּשֵׂעִיר
וְהַמּוֹאָבִים הַיֹּשְׁבִים בְּעָר עַד אֲשֶׁר־אֶעֱבֹר אֶת־הַיַּרְדֵּן אֶל־הָאָרֶץ אֲשֶׁר־
ל יהוה אֱלֹהֵינוּ נֹתֵן לָנוּ׃ וְלֹא אָבָה סִיחֹן מֶלֶךְ חֶשְׁבּוֹן הַעֲבִרֵנוּ בּוֹ כִּי־
הִקְשָׁה יהוה אֱלֹהֶיךָ אֶת־רוּחוֹ וְאִמֵּץ אֶת־לְבָבוֹ לְמַעַן תִּתּוֹ בְיָדְךָ כַּיּוֹם
ששי לא הַזֶּה׃ וַיֹּאמֶר יהוה אֵלַי רְאֵה הַחִלֹּתִי תֵּת לְפָנֶיךָ אֶת־סִיחֹן
לב וְאֶת־אַרְצוֹ הָחֵל רָשׁ לָרֶשֶׁת אֶת־אַרְצוֹ׃ וַיֵּצֵא סִיחֹן לִקְרָאתֵנוּ הוּא וְכָל־
לג עַמּוֹ לַמִּלְחָמָה יָהְצָה׃ וַיִּתְּנֵהוּ יהוה אֱלֹהֵינוּ לְפָנֵינוּ וַנַּךְ אֹתוֹ וְאֶת־בָּנָו
לד וְאֶת־כָּל־עַמּוֹ׃ וַנִּלְכֹּד אֶת־כָּל־עָרָיו בָּעֵת הַהִוא וַנַּחֲרֵם אֶת־כָּל־עִיר
לה מְתִם וְהַנָּשִׁים וְהַטָּף לֹא הִשְׁאַרְנוּ שָׂרִיד׃ רַק הַבְּהֵמָה בָּזַזְנוּ לָנוּ וּשְׁלַל
לו הֶעָרִים אֲשֶׁר לָכָדְנוּ׃ מֵעֲרֹעֵר אֲשֶׁר עַל־שְׂפַת־נַחַל אַרְנֹן וְהָעִיר אֲשֶׁר־
בַּנַּחַל וְעַד־הַגִּלְעָד לֹא הָיְתָה קִרְיָה אֲשֶׁר שָׂגְבָה מִמֶּנּוּ אֶת־הַכֹּל נָתַן
לז יהוה אֱלֹהֵינוּ לְפָנֵינוּ׃ רַק אֶל־אֶרֶץ בְּנֵי־עַמּוֹן לֹא קָרָבְתָּ כָּל־יַד נַחַל יַבֹּק
ג א וְעָרֵי הָהָר וְכֹל אֲשֶׁר־צִוָּה יהוה אֱלֹהֵינוּ׃ וַנֵּפֶן וַנַּעַל דֶּרֶךְ הַבָּשָׁן וַיֵּצֵא עוֹג
ב מֶלֶךְ־הַבָּשָׁן לִקְרָאתֵנוּ הוּא וְכָל־עַמּוֹ לַמִּלְחָמָה אֶדְרֶעִי׃ וַיֹּאמֶר יהוה אֵלַי
אַל־תִּירָא אֹתוֹ כִּי בְיָדְךָ נָתַתִּי אֹתוֹ וְאֶת־כָּל־עַמּוֹ וְאֶת־אַרְצוֹ וְעָשִׂיתָ
ג לּוֹ כַּאֲשֶׁר עָשִׂיתָ לְסִיחֹן מֶלֶךְ הָאֱמֹרִי אֲשֶׁר יוֹשֵׁב בְּחֶשְׁבּוֹן׃ וַיִּתֵּן יהוה
אֱלֹהֵינוּ בְּיָדֵנוּ גַּם אֶת־עוֹג מֶלֶךְ־הַבָּשָׁן וְאֶת־כָּל־עַמּוֹ וַנַּכֵּהוּ עַד־בִּלְתִּי
ד הִשְׁאִיר־לוֹ שָׂרִיד׃ וַנִּלְכֹּד אֶת־כָּל־עָרָיו בָּעֵת הַהִוא לֹא הָיְתָה קִרְיָה
אֲשֶׁר לֹא־לָקַחְנוּ מֵאִתָּם שִׁשִּׁים עִיר כָּל־חֶבֶל אַרְגֹּב מַמְלֶכֶת עוֹג בַּבָּשָׁן׃
ה כָּל־אֵלֶּה עָרִים בְּצֻרֹת חוֹמָה גְבֹהָה דְּלָתַיִם וּבְרִיחַ לְבַד מֵעָרֵי הַפְּרָזִי
ו הַרְבֵּה מְאֹד׃ וַנַּחֲרֵם אוֹתָם כַּאֲשֶׁר עָשִׂינוּ לְסִיחֹן מֶלֶךְ חֶשְׁבּוֹן הַחֲרֵם כָּל־

30. כִּי הִקְשָׁה ה׳ אֱלֹהֶיךָ אֶת רוּחוֹ — *For HASHEM your God hardened his spirit* ... not to allow the Israelites to pass his border.

NOTES

mentioned above, if any of these territories were conquered by other nations, Israel was permitted to wage war against them and take the land for themselves. The Torah already told us that this was the reason Israel was permitted to take Cheshbon from Sichon although originally it had belonged to Moab (*Numbers* 21:26). The *Sforno* explains that the same holds true for the land originally inhabited by the Avim, whom they were not permitted to displace, but which now was inhabited by the Caphtorim who were an Egyptian people. Just as Sichon the Emorite took over Cheshbon, so the Caphtorim took over the villages as far as Gaza ...

30. ... כִּי הִקְשָׁה ה׳ אֱלֹהֶיךָ ... וְאִמֵּץ ... — *For HASHEM your God hardened ... and made obstinate ...* The *Sforno* explains that these two expressions, הִקְשָׁה, *hardened*, and אִמֵּץ, *made obstinate*, are not

in open cities until Gaza, the Caphtorim who went out of Caphtor destroyed
them, and dwelled in their place. 24 *Rise up and cross Arnon Brook; see! into*
your hand have I delivered Sihon king of Heshbon, the Amorite, and his
land; begin to possess it, and provoke war with him. 25 *This day I shall begin*
to place dread and fear of you on the peoples under the entire heaven, when
they hear of your reputation, and they will tremble and be anxious before
you."

26 *I sent messengers from the Wilderness of Kedemoth to Sihon king of*
Heshbon, words of peace, saying, 27 *"Let me pass through your land; only on*
the road shall I go; I will not stray right or left. 28 *Food shall I purchase for*
money as provisions, and I will eat; and you will give me water for money,
and I shall drink — only let me pass with my foot-goers; 29 *as the children*
of Esau who dwell in Seir did for me, and the Moabites who dwell in Ar —
until I cross the Jordan to the Land that HASHEM, our God, gives us." 30 *But*
Sihon king of Heshbon was not willing to let us pass through it, for HASHEM,
your God, hardened his spirit and made his heart stubborn, in order to give
him into your hand, like this very day.

31 *HASHEM said to me: See, I have begun to deliver before you Sihon and*
his land; begin to drive out, to possess his land.

32 *Sihon went out toward us — he and his entire people — for battle, to*
Jahaz. 33 *HASHEM, our God, gave him before us, and we smote him and his*
sons and his entire people. 34 *We occupied all his cities at that time, and we*
destroyed every populated city, with the women and small children; we did
not leave a survivor. 35 *Only the animals did we loot for ourselves, and the*
booty of the cities that we occupied: 36 *from Aroer, which is by the shore of*
Arnon Brook, and the city that is by the brook, and until Gilead — there was
no city that was too strong for us; HASHEM, our God, gave everything before
us. 37 *Only to the land of the children of Ammon did you not draw near,*
everywhere near Jabbok Brook and the cities of the mountain, and every-
where that HASHEM, our God, commanded us.

3 1 *We turned and ascended by way of the Bashan, and Og king of*
Bashan went out toward us, he and his entire people, for war at Edrei.
2 *HASHEM said to me: Do not fear him, for in your hand have I given him and*
his entire people and his land, and you shall do to him as you did to Sihon
king of the Amorite, who dwells in Heshbon. 3 *HASHEM, our God, gave into*
our hand also Og king of the Bashan and his entire people, and we smote him
until no survivor was left of him. 4 *We occupied all his cities at that time;*
there was no city that we did not take from them — sixty cities, the entire
region of Argob — the kingdom of Og in the Bashan. 5 *All these were fortified*
cities, with a high wall, doors and bar, aside from open cities, very many.
6 *We destroyed them, as we did to Sihon king of Heshbon, destroying every*

וְאִמֵּץ אֶת לְבָבוֹ — *And made his heart obstinate* ... to wage war against them.

NOTES

redundant. The former refers to Sichon's refusal to allow Israel to pass through his land while the latter speaks of his decision to wage war against them.

ז־ח עִיר מְתִם הַנָּשִׁים וְהַטָּף: וְכָל־הַבְּהֵמָה וּשְׁלַל הֶעָרִים בַּזּוֹנוּ לָנוּ: וַנִּקַּח בָּעֵת
הַהִוא אֶת־הָאָרֶץ מִיַּד שְׁנֵי מַלְכֵי הָאֱמֹרִי אֲשֶׁר בְּעֵבֶר הַיַּרְדֵּן מִנַּחַל אַרְנֹן
ט עַד־הַר חֶרְמוֹן: צִידֹנִים יִקְרְאוּ לְחֶרְמוֹן שִׂרְיֹן וְהָאֱמֹרִי יִקְרְאוּ־לוֹ שְׂנִיר:
י כֹּל ׀ עָרֵי הַמִּישֹׁר וְכָל־הַגִּלְעָד וְכָל־הַבָּשָׁן עַד־סַלְכָה וְאֶדְרֶעִי עָרֵי
יא מַמְלֶכֶת עוֹג בַּבָּשָׁן: כִּי רַק־עוֹג מֶלֶךְ הַבָּשָׁן נִשְׁאַר מִיֶּתֶר הָרְפָאִים הִנֵּה
עַרְשׂוֹ עֶרֶשׂ בַּרְזֶל הֲלֹה הִוא בְּרַבַּת בְּנֵי עַמּוֹן תֵּשַׁע אַמּוֹת אָרְכָּהּ וְאַרְבַּע
יב אַמּוֹת רָחְבָּהּ בְּאַמַּת־אִישׁ: וְאֶת־הָאָרֶץ הַזֹּאת יָרַשְׁנוּ בָּעֵת הַהִוא
מֵעֲרֹעֵר אֲשֶׁר־עַל־נַחַל אַרְנֹן וַחֲצִי הַר־הַגִּלְעָד וְעָרָיו נָתַתִּי לָראוּבֵנִי
יג וְלַגָּדִי: וְיֶתֶר הַגִּלְעָד וְכָל־הַבָּשָׁן מַמְלֶכֶת עוֹג נָתַתִּי לַחֲצִי שֵׁבֶט הַמְנַשֶּׁה
יד כֹּל חֶבֶל הָאַרְגֹּב לְכָל־הַבָּשָׁן הַהוּא יִקָּרֵא אֶרֶץ רְפָאִים: יָאִיר בֶּן־מְנַשֶּׁה
לָקַח אֶת־כָּל־חֶבֶל אַרְגֹּב עַד־גְּבוּל הַגְּשׁוּרִי וְהַמַּעֲכָתִי וַיִּקְרָא אֹתָם עַל־
שביעי טו שְׁמוֹ אֶת־הַבָּשָׁן חַוֺּת יָאִיר עַד הַיּוֹם הַזֶּה: וּלְמָכִיר נָתַתִּי אֶת־הַגִּלְעָד:
טז וְלָראוּבֵנִי וְלַגָּדִי נָתַתִּי מִן־הַגִּלְעָד וְעַד־נַחַל אַרְנֹן תּוֹךְ הַנַּחַל וּגְבֻל וְעַד
יז יַבֹּק הַנַּחַל גְּבוּל בְּנֵי עַמּוֹן: וְהָעֲרָבָה וְהַיַּרְדֵּן וּגְבֻל מִכִּנֶּרֶת וְעַד יָם הָעֲרָבָה
יח יָם הַמֶּלַח תַּחַת אַשְׁדֹּת הַפִּסְגָּה מִזְרָחָה: וָאֲצַו אֶתְכֶם בָּעֵת הַהִוא לֵאמֹר
יהוה אֱלֹהֵיכֶם נָתַן לָכֶם אֶת־הָאָרֶץ הַזֹּאת לְרִשְׁתָּהּ חֲלוּצִים תַּעַבְרוּ
יט לִפְנֵי אֲחֵיכֶם בְּנֵי־יִשְׂרָאֵל כָּל־בְּנֵי־חָיִל: רַק נְשֵׁיכֶם וְטַפְּכֶם וּמִקְנֵכֶם
מפטיר כ יָדַעְתִּי כִּי־מִקְנֶה רַב לָכֶם יֵשְׁבוּ בְּעָרֵיכֶם אֲשֶׁר נָתַתִּי לָכֶם: עַד אֲשֶׁר־
יָנִיחַ יהוה ׀ לַאֲחֵיכֶם כָּכֶם וְיָרְשׁוּ גַם־הֵם אֶת־הָאָרֶץ אֲשֶׁר יהוה אֱלֹהֵיכֶם
כא נֹתֵן לָהֶם בְּעֵבֶר הַיַּרְדֵּן וְשַׁבְתֶּם אִישׁ לִירֻשָּׁתוֹ אֲשֶׁר נָתַתִּי לָכֶם: וְאֶת־
יְהוֹשׁוּעַ צִוֵּיתִי בָּעֵת הַהִוא לֵאמֹר עֵינֶיךָ הָרֹאֹת אֵת כָּל־אֲשֶׁר עָשָׂה יהוה
אֱלֹהֵיכֶם לִשְׁנֵי הַמְּלָכִים הָאֵלֶּה כֵּן־יַעֲשֶׂה יהוה לְכָל־הַמַּמְלָכוֹת אֲשֶׁר
כב אַתָּה עֹבֵר שָׁמָּה: לֹא תִּירָאוּם כִּי יהוה אֱלֹהֵיכֶם הוּא הַנִּלְחָם לָכֶם:

III

11. כִּי רַק עוֹג מֶלֶךְ הַבָּשָׁן נִשְׁאַר מִיֶּתֶר הָרְפָאִים — *For only Og king of Bashan remained of the remnant of the Rephaim.* Now the reason Og reigned in that district was because he alone *remained of the remnant of the Rephaim,* for in the battle with Amraphel (אַמְרָפֶל) and his allies when the Rephaim were smitten in Ashteros Karnaim, many Rephaim survived, but that remnant was smitten by the children of Ammon as explained above (2:20,21), and from that battle with Ammon he alone remained, and since he was mighty, as are all Rephaim, he became the king.

בְּאַמַּת אִישׁ — *After the cubit of a man . . .* (This means to say) a cubit according to the measurement of each one of those Rephaim. The phrase אִישׁ, *man,* indicates each and

NOTES

III

11. בְּאַמַּת אִישׁ — *After the cubit of a man.* An אַמָּה, *cubit,* is a linear measure equal to the distance from the elbow to the tip of the middle finger. Obviously, the length of that distance depends upon the size of the individual. This is what the *Sforno* means when he says that the nine cubits recorded in the Torah was according to the cubit of each one of these giantlike men. Were this bedstead to have been measured by the measurement of "elbow to tip of finger" of the average man, it would be far more than nine cubits! The only reason the Torah

populated city, the women and small children. 7 *And all the animals and the*
booty of the cities we looted for ourselves. 8 *At that time we took the land*
from the hand of the two kings of the Amorite that were on the other side
of the Jordan, from Arnon Brook to Mount Hermon — 9 *Sidonians would refer*
to Hermon as Sirion, and the Amorites would call it Senir — 10 *all the cities*
of the plain, the entire Gilead, and the entire Bashan until Salcah and Edrei,
the kingdom of Og in the Bashan. 11 *For only Og king of the Bashan was left*
of the remaining Rephaim — behold! his bed was an iron bed, in Rabbah of
the children of Ammon — nine cubits was its length and four cubits its width,
by the cubit of that man.
12 *And we possessed that land at that time; from Aroer, which is by Arnon*
Brook, and half of the mountain of Gilead and its cities did I give to the
Reubenite and the Gadite. 13 *The rest of the Gilead and the entire Bashan, the*
kingdom of Og, did I give to half the tribe of Manasseh, the entire region of
the Argov of the entire Bashan, that is called the land of Rephaim. 14 *Jair son*
of Manasseh took the entire region of Argov until the border of the Geshurite
and the Maacathite, and he named them, the Bashan, after himself,
"Havvoth-jair," until this day. 15 *To Machir I gave the Gilead.* 16 *To the*
Reubenite and the Gadite I gave from the Gilead until Arnon Brook, the
midst of the brook and the border, until Jabbok Brook, the border of the
children of Ammon, 17 *and the Arabah and the Jordan and its border, from*
Kinnereth to the Arabah Sea, the Salt Sea, below the waterfalls from the
mountaintop, eastward.
18 *I commanded you at that time, saying, "HASHEM, your God, gave you*
this Land for a possession, armed shall you cross over before your brethren,
the Children of Israel, all the men of accomplishment. 19 *Only your wives,*
small children, and livestock — I know that you have abundant livestock —
shall dwell in your cities that I have given you. 20 *Until HASHEM shall give*
rest to your brethren like yourselves, and they, too, shall possess the Land
that HASHEM, your God, gives them on the other side of the Jordan; then you
shall return, every man to his inheritance that I have given you."
21 *I commanded Joshua at that time, saying, "Your eyes have seen every-*
thing that HASHEM, your God, has done to these two kings; so will HASHEM
do to all the kings where you cross over. 22 *You shall not fear them, for*
HASHEM, your God — He shall wage war for you."

---

every one, similar to אִישׁ לְבִצְעוֹ מִקָּצֵהוּ, *Each one to his gain, one and all* (*Isaiah* 56:11) and וַיַּכּוּ אִישׁ אִישׁוֹ, *And they slew each one his man* (*I Kings* 20:20), and other such similar expressions. (The verse) says that although that bedstead was תֵּשַׁע אַמּוֹת אָרְכָּהּ, *nine cubits the length thereof*, according to the cubit of each of them, and according to the cubit measurement of the average person, it was without a doubt much larger than nine cubits, so we can then understand the great size of those giants and their strength. Yet, nonetheless, the children of Ammon destroyed them by the decree of God, the Blessed One, as explained above (2:21).

NOTES

tells us this interesting, but seemingly nonvital piece of information, is to underscore that the conquest of these people by Ammon was accomplished only through the will of God.

פרשת ואתחנן

כג-כד וָאֶתְחַנַּן אֶל־יְהוָה בָּעֵת הַהִוא לֵאמֹר: אֲדֹנָי יֱהוִה אַתָּה הַחִלּוֹתָ
לְהַרְאוֹת אֶת־עַבְדְּךָ אֶת־גָּדְלְךָ וְאֶת־יָדְךָ הַחֲזָקָה אֲשֶׁר מִי־אֵל בַּשָּׁמַיִם
כה וּבָאָרֶץ אֲשֶׁר־יַעֲשֶׂה כְמַעֲשֶׂיךָ וְכִגְבוּרֹתֶךָ: אֶעְבְּרָה־נָּא וְאֶרְאֶה אֶת־
כו הָאָרֶץ הַטּוֹבָה אֲשֶׁר בְּעֵבֶר הַיַּרְדֵּן הָהָר הַטּוֹב הַזֶּה וְהַלְּבָנֹן: וַיִּתְעַבֵּר
יְהוָה בִּי לְמַעַנְכֶם וְלֹא שָׁמַע אֵלָי וַיֹּאמֶר יְהוָה אֵלַי רַב־לָךְ אַל־תּוֹסֶף
כז דַּבֵּר אֵלַי עוֹד בַּדָּבָר הַזֶּה: עֲלֵה | רֹאשׁ הַפִּסְגָּה וְשָׂא עֵינֶיךָ יָמָּה וְצָפֹנָה
כח וְתֵימָנָה וּמִזְרָחָה וּרְאֵה בְעֵינֶיךָ כִּי־לֹא תַעֲבֹר אֶת־הַיַּרְדֵּן הַזֶּה: וְצַו
אֶת־יְהוֹשֻׁעַ וְחַזְּקֵהוּ וְאַמְּצֵהוּ כִּי־הוּא יַעֲבֹר לִפְנֵי הָעָם הַזֶּה וְהוּא יַנְחִיל
כט אוֹתָם אֶת־הָאָרֶץ אֲשֶׁר תִּרְאֶה: וַנֵּשֶׁב בַּגָּיְא מוּל בֵּית פְּעוֹר:
ד א וְעַתָּה יִשְׂרָאֵל שְׁמַע אֶל־הַחֻקִּים וְאֶל־הַמִּשְׁפָּטִים אֲשֶׁר אָנֹכִי מְלַמֵּד
אֶתְכֶם לַעֲשׂוֹת לְמַעַן תִּחְיוּ וּבָאתֶם וִירִשְׁתֶּם אֶת־הָאָרֶץ אֲשֶׁר יְהוָה
ב אֱלֹהֵי אֲבֹתֵיכֶם נֹתֵן לָכֶם: לֹא תֹסִפוּ עַל־הַדָּבָר אֲשֶׁר אָנֹכִי מְצַוֶּה
אֶתְכֶם וְלֹא תִגְרְעוּ מִמֶּנּוּ לִשְׁמֹר אֶת־מִצְוֺת יְהוָה אֱלֹהֵיכֶם אֲשֶׁר אָנֹכִי
ג מְצַוֶּה אֶתְכֶם: עֵינֵיכֶם הָרֹאוֹת אֵת אֲשֶׁר־עָשָׂה יְהוָה בְּבַעַל פְּעוֹר כִּי

---

24. וְאֶת יָדְךָ הַחֲזָקָה — *And Your strong hand* . . . to alter the nature of the imperishables (i.e., the forces of nature) which none but You can do. Now all this You did in order to bring Israel into the Land (of Canaan) and therefore, it is fitting (that I) attempt to secure their residence in it.

25. אֶעְבְּרָה נָּא — *Let me please cross over* . . . to destroy all the inhabitants of Canaan, so that Israel will never be exiled from it.

וְאֶרְאֶה אֶת הָאָרֶץ הַטּוֹבָה — *And see the good land.* I will gaze upon it for good (which shall result) from my blessing, bringing everlasting benefit for Israel.

26. וַיִּתְעַבֵּר ה׳ בִּי לְמַעַנְכֶם — *But HASHEM was angry with me for your sake* . . . because I desired to insure your existence in it so that you should never be exiled from it; (but) He had already sworn to *cast out your seed among the nations* (based on *Psalms* 106:27).

NOTES

24. וְאֶת יָדְךָ הַחֲזָקָה — *And Your strong hand*. The *Sifre* states that יָדְךָ הַחֲזָקָה, *Your strong hand*, refers to the Ten Plagues visited upon Egypt by the Almighty. These מַכּוֹת, *plagues*, in many instances affected and altered the laws of nature, as the *Sforno* points out; hence, they are called God's *strong hand*. The very fact that God was prepared to resort to these supernatural acts reflects the importance He attached to Israel's exodus from Egypt and their ultimate entry into the Promised Land. Moses therefore argues that he be permitted to enter with them so as to insure their permanent possession of the Land.

25. אֶעְבְּרָה נָּא וְאֶרְאֶה — *Let me please cross over and see*. Moses presents two arguments to God that He relent and permit him to enter *Eretz Yisrael* with his people. One is a practical reason: As a mighty warrior and military leader, he will be able to lead the Israelites in vanquishing the inhabitants of the Land. The second reason is that by viewing the Land from a perspective of "good," he will be able to have a positive impact upon it for the "good" of Israel, and that will have an everlasting and indelible influence upon Israel's security and well-being in the Land. According to the *Sforno's* interpretation, the expression וְאֶרְאֶה, *and see*, is not simply a request *to see*, in the usual sense, but to effectuate a major influence upon Israel's permanent residence and success in *Eretz Yisrael*.

26. וַיִּתְעַבֵּר ה׳ בִּי לְמַעַנְכֶם — *But HASHEM was angry with me for your sake*. See the *Sforno's* commentary in chapter 1, verse 37, and the explanatory note on his commentary for clarification of the *Sforno* on this verse.

PARASHAS VAESCHANAN

*23 I implored HASHEM at that time, saying, 24 "My Lord, HASHEM/ELOHIM,
you have begun to show Your servant Your greatness and Your strong
hand, for what power is there in the heaven or on the earth that can perform
according to Your deeds and according to Your mighty acts? 25 Let me now
cross and see the good Land that is on the other side of the Jordan, this good
mountain and the Lebanon."*

*26 But HASHEM became angry with me because of you, and He did not
listen to me; HASHEM said to me, "It is too much for you! Do not continue to
speak to Me further about this matter. 27 Ascend to the top of the cliff and
raise your eyes westward, northward, southward, and eastward, and see
with your eyes, for you shall not cross this Jordan. 28 But you shall command
Joshua, and strengthen him and give him resolve, for he shall cross before
the people and he shall cause them to inherit the Land that you will see."*
29 So we remained in the valley, opposite Beth-peor.

4 *1 Now, O Israel, listen to the decrees and to the ordinances that I teach
you to perform, so that you may live, and you will come and possess
the Land that HASHEM, the God of your forefathers, gives you. 2 You
shall not add to the word that I command you, nor shall you subtract
from it, to observe the commandments of HASHEM, your God, that I command you. 3 Your eyes have seen what HASHEM did with Baal-peor, for*

IV

1. וְעַתָּה יִשְׂרָאֵל — *And now Israel.* Since you see that the decree of God, the Blessed One, is to exile you if you sin, be careful not to transgress, but (rather to) observe the commandments without adding or diminishing, for any addition to or diminishment from (the word of God) will bring you to ultimate ruination.

2. וְלֹא תִגְרְעוּ מִמֶּנּוּ לִשְׁמֹר — *Neither shall you diminish from it, that you may keep.* One should not think that once the cause (reason) of the prohibition is removed, then it is not sinful to diminish, as King Solomon thought (when he said), אֲנִי אַרְבֶּה וְלֹא אָסוּר, אֲנִי אַרְבֶּה וְלֹא אָשִׁיב, *I will multiply but my heart will not be turned away, I will multiply but not cause the people to return* (*Sanhedrin* 21b).

3. עֵינֵיכֶם הָרֹאוֹת — *Your eyes have seen.* Behold, that which you saw happening regarding Baal-Peor attests to this, for indeed, those who sinned with idolatry did not

NOTES

IV

2. וְלֹא תִגְרְעוּ מִמֶּנּוּ לִשְׁמֹר — *Neither shall you diminish from it, that you may keep.* The words of our Sages cited by the *Sforno* refer to the prohibitions imposed by the Torah upon a Jewish king. In *Deut.* 17:16,17, the king is admonished not to *multiply horses to himself* lest he cause the people to return to Egypt where horses were obtained. He is also cautioned not to *multiply wives to himself*, lest they turn his heart to sensual passions, as the *Ibn Ezra* explains. In most instances, the Torah does not give explicit reasons for prohibitions. This case here is an exception to the rule, and as a result King Solomon reasoned that if the cause for the Torah's apprehension is removed, so is the prohibition. He was confident that he would not be misled by his many wives nor would he be tempted to return to Egypt to purchase more horses. Unfortunately, he was wrong. This verse is interpreted by the *Sforno* as applying not only to subtracting laws from the Torah but also to any rationalization which will prove to be the cause of one's downfall, as was the case with Solomon.

3. עֵינֵיכֶם הָרֹאוֹת — *Your eyes have seen.* The *Sforno* interprets the citing of the event at Peor by Moses as a perfect example how a seemingly

כָּל־הָאִישׁ אֲשֶׁר הָלַךְ אַחֲרֵי בַעַל־פְּעוֹר הִשְׁמִידוֹ יהוה אֱלֹהֶיךָ מִקִּרְבֶּךָ׃
*שני ד־ה וְאַתֶּם הַדְּבֵקִים בַּיהוה אֱלֹהֵיכֶם חַיִּים כֻּלְּכֶם הַיּוֹם׃ *רְאֵה ׀ לִמַּדְתִּי
אֶתְכֶם חֻקִּים וּמִשְׁפָּטִים כַּאֲשֶׁר צִוַּנִי יהוה אֱלֹהָי לַעֲשׂוֹת כֵּן בְּקֶרֶב
ו הָאָרֶץ אֲשֶׁר אַתֶּם בָּאִים שָׁמָּה לְרִשְׁתָּהּ׃ וּשְׁמַרְתֶּם וַעֲשִׂיתֶם כִּי הִוא
חָכְמַתְכֶם וּבִינַתְכֶם לְעֵינֵי הָעַמִּים אֲשֶׁר יִשְׁמְעוּן אֵת כָּל־הַחֻקִּים
ז הָאֵלֶּה וְאָמְרוּ רַק עַם־חָכָם וְנָבוֹן הַגּוֹי הַגָּדוֹל הַזֶּה׃ כִּי מִי־גוֹי גָּדוֹל
ח אֲשֶׁר־לוֹ אֱלֹהִים קְרֹבִים אֵלָיו כַּיהוה אֱלֹהֵינוּ בְּכָל־קָרְאֵנוּ אֵלָיו׃ וּמִי
גּוֹי גָּדוֹל אֲשֶׁר־לוֹ חֻקִּים וּמִשְׁפָּטִים צַדִּיקִם כְּכֹל הַתּוֹרָה הַזֹּאת אֲשֶׁר
ט אָנֹכִי נֹתֵן לִפְנֵיכֶם הַיּוֹם׃ רַק הִשָּׁמֶר לְךָ וּשְׁמֹר נַפְשְׁךָ מְאֹד פֶּן־תִּשְׁכַּח
אֶת־הַדְּבָרִים אֲשֶׁר־רָאוּ עֵינֶיךָ וּפֶן־יָסוּרוּ מִלְּבָבְךָ כֹּל יְמֵי חַיֶּיךָ וְהוֹדַעְתָּם

---

initially intend to do so, but their original intent was (only) to commit harlotry, as it says, וַיָּחֶל הָעָם לִזְנוֹת, *and the people began to commit harlotry* (*Numbers* 25:1). And although the Torah prohibited this because of the fear that (harlotry) will lead to idolatry, as it says, וְזָנוּ בְנֹתָיו . . . וְהִזְנוּ אֶת בָּנֶיךָ, *and their daughters go astray . . . and make your sons go astray* (*Exodus* 34:16), nonetheless, each one of them thought that it would never happen to him, but behold, the opposite occurred.

כִּי כָל הָאִישׁ אֲשֶׁר הָלַךְ אַחֲרֵי בַעַל פְּעוֹר — *For all the men that followed the Baal-Peor . . .* to cleave unto his daughters, not one of them with all his wisdom was able to avoid stumbling into the sin of idolatry until הִשְׁמִידוֹ ה׳ אֱלֹהֶיךָ, *HASHEM your God destroyed him.*

4. וְאַתֶּם הַדְּבֵקִים בַּה׳ אֱלֹהֵיכֶם חַיִּים כֻּלְּכֶם הַיּוֹם — *But you who did cleave unto HASHEM your God are alive every one of you this day.* You were all wise enough to avoid the pitfall of idolatry.

6. כִּי הִוא חָכְמַתְכֶם — *For this is your wisdom . . .* (and) with it you will be able to answer the non-believers with reasoned proof.

7. כִּי מִי גוֹי גָּדוֹל אֲשֶׁר לוֹ אֱלֹהִים קְרֹבִים אֵלָיו — *For what great nation is there that has God so close to him.* It is proper to be particularly (concerned) that you be considered wise and understanding in the eyes of the nations because God, the Blessed One, is nigh unto you בְּכָל קָרְאֵנוּ אֵלָיו, *whensoever we call upon Him,* and this demonstrates that He chose us

NOTES

minor infraction which is, nonetheless, a transgression can lead to a far more serious one. To add to, or subtract from, the *mitzvos* and prohibitions of the Torah will result in the unraveling of the fabric of observance in an uncontrollable manner, just as harlotry led to idolatry which is one of the cardinal sins.

6. כִּי הִוא חָכְמַתְכֶם — *For this is your wisdom.* The observance of *mitzvos* enables one to understand the profound teachings of Torah which, in turn, mold the mind of the observant Israelite. The result is a person who, with this wisdom gained from the Torah, will be able to convey the truth of Torah in a logical, clear and reasoned manner which the *Sforno* believes is the way to answer the unbeliever (דַע מַה שֶּׁתָּשִׁיב לְאֶפִּיקוֹרס).

7. כִּי מִי גוֹי גָּדוֹל — *For what great nation is there.* The prophet Ezekiel teaches us that since Israel is the Chosen People of God, their status, condition and qualities — or lack of them — reflect upon God Himself. The actions of Israel either sanctify Him (קִדּוּשׁ הַשֵּׁם) or profane His great Name (חִלּוּל הַשֵּׁם). When Israel is driven out of the Land because of their sins and scattered among the nations, it causes a חִלּוּל הַשֵּׁם and it is that tragic condition to which Ezekiel addresses himself in the chapter cited by the *Sforno.* This is the reason for Moses' concern that their image among the nations be that of a wise people, for since they are recognized as "the People of God," the respect and admiration which they evoke as a result of their wisdom brings glory and praise to the Almighty as well. This perception of Israel as a wise people results from Israel's observance of the Torah's statutes and ordinances, as explained in the following verse.

8. וּמִי גוֹי גָּדוֹל — *And what great nation is there.*

every man that followed Baal-peor — HASHEM, your God, destroyed him from your midst. 4 *But you who cling to HASHEM, your God — you are all alive today.*

5 *See, I have taught you decrees and ordinances, as HASHEM, my God, has commanded me, to do so in the midst of the Land to which you come, to possess it.* 6 *You shall safeguard and perform them, for it is your wisdom and discernment in the eyes of the peoples, who shall hear all these decrees and who shall say, "Surely a wise and discerning people is this great nation!"* 7 *For which is a great nation that has a God Who is close to it, as is HASHEM, our God, whenever we call to Him?* 8 *And which is a great nation that has righteous decrees and ordinances, such as this entire Torah that I place before you this day?* 9 *Only beware for yourself and greatly beware for your soul, lest you forget the things that your eyes have beheld and lest you remove them from your heart all the days of your life, and make them*

---

from all the nations, and if you are considered unwise by the nations it would be a desecration of God, when they would say to you (derisively), עַם ה׳ אֵלֶּה, *These are the people of HASHEM* (*Ezekiel* 36:20).

8. וּמִי גּוֹי גָּדוֹל אֲשֶׁר לוֹ חֻקִּים — *And what great nation is there that has statutes.* You are considered wise in the eyes of the nations when you observe the statutes of God and His teachings because there is no other nation in existence which has statutes that demonstrate the existence of God and His ways *and ordinances so righteous*, which do not profit the judges nor reward their officials and scribes, but are solely (to dispense) justice and righteousness, as our Sages say: מִשְׁפָּט לָזֶה וּצְדָקָה לָזֶה, מִשְׁפָּט לָזֶה שֶׁהֶחְזִיר לוֹ אֶת שֶׁלּוֹ וּצְדָקָה לָזֶה שֶׁהוֹצִיא גְזֵלָה מִתַּחַת יָדוֹ, *Justice to one and righteousness to the other. Justice to the one to whom we return his due and righteousness to the other by removing an ill-gotten thing from his possession* (*Sanhedrin* 6b).

9. רַק הִשָּׁמֶר לְךָ — *Only take heed to yourself.* Although I have told you that it is fitting that you be considered wise in the eyes of the nations, (nonetheless) take heed (not to be influenced) by the philosophy of their wise men who deny the existence, power and providence of God, the Blessed One, and who attempt to prove all this with reasoned proof.

פֶּן תִּשְׁכַּח אֶת הַדְּבָרִים אֲשֶׁר רָאוּ עֵינֶיךָ — *Lest you forget the things which your eyes saw.* And the reason I cautioned you to take great heed of this is because there is reason to be concerned that you may forget what your own physical eyes saw at Sinai, and (what) your

NOTES

The Talmudic selection from Tractate *Sanhedrin* quoted by the *Sforno* is the conclusion of the Sages' interpretation of a verse in *II Samuel* 8:15 which speaks of King David. The verse states וַיְהִי דָוִד עֹשֶׂה מִשְׁפָּט וּצְדָקָה לְכָל עַמּוֹ, *and David executed judgment and righteousness to all his people.* The Sages comment, "Are these two not mutually contradictory? — If there is justice, then there cannot be righteousness, and if there is righteousness, then there cannot be justice." For justice is the strict application of the letter of the law while righteousness implies a charitable, lenient interpretation of the spirit of the law. The answer given is that which the *Sforno* quotes in his commentary, namely the execution of both justice *and* righteousness which evokes the admiration and respect of the nations.

9. פֶּן תִּשְׁכַּח ... אֲשֶׁר רָאוּ עֵינֶיךָ — *Lest you forget . . . which your eyes saw.* "To see" is to perceive with the eyes and also to perceive mentally, i.e., to grasp and comprehend. The generation that was delivered from Egypt and received the Torah at Sinai was granted this twofold רְאִיָּה — "seeing." They saw the miracles with their own eyes and they were also granted the power of prophecy (as explained in *parashas Yisro*) and a clear comprehension of the Divine. Their children, however, did not see this revelation at Sinai and therefore, it is incumbent upon the previous generation, who did so, to make it *known to their children,* through reasoned proof.

לְבָנֶ֖יךָ וְלִבְנֵ֥י בָנֶֽיךָ׃ י יֹ֗ום אֲשֶׁ֨ר עָמַ֜דְתָּ לִפְנֵ֨י יהוה אֱלֹהֶ֙יךָ֙ בְּחֹרֵ֔ב בֶּאֱמֹ֨ר יהוה אֵלַ֗י הַקְהֶל־לִי֙ אֶת־הָעָ֔ם וְאַשְׁמִעֵ֖ם אֶת־דְּבָרָ֑י אֲשֶׁ֨ר יִלְמְד֜וּן לְיִרְאָ֣ה אֹתִ֗י כָּל־הַיָּמִים֙ אֲשֶׁ֨ר הֵ֤ם חַיִּים֙ עַל־הָ֣אֲדָמָ֔ה וְאֶת־בְּנֵיהֶ֖ם יְלַמֵּדֽוּן׃ יא וַתִּקְרְב֥וּן וַתַּֽעַמְד֖וּן תַּ֣חַת הָהָ֑ר וְהָהָ֞ר בֹּעֵ֤ר בָּאֵשׁ֙ עַד־לֵ֣ב הַשָּׁמַ֔יִם חֹ֖שֶׁךְ עָנָ֥ן וַעֲרָפֶֽל׃ יב וַיְדַבֵּ֧ר יהוה אֲלֵיכֶ֛ם מִתֹּ֥וךְ הָאֵ֖שׁ קֹ֣ול דְּבָרִים֙ אַתֶּ֣ם שֹׁמְעִ֔ים וּתְמוּנָ֛ה אֵינְכֶ֥ם רֹאִ֖ים זֽוּלָתִ֥י קֹֽול׃ יג וַיַּגֵּ֣ד לָכֶ֗ם אֶת־בְּרִיתֹו֙ אֲשֶׁ֨ר צִוָּ֤ה אֶתְכֶם֙ לַעֲשֹׂ֔ות עֲשֶׂ֖רֶת הַדְּבָרִ֑ים וַֽיִּכְתְּבֵ֔ם עַל־שְׁנֵ֖י לֻחֹ֥ות אֲבָנִֽים׃ יד וְאֹתִ֞י צִוָּ֤ה יהוה֙ בָּעֵ֣ת הַהִ֔וא לְלַמֵּ֣ד אֶתְכֶ֔ם חֻקִּ֖ים וּמִשְׁפָּטִ֑ים לַעֲשֹׂתְכֶ֣ם אֹתָ֔ם בָּאָ֕רֶץ אֲשֶׁ֥ר אַתֶּ֛ם עֹבְרִ֥ים שָׁ֖מָּה לְרִשְׁתָּֽהּ׃ טו וְנִשְׁמַרְתֶּ֥ם מְאֹ֖ד לְנַפְשֹֽׁתֵיכֶ֑ם כִּ֣י לֹ֤א רְאִיתֶם֙ כָּל־תְּמוּנָ֔ה בְּיֹ֗ום דִּבֶּ֨ר יהוה אֲלֵיכֶ֛ם בְּחֹרֵ֖ב מִתֹּ֥וךְ הָאֵֽשׁ׃ טז פֶּ֨ן־תַּשְׁחִת֔וּן וַעֲשִׂיתֶ֥ם לָכֶ֛ם פֶּ֖סֶל תְּמוּנַ֣ת כָּל־סָ֑מֶל תַּבְנִ֥ית זָכָ֖ר אֹ֥ו נְקֵבָֽה׃ יז תַּבְנִ֕ית כָּל־בְּהֵמָ֖ה אֲשֶׁ֣ר בָּאָ֑רֶץ תַּבְנִית֙ כָּל־צִפֹּ֣ור כָּנָ֔ף אֲשֶׁ֥ר תָּע֖וּף בַּשָּׁמָֽיִם׃ יח תַּבְנִ֕ית כָּל־רֹמֵ֖שׂ בָּאֲדָמָ֑ה תַּבְנִ֛ית כָּל־דָּגָ֥ה אֲשֶׁר־בַּמַּ֖יִם מִתַּ֥חַת לָאָֽרֶץ׃ יט וּפֶן־תִּשָּׂ֨א עֵינֶ֜יךָ הַשָּׁמַ֗יְמָה וְֽרָאִ֣יתָ אֶת־הַשֶּׁ֡מֶשׁ וְאֶת־הַיָּרֵ֨חַ וְאֶת־הַכּֽוֹכָבִ֜ים כֹּ֣ל צְבָ֣א הַשָּׁמַ֗יִם וְנִדַּחְתָּ֙ וְהִשְׁתַּחֲוִ֤יתָ לָהֶם֙ וַעֲבַדְתָּ֔ם אֲשֶׁ֣ר חָלַ֜ק כ יהוה אֱלֹהֶ֣יךָ אֹתָ֗ם לְכֹל֙ הָֽעַמִּ֔ים תַּ֖חַת כָּל־הַשָּׁמָֽיִם׃ וְאֶתְכֶם֙ לָקַ֣ח יהוה וַיּוֹצִ֥א אֶתְכֶ֛ם מִכּ֥וּר הַבַּרְזֶ֖ל מִמִּצְרָ֑יִם לִהְיֹ֥ות לֹ֛ו לְעַ֥ם נַחֲלָ֖ה כַּיֹּ֥ום הַזֶּֽה׃

---

discerning eyes (see) in the interpretation of Torah, wherein you were shown that you may know, with reasoned proof, the opposite of their philosophy.

וְהוֹדַעְתָּם לְבָנֶיךָ — *And make them known to your children.* To those children who did not see (the revelation at Sinai) make it known through reasoned proof.

15. כִּי לֹא רְאִיתֶם כָּל תְּמוּנָה — *For you saw no manner of form . . .* and this is the reverse of the doctrine of the Sabians who thought that there is nothing in existence superior to the heavenly bodies (lit. "causes"), and that they alone preceded (everything) (and are) first and eternal.

16. תְּמוּנַת כָּל סָמֶל — *The form of any figure . . .* (as was) the practice of those who believed that every existing perishable (thing) began with a primeval cause and so they would fashion a form of that perishable (object) to indicate (i.e., reflect or symbolize) that which they thought was the generator and beginning (i.e., cause) of that form or figure. They

NOTES

15. כִּי לֹא רְאִיתֶם כָּל תְּמוּנָה — *For you saw no manner of form.* The *Rambam* in his *Guide* (III 29) speaks of the Sabians "whose doctrine is that there is no deity but the stars." The *Rambam* continues his discussion of the Sabians and tells us that "in conformity with these opinions, the Sabians set up statues for the planets; golden ones for the sun and silver ones for the moon." This is what the *Sforno* is referring to in his commentary on this verse where the Torah reminds Israel that no manner of form was seen and therefore they are to make no graven image or the form of any figure.

16. תְּמוּנַת כָּל סָמֶל — *The form of any figure.* The term "נִמְצָא נִפְסָד — perishable existent" is used by

the *Sforno* when referring to that which is "subject to generation and corruption," to quote the expression of the *Rambam.* The school of Plato believed (as the *Sforno* states here) that the world of matter (עֲשִׂיָּה), i.e., the material world which we experience and know, reflects the world of emanations (אֲצִילוּת) taking on form (צוּרָה). Hence, as the *Sforno* explains, they believed that every material form (i.e., "perishable" — for it cannot last) comes from a higher spiritual force. By worshiping this material form, one causes the originator or cause (קַדְמוֹן) to influence the material world in a beneficial manner for man. That is why the Torah cautions us not to be misled into making the form of

known to your children and your children's children — [10] *the day that you stood before* HASHEM, *your God, at Horeb, when* HASHEM *said to me, "Gather the people to Me and I shall let them hear My words, so that they shall learn to fear Me all the days that they live on the earth, and they shall teach their children."*

[11] *So you approached and stood at the foot of the mountain, and the mountain was burning with fire up to the heart of heaven, darkness, cloud, and thick cloud.*

[12] HASHEM *spoke to you from the midst of the fire; you were hearing the sound of words, but you were not seeing a form, only a sound.* [13] *He told you of His covenant that He commanded you to observe, the Ten Declarations, and He inscribed them on two stone Tablets.* [14] HASHEM *commanded me at that time to teach you decrees and ordinances, that you shall perform them in the Land to which you cross, to possess it.* [15] *But you shall greatly beware for your souls, for you did not see any likeness on the day* HASHEM *spoke to you at Horeb, from the midst of the fire,* [16] *lest you act corruptly and make yourselves a carved image, a likeness of any shape; a form of a male or a female;* [17] *a form of any animal on the earth; a form of any winged bird that flies in the heaven;* [18] *a form of anything that creeps on the ground, a form of any fish that is in the water under the earth;* [19] *and lest you raise your eyes to the heaven and you see the sun, and the moon, and the stars — the entire legion of heaven — and you be drawn astray and bow to them and worship them, which* HASHEM, *your God, has apportioned to all the peoples under the entire heaven!* [20] *But* HASHEM *has taken you and withdrawn you from the iron crucible, from Egypt, to be a nation of heritage for Him, as this very day.*

---

would (then) worship that form in order to cause that primeval (force) to influence and have some impact upon them to a degree.

19. אֲשֶׁר חָלַק ה׳ אֱלֹהֶיךָ אֹתָם לְכֹל הָעַמִּים — *Which* HASHEM *your God has allotted unto all the peoples.* He arranged them in a fitting order to meet the need of each part of the earth according to the diversity of each land and the people who inhabit it. Now this order demonstrates the reverse of the doctrine of those who err, because it shows perforce that there is One Who exists Who arranges all for a purpose designated by Him, and they exist according to a plan and certainly not by chance, in order to attain some goal (purpose) by their (very) being and their order.

20. וְאֶתְכֶם לָקַח ה׳ — *But* HASHEM *has taken you . . .* to walk in His ways and to cleave to Him, therefore you are not to pay heed to the conduct of the hosts of heaven and their order, as do other nations.

NOTES

any figure for this erroneous purpose, since God is the Creator of all and there is no need to worship Him through intermediaries.

19-20. אֲשֶׁר חָלַק ה׳ אֱלֹהֶיךָ לְכֹל הָעַמִּים . . . וְאֶתְכֶם לָקַח ה׳ — *Which* HASHEM *your God has allotted unto all the peoples. . . But* HASHEM *has taken you.* The Rambam in his *Guide* 2:20 refutes the theory of spontaneity and chance bringing about the existence of the heavenly bodies. He also emphasizes the elements of cause and purpose in their creation. All this the *Sforno* incorporates into his commentary on these verses, adding that the purpose of God's creation of the various stars and planets was, in some mysterious way, to place the nations of the earth under their influence according to some Divine plan and order. The exception is Israel, regarding whom we are taught, אֵין מַזָּל לְיִשְׂרָאֵל, *Israel's fate is not determined by the stars* (*Shabbos* 156b).

כא וַיהוָה הִתְאַנֶּף־בִּי עַל־דִּבְרֵיכֶם וַיִּשָּׁבַע לְבִלְתִּי עָבְרִי אֶת־הַיַּרְדֵּן
כב וּלְבִלְתִּי־בֹא אֶל־הָאָרֶץ הַטּוֹבָה אֲשֶׁר יְהוָה אֱלֹהֶיךָ נֹתֵן לְךָ נַחֲלָה׃ כִּי
אָנֹכִי מֵת בָּאָרֶץ הַזֹּאת אֵינֶנִּי עֹבֵר אֶת־הַיַּרְדֵּן וְאַתֶּם עֹבְרִים וִירִשְׁתֶּם
כג אֶת־הָאָרֶץ הַטּוֹבָה הַזֹּאת׃ הִשָּׁמְרוּ לָכֶם פֶּן־תִּשְׁכְּחוּ אֶת־בְּרִית יְהוָה
אֱלֹהֵיכֶם אֲשֶׁר כָּרַת עִמָּכֶם וַעֲשִׂיתֶם לָכֶם פֶּסֶל תְּמוּנַת כֹּל אֲשֶׁר צִוְּךָ
כד יְהוָה אֱלֹהֶיךָ׃ כִּי יְהוָה אֱלֹהֶיךָ אֵשׁ אֹכְלָה הוּא אֵל קַנָּא׃
כה כִּי־תוֹלִיד בָּנִים וּבְנֵי בָנִים וְנוֹשַׁנְתֶּם בָּאָרֶץ וְהִשְׁחַתֶּם וַעֲשִׂיתֶם פֶּסֶל
כו תְּמוּנַת כֹּל וַעֲשִׂיתֶם הָרַע בְּעֵינֵי יְהוָה־אֱלֹהֶיךָ לְהַכְעִיסוֹ׃ הַעִידֹתִי בָכֶם
הַיּוֹם אֶת־הַשָּׁמַיִם וְאֶת־הָאָרֶץ כִּי־אָבֹד תֹּאבֵדוּן מַהֵר מֵעַל הָאָרֶץ אֲשֶׁר
אַתֶּם עֹבְרִים אֶת־הַיַּרְדֵּן שָׁמָּה לְרִשְׁתָּהּ לֹא־תַאֲרִיכֻן יָמִים עָלֶיהָ כִּי
כז הִשָּׁמֵד תִּשָּׁמֵדוּן׃ וְהֵפִיץ יְהוָה אֶתְכֶם בָּעַמִּים וְנִשְׁאַרְתֶּם מְתֵי מִסְפָּר בַּגּוֹיִם
כח אֲשֶׁר יְנַהֵג יְהוָה אֶתְכֶם שָׁמָּה׃ וַעֲבַדְתֶּם־שָׁם אֱלֹהִים מַעֲשֵׂה יְדֵי אָדָם עֵץ
כט וָאֶבֶן אֲשֶׁר לֹא־יִרְאוּן וְלֹא יִשְׁמְעוּן וְלֹא יֹאכְלוּן וְלֹא יְרִיחֻן׃ וּבִקַּשְׁתֶּם
מִשָּׁם אֶת־יְהוָה אֱלֹהֶיךָ וּמָצָאתָ כִּי תִדְרְשֶׁנּוּ בְּכָל־לְבָבְךָ וּבְכָל־נַפְשֶׁךָ׃
ל בַּצַּר לְךָ וּמְצָאוּךָ כֹּל הַדְּבָרִים הָאֵלֶּה בְּאַחֲרִית הַיָּמִים וְשַׁבְתָּ עַד־יְהוָה

22. כִּי אָנֹכִי מֵת — *But I must die.* I need to caution you exceedingly since I will not be going over with you, as it says, *For I know that after my death you will deal corruptly* (31:29).

24. אֵשׁ אֹכְלָה הוּא — *A devouring fire.* Fire which consumes fire, and as such will devour the soul with the flesh.

אֵל קַנָּא — *A jealous God.* Because there is naught in existence which is comparable to Him and His existence whatsoever; hence, whoever serves another (deity) gives to him what is only fitting to be offered to (God) alone, and this is comparable to a married woman who gives to another man that which is only fitting for her husband alone, and because of this He is a jealous (God).

25. לְהַכְעִיסוֹ — *To provoke Him . . .* to remove the Divine Presence from Israel in order to be like unto the nations of the world and not be subject to the Torah and the commandments of God, the Blessed One.

28. וַעֲבַדְתֶּם שָׁם אֱלֹהִים — *And there you shall serve gods . . .* (as the Talmud teaches) "Israelites who reside outside the Land (of Israel) serve idols, though in pure innocence" (*Avodah Zarah* 8a).

NOTES

24. אֵשׁ אֹכְלָה הוּא — *A devouring fire*. The fire which came forth from heaven and devoured Nadav and Avihu (*Leviticus* 10:2) consumed their souls as well as their bodies, according to our Sages. Such is the nature of the Divine fire. Therefore, the *Sforno* interprets the phrase *a devouring fire* as meaning the devouring of the soul together with the flesh.

אֵל קַנָּא — *A jealous God*. The word קִנְאָה, *jealousy*, is found in the *parashah* of the סוֹטָה, *a woman suspected of infidelity*. The sin of adultery is one wherein a woman grants to a man other than her husband that which is exclusively his. The *Sforno* interprets the phrase אֵל קַנָּא, *a jealous God*, in a similar sense; man's observance, service and worship belongs to God alone. The worship of a פֶּסֶל, *graven image*, or the form of any figure is an act of infidelity; hence the term used is אֵל קַנָּא, similar to the expression used in reference to a husband whose wife is unfaithful.

25. לְהַכְעִיסוֹ — *To provoke Him*. When God is angered by man's misbehavior, the שְׁכִינָה — His Presence — departs. The *Sforno* states this principle here, as well as in *Deut.* 32:16. The source may well be in *Numbers* 12:9 where the Torah tells us that when God became angry with Miriam

[21] *HASHEM became angry with me because of you, and He swore that I would not cross the Jordan and not come to the good Land that HASHEM, your God, gives you as a heritage.* [22] *For I will die in this land; I am not crossing the Jordan — but you are crossing and you shall possess this good Land.* [23] *Beware for yourselves lest you forget the covenant of HASHEM, your God, that He has sealed with you, and you make yourselves a carved image, a likeness of anything, as HASHEM, your God, has commanded you.* [24] *For HASHEM, your God — He is a consuming fire, a jealous God.*

[25] *When you beget children and grandchildren and will have been long in the Land, you will grow corrupt and make a carved image of anything, and you will do evil in the eyes of HASHEM, your God, to anger Him.* [26] *I appoint heaven and earth this day to bear witness against you that you will surely perish quickly from the Land to which you are crossing the Jordan to possess; you shall not have lengthy days upon it, for you will be destroyed.* [27] *HASHEM will scatter you among the peoples, and you will be left few in number among the nations where HASHEM will lead you.* [28] *There you will serve gods, the handiwork of man, of wood and stone, which do not see, and do not hear, and do not eat, and do not smell.*

[29] *From there you will seek HASHEM, your God, and you will find Him, if you search for Him with all your heart and all your soul.* [30] *When you are in distress and all these things have befallen you, at the end of days, you will*

אֲשֶׁר לֹא יִרְאוּן — *Which neither see*. These (idols) have no power of will, as their worshipers thought (and who therefore) crafted images with organs that function (in man) at will, in order to demonstrate that the primeval cause they believed in could activate these organs by their will. Hence, they would worship it and pray to it to attain fulfillment of their requests. However, behold that there is naught which exists except God, the Blessed One, and living man who possesses the power of free will, whereas the action of all others (i.e., living creatures and the elements) are caused by (the laws) of nature as ordered by God, the Blessed One.

29. וּמָצָאתָ — *And you shall find Him* . . . even though there is neither a Temple nor sacred vessels (or furnishings) there.

כִּי תִדְרְשֶׁנּוּ בְּכָל לְבָבְךָ וּבְכָל נַפְשֶׁךָ — *Because you will search for Him with all your heart and soul.* The reason you will find Him is because you will seek Him with all your heart due to the great distress (which you will experience).

30. בְּאַחֲרִית הַיָּמִים — *In the latter days* . . . at the end of days as (the Torah) attests to saying: *And it shall come to pass when all these things are come upon you . . . and you shall return to HASHEM your God and hearken to His voice* (30:1-2).

NOTES

and Aaron, He departed.

28. וַעֲבַדְתֶּם שָׁם אֱלֹהִים — *And there you shall serve gods*. It is difficult to understand the sense of certainty reflected in this verse, that Israel's presence in exile must lead to idolatry. The *Sforno* therefore cites the saying of our Sages that when Israel dwells outside *Eretz Yisrael*, their cultural and social environment causes them to conduct themselves, albeit innocently, in a non-Jewish manner, which the Torah equates with the serving of strange gods. The *Ramban* interprets this verse in a similar fashion, quoting the Talmud in *Kesubos* 110b where our Sages say, "Whoever dwells outside the Holy Land is regarded as if he worships idols."

אֲשֶׁר לֹא יִרְאוּן — *Which neither see.* See the notes or verses 15-16.

לא אֱלֹהֶיךָ וְשָׁמַעְתָּ בְּקֹלוֹ: כִּי אֵל רַחוּם יְהוָה אֱלֹהֶיךָ לֹא יַרְפְּךָ וְלֹא יַשְׁחִיתֶךָ
לב וְלֹא יִשְׁכַּח אֶת־בְּרִית אֲבֹתֶיךָ אֲשֶׁר נִשְׁבַּע לָהֶם: כִּי שְׁאַל־נָא לְיָמִים
רִאשֹׁנִים אֲשֶׁר־הָיוּ לְפָנֶיךָ לְמִן־הַיּוֹם אֲשֶׁר בָּרָא אֱלֹהִים ׀ אָדָם עַל־הָאָרֶץ
וּלְמִקְצֵה הַשָּׁמַיִם וְעַד־קְצֵה הַשָּׁמָיִם הֲנִהְיָה כַּדָּבָר הַגָּדוֹל הַזֶּה אוֹ הֲנִשְׁמַע
לג כָּמֹהוּ: הֲשָׁמַע עָם קוֹל אֱלֹהִים מְדַבֵּר מִתּוֹךְ־הָאֵשׁ כַּאֲשֶׁר־שָׁמַעְתָּ אַתָּה
לד וַיֶּחִי: אוֹ ׀ הֲנִסָּה אֱלֹהִים לָבוֹא לָקַחַת לוֹ גוֹי מִקֶּרֶב גּוֹי בְּמַסֹּת בְּאֹתֹת
וּבְמוֹפְתִים וּבְמִלְחָמָה וּבְיָד חֲזָקָה וּבִזְרוֹעַ נְטוּיָה וּבְמוֹרָאִים גְּדֹלִים כְּכֹל
לה אֲשֶׁר־עָשָׂה לָכֶם יְהוָה אֱלֹהֵיכֶם בְּמִצְרַיִם לְעֵינֶיךָ: אַתָּה הָרְאֵתָ לָדַעַת כִּי
לו יְהוָה הוּא הָאֱלֹהִים אֵין עוֹד מִלְּבַדּוֹ: מִן־הַשָּׁמַיִם הִשְׁמִיעֲךָ אֶת־קֹלוֹ
לְיַסְּרֶךָּ וְעַל־הָאָרֶץ הֶרְאֲךָ אֶת־אִשּׁוֹ הַגְּדוֹלָה וּדְבָרָיו שָׁמַעְתָּ מִתּוֹךְ הָאֵשׁ:
לז וְתַחַת כִּי אָהַב אֶת־אֲבֹתֶיךָ וַיִּבְחַר בְּזַרְעוֹ אַחֲרָיו וַיּוֹצִאֲךָ בְּפָנָיו בְּכֹחוֹ
לח הַגָּדֹל מִמִּצְרָיִם: לְהוֹרִישׁ גּוֹיִם גְּדֹלִים וַעֲצֻמִים מִמְּךָ מִפָּנֶיךָ לַהֲבִיאֲךָ
לט לָתֶת־לְךָ אֶת־אַרְצָם נַחֲלָה כַּיּוֹם הַזֶּה: וְיָדַעְתָּ הַיּוֹם וַהֲשֵׁבֹתָ אֶל־לְבָבֶךָ

32. כִּי שְׁאַל נָא — *For ask now.* The proof of what I said that the covenant of the fathers will not be forgotten (v. 31) is in what He did for all of Israel at the (time) of the giving of the Torah when you all merited the attainment of such (a high) level of prophecy. This occurred for the purpose of taking you unto Him as a people because of the covenant with the Patriarchs, since each of you (individually) was certainly not worthy (to attain this exalted status), for although it did occur at times that individuals prophesied, (nonetheless,) this never happened to any other (entire) people.

34. אוֹ הֲנִסָּה אֱלֹהִים — *Or has God proved himself.* Although it has happened that an individual or individuals have escaped from among the wicked, nonetheless this never happened to an entire nation.

בְּמַסֹּת בְּאֹתֹת — *By trials, by signs* . . . which indicate that this did not happen by chance, but by the (deliberate) intent of a פּוֹעֵל רְצוֹנִי, *one according to His will.*

וּבִזְרוֹעַ נְטוּיָה — *And by an outstretched arm* . . . prepared to smite again, (thereby) teaching that if the sinner does not repent He will continue to smite (him).

35. אַתָּה הָרְאֵתָ — *To you it was shown.* All this God, the Blessed One, showed you . . . לָדַעַת — *That you might know.* So that you might contemplate and know, without a doubt, כִּי ה׳ הוּא הָאֱלֹהִים — *that HASHEM, He is God;* He is perforce the First Cause.

36. לְיַסְּרֶךָּ — *That He might instruct you* . . . to bring you to a (high) level of prophecy

NOTES

32. כִּי שְׁאַל נָא — *For ask now.* The previous verse (31) states that God will not forget the covenant of the fathers (בְּרִית אָבוֹת). In verse 37, Moses tells Israel that all the signs and wonders witnessed by them in Egypt and at Mt. Sinai were wrought because God loved their fathers. The *Sforno*, in his commentary, explains that there is a theme which links all these verses together, namely the merit of בְּרִית אָבוֹת. Because of this covenant, the entire nation was delivered; an entire people was elevated to the highest level of prophecy, and ultimately given a special land conducive to the perfection of man's mind and spirit.

37. וַיּוֹצִיאֲךָ בְּפָנָיו — *And brought you out with His presence. The expressions* פָּנִים, *face,* and אָחוֹר, *back,* in relationship to God appear in *Exodus* 33:23 where God tells Moses, *You shall see My back, but My face shall not be seen.* The *Sforno* translates the word בְּפָנָיו in our verse literally: God brought us out of Egypt through supernatural means, indicated by the expression *face,* for He graciously showed us His face of concern and love, as opposed to His "back" which implies acts regulated only by the laws of nature. In *Exodus*, the *Sforno* offers a different interpretation. See his commentary on that verse and the explanatory note.

return unto HASHEM, your God, and hearken to His voice. [31] *For HASHEM, your God, is a merciful God, He will not abandon you nor destroy you, and He will not forget the covenant of your forefathers that He swore to them.* [32] *For inquire now regarding the early days that preceded you, from the day when HASHEM created man on the earth, and from one end of heaven to the other end of heaven: Has there ever been anything like this great thing or has anything like it been heard?* [33] *Has a people ever heard the voice of God speaking from the midst of the fire as you have heard, and survived?* [34] *Or has any god ever miraculously come to take for himself a nation from amidst a nation, with challenges, with signs, and with wonders, and with war, and with a strong hand, and with an outstretched arm, and with greatly awesome deeds, such as everything that HASHEM, your God, did for you in Egypt before your eyes?* [35] *You have been shown in order to know that HASHEM, He is the God! There is none beside Him!*

[36] *From heaven He caused you to hear His voice in order to teach you, and on earth He showed you His great fire, and you heard His words from the midst of the fire,* [37] *because He loved your forefathers, and He chose his offspring after him, and took you out before Himself with His great strength from Egypt;* [38] *to drive away before you nations that are greater and mightier than you, to bring you, to give you their land as an inheritance, as this very day.* [39] *You shall know this day and take to your heart that*

---

at the (time) of the giving of the Torah, similar to (the episode) of Elijah, וְהִנֵּה . . . וְרוּחַ גְּדוֹלָה וְחָזָק, *and behold . . . and a great strong wind* (*I Kings* 19:11), and also, וְעַל הָאָרֶץ הֶרְאֲךָ אֶת אִשּׁוֹ, *And upon the earth He made you see His great fire*, as we (also) find there, where (the verse) states: וְאַחַר הָרַעַשׁ אֵשׁ, *And after the earthquake a fire* (*I Kings* 19:12).

37. וְתַחַת כִּי אָהַב אֶת אֲבֹתֶיךָ — *And because He loved your fathers . . .* and since He did all this because He loved your fathers.

וַיִּבְחַר בְּזַרְעוֹ — *And chose his seed . . .* of only one, namely the seed of Jacob.

וַיּוֹצִיאֲךָ בְּפָנָיו — *And brought you out with His Presence . . .* through actions which emanate from His Presence (lit. face), i.e., transcending nature; not from His "back," (which denotes) actions within nature.

38. לְהוֹרִישׁ — *To drive out.* His intent was to deliver you from bondage, (a state wherein) you were not able to contemplate.

לָתֶת לְךָ אֶת אַרְצָם — *To give you their land . . .* which is God's land, conducive (lit. "prepared") to attain the desired perfection (of mind and spirit).

39. וְיָדַעְתָּ הַיּוֹם — *And you shall know this day.* Therefore, it is, without a doubt, fitting that you contemplate and know (all the) contradictory parts (of theological speculation).

וַהֲשֵׁבֹתָ אֶל לְבָבֶךָ — *And bring it back to your heart.* And after such reflection you will place

NOTES

39. וְיָדַעְתָּ הַיּוֹם — *And you shall know this day.* The *Sforno* views this verse as a major fundamental doctrine of Judaism. Following in the path of the *Rambam*, he emphasizes the need to study and contemplate the truth of God's existence, to examine and analyze all alternatives, resulting in the conviction that the Almighty is one, non-corporeal, the First Cause, and the Source of all existence. He submits that proof of a Creator is derived from nature — its order, harmony and manifestation of a higher purpose. His interpretation of the phrase, אֵין עוֹד, *there is none else*, is a succinct summary of the *Rambam's* arguments in his *Guide* (II,1) expressing belief in the unity and uniqueness of God.

כִּי יְהוָה הוּא הָאֱלֹהִים בַּשָּׁמַיִם מִמַּעַל וְעַל־הָאָרֶץ מִתָּחַת אֵין עוֹד׃
מ וְשָׁמַרְתָּ אֶת־חֻקָּיו וְאֶת־מִצְוֹתָיו אֲשֶׁר אָנֹכִי מְצַוְּךָ הַיּוֹם אֲשֶׁר יִיטַב לְךָ
וּלְבָנֶיךָ אַחֲרֶיךָ וּלְמַעַן תַּאֲרִיךְ יָמִים עַל־הָאֲדָמָה אֲשֶׁר יְהוָה אֱלֹהֶיךָ נֹתֵן
לְךָ כָּל־הַיָּמִים׃
*שלישי מא־מב *אָז יַבְדִּיל מֹשֶׁה שָׁלֹשׁ עָרִים בְּעֵבֶר הַיַּרְדֵּן מִזְרְחָה שָׁמֶשׁ׃ לָנֻס שָׁמָּה
רוֹצֵחַ אֲשֶׁר יִרְצַח אֶת־רֵעֵהוּ בִּבְלִי־דַעַת וְהוּא לֹא־שֹׂנֵא לוֹ מִתְּמֹל
מג שִׁלְשֹׁם וְנָס אֶל־אַחַת מִן־הֶעָרִים הָאֵל וָחָי׃ אֶת־בֶּצֶר בַּמִּדְבָּר בְּאֶרֶץ
הַמִּישֹׁר לָראוּבֵנִי וְאֶת־רָאמֹת בַּגִּלְעָד לַגָּדִי וְאֶת־גּוֹלָן בַּבָּשָׁן לַמְנַשִּׁי׃
מד־מה וְזֹאת הַתּוֹרָה אֲשֶׁר־שָׂם מֹשֶׁה לִפְנֵי בְּנֵי יִשְׂרָאֵל׃ אֵלֶּה הָעֵדֹת וְהַחֻקִּים
מו וְהַמִּשְׁפָּטִים אֲשֶׁר דִּבֶּר מֹשֶׁה אֶל־בְּנֵי יִשְׂרָאֵל בְּצֵאתָם מִמִּצְרָיִם׃ בְּעֵבֶר
הַיַּרְדֵּן בַּגַּיְא מוּל בֵּית פְּעוֹר בְּאֶרֶץ סִיחֹן מֶלֶךְ הָאֱמֹרִי אֲשֶׁר יוֹשֵׁב
מז בְּחֶשְׁבּוֹן אֲשֶׁר הִכָּה מֹשֶׁה וּבְנֵי יִשְׂרָאֵל בְּצֵאתָם מִמִּצְרָיִם׃ וַיִּירְשׁוּ
אֶת־אַרְצוֹ וְאֶת־אֶרֶץ ׀ עוֹג מֶלֶךְ־הַבָּשָׁן שְׁנֵי מַלְכֵי הָאֱמֹרִי אֲשֶׁר בְּעֵבֶר
מח הַיַּרְדֵּן מִזְרַח שָׁמֶשׁ׃ מֵעֲרֹעֵר אֲשֶׁר עַל־שְׂפַת־נַחַל אַרְנֹן וְעַד־הַר שִׂיאֹן
מט הוּא חֶרְמוֹן׃ וְכָל־הָעֲרָבָה עֵבֶר הַיַּרְדֵּן מִזְרָחָה וְעַד יָם הָעֲרָבָה תַּחַת
אַשְׁדֹּת הַפִּסְגָּה׃

---

in your heart those parts of these philosophical (searchings) which are true, that being (the certainty . . .).

כִּי ה׳ הוּא הָאֱלֹהִים — *That HASHEM is God.* The well-known, eternal (Master) Who orders (all that is . . .).

בַּשָּׁמַיִם מִמַּעַל וְעַל הָאָרֶץ מִתָּחַת — *In heaven above and upon the earth below . . .* because God's mastery is demonstrated by their order, connection and the purpose manifested by them, which cannot be realized except through them, and thereby it becomes known that there is an Existent Who directs (the cosmos) Who created all this for a specific purpose, which comes from Him.

אֵין עוֹד — *There is none else . . .* and from all this it is made known that there is none else, because perforce all this cannot be except through the power of some Creator who is separated from matter (incorporeal) and elevated to the greatest possible degree. It is (also) impossible that there is more than one on the same level of elevation among those separated from matter, and therefore there can be none comparable to Him.

NOTES

40. וְשָׁמַרְתָּ אֶת חֻקָּיו — *And you shall keep His statutes.* The *Sforno* in his interpretation of this verse reflects the *Rambam* in *Mishneh Torah, Yesodai HaTorah* 2:2, where he states that man is commanded to love and revere God. The way to attain this love and reverence is by contemplating His greatness manifested through His wondrous creation which reveals His infinite and incomparable wisdom. The knowledge of all this will bring man to a passionate desire to *know His great Name.*

אֲשֶׁר אָנֹכִי מְצַוְּךָ . . . כָּל הַיָּמִים — *Which I command you . . . all the days.* The brief commentary of the *Sforno* on this portion of the verse reflects the ninth principle of the *Rambam's* Thirteen Principles of Faith: "I believe with complete faith that this Torah will not be exchanged nor will there be another Torah from the Creator, Blessed is His Name." The *Sforno* derives this from the concluding words of this verse כָּל הַיָּמִים, *all the days,* which revert back to the phrase אֲשֶׁר אָנֹכִי מְצַוְּךָ, *which I command you,* viz., that which I command you in this Torah is for all days.

41. אָז יַבְדִּיל — *Then Moses separated.* The *Sforno* explains the connection of this act to the preceding verses in this chapter. The philosophical, analyti-

HASHEM, He is the God — in heaven above and on the earth below — there is none other. 40 *You shall observe His decrees and His commandments that I command you this day, so that He will do good to you and to your children after you, and so that you will prolong your days on the Land that HASHEM, your God, gives you, for all the days.*

41 *Then Moses set aside three cities on the bank of the Jordan, toward the rising sun,* 42 *for a murderer to flee there, who will have killed his fellow without knowledge, but who was not an enemy of his from yesterday and before yesterday — then he shall flee to one of these cities and live:* 43 *Bezer in the wilderness, in the land of the plain, of the Reubenite; Ramoth in the Gilead, of the Gadite; and Golan in the Bashan, of the Manassite.*

44 *This is the teaching that Moses placed before the Children of Israel.* 45 *These are the testimonies, the decrees, and the ordinances that Moses spoke to the Children of Israel, when they left Egypt,* 46 *on the bank of the Jordan, in the valley, opposite Beth-peor, in the land of Sihon, king of the Amorite, who dwells in Heshbon, whom Moses and the Children of Israel smote when they went out of Egypt.* 47 *They possessed his land and the land of Og the king of Bashan, two kings of the Amorite, which are on the bank of the Jordan, where the sun rises;* 48 *from Aroer that is by the shore of Arnon Brook until Mount Sion, which is Hermon,* 49 *and the entire Arabah, the eastern bank of the Jordan until the Sea of Aravah, under the waterfalls of the cliffs.*

---

40. וְשָׁמַרְתָּ אֶת חֻקָּיו — *And you shall keep His statutes* ... and when you know Him, without a doubt, you will keep His statutes, as it says, מִי לֹא יִרָאֲךָ מֶלֶךְ הַגּוֹיִם, *Who would not fear You, King of the nations?* (*Jeremiah* 10:7).

וְאֶת מִצְוֹתָיו אֲשֶׁר אָנֹכִי מְצַוְּךָ הַיּוֹם ... כָּל הַיָּמִים — *And His commandments which I command you this day ... all the days ...* because there shall never be any new law (religion).

41. אָז יַבְדִּיל מֹשֶׁה שָׁלֹשׁ עָרִים — *Then Moses separated* (*set aside*) *three cities.* After he completed the introduction to his explanation of the Torah, he separated the cities (of refuge) to teach Israel how important (lit. "distinguished") the fulfillment of the commandments are; that he was so particular to observe even a small part of (this) positive commandment.

44. וְזֹאת הַתּוֹרָה — *And this is the Torah* (*law*). The analytical portion (חֵלֶק הָעִיּוּנִי).

45. אֵלֶּה הָעֵדֹת — *These are the testimonies.* That portion which is attested to by (reasoned) proof.

47. וַיִּירְשׁוּ אֶת אַרְצוֹ — *And they took his land in possession.* After they conquered inhabited lands and were able to keep the *mitzvos* without fear, he (Moses) began to expound the Torah and commandments and caution (Israel) regarding them.

NOTES

cal, theoretical verses of this chapter, as the *Sforno* has explained them, important and vital as they may be, are equaled in importance by the action of Moses in commencing the concrete implementation of the commandment to establish cities of refuge. Although these cities would not be operative until those on the west side of the Jordan were established, nonetheless, Moses set aside these cities. He did so to demonstrate the importance of implementing God's command, be it ever so modest an act, even though it is only a partial, non-operative fulfillment of a *mitzvah!*

ה רביעי א וַיִּקְרָא מֹשֶׁה אֶל־כָּל־יִשְׂרָאֵל וַיֹּאמֶר אֲלֵהֶם שְׁמַע יִשְׂרָאֵל אֶת־הַחֻקִּים
וְאֶת־הַמִּשְׁפָּטִים אֲשֶׁר אָנֹכִי דֹּבֵר בְּאָזְנֵיכֶם הַיּוֹם וּלְמַדְתֶּם אֹתָם
ב־ג וּשְׁמַרְתֶּם לַעֲשֹׂתָם: יהוה אֱלֹהֵינוּ כָּרַת עִמָּנוּ בְּרִית בְּחֹרֵב: לֹא
אֶת־אֲבֹתֵינוּ כָּרַת יהוה אֶת־הַבְּרִית הַזֹּאת כִּי אִתָּנוּ אֲנַחְנוּ אֵלֶּה פֹה
ד־ה הַיּוֹם כֻּלָּנוּ חַיִּים: פָּנִים | בְּפָנִים דִּבֶּר יהוה עִמָּכֶם בָּהָר מִתּוֹךְ הָאֵשׁ: אָנֹכִי
עֹמֵד בֵּין־יהוה וּבֵינֵיכֶם בָּעֵת הַהִוא לְהַגִּיד לָכֶם אֶת־דְּבַר יהוה כִּי
ו יְרֵאתֶם מִפְּנֵי הָאֵשׁ וְלֹא־עֲלִיתֶם בָּהָר לֵאמֹר: אָנֹכִי יהוה
ז אֱלֹהֶיךָ אֲשֶׁר הוֹצֵאתִיךָ מֵאֶרֶץ מִצְרַיִם מִבֵּית עֲבָדִים: לֹא־יִהְיֶה לְךָ
ח אֱלֹהִים אֲחֵרִים עַל־פָּנָי: לֹא־תַעֲשֶׂה לְךָ פֶסֶל כָּל־תְּמוּנָה אֲשֶׁר בַּשָּׁמַיִם
ט מִמַּעַל וַאֲשֶׁר בָּאָרֶץ מִתָּחַת וַאֲשֶׁר בַּמַּיִם מִתַּחַת לָאָרֶץ: לֹא־תִשְׁתַּחֲוֶה
לָהֶם וְלֹא תָעָבְדֵם כִּי אָנֹכִי יהוה אֱלֹהֶיךָ אֵל קַנָּא פֹּקֵד עֲוֹן אָבוֹת
י עַל־בָּנִים וְעַל־שִׁלֵּשִׁים וְעַל־רִבֵּעִים לְשֹׂנְאָי: וְעֹשֶׂה חֶסֶד לַאֲלָפִים לְאֹהֲבַי
°מִצְוֹתָי ק׳ יא וּלְשֹׁמְרֵי °מצותו: לֹא תִשָּׂא אֶת־שֵׁם־יהוה אֱלֹהֶיךָ לַשָּׁוְא
יב כִּי לֹא יְנַקֶּה יהוה אֵת אֲשֶׁר־יִשָּׂא אֶת־שְׁמוֹ לַשָּׁוְא: שָׁמוֹר
יג אֶת־יוֹם הַשַּׁבָּת לְקַדְּשׁוֹ כַּאֲשֶׁר צִוְּךָ יהוה אֱלֹהֶיךָ: שֵׁשֶׁת יָמִים תַּעֲבֹד
יד וְעָשִׂיתָ כָּל־מְלַאכְתֶּךָ: וְיוֹם הַשְּׁבִיעִי שַׁבָּת לַיהוה אֱלֹהֶיךָ לֹא־תַעֲשֶׂה
כָל־מְלָאכָה אַתָּה | וּבִנְךָ־וּבִתֶּךָ וְעַבְדְּךָ־וַאֲמָתֶךָ וְשׁוֹרְךָ וַחֲמֹרְךָ וְכָל־
טו בְּהֶמְתֶּךָ וְגֵרְךָ אֲשֶׁר בִּשְׁעָרֶיךָ לְמַעַן יָנוּחַ עַבְדְּךָ וַאֲמָתְךָ כָּמוֹךָ: וְזָכַרְתָּ כִּי
עֶבֶד הָיִיתָ בְּאֶרֶץ מִצְרַיִם וַיֹּצִאֲךָ יהוה אֱלֹהֶיךָ מִשָּׁם בְּיָד חֲזָקָה וּבִזְרֹעַ

V

3. הַיּוֹם כֻּלָּנוּ חַיִּים — *All of us alive this day.* Therefore, you who have made the covenant (with God) and are about to enter the Land, arrange your affairs in such a manner that coming generations who were not present when this covenant was established will (still) fulfill that which you accepted upon yourselves.

4-6. פָּנִים בְּפָנִים — *Face to face* . . . not in a dream or a night vision, but while you were in command of your senses — דִּבֶּר ה׳ עִמָּכֶם, *HASHEM spoke with you* — לֵאמֹר אָנֹכִי ה׳ וכו׳, *saying, I am HASHEM etc.*, as explained above. וַיְדַבֵּר אֱלֹהִים אֵת כָּל הַדְּבָרִים הָאֵלֶּה לֵאמֹר: אָנֹכִי ה׳, *And God spoke all these words, saying: I am HASHEM* (Exodus 20:1-2). However, my standing *between HASHEM and you* was (for this purpose): לְהַגִּיד לָכֶם אֶת דְּבַר ה׳, כִּי יְרֵאתֶם, *to declare unto you the word of HASHEM because you were afraid.*

NOTES

V

3. הַיּוֹם כֻּלָּנוּ חַיִּים — *All of us alive this day*. Moses stresses that the generation he is speaking to witnessed the giving of Torah at Sinai and heard the voice of God. They are therefore charged with the responsibility of transmitting this evidence to the next generation, so as to insure their compliance with the covenant between God and Israel.

4-6. פָּנִים בְּפָנִים . . . — *Face to face* . . . The first two commandments of the Decalogue, אָנֹכִי ה׳ אֱלֹהֶיךָ, *I am HASHEM your God*, and לֹא יִהְיֶה לְךָ אֱלֹהִים אֲחֵרִים, *You shall have no other gods*, were heard by Israel directly from God. However, the balance of the Ten Commandments was transmitted to them by Moses. Because the people of Israel were afraid to listen to the Almighty directly, they had asked Moses to be their intermediary. The *Sforno* explains that the expression "face to face" refers to the first two commandments, since God spoke to all the people of Israel in this manner, whereas the statement of Moses, that he stood between God and Israel, refers to the subsequent commandments.

12. כַּאֲשֶׁר צִוְּךָ ה׳ אֱלֹהֶיךָ — *As HASHEM your God commanded you*. The expression *as HASHEM* . . .

5 *1 Moses called all of Israel and said to them: Hear, O Israel, the decrees
and the ordinances that I speak in your ears today; learn them, and
be careful to perform them. 2 HASHEM, our God, sealed a covenant with us
at Horeb. 3 Not with our forefathers did HASHEM seal this covenant, but
with us — we who are here, all of us alive today. 4 Face to face did HASHEM
speak with you on the mountain, from amid the fire. 5 I was standing
between HASHEM and you at that time, to relate the word of HASHEM to you
— for you were afraid of the fire and you did not ascend the mountain —
saying:*

*6 I am HASHEM, your God, Who has taken you out of the land of Egypt,
from the house of slavery.*

7 You shall not recognize the gods of others in My Presence.

*8 You shall not make yourself a carved image of any likeness of that
which is in the heavens above or on the earth below or in the water beneath
the earth. 9 You shall not prostrate yourself to them nor worship them, for
I am HASHEM, your God — a jealous God, Who visits the sin of fathers upon
children to the third and fourth generations, for My enemies; 10 but Who
shows kindness for thousands [of generations], to those who love Me and
observe My commandments.*

*11 You shall not take the Name of HASHEM, your God, in vain, for
HASHEM will not absolve anyone who takes His Name in vain.*

*12 Safeguard the Sabbath day to sanctify it, as HASHEM, your God, has
commanded you. 13 Six days shall you labor and accomplish all your work;
14 but the seventh day is Sabbath to HASHEM, your God; you shall not do
any work — you, your son, your daughter, your slave, your maidservant,
your ox, your donkey, and your every animal, and your convert within
your gates, in order that your slave and your maidservant may rest like
you. 15 And you shall remember that you were a slave in the land of Egypt,
and HASHEM, your God, has taken you out from there with a strong hand*

---

12. כַּאֲשֶׁר צִוְּךָ ה׳ אֱלֹהֶיךָ — *As HASHEM your God commanded you* ... in the manner commanded you at Marah, because indeed, when He charged you regarding the Sabbath there, He informed you that it is not sufficient to sanctify it by abstaining from labor, but also to occupy yourselves with Torah and *mitzvos*, as it says, וְהַיָּשָׁר בְּעֵינָיו תַּעֲשֶׂה וְהַאֲזַנְתָּ לְמִצְוֹתָיו, *and do that which is right in His eyes and give ear to His commandments* (*Exodus* 15:26).

14-15. לְמַעַן יָנוּחַ עַבְדְּךָ וַאֲמָתְךָ כָּמוֹךָ: וְזָכַרְתָּ כִּי עֶבֶד הָיִיתָ — *That your man-servant and your maid-servant may rest as you do: And you shall remember that you were a slave.* Behold, the commandment that the animal should also rest was given so that the servant should rest, and this *mitzvah* (that the servant should rest) was given in order to remember the Exodus from Egypt whereby the Holy One, Blessed is He, caused the slaves to cease their labors.

NOTES

commanded you must refer to a previous period when God spoke to Israel regarding the Sabbath. The Sages, indeed, comment: כַּאֲשֶׁר צִוְּךָ בְּמָרָה, "as He commanded you at Marah" (see *Exodus* 15). The *Sforno*, however, adds that this phrase refers not only to the commandment per se of Sabbath observance, but also to the manner and spirit of its observance, which was alluded to at Marah when the Almighty said *and do what is right etc.*, as the *Sforno* explains here in his commentary.

טז נְטוּיָ֑ה עַל־כֵּ֗ן צִוְּךָ֙ יהו֣ה אֱלֹהֶ֔יךָ לַעֲשׂ֖וֹת אֶת־י֥וֹם הַשַּׁבָּֽת: כַּבֵּ֣ד
אֶת־אָבִ֣יךָ וְאֶת־אִמֶּ֗ךָ כַּאֲשֶׁ֤ר צִוְּךָ֙ יהו֣ה אֱלֹהֶ֔יךָ לְמַ֣עַן ׀ יַאֲרִיכֻ֣ן יָמֶ֗יךָ
יז וּלְמַ֨עַן֙ יִ֣יטַב לָ֔ךְ עַ֚ל הָֽאֲדָמָ֔ה אֲשֶׁר־יהו֥ה אֱלֹהֶ֖יךָ נֹתֵ֥ן לָֽךְ:   לֹ֥א
תִּרְצָ֖ח   וְלֹ֣א תִּנְאָ֑ף   וְלֹ֣א תִּגְנֹֽב   וְלֹא־תַעֲנֶ֥ה
יח בְרֵעֲךָ֖ עֵ֣ד שָֽׁוְא: וְלֹ֥א תַחְמֹ֖ד אֵ֣שֶׁת רֵעֶ֑ךָ   וְלֹ֣א
תִתְאַוֶּ֜ה בֵּ֣ית רֵעֶ֗ךָ שָׂדֵ֜הוּ וְעַבְדּ֤וֹ וַֽאֲמָתוֹ֙ שׁוֹר֣וֹ וַחֲמֹר֔וֹ וְכֹ֖ל אֲשֶׁ֥ר
יט לְרֵעֶֽךָ:   אֶֽת־הַדְּבָרִ֣ים הָאֵ֡לֶּה דִּבֶּר֩ יהו֨ה אֶל־כָּל־קְהַלְכֶ֜ם
בָּהָ֗ר מִתּ֤וֹךְ הָאֵשׁ֙ הֶֽעָנָ֣ן וְהָֽעֲרָפֶ֔ל ק֥וֹל גָּד֖וֹל וְלֹ֣א יָסָ֑ף וַֽיִּכְתְּבֵ֗ם עַל־שְׁנֵי֙
כ לֻחֹ֣ת אֲבָנִ֔ים וַֽיִּתְּנֵ֖ם אֵלָֽי: וַיְהִ֗י כְּשָׁמְעֲכֶ֤ם אֶת־הַקּוֹל֙ מִתּ֣וֹךְ הַחֹ֔שֶׁךְ וְהָהָ֖ר
כא בֹּעֵ֣ר בָּאֵ֑שׁ וַתִּקְרְב֣וּן אֵלַ֗י כָּל־רָאשֵׁ֥י שִׁבְטֵיכֶ֖ם וְזִקְנֵיכֶֽם: וַתֹּֽאמְר֗וּ הֵ֣ן
הֶרְאָ֜נוּ יהו֤ה אֱלֹהֵ֨ינוּ֙ אֶת־כְּבֹד֣וֹ וְאֶת־גָּדְל֔וֹ וְאֶת־קֹל֥וֹ שָׁמַ֖עְנוּ מִתּ֣וֹךְ
כב הָאֵ֑שׁ הַיּ֤וֹם הַזֶּה֙ רָאִ֔ינוּ כִּֽי־יְדַבֵּ֧ר אֱלֹהִ֛ים אֶת־הָֽאָדָ֖ם וָחָֽי: וְעַתָּה֙ לָ֣מָּה
נָמ֔וּת כִּ֣י תֹֽאכְלֵ֔נוּ הָאֵ֥שׁ הַגְּדֹלָ֖ה הַזֹּ֑את אִם־יֹֽסְפִ֣ים ׀ אֲנַ֗חְנוּ לִשְׁמֹ֨עַ
כג אֶת־ק֨וֹל יהו֧ה אֱלֹהֵ֛ינוּ ע֖וֹד וָמָֽתְנוּ: כִּ֣י מִ֣י כָל־בָּשָׂ֗ר אֲשֶׁ֣ר שָׁמַ֣ע קוֹל֩
כד אֱלֹהִ֨ים חַיִּ֜ים מְדַבֵּ֧ר מִתּֽוֹךְ־הָאֵ֛שׁ כָּמֹ֖נוּ וַיֶּֽחִי: קְרַ֤ב אַתָּה֙ וּֽשֲׁמָ֔ע אֵ֛ת
כָּל־אֲשֶׁ֥ר יֹאמַ֖ר יהו֣ה אֱלֹהֵ֑ינוּ וְאַ֣תְּ ׀ תְּדַבֵּ֣ר אֵלֵ֗ינוּ אֵת֩ כָּל־אֲשֶׁ֨ר יְדַבֵּ֜ר
כה יהו֤ה אֱלֹהֵ֨ינוּ֙ אֵלֶ֔יךָ וְשָׁמַ֖עְנוּ וְעָשִֽׂינוּ: וַיִּשְׁמַ֤ע יהו֙ה אֶת־ק֣וֹל דִּבְרֵיכֶ֔ם
בְּדַבֶּרְכֶ֖ם אֵלָ֑י וַיֹּ֨אמֶר יהו֜ה אֵלַ֗י שָׁ֠מַעְתִּי אֶת־ק֨וֹל דִּבְרֵ֜י הָעָ֤ם הַזֶּה֙ אֲשֶׁ֣ר
כו דִּבְּר֣וּ אֵלֶ֔יךָ הֵיטִ֖יבוּ כָּל־אֲשֶׁ֥ר דִּבֵּֽרוּ: מִֽי־יִתֵּ֡ן וְהָיָה֩ לְבָבָ֨ם זֶ֜ה לָהֶ֗ם
לְיִרְאָ֥ה אֹתִ֛י וְלִשְׁמֹ֥ר אֶת־כָּל־מִצְוֺתַ֖י כָּל־הַיָּמִ֑ים לְמַ֨עַן יִיטַ֥ב לָהֶ֛ם
כז־כח וְלִבְנֵיהֶ֖ם לְעֹלָֽם: לֵ֥ךְ אֱמֹ֖ר לָהֶ֑ם שׁ֥וּבוּ לָכֶ֖ם לְאָֽהֳלֵיכֶֽם: וְאַתָּ֗ה פֹּה֮ עֲמֹ֣ד
עִמָּדִי֒ וַֽאֲדַבְּרָ֣ה אֵלֶ֗יךָ אֵ֧ת כָּל־הַמִּצְוָ֛ה וְהַֽחֻקִּ֥ים וְהַמִּשְׁפָּטִ֖ים אֲשֶׁ֣ר
כט תְּלַמְּדֵ֑ם וְעָשׂ֣וּ בָאָ֔רֶץ אֲשֶׁ֧ר אָֽנֹכִ֛י נֹתֵ֥ן לָהֶ֖ם לְרִשְׁתָּֽהּ: וּשְׁמַרְתֶּ֣ם לַֽעֲשׂ֔וֹת
ל כַּֽאֲשֶׁ֥ר צִוָּ֛ה יהו֥ה אֱלֹהֵיכֶ֖ם אֶתְכֶ֑ם לֹ֣א תָסֻ֔רוּ יָמִ֖ין וּשְׂמֹֽאל: בְּכָל־הַדֶּ֗רֶךְ
אֲשֶׁ֨ר צִוָּ֜ה יהו֤ה אֱלֹֽהֵיכֶם֙ אֶתְכֶ֔ם תֵּלֵ֑כוּ לְמַ֨עַן֙ תִּֽחְי֔וּן וְט֥וֹב לָכֶ֖ם

---

16. וּלְמַעַן יִיטַב לָךְ — *And that it may go well with you* . . . even in this world, as our Sages
say: דְּבָרִים שֶׁאָדָם אוֹכֵל פֵּרוֹתֵיהֶם בָּעוֹלָם הַזֶּה וְהַקֶּרֶן קַיֶּמֶת לוֹ לָעוֹלָם הַבָּא . . . כִּבּוּד אָב וָאֵם וכו׳,
*Precepts whose fruits a person enjoys in This World but whose principal remains intact
for him in the World to Come . . . honor due to father and mother, etc. (Peah 1:1).*

24. וְאַתְּ תְּדַבֵּר אֵלֵינוּ — *And you shall speak to us* . . . although your speaking (to us) will
be inferior in quality to God's speaking (to us).

29. וּשְׁמַרְתֶּם לַעֲשׂוֹת — *And you shall observe to do* . . . and since the matter developed
thus, it is proper that you observe (what I shall relate to you).

NOTES

24. וְאַתְּ תְּדַבֵּר — *And you shall speak.* This
commentary of the *Sforno* is suggested by the
feminine form of וְאַתְּ, *and you,* which implies a
weaker, lesser level of communication.

29. וּשְׁמַרְתֶּם לַעֲשׂוֹת . . . לֹא תָסֻרוּ יָמִין וּשְׂמֹאל —
And you shall observe to do . . . you shall not turn
aside to the right hand or to the left. Originally,
it was God's intent that Israel should hear all
the commandments directly from Him. Had
that come to pass, there would have been no doubt
in the mind of the people that these commandments were authentic, since they emanated

and an outstretched arm; therefore HASHEM, your God, has commanded you to make the Sabbath day.

16 *Honor your father and your mother, as HASHEM, your God, commanded you, so that your days will be lengthened and so that it will be good for you, upon the land that HASHEM, your God, gives you.*

17 *You shall not kill; and you shall not commit adultery; and you shall not steal; and you shall not bear vain witness against your fellow.*

18 *And you shall not covet your fellow's wife, you shall not desire your fellow's house, his field, his slave, his maidservant, his ox, his donkey, or anything that belongs to your fellow.*

19 *These words HASHEM spoke to your entire congregation on the
mountain, from the midst of the fire, the cloud, and the thick cloud — a great
voice, never to be repeated — and He inscribed them on two stone Tablets
and gave them to me.*
20 *It happened that when you heard the voice from the
midst of the darkness and the mountain was burning in fire, that all the
heads of your tribes and your elders approached me.*

21 *They said, "Behold! HASHEM, our God, has shown us His glory and His
greatness, and we have heard His voice from the midst of the fire; this day
we saw that HASHEM will speak to a person and he can live.*
22 *But now, why
should we die when this great fire consumes us? If we continue to hear the
voice of HASHEM, our God, any longer, we will die!*
23 *For is there any human
that has heard the voice of the Living God speaking from the midst of the
fire, as we have, and lived?*
24 *You should approach and hear whatever
HASHEM, our God, will say, and you should speak to us whatever HASHEM,
our God, will speak to you — then we shall hear and we shall do."*

25 *HASHEM heard the sound of your words when you spoke to me, and
HASHEM said to me, "I heard the sound of the words of this people, that they
have spoken to you; they did well in all that they spoke.*
26 *Who can assure
that this heart should remain theirs, to fear Me and observe all My
commandments all the days, so that it should be good for them and for their
children forever?*
27 *Go say to them, 'Return to your tents.'*
28 *But as for you,
stand here with Me and I shall speak to you the entire commandment, and
the decrees, and the ordinances that you shall teach them and they shall
perform in the Land that I give them, to possess it."*

29 *You shall be careful to act as HASHEM, your God, commanded you, you
shall not stray to the right or left.*
30 *On the entire way that HASHEM, your
God, commanded you shall you go, so that you shall live and it will be good*

לֹא תָסֻרוּ יָמִין וּשְׂמֹאל — *You shall not turn aside to the right hand or to the left.* You shall neither add (that) which you think will improve (them) nor diminish from them whatsoever.

30. לְמַעַן תִּחְיוּן וְטוֹב לָכֶם — *That you may live and that it may be well with you . . .* so

NOTES

from the Almighty. However, since the subsequent eight commandments were transmitted by Moses, there was a danger that they might question their authenticity. Therefore, it was necessary for Moses to caution them that they must observe *all* of the commandments, including those they heard through him, and not deviate from them.

ו א וְהַאֲרַכְתֶּם יָמִים בָּאָרֶץ אֲשֶׁר תִּירָשׁוּן׃ וְזֹאת הַמִּצְוָה הַחֻקִּים וְהַמִּשְׁפָּטִים
אֲשֶׁר צִוָּה יְהוָה אֱלֹהֵיכֶם לְלַמֵּד אֶתְכֶם לַעֲשׂוֹת בָּאָרֶץ אֲשֶׁר אַתֶּם
ב עֹבְרִים שָׁמָּה לְרִשְׁתָּהּ׃ לְמַעַן תִּירָא אֶת־יְהוָה אֱלֹהֶיךָ לִשְׁמֹר אֶת־כָּל־
חֻקֹּתָיו וּמִצְוֹתָיו אֲשֶׁר אָנֹכִי מְצַוֶּךָּ אַתָּה וּבִנְךָ וּבֶן־בִּנְךָ כֹּל יְמֵי חַיֶּיךָ
ג וּלְמַעַן יַאֲרִכֻן יָמֶיךָ׃ וְשָׁמַעְתָּ יִשְׂרָאֵל וְשָׁמַרְתָּ לַעֲשׂוֹת אֲשֶׁר יִיטַב לְךָ
וַאֲשֶׁר תִּרְבּוּן מְאֹד כַּאֲשֶׁר דִּבֶּר יְהוָה אֱלֹהֵי אֲבֹתֶיךָ לָךְ אֶרֶץ זָבַת
חָלָב וּדְבָשׁ׃
*ע' וד' רבתי
ששי ד־ה שְׁמַע* יִשְׂרָאֵל יְהוָה אֱלֹהֵינוּ יְהוָה ׀ אֶחָד*׃ וְאָהַבְתָּ אֵת יְהוָה אֱלֹהֶיךָ

---

that you may (merit) eternal life, in a good and happy manner.

וְהַאֲרַכְתֶּם יָמִים בָּאָרֶץ אֲשֶׁר תִּירָשׁוּן — *That you may prolong your days in the land which you shall possess* . . . and that you may acquire length of days in the world which is כֻּלּוֹ אָרוּךְ, *wholly long* (based on *Kiddushin* 39b), as a result of your dwelling in the land without pain, free from anxiety and impediments.

VI

1. וְזֹאת הַמִּצְוָה — *Now this is the commandment* . . . the intent of (God), the Blessed One, Who commanded these precepts which are linked to the Land (הַתְּלוּיוֹת בָּאָרֶץ) when you enter it (is) . . .

2. לְמַעַן תִּירָא אֶת ה׳ אֱלֹהֶיךָ — *That you might fear* HASHEM *your God* . . . that you shall remember that the Land is His, and that you are (but) *strangers and settlers with Him* (based on *Leviticus* 25:23).

אַתָּה וּבִנְךָ וּבֶן בִּנְךָ — *You, your son and your son's son* . . . so that those generations who did not see the great works of God will also fear Him, when they accept these commandments from you who did witness them (i.e., the great deeds of God).

וּלְמַעַן יַאֲרִכֻן יָמֶיךָ — *And that your days may be prolonged* . . . and so that these commandments shall grant you life which is כֻּלּוֹ אָרוּךְ, *everlasting*.

3. וְשָׁמַעְתָּ יִשְׂרָאֵל — *And you shall hear, O Israel* . . . and being that this is the intended purpose of God, the Blessed One, (because of) His great lovingkindness for you, it is fitting that you listen and understand the intent of God, the Blessed One, regarding all these (*mitzvos*).

NOTES

30. וְהַאֲרַכְתֶּם יָמִים בָּאָרֶץ אֲשֶׁר תִּירָשׁוּן — *That you may prolong your days in the land which you shall possess*. The *Sforno*, consistent with his oft-expressed views, is of the opinion that man requires tranquility, a sense of well-being and security, in order to develop his intellect and attain spiritual perfection, which in turn insures the attainment of one's portion of eternal life. The expression כּוּלוֹ אָרוּךְ, *wholly long*, in his commentary is taken from the expression in the Torah regarding the reward given for honoring one's parents (לְמַעַן יַאֲרִיכֻן יָמֶיךָ).

VI

2. לְמַעַן תִּירָא . . . וּלְמַעַן יַאֲרִכֻן יָמֶיךָ — *That you might fear . . . and that your days may be prolonged*. The *Sforno* explains that the מִצְוֹת הַתְּלוּיוֹת בָּאָרֶץ, the commandments which are associated exclusively with the Land, and are not obligatory outside *Eretz Yisrael*, serve a twofold purpose. One, as stated in this verse, is to impress upon the Israelite that he is but a sojourner in the land which belongs to God alone. The second is to reward him with the blessing of eternal life. As the *Sforno* explains in the next verse, the exceptional character of *Eretz Yisrael*, a land which flows with milk and honey, was given to Israel because it decreased the need for strenuous physical labor while improving those conditions which enhance the mental and spiritual growth of its inhabitants.

4. שְׁמַע יִשְׂרָאֵל ה׳ אֱלֹהֵינוּ — *Hear, O Israel,* HASHEM *Our God*. The sense of the *Sforno's* commentary regarding this major declaration of faith is: It is

for you, and you shall prolong your days in the Land that you shall possess.

6 [1] *This is the commandment, and the decrees, and the ordinances that HASHEM, your God, commanded to teach you, to perform in the Land to which you are crossing, to possess it,* [2] *so that you will fear HASHEM, your God, to observe all His decrees and commandments that I command you — you, your child, and your grandchild — all the days of your life, so that your days will be lengthened.* [3] *You shall hearken, O Israel, and beware to perform, so that it will be good for you, and so that you will increase very much, as HASHEM, the God of your forefathers, spoke for you — a land flowing with milk and honey.*

[4] *Hear, O Israel: HASHEM is our God, HASHEM is the One and Only.* [5] *You*

וְשָׁמַרְתָּ לַעֲשׂוֹת אֲשֶׁר יִיטַב לְךָ — *And observe to do it that it may be well with you.* You will then attempt to do God's will with love and to find favor (in His eyes), which will insure that it shall be well with you and you will be granted eternal happiness. Also by observing to do it, you will "increase mightily," all this resulting from your observance of righteousness and justice done in His honor.

כַּאֲשֶׁר דִּבֶּר ה׳ אֱלֹהֵי אֲבֹתֶיךָ לָךְ אֶרֶץ זָבַת חָלָב וּדְבָשׁ — *As HASHEM the God of your fathers promised you, a land flowing with milk and honey.* As He spoke to you, (He will give you) a land flowing with milk and honey, prepared for those who serve Him for this purpose, that you may earn your livelihood without pain and (thereby) have time for analytical (study) and for (good) deeds, (as well) as being fruitful and multiplying.

4. שְׁמַע יִשְׂרָאֵל — *Hear, O Israel.* Contemplate and understand this.

ה׳ — *HASHEM.* Who gives existence and is the Creator.

אֱלֹהֵינוּ — *Our God.* He is the Chosen One of all who are separated (from matter), and our hope is to attain our desires from Him (alone), not through any intermediary. And being that He is exalted (and superior) in His power of creativity, hence it is fitting to bow down to Him alone. And since our hope lies in Him (alone), without need for any intermediary, it is proper that we pray to and serve Him alone.

ה׳ אֶחָד — *HASHEM is One.* Now, being that He granted existence from total nothingness (יֵשׁ מֵאַיִן), it is understood (lit. "explained") that there does not exist any kind similar to Him and that He is separated in kind from all that exists in the world of נִפְסָדִים, *perishables,* and all that exists in the world of the spheres, and all that exists in the world of angels, in such a manner that He is (singular) and alone in His fourth world. Now it seems to me that this is alluded to in the fact that the letter *daled* of the word אֶחָד, *echad,* is larger and that the letter *ayin* of the word שְׁמַע, *hear,* is (also) larger, teaching us that it is fitting that

NOTES

imperative that the Israelite contemplate and understand that God is the First Cause, Who grants the power of being to every aspect of creation and without Him one cannot conceive of any existence. He is our God in the sense that whereas other nations have their heavenly princes (שָׂרִים) and guardian angels, we Israelites are under His direct supervision and Divine Providence without the need of any intermediary. Hence, we must place all our hopes in Him alone, and pray to and worship Him alone. This is the meaning of the word אֱלֹהֵינוּ — *our* God.

ה׳ אֶחָד — *HASHEM is One.* (a) According to Kabbalistic doctrine there are four "worlds": עוֹלָם הָאֲצִילוּת, *the world of emanations;* עוֹלָם הַבְּרִיאָה, *the world of creation;* עוֹלָם הַיְצִירָה, *the world of formation;* and עוֹלָם הָעֲשִׂיָּה, *the world of creative matter.* The aforementioned emanations are also known as the ten סְפִירוֹת, *sefiros,* ranging from כֶּתֶר, *Crown,* to מַלְכוּת, *Kingship,* all these being incorporated in the עוֹלָם הָאֲצִילוּת, which is the most spiritual of the four "worlds." As such, the Almighty is "near" or "close by" these ten *sefiros* and the word אֲצִילוּת is derived from אֵצֶל, i.e.,

ו בְּכָל־לְבָבְךָ וּבְכָל־נַפְשְׁךָ וּבְכָל־מְאֹדֶךָ: וְהָיוּ הַדְּבָרִים הָאֵלֶּה אֲשֶׁר אָנֹכִי
ז מְצַוְּךָ הַיּוֹם עַל־לְבָבֶךָ: וְשִׁנַּנְתָּם לְבָנֶיךָ וְדִבַּרְתָּ בָּם בְּשִׁבְתְּךָ בְּבֵיתֶךָ
ח וּבְלֶכְתְּךָ בַדֶּרֶךְ וּבְשָׁכְבְּךָ וּבְקוּמֶךָ: וּקְשַׁרְתָּם לְאוֹת עַל־יָדֶךָ וְהָיוּ לְטֹטָפֹת
ט־י בֵּין עֵינֶיךָ: וּכְתַבְתָּם עַל־מְזֻזוֹת בֵּיתֶךָ וּבִשְׁעָרֶיךָ: וְהָיָה
כִּי־יְבִיאֲךָ | יהוה אֱלֹהֶיךָ אֶל־הָאָרֶץ אֲשֶׁר נִשְׁבַּע לַאֲבֹתֶיךָ לְאַבְרָהָם
יא לְיִצְחָק וּלְיַעֲקֹב לָתֶת לָךְ עָרִים גְּדֹלֹת וְטֹבֹת אֲשֶׁר לֹא־בָנִיתָ: וּבָתִּים
מְלֵאִים כָּל־טוּב אֲשֶׁר לֹא־מִלֵּאתָ וּבֹרֹת חֲצוּבִים אֲשֶׁר לֹא־חָצַבְתָּ
יב כְּרָמִים וְזֵיתִים אֲשֶׁר לֹא־נָטָעְתָּ וְאָכַלְתָּ וְשָׂבָעְתָּ: הִשָּׁמֶר לְךָ פֶּן־תִּשְׁכַּח
יג אֶת־יהוה אֲשֶׁר הוֹצִיאֲךָ מֵאֶרֶץ מִצְרַיִם מִבֵּית עֲבָדִים: אֶת־יהוה אֱלֹהֶיךָ
יד תִּירָא וְאֹתוֹ תַעֲבֹד וּבִשְׁמוֹ תִּשָּׁבֵעַ: לֹא תֵלְכוּן אַחֲרֵי אֱלֹהִים אֲחֵרִים
טו מֵאֱלֹהֵי הָעַמִּים אֲשֶׁר סְבִיבוֹתֵיכֶם: כִּי אֵל קַנָּא יהוה אֱלֹהֶיךָ בְּקִרְבֶּךָ פֶּן־
טז יֶחֱרֶה אַף־יהוה אֱלֹהֶיךָ בָּךְ וְהִשְׁמִידְךָ מֵעַל פְּנֵי הָאֲדָמָה: לֹא
יז תְנַסּוּ אֶת־יהוה אֱלֹהֵיכֶם כַּאֲשֶׁר נִסִּיתֶם בַּמַּסָּה: שָׁמוֹר תִּשְׁמְרוּן
יח אֶת־מִצְוֹת יהוה אֱלֹהֵיכֶם וְעֵדֹתָיו וְחֻקָּיו אֲשֶׁר צִוָּךְ: וְעָשִׂיתָ הַיָּשָׁר
וְהַטּוֹב בְּעֵינֵי יהוה לְמַעַן יִיטַב לָךְ וּבָאתָ וְיָרַשְׁתָּ אֶת־הָאָרֶץ הַטֹּבָה
יט אֲשֶׁר־נִשְׁבַּע יהוה לַאֲבֹתֶיךָ: לַהֲדֹף אֶת־כָּל־אֹיְבֶיךָ מִפָּנֶיךָ כַּאֲשֶׁר
כ דִּבֶּר יהוה: כִּי־יִשְׁאָלְךָ בִנְךָ מָחָר לֵאמֹר מָה הָעֵדֹת וְהַחֻקִּים

we pay attention and increase our analysis of all this, as our Sages said: "... Providing that one prolongs (the utterance) of the (letter) *daled* of *echad*" so that one might concentrate (his thoughts) regarding (all) this.

5. וְאָהַבְתָּ — *And you shall love.* You shall rejoice to do that which is good in His eyes once you discern that there is no nobler goal than this.

6. עַל לְבָבֶךָ — *Upon your heart.* You shall constantly remember to direct your deeds toward this goal.

7. וְשִׁנַּנְתָּם לְבָנֶיךָ — *And you shall teach them diligently to your children.* Teach them by constant review and with sharpness, (resulting in) reasoned proof.

וְדִבַּרְתָּ בָּם — *And you shall talk of them* ... for by such constant repetition, you (and they) will always remember them.

NOTES

"near," according to the *Ramban*. The *Sforno* is of the opinion that God is singular and unique in this "fourth world," which explains why the letter ד is written large at the end of the word אֶחָד according to the *Mesorah* to call our attention to this concept, being that ד is the numerical equivalent of four. The letter ע is also written large at the end of the word שְׁמַע, implying that we should look and see ("*ayin*" meaning "eye"), the significance of God's transcendence over the four worlds, for He is the אֵין סוֹף, *the Limitless and Boundless One* — as the Kabbalists refer to God.

(b) The "world of spheres," mentioned by the *Sforno*, is part of the "world of emanations" or of "creative matter," depending upon the opinion of various Kabbalistic schools, while the "world of angels" is part of the "world of formation." They are not separate worlds. The *Sforno* refers to עוֹלָם הָעֲשִׂיָּה, *the world of matter*, as the world of הַנִּפְסָדִים, the *perishable* or the *destructible*. This material world is comprised of four basic elements or substances — earth, air, water and fire.

5. וְאָהַבְתָּ — *And you shall love*. Many commentators have pointed out that the phrase *and you shall love* cannot be interpreted as a command, for how can the emotion of love be commanded? The *Sforno* resolves this difficulty by interpreting the phrase וְאָהַבְתָּ as a promise and assurance, i.e., you *will* love. When man arrives at a clear and complete understanding of God, he will then appreciate His

shall love HASHEM, *your God, with all your heart, with all your soul, and with all your resources.* [6] *And these matters that I command you today shall be upon your heart.* [7] *You shall teach them thoroughly to your children and you shall speak of them while you sit in your home, while you walk on the way, when you retire and when you arise.* [8] *Bind them as a sign upon your arm and let them be ornaments between your eyes.* [9] *And write them on the doorposts of your house and upon your gates.*

[10] *It shall be that when* HASHEM, *your God, brings you to the Land that* HASHEM *swore to your forefathers, to Abraham, to Isaac, and to Jacob, to give you — great and good cities that you did not build,* [11] *houses filled with every good thing that you did not fill, chiseled cisterns that you did not chisel, orchards and olive trees that you did not plant — and you shall eat and be satisfied —* [12] *beware for yourself lest you forget* HASHEM *Who took you out of the land of Egypt, from the house of slavery.* [13] HASHEM, *your God, shall you fear, Him shall you serve, and in His Name shall you swear.* [14] *You shall not follow after gods of others, of the gods of the peoples that are around you.* [15] *For a jealous God is* HASHEM, *your God, among you — lest the wrath of* HASHEM, *your God, will flare against you and He destroy you from upon the face of the earth.*

[16] *You shall not test* HASHEM, *your God, as you tested Him at Massah.* [17] *You shall surely observe the commandments of* HASHEM, *your God, and His testimonies and His decrees that He commanded you.* [18] *You shall do what is fair and good in the eyes of* HASHEM, *so that it will be good for you, and you shall come and possess the good Land that* HASHEM *swore to your forefathers,* [19] *to thrust away all your enemies from before you, as* HASHEM *spoke.*

[20] *If your child asks you tomorrow, saying, "What are the testimonies*

10-11. אֲשֶׁר לֹא בָנִיתָ: וּבָתִּים מְלֵאִים כָּל טוּב אֲשֶׁר לֹא מִלֵּאתָ — *Which you did not build. And houses full of all good things which you did not fill* . . . for you will acquire wealth without toil.

12. הִשָּׁמֶר לְךָ פֶּן תִּשְׁכַּח — *Beware lest you forget.* For wealth acquired in this fashion, in most cases, results in unrestrained lust, and thus man forgets his Maker.

20. מָה הָעֵדֹת — *What do the testimonies mean?* . . . that part (of Torah) which is analytical and is proven testimony (of its truth).

NOTES

greatness and kindness which will bring him sincere joy, and this in turn will evoke a profound feeling of love for God. The *Rambam,* in *Hilchos Teshuvah* 10:2, interprets the word וְאָהַבְתָּ thus: "Whoever serves God out of love and occupies himself with the study of Torah and the fulfillment of commandments and walks in the path of wisdom . . . ultimately happiness comes to him as a result of his conduct . . . This is the standard which God, through Moses, bids us to achieve, as it is said, וְאָהַבְתָּ אֵת ה׳ אֱלֹהֶיךָ, *And you shall love* HASHEM *your God."*

6. עַל לְבָבֶךָ — *Upon your heart.* The expression *upon your heart* means to commit something to memory. Israel is urged to take heed of God's words and to remember them ever for the purpose of translating them into action. We find a similar expression in *Proverbs* 3:3, כָּתְבֵם עַל לוּחַ לִבֶּךָ, *Write them* (i.e., the commandments of God) *on the tablet of your heart.* In the next verse, the Torah tells us how to insure memory by constant review and repetition.

11-12. וּבָתִּים מְלֵאִים כָּל טוּב . . . הִשָּׁמֶר לְךָ פֶּן תִּשְׁכַּח — *And houses full of all good things which you did not fill . . . Beware lest you forget.* Wealth so easily acquired is liable to produce unlimited desires in man which eventually result in his rejecting the sovereignty of God.

כא וְהַמִּשְׁפָּטִים אֲשֶׁר צִוָּה יְהוָה אֱלֹהֵינוּ אֶתְכֶם: וְאָמַרְתָּ לְבִנְךָ עֲבָדִים הָיִינוּ
כב לְפַרְעֹה בְּמִצְרָיִם וַיֹּצִיאֵנוּ יְהוָה מִמִּצְרַיִם בְּיָד חֲזָקָה: וַיִּתֵּן יְהוָה אוֹתֹת
כג וּמֹפְתִים גְּדֹלִים וְרָעִים | בְּמִצְרַיִם בְּפַרְעֹה וּבְכָל־בֵּיתוֹ לְעֵינֵינוּ: וְאוֹתָנוּ
הוֹצִיא מִשָּׁם לְמַעַן הָבִיא אֹתָנוּ לָתֶת לָנוּ אֶת־הָאָרֶץ אֲשֶׁר נִשְׁבַּע
כד לַאֲבֹתֵינוּ: וַיְצַוֵּנוּ יְהוָה לַעֲשׂוֹת אֶת־כָּל־הַחֻקִּים הָאֵלֶּה לְיִרְאָה אֶת־יְהוָה
כה אֱלֹהֵינוּ לְטוֹב לָנוּ כָּל־הַיָּמִים לְחַיֹּתֵנוּ כְּהַיּוֹם הַזֶּה: וּצְדָקָה תִּהְיֶה־לָּנוּ
כִּי־נִשְׁמֹר לַעֲשׂוֹת אֶת־כָּל־הַמִּצְוָה הַזֹּאת לִפְנֵי יְהוָה אֱלֹהֵינוּ כַּאֲשֶׁר
ז שביעי א צִוָּנוּ: כִּי יְבִיאֲךָ יְהוָה אֱלֹהֶיךָ אֶל־הָאָרֶץ אֲשֶׁר־אַתָּה בָא־שָׁמָּה
לְרִשְׁתָּהּ וְנָשַׁל גּוֹיִם־רַבִּים | מִפָּנֶיךָ הַחִתִּי וְהַגִּרְגָּשִׁי וְהָאֱמֹרִי וְהַכְּנַעֲנִי
ב וְהַפְּרִזִּי וְהַחִוִּי וְהַיְבוּסִי שִׁבְעָה גוֹיִם רַבִּים וַעֲצוּמִים מִמֶּךָּ: וּנְתָנָם יְהוָה
אֱלֹהֶיךָ לְפָנֶיךָ וְהִכִּיתָם הַחֲרֵם תַּחֲרִים אֹתָם לֹא־תִכְרֹת לָהֶם בְּרִית וְלֹא
ג־ד תְחָנֵּם: וְלֹא תִתְחַתֵּן בָּם בִּתְּךָ לֹא־תִתֵּן לִבְנוֹ וּבִתּוֹ לֹא־תִקַּח לִבְנֶךָ: כִּי־
יָסִיר אֶת־בִּנְךָ מֵאַחֲרַי וְעָבְדוּ אֱלֹהִים אֲחֵרִים וְחָרָה אַף־יְהוָה בָּכֶם
ה וְהִשְׁמִידְךָ מַהֵר: כִּי־אִם־כֹּה תַעֲשׂוּ לָהֶם מִזְבְּחֹתֵיהֶם תִּתֹּצוּ וּמַצֵּבֹתָם
ו תְּשַׁבֵּרוּ וַאֲשֵׁירֵהֶם תְּגַדֵּעוּן וּפְסִילֵיהֶם תִּשְׂרְפוּן בָּאֵשׁ: כִּי עַם קָדוֹשׁ אַתָּה
לַיהוָה אֱלֹהֶיךָ בְּךָ בָּחַר | יְהוָה אֱלֹהֶיךָ לִהְיוֹת לוֹ לְעַם סְגֻלָּה מִכֹּל

וְהַחֻקִּים וְהַמִּשְׁפָּטִים — *And the statutes and the ordinances.* The part (of Torah) which (demands) deeds.

אֲשֶׁר צִוָּה ה׳ אֱלֹהֵינוּ אֶתְכֶם — *Which HASHEM our God has commanded you* ... the commandments given to the sons of Noach (בְּנֵי נֹחַ) being insufficient.

21. עֲבָדִים הָיִינוּ — *We were slaves.* And being that in our servitude (to Pharaoh) we were incapable of attaining the perfection intended for us (by God), He wondrously delivered us and brought us to the land so that we might be able to acquire that perfection (completeness) (residing) in it.

24. וַיְצַוֵּנוּ ה׳ לַעֲשׂוֹת אֶת כָּל הַחֻקִּים הָאֵלֶּה — *And HASHEM commanded us to do all these statutes* ... so that we might understand through observing them ...

לְיִרְאָה אֶת ה׳ אֱלֹהֵינוּ — *To fear HASHEM our God.* And this will result when we contemplate and recognize His greatness. Now, all this He wanted לְטוֹב לָנוּ כָּל הַיָּמִים, *for our good all the days,* for He desires to perform (deeds of) lovingkindness, not for His own sake (but rather for our benefit).

לְחַיֹּתֵנוּ כְּהַיּוֹם הַזֶּה — *That He might preserve us alive as it is this day.* (This refers to) transitory life (lit., life of the hour), and that there be *righteousness to us* and merit *before Hashem, our God*, (refers to) the everlasting world.

NOTES

20. אֲשֶׁר צִוָּה ה׳ אֱלֹהֵינוּ אֶתְכֶם . . . — *Which HASHEM our God has commanded you.* The son is puzzled by the multiplicity of laws given to Israel, whereas the other nations are only required to observe the basic laws of humanity, known as "the seven laws of the sons of Noah," viz. not to worship idols, not to blaspheme the Name of God, to establish courts of justice, not to kill, not to commit adultery, not to rob and not to eat flesh cut from a living animal. The answer to this question is given in verses 24-25.

24-25. לְטוֹב לָנוּ כָּל הַיָּמִים . . . וּצְדָקָה תִּהְיֶה לָּנוּ — *For our good all the days ... And it shall be righteousness unto us.* The *Sforno* interprets כָּל הַיָּמִים, *all the days,* as indicating This World and the World to Come. The expression לְטוֹב לָנוּ, *for our good,* means it is for our benefit and not for the benefit of God. The phrase לְחַיֹּתֵנוּ כְּהַיּוֹם הַזֶּה, *that He might preserve us alive as it is this day,* refers to man's happiness and fulfillment in This World, while the expression וּצְדָקָה תִּהְיֶה לָּנוּ, *and it shall be righ-*

*and the decrees and the ordinances that HASHEM, our God, commanded
you?"*
*21 You shall say to your child, "We were slaves to Pharaoh in Egypt, and
HASHEM took us out of Egypt with a strong hand. 22 HASHEM placed signs and
wonders, great and harmful, against Egypt, against Pharaoh and against his
entire household, before our eyes. 23 And He took us out of there in order to
bring us, to give us the Land that He swore to our forefathers. 24 HASHEM
commanded us to perform all these decrees, to fear HASHEM, our God, for our
good, all the days, to give us life, as this very day. 25 And it will be a merit
for us if we are careful to perform this entire commandment before HASHEM,
our God, as He commanded us.*

7 *1 When HASHEM, your God, will bring you to the Land to which you
come to possess it, and many nations will be thrust away from
before you — the Hittite, the Girgashite, the Amorite, the Canaanite, the
Perizzite, the Hivvite, and the Jebusite — seven nations greater and
mightier than you, 2 and HASHEM, your God, will deliver them before you,
and you will smite them — you shall utterly destroy them; you shall not
seal a covenant with them nor shall you show them favor. 3 You shall not
intermarry with them; you shall not give your daughter to his son, and you
shall not take his daughter for your son, 4 for he will cause your child to
turn away from after Me and they will worship the gods of others; then
HASHEM's wrath will burn against you, and He will destroy you quickly.
5 Rather, so shall you do to them: Their altars shall you break apart; their
pillars shall you smash; their sacred trees shall you cut down; and their
carved images shall you burn in fire.*
*6 For you are a holy people to HASHEM, your God; HASHEM, your God,
has chosen you to be for Him a treasured people above all the peoples*

25. וּצְדָקָה תִּהְיֶה לָּנוּ — *And it shall be righteousness unto us* . . . and when I said to you *for our good all the days,* I meant to say by that it should be for our good in This World (עוֹלָם הַזֶּה) and in the World to Come (עוֹלָם הַבָּא).

VII

6. כִּי עַם קָדוֹשׁ אַתָּה — *For you are a holy people.* And it is not fitting to profane your holiness by marrying women who serve strange gods, thereby giving birth to disqualified offspring, as it says, כִּי חִלֵּל יְהוּדָה קֹדֶשׁ ה׳ אֲשֶׁר אָהֵב וּבָעַל בַּת אֵל נֵכָר, *for Judah has profaned the holiness of HASHEM which he loved, and has married the daughter of a strange god* (*Malachi* 2:11).

בְּךָ בָּחַר ה׳ — *HASHEM has chosen you* . . . but not unfit offspring, as our Sages say, "The Divine Presence comes to rest only upon families of pure birth in Israel" (*Kiddushin* 70b).

NOTES

teousness unto us, implies the merits earned by man in This World which will be rewarded eventually in the eternal, everlasting world.

VII

6. כִּי עַם קָדוֹשׁ אַתָּה — *For you are a holy people.* The *Sforno* interprets the statement as the source for the prohibition of intermarriage. Because Israel is holy, they must not marry gentile women who practice idolatry. The verse from *Malachi* quoted by the *Sforno* proves that such behavior profanes the holiness of God. [This does not mean that the prohibition against intermarriage is limited to women addicted to idolatry. All gentile women are forbidden to Jewish men. The verse only gives this reason as a generalization.]

ז הָעַמִּים אֲשֶׁר עַל־פְּנֵי הָאֲדָמָה: לֹא מֵרֻבְּכֶם מִכָּל־הָעַמִּים חָשַׁק יהוה
ח בָּכֶם וַיִּבְחַר בָּכֶם כִּי־אַתֶּם הַמְעַט מִכָּל־הָעַמִּים: כִּי מֵאַהֲבַת יהוה
אֶתְכֶם וּמִשָּׁמְרוֹ אֶת־הַשְּׁבֻעָה אֲשֶׁר נִשְׁבַּע לַאֲבֹתֵיכֶם הוֹצִיא יהוה
מפטיר ט אֶתְכֶם בְּיָד חֲזָקָה וַיִּפְדְּךָ מִבֵּית עֲבָדִים מִיַּד פַּרְעֹה מֶלֶךְ־מִצְרָיִם: וְיָדַעְתָּ
כִּי־יהוה אֱלֹהֶיךָ הוּא הָאֱלֹהִים הָאֵל הַנֶּאֱמָן שֹׁמֵר הַבְּרִית וְהַחֶסֶד
י לְאֹהֲבָיו וּלְשֹׁמְרֵי מִצְוֹתָו לְאֶלֶף דּוֹר: וּמְשַׁלֵּם לְשֹׂנְאָיו אֶל־פָּנָיו
יא לְהַאֲבִידוֹ לֹא יְאַחֵר לְשֹׂנְאוֹ אֶל־פָּנָיו יְשַׁלֶּם־לוֹ: וְשָׁמַרְתָּ אֶת־הַמִּצְוָה
וְאֶת־הַחֻקִּים וְאֶת־הַמִּשְׁפָּטִים אֲשֶׁר אָנֹכִי מְצַוְּךָ הַיּוֹם לַעֲשׂוֹתָם:

---

7. לֹא מֵרֻבְּכֶם — *Not because you were more in number* . . . not for the purpose of gaining honor through their large populace (did God choose them).

8. כִּי מֵאַהֲבַת ה׳ אֶתְכֶם — *But out of HASHEM's love for you* . . . because you are the seed of (those) who loved Him and acknowledged His Name moreso than other nations.

9. הָאֵל הַנֶּאֱמָן — *The faithful God* . . . who unswervingly (keeps His word) and is unchanging.

9-10. שֹׁמֵר הַבְּרִית . . . וּמְשַׁלֵּם לְשֹׂנְאָיו — *Who keeps the covenant . . . and repays them who hate Him.* The reason (that we find) רָשָׁע וְטוֹב לוֹ, *a wicked man who prospers* (*Berachos*

NOTES

8. כִּי מֵאַהֲבַת ה׳ אֶתְכֶם — *But out of HASHEM's love for you*. When the Almighty brought Israel forth from Egypt with a mighty hand, they were not worthy on their own to be delivered. It was only because God had sworn to the Patriarchs and he was obligated to keep His oath, as this verse explicitly states. Hence, the *Sforno* interprets this phrase as also referring to the seed of the Patriarchs, especially Abraham, who is called זֶרַע אַבְרָהָם אֹהֲבִי, *The offspring of Abraham who loved Me* (*Isaiah* 41:8). Indeed, the phraseology used by the *Sforno* here is based on the verse in *Isaiah*.

9. הָאֵל הַנֶּאֱמָן — *The faithful God*. The word נֶאֱמָן, *faithful*, also means "something that is sure and secure," as we find in *Isaiah* 22:23, בְּמָקוֹם נֶאֱמָן, *in*

that are on the face of the earth. [7] *Not because you are more numerous than all the peoples did* HASHEM *desire you and choose you, for you are the fewest of all the peoples.* [8] *Rather, because of* HASHEM'*s love for you and because He observes the oath that He swore to your forefathers did He take you out with a strong hand and redeem you from the house of slavery, from the hand of Pharaoh, king of Egypt.* [9] *You must know that* HASHEM, *your God — He is the God, the faithful God, Who safeguards the covenant and the kindness for those who love Him and for those who observe His commandments, for a thousand generations.* [10] *And He repays His enemies in his lifetime to make him perish; He shall not delay for His enemy — in his lifetime He shall repay him.* [11] *You shall observe the commandment, and the decrees and the ordinances that I command you today, to perform them.*

7a), is twofold. One part is due to the merit of (his) fathers, as we find by Ishmael, כִּי זַרְעֲךָ הוּא, *because he is your seed* (*Genesis* 21:13), and the second is due to some merit that the wicked person himself possesses, which is insufficient for him to merit everlasting life but is enough for him to be compensated in this world, for "the Holy One, Blessed is He, does not withhold the reward of any creature" (*Pesachim* 118a).

11. וְשָׁמַרְתָּ . . . הַיּוֹם לַעֲשׂוֹתָם — *And you shall keep . . . this day to do them.* And let it not trouble you if you do not receive reward for them in This World.

NOTES

a sure place. The *Sforno* interprets it similarly here.

10. וּמְשַׁלֵּם לְשֹׂנְאָיו — *And repays them who hate Him.* Ishmael is blessed by God to become a nation because he is the son of Abraham. Thus, the wicked may at times prosper in the merit of righteous fathers.

11. הַיּוֹם לַעֲשׂוֹתָם — *This day to do them.* Compare to *Rashi* who comments, "And tomorrow, in the World to Come, to receive reward for them," based on *Eruvin* 22b.

פרשת עקב

יב וְהָיָ֣ה | עֵ֣קֶב תִּשְׁמְע֗וּן אֵ֤ת הַמִּשְׁפָּטִים֙ הָאֵ֔לֶּה וּשְׁמַרְתֶּ֥ם וַעֲשִׂיתֶ֖ם אֹתָ֑ם וְשָׁמַר֩ יהוָ֨ה אֱלֹהֶ֜יךָ לְךָ֗ אֶֽת־הַבְּרִית֙ וְאֶת־הַחֶ֔סֶד אֲשֶׁ֥ר נִשְׁבַּ֖ע לַאֲבֹתֶֽיךָ:

יג וַאֲהֵ֣בְךָ֔ וּבֵֽרַכְךָ֖ וְהִרְבֶּ֑ךָ וּבֵרַ֣ךְ פְּרִֽי־בִטְנְךָ֣ וּפְרִֽי־אַדְמָתֶ֗ךָ דְּגָֽנְךָ֤ וְתִירֽשְׁךָ֙ וְיִצְהָרֶ֔ךָ שְׁגַר־אֲלָפֶ֖יךָ וְעַשְׁתְּרֹ֣ת צֹאנֶ֑ךָ עַ֚ל הָֽאֲדָמָ֔ה אֲשֶׁר־נִשְׁבַּ֥ע

יד לַֽאֲבֹתֶ֖יךָ לָ֥תֶת לָֽךְ: בָּר֥וּךְ תִּֽהְיֶ֖ה מִכָּל־הָֽעַמִּ֑ים לֹא־יִֽהְיֶ֥ה בְךָ֛ עָקָ֥ר וַֽעֲקָרָ֖ה

טו וּבִבְהֶמְתֶּֽךָ: וְהֵסִ֧יר יהוָ֛ה מִמְּךָ֖ כָּל־חֹ֑לִי וְכָל־מַדְוֵי֩ מִצְרַ֨יִם הָֽרָעִים֙ אֲשֶׁ֣ר

טז יָדַ֔עְתָּ לֹ֥א יְשִׂימָ֖ם בָּ֑ךְ וּנְתָנָ֖ם בְּכָל־שֽׂנְאֶֽיךָ: וְאָֽכַלְתָּ֣ אֶת־כָּל־הָֽעַמִּ֗ים אֲשֶׁ֨ר יהוָ֤ה אֱלֹהֶ֨יךָ֙ נֹתֵ֣ן לָ֔ךְ לֹֽא־תָח֥וֹס עֵֽינְךָ֖ עֲלֵיהֶ֑ם וְלֹ֤א

12. וְהָיָ֣ה עֵ֣קֶב תִּשְׁמְע֗וּן — *And it shall come to pass because you hearken.* Behold, the King (i.e., the Almighty) has commanded all this in order that you may merit His keeping of the covenant, and His kindness. Thus, (if) you keep this day (i.e., in this world) His *mitzvos* and observe them out of love and not on the condition of receiving reward immediately, He, in turn, will keep the covenant and show His kindness to you.

אֵ֤ת הַמִּשְׁפָּטִים֙ — *These ordinances ...* because בְּמִשְׁפָּט יַעֲמִיד אָֽרֶץ, *(The king) by justice establishes the land* (based on *Proverbs* 29:4).

וּשְׁמַרְתֶּם — *And you will keep.* This refers to Mishnah.

וַעֲשִׂיתֶ֖ם אֹתָ֑ם — *And you will do them.* And in this manner you will do them correctly.

וְשָׁמַר֩ ה' אֱלֹהֶ֜יךָ לְךָ֗ אֶֽת הַבְּרִית֙ — *and* HASHEM *your God shall keep the covenant with you ...* which He swore when He said, וַהֲקִמֹתִי אֶת בְּרִיתִי בֵּינִי וּבֵינֶךָ וּבֵין זַרְעֲךָ אַחֲרֶיךָ לְדֹרֹתָם לִבְרִית, עוֹלָם לִהְיוֹת לְךָ לֵאלֹהִים וּלְזַרְעֲךָ אַחֲרֶיךָ, *And I will establish My covenant between Myself and you and your seed after you, throughout their generations for an everlasting covenant to be a God unto you and to your seed after you* (*Genesis* 17:7). Because He is a God unto us without any intermediary, hence everlasting existence flows from God to Israel, emanating from Him directly without any intermediary as it says, כִּי כָּל אֲשֶׁר יַעֲשֶׂה הָאֱלֹהִים, הוּא יִהְיֶה לְעוֹלָם, *Whatever God does shall be forever* (*Ecclesiastes* 3:14), whereas the existence of the perishable, without a doubt, emanates from Him through intermediaries.

וְאֶת הַחֶסֶד — *And the lovingkindness.* As it says, וְנָתַתִּי לְךָ וּלְזַרְעֲךָ אַחֲרֶיךָ אֵת אֶרֶץ מְגֻרֶיךָ, *And I will give you and your seed after you the land of your sojournings* (*Genesis* 17:8); because, indeed, the good granted to the righteous in This World is a result of (God's)

NOTES

12. וְהָיָ֣ה עֵ֣קֶב תִּשְׁמְע֗וּן ... וּשְׁמַרְתֶּם ... וְשָׁמַר֩ ה' אֱלֹהֶיךָ — *And it shall come to pass because you hearken ... and you will keep ... and* HASHEM *your God shall keep ...* This verse must be understood as a continuation of verses 9 and 11 at the conclusion of *parashas Vaeschanan.* In verse 9, the Torah tells us that the Almighty will faithfully keep the covenant He entered into with Israel, and will also bestow His lovingkindness upon them, providing they keep their part of the covenant by observing His commandments. In verse 11, another concept is introduced with the phrase הַיּוֹם לַעֲשׂוֹתָם, *to do them this day*, and *Rashi* comments, "But tomorrow, in the World to Come, you will be rewarded."

The *Sforno* explains that this opening verse of *Eikev* is to be understood as God's reason for keeping the covenant, resulting from Israel's willingness to observe the commandments even though they will not receive reward in This World but in the World to Come. The *Sforno* explains that this postponed reward is due to the fact that the Almighty's covenant with Israel was originally entered into with Abraham, and continues with his offspring in such a manner that our very existence flows *directly* from the Eternal. As such, we are an eternal people, and therefore our just reward which is everlasting must be given in a world which is also everlasting. On the other hand, those whose existence is temporal and perishable (נִפְסָד), coming through intermediary forces, are properly rewarded in this transitory world.

The final point made by the *Sforno* is that since a covenant imposes responsibilities which are binding on both parties, it cannot correctly be

PARASHAS EIKEV

12 *This shall be the reward when you hearken to these ordinances, and you observe and perform them; HASHEM, your God, will safeguard for you the covenant and the kindness that He swore to your forefathers.* 13 *He will love you, bless you and multiply you, and He will bless the fruit of your womb and the fruit of your Land; your grain, your wine, and your oil; the offspring of your cattle and the flocks of your sheep and goats; on the Land that He swore to your forefathers to give you.* 14 *You will be the most blessed of all the peoples; there will be no infertile male or infertile female among you nor among your animals.* 15 *HASHEM will remove from you every illness; and all the bad maladies of Egypt that you knew — He will not put them upon you, but will put them upon all your foes.* 16 *You will devour all the peoples that HASHEM, your God, will deliver to you; your eye shall not pity them; you*

---

lovingkindness, and not compensation for their deeds.

13. וְאֲהֵבְךָ — *And He will love you* ... being that you are (His) "children" (created) in His form and image, as our Sages say, חֲבִיבִין יִשְׂרָאֵל שֶׁנִּקְרְאוּ בָנִים לַמָּקוֹם, *Beloved is Israel for they are called children of God* (*Avos* 3:14), and thus the everlasting (nature of the) covenant shall be a felicitous (complete) one.

וּבֵרַכְךָ — *And bless you* ... with material wealth for transitory life (This World) and thus He shall (insure) the (condition of) goodness and grace which (He promised) when He swore that you would (dwell) in the Land in a blessed (lit. happy) manner.

15. כָּל חֹלִי — *All sickness* ... even ordinary ailments which afflict (people) through the (heavenly) bodies (lit. order).

הָרָעִים — *The evil (diseases)* ... contagious (ailments).

אֲשֶׁר יָדַעְתָּ — *Which you know* ... With which (the Egyptians) were smitten at the sea, as explained above (*Exodus* 14:31).

לֹא יְשִׂימָם בָּךְ וּנְתָנָם בְּכָל שֹׂנְאֶיךָ — *Will not put them upon you, but will visit them upon all that hate you.* Although He will visit them upon your enemies, they will not infect you, similar to, יִפֹּל מִצִּדְּךָ אֶלֶף ... אֵלֶיךָ לֹא יִגָּשׁ, *A thousand shall fall at your side ... but it shall not come near you* (*Psalms* 91:7).

16. לֹא תָחוֹס עֵינְךָ עֲלֵיהֶם וְלֹא תַעֲבֹד אֶת אֱלֹהֵיהֶם — *Your eye shall not pity them so that you not serve their gods.* If *your eye will not pity them* then *you will not serve their gods,* but if you pity them, then, without a doubt, they will mislead you (into sin).

NOTES

termed a *chesed,* an act of mercy or lovingkindness, when one party compensates the other! Why then does the verse speak of God's *chesed* in addition to His covenant? The *Sforno* answers this question by explaining that *chesed* refers to the good granted to us in This World, bestowed by God in His kindness, since the ultimate reward for our good deeds which we have earned will only be given to us in the World to Come.

13. וְאֲהֵבְךָ וּבֵרַכְךָ — *And He will love you and bless you.* God's manifestation of love for us is a reciprocal act evoked by our love for Him. As mentioned in the previous note, these verses are linked to verse 9 where the Torah speaks of those who love Him. Hence this represents an example of מִדָּה כְּנֶגֶד מִדָּה, *measure for measure.* In addition to this love that God, our Heavenly Father, has for us, He will also bless us with material well-being in the Land of Israel. The phrase וּבֵרַכְךָ, *and bless you,* is similar to the opening phrase of the priestly blessing יְבָרֶכְךָ, *May (HASHEM) bless you,* which is interpreted to mean בְּמָמוֹן, *with wealth* (see *Rashi* and the *Sforno* on *Bamidbar* 6:24).

15. כָּל חֹלִי ... הָרָעִים — *All sickness ... the evil (diseases).* God promised that He would not permit even common illness to be visited upon Israel, nor would the diseases visited upon the Egyptians at the sea infect them, in spite of their being contagious, for Israel would be immune to them.

יז תַעֲבֹד אֶת־אֱלֹהֵיהֶם כִּי־מוֹקֵשׁ הוּא לָךְ׃ כִּי תֹאמַר בִּלְבָבְךָ
יח רַבִּים הַגּוֹיִם הָאֵלֶּה מִמֶּנִּי אֵיכָה אוּכַל לְהוֹרִישָׁם׃ לֹא תִירָא מֵהֶם זָכֹר
יט תִּזְכֹּר אֵת אֲשֶׁר־עָשָׂה יהוה אֱלֹהֶיךָ לְפַרְעֹה וּלְכָל־מִצְרָיִם׃ הַמַּסֹּת
הַגְּדֹלֹת אֲשֶׁר־רָאוּ עֵינֶיךָ וְהָאֹתֹת וְהַמֹּפְתִים וְהַיָּד הַחֲזָקָה וְהַזְּרֹעַ הַנְּטוּיָה
אֲשֶׁר הוֹצִאֲךָ יהוה אֱלֹהֶיךָ כֵּן־יַעֲשֶׂה יהוה אֱלֹהֶיךָ לְכָל־הָעַמִּים אֲשֶׁר־
כ אַתָּה יָרֵא מִפְּנֵיהֶם׃ וְגַם אֶת־הַצִּרְעָה יְשַׁלַּח יהוה אֱלֹהֶיךָ בָּם עַד־אֲבֹד
כא הַנִּשְׁאָרִים וְהַנִּסְתָּרִים מִפָּנֶיךָ׃ לֹא תַעֲרֹץ מִפְּנֵיהֶם כִּי־יהוה אֱלֹהֶיךָ
כב בְּקִרְבֶּךָ אֵל גָּדוֹל וְנוֹרָא׃ וְנָשַׁל יהוה אֱלֹהֶיךָ אֶת־הַגּוֹיִם הָאֵל מִפָּנֶיךָ מְעַט
כג מְעָט לֹא תוּכַל כַּלֹּתָם מַהֵר פֶּן־תִּרְבֶּה עָלֶיךָ חַיַּת הַשָּׂדֶה׃ וּנְתָנָם יהוה
כד אֱלֹהֶיךָ לְפָנֶיךָ וְהָמָם מְהוּמָה גְדֹלָה עַד הִשָּׁמְדָם׃ וְנָתַן מַלְכֵיהֶם בְּיָדֶךָ
וְהַאֲבַדְתָּ אֶת־שְׁמָם מִתַּחַת הַשָּׁמָיִם לֹא־יִתְיַצֵּב אִישׁ בְּפָנֶיךָ עַד הִשְׁמִדְךָ
כה אֹתָם׃ פְּסִילֵי אֱלֹהֵיהֶם תִּשְׂרְפוּן בָּאֵשׁ לֹא־תַחְמֹד כֶּסֶף וְזָהָב עֲלֵיהֶם
כו וְלָקַחְתָּ לָךְ פֶּן תִּוָּקֵשׁ בּוֹ כִּי תוֹעֲבַת יהוה אֱלֹהֶיךָ הוּא׃ וְלֹא־תָבִיא
תוֹעֵבָה אֶל־בֵּיתֶךָ וְהָיִיתָ חֵרֶם כָּמֹהוּ שַׁקֵּץ ׀ תְּשַׁקְּצֶנּוּ וְתַעֵב ׀ תְּתַעֲבֶנּוּ
כִּי־חֵרֶם הוּא׃
ח א כָּל־הַמִּצְוָה אֲשֶׁר אָנֹכִי מְצַוְּךָ הַיּוֹם תִּשְׁמְרוּן לַעֲשׂוֹת לְמַעַן תִּחְיוּן וּרְבִיתֶם

כִּי מוֹקֵשׁ הוּא לָךְ — *Because it will be a snare unto you.* Because if you do pity them they will be a snare unto you, for they will entice you to worship their gods.

17-18. כִּי תֹאמַר ... אֵיכָה אוּכַל לְהוֹרִישָׁם. לֹא תִירָא מֵהֶם — *If you say ... "How can I dispossess them?" Be not afraid of them.* When you say, "How can I dispossess them since they are more numerous than I am," do not say so because you fear them, but because you recognize that this would, indeed, be impossible were it not for God's help, and this is the meaning of *you shall well remember what God your God did to Pharaoh and all Egypt,* who were more numerous and far more mighty than you.

24. וְנָתַן מַלְכֵיהֶם בְּיָדֶךָ וְהַאֲבַדְתָּ אֶת שְׁמָם — *And He shall deliver their kings into your hand, and you shall destroy their name.* Because if one permits the seed of the royal enemy to survive, they will be adversaries for all time, as was the case with Hadad who was a young lad of the seed of the Edomite king and rose up as an adversary against Solomon (see *King* 1, 11:14).

25. פֶּן תִּוָּקֵשׁ בּוֹ — *Lest you be ensnared therein.* Because, at times, it may happen that you will prosper with the silver and gold which were taken from them and you will attribute (this success) to the power of that idol, whence (this silver and gold) was taken.

NOTES

17-18. כִּי תֹאמַר ... אֵיכָה אוּכַל לְהוֹרִישָׁם. לֹא תִירָא מֵהֶם — *If you say ... "How can I dispossess them?" Be not afraid of them.* When one asks, "How can I dispossess them?" there can be two reasons for posing such a question. One is because you fear them, and that would be improper, for it implies a lack of faith in God. The other reason is because you recognize that you cannot hope to dispossess them without God's help. This is proper and commendable, for it demonstrates a recognition of one's inadequacy coupled with trust and faith in the Almighty. The meaning, therefore, of these two verses is to be understood as follows: Let not your doubts and apprehensions be due to your fear of the enemy, rather let it be an acknowledgment that without the help of God, the task is impossible. When you come to this realization, there will, indeed, be no reason for you to fear them.

24. וְהַאֲבַדְתָּ אֶת שְׁמָם — *And you shall destroy their name.* The *Sforno* cites the story of Hadad the Edomite, who escaped when David and Joab smote the Edomites, as an example of the threat

shall not worship their gods, for it is a snare for you.
[17] *Perhaps you will say in your heart, "These nations are more numerous than I; how will I be able to drive them out?"*
[18] *Do not fear them! You shall remember what HASHEM, your God, did to*
Pharaoh and to all of Egypt. [19] *The great tests that your eyes saw, and the*
signs, the wonders, the strong hand, and the outstretched arm with which HASHEM, your God, took you out — so shall HASHEM, your God, do to all the peoples before whom you fear. [20] *Also the hornet-swarm will HASHEM, your*
God, send among them, until the survivors and hidden ones perish before
you. [21] *You shall not be broken before them, for HASHEM, your God, is among you, a great and awesome God.*
[22] *HASHEM, your God, will thrust these nations from before you little by little; you will not be able to annihilate them quickly, lest the beasts of the*
field increase against you. [23] *HASHEM, your God, will deliver them before you,*
and will confound them with great confusion, until their destruction. [24] *He*
will deliver their kings into your hand and you shall cause their name to perish from under the heaven; no man will stand up against you until you
have destroyed them. [25] *The carved images of their gods you shall burn in the fire; you shall not covet and take for yourself the silver and gold that is on them, lest you be ensnared by it, for it is an abomination of HASHEM, your*
God. [26] *And you shall not bring an abomination into your home and become banned like it; you shall surely loathe it and you shall surely abominate it, for it is banned.*

8 [1] *The entire commandment that I command you today you shall observe to perform, so that you may live and increase, and come and possess*

---

26. תְּתַעֲבֶנּוּ כִּי חֵרֶם הוּא — *You shall abhor it, for it is a banned thing.* You shall abhor the silver and gold of abomination, כִּי חֵרֶם הוּא, *for it is a banned (accursed) thing,* and not only will it not bring you success but it will destroy the rest of your possessions.

VIII

1. כָּל הַמִּצְוָה אֲשֶׁר אָנֹכִי מְצַוְּךָ הַיּוֹם תִּשְׁמְרוּן לַעֲשׂוֹת — *All the commandment which I command you this day shall you observe to do.* Behold, the purpose of all who worship strange gods (idols) is to attain temporary success which is threefold — length of days, children and money. Now, by observing the commandments you shall attain all of these, therefore take care to do them ...

לְמַעַן תִּחְיוּן — *That you may live.* Because the intent of God, the Blessed One, when He

NOTES

posed by a royal survivor. Ultimately, Hadad returned to his land and became a dangerous adversary of Solomon and Israel.

25. פֶּן תִּוָּקֵשׁ בּוֹ — *Lest you be ensnared therein.* The *Sforno's* commentary reflects the powerful attraction idolatry held for people in ancient times. Although these graven images were powerless to prevent their being taken by the Israelites, nonetheless when the gold and silver would bring prosperity to the Israelites there was concern that they might believe it was due to the magical power of these idols!

26. כִּי חֵרֶם הוּא — *For it is a banned thing.* These graven images are not only an abomination but they also bring with them a curse. The gold and silver would not only fail to bring prosperity, but would lead to the destruction of Israel's other possessions.

VIII

1. כָּל הַמִּצְוָה — *All the commandment.* Our Sages teach us that longevity, children and wealth depend not on *z'chus*, merit, but rather on *mazal*,

ב וּבָאתֶם וִירִשְׁתֶּם אֶת־הָאָרֶץ אֲשֶׁר־נִשְׁבַּע יהוה לַאֲבֹתֵיכֶם: וְזָכַרְתָּ אֶת־
כָּל־הַדֶּרֶךְ אֲשֶׁר הוֹלִיכְךָ יהוה אֱלֹהֶיךָ זֶה אַרְבָּעִים שָׁנָה בַּמִּדְבָּר לְמַעַן
ג עַנֹּתְךָ לְנַסֹּתְךָ לָדַעַת אֶת־אֲשֶׁר בִּלְבָבְךָ הֲתִשְׁמֹר מִצְוֺתָו אִם־לֹא: וַיְעַנְּךָ
וַיַּרְעִבֶךָ וַיַּאֲכִלְךָ אֶת־הַמָּן אֲשֶׁר לֹא־יָדַעְתָּ וְלֹא יָדְעוּן אֲבֹתֶיךָ לְמַעַן
הוֹדִיעֲךָ כִּי לֹא עַל־הַלֶּחֶם לְבַדּוֹ יִחְיֶה הָאָדָם כִּי עַל־כָּל־מוֹצָא פִי־יהוה
ד יִחְיֶה הָאָדָם: שִׂמְלָתְךָ לֹא בָלְתָה מֵעָלֶיךָ וְרַגְלְךָ לֹא בָצֵקָה זֶה אַרְבָּעִים
ה שָׁנָה: וְיָדַעְתָּ עִם־לְבָבֶךָ כִּי כַּאֲשֶׁר יְיַסֵּר אִישׁ אֶת־בְּנוֹ יהוה אֱלֹהֶיךָ
ו מְיַסְּרֶךָּ: וְשָׁמַרְתָּ אֶת־מִצְוֺת יהוה אֱלֹהֶיךָ לָלֶכֶת בִּדְרָכָיו וּלְיִרְאָה אֹתוֹ:
ז כִּי יהוה אֱלֹהֶיךָ מְבִיאֲךָ אֶל־אֶרֶץ טוֹבָה אֶרֶץ נַחֲלֵי מָיִם עֲיָנֹת וּתְהֹמֹת
ח יֹצְאִים בַּבִּקְעָה וּבָהָר: אֶרֶץ חִטָּה וּשְׂעֹרָה וְגֶפֶן וּתְאֵנָה וְרִמּוֹן אֶרֶץ־זֵית
ט שֶׁמֶן וּדְבָשׁ: אֶרֶץ אֲשֶׁר לֹא בְמִסְכֵּנֻת תֹּאכַל־בָּהּ לֶחֶם לֹא־תֶחְסַר כֹּל
י בָּהּ אֶרֶץ אֲשֶׁר אֲבָנֶיהָ בַרְזֶל וּמֵהֲרָרֶיהָ תַּחְצֹב נְחֹשֶׁת: וְאָכַלְתָּ וְשָׂבָעְתָּ

---

commanded you to fulfill His commandments was that you might attain longevity, albeit in this transitory world.

וּרְבִיתֶם — *And multiply* ... (and) that you shall have many children.

וּבָאתֶם וִירִשְׁתֶּם — *And come and possess* ... and that you shall attain riches and honor through (inheritance) of the land.

2. וְזָכַרְתָּ אֶת כָּל הַדֶּרֶךְ — *And you shall remember the whole way* ... when He provided you with bread to eat and clothes to wear in a miraculous manner.

לְנַסֹּתְךָ — *To test you* ... (to see) if you will do His will (even) when you are able to attain bread and clothing without pain (i.e., without effort).

לָדַעַת אֶת אֲשֶׁר בִּלְבָבְךָ — *To know what was in your heart* ... in order that what is in your heart (the potential) shall be (translated) into the actual, so that every angel may know that your elevated status, superior to that of the ministering angels, is justified. (You, in turn), will come to (recognize) His knowledge, which functions for the good (of man) as is fitting for that which is found in actuality.

5. מְיַסְּרֶךָּ — *Instructs you.* Through His commandments, He grants you instruction befitting (the purpose of reaching) the perfection which is intended by Him.

7. אֶל אֶרֶץ טוֹבָה — *Into a good land* ... (a land) in which all kinds of excellence and goodness is concentrated, such as cannot be found in any other (geographical) area. (The verses) relate five kinds of (superior) goodness, and regarding each one of them, the word

NOTES

destiny (*Moed Katan* 28a). The *Sforno*, nonetheless, interprets this verse as meaning that as a consequence of observing *mitzvos*, God will grant these three blessings of life, progeny and wealth. This assurance is meant to wean Israel away from idolatry, being that in those days the worship of gods was considered to be the only way to insure this threefold blessing.

2. לְנַסֹּתְךָ — *To test you*. The intent of God was to give you the test of easily attained physical needs, to see whether this would affect your faith. The *Sforno* interprets the phrase *and that He might test you* (v. 16) similarly.

לָדַעַת אֶת אֲשֶׁר בִּלְבָבְךָ — *To know what was in your heart*. The Almighty knows what is in man's heart. An angel does not. The verse here speaks of man's potential (i.e., what is in his heart), which is unknown both to him and to angels as well. When life's demands bring forth the potential into the actual, man's ability and superiority to the angels is revealed — both to the angels and to man himself. This is the sense of the phrase, *to know what was in your heart*. Man's superiority to the angels is also discussed in the *Sforno*'s explanation of עַתָּה יָדַעְתִּי, *for now I know* (*Genesis* 22:12).

When the Torah speaks of God's "knowledge,"

the Land that HASHEM swore to your forefathers. [2] *You shall remember the entire road on which HASHEM, your God, led you these forty years in the Wilderness so as to afflict you, to test you, to know what is in your heart, whether you would observe His commandments or not.* [3] *He afflicted you and let you hunger, then He fed you the manna that you did not know, nor did your forefathers know, in order to make you know that not by bread alone does man live, rather by everything that emanates from the mouth of God does man live.* [4] *Your garment did not wear out upon you and your feet did not swell, these forty years.* [5] *You should know in your heart that just as a father will chastise his son, so HASHEM, your God, chastises you.* [6] *You shall observe the commandments of HASHEM, your God, to go in his ways and fear him.* [7] *For HASHEM, your God, is bringing you to a good Land: a Land with streams of water, of springs and underground water coming forth in valley and mountain;* [8] *a Land of wheat, barley, grape, fig, and pomegranate; a Land of oil-olives and date-honey;* [9] *a Land where you will eat bread without poverty — you will lack nothing there; a Land whose stones are iron and from whose mountains you will mine copper.* [10] *You will eat and you will be satisfied,*

אֶרֶץ, *land*, is used: The first is אֶרֶץ נַחֲלֵי מָיִם עֲיָנֹת וּתְהֹמֹת, *a land of brooks of water, of fountains and depths,* not muddy (lit., bad) pools and canals, i.e., the opposite of וְהַמַּיִם רָעִים וְהָאָרֶץ מְשַׁכָּלֶת, *The water is bad and the ground causes untimely births* (*II Kings* 2:19). The second is . . .

8. אֶרֶץ חִטָּה וּשְׂעֹרָה — *A land of wheat and barley* . . . which are necessary for sustenance. The third is אֶרֶץ זֵית שֶׁמֶן וּדְבָשׁ, *a land of olive trees and honey*, which are royal delicacies. The fourth is . . .

9. אֶרֶץ אֲשֶׁר לֹא בְמִסְכֵּנֻת תֹּאכַל בָּהּ לֶחֶם — *A land wherein you shall not eat bread parsimoniously*. They will find that the price of bread is cheap there, as it says, וַתִּמָּלֵא אַרְצוֹ כֶּסֶף וְזָהָב וְאֵין קֵצֶה לְאֹצְרֹתָיו, *His land is full of silver and gold, neither is there any end of His treasures* (*Isaiah* 2:7), because a scarcity of money is more difficult (to accept) than a scarcity of produce, as (our Sages) state, "This is the case (that we wait to sound the alarm) when money is plentiful and food is scarce but if money is scarce and food is plentiful then the alarm is sounded at once" (*Taanis* 19b). The fifth is אֶרֶץ אֲשֶׁר אֲבָנֶיהָ בַרְזֶל, *a land whose stones are iron*, for in it are found plentiful hard and bright stones, suitable and good for building (purposes).

תַּחְצֹב נְחֹשֶׁת — *You may dig copper*. Brass; good metal which is bright, and fit for building and (also) for vessels.

NOTES

it means His will and creative power. In *Genesis* 1:4, where the Torah uses the expression, *And HASHEM saw that the light was good*, the *Sforno* explains that when God perceives that something is good for the world and its inhabitants, He brings it into existence through His יְדִיעָה, *knowledge*, which is פּוֹעֶלֶת, i.e., "the efficient cause." The meaning, therefore, of the expression *to know what was in your heart*, according to *Sforno* is a twofold one. First, that the angels shall recognize your superiority over them, and secondly, that you shall recognize the power of God's knowledge that can alone translate the potential into reality.

5. מְיַסְּרֶךָּ — *Instructs you*. Although the word יָסַר can mean *to inflict pain* and *to chasten*, the *Sforno* interprets it to mean *instruction*, akin to מוּסַר אָבִיךָ, *the instruction of your father* (*Proverbs* 1:8); compare to 4:36.

7-9. אֶל אֶרֶץ טוֹבָה . . . אֶרֶץ חִטָּה וּשְׂעֹרָה . . . אֶרֶץ אֲשֶׁר לֹא בְמִסְכֵּנֻת תֹּאכַל בָּהּ לֶחֶם . . . — *Into a good land . . . A land of wheat and barley . . . A land wherein you shall not eat bread parsimoniously . . .* The first mention of אֶרֶץ, *land*, is an introductory one. The Torah tells us that *Eretz Yisrael* is a good land, of superior quality. The repetition of the word אֶרֶץ is meant to underscore the various aspects of

שני יא וּבֵרַכְתָּ אֶת־יהוה אֱלֹהֶיךָ עַל־הָאָרֶץ הַטֹּבָה אֲשֶׁר נָתַן־לָךְ: הִשָּׁמֶר לְךָ
פֶּן־תִּשְׁכַּח אֶת־יהוה אֱלֹהֶיךָ לְבִלְתִּי שְׁמֹר מִצְוֹתָיו וּמִשְׁפָּטָיו וְחֻקֹּתָיו
יב אֲשֶׁר אָנֹכִי מְצַוְּךָ הַיּוֹם: פֶּן־תֹּאכַל וְשָׂבָעְתָּ וּבָתִּים טֹבִים תִּבְנֶה וְיָשָׁבְתָּ:
יג-יד וּבְקָרְךָ וְצֹאנְךָ יִרְבְּיֻן וְכֶסֶף וְזָהָב יִרְבֶּה־לָּךְ וְכֹל אֲשֶׁר־לְךָ יִרְבֶּה: וְרָם
לְבָבֶךָ וְשָׁכַחְתָּ אֶת־יהוה אֱלֹהֶיךָ הַמּוֹצִיאֲךָ מֵאֶרֶץ מִצְרַיִם מִבֵּית עֲבָדִים:
טו הַמּוֹלִיכְךָ בַּמִּדְבָּר | הַגָּדֹל וְהַנּוֹרָא נָחָשׁ | שָׂרָף וְעַקְרָב וְצִמָּאוֹן אֲשֶׁר אֵין־
*ב׳ טעמים טז מָיִם הַמּוֹצִיא לְךָ מַיִם מִצּוּר הַחַלָּמִישׁ: *הַמַּאֲכִלְךָ מָן בַּמִּדְבָּר אֲשֶׁר לֹא־
יָדְעוּן אֲבֹתֶיךָ לְמַעַן עַנֹּתְךָ וּלְמַעַן נַסֹּתֶךָ לְהֵיטִבְךָ בְּאַחֲרִיתֶךָ: וְאָמַרְתָּ
יז-יח בִּלְבָבֶךָ כֹּחִי וְעֹצֶם יָדִי עָשָׂה לִי אֶת־הַחַיִל הַזֶּה: וְזָכַרְתָּ אֶת־יהוה אֱלֹהֶיךָ
כִּי הוּא הַנֹּתֵן לְךָ כֹּחַ לַעֲשׂוֹת חָיִל לְמַעַן הָקִים אֶת־בְּרִיתוֹ אֲשֶׁר־נִשְׁבַּע
לַאֲבֹתֶיךָ כַּיּוֹם הַזֶּה:
יט וְהָיָה אִם־שָׁכֹחַ תִּשְׁכַּח אֶת־יהוה אֱלֹהֶיךָ וְהָלַכְתָּ אַחֲרֵי אֱלֹהִים אֲחֵרִים
כ וַעֲבַדְתָּם וְהִשְׁתַּחֲוִיתָ לָהֶם הַעִדֹתִי בָכֶם הַיּוֹם כִּי אָבֹד תֹּאבֵדוּן: כַּגּוֹיִם
אֲשֶׁר יהוה מַאֲבִיד מִפְּנֵיכֶם כֵּן תֹּאבֵדוּן עֵקֶב לֹא תִשְׁמְעוּן בְּקוֹל
יהוה אֱלֹהֵיכֶם:
ט א שְׁמַע יִשְׂרָאֵל אַתָּה עֹבֵר הַיּוֹם אֶת־הַיַּרְדֵּן לָבֹא לָרֶשֶׁת גּוֹיִם גְּדֹלִים
ב וַעֲצֻמִים מִמֶּךָּ עָרִים גְּדֹלֹת וּבְצֻרֹת בַּשָּׁמָיִם: עַם־גָּדוֹל וָרָם בְּנֵי עֲנָקִים
ג אֲשֶׁר אַתָּה יָדַעְתָּ וְאַתָּה שָׁמַעְתָּ מִי יִתְיַצֵּב לִפְנֵי בְּנֵי עֲנָק: וְיָדַעְתָּ
הַיּוֹם כִּי יהוה אֱלֹהֶיךָ הוּא הָעֹבֵר לְפָנֶיךָ אֵשׁ אֹכְלָה הוּא יַשְׁמִידֵם
וְהוּא יַכְנִיעֵם לְפָנֶיךָ וְהוֹרַשְׁתָּם וְהַאֲבַדְתָּם מַהֵר כַּאֲשֶׁר דִּבֶּר יהוה לָךְ:

---

10. וּבֵרַכְתָּ אֶת ה׳ אֱלֹהֶיךָ — *And bless* HASHEM *your God* ... that you may remember that all this comes from Him.

15. מִצּוּר הַחַלָּמִישׁ — *Out of the rock of flint* ... which was transformed into water, as it says, הַהֹפְכִי הַצּוּר אֲגַם מָיִם חַלָּמִישׁ לְמַעְיְנוֹ מָיִם, *Who turned the rock into a pool of water, the flint into a fountain of waters* (*Psalms* 114:8).

16. לְמַעַן עַנֹּתְךָ — *That He might afflict you* ... that you shall fulfill (God's will) in a state of affliction with the worry of "one who has no loaf in his basket."

וּלְמַעַן נַסֹּתֶךָ — *And that He might test you* ... whether you would do His will when He grants you sustenance without pain (without effort).

לְהֵיטִבְךָ — *To do good for you* ... more so than (what he does for) the ministering angels, as befits one who is tested by Him.

NOTES

excellence which define this superiority — its water, produce, delicacies, plentiful bread and materials for building.

15. מִצּוּר הַחַלָּמִישׁ — *Out of the rock of flint*. The *Sforno* stresses that the water did not come forth *from* the rock, but the rock became *transformed* into water, which is a far-greater miracle.

16. לְמַעַן עַנֹּתְךָ וּלְמַעַן נַסֹּתֶךָ — *That He might afflict you and that He might test you*. There are two kinds of tests given to man — one is נִסָּיוֹן מֵעֹשֶׁר, *the test of riches*, while the second is נִסָּיוֹן מֵעֹנִי, *the test of poverty*. Will man do God's will when he is prosperous and will he obey Him when he is impoverished? Israel was put to both tests in the wilderness when they were given the manna from heaven each day. On the one hand, their sustenance was given without suffering, while on the other hand, since it could not be stored, each day they were in a state of uncertainty as to whether they would have food the next day. Now, since angels are never put to such tests, it follows that

and bless HASHEM, your God, for the good Land that He gave you.
11 *Take care lest you forget HASHEM, your God, by not observing His*
commandments, His ordinances, and His decrees, which I command you
today, 12 *lest you eat and be satisfied, and you build good houses and settle,*
13 *and your cattle and sheep and goats increase, and you increase silver and*
gold for yourselves, and everything that you have will increase — 14 *and*
your heart will become haughty and you will forget HASHEM, your God, Who
took you out of the land of Egypt from the house of slavery, 15 *Who leads you*
through the great and awesome Wilderness — of snake, fiery serpent, and
scorpion, and thirst where there was no water — who brings forth water for
you from the rock of flint, 16 *Who feeds you manna in the Wilderness, which*
your forefathers knew not, in order to afflict you and in order to test you, to
do good for you in your end. 17 *And you may say in your heart, "My strength*
and the might of my hand made me all this wealth!" 18 *Then you shall*
remember HASHEM, your God: that it was He Who gave you strength to
make wealth, in order to establish His covenant that He swore to your
forefathers, as this day.
19 *It shall be that if you forget HASHEM, your God, and go after the gods*
of others, and worship them and prostrate yourself to them — I testify
against you today that you will surely perish, 20 *like the nations that*
HASHEM causes to perish before you, so will you perish because you will not
have hearkened to the voice of HASHEM, your God.

9 1 *Hear, O Israel, today you cross the Jordan, to come and drive out*
nations that are greater and mightier than you, cities that are great
and fortified up to the heavens, 2 *a great and lofty people, children of giants,*
that you knew and of whom you have heard, "Who can stand up against the
children of the giant?" 3 *But you know today that HASHEM, your God — He*
crosses before you, a consuming fire; He will destroy them and He will
subjugate them before you; you will drive them out and cause them to perish
quickly, as HASHEM spoke to you.

---

19. וְהָיָה אִם שָׁכֹחַ תִּשְׁכַּח — *And it shall be if you forget* ... and this will occur when you attribute your success to your own might and fail to bless Him for it.

כִּי אָבֹד תֹּאבֵדוּן — *That you will surely perish* ... from two worlds.

20. עֵקֶב לֹא תִשְׁמְעוּן — *Because you will not hearken* ... and all this shall come to pass when you do not bless (God) as commanded above (v. 10).

NOTES

Israel deserves to be the recipient of God's *good* mentioned here.

19. כִּי אָבֹד תֹּאבֵדוּן — *That you will surely perish*. At the beginning of this *sedrah* (7:12), the *Sforno* explains that God's promise to keep the covenant assures Israel's prosperity in This World, and their inheritance of the World to Come. Conversely, if we fail to keep His commandments the loss will be a twofold one. Hence, the double expression אָבֹד תֹּאבֵדוּן (lit., *you will be lost — be lost*) is most fitting.

20. עֵקֶב לֹא תִשְׁמְעוּן — *Because you will not hearken*. This phrase links the beginning of this *parashah* (עֵקֶב תִּשְׁמְעוּן) with the conclusion of the chapter (עֵקֶב לֹא תִשְׁמְעוּן). *If you hearken*, the reward will be twofold and if *you fail to hearken*, your loss will be twofold, as explained above. Now the reason for your refusal to listen to God will be due to your failure to recognize God's Providence and the erroneous assumption that your prosperity is due to your own strength and talent (v. 19).

שלישי ד אַל־תֹּאמַר בִּלְבָבְךָ בַּהֲדֹף יהוה אֱלֹהֶיךָ אֹתָם ׀ מִלְּפָנֶיךָ לֵאמֹר בְּצִדְקָתִי
הֱבִיאַנִי יהוה לָרֶשֶׁת אֶת־הָאָרֶץ הַזֹּאת וּבְרִשְׁעַת הַגּוֹיִם הָאֵלֶּה יהוה
ה מוֹרִישָׁם מִפָּנֶיךָ: לֹא בְצִדְקָתְךָ וּבְיֹשֶׁר לְבָבְךָ אַתָּה בָא לָרֶשֶׁת
אֶת־אַרְצָם כִּי בְּרִשְׁעַת ׀ הַגּוֹיִם הָאֵלֶּה יהוה אֱלֹהֶיךָ מוֹרִישָׁם מִפָּנֶיךָ
וּלְמַעַן הָקִים אֶת־הַדָּבָר אֲשֶׁר נִשְׁבַּע יהוה לַאֲבֹתֶיךָ לְאַבְרָהָם לְיִצְחָק
ו וּלְיַעֲקֹב: וְיָדַעְתָּ כִּי לֹא בְצִדְקָתְךָ יהוה אֱלֹהֶיךָ נֹתֵן לְךָ אֶת־הָאָרֶץ
ז הַטּוֹבָה הַזֹּאת לְרִשְׁתָּהּ כִּי עַם־קְשֵׁה־עֹרֶף אָתָּה: זְכֹר אַל־תִּשְׁכַּח אֵת
אֲשֶׁר־הִקְצַפְתָּ אֶת־יהוה אֱלֹהֶיךָ בַּמִּדְבָּר לְמִן־הַיּוֹם אֲשֶׁר־יָצָאתָ ׀ מֵאֶרֶץ
ח מִצְרַיִם עַד־בֹּאֲכֶם עַד־הַמָּקוֹם הַזֶּה מַמְרִים הֱיִיתֶם עִם־יהוה: וּבְחֹרֵב
ט הִקְצַפְתֶּם אֶת־יהוה וַיִּתְאַנַּף יהוה בָּכֶם לְהַשְׁמִיד אֶתְכֶם: בַּעֲלֹתִי הָהָרָה
לָקַחַת לוּחֹת הָאֲבָנִים לוּחֹת הַבְּרִית אֲשֶׁר־כָּרַת יהוה עִמָּכֶם וָאֵשֵׁב
בָּהָר אַרְבָּעִים יוֹם וְאַרְבָּעִים לַיְלָה לֶחֶם לֹא אָכַלְתִּי וּמַיִם לֹא שָׁתִיתִי:

IX

4. אַל תֹּאמַר בִּלְבָבְךָ בַּהֲדֹף — *Do not say in your heart when HASHEM thrusts out.* When you will see that you are able to conquer them in an unnatural fashion (lit. "not according to the custom of the world"), and thereby you will recognize that it is due to Divine intervention, do not think mistakenly that *because of my righteousness God brought me in to possess this land,* so that I might possess the Land quickly, and because of my merit He thrust them out quickly.

וּבְרִשְׁעַת הַגּוֹיִם הָאֵלֶּה ה׳ מוֹרִישָׁם מִפָּנֶיךָ — *Because of the wickedness of these nations did HASHEM drive them out before you.* Behold, the reason He battles against them is because of their wickedness, and not in order that you inherit (the Land) quickly.

5. לֹא בְצִדְקָתְךָ וּבְיֹשֶׁר לְבָבְךָ אַתָּה בָא לָרֶשֶׁת — *Not because of your righteousness do you go in to possess.* Because, indeed, your inheriting the Land is not due to your merit, for you are not worthy that God battle on your behalf so that you might inherit quickly.

כִּי בְּרִשְׁעַת הַגּוֹיִם הָאֵלֶּה ה׳ אֱלֹהֶיךָ מוֹרִישָׁם מִפָּנֶיךָ — *But because of the wickedness of these nations, HASHEM your God drives them out before you.* He wanted His revenge to be taken from them through you — that you should destroy them for their iniquities, as it says, וַיֹּאמֶר הַשְׁמֵד, *and said: Destroy* (33:27), as opposed to וּבְיַד אָדָם אַל אֶפֹּלָה, *and let me not fall into the hand of man* (*II Samuel*, 24:14).

וּלְמַעַן הָקִים — *And that He may fulfill.* So that by fulfilling His command, you will merit to inherit, akin to כְּכֹל אֲשֶׁר בִּלְבָבִי עָשִׂיתָ לְבֵית אַחְאָב בְּנֵי רְבִעִים יֵשְׁבוּ לְךָ עַל כִּסֵּא יִשְׂרָאֵל, *And*

NOTES

IX

4. אַל תֹּאמַר ... וּבְרִשְׁעַת הַגּוֹיִם — *Do not say ... because of the wickedness of these nations.* There are two reasons the Almighty intervenes in the affairs of people. One is because a nation merits His involvement and aid, while another is because the wickedness of their adversary demands Divine retribution. Moses tells Israel that their conquest of *Eretz Yisrael* is due to the latter reason.

5. לֹא בְצִדְקָתְךָ ... כִּי בְּרִשְׁעַת ... וּלְמַעַן הָקִים — *Not because of your righteousness ... but because of the wickedness ... and that He may fulfill.* Although this verse seems repetitious, the *Sforno* explains the significance of this statement as follows: As stated above, the Israelites were not worthy that God should battle on their behalf, nonetheless He desired to fulfill the promise made to the Patriarchs regarding the inheritance of the Land by their children. He therefore is willing to use them as His instrument to punish the inhabitants of Canaan, and by doing so they will fulfill His will and merit His aid and intervention. The *Sforno* proves this thesis from the story of Yahu who

4 *Do not say in your heart, when* HASHEM *pushes them away from before you, saying, "Because of my righteousness did* HASHEM *bring me to possess this Land and because of the wickedness of these nations did* HASHEM *drive them away from before you."* 5 *Not because of your righteousness and the uprightness of your heart are you coming to possess their Land, but because of the wickedness of these nations does* HASHEM, *your God, drive them away from before you, and in order to establish the word that* HASHEM *swore to your forefathers, to Abraham, to Isaac, and to Jacob.* 6 *And you should know that not because of your righteousness does* HASHEM, *your God, give you this good Land to possess it, for you are a stiff-necked people.*

7 *Remember, do not forget, that you provoked* HASHEM, *your God, in the Wilderness; from the day you left the land of Egypt until your arrival at this place, you have been rebels against* HASHEM. 8 *And in Horeb you provoked* HASHEM, *and* HASHEM *became angry with you to destroy you.* 9 *Then I ascended the mountain to receive the Tablets of stone, the Tablets of the covenant that* HASHEM *sealed with you, and I remained on the mountain for forty days and forty nights; bread I did not eat, and water I did not drink.*

---

you have done to the house of Ahab according to all that was in my heart, your children of the fourth generation shall sit on the throne of Israel (*II Kings* 10:30). And all this He did to fulfill that which He swore to the Patriarchs.

6. כִּי עַם קְשֵׁה עֹרֶף אָתָּה — *For you are a stiff necked people.* It is impossible to have righteousness and an upright heart if one is stiff necked, for he who is stiff necked follows the stubbornness of his heart and mind, and even though a righteous teacher may demonstrate (lit. "tell") with clear proof that his thoughts are improper and will lead to loss, (he still refuses to listen). This is (due to the fact) that he does not turn (his attention) to the teacher — as though his neck were hard, akin to an iron sinew, in such a manner that he cannot turn (his neck) in any direction — but follows the stubbornness of his heart as before.

7. זְכֹר אַל תִּשְׁכַּח — *Remember, forget not* ... because your constant backsliding which angered (God), similar to *a dog who returns to his vomit* (based on *Proverbs* 26:11), testifies to your being a stiff-necked people. (And this you did) although each time you (suffered) the chastisement of God your God and saw His greatness!

8. וּבְחֹרֵב הִקְצַפְתֶּם — *And in Horeb you angered.* And the proof of the evil nature of your stiffneckedness was that when you angered God at Horeb, His decision to destroy you was only because you were a stiff-necked people, as the Blessed One said, *I have seen this people, and behold, it is a stiff-necked people; leave Me alone that I may destroy them* (9:13,14). And the reason is because (when one) is stiff necked, it removes all hope of repentance.

NOTES

destroyed the house of Ahab, which fulfilled the intent of the Almighty, and thereby Yahu merited to reign over Israel for four generations.

6. עַם קְשֵׁה עֹרֶף אָתָּה — *You are a stiff-necked people.* A stubborn person is convinced that his way is correct and proper, and rivets his attention upon a course from which he refuses to deviate. Were he flexible in his opinions, he would be willing to consider different viewpoints and other options. One who is stiff necked, however, cannot turn left or right — he is inflexible. This is the sense of the *Sforno's* explanation of the simile used in this verse, as well as in *Exodus* 32:9, and verse 13 in this chapter.

7-8. זְכֹר אַל תִּשְׁכַּח . . . וּבְחֹרֵב הִקְצַפְתֶּם — *Remember, forget not* ... *And in Horeb you angered.* The *Sforno* explains these verses as proof of Israel's stiffneckedness. The verse quoted from *Proverbs* is a colorful one which illustrates the foolish tendency of man to backslide and repeat his sins over and over again even though they are malodorous.

י וַיִּתֵּן יהוה אֵלַי אֶת־שְׁנֵי לוּחֹת הָאֲבָנִים כְּתֻבִים בְּאֶצְבַּע אֱלֹהִים וַעֲלֵיהֶם
יא כְּכָל־הַדְּבָרִים אֲשֶׁר דִּבֶּר יהוה עִמָּכֶם בָּהָר מִתּוֹךְ הָאֵשׁ בְּיוֹם הַקָּהָל: וַיְהִי
מִקֵּץ אַרְבָּעִים יוֹם וְאַרְבָּעִים לָיְלָה נָתַן יהוה אֵלַי אֶת־שְׁנֵי לֻחֹת הָאֲבָנִים
יב לֻחוֹת הַבְּרִית: וַיֹּאמֶר יהוה אֵלַי קוּם רֵד מַהֵר מִזֶּה כִּי שִׁחֵת עַמְּךָ אֲשֶׁר
הוֹצֵאתָ מִמִּצְרָיִם סָרוּ מַהֵר מִן־הַדֶּרֶךְ אֲשֶׁר צִוִּיתִם עָשׂוּ לָהֶם מַסֵּכָה:
יג וַיֹּאמֶר יהוה אֵלַי לֵאמֹר רָאִיתִי אֶת־הָעָם הַזֶּה וְהִנֵּה עַם־קְשֵׁה־עֹרֶף הוּא:
יד הֶרֶף מִמֶּנִּי וְאַשְׁמִידֵם וְאֶמְחֶה אֶת־שְׁמָם מִתַּחַת הַשָּׁמָיִם וְאֶעֱשֶׂה אוֹתְךָ
טו לְגוֹי־עָצוּם וָרָב מִמֶּנּוּ: וָאֵפֶן וָאֵרֵד מִן־הָהָר וְהָהָר בֹּעֵר בָּאֵשׁ וּשְׁנֵי לוּחֹת
טז הַבְּרִית עַל שְׁתֵּי יָדָי: וָאֵרֶא וְהִנֵּה חֲטָאתֶם לַיהוה אֱלֹהֵיכֶם עֲשִׂיתֶם לָכֶם
יז עֵגֶל מַסֵּכָה סַרְתֶּם מַהֵר מִן־הַדֶּרֶךְ אֲשֶׁר־צִוָּה יהוה אֶתְכֶם: וָאֶתְפֹּשׂ בִּשְׁנֵי
יח הַלֻּחֹת וָאַשְׁלִכֵם מֵעַל שְׁתֵּי יָדָי וָאֲשַׁבְּרֵם לְעֵינֵיכֶם: וָאֶתְנַפַּל לִפְנֵי יהוה
כָּרִאשֹׁנָה אַרְבָּעִים יוֹם וְאַרְבָּעִים לַיְלָה לֶחֶם לֹא אָכַלְתִּי וּמַיִם לֹא
שָׁתִיתִי עַל כָּל־חַטַּאתְכֶם אֲשֶׁר חֲטָאתֶם לַעֲשׂוֹת הָרַע בְּעֵינֵי יהוה
יט לְהַכְעִיסוֹ: כִּי יָגֹרְתִּי מִפְּנֵי הָאַף וְהַחֵמָה אֲשֶׁר קָצַף יהוה עֲלֵיכֶם לְהַשְׁמִיד
כ אֶתְכֶם וַיִּשְׁמַע יהוה אֵלַי גַּם בַּפַּעַם הַהִוא: וּבְאַהֲרֹן הִתְאַנַּף יהוה מְאֹד
כא לְהַשְׁמִידוֹ וָאֶתְפַּלֵּל גַּם־בְּעַד אַהֲרֹן בָּעֵת הַהִוא: וְאֶת־חַטַּאתְכֶם אֲשֶׁר־
עֲשִׂיתֶם אֶת־הָעֵגֶל לָקַחְתִּי וָאֶשְׂרֹף אֹתוֹ | בָּאֵשׁ וָאֶכֹּת אֹתוֹ טָחוֹן הֵיטֵב
עַד אֲשֶׁר־דַּק לְעָפָר וָאַשְׁלִךְ אֶת־עֲפָרוֹ אֶל־הַנַּחַל הַיֹּרֵד מִן־הָהָר:
כב־כג וּבְתַבְעֵרָה וּבְמַסָּה וּבְקִבְרֹת הַתַּאֲוָה מַקְצִפִים הֱיִיתֶם אֶת־יהוה: וּבִשְׁלֹחַ
יהוה אֶתְכֶם מִקָּדֵשׁ בַּרְנֵעַ לֵאמֹר עֲלוּ וּרְשׁוּ אֶת־הָאָרֶץ אֲשֶׁר נָתַתִּי
לָכֶם וַתַּמְרוּ אֶת־פִּי יהוה אֱלֹהֵיכֶם וְלֹא הֶאֱמַנְתֶּם לוֹ וְלֹא שְׁמַעְתֶּם
כד־כה בְּקֹלוֹ: מַמְרִים הֱיִיתֶם עִם־יהוה מִיּוֹם דַּעְתִּי אֶתְכֶם: וָאֶתְנַפַּל לִפְנֵי
יהוה אֵת אַרְבָּעִים הַיּוֹם וְאֶת־אַרְבָּעִים הַלַּיְלָה אֲשֶׁר הִתְנַפָּלְתִּי כִּי־
כו אָמַר יהוה לְהַשְׁמִיד אֶתְכֶם: וָאֶתְפַּלֵּל אֶל־יהוה וָאֹמַר אֲדֹנָי יֱהֹוִה אַל־
תַּשְׁחֵת עַמְּךָ וְנַחֲלָתְךָ אֲשֶׁר פָּדִיתָ בְּגָדְלֶךָ אֲשֶׁר־הוֹצֵאתָ מִמִּצְרַיִם
כז בְּיָד חֲזָקָה: זְכֹר לַעֲבָדֶיךָ לְאַבְרָהָם לְיִצְחָק וּלְיַעֲקֹב אַל־תֵּפֶן אֶל־קְשִׁי

---

15. וְהָהָר בֹּעֵר בָּאֵשׁ — *And the mount burned with fire* . . . and you sinned while *the King was reclining at His table* (based on *Shir Hashirim* 1:12).

22. וּבְתַבְעֵרָה וּבְמַסָּה — *And at Taberah and at Massah.* Although you saw that by angering God, the Blessed One, the tablets of law were shattered, and I had to pray and

NOTES

15. וְהָהָר בֹּעֵר בָּאֵשׁ — *And the mount burned with fire*. The *Sforno* explains why Moses found it necessary to tell them that the mount "was burning." He wished to emphasize that while the mount was still on fire, meaning that the majestic experience of מַתַּן תּוֹרָה, *the giving of the Torah*, was so fresh, they sinned with the Golden Calf. The expression used by the *Sforno*, בְּעוֹד שֶׁהַמֶּלֶךְ בִּמְסִבּוֹ, *while the King was reclining at His table*, is based on *Shir Hashirim* 1:12. That verse refers to God's presence at Sinai. The Talmud (*Shabbos* 88b) states, "shameless is the bride that is unfaithful within her bridal canopy." Our Sages were commenting on Israel's sin of the Golden Calf, which they committed when they were so fresh from their acceptance of the Torah, which was considered as Israel's betrothal to the Almighty.

22. וּבְתַבְעֵרָה וּבְמַסָּה וּבְקִבְרֹת הַתַּאֲוָה — *And at Taberah and at Massah and at Kibros Hataavah*. Taberah refers to the מִתְאֹנְנִים, *the murmurers*,

10 And HASHEM gave me the two stone Tablets, inscribed with the finger of
HASHEM, and on them were all the words that HASHEM spoke with you on the
mountain from the midst of the fire, on the day of the congregation.
11 It was at the end of forty days and forty nights that HASHEM gave me
the two stone Tablets, the Tablets of the covenant. 12 Then HASHEM said to
me, "Arise, descend quickly from here, for the people that you took out of
Egypt has become corrupt; they have strayed quickly from the way that I
commanded them; they have made themselves a molten image."
13 HASHEM said to me, saying, "I have seen this people, and behold! it is a
stiff-necked people. 14 Release Me, and I shall destroy them and erase their
name from under the heavens, and I shall make you a mightier, more
numerous nation than they!" 15 So I turned and descended from the mountain
as the mountain was burning in fire, and the two Tablets of the covenant were
in my two hands.
16 Then I saw and behold! you had sinned to HASHEM, your God; you made
yourselves a molten calf; you strayed quickly from the way that HASHEM
commanded you. 17 I grasped the two Tablets and threw them from my two
hands, and I smashed them before your eyes. 18 Then I threw myself down
before HASHEM as the first time — forty days and forty nights — bread I did
not eat and water I did not drink, because of your entire sin that you commit-
ted, to do that which is evil in the eyes of HASHEM, to anger Him, 19 for I was
terrified of the wrath and blazing anger with which HASHEM had been pro-
voked against you to destroy you; and HASHEM hearkened to me that time,
as well. 20 HASHEM became very angry with Aaron to destroy him, so I prayed
also for Aaron at that time. 21 Your sin that you committed — the calf — I took
and burned it in fire, and I pounded it, grinding it well, until it was fine as
dust, and I threw its dust into the brook that descended from the mountain.
22 And in Taberah, in Massah, and in Kibroth-hattaavah you were pro-
voking HASHEM, 23 and when HASHEM sent you from Kadesh-barnea, saying,
"Go up and possess the Land that I gave you" — then you rebelled against
the word of HASHEM, your God; you did not believe Him and you did not
hearken to His voice. 24 You have been rebels against HASHEM from the day
that I knew you!
25 I threw myself down before HASHEM for the forty days and the forty
nights that I threw myself down, for HASHEM had intended to destroy you.
26 I prayed to HASHEM and said, "My Lord, HASHEM/ELOHIM, do not destroy
Your people and Your heritage that You redeemed in Your greatness, that
You took out of Egypt with a strong hand. 27 Remember for the sake of Your
servants, for Abraham, for Isaac, and for Jacob; do not turn to the stubborn-

---

fast forty days on your behalf, (still) you continued to anger (Him) at Taberah and at Massah when you cried in His hearing to test (Him).

וּבְקִבְרֹת הַתַּאֲוָה — *And at Kibros Hataavah* ... when you asked for meat.

NOTES

recorded in *Bamidbar* 11:1; Massah to the people's complaint regarding the lack of water (*Exodus* 17:7), and Kibros Hataavah to their request for meat (*Bamidbar* 11:34).

כח הָעָם הַזֶּה וְאֶל־רִשְׁעוֹ וְאֶל־חַטָּאתוֹ: פֶּן־יֹאמְרוּ הָאָרֶץ אֲשֶׁר הוֹצֵאתָנוּ
מִשָּׁם מִבְּלִי יְכֹלֶת יהוה לַהֲבִיאָם אֶל־הָאָרֶץ אֲשֶׁר־דִּבֶּר לָהֶם וּמִשִּׂנְאָתוֹ
כט אוֹתָם הוֹצִיאָם לַהֲמִתָם בַּמִּדְבָּר: וְהֵם עַמְּךָ וְנַחֲלָתֶךָ אֲשֶׁר הוֹצֵאתָ בְּכֹחֲךָ
הַגָּדֹל וּבִזְרֹעֲךָ הַנְּטוּיָה:
י רביעי א בָּעֵת הַהִוא אָמַר יהוה אֵלַי פְּסָל־לְךָ שְׁנֵי־לוּחֹת אֲבָנִים כָּרִאשֹׁנִים וַעֲלֵה
ב אֵלַי הָהָרָה וְעָשִׂיתָ לְּךָ אֲרוֹן עֵץ: וְאֶכְתֹּב עַל־הַלֻּחֹת אֶת־הַדְּבָרִים אֲשֶׁר
ג הָיוּ עַל־הַלֻּחֹת הָרִאשֹׁנִים אֲשֶׁר שִׁבַּרְתָּ וְשַׂמְתָּם בָּאָרוֹן: וָאַעַשׂ אֲרוֹן עֲצֵי
שִׁטִּים וָאֶפְסֹל שְׁנֵי־לֻחֹת אֲבָנִים כָּרִאשֹׁנִים וָאַעַל הָהָרָה וּשְׁנֵי הַלֻּחֹת
ד בְּיָדִי: וַיִּכְתֹּב עַל־הַלֻּחֹת כַּמִּכְתָּב הָרִאשׁוֹן אֵת עֲשֶׂרֶת הַדְּבָרִים אֲשֶׁר
ה דִּבֶּר יהוה אֲלֵיכֶם בָּהָר מִתּוֹךְ הָאֵשׁ בְּיוֹם הַקָּהָל וַיִּתְּנֵם יהוה אֵלָי: וָאֵפֶן
וָאֵרֵד מִן־הָהָר וָאָשִׂם אֶת־הַלֻּחֹת בָּאָרוֹן אֲשֶׁר עָשִׂיתִי וַיִּהְיוּ שָׁם כַּאֲשֶׁר
ו צִוַּנִי יהוה: וּבְנֵי יִשְׂרָאֵל נָסְעוּ מִבְּאֵרֹת בְּנֵי־יַעֲקָן מוֹסֵרָה שָׁם מֵת אַהֲרֹן
ז וַיִּקָּבֵר שָׁם וַיְכַהֵן אֶלְעָזָר בְּנוֹ תַּחְתָּיו: מִשָּׁם נָסְעוּ הַגֻּדְגֹּדָה וּמִן־הַגֻּדְגֹּדָה
ח יָטְבָתָה אֶרֶץ נַחֲלֵי מָיִם: בָּעֵת הַהִוא הִבְדִּיל יהוה אֶת־שֵׁבֶט הַלֵּוִי
לָשֵׂאת אֶת־אֲרוֹן בְּרִית־יהוה לַעֲמֹד לִפְנֵי יהוה לְשָׁרְתוֹ וּלְבָרֵךְ בִּשְׁמוֹ
ט עַד הַיּוֹם הַזֶּה: עַל־כֵּן לֹא־הָיָה לְלֵוִי חֵלֶק וְנַחֲלָה עִם־אֶחָיו יהוה הוּא
י נַחֲלָתוֹ כַּאֲשֶׁר דִּבֶּר יהוה אֱלֹהֶיךָ לוֹ: וְאָנֹכִי עָמַדְתִּי בָהָר כַּיָּמִים
הָרִאשֹׁנִים אַרְבָּעִים יוֹם וְאַרְבָּעִים לָיְלָה וַיִּשְׁמַע יהוה אֵלַי גַּם בַּפַּעַם
יא הַהִוא לֹא־אָבָה יהוה הַשְׁחִיתֶךָ: וַיֹּאמֶר יהוה אֵלַי קוּם לֵךְ לְמַסַּע לִפְנֵי

X

1. בָּעֵת הַהִוא אָמַר ה׳ אֵלַי פְּסָל לְךָ — *At that time HASHEM said to me, "Hew out."* Behold, that with all my prayers, the forgiveness (lit., repair) was incomplete, because in place of the (first) tablets which were the work of God, He (now) told me, *Hew out yourself etc.*

6. וּבְנֵי יִשְׂרָאֵל נָסְעוּ — *And the Children of Israel journeyed.* Although they saw that the prayers of a righteous person (succeeds) in protecting his generation, and that it was (therefore) fitting to lament his passing (,nonetheless the following occurred). Some or most of those who were tending their flocks in the wilderness journeyed to Mossarah, to seek out water and grazing land for their sheep, and while there Aaron died and was buried, and his son Elazar succeeded him. Yet, they did not return to grieve his death, nor to mourn at his burial, nor were they concerned to honor Elazar who became the *Kohen* in his stead, but . . .

7. מִשָּׁם נָסְעוּ הַגֻּדְגֹּדָה — *From there, they journeyed to Gudgod* . . . to tend their sheep.

NOTES

X

1. פְּסָל לְךָ — *"Hew out."* The *Ramban* states that this verse is a continuation of the admonition recorded in the previous chapter. The *Sforno* interprets this verse in the same vein, pointing out that whereas the first tablets were מַעֲשֵׂה אֱלֹהִים, *the work of God (Exodus 2:16)*, these second tablets were the work of man. This indicates that the original קְדוּשָׁה, *holiness*, was not recaptured.

6-7. וּבְנֵי יִשְׂרָאֵל נָסְעוּ . . . מִשָּׁם נָסְעוּ הַגֻּדְגֹּדָה . . . אֶרֶץ נַחֲלֵי מָיִם — *And the Children of Israel journeyed . . . From there, they journeyed to Gudgod . . . a land of brooks of water*. Moses continues to admonish Israel for the insensitivity demonstrated by many when Aaron died and Elazar succeeded him. They were less concerned over Aaron's death than in hurrying on to places with a good supply of water, nor did they feel the need to pay honor to Elazar, the new *Kohen Gadol*.

8. בָּעֵת הַהִוא הִבְדִּיל ה׳ — *At that time, HASHEM separated*. The reason Moses inserts the selection of the Levites for the Divine Service at this point

ness of this people, and to its wickedness and to its sin, [28] lest the land from which You took them out will say, 'For lack of HASHEM's ability to bring them to the Land of which He spoke to them, and because of His hatred of them did He take them out to let them die in the Wilderness.' [29] Yet they are Your people and Your heritage, whom You took out with Your great strength and Your outstretched arm."

10 *[1] At that time HASHEM said to me, "Carve for yourself two stone Tablets like the first ones, and ascend to Me to the mountain, and make a wooden Ark for yourself. [2] And I shall inscribe on the Tablets the words that were on the first Tablets that you smashed, and you shall place them in the Ark."*

[3] So I made an Ark of cedarwood and I carved out two stone Tablets like the first ones; then I ascended the mountain with the two Tablets in my hand. [4] He inscribed on the Tablets according to the first script, the Ten Statements that HASHEM spoke to you on the mountain from the midst of the fire, on the day of the congregation, and HASHEM gave them to me. [5] I turned and descended from the mountain, and I placed the Tablets in the Ark that I had made, and they remained there as HASHEM had commanded.

[6] The Children of Israel journeyed from Beeroth-bene-jaakan to Moserah; there Aaron died and he was buried there, and Elazar his son ministered in his place. [7] From there they journeyed to Gudgod, and from Gudgod to Jotbah, a land of brooks of water. [8] At that time, HASHEM set apart the tribe of Levi to carry the Ark of the covenant of HASHEM, to stand before HASHEM to minister to Him and to bless in His Name until this day. [9] Therefore, Levi did not have a share and a heritage with his brethren; HASHEM is his heritage, as HASHEM, your God, had spoken of him.

[10] I remained on the mountain as on the first days — forty days and forty nights — and HASHEM listened to me this time, as well, and HASHEM did not wish to destroy you. [11] HASHEM said to me, "Arise, go on the journey before

וּמִן הַגֻּדְגֹּדָה יָטְבָתָה אֶרֶץ נַחֲלֵי מָיִם — *And from Gudgod to Jotbah, a land of brooks of water.* All the places mentioned here were areas which had abundant brooks to water the sheep, and they did not even consider the loss (lit., harm) suffered by the death of the righteous man (i.e., Aaron), nor (concern themselves) with his honor nor the honor (due) his son.

8. בָּעֵת הַהִוא הִבְדִּיל ה׳ — *At that time, HASHEM separated.* Now since God, the Blessed One, already separated one tribe for the sacred service, and you (the people at large) were not considered worthy (enough) to occupy yourselves with (this service), and in spite of this (punishment), I could only attain through my prayers the (willingness of God) not to destroy you. He then said to me . . .

11. קוּם לֵךְ לְמַסַּע — *Arise, go and cause (them) to journey*, (לְמַסַּע should be interpreted as) לְמַסִּיעַ, *causing others to journey*, similar to וּלְמַסַּע אֶת הַמַּחֲנוֹת, *and for causing the camps to set forward* (Numbers 10:2).

NOTES

was to remind the people that, as a consequence of the sin of the Golden Calf, Israel as a people was no longer considered worthy to serve God through this service as had been God's original intent. Indeed, their transgression was so great that, at best, Moses was only able to prevail upon God not to destroy them (v. 10), but was unable to restore them to the exalted level they had attained at Sinai when they accepted the Torah.

11. קוּם לֵךְ לְמַסַּע . . . אֶת הָאָרֶץ אֲשֶׁר נִשְׁבַּעְתִּי — *Arise, go and cause (them) to journey . . . the land which I swore.* Continuing the theme of the previous

הָעָם וְיָבֹאוּ וְיִירְשׁוּ אֶת־הָאָרֶץ אֲשֶׁר־נִשְׁבַּעְתִּי לַאֲבֹתָם לָתֵת לָהֶם׃
חמישי יב וְעַתָּה יִשְׂרָאֵל מָה יהוה אֱלֹהֶיךָ שֹׁאֵל מֵעִמָּךְ כִּי אִם־לְיִרְאָה אֶת־יהוה
אֱלֹהֶיךָ לָלֶכֶת בְּכָל־דְּרָכָיו וּלְאַהֲבָה אֹתוֹ וְלַעֲבֹד אֶת־יהוה אֱלֹהֶיךָ
יג בְּכָל־לְבָבְךָ וּבְכָל־נַפְשֶׁךָ׃ לִשְׁמֹר אֶת־מִצְוֹת יהוה וְאֶת־חֻקֹּתָיו אֲשֶׁר
יד אָנֹכִי מְצַוְּךָ הַיּוֹם לְטוֹב לָךְ׃ הֵן לַיהוה אֱלֹהֶיךָ הַשָּׁמַיִם וּשְׁמֵי הַשָּׁמָיִם
טו הָאָרֶץ וְכָל־אֲשֶׁר־בָּהּ׃ רַק בַּאֲבֹתֶיךָ חָשַׁק יהוה לְאַהֲבָה אוֹתָם וַיִּבְחַר
טז בְּזַרְעָם אַחֲרֵיהֶם בָּכֶם מִכָּל־הָעַמִּים כַּיּוֹם הַזֶּה׃ וּמַלְתֶּם אֵת עָרְלַת
יז לְבַבְכֶם וְעָרְפְּכֶם לֹא תַקְשׁוּ עוֹד׃ כִּי יהוה אֱלֹהֵיכֶם הוּא אֱלֹהֵי
הָאֱלֹהִים וַאֲדֹנֵי הָאֲדֹנִים הָאֵל הַגָּדֹל הַגִּבֹּר וְהַנּוֹרָא אֲשֶׁר לֹא־יִשָּׂא פָנִים

וְיָבֹאוּ וְיִירְשׁוּ אֶת הָאָרֶץ אֲשֶׁר נִשְׁבַּעְתִּי — *That they may go in and possess the land which I swore ...* because were it not for the oath, you would not be worthy to (possess) it due to your frequent revolts.

12. וְעַתָּה יִשְׂרָאֵל — *And now, Israel.* Therefore, you Israel, attempt now to correct your crookedness henceforth and consider *what God your God requires of you,* for He does not ask anything for His own sake, כִּי אִם לְיִרְאָה, *but to fear* — and this (level) you shall reach when you reflect in such a manner that you will come to recognize His greatness.

וּלְאַהֲבָה אֹתוֹ — *And to love Him.* And this (love) you shall attain when you consider His Goodness. All this He asks לְטוֹב לָךְ, *for your good* (v. 13) — in order that you may merit eternal life.

14. הֵן לַה׳ אֱלֹהֶיךָ הַשָּׁמַיִם — *Behold, unto HASHEM your God belong the heavens.* And the proof that He seeks that which is *for your good* is because, indeed, heaven and earth are His, and even though they are exalted and non-perishable — (nonetheless) ...

15. רַק בַּאֲבֹתֶיךָ חָשַׁק ה׳ — *Only in your forefathers did HASHEM find pleasure.* And He altered (the laws of) nature of these exalted (creations) on your behalf in the merit of the Patriarchs which without a doubt was done to attain something of greater value than heaven and earth, namely the perfect man who is similar to his Creator, to the greatest extent possible, as it says: בְּצַלְמֵנוּ כִּדְמוּתֵנוּ, *in our image after our likeness* (*Genesis* 1:26).

NOTES

verses, Moses tells the people that the Almighty removed Himself from their midst and commanded him to *cause them to journey,* which represented a far lesser degree of הַשְׁגָּחַת ה׳, *Hashem's providence and concern.* Indeed, were it not for the oath He had taken to grant the Land to them as the descendants of the Patriarchs, He would not have allowed them to enter and conquer *Eretz Yisrael,* because of their frequent revolts.

12. וְעַתָּה יִשְׂרָאֵל — *And now, Israel ...* The expression וְעַתָּה, *and now,* links this verse to the previous ones (8-11). The *Sforno* interprets this verse in the following manner: Since you are guilty of many sins and frequent rebellion against God, it is imperative that you mend your ways and alter your attitude. This can only be accomplished by considering the greatness of God which will bring you to יִרְאָה — *awe and reverance* which deters sin — and by considering God's goodness and kindness which brings one to אַהֲבָה — *love of God.*

The next verse states, לְטוֹב לָךְ, *for your good.* Man's attainment of יִרְאַת ה׳, *reverence of God,* and אַהֲבַת ה׳, *love of God,* is for his own benefit, because through these two traits he will merit eternal life. Hence, this is לְטוֹב לָךְ, *for your good.* The *Sforno* explains in the next verse (14) that God's request that Israel revere and love Him is certainly not for His benefit, since He is the Master of heaven and earth. Hence, it can only be for Israel's benefit that they may merit everlasting life.

15. רַק בַּאֲבֹתֶיךָ חָשַׁק ה׳ — *Only in your forefathers did HASHEM find pleasure.* The fact that God disrupted the laws of nature and altered the nature of heaven and earth proves how great His love for the Patriarchs was, and this Divine willingness also indicates the greatness and exalted nature of the "perfect man" on whose behalf the suspension of the laws of nature took place. This can only be because

the people; let them come and possess the Land that I swore to their forefathers to give them."

[12] *Now, O Israel, what does HASHEM, your God, ask of you? Only to fear HASHEM, your God, to go in all His ways and to love Him, and to serve HASHEM, your God, with all your heart and with all your soul,* [13] *to observe the commandments of HASHEM and His decrees, which I command you today, for your benefit.* [14] *Behold! To HASHEM, your God, are the heaven and highest heaven, the earth and everything that is in it.* [15] *Only your forefathers did HASHEM cherish to love them, and He chose their offspring after them — you — from among all the peoples, as this day.* [16] *You shall cut away the barrier of your heart and no longer stiffen your neck.* [17] *For HASHEM, your God — He is the God of the powers and the Lord of the lords, the great, mighty, and awesome God, Who does not show favor and Who*

---

16. וּמַלְתֶּם אֵת עָרְלַת לְבַבְכֶם — *And circumcise therefore the foreskin of your heart.* Therefore, it is fitting that you remove the foreskin (covering) of your intelligence, by examining and eliminating the errors (of your thinking) which give birth to false ideas (philosophies).

וְעָרְפְּכֶם לֹא תַקְשׁוּ עוֹד — *And be no more stiff necked.* And when you remove the stiffness of your neck, which prevents you from turning to that which is proper, you will come to a recognition of your Creator, and realize that it is evil and bitter to forsake Him. And this (will come about) when you consider . . .

17. כִּי ה' אֱלֹהֵיכֶם הוּא אֱלֹהֵי הָאֱלֹהִים — *For HASHEM your God, He is God of gods* . . . the Eternal (One) over all the eternal ones who are separated from matter, because the eternal nature of all others stems from His eternity.

וַאֲדֹנֵי הָאֲדֹנִים — *And the Lord of lords* . . . the conductor of all (heavenly) conductors, these being the celestial spheres (גַּלְגַּלִּים) and their moving forces, whose actions are all intended to attain the end purpose of His intent, similar to individual labors that are directed toward the primary goal.

הָאֵל הַגָּדֹל — *The great God.* There is none in existence equal to His level of existence in *kind.*

הַגִּבֹּר — *The mighty* . . . Who grants (establishes and insures) existence, through His existence, to all that exist, as it says: וְאַתָּה מְחַיֶּה אֶת כֻּלָּם, *and You preserve them all* (*Nehemiah* 9:6).

וְהַנּוֹרָא — *And the* awesome (*God*). He oversees (all) to reward and to punish, in such a manner that it is fitting (for man) to fear His Presence.

אֲשֶׁר לֹא יִשָּׂא פָנִים — *Who favors no person* . . . (including) the unrestrained (wild) son for

NOTES

"perfect man" represents and reflects, at his best, the "image and likeness" of God and the angels.

16. וּמַלְתֶּם . . . וְעָרְפְּכֶם לֹא תַקְשׁוּ עוֹד — *And circumcise . . . and be no more stiff necked.* Moses argues that since man was created in the image of God, he is good inherently and also is straightforward in his thinking. Unfortunately, his physical appetites and weaknesses divert him from the proper path. It is therefore imperative for him to remove the barrier, symbolically called the "foreskin," which exists between him and God and to be flexible enough to consider his errors and return to the Almighty.

17. הוּא אֱלֹהֵי הָאֱלֹהִים — *He is God of gods.* The *Sforno* painstakingly defines every term used in this verse to describe God, explaining that each appellation is distinctive and not repetitious: He is the source of existence; the first and continuous cause; He is unique, omnipotent and omniscient, and He rewards and punishes, showing no favoritism. Man, in turn, is accountable and will reap what he sows through his actions. Nonetheless, sincere repentance will grant him salvation.

יח וְלֹא יִקַּח שֹׁחַד: עֹשֶׂה מִשְׁפַּט יָתוֹם וְאַלְמָנָה וְאֹהֵב גֵּר לָתֶת לוֹ לֶחֶם
יט־כ וְשִׂמְלָה: וַאֲהַבְתֶּם אֶת־הַגֵּר כִּי־גֵרִים הֱיִיתֶם בְּאֶרֶץ מִצְרָיִם: אֶת־יְהוָה
כא אֱלֹהֶיךָ תִּירָא אֹתוֹ תַעֲבֹד וּבוֹ תִדְבָּק וּבִשְׁמוֹ תִּשָּׁבֵעַ: הוּא תְהִלָּתְךָ וְהוּא
אֱלֹהֶיךָ אֲשֶׁר־עָשָׂה אִתְּךָ אֶת־הַגְּדֹלֹת וְאֶת־הַנּוֹרָאֹת הָאֵלֶּה אֲשֶׁר רָאוּ
כב עֵינֶיךָ: בְּשִׁבְעִים נֶפֶשׁ יָרְדוּ אֲבֹתֶיךָ מִצְרָיְמָה וְעַתָּה שָׂמְךָ יְהוָה אֱלֹהֶיךָ
יא א כְּכוֹכְבֵי הַשָּׁמַיִם לָרֹב: וְאָהַבְתָּ אֵת יְהוָה אֱלֹהֶיךָ וְשָׁמַרְתָּ מִשְׁמַרְתּוֹ
ב וְחֻקֹּתָיו וּמִשְׁפָּטָיו וּמִצְוֹתָיו כָּל־הַיָּמִים: וִידַעְתֶּם הַיּוֹם כִּי | לֹא אֶת־בְּנֵיכֶם
אֲשֶׁר לֹא־יָדְעוּ וַאֲשֶׁר לֹא־רָאוּ אֶת־מוּסַר יְהוָה אֱלֹהֵיכֶם אֶת־גָּדְלוֹ אֶת־
ג יָדוֹ הַחֲזָקָה וּזְרֹעוֹ הַנְּטוּיָה: וְאֶת־אֹתֹתָיו וְאֶת־מַעֲשָׂיו אֲשֶׁר עָשָׂה בְּתוֹךְ
ד מִצְרָיִם לְפַרְעֹה מֶלֶךְ־מִצְרַיִם וּלְכָל־אַרְצוֹ: וַאֲשֶׁר עָשָׂה לְחֵיל מִצְרַיִם
לְסוּסָיו וּלְרִכְבּוֹ אֲשֶׁר הֵצִיף אֶת־מֵי יַם־סוּף עַל־פְּנֵיהֶם בְּרָדְפָם אַחֲרֵיכֶם
ה וַיְאַבְּדֵם יְהוָה עַד הַיּוֹם הַזֶּה: וַאֲשֶׁר עָשָׂה לָכֶם בַּמִּדְבָּר עַד־בֹּאֲכֶם עַד־
ו הַמָּקוֹם הַזֶּה: וַאֲשֶׁר עָשָׂה לְדָתָן וְלַאֲבִירָם בְּנֵי אֱלִיאָב בֶּן־רְאוּבֵן אֲשֶׁר
פָּצְתָה הָאָרֶץ אֶת־פִּיהָ וַתִּבְלָעֵם וְאֶת־בָּתֵּיהֶם וְאֶת־אָהֳלֵיהֶם וְאֵת כָּל־
ז הַיְקוּם אֲשֶׁר בְּרַגְלֵיהֶם בְּקֶרֶב כָּל־יִשְׂרָאֵל: כִּי עֵינֵיכֶם הָרֹאֹת אֶת כָּל־
ח מַעֲשֵׂה יְהוָה הַגָּדֹל אֲשֶׁר עָשָׂה: וּשְׁמַרְתֶּם אֶת־כָּל־הַמִּצְוָה אֲשֶׁר אָנֹכִי
מְצַוְּךָ הַיּוֹם לְמַעַן תֶּחֶזְקוּ וּבָאתֶם וִירִשְׁתֶּם אֶת־הָאָרֶץ אֲשֶׁר אַתֶּם עֹבְרִים
ט שָׁמָּה לְרִשְׁתָּהּ: וּלְמַעַן תַּאֲרִיכוּ יָמִים עַל־הָאֲדָמָה אֲשֶׁר נִשְׁבַּע יְהוָה

---

the sake of his righteous father, even though He is slow to anger in the merit of the father.

וְלֹא יִקַּח שֹׁחַד — *And takes no bribe.* He will not reduce the punishment for a transgression because of the merit of a *mitzvah* which the sinner performed, as our Sages say, שֶׁאֵין מִצְוָה מְכַבָּה עֲבֵרָה, *A mitzvah shall not extinguish a transgression* (*Sotah* 21a). And all this teaches us that if we sin, we cannot rely on any merit to save us from punishment — except perfect repentance.

21. הוּא תְהִלָּתְךָ — *He is your glory.* It is praiseworthy that you be a servant of the One Who reigns over all existence.

XI

2. כִּי לֹא אֶת בְּנֵיכֶם — *For (I speak not) to your children.* Therefore, you who did see (the miracles and wonders) must make signs when you enter (the Land) which will bear witness for (future) generations.

וּזְרֹעוֹ הַנְּטוּיָה — *And His outstretched arm* . . . which is prepared to smite whoever returns to sin.

NOTES

21. הוּא תְהִלָּתְךָ — *He is your glory*. The *Sforno* explains that the verse does not refer to man's praise of God. Rather, it means that Israel is praiseworthy for having been granted the privilege to be the servants of God!

XI

2. כִּי לֹא אֶת בְּנֵיכֶם — *For (I speak not) to your children*. The *Sforno* explains the sequence of verses 2-8 thus: God speaks to this generation that witnessed the greatness of God, His signs and wonders, as well as the punishment of the Egyptians and of those who rebelled against Moses. Since they actually beheld this with their own eyes it is their responsibility to transmit this testimony to their children who did not experience it. This was to be done by writing the words of Torah on great stones when they passed over the Jordan, setting them up on Mt. Ebal as we read in chapter 27:2-4.

4. עַד הַיּוֹם הַזֶּה — *Unto this day*. The *Sforno* inter-

does not accept a bribe. [18] *He carries out the judgment of orphan and widow, and loves the proselyte to give him bread and garment.* [19] *You shall love the proselyte for you were strangers in the land of Egypt.* [20] *HASHEM, your God, shall you fear, Him shall you serve, to Him shall you cleave, and in His Name shall you swear.* [21] *He is your praise and He is your God, Who did for you these great and awesome things that your eyes saw.* [22] *With seventy souls did your ancestors descend to Egypt, and now HASHEM, your God, has made you like the stars of heaven for abundance.*

11

[1] *You shall love HASHEM, your God, and you shall safeguard His charge, His decrees, His ordinances, and His commandments, all the days.* [2] *You should know today that it is not your children who did not know and who did not see the chastisement of HASHEM, your God, His greatness, His strong hand, and His outstretched arm;* [3] *His signs and His deeds that He performed in the midst of Egypt, to Pharaoh, king of Egypt, and to all his land;* [4] *and what He did to the army of Egypt, to its horses and its riders, over whom He swept the waters of the Sea of Reeds when they pursued you, and HASHEM caused them to perish until this day;* [5] *and what He did for you in the Wilderness, until you came to this place;* [6] *and what He did to Dathan and Abiram the sons of Eliab son of Reuben, when the earth opened its mouth wide and swallowed them, and their households, and their tents, and all the fortunes at their feet, in the midst of all Israel.* [7] *Rather it is your own eyes that see all the great work of HASHEM, which He did.*

[8] *So you shall observe the entire commandment that I command you today, so that you will be strong, and you will come and possess the Land to which you are crossing the Jordan, to possess it,* [9] *and so that you will prolong your days on the Land that HASHEM swore to your forefathers*

4. וַיְאַבְּדֵם ה׳ עַד הַיּוֹם הַזֶּה — *And HASHEM has destroyed them unto this day* ... because the drowning of the captains of Egypt and their soldiers (caused) a loss which was felt forty years later since they were the mighty ones, and there were none to replace them.

7. כִּי עֵינֵיכֶם הָרֹאֹת אֵת כָּל מַעֲשֵׂה ה׳ — *But your eyes have seen all the work of HASHEM.* Who did such great (deeds) against those who rebelled against Him; to Pharaoh and the Egyptians in Egypt, and at the sea; to the rebels in the wilderness, and to Dathan and Abiram (as well). Hence, it is (incumbent) upon you to caution the children who did not see all this — therefore ...

8. וּשְׁמַרְתֶּם אֶת כָּל הַמִּצְוָה אֲשֶׁר אָנֹכִי מְצַוְּךָ הַיּוֹם — *And you shall keep all the commandment which I command you this day* ... the commandment of the stones which you shall erect in the Jordan, and which you shall take from the midst of the Jordan, and write on them the Torah, which shall bear witness for (all) generations (coming) from you, who did see (all these wonders).

9. וּלְמַעַן תַּאֲרִיכוּ יָמִים עַל הָאֲדָמָה — *And that you may prolong your days upon the land* ... for if your children will not keep the commandments, they will be exiled from (the Land) quickly, (even) before (the period of) וְנוֹשַׁנְתֶּם בָּאָרֶץ, *and you shall have been long*

NOTES

prets this phrase as meaning that Egypt never recovered from this disaster.

8. וּשְׁמַרְתֶּם אֶת כָּל הַמִּצְוָה — *And you shall keep all the commandment*. See note on verse 2.

9. וּלְמַעַן תַּאֲרִיכוּ יָמִים — *And that you may prolong your days*. The *Sforno's* quote of וְנוֹשַׁנְתֶּם, *and you*

ששי י לַאֲבֹתֵיכֶם לָתֵת לָהֶם וּלְזַרְעָם אֶרֶץ זָבַת חָלָב וּדְבָשׁ׃ כִּי הָאָרֶץ
אֲשֶׁר אַתָּה בָא־שָׁמָּה לְרִשְׁתָּהּ לֹא כְאֶרֶץ מִצְרַיִם הִוא אֲשֶׁר יְצָאתֶם
יא מִשָּׁם אֲשֶׁר תִּזְרַע אֶת־זַרְעֲךָ וְהִשְׁקִיתָ בְרַגְלְךָ כְּגַן הַיָּרָק׃ וְהָאָרֶץ אֲשֶׁר
אַתֶּם עֹבְרִים שָׁמָּה לְרִשְׁתָּהּ אֶרֶץ הָרִים וּבְקָעֹת לִמְטַר הַשָּׁמַיִם תִּשְׁתֶּה־
יב מָּיִם׃ אֶרֶץ אֲשֶׁר־יְהוָה אֱלֹהֶיךָ דֹּרֵשׁ אֹתָהּ תָּמִיד עֵינֵי יְהוָה אֱלֹהֶיךָ בָּהּ
יג מֵרֵשִׁית הַשָּׁנָה וְעַד אַחֲרִית שָׁנָה׃ וְהָיָה אִם־שָׁמֹעַ תִּשְׁמְעוּ
אֶל־מִצְוֺתַי אֲשֶׁר אָנֹכִי מְצַוֶּה אֶתְכֶם הַיּוֹם לְאַהֲבָה אֶת־יְהוָה אֱלֹהֵיכֶם
יד וּלְעָבְדוֹ בְּכָל־לְבַבְכֶם וּבְכָל־נַפְשְׁכֶם׃ וְנָתַתִּי מְטַר־אַרְצְכֶם בְּעִתּוֹ יוֹרֶה
טו וּמַלְקוֹשׁ וְאָסַפְתָּ דְגָנֶךָ וְתִירֹשְׁךָ וְיִצְהָרֶךָ׃ וְנָתַתִּי עֵשֶׂב בְּשָׂדְךָ לִבְהֶמְתֶּךָ
טז וְאָכַלְתָּ וְשָׂבָעְתָּ׃ הִשָּׁמְרוּ לָכֶם פֶּן־יִפְתֶּה לְבַבְכֶם וְסַרְתֶּם וַעֲבַדְתֶּם אֱלֹהִים
יז אֲחֵרִים וְהִשְׁתַּחֲוִיתֶם לָהֶם׃ וְחָרָה אַף־יְהוָה בָּכֶם וְעָצַר אֶת־הַשָּׁמַיִם וְלֹא־
יִהְיֶה מָטָר וְהָאֲדָמָה לֹא תִתֵּן אֶת־יְבוּלָהּ וַאֲבַדְתֶּם מְהֵרָה מֵעַל הָאָרֶץ
יח הַטֹּבָה אֲשֶׁר יְהוָה נֹתֵן לָכֶם׃ וְשַׂמְתֶּם אֶת־דְּבָרַי אֵלֶּה עַל־לְבַבְכֶם וְעַל־
נַפְשְׁכֶם וּקְשַׁרְתֶּם אֹתָם לְאוֹת עַל־יֶדְכֶם וְהָיוּ לְטוֹטָפֹת בֵּין עֵינֵיכֶם׃
יט וְלִמַּדְתֶּם אֹתָם אֶת־בְּנֵיכֶם לְדַבֵּר בָּם בְּשִׁבְתְּךָ בְּבֵיתֶךָ וּבְלֶכְתְּךָ בַדֶּרֶךְ
כ־כא וּבְשָׁכְבְּךָ וּבְקוּמֶךָ׃ וּכְתַבְתָּם עַל־מְזוּזוֹת בֵּיתֶךָ וּבִשְׁעָרֶיךָ׃ לְמַעַן יִרְבּוּ
יְמֵיכֶם וִימֵי בְנֵיכֶם עַל הָאֲדָמָה אֲשֶׁר נִשְׁבַּע יְהוָה לַאֲבֹתֵיכֶם לָתֵת לָהֶם

---

in the Land (4:25), as (the Torah) testifies, saying, *and the heaven shall be shut up . . . and you perish quickly* (v. 17).

10. כִּי הָאָרֶץ אֲשֶׁר אַתָּה בָא שָׁמָּה לְרִשְׁתָּהּ לֹא כְאֶרֶץ מִצְרַיִם הִוא — *For the land which you go in, to possess, is not as the land of Egypt* . . . Which does not require rain.

11. לִמְטַר הַשָּׁמַיִם תִּשְׁתֶּה מָּיִם — *By rain from heaven, it consumes water.* There are insufficient rivers to water the Land, and it needs rainwater.

12. דֹּרֵשׁ אֹתָהּ — *Cares for (it)* . . . observing the deeds of its inhabitants (to see) if they are worthy (to have) rain or not. Therefore, know this that indeed . . .

13-14. אִם שָׁמֹעַ תִּשְׁמְעוּ . . . וְנָתַתִּי מְטַר אַרְצְכֶם — *If you shall hearken . . . that I will give the rain of your land* . . . in a manner that you will find sustenance without pain (effort) and will be able to serve Him. And if not, He will give you no rain at all and you will have no food to sustain you.

NOTES

shall have been long, is most significant. Our Sages tell us that the numerical equivalent of this phrase is 852, indicating that Israel was destined to go into exile after that number of years (*Sanhedrin* 35). In our verse, Israel is cautioned that if the *mitzvos* are not observed, the time of exile will be hastened. The *Sforno* aptly concludes by quoting verse 17 where Israel is warned that they will be dispossessed *quickly*, i.e., before the ordained time.

12. דֹּרֵשׁ אֹתָהּ — *Cares for* (it). The commentary of the *Sforno* is best understood by the phrase that follows, *"the eyes of HASHEM your God are always upon it."* Since *Eretz Yisrael* is special, God observes the deeds of its inhabitants, sending or withholding rain according to their actions, be they good or evil. The *Sifri* comments, "The land of Egypt has water whether its inhabitants fulfill the will of God or not. *Eretz Yisrael* is not so; if they fulfill God's will, they shall dwell in the Land, and if not, they will go into exile."

13-14. אִם שָׁמֹעַ תִּשְׁמְעוּ . . . וְנָתַתִּי מְטַר אַרְצְכֶם — *If you shall hearken . . . that I will give the rain of your land*. The Torah states that if Israel will *hearken* to God's commandments and *love* Him and *serve* Him, they will be granted rain and the blessing of plenty. The *Sforno* adds that this prosperity will result without great physical exertion

to give them and to their offspring — a land flowing with milk and honey.
10 For the Land to which you come, to possess it — it is not like the land
of Egypt that you left, where you would plant your seed and water it on foot
like a vegetable garden. 11 But the Land to which you cross over to possess
it is a Land of hills and valleys; from the rain of heaven will it drink water;
12 a Land that HASHEM, your God, seeks out; the eyes of HASHEM, your God,
are always upon it, from the beginning of the year to year's end.
13 It will be that if you hearken to My commandments that I command
you today, to love HASHEM, your God, and to serve Him with all your heart
and with all your soul, 14 then I shall provide rain for your Land in its proper
time, the early and the late rains, that you may gather in your grain, your
wine, and your oil. 15 I shall provide grass in your field for your cattle and
you will eat and you will be satisfied. 16 Beware for yourselves, lest your
heart be seduced and you turn astray and serve gods of others and prostrate
yourselves to them. 17 Then the wrath of HASHEM will blaze against you; He
will restrain the heaven so there will be no rain, and the ground will not
yield its produce; and you will be swiftly banished from the goodly Land
that HASHEM gives you. 18 You shall place these words of Mine upon your
heart and upon your soul; you shall bind them for a sign upon your arm and
let them be an ornament between your eyes. 19 You shall teach them to your
children to discuss them, while you sit in your home, while you walk on the
way, when you retire and when you arise. 20 And you shall write them on
the doorposts of your house and upon your gates. 21 In order to prolong your
days and the days of your children upon the Land that HASHEM has sworn
to your forefathers to give them, like the days of the heaven over the earth.

---

17. וַאֲבַדְתֶּם מְהֵרָה — *And you will perish quickly* . . . through famine which is far worse than the sword — therefore, הִשָּׁמְרוּ לָכֶם, *take heed to yourselves* (v. 16).

18. וְשַׂמְתֶּם אֶת דְּבָרַי אֵלֶּה עַל לְבַבְכֶם — *And you shall place these words of Mine on your heart* . . . to reflect upon them.

וְעַל נַפְשְׁכֶם — *And in your soul* . . . to fulfill them willingly.

19. וְלִמַּדְתֶּם אֹתָם אֶת בְּנֵיכֶם — *And teach them to your children* . . . to train your children in the commandments.

לְדַבֵּר בָּם בְּשִׁבְתְּךָ בְּבֵיתֶךָ — *To speak of them when you sit in your house* . . . so as to speak of them constantly.

NOTES

so that they will be able to serve Him (וּלְעָבְדוֹ). The alternative is lack of rain and ultimately famine (v. 17).

17. וַאֲבַדְתֶּם מְהֵרָה — *And you will perish quickly.* The statement by the *Sforno* that famine is more severe than the sword is based upon the Talmudic saying, "Famine is harder than the sword" (*Bava Basra* 8b), which in turn is derived from the verse in *Lamentations* 4:9, *They that were slain with the sword are better than they that were slain with hunger.*

18. עַל לְבַבְכֶם וְעַל נַפְשְׁכֶם — *On your heart and in your soul.* Reflection stems from the heart, while desire comes from the soul.

19. וְלִמַּדְתֶּם . . . לְדַבֵּר בָּם — *And teach them . . . to speak of them.* To teach is not sufficient; one must *train* his children to do the *mitzvos*, for only through practice will it become second nature. The study of Torah, in turn, cannot be sporadic and occasional but must be constant and continual — in one's home, on the road, by day and by night.

כב כִּימֵ֥י הַשָּׁמַ֖יִם עַל־הָאָֽרֶץ׃   כִּי֩ אִם־שָׁמֹ֨ר תִּשְׁמְר֜וּן אֶת־כָּל־
הַמִּצְוָ֣ה הַזֹּ֗את אֲשֶׁ֧ר אָנֹכִ֛י מְצַוֶּ֥ה אֶתְכֶ֖ם לַעֲשֹׂתָ֑הּ לְאַהֲבָ֞ה אֶת־יְהוָ֤ה
כג אֱלֹֽהֵיכֶם֙ לָלֶ֣כֶת בְּכָל־דְּרָכָ֔יו וּלְדָבְקָה־בֽוֹ׃ וְהוֹרִ֧ישׁ יְהוָ֛ה אֶת־כָּל־הַגּוֹיִ֖ם
כד הָאֵ֑לֶּה מִלִּפְנֵיכֶ֑ם וִירִשְׁתֶּ֣ם גּוֹיִ֔ם גְּדֹלִ֥ים וַעֲצֻמִ֖ים מִכֶּֽם׃ כָּל־הַמָּק֗וֹם אֲשֶׁ֨ר
תִּדְרֹ֧ךְ כַּף־רַגְלְכֶ֛ם בּ֖וֹ לָכֶ֣ם יִהְיֶ֑ה מִן־הַמִּדְבָּ֣ר וְֽהַלְּבָנ֗וֹן מִן־הַנָּהָ֤ר נְהַר־פְּרָ֔ת
כה וְעַ֖ד הַיָּ֣ם הָאַחֲר֑וֹן יִהְיֶ֖ה גְּבֻלְכֶֽם׃ לֹא־יִתְיַצֵּ֥ב אִ֛ישׁ בִּפְנֵיכֶ֖ם פַּחְדְּכֶ֣ם
וּמֽוֹרַאֲכֶ֗ם יִתֵּ֣ן ׀ יְהוָ֣ה אֱלֹֽהֵיכֶ֗ם עַל־פְּנֵ֤י כָל־הָאָ֙רֶץ֙ אֲשֶׁ֣ר תִּדְרְכוּ־בָ֔הּ
כַּאֲשֶׁ֖ר דִּבֶּ֥ר לָכֶֽם׃

22. כִּי אִם שָׁמֹר תִּשְׁמְרוּן ... לְאַהֲבָה — *For if you shall diligently guard . . . to love . . .* to occupy yourselves with Torah in order to recognize the lovingkindness of God, the Exalted One, for from this (knowledge) does love flow.

לָלֶכֶת בְּכָל דְּרָכָיו — *To walk in all His ways . . .* to conduct yourselves in those ways with which He conducts His world, namely righteousness and justice.

NOTES

22. כִּי אִם שָׁמֹר תִּשְׁמְרוּן ... לְאַהֲבָה ... לָלֶכֶת בְּכָל דְּרָכָיו — *For if you shall diligently guard . . . to love . . . to walk in all His ways.* The *Sforno* at the beginning of this *sedrah* (7:12) interprets the word וּשְׁמַרְתֶּם as meaning "Mishnah." Similarly, he explains the term שָׁמֹר תִּשְׁמְרוּן, *to diligently guard,* as meaning the study of Torah which causes man to recognize and appreciate the חַסְדֵּי ה', *the loving* kindness of God, which, in turn, brings man to the love of God, as we see in the *Sforno's* commentary on the phrase וּלְאַהֲבָה אֹתוֹ, *and to love Him* (10:12). To walk in the ways of God is always interpreted as meaning to imitate His attributes. *Rashi* gives a similar interpretation, *and Rashi* also explains the expression of שָׁמֹר תִּשְׁמְרוּן as referring to the continuous study of Torah that it not be forgotten.

22 *For if you will observe this entire commandment that I command you, to perform it, to love* HASHEM, *your God, to walk in all His ways and to cleave to Him,* 23 HASHEM *will drive out all these nations from before you, and you will drive out greater and mightier nations than yourselves.*
24 *Every place where the sole of your foot will tread shall be yours— from the Wilderness and the Lebanon, from the river, the Euphrates River, until the western sea shall be your boundary.* 25 *No man will stand up against you;* HASHEM, *your God, will set your terror and fear on the entire face of the earth where you will tread, as He spoke to you.*

וּלְדָבְקָה בוֹ — *And to cleave to Him* . . . that all your actions have as their aim the doing of His will, as it says, בְּכָל דְּרָכֶיךָ דָעֵהוּ, *In all your ways know Him* (*Proverbs* 3:6).

23. וְהוֹרִישׁ ה׳ — *And* HASHEM *will drive out.* He will grant you a place in which to earn your livelihood without pain, so that you shall be able to do His will.

25. לֹא יִתְיַצֵּב אִישׁ בִּפְנֵיכֶם — *No man shall stand against you* . . . even outside the Land.

NOTES

23. וְהוֹרִישׁ ה׳ — *And* HASHEM *will drive out.* By driving out the enemy, God will grant Israel the opportunity to realize their material well-being without excessive exertion, thereby enabling them to serve God in tranquility.

25. לֹא יִתְיַצֵּב אִישׁ בִּפְנֵיכֶם — *No man shall stand against you.* In the previous verse, the borders of the Land are delineated; hence the expression in this verse עַל פְּנֵי כָל הָאָרֶץ, *upon all the land,* seems redundant. The *Sforno,* however, explains that the Torah assures the Israelites that they will enter *Eretz Yisrael* unchallenged, for God will cause the nations to fear and dread their might. This fear of the Israelites will extend to the geographical area outside the Land as well. This explains the use of the term כָּל הָאָרֶץ which is all inclusive.

פרשת ראה

כו־כז רְאֵה אָנֹכִי נֹתֵן לִפְנֵיכֶם הַיּוֹם בְּרָכָה וּקְלָלָה: אֶת־הַבְּרָכָה אֲשֶׁר תִּשְׁמְעוּ
כח אֶל־מִצְוֹת יהוה אֱלֹהֵיכֶם אֲשֶׁר אָנֹכִי מְצַוֶּה אֶתְכֶם הַיּוֹם: וְהַקְּלָלָה
אִם־לֹא תִשְׁמְעוּ אֶל־מִצְוֹת יהוה אֱלֹהֵיכֶם וְסַרְתֶּם מִן־הַדֶּרֶךְ אֲשֶׁר
אָנֹכִי מְצַוֶּה אֶתְכֶם הַיּוֹם לָלֶכֶת אַחֲרֵי אֱלֹהִים אֲחֵרִים אֲשֶׁר לֹא־
כט יְדַעְתֶּם: וְהָיָה כִּי יְבִיאֲךָ יהוה אֱלֹהֶיךָ אֶל־הָאָרֶץ אֲשֶׁר־
אַתָּה בָא־שָׁמָּה לְרִשְׁתָּהּ וְנָתַתָּה אֶת־הַבְּרָכָה עַל־הַר גְּרִזִּים וְאֶת־
ל הַקְּלָלָה עַל־הַר עֵיבָל: הֲלֹא־הֵמָּה בְּעֵבֶר הַיַּרְדֵּן אַחֲרֵי דֶּרֶךְ מְבוֹא
לא הַשֶּׁמֶשׁ בְּאֶרֶץ הַכְּנַעֲנִי הַיֹּשֵׁב בָּעֲרָבָה מוּל הַגִּלְגָּל אֵצֶל אֵלוֹנֵי מֹרֶה: כִּי
אַתֶּם עֹבְרִים אֶת־הַיַּרְדֵּן לָבֹא לָרֶשֶׁת אֶת־הָאָרֶץ אֲשֶׁר־יהוה אֱלֹהֵיכֶם
לב נֹתֵן לָכֶם וִירִשְׁתֶּם אֹתָהּ וִישַׁבְתֶּם־בָּהּ: וּשְׁמַרְתֶּם לַעֲשׂוֹת אֵת כָּל־
יב א הַחֻקִּים וְאֶת־הַמִּשְׁפָּטִים אֲשֶׁר אָנֹכִי נֹתֵן לִפְנֵיכֶם הַיּוֹם: אֵלֶּה הַחֻקִּים
וְהַמִּשְׁפָּטִים אֲשֶׁר תִּשְׁמְרוּן לַעֲשׂוֹת בָּאָרֶץ אֲשֶׁר נָתַן יהוה אֱלֹהֵי
ב אֲבֹתֶיךָ לְךָ לְרִשְׁתָּהּ כָּל־הַיָּמִים אֲשֶׁר־אַתֶּם חַיִּים עַל־הָאֲדָמָה: אַבֵּד
תְּאַבְּדוּן אֶת־כָּל־הַמְּקֹמוֹת אֲשֶׁר עָבְדוּ־שָׁם הַגּוֹיִם אֲשֶׁר אַתֶּם יֹרְשִׁים
אֹתָם אֶת־אֱלֹהֵיהֶם עַל־הֶהָרִים הָרָמִים וְעַל־הַגְּבָעוֹת וְתַחַת כָּל־

26. רְאֵה — *Behold.* Look and perceive that your affairs (as a people) are not of an intermediate nature (i.e., the mean or average) as is the case with other nations because, indeed, (in your case) *I set before you this day a blessing and a curse,* which are two extremes since the blessing represents good fortune beyond what is sufficient (or adequate) (for it is) exceedingly good, (whereas) the curse is one which brings diminishment and (even a state of) sufficiency becomes unattainable. Both of these (blessing and curse) are לִפְנֵיכֶם, *before you,* i.e., attainable according to your choice.

29. וְנָתַתָּה אֶת הַבְּרָכָה — *And you shall set the blessing.* You shall bless those who guard (observe) the commandments.

וְאֶת הַקְּלָלָה — *And the curse* ... (upon) those who transgress them.

30. הֲלֹא הֵמָּה בְּעֵבֶר הַיַּרְדֵּן — *Are they not beyond the Jordan.* (This refers to) when you first enter the Land, in order to publicize as you begin to enter (*Eretz Yisrael*) that your

NOTES

26. רְאֵה — *Behold.* The fate of other nations is not one marked by full prosperity or complete devastation. Theirs is not a condition of extremes — blessing or curse. Moses cautions Israel that they, however, are unlike other peoples. Their lot as the people of God is destined to be most uncommon; there will be no middle course, for they will either be blessed or cursed! This is the significance of the introductory word רְאֵה, *see* or *behold,* which indicates something new and different, as we find in *Koheles* 1:10, *See, this is new.* The *Sforno* explains that Moses warned the people of Israel that this unique fate which lies in store for them, of extreme good fortune or total diminishment, is dependent upon their choice (לִפְנֵיכֶם); whether they choose to hearken to the commandments of God or not. According to the *Sforno*, for the people of Israel there can be no moderate stance because Torah brooks no compromise. God demands total commitment and offers two extreme options — a blessing or a curse. Unlike other commentators, the *Sforno* does not interpret the "blessing" and "curse" as referring to those pronounced on Mount Gerizim and Mount Ebal. He does, however, agree that those blessings and curses listed in chapter 27 emphasize the fact that Israel's destiny in *Eretz Yisrael* will be dependent upon their conduct and behavior as the Chosen People. This we must conclude from his commentary on verse 30.

PARASHAS RE'EH

[26] *See, I present before you today a blessing and a curse.* [27] *The blessing:*
that you hearken to the commandments of H*ASHEM, your God, that I*
command you today. [28] *And the curse: if you do not hearken to the*
commandments of H*ASHEM, your God, and you stray from the path that I*
command you today, to follow gods of others, that you did not know.
[29] *It shall be that when* H*ASHEM, your God, brings you to the Land to which*
you come, to possess it, then you shall deliver the blessing on Mount Gerizim
and the curse on Mount Ebal. [30] *Are they not on the other side of the Jordan,*
far, in the direction of the sunset, in the land of the Canaanite, that dwells
in the plain, far from Gilgal, near the plain of Moreh? [31] *For you are crossing*
the Jordan to come and possess the Land that H*ASHEM, your God, gives you;*
you shall possess it and you shall settle in it. [32] *You shall be careful to*
perform all the decrees and the ordinances that I present before you today.

12 [1] *These are the decrees and the ordinances that you shall observe to per-*
form in the Land that H*ASHEM, the God of your forefathers, has given*
you, to possess it, all the days that you live on the Land. [2] *You shall utterly*
destroy all the places where the nations that you are driving away wor-
shiped their gods: on the high mountains and on the hills, and under every

---

dwelling in it will not be in a moderate, average manner but rather it will be either in a successful manner or an accursed one.

XII

1. אֵלֶּה הַחֻקִּים וְהַמִּשְׁפָּטִים אֲשֶׁר תִּשְׁמְרוּן לַעֲשׂוֹת... לְרִשְׁתָּהּ כָּל הַיָּמִים — *These are the statutes and ordinances which you shall observe to do . . . to possess it all the days.* Included in these commandments which you must observe, and through the fulfillment of which you shall possess the Land all the days, (is the commandment) to destroy the place of every idol (v. 2), and (also) that you shall not conduct yourself in like manner regarding God, the Exalted One (v. 4), namely, to sacrifice to Him, in every place. Rather, you shall designate a specific place to sacrifice to Him, that place being the one *which* H*ASHEM your God shall choose out of all your tribes* (v. 5).

NOTES

29. וְנָתַתָּה אֶת הַבְּרָכָה... וְאֶת הַקְּלָלָה — *And you shall set the blessing . . . and the curse*. The *Sforno* explains that the setting of the blessing on Mt. Gerizim and the curse on Mt. Ebal is not meant to bless or curse these mountains. The purpose is to bless those who keep God's commandments and curse those who violate them. As *Rashi* explains (and the *Sforno* certainly concurs), those who pronounced the blessing were to face Mt. Gerizim after which they were to turn toward Mt. Ebal with the corresponding curse.

30. הֲלֹא הֵמָּה בְּעֵבֶר הַיַּרְדֵּן — *Are they not beyond the Jordan*. See note on verse 26. The *Sforno* emphasizes that the pronouncement of the blessing and curse was to be done immediately upon entering the land, thereby informing one and all that their dwelling in *Eretz Yisrael* was meant to be unique — either a prosperous or an accursed one. The *Sifri* comments on וְהָיָה, *and it shall be* (which is the opening word in verse 29): אֵין וְהָיָה אֶלָּא מִיַּד, "The expression וְהָיָה indicates immediacy." This supports the commentary of the *Sforno* on this verse.

XII

1. אֵלֶּה הַחֻקִּים וְהַמִּשְׁפָּטִים — *These are the statutes and ordinances*. This statement appears to be all inclusive but the following verses command Israel to destroy the idols of the inhabitants of the land, and to refrain from offering sacrifices to God everywhere, indiscriminately. The *Sforno*, therefore, explains the phrase, *These are the statutes etc.*, as meaning that these two commandments are included among the statutes which they are to observe when they enter the land, and in the merit of observing them Israel will possess the land all the days.

ג עֵץ רַעֲנָן: וְנִתַּצְתֶּם אֶת־מִזְבְּחֹתָם וְשִׁבַּרְתֶּם אֶת־מַצֵּבֹתָם וַאֲשֵׁרֵיהֶם
תִּשְׂרְפוּן בָּאֵשׁ וּפְסִילֵי אֱלֹהֵיהֶם תְּגַדֵּעוּן וְאִבַּדְתֶּם אֶת־שְׁמָם מִן־הַמָּקוֹם
ד־ה הַהוּא: לֹא־תַעֲשׂוּן כֵּן לַיהוָה אֱלֹהֵיכֶם: כִּי אִם־אֶל־הַמָּקוֹם אֲשֶׁר־יִבְחַר
יהוָה אֱלֹהֵיכֶם מִכָּל־שִׁבְטֵיכֶם לָשׂוּם אֶת־שְׁמוֹ שָׁם לְשִׁכְנוֹ תִדְרְשׁוּ וּבָאתָ
ו שָׁמָּה: וַהֲבֵאתֶם שָׁמָּה עֹלֹתֵיכֶם וְזִבְחֵיכֶם וְאֵת מַעְשְׂרֹתֵיכֶם וְאֵת תְּרוּמַת
ז יֶדְכֶם וְנִדְרֵיכֶם וְנִדְבֹתֵיכֶם וּבְכֹרֹת בְּקַרְכֶם וְצֹאנְכֶם: וַאֲכַלְתֶּם־שָׁם לִפְנֵי
יהוָה אֱלֹהֵיכֶם וּשְׂמַחְתֶּם בְּכֹל מִשְׁלַח יֶדְכֶם אַתֶּם וּבָתֵּיכֶם אֲשֶׁר בֵּרַכְךָ
ח יהוָה אֱלֹהֶיךָ: לֹא תַעֲשׂוּן כְּכֹל אֲשֶׁר אֲנַחְנוּ עֹשִׂים פֹּה הַיּוֹם אִישׁ כָּל־
ט הַיָּשָׁר בְּעֵינָיו: כִּי לֹא־בָאתֶם עַד־עָתָּה אֶל־הַמְּנוּחָה וְאֶל־הַנַּחֲלָה אֲשֶׁר־
י יהוָה אֱלֹהֶיךָ נֹתֵן לָךְ: וַעֲבַרְתֶּם אֶת־הַיַּרְדֵּן וִישַׁבְתֶּם בָּאָרֶץ אֲשֶׁר־יהוָה
אֱלֹהֵיכֶם מַנְחִיל אֶתְכֶם וְהֵנִיחַ לָכֶם מִכָּל־אֹיְבֵיכֶם מִסָּבִיב וִישַׁבְתֶּם־בֶּטַח:
שני יא וְהָיָה הַמָּקוֹם אֲשֶׁר־יִבְחַר יהוה אֱלֹהֵיכֶם בּוֹ לְשַׁכֵּן שְׁמוֹ שָׁם שָׁמָּה תָבִיאוּ
אֵת כָּל־אֲשֶׁר אָנֹכִי מְצַוֶּה אֶתְכֶם עוֹלֹתֵיכֶם וְזִבְחֵיכֶם מַעְשְׂרֹתֵיכֶם וּתְרֻמַת
יב יֶדְכֶם וְכֹל מִבְחַר נִדְרֵיכֶם אֲשֶׁר תִּדְּרוּ לַיהוָה: וּשְׂמַחְתֶּם לִפְנֵי יהוָה
אֱלֹהֵיכֶם אַתֶּם וּבְנֵיכֶם וּבְנֹתֵיכֶם וְעַבְדֵיכֶם וְאַמְהֹתֵיכֶם וְהַלֵּוִי אֲשֶׁר
יג בְּשַׁעֲרֵיכֶם כִּי אֵין לוֹ חֵלֶק וְנַחֲלָה אִתְּכֶם: הִשָּׁמֶר לְךָ פֶּן־תַּעֲלֶה עֹלֹתֶיךָ
יד בְּכָל־מָקוֹם אֲשֶׁר תִּרְאֶה: כִּי אִם־בַּמָּקוֹם אֲשֶׁר־יִבְחַר יהוה בְּאַחַד שְׁבָטֶיךָ
טו שָׁם תַּעֲלֶה עֹלֹתֶיךָ וְשָׁם תַּעֲשֶׂה כֹּל אֲשֶׁר אָנֹכִי מְצַוֶּךָּ: רַק בְּכָל־אַוַּת
נַפְשְׁךָ תִּזְבַּח | וְאָכַלְתָּ בָשָׂר כְּבִרְכַּת יהוָה אֱלֹהֶיךָ אֲשֶׁר נָתַן־לְךָ בְּכָל־
טז שְׁעָרֶיךָ הַטָּמֵא וְהַטָּהוֹר יֹאכְלֶנּוּ כַּצְּבִי וְכָאַיָּל: רַק הַדָּם לֹא תֹאכֵלוּ עַל־
יז הָאָרֶץ תִּשְׁפְּכֶנּוּ כַּמָּיִם: לֹא־תוּכַל לֶאֱכֹל בִּשְׁעָרֶיךָ מַעְשַׂר דְּגָנְךָ וְתִירֹשְׁךָ
וְיִצְהָרֶךָ וּבְכֹרֹת בְּקָרְךָ וְצֹאנֶךָ וְכָל־נְדָרֶיךָ אֲשֶׁר תִּדֹּר וְנִדְבֹתֶיךָ וּתְרוּמַת
יח יָדֶךָ: כִּי אִם־לִפְנֵי יהוָה אֱלֹהֶיךָ תֹּאכְלֶנּוּ בַּמָּקוֹם אֲשֶׁר יִבְחַר יהוָה אֱלֹהֶיךָ
בּוֹ אַתָּה וּבִנְךָ וּבִתֶּךָ וְעַבְדְּךָ וַאֲמָתֶךָ וְהַלֵּוִי אֲשֶׁר בִּשְׁעָרֶיךָ וְשָׂמַחְתָּ לִפְנֵי
יט יהוָה אֱלֹהֶיךָ בְּכֹל מִשְׁלַח יָדֶךָ: הִשָּׁמֶר לְךָ פֶּן־תַּעֲזֹב אֶת־הַלֵּוִי כָּל־יָמֶיךָ

---

5. לְשִׁכְנוֹ — *Unto His habitation* . . . where the dwelling place of His name (shall be). This refers to Shiloh or the Holy Temple (in Jerusalem).

תִּדְרְשׁוּ — *Shall you seek*. You shall seek to bow down and sacrifice in that chosen place, similar to אֵלָיו גּוֹיִם יִדְרֹשׁוּ, *to it shall the nations seek* (*Isaiah* 11:10).

וּבָאתָ שָׁמָּה — *And there you shall come*. But the dwelling place of His Name shall not come to you in every place, as is the custom of idolaters and their gods.

7. וַאֲכַלְתֶּם שָׁם לִפְנֵי ה׳ אֱלֹהֵיכֶם וּשְׂמַחְתֶּם — *And there you shall eat before* HASHEM *your God and rejoice*. עִבְדוּ אֶת ה׳ בְּשִׂמְחָה, *Serve* HASHEM *with gladness* (*Psalms* 100:2), as befits all who serve with love.

NOTES

5. וּבָאתָ שָׁמָּה — *And there you shall come*. The Sanctuary was to be established in one place, and the people were enjoined to go there to worship and bring sacrifices. The *Sforno* may well be alluding to practices in his time, when he comments almost parenthetically, "As is the custom of idolaters." It was common for the priest to transport idols or religious articles from place to place wherever their religious adherents gathered.

leafy tree. 3 You shall break apart their altars; you shall smash their pillars;
and their sacred trees shall you burn in the fire; their carved images shall
you cut down; and you shall obliterate their names from that place.
4 You shall not do this to HASHEM, your God. 5 Rather, only at the place
that HASHEM, your God, will choose from among all your tribes to place His
Name shall you seek out His Presence and come there. 6 And there shall you
bring your elevation-offerings and feast-offerings, your tithes and what you
raise up with your hands, your vow offerings and your free-will offerings,
and the firstborn of your cattle and your flocks. 7 You shall eat there before
HASHEM, your God, and you shall rejoice with your every undertaking, you
and your households, as HASHEM, your God, has blessed you.
8 You shall not do everything that we do here today — [rather,] every man
what is proper in his eyes — 9 for you will not yet have come to the resting
place or to the heritage that HASHEM, your God, gives you.
10 You shall cross the Jordan and settle in the Land that HASHEM, your
God, causes you to inherit, and He will give you rest from all your enemies
all around, and you will dwell securely.
11 It shall be that the place where HASHEM, your God, will choose to rest
His Name — there shall you bring everything that I command you: your
elevation-offerings and your feast-offerings, your tithes and what you raise
up with your hands, and the choicest of your vow offerings that you will
vow to HASHEM. 12 You shall rejoice before HASHEM, your God — you, your
sons and your daughters, your slaves and your maidservants, and the Levite
who is in your cities, for he has no share and inheritance with you. 13 Beware
for yourself lest you bring up your elevation-offerings in any place that you
see. 14 Rather, only in the place that HASHEM will choose, among one of your
tribes, there shall you bring up your elevation-offerings, and there shall you
do all that I command you.
15 However, to your heart's desire you may slaughter and eat meat,
according to the blessing that HASHEM, your God, will have given you in all
your cities; the contaminated one and the pure one may eat it, like the deer
and the hart. 16 But you shall not eat the blood; you shall pour it onto the
earth, like water.
17 In your cities, you may not eat: the tithe of your grain, and your wine,
and your oil; the firstborn of your cattle and your flocks; all your vow
offerings that you vow and your free-will offerings; and what you raise
up with your hands. 18 Rather you shall eat them before HASHEM, your
God, in the place that HASHEM, your God, will choose — you, your son,
your daughter, your slave, your maidservant, and the Levite who is in your
cities — and you shall rejoice before HASHEM, your God, in your every
undertaking. 19 Beware for yourself lest you forsake the Levite, all your days

---

בְּכֹל מִשְׁלַח יֶדְכֶם — *In all to which you put your hand* . . . for then you shall make your ways prosperous and you shall have good success (based on *Joshua* 1:8).

NOTES

7. וּשְׂמַחְתֶּם — *And rejoice.* Although fear of the Almighty is of paramount importance in the service of God, it is שִׂמְחָה, *gladness,* which brings man to the love of God.

כ עַל־אַדְמָתֶךָ: כִּי־יַרְחִיב יְהוָה אֱלֹהֶיךָ אֶת־גְּבֻלְךָ כַּאֲשֶׁר
דִּבֶּר־לָךְ וְאָמַרְתָּ אֹכְלָה בָשָׂר כִּי־תְאַוֶּה נַפְשְׁךָ לֶאֱכֹל בָּשָׂר בְּכָל־אַוַּת
כא נַפְשְׁךָ תֹּאכַל בָּשָׂר: כִּי־יִרְחַק מִמְּךָ הַמָּקוֹם אֲשֶׁר יִבְחַר יְהוָה אֱלֹהֶיךָ
לָשׂוּם שְׁמוֹ שָׁם וְזָבַחְתָּ מִבְּקָרְךָ וּמִצֹּאנְךָ אֲשֶׁר נָתַן יְהוָה לְךָ כַּאֲשֶׁר
כב צִוִּיתִךָ וְאָכַלְתָּ בִּשְׁעָרֶיךָ בְּכֹל אַוַּת נַפְשֶׁךָ: אַךְ כַּאֲשֶׁר יֵאָכֵל אֶת־הַצְּבִי
כג וְאֶת־הָאַיָּל כֵּן תֹּאכְלֶנּוּ הַטָּמֵא וְהַטָּהוֹר יַחְדָּו יֹאכְלֶנּוּ: רַק חֲזַק לְבִלְתִּי
כד אֲכֹל הַדָּם כִּי הַדָּם הוּא הַנָּפֶשׁ וְלֹא־תֹאכַל הַנֶּפֶשׁ עִם־הַבָּשָׂר: לֹא
כה תֹּאכְלֶנּוּ עַל־הָאָרֶץ תִּשְׁפְּכֶנּוּ כַּמָּיִם: לֹא תֹּאכְלֶנּוּ לְמַעַן יִיטַב לְךָ וּלְבָנֶיךָ
כו אַחֲרֶיךָ כִּי־תַעֲשֶׂה הַיָּשָׁר בְּעֵינֵי יְהוָה: רַק קָדָשֶׁיךָ אֲשֶׁר־יִהְיוּ לְךָ וּנְדָרֶיךָ
כז תִּשָּׂא וּבָאתָ אֶל־הַמָּקוֹם אֲשֶׁר־יִבְחַר יְהוָה: וְעָשִׂיתָ עֹלֹתֶיךָ הַבָּשָׂר וְהַדָּם
עַל־מִזְבַּח יְהוָה אֱלֹהֶיךָ וְדַם־זְבָחֶיךָ יִשָּׁפֵךְ עַל־מִזְבַּח יְהוָה אֱלֹהֶיךָ
כח וְהַבָּשָׂר תֹּאכֵל: שְׁמֹר וְשָׁמַעְתָּ אֵת כָּל־הַדְּבָרִים הָאֵלֶּה אֲשֶׁר אָנֹכִי מְצַוֶּךָּ
לְמַעַן יִיטַב לְךָ וּלְבָנֶיךָ אַחֲרֶיךָ עַד־עוֹלָם כִּי תַעֲשֶׂה הַטּוֹב וְהַיָּשָׁר בְּעֵינֵי
שלישי כט יְהוָה אֱלֹהֶיךָ: כִּי־יַכְרִית יְהוָה אֱלֹהֶיךָ אֶת־הַגּוֹיִם אֲשֶׁר אַתָּה
ל בָא־שָׁמָּה לָרֶשֶׁת אוֹתָם מִפָּנֶיךָ וְיָרַשְׁתָּ אֹתָם וְיָשַׁבְתָּ בְּאַרְצָם: הִשָּׁמֶר
לְךָ פֶּן־תִּנָּקֵשׁ אַחֲרֵיהֶם אַחֲרֵי הִשָּׁמְדָם מִפָּנֶיךָ וּפֶן־תִּדְרֹשׁ לֵאלֹהֵיהֶם
לֵאמֹר אֵיכָה יַעַבְדוּ הַגּוֹיִם הָאֵלֶּה אֶת־אֱלֹהֵיהֶם וְאֶעֱשֶׂה־כֵּן גַּם־אָנִי:

---

20. וְאָמַרְתָּ אֹכְלָה בָשָׂר — *And you shall say, "I will eat meat"* ... without the need to trouble myself to bring it (the animal) up to the Temple.

כִּי תְאַוֶּה נַפְשְׁךָ לֶאֱכֹל בָּשָׂר — *Because your soul desires to eat meat* ... and also when you desire to eat that portion which is given to the *Kohanim* from the sacrifice.

בְּכָל אַוַּת נַפְשְׁךָ תֹּאכַל בָּשָׂר — *You may eat meat after all the desire of your soul* ... but not the (prohibited) fat or blood even though it is non-sacred.

22. אַךְ כַּאֲשֶׁר יֵאָכֵל אֶת הַצְּבִי — *Even as the deer is eaten* ... not in a hallowed place.

23. רַק חֲזַק לְבִלְתִּי אֲכֹל הַדָּם — *Only be steadfast in not eating the blood.* Even though by eating it you hope to (be accepted) into the company of שֵׁדִים, *demons,* who will reveal the future to you, as our Sages say, "They know what will happen like ministering angels" (*Chagigah* 16a), (nonetheless) do not eat the blood in order to fraternize with them.

24. לֹא תֹאכְלֶנּוּ עַל הָאָרֶץ תִּשְׁפְּכֶנּוּ כַּמָּיִם — *You shall not eat it; you shall pour it out upon the earth as water.* Treat it in such a manner that it is rendered unfit for consumption, and

NOTES

20. וְאָמַרְתָּ אֹכְלָה בָשָׂר ... לֶאֱכֹל בָּשָׂר ... תֹּאכַל בָּשָׂר — *And you shall say, "I will eat meat" ... to eat meat ... you may eat meat.* The word בָּשָׂר, *meat*, appears three times in this verse. The first is permissive; once their borders are enlarged and it is difficult to bring every animal to the Sanctuary, permission is granted to slaughter animals for food anywhere. The second is inclusive; although certain parts of the animal must be given to the *Kohen* when a sacrifice is offered (the breast and thigh), such is not the case if the animal is חולין, *non-sacred.* The third is exclusive; although restrictions are removed regarding place and priestly gifts when one slaughters an animal outside the Sanctuary, nonetheless the prohibition of fat and blood is still applicable.

22. כַּאֲשֶׁר יֵאָכֵל אֶת הַצְּבִי — *As the deer is eaten.* A deer is not qualified to be brought on the Altar as a sacrifice. Hence, comparing the animals slaughtered for ordinary consumption to the deer is apt; both can be eaten by the *tamei* as well as the *tahor.*

23. רַק חֲזַק לְבִלְתִּי אֲכֹל הַדָּם — *Only be steadfast in not eating the blood.* The *Sforno* explains why it is

on your Land.
[20] *When* H*ASHEM*, *your God, will broaden your boundary as He spoke to*
you, and you say, "I would eat meat," for you will have a desire to eat meat,
to your heart's entire desire may you eat meat. [21] *If the place that* H*ASHEM*,
your God, will choose to place His Name will be far from you, you may
slaughter from your cattle and your flocks that H*ASHEM* *has given you, as*
I have commanded you, and you may eat in your cities according to your
heart's entire desire. [22] *Even as the deer and the hart are eaten, so may you*
eat it, the contaminated one and the pure one may eat it together. [23] *Only be*
strong not to eat the blood — for the blood, it is the life — and you shall not
eat the life with the meat. [24] *You shall not eat it, you shall pour it onto the*
ground like water. [25] *You shall not eat it, in order that it be well with you and*
your children after you, when you do what is right in the eyes of H*ASHEM*.
[26] *Only your sanctities that you will have and your vow offerings shall*
you carry, and come to the place that H*ASHEM* *will choose.* [27] *You shall*
perform your elevation-offerings, the flesh and the blood, upon the Altar of
H*ASHEM*, *your God; and the blood of your feast-offerings shall be poured*
upon the Altar of H*ASHEM*, *your God, and you shall eat the flesh.*
[28] *Safeguard and hearken to all these words that I command you, in order*
that it be well with you and your children after you forever, when you do
what is good and right in the eyes of H*ASHEM*, *your God.*
[29] *When* H*ASHEM*, *your God, will cut down the nations where you come to*
drive them away before you, and you drive them away and settle in their
land, [30] *beware for yourself lest you be attracted after them after they*
have been destroyed before you, and lest you seek out their gods, saying,
"How did these nations worship their gods, and even I will do the same."

---

this (shall be done) by pouring it on the earth as water. Do not store it as wine, oil and other beverages are stored for consumption.

25. לֹא תֹאכְלֶנּוּ . . . כִּי תַעֲשֶׂה הַיָּשָׁר בְּעֵינֵי ה׳ — *You shall not eat it . . . when you shall do that which is right in the eyes of* H*ASHEM*. Do not refrain from eating it because you abhor it, but because you are doing what is right in God's eyes, as our Sages say, "Let not man say, 'My soul loathes the meat of swine,' but let him say, 'I desire it but my Father in heaven has decreed (that it is forbidden)' " (*Sifra*).

30. וְאֶעֱשֶׂה כֵּן גַּם אָנִי — *I will do likewise.* I will also serve God, the Blessed One, with the same means of service with which they (the idolaters) worship their strange gods.

NOTES

necessary for the Torah to strengthen the resolve of the Israelite not to partake of blood. After all, blood is not that appetizing and tempting that we must be urged to be steadfast and resist the desire to eat it. The answer, however, is that there was a belief that through eating blood one could cultivate the companionship of שֵׁדִים, *demons*. This was greatly desired for many believed that these demons possessed great powers which would benefit those who were close to them, as the *Sforno* explains in *Leviticus* 17:7. See his commentary there and the notes on that verse.

25. לֹא תֹאכְלֶנּוּ . . . — *You shall not eat it . . . .* The *Sforno* explains why this prohibition is repeated, considering that it was already stated in the previous verse. The reason for this apparent redundancy is to teach us that our motivation for abstaining from any practice should not be because it repels us but because God has forbidden it. On the contrary, one should say, "אֶפְשִׁי וְאֶפְשִׁי, I indeed desire to do it, but I am disciplined and shall refrain because God has forbidden it." *Rashi* to *Leviticus* 20:26 quotes this concept from the *Sifra*.

לא לֹא־תַעֲשֶׂה כֵּן לַיהוָה אֱלֹהֶיךָ כִּי כָל־תּוֹעֲבַת יהוה אֲשֶׁר שָׂנֵא עָשׂוּ
יג א לֵאלֹהֵיהֶם כִּי גַם אֶת־בְּנֵיהֶם וְאֶת־בְּנֹתֵיהֶם יִשְׂרְפוּ בָאֵשׁ לֵאלֹהֵיהֶם: אֵת
כָּל־הַדָּבָר אֲשֶׁר אָנֹכִי מְצַוֶּה אֶתְכֶם אֹתוֹ תִשְׁמְרוּ לַעֲשׂוֹת לֹא־תֹסֵף עָלָיו
וְלֹא תִגְרַע מִמֶּנּוּ:
ב כִּי־יָקוּם בְּקִרְבְּךָ נָבִיא אוֹ חֹלֵם חֲלוֹם וְנָתַן אֵלֶיךָ אוֹת אוֹ מוֹפֵת:
ג וּבָא הָאוֹת וְהַמּוֹפֵת אֲשֶׁר־דִּבֶּר אֵלֶיךָ לֵאמֹר נֵלְכָה אַחֲרֵי אֱלֹהִים אֲחֵרִים
ד אֲשֶׁר לֹא־יְדַעְתָּם וְנָעָבְדֵם: לֹא תִשְׁמַע אֶל־דִּבְרֵי הַנָּבִיא
הַהוּא אוֹ אֶל־חוֹלֵם הַחֲלוֹם הַהוּא כִּי מְנַסֶּה יהוה אֱלֹהֵיכֶם אֶתְכֶם
לָדַעַת הֲיִשְׁכֶם אֹהֲבִים אֶת־יהוה אֱלֹהֵיכֶם בְּכָל־לְבַבְכֶם וּבְכָל־
ה נַפְשְׁכֶם: אַחֲרֵי יהוה אֱלֹהֵיכֶם תֵּלֵכוּ וְאֹתוֹ תִירָאוּ וְאֶת־מִצְוֹתָיו תִּשְׁמֹרוּ

31. כִּי כָל תּוֹעֲבַת ה׳ אֲשֶׁר שָׂנֵא עָשׂוּ לֵאלֹהֵיהֶם — *For every abomination to* HASHEM *which He hates, have they done to their gods* . . . because among the practices with which they serve strange gods are acts that are repugnant to God, the Blessed One.

XIII

1. לֹא תֹסֵף עָלָיו — *You shall not add thereto* . . . lest you add something which is repugnant as it may well be if you add certain kinds of service to God, the Blessed One, the addition of which, at times, might be repugnant to Him, the Blessed One, such as the burning of children.

וְלֹא תִגְרַע מִמֶּנּוּ — *Nor diminish from it* . . . even if the reason for the commandment no longer applies (lit., is removed) in your eyes, as we find with (King) Solomon when he said, "I will multiply (women) but not be turned away" (*Sanhedrin* 21b).

3. אֲשֶׁר לֹא יְדַעְתָּם — *Which you have not known* . . . for which no proof was ever given to establish their existence, because those (forces), which are known (to us) by sense or wonder, are known to function continually and uniformly, in such a manner that (we know) they are natural forces without a (free) will of their own, and therefore it avails naught to pray to them or serve them.

4. לֹא תִשְׁמַע אֶל דִּבְרֵי הַנָּבִיא הַהוּא — *Do not hearken to the words of that prophet.* Do not pay attention to his words to see if there is some substance (to them) because, without a

NOTES

30-31. וְאֶעֱשֶׂה כֵּן גַּם אָנִי. כִּי כָל תּוֹעֲבַת ה׳ . . . — *I will do likewise. For every abomination to* HASHEM . . . The *Sforno* explains that the Israelites will not necessarily be tempted to actually serve strange gods but rather to adopt the practices of the idolaters and use them in the service of God. The Torah warns them not to do so because even though there are aspects of religious service common to both idol worship and Divine service, there are also certain abominable acts which are totally repugnant to God, such as offering one's children as fire offerings to their gods, and therefore it is imperative that we reject the adoption of *any* of their practices.

XIII

1. לֹא תֹסֵף עָלָיו — *You shall not add to.* Although this prohibition is recorded in chapter 4:2, it is repeated here to teach us that the addition of any kind of service to God is included, since it may be repugnant to Him.

וְלֹא תִגְרַע מִמֶּנּוּ — *Nor diminish from it.* See the *Sforno's* commentary on 4:2.

3. אֲשֶׁר לֹא יְדַעְתָּם — *Which you have not known.* The attempt to convince people to serve strange gods can only succeed through the introduction of new, *unknown* ones, since those heavenly bodies and other forces of nature already known to man present no danger to man's pure and established belief, being that they are recognized as forces of nature, and as such are the creation of the One God. Since they have no independent power of their own, people realize that there is no purpose in praying to them or serving them.

4. לֹא תִשְׁמַע אֶל דִּבְרֵי הַנָּבִיא הַהוּא אוֹ אֶל חוֹלֵם הַחֲלוֹם הַהוּא — *Do not hearken to the words of that prophet*

31 *You shall not do so to HASHEM, your God, for everything that is an abomination of HASHEM, that He hates, have they done to their gods; for even their sons and their daughters have they burned in the fire for their gods.*

13

1 *The entire word that I command you, that shall you observe to do; you shall not add to it and you shall not subtract from it.*

2 *If there should stand up in your midst a prophet or a dreamer of a*
dream, and he will produce to you a sign or a wonder, 3 *and the sign or the*
wonder comes about, of which he spoke to you, saying, "Let us follow gods
of others that you did not know and we shall worship them!" — 4 *do not*
hearken to the words of that prophet or to that dreamer of a dream, for HASHEM, your God, is testing you to know whether you love HASHEM, your
God, with all your heart and with all your soul. 5 *HASHEM, your God, shall*
you follow and Him shall you fear; His commandments shall you observe

doubt, all his words are false, concocted in his heart for evil (purposes) as it says, *Because he has spoken perversion against HASHEM* (v. 6). And (as for) the sign and wonder, it was done through witchcraft, a contrivance or some other (device), and not by the power of any prophecy which (he claims) came to him.

או אֶל חוֹלֵם הַחֲלוֹם הַהוּא — *Or unto the dreamer of that dream* . . . (nor should you) examine to see whether part of his dream is true — but you should know, without doubt, that he did not dream a single thing which he said, but invented it all from his heart in order to lead you astray.

כִּי מְנַסֶּה ה׳ אֱלֹהֵיכֶם אֶתְכֶם — *For HASHEM your God is testing you* . . . because, by considering the person who speaks against your God as an enemy, you will be proven in His sight, as one who loves (God).

לָדַעַת — *To know* . . . so that as a consequence of your love (of God), proven in actuality, God's knowledge, which always functions for good, will in turn become actual, as is proper whenever one is prepared to receive the overflow of His goodness.

5. אַחֲרֵי ה׳ אֱלֹהֵיכֶם תֵּלֵכוּ — *After HASHEM your God shall you walk.* Similar to וְהָלַכְתָּ בִּדְרָכָיו,

NOTES

or unto the dreamer of that dream. The *Sforno* interprets this admonition thus: The Torah is not concerned lest we give total credence to the words of the false prophet and dreamer. The Torah is concerned lest we believe *part* of the dream or a *portion* of his words. We are told here that *all* his words are false and that his dream is totally a figment of his imagination.

כִּי מְנַסֶּה ה׳ אֱלֹהֵיכֶם אֶתְכֶם — *For HASHEM your God is testing you.* The *Sforno's* expression "as an enemy" is based on *Psalms* 139:21,22: *Do I not hate them, HASHEM, that hate you . . . I regard them as my enemies.*

לָדַעַת — *To know*. In a number of places, the *Sforno* explains this word, in regard to God, as meaning knowledge which is manifested in action through the performance of a deed. In general, דַּעַת, *knowledge*, implies potentiality. Regarding God, however, the potentiality and reality are one, unlike man where the intent and the action are separate and distinct. Man may have the potential to do something, but it must be translated into action in order to become *real*. Also, the expression *to know* in its usual sense is inapplicable regarding God, for it implies a lack of knowledge originally, which only becomes known to Him through some action of man.

The *Sforno*, in his commentary on *Genesis* 22:1, *Numbers* 7:89, and *Deuteronomy* 2:7, expresses this thought, as he does in his commentary on this verse. The sense therefore of this verse according to the *Sforno* is: The blandishments of the false prophet put Israel's love of God to the test, not theoretically but practically. By withstanding this test, they are now worthy and prepared to receive the overflow of God's goodness, for *their* act of faith and love causes God's love and goodness to be actuated as well. God's יְדִיעָה, *knowledge*, becomes a פְּעוּלָה, *actuality*, when there are those prepared to receive the beneficial consequences of that knowledge, "those" being the people of Israel.

5. אַחֲרֵי ה׳ אֱלֹהֵיכֶם תֵּלֵכוּ — *After HASHEM your God*

ו וּבְקֹלוֹ תִשְׁמָעוּ וְאֹתוֹ תַעֲבֹדוּ וּבוֹ תִדְבָּקוּן: וְהַנָּבִיא הַהוּא אוֹ חֹלֵם הַחֲלוֹם
הַהוּא יוּמָת כִּי דִבֶּר־סָרָה עַל־יְהוָה אֱלֹהֵיכֶם הַמּוֹצִיא אֶתְכֶם | מֵאֶרֶץ
מִצְרַיִם וְהַפֹּדְךָ מִבֵּית עֲבָדִים לְהַדִּיחֲךָ מִן־הַדֶּרֶךְ אֲשֶׁר צִוְּךָ יְהוָה אֱלֹהֶיךָ
ז לָלֶכֶת בָּהּ וּבִעַרְתָּ הָרָע מִקִּרְבֶּךָ: כִּי יְסִיתְךָ אָחִיךָ בֶן־אִמֶּךָ
אוֹ־בִנְךָ אוֹ־בִתְּךָ אוֹ | אֵשֶׁת חֵיקֶךָ אוֹ רֵעֲךָ אֲשֶׁר כְּנַפְשְׁךָ בַּסֵּתֶר לֵאמֹר
ח נֵלְכָה וְנַעַבְדָה אֱלֹהִים אֲחֵרִים אֲשֶׁר לֹא יָדַעְתָּ אַתָּה וַאֲבֹתֶיךָ: מֵאֱלֹהֵי
הָעַמִּים אֲשֶׁר סְבִיבֹתֵיכֶם הַקְּרֹבִים אֵלֶיךָ אוֹ הָרְחֹקִים מִמֶּךָּ מִקְצֵה הָאָרֶץ
ט וְעַד־קְצֵה הָאָרֶץ: לֹא־תֹאבֶה לוֹ וְלֹא תִשְׁמַע אֵלָיו וְלֹא־תָחוֹס עֵינְךָ

and walk in His ways (28:9), and not in new (incorrect) ways that the prophet or dreamer shows (lit., says), with the intent of leading you astray from the (proper) way.

וְאֹתוֹ תִירָאוּ — *And Him shall you fear.* Even though that prophet was already (accepted) among you as an important and revered person, (yet if) he now exaggerates (his prophetic powers), then nullify your reverence of this prophet before the reverence of God, the Blessed One.

וְאֶת מִצְוֹתָיו תִּשְׁמֹרוּ — *And His commandments you shall keep* ... but not new commandments devised by a prophet, especially idolatry which is contradictory to all the commandments of God, the Exalted One, because He commanded His covenant forever, (and) He will not exchange it or change it.

וּבְקֹלוֹ תִשְׁמָעוּ — *And to His voice shall you hearken* ... that which He commands you through His prophets, in order to preserve His Torah and sanctify His name, as we find with Elijah on Mt. Carmel — but (one is not to hearken) to the voice of he who nullifies all the commandments of God, the Exalted One.

וְאֹתוֹ תַעֲבֹדוּ — *And Him shall you serve* ... Him alone and none other with Him, as it says, זֹבֵחַ לָאֱלֹהִים יָחֳרָם, *He that sacrifices unto the gods ... shall be utterly destroyed* (Exodus 22:19), as explained there.

וּבוֹ תִדְבָּקוּן — *And unto Him you shall cleave.* The purpose of all your actions shall be to do His will, and your animosity toward this (false prophet) shall not be motivated by a prior hatred.

6. יוּמָת כִּי דִבֶּר סָרָה עַל ה׳ — *Shall be put to death, because he spoke untruth about* HASHEM. Although he spoke in the name of God, and not in the name of strange gods, and therefore it would appear that he should not be put to death, similar to the elders' decision regarding Jeremiah when they said, אֵין לָאִישׁ הַזֶּה מִשְׁפַּט מָוֶת, כִּי בְּשֵׁם ה׳ אֱלֹקֵינוּ דִּבֶּר אֵלֵינוּ, *This man*

NOTES

shall you walk. The expression "to walk in His ways" denotes the practical application of the commandments in deed. Hence, the verse means to say that we are urged to follow the ways (i.e., commandments) only of God, and not new commandments devised by a false prophet which contradict the law of God.

וְאֶת מִצְוֹתָיו תִּשְׁמֹרוּ — *And His commandments you shall keep*. The expression used by the *Sforno*, לֹא יַחֲלִיפֶנּוּ, *He will not exchange it*, is used by the *Rambam* in the 9th principle of his Thirteen Principles of Faith: "I believe with complete faith that this Torah will not be exchanged." The phrase וְלֹא יָמִיר, *and not change it*, is based on *Leviticus* 27:33.

וְאֹתוֹ תִירָאוּ — *And Him shall you fear*. The admonition *Him shall you fear* implies that there is a competing fear which is to be rejected. The *Sforno's* commentary clarifies this phrase. Fear only Him, not the great man who heretofore deserved your reverence but who has now forfeited it because of his deviant conduct.

וּבְקֹלוֹ תִשְׁמָעוּ... וְאֹתוֹ תַעֲבֹדוּ... וּבוֹ תִדְבָּקוּן — *And to His voice shall you hearken ... and Him shall you serve ... and unto Him you shall cleave*. The *Sforno* explains that these three statements do not repeat a single idea, namely to be loyal to God, but represent three distinct concepts. *Shall you hearken to His voice* means that God will make His will

and to His voice shall you hearken; Him shall you serve and to Him shall you cleave. [6] *And that prophet and that dreamer of a dream shall be put to death, for he had spoken perversion against HASHEM, your God, Who takes you out of the land of Egypt, and Who redeems you from the house of slavery, to make you stray from the path on which HASHEM, your God, has commanded you to go; and you shall destroy the evil from your midst.*

[7] *If your brother, the son of your mother, or your son or your daughter, or the wife of your bosom, or your friend who is like your own soul will entice you secretly, saying, "Let us go and worship the gods of others" — that you did not know, you nor your forefathers,* [8] *from the gods of the peoples that are all around you, those near to you or those far from you, from one end of the earth to the other end of the earth —* [9] *you shall not accede to him and not hearken to him; your eye shall not take pity*

---

is not worthy to die, for he has spoken to us in the name of HASHEM our God (Jeremiah 26:16); however, (in this case) he deserves to die because he spoke an untruth in His name.

לְהַדִּיחֲךָ מִן הַדֶּרֶךְ — *To draw you aside out of the way.* Even though he did not attempt to draw you away from God, since he said in the name of God that you should serve strange gods according to His command, nonetheless he sought *to draw you aside out of the way which God your God had commanded you.*

8. הַקְּרֹבִים אֵלֶיךָ — *Close to you . . .* although due to their close proximity you know (full well) their falsity, and (hence) there is no (reason) to fear that you will be misled by them.

אוֹ הָרְחֹקִים מִמֶּךָּ מִקְצֵה הָאָרֶץ — *Or far from you, from one end of the earth* (*to the other end*) . . . even though due to the great distance one need not fear that you will go there to serve them.

9. לֹא תֹאבֶה לוֹ — *Do not accede to him . . .* by saying that you will investigate and find out whether his claims (lit., words) are correct, that a particular false god does good thus and bad thus.

וְלֹא תִשְׁמַע אֵלָיו — *Nor hearken to him.* In this manner (i.e., by not acceding to him), you will not listen to him, and you will not accept (his invitation) to serve (this "deity"). For if the matter is in doubt whether he is worthy (to be listened to), eventually you will hearken to him, for such doubt can only come from (your) lack of reflection regarding the greatness of God, the Blessed One, and His order in the world.

NOTES

known to us through the voice of His true prophets; *and Him shall you serve* is a warning against שִׁתּוּף, the prohibition of associating other deities with the one true God (i.e., polytheism), while *and unto Him you shall cleave* teaches us that personal animus must never motivate us in the punishment of the false prophet. It must be done only for the purpose of fulfilling God's will.

6. כִּי דִבֶּר סָרָה עַל ה׳ — *Because he spoke untruth about HASHEM.* The *Sforno* cites the episode recorded in *Jeremiah* 26 regarding the prophet Jeremiah who was sent by God to warn Jerusalem that unless the people mended their ways and returned to God, the Temple and the city would be destroyed. The *Kohanim* and false prophets demanded that Jeremiah be put to death, but the princes of Judah refused to do so asserting that he had spoken in the name of God. The *Sforno* explains that the argument used by the princes of Judah is not applicable to the false prophet, for even though he claims to speak in His name, and not in the name of a false God, nonetheless he utters falsehoods in the name of the true God, unlike Jeremiah who spoke the truth in the name of God.

9. לֹא תֹאבֶה לוֹ וְלֹא תִשְׁמַע אֵלָיו — *Do not accede to him, nor hearken to him.* The Torah cautions the people of Israel not to permit the false prophet to entice them into examining the powers of this false god, even though they will not worship him, for by doing so they will be taking the first step that may ultimately lead to their complete defection. He who is firm and resolute in his faith has no doubts and will in no way accede to this false prophet, nor

י עָלָיו וְלֹא־תַחְמֹל וְלֹא־תְכַסֶּה עָלָיו׃ כִּי הָרֹג תַּהַרְגֶנּוּ יָדְךָ תִּהְיֶה־בּוֹ
יא בָרִאשׁוֹנָה לַהֲמִיתוֹ וְיַד כָּל־הָעָם בָּאַחֲרֹנָה׃ וּסְקַלְתּוֹ בָאֲבָנִים וָמֵת כִּי
בִקֵּשׁ לְהַדִּיחֲךָ מֵעַל יְהוָה אֱלֹהֶיךָ הַמּוֹצִיאֲךָ מֵאֶרֶץ מִצְרַיִם מִבֵּית
יב עֲבָדִים׃ וְכָל־יִשְׂרָאֵל יִשְׁמְעוּ וְיִרָאוּן וְלֹא־יוֹסִפוּ לַעֲשׂוֹת כַּדָּבָר הָרָע הַזֶּה
יג בְּקִרְבֶּךָ׃ כִּי־תִשְׁמַע בְּאַחַת עָרֶיךָ אֲשֶׁר יְהוָה אֱלֹהֶיךָ נֹתֵן לְךָ
יד לָשֶׁבֶת שָׁם לֵאמֹר׃ יָצְאוּ אֲנָשִׁים בְּנֵי־בְלִיַּעַל מִקִּרְבֶּךָ וַיַּדִּיחוּ אֶת־יֹשְׁבֵי
טו עִירָם לֵאמֹר נֵלְכָה וְנַעַבְדָה אֱלֹהִים אֲחֵרִים אֲשֶׁר לֹא־יְדַעְתֶּם׃ וְדָרַשְׁתָּ
וְחָקַרְתָּ וְשָׁאַלְתָּ הֵיטֵב וְהִנֵּה אֱמֶת נָכוֹן הַדָּבָר נֶעֶשְׂתָה הַתּוֹעֵבָה הַזֹּאת
טז בְּקִרְבֶּךָ׃ הַכֵּה תַכֶּה אֶת־יֹשְׁבֵי הָעִיר הַהִוא לְפִי־חָרֶב הַחֲרֵם אֹתָהּ וְאֶת־
יז כָּל־אֲשֶׁר־בָּהּ וְאֶת־בְּהֶמְתָּהּ לְפִי־חָרֶב׃ וְאֶת־כָּל־שְׁלָלָהּ תִּקְבֹּץ אֶל־תּוֹךְ
רְחֹבָהּ וְשָׂרַפְתָּ בָאֵשׁ אֶת־הָעִיר וְאֶת־כָּל־שְׁלָלָהּ כָּלִיל לַיהוָה אֱלֹהֶיךָ
יח וְהָיְתָה תֵּל עוֹלָם לֹא תִבָּנֶה עוֹד׃ וְלֹא־יִדְבַּק בְּיָדְךָ מְאוּמָה מִן־הַחֵרֶם
לְמַעַן יָשׁוּב יְהוָה מֵחֲרוֹן אַפּוֹ וְנָתַן־לְךָ רַחֲמִים וְרִחַמְךָ וְהִרְבֶּךָ כַּאֲשֶׁר
יט נִשְׁבַּע לַאֲבֹתֶיךָ׃ כִּי תִשְׁמַע בְּקוֹל יְהוָה אֱלֹהֶיךָ לִשְׁמֹר אֶת־כָּל־מִצְוֺתָיו
יד רביעי א אֲשֶׁר אָנֹכִי מְצַוְּךָ הַיּוֹם לַעֲשׂוֹת הַיָּשָׁר בְּעֵינֵי יְהוָה אֱלֹהֶיךָ׃ בָּנִים
אַתֶּם לַיהוָה אֱלֹהֵיכֶם לֹא תִתְגֹּדְדוּ וְלֹא־תָשִׂימוּ קָרְחָה בֵּין עֵינֵיכֶם לָמֵת׃

11. כִּי בִקֵּשׁ לְהַדִּיחֲךָ — *Because he sought to lead you away.* Although he did not (succeed) in doing damage, as (in the case) of those who lead astray the condemned city (עִיר הַנִּדַּחַת), nonetheless he deserves to die because he did seek to lead you away (from God), and by executing him you will attain (the end) that he will not be able to mislead others, but if you do not kill him, perhaps he, or another, will lead others astray and succeed.

12. וְכָל יִשְׂרָאֵל יִשְׁמְעוּ וְיִרָאוּן וְלֹא יוֹסִפוּ — *And all of Israel shall hear and fear and shall do no more ...* neither he nor any other (person).

16. וְאֶת בְּהֶמְתָּהּ לְפִי חָרֶב — *And the cattle by the sword ...* to blot out their remembrance, thereby revenging (the honor) of God, the Blessed One, similar to Amalek of whom it is said, תִּמְחֶה אֶת זֵכֶר עֲמָלֵק, *blot out the remembrance of Amalek* (25:19), and so the prophet elaborated when he said, וְהֵמַתָּה מֵאִישׁ עַד אִשָּׁה מֵעֹלֵל וְעַד יוֹנֵק מִשּׁוֹר וְעַד שֶׂה מִגָּמָל וְעַד חֲמוֹר, *but slay both man and woman, infant and suckling, ox and sheep, camel and ass* (*I Samuel*, 15:3).

18. וְלֹא יִדְבַּק בְּיָדְךָ מְאוּמָה מִן הַחֵרֶם — *And nothing of that which is banned shall cleave to your hand ...* lest it become a snare, similar to the ornaments of the strange gods of

NOTES

will he give any credence to the possible efficacy of any false god. The sense of this verse, according to the *Sforno*, is: *Do not accede to him* at all, for only by rejecting him immediately and completely will you insure that you will *not hearken to him.*

16. וְאֶת בְּהֶמְתָּהּ לְפִי חָרֶב — *And the cattle by sword.* The Torah states (*Leviticus* 20:15) that if a man lies with a beast, both he and the beast shall be put to death. Our Sages ask, "If man sinned, how did the animal sin?" (*Sanhedrin* 54b). One of the answers given is, "So that the animal should not pass by in the market place and people will say, this is the animal who brought about the execution of that person." By eliminating the animal, we eliminate added shame. The *Sforno* gives a similar explanation here as to why we destroy the cattle of the עִיר הַנִּדַּחַת, *the city drawn away from God*. By erasing everything which can cause people to remember the idolatry of an entire city, we safeguard the honor of God and prevent added desecration of His Name.

18. וְלֹא יִדְבַּק בְּיָדְךָ מְאוּמָה מִן הַחֵרֶם — *And nothing of that which is banned shall cleave to your hand.* The prohibition of taking aught from the spoil of

on him, you shall not be compassionate nor conceal him. [10] *Rather, you shall*
surely kill him; your hand shall be the first against him to kill him, and the
hand of the entire people afterwards. [11] *You shall pelt him with stones and*
he shall die, for he sought to make you stray from near HASHEM, your God,
Who takes you out of Egypt, from the house of slavery. [12] *All Israel shall*
hear and fear, and they shall not again do such an evil thing in your midst.
[13] *If, in one of your cities that HASHEM, your God, gives you in which to*
dwell, you hear, saying, [14] *"Lawless men have emerged from your midst,*
and they have caused the dwellers of their city to go astray, saying, 'Let us
go and worship the gods of others, that you have not known' " — [15] *you*
shall seek out and investigate, and inquire well, and behold! it is true, the
word is correct, this abomination was committed in your midst. [16] *You shall*
smite the inhabitants of that city with the edge of the sword; lay it waste
and everything that is in it, and its animals, with the edge of the sword.
[17] *You shall gather together all its booty to the midst of its open square, and*
you shall burn in fire completely the city and all its booty to HASHEM, your
God, and it shall be an eternal heap, it shall not be rebuilt. [18] *No part of the*
banned property may adhere to your hand, so that HASHEM will turn back
from His burning wrath; and He will give you mercy and be merciful to you
and multiply you, as He swore to your forefathers, [19] *when you hearken to*
the voice of HASHEM, your God, to observe all His commandments that I
command you today, to do what is right in the eyes of HASHEM, your God.

14 [1] *You are children to HASHEM, your God — you shall not cut yourselves and*
you shall not make a bald spot between your eyes for a dead person.

---

which (the verse) says, *You shall not covet the silver or the gold that is on them, nor take it for yourself, lest you be ensnared therein* (7:25), as it is explained there.

XIV

1. בָּנִים אַתֶּם לַה׳ אֱלֹהֵיכֶם לֹא תִתְגֹּדְדוּ — *You are the children of HASHEM your God; you shall not cut yourselves.* It is not proper (for you) to show extreme concern and pain for the death of a relative, when a more honorable and distinguished relative still remains, in whom there is hope for (ultimate) good. Therefore, since you are children of God, Who is your eternal Father, it is unseemly that you should worry and mourn excessively over the death of anyone.

וְלֹא תָשִׂימוּ קָרְחָה בֵּין עֵינֵיכֶם לָמֵת — *Nor shall you make any baldness between your eyes for the dead.* And also you must not be greatly pained for the harm caused to the deceased in his death . . .

NOTES

the עִיר הַנִּדַּחַת is for the same reason given by the *Sforno* in his commentary on 7:25. If we were to prosper with the precious material taken from the spoil of this banned city we might attribute it to the power of the idols whom the inhabitants served.

XIV

1. בָּנִים אַתֶּם לַה׳ אֱלֹהֵיכֶם לֹא תִתְגֹּדְדוּ וְלֹא תָשִׂימוּ קָרְחָה — *You are the children of HASHEM your God; you shall not cut yourselves, nor shall you make any baldness.* Excessive mourning is caused by two factors. One is deep concern for the fate of the deceased, while the other is the profound sense of loss experienced by the surviving relatives. The Torah comforts Israel on both counts. Since we are a holy people each of us is insured a share in the World to Come, hence there is no reason to be concerned for the welfare of the deceased. As for one's great feeling of loss, since we are God's children, we must find comfort, support and strength in the

ב כִּי עַם קָדוֹשׁ אַתָּה לַיהוָה אֱלֹהֶיךָ וּבְךָ בָּחַר יהוה לִהְיוֹת לוֹ לְעַם סְגֻלָּה
ג מִכֹּל הָעַמִּים אֲשֶׁר עַל־פְּנֵי הָאֲדָמָה: לֹא תֹאכַל כָּל־
ד־ה תּוֹעֵבָה: זֹאת הַבְּהֵמָה אֲשֶׁר תֹּאכֵלוּ שׁוֹר שֵׂה כְשָׂבִים וְשֵׂה עִזִּים: אַיָּל
ו וּצְבִי וְיַחְמוּר וְאַקּוֹ וְדִישֹׁן וּתְאוֹ וָזָמֶר: וְכָל־בְּהֵמָה מַפְרֶסֶת פַּרְסָה וְשֹׁסַעַת
ז שֶׁסַע שְׁתֵּי פְרָסוֹת מַעֲלַת גֵּרָה בַּבְּהֵמָה אֹתָהּ תֹּאכֵלוּ: אַךְ אֶת־זֶה לֹא
תֹאכְלוּ מִמַּעֲלֵי הַגֵּרָה וּמִמַּפְרִיסֵי הַפַּרְסָה הַשְּׁסוּעָה אֶת־הַגָּמָל וְאֶת־
הָאַרְנֶבֶת וְאֶת־הַשָּׁפָן כִּי־מַעֲלֵה גֵרָה הֵמָּה וּפַרְסָה לֹא הִפְרִיסוּ טְמֵאִים
ח הֵם לָכֶם: וְאֶת־הַחֲזִיר כִּי־מַפְרִיס פַּרְסָה הוּא וְלֹא גֵרָה טָמֵא הוּא לָכֶם
ט מִבְּשָׂרָם לֹא תֹאכֵלוּ וּבְנִבְלָתָם לֹא תִגָּעוּ: אֶת־זֶה תֹּאכְלוּ
י מִכֹּל אֲשֶׁר בַּמָּיִם כֹּל אֲשֶׁר־לוֹ סְנַפִּיר וְקַשְׂקֶשֶׂת תֹּאכֵלוּ: וְכֹל אֲשֶׁר
יא אֵין־לוֹ סְנַפִּיר וְקַשְׂקֶשֶׂת לֹא תֹאכֵלוּ טָמֵא הוּא לָכֶם: כָּל־
יב צִפּוֹר טְהֹרָה תֹּאכֵלוּ: וְזֶה אֲשֶׁר לֹא־תֹאכְלוּ מֵהֶם הַנֶּשֶׁר וְהַפֶּרֶס וְהָעָזְנִיָּה:
יג־טו וְהָרָאָה וְאֶת־הָאַיָּה וְהַדַּיָּה לְמִינָהּ: וְאֵת כָּל־עֹרֵב לְמִינוֹ: וְאֵת בַּת הַיַּעֲנָה
טז וְאֶת־הַתַּחְמָס וְאֶת־הַשָּׁחַף וְאֶת־הַנֵּץ לְמִינֵהוּ: אֶת־הַכּוֹס וְאֶת־הַיַּנְשׁוּף
יז־יח וְהַתִּנְשָׁמֶת: וְהַקָּאָת וְאֶת־הָרָחָמָה וְאֶת־הַשָּׁלָךְ: וְהַחֲסִידָה וְהָאֲנָפָה
יט לְמִינָהּ וְהַדּוּכִיפַת וְהָעֲטַלֵּף: וְכֹל שֶׁרֶץ הָעוֹף טָמֵא הוּא לָכֶם לֹא יֵאָכֵלוּ:
כ־כא כָּל־עוֹף טָהוֹר תֹּאכֵלוּ: לֹא תֹאכְלוּ כָל־נְבֵלָה לַגֵּר אֲשֶׁר־בִּשְׁעָרֶיךָ
תִּתְּנֶנָּה וַאֲכָלָהּ אוֹ מָכֹר לְנָכְרִי כִּי עַם קָדוֹשׁ אַתָּה לַיהוָה אֱלֹהֶיךָ
לֹא־תְבַשֵּׁל גְּדִי בַּחֲלֵב אִמּוֹ:

---

2. כִּי עַם קָדוֹשׁ אַתָּה — *For you are a holy people* ... destined (to share) in the life of the World to Come, where one hour of spiritual bliss is better than the entire life of This World (based on *Avos* 4:22).

סְגֻלָּה מִכֹּל הָעַמִּים — *A treasure out of all peoples* . . . and therefore, He only prohibits (these practices) to you, but not to the "sons of Noah" who are not His treasure to the same extent.

3. לֹא תֹאכַל כָּל תּוֹעֵבָה — *You shall not eat any abominable thing.* Behold, before the Torah was given, the difference between clean (kosher) and unclean (non-kosher) animals was (already) known, as explained regarding Noah; nonetheless, when God, the Blessed One, permitted Noah and his children to consume living creatures, no differentiation was made between the clean and the unclean. However, being that you are a holy treasure out of all the peoples, it is improper for you to be nourished from the unclean and the abominable,

NOTES

realization that we still have our Father in heaven, Who is our most dear and distinguished "relative."

2. סְגֻלָּה מִכֹּל הָעַמִּים — *A treasure out of all peoples*. This expression is interpreted by the *Sforno* to mean that although all mankind is precious to God, the people of Israel are considered to be a special treasure among the human race and therefore, their exalted level requires the observance of these prohibitions. See his commentary on *Exodus* 19:5.

3. לֹא תֹאכַל כָּל תּוֹעֵבָה — *You shall not eat any abominable thing*. In *parashas Noach*, we find mention made of animals which are both clean and unclean (*Genesis* 7:8). After the flood, mankind was permitted to eat the flesh of *all* animals, and no differentiation was made. A distinction was made between them only regarding sacrifices. However, after the Torah was given, the people of Israel were allowed to eat those animals, fowl and fish enumerated in the subsequent verses. The *Sforno* links this verse to the expression in verse 2, סְגֻלָּה מִכֹּל הָעַמִּים, *a treasure out of all peoples*. Since Israel is a special, unique people, they are not permitted to eat that which is considered unclean and abominable by God, lest it affect

[2] *For you are a holy people to HASHEM, your God, and HASHEM has chosen you for Himself to be a treasured people, from among all the peoples on the face of the earth.*

[3] *You shall not eat any abomination.* [4] *These are the animals that you may eat: the ox, sheep, and goat;* [5] *the hart, deer, and the yachmur, the akko, dishon, the teo, and the zamer.* [6] *And every animal that has a split hoof, which is completely separated in two hooves, that brings up its cud among animals — it may you eat.* [7] *But this shall you not eat from among those that bring up their cud or have a completely separated split hoof: the camel, the hare, and the hyrax, for they bring up their cud, but their hoof is not split — they are unclean to you;* [8] *and the pig, for it has a split hoof, but not the cud — it is unclean to you; from their flesh you shall not eat and you shall not touch their carcasses.*

[9] *This you may eat of everything that is in the water: anything that has fins and scales you may eat.* [10] *And anything that does not have fins or scales you shall not eat; it is unclean to you.*

[11] *Every clean bird, you may eat.* [12] *This is what you shall not eat from among them: the nesher, the peres, the ozniah;* [13] *the raah, the ayah, and the dayah according to its kind;* [14] *and every oreiv according to its kind;* [15] *the bas haya'anah, the tachmos, the shachaf, and the netz, according to its kind;* [16] *the kos, the yanshuf, and the tinshemes;* [17] *the ka'as, the rachamah, and the shalach;* [18] *the chasidah, and the anafah according to its kind, the duchifas and the atalef.* [19] *And every flying swarming creature is unclean to you; they shall not be eaten.* [20] *Every clean bird may you eat.* [21] *You shall not eat any carcass; to the stranger who is in your cities shall you give it that he may eat it, or sell it to a gentile, for you are a holy people to HASHEM, your God; you shall not cook a kid in its mother's milk.*

(for through such ingestion) you will become similar (to them) in temperament.

21. לֹא תֹאכְלוּ כָל נְבֵלָה — *You shall not eat anything that dies of itself* ... even of a clean species.

כִּי עַם קָדוֹשׁ אַתָּה לַה׳ אֱלֹהֶיךָ — *For you are a holy people unto HASHEM your God.* Although that which dies of itself is suitable for human food, such as for the stranger or foreigner, it is not suitable food (for) a holy people, designated to attain an intended perfection from God, the Blessed One.

לֹא תְבַשֵּׁל גְּדִי — *You shall not cook a kid.* As was the practice of the nations, who thought that through this act, they would increase their cattle, and their possessions and their animals.

NOTES

their character and personality. This is perhaps the origin of the saying, "You are what you eat."

21. לֹא תֹאכְלוּ כָל נְבֵלָה — *You shall not eat anything that dies of itself.* Although a נְבֵלָה, *an animal that dies of itself*, is not in itself an abomination, since this term applies to a clean animal as well and is fit for consumption by the stranger and foreigner (נָכְרִי and גֵּר), nonetheless you are not permitted to eat it because you are a holy people and as such, must avoid those foods which might impair the attainment of the perfection intended for you.

21-22. לֹא תְבַשֵּׁל גְּדִי... עַשֵּׂר תְּעַשֵּׂר — *You shall not cook a kid ... You shall surely tithe.* This prohibition appears twice in *Exodus* (23:19 and 34:26). In those two verses, the commandment to bring the first fruits of one's land to the Temple precedes this prohibition. Here, in the Book of *Deuteronomy,*

חמישי כב־כג עַשֵּׂר תְּעַשֵּׂר אֵת כָּל־תְּבוּאַת זַרְעֶךָ הַיֹּצֵא הַשָּׂדֶה שָׁנָה שָׁנָה: וְאָכַלְתָּ
לִפְנֵי | יהוה אֱלֹהֶיךָ בַּמָּקוֹם אֲשֶׁר־יִבְחַר לְשַׁכֵּן שְׁמוֹ שָׁם מַעְשַׂר דְּגָנְךָ
תִּירֹשְׁךָ וְיִצְהָרֶךָ וּבְכֹרֹת בְּקָרְךָ וְצֹאנֶךָ לְמַעַן תִּלְמַד לְיִרְאָה אֶת־יהוה
כד אֱלֹהֶיךָ כָּל־הַיָּמִים: וְכִי־יִרְבֶּה מִמְּךָ הַדֶּרֶךְ כִּי לֹא תוּכַל שְׂאֵתוֹ כִּי־
יִרְחַק מִמְּךָ הַמָּקוֹם אֲשֶׁר יִבְחַר יהוה אֱלֹהֶיךָ לָשׂוּם שְׁמוֹ שָׁם כִּי יְבָרֶכְךָ
כה יהוה אֱלֹהֶיךָ: וְנָתַתָּה בַּכָּסֶף וְצַרְתָּ הַכֶּסֶף בְּיָדְךָ וְהָלַכְתָּ אֶל־הַמָּקוֹם
כו אֲשֶׁר יִבְחַר יהוה אֱלֹהֶיךָ בּוֹ: וְנָתַתָּה הַכֶּסֶף בְּכֹל אֲשֶׁר־תְּאַוֶּה נַפְשְׁךָ
בַּבָּקָר וּבַצֹּאן וּבַיַּיִן וּבַשֵּׁכָר וּבְכֹל אֲשֶׁר תִּשְׁאָלְךָ נַפְשֶׁךָ וְאָכַלְתָּ שָּׁם
כז לִפְנֵי יהוה אֱלֹהֶיךָ וְשָׂמַחְתָּ אַתָּה וּבֵיתֶךָ: וְהַלֵּוִי אֲשֶׁר־בִּשְׁעָרֶיךָ לֹא
כח תַעַזְבֶנּוּ כִּי אֵין לוֹ חֵלֶק וְנַחֲלָה עִמָּךְ: מִקְצֵה | שָׁלֹשׁ שָׁנִים
כט תּוֹצִיא אֶת־כָּל־מַעְשַׂר תְּבוּאָתְךָ בַּשָּׁנָה הַהִוא וְהִנַּחְתָּ בִּשְׁעָרֶיךָ: וּבָא
הַלֵּוִי כִּי אֵין־לוֹ חֵלֶק וְנַחֲלָה עִמָּךְ וְהַגֵּר וְהַיָּתוֹם וְהָאַלְמָנָה אֲשֶׁר
בִּשְׁעָרֶיךָ וְאָכְלוּ וְשָׂבֵעוּ לְמַעַן יְבָרֶכְךָ יהוה אֱלֹהֶיךָ בְּכָל־מַעֲשֵׂה יָדְךָ
טו ששי א־ב אֲשֶׁר תַּעֲשֶׂה: מִקֵּץ שֶׁבַע־שָׁנִים תַּעֲשֶׂה שְׁמִטָּה: וְזֶה דְּבַר
הַשְּׁמִטָּה שָׁמוֹט כָּל־בַּעַל מַשֵּׁה יָדוֹ אֲשֶׁר יַשֶּׁה בְּרֵעֵהוּ לֹא־יִגֹּשׂ
ג אֶת־רֵעֵהוּ וְאֶת־אָחִיו כִּי־קָרָא שְׁמִטָּה לַיהוה: אֶת־הַנָּכְרִי תִּגֹּשׂ וַאֲשֶׁר
ד יִהְיֶה לְךָ אֶת־אָחִיךָ תַּשְׁמֵט יָדֶךָ: אֶפֶס כִּי לֹא יִהְיֶה־בְּךָ אֶבְיוֹן כִּי־

22. עַשֵּׂר תְּעַשֵּׂר — *You shall surely tithe.* Because by tithing the grain produce and animals, you will increase your produce and cattle, as our Sages state, עַשֵּׂר בִּשְׁבִיל שֶׁתִּתְעַשֵּׁר, *Tithe so that you will become affluent* (*Shabbos* 119a).

23. לְמַעַן תִּלְמַד לְיִרְאָה אֶת ה׳ — *That you may learn to fear* HASHEM. Because in that place chosen for the Holy Temple, the Great Court (Sanhedrin) will be (present) to achieve understanding and to teach.

XV

2. וְזֶה דְּבַר הַשְּׁמִטָּה — *And this is the manner of the release* (*shemittah*). When God, the Blessed One, said, וְהַשְּׁבִיעִת תִּשְׁמְטֶנָּה, *but the seventh year you shall release* (*Exodus* 23:11), the intent was to institute the release of money (i.e., cancellation of debts).

NOTES

this prohibition is followed by the commandment of tithing. In his commentary on the two verses in *Exodus*, the *Sforno* explains that whereas the heathens would cook a kid in its mother's milk to appease the gods in the hope of having their flocks and produce blessed, Israel was told to bring their first fruits to God in recognition of His granting them heavenly blessings and due to the merit of this *mitzvah*, He would continue to bless them. Similarly in these verses, the *Sforno* explains that as opposed to the pagans who resort to this act of cooking a kid in its mother's milk, let the Israelite tithe and as a result he will be granted riches. עַשֵּׂר בִּשְׁבִיל שֶׁתִּתְעַשֵּׁר, *tithe so that you will be rewarded with wealth*, is a play on the word עשר, which can be read as עַשֵּׂר, *tithe*, or עֹשֶׁר, *riches*, depending on the use of the letter שׂ or שׁ.

23. לְמַעַן תִּלְמַד לְיִרְאָה — *That you may learn to fear*. The *Sforno* is of the opinion that fear and reverence of God stems from man's knowledge of Him. To gain this knowledge, one needs instruction which he can receive from the teachers of Israel who reside in Jerusalem. Indeed, the purpose of bringing the second tithe to Jerusalem was to afford them the opportunity to learn God's will and His teachings, which, in turn, would bring one to יִרְאַת שָׁמַיִם *the fear of heaven*, as it says, רֵאשִׁית חָכְמָה יִרְאַת ה׳, *The beginning of wisdom is the fear of* HASHEM (*Psalms* 111:10).

XV

2. וְזֶה דְּבַר הַשְּׁמִטָּה — *And this is the manner of the release* (*shemittah*). The *Sforno* in his commentary on *Exodus* 23:11, וְהַשְּׁבִיעִת תִּשְׁמְטֶנָּה וּנְטַשְׁתָּהּ, *but the*

22 *You shall tithe the entire crop of your planting, the produce of the field,*
year by year. 23 *And you shall eat before HASHEM, your God, in the place*
that He will choose to rest His Name — the tithe of your grain, your wine,
and your oil, and the firstborn of your cattle and your flocks, so that you
will learn to fear HASHEM, your God, all the days. 24 *If the road will be too*
long for you, so that you cannot carry it, because the place that HASHEM,
your God, will choose to place His Name there is far from you, for HASHEM,
your God, will have blessed you — 25 *then you may exchange it for money,*
wrap up the money in your hand, and go to the place that HASHEM, your
God, will choose. 26 *You may spend the money for whatever your heart*
desires — for cattle, for flocks, for wine, or for alcoholic beverage, or
anything that your soul wishes; you shall eat it there before HASHEM, your
God, and rejoice — you and your household. 27 *You shall not forsake the*
Levite who is in your cities, for he has no portion or inheritance with you.
28 *At the end of three years you shall take out every tithe of your crop in*
that year and set it down within your cities. 29 *Then the Levite can come —*
for he has no portion or inheritance with you — and the proselyte, the
orphan, and the widow who are in your cities, so they may eat and be
satisfied, in order that HASHEM, your God, will bless you in all your
handiwork that you may undertake.

15 1 *At the end of seven years you shall institute a remission.* 2 *This is the*
matter of the remission: Every creditor shall remit his authority
over what he has lent his fellow; he shall not press his fellow or his
brother, for He has proclaimed a remission for HASHEM. 3 *You may press*
the gentile; but over what you have with your brother, you shall remit
your authority. 4 *However, may there be no destitute among you; rather,*

שָׁמוֹט כָּל בַּעַל מַשֵּׁה יָדוֹ — *Every creditor shall release from his hand ...* because God, the Blessed One, proclaimed *shemittah*, release, when He said, תִּשְׁמְטֶנָּה, *you shall release* (*Exodus* 23:11).

4. אֶפֶס כִּי לֹא יִהְיֶה בְּךָ אֶבְיוֹן — *However, there shall be no needy among you.* Although I told you to *release your hand*, behold there shall be no borrowers among you that will necessitate the release (of debts). This, without a doubt, transpired with the generation that entered the Land *all the days of Joshua and all the days of the elders who outlived Joshua* (*Joshua* 24:31).

NOTES

seventh year you shall release and abandon, interprets the first verb, תִּשְׁמְטֶנָּה, as meaning the release of all debts which are canceled, while the second verb, וּנְטַשְׁתָּהּ, refers to the land that cannot be sown and the produce of that land which may be eaten by all. In his commentary on this verse, he refers back to the verse in *Exodus*, explaining that the word הַשְּׁמִטָּה, *the shemittah* (using the definite article), only refers to the cancellation of debts (i.e., the first verb in *Exodus* 23:11). Indeed, the subsequent verses here specifically refer to cancellation of debts, and not to the *shemittah* of land.

שָׁמוֹט כָּל בַּעַל מַשֵּׁה יָדוֹ — *Every creditor shall release from his hand.* The *Sforno's* comment on this phrase is based on the concluding part of this verse, *'because a release has been proclaimed to HASHEM.'*

4. אֶפֶס כִּי לֹא יִהְיֶה בְּךָ אֶבְיוֹן — *However, there shall be no needy among you.* In this verse, we are told that there will be no needy among us. In verse 11, however, the Torah tells us that *the needy will never cease.* To reconcile these two verses, the *Sforno* explains that it all depends upon Israel's obedience, or disobedience, to God's laws. While this answer is given by many other commentators, he expands on this classic answer by citing two

בָּרֵךְ יְבָרֶכְךָ֮ יהוה֒ בָּאָ֗רֶץ אֲשֶׁר֙ יהוה אֱלֹהֶ֔יךָ נֹתֵֽן־לְךָ֥ נַחֲלָ֖ה לְרִשְׁתָּֽהּ:

ה   רַ֚ק אִם־שָׁמ֣וֹעַ תִּשְׁמַ֔ע בְּק֖וֹל יהוה אֱלֹהֶ֑יךָ לִשְׁמֹ֣ר לַֽעֲשׂוֹת֙ אֶת־כָּל־

ו הַמִּצְוָ֣ה הַזֹּ֔את אֲשֶׁ֛ר אָֽנֹכִ֥י מְצַוְּךָ֖ הַיּֽוֹם: כִּֽי־יהוה אֱלֹהֶ֨יךָ֙ בֵּֽרַכְךָ֔ כַּֽאֲשֶׁ֖ר דִּבֶּר־לָ֑ךְ וְהַֽעֲבַטְתָּ֞ גּוֹיִ֣ם רַבִּ֗ים וְאַתָּה֙ לֹ֣א תַֽעֲבֹ֔ט וּמָֽשַׁלְתָּ֙ בְּגוֹיִ֣ם רַבִּ֔ים וּבְךָ֖

ז לֹ֥א יִמְשֹֽׁלוּ: כִּֽי־יִֽהְיֶה֩ בְךָ֨ אֶבְי֜וֹן מֵֽאַחַ֤ד אַחֶ֨יךָ֙ בְּאַחַ֣ד שְׁעָרֶ֔יךָ בְּאַ֨רְצְךָ֔ אֲשֶׁר־יהוה אֱלֹהֶ֖יךָ נֹתֵ֣ן לָ֑ךְ לֹ֧א תְאַמֵּ֣ץ אֶת־לְבָֽבְךָ֗ וְלֹ֤א

ח תִקְפֹּץ֙ אֶת־יָ֣דְךָ֔ מֵֽאָחִ֖יךָ הָֽאֶבְיֽוֹן: כִּֽי־פָתֹ֧חַ תִּפְתַּ֛ח אֶת־יָֽדְךָ֖ ל֑וֹ וְהַֽעֲבֵט֙

ט תַּֽעֲבִיטֶ֔נּוּ דֵּ֚י מַחְסֹר֔וֹ אֲשֶׁ֥ר יֶחְסַ֖ר לֽוֹ: הִשָּׁ֣מֶר לְךָ֡ פֶּן־יִֽהְיֶ֣ה דָבָר֩ עִם־לְבָֽבְךָ֨ בְלִיַּ֜עַל לֵאמֹ֗ר קָֽרְבָ֣ה שְׁנַֽת־הַשֶּׁ֘בַע֮ שְׁנַ֣ת הַשְּׁמִטָּה֒ וְרָעָ֣ה עֵֽינְךָ֗ בְּאָחִ֨יךָ֙

י הָֽאֶבְי֔וֹן וְלֹ֥א תִתֵּ֖ן ל֑וֹ וְקָרָ֤א עָלֶ֨יךָ֙ אֶל־יהוה וְהָיָ֥ה בְךָ֖ חֵֽטְא: נָת֤וֹן תִּתֵּן֙ ל֔וֹ וְלֹֽא־יֵרַ֥ע לְבָֽבְךָ֖ בְּתִתְּךָ֣ ל֑וֹ כִּ֞י בִּגְלַ֣ל | הַדָּבָ֣ר הַזֶּ֗ה יְבָֽרֶכְךָ֙ יהוה אֱלֹהֶ֔יךָ

יא בְּכָֽל־מַֽעֲשֶׂ֔ךָ וּבְכֹ֖ל מִשְׁלַ֥ח יָדֶֽךָ: כִּ֛י לֹֽא־יֶחְדַּ֥ל אֶבְי֖וֹן מִקֶּ֣רֶב הָאָ֑רֶץ עַל־כֵּ֞ן אָֽנֹכִ֤י מְצַוְּךָ֙ לֵאמֹ֔ר פָּ֠תֹ֠חַ תִּפְתַּ֨ח אֶת־יָֽדְךָ֜ לְאָחִ֧יךָ לַֽעֲנִיֶּ֛ךָ וּלְאֶבְיֹֽנְךָ֖

יב בְּאַרְצֶֽךָ: כִּֽי־יִמָּכֵ֨ר לְךָ֜ אָחִ֣יךָ הָֽעִבְרִ֗י א֚וֹ הָֽעִבְרִיָּ֔ה וַֽעֲבָֽדְךָ֖ שֵׁ֣שׁ

יג שָׁנִ֑ים וּבַשָּׁנָה֙ הַשְּׁבִיעִ֔ת תְּשַׁלְּחֶ֥נּוּ חָפְשִׁ֖י מֵֽעִמָּֽךְ: וְכִֽי־תְשַׁלְּחֶ֥נּוּ חָפְשִׁ֖י מֵֽעִמָּ֑ךְ

יד לֹ֥א תְשַׁלְּחֶ֖נּוּ רֵיקָֽם: הַֽעֲנֵ֤יק תַּֽעֲנִיק֙ ל֔וֹ מִצֹּ֣אנְךָ֔ וּמִֽגָּרְנְךָ֖ וּמִיִּקְבֶ֑ךָ אֲשֶׁ֧ר

טו בֵּֽרַכְךָ֛ יהוה אֱלֹהֶ֖יךָ תִּתֶּן־לֽוֹ: וְזָ֣כַרְתָּ֗ כִּ֣י עֶ֤בֶד הָיִ֨יתָ֙ בְּאֶ֣רֶץ מִצְרַ֔יִם וַֽיִּפְדְּךָ֖

טז יהוה אֱלֹהֶ֑יךָ עַל־כֵּ֞ן אָֽנֹכִ֧י מְצַוְּךָ֛ אֶת־הַדָּבָ֥ר הַזֶּ֖ה הַיּֽוֹם: וְהָיָה֙ כִּֽי־יֹאמַ֣ר

יז אֵלֶ֔יךָ לֹ֥א אֵצֵ֖א מֵֽעִמָּ֑ךְ כִּ֤י אֲהֵֽבְךָ֙ וְאֶת־בֵּיתֶ֔ךָ כִּי־ט֥וֹב ל֖וֹ עִמָּֽךְ: וְלָֽקַחְתָּ֣ אֶת־הַמַּרְצֵ֗עַ וְנָֽתַתָּ֤ה בְאָזְנוֹ֙ וּבַדֶּ֔לֶת וְהָיָ֥ה לְךָ֖ עֶ֣בֶד עוֹלָ֑ם וְאַ֖ף לַֽאֲמָֽתְךָ֥

יח תַּֽעֲשֶׂה־כֵּֽן: לֹֽא־יִקְשֶׁ֣ה בְעֵינֶ֗ךָ בְּשַׁלֵּֽחֲךָ֙ אֹת֤וֹ חָפְשִׁי֙ מֵֽעִמָּ֔ךְ כִּ֗י מִשְׁנֶה֙ שְׂכַ֣ר שָׂכִ֔יר עֲבָֽדְךָ֖ שֵׁ֣שׁ שָׁנִ֑ים וּבֵֽרַכְךָ֙ יהוה אֱלֹהֶ֔יךָ בְּכֹ֖ל אֲשֶׁ֥ר תַּֽעֲשֶֽׂה:

יט כָּֽל־הַבְּכ֡וֹר אֲשֶׁר֩ יִוָּלֵ֨ד בִּבְקָֽרְךָ֤ וּבְצֹֽאנְךָ֙ הַזָּכָ֔ר תַּקְדִּ֕ישׁ לַֽיהוה אֱלֹהֶ֑יךָ

שביעי

---

11. כִּי לֹא יֶחְדַּל אֶבְיוֹן — *For the needy will never cease.* This refers (to the period of), *For I know that after my death you will fall into great corruption* (31:29).

15. וְזָכַרְתָּ כִּי עֶבֶד הָיִיתָ — *And you shall remember that you were a slave.* Not only did He deliver you and free you from bondage but (also) furnished you liberally with the money of those who subjugated you.

18. לֹא יִקְשֶׁה בְעֵינֶךָ — *And this shall not seem hard in your eyes* . . . to furnish him liberally when you set him free because he is worthy (to be so compensated), and you will not lack aught (by doing so).

וּבֵרַכְךָ ה׳ אֱלֹהֶיךָ — *And* HASHEM *your God will bless you.* (Hence) it is from Him that you give it.

NOTES

verses which reflect different periods in Jewish history. Moses predicted that a time would come when Israel would turn away from God. During such a period the needy would never cease. During the time of Joshua and the Elders, however, when Israel first entered *Eretz Yisrael* the people followed in the ways of God and poverty was unknown. Of such a time the Torah states, *there shall be no needy among you.*

15-18. וְזָכַרְתָּ כִּי עֶבֶד הָיִיתָ . . . וּבֵרַכְךָ ה׳ אֱלֹהֶיךָ — *And you shall remember that you were a slave . . . and* HASHEM *your God will bless you.* As the *Sforno* explains, these verses were meant to encourage the master to give הַעֲנָקָה, *compensation,* to a slave

*HASHEM will surely bless you in the Land that HASHEM, your God, will give
you as an inheritance, to possess it, 5 only if you will hearken to the voice of
HASHEM, your God, to observe, to perform this entire commandment that I
command you today. 6 For HASHEM, your God, has blessed you as He has
told you; you will lend to many nations, but you will not borrow; and you
will dominate many nations, but they will not dominate you.*

*7 If there shall be a destitute person among you, any of your brethren in
any of your cities, in the Land that HASHEM, your God, gives you, you shall
not harden your heart or close your hand against your destitute brother.
8 Rather, you shall open your hand to him; you shall lend him his
requirement, whatever is lacking to him. 9 Beware lest there be a lawless
thought in your heart, saying, "The seventh year approaches, the remission
year," and you will look malevolently upon your destitute brother and
refuse to give him — then he may appeal against you to HASHEM, and it will
be a sin upon you. 10 You shall surely give him, and let your heart not feel
bad when you give him, for in return for this matter, HASHEM, your God,
will bless you in all your deeds and in your every undertaking. 11 For
destitute people will not cease to exist within the Land; therefore I
command you, saying, "You shall surely open your hand to your brother, to
your poor, and to your destitute in your Land."*

*12 If your brother, a Hebrew man or a Hebrew woman, will be sold to you,
he shall serve you for six years, and in the seventh year you shall send him
away from you free. 13 But when you send him away free, you shall not
send him away empty-handed. 14 Adorn him generously from your flocks,
from your threshing floor, and from your wine-cellar; as HASHEM, your
God, has blessed you, so shall you give him. 15 You shall remember that you
were a slave in the land of Egypt, and HASHEM, your God, redeemed you;
therefore, I command you regarding this matter today.*

*16 In the event he will say to you, "I will not leave you," for he loves you
and your household, for it is good for him with you, 17 then you shall take
the awl and put it through his ear and the door, and he shall be for you an
eternal slave; even to your maidservant shall you do the same. 18 It shall not
be difficult in your eyes when you send him away free from you, for twice
as much as a hired hand — six years — has he served you; and HASHEM,
your God, will bless you in all that you do.*

19 Every firstborn male that is born in your cattle and in your flock, you

19. כָּל הַבְּכוֹר — *All the firstlings.* After (the Torah) explains the various aspects of *chesed*, lovingkindness, regarding grain produce such as the tithe for the poor, and regarding money such as charity, and the release of debts and regarding other possessions through

NOTES

leaving his service. The Torah first reminds us that we were also slaves and God gave us great treasures when we departed Egypt, treasures taken from our masters! Secondly, we are reassured by the Almighty that He will compensate us for our generosity; hence, it will in no way diminish our wealth.

19. כָּל הַבְּכוֹר — *All the firstlings.* The *Sforno's* commentary on this verse is meant to explain the logical order of the remainder of the *parashah*, and the link to the preceding portion (chapter 14:22 to 15:18). He also answers the question, "Why doesn't the Torah mention the specific month and day of each festival?" He explains that here the Torah is

כ לֹא תַעֲבֹד בִּבְכֹר שׁוֹרֶךָ וְלֹא תָגֹז בְּכוֹר צֹאנֶךָ: לִפְנֵי יהוה אֱלֹהֶיךָ
כא תֹאכְלֶנּוּ שָׁנָה בְשָׁנָה בַּמָּקוֹם אֲשֶׁר־יִבְחַר יהוה אַתָּה וּבֵיתֶךָ: וְכִי־יִהְיֶה בוֹ
כב מוּם פִּסֵּחַ אוֹ עִוֵּר כֹּל מוּם רָע לֹא תִזְבָּחֶנּוּ לַיהוה אֱלֹהֶיךָ: בִּשְׁעָרֶיךָ
כג תֹּאכְלֶנּוּ הַטָּמֵא וְהַטָּהוֹר יַחְדָּו כַּצְּבִי וְכָאַיָּל: רַק אֶת־דָּמוֹ לֹא תֹאכֵל
עַל־הָאָרֶץ תִּשְׁפְּכֶנּוּ כַּמָּיִם:

טז א שָׁמוֹר אֶת־חֹדֶשׁ הָאָבִיב וְעָשִׂיתָ פֶּסַח לַיהוה אֱלֹהֶיךָ כִּי בְּחֹדֶשׁ הָאָבִיב
ב הוֹצִיאֲךָ יהוה אֱלֹהֶיךָ מִמִּצְרַיִם לָיְלָה: וְזָבַחְתָּ פֶּסַח לַיהוה אֱלֹהֶיךָ צֹאן
ג וּבָקָר בַּמָּקוֹם אֲשֶׁר יִבְחַר יהוה לְשַׁכֵּן שְׁמוֹ שָׁם: לֹא־תֹאכַל עָלָיו חָמֵץ
שִׁבְעַת יָמִים תֹּאכַל־עָלָיו מַצּוֹת לֶחֶם עֹנִי כִּי בְחִפָּזוֹן יָצָאתָ מֵאֶרֶץ מִצְרַיִם

הַעֲנָקָה, the liberal furnishing of a Hebrew slave (when he is freed), it now explains those commandments which represent thanksgiving to God, the Exalted One, and they are: the offering of the firstlings, for it is proper that owners of cattle thank (Him) because our cattle comes from His hand; and the Festival of Matzos, unleavened bread, to thank (Him) for freedom through the sacrifice of the *Pesach* lamb and the matzos; and for the *Aviv* through the *omer* (measure of barley) which is waved; and the Festival of Shevuos to thank Him for keeping שְׁבֻעֹת חֻקּוֹת קָצִיר, *the appointed weeks of the harvest* (*Jeremiah* 5:24), on our behalf; and the Festival of Ingathering (Succos) to thank Him for the ingathering. On each of these (occasions), we are to bring some gift to the Master, as it says, *and they shall not appear before HASHEM empty* (16:16). Therefore, the Torah does not mention in which month, nor the date of the month, they will occur, but mentions the *Aviv*, (and the Festivals of) the Weeks and the Ingathering.

XVI

1. שָׁמוֹר אֶת חֹדֶשׁ הָאָבִיב — *Observe the month of Aviv.* Guard with constant care that Nissan coincide with the month of *Aviv*, by intercalating the months and years so that the lunar and solar year are equal.

וְעָשִׂיתָ פֶּסַח — *And you shall make the Pesach* ... on the eve of the Festival of Matzos.

כִּי בְּחֹדֶשׁ הָאָבִיב הוֹצִיאֲךָ — *For in the month of Aviv, (God) brought you forth.* His intent and desire was that your departure (from Egypt) be at a time when the renewal of *Aviv* is complete, (a time) of contrast being that (the sign of) the ram, the deity of Egypt, (then

NOTES

only telling us the rationale for these festivals, namely an expression of our thanks to God, and not the details of their time and manner of observance.

XVI

1. שָׁמוֹר אֶת חֹדֶשׁ הָאָבִיב — *Observe the month of Aviv. Aviv* is the season of the ripening of the ears. Israel is cautioned to take care that Pesach should always coincide with this month. Since Israel's is a lunar year, which is eleven days shorter than the solar year, it is bound to bring about a shifting of its festivals from their proper seasons in the course of time; hence, the need to intercalate the year by adding an extra month (*Adar Sheini*) seven times in every cycle of nineteen years. The Torah, therefore, enjoins us to *guard* (שָׁמוֹר) that Nissan fall in the month of *Aviv*, as the *Sforno* explains.

וְעָשִׂיתָ פֶּסַח — *And offer the Pesach*. In the terminology of the Torah, the term פֶּסַח refers to the *Pesach* lamb which is brought on the 14th day of *Nissan* — the eve of חַג הַמַּצּוֹת, *the Festival of Matzos.*

כִּי בְּחֹדֶשׁ הָאָבִיב הוֹצִיאֲךָ . . . לָיְלָה — *For in the month of Aviv, (God) brought you forth ... by night*. In ancient times, every nation identified with a certain planet, constellation or sign of the zodiac, which was considered their deity. Egypt's constellation was Aries the Ram. According to astrology, each month corresponds to a different sign of the zodiac indicating the ascendancy of a particular planet during that month. The *mazal*, planet, which represents Egypt ascends in the month of Nissan which is *Aviv*. Symbolically, this means that Egypt's strength and influence was then at its zenith. Conversely, the fortune of Israel, which is

shall sanctify to HASHEM, *your God; you shall not work with the firstborn*
of your bull nor shall you shear the firstborn of your flock. [20] *Before*
HASHEM, *your God, shall you eat it, year by year, in the place that* HASHEM
will choose, you and your household. [21] *If it shall have a blemish —*
lameness or blindness or any serious blemish — you shall not slaughter it to
HASHEM, *your God.* [22] *In your cities shall you eat it, the contaminated one*
and the pure one alike, like the deer and the hart. [23] *However you shall not*
eat the blood; you shall pour it onto the ground like water.

16 [1] *You shall observe the month of springtime and perform the pesach-*
offering for HASHEM, *your God, for in the month of springtime*
HASHEM, *your God, took you out of Egypt at night.* [2] *You shall slaughter the*
pesach-offering to HASHEM, *your God, from the flock, [and also offer] cattle,*
in the place where HASHEM *will choose to rest His Name.* [3] *You shall not*
eat leavened bread with it, for seven days you shall eat matzos because
of it, bread of affliction, for you departed from the land of Egypt in haste —

---

goes up) with the sun in its strength (while) the moon's (state) is the opposite.

לַיְלָה — *By night.* That contrast was at night, but being that no sacrifice can be offered at night it was necessary to advance it to the day previous to that contrast, and in remembrance of this it was established so for (future) generations.

2. וּבָקָר — *And the herd* . . . for the *chagigah*, festival offering; even though this (i.e., the *chagigah)* was not brought with the *Pesach* (sacrifice) in Egypt.

3. לֹא תֹאכַל עָלָיו חָמֵץ שִׁבְעַת יָמִים — *You shall eat no leavened bread with it; seven days* . . . even though the prohibition of leavened bread at the Egyptian Pesach was only for one day, as our Sages mention (*Pesachim* 96a).

NOTES

compared to the moon, is then at its nadir since the full moon appears in successive parts of the heaven each month, and in Nissan it is at the farthest point from the earth (180 degrees) implying that its influence on Israel's affairs is at its lowest point. Hence, logically, the night of the 15th of Nissan was the time least propitious for Israel to leave Egypt. Nonetheless, God ordained that it be done at that time to demonstrate that His power transcends the heavenly forces. Now the proper time to bring the *Pesach* offering should have been that *night*, but since sacrifices can only be brought during the day we were commanded to bring the *Pesach* lamb on the 14th day of Nissan, the eve of the 15th.

See *Rashi* in tractate *Rosh Hashanah* 11b for a full description of the 12 constellations and their positions in the zodiac at various times of the year. It is important to note that our Sages teach us that, unlike other nations, אֵין מַזָּל לְיִשְׂרָאֵל, *Israel has no constellation* and is not subject to planetary influences (*Shabbos* 15a). However, we are *compared* to the moon, which explains the *Sforno's* commentary on this verse.

2. וּבָקָר — *And the herd*. The *Sforno* points out here, as he does in subsequent verses (3,4 and 5), that the Torah in the Book of *Deuteronomy* repeats certain laws of Pesach to teach us that there are basic differences between the law of the פֶּסַח in Egypt and of the *Pesach* sacrifice and festival observance in later generations. In this verse, we learn that a *chagigah, a festival offering from the herd*, is to be brought and eaten before one partakes of the *Pesach* lamb on Passover night so that the latter be eaten עַל הַשּׂוֹבַע, *when one is satisfied*, and not ravenously hungry. In this manner he will be able to observe the prohibition against breaking any bones of the *Pesach* offering. In verse 3, the Torah prohibits the eating of leaven for seven days, whereas in Egypt it was only prohibited for one day. In verse 4, the Torah enjoins us to remove leaven in our possession for seven days, an interdiction which did not apply in Egypt. In verse 5, we are told that the *Pesach* can only be brought in the Holy Temple, even though the first *Pesach* sacrifice was brought in Egypt where there was no temple and altar.

3. לֹא תֹאכַל עָלָיו חָמֵץ ... תֹּאכַל עָלָיו מַצּוֹת ... כִּי בְחִפָּזוֹן יָצָאתָ — *You shall eat no leavened bread with it . . . you shall eat unleavened bread with it . . . for in haste you came forth.* The *Sforno* points out that the characteristics of bread and matzoh are diamet-

ד לְמַעַן תִּזְכֹּר אֶת־יוֹם צֵאתְךָ מֵאֶרֶץ מִצְרַיִם כֹּל יְמֵי חַיֶּיךָ: וְלֹא־יֵרָאֶה
לְךָ שְׂאֹר בְּכָל־גְּבֻלְךָ שִׁבְעַת יָמִים וְלֹא־יָלִין מִן־הַבָּשָׂר אֲשֶׁר תִּזְבַּח
ה בָּעֶרֶב בַּיּוֹם הָרִאשׁוֹן לַבֹּקֶר: לֹא תוּכַל לִזְבֹּחַ אֶת־הַפָּסַח בְּאַחַד שְׁעָרֶיךָ
ו אֲשֶׁר־יְהוָה אֱלֹהֶיךָ נֹתֵן לָךְ: כִּי אִם־אֶל־הַמָּקוֹם אֲשֶׁר־יִבְחַר יְהוָה
אֱלֹהֶיךָ לְשַׁכֵּן שְׁמוֹ שָׁם תִּזְבַּח אֶת־הַפֶּסַח בָּעֶרֶב כְּבוֹא הַשֶּׁמֶשׁ מוֹעֵד
ז צֵאתְךָ מִמִּצְרָיִם: וּבִשַּׁלְתָּ וְאָכַלְתָּ בַּמָּקוֹם אֲשֶׁר יִבְחַר יְהוָה אֱלֹהֶיךָ בּוֹ
ח וּפָנִיתָ בַבֹּקֶר וְהָלַכְתָּ לְאֹהָלֶיךָ: שֵׁשֶׁת יָמִים תֹּאכַל מַצּוֹת וּבַיּוֹם הַשְּׁבִיעִי
ט עֲצֶרֶת לַיהוָה אֱלֹהֶיךָ לֹא תַעֲשֶׂה מְלָאכָה: שִׁבְעָה
שָׁבֻעֹת תִּסְפָּר־לָךְ מֵהָחֵל חֶרְמֵשׁ בַּקָּמָה תָּחֵל לִסְפֹּר שִׁבְעָה שָׁבֻעוֹת:
י וְעָשִׂיתָ חַג שָׁבֻעוֹת לַיהוָה אֱלֹהֶיךָ מִסַּת נִדְבַת יָדְךָ אֲשֶׁר תִּתֵּן כַּאֲשֶׁר

תֹּאכַל עָלָיו מַצּוֹת — *You shall eat unleavened bread with it.* Because, being that it is an offering of remembrance for the redemption which occurred in a brief moment, it is not fitting to eat leavened bread with it, since bread requires (considerable) time to prepare, from the time of the kneading of the dough until it is leavened (based on *Hosea* 7:4).

לֶחֶם עֹנִי — *The bread of affliction* ... bread which they ate in their affliction, and because of the pressure of their oppressors they had no time to wait for their dough to become leavened.

כִּי בְחִפָּזוֹן יָצָאתָ — *For in haste you came forth.* And the reason (we are told) to recall the haste (connected) with the bread is (to teach us) that in exchange for the haste of affliction you were then (granted) the haste of redemption, similar to, וְהָפַכְתִּי אֶבְלָם לְשָׂשׂוֹן, *I will turn their mourning to joy* (*Jeremiah* 31:12).

לְמַעַן תִּזְכֹּר אֶת יוֹם צֵאתְךָ מֵאֶרֶץ מִצְרַיִם כֹּל יְמֵי חַיֶּיךָ — *That you may remember the day you came out of the land of Egypt all the days of your life.* And the reason I commanded (you) to take care that the lunar year be analogous to the solar year through intercalation was in order that Nissan would always be the month of *Aviv*. And (the reason) I did not command you to count (the festival) according to the solar months, which would not necessitate intercalation, was so that you would remember the Exodus from Egypt *all the days of your life*, because each time you intercalate the year or the month, so as to insure that Nissan would be in the month of *Aviv*, you will remember that it is being done because of the Exodus from Egypt.

4. וְלֹא יֵרָאֶה לְךָ שְׂאֹר בְּכָל גְּבֻלְךָ שִׁבְעַת יָמִים — *And there shall be no leaven seen with you in all your borders seven days* ... although this was not necessary at the time of the *Pesach* (offering) in Egypt.

NOTES

rically opposed. For example, the former requires more time for baking, while the latter is baked quickly. The significance of the brief time required to bake matzoh is that it symbolizes the swiftness of God's redemption of Israel from Egypt. This theme of haste is continued in the *Sforno's* explanation of the balance of this verse. When they were slaves, the Israelites had no time to bake bread because their taskmasters gave them little respite from their labors. As compensation for that callous haste, the Almighty redeemed them swiftly, as He shall do once again in the future, as the prophet Malachi says, *And the Lord Whom you seek shall suddenly come to His Temple* (*Malachi* 3:1).

לְמַעַן תִּזְכֹּר — *That you may remember.* The *Sforno* interprets this phrase as referring back to verse 1. The reason Israel is to take care that this festival falls in the month of "the ripe ears" (*Aviv*) is so that they will always be mindful, when they intercalate the year, that this is being done to insure that this festival is celebrated during the same season that they departed from Egypt. In this manner, even the intercalation of the year (עִבּוּר שָׁנָה) becomes part of the yearly remembrance of that departure.

so that you will remember the day of your departure from the land of Egypt all the days of your life.

4 *No leaven of yours shall be seen throughout your boundary for seven days, nor shall any of the flesh that you offer on the afternoon before the first day remain overnight until morning.*
5 *You may not slaughter the pesach-offering in one of your cities that HASHEM, your God, gives you;*
6 *except at the place that HASHEM, your God, will choose to rest His Name, there shall you slaughter the pesach-offering in the afternoon, when the sun descends, the appointed time of your departure from Egypt.*
7 *You shall roast it and eat it in the place that HASHEM, your God, will choose, and in the morning you may turn back and go to your tents.*
8 *For a six-day period you shall eat matzos and on the seventh day shall be an assembly to HASHEM, your God; you shall not perform any labor.*

9 *You shall count seven weeks for yourselves; from when the sickle is first put to the standing crop shall you begin counting seven weeks.*
10 *Then you shall observe the festival of Shavuos for HASHEM, your God; the voluntary offerings that you give should be commensurate with how much*

וְלֹא יָלִין מִן הַבָּשָׂר — *Neither shall any of the meat remain.* Do not think that the prohibition of "remaining" (נוֹתָר) only applied to the *Pesach* sacrifice in Egypt, because they were leaving in haste and (this prohibition) would serve to prevent any (part) of it from remaining in the hands of the non-Israelites (i.e., Egyptians).

5. לֹא תוּכַל לִזְבֹּחַ אֶת הַפָּסַח — *You may not sacrifice the Pesach offering.* Although the *Pesach* sacrifice in Egypt was offered without altar or Sanctuary, this is not (permitted) to be done in the future.

8. וּבַיּוֹם הַשְּׁבִיעִי עֲצֶרֶת — *And on the seventh day shall be an assembly.* All Israel convened together in the service of God, the Blessed One, and sang a song unto Him on the seventh day of the Festival of Matzos — therefore, that day became sanctified.

לֹא תַעֲשֶׂה מְלָאכָה — *You shall do no work.* Were it not for this (the convening together to sing a song), the seventh day would not be holy at all, similar to the Festival of Succos when the seventh day is not a holy convocation (מִקְרָא קֹדֶשׁ).

9. מֵהָחֵל חֶרְמֵשׁ בַּקָּמָה — *From the time the sickle is first put to the standing (barley).* (This refers to) the standing barley of the *omer*, כִּי הַשְּׂעֹרָה אָבִיב, *for the barley was in the ear* (*Exodus* 9:31), and from the *Aviv* to the harvest you shall count seven weeks, *the appointed (weeks) of the harvest* (based on *Jeremiah* 5:24).

NOTES

4. וְלֹא יָלִין מִן הַבָּשָׂר — *Neither shall any of the meat remain.* The laws pertaining to the פֶּסַח הַדּוֹרוֹת, *Pesach of generations*, are different in many respects from those of פֶּסַח מִצְרַיִם, *the Pesach of Egypt*, as explained in the note to verse 2. It is, therefore, necessary for the Torah to tell us that the prohibition of נוֹתָר, *allowing the meat of the sacrifice to remain overnight*, is common to both, even though the circumstances surrounding the *Pesach* in Egypt are not the same as the circumstances of the *Pesach* for generations.

8. וּבַיּוֹם הַשְּׁבִיעִי עֲצֶרֶת... לֹא תַעֲשֶׂה מְלָאכָה — *And on the seventh day shall be an assembly ... you shall do no work.* The word עֲצֶרֶת can be translated as "stoppage" or "to cease." If so, it is meant as an injunction against working on the seventh day of the festival, as stated specifically at the conclusion of the verse. The *Sforno*, however, interprets עֲצֶרֶת in this verse as "an assembly" and thus the term is meant as an explanation of the historic *cause* and *reason* for prohibiting labor on the seventh day of Pesach. Since Israel assembled (עֲצֶרֶת) together at the Sea of Reeds (יַם סוּף) and sang the Song of the Sea (שִׁירַת הַיָּם) on the seventh day, praising God for the miracle of dividing the waters, it was therefore ordained to mark this day by cessation of labor, as is the case when a holy festival is observed.

יא יְבָרֶכְךָ֗ יהוה אֱלֹהֶ֑יךָ: וְשָׂמַחְתָּ֞ לִפְנֵ֣י | יהוה אֱלֹהֶ֗יךָ אַתָּ֨ה וּבִנְךָ֣ וּבִתֶּ֜ךָ
וְעַבְדְּךָ֣ וַאֲמָתֶ֗ךָ וְהַלֵּוִי֙ אֲשֶׁ֣ר בִּשְׁעָרֶ֔יךָ וְהַגֵּ֛ר וְהַיָּת֥וֹם וְהָאַלְמָנָ֖ה אֲשֶׁ֣ר
יב בְּקִרְבֶּ֑ךָ בַּמָּק֗וֹם אֲשֶׁ֤ר יִבְחַר֙ יהוה אֱלֹהֶ֔יךָ לְשַׁכֵּ֥ן שְׁמ֖וֹ שָֽׁם: וְזָכַרְתָּ֗
כִּי־עֶ֤בֶד הָיִ֨יתָ֙ בְּמִצְרָ֔יִם וְשָׁמַרְתָּ֣ וְעָשִׂ֔יתָ אֶת־הַֽחֻקִּ֖ים הָאֵֽלֶּה:

מפטיר יג־יד חַ֧ג הַסֻּכֹּ֛ת תַּֽעֲשֶׂ֥ה לְךָ֖ שִׁבְעַ֣ת יָמִ֑ים בְּאָ֨סְפְּךָ֔ מִֽגָּרְנְךָ֖ וּמִיִּקְבֶֽךָ: וְשָֽׂמַחְתָּ֞
בְּחַגֶּ֗ךָ אַתָּ֨ה וּבִנְךָ֤ וּבִתֶּ֨ךָ֙ וְעַבְדְּךָ֣ וַאֲמָתֶ֔ךָ וְהַלֵּוִ֗י וְהַגֵּ֛ר וְהַיָּת֥וֹם וְהָאַלְמָנָ֖ה
טו אֲשֶׁ֥ר בִּשְׁעָרֶֽיךָ: שִׁבְעַ֣ת יָמִ֗ים תָּחֹג֙ לַֽיהוה אֱלֹהֶ֔יךָ בַּמָּק֖וֹם אֲשֶׁר־יִבְחַ֣ר
יהוה כִּ֣י יְבָרֶכְךָ֞ יהוה אֱלֹהֶ֗יךָ בְּכֹ֤ל תְּבוּאָֽתְךָ֙ וּבְכֹל֙ מַֽעֲשֵׂ֣ה יָדֶ֔יךָ וְהָיִ֖יתָ
טז אַ֖ךְ שָׂמֵֽחַ: שָׁל֣וֹשׁ פְּעָמִ֣ים | בַּשָּׁנָ֡ה יֵרָאֶ֨ה כָל־זְכ֣וּרְךָ֗ אֶת־פְּנֵ֣י | יהוה
אֱלֹהֶ֨יךָ֙ בַּמָּק֣וֹם אֲשֶׁ֣ר יִבְחָ֔ר בְּחַ֧ג הַמַּצּ֛וֹת וּבְחַ֥ג הַשָּֽׁבֻע֖וֹת וּבְחַ֣ג הַסֻּכּ֑וֹת
יז וְלֹ֧א יֵֽרָאֶ֛ה אֶת־פְּנֵ֥י יהוה רֵיקָֽם: אִ֖ישׁ כְּמַתְּנַ֣ת יָד֑וֹ כְּבִרְכַּ֛ת יהוה אֱלֹהֶ֖יךָ
אֲשֶׁ֥ר נָֽתַן־לָֽךְ:

---

11. וְהַגֵּר וְהַיָּתוֹם וְהָאַלְמָנָה — *The stranger, the orphan and the widow.* They will rejoice during the festival of the harvest with לֶקֶט, *the gleaning,* and the פֵּאָה (*the corner* of the field), which is available at the harvest. These are mentioned in conjunction with this Festival (of Weeks) in *parashas Emor* (*Leviticus* 23:22).

12. וְזָכַרְתָּ כִּי עֶבֶד הָיִיתָ — *And you shall remember that you were a slave . . .* at which time you possessed no money of your own because, מַה שֶּׁקָּנָה עֶבֶד קָנָה רַבּוֹ, *Whatever a slave owns, his master owns* (Pesachim 88b).

וְשָׁמַרְתָּ וְעָשִׂיתָ אֶת הַחֻקִּים הָאֵלֶּה — *And you shall observe and do these statutes . . .* (namely) the giving of gleanings and the corner of the field (to the needy) in accordance with the will of God who took you forth from there (Egypt) and gave you riches and possessions.

13. בְּאָסְפְּךָ מִגָּרְנְךָ וּמִיִּקְבֶךָ — *When you gather in from the threshing-floor and from your wine-press . . .* when you gather the produce into your house from the threshing-floor and from the wine-press.

NOTES

11. וְהַגֵּר וְהַיָּתוֹם וְהָאַלְמָנָה — *The stranger, the orphan and the widow.* Although the Torah does not mention the gifts for the poor (the "gleaning" and "corner" — לֶקֶט וּפֵאָה) in this chapter, they are mentioned in *parashas Emor* (*Leviticus* 23:22) in the same chapter which speaks of Shevuos. The *Sforno* explains that the reason for the rejoicing of the widow, orphan and stranger stated here is

HASHEM, your God, will have blessed you. 11 *You shall rejoice before*
HASHEM, your God — you, your son, your daughter, your slave, your maidservant, the Levite who is in your cities, the proselyte, the orphan, and the widow who are among you — in the place that HASHEM, your God, will choose to rest His Name.
12 *You shall remember that you were a slave in Egypt, and you shall observe and perform these decrees.*

13 *You shall make the festival of Succos for a seven-day period, when you gather in from your threshing floor and from your wine cellar.*
14 *You shall rejoice on your festival — you, your son, your daughter, your slave, your maidservant, the Levite, the proselyte, the orphan, and the widow who are in your cities.*
15 *A seven-day period shall you celebrate to HASHEM, your God, in the place that HASHEM, your God, will choose, for HASHEM will have blessed you in all your crop and in all your handiwork, and you will be completely joyous.*

16 *Three times a year all your males should appear before HASHEM, your God, in the place that He will choose: on the Festival of Matzos, the Festival of Shavuos, and the Festival of Succos; and he shall not appear before HASHEM empty-handed,*
17 *everyone according to what he can give, according to the blessing that HASHEM, your God, gives you.*

---

14. וְהַגֵּר וְהַיָּתוֹם וְהָאַלְמָנָה — *And the stranger, and the orphan and the widow.* They will rejoice with פֶּרֶט (grapes fallen off during cutting) and gleanings, and the gifts (for the poor) from the fruit-trees.

15. כִּי יְבָרֶכְךָ — *Because HASHEM your God shall bless you.* You will have a bountiful harvest, and the needy will have many gifts (מַתְּנַת עֲנִיִּים).

אַךְ שָׂמֵחַ — *Altogether joyful.* You will be only joyful and no sorrow will intermingle with your joy.

17. אִישׁ כְּמַתְּנַת יָדוֹ — *Every man shall give as he is able.* He should not give away all that he has, thereby becoming dependent upon others, as is the practice of the foolish among the nations, as our Sages say, הַמְבַזְבֵּז אַל יְבַזְבֵּז יוֹתֵר מֵחֹמֶשׁ, *If a man wishes to spend liberally (for charity), he should not spend more than a fifth* (Kesubos 50a).

NOTES

because during the wheat harvest they enjoy the מַתְּנַת עֲנִיִּים — the gifts for the poor which are mentioned in *Leviticus*.

15. אַךְ שָׂמֵחַ — *Altogether joyful*. The word אַךְ denotes מִעוּט — a limitation. What is the Torah limiting in our case? The *Sforno* explains that God assures us that the festival will be limited to joy exclusively, without any intermingling of grief or sorrow.

17. אִישׁ כְּמַתְּנַת יָדוֹ — *Every man shall give as he is able*. The Torah cautions us not to be excessively open handed to such a degree that one impoverishes himself. As an aside, he criticizes those adherents of other faiths who take a vow of poverty or give away everything they own as a religious act. Judaism frowns on such practices.

פרשת שופטים

יח שֹׁפְטִים וְשֹׁטְרִים תִּתֶּן־לְךָ בְּכָל־שְׁעָרֶיךָ אֲשֶׁר יהוה אֱלֹהֶיךָ נֹתֵן לְךָ
יט לִשְׁבָטֶיךָ וְשָׁפְטוּ אֶת־הָעָם מִשְׁפַּט־צֶדֶק: לֹא־תַטֶּה מִשְׁפָּט לֹא תַכִּיר
פָּנִים וְלֹא־תִקַּח שֹׁחַד כִּי הַשֹּׁחַד יְעַוֵּר עֵינֵי חֲכָמִים וִיסַלֵּף דִּבְרֵי צַדִּיקִם:
כ צֶדֶק צֶדֶק תִּרְדֹּף לְמַעַן תִּחְיֶה וְיָרַשְׁתָּ אֶת־הָאָרֶץ אֲשֶׁר־יהוה אֱלֹהֶיךָ
כא נֹתֵן לָךְ: לֹא־תִטַּע לְךָ אֲשֵׁרָה כָּל־עֵץ אֵצֶל מִזְבַּח
כב יהוה אֱלֹהֶיךָ אֲשֶׁר תַּעֲשֶׂה־לָּךְ: וְלֹא־תָקִים לְךָ מַצֵּבָה אֲשֶׁר שָׂנֵא יהוה

18. שֹׁפְטִים וְשֹׁטְרִים — *Judges and officers.* Following the commandments given to the masses, He now commands regarding the affairs of the leaders, these being the judges and kings, *Kohanim* and prophets, through whose correct (behavior) the affairs of the masses will be improved, and through whose corrupt (behavior) the (needs of the populace) will be damaged, which the prophet attests to saying, שָׂרֶיהָ בְקִרְבָּהּ אֲרָיוֹת שֹׁאֲגִים, שֹׁפְטֶיהָ זְאֵבֵי עֶרֶב לֹא גָרְמוּ לַבֹּקֶר. נְבִיאֶיהָ פֹּחֲזִים אַנְשֵׁי בֹּגְדוֹת כֹּהֲנֶיהָ חִלְּלוּ קֹדֶשׁ חָמְסוּ תּוֹרָה, *Her princes within her are roaring lions; her judges are wolves at evening, they gnaw no bones in the morning. Her prophets are worthless, treacherous persons; her Kohanim have polluted the Sanctuary, they have violently perverted Torah* (Zephaniah 3:3,4).

נֹתֵן לְךָ לִשְׁבָטֶיךָ — *Gives to your tribes.* In your gates which He *gives to you* to be divided among your tribes, but not (the land) which you may conquer outside the Land (of Israel) which is not divided (among) the tribes, as our Sages state, "Outside the Land you seat judges in each district but not in each city" (*Makos* 7a). This would apply to Syria and other such (neighboring) lands.

מִשְׁפַּט צֶדֶק — *Righteous judgment.* Let the hearing of testimony (lit., claims) be in such a manner that the judicial decision be righteous. (The judge) must not be lenient with one and harsh to the other (based on *Kesuvos* 46a).

20. צֶדֶק צֶדֶק תִּרְדֹּף — *Justice, justice shall you follow.* When you choose and appoint judges, select only those who are the most likely to judge with righteousness, even though they may not possess other characteristics befitting a judge, such as perfection in matters of possession, and perfection of physical appearance. This is similar to אַל תַּבֵּט אֶל מַרְאֵהוּ

NOTES

18. שֹׁפְטִים וְשֹׁטְרִים — *Judges and officers.* The previous chapters include numerous commandments addressed to the people of Israel as a whole. For example in *parashas Re'eh*, the Torah speaks of Israel's responsibility to rid its land of idolatry. It also commands the establishment of a central Sanctuary, the prohibition of eating blood, the laws of tithes, the dietary laws, the nullification of debts at the end of the seventh year, the punishment of the false prophet and of a city guilty of idol worship, as well as discussing the various festivals. Now, at the beginning of *parashas Shoftim*, the Torah directs its attention to personalities rather than concepts, namely to the king, the judge, the *Kohen* and the prophet who fill the roles of leadership and authority in Israel. The *Sforno* emphasizes, as he does in numerous other places, that the proper behavior of the leader will affect not only the spiritual state of Jewish society but also its material well-being.

נֹתֵן לְךָ לִשְׁבָטֶיךָ — *Gives to your tribes.* The *Sforno* interprets the word לִשְׁבָטֶיךָ, *to your tribes* as a מִעוּט, *a limitation.* Only in *Eretz Yisrael*, which is divided among your tribes, shall you establish courts in each city, but not outside the land. This law applies even in territory which may be conquered by a Jewish king if that conquest is not sanctioned by the Sanhedrin, such as Syria which was conquered by King David (See *Bava Basra* 90b and *Tosfos* there).

מִשְׁפַּט צֶדֶק — *Righteous judgment.* Can there be a מִשְׁפָּט, *judgment*, which is not צֶדֶק, *righteous*? The *Sforno* explains that this does not refer to the *decision* of the judges but to their *manner* of judging. It must be *righteous* in the sense of being impartial and evenhanded.

20. צֶדֶק צֶדֶק תִּרְדֹּף — *Justice, justice shall you follow.* The *Sforno* interprets the repetition of the word צֶדֶק, *justice*, to mean that in choosing a

PARASHAS SHOFTIM

18 Judges and officers shall you appoint in all your cities — which HASHEM,
your God, gives you — for your tribes; and they shall judge the people
with righteous judgment. 19 You shall not pervert judgment, you shall
not respect someone's presence, and you shall not accept a bribe, for the
bribe will blind the eyes of the wise and make just words crooked.
20 Righteousness, righteousness shall you pursue, so that you will live and
possess the Land that HASHEM, your God, gives you.
21 You shall not plant for yourselves an idolatrous tree — any tree — near
the Altar of HASHEM, your God, that you shall make for yourself. 22 And you
shall not erect for yourselves a pillar, which HASHEM, your God, hates.

וְאֶל גְּבֹהַּ קוֹמָתוֹ, *Look not on his countenance, nor on the height of his stature* (*I Samuel* 16:7).

לְמַעַן תִּחְיֶה וְיָרַשְׁתָּ — *That you may live and inherit (the land).* There is need for this (justice) more so in the Land (of Israel), because the lack of it will impede the possession of (the Land), as it says, בַּעֲוֹן בִּצְעוֹ קָצַפְתִּי וְאַכֵּהוּ, *For the iniquity of his covetousness was I wrathful and smote him* (*Isaiah* 57:17).

21-22. לֹא תִטַּע לְךָ אֲשֵׁרָה ... וְלֹא תָקִים לְךָ מַצֵּבָה — *You shall not plant an Asherah ... Neither shall you set up a pillar.* The Torah cites three instances of similar things which are beautiful and appealing to the senses, but are abhorrent (to God) for they are spiritually blemished. The first is an Asherah, which is used to beautify palaces, but nonetheless, is abhorrent if used in a holy place because it is customarily used for idolatrous services. (Similarly) we grant preference to the spirit of righteousness and justice of the judge over his physical perfection, which is material and (appeals) to the physical senses.

Secondly, although a pillar was acceptable prior to the giving of the Torah, as it says, וּשְׁתֵּים עֶשְׂרֵה מַצֵּבָה, *And twelve pillars* (*Exodus* 24:4), the reason being because symbolically it is as though the one who brings an offering stands continually before the Holy, similar to שִׁוִּיתִי ה׳ לְנֶגְדִּי תָמִיד, *I have set HASHEM always before me* (*Psalms* 16:8); — (however), they (i.e., the pillars) fell from that (elevated) level when (Israel sinned) with the Golden Calf, as it says, כִּי לֹא אֶעֱלֶה בְּקִרְבְּךָ, *For I will not go up in your midst* (*Exodus* 33:3). Similarly, regarding an elder (i.e., a judge or leader) whose lifetime has not been well spent and who has a bad name due to youthful (indiscretion), (such a judge should be rejected) when you can find an elder whose lifetime has been well spent.

Thirdly, the Torah cites the case of an abhorrent blemish ...

NOTES

judge, judicial temperament and a sense of fairness is of paramount importance, more so than a dignified bearing and imposing presence. Appearance is not as important as substance. The verse quoted by the *Sforno* to prove this scale of priorities is most appropriate. When the prophet Samuel went to the house of Jesse to select a king of Israel, he was impressed by the appearance of Eliav, but God cautioned him not to be misled by his physical stature, saying, "*Do not look at his countenance nor the height of his stature because I have rejected him; for it is not as a man sees; for a man looks at the outward appearance but God looks at the heart*" (*I Samuel* 16).

The *Sforno* uses the expression שְׁלֵמוּת הַקִּנְיָן וּשְׁלֵמוּת הַגּוּף, *perfection in matters of possession,* meaning material wealth attained honestly and used properly, and *perfection of physical stature* — which so impressed Samuel when he saw Eliav.

לְמַעַן תִּחְיֶה — *That you may live*. The *Sforno* explains that there is no greater danger to the stability of national life in *Eretz Yisrael* than injustice.

21-22,17:1. לֹא תִטַּע לְךָ אֲשֵׁרָה ... וְלֹא תָקִים לְךָ מַצֵּבָה ... לֹא תִזְבַּח — *You shall not plant an Asherah ... Neither shall you set up a pillar ... You shall not sacrifice*. The *Sforno* cites three examples of judges who are not qualified to serve on a Jewish court and compares them to three prohibitions, namely the planting of an *Asherah*, the setting up of a pillar and the offering of a blemished animal. The first is an example of something

יז א אֱלֹהֶיךָ: לֹא־תִזְבַּח לַיהוָה אֱלֹהֶיךָ שׁוֹר וָשֶׂה אֲשֶׁר יִהְיֶה
ב בוֹ מוּם כֹּל דָּבָר רָע כִּי תוֹעֲבַת יְהוָה אֱלֹהֶיךָ הוּא: כִּי־
יִמָּצֵא בְקִרְבְּךָ בְּאַחַד שְׁעָרֶיךָ אֲשֶׁר־יְהוָה אֱלֹהֶיךָ נֹתֵן לָךְ אִישׁ אוֹ־אִשָּׁה
ג אֲשֶׁר יַעֲשֶׂה אֶת־הָרַע בְּעֵינֵי יְהוָה־אֱלֹהֶיךָ לַעֲבֹר בְּרִיתוֹ: וַיֵּלֶךְ וַיַּעֲבֹד
אֱלֹהִים אֲחֵרִים וַיִּשְׁתַּחוּ לָהֶם וְלַשֶּׁמֶשׁ ׀ אוֹ לַיָּרֵחַ אוֹ לְכָל־צְבָא הַשָּׁמַיִם
ד אֲשֶׁר לֹא־צִוִּיתִי: וְהֻגַּד־לְךָ וְשָׁמָעְתָּ וְדָרַשְׁתָּ הֵיטֵב וְהִנֵּה אֱמֶת נָכוֹן
ה הַדָּבָר נֶעֶשְׂתָה הַתּוֹעֵבָה הַזֹּאת בְּיִשְׂרָאֵל: וְהוֹצֵאתָ אֶת־הָאִישׁ הַהוּא אוֹ
אֶת־הָאִשָּׁה הַהִוא אֲשֶׁר עָשׂוּ אֶת־הַדָּבָר הָרָע הַזֶּה אֶל־שְׁעָרֶיךָ אֶת־
ו הָאִישׁ אוֹ אֶת־הָאִשָּׁה וּסְקַלְתָּם בָּאֲבָנִים וָמֵתוּ: עַל־פִּי ׀ שְׁנַיִם עֵדִים אוֹ
ז שְׁלֹשָׁה עֵדִים יוּמַת הַמֵּת לֹא יוּמַת עַל־פִּי עֵד אֶחָד: יַד הָעֵדִים תִּהְיֶה־בּוֹ

XVII

1. לֹא תִזְבַּח ... אֲשֶׁר יִהְיֶה בוֹ מוּם — *You shall not sacrifice ... wherein is a blemish.* Although the animal is comely to the senses and fat, its worth being a thousand *zuz,* nonetheless, it is disqualified for sacred use because of its blemish, (although) it does not decrease in value. (On the other hand,) if an ox (only) worth a *sela* is unblemished, it is acceptable to be offered (to God). Similarly, if an elder possesses disgraceful vices and you find one who is superior to him in perfection of his attributes, (select him as a judge) even though he is not as rich and (physically) handsome as the other.

2. כִּי יִמָּצֵא בְקִרְבְּךָ — *If there be found in your midst.* After (the Torah) commands the appointment of judges in every city so that each court should judge the inhabitants of its (own) city, it now mentions the judging of an idolater who is not judged in his city but is judged in the city where he served (the strange god). Following this, (the Torah) speaks of differences of opinion (among the judges) of a court, which is also adjudicated in a different city, namely in the place *which* HASHEM *your God shall choose* (v. 8), and so also (the case) of a זָקֵן מַמְרֵא, *a rebellious scholar* (lit., elder).

לַעֲבֹר בְּרִיתוֹ — *Transgressing His covenant* ... the covenant which was entered into regarding all the commandments, because, indeed, one who serves strange gods (is considered as though) he denies all the commandments and nullifies them.

3. אֱלֹהִים אֲחֵרִים — *Other gods* ... beings separated from matter, except for God, the Blessed One.

וְלַשֶּׁמֶשׁ או לַיָּרֵחַ — *Or to the sun or the moon* ... which are corporeal.

NOTES

which is aesthetically appealing but spiritually objectionable. The second is an example of something which changes with time, and the third is an example of that which may seem to be valuable but is unacceptable by the standards of Torah. Conversely, that which appears to be without great value may be priceless by the Torah's yardstick. The Asherah represents the first, as does a judge who is physically impressive but deficient in virtues. The pillar represents the second, as does a judge whose past is checkered, while a blemished animal represents the third, similar to a judge who is rich and handsome but whose character is flawed.

XVII

2. כִּי יִמָּצֵא בְקִרְבְּךָ — *If there be found in your midst.* The *Sforno* explains the reason for the juxtaposition of these verses (2-13) which deal with the worshiping of other gods, a difference of opinion among judges of a local court and the punishment of an elder who defies the decision of the High Court in Jerusalem. The common denominator is that they are not judged by their local courts but by the court of the city where the transgression occurred or by the Supreme Court in Jerusalem.

לַעֲבֹר בְּרִיתוֹ — *Transgressing His covenant.* Compare to *Rashi* 11:28, who cites the *Sifri,* that he who

17 [1] *You shall not slaughter for HASHEM, your God, an ox or a lamb or kid in
which there will be a blemish, any bad thing, because that is an
abomination of HASHEM, your God.*
[2] *If there will be found among you in one of your cities, which HASHEM,
your God, gives you, a man or woman who commits what is evil in the eyes
of HASHEM, your God, to violate His covenant,* [3] *and he will go and serve
gods of others and prostrate himself to them, or to the sun or the moon or to
any host of heaven, which I have not commanded,* [4] *and it will be told to
you and you will hear; then you shall investigate well, and behold! it is true,
the testimony is correct — this abomination was done in Israel —* [5] *then you
shall remove that man or that woman who did this evil thing to your cities
— the man or the woman — and you shall pelt them with stones, so that
they will die.* [6] *By the testimony of two witnesses or three witnesses shall
the condemned person be put to death; he shall not be put to death by the
testimony of a single witness.* [7] *The hand of the witnesses shall be upon him*

אֲשֶׁר לֹא צִוִּיתִי — *Which I have not commanded.* Whom I have not appointed, by any designation, (as having) the power of choice that would (permit them) to function according to their own will. Rather, I ordained unto them immutable laws contrary to the thinking of the idolaters who thought that every city had its (heavenly) lord who could do good or evil according to his will, (and) who benefits those who serve him.

5. אֶת הָאִישׁ הַהוּא אוֹ אֶת הָאִשָּׁה הַהִוא — *That man or that woman.* And we do not say that she was seduced and knew nothing, and therefore it is unnecessary to judge her in the gate (of the city) where she served (the strange gods) so as to demonstrate the error of her opinions.

אֶל שְׁעָרֶיךָ — *Unto your gates* ... the gate (of the city) where the idol was worshiped, to demonstrate that this alien god has no power to save its worshiper who thought that he would be saved by (his god).

6. עַל פִּי שְׁנַיִם עֵדִים אוֹ שְׁלֹשָׁה — *At the mouth of two witnesses or three.* Even in the case of idolatry the entire set of witnesses is disqualified if one of them is found to be (a relative) or unqualified, and we are not to presume that the testimony shall take place through the rest (of the witnesses).

NOTES

serves strange gods is considered as one who denies the entire Torah.

3. אֱלֹהִים אֲחֵרִים ... וְלַשֶּׁמֶשׁ אוֹ לַיָּרֵחַ — *Other gods ... or to the sun or the moon.* The *Sforno* explains that these are two distinct and separate modes of proscribed worship. The former refers to angels who are spiritual beings while the heavenly bodies are corporeal. Both are prohibited to be considered deities.

5. אוֹ אֶת הָאִשָּׁה הַהִוא — *Or that woman.* The *Sforno* explains the reason why the Torah specifically mentions a woman in this verse. Since a woman is more prone to he misled by certain blandishments, signs and wonders, one might think that she is not responsible for her actions, therefore it is necessary to teach us that this is an incorrect assumption. See the *Ramban* who explains this verse in a similar fashion.

אֶל שְׁעָרֶיךָ — *Unto your gates.* The reason that punishment is exacted in the gates of the city where the idol was worshiped is to demonstrate that the idol has no power to save its worshiper.

6. עַל פִּי שְׁנַיִם עֵדִים אוֹ שְׁלֹשָׁה — *At the mouth of two witnesses or three.* According to Rabbinic teaching, the evidence of two witnesses is considered as one unit of testimony and if one witness is disqualified, the testimony is disallowed. So too is the testimony of three or more witnesses considered as a single unit and if one is rendered unfit, the testimony likewise is rejected. Lest one think that given the severity of the sin of idolatry we should waive this technicality and punish the accused, the Torah cautions us not to do so.

בָּרִאשֹׁנָה לַהֲמִיתוֹ וְיַד כָּל־הָעָם בָּאַחֲרֹנָה וּבִעַרְתָּ הָרָע מִקִּרְבֶּךָ׃
ח כִּי יִפָּלֵא מִמְּךָ דָבָר לַמִּשְׁפָּט בֵּין־דָּם ׀ לְדָם בֵּין־דִּין לְדִין וּבֵין נֶגַע לָנֶגַע
דִּבְרֵי רִיבֹת בִּשְׁעָרֶיךָ וְקַמְתָּ וְעָלִיתָ אֶל־הַמָּקוֹם אֲשֶׁר יִבְחַר יהוה אֱלֹהֶיךָ
ט בּוֹ׃ וּבָאתָ אֶל־הַכֹּהֲנִים הַלְוִיִּם וְאֶל־הַשֹּׁפֵט אֲשֶׁר יִהְיֶה בַּיָּמִים הָהֵם
י וְדָרַשְׁתָּ וְהִגִּידוּ לְךָ אֵת דְּבַר הַמִּשְׁפָּט׃ וְעָשִׂיתָ עַל־פִּי הַדָּבָר אֲשֶׁר יַגִּידוּ
לְךָ מִן־הַמָּקוֹם הַהוּא אֲשֶׁר יִבְחַר יהוה וְשָׁמַרְתָּ לַעֲשׂוֹת כְּכֹל אֲשֶׁר יוֹרוּךָ׃
יא עַל־פִּי הַתּוֹרָה אֲשֶׁר יוֹרוּךָ וְעַל־הַמִּשְׁפָּט אֲשֶׁר־יֹאמְרוּ לְךָ תַּעֲשֶׂה לֹא
יב תָסוּר מִן־הַדָּבָר אֲשֶׁר־יַגִּידוּ לְךָ יָמִין וּשְׂמֹאל׃ וְהָאִישׁ אֲשֶׁר־יַעֲשֶׂה בְזָדוֹן
לְבִלְתִּי שְׁמֹעַ אֶל־הַכֹּהֵן הָעֹמֵד לְשָׁרֶת שָׁם אֶת־יהוה אֱלֹהֶיךָ אוֹ אֶל־
יג הַשֹּׁפֵט וּמֵת הָאִישׁ הַהוּא וּבִעַרְתָּ הָרָע מִיִּשְׂרָאֵל׃ וְכָל־הָעָם יִשְׁמְעוּ וְיִרָאוּ
שני יד וְלֹא יְזִידוּן עוֹד׃ כִּי־תָבֹא אֶל־הָאָרֶץ אֲשֶׁר יהוה אֱלֹהֶיךָ
נֹתֵן לָךְ וִירִשְׁתָּהּ וְיָשַׁבְתָּה בָּהּ וְאָמַרְתָּ אָשִׂימָה עָלַי מֶלֶךְ כְּכָל־הַגּוֹיִם
טו אֲשֶׁר סְבִיבֹתָי׃ שׂוֹם תָּשִׂים עָלֶיךָ מֶלֶךְ אֲשֶׁר יִבְחַר יהוה אֱלֹהֶיךָ בּוֹ
מִקֶּרֶב אַחֶיךָ תָּשִׂים עָלֶיךָ מֶלֶךְ לֹא תוּכַל לָתֵת עָלֶיךָ אִישׁ נָכְרִי אֲשֶׁר
טז לֹא־אָחִיךָ הוּא׃ רַק לֹא־יַרְבֶּה־לּוֹ סוּסִים וְלֹא־יָשִׁיב אֶת־הָעָם מִצְרַיְמָה

---

8. כִּי יִפָּלֵא מִמְּךָ דָבָר — *If there arise a matter too hard.* Although you appointed judges for each city so that each court shall judge its city, nevertheless if a doubt arises regarding the traditional teaching, the court of that city shall not decide according to its (own) deliberation, but the decision shall be made according to the deliberation of the majority of the High Court (in Jerusalem). (This is also the case) when (the local court) cannot reach a majority opinion.

12. וְהָאִישׁ אֲשֶׁר יַעֲשֶׂה בְזָדוֹן — *And the man that does presumptuously* ... who issues a halachic decision, in fact, contrary to the decision of the High Court.

וּמֵת הָאִישׁ הַהוּא — *That man shall die* ... through the High Court, and thus *the people shall hear and fear* (v. 13).

14. אָשִׂימָה עָלַי מֶלֶךְ כְּכָל הַגּוֹיִם — *I will set a king over me like all the nations* ... a hereditary monarchy, unlike (the system) of judges where only the judge ruled but not his children after him. Now, they were commanded regarding the appointment of a judge as a king in such a manner when they came to the Land (of Israel), as it says, וְלֹא תִהְיֶה עֲדַת ה׳ כַּצֹּאן אֲשֶׁר אֵין לָהֶם רֹעֶה, *That the congregation of* Hashem *be not as sheep which have no shepherd* (*Numbers* 27:17). However, (in regard to) appointing a king, such as one (who rules among) the nations who claims the monarchy for himself and his children, (such a

NOTES

8. כִּי יִפָּלֵא מִמְּךָ דָבָר — *If there arise a matter too hard*. The expression מִפִּי הַשְּׁמוּעָה, *traditional teaching*, is based on *Sanhedrin* 88a, in accordance with the opinion of Rabbi Elazar.

12. וְהָאִישׁ אֲשֶׁר יַעֲשֶׂה בְזָדוֹן — *And the man that does presumptuously*. The *Sforno's* commentary is based on tractate *Sanhedrin* 86b. Our Sages teach us that a זָקֵן מַמְרֵא, *rebellious scholar*, is only liable to the death penalty if he renders a decision meant to be implemented (הֲלָכָה לְמַעֲשֶׂה) — not a theoretical one.

וּמֵת הָאִישׁ הַהוּא — *That man shall die*. The *Sforno* reflects in his commentary the Talmudic statement (*Sanhedrin* 89a) that the execution of a rebellious scholar is not held in his city but in Jerusalem, at the time when Israel gathers together at the festival period, so that *all the people shall hear and fear*. *Rashi* explains this verse in a similar manner.

14. אָשִׂימָה עָלַי מֶלֶךְ — *I will set a king over me*. The *Sforno's* commentary on this verse explains the Torah's antipathy to the institution of a monarchy

first to put him to death, and the hand of the entire people afterward, and you shall destroy the evil from your midst.

[8] *If a matter of judgment is hidden from you, between blood and blood, between verdict and verdict, between plague and plague, matters of dispute in your cities — you shall rise up and ascend to the place that HASHEM, your God, shall choose.* [9] *You shall come to the Kohanim, the Levites, and to the judge who will be in those days; you shall inquire and they will tell you the word of judgment.* [10] *You shall do according to the word that they will tell you, from that place that HASHEM will choose, and you shall be careful to do according to everything that they will teach you.* [11] *According to the teaching that they will teach you and according to the judgment that they will say to you, shall you do; you shall not deviate from the word that they will tell you, right or left.* [12] *And the man that will act with willfulness, not listening to the Kohen who stands there to serve HASHEM, your God, or to the judge, that man shall die, and you shall destroy the evil from among Israel.* [13] *The entire nation shall listen and fear, and they shall not act willfully any more.*

[14] *When you come to the Land that HASHEM, your God, gives you, and possess it, and settle in it, and you will say, "I will set a king over myself, like all the nations that are around me."* [15] *You shall surely set over yourself a king whom HASHEM, your God, shall choose; from among your brethren shall you set a king over yourself; you cannot place over yourself a foreign man, who is not your brother.* [16] *Only he shall not have too many horses for himself, so that he will not return the people to Egypt*

---

reign) is abhorrent to God, the Blessed One. But He did command that if they would stubbornly insist to have such a monarch, they should choose only a fit person, chosen by God, so that he not lead Israel away from their faith. (Also,) he may not be a foreigner, even though he be a fit, decent person and a mighty man of war. Now, when they sinned by requesting a king who would rule, he and his children after him, similar to all other nations, their punishment was through disasters which befell the masses on account of the king, as it says, וּזְעַקְתֶּם בַּיּוֹם הַהוּא מִלִּפְנֵי מַלְכְּכֶם אֲשֶׁר בְּחַרְתֶּם לָכֶם וְלֹא יַעֲנֶה ה׳ אֶתְכֶם בַּיּוֹם הַהוּא, *And you will cry out on that day because of your king who you will have chosen for yourselves, and HASHEM will not answer you on that day* (*I Samuel* 8:18), and as it says, אֶתֶּן לְךָ מֶלֶךְ בְּאַפִּי וְאֶקַּח בְּעֶבְרָתִי, *I give you a king in My anger, and take him away in My wrath* (*Hosea* 13:11). The permission granted (to Israel) to appoint a king is similar to the permission granted to take אֵשֶׁת יְפַת תֹּאַר, *the woman of goodly form* (21:11), where (the Torah) indicates that eventually he will hate her and a rebellious son will be born to her, as it happened with David and Absalom.

NOTES

in Israel. When Moses asked God to appoint a leader over the Jewish people who would lead them after his demise (*Numbers* 27:16), it was the appointment of a judge that he requested and not a king whose children would inherit the monarchy. Although the Torah speaks here of a Jewish king, it is a concession made reluctantly, similar in nature to the law of אֵשֶׁת יְפַת תֹּאַר, *the woman of goodly form*, taken captive in battle, who is allowed to be taken as a concubine. Indeed, our Sages say that *the Torah only speaks thus to appease the evil inclination* in man. The *Sforno* explains that a hereditary monarchy will, in most cases, bring in its wake trouble and anguish, as is the case of *the woman of goodly form* who will usually produce a child that will be a בֵּן סוֹרֵר וּמוֹרֶה, *a stubborn rebellious son*. The *Sforno* links these two together — i.e., Jewish monarchy and the captive woman — by citing the example of David's son Absalom who was the son of Maacha, daughter of Ptolemy, king of Geshur, taken captive in battle by David.

לְמַ֫עַן הַרְבּ֣וֹת ס֑וּס וַֽיהוָה֙ אָמַ֣ר לָכֶ֔ם לֹ֣א תֹסִפ֗וּן לָשׁ֛וּב בַּדֶּ֥רֶךְ הַזֶּ֖ה עֽוֹד׃
יז וְלֹ֤א יַרְבֶּה־לּוֹ֙ נָשִׁ֔ים וְלֹ֥א יָס֖וּר לְבָב֑וֹ וְכֶ֣סֶף וְזָהָ֔ב לֹ֥א יַרְבֶּה־לּ֖וֹ מְאֹֽד׃
יח וְהָיָ֣ה כְשִׁבְתּ֔וֹ עַ֖ל כִּסֵּ֣א מַמְלַכְתּ֑וֹ וְכָ֨תַב ל֜וֹ אֶת־מִשְׁנֵ֨ה הַתּוֹרָ֤ה הַזֹּאת֙
יט עַל־סֵ֔פֶר מִלִּפְנֵ֖י הַכֹּהֲנִ֥ים הַלְוִיִּֽם׃ וְהָיְתָ֣ה עִמּ֔וֹ וְקָ֥רָא ב֖וֹ כָּל־יְמֵ֣י חַיָּ֑יו לְמַ֣עַן
יִלְמַ֗ד לְיִרְאָה֙ אֶת־יְהוָ֣ה אֱלֹהָ֔יו לִ֠שְׁמֹר אֶֽת־כָּל־דִּבְרֵ֞י הַתּוֹרָ֥ה הַזֹּ֛את
כ וְאֶת־הַחֻקִּ֥ים הָאֵ֖לֶּה לַעֲשֹׂתָֽם׃ לְבִלְתִּ֤י רוּם־לְבָבוֹ֙ מֵֽאֶחָ֔יו וּלְבִלְתִּ֛י ס֥וּר
*מלא ו מִן־הַמִּצְוָ֖ה יָמִ֣ין וּשְׂמֹ֑אול לְמַעַן֩ יַאֲרִ֨יךְ יָמִ֧ים עַל־מַמְלַכְתּ֛וֹ ה֥וּא וּבָנָ֖יו
יח שלישי א בְּקֶ֥רֶב יִשְׂרָאֵֽל׃ לֹֽא־יִהְיֶ֜ה לַכֹּהֲנִ֣ים הַלְוִיִּ֗ם כָּל־שֵׁ֥בֶט לֵוִ֛י
ב חֵ֥לֶק וְנַחֲלָ֖ה עִם־יִשְׂרָאֵ֑ל אִשֵּׁ֧י יְהוָ֛ה וְנַחֲלָת֖וֹ יֹאכֵלֽוּן׃ וְנַחֲלָ֥ה לֹא־יִֽהְיֶה־
ג לּ֖וֹ בְּקֶ֣רֶב אֶחָ֑יו יְהוָה֙ ה֣וּא נַחֲלָת֔וֹ כַּאֲשֶׁ֖ר דִּבֶּר־לֽוֹ׃ וְזֶ֡ה
יִהְיֶה֩ מִשְׁפַּ֨ט הַכֹּהֲנִ֜ים מֵאֵ֣ת הָעָ֗ם מֵאֵ֛ת זֹבְחֵ֥י הַזֶּ֖בַח אִם־שׁ֣וֹר אִם־שֶׂ֑ה
ד וְנָתַן֙ לַכֹּהֵ֔ן הַזְּרֹ֥עַ וְהַלְּחָיַ֖יִם וְהַקֵּבָֽה׃ רֵאשִׁ֨ית דְּגָנְךָ֜ תִּירֹשְׁךָ֣ וְיִצְהָרֶ֗ךָ
ה וְרֵאשִׁ֛ית גֵּ֥ז צֹאנְךָ֖ תִּתֶּן־לּֽוֹ׃ כִּ֣י ב֗וֹ בָּחַ֛ר יְהוָ֥ה אֱלֹהֶ֖יךָ מִכָּל־שְׁבָטֶ֑יךָ
רביעי ו לַעֲמֹ֨ד לְשָׁרֵ֧ת בְּשֵׁם־יְהוָ֛ה ה֥וּא וּבָנָ֖יו כָּל־הַיָּמִֽים׃ וְכִֽי־
יָבֹ֨א הַלֵּוִ֜י מֵאַחַ֤ד שְׁעָרֶ֙יךָ֙ מִכָּל־יִשְׂרָאֵ֔ל אֲשֶׁר־ה֖וּא גָּ֣ר שָׁ֑ם וּבָא֙ בְּכָל־
ז אַוַּ֣ת נַפְשׁ֔וֹ אֶל־הַמָּק֖וֹם אֲשֶׁר־יִבְחַ֥ר יְהוָֽה׃ וְשֵׁרֵ֕ת בְּשֵׁ֖ם יְהוָ֣ה אֱלֹהָ֑יו
ח כְּכָל־אֶחָיו֙ הַלְוִיִּ֔ם הָעֹמְדִ֥ים שָׁ֖ם לִפְנֵ֥י יְהוָֽה׃ חֵ֥לֶק כְּחֵ֖לֶק יֹאכֵ֑לוּ לְבַ֥ד
ט מִמְכָּרָ֖יו עַל־הָאָבֽוֹת׃ כִּ֛י אַתָּה֙ בָּ֣א אֶל־הָאָ֔רֶץ אֲשֶׁר־
יְהוָ֥ה אֱלֹהֶ֖יךָ נֹתֵ֣ן לָ֑ךְ לֹֽא־תִלְמַ֣ד לַעֲשׂ֔וֹת כְּתוֹעֲבֹ֖ת הַגּוֹיִ֥ם הָהֵֽם׃
י לֹֽא־יִמָּצֵ֣א בְךָ֔ מַעֲבִ֥יר בְּנֽוֹ־וּבִתּ֖וֹ בָּאֵ֑שׁ קֹסֵ֣ם קְסָמִ֔ים מְעוֹנֵ֥ן וּמְנַחֵ֖שׁ

---

19. לְמַעַן יִלְמַד לְיִרְאָה אֶת ה׳ — *That he may learn to fear* HASHEM. Through the knowledge of the contemplative portion of (the Torah) which teaches clearly the greatness and providence of God, the Exalted One, he will perforce be brought to the fear (of God).

XVIII

5. כִּי בוֹ בָּחַר ה׳ אֱלֹהֶיךָ מִכׇּל שְׁבָטֶיךָ — *For* HASHEM *your God has chosen him out of all your tribes.* It is (therefore) fitting that you give him bread and clothing so that he be able to stand to minister.

8. לְבַד מִמְכָּרָיו עַל הָאָבוֹת — *Besides that which can be sold* (i.e., *exchanged*) *according to the fathers' houses.* The fathers could only divide among the priestly watches (מִמְכָּרָיו) that which could be sold through an exchange by every watch to their fellow *Kohanim,* namely the offerings of all the days of the year. Every watch (was permitted) to exchange

NOTES

19. לְמַעַן יִלְמַד לְיִרְאָה אֶת ה׳ — *That he may learn to fear* HASHEM. Kingship, by its very nature, often leads to corruption of the monarch's moral character, and also limits the freedom of the people over whom he rules. It is therefore imperative for the Torah to teach that the king of Israel be restrained and guided by the laws and discipline of God's Torah. Hopefully, by studying and obeying it, he will learn to fear God, and thus control his appetite for power which tends to corrupt man.

XVIII

8. לְבַד מִמְכָּרָיו עַל הָאָבוֹת — *Besides that which can be sold according to the fathers' houses.* The priestly families were divided into twenty-four watches (מִשְׁמָרוֹת) at the time of Samuel and David, each serving in the Temple for a period of one week. The various מַתְּנוֹת כְּהוּנָה, *priestly gifts,* belonged to the watch of that week. However, as the *Sforno* points out, they were permitted to exchange these gifts with other priestly families,

in order to increase horses, for HASHEM has said to you, "You shall no longer
return on this road again." 17 *And he shall not have too many wives, so that*
his heart not turn astray; and he shall not greatly increase silver and gold for
himself. 18 *It shall be that when he sits on the throne of his kingdom, he shall*
write for himself two copies of this Torah in a book, from before the Kohanim,
the Levites. 19 *It shall be with him, and he shall read from it all the days of*
his life, so that he will learn to fear HASHEM, his God, to observe all the words
of this Torah and these decrees, to perform them, 20 *so that his heart does not*
become haughty over his brethren and not turn from the commandment right
or left, so that he will prolong years over his kingdom, he and his sons amid
Israel.

18 1 *There shall not be for the Kohanim, the Levites — the entire tribe of Levi*
— a portion and an inheritance with Israel; the fire-offerings of HASHEM
and His inheritance shall they eat. 2 *He shall not have an inherit-*
ance among his brethren; HASHEM is his inheritance, as He spoke to him.
3 *This shall be the due of the Kohanim from the people, from those who*
perform a slaughter, whether of an ox or of the flock: he shall give the Kohen
the foreleg, the jaw, and the maw. 4 *The first of your grain, wine, and oil, and*
the first of the shearing of your flock shall you give him. 5 *For him has*
HASHEM chosen from among all your tribes, to stand and minister in the name
of HASHEM, him and his sons, all the days.
6 *When the Levite will come from one of your cities, from all of Israel, where*
he sojourns, and he comes with all the desire of his soul to the place that
HASHEM will choose, 7 *then he shall minister in the name of HASHEM, his God,*
like all of his brethren, the Levites, who stand there before HASHEM. 8 *Portion*
for portion shall they eat, except for what was transacted by the forefathers.
9 *When you come to the Land that HASHEM, your God, gives you, you shall*
not learn to act according to the abominations of those nations. 10 *There shall*
not be found among you one who causes his son or daughter to pass through
the fire, one who practices divinations, an astrologer, one who reads omens,

---

their portion of the regular offerings during the year with their fellow (*Kohanim*) who would give them (in turn) their portion of a week or two (from their watch). However, the festival offerings, for which there could be no exchange and were not included in מִמְכָּרָיו, that which the fathers could divide among the watches, (regarding these we say) חֵלֶק כְּחֵלֶק יֹאכֵלוּ, *they shall have like portions to eat.*

10. לֹא יִמָּצֵא בְךָ — *There shall not be found among you . . .* even one who is from a foreign people such as the בַּעֲלַת אוֹב — necromanceress — who remained in En-dor (*I Samuel* 28:7).

NOTES

who in turn would repay them with their portion during the week of their service. However, the priestly gifts from the offerings brought during the festivals were not allocated to the *watch* of that week, but belonged to all the *Kohanim* who were in Jerusalem at that time. (See Tractate *Succah* 56a and compare to *Rashi* on this verse.)

10. לֹא יִמָּצֵא בְךָ — *There shall not be found among you*. The *Sforno* interprets the expression *there shall not be found among you* as a cautionary command not to permit such soothsayers and sorcerers to reside in the midst of Israel even if they are aliens and not Israelites. The *Sforno* is of the opinion that the necromanceress of En-dor was not a Jewess, contrary to the commentary of *Radak* in *I Samuel*, chapter 28, who quotes a Midrash that she was the mother of Abner.

יא־יב וּמְכַשֵּׁף: וְחֹבֵר חָבֶר וְשֹׁאֵל אוֹב וְיִדְּעֹנִי וְדֹרֵשׁ אֶל־הַמֵּתִים: כִּי־תוֹעֲבַת
יהוה כָּל־עֹשֵׂה אֵלֶּה וּבִגְלַל הַתּוֹעֵבֹת הָאֵלֶּה יהוה אֱלֹהֶיךָ מוֹרִישׁ
*חמישי יג־יד אוֹתָם מִפָּנֶיךָ: תָּמִים תִּהְיֶה עִם יהוה אֱלֹהֶיךָ: * כִּי ׀ הַגּוֹיִם הָאֵלֶּה אֲשֶׁר
אַתָּה יוֹרֵשׁ אוֹתָם אֶל־מְעֹנְנִים וְאֶל־קֹסְמִים יִשְׁמָעוּ וְאַתָּה לֹא כֵן נָתַן
טו לְךָ יהוה אֱלֹהֶיךָ: נָבִיא מִקִּרְבְּךָ מֵאַחֶיךָ כָּמֹנִי יָקִים לְךָ יהוה אֱלֹהֶיךָ
טז אֵלָיו תִּשְׁמָעוּן: כְּכֹל אֲשֶׁר־שָׁאַלְתָּ מֵעִם יהוה אֱלֹהֶיךָ בְּחֹרֵב בְּיוֹם
הַקָּהָל לֵאמֹר לֹא אֹסֵף לִשְׁמֹעַ אֶת־קוֹל יהוה אֱלֹהָי וְאֶת־הָאֵשׁ הַגְּדֹלָה
יז הַזֹּאת לֹא־אֶרְאֶה עוֹד וְלֹא אָמוּת: וַיֹּאמֶר יהוה אֵלָי הֵיטִיבוּ אֲשֶׁר
יח דִּבֵּרוּ: נָבִיא אָקִים לָהֶם מִקֶּרֶב אֲחֵיהֶם כָּמוֹךָ וְנָתַתִּי דְבָרַי בְּפִיו וְדִבֶּר
יט אֲלֵיהֶם אֵת כָּל־אֲשֶׁר אֲצַוֶּנּוּ: וְהָיָה הָאִישׁ אֲשֶׁר לֹא־יִשְׁמַע אֶל־דְּבָרַי
כ אֲשֶׁר יְדַבֵּר בִּשְׁמִי אָנֹכִי אֶדְרֹשׁ מֵעִמּוֹ: אַךְ הַנָּבִיא אֲשֶׁר יָזִיד לְדַבֵּר
דָּבָר בִּשְׁמִי אֵת אֲשֶׁר לֹא־צִוִּיתִיו לְדַבֵּר וַאֲשֶׁר יְדַבֵּר בְּשֵׁם אֱלֹהִים
כא אֲחֵרִים וּמֵת הַנָּבִיא הַהוּא: וְכִי תֹאמַר בִּלְבָבֶךָ אֵיכָה נֵדַע אֶת־הַדָּבָר
כב אֲשֶׁר לֹא־דִבְּרוֹ יהוה: אֲשֶׁר יְדַבֵּר הַנָּבִיא בְּשֵׁם יהוה וְלֹא־יִהְיֶה הַדָּבָר
וְלֹא יָבֹא הוּא הַדָּבָר אֲשֶׁר לֹא־דִבְּרוֹ יהוה בְּזָדוֹן דִּבְּרוֹ הַנָּבִיא לֹא
יט א תָּגוּר מִמֶּנּוּ: כִּי־יַכְרִית יהוה אֱלֹהֶיךָ אֶת־הַגּוֹיִם אֲשֶׁר
יהוה אֱלֹהֶיךָ נֹתֵן לְךָ אֶת־אַרְצָם וִירִשְׁתָּם וְיָשַׁבְתָּ בְעָרֵיהֶם וּבְבָתֵּיהֶם:
ב שָׁלוֹשׁ עָרִים תַּבְדִּיל לָךְ בְּתוֹךְ אַרְצְךָ אֲשֶׁר יהוה אֱלֹהֶיךָ נֹתֵן לְךָ

13. תָּמִים תִּהְיֶה — *You shall be wholehearted* ... perfect and complete with Him. Even when you seek to inquire as to the future you shall inquire of none other than Him, through a prophet or the *Urim and Tumim.*

14. וְאַתָּה לֹא כֵן נָתַן לְךָ — *But as for you,* (*God*) *has not given you* (*permission*) *as such* ... for the words of the diviners and soothsayers regarding you will not be fulfilled as our Sages say, אֵין מַזָּל לְיִשְׂרָאֵל, *Israel is not affected by planetary influences* (*Shabbos* 156a).

15. אֵלָיו תִּשְׁמָעוּן — *Unto him shall you hearken* ... if he commands you a commandment which is temporary.

21. אֵיכָה נֵדַע אֶת הַדָּבָר — *How shall we know the word* ... when (the prophet) commands the performance of an (extraordinary) temporary commandment, as Elijah did on Mount Carmel (*I Kings*, ch. 18), and as Joshua did when he surrounded Jericho on the Sabbath, and when he commanded the *Kohanim* to carry the Ark into the Jordan and stand there until the people crossed over (*Joshua* 6:4-15).

22. וְלֹא יִהְיֶה הַדָּבָר — *If the thing follow not.* Because, even temporarily, no new

NOTES

13. תָּמִים תִּהְיֶה — *You shall be wholehearted.* The *Urim and Tumim,* cited by the *Sforno,* are mentioned in *Exodus* 28:30. *Urim* means *light* and *Tumim* means *perfect.* The שֵׁם הַמְפוֹרָשׁ, *the Ineffable Name of God,* was inscribed on some material and placed in the fold of the חֹשֶׁן, *breastplate,* worn by the *Kohen Gadol.* The will of God was revealed clearly (like the "light") and His promises "made perfect," i.e., verified through the letters inscribed on the breastplate.

14. וְאַתָּה לֹא כֵן נָתַן לְךָ — *But as for you,* (*God*) *has not given you* (*permission*) *as such.* The *Sforno* does not interpret this phrase as meaning "God, your God has not given you" the right or need to listen to soothsayers and diviners as do other nations. Rather, he explains the sense of the verse thus: Whereas the destiny of other nations is determined by the stars, and therefore they consult stargazers and diviners, the people of Israel are not affected by these heavenly, planetary forces for

a sorcerer; 11 *or an animal charmer, one who inquires of Ov or Yidoni, or one*
who consults the dead. 12 *For anyone who does these is an abomination of*
HASHEM, and because of these abominations HASHEM, your God, banishes
[the nations] from before you. 13 *You shall be wholehearted with HASHEM,*
your God. 14 *For these nations that you are possessing — they hearkened to*
astrologers and diviners; but as for you — not so has HASHEM, your God,
given for you.
15 *A prophet from your midst, from your brethren, like me, shall HASHEM,*
your God, establish for you — to him shall you hearken. 16 *According to all*
that you asked of HASHEM, your God, in Horeb on the day of the
congregation, saying, "I can no longer hear the voice of HASHEM, my God,
and this great fire I can no longer see, so that I shall not die."
17 *Then HASHEM said to me: They have done well in what they have said.*
18 *I will establish a prophet for them from among their brethren, like you,*
and I will place My words in his mouth; He shall speak to them everything
that I will command him. 19 *And it shall be that the man who will not*
hearken to My words that he shall speak in My name, I will exact from
him. 20 *But the prophet who willfully shall speak a word in My name, that*
which I have not commanded him to speak, or who shall speak in the name
of the gods of others — that prophet shall die.
21 *When you say in your heart, "How can we know the word that*
HASHEM has not spoken?" 22 *If the prophet will speak in the Name of*
HASHEM and that thing will not occur and not come about — that is the
word that HASHEM has not spoken; with willfulness has the prophet spoken
it, you should not fear him.

19 1 *When HASHEM, your God, will cut down the nations whose Land*
HASHEM, your God, gives you, and you will possess them, and you
will settle in their cities and in their houses, 2 *you shall separate three cities*
for yourselves in the midst of your Land, which HASHEM, your God, gives

commandment will be introduced to the masses unless it is accompanied (substantiated) by some sign. For example, (regarding) Joshua, the Jordan divided (*Joshua*, ch. 3) and the walls of Jericho fell (ibid. 6:20). As for Elijah, fire descended from heaven (*I Kings* 18:38). However, regarding the command of the prophet who said to his colleague, הַכֵּינִי נָא, *smite me* (*I Kings* 20:35), that was said to his fellow prophet, who knew it was the word of God; therefore, he was punished when he refused (to obey).

XIX

2. שָׁלוֹשׁ עָרִים תַּבְדִּיל — *You shall separate three cities.* After (the Torah) explains the

NOTES

they are ruled only by God and transcend the מַזָּלוֹת, *planets*. Hence, they are not subject (לֹא כֵן) to the words of the diviners.

21-22. אֵיכָה נֵדַע...וְלֹא יִהְיֶה הַדָּבָר — *How shall we know . . . if the thing follow not*. The *Sforno* interprets these verses as referring to הוֹרָאַת שָׁעָה, *a temporary ruling*, of a Jewish leader, scholar or prophet. He explains that in order to substantiate the validity of such a ruling, it must be accompanied by some special sign, unless the one who is commanded to do a certain act is himself a prophet who is aware that what is being ordered is indeed the word of God.

XIX

2. שָׁלוֹשׁ עָרִים תַּבְדִּיל — *You shall separate three cities*. The *Sforno* explains the continuity of the

ג לִרְשְׁתָּהּ: תָּכִין לְךָ הַדֶּרֶךְ וְשִׁלַּשְׁתָּ אֶת־גְּבוּל אַרְצְךָ אֲשֶׁר יַנְחִילְךָ יהוה
ד אֱלֹהֶיךָ וְהָיָה לָנוּס שָׁמָּה כָּל־רֹצֵחַ: וְזֶה דְּבַר הָרֹצֵחַ אֲשֶׁר־יָנוּס שָׁמָּה וָחָי
אֲשֶׁר יַכֶּה אֶת־רֵעֵהוּ בִּבְלִי־דַעַת וְהוּא לֹא־שֹׂנֵא לוֹ מִתְּמֹל שִׁלְשֹׁם:
ה וַאֲשֶׁר יָבֹא אֶת־רֵעֵהוּ בַיַּעַר לַחְטֹב עֵצִים וְנִדְּחָה יָדוֹ בַגַּרְזֶן לִכְרֹת הָעֵץ
וְנָשַׁל הַבַּרְזֶל מִן־הָעֵץ וּמָצָא אֶת־רֵעֵהוּ וָמֵת הוּא יָנוּס אֶל־אַחַת
ו הֶעָרִים־הָאֵלֶּה וָחָי: פֶּן־יִרְדֹּף גֹּאֵל הַדָּם אַחֲרֵי הָרֹצֵחַ כִּי יֵחַם לְבָבוֹ
וְהִשִּׂיגוֹ כִּי־יִרְבֶּה הַדֶּרֶךְ וְהִכָּהוּ נָפֶשׁ וְלוֹ אֵין מִשְׁפַּט־מָוֶת כִּי לֹא שֹׂנֵא
ז הוּא לוֹ מִתְּמוֹל שִׁלְשׁוֹם: עַל־כֵּן אָנֹכִי מְצַוְּךָ לֵאמֹר שָׁלֹשׁ עָרִים תַּבְדִּיל
ח לָךְ: וְאִם־יַרְחִיב יהוה אֱלֹהֶיךָ אֶת־גְּבֻלְךָ כַּאֲשֶׁר נִשְׁבַּע לַאֲבֹתֶיךָ וְנָתַן
ט לְךָ אֶת־כָּל־הָאָרֶץ אֲשֶׁר דִּבֶּר לָתֵת לַאֲבֹתֶיךָ: כִּי־תִשְׁמֹר אֶת־כָּל־
הַמִּצְוָה הַזֹּאת לַעֲשֹׂתָהּ אֲשֶׁר אָנֹכִי מְצַוְּךָ הַיּוֹם לְאַהֲבָה אֶת־יהוה
אֱלֹהֶיךָ וְלָלֶכֶת בִּדְרָכָיו כָּל־הַיָּמִים וְיָסַפְתָּ לְךָ עוֹד שָׁלֹשׁ עָרִים עַל
י הַשָּׁלֹשׁ הָאֵלֶּה: וְלֹא יִשָּׁפֵךְ דָּם נָקִי בְּקֶרֶב אַרְצְךָ אֲשֶׁר יהוה אֱלֹהֶיךָ נֹתֵן
לְךָ נַחֲלָה וְהָיָה עָלֶיךָ דָּמִים:
יא וְכִי־יִהְיֶה אִישׁ שֹׂנֵא לְרֵעֵהוּ וְאָרַב לוֹ וְקָם עָלָיו וְהִכָּהוּ נֶפֶשׁ וָמֵת וְנָס
יב אֶל־אַחַת הֶעָרִים הָאֵל: וְשָׁלְחוּ זִקְנֵי עִירוֹ וְלָקְחוּ אֹתוֹ מִשָּׁם וְנָתְנוּ אֹתוֹ
יג בְּיַד גֹּאֵל הַדָּם וָמֵת: לֹא־תָחוֹס עֵינְךָ עָלָיו וּבִעַרְתָּ דַם־הַנָּקִי מִיִּשְׂרָאֵל
יד וְטוֹב לָךְ: ששי לֹא תַסִּיג גְּבוּל רֵעֲךָ אֲשֶׁר גָּבְלוּ רִאשֹׁנִים בְּנַחֲלָתְךָ
טו אֲשֶׁר תִּנְחַל בָּאָרֶץ אֲשֶׁר יהוה אֱלֹהֶיךָ נֹתֵן לְךָ לְרִשְׁתָּהּ: לֹא־
יָקוּם עֵד אֶחָד בְּאִישׁ לְכָל־עָוֹן וּלְכָל־חַטָּאת בְּכָל־חֵטְא אֲשֶׁר יֶחֱטָא
טז עַל־פִּי | שְׁנֵי עֵדִים אוֹ עַל־פִּי שְׁלֹשָׁה־עֵדִים יָקוּם דָּבָר: כִּי־יָקוּם
יז עֵד־חָמָס בְּאִישׁ לַעֲנוֹת בּוֹ סָרָה: וְעָמְדוּ שְׁנֵי־הָאֲנָשִׁים אֲשֶׁר־לָהֶם הָרִיב

---

subject of the judges and of the king, the *Kohanim* and the prophets (in the preceding chapters), it now relates the commandments which are the responsibility of the judges and these are: setting aside the cities of refuge, setting the boundaries (of the tribes) (v. 14), the examination of witnesses and the acceptance of their testimony (vs. 15-21). (The *parashah* then speaks of) the commandments which are the responsibility of the king, these being *when you go forth to do battle* (20:1-9), *when you draw close to a city* (20:10-18), *when you shall besiege a city* (20:19-20). (The Torah than proceeds to tell us) of the (responsibility) placed upon the *Kohanim* and judges jointly, namely the matter of the עֶגְלָה עֲרוּפָה — *the heifer whose neck is broken* (21:1-9).

13. וּבִעַרְתָּ דַם הַנָּקִי מִיִּשְׂרָאֵל — *But you shall do away with the blood of the innocent from*

NOTES

topics presented from this point until the end of the *sedrah.* The responsibilities of the judges, the king and the *Kohanim* are the unifying theme of these chapters and verses comprising the balance of *parashas Shoftim.* The determination whether a killing was murder or manslaughter, the settling of disputes over boundaries and the subject of witnesses are all matters to be decided by the judges. The waging of war is the responsibility of the king while the ritual of the עֶגְלָה עֲרוּפָה, *the heifer whose neck is broken*, is the responsibility of both the judges and the *Kohanim* (21:4-8).

13. וּבִעַרְתָּ דַם הַנָּקִי מִיִּשְׂרָאֵל וְטוֹב לָךְ — *But you shall do away with the blood of the innocent . . . that it may go well with you.* The *Sforno* explains the phrase *the blood of the innocent* as referring to the

you to possess it. 3 *Prepare the way for yourself, and divide into three parts*
the boundary of the Land that HASHEM, *your God, causes you to inherit;*
and it shall be for any murderer to flee there. 4 *This is the matter of the*
murderer who shall flee there and live: One who will strike his fellow
without knowledge, and he did not hate him from yesterday or before
yesterday; 5 *or who will come with his fellow into the forest to hew trees,*
and his hand swings the axe to cut the tree, and the iron slips from the wood
and finds his fellow and he dies, he shall flee to one of these cities and live,
6 *lest the redeemer of the blood will chase after the murderer, for his heart*
will be hot, and he will overtake him for the way was long, and he shall
strike him mortally — and there is no judgment of death upon him, for he
did not hate him from yesterday and before yesterday. 7 *Therefore I*
command you, saying: You shall separate three cities for yourselves.

8 *When* HASHEM *will broaden your boundary, as He swore to your*
forefathers, and He will give you the entire Land that he spoke to your
forefathers to give, 9 *when you observe this entire commandment to*
perform it — which I command you today — to love HASHEM, *your God, and*
to walk in His ways all the years, then you shall add three more cities to
these three. 10 *Innocent blood shall not be shed in the midst of your Land*
that HASHEM, *your God, gives as an inheritance, for then blood will be upon*
you.

11 *But if there will be a man who hates his fellow, and ambushes him and*
rises up against him, and strikes him mortally and he dies, and he flees to
one of these cities — 12 *then the elders of his city shall send and take him*
from there and place him in the hand of the redeemer of the blood, and he
shall die. 13 *Your eye shall not pity him; you shall remove the innocent blood*
from Israel; and it shall be good for you.

14 *You shall not move a boundary of your fellow, which the early ones*
marked out, in your inheritance that you shall inherit, in the Land that
HASHEM, *your God, gives you to possess it.*

15 *A single witness shall not stand up against any man for any iniquity or*
for any error, regarding any sin that he may commit; according to two
witnesses or according to three witnesses shall a matter be confirmed.
16 *If a false witness stands against a man to speak up spuriously against*
him, 17 *then the two men [and those] who have the grievance shall stand*

Israel . . . the punishment for (shedding) innocent blood, as it says, וְלָאָרֶץ לֹא יְכֻפַּר לַדָּם אֲשֶׁר שֻׁפַּךְ בָּהּ כִּי אִם בְּדַם שֹׁפְכוֹ, *and no expiation can be made for the land for the blood that is shed therein, but by the blood of him that shed it* (*Bamidbar* 35:33).

וְטוֹב לָךְ — *That it may go well with you.* For the murderer will not be able to murder others, וְהַנִּשְׁאָרִים יִשְׁמְעוּ וְיִרָאוּ, *and those that remain shall hear and fear* (v. 20).

NOTES

Divine punishment which will be visited upon innocent inhabitants of *Eretz Yisrael* if a murderer is not punished. As he proves from the verse in the Book of *Numbers*, when murder goes unpunished, the Land and its inhabitants suffer the consequences, for the blemish of bloodshed is not expiated until the murderer is put to death. Regarding the phrase *that it may go well with you*, the *Sforno* points out that the execution of the murderer will benefit society in a two-fold manner; it will remove a menace from society, and also serve as a deterrent to others.

יח לִפְנֵי יְהוָה לִפְנֵי הַכֹּהֲנִים וְהַשֹּׁפְטִים אֲשֶׁר יִהְיוּ בַּיָּמִים הָהֵם: וְדָרְשׁוּ
יט הַשֹּׁפְטִים הֵיטֵב וְהִנֵּה עֵד־שֶׁקֶר הָעֵד שֶׁקֶר עָנָה בְאָחִיו: וַעֲשִׂיתֶם לוֹ
כ כַּאֲשֶׁר זָמַם לַעֲשׂוֹת לְאָחִיו וּבִעַרְתָּ הָרָע מִקִּרְבֶּךָ: וְהַנִּשְׁאָרִים יִשְׁמְעוּ
כא וְיִרָאוּ וְלֹא־יֹסִפוּ לַעֲשׂוֹת עוֹד כַּדָּבָר הָרָע הַזֶּה בְּקִרְבֶּךָ: וְלֹא תָחוֹס עֵינֶךָ
א נֶפֶשׁ בְּנֶפֶשׁ עַיִן בְּעַיִן שֵׁן בְּשֵׁן יָד בְּיָד רֶגֶל בְּרָגֶל: כִּי־
כ
תֵצֵא לַמִּלְחָמָה עַל־אֹיְבֶךָ וְרָאִיתָ סוּס וָרֶכֶב עַם רַב מִמְּךָ לֹא תִירָא
ב מֵהֶם כִּי־יְהוָה אֱלֹהֶיךָ עִמָּךְ הַמַּעַלְךָ מֵאֶרֶץ מִצְרָיִם: וְהָיָה כְּקָרָבְכֶם
ג אֶל־הַמִּלְחָמָה וְנִגַּשׁ הַכֹּהֵן וְדִבֶּר אֶל־הָעָם: וְאָמַר אֲלֵהֶם שְׁמַע יִשְׂרָאֵל
אַתֶּם קְרֵבִים הַיּוֹם לַמִּלְחָמָה עַל־אֹיְבֵיכֶם אַל־יֵרַךְ לְבַבְכֶם אַל־תִּירְאוּ
ד וְאַל־תַּחְפְּזוּ וְאַל־תַּעַרְצוּ מִפְּנֵיהֶם: כִּי יְהוָה אֱלֹהֵיכֶם הַהֹלֵךְ עִמָּכֶם
ה לְהִלָּחֵם לָכֶם עִם־אֹיְבֵיכֶם לְהוֹשִׁיעַ אֶתְכֶם: וְדִבְּרוּ הַשֹּׁטְרִים אֶל־הָעָם
לֵאמֹר מִי־הָאִישׁ אֲשֶׁר בָּנָה בַיִת־חָדָשׁ וְלֹא חֲנָכוֹ יֵלֵךְ וְיָשֹׁב לְבֵיתוֹ
ו פֶּן־יָמוּת בַּמִּלְחָמָה וְאִישׁ אַחֵר יַחְנְכֶנּוּ: וּמִי־הָאִישׁ אֲשֶׁר נָטַע כֶּרֶם וְלֹא
חִלְּלוֹ יֵלֵךְ וְיָשֹׁב לְבֵיתוֹ פֶּן־יָמוּת בַּמִּלְחָמָה וְאִישׁ אַחֵר יְחַלְּלֶנּוּ:
ז וּמִי־הָאִישׁ אֲשֶׁר אֵרַשׂ אִשָּׁה וְלֹא לְקָחָהּ יֵלֵךְ וְיָשֹׁב לְבֵיתוֹ פֶּן־יָמוּת
ח בַּמִּלְחָמָה וְאִישׁ אַחֵר יִקָּחֶנָּה: וְיָסְפוּ הַשֹּׁטְרִים לְדַבֵּר אֶל־הָעָם וְאָמְרוּ
מִי־הָאִישׁ הַיָּרֵא וְרַךְ הַלֵּבָב יֵלֵךְ וְיָשֹׁב לְבֵיתוֹ וְלֹא יִמַּס אֶת־לְבַב אֶחָיו
ט כִּלְבָבוֹ: וְהָיָה כְּכַלֹּת הַשֹּׁטְרִים לְדַבֵּר אֶל־הָעָם וּפָקְדוּ שָׂרֵי צְבָאוֹת

---

18. וְהִנֵּה עֵד שֶׁקֶר הָעֵד שֶׁקֶר עָנָה בְאָחִיו — *And behold, if the witness is a false witness and has testified falsely against his brother.* His testimony was false and his intent was to testify falsely against his brother. It was not done mistakenly or inadvertently, as is the case of mistaken testimony regarding the hour on a cloudy day, or regarding the intercalation of a month.

XX

1. כִּי תֵצֵא לַמִּלְחָמָה — *When you go forth to battle* . . . outside the Land (of Israel), for were it a מִלְחֶמֶת מִצְוָה, *a war in fulfillment of a commandment*, none would be exempted from military service (lit., return from the order of battle), for even יֵצֵא חָתָן מֵחֶדְרוֹ וְכַלָּה מֵחֻפָּתָהּ, *the bridegroom (would) go forth from his chamber and the bride out of her pavilion* (based on *Joel* 1:16 and tractate *Sotah* 44b).

NOTES

18. וְהִנֵּה עֵד שֶׁקֶר הָעֵד שֶׁקֶר עָנָה בְאָחִיו — *And behold, if the witness is a false witness and has testified falsely againt his brother*. The *Sforno* explains the reason for the repetition of the word שֶׁקֶר, *falsehood*, in this verse. The first refers to the actual testimony of the witness, while the second refers to his motivation.

XX

1. כִּי תֵצֵא לַמִּלְחָמָה — *When you go forth to battle*. The Talmud in tractate *Sotah* (44b) lists three categories of war. One is מִלְחֶמֶת חוֹבָה, *a war of duty*, such as Joshua's conquest of *Eretz Yisrael*. Another is called מִלְחֶמֶת מִצְוָה, *a war in fulfillment of a commandment*, such as the defense of the Land of Israel or a preemptive strike against Israel's enemies. Finally, there is מִלְחֶמֶת רְשׁוּת, *an optional war of political nature*, such as the battles of King David against Syria for the purpose of expanding Israel's territory.

The *Sforno* observes that the expression used in this verse כִּי תֵצֵא, *when you go forth*, implies מִלְחֶמֶת רְשׁוּת, an optional war, and only then are the exemptions listed in this *parashah* granted, but were it מִלְחֶמֶת מִצְוָה, a *commanded war*, these exemptions would not be operative, for then everyone must go to war to defend the land and its people.

before HASHEM, before the Kohanim and the judges who will be in those
days. [18] *The judges shall inquire thoroughly, and behold! the testimony was*
false testimony; he spoke up falsely against his fellow. [19] *You shall do to him*
as he conspired to do to his fellow, and you shall destroy the evil from your
midst. [20] *And those who remain shall hearken and fear; and they shall not*
continue again to do such an evil thing in your midst. [21] *Your eye shall not*
pity; life for life, eye for eye, tooth for tooth, hand for hand, foot for foot.

20 [1] *When you go out to the battle against your enemy, and you see horse*
and chariot — a people more numerous than you — you shall not
fear them, for HASHEM, your God, is with you, Who brought you up from the
land of Egypt. [2] *It shall be that when you draw near to the war, the Kohen*
shall approach and speak to the people.
[3] *He shall say to them, "Hear, O Israel, you are coming near to the battle*
against your enemies; let your heart not be faint; do not be afraid, do not
panic, and do not be broken before them. [4] *For HASHEM, your God, is the One*
Who goes with you, to fight for you with your enemies, to save you."
[5] *Then the officers shall speak to the people, saying, "Who is the man who*
has built a new house and has not inaugurated it? Let him go and return to
his house, lest he die in the war and another man will inaugurate it. [6] *And*
who is the man who has planted a vineyard and not redeemed it? Let him
go and return to his house, lest he die in the war and another man will
redeem it. [7] *And who is the man who has betrothed a woman and not*
married her? Let him go and return to his house, lest he die in the war and
another man will marry her."
[8] *The officers shall continue speaking to the people and say, "Who is the*
man who is fearful and fainthearted? Let him go and return to his house, and
let him not melt the heart of his fellows, like his heart." [9] *When the officers*
have finished speaking to the people, the leaders of the legions shall take

5. פֶּן יָמוּת בַּמִּלְחָמָה וְאִישׁ אַחֵר יַחְנְכֶנּוּ — *Lest he die in battle and another man dedicate it.* Perhaps he is guilty of a transgression, the penalty for which is this particular punishment, as explained in the תּוֹכָחָה, *admonition* (28:30). (This, in turn,) will bring harm to his brothers (in battle), for it will turn away their hearts and cause other similar (demoralization).

9. וּפָקְדוּ שָׂרֵי צְבָאוֹת — *And they appointed captains of hosts . . .* (only) after the return (exemption) of the returnees, lest one of those chosen as a captain of hosts would be among the ones who return which would cause the hearts of his legion to melt (in fear), as it says,

NOTES

5. פֶּן יָמוּת בַּמִּלְחָמָה — *Lest he die in battle*. The section of admonition (פָּרָשַׁת הַתּוֹכָחָה) appears in the portion of *Ki Savo*. The Torah there (28:30) speaks of three misfortunes which will befall Israel, and these three experiences are precisely those mentioned in our chapter regarding exemption from military service. One is the betrothal of a woman who is then taken as a wife by another; the second is regarding one who builds a house and another man ultimately dwells in it; and the third speaks of a man who plants a vineyard and another man eventually eats its fruit. The *Sforno* explains that the reason these men are excused is because if one of them were to fall in battle it would be viewed as the fulfillment of the terrible admonition recorded later in the Book of *Deuteronomy* and would arouse fear, dismay and panic in the hearts of the Jewish army. Hence, it is far better that these soldiers be excused, for the sake of the morale of the other soldiers.

9. וּפָקְדוּ שָׂרֵי צְבָאוֹת — *And they appointed captains of hosts*. The *Sforno* explains why the cap-

שביעי
י בְּרֹאשׁ הָעָם: כִּי־תִקְרַב אֶל־עִיר לְהִלָּחֵם עָלֶיהָ וְקָרָאתָ
יא אֵלֶיהָ לְשָׁלוֹם: וְהָיָה אִם־שָׁלוֹם תַּעַנְךָ וּפָתְחָה לָךְ וְהָיָה כָּל־הָעָם
יב הַנִּמְצָא־בָהּ יִהְיוּ לְךָ לָמַס וַעֲבָדוּךָ: וְאִם־לֹא תַשְׁלִים עִמָּךְ וְעָשְׂתָה עִמְּךָ
יג מִלְחָמָה וְצַרְתָּ עָלֶיהָ: וּנְתָנָהּ יהוה אֱלֹהֶיךָ בְּיָדֶךָ וְהִכִּיתָ אֶת־כָּל־זְכוּרָהּ
יד לְפִי־חָרֶב: רַק הַנָּשִׁים וְהַטַּף וְהַבְּהֵמָה וְכֹל אֲשֶׁר יִהְיֶה בָעִיר כָּל־שְׁלָלָהּ
טו תָּבֹז לָךְ וְאָכַלְתָּ אֶת־שְׁלַל אֹיְבֶיךָ אֲשֶׁר נָתַן יהוה אֱלֹהֶיךָ לָךְ: כֵּן
תַּעֲשֶׂה לְכָל־הֶעָרִים הָרְחֹקֹת מִמְּךָ מְאֹד אֲשֶׁר לֹא־מֵעָרֵי הַגּוֹיִם־הָאֵלֶּה
טז הֵנָּה: רַק מֵעָרֵי הָעַמִּים הָאֵלֶּה אֲשֶׁר יהוה אֱלֹהֶיךָ נֹתֵן לְךָ נַחֲלָה לֹא
יז תְחַיֶּה כָּל־נְשָׁמָה: כִּי־הַחֲרֵם תַּחֲרִימֵם הַחִתִּי וְהָאֱמֹרִי הַכְּנַעֲנִי וְהַפְּרִזִּי
יח הַחִוִּי וְהַיְבוּסִי כַּאֲשֶׁר צִוְּךָ יהוה אֱלֹהֶיךָ: לְמַעַן אֲשֶׁר לֹא־יְלַמְּדוּ אֶתְכֶם
לַעֲשׂוֹת כְּכֹל תּוֹעֲבֹתָם אֲשֶׁר עָשׂוּ לֵאלֹהֵיהֶם וַחֲטָאתֶם לַיהוה
יט אֱלֹהֵיכֶם: כִּי־תָצוּר אֶל־עִיר יָמִים רַבִּים לְהִלָּחֵם עָלֶיהָ
לְתָפְשָׂהּ לֹא־תַשְׁחִית אֶת־עֵצָהּ לִנְדֹּחַ עָלָיו גַּרְזֶן כִּי מִמֶּנּוּ תֹאכֵל וְאֹתוֹ
כ לֹא תִכְרֹת כִּי הָאָדָם עֵץ הַשָּׂדֶה לָבֹא מִפָּנֶיךָ בַּמָּצוֹר: רַק עֵץ
אֲשֶׁר־תֵּדַע כִּי לֹא־עֵץ מַאֲכָל הוּא אֹתוֹ תַשְׁחִית וְכָרָתָּ וּבָנִיתָ מָצוֹר
עַל־הָעִיר אֲשֶׁר־הִוא עֹשָׂה עִמְּךָ מִלְחָמָה עַד רִדְתָּהּ:
כא א כִּי־יִמָּצֵא חָלָל בָּאֲדָמָה אֲשֶׁר יהוה אֱלֹהֶיךָ נֹתֵן לְךָ לְרִשְׁתָּהּ נֹפֵל בַּשָּׂדֶה
ב לֹא נוֹדַע מִי הִכָּהוּ: וְיָצְאוּ זְקֵנֶיךָ וְשֹׁפְטֶיךָ וּמָדְדוּ אֶל־הֶעָרִים אֲשֶׁר סְבִיבֹת

הַךְ הַכַּפְתּוֹר וְיִרְעֲשׁוּ הַסִּפִּים, *Smite the capitals that the thresholds may shake* (*Amos* 9:1).

15. הָרְחֹקֹת מִמְּךָ מְאֹד — *Which are very far off from you . . .* far from the place where the camp of Israel is situated, because the boundary of Israel is far from it on all sides.

19. לֹא תַשְׁחִית אֶת עֵצָהּ לִנְדֹּחַ עָלָיו גַּרְזֶן — *You shall not destroy its trees, wielding an axe against them.* Do not destroy the tree (just) to wield an axe of destruction upon it, i.e., (for the sole purpose) of doing harm to the inhabitants of that city.

כִּי מִמֶּנּוּ תֹאכֵל — *Because from it you shall eat.* Because the cutting down of trees in a destructive manner is done by armies to harm (the enemy) when they are not certain that they will be victorious and dwell in the land. However, you, who are assured that you will conquer the land and settle in it, must not destroy the fruit-bearing trees.

כִּי מִמֶּנּוּ תֹאכֵל — *Because from it you shall eat.* Without a doubt, you will conquer the land and (ultimately) eat from its trees, provided you do not destroy them.

כִּי הָאָדָם עֵץ הַשָּׂדֶה — *Is then the tree of the field a man?* Is then the tree of the field a man who is capable of submitting to you that the city be besieged on its account, and be forced to surrender because of the siege? This is (obviously) not so, and although it is acceptable to inflict damage upon the inhabitants of a city with implements of war and other kinds

NOTES

tains were appointed *after* those who were disqualified were discharged. Otherwise, the captain chosen might be discharged for one of the reasons mentioned above, which would have a devastating effect upon the entire army.

19. לֹא תַשְׁחִית אֶת עֵצָהּ . . . כִּי הָאָדָם עֵץ הַשָּׂדֶה — *You shall not destroy its trees . . . is then the tree of the field a man?* The *Sforno* interprets this verse, which prohibits the wanton destruction of fruit-bearing trees when a city is under siege, as a reasoned two-fold argument. It would be foolhardy to deprive oneself of the produce of the land which is beneficial for the sustenance of its inhabitants, and since Israel is assured of conquering and settling the land, there would be no reason to

command at the head of the people.

[10] *When you draw near to a city to wage war against it, you shall call out to it for peace.* [11] *It shall be that if it responds to you in peace and opens for you, then the entire people found within it shall be as tribute for you, and they shall serve you.* [12] *But if it does not make peace with you, but makes war with you, you shall besiege it.* [13] *HASHEM shall deliver it into your hand, and you shall smite all its males by the blade of the sword.* [14] *Only the women, the small children, the animals, and everything that will be in the city — all its booty — may you plunder for yourselves; you shall eat the booty of your enemies, which HASHEM, your God, gave you.* [15] *So shall you do to all the cities that are very distant from you, which are not of the cities of these nations.* [16] *But from the cities of these peoples that HASHEM, your God, gives you as an inheritance, you shall not allow any person to live.* [17] *Rather you shall utterly destroy them: the Hittite, the Amorite, the Canaanite, the Perizzite, the Hivvite, and the Jebusite, as HASHEM, your God has commanded you,* [18] *so that they will not teach you to act according to all their abominations that they performed for their gods, so that you will sin to HASHEM, your God.*

[19] *When you besiege a city for many days to wage war against it to seize it, do not destroy its trees by swinging an axe against them, for from it you will eat, and you shall not cut it down; is the tree of the field a man that it should enter the siege before you?* [20] *Only a tree that you know is not a food tree, it you may destroy and cut down, and build a bulwark against the city that makes war with you, until it is conquered.*

21 [1] *If a corpse will be found on the land that HASHEM, your God, gives you to possess it, fallen in the field, it was not known who smote him,* [2] *your elders and judges shall go out and measure toward the cities that are around*

of (tactics) so as to besiege the city, since you will not attain (this goal) by destroying the trees, it is improper to destroy them. (Yet, it is still) proper that you destroy the people who dwell in the city.

לָבֹא מִפָּנֶיךָ בַּמָּצוֹר — *To bring under siege before you.* In order that you bring the city under siege before you in a manner that they will (be forced) to give themselves over into your hand.

20. רַק עֵץ אֲשֶׁר תֵּדַע כִּי לֹא עֵץ מַאֲכָל הוּא — *Only a tree which you know is not a tree for food.* Although it is a species of tree which is meant for food, if you know that it is old or spoiled (deficient) to such an extent that it cannot produce fruit, and that it is not worthwhile for one to exert himself on its behalf (given its meager productivity), *you may destroy it.*

NOTES

destroy these fruit-bearing trees. To do so would demonstrate a lack of faith and trust in God's promise that they will conquer *Eretz Yisrael*. Secondly, the Torah argues that a tree, unlike a person, cannot be intimidated into surrendering; hence, what will be accomplished by destroying it? The sense of the words כִּי הָאָדָם עֵץ הַשָּׂדֶה is, "Certainly a tree is not a person whose destruction can be justified."

20. רַק עֵץ אֲשֶׁר תֵּדַע כִּי לֹא עֵץ מַאֲכָל הוּא — *Only a tree which you know is not a tree for food*. Based upon the Talmud (*Bava Kama* 91b), the *Sforno* interprets the phrase *which you know is not a tree for food* as meaning: Although it is a fruit-bearing tree, its yield is so meager or its fruit of such inferior quality that even under ordinary circumstances such a tree would be cut down. Therefore, one is permitted to destroy such a tree.

ג הֶחָלָל: וְהָיָה הָעִיר הַקְּרֹבָה אֶל־הֶחָלָל וְלָקְחוּ זִקְנֵי הָעִיר הַהִוא עֶגְלַת
ד בָּקָר אֲשֶׁר לֹא־עֻבַּד בָּהּ אֲשֶׁר לֹא־מָשְׁכָה בְּעֹל: וְהוֹרִדוּ זִקְנֵי הָעִיר
הַהִוא אֶת־הָעֶגְלָה אֶל־נַחַל אֵיתָן אֲשֶׁר לֹא־יֵעָבֵד בּוֹ וְלֹא יִזָּרֵעַ
ה וְעָרְפוּ־שָׁם אֶת־הָעֶגְלָה בַּנָּחַל: וְנִגְּשׁוּ הַכֹּהֲנִים בְּנֵי לֵוִי כִּי בָם בָּחַר יהוה
אֱלֹהֶיךָ לְשָׁרְתוֹ וּלְבָרֵךְ בְּשֵׁם יהוה וְעַל־פִּיהֶם יִהְיֶה כָּל־רִיב וְכָל־נָגַע:
ו וְכֹל זִקְנֵי הָעִיר הַהִוא הַקְּרֹבִים אֶל־הֶחָלָל יִרְחֲצוּ אֶת־יְדֵיהֶם עַל־הָעֶגְלָה
°שָׁפְכוּ ק׳ מפטיר ז הָעֲרוּפָה בַנָּחַל: וְעָנוּ וְאָמְרוּ יָדֵינוּ לֹא °שפכה אֶת־הַדָּם הַזֶּה וְעֵינֵינוּ לֹא
ח רָאוּ: כַּפֵּר לְעַמְּךָ יִשְׂרָאֵל אֲשֶׁר־פָּדִיתָ יהוה וְאַל־תִּתֵּן דָּם נָקִי בְּקֶרֶב
ט עַמְּךָ יִשְׂרָאֵל וְנִכַּפֵּר לָהֶם הַדָּם: וְאַתָּה תְּבַעֵר הַדָּם הַנָּקִי מִקִּרְבֶּךָ
כִּי־תַעֲשֶׂה הַיָּשָׁר בְּעֵינֵי יהוה:

XXI

4. אֶל נַחַל אֵיתָן — *To a hard* (*rough*) *ravine* ... where there are no wayfarers.

וְעָרְפוּ . . . אֶת הָעֶגְלָה — *And break the heifer's neck.* This is a death (killing) which is hidden from the eyes of the slain one (i.e., the heifer), to teach us that the killing (of the victim) was, without a doubt, in a place concealed from the eyes of people, and committed by a murderer unknown as a killer to the court, for were he known to them as a murderer, they would have eliminated him (from their midst).

5. לְשָׁרְתוֹ וּלְבָרֵךְ — *To minister unto Him, and to bless* ... and through them, there will be atonement for the innocent blood and a blessing for the Land.

וְעַל פִּיהֶם יִהְיֶה כָּל רִיב וְכָל נָגַע — *And according to their word shall every controversy and every plague be* ... (and) in this manner they are knowledgeable experts in the temperament and ways of man, (being that) they and their fathers have constantly observed human behavior, and perhaps through their knowledge of his ways and deeds, they will recognize who might be sullied by this sin, and (thus) the matter will be revealed.

7. יָדֵינוּ לֹא שָׁפְכוּ — *Our hands have not shed.* We did not allow any known murderer to remain in the land.

NOTES

XXI

4. אֶל נַחַל אֵיתָן . . . וְעָרְפוּ . . . אֶת הָעֶגְלָה — *To a hard* (*rough*) *ravine . . . and break the heifer's neck*. The *Sforno* interprets the act of beheading the heifer from the *back* symbolically. Just as the heifer is slain in a manner whereby the one who kills him is not seen, so the murder victim was taken unawares and killed by one whom he did not see, and who was also unknown to the court, and hidden from the eyes of witnesses.

5. לְשָׁרְתוֹ וּלְבָרֵךְ — *To minister unto Him, and to bless*. This phrase seems to be gratuitous in the context of the verse. Why is it necessary to tell us the function of the *Kohen* in connection with the ceremony of the עֶגְלָה עֲרוּפָה? The *Sforno* explains that the Torah is telling us that the *Kohanim* who had been chosen to serve God and bring blessing to the people are best fit to make atonement for the shedding of innocent blood.

וְעַל פִּיהֶם — *And according to their word.* The sense of the *Sforno's* interpretation is that since the *Kohanim* in their various duties constantly come into contact with different people, and are aware of people's weaknesses, hence they may be able to detect the murderer.

7. יָדֵינוּ לֹא שָׁפְכוּ — *Our hands have not shed*. *Rashi* explains that the elders state that the victim was not sent away from the city without

the corpse. [3] *It shall be that the city nearest the corpse, the elders of that city shall take a heifer, with which no work has been done, which has not pulled with a yoke.* [4] *The elders of that city shall bring the heifer down to a harsh valley, which cannot be worked and cannot be sown, and they shall axe the back of its neck in the valley.* [5] *The Kohanim, the offspring of Levi, shall approach, for them has HASHEM, your God, chosen to minister to Him and to bless with the Name of HASHEM, and according to their word shall be every grievance and every plague.*

[6] *All the elders of that city, who are closest to the corpse, shall wash their hands over the heifer that was axed in the valley.* [7] *They shall speak up and say, "Our hands have not spilled this blood, and our eyes did not see.* [8] *Atone for Your people Israel that You have redeemed, O HASHEM: Do not place innocent blood in the midst of Your people Israel!" Then the blood shall be atoned for them.*

[9] *But you shall remove the innocent blood from your midst when you do what is upright in the eyes of HASHEM.*

וְעֵינֵינוּ לֹא רָאוּ — *Neither have our eyes seen it.* It did not occur in a place where it could be seen, for if there were those who saw (it happen), they would have risen up and testified.

8. כַּפֵּר לְעַמְּךָ — *Grant atonement to Your people.* (May) You grant atonement by the blood of he who shed it, as our Sages say, 'He, who would have been sentenced to execution by the sword, is either delivered to the government or robbers come upon him' (*Kesuvos* 30b).

וְנִכַּפֵּר לָהֶם הַדָּם — *And the blood shall be atoned for them.* It shall be atoned by the law of heaven through the blood of he who shed it, in such a manner that it appears as though he atones by himself.

9. וְאַתָּה תְּבַעֵר — *And you shall purge.* Behold, God the Blessed One, will atone if you do not know who (the killer) is; but if you do know, you must remove him before the law of heaven is effectuated.

NOTES

food or without being accompanied part of the way. The *Sforno*, however, explains their disclaimer differently. The elders and *Kohanim* proclaim that they did not permit any murderer to remain in the land, but justice was always served and murderers were punished so as to protect society. Hence, this man's blood is not on their hands.

8. כַּפֵּר לְעַמְּךָ — *Grant atonement to Your people.* The Talmud in tractate *Kesuvos* (30b) states that although the Sanhedrin no longer functions, nonetheless, the four forms of capital punishment have not ceased. By this, our Sages mean that a person who is guilty of a crime or transgression punishable by death will be dealt with accordingly through some *apparent* natural method of death. Since a murderer received the punishment of הֶרֶג (execution by the sword) when the court had the authority to impose it, in our case, this man who slew the victim may be executed by the government or killed by robbers — both of whom will do so by the sword. In this manner, he will receive his due through a decree from Heaven.

9. וְאַתָּה תְּבַעֵר — *And you shall purge.* Although the previous verse states that the blood of the victim will be atoned for by the law of heaven, i.e., the murderer will meet his death through Divine justice, nonetheless this is so only if the court cannot ascertain the identity of the killer. If they know his identity they must punish him even though the heifer has been brought and the ritual of atonement performed. The Jerusalem Talmud (*Sotah* 9:6) says: It is written (v. 8), *"and the blood shall be atoned for them,"* (followed by) *"and you shall purge the innocent blood from your midst"* (v. 9). This teaches us that if the murderer is detected after the heifer has been beheaded, nevertheless (the court) shall execute him.

פרשת כי תצא

י כִּֽי־תֵצֵא לַמִּלְחָמָה עַל־אֹיְבֶיךָ וּנְתָנוֹ יְהוָה אֱלֹהֶיךָ בְּיָדֶךָ וְשָׁבִיתָ שִׁבְיוֹ׃
יא וְרָאִיתָ בַּשִּׁבְיָה אֵשֶׁת יְפַת־תֹּאַר וְחָשַׁקְתָּ בָהּ וְלָקַחְתָּ לְךָ לְאִשָּׁה׃
יב וַהֲבֵאתָהּ אֶל־תּוֹךְ בֵּיתֶךָ וְגִלְּחָה אֶת־רֹאשָׁהּ וְעָשְׂתָה אֶת־צִפָּרְנֶיהָ׃
יג וְהֵסִירָה אֶת־שִׂמְלַת שִׁבְיָהּ מֵעָלֶיהָ וְיָשְׁבָה בְּבֵיתֶךָ וּבָכְתָה אֶת־אָבִיהָ
וְאֶת־אִמָּהּ יֶרַח יָמִים וְאַחַר כֵּן תָּבוֹא אֵלֶיהָ וּבְעַלְתָּהּ וְהָיְתָה לְךָ לְאִשָּׁה׃
יד וְהָיָה אִם־לֹא חָפַצְתָּ בָּהּ וְשִׁלַּחְתָּהּ לְנַפְשָׁהּ וּמָכֹר לֹא־תִמְכְּרֶנָּה בַּכָּסֶף
טו לֹא־תִתְעַמֵּר בָּהּ תַּחַת אֲשֶׁר עִנִּיתָהּ׃ כִּֽי־תִהְיֶיןָ לְאִישׁ שְׁתֵּי
נָשִׁים הָאַחַת אֲהוּבָה וְהָאַחַת שְׂנוּאָה וְיָלְדוּ־לוֹ בָנִים הָאֲהוּבָה וְהַשְּׂנוּאָה
טז וְהָיָה הַבֵּן הַבְּכֹר לַשְּׂנִיאָה׃ וְהָיָה בְּיוֹם הַנְחִילוֹ אֶת־בָּנָיו אֵת אֲשֶׁר־יִהְיֶה
יז לוֹ לֹא יוּכַל לְבַכֵּר אֶת־בֶּן־הָאֲהוּבָה עַל־פְּנֵי בֶן־הַשְּׂנוּאָה הַבְּכֹר׃ כִּי
אֶת־הַבְּכֹר בֶּן־הַשְּׂנוּאָה יַכִּיר לָתֶת לוֹ פִּי שְׁנַיִם בְּכֹל אֲשֶׁר־יִמָּצֵא לוֹ
יח כִּי־הוּא רֵאשִׁית אֹנוֹ לוֹ מִשְׁפַּט הַבְּכֹרָה׃ כִּֽי־יִהְיֶה לְאִישׁ בֵּן
סוֹרֵר וּמוֹרֶה אֵינֶנּוּ שֹׁמֵעַ בְּקוֹל אָבִיו וּבְקוֹל אִמּוֹ וְיִסְּרוּ אֹתוֹ וְלֹא יִשְׁמַע
יט אֲלֵיהֶם׃ וְתָפְשׂוּ בוֹ אָבִיו וְאִמּוֹ וְהוֹצִיאוּ אֹתוֹ אֶל־זִקְנֵי עִירוֹ וְאֶל־שַׁעַר

10. כִּי תֵצֵא — *When you go forth (to battle)* . . . outside the Land.

13. וּבָכְתָה אֶת אָבִיהָ וְאֶת אִמָּהּ — *And weep for her father and her mother* . . . so that she relinquish them and thereby find composure (peace of mind) and not think of them any longer, similar to, וְשִׁכְחִי עַמֵּךְ וּבֵית אָבִיךְ, *forget your people and your father's house* (*Psalms* 45:11). But (her) weeping is not for their death, for we would (certainly) not kill her mother.

15. כִּי תִהְיֶיןָ לְאִישׁ שְׁתֵּי נָשִׁים — *If a man have two wives.* Following the military victory, (the Torah) speaks of affairs (affecting) the citizenry of the state. These are: the case of the women and their sons (verse 18) and of livestock (22:1) and ornaments (22:5) and game (22:6) and a building (22:8) and farming and the wearing of garments (22:9-12).

16. לֹא יוּכַל לְבַכֵּר אֶת בֶּן הָאֲהוּבָה עַל פְּנֵי בֶן הַשְּׂנוּאָה הַבְּכֹר — *He may not make the son of the beloved the firstborn before the son of the hated who is the firstborn.* He cannot transfer the birthright of the firstborn from the (rightful) son due to his hatred of this one or the love of that one. However, if he does so because of the wickedness of the firstborn son,

NOTES

10. כִּי תֵצֵא — *When you go forth (to battle).* The expression כִּי תֵצֵא, *when you go forth,* is identical to the phrase used in chapter 20, verse 1. The *Sforno* there comments, as he does here, "outside the Land" i.e., of Israel. Just as the rules set forth there regarding military exemptions only apply to a מִלְחֶמֶת רְשׁוּת, *an optional, political war,* so does the law of the אֵשֶׁת יְפַת תֹּאַר, *the woman of goodly form,* only apply to this type of war, as *Rashi* explains in his commentary on this verse. If the battle is conducted in defense of the Land of Israel or to conquer it, then it is a war in fulfillment of a religious imperative (מִלְחֶמֶת מִצְוָה), and under such circumstances neither of these laws (exemption and the woman captive) apply.

13. וּבָכְתָה אֶת אָבִיהָ וְאֶת אִמָּהּ — *And weep for her father and her mother.* The *Ramban* in his commentary on this verse cites the *Rambam* in his *Guide* 3:41, where he explains that "she should not be forbidden to grieve . . . for those who grieve find solace in weeping and in arousing their sorrow." The *Sforno* interprets this verse in a similar vein. He also adds that it cannot mean that she weeps for the death of her parents, for her mother was certainly not put to death in battle by the Israelites, even though her father may have fallen in battle. Hence, her grieving is for being taken from her home and family. In all probability, with the passage of time and the catharsis of weeping, she will make peace with her fate.

PARASHAS KI SEITZEI

10 When you will go out to war against your enemies, and HASHEM, your God, will deliver them into your hand, and you will capture its captivity; 11 and you will see among its captivity a woman who is beautiful of form, and you will desire her, you may take her to yourself for a wife.
12 You shall bring her to the midst of your house; she shall shave her head and let her nails grow. 13 She shall remove the garment of her captivity from upon herself and sit in your house and she shall weep for her father and her mother for a full month; thereafter you may come to her and live with her, and she shall be a wife to you. 14 But it shall be that if you do not desire her, then you shall send her on her own, but you may not sell her for money; you shall not enslave her, because you have afflicted her.

15 If a man will have two wives, one beloved and one hated, and they bear him sons, the beloved one and the hated one, and the firstborn son is the hated one's; 16 then it shall be that on the day that he causes his sons to inherit whatever will be his, he cannot give the right of the firstborn to the son of the beloved one ahead of the son of the hated one, the firstborn.
17 Rather, he must recognize the firstborn, the son of the hated one, to give him the double portion in all that is found with him; for he is his initial vigor, to him is the right of the firstborn.

18 If a man will have a wayward and rebellious son, who does not hearken to the voice of his father and the voice of his mother, and they discipline him, but he does not hearken to them; 19 then his father and mother shall grasp him and take him out to the elders of his city and the gate of

---

then it is proper to transfer it (to another son), as our Sages say, "If his children did not conduct themselves in a proper manner (and that is why he transferred it) he will be remembered for good" (*Bava Basra* 133b). And apparently, this our father Jacob did, as it says, וּבְחַלְּלוֹ יְצוּעֵי אָבִיו נִתְּנָה בְּכֹרָתוֹ לִבְנֵי יוֹסֵף בֶּן יִשְׂרָאֵל, *But since he defiled his father's bed, his birthright was given to the sons of Joseph, the son of Israel* (*I Chronicles* 5:1).

18. סוֹרֵר וּמוֹרֶה — *Disobedient and rebellious* ... because his rebellious (nature) frustrates any hope that he may repent his disobedience.

NOTES

15. כִּי תִהְיֶיןָ לְאִישׁ — *If a man have*. The *Sforno* explains the continuity of this *parashah*. After discussing the laws of war in chapters 20-21, the Torah now turns its attention to a variety of laws as they affect society in peacetime, these being the law of the firstborn, the disobedient and rebellious son, lost animals and articles, the prohibition of garbing oneself in clothes of the opposite sex, the law of sending away the mother bird before taking the young ones, building a parapet on one's roof, the prohibition of כִּלְאַיִם (mixture of seeds, animals or material) and the commandment of צִיצִית, *fringes*. These are all civil, social and personal regulations and laws.

16. לֹא יוּכַל לְבַכֵּר אֶת בֶּן הָאֲהוּבָה — *He may not make the son of the beloved the firstborn*. The feelings of the father toward the two mothers cannot determine the status of their sons, but the behavior of the sons may well affect their inheritance. The Mishnah cited by the *Sforno* is according to the opinion of R' Simeon ben Gamliel. The Rabbis, however, disagree and are of the opinion that one should not disinherit even a bad son. Note that the *Sforno* in *Genesis* 48:22 gives a different reason for Jacob's decision to grant Joseph a double inheritance which was due Reuben, his firstborn son.

18. סוֹרֵר וּמוֹרֶה — *Disobedient and rebellious*. The *Sforno* explains why the son who is so severely punished is characterized as both *disobedient and rebellious*. Were he not rebellious, there might be hope that he would repent his evil ways. However, his rebellious spirit will prevent him from ever doing so. *Rashi* explains סוֹרֵר as meaning "turning away from the proper path."

כ מְקֹמוֹ: וְאָמְרוּ אֶל־זִקְנֵי עִירוֹ בְּנֵנוּ זֶה סוֹרֵר וּמֹרֶה אֵינֶנּוּ שֹׁמֵעַ בְּקֹלֵנוּ זוֹלֵל
כא וְסֹבֵא: וּרְגָמֻהוּ כָּל־אַנְשֵׁי עִירוֹ בָאֲבָנִים וָמֵת וּבִעַרְתָּ הָרָע מִקִּרְבֶּךָ
שני כב וְכָל־יִשְׂרָאֵל יִשְׁמְעוּ וְיִרָאוּ: וְכִי־יִהְיֶה בְאִישׁ חֵטְא מִשְׁפַּט־
כג מָוֶת וְהוּמָת וְתָלִיתָ אֹתוֹ עַל־עֵץ: לֹא־תָלִין נִבְלָתוֹ עַל־הָעֵץ כִּי־קָבוֹר
תִּקְבְּרֶנּוּ בַּיּוֹם הַהוּא כִּי־קִלְלַת אֱלֹהִים תָּלוּי וְלֹא תְטַמֵּא אֶת־אַדְמָתְךָ
כב א אֲשֶׁר יהוה אֱלֹהֶיךָ נֹתֵן לְךָ נַחֲלָה: לֹא־תִרְאֶה אֶת־שׁוֹר
אָחִיךָ אוֹ אֶת־שֵׂיוֹ נִדָּחִים וְהִתְעַלַּמְתָּ מֵהֶם הָשֵׁב תְּשִׁיבֵם לְאָחִיךָ:
ב וְאִם־לֹא קָרוֹב אָחִיךָ אֵלֶיךָ וְלֹא יְדַעְתּוֹ וַאֲסַפְתּוֹ אֶל־תּוֹךְ בֵּיתֶךָ וְהָיָה
ג עִמְּךָ עַד דְּרֹשׁ אָחִיךָ אֹתוֹ וַהֲשֵׁבֹתוֹ לוֹ: וְכֵן תַּעֲשֶׂה לַחֲמֹרוֹ וְכֵן תַּעֲשֶׂה
לְשִׂמְלָתוֹ וְכֵן תַּעֲשֶׂה לְכָל־אֲבֵדַת אָחִיךָ אֲשֶׁר־תֹּאבַד מִמֶּנּוּ וּמְצָאתָהּ
ד לֹא תוּכַל לְהִתְעַלֵּם: לֹא־תִרְאֶה אֶת־חֲמוֹר אָחִיךָ אוֹ
ה שׁוֹרוֹ נֹפְלִים בַּדֶּרֶךְ וְהִתְעַלַּמְתָּ מֵהֶם הָקֵם תָּקִים עִמּוֹ: לֹא־
יִהְיֶה כְלִי־גֶבֶר עַל־אִשָּׁה וְלֹא־יִלְבַּשׁ גֶּבֶר שִׂמְלַת אִשָּׁה כִּי תוֹעֲבַת יהוה
אֱלֹהֶיךָ כָּל־עֹשֵׂה אֵלֶּה:
ו כִּי יִקָּרֵא קַן־צִפּוֹר ׀ לְפָנֶיךָ בַּדֶּרֶךְ בְּכָל־עֵץ ׀ אוֹ עַל־הָאָרֶץ אֶפְרֹחִים אוֹ
בֵיצִים וְהָאֵם רֹבֶצֶת עַל־הָאֶפְרֹחִים אוֹ עַל־הַבֵּיצִים לֹא־תִקַּח הָאֵם עַל־
ז הַבָּנִים: שַׁלֵּחַ תְּשַׁלַּח אֶת־הָאֵם וְאֶת־הַבָּנִים תִּקַּח־לָךְ לְמַעַן יִיטַב לָךְ
שלישי ח וְהַאֲרַכְתָּ יָמִים: כִּי תִבְנֶה בַּיִת חָדָשׁ וְעָשִׂיתָ מַעֲקֶה לְגַגֶּךָ

20. זולל וְסֹבא — *He is a glutton and a drunkard.* Since a glutton and drunkard becomes impoverished, he (will eventually) rob to satisfy his appetite (lit., "soul").

23. כִּי קִלְלַת אֱלֹהִים תָּלוּי — *For he that is hung is a reproach to* (*the image*) *of God.* Behold, every object that is separated from matter is called *Elohim,* and regarding this species (i.e., man), the essence of the intelligent soul is called צֶלֶם אֱלֹהִים, *the image of God* (*Genesis* 1:27). In a similar manner, the necromanceress said to Saul, אֱלֹהִים רָאִיתִי עֹלִים, *I saw Elohim ascending* (*I Samuel* 28:13). The disgrace brought upon a deceased person after death is shameful to his intelligent soul, which is considered as the essence separated (from matter) that remains after the death of the body; hence it states that it is a reproach to *Elohim,* because allowing the hanging body to remain overnight without burial is shameful to that everlasting essence called *Elohim.*

וְלֹא תְטַמֵּא — *That you not defile* . . . by causing a spirit of impurity to rest in the place of the unburied dead person.

NOTES

23. כִּי קִלְלַת אֱלֹהִים תָּלוּי — *For he that is hung is a reproach to* (*the image*) *of God.* The *Sforno* explains that it is an affront to the soul of man to allow the body which housed that נֶפֶשׁ שִׂכְלִית, *intelligent soul* (also called *Elohim,* reflecting the image of the Divine), to remain in such a disrespectful manner overnight. In his commentary on *Genesis* 1:27, the *Sforno* states that if one attains the level of perfection which is possible to man, then this *image of God* exists even after death. This explains the expression used by the medium of En-dor regarding Samuel when she said, "*I saw Elohim ascending,*" referring to his עֶצֶם נֶפֶשׁ הַשִּׂכְלִית, *the essence of his intelligent soul*, which is immortal. The *Rambam* in his *Guide* (1:70 and 3:27) teaches that the immortality of the soul is achieved by the special knowledge of God attained through man's intellectual power. This is similar to the concept referred to by the *Sforno*, here and in *Genesis.*

XXII

3. וְכֵן תַּעֲשֶׂה לְשִׂמְלָתוֹ — *And so shall you do with his garment*. The first two verses of this chapter

his place. [20] *They shall say to the elders of his city, "This son of ours is*
wayward and rebellious; he does not hearken to our voice; he is a glutton
and a drunkard." [21] *All the men of his city shall pelt him with stones and*
he shall die; and you shall remove the evil from your midst; and all Israel
shall hear and they shall fear.

[22] *If a man shall have committed a sin whose judgment is death, he shall*
be put to death, and you shall hang him on a gallows. [23] *His body shall not*
remain for the night on the gallows, rather you shall surely bury him on that
day, for a hanging person is a curse of God, and you shall not contaminate
your Land, which H*ASHEM*, *your God, gives you as an inheritance.*

22 [1] *You shall not see the ox of your brother or his sheep or goat cast off, and*
hide yourself from them; you shall surely return them to your brother.
[2] *If your brother is not near you and you do not know him, then gather it*
inside your house, and it shall remain with you until your brother inquires
after it, and you return it to him. [3] *So shall you do for his donkey, so shall you*
do for his garment, and so shall you do for any lost article of your brother
that may become lost from him and you find it; you shall not hide yourself.
[4] *You shall not see the donkey of your brother or his ox falling on the road*
and hide yourself from them; you shall surely stand them up, with him.
[5] *Male garb shall not be on a woman, and a man shall not wear a feminine*
garment, for anyone who does so is an abomination of H*ASHEM*.
[6] *If a bird's nest happens to be before you on the road, on any tree or on*
the ground — young birds or eggs — and the mother is roosting on the young
birds or the eggs, you shall not take the mother with the young. [7] *You shall*
surely send away the mother and take the young for yourself, so that it will
be good for you and will prolong your days.
[8] *If you build a new house, you shall make a fence for your roof, so that*

XXII

3. וְכֵן תַּעֲשֶׂה לְשִׂמְלָתוֹ — *And so shall you do with his garment.* Even though the loss (of a garment) is not as common (as that of animals), do not consider it a deliberate loss (אֲבֵדָה מְדַעַת).

7. לְמַעַן יִיטַב לָךְ וְהַאֲרַכְתָּ יָמִים — *That it may be well with you and that you may prolong your days.* Behold, by sending away (the mother bird) from the nest, one performs an act of lovingkindness benefiting the masses, (namely) the preservation of the birds of the field who are ownerless property. This is (accomplished) by sending forth the mother (bird). (The Torah therefore) says that even for such a minor act of lovingkindness, (one will be

NOTES

speak of livestock that are lost and found. We are commanded to care for these animals and return them to their owner. Now, while it is quite common for animals to wander off, a garment, on the other hand, is rarely *lost* but may well be *abandoned*. If this were the case there is no commandment of הֲשָׁבַת אֲבֵדָה, *return of lost property*, since the owner did so deliberately. This is known as אֲבֵדָה מְדַעַת, *a conscious loss*. The *Sforno* explains that this is why the Torah uses the word וְכֵן, *"and so" shall you do with his garment;* i.e., do not assume that this article was abandoned and that you are absolved of returning it. Rather, it must be treated as an אֲבֵדָה, *lost property*, and the commandment to return it is applicable.

7. לְמַעַן יִיטַב לָךְ וְהַאֲרַכְתָּ יָמִים — *That it may be well with you and that you may prolong your days.* The Talmud teaches us that there are *precepts whose fruits a person enjoys in This World but whose*

ט וְלֹא־תָשִׂים דָּמִים בְּבֵיתֶךָ כִּי־יִפֹּל הַנֹּפֵל מִמֶּנּוּ׃ לֹא־תִזְרַע כַּרְמְךָ כִּלְאָיִם
י פֶּן־תִּקְדַּשׁ הַמְלֵאָה הַזֶּרַע אֲשֶׁר תִּזְרָע וּתְבוּאַת הַכָּרֶם׃ לֹא־
יא תַחֲרֹשׁ בְּשׁוֹר־וּבַחֲמֹר יַחְדָּו׃ לֹא תִלְבַּשׁ שַׁעַטְנֵז צֶמֶר וּפִשְׁתִּים
יב יַחְדָּו׃ גְּדִלִים תַּעֲשֶׂה־לָּךְ עַל־אַרְבַּע כַּנְפוֹת כְּסוּתְךָ אֲשֶׁר
יג־יד תְּכַסֶּה־בָּהּ׃ כִּי־יִקַּח אִישׁ אִשָּׁה וּבָא אֵלֶיהָ וּשְׂנֵאָהּ׃ וְשָׂם
לָהּ עֲלִילֹת דְּבָרִים וְהוֹצִא עָלֶיהָ שֵׁם רָע וְאָמַר אֶת־הָאִשָּׁה הַזֹּאת
טו לָקַחְתִּי וָאֶקְרַב אֵלֶיהָ וְלֹא־מָצָאתִי לָהּ בְּתוּלִים׃ וְלָקַח אֲבִי הַנַּעֲרָ וְאִמָּהּ
טז וְהוֹצִיאוּ אֶת־בְּתוּלֵי הַנַּעֲרָ אֶל־זִקְנֵי הָעִיר הַשָּׁעְרָה׃ וְאָמַר אֲבִי הַנַּעֲרָ
יז אֶל־הַזְּקֵנִים אֶת־בִּתִּי נָתַתִּי לָאִישׁ הַזֶּה לְאִשָּׁה וַיִּשְׂנָאֶהָ׃ וְהִנֵּה־הוּא
שָׂם עֲלִילֹת דְּבָרִים לֵאמֹר לֹא־מָצָאתִי לְבִתְּךָ בְּתוּלִים וְאֵלֶּה בְּתוּלֵי
יח בִתִּי וּפָרְשׂוּ הַשִּׂמְלָה לִפְנֵי זִקְנֵי הָעִיר׃ וְלָקְחוּ זִקְנֵי הָעִיר־הַהִוא
יט אֶת־הָאִישׁ וְיִסְּרוּ אֹתוֹ׃ וְעָנְשׁוּ אֹתוֹ מֵאָה כֶסֶף וְנָתְנוּ לַאֲבִי הַנַּעֲרָה
כִּי הוֹצִיא שֵׁם רָע עַל בְּתוּלַת יִשְׂרָאֵל וְלוֹ־תִהְיֶה לְאִשָּׁה לֹא־יוּכַל
כ לְשַׁלְּחָהּ כָּל־יָמָיו׃ וְאִם־אֱמֶת הָיָה הַדָּבָר הַזֶּה לֹא־נִמְצְאוּ
כא בְתוּלִים לַנַּעֲרָ׃ וְהוֹצִיאוּ אֶת־הַנַּעֲרָ אֶל־פֶּתַח בֵּית־אָבִיהָ וּסְקָלוּהָ
אַנְשֵׁי עִירָהּ בָּאֲבָנִים וָמֵתָה כִּי־עָשְׂתָה נְבָלָה בְּיִשְׂרָאֵל לִזְנוֹת בֵּית
כב אָבִיהָ וּבִעַרְתָּ הָרָע מִקִּרְבֶּךָ׃ כִּי־יִמָּצֵא אִישׁ שֹׁכֵב ׀
עִם־אִשָּׁה בְעֻלַת־בַּעַל וּמֵתוּ גַּם־שְׁנֵיהֶם הָאִישׁ הַשֹּׁכֵב עִם־הָאִשָּׁה
כג וְהָאִשָּׁה וּבִעַרְתָּ הָרָע מִיִּשְׂרָאֵל׃ כִּי יִהְיֶה נַעֲרָ בְתוּלָה
כד מְאֹרָשָׂה לְאִישׁ וּמְצָאָהּ אִישׁ בָּעִיר וְשָׁכַב עִמָּהּ׃ וְהוֹצֵאתֶם אֶת־שְׁנֵיהֶם
אֶל־שַׁעַר ׀ הָעִיר הַהִוא וּסְקַלְתֶּם אֹתָם בָּאֲבָנִים וָמֵתוּ אֶת־הַנַּעֲרָ עַל־

rewarded) by enjoying the fruits thereof in This World, while the principal remains intact in the World to Come.

8. וְלֹא תָשִׂים דָּמִים בְּבֵיתֶךָ כִּי יִפֹּל הַנֹּפֵל — *That you shall not bring blood upon your house if any man falls from there.* Should it happen that anyone falls from there (i.e., the roof), you will not be (considered) the cause, bringing about that the punishment for (this) blood would be in your house.

13. כִּי יִקַּח אִישׁ אִשָּׁה — *If a man takes himself a wife.* Following the verses regarding society, (the Torah now) speaks of those cautionary laws which are obligatory (to insure) the dwelling of the *Shechinah* (Divine presence) in Israel. (We are to) guard against blemished offspring which causes (the *Shechinah*) to depart, due to unchastity and to the intermingling of disqualified nations (in Israel), (and also) due to the defiling of the camp

NOTES

principal remains intact for him in the World to Come (*Shabbos* 127a). Included in these precepts is *gemilas chasadim*, the performance of acts of loving kindness. The *Sforno* interprets the dual expression of לְמַעַן יִיטַב, *that it may be well*, and וְהַאֲרַכְתָּ יָמִים, *and that you may prolong your days*, as reflecting this reward of eating the fruits of one's *mitzvos* in this life and also receiving reward in the World to Come. He explains that sending the mother bird away insures the propagation of the birds of the field which benefits all, for whoever wishes can take them since they are not owned by anyone. The Torah considers this a *chesed*, an act of kindness, and therefore promises the reward of טוֹב, *well-being*, and also that of אֲרִיכוּת יָמִים, *longevity*, which the *Sforno* always interprets to mean the World to Come, i.e., a time of never-ending days.

you will not place blood in your house if a fallen one falls from it.
9 *You shall not sow your vineyard with a mixture, lest the growth of the seed that you plant and the produce of the vineyard become forbidden.*
10 *You shall not plow with an ox and a donkey together.* 11 *You shall not wear combined fibers, wool and linen together.*
12 *You shall make for yourselves twisted threads on the four corners of your garment with which you cover yourself.*
13 *If a man marries a wife, and comes to her and hates her,* 14 *and he makes a wanton accusation against her, spreading a bad name against her, and he said, "I married this woman, and I came near to her and I did not find signs of virginity on her,"* 15 *then the father of the girl and her mother should take and bring proofs of the girl's virginity to the elders of the city, to the gate.*
16 *The father of the girl should say to the elders, "I gave my daughter to this man as a wife, and he hated her.* 17 *Now, behold! he made a wanton accusation against her, saying, 'I did not find signs of virginity on your daughter' — but these are the signs of virginity of my daughter!" And they should spread out the sheet before the elders of the city.*
18 *The elders of the city shall take that man and punish him.* 19 *And they shall fine him one hundred silver [shekels] and give them to the father of the girl, for he had issued a slander against a virgin of Israel, and she shall remain with him as a wife; he cannot divorce her all his days.*
20 *But if this matter was true — signs of virginity were not found on the girl —* 21 *then they shall take the girl to the entrance of her father's house and the people of her city shall pelt her with stones and she shall die, for she had committed an outrage in Israel, to commit adultery in her father's house, and you shall remove the evil from your midst.*
22 *If a man will be found lying with a woman who is married to a husband, then both of them shall die, the man who lay with the woman and the woman; and you shall remove the evil from Israel.*
23 *If there will be a virgin girl who is betrothed to a man, and a man finds her in the city and lies with her,* 24 *then you shall take them both to the gate of that city and pelt them with stones and they shall die: the girl because of*

(of Israel) as it says, *And your camp shall be holy so that He see no unclean thing among you and turn away from your back* (23:15).

24. אֲשֶׁר עִנָּה אֶת אֵשֶׁת רֵעֵהוּ — *Because he degraded his neighbor's wife.* He oppressed and degraded her from her (status) of fitness and disqualified her from her worthiness (as a wife) to her husband who is his neighbor, similar to נְשֵׁי עַמִּי תְּגָרְשׁוּן מִבֵּית תַּעֲנֻגֶיהָ, *The women of my people you cast out from their pleasant houses* (Micah 2:9).

NOTES

8. וְלֹא תָשִׂים דָּמִים בְּבֵיתֶךָ כִּי יִפֹּל הַנֹּפֵל — *That you shall not bring blood upon your house if any man falls from there.* The *Sforno* explains the word דָּמִים, *blood,* as meaning the "punishment for blood" that was shed by the victim who fell from one's roof. Since you built a parapet you are no longer responsible. The sense of the verse is: Make a parapet for your roof and in this manner, you will not be liable for the blood spilled.

13. כִּי יִקַּח אִישׁ אִשָּׁה — *If a man takes himself a wife.* The "blemished offspring" mentioned by the *Sforno* refers to verses 21-24. The "intermingling of disqualified nations" refers to chapter 23, verses 4-9 regarding Ammonites and Moabites (prohibited forever), and Edomites and Egyptians (prior to the third generation).

דְּבַר אֲשֶׁר לֹא־צָעֲקָה בָעִיר וְאֶת־הָאִישׁ עַל־דְּבַר אֲשֶׁר־עִנָּה אֶת־אֵשֶׁת
כה רֵעֵהוּ וּבִעַרְתָּ הָרָע מִקִּרְבֶּךָ: וְאִם־בַּשָּׂדֶה יִמְצָא הָאִישׁ
אֶת־הַנַּעֲרָ הַמְאֹרָשָׂה וְהֶחֱזִיק־בָּהּ הָאִישׁ וְשָׁכַב עִמָּהּ וּמֵת הָאִישׁ אֲשֶׁר־
כו שָׁכַב עִמָּהּ לְבַדּוֹ: וְלַנַּעֲרָ לֹא־תַעֲשֶׂה דָבָר אֵין לַנַּעֲרָ חֵטְא מָוֶת כִּי
כז כַּאֲשֶׁר יָקוּם אִישׁ עַל־רֵעֵהוּ וּרְצָחוֹ נֶפֶשׁ כֵּן הַדָּבָר הַזֶּה: כִּי בַשָּׂדֶה מְצָאָהּ
כח צָעֲקָה הַנַּעֲרָ הַמְאֹרָשָׂה וְאֵין מוֹשִׁיעַ לָהּ: כִּי־יִמְצָא אִישׁ
כט נַעֲרָ בְתוּלָה אֲשֶׁר לֹא־אֹרָשָׂה וּתְפָשָׂהּ וְשָׁכַב עִמָּהּ וְנִמְצָאוּ: וְנָתַן הָאִישׁ
הַשֹּׁכֵב עִמָּהּ לַאֲבִי הַנַּעֲרָ חֲמִשִּׁים כָּסֶף וְלוֹ־תִהְיֶה לְאִשָּׁה תַּחַת אֲשֶׁר
כג א עִנָּהּ לֹא־יוּכַל שַׁלְּחָהּ כָּל־יָמָיו: לֹא־יִקַּח אִישׁ אֶת־אֵשֶׁת
ב אָבִיו וְלֹא יְגַלֶּה כְּנַף אָבִיו: לֹא־יָבֹא פְצוּעַ־דַּכָּא וּכְרוּת שָׁפְכָה בִּקְהַל
ג יהוה: לֹא־יָבֹא מַמְזֵר בִּקְהַל יהוה גַּם דּוֹר עֲשִׂירִי לֹא־
ד יָבֹא לוֹ בִּקְהַל יהוה: לֹא־יָבֹא עַמּוֹנִי וּמוֹאָבִי בִּקְהַל יהוה
ה גַּם דּוֹר עֲשִׂירִי לֹא־יָבֹא לָהֶם בִּקְהַל יהוה עַד־עוֹלָם: עַל־דְּבַר אֲשֶׁר
לֹא־קִדְּמוּ אֶתְכֶם בַּלֶּחֶם וּבַמַּיִם בַּדֶּרֶךְ בְּצֵאתְכֶם מִמִּצְרָיִם וַאֲשֶׁר שָׂכַר
ו עָלֶיךָ אֶת־בִּלְעָם בֶּן־בְּעוֹר מִפְּתוֹר אֲרַם נַהֲרַיִם לְקַלְלֶךָּ: וְלֹא־אָבָה
יהוה אֱלֹהֶיךָ לִשְׁמֹעַ אֶל־בִּלְעָם וַיַּהֲפֹךְ יהוה אֱלֹהֶיךָ לְּךָ אֶת־הַקְּלָלָה
ז לִבְרָכָה כִּי אֲהֵבְךָ יהוה אֱלֹהֶיךָ: לֹא־תִדְרֹשׁ שְׁלֹמָם וְטֹבָתָם כָּל־יָמֶיךָ

26. אֵין לַנַּעֲרָ חֵטְא מָוֶת — *The girl has no sin worthy of death* . . . even though the end (of the act) was with (her) consent, since the beginning was under duress, she is absolved (of sin) because when she began (to engage) in an unlawful act, her desire compelled her (to continue), as (our Sages) say, "Even if she said, 'Leave him alone, for if he had not (violated me) I would have hired him' " (*Kesubos* 51b).

כִּי כַּאֲשֶׁר יָקוּם אִישׁ עַל רֵעֵהוּ וּרְצָחוֹ — *For as a man rises up against his neighbor and slays him.* This is not similar to the case of an animal with whom a man lies, of which it is written, וְאֶת הַבְּהֵמָה תַּהֲרֹגוּ, *And you shall slay the animal* (*Lev.* 20:15), because the animal did not resist at all, but this (girl) who was assaulted resisted to the extent of her capability; hence that which occurred to her is akin to that which happens to a murder victim through whom a sin is committed against his will. Therefore, she has no part in this sin at all.

27. צָעֲקָה הַנַּעֲרָ — *The girl cried out.* We judge her favorably.

NOTES

26. אֵין לַנַּעֲרָ חֵטְא מָוֶת — *The girl has no sin worthy of death.* Considering that the verse just stated, *But unto the girl you shall do nothing,* why is it necessary to add these words? The *Sforno* resolves this difficulty by explaining that this is meant to teach us an important principle in Jewish law, namely that תְּחִלָּתָהּ בְּאוֹנֶס וְסוֹפָהּ בְּרָצוֹן פְּטוּרָה, *an act which begins under compulsion, though it terminated with consent, is non-punishable* (*Kesubos* 51b). This is in accordance with the opinion of *Rava* who says that she is a victim of uncontrollable passion aroused by the act. According to the *Sforno*, the Torah alludes to this reasoning in our verse in saying that she is not considered responsible for her action.

כִּי כַּאֲשֶׁר יָקוּם — *For as a man rises up.* The *Sforno* explains the reason for comparing the act of rape to that of murder. The Torah in *Leviticus* 20:15 commands us to destroy the animal with whom sodomy has been committed. Why then should the betrothed girl, with whom a sin has been committed, be absolved? In what way is she different than the case of the animal with whom a man did lie? The *Sforno* answers that whereas the animal did not resist, it is difficult to imagine that the assaulted girl did not resist, just as we assume that a murder victim does not passively allow himself to be slain. This explains the reason for the Torah's comparison of the rape victim to the murder victim.

the fact that she did not cry out in the city, and the man because of the fact
that he afflicted the wife of his fellow; and you shall remove the evil from
your midst.
25 *But if it is in the field that the man will find the betrothed girl, and the*
man will seize her and lie with her, only the man who lies with her shall die.
26 *But you shall do nothing to the girl, for the girl has committed no capital*
sin, for like a man who rises up against his fellow and murders him, so is
this thing; 27 *for he found her in the field, the betrothed girl cried out, but*
she had no savior.
28 *If a man will find a virgin maiden who was not betrothed, and takes*
hold of her and lies with her, and they are discovered, 29 *then the man who*
lay with her shall give the father of the girl fifty silver [shekels], and she
shall become his wife, because he had afflicted her; he cannot divorce her
all his life.

23 1 *A man shall not marry the wife of his father; and he shall not uncover*
the robe of his father. 2 *A man with crushed testicles or a severed*
organ shall not enter the congregation of HASHEM.
3 *A mamzer shall not enter the congregation of* HASHEM, *even his tenth*
generation shall not enter the congregation of HASHEM.
4 *An Ammonite or Moabite shall not enter the congregation of* HASHEM,
even their tenth generation shall not enter the congregation of HASHEM, *to*
eternity, 5 *because of the fact that they did not greet you with bread and*
water on the road when you were leaving Egypt, and because he hired
against you Balaam son of Beor, of Pethor, Aram Naharaim, to curse you.
6 *But* HASHEM, *your God, refused to listen to Balaam, and* HASHEM, *your*
God, reversed the curse to a blessing for you, because HASHEM, *your God,*
loved you. 7 *You shall not seek their peace or welfare, all your days, forever.*

XXIII

5. אֲשֶׁר לֹא קִדְּמוּ אֶתְכֶם — *They did not (come forth) to meet you.* Both (Ammon and Moab) did not come forth to meet you. However the Moabites did sell them bread and water for money, as it says, *You shall sell me food for money . . . as the children of Esau that dwell in Seir, and the Moabites that dwell in Ar did for me* (2:28,29). The Ammonites did not do so. Nevertheless, the Moabites added transgression to their sin *because they hired against you Balaam,* and therefore . . .

7. לֹא תִדְרֹשׁ שְׁלֹמָם — *You shall not seek their peace . . .* (because) both did not come forth to meet you. Ammon did not even sell you (food) for money, while Moab who did sell (you food) hired Balaam (to curse you).

NOTES

27. צָעֲקָה הַנַּעֲרָ — *The girl cried out.* There is no proof that the girl cried out. It is presumed, however, that she did so, for we always give a person the benefit of the doubt and judge one favorably.

XXIII

5-7. אֲשֶׁר לֹא קִדְּמוּ אֶתְכֶם ... לֹא תִדְרֹשׁ שְׁלֹמָם — *They did not (come forth) to meet you . . . You shall not seek their peace.* Both Ammon and Moab, who were related to the Israelites, refused them hospitality when they journeyed from Egypt to the Promised Land. In one respect, however, the Moabites were more cooperative than the Ammonites. They were at least willing to sell food and water to the Jewish people which the Ammonites refused to do. On the other hand, the Moabites were guilty of hiring Balaam to curse the people of Israel (*Numbers* 22). Hence, each of these nations

רביעי

ח לְעוֹלָם׃ לֹא־תְתַעֵב אֲדֹמִי כִּי אָחִיךָ הוּא לֹא־תְתַעֵב
ט מִצְרִי כִּי־גֵר הָיִיתָ בְאַרְצוֹ׃ בָּנִים אֲשֶׁר־יִוָּלְדוּ לָהֶם דּוֹר שְׁלִישִׁי יָבֹא
י לָהֶם בִּקְהַל יהוה׃ כִּי־תֵצֵא מַחֲנֶה עַל־אֹיְבֶיךָ וְנִשְׁמַרְתָּ
יא מִכֹּל דָּבָר רָע׃ כִּי־יִהְיֶה בְךָ אִישׁ אֲשֶׁר לֹא־יִהְיֶה טָהוֹר מִקְּרֵה־לָיְלָה
יב וְיָצָא אֶל־מִחוּץ לַמַּחֲנֶה לֹא יָבֹא אֶל־תּוֹךְ הַמַּחֲנֶה׃ וְהָיָה לִפְנוֹת־עֶרֶב
יג יִרְחַץ בַּמָּיִם וּכְבֹא הַשֶּׁמֶשׁ יָבֹא אֶל־תּוֹךְ הַמַּחֲנֶה׃ וְיָד תִּהְיֶה לְךָ מִחוּץ
יד לַמַּחֲנֶה וְיָצָאתָ שָׁמָּה חוּץ׃ וְיָתֵד תִּהְיֶה לְךָ עַל־אֲזֵנֶךָ וְהָיָה בְּשִׁבְתְּךָ חוּץ
טו וְחָפַרְתָּה בָהּ וְשַׁבְתָּ וְכִסִּיתָ אֶת־צֵאָתֶךָ׃ כִּי יהוה אֱלֹהֶיךָ מִתְהַלֵּךְ ׀
בְּקֶרֶב מַחֲנֶךָ לְהַצִּילְךָ וְלָתֵת אֹיְבֶיךָ לְפָנֶיךָ וְהָיָה מַחֲנֶיךָ קָדוֹשׁ וְלֹא־
טז יִרְאֶה בְךָ עֶרְוַת דָּבָר וְשָׁב מֵאַחֲרֶיךָ׃ לֹא־תַסְגִּיר עֶבֶד
יז אֶל־אֲדֹנָיו אֲשֶׁר־יִנָּצֵל אֵלֶיךָ מֵעִם אֲדֹנָיו׃ עִמְּךָ יֵשֵׁב בְּקִרְבְּךָ בַּמָּקוֹם
יח אֲשֶׁר־יִבְחַר בְּאַחַד שְׁעָרֶיךָ בַּטּוֹב לוֹ לֹא תּוֹנֶנּוּ׃ לֹא־
יט תִהְיֶה קְדֵשָׁה מִבְּנוֹת יִשְׂרָאֵל וְלֹא־יִהְיֶה קָדֵשׁ מִבְּנֵי יִשְׂרָאֵל׃ לֹא־תָבִיא
אֶתְנַן זוֹנָה וּמְחִיר כֶּלֶב בֵּית יהוה אֱלֹהֶיךָ לְכָל־נֶדֶר כִּי תוֹעֲבַת יהוה
כ אֱלֹהֶיךָ גַּם־שְׁנֵיהֶם׃ לֹא־תַשִּׁיךְ לְאָחִיךָ נֶשֶׁךְ כֶּסֶף נֶשֶׁךְ

15. וְהָיָה מַחֲנֶיךָ קָדוֹשׁ — *And your camp shall be holy* ... (uncontaminated by) impurity and repulsiveness.

וְלֹא יִרְאֶה בְךָ עֶרְוַת דָּבָר — *So that He see no unclean thing among you* ... impurity, or body wastes or blemished offspring, as (our Sages) state, "The Divine Presence (*Shechinah*) only rests upon families of pure birth in Israel" (*Kiddushin* 70b), and (for this reason) they said that all who are recorded in the army list of the kings of the House of David were, without a doubt, of distinguished descent.

וְשָׁב מֵאַחֲרֶיךָ — *And turn away from your back* ... when you will turn your back on Him and not be concerned for His honor, (by your unseemly conduct) in one of these (areas).

16. לֹא תַסְגִּיר עֶבֶד אֶל אֲדֹנָיו — *You shall not deliver a slave to his master.* After discussing (laws) regarding the army camp, (the Torah) now speaks of matters which occur therein, such as the slave that fled (his master) and the subject of harlots found there (verse 18), so that you may rectify these matters.

NOTES

was guilty of two offenses. Both failed to come forth to meet them and extend a helping hand to the Israelites. In addition the Ammonites refused to even sell them provisions while the Moabites attempted to destroy the people of Israel through Balaam. Therefore, the Torah tells us that we may *not seek their peace* because their cruel behavior severed their bond of kinship with Israel.

15. וְהָיָה מַחֲנֶיךָ קָדוֹשׁ — *And your camp shall be holy*. The *Sforno* explains that a state of sanctity cannot exist in an environment of טוּמְאָה — impurity — or מְאוּס — that which is abhorrent and loathsome. The former phrase refers to verse 12 which speaks of a man who had a nocturnal emission causing uncleanness. The latter phrase refers to verse 14 which speaks of the need for hygienic practice in the army camp of Israel when they are in the field.

וְלֹא יִרְאֶה בְךָ עֶרְוַת דָּבָר — *So that He see no unclean thing among you*. The Torah teaches us that when the Jewish army goes forth to do battle against their enemies, God accompanies them. His presence in their midst is their source of strength and protection; hence they must refrain from any unseemly behavior which might drive the *Shechinah* away. The *Sforno* explains that עֶרְוַת דָּבָר, usually translated nakedness, means *an unclean thing*, and encompasses impurity in the ritual sense (טוּמְאָה), unhygienic conditions and פְּסוּלֵי זֶרַע, i.e., flaws in the pedigree of Jewish families. Our Sages have taught us that God's Presence in the camp of Israel depends upon the pure geneology of its armed

[8] *You shall not reject an Edomite, for he is your brother; you shall not
reject an Egyptian, for you were a sojourner in his land.* [9] *Children who are
born to them in the third generation may enter the congregation of* HASHEM.
[10] *When a camp goes out against your enemies, you shall guard against
anything evil.* [11] *If there will be among you a man who will not be clean
because of a nocturnal occurrence, he shall go outside the camp; he shall not
enter the midst of the camp.* [12] *When it will be toward evening, he shall
immerse himself in the water, and when the sun sets, he may enter the
midst of the camp.* [13] *You shall have a place outside the camp, and to it you
shall go out.* [14] *You shall have a shovel in addition to your weapons, and it
will be that when you sit outside, you shall dig with it; you shall go back
and cover your excrement.* [15] *For* HASHEM, *your God, walks in the midst of
your camp to rescue you and to deliver your enemies before you; so your
camp shall be holy, so that He will not see a shameful thing among you and
turn away from behind you.*
[16] *You shall not turn over to his master a slave who is rescued from his
master to you.* [17] *He shall dwell with you in your midst, in whatever place
he will choose in one of your cities, which is beneficial to him; you shall not
taunt him.*
[18] *There shall not be a promiscuous woman among the daughters of
Israel, and there shall not be a promiscuous man among the sons of Israel.*
[19] *You shall not bring a harlot's hire or the exchange for a dog to the House
of* HASHEM, *your God, for any vow, for both of them are an abomination of*
HASHEM, *your God.*
[20] *You shall not cause your brother to take interest, interest of money*

20. לֹא תַשִּׁיךְ לְאָחִיךָ — *You shall not give interest to your brother.* After admonishing us to guard against those things which cause the *Shechinah* (Divine Presence) to depart from Israel, (the Torah) now advocates diverse acts of kindness which cause (the *Shechinah*) to dwell in Israel — these being the matters of interest and vows (verse 22), including charity that one is obligated to fulfill promptly since the poor are ever present. (Also included are) the subject of the laborer's eating (rights) (verses 25-26) and the matter of a גֵּט, *bill of divorce*, which should properly be given only because of (a wife's) immoral behavior (chapter 24, verse 1) so as to remove the obstacle of bastardy, but not for other reasons (of

NOTES

forces. Indeed, the officers' corps of the king's army was so carefully screened that the very fact that one was chosen was proof that there was no blemish in his family tree.

וְשָׁב מֵאַחֲרֶיךָ — *And turn away from your back.* The *Sforno* interprets the word אַחֲרֶיךָ as meaning *your back*. He therefore explains the verse thus: When you will be insensitive to your moral conduct on the field of battle, it is tantamount to turning your back on God. He will then, in turn, leave your midst and abandon you.

16. לֹא תַסְגִּיר עֶבֶד — *You shall not deliver a slave.* The *Sforno* clarifies the continuity of these verses (16-18) with the preceding one, which has as its theme the sanctity of the Jewish camp. It apparently was not unusual for a slave who accompanied his master into battle to use that opportunity to flee and seek refuge in the enemy's camp. It also was quite common for an army to have "camp followers", which is alluded to in verse 18. The *Sforno* explains that the Torah cautions us to give sanctuary to the fugitive slave, and also to remove "camp followers" from the midst of our camp, so as to insure the high moral standards governing a Jewish army.

20. לֹא תַשִּׁיךְ לְאָחִיךָ — *You shall not give interest to your brother*. Similar to his commentary on 21:15 and 22:13, the *Sforno's* intent is to explain the thematic continuity of the balance of this chapter, as well as the chapters which follow. A superficial

כא אַכַל נֶשֶׁךְ כָּל־דָּבָר אֲשֶׁר יִשָּׁךְ: לַנָּכְרִי תַשִּׁיךְ וּלְאָחִיךָ לֹא תַשִּׁיךְ לְמַעַן
יְבָרֶכְךָ יהוה אֱלֹהֶיךָ בְּכֹל מִשְׁלַח יָדֶךָ עַל־הָאָרֶץ אֲשֶׁר־אַתָּה בָא־שָׁמָּה
כב לְרִשְׁתָּהּ: כִּי־תִדֹּר נֶדֶר לַיהוה אֱלֹהֶיךָ לֹא תְאַחֵר לְשַׁלְּמוֹ
כג כִּי־דָרֹשׁ יִדְרְשֶׁנּוּ יהוה אֱלֹהֶיךָ מֵעִמָּךְ וְהָיָה בְךָ חֵטְא: וְכִי תֶחְדַּל לִנְדֹּר
כד לֹא־יִהְיֶה בְךָ חֵטְא: מוֹצָא שְׂפָתֶיךָ תִּשְׁמֹר וְעָשִׂיתָ כַּאֲשֶׁר נָדַרְתָּ לַיהוה
חמישי כה אֱלֹהֶיךָ נְדָבָה אֲשֶׁר דִּבַּרְתָּ בְּפִיךָ: כִּי תָבֹא בְּכֶרֶם רֵעֶךָ
כו וְאָכַלְתָּ עֲנָבִים כְּנַפְשְׁךָ שָׂבְעֶךָ וְאֶל־כֶּלְיְךָ לֹא תִתֵּן: כִּי
תָבֹא בְּקָמַת רֵעֶךָ וְקָטַפְתָּ מְלִילֹת בְּיָדֶךָ וְחֶרְמֵשׁ לֹא תָנִיף עַל קָמַת
כד א רֵעֶךָ: כִּי־יִקַּח אִישׁ אִשָּׁה וּבְעָלָהּ וְהָיָה אִם־לֹא תִמְצָא־
חֵן בְּעֵינָיו כִּי־מָצָא בָהּ עֶרְוַת דָּבָר וְכָתַב לָהּ סֵפֶר כְּרִיתֻת וְנָתַן בְּיָדָהּ
ב־ג וְשִׁלְּחָהּ מִבֵּיתוֹ: וְיָצְאָה מִבֵּיתוֹ וְהָלְכָה וְהָיְתָה לְאִישׁ־אַחֵר: וּשְׂנֵאָהּ
הָאִישׁ הָאַחֲרוֹן וְכָתַב לָהּ סֵפֶר כְּרִיתֻת וְנָתַן בְּיָדָהּ וְשִׁלְּחָהּ מִבֵּיתוֹ אוֹ כִי
ד יָמוּת הָאִישׁ הָאַחֲרוֹן אֲשֶׁר־לְקָחָהּ לוֹ לְאִשָּׁה: לֹא־יוּכַל בַּעְלָהּ הָרִאשׁוֹן
אֲשֶׁר־שִׁלְּחָהּ לָשׁוּב לְקַחְתָּהּ לִהְיוֹת לוֹ לְאִשָּׁה אַחֲרֵי אֲשֶׁר הֻטַּמָּאָה

incompatibility), as it says, כִּי ה׳ הֵעִיד בֵּינְךָ וּבֵין אֵשֶׁת נְעוּרֶיךָ אֲשֶׁר אַתָּה בָּגַדְתָּה בָּהּ, *Because* HASHEM *has been witness between you and the wife of your youth against whom you dealt treacherously* (*Malachi* 2:14). (Also mentioned are) the kindness due a new wife which is to cheer her (24:5) and the act of kindness by not taking *the lower or the upper millstone for a pledge* (24:6) and guarding against those who harm the public, namely kidnappers who commonly abduct minors (24:7). (Furthermore, we are cautioned) to take heed regarding the plague of leprosy by isolating the lepers so that their affliction does not harm (society) through contagion; and to guard against talebearing and slander (24:9); and the kindness due a borrower (24:10-13), a hired servant (24:14-15) and the poor during the harvest (24:19-21). (Likewise, we are told about) pity shown to the one who receives stripes (25:2-3); and (the compassion shown) to an animal when he treads out the corn, and (concern) for one who dies without offspring that his name not be wiped out (25:5-10).

21. לַנָּכְרִי תַשִּׁיךְ — *Unto a stranger you may give interest.* Give him the interest if you made such a condition with him, and do not renege.

וּלְאָחִיךָ לֹא תַשִּׁיךְ — *But to your brother you shall not give interest.* Even though you made such a condition with him and agreed to pay him (interest), it is forbidden for you to give him interest.

NOTES

reading of these verses gives one an impression of a series of disjointed verses. The *Sforno* however teaches us that, beginning with this verse, and continuing through chapter 25, the Torah is presenting a blueprint for moral excellence and ethical behavior, which will insure God's presence in our midst. These precepts are varied and manifold, including, among others, sensitivity to the financial problems confronting a borrower, concern for the laborer and for the poor, proper grounds for divorce, regard for the happiness of one's wife, compassion for a person punished by the court and pity for an animal treading corn. All these are meant to refine one's character and heighten one's sense of righteousness, compassion, and social responsibility. The unifying theme of these varied verses is that of *chesed*, loving-kindness, in the community of Israel, which will cause the *Shechinah* to dwell in their midst.

21. לַנָּכְרִי תַשִּׁיךְ — *Unto a stranger you may give interest*. The phrase לַנָּכְרִי תַשִּׁיךְ is translated by some as meaning "unto a stranger (i.e., a non-Jew) you may lend with interest." *Rashi*, based on the Talmud (*Bava Metzia* 70), interprets this phrase as adding a prohibition against lending a fellow Jew money on interest (לָאו הַבָּא מִכְּלַל עֲשֵׂה). The *Sforno*, however, interprets this phrase to mean that if a

or interest of food, interest of anything that he may take as interest. 21 *You may cause a gentile to take interest, but you may not cause your brother to take interest, so that* HASHEM, *your God, will bless you in your every undertaking on the Land to which you are coming, to possess it.*

22 *When you make a vow to* HASHEM, *your God, you shall not be late in paying it, for* HASHEM, *your God, will demand it of you, and there will be a sin in you.* 23 *If you refrain from vowing, there will be no sin in you.* 24 *You shall observe and carry out what emerges from your lips, just as you vowed a voluntary gift to* HASHEM, *your God, whatever you spoke with your mouth.*

25 *When you come into the vineyard of your fellow, you may eat grapes as is your desire, to your fill, but you may not put into your vessel.*

26 *When you come into the standing grain of your fellow, you may pluck ears with your hand, but you may not lift a sickle against the standing grain of your fellow.*

24

1 *If a man marries a woman and lives with her, and it will be that she will not find favor in his eyes, for he found in her a matter of immorality, and he wrote her a bill of divorce and presented it into her hand, and sent her from his house,* 2 *and she left his house and went and married another man,* 3 *and the latter man hated her and wrote her a bill of divorce and presented it into her hand and sent her from his house, or the latter man who married her to himself will die —* 4 *her first husband who divorced her shall not again take her to become his wife, after she had been defiled,*

לְמַעַן יְבָרֶכְךָ ה׳ אֱלֹהֶיךָ — *So that* HASHEM *your God may bless you . . .* when you will not act treacherously with the stranger and (thus) not profane the Name of God.

22. כִּי תִדֹּר נֶדֶר לַה׳ אֱלֹהֶיךָ — *When you make a vow to* HASHEM *your God.* Behold, it is proper that your word be trustworthy with all. However, that which you vow to God your God, not only are you obligated to pay it, but, in addition, the payment must be made without delay.

כִּי דָרֹשׁ יִדְרְשֶׁנּוּ — *For* (*God your God*) *will surely require it* (*of you*). For if you delay payment, He will collect it from you against your will.

וְהָיָה בְךָ חֵטְא — *And it will be* (*reckoned*) *as a sin to you.* And that which you do pay in this manner will still carry with it punishment for the delay.

NOTES

Jew borrowed money from a non-Jew and agreed to pay him interest (which is permissible), he is bound to do so and must not go back on his word.

וּלְאָחִיךָ לֹא תַשִּׁיךְ — *But to your brother you shall not give interest.* This prohibition seems to be a repetition of that which is already written in verse 20. The *Sforno,* however, explains that the purpose of this added prohibition is to teach us that even if there was a mutual agreement between the lender and borrower, nonetheless it is prohibited for one Jew to pay interest to another Jew.

לְמַעַן יְבָרֶכְךָ — *So that* HASHEM *your God may bless you.* The *Sforno* explains that the blessing of God is not a reward for refraining from paying interest to a fellow Jew or accepting it, but for meeting your obligation by paying the stranger what you have pledged. By so doing, you earn God's blessing because if you were to deal dishonestly in this situation, you would be desecrating His Name.

22. וְהָיָה בְךָ חֵטְא — *And it will be* (*reckoned*) *as a sin to you.* Since God exacts payment for a vow, even against the will of the person who made that vow, why then does the Torah say that, nevertheless, it is reckoned as a sin? The *Sforno* explains that the sin is for the *delay* in redeeming one's pledge, which is an added violation regarding a vow made to God, unlike a vow made to man which does not carry this penalty.

כִּֽי־תוֹעֵבָה הִוא לִפְנֵי יְהוָה וְלֹא תַחֲטִיא אֶת־הָאָרֶץ אֲשֶׁר יְהוָה אֱלֹהֶיךָ
ששי ה נֹתֵן לְךָ נַחֲלָה׃ כִּֽי־יִקַּח אִישׁ אִשָּׁה חֲדָשָׁה לֹא יֵצֵא
בַּצָּבָא וְלֹא־יַעֲבֹר עָלָיו לְכָל־דָּבָר נָקִי יִהְיֶה לְבֵיתוֹ שָׁנָה אֶחָת
ו וְשִׂמַּח אֶת־אִשְׁתּוֹ אֲשֶׁר־לָקָח׃ לֹא־יַחֲבֹל רֵחַיִם וָרָכֶב כִּֽי־נֶפֶשׁ הוּא
ז חֹבֵל׃ כִּֽי־יִמָּצֵא אִישׁ גֹּנֵב נֶפֶשׁ מֵאֶחָיו מִבְּנֵי יִשְׂרָאֵל וְהִתְעַמֶּר־
ח בּוֹ וּמְכָרוֹ וּמֵת הַגַּנָּב הַהוּא וּבִעַרְתָּ הָרָע מִקִּרְבֶּךָ׃ הִשָּׁמֶר
בְּנֶגַע־הַצָּרַעַת לִשְׁמֹר מְאֹד וְלַעֲשׂוֹת כְּכֹל אֲשֶׁר־יוֹרוּ אֶתְכֶם הַכֹּהֲנִים
ט הַלְוִיִּם כַּאֲשֶׁר צִוִּיתִם תִּשְׁמְרוּ לַעֲשׂוֹת׃ זָכוֹר אֵת אֲשֶׁר־עָשָׂה יְהוָה
י אֱלֹהֶיךָ לְמִרְיָם בַּדָּרֶךְ בְּצֵאתְכֶם מִמִּצְרָיִם׃ כִּֽי־תַשֶּׁה
יא בְרֵעֲךָ מַשַּׁאת מְאוּמָה לֹא־תָבֹא אֶל־בֵּיתוֹ לַעֲבֹט עֲבֹטוֹ׃ בַּחוּץ
תַּעֲמֹד וְהָאִישׁ אֲשֶׁר אַתָּה נֹשֶׁה בוֹ יוֹצִיא אֵלֶיךָ אֶת־הָעֲבוֹט הַחוּצָה׃
יב־יג וְאִם־אִישׁ עָנִי הוּא לֹא תִשְׁכַּב בַּעֲבֹטוֹ׃ הָשֵׁב תָּשִׁיב לוֹ אֶת־הָעֲבוֹט
כְּבוֹא הַשֶּׁמֶשׁ וְשָׁכַב בְּשַׂלְמָתוֹ וּבֵרְכֶךָּ וּלְךָ תִּהְיֶה צְדָקָה לִפְנֵי יְהוָה
שביעי יד אֱלֹהֶיךָ׃ לֹא־תַעֲשֹׁק שָׂכִיר עָנִי וְאֶבְיוֹן מֵאַחֶיךָ אוֹ מִגֵּרְךָ
טו אֲשֶׁר בְּאַרְצְךָ בִּשְׁעָרֶיךָ׃ בְּיוֹמוֹ תִתֵּן שְׂכָרוֹ וְלֹא־תָבוֹא עָלָיו הַשֶּׁמֶשׁ
כִּי עָנִי הוּא וְאֵלָיו הוּא נֹשֵׂא אֶת־נַפְשׁוֹ וְלֹא־יִקְרָא עָלֶיךָ אֶל־יְהוָה
טז וְהָיָה בְךָ חֵטְא׃ לֹא־יוּמְתוּ אָבוֹת עַל־בָּנִים וּבָנִים לֹא־

XXIV

4. כִּי תוֹעֵבָה הִוא — *For it is an abomination* . . . because this is a (subtle) way of introducing adultery; the husband divorces his wife at the request of the adulterer so that he may take her for a period of time, (after which) her first husband will take her back.

10. מַשַּׁאת מְאוּמָה — *Any matter of loan* . . . even a porter's fee or similar (payment for service), if converted into a loan, as our Sages have received the tradition (regarding this prohibition) (*Bava Metzia* 115a).

16. לֹא יוּמְתוּ אָבוֹת עַל בָּנִים וּבָנִים לֹא יוּמְתוּ עַל אָבוֹת — *The fathers shall not be put to death for the children, neither shall the children be put to death for the fathers* . . . even for the sin of rebellion against the monarchy, where customarily the king executed the children (of the rebels) so that they should not rise up against the monarchy in (a spirit) of enmity, as we find, הָכִינוּ לְבָנָיו מַטְבֵּחַ בַּעֲוֹן אֲבוֹתָם בַּל יָקֻמוּ וְיָרְשׁוּ אָרֶץ וּמָלְאוּ פְנֵי תֵבֵל עָרִים, *Prepare slaughter for his children, for the iniquity of their fathers; that they rise not up and possess the earth, and fill the face of the world with enemies* (*Isaiah* 14:21), the meaning of עָרִים being *enemies,* similar to וַיְהִי עָרֶךָ, *has become your enemy* (*I Samuel* 28:16).

NOTES

XXIV

4. כִּי תוֹעֵבָה הִוא — *For it is an abomination*. The *Sforno* explains why the Torah is so adamantly opposed to the remarriage of a woman to her first husband, after she has married another man and subsequently been divorced by him. Because of collusion or pressure, this could be but a subterfuge for the transfer of a woman for a limited period of time to another man, which would still be adultery cloaked in 'legitimacy' and therefore an act of abomination in the eyes of God.

10. מַשַּׁאת מְאוּמָה — *Any matter of loan*. The *Sforno* in his commentary is referring to our Sages' interpretation of this verse, *You shall not go into his house to take his pledge.* They exclude from this prohibition the seizing and holding of goods in pledge in order to obtain satisfaction of a claim for services rendered, as opposed to collection of a debt by the lender. The latter is prohibited while the former is permitted. However, if one's obligation for services rendered, such as porterage, rent or repairs was converted into a loan, then it is covered

for it is an abomination before HASHEM. You shall not bring sin upon the Land that HASHEM, your God, gives you as an inheritance.

5 *When a man marries a new wife, he shall not go out to the army, nor shall it obligate him for any matter; he shall be free for his home for one year, and he shall gladden his wife whom he has married.*

6 *One shall not take an upper or lower millstone as a pledge, for he would be taking a life as a pledge.*

7 *If a man is found kidnaping a person of his brethren among the Children of Israel, and he enslaves him and sells him, that kidnaper shall die, and you shall remove the evil from your midst.*

8 *Beware of a tzaraas affliction, to be very careful and to act; according to everything that the Kohanim, the Levites, shall teach you — as I have*
commanded them — you shall be careful to perform. 9 *Remember what*
HASHEM, your God, did to Miriam on the way, when you were leaving Egypt.

10 *When you make your fellow a loan of any amount, you shall not enter*
his home to take security for it. 11 *You shall stand outside; and the man to*
whom you lend shall bring the security to you outside. 12 *If that man is poor,*
you shall not sleep with his security. 13 *You shall return the security to him*
when the sun sets, and he will sleep in his garment and bless you, and for you it will be an act of righteousness before HASHEM, your God.

14 *You shall not cheat a poor or destitute hired person among your*
brethren, or a proselyte who is in your Land, or one who is in your cities. 15 *On*
that day shall you pay his hire; the sun shall not set upon him, for he is poor, and his life depends on it; let him not call out against you to HASHEM, for it shall be a sin in you.

16 *Fathers shall not be put to death because of sons, and sons shall not be*

Nonetheless, the Torah prohibits our kings to slay (sons) in this manner (lit., this for this), for God has pity on His people. Now, King Amaziah of Judah fulfilled this (law), as it says, וַיְהִי כַּאֲשֶׁר חָזְקָה הַמַּמְלָכָה עָלָיו וַיַּהֲרֹג אֶת עֲבָדָיו הַמַּכִּים אֶת הַמֶּלֶךְ אָבִיו. וְאֶת בְּנֵיהֶם לֹא הֵמִית כִּי כַכָּתוּב בַּתּוֹרָה בְּסֵפֶר מֹשֶׁה אֲשֶׁר צִוָּה ה׳ לֵאמֹר לֹא יָמוּתוּ אָבוֹת עַל בָּנִים וּבָנִים לֹא יָמוּתוּ עַל אָבוֹת, *Now it came to pass when the kingdom was established unto him that he slew his servants who had killed the king, his father. But he did not put their children to death but did according to that which is written in the law in the Book of Moses, as HASHEM commanded saying, "The fathers shall not die for the children and children shall not die for the fathers"* (*II Chronicles* 25:3,4).

NOTES

by the prohibition set forth in our verse. This they learn from the expression מְאוּמָה — *any matter* — of loan.

16. וּבָנִים לֹא יוּמְתוּ עַל אָבוֹת — *Neither shall the children be put to death for the fathers.* The *Sforno* cites the verse from *Isaiah* to prove his thesis that it was common for a king to wipe out the entire family of a rebel leader. The word עָרִים usually means "cities"; however, in the context of this particular verse it means *enemies*, as the *Sforno* stresses. Other commentators translate the word עָרֶךָ in *I Samuel* 28:16, where Samuel tells Saul that God has become his enemy, to mean "the supporter of your adversary." This interpretation would be appropriate for the verse in *Isaiah* as well, for it would mean that the survivors of a man executed by the king for treason would someday vigorously support another rebellion.

The verses cited by the *Sforno* from *Chronicles* relate the story of Amaziah, whose father Joash, King of Judah, was assassinated by his own servants to avenge the blood of the sons of Jehoida, the *Kohen Gadol*, who were slain at his behest. Amaziah, in turn, executed the murderers of his father, but spared the lives of their sons, in accordance with the teaching of the Torah.

יז יוּמְתוּ עַל־אָבוֹת אִישׁ בְּחֶטְאוֹ יוּמָתוּ׃ לֹא תַטֶּה מִשְׁפַּט
יח גֵּר יָתוֹם וְלֹא תַחֲבֹל בֶּגֶד אַלְמָנָה׃ וְזָכַרְתָּ כִּי עֶבֶד הָיִיתָ בְּמִצְרַיִם
וַיִּפְדְּךָ יהוה אֱלֹהֶיךָ מִשָּׁם עַל־כֵּן אָנֹכִי מְצַוְּךָ לַעֲשׂוֹת אֶת־הַדָּבָר
יט הַזֶּה׃ כִּי תִקְצֹר קְצִירְךָ בְשָׂדֶךָ וְשָׁכַחְתָּ עֹמֶר בַּשָּׂדֶה לֹא
תָשׁוּב לְקַחְתּוֹ לַגֵּר לַיָּתוֹם וְלָאַלְמָנָה יִהְיֶה לְמַעַן יְבָרֶכְךָ יהוה אֱלֹהֶיךָ
כ בְּכֹל מַעֲשֵׂה יָדֶיךָ׃ כִּי תַחְבֹּט זֵיתְךָ לֹא תְפַאֵר אַחֲרֶיךָ
כא לַגֵּר לַיָּתוֹם וְלָאַלְמָנָה יִהְיֶה׃ כִּי תִבְצֹר כַּרְמְךָ לֹא תְעוֹלֵל אַחֲרֶיךָ לַגֵּר
כב לַיָּתוֹם וְלָאַלְמָנָה יִהְיֶה׃ וְזָכַרְתָּ כִּי־עֶבֶד הָיִיתָ בְּאֶרֶץ מִצְרָיִם עַל־כֵּן אָנֹכִי
כה א מְצַוְּךָ לַעֲשׂוֹת אֶת־הַדָּבָר הַזֶּה׃ כִּי־יִהְיֶה רִיב בֵּין אֲנָשִׁים
וְנִגְּשׁוּ אֶל־הַמִּשְׁפָּט וּשְׁפָטוּם וְהִצְדִּיקוּ אֶת־הַצַּדִּיק וְהִרְשִׁיעוּ אֶת־הָרָשָׁע׃
ב וְהָיָה אִם־בִּן הַכּוֹת הָרָשָׁע וְהִפִּילוֹ הַשֹּׁפֵט וְהִכָּהוּ לְפָנָיו כְּדֵי רִשְׁעָתוֹ
ג בְּמִסְפָּר׃ אַרְבָּעִים יַכֶּנּוּ לֹא יֹסִיף פֶּן־יֹסִיף לְהַכֹּתוֹ עַל־אֵלֶּה מַכָּה רַבָּה
ד-ה וְנִקְלָה אָחִיךָ לְעֵינֶיךָ׃ לֹא־תַחְסֹם שׁוֹר בְּדִישׁוֹ׃ כִּי־יֵשְׁבוּ
אַחִים יַחְדָּו וּמֵת אַחַד מֵהֶם וּבֵן אֵין־לוֹ לֹא־תִהְיֶה אֵשֶׁת־הַמֵּת הַחוּצָה
ו לְאִישׁ זָר יְבָמָהּ יָבֹא עָלֶיהָ וּלְקָחָהּ לוֹ לְאִשָּׁה וְיִבְּמָהּ׃ וְהָיָה הַבְּכוֹר אֲשֶׁר

---

17. לֹא תַטֶּה מִשְׁפַּט גֵּר יָתוֹם — *You shall not pervert the justice due to a stranger or to an orphan.* At the time of argument, be careful (in dealing with) these (litigants) that their claims not be "closed off" due to their humble standing. (Indeed,) under proper circumstances (you should fulfill the precept of) פְּתַח פִּיךָ לְאִלֵּם, *Open your mouth for the dumb* (*Proverbs* 31:8).

18. וַיִּפְדְּךָ ה׳ אֱלֹהֶיךָ מִשָּׁם — *And* HASHEM *your God redeemed you from there.* He observed your humble situation and acted toward you (leniently) לִפְנִים מִשּׁוּרַת הַדִּין, *not according to the strict letter of the law,* so as to redeem you, as it says, *and He saw our affliction, and our toil and our oppression* (26:7).

22. וְזָכַרְתָּ כִּי עֶבֶד הָיִיתָ — *And you shall remember that you were a slave.* And then (in Egypt) you (also) needed gleanings at harvest time.

XXV

2. וְהִפִּילוֹ הַשֹּׁפֵט — *And the judge shall cause him to be bound.* He shall be bound to a pillar (for flogging).

NOTES

17. לֹא תַטֶּה מִשְׁפַּט גֵּר יָתוֹם — *You shall not pervert the justice due to a stranger or to an orphan.* Although the Torah already cautioned the court not "to twist judgment" (16:19), the *Sforno* explains that this is a special warning to the judge not to embarrass or intimidate people of humble standing in any way, lest it lead to the perversion of justice. Indeed, just the opposite is demanded of the court — to assist unfortunate and humble people in presenting their case properly. This concept is found in the Talmud in a number of cases such as a woman's claim for payment of her *kesubah* (*Kesubos* 36a), and in suggesting to one in possession of property that he should claim he had a שְׁטָר, *deed*, but lost it (*Bava Basra* 41a), and also in suggesting to a creditor that he write a *pruzbul* which would permit him to collect a debt after the Sabbatical year (*Gittin* 37b). The responsibility of the court to suggest these claims to one of these parties, if they are otherwise unaware of these suggestions, is based on the verse in *Proverbs* quoted by the *Sforno*, פְּתַח פִּיךָ לְאִלֵּם, *Open your mouth for the dumb.*

18. וַיִּפְדְּךָ ה׳ אֱלֹהֶיךָ — *And* HASHEM *your God redeemed you.* The *Sforno* explains the sequence of verses 17-18 thus: You are obligated to be concerned for, and helpful to, the weak and unfortunate, even to the extent of arguing their case in court.

put to death because of fathers; a man should be put to death for his own sin.

[17] You shall not pervert the judgment of a proselyte or orphan, and you shall not take the garment of a widow as a pledge. [18] You shall remember that you were a slave in Egypt, and HASHEM, *your God, redeemed you from there; therefore I command you to do this thing.*

[19] When you reap your harvest in your field, and you forget a bundle in the field, you shall not turn back to take it; it shall be for the proselyte, the orphan, and the widow, so that HASHEM, *your God, will bless you in all your handiwork.*

[20] When you beat your olive tree, do not remove all the splendor behind you; it shall be for the proselyte, the orphan, and the widow. [21] When you harvest your vineyard, you shall not glean behind you; it shall be for the proselyte, the orphan, and the widow. [22] You shall remember that you were a slave in the land of Egypt, therefore I command you to do this thing.

25 *[1] When there will be a grievance between people, and they approach the court, and they judge them, and they vindicate the righteous one and find the wicked one guilty; [2] it will be that if the wicked one is liable to lashes, the judge shall cast him down and strike him, before him, according to his wickedness, by a count. [3] Forty shall he strike him, he shall not add; lest he strike him an additional blow beyond these, and your brother will be degraded in your eyes. [4] You shall not muzzle an ox in its threshing.*

[5] When brothers dwell together and one of them dies, and he has no child, the wife of the deceased shall not marry outside to a strange man; her brother-in-law shall come to her, and take her to himself as a wife, and perform levirate marriage. [6] It shall be that the firstborn — if she can

3. מַכָּה רַבָּה — *With many stripes . . .* which he is unable to bear.
וְנִקְלָה אָחִיךָ — *Then your brother would be degraded.* He may become soiled with excrement or water (urine) due to the great pain.

5. וְיִבְּמָהּ — *And he shall remove her "yevamah" status.* (This word means) he shall remove her status of יְבָמָה, *deceased brother's wife*, and she will become his wife regarding

NOTES

Although this may seem to be bending evenhanded justice, nonetheless, we do not always follow the strict letter of the law, just as God tempered justice in Egypt. We did not deserve redemption, but even so, God saw our difficulties and redeemed us.

XXV

2. וְהִפִּילוֹ הַשֹּׁפֵט — *And the judge shall cause him to be bound. Rashi,* based on the Talmud in *Makos* 22b, explains that the accused is whipped "neither standing (erect) or sitting but bending over." The Sages state that he is bound to a pole and leans over it while receiving the stripes. This is also the intent of the *Sforno* in his interpretation of the expression וְהִפִּילוֹ הַשֹּׁפֵט, which should not be translated "cause him to lie down" (A.V.) but "*cause him to be bound* to a pillar."

3. מַכָּה רַבָּה וְנִקְלָה אָחִיךָ — *With many stripes then your brother would be degraded.* According to our Sages, the accused's physical condition must be evaluated to determine whether he can reasonably and safely receive the full number of thirty-nine lashes. Otherwise, he is only given the maximum amount that he can bear. Were he to be whipped excessively, he may not be able to withstand the lashes, and he may also be unable to control his bodily functions, thereby causing him public embarrassment and shame. This is not the intent of מַלְקוֹת, *lashes,* which are meant to punish him and not to degrade him.

5. וְיִבְּמָהּ — *And he shall remove her "yevamah" status.* The word וְיִבְּמָהּ is written after the phrase, וּלְקָחָהּ לוֹ לְאִשָּׁה, *and take her unto himself as a*

ז תֵּלֵד יָקוּם עַל־שֵׁם אָחִיו הַמֵּת וְלֹא־יִמָּחֶה שְׁמוֹ מִיִּשְׂרָאֵל: וְאִם־לֹא
יַחְפֹּץ הָאִישׁ לָקַחַת אֶת־יְבִמְתּוֹ וְעָלְתָה יְבִמְתּוֹ הַשַּׁעְרָה אֶל־הַזְּקֵנִים
ח וְאָמְרָה מֵאֵן יְבָמִי לְהָקִים לְאָחִיו שֵׁם בְּיִשְׂרָאֵל לֹא אָבָה יַבְּמִי: וְקָרְאוּ־
ט לוֹ זִקְנֵי־עִירוֹ וְדִבְּרוּ אֵלָיו וְעָמַד וְאָמַר לֹא חָפַצְתִּי לְקַחְתָּהּ: וְנִגְּשָׁה
יְבִמְתּוֹ אֵלָיו לְעֵינֵי הַזְּקֵנִים וְחָלְצָה נַעֲלוֹ מֵעַל רַגְלוֹ וְיָרְקָה בְּפָנָיו וְעָנְתָה
י וְאָמְרָה כָּכָה יֵעָשֶׂה לָאִישׁ אֲשֶׁר לֹא־יִבְנֶה אֶת־בֵּית אָחִיו: וְנִקְרָא שְׁמוֹ
יא בְּיִשְׂרָאֵל בֵּית חֲלוּץ הַנָּעַל: כִּי־יִנָּצוּ אֲנָשִׁים יַחְדָּו אִישׁ
וְאָחִיו וְקָרְבָה אֵשֶׁת הָאֶחָד לְהַצִּיל אֶת־אִישָׁהּ מִיַּד מַכֵּהוּ וְשָׁלְחָה יָדָהּ
יב־יג וְהֶחֱזִיקָה בִּמְבֻשָׁיו: וְקַצֹּתָה אֶת־כַּפָּהּ לֹא תָחוֹס עֵינֶךָ: לֹא־
יד יִהְיֶה לְךָ בְּכִיסְךָ אֶבֶן וָאָבֶן גְּדוֹלָה וּקְטַנָּה: לֹא־יִהְיֶה לְךָ בְּבֵיתְךָ אֵיפָה
טו וְאֵיפָה גְּדוֹלָה וּקְטַנָּה: אֶבֶן שְׁלֵמָה וָצֶדֶק יִהְיֶה־לָּךְ אֵיפָה שְׁלֵמָה וָצֶדֶק
יִהְיֶה־לָּךְ לְמַעַן יַאֲרִיכוּ יָמֶיךָ עַל הָאֲדָמָה אֲשֶׁר־יהוה אֱלֹהֶיךָ נֹתֵן לָךְ:
טז כִּי תוֹעֲבַת יהוה אֱלֹהֶיךָ כָּל־עֹשֵׂה אֵלֶּה כֹּל עֹשֵׂה עָוֶל:
מפטיר יז־יח זָכוֹר אֵת אֲשֶׁר־עָשָׂה לְךָ עֲמָלֵק בַּדֶּרֶךְ בְּצֵאתְכֶם מִמִּצְרָיִם: אֲשֶׁר
קָרְךָ בַּדֶּרֶךְ וַיְזַנֵּב בְּךָ כָּל־הַנֶּחֱשָׁלִים אַחֲרֶיךָ וְאַתָּה עָיֵף וְיָגֵעַ וְלֹא

all matters, even (to the point of) necessitating a divorce through a bill of divorcement and her return to him (through remarriage).

6. וְלֹא יִמָּחֶה שְׁמוֹ מִיִּשְׂרָאֵל — *That his name not be blotted out of Israel* . . . for (regarding) the child (born of this union), God, the Exalted One, will consider it as if (the *mitzvah*) of "be fruitful and multiply" was fulfilled by the deceased, since he was born as a result of the (original) marriage of the deceased, and the deceased's brother (יָבָם) does not have to remarry her. This commandment was rejected by Onen because of the animosity he had toward his brother, and because of this the anger (of God) was poured out on him.

9. כָּכָה יֵעָשֶׂה לָאִישׁ אֲשֶׁר לֹא יִבְנֶה אֶת בֵּית אָחִיו — *So shall it be done to the man who does not build up his brother's house.* He is worthy of this disgrace since he refused to complete the building up of the house which his brother began by marrying (this woman), as our Sages say, "I never called my wife, 'my wife' but I called my wife 'my house' " (*Shabbos* 118b).

11. וְקָרְבָה אֵשֶׁת הָאֶחָד לְהַצִּיל אֶת אִישָׁהּ — *And the wife of one approached to save her husband.* Even though it is a religious duty for a יְבָמָה (sister-in-law of the brother — יָבָם) to disgrace the brother of her husband who was not concerned for her husband (to honor his name), (nonetheless) a woman is not permitted to shame (the man) who is fighting with her husband.

NOTES

wife; hence it cannot mean יִבּוּם, the act of levirate marriage. The *Sforno* therefore explains it to mean that he has changed her status from that of יְבָמָה to that of wife by continuing the previous marriage of his brother. A new act of קִידוּשִׁין, *marriage*, is not necessary, and she now becomes his wife in the full sense of the law. To dissolve this relationship, a divorce will be necessary and not *chalitzah* (the ceremony of the removal of the shoe), which is done to dissolve the levirate bonds of a couple that does not perform *yibum*.

6. וְלֹא יִמָּחֶה שְׁמוֹ מִיִּשְׂרָאֵל — *That his name not be blotted out of Israel.* As mentioned in the previous note, when the brother of the deceased takes his sister-in-law in levirate marriage, it is unnecessary to perform another act of קִידוּשִׁין (marriage). This indicates that their relationship is considered to be a continuation of the original marriage; hence the child born of their union is considered as the child of the deceased brother. The *Sforno* brings proof of this by citing the story of Er and Onen, the sons of Judah. After Er's death,

bear — shall succeed to the name of his dead brother, so that his name not be blotted out from Israel. 7 But if the man will not wish to marry his sister-in law, then his sister-in-law shall ascend to the gate, to the elders, and she shall say, "My brother-in-law refuses to establish a name for his brother in Israel, he did not consent to perform levirate marriage with me."
8 Then the elders of his city shall summon him and speak to him, and he shall stand and say, "I do not wish to marry her."
9 Then his sister-in-law shall approach him before the eyes of the elders; she shall remove his shoe from on his foot and spit before him; she shall speak up and say, "So is done to the man who will not build the house of his brother." 10 Then his name shall be proclaimed in Israel, "The house of the one whose shoe was removed!"
11 If men fight with one another, a man and his brother, and the wife of one of them approaches to rescue her husband from the hand of the one who is striking him, and she stretches out her hand and grasps his embarrassing place, 12 you shall cut off her hand; your eye shall not show pity.
13 You shall not have in your pouch a weight and a weight — a large one and a small one. 14 And you shall not have in your house a measure and a measure — a large one and a small one. 15 A perfect and honest weight shall you have, a perfect and honest measure shall you have, so that your days shall be lengthened on the Land that HASHEM, your God, gives you. 16 For an abomination of HASHEM, your God, are all who do this, all who act corruptly.
17 Remember what Amalek did to you, on the way when you were leaving Egypt, 18 that he happened upon you on the way, and he struck those of you who were hindmost, all the weaklings at your rear, when you were faint and

14. לֹא יִהְיֶה לְךָ בְּבֵיתְךָ אֵיפָה וְאֵיפָה — *You shall not have in your house two kinds of measures.* After mentioning the ways by which the *Shechinah* (Divine Presence) comes to dwell in Israel, (the Torah now) warns that God not only hates perversion of justice but He also hates the one who has (in his house) implements whose purpose are to perpetrate injustice. (Therefore), it is necessary to remove those articles, lest His spirit abhor us, as it says, *for all that do such things are an abomination to HASHEM your God* (verse 16).

NOTES

Onen refused to impregnate his brother's wife, because he *knew that the seed would not be his* (*Genesis* 38:9). The *Sforno* explains that Onen's refusal was motivated by his hostility toward his brother.

9. בֵּית אָחִיו — *His brother's house.* The *Sforno* interprets the word בַּיִת, *house,* as meaning *wife.* The sense of the verse is that this man (the יָבָם), by refusing to perform a levirate marriage (יבום), failed to continue and complete the marriage of his deceased brother with this woman. She is called בֵּית אָחִיו, *his brother's house,* in keeping with Rabbi Yosi's statement that he always referred to his wife as *his house,* because she was the principal figure of the household, as *Rashi* explains there (*Shabbos* 118b).

11. וְקָרְבָה אֵשֶׁת הָאֶחָד — *And the wife of one approached.* The *Sforno's* commentary on this verse explains the juxtaposition of this law, regarding the wife who comes to the defense of her husband, to the ceremony of removing the shoe of the יָבָם and spitting on the ground in front of his face (חֲלִיצָה). Though the latter act is prescribed by Jewish law, the former is inexcusable and the woman must pay monetary compensation for the shame she caused to that man.

14. לֹא יִהְיֶה לְךָ בְּבֵיתְךָ אֵיפָה וְאֵיפָה — *You shall not have in your house two kinds of measures.* The *Sforno's* commentary clarifies the meaning of the phrases כָּל עֹשֵׂה אֵלֶּה, *all who do these (things),* and כֹּל עֹשֵׂה עָוֶל, *all that do unrighteousness,* both found in verse 16. The former refers to the *means* of committing fraud, while the latter refers to the actual *act* of injustice.

יט יָרֵ֖א אֱלֹהִֽים׃ וְהָיָ֡ה בְּהָנִ֣יחַ יְהוָ֣ה אֱלֹהֶ֣יךָ ׀ לְ֠ךָ֠ מִכׇּל־אֹ֨יְבֶ֜יךָ מִסָּבִ֗יב בָּאָ֙רֶץ֙
אֲשֶׁ֣ר יְהוָֽה־אֱ֠לֹהֶ֠יךָ נֹתֵ֨ן לְךָ֤ נַחֲלָה֙ לְרִשְׁתָּ֔הּ תִּמְחֶה֙ אֶת־זֵ֣כֶר עֲמָלֵ֔ק
מִתַּ֖חַת הַשָּׁמָ֑יִם לֹ֖א תִּשְׁכָּֽח׃

---

19. תִּמְחֶה אֶת זֵכֶר עֲמָלֵק — *Blot out the remembrance of Amalek . . . ox and sheep, camel and ass*, as was commanded to Saul (*I Samuel* 15:3). (This is commanded) in order to take

NOTES

19. תִּמְחֶה אֶת זֵכֶר עֲמָלֵק — *Blot out the remembrance of Amalek*. To *blot out the remembrance* denotes total annihilation, including livestock, which the *Sforno* proves from the verse in the Book of *Samuel*. The expression "arrogant behavior" reflects the teaching of our Sages

exhausted, and he did not fear God. 19 *It shall be that when HASHEM, your God, gives you rest from all your enemies all around, in the Land that HASHEM, your God, gives you as an inheritance to possess it, you shall wipe out the memory of Amalek from under the heaven — you shall not forget!*

---

revenge of Amalek for their arrogant behavior toward God, the Exalted One, (in the manner of those who) act zealously on behalf of His Honor.

NOTES

regarding Amalek. They were the first nation to challenge God's people after the Exodus from Egypt. The *Sforno*, therefore, states that it is incumbent upon Israel to remember what Amalek did, and to avenge God's honor by blotting them out.

פרשת כי תבוא

כו א וְהָיָה כִּי־תָבוֹא אֶל־הָאָרֶץ אֲשֶׁר יְהוָה אֱלֹהֶיךָ נֹתֵן לְךָ נַחֲלָה וִירִשְׁתָּהּ
ב וְיָשַׁבְתָּ בָּהּ׃ וְלָקַחְתָּ מֵרֵאשִׁית ׀ כָּל־פְּרִי הָאֲדָמָה אֲשֶׁר תָּבִיא מֵאַרְצְךָ
אֲשֶׁר יְהוָה אֱלֹהֶיךָ נֹתֵן לָךְ וְשַׂמְתָּ בַטֶּנֶא וְהָלַכְתָּ אֶל־הַמָּקוֹם אֲשֶׁר יִבְחַר
ג יְהוָה אֱלֹהֶיךָ לְשַׁכֵּן שְׁמוֹ שָׁם׃ וּבָאתָ אֶל־הַכֹּהֵן אֲשֶׁר יִהְיֶה בַּיָּמִים הָהֵם
וְאָמַרְתָּ אֵלָיו הִגַּדְתִּי הַיּוֹם לַיהוָה אֱלֹהֶיךָ כִּי־בָאתִי אֶל־הָאָרֶץ אֲשֶׁר
ד נִשְׁבַּע יְהוָה לַאֲבֹתֵינוּ לָתֶת לָנוּ׃ וְלָקַח הַכֹּהֵן הַטֶּנֶא מִיָּדֶךָ וְהִנִּיחוֹ לִפְנֵי
ה מִזְבַּח יְהוָה אֱלֹהֶיךָ׃ וְעָנִיתָ וְאָמַרְתָּ לִפְנֵי ׀ יְהוָה אֱלֹהֶיךָ אֲרַמִּי אֹבֵד אָבִי
ו וַיֵּרֶד מִצְרַיְמָה וַיָּגָר שָׁם בִּמְתֵי מְעָט וַיְהִי־שָׁם לְגוֹי גָּדוֹל עָצוּם וָרָב׃ וַיָּרֵעוּ
ז אֹתָנוּ הַמִּצְרִים וַיְעַנּוּנוּ וַיִּתְּנוּ עָלֵינוּ עֲבֹדָה קָשָׁה׃ וַנִּצְעַק אֶל־יְהוָה אֱלֹהֵי
אֲבֹתֵינוּ וַיִּשְׁמַע יְהוָה אֶת־קֹלֵנוּ וַיַּרְא אֶת־עָנְיֵנוּ וְאֶת־עֲמָלֵנוּ וְאֶת־לַחֲצֵנוּ׃
ח וַיּוֹצִאֵנוּ יְהוָה מִמִּצְרַיִם בְּיָד חֲזָקָה וּבִזְרֹעַ נְטוּיָה וּבְמֹרָא גָּדֹל וּבְאֹתוֹת

XXVI

2. מֵרֵאשִׁית כָּל פְּרִי הָאֲדָמָה אֲשֶׁר תָּבִיא מֵאַרְצְךָ — *The choicest of all the fruit of the ground which you shall bring in from your land* . . . the choicest of all its fruits, similar to, וְרֵאשִׁית שְׁמָנִים יִמְשָׁחוּ, *and anoint themselves with chief* (רֵאשִׁית) *ointments* (*Amos* 6:6), and נְקֻבֵי רֵאשִׁית הַגּוֹיִם, *who are named chief* (רֵאשִׁית) *of the nations* (ibid. 6:1). Now, the choicest (fruit) are the seven species with which *Eretz Yisrael* is praised, as we learn from tradition (*Bikurim* 1:3). This (verse) is an explanation of that which is written in *Exodus* 23:19, רֵאשִׁית בִּכּוּרֵי אַדְמָתְךָ תָּבִיא, *The choicest first fruits of your land shall you bring.* (The Torah now) explains that when it is written, *the choicest first fruits of your land*, the intent was that you bring the first of the choicest fruits of your land, namely from the seven species for which it is praised.

3. אֶל הַכֹּהֵן אֲשֶׁר יִהְיֶה בַּיָּמִים הָהֵם — *To the Kohen that shall be in those days.* Even though he is not great in wisdom, you shall not refrain from addressing him with honor by saying, ה׳ אֱלֹהֶיךָ, *HASHEM your God*, and although this (expression) is not used except for men of renown such as kings and prophets, nonetheless it is proper to speak to him with deference since when you bring the first fruits to him, it is as though you are offering a gift to God, the Exalted One, Who is the owner of the land.

הִגַּדְתִּי הַיּוֹם — *I have declared this day.* I declared to all through this action (of bringing the first fruits), similar to, כִּי הִגַּדְתָּ הַיּוֹם כִּי אֵין לְךָ שָׂרִים וַעֲבָדִים, *for you have declared this day that you regard neither princes or servants* (*II Samuel* 19:7).

כִּי בָאתִי אֶל הָאָרֶץ — *That I have come to the Land* . . . that I came from another land to this land.

NOTES

XXVI

2. מֵרֵאשִׁית כָּל פְּרִי הָאֲדָמָה — *The choicest of all the fruit of the ground. Rashi* points out that the expression "*of* the first" rather than "*the* first" implies that not all fruits are subject to this law of בִּכּוּרִים, *first fruits.* This commandment only applies to the seven species for which *Eretz Yisrael* is praised, i.e., wheat, barley, grapes, figs, pomegrantes, olives and dates, which are listed in *Deut.* 8:8 (See *Bikurim* 1:3). The *Sforno*, however, interprets the word רֵאשִׁית as meaning *choicest* while בִּכּוּרִים means *first*. Our verse is an amplification of the verse in *Exodus* 23:19 where the Torah commands us to bring the choicest first fruits to the Temple in Jerusalem. Indeed, the verses from *Amos* quoted by the *Sforno* in his commentary on this verse are identical to those cited by him in his commentary on the verse in *Exodus*. The usage of the word רֵאשִׁית in *Amos* substantiates that its meaning is not *first* or *beginning* but *choicest*.

PARASHAS KI SAVO

26 [1] *It will be when you enter the Land that* HASHEM, *your God, gives you as
an inheritance, and you possess it, and dwell in it,* [2] *that you shall take
of the first of every fruit of the ground that you bring in from your Land that*
HASHEM, *your God, gives you, and you shall put it in a basket and go to the
place that* HASHEM, *your God, will choose, to make His Name rest there.*
[3] *You shall come to whomever will be the Kohen in those days, and you
shall say to him, "I declare today to* HASHEM, *your God, that I have come to
the Land that* HASHEM *swore to our forefathers to give us."* [4] *The Kohen
shall take the basket from your hand, and lay it before the Altar of* HASHEM,
your God.
[5] *Then you shall call out and say before* HASHEM, *your God, "An
Aramean tried to destroy my forefather. He descended to Egypt and
sojourned there, few in number, and there he became a nation — great,
strong, and numerous.* [6] *The Egyptians mistreated us and afflicted us, and
placed hard work upon us.* [7] *Then we cried out to* HASHEM, *the God of our
forefathers, and* HASHEM *heard our voice and saw our affliction, our travail,
and our oppression.* [8] HASHEM *took us out of Egypt with a strong hand
and with an outstretched arm, with great awesomeness, and with signs*

אֲשֶׁר נִשְׁבַּע ה׳ לַאֲבֹתֵינוּ לָתֶת לָנוּ — *Which* HASHEM *swore to our fathers to give to us . . .* As it says, וְנָתַתִּי לְךָ וּלְזַרְעֲךָ אַחֲרֶיךָ, *And I will give unto you and your seed after you* (*Genesis* 17:8). Therefore, I, the stranger, who came to this land as a sojourner by virtue of His gift, have brought the first fruits as befitting one who gives land to another as a gift or as a tenancy.

4. וְהִנִּיחוֹ לִפְנֵי מִזְבַּח ה׳ אֱלֹהֶיךָ — *And set it down before the Altar of* HASHEM *your God . . .* to demonstrate and declare that the first fruits are not brought to the *Kohen* but to God the Blessed One, and He in turn gives them to the *Kohen*, together with the other priestly gifts.

5. אֲרַמִּי אֹבֵד אָבִי — *A wandering Aramean was my father.* Behold, my father Jacob was, for a period, a wandering Aramean (a wanderer in Aram) who had no permanent home, and therefore he was not prepared to establish a nation fit to inherit a land.

6. וַיְעַנּוּנוּ וַיִּתְּנוּ עָלֵינוּ עֲבֹדָה קָשָׁה — *And afflicted us and placed upon us hard labor.* And even after they became a nation, they were unfit to receive any gift because they were slaves, and "whatsoever a slave possesses belongs to his master" (*Pesachim* 88b).

NOTES

3. אֶל הַכֹּהֵן אֲשֶׁר יִהְיֶה . . . אֲשֶׁר נִשְׁבַּע ה׳ לַאֲבֹתֵינוּ לָתֶת לָנוּ — *To the Kohen that shall be . . . which* HASHEM *swore to our fathers to give to us*. The *Sforno* explains that the first fruits are not meant to be a gift for the *Kohen*, but symbolically are an offering of thanksgiving to the Almighty for giving us the Land of Israel. This act is meant to declare our recognition that God is the master of the Land and had He not given us *Eretz Yisrael*, we would have no legitimate right to it. This thought is developed further in the following verses.

5. אֲרַמִּי אֹבֵד אָבִי — *A wandering Aramean was my father*. *Rashi*, based on Onkelos, interprets this to mean, "an Aramean (Laban) planned to destroy my father (Jacob)." The *Sforno*, however, as does Ibn Ezra, interprets this expression as meaning, "While living in Aram, my father Jacob was destitute and without a permanent home." This statement is included in the *Bikurim* ceremony, to indicate that the forging of Jacob's family into a nation and their eventual inheritance of the Land of Israel was not a natural, logical development, but came to pass because it was the will of the Almighty. This thought is further expanded upon in the *Sforno's* commentary on verses 6 and 9.

ט וּבְמֹפְתִים: וַיְבִאֵנוּ אֶל־הַמָּקוֹם הַזֶּה וַיִּתֶּן־לָנוּ אֶת־הָאָרֶץ הַזֹּאת אֶרֶץ
י זָבַת חָלָב וּדְבָשׁ: וְעַתָּה הִנֵּה הֵבֵאתִי אֶת־רֵאשִׁית פְּרִי הָאֲדָמָה
אֲשֶׁר־נָתַתָּה לִּי יהוה וְהִנַּחְתּוֹ לִפְנֵי יהוה אֱלֹהֶיךָ וְהִשְׁתַּחֲוִיתָ לִפְנֵי
יא יהוה אֱלֹהֶיךָ: וְשָׂמַחְתָּ בְכָל־הַטּוֹב אֲשֶׁר נָתַן־לְךָ יהוה אֱלֹהֶיךָ וּלְבֵיתֶךָ
שני יב אַתָּה וְהַלֵּוִי וְהַגֵּר אֲשֶׁר בְּקִרְבֶּךָ: כִּי תְכַלֶּה לַעְשֵׂר
אֶת־כָּל־מַעְשַׂר תְּבוּאָתְךָ בַּשָּׁנָה הַשְּׁלִישִׁת שְׁנַת הַמַּעֲשֵׂר וְנָתַתָּה
יג לַלֵּוִי לַגֵּר לַיָּתוֹם וְלָאַלְמָנָה וְאָכְלוּ בִשְׁעָרֶיךָ וְשָׂבֵעוּ: וְאָמַרְתָּ לִפְנֵי
יהוה אֱלֹהֶיךָ בִּעַרְתִּי הַקֹּדֶשׁ מִן־הַבַּיִת וְגַם נְתַתִּיו לַלֵּוִי וְלַגֵּר לַיָּתוֹם
וְלָאַלְמָנָה כְּכָל־מִצְוָתְךָ אֲשֶׁר צִוִּיתָנִי לֹא־עָבַרְתִּי מִמִּצְוֹתֶיךָ וְלֹא
יד שָׁכָחְתִּי: לֹא־אָכַלְתִּי בְאֹנִי מִמֶּנּוּ וְלֹא־בִעַרְתִּי מִמֶּנּוּ בְּטָמֵא וְלֹא־נָתַתִּי
מִמֶּנּוּ לְמֵת שָׁמַעְתִּי בְּקוֹל יהוה אֱלֹהָי עָשִׂיתִי כְּכֹל אֲשֶׁר צִוִּיתָנִי:
טו הַשְׁקִיפָה מִמְּעוֹן קָדְשְׁךָ מִן־הַשָּׁמַיִם וּבָרֵךְ אֶת־עַמְּךָ אֶת־יִשְׂרָאֵל וְאֵת
הָאֲדָמָה אֲשֶׁר נָתַתָּה לָנוּ כַּאֲשֶׁר נִשְׁבַּעְתָּ לַאֲבֹתֵינוּ אֶרֶץ זָבַת חָלָב

9. וַיִּתֶּן לָנוּ אֶת הָאָרֶץ הַזֹּאת — *And gave us this land.* And after we came forth into freedom, we had no portion of land wherein to dwell, (but) He gave us this (land), which is a choice land flowing with milk and honey.

10. וְעַתָּה — *And now.* Now that I know how great is Your goodness and kindness to us, that You made us into a nation worthy to inherit a land, and delivered us into freedom in a manner that we are able to receive a gift which will be ours, and You gave us this (land) which is the most lovely of all lands and the choicest of all places.

הִנֵּה הֵבֵאתִי אֶת רֵאשִׁית פְּרִי הָאֲדָמָה אֲשֶׁר נָתַתָּה לִּי ה׳ — *Behold, I have brought the first of the fruit of the land which You, HASHEM, have given me.* I have brought the choicest fruit of that land which You gave unto me, to offer thanks to Your Name for it.

13. בִּעַרְתִּי הַקֹּדֶשׁ מִן הַבַּיִת — *I have removed the sacred things from the house.* (Because) of our sins and the wicked deeds of our fathers, the sacred service was denied to the firstborn (of Israel), who were originally deemed worthy to receive the offerings (תְּרוּמָה) and tithes (מַעְשְׂרוֹת), as it says, וָאֲטַמֵּא אוֹתָם בְּמַתְּנוֹתָם בְּהַעֲבִיר כָּל פֶּטֶר רָחַם, *And I defiled them by their gifts in that they caused all that opens the womb to pass (through the fire)* (*Ezekiel* 20:26). This is the וִדּוּי מַעֲשֵׂר, *confession of the tithe,* mentioned by our Sages (*Maaser Shani* 5:10).

NOTES

10. וְעַתָּה — *And now.* The *Sforno* explains that three concepts are incorporated in this one word וְעַתָּה, *and now,* pronounced by the Israelite when he brings his offering of first fruits to God. They are: 1) that He fashioned us into a nation; 2) that He liberated us so that as free men we were capable of receiving a gift, unlike a slave who has no such legal right; and 3) that He gave us this outstanding beautiful land.

13. בִּעַרְתִּי הַקֹּדֶשׁ מִן הַבַּיִת וְגַם נְתַתִּיו לַלֵּוִי — *I have removed the sacred things from the house and although I have given it to the Levite etc.* The expression קֹדֶשׁ, *sacred things,* refers to the מַעֲשֵׂר שֵׁנִי, *second tithe,* and כֶּרֶם רְבָעִי, *the growth of the vineyard in the fourth year,* which must be removed from the house in the fourth year of the Sabbatical cycle. It also refers to מַעֲשֵׂר רִאשׁוֹן, the *first tithe,* and the מַעֲשֵׂר עָנִי, *tithe for the poor.* The Sages call the statement made at the time of בִּעוּר, *removal,* by the term וִדּוּי מַעַשְׂרוֹת, *confession.* Since the term וִדּוּי means "confession of sins," it is difficult to understand why this term is applied to a statement of one's fulfillment of his obligations, including the careful observance of the order and manner of the disposal of these tithes (see *Rashi's* commentary on this verse). The *Sforno* explains the reason for the term וִדּוּי. The original intent of God was that the firstborn in Israel be the ones to serve Him. Only after the sin of the Golden Calf was this privilege and responsibility transferred to

and with wonders. 9 *He brought us to this place, and He gave us this Land,*
a Land flowing with milk and honey. 10 *And now, behold! I have brought the*
first fruit of the ground that You have given me, O HASHEM!" And you shall lay it before HASHEM, your God, and you shall prostrate yourself before HASHEM, your God.

11 *You shall be glad with all the goodness that HASHEM, your God, has given you and your household — you and the Levite and the proselyte who is in your midst.*

12 *When you have finished tithing every tithe of your produce in the third year, the year of the tithe, you shall give to the Levite, to the proselyte, to the orphan, and to the widow, and they shall eat in your cities and be satisfied.*
13 *Then you shall say before HASHEM, your God, "I have removed the holy things from the house, and I have also given it to the Levite, to the proselyte, to the orphan, and to the widow, according to whatever commandment You commanded me; I have not transgressed any of your commandments, and*
I have not forgotten. 14 *I have not eaten of it in my intense mourning, I did not consume it in a state of contamination, and I did not give of it for the needs of the dead; I have hearkened to the voice of HASHEM, my God; I have*
acted according to everything You commanded me. 15 *Gaze down from*
Your holy abode, from the heavens, and bless Your people Israel, and the ground that You gave us, as You swore to our forefathers, a Land flowing with milk and honey."

וְגַם נְתַתִּיו לַלֵּוִי — *And although I have given it to the Levite.* The meaning of גַּם (in this verse) is akin to the meaning of although, similar to, גַּם הָיִיתִי הַלַּיְלָה לְאִישׁ וְגַם יָלַדְתִּי בָנִים, *even if I should be this night with a man and even should I bear sons* (*Ruth* 1:12). Therefore, this is what he says: I confess that my transgression is great (and) I have caused the sacred things to be removed from the house, and although I have given them to the Levites and to others according to Your commandment, (nonetheless) I pray that You look down (from heaven) for good and not for evil, which, considering my transgression, would be fitting.

15. וּבָרֵךְ אֶת עַמְּךָ . . . וְאֵת הָאֲדָמָה אֲשֶׁר נָתַתָּה לָנוּ — *And bless Your people . . . and the land which You have given us . . .* in the manner that *You did swear to our fathers* when You said, אַעֲלֶה אֶתְכֶם מֵעֳנִי מִצְרַיִם אֶל אֶרֶץ, *I will bring you up out of the affliction of Egypt to the Land* (*Exodus* 3:17).

NOTES

the Levites and *Kohanim* (see *Sforno* on *Numbers* 3:13). Hence, had Israel not sinned, both *terumah* and *maaseros* would not have been given to the *Kohanim* and Levites, but would have remained in each Jewish home for it would have rightfully belonged to the בְּכוֹר, *firstborn*, of each household. The fact that there must be removal is an indication of this failing, an acknowledgement of the sin of Israel in worshiping the Golden Calf. Therefore, this statement is called וִדּוּי — confession. The *Sforno* points out that the word גַּם, in our verse, does not mean *also* but *although*. The sense of the phrase וְגַם נְתַתִּיו לַלֵּוִי is that, although I confess that my giving the tithe to the Levite is an admission of the sin of my fathers, nonetheless הַשְׁקִיפָה, *look down*, from heaven and bless me (v. 15), even though I may not be worthy of this heavenly blessing, considering my transgressions and those of my ancestors as well.

The verse in *Ezekiel* cited by the *Sforno* is to be understood in the following manner. The gift which I gave to all Israel originally, namely that the firstborn of each family be sanctified, which also entitled them to receive the offerings and tithes, was defiled through their sins. This included not only the passivity of the firstborn at the time of the sin of the Golden Calf but also the sacrificing of the firstborn by their fathers to the Moloch. See the commentaries on chapter 20, verse 26 in the Book of *Ezekiel*.

שלישי
טז וּדְבָשׁ: הַיּוֹם הַזֶּה יְהוָה אֱלֹהֶיךָ מְצַוְּךָ לַעֲשׂוֹת אֶת־הַחֻקִּים
הָאֵלֶּה וְאֶת־הַמִּשְׁפָּטִים וְשָׁמַרְתָּ וְעָשִׂיתָ אוֹתָם בְּכָל־לְבָבְךָ וּבְכָל־
יז נַפְשֶׁךָ: אֶת־יְהוָה הֶאֱמַרְתָּ הַיּוֹם לִהְיוֹת לְךָ לֵאלֹהִים וְלָלֶכֶת בִּדְרָכָיו
יח וְלִשְׁמֹר חֻקָּיו וּמִצְוֹתָיו וּמִשְׁפָּטָיו וְלִשְׁמֹעַ בְּקֹלוֹ: וַיהוָה הֶאֱמִירְךָ הַיּוֹם
יט לִהְיוֹת לוֹ לְעַם סְגֻלָּה כַּאֲשֶׁר דִּבֶּר־לָךְ וְלִשְׁמֹר כָּל־מִצְוֹתָיו: וּלְתִתְּךָ
עֶלְיוֹן עַל כָּל־הַגּוֹיִם אֲשֶׁר עָשָׂה לִתְהִלָּה וּלְשֵׁם וּלְתִפְאָרֶת וְלִהְיֹתְךָ
עַם־קָדֹשׁ לַיהוָה אֱלֹהֶיךָ כַּאֲשֶׁר דִּבֵּר:

16. הַיּוֹם הַזֶּה — *This day* . . . the day you enter into a covenant with Him. Behold, the covenant is that God, the Blessed One, commands you to do these statutes and judgments for your (own) good, which He has not done with any other people, and you (in turn) accept upon yourself to observe them.

בְּכָל לְבָבְךָ — *With all your heart* . . . that you shall recognize, without any doubt, that it is fitting to do His will.

וּבְכָל נַפְשְׁךָ — *And with all your soul*. That your powerful desires shall not deter you (from serving God), because you recognize the superiority of He who commanded you (to observe His commandments), and their benefit — and thus . . .

17. אֶת ה׳ הֶאֱמַרְתָּ הַיּוֹם — *You have exalted* HASHEM *this day*. When you accepted upon yourself through an oath, which carried with it a curse, to enter into the covenant whereby you would forfeit all material well being if you would violate it — הֶאֱמַרְתָּ, you thereby exalted and elevated God, the Blessed One, (acknowledging) that the fulfillment of His will would be more honorable to you than all material good.

לִהְיוֹת לְךָ לֵאלֹהִים — *To be unto you Elohim* . . . that He shall be unto you the most honored of all objects separated (from matter), and from Him (emanates) the direction and existence of all your affairs, without any intermediary as befits (One) who is Eternal. (Therefore,) in this manner it is fitting that you serve and be subservient to Him alone, as is proper for the One above (i.e., He Who is) your Leader, and that you pray only to Him, being that He alone is your Guide.

NOTES

16. בְּכָל לְבָבְךָ וּבְכָל נַפְשְׁךָ — *With all your heart and with all your soul*. The *Sforno* interprets לְבָבְךָ, *your heart*, as referring to man's intellectual powers, while נַפְשְׁךָ, *your soul*, alludes to his normal appetites and desires which must be disciplined and controlled.

17. אֶת ה׳ הֶאֱמַרְתָּ — *You have exalted* HASHEM. The word הֶאֱמַרְתָּ is interpreted in a variety of ways by the commentators. *Rashi* explains it to mean that Israel selected God from among the strange gods — i.e., they singled Him out. The Sages in *Berachos* 6a expound on this expression, stating that we made of God a "unique entity" or "the object of our love" (חֲטִיבָה אַחַת), and He, in turn, made us a "unique entity" in the world. Ibn Ezra translates it as "to exalt" and the *Sforno*, similarly, interprets it to mean elevation. The sense of the *Sforno's* commentary is: By entering into a covenant with God, we affirmed that the רְצוֹן ה׳, *God's will*, is paramount, and there is naught in this world more important than the fulfillment of God's will. We have elevated Him above all other considerations and all other claims to our time, energies and means.

לִהְיוֹת לְךָ לֵאלֹהִים — *To be unto you Elohim*. The *Sforno* explains that this phrase has a two-fold implication. As he commented at the very beginning of *Genesis* (1:1), the term *Elohim* can also be applied to angels who are separated from matter, and even to judges who reflect Divine intelligence. However, man must recognize that the Almighty is the One Who is unique and from Whom emanates the existence of all — including those who are "separated from matter" such as the angels. He also stresses that man's destiny is determined and directed by God alone, and only to Him shall one's prayers be addressed. This latter thought is incorporated in the word לְךָ, *unto you*.

וְלָלֶכֶת בִּדְרָכָיו — *And to walk in His ways*. The *Sforno* interprets this phrase in the sense of endeavoring to follow and imitate the ways of God, as the Talmud teaches us, "As He is gracious and

16 *This day, HASHEM, your God, commands you to perform these decrees and the statutes, and you shall observe and perform them with all your heart and with all your soul.* 17 *You have distinguished HASHEM today to be a God for you, and to walk in His ways, and to observe His decrees, His commandments, and His statutes, and to hearken to His voice.* 18 *And HASHEM has distinguished you today to be for Him a treasured people, as He spoke to you, and to observe all His commandments,* 19 *and to make you supreme over all the nations that He made, for praise, for renown, and for splendor, and so that you will be a holy people to HASHEM, your God, as He spoke.*

וְלָלֶכֶת בִּדְרָכָיו — *And to walk in His ways.* To be like the One Who is honored above all else that exists.

וְלִשְׁמֹעַ בְּקֹלוֹ — *And hearken to His voice . . .* as befits His servants.

18. וַה׳ הֶאֱמִירְךָ הַיּוֹם — *And HASHEM has exalted you this day.* By entering into a covenant with you, (an act) which He has done with no other people, (and thus) He has given you this preeminence.

לִהְיוֹת לוֹ לְעַם סְגֻלָּה — *To be unto Him a treasured people.* So as to realize, through you, that which He desired to attain with human kind [as it says, נַעֲשֶׂה אָדָם בְּצַלְמֵנוּ כִּדְמוּתֵנוּ, *Let us make man in our image after our likeness* (*Genesis* 1:26).]

וְלִשְׁמֹר כָּל מִצְוֹתָיו — *And to keep all His commandments.* And He also gave you preeminence in that He chose you to keep all His commandments through which you will find favor in His eyes. [All other nations are unprepared and unworthy in His (sight) for this (gift of Torah), as our Sages teach us, "A non-Jew that observes the Sabbath is guilty of a capital (crime)" (*Sanhedrin* 58b), and they are unfit to keep all His commandments except for those which are the Noachide laws.]

19. וּלְתִתְּךָ עֶלְיוֹן עַל כָּל הַגּוֹיִם — *And to make you high above all nations . . .* to understand and to teach, as it says, וְאַתֶּם תִּהְיוּ לִי מַמְלֶכֶת כֹּהֲנִים, *And you shall be to Me a kingdom of Kohanim* (*Exodus* 19:6).

NOTES

compassionate, so shall you be gracious and compassionate" (*Shabbos* 133b). This concept reflects the teaching of Abba Saul, who interprets the verse in *Exodus* 15:2, זֶה אֵלִי וְאַנְוֵהוּ, *This is my God and I will glorify Him*, as meaning אֲנִי וָהוּא, *I and He*, indicating that man is to emulate the attributes of God. The *Sforno* interprets the phrase לָלֶכֶת בִּדְרָכָיו, *to walk in His ways*, in a similar fashion.

18. וַה׳ הֶאֱמִירְךָ הַיּוֹם לִהְיוֹת לוֹ לְעַם סְגֻלָּה . . . וְלִשְׁמֹר כָּל מִצְוֹתָיו — *And HASHEM has exalted you this day to be unto Him a treasured people . . . and to keep all His commandments.* It is interesting to note that the text of the *Sforno* in many editions of the מִקְרָאוֹת גְּדוֹלוֹת (the standard version of the *Chumash*) does not include some of his commentary that appears in the Mosad HaRav Kook edition, which is based on various manuscripts. It is apparent that the censor deleted certain words, phrases and quotations. For example, the phrase "which He has done with no other people" (לֹא עָשָׂה כֵן לְכָל גּוֹי) is missing. The quote from *Genesis* 1:26 regarding the creation of man in God's image is also deleted. Finally, the entire paragraph which speaks of the nations being "unprepared and unworthy . . . for the gift of Torah" and the statement of our Sages from tractate *Sanhedrin* 58b is excised. Obviously, the censor did not want to permit the troublesome statements: (a) that the covenant between God and Israel excludes the גּוֹיִם, *the gentile nations*; (b) that only the people of Israel represent the fulfillment of God's goal of creating mankind in His image and likeness; and (c) that only Israel was capable of accepting the yoke of all the commandments, while others are only required to observe the seven basic commandments (שֶׁבַע מִצְוֹת בְּנֵי נֹחַ).

19. וּלְתִתְּךָ עֶלְיוֹן — *And to make you high.* The *Sforno* carefully defines the various phrases used in this verse. The expression עֶלְיוֹן, *high* or *elevated*, refers to our role as teachers and guides of mankind. The *Kohen* is normally given this mission, therefore he quotes the verse from *Exodus* where God charges us to be "*a kingdom of Kohanim.*" Israel, however, is not to glorify itself because of this special role which God has given to them. Rather, God is glorified through us, as the prophet says.

כז רביעי א וַיְצַו מֹשֶׁה וְזִקְנֵי יִשְׂרָאֵל אֶת־הָעָם לֵאמֹר שָׁמֹר אֶת־כָּל־הַמִּצְוָה אֲשֶׁר
ב אָנֹכִי מְצַוֶּה אֶתְכֶם הַיּוֹם: וְהָיָה בַּיּוֹם אֲשֶׁר תַּעַבְרוּ אֶת־הַיַּרְדֵּן אֶל־הָאָרֶץ
אֲשֶׁר־יהוה אֱלֹהֶיךָ נֹתֵן לָךְ וַהֲקֵמֹתָ לְךָ אֲבָנִים גְּדֹלוֹת וְשַׂדְתָּ אֹתָם
ג בַּשִּׂיד: וְכָתַבְתָּ עֲלֵיהֶן אֶת־כָּל־דִּבְרֵי הַתּוֹרָה הַזֹּאת בְּעָבְרֶךָ לְמַעַן אֲשֶׁר
תָּבֹא אֶל־הָאָרֶץ אֲשֶׁר־יהוה אֱלֹהֶיךָ | נֹתֵן לְךָ אֶרֶץ זָבַת חָלָב וּדְבַשׁ
ד כַּאֲשֶׁר דִּבֶּר יהוה אֱלֹהֵי־אֲבֹתֶיךָ לָךְ: וְהָיָה בְּעָבְרְכֶם אֶת־הַיַּרְדֵּן תָּקִימוּ
אֶת־הָאֲבָנִים הָאֵלֶּה אֲשֶׁר אָנֹכִי מְצַוֶּה אֶתְכֶם הַיּוֹם בְּהַר עֵיבָל וְשַׂדְתָּ
ה אוֹתָם בַּשִּׂיד: וּבָנִיתָ שָּׁם מִזְבֵּחַ לַיהוה אֱלֹהֶיךָ מִזְבַּח אֲבָנִים לֹא־תָנִיף
ו עֲלֵיהֶם בַּרְזֶל: אֲבָנִים שְׁלֵמוֹת תִּבְנֶה אֶת־מִזְבַּח יהוה אֱלֹהֶיךָ וְהַעֲלִיתָ
ז עָלָיו עוֹלֹת לַיהוה אֱלֹהֶיךָ: וְזָבַחְתָּ שְׁלָמִים וְאָכַלְתָּ שָּׁם וְשָׂמַחְתָּ לִפְנֵי
ח יהוה אֱלֹהֶיךָ: וְכָתַבְתָּ עַל־הָאֲבָנִים אֶת־כָּל־דִּבְרֵי הַתּוֹרָה הַזֹּאת בַּאֵר
ט הֵיטֵב: וַיְדַבֵּר מֹשֶׁה וְהַכֹּהֲנִים הַלְוִיִּם אֶל־כָּל־יִשְׂרָאֵל לֵאמֹר
י הַסְכֵּת | וּשְׁמַע יִשְׂרָאֵל הַיּוֹם הַזֶּה נִהְיֵיתָ לְעָם לַיהוה אֱלֹהֶיךָ: וְשָׁמַעְתָּ
בְּקוֹל יהוה אֱלֹהֶיךָ וְעָשִׂיתָ אֶת־מִצְוֹתָו וְאֶת־חֻקָּיו אֲשֶׁר אָנֹכִי מְצַוְּךָ
חמישי יא־יב הַיּוֹם: וַיְצַו מֹשֶׁה אֶת־הָעָם בַּיּוֹם הַהוּא לֵאמֹר: אֵלֶּה יַעַמְדוּ

לִתְהִלָּה וּלְשֵׁם וּלְתִפְאָרֶת — *In praise, in name and in glory* . . . to God, the Blessed One, as it says, יִשְׂרָאֵל אֲשֶׁר בְּךָ אֶתְפָּאָר, *Israel in whom I will be glorified* (*Isaiah* 49:3).

וְלִהְיֹתְךָ עַם קָדֹשׁ — *That you may be a holy people* . . . everlasting, (bringing you) to the life of the World to Come.

כַּאֲשֶׁר דִּבֵּר — *As He has spoken* . . . when He said, וְאַתֶּם תִּהְיוּ לִי מַמְלֶכֶת כֹּהֲנִים, *And you shall be to Me a kingdom of Kohanim and a holy nation* (*Exodus* ibid.).

XXVII

1. וַיְצַו מֹשֶׁה וְזִקְנֵי יִשְׂרָאֵל — *And Moses and the elders of Israel commanded.* He included the elders with him, because they would be present with him when they (Israel) crossed the Jordan River.

7. וְשָׂמַחְתָּ לִפְנֵי ה׳ אֱלֹהֶיךָ — *And you shall rejoice before* HASHEM *your God* . . . because you

NOTES

וְלִהְיֹתְךָ עַם קָדֹשׁ . . . כַּאֲשֶׁר דִּבֵּר — *That you may be a holy people* . . . *as He has spoken.* In addition to being mankind's mentors, a duty expressed in the phrase מַמְלֶכֶת כֹּהֲנִים, *a kingdom of Kohanim,* Israel is also told to be a גוֹי קָדוֹשׁ, *a holy people* (*Exodus* 19:6) — which is the same as עַם קָדוֹשׁ, the phrase used here. By so doing, they insure their eternal, everlasting existence, for as the *Sforno* explains elsewhere (*Exodus* 19:6), holiness insures נִצְחִיּוּת, *eternity.* All this was already told to Israel prior to the giving of the Torah at Sinai, and this is the meaning of the words כַּאֲשֶׁר דִּבֵּר, *as He has spoken.* Thus, the *Sforno* explains the Torah's precise choice of words in this section.

XXVII

1. וַיְצַו מֹשֶׁה וְזִקְנֵי יִשְׂרָאֵל — *And Moses and the elders of Israel commanded.* The *Sforno* explains why Moses included the elders when he went to command the Israelites regarding the setting up of the great stones after they cross the Jordan, while in verse 9 Moses included the *Kohanim* and Levites when he spoke to the people and urged them to listen to God and observe His commandments. The reason given by the *Sforno* is that the elders, as the leaders of the people, would be directly involved in the setting up of these stones upon which the commandments contained in the Torah were inscribed, while the *Kohanim,* whose function it was to instruct the people in the laws, were better suited to be associated with Moses in this second area of admonishing the people to learn, obey and follow the teachings of the Torah.

7. וְשָׂמַחְתָּ — *And you shall rejoice.* The *Sforno* explains that the renewed covenant between God and Israel, entered into on Mount Gerizim and

27 [1] *Moses and the elders of Israel commanded the people, saying, "Ob-*
serve the entire commandment that I command you this day. [2] *It*
shall be on the day that you cross the Jordan to the Land that HASHEM, *your*
God, gives you, you shall set up great stones and you shall coat them with
plaster. [3] *You shall inscribe on them all the words of this Torah, when you*
cross over, so that you may enter the Land that HASHEM, *your God, gives*
you, a Land flowing with milk and honey, as HASHEM, *the God of your*
forefathers, spoke about you. [4] *It shall be that when you cross the Jordan,*
you shall erect these stones, of which I command you today, on Mount Ebal,
and you shall coat them with plaster. [5] *There you shall build an altar for*
HASHEM, *your God, an altar of stones; you shall not raise iron upon them.*
[6] *Of whole stones shall you build the altar of* HASHEM, *your God, and you*
shall bring upon it elevation-offerings to HASHEM, *your God.* [7] *You shall*
slaughter peace-offerings and eat there, and you shall be glad before
HASHEM, *your God.* [8] *You shall inscribe on the stones all the words of this*
Torah, well clarified."
[9] *Moses and the Kohanim, the Levites, spoke to all Israel, saying, "Be*
attentive and hear, O Israel: This day you have become a people to HASHEM,
your God. [10] *You shall hearken to the voice of* HASHEM, *your God, and you*
shall perform all His commandments and His decrees, which I command
you today."
[11] *Moses commanded the people on that day, saying,* [12] *"These shall stand*

---

will enter into a covenant with Him at that time, on Mount Gerizim and Mount Ebal.

9. וַיְדַבֵּר מֹשֶׁה וְהַכֹּהֲנִים הַלְוִיִּם — *And Moses and the Kohanim the Levites spoke.* He included the *Kohanim* with him to caution (them) regarding the analytical study of Torah, being that the (responsibility) to teach knowledge (of Torah) to the people rested on the *Kohanim*, as it says, *They shall teach Jacob Your ordinances* (33:10).

הַסְכֵּת — *Imagine.* Imagine (portray) in your mind, similar to, אֵת סִכּוּת מַלְכְּכֶם, *Sikkus (the image of) your king* (*Amos* 5:26).

וּשְׁמַע — *And hear.* And consider (observe).

10. וְשָׁמַעְתָּ בְּקוֹל ה׳ אֱלֹהֶיךָ — *And you will hearken to the voice of* HASHEM *your God.* When you conjure this up (in your mind) and comprehend, then without a doubt you will listen to His voice.

NOTES

Mount Ebal, was indeed an occasion for rejoicing. There can be no greater *simchah* than the realization that the Almighty has chosen Israel as His people, as it says, *This day you have become a people to God your God* (v. 9).

9-10. הַסְכֵּת וּשְׁמַע . . . וְשָׁמַעְתָּ — *Imagine and hear . . . and you will hearken.* The *Sforno* explains the sequence of these two verses. First, you must conjure up the image of God's relationship to Israel and their commitment to Him and impress this upon your mind. Then you must consider and contemplate the meaning of this covenant between Israel and God, its deeper meaning and significance. If you do this, then it will result in your listening to the voice of God. The word וְשָׁמַעְתָּ, *and you will hearken*, is not an additional commandment, but an assurance that the result of הַסְכֵּת, *imagine*, and שְׁמַע, *hear*, will be וְשָׁמַעְתָּ, *and you will hearken.* The *Sforno's* interpretation of the word הַסְכֵּת is unique. *Rashi*, based on *Onkelos*, interprets it as *listen*. S.R. Hirsch translates it as *pay attention.* Our Sages interpret it in a variety of ways (see *Berachos* 63b). The *Sforno*, however, understands it to mean "imagine in your mind," let there be a full impact upon you of the realization that you are God's people. The verse cited from *Amos* speaks of people carrying and clutching their idols closely to their hearts. So should Israel be suffused with their belief in God and hold their loyalty to the covenant close to their heart.

לְבָרֵךְ אֶת־הָעָם עַל־הַר גְּרִזִּים בְּעָבְרְכֶם אֶת־הַיַּרְדֵּן שִׁמְעוֹן וְלֵוִי וִיהוּדָה
יג וְיִשָּׂשכָר וְיוֹסֵף וּבִנְיָמִן: וְאֵלֶּה יַעַמְדוּ עַל־הַקְּלָלָה בְּהַר עֵיבָל רְאוּבֵן גָּד
יד וְאָשֵׁר וּזְבוּלֻן דָּן וְנַפְתָּלִי: וְעָנוּ הַלְוִיִּם וְאָמְרוּ אֶל־כָּל־אִישׁ יִשְׂרָאֵל קוֹל
טו רָם: אָרוּר הָאִישׁ אֲשֶׁר יַעֲשֶׂה פֶסֶל וּמַסֵּכָה תּוֹעֲבַת יהוה מַעֲשֵׂה
טז יְדֵי חָרָשׁ וְשָׂם בַּסָּתֶר וְעָנוּ כָל־הָעָם וְאָמְרוּ אָמֵן: אָרוּר מַקְלֶה
יז אָבִיו וְאִמּוֹ וְאָמַר כָּל־הָעָם אָמֵן: אָרוּר מַסִּיג
יח גְּבוּל רֵעֵהוּ וְאָמַר כָּל־הָעָם אָמֵן: אָרוּר מַשְׁגֶּה
יט עִוֵּר בַּדָּרֶךְ וְאָמַר כָּל־הָעָם אָמֵן: אָרוּר מַטֶּה
כ מִשְׁפַּט גֵּר־יָתוֹם וְאַלְמָנָה וְאָמַר כָּל־הָעָם אָמֵן: אָרוּר שֹׁכֵב עִם־אֵשֶׁת
כא אָבִיו כִּי גִלָּה כְּנַף אָבִיו וְאָמַר כָּל־הָעָם אָמֵן: אָרוּר שֹׁכֵב
כב עִם־כָּל־בְּהֵמָה וְאָמַר כָּל־הָעָם אָמֵן: אָרוּר שֹׁכֵב עִם־אֲחֹתוֹ
כג בַּת־אָבִיו אוֹ בַת־אִמּוֹ וְאָמַר כָּל־הָעָם אָמֵן: אָרוּר שֹׁכֵב
כד עִם־חֹתַנְתּוֹ וְאָמַר כָּל־הָעָם אָמֵן: אָרוּר מַכֵּה
כה רֵעֵהוּ בַּסָּתֶר וְאָמַר כָּל־הָעָם אָמֵן: אָרוּר לֹקֵחַ שֹׁחַד
כו לְהַכּוֹת נֶפֶשׁ דַּם נָקִי וְאָמַר כָּל־הָעָם אָמֵן: אָרוּר אֲשֶׁר
לֹא־יָקִים אֶת־דִּבְרֵי הַתּוֹרָה־הַזֹּאת לַעֲשׂוֹת אוֹתָם וְאָמַר כָּל־הָעָם אָמֵן:

15. אָרוּר הָאִישׁ — *Cursed be the man.* Behold, all the curses were preceded with the language of *blessed be*, as we have received in our tradition (*Sotah* 32a); therefore, it says, *These shall stand to bless the people* (v. 12). However, the Torah only mentions the language of curse, because the main purpose of these imprecations was to curse those who transgressed these (laws) so that they alone should bear the consequences of their wicked acts, but the rest of the people would not be responsible for them. The (reason) for this is that these sins, in the majority of cases, were committed by the leaders of the people and the common people had (no power) to protest, as Ezekiel attests, saying, נְשִׂיאֵי יִשְׂרָאֵל אִישׁ לִזְרֹעוֹ הָיוּ בָךְ לְמַעַן שְׁפָךְ דָּם. אָב וָאֵם הֵקַלּוּ בָךְ . . ., *The princes of Israel, every man for his own power were they within you, for the sake of bloodshed. Father and mother have they slighted within you . . .* (*Ezekiel* 22:6,7). Now, in that chapter the prophet mentions most, if not all, of these maledictions, and says that these wicked acts were performed in Jerusalem, not that the entire city sinned but those who transgressed were the princes. However, when he mentions the wicked acts of the community, he does accuse the (entire) city, as it says, קָדָשַׁי בָּזִית וְאֶת שַׁבְּתֹתַי חִלָּלְתְּ, *My sanctities you spurned, My Sabbaths you desecrated* (ibid. v. 8).

NOTES

15. אָרוּר הָאִישׁ — *Cursed be the man*. The Talmud in tractate *Sotah* 31a describes how the tribes stood on the two mounts of Gerizim and Ebal while the *Kohanim* and Levites stood in the valley between these mountains and pronounced the blessings and curses, beginning in each instance with בָּרוּךְ, *blessed*, followed by אָרוּר, *cursed*. The *Sforno* quotes verse 12 in our chapter, which speaks of blessing, to prove that, indeed, each curse (not mentioned until verse 13) was preceded by a blessing. He explains that the twelve transgressions listed were not evil acts of the community, but those of certain powerful leaders, as we see from the verses cited in *Ezekiel* which mirror all the sins recorded in our *parashah*. Therefore, the Torah curses only the leaders and not the masses, for they were blameless, given their inability to prevent these mighty men from sinning. The wicked acts enumerated both here and in *Ezekiel* are the cardinal sins of bloodshed, idolatry and sexual immorality, as well as oppression of the weak and the accepting of bribes. All these are associated with the ruling class. For these acts, the populace would not be punished, although all Israel is responsible one for another, but that is true only when one has the power to protest and fails to do so (see tractate *Shabbos* 54b). The *Sforno*, however, points out that those sins mentioned in the Book of *Ezekiel* (but

to bless the people on Mount Gerizim, when you have crossed the Jordan:
Simeon, Levi, Judah, Issachar, Joseph, and Benjamin. 13 *And these shall*
stand for the curse on Mount Ebal: Reuben, Gad, Asher, Zebulun, Dan, and
Naphtali. 14 *The Levites shall speak up and say to every man of Israel, in a*
loud voice:
15 *'Accursed is the man who will make a graven or molten image, an*
abomination of HASHEM, *a craftsman's handiwork, and emplace it in secret.'*
And the entire people shall speak up and say, 'Amen.'
16 *'Accursed is one who degrades his father or mother.' And the entire*
people shall say, 'Amen.'
17 *'Accursed is one who moves the boundary of his fellow.' And the entire*
people shall say, 'Amen.'
18 *'Accursed is one who causes a blind person to go astray on the road.'*
And the entire people shall say, 'Amen.'
19 *'Accursed is one who perverts a judgment of a proselyte, orphan, or*
widow.' And the entire people shall say, 'Amen.'
20 *'Accursed is one who lies with the wife of his father, for he will have*
uncovered the robe of his father.' And the entire people shall say, 'Amen.'
21 *'Accursed is one who lies with any animal.' And the entire people shall*
say, 'Amen.'
22 *'Accursed is one who lies with his sister, the daughter of his father or*
the daughter of his mother.' And the entire people shall say, 'Amen.'
23 *'Accursed is one who lies with his mother-in-law.' And the entire*
people shall say, 'Amen.'
24 *'Accursed is one who strikes his fellow stealthily.' And the entire*
people shall say, 'Amen.'
25 *'Accursed is one who takes a bribe to kill a person of innocent blood.'*
And the entire people shall say, 'Amen.'
26 *'Accursed is one who will not uphold the words of this Torah, to*
perform them.' And the entire people shall say, 'Amen.' "

---

25. לֹקֵחַ שֹׁחַד לְהַכּוֹת — *That takes a bribe to slay* . . . such as Doeg the Edomite and the Ziphim, (who acted) to gain favor in the eyes of the king or to profit.

26. אֲשֶׁר לֹא יָקִים אֶת דִּבְרֵי הַתּוֹרָה הַזֹּאת לַעֲשׂוֹת אוֹתָם — *That does not confirm the words of this Torah to do them* . . . who does not fulfill and confirm that it is proper to do them *all*,

NOTES

not here), such as desecration of the Sabbath and the spurning of the holy, was practiced by many of the masses and therefore they would also be punished. The prophet indicates this liability and guilt of all the people by using the term עִיר, *city*.

25. לֹקֵחַ שֹׁחַד לְהַכּוֹת — *That takes a bribe to slay*. The *Sforno* realizes that this phrase cannot be interpreted literally, for then he would be guilty of murder, which is far more serious than bribery, hence why mention שֹׁחַד, *bribe*, at all? He therefore explains that this verse alludes to one whose actions are motivated by a desire to find favor in the eyes of another, which results in bloodshed. He gives two examples, which are recorded in *I Samuel*, chapters 22, 23. Doeg the Edomite informed King Saul that the *Kohanim* in the city of Nob had given David food and assisted him. As a result of this information, the *Kohanim* were executed. The Ziphim told the king that David was hiding in the hills of Hakhilah. In both instances, the reason for informing on David was to gain favor with Saul whose heart was filled with hatred for him. It is this form of bribery that the Torah speaks of and curses.

26. אֲשֶׁר לֹא יָקִים — *That does not confirm*. The *Sforno* interprets this verse to mean that even one

כח

א וְהָיָה אִם־שָׁמוֹעַ תִּשְׁמַע בְּקוֹל יהוה אֱלֹהֶיךָ לִשְׁמֹר לַעֲשׂוֹת אֶת־כָּל־
מִצְוֹתָיו אֲשֶׁר אָנֹכִי מְצַוְּךָ הַיּוֹם וּנְתָנְךָ יהוה אֱלֹהֶיךָ עֶלְיוֹן עַל כָּל־גּוֹיֵי
ב הָאָרֶץ: וּבָאוּ עָלֶיךָ כָּל־הַבְּרָכוֹת הָאֵלֶּה וְהִשִּׂיגֻךָ כִּי תִשְׁמַע בְּקוֹל יהוה
ג־ד אֱלֹהֶיךָ: בָּרוּךְ אַתָּה בָּעִיר וּבָרוּךְ אַתָּה בַּשָּׂדֶה: בָּרוּךְ פְּרִי־בִטְנְךָ וּפְרִי
ה אַדְמָתְךָ וּפְרִי בְהֶמְתֶּךָ שְׁגַר אֲלָפֶיךָ וְעַשְׁתְּרוֹת צֹאנֶךָ: בָּרוּךְ טַנְאֲךָ
ששי ו־ז וּמִשְׁאַרְתֶּךָ: בָּרוּךְ אַתָּה בְּבֹאֶךָ וּבָרוּךְ אַתָּה בְּצֵאתֶךָ: *יִתֵּן יהוה אֶת־
אֹיְבֶיךָ הַקָּמִים עָלֶיךָ נִגָּפִים לְפָנֶיךָ בְּדֶרֶךְ אֶחָד יֵצְאוּ אֵלֶיךָ וּבְשִׁבְעָה
ח דְרָכִים יָנוּסוּ לְפָנֶיךָ: יְצַו יהוה אִתְּךָ אֶת־הַבְּרָכָה בַּאֲסָמֶיךָ וּבְכֹל מִשְׁלַח
ט יָדֶךָ וּבֵרַכְךָ בָּאָרֶץ אֲשֶׁר־יהוה אֱלֹהֶיךָ נֹתֵן לָךְ: יְקִימְךָ יהוה לוֹ לְעַם
קָדוֹשׁ כַּאֲשֶׁר נִשְׁבַּע־לָךְ כִּי תִשְׁמֹר אֶת־מִצְוֹת יהוה אֱלֹהֶיךָ וְהָלַכְתָּ
י בִּדְרָכָיו: וְרָאוּ כָּל־עַמֵּי הָאָרֶץ כִּי שֵׁם יהוה נִקְרָא עָלֶיךָ וְיָרְאוּ מִמֶּךָּ:
יא וְהוֹתִרְךָ יהוה לְטוֹבָה בִּפְרִי בִטְנְךָ וּבִפְרִי בְהֶמְתְּךָ וּבִפְרִי אַדְמָתֶךָ עַל
יב הָאֲדָמָה אֲשֶׁר נִשְׁבַּע יהוה לַאֲבֹתֶיךָ לָתֶת לָךְ: יִפְתַּח יהוה | לְךָ
אֶת־אוֹצָרוֹ הַטּוֹב אֶת־הַשָּׁמַיִם לָתֵת מְטַר־אַרְצְךָ בְּעִתּוֹ וּלְבָרֵךְ אֵת
יג כָּל־מַעֲשֵׂה יָדֶךָ וְהִלְוִיתָ גּוֹיִם רַבִּים וְאַתָּה לֹא תִלְוֶה: וּנְתָנְךָ יהוה

---

but there will be a commandment which he will nullify; this refers to one who is an apostate (even) regarding one thing (commanded by God).

XXVIII

2. וּבָאוּ עָלֶיךָ כָּל הַבְּרָכוֹת הָאֵלֶּה וְהִשִּׂיגֻךָ — *And all these blessings shall come upon you and overtake you* . . . even though you will make no effort to attain them.

כִּי תִשְׁמַע בְּקוֹל ה' אֱלֹהֶיךָ — *If you shall listen to the voice of* H*ASHEM your God.* And this (shall come to pass) when your study of Torah will be your main concern (קֶבַע), and your ordinary work subsidiary (עֲרַאי) to it (based on *Berachos* 35b), and therefore the blessings shall overtake you without any effort (on your part). (Now,) behold, the blessings of the First Temple period are mentioned here, and (the Torah) tells us that they will merit them as long as they keep the commandments. (This section continues until) the verse, *HASHEM will establish you for a holy people to Himself* (v. 9), which refers to the early period of

NOTES

who accepts the entire Torah, except for one commandment which he denies and rejects, is guilty of not confirming the words of Torah and is therefore cursed. He bases this concept on the teaching of our Sages that one who professes that the entire Torah is of Divine origin except for one verse is guilty of heresy (*Sanhedrin* 99b). The *Rambam* in *Hilchos Teshuvah* 3:8 lists three כּוֹפְרִים, *heretics*; and included among them is one who denies the validity of "one verse or one letter" of the Torah.

XXVIII

2. וְהִשִּׂיגֻךָ כִּי תִשְׁמַע בְּקוֹל ה' אֱלֹהֶיךָ — *And overtake you if you shall listen to the voice of* H*ASHEM your God*. The difficulty with the word וְהִשִּׂיגֻךָ, *overtake you,* regarding a blessing is obvious. What person flees from a blessing that it should be necessary for the blessing to overtake him? The *Sforno* answers this question, explaining that the sense of the verse is as follows. Normally, one pursues success and material blessings. We, however, are promised that this will be unnecessary, for the blessings will find us without any effort on our part, providing we hearken to the voice of God and observe His commandments.

The *Sforno* is of the opinion that these verses of blessing (1-13) refer to the period of the First Temple, before the people of Israel sinned and deviated from the path of God. They refer also to the early period of the Second Temple during the forty years that Simeon the Righteous ministered as the *Kohen* Gadol and many blessings were showered on Israel and numerous miracles occurred in the Temple. The Mishnah (*Yoma* 39a) records a number of them including the following: The lot drawn on Yom Kippur with the Name of

28 1 *It shall be that if you hearken to the voice of HASHEM, your God, to
observe, to perform all of His commandments that I command you this
day, then HASHEM, your God, will make you supreme over all the nations of
the earth.* 2 *All these blessings will come upon you and overtake you, if you
hearken to the voice of HASHEM, your God:*
3 *Blessed shall you be in the city and blessed shall you be in the field.*
4 *Blessed shall be the fruit of your womb, and the fruit of your ground, and
the fruit of your animals; the offspring of your cattle and the flocks of your
sheep and goats.* 5 *Blessed shall be your fruit basket and your kneading bowl.*
6 *Blessed shall you be when you come in and blessed shall you be when you
go out.* 7 *HASHEM shall cause your enemies who rise up against you to be
struck down before you; on one road will they go out toward you and on
seven roads will they flee before you.* 8 *HASHEM will command the blessing
for you in your storehouses and your every undertaking; and He will bless
you in the Land that HASHEM, your God, gives you.* 9 *HASHEM will confirm
you for Himself as a holy people, as He swore to you — if you observe the
commandments of HASHEM, your God, and you go in His ways.* 10 *Then all
the peoples of the earth will see that the Name of HASHEM is proclaimed over
you, and they will revere you.* 11 *HASHEM shall give you bountiful goodness,
in the fruit of your womb and the fruit of your animals and the fruit of your
ground, on the ground that HASHEM swore to your forefathers to give you.*
12 *HASHEM shall open for you His storehouse of goodness, the heavens, to provide rain for your Land in its time, and to bless all your handiwork; you shall
lend to many nations, but you shall not borrow.* 13 *HASHEM shall place you*

---

the Second Temple, as our Sages tell us regarding the blessings (in the time) of Simeon the Righteous and the miracles which transpired in the Holy Temple in his lifetime.

10. וְרָאוּ כָּל עַמֵּי הָאָרֶץ — *And all the peoples of the earth shall see . . .* as our Sages tell us regarding Alexander who bowed down to Simeon (the Righteous).

11. וְהוֹתִרְךָ ה' לְטוֹבָה — *And HASHEM shall make you plenteous in goods.* Your material prosperity will be greater than that of others who (also) succeed materially. With these blessings, which occurred during the period of the Second Temple, this section concludes.

NOTES

God on it constantly came up in the right hand of the *Kohen*, which was considered an omen of good fortune; the crimson-colored strap tied on Yom Kippur between the horns of the bull turned white signifying that the sins of Israel were forgiven, and the light on the far right of the menorah was never extinguished. During this period of the Second Temple, a blessing was bestowed from on High on the *omer* (the measure of barley offered on the 16th day of Nissan), and upon the שְׁתֵּי הַלֶּחֶם (the two loaves of bread offered on Shevuos) and on the לֶחֶם הַפָּנִים (the "showbread" which was changed weekly in the Temple). All this occurred only sporadically after Simeon's death.

10. וְרָאוּ כָּל עַמֵּי הָאָרֶץ — *And all the peoples of the earth shall see.* The Sforno interprets the phrase, *that the Name of God is called upon you,* as referring to the awe and reverence aroused in powerful leaders of the nations upon seeing the radiance of sanctity shining forth from the pious men of Israel. He cites the episode recorded in *Yoma* 69a regarding Alexander the Macedonian and Simeon the Righteous. The Cutheans demanded that the Temple in Jerusalem be given to them so that they could destroy it. When Simeon the Righteous heard of this wicked plot, he put on his priestly garments and came to see Alexander the Great. When Alexander beheld Simeon approaching, he descended from his carriage and bowed before him. When he was asked why he did so, he responded, "It is his image which wins for me in all my battles." Looking at Simeon the *Kohen Gadol*, he saw the "Name of God" radiating from his face, and paid homage to him.

לְרֹאשׁ וְלֹא לְזָנָב וְהָיִיתָ רַק לְמַעְלָה וְלֹא תִהְיֶה לְמָטָּה כִּי־תִשְׁמַע
יד אֶל־מִצְוֺת | יהוה אֱלֹהֶיךָ אֲשֶׁר אָנֹכִי מְצַוְּךָ הַיּוֹם לִשְׁמֹר וְלַעֲשׂוֹת: וְלֹא
תָסוּר מִכָּל־הַדְּבָרִים אֲשֶׁר אָנֹכִי מְצַוֶּה אֶתְכֶם הַיּוֹם יָמִין וּשְׂמֹאול
לָלֶכֶת אַחֲרֵי אֱלֹהִים אֲחֵרִים לְעָבְדָם:
טו וְהָיָה אִם־לֹא תִשְׁמַע בְּקוֹל יהוה אֱלֹהֶיךָ לִשְׁמֹר לַעֲשׂוֹת אֶת־
כָּל־מִצְוֺתָיו וְחֻקֹּתָיו אֲשֶׁר אָנֹכִי מְצַוְּךָ הַיּוֹם וּבָאוּ עָלֶיךָ כָּל־הַקְּלָלוֹת
טז־יז הָאֵלֶּה וְהִשִּׂיגוּךָ: אָרוּר אַתָּה בָּעִיר וְאָרוּר אַתָּה בַּשָּׂדֶה: אָרוּר
יח טַנְאֲךָ וּמִשְׁאַרְתֶּךָ: אָרוּר פְּרִי־בִטְנְךָ וּפְרִי אַדְמָתֶךָ שְׁגַר אֲלָפֶיךָ
יט־כ וְעַשְׁתְּרֹת צֹאנֶךָ: אָרוּר אַתָּה בְּבֹאֶךָ וְאָרוּר אַתָּה בְּצֵאתֶךָ: יְשַׁלַּח יהוה |

14. וְלֹא תָסוּר מִכָּל הַדְּבָרִים אֲשֶׁר אָנֹכִי מְצַוֶּה אֶתְכֶם הַיּוֹם יָמִין וּשְׂמֹאול — *And you shall not turn aside from any of the words which I command you this day, to the right or to the left.* They shall not change the commandments of God, the Blessed One, especially regarding the judgments, nor exchange the other commandments with secular customs and with *commandments learned by rote* (מִצְוַת אֲנָשִׁים מְלֻמָּדָה — *Isaiah* 29:13). This is especially so when these are done in honor of the ancients who instituted these customs and not in honor of their Maker, nor for the purpose of strengthening the observance of His commandments. [For in such a manner you will *go after other gods to serve them*, and even more serious than this (practice) is the institution of a new religion in honor of the ancients who were considered as Elohim — judges in the land.] Now the curses and punishments up to the verse, *HASHEM will bring you and your king* (v. 36), occurred during the (period) of the Second Temple, in the days of the Greeks and others, until the kings of the House of the Hasmoneans besieged one another, and one of them (Aristobulos) was exiled at the behest of Pompey to Rome. From that verse, and until the verse, *You shall be plucked from off the land* (v. 63), (the Torah) refers to the period (culminating with) the destruction of the Temple at the hands of the Romans. From (that verse) on are the admonitions occurring in exile and related to it.

Now he begins the curse and rebuke (תּוֹכָחָה) saying, *It shall come to pass, if you will not listen to the voice of HASHEM your God to observe and do all His commandments and His statutes which I command you this day* (v. 15), this doubtless being when the observance of the *mitzvos* of the Torah were exchanged for various customs, and justice retrogressed. Now after (the Torah) says, *HASHEM will bring you and your king* (v. 36),

NOTES

14. וְלֹא תָסוּר מִכָּל הַדְּבָרִים — *And you shall not turn aside from any of the words.* The תּוֹכָחָה, *admonition,* is written in the Book of *Leviticus* and repeated in our *parashah.* A cursory examination of the two will reveal a number of differences. Our Sages tell us that the admonition recorded in *Leviticus* came directly from God, while the one recorded in our *parashah* was uttered by Moses in his own name. In the former, Israel is addressed in the plural, while in the latter they are addressed in the singular (*Megillah* 31b). The chastisements uttered by Moses are more numerous than those uttered in the name of God (*Bava Basra* 88b). The early Bible commentators are of the opinion that these chastisements are not simply admonitions and warnings, but a prophetic vision of events which would transpire during various periods. The *Ramban* states that the תּוֹכָחָה in *Leviticus* speaks of the First Temple period, while the admonition in *Ki Savo* alludes to the period of the Second Temple. The *Abarbanel,* on the other hand, does not divide the two chapters of curses and punishments in this manner, but is of the opinion that they are part of one whole, covering the period from the destruction of the First Temple to the ultimate exile from the Land following the destruction of the Second Temple.

The *Sforno,* in his commentary on *Leviticus* 26:16-33, interprets those verses as referring to the period following the leadership of Deborah, the destruction of the Sanctuary at Shiloh, the exile of the Ten Tribes and finally, the destruction of the First Temple. He interprets the later verses (ibid. 42-45) as alluding to the Second Temple and

as a head and not as a tail; you shall be only above and you shall not be below — if you hearken to the commandments of HASHEM, *your God, that I command you today, to observe and to perform;*
14 *and you do not turn away from any of the words that I command you this day, right or left, to follow gods of others, to worship them.*
15 *But it will be that if you do not hearken to the voice of* HASHEM, *your God, to observe, to perform all His commandments and all His decrees that I command you today, then all these curses will come upon you and overtake you:*
16 *Accursed will you be in the city and accursed will you be in the field.*
17 *Accursed will be your fruit basket and your kneading bowl.*
18 *Accursed will be the fruit of your womb and the fruit of your ground, the offspring of your cattle and the flocks of your sheep and goats.*
19 *Accursed will you be when you come in and accursed will you be when you go out.*
20 HASHEM *will send*

---

which is the second part (of the תּוֹכָחָה), it repeats (the reason), *because you did not listen to the voice of* HASHEM *your God to keep His commandments and His statutes which He commanded you* (v. 45) — meaning that you did (however) keep that which was commanded or instituted as customs by others (which are) not in (keeping) with His Torah, as our Sages have told us that they ceased giving תְּרוּמָה, *the heave offering*, and מַעַשְׂרוֹת, *tithes*, which necessitated Jochanan the *Kohen Gadol* to institute the law of דְּמַאי (the produce of an *am haaretz* which had to be tithed), and Hillel had to institute the *pruzbul* because "the door was being closed" to borrowers for fear of the Sabbatical year (cancellation of debts). Also, due to the increase of iniquity at the end of the Second Temple period, the ritual of the water of the suspected adulteress (סוֹטָה) and the ceremony of the heifer whose neck was broken (עֶגְלָה עֲרוּפָה) were discontinued (*Sotah* 47a), and the Sanhedrin ceased to function (ibid. 48a), in a manner that all justice was nullified, as our Sages tell us, *Men of violence grew powerful* (ibid. 49a), and thus, they and their possessions were confiscated (lost). [Similar to the condition prevalent today in all our exiles and our debasement, when wealthy people, especially those who are liable according to (Torah) law, reject the Torah of God, the Blessed One, and the laws of His mouth, and through the medium of gentiles and their courts boldly pervert (justice) in their disputes with others.] And with these (verses), the cause of the destruction of the Second Temple is explained, and the continuance of the Exile due to the continuance of its cause.

NOTES

the return from Babylonia to the Land of Israel. In his commentary on our *parashah*, the *Sforno* interprets the blessings at the beginning of this chapter as applying to the early period of the Second Temple, a time when blessings and miracles would occur and the prosperity of Israel would be very great. The curses and punishments, according to him, would take place at a later period, after the death of Simeon the *Kohen Gadol*, when Israel would sin and deviate from the path of God. During that period, a variety of תַּקָּנוֹת, *ordinances*, would be instituted, necessitated by the weakening of Israel's commitment to the law and an erosion of their faith in the Almighty. Toward the end of the Second Temple period, a number of Biblical rituals and ceremonies would also be suspended, due to the misconduct of the Jewish people. The Mishnah (*Sotah* 47a) states: "When adulterers multiplied, the ceremony of the bitter waters (מֵי סוֹטָה) was discontinued and when murderers multiplied, the ceremony of the breaking of the heifer's neck (עֶגְלָה עֲרוּפָה) was discontinued." The Sanhedrin ceased to function when "men of violence grew powerful" (ibid. 49a). All this, according to the *Sforno*, is reflected in this *parashah*.

It is interesting to note that the *Sforno's* commentary, as printed in the מִקְרָאוֹת גְּדוֹלוֹת (the standard edition of the *Chumash*), was apparently censored and a number of sentences which appear in the Mosad Harav Kook edition were eliminated, since they refer in one case to the Christian faith and in another to powerful, rich Jews of his generation. These sentences are bracketed in this edition, and the perceptive reader can see why the censor chose to delete them.

בְּךָ֗ אֶת־הַמְּאֵרָה֙ אֶת־הַמְּהוּמָה֙ וְאֶת־הַמִּגְעֶ֔רֶת בְּכָל־מִשְׁלַ֥ח יָדְךָ֖
אֲשֶׁ֣ר תַּעֲשֶׂ֑ה עַ֣ד הִשָּֽׁמֶדְךָ֞ וְעַד־אֲבָדְךָ֣ מַהֵ֔ר מִפְּנֵ֛י רֹ֥עַ מַעֲלָלֶ֖יךָ אֲשֶׁ֥ר
כא עֲזַבְתָּֽנִי׃ יַדְבֵּ֧ק יְהוָ֛ה בְּךָ֖ אֶת־הַדָּ֑בֶר עַ֚ד כַּלֹּת֣וֹ אֹֽתְךָ֔ מֵעַל֙ הָאֲדָמָ֔ה
כב אֲשֶׁר־אַתָּ֥ה בָא־שָׁ֖מָּה לְרִשְׁתָּֽהּ׃ יַכְּכָ֣ה יְ֠הוָה בַּשַּׁחֶ֨פֶת וּבַקַּדַּ֜חַת
כג וּבַדַּלֶּ֗קֶת וּבַֽחַרְחֻר֙ וּבַחֶ֔רֶב וּבַשִּׁדָּפ֖וֹן וּבַיֵּרָק֑וֹן וּרְדָפ֖וּךָ עַ֥ד אָבְדֶֽךָ׃ וְהָי֥וּ
כד שָׁמֶ֛יךָ אֲשֶׁ֥ר עַל־רֹאשְׁךָ֖ נְח֑שֶׁת וְהָאָ֥רֶץ אֲשֶׁר־תַּחְתֶּ֖יךָ בַּרְזֶֽל׃ יִתֵּ֧ן יְהוָ֛ה
כה אֶת־מְטַ֥ר אַרְצְךָ֖ אָבָ֣ק וְעָפָ֑ר מִן־הַשָּׁמַ֙יִם֙ יֵרֵ֣ד עָלֶ֔יךָ עַ֖ד הִשָּֽׁמְדָֽךְ׃ יִתֶּנְךָ֨
יְהוָ֥ה ׀ נִגָּף֮ לִפְנֵ֣י אֹיְבֶ֒יךָ֒ בְּדֶ֤רֶךְ אֶחָד֙ תֵּצֵ֣א אֵלָ֔יו וּבְשִׁבְעָ֥ה דְרָכִ֖ים תָּנ֣וּס
כו לְפָנָ֑יו וְהָיִ֣יתָ לְזַעֲוָ֔ה לְכֹ֖ל מַמְלְכ֥וֹת הָאָֽרֶץ׃ וְהָיְתָ֤ה נִבְלָֽתְךָ֙ לְמַאֲכָ֔ל
כז לְכָל־ע֥וֹף הַשָּׁמַ֖יִם וּלְבֶהֱמַ֣ת הָאָ֑רֶץ וְאֵ֖ין מַחֲרִֽיד׃ יַכְּכָ֨ה יְהוָ֜ה בִּשְׁחִ֤ין
כח מִצְרַ֙יִם֙ °ובעפלים וּבַגָּרָ֖ב וּבֶחָ֑רֶס אֲשֶׁ֥ר לֹא־תוּכַ֖ל לְהֵרָפֵֽא׃ יַכְּכָ֣ה °וּבַטְּחֹרִים ק׳
כט יְהוָ֔ה בְּשִׁגָּע֖וֹן וּבְעִוָּר֑וֹן וּבְתִמְה֖וֹן לֵבָֽב׃ וְהָיִ֜יתָ מְמַשֵּׁ֣שׁ בַּֽצָּהֳרַ֗יִם כַּאֲשֶׁ֨ר
יְמַשֵּׁ֤שׁ הָֽעִוֵּר֙ בָּאֲפֵלָ֔ה וְלֹ֥א תַצְלִ֖יחַ אֶת־דְּרָכֶ֑יךָ וְהָיִ֜יתָ אַ֣ךְ עָשׁ֧וּק וְגָז֛וּל
ל כָּל־הַיָּמִ֖ים וְאֵ֥ין מוֹשִֽׁיעַ׃ אִשָּׁ֣ה תְאָרֵ֗שׂ וְאִ֤ישׁ אַחֵר֙ °ישגלנה בַּ֥יִת °יִשְׁכָּבֶנָּה ק׳
לא תִּבְנֶ֖ה וְלֹא־תֵשֵׁ֣ב בּ֑וֹ כֶּ֥רֶם תִּטַּ֖ע וְלֹ֥א תְחַלְּלֶֽנּוּ׃ שֽׁוֹרְךָ֞ טָב֣וּחַ לְעֵינֶ֗יךָ
וְלֹ֣א תֹאכַל֮ מִמֶּ֒נּוּ֒ חֲמֹֽרְךָ֙ גָּז֣וּל מִלְּפָנֶ֔יךָ וְלֹ֥א יָשׁ֖וּב לָ֑ךְ צֹֽאנְךָ֙ נְתֻנ֣וֹת
לב לְאֹיְבֶ֔יךָ וְאֵ֥ין לְךָ֖ מוֹשִֽׁיעַ׃ בָּנֶ֨יךָ וּבְנֹתֶ֜יךָ נְתֻנִ֨ים לְעַ֤ם אַחֵר֙ וְעֵינֶ֣יךָ
לג רֹא֔וֹת וְכָל֥וֹת אֲלֵיהֶ֖ם כָּל־הַיּ֑וֹם וְאֵ֖ין לְאֵ֥ל יָדֶֽךָ׃ פְּרִ֤י אַדְמָֽתְךָ֙
וְכָל־יְגִ֣יעֲךָ֔ יֹאכַ֥ל עַ֖ם אֲשֶׁ֣ר לֹא־יָדָ֑עְתָּ וְהָיִ֗יתָ רַ֛ק עָשׁ֥וּק וְרָצ֖וּץ
לד־לה כָּל־הַיָּמִֽים׃ וְהָיִ֖יתָ מְשֻׁגָּ֑ע מִמַּרְאֵ֥ה עֵינֶ֖יךָ אֲשֶׁ֥ר תִּרְאֶֽה׃ יַכְּכָ֨ה יְהוָ֜ה
בִּשְׁחִ֣ין רָ֗ע עַל־הַבִּרְכַּ֙יִם֙ וְעַל־הַשֹּׁקַ֔יִם אֲשֶׁ֥ר לֹא־תוּכַ֖ל לְהֵרָפֵ֑א מִכַּ֥ף
לו רַגְלְךָ֖ וְעַ֥ד קָדְקֳדֶֽךָ׃ יוֹלֵ֨ךְ יְהוָ֜ה אֹֽתְךָ֗ וְאֶֽת־מַלְכְּךָ֙ אֲשֶׁ֣ר תָּקִ֣ים עָלֶ֔יךָ
אֶל־גּ֕וֹי אֲשֶׁ֥ר לֹא־יָדַ֖עְתָּ אַתָּ֣ה וַאֲבֹתֶ֑יךָ וְעָבַ֥דְתָּ שָּׁ֛ם אֱלֹהִ֥ים אֲחֵרִ֖ים
לז עֵ֥ץ וָאָֽבֶן׃ וְהָיִ֣יתָ לְשַׁמָּ֔ה לְמָשָׁ֖ל וְלִשְׁנִינָ֑ה בְּכֹל֙ הָֽעַמִּ֔ים אֲשֶׁר־יְנַהֶגְךָ֥
לח יְהוָ֖ה שָֽׁמָּה׃ זֶ֥רַע רַ֖ב תּוֹצִ֣יא הַשָּׂדֶ֑ה וּמְעַ֣ט תֶּאֱסֹ֔ף כִּ֥י יַחְסְלֶ֖נּוּ הָאַרְבֶּֽה׃
לט כְּרָמִ֥ים תִּטַּ֖ע וְעָבָ֑דְתָּ וְיַ֤יִן לֹא־תִשְׁתֶּה֙ וְלֹ֣א תֶאֱגֹ֔ר כִּ֥י תֹאכְלֶ֖נּוּ
מ הַתֹּלָֽעַת׃ זֵיתִ֛ים יִהְי֥וּ לְךָ֖ בְּכָל־גְּבוּלֶ֑ךָ וְשֶׁ֙מֶן֙ לֹ֣א תָס֔וּךְ כִּ֥י יִשַּׁ֖ל זֵיתֶֽךָ׃
מא־מב בָּנִ֥ים וּבָנ֖וֹת תּוֹלִ֑יד וְלֹא־יִהְי֣וּ לָ֔ךְ כִּ֥י יֵלְכ֖וּ בַּשֶּֽׁבִי׃ כָּל־עֵצְךָ֖ וּפְרִ֣י
מג אַדְמָתֶ֑ךָ יְיָרֵ֖שׁ הַצְּלָצַֽל׃ הַגֵּר֙ אֲשֶׁ֣ר בְּקִרְבְּךָ֔ יַעֲלֶ֥ה עָלֶ֖יךָ מַ֣עְלָה מָּ֑עְלָה
מד וְאַתָּ֥ה תֵרֵ֖ד מַ֥טָּה מָּֽטָּה׃ ה֣וּא יַלְוְךָ֔ וְאַתָּ֖ה לֹ֣א תַלְוֶ֑נּוּ ה֚וּא יִהְיֶ֣ה לְרֹ֔אשׁ
מה וְאַתָּ֖ה תִּהְיֶ֥ה לְזָנָֽב׃ וּבָ֨אוּ עָלֶ֜יךָ כָּל־הַקְּלָל֣וֹת הָאֵ֗לֶּה וּרְדָפ֙וּךָ֙ וְהִשִּׂיג֔וּךָ
עַ֖ד הִשָּֽׁמְדָ֑ךְ כִּי־לֹ֣א שָׁמַ֗עְתָּ בְּקוֹל֙ יְהוָ֣ה אֱלֹהֶ֔יךָ לִשְׁמֹ֛ר מִצְוֺתָ֥יו
מו־מז וְחֻקֹּתָ֖יו אֲשֶׁ֥ר צִוָּֽךְ׃ וְהָי֣וּ בְךָ֔ לְא֖וֹת וּלְמוֹפֵ֑ת וּֽבְזַרְעֲךָ֖ עַד־עוֹלָֽם׃ תַּ֗חַת
אֲשֶׁ֤ר לֹא־עָבַ֙דְתָּ֙ אֶת־יְהוָ֣ה אֱלֹהֶ֔יךָ בְּשִׂמְחָ֖ה וּבְט֣וּב לֵבָ֑ב מֵרֹ֖ב כֹּֽל׃

in your midst attrition, confusion, and worry, in your every undertaking that you
will do, until you are destroyed, and until you are quickly annihilated, because
of the evil of your deeds, for having forsaken Me. 21 HASHEM will attach the plague
to you, until it consumes you from upon the ground to which you are coming, to
possess it. 22 HASHEM will strike you with swelling lesions, with fever, with
burning heat, with thirst, and with sword; and with wind blasts and with
withering — and they will pursue you until your destruction. 23 Your heavens over
your head will be copper and the land beneath you will be iron. 24 HASHEM will
make the rain of your Land dust and dirt; from the heaven it will descend upon
you until you are destroyed. 25 HASHEM will cause you to be struck down before
your enemies; on one road you will go out against him, but on seven roads will you
flee before him; and you will be a cause of terror to all the kingdoms of the earth.
26 Your carcass will be food for every bird of the sky and animal of the
earth, and nothing will frighten them. 27 HASHEM will strike you with the boils
of Egypt, with hemorrhoids, with wet boils and dry boils, of which you cannot be
cured. 28 HASHEM will strike you with madness and with blindness, and with
confounding of the heart. 29 You will grope at noontime as a blind man gropes in
the darkness, but you will not succeed on your way; you will be only cheated and
robbed all the days, and there will be no savior. 30 You will betroth a woman, but
another man will lie with her; you will build a house, but you will not dwell in it;
you will plant a vineyard, but you will not redeem it. 31 Your ox will be slaughtered
before your eyes, but you will not eat from it; your donkey will be robbed from
before you, but it will not return to you; your flocks will be given to your enemies,
and you will have no savior. 32 Your sons and daughters will be given to another
people — and your eyes will see and pine in vain for them all day long, but your
hand will be powerless. 33 A nation unknown to you will devour the fruit of your
ground and all your labor, and you will be only cheated and downtrodden all the
days. 34 You will go mad from the sight of your eyes that you will see. 35 HASHEM
will strike you with a foul boil, on the knees and on the legs, that cannot be cured,
from the sole of your foot to your crown. 36 HASHEM will lead you and your king
whom you will set up over yourself to a nation you never knew — neither you
nor your forefathers — and there you will work for the gods of others — of wood
and of stone. 37 You will be a source of astonishment, a parable, and a conversation
piece, among all the peoples where HASHEM will lead you. 38 You will take
abundant seed out to the field, but you will harvest little, for the locust will devour
it. 39 You will plant vineyards and work them, but you will not drink and you will
not gather in, for the worm will eat it. 40 You will have olive trees throughout your
boundaries, but you will not anoint with oil, for your olives will drop. 41 You will
bear sons and daughters, but they will not be yours, for they will go into captivity.
42 All your trees and the fruits of your ground, the chirping locust will impoverish.
43 The stranger who is among you will ascend higher and higher, while you will
descend lower and lower. 44 He will lend to you, but you will not lend to him;
he will be a head, but you will be a tail. 45 All these curses will come upon you
and pursue you and overtake you, until you are destroyed, because you will not
have hearkened to the voice of HASHEM, your God, to observe His commandments and decrees that He commanded you. 46 They will be a sign and a wonder,
in you and in your offspring, forever, 47 because you did not serve HASHEM, your
God, amid gladness and goodness of heart, when everything was abundant.

מח וְעָבַדְתָּ אֶת־אֹיְבֶיךָ אֲשֶׁר יְשַׁלְּחֶנּוּ יהוה בָּךְ בְּרָעָב וּבְצָמָא וּבְעֵירֹם וּבְחֹסֶר
מט כֹּל וְנָתַן עֹל בַּרְזֶל עַל־צַוָּארֶךָ עַד הִשְׁמִידוֹ אֹתָךְ׃ יִשָּׂא יהוה עָלֶיךָ גּוֹי
נ מֵרָחֹק מִקְצֵה הָאָרֶץ כַּאֲשֶׁר יִדְאֶה הַנָּשֶׁר גּוֹי אֲשֶׁר לֹא־תִשְׁמַע לְשֹׁנוֹ׃ גּוֹי
נא עַז פָּנִים אֲשֶׁר לֹא־יִשָּׂא פָנִים לְזָקֵן וְנַעַר לֹא יָחֹן׃ וְאָכַל פְּרִי בְהֶמְתְּךָ
וּפְרִי־אַדְמָתְךָ עַד הִשָּׁמְדָךְ אֲשֶׁר לֹא־יַשְׁאִיר לְךָ דָּגָן תִּירוֹשׁ וְיִצְהָר שְׁגַר
נב אֲלָפֶיךָ וְעַשְׁתְּרֹת צֹאנֶךָ עַד הַאֲבִידוֹ אֹתָךְ׃ וְהֵצַר לְךָ בְּכָל־שְׁעָרֶיךָ עַד
רֶדֶת חֹמֹתֶיךָ הַגְּבֹהֹת וְהַבְּצֻרוֹת אֲשֶׁר אַתָּה בֹּטֵחַ בָּהֵן בְּכָל־אַרְצֶךָ וְהֵצַר
נג לְךָ בְּכָל־שְׁעָרֶיךָ בְּכָל־אַרְצְךָ אֲשֶׁר נָתַן יהוה אֱלֹהֶיךָ לָךְ׃ וְאָכַלְתָּ פְרִי־
בִטְנְךָ בְּשַׂר בָּנֶיךָ וּבְנֹתֶיךָ אֲשֶׁר נָתַן־לְךָ יהוה אֱלֹהֶיךָ בְּמָצוֹר וּבְמָצוֹק
נד אֲשֶׁר־יָצִיק לְךָ אֹיְבֶךָ׃ הָאִישׁ הָרַךְ בְּךָ וְהֶעָנֹג מְאֹד תֵּרַע עֵינוֹ בְאָחִיו
נה וּבְאֵשֶׁת חֵיקוֹ וּבְיֶתֶר בָּנָיו אֲשֶׁר יוֹתִיר׃ מִתֵּת ׀ לְאַחַד מֵהֶם מִבְּשַׂר בָּנָיו
אֲשֶׁר יֹאכֵל מִבְּלִי הִשְׁאִיר־לוֹ כֹּל בְּמָצוֹר וּבְמָצוֹק אֲשֶׁר יָצִיק לְךָ אֹיִבְךָ
נו בְּכָל־שְׁעָרֶיךָ׃ הָרַכָּה בְךָ וְהָעֲנֻגָּה אֲשֶׁר לֹא־נִסְּתָה כַף־רַגְלָהּ הַצֵּג עַל־
נז הָאָרֶץ מֵהִתְעַנֵּג וּמֵרֹךְ תֵּרַע עֵינָהּ בְּאִישׁ חֵיקָהּ וּבִבְנָהּ וּבְבִתָּהּ׃ וּבְשִׁלְיָתָהּ
הַיּוֹצֵת ׀ מִבֵּין רַגְלֶיהָ וּבְבָנֶיהָ אֲשֶׁר תֵּלֵד כִּי־תֹאכְלֵם בְּחֹסֶר־כֹּל בַּסָּתֶר
נח בְּמָצוֹר וּבְמָצוֹק אֲשֶׁר יָצִיק לְךָ אֹיִבְךָ בִּשְׁעָרֶיךָ׃ אִם־לֹא תִשְׁמֹר לַעֲשׂוֹת
אֶת־כָּל־דִּבְרֵי הַתּוֹרָה הַזֹּאת הַכְּתֻבִים בַּסֵּפֶר הַזֶּה לְיִרְאָה אֶת־הַשֵּׁם
נט הַנִּכְבָּד וְהַנּוֹרָא הַזֶּה אֵת יהוה אֱלֹהֶיךָ׃ וְהִפְלָא יהוה אֶת־מַכֹּתְךָ וְאֵת
ס מַכּוֹת זַרְעֶךָ מַכּוֹת גְּדֹלֹת וְנֶאֱמָנוֹת וָחֳלָיִם רָעִים וְנֶאֱמָנִים׃ וְהֵשִׁיב בְּךָ אֵת
סא כָּל־מַדְוֵה מִצְרַיִם אֲשֶׁר יָגֹרְתָּ מִפְּנֵיהֶם וְדָבְקוּ בָּךְ׃ גַּם כָּל־חֳלִי וְכָל־מַכָּה
אֲשֶׁר לֹא כָתוּב בְּסֵפֶר הַתּוֹרָה הַזֹּאת יַעְלֵם יהוה עָלֶיךָ עַד הִשָּׁמְדָךְ׃
סב וְנִשְׁאַרְתֶּם בִּמְתֵי מְעָט תַּחַת אֲשֶׁר הֱיִיתֶם כְּכוֹכְבֵי הַשָּׁמַיִם לָרֹב כִּי־לֹא
סג שָׁמַעְתָּ בְּקוֹל יהוה אֱלֹהֶיךָ׃ וְהָיָה כַּאֲשֶׁר־שָׂשׂ יהוה עֲלֵיכֶם לְהֵיטִיב
אֶתְכֶם וּלְהַרְבּוֹת אֶתְכֶם כֵּן יָשִׂישׂ יהוה עֲלֵיכֶם לְהַאֲבִיד אֶתְכֶם וּלְהַשְׁמִיד
סד אֶתְכֶם וְנִסַּחְתֶּם מֵעַל הָאֲדָמָה אֲשֶׁר־אַתָּה בָא־שָׁמָּה לְרִשְׁתָּהּ׃ וֶהֱפִיצְךָ
יהוה בְּכָל־הָעַמִּים מִקְצֵה הָאָרֶץ וְעַד־קְצֵה הָאָרֶץ וְעָבַדְתָּ שָּׁם אֱלֹהִים
סה אֲחֵרִים אֲשֶׁר לֹא־יָדַעְתָּ אַתָּה וַאֲבֹתֶיךָ עֵץ וָאָבֶן׃ וּבַגּוֹיִם הָהֵם לֹא תַרְגִּיעַ
וְלֹא־יִהְיֶה מָנוֹחַ לְכַף־רַגְלֶךָ וְנָתַן יהוה לְךָ שָׁם לֵב רַגָּז וְכִלְיוֹן עֵינַיִם
סו וְדַאֲבוֹן נָפֶשׁ׃ וְהָיוּ חַיֶּיךָ תְּלֻאִים לְךָ מִנֶּגֶד וּפָחַדְתָּ לַיְלָה וְיוֹמָם וְלֹא תַאֲמִין
סז בְּחַיֶּיךָ׃ בַּבֹּקֶר תֹּאמַר מִי־יִתֵּן עֶרֶב וּבָעֶרֶב תֹּאמַר מִי־יִתֵּן בֹּקֶר מִפַּחַד
סח לְבָבְךָ אֲשֶׁר תִּפְחָד וּמִמַּרְאֵה עֵינֶיךָ אֲשֶׁר תִּרְאֶה׃ וֶהֱשִׁיבְךָ יהוה ׀ מִצְרַיִם
בָּאֳנִיּוֹת בַּדֶּרֶךְ אֲשֶׁר אָמַרְתִּי לְךָ לֹא־תֹסִיף עוֹד לִרְאֹתָהּ וְהִתְמַכַּרְתֶּם

68. וְהִתְמַכַּרְתֶּם — *And you shall attempt to sell.* You will attempt to do a variety of labors to sustain yourself in the midst of the nations.

NOTES

68. וְהִתְמַכַּרְתֶּם וְאֵין קֹנֶה — *And you shall attempt to sell and none will purchase*. The *Sforno* explains that even at a time when slavery would no longer prevail, this verse will still be relevant. The meaning of the verse is that the attitude of gentile society toward the Jew will be such, that any

48 *So you will serve your enemies whom HASHEM will send against you, in hunger
and in thirst, in nakedness and without anything; and he will put an iron yoke on
your neck, until he destroys you.* 49 *HASHEM will carry against you a nation from
afar, from the end of the earth, as an eagle will swoop, a nation whose language you
will not understand,* 50 *a brazen nation that will not be respectful to the old nor
gracious to the young.* 51 *It will devour the fruit of your animals and the fruit of
your ground, until you are destroyed — it will not leave you grain, wine, or oil,
offspring of your cattle or flocks of your sheep and goats — until it causes you to
perish.* 52 *It will besiege you in all your cities, until the collapse of your high and
fortified walls in which you trusted throughout your Land; it will besiege you in all
your cities, in all your Land, which HASHEM, your God, has given you.* 53 *You will
eat the fruit of your womb — the flesh of your sons and daughters, which HASHEM,
your God, had given you — in the siege and distress that your enemy will distress
you.* 54 *The man among you who is tender and very delicate will turn selfish
against his brother and the wife of his bosom, and against the remaining children
that he has let survive,* 55 *not to give even one of them of the flesh of his children
that he will eat, not leaving anything for him, in the siege and distress that your
enemy will distress you in all your cities.* 56 *The tender and delicate woman among
you, who had never tried to set the sole of her foot on the ground, because of
delicacy and tenderness, will turn selfish against the husband of her bosom, and
against her son and daughter,* 57 *against the afterbirth that emerges from between
her legs, and against her children whom she will bear — for she will eat them in
secret for lack of anything, in the siege and distress that your enemy will distress
you in your cities.* 58 *If you will not be careful to perform all the words of this Torah
that are written in this Book, to fear this honored and awesome Name: HASHEM,
your God,* 59 *then HASHEM will make extraordinary your blows and the blows of
your offspring — great and faithful blows, and evil and faithful illnesses.* 60 *He will
bring back upon you all the sufferings of Egypt, of which you were terrified, and
they will cleave to you.* 61 *Even any illness and any blow that is not written in this
Book of the Torah, HASHEM will bring upon you, until you are destroyed.* 62 *You will
be left few in number, instead of having been like the stars of heaven in abundance,
for you will not have hearkened to the voice of HASHEM, your God.* 63 *And it will be
that just as HASHEM rejoiced over you to benefit you and multiply you, so HASHEM
will cause them to rejoice over you to make you perish and to destroy you; and you
will be torn from upon the ground to which you come to possess it.* 64 *HASHEM will
scatter you among all the peoples, from the end of the earth to the end of the earth,
and there you will work for gods of others, whom you did not know — you or your
forefathers — of wood and of stone.* 65 *And among those nations you will not be
tranquil, there will be no rest for the sole of your foot; there HASHEM will give
you a trembling heart, longing of eyes, and suffering of soul.* 66 *Your life will
hang in the balance, and you will be frightened night and day, and you will not be
sure of your livelihood.* 67 *In the morning you will say, "Who can give back last
night!" And in the evening you will say, "Who can give back this morning!" —
for the fright of your heart that you will fear and the sight of your eyes that you
will see.* 68 *HASHEM will return you to Egypt in ships, on the road of which I said
to you, "You shall never again see it!" And there you will offer yourselves for sale*

NOTES

attempt by Jews to earn an honest livelihood will be thwarted by the refusal of their gentile neighbors to utilize their services or patronize their business establishments. This will be motivated by

סט שָׁם לְאֹיְבֶיךָ לַעֲבָדִים וְלִשְׁפָחוֹת וְאֵין קֹנֶה׃ אֵלֶּה דִבְרֵי
הַבְּרִית אֲשֶׁר־צִוָּה יהוה אֶת־מֹשֶׁה לִכְרֹת אֶת־בְּנֵי יִשְׂרָאֵל בְּאֶרֶץ מוֹאָב
מִלְּבַד הַבְּרִית אֲשֶׁר־כָּרַת אִתָּם בְּחֹרֵב׃

כט שביעי א וַיִּקְרָא מֹשֶׁה אֶל־כָּל־יִשְׂרָאֵל וַיֹּאמֶר אֲלֵהֶם אַתֶּם רְאִיתֶם אֵת
כָּל־אֲשֶׁר עָשָׂה יהוה לְעֵינֵיכֶם בְּאֶרֶץ מִצְרַיִם לְפַרְעֹה וּלְכָל־עֲבָדָיו
ב וּלְכָל־אַרְצוֹ׃ הַמַּסּוֹת הַגְּדֹלֹת אֲשֶׁר רָאוּ עֵינֶיךָ הָאֹתֹת וְהַמֹּפְתִים
ג הַגְּדֹלִים הָהֵם׃ וְלֹא־נָתַן יהוה לָכֶם לֵב לָדַעַת וְעֵינַיִם לִרְאוֹת וְאָזְנַיִם
ד לִשְׁמֹעַ עַד הַיּוֹם הַזֶּה׃ וָאוֹלֵךְ אֶתְכֶם אַרְבָּעִים שָׁנָה בַּמִּדְבָּר לֹא־בָלוּ
ה שַׂלְמֹתֵיכֶם מֵעֲלֵיכֶם וְנַעַלְךָ לֹא־בָלְתָה מֵעַל רַגְלֶךָ׃ לֶחֶם לֹא אֲכַלְתֶּם
מפטיר ו וְיַיִן וְשֵׁכָר לֹא שְׁתִיתֶם לְמַעַן תֵּדְעוּ כִּי אֲנִי יהוה אֱלֹהֵיכֶם׃ וַתָּבֹאוּ
אֶל־הַמָּקוֹם הַזֶּה וַיֵּצֵא סִיחֹן מֶלֶךְ־חֶשְׁבּוֹן וְעוֹג מֶלֶךְ־הַבָּשָׁן לִקְרָאתֵנוּ
ז לַמִּלְחָמָה וַנַּכֵּם׃ וַנִּקַּח אֶת־אַרְצָם וַנִּתְּנָהּ לְנַחֲלָה לָראוּבֵנִי וְלַגָּדִי וְלַחֲצִי
ח שֵׁבֶט הַמְנַשִּׁי׃ וּשְׁמַרְתֶּם אֶת־דִּבְרֵי הַבְּרִית הַזֹּאת וַעֲשִׂיתֶם אֹתָם לְמַעַן
תַּשְׂכִּילוּ אֵת כָּל־אֲשֶׁר תַּעֲשׂוּן׃

וְאֵין קֹנֶה — *And none will purchase.* Not one of them will want (to pay for) your labors, so that you will be unable to earn a livelihood from it.

XXIX

3. וְלֹא נָתַן ה׳ לָכֶם לֵב לָדַעַת — *But HASHEM has not given you a heart to know.* Even though He, the Exalted One, attempted through His teachings and wonders to give you *a heart to know* as it says, וּלְמַעַן תְּסַפֵּר . . . וִידַעְתֶּם כִּי אֲנִי ה׳, *That you may tell . . . that you may know that I am HASHEM* (*Exodus* 10:2), (nonetheless) this intended (goal) was not realized because of your numerous insubordinations.

4. וָאוֹלֵךְ אֶתְכֶם — *And I led you.* However, after you have seen the many kindnesses done

NOTES

their animosity toward Israel.

XXIX

3. וְלֹא נָתַן ה׳ לָכֶם לֵב לָדַעַת — *But HASHEM has not given you a heart to know.* The verse cannot be understood as meaning that God did not give them the *ability* to understand. Rather, it means that they did not have the *will* to do so. The *Sforno* proves this point by citing the verse in *Exodus* 10:2, where the Almighty tells Moses that He purposely hardened Pharaoh's heart so that He might show His signs and wonders to Israel for the express purpose of educating generations of Israel that they *may know* that He is God. In spite of this effort, the people of Israel did not reach that level of knowledge until *this day* — forty years later! The *Sforno's* commentary explains the link between this verse and the previous two verses (1-2) which speak of the deeds wrought by God in Egypt and the signs and wonders winessed by Israel.

to your enemies as slaves and maidservants — but there will be no buyer!
69 *These are the words of the covenant that HASHEM commanded Moses*
to seal with the Children of Israel in the land of Moab, beside the covenant
that He sealed with them in Horeb.

29 1 *Moses summoned all of Israel and said to them, "You have seen*
everything that HASHEM did before your eyes in the land of Egypt, to
Pharaoh and to all his servants and to all his land — 2 *the great trials that*
your eyes beheld, those great signs and wonders. 3 *But HASHEM did not give*
you a heart to know, or eyes to see, or ears to hear until this day. 4 *I led you*
for forty years in the Wilderness, your garment did not wear out from on
you, and your shoe did not wear out from on your foot. 5 *Bread you did not*
eat and wine or intoxicant you did not drink, so that you would know that
I am HASHEM, your God. 6 *Then you arrived at this place, and Sihon, king of*
Heshbon, and Og, king of Bashan, went out toward us to battle, and we
smote them. 7 *We took their land and gave it as an inheritance to the*
Reubenite, the Gadite, and to half the tribe of the Manassite. 8 *You shall*
observe the words of this covenant, so that you will succeed in all that you
do."

---

on your behalf in the wilderness *that you might know* (v. 5), and now that He brought you to the land of Sichon and Og where you have an inheritance in the land so that you can (now) establish in them the intended (purpose of your settlement), it is proper that from now on you should apply your heart to know.

8. וּשְׁמַרְתֶּם אֶת דִּבְרֵי הַבְּרִית הַזֹּאת — *And you shall observe the words of this covenant . . .* which you shall accept upon yourselves on Mount Gerizim and Mount Ebal.

לְמַעַן תַּשְׂכִּילוּ אֵת כָּל אֲשֶׁר תַּעֲשׂוּן — *That you may succeed in all your doings . . .* that you achieve, through your deeds, the intended purpose (of Israel) and (attain) eternal life and temporal life.

NOTES

4. וָאוֹלֵךְ אֶתְכֶם — *And I led you*. The *Sforno* links this verse with the following one (v. 5) which concludes with the words, *that you might know that I am HASHEM your God*. Moses argues that even if the many miracles and wonders in Egypt did not succeed in implanting the knowledge of God in the hearts of Israel, surely it is now time, as they consider the providential care for them in the wilderness (vs. 4-5), and after acquiring the territories of Sichon and Og, that they acknowledge God's greatness and their obligation to accept and observe His commandments.

8. אֵת כָּל אֲשֶׁר תַּעֲשׂוּן — *In all your doings*. The *Sforno* takes note of the word כָּל, *all*, which is all-inclusive. He interprets the verse to mean that by keeping the covenant, Israel will merit success in This World and reward in the World to Come. See the *Sforno's* commentary on the phrase לְטוֹב לָנוּ כָּל הַיָּמִים, *for our good all the days* (6:24), where he also explains it to mean This World and the Eternal One.

פרשת נצבים

ט אַתֶּם נִצָּבִים הַיּוֹם כֻּלְּכֶם לִפְנֵי יהוה אֱלֹהֵיכֶם רָאשֵׁיכֶם שִׁבְטֵיכֶם זִקְנֵיכֶם
י וְשֹׁטְרֵיכֶם כֹּל אִישׁ יִשְׂרָאֵל: טַפְּכֶם נְשֵׁיכֶם וְגֵרְךָ אֲשֶׁר בְּקֶרֶב מַחֲנֶיךָ
יא מֵחֹטֵב עֵצֶיךָ עַד שֹׁאֵב מֵימֶיךָ: לְעָבְרְךָ בִּבְרִית יהוה אֱלֹהֶיךָ וּבְאָלָתוֹ
שני יב אֲשֶׁר יהוה אֱלֹהֶיךָ כֹּרֵת עִמְּךָ הַיּוֹם: לְמַעַן הָקִים־אֹתְךָ הַיּוֹם לוֹ לְעָם וְהוּא
יִהְיֶה־לְּךָ לֵאלֹהִים כַּאֲשֶׁר דִּבֶּר־לָךְ וְכַאֲשֶׁר נִשְׁבַּע לַאֲבֹתֶיךָ לְאַבְרָהָם
יג לְיִצְחָק וּלְיַעֲקֹב: וְלֹא אִתְּכֶם לְבַדְּכֶם אָנֹכִי כֹּרֵת אֶת־הַבְּרִית הַזֹּאת
יד וְאֶת־הָאָלָה הַזֹּאת: כִּי אֶת־אֲשֶׁר יֶשְׁנוֹ פֹּה עִמָּנוּ עֹמֵד הַיּוֹם לִפְנֵי יהוה
שלישי טו אֱלֹהֵינוּ וְאֵת אֲשֶׁר אֵינֶנּוּ פֹּה עִמָּנוּ הַיּוֹם: כִּי־אַתֶּם יְדַעְתֶּם אֵת אֲשֶׁר־
יָשַׁבְנוּ בְּאֶרֶץ מִצְרָיִם וְאֵת אֲשֶׁר־עָבַרְנוּ בְּקֶרֶב הַגּוֹיִם אֲשֶׁר עֲבַרְתֶּם:
טז־יז וַתִּרְאוּ אֶת־שִׁקּוּצֵיהֶם וְאֵת גִּלֻּלֵיהֶם עֵץ וָאֶבֶן כֶּסֶף וְזָהָב אֲשֶׁר עִמָּהֶם: פֶּן־
יֵשׁ בָּכֶם אִישׁ אוֹ־אִשָּׁה אוֹ מִשְׁפָּחָה אוֹ־שֵׁבֶט אֲשֶׁר לְבָבוֹ פֹנֶה הַיּוֹם מֵעִם

---

9. אַתֶּם נִצָּבִים הַיּוֹם כֻּלְּכֶם לִפְנֵי ה׳ אֱלֹהֵיכֶם — *You are standing this day, all of you, before* H*ASHEM your God.* And whoever might mislead me cannot mislead Him, and it is according to His understanding (of your sincerity) that you accept (the covenant) upon yourselves.

רָאשֵׁיכֶם שִׁבְטֵיכֶם זִקְנֵיכֶם וְשֹׁטְרֵיכֶם — *Your leaders, elders (judges) and your officers.* Your *leaders* who are שִׁבְטֵיכֶם, i.e., those who (are entrusted with) the scepter of one who rules. (This refers) to those who are princes and chiefs in whose hands is the scepter of a ruler; and *your elders* — these are the judges; and *your officers* have the power to force the litigants (to accept the court's decision). It is incumbent upon these leaders to instruct the masses (as to) what is beneficial to accept upon themselves and what they should reject.

10. טַפְּכֶם נְשֵׁיכֶם — *Your little children and your wives . . .* for it is proper that their deeds be in accordance with the consent of their fathers and husbands.

מֵחֹטֵב עֵצֶיךָ עַד שֹׁאֵב מֵימֶיךָ — *From the hewer of your wood to the drawer of your water . . .* from the first of the hewers to the last of the drawers, similar to, מֵעֹלֵל וְעַד יוֹנֵק מִשּׁוֹר וְעַד שֶׂה מִגָּמָל וְעַד חֲמוֹר, *from infant to suckling, from ox to sheep, from camel to ass* (*I Samuel* 15:3).

11. לְעָבְרְךָ בִּבְרִית — *So that you pass over into the covenant.* You stand (here) with all this order and (united) consent, prepared to pass over into the covenant, and thus it is apparent that you are all desirous to accept (this covenant) upon yourselves wholeheartedly.

11-12. אֲשֶׁר ה׳ אֱלֹהֶיךָ כֹּרֵת עִמְּךָ הַיּוֹם. לְמַעַן הָקִים אֹתְךָ הַיּוֹם לוֹ לְעָם — *Which* H*ASHEM your*

NOTES

9. לִפְנֵי ה׳ אֱלֹהֵיכֶם — *Before* H*ASHEM your God.* Since God's presence is everywhere, obviously Israel stands "before God." The *Sforno* explains that Moses cautioned them that God knows the innermost thoughts of man, and therefore, when they enter into the covenant with Him, they cannot do so with their lips alone, while rejecting it in their hearts, as he explains in verses 17-18. Man can be deceived — not so God.

רָאשֵׁיכֶם שִׁבְטֵיכֶם — *Your leaders, elders (judges) and your officers. Rashi* interprets this phrase (רָאשֵׁיכֶם שִׁבְטֵיכֶם) as meaning "the heads of your tribes." The *Sforno*, however, explains it to mean "your heads who are leaders that wield the scepter of rulership." The word שֵׁבֶט is translated as "scepter" (*Genesis* 49:10), and in our verse the word שִׁבְטֵיכֶם doesn't mean "your tribes" but "your scepters." According to the *Sforno*, three categories of leadership are listed in this verse: leaders who have authority; judges and officers who enforce the law.

10. טַפְּכֶם נְשֵׁיכֶם — *Your little children and your wives.* Whereas the leaders of Israel have the responsibility to instruct the adult community, the guidance of women and children is the responsibil-

PARASHAS NITZAVIM

9 *You are standing today, all of you, before HASHEM, your God: the heads
of your tribes, your elders, and your officers — all the men of Israel;
10 your small children, your women, and your proselyte who is in the midst
of your camp, from the hewer of your wood to the drawer of your water,
11 for you to pass into the covenant of HASHEM, your God, and into His
imprecation that HASHEM, your God, seals with you today, 12 in order to
establish you today as a people to Him and that He be a God to you, as He
spoke to you and as He swore to your forefathers, to Abraham, to Isaac, and
to Jacob. 13 Not with you alone do I seal this covenant and this imprecation,
14 but with whoever is here, standing with us today before HASHEM, our
God, and with whoever is not here with us today.*

*15 For you know how we dwelled in the land of Egypt and how we passed
through the midst of the nations through whom you passed. 16 And you saw
their abominations and their detestable idols — of wood and stone, of silver
and gold that were with them. 17 Perhaps there is among you a man or
woman, or a family or tribe, whose heart turns away today from being with*

God makes with you this day, that He may establish you this day unto Himself for a people. Behold, the intent of God, the Blessed One, in entering the covenant is to establish you unto Himself for a people so that He shall be unto you as a God and thereby you will acquire eternal life. Now being that the purpose of this covenant is so distinguished, your acceptance should be with complete whole-heartedness.

14. וְאֵת אֲשֶׁר אֵינֶנּוּ פֹּה עִמָּנוּ הַיּוֹם — *And also with them who are not here with us this day. They* refers to future generations. Therefore, you must inform them that the gift of the Land and other (possessions) is given to you on the condition that you keep the covenant, and contingent upon that condition (is the fact that) they will inherit the Land from you.

15. כִּי אַתֶּם יְדַעְתֶּם אֵת אֲשֶׁר יָשַׁבְנוּ — *For you know how we dwelt* ... and therefore it is fitting to be apprehensive ...

17. פֶּן יֵשׁ בָּכֶם אִישׁ אוֹ אִשָּׁה — *Lest there should be among you man or woman.* Lest their hearts have been seduced by the vanities of the nations, when they dwelt among them, and they will consider nullifying the acceptance of the covenant. Therefore, I have said that all of you stand before God, who examines the innermost thoughts in the heart (of man), and you cannot mislead Him.

NOTES

ity of their husbands and parents.

11-12. לְעָבְרְךָ בִּבְרִית... לְמַעַן הָקִים אֹתְךָ הַיּוֹם לוֹ לְעָם — *So that you pass over into the covenant ... that He may establish you this day unto Himself for a people.* The preceding two verses (9-10), together with these two, are meant to indicate that the whole nation, from the most superior elements to the lowest class, eagerly awaited the opportunity to enter into a covenant with God. This was because they understood the special privilege and status granted to them as the people of God. Hence, their acceptance of the covenant was without reservation or qualification. He calls this שְׁלֵמוּת, *a perfect, complete* acceptance. See the *Sforno's* commentary on *Leviticus* 26:12.

14. וְאֵת אֲשֶׁר אֵינֶנּוּ פֹּה — *And also with them who are not here.* How can those *who are not here this day* be parties to this covenant? The *Sforno* explains that those who were present were obligated to instruct future generations that the possession of the Land of Israel was contingent upon their continued obedience to the covenant.

15. כִּי אַתֶּם יְדַעְתֶּם — *For you know.* The *Sforno* interprets this verse as an introduction to the following verses. The reason the Torah cautions Israel to be concerned and wary of certain elements in their midst, whose heart may turn them away from God, is because Israel's exposure to idolatrous practice in Egypt may have adversely influenced them, and made them susceptible to idolatry.

יְהוָה אֱלֹהֵינוּ לָלֶכֶת לַעֲבֹד אֶת־אֱלֹהֵי הַגּוֹיִם הָהֵם פֶּן־יֵשׁ בָּכֶם שֹׁרֶשׁ פֹּרֶה
יח רֹאשׁ וְלַעֲנָה: וְהָיָה בְּשָׁמְעוֹ אֶת־דִּבְרֵי הָאָלָה הַזֹּאת וְהִתְבָּרֵךְ בִּלְבָבוֹ
לֵאמֹר שָׁלוֹם יִהְיֶה־לִּי כִּי בִּשְׁרִרוּת לִבִּי אֵלֵךְ לְמַעַן סְפוֹת הָרָוָה אֶת־
יט הַצְּמֵאָה: לֹא־יֹאבֶה יְהוָה סְלֹחַ לוֹ כִּי אָז יֶעְשַׁן אַף־יְהוָה וְקִנְאָתוֹ בָּאִישׁ
הַהוּא וְרָבְצָה בּוֹ כָּל־הָאָלָה הַכְּתוּבָה בַּסֵּפֶר הַזֶּה וּמָחָה יְהוָה אֶת־שְׁמוֹ
כ מִתַּחַת הַשָּׁמָיִם: וְהִבְדִּילוֹ יְהוָה לְרָעָה מִכֹּל שִׁבְטֵי יִשְׂרָאֵל כְּכֹל אָלוֹת
כא הַבְּרִית הַכְּתוּבָה בְּסֵפֶר הַתּוֹרָה הַזֶּה: וְאָמַר הַדּוֹר הָאַחֲרוֹן בְּנֵיכֶם אֲשֶׁר
יָקוּמוּ מֵאַחֲרֵיכֶם וְהַנָּכְרִי אֲשֶׁר יָבֹא מֵאֶרֶץ רְחוֹקָה וְרָאוּ אֶת־מַכּוֹת הָאָרֶץ
כב הַהִוא וְאֶת־תַּחֲלֻאֶיהָ אֲשֶׁר־חִלָּה יְהוָה בָּהּ: גָּפְרִית וָמֶלַח שְׂרֵפָה כָל־
אַרְצָהּ לֹא תִזָּרַע וְלֹא תַצְמִחַ וְלֹא־יַעֲלֶה בָהּ כָּל־עֵשֶׂב כְּמַהְפֵּכַת סְדֹם
כג וַעֲמֹרָה אַדְמָה °וצביים אֲשֶׁר הָפַךְ יְהוָה בְּאַפּוֹ וּבַחֲמָתוֹ: וְאָמְרוּ כָּל־הַגּוֹיִם   °וּצְבוֹיִם ק׳
כד עַל־מֶה עָשָׂה יְהוָה כָּכָה לָאָרֶץ הַזֹּאת מֶה חֳרִי הָאַף הַגָּדוֹל הַזֶּה: וְאָמְרוּ
עַל אֲשֶׁר עָזְבוּ אֶת־בְּרִית יְהוָה אֱלֹהֵי אֲבֹתָם אֲשֶׁר כָּרַת עִמָּם בְּהוֹצִיאוֹ
כה אֹתָם מֵאֶרֶץ מִצְרָיִם: וַיֵּלְכוּ וַיַּעַבְדוּ אֱלֹהִים אֲחֵרִים וַיִּשְׁתַּחֲווּ לָהֶם
כו אֱלֹהִים אֲשֶׁר לֹא־יְדָעוּם וְלֹא חָלַק לָהֶם: וַיִּחַר־אַף יְהוָה בָּאָרֶץ הַהִוא

פֶּן יֵשׁ בָּכֶם שֹׁרֶשׁ פֹּרֶה רֹאשׁ וְלַעֲנָה — *Lest there be among you a root which will bear as fruit a poisonous herb and wormwood . . .* (one) who thinks to lead many astray by accepting his destructive opinions.

18. וְהִתְבָּרֵךְ בִּלְבָבוֹ — *That he bless himself in his heart.* He will accept the curse with his mouth but *bless himself in his heart* by nullifying it.

לֵאמֹר שָׁלוֹם יִהְיֶה לִּי כִּי בִּשְׁרִרוּת לִבִּי אֵלֵךְ — *Saying, "I shall have peace though I walk in the stubborness of my heart."* The expression, *bless himself in his heart,* means, that he will say, "Although I accept the curse with my mouth, I nullify it in my heart and thereby *I shall have peace."*

לְמַעַן סְפוֹת הָרָוָה אֶת הַצְּמֵאָה — *That the watered* (*soul*) *be added* (*linked*) *to the thirsty* (*ones*). The reason that he will accept the curse with his mouth is so that he might add his soul, which is watered and saturated with (the fulfillment of) all desires, to the congregation of God that thirsts (for the spiritual), and is separated from the physical, material desires. (This is all) so that he may rejoice (together) with them in their blessings.

NOTES

17. שֹׁרֶשׁ פֹּרֶה רֹאשׁ וְלַעֲנָה — *A root which will bear as fruit a poisonous herb and wormwood.* The *Ramban* explains that the root of evil was already present among some in this generation, and the fear expressed here is that this root might develop into poisonous fruit. The *Sforno's* commentary reflects this explanation of the *Ramban.*

18. לְמַעַן סְפוֹת הָרָוָה אֶת הַצְּמֵאָה — *That the watered* (*soul*) *be added* (*linked*) *to the thirsty* (*ones*). The commentators have interpreted this difficult passage in a variety of ways. Some interpret רָוָה, *watered,* as meaning "drunkenness," implying a condition of irresponsibility, while conversely others interpret it as a metaphor for the righteous. Similarly, the phrase צְמֵאָה, *dry* or *thirsty*, is interpreted as being descriptive of an act לְתַאֲבוֹן, i.e., a transgression motivated by desire; alternatively, others explain it to be a metaphor for the wicked. The verb סְפוֹת is translated by some as "swept away" while the *Ibn Ezra* translates it to mean "to add." The *Sforno* agrees with this interpretation of the verb סְפוֹת but explains the words רָוָה and צְמֵאָה as meaning one whose desires are fulfilled and appetites satiated (רָוָה), as opposed to one who is thirsty because he suppresses his lusts and appetites (צְמֵאָה). The sense of the verse is that there will be those who will accept the oath and curse with their lips but in reality spurn and reject it. The only reason they make a pretense of accepting the covenant is because they wish to *be added* to the

HASHEM, our God, to go and serve the gods of those nations; perhaps there
is among you a root flourishing with gall and wormwood. 18 *And it will be*
that when he hears the words of this imprecation, he will bless himself in
his heart, saying, "Peace will be with me, though I walk as my heart sees
fit" — thereby adding the watered upon the thirsty.
19 *HASHEM will not be willing to forgive him, for then HASHEM's anger and*
jealousy will smoke against that man, and the entire imprecation written in
this Book will come down upon him, and HASHEM will erase his name from
under heaven. 20 *HASHEM will set him aside for evil from among all the*
tribes of Israel, like all the imprecations of the covenant that is written in
this Book of the Torah.
21 *The later generation will say — your children who will arise after you*
and the foreigner who will come from a distant land — when they will see
the plagues of that Land and its illnesses with which HASHEM has afflicted
it: 22 *"Sulphur and salt, a conflagration of the entire Land, it cannot be sown*
and it cannot sprout, and no grass shall rise up on it; like the upheaval of
Sodom and Gomorrah, Admah and Zeboiim, which HASHEM overturned in
His anger and wrath." 23 *And all the nations will say, "For what reason did*
HASHEM do so to this Land; why this wrathfulness of great anger?"
24 *And they will say, "Because they forsook the covenant of HASHEM,*
the God of their forefathers, that He sealed with them when He took
them out of the land of Egypt; 25 *and they went and served the gods of*
others and prostrated themselves to them — gods that they knew not and
He did not apportion to them. 26 *So God's anger flared against that land,*

19. לֹא יֹאבֶה ה׳ סְלֹחַ לוֹ — *HASHEM will not be willing to pardon him . . .* for profaning the oath and curse which he accepted with his mouth, even though he nullified it in his heart.

22. גָּפְרִית וָמֶלַח . . . כְּמַהְפֵּכַת סְדֹם וַעֲמֹרָה . . . אֲשֶׁר הָפַךְ ה׳ — *Brimstone and salt . . . like the overthrow of Sodom and Amorah . . . which HASHEM overthrew.* They will recognize that this is not an accident but the finger of God, for it is similar to that which He did in Sodom, where it was evident that He destroyed it.

23. וְאָמְרוּ כָּל הַגּוֹיִם — *And all the nations shall say . . .* when (Israel) will be exiled among them.

25. אֱלֹהִים אֲשֶׁר לֹא יְדָעוּם — *Gods that they knew not . . .* whose existence was unknown to them in every way, (while) forsaking their God Who is the authentic God, whose existence, omnipotence and providence has been proven.

וְלֹא חָלַק לָהֶם — *And that He had not allotted to them.* For they will see (realize) that there is no constellation (or planet) which controls their fate, as it says, *Which HASHEM your God*

NOTES

congregation of Israel and enjoy the blessings of God, Who will bless Israel in the merit of those who discipline and deny themselves (which the Torah terms צְמֵאָה (thirsty). At the same time they, the wicked, indulge themselves in all their desires (which the Torah calls רָוָה). Their hope, however, will be frustrated, as the Torah states in the next verse.

22. כְּמַהְפֵּכַת סְדֹם וַעֲמֹרָה . . . אֲשֶׁר הָפַךְ ה׳ — *Like the overthrow of Sodom and Amorah . . . which HASHEM overthrew.* From the nature of the destruction and the catastrophe visited upon *Eretz Yisrael*, it will be evident that it was an act of God, similar to that which happened to Sodom. The verse does not have to be understood in the literal sense of *brimstone and salt;* rather it is meant in the sense of destruction which is not accidental but is the result of Divine punishment. This will be as apparent as the brimstone and fire showered upon Sodom (*Genesis* 19:24).

25. וְלֹא חָלַק לָהֶם — *And that He had not allotted to them.* The *Sforno* in his commentary on 4:19,20

כז לְהָבִיא עָלֶיהָ אֶת־כָּל־הַקְּלָלָה הַכְּתוּבָה בַּסֵּפֶר הַזֶּה: וַיִּתְּשֵׁם יהוה מֵעַל
אַדְמָתָם בְּאַף וּבְחֵמָה וּבְקֶצֶף גָּדוֹל וַיַּשְׁלִכֵם אֶל־אֶרֶץ אַחֶרֶת כַּיּוֹם הַזֶּה:
*י"א נקודות כח הַנִּסְתָּרֹת לַיהוה אֱלֹהֵינוּ וְהַנִּגְלֹת *לָנוּ וּלְבָנֵינוּ עַד־עוֹלָם לַעֲשׂוֹת אֶת־כָּל־
ל רביעי [שני] א דִּבְרֵי הַתּוֹרָה הַזֹּאת: וְהָיָה כִי־יָבֹאוּ עָלֶיךָ כָּל־הַדְּבָרִים הָאֵלֶּה
הַבְּרָכָה וְהַקְּלָלָה אֲשֶׁר נָתַתִּי לְפָנֶיךָ וַהֲשֵׁבֹתָ אֶל־לְבָבֶךָ בְּכָל־הַגּוֹיִם אֲשֶׁר
ב הִדִּיחֲךָ יהוה אֱלֹהֶיךָ שָׁמָּה: וְשַׁבְתָּ עַד־יהוה אֱלֹהֶיךָ וְשָׁמַעְתָּ בְקֹלוֹ כְּכֹל
ג אֲשֶׁר־אָנֹכִי מְצַוְּךָ הַיּוֹם אַתָּה וּבָנֶיךָ בְּכָל־לְבָבְךָ וּבְכָל־נַפְשֶׁךָ: וְשָׁב יהוה
אֱלֹהֶיךָ אֶת־שְׁבוּתְךָ וְרִחֲמֶךָ וְשָׁב וְקִבֶּצְךָ מִכָּל־הָעַמִּים אֲשֶׁר הֱפִיצְךָ יהוה
ד אֱלֹהֶיךָ שָׁמָּה: אִם־יִהְיֶה נִדַּחֲךָ בִּקְצֵה הַשָּׁמָיִם מִשָּׁם יְקַבֶּצְךָ יהוה אֱלֹהֶיךָ
ה וּמִשָּׁם יִקָּחֶךָ: וֶהֱבִיאֲךָ יהוה אֱלֹהֶיךָ אֶל־הָאָרֶץ אֲשֶׁר־יָרְשׁוּ אֲבֹתֶיךָ וִירִשְׁתָּהּ
ו וְהֵיטִבְךָ וְהִרְבְּךָ מֵאֲבֹתֶיךָ: וּמָל יהוה אֱלֹהֶיךָ אֶת־לְבָבְךָ וְאֶת־לְבַב
זַרְעֶךָ לְאַהֲבָה אֶת־יהוה אֱלֹהֶיךָ בְּכָל־לְבָבְךָ וּבְכָל־נַפְשְׁךָ לְמַעַן חַיֶּיךָ:

---

has allotted unto all the peoples . . . but you HASHEM have taken . . . to be unto Him a people (4:19,20).

28. הַנִּסְתָּרֹת לַה' אֱלֹהֵינוּ — *The hidden things belong to HASHEM our God.* Although I said that *you stand this day, all of you, before HASHEM* (verse 9), and that no person can mislead Him, and that He will punish the betrayer, behold this applies only to that which is hidden (unknown to man).

וְהַנִּגְלֹת לָנוּ וּלְבָנֵינוּ עַד עוֹלָם — *But the revealed things belong to us and our children forever.* But (as for) revealed (sins), it is incumbent upon us and our children (to punish the sinner) and it is proper that *we do all the words of this law,* to exact revenge from the sinners and do unto them the judgment that is written.

XXX

1. וַהֲשֵׁבֹתָ אֶל לְבָבֶךָ — *And you will ponder in your heart.* When you carefully examine and consider the conflicting aspects (of your concepts and actions), and call them all to mind so as to distinguish truth from falsehood, then you will recognize (realize) how far you have distanced yourself from God, the Blessed One, in your opinions and behavior which are contrary to His Torah.

בְּכָל הַגּוֹיִם — *Among all the nations . . .* while you are still in exile.

NOTES

explains that whereas the destiny of all other nations is affected by planetary influences, Israel is unaffected by "the hosts of heaven and their order." See the note on those verses which clarify this concept, based on the opinion of our Sages, that the nations of the earth are under the influence of stars, planets and constellations but Israel is not, as we are taught, אֵין מַזָּל לְיִשְׂרָאֵל (*Shabbos* 156a), *Israel's fate is not determined by the stars.* This is the thrust of the *Sforno*'s commentary on the phrase וְלֹא חָלַק לָהֶם — God has not allotted to Israel heavenly forces to control their destiny.

28. הַנִּסְתָּרֹת לַה' אֱלֹהֵינוּ וְהַנִּגְלֹת לָנוּ — *The hidden things belong to HASHEM our God but the revealed things belong to us.* Similar to other commentators (*Rashi, Rashbam, Ibn Ezra*), the *Sforno* explains this verse in the following manner: The terrible Divine retribution mentioned in the preceding verses apply only to those who violate the covenant in secret, hidden from the sight of man and known only to God. But those who defy the commandments openly must be tried and punished by the community, for the responsibility of bringing them to justice rests upon the whole nation.

XXX

1. וַהֲשֵׁבֹתָ אֶל לְבָבֶךָ בְּכָל הַגּוֹיִם — *And you will ponder in your heart among all the nations.* As a result of the experiences of Israel in exile, they will at some time realize that their defection from God and His Torah has caused them to be cursed and oppressed. This, in turn, will result in serious self-examination which the Torah calls "the pondering of the heart," and which the *Sforno* interprets as one's consideration of the inner conflict between good and evil, the truth and falsehood in

to bring upon it the entire curse that is written in this Book; [27] *and* HASHEM
removed them from upon their soil, with anger, with wrath, and with great
fury, and He cast them to another land, as this very day!"
[28] *The hidden [sins] are for* HASHEM, *our God, but the revealed [sins] are for*
us and our children forever, to carry out all the words of this Torah.

30 [1] *It will be that when all these things come upon you — the blessing and the*
curse that I have presented before you — then you will take it to your heart
among all the nations where HASHEM, *your God, has dispersed you;* [2] *and you*
will return unto HASHEM, *your God, and listen to His voice, according to every-*
thing that I command you today, you and your children, with all your heart
and all your soul. [3] *Then Hashem, your God, will bring back your captivity*
and have mercy upon you, and He will gather you in from all the peoples to
which HASHEM, *your God, has scattered you.* [4] *If your dispersed will be at the*
ends of heaven, from there HASHEM, *your God, will gather you in and from*
there He will take you. [5] HASHEM, *your God, will bring you to the Land that*
your forefathers possessed and you shall possess it; He will do good to you
and make you more numerous than your forefathers. [6] HASHEM, *your God,*
will circumcise your heart and the heart of your offspring, to love HASHEM,
your God, with all your heart and with all your soul, that you may live.

---

2. וְשַׁבְתָּ עַד ה' אֱלֹהֶיךָ — *And you shall return unto* HASHEM *your God.* Your return (repentance) will be exclusively to do the will of your Creator, and it is this repentance of which our Sages say, שֶׁמַּגַּעַת עַד כִּסֵּא הַכָּבוֹד, *It reaches to the Throne of Glory* (*Yoma* 86a).

וְשָׁמַעְתָּ בְקֹלוֹ כְּכֹל אֲשֶׁר אָנֹכִי מְצַוְּךָ הַיּוֹם — *And you shall listen to His voice according to all that I command you this day* . . . and not as *commandments of men performed by rote* (*Isaiah* 29:13), as you have done heretofore.

אַתָּה וּבָנֶיךָ — *You and your children.* The younger members of the generation will also recognize this (truth), as it says, כִּי כוּלָּם יֵדְעוּ אוֹתִי לְמִקְּטַנָּם וְעַד גְּדוֹלָם, *For they shall all know Me, from the least of them to the greatest of them* (*Jeremiah* 31:33).

בְּכָל לְבָבְךָ — *With all your heart.* You will have no doubts regarding this.

וּבְכָל נַפְשְׁךָ — *And with all your soul.* The lustful spirit will not deter you, for you will recognize the importance of the matter.

3. וְשָׁב וְקִבֶּצְךָ — *And return and gather you* . . . through the ingathering of the exiles.

6. וּמָל ה' אֱלֹהֶיךָ אֶת לְבָבְךָ וְאֶת לְבַב זַרְעֶךָ לְאַהֲבָה — *And* HASHEM *your God will circumcise*

NOTES

man's heart, which he always attempts to resolve. Repentance will follow when man recognizes the folly of his ways and chooses to return to God. The *Sforno* stresses that this reflection and repentance will come to pass while Israel is still in exile, for it is in the merit of this repentance that Israel will be redeemed. See his commentary on verse 11.

2. וְשַׁבְתָּ עַד ה' אֱלֹהֶיךָ . . . אַתָּה וּבָנֶיךָ . . . בְּכָל לְבָבְךָ . . . וּבְכָל נַפְשְׁךָ — *And you shall return unto* HASHEM *your God . . . you and your children . . . with all your heart and with all your soul . . .* The *Sforno* carefully interprets each phrase in this verse. The word עַד, *unto,* is used by the prophet *Hosea* (14:2) when he calls upon Israel to repent — שׁוּבָה יִשְׂרָאֵל עַד ה' אֱלֹהֶיךָ, *Return, O Israel, unto* HASHEM *your God.* The Talmud in *Yoma* (86a), commenting on this verse, states: "Great is repentance for it reaches unto the Throne of Glory." The *Sforno* interprets the term עַד as implying that the repentance spoken of in our verse is similar to the *teshuvah* of which *Hosea* speaks. Such sincere repentance can only result from a substantial meaningful hearkening to God's voice; not a superficial one. He therefore explains that Israel, at the time of their return, will not perform *mitzvos* in a perfunctory fashion but will do so with a profound appreciation of their significance. This return to God will be a total one, including young and old alike, and it will represent total commitment to *mitzvos*, performed with one's entire *heart and soul.*

חמישי [שלישי] ז וְנָתַן יְהוָה אֱלֹהֶיךָ אֵת כָּל־הָאָלוֹת הָאֵלֶּה עַל־אֹיְבֶיךָ וְעַל־שֹׂנְאֶיךָ אֲשֶׁר
ח רְדָפוּךָ: וְאַתָּה תָשׁוּב וְשָׁמַעְתָּ בְּקוֹל יְהוָה וְעָשִׂיתָ אֶת־כָּל־מִצְוֹתָיו אֲשֶׁר
ט אָנֹכִי מְצַוְּךָ הַיּוֹם: וְהוֹתִירְךָ יְהוָה אֱלֹהֶיךָ בְּכֹל | מַעֲשֵׂה יָדֶךָ בִּפְרִי בִטְנְךָ
וּבִפְרִי בְהֶמְתְּךָ וּבִפְרִי אַדְמָתְךָ לְטֹבָה כִּי | יָשׁוּב יְהוָה לָשׂוּשׂ עָלֶיךָ
י לְטוֹב כַּאֲשֶׁר־שָׂשׂ עַל־אֲבֹתֶיךָ: כִּי תִשְׁמַע בְּקוֹל יְהוָה אֱלֹהֶיךָ לִשְׁמֹר
מִצְוֹתָיו וְחֻקֹּתָיו הַכְּתוּבָה בְּסֵפֶר הַתּוֹרָה הַזֶּה כִּי תָשׁוּב אֶל־יְהוָה אֱלֹהֶיךָ
ששי יא בְּכָל־לְבָבְךָ וּבְכָל־נַפְשֶׁךָ: כִּי הַמִּצְוָה הַזֹּאת
יב אֲשֶׁר אָנֹכִי מְצַוְּךָ הַיּוֹם לֹא־נִפְלֵאת הִוא מִמְּךָ וְלֹא־רְחֹקָה הִוא: לֹא
בַשָּׁמַיִם הִוא לֵאמֹר מִי יַעֲלֶה־לָּנוּ הַשָּׁמַיְמָה וְיִקָּחֶהָ לָּנוּ וְיַשְׁמִעֵנוּ אֹתָהּ

---

your heart and the heart of your children to love. He will open your eyes so that you might turn away from errors which confuse (man's) understanding and knowledge of the truth. (This shall occur) when you attempt to cleave to Him in such a manner that you will recognize His goodness and perforce love Him. This you shall do *that you may live* forevermore.

7. עַל אֹיְבֶיךָ וְעַל שֹׂנְאֶיךָ — *Upon your enemy and upon those who hate you* ... upon them that rise up against you and those who harbor hatred for you in their heart, as it says, כִּי אֶעֱשֶׂה כָלָה בְּכָל הַגּוֹיִם, *for I will make a full end of all the nations* (*Jeremiah* 30:11).

8. וְאַתָּה תָשׁוּב — *And you shall be at ease.* You shall rest, similar to בְּשׁוּבָה וָנַחַת, *In ease and rest* (*Isaiah* 30:15). This will (come to pass) when Messiah the Righteous One will reveal himself following the destruction of the nations; that is, they will be destroyed but you will survive in ease and rest and no longer be exiled, as the prophet explains, saying, אִם תָּשׁוּב יִשְׂרָאֵל ... אֵלַי תָּשׁוּב ... וְלֹא תָנוּד, *If you will return, O Israel ... return to Me ... and you will not wander* (*Jeremiah* 4:1).

וְעָשִׂיתָ אֶת כָּל מִצְוֹתָיו אֲשֶׁר אָנֹכִי מְצַוְּךָ הַיּוֹם — *And do all His commandments which I command you this day* ... for the faith (religion) will never be changed (lit., made new).

9-10. וְהוֹתִירְךָ ה׳ — *And HASHEM will make you plenteous.* He will grant you success greater than all former successes.

לְטֹבָה ... הַכְּתוּבָה בְּסֵפֶר הַתּוֹרָה הַזֶּה — *For good ... which are written in this book of the law* ... as it says, וְהִתְהַלַּכְתִּי בְּתוֹכְכֶם וְהָיִיתִי לָכֶם לֵאלֹהִים, *And I will walk among you and will be your God and you shall be My people.* Now this He shall do when *He will again rejoice over you for good as He rejoiced over your fathers* (*Leviticus* 26:12), but it will not be in the merit

NOTES

6. וּמָל ה׳ אֱלֹהֶיךָ — *And HASHEM your God will circumcise.* As explained above (6:5), love of God cannot be commanded, nor can reverence, as our Sages state, הַכֹּל בִּידֵי שָׁמַיִם חוּץ מִיִּרְאַת שָׁמַיִם, *All is in the hands of heaven except for fear of heaven* (*Berachos* 33b). The *Sforno*, therefore, explains this verse as meaning that the Almighty will assist man to open his eyes to the truth, and sensitize him to an awareness of God's preeminent role in the universe and to His goodness. This, in turn, will bring man, of his own free will, to the love and fear of God.

7. עַל אֹיְבֶיךָ וְעַל שֹׂנְאֶיךָ — *Upon your enemy and upon those who hate you.* Two words are used in this verse — אוֹיֵב, *one who persecutes,* and שׂוֹנֵא, *one who hates.* The *Sforno* explains the former to mean one who manifests his enmity through overt action, whereas the latter is applicable to one who harbors hatred for Israel in his heart.

8. וְאַתָּה תָשׁוּב — *And you shall be at ease.* In verse 2 we read וְשַׁבְתָּ, *and you shall return,* meaning repentance. Hence the phrase וְאַתָּה תָשׁוּב cannot mean "and you shall return" which would be repetitious. The *Sforno* therefore explains it as meaning a promise and assurance that Israel will survive and be at rest, dwelling tranquilly in their land, never again to be forced into exile.

אֲשֶׁר אָנֹכִי מְצַוְּךָ הַיּוֹם — *Which I command you this day.* One of the fundamentals of the Jewish faith is the principle that the Torah given to us by God through Moses "will never be exchanged nor will

7 HASHEM, your God, will place all these imprecations upon your enemies and those who hate you, who pursued you. 8 You shall return and listen to the voice of HASHEM, and perform all His commandments that I command you today. 9 HASHEM will make you abundant in all your handiwork — in the fruit of your womb, the fruit of your animals, and the fruit of your Land — for good, when HASHEM will return to rejoice over you for good, as He rejoiced over your forefathers, 10 when you listen to the voice of HASHEM, your God, to observe His commandments and His decrees, that are written in this Book of the Torah, when you shall return to HASHEM, your God, with all your heart and all your soul.

11 For this commandment that I command you today — it is not hidden from you and it is not distant. 12 It is not in heaven, [for you] to say, "Who can ascend to the heaven for us and take it for us, so that we can listen to

---

of the fathers, rather because your repentance will be with all your heart and all your soul, in such a manner that all your iniquities will be counted as though they were merits (based on *Yoma* 86b). Thereby, you will find favor before Me as did your fathers.

11. כִּי הַמִּצְוָה הַזֹּאת — *For this commandment.* Now the reason I stated, *You will ponder it in your heart among all the nations* (verse 1), is that it is necessary for you to repent while still in exile so that through (this repentance) you will be saved. This is because, indeed, the commandment of repentance which I command you this day (is in your hands alone), as it says in *parashas Vayikra* regarding all sins, וְאָשֵׁם, *and be guilty*, or וְאַשָׁמוֹ, *and his guilt offering*. The intent of this is that man shall come to recognize his transgression (and confess to it) as it explicitly states subsequently, וְהָיָה כִי יֶאְשַׁם לְאַחַת מֵאֵלֶּה וְהִתְוַדָּה אֲשֶׁר חָטָא עָלֶיהָ, *And it shall be when he is guilty of one of these things that he shall confess that wherein he has sinned* (*Leviticus* 5:5), and also when it says, אִישׁ אוֹ אִשָּׁה כִּי יַעֲשׂוּ מִכָּל חַטֹּאת הָאָדָם . . . וְאָשְׁמָה הַנֶּפֶשׁ הַהִוא. וְהִתְוַדּוּ אֶת חַטָּאתָם . . ., *When a man or a woman shall commit any sin that men commit . . . and that soul shall be guilty. Then they shall confess their sin* (*Numbers* 5:6,7) . . .

לֹא נִפְלֵאת הִוא מִמְּךָ — *Is not beyond your understanding* . . . that you should have need for prophets (to explain the way of repentance).

וְלֹא רְחֹקָה הִוא — *Nor is it far away* . . . that there be need for the wise men of the generation, who are far away, to expound it for you, in such a manner that you may be able to do it while still in exile; and this he explains by saying . . .

12. לֹא בַשָּׁמַיִם הִוא — *It is not in heaven.* There is no aspect of repentance which necessitates the amplification (lit., telling) of a prophet.

NOTES

there be another Torah," as stated by *Maimonides* in his 9th Principle of Faith. The *Sforno* reads this basic concept into the words of this verse. He may well be implying that the addition of the word הַיּוֹם, *today*, is meant to reflect the saying of our Sages that *each day* Torah is to be considered as new and fresh, בְּכָל יוֹם יִהְיוּ בְעֵינֶיךָ כַּחֲדָשִׁים, *each day it shall be new in your eyes*, therefore it is unnecessary for it to be exchanged.

9. וְהוֹתִירְךָ ה׳ — *And HASHEM will make you plenteous*. The expression וְהוֹתִירְךָ, *will make you plenteous*, also appears in chapter 28, verse 11. The *Sforno's* interpretation there is similar to the one he gives here; however, in *Ki Savo*, the verse compares Israel's prosperity to that of other nations, while here Israel's present success is compared to their own previous successes.

9-10. לְטֹבָה . . . הַכְּתוּבָה בְּסֵפֶר הַתּוֹרָה הַזֶּה — *For good . . . which are written in this book of the law.* The *Sforno* links these two verses together. He is of the opinion that the greatest good which God can grant Israel is for Him to dwell in their midst, thereby demonstrating that He is the God of Israel and they are His people. This blessing of טוֹב, *good*, will result from Israel's sincere return to God, as stated at the conclusion of verse 10. The *Sforno* stresses that God's joy will be evoked by the actions of Israel and their wholehearted repentance, and not because of זְכוּת אָבוֹת, *the merits of the fathers*.

יג וְנַעֲשֶֽׂנָּה׃ וְלֹֽא־מֵעֵ֥בֶר לַיָּ֖ם ה֑וא לֵאמֹ֗ר מִ֣י יַעֲבָר־לָ֜נוּ אֶל־עֵ֤בֶר הַיָּם֙ וְיִקָּחֶ֣הָ
יד לָּ֔נוּ וְיַשְׁמִעֵ֥נוּ אֹתָ֖הּ וְנַעֲשֶֽׂנָּה׃ כִּֽי־קָר֥וֹב אֵלֶ֛יךָ הַדָּבָ֖ר מְאֹ֑ד בְּפִ֥יךָ וּבִֽלְבָבְךָ֖
שביעי ומפטיר טו לַעֲשֹׂתֽוֹ׃ רְאֵ֨ה נָתַ֤תִּי לְפָנֶ֙יךָ֙ הַיּ֔וֹם אֶת־הַֽחַיִּ֖ים וְאֶת־הַטּ֑וֹב
[רביעי] טז וְאֶת־הַמָּ֖וֶת וְאֶת־הָרָֽע׃ אֲשֶׁ֨ר אָנֹכִ֣י מְצַוְּךָ֮ הַיּוֹם֒ לְאַהֲבָ֞ה אֶת־יְהוָ֤ה אֱלֹהֶ֙יךָ֙
לָלֶ֣כֶת בִּדְרָכָ֔יו וְלִשְׁמֹ֛ר מִצְוֺתָ֥יו וְחֻקֹּתָ֖יו וּמִשְׁפָּטָ֑יו וְחָיִ֣יתָ וְרָבִ֔יתָ וּבֵֽרַכְךָ֙
יז יְהוָ֣ה אֱלֹהֶ֔יךָ בָּאָ֕רֶץ אֲשֶׁר־אַתָּ֥ה בָא־שָׁ֖מָּה לְרִשְׁתָּֽהּ׃ וְאִם־יִפְנֶ֥ה לְבָבְךָ֖
יח וְלֹ֣א תִשְׁמָ֑ע וְנִדַּחְתָּ֗ וְהִשְׁתַּחֲוִ֛יתָ לֵאלֹהִ֥ים אֲחֵרִ֖ים וַעֲבַדְתָּֽם׃ הִגַּ֤דְתִּי לָכֶם֙
הַיּ֔וֹם כִּ֥י אָבֹ֖ד תֹּאבֵד֑וּן לֹא־תַאֲרִיכֻ֤ן יָמִים֙ עַל־הָ֣אֲדָמָ֔ה אֲשֶׁ֨ר אַתָּ֤ה עֹבֵר֙
יט אֶת־הַיַּרְדֵּ֔ן לָב֥וֹא שָׁ֖מָּה לְרִשְׁתָּֽהּ׃ הַעִדֹ֨תִי בָכֶ֣ם הַיּוֹם֮ אֶת־הַשָּׁמַ֣יִם וְאֶת־
הָאָרֶץ֒ הַחַיִּ֤ים וְהַמָּ֙וֶת֙ נָתַ֣תִּי לְפָנֶ֔יךָ הַבְּרָכָ֖ה וְהַקְּלָלָ֑ה וּבָֽחַרְתָּ֙ בַּֽחַיִּ֔ים לְמַ֥עַן
כ תִּחְיֶ֖ה אַתָּ֥ה וְזַרְעֶֽךָ׃ לְאַהֲבָה֙ אֶת־יְהוָ֣ה אֱלֹהֶ֔יךָ לִשְׁמֹ֥עַ בְּקֹל֖וֹ וּלְדָבְקָה־ב֑וֹ
כִּ֣י ה֤וּא חַיֶּ֙יךָ֙ וְאֹ֣רֶךְ יָמֶ֔יךָ לָשֶׁ֣בֶת עַל־הָאֲדָמָ֗ה אֲשֶׁר֩ נִשְׁבַּ֨ע יְהוָ֧ה לַאֲבֹתֶ֛יךָ
לְאַבְרָהָ֛ם לְיִצְחָ֥ק וּֽלְיַעֲקֹ֖ב לָתֵ֥ת לָהֶֽם׃

---

13. וְלֹא מֵעֵבֶר לַיָּם הוּא — *Neither is it beyond the sea.* You also have no need for the wise men of the generation, who are far away, to expound it for you in such a manner that it will be possible for you (to do it) in exile. Hence, it is not difficult for you (to perform), as (sometimes) occurs with a commandment that needs the interpretation of the wise men of the generation to clarify doubts which arise (regarding its observance), or (certain *mitzvos*) which cannot possibly be fulfilled in exile.

14. בְּפִיךָ וּבִלְבָבְךָ לַעֲשֹׂתוֹ — *In your mouth and in your heart that you may do it* ... to recognize your sin in your heart, that you sinned against God, the Blessed One, and to regret it and confess to it by words of your mouth.

15. אֶת הַחַיִּים — *Life* ... forever.

וְאֶת הַטּוֹב — *And good* ... the sweetness of this transitory world.

וְאֶת הַמָּוֶת — *And death* ... forever.

וְאֶת הָרָע — *And evil* ... suffering in this transitory world.

16. וְחָיִיתָ — *Then you shall live* ... forever.

18. אָבֹד תֹּאבֵדוּן — *You will surely perish* ... forever.

NOTES

11-14. כִּי הַמִּצְוָה הַזֹּאת ... לֹא נִפְלֵאת הִוא מִמְּךָ ... בְּפִיךָ וּבִלְבָבְךָ לַעֲשׂתוֹ — *For this commandment* ... *is not beyond your understanding* ... *in your mouth and in your heart that you may do it*. The *Sforno* interprets the phrase הַמִּצְוָה הַזֹּאת, *this commandment*, as referring to the *mitzvah* of תְּשׁוּבָה, repentance. His commentary on this verse and verses 12-14 must be joined together, the sense of these verses being: Man's ability to repent is a privilege and gift granted to him by God. It is an act which can be performed by anyone and is not conditional upon place or time, nor does it require great wisdom or knowledge. When man sins, he can atone for that sin through sincere regret for having transgressed, combined with confession to God, and by accepting upon himself never to sin again (חֲרָטָה, וִדּוּי, קַבָּלָה). There is no need for a prophet or a wise man to reveal to him or teach him how this is to be done for it is totally within the capacity of man. The sequence of repentance is explained by the *Sforno* in verse 14; recognition of one's sins, regret, and confession which must be expressed. See the *Rambam* in *Hilchos Teshuvah* 1:1 and 2:2,3 where these principles are clearly stated. The *Sforno* explains that the Torah in verse 11 makes two statements regarding the nature of repentance — one that it is not beyond man's understanding necessitating the guidance of a prophet, and second that it is not beyond comprehension, necessitating the teaching and interpretation of a wise man. These two ideas are then expanded upon in verses 12-13, while verse 14 teaches us that each

it and perform it?" 13 Nor is it across the sea, [for you] to say, "Who can
cross to the other side of the sea for us and take it for us, so that we can
listen to it and perform it?" 14 Rather, the matter is very near to you — in
your mouth and your heart — to perform it.
15 See — I have placed before you today the life and the good, and the
death and the evil, 16 that which I command you today, to love HASHEM*,*
your God, to walk in His ways, to observe His commandments, His decrees,
and His ordinances; then you will live and you will multiply, and HASHEM*,*
your God, will bless you in the Land to which you come, to possess it. 17 But
if your heart will stray and you will not listen, and you are led astray, and
you prostrate yourself to strange gods and serve them, 18 I tell you today
that you will surely be lost; you will not lengthen your days upon the Land
that you cross the Jordan to come there, to possess it. 19 I call heaven and
earth today to bear witness against you: I have placed life and death before
you, blessing and curse; and you shall choose life, so that you will live, you
and your offspring — 20 to love HASHEM*, your God, to listen to His voice and*
to cleave to Him, for He is your life and the length of your days, to dwell
upon the land that HASHEM *swore to your forefathers, to Abraham, to Isaac,*
and to Jacob, to give them.

---

19. וּבָחַרְתָּ בַּחַיִּים — *Therefore choose life ...* everlasting life.

19-20. לְמַעַן תִּחְיֶה אַתָּה וְזַרְעֶךָ. לְאַהֲבָה אֶת ה׳ אֱלֹהֶיךָ — *That you may live, you and your seed. To love* HASHEM *your God.* And I said that you should choose life, not as one who serves for the sake of receiving a reward, rather, I said (i.e., meant) that you should choose only what is *real* life, by desiring (to utilize) transitory life for this purpose alone, namely to love God your God, recognizing His goodness and greatness.

וּלְדָבְקָה בוֹ — *And to cleave to Him ...* that all your actions be in His name.

כִּי הוּא חַיֶּיךָ — *For that is your life ...* the cleaving to Him results in everlasting life.

וְאֹרֶךְ יָמֶיךָ לָשֶׁבֶת עַל הָאֲדָמָה — *And the length of your days that you may dwell on the land.* And this will also bring you length of days to dwell on the land in this transitory life, through which you will merit everlasting life, as a result of careful examination and performance of good deeds (i.e., *mitzvos*), as our Sages say, הַתְקֵן עַצְמְךָ בִּפְרוֹזְדוֹר כְּדֵי שֶׁתִּכָּנֵס לַטְּרַקְלִין, *Prepare yourself in the anteroom that you may enter the banquet hall* (*Avos* 4:21).

NOTES

person possesses the ability to repent.

15-19. אֶת הַחַיִּים וְאֶת הַטּוֹב ... וְחָיִיתָ ... אָבֹד תֹּאבֵדוּן ... וּבָחַרְתָּ בַּחַיִּים לְמַעַן תִּחְיֶה אַתָּה וְזַרְעֶךָ — *Life and good ... then you shall live ... you will surely perish ... therefore choose life that you may live, you and your seed*. The *Sforno* explains these verses in alternate sequence. Moses speaks to Israel of the transitory and the permanent, of this world and eternity. "Life" in the context of these verses refers to eternal life while "death" is eternal death. "Good" and "evil" refer to man's condition in this world.

20. לְאַהֲבָה אֶת ה׳ אֱלֹהֶיךָ — *To love* HASHEM *your God*. Since the term חַיִּים, *life*, as mentioned in the previous note, refers to everlasting life, it is necessary to clarify that the phrase לְמַעַן תִּחְיֶה, *that you may live* (verse 19), refers to life in *this world* and is linked to the words in this verse *to love* HASHEM *your God* (verse 20). The *Sforno* explains that life in this world is of great importance and paramount value, providing man utilizes it for fulfillment of God's will and appreciates and acknowledges God's kindness and goodness which is manifested in this world.

כִּי הוּא חַיֶּיךָ וְאֹרֶךְ יָמֶיךָ — *For that is your life and the length of your days*. The *Sforno* amplifies the concept that one's life experience in this world has impact upon everlasting life in the World to Come. By cleaving to God, Israel will be granted length of days in *Eretz Yisrael*, enabling them to serve God through Torah study and *mitzvos*, thereby meriting eternal life.

פרשת וילך

לא

א־ב וַיֵּ֖לֶךְ מֹשֶׁ֑ה וַיְדַבֵּ֛ר אֶת־הַדְּבָרִ֥ים הָאֵ֖לֶּה אֶל־כָּל־יִשְׂרָאֵֽל: וַיֹּ֣אמֶר אֲלֵהֶ֗ם בֶּן־מֵאָ֨ה וְעֶשְׂרִ֥ים שָׁנָ֛ה אָנֹכִ֖י הַיּ֑וֹם לֹא־אוּכַ֥ל ע֖וֹד לָצֵ֣את וְלָב֑וֹא וַֽיהֹוָה֙

ג אָמַ֣ר אֵלַ֔י לֹ֥א תַֽעֲבֹ֖ר אֶת־הַיַּרְדֵּ֣ן הַזֶּֽה: יְהֹוָ֨ה אֱלֹהֶ֜יךָ ה֣וּא ׀ עֹבֵ֣ר לְפָנֶ֗יךָ הֽוּא־יַשְׁמִ֞יד אֶת־הַגּוֹיִ֥ם הָאֵ֛לֶּה מִלְּפָנֶ֖יךָ וִֽירִשְׁתָּ֑ם יְהוֹשֻׁ֗עַ ה֚וּא עֹבֵ֣ר לְפָנֶ֔יךָ

שני

ד כַּֽאֲשֶׁ֖ר דִּבֶּ֥ר יְהֹוָֽה: וְעָשָׂ֤ה יְהֹוָה֙ לָהֶ֔ם כַּֽאֲשֶׁ֣ר עָשָׂ֗ה לְסִיח֤וֹן וּלְע֛וֹג

ה מַלְכֵ֥י הָֽאֱמֹרִ֖י וּלְאַרְצָ֑ם אֲשֶׁ֥ר הִשְׁמִ֖יד אֹתָֽם: וּנְתָנָ֥ם יְהֹוָ֖ה לִפְנֵיכֶ֑ם

ו וַֽעֲשִׂיתֶ֣ם לָהֶ֔ם כְּכָ֨ל־הַמִּצְוָ֔ה אֲשֶׁ֥ר צִוִּ֖יתִי אֶתְכֶֽם: חִזְק֣וּ וְאִמְצ֗וּ אַל־תִּֽירְא֤וּ וְאַל־תַּֽעַרְצ֣וּ מִפְּנֵיהֶ֑ם כִּ֣י ׀ יְהֹוָ֣ה אֱלֹהֶ֗יךָ ה֚וּא הַֽהֹלֵ֣ךְ עִמָּ֔ךְ לֹ֥א יַרְפְּךָ֖ וְלֹ֥א יַֽעַזְבֶֽךָּ:

שלישי [חמישי]

ז וַיִּקְרָ֨א מֹשֶׁ֜ה לִֽיהוֹשֻׁ֗עַ וַיֹּ֨אמֶר אֵלָ֜יו לְעֵינֵ֣י כָל־יִשְׂרָאֵל֮ חֲזַ֣ק וֶֽאֱמָץ֒ כִּ֣י אַתָּ֗ה תָּבוֹא֙ אֶת־הָעָ֣ם הַזֶּ֔ה אֶל־הָאָ֕רֶץ אֲשֶׁ֨ר נִשְׁבַּ֧ע

ח יְהֹוָ֛ה לַֽאֲבֹתָ֖ם לָתֵ֣ת לָהֶ֑ם וְאַתָּ֖ה תַּנְחִילֶ֥נָּה אוֹתָֽם: וַֽיהֹוָ֞ה ה֣וּא ׀ הַֽהֹלֵ֣ךְ לְפָנֶ֗יךָ ה֚וּא יִֽהְיֶ֣ה עִמָּ֔ךְ לֹ֥א יַרְפְּךָ֖ וְלֹ֣א יַֽעַזְבֶ֑ךָּ לֹ֥א תִירָ֖א וְלֹ֥א תֵחָֽת:

XXXI

1. וַיֵּלֶךְ מֹשֶׁה — *And Moses went.* He roused himself to do so, similar to וַיֵּלֶךְ אִישׁ מִבֵּית לֵוִי, *And there went a man out of the house of Levi* (Exodus 2:1), and וַיֵּלֶךְ וַיַּעֲבֹד, *And he went and served* (17:3), and other (such verses). This (is to say) that after he concluded the matter of completing the covenant (between God and Israel), he roused himself to comfort Israel regarding his death, so that the joy of the covenant which was meant to be accepted with rejoicing — as it states, יִשְׂמַח יִשְׂרָאֵל בְּעֹשָׂיו, *Let Israel rejoice in Him Who made them* (Psalms 149:2), and as it says, וְזָבַחְתָּ שְׁלָמִים וְאָכַלְתָּ שָּׁם וְשָׂמַחְתָּ לִפְנֵי ה' אֱלֹהֶיךָ, *And you shall sacrifice peace-offerings and shall eat there and you shall rejoice before HASHEM your God* (27:7) — should not be impaired [lit., confounded] (by the sorrow of Moses' imminent death).

2. בֶּן מֵאָה וְעֶשְׂרִים שָׁנָה אָנֹכִי הַיּוֹם — *I am a hundred and twenty years old this day.* And therefore do not grieve over my death, for according to nature I should no longer be able to live.

לֹא אוּכַל עוֹד לָצֵאת וְלָבוֹא — *I can no longer go out and come in.* And even were I to live, I would not be able to go out and come in on your behalf in my old age.

וַה' אָמַר אֵלַי לֹא תַעֲבֹר — *And HASHEM has said to me, you shall not cross over.* And even were I able to go out and come in , behold God has said to me that I am not to go over

NOTES

1. וַיֵּלֶךְ מֹשֶׁה — *And Moses went.* The word וַיֵּלֶךְ, *and went,* in the context of this verse lends itself to various interpretations. Where did Moses go? The verses that follow record his words but not any departure from one place and arrival at another. Some commentators say that he walked vigorously before the people to demonstrate that his powers and vitality were unimpaired. Others say that Moses went to each tribe separately to bid them farewell. The *Midrash Tanchuma* states, *The term* וַיֵּלֶךְ *implies admonition.* The *Sforno,* however, explains this word as indicating arousal, animation, or stirring oneself to action. Moses felt it necessary to comfort and encourage the people

of Israel who were devastated by the knowledge that he was leaving them forever. His imminent death threatened to cast them into a state of despair, whereas they should have been in a state of great joy and happiness, having entered into a covenant with God. He therefore roused himself to strengthen their resolve and elevate their spirits, reassuring them that God would not forsake them and will lead them to *Eretz Yisrael* under the leadership of Joshua.

2. בֶּן מֵאָה וְעֶשְׂרִים שָׁנָה ... וַה' אָמַר אֵלַי — *I am a hundred and twenty years old ... and HASHEM has said to me.* Moses gives three reasons why they

PARASHAS VAYEILECH

31 *[1] Moses went and spoke these words to all of Israel. [2] He said to them, "I
am a hundred and twenty years old today; I can no longer go out and
come in, for HASHEM has said to me, 'You shall not cross this Jordan.'
[3] HASHEM, your God — He will cross before you; He will destroy these nations
from before you, and you shall possess them; Joshua — he shall cross over
before you, as HASHEM has spoken. [4] HASHEM will do to them as He did to
Sihon and Og, the kings of the Amorite, and their land, which He destroyed,
[5] and HASHEM gave them before you; and you shall do to them according to
the entire commandment that I have commanded you. [6] Be strong and
courageous, do not be afraid and do not be broken before them, for HASHEM,
your God — it is He Who goes before you, He will not release you nor will He
forsake you."*

*[7] Moses summoned Joshua and said to him before the eyes of all Israel, "Be
strong and courageous, for you shall come with this people to the Land that
HASHEM swore to give them, and you shall cause them to inherit it. [8] HASHEM
— it is He Who goes before you; He will be with you; He will not release you
nor will He forsake you; do not be afraid and do not be dismayed."*

(the Jordan), therefore it is better for you that I die, so that you will be able to go over (into the land).

3. ה׳ אֱלֹהֶיךָ הוּא עֹבֵר לְפָנֶיךָ — *HASHEM your God, He will go over before you.* Nor should you grieve over the fact that you will have lost my leadership, because indeed, *HASHEM your God will go over before you,* and thereby you will merit a leadership which is far better than mine.

יְהוֹשֻׁעַ הוּא עֹבֵר לְפָנֶיךָ כַּאֲשֶׁר דִּבֶּר ה׳ — *Joshua shall go over before you, as HASHEM has spoken* . . . because indeed Joshua is not the leader, but he goes over before you at the command of God, the Exalted One, Who is (the actual) leader.

6. לֹא יַרְפְּךָ — *He will not fail you.* Because He will strengthen your hands in time of war.

וְלֹא יַעַזְבֶךָּ — *And He will not forsake you.* Afterward, for He will not remove (lit., "diminish") His watchful eye (providence) from you, and those surrounding you will not rise up (against you).

7. כִּי אַתָּה תָּבוֹא — *For you shall go (with this people)* . . . even though I was not privileged to do so.

NOTES

should not mourn his passing exceedingly: (1) He has lived a long life; (2) even were he to continue to live, his advanced age would prevent him from maintaining his vigorous leadership; (3) since the heavenly decree was that he would not be permitted to enter *Eretz Yisrael*, then were he to continue to live, it would delay their crossing over into the Promised Land.

3. ה׳ אֱלֹהֶיךָ הוּא עֹבֵר . . . יְהוֹשֻׁעַ הוּא עֹבֵר — *HASHEM your God, He will go over . . . Joshua shall go over.* The verse seems to be self-contradictory. First we are told that God will go over before Israel and then we are told that Joshua will bring them across! The *Sforno* explains that God is the actual leader, whereas Joshua is but His messenger.

6. לֹא יַרְפְּךָ וְלֹא יַעַזְבֶךָּ — *He will not fail you and He will not forsake you.* The *Sforno* explains that these two expressions, "to fail" and "to forsake," are not redundant. The first speaks of a time of war while the second refers to a period of peace, which nonetheless requires the protection of God to secure Israel's well-being in the land.

7. כִּי אַתָּה תָּבוֹא — *For you shall go. Sforno* stresses the significance of the added word אַתָּה, *you.* Moses says to Joshua: "You will merit to cross over the Jordan River and lead Israel into the Promised Land, a privilege denied to me."

ט וַיִּכְתֹּב מֹשֶׁה אֶת־הַתּוֹרָה הַזֹּאת וַיִּתְּנָהּ אֶל־הַכֹּהֲנִים בְּנֵי לֵוִי הַנֹּשְׂאִים
רביעי י אֶת־אֲרוֹן בְּרִית יהוה וְאֶל־כָּל־זִקְנֵי יִשְׂרָאֵל: וַיְצַו מֹשֶׁה אוֹתָם לֵאמֹר
יא מִקֵּץ ׀ שֶׁבַע שָׁנִים בְּמֹעֵד שְׁנַת הַשְּׁמִטָּה בְּחַג הַסֻּכּוֹת: בְּבוֹא כָל־יִשְׂרָאֵל
לֵרָאוֹת אֶת־פְּנֵי יהוה אֱלֹהֶיךָ בַּמָּקוֹם אֲשֶׁר יִבְחָר תִּקְרָא אֶת־הַתּוֹרָה
יב הַזֹּאת נֶגֶד כָּל־יִשְׂרָאֵל בְּאָזְנֵיהֶם: הַקְהֵל אֶת־הָעָם הָאֲנָשִׁים וְהַנָּשִׁים
וְהַטַּף וְגֵרְךָ אֲשֶׁר בִּשְׁעָרֶיךָ לְמַעַן יִשְׁמְעוּ וּלְמַעַן יִלְמְדוּ וְיָרְאוּ אֶת־יהוה
יג אֱלֹהֵיכֶם וְשָׁמְרוּ לַעֲשׂוֹת אֶת־כָּל־דִּבְרֵי הַתּוֹרָה הַזֹּאת: וּבְנֵיהֶם אֲשֶׁר
לֹא־יָדְעוּ יִשְׁמְעוּ וְלָמְדוּ לְיִרְאָה אֶת־יהוה אֱלֹהֵיכֶם כָּל־הַיָּמִים אֲשֶׁר
אַתֶּם חַיִּים עַל־הָאֲדָמָה אֲשֶׁר אַתֶּם עֹבְרִים אֶת־הַיַּרְדֵּן שָׁמָּה לְרִשְׁתָּהּ:
חמישי [ששי] יד וַיֹּאמֶר יהוה אֶל־מֹשֶׁה הֵן קָרְבוּ יָמֶיךָ לָמוּת קְרָא אֶת־יְהוֹשֻׁעַ וְהִתְיַצְּבוּ
בְּאֹהֶל מוֹעֵד וַאֲצַוֶּנּוּ וַיֵּלֶךְ מֹשֶׁה וִיהוֹשֻׁעַ וַיִּתְיַצְּבוּ בְּאֹהֶל מוֹעֵד:
טו וַיֵּרָא יהוה בָּאֹהֶל בְּעַמּוּד עָנָן וַיַּעֲמֹד עַמּוּד הֶעָנָן עַל־פֶּתַח הָאֹהֶל:
טז וַיֹּאמֶר יהוה אֶל־מֹשֶׁה הִנְּךָ שֹׁכֵב עִם־אֲבֹתֶיךָ וְקָם הָעָם הַזֶּה
וְזָנָה ׀ אַחֲרֵי ׀ אֱלֹהֵי נֵכַר־הָאָרֶץ אֲשֶׁר הוּא בָא־שָׁמָּה בְּקִרְבּוֹ וַעֲזָבַנִי

9. אֶת הַתּוֹרָה הַזֹּאת — *This law.* (This refers to) the פָּרָשַׁת הַמֶּלֶךְ, *the section relating to the king*, which he now commanded to be read at הַקְהֵל (the assembly held every seven years).

וַיִּתְּנָהּ אֶל הַכֹּהֲנִים בְּנֵי לֵוִי — *And gave it to the Kohanim the sons of Levi.* For from their hand the king shall receive it to be read, as we learned, *The deputy hands it to the Kohen Gadol, and the Kohen Gadol (hands it) to the king* (*Sotah* 41a).

הַנֹּשְׂאִים אֶת אֲרוֹן — *Who carry the Ark ...* who carried (the Ark) when special miracles occurred.

וְאֶל כָּל זִקְנֵי יִשְׂרָאֵל — *And to the elders of Israel ...* from whose hand the *Kohanim* would receive the Torah at the Assembly, as we learn, "The *chazan* (attendant) of the synagogue gives it to the head of the synagogue, and the head of the synagogue to the deputy" (*Sotah* 41a).

12. לְמַעַן יִשְׁמְעוּ — *That they may hear ...* (that) the wise men of the people may understand.

NOTES

9. אֶת הַתּוֹרָה הַזֹּאת — *This law. Rashi* and *Ramban* understand this to mean the entire Torah, which was entrusted to the tribe of Levi to deposit in the Ark next to the tablets of law (v. 24). This interpretation, however, presents a problem, since here the *Kohanim* are mentioned, whereas in verse 24 the Levites are mentioned. *Ibn Ezra* attempts to resolve this difficulty by explaining that the *Kohanim* were responsible to teach the Torah to Israel and that the expression in verse 24, "the Levites," is an abbreviation for *the Kohanim the sons of Levi* written in our verse. The *Sforno*, however, defines the term אֶת הַתּוֹרָה הַזֹּאת, *this law*, as meaning the special section relating to the monarchy, i.e., that which was read by the king at the *Hakhel* ceremony. This was given to the *Kohanim* rather than to the Levites, for as the Mishnah teaches us (*Sotah* 41a), the *Kohen Gadol* would hand the Scroll to the king to be read on that occasion. The king would read selections from the Book of *Deuteronomy* including the section dealing with the monarchy (פָּרָשַׁת הַמֶּלֶךְ).

הַנֹּשְׂאִים אֶת אֲרוֹן — *Who carry the Ark.* Normally the Ark of the covenant was carried by the Kehathites of the tribe of Levi and not by the *Kohanim*. Our Sages tell us that "on three occasions the *Kohanim* carried the Ark; when they crossed the Jordan, when they walked around Jericho and when they deposited the Ark in its place (in the holy Temple)" (*Sotah* 33b). The *Sforno's* commentary reflects this saying of our Sages.

וְאֶת כָּל זִקְנֵי יִשְׂרָאֵל — *And to the elders of Israel.* Consistent with his explanation that "this law" refers to the Scroll read by the king at *Hakhel*, the *Sforno* explains the reason for including the elders of Israel. Since they were also involved in the ceremony of handing the Torah to the king on this

9 *Moses wrote this Torah and gave it to the Kohanim, the sons of Levi, the bearers of the Ark of the covenant of HASHEM, and to all the elders of Israel.*
10 *Moses commanded them, saying, "At the end of seven years, at the time of the Sabbatical year, during the Succos festival,*
11 *when all Israel comes to appear before HASHEM, your God, in the place that He will choose, you shall read this Torah before all Israel, in their ears,*
12 *Gather together the people — the men, the women, and the small children, and your stranger who is in your cities — so that they will hear and so that they will learn, and they shall fear HASHEM, your God, and be careful to perform all the words of this Torah.*
13 *And their children who do not know — they shall hear and they shall learn to fear HASHEM, your God, all the days that you live on the land to which you are crossing the Jordan, to possess it."*
14 *HASHEM spoke to Moses, "Behold, your days are drawing near to die; summon Joshua, and both of you shall stand in the Tent of Meeting, and I shall instruct him." So Moses and Joshua went and stood in the Tent of Meeting.*
15 *HASHEM appeared in the Tent, in a pillar of cloud, and the pillar of cloud stood by the entrance of the Tent.*
16 *HASHEM said to Moses, "Behold, you will lie with your forefathers, but this people will rise up and stray after the gods of the foreigners of the Land, in whose midst it is coming, and it will forsake*

וּלְמַעַן יִלְמְדוּ — *And that they may learn* ... so that they who do not understand shall (in turn) learn from them.

וְיָרְאוּ אֶת ה׳ אֱלֹהֵיכֶם — *To fear HASHEM your God* ... by understanding (appreciating) His greatness, as reflected in the reasoned proof of His Torah.

13. וּבְנֵיהֶם אֲשֶׁר לֹא יָדְעוּ — *And their children who have not known* . . . who were incapable of asking when they were little ones.

יִשְׁמְעוּ — *May hear* . . . a (superficial) hearing of the ear, i.e., they will hear that something is being said.

וְלָמְדוּ — *And learn.* When they grow older, they will inquire and learn from those who do understand.

NOTES

occasion (*Sotah* 41a), Moses gave it to them, as well as to the *Kohanim*.

12. לְמַעַן יִשְׁמְעוּ וּלְמַעַן יִלְמְדוּ — *That they may hear and that they may learn.* The previous verse (11) already states that the Torah was to be read by the king to Israel, בְּאָזְנֵיהֶם, *in their ears.* Why then is it necessary to state in this verse לְמַעַן יִשְׁמְעוּ, *that they may hear?* The *Sforno* explains that the previous verse speaks of listening superficially, without necessarily absorbing and understanding. Our verse speaks of the intelligent listener who understands the significance of the Torah's words, and in turn can teach it to others.

13. וּבְנֵיהֶם אֲשֶׁר לֹא יָדְעוּ יִשְׁמְעוּ וְלָמְדוּ — *And their children who have not known may hear and learn.* The *Sforno* continues the interpretation of this verse in the same vein as that of the previous verse. The young children assembled at the time of *Hakhel,* who are incapable of appreciating the words read by the king, will nonetheless sense that something of importance is transpiring. Eventually, they will inquire and learn as they mature, for their curiosity and desire to know will have been aroused. Hence, their attendance at *Hakhel* will serve an important purpose. The *Sforno's* explanation clarifies the question, "Why should the little ones come?" to which the Sages answer, "To reward those who bring them" (*Chagigah* 3). The bringing of the little ones must serve some purpose for which the adults will be rewarded. The *Sforno's* commentary illuminates the practical benefit of their presence at *Hakhel*. This experience will ultimately cause them to pursue the teachings of Torah when they mature and will be old enough to understand. And it is for enabling the children to have this experience that their parents are rewarded.

יז וְהֵפֵר אֶת־בְּרִיתִי אֲשֶׁר כָּרַתִּי אִתּוֹ: וְחָרָה אַפִּי בוֹ בַיּוֹם־הַהוּא וַעֲזַבְתִּים
וְהִסְתַּרְתִּי פָנַי מֵהֶם וְהָיָה לֶאֱכֹל וּמְצָאֻהוּ רָעוֹת רַבּוֹת וְצָרוֹת וְאָמַר בַּיּוֹם
יח הַהוּא הֲלֹא עַל כִּי־אֵין אֱלֹהַי בְּקִרְבִּי מְצָאוּנִי הָרָעוֹת הָאֵלֶּה: וְאָנֹכִי
הַסְתֵּר אַסְתִּיר פָּנַי בַּיּוֹם הַהוּא עַל כָּל־הָרָעָה אֲשֶׁר עָשָׂה כִּי פָנָה אֶל־
יט אֱלֹהִים אֲחֵרִים: וְעַתָּה כִּתְבוּ לָכֶם אֶת־הַשִּׁירָה הַזֹּאת וְלַמְּדָהּ אֶת־בְּנֵי־
יִשְׂרָאֵל שִׂימָהּ בְּפִיהֶם לְמַעַן תִּהְיֶה־לִּי הַשִּׁירָה הַזֹּאת לְעֵד בִּבְנֵי יִשְׂרָאֵל:
ששי [שביעי] כ כִּי־אֲבִיאֶנּוּ אֶל־הָאֲדָמָה | אֲשֶׁר־נִשְׁבַּעְתִּי לַאֲבֹתָיו זָבַת חָלָב וּדְבַשׁ
וְאָכַל וְשָׂבַע וְדָשֵׁן וּפָנָה אֶל־אֱלֹהִים אֲחֵרִים וַעֲבָדוּם וְנִאֲצוּנִי וְהֵפֵר אֶת־
כא בְּרִיתִי: וְהָיָה כִּי־תִמְצֶאןָ אֹתוֹ רָעוֹת רַבּוֹת וְצָרוֹת וְעָנְתָה הַשִּׁירָה הַזֹּאת
לְפָנָיו לְעֵד כִּי לֹא תִשָּׁכַח מִפִּי זַרְעוֹ כִּי יָדַעְתִּי אֶת־יִצְרוֹ אֲשֶׁר הוּא עֹשֶׂה
כב הַיּוֹם בְּטֶרֶם אֲבִיאֶנּוּ אֶל־הָאָרֶץ אֲשֶׁר נִשְׁבָּעְתִּי: וַיִּכְתֹּב מֹשֶׁה אֶת־
כג הַשִּׁירָה הַזֹּאת בַּיּוֹם הַהוּא וַיְלַמְּדָהּ אֶת־בְּנֵי יִשְׂרָאֵל: וַיְצַו אֶת־יְהוֹשֻׁעַ
בִּן־נוּן וַיֹּאמֶר חֲזַק וֶאֱמָץ כִּי אַתָּה תָּבִיא אֶת־בְּנֵי יִשְׂרָאֵל אֶל־הָאָרֶץ
כד אֲשֶׁר־נִשְׁבַּעְתִּי לָהֶם וְאָנֹכִי אֶהְיֶה עִמָּךְ: וַיְהִי | כְּכַלּוֹת מֹשֶׁה לִכְתֹּב
שביעי כה אֶת־דִּבְרֵי הַתּוֹרָה־הַזֹּאת עַל־סֵפֶר עַד תֻּמָּם: וַיְצַו מֹשֶׁה אֶת־הַלְוִיִּם

---

17. וַעֲזַבְתִּים — *And I will forsake them* ... into the hands of their enemies who will prevail over them.

וְהִסְתַּרְתִּי פָנַי מֵהֶם — *And I will hide my face from them.* After they will be (given over into) the hands of the nations who will deal with them in an ill fashion and afflict them, I will avert my merciful eye from them as though I do not see their troubles.

עַל כִּי אֵין אֱלֹהַי בְּקִרְבִּי מְצָאוּנִי הָרָעוֹת הָאֵלֶּה — *These evils have come upon me because my God is not in my midst.* Because He removed His *Shechinah,* Divine Presence, from our midst, all these (evils) have befallen us. And by so thinking, you will not turn to Him in prayer or repent.

18. וְאָנֹכִי הַסְתֵּר אַסְתִּיר פָּנַי — *And I will surely hide My face.* It is not as they thought when they said that I am not in their midst, because (in reality) wherever they may be, My *Shechinah* is to be found there, as our Sages said, "Wherever Israel was exiled, the *Shechinah* was with them" (*Megillah* 29a). Rather, I shall but *hide* My face (and refrain) from saving them.

עַל כָּל הָרָעָה אֲשֶׁר עָשָׂה — *For all the evil which they have done* ... to themselves.

NOTES

17-18. וְהִסְתַּרְתִּי פָנַי מֵהֶם ... עַל כִּי אֵין אֱלֹהַי בְּקִרְבִּי ... — וְאָנֹכִי הַסְתֵּר אַסְתִּיר ... כִּי פָנָה אֶל אֱלֹהִים אֲחֵרִים — *And I will hide my face from them ... because my God is not in my midst ... and I will surely hide ... because they turned to other gods.* The expression הַסְתָּרַת פָּנִים means "the concealment of God's face," which the *Sforno* explains as the removal of His merciful concern for the people of Israel, as though He is averting His eyes and refuses to look at their troubles. This does not mean, however, that God has left their midst as Israel may think (*because God is not in our midst*). The *Sforno* quotes the statement of our Sages, which is a fundamental belief of our faith, that the *Shechinah,* Divine Presence, accompanies Israel into their various exiles. This error on the part of Israel will deter them from repenting, and therefore it is necessary for God to reassure them that although He has permitted their enemies to prevail and has hidden His face, nonetheless, He has not left them and therefore their prayers will still be heard and their repentance accepted.

21. כִּי יָדַעְתִּי אֶת יִצְרוֹ — *For I know their inclinations.* Moses laments that instead of Israel entering *Eretz Yisrael* to realize and develop their spiritual

Me and annul My covenant that I have sealed with it. [17] *My anger will flare against it on that day and I will forsake them; and I will conceal My face from them and they will become prey, and many evils and distresses will encounter it. It will say on that day, 'Is it not because my God is not in my midst that these evils have come upon me?'* [18] *But I will surely have concealed My face on that day because of all the evil that it did, for it had turned to gods of others.* [19] *So now, write this song for yourselves, and teach it to the Children of Israel, place it in their mouth, so that this song shall be for Me a witness against the Children of Israel.*

[20] *"For I shall bring them to the Land that I swore to their forefathers, which flows with milk and honey, but it will eat, be sated, and grow fat, and turn to gods of others and serve them, it will provoke Me and annul My covenant.* [21] *It shall be that when many evils and distresses come upon it, then this song shall speak up before it as a witness, for it shall not be forgotten from the mouth of its offspring, for I know its inclination, what it does today, before I bring them to the Land that I have sworn."* [22] *Moses wrote this song on that day, and he taught it to the Children of Israel.* [23] *He commanded Joshua son of Nun, and said, "Be strong and courageous, for you shall bring the Children of Israel to the Land that I have sworn to them, and I shall be with you."*

[24] *So it was that when Moses finished writing the words of this Torah onto a book, until their conclusion:* [25] *Moses commanded the Levites,*

כִּי פָנָה אֶל אֱלֹהִים אֲחֵרִים — *Because they turned to other gods.* Because when troubles befell them due to their sins, they did not turn to Me to help them (through) prayer and repentance, but (instead), they turned to those who serve other gods to be rescued through them.

21. כִּי יָדַעְתִּי אֶת יִצְרוֹ אֲשֶׁר הוּא עֹשֶׂה הַיּוֹם — *For I know their inclinations which they form this day.* They do not anticipate entering the Land so as to serve Me, which is My intent, as it says, וַיִּתֵּן לָהֶם אַרְצוֹת גּוֹיִם ... בַּעֲבוּר יִשְׁמְרוּ חֻקָּיו, *And He gave them the lands of the nations ... that they might keep His statutes* (*Psalms* 105:44,45). Rather, they look to it (the Land) to satisfy the (base) desires of their souls, and because of this (attitude) the prophesied evil will come to pass, as it says, *But Jeshurun waxed fat and kicked* (32:15).

23. וַיְצַו אֶת יְהוֹשֻׁעַ — *And He appointed Joshua.* God, the Blessed One, then appointed Joshua as ruler, similar to, צִוִּיתִי שֹׁפְטִים, *I appointed judges* (*II Samuel* 7:11), and וַיְצַוְּךָ לְנָגִיד, *And have appointed you ruler* (*I Samuel* 25:30) and such similar (verses).

24. עַל סֵפֶר עַד תֻּמָּם — *In a book until they were finished* ... including the portion of *Haazinu* and the portion of *Vezos HaBerachah.*

NOTES

potential, which was the primary purpose of God's granting them the Land, they will settle in it to enjoy material wealth and physical comfort.

23. וַיְצַו אֶת יְהוֹשֻׁעַ — *And He appointed Joshua.* As the *Sforno* pointed out in his commentary on *Exodus* 6:13 regarding Moses and Aaron — וַיְצַוֵּם אֶל בְּנֵי יִשְׂרָאֵל, *And He charged them over the Children of Israel* — the meaning is He *appointed* them as leaders. So too, in our verse, the word וַיְצַו does not mean *He commanded* but rather, *He appointed* Joshua as a ruler (see also *Sforno, Genesis* 36:31).

24. עַל סֵפֶר עַד תֻּמָּם — *In a book until they were finished.* The *Sforno* explains that the reference here is to the completion of the entire Torah from beginning to end, including the two portions of *Haazinu* and *Vezos HaBerachah,* which appear following this *sedrah.* The שִׁירָה, *song* or *poem,* mentioned in verse 30, however, which includes the same expression עַד תֻּמָּם, *until they were finished,* only refers to the song of *Haazinu,* which Moses recited to the people prior to his death.

כו נֹשְׂאֵי אֲרוֹן בְּרִית־יְהוָה לֵאמֹר: לָקֹחַ אֵת סֵפֶר הַתּוֹרָה הַזֶּה וְשַׂמְתֶּם אֹתוֹ
כז מִצַּד אֲרוֹן בְּרִית־יְהוָה אֱלֹהֵיכֶם וְהָיָה־שָׁם בְּךָ לְעֵד: כִּי אָנֹכִי יָדַעְתִּי
אֶת־מֶרְיְךָ וְאֶת־עָרְפְּךָ הַקָּשֶׁה הֵן בְּעוֹדֶנִּי חַי עִמָּכֶם הַיּוֹם מַמְרִים הֱיִתֶם
מפטיר כח עִם־יְהוָה וְאַף כִּי־אַחֲרֵי מוֹתִי: הַקְהִילוּ אֵלַי אֶת־כָּל־זִקְנֵי שִׁבְטֵיכֶם
וְשֹׁטְרֵיכֶם וַאֲדַבְּרָה בְאָזְנֵיהֶם אֵת הַדְּבָרִים הָאֵלֶּה וְאָעִידָה בָּם אֶת־
כט הַשָּׁמַיִם וְאֶת־הָאָרֶץ: כִּי יָדַעְתִּי אַחֲרֵי מוֹתִי כִּי־הַשְׁחֵת תַּשְׁחִתוּן וְסַרְתֶּם
מִן־הַדֶּרֶךְ אֲשֶׁר צִוִּיתִי אֶתְכֶם וְקָרָאת אֶתְכֶם הָרָעָה בְּאַחֲרִית הַיָּמִים
ל כִּי־תַעֲשׂוּ אֶת־הָרַע בְּעֵינֵי יְהוָה לְהַכְעִיסוֹ בְּמַעֲשֵׂה יְדֵיכֶם: וַיְדַבֵּר מֹשֶׁה
בְּאָזְנֵי כָּל־קְהַל יִשְׂרָאֵל אֶת־דִּבְרֵי הַשִּׁירָה הַזֹּאת עַד תֻּמָּם:

26. וְהָיָה שָׁם בְּךָ לְעֵד — *That it remain there as a witness against you.* It will bear testimony that I knew you would forsake the Torah of God, the Blessed One, and therefore, I had to place a Torah Scroll in a (secure) place where no man could enter, except for the *Kohen Gadol*, and he only once a year. This Scroll will bear testimony that all that is written in the Torah, which is in the hands of the righteous of the generation, are the words which were spoken to Moses at Sinai, without (any) addition or diminishment, and thus no doubts will arise among you regarding them (i.e., the words of Torah). However, as for the Scroll found by Chilkeyahu (*II Kings* 22:8), it would seem to me that it was the Scroll given by Moses to the *Kohanim* who carried the Ark of the Covenant of God, as mentioned above, which contained only the portion of the king (פָּרָשַׁת הַמֶּלֶךְ). In it, Joshua (also) wrote the covenant which he renewed with Israel in Shechem (*Joshua* 24:25,26) when they accepted to serve God, the Exalted One, in truth and integrity (תְּמִים), (meaning) with contemplation and deed. When Josiah read from this Scroll and realized that they had strayed from it, he trembled and inquired of God (for guidance) therein (i.e., in regard to this defection).

NOTES

26. וְהָיָה שָׁם בְּךָ לְעֵד — *That it remain there as a witness against you*. The Midrash says that on the day Moses passed away, he wrote thirteen Torah Scrolls. He gave one to each of the twelve tribes and the thirteenth he delivered into the hands of the Levites for safekeeping. They placed it *on the side of the Ark of the covenant*. The *Sforno* explains that this was done so that there would always be an authentic, authoritative copy of the Torah in a secure place thus preventing any attempt to falsify it or to produce a counterfeit one. The Levites were entrusted with this Torah for it was they who carried the Ark. However, the Scroll mentioned in verse 9, which contained the פָּרָשַׁת הַמֶּלֶךְ, *the portion of the king*, was entrusted to the *Kohanim*, for the reason given by the *Sforno* in his commentary on that verse. In the opinion of the *Sforno*, it is this latter Torah which Chilkeyahu the *Kohen Gadol* discovered in the reign of King Josiah, as recorded in *II Kings* 22:8, and not the 13th Torah mentioned by the Midrash. In that chapter, we read that Josiah ordered that the Temple be repaired and in the process a Torah Scroll was found which had been hidden in defiance of King Ahaz' order that all Torah Scrolls be burned. When this *Sefer Torah* was read to Josiah, he rent his clothes, for he realized that Israel was guilty of violating God's teachings. Subsequently, he gathered the people and read from the Scroll and renewed the covenant between Israel and God. The *Sforno* is of the opinion that this particular Scroll contained only "the portion of the king" which was read by the king at *Hakhel*. This public assembly took place every seven years at the conclusion of the Succos festival following each Sabbatical year.

The basis for the *Sforno's* thesis may well be the Mishnah in tractate *Sotah* (41a), which states that included in the פָּרָשַׁת הַמֶּלֶךְ are the blessings and

the bearers of the Ark of the covenant of HASHEM, saying, 26 *"Take this book of the Torah and place it at the side of the Ark of the covenant of HASHEM, and it shall be there for you as a witness.* 27 *For I know your rebelliousness and your stiff neck; behold! while I am still alive with you today, you have been rebels against God — and surely after my death.* 28 *Gather to me all the elders of your tribes and your officers, and I shall speak these words into their ears, and call heaven and earth to bear witness against them.* 29 *For I know that after my death you will surely act corruptly, and you will stray from the path that I have commanded you, and evil will befall you at the end of days, if you do what is evil in the eyes of HASHEM, to anger Him through your handiwork."*

30 *Moses spoke the words of this song into the ears of the entire congregation of Israel, until their conclusion.*

---

28. וַאֲדַבְּרָה בְאָזְנֵיהֶם אֵת הַדְּבָרִים הָאֵלֶּה — *That I may speak these words in their ears ...* the song of *Haazinu.*

וְאָעִידָה בָּם אֶת הַשָּׁמַיִם וְאֶת הָאָרֶץ — *And call heaven and earth to witness against them ...* as it says, *Give ear, O heavens etc.* (32:1).

29. כִּי יָדַעְתִּי — *For I know.* I shall relate with this song, and bear testimony against you, that I knew you would act in such a manner that evil would be brought upon you. (This was) in order that you shall not attribute future (events) simply to chance but rather you will attribute it to your corrupt behavior, and (thereby) consider returning (to God), similar to, וָאַגִּיד לְךָ מֵאָז בְּטֶרֶם תָּבוֹא הִשְׁמַעְתִּיךָ פֶּן תֹּאמַר עָצְבִּי עָשָׂם, *Therefore I have declared it to you from of old, before it came to pass I announced it to you, lest you say my idol has done them* (*Isaiah* 48:5).

30. אֵת דִּבְרֵי הַשִּׁירָה הַזֹּאת עַד תֻּמָּם — *The words of this song, until they were complete ...* including the portion of *For HASHEM will judge* (32:36) and *For I lift up My hand* (32:40), even though these are not part of the words of the testimony.

NOTES

curses as recorded in *parashas Ki Savo* (chapter 27). Josiah was deeply alarmed when he read these curses, and the fact that he later read from this Scroll to the people whom he had assembled, and also renewed the covenant between Israel and God, is reasonable proof that it was indeed the פָּרָשַׁת הַמֶּלֶךְ which had been found, since the "blessing and curses" are the prelude to the covenant between Israel and God, as stated in *Nitzavim* (29:11).

The *Sforno* is also of the opinion that when Joshua, before his death, renewed the covenant between the people and God, he recorded it *in the book of God's Torah* (*Joshua* 24:26), namely, the Scroll of פָּרָשַׁת הַמֶּלֶךְ. This is his theory even though the Talmud (*Makos* 11a) tells us that one Sage is of the opinion that this act of writing by Joshua refers to the last eight verses of the Torah. Since they speak of Moses' death, Moses could not have written them. Thus, God bid Joshua to write these verses. Another Sage states that it refers to the list of cities of refuge recorded in the Book of *Joshua.* Nonetheless, the *Sforno* is of the opinion that Joshua would never have added anything to the Torah itself, but did feel free to add the confirmation of the covenant in his time to the special book of פָּרָשַׁת הַמֶּלֶךְ. When Josiah read of the renewal of the covenant in the time of Joshua, he decided to do likewise, as recorded in *II Kings* 23.

29. כִּי יָדַעְתִּי — *For I know.* The tendency of people is to attribute events to blind chance — a happenstance. Moses cautions the people to avoid this error, and to recognize that their fate is always the consequence of their behavior, and a heavenly judgment from God. The poem of *Haazinu* foretells the history of Israel and thereby bears testimony to God's Providence and His Divine system of reward and punishment.

פרשת האזינו

לב

א הַאֲזִינוּ הַשָּׁמַיִם וַאֲדַבֵּרָה וְתִשְׁמַע הָאָרֶץ אִמְרֵי־פִי׃
ב יַעֲרֹף כַּמָּטָר לִקְחִי תִּזַּל כַּטַּל אִמְרָתִי
כִּשְׂעִירִם עֲלֵי־דֶשֶׁא וְכִרְבִיבִים עֲלֵי־עֵשֶׂב׃
ג כִּי שֵׁם יהוה אֶקְרָא הָבוּ גֹדֶל לֵאלֹהֵינוּ׃
ד הַצּוּר תָּמִים פָּעֳלוֹ כִּי כָל־דְּרָכָיו מִשְׁפָּט
אֵל אֱמוּנָה וְאֵין עָוֶל צַדִּיק וְיָשָׁר הוּא׃
ה שִׁחֵת לוֹ לֹא בָּנָיו מוּמָם דּוֹר עִקֵּשׁ וּפְתַלְתֹּל׃

XXXII

2. יַעֲרֹף כַּמָּטָר לִקְחִי — *My Torah shall drop as the rain.* Behold, my teaching (lit., my Torah) shall drop and stream as the rain unto those who understand and are prepared to receive the flow from the fount of wisdom.

תִּזַּל כַּטַּל אִמְרָתִי — *My speech shall flow gently like the dew.* And it (i.e., my Torah) shall also grant some knowledge to the common man, according to its apparent (lit., revealed) teaching, for although it is small in quantity it is exceedingly good, similar to the dew. In such a manner, it (the teaching of Moses) shall be as *the stormy showers upon the herbage,* (meaning) that the intelligent ones shall see the wonders in it (i.e., the Torah); *and as the drops of rain upon the grass,* (meaning) that the common people will also attain some knowledge from it, learning to recognize their Creator to some extent through its (study). Therefore to you, Israel, who have received it, (I now say) . . .

3. כִּי שֵׁם ה׳ אֶקְרָא — *When I proclaim the Name of HASHEM.* Behold, a קוֹרֵא שֵׁם ה׳, *one who proclaims the Name of God,* is he who prays, as it says קָרָאתִי שִׁמְךָ ה׳ מִבּוֹר תַּחְתִּיּוֹת, *I called upon Your Name, HASHEM, out of the nethermost pit* (*Lamentations* 3:55); and also וּשְׁמוּאֵל בְּקֹרְאֵי שְׁמוֹ קֹרְאִים אֶל ה׳ וְהוּא יַעֲנֵם, *and Samuel among those who call upon His Name; they called upon HASHEM and He answered them* (*Psalms* 99:6). (Moses) therefore says: When I pray regarding the ingathering of the exiles, saying, *As an eagle that stirs up her nest* (v. 11), and also regarding the coming of Messiah saying, *HASHEM alone did lead him* (v. 12), and also at the conclusion of the song, when I say, *Sing aloud, you nations, of His people* (v. 43), you who know of His greatness through reasoned proof, as explained in His Torah . . .

הָבוּ גֹדֶל לֵאלֹהֵינוּ — *Give greatness to our God.* Do not attribute any change to Him (as a result) of what will be related in this song regarding the future of Israel, or (think) that He

NOTES

XXXII

2. כַּמָּטָר . . . כַּטַּל — *As the rain . . . like the dew.* Moses uses the simile of מָטָר, *rain*, and also of טַל, *dew*. Linked to the former is the expression שְׂעִירִם, which *Rashi* explains as meaning a stormy wind, whereas the phrase רְבִיבִים, meaning drops of rain, is linked to the latter. The *Sforno* explains the verse thus: God's Torah can be comprehended by simple folk as well as by scholars, but their understanding and grasp of its teachings and profound wisdom are on different levels. The common, average individual understands the Torah's instruction superficially. He absorbs and appreciates it within certain limitations. The Torah compares this to dew and drops of rain. However, the intelligent, advanced student of Torah plummets the depths and unravels its profound mysteries; this is compared to the rain and the stormy wind, because it overwhelms the mind and permeates the soul of wise men who are capable of appreciating the wonders of God's teaching.

3-4. כִּי שֵׁם ה׳ אֶקְרָא . . . כִּי כָל דְּרָכָיו מִשְׁפָּט . . . צַדִּיק וְיָשָׁר הוּא — *When I proclaim the Name of HASHEM . . . for all His ways are justice . . . righteous and right is He.* The *Sforno* interprets the sense of these two verses thus: Although you may well surmise from my prayer and song that trouble will befall the people of Israel, including persecution and

PARASHAS HAAZINU

32 [1] Give ear, O heavens, and I will speak; and may the earth hear the words of my mouth.
[2] May my teaching drop like the rain, may my utterance flow like the dew; like storm winds upon vegetation and like raindrops upon blades of grass.
[3] When I call out the Name of HASHEM, ascribe greatness to our God.
[4] The Rock! — perfect is His work, for all His paths are justice; a God of faith without iniquity, righteous and fair is He.
[5] Corruption is not His — the blemish is His children's, a perverse and twisted generation.

---

will become an enemy to them (i.e., Israel), because you know, through proof from His Torah, that He is *the Rock* Who is unchanging, and His hand is (never) incapable of saving, (nor) His ear incapable of hearing. Also, you shall not attribute to Him iniquity, considering that you know with certainty that *His work is perfect* (v. 4) as is (His) existence, and nothing can be added to it (i.e., *His work*) nor can anything be subtracted from it, and thus (we) know ...

4. כִּי כָל דְּרָכָיו מִשְׁפָּט — *For all His ways are justice.* His ways of goodness and His attributes of law are all just, without any doubt.

אֵל אֱמוּנָה — *A God of faithfulness.* He will faithfully (fulfill) that which He swore to the Patriarchs, i.e., to be good to (their) descendants in the merit of their fathers.

וְאֵין עָוֶל — *And without iniquity* ... when He brings punishment.

צַדִּיק — *Righteous.* He loves righteousness, and because of His righteousness He will not cast off His people in exile.

וְיָשָׁר הוּא — *And right is He* ... never denying the reward of any human being. (He) repays His enemies before Him, and therefore prolongs (their existence) and is good to the nations in This World.

5. שִׁחֵת לוֹ לֹא בָּנָיו מוּמָם דּוֹר עִקֵּשׁ וּפְתַלְתֹּל — *A generation crooked and perverse, that are not His children, has corrupted His ways (and this is) their blemish.* But a generation (that is) crooked and perverse are not His children, who are (characterized by) perfection, for behold, their blemish (manifested) through the (sin) of the calf corrupted the intent of God, the Exalted One, as it says כִּי שִׁחֵת עַמְּךָ, *for your people have dealt corruptly* (*Exodus* 32:7). Because He indeed intended to sanctify Israel and to sanctify His Name through them in His world, that they should be luminaries for human kind, to understand and to instruct, as it says כִּי לִי כָּל הָאָרֶץ וְאַתֶּם תִּהְיוּ לִי מַמְלֶכֶת כֹּהֲנִים, *For all the earth is Mine; and you shall be unto Me a kingdom of Kohanim* (ibid 19:5,6), (but) they perverted all this through idolatry.

NOTES

exile, do not despair, for God is unchanging as a Rock and He is unswerving in His love for Israel, ever committed to preserve them. He is also a God of justice and faithfulness, Who rewards the righteous and punishes the wicked. This may not be perceived by man at the beginning, but God is patient — as we must also be — and eventually there is Divine accountability, be it for evil or for good. Compare this commentary to *Rashi* on verse 4.

5. שִׁחֵת לוֹ — *Has corrupted His ways.* The expression שִׁחֵת is used in this verse and also at the episode of the Golden Calf. It indicates turning away from the correct and proper way. The *Sforno* interprets our verse as referring to the sin of idolatry at Mt. Sinai, which vitiated the plan of God for Israel — to be a light unto the nations. See the *Sforno's* commentary on *Exodus* 19:5,6 where he explains that mankind as a whole is precious to God, but Israel is His unique treasure whose mis-

*ה' רבתי והיא תיבה לעצמה

ו הַ֨לְיהוָ֙ה תִּגְמְלוּ־זֹ֔את עַ֥ם נָבָ֖ל וְלֹ֣א חָכָ֑ם
הֲלוֹא־הוּא֙ אָבִ֣יךָ קָּנֶ֔ךָ ה֥וּא עָֽשְׂךָ֖ וַֽיְכֹנְנֶֽךָ׃

שני ז זְכֹר֙ יְמ֣וֹת עוֹלָ֔ם בִּ֖ינוּ שְׁנ֣וֹת דֹּר־וָדֹ֑ר
שְׁאַ֤ל אָבִ֙יךָ֙ וְיַגֵּ֔דְךָ זְקֵנֶ֖יךָ וְיֹ֥אמְרוּ לָֽךְ׃

ח בְּהַנְחֵ֤ל עֶלְיוֹן֙ גּוֹיִ֔ם בְּהַפְרִיד֖וֹ בְּנֵ֣י אָדָ֑ם
יַצֵּב֙ גְּבֻלֹ֣ת עַמִּ֔ים לְמִסְפַּ֖ר בְּנֵ֥י יִשְׂרָאֵֽל׃

6. הַלַה׳ תִּגְמְלוּ זֹאת — *Do you thus repay HASHEM?* Considering that His intent was to elevate you above all the nations, is it then proper that you repay Him thus, impairing His intent by desecrating his Holy Name, and thereby preventing the attainment of (His) purpose which He intended (when) He said, נַעֲשֶׂה אָדָם בְּצַלְמֵנוּ כִּדְמוּתֵנוּ, *Let us make man in our image after our likeness* (*Genesis* 1:26)?

עַם נָבָל — *A vile people.* Contemptible, in that you are ingrates who repay with evil (the One) Who does good, as opposed to the honored noble (generous) One, Who does good even to those who never did good unto Him.

וְלֹא חָכָם — *And unwise.* (Unwise) in statesmanship so as to understand what the end result will be and what will (eventually) be attained.

הֲלוֹא הוּא אָבִיךָ קָּנֶךָ — *Is He not your Father Who has acquired you?* (He) is not a natural father who causes existence by chance, but a Father by choice Who granted you existence that you might be His possession, prepared to attain His desire through you, and that you shall be His treasured people. (And thus) He made you into a nation, because (otherwise) you would not have been considered a nation at all.

וַיְכֹנְנֶךָ — *And prepared you.* He gave you preparatory (powers) that you might be predisposed through them to be a treasured (chosen) people unto Him.

7. זְכֹר יְמוֹת עוֹלָם — *Remember the days of old.* After he completed the introductory section of the song wherein he proclaimed his intent to tell of the righteousness of the Exalted God; that He is a faithful God Who does good for Israel, Who has "blessed and will not reverse it" (based on *Numbers* 23:20), and that there is no iniquity in the measure of His judgment against them, Moses (now) begins to explain this by relating the (events) of the past and the future, telling us (the following): First, the intent of God, the Blessed

NOTES

sion it is to instruct mankind in the ways of God. Through their sinful actions, they thwarted His plan and frustrated His intent, as the *Sforno* states in the next verse.

6. עַם נָבָל וְלֹא חָכָם ... אָבִיךָ קָּנֶךָ ... וַיְכֹנְנֶךָ — *A vile people and unwise ... your Father Who has acquired you ... and prepared you.* Similar to other commentators, among them the *Ramban*, the *Sforno* interprets the word נָבָל to mean one whose vile nature is manifested in a lack of gratitude for past favors and לֹא חָכָם, *unwise*, as one who has demonstrated his failure to understand that any future assistance from the same source is jeopardized by such ingratitude. The word קָנֶךָ, *Who has acquired you*, qualifying the word אָבִיךָ, *your Father*, is explained as meaning a conscious choice by God to acquire Israel as His people and prepare them to be an עַם סְגוּלָה, *a treasured people* (*Exodus* 19:5). Unlike *Rashi* who interprets וַיְכֹנְנֶךָ as being derived from the root כֵּן, *base*, the *Sforno* interprets it in the sense of הֲכָנָה, *preparation*.

7. זְכֹר יְמוֹת עוֹלָם — *Remember the days of old*. The Talmud (*Rosh Hashanah* 31a) explains why specific psalms were chanted by the Levites each day in the Temple as part of the morning service. At the *Mussaf* service on *Shabbos* they would recite the *parashah* of *Haazinu*, which was divided into six parts and recited over a period of six weeks.

The *Sforno* explains the division of the *parashah* into six sections in the following manner. Verses 1-6 are the introductory remarks of Moses where he assures Israel that God is faithful and concerned for their welfare. This section beginning with the letter ה׳ was read in the Temple as one unit and in the synagogue today is the portion read by the *Kohen*. The second section, read by the Levi (verses 7-12), begins with the letter ז׳ and discusses God's original plan for mankind. This

[6] *Is it to HASHEM that you do this, O vile and unwise people? Is He not your Father, your Master? Has He not created you and firmed you?*
[7] *Remember the days of yore, understand the years of generation after generation. Ask your father and he will relate it to you, and your elders and they will tell you.*
[8] *When the Supreme One gave the nations their inheritance, when He separated the children of man, He set the borders of the peoples according to the number of the Children of Israel.*

One, was to attain this goal (purpose) through all of humankind "in days of old and the years of many generations," and when this did not succeed, God did great wonders with Israel by elevating them to the heights, as He shall do at the "end of days" with the remnants (of Israel) whom He will call upon.

Second, He gave them an appropriate place in which to serve Him in joy and goodness of heart, with an abundance (of material blessings), but they rebelled and repaid evil for good. And he who frustrated this intent (of God) is, without a doubt, deserving of severe punishment.

Third, because of the magnitude of their sins they fell into the net of the wicked and were deserving of complete destruction, were it not for the desecration of God's honor which prevented it.

Fourth, he informs (us) the cause (reason) for which they will be redeemed at the end of days.

Fifth, he describes the manner of (Israel's) redemption, and the revenge that God, the Blessed One, (will exact) against the oppressors of His people. (Now) these are the (various) parts of *parashas Haazinu* mentioned by our Sages (*Rosh Hashanah* 31a) who designated (special) signs for them: הזי״ו ל״ך (these being the first letters of these six sections). He therefore says, *Remember the days of old,* and you will understand the goodness of His ways and how He intended to benefit humankind in general, when you recall how at first He was good to Adam at the beginning of time (lit., the days of old), placing him in the Garden of Eden, but (Adam) spoiled the state of (his affairs). Secondly, *Consider the years of many generations* and you will understand how, prior to the Flood, He was good to many generations but they corrupted (their ways); and thirdly, (His goodness) from the time of the Flood to (the generations of) dispersal, and (how) they perverted (their ways).

8. יַצֵּב גְּבֻלֹת עַמִּים — *He set the borders of the peoples.* And He set the borders of the

NOTES

plan was frustrated as a result of man's transgressions, resulting in the Almighty's choice of one people (Israel) through whom He hoped to effectuate His original plan for mankind. The third section (verses 15-18) tells us that a special land (*Eretz Yisrael*) was given to Israel, and was blessed with material and spiritual goodness, but they rebelled against Him and were consequently punished. This unit begins with the letter 'י and is שְׁלִישִׁי — the third *aliyah* read on *Shabbos Haazinu.* The fourth unit (verses 19-28) beginning with the letter 'ו, speaks of Israel's punishment which was tempered lest their destruction cause a חִלּוּל הַשֵּׁם, *profanation of God's Name.* The fifth section, beginning with the letter 'ל (verses 29-39), speaks of God's concern and compassion for Israel, His revenge against the nations who had persecuted the Jewish people, and of Israel's ultimate redemption. The sixth and concluding unit (verses 40-43) begins with the letter 'כ and tells us the manner of God's revenge and of the redemption of Israel. The Sages refer to these six units as הזי״ו ל״ך, an acrostic composed of the first letter of each of the first words of the six portions. The *Sforno* in his commentary lists only five sections since he considers the first part of הַאֲזִינוּ as an introduction and not part of the body of the poem. The *Rambam* explains that this *parashah* was read at the Temple *Mussaf* service on the Sabbath because 'they are words encouraging the people to repent.' (See *Orach Chaim* 428:5 and the *Mishnah Berurah* 11.)

ט כִּי חֵלֶק יְהוָה עַמּוֹ — יַעֲקֹב חֶבֶל נַחֲלָתוֹ׃
י יִמְצָאֵהוּ בְּאֶרֶץ מִדְבָּר — וּבְתֹהוּ יְלֵל יְשִׁמֹן
יְסֹבְבֶנְהוּ יְבוֹנְנֵהוּ — יִצְּרֶנְהוּ כְּאִישׁוֹן עֵינוֹ׃
יא כְּנֶשֶׁר יָעִיר קִנּוֹ — עַל־גּוֹזָלָיו יְרַחֵף
יִפְרֹשׂ כְּנָפָיו יִקָּחֵהוּ — יִשָּׂאֵהוּ עַל־אֶבְרָתוֹ׃
יב יְהוָה בָּדָד יַנְחֶנּוּ — וְאֵין עִמּוֹ אֵל נֵכָר׃
°בָּמֳתֵי ק׳ שלישי יג יַרְכִּבֵהוּ עַל־°בָּמוֹתֵי אָרֶץ — וַיֹּאכַל תְּנוּבֹת שָׂדָי
וַיֵּנִקֵהוּ דְבַשׁ מִסֶּלַע — וְשֶׁמֶן מֵחַלְמִישׁ צוּר׃

peoples (at the time of) the Separation (הַפְּלָגָה) but did not destroy them completely which, in reality, they deserved.

לְמִסְפַּר בְּנֵי יִשְׂרָאֵל — *According to the number of the Children of Israel* . . . for the sake of the Children of Israel who were few in number, but who would ultimately come forth from those people — and the proof of this is . . .

9. כִּי חֵלֶק ה׳ עַמּוֹ — *For the portion of* HASHEM *is His people* . . . because God, the Blessed One, has no portion among humankind except for His people, because all other nations are children of strange gods. Hence, it is clear that were it not for His people who were destined to come forth from those nations, He would have destroyed them due to the (sin) of the (Generation) of Separation.

יַעֲקֹב חֶבֶל נַחֲלָתוֹ — *Jacob the lot of His inheritance.* For he and his children are servants of God, the Exalted One, but among the nations of the world, (even) if there is to be found among them a righteous (pious) one, it is not passed on to his children.

10. יִמְצָאֵהוּ בְּאֶרֶץ מִדְבָּר — *He found him in a desert land.* He found the heart of His portion (Israel), trustworthy before Him in the desert, as it says, לֶכְתֵּךְ אַחֲרַי בַּמִּדְבָּר, *Going after Me in the wilderness* (Jeremiah 2:2).

יְסֹבְבֶנְהוּ — *He compassed it about* . . . i.e., the mountain of Sinai, as it says, וְהִגְבַּלְתָּ אֶת הָעָם סָבִיב, *And you shall set bounds for the people round about* (Exodus 19:12).

יְבוֹנְנֵהוּ — *He instructed him.* As it says, וְהַתּוֹרָה וְהַמִּצְוָה אֲשֶׁר כָּתַבְתִּי לְהוֹרֹתָם, *And the Torah and the commandment which I have written that you may teach them* (ibid. 24:12).

יִצְּרֶנְהוּ — *He protected him* . . . from the bondage of Egypt and the angel of death [as the Sages say, (The verse) חָרוּת עַל הַלֻּחֹת, *engraved on the tablets* (Exodus 32:16), (implies) freedom from the angel of death and freedom from the bondage of the nations].

NOTES

8. יַצֵּב גְּבֻלֹת עַמִּים לְמִסְפַּר בְּנֵי יִשְׂרָאֵל — *He sets the borders of the peoples according to the number of the Children of Israel*. The *Sforno* reflects the commentary of *Rashi* who states, "He let them (the peoples) remain in existence and did not destroy them because of the number of the Children of Israel that were to descend from Shem's sons in the future."

9. כִּי חֵלֶק ה׳ עַמּוֹ יַעֲקֹב חֶבֶל נַחֲלָתוֹ — *For the portion of* HASHEM *is His people; Jacob the lot of His inheritance*. The *Sforno* may well be explaining the reason for the choice of the word חֵלֶק, *portion*, in the first part of the verse, and חֶבֶל, *rope*, in the second part. Although the *Sforno* in *Genesis* and *Exodus* emphasizes that all humanity is cherished by God, this love is removed when they serve strange gods. When this occurs, only *His people* (Israel) who are loyal to Him are considered to be *His portion* among the nations. And if one should demur and argue that there are among the nations those who also believe in the One God, nonetheless there is no continuity and later generations generally defect. The nation of Jacob, however, in which the belief in the One God is transmitted from father to son, ties each subsequent generation to the preceding one by חֶבֶל, *a strong rope*, as it were. Hence they alone are His inheritance.

10. יִמְצָאֵהוּ — *He found him*. Israel was not "lost" that it should be necessary for them to be found by God! The *Sforno* explains that the word *found* refers to the "heart" or character of this people

9 *For* HASHEM*'s portion is His people; Jacob is the measure of His inheritance.*
10 *He discovered him in a desert land, in desolation, a howling wilderness; He encircled him, He granted him discernment, He preserved him like the pupil of His eye.*
11 *He was like an eagle arousing its nest, hovering over its young, spreading its wings and taking them, carrying them on its pinions.*
12 HASHEM *alone guided them, and no other power was with them.*
13 *He would make him ride on the heights of the Land and have him eat the ripe fruits of the fields; He would suckle him with honey from a stone, and oil from a flinty rock;*

כְּאִישׁוֹן עֵינוֹ — *As the pupil of his eye . . .* just as He guarded the pupil of man's eye when He formed him, by surrounding the eye with a cloak of skin (the eyelid) that it not be damaged, being that it is prone to be injured.

11. כְּנֶשֶׁר יָעִיר קִנּוֹ — *As an eagle stirs up his nest.* May it be His will that He will do (for you) in the future that which He planned to do at Sinai had (Israel) not sinned with the calf. And (indeed) God, the Blessed One, accepted his prayer, as it says, אֶשְׁרְקָה לָהֶם וַאֲקַבְּצֵם כִּי פְדִיתִים, *I will whistle to them and gather them, for I have redeemed them* (*Zechariah* 10:8).

עַל גּוֹזָלָיו יְרַחֵף — *Hovering over her young . . .* as it says: הִנֵּה אֶשָּׂא אֶל גּוֹיִם יָדִי וְאֶל עַמִּים אָרִים נִסִּי וְהֵבִיאוּ בָנַיִךְ בְּחֹצֶן, *Behold, I will lift up my hand to the nations and set up my standard to the peoples, and they shall bring your sons in their arms* (*Isaiah* 49:22).

יִפְרֹשׂ כְּנָפָיו יִקָּחֵהוּ — *Spreading out her wings, takes them . . .* as it says, וְאַתֶּם תְּלֻקְּטוּ לְאַחַד אֶחָד בְּנֵי יִשְׂרָאֵל, *And you shall be gathered up one by one, O Children of Israel* (ibid. 27:12).

יִשָּׂאֵהוּ עַל אֶבְרָתוֹ — *Bearing them on her pinions . . .* as it says, מִי אֵלֶּה כָּעָב תְּעוּפֶינָה, *Who are these who fly as a cloud* (ibid. 60:8).

12. ה׳ בָּדָד יַנְחֶנּוּ — HASHEM *alone did guide him.* As it says, כִּי אֶעֱשֶׂה כָלָה בְּכָל הַגּוֹיִם . . . וְאֹתְךָ לֹא אֶעֱשֶׂה כָלָה, *For I will make full end of all the nations . . . but I will not make a full end of you* (*Jeremiah* 46:28).

וְאֵין עִמּוֹ אֵל נֵכָר — *And there is no strange god with Him . . .* as it says, כִּי אָז אֶהְפֹּךְ אֶל עַמִּים שָׂפָה בְרוּרָה לִקְרֹא כֻלָּם בְּשֵׁם ה׳, *For then I will convert the peoples to a purer language, that they may all call upon the name of* HASHEM (*Zephaniah* 3:9), and, as it says, אֱלֹהֵי כָל הָאָרֶץ יִקָּרֵא, *He is called the God of the whole world* (*Isaiah* 54:5).

13. יַרְכִּבֵהוּ עַל בָּמֳתֵי אָרֶץ — *He made him ride on the high places of the earth.* This He will do because He did not attain His desired (goal) through the giving of the Torah mentioned

NOTES

which proved to be trustworthy, similar to the expression, *You found his heart faithful before you* (*Nechemiah* 9:8), which refers to Abraham.

יִצְּרֶנְהוּ — *He protected him.* The Mosad Harav Kook edition adds, "As our Sages say: *Engraved upon the tablets* (*Exodus* 32:16), i.e., freedom from the angel of death and the bondage of Egypt." The *Sforno's* intent is to teach us that Torah grants freedom (a play on words — חָרוּת, *engraved*, and חֵרוּת, *freedom*) from the angel of death, and freedom from the bondage of the nations (based on *Eruvin* 54a and the *Tanchuma*).

11. כְּנֶשֶׁר יָעִיר קִנּוֹ — *As an eagle stirs up his nest.* As the *Sforno* explained in his commentary on verse 3, Moses is reviewing the history of the Jewish people, of early mankind, and is prophesying about the future in this song. He is also *praying* to God on behalf of Israel. This verse is an example of how he entreats God for his people; in effect saying, "May it be Your will that You spread Your wings over Your children and bear them on Your pinions as an eagle carries its young."

יד חֶמְאַת בָּקָר וַחֲלֵב צֹאן עִם־חֵלֶב כָּרִים
וְאֵילִים בְּנֵי־בָשָׁן וְעַתּוּדִים עִם־חֵלֶב כִּלְיוֹת חִטָּה
טו וְדַם־עֵנָב תִּשְׁתֶּה־חָמֶר: וַיִּשְׁמַן יְשֻׁרוּן וַיִּבְעָט
שָׁמַנְתָּ עָבִיתָ כָּשִׂיתָ וַיִּטֹּשׁ אֱלוֹהַ עָשָׂהוּ
טז וַיְנַבֵּל צוּר יְשֻׁעָתוֹ: יַקְנִאֻהוּ בְּזָרִים
יז בְּתוֹעֵבֹת יַכְעִיסֻהוּ: יִזְבְּחוּ לַשֵּׁדִים לֹא אֱלֹהַ
אֱלֹהִים לֹא יְדָעוּם חֲדָשִׁים מִקָּרֹב בָּאוּ
י׳ זעירא יח לֹא שְׂעָרוּם אֲבֹתֵיכֶם: צוּר יְלָדְךָ תֶּשִׁי

above (v. 10), so He will (now) seek again to perfect them by giving them the Land בַּעֲבוּר יִשְׁמְרוּ חֻקָּיו, *that they might observe His statutes* (*Psalms* 105:45), and by making them ride on a portion of the earth which is superior in location and in quality over all other lands, as it says, צְבִי הִיא לְכָל הָאֲרָצוֹת, *which is an ornament for all the lands* (*Ezekiel* 20:6). And this (will occur) now, when they enter the Land.

וַיֹּאכַל תְּנוּבֹת שָׂדָי — *And he ate the produce of the fields* . . . (produce) for which they did not exert themselves as it says, כְּרָמִים וְזֵיתִים אֲשֶׁר לֹא נְטַעְתֶּם אַתֶּם אֹכְלִים, *of vineyards and oliveyards which you did not plant do you eat* (*Joshua* 24:13).

14. וְדַם עֵנָב תִּשְׁתֶּה חָמֶר — *And you did drink wine of the pure blood of the grape.* The juice of the grape was fit to be drunk without need for excessive labor to produce it; hence, they were provided for without pain, and this was done for them by God, the Blessed One, in order that they might have (ample) opportunity to occupy themselves with Torah and *mitzvos.*

15. וַיִּשְׁמַן יְשֻׁרוּן וַיִּבְעָט — *But Jeshurun grew fat and kicked.* Behold, even those who are the scholars and philosophers (בַּעֲלֵי עִיוּן) among them who are called יְשֻׁרוּן, derived from אֲשׁוּרֶנּוּ וְלֹא קָרוֹב, *I behold him but not close* (*Numbers* 24:17), acted as animals that kick those who give them food.

שָׁמַנְתָּ עָבִיתָ כָּשִׂיתָ — *You are waxen fat, grown thick and covered with fatness.* Behold, you Jeshurun, the congregation of Torah adherents and men who are scholars and philosophers, have turned to material pleasures and *grown thick,* (incapable) of understanding subtle truths, as it says, וְגַם אֵלֶּה בַּיַּיִן שָׁגוּ וּבַשֵּׁכָר תָּעוּ כֹּהֵן וְנָבִיא, *But these also reel through wine and stagger through strong drink, the Kohen and the prophet* (*Isaiah* 28:7). (You are also) *covered with fatness* as it says, כִּי טַח מֵרְאוֹת עֵינֵיהֶם מֵהַשְׂכִּיל לִבֹּתָם, *for He has shut their eyes that they cannot see and their hearts that they cannot understand* (ibid. 44:18).

וַיִּטֹּשׁ אֱלוֹהַ עָשָׂהוּ — *Then he forsook God Who made him.* Therefore, the multitude forsook

NOTES

13-14. יַרְכִּבֵהוּ עַל בָּמֳתֵי אָרֶץ . . . וְדַם עֵנָב תִּשְׁתֶּה חָמֶר — *He made him ride on the high places of the earth . . . and you did drink wine of the pure blood of the grape.* The *Sforno* does not mean to imply that had Israel attained the desired perfection through their acceptance of the Torah they would not have been given the Land. God had already promised *Eretz Yisrael* to Abraham and his seed. What the *Sforno* means is that although the prime factor in fashioning Israel into a people was the Torah, which is universal, their flowering and development as a people of Torah could only be realized in the Land of Israel which is especially conducive to the implementation of its *mitzvos* and the mastering of its wisdom. Although Israel had sinned at Sinai and did not reach the level of holiness hoped for, nonetheless the Almighty brought them into the holy land for the very purpose of reaching that original goal. They were to observe His statutes and reach the heights of sanctity and ultimate perfection, as indicated by the verses quoted from *Psalms* and *Ezekiel.* God brought Israel into a land which possessed material plenty and was so blessed that one could attain his material needs with little effort, thereby allowing them time for the study of Torah and the fulfillment of its *mitzvos.*

14 *Butter of cattle and milk of sheep with fat of lambs, rams born in Bashan and he-goats, with wheat as fat as kidneys; and you would drink blood of grapes like delicious wine.*
15 *Jeshurun became fat and kicked. You became fat, you became thick, you became corpulent — and it deserted God its Maker, and was contemptuous of the Rock of its salvation.*
16 *They would provoke His jealousy with strangers; they would anger Him with abominations.*
17 *They would slaughter to demons without power, gods whom they knew not, newcomers recently arrived, whom your ancestors did not dread.*
18 *You ignored the Rock Who gave birth to you, and forgot God Who*

God Who made *them.*

וַיְנַבֵּל צוּר יְשֻׁעָתוֹ — *And was contemptuous to the Rock of his salvation.* They (treated Him) with contempt, because they progressed from evil to evil.

16. בְּתוֹעֵבֹת יַכְעִיסֻהוּ — *With abomination they provoked Him to anger* ... causing the *Shechinah* to leave Israel, (and thus causing them) to become as the nations of the world.

17. לַשֵּׁדִים לֹא אֱלֹהַ — *To demons, no-gods* ... who are not everlasting (immortal), as our Sages say regarding demons, "*They perish similar to humans*" (*Chagigah* 16a).

אֱלֹהִים לֹא יְדָעוּם חֲדָשִׁים מִקָּרֹב בָּאוּ — *Gods whom they knew not, to new gods that newly arrived.* When they would see a certain species of whose existence they heretofore had no knowledge, they thought that there was some ancient primeval cause (i.e., power) unique to that creature (which created it), and they would therefore worship it (i.e., that power).

18. צוּר יְלָדְךָ תֶּשִׁי — *Of the Rock Who begot you, you are unmindful.* And also, you Jeshurun, the scholarly and philosophical ones, by turning to the pleasures (of life), forgot your wisdom and the knowledge of His greatness.

וַתִּשְׁכַּח אֵל מְחֹלְלֶךָ — *And you have forgotten God Who formed you* ... Who was good to you, as it says, אָנֹכִי הוּא מְנַחֶמְכֶם ... וַתִּשְׁכַּח ה׳ עֹשֶׂךָ נוֹטֶה שָׁמַיִם, *I am He Who comforts you ... and you have forgotten* H*ASHEM your Maker Who stretches forth the heavens* (*Isaiah* 51:12,13).

NOTES

15. וַיִּשְׁמַן יְשֻׁרוּן וַיִּבְעָט ... וַיִּטֹּשׁ אֱלוֹהַּ עָשָׂהוּ — *But Jeshurun grew fat and kicked ... then he forsook God Who made him*. When those who are intelligent, refined leaders of the people set a bad example, the masses will follow their lead and even compound the evil ways of their superiors. Those who are called יְשֻׁרוּן — the scholars and intellectuals — "wax fat" and become materialistic, thereby becoming coarse and insensitive. The masses retrogress further; they forsake God and treat all that is important and sacred with contempt. This is the meaning of the *Sforno's* comment, "from evil to evil."

17. לַשֵּׁדִים לֹא אֱלֹהַ — *To demons, no-gods*. See the *Sforno's* commentary on *Genesis* 1:1.

17-18. חֲדָשִׁים מִקָּרֹב בָּאוּ ... צוּר יְלָדְךָ תֶּשִׁי — *To new gods that newly arrived ... Of the Rock Who begot you, you are unmindful*. *Rashi* interprets this verse to mean that they would worship gods unknown to other nations, gods which were certainly unknown to their own ancestors. The *Sforno*, however, interprets this verse to mean that when they would observe any exotic creature whose existence they were unaware of heretofore, their initial amazement was transformed ultimately into reverence, not for the creature itself but for the force and power who created it. This they attributed not to the Creator but to some primeval, unique force whom they deified by worshiping his handiwork, namely this exotic creature. Verses 16 and 17 speak of the masses who abandoned God and became idolaters, whereas verse 18 addresses itself to יְשֻׁרוּן, the scholars who do not reject God but whose wisdom is adulterated by their pursuit of physical pleasures and material riches. Their "forgetting" is a twofold one; they forget what they have learned and also are unmindful of past history. That is why the verse uses two words for "forgetfulness" — תֶּשִׁי and וַתִּשְׁכַּח.

רביעי
יט וַתִּשְׁכַּח אֵל מְחֹלְלֶךָ: וַיַּרְא יהוה וַיִּנְאָץ
כ מִכַּעַס בָּנָיו וּבְנֹתָיו: וַיֹּאמֶר אַסְתִּירָה פָנַי מֵהֶם
אֶרְאֶה מָה אַחֲרִיתָם כִּי דוֹר תַּהְפֻּכֹת הֵמָּה
כא בָּנִים לֹא־אֵמֻן בָּם: הֵם קִנְאוּנִי בְלֹא־*אֵל
כִּעֲסוּנִי בְּהַבְלֵיהֶם וַאֲנִי אַקְנִיאֵם בְּלֹא־עָם
כב בְּגוֹי נָבָל אַכְעִיסֵם: כִּי־אֵשׁ קָדְחָה בְאַפִּי
וַתִּיקַד עַד־שְׁאוֹל תַּחְתִּית וַתֹּאכַל אֶרֶץ וִיבֻלָהּ
כג וַתְּלַהֵט מוֹסְדֵי הָרִים: אַסְפֶּה עָלֵימוֹ רָעוֹת
כד חִצַּי אֲכַלֶּה־בָּם: מְזֵי רָעָב וּלְחֻמֵי רֶשֶׁף
וְקֶטֶב מְרִירִי וְשֶׁן־בְּהֵמֹת אֲשַׁלַּח־בָּם
כה עִם־חֲמַת זֹחֲלֵי עָפָר: מִחוּץ תְּשַׁכֶּל־חֶרֶב
וּמֵחֲדָרִים אֵימָה גַּם־בָּחוּר גַּם־בְּתוּלָה

*חול

19. וַיִּנְאָץ מִכַּעַס בָּנָיו וּבְנֹתָיו — *And He abhorred them because of the provocation of His sons and of His daughters.* And after He did not attain the perfection (of Israel) in the Land, He chose a third (way), namely to refine them in Exile. He did this by shaming and making loathsome His sons and daughters through His anger with no mercy shown for the young ones, nor for the honor of the daughters.

20. אַסְתִּירָה פָנַי מֵהֶם — *I will hide My face from them* . . . from the sons and the daughters.

אֶרְאֶה מָה אַחֲרִיתָם — *I will see what their end shall be.* I see that there is no hope that they will eventually repent.

כִּי דוֹר תַּהְפֻּכֹת הֵמָּה — *For they are a perverse generation.* They had a change of heart, turning aside from the ways of God, the Blessed One.

בָּנִים לֹא אֵמֻן בָּם — *Children in whom there is no faith* . . . for they did not learn truth from their fathers.

21. הֵם קִנְאוּנִי בְלֹא אֵל — *They have moved Me to jealousy with a no-god.* The fathers moved Me to jealousy with a *no-god* (during the period of) the First Temple.

כִּעֲסוּנִי בְּהַבְלֵיהֶם — *Provoked Me to anger with their vanities.* . . (during the period of) the Second Temple.

וַאֲנִי אַקְנִיאֵם בְּלֹא עָם — *And I will move them to jealousy with a no-people* . . . (during the time) of the First Temple, which was destroyed by the Chaldeans of whom it is said, הֵן אֶרֶץ כַּשְׂדִּים זֶה הָעָם לֹא הָיָה, *Behold the land of Kasdim (Chaldea), this people was not* (*Isaiah* 23:13).

NOTES

19. וַיִּנְאָץ מִכַּעַס בָּנָיו וּבְנֹתָיו — *And He abhorred them because of the provocation of His sons and of His daughters*. The expression "a third way" used by the *Sforno* means that the Almighty had already tried two previous methods of instruction in the hope of perfecting Israel; one was by giving them the Torah and the second was by bringing them into the Land of Israel. Both of these methods had failed, so He now attempts Exile as a way to purge, cleanse and refine them.

20. אֶרְאֶה מָה אַחֲרִיתָם — *I will see what their end shall be*. This expression in the view of the *Sforno* does not mean as *Rashi* explains, "what will come upon them in the end." Rather, the Almighty says "I see" (akin to רוֹאֶה אֲנִי) that even in the end there will be no improvement (the word מָה is to be understood as אֶפֶס, *naught*, for they will not repent).

21. הֵם קִנְאוּנִי . . . כִּעֲסוּנִי . . . וַאֲנִי אַקְנִיאֵם . . . בְּגוֹי נָבָל אַכְעִיסֵם — *They have moved Me to jealousy* . . . *provoked Me to anger* . . . *and I will move them to jealousy* . . . *I will provoke them to anger with a vile people*. The *Sforno* sees a symmetry in this verse, where the concluding portion which speaks of God's response and retribution corresponds to the

brought you forth.
19 *HASHEM will see and be provoked by the anger of His sons and daughters,*
20 *and He will say, "I shall hide My face from them and see what their end will be — for they are a generation of reversals, children whose upbringing is not in them.*
21 *They provoked Me with a non-god, angered Me with their vanities; so shall I provoke them with a non-people, with a vile nation shall I anger them.*
22 *For fire will have been kindled in My nostrils and blaze to the lowest depths. It shall consume the earth and its produce, and set ablaze what is founded on mountains.*
23 *I shall accumulate evils against them, My arrows shall I use up against them;*
24 *bloating of famine, battles of flaming demons, cutting down by the noontime demon, and the teeth of beasts shall I dispatch against them, with the venom of those that creep on the earth.*
25 *On the outside, the sword will bereave, while indoors there will be dread*

בְּגוֹי נָבָל אַכְעִיסֵם — *I will provoke them to anger with a vile people . . .* (at the time of) the Second Temple, which was destroyed by a kingdom that was unworthy and which had no alphabet or language.

22. כִּי אֵשׁ קָדְחָה בְאַפִּי — *For a fire is kindled in My anger . . .* when I afflicted them so that they should repent.

וַתִּיקַד עַד שְׁאוֹל תַּחְתִּית — *And shall burn to the nethermost parts of the earth.* They rebelliously added to their sin in such a manner that My anger was sufficiently kindled to bring them down to the nethermost abyss, as it says of Achaz, וּבְעֵת הָצֵר לוֹ וַיּוֹסֶף לִמְעוֹל בַּה׳, *And in the time of his distress he trespassed still more against HASHEM* (*II Chronicles* 28:22).

וַתְּלַהֵט מוֹסְדֵי הָרִים — *And set on fire the leaders of the people.* He will remove from them all the leaders of the people, as it says, מֵסִיר מִירוּשָׁלַםִ וּמִיהוּדָה מַשְׁעֵן וּמַשְׁעֵנָה . . . גִּבּוֹר וְאִישׁ מִלְחָמָה . . . וְנָבִיא . . . וְיוֹעֵץ, *He takes away from Jerusalem and from Judah the stay and the staff . . . the mighty man and the man of war . . . the prophet . . . and the counselor* (*Isaiah* 3:1-3).

25. וּמֵחֲדָרִים אֵימָה גַּם בָּחוּר גַּם בְּתוּלָה — *And terror within,* (*shall destroy*) *both the young man and the virgin.* And from within, the terror shall destroy the young men and the virgins.

NOTES

initial part of the verse which speaks of Israel's provocation. They moved God to jealousy during the period of the First Temple by serving idols who were no-gods; therefore He responded by bringing about their destruction through a people who were nonentities. In the time of the Second Temple, they provoked the Almighty with their vanities, therefore He, in turn, punished them through a people who were uncultured, a vile people who were used by God to destroy a people guilty of vanity.

22. כִּי אֵשׁ קָדְחָה בְאַפִּי . . . וַתְּלַהֵט מוֹסְדֵי הָרִים — *For a fire is kindled in My anger . . . and set on fire the leaders of the people.* The sense of this verse acording to the *Sforno* is as follows: Affliction is meant to arouse people and thus bring them to repentance, but at times the more one suffers the greater becomes one's resistance to repentance, as we find in the case of King Achaz who increased his trespassing at the time of his distress. This stubbornness added fuel to the fire of God's wrath, resulting in the punishment of the people's leaders whom God holds responsible for the evil ways of the masses.

כו יוֹנֵק עִם־אִישׁ שֵׂיבָה:　　אָמַרְתִּי אַפְאֵיהֶם
כז אַשְׁבִּיתָה מֵאֱנוֹשׁ זִכְרָם:　　לוּלֵי כַּעַס אוֹיֵב אָגוּר
פֶּן־יְנַכְּרוּ צָרֵימוֹ　　פֶּן־יֹאמְרוּ יָדֵנוּ רָמָה
כח וְלֹא יְהוָה פָּעַל כָּל־זֹאת:　　כִּי־גוֹי אֹבַד עֵצוֹת הֵמָּה
חמישי כט וְאֵין בָּהֶם תְּבוּנָה:　　לוּ חָכְמוּ יַשְׂכִּילוּ זֹאת
ל יָבִינוּ לְאַחֲרִיתָם:　　אֵיכָה יִרְדֹּף אֶחָד אֶלֶף
וּשְׁנַיִם יָנִיסוּ רְבָבָה　　אִם־לֹא כִּי־צוּרָם מְכָרָם
לא וַיהוָה הִסְגִּירָם:　　כִּי לֹא כְצוּרֵנוּ צוּרָם
לב וְאֹיְבֵינוּ פְּלִילִים:　　כִּי־מִגֶּפֶן סְדֹם גַּפְנָם

26. אָמַרְתִּי אַפְאֵיהֶם — *I said I will leave over a corner.* I will leave over some פֵּאָה (corner) while destroying the rest of them, similar to that which I shall do at the end of days, since I did not attain (through them) the perfection (I had hoped for), be it through the giving of the Torah, or *Eretz Yisrael*, or through Exile, as it says, כִּי בְּהַר צִיּוֹן וּבִירוּשָׁלַם תִּהְיֶה פְלֵיטָה כַּאֲשֶׁר אָמַר ה׳ וּבַשְּׂרִידִים אֲשֶׁר ה׳ קֹרֵא, *For in Mount Zion and in Jerusalem there shall be those that escape, as HASHEM has said, and among the remnant those whom HASHEM shall call* (*Joel* 3:5).

27. לוּלֵי כַּעַס אוֹיֵב אָגוּר — *Were it not for the heaped-up wrath of the enemy.* Because of the wrath of the nations (directed) against this remnant (of Israel), there is concern ...

פֶּן יְנַכְּרוּ צָרֵימוֹ — *Lest their adversaries estrange them* ... lest they draw away the hearts of this remnant to become estranged (from God) as they (i.e., the adversaries) are.

פֶּן יֹאמְרוּ — *Lest they should say* ... to that remnant.

יָדֵנוּ רָמָה — *Our hand is high* ... (capable of) exterminating Israel as a nation, and you will (then) remain few in number.

וְלֹא ה׳ פָּעַל כָּל זֹאת — *And HASHEM has not done all this.* And you should not believe that you can escape through His (help). However, being that Israel is numerous and widely dispersed among many nations, not *all* of the nations will attempt to do so (i.e., to mislead them), as our Sages said: "What is the meaning of the verse, צִדְקֹת פִּרְזוֹנוֹ בְּיִשְׂרָאֵל, *even the righteous acts of His rule in Israel* (*Judges* 5:11)? The Holy One, Blessed is He, showed righteousness (mercy) to Israel by scattering them among the nations" (*Pesachim* 87b).

NOTES

26. אָמַרְתִּי אַפְאֵיהֶם — *I said I will leave over a corner. Rashi* also explains the phrase אַפְאֵיהֶם to mean, "I would make them as פֵּאָה — as grain left in the corner of the field." However, he interprets this to mean that God will cast away Israel as הֶפְקֵר, something which is free to all devoid of ownership. The *Sforno*, however, interprets this phrase as one of encouragement and hope. Although large numbers of Israel shall be destroyed, God assures us that there will always be a saving remnant whom the Torah characterizes as פֵּאָה — that *corner* of the field which *remains*! So it shall be at the end of days.

27. פֶּן יְנַכְּרוּ צָרֵימוֹ ... וְלֹא ה׳ פָּעַל כָּל זֹאת — *Lest their adversaries estrange them ... and HASHEM has not done all this.* The word יְנַכְּרוּ comes from the root נֵכָר, *a stranger. Rashi* therefore interprets this phrase to mean that the enemy will attribute their success against Israel to a strange power and not to God. The *Sforno* however interprets this phrase to mean that the nations will attempt to wean Israel away from God and estrange them from the true God to become idolaters as they are. However, God will not permit this to happen, for even in Exile the Jewish people will not be concentrated in one place, and although some nations will indeed attempt to exterminate Israel, others will not, and thus their dispersal will prove to be their salvation. That is why our Sages say that the righteousness of God is manifested in the fact that Israel is scattered far and wide; hence, though one part of the Jewish people may be subjected to persecution and even destruction, other parts will be spared and they will become the saving remnant.

— even a young man, even a virgin, a suckling with the gray-haired man.
26 *I had said, 'I will scatter them, I will cause their memory to cease from man' —*
27 *were it not that the anger of the enemy was pent up, lest the tormenter misinterpret; lest they say, 'Our hand was raised in triumph, and it was not* HASHEM *Who accomplished all this!'*
28 *For they are a nation bereft of counsel, and there is no discernment in them.*
29 *Were they wise they would comprehend this, they would discern it from their end.*
30 *For how could one pursue a thousand, and two cause a myriad to flee, if not that their Rock had sold them out, and* HASHEM *had delivered them?*
31 *— for not like our Rock is their rock — yet our enemies judge us!*
32 *For their vineyard is from the vineyard of Sodom, and from the fields*

28. כִּי גוֹי אֹבַד עֵצוֹת הֵמָּה — *For they are a nation void of counsel . . .* the various (peoples) of the world.

29. לוּ חָכְמוּ יַשְׂכִּילוּ זֹאת — *Were they wise they would understand this . . .* that Israel fell into their hands in such an unnatural fashion, because of their (i.e., Israel's) sins!

יָבִינוּ לְאַחֲרִיתָם — *They would consider their latter end.* And thus the nations would understand what *their* latter end will be as a result of their many rebellious transgressions.

30. אֵיכָה יִרְדֹּף אֶחָד אֶלֶף — *How can one man chase a thousand.* They should have understood that it is unnatural for one to pursue a thousand . . .

אִם לֹא כִּי צוּרָם מְכָרָם — *Unless their Rock had sold them.* (It is) He who does battle against them and has removed their strength. Therefore, their might has become warped and they are (weak) as women.

31. כִּי לֹא כְצוּרֵנוּ צוּרָם — *For their rock is not as our Rock.* And this occurred without a doubt because their rock is not like our Rock, because indeed every nation succeeds during the time that its (heavenly) prince or *mazal* (planet) rules, and that heavenly prince will never be transformed into an enemy of his people. However, they will eventually fall when their heavenly prince no longer rules (lit., is turned away), and the prince of another people comes to power, according to the order which God, the Blessed One, has decreed. Therefore, they will never be destroyed in such an unnatural manner that one will pursue a thousand.

וְאֹיְבֵינוּ — *And our enemies.* Although there are nations who are the enemies of God and the enemies of His people, as the (Torah) attests, *Were it not for the heaped-up wrath of*

NOTES

28. כִּי גוֹי אֹבַד עֵצוֹת הֵמָּה — *For they are a nation void of counsel*. The *Sforno*, as do most commentators, explains that the word "nation" refers to the peoples of the world, not to Israel. It is interesting to note that in the מִקְרָאוֹת גְּדוֹלוֹת (standard version) the phrase "peoples of the world" reads "Babylonians." This is but one example of revisions and excisions made by the censor in this *parashah*, lest the *Sforno's* commentary reflect in an adverse manner upon the church and government of Italy and other European nations of the 16th century.

29-30. לוּ חָכְמוּ . . . יָבִינוּ לְאַחֲרִיתָם . . . אֵיכָה יִרְדֹּף אֶחָד אֶלֶף — *Were they wise . . . they would consider their latter end . . . How can one man chase a thousand*. The sense of the *Sforno's* commentary is that had God not decided to punish and weaken Israel, the nations of the world would be powerless against them. Hence it is not their strength but the weakness of Israel generated by God which accounts for the abnormal vulnerability of the Jewish people and the unnatural superiority of their enemies.

31. כִּי לֹא כְצוּרֵנוּ צוּרָם וְאֹיְבֵינוּ — *For their rock is not as our Rock, and our enemies.* Unlike Israel, whose fate and destiny are determined solely by God and not by any planetary influence, that of the nations

וּמִשַּׁדְמֹת עֲמֹרָה　　עֲנָבֵמוֹ עִנְּבֵי־רוֹשׁ
לג אַשְׁכְּלֹת מְרֹרֹת לָמוֹ׃　　חֲמַת תַּנִּינִם יֵינָם
לד וְרֹאשׁ פְּתָנִים אַכְזָר׃　　הֲלֹא־הוּא כָּמֻס עִמָּדִי
לה חָתוּם בְּאוֹצְרֹתָי׃　　לִי נָקָם וְשִׁלֵּם
לְעֵת תָּמוּט רַגְלָם　　כִּי קָרוֹב יוֹם אֵידָם
לו וְחָשׁ עֲתִדֹת לָמוֹ׃　　כִּי־יָדִין יהוה עַמּוֹ
וְעַל־עֲבָדָיו יִתְנֶחָם　　כִּי יִרְאֶה כִּי־אָזְלַת יָד

---

the enemy (v. 27), and as it says, *With the head of the wild bands of the enemy* (v. 42) — they are פְּלִילִים, *men of judgment*, thinkers and intelligent men (in the area) of political science, as it says, וְהַאֲבַדְתִּי חֲכָמִים מֵאֱדוֹם, *And I will destroy the wise men out of Edom* (*Ovadiah* 1:8), which implies that there are (wise men among them). (See *Eichah Rabbah* 2:13.) [Why, then, are they so blind regarding Israel?]

32. כִּי מִגֶּפֶן סְדֹם גַּפְנָם — *For their vine is the vine of Sodom.* The reason they lack understanding regarding this matter is because they are proud of their great tranquility and turn their attention to the attainment of their physical pleasures, as did the people of Sodom. In order to realize this they (rejected and) abhorred all acts of kindness, as the prophet attests saying, הִנֵּה זֶה הָיָה עֲוֹן סְדֹם אֲחוֹתֵךְ גָּאוֹן שִׂבְעַת לֶחֶם וְשַׁלְוַת הַשְׁקֵט הָיָה לָהּ וְלִבְנוֹתֶיהָ וְיַד עָנִי וְאֶבְיוֹן לֹא הֶחֱזִיקָה, *Behold this was the iniquity of your sister Sodom; she and her daughters had pride, surfeit of bread and abundance of idleness and yet she did not strengthen the hand of the poor and needy* (*Ezekiel* 16:49).

עֲנָבֵמוֹ עִנְּבֵי רוֹשׁ — *Their grapes are grapes of gall.* And from this vine shall grow *grapes of gall,* (meaning) evil deeds which harm society, and all this results from their efforts to attain unjust gains, and because they shed innocent blood in order to rule haughtily.

אַשְׁכְּלֹת מְרֹרֹת לָמוֹ — *Their clusters are bitter.* And thus they develop evil and false opinions, speaking against God perversely, saying, *God will not see* (based on *Psalms* 94:7).

33. חֲמַת תַּנִּינִם יֵינָם — *Their wine is the fierceness of crocodiles.* And behold, stored in those clusters of the grapes is to be found wine which is *fierce as crocodiles,* meaning punishment which they deserve according to the attribute of justice. It will be guarded (within the grapes) until God, the Blessed One, will bring it forth and cause them to drink (this wine of punishment) as it says, פּוּרָה דָּרַכְתִּי לְבַדִּי, *I have trodden the winepress alone* (*Isaiah* 63:3).

NOTES

of the world is controlled by constellations and planets, and as such their rise and fall follows a steady, even course. Only Israel is subject to abrupt, sudden changes in their status which result from their actions and their relationship to God. His Providence is present to protect His people when they are worthy, or when God forbid undeserving, to punish them. Hence their downfall is marked by abnormal events — as is their success and ultimately their redemption. All this, the nations, who normally are wise and perceptive, fail to understand. The reason for this unusual lack of comprehension is given in the next verse.

32. עֲנָבֵמוֹ עִנְּבֵי רוֹשׁ אַשְׁכְּלֹת מְרֹרֹת לָמוֹ — *Their grapes are grapes of gall, their clusters are bitter.* The *Sforno* explains that these two phrases are not redundant. The first refers to evil actions and deeds, while the second speaks of false concepts and ideas which fashion their evil, corrupt ideology. Within these clusters of grapes, the wine of God's wrath and punishment is stored, as the *Sforno* explains in the following verse.

33. חֲמַת תַּנִּינִם יֵינָם — *Their wine is the fierceness of crocodiles.* In the standard version of *Sforno* in the מִקְרָאוֹת גְּדוֹלוֹת, the entire section beginning from the word "punishment" has been excised by the censor. It does appear in the Mosad Harav Kook edition which is based upon a number of original manuscripts. The prophesy of Moses regarding the eventual Divine retribution against the nations who persecuted Israel was considered unacceptable by the censor, who in most cases was

of Gomorrah; their grapes are grapes of gall, so clusters of bitterness were given them.

33 *Serpents' venom is their wine, the poison of cruel vipers.*

34 *Is it not revealed with Me, sealed in My treasuries?*

35 *Mine is vengeance and retribution at the time when their foot will falter, for the day of their catastrophe is near, and future events are rushing at them."*

36 *When* HASHEM *will have judged His people, He shall relent regarding His servants, when He sees that enemy power progresses,*

---

34. הֲלֹא הוּא כָּמֻס עִמָּדִי — *Is this not laid up with Me?* ... as it says, כִּי יוֹם נָקָם בְּלִבִּי, *For the day of vengeance is in my heart* (ibid. 63:4).

חָתוּם בְּאוֹצְרֹתָי — *And sealed up among My treasures* ... as it says, כִּי סְתֻמִים וַחֲתֻמִים הַדְּבָרִים, *for the words are closed up and sealed* (Daniel 12:9).

35. לִי נָקָם — *To Me belongs vengeance.* It is incumbent upon Me to take revenge from my enemies.

וְשִׁלֵּם — *And recompense.* And also to repay measure for measure.

לְעֵת תָּמוּט רַגְלָם — *When their foot slides* ... when their measure is full and they fall and break.

[כִּי קָרוֹב יוֹם אֵידָם — *For the day of their calamity is at hand.* Because, indeed, the day of calamity for the nations is nigh when HASHEM *will judge His people* (v. 36), as it says, וּבָרוֹתִי מִכֶּם הַמֹּרְדִים וְהַפּוֹשְׁעִים, *And I will purge out from among you the rebels, and the transgressors* (Ezekiel 20:38), because the other nations will then quickly be destroyed.]

36. וְעַל עֲבָדָיו יִתְנֶחָם — *And repent Himself for His servants.* He will repent Himself for the evil He properly (visited) upon His people, and will have mercy upon them, (in the merit) of His servants who are among them, as it says, כֵּן אֶעֱשֶׂה לְמַעַן עֲבָדַי לְבִלְתִּי הַשְׁחִית הַכֹּל, *So will I do for My servants' sake, that I may not destroy them all* (Isaiah 65:8).

כִּי יִרְאֶה כִּי אָזְלַת יָד — *When He sees that their power is gone.* And the reason that He will then repent Himself of the evil properly (visited) upon His people, doing so (in the merit) of His servants [even though this was not done all the days of Exile — is because He will observe that Israel (will have reached) the ultimate affliction and oppression in their Exile, in such a manner that they can no longer exist in it (i.e., Exile), as was the case in Egypt where it says, *And He saw our affliction, and our toil and our oppression* (26:7)].

NOTES

a convert to Christianity. Such deletions abound in this *parashah* and among them are parts of the commentary on verses 34, 35, and 36. Especially significant among the omissions is the *Sforno's* commentary on verse 37, which is totally removed from the standard edition of the מִקְרָאוֹת גְּדוֹלוֹת, as is the concluding part of verse 41, all of 42 and a major part of 43. Careful examination of the *Sforno's* commentary on these verses, which we have included in brackets in this edition, will readily reveal what aroused the ire of the censor.

35. לִי נָקָם ... לְעֵת תָּמוּט רַגְלָם — *To Me belongs vengeance ... when their foot slides.* Rashi in his commentary on this verse states, "So far Moses exhorted them (i.e., Israel) with words of reproof ... from here onwards (i.e., starting with verse 36) he consoles them with a statement of comfort." The *Sforno*, however, interprets the previous verses, as well as this one, as referring to the nations of the world who will be punished by God for their wickedness towards Israel. God will take revenge from His enemies when their measure is full and as the day of reckoning draws near He will judge His people and have mercy upon them, as the following verse states.

36. וְעַל עֲבָדָיו יִתְנֶחָם כִּי יִרְאֶה כִּי אָזְלַת יָד וְאֶפֶס עָצוּר וְעָזוּב — *And repent Himself for His servants when He sees that their power is gone and there is nothing retained or left.* Although the majority of the people of Israel are worthy of punishment, God will save them in the merit of the righteous ones among them. He will do so not only in their merit

לז וְאֶפֶס עָצוּר וְעָזוּב׃ וְאָמַר אֵי אֱלֹהֵימוֹ
לח צוּר חָסָיוּ בוֹ׃ אֲשֶׁר חֵלֶב זְבָחֵימוֹ יֹאכֵלוּ
יִשְׁתּוּ יֵין נְסִיכָם יָקוּמוּ וְיַעְזְרֻכֶם
לט יְהִי עֲלֵיכֶם סִתְרָה׃ רְאוּ | עַתָּה כִּי אֲנִי אֲנִי הוּא
וְאֵין אֱלֹהִים עִמָּדִי אֲנִי אָמִית וַאֲחַיֶּה
מָחַצְתִּי וַאֲנִי אֶרְפָּא וְאֵין מִיָּדִי מַצִּיל׃
ששי מ כִּי־אֶשָּׂא אֶל־שָׁמַיִם יָדִי וְאָמַרְתִּי חַי אָנֹכִי לְעֹלָם׃
מא אִם־שַׁנּוֹתִי בְּרַק חַרְבִּי וְתֹאחֵז בְּמִשְׁפָּט יָדִי
אָשִׁיב נָקָם לְצָרָי וְלִמְשַׂנְאַי אֲשַׁלֵּם׃
מב אַשְׁכִּיר חִצַּי מִדָּם וְחַרְבִּי תֹּאכַל בָּשָׂר

וְאֶפֶס עָצוּר וְעָזוּב — *And there is nothing retained or left.* And He shall see that they have no money retained in their homes or left in the field.

[**37.** וְאָמַר — *And He shall say.* God, the Blessed One, will say to Israel ...

אֵי אֱלֹהֵימוֹ — *Where are their gods?* ... (the gods) of the nations of the world, because then indeed the mastery of the heavenly and temporal princes (the heavenly representatives of the nations) will be removed, as it says, יִפְקֹד ה׳ עַל צְבָא הַמָּרוֹם בַּמָּרוֹם וְעַל מַלְכֵי הָאֲדָמָה עַל הָאֲדָמָה, *HASHEM will punish the host of the high ones on high and the kings of the earth upon the earth* (*Isaiah* 24:21).

38. יָקוּמוּ וְיַעְזְרֻכֶם — *Let them rise up and help you.* And similarly, the Almighty will say to Israel, "Where are the nations and their kings who will rise up and protect (lit., "assist") you from My judgment, as you thought when you were in exile, relying upon their protection?"]

39. רְאוּ עַתָּה כִּי אֲנִי אֲנִי הוּא — *See now that I, even I, am He* ... who brought punishment upon you in Exile.

וְאֵין אֱלֹהִים עִמָּדִי — *And there is no god with Me* ... and it did not emanate from the power of princes above or heavenly hosts.

אֲנִי אָמִית וַאֲחַיֶּה — *I kill and I make alive* ... as it says, וְהַעֲלֵיתִי אֶתְכֶם מִקִּבְרוֹתֵיכֶם, *And cause you to come up out of your graves* (*Ezekiel* 37:12).

מָחַצְתִּי — *I wound* ... with the punishment of being a fugitive and wanderer, as it says, וְהִכָּה ה׳ אֶת יִשְׂרָאֵל כַּאֲשֶׁר יָנוּד הַקָּנֶה בַּמַּיִם, *For HASHEM will smite Israel as a reed is shaken in the water* (*I Kings* 14:15).

וַאֲנִי אֶרְפָּא — *And I heal* ... as it says, בְּיוֹם חֲבֹשׁ ה׳ אֶת שֶׁבֶר עַמּוֹ וּמַחַץ מַכָּתוֹ יִרְפָּא, *On the day*

NOTES

but because Israel will have reached the limit of their endurance and if not rescued they would, God forbid, be wiped away. The expression עָצוּר, *guarded* or *retained*, is applicable to one's monetary wealth, kept in one's home, whereas the word עָזוּב, *forsaken*, is applicable to one's property in the field.

37-38. וְאָמַר אֵי אֱלֹהֵימוֹ ... יָקוּמוּ וְיַעְזְרֻכֶם — *And He shall say, Where are their gods ... let them rise up and help you.* The Almighty says to Israel: In Exile, you placed your faith and trust in the gods of the nations of the world, as well as in the nations themselves. Now you will realize that these gods are worthless and the nations upon whom you relied are powerless. *Sforno* interprets these verses as a straightforward statement, unlike *Rashi* who interprets it as a mocking rebuke.

39. אֲנִי אָמִית וַאֲחַיֶּה מָחַצְתִּי וַאֲנִי אֶרְפָּא — *I kill and I make alive, I wound and I heal.* The *Sforno* finds in this verse a source from the Torah for our belief in תְּחִיַּת הַמֵּתִים, *the resurrection of the dead*, linking this assurance to the verse in *Ezekiel* which speaks of the dry bones brought back to life. He also is of the opinion that the "wounding" men-

and none is saved or assisted.
37 *He will say, "Where is their god, the rock in whom they sought refuge,*
38 *the fat of whose offerings they would eat, they would drink the wine of their libations? Let them stand and help you! Let them be a shelter for you!*
39 *"See, now, that I, I am He — and no god is with Me. I put to death and I bring life, I struck down and I will heal, and there is no rescuer from My hand.*
40 *"For I shall raise My hand to heaven and say, 'As I live forever,*
41 *if I sharpen My flashing sword and My hand grasps judgment, I shall return vengeance upon My enemies and upon those that hate Me shall I bring retribution.*
42 *I shall intoxicate My arrows with blood and My sword shall devour*

---

that H*ASHEM* *binds up the breach of His people and heals the wound of their bruise* (*Isaiah* 30:26).

40. כִּי אֶשָּׂא אֶל שָׁמַיִם יָדִי — *For I lift My hand to heaven* . . . to take an oath, similar to, וַיָּרֶם יְמִינוֹ וּשְׂמֹאלוֹ אֶל הַשָּׁמַיִם, *When He lifted up his right hand and his left hand to heaven* (*Daniel* 12:7).

וְאָמַרְתִּי חַי אָנֹכִי לְעֹלָם — *And say, I live for ever.* I shall swear, just as I live forever, similar to His saying, וַיִּשָּׁבַע בְּחֵי הָעוֹלָם, *And swore by the One Who lives forever* (ibid.).

41. אִם שַׁנּוֹתִי — *If I sharpen.* Although I sharpened the luster of My sword against Israel during the period of Exile, I did not (sharpen) the *edge* of My sword.

וְתֹאחֵז בְּמִשְׁפָּט יָדִי — *And My hand take hold of judgment* . . . and even though My hand will afterward *take hold of judgment* against them, *for* H*ASHEM* *will pronounce judgment on His people* (v. 36); nonetheless . . .

אָשִׁיב נָקָם לְצָרָי — *I will render vengeance to My adversaries* . . . the vengeance which they dealt upon Israel, as it says, יַעַן עֲשׂוֹת אֱדוֹם בִּנְקֹם נָקָם לְבֵית יְהוּדָה, *Because Edom has dealt against the house of Judah by taking vengeance* (*Ezekiel* 25:12), I shall bring the same vengeance upon them, as it says, וְנָתַתִּי אֶת נִקְמָתִי בֶּאֱדוֹם בְּיַד עַמִּי יִשְׂרָאֵל, *And I will lay My vengeance upon Edom by the hand of My people Israel* (ibid. v. 14).

וְלִמְשַׂנְאַי אֲשַׁלֵּם — *And will repay those who hate Me* . . . the payment of "measure for measure" as it says, כַּאֲשֶׁר עָשִׂיתָ יֵעָשֶׂה לָּךְ גְּמֻלְךָ יָשׁוּב בְּרֹאשֶׁךָ, *As you have done, it shall be done to you; may your recompense return upon your head* (*Obadiah* 1:15).

42. אַשְׁכִּיר חִצַּי מִדָּם וְחַרְבִּי תֹּאכַל בָּשָׂר — *I will make My arrows drunk with blood, and My sword shall devour flesh* . . . as it says, כִּי בָאֵשׁ ה׳ נִשְׁפָּט וּבְחַרְבּוֹ אֶת כָּל בָּשָׂר, *For by fire will* H*ASHEM* *execute judgment and with his sword upon all flesh* (*Isaiah* 66:16).

NOTES

tioned in this verse refers to the wandering of Israel in Exile, which is the severest wound that can be inflicted upon a people. However, God comforts them and promises to heal this historic hurt by redeeming them and returning them to their land.

41. אִם שַׁנּוֹתִי — *If I sharpen.* When a warrior whets his sword it can be for one of two reasons — to shine it so that it might glow, or to sharpen it for use against his enemy. God reassures Israel that although He brandished His sword against them in Exile, it was meant to caution and frighten them so that they would return to Him, but the intent was not to destroy them.

אָשִׁיב נָקָם לְצָרָי וְלִמְשַׂנְאַי אֲשַׁלֵּם — *I will render vengeance to My adversaries and will repay those who hate Me.* These are two expressions, each with a distinct meaning. The vengeful actions of the nations against Israel will be redirected against *them* by God, and the evil inflicted by Israel's enemies upon them will be repaid — measure for measure. Hence two words — אָשִׁיב and אֲשַׁלֵּם — are used to indicate this twofold retribution.

מִדַּם חָלָל֙ וְשִׁבְיָ֔ה　　מֵרֹ֖אשׁ פַּרְע֥וֹת אוֹיֵֽב׃
מג הַרְנִ֤ינוּ גוֹיִם֙ עַמּ֔וֹ　　כִּ֥י דַם־עֲבָדָ֖יו יִקּ֑וֹם
וְנָקָם֙ יָשִׁ֣יב לְצָרָ֔יו　　וְכִפֶּ֥ר אַדְמָת֖וֹ עַמּֽוֹ׃

שביעי מד וַיָּבֹ֣א מֹשֶׁ֗ה וַיְדַבֵּ֛ר אֶת־כָּל־דִּבְרֵ֥י הַשִּׁירָֽה־הַזֹּ֖את בְּאָזְנֵ֣י הָעָ֑ם ה֖וּא וְהוֹשֵׁ֥עַ
מה בִּן־נֽוּן׃ וַיְכַ֣ל מֹשֶׁ֗ה לְדַבֵּ֛ר אֶת־כָּל־הַדְּבָרִ֥ים הָאֵ֖לֶּה אֶל־כָּל־יִשְׂרָאֵֽל׃
מו וַיֹּ֤אמֶר אֲלֵהֶם֙ שִׂ֣ימוּ לְבַבְכֶ֔ם לְכָל־הַ֨דְּבָרִ֔ים אֲשֶׁ֧ר אָנֹכִ֛י מֵעִ֥יד בָּכֶ֖ם הַיּ֑וֹם
אֲשֶׁ֤ר תְּצַוֻּם֙ אֶת־בְּנֵיכֶ֔ם לִשְׁמֹ֣ר לַעֲשׂ֔וֹת אֶת־כָּל־דִּבְרֵ֖י הַתּוֹרָ֥ה הַזֹּֽאת׃
מז כִּ֠י לֹֽא־דָבָ֨ר רֵ֥ק הוּא֙ מִכֶּ֔ם כִּי־ה֖וּא חַיֵּיכֶ֑ם וּבַדָּבָ֣ר הַזֶּ֗ה תַּאֲרִ֤יכוּ יָמִים֙
עַל־הָ֣אֲדָמָ֔ה אֲשֶׁ֨ר אַתֶּ֜ם עֹבְרִ֧ים אֶת־הַיַּרְדֵּ֛ן שָׁ֖מָּה לְרִשְׁתָּֽהּ׃
מפטיר מח־מט וַיְדַבֵּ֤ר יהוה֙ אֶל־מֹשֶׁ֔ה בְּעֶ֛צֶם הַיּ֥וֹם הַזֶּ֖ה לֵאמֹֽר׃ עֲלֵ֡ה אֶל־הַר֩ הָעֲבָרִ֨ים
הַזֶּ֜ה הַר־נְב֗וֹ אֲשֶׁר֙ בְּאֶ֣רֶץ מוֹאָ֔ב אֲשֶׁ֖ר עַל־פְּנֵ֣י יְרֵח֑וֹ וּרְאֵה֙ אֶת־אֶ֣רֶץ כְּנַ֔עַן

מִדַּם חָלָל וְשִׁבְיָה — *With the blood of the slain and of the captives* ... as it says, וְרַבּוּ חַלְלֵי ה׳, *And the slain of* HASHEM *shall be many* (ibid.).]

43. הַרְנִינוּ גוֹיִם — *Rejoice, O nations.* You, the arrows and sword of God, *make the nations rejoice,* for they will all recognize that God is just in Whom there is no wrong (based on *Psalms* 92), as it says, יִשְׂמְחוּ וִירַנְּנוּ לְאֻמִּים כִּי תִשְׁפֹּט עַמִּים מִישֹׁר, *let the nations be glad and sing for joy, for You shall judge the peoples with equity* (*Psalms* 67:5).

עַמּוֹ — *His people* ... and cause His people to rejoice, that they shall give thanks with the voice of song, because ...

[דַּם עֲבָדָיו יִקּוֹם וְנָקָם יָשִׁיב לְצָרָיו — *The blood of His servants will He avenge and He will render vengeance to His adversaries.* The rejoicing of His people will be for the vengeance of His servant's blood, and for (the punishment) imposed on His adversaries, because of that which they did to Israel in a vengeful manner.]

וְכִפֶּר אַדְמָתוֹ — *And He will atone for His land* ... (when the Land) will have been left desolate by them, (because) of that which was done therein.

עַמּוֹ — *And His people.* And He will also atone for His people for all (the sins) they have done in Exile (in) desecrating the Name of God and similar (sins). (This atonement will be) because of their sufferings in Exile, in such a manner that the *Shechinah* will return (and

NOTES

43. הַרְנִינוּ גוֹיִם עַמּוֹ — *Rejoice, O nations, His people. Rashi* explains this phrase as meaning that the nations will praise "His people" for cleaving to Him amidst all their troubles. The *Sforno,* however, links the verb הַרְנִינוּ, *exult with singing,* to the words "nations" and "His people." The nations will sing a song of praise and recognition to God attesting to His just ways. Israel will sing a song of thanksgiving for their deliverance, for the avenging of the blood of their martyrs and for the just punishment meted out to the enemies of Israel. Here again, for obvious reasons, the censor deleted much of the *Sforno's* commentary on this verse.

וְכִפֶּר אַדְמָתוֹ עַמּוֹ — *And He will atone for His land and His people.* Two phases of atonement are implied in this verse. The first concerns the fact that when Israel dwelt in the Land, they failed to observe the Sabbatical and Jubilee years properly. As a result of this transgression they were exiled, and expiation for this sin came only because *Eretz Yisrael* lay desolate for many years. See *Leviticus* 26:34 and the *Sforno's* commentary there. The *Sforno* alludes to this when he states that atonement for the Land was attained through its desolation. The word עַמּוֹ, *His people,* conveys a second thought. The people of Israel sinned in Exile through actions which profaned God's Holy Name. The expiation for these sins will come through their great suffering in their state of exile. The atonement for both of these sins, that of

flesh, because of the blood of corpse and captive, because of the earliest depredations of the enemy.' "

43 *O nations — sing the praises of His people, for He will avenge the blood of His servants; He will bring retribution upon His foes, and He will appease His Land and His people.*

44 *Moses came and spoke all the words of this Song in the ears of the people, he and Hoshea son of Nun.*
45 *Moses concluded speaking all these words to all Israel.*
46 *He said to them, "Apply your hearts to all the words that I testify against you today, with which you are to instruct your children, to be careful to perform all the words of this Torah,*
47 *for it is not an empty thing for you, for it is your life, and through this matter shall you prolong your days on the Land to which you cross the Jordan, to possess it."*

48 *HASHEM spoke to Moses on that very day, saying,*
49 *"Ascend to this mount of Abarim, Mount Nebo, which is in the land of Moab, which is before Jericho, and see the Land of Canaan that I give to*

---

dwell) in their midst, as it says, יַחְדָּו יְרַנֵּנוּ כִּי עַיִן בְּעַיִן יִרְאוּ בְּשׁוּב ה׳ צִיּוֹן, *Together shall they sing, for they shall see, eye to eye, HASHEM returning to Zion (Isaiah 52:8).*

46. אֲשֶׁר אָנֹכִי מֵעִיד בָּכֶם הַיּוֹם — *Which I testify among you this day* . . . through the song of *Haazinu* by which I testify and caution Israel that just as God, the Blessed One, gave them sustenance without suffering so that they might serve Him, so will He destroy them if they frustrate His intent.

אֲשֶׁר תְּצַוֻּם אֶת בְּנֵיכֶם — *Which you shall command your children.* At the end of your days, you shall make mention of all these words to your children in your last will and testament and command them to guard their souls, lest they become corrupted, just as David (before his death) commanded his son Solomon.

לִשְׁמֹר לַעֲשׂוֹת — *To observe to do* . . . so that the children will observe and do.

47. כִּי הוּא חַיֵּיכֶם — *Because it is your life* . . . eternal perfection, (the condition) in which one lives after the death of the body.

49. וּרְאֵה אֶת אֶרֶץ — *And see the land* . . . so as to grant your blessing therein.

NOTES

rejecting the laws of *Shemittah* in *Eretz Yisrael* and the transgressions committed in Exile, will eventually result in the return of the Divine Presence to Israel.

46. אֲשֶׁר אָנֹכִי מֵעִיד בָּכֶם הַיּוֹם — *Which I testify among you this day*. The testimony of *Haazinu* is such that Israel would do well to hearken to it most carefully. It is a poem of promise and warning. In verses 13-14, they are told that God will grant them a land filled with material good which they have not worked for and even later the earth will produce its blessings with a minimum of toil. However, by the same token, they are cautioned that if they fail to keep the covenant with God they will be severely punished.

אֲשֶׁר תְּצַוֻּם אֶת בְּנֵיכֶם — *Which you shall command your children*. The *Sforno* interprets the word תְּצַוֻּם as meaning not only *to command* but also in the sense of צַוָּאָה — a last will and testament. What is said by a father to his children on his deathbed is of the utmost importance, and children will treat such instructions with great seriousness and respect. By adjuring one's children before passing away to keep the Torah and observe its *mitzvos*, the probability of their doing so is greatly enhanced.

49. וּרְאֵה אֶת אֶרֶץ — *And see the land*. In *Genesis* 48:10, the *Sforno* comments on Jacob's inability to see Ephraim and Menasseh due to his blindness, and states that one must see the object of his blessing in order for that blessing to be effective. He cites as an example the fact that Balak brought Bilaam to the heights to see the camp of Israel in order to curse them, because a blessing and curse are closely related! He also cites *Deut.* 34:1 where God shows Moses the Land of Israel for the purpose of blessing it. The *Sforno's* comment on this verse echoes this idea.

נ אֲשֶׁר אֲנִי נֹתֵן לִבְנֵי יִשְׂרָאֵל לַאֲחֻזָּה: וּמֻת בָּהָר אֲשֶׁר אַתָּה עֹלֶה שָׁמָּה
וְהֵאָסֵף אֶל־עַמֶּיךָ כַּאֲשֶׁר־מֵת אַהֲרֹן אָחִיךָ בְּהֹר הָהָר וַיֵּאָסֶף אֶל־עַמָּיו:
נא עַל אֲשֶׁר מְעַלְתֶּם בִּי בְּתוֹךְ בְּנֵי יִשְׂרָאֵל בְּמֵי־מְרִיבַת קָדֵשׁ מִדְבַּר־צִן
נב עַל אֲשֶׁר לֹא־קִדַּשְׁתֶּם אוֹתִי בְּתוֹךְ בְּנֵי יִשְׂרָאֵל: כִּי מִנֶּגֶד תִּרְאֶה
אֶת־הָאָרֶץ וְשָׁמָּה לֹא תָבוֹא אֶל־הָאָרֶץ אֲשֶׁר־אֲנִי נֹתֵן לִבְנֵי יִשְׂרָאֵל:

50. וּמֻת בָּהָר — *And accept your death in the mount.* Accept death upon yourself as an atonement for having acted faithlessly.

NOTES

50. וּמֻת בָּהָר — *And accept your death.* The word does not mean *die.* Rather it means *accept death* as a consequence of the sin you committed when you smote the rock rather than speaking to it in defi-

the Children of Israel as an inheritance, [50] *and die on the mountain where you will ascend, and be gathered to your people, as Aaron your brother died on Mount Hor, and was gathered to his people,* [51] *because you trespassed against Me among the Children of Israel at the waters of Meribath-kadesh, in the wilderness of Zin; because you did not sanctify Me among the Children of Israel.* [52] *For from a distance shall you see the Land, but you shall not enter there, into the Land that I give to the Children of Israel."*

וְהֵאָסֵף אֶל עַמֶּיךָ — *And be gathered to your people.* And thus, you will be gathered in the bond of life, (together) with those who are as fitting and proper as you are.

NOTES

ance of God. When one accepts punishment willingly, it atones for the sin committed.

וְהֵאָסֵף אֶל עַמֶּיךָ — *And be gathered to your people.* See *Sforno* on *Genesis* 25:8 and the note.

פרשת וזאת הברכה

לג א וְזֹאת הַבְּרָכָה אֲשֶׁר בֵּרַךְ מֹשֶׁה אִישׁ הָאֱלֹהִים אֶת־בְּנֵי יִשְׂרָאֵל לִפְנֵי
ב מוֹתוֹ: וַיֹּאמַר יהוה מִסִּינַי בָּא וְזָרַח מִשֵּׂעִיר לָמוֹ הוֹפִיעַ מֵהַר פָּארָן וְאָתָה
°אֵשׁ דָּת ק׳ ג מֵרִבְבֹת קֹדֶשׁ מִימִינוֹ °אשדת לָמוֹ: אַף חֹבֵב עַמִּים כָּל־קְדֹשָׁיו בְּיָדֶךָ
ד וְהֵם תֻּכּוּ לְרַגְלֶךָ יִשָּׂא מִדַּבְּרֹתֶיךָ: תּוֹרָה צִוָּה־לָנוּ מֹשֶׁה מוֹרָשָׁה קְהִלַּת

XXXIII

1. וְזֹאת הַבְּרָכָה אֲשֶׁר בֵּרַךְ מֹשֶׁה — *And this is the blessing wherewith Moses blessed ...* when God, the Blessed One, showed him all the Land (of Israel) before his death, so that he might bless the Land and Israel (who dwelt) therein, as was the intent (of Moses) when he said, אֶעְבְּרָה נָּא וְאֶרְאֶה, *Let me go over, please* (3:25). And this was also God's intent when He said to him, וּרְאֵה אֶת הָאָרֶץ, *And behold the Land* (*Numbers* 27:12). (Now) this is that blessing which he (Moses) did bless (Israel and the Land).

2. וַיֹּאמַר — *And he said.* Before he began the blessing (proper), which begins with *Iron and brass shall be your locks* (verse 25), he recited this introduction and prayed for the tribes, so that his blessing might come to pass; because, indeed, words of blessing are always said when speaking (directly) to the (one) who is being blessed, as it says אָמוֹר לָהֶם, *You shall say to them* (*Numbers* 6:23). (Now) all his words from *iron and brass* until *shall tread upon their high places* (verse 29) were (spoken) with Israel, but his previous words (i.e., verses 2-24) were (directed) to God, beseeching Him on behalf of His people.

ה׳ — *God!* (This is) an expression of calling.

מִסִּינַי בָּא וְזָרַח ... אֵשׁ דָּת לָמוֹ — *HASHEM came from Sinai and rose ... a fiery law unto them.* He mentioned the merit of Israel in order that his prayer be accepted and that his blessing should rest upon (them). He said to God, the Blessed One, "Behold, You came from Sinai and rose and shone from various places unto Israel (radiating) the holiness of the fiery law." (This) refers to the speculative-theoretical part of the Torah (חֵלֶק הָעִיּוּנִי) which emanates from the *myriad of holiness,* (meaning) the "right side of holiness," because indeed (that portion) was given through a mirror of clarity (אַסְפַּקְלַרְיָה הַמְּאִירָה).

3. אַף חֹבֵב עַמִּים — *Although He loves the peoples.* Although You love (all) people, as You said, וִהְיִיתֶם לִי סְגֻלָּה מִכָּל הָעַמִּים, *And you shall be My own treasure from among all peoples*

NOTES

XXXIII

1. וְזֹאת הַבְּרָכָה — *And this is the blessing.* This expression implies that a specific previously mentioned blessing is being referred to. The *Sforno* therefore explains that when God showed Moses the Land, as stated in a number of places (*Numbers* 27:12, *Deut.* 32:49, 34:4), and when Moses requested permission to cross over and see the Land (*Deut.* 3:25), the purpose was to see it and bless it. As explained in *Genesis* 48:10, and in the note on verse 49 in the previous chapter, one must see the object or the recipient of the blessing for the blessing to be effective. This then is *the blessing* which was given by Moses, in keeping with his and God's desire.

2. וַיֹּאמַר — *And he said.* A blessing is always given in the presence of the recipient, in a direct manner. It is for this reason that one must see the object of his blessing, as mentioned in the previous note. The *Sforno* points out that all the verses preceding verse 25 are not written in the second person. Only verses 25 through 29 are to be considered a בְּרָכָה, *a blessing,* whereas the opening verses are to be understood as praise of God and prayers uttered by Moses on behalf of the tribes that they may be worthy to receive God's blessing. Also, these opening verses speak of individual tribes, while the verses of actual blessing (25-29) are directed to the people of Israel collectively.

מִסִּינַי בָּא וְזָרַח ... — *HASHEM came from Sinai and rose etc. Rashi* in his commentary states: "(Moses) began with praise of the Omnipotent ... but in the praise of God there is also mention of Israel's merit." The *Sforno* reflects this latter part of *Rashi's* interpretation, after which he proceeds to explain

PARASHAS VEZOS HABERACHAH

33 [1] *And this is the blessing that Moses, the man of God, bestowed upon the Children of Israel before his death.* [2] *He said:* HASHEM *came from Sinai — having shone forth to them from Seir, having appeared from Mount Paran, and then approached with some of the holy myriads — from His right hand He presented the fiery Torah to them.* [3] *Indeed, You loved the tribes greatly, all its holy ones were in Your hands; for they planted themselves at Your feet, bearing [the yoke] of Your utterances:* [4] *"The Torah that Moses commanded us is the heritage of the Congregation of*

(*Exodus* 19:5), and thus You made it known that all humanity is considered as a treasure to You, as (our Sages) state, חָבִיב אָדָם שֶׁנִּבְרָא בְצֶלֶם, *Precious is man who was created in the Image* (*Avos* 3:18), still כָּל קְדֹשָׁיו בְּיָדֶךָ, *all His holy ones are in Your hand;* You have stated that all His holy ones sanctified by the holiness of the fiery law are in Your hand akin to a bag of silver. [For they (i.e., Israel) are more precious to You than all other human beings as it says, וְאַתֶּם תִּהְיוּ לִי מַמְלֶכֶת כֹּהֲנִים וְגוֹי קָדוֹשׁ, *And you shall be unto Me a kingdom of Kohanim and a holy nation* (*Exodus* 19:6), and as our Sages state, חֲבִיבִין יִשְׂרָאֵל שֶׁנִּקְרְאוּ בָנִים לַמָּקוֹם, *Beloved are Israel for they are called children of the Omnipresent* (*Avos* 3:14).]

וְהֵם תֻּכּוּ — *And they (pray) with broken spirit ...* (תֻּכּוּ) meaning broken, similar to וְאִישׁ תְּכָכִים, *A man who breaks (the oppressor)* (*Proverbs* 29:13). They prayed with a broken, contrite spirit.

לְרַגְלֶךָ — *At Your feet.* At Your footstool on Sinai (based on *Psalms* 99:5).

3.-4. יִשָּׂא מִדַּבְּרֹתֶיךָ ... תּוֹרָה צִוָּה לָנוּ מֹשֶׁה — *He will bear Your words ... the Torah that Moses commanded us.* They said to God, the Blessed One, "Moses *will bear Your words* to us, which is the Torah commanded to us." The phrase מִדַּבְּרֹתֶיךָ is used (as opposed to דְּבָרֶיךָ), similar to (the verse), וַיִּשְׁמַע אֶת הַקּוֹל מִדַּבֵּר אֵלָיו, *And he heard the Voice speaking to him* (*Numbers* 7:89).

מוֹרָשָׁה קְהִלַּת יַעֲקֹב — *An inheritance of the congregation of Jacob.* And this shall be an inheritance to the congregation of Jacob, accepted by us and our children as an inheritance.

NOTES

that the light of revelation at Sinai which shone upon Israel was of such a nature that it emanated from the strongest source of holiness, the "right" which represents strength as opposed to the "left," representing the speculative-theoretical part of Torah which becomes clear and understandable when one reaches the exalted level of פָּנִים אֶל פָּנִים, *face to face*, as Israel did at Sinai. (See the *Sforno* on *Exodus* 19:9.) The word רִבְבוֹת comes from רְבָבָה, *ten thousand*, which represents a myriad of light. The phrase אֶלֶף, *a thousand*, is a lesser degree of God's radiance; hence, the former is called יָמִין, *right*, while the latter is referred to as שְׂמֹאל, *left*.

3. אַף חֹבֵב עַמִּים — *Although He loves the peoples.* In his commentary on *Exodus*, chapter 19, the *Sforno* stresses the importance and dignity of mankind in general, although he also underscores the unique, special role played by Israel. Man is beloved, but Israel alone are called the children of God. He repeats this concept here, adding one moving thought: The people of Israel, called *His holy ones*, are so precious that they are not even placed in the king's treasure house but are held in *His hand!* It is interesting to note that in the מִקְרָאוֹת גְּדוֹלוֹת, that part of the *Sforno's* commentary which states, "For they are more precious to you etc.," the quote from *Exodus* 19:6 as well as the Mishnah in *Avos* are deleted. The censor apparently could not accept such an expression of elitism.

מִדַּבְּרֹתֶיךָ — *Your words. Sforno* explains the word מְדַבֵּר similar to *Rashi*, as meaning to speak to oneself (מִתְדַּבֵּר); see the *Sforno's* commentary on *Numbers* 7:89 and the note there. God speaks, as it were, to Himself but makes it audible and understandable to Moses so that he, in turn, might transmit the word of God to Israel. Hence, the word מִדַּבְּרֹתֶיךָ and not דְּבָרֶיךָ.

ה־ו יַעֲקֹב: וַיְהִי בִישֻׁרוּן מֶלֶךְ בְּהִתְאַסֵּף רָאשֵׁי עָם יַחַד שִׁבְטֵי יִשְׂרָאֵל: יְחִי
ז רְאוּבֵן וְאַל־יָמֹת וִיהִי מְתָיו מִסְפָּר: וְזֹאת לִיהוּדָה וַיֹּאמַר
שְׁמַע יהוה קוֹל יְהוּדָה וְאֶל־עַמּוֹ תְּבִיאֶנּוּ יָדָיו רָב לוֹ וְעֵזֶר מִצָּרָיו תִּהְיֶה:
שני ח וּלְלֵוִי אָמַר תֻּמֶּיךָ וְאוּרֶיךָ לְאִישׁ חֲסִידֶךָ אֲשֶׁר נִסִּיתוֹ בְּמַסָּה
ט תְּרִיבֵהוּ עַל־מֵי מְרִיבָה: הָאֹמֵר לְאָבִיו וּלְאִמּוֹ לֹא רְאִיתִיו וְאֶת־
אֶחָיו לֹא הִכִּיר וְאֶת־בָּנָו לֹא יָדָע כִּי שָׁמְרוּ אִמְרָתֶךָ וּבְרִיתְךָ יִנְצֹרוּ:

5. וַיְהִי בִישֻׁרוּן מֶלֶךְ — *And there was a King in Jeshurun.* And then He Who was King in Jeshurun, namely God the Blessed One, Who was King among those who delved into and held fast to the Torah.

בְּהִתְאַסֵּף רָאשֵׁי עָם — *When the heads of the people gathered . . .* at the time of the giving of the Torah, as it says, *All the heads of your tribes and your elders came near to me* (5:20), and as it says, *HASHEM our God has shown us His glory* (ibid. v. 21).

יַחַד שִׁבְטֵי יִשְׂרָאֵל — *All the tribes of Israel together.* He was then King over all the tribes of Israel together, for it was then that they accepted and affirmed His Kingship, as it says, *and you shall speak unto us all that HASHEM our God speaks to you and we will hear it and do it* (ibid. v. 24).

6. יְחִי רְאוּבֵן — *Let Reuben live.* Even though Reuben chose an unclean land on the other side of the Jordan which was not the land of God, as it says, וְאַךְ אִם טְמֵאָה אֶרֶץ אֲחֻזַּתְכֶם, *However, if the land of your possession is unclean* (*Joshua* 22:19), and therefore it is not so conducive (lit., prepared) in which to merit everlasting life, nonetheless let his heart live forever.

וְאַל יָמֹת וִיהִי מְתָיו מִסְפָּר — *And not die, nor his number be diminished* (lit., few). And let him not die in this world in such a manner that his men be few, similar to וַאֲנִי מְתֵי מִסְפָּר, *And I am few in number* (*Genesis* 34:30). (And may this be) even though it is written, *That your days may be multiplied . . . upon the land* (11:21).

7. וְזֹאת לִיהוּדָה — *And this for Judah.* And this request I also ask and pray on behalf of the land of Judah, wherein the inheritance of Simeon is scattered (as well), that they do not perish in battle — because they went forth to battle together.

וַיֹּאמַר שְׁמַע ה׳ קוֹל יְהוּדָה — *And he said, "Hear, HASHEM, the voice of Judah."* Besides his saying, וְזֹאת לִיהוּדָה, *and this for Judah,* he also said, *Hear, HASHEM, the voice of Judah,*

NOTES

5. וַיְהִי בִישֻׁרוּן מֶלֶךְ . . . יַחַד שִׁבְטֵי יִשְׂרָאֵל — *And there was a King in Jeshurun . . . all the tribes of Israel together*. The *Sforno,* in his commentary on 32:15, translates the term יְשֻׁרוּן as meaning those who are of superior intelligence and understanding. The sense of our verse is: God, Who was initially recognized as King by these men of excellence (Jeshurun), was subsequently recognized and accepted as King by the tribes of Israel at large when they experienced the revelation at Sinai. However, the *Sforno* himself gives a different interpretation of this verse in his commentary on *Numbers* 7:3. There he explains it to mean that only when unity reigns among the leaders of Israel is God their King.

6. יְחִי רְאוּבֵן — *Let Reuben live. Rashi* interprets this phrase as referring to This World, and *and let him not die* as alluding to the World to Come. The *Sforno* interprets these phrases in reverse fashion. The former speaks of חַיֵּי עוֹלָם, *everlasting life,* which is endangered because Reuben will not reside in *Eretz Yisrael,* a land that is more conducive to insure the spiritual reward of eternal life, while the latter phrase refers to long life here on earth. This prayer was necessary for Reuben, since the blessing of lengthy days (אֲרִיכַת יָמִים) was bestowed in *Eretz Yisrael* and not Trans-Jordan where his tribe resided.

7. וְזֹאת לִיהוּדָה — *And this for Judah*. Both *Rashi* and the *Sforno* explain that the prayer for Simeon, who is not mentioned explicitly in this *parashah,* is alluded to in this verse. The *Sforno,* however, reads it into the phrase, *And this for Judah,* while *Rashi* finds the allusion in the phrase, *Hear, HASHEM, the voice of Judah. Sforno* apparently interprets וְזֹאת, *and this,* as a רִבּוּי — a word meant

Jacob." 5 *He became King over Jeshurun when the numbers of the nation gathered — the tribes of Israel in unity.*

6 *May Reuben live and not die, and may his population be included in the count.*

7 *And this to Judah, and he said: Hearken, O* Hashem, *to Judah's voice, and return him to his people; may his hands fight his grievance and may You be a Helper against his enemies.*

8 *Of Levi he said: Your Tumim and Your Urim befit Your devout one, whom You tested at Massah, and whom You challenged at the waters of Meribah.*
9 *The one who said of his father and mother, "I have not favored him"; his brothers he did not give recognition and his children he did not know; for they [the Levites] have observed Your word and Your covenant they preserved.*

---

when he will beseech you in (time of) war or other (times of need).

יָדָיו רָב לוֹ וְעֵזֶר מִצָּרָיו תִּהְיֶה — *You will be his hands, contend for him and help him against his adversaries.* (May) You be *his hands* to battle on his behalf and also contend for him and exact revenge (on his behalf), and also be a help against his enemies when they do battle against him.

8. תֻּמֶּיךָ וְאוּרֶיךָ לְאִישׁ חֲסִידֶךָ — *Your Tumim and Urim (You gave) to the leader of Your pious ones.* Behold, the *Tumim* and *Urim* You did give to Aaron who was the אִישׁ, *man*, and head of the pious tribe, namely the tribe of Levi. Thus it became evident that he (i.e., Aaron) spoke, inspired by the Holy Spirit, and the *Shechinah* dwelt on him, as our Sages state, "No *Kohen* is inquired of (by the Israelites) through the *Urim* and *Tumim* who does not speak by means of the Holy Spirit and upon whom the *Shechinah* does not rest" (*Yoma* 73b).

אֲשֶׁר נִסִּיתוֹ בְּמַסָּה — *Whom You did prove at the time of testing.* The tribe of Levi did not test Him at those times when Israel tested God, the Blessed One, as it says וַיְנַסּוּ אֹתִי זֶה עֶשֶׂר פְּעָמִים, *You have tested Me these ten times* (*Numbers* 14:22), and therefore the decree (against) the spies was not issued against them.

תְּרִיבֵהוּ עַל מֵי מְרִיבָה — *And with whom You strove at the waters of Meribah.* You eliminated their two leaders, Moses and Aaron, because of the waters of strife.

9. הָאֹמֵר לְאָבִיו — *Who said of his father ...* in the matter of the (Golden) Calf.

וְאֶת בָּנָו לֹא יָדָע כִּי שָׁמְרוּ אִמְרָתֶךָ — *Nor regarded his own children, for they observed Your word.* He was not concerned for the safety (lit., life) of his sons in the wilderness, so that

NOTES

to expand upon the term לִיהוּדָה; hence, it is meant to add Simeon to Judah, which is a reasonable interpretation since Simeon took his portion from amongst Judah's lot (see *Rashi*) and they went forth to do battle together.

יָדָיו רָב לוֹ וְעֵזֶר מִצָּרָיו תִּהְיֶה — *You will be his hands, contend for him and help him against his adversaries.* The *Sforno* explains that these three terms refer to three different circumstances when God's assistance is requested and needed. יָדָיו, *His hands,* refers to God's intervention on behalf of Judah and Simeon when they do battle; רָב לוֹ, *contend for him,* is a request that God avenge Judah when he may have suffered defeat, while עֵזֶר, *help,* speaks of lending assistance in his defense when the enemy attacks Judah.

8. לְאִישׁ חֲסִידֶךָ — *To the leader of Your pious ones.* The term אִישׁ, *man,* in the singular is difficult to understand in the context of this verse. The *Sforno,* however, explains it as referring to Aaron who was the head of the tribe of Levi and who was so worthy that God would make His wishes known through him as the leader of the pious ones.

אֲשֶׁר נִסִּיתוֹ בְּמַסָּה תְּרִיבֵהוּ עַל מֵי מְרִיבָה — *Whom You did prove at the time of testing and with whom You strove at the waters of Meribah.* Unlike the Israelites who tested God on ten different occasions, the Levites never put God or Moses to the test. The one time this tribe faltered was, ironically, when their great leaders, Moses and Aaron, failed to carry out God's directive *at the waters of Meribah.*

9. וְאֶת בָּנָו לֹא יָדָע כִּי שָׁמְרוּ אִמְרָתֶךָ — *Nor regarded his own children, for they observed Your word.* The commentators are hard put to explain this

י יוֹר֤וּ מִשְׁפָּטֶ֙יךָ֙ לְיַעֲקֹ֔ב וְתוֹרָתְךָ֖ לְיִשְׂרָאֵ֑ל יָשִׂ֤ימוּ קְטוֹרָה֙ בְּאַפֶּ֔ךָ וְכָלִ֖יל עַל־
יא מִזְבְּחֶֽךָ׃ בָּרֵ֤ךְ יהוה֙ חֵיל֔וֹ וּפֹ֥עַל יָדָ֖יו תִּרְצֶ֑ה מְחַ֨ץ מָתְנַ֤יִם קָמָיו֙ וּמְשַׂנְאָ֔יו
יב מִן־יְקוּמֽוּן׃   לְבִנְיָמִ֣ן אָמַ֔ר יְדִ֣יד יהוה יִשְׁכֹּ֥ן לָבֶ֖טַח עָלָ֑יו חֹפֵ֤ף
יג עָלָיו֙ כָּל־הַיּ֔וֹם וּבֵ֥ין כְּתֵפָ֖יו שָׁכֵֽן׃   וּלְיוֹסֵ֣ף אָמַ֔ר מְבֹרֶ֥כֶת יהוה
יד אַרְצ֑וֹ מִמֶּ֤גֶד שָׁמַ֙יִם֙ מִטָּ֔ל וּמִתְּה֖וֹם רֹבֶ֥צֶת תָּֽחַת׃ וּמִמֶּ֖גֶד תְּבוּאֹ֣ת שָׁ֑מֶשׁ
טו־טז וּמִמֶּ֖גֶד גֶּ֥רֶשׁ יְרָחִֽים׃ וּמֵרֹ֖אשׁ הַרְרֵי־קֶ֑דֶם וּמִמֶּ֖גֶד גִּבְע֣וֹת עוֹלָֽם׃ וּמִמֶּ֜גֶד
אֶ֣רֶץ וּמְלֹאָ֗הּ וּרְצ֤וֹן שֹׁכְנִ֣י סְנֶ֔ה תָּב֙וֹאתָה֙ לְרֹ֣אשׁ יוֹסֵ֔ף וּלְקָדְקֹ֖ד נְזִ֥יר אֶחָֽיו׃

---

he might observe Your word, i.e., the commandment regarding the circumcision of the sons, even though many of them perished, as our Sages say, "Because the North wind did not blow upon them" (*Yevamos* 72a).

וּבְרִיתְךָ֣ יִנְצֹ֑רוּ — *And they kept Your covenant* . . . as our Sages say, "The tribe of Levi did not participate in the idolatry (of the Golden Calf)" (*Yoma* 66b), and this was true both in Egypt and in the wilderness.

10. יוֹר֤וּ מִשְׁפָּטֶ֙יךָ֙ לְיַעֲקֹ֔ב — *May they be worthy to teach Your laws to Jacob.* Since they are a proper, fit tribe, grant them favor and good understanding that they may teach Your laws to Jacob, as our Sages say, "If the *Rav* is like unto a messenger of God, the Lord of Hosts, they will seek Torah from his mouth" (*Moed Katan* 17a).

11. בָּרֵךְ ה' חֵילוֹ — *Bless, HASHEM, his substance.* Bless their property in such a manner that a minimum of effort will suffice, so that they will have time to understand and teach (Torah).

וּפֹעַל יָדָיו תִּרְצֶה — *And accept the work of his hands.* (May) their service in the Sanctuary be acceptable to You.

מִן יְקוּמוּן — *That they not rise again* . . . that those who (challenge them) not be able to rise up against them, such as occurred with Korach and Uzziah.

12. יְדִיד ה' — *The beloved of HASHEM.* As our Sages state, Benjamin died בְּעֶטְיוֹ שֶׁל נָחָשׁ, *through the serpent's machinations* (*Shabbos* 55b). Moses mentions this merit to God.

יִשְׁכֹּן לָבֶטַח עָלָיו — *Shall dwell securely with Him.* He will not rebel against his king (as did) the ten tribes.

NOTES

phrase since the "sons" of the tribe were also Levites, and none of them were guilty of idolatry during the episode of the Golden Calf (see *Rashi's* explanation here). The *Sforno*, however, interprets this phrase as extolling the sacrificial commitment of the Levites to the *mitzvah* of בְּרִית מִילָה, *circumcision,* which they performed even in the wilderness even though the environmental and climatic conditions were not suitable for circumcision. See the *Sforno* (*Exodus* 32:29) on the phrase, כִּי אִישׁ בִּבְנוֹ, *for every man through his son,* and the note there. The *Sforno's* interpretation clarifies the subsequent expression, *for they observed Your word,* i.e., they observed Your word (commandment) regarding circumcision, even under the most difficult circumstances.

10. יוֹרוּ מִשְׁפָּטֶיךָ — *May they be worthy to teach Your laws.* As mentioned above, these verses are not a blessing but a prayer to God. Hence, the

phrase יוֹרוּ מִשְׁפָּטֶיךָ is interpreted by the *Sforno* not as a statement or a blessing that they will teach the laws of God to the people; rather it is a devout wish that they be granted the qualities and character of the ideal Torah teacher, one whose piety and sincerity is such that people will seek him out and listen to him, as though he were a messenger of God.

11. בָּרֵךְ ה' חֵילוֹ וּפֹעַל יָדָיו תִּרְצֶה — *Bless, HASHEM, his substance and accept the work of his hands.* Although the tribe of Levi did not receive a portion in *Eretz Yisrael,* nonetheless, they were given 48 cities in which to dwell and also open land around these cities. Their primary mission was to serve in God's Temple and to be the teachers of His law. Hence the prayer was that they be spared arduous and time-consuming labor so that they might be free to pursue their calling. See the *Sforno's* commentary on *Genesis* 49:13 regarding the gifts given to the *Kohanim* and Levites.

[10] *They shall teach Your ordinances to Jacob and Your Torah to Israel; they shall place incense before Your presence, and burnt offerings on Your Altar.*
[11] *Bless, O HASHEM, his resources, and favor the work of his hands; smash the loins of his foes and his enemies, that they may not rise.*
[12] *Of Benjamin he said: May HASHEM's beloved dwell securely by Him; He hovers over him all day long; and rests between his shoulders.*
[13] *Of Joseph he said: Blessed by HASHEM is his land — with the heavenly bounty of dew, and with the deep waters crouching below;* [14] *with the bounty of the sun's crops, and with the bounty of the moon's yield;* [15] *with the quick-ripening crops of the early mountains, and with the bounty of eternal hills;* [16] *with the bounty of the land and its fullness, and by the favor of Him Who rested upon the thornbush; may this blessing rest upon Joseph's head, and upon the crown of him who was separated from his brothers.*

---

13. מְבֹרֶכֶת ה׳ אַרְצוֹ — *Blessed of HASHEM is his land.* Behold, the portion of Joseph is naturally blessed.

מִמֶּגֶד שָׁמַיִם מִטָּל — *From the dew of heaven precious things (shall come).* And behold, I pray that the blessing (of his land) shall also be through the choice fruits which ripen due to the power of heaven (through the medium) of dew, even without rain — and *from the deep* and *the choice fruits of the sun* (verse 14).

16. וּרְצוֹן שֹׁכְנִי סְנֶה — *And by the will of Him Who dwelt in the bush . . .* and also by the will of God Who revealed Himself in the bush, thereby demonstrating to Israel that עִמּוֹ אָנֹכִי בְצָרָה, *I will be with him in trouble* (*Psalms* 91:15). All this . . .

תָּבוֹאתָה לְרֹאשׁ יוֹסֵף — *Let (the blessing) come upon the head of Joseph.* Besides those blessings which he receives together with the congregation (of Israel), let blessings come from God on high on his head (i.e., directly), without any intermediary.

וּלְקָדְקֹד נְזִיר אֶחָיו — *And upon the crown of the head of him that is prince among his brothers.* Indeed, he is worthy of all this because he was a prince who wore the crown of kingship in the midst of his brothers and conducted himself with lovingkindness toward all of them.

NOTES

מִן יְקוּמוּן — *That they rise not again.* Korach challenged the legitimacy of Aaron's priesthood. King Uzziah entered the Holy to offer incense on the golden Altar even though he was not a *Kohen;* he became a leper as a consequence of this willful illegal act. Moses prays that the authority and special rank of the Levites and *Kohanim* not be challenged but accepted as the will of God Who chose them to act as His servants.

12. יְדִיד ה׳ — *The beloved of HASHEM.* The Talmud (*Shabbos* 55b) tells us that there were four righteous men who never sinned and hence never would have died. Their deaths were due to the decree of death issued by God as a consequence of Adam and Eve's eating of the fruit of the Tree of Knowledge at the instigation of the serpent. This is the meaning of עֲטָיו שֶׁל נָחָשׁ, *the serpent's machinations.* Benjamin was one of the four and is therefore called *the beloved of God.* The other three were Amram the father of Moses, Jesse the father of David and Caleb the son of David.

16. וּרְצוֹן שֹׁכְנִי סְנֶה — *And by the will of Him Who dwelt in the bush.* Moses invokes the "will of God" Who revealed Himself to Moses in the bush (*Exodus* 3:2). The *Sforno* explains that he chose to recall an event which symbolizes God's concern for Israel in times of trouble because similarly, God was with Joseph during his time of trouble in Egypt.

תָּבוֹאתָה לְרֹאשׁ יוֹסֵף וּלְקָדְקֹד נְזִיר אֶחָיו — *Let (the blessing) come upon the head of Joseph and upon the crown of the head of him that is prince among his brothers.* The *Sforno,* in *Genesis* 49:25, explains that when Jacob blessed Joseph he asked that God bless him Himself, without an intermediary. This is the highest level of Divine blessing. He interprets the prayer of Moses regarding Joseph in a similar vein. Moses adds the thought that since Joseph conducted himself toward his brothers לִפְנִים מִשּׁוּרַת הַדִּין, *beyond that which the law of*

יז בְּכוֹר שׁוֹרוֹ הָדָר לוֹ וְקַרְנֵי רְאֵם קַרְנָיו בָּהֶם עַמִּים יְנַגַּח יַחְדָּו אַפְסֵי־אָרֶץ
רביעי יח וְהֵם רִבְבוֹת אֶפְרַיִם וְהֵם אַלְפֵי מְנַשֶּׁה: וְלִזְבוּלֻן אָמַר
יט שְׂמַח זְבוּלֻן בְּצֵאתֶךָ וְיִשָּׂשכָר בְּאֹהָלֶיךָ: עַמִּים הַר־יִקְרָאוּ שָׁם יִזְבְּחוּ
כ זִבְחֵי־צֶדֶק כִּי שֶׁפַע יַמִּים יִינָקוּ וּשְׂפֻנֵי טְמוּנֵי חוֹל: וּלְגָד
כא אָמַר בָּרוּךְ מַרְחִיב גָּד כְּלָבִיא שָׁכֵן וְטָרַף זְרוֹעַ אַף־קָדְקֹד: וַיַּרְא רֵאשִׁית
לוֹ כִּי־שָׁם חֶלְקַת מְחֹקֵק סָפוּן וַיֵּתֵא רָאשֵׁי עָם צִדְקַת יהוה עָשָׂה
חמישי כב וּמִשְׁפָּטָיו עִם־יִשְׂרָאֵל: וּלְדָן אָמַר דָּן גּוּר אַרְיֵה יְזַנֵּק מִן־

17. בְּכוֹר שׁוֹרוֹ — *The firstborn* (*called*) *His ox*. And he, Joseph, is the firstborn (called) the ox of *He Who dwelt in the bush*. For although kingship belongs to Judah, and he is called "lion," following him in rank will be Joseph, just like the ox comes after the lion, as our Sages say, "The king of the wild animals is the lion; the king of the cattle is the ox" (*Chagigah* 13b). And thus the tribe of Joseph was first among the tribes, after the tribe of Judah, as it says, כְּדַבֵּר אֶפְרַיִם רְתֵת, *When Ephraim spoke there was trembling* (*Hosea* 13:1).

הָדָר לוֹ — *Glory is his*. Although he does not possess הוֹד, *the majesty of kingship*, he is worthy of הָדָר, *glory and elevated rank*.

בָּהֶם עַמִּים יְנַגַּח יַחְדָּו — *With them he shall gore the nations all together*. Together with the ruling tribe (Judah) he will gore and destroy many peoples as it says, וְסָרָה קִנְאַת אֶפְרַיִם וְצֹרְרֵי יְהוּדָה יִכָּרֵתוּ . . . וְעָפוּ בְכָתֵף פְּלִשְׁתִּים יָמָּה יַחְדָּו יָבֹזּוּ אֶת בְּנֵי קֶדֶם, *The envy of Ephraim shall depart and the adversaries of Judah shall be cut off . . . And they shall fly on the shoulders of the Philistines toward the sea; they shall spoil the children of the east together* (*Isaiah* 11:13,14).

19. עַמִּים הַר יִקְרָאוּ — *They shall call peoples to the mountain*. Issachar and Zebulun will call (draw) the nations of the world to the "good mountain" (Jerusalem) through their various wares that are unattainable among the nations.

שָׁם יִזְבְּחוּ זִבְחֵי צֶדֶק — *There they shall offer sacrifices of righteousness*. The merchants of the nations, who all their days sacrificed זִבְחֵי מֵתִים, *sacrifices of the dead* (based on *Psalms* 106:28), will also bring sacrifices of righteousness when they come to the "good mountain."

כִּי שֶׁפַע יַמִּים יִינָקוּ — *For they shall suck the abundance of the seas*. Issachar and Zebulun will have all sorts of merchandise which come from the sea, and some which are hidden in the sand, such as the blood (or juice) of the snail and milk glass made from glass sand.

20. בָּרוּךְ מַרְחִיב גָּד — *Blessed is He that enlarges Gad*. For he was given a larger portion than all the other tribes in Trans-Jordan because the land of Sichon and Og was larger

NOTES

God required of him, he earned this special privilege to be the recipient of God's *direct* blessing.

17. בְּכוֹר שׁוֹרוֹ הָדָר לוֹ — *The firstborn* (*called*) *His ox, glory is his*. *Rashi* states that there is a usage of the word בְּכוֹר that denotes "greatness and sovereignty" rather than "firstborn." He also says that the simile *ox* refers to Joshua who was descended from Joseph and was indeed, strong and mighty as an ox. The *Sforno*, however, explains the word בְּכוֹר in the sense that Joseph was first among the tribes, second only to Judah insofar as kingship was concerned. Judah is compared to a lion who is the king of the beasts; Joseph to an ox who is king of the domestic animals. He also draws a fine distinction between the word הָדָר, *glory*, and הוֹד, *majesty*. The latter is Judah's exclusively, but Joseph possesses the former — hence, the phrase in this verse הָדָר לוֹ, *glory is his*.

19. עַמִּים הַר יִקְרָאוּ — *They shall call peoples to the mountain*. Zebulun is a seafaring tribe with access to a variety of treasures which are cherished and desired by all. Since both Zebulun and Issachar

*17 A sovereignty is his ox-like one — majesty is his, and his glory will be
like the horns of a re'eim; with them shall he gore nations together, to the
ends of the Land; they are the myriads of Ephraim, and the thousands of
Manasseh.*
*18 Of Zebulun he said: Rejoice, O Zebulun, in your excursions, and
Issachar in your tents.*
*19 The tribes will assemble at the mount, there they
will slaughter offerings of righteousness, for by the riches of the sea they will
be nourished, and by the treasures concealed in the sand.*
*20 Of Gad he said: Blessed is He Who broadens Gad; he dwells like a lion,
tearing off arm and even head.*
*21 He chose the first portion for himself, for
that is where the lawgiver's plot is hidden; he came at the head of the nation,
carrying out HASHEM's justice and His ordinances with Israel.*
22 Of Dan he said: Dan is a lion cub, leaping forth from the Bashan.

---

quantitatively, even though it was not flowing with milk and honey as was the (west) side of the Jordan (i.e., *Eretz Yisrael* proper).

כְּלָבִיא שָׁכֵן — *He dwells as a lioness.* He is worthy of this enlarged territory because he dwells among the nations as a lion, (capable) of conquering all those around him.

21. וַיַּרְא רֵאשִׁית לוֹ — *And he saw* (*chose*) *the first part for himself.* And he was also worthy to receive this (particular portion) because when Gad chose the land of Sichon and Og, (he knew) it was not as holy as Trans-Jordan, but his intent was to obtain something essential to him, for there in the land of Sichon and Og, the *portion of the lawgiver was reserved,* the portion where the lawgiver, namely Moses, was to be buried.

וַיֵּתֵא רָאשֵׁי עָם — *And there he came, the head of the people.* And there, in the land of Sichon and Og, the lawgiver came at the head of the people to conquer the land.

צִדְקַת ה׳ עָשָׂה וּמִשְׁפָּטָיו עִם יִשְׂרָאֵל — *He executed the righteousness of HASHEM and His ordinances with Israel.* And there the lawgiver executed *the righteousness of God* with Israel by explaining His Torah, and there he exhorted Israel and discussed the judgments and laws of God with them, as did Samuel when he said, הִתְיַצְּבוּ וְאִשָּׁפְטָה אִתְּכֶם . . . אֵת כָּל צִדְקוֹת ה׳, *Now stand there and I will judge with you . . . concerning all the righteous acts of HASHEM* (*I Samuel* 12:7).

22. גּוּר אַרְיֵה יְזַנֵּק מִן הַבָּשָׁן — *A lion's whelp that leaps forth from the Bashan.* Behold, the lion does not (usually) spring forth from the Bashan, which is a choice fertile place for cattle, as it says, אַבִּירֵי בָשָׁן, *strong bulls of Bashan* (*Psalms* 22:13), and פָּרוֹת הַבָּשָׁן, *cows of Bashan* (*Amos* 4:1), unless he is confident that he will find prey outside the Bashan. So Dan will be confident that he can conquer his surroundings and (therefore) he will go out against them, secure (in his success).

NOTES

come into contact with merchants of many nations, they are able to attract many strangers to Jerusalem and awaken their interest in the Almighty to such an extent that these heathens will eventually bring sacrifices to the Holy Temple.

20-21. בָּרוּךְ מַרְחִיב גָּד כְּלָבִיא שָׁכֵן . . . וַיַּרְא רֵאשִׁית לוֹ . . . צִדְקַת ה׳ עָשָׂה . . . — *Blessed is He that enlarges Gad, he dwells as a lioness . . . And he saw* (*chose*) *the first part for himself . . . he executed the righteousness of HASHEM.* The *Sforno* explains that Gad was worthy to be granted a larger portion of land than any other tribe because of two reasons. First, his strength and valor enabled him to conquer and protect a vast territory on the border. Second, his motivation to acquire this particular area was an honorable and praiseworthy one, namely to be privileged to have Moses buried in his portion. The concluding part of verse 21, *he executed the righteousness, etc.,* speaks not of Gad but of Moses, who is interred in the portion of Gad. See *Sotah* 13, the *Sifri* and *Rashi* on this verse (21).

כג הַבָּשָׁן: וּלְנַפְתָּלִי אָמַר נַפְתָּלִי שְׂבַע רָצוֹן וּמָלֵא בִּרְכַּת יְהוָה יָם וְדָרוֹם
כד יְרָשָׁה: וּלְאָשֵׁר אָמַר בָּרוּךְ מִבָּנִים אָשֵׁר יְהִי רְצוּי אֶחָיו וְטֹבֵל
כה־כו בַּשֶּׁמֶן רַגְלוֹ: בַּרְזֶל וּנְחֹשֶׁת מִנְעָלֶךָ וּכְיָמֶיךָ דָּבְאֶךָ: אֵין כָּאֵל יְשֻׁרוּן רֹכֵב
חתן תורה כז שָׁמַיִם בְּעֶזְרֶךָ וּבְגַאֲוָתוֹ שְׁחָקִים: מְעֹנָה אֱלֹהֵי קֶדֶם וּמִתַּחַת זְרֹעֹת עוֹלָם

23. נַפְתָּלִי שְׂבַע רָצוֹן וּמָלֵא בִּרְכַּת ה׳ יָם וְדָרוֹם יְרָשָׁה — *Naphtali, satisfied with favor, and full with the blessings of* HASHEM, *you possess the west and the south.* You, Naphtali, who possess the west and south, are satisfied and full of God's blessings, and I need not pray that your land be blessed, because in this portion are the fruits of Genossar, the first to ripen, and from them are brought בִּכּוּרִים, *the first fruits,* which are accepted with favor by Him (i.e., God).

24. בָּרוּךְ מִבָּנִים אָשֵׁר — *Blessed be Asher by sons (his brothers).* Behold, Asher will be blessed above all others in that he will *be the favored of his brethren.* Although (normally) there is jealousy of brothers toward their rich (brother) and even a degree of animosity, the opposite (will be true) of the tribe of Asher.

וְטֹבֵל בַּשֶּׁמֶן רַגְלוֹ — *And he dips his foot in oil.* (He is favored) because he sells (lit., "gives") oil cheaply to his brothers since he has such an abundance of (olive oil).

25-26. בַּרְזֶל וּנְחֹשֶׁת מִנְעָלֶךָ וּכְיָמֶיךָ דָּבְאֶךָ. אֵין כָּאֵל יְשֻׁרוּן — *Iron and brass shall be your locks, and as your early days so shall your strength be. There is none like God, Jeshurun.* After he concludes his prayer for the tribes, he begins to bless Israel collectively, saying, "You, Jeshurun, being that there is none like (your) God Who is immutable and omnipotent, Who rules over all, your kingdom will be different from other kingdoms on two counts: First, no nation will enter your land to do battle and none will covet your land for fear of you, as indeed it was, כֹּל יְמֵי יְהוֹשֻׁעַ וְכֹל יְמֵי הַזְּקֵנִים אֲשֶׁר הֶאֱרִיכוּ יָמִים אַחֲרֵי יְהוֹשֻׁעַ, *All the days of Joshua and all the days of the elders that outlived Joshua* (Joshua 24:31) — as if the Land was locked with bars of iron and brass. Second, your kingdom will not rise and fall as do the kingdoms of the nations of the world who ascend when their מַזָּל, *constellation,*

NOTES

24. בָּרוּךְ מִבָּנִים אָשֵׁר — *Blessed be Asher by sons (his brothers).* The *Sforno* does not translate the word מִבָּנִים as *above sons,* which is the accepted translation, but *by sons.* Asher will be blessed by the other tribes, the *sons* of Jacob, for he will be generous and gracious in sharing his blessing of oil with all of them.

25-26. בַּרְזֶל וּנְחֹשֶׁת מִנְעָלֶךָ וּכְיָמֶיךָ דָּבְאֶךָ. אֵין כָּאֵל יְשֻׁרוּן רֹכֵב שָׁמַיִם בְּעֶזְרֶךָ — *Iron and brass shall be your locks, and as your early days so shall your strength be. There is none like God, Jeshurun, Who rides upon the heaven and is your help.* As the *Sforno* said in his commentary on verse 2, the blessings of Moses (as opposed to his prayer) begin with these verses. The opening section of the second verse (26) is interpreted by the *Sforno* as an introduction in retrospect to the previous verse (25). Moses addresses Israel using the title Jeshurun and begins by stating that the God of Israel is unique, all-powerful and everlasting. As such, the kingdom He established for them in *Eretz Yisrael* will be secure and safe under His protection and, unlike other nations and kingdoms, their destiny as a people will not be dependent upon the heavenly hosts, planets and constellations which comprise the zodiac. As such, just as God is everlasting and unchanging, so shall Israel be an eternal people and retain their youthful vigor.

The theory of the Sabians, that there is no Divine power superior to the heavenly hosts, is mentioned by Maimonides in his *Guide* and refuted by him, as does the *Sforno* in a number of places in his commentary. Here he reads this refutation into the phrase, *Who rides upon the heaven,* i.e., the Almighty transcends and rules over the stars and planets. Since Israel has no מַזָּל, but is totally dependent upon God and ruled by Him; hence, there shall be no national rise and decline for them as is the case with other nations, whose rise and fall correspond to that of their heavenly representatives.

26-27. וּבְגַאֲוָתוֹ שְׁחָקִים. מְעֹנָה — *And in His majesty on the skies. The dwelling place.* The *Rambam* (*Mishnah Torah, Yesodai HaTorah* 3:1-7) states that there are nine גַּלְגַּלִּים, *spheres,* which encircle the universe, eight of which contain stars or planets that move and control them, such as Mercury, Venus, Mars, Jupiter and Saturn. The ninth sphere, however, which encompasses the universe

23 *Of Naphtali he said: Naphtali, satiated with favor, and filled with HASHEM's blessing; go possess the sea and its south shore.*
24 *Of Asher he said: The most blessed of children is Asher; he shall be pleasing to his brothers, and dip his feet in oil.*
25 *May your borders be sealed like iron and copper, and like the days of your prime, so may your old age be.* 26 *There is none like God, O Jeshurun; He rides across heaven to help you, and in His majesty through the upper heights.*
27 *That is the abode of God immemorial, and below are the world's mighty*

---

rises, and descend when it falls, because they are subject to the hosts of heaven. You, however, כְּיָמֶיךָ, *as your days,* referring to the days of youth when you first entered the Land, דָּבְאֶךָ, *so shall your strength be,* referring to the days of your old age *when you will beget children and children's children and become old in the Land* (based on 4:25). This blessing of mine shall come to pass since *there is none like God* Who conducts your affairs."

רֹכֵב שָׁמַיִם בְּעֶזְרֶךָ — *Who rides upon the heaven and is your Help.* Indeed, God Who is your Helper, He rides upon the heaven, (meaning that) He is supreme, ruling over them (i.e., the planets and constellations) as opposed to the opinion of the Sabians who said that there is none superior (lit., more honored) than the heavens (and their hosts). Therefore, a kingdom which is established by Him does not ascend or decline when the constellations rise and fall.

26-27. וּבְגַאֲוָתוֹ שְׁחָקִים. מְעֹנָה — *And in His majesty on the skies. The dwelling place.* And in His supremacy He rides the skies; this refers to the daily sphere which contains no star or form and its moving (force) is an invisible power, similar to the dwelling place (den) of the lion in which there is great hidden strength.

אֱלֹהֵי קֶדֶם — *The ancient God . . .* the ancient, primeval God, whereas all others are created (lit., renewed) by Him.

וּמִתַּחַת זְרֹעֹת עוֹלָם — *And underneath (the heavens,) the everlasting might.* And below

NOTES

and revolves around the earth every twenty-four hours, "has no division nor any of these forms nor any star," as do the other eight. This ninth sphere is called the גַּלְגַּל חוֹזֵר, *revolving sphere,* which is all-encompassing. According to Maimonides, each sphere "has a soul and is endowed with knowledge and intelligence," but since the ninth sphere has neither star nor form (צוּרָה) within it, its force is hidden and apparently moved, guided and controlled by the direct influence of the Almighty.

The *Sforno,* in his commentary here, reflects this theory of the *Rambam,* while linking the conclusion of verse 26 (וּבְגַאֲוָתוֹ שְׁחָקִים) with the first word (מְעֹנָה) of verse 27. The meaning of his commentary is that the Almighty rides upon the heaven and traverses the skies by guiding the ninth sphere with His direct power. This sphere is called the *daily sphere,* since it revolves around the planet earth from east to west every twenty-four hours. This force of God is concealed in the sense that, unlike the other eight spheres which contain stars and planets moving them, the ninth sphere contains none. The *Sforno* compares this hidden power to a lion in his den who is not seen, but everyone is aware that there is great strength lurking in his "dwelling place." This imagery of a lion in his den is found in *Psalms* 10:9, *He lies in wait secretly like a lion in his den.* The phrase מְעֹנָה is used regarding the lion's den as we find in the verse, *Where is the den of the lions* (*Nachum* 2:12). The meaning of the concluding portion of verse 26, linked with the beginning of verse 27, is "God in His majesty and power is manifested in the daily sphere, which is the ninth sphere, and this power is invisible, as is the power of the lion in his den or dwelling place." (I am indebted to Dr. Sid Leiman for his assistance in the preparation of this note.)

אֱלֹהֵי קֶדֶם — *The ancient God.* In Jewish tradition, God is referred to as קַדְמוֹנוֹ שֶׁל עוֹלָם, *the One Who preceded the world.* The word *ancient,* when applied to the Almighty, does not mean "old" or that which existed many eons ago. God is above time and place. As the *Sforno* states, God is primeval and He is the One Who brought all the forces and powers of the universe into existence; hence, He is referred to as קֶדֶם.

כח וַיְגָרֶשׁ מִפָּנֶיךָ אוֹיֵב וַיֹּאמֶר הַשְׁמֵד: וַיִּשְׁכֹּן יִשְׂרָאֵל בֶּטַח בָּדָד עֵין יַעֲקֹב אֶל־
כט אֶרֶץ דָּגָן וְתִירוֹשׁ אַף־שָׁמָיו יַעַרְפוּ טָל: אַשְׁרֶיךָ יִשְׂרָאֵל מִי כָמוֹךָ עַם נוֹשַׁע
בַּיהוָה מָגֵן עֶזְרֶךָ וַאֲשֶׁר־חֶרֶב גַּאֲוָתֶךָ וְיִכָּחֲשׁוּ אֹיְבֶיךָ לָךְ וְאַתָּה עַל־בָּמוֹתֵימוֹ

---

the heavens, He is the God of might Who directs all existing (things) of the world, (meaning) that which exists but perishes with the passage of time such as the quality of the (primary) elements and the (forces) of nature which nourish, promote growth and reproduction, and the formative power in plant life and living creatures.

וַיְגָרֶשׁ מִפָּנֶיךָ אוֹיֵב וַיֹּאמֶר הַשְׁמֵד — *And He thrust out the enemy from before you and said, "Destroy."* And behold, He drove out the enemies before you who were the inhabitants of the Land, and He said to you, "Destroy!" Because you did not conquer the Land by your sword that you should think when your strength leaves you, with the passage of time, or when other (enemies) replace them, that they will overpower you. Because indeed He was the One Who cast them out and how shall others enter (the Land) against His will?

28. וַיִּשְׁכֹּן יִשְׂרָאֵל בֶּטַח — *And Israel dwells securely* . . . as it says, וְהָאָרֶץ שָׁקְטָה מִמִּלְחָמָה, *And the Land had rest from war* (*Joshua* 11:23).

בָּדָד עֵין יַעֲקֹב אֶל אֶרֶץ דָּגָן וְתִירוֹשׁ אַף שָׁמָיו יַעַרְפוּ טָל — *The fountain of Jacob (shall dwell) alone upon a land of corn and wine, also His heavens shall drop down dew.* May it be Your will at the end of days (that) *the Fountain of Jacob*, Who is *the Lord that you seek* (based on *Malachi* 3:1), and Who (will be) the Fountain of Israel at the end (lit., the heel) of time, and (regarding Whom the verse states,) *His heavens shall drop dew*, that there will flow an abundance of dew *upon a land of corn and wine*. This indicates that the teaching of the Messiah will drop as the dew which all rejoice in and the heavens shall also (literally) flow with abundant dew *upon the land of corn and wine*, as was the case at the time of the six days of creation before the sin of Adam, כִּי לֹא הִמְטִיר . . . וְאָדָם אַיִן לַעֲבֹד . . . וְאֵד יַעֲלֶה . . . וְהִשְׁקָה, *For (God) had not caused it to rain . . . and there was not a man to till . . . but a mist went up . . . and watered* (*Genesis* 2:5,6), in such a manner that the earth itself will (produce) corn and wine when the dew will drop down and bless it. In this way, its inhabitants will attain their livelihood without pain as was the (original) intent before the sin, that Adam's needs would be met (without great toil), as our Sages say, "There will come a time when *Eretz Yisrael* will produce baked cakes and silk garments" (*Shabbos* 30b).

NOTES

וּמִתַּחַת זְרֹעֹת עוֹלָם — *And underneath (the heavens,) the everlasting might*. The expression זְרֹעֹת עוֹלָם translates literally as *the arms of the world*. God, as it were, holds the world in His arms — guiding, directing and protecting it. As the *Sforno* states, this concern and control of God *underneath the heavens* extends to all the forces of nature which guarantee the continuity of the בְּרִיאָה, *creation*.

וַיְגָרֶשׁ . . . וַיֹּאמֶר הַשְׁמֵד — *And He thrust out . . . and said, "Destroy."* Israel is depicted as being the instrument of God in the conquest of *Eretz Yisrael*. God is the true conqueror while Israel is but the medium chosen by Him to drive out the inhabitants of Canaan, whom they will replace. Hence, there is no fear that eventually the Jews will in turn be replaced by others, for they are not subject to the normal pattern of rise, decline and fall as are other nations since God is the source of their strength and security.

28. בָּדָד עֵין יַעֲקֹב . . . אַף שָׁמָיו יַעַרְפוּ טָל — *The fountain of Jacob (shall dwell) alone . . . also His heavens shall drop down dew*. The *Sforno* explains why this verse, which he interprets as being a prayer instead of a blessing, uses the term עֵין יַעֲקֹב, *fountain of Jacob*, rather than יִשְׂרָאֵל, *Israel*. As the *Sforno* points out in *Genesis* 25:26, the name יַעֲקֹב, which stems from עָקֵב, *heel*, implies אַחֲרִית הַיָּמִים, *the end of days*. In our verse, the word *fountain*, the source of life-giving and refreshing waters, refers to מָשִׁיחַ, *the Messiah*, whose teachings will be readily understood, accepted and appreciated by one and all. He explains the phrase יַעַרְפוּ טָל, *shall drop down dew*, as having a two-fold meaning. One is symbolic, referring to the Messiah and his teachings, while the second is a literal one, promis-

ones; He drove the enemy away from before you, and He said, "Destroy!"
28 *Thus Israel shall dwell secure, solitary, in the likeness of Jacob, in a land of grain and wine; even his heavens shall drip with dew.*
29 *Fortunate are you, O Israel: Who is like you! O people delivered by HASHEM, the Shield of your help, Who is the Sword of your grandeur; your foes will try to deceive you, but you will trample their haughty ones.*

---

29. אַשְׁרֶיךָ יִשְׂרָאֵל — *Happy are you, O Israel.* And then you will reach that (degree) of happiness which is the highest level (of contentment) possible for a people (to attain).

מִי כָמוֹךָ — *Who is like unto you?* No other people will be found like unto you (in this respect), as it says, וְאִשְּׁרוּ אֶתְכֶם כָּל הַגּוֹיִם, *And all nations shall call you happily blessed* (*Malachi* 3:12).

עַם נוֹשַׁע בַּה׳ — *A people saved by HASHEM.* Your salvation will not be secured by the battles you wage but rather God will do battle on your behalf.

מָגֵן עֶזְרֶךָ — *The shield of your help.* He is the One Who helped you in Exile, (insuring) that you not be annihilated, as it says, לוּלֵי ה׳ שֶׁהָיָה לָנוּ ... אֲזַי הַמַּיִם שְׁטָפוּנוּ ... עֶזְרֵנוּ בְּשֵׁם ה׳, *If not for HASHEM Who was with us . . . then the waters would have overwhelmed us . . . Our help is in the Name of HASHEM* (*Psalms* 124:2,4,8).

וַאֲשֶׁר חֶרֶב גַּאֲוָתֶךָ — *And the sword of your majesty.* His will be the sword that will be elevated over the nations when He battles against them as it says כִּי בָאֵשׁ ה׳ נִשְׁפָּט, וּבְחַרְבּוֹ אֶת כָּל בָּשָׂר, *For by fire will HASHEM execute judgment, and with His sword upon all flesh* (*Isaiah* 66:16).

וְיִכָּחֲשׁוּ אֹיְבֶיךָ לָךְ — *And your enemies shall submit to you.* Those who shamed you (in the past) will now submit to you when you will be honored, as it says, וְהִשְׁתַּחֲווּ עַל כַּפּוֹת רַגְלַיִךְ כָּל מְנַאֲצָיִךְ, *And those who despised you shall bow down at the soles of your feet* (*Isaiah* 60:14).

וְאַתָּה עַל בָּמוֹתֵימוֹ תִדְרֹךְ — *And you shall tread upon their high places.* Even their kings will humble themselves (before) you, as it says, וְהָיוּ מְלָכִים אֹמְנַיִךְ ... אַפַּיִם אֶרֶץ יִשְׁתַּחֲווּ לָךְ, *And kings shall be your foster parents . . . they shall bow down to you with their faces toward the earth* (*Isaiah* 49:23).

NOTES

ing that Israel will at that time in their history be granted פַּרְנָסָה, *livelihood,* which will be easily acquired, permitting them to pursue the study and mastery of Torah.

29. אַשְׁרֶיךָ יִשְׂרָאֵל מִי כָמוֹךָ — *Happy are you, O Israel; who is like unto you?* Moses is not praising or complimenting Israel, rather he is stating a fact regarding their future. He asserts that ultimately they will reach a level of happiness that will be unique and unsurpassed by other nations, and this special condition will be recognized by all the nations, as Malachi prophesied.

עַם נוֹשַׁע בַּה׳ מָגֵן עֶזְרֶךָ וַאֲשֶׁר חֶרֶב גַּאֲוָתֶךָ — *A people saved by HASHEM, the shield of your help and the sword of your majesty.* The *Sforno* explains these three distinct phrases in the following manner: Israel's salvation is not secured by their own military might but through God Who battles on their behalf. In fact, through the years in Exile, were it not for the fact that God was their *shield of help,* they would have been destroyed. And at that time in Israel's history, when they will again do battle against their enemies at the conclusion of their exile, God will serve as their *sword of majesty.*

וְיִכָּחֲשׁוּ אֹיְבֶיךָ לָךְ וְאַתָּה עַל בָּמוֹתֵימוֹ תִדְרֹךְ — *And your enemies shall submit to you and you shall tread upon their high places.* The *Sforno* explains that these two concluding phrases refer to the high regard, esteem and respect that the nations and their leaders will have for the people of Israel. Those nations who were their enemies, mocking and shaming them over the years, will eventually submit to them and be subservient to them, and the leaders of those nations will likewise humble themselves before Israel.

לד

א תִּדְרֹךְ: וַיַּעַל מֹשֶׁה מֵעַרְבֹת מוֹאָב אֶל־הַר נְבוֹ רֹאשׁ
הַפִּסְגָּה אֲשֶׁר עַל־פְּנֵי יְרֵחוֹ וַיַּרְאֵהוּ יהוה אֶת־כָּל־הָאָרֶץ אֶת־הַגִּלְעָד
ב עַד־דָּן: וְאֵת כָּל־נַפְתָּלִי וְאֶת־אֶרֶץ אֶפְרַיִם וּמְנַשֶּׁה וְאֵת כָּל־אֶרֶץ יְהוּדָה
ג עַד הַיָּם הָאַחֲרוֹן: וְאֶת־הַנֶּגֶב וְאֶת־הַכִּכָּר בִּקְעַת יְרֵחוֹ עִיר הַתְּמָרִים
ד עַד־צֹעַר: וַיֹּאמֶר יהוה אֵלָיו זֹאת הָאָרֶץ אֲשֶׁר נִשְׁבַּעְתִּי לְאַבְרָהָם
לְיִצְחָק וּלְיַעֲקֹב לֵאמֹר לְזַרְעֲךָ אֶתְּנֶנָּה הֶרְאִיתִיךָ בְעֵינֶיךָ וְשָׁמָּה לֹא
ה־ו תַעֲבֹר: וַיָּמָת שָׁם מֹשֶׁה עֶבֶד־יהוה בְּאֶרֶץ מוֹאָב עַל־פִּי יהוה: וַיִּקְבֹּר
אֹתוֹ בַגַּי בְּאֶרֶץ מוֹאָב מוּל בֵּית פְּעוֹר וְלֹא־יָדַע אִישׁ אֶת־קְבֻרָתוֹ
ז עַד הַיּוֹם הַזֶּה: וּמֹשֶׁה בֶּן־מֵאָה וְעֶשְׂרִים שָׁנָה בְּמֹתוֹ לֹא־כָהֲתָה עֵינוֹ
ח וְלֹא־נָס לֵחֹה: וַיִּבְכּוּ בְנֵי יִשְׂרָאֵל אֶת־מֹשֶׁה בְּעַרְבֹת מוֹאָב שְׁלֹשִׁים
ט יוֹם וַיִּתְּמוּ יְמֵי בְכִי אֵבֶל מֹשֶׁה: וִיהוֹשֻׁעַ בִּן־נוּן מָלֵא רוּחַ חָכְמָה כִּי־
סָמַךְ מֹשֶׁה אֶת־יָדָיו עָלָיו וַיִּשְׁמְעוּ אֵלָיו בְּנֵי־יִשְׂרָאֵל וַיַּעֲשׂוּ כַּאֲשֶׁר צִוָּה
י יהוה אֶת־מֹשֶׁה: וְלֹא־קָם נָבִיא עוֹד בְּיִשְׂרָאֵל כְּמֹשֶׁה אֲשֶׁר יְדָעוֹ יהוה

XXXIV

4. הֶרְאִיתִיךָ בְעֵינֶיךָ — *I have caused you to see it with your eyes* . . . so that you may bless it.

וְשָׁמָּה לֹא תַעֲבֹר — *But you shall not go over there* . . . lest your blessing will (firmly) take hold in such a manner that (the Land) will not be destroyed at the end, as it was decreed (to occur) when their measure (of evil) would be full.

6. וַיִּקְבֹּר אֹתוֹ — *And he was buried.* If he (Moses) buried himself, as is the opinion of some of our Sages, then (we must say) that his separated soul did it, because he died on the mountain on the top of Pisgah, from whence he saw the Land, as it states, *And Moses died there* (v. 5), whereas the burial was in the valley.

8-9. וַיִּתְּמוּ יְמֵי בְכִי אֵבֶל מֹשֶׁה. וִיהוֹשֻׁעַ בִּן נוּן מָלֵא רוּחַ חָכְמָה — *The days of weeping in the mourning for Moses ended. And Joshua the son of Nun was full of the spirit of wisdom* . . . because in the days of weeping, there is no wisdom and no counsel.

NOTES

XXXIV

4. הֶרְאִיתִיךָ בְעֵינֶיךָ — *I have caused you to see it with your eyes*. See *Genesis* 48:10 and the note there; also *Numbers* 27:12 and *Deut.* 32:49.

וְשָׁמָּה לֹא תַעֲבֹר — *But you shall not go over there*. Rabbinic tradition has it that whatever Moses himself did was destined to last forever. Had he himself entered the Land of Israel and conquered it, *Eretz Yisrael* would never have been destroyed, nor would the Jewish people have been exiled from it. The *Sforno* established this concept above in chapter 1:37 and chapter 3:25. God, however, had decreed that if Israel sinned they would be punished with Exile; hence, Moses was not permitted to enter the Land since this would frustrate the Divine plan. In some ways this was also beneficial to the Jewish people, for had the Land not been destroyed and the people exiled, then when their sins would multiply greatly and God could no longer be forbearing with them, they would be subject to total annihilation. Hence, their exile allowed them to survive as a people and God's wrath was poured out on the Land, and in the case of the Temple, on "the wood and stones."

6. וַיִּקְבֹּר אֹתוֹ — *And he was buried*. See *Rashi's* commentary on this verse.

8-9. וַיִּתְּמוּ יְמֵי בְכִי אֵבֶל מֹשֶׁה. וִיהוֹשֻׁעַ בִּן נוּן מָלֵא רוּחַ חָכְמָה — *The days of weeping in the mourning for Moses ended. And Joshua the son of Nun was full of the spirit of wisdom*. The Sages have taught us that the *Shechinah*, the Divine Presence, including the gift of prophecy, can only dwell upon a person when a spirit of joy prevails (*Shabbos* 30b). Depression and sadness caused by mourning inhibits the power of prophecy and the gift of Divinely inspired wisdom as well. The *Sforno* therefore links

34 1 *Moses ascended from the plains of Moab, to Mount Nebo, to the summit*
of the cliff that faces Jericho, and HASHEM showed him the entire
Land: the Gilead as far as Dan; 2 *all of Naphtali, and the land of Ephraim*
and Manasseh; the entire land of Judah as far as the western sea; 3 *the Negev*
and the Plain — the valley of Jericho, city of date palms — as far as Zoar.
4 *And HASHEM said to him, "This is the land which I swore to Abraham,*
to Isaac, and to Jacob, saying, 'I will give it to your offspring.' I have let you
see it with your own eyes, but you shall not cross over to there."
5 *So Moses, servant of HASHEM, died there, in the land of Moab, by the*
mouth of HASHEM. 6 *He buried him in the depression, in the land of Moab,*
opposite Beth-peor, and no one knows his burial place to this day. 7 *Moses*
was one hundred and twenty years old when he died; his eye had not
dimmed, and his vigor had not diminished. 8 *The Children of Israel bewailed*
Moses in the plains of Moab for thirty days; then the days of tearful
mourning for Moses ended.
9 *Joshua son of Nun was filled with the spirit of wisdom, because Moses*
had laid his hands upon him, so the Children of Israel obeyed him and did
as HASHEM had commanded Moses.
10 *Never again has there arisen in Israel a prophet like Moses, whom*

כַּאֲשֶׁר צִוָּה ה׳ אֶת מֹשֶׁה — *As HASHEM commanded Moses* . . . according to all that God had commanded Moses, as it says, וְשָׁאַל לוֹ בְּמִשְׁפַּט הָאוּרִים לִפְנֵי ה׳ עַל פִּיו יֵצְאוּ וְעַל פִּיו יָבֹאוּ הוּא וְכָל בְּנֵי יִשְׂרָאֵל אִתּוֹ וְכָל הָעֵדָה, *They shall inquire of him by the judgment of the Urim before HASHEM; at his word shall they go out and at his word they shall come in, both he and all the Children of Israel with him and all the congregation* (*Numbers* 27:21).

10. וְלֹא קָם נָבִיא עוֹד בְּיִשְׂרָאֵל כְּמֹשֶׁה — *And there did not arise a prophet in Israel like Moses since.* No other prophet ever reached his level of prophecy and thus it is clear that no prophet is permitted to institute new laws, as our Sages say, "One *Beis Din* cannot annul the ordinances of another unless it is superior to it in number and in wisdom" (*Megillah* 2a).

אֲשֶׁר יְדָעוֹ ה׳ — *Whom HASHEM's knowledge (he absorbed).* Behold, when a prophet prophesies, without a doubt, he acquires an added (dimension) of intellectual light, emanating from the light (radiance) of the King's countenance, as it says, וְהִתְנַבִּיתָ עִמָּם וְנֶהְפַּכְתָּ לְאִישׁ אַחֵר, *And you shall prophesy with them and shall be turned into another man* (*I Samuel* 10:6). That is also why (the prophet) tells us of the lovingkindness shown

NOTES

together the concluding phrase of verse 8 with the opening statement of verse 9. Only after the days of weeping and mourning were over could Joshua be the recipient of *the spirit of wisdom.*

10. וְלֹא קָם נָבִיא — *And there did not arise a prophet.* The *Sforno* stresses that the Torah given by Moses is a permanent and unchanging one. The claim by the Church that Christianity was the "New Israel" supplanting the old, and that the New Testament replaced the Tanach, had to be refuted. Maimonides, his contemporaries and many who followed, such as the *Sforno*, emphasized the everlasting character of God's covenant with Israel and the unchanging nature of Torah. (See the *Rambam's* ninth Principle of Faith.) *Sforno* interprets the opening phrase of this verse, *And there did not arise a prophet like Moses,* as an added argument against the attempt made by those who would amend the original covenant and the Torah given through Moses our Teacher. Since a later court that is inferior to a previous one has no power to override the decision of that court, and since no prophet ever arose who was the equal, let alone the superior, of Moses, how then could any *prophet* abrogate the teachings of Moses and legitimately establish a new covenant or testament? It is for this reason that the Torah emphasizes that no prophet ever rose to his level.

יא פָּנִים אֶל־פָּנִים: לְכָל־הָאֹתֹת וְהַמּוֹפְתִים אֲשֶׁר שְׁלָחוֹ יהוה לַעֲשׂוֹת
יב בְּאֶרֶץ מִצְרָיִם לְפַרְעֹה וּלְכָל־עֲבָדָיו וּלְכָל־אַרְצוֹ: וּלְכֹל הַיָּד הַחֲזָקָה
וּלְכֹל הַמּוֹרָא הַגָּדוֹל אֲשֶׁר עָשָׂה מֹשֶׁה לְעֵינֵי כָּל־יִשְׂרָאֵל:

---

by God to His people (and it therefore) says, וָאָקִים מִבְּנֵיכֶם לִנְבִיאִים, *And I will rise up your sons for prophets* (*Amos* 2:11). Now, being that all actions of God, the Blessed One, are executed solely through His own knowledge of self, it says, אֲשֶׁר יְדָעוֹ, *Whom* (*HASHEM'S*) *knowledge*, teaching (us) that He acted upon him through His knowledge for good, similar to, מָה אָדָם וַתֵּדָעֵהוּ, *What is man that you make him to know* (*Psalms* 144:3), and וָאֵדָעֲךָ בְשֵׁם, *and I know you by name* (*Exodus* 33:17), and וַיֵּדַע אֱלֹהִים, *And God knew* (ibid. 2:25), and יוֹדֵעַ ה׳ דֶּרֶךְ צַדִּיקִים, *HASHEM knows the way of the righteous* (*Psalms* 1:6), and many such similar (passages).

פָּנִים אֶל פָּנִים — *Face to face* . . . while he still made use of his senses (faculties).

11. לְכָל הָאֹתֹת — *In all the signs.* And this knowledge (of God) *face to face* was granted to him when God sent him to perform signs and wonders in Egypt, because indeed the vision revealed to him at the bush did not take place in this manner as it says, כִּי יָרֵא מֵהַבִּיט אֶל הָאֱלֹהִים, *For he was afraid to look upon God* (*Exodus* 3:6) as compared to, וּתְמֻנַת ה׳ יַבִּיט, *And the similitude of HASHEM he beholds* (*Numbers* 12:8).

NOTES

אֲשֶׁר יְדָעוֹ ה׳ — *Whom HASHEM's knowledge*. The *Sforno* explains this expression as meaning that the Almighty, Whose knowledge is not external to Himself, but rather "He . . . and His knowledge are One" (*Rambam, Mishnah Torah, Hilchos Teshuvah* 5:5), acted upon Moses until he became influenced and instructed by this Divine knowledge, thereby expanding his own knowledge. See the *Sforno's* commentary on *Numbers* 7:89 and *Deut.* 2:7 and the notes on those verses for further clarification.

פָּנִים אֶל פָּנִים — *Face to face*. See the *Sforno* on *Exodus* 19:19 and 33:11 and the notes on those verses regarding the meaning of פָּנִים אֶל פָּנִים, *face to face*.

11-12. לְכָל הָאֹתֹת ... וּלְכֹל הַיָּד הַחֲזָקָה ... וּלְכֹל הַמּוֹרָא הַגָּדוֹל אֲשֶׁר עָשָׂה מֹשֶׁה לְעֵינֵי כָּל יִשְׂרָאֵל — *In all the signs . . . and in all that mighty hand . . . and in all the great awesomeness which Moses performed in the sight of all Israel. Rashi* interprets *mighty hand* as referring to the giving of the Torah, while

HASHEM had known face to face, [11] *as evidenced by all the signs and wonders that HASHEM sent him to perform in the land of Egypt, against Pharaoh and all his courtiers and all his land,* [12] *and by all the strong hand and awesome power that Moses performed before the eyes of all Israel.*

12. וּלְכֹל הַיָּד הַחֲזָקָה — *And in all that mighty hand* ... which God wrought through him, changing the nature of permanent (aspects of creation), such as the splitting of the (waters) of the Sea (of Reeds) (*Exodus* 14:21) and the earth opening its mouth (*Numbers* 16:31) and bringing down manna from heaven (*Exodus* 16:4) and other such (phenomena).

וּלְכֹל הַמּוֹרָא הַגָּדוֹל — *And in all the great awesomeness* ... of the giving of the Torah.

אֲשֶׁר עָשָׂה מֹשֶׁה לְעֵינֵי כָּל יִשְׂרָאֵל — *Which Moses performed in the sight of all Israel.* When they (Israel) stood from afar at the time the Torah was given, they saw how Moses drew nigh to the thick darkness (*Exodus* 20:18), because he then attained the highest level of prophecy (characterized as) *face to face*, and Moses then became נוֹרָא, *awesome*, through the "rays of glory."

לְעֵינֵי כָּל יִשְׂרָאֵל — *In the sight of all Israel* ... as it says, וַיַּרְא אַהֲרֹן וְכָל בְּנֵי יִשְׂרָאֵל אֶת מֹשֶׁה וְהִנֵּה קָרַן עוֹר פָּנָיו וַיִּירְאוּ מִגֶּשֶׁת אֵלָיו, *And when Aaron and all the Children of Israel saw Moses, and behold the skin of his face sent forth beams, they were afraid to come near him* (*Exodus* 34:30).

NOTES

and in all the great awesomeness refers to the miracles and mighty deeds wrought by God in the terrible wilderness. *Sforno*, however, interprets *mighty hand* to mean the supernatural acts of God in Egypt and at the Sea of Reeds, executed through the hand of Moses, while *the great awsomeness* refers to the giving of the Torah. The latter occasion caused Israel to be in awe of Moses who drew nigh to Sinai when all others stood from afar, and who ultimately came down to the people with "rays of glory" shining from his face. The *Sforno*, in his commentary on verse 11, links the unique stature of Moses and his ability to communicate with God *face to face* (verse 10) with his worthiness to be chosen to perform signs and wonders in Egypt at the behest of God. This level of prophecy was not reached at once but evolved gradually, for at the bush he had not as yet attained such an exalted station, but with time he merited to speak with God while still in command of his faculties.